Proceedings

of the

International Joint Conference on Neural Networks 2003

Co-Sponsored by:

The International Neural
Network Society

The IEEE Neural
Networks Society

Doubletree Hotel – Jantzen Beach

Portland, Oregon

July 20 – 24, 2003

Volume 3

IJCNN 2003 Conference Proceedings

Copyright and Reprint Permissions: Abstracting is permitted with credit to the source. Libraries are permitted to photocopy beyond the limits of U.S. copyright law for private use of patrons those articles in this volume that carry a code at the bottom of the first page, provided the per-copy fee indicated in the code is paid through the Copyright Clearance Center, 222 Rosewood Drive, Danvers, MA, 01923 USA. For other copying, reprint or republication permission, write to IEEE Copyrights Manager, IEEE Service Center, 445 Hoes Lane, PO Box 1331, Piscataway, NJ, 08855-1331 USA. All rights reserved. Copyright © 2003 by The Institute of Electrical and Electronics Engineers, Inc.

Papers are printed as received from the authors.

All opinions expressed in the Proceedings are those of the authors and are not binding on The Institute of Electrical and Electronics Engineers, Inc.

Additional copies may be ordered from:
IEEE Order Dept.
445 Hoes Lane / PO Box 1331
Piscataway, NJ 08855 USA
Phone (Toll Free): +1-800-678-4333
email: customer.services@ieee.org
Web: shop.ieee.org

IEEE Catalog No. 03CH37464
ISBN 0-7803-7898-9   Bound Edition
ISSN 1098-7576

IEEE Catalog No. 03CH37464C   CD Edition
ISBN 0-7803-7899-7   CD Edition

Preface

IJCNN is the flagship conference of the INNS, as well as the IEEE Neural Networks Society. It has arguably been the preeminent conference in the field, even as neural network conferences have proliferated and specialized. As the number of conferences has grown, its strongest competition has migrated away from an emphasis on neural networks. IJCNN, on the other hand, has always welcomed your neural networks research contributions, while embracing the proliferation of spin-off and related fields. (See the topic list below.) Still, you won't need to call your neural network by some other name, merely to get it accepted at IJCNN.

While being an inclusive conference, IJCNN has strict, documented standards for acceptance, including literature review; quality of English; and reproducibility, accuracy and meaningfulness of results. All papers, even invited papers, were subject to a minimum of two reviews -- and many papers received up to five. We rejected 15% of submitted papers. The topics cover most of the major areas of research in neural networks, including: self-organizing maps, reinforcement learning, support vector machines, adaptive resonance theory, principal component analysis and independent component analysis, as well as numerous engineering applications and detailed biological models of the function of neural circuits.

IJCNN '03 has, at this writing, surpassed expectations in every capacity. We got all our first choices of plenary speakers: Kunihiko Fukushima, Earl Miller, Terrence Sejnowski, Vladimir Vapnik, and Christoph von der Malsburg; an extraordinary slate of tutorial presenters, and 730 submitted articles -- 33% over projections. We will also have several distinguished award recipients.

An event of this magnitude does not occur spontaneously. We owe a tremendous debt of gratitude to the following:
- The sponsoring societies: INNS (lead society in odd-numbered years), and the new IEEE Neural Networks Society. We drew on expertise of several past society presidents, conference chairs, program chairs, and numerous other dedicated volunteers. The INNS Board of Governors and IEEE NNS AdCom are listed later in this program.
- The generous conference co-Sponsors: Boeing, Portland State University, and the Applied Computational Intelligence Laboratory of the University of Missouri-Rolla (so far, as this program went to press).
- Portland Oregon Visitors' Association.
- Talley Management Company: especially Anthony Celenza, Tom Sims, Darla Dobson, Stacy Blackshaw, Bob Talley, as well as numerous other support staffers.
- The Program Committee, listed later in this program.
- The Review Committee, listed later in this program.
- The Organizing Committee, listed later in this program. Their contributions were so essential as to justify further clarification here:
  - Mike Hasselmo did the Herculean feat of serving as Program Chair and INNS President simultaneously! We need to thank not only him, but his family, for tolerating this. He's much too modest to admit it, but his role was pivotal.
  - DeLiang Wang and Kumar Venayagamoorthy were the kind of Program Co-Chairs who took huge chunks of responsibility and executed the tasks flawlessly. Mike and I never once needed to revisit something they took on, no matter how critical. They'd be ideal candidates for General Chair in the future!
  - Harold Szu and Carlo Morabito attracted an amazing slate of tutorial speakers.

- o George Lendaris mobilized an outstanding local arrangement committee, and secured the conference Co-sponsorship of Portland State University.
  - o Derong Liu created the web interface, distributed posters, and many other things.
  - o Tomasz Cholewo cut work in half for nearly every other person involved in this meeting, with what is perhaps the best conference management software in the business – plus exceptional around-the-clock volunteer support.
  - o You're sure to like the improved Exhibits area this year – so thank Karl Mathia, Exhibits Chair.
  - o Slawo Wesolkowski coordinated the student travel grants, an enormous task.
  - o The International Liaison, Bill Howell, and his committee, Asian Liaison M.H. Lim and European Liaison Tulay Yildrim, had to deal with a deluge of invitation requests, faxes, letters, SARS cancellations, intransigent embassies and consulates, and more.
- Last but not least, a heartfelt thanks to YOU – the reader. Whether you attended the meeting in person, or are just reading these proceedings to enhance your knowledge in the field, it is for your consumption that this knowledge is being disseminated. We encourage you to read and refer to IJCNN papers frequently in your work, and hope to see you at future IJCNN's.

Sincerely,

Donald C. Wunsch II, University of Missouri-Rolla
General Chair, IJCNN '03

2003 International Joint Conference on Neural Networks

TOPIC LIST

A. PERCEPTUAL AND MOTOR FUNCTION
- Vision and image processing
- Pattern recognition
  - Face recognition
  - Handwriting recognition
  - Other pattern recognition
- Auditory and speech processing
  - Audition
- Speech recognition
  - Speech production
  - Other perceptual systems
  - Motor control and response

B. COGNITIVE FUNCTION
- Cognitive information processing
- Learning and memory
- Spatial Navigation
- Conditioning, Reward and Behavior
- Mental disorders
- Attention and Consciousness
- Language
- Emotion and Motivation

C. COMPUTATIONAL NEUROSCIENCE
- Models of neurons and local circuits
- Systems neurobiology and neural modeling
- Spiking neurons

D. INFORMATICS
- Neuroinformatics
- Bioinformatics
- Artificial immune systems
- Data mining

E. HARDWARE
- Neuromorphic hardware and implementations
- Embedded neural networks

F. REINFORCEMENT LEARNING AND CONTROL
- Reinforcement learning
- Approximate/Adaptive dynamic programming
- Control
- Reconfigurable systems
- Robotics
- Fuzzy neural systems
- Optimization

G. DYNAMICS
- Neurodynamics
- Recurrent networks
- Chaos and learning theory

H. THEORY
- Mathematics of Neural Systems
- Support vector machines
- Extended Kalman filters
- Mixture models, EM algorithms and ensemble learning
- Radial basis functions
- Self-organizing maps
- Adaptive resonance theory
- Principal component analysis and independent component analysis
- Probabilistic and information-theoretic methods
- Neural Networks and Evolutionary Computation

I. APPLICATIONS
- Signal Processing
- Telecommunications Applications
- Time Series Analysis
- Biomedical Applications
- Financial Engineering
- Biomimetic applications
- Computer security applications
- Power system applications
- Aeroinformatics
- Diagnostics and Quality Control
- Other applications

Message from the President of the International Neural Network Society,

Dear colleagues,

As President of the International Neural Network Society (INNS), I am pleased to welcome you to the International Joint Conference on Neural Networks (IJCNN 2003). As you know, this conference is jointly sponsored by the INNS and the IEEE Neural Network Society, with INNS organizing the conference this year. We look forward to your participation in this excellent conference program.

I'd like to thank the General Chair, Donald C. Wunsch II for his outstanding work in organizing a highly successful conference. His skill and experience with conference organization was essential. As Program Chair of the conference, I would like to thank the Program Co-chairs, DeLiang Wang and Ganesh Kumar Venayagamoorthy for their excellent work in helping me to oversee the review process and assemble the program. Thanks also to the dedicated Program Committee for this conference (listed on a later page), who helped us assign reviewers, review articles and make the acceptance decisions. I would also like to thank all the individuals whom Don lists in his message.

Over 730 articles were submitted to the conference. I'd like to thank the Review Committee of about 200 reviewers (listed on a later page) who participated in reviewing these articles. Each article received a minimum of two reviews, and many received more. This allowed for selection of highly ranked articles for the conference. About 15% of articles were rejected. This rigorous peer review enhances the status of the conference presentations. The articles from this conference will appear in the proceedings published by IEEE. In addition, the authors of 52 highly rated papers from this conference were invited to submit separate articles which are appearing in a special issue of the journal Neural Networks this summer.

The sessions in IJCNN 2003 cover the full range of vital topics in this field, ranging from the Dynamics of Neural Networks to Support Vector Machines to Reinforcement Learning. The conference is organized into parallel oral sessions, which fall into the broad categories of Biological/Cognitive, Theoretical and Applications, with an additional series of Special Sessions containing peer reviewed articles assembled on a specific topic by session chairs.

I hope that you will enjoy hearing about this research as much as I have enjoyed reading the articles. We encourage all conference attendees to become members of the International Neural Network Society and join in our mission to further research and education in Neural Networks (take a look at our society web pages at www.inns.org). We also welcome your participation in future conferences.

With best regards,

Michael E. Hasselmo
President, International Neural Network Society
Program Chair, IJCNN 2003

2003 International Neural Network Society Officers

President
Michael Hasselmo
Boston University

President Elect
Jose C. Principe
University of Florida

Past President
Lee Feldkamp
Ford Research Laboratory

Secretary
Francesco Carlo Morabito
University "Mediterranea" of Reggio Calabria

Treasurer
David G. Brown
Food and Drug Administration

2003 Board of Governors

Gail Carpenter
Boston University Center for Adaptive Systems

David Casasent
Carnegie Mellon University

Wlodzislaw Duch
Nicholas Copernicus University

Dario Floreano
Swiss Federal Institute of Technology (EPFL)

Walter Freeman
University of Cal. - Berkeley

Kunihiko Fukushima
Tokyo University of Technology

Stan Gielen
University of Nymegen

Stephen Grossberg
Boston University

Bart Kosko
University of Southern California

George Lendaris
Portland State University

Daniel S. Levine
University of Texas at Arlington

William Levy
University of Virginia Health Science Center

Erkki Oja
Helsinki University of Technology

Harold Szu
Office of Naval Research

John G. Taylor
Kings College London

Shiro Usui
Toyohashi University of Technology

Deliang Wang
Ohio State University

Paul Werbos
US National Science Foundation

Bernard Widrow
Stanford University

Donald C. Wunsch
University of Missouri-Rolla

Lei Xu, Professor
Chinese University of Hong Kong

Lotfi A. Zadeh
University of California at Berkeley

IJCNN 2003 ORGANIZING COMMITTEE

General Chair:
Donald C. Wunsch II, University of Missouri – Rolla

Program Chair:
Michael E. Hasselmo, Boston University

Program Co-Chair:
DeLiang Wang, Ohio State University

Program Co-Chair:
Ganesh K. Venayagamoorthy, University of Missouri – Rolla

Web Chair: Tomasz Cholewo, Lexmark International Inc., Kentucky

Local Arrangements Chair: George Lendaris, Portland State University

Publicity Chair: Derong Liu, University of Illinois at Chicago

Tutorial Chair: Harold Szu, Office of Naval Research

Tutorial Co-Chair: F. Carlo Morabito, University of "Mediterranea" Reggio Calabria, Italy

Exhibits Chair: Karl Mathia, Brooks-PRI Automation Inc., California

Student Travel and Volunteer Chair: Slawo Wesolkowski, University of Waterloo, Canada

International Liaison: William N. Howell, Mining and Mineral Sciences Laboratories, Canada

Asian Liaison: Meng-Hiot Lim, Nanyang Technological University, Singapore

European Liaison: Tulay Yildirim, Yildiz Technical University, Turkey

PROGRAM COMMITTEE MEMBERS

David Brown,
Food and Drug Administration

David Casasent,
Carnegie Mellon University

Ke Chen,
University of Birmingham, UK

Michael Denham,
University of Plymouth, UK

Tom Dietterich,
Oregon State University

Lee Feldkamp,
Ford Motor Company

Kunihiko Fukushima,
Tokyo University of Technology, Japan

Joydeep Ghosh,
University of Texas at Austin

Stephen Grossberg,
Boston University

Fred Ham,
Florida Institute of Technology

Ron Harley,
Georgia Institute of Technology

Bart Kosko,
University of Southern California

Robert Kozma, University of Memphis

Dan Levine,
University of Texas at Arlington

Xiuwen Liu,
Florida State University

F. Carlo Morabito,
Universita di Reggio Calabria, Italy

Ali Minai,
University of Cincinnati

Catherine Myers,
Rutgers University

Erkki Oja,
Helsinki University of Technology, Finland

Jose Principe,
University of Florida

Danil Prokhorov,
Ford Motor Company

Harold Szu,
Office of Naval Research

John Gerald Taylor,
University College, London, UK

Shiro Usui,
Toyohashi Univ. of Technology, Japan

Bernie Widrow,
Stanford University

Lei Xu,
The Chinese University of Hong Kong

Gary Yen,
Oklahoma State University

Lotfi Zadeh,
University of California, Berkeley

REVIEW COMMITTEE

Ashraf Abdelbar
Corey Acker
Amit Agarwal
Igor Aleksander
Georgios Anagnostopoulos
Sameer Antani
Amir Assadi
Leemon Baird
David Balya
Eduardo Bayro-Corrochano
Elizabeth Behrman
Brian Blaha
Zvi Boger
Jonathan Boswell
Abdesselam Bouzerdoum
David Brown
Gavin Brown
John Bullinaria
Dan Bullock
Bruce Burton
Xindi Cai
P. Campadelli
Robert Cannon
Gail Carpenter
David Casasent
Gavin Cawley
Antonio Chella
Ke Chen
Lei Cheng
Yiu Ming Cheung
Ratna Babu Chinnam
K.C. Chiu
Tomasz Cholewo
Mo-Yuen Chow
Thomas Cleland
Fernando Corinto
Ernesto Cuadros-Vargas
Alexandre da Silva
Nathaniel Daw
Michael Denham
Chris Diehl
Thomas G. Dietterich
Simona Doboli
Tim Draelos
Rohit Dua
Wlodzislaw Duch
Witali Dunin-Barkowski
R. Eckmiller
Mehmet Onder Efe
Mohamed El-Sharkawi
Malik Elbuluk
Mark J. Embrechts
David L. Enke
Steven Epstein
Peter Erdi
Deniz Erdogmus
Djalma Falcao
Lee Feldkamp
Aaron Flores
Peter Foldesy
Tyler C. Folsom
Kunihiko Fukushima
Cesare Furlanello
John Q. Gan
M. Georgiopoulos
Joydeep Ghosh

Lee Giles
Mark van Gils
Nils Goerke
Alexander Gorban
Anatoli Gorchetchnikov
Poobalan Govender
Stephen Grossberg
Venu Gopal Gudise
Fredric Ham
Barbara Hammer
Thomas Hanselmann
Ron Harley
Michael Hasselmo
Jonathan Hay
Kenneth Hild
James Hornell
Barry Horwitz
Xinwen Hou
Bill Howell
Xiao Hu
De-Shuang Huang
Andreas Ioannides
Richard Ivey
Nathalie Japkowicz
Jae-Byung Jung
Jeevan Kalanithi
Mohamed Kamel
Max Kamenetsky
Nick Karayiannis
Juha Karhunen
Nik Kasabov
Ioannis Kassabalidis
Okyay Kaynak
Laszlo Kek
Paul E. Keller
Randal Koene
B. Kosko
Ivica Kostanic
Robert Kozma
Vladik Kreinovich
David Krout
Naoyuki Kubota
Suwat Kuntanapreeda
Vera Kurkova
Ernst Kussul
Steffen Lange
Ian Lee
Soo-Young Lee
George Lendaris
Dan Levine
William B. "Chip" Levy
Shuhui Li
Ngin-Choo Lim
Chih-Jen Lin
Li-Ju Lin
Derong Liu
Wenxin Liu
Xiuwen Liu
Yong Liu
James T. Lo
Rodney Long
Teresa Bernarda Ludermir
Jinwen Ma
Marco Maggini
Aleksander Malinowski
Marcus Maloof

Tobias Mann
Robert J. J. Marks
Tony R. Martinez
Weber Martins
Francesco Masulli
Marius van der Meer
Martijn Meeter
Eduardo Mercado
Marta Milo
Ali Minai
Sanya Mitaim
Salman Mohagheghi
Carlo Francesco Morabito
Sam Mulder
Yi Lu Murphey
Catherine Myers
Bashan Naidoo
Theoden Netoff
Dagmar Niebur
Ken Norman
Alexander Novokhodko
Andreas Nuernberger
Se-Young Oh
Erkki Oja
Pekka Orponen
Ari Paasio
Alberto Paccanaro
Andrzej Pacut
Kalyani Padma
Francesco Palmieri
Jung-Wook Park
Sungjin Park
Alexander G. Parlos
Mary Pastel
Ashok Patel
W. Pedrycz
Istvan Petras
Nicholas Petrick
Robi Polikar
Massimiliano Pontil
Jose Principe
Danil Prokhorov
Yadunandana Rao
Larry Reeker
Jose Restrepo
Leonardo Reyneri
Gerhard Ritter
Stefano Rovetta
A. Roy
Stuart RubinMichele Rucci
Emad Saad
Ralf Salomon
Brian Scassellati
Gursel Serpen
Raymond Shen
Bertram Shi
Jeong-Yon Shim
Hyunjung Shin
Marcelo Simoes
Patrick K. Simpson
Scott Smith
A. Sperduti
Olaf Sporns
Jim Steck
Johan Suykens
K. Shanti Swarup

Harold Szu	Patrick van der Smagt	Jingyan Xu
Rod Taber	Rao Vemuri	Lei Xu
Roberto Tagliaferri	Ganesh Kumar Venayagamoorthy	Rui Xu
Ranga Tallam		Koichiro Yamauchi
Anya Tascillo	Nikita Visnevski	Simon X. Yang
John G. Taylor	DeLiang Wang	Li Yao
George Thoma	Christopher Waring	Xin Yao
Benjamin Thompson	John Weng	Gary G. Yen
Gergely Timar	Paul Werbos	A. Steven Younger
Georgia Tourassi	Stefan Wermter	Anthony Zaknich
Theodore Trafalis	John White	Nian Zhang
Shiro Usui	Bernard Widrow	Qiang Zhang
Gancho Vachkov	Mingyang Wu	Mingsheng Zhao
Giorgio Valentini	Don Wunsch	Qiangfu Zhao

IEEE NNS President's message

It is a great pleasure to write these lines as the president of the IEEE Neural Networks Society, to welcome you all at the 2003 International Joint Conference on Neural Networks.

As it has been in the past, the field of interest of this conference covers *the theory, design, application and development of biologically and linguistically motivated computational paradigms emphasizing neural networks, including connectionist systems, genetic algorithms, evolutionary programming, fuzzy systems and hybrid intelligent systems in which these paradigms are contained.*

The IEEE Neural Networks Society, has several publications and more conferences that cover these subjects. Our new newsletter along with our three already established Transactions play an important role in the progress and development of our society, by summarizing and publishing exciting new developments in our field. New ideas for emerging technologies might come about from discussions in our already active Technical Committees (TCs), as well as some newly established ones. These committees are formed depending on the need to examine potential new areas that have as a scope the use of Neural Networks, Fuzzy Logic and Evolutionary Computation or in short and inclusive of all, Computational Intelligence. The newsletter will be part of our continuous efforts to increase the IEEE/NNS membership and your participation to our conferences. Throughout my presidency, I will encourage all of you to actively participate in the society activities and issues, express your concerns if any and offer your expertise for further development of our field. Do not hesitate to talk to us about any problems you might see. We need your input in order to make our main conferences better, provide you with more services and products that may serve you better.

I have been involved with this community since its inception in the late 80s. It was then that a few of us interested in biological and artificial neural networks formed a committee, the neural network committee, and precursor of the neural networks council. The purpose of this committee was to promote the interests of those few working in the field and to develop a cohesive plan for its development. A couple of years later, the neural networks council (NNC) was created. Through the constant and untiring efforts of those involved, the NNC was gaining more and more in the leadership and advancement of the field. Finally, last year we became a society. This new society is not by any means the end of the race. It is a new beginning for all of us.

Computational intelligence is the basis of operation of many everyday products. We should not only be aware of their importance but also remind ourselves continuously to inform and remind others what is our field of interest. One step towards that direction is to "educate" the rest of the scientific world by expanding our conferences and the subjects covered. Special sessions, workshops, and symposia on emerging technologies, plenary talks that introduce important findings on various subjects are encouraged. We will be "inclusive" of anybody who can offer something to our society. Welcoming new members from different backgrounds and cultures will not only give us the ability to increase our membership but also to benefit our scientific community. This year will also be a year of promoting women in Computational Intelligence. To this end, we have established a new committee to encourage women to get involved more actively in conferences and other activities of the society.

The NNS is also trying to function as an incubator for emerging technologies that are germane to our field of interest, such as evolutionary multi-objective optimization, particle swarm optimization, data mining and knowledge extraction, neuro-informatics, computational neuroscience, artificial life and artificial immune systems, etc. We have devoted special issues of our transactions to some of these topics, organized special tracks at our conferences, and sponsored specialized symposia, workshops, and satellite conferences and symposia to provide a nurturing environment for these new fields.

We would also like to extend to you an invitation to become a member of the IEEE Neural Networks Society for 2003. Our yearly membership fee of $10.00 for IEEE members or IEEE affiliates will allow you to take full advantage of our high-quality educational product offerings. Next year's membership benefits will include a newsletter, access to all our current and archival electronic publications (for a subscription fee of $15.00), and the opportunity to buy the "computational intelligence package" that contains all three paper transactions (TNN, TEC, TFS) at a bundled price of $50.00 (a $24.00 discount). As a member, you may also have an active participation in the operations of the IEEE Neural Networks Society, by running for an AdCom representative position, nominating candidates, and voting for the candidates. Membership renewal for 2004 will start around September 2003. Become a member, get involved, help your field by assuming an active role today.

I would like to thank the organizers of the 2003 IJCNN for their hard work in making it what we believe will be: a huge success. I would also like to thank you, the participants, and please keep sending your papers and come to our conferences in the years to come. They have become the forra for exchange of ideas, the test beds of emerging technologies that may flourish in the future.

I welcome your comments and suggestions at any time. Enjoy the conference.

Evangelia Micheli-Tzanakou

President, IEEE Neural Networks Society

IEEE Neural Networks Society Officers

President
Evangelia Micheli-Tzanakou
Rutgers University

President-Elect
Jacek M. Zurada
University of Louisville

Past President
Piero Bonissone
General Electric Company

Vice President - Finances
Bogdan (Dan) M. Wilamowski
University of Idaho at Boise

Vice President - Conferences
Marios M. Polycarpou
University of Cincinnati

Vice President - Membership
Vincenzo Piuri
University of Milan

Vice President - Publications
David B. Fogel
Natural Selection, Inc.

Vice President - Technical Activities
Mohamed El-Sharkawi
University of Washington

Secretary
Ann Johnston
SRI International

General Information

Registration Hours

Sunday	July 20, 2003	7:00am	-	6:00pm
Monday	July 21, 2003	7:00am	-	6:00pm
Tuesday	July 22, 2003	7:00am	-	6:00pm
Wednesday	July 23, 2003	7:00am	-	6:00pm
Thursday	July 24, 2003	7:00am	-	4:00pm

Exhibits: Grand Ballroom

Monday,	10:00 am – 6:00 pm
Tuesday,	10:00 am – 6:00 pm
Wednesday,	10:00 am – 6:00 pm

Posters: Grand Ballroom / Poster Hours

Monday,	10:00 am – 10:00 pm
Tuesday	10:00 am – 10:00 pm

Poster Set-up: Monday Posters – 7:00 am – 10:00 am
Tuesday Posters - 7:00 am – 10:00 am

Poster Breakdown: Please do this from **10:00pm-12:00 Midnight** each day.

Speaker Ready Room: Located in Pendleton Room

- Smoking is prohibited at all conference events.

- Your conference badge is your admission to all events and educational sessions.

IJCNN 2003 Meeting Management

Anthony Celenza, Meeting Manager
International Neural Network Society
19 Mantua Road
Mt. Royal, New Jersey 08061
856-423-7222   856-423-3420 (fax)
innsmtg@talley.com

IJCNN EXHIBITOR DIRECTORY 2003

Books and Books Browse Table
P.O. Box 11283
Boulder, CO 80301-003
PH: 303.661.9942
FX: 303.665.8264

Books and Books will provide a combined book display with titles from several different publishers.

The Boeing Company Booth 5
100 North Riverside
Washington, D.C. 60606
312-544-2000
www.boeing.com

The Boeing Company is the world's leading aerospace company, with it's heritage mirroring the history of flight. Boeing Phantom Workds innovators work across the Global Enterprise to create the future of aerospace.

Cardiff University Booth 2
2095 Rattler Ridge Road
Mosler, OR 97040
PH: 541.478.2444
FX: 541.478.2555

The Gamma Test has been called "the holy grail of nonlinear modeling." Among other things, it definitively solves the overtraining problem in neural network building.

Elsevier Booth 1
360 Park Avenue South
New York, NY 10010
PH: 212-633-3758
FX: 212-633-3112
www.elsevier.com

Elsevier is the leading publisher of the scientific and technical books, journals and online products. www.ElsevierComputerScience.com is an online platform offering access to abstracts and full text articles of over 110 leading computer science journals and services. Elsevier is the publisher of Neural Networks; The Official Journal of the International Neural Network Society, European Neural Network Society and Japanese Neural Network Society. Visit our booth for more information or free sample copies.

Microsoft Tablet PC Booth 6
One Microsoft Way
Redmond, WA 98052
425-706-8578
www.tabletpc.com

The evolution of the notebook PC. WindowsXP Professional was extended to support, pen, ink and handwriting recognition on a digitizing screen.

Portland State University Booth 4
DNWCIL: NW Computational Intelligence Laboratory

Display of work accomplished at NW Computational Intelligence Laboratory, with focus on Adaptive Critic control related projects, including neural network, Fuzzy, and evolutionary implementations.

StatSoft Inc.   **Browse Table**
2300 E 14th Street
Tulsa, OK 74104
PH: 918.749.1119
FX: 918.749.2217
www.statsoft.com

StatSoft Inc. is one of the largest developers of enterprise-wide and single-user software for Data Analysis, Data Mining, Quality Control/Six Sigma, and Web-based Analytics worldwide. Statsoft's STATISTICA has received the highest rating in every comparative review of Statistics Software since its first release (1993)- a record unmatched in the industry.

University of Missouri-Rolla   **Booth 3**
131 Emerson Electric Co. Hall
Rolla, MO 65409
PH: 573.341.4521
FX: 573.341.4532
www.ece.umr.edu/-dwunsch

The Applied Computational Intelligence Laboratory (www.ece.umr.edu/acil) at UMR pursues a variety of computational intelligence research projects, especially in the context of reinforcement and unsupervised learning.

Hotel Floor Plans

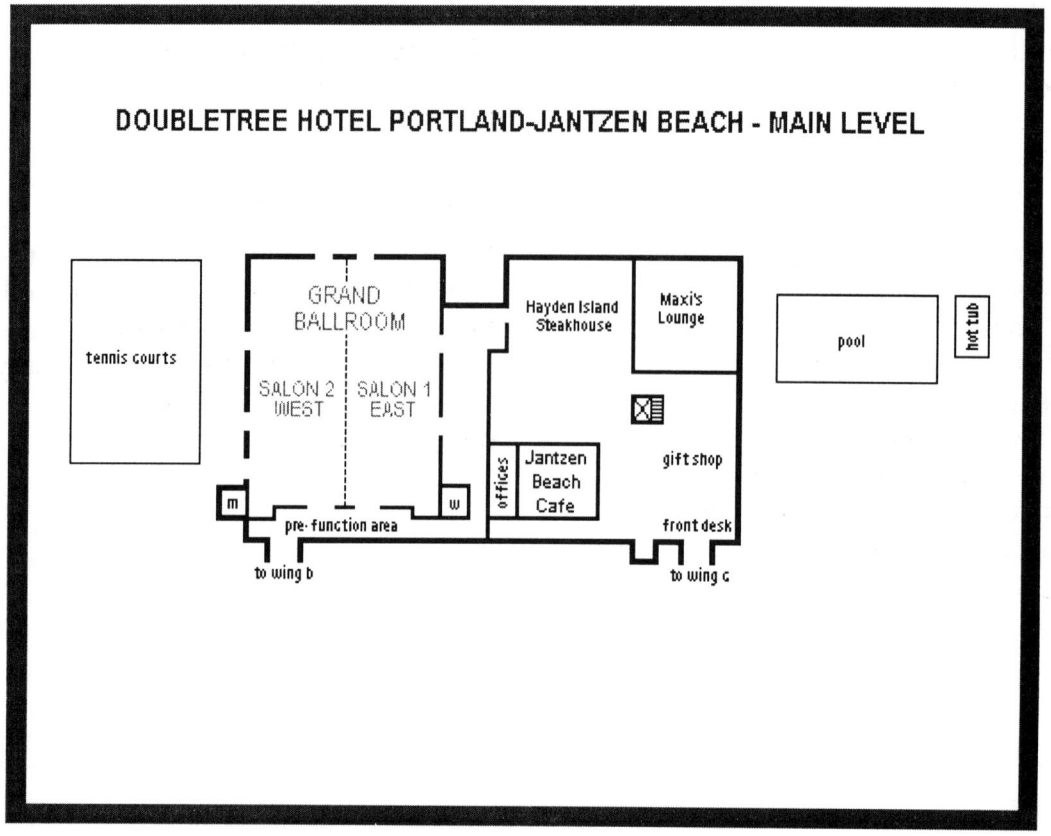

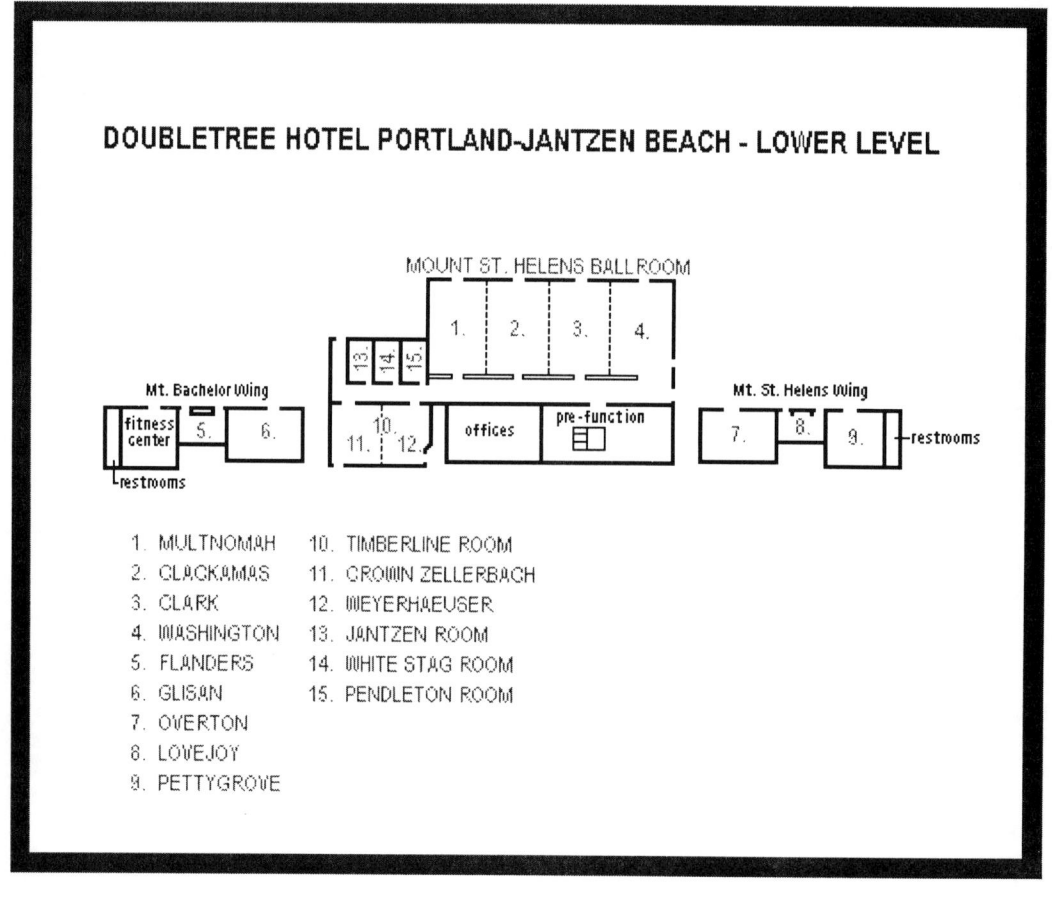

xviii

SCHEDULE AT A GLANCE

Monday, July 21, 8:00AM-9:00AM
Plenary Talk: The prefrontal cortex: Categories, concepts, and executive control, Speaker: Earl K. Miller, Room: Mount Saint Helens Ballroom
Monday, July 21, 9:20AM-12:00PM
Special Session: Visual cortex: How illusions represent reality, Room: Multnomah
Monday, July 21, 9:20AM-10:40AM
Self-organizing maps, Room: Clark
Neurodynamics, Room: Clackamas
Biomedical applications, Room: Washington
Monday, July 21, 10:50AM-12:10PM
Radial basis functions, Room: Clark
Vision and Image Processing, Room: Clackamas
Biomedical Applications, Room: Washington
Monday, July 21, 1:20PM-3:00PM
Special Session: Knowledge Discovery, and Image and Signal Processing in Medicine, Room: Multnomah
Vision and Image Processing, Room: Clark
Learning and Memory, Room: Clackamas
Optimization and Forecasting, Room: Washington
Monday, July 21, 3:20PM-5:20PM
Special Session: Attention and Consciousness in Normal Brains, Room: Multnomah
Fuzzy Neural Systems, Room: Clark
Chaos and Dynamics, Room: Clackamas
Hardware, Room: Washington
Monday, July 21, 7:00PM-10:00PM
Plenary Poster Session: Room: Grand Ballroom
Plenary Poster Session: Neural Networks and Evolutionary Computation, Room: Grand Ballroom
Plenary Poster Session: Probabilistic and IT methods, Mixture Models, RBFs, EM Algorithms and Ensemble Learning, Room: Grand Ballroom
Plenary Poster Session: Biomimetic and biomedical applications, Room: Grand Ballroom
Plenary Poster Session: Auditory and Speech Processing, Room: Grand Ballroom
Plenary Poster Session: SOM and Component Analyses, Dynamics, Room: Grand Ballroom
Plenary Poster Session: Hardware, Room: Grand Ballroom
Plenary Poster Session: Signal Processing, Room: Grand Ballroom
Plenary Poster Session: Telecommunications and Other Applications, Room: Grand Ballroom
Plenary Poster Session: Vision and Image Processing, Room: Grand Ballroom
Tuesday, July 22, 8:00AM-9:00AM
Plenary Talk: Empirical inference problems, Speaker: Vladimir Vapnik, Room: Mount Saint Helens Ballroom
Tuesday, July 22, 9:20AM-10:40AM
Special Session: Applications in Underwater Acoustics, Room: Multnomah
Principal Component Analysis, Room: Clark
Spatial Navigation, Room: Clackamas
Signal Processing and Telecommunications, Room: Washington
Tuesday, July 22, 10:50AM-12:10PM
Special Session: Dynamical Aspects of Information Encoding in Neural Networks, Room: Multnomah
Adaptive resonance theory, Room: Clark
Pattern recognition, Room: Clackamas
Signal Processing and Telecommunications, Room: Washington
Tuesday, July 22, 1:20PM-3:00PM
Special Session: Dynamical Aspects of Information Encoding in Neural Networks, Room: Multnomah
Special Session: Cellular visual microprocessors, Room: Clark
Pattern Recognition, Room: Clackamas

Control, Room: Washington
Tuesday, July 22, 3:20PM-5:40PM
Dynamical Aspects of Information Encoding in Neural Networks, Room: Multnomah
Support vector machines, Room: Clark
Special Session: Discussion Panel: Biologically inspired/motivated computational models, Room: Washington
Tuesday, July 22, 7:00PM-10:00PM
Plenary Poster Session. Room: Grand Ballroom
Plenary Poster Session: Neurodynamics, Learning and Memory, Informatics, Room: Grand Ballroom
Plenary Poster Session: Reinforcement Learning and Control, Room: Grand Ballroom
Plenary Poster Session: Adaptive Resonance Theory and Mathematics of Neural Systems, Room: Grand Ballroom
Plenary Poster Session: Support vector machines, Room: Grand Ballroom
Plenary Poster Session: Power System Applications, Room: Grand Ballroom
Plenary Poster Session: Pattern recognition, Room: Grand Ballroom
Plenary Poster Session: Optimization and Control, Room: Grand Ballroom
Plenary Poster Session: Time Series Analysis and Financial Engineering, Room: Grand Ballroom
Plenary Poster Session: Learning and memory, Room: Grand Ballroom
Plenary Poster Session: Computational Neuroscience, Room: Grand Ballroom
Plenary Poster Session: Cognitive Information Processing, Room: Grand Ballroom
Wednesday, July 23, 8:00AM-9:00AM
Plenary Talk: Neural network models for vision, Speaker: Kunihiko Fukushima, Room: Mount Saint Helens Ballroom
Wednesday, July 23, 9:20AM-10:20AM
Special Session: Patient Care and Clinical Decision Support, Room: Multnomah
Mixture models, EM algorithms and ensemble learning, Room: Clark
Diagnostics and Quality Control, Room: Clackamas
Special Session: Incremental Learning, Room: Washington
Wednesday, July 23, 10:30AM-11:50AM
Special Session: Autonomous Mental Development, Room: Multnomah
Probabilistic and Information-Theoretic Methods, Room: Clark
Auditory Processing, Room: Clackamas
Incremental Learning, Room: Washington
Wednesday, July 23, 1:20PM-3:00PM
Special Session: Autonomous Mental Development, Room: Multnomah
Recurrent Networks, Room: Clark
Spiking Neurons, Room: Clackamas
Time Series Analysis and Financial Engineering, Room: Washington
Wednesday, July 23, 3:20PM-5:00PM
Special Session: Geometric Neurocomputing, Room: Multnomah
Reinforcement Learning and Adaptive Dynamic Programming, Room: Clark
Bioinformatics, Room: Clackamas
Power System Applications, Room: Washington
Wednesday, July 23, 5:00PM-7:00PM
Panel Session: International Research, Room: Multnomah
Wednesday, July 23, 7:00PM-9:00PM
Plenary Talk: Banquet and Award Presentations, Speaker: Donald C. Wunsch II and Michael E. Hasselmo, Room: Riverview Ballroom – Doubletree Hotel – Columbia River
Wednesday, July 23, 9:00PM-10:00PM
Panel Session: Funding resources, Room: Multnomah
Thursday, July 24, 8:00AM-9:00AM
Plenary Talk: On the importance of binding, Speaker: Christoph von der Malsburg, Room: Mount Saint Helens Ballroom
Thursday, July 24, 9:20AM-10:40AM
Special Session: Applications in Aerospace, Room: Multnomah
Recurrent networks, Room: Clark
Learning and memory, Room: Clackamas
Applications, Room: Washington

Thursday, July 24, 10:50AM-12:10PM
Special Session: Bioinformatics, Room: Multnomah
Mathematics of Neural Systems, Room: Clark
Speech Recognition and Production, Room: Clackamas
Robotics, Motor Control and Response, Room: Washington
Thursday, July 24, 1:20PM-3:00PM
Biomimetic applications, Room: Multnomah
Neural Networks and Evolutionary Computation, Room: Clark
Pattern Recognition, Room: Clackamas
Data Mining, Room: Washington
Thursday, July 24, 3:10PM-4:10PM
Plenary Talk: Combinatorial representation of color in visual cortex, Speaker: Terrence Sejnowski, Room: Mount Saint Helens Ballroom

IJCNN 2003 Tutorials
Sunday, July 20

Biomedical Applications:

Multnomah Room

7:45-9:45 a.m.	1.	Prediction of Protein Structures on a Proteomics Scale Using Machine Learning Approaches *Pierre Baldi*
10:00 –12:00 noon	2.	Data Mining and Knowledge Discovery Using Adaptive Neural Networks *Nik Kasabov*
1:00-3:00 p.m.	3.	Neuropercolation: Dynamical Memory Neural Networks - Biological Systems and Computer Implementations *Robert Kozma and Walter J Freeman*
3:15-5:15 pm	4.	A survey of blind source separation techniques applied to clinical data *Martin McKeown*
6:15-8:15 pm	5.	Evolutionary Autonomous Agents: A Novel Neuroscience Research Paradigm *Eytan Ruppin*
8:15-10:15 pm	6.	Attention and Consciousness as Control System Components in the Brain *John G. Taylor*

Engineering Applications:

Clackamas Room

7:45-9:45 a.m.	7.	Linear Attractor Networks for solving linear equations and optimization problems *Evgeny E. Dudnikov*
10:00 –12:00 noon	8.	Learning with multiple machines: ECOC models vs Bayesian Framework *Antonio Eleuteri, Francesco Masulli, Roberto Tagliaferro*

1:00-3:00 p.m.	9.	Fuzzy Logic and Expert Systems: An Introduction with BioMedical Applications *Amie J. O'Brien*
3:15-5:15 pm	10.	AI's Best Bet: The Creativity Machine Paradigm *Stephen Thaler*
6:15-8:15 pm	11.	Processing of audio signal by neural networks *Aurelio Uncini*
8:15-10:15 pm	12.	Neural control systems *Bernard Widrow*

Learning Algorithms:

Clark Room

7:45-9:45 a.m.	14.	Threshold Logic From TTL To Quantum Computing *V. Beiu, J.M. Quintana, M.J. Avedillo*
10:00 –12:00 noon	15.	Information Theoretic Learning *Ken Hild*
1:00-3:00 p.m.	16.	Autonomous Learning: the New Connectionist Algorithms *Asim Roy*
3:15-5:15 pm	17.	Least Squares Support Vector Machines *Johan Suykens*
6:15-8:15 pm	18.	Signal and image denoising using VC learning theory *Vladimir Cherkassky*
8:15-10:15 pm	19.	Dependence Structure Mining, Statistical Approaches, and Bayesian Ying-Yang Learning *Lei Xu*

IJCNN 2003 Sessions and Papers

Volume I

Monday, July 21, 8:00AM-9:00AM

Plenary Talk:
Speaker: Earl K. Miller .... Room: Mount Saint Helens Ballroom

The prefrontal cortex: Categories, concepts, and executive control... 1

Monday, July 21, 9:20AM-12:00PM

Special Session: Visual Cortex: How illusions Represent Reality
Chair: Stephen Grossberg.. Room: Multnomah

Perceptual processes that create objects from fragments 2
  P. J. Kellman

Cortical dynamics of form perception 8
  Stephen Grossberg

Moving in a Fog: stimulus contrast affects the perceived speed and direction of motion 11
  Stuart Anstis

Cortical dynamics of motion integration and segmentation... 16
  Ennio Mingol

Monday, July 21, 9:20AM-10:40AM

Self-organizing Maps
Chair: Erkki Oja .... Room: Clark

Self-organisation of language instruction for robot action control..22
  Mark Elshaw, Stefan Wermter, and Peter Watt

Fusion of structure adaptive self-organizing maps using fuzzy integral 28
  Kyung-Joong Kim and Sung-Bae Cho

A local linear modeling paradigm with a modified counterpropagation network 34
  Jeongho Cho, Jose C. Principe, and Mark A. Motter

Adaptive double self-organizing map and its application in clustering gene expression data.....39
  Habtom Ressom, Dali Wang, and Padma Natarajan

Neurodynamics
Chair: Ali Minai..Room: Clackamas

A new design method for complex-values multistate Hopfield associative memory...................45
  Mehmet Kerem Muezzinoglu, Cuneyt Guzelis, and Jacek M. Zurada

A two-processing element adaptable linear oscillating recurrent system with single-weight plasticity 51
  Michael R. Johnson and Jose C. Principe

Annealed imitation: Fast dynamics for maximum clique 55
   Marcello Pelillo

Dynamic properties of a class of cellular neural networks: Model, stability analysis and
design method 61
   Giuseppe Grassi and Donato Cafagna

Biomedical Applications
Chair: David Brown... Room: Washington

Modeling the relation from motor cortical neuronal firing to hand movements using
competitive linear filters and a MLP...66
   *Sung-Phil Kim, Justin C. Sanchez, Deniz Erdogmus, Yadunandana N. Rao,
   Jose C. Principe, and Miguel Nicolelis*

Artficial neural network based pharmacodynamic population analysis in chronic renal
failure..71
   Adam E. Gaweda, Alfred A. Jacobs, Michael E. Brier, and Jacek M. Zurada

Identifying riskier combinations of risky behavior using a self-organizing map...........................75
   Susan B. Garavaglia

Local features in biomedical image clusters extracted with independent component
analysis..81
   Christoph Bauer, Fabian J. Theis, Wolfgang Baumler, and Elmar W. Lang

Monday, July 21, 10:50AM-12:10PM

Radial Basis Functions
Chair: Lei Xu... Room: Clark

Numerical solution of elliptic partial differential equation by growing radial basis function
neural networks...85
   Jianyu Li, Siwei Luo, Yingjian Qi, and Yaping Huang

Automatic basis selection for RBF networks using Stein's unbiased risk estimator...................91
   Ali Ghodsi and Dale Schuurmans

Cosine radial basis function neural networks...96
   Mary M. Randolph-Gips and Nicolaos B. Karayiannis

A fast incremental learning algorithm of RBF networks with long-term memory......................102
   Keisuke Okamoto, Seiichi Ozawa, and Shigeo Abe

Vision and Image Processing
Chair: Kunihiko Fukushima...Room: Clackamas

Color image segmentation using rival penalization controlled competitive learning 108
   Lap-Tak Law and Yiu-Ming Cheung

Texture discrimination based on neural dynamics of visual perception....................................113
   Vidya Manian and Ramon Vasquez

Face detection using biologically motivated saliency map model 119
   Sang-Woo Ban, Jang-Kyoo Shin, and Minho Lee

An association architecture for the detection of objects with changing topologies 125
   J. Teichert and R. Malaka

Biomedical Applications
Chair: David Brown... Room: Washington

Protecting multimedia authenticity with ICA vaccination of digital bacteria watermarks 131
   Harold H. Szu, S. Noel, S.-B. Yim, J. Willey, and J. Landa

Artificial intelligence approach to determine minimum dose of haemodialysis 137
   Monika Ray and Uvais Qidwai

Neural networks for odor recognition in artificial noses.. 143
   Teresa B. Ludermir and Akio Yamazaki

Principal component analysis for poultry tumor inspection using hyperspectral
fluorescence imaging 149
   John T. Fletcher and Seong G. Kong

Monday, July 21, 1:20PM-3:00PM

Special Session: Knowledge Discovery, and Image and Signal Processing in Medicine
Chairs: F. Carlo Morabito and Sameer Antani.................... Room: Multnomah

Adaptive neural networks control of drug dosage regimens in cancer chemotherapy............. 154
   A. G. Floares, Carmen Floares, M. Cucu, and L. Lazar

Vertebra shape classification using MLP for content-based image retrieval 160
   Sameer Antani, L. Rodney Long, George R. Thoma, and R. Joe Stanley

A Morlet wavelet classification technique for ICA filtered sEMG experimental data 166
   D. Costantino, A. Greco, F. C. Morabito, and M. Versaci

Time-frequency characterization of multi-channel dynamic semg recordings by neural
networks 172
   B. Azzerboni, G. Finocchio, M. Ipsale, F. La Foresta, and F. C. Morabito

Knowledge discovery in support of early diagnosis of hepatocellular carcinoma 177
   F. Ciocchetta, R. Dell'Anna, F. Demichelis, A. Dhillon, A. P. Dhillon, A. Godfrey,
   A. Quaglia, and A. Sboner

Vision and Image Processing
Chair: Kunihiko Fukushima... Room: Clark

On intrinsic generalization of low dimensional representations of images for recognition 182
   Xiuwen Liu, Anuj Srivastava, and DeLiang Wang

Effects of temporal frequency on speed discrimination and perceived speed 188
   Haoming Shen, Yoshifumi Shimodaira, and Gosuke Ohashi

CBP neural network for objective assessment of image quality.. 194
   Paolo Gastaldo, Rodolfo Zunino, Elena Vicario, and Ingrid Heynderickx

Intensity-invariant color image segmentation using MPC algorithm 200
   Slawo Wesolkowski, and M. Jernigan

Detecting salient contours using orientation energy distribution 206
   Hyeon-Cheol Lee and Yoonsuck Choe

Learning and Memory
Chairs: Michael E. Hasselmo and Daniel S. Levine .... Room: Clackamas

Computational modeling of human performance in a sequence learning experiment 212
   Rainer Spiegel and I. P. L. McLaren

Presynaptic modulation as fast synaptic switching: State-dependent modulation of task performance..218
   Gabriele Scheler and Johann Schumann

Using temporal binding for connectionist recruitment learning over delayed lines 224
   Cengiz Gunay and Anthony S. Maida

Universal computation by networks of model cortical columns 230
   Patrick Simen, Thad Polk, Rick Lewis, and Eric Freedman

Binary autoassociative morphological memories derived from the kernel method and the dual kernel method...236
   Peter Sussner

Optimization and Forecasting
Chair: Danil V. Prokhorov .... Room: Washington

On sparsity-exploiting memory-efficient trust-region regularized nonlinear least squares algorithms for neural-network learning 242
   Eiji Mizutani and James W. Demmel

A comparison of dual heuristic programming (DHP) and neural network based stochastic optimization approach on collective robotic search problem...248
   Nian Zhang and Donald C. Wunsch II

A study of non-periodic short-term random walk forecasting based on RBFNN, ARMA, or SVR-GM(1,1,tau) approach..254
   Bao Rong Chang

Forecasting stock index increments using neural networks with trust region methods.............260
   Paul Kang Hoh Phua, Xiaotian Zhu, and Chung-Haur Koh

Decentralized algorithms for sensor registration...266
   Valentino Crespi and George Cybenko

Monday, July 21, 3:20PM-5:20PM

Special Session: Attention and Consciousness in Normal Brains
Chairs: Andreas A. Ioannides and John G. Taylor............. Room: Multnomah

Modeling orbitofrontal involvement in decision making on a gambling task 272
   Daniel S. Levine, Britain Mills, Steven Estrada, Carson Clanton, and Stephen Denton

Consciousness and its correlates in awake condition, in different sleep stages and in epilepsy...276
   P. B. C. Fenwick, G. K. Kostopoulos, L. C. Liu, and A. A. Ioannides

Early striate activity related to attention in a choice reaction task 282
    V. Poghosyan, T. Shibata, P. B. C. Fenwick, L. C. Liu, and A. A. Ioannides

Testing models of attention with MEG 287
    A. A. Ioannides and J. G. Taylor

The CODAM model of attention and consciousness 292
    J. G. Taylor

Simulations of attention control models in sensory and motor paradigms 298
    J. G. Taylor and N. Fragopanagos

Fuzzy Neural Systems
Chairs: Bart Kosko and Lotfi Zadeh .... **Room: Clark**

Multi-objective optimal control of batch processes using recurrent neuro-fuzzy networks 304
    Jie Zhang

Stability analysis of fuzzy robot control without fuzzy rule base 310
    Josip Kasac, Branko Novakovic, Dubravko Majetic, and Danko Brezak

Enhancing multi-neural systems through the use of hybrid structures 316
    Anne Canuto, Michael Fairhurst, and Gareth Howells

A hierarchical neuro-fuzzy system based on s-implications 321
    Robert Nowicki, Rafal Scherer, and Leszek Rutkowski

A fuzzy autoassociative morphological memory 326
    Peter Sussner

Chaos and Dynamics
Chairs: DeLiang Wang and Robert Kozma .... **Room: Clackamas**

Simulation of the Freeman model of the olfactory cortex: A quantitative performance
analysis for the DSP approach 332
    Mustafa C. Ozturk, Jose C. Principe, Bryan A. Davis, and Deniz Erdogmus

Clustering in coupled maps on small-world networks 337
    Rogério de Oliveira and Luiz H. A. Monteiro

Coherent oscillations as a neural code in a model of the olfactory system 341
    A. Gutierrez-Galvez and R. Gutierrez-Osuna

A dynamic neural network method for time series prediction using the KIII model 347
    Haizhon Li and Robert Kozma

Neural networks with chaotic recursive nodes: Design of associative memories,
performance analysis, and contrast with traditional Hopfield architectures 353
    Emilio Del Moral Hernandez

Trajectory tracking via adaptive recurrent neural control with input saturation 359
    Edgar N. Sanchez and Luis J. Ricalde

Hardware
Chair: Fred Ham .... **Room: Washington**

Possible nanoelectronic implementation of neuromorphic networks 365
    Ozgur Turel, Ibrahim Muckra, and Konstantin Likharev

The design of a bionic sensory chip based on the CNN model derived from the mammalian retina 371
Wen-Chia Yang, Li-Ju Lin, and Chung-Yu Wu

An analog VLSI system for computing depth from motion parallax 376
Sirisha S. Karri and Albert H. Titus

Predicting protein cellular localization sites with a hardware analog neural network 381
S. G. Hohmann, J. Schemmel, F. Schurmann, and K. Meier

An analog silicon retina with multi-chip configuration 387
Seiji Kameda and Tetsuya Yagi

The H1 neural network trigger 393
Christian Kiesling

Monday, July 21, 7:00PM-10:00PM (Posters on display all day 10 a.m. to 10 p.m.)

Plenary Poster Session: Neural Networks and Evolutionary Computation
Room: Grand Ballroom

Extension neural network 399
M. H. Wang and Chin-Pao Hung

Determination of tea quality by using a neural network based electronic nose 404
Ritaban Dutta, J. W. Gardner, K. R. Kashwan, and M. Bhuyan

Global optimization for fast multilayer perceptron training 410
Jaewook Lee

Evolutionary optimization of radial basis function networks for intrusion detection 415
Alexander Hofmann and Bernhard Sick

Quantitative feature evaluation using hybrid neural network and fuzzy logic approach 421
Hao Jiang and Xin Feng

A genetically optimized ensemble of s-FLNMAP neural classifiers based on non-parametric probability distributions functions 426
Vassilis G. Kaburlasos, S. E. Papadakis, and S. Kazarlis

A genetic learning of functional link network 432
C. Bhumireddy and C. L. Philip Chen

Evolutionary computation for parameter optimisation of evolving connectionist systems for on-line prediction of time series with changing dynamics 438
Nikola Kasabov, Qun Song, and Ikuko Nishikawa

Finding optimal neural network basis function subsets using the Schmidt procedure 444
Francisco J. Maldonado, Michael T. Manry, and Tae-Hoon Kim

A multi-core learning algorithm for Boolean neural networks 450
Di Wang and Narendra S. Chaudhari

Solving the puzzle problem using Hopfield neural network in conjunction with tree search algorithm 456
Javid Taheri

Implementing evolutionary self-organizing maps with the genetic operations of graph evolution theory 462
Maiga Chang and Jia-Sheng Heh

Evolving digtal circuits using particle swarm 468
V. G. Gudise and Ganesh K. Venayagamoorthy

Representation and training of vector graphics with NRAAM networks 473
Mark Schaefer and Werner Dilger

Evolution and adaptation of neural networks 478
Paulito P. Palmes, Taichi Hayasaka, and Shiro Usui

Discriminative training of Bayesian Chow-Liu multinet classifiers 484
Kaizhu Huang, Irwin King, and Michael R. Lyu

Fault tolerance of feedforward artificial neural networks - A framework of study 489
Pravin Chandra and Yogesh Singh

Plenary Poster Session: Probabilistic and IT Methods, Mixture Models, RBFs, EM Algorithms and Ensemble Learning
Room: Grand Ballroom

Multioutput feedforward neural network selection: A Bayesian approach 495
Jean-Pierre Vila and Vivien Rossi

Threshold-based dynamic annealing for multi-thread DAEM and its extreme 501
Masaharu Takada and Ryohei Nakano

True risk bounds for the regression of real-valued functions 507
Rhee Man Kil and Imhoi Koo

A divide-and-conquer based radial basis function network with application to recurrent function modelling 513
Rongbo Huang, Yiu-Ming Cheung, and Lap-Tak Law

Handling class overlap with variance-controlled neural networks 517
Ralf Kretzschmar, Nicolaos B. Karayiannis, and Fritz Eggimann

Clustering using Renyi's entropy 523
Robert Jenssen, Kenneth E. Hild II, Deniz Erdogmus, Jose C. Principe, and Torbjorn Eltoft

Faithful feature extraction by greedy network-growing algorithm 529
Ryotaro Kamimura, and Osamu Uchida

How hierarchies of objects and constraints reduce complexity 535
Blaga N. Iordanova

A unified view of probabilistic PCA and regularized linear fuzzy clustering 541
Yoshio Mori, Katsuhiro Honda, Akihiro Kanda, and Hidetomo Ichihashi

Ensemble neural network methods for satellite-derived estimation of chlorophyll a 547
Wayne H. Slade Jr., Richard L. Miller, Habtom Ressom, and Padma Natarajan

An ensemble of classifiers approach for the missing feature problem 553
Stefan Krause and Robi Polikar

A dual-phase technique for pruning constructive networks 559
J. P. Thivierge, F. Rivest, and T. R. Shultz

How many neighbors to consider in pattern pre-selection for support vector classifiers?..........565
   Hyunjung Shin and Sungzoon Cho

Modular adaptive RBF-type neural networks for letter recognition..571
   Gao Daqi, Lin Chengyin, and Li Changwu

A novel vector quantizer for pattern classification tasks...577
   V. Shiv Naga Prasad, B. Yegnanarayana, and S. Guruprasad

Plenary Poster Session: Biomimetic and Biomedical Applications
Room: Grand Ballroom

The use of artificial neural networks to diagnose mastitis in dairy cattle 582
   M. Lopez-Benavides, S. Samarasinghe, and J. G. H. Hickford

Artificial neural networks for diagnosis of hepatitis disease 586
   Lale Ozyilmaz and Tulay Yildirim

Neural network-based estimation of light attenuation coefficient 590
   Siva Srirangam, Habtom Ressom, Padma Natarajan, Mohamad T. Musavi,
   Robert W. Virnstein, Lori J. Morris, and Wendy Tweedale

Improved Bayesian MRI reconstruction involving neural priors based on a regularization
approach 596
   D. A. Karras, B. G. Mertzios, D. Graveron-Demilly, and D. van Ormondt

Topographic independent component analysis for fMRI signal detection 601
   Anke Meyer-Baese, Dorothee Auer, and Axel Wismueller

Comparison and hybridization of neural networks and fuzzy logic in biomedical
applications 606
   Amy J. O'Brien

An intelligent system for detection of nematodes in digital images 612
   Carlos A. Silva, Kaiser M. C. Magalhaes, and Adriao Duarte Doria Neto

Classifying hemodynamics of MR brain perfusion images using independent component
analysis (ICA)..616
   Yu-Te Wu, Yi-Hsuan Kao, Wan-Yuo Guo, Tzu-Chen Yeh, Jen-Chuen Hsieh, and
   Michael Mu Huo Teng

Raman spectra calibration, extraction and neural network based training for sample
identification 622
   Zhengmao Ye, Prasad Manda, and Gregory Auner

Systolic blood pressure classification 627
   Sukru Colak and Can Isik

Application of biomimetics intelligence for smart sensor surveillance system in legacy
powerline network 631
   Pornchai Chanyagorn, Harold H. Szu, and Ivica Kopriva

Discrete feature weighting and selection algorithm...636
   Norbert Jankowski

Estimation of cutting torque in drilling system based on flexible neural network 642
   Myeonghee Kim, Nobutomo Matsunaga, and Shigeyasu Kawaji

Neural networks in comparing USN and Wageningen b-series marine propellers 648
    C. Neocleous and Chr. Schizas

Bayesian regularized neural network for multiple gene expression pattern classification.........654
    Arpad Kelemen and Yulan Liang

Quo vadis neurocomputing? Neural computation at the edge to new perspectives 660
    Nils Goerke

Plenary Poster Session: Auditory and Speech Processing
Room: Grand Ballroom

Using dynamic synapse based neural networks with wavelet preprocessing for speech
applications 666
    Sageev George, Alireza A. Dibazar, Vishal Desai, and Theodore W. Berger

High performance arabic digits recognizer using neural networks 670
    Yousef A. Alotaibi

Speech segmentation using probabilistic phonetic feature hierarchy and support vector
machines...675
    Amit Juneja and Carol Espy-Wilson

An entropy based robust speech boundary detection algorithm for realistic noisy
environments 680
    Kim Weaver, Khurram Waheed, and Fathi M. Salem

Combining evidence from multiple modular networks for recognition of consonant-vowel
units of speech..686
    Suryakanth V. Gangashetty, K. Sreenivasa Rao, A. Nayeemulla Khan,
    C. Chandra Sekhar, and B. Yegnanarayana

AANN models for speaker recognition based on difference cepstrals....................................692
    S. Guruprasad, N. Dhananjaya, and B. Yegnanarayana

Phoneme transcription based om sampa for Norwegian 698
    Terje Kristensen, Bernd Treeck, and Ronny Falck-Olsen

Plenary Poster Session: SOM and Component Analyses
Room: Grand Ballroom

Genetic algorithm applied to ICA feature selection 704
    Yaping Huang, and Siwei Lou

Amplitude and permutation indeterminacies in frequency domain convolved ICA 708
    Angelo Ciaramella and Roberto Tagliaferri

Parallel structured independent component analysis for SIMO-model-based blind
separation and deconvolution of convolutive speech mixture 714
    Hiroshi Saruwatari, Hiroaki Yamajo, Tomoya Takatani, Tsuyoki Nishikawa, and Kiyohiro
    Shikano

Adaptive and heuristic approaches for nonlinear source separation.......................................720
    F. Rojas, M. R. Alvarez, M. Salmeron, Carlos G. Puntonet, and Ruben Martin-Clemente

Neural net with two hidden layers for non-linear blind source separation 726
    Ruben Martin-Clemente, S. Hornillo-Mellado, Jose I. Acha, and Carlos G. Puntonet

Robust local principal component analyzer with fuzzy clustering ... 732
  Katsuhiro Honda, Nobukazu Sugiura, and Hidetomo Ichihashi

Stability analysis of blind signals separation algorithms ... 738
  Tianping Chen and Wenlian Lu

Integrated learning of linear representations ... 742
  Xiuwen Liu and Anuj Srivastava

Cauchy machine for blind inversion in linear space-variant imaging ... 747
  Harold H. Szu and Ivica Kopriva

Hierarchical and dynamic SOM applied to image compression ... 753
  Jose Marinho Barbalho Jose Alfredo, F. Costa, A. Duarte D. Neto, and
  Marcio L. A. Netto

Simplified nonlinear principal component analysis ... 759
  Beiwei Lu and William W. Hsieh

Identification of dynamical systems using GMM with VQ initialization ... 764
  Jing Lan, Jose C. Principe, and Mark A. Motter

PCA and ICA neural implementations for source separation - A comparative study ... 769
  Radu Mutihac and Marc M. Van Hulle

Algebraic independent component analysis: An approach for separation of overcomplete
speech mixtures ... 775
  Khurram Waheed and Fathi M. Salem

The self-organization by lateral inhibition model: Validation of clustering ... 781
  Bin Tang, Malcolm I. Heywood, and Michael Shepherd

A simple learning algorithm for growing self-organizing maps and its application to the
skeletonization ... 787
  Hiroki Sasamura and Toshimichi Saito

The graded possibilistic clustering model ... 791
  Francesco Masulli and Stefano Rovetta

An accurate and fast neural method for PCA extraction ... 797
  J. B. O. Souza Filho, L. P. Caloba, and J. M. Seixas

Support vector visualization and clustering using self-organizing map and support vector
one-class classification ... 803
  Sitao Wu and Tommy W. S. Chow

Modeling CMOS gate charachteristics using independent component analysis ... 809
  Thaddeus T. Shannon, David Abercrombie, and James McNames

Sunspot number prediction by a conditional distribution discrimination tree ... 814
  Marc C. Girod Genet and Alain G. Petrowski

Exploiting PCA classifiers to speaker recognition ... 820
  Wanfeng Zhang, Yingchun Yang, and Zhaohui Wu

Volume 2

Plenary Poster Session: Dynamics
Room: Grand Ballroom

A hybrid dynamical system as an automaton on the fractal set 825
   Jun Nishikawa and Kazutoshi Gohara

Phase transitions in a probabilistic cellular neural network model having local and remote connections 831
   Marko Puljic and Robert Kozma

Function complexity estimation and its application to the optimum tie of geophysical data using ANNs 836
   Zhengping Liu

Chaotic associative recalls for fixed point attractor patterns 841
   Liang Zhao, Juan C. G. Caceres, and Harold H. Szu

Improved chaotic associative memory using distributed patterns for image retrieval 846
   Yuko Osana

Incremental learning by VSF network and its chaotic effects 852
   Yoshitsugu Kakemoto and Shinichi Nakasuka

Convergence analysis of chaotic dynamic neuron 858
   Sang-Hee Kim

A chaotic neural network for reducing the peak-to-average power ratio of multicarrier modulation 864
   Masaya Ohta and Katsumi Yamashita

Diagnostic monitoring of internal combustion engines by use of independent component analysis and neural networks 869
   J. P. Barnard and C. Aldrich

Yet another "optimal" neural representation for combinatorial optimization 873
   Satoshi Matsuda

A neural network model for general minimax problem 879
   Zheng Yong-Ling, Ma Long-hua, and Qian Ji-Xin

A synthesis procedure for associative memories using cellular neural networks with space-invariant cloning template library 885
   Takeshi Kamio and Mititada Morisue

A winner-take-all circuit based on second order Hopfield neural networks as building blocks 891
   P. Tymoshchuk and E. Kaszkurewicz

Relaxing in a warped space: An effect due to the cooperation of static and dynamical neurons 897
   Kazuyoshi Tsutsumi

New results on exponential periodicity of delayed neural networks 902
   Changyin Sun, Derong Liu, and Chun-Bo Feng

Relating bayesian learning to training in recurrent networks 908
  Rainer Spiegel

Adaptive parallel identification of dynamical systems by adaptive recurrent neural
networks 914
  James T. Lo and Devasis Bassu

Implicit de-noising in hybrid recurrent nets for meta knowledge abduction 919
  David Al-Dabass, David Evans, and Siva Sivayoganathan

Two–cell cellular neural networks: Generation of new hyperchaotic multiscroll attractors 924
  Donato Cafagna and Giuseppe Grassi

Feedforward dynamic neural network technique for modeling and design of nonlinear
telecommunication circuits and systems 930
  Jianjun Xu, Mustapha C. E. Yagoub, Runtao Ding, and Q. J. Zhang

Plenary Poster Session: Hardware
Room: Grand Ballroom

Toward an analog VLSI implementation of adaptive resonance theory (ART2) 936
  Senthil Kumar Ganapathy and Albert H. Titus

Integrated pulse neuron circuit for asynchronous pulse neural networks 942
  Takuya Taniguchi, Yoshihiko Horio, and Kazuyuki Aihara

Architecture research and hardware implementation on simplified neural computing
system for face identification 948
  Xu Jian, Li Weijun, Qu Yanfeng, Qin Hong, and Wang Shoujue

Hardware design of CMAC neural network for control applications 953
  Chan-Mo Kim, Kwang-Ho Choi, and Yong B. Cho

A model-selection approach to the VLSI design of vector quantizers 959
  Massimiliano Bracco, Sandro Ridella, and Rodolfo Zunino

Silicon approximation to biological neuron 965
  Vladimir A. Gorelik

A VLSI implementation of mixed-signal mode bipolar neuron circuitry 971
  Dong Pan and Bogdan M. Wilamowski

A VLSI hamming artificial neural network with k-winner-take-all and k-looser-take-all
capability 977
  Stephane Badel, Alexandre Schmid, and Yusuf Leblebici

An analog neural oscillator circuit for locomotion control in quadruped walking robot 983
  Kazuki Nakada, Tetsuya Asai, and Yoshihito Amemiya

A survey of perceptron circuit complexity results 989
  Valeriu Beiu

Platform performance comparison of PALM network on Pentium 4 and FPGA 995
  Changjian Gao, and Dan Hammerstrom

Neural network for LIDAR detection of fish 1001
  V. Mitra, C. Wang, and G. Edwards

Plenary Poster Session: Signal Processing, Telecommunications and Other Applications
Room: Grand Ballroom

Suppression of maternal ECG from fetal ECG using neuro fuzzy logic technique 1007
   C. Kezi Selva Vijila, S. Renganathan, and Stanley Johnson

Eggplant classification using artificial neural network 1013
   Yasuo Saito, Toshiharu Hatanaka, Katsuji Uosaki, and Kazuhide Shigeto

Monitoring seagrass health using neural networks 1019
   Habtom Ressom, Suzanne K. Fyfe, Padma Natarajan, and Siva Srirangam

A strategy for an efficient training of radial basis function networks for classification
applications 1025
   Oliver Buchtala, Peter Neumann, and Bernhard Sick

Image proessing techniques and neural network models for predicing of plant nitrate using
aerial images 1031
   Ramesh K. Gautam and Suranjan Panigrahi

Failure analysis of transmission devices using self-organizing map 1037
   Bingchen Wang, Sigeru Omatu, and Toshiro Abe

Application of neural network on LTCC fine line screen printing process 1043
   Kuo-Chuang Chiu

Effect of regularization term upon fault tolerant training 1048
   Haruhiko Takase, Hidehiko Kita, and Terumine Hayashi

The application of neural network soft sensor technology to an advanced control system
of distillation operation 1054
   C. M. Bo, J. Li, S. Zhang, C. Y. Sun, and Y. R. Wang

Explaining how a multi-layer perceptron predicts helicopter airframe load spectra from
continuously valued flight parameter data 1059
   M. L. Vaughn and J. G. Franks

Artiificial nueral networks methods applied to conductometric microhotplate data for the
identification of the type and relative concentration of chemical warfare agents 1065
   Zvi Boger, D. C. Meier, R.E. Cavicchi, and S. Semancik

Multi-scale high-speed network traffic prediction using combination of neural networks 1071
   Alireza Khotanzad and Nayera Sadek

Neural network based benchmarks in the quality assessment of message digest
algorithms for digital signatures based secure internet communications 1076
   D. A. Karras and V. Zorkadis

Single-trial analysis of post-movement MEG beta synchronization using independent
component analysis (ICA) 1081
   *P. L. Lee, Y. T. Wu, L. F. Chen, S. S. Chen, Tzu-Chen Yeh, L. T. Ho, and
   Jen-Chuen Hsieh*

A hybrid HMM-neural network with gradient descent parameter training 1086
   Jaime Salazar, Marc Robinson, and Mahmood R. Azimi-Sadjadi

A learning algorithm with adaptive exponential stepsize for blind source separation of convolutive mixtures with reverberations 1092
Kenji Nakayama, Akihiro Hirano, and Akihide Horita

Finding the ordered roots of arbitrary polynomials using constrained partitioning neural networks 1098
De-Shuang Huang, H. S. Horace, C. K. Law Ken, and H. S. Wong

Improved multiuser detectors employing genetic algorithms in a space-time block coding system 1104
Yinggang Du and K. T. Chan

A music retrieval system based on the extraction of non-trivial recurrent themes and neural classification 1110
Barbara Colaiocco and Francesco Piazza

Support vector machines for multi-class signal classification with unbalanced samples 1116
Peng Xu and Andrew K. Chan

Inheritance of information in multi-layer sigma-pi neural networks 1120
R. S. Neville

Piecewise-linear modeling of analog circuits using trained feed-forward neural networks and adaptive clustering of hidden neurons 1126
Simona Doboli, Gaurav Gothoskar, and Alex Doboli

Interpretation of geophysical surveys of archaeological sites using artificial neural networks 1132
David J. Bescoby, Gavin C. Cawley, and P. Neil Chroston

Solving quadratic programming problems with linear Hopfield networks 1138
Evgeny Dudnikov

Model selection for k-nearest neighbors regression using VC bounds 1143
Vladimir Cherkassky, Yunqian Ma, and Jun Tang

Binary image coding using cellular neural networks 1149
Dirk Feiden and Ronald Tetzlaff

Accoustic recurrent neural networks echo cancellers 1153
Pedro H. G. Coelho and Luiz Biondi Neto

Identification of a typical CD player arm using a two-layer perceptron neural network model 1157
S. V. Dudul and A. A. Ghatol

Rectilinear floorplanning of FPGAs using Kohonen map 1163
Morteza Saheb Zamani and Masoud Soleimani

RLS lattice algorithm using gradient based variable forgetting factor 1168
C. F. So, S. C. Ng, and S. H. Leung

On the transformation mechanisms of multilayer perceptrons with sigmoid activation functions for classifications 1173
Gao Daqi, Zhu Haijun, and Nie Guiping

Plenary Poster Session: Vision and Image Processing
Room: Grand Ballroom

Pulse coupled neural network for motion detection 1179
    Bo Yu and Liming Zhang

High performance associative memory with distance based training algorithm for character recognition 1185
    Ming-Jung Seow and Vijayan K. Asari

Simulation of the visual cortex with laterally connected spiking neural networks 1189
    Jianguo Xin and Mark J. Embrechts

License plate location based on a dynamic PCNN scheme 1195
    Mario I. Chacon M. and Alejandro Zimmerman S.

Automated tracking and classification of infrared images 1201
    J. S. Shaik and Khan M. Iftekharuddin

A method for selective color images compression 1207
    Diego de Miranda Gomes, Wedson T. de Almeida Filho, and Adriao Duarte Doria Neto

Real-time image transmission on the TCP/IP network using wavelet transform and neural network 1213
    Jeong Ha Kim, Hyoung Bae Kim, and Boo Hee Nam

Image edge detection using adaptive morphology Meyer wavelet-CNN 1219
    Young-Hyun Baek, Oh-Sung Byun, and Sung-Rung Moon

The effects of training algorithms in MLP network on image classification 1223
    Nihan Coskun and Tulay Yildirim

A design of the object detection system using the RGA 1227
    Seiki Yoshimori, Yasue Mitsukura, Minoru Fukumi, and Norio Akamatsu

Exploitation of sparse properties of support vector machines in image compression 1232
    Jonathan Robinson and Vojislav Kecman

Unsupervised clustering of texture features using SOM and fourier transform 1237
    Brijesh Verma, Vallipuram Muthukkumarasamy, and Changming He

Edge-preserving nonlinear image restoration using adaptive components-based radial basis function neural networks 1243
    Dianhui Wang, Alex Talevski, and Tharam S. Dillon

Retina encoder tuning and data encryption for learning retina implants 1249
    Oliver Baruth, Rolf Eckmiller, and Dirk Neumann

Face detection and emotional extraction system using double structure neural networks 1253
    Yasue Mitsukura, Hironri Takimoto, Minoru Fukumi, and Norio Akamatsu

A reliable method for recognition of paper currency by approach to local PCA 1258
    Ali Ahmadi, Sigeru Omatu, and Toshihisa Kosaka

Spectral histogram based face detection 1263
    Christopher Waring and Xiuwen Liu

Scaling, rotation, and translation invariant image recognition using competing multiple subspaces 1268
    Noriji Kato, Hitoshi Ikeda, Hirotsugu Kashimura, and Masaaki Shimizu

Firing correlations improve detection of moving bars 1274
Garrett Kenyon, Bartlett Moore, Janelle Jeffs, James Theiler, Bryan Travis, and David Marshak

Location of coffee beans using Hopfield-type neural network 1280
David R. Arellano-Baez, Edgar N. Sanchez, and Flavio A. Prieto-Ortiz

Comments on using MLP and FFT for fast object/face detection 1284
Hazem Mokhtar El-Bakry

Tuesday, July 22, 8:00AM-9:00AM

Plenary Talk
Speaker: Vladimir Vapnik .... Room: Mount Saint Helens Ballroom

Empirical inference problems 1289

Tuesday, July 22, 9:20AM-10:40AM

Special Session: Applications in Underwater Acoustics
Chairs: Warren Fox and Mohamed A. El-Sharkawi .... Room: Multnomah

Orthogonal transformation of output principal components for improved tolerance to error ... 1290
T. P. Mann, C. Eggen, Warren L. J. Fox, D. Krout, G. Anderson, M. A. El Sharkawi, and Robert J. Marks II

Initial species discrimination experiments with riverine salmonids 1295
Jae-Byung Jung, James H. Jacobs, George A. Dowding, and Patrick K. Simpson

Inversion of neural network underwater acoustic model for estimation of bottom parameters using modified particle swarm optimizers 1301
Benjamin B. Thompson, Robert J. Marks II, Mohamed A. El-Sharkawi, Warren L. J. Fox, and Robert T. Miyamoto

Broadband sonar target classification: Pool experiments 1307
Jae-Byung Jung, James H. Jacobs, Gerald F. Denny, and Patrick K. Simpson

Principal Component Analysis
Chair: Erkki Oja .... Room: Clark

A canonical coordinate decomposition network 1313
Ali Pezeshki, Mahmood R. Azimi-Sadjadi, and Louis L. Scharf

SOMICA: An application of self-organizing maps to geometric independent component analysis 1318
Fabian J. Theis, Carlos G. Puntonet, and Elmar W. Lang

Sparse linear representations for recognition 1324
Lei Cheng and Xiuwen Liu

Spatial Navigation
Chair: Michael E. Hasselmo .... Room: Clackamas

Goal-directed spatial navigation of the rat depends on phases of theta oscillation in hippocampal circuitry 1328
Randal A. Koene, Robert C. Cannon, and Michael E. Hasselmo

Building and using a hierarchical representation of space 1334
   Horatiu Voicu

Reinforcement learning for hierarchical and modular neural network in autonomous robot navigation..1340
   Rodrigo Calvo and Mauricio Figueiredo

Reinforcement learning in associative memory 1346
   Shaojuan Zhu and Dan Hammerstrom

Signal Processing and Telecommunications
Chair: Bernard Widrow .... Room: Washington

A recursive neural network model for processing directed acyclic graphs with labeled edges..1351
   Marco Gori, Marco Maggini, and Lorenzo Sarti

A hierarchical Bayesian learning scheme for autoregressive neural networks.......................1356
   Fausto Acernese, Fabrizio Barone, Rosario De Rosa, Antonio Eleuteri, Leopoldo Milano, and Roberto Tagliaferri

Real-time surface meshing through HRBF networks..1361
   N. A. Borghese, S. Ferrari, and V. Piuri

Improving pseudorandom bit sequence generation and evaluation for secure internet communications using neural network techniques..1367
   D. A. Karras and V. Zorkadis

Tuesday, July 22, 10:50AM-12:10PM

Special Session: Dynamical Aspects of Information Encoding in Neural Networks (part 1)
Chairs: Robert Kozma, Ali Minai, and DeLiang Wang .... Room: Multnomah

A neurobiological theory of meaning in perception 1373
   Walter J. Freeman

The role of temporal coding in the processing of relational information in the mind-brain 1379
   Lokendra Shastri

Understanding neural computation in terms of pattern languages..1385
   Peter Andras

On a pulse-coupled network of spiking neurons having quantized state................................1391
   Hiroyuki Torikai and Toshimichi Saito

Adaptive resonance Theory
Chair: Gail Carpenter .... Room: Clark

Default ARTMAP...1396
   Gail A. Carpenter

Evaluating quality of text clustering with ART1 1402
   Louis Massey

Using adaptive resonance theory and local optimization to divide and conquer large scale traveling salesman problems 1408
Samuel Mulder and Donald C. Wunsch II

Snap-drift: Real-time, performance-guided learning 1412
Sin Wee Lee, Dominic Palmer-Brown, Jonathan Tepper, and Christopher Roadknight

Bidirectional ARTMAP: An artificial mirror neuron system 1417
Martin V. Butz and Sylvian Ray

Pattern Recognition
Chair: David Casasent .... Room: Clackamas

Confidence-clustering supervised radial basis function neural networks 1423
David Casasent and Xue-wen Chen

A generalized feedforward neural network classifier..1429
Ganesh Arulampalam and Abdesselam Bouzerdoum

Transductive confidence machine for active learning 1435
Shen-Shyang Ho and Harry Wechsler

Associative memories for handwritten pattern recognition..1441
Francisco J. Lopez-Aligue, Isabel Acevedo-Sotoca, Carlos Garcia-Orellana, and Horacio Gonzalez-Velasco

Signal Processing and Telecommunications
Chair: Bernard Widrow .... Room: Washington

Error whitening criterion for linear filter estimation...1447
Yadunandana N. Rao, Deniz Erdogmus, and Jose C. Principe

Blind dereverberation of speech signals using independence transform matrix....................1453
Jong-Hwan Lee and Soo-Young Lee

Employing adaptive functions and maximum entropy principle for nonlinear blind source deconvolution...1458
E. Corinti, V. Amadio, G. Tummarello, and Francesco Piazza

An adaptive sub-space filter model 1464
Anthony Zaknich

Tuesday, July 22, 1:20PM-3:00PM

Special Session: Dynamical Aspects of Information Encoding in Neural Networks (part 2)
Chairs: Robert Kozma, Ali Minai, and DeLiang Wang .... Room: Multnomah

Some dynamics arising from learning in a hippocampal model 1469
William B. Levy

Theta theory: Requirements for encoding events and task rules explain theta phase relationships in hippocampus and neocortex...1470
Michael E. Hasselmo

Learning spatial navigation using chaotic neural network model 1476
Robert Kozma and Prashant Ankaraju

Processing of analogy in the thalamocortical circuit 1480
  Yoonsuck Choe

Special Session: Cellular Visual Microprocessors
Chairs: Csaba Rekeczky and Tamas Roska .... **Room: Clark**

Design and synthesis methods for cellular neural networks 1486
  Marco Gilli, Fernando Corinto, and Pierpaolo Civalleri

Feature guided visual attention with topographic array processing and neural network-based classification 1492
  G. Timar, D. Balya, I. Szatmari, and Cs. Rekeczky

A new structure of large-neighborhood cellular nonlinear network (LN-CNN) 1497
  Chiu-Hung Cheng, Sheng-Hao Chen, Li-Ju Lin, Kuan-Hsun Huang, and Chung-Yu Wu

High speed cellular array computer realizations for low power applications 1502
  Mika Laiho, Asko Kananen, Ari Paasio, and Kari Halonen

Cortically-inspired visual processing with a four layer cellular neural network 1506
  Bertram E. Shi

Pattern Recognition
Chair: David Casasent .... **Room: Clackamas**

RBF-based real-time hierarchical intrusion detection systems 1512
  Ju Jiang, Chunlin Zhang, and Mohamed Kamel

Centroid stability with k-means fast learning artificial neural networks 1517
  Wong Lai Ping and Alex Tay Leng Phuan

Refine decision boundaries of a statistical ensemble by active learning 1523
  Dingsheng Luo and Ke Chen

Invariant feature representation by sparse vectors using adaptive subspace self-organizing maps 1529
  Thomas Zheng

Control
Chair: Gary Yen .... **Room: Washington**

Neuro emission controller for minimizing cyclic dispersion in spark ignition engines 1535
  Pingan He

Mathematical underpinning of adaptive capability of recurrent neural networks with fixed weights 1541
  James T. Lo

A design of model driven cascade PID controllers using a neural network 1547
  Kenji Takao, Toru Yamamoto, and Takao Hinamoto

Adaptive series-parallel identification of dynamical systems with uncertain bifurcations and chaos 1553
  James T. Lo, Feng Li, and Devasis Bassu

Intelligent control of non-linear plants using Type-2 fuzzy logic and neural networks 1558
  Patricia Melin and Oscar Castillo

Tuesday, July 22, 3:20PM-5:40PM

Dynamical Aspects of Information Encoding in Neural Networks (part 3)
Chairs: Robert Kozma, Ali Minai, and DeLiang Wang .... Room: Multnomah

Dynamic cortical cooperation related to visual perception 1563
  R. Eckhorn, A. Gail, A. Bruns, and B. Al-Shaikhli

A dynamical model for multi-scale pixel clustering 1569
  Liang Zhao, Antonio P. G. Damiance Jr., Rogerio A. Furukawa, and
  Andre C. P. L. F. Carvalho

Monaural speech segregation and oscillatory correlation 1574
  DeLiang Wang

Recurrent timing nets for auditory scene analysis 1575
  Peter Cariani

Discussion: Support Vector Machines
Chair: Ke Chen .... Room: Clark

Multiple model classification using SVM-based approach 1581
  Yunqian Ma and Vladimir Cherkassky

Training support vector machines: A quantum-computing perspective 1587
  Davide Anguita, Sandro Ridella, Fabio Rivieccio, and Rodolfo Zunino

Training support vector machines with particle swarms 1593
  U. Paquet and A. P. Engelbrecht

Fuzzy least squares support vector machines 1599
  Daisuke Tsujinishi and Shigeo Abe

Reordering adaptive directed acyclic graphs: An improved algorithm for multiclass support
vector machines 1605
  Thimaporn Phetkaew, Boonserm Kijsirikul, and Wanchai Rivepiboon

Support vector machines for class representation and discrimination 1611
  Chao Yuan and David Casasent

Using support vector machines in optimization for black-box objective functions 1617
  Hirotaka Nakayama, Masao Arakawa, and Koji Washino

Special Session: Discussion Panel: Biologically Inspired/Motivated Computational Models
Chair: Mitra Basu, Room: Washington

Discussion on Biologically Motivated Computational Models 1623
  Organizer: Mitra Basu.
  Panelists: Jon Timmis, Dipankar Dasgupta, Daniel D. Lee, Guang R. Gao,
  Kwabena A. Boahen

Volume 3

Tuesday, July 22, 7:00PM-10:00PM (Posters on display all day 10 a.m. to 10 p.m.)

Plenary Poster Session: Neurodynamics, Learning and Memory
Room: Grand Ballroom

Synaptic modification of interneuron afferents in a hippocampal CA3 model prevents activity oscillations 1625
  David W. Sullivan and William B. Levy

Defining time in a minimal hippocampal CA3 model by matching time-span of associative synaptic modification and input pattern duration 1631
  Kurt E. Mitman, Patryk A. Laurent, and William B. Levy

Timing of consecutive traveling pulses in a model of entorhinal cortex 1637
  Anatoli Gorchetchnikov and Michael E. Hasselmo

Latent attractor selection for variable length episodic context stimuli with distractors 1643
  Simona Doboli and Ali A. Minai

Consecutive face recognition by association cortex - entorhinal cortex - hippocampal formation model 1649
  K. Nakamura, J. Nitta, H. Takano, and M. Yamazaki

T-maze training of a recurrent CA3 model reveals the necessity of novelty-based modulation of LTP in hippocampal region CA3 1655
  J. D. Monaco and William B. Levy

Plenary Poster Session: Informatics
Room: Grand Ballroom

The importance of stop word removal on recall values in text categorization 1661
  Catarina Silva and Bernardete Ribeiro

Training and holistic computation of vector graphics with Hebbian bases in contrast to RAAM networks 1667
  Mark Schaefer and Werner Dilger

Fault detection system in gas lift well based on artificial immune system 1673
  Mariana Araujo, Jose Aguilar, and Hugo Aponte

An investigation into the source of power for AIRS, an artificial immune classification system 1678
  Donald Goodman, Lois Boggess, and Andrew Watkins

Self-organizing neural networks for efficient clustering of gene expression data 1684
  Ji He, Ah-Hwee Tan, and Chew-Lim Tan

Membership scoring via independent feature subspace analysis for grouping co-expressed genes 1690
  Hyejin Kim, Seungjin Choi, and Sung-Yang Bang

Probabilistic neural networks for multi-class tissue discrimination with gene expression data 1696
  Rui Xu and Donald C. Wunsch II

Genetic search for optimal ensemble of feature-classifier pairs in DNA gene expression pfofiles 1702
    Chanho Park and Sung-Bae Cho

Paired neural network with negatively correlated features for cancer classification in DNA gene expression profiles 1708
    Hong-Hee Won and Sung-Bae Cho

Probabilistic neural network classification for microarray data..1714
    Barbara Comes and Arpad Kelemen

Classification of eukaryotic and prokaryotic cells by a backpropagation network...................1718
    Terje Kristensen and Ruben Patel

Integrated gene expression analysis of multiple microarray data sets based on a normalization technique and on adaptive connectionist model 1724
    Liang Goh and Nikola Kasabov

Robust regression under asymmetric or/and non-constant variance error by simultaneously training conditional quantiles...1729
    Ichiro Takeuchi, Noriyuki Yamanaka, and Takeshi Furuhashi

Coloring black boxes: Visualization of neural network decisions 1735
    Wlodzislaw Duch

Time series novelty detection using one class support vector machines 1741
    Junshui Ma and Simon Perkins

Data mining for building neural protein sequence classification systems with improved performance...1746
    Dianhui Wang, Nung Kion Lee, and Tharam S. Dillon

Interval arithmetic inversion: A new rule extraction algorithm 1752
    Carlos Hernandez-Espinosa, Mercedes Fernandez-Redondo, and Mamen Ortiz-Gomez

Relevance feedback with active learning for document retrieval..1757
    Takashi Onoda, Hiroshi Murata, and Seiji Yamada

A SOM projection technique with the growing structure for visualizing high-dimensional data..1763
    Zheng Wu and Gary G. Yen

Naive Bayesian classifier for microarray data...1769
    Arpad Kelemen, Hong Zhou, Pamela Lawhead, and Yulan Liang

Efficient realization of classification using modified Haar DWT..1774
    Rory Mulvaney and Dhananjay S. Phatak

Predicting intrusions with local linear models 1780
    PingZhao Hu and Malcolm I. Heywood

A comparison of SOM based document categorization systems 1786
    Xiao Luo and A. Nur Zincir-Heywood

Neural networks for web page classification based on augmented PCA 1792
    Ali Selamat and Sigeru Omatu

Neural networks mine for gold at the greyhound racetrack..1798
    Ulf Johansson and Cecilia Sonstrod

Learning classifier systems for data mining: A comparison of XCS with other classifiers for the forest cover data set 1802
    A. J. Bagnall and Gavin C. Cawley

On the capability of an SOM based intrusion detection system 1808
    H. Gunes Kayacik, A. Nur Zincir-Heywood, and Malcolm I. Heywood

Mineral potential mapping using feed-forward neural networks 1814
    Andrew Skabar

Intrusion detection using radial basis function network on sequences of system calls 1820
    Arvind Rapaka, Alexander Novokhodko, and Donald C. Wunsch II

Application of the method of elastic maps in analysis of genetic texts 1826
    A. N. Gorban, A. Yu. Zinovyev, and Donald C. Wunsch II

Towards a tactile communication system with dialog-based tuning 1832
    Carsten Wilks, Thomas Schieder, and Rolf Eckmiller

Unsupervised similarity-based feature selection using heuristic Hopfield neural networks 1838
    S. Y. M. Shi and P. N. Suganthan

Bagged ensembles of support vector machines for gene expression data analysis 1844
    Giorgio Valentini, Marco Muselli, and Francesca Ruffino

Improved fuzzy lattice neurocomputing (FLN) for semantic neural computing 1850
    Vassilis G. Kaburlasos

A cascade form blind source separation connecting source separation and linearization for nonlinear mixtures 1856
    Kenji Nakayama, Akihiro Hirano, and Takayuki Nishiwaki

Natural gradient based blind multi user detection in QPSK DS-CDMA systems 1862
    Khurram Waheed, Keyur Desai, and Fathi M. Salem

Plenary Poster Session: Reinforcement Learning and Control
Room: Grand Ballroom

The further discussions on constrained learning algorithms 1868
    De-Shuang Huang

Acceleration of Levenberg-Marquardt training of neural networks with variable decay rate ... 1873
    Tai-Cong Chen, Da-jian Han, Francis T. K. Au, and L. G. Tham

Adaptive critic designs and their implementations on different neural network architectures . 1879
    Jung-Wook Park, Ganesh K. Venayagamoorthy, and Ronald G. Harley

Combination of on-line clustering and q-value based genetic reinforcement learning for fuzzy network design 1885
    Chia-Feng Juang, and Chun-Feng Lu

Approximate dynamic programming based optimal neurocontrol synthesis of a chemical reactor process using proper orthogonal decomposition 1891
    Radhakant Padhi and S. N. Balakrishnan

A performance comparison of TRACA - An incremental on-line learning algorithm 1897
    Matthew W. Mitchell

Fast convergence for back-propagation network with magnified gradient function 1903
    S. C. Ng, C. C. Cheung, S. H. Leung, and Andrew Luk

Competitive reinforcement learning in continuous control tasks 1909
   Myriam Abramson, Peter Pachowicz, and Harry Wechsler

A neural cascade architecture for document retrieval 1915
   Abdelhamid Bouchachia and Roland Mittermeir

A wavelet-based neuro-fuzzy system and its applications 1921
   Cheng-Jian Lin, Cheng-Chung Chun, and Cheng-Ling Lee

Feature extraction for neural-fuzzy inference system 1927
   Chai Quek, Geok See Ng, and Abdul Wahab

A PID neural network controller 1933
   Yu Yongquan, Huang Ying, and Zeng Bi

Modular fuzzy hyperline segment neural network 1939
   P. M. Patil, U. V. Kulkarni, and T. R. Sontakke

Multivariate time series model discovery with similarity-based neuro-fuzzy networks and
genetic algorithms 1945
   Julio J. Valdes and Alan J. Barton

Adaptive fuzzy-neural control for uncertain time-delayed systems 1951
   Wen-Shyong Yu

Three improved fuzzy lattice neurocomputing (FLN) classifiers 1957
   Al Cripps, N. Nguyen, and Vassilis G. Kaburlasos

Parameter sensitivities of a neuro-based adaptive controller with guaranteed stability 1963
   M. B. Menhaj and Swakshar Ray

Plenary Poster Session: Adaptive Resonance Theory and Mathematics of Neural Systems
Room: Grand Ballroom

A comparative study of the category choice of the fuzzy art with the L-1 norm 1969
   Issam Dagher

Fuzzy ARTMAP with relevance factor 1975
   Razvan Andonie, Lucian Sasu, and Valeriu Beiu

From categorical semantics to neural network design 1981
   Michael J. Healy, Thomas P. Caudell, and Yunhai Xiao

Universal approximation with fuzzy ART and fuzzy ARTMAP 1987
   Stephen J. Verzi, Gregory L. Heileman, Michael Georgiopoulos, and Georgios C. Anagnostopoulos

Perceptron learning in the domain of graphs 1993
   Brijnesh J. Jain and Fritz Wysotzki

A novel approach for training small-sized multi-layer perceptrons 1999
   Deepak P. Chermakani

Accurate initialization of neural network weights by backpropagation of the desired
response 2005
   Deniz Erdogmus, Oscar Fontenla-Romero, Jose C. Principe, Amparo Alonso-Betanzos, Enrique Castillo, and Robert Jenssen

New learning factor and testing methods for conjugate gradient training algorithm 2011
  Tae-Hoon Kim, Michael T. Manry, and Javier F. Maldonado

On variable sizes and sigmoid activation functions of multilayer perceptrons 2017
  Gao Daqi, Liu Hua, and Li Changwu

Improve neural network training using redundant structure 2023
  Yingjie Yang, Chris Hinde, and David Gillingwater

An efficient learning algorithm with second-order convergence for multilayer neural networks 2028
  Hiroshi Ninomiya, Chikahiro Tomita, and Hideki Asai

A novel min-max feature value based neural architecture and learning algorithm for classification of microcalcifications 2033
  Brijesh Verma, Rinku Panchal, and Kuldeep Kumar

Plenary Poster Session: Support Vector Machines
Room: Grand Ballroom

Robust optimization in support vector machine training with bounded errors 2039
  Theodore B. Trafalis and Samir A. Alwazzi

A kernel fuzzy classifier with ellipsoidal regions 2043
  Kenichi Kaieda and Shigeo Abe

A role of total margin in support vector machines 2049
  Min Yoon, Yeboon Yun, and Hirotaka Nakayama

Comparison of L1 and L2 support vector machines 2054
  Yoshiaki Koshiba and Shigeo Abe

Fast linear stationary methods for automatically biased support vector machines 2060
  D. Lai, M. Palaniswami, and N. Mani

Identification of chaotic process systems with least squares support vector machines ..2066
  G. T. Jemwa and C. Aldrich

SVM learning with fixed-point math 2072
  Davide Anguita, Andrea Boni, and Sandro Ridella

Optimizing support vector regression hyperparameters based on cross-validation 2077
  Kentaro Ito and Ryohei Nakano

Design of support vector machine by adaptive aggregation 2083
  Oscar Chacon, Igor Litvintchev, Ada Alvarez, and Ernesto Vazquez

SMO algorithm for least squares SVM 2088
  S. Sathiya Keerthi and Shirish K. Shevade

Plenary Poster Session: Power System Applications
Room: Grand Ballroom

Power system security evaluation using ANN: Feature selection using divergence 2094
  K. R. Niazi, C. M. Arora, and S. L. Surana

Evaluation of cosine radial basis function neural networks on electric power load forecasting 2100
  Nicolaos B. Karayiannis, Mahesh Balasubramanian, and Heidar A. Malki

Direct torque control of induction motors by use of the GMR neural network................2106
   G. Cirrincione, M. Cirrincione, C. Lu, and M. Pucci

Neuro-Hybrid genetic algorithm based economic dispatch for utility system................2112
   N. Kumarappan and M. R. Mohan

Self-organizing neural-based fuzzy controller for transient stability of multimachine power systems using flywheel battery................2118
   M. H. Wang and Chin-Pao Hung

Neural systems for solving the inverse problem about recovering the primary signal waveform in potential transformers 2124
   Nikola Kasabov, Gancho Venkov, and Stefan Minchev

Plenary Poster Session: Pattern Recognition
Room: Grand Ballroom

Recognition system for EMG signals by using non-negative matrix factorization................2130
   Yuuki Yazama, Yasue Mitsukura, Minoru Fukumi, and Norio Akamatsu

Human head detection using multi-modal object features 2134
   Yun Luo, Yi Lu Murphey, and Farid Khairallah

Local voting networks for human face recognition................2140
   Metin Artiklar, Xiaoyan Mu, Mohamad H. Hassoun, and Paul Watta

Application of four-layer neural network on information extraction................2146
   Min Han, Lei Cheng, and Hua Meng

Submodular neural network is better than modular neural network and support vector machines for personal verification 2152
   Takashi Nagano, Makoto Hirahara, and Hideo Eguchi

A new class of convolutional neural networks (SICoNNets) and their application to face detection 2157
   F. H. C. Tivive and Abdesselam Bouzerdoum

Permutative coding technique for handwritten digit recognition system................2163
   E. Kussul and T. Baidyk

3D face recognition by profile and surface matching 2169
   Gang Pan, Yijun Wu, Zhaohui Wu, and Wenyao Liu

Various decomposition methods applied to face recognition 2175
   Jaepil Ko, Eunju Kim, and Hyeran Byun

Feature selection forcing overtraining may help to improve performance................2181
   Enrique Romero, Josep M. Sopena, Gorka Navarrete, and René Alquézar

Pattern recognition device using scalar vector graphics 2187
   Rex Sandwith

A novel electromyography (EMG) based classification approach for arabic handwriting........2193
   Azzedine Lansari, Faouzi Bouslama, Mohammed Khasawneh, and Akram Al-Rawi

An adaptive sparse distributed memory 2197
   Jose Aguilar

Modular neural networks for solving high complexity problems 2202
   Hazem Mokhtar El-Bakry

Human face recognition based on radial basis probabilistic neural network 2208
  Lin Guo and De-Shuang Huang

Classification of the italian liras using the LVQ method 2212
  Sigeru Omatu, Toshihisa Kosaka, and Masaru Teranisi

A method of biomimetic pattern recognition for face recognition 2216
  Wang Zhi-hai, Mo Hua-Yi, Lu Hua-Xiang, and Wang Shou-Jue

Neural interpolator for image recognition in the process of microdevice assembly 2222
  O. Makeyev

A neuro-fuzzy graphic object classifier with modified distance measure estimator 2227
  R. A. Aliev, B. G. Guirimov, and R. R. Aliev

Combinative neural-network-based classifiers for optical handwritten character and letter
recognition 2232
  Gao Daqi, Xie Chao, and Nie Guiping

Document clustering using hierarchical SOMART neural network 2238
  M. F. Hussin and Mohamed Kamel

Facial expression recognition combined with robust face detection in a convolutional
neural network 2243
  Masakazu Matsugu, Katsuhiko Mori, Yusuke Mitarai, and Yuji Kaneda

Hierarchical learning of optimal linear representations 2247
  Qiang Zhang and Xiuwen Liu

GA-SVM wrapper approach for feature subset selection in keystroke dynamics identity
verification 2253
  Enzhe Yu and Sungzoon Cho

Biomimetic (topological) pattern recognition: A new model of pattern recognition theory
and its application 2258
  Wang Shou-jue Chen Xu

A feature extraction of the EEG during listening to the music using the factor analysis and
neural networks 2263
  Shin-ichi Ito, Yasue Mitsukura, Minoru Fukumi, and Norio Akamatsu

Gene expression data analysis using support vector machines 2268
  Feng Chu and Lipo Wang

Robust recognition based on adaptive combination of weak classifiers 2272
  Guoping Wang, Misha Pavel, and Xubo Song

Optimizing radial basis probabilistic neural networks using recursive orthogonal least
squares algorithms combined with micro-genetic algorithms 2277
  Wenbo Zhao, De-Shuang Huang, and Lin Guo

Using artificial neural networks to identify headings in newspaper documents 2283
  Wei Zhange and Timothy L. Andersen

"Freecell" neural network heuristics 2288
  Alphonsus Dunphy and Malcolm I. Heywood

Layered neural network training with model switching and hidden layer feature
regularization 2294
  Keisuke Kameyama and Kei Taga

Multi class support vector machine implementation to intrusion detection 2300
   Tarun Ambwani

On the efficiency of orthogonal least squares reduced probabilistic neural networks for
aircraft-flare discrimination 2306
   Gilles Labonte

A multivalent logic approach to risk estimation of learning machines 2312
   Bojan Novak

Toward a modular connectionist model of local chlorophyll concentration from satellite
images 2317
   E. Trentin, L. Magnoni, and A. Andronico

Improved defect detection using support vector machines and wavelet feature extraction
based on vector quantization and SVD techniques 2322
   D. A. Karras

Three heuristics for receptive field optimization for ensemble encoding 2328
   Ashraf M. Abdelbar, Deena O. Hassan, Gene A. Tagliarini, and Sridhar Narayan

Plenary Poster Session: Optimization and Control
Room: Grand Ballroom

A general projection neural network for solving optimization and related problems 2334
   Youshen Xia and Jun Wang

Extended simulated annealing for augmented TSP and multisalesmen TSP 2340
   Chi-Hwa Song, Kyunghee Lee, and Won Don Lee

Support vector machines and the electoral college 2344
   Alexander Malyscheff and Theodore B. Trafalis

Mixed analog/digital system for quadratic assignment problems 2349
   *Yukihiro Kobayashi, Takehiko Koyama, Satoshi Matsui, Yoshihiko Horio, and
   Kazuyuki Aihara*

Distribution approximation, combinatorial optimization, and Lagrange-barrier 2354
   Lei Xu

Synthesis of a k-winners-take-all neural network using linear programming with bounded
variables 2360
   L. V. Ferreira, E. Kaszkurewicz, and A. Bhaya

Regularization and feedforward artificial neural network training with noise 2366
   Pravin Chandra and Yogesh Singh

Hybrid adaptive fuzzy control wing rock motion system with H8 robust performance 2372
   Chin-Teng Lin, Tsu-Tian Lee, Chun-Fei Hsu, and Chih-Min Lin

Parameter plane analysis of neurocontrol vehicle systems for limit cycle prediction 2378
   Bing-Fei Wu, Jau-Woei Perng, and Tsu-Tian Lee

Parameter sensitivities of a neuro-based adaptive controller with guaranteed stability 2382
   M. B. Menhaj and Swakshar Ray

Maximum entropy utility equilibrium of mobile agents with aggregated statistical
behaviours 2388
   Alexandru Murgu

Robust tracking control of uncertain nonlinear systems with an input time delay 2394
   Chiang-Cheng Chiang and Tzu-Ching Tung

Development of autonomous flight control system for unmanned helicopter by use of neural networks...2400
   Hiroaki Nakanishi and Koichi Inoue

Constructive neural network in model-based control of a biotechnological process...............2406
   L. A. C. Meleiro, R. Maciel Filho, and F. J. Von Zuben

Lyapunov stability analysis of the quantization error for DCS neural networks 2412
   Sampath Yerramalla, Edgar Fuller, and Bojan Cukic

An in-vehicle virtual driving assistant using neural nets..2418
   Anya Tascillo and Ronald Miller

Transition between position-matching control and rhythm-matching control in hand tracking task is explained by a phase model for hand motion..2424
   Fumihiko Ishida, Yoshiki Kuramoto, and Yasuji Sawada

Applying guided evolutionary simulated annealing to cost-based abduction..........................2428
   Ashraf M. Abdelbar and Heba Amer

Volume 4

Plenary Poster Session: Time Series Analysis and Financial Engineering
Room: Grand Ballroom

Radial basis network approach for non linear filtering in discrete time...................................2433
   Vivien Rossi and Jean-Pierre Vila

Stock market prediction using neural networks: Does trading volume help in short-term prediction? 2438
   Xiaohua Wang, Paul Kang Hoh Phua, and Weidong Lin

An adaptive detection of anomalies in user's behavior 2443
   Artem M. Sokolov

Neural networks and Cao's method: A novel approach for air pollutants time series forecasting 2448
   S. Marra, F. C. Morabito, and M. Versaci

Time series identifying and modeling with neural networks 2454
   Dayong Gao, Y. Kinouchi, K. Ito, and Xueli Zhao

Prediction of white noise time series using artificial neural networks and asymmetric cost functions 2460
   Sven F. Crone

Autonomous diagnostics and prognostics through competitive learning driven HMM-based clustering..2466
   Ratna Babu Chinnam and Pundarikaksha Baruah

Improving data based nonlinear process modelling through Bayesian combination of multiple neural networks...2472
   Zainal Ahmad and Jie Zhang

Robust short term prediction using combination of linear regression and modified probabilistic neural network model 2478
Tony Jan

Fast and efficient second-order training of the dynamic neural network paradigm 2482
Christian Gruber and Bernhard Sick

Apply decision tree and support vector regression to predict the gold price 2488
Pedrudee Ongsritrakul and Nuanwan Soonthornphisaj

Neural smoothing transition coefficients for nonlinear processes in mean and variance 2493
Maria Luiza F. Velloso, Marley M. B. R. Vellasco, Marco Aurelio P. Cavalcante, and Cristiano Fernandes

Adaptive vs. accommodative neural networks for adaptive system identification: Part II 2497
James T. Lo and Devasis Bassu

Plenary Poster Session: Learning and Memory
Room: Grand Ballroom

A neural network for the typicality effects 2502
Makoto Hirahara and Takashi Nagano

Detecting rare events with lotto-type competitive learning 2506
Andrew Luk and Sandra Lien

Growing neural network for aqcuisition of 2-layer structure 2512
Ryusuke Kurino, Masanori Sugisaka, and Katsunari Shibata

Associative memory using ratio rule for multi-valued pattern association 2518
Ming-Jung Seow and Vijayan K. Asari

Learning-possibility of neuron model can recognize depth-rotation in three-dimension space 2523
Qianyi Wang, Yasuhiro Sekiya, and Hirosato Nomura

Generalized associative memory models for data fusion 2528
Teddy N. Yap Jr. and Arnulfo P. Azcarraga

Noise supplement learning algorithm for associative memories using multilayer perceptrons and sparsely interconnected neural networks 2534
Yusuke Magori, Takeshi Kamio, Hisato Fujisaka, and Mititada Morisue

A study on on-line learning of Nntrees 2540
Takeda Takaharu, Qiangfu Zhao, and Yong Liu

Solving parity–n problems with feedforward neural networks 2546
Bogdan M. Wilamowski, David Hunter, and Aleksander Malinowski

An RCE-based associative memory with application to human face recognition 2552
Xiaoyan Mu, Mehmet Artiklar, Mohamad H. Hassoun, and Paul Watta

Plenary Poster Session: Computational Neuroscience
Room: Grand Ballroom

Supervised synaptic weight adaptation for a spiking neuron 2558
Bryan A. Davis, Deniz Erdogmus, Yadunandana N. Rao, and Jose C. Principe

Different inhibitory effects by dopaminergic modulation and global suppression of activity....2563
Takuji Hayashi, Osamu Araki, and Tohru Ikeguchi

Synchronization phenomena of a mutually pulse-coupled network of integrate-and-fire circuits..2569
Masanao Shimazaki, Hiroyuki Torikai, and Toshimichi Saito

A neural network model for chemotaxis in Caenorhabditis Elegans 2574
N. A. Dunn, J. S. Conery, and S. R. Lockery

Associative memories with "killed" neurons: The methods of recovery................................2579
A. M. Reznik, A. S. Sitchov, O. K. Dekhtyarenko, and D. W. Nowicki

Incremental learning in dynamic environments using neural network with long-term memory..2583
Kenji Tsumori and Seiichi Ozawa

Plenary Poster Session: Cognitive Information Processing
Room: Grand Ballroom

Quantum generation of neural networks..2589
Hugo de Garis, Ravichandra Sriram, and Zijun Zhang

Emotion recognition and acoustic analysis from speech signal 2594
Chang-Hyun Park and Kwee-Bo Sim

Phrase detection and the associative memory neural network 2599
Richard C. Murphy

Working of the brain and rationality in economic behavior...2604
Kazuo Nshimura and Yoshikazu Tobinaga

Systemic intelligence: Methods for growing up artefacts that live 2609
Nils Goerke

A self-organizing neural structure for concept formation from incomplete observation 2615
Noriyasu Homma and Madan M. Gupta

Hidden representation after reinforcement learning of hand reaching movement with variable link length 2619
Katsunari Shibata and Koji Ito

Wednesday, July 23, 8:00AM-9:00AM

Plenary Talk
Speaker: Kunihiko Fukushima .... Room: Mount Saint Helens Ballroom

Neural network models for vision 2625

Wednesday, July 23, 9:20AM-10:20AM

Special Session: Patient Care and Clinical Decision Support
Chair: Jim DeLeo and Roberto Tagliaferri......................... Room: Multnomah

Survival analysis and neural networks..2631
Antonio Eleuteri, Roberto Tagliaferri, Leopoldo Milano, S. De Placido, and M. De Laurentiis, Gennaro Sansome, and Diego D. Agostino

Application of probabilistic neural networks to population pharmacokinetics 2637
   E. Berno, L. Brambilla, R. Canaparo, F. Casale, M. Costa, C. Della Pepa, M. Eandi, and E. Pasero

Finding patient cluster attributes using auto-associative ANN modeling 2643
   Zvi Boger

Mixture models, EM Algorithms and Ensemble Learning
Chair: Lei Xu .... **Room: Clark**

Data-smoothing regularization, normalization regularization, and competition-penalty mechanism for statistical learning and multi-agents 2649
   Lei Xu

A comparison of ensemble methods for multilayer feedforward networks 2655
   Carlos Hernandez-Espinosa, Mercedes Fernandez-Redondo, and Mamen Ortiz-Gomez

MMI-based training for a probabilistic neural network 2661
   Nan Bu, Toshio Tsuji, and Osamu Fukuda

Diagnostics and Quality Control
Chair: F. Carlo Morabito .... **Room: Clackamas**

Intelligent strain sensing on a smart composite wing using extrinsic Fabry-Perot interferometric sensors and neural networks 2667
   Rohit Dua, Vicki Eller, Kakkattukuzhy M. Isaac, Steve E. Watkins, and Donald C. Wunsch II

A novel approach to fault classification using sparse sets of exemplars 2673
   Erik M. Laxdal and Nikitas J. Dimopoulos

Case base reasoning in vehicle fault diagnostics 2679
   Ziyan Wen, Jacob Crossman, John Cardillo, and Yi Lu Murphey

Special Session: Incremental Learning   Chair: Robi Polikar, Room: Washington

SVM incremental learning, adaptation and optimization 2685
   Christopher P. Diehl and Gert Cauwenberghs

Formal models of incremental learning and their analysis 2691
   Steffen Lange and Sandra Zilles

Competitive learning mechanisms for scalable, incremental and balanced clustering of streaming texts 2697
   Arindam Banerjee and Joydeep Ghosh

Wednesday, July 23, 10:30AM-11:50AM

Special Session: Autonomous Mental Development (part 1)
Chairs: John Weng and Olaf Sporns .... **Room: Multnomah**

Early integration of vision and manipulation 2703
   Giorgio Metta and Paul Fitzpatrick

Investigating models of social development with a humanoid robot 2704
   Brian Scassellati

Developing early senses about the world: "object permanence" and visuoauditory real-time learning 2710
Juyang Weng, Yilu Zhang, and Yi Chen

Automatic language acquisition by an autonomous robot 2716
Stephen Levinson, Weiyu Zhu, Danfeng Li, Kevin Squire, Ruei-sung Lin, Matthew Kleffner, Matthew McClain, and Johnny Lee

Probabilistic and Information-Theoretic Methods
Chair: Lei Xu .... Room: Clark

Evaluation of neural and entropy-constrained routing of communication networks 2722
Nicolaos B. Karayiannis, Nagabhushan Kaliyur S. M., and Heidar A. Malki

Non-information-maximizing neural coding 2728
Michael Stiber

Flexible self-organizing maps by information maximization 2734
Ryotaro Kamimura and Haruhiko Takeuchi

Almost all noise types can improve the mutual information of threshold neurons that detect subthreshold signals 2740
B. Kosko and S. Mitaim

Auditory Processing
Chair: DeLiang Wang .... Room: Clackamas

Cognitive modeling of symbolic-like relationships with the adaptive neural network associator (ANNA) 2746
Rainer Spiegel

A hypothetical mechanism of auditory processing for extraction of directional cues: Integration with oculomotor function 2752
Vladimir A. Gorelik

Discovering hierarchical speech features using convolutional non-negative matrix factorization 2758
Sven Behnke

Incremental Learning
Chair: Robi Polikar .... Room: Washington

Incremental rule learning with partial instance memory for changing concepts 2764
Marcus A. Maloof

Ensemble of classifiers based incremental learning with dynamic voting weight update 2770
Robi Polikar, Stefan Krause, and Lyndsay Burd

Incremental learning with sleep: Function approximation and classification 2776
Koichiro Yamauchi

Exemplar-based pattern recognition via semi-supervised learning 2782
Georgios C. Anagnostopoulos, Madan Bharadwaj, Michael Georgiopoulos, Stephen J. Verzi, and Gregory L. Heileman

Wednesday, July 23, 1:20PM-3:00PM

Special Session: Autonomous Mental Development (part 2)
Chair: John Weng and Olaf Sporns .... **Room: Multnomah**

Investigating the emergence of shared attention through an embodied computational modeling approach: A progress report 2788
Jochen Triesch, Eric Carlson, Gedeon Deak, and Javier Movellan

Neuromodulation in a learning robot: Interactions between neural plasticity and behavior 2789
Olaf Sporns and William H. Alexander

Lessons from ethology for computational models of development 2795
Bruce Blumberg, Matt Berlin, Daphna Buchsbaum, Marc Downie, Derek Lyons, and Jennie Cochran

Generating structure in sensory data through coordinated motor activity 2796
Olaf Sporns and Teresa Pegors

Learning communities: Connectivity and dynamics of interacting agents 2797
Tanzeem Choudhury, Brian Clarkson, Sumit Basu, and Alex Pentland

Recurrent Networks
Chair: Lee Feldkamp .... **Room: Clark**

Finding least cost proofs using high order recurrent networks 2803
Ashraf M. Abdelbar, Emad A. M. Andrews, and Gene A. Tagliarini

Feature selection assessment and comparison using two saliency measures in an Elman recurrent neural network 2807
Trevor I. Laine and Kenneth W. Bauer

Prediction of pitch and yaw head movements via recurrent neural networks 2813
M. Aguilar, Y. Barniv, and A. Garrett

Attempting to reduce the vanishing gradient problem through a novel recurrent multiscale architecture 2819
Stefano Squartini, Amir Hussain, and Francesco Piazza

Spiking Neurons
Chair: William B. Levy .... **Room: Clackamas**

BSA, a fast and accurate spike train encoding scheme 2825
Benjamin Schrauwen and Jan Van Campenhout

Electrotonic effects on spike response model dynamics 2831
Giorgio A. Ascoli

An automated method for neuronal spike source identification 2837
Roberto A. Santiago, James McNames, Kim Burchiel, and George G. Lendaris

Statistical approach to unsupervised recognition of spatio-temporal patterns by spiking neurons 2843
M. V. Kiselev

Trust region nonlinear optimization learning method for dynamic synapse neural networks ..2848
Hassan H. Namarvar and Theodore W. Berger

Time Series Analysis and Financial Engineering
Chair: Fred Ham .... **Room: Washington**

Analyzing dividend events with neural network rule extraction 2854
Ming Dong and Xu-Shen Zhou

SVM learning from large training data set 2860
Yi Lu Murphey, ZhiHang Chen, May Putrus, and Lee A. Feldkamp

Neural networks and rule extraction for prediction and explanation in the marketing domain 2866
Ulf Johansson, Cecilia Sonstrod, Rikard Konig, and Lars Niklasson

On the statistical efficiency of the LMS family of adaptive algorithms 2872
Bernard Widrow and Max Kamenetsky

Wednesday, July 23, 3:20PM-5:00PM

Special Session: Geometric Neurocomputing
Chair: Eduardo Bayro-Corrochano .... **Room: Multnomah**

The role of the quaternion Fourier descriptors for preprocessing in neuralcomputing 2881
Eduardo Bayro-Corrochano, Noel Trujillo, and Michel Naranjo

Single layer feedforward neural network based on lattice algebra 2887
Gerhard X. Ritter and Laurentiu Iancu

Design of kernels for support multivector machines involving the clifford gometric product and the conformal geometric neuron 2893
Eduardo Bayro-Corrochano, Nancy Arana, and Refugio Vallejo

A computational model of visual perception of surfaces 2899
Hamid Eghbalnia and Amir Assadi

Reinforcement Learning and Adaptive Dynamic Programming
Chair: Danil V. Prokhorov .... **Room: Clark**

An enhanced least-squares approach for reinforcement learning 2905
Hailin Li and Cihan H. Dagli

Tabu search exploration for on-policy reinforcement learning 2910
Myriam Abramson and Harry Wechsler

Dynamic pricing and reinforcement learning 2916
Alexandre X. Carvalho and Martin L. Puterman

Accelerating critic learning in approximate dynamic programming via value templates and perceptual learning 2922
Thaddeus T. Shannon, Roberto A. Santiago, and George G. Lendaris

Autonomous mental development in high dimensional state and action spaces 2928
Ameet Joshi and Juyang Weng

Bioinformatics
Chair: Shiro Usui .... **Room: Clackamas**

Train-spotting: Building classifiers for microarrays 2934
Yuxuan Lan, Gavin C. Cawley, and Richard Harvey

Statistical learning for detecting protein-DNA-binding sites 2940
    Thomas Martinetz, Jan E. Gewehr, and Jan T. Kim

Transductive support vector machines for classification of microarray gene expression data..2946
    R. Semolini and F. J. Von Zuben

PCA feature extraction for protein structure prediction 2952
    Jeane C. B. Melo, George D. C. Cavalcanti, and Katia S. Guimaras

Modelling the growth domain of clostridium botulinum via kernel survival analysis................2958
    Robert J. Foxall, Gavin C. Cawley, and Michael W. Peck

Power System Applications
Chair: Ron Harley.. Room: Washington

An adaptive neural network identifier for effective control of a static compensator connected to a power system..2964
    Salman Mohagheghi, Jung-Wook Park, Ronald G. Harley, Ganesh K. Venayagamoorthy, and Mariesa L. Crow

Adaptive neural network based power system stabilizer design 2970
    W. Liu, Ganesh K. Venayagamoorthy, and Donald C. Wunsch II

A novel dual heuristic programming based optimal control of a series compensator in the electric power transmission system..2976
    Jung-Wook Park, Ronald G. Harley, and Ganesh K. Venayagamoorthy

A continually online trained neurocontroller for the series branch control of the UPFC..........2982
    R. P. Kalyani and Ganesh K. Venayagamoorthy

Fault diagnosis of steam turbine-generator using CMAC neural network approach...............2988
    Chin-Pao Hung, Mang-Hui Wang, Chin-Hsing Cheng, and Wen-Lang Lin

Wednesday, July 23, 5:00PM-7:00PM

Panel Session: International Research
Chair: Harold H. Szu.. Room: Multnomah

Wednesday, July 23, 7:00PM-9:00PM

Banquet and Award Presentations
Hosts: Donald C. Wunsch II and Michael E. Hasselmo

Room: Riverview Ballroom - Doubletree Hotel Columbia River (adjacent hotel)

Wednesday, July 23, 9:00PM-10:00PM

Panel Session: Funding Resources
Chair: Paul Werbos.. Room: Multnomah

Thursday, July 24, 8:00AM-9:00AM

Plenary Talk:
Speaker: Christoph von der Malsburg.. Room: Mount Saint Helens Ballroom

On the importance of binding 2994

Thursday, July 24, 9:20AM-10:40AM

Special Session: Applications in Aerospace
Chair: Robert J. Marks and John Vian .... Room: Multnomah

Layered URC fuzzy systems: A novel link between fuzzy systems and neural networks 2995
  Jeffrey J. Weinschenk, Robert J. Marks II, and W. E. Combs

Vibration analysis via neural network inverse models to determine aircraft engine
unbalance condition 3001
  Xiao Hu, John Vian, Joseph R. Slepski, and Donald C. Wunsch II

Missing sensor data restoration for vibration sensors on a jet aircraft engine 3007
  Sreeram Narayanan, John Vian, Jai Choi, Robert J. Marks II, Mohamed A. El-Sharkawi, and Benjamin B. Thompson

On the contractive nature of autoencoders: Application to missing sensor restoration 3011
  Benjamin B. Thompson, Robert J. Marks II, and Mohamed A. El-Sharkawi

Recurrent Networks
Chair: Lee Feldkamp .... Room: Clark

Conditioned adaptive behavior from Kalman filter trained recurrent networks 3017
  Lee A. Feldkamp, Danil V. Prokhorov, and Timothy M. Feldkamp

Using reconstructability analysis to select input variables for artificial neural networks 3022
  Stephen Shervais and Martin Zwick

Fascinating rhythms by chaotic Hopfield networks 3027
  Colin Molter and Hugues Bersini

Modular neural associative memory capable of storage of large amounts of data 3031
  A. M. Reznik and O. K. Dekhtyarenko

Learning and Memory
Chair: Daniel S. Levine .... Room: Clackamas

Implicant network: An associative memory model 3036
  Diego Federici

Improving generalization by teacher-directed learning 3042
  Ryotaro Kamimura

eLoom: A specification, simulation and visualization engine for modeling arbitrary
hierarchical neural architectures 3048
  Yunhai Xiao, Thomas Preston Caudell, and Michael J. Healy

Multi-map self-organization for sensorimotor learning: A cortical approach 3054
  Olivier Menard and Herve Frezza-Buet

Applications
Chair: Joydeep Ghosh .... Room: Washington

Image restoration using chaotic simulated annealing 3060
Leipo Yan and Lipo Wang

Fuzzy Markov predictor in multi-step electric load forecasting 3065
Marcelo Teixeira and Gerson Zaverucha

Neural networks applied to classification of data based on Mahalanobis metrics 3071
Allan de Medeiros Martins, Adriao Duarte Doria Neto, and Jorge Dantas de Melo

Thursday, July 24, 10:50AM-12:10PM

Special Session: Bioinformatics
Chair: Francesco Masulli and Larry Reeker .... Room: Multnomah

Gene selection and classification by entropy-based recursive feature elimination 3077
C. Furlanello, M. Serafini, S. Merler, and G. Jurman

Spectral clustering of protein sequences 3083
Alberto Paccanaro, Chakra Chennubhotla, James A. Casbon, and Mansoor A. S. Saqi

An ensemble approach to variable selection for classification of DNA microarray data 3089
Francesco Masulli and Stefano Rovetta

Artificial neural networks methods for the identification of the most relevant genes from gene expression array data 3095
Zvi Boger

Mathematics of Neural Systems
Chair: George G. Lendaris... Room: Clark

Flow invariance for competitive neural networks for different time-scales 3101
Anke Meyer-Baese and Sergei S. Pilyugin

A novel neural approach to inverse problems with discontinuities (the GMR neural network) 3106
G. Cirrincione, M. Cirrincione, C. Lu, and S. Van Huffel

Artificial neural network implementation using many-valued quantum computing 3112
Anas N. Al-Rabadi and George G. Lendaris

Incorporating invariants in Mahalanobis distance based classifiers: Application to face recognition 3118
Andrew M. Fraser, Nicolas W. Hengartner, Kevin R. Vixie, and Brendt E. Wohlberg

Networks of width one are universal classifiers 3124
Raul Rojas

Speech Recognition and Production
Chair: Ke Chen .... Room: Clackamas

Sub auditory speech recognition based on EMG signals... 3128
Chuck Jorgensen, Diana Lee, and Shane Agabon

Robust command recognition using kernel learning algorithms 3134
Hassan H. Namarvar and Theodore W. Berger

Mel-frequency cepstrum coefficients extraction from infant cry for classification of normal
and pathological cry with feed-forward neural networks 3140
   Jose Orozco García and Carlos A. Reyes García

A new approach for isolated word recognition using dynamic synapse neural networks 3146
   Alireza A. Dibazar, Hassan H. Namarvar, and Theodore W. Berger

Robotics, Motor Control and Response
Chair: Gary Yen .... **Room: Washington**

A sensory network for perception-based robotics using neural networks 3151
   Naoyuki Kubota, Setsuo Hashimoto, and Fumio Kojima

A RAM-based neural network for collision avoidance in a mobile robot 3157
   Qiang Yao, Daryl Beetner, Donald C. Wunsch II, and Bjorn Osterloh

Stability analysis of decentralized cerebellum motor control 3161
   Aiko Miyamura and Kazuyuki Aihara

A model of cerebellar adaptation of grip forces during lifting 3167
   Antonio Ulloa, Daniel Bullock, and Bradley J. Rhodes

Controller design via adaptive critic and model reference methods 3173
   George G. Lendaris, Roberto A. Santiago, J. McCarthy, and M. Carroll

Thursday, July 24, 1:20PM-3:00PM

Biomimetic Applications
Chair: Harold H. Szu .... **Room: Multnomah**

Theoretical confirmation of simple cell's receptive field of animal's visual systems and
efficient navigation applications 3179
   Liming Zhang and Jianfeng Mei

Early stage fire detection using reliable metal oxide gas sensor and artificial neural
networks 3185
   Bancha Charumporn, Michifumi Yoshioka, Toru Fujinaka, and Sigeru Omatu

Biomimetics speaker identification systems for network security gatekeepers 3189
   Xihong Wu, Dingsheng Luo, Huisheng Chi, and Harold H. Szu

An EMG-controlled omnidirectional pointing device using a HMM-based neural network 3195
   Osamu Fukuda, Jun Arita, and Toshio Tsuji

A self-aiming camera based on neurophysical principles 3201
   Samarth Swarup, Tuna Oezer, Sylvian Ray, and Thomas Anastasio

Thursday, July 24, 1:20PM-2:20PM

Neural Networks and Evolutionary Computation
Chair: Xin Yao .... **Room: Clark**

Optimizing the learning of binary mappings 3207
   John A. Bullinaria

The optimization of radial basis probabilistic neural networks based on genetic algorithms .. 3213
   Lin Guo, De-Shuang Huang, and Wenbo Zhao

Combining evolving neural network classifiers using bagging 3218
Sunghwan Sohn and Cihan H. Dagli

Thursday, July 24, 1:20PM-3:00PM

Pattern Recognition
Chair: Xiuwen Liu..Room: Clackamas

Classifiability based omnivariate decision trees... 3223
Ming Dong and Yuanhong Li

An efficient algorithm on multi-class support vector machine model selection 3229
Peng Xu and Andrew K. Chan

Enhancement of categorizing and learning module (CALM) - embedded detection of
signal change 3233
Jan Koutnik and Miroslav Snorek

A computational model of visual attention 3238
Teuvo Kohonen

Thursday, July 24, 1:20PM-2:20PM

Data Mining
Chair: Joydeep Ghosh ....Room: Washington

Knowledge-oriented clustering for decision support 3244
Charlotte Bean and Chandra Kambhampati

Unsupervised clustering of symbol strings.. 3250
John A. Flanagan

A new method for explaining neural network reasoning 3256
Yingjie Yang, Chris Hinde, and David Gillingwater

Thursday, July 24, 3:10PM-4:10PM

Plenary Talk
Speaker: Terrence Sejnowski................Room: Mount Saint Helens Ballroom

Combinatorial representation of color in visual cortex 3261

Synaptic Modification of Interneuron Afferents in a Hippocampal CA3 Model Prevents Activity Oscillations

David W. Sullivan and William B Levy

Department of Neurosurgery, University of Virginia
P.O. Box 800420, Charlottesville, VA 22908

Abstract – In recurrent neural networks, excessive activity oscillations can be very disruptive to successful learning performance. Inhibitory feedback can be used to offset a dominating positive feedback; however, synaptic modification at excitatory synapses would seem to require synaptic modification at inhibitory synapses if activity is to be controlled during training. Here, we present a novel synaptic modification rule that governs the synaptic strength of afferents (inputs) to activity controlling inhibitory interneurons. A hippocampal CA3 model incorporating this rule can avoid certain performance destroying activity oscillations. In the minimal model used here, this new rule for synaptic modification implements an error-correcting-like procedure at each excitatory input to a global feedback inhibitory interneuron. Simulations that include this novel modification rule demonstrate robust sequence learning as well as the elimination of major activity fluctuations that are outside the biologically plausible range. Importantly, simulations using this rule are able to adapt quickly and selectively to large, discontinuous jumps in the training sequences.

I. INTRODUCTION

Control of activity in the hippocampus is known to be delicate. If inhibition is reduced, uncontrollable electrical activity called epilepsy can result, which is unsurprising given the dominance of positive feedback in hippocampal region CA3. Similarly, activity control is a critical issue for a minimal model of the CA3. Although the organization of the hippocampus is very simple, there are multiple types of interneurons, multiple forms of synaptic modification, and multiple potassium conductances, all of which are likely to help control activity. But as Nature employs, or potentially employs, such complexity to maintain control of the appropriate activity, there is a severe problem for minimal modeling, i.e., which biological-based mechanisms should be used?

In the absence of synaptic modification, Smith et al. solved the problem of activity control by adding a shunting conductance to each neuron [1]. However, with synaptic modification enabled and as training progresses, the equations described in [1] are no longer valid, and uncontrolled firing is often observed in larger networks run with low activity settings.

Polyn and Levy [2] demonstrated that nonspecific modification of the inhibitory synapse onto the primary neurons (termed Dynamic Automatic Scaling Inhibition, or DAS inhibition) can improve sequence learning in our minimal model. Specifically, DAS inhibition improves sequence learning by lowering trial-to-trial fluctuations of activity and by steering activity levels toward a prespecified desirable value.

A major focus of our research has been the application of our model to the learning of hippocampally dependent cognitive tasks; specifically, the Transverse Patterning and Transitive Inference tasks [3-7]. Simulations of these tasks require multi-sequence learning using a massed (or *blocked*) training paradigm, in which the input sequence is switched multiple times. Unpublished observations show that large trial-to-trial activity oscillations frequently occur whenever the input sequence is switched. These oscillations are destructive to successful learning of the cognitive task. Other research questions also motivate better activity control.

In order to achieve more biological parameterizations in our minimal hippocampal model, recent work by this lab has incorporated quantal synaptic failures, more neurons, and lower activity settings [7]. However, a key obstacle to producing successful learning while incorporating the additional biology has been the appearance of within-trial activity oscillations.

Although we have shown that a limited amount of within-trial fluctuation of activity can be beneficial for learning [5], overly large, within-trial activity oscillations can disrupt learning by preventing the emergence of repetitive recurrent firing (local context neurons [8]) that encodes subsequences. Because the disruption of learning by these activity oscillations can be of such severity, Sullivan and Levy switched inhibition in the model to the less biological competitive (or k-winners-take-all) inhibition rule so that simulations with other more biological parameters could be investigated. However in keeping with our philosophy of minimal, yet biologically realistic neural modeling, we want a more robust method of activity control that is also biologically valid.

Here, we present a rule for synaptic modification of afferents to inhibitory neurons (PyrToInt) that allows robust sequence learning. This robust learning occurs in simulations that include synaptic failures, divisive inhibition, massed training, many neurons, and relatively low activity settings. The distinction between this rule and DAS is notable. That is, this new rule achieves activity control through the modification of individual excitatory synapses from each pyramidal neuron to the inhibitory interneurons and is arguably complementary to, not contradictory of, DAS.

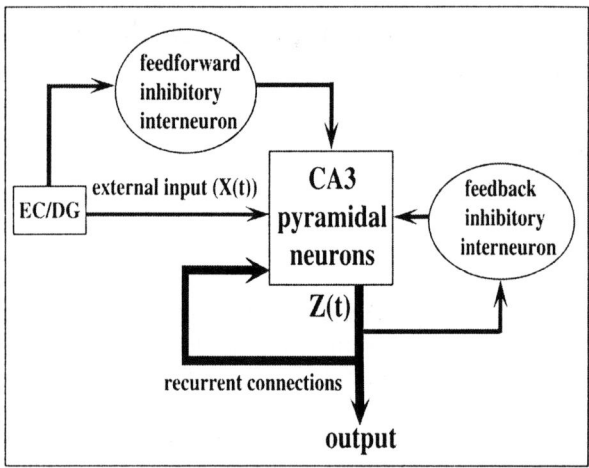

Fig. 1. The hippocampal model. The sparse, excitatory external input to CA3 represents a combination of connections from dentate gyrus (DG) and entorhinal cortex (EC). Recurrent excitation fires more neurons than external input. Inhibitory interneurons accompany both the external and recurrent inputs.

TABLE I
SYMBOLS USED IN EQUATIONS

Symbol	Description
$Y_j(t)$	[0,1] Excitation of pyramidal neuron i
$Z_i(t)$	{0,1} Firing state of neuron i
C_{ij}	{0,1} Indicator of connection from neuron i to neuron j (static after simulation begins)
W_{ij}	[0,1] Strength of synaptic connection from neuron i to neuron j
$X_i(t)$	{0,1} External input line to neuron i
Φ_{ij}	Synaptic failure channel for the connection from neuron i to neuron j
D_i	$(-\infty, \infty)$ Weight of excitatory connection from neuron i to the feedback interneuron

TABLE II
SIMULATION PARAMETERS

Parameter	Description
N = 4096	Number of neurons in the network
Desired Act = 0.05	Desired fraction of recurrent neurons active per time step
K_R = 0.0276	Feedback inhibition scaling factor
K_I = 0.012	Feedforward inhibition scaling constant
K_0 = 0.126	Shunting inhibition constant
μ = 0.05	Pyramidal-pyramidal synaptic modification rate constant
λ = 0.8	Pyramidal-interneuron synaptic modification rate constant
ξ = 0.05	Interneuron-pyramidal synaptic modification rate constant
T = 9	Number of time steps per trial
θ = 0.5	Firing threshold constant

II. METHODS

A. The Model

Our minimal model of hippocampal region CA3 consists of a sparse, recurrent network of McCulloch-Pitts neurons, with connections modifiable by an asymmetric time spanning Hebbian rule, and forcing input lines representing afferent connections from the entorhinal cortex and dentate gyrus. Fig. 1 illustrates the organization of our model. Time is discrete, with each time step representing approximately 30 ms in the simulations used here [9]. Synaptic failure is modeled as an independent Bernoulli process at each synapse. In the simulations here, the probability of synaptic failure is 40% (i.e., Prob($\Phi_{ij}(Z_i(t)=1)=0$) = 0.4). All simulations use 10% connectivity (i.e., Prob(C_{ij} = 1) = 0.1), and N=4096. Pyramidal-pyramidal weights are initialized to 0.4. Table I defines the symbols used in the equations and gives their domains, Table II defines the parameters used in simulations (unless noted otherwise), and Table III contains the equations that govern the operation of the model.

Inhibition, as seen in equation (1) is divisive [10]. We model inhibitory input to pyramidal cells as the sum of contributions from three sources: a global feedback interneuron, a global feedforward interneuron, and a static shunting inhibition. The inhibitory contribution of the interneurons operates on the same time scale as the pyramidal cells.

TABLE III
MODEL EQUATIONS

Somato-Dendritic Excitation/Inhibition

$$Y_j(t) = \frac{\sum_{i=1}^{N} \Phi(Z_i(t-1)) C_{ij} W_{ij}(t-1)}{\sum_{i=1}^{N} \Phi(Z_i(t-1)) C_{ij} W_{ij}(t-1) + K_R \left(\sum_{i=1}^{N} D_i(t-1) Z_i(t-1) \right) + K_I \sum_{i=1}^{N} X_i(t) + K_0} \quad (1)$$

Output

$$Z_i(t) = \begin{cases} 1 & \text{if } Y_i(t) \geq \theta \text{ or } X_i(t) = 1 \\ 0 & \text{otherwise} \end{cases} \quad (2)$$

Pyramidal-Pyramidal Synaptic Modification Rule

$$W_{ij}(t+1) = W_{ij}(t) + \mu(Z_j(t)) \left(\Phi(Z_i(t-1)) - W_{ij}(t) \right) \quad (3)$$

Rule for Modification of Interneuron Afferents (PyrToInt)

$$D_i(t) = D_i(t-1) + \lambda(Z_i(t-1)) \left(\frac{\sum_{j=1}^{N} Z_j(t)}{N} - \text{Desired Act} \right) \quad (4)$$

Rule for Modification of Global Feedback Inhibitory Input onto the Pyramidal Cells (DAS)

$$K_R(\tau) = K_R(\tau-1) + \xi \left(\frac{\sum_{t=1}^{T} \sum_{i=1}^{N} Z_i(t)}{NT} \right) \left(\frac{\sum_{t=1}^{T} \sum_{i=1}^{N} Z_i(t)}{NT} - \text{Desired Act} \right) \quad (5)$$

B. Inhibitory Synaptic Modification Rules

Modification of global feedback inhibitory input onto the pyramidal cells (DAS) operates through an error-correcting rule that adjusts the value of the feedback inhibition scaling factor, K_R (5). The DAS rule updates K_R once after every training trial. Whenever DAS is used in isolation, PyrToInt is turned off by setting λ to 0 and all D_i to 1.0.

The model using PyrToInt (4) is more complicated. Like our pyramidal-pyramidal synaptic modification rule (3), the PyrToInt rule has a time-spanning property. Synaptic modification is dependent on firing of the presynaptic pyramidal neuron: if the presynaptic neuron fires, its weight modifies according to a factor that is the product of a scaling constant (λ) and the error between activity on the following time step and the desired activity. Thus, over the course of a simulation, neurons that tend to contribute to activity that is too high will have increased weights, and vice-versa. The PyrToInt rule updates the weights onto the inhibitory interneuron after every time step during all training trials.

For both PyrToInt and DAS, we selected a synaptic modification rate constant that produced the best performance on a basic sequence completion task (see C below). These rate constants were used for all simulations discussed in this paper unless noted otherwise.

C. Sequence Completion

The sequence completion task used here requires the network to learn both of two distinct sequences sufficiently well such that the network, when prompted with the initial firing pattern of one of the sequences, will recall the rest of the sequence in the absence of further external input. Each sequence consists of 3 orthogonal (non-overlapping) patterns. Each pattern, which is defined as a set of 164 neurons, is presented for 3 consecutive time steps (~100 ms). On each time step, noise is applied to the input pattern (quantal failures of inputs), such that each neuron that is a member of the input pattern has a 50% probability of receiving forcing external input. Thus, an external input pattern fires approximately 82 neurons on each time step. Importantly, some externally activated neurons will fire even in the case that recurrent activity drops to 0%.

Simulations consisted of 180 training trials followed by 2 test trials. Training followed a massed procedure: the first sequence was presented for 60 trials, then the second sequence was presented for 60 trials, followed by an additional 60 trials of training on the first sequence. We test sequence learning by observing the network's output following the presentation of an abbreviated version of the training input sequence that consists of only the first three time steps (i.e., the first pattern in the sequence). Sequence completion is then quantified by performing cosine comparisons between firing on corresponding time steps of testing and training [11]. For the first input sequence, firing during trial 180 forms the basis of this comparison, whereas for the second input sequence, the comparison is made against firing during trial 120. The value of this cosine comparison, averaged over time steps 4-9, is considered the measure of sequence learning performance.

III. RESULTS

A. Pyramidal-to-Interneuron Synaptic Modification Best Controls Trial-to-Trial Activity Levels

The type of inhibitory modification used in simulations greatly affects trial-to-trial activity oscillations. Fig. 2 compares trial-to-trial activity levels for three configurations of the model: modification of the excitatory afferents onto the interneuron (PyrToInt), modification of the inhibitory inputs onto the pyramidal cells (DAS), and a control configuration (no inhibitory synaptic modification). In the control configuration, activity experiences a steady decline at the early stages of training and plateaus at approximately 2%. Because the network has no way of decreasing inhibition, it is effectively stuck at this low activity value. Introducing a novel sequence at trial 60 only exacerbates this problem, with recurrent activity dropping to 0%.

With the DAS configuration, the simulation demonstrates some control over trial-to-trial activity. Although activity initially drops to 3%, modification of the feedback inhibition scaling constant (K_R) drives activity back towards the desired value of 5%. DAS inhibition also allows recovery from activity disruptions due to introduction of a novel sequence. However, there are some problems with DAS. First, the recovery after trial 60 is slow; activity does not reach the desired value until trial 97. Second, this recovery is imprecise, with activity briefly rising above the desired value (trials 100-120). Increasing the DAS rate constant (ξ) from 0.2 to 0.8 leads to a faster recovery from the activity disruption at trial 60 (Fig. 3). While this may seem beneficial, the system borders on instability. Note that at the higher rate constant there is a large, non-physiological activity oscillation at trial 70.

PyrToInt produces the better control of trial-to-trial activity fluctuations. During training on the initial sequence (trials 1-60), activity behaves similar to the simulation with the DAS configuration. In contrast, recovery from the activity disruption at trial 60 is much faster than in the simulation with DAS, as activity reaches the desired value by trial 77; moreover, this return to desired activity occurs without the violent overshoot that characterizes DAS when set to return as quickly. A small dip in activity upon the reintroduction of the original sequence at trial 120 is quickly corrected by the PyrToInt governed network.

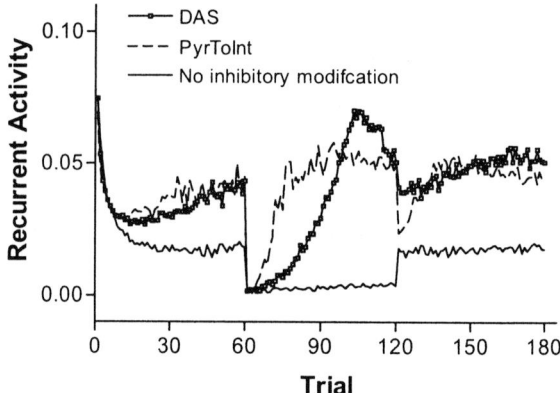

Fig. 2. Recurrent activity over training as a function of inhibition. Without modification of inhibitory synaptic strength, activity is very poorly controlled; note the large fluctuation away from the desired activity of 5%. With inhibitory modification turned off (solid line), average activity decreases as training progresses, and by trial 30 stabilizes at approximately 2%, which is well below the desired value of 5%. Introducing a novel sequence at trial 60 causes activity to drop to 0%, at which recurrent firing has ceased and consequentially, learning cannot occur. Activity does not recover significantly during trials 60-120. The two types of inhibitory modification differ in their ability to control trial-to-trial activity. If modification of the inhibitory synapses onto the pyramidal neurons is used (dark line), activity approaches the desired value during trials 15-60. However, the introduction of the new input sequence at trial 60 causes a precipitous decline in activity, which the network recovers from, albeit this recovery is slow and imprecise, resulting in a period during which activity is higher than the desired value. On the other hand, if modification of the excitatory synapses onto the interneuron is used, the activity quickly recovers from the decline caused by the introduction of a novel training sequence. Reintroduction of the original training sequence at trial 120 causes a second, smaller drop in activity, which is followed by a quick recovery back to the desired 5% value.

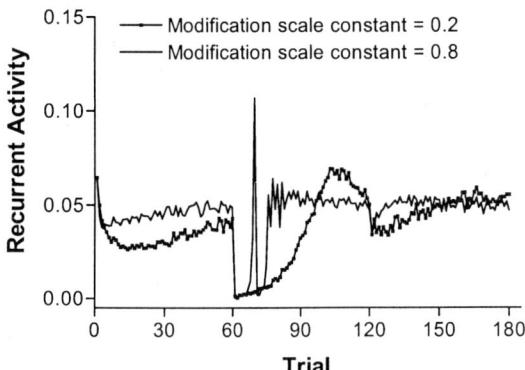

Fig. 3. Recurrent activity over training as a function of DAS inhibitory modification scale constant. Increasing the scale constant from 0.2 (as plotted in Fig. 2) to 0.8 allows a recovery from the activity fluctuation at trial 60 that is nearly as fast as when PyrToInt is used. However, increasing the modification scale constant brings the unwanted side effect of a large activity fluctuation at trial 70.

B. *Combining PyrToInt and DAS Leads to Superior Trial-to-Trial Activity Control*

So far, we have demonstrated that both PyrToInt and DAS allow control over trial-to-trial activity fluctuations, but that each rule has drawbacks: DAS results in a slow recovery from the activity disruption at trial 60, and PyrToInt suffers from a dip in activity at trial 120. Here, we examine the effects of using PyrToInt and DAS in combination.

Fig. 4 plots activity over training for both PyrToInt alone and DAS and PyrToInt in combination. Activity is similar for the first 60 trials, with the combined rules performing slightly better than PyrToInt alone. Recovery from the decline in activity at trial 60 is slightly faster with the combined rules than with PyrToInt alone. Using DAS and PyrToInt in combination leads to an improvement in activity control at trial 120, where with PyrToInt alone, the reintroduction of the original input sequence causes recurrent activity to drop from 4.9% to 2.3%. In contrast, when DAS and PyrToInt are used in combination, switching sequences at trial 120 does not cause an activity disruption.

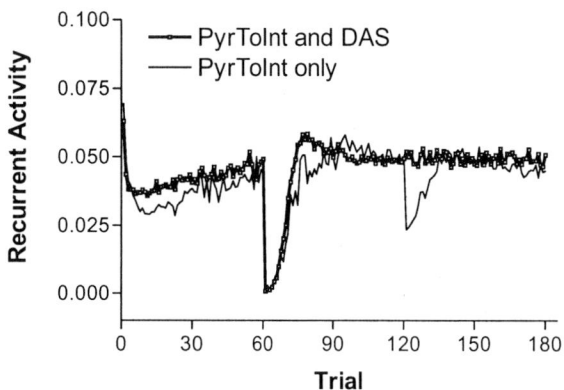

Fig. 4. Recurrent activity over training in a combined model. The combination of PyrToInt and DAS is better than PyrToInt alone. The combination returns nearly to the desired activity level during the initial training sequence (trials 1-59) while the model incorporating PyrToInt along lags behind. There is no great improvement for trials 60-119, but the combined model is marginally better. Finally in the third training block (120-180), the combined model maintains near perfect activity control while the PyrToInt alone model only is subject to an early fluctuation after the change at trial 120. Simulation parameters: $\lambda = 0.8$, $\xi = 0.4$, all others as described in Table II.

C. *PyrToInt Provides Robust Control of Within-Trial Activity Oscillations*

Within-trial activity oscillations pose two serious problems for our minimal model. First, if the low activity value of the oscillation is too low, information will not propagate across time. Similarly, if the high activity component of a large oscillation is too high, information from earlier in the sequence is corrupted by less meaningful neural firing.

Fig. 5 shows an extreme contrast between within-trial activity (values are from trial 180) for the different types of activity control. With no inhibitory modification, activity oscillates between 0% and 5% (external input allows recovery from the minimal activity portion of the oscillation). While DAS produces an average activity that is near the desired value (Fig. 2), the within-trial activity produced by DAS is characterized by two large oscillations. In contrast, PyrToInt simulations are very well controlled in terms of within-trial activity; for example in Figure 5, on time steps 2-9, activity does not deviate from the desired value by more than 16% of the desired value(32 neurons).

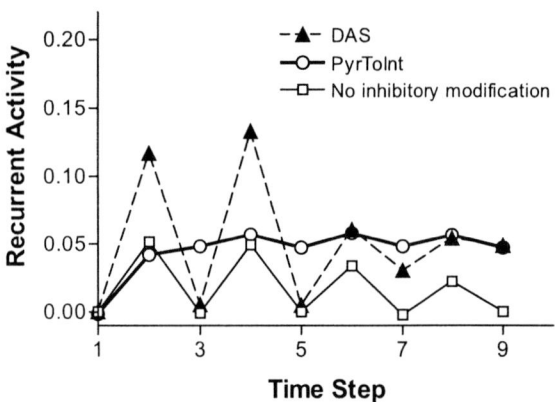

Fig. 5. Recurrent activity over a single trial as a function of inhibition. With inhibitory modification disabled, recurrent activity oscillates between 0%, and the desired activity, 5%. This oscillation prevents sequence learning, as recurrent firing is required during testing and in this case – without external activity – there is no recovery from zero activity. When DAS inhibition is used, the average activity is near the desired 5%. However, the extreme oscillations during the initial 5 time steps prevent sequence learning. In contrast, when PyrToInt is incorporated into the model instead of DAS, within-trial activity stays relatively free of oscillations and sequence completion occurs when the trained network is tested.

IV. Discussion

In summary, there are oscillations at two time scales in our minimal CA3 model that lacks synaptic modification involving an inhibitory interneuron. These two time scales of oscillation are within trials and between trials – whenever the training trial information changes. Modification of inhibitory synapses upon excitatory cells, DAS, helps a little bit but modification of the excitatory synapses upon the inhibitory interneuron (PyrToInt) is superior in terms of controlling both types of activity oscillations. As one suspects from the biology, the two modification rules are complementary. That is, the model that combines DAS and PyrToInt shows even less between trial activity fluctuations than the model using either synaptic modification rule alone.

Acknowledgments

This work was supported by NIH MH48161, MH63855 and RR15205 to WBL; and NSF NGSEIA-9974968, NPACI ASC-96-10920, and NGS ACI-0203960 to Marty Humphrey.

References

[1] A. C. Smith, X. B. Wu, and W. B Levy, Controlling activity fluctuations in large, sparsely connected random networks, *Network*, vol. 11, pp. 63-81, 2000.

[2] S. Polyn and W. B Levy, Dynamic control of inhibition improves performance of a hippocampal model, *Neurocomputing*, vol. 38-40, pp. 823-829, 2001.

[3] X. B. Wu, J. Tyrcha, and W. B Levy, A neural network solution to the transverse-patterning problem depends on repetition of the input code, *Biol. Cybern.*, vol. 79, pp. 203-213, 1998.

[4] X. B. Wu and W. B Levy, A hippocampal-like neural network model solves the transitive inference problem, In: *Computational Neuroscience: Trends in Research*, (J. M. Bower, Ed.) New York: Plenum Press, 1998, pp. 567-572.

[5] W. B Levy and X. B. Wu, Some randomness benefits a model of hippocampal function, in: *Disorder versus Order in Brain Function*, P. Århem, C. Blomberg, and H. Liljenström (Editors), World Scientific Publishing Co., 2000, pp.221-237.

[6] A. P. Shon, X. B. Wu, D. W. Sullivan, and W.B Levy, Initial state randomness improves sequence learning in a model hippocampal network, *Physical Review E*, Vol 65, 031914, 2002.

[7] D. W. Sullivan and W. B Levy, Quantal synaptic failures improve performance in a sequence learning model of hippocampal CA3, *Neurocomputing*, in press.

[8] X. B. Wu, R. A. Baxter, and W. B Levy, Context codes and the effect of noisy learning on a simplified hippocampal CA3 model, *Biol. Cybern.*, vol. 74, pp. 159-165, 1996.

[9] K. E. Mitman, P. A. Laurent, and W. B Levy, Defining time in a minimal hippocampal CA3 model by matching time-span of associative synaptic modification and input pattern duration, *These Proceedings*.

[10] A. A. Minai, and Levy, W. B, Predicting complex behavior in sparse asymmetric networks, *Neural Information Processing Systems 5: Natural and Synthetic*, pp. 556-563, 1993.

[11] W. B Levy, X. B. Wu, and R. A. Baxter, Unification of hippocampal function via computational/encoding considerations, In: *Proc. Third Workshop on Neural Networks: from Biology to High Energy Physics*, Intl. J. Neural Sys., 6, (Supp.), (D. J. Amit, P. del Guidice, B. Denby, E. T. Rolls & A. Treves, Eds.), Singapore:World Scientific Publishing, 1995, pp. 71-80.

Defining Time in a Minimal Hippocampal CA3 Model by Matching Time-span of Associative Synaptic Modification and Input Pattern Duration

Kurt E. Mitman[1], Patryk A. Laurent[1], William B Levy[2]
Department of Neurosurgery[2], College of Arts and Sciences[1], University of Virginia
P.O. Box 800420, Charlottesville, VA 22908

Abstract – This paper quantifies the time shifting of neuronal codes in a sparse, randomly connected neural network model of hippocampal region CA3. As this network is trained to learn a sequence, the neurons that encode portions of this sequence characteristically fire earlier and earlier over the course of training. Here we systematically investigate the effects of the N-methyl-D-aspartate(NMDA)-governed time-span of synaptic associativity on this shifting process and how this time-span interacts with the duration of each successive external input. The results show that there is an interaction between this synaptic time-span and externally applied pattern duration such that the early shifting effect approaches a maximum asymptotically and that this maximum is very nearly produced when the e-fold decay time-span of synaptic associativity is matched to the duration of individual input patterns. The performance of this model as a sequence prediction device varies with the time-span selected. If too long a time-span is used, overly strong attractors evolve and destroy the sequence prediction ability of the network. Local context cell firing – the learned repetitive firing of neurons that code for a specific subsequence – also varies in duration with these two parameters. Importantly, if the associative time-span is matched to the longevity of each individual external pattern and if time-shifting and local context length are normalized by this same external pattern duration, then time-shifting and local context length are constant across simulations with different parameters. This constancy supports the idea that real time can be mapped into a network of McCulloch-Pitts neurons that lack a time scale for excitation and resetting.

I. Introduction

The sequence learning, recoding theory of hippocampal function [1] depends heavily on a temporally asymmetric rule governing associative synaptic modification. This temporal asymmetry plays a critical role for a special kind of sequence completion: it allows learning that produces timely predictions [2]. That is, it enables the network to meet an important requirement – use an early part of a sequence to generate the rest of the sequence before the rest of the sequence occurs. The asymmetric associative temporal characteristic of synaptic modification arises from the on- and off-rate properties of the NMDA receptor [3].

The recoding process itself has been predicted as time-shifting to earlier firings [1,4] resulting in a somewhat loosely overlapping code (see "rough-counting" in [1]). In this way a sequence of neural firing resembles an incrementing, shifting binary counter when the neurons are visualized via re-ordering by the temporal order in which they fire. In terms of biology, the earlier or backwards shifting of firing in the model is similar to that recently demonstrated in vivo [5] where it was complemented by a negative skew in the activity of a large portion of the neurons [6]. The combination of earlier-shifting of firing with the formation and lengthening of place-cell type firing results in a neural code for the present input which becomes increasingly similar to the future patterns. This similarity is what allows timely predictions [1].

When the model learns a nonspatial task, cell firing resembling place cells occurs, and these neurons are called local context neurons because they identify a particular subsequence of a longer sequence. The average duration of such place-cell type firings is denoted E[L], the average local context length. When training the model to learn cognitive tasks, an intermediate to high value of E[L] correlates with good performance (e.g., [7,8]). However, if E[L] becomes excessively large, the network state can be drawn into a noisy attractor, which could prevent the appropriate sequence recall. This motivates us to study E[L] as a function of parameters such as the time constant of synaptic associativity. As an expected result, we find that E[L] increases with increasing values of the time constant of associativity.

A central finding of this paper is a matching between the time-span of associative modification and the duration of the inputs (stutter length) to the network. We show that this matching produces a compromise between the predictive component of the neuronal codes developed during learning and performance. *Specifically increasing the LTP time-span beyond this compromise does in fact marginally increase the predictive component of the neuronal codes, but it also degrades performance and the robustness of the codes.* That is, too large of a time-span can cause the formation of performance-destroying stable attractors. The other important observation here concerns the mapping of time between computational cycles of the simulations and real time.

By ratioing against input pattern longevity (stutter length), the neuronal codes developed by training are constant across parametric changes of the NMDA receptor off-rate time constant that maps the model into real time. Thus, the longevity of neuronal firings and the time shifts measured are also mapped into real time.

II. Methods

A. The Model

The model simulates the CA3 region of the hippocampus, an area sometimes thought to be the center of associative memory due to the presence of recurrent connectivity [9,10]. Because we implement an asymmetric synaptic modification rule [11], the CA3 region is also able to make associations across time. Therefore, context-dependent sequence learning takes place in this model (see [12], for a review).

The model reflects the biology of the hippocampus, yet at the same time aiming for easy interpretation via minimality. The network is comprised of McCulloch-Pitts binary neurons. The recurrent connectivity between neurons is random and sparse. The connections to the CA3 region from the entorhinal cortex and dentate gyrus are combined and represented as a single input vector. In contrast to the visual model, here inhibition is implemented using a *k-winners-take-all* competitive rule. The following equations illustrate the dynamics of the model:

For neuronal excitation,

$$y_j(t) = \sum_{i=1}^{n} c_{ij} \times W_{ij} \times Z_i(t-1);$$

for output,

$$Z_j(t) = \begin{cases} 1 & \text{if } y_j(t) \geq \theta \quad x_j(t) = 1 \\ 0 & \text{otherwise,} \end{cases}$$

where $y_j(t)$ is the net excitation for the jth neuron at time t, for $j \in \{1,...,n\}$ neurons, $Z_j(t)$ is the output, $W_{ij}(t)$ is the weight of the connection from neuron i to j; $c_{ij} \in \{0, 1\}$ is the connection indicator, $x_i \in \{0, 1\}$ indicates which neuron are activated by the entorhinal cortex/dentate gyrus (externals), and θ is the threshold, determined each time step such that only the 7.5% of neurons with the highest activity have an output of 1.

Synaptic weights are modified in accordance with a temporally asymmetric Hebbian rule [11,13,14] and have a time-spanning associative capability that models a saturation-decay model of the NMDA receptor. The equations are as follows:

For time-span associativity a saturate and decay variable $\bar{Z}_i(t)$ is used,

$$\bar{Z}_i(t) = \begin{cases} 1 & \text{if } Z_i(t) = 1, \text{ and} \\ \alpha \times \bar{Z}_i(t-1) & \text{otherwise} \end{cases}$$

for synaptic modification,

$$W_{ij}(t+1) = W_{ij}(t) + \mu Z_j(t)\left(\bar{Z}_i(t-1) - W_{ij}(t)\right).$$

The term μ in the weight modification equation is the learning rate constant for weight changes and depends on stutter length, $\mu = [(1.05)^{1/\text{stutter}} - 1]$. The term α in the presynaptic updating of $\bar{Z}_i(t)$ is the decay time constant of the NMDA receptor. We assume e-fold decay in the NMDA receptor after 100 ms. We can represent this decay in discrete time as the number of time steps it takes for $\bar{Z}_i$ to reach $1/e$ if no further excitation arrives on input line i. Thus, the length of real time represented by each time step (in ms) = $-100 / [\log(\alpha) \times e]$.

All simulations used 8% connectivity (e.g. $P(c_{ij} = 1) = .08$), where self connections are not allowed and n=4096. This value of connectivity is inferred from the projections of the roughly 83,000 neurons in the septal one-third of CA3 of the rat hippocampus. Random synaptic transmission failures occur at each synapse at a rate of 20%. The results presented, however, are not significantly different from those where synaptic transmission failures were absent from the network model.

B. Inputs

The network was trained on sequences of ten orthogonal (non-overlapping) patterns. Each pattern was presented for multiple time steps. The number of time steps each pattern is activated is called "stutter length." An input pattern on one time step activated 64 neurons randomly chosen from sets of 96 neurons. That is, on each time step, a random 67% of the neurons of the appropriate external input pattern fire (see Fig. 1, top graph).

There are two types of sequences which are simulated: training trials, in which the entire externally driven sequence is presented and synaptic modification is allowed to occur and testing trials, in which part or all of the sequence is presented and no synaptic modification is allowed to occur.

C. Determining Shift

Shift is a measure of the change in temporal position of neural firing as a function of training. The metric used here compares neuronal firing after an "early" training trial to the final training trial. The "early" training trial is determined to be that when the network has achieved a stable initial firing distribution across time-steps even though firing is still mostly random at the beginning of training due to the random connectivity (See Fig. 1). We find that after 5 training trials most neuronal initial firing times can be reliably predicted across the sequence. We ignore, however, neurons from the final two patterns of the sequence because of a nonrepresentative end of sequence effect.

When α is non-zero, shift always tends to be in the earlier direction for the neurons in a network. We do find that some neurons which originally fired at the beginning of sequences appear to shift later (towards the end of the sequence) by large numbers of time steps. This "later shifting", however, is unrelated to the earlier-shifting phenomenon being studied. We hypothesized these neurons, which can later-shift by as much as 75% of the sequence, are inefficient coding neurons from the early patterns which through the process of synaptic modification are depotentiated, cease firing, and then are recruited later to code for patterns in the middle or at the end of the sequence. Also, in the case of neurons which have inputs from externals as well as recurrents driven by those same externals marginal forward shifting is possible, representing a different mechanism. A more detailed analysis of these other mechanisms is still necessary.

D. Measuring Performance

Successful learning is defined as a simulation being able to complete 80% of the training sequence during recall testing (only the first input pattern is externally activated) and doing so without skipping more than two patterns and without reaching an inappropriate stable state before the end of the sequence (see Fig. 2).

To determine which external pattern is being represented at each time step of recall, the neuronal firing is compared to the previously recorded neuronal firing on every time step of training (where all patterns were externally activated). The time step of training which is most similar to that of the network state at time t of recall (as determined by an inner product of the firing) is the input represented by the network during recall at time t.

E. Measuring E(L)

Local context firing length measures the contiguous period of time over which neurons fire. Published findings from our laboratory show that an intermediate to high average value of local context length, $E(L)$, is a good predictor of learning (e.g., [7,8]). We measure local context length using externally driven sequences and then count the period of time from a neuron's first time-step of firing to its last time-step of contiguous firing. Temporally contiguous firing is defined as two firings with less than three non-firing time-steps between the firings (e.g. on-off-off-on are temporally contiguous, on-off-off-off-on are not).

Because failure prone synaptic transmission and noisy inputs are being used here, some neurons flicker on-off-on while still being a local context neuron. The entire length was used to value such a neuron (e.g., on-off-on implies a length of 3). Some other neurons are randomly activated by the random processes just mentioned and are not strongly associated with any particular subsequence, or time-step, of the training sequence. These neurons were characterized by wide gaps between firing times and lack of temporally adjacent firings. Such neurons are categorized as unused.

III. RESULTS

For the first two or three training trials neural firing is almost entirely random. However, by trial five it is possible to reliably identify a particular time step with the firing of a particular neuron. With additional training trials the firing of the neurons begins to shift earlier in the sequence. Earlier shifting is clearly demonstrated by the externally activated neurons (see Fig. 1). The average shift of the externally activated neurons at the end of training is around fourteen time steps or 154 ms or just over one and a half patterns.

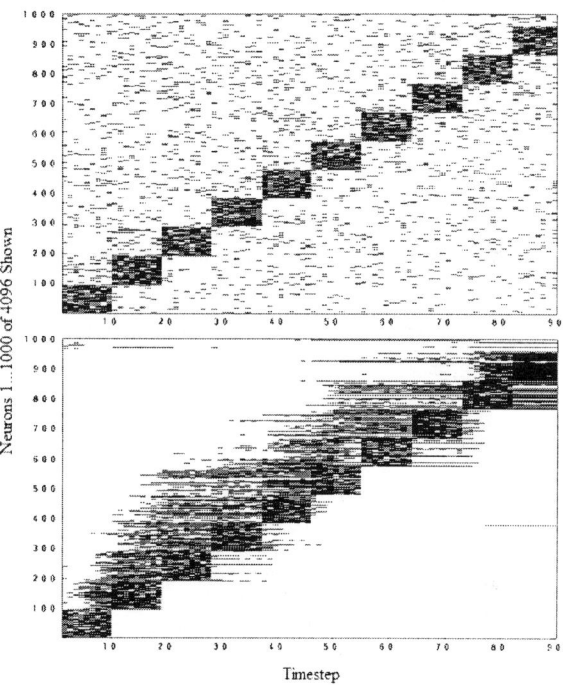

Fig. 1. **Training produces time shifting to earlier positions of externally activated neurons by extending context length.** Firing of the first 1000 neurons of the 4096 total neurons in a network during the fifth (upper figure) and 250th (lower figure) training trials. The external inputs to the network include neurons 1 through 960. Neurons 961 through 1000 are recurrently activated if they fire. The inputs are a sequence of orthogonal patterns, each on for nine time-steps (stutter=9). The rectangular blocks along the diagonal in the upper figure are the externally activated neurons. These rectangles are not solid because of input noise that randomly deselects external activation.

Typically, however, the time-shifting of the externally activated neurons tends to be less pronounced than that of purely, recurrently-activated neurons. Because an externally activated neuron is turned regardless of other activity, there is strong depotentiation of the recurrent inputs to these neurons, synaptic weakening beyond a reclaimable weight value. Thus, such a neuron tends toward a functional disconnection from most other neurons, thereby decreasing the likelihood that it can be activated earlier.

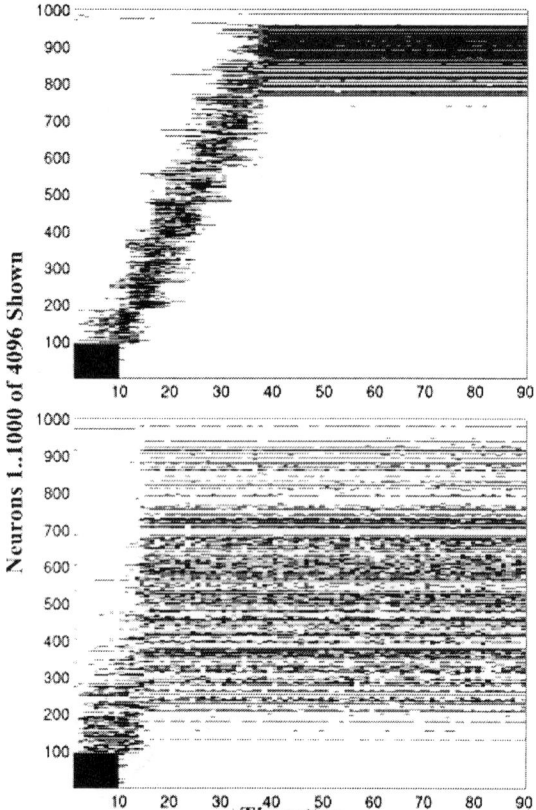

Fig. 2. **Example of a simulation that satisfies (top) and fails (bottom) to meet the 80% learning criterion on recall.** Both graphs are testing trials after 250 training trials. During the testing trial the first pattern is presented (dark rectangle) and then the network is allowed the free run. The top graph has a matched value of α to the stutter (note, on recall the sequence is compressed by a factor ~ 2). The bottom graph has a value of α above the matching value and falls into a steady state attractor.

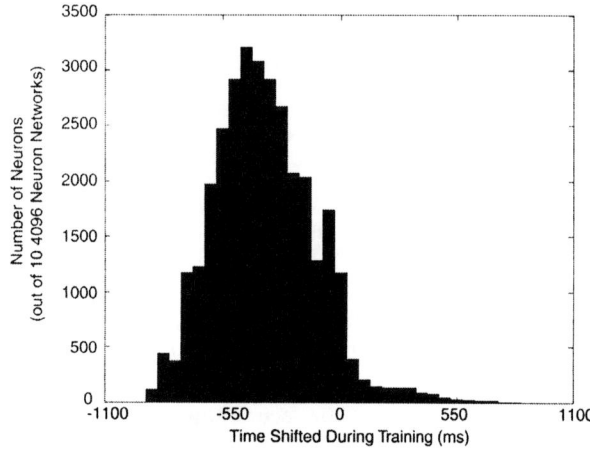

Fig. 3. **Time shift histogram** of the recurrent neurons in 10 networks with externally activated neurons excluded. Shift for each neuron is defined as the change in onset time of its initial firing after trial 5 vs. trial 250 (see Methods). Temporal shifting in the network during learning is predominantly in the earlier direction. The median total shift is approximately -34 time steps. However, this figure does not take context length, E(L), into account, and so does not fully reflect the skewing of place fields. The stutter was 9 and α was matched to this stutter length.

The earlier shifting seems to exhibit asymptotic behavior, that is by trial 150 neurons are reliably firing to a particular subsequence of the training sequence and shift only slightly as training proceeds. The average number of time steps shifted at the end of training is quite sensitive to the value of α, particularly when $-\log(\alpha) > 1/stutter$ (See Fig. 3). While there is no local minimum at e-fold decay ($\alpha^{stutter} = e^{-1} \approx 0.3679$), beyond e-fold decay rates, earlier-shifting approaches an asymptotic value (See Fig. 4). The mean amount of earlier-shifting appropriately reaches the maximum backward shift by setting the time-span of associativity to the e-fold decay value suggested by biology. The results show that the e-fold decay rate yields the maximum earlier-shifting with the minimal amount of code and learning degradation (only 15% of networks fail to complete the sequence on recall). Increasing α even slightly beyond the e-fold decay rate results in network failure in more than 50% of networks (See Fig. 4). Therefore, matching the time-span of associativity to the input pattern duration (in the model, matching the parameter alpha to the parameter stutter) is arguably a useful compromise for the model and, as a hypothesis, explains the similarity between the time of a theta cycle and the NMDA-R off-rate time constant in rats.

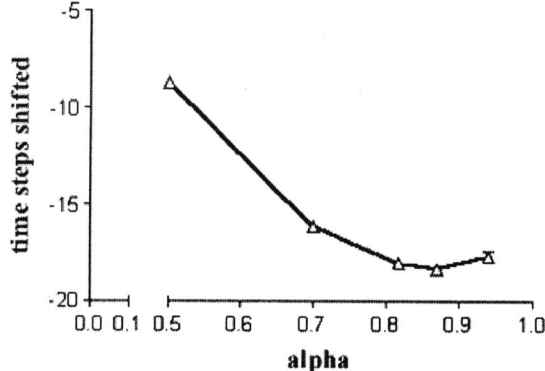

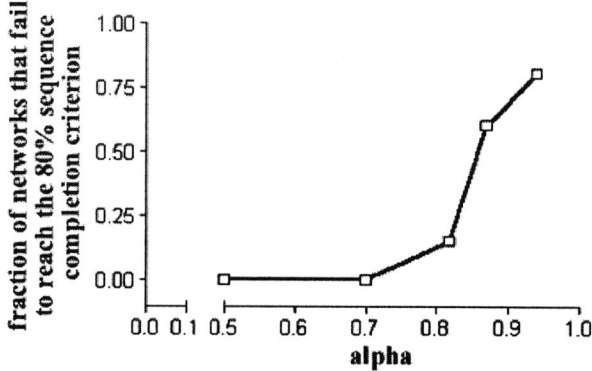

Fig. 4. **The effects of α on performance and shift at stutter-length five.** When α is matched to stutter-length (= 0.82), the time shift (upper figure) has essentially achieved its maximum backward value. However, at this value an overly strong attractor is beginning to develop to the detriment of performance (lower figure), at least for the competitive networks used here. Each point represents the average of 20 randomly connected networks.

At the beginning of training, the randomness in connectivity and random neural firing imply that, besides the externally activated neurons, almost no place-cell type firing (local context firing) is present in the network. However, after five training trials, such local context firing begins to emerge. These regular firings are typically on the order of one or two time steps in duration. With repeated training trials the firing length for context neurons increases, and non-context neurons begin to stop firing altogether. We find that $E(L)$ at the end of training is sensitive to α, increasing almost linearly with increasing α. This result is closely related to the earlier-shifting of neurons. That is, neurons not only begin their context firing earlier in each trial as training progresses, but they maintain part of their previous firing times. As a result, overall local context firing times lengthen for such neurons. At the matching e-fold decay rates, $E(L)$ is typically 1.9 times the input pattern duration (see Fig. 5).

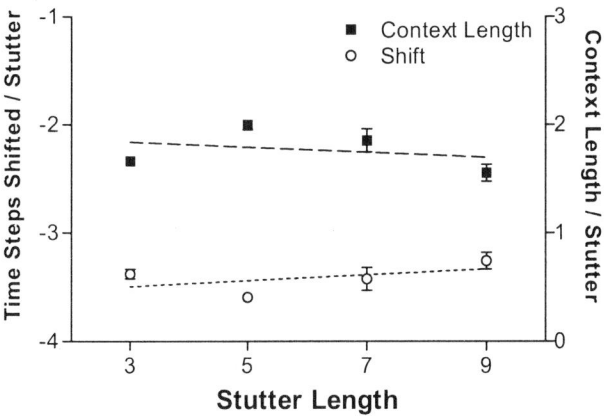

Fig. 5. **Normalized time shifting and normalized context length are constants.** Mean time shifting divided by stutter length and median context length divided by stutter length are plotted for four different values of stutter with each stutter length matched by the e-fold, decay constant α. Because a constant value is produced, time may be physically and consistently represented in the model by the ratioing and matching α to stutter. Each point is the average of ten random networks. The slopes of the two regression lines is approximately 0.01 and do not represent a significant deviation from zero in the slope.

The meaningfulness of matching stutter length to the associative time span is emphasized by normalized measurements of average time shifting and of average context length and is illustrated by the mean zero slope lines of Fig. 5. That is, if we divide training-induced average context length by stutter length when training at the matched time span, the model becomes parameter independent. Thus the matching of stutter length and time span becomes an explicit definition of time in the model because the associative time span is measurable and available from experimental work. Moreover, the normalized shift value and the normalized context length, $E(L)$, are a physiological prediction if we assume one complete pattern cycle is one complete theta cycle. And there is another prediction: slow animals – like humans – have a slower NMDA-R off-rate time constant in CA3 than fast, small animals like rats and mice.

IV. DISCUSSION

Most of these paragraphs address the origin of the earlier-shifting phenomenon across training. The last paragraph points out a general hypothesis about the evolved function and parameterization of the hippocampus.

Because of the direct externally activated excitation and because of indirect external excitation through recurrent neurons, any one recurrent neuron will be variously biased to fire as a function of time within a training trial (at the outset of training). Because the external activation is stuttered, the bias of any one, particular recurrent neuron is also stuttered. That is, an approximately constant bias covers a more-or-less contiguous time interval equal to the stutter-length for such a neuron. Now hypothesize random firing of recurrent neurons reflecting such biases, then we claim that the temporally asymmetric synaptic modification rule produces a tendency for such neurons to fire earlier over the course of training for two reasons:

First, because of the temporal asymmetry of the synaptic modification rule, only those inputs turning on somewhat before a postsynaptic neuron fires, or would tend to fire due to a strong bias, will on average potentiate. Contrariwise, those inputs tending to turn on afterward or not turn on at all will, on average, have their synapses weakened. Thus, the inputs that get strengthened are the ones that turn on earlier. But again recall, these inputs too are biased to turn on for several steps just as the relevant postsynaptic neuron is biased toward firing for several time-steps. So as these inputs strengthen, the postsynaptic neuron will begin to fire earlier. These ideas, however, need to be generalized.

Consider now two sets of equal biases that excite the same postsynaptic neuron but are at different noncontiguous places in the sequence. Just by chance one bias will grow stronger than the other because of synaptic modification and the random aspects of the inputs. Then this stronger bias will tend to wipe out the weaker bias by virtue of the synaptic modification rule weakening the synaptic inputs through which the weaker bias is expressed.

Second, if any one particular neuron is biased strongly enough so it begins to fire with regularity in response to a particular subsequence, this neuron will contribute to the bias of other neurons just as if it were an externally activated neuron. The fact that this particular neuron is shifting earlier, in accordance with the reasons just above, results in a *cascade* of earlier shifting. That is, as a set of temporally associated neurons shift earlier so will the neurons they activate. Thus, it makes sense to refer to an earlier-shift or backward cascade that can propagate through assemblies of coding neurons over successive trials.

The earlier shifting of neurons can be controlled by the value of α. We take α to be the rate constant for the unbinding of glutamate from the NMDA receptor. We propose that the role of hippocampal recoding is a compromise between maximizing the predictive value of the codes developed while preserving the ability of the CA3 to sequence. However, as we increase α we find that there is a point at which overly strong associations create noisy stable attractors, destroying the sequencing capabilities of the sparsely connected recurrent network.

Neurophysiological findings are consistent with an e-fold decay rate in which the presynaptic neuron's contribution to LTP decreases. Presumably the e-fold decay rate arises from the unbinding of a glutamate saturated NMDA-R system. As such, we can write the unbinding as proportional to $e^{-t \cdot constant}$, for some constant that we set to one. Suppose at t = 0, the saturated system has a value of one. Then on the next timestep, Δt, its value is α; that is, $\alpha = e^{-\Delta t}$. But Δt is 1/(stutter length) because stimulus longevity is constant no matter how temporally refined it is represented. The central result is that simulations of our model imply this theoretical relationship to be optimal for sequence learning, a result foreshadowed by the compression result in [15].

ACKNOWLEDGMENT

This work was supported by David A. Harrison III research grants to K.E.M and P.L., by NIH MH48161, MH63855 and RR15205 to WBL; and NSF NGSEIA-9974968, NPACI ASC-96-10920, and NGS ACI-0203960 to Marty Humphrey. We also thank Aaron Shon, Sean Polyn, David Sullivan, and Xiangbao Wu for their comments on early versions of the text.

REFERENCES

[1] W.B Levy, "A computational approach to hippocampal function," in *Computational modeling of learning in simple neural systems*, R. D. Hawkins and G. H. Bower, Eds. Orlando, FL: Academic Press, 1989, pp. 243 - 305.

[2] W.B Levy, X.B. Wu, and R.A. Baxter, "Unification of hippocampal function via computational/encoding considerations." in Proc. Third Workshop on Neural Networks: from Biology to High Energy Physics. *Intl. J. Neural Sys.*, vol. 6, (Supp.), (D. J. Amit, P. del Guidice, B. Denby, E. T. Rolls and A. Treves, Eds.), Singapore:World Scientific Publishing, 1995, pp. 71-80.

[3] W.R. Holmes and W.B Levy, "Insights into associative long-term potentiation from computational models of NMDA receptor-mediated calcium influx and intracellular calcium concentration changes," *J. Neurophysiol.*, vol. 63(5), pp.1148-68, 1990.

[4] K.I. Blum and L.F. Abbott, "A model of spatial map formation in the hippocampus of the rat," *Neural Comput.*, 8, pp. 85-93. 1996.

[5] M.R. Mehta, C.A. Barnes, and B.L. McNaughton, "Experience-dependent, asymmetric expansion of hippocampal place fields," *Proc. National Acad. Sci.*, USA, 94, pp.8918-8921. 1997.

[6] M.R. Mehta, M.C. Quirk, and M.A. Wilson, "Experience-dependent, asymmetric shape of hippocampal receptive fields," *Neuron*, 25, pp.707 -715. 2000.

[7] A.P. Shon, X.B. Wu, D.W. Sullivan and W.B Levy, "Initial state randomness improves sequence learning in a model hippocampal network," *Phys. Rev. E*, vol 65, 031914. 2002.

[8] X.B. Wu, J. Tyrcha, and W.B Levy, "A neural network solution to the transverse-patterning problem depends on repetition of the input code," *Biol. Cybern.*, 79, 1998, 203-213.

[9] D. Marr, "Simple memory, a theory for archicortex," *Phil. Trans. Roy. Soc. London*, 262, 23-81, 1971

[10] E.T. Rolls, "A theory of hippocampal function in memory," *Hippocampus*, 6, pp. 601-620. 1996.

[11] W.B Levy, and O. Steward, "Temporal contiguity requirements for long-term associative potentiation/depression in the hippocampus," *Neuroscience*, 8, pp.791-797. 1983.

[12] W.B Levy, "A sequence predicting CA3 is a flexible associator that learns and uses context to solve hippocampal-like tasks," *Hippocampus*, 6(6), pp. 579 - 591. 1996.

[13] W.B Levy, and P. Sederberg, "A neural network model of hippocampally mediated trace conditioning," in *IEEE International Conference on Neural Networks*, vol. 1, pp. 372-376. Piscataway, NJ: Institute of Electrical and Electronics Engineers. 1997.

[14] P. Rodriguez, and W.B Levy, "A model of hippocampal activity in trace conditioning: Where's the trace?" *Behav. Neurosci.* 115, 2001, 1224-1238.

[15] D.A. August, and W. B Levy, "Temporal sequence compression by an integrate-and-fire model of hippocampal area CA3." *J. Computational Neurosci.*, 6, 1999, 71-90.

Timing of consecutive traveling pulses in a model of entorhinal cortex

Anatoli Gorchetchnikov
Dept of Cognitive and Neural Systems,
Boston University,
677 Beacon St, Boston, MA 02215, USA
Email: anatoli@cns.bu.edu

Michael E. Hasselmo
Dept of Psychology,
Boston University,
64 Cummington St, Boston, MA 02215, USA
Email: hasselmo@bu.edu

Abstract—Previous work described a detailed spiking model of interactions between the hippocampus and entorhinal cortex in guiding rat spatial navigation behavior [1]. The timing of spiking activity in the entorhinal cortex is critical for the proper functioning of that model. Here we investigate the influence of several parameters of the model on the spike timing of consecutive traveling pulses within the network of spiking neurons with biologically realistic synaptic parameters. The results suggest that the local properties of the circuit consisting of pyramidal cell and interneuron affect the time interval between consecutive traveling pulses, while the strength of excitatory coupling between these circuits has little influence unless this strength is too small. These results can be generalized to other models of similar architecture that exhibit traveling pulses behavior, and also serve as a basis of further development of full scale realistic implementation of the formal model of spatial navigation [1].

I. INTRODUCTION

In the model of spatial navigation by Hasselmo et al [1] the navigation task is solved by interaction between the knowledge about desired destination and knowledge about current location. This interaction takes place in hippocampal area CA1 using two converging inputs. The input from the hippocampal area CA3 represents the activity spreading forward along the path from the current location. The input from entorhinal cortex layer III (ECIII) represents the spread of activity from the goal location in the direction reverse to movement. The plots of neuronal activity illustrating the interaction between involved brain areas over a single theta cycle are presented in Figure 2. Numerical simulations showed that this mechanism allows the model to navigate successfully toward a known reward location, or visit several reward locations sequentially [2].

Implementation of this model with spiking neural network [3] led to conclusion that successful performance requires the arrival of spikes from two principal inputs, the hippocampal area CA3 and the layer III of entorhinal cortex within a narrow (about 15ms) time window from each other. Such precise timing requires full understanding of the influence of various parameters of the model on two time courses: interpulse interval between consecutive spikes of the same cell in ECIII (shown in Figure 2 by red arrow), and propagating of the activity through ECIII, ECII and CA3 (shown in Figure 2 by a set of blue arrows). Previously presented simulations used a set of biologically realistic parameters, which allowed the proper timing [3], but a detailed parametric study was not conducted. Here we concentrate on the timing of interpulse interval within the ECIII (red arrow in Figure 2).

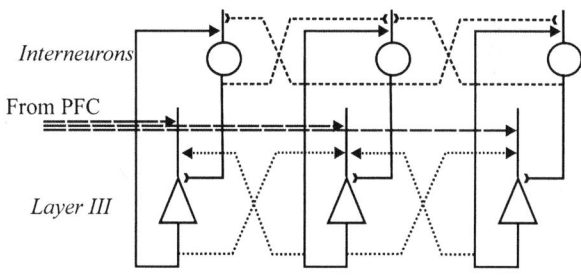

Fig. 1. Sketch of the connectivity within the model. Solid lines represent connections within a circuit for a single location; dotted lines – excitatory interactions between locations (only nearest neighbor connections are shown); dashed lines – inhibitory interactions between locations (weak); long-dashed lines – input projections. Arrowheads stand for excitatory synapses, archeads for inhibitory synapses.

To simplify the computation, in this study all populations of the original model [3] except ECIII were removed from the network. The resulting architecture of the ECIII is presented in Figure 1. Both pyramidal cells and interneurons are quiescent without input. Note, that in the case of constant external input to all pyramidal cells this model can be classified as a network of coupled neuronal oscillators, where each oscillator consists of a pair made up of pyramidal cell and interneuron. The properties of traveling pulses in this type of networks were studied by Ermentrout and Kleinfeld [4]. The model presented here has two significant differences, which might render the analysis in [4] inapplicable. Firstly, the coupling between the circuits is strong enough not to satisfy the definition of weak coupling from [4]. Secondly, there is no constant input to the circuits, and, therefore, they are only potential oscillators. Therefore, one can probably disregard the oscillatory nature of the circuit and collapse it into a single cell with long refractory period. The period of oscillations in the network of such cells was shown to scale linearly with the length of the refractory period [5], but traveling solutions were not investigated there.

In our full circuit model of spatial navigation [1] the input from prefrontal cortex to ECIII activates only the cells that correspond to goal locations. To replicate that, here the input

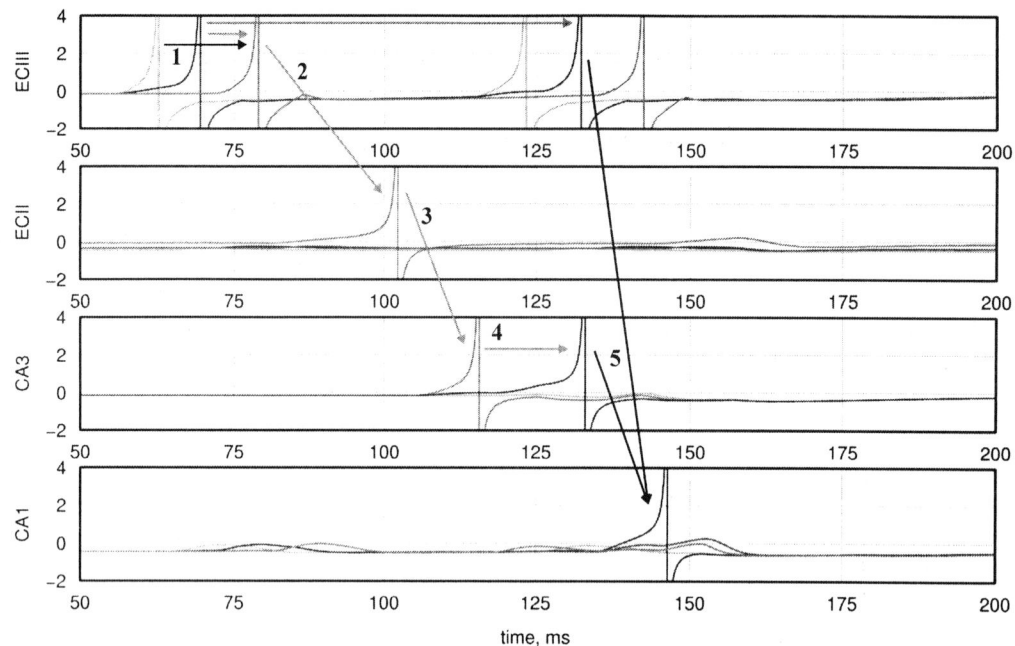

Fig. 2. Sketch of neuronal activity within a spiking model guiding the movement of a virtual rat during one step on the linear track. The animal starts two locations from the goal. Numbers next to arrows correspond to the following steps in the process. 1) The reverse spread of activity from the cell representing the goal location (cell activity in pink) through the cell representing the next desired location (cell activity in green) to the cell representing the current location (cell activity in blue). 2 and 3) Activation of the cell representing the current location in ECIII leads to consecutive activation of the cells representing the current location in ECII and CA3. 4) The forward spread of activity from current location in CA3. 5) Convergence between the forward spread and the second wave of the reverse spread leads to selection of the next desired location by the corresponding activity in CA1. Two time courses important for proper convergence are represented by blue and red arrows.

was limited to a single pyramidal cell, and this cell initiates the consecutive traveling pulses through the network. The activity spreads along excitatory connectivity between neighboring pyramidal cells, which follows the Gaussian profile. Therefore, the model falls within a class of networks with spatially decaying connectivity. Golomb and Ermentrout [6] analyzed the traveling solutions in this class of networks, but they studied the propagation of a single pulse and did not consider the interpulse interval, which is critical for our model of spatial navigation [1] and is the subject of this study.

II. METHODS

The model uses the KDE Integrated Neuro-Simulation Software (KInNeSS) version 0.2.2alpha1[1], which allows the creation of the virtual environment for the model, and provides input from this environment in the form of depolarizing current injections to the respective input cells of the model. The environment was a horizontal linear track of length 14 and width 1 location/cell, surrounded by walls one location/cell thick to emulate a one-dimensional case.

Entorhinal neuronal populations in the model use two-compartmental cell representation with an output delay line representing the action potential traveling time through an axon. A population of neuronal elements representing prefrontal cortex provides the information about the goal location that initiates the traveling pulse in ECIII. These cells do not receive synaptic input, and, therefore, do not use dendritic compartment. The driving input was provided as a current injection to the prefrontal cell connected to the ECIII cell corresponding to the leftmost location on the track. Detailed descriptions of the compartments and parameters of the simulations are presented in the Appendix.

The first experiment consisted of multiple simulations where the strength of one-to-one inhibitory connections from interneurons to respective pyramidal cells varied from 1 to 10 with step 1 (in units corresponding to the density of synaptic channels, see Appendix), and the strength of excitatory connections between neighboring pyramidal cells varied as follows. The base profile was a Gaussian, scaled so that the peak value was equal to a numeric value from 1 to 10 with step 1 (called excitatory strength henceforth), and $\sigma = 0.6d$, where $d = 1$ for adjacent pyramidal cells. This profile was applied to the model by assigning the synaptic weights to connections between neighboring cells, with exclusion of the cell's projection to itself and all projections that had weight below 10^{-3}.

For each set of synaptic weights, the interspike intervals were recorded during 500 simulated milliseconds (3–10 spikes per cell depending on the parameters). The first four cells including the driving cell were excluded from the analysis to avoid the unstable pulses that occur close to the driving cell under some parameter settings. From the remaining ten cells all interspike intervals were combined in a sample (30–50 intervals per sample), and sample average, standard deviation

[1] Available for download at *http://temporal.bu.edu*.

and coefficient of variation were calculated.

In the second set of simulations the decay time constant of inhibitory synapse was varied from 6 to 8 ms with the step 0.2 ms, the excitatory and inhibitory connection strengths were fixed at 6 and 8, respectively. As a reference point for this experiment the dependency of intrinsic frequency of single uncoupled oscillatory circuit (pyramidal cell and corresponding interneuron) henceforth called local circuit frequency was measured for the same values of time constant. Since the local circuit frequency depends on the injected current, the current amplitude was adjusted to provide interspike intervals similar to these received in the network simulations.

Finally, the dependency of local circuit oscillatory frequency on the inhibitory strength was measured in an isolated circuit for two values of injected current, also adjusted to provide interspike intervals similar to the ones received in previous experiments.

III. RESULTS

The results of the first simulation are summarized in Figure 5. The plateau of almost constant interpulse intervals for the strong local interneuron-to-pyramidal inhibition (panel A) together with lower standard deviation and coefficient of variance in the same parameter ranges (panels B and C) can be of critical importance for learning in the networks of similar architecture.

In some cases the excitation was strong enough to allow the spread of the activity to the cells corresponding to locations inside the walls of the environment. These cases were disregarded for three reasons. Firstly, the spread within the walls of the environment violated the emulation of one-dimensional setting and caused a pattern of network activation that differed from all presented in Figure 5 cases and, therefore, should be analyzed separately. Secondly, in the model of spatial navigation [3] the spread of activity in restricted locations like the walls renders the model inoperable. Finally, in two-dimensional case the domination of excitatory strengths over inhibitory strengths leads to seizure-like oscillatory solutions instead of traveling pulse solutions. Simulations that expressed such behavior were terminated as soon as the excessive spread of activity happened, and the respective data is omitted from Figure 5.

All runs with the excitatory strength of 1 were disregarded, since no traveling pulses were generated at this level of excitation. For low excitation (strength 2 and 3, left back part of the plot), the generation of next pulse often happened before the previous one moved far enough along the network. This led the network to skip the second pulse occasionally, and, therefore, to longer interspike intervals and higher variability of these intervals.

The results of the second and third simulations are plotted in Figures 3 and 4, respectively. The local circuit frequency in Figure 3 and the interval between consecutive traveling pulses in Figure 4 are plotted on the same graphs, but can only be used for the reference, since the experimental settings were different for these measurements. In both plots the error

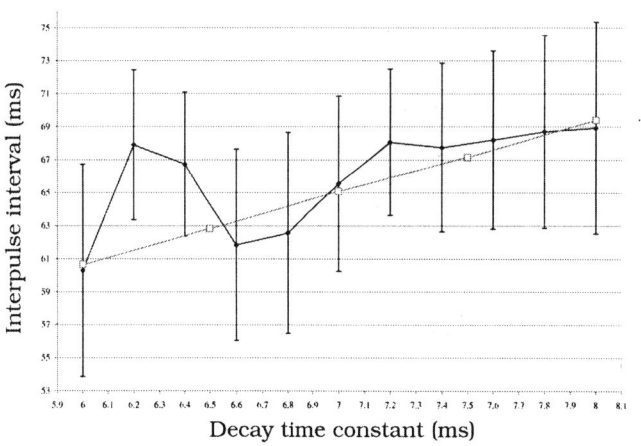

Fig. 3. Interval between consecutive traveling pulses as a function of the decay time constant of inhibitory synapse is shown in blue. For the reference, the gray line indicates the dependency of local circuit oscillatory frequency on the decay time constant.

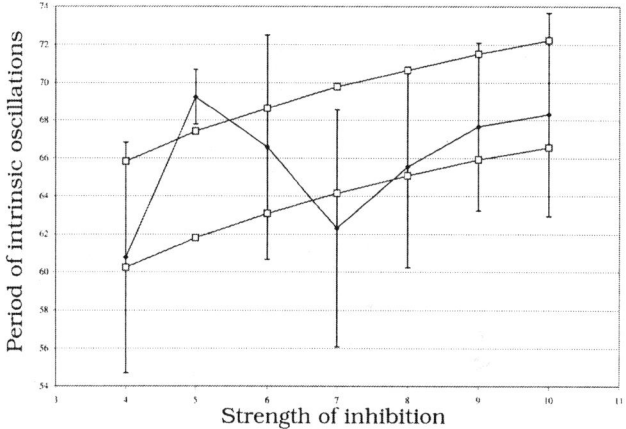

Fig. 4. Circuit intrinsic oscillatory frequency as a function of the strength of inhibitory connection. Two values of input current are plotted in red, the higher plot corresponds to the smaller value of the current. For the reference, the blue plot indicates the dependency of interval between consecutive traveling pulses on the strength of inhibitory connections.

of local circuit frequency measurements was negligible and mostly due to the discretization error, therefore it is omitted from the plots.

IV. DISCUSSION

We investigated the influence of several parameters on the interpulse interval of consecutive traveling spikes in the network sketched in Figure 1 looking for the parameter ranges where the interspike interval stays approximately constant. As shown in Figure 5, such parameter regime exists and spans over wide range of medium to high strength of excitatory connections between pyramidal cells in Figure 1 as long as the strength of inhibitory connections from interneurons to pyramidal cells is high enough. This regime will be referred to as "persistent" in the following discussion.

The network can also be in two other regimes. One is the seizure-like oscillatory activity that occur when the level of

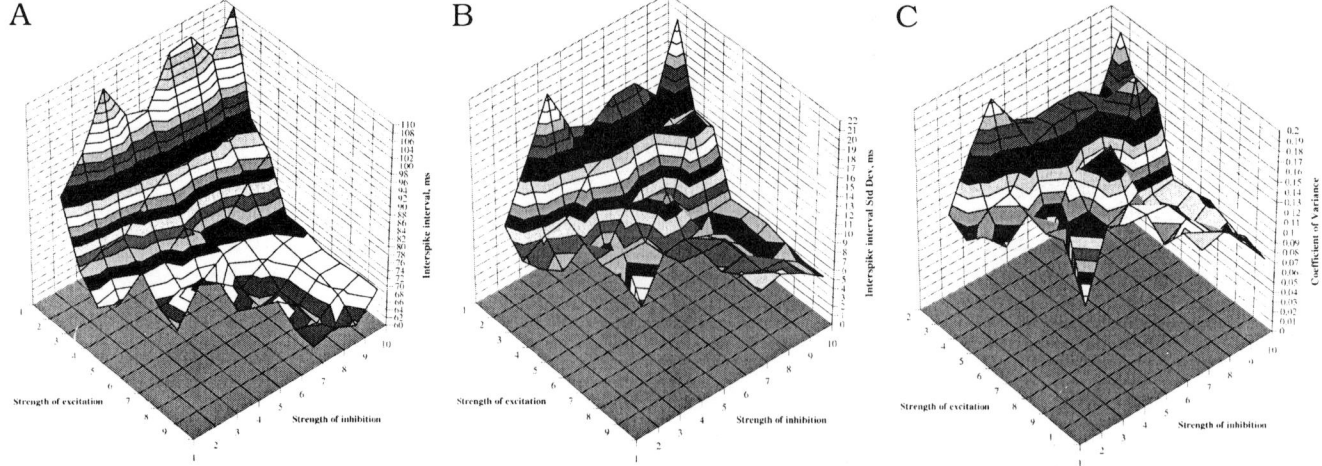

Fig. 5. Interval between consecutive traveling pulses as a function of the strength of inhibitory and excitatory connections. Inhibitory strength is on X axis, excitatory strength on Y axis. Missing front corners in each panel correspond to cases when the excitation is too strong compared to inhibition (see text). Panel A – average interspike interval; note the flattening of the plot for strong inhibitory values. Panel B – standard deviation of the interspike interval; note that it is the lowest for the flat part of panel A. Panel C – coefficient of variation; note that it is also the lowest for the flat part of panel A.

excitatory strength is too high comparing to the inhibition. In this parameter range traveling solution does not exist, and the results were omitted from Figure 5 to avoid confusion. The last regime (henceforth called "volatile") exists at low levels of excitatory connection strengths and shows as a ridge in panel A of Figure 5.

The difference in behavior between persistent and volatile regimes resulted from the relation between the wave speed and local circuit frequency. In the volatile regime, the wave speed was slower than the local circuit frequency (or the refractory period of the circuit), which led to the attempt to generate a new wave before it could spread without collapsing on the previous wave. This led to occasional skipping pulses during the simulations as well as to strong dependency of the interpulse interval on the strength of excitation (through its influence on the wave speed). For high values of excitation strength the wave speed was faster than the refractory period, therefore the latter controlled the interpulse interval leading to persistent regime as discussed below.

The dependency of the interspike interval on the decay time constant of the inhibitory synapse appears to follow a similar trend to the dependency of local circuit frequency for the pair consisting of pyramidal cell and interneuron. This similarity suggests that the local circuit frequency at least in part determines the interspike interval in the model. The local circuit frequency scales linearly with the decay time constant both in our numeric simulations presented here and in theoretical analysis of similar circuits [5]. The interpulse interval in Figure 3 appears to saturate, but more data is necessary to determine whether it is a significant trend.

The dependency of local circuit frequency on the strength of inhibition follows the exponential decay due to the dual exponential synaptic implementation in the model. The interpulse interval follows a similar trend (see Figure 4). Together, the results plotted in Figures 3 and 4 suggest that the local

TABLE I
LOCAL CIRCUIT OSCILLATION PERIOD AS A FUNCTION OF INHIBITORY STRENGTH IN ISOLATED CIRCUIT.

Inhibitory strength	0	0.1	1	5	10
Period, ms	31.2	35.7	55.6	66.1	71.4

properties of the circuit consisting of pyramidal cell and interneuron are the major factor that determines the interpulse interval when the model is in persistent regime[2].

The increase of inhibitory connections strength within the local circuit influences the interpulse interval through the change of local circuit frequency described above. Note that only the slow changing tail of this exponent falls into the range of inhibitory strengths studied here. Lower values of inhibitory strength showed much higher influence on local circuit frequency, when the isolated circuit was studied (see Table I), but they also led the network into epilepsy-like oscillatory behavior instead of traveling pulse solutions, when these circuits were combined together. Therefore, in the network the increase of inhibitory strength leads only to a minor increase in interspike interval between consecutive traveling pulses.

A more important effect of the inhibitory strength increase in the studied range is the stabilization of interpulse interval for a range of excitatory strengths. The width of this range increases with the strength of inhibition, as shown in Figure 5 and creates the persistent regime. Note that not only the interpulse interval becomes approximately constant (light blue flat part of the panel A towards the right back of the panel), but also the variance became smaller in this parameter regime

[2]This is only true, if the driving input is either constant current or very high frequency (much higher than the local circuit frequency) low amplitude stimulation used in simulations presented here. Low frequency stimulation will affect the interpulse interval by driving the activity in the network.

(panels B and C). Stabilized timing in the network over the range of excitatory strengths can allow better learning in the network, since the modification of the excitatory connections and redistribution of the network activation will not cause disruption of the overall timing of the network activity, and, therefore will reduce any negative effect learning can induce on communication between populations in the network.

Applying these results to the model of spatial navigation [1], one can conclude that the balance of excitatory and inhibitory strengths should not matter much for the behavior of the model as long as both strengths stay not lower than 4. In this case the interspike interval falls mostly within 60–70ms. The actual simulations of [3] used 4 and 5 for excitatory and inhibitory strengths, respectively, and showed that this interval allows proper behavior. The results from Figure 5 show that a wide variety of parameter settings can achieve a similar interval. Out of this variety the strongest inhibition is preferable if learning is enabled in the excitatory lateral connectivity of the model.

ACKNOWLEDGMENTS

This research was supported by NIH grants MH60013, MH61492, MH60450, and DA16454.

APPENDIX

A. Dendritic compartment

Dendritic compartment representation is derived from the standard approximation of the cable equation [7]:

$$C_m \frac{dV_m}{dt} = \sum_{Ch} g_{Ch}(E_{Ch} - V_m) + g_a(V_{m+1} + V_{m-1} - 2V_m) - g_l V_m \quad (1)$$

where V_m is a membrane potential in this compartment $[mV]$, $V_{m\pm1}$ are membrane potentials in neighboring compartments $[mV]$, g_{Ch} is a conductance of ligand gated ion channel $[mS]$, g_l is a leakage conductance $[mS]$, g_a is an axial conductance $[mS]$, and C_m is a membrane capacitance $[\mu F]$.

Equation (1) can be simplified for the purpose of this study to

$$C_m \frac{dV_m}{dt} = \sum_{Ch} g_{Ch}(E_{Ch} - V_m) + g_a(V_{m+1} - V_m) - g_l V_m \quad (2)$$

since there is only one neighboring compartment. Further more, to convert the actual capacitance and conductances to their dimension independent counterparts, we divide both sides by πdl to obtain

$$C_M \frac{dV_m}{dt} = \sum_{Ch} \frac{g_{Ch}}{\pi dl}(E_{Ch} - V_m) + \frac{dg_A}{4l^2}(V_{m+1} - V_m) - g_L V_m \quad (3)$$

are $C_M = 1\mu F/cm^2$. Current version of KInNeSS allows to set

$$z = \frac{dg_A}{4l^2} \left[\frac{mS}{cm^2}\right] \quad (4)$$

directly.

For the ligand-gated channels, the value $\sum_{Ch} \frac{g_{Ch}}{\pi dl}$ is represented as individual channel conductances $g_{Ch}[nS]$ times the synaptic weight $w = \frac{N_{Ch}}{\pi dl}\left[\frac{10^6}{cm^2}\right]$ corresponding to a channel density in millions of channels per cm^2 of the membrane. Channel conductance is calculated according to a dual-exponential equation

$$g_{Ch} = \frac{\bar{g}_{Ch} p}{\tau_f - \tau_r}(e^{-\frac{t}{\tau_f}} - e^{-\frac{t}{\tau_r}}) \quad (5)$$

if $\tau_f \neq \tau_r$, and according to the alpha function

$$g_{Ch} = \bar{g}_{Ch} \frac{t}{\tau_f} e^{(1-\frac{t}{\tau_f})} \quad (6)$$

if $\tau_f = \tau_r$. In both cases $\bar{g}_{Ch}[nS]$ is the maximal conductance, and t is time since presynaptic action potential. In (5) p is a scaling coefficient that enforces

$$\max\left(\frac{p}{\tau_f - \tau_r}(e^{-\frac{t}{\tau_f}} - e^{-\frac{t}{\tau_r}})\right) = 1 \quad (7)$$

Note that setting of the synaptic weight w to a experimentally measured channel density in the synapse would not be correct. It should accommodate the non-uniform distribution of ligand-gated channels in the compartment by averaging out the total number of channels in respective synapses over the membrane area of a *whole* compartment, not just the area of the synapse.

B. Somatic compartment

To lower the computational complexity of the model, the generation of action potentials is simulated using the reduced version of Hodgkin-Huxley equation also known as the theta-neuron or canonical Type I equation [8], [9]. This equation was modified to take the form

$$\begin{cases} \frac{d\theta}{dt} = [1 - \cos(\theta) + \\ \qquad + (1 + \cos(\theta))(qI - r)]\tau & \text{if } \theta \leq 3.125 \\ \theta = -3.04 & \text{otherwise} \end{cases} \quad (8)$$

where the numerical limits for θ were set so that membrane potential

$$V_m = \tan\left(\frac{\theta}{2}\right) \quad (9)$$

changes between approximately -20 and 120 mV. This allows us to replace the reduced representation with a complete Hodgkin-Huxley type equation without affecting the rest of the model if the need arises. The dimensionless parameter r is the original threshold controlling the dynamics of the cell. In the absence of input, the negative value of r sets the cell in excitable state, when a certain excitatory input is necessary to make it fire, while a positive value of r sets the neuron to a constantly firing state, when the excitatory input only modifies the firing frequency, but the inhibitory input can force it to cease firing. For more detailed discussion of this parameter influence see [9].

Additional modifications over the original version of reduced equation discussed in [9] include two dimensionless

TABLE II
POPULATION-SPECIFIC PARAMETERS OF THE MODEL.

Population	$\bar{g}_{AMPA}$, nS	r	Axonal delay, ms
Prefrontal cortex	n/a	-0.01	0.1
EC III interneurons	0.15	-0.01	0.1
EC III pyramidals (from PFC) (recurrent)	0.247 0.15	-0.02	2.0

TABLE III
CONNECTION STRENGTHS.

Target	Type	Source	Weight(σ)
EC III interneurons	AMPA GABA	EC III pyr recurrent	9.0 0.25 (0.8)[a]
EC III pyramidals	AMPA	PFC	1.0 (0.6)

[a]Recurrent projections exclude the connection from cell to itself.

scaling factors: q – overall voltage gain factor that allows scaling of realistic synaptic potentials provided by (3) to values fit for use by (8); τ – time scaling factor that allows to adjust behavior of (8) to the same timescale as the rest of the model.

The input current is calculated according to a simplified version of the second term in (3)

$$I = zV_{m-1} \quad (10)$$

Comparing to (3) $V_m = 0$ here, because due to the specific nature of the reduced representation, the value of V_m stays within $[-0.6, 0.6]$ mV unless the spike is generated (in which case the influence of the input on the cell dynamics is minimal), while the value of V_{m-1} is of the order of tens mV. Parameter z is defined in (4).

C. Parameters of the simulations

For simplicity, all of the populations use only two types of synaptic channels: AMPA receptor and GABA$_A$ receptor with the parameters as described in [10]. Unless the parameter was under study in specific experiment, the following values were used. For AMPA channels $E_{Ch} = 0mV$, $\tau_r = 2ms$, $\tau_f = 2ms$, $\bar{g}_{Ch}$ varied from population to population and is listed in Table II. Parameters for $GABA_A$ channels were $E_{Ch} = -70mV$, $\tau_r = 1ms$, $\tau_f = 7ms$, $\bar{g}_{Ch} = 2.461nS$. Parameters in equation (8) were: $q = 10$, $s = 0.45$, and threshold r was population specific and is listed in Table II.

KInNeSS does not allow to set different axonal delays for different outputs of the same cell. To compensate for this problem, the axonal delay for pyramidal cells was set to the pyramidal-to-pyramidal value, and axonal delay of the interneurons was artificially reduced to accommodate smaller pyramidal-to-interneuron delay. The axonal delay of prefrontal cells does not influence the system dynamics, since they do not receive any recurrent input. In equations (3-4) for simplicity $z = 3.0$ and $g_l = 0$ for all cells. Synaptic connection strengths that did not change across experiments are listed in Table III.

REFERENCES

[1] M. E. Hasselmo, J. Hay, M. Ilyn, and A. Gorchetchnikov, "Neuromodulation, theta rhythm, and rat spatial navigation," *Neural Netw*, vol. 15, no. 4-6, pp. 689–707, 2002.

[2] A. Gorchetchnikov and M. E. Hasselmo, "A model of hippocampal circuitry mediating goal-driven navigation in a familiar environment," *Neurocomputing*, vol. 44-46, pp. 423–427, 2002.

[3] ——, "A model of septal, entorhinal and hippocampal interactions to solve multiple goal navigation tasks," *Soc Neurosci Abstr*, vol. 32, p. 676.16, 2002.

[4] G. B. Ermentrout and D. Kleinfeld, "Traveling electrical waves in cortex: Insights from phase dynamics and speculation on a computational role," *Neuron*, vol. 29, no. 1, pp. 33–44, 2001.

[5] R. Curtu and G. B. Ermentrout, "Oscillations in a refractory neural net," *J Math Biol*, vol. 43, pp. 81–100, 2001.

[6] D. Golomb and G. B. Ermentrout, "Effect of delay on the type and velocity of travelling pulses in neuronal networks with spatially decaying connectivity," *Network: Comput Neural Syst*, vol. 11, pp. 221–246, 2000.

[7] J. B. Bower and D. Beeman, *The Book of GENESIS. Exploring Realistic Neural Models with the GEneral NEural SImulation System*. New York: Springer-Verlag, 1995.

[8] G. B. Ermentrout and N. Kopell, "Parabolic bursting in an excitable system coupled with slow oscillation," *SIAM J Appl Math*, vol. 46, pp. 233–252, 1986.

[9] F. C. Hoppensteadt and E. M. Izhikevich, *Weakly Connected Neural Networks*. New York: Springer-Verlag, 1998.

[10] E. Fransen, A. A. Alonso, and M. E. Hasselmo, "Simulations of the role of the muscarinic-activated calcium-sensitive nonspecific cation current i_{NCM} in entorhinal neuronal activity during delayed matching tasks," *J Neurosci*, vol. 22, no. 3, pp. 1081–1097, 2002.

Latent Attractor Selection for Variable Length Episodic Context Stimuli with Distractors

Simona Doboli
Computer Science Department
Hofstra University
Hempstead, NY 11549

Ali A. Minai
Complex Adaptive Systems Laboratory
ECECS Department
University of Cincinnati
Cincinnati, OH 45221

Abstract

Latent attractor networks have been proposed as a possible mechanism for representing episodic context in the hippocampus [5], and as general purpose models of episodic context-dependent encoding in neural networks [3]. These are recurrent neural networks with attractors that never fully manifest themselves, but bias the network's response to external stimuli. While each attractor in the original latent attractor model was triggered by unique *context patterns* specific to the context, this model was later extended to the case where contexts were triggered progressively by the sequential presentation of several stimulus patterns without regard to order, simulating the more realistic situation where a context is identified by a sequentially scanned combination of landmarks. In this paper, we describe a network model that can select among contexts identified by overlapping sequences of different lengths, even if the relevant stimulus patterns are interspersed among patterns irrelevant to context selection.

I. INTRODUCTION

In most realistic situations facing a cognitive system, the meaning of stimuli depends on context. It is possible to distinguish between two types of contexts, depending on how far in the past the context information is given *relative to the current time*. The first one — which we call *Type I Context* — comprises the cases where the system's response at time t depends on stimuli presented in an immediately preceding time window. Examples of such context occur in applications such as speech processing and word recognition. It is embodied in autoregressive models or finite-state machines and can be learned by recurrent neural networks where past states are fed back to the network [12, 14, 13].

The second type of context, which we term *Type II* or *episodic context*, arises when the information identifying context is given transiently at *a particular time* — typically at the beginning of an episode. Examples of such context occur in the recognition of spatial environments, social situations and in task planning, etc., where the context identified at the beginning of the episode continues to be in force for its entire duration. For example, upon entering a room, one recognizes it based on the presence of certain objects and/or persons, setting the context for future behavior in that room even if the identifying stimuli disappear subsequently. Episodic context dependence is more difficult for neural networks because the information on context is specified at a fixed time which grows increasingly remote from the present. This requires the system to "latch" information which is difficult to achieve by simple recurrence [1, 13].

The hippocampal region of the brain in rodents appears to construct distinct representations of similar — even identical — environments based on episodic context [21, 22]. We have previously proposed a class of networks called *latent attractor networks* to explain how episodic context-dependent representations can arise in a hippocampus-like system without resorting to off-line or external biasing [19, 5, 3, 6]. Latent attractor networks are recurrent neural networks with competitive firing that embed patterns of activity as attractors using associative Hebbian learning. However, the recurrent connections are not strong enough to sustain the activity patterns autonomously. Each attractor is associated with a specific external stimulus pattern called a *context pattern*. When the context pattern is presented to the network, it disproportionately activates neurons that are supposed to be active in the associated attractor. This then produces a stable bias onto this set through the recurrent connections so that subsequent external inputs — not explicitly associated with any particular attractor — also produce response patterns whose activity lies mainly in the active set of the chosen attractor, thus conditioning the system's responses to stimuli by the original context pattern long after the pattern itself is gone. This situation persists until an external stimulus associated with another context/attractor is presented to the network [5].

In the paradigm described above, the context patterns are unitary stimuli (e.g., looking at the number on a door or seeing a single identifying landmark). However, in realistic situations, context is not set by a single stimulus, but by a conjunction of stimuli (e.g., objects in a room). For each episode with the same context, these stimuli would typically be apprehended in different order depending on their location and the viewer's actions, and may be interspersed with other irrelevant stimuli, termed *distractors*. Furthermore, each individual stimulus may be part of the identifying combination for multiple contexts; it is the combination as a whole that indicates the specific context. Thus, as the context-setting stimuli are scanned, a unique context identification would only emerge gradually rather than instantaneously, and, until the context is uniquely identified, the system's response may be compatible with several choices.

In previous studies, we have considered the gradual activation of latent attractors by the presentation of a stimulus sequence including distractor stimuli [8, 9]. However, it was implicitly assumed that each stimulus sequence contained the same number of relevant stimuli. This is, of course, a rather artificial assumption, and we now report on a model that removes it. As noted in our earlier work, the problem of gradual convergence in response to temporally presented stimuli is relevant to tasks other than context selection, e.g., representation of hierarchical information structures in neural networks.

Previous studies have considered the gradual activation of attractors by sequences of stimuli [15, 2]. However, in these cases, the order of stimuli is fixed, while we focus on the equally — perhaps more — natural case where the order is explicitly irrelevant. This is closer in spirit to the problem of encoding and recovering hierarchical information structures in modular neural networks [10, 11]. In these networks, higher level categories are represented by the simultaneous activation of lower level concepts represented by activity in different modules. However, these networks learn specially designed hierarchical patterns [10, 11]. We do not use such patterns.

II. PROBLEM DEFINITION

The network is presented with η different external stimulus sequences in discrete time. Each sequence, S^q, of length n_q

$$S^q = C_1^q[R^q]C_2^q[R^q]...[R^q]C_{m_q}^q[R^q] \quad q = 1, 2, ..., \eta \quad (1)$$

begins with a sub-sequence of r_q patterns – the *context sequence* – comprising m_q context patterns, C_i^q, interspersed with varying numbers of non-context patterns, indicated by $[R^q]$. The last $[R^q]$ is a sub-sequence of $n_q - r_q$ non-context stimuli termed the *regular sequence*. The context patterns, C_i^q are drawn from a set of patterns called the *context set*, $C = \{C_k\}$, and the remaining patterns are drawn from the set, $R = \{R_k\}$. Both $C_k, R_k \in I$, where I is the input space of dimension N_I. We use binary stimulus patterns, so $I \equiv \{0, 1\}^{N_I}$. For purposes of simulation, patterns in both sets are generated randomly, but mutually exclusive.

A total of ν possible contexts are defined, each context, c^k, specified by a unique set of μ_k context patterns drawn randomly without repetition from C. Each episode sequence, S^q, has a unique context, c^{k_q}, drawn from among the $\{c^k\}$. The context sequence for S^q includes the $m_q = \mu_{k_q}$ context patterns for c^{k_q} in random order mixed with $n_q - m_q$ non-context patterns. The regular sequence patterns for S^q are chosen randomly from R.

At the beginning of an episode, as context patterns are presented, each context pattern identifies the correct attractor with increasing specificity until, at the end of the context sequence, the attractor is uniquely identified. Correspondingly, the network activity should gradually become confined to the active set of the correct latent attractor and remain confined during the presentation of the regular stimulus patterns.

III. METHOD

The core of the system is a latent attractor network composed of two layers: the *response layer*, L_R, and the *intermediary layer*, L_H. The input patterns are projected to the response layer through the *stimulus layer*, L_S. An additional layer called the *biasing layer*, L_B, receives input from the stimulus layer and projects back to the response layer. The network structure is presented in Figure 1.

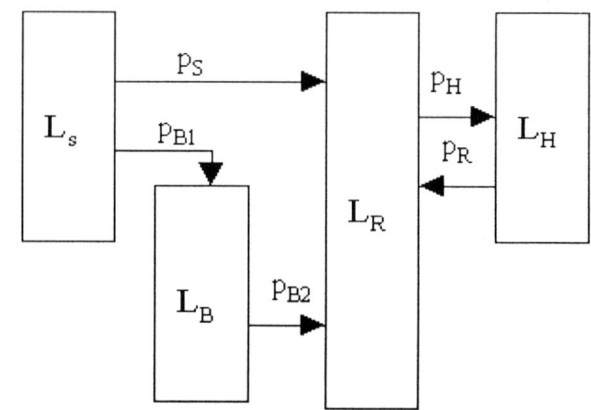

Figure 1: Network architecture

The *stimulus layer*, L_S, has N_S neurons that project the input stimuli to the *response layer*, L_R. The connections from L_S to L_R are set randomly with probability p_S of connection. Only K_S neurons in the input layer are active at one time. The *biasing layer* L_B has N_B neurons that receive input from the stimulus layer L_S and project to the response layer. The input connections from L_S to L_B layer are chosen randomly, with a high probability of connection p_{B1}. The output connections from L_B to L_R

layer are also chosen randomly with a high probability of connection (p_{B2}).

The response layer, with N_R neurons, also receives a disynaptic recurrent connection through the *intermediary layer*, L_H with N_H neurons. The latent attractors are stored in the recurrent connections between the L_R and L_H layers. There are M attractors, each comprising two binary patterns, one in layer L_R and the other in layer L_H. The patterns have G_R and G_H active neurons, respectively in L_R and L_H, called the *active sets* of the attractor. The connections between L_R and L_H layers are chosen randomly with probability of connections p_R (L_H to L_R) and p_H (L_R to L_H). The attractors are stored in the connections using a clipped binary Hebbian rule first proposed by Willshaw: The connections between neurons active in the two patterns of any attractor are set to high values, while the rest are set to low values [23]. In this way, the M pairs of patterns are set as attractors or fixed points in the in the 2-layer network. The attractors are called latent because they are never fully activated.

The network activity is determined as follows. The excitation to a layer L_R neuron, i, at time t is given by:

$$y_i^R(t) = \sum_{j \in L_S} w_{ij}^{SR} x_j(t) + g_i(t) \sum_{j \in L_H} w_{ij}^{HR} z_j(t-1) + g_{bias} \sum_{j \in L_B} w_{ij}^{BR} u_j(t-1) \quad (2)$$

where $w_{ij}^{(\cdot)}$ denote connection weights, $x_j(t)$ is the jth bit of the external stimulus patterns at time t, $z_j(t)$ is the output of neuron $j \in L_H$, $u_j(t)$ is the output of neuron $j \in L_B$, $g_i(t)$ is the (modifiable) recurrent gain of neuron i, and g_{bias} is the gain from the biasing layer L_B to the response layer L_R.

The synaptic input to a layer L_H neuron, i, is given by:

$$y_i^H(t) = \sum_{j \in L_R} w_{ij}^{RH} v_j(t) \quad (3)$$

where $v_j(t)$ is the output of $j \in L_R$.

Firing in both L_R and L_H is competitive: The output of the K_R (K_H) most excited neurons in L_R (L_H) at time t is set to 1, while the rest of the neurons output 0. This is a K-winner take all competitive firing rule. The number of neurons allowed to fire - K_R and K_H respectively - are much smaller than the size of the attractors - G_R and G_H.

The input onto a layer L_B neuron i is:

$$y_i^B(t) = \sum_{j \in L_S} w_{ij}^{SB} x_j(t) \quad (4)$$

where $x_j(t)$ is the output of neuron $j \in L_S$. Neurons in L_B fire when their synaptic input exceeds a threshold level, θ_B. This corresponds to the recognition of a pattern in the L_S layer. Once a biasing neuron starts firing, it will remain active until the end of a context sequence. The prolonged activity of neurons in the biasing layer simulates the role of a short-term memory. It can be obtained by recurrent self-excitation, currently not included in the model.

Latent attractors are associated with stimulus sequences as follows: The connections between L_S and L_R layers are modified such that each context pattern in a sequence excites primarily neurons in the active set of the corresponding attractor in the L_R layer.

The system is faced with the following three problems: (1) the network's state should not become confined to any attractor until it has received enough evidence to uniquely identify the context (i.e. until all context patterns have been presented at the stimulus layer), (2) the activity of the network should not change during the presentation of distractor inputs, and (3) the length of a context (μ_k) should not influence its recognition.

The first problem is addressed by a process called *incremental competitive positive feedback* [8, 9]. The stability of any attractor in the network is controlled by its recurrent gain, g_i, which sets the relative strength of the recurrent excitation versus the external one. For a latent attractor to be stable, neurons in its active set must be above a minimum limit of g_i [6]. When g_i is small compared to the strength of the external stimulus, activity in the network is dictated by the external, feed-forward pathway. Neurons which receive stronger excitation by the stimulus will tend to win the competition for firing among L_R neurons, independent of the distribution of activity in the network. If g_i are large, the recurrent path dominates and the network's activity is determined by the competitive firing between attractors in L_R and L_H.

In our system, all g_i are set to a small value at the beginning of an episode, so that attractors that are associated with the early context patterns are likely to be activated a bit more than others due to feed-forward association. As the presentation of context patterns proceeds, g_i for neurons that belong to the active sets of attractors with more current activity is increased gradually, priming these attractors for possible persistence if reinforced by subsequent context stimuli. Thus, at each stage, activity is distributed among those attractors that are consistent with the context stimuli received thus far. As each new context stimulus is presented, some of these candidate attractors are reinforced further at the expense of others until, finally, only one is left. When the stimulus is not a context pattern, it causes no significant change in the bias for any attractor, and the biasing neurons keep activity distributed among the attractors as at the previous step. The recurrent gain is not allowed to change during presentation of irrelevant inputs. Since these stimuli do not represent any positive or negative reinforcement about the correct context, they should not modify the balance of activity in the network, by allowing the recurrent gain to vary.

The equation governing the modulation of recurrent gain is [9]:

$$\hat{g}_i(t) = g_{min} + \frac{g_{max} - g_{min}}{(1 + e^{-\alpha(a_l(t)-\beta)})}$$

$$d_i(t) = \hat{g}_i(t) - g_i(t-1)$$

$$g_i(t) = \begin{cases} \hat{g}_i(t) & if \ |d_i(t)| < \Delta g_{max} \\ g_i(t-1) + \Delta g_{max} sgn(d_i(t)) & otherwise \end{cases} \quad (5)$$

where α is a rate of change parameter, β is an offset parameter, l is the index of the attractor for which i is in the active set, $a_l(t)$ is the total number of active neurons in the L_R active set of attractor l at time t, g_{min} and g_{max} are the minimum and maximum possible values of the recurrent gain. Thus, the gain is $\hat{g}_i(t)$, but the absolute change in gain is bounded by Δg_{max} ($\Delta g_{max} > 0$).

The modulation of recurrent gain on individual neurons is motivated by several biological considerations:

1. Projections to neurons in most cortical regions are segregated on the dendritic tree, making the selective modulation of gain on input from individual sources quite feasible [17].

2. It is well known that, in the hippocampal region, which is the basis for our model, animals are especially attentive at the beginning of an episode, as indicated by the change in the EEG theta rhythm. This leads to, for example, greater spike synchronization, lower firing latency, and other phenomena [20].

3. In the granule cells of the dentate gyrus, which, we hypothesize, corresponds roughly to our layer L_R, there is both anatomical and physiological evidence [16, 18] of an intricate and highly specific system of excitability modulation based on motivation and attention [20].

The second problem - the preservation of the network's state during irrelevant inputs - is addressed by the functionality of the biasing layer. The role of the biasing layer L_B is to sustain the level of activity in candidate latent attractors during the presentation of irrelevant patterns in the context sequence. Each neuron in L_B corresponds to one context pattern. When a context pattern is presented at the stimulus layer L_S, the associated neuron in the biasing layer becomes active. The active biasing neuron, in turn, projects back a higher excitation to the L_R neurons in the active sets of the attractors with which that context pattern is associated. Thus, in between context patterns, the activity in the latent attractors tends to be preserved until a new context pattern is presented at the input. The activity of the biasing neurons is reset after a latent attractor has been fully activated (i.e. at the end of a context sequence). The biasing layer plays the role of a short-term memory by sustaining the effect of context patterns until the context sequence is complete.

The weights of the connections between the biasing layer and the response layer (w_{ij}^{BR}) are set as follows:

$$w_{ij}^{BR} = \begin{cases} 1/\mu_k & , \ i, j \in c^k \\ 0 & , \ otherwise \end{cases} \quad (6)$$

The weights from a biasing neuron to the active set of an attractor in the L_R layer are normalized by the length of the context set (μ_k) which is associated with that attractor. Thus, neurons in the active set of an attractor corresponding to a context (c^k) of length μ_k, receive connections from μ_k biasing neurons. The weight of these connections is inverse proportional with the length of the context. The rule normalizes the total synaptic input coming from the biasing layer into a L_R neuron. At the end of a context sequence only the active set of the correct attractor will receive full excitation from the biasing layer. The normalization rule addresses the third problem of the system - independent context recognition behavior with respect to the length of a context μ_k. The rule ensures that shorter contexts have the same chance as longer ones to be recognized. A biological motivation for the normalization rule is the limited number of synaptic sites which constrains the total change in synaptic strength by the number of connections a neuron receives [15].

IV. SIMULATION RESULTS

Simulation were done using a four layer latent attractor network with the following parameters: $N_S = 400$, $K_S = 40$, $p_S = 0.4$, $N_B = 20$, $p_{B1} = 0.9$, $p_{B2} = 0.9$, $N_R = 2000$, $G_R = 200$, $K_R = 40$, $p_R = 0.4$, $N_H = 500$, $G_H = 50$, $K_H = 45$, $p_H = 0.8$. There are $M = 10$ attractors embedded in the connections between L_R and L_H layers. The modulation rate for recurrent gain g_i is $\alpha = 0.3$ and $\beta = 25$. The gain of the L_B to L_R projection is $g_{bias} = 24$.

The context set C has 20 distinct patterns, from which $\nu = 5$ context sets are selected. Each c^k consists of μ_k distinct patterns picked randomly without repetition from C. The length of each sequence is chosen uniformly in the interval $\mu_k^{min} = 2$ and $\mu_k^{max} = 6$. Context patterns in distinct c^k's are not mutually exclusive, but context sets completely included in another context set are excluded. Each c^k set of context patterns is associated with a randomly chosen attractor: The connections from L_S to L_R layers are potentiated such that patterns in c^k are associated with the neurons in the active set of the appropriate attractor. Also, each individual context pattern is associated with a neuron in the biasing layer through Hebbian potentiation of the connections from the stimulus layer L_S and the L_B layer. In turn, each biasing neuron, provides excitation to neurons in the active sets of those latent attractors whose context sequences include that context pattern.

At the beginning of each sequence, S^q, the recurrent gain for all L_R neurons is set to a low value. Depending on how many context groups are simultaneously stimulated by the incoming context patterns from c^{k_q}, the activity in L_R and L_H is distributed among the excited attractors. The recurrent gain of neurons in these attractors goes up, while that of other neurons decreases. At the end of a context sequence, only one attractor is consistent with the whole set of context stimuli in c^{k_q}, and almost all activity should be concentrated in its active set.

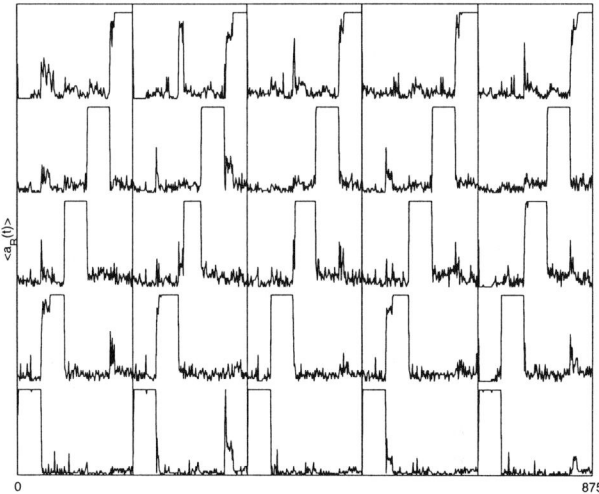

Figure 3: Five repeats of the run in Figure 1, with different context pattern order each time. Each context sequence is followed by a regular sequence of 10 patterns.

In the second set of simulations is presented the mean activity in L_R context attractors over five different networks, five different order presentations of the same context sequence. In Figure 3, the mean activity during the presentation of the context sequence is plotted as a function of time. The level of activity slowly goes up as more evidence is presented during the context sequence. The mean activity is averaged over all context sequences, independent of their length. Figure 4 shows the mean activity in the correct attractor with respect to the length, m_q, of the context set. The mean is averaged over the regular sequence patterns - the last 10 irrelevant patterns at the end of a context sequence. The plot shows that the correct attractor is active at the end of a context sequence and that it remains stable in face of noisy external inputs, independent of the length of the context set.

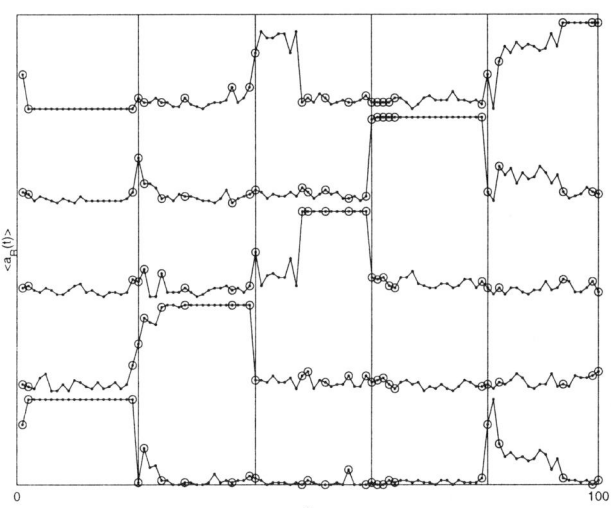

Figure 2: The activity level in the selected L_R attractors with respect to time. Every $r_q = 20$ time steps a different context sequence starts. The activity is normalized with respect to K_R. The time steps when context patterns are presented is denoted with circles.

In the first set of simulations, the context patterns are presented in a random order at the stimulus layer interleaved with irrelevant patterns. The total length of the context sequence is fixed to $r_q = 20$, but the position of the m_q context patterns and of the $r_q - m_q$ irrelevant patterns is not fixed. Figure 1 shows the result of a single network simulation, during one presentation of each context sequence. Each graph represents the normalized activity within the active set of an attractor in the L_R layer. It can be seen that, for each context sequence, the activity in only one of the attractors goes up steadily. In all other attractors the activity might increase for a few time steps, but it finally shuts down. In between consecutive context patterns, the activity is spread approximately equally between the candidate attractors. Figure 2 shows the results when the simulation is repeated with the same 5 context sequences but with the context patterns presented in different order each time. Each context sequence is followed by 10 regular patterns. It is clear that the activity remains confined within the chosen attractor even though the regular patterns have no association with any attractor. It can be seen that sometimes a wrong attractor almost wins the competition (the spikes) in the middle of a context sequence, but it is finally shut down.

V. CONCLUSIONS

We have demonstrated a mechanism by which a latent attractor can be activated progressively by a set of context-setting stimuli presented sequentially in a random order interspersed with a variable number irrelevant stimuli. The system is able to select and activate the right attractor progressively even though individual input patterns are associated with multiple attractors. The system overcomes the disrupting effect of the irrelevant patterns by trying to maintain the state of attractor participation until a new relevant pattern is encountered. This requires a subtle gain control scheme consistent with experimental evidence in the hippocampus, but whose precise neural

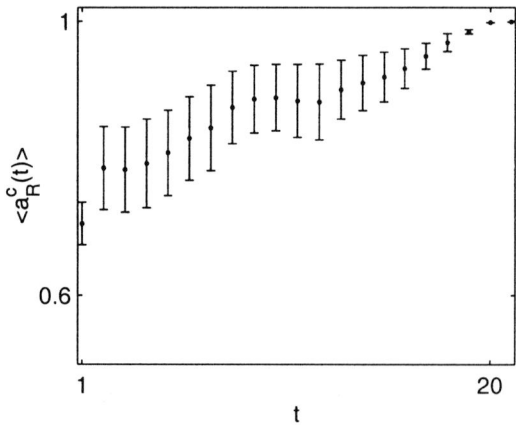

Figure 4: The graph presents the mean activity in the context attractors of the L_R layer as it varies in time, during the presentation of the context sequence.

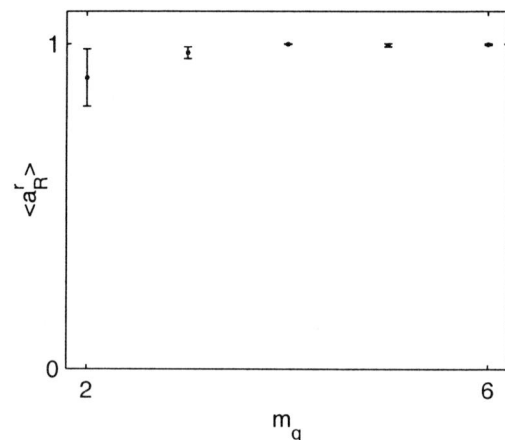

Figure 5: The plot shows the mean and the standard deviation of the activity in the correct attractor in the L_R layer with respect to the length of a context set (m_q). The mean is computed over five different networks, five different order presentations of the context patterns, and over the last 10 regular patterns at the end of each context sequence.

correlates remain to be fully explored. This will be discussed in future papers.

References

[1] Y. Bengio, P. Simard, and P. Frasconi, "Learning long-term dependencies with gradient descent is difficult," *IEEE Trans. on Neural Networks*, vol. Vol. 5, No. 2, pp. 157–166, 1994.

[2] G. Bradski, G.A. Carpenter and S. Grossberg. STORE working memory networks for storage ad recall of arbitrary temporal sequences. *Biological Cybernetics* 71:469–480, 1994.

[3] S. Doboli, A.A. Minai and P.J. Best. Generating smooth context-dependent representations. *Proc. of IJCNN'1999*, 1999.

[4] S. Doboli, A.A. Minai, and P.J. Best. A latent attractors model of context-selection in the dentate gyrus-hilus system. *Neurocomputing* 26-27:671–676, 1999.

[5] S. Doboli, A.A. Minai and P.J. Best. Latent attractors: a model for context-dependence place representations in the hippocampus. *Neural Computation* 12:1009–1043, 2000.

[6] S. Doboli and A.A. Minai. Network capacity for network attractor computation. *Proc. IJCNN'2000* 222-228, 2000.

[7] S. Doboli, A.A. Minai, and P.J. Best, A comparison of context-dependent hippocampal place codes in 1-layer and 2-layer recurrent networks, *Neurocomputing*, 3-33:353–358, 2000.

[8] S. Doboli, A.A. Minai, Progressive attractor selection in latent attractor networks, *Proc. IJCNN'2001*, Washington, USA, 2001.

[9] S. Doboli, A.A. Minai, Latent attractor selection in the presence of irrelevant stimuli, Proc. IJCNN'2002, Hawaii, USA, 2002.

[10] D.R.C. Dominguez. Information capacity of a hierarchical neural network. *Phys. Rev. E* 58:4811–4815, 1998.

[11] V.S. Dotsenko. Hierarchical model of memory. *Physica A*, 410–415, 1986.

[12] J.L. Elman, "Finding structure in time," *Cognitive Science.*, vol. 14, pp. 179–211, 1990.

[13] P. Frasconi and M. Gori, "Computational capabilities of local-feedback recurrent networks acting as finite-state machines," *IEEE Trans. on Neural Networks*, vol. Vol. 7, No. 6, pp. 1521–1525, 1996.

[14] C.L. Giles, C.B. Miller, D. Chen, H.H. Chen, G.Z. Sun, and Y.C. Lee, "Learning and extracting finite state automata with second-order recurrent neural networks," *Neural Computation*, vol. 4, pp. 393–405, 1992.

[15] S. Grossberg and C. W. Myers. The resonant dynamics of speech perception: Interword integration and duration-dependent backward effects. *Psychological Review*, 2000.

[16] Z.-S. Han, E.H. Buhl, Z. Lörinczi, and P. Somogyi, A high degree of spatial selectivity in the axonal and dendritic domains of physiologically identified local-circuit neurons in the dentate gyrus of the rat hippocampus. *Eur. J. Neurosci.* 5, 395–410, 1993.

[17] M.E. Hasselmo, E. Schnell, and E. Barkai. Dynamics of learning and recall at excitatory recurrent synapses and cholinergic modulation in hippocampal region CA3. *J. Neurosci.*, 15:5249–5262, 1995.

[18] M.B. Jackson and H.E. Scharfman, Positive feedback from hilar mossy cells to granule cells in the dentate gyrus revealed by voltage-sensitive dye and microelectrode recording. *J. Neurophysiol.* 76, 601–616, 1996.

[19] A.A. Minai and P.J. Best. Encoding spatial context: A hypothesis on the function of the dentate gyrus-hilus system. *Proc. of IJCNN'1998* 587-598, 1998.

[20] E.I. Moser. Altered inhibition of granule cells during spatial learning in an exploration task. *J. Neurosci.* 16:1247-1259, 1996.

[21] Quirk, G.J. and Muller, R.U. and Kubie, J.L. The firing of hippocampal place cells in the dark depends on the rat's recent experience *J. Neurosci.* 10:2008-2017, 1990.

[22] Rotenberg, A. and Muller, R.U. Variable place-cell coupling to a continuously viewed stimulus: Evidence that the hippocampus acts as a perceptual system *Phil. Trans. R. Soc. Lond. B*, 352:1505-1513, 1997.

[23] D. Willshaw, O.P. Buneman and H.C. Longuet-Higgins. Non-holographic associative memory. *Nature* 222:960-962, 1969.

Consecutive Face Recognition by Association Cortex - Entorhinal Cortex - Hippocampal Formation Model

K. Nakamura, J. Nitta, H. Takano and M. Yamazaki
Graduate School of Engineering, Toyama Prefectural University
5180 Kurokawa, Kosugi-town, Toyama 939-0398, JAPAN

Abstract - In this paper, we propose a neural network model which incorporates neurophysiological knowledge into Jones's hypothesis, i.e. the association cortex - entorhinal cortex - hippocampal formation model (AEH model). In this model, the inhibitory action from the inferotemporal cortex to parietal cortex has a gating role for activation of the reverberatory closed circuit between the entorhinal cortex and hippocampal formation. The successive recognition performance of the AEH model was tested using human face images. In the experiments, face images were presented to the AEH model twice. Twenty human faces were tested to learn and recollect successively either in a series or in a block. In both tests, the recognition performance of the AEH model was nearly 100 percent. In the memory consolidation experiments, when face images were presented five times in series, potentiation of long-term memory occurred without any distortions.

1 INTRODUCTION

Our understanding of how the information processing of seeing things, memorizing, and recollecting is carried out in the brain remains limited. When a human sees several novel faces in series he can easily memorize the respective faces by using the visual information processing system in the brain, and can recollect the respective faces when he sees the faces again. In the human brain, it is thought that two information processing systems, i.e. shape and spatial recognition systems, work in parallel. The information processing for shape recognition primarily depends on the visual cortex (VC) - inferotemporal cortex (IT) - entorhinal cortex (EC) to hippocampal formation (HF) neural axis and that of spatial recognition primarily depends on the VC - parietal cortex (PG) - EC to HF neural axis [1].

In the present study, we developed an association cortex to EC - HF neural network model (AEH model) based on neurophysiological findings and Jones' hypothesis [2]. In this model, the inhibitory action from IT to PG has a gating role for the activation of the reverberatory closed circuit between EC and HF. In order to artificially simulate learning and recognition operation in the brain, serial learning and recognition experiments with model using human faces as the recognition object were carried out. We evaluated the recognition performance of the AEH model.

2 RELATION AMONG VISUAL, TEMPORAL AND PARIETAL CORTICES

It is well known that there are strong inter-connections between the association cortices. From neurophysiological experiments, it is reported that neurons in the monkey IT barely respond to novel stimuli but respond strongly to well-known stimuli [3]. Some neurons in the IT also respond highly selectively to faces [4][5]. The various face components, i.e. eyes, mouth deeply affect the responses of the face responsive neurons. It is proposed that the object image is coded by combinations of the particular partial features in the image [4]. On the other hand, it is reported that neurons in PG respond to spatial stimuli [6][7]. Some neurons in the posterior PG of the rat also respond to novel stimuli much more strongly (4.3 times) than to well-known stimuli (1.3 times) [7]. Although this result concerns the auditory sense, it seems to apply to the visual sense also, since the posterior parietal association area is a multimodal sensory area which integrates visual sense, auditory sense and somatosensation. Taking the above into consideration, it is reasonable to consider that there is an inhibitory effect in the interconnection between cortices in the parietal association area and temporal association area.

An inhibitory effect from the temporal association area to the parietal association area was thus set in the AEH model. Fig.1 shows an outline of the AEH model. In the AEH model, the inhibitory effect works more strongly when learned stimulation is presented than when novel stimulation is presented.

3 ENTORHINAL CORTEX - HIPPOCAMPAL FORMATION SYSTEM

3.1 Memory Consolidation

The HF and its surrounding areas (e.g. EC - HF system) are considered to be the medial temporal memory consolidation system [1]. Multimodal sensory inputs from the cerebral sensory association cortex (i.e. IT, PG and prefrontal association cortex) converge into these areas. It is reported that anterograde amnesia and age-dependent retrograde amnesia occur by the destruction of the HF and surrounding areas. The age dependency is different between animals, i.e. $2 \sim 3$ years in humans, $2 \sim 3$ months in monkeys and $2 \sim 3$ weeks in rats. From these facts, the HF and its surrounding areas are considered to be intermediate memory storage areas to convert temporary memory into the long-term memory in the cerebral association cortex [1]. On the other hand, it is reported that neurons in the monkey HF are related to both ob-

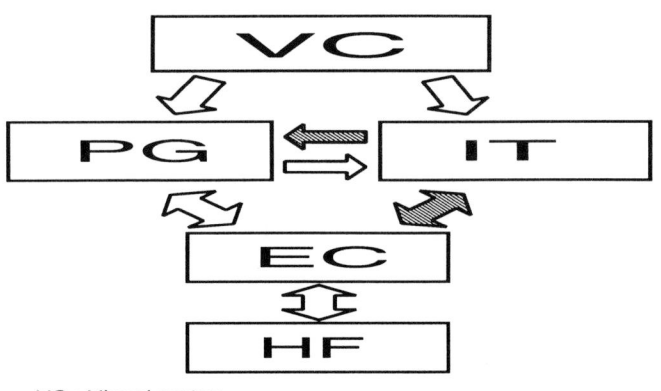

Figure 1: Fundamental structure of an AEH model.

VC : Visual cortex
PG : Parietal cortex
HF : Hippocampal formation
IT : Inferotemporal cortex
EC : Entorhinal cortex

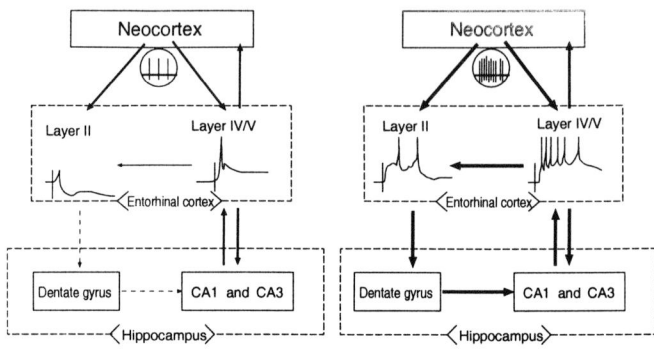

Figure 2: Jones' hypothesis. Activation of reverberatory closed circuit between the entorhinal cortex and hippocampal formation is dependent on an input from neocortex.

ject shape and spatial recognition [8][9]. These neurons are distributed sparsely in the HF. These facts indicate that both object and spatial information converge in HF and new associative or episodic learning occurs.

Neural models of recall and recognition take seriously the interaction between EC and HF [10][11]. The rich recollection process may depend on the HF, whereas the familiarity sense may depend on other cortical areas. It is reported that perirhinal neurons signal the prior occurrence of stimuli by a decrease of this response [12].

3.2 Jones' Hypothesis

There is a reverberatory closed circuit between the EC and HF. As shown in Fig.2, this is a feedback circuit, i.e. EC (II) → Dentate gyrus → HF(CA3 → CA1) → EC (IV/V) → EC (II) [2][8]. The neural activity in the EC - HF circuit is dependent on the input from the cerebral neocortex, and it is thought that the activity of the reverberatory closed circuit is deeply concerned with memory consolidation [2]. Jones hypothesized that the reverberatory closed circuit did not work when EC received low frequency inputs from the neocortex because of the activation of inhibitory interneurons in layer II of EC (Fig.2 left) [2]. On the other hand, the reverberatory closed circuit worked by activating the excitatory neurons in layer II of EC when the EC received high frequency inputs from the neocortex (Fig.2 right). Consequently, the activation of the closed circuit induces long-term potentiation in the HF and is connected with the formation of long-term memory in the cerebral neocortex.

4 AEH MODEL

4.1 Detailed Structure of AEH Model

The fundamental structure of the AEH model is shown in Fig.3. The model consists of five areas; visual cortex (VC), parietal cortex (PG), inferior temporal cortex (IT), entorhinal cortex (EC) and hippocampal formation (HF). The VC is separated into three layers, i.e. V1, V2·V3 and V4·TEO layers. The V1 receives input from both eyes via the lateral genuculate body, and sends the output to V2·V3 layers. The V2·V3 layers output positional information of the full face to PG and shape information of face part components (eyebrows, eyes, nose and mouth) to the V4·TEO layers. Each of four V4·TEO layers corresponding to four face parts is composed of 60 neurons. The V4·TEO layers output part code information on the respective face parts to IT.

The IT is composed of three layers, i.e. PIT (posterior IT), LTM (long-term memory), and STM(short term memory) layers. Although the STM layer is included in the IT in the present model aiming for actual application, readers should consider the STM layer to be a part of the EC layer (i.e. layer IV/V in EC). Each of the four PIT layers corresponding to the four face parts is composed of 30 neurons. The LTM and STM layers are composed of the same number of 30 neurons. Each layer in the PIT engages in individual recognition based only on the face part code input from the respective V4·TEO layer. The LTM neurons finally recognize the individual by the whole face, combining the respective recognition results of the four PIT layers. The STM layer receives a sparse code signal from the HF to produce a new memory cell (i.e. grandmother cell) and sends the output to both PIT and LTM layers.

The EC layers (layer II) are composed of inhibitory interneuron EN0 and excitatory output neuron EN1, based on Jones' hypothesis. The HF layer is composed of 1000 neurons in the present model. The HF layer produces sparse code when a new episode occurs, i.e. a novel face is presented.

4.2 Operation of AEH Model

The visual image of a human face on the retina goes to the V1 layer in VC via a lateral geniculate body. The outputs from the V1 layer are sent to the V2·V3 layers in VC, and are divided into four face parts; eyebrows, eyes, nose and mouth. Between the V1 and V2·V3 layers, the input face image is passed through a Laplacian filter to enhance the image contrast. In the V2·V3 layer, the feature vectors of the four face parts are calculated by subtracting the average face information and then normalizing.

There are two pathways from the V2·V3 layer. One of

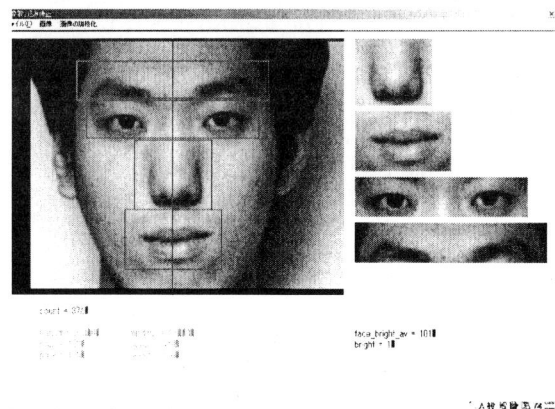

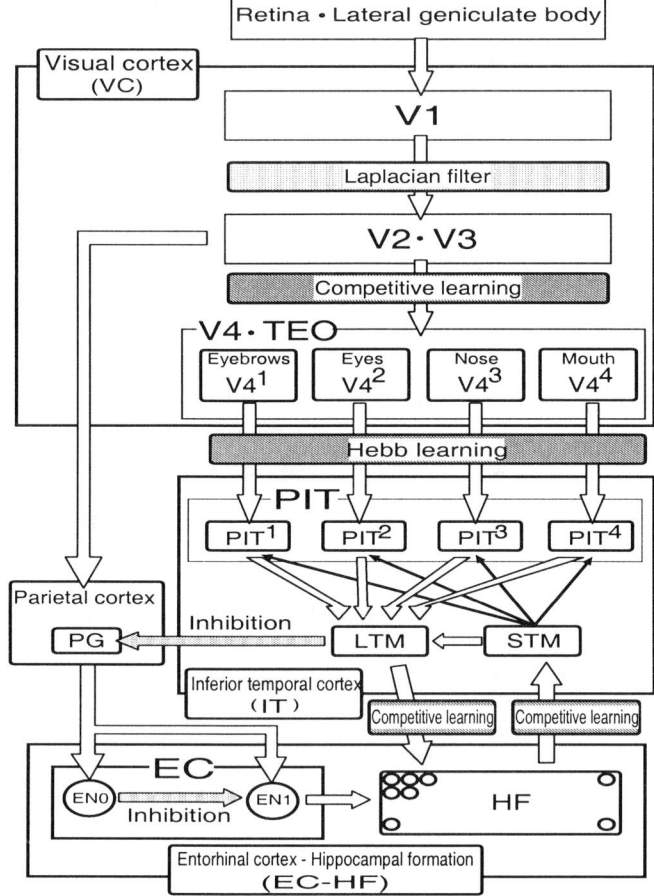

Figure 3: Detailed structure and information flow of the AEH model.

Figure 4: Automatical separation to face part components (eyebrows, eyes, nose and mouth).

them is the positional information pathway to PG where the position of the whole face is recognized. The other goes to the V4·TEO layers for shape recognition. In the V4·TEO layers, the feature vector data of face parts is converted to respective part codes. The part code data from V4·TEO layers is sent to the respective PIT layers in IT. Each PIT layer identifies a person by each face part code. The results of identification are put together into the LTM (long-term memory) layer in IT, and the LTM layer identifies the whole face.

At this point, if the input face is novel, all neurons in the LTM layer have small outputs, and suppression to the PG layer does not work. Therefore, both an inhibitory interneuron EN0 and an excitatory neuron EN1 in layer II of EC receive strong input from PG. The activating threshold of the EN0 neuron is set lower than that of the EN1 neuron. Since the interneuron EN0 neuron inhibits the EN1 neuron, a strong input from PG is needed to activate the EN1 neuron. The output of the EN1 neuron is sent to the HF layer. If the activity of the EN1 neuron is above a predetermined value, a sparse code is generated in HF. At the same time, competitive learning occurs between the HF and STM layers, and the winner output of the STM layer is sent to both the PIT and LTM layers. After that, the learning occurs in cascade. The sparse code in the HF is consolidated by competitive learning between the HF and LTM layers. Individual recognition in the PIT is then consolidated by Hebb learning between the PIT and V4·TEO layers. Finally, each part code in the V4·TEO layers is consolidated by competitive learning between the V2·V3 and V4·TEO layers.

In contrast, if the input face is familiar, some neuron(s) in the LTM layer have large output and suppression to the PG layer works strongly. Since both the EN0 and EN1 neurons receive weak inputs from the PG layer and the EN1 neuron is inhibited by the EN0 neuron, the output of the EN1 neuron is either under the predetermined value or zero. In the HF, therefore, the new sparse code is not produced. Instead, the previously memorized sparse code in the HF is recollected by the strong input for the LTM layer. After that, long-term potentiation of the memory in the HF is realized and the memory consolidation process occurs again in cascade as previously described.

5 RECOGNITION EXPERIMENTS

Face pictures taken by a digital video camera under the same lighting conditions and the same distance between face and camera were used as recognition images for the AEH model (the input image to V1 layer). The color images were transformed to gray scaled images of 256 levels. The face pictures were separated into four face parts, i.e. eyebrow, eye, nose and mouth (processing in V2·V3 layer). The face part separation was done manually at the beginning of the research, but was improved to be done automatically using an eye tracking system. An example of the separated face parts is shown in Fig.4. In order to apply them to a practical face recognition system, the brightness of the face including four face parts was normalized.

The edge components of the face part images were emphasized by a Laplacian filter (processing in V2·V3 layer). Each face part was subtracted by the average of all face parts and then normalized to produce the feature vector of each face part. In the experiment, the average of all face parts was calculated across an optional number L(=12) of faces, beforehand. The feature vector of each face part was the output of the V2·V3 layer, and these were sent to V4·TEO layer to produce the part code. Competitive learning was used for the production of part code in the V4·TEO layer. In competitive learning of the V4·TEO layer, a predetermined number (q=3) or less of neurons that had strong and positive outputs were selected to reinforce the connection weights from the input V2·V3 layers. The neuron outputs from respective V4·TEO layers were used for part codes.

In order to memorize and recognize the face correctly, it is important to set appropriate relational equations among the V4·TEO - PIT, PIT - LTM, LTM - PG, PG - EC, EC - HF, HF - STM and LTM - HF layers. Since space does not allow full descriptions, some important relational equations between these layers are described.

LTM - PG and PG - EC layers: Neurons in the PG layer output positional information. In the model, it was postulated that the positional information of the full face was already obtained by some other method, e.g. by the SSAN net developed previously [13]. Thus, the V2·V3 layer output to the PG layer was fixed (either 1 or 0 according to the face input). The PG layer is inhibited by the LTM layer. The output of the PG neuron is expressed by (1).

$$y_{pg} = 1 - LTM_{max} \cdot \beta_{ltm} \quad (1)$$

Here, LTM_{max} is a maximum value among the LTM neuron outputs, and β_{ltm} is the inhibitory connection weight from LTM to PG layers.

The output of the PG layer is sent to both EN0 and EN1 neurons in the EC layer. The outputs of EN0 and EN1 neurons are expressed in (2) and (3).

$$y_{en0} = y_{pg} \cdot w_{en0} - \Theta_{en0} \quad (2)$$
$$y_{en1} = y_{pg} \cdot w_{en1} - \Theta_{en1} - y_{en0} \quad (3)$$

Here, w_{en0} is the connection weight between PG and EN0 neurons, $\Theta_{en0}(=0.05)$ is the threshold of the EN0 neuron, and w_{en1} is the connection weight between PG and EN1 neurons, $\Theta_{en1}(=0.1)$ is the threshold of the EN1 neuron.

EC - HF layers: Neurons in the HF layer are activated when the input to the HF layer from the EN1 neuron in the EC layer goes over the predetermined value Θ_{hf}. If the condition in (4) is satisfied, a sparse code is generated in the HF layer by the activation of several HF neurons (4 of 1000 HF neurons).

$$y_{en1} > \Theta_{hf} \quad (4)$$

HF - STM and LTM - HF layers: These layers are composed of a competitive learning neural network. If we set x_i as any input from the HF layer and y_j as any output of the STM layer, then y_j can be expressed as (5) and (6).

$$\frac{du_j}{dt} = \frac{1}{\tau} \cdot \left(-u_j(t) + \sum_{i=1}^{P} x_i(t) \cdot w_{ji} - h - \sum_{l \neq j} y_l(t) \cdot \gamma_{jl} \right) \quad (5)$$

$$y_j(t + \Delta t) = max[u_j(t + \Delta t), 0] \quad (6)$$

Here, $\tau(=3)$ is a time constant, u_j is the membrane potential w_{ji} is the connecting weight from the HF to LTM

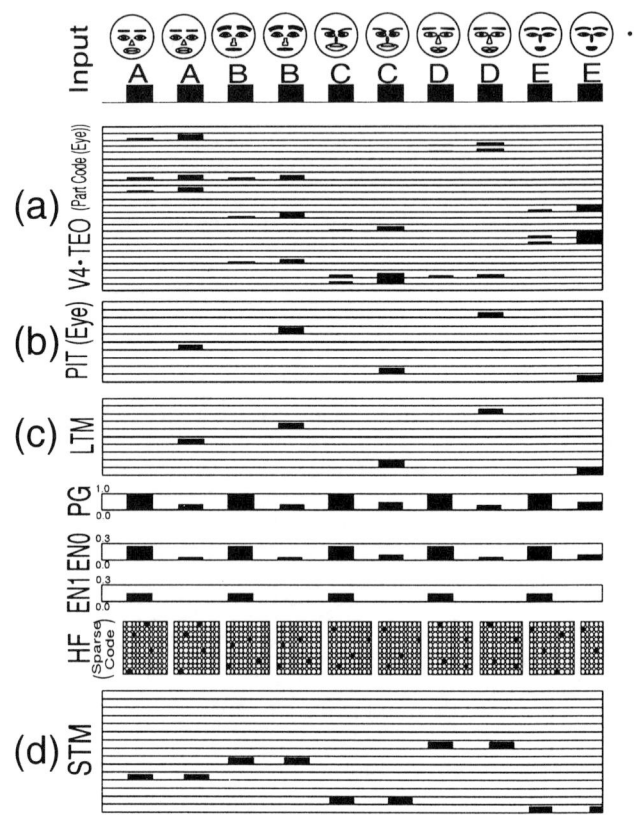

Figure 5: Neural output in respective layers of the AEH model.

layer, h is the threshold, and γ_{jl} is the lateral inhibition in the STM layer. We use (7) to reinforce the weights, and (8) for normalization.

$$(w_{ji}(t + \Delta t))' = w_{ji}(t) + \alpha \cdot x_i \cdot y_j(t + \Delta t) \quad (7)$$

$$w_{ji}(t + \Delta t) = \frac{(w_{ji}(t + \Delta t))'}{||(w_j(t + \Delta t))'||} \cdot w_{length} \quad (8)$$

Here, $\alpha(=3)$ is a learning coefficient, and w_{length} is a fixed number to decide the sum of connecting weights.

The competitive learning between LTM -HF layers is similar to the above description.

Fig.5 shows an example of neuron output in each layer of the AEH model. The abscissa is the time course and the vertical axis is the output of each neurons. The top of Fig.5 is the sequence of the input face images. The part codes produced by part eye in V4·TEO layer are shown in Fig.5(a). In general, each V4·TEO layer successfully made an almost orthogonal part code for each input of the face part. Some overlapping, however, occasionally occurred. The output of PIT layer neurons corresponding to part eye is shown in Fig.5(b). The outputs of LTM and STM layer neurons are shown in Fig.5(c) and (d), respectively. Between Fig.5(c) and (d), the outputs of PG, EN0, EN1, and HF neurons are shown, respectively.

In the first presentation trial of each face, since the output of EN1 neuron exceeded the predetermined threshold, the sparse code was generated in the HF. The sparse

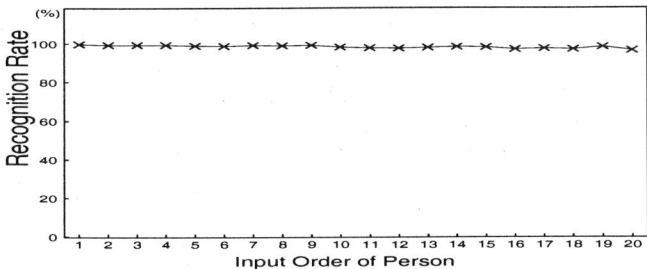

Figure 6: Recognition rate in the presentation method 1 ("AABBCC···"). Each of 20 human faces was presented twice in series.

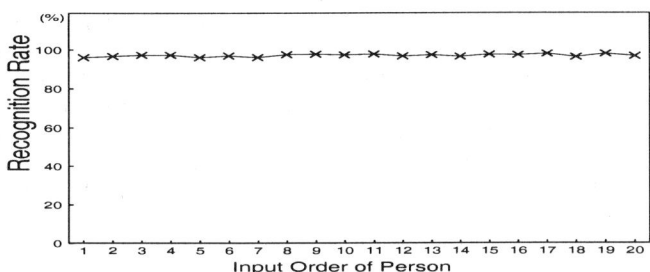

Figure 7: Recognition rate in the presentation method 2 ("ABCD···ABCD···"). Twenty human faces in a block were presented twice.

code generated corresponded to 4 randomly selected neurons among 1000 HF neurons. As a result, the output of the LTM neuron was bigger the second time than the first time for each face. On the other hand, the output of the PG neuron was bigger the first time than the second time because of inhibition from the LTM layer. At the second presentation of each face, since the output of the PG layer was weak, the output of the EN1 neuron did not exceed the activation threshold for the generation of sparse code in the HF layer. Instead, the previously learned sparse code was recollected in the HF, and memory consolidation occurred in the respective layers of the AEH model.

6 RECOGNITION EVALUATION

We used 20 human faces for learning and recollection. We determined the AEH model to have recognized each face correctly if the AEH model learned (stored) the face the first time and recognized (identified) it the second time.

Each face was presented to the AEH model twice by two different methods. In the first method, each of the 20 images was presented twice in succession, i.e. "AABBCC···" as shown in Fig.5 (presentation method 1). The respective A,B,C,··· indicate different human faces for convenience. In the second method, the 20 images were presented successively in a block the first time, and then the same 20 faces were presented successively in a block the second time, i.e. "ABCD···ABCD···" (presentation method 2). In order to eliminate dependency on the input order of the face, the input order was randomized. In both presentation methods, one thousand conditions of input order were tested for 20 human faces among all presentation orders. Figs.6 and 7 show the average recognition rate by the two methods. In Figs.6 and 7, the vertical axis indicates the recognition rate and the horizontal axis indicates the input order. Recognition rates in the two methods were nearly 100 percent correct (more than 95 percent correct in both). In the first presentation method (Fig.6), although the recognition rate for the first person was 100 percent correct, the recognition rate became gradually lower as the number of persons to be recognized increased. This gradual reduction of the recognition rate would be caused by the partial overlapping of sparse code in the HF which occurred during the later consecutive recognition of the persons in the series. In the second presentation method (Fig.7), the recognition rate even for the first person was not perfectly 100 percent correct. This would be because there were already 20 persons' sparse codes in the HF before the second presentation of the same person in a block. In this situation, there would be the same kind of overlapping of the sparse code in the HF as described above. We think the overlapping problem should be easily overcome if the number of HF neurons is increased.

In the next experiment, we examined whether the original sparse codes which were generated in the first presentation were retrieved in the HF, and whether consolidation of long-term memory in the LTM occurred when images of the same persons were presented more than twice, repeatedly. In the experiment, 8 human face images were presented five times in series, i.e. "AAAAABBBBBCCCCC ···". There were no errors of the sparse code retrieval in the HF during the consecutive presentation trials. Fig. 8 is the average of LTM neuron outputs during the consecutive presentation trials across 8 persons. The Target neurons were neurons that learned respective person faces in the first time presentation and should output also in the second and subsequent presentations of the same person. All the other neurons were Non-target neurons. The average output and standard deviation of the Target and Non-target neurons were examined. As shown in Fig.8, the average output of the Target neurons became gradually larger in the second and subsequent presentation trials, and the difference between Target and Non-target neurons also became larger. This finding means that not only the difference among the learned person faces but also the difference between the learned and newly presented persons became more clear by consecutive learning during the second and later presentation trials. This also indicates that the consolidation of long-term memory occurred gradually. Thus the operation of the AEH model is similar to human recognition, since humans also clarify their memory of objects by repeatedly looking at the same objects.

7 CONSIDERATIONS

Recent models of memory function have addressed issues concerning recall and recognition dynamics, sequences of activity patterns as the unit of memory storage, and consolidation of the intermediate-term episodic memory into

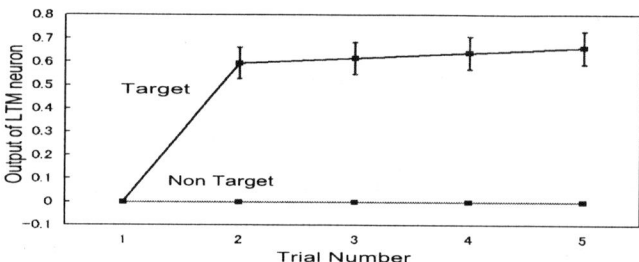

Figure 8: Outputs of a target neuron and non-target neurons in LTM layer during consecutive presentation trials.

long-term memory [10][11][14].

The function of storage vs. recall switching by novelty detection has been extensively modeled by the interaction between EC and HF. In one model, the EC input, synaptic currents, and potentiation or depotentiation arising from CA3 should have a specific phase adjustment to theta rhythm in the reversal learning in a T-maze place-reward association task [14]. The phenomenon of theta phase precession is also suggestive of sequence storage models in the HF.

As for the consolidation of memory, many neural models take seriously the interaction between neocortex and HF. They have explicitly addressed the two-stage process of memory formation. During a period of no external input, the spread of the activity of the attractor states initially formed in HF reactivates components of the association in the neocortex, allowing gradual strengthening of the representation in the neocortex. But they do not directly address the differences in the nature of representation in the two structures. In one model, the initial encoding in the HF has been proposed to take place during theta rhythm oscillations, and the subsequent transfer to the neocortex during sharp waves (SPW) during quiet waking and slow-wave sleep [11]. The SPW may serve and trigger LTP in the deep layer neurons in EC. In this model, the HF is conceived as an association-feedback device which potentiates the neocortical representation. However, the two stage memory model has not demonstrated the fidelity of the reafferent copy in the associational areas in the neocortex, and the role of the SPW in modifying their neural patterns.

For recognition performance, the most important parts of the AEH model are the gating of PG layer to activate the medial temporal memory consolidation (EC - HF) system, the sparse code generation in the HF, and competitive learning between HF and STM. Although the STM is included in the IT in the present model, readers should consider the STM as the deep layer (layer IV/V) in EC.

The key point concerns the implementation of Jones' hypothesis by taking a role of the PG layer in gating an EC - HF loop. This function of "gating" is not only switching the HF between storage and recognition modes but also consolidating the HF sparse code representation into the association cortex representation such that the coded information is effectively transferred without distortion.

8 CONCLUSIONS

In the present study, an association cortex - entorhinal cortex - hippocampal formation neural network model (AEH model) which incorporated neurophysiological knowledge into Jones's hypothesis was proposed, and the recognition performance was examined using human faces. Twenty human faces were used in the recognition experiment. In the experiments, each face was presented twice either in a series or in a block. The recognition performances of the model were nearly 100 percent correct in both experiments indicating the effectiveness of the representation and transformation algorithm of the model. The retrieval of previously encoded associations was almost perfect even after 20 new encodings. Consolidation of long-term memory occurred gradually without any distortions of previously learned memory when the learned faces were repeatedly presented five times in series. Humans memorize a person's face when they meet the person for the first time, and recollect the person's face upon subsequent encounters. Thus the AEH model closely approximates the behavior of human visual learning and recollection.

In future studies, we will evaluate the recognition performance of the AEH model using many more (up to 1000) human faces, including facial expression changes. We will also apply the AEH model to a real-time individual authentication system from the input image of video camera.

References

[1] Squire, L.R., "Memory and Brain", Oxford University Press, New York, 1987.

[2] Jones, R. S., "Entorhinal-hippocampal connections : a speculative view of their function", Trends Neurosci., Vol. 16, pp. 58 - 64, (1993).

[3] Miyashita, Y., "Neural correlate of visual associative long-term memory in the primate temporal cortex", Nature, Vol. 335, pp. 817 - 820, (1988).

[4] Tanaka, K., Saito, H., Fukuda, Y. and Moriya, M., "Coding visual images of objects in the inferotemporal cortex of the macaque monkey", J. Neurophysiol., Vol. 66, pp. 170 - 189, (1991).

[5] Desimone, R., "Face-selective cells in the temporal cortex of monkeys", J. Cognitive Neurosci., Vol. 3, pp. 1 - 8, (1991).

[6] Andersen, R. A., Essick, G. K. and Siegel, R. M., "Encoding of spatial location by posterior parietal neurons", Science, Vol. 230, pp. 456 - 458, (1980).

[7] Nakamura, K., "Auditory spatial discriminatory and mnemonic neurons in rat posterior parietal cortex", J. Neurophysiol., Vol. 82, pp. 2503 - 2517, (1999).

[8] Rolls, E. T., "Information representation, processing, and storage in the brain: analysis at the single neuron level", in The Neural and Molecular Bases of Learning, edited by J. -P. Changeux and M. Konishi, John Wiley and Sons, pp. 503 - 540, (1987).

[9] Ono, T., Nakamura, K., Nishijo, H. and Eifuku, S., "Monkey hippocampal neurons related to spatial and nonspatial functions", J. Neurophysiol., Vol. 70, No. 4, pp. 1516 - 1529, (1993).

[10] Hasselmo, M.E. and McClelland, J.L. "Neural models of memory.", Current Opinion in Neurobiol., Vol. 9, pp.184-188, (1999).

[11] Buzsaki, G., "Two-stage model of memory trace formation: a role for "noisy" brain states.", Neuroscience, 31, pp.551-570, (1989).

[12] Brown, M.W. and Xiang, J.-Z., "Recognition memory: neuronal substrates of the judgement of prior occurrence.", Prog. in Neurobiol., Vol. 55, pp.149-189, (1998).

[13] Nakamura, K., Kinoshita, N. and Kanayama H., "2D spreading associative neural network simultaneously recognizes object position and shape in 2D space", Systems and Computers in Japan, Vol. 33, No. 13, pp.11 - 23, (2002).

[14] Hasselmo, M.E., Bodelon, C. and Wyble, B.P. "A proposed function for hippocampal theta rhythm: separate phases of encoding and retrieval enhance reversal of prior learning.", Neural Computation, Vol. 14, pp.793-817, (2002).

T-maze Training of a Recurrent CA3 Model Reveals the Necessity of Novelty-Based Modulation of LTP in Hippocampal Region CA3

J. D. Monaco and W. B Levy
Dept. of Neurological Surgery
University of Virginia
P.O. Box 800420
Charlottesville, VA 22908-0420

Abstract-The rat hippocampus has been shown to mediate a large set of spatial navigation tasks such as the simple T-maze. We investigated the performance of a minimal computational, but biologically based, model of CA3 on this task. For successful performance, the model needs to generate and maintain neuronal codes for each of the two arms of the T-maze. Moreover, each code must be distinctively recalled in a goal-dependent manner. The development of such neuronal codes is aided by the appearance of repetitively firing recurrent neurons – known as local context units, analogous to hippocampal place cells – which promote spatiotemporal association within the T-maze training sequences. The number, longevity, and connectivity of local context units exclusively coding for each arm of the maze grow with training. Although with too much training, the coding for one arm uncontrollably dominates over the other code, and goal appropriate choice-behavior is lost. That is, successful network codes can easily deteriorate with overtraining. The amount of training that produces this deterioration in performance depends on other network parameters. Rather than a failure of the model, we believe these results tell us something important about the biology of the hippocampal system. That is, this result provides support for the hypothesis of a hippocampal afferent system which down-regulates LTP once a task has been successfully learned. Modulatory systems (e.g., dopaminergic, generally D1/D5r) exist which are candidates for this functional role.

I. INTRODUCTION

The T-maze task has a long history as an important tool of behavioral psychology [1-5]. Tolman studied rats running complex T-mazes and systematized the theory of cognitive maps [1,6]. Others have used it to investigate behaviors in rats ranging from odor discrimination [4] to height aversion on an elevated maze [7]. It is also one of the simplest spatial navigation paradigms, and as such is a good minimal case for studying goal-dependent sequence learning and recall in hippocampal memory formation. Positive reinforcement tasks provide food or a more pleasant odor at one of the arms of the T-maze more often than the other [1-5], and the rats learn quickly where to go. That is, the animals have both a goal in mind and a learned spatial map allowing them to get there when being tested. In this paper, we apply an established computational model [8-11] of the CA3 region of the rat hippocampus to goal finding in a T-maze scenario.

Many recent studies have investigated the modulatory effect of novelty on hippocampal plasticity and the strength of memory formation. Even brief exposure to novelty for neonatal rats was shown to elicit a lasting enhancement of hippocampal long-term potentiation (LTP) [12]. Physiologically, novel environments were shown to increase the rate of phosphorylation of the protein CREB in pyramidal cells [13]; this process seems to lead to the generation of new dendritic spines in female rats [14]. Increases in postsynaptic spine density might serve to enhance hippocampal excitability as well as LTP. Such observations suggest that stronger hippocampal memories are formed in novel situations than familiar ones. Indeed, exposure to a novel environment just prior to a single trial avoidance task has a significant enhancing effect on task recall [15]. The hippocampal formation receives projections, primarily at D1/D5 receptors, that possibly modulate long-term synaptic modification [16]. It then projects directly to nucleus accumbens (N.Acc) from the ventral subiculum [17]; this projection is activated within the hippocampal formation by novel stimuli and increases extracellular dopamine in the N.Acc [18].

The implication of hippocampal involvement in a novelty-reward pathway is clear with regard to the learning of various cognitive tasks. Novel stimuli, such as those at the beginning of a training session, both reward the animal and enhance the hippocampal LTP necessary to learn the task. A reasonable hypothesis then emerges regarding continued training on the same task: there will be a point at which more training is unnecessary and may even be detrimental. This is the point at which the animal becomes bored with the exercise, as it is no longer stimulating its dopamine system, and the heightened plasticity of the hippocampus is down-regulated. That is, learning is effectively turned off once the task is learned. The demonstration of a simple hippocampal-mediated task whose solution requires LTP down-regulation would provide strong support for this hypothesis. As described above, the necessary novelty-reward mechanisms are in place [12-18].

In the present report, we find that overtraining of this CA3 model on the T-maze task leads to increased similarity between the recurrent neuronal firing that codes for each of the two arm subsequences. Such similarity destroys previously successful learning. That is, we found a large class of biologically reasonable networks which are successful T-maze learners after a given number of training trials, but then fail at some point if training is continued. Since rats quickly learn T-mazes [1-6], the model predicts that the hippocampal aspect of this learning be down-regulated as learning proceeds.

Overview of the Model

The CA3 model is a sparsely connected, asymmetric, recurrent neural network composed of McCulloch-Pitts units [8]. As described in [9], synaptic modification is based on a local Hebbian rule with a time-spanning associative capability. The total network activity comes from both externally driven input units and recurrent processing units, with the majority of network activity resulting from the latter. As such, the model processes spatiotemporal sequences of entorhinal cortex/dentate gyrus input.

Two sequence learning tasks that the model successfully solves are subsequence disambiguation and goal finding [9,19]. They are complementary in the sense that they are trained identically yet tested differently. In these tasks, the network is trained on two sequences which share a middle subsequence (see Fig. 2b in [9]). In testing for disambiguation, the proper sequence must be recalled when prompted with the beginning of either sequence. In testing goal finding, a goal code is present which represents the end of one sequence, and recall for both sequences must be completely dependent on the goal code. Behaviorally, a rat learns to associate the end of one of the two sequences with a reward, such as food. During testing, the animal is motivated by a goal, such as hunger, and finds the path to the spatial location that it associated with food during training. In this form of the goal finding task, a novel path to the goal must be found. That is, for success, a goal code must cause a simulated network to recall its respective goal pattern.

The T-maze task is similar to the above goal finding task, except that there are only two subsequences. Each of the two training sequences are composed of a shared "stem" subsequence followed by one of two nonshared (i.e., orthogonal) "arm" subsequences. These are analogous to the stem and arm pathways on a physical T-maze, where the final patterns of each of the two arms are the goal boxes. Simulations, to be successful, must demonstrate flexible, goal-code-dependent recall. Successive patterns of recurrent activity called local context codes are characteristic of our CA3 model's ability to resolve the inherent ambiguity of this task [20]. Local context neurons are recurrent neurons that identify a subsequence of a larger sequence, usually by firing repetitively in response to its particular input subsequence [9]. Accordingly, these neurons are analogous to hippocampal place cells (for review, see [21]). By firing continuously over more than one pattern in the sequence, they allow time-spanning associativity to flexibly associate temporally nonadjacent input patterns [9]. This repetitive firing of the model allows us to talk about attractors in the state space of neuronal codes [9]. Indeed, the neuronally encoded goals at the end of each T-maze arm are two fixed-point attractors learned by the network. The task then tests the network's ability to induce one or the other attractor.

II. MODEL AND METHODS

A. The Network Model

The hippocampal CA3 model is a sparsely and randomly connected recurrent network. The probability of a recurrent interconnection is 10%. The neurons are simple McCulloch-Pitts binary units. Synaptic weights are modified using a temporally asymmetric rule of association [22]. This asymmetry allows the recurrent network model to form context codes, which are critical to its problem-solving capabilities [8,9,20]. The Hebbian-like learning rule is

$$W_{ij}(t+1) = W_{ij}(t) + \mu Z_j(t)\left(\overline{Z}_i(t-1) - W_{ij}(t)\right), \quad (1)$$

where W_{ij} is the weight of the synapse from neuron i to neuron j, μ is the learning rate constant, Z_j is a binary indicator of the firing state of neuron j, and $\overline{Z}_i(t)$ is the neuronal signal decay of neuron i at timestep t such that

$$\overline{Z}_i(t) = \begin{cases} 1, & \text{if } Z_i(t) = 1 \\ \alpha \cdot \overline{Z}_i(t-1), & \text{otherwise} \end{cases}, \quad (2)$$

where α determines the off-rate time constant of the NMDA receptor. For the data in this report, we used $\alpha = 0.4$ and a learning rate constant of $\mu = 0.5$. Also, all neuronal firing was determined using a *k-winners-take-all* competitive paradigm. All externally driven neurons for a given timestep t are indicated by the binary vector $x(t)$, and $Z_i(t) = 1$ whenever $x_i(t) = 1$. The internal excitation for neuron j is

$$y_j(t) = \sum_{i=1}^{n} c_{ij} \cdot W_{ij}(t-1) \cdot Z_i(t-1), \quad (3)$$

where c_{ij} is a binary indicator of a synaptic connection from neuron i to neuron j. For recurrently excited neuron j, $y_j(t)$ determines that $Z_i(t) = 1$ if it is among the k largest neural excitations. Otherwise, $Z_i(t) = 0$.

The value k is the number of neurons that need to be active in order to maintain the predetermined network activity level a, which includes externally driven activity. For a network of size n, k is the largest integer less than na. If the lowest excitation value of the *k-winners* is shared among several neurons, not all of which are allowed to fire, then a random subset of these neurons is fired.

B. Input Sequences, Training, and Testing

There are two training sequences for the T-maze task, one each for the "left path" and "right path" of the maze. They share the same stem subsequence. The stem is 6 patterns long, while each of the arms is 4 patterns. The number of neurons in each input pattern in a sequence is the same, and is determined by the network size (n), total network activity level (a), and external fraction of activity (m_e). The variable a, as a fraction of the network size, determines how many neurons, both recurrent and externally driven, are active per timestep. The variable m_e specifies the number of neurons assigned to any given external input pattern as a fraction of the number of active neurons. For all data in this report, network size is constant at $n = 4096$, but a and m_e are independently variable.

Input firing patterns within subsequences are slowly shifting. That is, temporally adjacent patterns are spatially adjacent in that they share one third of their neurons. However, the three input subsequences that constitute the T-maze (i.e., stem, "left side" arm, and "right side" arm) are mutually orthogonal. Also, each of the 10 patterns in a training sequence are repeated ("stuttered") for 3 timesteps [10]. So, each input sequence is 30 timesteps long, with the arm subsequences beginning at $t = 19$.

A single training trial consists of the presentation of both training sequences to the network. The network is initialized for every sequence presentation with a random firing vector at the network activity level. Synaptic modification is turned off during the testing trials. Testing consists of two sequence trials in which the stem input subsequence is presented to the network. This is analogous to a rat physically moving though the T-maze up to the point where a decision must be made. From the beginning of the sequence and up to the final goal pattern in the first trial, 25% of the external neurons representing the goal pattern of the "left side" arm subsequence are also turned on. This is the goal code [9]. A normalized cosine of the activity of the external input neurons determines whether or not the network recalls the "left side" goal. The same process is done for the "right side" arm subsequence. If both the "left" and "right" goals are appropriately recalled, for at least 8 out of 10 pairs of random goal codes, then this network learned the T-maze.

III. CODE SIMILARITY AND T-MAZE PERFORMANCE

Successful learning of the T-maze task is mediated by the development during training of learned firing patterns, called local context codes [9]. The number of local context (LC) neurons in any particular simulation for a given input sequence depends on many different factors, the most general being the proportion of recurrent to externally driven activity [19]. The firing patterns of LC neurons allow the network to flexibly learn the two paths leading away from the end of the T-maze stem. However, T-maze performance is not linearly correlated with either the average length of context codes or the number of LC neurons (data not shown).

When we discuss the "codes" developed during a simulation, we are referring to the sequences of recurrent neuronal firing that occur during the presentation of the two input sequences within a given training trial. If we restrict the discussion to the "codes" for the arm subsequences, then we are only interested in the sequences of recurrent firing in the range of timesteps from $t = 19$ to $t = 30$. So, the codes recalled during a training trial always consist of both "left side" sequence codes and "right side" sequence codes, regardless of which subsequences are being discussed. Given this, it is always possible to refer to the degree of similarity between the "left" and "right" training codes, which we term the "between-sequence similarity". Of course, this similarity is timestep dependent, since it is possible for the "left" codes to be very similar to the "right" codes during one range of timesteps of a trial and orthogonal to them during another range.

A. Arm Subsequence Similarity

This CA3 model develops an end of sequence attractor [9]. In the language of attractors, a successful simulation has developed two noisy fixed-point goal attractors. When tested, perturbations in the direction of one or the other goal attractor are able to influence the otherwise free recall of the network. The recall trajectory, through the state space of neuronal firing vectors, then falls into the basin of attraction of the appropriate goal attractor. This is what is meant by a goal code's ability to "induce" a goal attractor. The network training codes for the two goal patterns must be nearly orthogonal since any similarity only decreases the efficacy of goal codes. That is, as the linear dependence of the attractor points increases, so does the probability that a random goal code will push the recall trajectory toward both goal attractors simultaneously. Successful simulations are those that have resolved such ambiguity.

So, successful T-maze learning requires very low similarity in the recurrent codes for each goal pattern. However, the solution requires flexibility in the associations between recurrent LC neurons and external neurons representing the patterns of the arms. That is, there must be a set of recurrent neurons which fire repeatedly over two or more nongoal patterns and which innervate, directly or indirectly, external neurons from both arm subsequences. These LC neurons must themselves be activated during both sequences in a training or testing trial. This can only happen if they are sufficiently innervated by externals in both arm subsequences or are activated by the end of the stem subsequence. There must be a set of such recurrent context neurons to develop the flexible goal associations necessary to the solution of this task. That is, substantial similarity between the recurrent codes at the beginning of the arm subsequences is necessary for good T-maze performance.

Thus, there is a tension between the two requirements: the recurrent codes that are goal attractors must be orthogonal, but there must be a substantial number of common LC neurons that fire at the beginning of both arm subsequences. For a simulation to be successful, then, there must be a progression in the between-sequence similarity of the arm subsequences from substantial similarity, starting around timestep $t = 19$, to orthogonality, occurring before timestep $t = 30$.

B. A Useful Measure of Between-Sequence Similarity

We define similarity in terms of a normalized cosine between two recurrent firing vectors. Let $z_L(t)$ and $z_R(t)$ be the recurrent network states at timestep t for the "left" and "right" training sequences, respectively, of a particular training trial. The timestep-dependent between-sequence similarity, $s(t)$, is

$$s(t) = \frac{z_L(t) \bullet z_R(t)^T}{na}, \forall t \in \{1,...,30\}. \quad (4)$$

A value of $s(t) = 1$ indicates that the "left" and "right" recurrent network states are identical at timestep t; between-sequence orthogonality is indicated by $s(t) = 0$. As discussed below and in the statement of our results, the timestep t at which the half-maximal similarity occurs will be important. First, define the maximal similarity between the "left side" and "right side" recurrent training codes,

$$m = \max_{t \in \{1,..,30\}} [s(t)]. \quad (5)$$

Then, define the timestep nearest the end of the sequence that produces half of that value,

$$B_{SIM} = \max \left[t: s(t) \geq \frac{m}{2} \right]. \quad (6)$$

Formally, we call this timestep the "similarity boundary". It measures the last time during the sequence, from the beginning to the end, when the recurrent codes for the "left side" and "right side" training sequences are mostly similar to each other.

According to the account of T-maze performance presented in III.A, the between-sequence similarity of the arm subsequences is critical. The maximal similarity m does not vary much and always occurs during the stem codes. That is, the stem codes are a trivial case during training since the network receives the same external inputs for the stem subsequence in both sequences. There is some variability in the similarity of the stem codes, due to the random processes in the network (i.e., competitive firing and sequence initialization), but m will always be very close to 1. So, the similarity boundary B_{SIM} is based on a the maximal similarity m of a given simulation as a normalizing factor.

However, for successful performance to be possible, the arm codes must diverge; that is, the arm codes must tend toward orthogonality as t approaches the end of the sequence. This requirement, coupled with the necessity of nonzero similarity at the beginning of the arm subsequence, implies that between-sequence similarity must decrease to 0 as the timestep increases to 30. Thus, for any given similarity value s, which is less than the maximum, we can find a timestep t_s such that all timesteps up to and including t_s yield between-sequence similarity greater than or equal to s, and all later timesteps yield similarity values less than s. This timestep can be considered a "boundary" dividing the sequence based on a chosen similarity value. Letting $s = m/2$, then, we can see that $t_s = B_{SIM}$, where m and B_{SIM} are defined in (5) and (6), respectively. So, B_{SIM} is a similarity boundary, a timestep that partitions an ordered sequence based on between-sequence similarity. Certainly, there are other possible measures of subsequence similarity. However, this particular definition allows a necessary, yet insufficient, condition for successful T-maze performance to be inferred, in the form of a critical range for B_{SIM} at the end of training.

C. Success and Failure Modes

We define a specific set of identically parameterized simulations to be successful if at least 80% of randomly seeded simulations successfully solve the given task. Every such set in this report is comprised of 15 simulations. Graphs of a typical T-maze success are shown in Figs. 1a-d. Note that in the two testing trials, Figs. 1b and 1c, the appropriate external arm subsequence neurons, up to the end of the sequence, are activated in each case. One of the cosine similarity diagrams used for network decoding is depicted in Fig. 1d. It is apparent that the first 3 patterns of each arm subsequence are active regardless of which goal code is present. However, the goal codes are able to influence recall during testing and induce the goal attractor for each of the arm subsequences.

There are two failure modes, each arising from opposing difficulties in solving the T-maze. The first, call it a Type I failure, is evident in parameterizations with a low number of active recurrents during training and testing. This reduces the number of possible LC

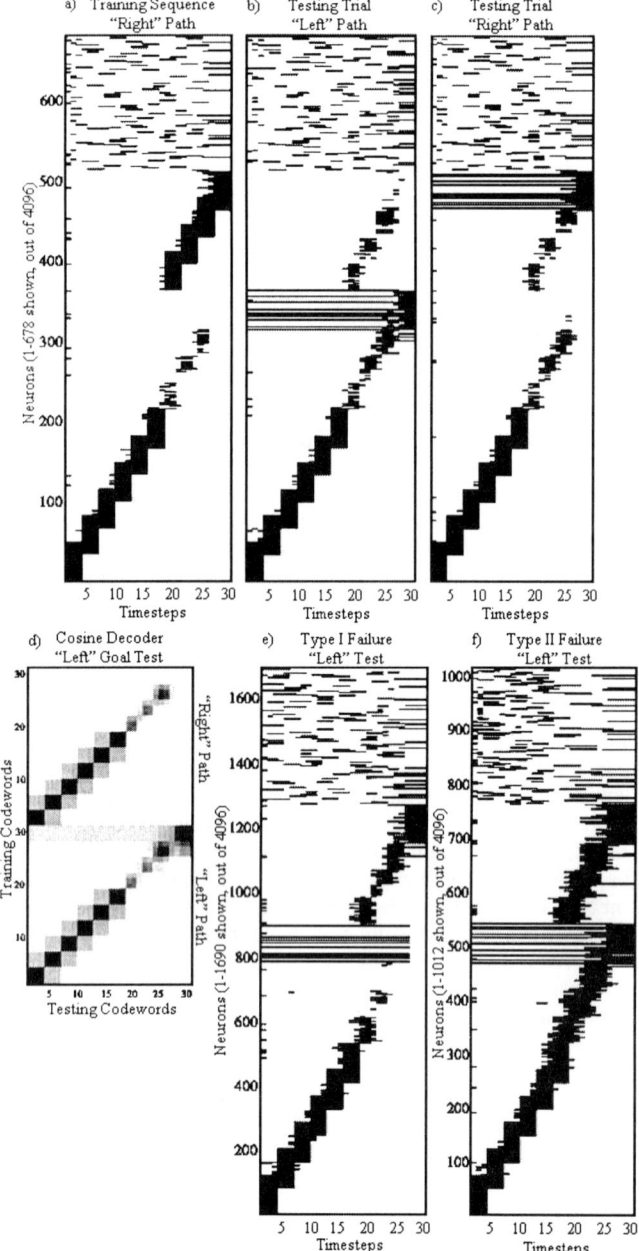

Fig. 1. Neuronal firing diagrams and an example cosine similarity matrix. Each of the firing diagrams shows all external neurons and a small subset of the recurrent neurons in the network. A "right path" training sequence for a typical successful network ($m_e = 0.15$, $a = 0.08$) is shown in (a). Note the concurrent "left side" arm firing that ceases around $t = 27$. The complete testing trial for this network is shown in (b) and (c). The horizontal lines are the fractional goal codes activated for the duration of the testing trial, except during the final pattern. The external neurons for both arm subsequences fire in both cases except for the appropriate goal pattern. The cosine similarities, as defined in (4), between the codewords recalled during the "left" testing sequence in (b) and the "left" and "right" training codewords are shown in the matrix (d). (In (d), a black cell indicates code identity, a white cell indicates orthogonality, and gray cells are intermediate.) This type of similarity matrix is used to decode network testing recall. Notice that the testing codewords at the end of the sequence are strongly similar to the final codewords of the "left" training sequence and orthogonal to those of the "right" training sequence. This is decoded as being a "left" choice. Finally, the neuronal firing diagrams for "left" testing sequences are shown for example Type I and II failure modes in (e) and (f), respectively.

neurons. Of those LC neurons, only a few, if any, will innervate the external neurons of both arm subsequences. As discussed above, this directly affects the ability of a network to have goal-code-dependent recall of both goals. Thus, a Type I failure mode occurs when a simul-ation predicts a single goal to either of the two test input sequences. For example, the simulation chooses the "right side" when the "right side" is the correct answer and when the "left side" is the correct answer. Fig. 1e contains a neur-onal firing diagram showing a Type I failure, in which this is the case.

All other failed simulations are Type II failures. A Type II failure results from parameterizations which activate a large number of recurrent neurons per timestep. A firing diagram of a typical Type II failure is shown in Fig. 1f. Due to the development of numerous LC neurons, training only serves to increase the between-sequence similarity of the recurrent codes for both arm subsequences, including the two goal patterns. The end result is that a single goal attractor is created at the end of the sequence, making the induction of separate goals impossible. A Type II failure mode occurs when a simulation predicts both goals simultaneously. In Fig. 1f, a single goal code is present, yet both external goal patterns are recalled.

IV. RESULTS

We examined the T-maze performance of a set of 15 network connectivities across broad ranges of both total network activity (a) and the external fraction of activity (m_e). We will show that robust T-maze performance necessarily depends on learned recurrent codes that correlate with having a similarity boundary within a critical range. Finally, we show that the value of the similarity boundary is training dependent. It tends to move towards the end of the sequence as training continues. As a result, overtraining destroys a previously learned solution.

A. Network Parameterization and Task Performance

We assessed the T-maze performance of a large set of network parameterizations, in which all simulations were trained for 40 trials. The results are shown as a contour plot in Fig. 2. The external fraction of activity, m_e, was tested from 0.100 to 0.300 in increments of 0.025. This is a broad, but reasonable, range of m_e for this CA3 model [19]. Total network activity was then tested from 0.06 to 0.13 in increments of 0.01 for each m_e. Similarly, this is a broad, yet biologically reasonable, range for the activity level in a 4096-neuron simulation [24]. There are no successful parameterizations with $m_e = 0.1$, and only the 7% activity level was successful with $m_e = 0.125$.

Similarly, only the 8% activity level produced successful simulations with $m_e = 0.15$. Lower activities result in Type I failures while at higher activities all failures were Type II. At 10% activity and up to 13%, none of the simulations learned the task. Now, consider parameterizations with $m_e = 0.175$, 0.200, and 0.225. These values of external activity are closer to those that lead to robust performance on the original goal finding task [19]. No simulations were able to learn at 6% activity, but all 15 performed successfully at 9% and 10% activity levels (except that only 11/15 of those with $m_e = 0.175$ at 10% activity learned the task). Again, the low activity failures are of Type I, and higher activity levels produce Type II failures. There is another region of successful parameterizations at higher external fractions of activity. Simulations with $m_e = 0.250$, 0.275, and 0.300 were successful at both 11% and 12% activity levels. Each simulation at 8% and lower activity levels was a Type I failure, and each simulation at 13% activity was a Type II failure.

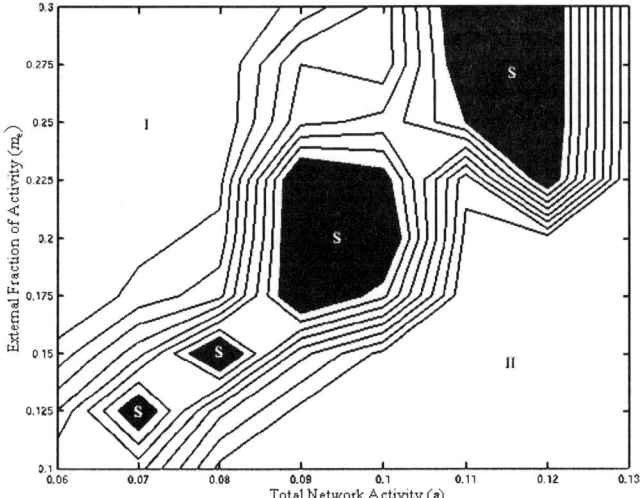

Fig. 2. T-maze success across both the total network activity (a) and the external fraction of activity (m_e). The two-dimensional parameter grid defined by $m_e = \{0.100, 0.125, ..., 0.300\}$ and $a = \{0.60, 0.70, ..., 0.13\}$ was tested for task performance after 40 training trials. A contour plot of this performance, as a fraction of successful simulations out of the 15 tested for each parameterization, is shown. The 80% contour is shaded in, representing the parameter values that lead to successful performance during testing. It should be noted that there are no data points between the apparently disjoint regions of success (i.e., those shaded in and marked "S"); that is, the evident division of the success region is an artifact of the interpolation necessary of a contour plot. The regions characterized by Type I or Type II failures are marked "I" and "II", respectively. There were 260 successful network simulations in the total 1,080 simulations of this data set.

B. Critical Range of the Similarity Boundary

Each of the 260 successful simulations in this data set of 1,080 total simulations has a similarity boundary in the range from $t = 21$ to $t = 30$. Fig. 3a shows the conditional probability of the success of a simulation given its similarity boundary at the end of 40 training trials. Each bar represents the fraction of simulations that learned successfully out of all simulations with a particular B_{SIM}. Task success correlates strongly with a similarity boundary between timesteps 24 and 26, with success most likely at $t = 25$. Specifically, 95.3% of simulations with a similarity boundary of $B_{SIM} = 25$ successfully learned the T-maze. Simulations having $B_{SIM} = 24$ and 26 have similarly high percentages of successes: 85.7% and 77.2%, respectively. Outside of that range, successful T-maze performance becomes very unlikely and much less robust. Specifically, no simulations having $B_{SIM} = 19$ or 20 solved the task. Also, simulations with similarity boundaries between timesteps 21 and 23 have less than a 40% probability of performing the task. Lastly, of the 388 simulations with codes such that the goals are similar, having $B_{SIM} = 30$, only one was successful. This correlation of performance with a small range of the similarity boundary timestep is especially significant considering that it emerged from a diverse set of simulations. With a narrow critical range, it becomes important to see how the similarity boundary can change over the course of training.

C. Similarity Boundary Dependence on Training

The similarity between the codes of the training sequences is related to the ability of these networks to perform the T-maze task. As measured by the similarity boundary B_{SIM}, this dynamic aspect of the networks can change greatly with training. An example of a network simulation, with 8% network activity and an external activity of $m_e = 0.15$, is shown in Fig. 3b. Both B_{SIM} and the performance of the network are plotted across 120 training trials. Performance is measured as the fraction out of 15 goal code pairs that recall their respective goals. At trial 0, and up to trial 20, the similarity boundary comes before timestep 24 and testing results in the Type I failure mode. Between trials 30 and 40, the similarity boundary is between timesteps 24 and 25, and 100% performance is achieved at both of those trials. After trial 50, B_{SIM} increases to timestep 30 and there is no successful performance from that point on. All of these failures are of Type II. Thus, there is a very small window in which this particular simulation learned the task. Continued training led to the deterioration of the encoding of the task that made successful T-maze performance possible.

A comparison of this data set to a similar set, where each simulation was trained for 65 trials, reveals that only a very small

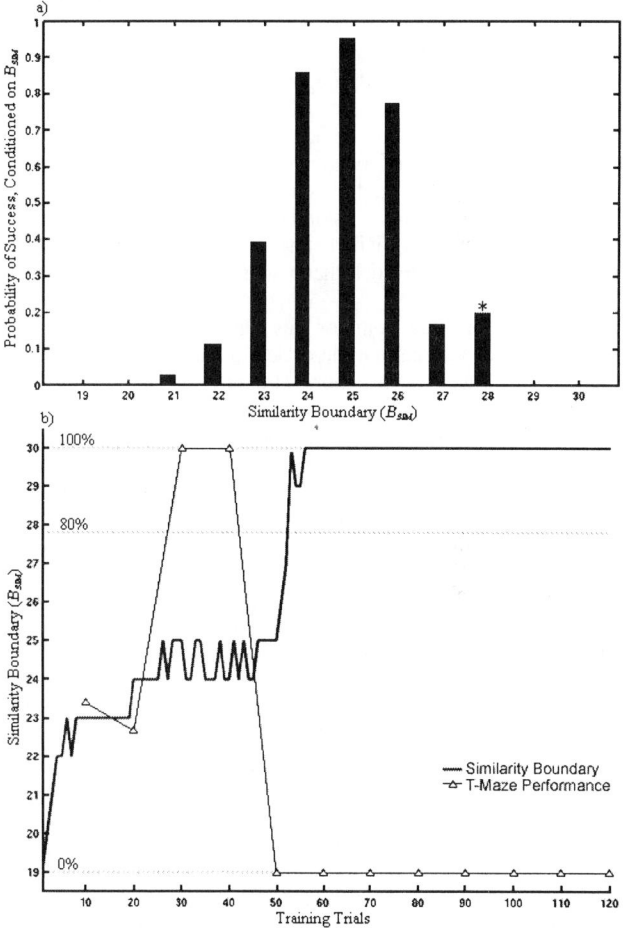

Fig. 3. T-maze performance depends critically upon the timestep at which the recurrent codes for the two arms of the maze cease to be mostly similar. This timestep, measured by the similarity boundary B_{SIM}, changes with the amount of training. Thus, the simulations can be overtrained such that the similarity boundary moves to the end of the sequence, destroying learned performance. A graph of the conditional probability of the success of a simulation, given the B_{SIM} of that simulation after training, is shown in (a). Thus, each bar in (a) represents the fraction of simulations, from the data set in Fig. 2, having a given B_{SIM} which are successful. (Only 5 simulations in the data set had $B_{SIM} = 28$, so the corresponding bar in (a) is due to only a single successful simulation.) A typical example of overtraining a simulation is shown in (b). In this figure, the changing value of B_{SIM} is shown, across training, along with the task performance of the simulation (measured every 10 training trials). At trials 10 and 20, this simulation is characterized by the Type I failure mode. The simulation is only successful for trials 30 and 40, for which $B_{SIM} = 24$ or 25. Additional training only serves to increase the similarity boundary to the point that task performance results in the Type II failure mode.

region (i.e., around the parameterization with $m_e = 0.225$, $a = 0.10$) that was successful at 40 training trials remained successful (data not shown). That is, a mere 15 additional trials of training effectively destroyed all of the successful learning evident after just 40 trials.

V. DISCUSSION

The T-maze problem is a special learning problem for a number of reasons. It is the simplest task requiring the induction of attractors, as in goal finding and other tasks (e.g., [19]). It is also a fundamental unit of many spatial learning and navigation tasks [2-5]. Tolman used a complex array of T-mazes to systematize the theory of cognitive maps [1,6], which laid the foundation for hippocampal place cell research [21]. In this report, we showed that a biologically reasonable, computational model of the rat CA3 can learn the T-maze over a wide range of parameterizations. Further, the task solution is critically dependent upon the similarity of the codes for the two arms of the maze. The neuronal codes for the stem of the T-maze will be identical, and local context codes facilitate the sharing of neurons at the beginning of the arm subsequences. However, this similarity must disappear at some point before the goal. In terms of the number of training trials, there is a narrow window when this between-sequence similarity transition is appropriate such that a simulation shows good learned performance.

We found that the point of this within trial transition in the sequence varies in a training dependent manner. This point comes increasingly later with more training, making successful performance more unlikely. This training dependent change in between-sequence similarity is mediated by local context codes, the very same coding feature which allows the network to solve the problem in the first place. Thus, there is a quantitative subtlety as to what constitutes a good encoding.

By documenting a large class of biologically reasonable parameterizations that learn the task well, but that can also be easily overtrained, we conjecture the necessity for a system capable of turning off hippocampal LTP once good learning has taken place.

There are plausible systems in place that could function in this role. For instance, the rat hippocampus receives dopaminergic projections from the ventral tegmental dopaminergic system [16], and projects to nucleus accumbens [17,18]. It is also known to function in the discrimination of novel experiences [13]. Additionally, novel stimuli have been shown to have modulatory effects on hippocampal LTP [12,15]. Therefore, the conjunction of the novelty and dopamine systems is at least a candidate for providing the hippocampal shut-off function necessitated by our study of the T-maze problem. That is, a rat that begins training on an unfamiliar task will be doing so with potentially stronger LTP, enabling it to learn reliably and fast. Training continues to the point at which the rat learns the task. Additional training serves to decrease the novelty of the situation, thus down-regulating LTP. This prevents the coding problem that destroyed, with overtraining, the learned solution developed by our networks. A rat that is familiar with the learned task, yet forced to continue training, will maintain its original solution.

This hypothesis seems reasonable, but certainly other possible systems exist which could serve this function. The primary result here is that the existence of such a system appears to be necessary to the maintenance of learned tasks in the rat hippocampus.

ACKNOWLEDGMENT

This work was supported by the John A. Harrison III Undergraduate Research Award of the University of Virginia Faculty Senate to J.D.M., and NIH MH48161, MH63855 and RR15205 to W.B.L.

REFERENCES

[1] E.C. Tolman, B.F. Ritchie, and D. Kalish, "Studies in spatial learning. I. Orientation and the short-cut," *J. Exp. Psychol.: General*, vol. 36, pp. 13-24, 1946.

[2] R.A. Littman, "Latent learning in a T-maze after two degrees of training," *J. Comp. Physiol. Psychol.*, vol. 43, pp. 135-147, 1950.

[3] J.R. Ison and H. Kniaz, "T-maze performance as a function of consummatory activity," *Psych. Rep.*, vol. 12, pp. 107-110, 1963.

[4] J. Mendelson and S.L. Chorover, "Lateral hypothalamic stimulation in satiated rats: T-maze learning for food," *Science*, vol. 149, pp. 559-561, 1965.

[5] P.F. Southall and C.J. Long, "Odor stimuli, training procedures, and performance in a T-maze," *Psychonomic Science*, vol. 24, pp. 4-6, 1971.

[6] E.C. Tolman, "Cognitive maps in mice and men," *Psychol. Rev.*, vol. 55, pp. 189-208, 1948.

[7] H. Zangrossi Jr., et al., "Serotonergic regulation of inhibitory avoidance and one-way escape in the rat elevated T-maze," *Neurosci. Biobehav.*, vol. 25, pp. 637-645, 2001.

[8] W.B. Levy, "A computational approach to hippocampal function," in *Computational Models of Learning in Simple Neural Systems*, R.D Hawkins and G.H. Bower, Eds. New York: Academic, 1989, pp. 243-305.

[9] W.B. Levy, "A sequence predicting CA3 is a flexible associator that learns and uses context to solve hippocampal-like tasks," *Hippocampus*, vol. 6, pp. 579-590, 1996.

[10] X.B. Wu, J. Tyrcha, and W.B. Levy, "A neural network solution to the transverse patterning problem depends on repetition of the input code," *Neurocomputing*, vol. 26, pp. 601-607, 1999.

[11] X.B. Wu and W.B. Levy, "Simulating the transverse non-patterning problem," *Neurocomputing*, vol. 44, pp. 1029-1034, 2002.

[12] H.E. Viola, et al., "Phosphorylated cAMP response element binding protein as a molecular marker of memory processing in rat hippocampus: effect of novelty," *J. Neurosci.*, vol. 20, art. no. RC112, 2000.

[13] A.C. Tang and B. Zou, "Neonatal exposure to novelty enhances long-term potentiation in CA1 of the rat hippocampus," *Hippocampus*, vol. 12, pp. 398-404, 2002.

[14] M. Segal and D.D. Murphy, "Estradiol induces formation of dendritic spines in hippocampal neurons: Functional correlates," *Horm. Behav.*, vol. 40, pp. 156-159, 2001.

[15] L.A. Izquierdo, et al., "Novelty enhances retrieval: molecular mechanisms involved in rat hippocampus," *Eur. J. Neurosci.*, vol. 13, pp. 1464-1467, 2001.

[16] S.L. Erickson, S.R. Sesack, and D.A. Lewis, "Dopamine innervation of monkey entorhinal cortex: postsynaptic targets of tyrosine hydroxylase-immunoreactive terminals," *Synapse*, vol. 36, pp. 47-56, 2000.

[17] C.D. Blaha, C.R. Yang, S.B. Floresco, A.M. Barr, and A.G. Philipps, "Stimulation of ventral subiculum of the hippocampus evokes glutamate-receptor mediated changes in dopamine efflux in the rat nucleus accumbens," *Eur. J. Neurosci.*, vol. 9, pp. 902-911, 1997.

[18] M. Legault and R.A. Wise, "Novelty-evoked elevations of nucleus accumbens dopamine: dependence on impulse flow from the ventral subiculum and glutamatergic neurotransmission in the ventral tegmental area," *Eur. J. Neurosci.*, vol. 13, pp. 819-828, 2001.

[19] S. Polyn, X.B. Wu, and W.B. Levy, "Entorhinal/dentate excitation of CA3: a critical variable in hippocampal models," *Neurocomputing*, vol. 32, pp. 493-499, 2000.

[20] X.B. Wu, R.A. Baxter, and W.B. Levy, "Context codes and the effect of noisy learning on a simplified hippocampal CA3 model," *Biol. Cybern.*, vol. 74, pp. 159-165, 1996.

[21] P.J. Best, A.M. White, and A.A. Minai, "Spatial processing in the brain: the activity of hippocampal place cells," *Annu. Rev. Neurosci.*, vol. 24, pp. 459-486, 2001.

[22] W.B. Levy and O. Steward, "Temporal contiguity requirements for long-term associative potentiation/depression in the hippocampus," *Neuroscience*, vol. 8, pp. 791-797, 1983.

[23] W.B. Levy and X.B. Wu, "The relationship of local context codes to sequence length memory capacity," *Network-Comp. Neural*, vol. 7, pp. 371-384, 1996.

[24] A.A. Minai and W.B. Levy, "Setting the activity level in sparse random networks," *Neural Comp.*, vol. 6, pp. 85-99, 1994.

The Importance of Stop Word Removal on Recall Values in Text Categorization

Catarina Silva[†‡], Bernardete Ribeiro[†]

[†]Departamento de Engenharia Informática, Centro de Informática e Sistemas, Universidade de Coimbra, 3030 Coimbra, Portugal

[‡]Escola Superior de Tecnologia e Gestão - Instituto Politécnico de Leiria - Portugal

email:{catarina,bribeiro}@dei.uc.pt

Abstract— Given a data set and a learning task such as classification, there are two prime motives for executing some kind of data set reduction. On one hand there is the possible algorithm performance improvement. On the other hand the decrease in the overall size of the data set can bring advantages in storage space used and time spent computing.

Our purpose is to determine the importance of several basic reduction techniques on Support Vector Machines, by comparing their relative performance improvement when applied on the standard REUTERS-21578 benchmark.

I. INTRODUCTION

Text classification is an important issue of any large scale information retrieval or text mining systems. With scopes such as the internet, it is often infeasible to use human categorization in most tasks. Nevertheless, there are still trained specialists that assign new items to categories in large taxonomies. As an example, conference papers, like this one, are still accompanied by a set of keywords, authors are asked to provide from a set of available categories. The applicability and generalization of this procedure to commercial collections is not practicable, since it is costly and time-consuming. Thus, interest is rising in tools that (semi) automate the task of text categorization, i.e., assign natural language texts to one or more pre-defined categories, based on their content [1].

This task is specially difficult because the number of features in each training example can be very large, since most systems use some version of the vector space model in order to parametrize a corpus of documents and allow for quantifiable calculations of similarity between documents [2].

This problem can be dealt with a set of pre-processing steps, whose importance can be determinant, which are the main focus of this paper. There is a great variety of pre-processing steps and they are definitely not independent. Therefore, one has to study their possible uses to assert of their individual influence in text categorization. The computational power, as well as the time effort employed have to be evaluated to determine their relative importance not only in space feature reduction, but also in categorization performance improvement. In this study, three major pre-processing steps were evaluated, namely the removal of words with low document frequency, the filtering of words in a stop word list and the use of stemming.

There has been an increasing interest in studying Support Vector Machines (SVMs), essentially due to the guarantee that an upper bound on generalization error can be effectively achieved. SVMs, proposed by Vapnik [3], have been applied to a wide range of classification, regression, time series prediction and density estimation problems [1], [4].

Section II will examine the text categorisation problem, setting guidelines for problem formulation. Section III will briefly enunciate the solid mathematical foundations of SVMs, stressing their application to classification tasks.

Section IV will address the application of SVMs to automatic text categorization with some state of the art examples.

Experimental results on Reuters-21578 corpus will be reported in Section V. Finally, in Section VI some concluding remarks are made and planned lines of research delineated.

II. TEXT CATEGORIZATION

Text categorization is a multi-label, multi-class problem and can be defined as the assignment of none, one or several categories to each text (document) in a data set.

The task can be split in several stages:
1) document representation;
2) space reduction/feature selection;
3) learning procedure;
4) categorization.

There has been given great relevance to the leaning procedure, since it constitutes the most important parcel of the four ones enumerated. However, the two first steps carry great relevance to the success of the learning procedure and consequently to categorization performance. These steps will be referred so on as text processing steps and will be analysed in the following subsection.

A. Text Processing

To accomplish automatic text categorization, one has first to convert the set of documents, typically strings of characters, to an acceptable representation that the learning machine can handle.

The most common, simple and successful document representation used so far is the vector space model, also known as the *Bag of Words*. Each document is indexed with the *bag* of the terms occurring in it, i.e., a vector with one component for each term occurring in the whole collection, having as value a representation of the number of times the term occurred in the document.

Each document is thus represented as a point in a vector space with one dimension for every term in the vocabulary. As the order of the words in each document is not stored with the *Bag*, word order information is lost. Joachims in [5] refers that this loss is not relevant since the it carries little information thus bringing unnecessary complexity, where categorization is concerned.

There are several possible representations for each word in a document. The simplest is simply a binary one: the word whether appears or does not appear in a document. This representation is usually replaced with the *term frequency* or tf, i.e., the number of times a term occurs in a document.

The method described here gives equal importance to all terms. It can be, however, more effective to weight terms according to their discriminative power within the document collection. This is usually done based on the idea that terms occurring in fewer documents are better selectors. The *document frequency* $df(t)$ of a term t is the number of documents in the collection in which the term occurs. The *inverse document frequency* or $idf(t)$ is (1):

$$idf(t) = \frac{|D|}{df(t)}, \qquad (1)$$

where $|D|$ is the number of documents in the collection. The idf of a term is lower the more documents it appears in [2] and therefore the less discriminative it becomes.

Vector components are weighted according to the idf of the corresponding term. Usually some monotonous function of the tf, such as the log or the square root, is used instead of the tf itself, to avoid giving more importance than appropriate to multiple occurrence of terms [6].

The most common, although not the simpler, weight used is the $tfidf$ representation (2):

$$tfidf = tf \times \log(idf) = tf \times \log\left(\frac{|D|}{df(t)}\right). \qquad (2)$$

Using the *Bag of Words* approach, and fairly all document representation schemes, a high dimensional space is reached, where the number of features is much larger than the number of documents available for training. This fact is inevitable, but can be mitigated by the use of some dimension reduction techniques, such as stop words and stemming.

In the simplest approach, a term is any space-separated word in a document[1]. However, there is a great number of non-informative words, such as articles, prepositions and conjunctions, called *stop words*. For this reason, a *stop-list* is usually built with words that should be filtered in the document representation process, since they have no distinguishing potential between categories. Words that are to be included in the *stop-list* are language and task dependent, existing however a set of general words that can be considered stop-words for almost all tasks, such as *and* and *or*.

Words that appear in very few examples (documents) are also filtered, because they will very unlikely represent a category.

[1]This a valid definition for English text, not for German or Finnish, for instance, where there are composite nouns.

Another commonly used method is *stemming*, where the word stem is derived from the occurrence of a word by removing case and inflection information. For example "computes", "computing" and "computer" are all mapped to the same stem "comput". Stemming does not alter significantly the information included in document representation, but it does avoid feature expansion.

B. Learning phase

The task of text categorization is a multi-class and multi-label problem, that is usually treated as several separate binary classification problems. There are two ways for categorize a corpus.

On one hand, using a category-pivoted approach, for each category a document either belongs or does not belong to it. On the other hand, each document belongs or not to each one of the available categories [6]. The approach to follow depends on the kind of application one is running. If the number of categories is fixed *a priori* and the objective is to categorize new documents then a category-pivoted categorization should be used. If you are in a category discovering phase, a document-pivoted categorization should be followed.

Having a suitable document representation, the goal is to find a mapping from the representation of documents into the class of possible labels. A classifier is a function that maps an input attribute vector $\mathbf{x} = (x_1, x_2, ... x_n)$ to the confidence that the input belongs to a class - that is $f(\mathbf{x}) = confidence(class)$. In the case of text categorization, attributes are words in the document and classes correspond to text categories.

The problem of inductive construction of a text classifier has been tackled in a variety of different ways, such as, Rule-Based Approach, k-Nearest Neighbor, Linear Models (like Rochio's method), Neural Networks and Probabilistic Models (like Bayesian classifiers). Kwok in [7] presents a synopsis of the representative machine-learning approaches for text categorization.

Although those approaches have been successfully applied in numerous problems they rely on dimension reduction as a pre-processing step which can rise up design classifier constraints while being computational expensive. Therefore, new methodologies for categorization of text (or hypertext) documents such as kernel based learning techniques, which circumvent those difficulties, have been recently developed and are one of the current focus in machine learning research.

III. SUPPORT VECTOR MACHINES

SVM are a learning method introduced by Vapnik [3] based on his statistical learning theory and Structural Minimization Principle. When using SVM for classification, the basic idea is to find the optimal separating hyperplane between the positive and negative examples. The optimal hyperplane is defined as the one giving the maximum margin between the training examples that are closest to the hyperplane. The group of examples (vectors) that lie closest to the separating hyperplane are referred to as support vectors. Once this hyperplane is found, new examples can be classified simply by checking which side of the hyperplane they fall on. Figure 1 shows a simple two-dimensional example, the optimal separating hyperplane and four support vectors.

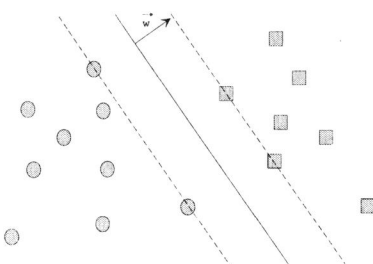

Fig. 1. Optimal Separating Hyperplane.

A. Foundations

The formulation of SVMs is constructed starting from a simple linear maximum margin classifier. A general two-class problem is posed as follows. Given an i.i.d. sample $(\mathbf{x}_1, y_1), ..., (\mathbf{x}_l, y_l)$, where $\mathbf{x}_i$ for $i = 1, ..., l$ is a feature vector of length l and $y_i = \{+1, -1\}$ is the class label for $\mathbf{x}_i$, find a classifier with the decision function $f(x)$, such that $y = f(x)$, where y is the class label for x.

The performance of the classifier is measured in terms of classification error, as defined in equation (3).

$$E(y, f(x)) = \begin{cases} 0 & if \quad y = f(x), \\ 1 & otherwise. \end{cases} \quad (3)$$

Usually, learning machines, SVMs included, have a set of adjustable parameters, λ. Given the above classification task, the machine will tune its parameters λ to learn the mapping $\mathbf{x} \to y$. This will result in a possible mapping $\mathbf{x} \to f(\mathbf{x}, \lambda)$, which defines the particular learning machine. The performance of this machine can be measured by the expectation of the test error, as shown in equation (4).

$$R(\lambda) = \int E(y, f(\mathbf{x}, \lambda)) \ dP(\mathbf{x}, y) \quad (4)$$

This is called the expected risk, or actual risk and requires that at least an estimate of $P(\mathbf{x}, y)$, which is not available for most classification tasks. Hence, one must settle for the empirical risk measure, defined in equation (5).

$$R_{emp} = \frac{1}{l} \sum_{i=1}^{l} E(y, f(\mathbf{x}, \lambda)). \quad (5)$$

This is just a measure of the mean error over the available training data. Most training algorithms for learning machines implement Empirical Risk Minimization (ERM), i.e., minimize the empirical error using maximum likelihood estimation for parameters λ. These conventional training algorithms do not consider the capacity of the learning machine and this can result in over fitting, i.e., using a learning machine with too much capacity for a particular problem.

In contrast with ERM, the goal of Structural Risk Minimization (SRM) [3] is to find the learning machine that yields a good trade-off between low empirical risk and small capacity. There are two major problems in achieving this goal: (i) SRM requires a measure of the capacity of a particular learning machine or, at least, an upper bound on this measure; (ii) an algorithm to select the desired learning machine according to SRM's goal is needed.

To address these two problems Vapnik and Chervonenkis [3] proposed the concepts of *Vapnik Chervonenkis (VC) confidence* and SVMs.

Putting no restrictions on f, it is possible to choose a function that classifies well training data, but does not generalize well on test or real data, i.e., therefore the real *Risk* (see 4) will not be minimized.

In *VC theory*, Vapnik and Chervonenkis prove that it is necessary to restrict the class of functions that f is chosen from to one with the *capacity* suitable for the amount of training data. VC theory provides bounds on the test error, circumventing the generalization problems presented earlier. Minimizing these bounds leads to the principle of *Structural Risk Minimization*. A function's capacity can take the form of VC *dimension*, defined as the largest number h of points that can be separated in all possible ways, using functions of the given class. If $h < l$ is the VC dimension of the class of functions that the learning machine can implement, then for all the functions of that class, with a probability of at least $1 - \eta$, the bound (6):

$$R(\lambda) \leq R_{emp}(\lambda) + \phi\left(\frac{h}{l}, \frac{\log(\eta)}{l}\right) \quad (6)$$

holds, where the *confidence term* ϕ is defined as (7):

$$\phi\left(\frac{h}{l}, \frac{\log(\eta)}{l}\right) = \sqrt{\frac{h(\log\frac{2l}{h} + 1) - \log(\frac{\eta}{4})}{l}} \quad (7)$$

B. Support Vector Classification

Although text categorization is a multi-class, multi-label problem, it can be broken into a number of binary class problems without loss of generality. This means that instead of classifying each document into all available categories, for each pair $\{document, category\}$ we have a two class problem: the document either belongs or does not to the category.

Although there are several linear classifiers that can separate both classes, only one, the Optimal Separating Hyperplane, maximizes the margin, i.e., the distance to the nearest data point of each class, thus presenting better generalization potential.

The output of a linear SVM is $u = \mathbf{w} \times \mathbf{x} - b$, where $\mathbf{w}$ is the normal vector to the hyperplane and $\mathbf{x}$ is the input vector. Maximizing the margin can be seen as an optimization problem:

$$\begin{aligned} minimize & \quad \frac{1}{2}\|\mathbf{w}\|^2, \\ subjected \ to & \quad y_i(\mathbf{w}.\mathbf{x} + b) \geq 1, \forall i, \end{aligned} \quad (8)$$

where x_i is the training example and y_i is the correct output for the ith training example, as represented in figure 1.

Intuitively the classifier with the largest margin will give low expected risk, and hence better generalization.

To deal with the constrained optimization problem in (8) it is appropriate to introduce Lagrange multipliers $\alpha_i \geq 0$ and the Lagrangian (9):

$$L_p \equiv \frac{1}{2}||\mathbf{w}||^2 - \sum_{i=1}^{l} \alpha_i(y_i(\mathbf{w}.\mathbf{x}+b)-1). \quad (9)$$

The Lagrangian has to be minimized with respect to the primal variables $\mathbf{w}$ and b and maximized with respect to the dual variables α_i (i.e. a saddle point has to be found) [8].

SVM are universal learners. In their basic form, shown so far, SVMs learn linear threshold functions. However, using an appropriate kernel function, they can be used to learn polynomial classifiers, radial-basis function networks and three layer sigmoid neural networks.

A note-worthy property of SVMs is that their ability to learn is independent of the dimensionality of the feature space. Complexity is based on the margin with which they separate the data, instead of the number of features.

IV. Automatic Text Categorization with SVMs

Text categorization has properties that make it a suitable SVM application field [9]:

- High dimensional input space: as already referred, fairly all document representation schemes have very high dimensional representation spaces (more that 10000 features). SVMs use is adequate since complexity is not proportional to the number of features.
- Few irrelevant features: the aforementioned dimensionality reduction techniques remove only non-informative words. It is easy to show by experiments almost all remaining features carry significant relevance to classification.
- Sparse document vectors: each vector representing a document has a very significant percentage of null values, since most words (all the words that appear in all the documents in the set) do not appear in each document.

V. Experimental Setup

A. Data set

An empirical study for evaluation of the importance of the testing conditions (see Table I) on text categorization performance has been accomplished using the Reuters-21578 collection with the ModApte split. The collection is publicly available at: http://kdd.ics.uci.edu/databases/reuters21578/reuters21578.html. Reuters-21578 is a financial corpus with news articles averaging 200 words each. Example categories are trade, earn or crude. In this corpus there are about 12000 classified stories into 118 possible categories.

The ModApte split was used, using 75% of the articles (9603 items) for training and 25% (3299 items) for testing.

Table I presents the ten most frequent categories and the number of training and test examples, comprising 75% of the items.

Category	Train	Test
Earn	2715	1044
Acquisitions	1547	680
Money-fx	496	161
Grain	395	138
Crude	358	176
Trade	346	113
Interest	313	121
Ship	186	89
Wheat	194	66
Corn	164	52

TABLE I

Number of training and test documents for ten most frequent categories.

Reuters is a very heterogeneous corpus, since the number of stories assigned to each category is very variable. There are stories not assigned to any of the categories and stories assigned to more than 10 categories.

On the other hand the number of documents assigned to each category is also not constant. There are categories with only one assigned document and others with thousands of assigned documents.

The pre-processing of documents was carried out with the Lemur Toolkit for Language Modelling and Information Retrieval. The toolkit is being developed as part of the Lemur Project, a collaboration between the Computer Science Department at the University of Massachusetts and the School of Computer Science at Carnegie Mellon University. This software is available at http://www-2.cs.cmu.edu/ lemur/.

B. Performance Criteria

For evaluating the simulation results besides accuracy, two other performance *criteria* were used: Recall and Precision. Take note that all these measures are computed in the test set for each category.

Recall is the percentage of total documents for the given topic that are correctly classified (10).

$$recall = \frac{categories\ found\ and\ correct}{total\ categories\ correct} \quad (10)$$

Precision is the percentage of predicted documents for the given topic that are correctly classified (11).

$$precision = \frac{categories\ found\ and\ correct}{total\ categories\ found} \quad (11)$$

An alternative representation is the use of true positives (f_{++}), false positives (f_{+-}) and false negatives (f_{-+}) as depicted in equations (12) and (13).

$$recall = \frac{f_{++}}{f_{++} + f_{-+}}, \quad (12)$$

$$precision = \frac{f_{++}}{f_{++} + f_{+-}}. \quad (13)$$

F1 measures were also considered. To compute F1 measure we have used (14).

$$F1 = \frac{2*precision*recall}{precision+recall}. \quad (14)$$

As the text categorization multi-class problem has been subdivided in several two-class problems, averaging has to be used to find total precision, recall and F1 values. There are two types of averaging: *micro-averaging* and *macro-averaging*. In *micro-averaging*, performance tables for each of the categories are added, and recall and precision are computed. In *macro-averaging*, performance measures are computed separately for each category and the mean of the resulting performance is taken. The results presented in this paper use macro-averaging.

C. Experimental conditions

To fulfil the objectives delineated, a set of eight test conditions was defined and is represented in Table II.

Test	Low freq. word removal	Stop word removal	Stemming
A	no	no	no
B	no	no	yes
C	no	yes	no
D	no	yes	yes
E	yes	no	no
F	yes	no	yes
G	yes	yes	no
H	yes	yes	yes

TABLE II
EIGHT TEST CONDITIONS DEFINED.

Table II presents three possible differences between the test conditions:
- Low frequency word removal: whether or not words that appeared in less than three documents were removed;
- Stop word removal: the removal or not of words in a stop word list;
- Stemming: whether Porter stemming was applied or not.

The documents were represented by the frequency of the terms that occurred in each one (term frequency - tf) and this representation was scaled to avoid result disturbance, but no further manipulations were carried out.

D. Results

Table III illustrates the accuracy, precision, recall and F1 results achieved for the eight test conditions defined in table II.

Test	Accuracy	Precision	Recall	F1
A	96.98 %	83.96%	55.66%	65.59%
B	97.01%	84.23%	55.92%	66.14%
C	96.54%	84.06%	62.81%	71.26%
D	97.30%	83.95%	62.54%	71.09%
E	97.00%	84.93%	58.05%	67.74%
F	97.05%	85.05%	56.05%	66.27%
G	97.32%	85.05%	63.06%	71.75%
H	97.31%	85.91%	62.54%	71.77%

TABLE III
ACCURACY, PRECISION, RECALL AND F1 VALUES FOR REUTERS CORPUS.

Comparing the results achieved it is clear that, where accuracy and precision are concerned, the results present only slight differences. This leads to the assertion that the conditions tested do not influence greatly these values.

However, in text categorization tasks recall values are usually more sensible due to the distribution of positive and negative examples. Usually the number of examples is large, but the number of positive examples is small (less than 5% in Reuters case). Hence, if a learning machine classifies all documents as not belonging to a category, it will still have a large accuracy, making the false negatives a problem to struggle against.

Thus, there is margin for improvement in the recall value, which is normally associated with the number of false negatives, as can be verified in equation (12).

Test	False Positives	False Negatives
A	22.90	62.90
B	22.40	62.50
C	23.30	55.00
D	22.20	54.60
E	22.60	62.60
F	21.80	62.20
G	23.00	53.30
H	22.00	54.50

TABLE IV
FALSE POSITIVE AND FALSE NEGATIVE VALUES FOR REUTERS CORPUS.

Table IV shows the average number of false negatives and false positives for each test. Examining these values, as expected, the false positive values do not present great divergence, while false negative exhibit substantial differences. The worst (largest) false negatives test values are those where stop word removal was not carried out, specially tests A, B, but also tests E and F, suggesting that preserving those words can be harmful to recall values.

Comparing G and H, which, respectively, correspond to tests without and with stemming, one can also conclude that stemming is not of major importance for recall values, but it can play an important role in precision matters.

While stop word removal alters significantly the contents of input data, stemming only alters its shape, i.e., the loss of information is not significative. We can therefore say that stemming is more relevant in terms of efficiency of the learning machine (the data is better organized, less redundant). The results achieved confirmed that Stop word removal removes information that could mislead the learning machine.

VI. CONCLUSIONS

SVMs present good results in automatic text categorization, since their objective is to maximize the margin between positive and negative examples for each class.

Several items that influence the categorization task were examined, to assert their importance in categorization performance. The items considered were mainly pre processing items.

It was concluded that the most significant of them was the stop word removal, whose influence was determinant and worthy of more research.

It remains to be studied how the word representation and the SVM parameters can positively influence the recall results, since there are still a significant number of false negatives.

Other work is also planed with new corpora, for result validation.

Acknowledgments

CISUC - Center of Informatics and Systems of University of Coimbra and Project POSI/SRI/41234/2001 are gratefully acknowledged for partial financing support.

References

[1] S. Dumais, J. Platt, D. Heckerman, "Inductive Learning Algorithms and Representations for Text Categorization", in Proceedings of the ACM-CIKM98, pp. 148-155, 1998.

[2] R. Cooley, "Classification of News Stories Using Support Vector Machines", in *Proceedings of the Sixteenth International Joint Conference on Artificial Intelligence Text Mining Workshop*, 1999.

[3] V. Vapnik, "The Nature of Statistical Learning Theory", 2nd edition, Springer, 1995.

[4] H. Drucker, C. Burges, L. Kaufman, A. Smola, V. Vapnik, "Support Vector Regression Machines", in *Neural Information Processing Systems*, Cambridge, MIT Press, 1997, Vol. 9.

[5] T. Joachims, "Learning to Classify Text Using Support Vector Machines - Methods, Theory and Algorithms", in The Kluwer International Series in Engineering and Computer Science, Kluwer Academic Publishers, 2001.

[6] F. Sebastiani, "A Tutorial on Automated Text Categorization", in Analia Amandi and Alejandro Zunino (eds.), Proceedings of ASAI-99, 1st Argentinian Symposium on Artificial Intelligence, Buenos Aires, AR, pp. 7-35, 1999.

[7] J. Kwok, "Automated Text Categorization Using Support Vector Machine", in Proceedings of the International Conference on Neural Information Processing (ICONIP'98), pp. 347-351, Kitakyushu, Japan, 1998.

[8] B. Schölkopf, C. Burges, A. Smola, "Advances in Kernel Methods - Introduction to Support Vector Learning", MIT Press, pp. 1-15, 1999.

[9] T. Joachims, "Text Categorization with Support Vector Machines: Learning with Many Relevant Features", in Proceedings of the European Conference on Machine Learning (ECML), Springer, pp. 137-142, Berlin, 1998.

[10] S. Gunn, "Support Vector Machines for Classification and Regression", Technical Report, Faculty of Engineering and Applied Science, Department of Electronics and Computer Science, 1998.

Training and Holistic Computation of Vector Graphics with Hebbian Bases in Contrast to RAAM Networks

Mark Schaefer and Werner Dilger
Chemnitz University of Technology
Chemnitz, Germany
Email: mark@markschaefer.de, dilger@informatik.tu-chemnitz.de

Abstract— Hebbian Learning is well-known for training of associative networks whereas RAAM learning uses auto-associative networks which are trained to represent structured information like parse trees of natural sentences or logical terms.
In this paper Hebbian learning is used for representing structured information in terms of vector graphic. The resulting networks are holistically computed. Furthermore a theorem relating bipolar Hebbian learning is proved.

I. INTRODUCTION

Recursive auto-associative memory (RAAM) networks were introduced by J.B. Pollack [5] for the purpose of learning representations of structured objects that do not increase with the size of the structures represented. RAAM networks were typically applied to syntactical structures like parse trees of natural language sentences [6] or logical expressions (cf. [4]). Hebbian learning was described 1949 by Donald Hebb as a learning rule for the weights in connectionist networks [3]. It can be used for one-step training of associative networks.

In this paper we will show that Hebbian learning is as suitable for representing structured information as RAAM networks are and that the learned information can be holistically modified.

In section II RAAM networks and their holistic modification are described, followed by a section which deals with the communities and differences of RAAM and Hebbian learning. In section III Hebbian bases are defined and a relating theorem is given and proved. The next section handles the holistic modification of matrices resulting from Hebbian learning and the results of concrete examples.

II. RAAM NETWORKS AND HOLISTIC MODIFICATION

A. Structure

Recursive auto-associative memory networks (RAAM) were developed by Pollack [5]. Figure 1 shows their basic structure. A RAAM is a three-layer feed-forward network. The input and output layer consist of k slots, the middle layer of only one. Each slot has n positions (or bits) and is independent from the other ones in the same layer. For short this is denoted as n-k-RAAM network or just n-k-RAAM.

The input neurons together with the hidden neurons are called encoder and the hidden neurons and the output neurons are called decoder. A RAAM is trained as an auto-associator, i.e. the network should reproduce each input vector at the output layer. When a training example has been learned successfully one can use the activation of the hidden neurons

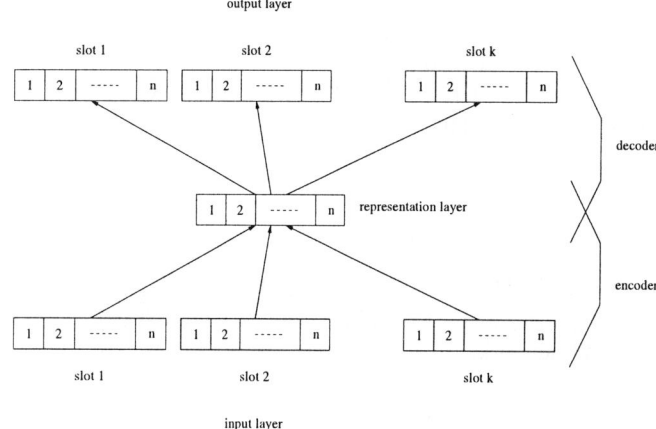

Fig. 1. RAAM basic structure

as a representation of the input/output vector. The input vector is encoded by the first layer of weights and the representation is decoded by the second one.

B. Structured Representation

After one knows a representation of an input vector it can be used as a part of another input vector, which is encoded into its own representation and so on. This is the essential feature of RAAMs. It can be used for subsymbolic representation of trees and their holistic computation, i.e. the computation of the whole RAAM network at once in order to gain another RAAM network which represents different information. It is important to bear in mind that the representation of every node changes during each training cycle which effects dependent nodes.

Once a RAAM has learned a tree, only the decoder part is needed to unfold it completely. Starting with the representation of the topmost node - which is now used as an input for the decoder network - all nodes are reconstructed.

C. Holistic Computation

If a RAAM network was trained to represent a tree, it can be computed holistically. There are three types of holistic computation: transformation, classification and matching. They have in common that

> ... holistic inference maps directly from the representation of a problem to the representation of an answer, in a gestalt fashion without accessing the constituent elements or relations within the data. [2]

For example holistic transformation was done by Chalmers who trained RAAM networks to represent 40 English sentences and their corresponding passive form [1]. The half of the active-passive pairs (in form of the representation of the topmost node) were used as training patterns for a so called transformation network. After training it was able to generate the passive form of 65% of the remaining sentences.

III. HEBBIAN LEARNING IN CONTRAST TO RAAM LEARNING

If a given tree is learned by a RAAM network the encoder part is not needed any longer. The remaining decoder part is an n-kn associative network. Such a network representing structured information can be build from scratch by using Hebbian learning.

A. Principles of Hebbian Learning

Donald Hebb [3] specified the following learning rule for the weight w_{xy} of a connection between two neurons x, y in a neural network.

$$\Delta w_{xy} = \eta \cdot x \cdot y \quad (1)$$

For an associative network and a training pattern (x_i, y_i)

$$x_i = (x_i^1, x_i^2, \ldots, x_i^n) \quad (2)$$
$$y_i = (y_i^1, y_i^2, \ldots, y_i^m) \quad (3)$$

we gain the following so called correlation matrix which is the outer product of the input and output vector:

$$W_i := x_i^T y_i \quad (4)$$

All correlation matrices are summed up to the final weight matrix of the associative network:

$$W = W_1 + W_2 + \ldots + W_k \quad (5)$$

The associated output vector y_i is retrieved by multiplying x_i with W:

$$x_i W = x_i W_i + x_i \sum_{\substack{j=1\ldots k \\ j \neq i}} W_j \quad (6)$$
$$= x_i(x_i^T y_i) + \sum_{\substack{j=1\ldots k \\ j \neq i}} x_i(x_j^T y_j) \quad (7)$$
$$= (x_i)^2 y_i + \sum_{\substack{j=1\ldots k \\ j \neq i}} (x_i x_j^T) y_j \quad (8)$$

We gain y_i multiplied with a positive constant plus a term called crosstalk. Obviously the crosstalk equals zero if $x_1, x_2, \ldots, x_k$ are piecewise orthogonal.

B. Learning of Structured Information with Hebbian Bases

Any information given by a tree can be trained using Hebbian learning similar to the process of RAAM learning described in section II. For training a tree a set of orthogonal vectors $X = \{x_1, x_2, \ldots, x_k\}$ is needed. Each node of the tree is represented by a unique vector $x_i \in X$ and for each of them a training pattern is build, consisting of the x_i as input and the representations of the children $c_{i1}, c_{i2}, \ldots, c_{ik}$ as output. The correlation matrix is built by multiplying x_i with the concatenated representations of the child nodes.

$$W_i = x_i^T \cdot (c_{i1} \mid c_{i2} \mid \ldots \mid c_{ik}) \quad (9)$$

This procedure is done for every node in the tree and the correlation matrices are added. Of course the representation of a node $x \in X$ can be used on the right side of (9) in order to represent a tree. This method of splitting a tree into training patterns is analogue to the one described for RAAM networks. In contrast to RAAM training the representations of the nodes are given from the beginning and only one training step must be performed. Furthermore no particular order for their training is prescribed.

Since the right signs of the associated vectors but not the vectors itself are returned, a binary bipolar encoding of the patterns is useful. Therefore a set of bipolar orthogonal vectors is needed, which is the subject of the next section.

C. Hebbian Bases

This subsection deals with orthogonal bipolar vectors. An algorithm for generating sets of orthogonal bipolar vectors called Hebbian bases is specified and the following theorem is proved: Hebbian bases only exist in dimensions $n = 2^k$. To do so we start with some basic definitions and lemmas.

1) Fundamentals:

Definition 3.1: Set $\mathbf{H} := \{-1, +1\}$. A vector $b \in \mathbf{H}^n$ is called bipolar. The j-th position of b is denoted as b^j. A set $B_n = \{b_1, b_2, \ldots, b_n\}$ of bipolar vectors $b_i \in \mathbf{H}^n$ is called Hebbian base if $\langle b_i, b_j \rangle = 0 \ \forall \ 1 \leq i < j \leq n$.

Definition 3.2: The hamming difference of two bipolar vectors $b_1, b_2 \in \mathbf{H}^n$ is defined as:

$$hdf(b_1, b_2) := \#\{i \mid b_1^i \neq b_2^i\} \quad (10)$$

Lemma 3.3: Two bipolar vectors $b_1, b_2 \in \mathbf{H}^n$ are orthogonal if and only if $hdf(b_1, b_2) = n/2$.

Proof:

$$b_1, b_2 \text{ are orthogonal} \quad (11)$$
$$\Leftrightarrow \langle b_1, b_2 \rangle = 0 \quad (12)$$
$$\Leftrightarrow 0 = \sum_{\substack{i=1,\ldots,n \\ b_1^i = b_2^i}} b_1^i b_2^i + \sum_{\substack{i=1,\ldots,n \\ b_1^i \neq b_2^i}} b_1^i b_2^i = \sum_{\substack{i=1,\ldots,n \\ b_1^i = b_2^i}} 1 - \sum_{\substack{i=1,\ldots,n \\ b_1^i \neq b_2^i}} \quad (13)$$
$$\Leftrightarrow \sum_{\substack{i=1,\ldots,n \\ b_1^i = b_2^i}} 1 = \sum_{\substack{i=1,\ldots,n \\ b_1^i \neq b_2^i}} 1 \quad (14)$$
$$\Leftrightarrow \#\{i \mid b_1^i = b_2^i\} = \#\{i \mid b_1^i \neq b_2^i\} \quad (15)$$
$$\Leftrightarrow hdf(b_1, b_2) = n/2 \quad \square \quad (16)$$

Definition 3.4: Let B_n be a Hebbian base and $b_1, b \in B_n$. The $\mathbf{b_1}$-notation of b resp. B_n is defined as:

$$b_1(b) := \begin{pmatrix} b_1^1 \cdot b^1 \\ b_1^2 \cdot b^2 \\ \vdots \\ b_1^n \cdot b^n \end{pmatrix} \quad (17)$$

$$b_1(B_n) := \{b_1(b) | b \in B_n\} \quad (18)$$

Lemma 3.5: Let $b \in \mathbf{H}^n$. B_n is a Hebbian base if and only if $b(B_n)$ is one also.

Proof:

$$B \text{ is a Hebbian base} \quad (19)$$
$$\Leftrightarrow \forall b_u, b_v \in B, u \neq v | \langle b_u, b_v \rangle = 0 \quad (20)$$
$$\Leftrightarrow \langle b(b_u), b(b_v) \rangle = \sum_{i=1}^n b^i b_u^i \cdot b^i b_v^i = \sum_{i=1}^n (b^i)^2 \cdot b_u^i b_v^i$$
$$= \sum_{i=1}^n b_u^i b_v^i = \langle b_u, b_v \rangle = 0 \quad (21)$$
$$\Leftrightarrow b(B) \text{ is a Hebbian base} \quad (22)$$

Definition 3.6: If σ is a permutation of $\{1, \ldots, n\}$, $\sigma(b), b \in \mathbf{H}^n$ is defined as:

$$\sigma(b) := \begin{pmatrix} b^{\sigma(1)} \\ b^{\sigma(2)} \\ \vdots \\ b^{\sigma(n)} \end{pmatrix} \quad (23)$$

and $\sigma(B_n)$ for a Hebbian base B_n:

$$\sigma(B_n) := \{\sigma(b) | b \in B_n\} \quad (24)$$

Lemma 3.7: Let σ be a permutation as in definition 3.6. B is a Hebbian base if and only if $\sigma(B)$ is one also.
Proof: Since all vectors are permuted equally the inner product is not affected. □

Definition 3.8: A structure of a bipolar vector b is a set $S = \{a, a+1, a+2, \ldots, e\} \subseteq \{1, 2, \ldots, n\}$ with $b^i = b^j \; \forall \, a \leq i < j \leq e$. A maximal structure of b is a structure $S = \{a, a+1, a+2, \ldots, e\}$ with $b^a \neq b^{a-1}$ if $a > 1$ and $b^b \neq b^{e+1}$ if $e < n$. $S(b)$ is the set of all maximal structures of b. The *structure size* of b is defined as:

$$s(b) := \min\{ord(s) | s \in S(b)\} \quad (25)$$

2) Dimension Restrictions of Hebbian Bases: At this point we are able to proof the following theorem:

Theorem 3.9: A Hebbian base B_n exists only for $n = 2^k, k = 0, 1, 2, \ldots$

Proof: At first we will prove that for $n = 2^k, k = 0, 1, 2, \ldots$ a Hebbian base exists. For this purpose an algorithm is defined which generates a Hebbian base for any $n = 2^k$.

In the second step a proof for the other direction is given which uses this algorithm in a special way.

1. The algorithm in figure 2 takes any bipolar vector $b_1 \in \mathbf{H}^n, n = 2^k \; k = 0, 1, 2, \ldots$ as input and returns a Hebbian base B containing b_1. To clarify the functionality

```
1:  B := {b_1}
2:  size:=n
3:  While |B| < n Do
4:    For each b_i ∈ B Do
5:      b_{|B|+i} := b_i
6:      For s:=1 To n Step size Do
7:        For t:=s+size/2 To s+size-1 Do
8:          b^t_{|B|+i} := -b^t_{|B|+i}
9:    B := B ∪ {b_{|B|+1}, b_{|B|+2}, ..., b_{2*|B|}}
10:   size:=size/2
```

Fig. 2. Algorithm for the Creation of Hebbian Bases

of the algorithm and other components of this proof, a new notation is introduced. A bipolar vector is written as a vertical bar with white sections denoting 1 and black ones denoting -1. The advantage of this notation is the independence from the actual dimension of the vector. As an example take a look at figure 3. Note that that the vectors a and c resp. b and d are

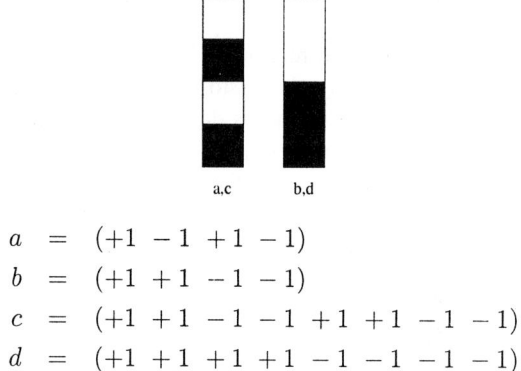

$a = (+1 \; -1 \; +1 \; -1)$
$b = (+1 \; +1 \; -1 \; -1)$
$c = (+1 \; +1 \; -1 \; -1 \; +1 \; +1 \; -1 \; -1)$
$d = (+1 \; +1 \; +1 \; +1 \; -1 \; -1 \; -1 \; -1)$

Fig. 3. Notation of Hebbian Vectors

denoted in the same way, but bear in mind that only vectors with the same dimension may be compared, e.g. a with b but not a with c. The progression of the algorithm is shown in figure 4. Note that not the vectors itself are drawn but their b_1-notation. The algorithm starts with setting $B = \{b_1\}$ (line 1). Of course b_1 is drawn entirely in white. In `size` the minimal structure size over all vectors which are currently elements of B is kept. As long as the size of the base $|B|$ does not reach n, the following steps take place.

Each vector of the base is copied to a new vector (lines 4 and 5). This new vector is modified in the following way: It is divided in parts with a length of `size/2`, every second one - starting with the first - leaved unchanged. The other ones are changed to the opposite sign (lines 6 to 8). After each vector from B has been copied and modified, the new vectors are added to the base (line 9). This results in the regular structure of the b_1-notation of B shown in figure 4.

After this short overview we will now examine the algorithm detailed. Before the first iteration of the while-loop $|B| = 1$ holds. Since for every vector in B a new one is added, in each iteration the size of B is doubled. After k iterations $|B| =$

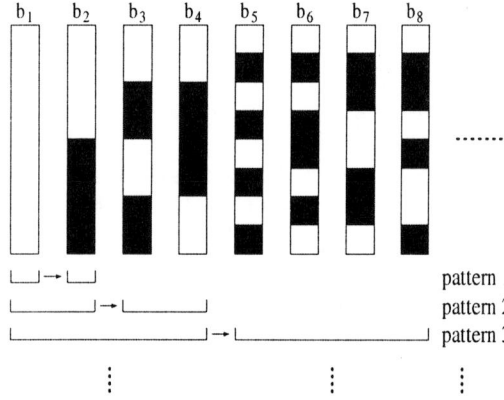

Fig. 4. Progression of Algorithm for Hebbian Bases

$2^k = n$ holds and the algorithm stops.

As $|B|$ doubles, size is divided by 2 at the end of each iteration. Since we assumed $n = 2^k$, at the end of the algorithm size=1 holds but in line 7 always size=0 mod 2 is valid.

So the algorithm is correct in the sense that he terminates and each step can always be performed. It remains to show that B is a Hebbian base what is done by induction.

For the following considerations only the b_1-notations as shown in figure 4 are used but for better reading not noted. According to lemma 3.5 they are equivalent to the original vectors, i.e. if the b_1-notation of B is a Hebbian base, B itself is one also.

Lets consider the state of the algorithm before the execution of line 9 and let $B' := \{b_{|B|+1}, b_{|B|+2}, \ldots, b_{2*|B|}\}$ the vectors to add. As a premise $\langle b_i, b_j \rangle = 0 \ \forall \ b_i, b_j \in B \ \forall \ b_i \neq b_j$ holds. Since this is valid for $B = \{b_1\}$ we have a starting point for the induction.

Let $b \in B, b' \in B'$. The intervals $(s, s+1, \ldots, s+size-1)$ chosen in line 6 to 8 correspond to structures of vectors in B. Since this intervals were generated by splitting larger intervals from other vectors of B, they do not overstep structure limits for b, i.e. $(b^s \ b^{s+1} \ \ldots \ b^{s+size-1}) = (1 \ 1 \ \ldots \ 1)$ or $(-1 \ -1 \ \ldots \ -1)$. Therefore each new generated pair of structures in b' (lines 8 to 9) corresponds to a structure of b leading to a hamming difference of $hdf(b, b') = n/2 \Rightarrow \langle b, b' \rangle = 0$.

Furthermore B is used as a pattern for generating B', i.e. a structure from a vector of b generates two new structures which can be imagined as a combination of two structures. There are two possible combinations: A $(+1 \ +1 \ \ldots \ +1)^T$ structure leads to a $((+1 \ +1 \ \ldots \ +1)(-1 \ -1 \ \ldots \ -1))^T$ combination and a $(-1 \ -1 \ \ldots \ -1)^T$ structure leads to a $((-1 \ -1 \ \ldots \ -1)(+1 \ +1 \ \ldots \ +1))^T$ combination. Concerning the inner product within B' the resulting combinations are equivalent to the former structures. From this point of view B' has the same configuration as B. $\Rightarrow b'_1, b'_2 \in B' \Rightarrow \langle b'_1, b'_2 \rangle = 0$. Altogether $B \cup B'$ meets the condition of the premise.

It might help to visualize the new generated pairs of structures with new colours, called white-black and black-white. A white section of B is transformed into a white-black section and a black one to black-white. Since two vectors are orthogonal if their hamming difference is $\frac{n}{2}$ or - by the means of their colours - if they have the same colour at the half of their elements, this transformation is leading to no change concerning the inner product.

As after k iterations of the while loop $|B| = n = 2^k$ holds and together with the previous conclusion it follows that B is a Hebbian base.

2. Let now an $n \neq 2^k, k = 0, 1, 2, \ldots$ be given. It will be shown that no Hebbian Base B_n exists.

We start with any vector $b_1 \in \mathbf{H}^n$ which is replaced by its b_1-notation as it is done for every following vector. We gain $b_1(b_1) = (1 \ 1 \ \ldots \ 1)^T$. For every vector b_2, which is orthogonal to b_1 we can specify the set $\Sigma_0 = \{\sigma_1, \sigma_2, \ldots, \sigma_p\}$ of all permutations which transforms b_2 into $\sigma_i(b_2) = (\underbrace{+1 \ +1 \ \ldots \ +1}_{n/2 \ times} \ \underbrace{-1 \ -1 \ \ldots \ -1}_{n/2 \ times})$ as shown in fig. 5. The applied permutation should not only affect given vectors but also ones which are added later, but for readability the permutation is not printed. At this point it is needed to decrease the structure size of a new vector b_3, because if not, $(\underbrace{-1 \ -1 \ \ldots \ -1}_{n/2 \ times} \ \underbrace{+1 \ +1 \ \ldots \ +1}_{n/2 \ times})$ would be the only possible value what is not orthogonal to b_2.

The inner product of b_2 and b_3 and of b_1 and b_3 has to result in 0:

$$0 = \langle b_2, b_3 \rangle = \sum_{i=0}^{n/2} b_3^i - \sum_{i=n/2+1}^{n} b_3^i \quad (26)$$

$$0 = \langle b_1, b_3 \rangle = \sum_{i=0}^{n/2} b_3^i + \sum_{i=n/2+1}^{n} b_3^i \quad (27)$$

Adding (26) and (27) leads to:

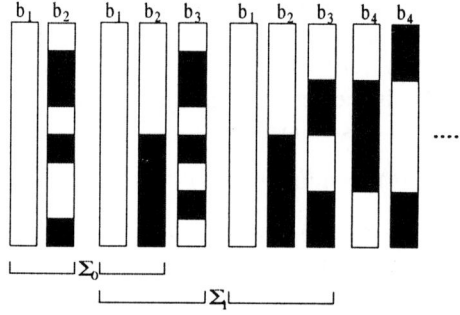

Fig. 5. Possibilities for Adding New Vectors to a Hebbian Base

$$0 = \sum_{i=0}^{n/2} b_3^i \quad (28)$$

$$0 = \sum_{i=n/2+1}^{n} b_3^i \quad (29)$$

This means that the first (second) half of b_3 is orthogonal to the first (second) half of b_2. Hence, it exists a set of permutations $\Sigma_1 \subset \Sigma_0$ which transforms b_3 to $(\underbrace{+1 \ldots +1}_{n/4\ times} \underbrace{-1 \ldots -1}_{n/4\ times} \underbrace{+1 \ldots +1}_{n/4\ times} \underbrace{-1 \ldots -1}_{n/4\ times})$ and leaving b_1 and b_2 unchanged, because the permutations take place on a lower structure size.

At this point we can exclude $n = 3$, because we had to divide b_3 in 4 parts in order to add a third vector. For the vector b_4 there are two possibilities as one can see from fig. 5. With the same reason as it was used for dividing b_3 in 4 parts, b_5 has to divided in 8 parts, excluding $n = 5, 6, 7$ and so on.

As it was shown it is always possible to perform such permutations that the resulting vectors look like as if they were generated by the algorithm. In its non deterministic version the algorithm could generate all possible vectors (figure 6). It remains to show that the structure size has to decreased

```
4b:      col:=true OR col:=false
         lines 6-8 replaced by
 6:      For s:=1 To n Step size Do
 7:         If col Then
 8:            For t:=s+size/2 To s+size-1 Do
 9:               b^t_{|B|+i} := -b^t_{|B|+i}
10:         Else
11:            For t:=s To s+size/2-1 Do
12:               b^t_{|B|+i} := -b^t_{|B|+i}
```

Fig. 6. Non-Deterministic Version of the Algorithm for the Creation of Hebbian Bases

for every $(2^k + 1)$-th vector. We have seen that new vectors are generated as the non-deterministic algorithm would do it. Therefore the vectors $B = \{b_1, \ldots, b_{2^k}\}$ are a pattern for the vectors $B' = \{b_{2^k+1}, \ldots, b_{2^{k+1}}\}$ and if B is maximal regarding the minimal structure size, B' is it also if the maximal structures are combined to pairs as it was shown before. Since we starting with $B = \{b_1 = (1\ 1\ \ldots\ 1)\}$ which is apparently maximal regarding the minimal structure size, every B' is it. In order to get n vectors the structure size has to been halved $\lceil log_2 n \rceil$ times leading to a necessary dimension greater than n for $n \neq 2^k, k = ,1,2\ldots$. □

Actually, a more general theorem was proved, namely:

Theorem 3.10: For any given $n \geq 1$, a maximum of 2^k bipolar vectors $b_i \in \mathbf{H}^n$ is piecewise orthogonal, with $k = max\{k|\ 2^k|n\}$.

The same proof can be used, with the difference that after the k-th decreasing of the structure size it is stopped leading to 2^k orthogonal vectors.

D. Vector Graphics

Since in the past only experiments with formal or natural language representations were performed, we decided to work with vector graphics. Until now we used ones with points defined by their coordinates, lines defined by their end points and circles defined by center and a point of the border.

For an example how the point (2,4) is denoted as a tree take a look at figure 7. A coordinate is a node with two sons, the left one denotes the type of the father (a bullet for a coordinate) and the right one the concrete value. A point is a node with two sons also, the left one denotes again the type of the father (a cross for a point), the right one is the father of the two coordinate subtrees. This is done analogue for the higher-level

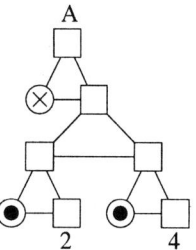

Fig. 7. Tree Format for Vector Graphics Training with Hebbian Bases

structures line and circle. Vector graphics in this form can be trained with Hebbian learning using Hebbian bases (as it was described before) resulting in $n-2n$ associative networks resp. matrices.

IV. RESULTS

Since the representation of any tree can always be given by a matrix of appropiate dimensions there is no need for experiments and we will describe only the ones with holistic computations. For more results see [7].

A. Transformation

Until now we worked with single points. In figure 8 one can see a grid of 25 points drawn in black and the corresponding image points shifted by $(2,1)$ and drawn in grey. All 50

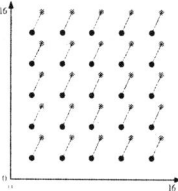

Fig. 8. Training patterns

points were represented by a matrix which was trained by Hebbian learning and then combined piecewise to training patterns. We used a 4 bit bipolar representation leading to 4×8 matrices. The transformation network was a 32-12-32 feed-forward network which was trained with backpropagation using no activation function. With a training rate of 0.0001 and a weight decay of 0.0001 the transformation network learned all 25 patterns with a squared error over all patterns of less than 0.01 in typical 80-100 cycles. Furthermore it was able to perform the shifting operation for unknown examples with a typical squared error of 3.0 to 5.0. In spite of the relative large error the vector graphic tree could be reconstructed. For a 32-8-32 transformation network about 150 cycles were needed.

B. Matching

For the matching experiments we used the two series of vector graphics shown in figure 9. Each of them was trained by a 16×32 matrix. These matrices were normalized and matched by their inner product. The results are printed in table I and II. Apparently the result is nearly independent of the orientation of the graphic. This could be used for image recognition.

	2	3	4	5	6
1	0.967	0.967	0.950	0.958	0.967
2		0.975	0.967	0.958	0.967
3			0.983	0.958	0.967
4				0.958	0.967
5					0.992

TABLE I
HEBBIAN BASES MATCHING - SERIES 1 RESULTS

	2	3	4	5	6
1	0.979	0.979	0.722	0.698	0.698
2		0.979	0.698	0.7222	0.698
3			0.698	0.698	0.722
4				0.972	0.972
5					0.972

TABLE II
HEBBIAN BASES MATCHING - SERIES 2 RESULTS

V. CONCLUSION

We have shown that structured information can be trained with Hebbian learning like it is done with RAAM networks. Furthermore the training process is much faster and - more important - always possible. The holistic transformation was possible for simple examples and it seems that holistic matching is orientation independent what is definitely worth further research.

REFERENCES

[1] Chalmers, D.J. (1990): Syntactic transformations on distributed representations. Connection Science, 2:53-62.
[2] Chrisman, L. (1991): Learning recursive distributed representations for holistic computation. Connection Science, 2(1-2):53-62
[3] Hebb, D.O. (1949): The Organization of Behaviour: A Neuropsychological Theory, Wiley, New York.
[4] Neumann, Jane (2001): Holistic Processing of Hierarchical Structures in Connectionist Networks, PhD, University of Edinburgh
[5] Pollack, J. B., (1988): Recursive auto.associative memory: Devising compositional distributed representations, Proceeding of the 10th Annual Conference of the Cognitive Science Society, 33-39, Hillsdale, NJ. Erlbaum
[6] Rummelhart, D.E. and McClelland, J.L. (1986): On learning past tenses of English verbs. In Rummlehart. D.E. and McClelland, J.L. editors, Parallel Distributed Processing: Explorations in the Microstructure of Cognition, Volume 2: Psychological and Biological Models, pages 216-271, MIT Press, Cambridge, MA.
[7] Schaefer, M. (2003): Learning and Computation of Vector Graphics with Distributed Representations. Diploma Thesis, Chemnitz University of Technology

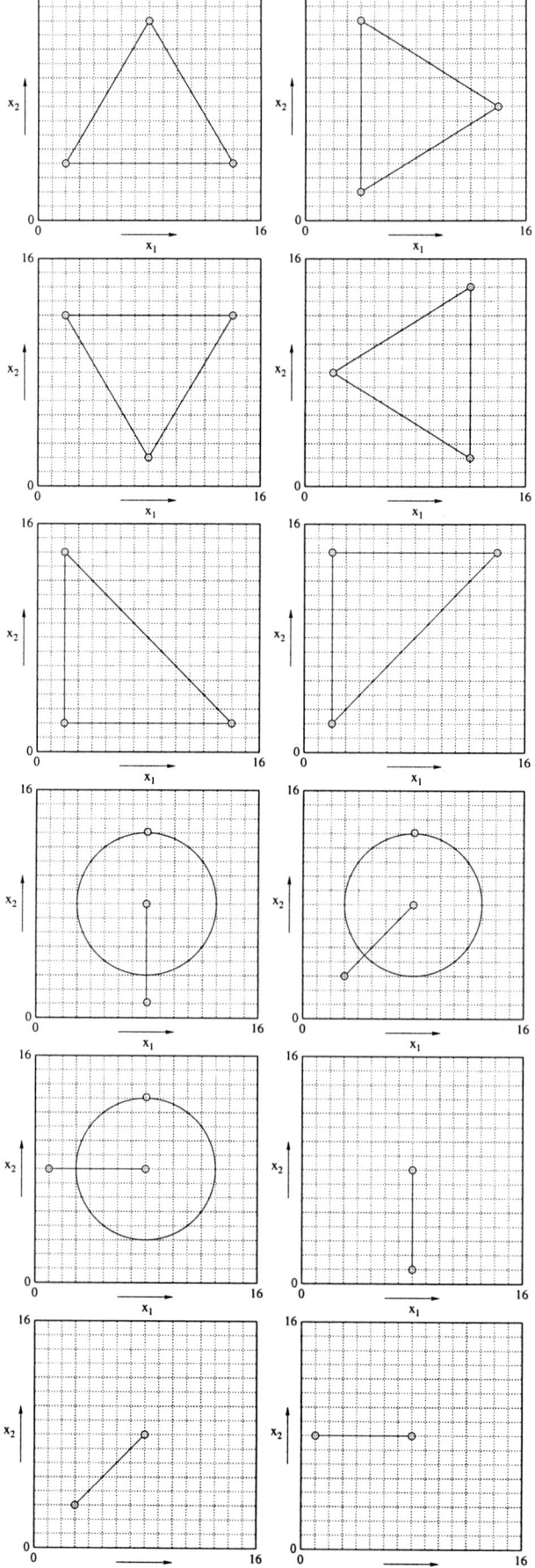

Fig. 9. Hebbian Bases Matching - Series 1 (triangles) and Series 2 (circles and lines)

Fault Detection System in Gas Lift Well based on Artificial Immune System

Mariana Araujo[1], Jose Aguilar[1], Hugo Aponte[2]

[1]CEMISID, Dpto. de Computación, Facultad de Ingeniería, Av. Tulio Febres. Universidad de los Andes, Mérida 5101, Venezuela
aguilar@ing.ula.ve
[2]Gerencia de Tecnología y Automatización Industrial
Petróleos de Venezuela. S.A., PDVSA
Chuao, Caracas, Venezuela

Abstract. **In this paper we propose an Artificial Immune System for fault detection in gas lift oil well. Our novel approach inspired by the Immune System allows the application of a pattern recognition model to perform fault detection. A significant feature of our approach is its ability to dynamically learning the fluid patterns of the 'self' and predicting new patterns of the 'non-self'**

I. INTRODUCTION

When the natural energy of an oil field is not enough to fluid lift, we need a secondary recovery procedure on the well (normally, this is called artificial lift) [1]. For this case, we can use different techniques such as artificial lift by gas (ALG) [1]. The idea of the ALG is to inject gas, and in this way to lighten the fluid. The design of this system must be made very carefully. One of the aspects to consider is the fault detection [1, 2]. On the other hand, the immune system is a collection of cells and organs able to perform tasks with characteristics such as pattern recognition, learning, noise tolerance, distributed detection, and memory, with the purpose of maintaining the physical integrity of an individual [6]. The problem that the immune system solves may be described as the distinction between self and non-self entities, being the self entities the internal cells and molecules produced by the body, while the non-self entities correspond to potentially harmful foreign entities such as viruses, parasites and bacteria. In recent years, some immunity based computational models have been successfully developed [2, 4, 6, 7, 8], showing an enormous potential for practical applications to other fields [4, 5]. In this paper we discuss an immuno-computational framework to define a fault detection system for a gas lift oil well.

II. THEORETICAL ASPECTS

A. Artificial Immune Systems

In the recent years, a novel approach has begun to emerge which is the use of concepts from immunology to solve problems [6]. The human immune system has a very distributed and adaptive, novel pattern recognition mechanism. In general, the purpose of the immune system is to protect the body against infection and includes a set of mechanisms collectively termed humoral immunity. The immune system uses learning, memory, matching, diversity, distributed control and associative retrieval to solve recognition and classification tasks. In particular, it learns to recognize relevant patterns, remember patterns that have been seen previously. The immune system also remembers successful responses to invasions and can re-use these responses if similar pathogens invade in the future. Diversity refers to the fact that, in order to achieve optimal antigen space coverage, antibody diversity must be encouraged. Cloning and hypermutation maintain the diversity of the antibody set. Distributed control means that there is no central controller, rather, the immune system is governed by local interactions between cells and antibodies. The antibodies are present through out the body without any central control and thus defend the body by this interaction in a distributed fashion. These remarkable information-processing abilities of the immune system provide several important inspirations to the field of computation [6]. There are many more features of the immune system, including adaptation, idiotypic network and protection against auto-immune attack.

In general, lymphocytes are subject to two types of selection process. Negative selection, which operates on lymphocytes maturing in the thymus (called T-cells), ensures that these lymphocytes do not respond to self-proteins. This is achieved by killing any T-cell that binds to a self protein while it is maturing. The second selection process, called clonal selection, operates on lymphocytes that have matured in the bone marrow (called B-cells). Any B-cell that binds to a pathogen is stimulated to copy itself. Thus, B-cells are selected for their success in detecting non-self. The combination of copying with mutation and selection amounts to an evolutionary algorithm that gives rise to B-cells that are increasingly specific to the invading pathogen.

B. Well Gas Lift

When we search oil (exploration), we need to use scientifique methods to determine the subsoil characteristic. In this way, we can know if there is a region with an accumulation of hydrocarbon. When the hydrocarbon has been detected, the exploitation of the oil field starts. It consists in bringing the oil to the surface using the natural energy of the oil field or other methods (for example gas artificial lift). Normally, at the beginning the natural energy of the oil field allow the oil lift, but when the oil field is old we need to use other techniques: gas artificial lift, mechanical pump, hydraulics pump, and so forth. The gas artificial lift technique is a technology based on the injection of gas to allow the fluid of the oil to go to the surface. The gas comes from compression plants, through a gas distribution system. The last part is composed by gas multiples (MLAG) and pressure high multiple (MAP). In general the gas goes to the oil well, and its injection is controlled by control equipment that is in the surface and subsoil. We need to inject the optimal quantity of gas to obtain the minimal pressure to allow the fluid lift. During the perforation, there is a cementation phase to glue a tube called 'casing'. Inside of it we include another tube called 'tubing'. This last tube is used to transport the oil from the oil field to the surface [1]. With the data from the pressure table of the "Casing" and "Tubing" we can determine the next information [1, 2]: 1. Surface Restriction: a high pressure of the "Tubing", 2. Freezing: a fault in the gas injection or small quantity of recovery fluid due to the freezing of the tubes, 3. Sandy or coat well: not continuos lift, 4. Frequent cycles of very fast lift: small pressure of the "Casing", 5. Far cycles with intermittent lift: small fall of the pressure of the "Casing", 6. Valve work bad: fall and climb of the pressure of the "Casing", 7. Valve does not work: the pressure of the "Casing" is smaller than the pressure of operation of the valve.

III. OUR FAULT DETECTION SYSTEM

Our approach works in two phases: at the beginning is generated the lymphocyte (outline operation phase). Then, our system is included in the environment (inline operation phase) to detect the anomalies.

A. Outline operation phase

This phase is based on the negative selection algorithm to generate lymphocytes. The macro-algorithm is: i) Recollection of data in normal state. ii) Pre-processing of data. iii) Representation of data. iv) Save the "self cells". v) Generation of detectors.

Recollection of data in normal state:

We use the normal and abnormal condition patterns presented in [1, 2] like reference model. Each pattern is a set of registers "Tubing-Casing". Some of the diagnostic with these patterns are: a) *Norma Operation*: small variation of the "Tubing" and "Casing" pressure. b) *Low Production*: The "Tubing" pressure increases and the "Casing" pressure is stabled. c) *Emulsion*: the "Tubing" and "Casing" pressures have small opposite tip. d) *Freezing Gas*: high variations of the "Tubing" pressure and the "Casing" pressure are stabled. For this phase, we have used the normal operation pattern to build the patterns to be used by the IAS.

Pre-processing of data:

We have defined a new representation of data, because our system uses information from different wells. In this way, we can unify the scale of the input values into the interval [-1,1]. We define a matrix (D[PxC]), where P is the number of data of each pattern (each data is a couple "Casing – Tubing" pressure) and C are the variables (in our case C=2, Casing and Tubing pressures). We use 80% of the normal condition patterns for generation of the detectors and 20% to test our system (to detect abnormal condition operations). The maximum and minimum value of each variable is determined using the set points of them. The parameters α and β define the fraction above or below of the set point that determine the maximum and minimum of each variable, respectively. Then, the transformation for each data of D is:

$$D^k_{ji} = 2 \times \left(\frac{D^k_{ji} - \min^k_i}{\max^k_i - \min^k_i} \right) - 1 \qquad (1)$$

where: D^k_{ji} is the value of the row j, column i, of the pattern k modified. with: $j \in (1,2,...P)$; $i \in (1,2)$; $k \in (1..3)$

$\max^k_i$ is the maximum value of the variable or column i of the pattern k:

[$\max^k_i = Op^k_i + \alpha_i \times Op^k_i \qquad 0 \le \alpha_i \le 1; i \in (1,2); k \in (1,3)$]

$\min^k_i$ is the minimum value of the variable or column i of the pattern k:

[$\min^k_i = Op^k_i - \beta_i \times Op^k_i \qquad 0 \le \beta_i \le 1; i \in (1,2); k \in (1..3)$]

Op^k_i is the set point of the variable i of the pattern k.

The value of α and β are: $\alpha_{Casing} = 0.15$, $\beta_{Casing} = 0.15$, $\alpha_{Tubing} = 0.5$, $\beta_{Tubing} = 0.5$

Representation of data:

With D, we have built a new vector of representation of data (X) over each variable using a sliding window with size ($2 \le l < P$) and sliding length ($1 \le shift < P$). $X^k_1 = [D^k_{11} \; D^k_{21} \; ... \; D^k_{P1}]$ is a vector with all the elements of column 1 of D^k, and $X^k_2 = [D^k_{12} \; D^k_{22} \; ... \; D^k_{P2}]$ is a vector with all the elements of column 2 of D^k. We build sliding windows for each vector X^k_i, with $i \in (1,2)$. Thus, we generate a matrix M^k_i for each variable i of each pattern

k where the number of rows represents the numbers of sliding windows generated from vector X^k_i. The size of each vector X^k_{ij} is l. The window is moved according to the sliding length to build a second window. When the sliding window matrix is built for each variable i of each pattern k, we unify the vectors that represent the same position of each variable for each pattern k. Now this matrix is called V with size h=2 x l for each pattern k. For example, the first vector of pattern k is:

$$V^k_1 = [D^k_{11} D^k_{21} \ldots D^k_{l1} D^k_{12} \ldots D^k_{l2}]$$

Then we determine the angle between contiguous data, and between the last element and the first element of this vector. That is, for the first vector of the pattern k we determine the angle as:

$$\tan(A^k_{1,1}) = D^k_{21} / D^k_{11} \qquad (2)$$

and the last angle is determined as:

$$\tan(A^k_{1,2 \times l}) = D^k_{11} / D^k_{l2} \qquad (3)$$

Where: A^k_g is the angle matrix of the pattern k, for the vector g, $g \in (1,\ldots,h)$ and $k \in (1,\ldots,n)$

Save the "self cells":

The "self" is the set of sliding windows represents by the angles obtain previously. So, the self set is represented by the k matrices of the angles of size h x (2x l), where the elements are angles inside of the interval [0, 2xΠ radians].

Generation of detectors:

Our system uses the negative selection algorithm. Each detector is an angle string generated randomly, which is defined as valid if it does not mate with the self (we avoid false positive). Now, we are going to present the negative selection algorithm used in this work, called the *Random generation of detectors*: We generate vectors (detectors) where theirs components are random angles inside of the interval [0, 2xΠ radians]. The number of detectors to generate and the coupling interval of the angle are given by the users. We search detectors that don't active them front the self set [3]. That is, we generate vectors (detectors) with random angles $B_1 = [B_{1,1} \ B_{1,2} \ \ldots \ B_{1,2 \times l}]$, and we compare them with all strings of the self set ($A_1 = [A_{1,1} \ A_{1,2} \ \ldots \ A_{1,2 \times l}]$). Each component of the detector B_1 has a sweep ΔB_1, and there is a coupling if: $B_{1,i} \leq A_{1,i} \leq B_{1,i} + \Delta B_1$ with $1 \leq i \leq 2 \times l$;

If a detector couples a string of the self set, then we eliminated this detector, we increase the counter of deleted detector and we generate another detector. We finish with a given sweep when a given number of detectors deleted is achieved. In this case, we increase the angle sweep, we reset the counter of deleted detectors and we restart the random generation of new detectors. When we achieve a number given of predefined detectors, then we stop the procedure of generation of detectors.

B. Online operation phase

In this phase the immune system must identify the self cells. It is composed by the next tasks: i) Recollection of new data (we test our system using the patterns of the work [1, 2]). ii) Pre-processing of data (we use the same procedure of the previous phase). iii) Representation of data (we use the same procedure like the previous phase to obtain vectors). iv) Define if the detectors can identify or not this new data (using each pattern of abnormal condition, we test the generated detectors in the previous phase).

IV. EXPERIMENTS

Because the Tubing and Casing registers have small opposite peak at the same time, we use that to divide a fault pattern in 11 sections. For intermittent injection, we divide this pattern in 7 sections that represent the fault regions by gas deficiency (Sections 1, 3, 5 y 7) and regions with quasi-stabilization (sections 2, 4 y 6). We follow a similar procedure to divide the rest of fault patterns (see [1, 2]). The performance measures to evaluate our system are: a) *Execution Time (seconds)*: is the CPU time of our system to generate the detectors. ii) Number of activated detectors by fault section. iii) Number of fault sections detected.

We use the next parameters for our algorithm: 1. Size of the sliding window (l) = {2, 3, 4}, 2. Length of the sliding window (*shift*) = 1, 3. Number of detectors to generate (*num*) = {50000, 60000, 70000}, 4. Coupling Interval (*asize*) = Π / 4. The standard case is: l=2, shift=1, num=5000, and asize=Π/4. We have not modified *shift* because when we have modified these parameters we have not obtained important changes at the level of the result [2]. We are going to show the main results, the rest of them can be seen in [2]. We have compare our algorithm with another one proposed in [2]. Table 1 shows the CPU time for each algorithm to generate the detectors for the low production fault pattern for different values of number of detectors. In general, if we increase the number of detectors, then the average of detection by fault section increase. The average of detection of our algorithm is bigger than algorithm [2]. We see in table 1 that the execution time of the algorithm [2] is smaller than our algorithm, but the number of fault sections detected by our algorithm is the biggest.

TABLE 1

EXECUTION TIME FOR BOTH ALGORITHMS

Parameters	Number of detectors	Execution Time (seconds)	
		Our Algorithm	Algorithm [2]
$l = 2$	50000	20605.77	4256.64
	60000	24184.565	5552.504
$l = 4$	50000	89538.891	52835.915

The table 2 shows the number of detectors activated for each algorithm in each fault section for the intermittent injection fault pattern for the standard case. Our detectors have detected the sections of the pattern. We can see more detectors activated by the algorithm 1. In all case, our algorithm has a bigger number of detectors activated by section than the algorithm [2].

TABLE 2

NUMBER OF DETECTORS GENERATED BY OUR ALGORITHM AND THE ALGORITHM PROPOSED IN [2] ACTIVATED IN EACH FAULT SECTION OF EMULSION

Emulsion Interval	Section size (minutes)	Our Algorithm Number of detectors activated	Algorithm [2] Number of detectors activated
Section 1	50	12	2
Section 2	90	39	5
Section 3	130	39	3
Section 4	220	70	8
Section 5	90	55	2
Section 6	170	54	8
Section 7	120	39	3

V. CONCLUSIONS

This paper presented an artificial immune model specially designed to solve the fault detection problem for LAG well. Our system has demonstrated to be capable of combining exploitation with exploration and showed a good performance. In contrast to existing error detection techniques that concentrate on single bit errors, and can sometimes fail to detect multiple errors, our immune system is adept to detecting this task. Particularly, we have generated detectors that determine deviation in the production process. This model can be used in system of high risk and real system, where we like to detect an abnormal condition operation very quickly. In the case of our algorithm, maybe there are a lot of detectors generated that cover the same class of fault problems. This model can be combined with other tools like a fault diagnostic system to classify the faults. In general, the model must be improved in: Add more dynamic (learning and memory systems) to avoid to use only the information catch outline; Use one algorithm to adapt the parameters of our system (coupling interval, etc.).

REFERENCES

[1] I. Albarran, "Una Aplicación de Redes Neuronales en la caracterización del proceso de Levantamiento Artificial de Petróleo por Gas". Technical Report, Univ. Central de Venezuela. Caracas, 2001.

[2] M. Araujo, J. Aguilar, H. Aponte, "Los Sistemas Inmunes Artificiales en problemas de Detección". Technical Report, CEMISID, Univ. de los Andes, 2002.

[3]. A. Avizienis, "Towards Systematic Design of Fault-Tolerant Systems", IEEE Computer, vol. 30:4, pp. 51-58, April 1997.

[4] D. Dasgupta (ed), *Artificial Immune Systems and their Applications,* Springer-Verlag, 1999

[5] D. Dasgupta S. Forrest, "An Anomaly Detection Algorithm Inspired by the Immune System", *in Artificial Immune Systems and Their Applications*, Springer-Verlag, 1999, pp 262-277.

[6] D. Dasgupta, N. Attoh-Okine, "Immunity-Based Systems: A Survey", IEEE International Conference on Systems, Man and Cybernetics, 1997

[7] L. de Castro, J. Timmis, *An Introduction to Artificial Immune Systems: A New Computational Intelligence Paradigm*, Springer-Verlag, 2002.

[8] L. de Castro, F. Von Zuben, "Learning and Optimization Using the Clonal Selection Principle", *IEEE Trans. On Evol. Comp*, Special Issue on Artificial Immune Systems, in press.

An Investigation into the Source of Power for AIRS, an Artificial Immune Classification System

Donald E. Goodman, Jr.[1], Lois Boggess[2], and Andrew Watkins[3]

[1]Department of Psychology, Mississippi State University
Mississippi State, MS 39762

[2]Department of Computer Science and Engineering, Mississippi State University
Mississippi State, MS 39762

[3]Computing Laboratory, University of Kent at Canterbury
Canterbury, Kent, England. U.K. CT2 7NF

Abstract - The AIRS classifier, based on metaphors from the field of artificial immune systems, has shown itself to be an effective general purpose classifier across a broad spectrum of classification problems. This research examines the new classifier empirically, replacing one of the two likely sources of its classification power with alternative modifications. The results are slightly less effective, but not statistically significantly so. We conclude that the modifications, which are computationally somewhat more efficient, provide fast test versions of AIRS for users to experiment with. We also conclude that the chief source of classification power of AIRS must lie in its replacement and maintenance of its memory cell population.

INTRODUCTION

Late in 2001, a new classifier was introduced, based on principles from the discipline of Artificial Immune Systems. The classifier was AIRS (Artificial Immune Recognition System), and it was interesting not only because it showed that Artificial Immune Systems could be used for classification but also because it was surprisingly successful as a general purpose classifier.

This paper empirically explores the possible sources of classification power of this new classifier. We believe such an exploration is important for the following reasons:

a) AIRS is effective in a broad array of different classification problems, including problems with large dimensioned feature space, problems with many classes, and problems with real-valued and discrete features.

b) Some general purpose classifiers perform poorly until an appropriate architecture for the classifier is determined by the researcher, and the search for the appropriate architecture may require substantial effort. For the majority of problems to which it has been applied, using the default parameters with which AIRS is delivered produces results which are within a couple of percentage points of the best results that AIRS obtains. And the best results that AIRS obtains are usually highly competitive.

c) AIRS is self-adjusting for the feature of its architecture that is most descriptive of the problem space. In fact, when another classifier, Kohonen's LVQ, was instructed to use the same number of cells that AIRS determined to be a good characterization of the problem space, the classification accuracy of LVQ improved [1]

d) Although we have experience with an array of general-purpose classifiers, none in our experience has performed as consistently strongly as AIRS across the same gamut of classification types.

AIRS was originally conceived in an attempt to demonstrate that Artificial Immune Systems were amenable to the task of classification. The AIRS algorithm was motivated in particular by resource limited Artificial Immune Systems [2][3]. Although the motivation was initially simply to show that classification was possible using this paradigm, the algorithm was tested a broad range of publicly-available classification tasks, and proved to be highly effective. It has been tested on problems with up to 279 features and on problems with up to 12 classes. [1][4][5][6][7].

[1] and [5] both investigated multiple-class problems in which the number of classes in the problem space was fairly large, and each encountered a widely-studied publicly available classification problem for which AIRS appears to be the most successful single general-purpose classifier for the problem.

This paper explores possible sources of the power of the AIRS algorithm. First, we briefly describe the basic classification algorithm, particularly the memory cell pool which is used for the actual classification task after training, and the "training" algorithm that derives this memory cell pool. Since this memory cell pool is in a sense the AIRS algorithm's depiction of the important parts of the problem space, we compare the characteristics of the members of the memory cell pool with the "antigens" - the training instances

- from the data for a variety of the classification problems. We then explore the effect of replacing the memory cell derivation algorithm of the original AIRS with a variety of plausible alternatives, observing any resulting changes in effectiveness in the overall AIRS classification performance. Finally, we apply our observations to the goal of deducing the source of power of the AIRS algorithm when applied to the problem of classification.

THE AIRS CLASSIFIER

As mentioned in the introduction, the initial intent in developing AIRS was to demonstrate that a classifier built on the principles of artificial immune systems could be an effective general purpose classifier suitable for a broad variety of classification tasks.

Artificial Immune Systems had already been applied successfully in other domains: in particular, Artificial Immune Systems are an appealing metaphor for applications in Computer Security. The ability to distinguish between Self and Non-self has considerable attraction in that field, and the immune system concept of negative selection of maturing recognizers based on response to Self has been successfully applied to systems whose purpose is to determine whether the integrity of data has been violated [8][9]. There is also considerable research into the application of such evolved recognizers in the field of Intrusion Detection, especially as applied to the question of whether traces of operating system calls correspond to normal behavior or not [10][11][12].

One previous system, [13], had been designed for the purpose of classification. However, it was devised by a medical professional, was highly complex, and was not sufficiently described to replicate. Work by Timmis and others on clustering using Artificial Immune Systems [3][14][15] was appealing, and the further development of that work using the concept of resource limitation [16] became the inspiration for AIRS.

LOOKING FOR THE SOURCE OF CLASSIFICATION POWER

The goal was to show that an Artificial Immune System could be an effective general purpose classifier; we did not actually expect it to be quite as effective as it proved to be. Table 1 on the next page shows the comparative effectiveness of the original AIRS algorithm [4] in terms of reported accuracy rates in the literature. The number reported in the table for AIRS is its average accuracy over multiple runs of 10-way cross-validation. The figures for the other classifiers are derived from [17] and [18] (which are themselves also normally averages of multiple runs of cross-validation), and indicate whether the accuracy was greater (positive) or less (negative) than the average accuracy for AIRS on the same problem.

In broad terms, training the AIRS classifier involves two interrelated processes. In nature, lymphocytes (B-cells and T-cells) respond to an invading antigen and those B-cells which match the invader closely enough begin mutating to generate even closer matches, as part of the process of attacking the invader. As a classifier-in-training, for any presenting antigen (training instance from the training data), AIRS uses a pool of B-cells, some of which are mutations of an existing B-cell which most closely resembles the presenting antigen, and some of which are simply randomly generated cells. In the current version of AIRS, stimulation is inversely proportional to distance in feature space: the smaller the Euclidean distance between antigen and B-cell, the greater the stimulation. The B-cells which are most highly stimulated by exposure to the antigen begin cloning and mutating. The least stimulated B-cells die out. The process continues over multiple generations, with the most-stimulated B-cells being retained and the least stimulated ones being eliminated. Once the average stimulation level of the entire B-cell population reaches a threshold, which can be determined by the user, the process stops, and the cell which is most stimulated by the antigen becomes a candidate for promotion to a memory cell.

The second training process referred to above is the selection and maintenance of the set of memory cells. In nature, most of the enormous number of lymphocytes generated in combating an invader die. But a relatively small number of the cells remain in the immune system indefinitely, with the result that any successive invasions by the same or similar antigens are met with an immediate response by the immune system. Although there is controversy over whether the cells themselves have an indefinite lifespan or whether the immune system has a method of replicating the actual cells, the net effect is the same - there are cells that represent a very long-term memory of invaders to the system. In AIRS, when a B-cell becomes a candidate for inclusion in the long-term memory cell population, it must first prove to be more stimulated by the current antigen than any other existing memory cell which responds to the classification class to which the antigen belongs. Provided that this is the case, the candidate cell is included in the memory cell population. Additionally, if the new memory cell is sufficiently similar to the memory cell which originally was most stimulated by the invading antigen (where the definition of "sufficiently similar" is controlled by a parameter which the user can adjust), the new memory cell actually replaces this other cell. This mechanism contributes both to the generalization capabilities of the AIRS classifier and to the data reduction capabilities of the classifier. Typically there are fewer than half as many memory cells in a trained AIRS system as there were training instances, and only a small fraction of the memory cell population is identical to the training instances which engendered them. For more details of the current AIRS algorithm, see [19].

Table 1.

Comparison of classifiers on the five classification tasks. Except for AIRS data, these results are taken from Duch [17][18]. When Duch's reported accuracy seems to disagree with Duch's ranking, both the ranking and the reported accuracy are retained.

	Cleveland heart disease		Iris		Ionosphere		Diabetes		Sonar	
1	IncNet	+6.8%	Grobian (rough)	+3.3%	3-NN + simplex	+3.8%	Logdisc	+3.6%	TAP MFT Bayesian	+8.3%
2	28-NN, stand, Euclid, 7 features	+2.6 - +1.6%	SSV	+1.3%	3-NN	+1.8%	IncNet	+3.5%	Naïve MFT Bayesian	+6.4%
3	Fisher discriminant analysis	+1%	C-MLP2LN	+1.3%	IB3	+1.8%	DIPOL92	+3.5%	SVM	+6.4%
4	LDA	+1.3%	PVM 2 rules	+1.3%	MLP + BP	+1.1%	Linear Discr. Anal.	+3.4 - +3.1%	Best 2-layer MLP + BP, 12 hidden	+6.4%
5	16-NN, stand, Euclid	+1.4 - +0.2%	PVM 1 rule	+0.6%	**AIRS**	**94.9%**	SMART	+2.7%	MLP+BP, 12 hidden	+0.7%
6	FSM, 82.4-84% on test only	+0.8%	**AIRS**	**96.7%**	C4.5	0%	GTO DT (5xCV)	+2.7%	MLP+BP, 24 hidden	+0.5%
7	Naïve Bayes	+0.2 - -0.7%	FuNe-I	0.0%	RIAC	-0.3%	ASI	+2.5%	1-NN, Manhatten	+0.2%
8	**AIRS**	**83.2%**	NEFCLASS	0.0%	SVM	-1.7%	Fischer discr. anal	+2.4%	**AIRS**	**84.0%**
9	SNB	-0.1%	CART	-0.7%	Non-linear perceptron	-2.9%	MLP+BP	+2.3%	MLP+BP, 6 hidden	-0.5%
10	LVQ	-0.3%	FUNN	-1.0%	FSM + rotation	-2.1%	LVQ	+1.7%	FSM - methodology?	-0.4%
11	kNN, k=27, Manh	+0.2 - -1.0%			1-NN	-2.8%	LFC	+1.7%	1-NN Euclidean	-1.8%
12	GTO DT (5xCV)	-0.7%			DB-CART	-3.6%	RBF	+1.6%	DB-CART, 10xCV	-2.2%
13	kNN, k=19, Euclidean	-0.3 - -1.9%			Linear perceptron	-4.2%	NB	+1.4- -0.3%	CART, 10xCV	-16.1%
14	LDA (all vectors, 85% on train)	-1.4%			OC1 DT	-5.4%	kNN, k=22, Manh	+1.4%		
15	SVM (5xCV)	-1.7%			CART	-6.0%	MML	+1.4%		
16	kNN (k=1?)	-1.7%			GTO DT	-8.9%	SNB	+1.3%		
...							...			
22							**AIRS**	**74.1%**		
23							C4.5	-0.9%		
	others below 16th rank include MLP with Backprop, CART, RBF, Gaussian EM, ASR, C4.5, and a number of WEKA tools, among others						11 others reported with lower scores, including Bayes, Kohonen, kNN, ID3 ...			

The experiments described in this paper test the hypothesis that the power of the AIRS classifier resides in the method of deriving a candidate memory cell from the B-cells. An empirical means of testing that conjecture is to replace that part of the AIRS algorithm with a function which directly generates a candidate memory cell drawn from some suitably constrained probability distribution, rather than filtering one from the random mutations of a population. (While the functions explored are not based on a natural metaphor, there may be natural justification for not using random mutation, since it appears that in nature the mutation of lymphocytes in response to an invader is not a random process.)

Frankly, we expected the performance of AIRS to drop off sharply when a function was substituted. When that was not the case with the first function that we experimented with, an elliptical probability distribution, we looked at how close in feature space the regular AIRS candidates for memory cell status were to the training vectors that caused them to be generated. That is, for each training vector presented to AIRS, a memory candidate cell is evolved. In general the feature space is high-dimensional, so it is not possible to look at a spatial representation of the training vectors and the resulting memory candidates. But it is possible to compute the distance between the training vectors and their respective candidate cells, and to plot a histogram of how many cells fall into respective distances from their training vectors.

Figure 1 is one of the resulting histograms. It shows the distribution of the distances of the memory cells from their respective training vectors for ten-way cross-validation, applying the normal AIRS algorithm (not the functional replacement) to the Pima Indian Diabetes classification problem [20]. AIRS normalizes the feature vector space so that all feature dimensions have the same range and so that the maximum Euclidean distance between any two vectors is 1.0. The farthest outliers of this set were slightly more than one quarter of this distance.

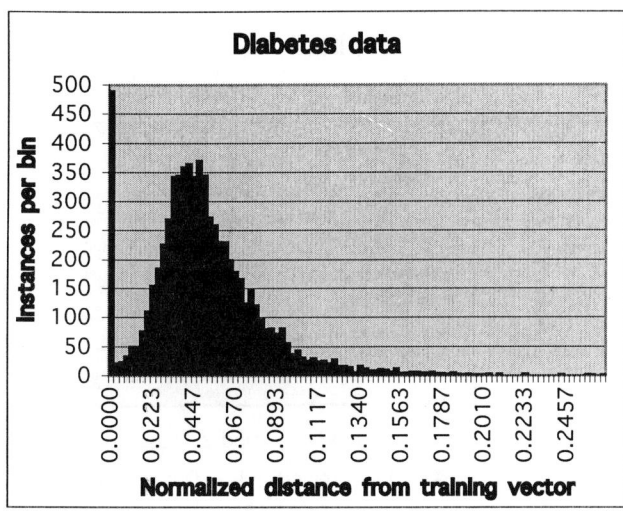

Figure 1. Distance of candidate memory cells from training antigen. Maximum normalized distance possible is 1.0. Y axis is number of antigens out of a total of 6920.

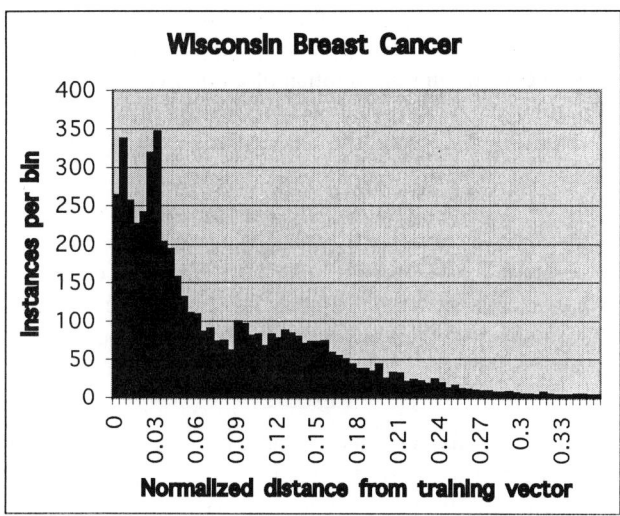

Figure 2. Two data sets were somewhat different from the preceding. Shown above is the distance of candidate memory cells from training antigen for Wisconsin Breast Cancer data.

In addition to the Diabetes data set, we also derived analogous histograms for the Wisconsin Breast Cancer data set, the balance scale data set, the credit.crx problem, iris, ionosphere and SPECT data sets, all from the University of California at Irvine Machine Learning Repository [20], and for an artificial three-class problem whose feature vectors are uniformly distributed over a subset of the real plane, with convoluted boundaries between the non-linearly separable classes (see [1] for a description of the latter data set). We hypothesized that the uniformly distributed nature of the training instances of the latter, in contrast to the "bursty" nature of feature vectors from naturally occurring classification problems, might affect how close the memory cells would be to their respective training antigens. However, the overall shape of the histograms was similar for all the problems except the balance scale problem, the breast cancer problem, and the SPECT problem. The histogram for the Wisconsin Breast Cancer data is shown in Figure 2.

Both the balance scale data and the Wisconsin Breast Cancer data produced histograms with no deep "valley" between the initial spike at zero and the first peak. They also both show a noticeable secondary rounded peak in the distribution. The histogram for SPECT is quite different from all other histograms and is shown in Figure 3. While it confirms that AIRS behaves differently for different data sets, it is also the case that AIRS's accuracy for SPECT is low. The distribution, which shows most of the memory cell candidates a distance of between 0.25 and 0.5 in a normalized space where the maximum distance between two entities is 1.0, may reflect a difficulty in distinguishing between training vectors on the basis of Euclidean distance in feature space.

We then experimented with three functions to replace the part of AIRS which generates candidate memory cells:

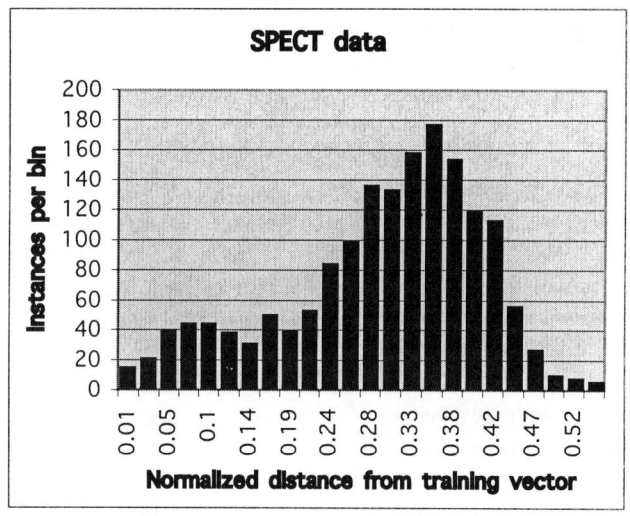

Figure 3. One distribution was markedly different from all the others. Above is the distribution of distances of candidate memory cells from the training antigens for the SPECT data set.

Function 1 (Mod 1): This was the initial function that we had created before looking at the histogram distributions. Since it had been more successful than expected, we retained it: for each antigen in the training set, generate a single cell mutated from the antigen whose distance from the antigen in feature space conforms to a hyperbolic (1/x) probability distribution with a constant multiplier which caused the distribution to tail off very rapidly. Consequently, most candidate memory cells were very close to their originating antigens.

Function 2 (Mod 2): The second function was also hyperbolic, with a multiplier which allowed more of the distributional mass to be in a tail, rather like figure 2, but without the secondary hump.

Function 3 (Mod 3): The probability distribution was derived from the actual probability distribution of AIRS's memory cells during the solution of a representative problem. In particular, we created a function by smoothing and interpolating the probability distribution for the memory candidate cells produced by AIRS during a ten-way cross-validation training run on the Ionosphere problem. This distribution was almost identical in shape to Figure 1, except that a thin tail extended out to 0.45, affording an opportunity for some cells generated by the function to be somewhat further away from their respective training antigens.

RESULTS

Figures 4, 5, 6, and 7 show results for four of the data sets which were tested. Mod 0 refers to the revision of AIRS described in [19] (the version of AIRS which is being distributed as of this writing). Mods 1, 2, and 3 refer to the modifications of that algorithm that replace candidate memory cell generation with the three functions described in the preceding section. While AIRS can be run pretty much "as delivered", it does have a number of user-specifiable parameters which can be modified to suit a given data set. The term "Unoptimized" in the figures refers to running the algorithm using the default values for its parameters. The term "Optimized" refers to systematically changing those parameters and observing whether average performance improves. The test runs in all cases are averages over three runs of 10-way validation using the parameters suggested by the optimization suite of tests. A number of trends are clear from examination of the performances of these unoptimized and "optimized" modifications of AIRS.

AIRS run "as delivered" with default parameters tends to deliver accuracy only a few percentage points below its optimum performance.

We note that the scales on Figures 4 and 5 are somewhat exaggerated. For the Wisconsin Breast Cancer data, the functions are marginally less effective than the original algorithm in both unoptimized and optimized cases, with the exception of the optimized version of the modification which used a smoothed function derived from the original AIRS' own candidate memory cell generation distribution. For the iris data, the unoptimized functions were slightly more accurate than the unoptimized unmodified AIRS, but the optimized original AIRS was slightly more accurate than the optimized functions. Both of these trends were observed in the remaining four data sets not illustrated in the figures which follow.

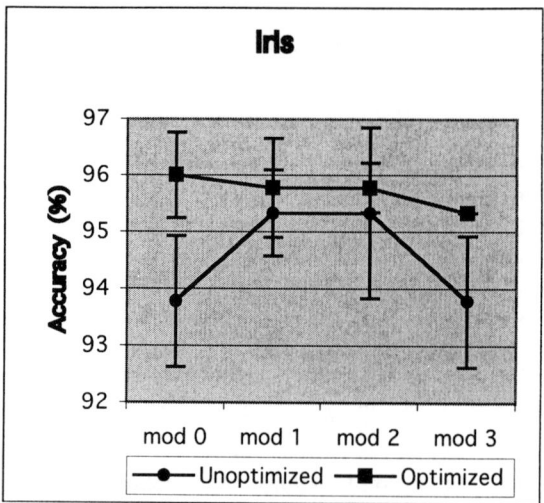

Figure 4.

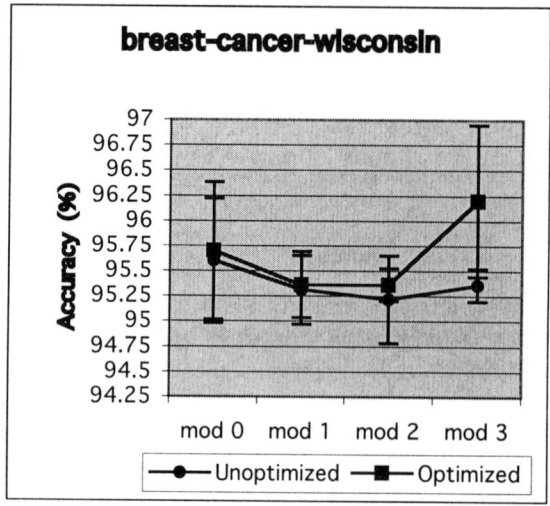

Figure 5.

It also tends to be the case that basing the functional distribution of the memory cell candidates on a prototypical distribution from AIRS's solutions to real-world problems is less effective than the other functional strategies; that is, the performance of mod 3 on the Iris data is more reflective of its general competitiveness than its performance on the Wisconsin Breast Cancer problem.

CONCLUSION

If we remove mod 3 from consideration, the differences between the functional modifications and normal AIRS, though observable, are not statistically significant. Hence we conclude that replacing the memory cell candidate generation portion of the AIRS algorithm has not changed the performance significantly. This leads us to hypothesize that the power of this classifier is in its approach to adding and replacing memory cells in the memory cell population. We are in the process of testing this conjecture.

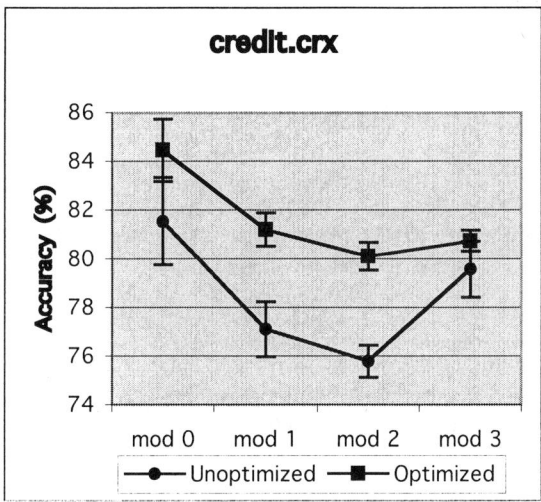

Figure 6.

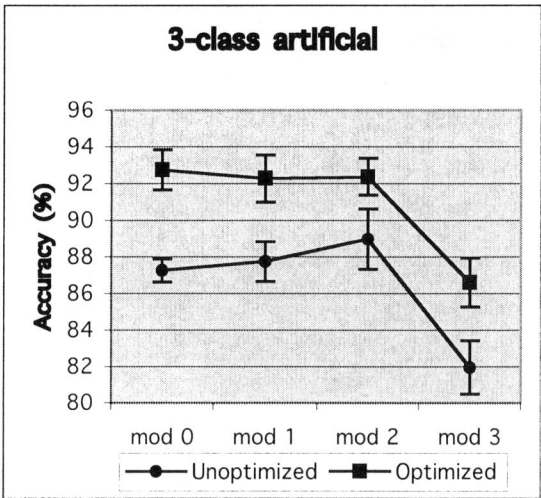

Figure 7. Comparison of the different modifications of AIRS on an artificially generated set of classes in the real plane R^2. The classes have convoluted boundaries and fill the subplane, and their instances are approximately uniformly distributed in the subspace.

We also note that the functional modifications to AIRS described in this paper are fast. In our experience they are not much faster than standard AIRS for most of the problems we have experimented with - one run of standard AIRS using five-way cross-validation takes less than five minutes on a 500MHz laptop for most of the datasets mentioned. However, we have encountered datasets for which certain combinations of user-set parameters caused AIRS to train for long periods before the population of B-cells reached the user-prescribed stimulation threshold, which allowed it to stop training. The function-based variations on AIRS are guaranteed not to have such problems, and do allow a user to get a reasonable estimate of how well AIRS works on the user's classification problem.

REFERENCES

[1] D. Goodman, L. Boggess, and A. Watkins, "Artificial Immune System classification of multiple-class problems," in *Proc. Artificial Neural Networks in Engineering (ANNIE-2002)*, St. Louis, Mo. Nov. 2002.

[2] L. N. de Castro and F. von Zuben, "An evolutionary immune network for data clustering," in *Proc. IEEE Brazilian Symposium on Neural Networks*, pp. 84-89, 2000.

[3] J. Timmis,, M. Neal, and J. E. Hunt, "An artificial immune system for data analysis," *Biosystems*, vol. 55, no. 1, pp. 143-150, 2000.

[4] A. Watkins, *AIRS: A Resource Limited Artificial Immune Classifier*. M.S. thesis, Department of Computer Science. Mississippi State University, 2001.

[5] A. Watkins and L. Boggess, "A new classifier based on resource limited Artificial Immune Systems," in *Proc. 2002 Congress on Evolutionary Computation (CEC2002)*, IEEE Press, Honolulu, Hawaii, May 2002.

[6] A. Watkins and L. Boggess, "A resource limited Artificial Immune classifier.," in *Proc. 2002 Congress on Evolutionary Computation (CEC2002)*, special session on Artificial Immune Systems. IEEE Press, Honolulu, Hawaii, May 2002.

[7] G. Marwah and L. C. Boggess, "Artificial Immune Systems for classification : Some issues," in *Proc. First Intl. Conf. Art. Immune Systems*, Canturbury, England, pp.149-153, Sep. 2002.

[8] S. Forrest, S. A. Hofmeyer, and A. Somayaji, "Computer immunology," *Communications of the ACM*, vol. 40, no. 10, pp.88-96, 1997.

[9] S. Forrest, A.S. Perelson, L. Allen, and R. Cherukuri, "Self-Nonself Discrimination in a Computer.". in *Proc. 1994 IEEE Symposium on Research in Security and Privacy*, Los Alamitos, CA: IEEE Computer Society Press, 1994. http://www.cs.unm.edu/~forrest/isa_papers.htm

[10] S. Hofmeyr, S. Forrest, and A. Somayaji, "Intrusion Detection Using Sequences of System Calls." *Journal of Computer Security* vol. 6, pp. 151-180, 1998. http://www.cs.unm.edu/~forrest/isa_papers.htm

[11] D. Dasgupta and S. Forrest, "Novelty detection in time series data using ideas from immunology," in *Proc. International Conference on Intelligent Systems*, 1999.
http://www.cs.unm.edu/~forrest/isa_papers.htm

[12] J. Kim and P. Bentley, "Towards an Artificial Immune System for network intrusion detection: An investigation of dynamic clonal selection," in *Proc. 2002 Congress on Evolutionary Computation*, IEEE Press, Honolulu, pp. 1015-1020, May 2002.

[13] Jerome Carter, "The immune system as a model for pattern recognition and classification," *J American Medical Informatics Association (JAMIA)*, vol. 7, no. 1, pp. 28-41, 2000.

[14] Jon Timmis, and Mark Neal, "Investigating the evolution and stability of a resource limited artificial immune system," in *Proc. Genetic and Evolutionary Computation Conference (GECCO)*, pp. 40-41, 2000.

[15] J. Timmis, *Artificial immune systems: A novel data analysis technique inspired by the immune network theory*, Ph.D. thesis, Department of Computer Science, University of Wales, Aberystwyth, Sep. 2000.

[16] J. Timmis and M. Neal, "A resource limited artificial immune system for data analysis," *Knowledge Based Systems*, vol. 14, nos. 3-4, pp. 121-130, 2001.

[17] Duch, W. 2000a. "Datasets used for classification: Comparison of results," http://www.phys.uni.torun.pl/kmk/projects/datasets.html.

[18] Duch, W. 2000b. "Logical rules extracted from data," http://www.phys.uni.torun.pl/kmk/projects/rules.html.

[19] A. Watkins and J. Timmis, "Artificial Immune Recognition System (AIRS): Revisions and refinements," in *Proc. 1st International Conf. on Artificial Immune Systems (ICARIS 2002)*, pp. 173-181, Sep. 2002.

[20] C. L. Blake, & C. J. Merz, *UCI repository of machine learning databases*, 1998. Retrieved 22 April 2002, from the University of California, Irvine Computer Science website: http://www.ics.uci.edu/~mlearn/MLRepository.html.

Self-organizing Neural Networks for Efficient Clustering of Gene Expression Data

Ji He*, Ah-Hwee Tan[†], and Chew-Lim Tan*
*School of Computing, National University of Singapore,
3 Science Drive 2, Singapore 117543
{heji,tancl}@comp.nus.edu.sg
[†]Institute for Infocomm Research,
21 Heng Mui Keng Terrace, Singapore 119613
ahhwee@i2r.a-star.edu.sg

Abstract—Clustering of gene expression patterns is of great value for the understanding of the various molecular biological processes. While a number of algorithms have been applied to gene clustering, there are relatively few studies on the application of neural networks to this task. In addition, there is a lack of quantitative evaluation of the gene clustering results. This paper proposes Adaptive Resonance Theory under Constraint (ART-C) for efficient clustering of gene expression data. We illustrate that ART-C can effectively identify gene functional groupings through a case study on rat CNS data. Based on a set of quantitative evaluation measures, we compare the performance of ART-C with those of K-Means, SOM, and conventional ART. Our comparative studies on the yeast cell cycle and the human hematopoietic differentiation data sets show that ART-C produces reasonably good quantitative performance. More importantly, compared with K-Means and SOM, ART-C shows a significantly higher learning efficiency, which is crucial for knowledge discovery from large scale biological databases.

I. INTRODUCTION

With the advances in molecular biology research, an increasing number of genes have been discovered and identified. To supplement traditional biological studies that collect expressions of individual genes, there is a natural need to analyze the gene expression data in a global fashion. Clustering of gene expressions (*gene clustering* in short) is one useful analysis technique. Specifically, the knowledge discovered by the clustering process is of great value for various molecular biological processes, such as correlating expression patterns, and mapping expressions data to sequence, structural and biochemical data [13].

While there exists a large number of clustering algorithms in the literature, only a few of them have been applied to analyze gene expression data in the recent half decade. These include K-Means [14], hierarchical clustering [5], graph theory based clustering [2], naive Bayesian clustering [1], and Gaussian mixture model based clustering [18]. There are very rare studies of neural networks on gene clustering, besides a few applications of the self-organizing map (SOM) [10], [15]. SOM however is not known as an efficient clustering algorithm, due to its high computational cost in maintaining the neighborhood relationship.

Adaptive Resonance Theory (ART) models is a family of self-organizing neural networks that performs online clustering of arbitrary input pattern sequences with a high level of efficiency [3]. However, a conventional ART model produces a varying number of output clusters in response to the distribution and the order of the inputs, mainly affected by a global *vigilance* parameter. This behavior may not be desirable for gene clustering, as a biologist would want to control the number of output clusters directly for the purpose of validation and inspection.

To address the above problem, this paper proposes a relatively new ART variance, known as Adaptive Resonance Theory under Constraint (ART-C), for efficient clustering of gene expression data. ART-C is capable of incorporating user-defined constraint when learning its category representation. Specifically it has been shown to produce clustering results equivalent to those of ART, with the added capability of self-adjusting its vigilance parameter to generate the desired number of categories (output clusters) [8]. We consider this capability of great value as it relieves the trial-and-error process of the user in suggesting a proper vigilance parameter.

The rest of this paper is organized as follows. Section II reviews several clustering algorithms used in our benchmark. Section III summarizes the ART-C learning algorithm. Section IV illustrates ART-C's capability in rediscovering gene functional groupings through case study on rat CNS data. Section V reports our comparative benchmark on the yeast cell cycle and the human hematopoietic differentiation data sets. The last section summarizes our conclusions and proposes the future work.

II. CLUSTERING ALGORITHMS: A BRIEF REVIEW

This section briefly reviews the clustering algorithms used in our benchmark. Detailed information of the algorithms can be found through the various references.

A. K-Means

K-Means [16] has been extensively studied and applied in the clustering literature due to its simplicity and robustness. The objective of the K-Means clustering method is to minimize the intra-cluster compactness of the output, in terms of the summed squared error. The algorithm randomly initializes k reference clusters and iteratively adjusts the prototype of each cluster as the mean of its cluster members. Learning is repeated until the cluster assignment of each input stabilizes. Though simple, K-Means can produce satisfactory clustering results by reaching one of its local optima. The deficiency of K-Means lies in its dependency on the availability of the entire input data set for batch processing, which could be memory intensive. In addition, K-Means is sensitive to the initialization of the reference clusters and the input noises.

B. Self-organizing Map

Self-organizing Map (SOM) proposed by Kohonen [12] is a family of self-organizing neural networks widely used for clustering and visualization. Similar to K-Means, the reference clusters in SOM are randomly initialized. SOM follows a *winner-take-part* competitive learning process. For each incremental input, the network identifies the winner cluster that is most similar to the input, and updates the weights of the winner as well as the winner's neighbors in order to incorporate the input. Although SOM adopts an online learning paradigm, it is not a fast clustering algorithm, due mainly to the extra computational cost in maintaining the neighborhood relationship and the slow learning rates. The advantage of SOM is the spatial map output in which similar clusters are placed close to each other. Specifically, 2-dimensional maps are widely used in various data visualization tasks.

C. Adaptive Resonance Theory

Besides SOM, Adaptive Resonance Theory (ART) [7] is another family of self-organizing neural architectures well-known by its *stability-plasticity* property. Unlike SOM that initializes a pre-specified number of reference clusters, the recognition categories (clusters) in ART are dynamically created using input samples. The network essentially follows a *winner-take-all* competitive learning process, with extra binary decision that triggers the network's state to either *resonance* or *reset* in response to each input, guided by a global *vigilance* parameter. If an input is dissimilar enough to the existing recognition categories in the network, such that the network fails to find a winner to reach a resonance, the input is inserted into the network as a new recognition category. This mechanism is effective in encoding distinct inputs and guarantees a high learning efficiency. The deficiency of ART is that the number of its output clusters is not directly determinable. In order to obtain a specific number of clusters over the input space, prior knowledge on the distribution of the data set is required to suggest a proper vigilance parameter.

There are a large number of ART variances, mainly depending on the pattern similarity measures used and the network's search process. The ART 2A [4] module, which uses dot product as the pattern similarity measure, is applied in our work due to its close relationship with K-Means and SOM.

III. ADAPTIVE RESONANCE THEORY UNDER CONSTRAINT

Adaptive Resonance Theory Under Constraint (ART-C) [8] is a relatively new ART variance that addresses the "undeterminable recognition field size" problem of ART. Unlike a conventional ART network that mainly controls its learning activity with a vigilance threshold, ART-C's learning is mainly guided by an intuitive constraint on the maximal number of recognition categories in the network. The solution introduces an extra *constraint reset* mechanism to the ART network, which self-adjusts the vigilance threshold through an adaptive estimation of the input distribution in response to the constraint. The dynamically adjusted vigilance threshold in turn drives the learning activities to satisfy the user-defined constraint. For a better understanding of this paper, the ART-C 2A learning paradigm, which is based on ART 2A [4], is reviewed with more details below.

Parameters
The ART-C 2A dynamics are determined by the constraint C on the maximal number of recognition categories and the learning rate $\eta \in [0, 1]$.

Network initialization
The category recognition layer is initialized with the null set $\emptyset$ (i.e. contains no recognition category). The vigilance ρ is initialized as 1.0.

Learning of each input representation
Learning of each input presentation follows the ART 2A learning paradigm [4].

Constraint checking
Constraint checking is performed after the learning of each input representation by comparing the number of existing recognition categories N with the predefined constraint C

$$\hbar = \begin{cases} 1 & \text{if } N > C \\ 0 & \text{otherwise.} \end{cases} \quad (1)$$

With $\hbar = 0$, the constraint is said to be satisfied, upon which the network carries on to learn the next input representation. Otherwise, *constraint reset* occurs, as described below.

Constraint reset
Constraint reset re-organizes the recognition categories in the network towards the satisfaction of the constraint and adjusts the ρ value based on the current category distribution. The process is introduced as follows.

1) *Searching of the nearest category pair:* For each category pair (i, j) in the category recognition layer, their similarity is defined by the dot product of their corresponding weights $\mathbf{w}_i$ and $\mathbf{w}_j$ such that

$$T_{(i,j)} \equiv \mathbf{w}_i \cdot \mathbf{w}_j. \quad (2)$$

The *nearest neighbor* of each category i, indexed as $J(i)$, is the category that has the maximal similarity with i:

$$T_{(i,J(i))} = \max\{T_{(i,j)} : j = 1, \ldots, N, j \neq i\}. \quad (3)$$

The *nearest neighbor similarity* of category i, marked as $\tau(i)$ then refers to the similarity between category i and its nearest neighbor $J(i)$:

$$\tau(i) \equiv T_{(i,J(i))}. \quad (4)$$

The *nearest category pair*, indexed as (I, J), is identified by the category I that has the minimal nearest neighbor similarity to its nearest neighbor J:

$$\tau(I) = T_{(I,J(I))} = \max\{T_{(i,J(i))} : i = 1, \ldots, N\}. \quad (5)$$

2) *Adjustment of the vigilance:* The vigilance value $\rho^{(new)}$ for subsequent learning is decreased according to:

$$\rho^{(new)} = \max\{\tau(i) : \text{all } i \text{ whose } \tau(i) < \rho^{(old)}\}. \quad (6)$$

3) *Merging of the nearest category pair:* Merging of the nearest category pair (I, J) is done by inserting a new

category L with the weight vector as the mean of these two categories:

$$\mathbf{w}_L = \Re(0.5\mathbf{w}_I + 0.5\mathbf{w}_J), \quad (7)$$

where $\Re$ is the Euclidean normalization as given by

$$\Re\mathbf{x} \equiv \frac{\mathbf{x}}{||\mathbf{x}||}. \quad (8)$$

In addition, the categories I and J are deleted from the network after the creation of the new category.

IV. CASE STUDY: INTERPRETATION OF ART-C 2A CLUSTERS

We applied ART-C 2A to the clustering problem of the rat CNS data set [17]. The rat CNS data set contains 112 gene expressions on nine time points, covering the embryonic development phase (E11, E13, E15, E18, and E21, time in days), the postnatal development phase (P0, P7, and P14) and the adult phase (A). Prior study by Wen et al [17] on the data set using the FITCH software summarized five major waves of the gene expression patterns. With the exception of the *constant wave*, they have shown high correlation with the four major functional categories identified using biological domain knowledge, namely *Neuroglial Markers*, *Neurotransmitter Receptors*, *Peptide Signaling*, and *Diverse*.

We replicated Wen et al's experiment with ART-C 2A and compared the output of ART-C 2A with that of the FITCH software as reported in Wen's study. The small size and the relatively distinct expression patterns of this data set enabled us to validate ART-C 2A's clustering results via visual inspection. We adopted a standard set of parameters for ART-C 2A. $C = 12$ is used for the purpose of analyzing the output clusters in satisfactory details. Figure 1 depicts the mean expression pattern of each cluster generated by ART-C 2A. The gene expressions grouped in each cluster are observed to have close similarity to each other (error bars corresponding to the deviations to the mean expressions are not plotted for a clearer illustration). Each pattern has showed a distinct group of gene expressions, identified by the variances of the expressions across all time points and the time point corresponding to the peak level. The ART-C 2A output is observed to have close relevancy with the output of the FITCH software as reported by Wen et al. The mapping of the clusters generated by ART-C 2A to the five major waves discovered by FITCH is summarized in Table I.

To further validate the ART-C 2A clusters, we investigated the correlation of genes in each cluster (Table II) with the major gene functional categories previously identified through human inspection (Table III) [17]. With the exception of cluster 1, which encodes a max of genes in *Peptide Signaling* and *Diverse* categories with relatively constant expressions (constant expressions normally are not of interests to biologists), the majority of the most clusters are dominated by genes of a single functional category. The best result is given by clusters 2 - 5, which clearly recognize the functional group *Neurotransmitter Receptors*. It is noted that, although cluster 6 and cluster 8 show relatively similar patterns (grouped into *wave1* in Wen et al's study), the majority of the genes in them

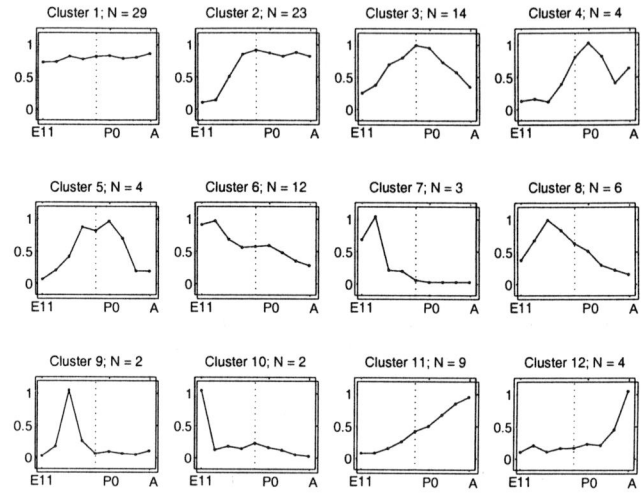

Fig. 1. The gene expression patterns of the rat CNS data set generated by ART-C 2A. N indicates the number of genes in each cluster.

TABLE I
MAPPING OF THE GENE PATTERNS GENERATED BY ART-C 2A TO THE PATTERNS DISCOVERED BY FITCH.

Cluster Pattern		
ART-C 2A	FITCH	Interpretation
Cluster 1	Constant Wave	Relatively constant levels across all time points.
Cluster 2	Wave 2	Ascending levels during E phase and relatively constant levels during P and A phases.
Clusters 3 - 5	Wave 3	Peak level during late E and early P phases.
Clusters 6 - 10	Wave 1	Peak level during early E phase.
Clusters 11 - 12	Wave 4	Ascending levels across all time points.

actually corresponded to two different gene functional groups *Peptide Signaling* and *Neuroglial Markers*. This shows that ART-C 2A is capable of identifying subtle differences between the sets of two patterns.

It is interesting that although cluster 8 and cluster 11 present very different patterns, they actually corresponded to the same functional group *Neuroglial Markers*. In addition, several small clusters, especially cluster 7, 9, and 10 clearly identify a number of noises who did not follow the correlation between their functions and expressions in the main stream. This reflected the underlying complexity of the gene expression data.

V. COMPARATIVE EXPERIMENTS

A. Cluster Validity Measures

The *quantitative* assessment of clustering results did not receive much attention from the biologists until recently. Among the few known studies that quantitatively evaluate the gene clustering results, Yeung et al. [19] used generalized Jaccard and Hurbert indices [11] to compare the performance of several clustering algorithms. The adjusted Rand index was

TABLE II
LISTING OF GENES GROUPED IN THE CLUSTERS GENERATED BY ART-C 2A.

Cluster	Genes in the cluster
1	GAP43, GAT1, ODC, GRa1, GRb3, BDNF, CNTF, trkB, trkC, CNTFR, PTN, PDGFa, FGFR, TGFR, Ins2, IGF I, IGFR1, CRAF, IP3R1, IP3R2, cyclin A, H2AZ, cjun, TCP, actin, DD63.2, SOD, CCO1, CCO2
2	MAP2, synaptophysin, neno, S100, pre-GAD67, GAD67, ACHE, GRa2, GRa3, GRa5, GRb1, GRg2, GRg3, mGluR3, mGluR5, mGluR7, NMDA1, NMDA2B, nAChRa7, mAChR2, 5HT1c, 5HT2, statin
3	L1, NFL, GAD65, NOS, GRa4, mGluR8, NMDA2D, nAChRa3, nAChRa4, mAChR3, 5HT1b, EGFR, InsR, SC2
4	mGluR4, NMDA2C, nAChRa2, EGF
5	GRb2, mGluR2, mGluR6, 5HT3
6	cellubrevin, nAChRa6, NT3, MK2, GDNF, PDGFR, IGF II, IGFR2, IP3R3, cyclin B, Brm, SC1
7	nAChRd, PDGFb, SC6
8	nestin, G67I80/86, G67I86, TH, nAChRa5, SC7
9	nAChRe, trk
10	keratin, Ins1
11	NFH, GFAP, MOG, ChAT, GRg1, mAChR4, bFGF, aFGF, cfos
12	NFM, mGluR1, NMDA2A, NGF

TABLE III
CORRELATION BETWEEN THE GENE CLUSTERS DISCOVERED BY ART-C 2A AND THE FUNCTIONAL GENE CATEGORIES IDENTIFIED THROUGH HUMAN INSPECTION. N IS THE TOTAL NUMBER OF GENES IN EACH CLUSTER. NM, NR, PS, DV ARE THE NUMBERS OF GENES IN FUNCTIONAL CATEGORY *Neuroglial Markers*, *Neurotransmitter Receptors*, *Peptide Signaling*, AND *Diverse* RESPECTIVELY. BOLDFACE NUMBERS IDENTIFY THE DOMINATE FUNCTIONAL CATEGORY IN EACH CLUSTER.

Cluster	N	Gene Class Distribution			
		NM	NR	PS	DV
1	29	3	2	**12**	**12**
2	23	7	**15**	0	1
3	14	4	**7**	2	1
4	4	0	**3**	1	0
5	4	0	**4**	0	0
6	12	1	1	**6**	4
7	3	0	1	1	1
8	6	**4**	1	0	1
9	2	0	1	1	0
10	2	1	0	1	0
11	9	**4**	2	2	1
12	4	1	**2**	1	0
Total	112	25	39	27	21

used in Yeung et al's recent work to evaluate their model-based clustering algorithm [18]. These evaluation measures are all based on the so-called *external* criteria, i.e. they require a *known optimal partition* of the data set as the reference result. Such an optimal partition however may not be available without extensive human knowledge on the problem domain. Therefore in our studies, we assess the clustering results through the distribution of the output clusters directly.

Since the target of clustering is to re-organize the input samples such that data points in the same cluster are more similar to each other than to points in a different cluster, it is natural to evaluate the intra-cluster homogeneity and the inter-cluster separation of the clustering output in a global fashion. We used two quantitative measures, namely *cluster compactness* and *cluster separation* for this purpose. The definitions of these two measures are summarized below. More discussions on these measures can be found in [9].

Cluster compactness

The cluster compactness measure is based on the generalized definition of the *variance* of a data set given by

$$v(\mathbf{X}) = \sqrt{\frac{1}{N}\sum_{i=1}^{N} d^2(\mathbf{x}_i, \overline{\mathbf{x}})} \quad (9)$$

where $d(\mathbf{x}_i, \mathbf{x}_j)$ is a distance metric between two vectors $\mathbf{x}_i$ and $\mathbf{x}_j$, N is the number of members in $\mathbf{X}$, and $\overline{\mathbf{x}} = \frac{1}{N}\sum_i \mathbf{x}_i$ is the mean of $\mathbf{X}$. The cluster compactness for the output clusters $\mathbf{c}_1, \mathbf{c}_2, \cdots, \mathbf{c}_C$ generated by a system is then defined as

$$Cmp = \frac{1}{C}\sum_i \frac{v(\mathbf{c}_i)}{v(\mathbf{X})} \quad (10)$$

where C is the number of clusters generated on the data set $\mathbf{X}$, $v(\mathbf{c}_i)$ is the variance of the cluster $\mathbf{c}_i$, and $v(\mathbf{X})$ is the variance of the data set $\mathbf{X}$.

Cluster separation

The cluster separation of a clustering system's output is defined by

$$Sep = \frac{1}{C(C-1)}\sum_{i=1}^{C}\sum_{j=1, j\neq i}^{C} \exp(-\frac{d^2(\mathbf{x}_{c_i}, \mathbf{x}_{c_j})}{2\sigma^2}) \quad (11)$$

where σ is a Gaussian constant, C is the number of clusters, $\mathbf{x}_{c_i}$ is the centroid of the cluster $\mathbf{c}_i$, and $d(\mathbf{x}_{c_i}, \mathbf{x}_{c_j})$ is the distance between the centroid of $\mathbf{c}_i$ and the centroid of $\mathbf{c}_j$.

It is understandable that for both measures, a smaller value indicates a better output quality.

B. Evaluation Paradigm

All the four clustering algorithms used a standard set of parameters. The reference clusters of K-Means and SOM were initialized with random vectors that slightly vary from the mean vector of the input set. Both K-Means and SOM utilized Euclidean distances. On SOM, different neighborhood degrees and various neighborhood decaying methods were tested. We obtained relatively faster convergence and marginally better quality when the neighborhood degree was zero. The results with such parameters are reported in this paper. Readers shall note that, as discussed in [6], with a zero neighborhood degree, SOM becomes equivalent to an online version of K-Means.

We utilized the Euclidean distance for the evaluation of cluster compactness (Cmp) and cluster separation (Sep). $2\sigma^2 = 1.0$ as in Equation 11 was used to simplify our evaluation. Multiple runs of experiments, each using randomly reshuffled sequence of input, are conducted in order to obtain a statistically valid comparison. t statistics was used to evaluate the statistical significance of our comparison observation when appropriate.

Note that a valid comparison of clustering systems using the two evaluation measures requires them to output the same (or at least comparable enough) number of clusters. In order to control the number of ART 2A output clusters, we manually tried various ρ values on one random input sequence, then used the ρ value which produced the pre-specified number of output clusters on this input sequence in the remaining runs. While the actual number of ART 2A output clusters may slightly vary from the pre-specified number using the same ρ value on different input sequences, we found the variance was within an acceptable level.

C. Data Sets

Our first batch of the experiments compared the performance of these four algorithms on two gene expression data sets, namely the yeast cell cycle data set (YEAST) and the human hematopoietic differentiation data set with features under mixed conditions (HL60_ U937_ NB4_ Jurkat).

The yeast cell cycle data set (YEAST) [1] consists of 6,601 gene expression data in 17 conditions. The 17 conditions are evenly divided into two panels, each one corresponding to a cell cycle, with the 9th condition as the intermediate point between the two cell cycles. Following a common procedure [15], we employed a variance filter to select genes with significant changes over conditions. The variance filter adjusted observation values into units range $[min, max]$ and eliminated genes which did not show a relative change of x times and an absolute change of y units across all conditions. Using the parameter settings $min = 20, max = 20,000, x = 3$, and $y = 150$, a sub-set of 1,109 genes was generated for use in our experiments. Expression levels were first normalized using the standard normal distribution with a mean of 0 and a standard variance of 1 within each panel. The intermediate 9th condition was excluded from our experiments for the ease of normalization. The remaining 16-dimensional vectors were further Euclidean normalized for our benchmark.

The human hematopoietic differentiation data set (HL60_ U937_ NB4_ Jurkat) [2], which consisted of 7,229 gene expression data in 17 conditions, was preprocessed with the same variance filter. Using settings $min = 20, max = 20,000, x = 3$, and $y = 100$, 1,423 genes passed through the variance filter. Expression levels were first normalized using the standard normal distribution over all conditions and then Euclidean normalized.

D. Results and Discussions

Both the two gene expression data sets are small scale, have a small number of features, and are densely distributed. Prior studies are capable of identifying a few number of expression patterns on these data sets only. Therefore on each data set, we set the target number of the output clusters to be relatively small. Table IV reports the four algorithms' cluster validity measures, together with the CPU time costs, when the target number of output clusters is 10 and 20 respectively.

[1] http://genomics.standford.edu.
[2] http://www-genome.wi.mit.edu/cgi-bin/cancer/datasets.cgi.

TABLE IV

EXPERIMENTAL RESULTS FOR ART-C 2A, ART 2A, SOM, AND K-MEANS ON THE YEAST AND THE HL60_U937_NB4_JURKAT DATA SETS, WHEN THE NUMBER OF CLUSTERS C WAS SET TO 10 AND 20. I, T, Cmp AND Sep INDICATE THE NUMBER OF LEARNING ITERATIONS, THE COST OF TRAINING TIME (IN ms), *cluster compactness* AND *cluster separation* RESPECTIVELY. ALL VALUES ARE SHOWN WITH THE MEAN AND THE STANDARD DEVIATION OVER TEN RUNS.

Method	I	T (ms)	Cmp	Sep
YEAST, $C = 10$				
ART-C 2A	2.6±0.5	12.0±4.2	**0.7469±0.0301**	0.1424±0.0057
ART 2A	2.0±0.0	10.0±0.0	0.7514±0.0135	**0.1408±0.0053**
SOM	7.9±1.4	52.1±10.3	0.7670±0.0071	0.1579±0.0044
K-Means	13.0±2.2	72.3±13.9	0.7583±0.0065	0.1639±0.0069
YEAST, $C = 20$				
ART-C 2A	3.0±0.0	19.0±8.9	0.7157±0.0107	**0.1587±0.0035**
ART 2A	3.0±0.0	18.0±4.2	0.7167±0.0123	0.1607±0.0024
SOM	14.3±0.9	196.5±14.6	0.6887±0.0250	0.1836±0.0048
K-Means	14.8±2.6	216.8±37.4	**0.6861±0.0136**	0.1858±0.0059
HL60_U937_NB4_Jurkat, $C = 10$				
ART-C 2A	2.6±0.5	11.0±3.2	0.7262±0.0316	0.1525±0.0073
ART 2A	2.0±0.0	10.0±0.0	0.7209±0.0161	**0.1462±0.0060**
SOM	10.3±1.8	84.8±16.5	**0.6983±0.0049**	0.1907±0.0033
K-Means	13.5±3.2	119.7±68.4	0.6985±0.0201	0.1963±0.0101
HL60_U937_NB4_Jurkat, $C = 20$				
ART-C 2A	3.0±0.0	23.0±4.8	0.6543±0.0192	**0.1675±0.0031**
ART 2A	3.0±0.0	20.0±4.7	0.6632±0.0197	0.1711±0.0048
SOM	17.0±2.6	279.7±45.6	0.6508±0.0194	0.2181±0.0090
K-Means	15.1±2.5	232.9±120.8	**0.6348±0.0123**	0.2174±0.0089

In all the four batches of experiments, the cluster validity measures produced by ART-C 2A, in terms of both cluster compactness and cluster separation, were very similar to those of ART 2A. Specifically, t-test did not suggest any significant difference between our observations on each evaluation measure. It is interesting that the performances of SOM and K-Means were rather similar to each other as well. This is surprising as some prior studies reported that SOM was notably worse than K-Means [6]. We should highlight that the good performance of SOM may be due to our use of zero neighborhood in the controlled experiments, which was extensively discussed in [6]. It is also noted that the initial reference clusters affect the outputs of both K-Means and SOM significantly. In our experiments, we used the same strategy to initialize the reference clusters for K-Means and SOM. This also partly explains the similarities in their outputs.

In terms of cluster compactness, the validity measures of these four algorithms did not show significant differences in experiments on YEAST with $C = 10$ and HL60_ U937_ NB4_ Jurkat with $C = 20$, although K-Means produced slightly lower scores than the remaining trio on HL60_ U937_ NB4_ Jurkat with $C = 20$. However, for YEAST with $C = 20$ and HL60_ U937_ NB4_ Jurkat with $C = 10$, both SOM and K-Means produced significantly lower scores than those of ART-C 2A and ART 2A. In general, across these four batches of observations, the cluster compactness scores of K-Means were slightly lower than those of SOM and significantly lower than those of ART-C 2A and ART 2A in some of our experiments.

This sounds reasonable, as K-Means, which uses the global distribution of the data set to reduce the overall error, should tend to outperform competitive learning systems that look at the input patterns one at a time. In addition, ART-C 2A and ART 2A tend to encode noises and produce clusters of uneven sizes. This in turn decreases the compactness of the large output clusters.

In terms of cluster separation, the validity measures of both ART-C 2A and ART 2A were significantly lower than those of SOM and K-Means. It may be that, whereas SOM and K-Means modify existing, randomly initialized cluster prototypes to encode new samples, ART-C 2A and ART 2A adaptively inserts recognition categories to encode new input samples that are significantly distinct from existing prototypes. The distinct reference clusters in turn make the output clusters to be more dissimilar to each other. This unique neuron initialization mechanism appears to be effective in representing diverse data patterns in the input set.

To sum up, the output quality of all the three self-organizing networks are quite satisfactory, comparable to that of K-Means. ART-C 2A and ART 2A tend to produce clusters that are more separated from each other, with slightly compromised cluster compactness.

In terms of efficiency, ART-C 2A incurred slightly more computational cost than ART 2A. However, the difference was not significant. More importantly, both ART-C 2A and ART 2A showed a significantly higher efficiency than SOM and K-Means. In all experiments, SOM and K-Means used three to five times more iterations and CPU times than those of ART-C 2A and ART 2A.

In addition to the above observations, it is necessary to highlight that ART-C 2A has a higher usability than ART 2A in our opinion. Given an unknown gene expression collection, it is desirable that the number of output clusters generated by a system is within a human controllable scale (and preferably fixed) for the ease of human inspection. Specifically, ART-C 2A removes the trial-and-try process of ART 2A in estimating a proper vigilance parameter for this purpose.

VI. Conclusions and Future Work

We have presented a novel neural architecture known as ART-C (Adaptive Resonance Theory under Constraints) for efficient clustering of gene expression data. Through a serial of experiments on three real-life data sets, namely the rat CNS data set, the yeast cell cycle data set, and the human hematopoietic differentiation data set, we compared the performance of ART-C with those of K-Means, SOM, and conventional ART. Our studies and comparative experiments on the three data sets indicate that:

- Through clustering of gene expressions, ART-C is capable of identifying inherent knowledge on functional groupings with a satisfactory level of quality. In addition, ART-C showed a high capability of identifying subtle differences between two pattern sets.
- Compared with SOM and K-Means, ART 2A and ART-C 2A showed a notably higher clustering efficiency. This is a crucial advantage for mining large scale gene expression data.
- Compared with ART 2A, ART-C 2A could have a greater ease of use for gene clustering, due to its capability of allowing the user to directly control the number of output cluster.

Our studies so far on several well-known data sets have produced satisfactory results, with respect to prior biological work. It would be interesting for biologists to apply these algorithms to *new* gene expression collections and explore what *new knowledge* can be discovered.

References

[1] Y. Barash and N. Friedman. Context-specific bayesian clustering for gene expression data. In *The Fifth Annual International Conference on Computational Molecular Biology (RECOMB)*, pages 12–21, 2001.

[2] A. Ben-Dor, R. Shamir, and Z. Yakhini. Clustering gene expression patterns. *Journal of Computational Biology*, 6(3/4):281–297, 1999.

[3] G. Carpenter and S. Grossberg. A massively parallel architecture for a self-organizing neural pattern recognition machine. *Computer Vision, Graphics, and Image processing*, 34:54–115, 1987.

[4] G. Carpenter, S. Grossberg, and D. Rosen. ART 2-A: An adaptive resonance algorithm for rapid category learning and recognition. *Neural Networks*, 4:493–504, 1991.

[5] M. Eisen, P. Spellman, D. Botstein, and P. Brown. Cluster analysis and display of genome-wide expression patterns. In *Proceedings of National Academy of Science USA*, volume 95, pages 14863–14867, 1998.

[6] A. Flexer. Limitations of self-organizing maps for vector quantization and multidimensional scaling. *Advances in Neural Information Processing Systems 9.*, pages 445–451, 1997.

[7] S. Grossberg. Adaptive pattern classification and universal recoding. I. parallel development and coding of neural feature detector. *Biological Cybernetics*, 23:121–134, 1976.

[8] J. He, A. Tan, and C. Tan. ART-C: A neural architecture for self-organization under constraints. In *Proceedings of International Joint Conference on Neural Networks (IJCNN)*, pages 2550–2555, 2002.

[9] J. He, A. Tan, C. Tan, and S. Sung. On quantitative evaluation of clustering systems. In W. Wu and H. Xiong, editors, *Information Retrieval and Clustering*. Kluwer Academic Publishers, 2002. in press.

[10] J. Herrero, A. Valencia, and J. Dopazo. A hierarchical unsupervised growing neural network for clustering gene expression patterns. *Bioinformatics*, 17(2):126–136, 2001.

[11] A. Jain and R. Dubes. *Algorithms for Clustering Data*. Prentice-Hall, Upper Saddle River, NJ, 1988.

[12] T. Kohonen. *Self-Organization and Associative Memory*. Springer-Verlag, Berlin, second edition, 1997.

[13] N. Luscombe, D. Greenbaum, and M. Gerstein. What is bioinformatics? An introduction and overview. *Yearbook of Medical Informatics*, pages 83–100, 2001.

[14] G. Michaels, D. Carr, M. Askenazi, S. Fuhrman, X. Wen, and R. Somogyi. Cluster analysis and data visualization of large-scale gene expression data. In *Pacific Symposium on Biocomputing*, 3, pages 42–53, 1998.

[15] P. Tamayo, D. Slonim, J. Mesirov, Q. Zhu, S. Kitareewan, E. Dmitrovsky, E. Lander, and T. Golub. Interpreting patterns of gene expression with self-organizing maps: Methods and application to homatopoietc differentiation. In *Proceedings of the National Academy of Science*, volume 96, pages 2907–2912, 1999.

[16] J. Tou and R. Gonzalez. *Pattern Recognition Principles*. Addison-Wesley, Massachusetts, 1974.

[17] X. Wen, S. Fuhrman, G. Michaels, D. Carr, S. Smith, G. Barker, and R. Somogyi. Large-scale temporal gene expression mapping of central nervous system development. In *Proceedings of the National Academy of Science*, pages 334–339, 1998.

[18] K. Yeung, C. Fraley, A. Raftery, and W. Ruzzo. Model-based clustering and data transformations for gene expression data. *Bioinformatics*, 17(10):977–987, 2001.

[19] K. Yeung, D. Haynor, and W. Ruzzo. Validating clustering for gene expression data. Technical Report UW-CSE-00-01-01, Department of Computer Science and Engineering, University of Washington, January 2000.

Membership Scoring via Independent Feature Subspace Analysis for Grouping Co-Expressed Genes

Heyjin Kim, Seungjin Choi, Sung-Yang Bang
Dept. of Computer Science and Engineering
POSTECH
San 31 Hyoja-dong, Nam-gu
Pohang 790-784, Korea
Email: {marisan, seungjin, sybang}@postech.ac.kr

Abstract—Linear decomposition models such as principal component analysis (PCA) and independent component analysis (ICA) were shown to be useful in analyzing high dimensional DNA microarray data, compared to clustering methods. Assuming that gene expression is controlled by a linear combination of uncorrelated/indepdendent latent variables, linear modes were shown to be related to some biological functions. However, grouping co-expressed genes using these methods is not quite successful since they take some biological dependence into account. In this paper, we employ the independent feature subspace analysis (IFSA) method [8] which finds phase- and shift-invariant features. We propose a new membership scoring method based on invariant features from IFSA and show its usefulness in grouping functionally-related genes in the presence of time-shift and expression phase variance. This is confirmed through *PathCalling*.

I. Introduction

Current DNA microarray technology produces a huge amount of high dimensional data and enables us to measure the expression levels of thousands of genes simultaneously. One interesting task in microarray data analysis is to monitor gene expression levels while a cell undergoes some biological process, in order to find co-expressed genes. One of exemplary data might be the yeast *Saccharomyces cerevisiae* whose genome sequences were revealed and the Open Reading Frames (ORFs) were already determined. Chu *et al.* [4] and Spellman *et al.* [14] studied cell cycle behavior using the microarray technique to analyze the roles of specific genes in the process.

A variety of methods have been employed for the analysis and interpretation of gene expression data. These include: (1) clustering methods such as hierarchical clustering and self-organizing map; (2) linear decomposition models such as PCA and ICA. Recently it was shown that linear models-based methods (especially ICA-based methods) are useful in DNA microarray data analysis [7], [10], [11], [13]. Linear models describe the expression levels of genes as linear functions of latent variables (hidden variables) which might be related to distinct biological causes of variation such as regulators of gene expression, cellular functions, or responses to experimental treatments [10]. Martoglio *et al.* [11] suggested to use a linear model in which each gene can participate, to varying degrees, in many independent patterns of covariation since each gene is expected to be influenced by several transcription factors, each of which influences several genes.

Grouping co-expressed genes is an important task [5] because co-expressed genes help us to explore regulatory networks, to find transcription factor binding sites, or to discover a certain biological function of a gene. Linear model methods find linear modes and influences. These linear modes are served as prototype patterns in order to find co-expressed genes. This is carried out through pattern matching. However a simple pattern matching is not always successful in grouping co-expressed genes. In a co-regulated system, some genes that are functionally related, do not share similar patterns and genes which do not have functional relations, show similar patterns. This is why grouping co-expressed genes is a difficult problem.

In this paper we take a close look at some biological dependency that linear model-based methods (such as PCA, ICA, and Bayes Decomposition) [10]–[13] overlooked. To this end, we employ the independent feature subspace analysis (IFSA) that was originally developed by Hyvärinen and Hoyer [8] in order to study a computational model for a complex cell in V1 (primary visual cortex). Since IFSA finds phase- and shift-invariant features, it is expected to grouping slightly time-delayed patterns as well as exactly matched pattern. Here we propose a new method for grouping co-expressed genes, which is based on membership scoring based on invariant features from IFSA. The usefulness of our method is verified by PathCalling and experimental evidence in [3], [6], [16].

II. Methods

A. Independent Feature Subspace Analysis

Linear decomposition model assumes that the data matrix $X = [x_{ij}]$ (where the element x_{ij} represents the expression level of gene i in the jth sample, $i = 1, \ldots, m, j = 1, \ldots, N$) is modelled as

$$X = SA, \qquad (1)$$

where $S \in \mathbb{R}^{m \times n}$ is a matrix consisting of latent variables and the row vectors of $A \in \mathbb{R}^{n \times N}$ are basis vectors (corresponding to *linear modes* in [10]).

ICA aims at finding a representation (1) with latent variables (contained in the columns of S) being statistically independent. The statistical independence among latent variables is a key assumption (as well as a limitation) in ICA. Multidimensional ICA [2] generalized the ICA by allowing

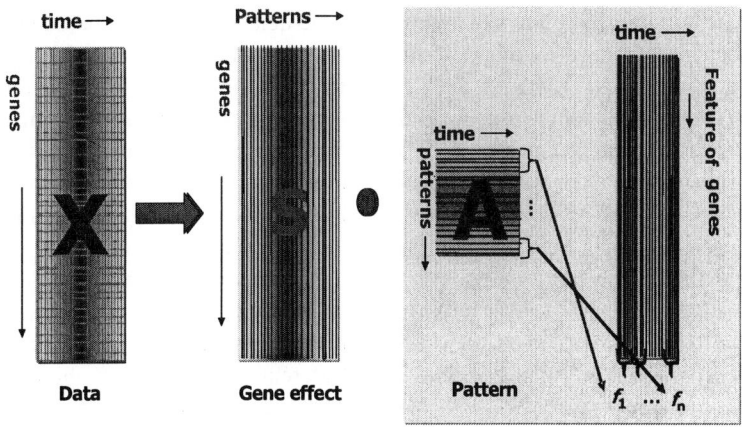

Fig. 1. The microarray data matrix X is decomposed into a product of two matrices S (gene effect) and A (linear modes). Invariant feature patterns $\{f_j\}_{j=1}^J$ (computed by (2)) play a critical role in grouping similar patterns with preserving shift- and phase-invariance.

the components in a p-tuple to be dependent but requiring different p-tuples to be independent. The IFSA [8] embedded the invariant feature subspaces in multidimensional ICA by considering the probability distributions for the p-tuples of latent variables that are spherically symmetric, i.e., depend only on the norm (see Fig. 1 for pictorial elucidation of IFSA as well as linear decomposition model). In contrast to ICA, the IFSA aims at finding a linear transformation W (which corresponds to the inverse system of A) such that feature subspaces (obtained by taking square root of sum of energy of responses) become independent but components in a feature subspace is allowed to be dependent.

We assume that the data matrix X is already whitened. In other words, the row vectors of A are confined to be orthogonal each other and to be normalized to have unit norm. Non-orthogonal factor is reflected in a whitening transform. In order to avoid an abuse of notations, we use the notation X for the whitened data matrix.

Let's denote by x_i, the ith row vector of X and by w_i, the ith column vector of W (which is the inverse system of A). Note that w_i corresponds to the ith row vector of A since orthogonal basis vectors are considered here. We consider the case where latent variables are divided into J number of p-tuples (where p represents the dimension of subspace). For the sake of simplicity, we assume identical dimension, p for every feature subspace. The jth feature subspace is denoted by $\mathcal{F}_j$. The value $f_j(x)$ in $\mathcal{F}_j$ with data vector x is given by

$$f_j(\boldsymbol{x}) = \sum_{i \in \mathcal{F}_j} \langle \boldsymbol{w}_i, \boldsymbol{x} \rangle^2, \qquad (2)$$

where $\langle \cdot, \cdot \rangle$ is the inner product. In fact $f_j(x)$ is a pooled energy.

With these notations, we can write the log-likelihood $\mathcal{L}$ of the data given the model as

$$\begin{aligned}\mathcal{L} &= \sum_{t=1}^{m}\sum_{j=1}^{J} \log p\left(\sum_{i \in \mathcal{F}_j} \langle \boldsymbol{w}_i, \boldsymbol{x}_t \rangle^2\right) \\ &\quad + m \log |\det \boldsymbol{W}|,\end{aligned} \qquad (3)$$

where $p\left(\sum_{i \in \mathcal{F}_j} s_i^2\right) = p_j(s_i, i \in \mathcal{F}_j)$ $(s_i = \langle \boldsymbol{w}_i, \boldsymbol{x} \rangle)$ represents the probability density inside the jth p-tuple of s_i.

The IFSA finds a linear transform W which maximizes the log-likelihood (3). Learning independent feature subspaces is carried out by a stochastic gradient ascent method, whose updating rule has the form

$$\Delta \boldsymbol{w}_i \propto \boldsymbol{x} \langle \boldsymbol{w}_i, \boldsymbol{x} \rangle \varphi\left(\sum_{r \in \mathcal{F}_{j(i)}} \langle \boldsymbol{w}_r, \boldsymbol{x} \rangle^2\right), \qquad (4)$$

where $j(i)$ is the index of the feature subspace which w_i belongs to and φ is the score function, i.e., $\varphi = \frac{p'}{p}$. More details on IFSA (including the description of hypothesize density p) can be found in [8].

B. Membership Scoring for Clustering

Linear model-based methods (such as Bayes Decomposition, PCA, and ICA) showed that linear modes (corresponding to basis vectors) might be related with certain biological functions such as phases of cell cycle or mating response, etc. [10], [12], [13]. For instance, Liebermeister [10] showed that linear modes that are estimated by ICA match B-cell activation and Lymph node, and so on. However these methods do not take some dependency among biological patterns into account. Here we focus on some connections between related functions with close time intervals and made a group of functionally linked patterns.

In contrast to ICA-based methods where only the influence of gene (S) was exploited for grouping similar patterns, we introduce a method of membership scoring which is described in details below. We normalize each row vector of the gene influence matrix S using l_1 norm and denote the resulting matrix by $\widetilde{S} = [\tilde{s}_{ij}]$. In other words, each row vector in $\widetilde{S}$ has unit l_1 norm. The feature value (which results from spatial pooling) $f_{ik} = \sum_{l \in \mathcal{F}_k} \langle w_l, x_i \rangle^2$ is also normalized over k. This normalized feature values are denoted by $\tilde{f}_{ik}$. With these normalized gene influences and feature values, we compute a membership scoring values ψ_{ik} by

$$\psi_{ik} = \tilde{f}_{ik} |\tilde{s}_{ij}|, \quad k = 1, \ldots, J \quad (5)$$

For each gene, J possible membership scoring values, $\{\psi_{i1}, \ldots, \psi_{iJ}\}$ are computed. Then, a maximal membership scoring, ψ_i^{max} is calculated over k, i.e.,

$$\psi_i^{max} = \max_k \psi_{ik}, \quad (6)$$

This maximal membership scoring ψ_i^{max} indicates an appropriate cluster that the ith gene is expected to belong to. In order to filter out some irrelevant genes, we threshold out genes which have relatively very low maximal membership scoring values. The level of threshold is decided, depending on how many relevant genes we want to group together.

Our results (see Sec. III) confirm that this new membership scoring method well explain the relationship between linked genes (that were already revealed by many experiments in biology domain)

III. RESULTS

We apply our membership scoring method based on IFSA to the yeast cell cycle data from Spellman *et al.* [14], which contains the expression of 6178 ORFs during the cell replication cycle in the budding yeast *Saccaromyces cerevisiae*. This data set contains 77 tissue samples in different experimental conditions such as α factor pheromone, cdc15, cdc28, elucidation, and so on.

Throughout several subsets of data, we confirm that our method is quite useful in grouping co-expressed genes. We also compared our results to PCA- or ICA-based methods, but due to the space limitation we do not include comparison results. These comparison results can be found in our supplement web site [1]. In grouping co-expressed genes, our method was quite successful, whereas PCA- or ICA-based methods were not. For fair comparison, we pre-processed the data by time warping [1], [9] and spline interpolation before we apply our method as well as ICA.

One of useful property in IFSA is that it finds a shift- and phase-invariant features. In gene expression time series, this invariant property produces a set of profiles containing slightly time-delayed patterns or some contrary patterns that show direction opposite to a main direction in a group. This invariance property is a key ingredient to our successful grouping, compared to previous linear model-based methods. In order to take this invariance property into account, we include slightly time-delayed patterns or some contrary patterns as well as exactly matched patterns in a group of co-expressed patterns. In other words, we let IFSA to find a statistical structure of gene expression data in an unsupervised fashion and rely on this result for grouping co-expressed genes. It turns out that this approach is able to consider some biological dependence in a task of grouping, whereas ICA-based methods do not take into account.

In general, it is not easy to interpret functional relations among several tens of genes. Hence we take a small size of data so that the interpretation become easier. We use 4 different test data sets (which is summarized in Table I). For graphical representation for gene interactions in test data sets in Table I, we used a web interface software, *PathCalling* [16], which provides information on putative protein interactions identified in the screens or reported in the literature. The output of PathCalling is remodelled in a form of undirected graph (see Fig. 2). Each node represents a gene and edges offer insight into novel interactions between proteins involved in the identical biological function.

Experiment 1: In the first experiment, we used the Test Data Set 1 and decomposed it into two groups (i.e., $J = 2$) with each group having two components ($p = 2$) by IFSA. The result is summarized in Table II. Every gene associated with the 1st component in Group 1 has its peak at G1 phase. Functions in group 1 mainly focus on DNA replication and G1/S cyclin. On the other hand, the genes in Group 2 are involved with G2/M cyclin. In this experiment we used a threshold value in the range between 10^{-4} and 10^{-5}. This threshold value is used in the rest of experiments.

Experiment 2: In this experiment, we investigated the effect of an extraneous gene YLR190W (which does not have any functional relation with other genes in the data set) whether our method is influenced by this artifact-like gene or not. The result summarized in Table III shows this unrelated gene is excluded, i.e., its maximal membership score value is below the threshold. The Data Set 2 was decomposed into three groups with dimension 2 (i.e., $J = 3$, $p = 2$). Genes associated with the 1st component in Group 1 are Pho85 cyclin family (PCL family) which activates Pho85 as a CDK [15]. PCL1, PCL2 and PCL9 are the only members expressed in a cell cycle-regulated pattern; PCL9 is activated by the transcription factor SWI5 and PCL1/PCL2 by SBF. One interesting point in this experiment is in PHO85. The gene PHO85 plays an important role in Group 3, the analysis method based on gene phase pattern (which is quite common method in the study of cell cycles) has difficulty in grouping this gene from only phase).

Experiment 3: In this experiment, we used Test Data Set 3 which contains all the genes in Test Data 1 and some other genes (see Table IV). Like the Experiment 1, we decomposed the data into 2 groups with dimension 2. The result is summarized in Table IV. We observed that our proposed

[1] http://home.postech.ac.kr/~marisan/Bioinformatics/ISAcycle.htm

TABLE I
DATA SETS USED IN EXPERIMENT 1-4. EACH DATA SET CONTAINS A SET OF GENES WHICH HAVE SOME INTERACTIONS. ONLY ONE GENE YLR190W (UNDERLINED) DOES NOT HAVE ANY RELATION WITH OTHER GENES. THESE DATA SETS ARE USED TO TEST THE VALIDITY OF OUR METHOD.

Data Set	Set I	Set II	Set III	Set IV
Gene Names (SGD)	CDC2 CDC6 CLB1 CLB2 CLB4 CLN1 CLN2 ELM1 POL32 SIC1	PCL9 SWI5 PCL2 DBF2 RDH54 TID3 PCL7 PHO85 PCL1 <u>YLR190W</u>	CDC2 CDC5 CDC6 CDC9 CLB1 CLB2 CLB4 CLN1 CLN2 CLN3 DBF2 ELM1 HYS2 POL1 POL32 SIC1 SPT16	CDC2 CDC5 CDC6 CDC9 CLB1 CLB2 CLB4 CLN1 CLN2 CLN3 DBF2 ELM1 HYS2 PCL1 PCL2 PCL7 PCL9 PHO85 POL1 POL32 RDH54 SIC1 SPT16 SWI5 TID3 <u>YLR190W</u>

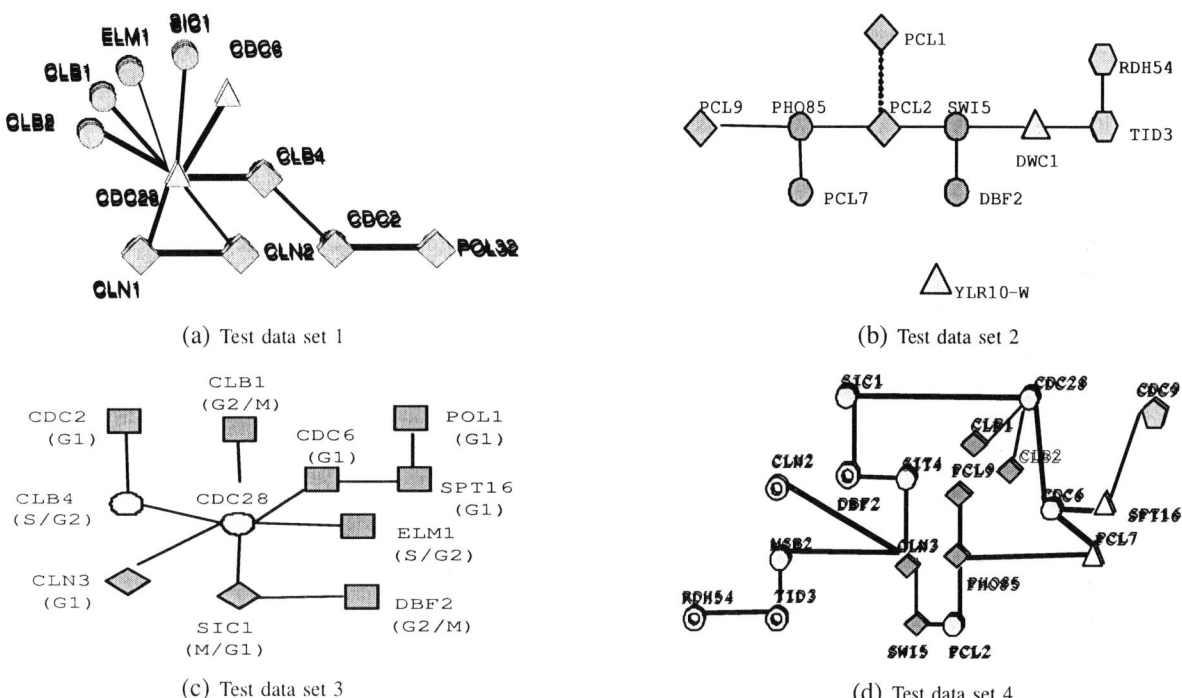

Fig. 2. Undirected graphical representation for gene interaction in each test data set summarized in Table I: (a) In test data set 1, circle and diamond indicate two different groups, mainly CLB families and CLN families, respectively. Triangle shape corresponds to genes that do not belong to anywhere.; (b) In addition to circle, diamond, and triangle (which represent the same meaning as those in (a)), two hexagons indicate another group, most of which are PCL families and their regulatory genes; (c) Square and diamond indicate two different groups and circle-shaped nodes represent genes that do not belong to these two groups. The erroneous gene DBF2 connected with CLN3 and SIC1 (a protein inhibitor), belong to another group, members of which function as a protein kinase; (d) Nodes with different shapes (except for circle-shaped nodes) represent different groups. The circle-shaped nodes indicate the genes which do not belong to any group. In Experiment 4, some genes belonging to the same group were successfully grouped by our method.

method were able to identify some contrary profiles that are usually considered as different patterns in existing methods. Expression profiles associated with genes POL1, CDC2, and CDC6, are in the opposite directions to those of ELM1, CLB1 and DBF2 (see Fig. the expression profiles for CLN3 and SIC 1 which were known to have similar patterns and to have peaks at G2/M and M/G1, respectively.

Experiment 4: The Test Data Set 4 contains genes in Test Data Set 1-3. Although we increased the data size, grouping based on our method was preserved. See the result in Table V. For instance, genes SWI5 and PHO85 were grouped together both in Experiment 2 and in Experiment 4.

IV. DISCUSSION

In this paper, we proposed a new method of grouping co-expressed genes using the membership scoring based on IFSA. In contrast to ICA-based methods, IFSA employed a linear decomposition with spatial pooling so that invariant features could be obtained. The invariant features (which are pooled energy) was nicely incorporated into our membership scoring. Our simulation results showed that the proposed method well matched the relationship between linked genes that were already known in biology community.

TABLE II

RESULT IN EXPERIMENT 1: CLB FAMILY, CLN FAMILY, AND SOME RELATED GENES.

Group	peak	ψ_i^{max}	SGD	Process	Function
1-1	G1	0.02239	CDC2	DNA replication	DNA polymerase δ catalytic 125kd subunit
	G1	0.03510	POL32	DNA replication	polymerase δ 55kd subunit
	G1	0.01233	CLN2	cell cycle	G1/S cyclin
1-2	G1	0.00195	CLN1	cell cycle	G1/S cyclin
2-1	S/G2	0.12880	ELM1	growth	protein kinase
	G2/M	0.00187	CLB1	cell cycle	G2/M cyclin
	G2/M	0.01579	CLB2	cell cycle	G2/M cyclin
	M/G1	0.07794	SIC1	cell cycle	Cdc28p-Clb5 protein kinase inhibitor

TABLE III

RESULT IN EXPERIMENT 2: EXTRANEOUS GENE, YLR10W AND PCL FAMILY.

Group	peak	ψ_i^{max}	SGD	Process	Function
1-1	G1	0.01790	PCL2	cell cycle	G1/S cyclin
	G1	0.00236	PCL1	cell cycle	G1/S cyclin
	M/G1	0.00152	PCL9	cell cycle	cyclin (Pho85p)
2-2	G1	0.00407	RDH54	meiosis	helicase
	S	0.00272	TID3	unknown	unknown
3-2	S/G2	0.01063	PCL7	cell cycle	cyclin
	G2/M	0.00060	SWI5	cell cycle	transcription factor, regulates HO
	G2/M	0.00212	DBF2	cell cycle	late mitosis; protein kinase
	U	0.00349	PHO85	cell cycle	cyclin-dependent protein kinase

TABLE IV

RESULT IN EXPERIMENT 3: PROTEIN KINASE VERSUS PROTEIN KINASE INHIBITOR.

Group	peak	ψ_i^{max}	SGD	Process	Function
1-1	G1	0.00057	SPT16	chromatin structure	non-histone protein
1-2	G1	0.21248	POL1	DNA replication	polymerase α 180kd subunit
	G1	0.00068	CDC2	DNA replication	polymerase δ 125kd subunit
	M/G1	0.00188	CDC6	DNA replication	pre-initiation complex formation
	S/G2	0.06263	ELM1	pseudohyphal growth	protein kinase
	G2/M	0.00116	CLB1	cell cycle	G2/M cyclin
	G2/M	0.01169	DBF2	cell cycle	late mitosis; protein kinase
2-1	G2/M	0.07817	CLN3	cell cycle	G1/S cyclin
	M/G1	0.03980	SIC1	cell cycle	Cdc28p-Clb5 protein kinase inhibitor

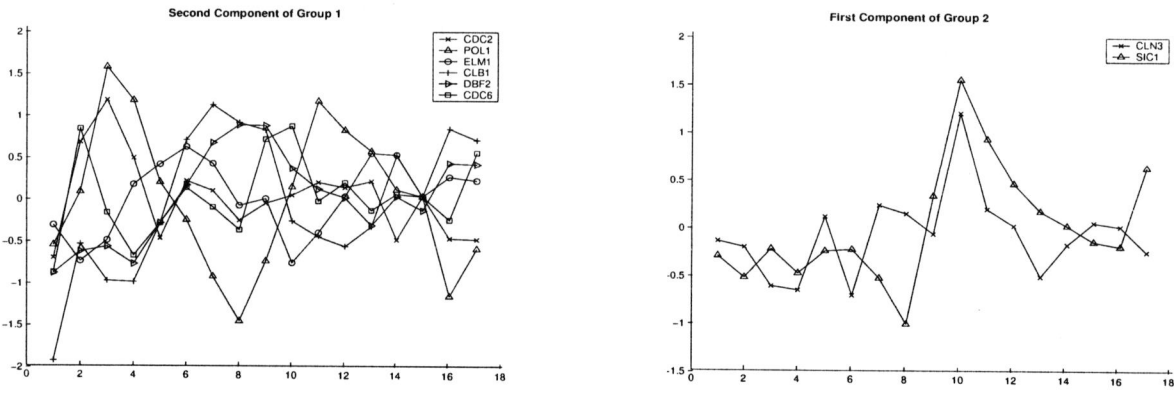

(a) Expression profiles which correspond to the second component in group 1. (b) Expression profiles which correspond to the first component in group 2.

Fig. 3. Expression Profiles in Experiment 3.

TABLE V
RESULT IN EXPERIMENT 4

Group	peak	ψ_i^{max}	SGD	Process	Function
2-2	G1	0.00240	SPT16	chromatin structure	non-histone protein
	S/G2	0.00278	PCL7	cell cycle	cyclin
3-1	G1	0.00146	CLN2	cell cycle	G1/S cyclin
	G1	0.00056	RDH54	meiosis	helicase
	S	0.00467	TID3	unknown	unknown
	G2/M	0.00190	DBF2	cell cycle	late mitosis, protein kinase
4-1	G1	0.00655	CDC9	DNA replication/repair	DNA ligase
6-1	G2/M	0.00181	CLN3	cell cycle	G1/S cyclin
	G2/M	0.00108	SWI5	G1 cell cycle	transcription factor, regulates HO
	U	0.00857	PHO85	cell cycle	cyclin-dependent protein kinase
6-2	G2/M	0.00087	CLB1	cell cycle	G2/M cyclin
	G2/M	0.00096	CLB2	cell cycle	G2/M cyclin
	M/G1	0.01411	PCL9	cell cycle	cyclin (Pho85p)

ACKNOWLEDGMENT

Authors would like to thank A. Hyvärinen and P. Hoyer for sharing their IFSA code. Portion of this work was carried out when S. Choi visited Advanced Brain Signal Processing Lab in RIKEN, Japan. This work was supported by Basic Science Research Center, POSTECH, by Korea Ministry of Science and Technology under Brain Science and Engineering Research Program and an International Cooperative Research Project, and by Ministry of Education of Korea for its financial support toward the Electrical and Computer Engineering Division at POSTECH through its BK21 program.

REFERENCES

[1] J. Aach and G. M. Church, "Aligning gene expression time series with time warping algorithms," *Bioinformatics*, vol. 17, no. 6, pp. 495–508, 2001.
[2] J. F. Cardoso, "Multidimensional independent component analysis," in *Proc. ICASSP*, Seattle, WA, 1998.
[3] J. M. Cherry, C. Ball, S. Weng, G. Juvik, R. Schmidt, C. Adler, B. Dunn, S. Dwight, L. Riles, R. K. Mortimer, and D. Botstein, "Genetic and physicalmaps of *saccharomyces cerevisiae*," *Nature*, vol. 387, pp. 67–73, May 1997.
[4] R. J. Cho, M. J. Campbell, E. A. Winzeler, L. Steinmetz, A. Conway, L. Wodicka, T. G. Wolfsberg, A. E. Gabrielian, D. Landsman, D. J. Lcokhart, and R. W. Davis, "A genome-wide transcriptional analysis of the mitotic cell cycle," *Mol. Cell*, vol. 2, pp. 65–73, 1998.
[5] L. J. Heyer, S. Kruglyak, and S. Yooseph, "Exploring expression data: Identification and analysis of coexpressed genes," *Genome Res.*, vol. 9, pp. 1106–1115, 1999.
[6] Y. Ho, A. Gruhler, A. Hellbut, G. D. Bader, L. Moore, S. L. Adams, A. Millar, P. Taylor, K. Bennett, K. Boutillier, L. Yang, C. Wolting, I. Donaldson, S. Schandorff, J. Shewarane, M. Vo, J. Taggart, M. Goudreault, B. Muskat, C. Alfarano, D. Dewar, Z. Lin, K. Michalickova, A. R. Willems, H. Sassi, P. A. Nielsen, K. J. Rasmussen, J. R. Andersen, L. E. Johansen, L. H. Hansen, H. Jespersen, A. Fodtelejnikov, E. Nielsen, J. Crawford, V. Poulsen, B. D. Serensen, J. Matthiesen, R. C. Hendrickson, F. Gleeson, T. Pawson, M. F. Moran, D. Durocher, M. Mann, C. W. V. Hogue, D. Figeys, and M. Tyers, "Systematic identification of protein complexes in *saccharomyces cerevisiae* by mass spectrometry," *Nature*, vol. 315, no. 10, pp. 180–183, Jan. 2002.
[7] G. Hori, M. Inoue, S. Nishimura, and H. Nakahara, "Blind gene classification based on ICA of microarray data," in *Proc. ICA*, San Diego, California, 2001.
[8] A. Hyvärinen and P. O. Hoyer, "Emergence of phase and shift invariant features by decomposition of natural images into independent feature subspaces," *Neural Computation*, vol. 12, no. 7, pp. 1705–1720, 2000.
[9] E. Keogh and M. Pazzani, "Derivative dynamic time warping," in *Proc. SIAM Int. Conf. Data Mining*, 2001.
[10] W. Liebermeister, "Linear modes of gene expression determined by independent component analysis," *Bioinformatics*, vol. 18, no. 1, pp. 51–60, 2002.
[11] A. M. Martoglio, J. W. Minskin, S. K. Smith, and D. J. C. MacKay, "A decomposition model to track gene expression signatures: Preview on observer-independent classification of ovarian cancer," *Bioinformatics*, vol. 18, no. 12, pp. 1617–1624, 2002.
[12] T. D. Moloshok, R. R. Klevecz, J. D. Grant, F. J. Manion, W. F. S. IV, and M. F. Ochs, "Application of bayesian decomposition for analysing microarray data," *Bioinformatics*, vol. 18, no. 4, pp. 566–575, 2002.
[13] S. Raychaudhuri, J. M. Stuart, and R. B. Altman, "Principal components analysis to summarize microarray experiments: Application to sporulation time series," in *Proc. Pacific Symp. Biocomputing*, 2000, pp. 452–463.
[14] P. T. Spellman, G. Sherlock, M. Q. Zhang, V. R. Iyer, K. Anders, M. B. Eisen, P. O. Brown, D. Botstein, and B. Futcher, "Comprehensive identification of cell cycle-regulated genes of the yeast *saccharomyces cerevisiae* by microarray hybridization," *Molecular Biology of the Cell*, vol. 9, pp. 3273–3297, Dec. 1998.
[15] C. N. Tennyson, J. Lee, and B. J. Andrews, "A role for the Pcl9-Pho85 cyclin-cdk complex at the M/G_1 boundary in *saccharomyces cerevisiae*," *Molecular Microbiology*, vol. 28, no. 1, pp. 69–79, 1998.
[16] P. Uetz, L. Gilot, G. Cagney, T. A. Mansfield, R. S. Judson, J. R. Knight, D. Lockshon, V. Narayan, M. Srinivasan, P. Pochart, A. Qureshi-Emili, Y. Li, B. Godwin, D. Conover, T. Kalbfleisch, G. Vijayadamodar, M. Yang, M. Johnston, S. Fields, and M. Rothberg, "A comprehensive analysis of protein-protein interactions in *saccharomyces cerevisiae*," *Nature*, vol. 403, pp. 623–631, Feb. 2000.

Probabilistic Neural Networks for Multi-class Tissue Discrimination with Gene Expression Data

Rui Xu and Donald C. Wunsch II
Applied Computational Intelligence Laboratory
Dept. of Electrical and Computer Engineering
University of Missouri - Rolla
Rolla, MO 65409-0249 USA
rxu@umr.edu, dwunsch@ece.umr.edu

Abstract – With the emergence and rapid advancement of DNA microarray technologies, construction of gene expression profiles for different cancer types has already become a promising means for cancer diagnosis and treatment. Most previous research has focused on binary classification. Here, we use a probabilistic neural network (PNN) for multi-classification of cancer data. The experimental results demonstrate the effectiveness of the PNN in addressing gene expression data.

I INTRODUCTION

With the emergence and rapid advancement of DNA microarray technologies [1-2], cancer classification through identifying the corresponding gene expression profiles has already attracted numerous efforts from a wide variety of research communities [3-16]. Cancer classification is important to the subsequent diagnosis and treatment. Without the correct identification of cancer types, it is rarely possible to provide useful therapies and achieve expecting effects. Traditional classification methods are largely dependent on morphological appearance of tumors, and their applications are limited by the existing uncertainties [3]. Tumors with similar appearance may have quite different origins and therefore respond differently for the same treatment therapy. For example, in diffuse large B-cell lymphoma (DLBCL), almost half of clinical cases fail to the treatment due to the existence of unknown subtypes that cannot be discriminated by their morphologic parameters [4]. DNA microarray technologies offer caner researchers a new way to investigate the pathologies of cancer from the molecular angle, and further, to make more accurate predictions in prognosis and treatment.

There exist different types of microarray technologies based on the nature of the attached DNA (cDNA with length varying from several hundred to thousand bases or oligonucleotides containing 20-30 bases). For cDNA technologies, a microarray consists of a solid substrate to which a large amount of cDNA clones are attached according to some certain order [1]. Fluorescently labeled cDNA, obtained from RNA samples of interest (e.g. tumor samples) through the process of reverse transcription, is hybridized with the array. A reference sample (e.g. normal samples) with a different fluorescent label is also required for the purpose of comparison. Image analysis techniques are then used to measure the fluorescence of each dye after the genes are washed off. The resulting ratio reflects relative levels of gene expression. For high-density oligonucleotide microarray, oligonucleotides are fixed on a chip through techniques like photolithography and solid-phase DNA synthesis [2]. With a wealth of gene expression data at hand, researchers have more opportunities, while inevitably facing new challenges. Gene expression data sets usually have features like high dimensionality, high redundancy and inherent noise, which ask for the computational analysis methods to have corresponding mechanism to deal with them. Research on gene expression data is summarized in three levels, according to the task complexity [17]. The bottom level investigates the activities of single genes under different conditions or tissues. The second level focuses on the relations and interactions among genes and conditions. The top level attempts to infer the whole genetic network that finally determines all the patterns we observed. The tumor classification researches based on gene expression data can be classified into the intermediate level, which explores the relations between types of tumors and gene markers.

This kind of research has already been reported in the literature with promising results [3-16]. Golub et al. deemed cancer classification as two challenges: class discovery and class prediction and used several strategies, including weighted voting, neighborhood analysis and self-organizing feature maps (SOFMs) to discriminate two types of human acute leukemias (ALL vs. AML) [3]. According to their results, two subsets of acute lymphoblastic leukemia (ALL), with different origin of lineage, are also well separated. Alizadeh et al. distinguished two molecularly distinct subtypes of diffuse large B-cell lymphoma by their gene expression profiles [4]. Alon et al. performed a two-way clustering for both colon tissues and genes and revealed the potential relations between them [5]. Other explorations include ovarian cancer [6], breast cancer [7], cutaneous melanoma [8], and so on. For most of the researches aforementioned, hierarchical clustering (HC) is employed. Although HC has the advantage such as informative visualization of the clustering results and the versatility, it lacks robustness and does not have favorable scalability properties. We have used a new family of neural network architecture – Ellipsoid ART and ARTMAP (EA/EAM) to analyze several publicly accessible data sets [11]. EA/EAM has the properties of fast, stable and finite learning and can create hyper-ellipsoidal clusters with complex nonlinear boundaries. Other examples include graph theory-based methods [10], singular value decomposition with Bayesian models [9], partial least squares combined with logic discrimination and quadratic discriminant analysis [14] and support vector machines (SVMs) [16].

In practice, it is common to discriminate more than two types of cancers. Ramaswamy et al. divided the multi-class problem as a series of binary classification sub-problems through either one-versus-all or all-pairs approach [18-19]. SVMs, weighted voting and k-nearest-neighbors algorithm were then used to perform binary classification and the final label was decided according to some confidence values. Khan trained perceptrons to categorize small round blue-cell tumors (SRBCTs) with 4 subclasses [12]. A nearest shrunken centroid method was proposed by Tibshirani et al. and was tested on the SRBCT data set with 100% accuracy [13]. Furthermore, Scherf et al. constructed a gene expression database to study the relationship between genes and drugs for 60 human cancer cell lines originating from 10 different tumors, which provides an important criterion for therapy selection and drug discovery [15].

In our study, we use the probabilistic neural network (PNN) [21] to address the problem of multiple tumor classification without the need to divide it into binary sub-problems. As a powerful tool developed to approximate the Bayesian decision rule, PNN has already shown appealing performance in a large number of applications [22-24]. Here, we further demonstrate the potential and effectiveness of PNN in addressing the challenges of gene expression data analysis with promising results based on several publicly accessible data sets on cancer researches.

The paper is organized as follows. Section II presents a brief introduction to PNN. Section III describes the data sets and experimental methods. The experimental results are presented and discussed in section IV and section V concludes the paper.

II. PROBABILISTIC NEURAL NETWORKS

Probabilistic neural networks were first introduced by Specht [21] as an implementation of nonparametric Pazen window estimation with feed-forward neural network architecture. A typical PNN architecture is illustrated in Fig. 1, which consists of three layers, known as input layer, pattern layer and category layer [20, 24]. The input layer works as a distribution mechanism and receives input components from the data set. Therefore, the number of nodes in this layer is equal to the dimension of the input vector. All of these nodes are fully connected with the nodes in the pattern layer, which is considered as the key of PNN. The PNN requires n pattern nodes if the total number of training patterns is n, so that each pattern node can be regarded as corresponding to a training pattern. Different from link between input and pattern layer, the nodes of pattern and category are sparsely connected. Each pattern node is only connected to the category node that correctly indicates the its associated class.

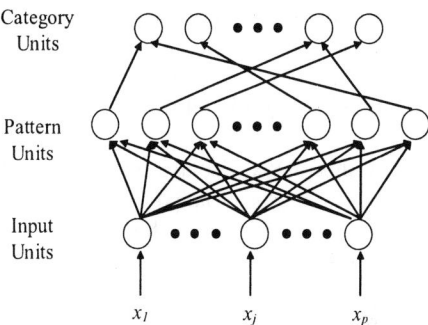

Fig. 1. PNN architecture. Each pattern node represents a pattern in the training set. The Bayesian posterior probability for each category is obtained as the output of the corresponding category node.

The PNN calculates the Bayesian posterior probability for each category. During the training phase, the weights connecting the input and pattern layer are simply set as the copy of input vectors, i.e. $\mathbf{w}_i = \mathbf{x}_i$, for $i = 1,...,n$. As mentioned before, each pattern node merely has connection with the category node representing the class of the corresponding pattern. The process is one of the fastest in known training strategies. However, the cost for the time efficiency is the storage complexity, one pattern unit is required for each pattern in the entire training set, which causes problems when dealing with large volume of data sets. One of potential solutions is to group training patterns into a series of clusters and only use the centroid of each cluster to supervise the network learning [25].

During the test or classification phase, each pattern node performs a dot product operation with a new pattern vector $\mathbf{x}$ and a weight vector $\mathbf{w}_i$, expressed as $P_i = \mathbf{x} \bullet \mathbf{w}_i$. The final output of pattern layer is obtained via a nonlinear transformation. Usually a Gaussian activation function, $\exp((P_i - 1)/\sigma^2)$, is used, though other alternatives are also available [21]. Here, σ is the smoothing parameter of the Gaussian kernel and is also the only one parameter that is dependent on the users to decide. It has great effect to the formation of resulting decision boundary and the strategy on how to select appropriate σ was discussed in details by Specht in [21]. Note that if both the training patterns (equivalent to weight vectors) and the new patterns are normalized to unit length, the output of pattern layer can be represented as

$$\exp((P_i - 1)/\sigma^2)$$
$$= \exp(-(\mathbf{x}^T\mathbf{x} + \mathbf{w}_i^T\mathbf{w}_i - 2\mathbf{x}^T\mathbf{w}_i)/2\sigma^2),$$
$$= \exp(-(\mathbf{x} - \mathbf{w}_i)^T(\mathbf{x} - \mathbf{w}_i)/2\sigma^2)$$

which is identical to the Parzen window function [21]. In this sense, each pattern node provides the corresponding category node with the class conditional probability given the training pattern. These values are then summed up in the category layer for each category as the estimated probability for the new pattern. The label of the pattern can be predicted by just choosing the maximum probability.

Due to its design, PNN displays many desirable properties and characteristics in the context of pattern classification. Among all of those features, the fast training is most appealing. The training rule is very simple and can be used in online learning. Only one pass of the training data is required under the training scheme. Though PNN sacrifices the space efficiency for it, the cost can be decreased to certain extent with the introduction of clustering techniques [25]. Also, the structure of PNN makes it very easy to achieve parallel implementation. Another important feature of PNN is the fewer user-dependent parameters compared with other classifiers. There is only one Gaussian kernel width parameter σ relying on the selection of the users. According to [21] and our experiments, it is not difficult to find appropriate σ and the experimental results are not sensitive to the small changes of σ. Moreover, PNN puts the nonparametric statistical approach into a neural network framework and provides the output of the neural network with a new interpretation, i.e. through the form of conditional probability density function. The resulting probability for each category makes it possible to investigate the confidence of assigning a new pattern to a class. Finally, PNN has the ability to approximate Bayesian optimal decision surfaces that can be arbitrarily complex.

III. DATA SETS AND EXPERIMENTS

We use two data sets to test PNN performance in multiple cancer classification.

SRBCT data set. This data set is on the diagnostic research of small round blue-cell tumors (SRBCTs) of childhood and consists of 83 samples from four categories, known as Burkitt lymphomas (BL), the Ewing family of tumors (EWS), neuroblastoma (NB) and rhabdomyosarcoma (RMS) [12]. 5 non-SRBCT samples are also included in the original data set for testing the ability of diagnosis rejection, but we do not use them in our study. Gene expression levels of 6567 genes were measured using cDNA microarray for each sample, 2308 of which passed the filter that requires the red intensity of a gene to be greater than 20 and were kept for further analyses. The relative red intensity (RRI) of a gene is defined as the ratio between the mean intensity of that particular spot and the mean intensity of all filtered genes and the ultimate expression levels measure is the natural logarithm of RRI. The data are expressed as a matrix $E = \{e_{i,j}\}_{83 \times 2308}$, where $e_{i,j}$ represents the expression level of gene j in tissue sample i.

GCM14 data set. This data set is available at http://www-genome.wi.mit.edu/cgi-bin/cancer/datasets.cgi. There are 14 different tumor types, consisting of breast, prostate, lung, colorectal, lymphoma, bladder, melanoma, uterus, leukemia, renal, pancreas, ovary, mesothelioma, and CNS cancer, with 218 samples. These samples are divided into three groups in the original research, 144 for training, 54 for testing, and the rest 20 as poorly differentiated (PD) tumors. Also, 90 normal tissue samples are included for the study of discriminating tumor and normal tissues. In our experiments, we only work on the 198 tumor samples in the original training and test sets. Gene expressions for 16,063 genes were measured using oligonucleotide microarrays. The final matrix is in the form of $E = \{e_{i,j}\}_{218 \times 16063}$.

Gene selection. From the above description of the two data sets used in the paper and other public data sets [3-8], it can be seen that one of the common feature is the overwhelming number of measures of gene expression levels compared with the number of samples. Not all of these genes are relevant to the discrimination of tumors and sometimes, only a small part of them is enough for correct classification [3, 11]. The existence of more genes that do not contribute to the distinction in the data sets not only increases the computational complexity, but impairs the effects of those relevant ones to some extent. Furthermore, cancer researches also require identifying the relation of tumors and their causes in the molecular level, which is imperative in determining appropriate therapy. Therefore, feature selection or extraction, also known as informative gene selection, is critically important in this context.

Principal component analysis (PCA) is a widely used tool for dimension reduction, which attempts to seek the projection that best interpret the variation of the data [20]. PCA has already been used in some applications on gene expression data [12]. But according to the experimental results in [26], PCA cannot always find the correct structure with just the first few principal components and therefore is not recommended under general cases. Several other methods based on ranking genes according to their expression differentiation under two different classes (represented as +1 and -1 here) have been proposed, examples including:
(1) Discrimination score [3]:
$$D(i) = \frac{\mu_+(i) - \mu_-(i)}{\sigma_+(i) + \sigma_-(i)},$$
where $\mu_+(i)$ and $\mu_-(i)$ are the mean values of gene i for the samples in class +1 and class -1, and $\sigma_+(i)$ and

$\sigma_-(i)$ are the standard deviations of gene i for the samples in class +1 and -1.

(2) *t*-statistics score [14]:
$$T(i) = \frac{\mu_+(i) - \mu_-(i)}{\sqrt{\sigma_+^2(i)/n_+ + \sigma_-^2(i)/n_-}},$$
where n_+ and n_1 are the sizes for samples in the two classes.

(3) TNoM score [10]:
$$TNoM(i,l) = \min_{d,t} Err(d,t \mid i,l),$$
where d is the class label parameter, t represents the threshold of the gene i, l_k is the label of the kth sample, and $Err(d,t \mid i,l) = \sum_k 1\{l_k \neq sign(d(e_{ki} - t))\}$ is the number of errors of a decision stump rule.

According to some experimental studies, most of these methods intend to choose the similar subsets of genes and do not greatly affect the performance of the classifiers. Thus, we employed the first criterion to select informative genes. The only change is that we just use the absolute value of the score. So it reflects the expression level difference between the two classes for each gene. Gene expresses itself most differently in two classes will have the highest score. Since our final goal is to classify multiple types of cancer, we utilize a one-versus-all strategy to seek gene predictors. In other words, for a *C*-class prediction problem, we compare a particular class with the other *C-1* classes that are considered as a whole. We can just select genes according to their contribution to distinguish each class, or the total score for each gene is summed over all *C* comparison and the top genes are selected with the highest scores. Of course, pairwise strategy can also be used, which performs $\binom{C}{2}$ comparisons between each pair of classes.

Experiment designs. Since the data sets consist of only a small number of samples, it is better to use the jackknife approach, which is also called leave one out cross validation (LOOCV), to examine the performance of the classifier. For a data set with *n* samples, the classifier is trained *n* times. Each time, a different single sample is left out as the test point and the other *n-1* samples are used to train the classifier. Performance evaluation of the classifier is estimated by considering the average accuracy of the *n* cross-validation experiments.

We summarize our experimental procedure with the following steps. First, normalize the input patterns to unit length. Then, two strategies are used. For the first strategy, we rank and select a set of informative genes with the aforementioned criterion across all samples, and perform the LOOCV operation with one sample left out for test and the others for training in the learning and prediction phase. This method does not consider the effect of bias for gene selection and is regarded as too optimistic [9]. The second strategy aims to overcome the bias by selecting informative genes at each step of LOOCV operation. Therefore, genes selected in the subset may be different for each stage. But generally, these gene subsets are highly overlapping, with only a small portion of difference observed. The experimental results are illustrated and depicted in the next section.

IV. RESULTS

Fig. 2 describes the classification accuracy for the SRBCT data set with the selection of different numbers of gene predictors. We illustrate the results for both the bias included and free strategy here. From the figure, we can see that there is just some minor decrease in the performance when bias free method was used. This shows that the effect of selection bias may not be very critical in the case of LOOCV procedure because of the high overlapping of gene subsets. We also can see the importance of informative genes selection in tumor classification. The PNN classifier can achieve 100% accuracy when only top 50 genes are chosen. If the subset is increased to include all genes in the data set or to another extreme, reduced to just comprise several genes, the accuracy will decrease in both cases, though not much. These suggest that too many or too few genes both deteriorate the performance of the classifier. Many genes are not related to the classification and including them in the data set will bring noise into the classification system. On the other hand, important information will be wrongly discarded with inadequate genes chosen. These results are consistent with those reported in [12] and [13].

Fig. 3 shows the effects of the smoothing parameter σ to the classification accuracy, when top 100 gene markers are selected with selection bias free strategy, or all genes are used. Obviously, it is not difficult to find a kernel width σ that can lead to a satisfying result. With the increase of the dimensionality, the effective σ tends to become larger in order to provide better interpolation.

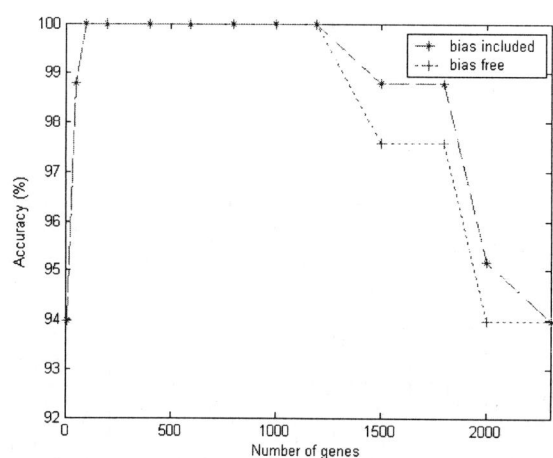

Fig. 2. The classification accuracy as a function of the number of informative genes.

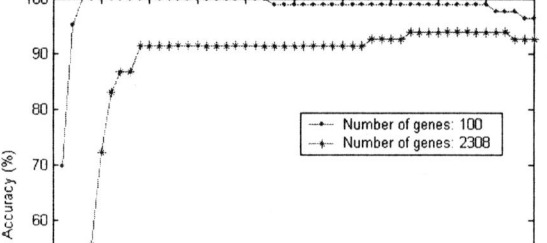

Fig. 3. The classification accuracy as a function of σ.

The best performance we obtain for the GCM14 data set is summarized in Table I, in which the numbers along the diagonal indicate the correct assignment of samples by PNN. For each one-versus-all comparison, top 10 genes are selected and the corresponding total number of genes is 138. The accuracy is around 75.3% and can be compared with the result reported in the original paper that constructs a multi-class prediction scheme consisting of 14 SVMs [18]. From the table, we also can observe that PNN can correctly classify most of cases for tumor types like colorectal, lymphoma, leukemia, mesothelioma and CNS. But for bladder, renal and ovary cancer, the classifier cannot effectively discriminate them from other tumor types. The analysis is also supported by other methods such as SOFMs and SVMs [18].

TABLE I. CONFUSION MATRIX OF PNN FOR 14 TUMOR TYPES: OVERALL ACCURACY IS 75.3%

	PNN Predicted Class													
Actual Class	BR	PR	LU	CO	LY	BL	ME	UT	LE	RE	PA	OV	ML	CNS
BR	7			1		3					1			
PR		10	1			1	1	1						
LU	3		7			2								
CO				10							1		1	
LY					22									
BL	5		1			4						1		
ME	2					1	6	1						
UT							2	7					1	
LE									29				1	
RE	1					1	1		4	1	3			
PA	2										8	1		
OV					2		2		1	1	6			
ML							1						10	
CNS													1	19

TABLE II. CLASSIFICATION CONFIDENCE

Cancer Type	Confidence			Percentage
	First	Second	Third	
BR	7	1	2	83.3%
PR	10	0	0	71.4%
LU	7	1	1	75%
CO	10	0	0	83.3%
LY	22	0	0	100%
BL	4	3	3	90.9%
ME	6	0	1	70%
UT	7	2	0	90%
LE	29	0	0	96.7%
RE	4	3	0	63.6%
PA	8	0	1	81.8%
OV	6	4	0	83.3%
ML	10	0	0	90.9%
CNS	19	1	0	100%

Since PNN has the mechanism that can estimate the confidence of the predictions, it provides us a way to evaluate the results by comprehensively considering these values. Table II lists the predicted results with the first three largest confidence values. Almost half of the errors are caused due to the reason that the confidence value for the correct category is ranked second or third by the classifier. This suggests that it is more effective and accurate to make predictions by combining the information of confidence values.

V. CONCLUSIONS

Cancer classification is critically important for prognosis and treatment. Microarray technologies provide a new and effective avenue to address the problem, while bringing many challenges. Here, we utilized the probabilistic neural network to distinguish tumor tissues with more than two categories, by analyzing gene expression profiling. Because of some limitations in conditions like sample collections, almost all of the publicly accessible data sets merely include a small set of samples for each tumor type, in contrast to the rapidly and persistently increasing capability of gene chip technologies that also follow the Moore's law [27]. The initial experimental results demonstrate the potential of PNN, combined with feature selection technique, in extracting useful information from these high-dimensional data sets. More experiments will be performed for further evaluation with richer data available. In the meantime, new feature selection approaches are required in order to find informative genes that are more efficient in prediction and prognosis.

Acknowledgment

The authors wish to thank Dr. Danil Prokhorov for helpful discussions. Partial support for this research from the National Science Foundation, and from the M.K. Finley Missouri endowment, is gratefully acknowledged.

References

[1] M. Eisen and P. Brown, "DNA Arrays for Analysis of Gene Expression," Methods Enzymol, vol. 303, pp. 179-205, 1999.

[2] R. Lipshutz, S. Fodor, T. Gingeras, and D. Lockhart, "High Density Synthetic Oligonucleotide Arrays," Nature Genetics, vol. 21, pp. 20-24, 1999.

[3] T.R. Golub, D.K. Slonim, P. Tamayo, C. Huard, M. Gaasenbeek, J.P. Mesirov, H. Coller, M. Loh, J.R. Downing, M.A. Caligiuri, C.D. Bloomfield, and E.S. Lander, "Molecular Classification of Cancer: Class Discovery And Class Prediction by Gene Expression Monitoring", Science, 286: 531-537,1999.

[4] A. Alizadeh, M. Eisen, R. Davis, C. Ma, I. Lossos, A. Rosenwald, J. Boldrick, H. Sabet, T. Tran, X. Yu, J. Powell, L. Yang, G. Marti, T. Moore, J. Hudson Jr, L. Lu, D. Lewis, R. Tibshirani, G. Sherlock W. Chan, T. Greiner, D. Weisenburger, J. Armitage, R. Warnke, R. Levy, W. Wilson, M. Grever, J. Byrd, D. Bostein, P. Brown, and L. Staudt, "Distinct Types of Diffuse Large B-cell Lymphoma Identified by Gene Expression Profiling", Nature, vol. 403, pp.503-511, 2000.

[5] U. Alon, N. Barkai, D. Notterman, K. Gish, S. Ybarra, D. Mack, and A. Levine, "Broad Patterns of Gene Expression Revealed by Clustering Analysis of Tumor And Normal Colon Tissues Probed by Oligonucleotide Arrays", Proc. Natl. Acad. Sci. USA 96, pp.6745-6750, 1999.

[6] M. Schummer, W. Ng, R. Bumgarner, P. Nelson, B. Schummer, D. Bednarski, L. Hassell, R. Baldwin, B. Karlan, and L. Hood, "comparative Hybridization of An Array of 21500 Ovarian cDNA for the discovery of Genes Overexpressed in Ovarian Carcinomas," Gene, vol. 238, pp. 375-385, 1999.

[7] C. Perou, T. Sørlie, M. Eisen, M. Rijn, S. Jeffrey, C. Rees, J. Pollack, D. Ross, J. Johnsent, L. Akslen, Ø. Fluge, A. Pergamenschlkov, C. Williams, S. Zhu, P. Lønning, A. Børresen-Dale, P. Brown, and D. Botstein, "Molecular Portraits of Human Breast Tumors," Nature, vol. 406, pp. 747-752, 2000.

[8] M. Bittner, P. Meltzer, Y. Chen, Y. Jiang, E. Seftor, M. Hendrix, M. Radmacher, R. Simon, Z. Yakhini, A. Ben-Dor, N. Sampas, E. Dougherty, E. Wang, F. Marincola, C. Gooden, J. Lueders, A. Glatfelter, P. Pollock, J. Carpten, E. Gillanders, D. Leja, K. Dietrich, C. Beaudry, , M. Berens, D. Alberts, V. Sondak, N. Hayward, and J. Trent, " Molecular Classification of Cutaneous Malignant Melanoma by Gene Expression Profiling," Nature, vol. 406, pp. 536-540, 2000.

[9] M. West, C. Blanchette, H. Dressman, E. Huang, S. Ishida, R. Spang, H. Zuzan, J. Olson, J. Marks, and J. Nevins, " Predicting the Clinical Status of Human Breast Cancer by Using Gene Expression Profiles," PNAS, vol. 98, no. 20, pp. 11462-11467, 2001.

[10] A. Ben-Dor, L. Bruhn, N. Friedman, I. Nachman, M. Schummer, and Z. Yakhini, "Tissue Classification with Gene Expression Profiles", Proceedings of the Fourth Annual International Conference on Computational Molecular biology, pp.598-583, 2000.

[11] R. Xu, G. Anagnostopoulos and D. Wunsch II, "Tissue Classification Through Analysis of Gene Expression Data Using A New Family of ART Architectures", IJCNN02, vol. 1, pp. 300-304, 2002.

[12] J. Khan, J. Wei, M. Ringnér, L. Saal, M. Ladanyi, F. Westermann, F. Berthold, M. Schwab, C. Antonescu, C. Peterson, and P. Meltzer, "Classification and Diagnostic Prediction of Cancers Using Gene Expression Profiling and Artificial Neural Networks," Nature Medicine, vol. 7, no. 6, pp. 673-679, 2001.

[13] R. Tibshirani, T. Hastie, B. Narasimhan, and G. Chu, "Diagnosis of Multiple Cancer Types by Shrunken Centroids of Gene Expression," PNAS, vol. 99, no. 10, pp. 6567-6572, 2002.

[14] D. Nguyen and D. Rocke, "Tumor Classification by Partial Least Squares using Microarray Gene Expression Data," Bioinformatics, vol. 18, no. 1, pp. 39-50, 2002.

[15] Uwe Scherf, Douglas T. Ross, Mark Waltham, Lawrence H. Smith, Jae K. Lee, Lorraine Tanabe, Kurt W. Kohn, William C. Reinhold, Timothy G. Myers, Darren T.Andrews, Dominic A. Scudiero, Michael B. Eisen, Edward A. Sausville, Yves Pommier, David Botstein, Patrick O. Brown, and John N. Weinstein, "A Gene Expression Database for The Molecular Pharmacology of Cancer", Nature Genetics, 24(3), pp.236-44, 2000.

[16] T. Furey, N. Cristianini, N. Duffy, D. Bednarski, M. Schummer, and D. Haussler, "support Vector Machine Classification and Validation of Cancer Tissue Samples Using Microarray Expression Data," Bioinformatics, vol. 16, no. 10, pp. 906-914, 2000.

[17] P. Baldi, A. D. Long, "A Bayesian Framework for The Analysis of Microarray Expression Data: Regularized t-test And Statistical Inferences of Gene Changes", Bioinformatics, 17:509-519, 2001.

[18] S. Ramaswamy, P. Tamayo, R. Rifkin, S. Mukherjee, C. Yeang, M. Angelo, C. Ladd, M. Reich, E. Latulippe, J. Mesirov, T. Poggio, W. Gerald, M. Loda, E. Lander, and T. Golub, 'Multiclass Cancer Diagnosis Using Tumor Gene Expression Signatures," PNAS, vol. 98, no. 26, pp. 15149-15154, 2001.

[19] C. Yeang, S. Ramaswamy, P. Tamayo, S. Mukherjee, R. Rifkin, M. Angelo, M. Reich, E. Lander, J. Mesirov, and T. Golub, "Molecular Classification of Multiple Tumor Types," Bioinformatics, vol. 17, pp. s316-s322, 2001.

[20] R. O. Duda, P. E. Hart and D. G. Stork, Pattern Classification, 2nd Ed., Wiley & Sons, New York, 2001.

[21] D. Specht, "Probabilistic Neural Networks," Neural Networks, vol. 3, pp. 109-118, 1990.

[22] E. Saad, D. Prokhorov, and D. Wunsch, "Comparative Study of Stock Trend Prediction Using Time Delay, Recurrent and Probabilistic Neural Networks," IEEE Transactions on Neural Networks, vol. 9, no. 6, pp. 1456-1470, 1998.

[23] D. Specht, "PNN: From Fast Training to Fast Running," In Computational Intelligence: A Dynamic System Perspective, IEEE Press, NY, pp. 246-258, 1995.

[24] S. Hart, R. Shaffer, S. Rose-pehrsson, and J. McDonald, "Using Physics-Based Modeler Outputs to Train Probabilistic Neural Networks for Unexploded Ordnance (UXO) Classification in Magnetometry Surveys," IEEE Transactions on Geoscience and Remote Sensing, vol. 39, no. 4, pp. 797-804, 2001.

[25] D. Specht, "Enhancement to Probabilistic Neural Networks," Proceedings of the IEEE International Joint Conference on Neural Networks, pp. 761-768, 1992.

[26] K. Yeung and W. Ruzzo, "Principal Component Analysis for Clustering Gene Expression Data," Bioinformatics, vol. 17, no. 9, pp. 763-774, 2001.

[27] S. Moore, "Making chips to probe genes," IEEE Spectrum, vol. 38, pp. 54-60, 2001.

Genetic Search for Optimal Ensemble of Feature-Classifier Pairs in DNA Gene Expression Profiles

Chanho Park
Yonsei University
Department of Computer Science
134 Shinchon-dong, Seodaemun-gu, Seoul Korea, 120-749.
cpark@candy.yonsei.ac.kr

Sung-Bae Cho
Yonsei University
Department of Computer Science
134 Shinchon-dong, Seodaemun-gu, Seoul Korea, 120-749
sbcho@cs.yonsei.ac.kr

Abstract-Gene expression profile is numerical data of gene expression levels from organism, measured on the microarray. In general, each specific tissue indicates different expression level in related genes, so that it is possible to classify disease by gene expression profile. For classification, it is needed to select related genes called feature selection, because all the genes are not useful for classification. We propose GA-based method for searching optimal ensemble of feature-classifier pairs of gene expression profile in seven feature selection methods based on correlation, distance, and information theory, and representative six classifiers. Experimental results on two gene expression profiles related to cancers show that GA finds good solution quickly. Especially, in Lymphoma dataset, GA finds the ensemble of 100% accuracy.

I. INTRODUCTION

Although earlier cancer detection and correct class discovery have been seriously studied over the past years, there has been no perfect way to work out this problem. It is because there are so many pathways causing cancer, and there exist tremendous number of varieties. Recently, array technologies have made it straightforward to monitor the expression patterns of thousands of genes during cellular differentiation and response [1]. These gene expression profiles, however, are just simple sequences of numbers, and the necessity of tools analyzing them to get useful information has risen sharply.

General procedure for classifying gene expression profile is divided into several steps. Because it does not fit to use raw data directly, normalization procedure is needed [2]. Then, we select informative genes by feature selection methods, because the number of genes is much greater than that of samples, and most of them do not help in classification [3]. After feature selection, classifier is trained by training samples with selected genes, so that input patterns yield right outputs. Trained classifier is evaluated the performance with test set or validation set [4, 5].

On the other hand, it is attempted to make ensemble classifiers, because it is hard to find perfect and general feature-classifier pair (combination of feature selection and classifier) [6]. Ensemble is to combine classifier pairs and it is generally known for yielding stable result. Ensemble can also search much wider solution space than individual classifiers. For ensemble various methods can be used such as majority voting, weighted voting, and weighted average.

One important problem of ensemble is that it takes long time to try all the ensembles because there are so many possible ensembles. If there are m feature selection methods and n classifiers, mn feature-classifier pairs are possible. In our case, mn is 42, so we can figure out the number of possible ensembles as follows.

$$\sum_{k=1}^{42} {}_{42}C_k \cong 4 \times 10^{12} \quad (1)$$

Even the newest Pentium 4 computer with 1 GB main memory would take several days to test all the ensembles. Moreover, the required time increases exponentially as feature selection methods or classifiers are added to the system.

In this paper, we propose a method based on genetic algorithm (GA) for finding optimal ensemble of feature-classifier pairs efficiently. We have used randomly selected initial chromosomes, and shown the tendency to the optimal ensemble by genetic operations. We have tried to test the proposed method in two benchmark cancer datasets, and systematically analyze its usefulness.

II. BACKGROUNDS

A. DNA Microarray

DNA microarray consists of a large number of DNA molecules spotted in a systemic order on a solid substrate. Especially, depending on the size of each DNA spot on the array, DNA microarray means the diameter of DNA spot is less than 250 microns. The arrays with the small solid substrate are also referred to as DNA chips. It is so powerful that we can investigate the gene information in short time, because at least hundreds of genes can be put on the DNA microarray to be analyzed.

DNA microarrays are composed of thousands of individual DNA sequences printed in a high density array on a glass microscope slide using a robotic arrayer. The relative abundance of these spotted DNA sequences in two DNA or RNA samples may be assessed by monitoring the differential hybridization of the two samples to the sequences on the array. For mRNA samples, the two samples are reverse-transcribed into cDNA, labeled using different fluorescent dyes mixed (red-fluorescent dye Cy5 and green-fluorescent dye Cy3). After the hybridization of these samples with the arrayed DNA probes, the slides are imaged using scanner that makes fluorescence measurements for each dye. The log ratio between the two intensities of each dye is used as the gene expression data [7].

$$gene\_expression = \log_2 \frac{Int(Cy5)}{Int(Cy3)} \quad (2)$$

Since at least hundreds of genes are put on the DNA microarray, it is so helpful that we can investigate the genome-wide information in short time.

B. Genetic Algorithm

Genetic algorithms are stochastic search methods that have been successfully applied in many search, optimization, and machine learning problems [8]. Unlike most other optimization techniques, GAs maintain a population of encoded solution candidates that are competitively manipulated by applying some variation operators to find a global optimum. A population consists of many chromosomes that can be a candidate solution. A chromosome is composed of bit strings that express a specific status or value.

A sequential GA proceeds in an iterative manner by generating new populations of strings from the old ones. Every string is the encoded (binary, real, ...) version of a candidate solution. An evaluation function associates a fitness measure to every string indicating its fitness to the problem. The standard GA applies genetic operators such as selection, crossover, and mutation on an initially random population in order to compute a whole generation of new strings.

C. Related Works

Many people have been studying about gene expression profile classification. They have used various feature selection methods to select informative genes, such as information gain, signal to noise ratio, t-statistics, Euclidean distance, Pearson correlation coefficient, principal component analysis, genetic algorithm, and so on [2, 3, 9, 10]. As classifiers, they have used MLP, kNN, SVM, Fisher's linear discriminant analysis, logistic discriminant, decision tree, and so on [3, 4, 5, 11]. It is summarized in Table I.

On the other hand, many researchers have been working on the ensemble of the multiple classifiers to improve the performance of classification. The ensemble classifier also produces stable results. The ensemble methods used are majority voting, Bayesian average, neural network, and so on [6, 12].

III. OPTIMAL ENSEMBLE CLASSIFIER

The classification architecture for DNA microarray is composed of a series of processes to classify samples. The architecture contains feature selection, classifier, and finding optimal ensemble using GA. The system is as shown in Fig. 1.

A. Gene Selection Methods

Seven feature selection methods are used to select informative genes based on statistical correlation, distance, or information theory. The genes are selected by rank.

1) Statistical approach: Using the statistical correlation analysis, we can see the linear relationship and the direction of relation between two variables. Correlation coefficient r varies from -1 to $+1$, so that the data distributed near the line biased to (+) direction will have positive coefficients, and the data near the line biased to (-) direction will have negative coefficients.

Suppose that we have a gene expression pattern g_i ($i = 1 \sim m$, where m is the number of genes). Each g_i is a vector of gene expression levels from n samples, $g_i = (e_1, e_2, e_3, ..., e_n)$. Some elements are examples of class 1, and the others are those from class 0. An ideal gene pattern that belongs to class 1 is defined by $g_{ideal\_c1} = (1, ..., 1, 0, ..., 0)$, so that all the elements from class 1's samples are 1 and the others are 0. In this paper, we have calculated the correlation coefficients between this g_{ideal} and the expression pattern of each gene. When we have two vectors X and Y that contain N elements, $r_{Pearson}$ (PC) and $r_{Spearman}$ (SC) are calculated as follows:

TABLE I
Relevant works on cancer classification

Authors	Dataset	Method		Accuracy [%]
		Feature selection	Classifier	
Furey *et al.*	Leukemia	Signal to noise ratio	SVM	94.1
	Colon			90.3
Li *et al.*	Lymphoma	Genetic Algorithm	KNN	84.6~
	Colon			94.1~
Dudoit *et al.*	Leukemia	The ratio of between-groups to within-groups sum of squares	Nearest neighbor	95.0~
	Lymphoma			95.0~
	Leukemia		Diagonal linear discriminant analysis	95.0~
	Lymphoma			95.0~
Nguyen *et al.*	Leukemia	Principal component analysis	Logistic discriminant	94.2
	Lymphoma			98.1
	Colon		Diagonal linear discriminant analysis	87.1
	Leukemia		Quadratic discriminant analysis	95.4
	Lymphoma		BoostCART	97.6
	Colon			87.1

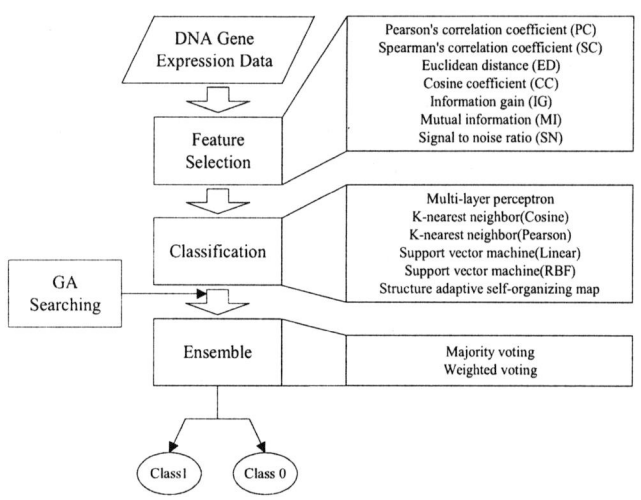

Fig. 1. The ensemble classification system

$$r_{Pearson} = \frac{\sum XY - \frac{\sum X \sum Y}{N}}{\sqrt{\left(\sum X^2 - \frac{(\sum X)^2}{N}\right)\left(\sum Y^2 - \frac{(\sum Y)^2}{N}\right)}} \quad (3)$$

$$r_{Spearman} = 1 - \frac{6\sum(D_x - D_y)^2}{N(N^2 - 1)} \quad (4)$$

where D_x and D_y are the rank matrices of X and Y, respectively.

2) Distance approach: The similarity between two input vectors X and Y can be thought of as distance. Distance is a measure on how far the two vectors are located, and the distance between g_{ideal_c1} and g_i tells us how much the g_i is likely to the class 1. Calculating the distance between them, if it is bigger than certain threshold, the gene g_i would belong to class 1, otherwise g_i belongs to class 0. In this paper, we have adopted Euclidean distance ($r_{Eclidean}$, ED) and cosine coefficient (r_{Cosine}, CC) represented by the following equations:

$$r_{Eclidean} = \sqrt{\sum(X-Y)^2} \quad (5)$$

$$r_{Cosine} = \frac{\sum XY}{\sqrt{\sum X^2 \sum Y^2}} \quad (6)$$

3) Information-theoretic approach: We have utilized the information gain and mutual information that are widely used in many fields such as text categorization and data mining. If we count the number of genes excited ($P(g_i)$) or not excited ($P(\bar{g}_i)$) in category c_j ($P(c_j)$), the coefficients of the information gain (IG) and mutual information (MI) become as follows:

$$IG(g_i, c_j) = P(g_i | c_j) \log \frac{P(g_i | c_j)}{P(c_j) \cdot P(g_i)} + P(\bar{g}_i | c_j) \log \frac{P(\bar{g}_i | c_j)}{P(c_j) \cdot P(\bar{g}_i)} \quad (7)$$

$$MI(g_i, c_j) = \log \frac{P(g_i, c_j)}{P(c_j) \cdot P(g_i)} \quad (8)$$

Mutual information tells us the dependency between two probabilistic variables of events. If two events are completely independent, the mutual information is 0. The more they are related, the higher the mutual information gets. Information gain is used when the features of samples are extracted by inducing the relationship between gene and class by the presence frequency of the gene in the sample. Information gain measures the goodness of gene using the presence and absence within the corresponding class.

For each gene g_i, some are from class 1, and some are from class 0. If we calculate the mean μ and standard deviation σ from the distribution of gene expressions within their classes, the signal to noise ratio of gene g_i, $SN(g_i)$, is defined by:

$$SN(g_i) = \frac{\mu_{c1}(g_i) - \mu_{c0}(g_i)}{\sigma_{c1}(g_i) + \sigma_{c0}(g_i)} \quad (9)$$

B. Classifiers

1) Multilayer perceptron: Error backpropagation neural network is a feed-forward multilayer perceptron (MLP) that is applied in many fields due to its powerful and stable learning algorithm [4]. The neural network learns the training examples by adjusting the synaptic weight of neurons according to the error occurred on the output layer. The power of the backpropagation algorithm lies in two main aspects: local for updating the synaptic weights and biases, and efficient for computing all the partial derivatives of the cost function with respect to these free parameters.

2) k-nearest neighbor: k-nearest neighbor (KNN) is one of the most common methods for memory based induction. Given an input vector, KNN extracts k closest vectors in the reference set based on similarity measures, and makes decision for the label of input vector using the labels of the k nearest neighbors [13].

Pearson's correlation and cosine coefficient have been used as the similarity measure. When we have an input X and a reference set $D = \{d_1, d_2, ..., d_N\}$, the probability that X may belong to class c_j, $P(X, c_j)$ is defined as follows:

$$P(X, c_j) = \sum_{d_i \in kNN} Sim(X, d_i) P(d_i, c_j) - b_j \quad (10)$$

where $Sim(X, d_i)$ is the similarity between X and d_i, and b_j is a bias term.

3) Support vector machine: Support vector machine (SVM) estimates the function classifying the data into two classes [6, 14]. SVM builds up a hyperplane as the decision surface in such a way to maximize the margin of separation between positive and negative examples. SVM achieves this by the structural risk minimization principle that the error rate of a learning machine on the test data is bounded by the sum of the training-error rate and a term that depends on the Vapnik-Chervonenkis (VC) dimension. Given a labeled set of M

training samples (X_i, Y_i), where $X_i \in R^N$ and Y_i is the associated label, $Y_i \in \{-1, 1\}$, the discriminant hyperplane is defined by:

$$f(X) = \sum_{i=1}^{M} Y_i \alpha_i k(X, X_i) + b \qquad (11)$$

where $k(\,.\,)$ is a kernel function and the sign of $f(X)$ determines the membership of X. Constructing an optimal hyperplane is equivalent to finding all the nonzero α_i (support vectors) and a bias b. We have used SVM^{light} module in this paper.

4) Structure adaptive SOM: Even though SOM is well known for its good performance of topology preserving, it is difficult to apply it to practical classification since the topology should be fixed before training. A structure adaptive self-organizing map (SASOM) was proposed to overcome this shortcoming [15]. SASOM starts with 4×4 map, and dynamically splits the output nodes of the map, where the data from different classes are mixed, trained with the LVQ learning algorithm.

C. Ensemble Classifier

It is hard to find the optimal method for classification, because there are many algorithms for the classification, and depending on the data, algorithms, features, and parameters used, the classifier would yield its result differently. To solve these problems, ensemble method is attempted and studied. It is informed that one can get improved result by combining classifiers that produce their own output.

If we just use one feature-classifier pair, we can get 42 results. However, we can get about 4-tera results by combining them. It means that we can search much wider solution space.

We have applied this idea to the classification framework as shown in Fig. 1. We have chosen majority voting and weighted voting method, among various methods for ensemble, and they are explained in the Table II.

D. Searching Optimal Ensemble Using GA

It takes so long time to test all possible ensembles. Moreover, if we added one feature-classifier pair, it would increase the necessary time exponentially. Therefore efficient method for finding optimal ensemble is needed, and we have proposed the method using GA. The structure of chromosome is as shown in Fig. 2.

TABLE II
Ensemble methods (when x is input, $C_{1i}(x) = 1$ if $e_i(x) = 1$, otherwise $C_{1i}(x) = 0$, $c_{0i}(x) = 1$ if $e_i(x) = 0$, otherwise $c_{0i}(x) = 0$, w_i is accuracy of $e_i(x)$, and $e_i(x)$ is element feature-classifier)

Ensemble method	Output	Condition
Majority voting	1	$\sum_i (c_{1i}(x)) > \sum_i (c_{0i}(x))$
	0	otherwise
Weighted voting	1	$\sum_i (c_{1i}(x) w_i) > \sum_i (c_{0i}(x) w_i)$
	0	otherwise

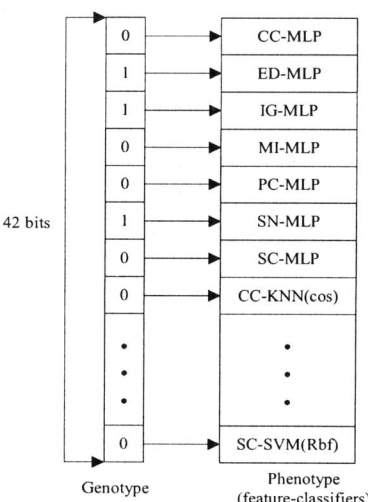

Fig. 2. Structure of chromosome

Each chromosome is composed of 42 bits string, and each bit indicates whether the corresponding feature-classifier pair is included or not. Each bit corresponding specific feature-classifier such as the first bit to CC-MLP, the second bit to ED-MLP, and so on. Fig. 2 shows the ensemble of second, third, and sixth feature-classifier pairs because their bits are 1.

After initial population is created, fitness is evaluated based on the performance of the ensemble.

IV. EXPERIMENTS

A. Experimental Dataset

There are several microarray datasets from published cancer gene expression studies. In this paper, we have used two representative datasets among them.

Lymphoma cancer dataset consists of 24 samples of GC B-like and 23 samples of activated B-like [16]. Each sample contains 4026 genes. 22 out of 47 samples were used as training data and the remaining were used as test data. (Available at: http://genome-www.stanford.edu/lymphoma)

Colon cancer dataset consists of 62 samples taken from colon-cancer patients. Each sample contains 2000 gene expression levels. 40 samples are colon cancer samples and the remaining are normal samples. Each sample was taken from tumors and normal healthy parts of the colons of the same patients [17]. 31 out of 62 samples were used as training data and the remaining were used as test data. (Available at: http://www.sph.uth.tmc.edu:8052/hgc/default.asp)

B. Experimental Environment

The experiment is composed of gene selection, classification, and searching optimal ensemble using GA. For gene selection, we rank the genes according to its feature score, and select 25 highly scored genes. For classifier, we have used a two-layered MLP with 8 hidden nodes, 2 output nodes, 0.01~0.50 of learning rate, 0.9 of momentum, 500 of maximum iterations, and 98% of target accuracy. In the case of *k*NN, we have set *k* from 1 to 8, and used Pearson correlation coefficient and cosine coefficient as similarity measures. We have used SVM with linear and RBF kernel function. In SASOM, we have used initial 4×4 map which has rectangular shape.

For GA, we have used roulette wheel rule for selection method. Preliminary results have indicated that it converges local minimum when we have used less than 100 chromosomes in a population. Stable result can be obtained when we use more than 100 chromosomes. In evaluation, a chromosome gets higher fitness when the number of feature-classifier pairs is smaller. Finally we have tested with crossover rates to 0.3, 0.5, 0.7 and 0.9, and mutation rates to 0.01 and 0.05.

C. Results of Element Feature-Classifier

Tables III and IV show the results of all element feature-classifier pairs for two datasets. In Lymphoma dataset, IG shows good performance for gene selection and *k*NN(Cosine) shows good accuracy for classification. Overall, feature selection methods based on information-theoretic approach show better performance than others in this dataset.

Also, *k*NN(Cosine) shows the best average performance in Colon dataset. However, the best performance of element feature-classifier pair, 83.9%, is worse compared with that in Lymphoma (92.0%) datasets. In the case of SASOM classifier, it has shown the worst performance that does not reach to 50% accuracy.

Table III
Recognition rates (%) of element feature-classifier pairs in Lymphoma dataset

	MLP	SASOM	SVM Linear	SVM RBF	KNN Cosine	KNN Pearson
PC	64.0	48.0	56.0	60.0	76.0	60.0
SC	60.0	68.0	44.0	44.0	60.0	60.0
ED	56.0	52.0	56.0	56.0	68.0	56.0
CC	68.0	52.0	56.0	56.0	72.0	60.0
IG	92.0	84.0	92.0	92.0	92.0	92.0
MI	72.0	64.0	64.0	64.0	64.0	80.0
SN	76.0	76.0	72.0	76.0	80.0	76.0
Avg.	69.7	63.4	62.9	63.4	73.1	69.1

Table IV
Recognition rates (%) of element feature-classifier pairs in Colon dataset

	MLP	SASOM	SVM Linear	SVM RBF	KNN Cosine	KNN Pearson
PC	74.2	74.2	64.5	64.5	77.4	71.0
SC	58.1	45.2	64.5	64.5	67.7	61.3
ED	67.8	67.6	64.5	64.5	83.9	83.9
CC	83.9	64.5	64.5	64.5	80.7	80.7
IG	71.0	71.0	71.0	71.0	80.7	74.2
MI	71.0	71.0	71.0	71.0	80.7	74.2
SN	64.5	45.2	64.5	64.5	71.0	64.5
Avg.	70.1	62.7	66.4	66.4	77.4	72.8

D. Results of Optimal Ensemble with GA

Before finding optimal ensemble, we investigate the change of average fitness to see if GA evolves, because optimal ensemble can be found by chance. Fig. 3 shows the change of average fitness in Lymphoma dataset. We can see that average fitness increases as iteration goes. It shows to converge after about 100 iterations, and it is similar in colon datasets.

We have not been able to obtain good performance with element feature-classifier pairs. It means that there exists high possibility to get improved performance, and GA practically finds outstanding ensembles that are better than any other element feature-classifier pairs.

In the case of Lymphoma dataset, GA finds the ensemble that shows the best performance. In this dataset, the accuracy of element feature-classifier pairs is 44~92%, leading to average of 67%. Nevertheless, GA finds the ensemble of 100% that is composed of complementary pairs of feature-classifier. Ensembles searched by GA are of 92~100% accuracy, and of 96.7% on average. Table V is some ensembles that show 100% accuracy.

Also, in the case of Colon dataset, GA finds the ensemble that shows higher performance than any other element feature-classifier pairs. The best accuracy of element feature-classifier pair is 83.9%, but the ensemble searched by GA is of 93.5% accuracy. Ensemble results in this dataset have ranged 87.1~93.5%, and average accuracy is 90.8%. These results are summarized in Fig. 4.

The practical usefulness of GA lies in its time-efficiency. We have experimented with all the ensembles that are composed of 7 feature-classifier pairs, and it takes about 3 hours. Therefore, it is almost impossible to test all the ensembles of 42. It takes less than 2 minutes using GA, however, when we use 2000 chromosomes with 500 iterations. We can find optimal ensemble in 100 iterations with 2000 chromosomes, and 900 iterations with 100 chromosomes. With these results, we can confirm that it is very efficient to use GA when searching space is very large.

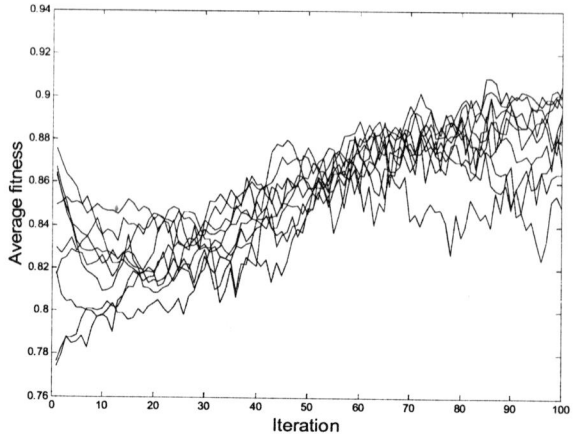

Fig. 3. Change of average fitness on Lymphoma dataset

Table V
Optimal ensembles of Lymphoma dataset

Methods	Feature-classifier pairs
Majority voting	CC-KNN(P), MI-KNN(C), SN-KNN(C), SS-SASOM, IG-SVM(L)
	IG-KNN(C), MI-KNN(C), PC-KNN(C), SN-KNN(P), SN-SASOM
Weighted voting	IG-KNN(C), IG-KNN(P), PC-KNN(P), SN-KNN(P), CC-SASOM
	IG-KNN(C), MI-KNN(C), SN-KNN(C), SN-KNN(P), CC-SASOM, IG-SASOM, PC-SVM(R)

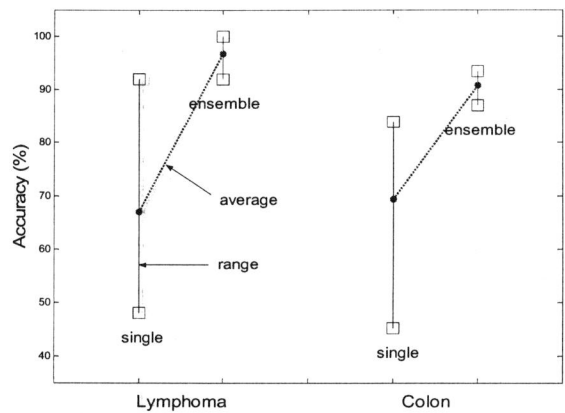

Fig. 4. Comparison of recognition rates for feature-classifier pairs (single) and ensemble (%)

V. CONCLUDING REMARKS

This paper uses GA that imitates the evolution of organism for efficiently finding the optimal ensemble classifier to analyze gene expression profiles. Experimental results show that GA finds ensembles that produce higher performance than any element feature-classifier pairs. Especially in Lymphoma dataset, GA finds the ensemble that yields 100% accuracy. GA finds optimal solution quickly, and it is more useful when the number of feature selection methods or classifiers is large. In addition, we can see that GA finds optimal solution through the increase of average fitness.

On the other hand, though we have just used simple GA and simple ensemble methods, we will investigate alternative methods later, such as rank-based or tournament selection method in GA and Bayesian ensemble method. Since we could not investigate the meaning of genes that do with the optimal ensemble found by GA, it might be interesting to see the biological implication.

ACKNOWLEDGEMENTS

This work was supported by Biometrics Engineering Research Center and a grant of Korea Health 21 R&D Project, Ministry of Health & Welfare, Republic of Korea.

REFERENCES

[1] T. R. Golub, *et al.* "Molecular classification of cancer: Class discovery and class prediction by gene expression monitoring," *Science*, vol. 286, pp. 531-537, 1999.
[2] Y. H. Yang, et al., "Normalization for cDNA microarray data," *SPIE Bios 2001*, San Jose, California, pp. 1-12, January 2001.
[3] L. Li, et al., "Gene selection for sample classification based on gene expression data: Study of sensitivity to choice of parameters of the GA/KNN method," *Bioinformatics*, vol. 17, no. 12, pp. 1131-1142, June 2001.
[4] J. Khan, et al., "Classification and diagnostic prediction of cancers using gene expression profiling and artificial neural networks," *Nature*, vol. 7, no. 6, pp. 673-679, June 2001.
[5] M. P. S. Brown, et al., "Support vector machine classification of microarray gene expression data," *USCS-CRL-99-09*, pp. 1-23, June 1999.
[6] S.-B. Cho, and J. Ryu, "Classifying gene expression data of cancer using classifier ensemble with mutually exclusive features," *Proc. of the IEEE*, vol. 90, no. 11, pp. 1744-1753, 2002.
[7] M. B. Eisen, et al., "Cluster analysis and display of genome-wide expression patterns," *Proc. of the Natl. Acad. of Sci. USA*, vol. 95, pp. 14863-14868, 1998.
[8] T. M. Mitchell, *Machine Learning*, Carnegie Mellon University, 1997.
[9] S. Fuhrman, et al., "The application of Shannon entropy in the identification of putative drug targets," *BioSystems*, vol. 55. pp. 5-14, 2000.
[10] D. V. Nguyen, et al., "Tumor classification by partial least squares using microarray gene expression data," *Bioinformatics*, vol. 18, no. 1, pp. 39-50, 2002.
[11] Y. Xu, et al., "Artificial neural networks and gene filtering distinguish between global gene expression profiles of Barrett's esophagus and esophageal cancer," *Cancer Research*, vol. 62, pp. 3493-3497, 2002.
[12] A. Ben-Dor, et al., "Tissue classification with gene expression profiles," *Journal of Computational Biology*, vol. 7. pp. 559-584, 2000.
[13] R. O. Duda, et al., *Pattern Classification*, 2nd Ed., Wiley Interscience, 2001.
[14] T. S. Furey, et al., "Support vector machine classification and validation of cancer tissue samples using microarray expression data," *Bioinformatics*, vol. 16, no. 10, pp. 906-914, 2000.
[15] H. D. Kim, and S.-B. Cho, "Genetic optimization of structure-adaptive self-organizing map for efficient classification," *Proc. of Int. Conf. on Soft Computing*, pp. 34-39, October 2000.
[16] A. A. Alizadeh, et al., "Distinct types of diffuse large B-cell lymphoma identified by gene expression profiling," *Nature*, vol. 403, pp. 503-511, February, 2000.
[17] U. Alon et al., "Broad patterns of gene expression revealed by clustering analysis of tumor and normal colon tissues probed by oligonucleotide arrays," *Proc. Natl. Acad. Sci. USA*. vol. 96, pp. 6745-6750, June 1999.

Paired Neural Network with Negatively Correlated Features for Cancer Classification in DNA Gene Expression Profiles

Hong-Hee Won
Yonsei University
Department of Computer Science
134 Shinchon-dong, Sudaemoon-ku, Seoul 120-749, Korea
cool@candy.yonsei.ac.kr

Sung-Bae Cho
Yonsei University
Department of Computer Science
134 Shinchon-dong, Sudaemoon-ku, Seoul 120-749, Korea
sbcho@cs.yonsei.ac.kr

Abstract-While several conventional techniques for diagnosis of cancer in clinical practice can be often incomplete or misleading, molecular level diagnostics with gene expression profiles can offer the methodology of precise, objective, and systematic cancer classification. Moreover, since accurate classification of cancer is very important issue for treatment of cancer, it is desirable to make a decision by combining the results of various basis classifiers rather than by deciding the result with only one classifier. Generally combining classifiers gives high performance and high confidence. In spite of many advantages of ensemble classifiers, ensemble with mutually error-correlated classifiers has a limit in the performance. In this paper, we propose the ensemble of neural network classifiers learned from negatively correlated features to precisely classify cancer, and systematically evaluate the performances of the proposed method using three benchmark datasets. Experimental results show that the ensemble classifier with negatively correlated features produces the best recognition rate on the three benchmark datasets.

I. INTRODUCTION

DNA microarray technology has advanced so much that we can simultaneously measure the expression levels of thousands of genes under particular experimental environments and conditions [1]. DNA microarray technology makes it possible to understand life on the molecular level. The development of DNA microarray technology enables to generate large-scale gene expression data. It has led to many statistical and analytical challenges from the problems in biology because it has been produced large amount of genes. We can analyze the gene information very rapidly and precisely by managing them at one time [2] using several statistical methods and machine learning.

Cancer classification in clinical practice relied on clinical and histopathological information can be often incomplete or misleading. DNA microarray technology has been applied to the field of accurate prediction and diagnosis of cancer and expected that it would help them. Molecular level diagnostics with gene expression profiles can offer the methodology of precise, objective, and systematic cancer classification. Especially accurate classification of cancer is very important issue for treatment of cancer. Since the gene expression data usually consist of huge number of genes, several researchers have been studying many problems of cancer classification using data mining methods, machine learning algorithms and statistical methods to efficiently analyze these data [3, 4].

However, most researchers have partly evaluated only the performance of the feature selection methods and classifiers. There was extensive work that not only evaluated the individual classifiers, but combined the individual classifiers based on a correlation of the features to improve the performance [5].

Many researchers have worked on the ensemble of the multiple classifiers to improve the performance of classification. The ensemble classifier increases not only the performance of the classification, but also the confidence of the results. Theoretically, the performance of the ensemble classifier grows larger when the combined classifiers are mutually independent. Representative ensemble methods such as average combination, voting, weighted voting, Bayesian approach and neural network have been applied to many fields of data mining and machine learning. However, these methods do not assure that the combined classifiers would be independent. On the other hand, the methods such as boosting (bootstrap resampling), bagging (bootstrap aggregating) and arcing (adaptively resampling and combining) produce diverse sample data, train heterogeneous classifiers with the data, and combine the classifiers [4, 6, 7, 8].

In this paper, we propose the method varying the data to create an effective ensemble [9]. For diagnosis of cancer, ensemble approach has been adapted to reduce false alarm rate with high detection rate [10]. While the breast cancer data consist of a number of samples and few features, our experimental data have a lot of features and few samples. Though creating an effective ensemble by varying the data is identical goal, the difference is that we vary features of data but they varied samples of data in the paper [10]. We use the negative correlation of the features for that purpose. We define two ideal feature vectors for a standard of good feature, and utilize the features selected by scoring the similarity with each ideal feature vector. Two ideal feature vectors are the one high in class *A* and low in class *B*, and the other one low in class *A* and high in class *B*. Since the vectors have negative correlation, the sets of genes similar to each ideal vector are also negatively correlated. The negatively correlated features represent two different aspects of classification boundary for gene expression data. We can search in a much wider solution space by combining classifiers learned from these features. In this paper, we propose the paired neural network classifier trained with negatively correlated features. We test the proposed method in three benchmark cancer datasets, and systematically analyze the usefulness of the negative correlation.

II. BACKGROUNDS

A. cDNA Microarray

DNA arrays consist of a large number of DNA molecules spotted in a systemic order on a solid substrate. Depending on the size of each DNA spot on the array, DNA arrays can be categorized as microarrays when the diameter of DNA spot is less than 250 microns, and macroarrays when the diameter is bigger than 300 microns. The arrays with the small solid substrate are also referred to as DNA chips. It is so powerful that we can investigate the gene information in short time, because at least hundreds of genes can be put on the DNA microarray to be analyzed.

DNA microarrays are composed of thousands of individual DNA sequences printed in a high density array on a glass microscope slide using a robotic arrayer. The relative abundance of these spotted DNA sequences in two DNA or RNA samples may be assessed by monitoring the differential hybridization of the two samples to the sequences on the array. For mRNA samples, the two samples are reverse-transcribed into cDNA, labeled using different fluorescent dyes mixed (red-fluorescent dye Cy5 and green-fluorescent dye Cy3). After the hybridization of these samples with the arrayed DNA probes, the slides are imaged using scanner that makes fluorescence measurements for each dye. The log ratio between the two intensities of each dye is used as the gene expression data [1].

$$gene\_expression = \log_2 \frac{Int(Cy5)}{Int(Cy3)} \quad (1)$$

where Int(Cy5) and Int(Cy3) are the intensities of red and green colors. Since at least hundreds of genes are put on the DNA microarray, we can investigate the genome-wide information in short time.

B. Oligonucleotide Microarray

Affymetrix (Inc, Santa Clara, CA) has developed GeneChip® oligonucleotide array. High-density oligonucleotide DNA probe array technology employs photolithography and solid-phase DNA synthesis.

High-density oligonucleotide chip arrays are made using spatially patterned, light-directed combinatorial chemical synthesis, and contain up to hundreds of thousands of different oligonucleotides on a small glass surface. Synthetic linkers, modified with a photochemically removable protecting groups, are attached to a glass surface, and light is directed through a photolithographic mask to a specific areas on the surface to produce localized deprotection. Specific hydroxyl-protected deoxynucleotides are incubated with the surface, and chemical coupling occurs at those sites that have been illuminated in the preceding step. As the chemical cycle is repeated, each spot on the array contains a short synthetic oligonucleotide, typically 20-25 bases long. The oligonucleotides are designed based on the knowledge of the DNA target sequences, to ensure high-affinity and specificity of each oligonucleotide to a particular gene. This allows cross-hybridization with the other similar sequenced gene and local background to be estimated and subtracted [1].

III. PAIRED NEURAL NETWORK WITH NEGATIVELY CORRELATED FEATURES

The framework of the proposed paired neural network with negatively correlated features is shown in Fig. 1. The basic idea of paired neural network scheme is to develop several pairs of trained neural networks with two ideal feature vectors, and to classify a given input pattern by utilizing combination methods. Then it naturally raises the question of obtaining a consensus on the results of each individual network.

The features are selected from DNA microarray data using two different ideal feature vectors, Ideal feature A and Ideal feature B. The neural network classifiers are trained with the selected features. MLP I is defined as the result of MLP trained by the feature set selected based on Ideal Gene A $(1,1,...,1,0,0,...,0)$ and MLP II is defined as the result of MLP trained by the feature set selected based on Ideal Gene B $(0,0,...,0,1,1,...,1)$. MLP I is $MLP_{A1} \sim MLP_{Ak}$ and MLP II is $MLP_{B1} \sim MLP_{Bk}$ in Fig. 1. Since the negatively correlated features represent two different aspects of data, the classifiers learned with two negatively correlated feature sets respectively are mutually complementary. Combining the heterogeneous classifiers helps increasing the performance of the classification.

A. Negative Correlation

Theoretically, the more features we may concern, the more

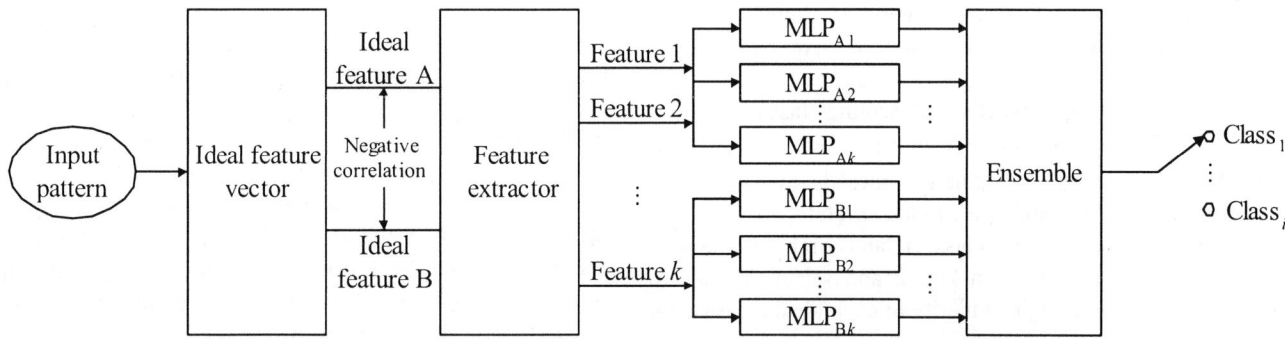

Fig. 1. Overview of the paired neural network with negatively correlated features

effective the classifier is to solve the problems [5]. But features that have overlapped in feature space may cause the redundancy of irrelevant information and result in the counter effect such as overfitting. When there are N feature selection methods, the set of non-linear transformation functions that change observation space into feature space is $\phi = \{\varphi_1, \varphi_2, \varphi_3, ..., \varphi_N\}$, and $\phi_k \in 2^\phi$, $I(\phi_k)$, the amount of classification information provided by the set of features ϕ_k, is defined as follows:

$$I(\phi_k) = \frac{a \sum A_i}{\frac{N}{2} \sum_{j=1, j \neq i}^{N} d_{ij}} + b \quad (2)$$

where d_{ij} is the dependency of the ith and the jth elements, A_i is the extent of the area which is occupied by the ith element from the feature space, and a and b are constant.

The higher dependency of a pair of features is, the smaller amount of classification information $I(\phi_k)$ is. As the extent of the area occupied by features is larger, the amount of classification information $I(\phi_k)$ is bigger. If we keep the number of features larger, the numerator of the equation is larger because the extent of the area occupied by features becomes wider. Although the numerator of the equation becomes larger, $I(\phi_k)$ will be mainly decreased without keeping d_{ij} small. Therefore, it is more desirable to use small number of mutually independent features than to unconditionally increase the number of features to enlarge $I(\phi_k)$, the amount of classification information provided to the classifier by the set of features. Correlation between feature sets can be induced from the distribution of feature numbers, or using mathematical analysis using statistics.

Therefore, it is more important to explore and utilize the informative features to train classifiers, rather than increase the number of features we use. The informative features are some genes highly related with particular classes for classification, which are called informative genes [11]. We have utilized the informative genes for the classification.

When there are $M \times N$ gene expression data having M samples and N genes and M samples are divided into two kinds of class, A and B, gene data g_i is defined as a vector as follows:

$$g_i = (e_1, e_2, e_3, \cdots, e_M), \quad i=1 \sim N \quad (3)$$

We want to know the locations of informative k features out of N. If it is possible to know representative vector g_{ideal} for class c_j, we can simply measure the correlation and similarity of g_i to classes, which tells the feature-goodness. Modeling g_{ideal}, we should use prior knowledge and intuitional experience about classes.

Suppose g_{ideal} is an ideal vector representing class c_j.

$$g_{ideal} = (e_1', e_2', e_3', \cdots, e_M') \quad (4)$$

In this paper, we attempt to define two ideal feature vectors as the one high in class A and low in class B $(1,1,...,1,0,0,...,0)$, and the other one low in class A and high in class B $(0,0,...,0,1,1,...,1)$ as shown in Fig. 2 and select the sets of informative genes with high similarity to each ideal gene vector.

Since Pearson's correlation coefficient of two ideal gene vectors is -1, two vectors are perfectly negatively correlated. The sets of gene vectors are also highly negatively correlated. The informative features selected by negative correlation represent two different aspects of training data. We can search in a much wider solution space by combining these features.

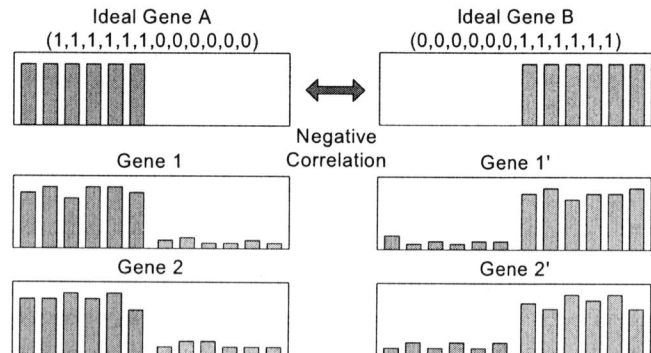

Fig. 2. Informative genes selected using negative correlation

B. Feature Selection Methods

Among thousands of genes whose expression levels are measured, not all are needed for classification. Microarray data consist of large number of genes in small samples. We need to select the informative genes for classification. This process is referred to as gene selection [11]. It is also called feature selection in machine learning. Informative genes highly correlated with class are selected generally using statistical correlation analysis, clustering method, etc. There have been various studies that extract the informative features for the classification using principal component analysis or genetic algorithm. The principal component analysis helps to extract the informative genes by transforming the feature space.

In this paper, informative genes are selected based on the similarity of gene vector g_i and ideal gene vectors A and B. The most similar 25 genes are used for classification. Correlation analysis and distance measure methods are used in order to measure the similarity of gene vector g_i and ideal gene vectors A and B.

Using the statistical correlation analysis, we can see the linear relationship and the direction of relation between two variables. Correlation coefficient r varies from -1 to $+1$, so that the data distributed near the line biased to $(+)$ direction will have positive coefficients, and the data near the line biased to $(-)$ direction will have negative coefficients. There are representative methods such as Pearson's correlation coefficient (PR) and Spearman's correlation coefficient (SP).

The similarity between two input vectors X and Y can be thought of as distance, which measures on how far the two vectors are located. The distance between g_{ideal_tumor} and g_i tells us how much likely the g_i is to the tumor class. Calculating the distance between them, if it is bigger than certain threshold, the gene g_i would belong to tumor class; otherwise g_i belong to normal class. We have adopted Euclidean distance (ED) and cosine coefficient (*CC*).

Feature selection methods are summarized in Table I: Pearson correlation coefficient (*PR*), Spearman correlation coefficient (*SP*), Euclidean distance (*ED*), and cosine coefficient (*CC*) are listed in order.

TABLE I
MATHEMATICAL FORMULA FOR EACH FEATURE SELECTION METHOD

$$PR(g_i, g_{ideal}) = \frac{\sum g_i g_{ideal} - \frac{\sum g_i \sum g_{ideal}}{N}}{\sqrt{\left(\sum g_i^2 - \frac{(\sum g_i)^2}{N}\right)\left(\sum g_{ideal}^2 - \frac{(\sum g_{ideal})^2}{N}\right)}} \quad (5)$$

$$SP(g_i, g_{ideal}) = 1 - \frac{6\sum(D_g - D_{ideal})^2}{N(N^2 - 1)} \quad (6)$$

(D_g and D_{ideal} are the rank matrices of g_i and g_{ideal})

$$ED(g_i, g_{ideal}) = \sqrt{\sum(g_i - g_{ideal})^2} \quad (7)$$

$$CC(g_i, g_{ideal}) = \frac{\sum g_i g_{ideal}}{\sqrt{\sum g_i^2 \sum g_{ideal}^2}} \quad (8)$$

C. Paired Neural Network

A feed-forward multilayer perceptron (MLP) is error backpropagation neural network that is applied in many fields due to its powerful and stable learning algorithm. A neural network can be considered as a mapping device between an input set and an output set. Mathematically, a neural network represents a function F that maps I into O; $F : I \rightarrow O$, or $y=f(x)$ where $y \in O$ and $x \in I$. Since the classification problem is a mapping from the feature space to some set of output classes, we can formalize the neural network as a classifier.

Suppose a two-layer neural network classifier with T neurons in the hidden layer, and c neurons in the output layer. Here T is the number of features, c is the number of classes, and H is an appropriately selected number. The network is fully connected between adjacent layers. The operation of this network can be thought of as a nonlinear decision-making process: Given an unknown input $X = (x_1, x_2, ..., x_T)$ and the class set $\Omega = \{w_1, w_2, ..., w_c\}$, each output neuron produces y_i of belonging to this class by

$$P(w_i | X) \approx y_i = f\left\{\sum_{k=1}^{H} w_{ik}^{om} f\left(\sum_{j=1}^{T} w_{kj}^{mi} x_j\right)\right\} \quad (9)$$

where w_{kj}^{mi} is a weight between the jth input neuron and the kth hidden neuron, w_{ik}^{om} is a weight from the kth hidden neuron to the ith class output, and f is a sigmoid function such as $f(x) = 1/(1 + e^{-x})$. The neuron having the maximum value is selected as the corresponding class.

The weight-update rule in backpropagation algorithm is defined as follows:

$$\Delta w_{ji}(n) = \eta \delta_j x_{ji} + \alpha \Delta w_{ji}(n-1) \quad (10)$$

where $\Delta w_{ji}(n)$ is the weight update performed during the nth iteration through the main loop of the algorithm, η is a positive constant called the learning rate, δ_j is the error term associated with j, x_{ji} is the input from neuron i to neuron j, and $0 \leq \alpha < 1$ is a constant called the *momentum*.

The network presented above trains on a set of example patterns and discovers relationships that distinguish the patterns. A network of a finite size, however, does not often load a particular mapping completely or it generalizes poorly. Increasing the size and number of hidden layers most often does not lead to any improvements.

We have chosen the Bayesian approach among several alternatives such as average combination, voting, weighted voting, Bayesian approach and neural network for final decision of the ensemble classifier. The Bayesian approach can solve the problem of tie-break in ensemble by using a priori knowledge of each combined classifier. While majority voting combines the classifiers with their results, Bayesian combination makes the error possibility of each classifier affect the final result. The method combines classifiers with different weights by using the previous knowledge of each classifier. Where k classifiers are combined, c_i, $i=1,...,m$, is the class of a sample, $c(classifier_j)$ is the class of the jth classifier, and w_i is a priori possibility of the class c_i, Bayesian combination is defined as follows:

$$c_{ensemble} = \arg\max_{1 \leq i \leq m} \left\{ w_i \prod_{j=1}^{k} P(c_i | c(classifier_j)) \right\} \quad (11)$$

IV. EXPERIMENTS

A. Experimental Environment

Three representative datasets, leukemia cancer dataset, colon cancer dataset and lymphoma cancer dataset, are used in this paper among several microarray datasets from published cancer gene expression studies. Leukemia dataset consists of 72 samples: 25 samples of acute myeloid leukemia (AML) and 47 samples of acute lymphoblastic leukemia (ALL). 38 out of 72 samples were used as training data and the remaining were used as test data. Each sample contains 7129 gene expression levels. Colon dataset consists of 62 samples of colon epithelial cells taken from colon-cancer patients. Each sample contains 2000 gene expression levels. 31 out of 62 samples were used as training data and the remaining were used as test data. Lymphoma dataset consists of 24 samples of GC B-like and 23 samples of activated B-like. 22 out of 47 samples were used as training data and the remaining were used as test data.

For feature selection, each gene is scored based on the feature selection methods described in Table I, and 25 top-ranked genes are chosen as the feature of the input pattern. There is no report on the optimal number of genes, but our previous study indicates that 25 is reasonable [5].

For classification, we have used 3-layered MLP with 5~15

hidden nodes, 2 output nodes, learning rate of 0.01~0.50 and momentum of 0.9 and finally chosen 8 hidden nodes and learning rate of 0.10 with high performance. The maximum learning iteration is fixed to 100 in order to prevent overfitting.

The negative correlation feature set consists of MLP I and MLP II. For comparative study, we have compared the result of the ensemble of the negatively correlated feature set to the result of the ensemble of MLP I and the result of the ensemble of MLP II. We have combined the classifiers learned with the negatively correlated feature set using Bayesian approach, analyzed the results and evaluated them. In case of the negatively correlated feature set, we have produced 8 feature-classifier combinations using 4 feature selection methods and 2 classifiers (MLP I and MLP II). We have tried to combine 2, 3 and 4 classifiers among 8 classifiers, and analyzed the results of ensemble. We have conducted all $_8C_k$ (k=2, 3 and 4) combinations of ensemble, and have investigated the best recognition rate and average recognition rate.

B. Result Analysis

Table II shows the recognition rate of the basis classifiers in each dataset. Column is the list of feature selection methods: Pearson's correlation coefficient (PR), Spearman's correlation coefficient (SP), Euclidean distance (ED) and cosine coefficient (CC). In Leukemia dataset, MLP I with Pearson's correlation coefficient and MLP I with information gain produce the best recognition rate, 97.1%, among the feature-classifier combinations. In Colon dataset, MLP I with cosine coefficient produces the best recognition rate, 83.9%. In Lymphoma dataset, MLP II with Spearman's correlation coefficient produces the best recognition rate, 88.0%.

The result of MLP I is different from that of MLP II on each dataset. While MLP I outperforms MLP II in Leukemia dataset and Colon dataset, MLP II outperforms MLP I in Lymphoma dataset. These results are caused by the characteristics of the datasets. We expect that it is more informative to use the set of genes selected using Ideal Gene A, so that MLP I can outperform MLP II. Table II shows that MLP I with Pearson's correlation coefficient and MLP I is superior to MLP II with Pearson's correlation coefficient.

TABLE II
RECOGNITION RATE WITH FEATURES AND CLASSIFIERS (%)

	Leukemia		Colon		Lymphoma	
	MLP I	MLP II	MLP I	MLP II	MLP I	MLP II
PR	97.1	79.4	74.2	77.4	64.0	72.0
SP	82.4	79.4	58.1	64.5	60.0	88.0
ED	91.2	61.8	67.8	77.4	56.0	72.0
CC	94.1	76.5	83.9	77.4	68.0	76.0
Mean	91.2	74.3	71.0	74.2	62.0	77.0

Fig. 3, 4 and 5 show the average recognition rates of the ensemble classifiers for benchmark datasets. The x-axis means the number of combined classifiers, and the y-axis means the recognition rate. In case of the negatively correlated feature set (MLP I + MLP II), 8 diverse feature sets have been produced with 2 ideal feature vectors (Ideal Gene A and Ideal Gene B) and 4 feature selection methods (Pearson's correlation coefficient, Spearman's correlation coefficient, Euclidean distance and cosine coefficient). The classifiers learned with 8 diverse feature sets have been combined using Bayesian approach. The average recognition rate means the average of all possible $_8C_k$ (k=2, 3 and 4) combinations of ensemble classifiers. As the number of combined classifiers is increasing, average recognition rate of the ensemble classifier is also increasing. The performance of the ensemble classifier is superior to the basis in all benchmark datasets. The best recognition rate of ensemble classifier is 97.1% in Leukemia dataset, 87.1% in Colon dataset, and 92.0% in Lymphoma dataset as shown in Table III. Compared with the best recognition rates of base classifiers, 97.1%, 83.9%, and 92.0% on the datasets respectively in Table II, the performance of ensemble is better.

Compared with the results of MLP I and MLP II, the negatively correlated features set (MLP I + MLP II) does not outperform in the average recognition rate, but outperforms in the best recognition rate. While the best recognition of the ensemble of MLP I and MLP II is decreasing as the number of combined classifiers is increasing, the best recognition of the ensemble of the negatively correlated coefficient feature set is increasing.

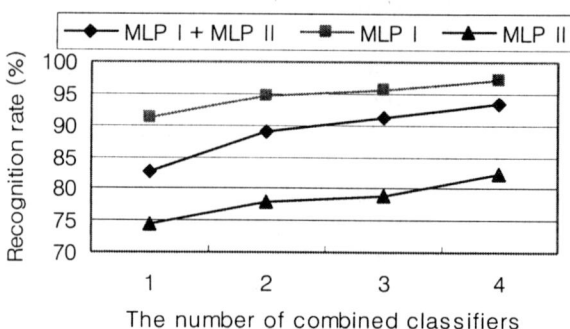

Fig. 3. Recognition rate of the ensemble in Leukemia

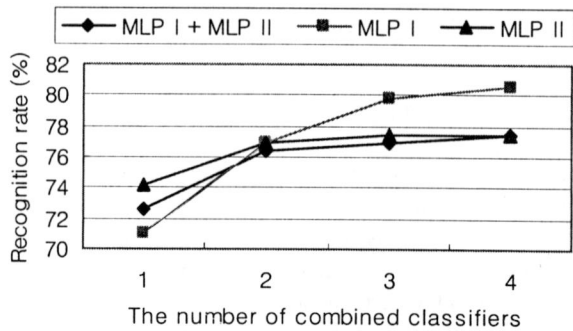

Fig. 4. Recognition rate of the ensemble in Colon

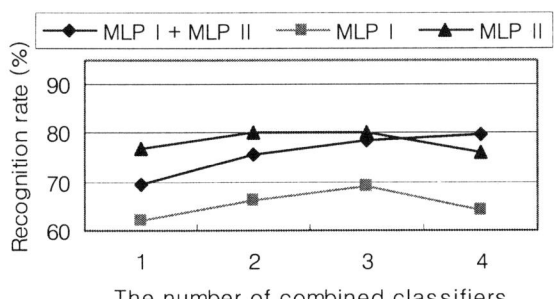

Fig. 5. Recognition rate of the ensemble in Lymphoma

TABLE III
THE BEST RECOGNITION RATE OF ENSEMBLE CLASSIFIERS (%)

	Generalization	Sensitivity	Specificity
Leukemia			
MLP I	97.1	92.9	100.0
MLP II	82.4	64.3	95.0
MLP I + MLP II	97.1	92.9	100.0
Colon			
MLP I	80.6	95.0	54.5
MLP II	77.4	95.0	45.5
MLP I + MLP II	87.1	95.0	72.7
Lymphoma			
MLP I	64	36.4	85.7
MLP II	76	72.7	78.6
MLP I + MLP II	92	90.9	92.9

This paper shows that the paired neural network classifier works and we can improve the classification performance by combining independent sets of classifiers learned from negatively correlated features, even when we use simple combination method like Bayesian approach.

V. CONCLUDING REMARKS

In this paper, we have proposed two ideal gene vectors to extract the informative genes for classification, selected the sets of genes based on the defined ideal gene vectors. We have combined the independent classifiers learned with the selected informative gene sets. In order to evaluate the usefulness of the proposed negative correlation, we have extracted the features using negative correlation and combined the neural network classifiers learned from negatively correlated features using Bayesian approach on three benchmark datasets.

The expression level of genes selected by negative correlation is clearly distinguishable between two classes. These patterns give enough information for the classification. The result of MLP I is different from that of MLP II on each dataset. While MLP I outperforms MLP II in Leukemia dataset and Colon dataset, MLP II outperforms MLP I in Lymphoma dataset. These results are caused by the characteristics of the dataset.

The experimental results show that the performance of the ensemble classifier is superior to the basis in all benchmark datasets. Moreover, the paired neural network classifier with negative correlation outperforms the ensemble classifiers without negative correlation. We have confirmed that negative correlation enables the ensemble classifier to work better by providing enough information for the classification to neural network classifiers.

ACKNOWLEDGEMENTS

This work was supported by Biometrics Engineering Research Center and a grant of Korea Health 21 R&D Project, Ministry of Health & Welfare, Republic of Korea.

REFERENCES

[1] Harrington, C. A., Rosenow, C., and Retief, J., "Monitoring gene expression using DNA microarrays," *Curr. Opin. Microbiol.*, vol. 3, pp. 285-291, 2000.
[2] Eisen, M. B. and Brown, P. O., "DNA arrays for analysis of gene expression," *Methods Enzymbol*, vol. 303, pp. 179-205, 1999.
[3] Dudoit, S., Fridlyand, J. and Speed, T. P., "Comparison of discrimination methods for the classification of tumors using gene expression data," *Technical Report 576*, Department of Statistics, University of California, Berkeley, 2000.
[4] Ben-Dor, A., Bruhn, L., Friedman, N., Nachman, I., Schummer, M. and Yakhini, N., "Tissue classification with gene expression profiles," *Journal of Computational Biology*, vol. 7, pp. 559-584, 2000.
[5] Cho, S.-B. and Ryu, J., "Classifying gene expression data of cancer using classifier ensemble with mutually exclusive features," *Proc. of the IEEE*, vol. 90, no. 11, pp. 1744-1753, 2002.
[6] Dettling, M. and Bühlmann, P., "How to use boosting for tumor classification with gene expression data," *Technical Report*, Department of Statistics, ETH Zürich, 2002.
[7] Parmanto, B., Munro, P. W. and Doyle, H. R., "Reducing variance of committee prediction with resampling techniques," *Connection Science*, vol. 8, pp. 405-426, 1996.
[8] Raviv, Y. and Intrator, N., "Bootstrapping with noise: An effective regularization techniques," *Connection Science*, vol. 8, pp. 355-372, 1996.
[9] Sharkey, A. J. C. and Sharkey, N. E., "Diversity, selection, and ensembles of artificial neural nets," *Proc. of Third Int. Conf. on Neural Networks and Their Applications, IUSPIM, France*, pp. 205-212, 1997.
[10] Sharkey, A. J. C., "Adapting an ensemble approach for the diagnosis of breast cancer," *Proc. Int. Conf. Artificial Neural Networks, Skövde, Sweden*, pp. 281-286, 1998.
[11] Li, L., Weinberg, C. R., Darden, T. A. and Pedersen, L. G., "Gene selection for sample classification based on gene expression data: Study of sensitivity to choice of parameters of the GA/KNN method," *Bioinformatics*, vol. 17, no. 12, pp. 1131-1142, 2001.

Probabilistic neural network classification for microarraydata

Barbara Comes, Arpad Kelemen
Department of Computer and Information Science
The University of Mississippi
University, MS 38677
Email: bjcomes@olemiss.edu

Abstract – We propose Probabilistic Neural Networks (PNN) to explore classifying microarray data patterns in gene expressions. The approach employs representative data that has patterns already identified to conduct training and testing of the classification capabilities of the PNN. Most supervised learning neural network models require multiple training cycles, whereas the PNN builds its model from just one training cycle. We hypothesize that the PNN is an ideal model to use for a quick analysis of a dataset and can be used as a tool to conduct a 'sanity check' on other classification models. Results show that a high-level classification rate can be achieved with this model with low time and model complexity. Comparison study with Bayesian Neural Network with structural learning has also been provided.

I. INTRODUCTION

DNA microarrays have allowed scientists to study the biological process of gene expression under many and varied conditions. The amount of data produced in conducting microarray gene testing presents an even bigger problem and that is the related microarry data analysis that follows. Now that microarray technology is producing more gene information than can be managed, scientists, and in particular, statisticians and computer scientists face the challenge of assisting the researcher in finding useful information from the vast arrays of collected gene data [1]. One area of interest is to detect patterns in gene expression data and the meaning behind these patterns. Another area of interest is the problem of dealing with the measurement errors produced due to the mechanics of conducting physical tests, i.e., dye inconsistencies, slight mechanical differences in measurement equipment, etc. These errors produce highly noisy data and present the problem of sorting out meaningful data in a noisy environment.

In this experiment we use gene expression data that identifies seven expression patterns during yeast sporulation as shown in Table I. The remaining gene expression patterns can be classified using the network model with the best results. Many gene expression classification studies have been conducted using some form of Bayesian neural networks or some form of Bayesian classifiers [2, 3, 4]. We explore the use of a probabilistic neural network to classify the gene expressions into the seven identified temporal patterns. The probabilistic neural network, introduced by Donald Specht in 1988, is a 3-layer network that uses a feed-forward, one-pass training algorithm to classify data [5]. The probabilistic neural network offers some of the same characteristics of the Bayesian neural network as it is based on Bayes theory [6]. A PNN offered by Mathworks Matlab and the Neural Network Toolbox is used to conduct the experiment. A PNN is typically easy to set up and eliminates lengthy and arduous network training iterations but still possesses good generalization characteristics. We want to explore and evaluate these characteristics.

TABLE I. THE SEVEN GENE EXPRESSION PATTERNS PRESENTED DURING YEAST SPORULATION.

Metabolic	Early	Early II	Early-Mid	Middle	Mid-Late	Late
ACS1	ZIP1	KGD2	YBL078C	YSW1	CDC27	SPS100
PYC1	YDR374C	AGA2	QRI1	SPR28	DIT2	YKL050C
SIP4	DMC1	YPT32	PDS1	SP82	DIT1	YMR322C
CAT2	HOP1	MRD1	APC4	YLR227C		YOR391C
Y0R100C	IME2	SPO18	KNR4	ORC3		
CAR1		NAB4	STU2	YLL005C		
		YPR182W	YNL013C	YLL012W		

The rest of the paper is divided as follows: in Section II we discuss the data acquisition and data preprocessing that we conducted. In Section III we describe the characteristics and architecture of the probabilistic neural network. Section IV presents the results based on cross-validation and multiple runs using the yeast microarray gene expression data. Section V discusses the further work that is needed to enhance this test and we conclude with Section VI by offering our thoughts on the uses of this model for this type of classification problem.

II. DATA ACQUISITION AND PREPROCESSING

The microarray data was obtained from an experiment described in Chu, et al [7] and published on the Stanford Genomic Resources website under Published Datasets. Of interest are genes that co-express under similar conditions (different drug dosages) at different times. This experiment used spotted DNA microarray tests that contained 97% of yeast genes of Saccharomyces cerevisiae yeast cells. The cells were studied and tested to explore temporal gene expression during meiosis and spore formulation (see fig 1). Yeast cells were induced to sporulation by placing them in a nitrogen-deficient substance and mRNA tests were taken at time points: 0, 30 min., and 2, 5, 7, 9, and 11.5 hours (see fig 2). For each measured time point, as visualized in fig. 2, a 'red' cDNA test was taken. At the beginning of the test, at time 0, a 'green' cDNA sample is prepared to serve as a baseline for this particular 'row' of timed tests [4]. Seven microarrays were used, each corresponding to each of the timed test points. Each time point produced was mixed with the green time 0 sample to provide a leveling effect.

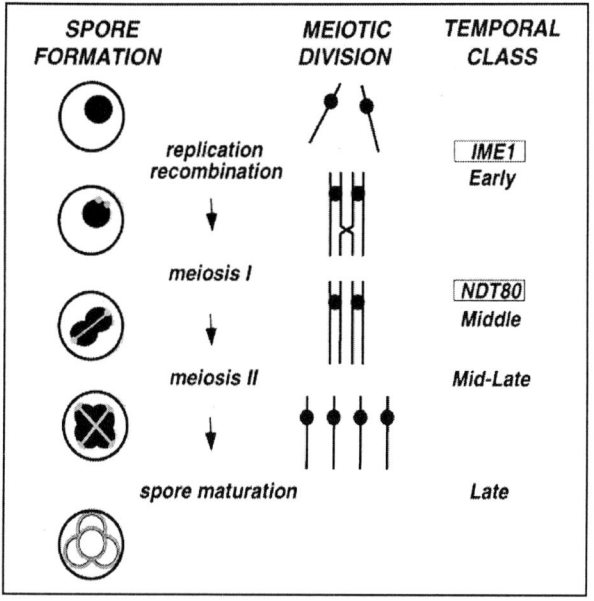

Fig 1. S. cerevisiae sporulation, meiotic division, and generated temporal class [7]

The data contains four quantitative measurements for each time point reading represented by red and green as shown in fig. 2. The four measurements for each time point are: red signal, red background, green signal, and green background. To convert the data into a format suitable for neural network processing, the four data points for each of the seven timed points were normalized in the following manner: log [(red signal – red background)/green signal – green background)].

The acquired dataset contained 6118 rows of which only 477 rows possessed temporal pattern profiles. The intent of this research is to test the PNN classification neural network and its capability to classify gene expression data into the seven known temporal profiles based on the seven time point gene patterns. Therefore, we used only the 477 rows of the data where their temporal pattern classification was already known to build and test the PNN model. The rest of the dataset could be run through the model for classification once the model is built and classification success rates determined. The 477 samples were ordered by temporal class and the temporal text class value was modified to a numerical value 1 through 7 (see Table II).

Within each of the seven temporal patterns, a group identification number was assigned to each row as 1, 2, 3 (and then repeated) for the entire class and each time a new class began, the sequence was started at 1 again. This technique provided the means to divide the training and testing data proportionately and allowed us to conduct multiple runs to verify the network's testing results. Three training and testing dataset groups were defined using the group id number using the following method: For Test 1, groups 1 and 3 (318 rows) were used for the training data and group 2 (159 rows) was used for the testing data. For Test 2, groups 1 and 2 (321 rows) were used for the training data and group 3 (156 rows) was used for testing. For Test 3, groups 2 and 3 (315 rows) were used for the training data and group 1 (162 rows) was used for the testing data.

TABLE II. SEVEN TEMPORAL GENE EXPRESSION PATTERNS CONVERTED TO NUMERICAL VALUES.

Metabolic	1
Early I	2
Early II	3
Early-Mid	4
Middle	5
Mid-Late	6
Late	7

The training data consisted of input/target pairs. Each input row consisted of the seven time point measurements normalized as discussed earlier. The matching target is the known temporal class that we are attempting to be able to predict for other gene expression patterns where the temporal classification is not known. The test dataset consisted of sample data where the temporal class pattern is known but not presented to the network model. The purpose of the test was to run the test dataset through the network model and to let the network model classify the test dataset based on previous training of the network.

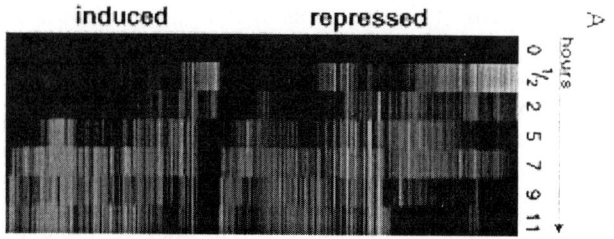

Fig 2. Visual representation of gene expression during sporulation. The red indicates the induced gene and the green represents a baseline gene. Each row represents the gene expressed at that point in time. Quantitatively there are 4 data points for each row [7]

III. DESIGN OF PROBABILISTIC NEURAL NETWORK

A PNN, a supervised neural network, may require more neurons than a standard feed-forward backpropagation network, but they require less set-up time and training time. PNN's work best when an adequate number of samples are available to train with and those samples possess good class distinctions. The PNN was chosen as the network model to use in this classification experiment. The PNN provides a general solution to pattern classification problems by using a statistical approach called Bayesian classifiers [6]. Bayes theory accounts for the relative frequency of already occurring events and the already learned patterns. Mathworks' Matlab and Neural Network Toolbox PNN model was used to conduct the classification experiment (see fig. 3).

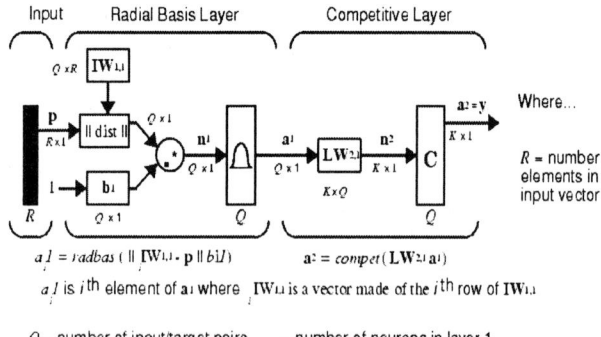

The PNN consists of two layers: a radial basis layer and a competitive layer. During training, the model reads in the

Fig 3. The architecture of a Probabilistic Neural Network[8]

input/target vector pairs and forms a pattern based on the pattern distinctions for that particular target. Weights are calculated based on input values as they are presented. The radial basis layer biases are all set to 0.8326/spread by default, where spread is a sensitivity factor - the distance between adjacent class patterns. The second layer of the network tracks the relative frequency or probability that a vector classifies to a particular target. The transfer function classifies the input vector into one of the target classes based on the pattern of the test input vector and the probability associated with this class. Matlab's PNN accepts a spread value which indicates the distance between class pattern vectors [8].

IV. EXPERIMENTAL RESULTS

The PNN model requires only one training cycle per training input/target dataset. Also, the order of the training input/target pairs does not affect the quality of the training nor does the order of the test dataset affect the outcome of its classification results.

Ten PNN models were trained each with varied spread values for each of the three different stratified training datasets for a resulting 30 tests in total. The test data for each of the three partitioned data groups was run through the trained PNN network and the number of pattern matches was recorded in a spreadsheet. For the purpose of clarity, Test 1 refers to the first training/testing dataset, Test 2 refers to the second training/testing dataset, and Test 3 refers to the third training/testing dataset. Table III shows the percentage of correct classifications for each dataset/spread combination network model that was created.

According to the results as shown in Table III, we can infer that the best spread value to use for the PNN for the overall classification of the temporal classes for this particular dataset is 0.08 or 0.1. The results between the 0.08 and 0.1 spread PNN are not significantly different and produced the best percentage of overall class matches at an accuracy rate of approximately 80%.

TABLE III. RESULTS OF THREE TEST DATASETS WITH VARYING SPREAD VALUES.

Spread Value	Test 1 % Match	Test 2 % Match	Test 3 % Match	Average % Match
0.009	64.15	65.39	67.90	65.81
0.01	66.04	66.03	69.75	67.27
0.03	75.47	78.85	78.40	77.57
0.05	76.10	78.85	79.01	77.78
0.08	77.99	79.49	80.86	79.45
0.1	77.99	80.77	79.63	79.46
0.5	62.26	63.46	67.28	64.33
1	40.25	39.10	40.12	39.82
1.8	33.33	32.69	32.72	32.91
2	33.33	32.69	32.72	32.91
Train n	318	321	315	
Test n	159	156	162	

Fig. 4 demonstrates the quickly declining correct classification rate beginning with the 0.5 spread value tests. It would be beneficial to conduct a statistical analysis of the data across the seven time points to determine the amount of disparity in the data. These seven time measurements determine the class distinctions that are ultimately used to select a classification.

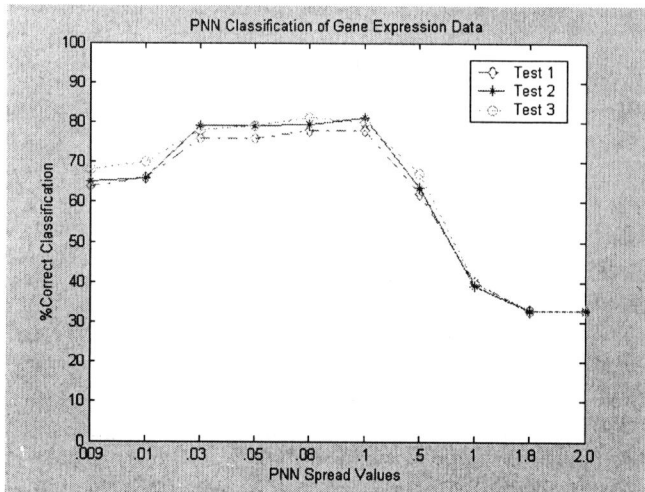

Fig 4. Line graph showing the 3 datasets used with PNN with varying spread values of .009, .01, .03, .05, .08, .1, .5, 1, 1.8, 2.

Fig. 5 depicts the percent of correct classification within each classification group (see Table II) for the PNN model with the best classification rate (0.1 spread) for the three different training/testing datasets. The rate of correct classification varies widely between some of the time points and only can be attributed to the variation in the training set and corresponding testing set. This indicates that either some of the data better differentiates a classification group or that the testing data better 'fits' the trained data. Further analysis of the data itself may be interesting and we may be able to better ascertain the important class distinctions.

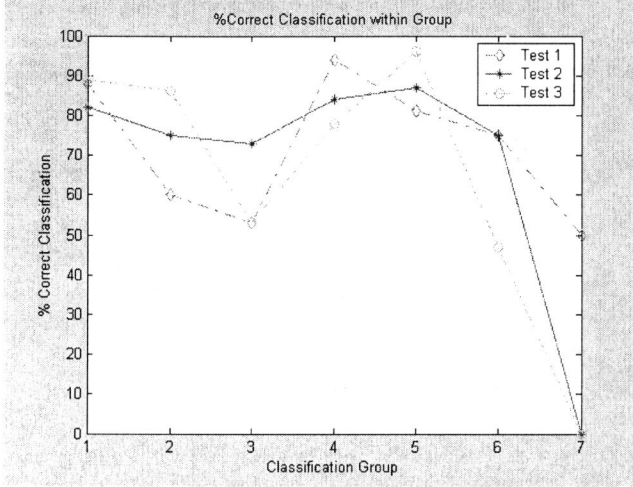

Fig 5. Line graph depicting the % correct classification within each classification group for the 0.1 spread value PNN model for the three different training/test datasets.

The PNN produces fairly good results with little time invested in training the network model. This experiment was conducted by selecting a spread value based on the previous run's results. Statistical analysis of the data could be done beforehand to determine the optimal spread value. Conducting this same test design with two other different datasets would further demonstrate the effectiveness of the PNN model. It would be interesting to see how the PNN model would perform on a dataset where the class distinctions are better differentiated than the subject dataset.

V. RELATED WORK

Many different classification techniques have been devised and tested by computer scientists and statisticians in an attempt to more accurately classify gene expression data to assist medical researchers in their studies using microarray data. For example, a Bayesian neural network (BNN) with structural learning was used by Liang, George, and Kelemen [4] on the same dataset with promising results. The model they developed was a supervised learning neural network that required on average 850 epochs even though as many as 5000 epochs were used to train the model. The best correct classification rate that they achieved was over 90%, but this was achieved with a much higher time complexity than the PNN model. In comparison, the PNN model achieved the best correct classification rate of higher than 80% with a much lower time complexity. The PNN model may be losing the essence of gene expression over time since the iterative training process is not a factor in the PNN model. The two models are similar in that they both use supervised learning algorithms and have Bayesian characteristics. Further research and experiments using these types of neural networks to classify gene expression data is needed in order to fine-tune and improve these models.

VI. CONCLUSION

The PNN demonstrated fairly good results with the testing conducted. A correct classification rate as high as 80.86% was achieved, with an average over 80%. The PNN model achieved only 10% lower classification rate than an earlier work done using a BNN, but with a significantly lower time and model complexity. Since the time and labor involved running the PNN is low (once the data is preprocessed) the PNN is an excellent classification technique to obtain quick statistics and ballpark figures. PNN can be used to obtain first hand knowledge about the data to be analyzed quickly and help to decide which classification model to be applied for further analysis. Statistical analysis of the data beforehand, could determine the data differences across the seven time points and could be used as a starting point in determining the spread value for the PNN.

REFERENCES

[1] Primer on Molecular Genetics", DOE Human Genome 1991-92 Program Report, Oak Ridge National Laboratory, Oak Ridge, TN, pp.1-43, June 1992.
[2] P. Baldi, A. Long, "A Bayesian framework for the analysis of microarry expression data: regularized t-test and statistical inferences of gene changes," Bioinformatics, Vol. 17(6), pp. 509-519, 2001.
[3] A. Keller, M. Schummer, W. Ruzzo, L. Hood, "Bayesian classification of DNA array expression data", Technical Report UW-CSE-2000-08-01, University of Washington, 2000.
[4] Y. Liang, E. George, A. Kelemen, "Bayesian neural network for microarray data," in the proceedings of the IEEE International Joint Conference on Neural Networks, Hawaii, pp. 193-198, 2002.
[5] Donald Specht, "Probabilistic neural networks," Neural Networks, Vol. 3, pp. 109-118, 1990.
[6] G. Paass, "Probabilistic reasoning and probabilistic neural networks," IJIS: International Journal of Intelligent Systems, pp. 1-6, 1992.
[7] S. Chu, J. DeRisi, M. Eisen, J. Mulholland, D. Bostein, P. O. Brown, I. Herskowitz, "The transcriptional program of sporulation in budding yeast," Science, Vol. 282, pp. 699-705, October 1998.
[8] Matlab6 User Manual, Release 12, Natick, MA: Mathworks, Inc., 2001.
[9] M. Craven, J. Shavlik, "Using neural networks for data mining," Future Generation Computer Systems, Vol 13, pp.211-229, 1997.
[10] J. Khan, J. Wei, R. Ringner, et al, "Classification and diagnostic prediction of cancers using gene expression profiling and artificial neural networks," Nature Medicine, Vol. 7, No 6, pp. 673-679, June 2001.
[11] J. Han, M. Kamber, Data Mining : Concepts and Techniques, Morgan Kaufman Publishers, San Francisco, 2001.

Classification of Eukaryotic and Prokaryotic Cells by a Backpropagation Network

TERJE KRISTENSEN
Departement of Computer Science,
Bergen University College, Nygårdsgaten 112,
N-5020, Bergen, Norway
E-mail: tkr@hib.no

RUBEN PATEL
Centre Of Marine Resources,
Institute of Marine Research, Nordnesgaten 33
N-5817, Bergen, Norway
E-mail: ruben@imr.no

Abstract

In this paper we show how a Backpropagation neural network is used to classify between eukaryotic and prokaryotic cells. The classification is based on their DNA (Deoxyribonuclei) sequences which are obtained from different databases available on the Internet. The sequences are first preprocessed using a sliding window technique to obtain sub-sequence frequencies, and then normalised to make them comparable.

Keywords: Backpropagation, prokaryotic and eukaryotic DNA-sequences, Matlab, Java, sliding window

1. Introduction

One of the research goals of molecular biology is to determine a complete genetic description of any organism. In the Human Genome Project [4] the goal is to decipher the exact sequence of about 3 billion nucleotides in the 46 human chromosomes. An important part of the genome project is the computational processing of data [2]. The data first have to be organised into databases, and then analysed to see what information they contain. Since the birth of the Human Genome Project, sequence analysis as a computational method has been used to infer biological information from the sequence data.

The classical approach to analysing sequences is by sequence matching using either single or multiple alignment techniques [7,8]. With these techniques one seeks to determine whether sequences are significantly similar or not.

Another approach is to use theories from neural computing to detect genetic information in the DNA sequences. Neural networks have been applied to various tasks such as automatic hyphenation of natural languages [11,12], edge detection [13], hand written Zip code recognition and DNA sequence recognition [1,14].

A Backpropagation (BP) neural network may learn to categorise between different types of bacteria cells related to the structure of their DNA-sequences. Such a method is based on pattern recognition analysis, and is built on the assumption that some underlying characteristics of the DNA-sequence can be used to identify its bacteria type.

A nucleotide sequence can be viewed as a language based on four letters: A, G, C and T where the number of A's is the same as the number of T's. This is the same for C's and G's. However, the relation of A(T) and G(C) can vary tremendously, and depends on the actual species that are studied. This fact can for instance be used in environmental research, where oil on the sea surface may contain many different types of species that can be identified on basis of their DNA sequence structure. Other neural network paradigms than a BP network may also be used to analyse DNA sequences [14,17].

In this paper, however, we will focus on how to use a BP network to distinguish between *eukaryotic* and *prokaryotic* sequences on basis of their nucleotide frequency structure [8]. Cells can be divided into two major groups, prokaryotic and eukaryotic cells. All prokaryotic cells are uni-cellular organisms and consist mostly of bacteria. The genome of a prokaryotic cell consists of one double helix DNA strand, floating freely in the cell. This double helix strand is often circular. The genome of the bacterium E.Coli for instance, consists of a circular strand of five and a half million bases.

Most eukaryotes are multicellular, but some are uni-cellular. The main difference between prokaryotic cells and eukaryotic cells is that eukaryotic cells contain a nucleus that is surrounded by a membrane. Prokaryotic cells do not have such a nucleus. In such cells the frequency distribution of pairs of nucleotides are different from those in prokaryotic cells [3].

2. The Backpropagation network

In a Backpropagation network the processing elements are organised in layers. Neurons in one layer receive signals from neurons in layers directly below, and send signals to neurons in the layer directly above. There is no connection between neurons in the same layer. The net input to each node is the weighted sum of outputs of the nodes in the previous layer. Each node is activated in accordance with the input to the node and the activation of the node. The net input to a node j in a layer is

$$S_j = \Sigma\, w_{ji}\, a_i \qquad (1)$$

where a_i is output from node i in the previous layer. The output of node j is then given by

$$a_j = f(S_j) \qquad (2)$$

where f usually is the *sigmodal* activation function given by (3).

$$f(S_j) = \frac{1}{1+e^{-S_j}} \quad (3)$$

In the learning phase we present patterns to the network, and the weights are adjusted so that the produced outputs from the output nodes are equal to the target. In fact, we want the network to find a single set of weights that will satisfy all the (input, output) pairs presented.

In general, the outputs $\{a_{pi}\}$ (p is the current pattern) of the nodes in the output layer will not be the same as the target or desired values $\{t_{pi}\}$. The system error or the cost function for the network is defined by:

$$E = \frac{1}{N}\frac{1}{2}\sum_p \sum_i (t_{pi} - a_{pi})^2 \quad (4)$$

where N is the total number of patterns. A gradient search should be based on minimisation of the expression in equation (4). The weight updating rule then becomes:

$$\Delta w_{ji} = -\alpha \delta_j a_i + \beta \Delta w_{ji} \quad (5)$$

where α is the learning rate, δ_j is the error for any node and β is the momentum constant. For a more thorough discussion see reference [9, 14].

3. Theory

Statistical analysis of several DNA sequences has shown that the distribution of nucleotides is far from random [17]. Some dinucleotide combinations in prokaryotic DNA sequences are more dominating than in eukaryotic cells. We will anticipate that this simple difference in data occurrence might be sufficient to allow species identification. We may then train a BP network to use the differences in the nucleotide distribution to discriminate between eukaryotic and prokaryotic cells. We assume there that the identification of the DNA sequence is based solely on the frequency of nucleotide sub-sequences.

A sliding window is used to count the number of nucleotide sub-sequences of the DNA sequence. In general the size of the window may vary, from one base wide to a user defined number w. By choosing a window of length one, we simply count the number of the different bases of the DNA sequence. The result will be four different frequencies, one for each base. A window of length two will give sixteen different ordered sub-sequences. The frequency of each sub-sequence is computed by counting the occurrence of each nucleotide pair in the DNA sequence.

The number of triplets or codon units of the DNA sequence, may be estimated by using a window of three bases wide. This results in 4^3 or 64 ordered triplets. This is maybe the most relevant sub-sequence to study because the codon itself has important meaning in the DNA sequence. In general, a window of w bases results in 4^w sub-sequences of length w to be counted.

For a sliding window of length two the frequency of sub-sequence AA is denoted as f_{AA}, for AC as f_{AC} and so on. These numbers are collected in a vector $\mathbf{F_n}$, where n denotes the number of DNA sub-sequences. For a sliding window of size two, n is equal to 16. The counting of the different nucleotide pairs is illustrated in figure 1. In the figure the counting of the nucleotide pair AC is shown. After counting the pair AC, the window is moved one letter to the right to cover the next nucleotide pair. This is done to the end of the DNA sequence.

|AC|ATGATGCTA...

A|CA|TGATGCTA...

AC|AT|GATGCTA...

ACA|TG|ATGCTA...

Figure 1. A sliding window consisting of two letters is used to count the occurrence of each ordered nucleotide pair.

The DNA sequences obtained on the Internet have different sequence length. The frequency of the different nucleotide pairs have to be normalised to compare and present them to the BP network. The normalisation condition of the frequency vector F_n is given by equation 6.

$$S_n = \frac{F_n}{|F_n|} \quad (6)$$

Here $|\mathbf{F_n}|$ means the Euclidean norm of the frequency vector. This non-linear transformation conserves the direction of the vector and enhances the differences among the input vectors. The geometric interpretation of the transformation is that the vector $\mathbf{F_n}$ is moved onto the hyper unit sphere.

The network is trained according to the BP algorithm [10,18]. A set of S_n vectors and their corresponding classification are presented to the network. During the training session the input to the network is alternately selected from the eukaryotic and prokaryotic cell class. After the training session is finished, the network is tested on a set of unknown S_n vectors. The output is recorded, and the performance of the network is computed.

The BP network used for window size two is shown in figure 2. The input layer consists of 16 input nodes, one for each component of $\mathbf{S_n} = (s_1, s_2, ..., s_n)$. Each p_{si} given in figure 2 is a 'relative frequency' of each nucleotide pair of a DNA sequence. This is not the conventional relative frequency, because the relative frequencies are not summed up to 1. In this case the 'relative frequency' is defined by the actual number of each nucleotide pair, divided by the square root of the total sum of the square of frequencies of all nucleotide pairs in the DNA sequence.

4. Materials and Methods

The different DNA sequences were obtained from several DNA databases on the Internet. The experiments were performed under Window 2000 and on a Pentium III processor running at 450 MHz. Software tools as Java and Matlab were also used in the experiments. Java classes for reading the EMBLM format, counting the sequences by use of the sliding window technique and normalisation of the frequency vectors, have been developed for use in the experiments. The Java classes developed were imported to Matlab, and Matlab's neural network toolbox was used in training and classification.

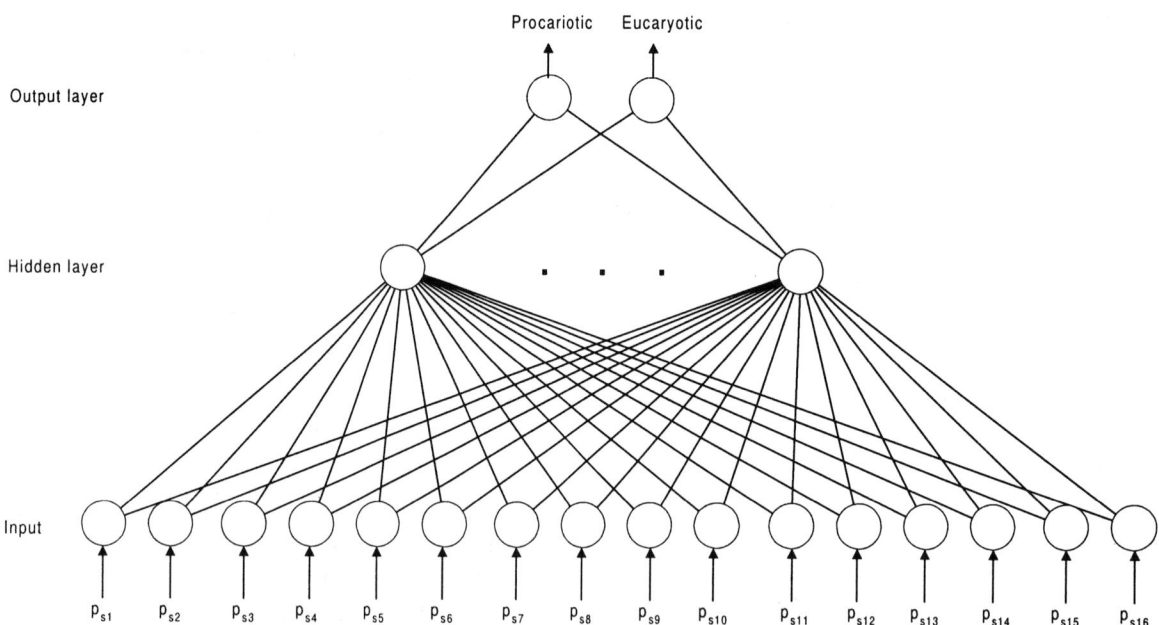

Fig. 2. Classification of eukaryotic and prokaryotic DNA-sequences by a BP network. Each p_{xi} is a 'relative frequency' of a nucleotide pair.

```
SQ   Sequence 691 BP; 135 A; 243 C; 192 G; 121 T; 0 other;
     CCTGAACCCG GTGTCCCCGG GTGGGGGGTG GGGACGCCAC GGCCGAAGCA GCTAGCTCCG       60
     TTCGTGATCC GGGAGCCTGG TGCCAGCGAG ACCTGGAATT TCCGGTCTGG TTGGTCTGGG      120
     GCCCCGCGGA GCCAGGTTGA TACCCTCACC TCCAACCCC  AGGCCCTCGG ATGCCCAGAA      180
     CCTGTAGGCC GCACCGTGGA CTTGTTCTTA ATCGAGGGGC ACTTCTACCC TAGCCGGGCC      240
     CAGCCCCCGA GCAGTGCAGC CTCCCGAGTG CAGAGTGCAG CCCCTGCCCG CCCTGGCCCA      300
     GCTGCCCATG TCTACCCTGC TGGATCCCAA GTAATGATGA TCCCTTCCCA GATCTCCTAC      360
     CCAGCCTCCC AGGGGGCCTA CTACATCCCT GGACAGGGGC GTTCCACATA CGTTGTCCCG      420
     ACACAGCAGT ACCCTGTGCA GCCAGGAGCC CCAGGCTTCT ATCCAGGTGC AAGCCCTACA      480
     GAATTTGGGA CCTACGCTGG CGCCTACTAT CCAGCCCAAG GGGTGCAGCA GTTTCCCACT      540
     GGCGTGGCCC CCGCCCCAGT TTTGATGAAC CAGCCACCCC AGATTGCTCC CAAGAGGGAG      600
     CGTAAGACGA TCCGAATTCG AGATCCAAAC CAAGGAGGAA AGGATATCAC AGAGGAGATC      660
     ATGTCTGGGG CCCGCACTGC CTCCACACCC A                                    691
```

Fig 3. A database entry of a eucaryotic DNA sequence from the EMBL database on the Internet. The length of the DNA-sequence is 691 bases. The DNA sequence is a protein found in human.

Some Matlab programs were also developed for plotting the frequency vectors and the global error during training. The EMBL format of a DNA sequence on the Internet looks like the one given in figure 3.

5. Feature Analysis

Before the training of the BP network started, a feature analysis of the training data was carried out. The training set consists of fifteen DNA sequences from each cell class. S_n vectors from the two classes were aligned to see if one could find similarities between them. The main relative frequency of corresponding sub-sequences in each class were computed and plotted in a graph. The main reason for doing these experiments was to make an analysis to see if the methodology used was adequate, and if there exist features that will make the DNA sequences different.

The correlation between the main relative frequency of eukaryotic and prokaryotic sub-sequences is given by the conventional linear correlation coefficient based on the usual covariance matrix.

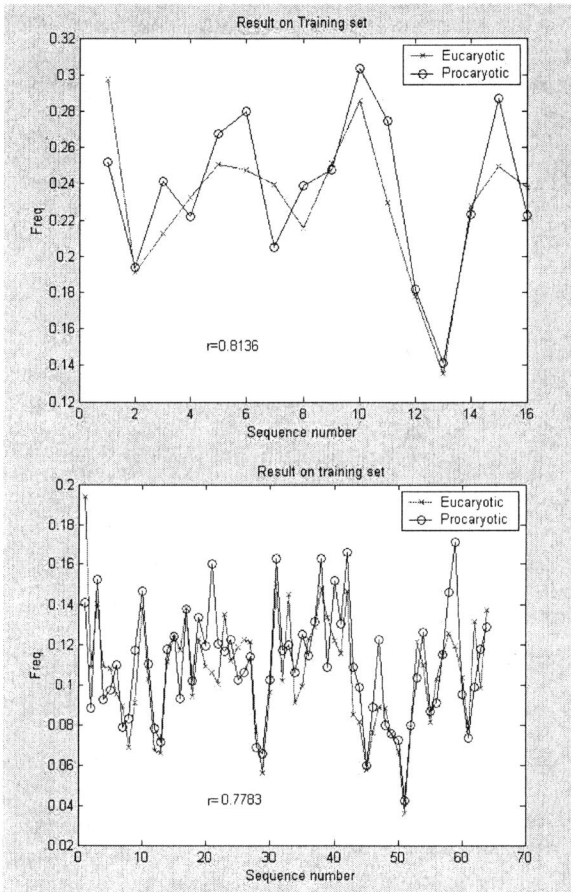

Fig. 4. The means of 'relative frequency' for corresponding sub-sequences of size 2 and 3 of eukaryotic and prokaryotic DNA sequences are compared.

The results of the comparison between eukaryotic and prokaryotic sequences in the training set are given in figure 4. The upper graph shows the correlation between the DNA sub-sequences when the size of the sliding window is *two*. The correlation coefficient r is then estimated to 0.82. The lower graph shows a comparison between eukaryotic and prokaryotic sequences when the window size is *three*. The correlation coefficient r is now 0.74.

Similar experiments were also carried out when the size of the window was greater than three. In figure 5 we notice that the correlation coefficient drops when the window size increases. This means that by using longer sub-sequences, the feature difference between the two DNA classes is getting more substantial. The classification accuracy between the different DNA sequences should then increase. However, longer sub-sequences will tend to identify one specific DNA strand. This can be understood by letting the window size approach the length of the DNA sequence. The feature extraction should then be harder and therefore make it more difficult for the network to generalise. A larger window will also generate more training data which in general will require more computer power and longer training times.

6. The Neural Network Approach

A DNA sequence taken from living material does not consist of one long strand, but rather of fragments. Fragment assembling is an ongoing research area in Bioinformatics, and one of the big tasks in this matter is to construct fast and accurate sequencing algorithms.

By using a BP neural network the classification task between the different DNA sequences might reduce the need for frequency aligning, and hence the classification time in general. From figure 5 we notice that for sub-sequences of length two to four bases, the correlation coefficient does not vary much. This should mean that for a window of length 2, 3 or 4 bases wide, the classification performance should not differ very much.

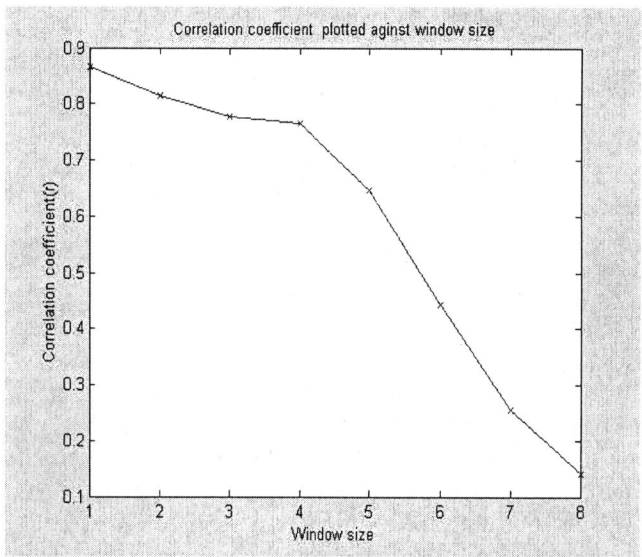

Fig. 5. The correlation coefficient between eukaryotic and prokaryotic DNA sequences drops when the window size increases.

If we want a neural network to fully automate the classification task of DNA sequences, we may get severe problems to solve. In general, both the training and testing (performance) of the network will depend on the window size. By changing the window size, the topology of the network will also change. The number of input nodes of the network is dependent on the window size. For a window size of length w the number of input nodes is equal to 4^w. By changing the number of input nodes, the number of neurons of the hidden layer must also change, to make the network topology optimal. However, a new network topology configuration in general would mean redefining of the learning rate α and momentum β of the learning algorithm. This will again influence the training time of the network. So when changing the network topology the different network's parameters should also be changed accordingly.

A full automation of the categorisation by a BP neural network for any size of sub-sequences, is a very difficult task to solve. To be able to compare the results of the different experiments on a general basis, we may plot the results in the 3D space for different parameter values. We could for instance represent this as a point in 3D where the axes are defined by the window size, learning rate and number of hidden neurons respectively.

A more detailed analysis may also take into account other parameters mentioned above. We could represent the different parameters as components of a vector in hyper space. However, the three parameters mentioned above are the most significant ones. We could also reduce the parameters by introducing some kind of a thumb rule, where for instance the number of neurons in the hidden layer could be defined in percent of number of neurons in the input layer.

7. Experiments and Results

The experiments so far have been carried out for a sliding window of size two. Several experiments have been done where the parameters mentioned in section 5 have been changed manually. Figure 2 shows the neural network which is used during the experiments.

The training set consisted only of 30 DNA sequences distributed equally between eukaryotes and prokaryotes. In one experiment only the number of hidden neurons were varied. The most optimal number was 30 hidden nodes. In another experiment the learning rate α and the momentum β were varied. The training time of the network was nearly 0.5 hour.

The training of the network is shown in figure 6. The number of iteration was set to 30 000. The global error was then estimated to about 10 %. In general this error is too high. However, the experiments showed that the generalisation of the network was then optimal. More training of the network resulted in that some over-training took place. The best results were achieved for the learning rate α = 0.07 and momentum β = 0.1. These parameter values are very small which could mean that the learning of the network must be slow in order to detect more detailed structures in the DNA sequences.

The performance of the network has been tested on 15 unknown DNA sequences found on the Internet. The best prediction was 80 %.

8. Conclusion and Further Work

A Backpropagation neural network program has been used to categorise between eukaryotic and prokaryotic DNA-sequences found in biological databases on the Internet. All the DNA sequences have been represented in the EMBL format. Programs in Java and Mathlab have been developed to carry out the experiments.

The experiments so far have shown that a Backpropagation network is able to distinguish between prokaryotes and eukaryotes by use of simple feature extraction technique. The performance of the network was estimated to 80 % in the best case.

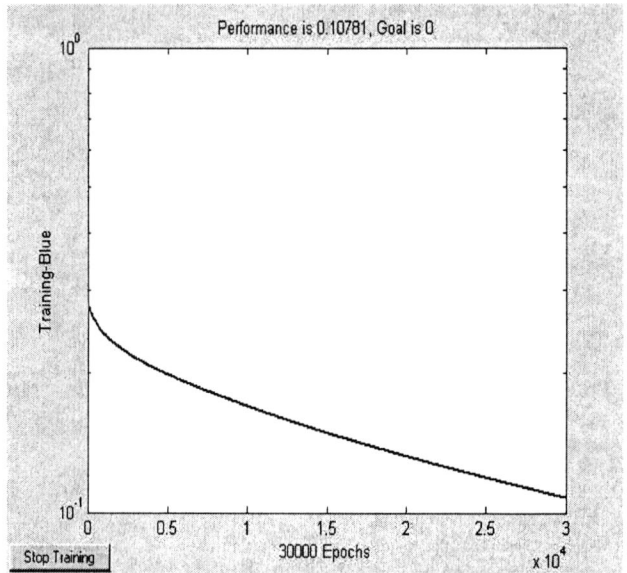

Fig 6. Training of the BP neural network. The training time is 30000 iterations.

Further work remains for a more fully exploration of this problem. So far the experiments have only been done for a sliding window of size two. Similar experiments are planned in the near future for a window of size three and four nucleotides. Specifically, we want to subdivide the DNA sequence by the codon unit (three nucleotides) because this unit has important coding interpretations (amino acids) in the DNA sequence.

We also want to explore if the categorisation depends on the window size, and if the analysis done in figure 4 can be verified. The experiments will also be extended to use a sliding window with length greater than four, to see if the graph in figure 5 can be explained from the experiments.

The number of DNA sequences used in the training set is at the moment too small. The experiments definitely have to be scaled up to make the conclusion more general. Short sequences in the data set may contain too little information to be of any value. Longer DNA sequences will give better performance. Further work is required to confirm this properly.

In a longer perspective a more general solution of the classification problem of DNA sequences should be established as indicated in the discussion at the end of section

5. This can be done by using an optimisation schedule for the different parameters in the network. This will require that the network has to be trained several times for different values of the parameters. In principle this is similar to search in a n-dimensional space where n is the number of parameters we want to optimise. One such optimisation technique is genetic algorithms that can be used. The experiments taught us that training of DNA data might take a long time. This also means that the optimisation of the neural network's parameters can be a time consuming process.

References

1. Allex,C.F.,Shavlik,J.W., Blattner,F.R. Neural Network Input Representations that Produce Accurate Consensus Sequences fram DNA Fragment Assemblies. Bioinformatics 15, 1999.
2. Claverie, J. (1997). Computational methods for the identification of genes in vertebrate genomic sequences. In Human Molecular Genetics, 6, 10, 1735-1744.
3. Campbell,N., Reece,J. Biology. Addison Wesley 2001 chapter 28, New York, USA.
4. Collins, F. and Galas, D. (1993). A new five-year plan for the U.S. Human Genome Project, *Science*, 262, 43-6.
5. Douzono,H., Hara, S., Noguchi,Y. An Application of Genetic Algorithm to DNA Sequencing by Oligonucleotide Hybridization. In Proceedings of IEEE International Joint Symposia on Intelligence and Systems, May 1998.
6. Douzono,H., Hara, S., Noguchi,Y. A Design Method of DNA chips for SNP Analysis Using Self Organising Maps. In Proceedings of IEEE International Joint Conference on Neural Computing, IJCNN 2001, Washington DC, USA.
7. Feng,F,F. , Dololitle,R.F. Progressive sequence alignment as a prerequisite to correct phylogenetic trees. In Journal of Molecular Evolution, 25, 1987.
8. Feng,D.,F., Doolitle,R.F. Progressive sequence alignment of amino acid sequences and construction of phylogenetic trees from them. Methods in Enzymology, 266, 1996.
9. Fickett, J.W., and Hatzigeorgiou, A.G. (1997). Eukaryotic promoter recognition. *Genome Res.*, 7, 861-878.
10. Haykin,S. Neural Networks. Prentice Hall, 1999.
11. Kristensen,T. A Neural Network Approach to Hyphenating Norwegian. In Proceedings of IEEE International Joint Conference on Neural Computing, IJCNN 2000, Como, Italy.
12. Kristensen,T., Langmyhr,D. Two Regimes for Computer Hyphenation – a Comparison. In Proceedings of IEEE International Joint Conference on Neural Computing, IJCNN 2001, Washington DC, USA.
13. Kristensen,T., Patel,R. Edge Detecting in a Lateral Inhibition Network. In Proceedings of IEEE World Congress on Computational Intelligence, WCCI 2002, Honolulu Hawai, USA 2002.
14. Kristensen,T. Prototypes of ANN Biomedical Pattern Recognition Systems. In Proceedings of IASTED International Conference on Applied Simulation and Modelling, ASM 2002, Crete, Greece.
15. LeCun,Y., Boser,B., Denker,J.S., Henderson,R., Howard,E., Hubbard,W., Jackel,L.D. Backpropagation Applied to Handwritten Zip Code Recognition. In Neural Computation 1, 1989.
16. Nusinov, R. Strong Preferences in Nucleotide Sequences of DNA Geometry. Journal of Molecular Evolution 20, 1984.
17. Potamias,G., Papanikolaou,E., Hatzigeorgiou,A. Knowledge-Based TDNN Architectures for Features Recognition in DNA Sequences. In Proceedings of IEEE International Joint Conference on Neural Computing, IJCNN 2001, Washington DC, USA.
18. Taylor,J.G. Neural networks. Alfred Waller Limited, Publishers. London, 1995.

Integrated Gene Expression Analysis of Multiple Microarray Data Sets Based on a Normalization Technique and on Adaptive Connectionist Model

Liang Goh, Nikola Kasabov
Knowledge Engineering and Discovery Research Institute (KEDRI)
Auckland University of Technology
Private Bag 92006, Auckland 1020, New Zealand
Email: liang.goh@aut.ac.nz; nkasabov@aut.ac.nz

Abstract- Research with microarray gene expression analysis has primarily been on expression profiling based on one set of microarray data. This paper presents a novel approach to integrated analysis and modeling of microarray data from multiple sources. Normalization method is applied to different data sets before they are used together in an adaptive connectionist classification system. The method is demonstrated on a bench-mark case study problem of classifying Diffuse Large B-cell lymphoma (DLBCL) and Follicular lymphoma (FL). For the purpose of comparison, different normalization techniques were applied and connectionist models were created from one or more microarray data sets and then tested on the others. The results show that with the use of proper normalization and modeling techniques, a model based on one set of data can be used to classify microarray data from totally different sources. For the modeling part, evolving connectionist systems (ECOS) are used that allow for new data to be added in an incremental way so that connectionist systems can be built for on-line adaptive learning where new data from various sources can be added into the system.

I. INTRODUCTION

This part explains the case study data for classifying two types of lymphoma tissues based on microarray gene expression data.

Diffuse Large B-cell lymphoma (DLBCL) is the most common subtype of non-Hodgkin's lymphoma, while Follicular lymphoma (FL) is a GC B-cell lymphoma. Both are of different presentations although FL, may over time, evolve to acquire the morphologic and clinical features of DLBCLs [9].

Microarray data from DLBCL and FL tissues [1, 8, 9] and from other tumors [7, 10, 11] have been explored quite extensively in the literature. The focus has been on the classification of certain tumors based on one set of microarray data. The research shows that tumor classification is possible with expression profiling obtained from one microarray data.

One problem with modeling gene expression for tumor classification is that often the microarray data set has too few data vectors. This is compounded by the thousands of gene variables for each vector (commonly known as the 'curse of dimensionality'), which makes the modeling process even more difficult. One approach to solving this problem is to reduce the set of gene variables through using feature extraction methods such as: signal-noise-ratio [8, 9], Fisher linear discriminant function [2], or statistical tools such as t-test or chi-square test [11]. Other approaches have used statistical techniques for data transformation as Principle Component Analysis [7], Discriminant analysis with variance [11] and hierarchical clustering [8, 9] to identify clusters of genes within the data.

The above techniques are valuable in some cases for solving the multi-variate problem in gene expression profiling, but do not address the issue of incremental learning from multiple sources of gene data. It is also necessary to have models that learn from multiple repeats of microarrays to overcome noise problems [6]. As the volume of the publicly available microarray databases increases, there is a need to have systems that can model expression profile incrementally and adaptively [3]. Can a classification model trained on one data set be used to classify another? Can we further train a model on another data set from a different source? Is there correlation between different gene expressions data sets related to a same problem? This paper attempts to answer these questions.

Other methods of modeling have been used for gene expression profiling, such as support vector machine [9], hierarchical clustering [1], and self organizing maps [8]. In this paper, ECOS was used for modeling due to its adaptive learning algorithm which optimizes in a continuous way its structure and performance [3, 5].

II. EVOLVING CONNECTIONIST SYSTEMS

Evolving connectionist systems (ECOS) are systems that evolve their structure and functionality over time from incoming information[3, 4]. The ECF (Evolving Classification Function) model used here is an ECOS for classification tasks [5]. This section gives a brief description of the principles of ECOS and the algorithm of ECF.

In principle, ECOS are multi-modular, connectionist architectures that facilitate modelling of evolving processes and knowledge discovery. An ECOS may consist of many evolving connectionist modules.

An ECOS is a neural network that operates continuously in time and adapts its structure and functionality through a continuous interaction with the environment and with other systems according to: (i) a set of parameters P that are subject to change during the system operation; (ii) an incoming continuous flow of information with unknown distribution; (iii) a goal (rationale) criteria (also subject to modification) that is applied to optimise the performance of the system over time. Fig. 1 shows the nodes and connectivity in ECF.

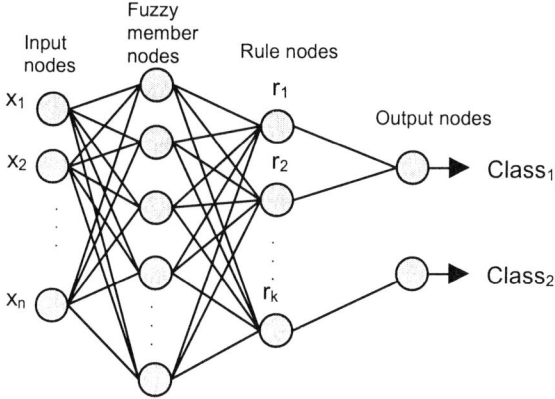

Fig. 1 Nodes and connectivity of ECF network.

ECOS have the following characteristics when compared with other connectionist models:
1) They evolve in an open space, not necessarily of fixed dimensions.
2) They learn in on-line, incremental, fast learning - possibly through one pass of data propagation.
3) They learn in a life-long learning mode.
4) They learn as both individual systems, and as part of an evolutionary population of such systems.
5) They have evolving structures and use constructive learning.
6) They learn locally and locally partition the problem space, thus allowing for a fast adaptation and tracing the evolving processes over time.
7) They facilitate different kind of knowledge representation and extraction, mostly - memory based, statistical and symbolic knowledge.

There are different models of ECOS [3]. The learning algorithm of the ECF model used in this paper is presented below as steps that are performed at each training iteration:
1) If all vectors have been inputted, finish the current iteration; otherwise, input a vector from the data set and calculate the distances between the vector and all rule nodes already created;
2) If all distances are greater than a max-radius parameter, a new rule node is created. The position of the new rule node is the same as the current vector in the input data space and the radius of its receptive field is set to the min-radius parameter, the algorithm goes to step 1; otherwise – next step:
3) If there is a rule node with a distance to the current input vector less then or equal to its radius and its class is the same as the class of the new vector, nothing will be changed; go to step 1; otherwise:
4) If there is a rule node with a distance to the input vector less then or equal to its radius and its class is different from those of the input vector, its influence field should be reduced. The radius of the new field is set to the larger value from the two numbers: distance minus the min-radius; min-radius. New node is created as in (2) to represent the new data vector.
5) If there is a rule node with a distance to the input vector less than or equal to the max-radius, and its class is the same as of the input vector's, enlarge the influence field by taking the distance as a new radius if only such enlarged field does not cover any other rule nodes which belong to a different class; otherwise, create a new rule node in the same way as in step 2, and go to step 1.

The recall procedure (classification of a new input vector) in the trained ECF is performed in the following way:
1) If the new input vector lies within the field of one or more rule nodes associated with one class, the vector belongs to this class;
2) If the input vector lies within the fields of two or more rule nodes associated with different classes, the vector will belong to the class corresponding to the closest rule node.
3) If the input vector does not lie within any field, then there are two cases: (i) one-of-n mode: the vector will belong to the class corresponding the closest rule node; (ii) m-of-n mode: take m highest activated by the new vector rule nodes, and calculate the average distances from the vector to the nodes with the same class; the vector will belong to the class corresponding the smallest average distance.

The ECF model used in the paper has the following parameter values: MaxField=0.6, MinField= 0.02, number of membership functions MF=1 (no fuzzy membership functions); number of rule nodes used to calculate the output value of the ECF when a new input vector is presented MofN=1; number of iterations for presenting each input vector Epochs=5.

III. CASE STUDY DATA

Data for the case study are taken from the databases created by Shipp et al. (data set A) and Ramaswamy et al. (data set B) [8, 9]. Ramaswamy's database contains gene expression levels for 90 normal tissue samples and 218 tumors samples from 14 common tumor types. Of all these, there are 11 DLBCL and 11 FL cases. In Shipp's database, there are 58 DLBCL and 19 FL samples.

In order to integrate the two data sets, the order of gene accession numbers must be the same for both data sets. Ramaswamy's data has 16,063 genes while Shipp's has 7129 genes. Only common genes from both databases are extracted (7129 of them). It is interesting to note that all the genes extracted by Shipp et al. were all present in Ramaswamy's.

The data sets can be downloaded from http://www.aut.ac.nz/research_showcase/research_activity_areas/kedri/research.shtml

The data is used to create a classification model to classify data in two classes based on certain set of genes (input variables) selected through a feature extraction procedure. As a general case in this paper, the feature sets used in different microarray gene expression sets can be different.

IV. NORMALIZATON

The data sets used were initially scanned on Affymetrix scanners and expression values for each gene were calculated using Affymetrix GENECHIP software. The data in the Ramaswamy's data set (data set B) were normalized by standardizing each gene to mean 0 and variance 1. Shipp's data (data set A) were re-scaled by using least square linear fit. To standardize the data from the two sources, normalization methods were applied. In our study five normalization techniques were explored as follows:

1) Conditional standard deviation: normalizing each gene by dividing each gene by its standard deviation. This will normalize each gene to variance of 1.
2) Linear-logarithmic: perform a linear standardization followed by natural logarithm. To avoid negative values, a value of 1 is added in a linear scale to obtain values from 1 to 2.
3) Logarithmic-linear: perform a logarithm normalization followed by linear normalization from 0 to 1.
4) Linear-min-max: dividing each gene by its min-max range.
5) Linear-mean-variance: normalized each gene so its mean is 0 and variance is 1.

Initial analysis of the 30 gene markers shows a high variance for gene 'V00594_s_at' for data sets. Variances of marker genes after normalization are shown in Fig. 2. A comparison of the variances for the various normalization techniques shows linear mean-variance does not standardize the data as well as the other methods. Gene 24 (i.e. 'V00594_s_at') still has a higher variance compared to the rest. In the other methods, the variances are more spread out.

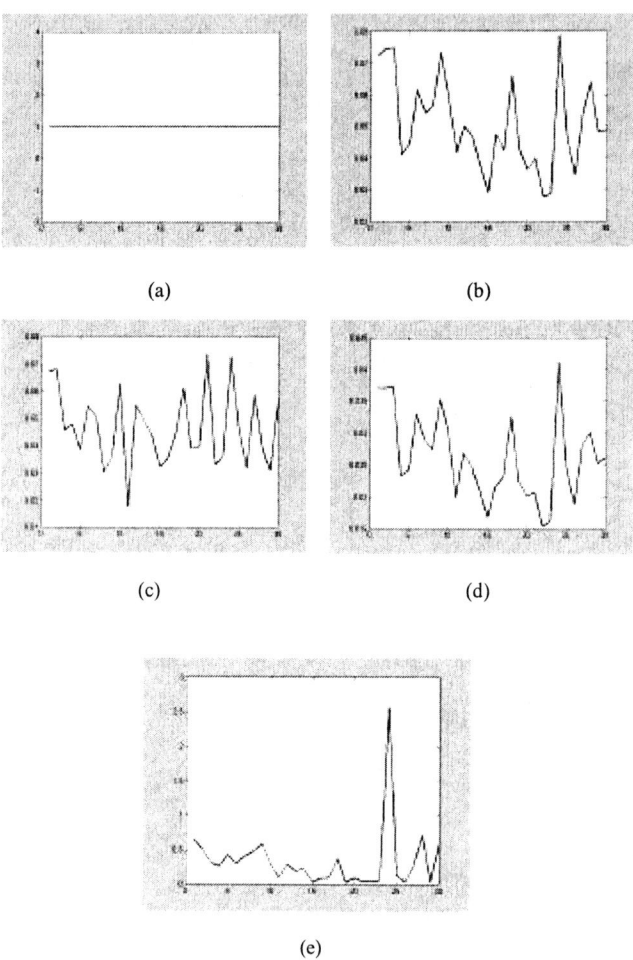

Fig. 2 Variances of the 30 genes for data set A after normalization. (a) conditional standard deviation (b) linear-logarithmic (c) logarithmic linear (d) linear min-max (e) linear mean-variance

V. FEATURE EXTRACTION

Feature extraction is an important phase. Several approaches have been explored, of which signal-to-noise ratio (SNR) [8, 9] has been proven robust. SNR is based on the idea that genes that are important to discriminate two classes will have a high value of the SNR.

A set of 30 gene markers were selected from data set A after ranking the SNR of all genes for the experiments. The genes selected are: 'X02152_at', 'M14328_s_at', 'J03909_at', 'X56494_at', 'L17131_rna1_at', 'M57710_at', 'HG1980-HT2023_at', 'M63138_at', 'HG417-HT417_s_at', 'HG2279-HT2375_at', 'D82348_at', 'M22382_at', 'J04173_at', 'M20471_at', 'U28386_at', 'X62078_at', 'L33842_rna1_at', 'X12447_at', 'L02426_at', 'X17620_at', 'D79997_at', 'X16396_at', 'D55716_at', 'V00594_s_at', 'X17567_s_at', 'HG4074-HT4344_at', 'X67951_at', 'L19686_rna1_at', 'M25753_at', and 'X15183_at'.

When the data sets A and B were combined in one of the experiments for the creation of a common model, 30 genes were extracted from each of the data sets. 23 of the 30 genes were the same in the two data sets. They were used for the common model.

VI. METHODS

The set of gene markers selected by SNR were used to extract the data from both microarray data sets. Four experiments were conducted:

1) Train ECF on data set A (77 vectors) and validate with data set B (22 vectors). Perform different normalization techniques on both data sets individually and repeat the same test.
2) Train/test ECF on data set A only using leave one out method. Perform different normalization techniques on the data set.
3) Train/test ECF on combined data sets A and B using leave one out method. Perform normalization techniques on combined data set and repeat.
4) Train/test ECF using leave one out method on combined data sets A and B that were normalized individually.

VII. RESULTS

The classification rates for all the experiments are shown in Fig. 3.

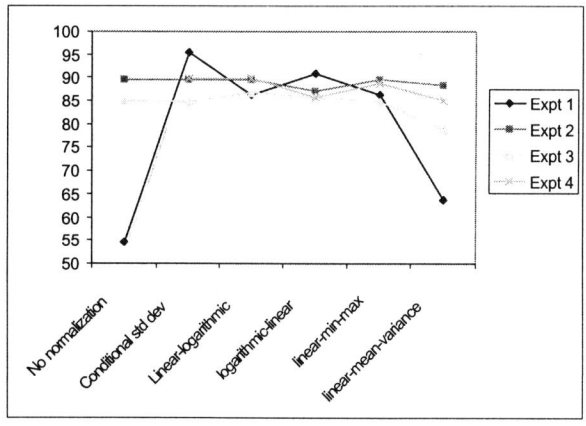

Fig. 3 Classification rate of DLBCL and FL with the use of various normalization methods and ECF model on two data sets A and B in experiments 1 to 4 as explained in the text.

The results show that:

1) When using ECOS, a model that was trained with one data set can still classify data from another set (experiment 1) subject to applying a proper normalization technique. This suggests that there is underlying correlation between different data sets for gene expression. This could mean that the sets of gene markers constitute significant profiles for classifying disease. ECF model performed consistently better using conditional standard deviation and logarithmic normalization methods.

2) When ECOS methods are used, a better performance is achieved when a model is trained on two (or several) data sets (experiments 3 and 4). That indicates that incremental training of a model on new data sets would be beneficial and it is possible to combine different sources of microarray data sets for a better profiling of diseases.

3) Interestingly enough, when a model is trained and tested on one data set only (experiment 2), the normalization method applied did not affect the results significantly. This points to a need for any new method suggested for gene expression data modeling to be tested on new data before applied in practice.

VIII. CONCLUSION

The paper presents a novel method for integrating gene expression data from multiple sources for building connectionist classification models with incremental learning. The method can be applied on gene expression data related to any types of tissue and disease thus making the creation of robust prognostic systems feasible in the future. Further research is currently being conducted on the integration of microarray data from multiple sources and clinical data related to the same problem.

ACKNOWLEDGEMENT

This research is fully supported by the NZ Foundation for Science, Research and technology FRST through a grant AUTX0201. The authors would like to acknowledge Dr Qun Song and Joyce D'Mello for their help and encouragement in this project.

REFERENCES

[1] A. A. Alizadeh, M. B. Elsen, R. E. Davis, C. Ma, and et al., "Distinct types of diffuse large B-cell lymphoma identified by gene expression profiling," *Nature*, vol. 403, pp. 503, 2000.
[2] C. Ambroise and G. J. McLachlan, "Selection bias in gene extraction on the basis of microarray gene-expression data," *Proceedings of the National Academy of Sciences of the United States of America*, vol. 99, pp. 6562, 2002.
[3] N. Kasabov, "Evolving connectionist systems for adaptive learning and knowledge discovery: methods, tools, applications VO - 1," presented at Intelligent Systems, 2002. Proceedings. 2002 First International IEEE Symposium, 2002.
[4] N. Kasabov, "Evolving fuzzy neural networks for supervised/unsupervised online knowledge-based learning," *IEEE Transactions on Systems Man and Cybernetics Part B- Cybernetics*, vol. 31, pp. 902-918, 2001.
[5] N. K. Kasabov, "Evolving Connectionist Systems, Methods and Applications in Bioinformatics, Brain Study and Intelligent Machines," 2002.
[6] L. D. Miller, P. M. Long, L. Wong, S. Mukherjee, L. M. McShane, and E. T. Liu, "Optimal gene expression analysis by microarrays," *Cancer Cell*, vol. 2, pp. 353-361, 2002.

[7] S. L. Pomeroy, P. Tamayo, M. Gaasenbeek, L. M. Sturla, and et al., "Prediction of central nervous system embryonal tumour outcome based on gene expression," *Nature*, vol. 415, pp. 426, 2002.

[8] S. Ramaswamy, P. Tamayo, R. Rifkin, S. Mukherjee, and et al., "Multiclass cancer diagnosis using tumor gene expression signatures," *Proceedings of the National Academy of Sciences of the United States of America*, vol. 98, pp. 15149, 2001.

[9] M. A. Shipp, K. N. Ross, P. Tamayo, A. P. Weng, J. L. Kutok, R. C. T. Aguiar, M. Gaasenbeek, M. Angelo, M. Reich, G. S. Pinkus, T. S. Ray, M. A. Koval, K. W. Last, A. Norton, T. A. Lister, J. Mesirov, D. S. Neuberg, E. S. Lander, J. C. Aster, and T. R. Golub, "Diffuse large B-cell lymphoma outcome prediction by gene-expression profiling and supervised machine learning," *Nature Medicine*, vol. 8, pp. 68-74, 2002.

[10] L. J. v. t. Veer, H. Dai, M. J. v. d. Vijver, Y. D. He, and et al., "Gene expression profiling predicts clinical outcome of breast cancer," *Nature*, vol. 415, pp. 530, 2002.

[11] E. J. Yeoh, M. E. Ross, S. A. Shurtleff, W. K. Williams, D. Patel, R. Mahfouz, F. G. Behm, S. C. Raimondi, M. V. Relling, A. Patel, C. Cheng, D. Campana, D. Wilkins, X. D. Zhou, J. Y. Li, H. Q. Liu, C. H. Pui, W. E. Evans, C. Naeve, L. S. Wong, and J. R. Downing, "Classification, subtype discovery, and prediction of outcome in pediatric acute lymphoblastic leukemia by gene expression profiling," Cancer Cell, vol. 1, pp. 133-143, 2002.

Robust Regression Under Asymmetric or/and Non-Constant Variance Error by Simultaneously Training Conditional Quantiles

Ichiro Takeuchi, Noriyuki Yamanaka and Takeshi Furuhashi
Dept. of Info. Engineering, Mie University, Tsu, Mie, 514-8507, Japan
Email: {takeuchi, yamanaka, furuhashi}@pa.info.mie-u.ac.jp

Abstract— We consider regression problems under asymmetric or/and non-constant variance error. We see this problem in several fields such as insurance premium estimation, medical cost analysis, etc. Applying the method of Least Squares (LS) to this problem yields unstable solution because of *outliers* that appears on one side of regression surfaces. Conventional robust techniques to deal with outliers, which intend to discard or down-weight the outliers equally from both sides of regression surfaces, does not help for asymmetric error. In this paper, we propose an robust regression estimator (an estimator of the conditional mean) under asymmetric or/and non-constant variance error by simultaneously training conditional quantiles in multi-layer perceptron (MLP). This is considered as a kind of *learning from hint* or *multitask learning* approach, i.e. we train the conditional quantile estimator as hints or extra tasks to improve generalization properties of the conditional mean estimator. Numerical experiments and an application to medical cost estimation problem have shown that our proposal has robustness and good generalization properties.

I. INTRODUCTION

We consider regression problems under asymmetric or/and non-constant variance error (see Figures 1 and 2). We see this problem in several fields such as insurance premium estimation, medical cost analysis, etc. Let us write the underlying regression system by

$$y = f(x) + \epsilon, \quad (1)$$

where x and y are covariates and response variables, f is a deterministic function and ϵ is error term with zero mean ($E[\epsilon] = 0$). We study robust estimation of f when the distribution of ϵ is possibly asymmetric or/and non-constant variance (the variance of ϵ depends on x).

It is well known that the method of Least Squares (LS) is the most efficient for regression problems under the normal constant variance error. But any violations of the assumptions (non-normality, non-constant variance) may cause LS estimates be less satisfactory and it is worthwhile to consider alternatives. Robust regression [1], [2] has long been studied to cope with such violations from standard assumptions. Their focus is especially on the cases where the distribution of ϵ has **symmetric heavy-tails**. Unfortunately, robust regressions yield bias in the estimation of f when the distribution of ϵ has **asymmetric heavy-tail**. Another approach to deal with non-normality or/and non-constant variance is transformation procedure such as Box-Cox transformation [3]. Unfortunately again, the straight forward use of transformation approach neither help because of so-called *transformation bias* [4].

We also studied this problem in [5]. We showed that, in many practical regression problems, the conditional mean $E[Y|x]$ and the conditional quantile $F_{Y|x}^{-1}(p), 0 < p < 1$, are *closely related* in the sense that their difference can be described with small number of parameters [1]. In light of the *close relationship* between those conditional moments, we proposed in [5] a two stage estimator. In the first stage, we estimates $F_{Y|x}^{-1}(p)$ using quantile regression [6], which is robust but biased as an estimate of $E[Y|x]$. In the second stage, the bias in the first stage is corrected using (non-robust) least squares, in which only small number of parameters are enough to be estimated due to the *close relationship* between $E[Y|x]$ and $F_{Y|x}^{-1}(p)$.

In this paper, we propose a similar in concept but different approach to regressions under asymmetric or/and non-constant variance error. In contrast to [5], we estimate the conditional mean $E[Y|x]$ and the conditional quantiles $F_{Y|x}^{-1}(p)$ simultaneously. This might be called *learning the conditional mean from the hints on the conditional quantiles* [7] or *multitask learning of the conditional mean and the conditional quantiles* [8] (see Figure 4). In particular, we consider multi-layer perceptron (MLP) with several output units, one of which is trained to approximate the conditional mean and the others are trained to approximate the conditional quantiles at various orders. A set of Monte-Carlo simulations and an application to medical cost analysis suggest that training these conditional moments simultaneously yields better generalization performance than training them individually.

II. CONVENTIONAL STUDIES AND THEIR DRAWBACKS

A. Traditional Robust Regression

Most of robust regression procedures have been designed for the cases when the distribution of the error term ϵ is symmetric and has heavier tails than the normal. *M-estimators* [1] are among the most successfully used for regression problems. It is defined in the form of minimization problem:

$$\hat{f} = \underset{f \in \mathcal{F}}{\operatorname{argmin}} \sum_i \rho(y_i - f(x_i)) \quad (2)$$

where $\hat{\ }$ denotes estimates, $\mathcal{F}$ is a set of functions, (x_i, y_i) is the i-th covariates-response sample, and ρ is a symmetric loss function, i.e., $\rho(-t) = \rho(t)$, with a unique minimum at zero.

---
[1]Throughout the paper, $F_W(\cdot)$ denotes the cumulative distribution function (cdf) of random variable W.

It is instructive to compare two spacial cases, $L_2 : \rho_{L2}(t) = \frac{1}{2}t^2$ and $L_1 : \rho_{L1}(t) = |t|$ loss functions [2]. When the error distribution $P(\epsilon)$ has heavy tails, samples around the tails are highly variable, and they have strong influences to estimators. The use of L_1 loss function is more *robust* than L_2 in the sense that L_1 gets less influences from those variable samples than L_2 does. M-estimators with L_1 and L_2 loss functions are, irrespective of the shape of distributions, consistent estimators of conditional median $F_{Y|x}^{-1}(0.5)$ and conditional mean $E[Y|x]$, respectively. When the error distribution $P(\epsilon)$ is **symmetric**, conditional median coincides with conditional mean and this is the why we can enjoy the robustness of L_1 even when we want to estimate $E[Y|x]$.

When the error distribution $P(\epsilon)$ is **asymmetric**, it is clear from the above consideration that conventional robust regressions are biased. Little attention has been paid to robust regression under asymmetric error distributions. Some considerations [9], [10] have been made, but they still impose several strong assumptions and not satisfactory in practical applications. See [5] for some empirical evidences on biases of conventional robust regressions.

B. Transformations

One commonly suggested solution is a transformation of response variable to symmetry (hopefully to the normal) or/and to constant variance. In practice, it is usually difficult to find appropriate transformation and we have to rely on techniques such as [3] to find it empirically.

When we want to estimate $E[Y|x]$, even when we succeeded in finding a good transformation, we still have a difficulty called *transformation bias* [4], [11], [12]. By an appropriate transformation, say h, the transformed response variable $\bar{y} = h(y)$ is supposed to follow a conditional distribution $P(\bar{Y}|x)$ with some good statistical properties. It leads to a good estimate of $E[\bar{Y}|x]$. To obtain an estimate of conditional mean of the original response $E[Y|x]$ from the estimate of conditional mean of the transformed response $E[\bar{Y}|x]$, *transformation bias* problem occurs. Applying the inverse transformation directly to $E[\bar{Y}|x]$ does not give unbiased estimate of $E[Y|x]$, i.e.

$$E[Y|x] \neq h^{-1}(E[h(Y)|x]). \quad (3)$$

Thus, it is usually difficult to get a robust estimate of $E[Y|x]$ through transformation techniques [3].

III. PROPOSED METHOD

A. Background

Figure 1 is a schematic illustration of a linear regression with **asymmetric** and **constant-variance** error. The solid and dotted lines indicate the conditional mean $E[Y|x]$ and the conditional median $F_{Y|x}^{-1}(0.5)$, respectively. Note that the mean and the median does not coincide in asymmetric distribution as discussed in II-A. In constant variance cases, it is clear from

[2] The use of L_2 loss function in (2) reduces to LS.
[3] See [11], [12] for the techniques to escape from transformation bias.

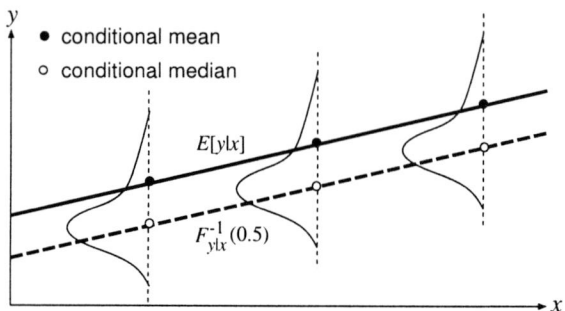

Fig. 1. Constant Variance Case: The difference between $E[Y|x]$ (solid line) and $F_{Y|x}^{-1}(0.5)$ (dotted line) is constant (does not depend on x).

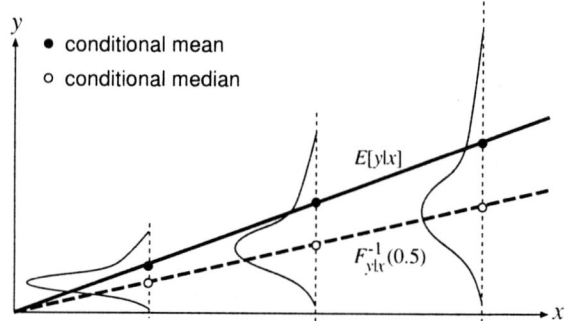

Fig. 2. A Simple Non-Constant Variance Case: The difference between $E[Y|x]$ (solid line) and $F_{Y|x}^{-1}(0.5)$ (dotted line) is linear in $E[Y|x]$.

the figure that the difference between $E[Y|x]$ and $F_{Y|x}^{-1}(0.5)$ is **constant** (does not depend on x), i.e.

$$E[y|x] = c_0 + F_{y|x}^{-1}(0.5). \quad (4)$$

Figure 2 is a schematic illustration of linear regression with **asymmetric** and **non-constant variance** error. The solid and dotted lines indicate $E[Y|x]$ and $F_{Y|x}^{-1}(0.5)$, respectively. In the case of Fig. 2 [4], it is clear that the difference between them is **linear in** $E[Y|x]$, i.e.

$$E[Y|x] = c_1 \cdot F_{Y|x}^{-1}(0.5). \quad (5)$$

As suggested from the formulations in (4) and (5), we can estimate the conditional mean $E[Y|x]$ by two-stage estimator:
1) estimate the conditional median $F_{Y|x}^{-1}(0.5)$,
2) estimate a single parameter c_0 in (4) or c_1 in (5).

This type of two-stage estimator formally described in [5] is able to provide robust estimates, because the majority of parameters may be estimated by robust L_1 estimator and only small number of parameters (only one parameter in the cases of (4) or (5)) are estimated by non-robust L_2 estimator.

Generalization of median regression $F_{Y|x}^{-1}(0.5)$ to quantile regression [6] $F_{Y|x}^{-1}(p), 0 < p < 1$ can widen the class of

[4] This type of non-constant variance error is called multiplicative error structure.

error structures to which the above two-stage estimator can be efficiently applied. Quantile regression is defined by an asymmetric loss function in (2)

$$\rho_{QR(p)}(t) = \begin{cases} pt, & t \geq 0, \\ -(1-p)t, & t < 0, \end{cases} \quad 0 < p < 1. \quad (6)$$

Quantile regression at order p is a consistent estimator of conditional p-th quantile $F_{Y|x}^{-1}(p)$ [13].

B. Proposed Method

We saw that the difference between the conditional mean $E[Y|x]$ and the conditional quantiles $F_{Y|x}^{-1}(p), 0 < p < 1$ can be described by small number of parameters. In other words, *conditional mean function* $f_{CM} : x \mapsto E[Y|x]$ and *conditional quantile function* $f_{CQ_p} : x \mapsto F_{Y|x}^{-1}(p)$ may *share* their majority of parameters and only small number of parameters are different each other. Thus, if these functions are characterized by finite set of parameters, we can write their parameters explicitly

conditional mean function $\quad f_{CM}(x; \theta, \kappa_0)$,
conditional p_1-th quantile function: $\quad f_{CQ_{p_1}}(x; \theta, \kappa_1)$,
conditional p_2-th quantile function: $\quad f_{CQ_{p_2}}(x; \theta, \kappa_2)$,
$\vdots$
conditional p_r-th quantile function: $\quad f_{CQ_{p_r}}(x; \theta, \kappa_r)$,

where θ is a set of *shared* parameters and $\kappa_i, i = 0, \cdots, r$ are sets of parameters that differs in each conditional moment.

Our main proposal in this paper is to train these functions simultaneously (Simultaneous Training: ST). We conjecture that simultaneous training might yield robust estimates of shared parameters θ. In particular, when we want to estimate $E[Y|x]$ under asymmetric or/and non-constant variance error, simultaneously trained conditional quantile functions (robust L_1 estimates) might bring some *benefits* for the robust estimation of θ.

In simultaneous training, we are to use multi-output $(1 + r$ outputs) function that has parametric form represented by: $\boldsymbol{f}(x; \theta, \kappa_0, \kappa_1, \cdots, \kappa_r)$. For notational convenience, we write $f_0(x)$ is one of the outputs of $\boldsymbol{f}(x)$ that is trained to approximate $E[Y|x]$ and $f_j(x), j = 1, \cdots, r$ is one of the outputs of $\boldsymbol{f}(x)$ that is trained to approximate $F_{Y|x}^{-1}(p_j)$.

Simultaneous training is realized by simply minimizing the sum of each criterion for each conditional moments. Namely, the entire error measure is given by

$$E = \sum_{i=1}^{N} \rho_{L2}(y_i - f_0(x_i)) + \sum_{l=1}^{r} \{ \sum_{i=1}^{N} \rho_{QR(p_l)}(y_i - f_l(x_i)) \} \quad (7)$$

The minimization of (7) contains a quadratic cost function and several conditional quantile cost functions defined by (6). No algorithm, as far as we know, has been developed for the minimization of (7) when models are nonlinear. In order to avert this, we approximated quantile regression cost functions

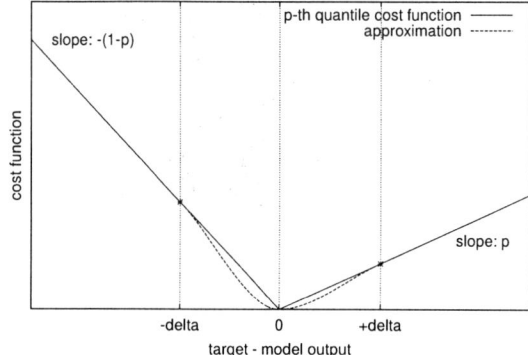

Fig. 3. Quantile Regression Cost Functions and An Approximation for Differentiability

(6) as

$$\tilde{\rho}_{QR(p)}(t) = \begin{cases} -(1-p)t, & t \leq -\delta, \\ \frac{2(1-p)}{\delta}t^2 + \frac{(1-p)}{\delta^2}t^3, & -\delta < t \leq 0, \\ \frac{2p}{\delta}t^2 - \frac{p}{\delta^2}t^3, & 0 < t \leq \delta, \\ pt, & \delta < t, \end{cases} \quad (8)$$

where δ is small value [5]. Figure 3 shows an example of quantile regression cost functions (6) and its approximation (8). Approximated cost function $\tilde{\rho}_{QR(p)}$ is designed so that $\tilde{\rho}_{QR(p)}(\pm\delta) = \rho_{QR(p)}(\pm\delta)$, $\tilde{\rho}'_{QR(p)}(\pm\delta) = \rho'_{QR(p)}(\pm\delta)$ and $\tilde{\rho}_{QR(p)}(0) = \tilde{\rho}'_{QR(p)}(0) = 0$.

C. MLP Implementation

There are many possible implementations of this simultaneous training strategy. In this paper, we focus on ordinary multilayer perception (MLP). The MLP implementation might be considered as a kind of *learning from hint* [7] or *multitask learning* [8]. In their terminologies, our proposal might be represented by "conditional mean estimator f_{CM} can be improved by the hints on the conditional quantile estimators $f_{CQ_{p_1}}, f_{CQ_{p_2}}, \cdots, f_{CQ_{p_r}}$" or "learning not only conditional mean estimator f_{CM} but also the conditional quantile estimators $f_{CQ_{p_1}}, f_{CQ_{p_2}}, \cdots, f_{CQ_{p_r}}$ can improve their generalization". The schematic illustration in Figure 4 illustrates this idea. An ordinary 3-layer MLP that has m input, q hidden and $1 + r$ output units is characterized by set of parameters $W = \{w_{kj}\}$ and $V = \{v_{lk}\}, j = 0, \cdots, m, k = 0, \cdots, q, l = 0, \cdots, r$, and given in the form:

$$z_l = v_{l0} + \sum_{k=1}^{q} v_{lk} \phi\{(w_{k0} + \sum_{j=1}^{m} w_{kj} u_j)\}, \quad l = 0, \cdots, r, \quad (9)$$

where $u = \{u_j, j = 1, \cdots, m\}$ is the input vector, $z = \{z_l, l = 0, \cdots, r\}$ is the output vector and ϕ is the transfer function. Let us specify output unit z_0 trains conditional mean function f_{CM} and $z_l, l = 1, \cdots, r$ trains conditional quantile

[5]We set $\delta = 10^{-6}$ in all the experiments in sections 4 and 5.

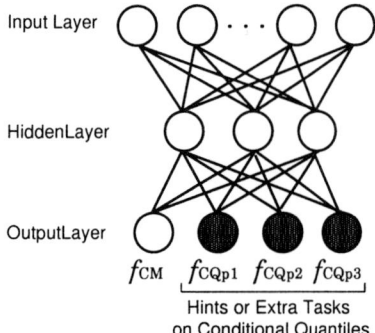

Fig. 4. MLP implementation of Simultaneous Training

function $f_{CQ_{p_l}}$. It follows that the sets of parameters defined above are expressed in MLP implementation by

$$\begin{aligned}
\theta &= \{w_{kj}, j = 0, \cdots, m, k = 0, \cdots, q\}, \\
\kappa_0 &= \{v_{0k}, k = 0, \cdots, q\}, \\
\kappa_1 &= \{v_{1k}, k = 0, \cdots, q\}, \\
\kappa_2 &= \{v_{2k}, k = 0, \cdots, q\}, \\
&\vdots \\
\kappa_r &= \{v_{rk}, k = 0, \cdots, q\}.
\end{aligned}$$

IV. MONTE-CARLO SIMULATION

We report a set of numerical experiments designed to see the generalization properties of *simultaneous training*. We considered 4 types of regression problems summarized in Table I. In experiments 1-1 and 1-2, we investigated asymmetric & constant variance error, and in experiments 2-1 and 2-2, we considered asymmetric & non constant variance error. In experiments 1-1 and 2-1, we estimated 9 conditional quantiles at the orders of $0.10, 0.20, \cdots, 0.90$, and in experiments 1-2 and 2-2, we also estimated conditional mean as well as the 9 conditional quantiles. In this section, simultaneous and individual trainings are abbreviated as ST and IT, respectively.

TABLE I
SUMMARY OF NUMERICAL EXPERIMENTS

	estimated moments	error term property
exp.1-1	quantiles	asymmetric & constant variance
exp.1-2	quantiles & mean	asymmetric & constant variance
exp.2-1	quantiles	asymmetric & non-constant variance
exp.2-2	quantiles & mean	asymmetric & non-constant variance

A. Experimental Setting

In each experiment, N training data pairs $(x_i, y_i), i = 1, \cdots, N$ were generated by

$$x_i \sim U[0,1]^2, \quad (10)$$
$$y_i = f(x_i) + \epsilon_i, \quad (11)$$

where f is among 4 nonlinear functions used in [14] [6] and ϵ_i is the error term from a log-normal distribution whose p.d.f.

[6] We used 4 functions: *franke1, franke2, simple interaction, radial* in [14].

is given by

$$p(\epsilon) = \frac{1}{\sqrt{2\pi\theta_2}\epsilon} \exp\{-\frac{(\log \epsilon - \theta_1)^2}{2\theta_2}\}. \quad (12)$$

Two parameters θ_1 and θ_2 were set so that $E[\epsilon] = 0$ and $F_\epsilon^{-1}(0) = 0.70$ [7]. By every possible combinations of 4 choices of f and $N \in \{100, 200, 500, 1000\}$, we considered 16 different *cases*. In each case, we generated 25 different datasets with different random seeds, and performed statistical comparisons.

We used MLP with one hidden layer in entire experiments. In every 4 types of experiments, we considered estimations of 9 conditional quantiles $F_{Y|x}^{-1}(p), p \in \{0, 10, 0.20, \cdots, 0.90\}$. Only in experiments 1-2 and 2-2, the conditional mean $E[Y|x]$ was also estimated. Thus, in IT, 9 in exp.1-1, 2-1 and 10 in exp.1-2, 2-2 *small* MLPs with 1 unit in output layer were constructed. In ST, one *big* MLP with 9 in exp.1-1, 2-1 and 10 in exp.1-2, 2-2 units in output layer were constructed. The model adequacies of each MLP were controlled by using 10,000 independent validation data. In particular, every combinations of 3 choices of number of units in hidden layer: $n_h \in \{1, 2, 5\}$ and 2 choices of starting values for nonlinear optimization[8] were tried and the best one was selected from those $3 \times 2 = 6$ candidates in terms of the performances on validation data [9].

The generalization performances were measured by (2) with (6) for conditional quantile functions and by mean-squared error for conditional mean function against independent 10,000 test data. In each 16 cases 25 performances on ST and on IT were statistically compared by paired t-test.

TABLE II
RESULT OF EXP.1-1

Integers in the table are the number of experimental settings in which the simultaneous training (ST) was significantly better/worse than individual training (IT) in several significance levels. Each of the 9 rows corresponds to the result on $0.10, 0.20, \cdots 0.90$ conditional quantile functions, respectively. **ST were, in most cases, better than IT especially in high order $(0.5 < p)$ conditional quantile functions.**

		worse (significance)				better (significance)			
	p	.01	.05	.10	N.S.	N.S.	.10	.05	.01
	.1	0	0	1	4	3	3	0	5
	.2	0	2	0	6	3	1	1	3
	.3	0	0	1	4	8	0	0	3
	.4	0	0	0	2	8	2	0	4
f_{CQ}	.5	0	0	0	1	4	0	4	7
	.6	0	0	0	1	2	0	1	12
	.7	0	0	0	0	0	1	0	15
	.8	0	0	0	0	0	0	0	16
	.9	0	0	0	0	0	0	1	15

p: the order of quantile regression, N.S: Not Significant

[7] It means that the mean of ϵ corresponds to the 0.70-th quantile, i.e. ϵ is asymmetric distribution with a long-tail toward the positive direction.
[8] We used Polack-Ribiele conjugate gradient method.
[9] In total, we trained (4 choices on N) × (4 choices on f) × (25 random seeds) × (10 small + 2 big MLPs) × (3 choices on n_h) × (2 choices on starting parameters) = 28,800 MLPs were trained.

TABLE III
RESULT OF EXP.1-2

See also the caption of tab. II. The last row added represents the performances on conditional mean function. **ST were always significantly better than IT in terms of conditional mean function. The significance of the difference slightly reduced in terms of conditional quantile functions compared with exp.1-1**.

		worse (significance)				better (significance)		
	p	.01	.05	.10	N.S.	N.S.	.10	.05	.01
f_{CQ}	.1	4	3	3	3	2	0	0	1
	.2	6	3	1	3	3	0	0	0
	.3	3	5	1	4	3	0	0	0
	.4	4	3	2	2	3	1	1	0
	.5	0	2	1	7	2	1	2	1
	.6	0	1	0	2	6	1	4	2
	.7	0	0	0	0	3	2	6	5
	.8	0	0	0	0	0	0	2	14
	.9	0	0	0	0	0	0	2	14
f_{CM}		0	0	0	0	0	0	0	16

p: the order of quantile regression, N.S: Not Significant

TABLE IV
RESULT OF EXP.2-1

See also the caption of tab. II. **ST were, in most cases, better than IT especially in high order ($0.5 < p$) conditional quantile functions**.

		worse (significance)				better (significance)		
	p	.01	.05	.10	N.S.	N.S.	.10	.05	.01
f_{CQ}	.1	0	0	0	3	4	1	3	5
	.2	0	0	0	0	1	0	6	9
	.3	0	0	0	0	1	0	5	10
	.4	0	0	0	0	0	0	3	13
	.5	0	0	0	0	0	0	3	13
	.6	0	0	0	0	2	0	2	12
	.7	0	0	0	0	3	1	3	9
	.8	0	0	0	1	1	2	1	11
	.9	0	0	0	0	0	4	3	9

p: the order of quantile regression, N.S: Not Significant

TABLE V
RESULT OF EXP.2-2

See also the caption of tab. II. **ST were always significantly better than IT in terms of conditional mean functions The significance of the difference was slightly reduced in terms of conditional quantile functions compared with exp.2-1**.

		worse (significance)				better (significance)		
	p	.01	.05	.10	N.S.	N.S.	.10	.05	.01
f_{CQ}	.1	0	1	1	2	4	2	3	3
	.2	0	0	0	1	1	2	4	8
	.3	0	0	0	0	1	0	4	11
	.4	0	0	0	0	0	0	4	12
	.5	0	0	0	0	0	0	2	14
	.6	0	0	0	0	1	2	1	12
	.7	0	0	0	1	2	1	3	9
	.8	0	0	0	1	2	2	2	9
	.9	0	0	0	3	3	0	6	4
f_{CM}		0	0	0	0	0	0	4	12

p: the order of quantile regression, N.S: Not Significant

B. Results

Tables II, III, IV and V show the results of exp.1-1, 1-2, 2-1 and 2-2, respectively. Integers in the tables are the number of experimental settings in which the ST was significantly better/worse than IT in several significance levels (The total number of experimental settings is 16, i.e. the sum of each row is 16). Each row of the tables represents the result in terms of each of 9 conditional quantile functions (and conditional mean function in tables III and V).

In the results on exps. 1-1 and 2-1, ST yields better performances than IT in most cases. The Significance of the difference increased as the order of quantiles approaches to one. This is because the noise imposed in the experiments is positive skewed (see footnote 6) and the conditional quantile samples at orders around $0.6 \sim 0.9$ are more variable than those around $0,1 \sim 0.5$. Consequently, conditional quantile functions at high orders received relatively more benefits than those at low orders.

In the results of exps. 1-2 and 2-2, ST was always significantly better than IT in terms of conditional mean function. In terms of simultaneously trained conditional quantile functions, ST was better than IT, but the significance of the difference decreases compared with corresponding results of exp.1-1 and 2-1.

V. APPLICATION TO PRACTICAL PROBLEMS

We present, in this section, an empirical illustration of the proposed method. We applied the proposed method to a medical cost estimation problem. The main objective of the experiment is to confirm the generalization performances and the robustness of simultaneous training compared with ordinary individual training. The summary of the dataset used in the experiment, the experimental setting and the results are as follows.

A. Dataset Description

The dataset is originally from 1992 National Health Interview Survey and used in [15]. The variables in the dataset are summarized in table VI.

TABLE VI
VARIABLES USED IN THE EXPERIMENT

Continuous Variables					
	label	mean	var.	skewness	kurtosis
age [yeas old]	x_1	42	123	.33	2.00
school [yeas]	x_2	13	8.5	-.69	4.84
visits [times]	y	6.4	205	9.8	156
Discrete Variables					
male	x_3	male:1, female:0			
white	x_4	white:1, other:0			
married	x_4	married:1, not married:0			
health	x_6	excellent:4, very good: 3, good: 2, fair: 1			

school: years of schooling, visits: the number of doctor visits within 12 months, health: health status chosen by interviewee

Our objective is to estimate $E[y|x_1, x_2, \cdots, x_6]$, i.e. the conditional mean of the number of doctor visits given individual's social and health status, which is one of the important factors to estimate the medical cost.

The original data contains 36,111 samples. We used only the data with $y > 0$ and the data which contains missing value were eliminated, which leads to 26,527 samples and 20,000 of them are used in the experiment.

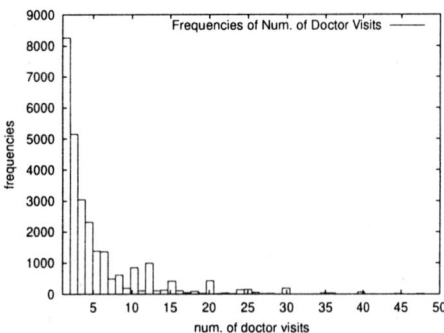

Fig. 5. The Unconditional Distribution of y

Note that the unconditional distribution of the response y, given in figure 5, is highly skewed and has a long-tail in the positive direction (skewness: 9.787, kurtosis: 156). We conjectured that the conditional distribution $P(y|x_1, \cdots, x_6)$ might also have similar characteristics (large skewness and kurtosis) and expected that our approach might work well for the robust estimation of $E[y|x_1, \cdots, x_6]$.

B. Experimental Setting

We divide 20,000 samples into 10 subsets, and each of them (2,000 samples) were further divided into three subsets, training set (1,000 samples), validation set (500 samples) and test set (500 samples). Training sets were used for parameter estimations of MLP, validation sets were used to select the hyper parameters (described later) and test sets were used to evaluate the final generalization performances.

We used MLP with one hidden layer in the experiment. The capacity of MLP was controlled by selecting the number of units in the hidden layer $n_h \in \{1, 2, 5\}$ and the coefficient of weight decay penalty terms $w_d \in \{0, 10^{-2}, 10^{-3}\}$ by the performances on validation set. The performance of MLP was measured by mean squared error (MSE) of the target and the MLP output.

C. Results

Table VII shows the results of 10 experiments on independent 10 data sets. The 2nd and the 3rd column of the table shows MSEs on the test set by individual training and by simultaneous training, respectively. The difference of them are given in the 4th column, where positive (negative) difference suggests that ST was better (worse) than IT.

Note, at first, that MSEs are variable from subset to subset because of outliers (many doctor visits). In such cases, the robust estimators are in demand. Simultaneous training (ST) was better than individual training (IT) in 7/10 cases. When ST was worse than IT, the differences are small. On the other hand, when ST was better than IT, the differences are, in some cases, very large (see experiments with subset 1, 4 and 10 marked with '*'). This illustrates the robustness of the proposed simultaneous training. The superiority of ST against IT with respect to the generalization performances was statistically significant in 0.05 level from Wilcoxon signed rank test (p-value: 0.0244).

TABLE VII
RESULTS

Simultaneous training (ST) was better than individual training (IT) in 7/10 cases. When ST was worse than IT, the differences are small. When ST was better than IT, the differences are, in some cases, very large (see experiments with subset 1, 4 and 10 marked with '*'). This illustrates the robustness of the proposed simultaneous training. The superiority of ST against IT with respect to the generalization performances was statistically significant in 0.05 level from Wilcoxon signed rank test.

subset	MSE (ind. train.)	MSE (sim. train.)	difference
1	134.071	129.318	4.753*
2	217.562	218.411	-0.849
3	242.436	242.771	-0.335
4	210.402	201.170	9.232*
5	93.780	93.800	-0.020
6	93.412	92.936	0.476
7	72.932	71.582	1.350
8	102.966	102.884	0.082
9	218.737	217.511	1.226
10	189.478	187.068	2.410*

ind.train.: individual training, sim.train.: simultaneous training

VI. CONCLUSION

In this paper, we proposed a robust estimation of conditional mean under asymmetric or/and non-constant variance error by simultaneously training conditional quantile estimators in MLP. Numerical experiments and an application to medical cost estimation problem have shown that our proposal has robustness and good generalization properties.

REFERENCES

[1] P.J. Huber. Robust regression: Asymptotics, conjectures and monte carlo. *Ann. Stat.*, 1:799–821, 1973.
[2] P.J. Rousseeuw and A.M. Leroy. *Robust Regression and Outlier Detection*. John Wiley & Sons Inc., 1987.
[3] G. E. P. Box and D. R. Cox. An analysis of transformations. *Journal of the Royal Statistical Society, Ser. B*, 26:211–246, 1964.
[4] J. Neyman and E. L. Scott. Correction for bias introduced by a transformation of variables. *Ann. Math. Stat.*, 31:643–655, 1960.
[5] I. Takeuchi, Y. Bengio, and T. Kanamori. Robust regression with asymmetric heavy-tail noise distributions. *Neural Computation*, 14(10):2469–2496, 2002.
[6] R. Koenker and G. Bassett Jr. Regression quantiles. *Econometrica*, 46(1):33–50, 1978.
[7] Y. S. Abu-Mostafa. A method for learning from hints. *Advances in Neural Information Processing Systems*, 2:598–605, 1990.
[8] R. Karuana. Multitask learning. *Machine Learning*, 28:41–75, 1997.
[9] R. J. Carroll. On estimating variances of robust estimators when the errors are asymmetric. *Journal of the American Statistical Association*, 74(357):674–679, 1979.
[10] R. J. Carroll and A. H. Welsh. A note on asymmetry and robustness in linear regression. *The American Statistician*, 42(4):285–287, 1988.
[11] N. Duan. Smearing estimate: A nonparametric retransformation method. *Journal of the American Statistical Association*, 78(383):605–610, 1983.
[12] D. M. Miller. Reducing transformation bias in curve fitting. *Am. Stat.*, 38:124–126, 1984.
[13] Saerens M. Building cost functions minimizaing to some summary statistics. *IEEE Trans. on Neural Networks*, 11(6):1263–1271, 2000.
[14] Roosen B. and Hastie T. J. Automatic smoothing spline projection pursuit. *Journal of Computational and Graphical Statistics*, 3:235–248, 1994.
[15] J. Mullahy. Much ado about two: reconsidering retransformation and the two-part model in health econometrics. *Journal of Health Economics*, 17:247–281, 1998.

Coloring black boxes: visualization of neural network decisions.

Włodzisław Duch

School of Computer Engineering, Nanyang Technological University, Singapore
& Dept. of Informatics, Nicholaus Copernicus University, Toruń, Poland
http://www.phys.uni.torun.pl/kmk

Abstract—Neural networks are commonly regarded as black boxes performing incomprehensible functions. For classification problems networks provide maps from high dimensional feature space to K-dimensional image space. Images of training vector are projected on polygon vertices, providing visualization of network function. Such visualization may show the dynamics of learning, allow for comparison of different networks, display training vectors around which potential problems may arise, show differences due to regularization and optimization procedures, investigate stability of network classification under perturbation of original vectors, and place new data sample in relation to training data, allowing for estimation of confidence in classification of a given sample. An illustrative example for the three-class Wine data and five-class Satimage data is described. The visualization method proposed here is applicable to any black box system that provides continuous outputs.

I. INTRODUCTION

In common opinion neural networks are black boxes that should not be used for safety-critical applications. Some understanding of network decisions may be found if the network is converted to logical rules [1]. This understanding always comes at a price. If network function is approximated decision borders provided by neural networks are severely distorted, since feature space has to be partitioned into hypercuboids (for crisp logical rules) or ellipsoids (for typical triangular or Gaussian fuzzy membership functions). An alternative is to convert the neural network itself to a simplified structure performing logical functions. Since neural networks are universal approximators, and regularization leads to low-complexity models that perform quite well providing estimation of posterior probabilities, approximation by logical rules always distorts the mapping found by the network. Although for some data classification accuracy obtained with optimized logical rules is higher than the accuracy obtained by neural networks, it seems to be an artifact of quantization of outputs (for example, forcing the patient into "healthy" or "sick" categories) [1].

What information do we get from a typical neural network? Estimation of the overall classification accuracy, mean square error (MSE), and sometimes estimation of the classification probability. The quality of two networks is compared only by looking at their accuracy, or at best at the Receiver Operator Characteristics (ROC) curves [2]. All such measures are global; they do not distinguish between easy and difficult cases. Overall classification accuracy is not a good estimator of the accuracy for the particular problem at hand, since all errors may be confined to a distant and localized region of the feature space. Multilayer Perceptron (MLP) networks provide outputs close to 0 and 1, making them overconfident in their predictions. There is a big difference between networks that make 10 errors, each time predicting wrong answer with probability close to 1, and networks that make the same wrong answers but with probability only slightly higher than that for the correct answer. Regularization may improve generalization [3] but since stochastic learning algorithms create networks with identical accuracy, but quite different weights and biases, which network should finally be choosen? Is the network hiding some strange behavior that may lead to completely wrong results for new data? Visualization of mappings performed by neural networks will certainly widen their range of applicability.

Since feature spaces are highly dimensional faithful presentation of the mapping learned by neural network is not possible. An interesting information is contained in perceived similarities of the training data samples. For classification problems with K categories these similarities may be displayed as a scatterogram in K-dimensional space. In the next section a linear projection method is introduced, projecting the network outputs into K vertices of a polygon. Section three presents a detailed case study using an MLP and RBF networks for the 3-class Wine dataset, and some examples for 5-class Satimage dataset. In the last section discussion and some remarks on the usefulness and further development of such visualization methods are given. Since the use of color makes it much easier to understand the figures the reader is advised to view the PDF version of the paper [4].

II. PROJECTION OF NETWORK OUTPUTS.

Assume that in K-class problem for each training vector $\mathbf{X}$ neural network outputs $o_i(\mathbf{X}) \in [0,1], i = 1\ldots K$ are given. They may come either from a single network, or K networks with single output that specialize in discrimination of vectors from a single class. The target output in a typical classification problem has $K-1$ zero outputs, and one $o_j(\mathbf{X}) = 1$ output that corresponds to the class C_j the input vector $\mathbf{X}$ belongs to. This requirement is in many cases artificial. The output classes may form continuum, rather then a small set of integer numbers, leading to a fuzzy "degree of membership" replacing crisp labeling. The outputs $o_i(\mathbf{X})$ may be treated as an estimation of this degree of membership, and in some caes as an estimation of similarity of the vector $\mathbf{X}$ to other vectors of the same class. In some network realizations the outputs are estimations of posterior probabilities $p(C_i|\mathbf{X};M)$, given the network M and the vector $\mathbf{X}$. Since probabilities sum to 1 the number of independent outputs is reduced to $K-1$. Networks outputs are K-dimensional images of inputs, created by the non-linear function that the network has learned. For vectors of different classes images created by neural networks that do not make any errors are separable clusters, otherwise these clusters will overlap.

Visualization of network decisions is possible in K-dimensional space, presenting images of all training vectors. For $K=2$, if the network outputs are independent (i.e. they do not sum to 1) the desired answers fall into $(1,0)$ and $(0,1)$ corners of a square in (o_1, o_2) coordinates. Images of vectors that belong to the overlapping regions may be close to $(1,1)$ vertex, while vectors that are not recognized are close to $(0,0)$ vertex. Vectors $\mathbf{X}$ that are far from decision borders and are classified correctly have scatterogram images $O(\mathbf{X})$ clustering around $(1,0)$ and $(0,1)$ corners. Images of vectors that are close to the decision borders fall closer to the middle of the square. Vectors from different classes are distinguished using different markers. Comparing such scatterograms for different networks will immediately show significant differences despite similar accuracies. The position of the image of a new vector $\mathbf{X}$ in relation to the images of training vectors shown in scatterogram allows for evaluation of the reliability of its classification.

Similar representation is possible for $K=3$, but for larger number of classes some projection on two or three dimensions is needed. Although all linear projections loose some information and more sophisticated projections could be devised, simple approach presented below is already quite useful. The hypercube corners that correspond to binary labels (from $(1,0,..,0)$ to $(0,0,..,1)$) will correspond to K corners of regular polygon in two dimensions. Coordinates of this polygon, with $(0,0)$ vertex corresponding to $(1,0,..,0)$ point, and $(0,1)$ vertex corresponding to $(0,1,..,0)$ point, are calculated from (see Fig. 1):

$$\begin{aligned} \phi &= -\frac{\pi}{2}-\frac{\pi}{K}, r = \frac{1}{2\cos(\frac{\pi}{2}-\frac{\pi}{K})} \\ x_j &= \frac{1}{2}+r\cos(\phi+\frac{2\pi j}{K}); \\ y_j &= \frac{1}{2}\tan(\frac{\pi}{2}-\frac{\pi}{K})+r\sin(\phi+\frac{2\pi j}{K}), j=0\ldots K-1 \end{aligned} \quad (1)$$

The transformation $\mathbf{x} = \mathbf{AO} + \mathbf{B}$ may be found by setting up $2K+2$ linear equations: $2K$ equations for projections of $(1,0,..,0)$ to $(0,0,..,1)$ unit vectors on (x_j, y_j) polygon vertices, and two equations for projection of $(1,1,...,1)$ point on the polygon center S, with coordinates $(x_c, y_c) = \left(\frac{1}{2}, \frac{1}{2}\tan(\frac{\pi}{2}-\frac{\pi}{K})\right)$.

This projection has several interesting features. For $K=3$ the center of the triangle corresponds to all (a,a,a) points (where a is arbitrary number) in 3 dimensions. Cases where all three outputs are 1 fall there, as well as cases where all three outputs are 0 (see Fig.2). Since all outputs are assumed to

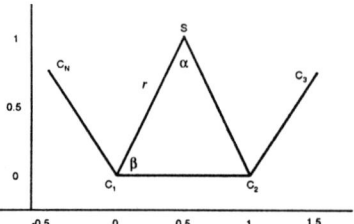

Fig. 1. Polygon used for projection of K-dimensional data.

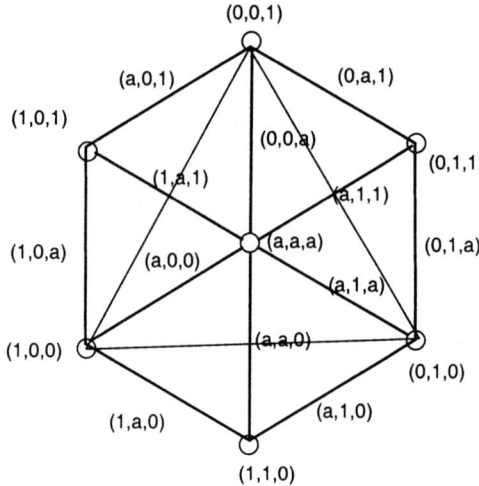

Fig. 2. Characteristic points and lines in the image space used for projection of 3-dimensional data.

lie in the unit interval $[0,1]$, all points will lie within hexagon, with corners corresponding to binary (o_1, o_2, o_3) values. The opposite corners of the hexagon have inverted bits, $\bar{o}_j = 1 - o_j$. Points corresponding to vectors that are weakly exciting o_1 output approach the center along the $(a,0,0)$ line, while points in the overlapping region of class two and three approach the center along the $(a,1,1)$ line.

III. CASE STUDY: WINE DATA

Chemical analysis of wines grown in the same region in Italy, but derived from three different cultivars, should be sufficient to recognize the source of the wine. The analysis determined 13 quantities, including alcohol content, hue, color intensity, and content 9 chemical compounds. The data is stored in UC Irvine repository of machine learning problems [5], where more details about it may be found. The number of data samples from Classes 1, 2, and 3 is 59, 71 and 48, respectively, so the data is rather small. It is possible to separate the classes perfectly using an MLP network with just 2 hidden neurons. The 3 classes are designated by +, o and x markers.

The NETLAB neural network package [6] written in Matlab has been used in the experiments described below. All MLP networks are trained with the scaled conjugate gradient pro-

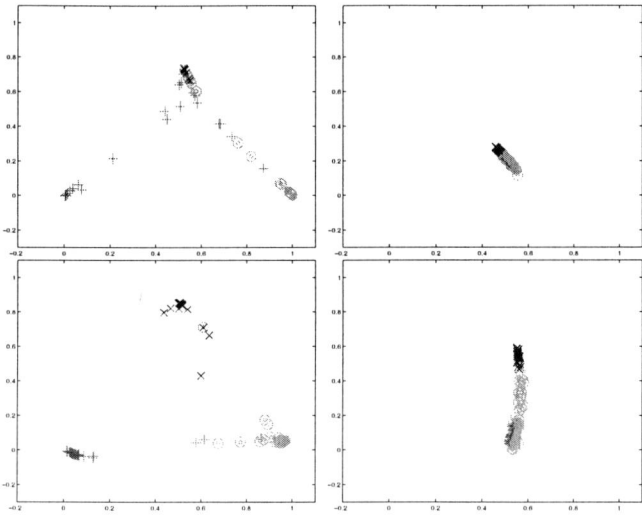

Fig. 3. Convergence of a network with 3 hidden neurons: top row - two solutions (27 and 107 errors) after 5 iterations, bottom row - two solutions (5 and 71 errors) after 10 iterations.

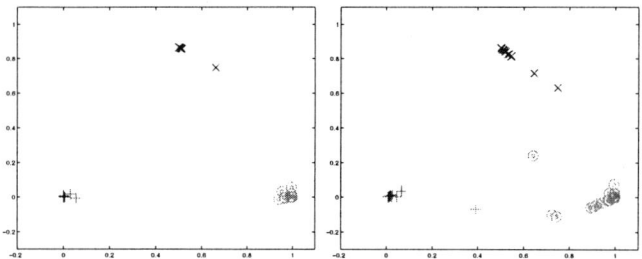

Fig. 4. Two converged solutions with zero errors after 30 iterations.

cedure, with a single hidden layer network. These networks are used to map 13-dimensional vectors into 3-dimensions and then project the result to 2-dimensions using the method introduced in the previous section. Using scatterograms of the training data created this way the following issues are addressed:

1) The dynamics of the neural learning.
2) Under and over-fitting effects.
3) Regularization effects.
4) Differences between networks of the same accuracy.

A. The dynamics of the neural learning

Three hidden neurons have been used in numerical experiments here. Since the network is initialized with small values of weights and biases after the first training epoch all output values are concentrated around 0.5. The first series of pictures (Fig. 3) shows the network performance after 5 and 10 iterations. Since each time the network is trained different solution is obtained two extreme cases were selected from 20 trials, the best network (lowest number of errors, on the left) and the worst network (largest number of errors, on the right). The vectors that are still not correctly handled are easily identified. In the lower left corner (0,0) most of the + class vectors are clustered. In the lower left part of figure 3 they are already well separated from other classes, although the hyperplane separating the o class vectors (clustered in the (0,1) corner) is still too close to the + class vectors. This is clear because 4 of these vectors have images close to the (0,1) corner. Further training should shift decision border for the o class vectors further away from the + class vectors.

The stochastic training algorithm changes network parameters along quite different trajectories in the parameter space, creating during learning very different networks, as is evident from the left and right subfigures of Fig. 3. After some initializations convergence is very fast, with emerging separation of vectors from different classes (left subfigures of Fig. 3. Sometimes the network gets stuck in a local minimum and inspection of the corresponding image will help to understand the problem. The lower right subfigure of Fig. 3 shows that vectors from the x class are well separated, but vectors from the two other classes have images close to the center of the triangle, extending into the lower part of the hexagon in Fig. 2. Evidently in the feature space data vectors from these two classes are covered by the sigmoidal functions with values close to 1. Instead of waiting for the learning algorithm to correct that problem (since gradients of saturated sigmoidal functions are small this would be slow), a few simple remedies may be applied: re-initializing the network, decreasing all network parameters to make the sigmoidal functions less saturated, or perturbing the weights by adding random numbers. Fig. 3 suggests another possibility: present as input only those vectors that correspond to images near the middle of $(a,a,0)$ line (Fig. 2), since the network response is then closer to 0.5 than to 0 or 1, therefore gradients are relatively large and learning may proceed faster, until the scatterogram becomes more like that on the left side of Fig. 3.

The final solutions may look similar, although the network weights significantly differ. The size of the network weights is reflected in concentration of vector images around the corners; at the end of training (Fig. 4) all images of training vectors cluster almost exactly in polygon's corners, indicating that the binary target values for the classes have been achieved. The number of errors is not a good indicator of the quality of solutions: both networks that were used to create Fig. 4 plots made no errors on the training data, but test results for the second network are significantly worse, since new data vectors close to the isolated + and o class vectors lead to several errors.

B. Under and over-fitting effects

Large number of errors may result from problems with convergence – for the Wine data some networks collapse images of all vectors into one cluster, evidently becoming trapped in a local minimum corresponding to a majority classifier. In such a case repeating the network training several times will lead to a better solution. The problem may also be due to the underfitting of the data, in which case repeating the calculation will not help. In classification problems this underfitting manifests itself with the inability of the network to create appropriate decision borders. Images of the training

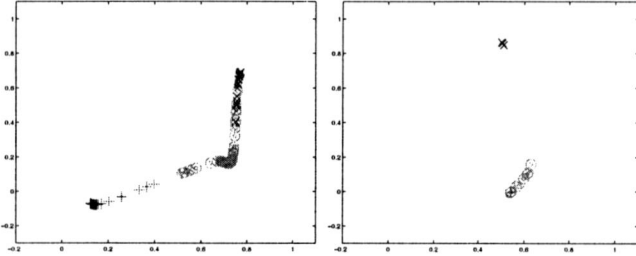

Fig. 5. Two converged solutions with too simple network.

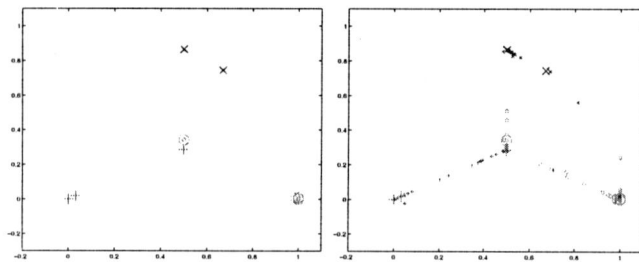

Fig. 6. Left plot – mapping by an MLP network that is too complex; right side – the same mapping applied to more vectors, created by adding small variance noise to the training vectors.

vectors in the scatterograms will not be clustered around the polygon vertices. In Fig. 5 images created by two networks with one hidden neuron are shown, one corresponding to a quite good solution with 6 errors only, and the other to a rather poor solution with 59 errors. In both cases images from one class appear in the triangle corner, while images from the two other classes appear somewhere in the middle of the triangle, showing the inability of the network to find a proper solution.

On the other hand networks may be too complex, overfitting the data. Training of the MLP network with 30 hidden neurons has been done on 2/3 of the randomly selected data, and results are displayed for all data. Although no errors have been made on the training partition, images of several test vectors appear near the center of the triangle, corresponding to vectors that the network does not recognize (all network outputs are quite small), indicating that the network does not generalize well. This is confirmed by adding noise to original data – in Fig. 6 small x, o and + are images of original data vectors, slightly perturbed with Gaussian distributed random vectors of unit variance multiplied by 0.02. The lines between the center and the triangle vertices show that some perturbed vectors are in regions of the feature space where all sigmoidal functions of the MLP network have small values.

C. Regularization effects

After convergence images of the training vectors may collapse into a single point, showing that the network is overconfident, and the images of vectors that are classified wrongly will be mapped into wrong vertices of the polygon. MLP networks behave in this way when weights become very large, creating almost step-like functions that correspond to sharp decision borders. Such decision borders may be brittle, and

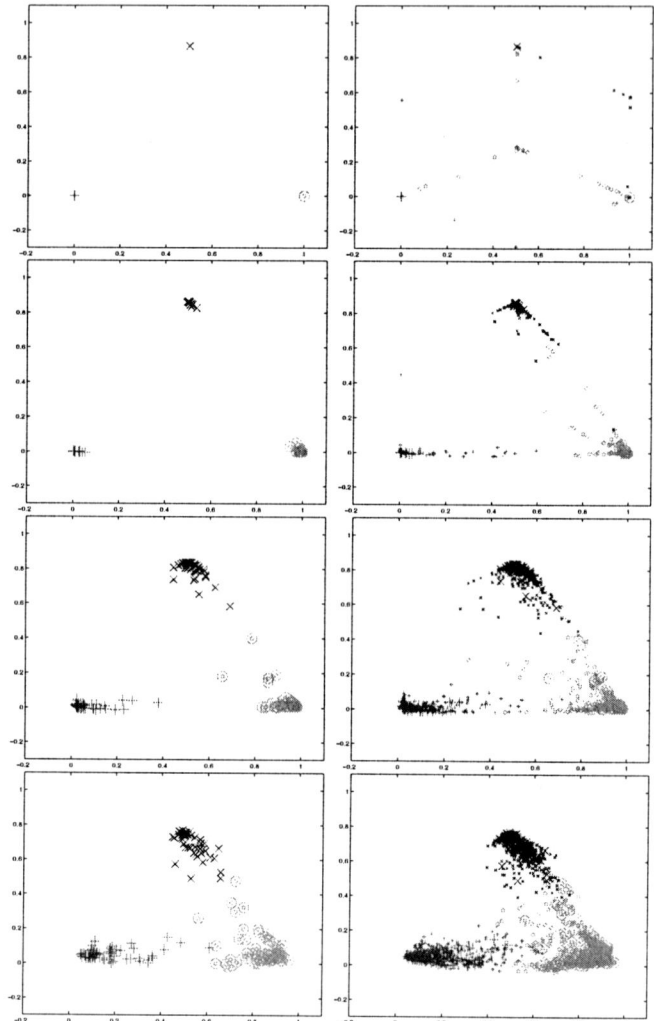

Fig. 7. Effects of regularization: top row - no regularization, second row $\alpha = 0.05$, third row $\alpha = 1.0$, and fourth row $\alpha = 5.0$. Figures on the right side are with 5% of Gaussian noise.

will lead to poor generalization of the network. Perturbing training vectors by adding some noise will show this effect clearly in scatterograms – lines connecting vertices with the polygon's center will appear, as in the right plot in Fig. 6, and the top right plot in Fig. 7. In fact adding noise to the input data is equivalent to a regularization procedure [3], making the solutions more robust and increasing classification margins.

Wide margin solutions are manifested by images of the training vectors concentrated near polygon vertices, but not collapsed into a single point. The network is not overconfident, i.e. the errors are closer to the center of the polygon or close to the midpoints of lines connecting polygon's vertices. This is shown in Fig. 7 for network with 3 hidden units that was able to perfectly separate the training data. Without regularization images of the training vectors generated by the network collapse into three vertices of the triangle, while images of some perturbed vectors (5% Gaussian noise) lie on the line joining vertices with centers, indicating that these vectors are in the region where no sigmoidal function has a large value

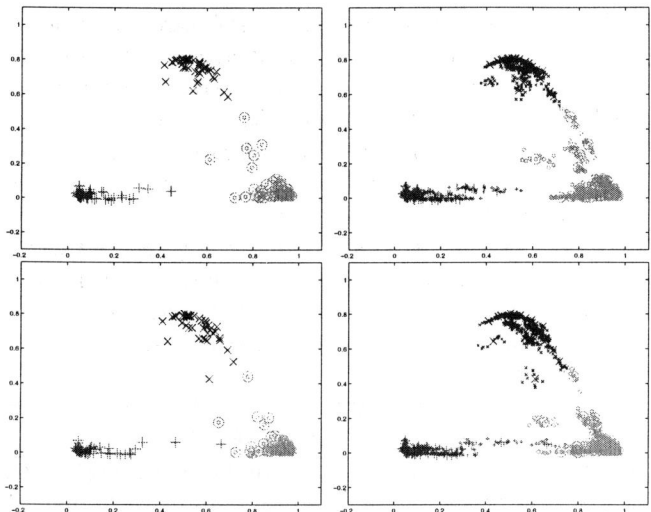
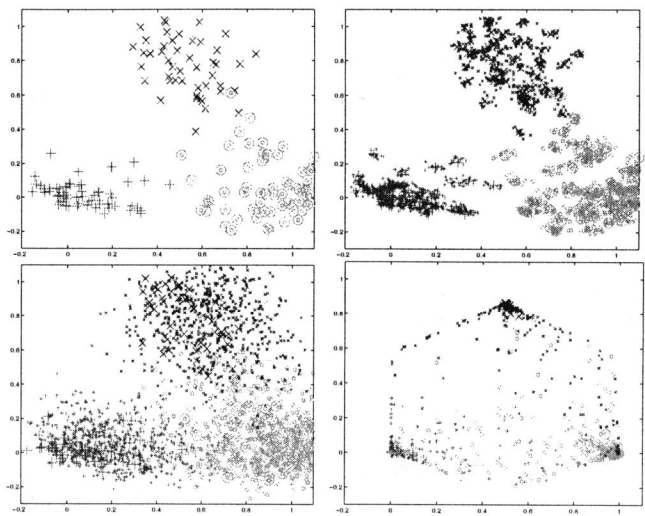

Fig. 8. Two networks, each making only one error on the training data; the first (top row) has higher chance to mix classes x and o more often, the second (bottom row) to mix classes + and o more often.

Fig. 9. Top row: RBF network solution with 6 Gaussian functions; right figure – same RBF network on slightly perturbed (2%) input vectors. Bottom row: comparison of RBF with MLP solutions for inputs perturbed by a strong noise (15%).

(Fig. 7, top row). Gaussian regularization prior added to the MLP error function scaled by a small $\alpha = 0.05$ hyperparameter partially removes this effect, making the corners more blurred and removing images of the perturbed vectors from the center, although the images of the training vectors are still very close to the triangle vertices. Increasing the regularization hyperparameter to $\alpha = 1.0$ and $\alpha = 5.0$ makes the network much less confident and shows more realistic predictions, because some samples of wines from the + class happen to be rather similar to samples from o class, and those from the o class are similar to samples from the x class. With very large regularization hyperparameter the network will start to make some errors, but even for $\alpha = 5.0$ images of almost all perturbed vectors are concentrated around correct corners of the triangle. Thus visualization may be useful to select the best network with proper regularization.

D. Differences between networks of the same accuracy

Two networks with similar MSE, making the same number of errors and having identical confusion matrices, may still significantly differ in some areas of the feature space. In the Wine example, vectors from + and o classes may be quite close to the decision surface, or vectors from x and o class may be close to the decision surface. Although in both cases same errors have been made so far, one network may be preferred over the other if the costs of mixing different classes are not equivalent. This is demonstrated in Fig. 8 by adding low variance noise (2%) to perturb original data.

Different gradient optimization procedures will also converge to different networks. These differences are visible even better if RBF network is used instead of an MLP. With 6 Gaussian functions RBF network also finds a solution with a single error. The images of the training vectors after mapping through the RBF network are much less localized, while the perturbed vectors are much closer to the unperturbed vectors (Fig. 9, top right) than for MLPs. Nonlinearities introduced by the RBF network are significantly smaller than those of the MLP network (especially with no regularization), therefore the RBF solution is more robust. Perturbing original vectors with noise with large variance will not elicit any unexpected behavior from the RBF network (bottom row, Fig. 9). MLP network with small regularization ($\alpha = 0.1$) and the same number of hidden units makes less errors, but places many perturbed vectors close to vertices corresponding to wrong classes (i.e. makes erros with high confidence). Images of vectors mapped by MLP show only how close these vectors are to the decision borders, while images obtained with RBF mapping show also similarities between vectors in feature spaces.

For easy problems, with well separated clusters, MLP with regularization provides quite robust solutions. MLP with 5 hidden neurons and strong regularization ($\alpha = 1$) creates images of vectors from 5 classes, clustered in vertices of a pentagon. The network mapping is quite robust, even after adding noise with 100% variance the network behavior is quite predictable, indicating that no strange kinks are hiding in its black box. The "arms" extending from one of the vertices to two other vertices simply indicate that the feature space vectors corresponding to these images belong to clusters that are relatively close together.

The Satimage data [5] originally contained images of six types of soil from the Landsat satellite multi-spectral scanner. The 3x3 neighborhoods of a central pixels from 4 different spectra re provided as feature vector (36 dimensions). The last, mixed soil class, has been removed to make small figures more legible, leaving 5 classes only and 3397 training samples. An MLP with 30 hidden nodes and 0.05 regularization coefficient has been trained on this data, providing good separation of most data points (left plot, Fig. 10). Most errors are due

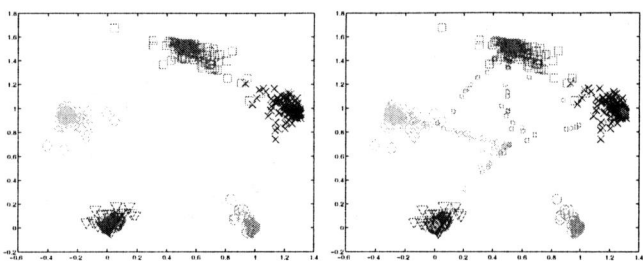

Fig. 10. Satimage data, first five classes, MLP with 30 hidden neurons and 0.05 regularization; right figure with additional 100 points for each class, generated by adding noise to selected vectors.

to mixing of the class 3 and 4 vectors. How stable is this solution? One point from each class has been selected, and 100 noise points generated by placing a Gaussian with 3% variance added, providing additional 500 points for display (right plot, Fig. 10). In some feature space areas reliability of classification is very high, with all 100 noise points staying within the cluster for triangles, circles and crosses. Many points generated near the vectors from the squares and diamonds class are in the region where none of the network outputs has strong value (center of Fig. 10). Other additional vectors are on the line between the corner representing wrong class, and the center, indicating that only one (wrong) output has value significantly greater than zero. Images of some vectors appear in the center of a wrong cluster, showing that the network is still too confident in its predictions, with sharp decision borders close to the data points. Recognizing the existence of such regions is obviously very important in safety critical applications.

IV. DISCUSSION AND CONCLUSIONS

Neural networks are used in various ways for data visualization. The activity of two hidden neurons of MLP or RBF networks may be displayed directly. Self-Organized-Maps and other competitive learning algorithms, neural Principal and Independent Component Analysis algorithms, autoassociative feedforward networks and Neuroscale algorithms are all aimed at using neural algorithms to reduce dimensionality of the data or to display it (for a summary of such visualization methods see [7]). The visualization method presented here is rather different, since neural networks are not modified or used to display multidimensional data directly, but rather a projection method is introduced to elucidate the network function. The method is applicable to any black box classification system that outputs some estimation of class memberships. Although linear projection cannot show all details of the higher dimensional data distribution (i.e. for more than 2 classes), it contains a lot of useful information. For two classes the images of data vectors appear in a square, with (1,0) and (0,1) corners coresponding to uniquely classified cases, (0,0) to unknown case (both outputs are close to zero), and (1,1) to cases in the overlapping regions. Such detailed information is unfortunately difficult to display in two dimensional plots for more than two-classes.

Images of the training data vectors mapped by MLP and RBF neural networks have been used here to show the dynamics of learning, to compare different network solution, inspecting the regions of the input space where potential problems may arise, to evaluate effects of regularization, to investigate stability of network classification under perturbation of original vectors and to place new data in relation to known data vectors, allowing for estimation of confidence that one may have in classification of a given vector. The best network solutions are not overconfident, but show large clusters of points around vertices of the polygon, without overlaps with clusters and with no vectors close to the center of the projection.

This type of visualization may also be combined with the Receiver Operator Characteristic (ROC) curves that show detection rates for a given false alarm rate [2]. Samples with images close to the polygon vertices correspond to the high probability assigned by the classifier. Leaving just those data vectors that are below the specified low detection rate will leave only images close to the polygon vertices. Moving to higher detection rates the number of errors observed is roughly inversely proportional to the slope of ROC curve. Scatterograms carry more information, showing what type of errors are made and allowing for quick identification of such data vectors. The common practice of selecting the largest network output value as the class indicator leads to optimal decision borders only for well separated images in scatterograms; more accurate decision boundaries in the image space may be selected.

A number of other options remains to be investigated, including applications to visualization of dynamic data. There is no reason why scatterogram images of the known data should not always be displayed as a part of the neural network output. Although such visualization may not open the black box completely, at least it adds some color to elucidate its function.

Acknowledgement. I am grateful to dr N. Jankowski for discussions on network function visualization, in particular for the idea to use polygon corners for projections. Initial version of the Matlab software used for simulations presented in this paper has been developed by Mr M. Orlowski as a part of his MSc thesis.

REFERENCES

[1] W. Duch, R. Adamczak and K. Grąbczewski, *Methodology of extraction, optimization and application of crisp and fuzzy logical rules.* IEEE Transactions on Neural Networks **12**: 277-306, 2001.
[2] J.A. Swets, *Measuring the accuracy of diagnostic systems.* Science **240**, 1285-93, 1988.
[3] C. Bishop, *Neural networks for pattern recognition.* Oxford: Clarendon Press, 1994.
[4] PDF version of this paper and the Matlab files are available at: http://www.phys.uni.torun.pl/kmk/publications.html
[5] C.L, Blake, C.J. Merz, UCI Repository of machine learning databases, http://www.ics.uci.edu/ mlearn/MLRepository.html. University of California, Irvine, Dept. of Information and Computer Science, 1998-2003.
[6] I. Nabnay and C. Bishop, NETLAB software, Aston University, Birmingham, UK, 1997. http://www.ncrg.aston.ac.uk/netlab/
[7] A. Naud, (1994): *Neural and statistical methods for the visualization of multidimensional data.* PhD thesis, Dept of Informatics, Nicholaus Copernicus University, 2001. Available from http://www.phys.uni.torun.pl/kmk/publications.html

Time-series Novelty Detection Using One-class Support Vector Machines

Junshui Ma and Simon Perkins

{junshui,s.perkins}@lanl.gov
Space and Remote Sensing Sciences, Los Alamos National Laboratory, Los Alamos, NM 87545

Abstract – Time-series novelty detection, or anomaly detection, refers to the automatic identification of novel or abnormal events embedded in normal time-series points. Although it is a challenging topic in data mining, it has been acquiring increasing attention due to its huge potential for immediate applications. In this paper, a new algorithm for time-series novelty detection based on one-class support vector machines (SVMs) is proposed. The concepts of phase and projected phase spaces are first introduced, which allows us to convert a time-series into a set of vectors in the (projected) phase spaces. Then we interpret novel events in time-series as outliers of the "normal" distribution of the converted vectors in the (projected) phase spaces. One-class SVMs are employed as the outlier detectors. In order to obtain robust detection results, a technique to combine intermediate results at different phase spaces is also proposed. Experiments on both synthetic and measured data are presented to demonstrate the promising performance of the new algorithm.

I. INTRODUCTION

Novelty detection, or anomaly detection, refers to automatic identification of unforeseen or abnormal phenomena embedded in a large amount of normal data [1, 10, 11]. One of its most attractive application scenarios is when time series are targeted [10, 11, 12, 13]. For example, in a safety-critical environment, it will be helpful to have an automatic supervising system to screen the time series generated by monitoring sensors, and to report abnormal observations. Meanwhile, novelty detection is a challenging topic, mainly because of the insufficient knowledge and inaccurate representative of the so-called "novelty" for a given system [1].

Despite its technical challenge, in the past over ten years novelty detection is a topic acquiring increasing attention, and a number of techniques have been proposed and investigated to address it. These techniques were experimentally proved to be effective in some cases, while they can fail in some other cases due to the assumptions and/or processes upon which they are based. For example, some were designed based on the assumption of possessing precise theoretical models of the underlying problem [2], or knowing the novelty conditions [3, 4, 5], which are unfortunately generally not true in real world. A wavelet-based signal trend shift detection method is proposed in [9]. Nevertheless, this method cannot detect short novel patterns embedded in normal signals. An interesting idea for novelty detection, inspired by the negative-selection mechanism of the immune system, was proposed in [10]. However, this method can potentially fail because the negative set will go to null with the increasing diversity of the normal set. The method, called TARZAN, proposed in [11] is based on converting the time series into a symbolic string. However, the procedure for discretizing and symbolizing real values in time series can potentially lose meaningful patterns in the original time series. The method presented in [15] is, strictly speaking, not novelty detection algorithm, because it requires knowing what kind of novelty is expecting.

In some other studies [6, 7, 8, 14], novel events were interpreted as outliers of the "normal" distribution function. The advantage of this direction is its theoretical tractability. Therefore, it leads to methods that can be well defined. This direction becomes especially appealing after an algorithm, called one-class SVMs, was proposed [6, 7], because the one-class SVMs can naturally detect outliers among a set of vectors. Following the direction of formulating novelty detection as outlier detection, this paper proposes a novelty detection algorithm for time series using one-class SVMs. As with other detection algorithms, it is impossible for this new algorithm to succeed in all scenarios. However, this algorithm can at least provide an alternative and complementary solution to some problems in which other available techniques may fail.

The main contributions of this paper are:
1) Introducing the (projected) phase space to allow one-class SVMs to be applied to time-series data;
2) Combining the one-class SVM outputs for different (projected) phase spaces to produce more robust novelty detection results.

The paper is organized as follows. Section II is devoted to a brief introduction to one-class SVMs. The conversion between a time series and a set of vectors in the (projected) phase space is proposed in Section III. The detection algorithm is presented in Section IV. Experiments on both synthetic and measured data are proposed in Section V to demonstrate the algorithmic performance.

II. A BRIEF INTRODUCTION TO ONE-CLASS SUPPORT VECTOR MACHINES

We briefly introduce the basic concepts of one-class SVMs in this section. Its more detailed presentation can be found in [6] and [7].

Given a set of vectors $T = \{\mathbf{x}_i, i = 1...l\}$, where $\mathbf{x}_i \in I \subseteq \mathbf{R}^E$, E is the dimension of I, and I is called the input space. A nonlinear function $\Phi(\mathbf{x})$ maps vector $\mathbf{x}$ from input space I into a huge, or even infinite, dimensional feature space F. We construct a hyper-plane in feature space F as

$$f(\mathbf{x}) = \mathbf{W}^T \Phi(\mathbf{x}) - \rho \quad (1)$$

to separate as many as possible of the mapped vectors $\{\Phi(\mathbf{x}_i), i = 1...l\}$ from the origin in feature space F. The $\mathbf{W}$ and ρ in (1) are obtained by solving an optimization problem:

$$\min_{\mathbf{W}, b} P = \frac{1}{2}\mathbf{W}^T\mathbf{W} + \frac{1}{\nu l}\sum_{i=1}^{l}\xi_i - \rho \quad (2)$$
$$s.t. \quad (\mathbf{W}^T\Phi(\mathbf{x}) - \rho) \geq -\xi_i, \quad \xi_i \geq 0$$

where $\nu \in (0,1)$, and it is a parameter to trade-off the smoothness of $f(\mathbf{x})$ and fewer falling on the same side of the hyper-plane (1) as the origin in F.

After introducing Lagrange multipliers α_i for each vector $\mathbf{x}_i$, the dual problem of the optimization problem of (2) can be obtained. Solving the dual problem leads to

$$\mathbf{W} = \sum_{i=1}^{l} \alpha_i \Phi(\mathbf{x}_i),$$

where $0 \leq \alpha_i \leq \frac{1}{\nu l}$.

The famous *kernel trick* is the procedure of using a kernel function in input space I to replace the inner product of two vectors in feature space F. Accordingly, the hyper-plane (1) in feature space F becomes a nonlinear function in the input space I

$$f(\mathbf{x}) = \sum_{i=1}^{l} \alpha_i K(\mathbf{x}_i, \mathbf{x}) - \rho, \quad (3)$$

where $K(\mathbf{x}_i, \mathbf{x}) = \Phi(\mathbf{x}_i)^T \Phi(\mathbf{x})$, and it is a kernel function in the input space I. There are many admissible choices for kernel function $K(\mathbf{x}_i, \mathbf{x})$. The most widely used one in one-class SVMs is the RBF kernel function. That is,

$$K(\mathbf{x}_i, \mathbf{x}) = \exp\{-\gamma \|\mathbf{x}_i - \mathbf{x}\|^2\}. \quad (4)$$

According to (2), any vector $\mathbf{x}$ with $f(\mathbf{x}) < 0$ is an outlier. Moreover, it can be proved that a vector $\mathbf{x}_i$ in the training set T is an outlier if and only if its α_i is $\frac{1}{\nu l}$.

It is proved that ν is the upper bound on the fraction of outliers over all training samples [6]. Therefore, the value of ν directly determines the sensitivity the outlier detection algorithm using one-class SVMs.

III. TIME SERIES VS. (PROJECTED) PHASE SPACE

According to Section II, one-class SVMs can only be applied to a set of vectors, and are not directly applicable to time-series type of data. Therefore, we have to figure out a method to convert the time series to a set of vectors. The most straightforward way is to unfold the time-series into a phase space using a time-delay embedding process [17].

More specifically, given a time series $x(t)$, $t = 1...N$, it can be unfolded into its phase space Q, where $Q \subseteq \mathbf{R}^E$, and E is called the *embedding dimension* using a time-delay embedding process:

$$\mathbf{x}_E(t) = [x(t-E+1) \quad x(t-E+2) \quad \cdots \quad x(t)], \quad (5)$$

where $\mathbf{x}_t \in Q$. Thus, a time series $x(t)$ can be converted to a set of vectors $T_E(N)$,

$$T_E(N) = \{\mathbf{x}_E(t), t = E \cdots N\}. \quad (6)$$

Note that when we use the concept of phase space, we only use its mathematical form, and ignore its implied physical meaning. Also, it is obvious that vectors in $T_E(N)$ fail to meet the i.i.d. condition. This fact can cause the outlier detection results obtained using one-class SVMs to lose some nice properties, such as the PAC performance bound [6]. However, it does not damage the validity of using one-class SVMs for outlier detection, because the formulation of one-class SVMs were not derived based on the assumption that the data set follows the i.i.d. condition.

In some cases, when a time series is mostly composed of low frequency components, in phase space Q the set of vectors converted from this time series distribute along the diagonal vector **1**, where $\mathbf{1} = \begin{bmatrix} 1 & 1 & \cdots & 1 \end{bmatrix}^T$. This point is demonstrated in Figure 1. If one-class SVMs are applied to a set of vectors like this, detection results will be heavily biased to the time-series points with either extremely large or extremely small values. Although novelty in many cases does appear in points with extreme values, this scenario potentially rules out the chance for detecting novel patterns formed by points with normal values. Therefore, the concept of *projected phase space* is introduced to cope with this bias.

The basic idea is to project all the vectors in a phase space to a subspace orthogonal to the diagonal vector **1**. That is, according to the projection theorem,

$$\mathbf{x}'_E(t) = (\mathbf{I} - \frac{1}{E}\mathbf{1}\mathbf{1}^T)\mathbf{x}_E(t), \quad (7)$$

where **I** is the identity matrix, and $\mathbf{x}'_E(t)$ is the projected vector in the projected phase space, denoted by Q'.

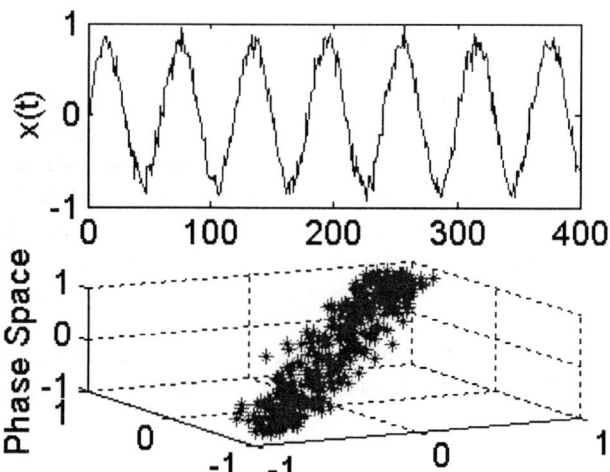

Fig. 1. A Time Series and Its Vector Set in a Phase Space (E=3)

Intuitively, the projection operation (7) is like applying a high-pass filter to the time series. The rationale of using this projection, instead of a high-pass filter, is that it can adaptively match the underlying data, and we need not specifically define any parameters, such as the cut-off frequency in high-pass filters.

Meanwhile, this projection operation is not guaranteed to be beneficial for every real world problem [19]. It is induced to enlarge our choices to handle situations where the one-class SVMs can be severely misled. In real world applications, whether the time series should be unfolded to phase spaces or to projected phase spaces is determined by both the property of the time series, and the kind of novelty we wish to detect. As suggested by other researchers, if we consider novelty detection as a problem of knowledge discovery and data mining, it should be an "iterative activity" [11], and "the discovery algorithm should be run several times with different parameter settings" [18].

IV. ONE-CLASS SVM-BASED NOVELTY DETECTION FOR TIME SERIES

After converting a time-series into a set of vectors in the (projected) phase space, a novelty detection algorithm for time series becomes readily available.

Given a time series $x(t)$, where $t = 1...N$, and its corresponding vector set $T_E(N) = \{\mathbf{x}_E^{()}(t), t = E \cdots N\}$ in the (projected) phase space, we denote $i(E,t)$, where $t = 1...N$, and $i(E,t) \in \{0,1\}$, as the detection results when the embedding dimension is E. $i(E,t) = 1$ suggests that $x(t)$ is considered as a novel point in the (projected) phase space with an embedding dimension of E. The value of $i(E,t)$ is set to 1 if its corresponding time-series point $x(t)$ is the element of any outlier detected using one-class SVMs. For example, if $\mathbf{x}_E^{()}(t)$ is detected as an outlier, all points from $i(E, t-E+1)$ to $i(E,t)$ are set to 1.

However, according to Section III, to unfold a time series into the (projected) phase space, one must first determine an embedding dimension E. Different embedding dimensions lead to different representations of the time series in phase spaces. Intuitively, if there is an intrinsic novel event happening, its novelty is supposed to manifest in its different representations.

In order to construct a robust novelty detection algorithm less dependent on a particular representation, we define $x(t)$ as a novel point only when the novelty indication function $I(t) = 1$, where $I(t) = \prod_{E \in S} i(E,t)$, and S is a set formed by a large range of embedding dimensions. The size of set S, along with the choice of its elements, plays an important role in trading-off between detection rate and false alarm.

V. EXPERIMENTS

Experiments based on both synthetic and measured data are presented to demonstrate the performance of our novelty detection algorithm.

A. Experiments Based on Synthetic Data

Two synthetic time series $x_1(t)$ and $x_2(t)$ are generated. $x_1(t)$ is a sinusoid signal with small additive noise, while $x_2(t)$ is the same as $x_1(t)$ except that it has a small segment of large additive noise. The algorithmic parameters are set as follows:
1) Embedding dimension range S,
   $S = [3\ 5\ 7\ \cdots\ 19]$;
2) One-class SVM parameter $\nu = 0.02$;
3) Kernel function used by one-class SVM
   $K(\mathbf{x}_i, \mathbf{x}_j) = \exp\{-|\mathbf{x}_i - \mathbf{x}_j|^2 / 10\}$;

The original signals $x_1(t)$ and $x_2(t)$ are plots in Figure 2, along with the novelty indication function $I(t)$ obtained when both time series are unfolded into the projected phase spaces.

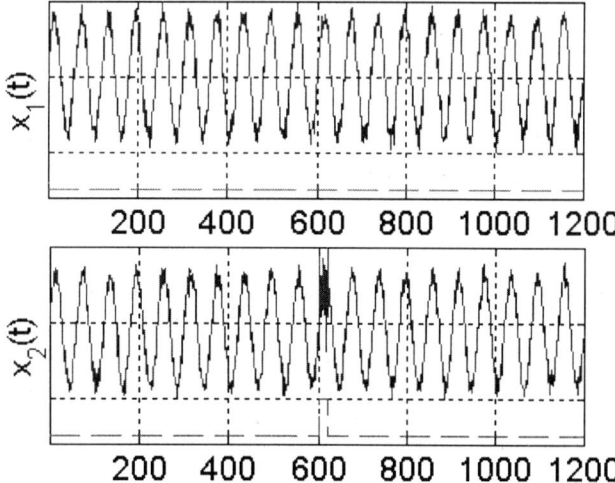

Fig. 2. Novelty Detection Results When Unfolded to Projected Phase Spaces

The solid curves in Figure 2 are the synthetic time series, and the dash-lines are the novelty indication function. Figure 2 shows that our detection algorithm successfully detects the novel points in $\mathbf{x}_2(t)$ without false alarms. Meanwhile, it also properly figures out that no part of $\mathbf{x}_1(t)$ can be considered as a novel point.

Because $x_1(t)$ and $x_2(t)$ are time series mainly composed of low frequency components, we predict that results obtained in projected phase spaces are more reliable. For comparison, the detection results obtained by unfolding both time series into the phase spaces are shown in Fig. 3. Compared with the result in Fig. 2, two false alarms are observed in this figure, which coincides with our prediction.

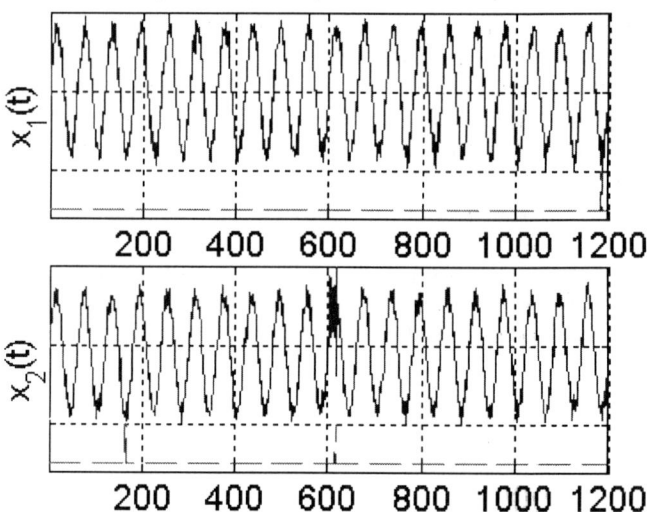

Fig. 3. Novelty Detection Results When Unfolded to Phase Spaces

B. An Experiment Based on Measured Data

The experiment is to apply the detection algorithm to the Santa Fe Institute Competition (SFIC) data [16], which is a 1000-point time series. The algorithmic parameters are set exactly the same as for the experiments in Subsection A, except that $\nu = 0.05$ is employed in this experiment. Because SFIC time series does not only have low frequent components, the novelty detection results obtained in phase spaces and project phased spaces are fairly similar. Therefore, we only plot out the result obtained in phase spaces in Figure 4. This result perfectly matches the human visual detection result.

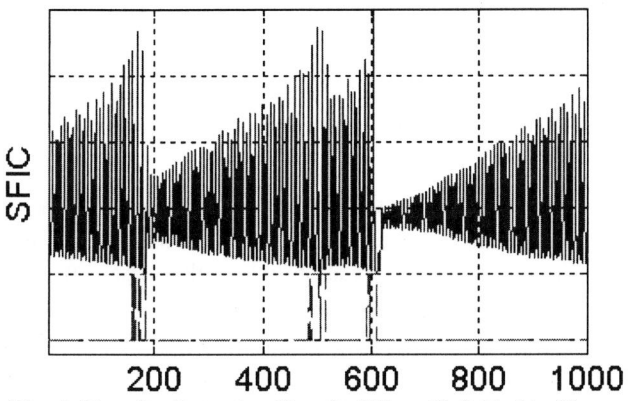

Fig. 4. Novelty Detection Results When Unfolded to Phase Spaces

VI. CONCLUSIONS

This paper proposes a new novelty detection algorithm for time series using one-class support vector machines. Experimental results demonstrate its promising performance. An interesting future direction related to this research is to find out the possible relationship between the value of ν and the confidence of the detected novelty.

ACKNOWLEDGEMENTS

This work is supported by the NASA project NRA-00-01-AISR-088 and by the Los Alamos Laboratory Directed Research and Development (LDRD) program.

REFERENCES

[1] Alexander Ypma and Rober P. Duin, Novelty Detection Using Self-Organizing Maps, in Progress in Connectionist-Based Information Systems, pp 1322-1325, London: Springer, 1997.

[2] R. Kozma, M. Kitamura, M. Sakuma, and Y. Yokoyama, Anomaly Detection by Neural Network Models and Statistical Time Series Analysis, in Proceedings of IEEE International Conference on Neural Networks, Orlando, Florida, June 27-29, 1994.

[3] Rolf Isermann, Process Fault Detection Based on Modeling and Estimation Method – A Survey, *Automatica*, vol. 20, pp.387-404, 1984.

[4] C. M. Bishop, Novelty Detection and Neural Network Validation, IEE Proceedings – Vision, Image and Signal Processing, vol. 141, no. 4, pp. 217-222, August, 1994.

[5] S.Roberts and L. Tarassenko. A Probabilistic Resource Allocating Network for Novelty Detection, Neural Computation, vol. 6, pp. 270-284, 1994.

[6] B. Schölkopf, R.C. Williamson, A.J. Smola, J. Shawe-Taylor, and J. Platt. Support vector method for novelty detection. In Neural Information Processing Systems, 2000.

[7] Colin Campbell, Kristin P. Bennett, A Linear Programming Approach to Novelty Detection, in Advances in Neural Information Processing Systems, vol 14, 2001.

[8] H. V. Jagadish, N. Kouda, and S. Muthukrishnan, Mining deviates in a time series database, in Proceedings of 25th International Conference on Very Large Data Bases, pp 102-113, 1999.

[9] C. Shahabi, X. Tian, and W. Zhao, Tsa-tree: A Wavelet-based Approach to Improve the Efficiency of Multi-level Surprise and Trend Queries. In Proceedings of 12th International Conference on Scientific and Statistical Database Management, 2000.

[10] Dipanker Dasgupta and Stephanie Forrest, Novelty Detection in Time Series Data Using Ideas from Immunology, In Proceedings of the 5th International Conference on Intelligent Systems, Reno, Nevada, June 19-21, 1996.

[11] E. Keogh, S Lonardi, and W Chiu, Finding Surprising Patterns in a Time Series Database In Linear Time and Space, In the 8th ACM SIGKDD International Conference on Knowledge Discovery and Data Mining, pp 550-556, Edmonton, Alberta, Canada, July 23 - 26, 2002.

[12] Valery Guralnik, Jaideep Srivastava, Event Detection from Time Series Data. In Proceedings of the International Conference Knowledge Discovery and Data Mining, San Diego, California, 1999.

[13] Tom Brotherton, Tom Johnson, and George Chadderdon, Classification and Novelty Detection Using Linear Models and a Class Dependent-Elliptical Basis Function Neural Network, in Proceedings of the International Conference on Neural Networks, Anchorage, May 1998.

[14] Martin Lauer, A Mixture Approach to Novelty Detection Using Training Data With Outliers, Lecture Notes in Computer Science, vol. 2167, pp. 300-310, 2001.

[15] Richard J. Povinelli, Xin Feng. (in press) "A New Temporal Pattern Identification Method For Characterization And Prediction Of Complex Time Series Events," IEEE Transactions on Knowledge and Data Engineering.

[16] A. S. Weigend, N. A. Gershenfeld, Ed., Time-series Prediction: Forcasting the future and Understanding the Past, Addison-Wesley, 1994.

[17] N. H. Packard, J. P. Crutchfield, J. D. Farmer, and R. S. Shaw, "Geometry from a Time Series", Physical Review Letters, vol. 45, pp. 712-716, 1980.

[18] G. Das, K.-I. Lin, H. Mannila, G. Renganathan, and P. Smyth. "Rule discovery from time series," in Proceedings of the 4th International Conference on Very Large Data Bases, pp. 606-617, 1998.

[19] J. Theiler, and S. Eubank, "Don't bleach chaotic data", Chaos, vol.3, pp. 771-782, 1993.

Data Mining for Building Neural Protein Sequence Classification Systems with Improved Performance

Dianhui Wang   Nung Kion Lee   Tharam S. Dillon

Department of Computer Science and Computer Engineering
La Trobe University, Melbourne, VIC 3083, Australia

Abstract - Traditionally, two protein sequences are classified into the same class if their feature patterns have high homology. These feature patterns were originally extracted by sequence alignment algorithms, which measure similarity between an unseen protein sequence and identified protein sequences. Neural network approaches, while reasonably accurate at classification, give no information about the relationship between the unseen case and the classified items that is useful to biologist. In contrast, in this paper we use a generalized radial basis function (GRBF) neural network architecture that generates fuzzy classification rules that could be used for further knowledge discovery. Our proposed techniques were evaluated using protein sequences with ten classes of super-families downloaded from a public domain database, and the results compared favorably with other standard machine learning techniques.

I. INTRODUCTION

A protein super-family consists of protein sequence members that are evolutionally related and therefore functionally and structurally relevant with each other [1,22]. One of the benefits from this category grouping is that some molecular analysis can be carried out within a particular super-family instead of individual protein sequence. It has also become apparent that the function of most genes is still unknown and classification into functionally related groups will provide valuable information on the protein function. Traditionally, two protein sequences are classified into the same class if they have high homology in terms of feature patterns extracted through sequence alignment algorithms. These algorithms, for instance, SAM[11], MEME[12], iPro-Class [9], compare an unseen protein sequence with all the identified protein sequences and provide a score based on similarity of sequences. As the size of the protein sequence databases are large, it is a very time consuming job to perform exhaustive comparison of existing protein sequences. Therefore, it is useful and helpful to build an intelligent classification system for effectively searching protein sequences in some large protein databases. Motivated by this, recently neural networks have been successfully applied in this domain and the results obtained demonstrate some merits of the methodology [1,13]. Neural networks (NNs) have been chosen as technical tools for the protein sequence classification task due to the following two reasons: (i) the extracted features of protein sequences are distributed in a high dimensional space with complex characteristics which is difficult to satisfactorily model using some statistical or parameterized approaches; and (ii) neural networks are able to use the raw continuous values as system inputs. Basically, there are two types of neural models applicable for protein sequences classification task, i.e., unsupervised self-organizing mapping (SOM) networks [8,13] and supervised feed-forward neural networks (FNNs) [14,15,16]. The use of the SOM networks is to discover relationships within a set of protein sequences by clustering them into different groups. In contrast, the FNN based classification systems emphasizes on matching patterns through supervised learning. Once off-line training of the neural network is accomplished, the resulting neural classifier is ready to be used for future protein sequence classification and only few seconds are needed to classify a new protein sequence. This saves a lot of time as compared to sequence alignment methods. Besides the direct protein classification, the supervised neural classifier could also been used to reduce the search scope of the sequence alignment program by only searching members of super-families [22].

Data mining is a process of transferring and analyzing available sets of specific data and extracting the information and knowledge in the form of relationships, patterns or clusters for decision-making, classification, prediction and control [17]. Construction typically involves clustering data points that are close to one another according to some metric or criteria [18]. Given a set of pre-classified examples described in terms of some attributes, the goal of data mining for classification tasks is to derive a set of IF-THEN rules that can be used to assign new events to the appropriate classes. To generate fuzzy classification rules, existing techniques can be categorized into two broad classes: a *direct* method and an *indirect* method. In the *direct* method, the cluster centers as linguistic concepts for fuzzy rules are derived from training data, then the relevant membership functions associated with these cluster centers are assigned by some parameters and further tuned optimally to satisfy some criteria [19]. The *indirect* method encodes domain knowledge expressed using linguistic concepts in various NN models, then updates the structures and weights of the NNs so that the final neural models may classify the given task effectively and efficiently. Note that this method can automatically generate one with explanatory functional fuzzy rules and has a fast inference process due to the connectionist models obtained [4]. For more details, readers may refer to a recent published survey paper [5].

The goal of this paper is to construct a generalized RBF network, which generates a set of fuzzy rules (the direct method), for protein sequence classification tasks. The rest of the paper is organized as follows: Section II discusses some issues on classifier design. Section III presents a novel objective function for classifier optimization. Section IV evaluates the performance of the proposed neural protein sequence classification system, where a data preprocessing description and a comparison are given. We conclude this work with some remarks in the last section.

II. Design Issues

Let the classification task contain n-class data sets, denoted by $\Theta_1, \Theta_2, \ldots, \Theta_n$, characterized by continuous attributes in the subset $[0,1]^m \subset R^m$. The data sets are divided into a training set denoted by S_{tra} and a test set denoted by S_{tes}, respectively. The training set will be used to initialize and optimize the rules, and the test set, unseen by the learning methods, will be used to stop the refinement process and evaluate the performance of the final fuzzy classifier.

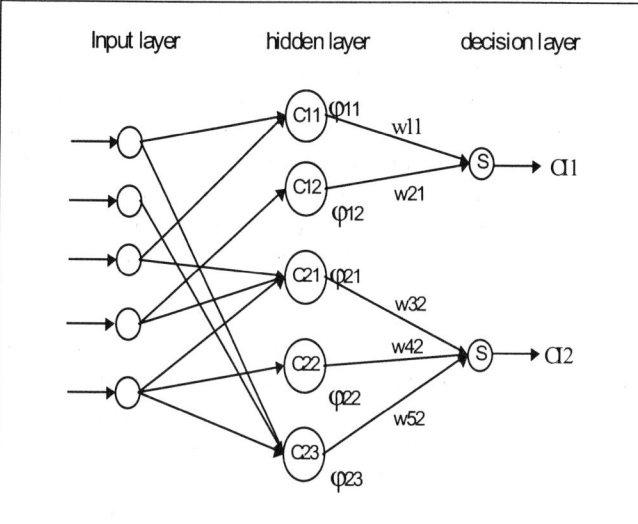

Figure 1. A typical GRBF network architecture

The network consists of m input features $X = [x_1, x_2, \ldots, x_m]^T$, M hidden units and n output units at the decision layer. The activation functions φ in the hidden units are the Gaussian functions defined by

$$\varphi(X_j) = \exp[-d(X_j, C_j)], \quad (1)$$

where $X_j = [x_{j1}, x_{j2}, \ldots, x_{jp}]^T$, $jp \leq m$, represents a subset or a projection of X onto a subspace of the feature space, which is the contributory input vector to the j-th hidden unit, C_j the corresponding cluster center of the unit, $d(X_j, C_j)$ represents the weighted Euclidean distance measure., i.e.,

$$d(X_j, C_j) = \sum_{k=1}^{p} (x_{jk} - c_{jk})^2 / \sigma_{jk}^2. \quad (2)$$

A fuzzy T-norm operator, namely, fuzzy plus operator $\oplus$, defined by

$$a \oplus b = a + b - ab, \quad (3)$$

is applied as the activation function at the output layer of the GRBF network. Therefore, each unit within a group in the hidden layer will contribute some certain classes disjunctively for classification decision-making. The network outputs, as classification indicator (*CI*), are given by

$$CI_P(X) = \sum_{k=1}^{N_p} (-1)^{k+1} \sum_{j_1 < \cdots < j_k} \alpha_{P_{j_1}} \cdots \alpha_{P_{j_k}}, \quad (4)$$

where $CI_P(X)$ represents the p-th output of the network for a given feature input X, N_p is the number of the neurons in the hidden layer connected with the p-th output, and α_{Pj} is given by

$$\alpha_{Pj} = W_{jP} \exp(-d(X_{Pj}, C_{Pj})), \quad (5)$$

which can be interpreted as a firing strength of the local fuzzy classification rules with confidence factor W_{jP}.

The classification criterion used in this paper follows the maximum component principle, that is, a given pattern X will be assigned to Class Q as

$$CI_Q(X) = \arg \max_P \{CI_P(X)\}. \quad (6)$$

A set of fuzzy rules for protein sequence classification can be directly extracted from the GRBF network described above. The following is a typical fuzzy rule:

R_{Pj}:   IF X_{Pj} is around C_{Pj}
        THEN $X \in \Theta_P$ with $CF = W_{jP}$

where *CF* represents a confidence factor of the fuzzy classification rule.

There are two core steps to build up the neural classifier, that is, the network structure determination and classifier parameters optimization. In the rest of this section, we discuss the first issue briefly and the second issue will be examined in the next section.

Structure identification contains two parts, i.e., initialization of a group of hidden units for each classes using supervised Expectation Maximization (EM) algorithm [20], and the input features selection for the hidden units. We omit the detailed description about the well-known EM algorithm and only outline a Feature Subset Selection (FSUBS) technique, which, in fact, is a modified version of the PROCLUS (Projected Clustering) [21] clustering subspace feature selection approach. Briefly, the FSUBS algorithm finds a partition of the points into clusters so that the points within each cluster are close to one another.

Description of FSUBS Algorithm

Procedure **FSUBS**(k, C_i, D_i) {*k is total number of clusters*}
{C_i: *cluster centers for $1 \leq i \leq k$*}
{D_i: *set of feature for C_i*}
{L_i: *set of points assigned to cluster i*}
CurrentBestObjective = -∞
    do
       BestObjective = CurrentBestObjective
       L_i=**AssignPoints**(k, C_i, D_i, T) {T is the training data}
       CurrentBestObjective = **FindDimensions**(C_i,D_i,L_i,k)
         while(CurrentBestObjective ≤ BestObjective)
         save D_i for $1 \leq i \leq k$
    end
Procedure **FindDimensions**(C_i, D_i, L_i, k)
{
{S_i *is the total number of feature in cluster center C_i*}
{X_{ij} *is the average distance from the points in L_i to cluster center of C_i along feature j*}
   Objectivevalue = **EvaluateObjective**(C_i, D_l)
for each cluster C_i do

$$Y_i = \frac{\sum_{j=1}^{S_i} X_{ij}}{S_i}, \ \gamma_i = \sqrt{\frac{\sum_{j=1}^{S_i}(X_{ij}-Y_i)^2}{S_i-1}} \qquad (7)$$

for each feature j do $Z_{i,j} = (X_{ij} - Y_i)/\gamma_i$
   Sort $Z_{i,j}$ in ascending order
   Remove feature Z_{i,S_i} from D_i
   ReducedObjective = **EvaluateObjective**(C_i,D_i)
   if (ReducedObjective > Objectivevalue)
   Restore feature Z_{i,S_i} into D_i {*don't remove it!*}
   else
   Remove feature Z_{i,S_i} permanently
   Objectivevalue = ReducedObjective {*best objective so far*}
   end if
end for
   Return Objectivevalue and ($D_1...D_k$)
}

The main loop in the FSUBS module calls the **FindDimensions** module to reduce the features associated to a cluster. Before the **FindDimensions** module is invoked, the **AssignPoints** module assigns each training data to the nearest cluster. The **FindDimensions** module calculates the average distance X_{ij}, between the points L_i assigned to a cluster C_i along each selected feature. The algorithm then calculates the average Y_i on these average distances X_{ij}. Finally, the error Z_{ij} between X_{ij} and Y_i are calculated on each feature. The features with the most negative Z_{ij} value are closer to the cluster center C_i at the j-th dimension. Thus, after sorted the Z_{ij} values in ascending order, the last value is the feature that has data points that are most dissimilar to the cluster center C_i. This feature is removed and the new performance is determined by using the **EvaluateObjective** module. If the performance is poorer than the best performance so far, then this feature is retained. Otherwise, it is removed permanently and the performance is updated.

The cost function for evaluating FSUBS is the classification rate (CR) of the training data. The CR of the training data is calculated after each removal of a feature from a cluster. The FSUBS algorithm differs from the PROCLUS feature selection in several aspects. In PROCLUS, the evaluation on the objective function is performed after selecting feature subsets for all clusters. In the FSUBS, the evaluation is done just after a feature is removed from a cluster. The reason for doing this is that the initial clusters are not formed by the training data sets. The FSUBS tries to reduce the misclassification by removing some features. The main objective of finding subspace feature using the PROCLUS is to increase the closeness between points assigned to a cluster. On the other hand, the objective of the FSUBS is to reduce overlap between clusters from different classes. As a result, the input features associated with each individual neuron in the hidden layer can be selected successively. To discard permanently a feature for a cluster, it is necessary to check out the CR value to ensure that the performance will not decrease largely.

III. CLASSIFIER OPTIMIZATION

Classifier optimization here refers to parameters refinement of the GRBF networks. The key for doing this is to define an objective function, which may characterizes the performance of the classifier. The commonly concerned performance index for neural classifiers is the misclassification rate (MR) for both training and test data sets. The MR for the training data set can be measured by

$$M_p(X) = \frac{\max_{q \neq p}\{CI_q(X)\}}{CI_p(X)}, X \in \Theta_p \cap S_{tra}. \qquad (8)$$

However, the expression above does not really demonstrate the Generalization Capability (GC) of the neural classification system, or equivalently, the MR index for the test data set. In order to embed this significant information into an objective function for the parameter tuning purpose, some indirect methods will be helpful and necessary although there is still a lack of rigorous theoretical basis. In this paper, we use the following mathematical formula to express this idea:

$$G_P(X) = CI_P(X) + \sum_{j=1}^{N_p}\sum_{k=1}^{P}\sigma_{jk}^2, X \in \Theta_p \cap S_{tra} \qquad (9)$$

The first term of the right hand side in (9) implies the CI quality or the reliability of the neural classifier, and the second term is associated with a geometric size constraint. As the ellipsoidal region tends to be large enough to enclose many training patterns for a certain category of data, the misclassification rate could be increased for this class. It could lead to lower recognition for other classes. On the other hand, if the size of region is reduced and only a small amount of training data for a class is enclosed, a good generalization ability of the rule cannot be expected because of over-fitting, also the recognition rate of this class could be reduced due to poor coverage. Thus, a larger value of this term implies a higher recognition possibility for unseen patterns, which have similar nature to the examples from class p. The higher the value $\sum_{X \in \Theta_p \cap S_{tra}} G_p(X)$ takes, the better the GC performance should be. Therefore, a tradeoff between the size of the ellipsoidal region to achieve good GC power and a low misclassification rate should be addressed. Finally, we define an objective function to refine the classification system as follows:

$$\psi_P(X) = (1-\lambda_p)M_P(X) + \lambda_p[G_P(X)]^{-1}, \qquad (10)$$

where $0 < \lambda_p < 1$ is a regularizing factor.

An overall cost function for optimizing the GRBF neural classifier is defined by

$$\psi(\lambda) = D_{tra}\sum_{p=1}^{n}\sum_{X \in (\Theta_p \cap S_{tra})}\psi_p(X), \qquad (11)$$

where

$$D_{tra} = \frac{1}{n}\sum_{k=1}^{n}c_k(X) \neq \hat{c}_k(X), \qquad (12)$$

and $c(X)$ and $\hat{c}(X)$ represent real class and predicted class for pattern X from the training data set, respectively.

Given a set of regularizing factors, minimization of the cost function (11) will result in a better classifier with improved performance. It must be mentioned that the regularizing factors allow us to balance the importance of misclassification against the generalization ability for each individual class. This importance comes from users and it is usually quite subjective. Within our best knowledge, so far, there is no better way to express the subjective nature and to assign the values of these regularizing factors satisfactorily. In this paper, all the regularizing factors take value of 0.5.

IV. Performance Evaluation

The protein sequences are transformed from DNA sequences using the predefined genome code. Protein sequences are more reliable than DNA sequence because of the redundancy of the genetic code [22]. Two protein sequences are believed to be functional and structurally related if they show similar sequence identity or homology. These conserved patterns are of interest for the protein classification task.

A protein sequence is made from combinations of variable length of 20 amino acids Σ = {A, C, D, E, F, G, H, I, K, L, M, N, P, Q, R, S, T, V, W, Y}. The n-grams or k-tuples [14] features will be extracted as an input vector of the neural network classifier. The n-gram features are a pair of values (v_i, c_i), where v_i is the feature i and c_i is the counts of this feature in a protein sequence for i = 1... 20^n. In general, a feature is the number of occurrences of an animal in a protein sequence. These features are all the possible combinations of n letters from the set Σ. For example, the 2-gram (400 in total) features are (AA, AC,...,AY, CA, CC,...,CY,...,YA, ...,YY). Consider a protein sequence VAAGTVAGT, the extracted 2-gram features are {(VA, 2), (AA, 1), (AG, 2), (GT, 2), (TV, 1)}. The 6-letter exchange group is another commonly used piece of information. The 6-letter group actually contains 6 combinations of the letters from the set Σ. These combinations are A={H,R,K}, B={D,E,N,Q}, C={C}, D={S,T,P,A,G}, E={M,I,L,V} and F={F,Y,W}. For example, the protein sequence VAAGTVAGT mentioned above will be transformed using 6-letter exchange group as EDDDDEDDD and their 2-gram features are {(DE, 1), (ED, 2), (DD, 5)}. We will use e_n and a_n to represent n-gram features from a 6-letter group and 20 letters set. Each sets of n-grams features, i.e., e_n and a_n, from a protein sequence will be scaled separately to avoid skew in the counts value using equation (13) below:

$$\bar{x} = \frac{x}{L-n+1}, \quad (13)$$

where x represents the count of generic gram feature, $\bar{x}$ is the normalized x, which will be the inputs of the neural networks; L is the length of the protein sequence and n is the size of n-gram features.

In this study, the protein sequences covering ten super-families (classes) were obtained from the PIR databases comprised by PIR1 and PIR2 [9]. The 949 protein sequences selected from PIR1 were used as the training data and the 533 protein sequences selected from PIR2 as the test data. The ten super-familes to be trained/classified in this study are: Cytochrome c (113/17), Cytochrome c6 (45/14), Cytochrome b (73/100), Cytochrome b5 (11/14), Triose-phosphate isomerase (14/44), Plastocyanin (42/56), Photosystem II D2 protein (30/45), Ferredoxin (65/33), Globin (548/204), and Cytochrome b6-f complex 4.2K(8/6). The 56 features were extracted and comprised by e_2 and a_1.

Table 1: Experiment Setup

EXP#	Experiments Description
EXPR1	The Principal Components Analysis (PCA) feature selection algorithm is applied to the e2, a1 features. The EM clustering algorithm is then applied to the training data with the selected feature subset. The GRBF model is then constructed and further optimized using the GA algorithm.
EXPR2	The FSUBS algorithm is applied to the clusters using the features selected in EXPR1. Then the optimization using GA algorithm is carried out.
EXPR3	The FSUBS algorithm is applied directly to the 56 features. The GRBF model is then optimized using GA algorithm.

Table 1 gives the setup of our experiment. A standard GA algorithm with parameter constraint is used to minimize the objective function (11). The GA population size and the maximum generation step are set as 30 and 1000, respectively, in our simulation studies. The crossover and mutation probability may be adjusted in different simulations to find the most suitable ones. In EXPR1, the mutation probability takes 0.01, the cross over probability is 0.95 and the replacement probability is 0.95. In EXPR3, the crossover probability is 0.90, the mutation probability is 0.01, and replacement probability is 0.85, respectively. It has been noticed that if the mutation probability is too high (e.g. > 0.5), the performance will become poor because the good genes are not preserved properly to the next generation. The optimization procedure terminates when the maximum generation index is met. The best solution with minimum objective value is recorded during optimization. Table 2 summarizes the clustering results. There are 43 and 48 clusters produced by the EM clustering algorithm, for EXPR1 and EXPR3, respectively. Figure 2 depicts the numbers of subset features of every cluster in EXPR 3.

In EXPR1, a PCA feature selection algorithm with 90% component rate is firstly applied to the e2 and a1 features respectively before using the EM algorithm. Then, the GA optimization process is applied to a GRBF network. To investigate whether the performance can be further improved from the new features, in EXPR2, the subspace feature selection method is applied to the 43 new features selected in EXPR1. The results observed show that the FSUBS can slightly improve the performance but not too much. Applying the FSUBS algorithm in EXPR3, an average of 43 features is selected, which reduces about 23.21% in feature number. It has been seen that less features are associated to the classes

TABLE 2: NUMBER OF CLUSTERS FOR EXPR1(2) AND EXPR3

Class	Number of Clusters for EXPR1 and EXPR2	Number of Clusters for EXPR3
1	7	7
2	5	2
3	5	6
4	3	4
5	3	4
6	3	2
7	2	2
8	3	4
9	11	16
10	1	1

TABLE 3: PERFORMANCE EVALUATION

EXP#	CR (%) before optimization		CR (%) after optimization	
	Training	Test	Training	Test
EXPR1	93.57 (888)	76.74 (409)	96.94 (920)	90.62 (483)
EXPR2	96.84 (919)	85.74 (457)	96.94 (920)	88.18 (470)
EXPR3	95.04 (902)	81.24 (433)	97.37 (924)	92.68 (494)

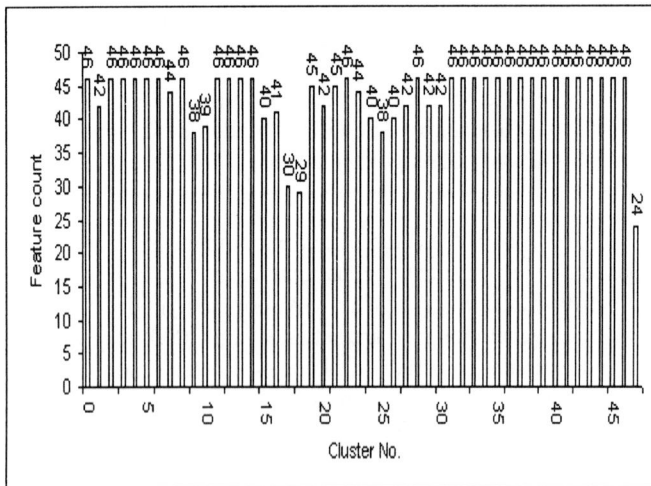

Figure 2. Features selected in each cluster for EXPR3

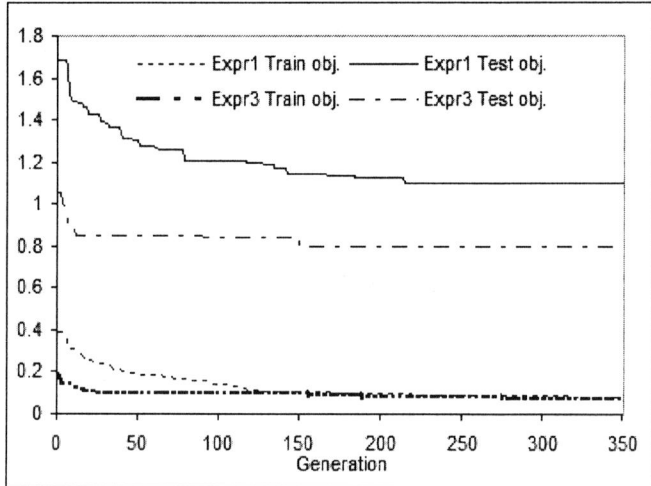

Figure 3. GRBF optimization progress for EXPR1 and EXPR2

TABLE 4: PERFORMANCE COMPARISON

Classifiers	CR for Training	CR for test
MLP-CE	99.16% (940)	90.81% (484)
MLP-MSE	99.37% (943)	91.37% (487)
RBF-CE	97.15% (922)	90.99% (485)
RBF-MSE	99.26% (942)	91.56% (488)
MRBF-CE	98.74% (937)	89.31% (476)
MRBF-MSE	99.89% (948)	87.62% (467)
C4.5	98.40% (934)	79.74% (425)

that have fewer number of clusters. The initial CR after the subspace feature selection is 95.04% (902) for the training data set and 81.24% (433) for the test data set, respectively. After refinement, the CR reaches 97.37% (924) for the training data set and 92.68% (494) for the test data set, respectively. This performance is the best one among all the experiments, but it required more GA generation as compared to the other two experiments. This is because the search space in EXPR3 is a little larger than other two cases. Table 3 demonstrates the performance of our presented neural classifier.

Figure 3 above shows the working progress of GA optimization for experiments EXPR1 and EXPR3 within the first 350 generations. It can be seen that the objective function values for both training and test data in EXPR3 are smaller than that in EXPR1. This indicates that the selected feature subsets using FSUBS in EXPR3 are more efficient to achieve the tradeoff objectives described in the objective function. The objective values for both data are decreasing quickly in the first 100 generations and slowly in the following generation.

To compare the performance of our GRBF network classifier with other classifiers, Table 4 gives the recognition rate of the standard RBF network, the MLP neural classifiers, Modular RBF (MRBF) network classifier with mean square error (MSE) and cross entropy (CE) learning criteria [16], and the well-known decision tree classifier C4.5 [10]. The C4.5 result is obtained using 10 trials and then average them to get to the final result.

The best performance is 92.68% reached by the proposed method in EXPR3 as compared to the best performance of 91.37% from the BP-MSE neural classifier. The C4.5 has the worst performance, CR=79.74%, for this classification task. From Table 4, we can see that training neural classifiers with MSE criterion function tends to over-fit the examples from the training data set easily, and the CE criterion for training neural classifiers seems to be able to perform better.

V. CONCLUSION

Building improved intelligent protein sequence classification systems for effectively searching large biological database is significant for developing competitive pharmacological products. This paper describes a methodology for constructing a neural protein classifier with various input features, rather than to train a neural classifier based on a given neural network architecture and some available data [6,7]. A set of fuzzy classification rules with confidence factors can be obtained directly after parameter refinement using GA programming. The feature selection and use of the new objective function for classifier refinement compromises between misclassification rate and generalization capability. Simulation studies are carried out using a 10-classes of super-family protein sequences. Experimental and comparative results demonstrate that our proposed method outperforms other neural classifiers for this data set.

The following issues will be studied in our further work:
- Learning strategies comparison [23,24];
- System quality improvement, for instance, increasing the recognition rate for super-families with low-probability items [25], reliability and robustness [16,26,27].

ACKNOWLEDGEMENT

This project was supported by the Victorian Partnership for Advanced Computing Expertise Program Grant Scheme.

REFERENCES

[1] Baldi P. and Brunak S., Bioinformatics: The Machine Learning Approach, (2nd edition), The MIT Press, 2001.

[2] Bishop C. M., Neural Networks for Pattern Recognition, Clarendon Press, Oxford, 1995.

[3] R. P. Lippmann, "Pattern classification using neural networks", IEEE Commun. Magazine, pp.47-64, 1989.

[4] S. Mitra, R. K. De and S. K. Pal, "Knowledge-based fuzzy MLP for classification and rule generation", IEEE Trans. On Neural Networks, pp. 1338-1350, 1998.

[5] K. Hirota and W. Pedrycz, "Fuzzy computing for data mining", Proceedings of the IEEE, 1999, pp.1575 –1600.

[6] J. Moody and C. Darken, "Faster learning in networks of locally-tuned processing units", Neural Computation. 1989, pp. 281-294.

[7] Y. S. Hwang, and Y. S. Bang, "An efficient method to construct a radial basis function neural network classifier", Neural Networks, 1997, pp.1495-1503.

[8] H. C Wang, Dapazo J., L. G. De La Fraga, Y. P. Zhu, Carazo J. M., Self-organizing tree-growing network for the classification of protein sequences, Protein Science, pp. 2613-2622, 1998.

[9] Protein Information Resources (PIR), http://pir.Georgetown.edu

[10] R., C4.5: programs for machine learning, San Mateo, CA Morgan Kaufmann, 1994.

[11] SAM: Sequence Alignment and Modeling Software System, Baskin Center for Computer Engineering and Science, http://www.cse.ucsc.edu/researchcompbio/

[12] MEME: Multiple EM for Motif Elicitation UCSD Computer Science and Engineeringhttp://meme.sdsc.edu

[13] H. C. Wang, J. Dopazo et al, Self-organizing tree-growing network for the classification of protein sequences, Protein Science, pp. 2613-2622, 1998.

[14] C. H. Wu, G. Whitson, J. McLarty, A. Ermongkonchai, T. C. Change, PROCANS: Protein Classification Artificial Neural System, Protein Science, pp. 667-677, 1992.

[15] C. H. Wu, Artificial neural networks for molecular sequence analysis, Computers Chemistry, pp. 237-256, 1997.

[16] D. H. Wang, N. K. Lee, T. S. Dillon and N. J. Hoogenraad, Protein sequences classification using Radial Basis Function (RBF) neural networks, R.I. McKay, J. Slaney (Eds.): AI 2002: Advances in Artificial Intelligence, Lecture Notes in Computer Science, LNAI 2557, pp. 477-486, Springer 2002.

[17] Sestito, S. and Dillon, T. S., Automated Knowledge Acquisition. Australia: Prentice Hall, 1995.

[18] Kennedy, R. L., Lee, Y., Roy, B. V., Reed C. D., and R. P. Lippmann, Solvong Data Mining Problems Through Pattern Recognition. Prentice Hall, PTR, Unica Technologies, Inc., 1998.

[19] M. Setnes and H. Roubos, GA-Fuzzy Modeling and Classification: Complexity and Performance, IEEE Transactions on Fuzzy Systems. No. 5, October 2000.

[20] A. P. Dempster, N. M. Laird and D. B. Rubin, Maximum likelihood from incomplete data via the EM algorithm. J. Royal Statiscal Soc., Serial *B*. Vol. 39, No. 1, pp 1-38, 1977.

[21] C. C. Aggarwal, C. Procopiuc, J. L. Wolf, P. S. Yu and J. S. Park, Fast algorithms for projected clustering. In SIGMOD'99, Philadephia, *PA*. June, 1999.

[22] Durbin, R., Eddy, S., Krogh, A. and Mitchison, G., Biological sequence analysis-Probabilistic models of proteins and nucleic acids, Cambridge University Press, 1998.

[23] E. Barnard and D. Casasent, Acomparison between criterion functions for linear classifiers, with application to neural nets, IEEE Trans. On SMC, Vol.19, No.5, pp.1030-1041, 1989.

[24] H. Ney, On the probabilistic interpretation of neural network classifiers and discriminative training criteria, IEEE Trans. On PAMI, Vol.17, No.2, pp.107-119,1995.

[25] D. J. Munro, O. K. Ersoy, M. R. Bell, and J. S.Sadowsky, Neural network learning of low-probability event, IEEE Trans. On AES, Vol.32, No.3, pp.898-910, 1996.

[26] L. P. Cordella, C. D. Stefano,F. Tortorella, and M. Vento, A method for improving classification reliability of multilayer perceptrons, IEEE Trans. On NN, Vol.6, No.5, pp.1140-1147, 1995.

[27] C. D. Stefano,F. Tortorella, and M. Vento, To reject or not to reject: that is the question-an answer in case of neural classifiers, IEEE Trans. On SMC, Part C: Applications and Review, Vol.30, No.1, pp.84-94, 2000.

Interval arithmetic inversion: A new rule extraction algorithm[†]

† Carlos Hernández-Espinosa † Mercedes Fernández-Redondo †Mamen Ortiz-Gómez.
† Universidad Jaume I, Campus de Riu Sec, D. de Ingeniería y Ciencia de los Computadores, 12071
Castellón, Spain. e-mail: espinosa@icc.uji.es

Abstract- **In this paper we propose a new algorithm for rule extraction from a trained Multilayer Feedforward network. The algorithm is based on an interval arithmetic network inversion for particular target outputs. The types of rules extracted are N-dimensional intervals in the input space. We have performed experiments with four databases and the results are very interesting. One rule extracted by the algorithm can cover 86% of the neural network output and in other cases sixty four rules cover 100% of the neural network output.**

I. INTRODUCTION

Neural networks have been applied to a great number of applications and one of the most widely used neural network paradigms is Multilayer Feedforward. However, in same applications it is not only sufficient a correct classification of an input, it is also necessary an explanation of the classification [1]. One example is the medical diagnosis field, in this case, we need to provide a correct classification of the symptoms (the disease) and an explanation of the classification for the doctor. The intelligent systems in this field are conceived as an aid for the doctor and not as a substitution of the doctor. Therefore, they should provide an explanation capability.

A fundamental problem of neural networks is that the information they encode can not be easily understood by humans, for example, it is difficult to give an explanation on how they solve a particular problem. The arithmetic operations of a neural network are complex and has no meaning for a human person.

One of the methods to solve this problem is rule extraction from a trained neural network. With this method, we tray to convert the information contained in a neural network in a set of rules that can be understood by a person.

There are many algorithm for rule extraction [2-8]. They differ in the type of rules extracted and many other characteristics. However, they lack from a common problem, the computational cost of the extraction of rules increases exponentially with the number of parameters in the neural network (weights or neurons). So, it is usually of crucial importance the application of pruning algorithms to reduce the size of the network previously to the application of the rule extraction method.

In this paper, we propose a new algorithm for rule extraction from a trained Multilayer Feedforward network based on interval arithmetic. The algorithm is based in a network inversion for a particular target using the interval arithmetic properties. The type of rules extracted are N-dimensional intervals in the input space.

This new algorithm has the problem of an exponential computational cost increase with the number of inputs in the network, but other parameters like the number of weights or hidden units does not affect significantly the computational cost.

The organization of the paper is the following. In section two we describe the interval arithmetic basis, the neural network inversion method and the rule extraction algorithm. In section three we present the experimental results with four databases and finally the conclusions are in section four.

II. THEORY

This section is divided in four subsection. The first one reviews the basic properties of interval arithmetic. The second explains how to calculate the output of a neural network for an interval input. Subsection three describes the interval arithmetic inversion algorithm, and finally in the fourth we explain the rule extraction algorithm.

A. Interval Arithmetic basis

First, we will review the basic operations of interval arithmetic used in this paper. They are sum of intervals, multiplication of an interval by a number and the exponential function of an interval [9].

The sum of two intervals is an interval whose upper limit is the sum of the upper limits of the intervals and whose lower limit is the sum of the lower limits of the intervals. See equation 1.

$$A + B = [a^L, a^U] + [b^L, b^U] = [a^L + b^L, a^U + b^U] \quad (1)$$

Where the superscripts L and U denote the lower and upper limits of the interval.

[†] This research work was supported by a Spanish CICYT project number TIC2000-1056.

The second property is the product of a real number by an interval. In this case the final interval depends on the sign of the real number. See equation 2.

$$m \cdot A = m \cdot [a^L, a^U] = \begin{cases} [m \cdot a^L, m \cdot a^U] & \text{if } m \geq 0 \\ [m \cdot a^U, m \cdot a^L] & \text{if } m < 0 \end{cases} \quad (2)$$

Another interesting property is the exponential function of an interval. It is interesting because it is often used in the transfer function of a neural network.

Since the exponential function is monotonically increasing the result is an interval whose lower limit is the exponential of the lower limit and whose upper limit is the exponential of the upper limit. See equation 3.

$$\exp(A) = \exp([a^L, a^U]) = [\exp(a^L), \exp(a^U)] \quad (3)$$

B. Interval output of Multilayer Feedforward for an input interval

With these three basic properties, we can calculate the output of the usual Multilayer Feedforward for an input interval, i.e., in the case we use intervals as the inputs of the neural network.

In this situation the output of the neural network becomes an N-dimensional interval where N is the number of output units.

Also, all the intermediate values of the neural network, like the output of the hidden units, become intervals.

The interval outputs of the hidden units can be calculated with equation 4.

$$H_{P,j} = [H^L_{P,j}, H^U_{P,j}] = f(Net_{P,j}) =$$
$$= f([net^L_{P,j}, net^U_{P,j}]) = [f(net^L_{P,j}), f(net^U_{P,j})]$$

where $Net_{P,j} = \sum_{i=1}^{Ninputs} w_{j,i} \cdot I_{P,i} + \theta_j$

$$Net_{P,i} = [net^L_{P,j}, net^U_{P,j}] \quad (4)$$

where

$$net^L_{P,j} = \sum_{i=1, w_{j,i} \geq 0}^{Ninputs} w_{j,i} \cdot I^L_{P,i} + \sum_{i=1, w_{j,i} < 0}^{Ninputs} w_{j,i} \cdot I^U_{P,i} + \theta_j$$

$$net^U_{P,j} = \sum_{i=1, w_{j,i} \geq 0}^{Ninputs} w_{j,i} \cdot I^U_{P,i} + \sum_{i=1, w_{j,i} < 0}^{Ninputs} w_{j,i} \cdot I^L_{P,i} + \theta_j$$

Where f is the standard sigmoid function, $I_{P,j}=[I_{P,j}^L, I_{P,j}^U]$ are the input intervals and $H_{P,j}=[H_{P,j}^L, H_{P,j}^U]$ are the output intervals of the hidden units.

In equation 4, we have to distinguish between positive and negative weights because of the same distinction in the property of multiplication of a real number by an interval.

Analogously for the interval outputs of the neural network we have the equation 5.

$$O_{p,k} = [O^L_{P,k}, O^U_{P,k}] = f(Net_{P,k}) =$$
$$= f([net^L_{P,k}, net^U_{P,k}])$$

where

$$net^L_{P,k} = \sum_{j=1, w_{k,j} \geq 0}^{Nhidden} w_{k,j} \cdot H^L_{P,j} + \sum_{j=1, w_{k,j} < 0}^{Nhidden} w_{k,j} \cdot H^U_{P,j} + \xi_k \quad (5)$$

and

$$net^U_{P,k} = \sum_{j=1, w_{k,j} \geq 0}^{Nhidden} w_{k,j} \cdot H^U_{P,j} + \sum_{j=1, w_{k,j} < 0}^{Nhidden} w_{k,j} \cdot H^L_{P,j} + \xi_k$$

Where f is the standard sigmoidal function and $O_{P,k}=[O_{P,k}^L, O_{P,k}^U]$ is the interval output of the neural network.

With these equations we can calculate the transformation of an interval in the inputs into an interval at the outputs across the neural network structure.

C. Network interval arithmetic inversion

The aim of a neural network inversion algorithm is to fix a particular output of the network and obtain an input or set of inputs whose output is the previously fixed output.

In the case of interval arithmetic inversion the objective is the same, but in this case the fixed output is an interval and obviously the obtained input will be an interval.

The algorithm for interval arithmetic inversion is basically the same algorithm of neural network inversion [10], but in this case, the target will be an interval vector, we have to consider the interval arithmetic properties and the error function will be the one of equation 6.

$$E_p = \frac{1}{4} \cdot \sum_{k=1}^{Noutput} \left\{ (t^U_{p,k} - o^U_{p,k})^2 + (t^L_{p,k} - o^L_{p,k})^2 \right\} \quad (6)$$

After we fix an interval output, the inversion is accomplished by selecting and initial interval vector as the initial input $\{[i^L_1(0), i^U_1(0)], [i^L_2(0), i^U_2(0)], ..., [i^L_N(0), i^U_N(0)]\}$ and applying an iterative gradient descent algorithm similar to Backpropagation that will minimize the error value by changing the initial input. The equations are basically in 7.

$$i^L_{P,k}(n) = i^L_{P,k}(n-1) - \eta \frac{\partial Error}{\partial i^L_{P,k}}$$
$$i^U_{P,k}(n) = i^U_{P,k}(n-1) - \eta \frac{\partial Error}{\partial i^U_{P,k}} \quad (7)$$

The process is iterative, we calculate the interval output of the neural network for the initial interval input. After that, we apply equations 7 and we obtain a new input interval. With this new input interval we can calculate again the output interval and iterate in this way the process.

The values of the partial derivates of equation 7 are in equations 8 and 9.

$$\frac{\partial Error}{\partial i_{P,k}^L} = -\frac{1}{2}\left\{\sum_{k=1}^{Noutput}(t_{P,k}^L - o_{P,k}^L)o_{P,k}^L(1-o_{P,k}^L)\cdot\right.$$
$$\left\{\sum_{i}^{w_{k,i}\geq 0, w_{i,l}\geq 0} w_{k,i}\cdot H_{P,i}^L\cdot(1-H_{P,i}^L)\cdot w_{i,l} + \right.$$
$$\left.\sum_{i}^{w_{k,i}<0, w_{i,l}<0} w_{k,i}\cdot H_{P,i}^U\cdot(1-H_{P,i}^U)\cdot w_{i,l}\right\} +$$
$$\sum_{k=1}^{Noutput}(t_{P,k}^U - o_{P,k}^U)o_{P,k}^U(1-o_{P,k}^U)\cdot$$
$$\left\{\sum_{i}^{w_{k,i}\geq 0, w_{i,l}<0} w_{k,i}\cdot H_{P,i}^U\cdot(1-H_{P,i}^U)\cdot w_{i,l} + \right.$$
$$\left.\left.\sum_{i}^{w_{k,i}<0, w_{i,l}\geq 0} w_{k,i}\cdot H_{P,i}^L\cdot(1-H_{P,i}^L)\cdot w_{i,l}\right\}\right\} \quad (8)$$

$$\frac{\partial Error}{\partial i_{P,k}^U} = -\frac{1}{2}\left\{\sum_{k=1}^{Noutput}(t_{P,k}^L - o_{P,k}^L)o_{P,k}^L(1-o_{P,k}^L)\cdot\right.$$
$$\left\{\sum_{i}^{w_{k,i}\geq 0, w_{i,l}<0} w_{k,i}\cdot H_{P,i}^L\cdot(1-H_{P,i}^L)\cdot w_{i,l} + \right.$$
$$\left.\sum_{i}^{w_{k,i}<0, w_{i,l}\geq 0} w_{k,i}\cdot H_{P,i}^U\cdot(1-H_{P,i}^U)\cdot w_{i,l}\right\}$$
$$+ \sum_{k=1}^{Noutput}(t_{P,k}^U - o_{P,k}^U)o_{P,k}^U(1-o_{P,k}^U)\cdot \quad (9)$$
$$\left\{\sum_{i}^{w_{k,i}\geq 0, w_{i,l}\geq 0} w_{k,i}\cdot H_{P,i}^U\cdot(1-H_{P,i}^U)\cdot w_{i,l} + \right.$$
$$\left.\left.\sum_{i}^{w_{k,i}<0, w_{i,l}<0} w_{k,i}\cdot H_{P,i}^L\cdot(1-H_{P,i}^L)\cdot w_{i,l}\right\}\right\}$$

Again in equations 8 and 9, we have to distinguish between positive and negative weights because of the same distinction in the property of multiplication of real number by an interval, equation 2.

D. Rule extraction algorithm

The type of rules we want to obtain are N-dimensional intervals in the input space like the following:

If $x_1 \subset [a_1^L, a_1^U]$, $x_2 \subset [a_2^L, a_2^U]$, ..., $x_N \subset [a_N^L, a_N^U]$ then $\{x_1, x_2, ..., x_N\} \in$ Class K.

If the input is contained in the N-dimensional interval $[a_i^L, a_i^U]$ the output is a particular class (class K in the example).

We should obtain the limits of the intervals a_i, b_i. They limit a N-dimensional interval in the input space and the whole N-dimensional interval has to be included in a classification class. An interval neural network inversion is used to get the intervals.

In order to obtain a rule, first, we will select a target value of the following type for one classification class (for example, class number 2): $\{[0,0.5]_{Class1}, [0.5,1.0]_{Class2}, [0,0.5]_{Class3}, ..., [0,0.5]_{ClassN}\}$. An output vector inside the above interval suppose a correct classification inside the class number 2 because neuron number 2 is activated and the rest of neurons are not, it is a strict rule of classification.

Second, we will apply the inversion algorithm for the target. We expect that the initial input interval will evolve to give an interval whose output is inside the target interval selected, in this case, the final input interval will correspond to a valid rule.

We have performed simulations with three types of initial intervals in several two dimensional examples. And the conclusion is that if the initial interval is a point correctly classified by the target interval, during the inversion, the point will expand to an interval. The final output limits of the interval input will generally touch the borders of the classification class and the final results will normally correspond to a valid rule. We can see several examples in Fig. 1, where A is the position of the initial input point correctly classified by the target, and B is the final interval as a consequence of the neural network inversion algorithm.

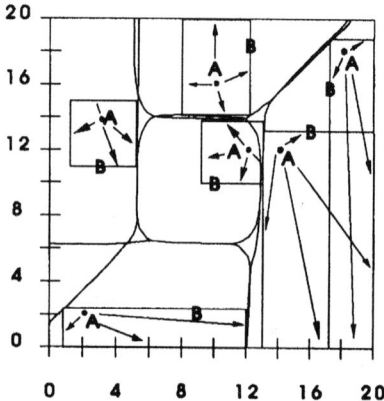

Fig. 1. Example of point expansion by interval arithmetic inversion. A is the initial point, B is the final interval.

As can be seen from the figure, the initial point input expands to an interval which is contained in the correct classification class and the limits of this interval usually touch the borders of the classification class.

It is obvious that we can exploit this behavior of this type of initial intervals in order to propose an algorithm which can convert the information contained in the neural network into rules. The algorithm can be resumed as follows:

a) Select an initial point and calculate the output of the neural network for this input.
b) Select a target of the type described above, this target should agree with the classification class of the output of the neural network for the initial point (the classification of the initial point should be correct).
c) Apply the inversion algorithm and extract a rule (the inversion algorithm will expand the initial point into an interval).
d) Select a new point which is not included in the rules that we have obtained before, and calculate the output of the neural network for this new point.
e) Select a target which agrees with the output of the neural network for this new point.
f) Apply the inversion algorithm and extract a new rule.
g) If we have not covered the whole input space with the appropriate accuracy go to step d).

In step d) we select a new point which is not included in the rules obtained before. This is a heuristic procedure to diminish the number of rules extracted.

As it can be seen in figure 1 the initial point of the interval arithmetic inversion is usually contained in the final rule. If we select initial points not covered by the rules the chance to get a new rule which cover a higher portion of the space not covered by previous rules is higher. This is the reason of this heuristic procedure.

In order to test whether we have covered the input space and select a new initial point we can scan the input space with equally spaced points and test if the points are included in the rules. The space between the points will also influence the final accuracy of the set of rules. This is confirmed by the experimental results.

The problem of this scanning method is that its yields a computational complexity increase with the increase of the number of inputs and it can not be used with a high number of inputs. The methods of input or feature selection will play an important role to apply this algorithm [11], usually only a lower part of the initial selected inputs are necessary to perform a good classification.

There are other specific characteristics of this method. A rule will always have an output interval inside the target described above, so there will not be incorrect classifications of points by the rule. Also another consequence is that there will not be overlapping among rules of different classes. And finally, the set of rules will not usually cover the total space of the neural network input, for example, the output {0.1, 0.8, 7} is not in the initial target intervals because two output units are activated and if an input has this output it will not be covered. We can say that the points where the classification of the neural network is not clear are not covered by the rules.

III. EXPERIMENTAL RESULTS

We have tested the neural network rule extraction algorithm with four database from the UCI repository of machine learning databases. The databases are Balance Scale (BALANCE), Liver Disorders (BUPA) and two of the Monk's Problems (MONK1 and MONK2). We have selected these databases because the input dimensionality is at most six (http://www.ics.uci.edu/~mlearn/MLRepository.html).

We have applied the rule extraction algorithm to ten networks for each database which were trained with different random initialization of weights and different partition of data among training, cross-validation and test.

In a rule extraction algorithm of this type we think that the two most important criteria for the results are the fidelity of the rules and the number of rules extracted. By fidelity of rules, we should understand how the results reproduced the behavior of the neural network.

In table I we have the results for the four databases.

The second column (Prec. Space) is the distance in the input space between the points generated to construct the rules. A lower number means a higher number of points and therefore a higher number of rules.

We have randomly generate 10.000 point inside the input space with the condition that only one output unit is activated. The third column (Percentage) is the mean percentage of points covered by the rules and the fourth column (Not Cover) the mean percentage of points which were not covered for the ten networks of each database.

Columns five and six are two mean percentages, in this case we have generated randomly 10.000 points without restriction inside the input space. The fifth column (Total Percentage) is the mean percentage of points covered by the rules and the sixth column (Total Not Cover) is the mean percentage of points not covered by the rules.

The seventh column (Number of Rules, Nrule) is the mean number of rules generated by the algorithm for the ten networks of each database. Column number eight is the minimum number of rules generated for a network and column number nine is the percentage of covering of this minimum number of rules.

We can see that, in general, the number of rules increases with the precision of the scanning space as it was expected. This is a normal behavior because we are using more points to extract rules.

But this is not the case in the percentage of covering (column number 3). In databases Bupa and Monk2 we increase the number of points (by increasing the "Prec. Space", the number of points to extract rules), but the percentage of covering (column number 3) decreases. We have to consider that we are approaching the decision surface of the neural networks by square N-dimensional intervals, and this approach depends on the particular situation of he points and in a neural networks, with a more squared decision surface the approach can be better than with other networks.

TABLE I.
RESULTS OF THE RULE EXTRACTION ALGORITHM.

Database	Prec. Space	Perc.	Not Cover	Total Perc.	Total Not Cover	Number of Rules (Nrule).	Nrule min.	Perc. Nrule min.
BALANCE	0.2	74.15	25.84	65.57	34.42	331.3	323	74.96
BALANCE	0.13	83.14	16.86	73.75	26.25	745.9	671	82.04
BUPA	0.2	92.59	7.41	92.59	7.41	6357.1	64	100
BUPA	0.13	85.11	14.89	85.11	14.89	19289.5	1	89.27
MONK1	0.2	81.10	18.90	81.10	18.90	8899.5	5036	82.44
MONK1	0.13	81.31	18.69	81.31	18.69	47211.4	35842	82.56
MONK2	0.2	93.21	6.79	93.21	6.79	7288	64	100
MONK2	0.13	83.16	16.84	82.69	17.31	12943.1	1	87.57

However, we can see very interesting results in the minimum number of rules, which means that for a particular network the rule extraction algorithm performed very well. For example, for the databases BUPA and MONK2 sixty four rules are enough to completely cover the input space and reproduce completely the behavior of the neural network. Also, in BUPA one rule covers the 89.27% of the input space and in MONK2 one rule covers more that 87% of the input space. These results are very interesting and better than other rule extraction algorithms.

As we commented before, the rules will only cover the input space where only one output unit is activated and the rest are not. We can evaluate the maximum percentage of points not covered by subtracting the columns "Percentage" and "Total Percentage", they are 8.58% for the database BALANCE, 0% for BUPA, 0% for MONK1 and 0.47% for MONK2. As we can see this effect is not so important in the experimental results and the input space is almost covered by the rules.

As commented before in the theory section there are no wrong classifications of the rules, this is confirmed by the experimental results. Also it is confirmed that there is no overlapping among rules of different classes. The classification of the rules with this method is perfect and we did not observe any error in the experimental results. This is a consequence of the targets selected for the interval arithmetic inversion.

The results of mean percentage of covering are in general good. But if we want to increase the percentage of covering we can generate random points outside the covering of the rules and extract new rules from these points. This is based in the following heuristic: in a rule the initial point is usually covered by the rule (see Fig. 1), therefore the new rule will usually cover part of the input space not covered by the rest of the rules (the initial point is not contained in any rule).

We have applied this technique with the database Balance which got the lower percentage of covering and the results are in Table 2, using 5000 new points not covered by the initial rules.

As we can see the mean percentage of covering by the rules (column three) increases from 74.15 to 95.15, so this is a good technique to increase the performance of our rule system. Also the mean number of rules increases from 323 to 2706, the new rules are covering the additional input space.

TABLE II.
RESULTS OF THE RULE EXTRACTION ALGORITHM ADITIONAL POINTS.

Database	Number of Points	Perc.	Not Cover	Total Perc.	Total Not Cover	Number of Rules (Nrule)	Nrule Min.	Perc. Nrule min.
BALANCE	5000	95.19	4.81	85.45	14.54	2963	2706	95.87

IV. CONCLUSIONS

We have presented a new algorithm for rule extraction from a trained Multilayer Feedforward neural network. The algorithm is based on an interval arithmetic network inversion for particular interval target outputs. The type of rules extracted are N-dimensional intervals in the input space. The experimental results are interesting, one rule extracted by the algorithm can cover 86% of the input space of the neural network, and in other cases 64 rules cover 100% of the neural network.

REFERENCES

[1] A. Maren, C. Harston y R. Pap, Handbook of Neural Computing Applications, Academic Press Inc., 1990.
[2] Lu, H., Setiono, R., Liu, H., "Effective Data Mining Using Neural Networks", IEEE Trans. on Knowledge and Data Engineering, vol. 8, no. 6, pp.957-961, 1996.
[3] Thrun, S., "Extracting Rules from Artificial Neural Networks with Distributed Representations", Advances in Neural Information Processing Systems 7, pp. 505-512, 1995.
[4] Gupta, A., Lam, S.M., "Generalized Analytic Rule Extraction for Feedforward Neural Networks", IEEE Trans. on Knowledge and Data Engineering, vol. 11, no. 6, pp. 985-991, 1999.
[5] Narazaki, H., Shigaki, I., Watanabe, T., "A Method for Extracting Approximate Rules from Neural Network", Proceedings of the IEEE International Conference on Fuzzy Systems, vol. 4, pp. 1865-1870, 1995.
[6] Palade, V., Neagu, D.C., Puscasu, G., "Rule extraction from neural networks by interval propagation", Fourth International Conference on Knowledge-Based Intelligent Engineering Systems and Alllied Technologies, pp. 217-220, 2000.
[7] Greczy, P., Usui, S., "Rule extraction from trained artificial neural networks", Behaviormetrika, vol. 26, no. 1, pp. 89-106, 1999.
[8] Taha, I.A., Ghosh, J., "Symbolic interpretation of artificial neural networks", IEEE Trans. on Knowledge and Data Engineering, vol. 11, no. 3, pp. 448-463, 1999.
[9] Alefeld, G., Herzberger, J., Introduction to Interval Computations, Academic Press, New York, 1983.
[10] Linden, A. and Kinderman, J., "Inversion of Multilayer Nets", in Proceedings of the International Conference on Neural Networks, Washington D.C., vol. 2, pp. 425-30, 1989.
[11] Fernandez, M., Hernandez, C., "Analysis of Input Selection Methods for Multilayer Feedforward", Journal Neural Network World, vol. 10, no. 3, pp. 389-406, 2000.

Relevance Feedback with Active Learning for Document Retrieval

Takashi Onoda[†] Hiroshi Murata[†] and Seiji Yamada[‡]

[†] Central Research Institute of Electric Power Industry, 2-11-1 Iwadokita, Komae-shi,
Tokyo, 201-8511 Japan

[‡] National Institute of Informatics, 2-1-2 Hitotsubashi, Chiyoda-ku, Tokyo 101-8430 Japan

{onoda,murata}@criepi.denken.or.jp, seiji@nii.ac.jp

Abstract— We investigate the following data mining problems from the document retrieval: From a large data set of documents, we need to find documents that relate to human interesting in as few iterations of human testing or checking as possible. In each iteration a comparatively small batch of documents is evaluated for relating to the human interesting. We apply active learning techniques based on Support Vector Machine for evaluating successive batches, which is called *relevance feedback*. Finally, our proposed approach is very useful for document retrieval with relevance feedback experimentally.

I. INTRODUCTION

As progression of the internet technology, accessible information by end users is explosively increasing. In this situation, we can now easily access a huge document database through the WWW. However it is hard for a user to retrieve relevant documents from which he/she can obtain useful information, and a lot of studies have been done in information retrieval), especially document retrieval [20]. Active works for such document retrieval have been reported in TREC(Text Retrieval Conference) [17] for English documents, IREX(Information Retrieval and Extraction Exercise) [4] and NTCIR(NII-NACSIS Test Collection for Information Retrieval System) [8] for Japanese documents.

In most frameworks for information retrieval, a Vector Space Model(which is called VSM) in which a document is described with a high-dimensional vector is used [13]. An information retrieval system using a vector space model computes the similarity between a query vector and document vectors by cosine of the two vectors and indicates a user a list of retrieved documents.

In general, since a user hardly describes a precise query in the first trial, interactive approach to modify the query vector by evaluation of the user on documents in a list of retrieved documents. This method is called *relevance feedback* [12] and used widely in information retrieval systems. In this method, a user directly evaluates whether a document is relevant or irrelevant in a list of retrieved documents, and a system modifies the query vector using the user evaluation. A traditional way to modify a query vector is a simple learning rule to reduce the difference between the query vector and documents evaluated as relevant by a user.

In another approach, relevant and irrelevant document vectors are considered as positive and negative examples, and relevance feedback is transposed to a binary classification problem [9]. For the binary classification problem, SVM shows the excellent ability. And some studies applied SVM to the text classification problems [16] and the information retrieval problems [3].

We propose a relevance feedback framework with SVM as *active learning*. In contrast that a conventional SVM based relevance feedback system indicates a user a list of the most relevant documents, our system provides a user a list of documents which are hard for SVM to classify them and may be relevant for the user. This is a kind of active learning approach and we consider it promising for relevance feedback.

Okabe and Yamada [9] proposed a frame work in which relational learning to classification rules was applied to interactive document retrieval. Since the learned classification rules is described with symbolic representation, they are readable to our human and we can easily modify the rules directly using a sort of editor. However we consider SVM dealing with continuous values can do more precise classification than symbolic classification rules.

The relevance feedback is similar to what is termed active learning in that we try to maximize test performance using the smallest number of documents in the training set [16]. From an active learning point of view, we are interested in maximizing learning performance. Tong et al. proposed SVM based text classification method from an active learning point of view. The method tries to maximize learning performance. Drucker et al. applied SVM to the information retrieval [3]. At each retrieval, their method tries to maximize the number of useful documents, which are displayed to users. But it does not consider the learning performance. Documents are generally represented by the vector space model for the information retrieval. In this method, term frequency(TF) and binary representation are used as the vector space model. However, the conventional relevance feedback information retrieval method is useful in term frequency inverse document frequency(TFIDF) representation [12]. We are interested in comparing the performance between SVM based relevance feedback method and the conventional method in TFIDF representation. The detail of this difference will be described in the third section. And we propose the SVM based relevance feedback method, which can give many relevant documents for users at each retrievaland keep the learning performance.

In the remaining parts of this paper, we explain a SVM

algorithm in the second section briefly, and an active learning with SVM for the relevance feedback in the third section. In the fourth section, in order to evaluate the effectiveness of our approach, we made experiments using a TREC data set of Los Angeles Times and discuss the experimental results. Eventually we conclude our work and discuss open problems in the fifth section.

II. SUPPORT VECTOR MACHINES

Formally, the Support Vector Machine (SVM) [18] like any other classification method aims to estimate a classification function $f : \mathcal{X} \to \{\pm 1\}$ using labeled training data from $\mathcal{X} \times \{\pm 1\}$. Moreover this function f should even classify unseen examples correctly.

In order to construct good classifiers by learning, two conditions have to be respected. First, the training data must be an unbiased sample from the same source (pdf) as the unseen test data. This concerns the experimental setup. Second, the size of the class of functions from which we choose our estimate f, the so-called capacity of the learning machine, has to be properly restricted according to statistical learning theory [18]. If the capacity is too small, complex discriminant functions cannot be approximated sufficiently well by any selectable function f in the chosen class of functions – the learning machine is too simple to learn well. On the other hand, if the capacity is too large, the learning machine bears the risk of overfitting.

In neural network training, overfitting is avoided by early stopping, regularization or asymptotic model selection [1], [7], [10], [11].

For SV learning machines that implement linear discriminant functions in feature spaces, the capacity limitation corresponds to finding a large margin separation between the two classes. The margin ϱ is the minimal distance of training points $(\mathbf{x}_1, y_1), \ldots, (\mathbf{x}_i, y_i), \mathbf{x}_i \in \mathbf{R}, y_i \in \{\pm 1\}$ to the separation surface, i.e.

$$\varrho = \min_{i=1,\ldots,\ell} \rho(\mathbf{z}_i, f) \quad (1)$$

where $\mathbf{z}_i = (\mathbf{x}_i, y_i)$ and

$$\rho(\mathbf{z}_i, f) = y_i f(\mathbf{x}_i), \quad (2)$$

and f is the linear discriminant function in some feature space

$$f(\mathbf{x}) = (\mathbf{w} \cdot \Phi(\mathbf{x})) + b = \sum_{i=1}^{\ell} \alpha_i y_i (\Phi(\mathbf{x}_i) \cdot \Phi(\mathbf{x})) + b, \quad (3)$$

with $\mathbf{w}$ expressed as $\mathbf{w} = \sum_{i=1}^{\ell} \alpha_i y_i \Phi(\mathbf{x}_i)$. The quantity Φ denotes the mapping from input space $\mathcal{X}$ by explicitly transforming the data into a feature space $\mathcal{F}$ using $\Phi : \mathcal{X} \to \mathcal{F}$. (see Figure 1). SVM can do so implicitly. In order to train and classify, all that SVMs use are dot products of pairs of data points $\Phi(\mathbf{x}), \Phi(\mathbf{x}_i) \in \mathcal{F}$ in feature space (cf. Eq. (3)). Thus, we need only to supply a so-called kernel function that can compute these dot products. A kernel function k allows to implicitly define the

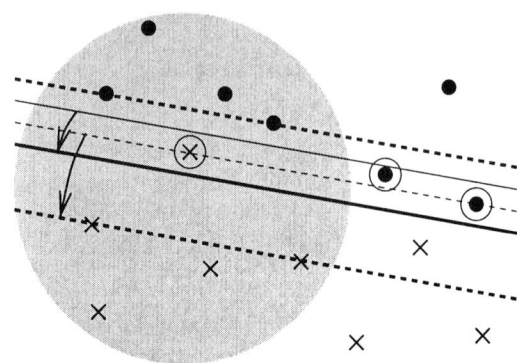

Fig. 1. A binary classification toy problem: This problem is to separate black circles from crosses. The shaded region consists of training examples, the other regions of test data. The training data can be separated with a margin indicated by the slim dashed line and the upper fat dashed line, implicating the slim solid line as discriminate function. Misclassifying one training example(a circled white circle) leads to a considerable extension(arrows) of the margin(fat dashed and solid lines) and this fat solid line can classify two test examples(circled black circles) correctly.

feature space (Mercer's Theorem, e.g. [2]) via

$$k(\mathbf{x}, \mathbf{x}_i) = (\Phi(\mathbf{x}) \cdot \Phi(\mathbf{x}_i)). \quad (4)$$

By using different kernel functions, the SVM algorithm can construct a variety of learning machines, some of which coincide with classical architectures:

Polynomial classifiers of degree d:

$$k(\mathbf{x}, \mathbf{x}_i) = (\kappa \cdot (\mathbf{x} \cdot \mathbf{x}_i) + \Theta)^d \quad (5)$$

Neural networks(sigmoidal):

$$k(\mathbf{x}, \mathbf{x}_i) = \tanh(\kappa \cdot (\mathbf{x} \cdot \mathbf{x}_i) + \Theta) \quad (6)$$

Radial basis function classifiers:

$$k(\mathbf{x}, \mathbf{x}_i) = \exp\left(-\frac{\|\mathbf{x} - \mathbf{x}_i\|^2}{\sigma}\right) \quad (7)$$

Note that there is no need to use or know the form of Φ, because the mapping is never performed explicitly The introduction of Φ in the explanation above was for purely didactical and not algorithmical purposes. Therefore, we can computationally afford to work in implicitly very large (e.g. 10^{10}- dimensional) feature spaces. SVM can avoid overfitting by controlling the capacity and maximizing the margin. Simultaneously, SVMs learn which of the features implied by the kernel k are distinctive for the two classes, i.e. instead of finding well-suited features by ourselves (which can often be difficult), we can use the SVM to select them from an extremely rich feature space.

With respect to good generalization, it is often profitable to misclassify some outlying training data points in order to achieve a larger margin between the other training points (see Figure 1 for an example).

This soft-margin strategy can also learn non-separable data. The trade-off between margin size and number of misclassified training points is then controlled by the regularization parameter C (softness of the margin). The following quadratic program (QP) (see e.g. [18], [15]):

$$\begin{aligned}\min \quad & \|\mathbf{w}\|^2 + C\sum_{i=1}^{\ell}\xi_i \\ \text{s.t.} \quad & \rho(\mathbf{z}_i, f) \geq 1 - \xi_i \quad \text{for all } 1 \leq i \leq \ell \\ & \xi_i \geq 0 \quad \text{for all } 1 \leq i \leq \ell\end{aligned} \quad (8)$$

leads to the SV soft-margin solution allowing for some errors.

III. Active Learning with SVM in Information Retrieval

In this section, we describe the information retrieval system using relevance feedback with SVM from an active learning point of view. Fig. 2 shows the concept of the relevance feedback document retrieval. In Fig. 2, the user makes the initial retrieval by inputing the query. The result of the initial retrieval consists of too many documents, which are ranked by similarity between the query and the documents. But the rank of the documents is not usually useful for the user. In the relevance feedback information retrieval, the user can see the top N ranked documents and evaluate whether the documents are relevant or not. Then the evaluated documents with the initial query are given to a supervised learning algorithm to produce a new classifier. The classifier is used to generate the new rank of the initial retrieved documents. The new ranking ranks the actual relevant documents at higher levels than the previous ranking does. This re-rank makes until finding useful documents iteratively. In Fig. 2, the iterative procedure is the gray arrows parts. In the relevance feedback method, the user have to judge the re-ranked documents. Hence, it is difficult to use a large number of user judged documents for supervised learning algorithms because the user can not overcome much effort to judge the many documents. The SVMs have a great ability to discriminate even if the training data is small. Consequently, we propose to apply SVMs as the classifier in relevance feedback method. The retrieval steps of proposed method perform as follows:

Step 1: **Preparation of documents for the first feedback**

The conventional information retrieval system based on vector space model displays the top N ranked documents along with a request query to the user. In our method, the top N ranked documents are selected by using cosine distance between the request query vector and each document vector for the first feedback iteration.

Step 2: **Judgement of documents**

The user then classifiers these N documents into relevant or irrelevant. The relevant documents and the irrelevant documents are labeled. For instance, the relevant documents have "+1" label and the irrelevant documents have "-1" label after the user's classification.

Step 3: **Determination of the optimal hyperplane**

The optimal hyperplane for classifying relevant and irrelevant documents is determined by using a SVM which is learned by labeled documents(see Figure 3).

Step 4: **Discrimination documents and information retrieval**

The documents, which are retrieved in the Step1, are mapped into the feature space. The SVM learned by the previous step classifies the documents as relevant or irrelevant. The documents, which are discriminated relevant and in the margin area of SVM are selected. From the selected documents, the top N ranked documents, which are ranked using the distance from the relevant documents area, are shown to user as the information retrieval results of the system(see Figure 4). If the number of feedback iterations is more than m, then go to next step. Otherwise, return to Step 2. The m is a maximal number of feedback iterations and is determined by the user.

Step 5: **Display of the final retrieved documents**

The retrieved documents are ranked by the distance between the documents and the hyper-plane which is the discriminant function determined by SVM. The retrieved documents are displayed based on this ranking(see Figure 5).

In the reference [3], Drucker et al. selects the higher ranked documents, which are relevant and far from the

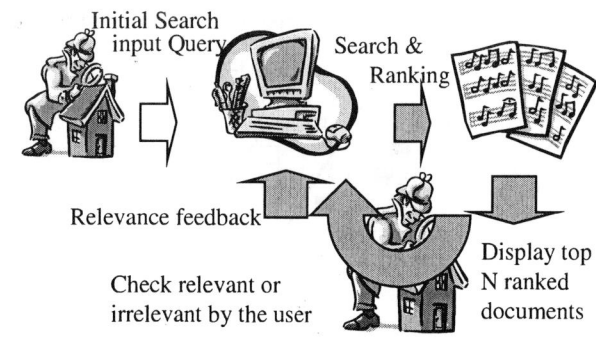

Fig. 2. Image of the relevance feedback documents retrieval: The gray arrow parts are made iteratively to retrieve useful documents for the user. This iteration is called feedback iteration in the information retrieval research area.

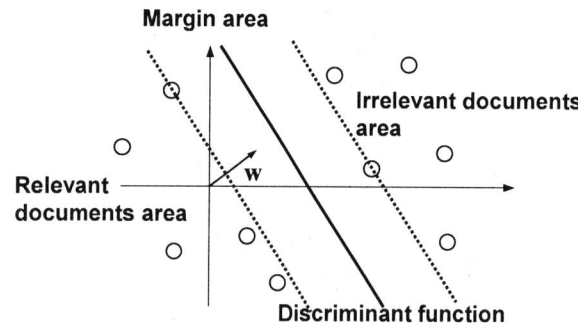

Fig. 3. Discriminant function for classifying relevant or irrelevant documents: Circles denote documents which are checked relevant or irrelevant by a user. The solid line denotes a discriminant function. The margin area is between dotted lines.

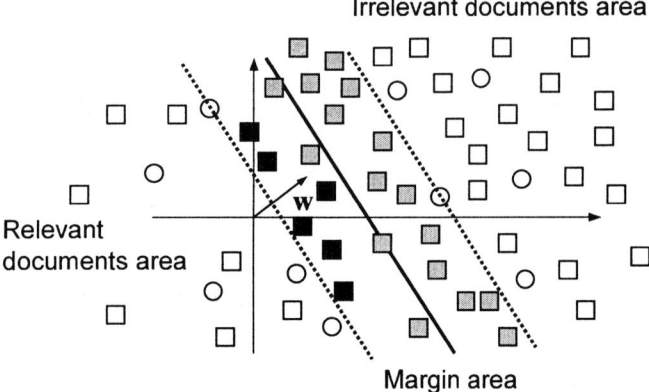

Fig. 4. Mapped non-checked documents into the feature space: Boxes denote non-checked documents which are mapped into the feature space. Circles denotes checked documents which are mapped into the feature space. Black and gray boxes are documents in the margin area. We show the documents which are represented by black boxes to a user for next iteration. These documents are in the margin area and near the relevant documents area.

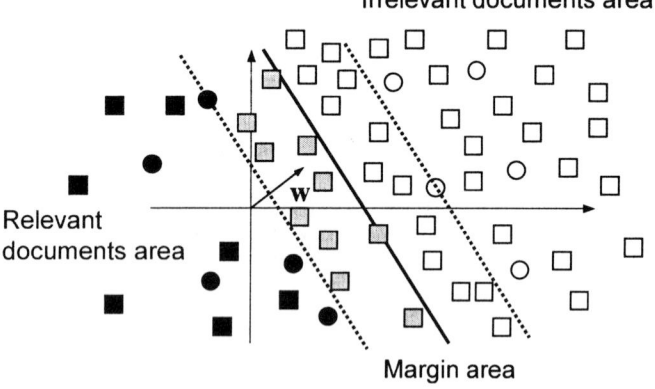

Fig. 5. Displayed documents as the result of document retrieval: Boxes denote non-checked documents which are mapped into the feature space. Circles denotes checked documents which are mapped into the feature space. The system displays the documents which are represented by black circles and boxes as the result of document retrieval to a user.

discriminant function. The selected documents do not neet to be in the margin area. The strategy may be able to show many relevant documents to the user. But it can not keep the efficient learning performance from an active learning point of view. Because the documents, which are on or near the discriminant function, should be selected to get the efficient learning performance [16]. In the reference [16], Tong et al. select the documents, which are on or near the discriminant function. This selection can make the efficient learning. However, users feel stress of the selection because it is difficult for the user to evaluate which the documents are relevant or irrelevant. The feature of our SVM based feedback is the selection of displayed documents to users in Step 4. Our proposed method selects the documents, which are discriminated in relevant and in the margin area, and near the relevant documents area. The documents may be the relevant documents for the user, because the documents are near the relevant area. And the documents may be able to keep the learning performance, because the documents are in the margin area and have the useful information to make good learning performance. The margin area means the obscurity area of classification. Therefore, our selection can be expected that the efficient learning can be kept and users do not need to feel stress.

IV. EXPERIMENTS

A. Experimental setting

We made experiments for evaluating the utility of our interactive document retrieval with active learning of SVM in section III. The document data set we used is a set of articles in the Los Angeles Times which is widely used in the document retrieval conference TREC [17]. The data set has about 130 thousands articles. The average number of words in a article is 526. This data set includes not only queries but also the relevant documents to each query. Thus we used the queries for experiments.

We used TFIDF [20], which is one of the most popular methods in information retrieval to generate document feature vectors, and the concrete equation [14] of a weight of a term t in a document d w_t^d are in the following.

$$w_t^d = L \times t \times u \qquad (9)$$
$$L = \frac{1 + \log(tf(t,d))}{1 + log(\text{average of } tf(t,d) ind)} \quad (tf)$$
$$t = \log(\frac{n+1}{df(t)}) \quad (idf)$$
$$u = \frac{1}{0.8 + 0.2\frac{uniq(d)}{\text{average of } uniq(d)}} \quad (normalization)$$

The notations in these equation denote as follows:
- w_t^d is a weight of a term t in a document d,
- $tf(t,d)$ is a frequency of a term t in a document d,
- n is the total number of documents in a data set,
- $df(t)$ is the number of documents including a term t,
- $uniq(d)$ is the number of different terms in a document d.

The size N of retrieved and displayed results developed in *Step 1* in section III was set as twenty. The feedback iterations m were 1, 2, 3 and 4. In order to investigate the influence of feedback iterations on accuracy of retrieval, we used plural feedback iterations.

In our experiments, we used the linear kernel for SVM learning, and found a discriminant function for the SVM classifier in this feature space. The VSM of documents is high dimensional space. Therefore, in order to classify the labeled documents into relevant or irrelevant, we do not need to use the kernel trick and the regularization parameter C (see section II). The VSM consists of TFIDF representation. Drucker et al. did not use TFIDF representation for SVM learning [3]. And we used LibSVM [6] as SVM software in our experiment.

For comparison with our approach, two information retrieval methods were used. The first is an information retrieval method that does not use a feedback. The second is an information retrieval method using conventional Rocchio-based relevance feedback [12] which is widely used in information retrieval research.

The Rocchio-based relevance feedback modifies a query vector Q_i by evaluation of a user using the following equation.

$$Q_{i+1} = Q_i + \alpha \sum_{x \in R_r} x - \beta \sum_{x \in R_n} x, \qquad (10)$$

where R_r is a set of documents which were evaluated as relevant documents by a user at the $i$the feedback, and R_n is a set of documents which were evaluated as irrelevant documents at the i feedback. α and β are weights for relevant and irrelevant documents respectively. In this experiment, we set $\alpha = 1.0$, $\beta = 0.5$ which are known adequate experimentally.

In general, retrieval accuracy significantly depends on the number of the feedback iterations. Thus we changed feedback iterations for 1, 2, 3, 4 and investigated the accuracy for each iteration.

We utilized *precision* and *recall* for evaluating the two information retrieval methods [5][19] and our approach. The following equations are used to compute *precision* and *recall*. Since a recall-precision curve is investigated to each query, we used the average recall-precision curve over all the queries as evaluation.

$$precision = \frac{\text{The No. of retrieved relevant doc.}}{\text{The No. of retrieved doc}},$$
$$recall = \frac{\text{The No. of retrieved relevant doc.}}{\text{The total No. of relevant doc.}}$$

B. Experimental results

B.1 Comparing of recall-precision performance curves

In this section, we investigated the effectiveness of proposed method, when the user judged the twenty higher ranked documents at each feedback iteration. In the first iteration, twenty higher ranked documents were retrieved using cosine distance between document vectors and a query vector in VSM, which is represented by TFIDF. The query vector was generated by a user's input of keywords. In the other iterations, the user does not need to input keywords for the information retrieval, and the user labels "+1" and "-1" as relevant and irrelevant documents respectively.

Figure 6 show a recall-precision performance curve of our SVM based method, after four feedback iterations. For comparison, this figure also show the recall-precision curves of the conventional feedback method (i.e., Rocchio-based method) and VSM (i.e., without feedback). The thick solid line is the proposed method, the broken line is the conventional feedback method, and the thin solid line was the VSM without feedback.

This figure shows that the retrieval effectiveness of both feedback methods, i.e., proposed and conventional feedback methods, is improved compared with that of the VSM without feedback. In this result, we could confirm that the

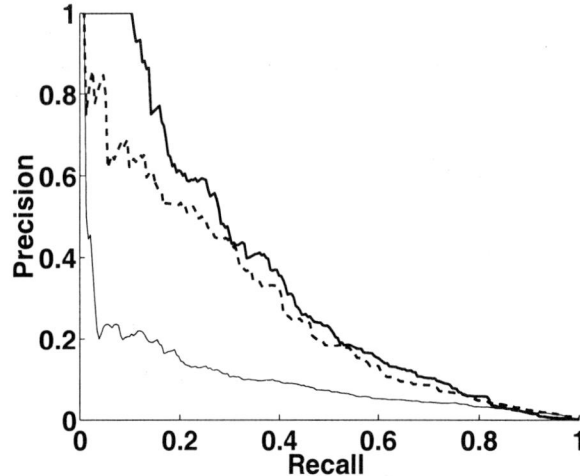

Fig. 6. The effectiveness of SVM based feedback: The lines show recall-precision performance curve by using twenty feedback documents on the set of articles in the Los Angeles Times after 4 feedback iterations. The wide solid line is proposed method, the broken line is conventional feedback method (i.e. Rocchio-based method), and the solid line is the VSM without feedback.

TABLE I
AVERAGE PRECISION USING SVM BASED FEEDBACK METHOD AND ROCCHIO-BASED FEEDBACK METHOD

| No. of feedback | Average precision | |
iterations	SVM	Rocchio
1	0.2625	0.2250
2	0.3500	0.2500
3	0.6125	0.2350
4	0.6375	0.2250

relevance feedback was useful technique for improving the performance of information retrieval in VSM.

Furthermore, this figure also shows that the proposed feedback method improves the performance compared with conventional feedback method at all recall points. Consequently, in this experiment, we conclude that the SVM is a useful relevant feedback technique improving performance of information retrieval in VSM, which is represented by TFIDF.

B.2 Relationships between the performance and the number of feedback iterations

Here, we describe the relationships between the performances of proposed method and the number of feedback iterations. Table I gave the average precision result as a function of the number of feedback iterations. We carried out twenty times document retrieval. At each feedback iteration, the system displays twenty higher ranked relevant documents in the margin area's documents for our proposed method. We also show the average precision of Rocchio-based method for comparing to proposed method in table I.

We can see from this table that the SVM based relevance feedback approach gives the higher performance in propor-

TABLE II

IN A SPECIAL CASE, THE RELATIONSHIP BETWEEN THE NUMBER OF FEEDBACK ITERATIONS AND THE NUMBER OF ACTUAL RELEVANT DOCUMENTS IN TWENTY HIGHER RANKED RELEVANT DOCUMENTS IN WHOLE DOCUMENTS.

No. of feedback iterations	No. of relevant documents	
	SVM	Rocchio
1	9	11
2	18	13
3	20	12
4	20	11

tion to increase the number of feedback iterations. On the other hand, the Rocchio-based relevance feedback method degrades the retrieval performance nevertheless the number of feedback iterations increased from three to four. In a case of VSM without feedback, the average precision is 0.15. Hence, we can consider that the more feedback iterations, the better relevance documents can be obtained by using SVM based feedback method. Especially, the proposed method can improve the performance of conventional feedback method at each feedback iteration. We believe that the reason of these results is that the SVM can find a more suitable hyperplane for discriminating between relevant and irrelevant documents as increasing the number of the feedback iterations. After all, we can believe that the proposed method can keep effective learning from active learning point of view.

Furthermore, we compare the performance of proposed method to that of Rocchio-based feedback method from an information retrieval point of view. Table II shows the relationship between the number of feedback iterations and the number of actual relevant documents in twenty higher ranked relevant documents in a special case. In this case, five documents were labeled as relevant documents in twenty documents at the first iteration. In almost case, one or two documents were labeled as relevant documents in twenty documents at the first iteration. We can see from this table that our SVM based feedback can increase the number of actual relevant documents, which are useful for the user in proportion to increase the number of feedback iterations. On the other hand, the Rocchio-based feedback method degrades the number of actual relevant documents nevertheless the number of feedback iterations increased from three to four. Hence, we can consider that the proposed method can give the suitable number of actual relevant documents to the user.

V. CONCLUSION

In this paper, we proposed the relevance feedback method with the support vector machine (SVM) for the information retrieval. Because the SVM has an excellent ability to discriminate even if the training data is small, we applied the SVM to relevance feedback method. Experimental results on a set of articles in the Los Angeles Times showed the proposed method gave a consistently better performance than the conventional feedback method. Therefore our proposed SVM based approach is very useful for the information retrieval with relevance feedback.

In our experiments, we used TFIDF documents representation as VSM. Drucker et al. used binary documents representation and TF representation for estimating the performance of their proposed method. We plan to apply our proposed method to the binary representation and TF representation and compare our method with other SVM based methods(Drucker's method and Tong's method) experimentally. And this paper proposed that the system should display the documents which are discriminated relevant and in the margin area of SVM at each feedback iteration. However, we do not discuss how the selection of documents influence both the effective learning and the performance of information retrieval theoretically. This point is also our future work.

REFERENCES

[1] C. Bishop, *Neural Networks for Pattern Recognition*. Oxford: Clarendon Press, 1995.
[2] B. Boser, I. Guyon, and V. Vapnik, "A training algorithm for optimal margin classifiers," in *5th Annual ACM Workshop on COLT*, (D. Haussler, ed.), (Pittsburgh, PA), pp. 144–152, ACM Press, 1992.
[3] H. Drucker, B. Shahrary, and D. C. Gibbon, "Relevance feedback using support vector machines," in *Proceedings of the Eighteenth International Conference on Machine Learning*, pp. 122–129, 2001.
[4] IREX http://cs.nyu.edu/cs/projects/ proteus/irex/.
[5] D. Lewis, "Evaluating text categorization," in *Proceedings of Speech and Natural Language Workshop*, pp. 312–318, 1991.
[6] K. Machines http://www.kernel-machines.org/.
[7] N. Murata, S. Yoshizawa, and S. Amari, "Network information criterion - determining the number of hidden units for an artificial neural network model," *IEEE Transactions on Neural Networks*, vol. 5, no. 6, pp. 865–872, 1994.
[8] NTCIR http://www.rd.nacsis.ac.jp/~ntcadm/.
[9] M. Okabe and S. Yamada, "Interactive document retrieval with relational learning," in *Proceedings of the 16th ACM Symposium on Applied Computing*, pp. 27–31, 2001.
[10] T. Onoda, "Neural network information criterion for the optimal number of hidden units," in *Proc. ICNN'95*, pp. 275–280, 1995.
[11] J. Orr and K.-R. Müller, eds., *Neural Networks: Tricks of the Trade*. LNCS 1524, Springer Verlag, 1998.
[12] G. Salton, ed., *Relevance feedback in information retrieval*, pp. 313–323. Englewood Cliffs, N.J.: Prentice Hall, 1971.
[13] G. Salton and J. McGili, *Introduction to modern information retrieval*. McGraw-Hill, 1983.
[14] R. Schapire, Y. Singer, and A. Singhal, "Boosting and rocchio applied to text filtering," in *Proceedings of the Twenty-First Annual International ACM SIGIR*, pp. 215–223, 1998.
[15] B. Schölkopf, A. Smola, R. Williamson, and P. Bartlett, "New support vector algorithms," Technical Report NC-TR-1998-031, Department of Computer Science, Royal Holloway, University of London, Egham, UK, 1998. *Neural Computation 2000*.
[16] S. Tong and D. Koller, "Support vector machine active learning with applications to text classification," in *Journal of Machine Learning Research*, pp. 45–66, 2001.
[17] TREC Web page http://trec.nist.gov/.
[18] V. Vapnik, *The Nature of Statistical Learning Theory*. Springer, 1995.
[19] I. Witten, A. Moffat, and T. Bell, *Managing Gigabytes: Compressing and Indexing Documents and Images*. New York: Van Nostrand Reinhold, 1994.
[20] R. B. Yates and B. R. Neto, *Modern Information Retrieval*. Addison Wesley, 1999.

A SOM PROJECTION TECHNIQUE WITH THE GROWING STRUCTURE FOR VISUALIZING HIGH-DIMENSIONAL DATA

Z. Wu   Gary G. Yen

Intelligent Systems and Control Laboratory
School of Electrical and Computer Engineering
Oklahoma State University
Stillwater, OK, 74078, USA

Abstract

The Self-Organizing Map (SOM) is an efficient tool for visualizing high-dimensional data. In this paper, an intuitive and effective SOM projection method is proposed for mapping high-dimensional data onto the two-dimensional SOM structure with a growing self-organizing map. In the learning phase, a growing SOM is trained and the growing cell structure is used as the baseline framework. After the learning phase, the new projection method is used to map the input vector so that the input data is mapped to the structure of the SOM without having to plot the weight values, resulting in easy visualization of the data. The projection method is demonstrated on two data sets with promising results and a significantly reduced network size.

1. INTRODUCTION

The Self-Organizing Map (SOM), originated by Kohonen [1], is an unsupervised, competitive learning algorithm that maps (or projects) high dimensional data onto a discrete network structure of lower dimensions (usually in two or three). Since the mapping of data from a high-dimensional space to a two- or three-dimensional grid makes the inter-relations among the data points perceptible, it provides a better insight into the data structure and clustering tendency. This feature capability has made the SOM an important tool in a wide range of applications such as data mining and information visualization.

Because of its implicit ability in dimensionality reduction, the SOM has been popularly used as a data clustering and visualization tool. One of the advantages of SOM mapping is its topology preserving ability. In the SOM, data vectors are clustered based on a similarity measure. Similar input vectors are mapped close to each other, while dissimilar ones are mapped far apart. In addition, the clusters are arranged in such a way that the neighborhood relations of the original high dimensional data is preserved. Therefore, not only are data vectors within the same cluster placed near each other, but members of closely related clusters are also expected to be nearby than those in remotely related clusters. Another advantage of SOM techniques is that the resulting map is generic in the sense that the shapes of the clusters need not to be assumed beforehand in constructing the SOM, while most other clustering algorithms are best suited to clusters of certain shapes [2].

In the SOM the input data is mapped to a low-dimensional discrete grid of neurons, which is usually rectangular or hexgonal shaped. The distance between two neurons on the grid indicates the degree of similarity of the data represented by the neurons. Thus, the cluster structure and other patterns of the data can be identified visually from the map created. It is a very intuitive and straightforward way to visualize the data structure.

However, when using the SOM, the network structure, namely the number of neurons and the height/width ratio of the grid, has to be predetermined. This often leads to a significant limitation on potential applications [3-6]. It is very likely that a predetermined size of the network is either too small or too big. In either case, the resulting map will be of poor quality and the complete learning process has to be repeated until an appropriate one is identified with satisfactory performance. In most cases, the user does not have much knowledge of the inherent data structure. So it is difficult to predefine a proper layout of the network. Another disadvantage of the fixed grid is that the projection made by the SOM is very crude [5]. Data vectors are mapped to (the locations of) corresponding best-matching neurons, but it is usually difficult to provide much information about the global distribution of the data by observing the raw map. In this paper, a SOM projection technique with a growing structure is proposed to help alleviate the constraints imposed by the fixed network structure.

The remainder of the paper is organized as follows. In Section 2, a brief review of the previous work on the SOM and its variations is introduced. The details of the proposed SOM projection method are then presented in Section 3. Section 4 provides illustrative examples demonstrating the principles of the algorithm and comparisons with other methods. Conclusions with pertinent observations are given in Section 5.

2. RELATED WORK

The Self-Organizing Map (SOM) is an unsupervised learning algorithm first introduced by Kohonen [1]. The SOM usually consists of a two-dimensional array of neurons. In the SOM, the input data is projected onto this two-dimensional space, which is called a map. An n-dimensional weight vector $w_i = [w_{i1}, w_{i2}, ..., w_{in}]^T$ is associated with each neuron, where n is the dimension of the input vectors. At each time step, one input vector x is drawn randomly and presented to the network. This input vector is compared with all the weight vectors. A best matching unit c can be found by calculating the Euclidean distance between the input vector x and the weight vector w_i, i.e.,

$$c = \arg \min_i \{\|x - w_i\|\}. \qquad (1)$$

The input vector is thus mapped to the location of the best match unit. Then the SOM updates the weight vectors of the neurons. The update rule of the weights is closely related to the k-means clustering. The weight vector of each neuron represents a cluster center. Like k-means, the weight of the best matching neuron (cluster center) is updated in a small step in the direction of the input vector x. However, unlike k-means, all neurons within a certain neighborhood are updated instead of a single unit according to

$$w_i(t+1) = w_i(t) + h_{ci}(t)[x(t) - w_i(t)] \qquad (2)$$

where $h_{ci}(t)$ is the neighborhood function. $h_{ci}(t)$ is a time decreasing function that converges to zero for large values of t. A typical smooth neighborhood function could be the Gaussian,

$$h_{ci}(t) = \alpha(t) \, exp \, \frac{-\|r_c - r_i\|^2}{2\sigma(t)^2} \qquad (3)$$

where $\alpha(t)$ is the learning rate function, $\sigma(t)$ is the width of the Gaussian kernel and $\|r_c - r_i\|^2$ is the distance between the winning neuron and the neuron i.

The learning process consists of winner selection by equation (1) and adaptation of the weight vectors by equation (2). After the training has been completed, the map should be topologically ordered so that similar data items are mapped onto nearby map units.

When using the SOM, the number of neurons and the layout of the neurons have to be determined before training. The need for predetermining the structure of the network results in a significant limitation on the final mapping [3, 4, 6, 7]. To overcome the problems introduced by the fixed structure of the classical SOM, several dynamic self-organizing network models have been developed recently. Some of the major variations are summarized as follows.

a. Growing Cell Structures (GCS): The GCS algorithm [6] is based on the SOM, but the basic two-dimensional grid of the SOM is replaced by a network of nodes whose basic building blocks are triangles. The GCS starts with 3 nodes forming a triangle. During the training process, there are not only new nodes added but also existing nodes deleted. Some measure of each node, e.g., a winner counter, is used to decide where to insert new nodes. The connections between nodes are adjusted in order to keep the triangular connectivity. The algorithm results in a network graph structure consisting of a set of nodes and the connections between them.

b. Growing Neural Gas Algorithm: The neural gas algorithm developed by Martinetz and Schulten [7] can also be categorized as an unsupervised self-generating neural network. Fritzke combined the GCS algorithm and the topology generation of *competitive Hebbian learning* [7] to form a growth mechanism. Starting with very few nodes, new nodes are inserted successively. Local error measures are used to determine where to grow new nodes. Each new node is inserted near the node with the most accumulated error.

c. Growing Grid: Fritzke developed the Growing Grid algorithm [8], which is an incremental variant of the SOM. Starting with 2×2 neurons, the network adds rows and columns of neurons during the training process. The heuristics used to both add and remove nodes and connections is the same as that used in Growing Cell Structures and Growing Neural Gas. The difference is that in Growing Grid all counters are set to zero after a row or column has been inserted.

d. Incremental Grid Growing (IGG): Starting from a small number of initial nodes, the IGG algorithm [7] generates new nodes only at the boundary of the map. This guarantees that the IGG network will always maintain a two-dimensional structure, which results in easy visualization. Another feature of IGG is that connections between neighboring map units may be added and removed according to a threshold value of the interunit weight differences. This may result in several disconnected subnetworks, which represent different clusters of input patterns.

e. Growing Self-organizing Maps (GSOM): The GSOM algorithm [3] is quite similar to the IGG in the way it adds new nodes but a spread factor is introduced to control the growing process of the map. Using manual intervention, the data analyst can select regions for further analysis hierarchically. This results in manually created hierarchical clusters.

After the data set is clustered using the SOM or its variations discussed above, the clusters as well as their spatial relationships can be acquired by visual display. One of the methods for visualizing the cluster structure of the SOM is the distance matrix technique [9, 10], especially the unified distance matrix (U-matrix). Another visualization method is to display the number of "hits" (input vectors mapped to each unit) in each map. Training of the SOM map units between clusters and thus obscures cluster borders. Those map units on the cluster borders have very few data items (hits) or none at all. This information can be utilized by using zero-hit units to indicate cluster borders. An example is the WebSOM by Kohonen *et al* [11]. Generic vector projection method can also be used. Such projection methods include multidimensional scaling algorithms [12] and Sammon's mapping [13].

The visualization approaches discussed above can be used to obtain an approximation of the structure of the input data, but they are computationally very expensive thus impractical for large datasets. In the following, we propose a SOM projection approach, which can efficiently cluster and map the input vectors with comparatively low computational complexity.

3. THE PROPOSED SOM-BASED VISUALIZATION METHOD

The proposed SOM projection method is implemented in two steps. In the learning phase, the high-dimensional input data is used to train a two-dimensional SOM. To overcome the limitations of the fixed structure of the classical SOM, a growing structure is selected. In this implementation, the GCS structure [6] is used as the growth mechanism. In the ordination phase, instead of projecting the input data directly onto top of the corresponding winning nodes, an easy and efficient projection method is proposed.

3.1 Learning Phase: A growing self-organizing map

The Growing Cell Structure is based on 2-dimensional Self-Organizing Maps, but the nodes are connected in a triangular way. The GCS network starts with only 3 nodes forming a triangle. During the training process, new nodes are added in areas receiving a high number of input signals. The connections are adjusted between nodes in order to keep the triangular connectivity. The basic GCS learning process is illustrated in Fig. 1. Starting with the initial triangle, a node is added after a certain number of training steps to allow a more accurate representation of input signals mapped onto that area. Training continues with more nodes being added.

During the training process, existing nodes may also be deleted, which receive no or only a few input signals. These nodes are removed together with all connections being part of the corresponding triangle.

Fig. 1. Illustration of the GCS growing process

The *GCS* learning procedure can be described as follows [6]:

a. Predefine the initial grid size (usually 3 units). Initialize the connection set so that the network keeps the triangular connectivity.
b. Initialize the weight vectors with randomly selected values according to the probability distribution of the input vectors. Reset error variables E_i for every unit i.
c. Train the map using randomly selected input vectors for a fixed number of iterations.
d. For every input vectors i increase the value of the corresponding error variables E_i by adding the squared distance between the input and its winner unit to E_i.
e. Identify the unit q with the maximum accumulated error.
f. Insert a new unit r by splitting the edge between q and its most dissimilar neighboring unit f. Insert the connections (q,r) and (r,f) and remove the original connection (q,f). Initialize the weight vector of r by averaging of the weight vectors of the neighboring units.
g. Decrease the error variables of all neighbors of r by a fraction.
h. Set the error variable of the new unit r to the mean value of its neighbors.
i. Decrease the error variables of all units by a fraction.
j. Continue with step c if a stopping criterion (e.g., net size or some performance measure) is not yet fulfilled.

3.2 Ordination Phase: Centroid method

After the learning phase, the weight vectors of the network span the input space. The weight matrix, W, and the x and y positions of the SOM units are retained.

Each column P of the input matrix A is one input vector. Pre-multiplying P by the weight matrix W results in a column vector of the projections of P with the individual weight vectors. The response $D = W \times P$ will be a column vector, each element of which is the inner product of the individual weight vectors with the document vector P. Therefore the magnitude of the elements in D represents the distance between the input vector P and the weights. D may be visualized as a spatial response across the nodes of the SOM, as shown in Fig. 2.

Since the map units are arranged in a two-dimensional grid, this response may be characterized as a two-dimensional histogram plotted across the map units.

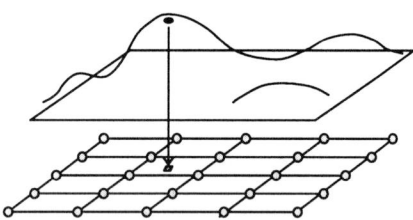

Fig. 2. Illustration of mapping an input vector by finding the centroid of the spatial response

The SOM ordination procedure continues with finding the centroid of this spatial response, by computing the weighted average of the various node coordinates with the node responses averaged over the total response. The negative elements of D must first be zeroed to stabilize the centroid calculation. The centroid is computed as follows: suppose N_{xy} is the $2 \times N$ matrix of the x and y coordinates of the N nodes, and $D = [d_1, d_2, ..., d_N]^T$ is the $N \times 1$ vector of spatial responses of the N nodes, the centroid of the various responses is $N_{xy} \times D / \sum d_i$. The complete process is illustrated in Fig. 3.

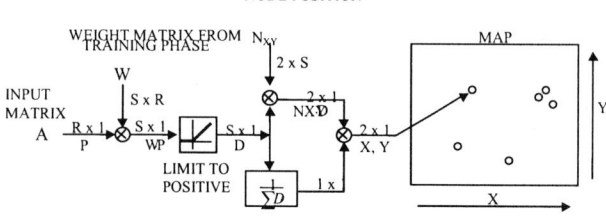

Fig. 3. Diagram of the ordination phase

Using the centroid method, the input vectors can be projected not only onto each node, but also to any locations across the SOM network, i.e., in between two nodes, thus introducing higher resolution of the display of the input data points. Also a comparably smaller network is required to cluster and map same number of input data.

4. SIMULATION RESULTS

This work was conducted using the Growing Cell Structure Visualization (GCSVIS) toolbox [12].

4.1 Animal Data Set

To test the operation of the proposed SOM projection method, first we present results for the animal data set, which was introduced by Ritter and Kohonen [14].

TABLE 1
Animal Data Set: Animal Names & Associated Binary Attributes

	dove	hen	duck	goose	owl	hawk	eagle	fox	dog	wolf	cat	tiger	lion	horse	zebra	cow
is																
small	1	1	1	1	1	1	0	0	0	1	0	0	0	0	0	0
medium	0	0	0	0	0	0	1	1	1	1	0	0	0	0	0	0
big	0	0	0	0	0	0	0	0	0	0	0	1	1	1	1	1
has																
2 legs	1	1	1	1	1	1	1	0	0	0	0	0	0	0	0	0
4 legs	0	0	0	0	0	0	0	1	1	1	1	1	1	1	1	1
hair	0	0	0	0	0	0	0	1	1	1	1	1	1	1	1	1
hooves	0	0	0	0	0	0	0	0	0	0	0	0	0	1	1	1
mane	0	0	0	0	0	0	0	0	0	1	0	0	1	1	1	0
feathers	1	1	1	1	1	1	1	0	0	0	0	0	0	0	0	0
likes to																
hunt	0	0	0	0	1	1	1	1	0	1	1	1	1	0	0	0
run	0	0	0	0	0	0	0	0	1	1	0	1	1	1	1	0
fly	1	0	0	1	1	1	1	0	0	0	0	0	0	0	0	0
swim	0	0	1	1	0	0	0	0	0	0	0	0	0	0	0	0

The data set comprises 16 artificial objects representing animals with 13 attributes. Table 1 shows the complete set of vectors. Ritter and Kohonen trained a planar SOM of 10×10 with the data set. After training, the map was manually partitioned into three regions, corresponding to birds, carnivores, and herbivores. Using the proposed new method, the network structure starts from three nodes connected in a triangular way. Eight new nodes are added during the learning process of the network. The number of new nodes to add here is an empirical value. Fig. 4 shows the final network structure used for the animal data set. The upper right triangle is the triangle the network starts with. Fig. 5 is the map generated by mapping each input vector to the centroids of the corresponding spatial responses across the two-dimensional cell structure. The small circles on the map represent the animals in the data set. The names of the animals are labeled manually.

The result shows meaningful clustering of the animals. Birds are mapped to the upper right corner of the map; predators gather in the right side; herbivores occupy the lower left corner. Within the big cluster of birds, further grouping is also discernible. From the spatial locations of the birds, it's apparent that the "hawk", "owl", and "eagle" form a subgroup, which is differentiated from the subgroup of "dove", "duck", "hen" and " goose". In the big cluster of the predators, similar phenomenon can be observed. "Lion" and "tiger" are mapped adjacent to each other, indicating significant similarity between the two. This mapping result shows similar data partition of the manual clustering by Ritter and Kohonen [14] but in our implementation the network size is much smaller, only 11 nodes are used compared to the 10×10 SOM used in [14].

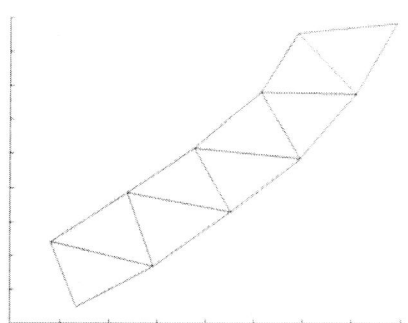

Fig. 4. The network structure used for the animal data

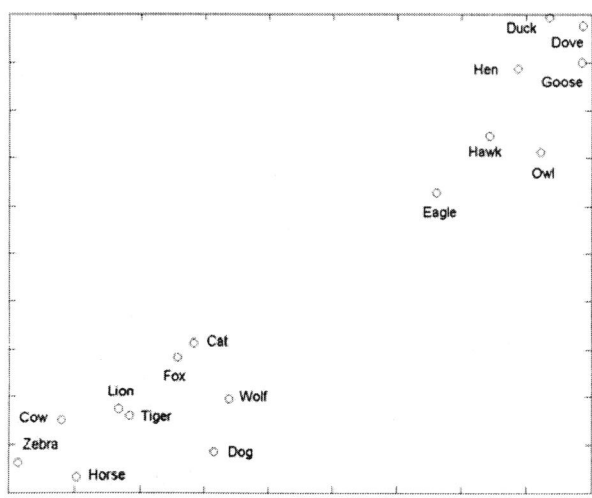

Fig. 5. Map of the animal data set

4.2 Patent Data Set

The second data set was constructed from a collection of oilfield polymer patents covering the subjects of polymer well cements and drilling muds. This collection was built starting with five key patents in the field of oilfield polymers [15]. The set was expanded to include the patents, which cite and are cited by the five key parents. There are totally 118 patents in the data set.

Patents are document collections that have some special characteristics that can be used for data analysis and exploration. In our implementation, document citation patterns are used to build the similarity matrix [15, 16], which describes the inter-document relationships among documents expressed as 'similarity' values. The similarity matrix is symmetric, each row or column of which represents one document and is used as an input vector to train the SOM.

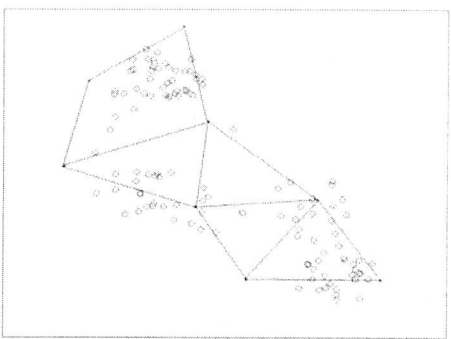

Fig. 6. The ordination result of patent data set.

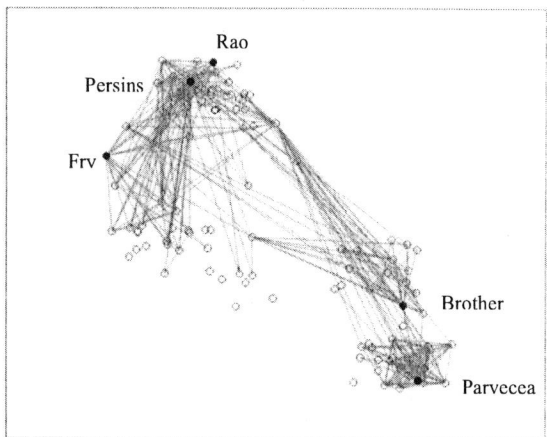

Fig. 7. Map of the patent data set with citations plotted.

Fig. 6 shows the final network structure after inserting 5 additional units. The patents are projected onto the map and plotted as dots on top of the network structure. Fig. 7 shows the citations between the patents. The five key patents used to build the data set are highlighted in the map, labeled with the inventor names. It is obvious that dense citation lines are connected to the key patents indicating they are cited frequently by other patents in the data set. The mapping is grouped into four main clusters grouped around the key patents.

Visually it appears that the proposed mapping approach has grouped the patents so that there are many citation lines between members of the same group and relatively few citation lines between groups, which implies more similarity between members within a cluster and less similarity between members of different clusters. This clustering results is similar to that in [15] where a 5×5 fixed-size SOM was used but only 16 nodes are used for the result herein.

5. CONCLUSION

Self-Organizing Maps can be a useful tool for data clustering and exploration. They cluster data vectors based on a similarity measure and consider also the similarities of neighboring clusters. The clusters are arranged in a low-dimensional topology that preserves the neighborhood relations of the corresponding high-dimensional data.

However, it has been noted that the predetermined size and structure of the classical SOM introduce limitations on the final mappings. In this paper, we use the Growing Cell Structure as the growing mechanism. This model automatically adapts the structure and size of the map during the learning process.

The projection implemented by the SOM is restricted to the junction of the map grid. Instead of using this crude mapping method, a SOM projection method is proposed to map the input data to the two-dimensional SOM network structure. Although simple, it reveals the overall shape and possible cluster structure of the data set. It has advantages over the projection implemented by the SOM, which is restricted to the junction of the map grid, and therefore very crude. Moreover, this method maps the input data to the grid of the SOM without having to plot the weight values, which greatly reduces the computational complexity and results in easy visualization of the data.

REFERENCES

[1] T. Kohonen, *Self-Organizing Maps*. Berlin, Germany: Springer-Verlag, 1995.

[2] S. Kaski, "Data exploration using self-organizing maps," in *Department of Computer Science and Engineering*: Helsinki University of Technology, 1997, pp. 57.

[3] D. Alahakoon, S. K. Halgarmuge, and B. Srinivasan, "Dynamic Self-Organizing Maps with Controlled Growth for Knowledge Discovery," *IEEE Transactions on Neural Networks*, vol. 11, pp. 601-614, 2000.

[4] B. Fritzke, "Growing grid - A self-organizing network with constant neighborhood range and adaption strength," *Neural Processing Letters*, vol. 2, pp. 9-13, 1995.

[5] J. Vesanto, "SOM-Based Data Visualization Methods," *Intelligent Data Analysis*, vol. 3, pp. 111-126, 1999.

[6] B. Fritzke, "Growing cell structures - a self-organizing network for unsupervised and supervised learning," *Neural Networks*, vol. 7, pp. 1441-1460, 1994.

[7] J. Blackmore and R. Miikkulainen, "Incremental grid growing: encoding high-dimensional structure into a two-dimensional feature map," presented at Int. Conf. Neural Networks, San Francisco, CA, 1993.

[8] M. Martinetz and K. J. Schulten, "A "neural-gas" network learns topologies," in *Artificial Neural Networks*, K. M. T. Kohonen, O. Simula, and J. Kangas, Ed. Amsterdam: North-Holland, 1991, pp. 397-402.

[9] A. Ultch and H. P. Siemon, "Kohonen's self-organizing feature maps for exploratory data analysis," presented at Proc. INNC'90, Int. Neural Network Conf., Dordrecht, Netherlands, 1990.

[10] M. A. Kraaijveld, J. Mao, and A. K. Jain, "A nonlinear projection method based on Kohonen's topology preserving maps," *IEEE Transactions on Neural Networks*, vol. 6, 1995.

[11] T. Kohonen, S. Kaski, K. Lagus, J. Salojärvi, J. Honkela, V. Paatero, and A. Saarela, *Self organization of a massive text document collection*. Amsterdam: Elsevier, 1999.

[12] M. L. Davison, *Multidimensional scaling*. New York, NY: John Wiley and Sons, 1983.

[13] J. W. Sammon, "A nonliear mapping for data structure analysis," *IEEE Transactions on Computers*, vol. 18, pp. 401-409, 1969.

[14] H. Ritter and T. Kohonen, "Self-organizing semantic maps," *Biological Cybernetics*, vol. 61, pp. 241-254, 1989.

[15] S. Morris, Z. Wu, and G. Yen, "A SOM Mapping Technique for Visualizing Documents in a Database," presented at International Joint Conference on Neural Networks, Washington D. C., U.S.A, 2001.

[16] S. Morris, C. Deyong, Z. Wu, S. Salman, and D. Yemenu, "DIVA: a visualization system for exploring document databases for technology forecasting," *Computer and Industrial Engineering*, vol. 43, pp. 841-862, 2002.

Naive Bayesian Classifier for Microarray Data

Arpad Kelemen[1], Hong Zhou[1], Pamela Lawhead[1], Yulan Liang[2]

[1]Department of Computer and Information Science
The University of Mississippi
University, MS 38677, USA

[2]Department of Social and Preventive Medicine
The State University of New York at Buffalo
Buffalo, NY 14214 USA
kelemen@cs.olemiss.edu

Abstract – Comparing with more sophisticated classifiers, the naive Bayesian classifier greatly simplifies learning by assuming that the attribute values are conditionally independent given the class. Although independence is a strong assumption, in practice naive Bayesian classifier often competes with other complex classifiers and naive Bayesian algorithm works well for classifying text documents. In this paper, we present our invented technique, called "attribute grouping" for data preprocessing. The naive Bayesian algorithm is implemented for classifying multiple gene expression patterns from microarray experiments. Results show that attribute grouping is very effective and that the naive Bayesian classifier becomes a suitable classification method for microarry data when the attribute grouping is used.

I. INTRODUCTION

cDNA microarrays and other high throughput genomic technologies are very important tools for the study of patterns of the gene expression and for understanding the regulation of the underlying biological processes. A microarray consists of multiple features of DNA, which will be used to determine the levels of mRNA expression in a collection of cells [1]. cDNA microarrays allow measurements of expression levels for thousands of genes under multiple of conditions simultaneously. It provides a huge challenge to comprehend and interpret the massive data due to the existence of the high level noise and uncertainties [2]. Gene researchers have been working on the use of microarrays to model the gene expressions and correlations for more than a decade. One crucial problem for gene researchers is gene discovery and prediction. Supervised classification approach is a typical form of data analysis that can be developed to extract the important information of the data classes or to predict future data trends [3].

Bayesian approach provides a way to deal with the uncertainties and also the noise features of the gene expressions. They start from the calculations of the probability of a hypothesis based on their prior probability, and then they update the posterior probabilities based on the observed data. Naive Bayesian classifier is a highly practical Bayesian learning method. In some domains its performance has been shown to be comparable with complex neural network and decision tree learning [4]. Naive Bayesian classifier assumes that the attribute values are conditionally independent given the class. The purpose of this assumption is to simplify the computation and, in this case, is considered naive [3].

Naive Bayesian classifier algorithm is known as an effective algorithm for classifying text documents [3], [4]. Yet, in this paper, we design a naive Bayesian classifier algorithm for classifying gene expression patterns with multiple classes from microarry experiments. We invented an approach called "attribute grouping" method for data preprocessing, which proved itself to be an important step for massive noisy data.

The rest of the paper is organized as follows. We describe how the data were acquired and some characteristics of the data in section II. In section III, first we introduce the method for data preprocessing, and the benefits for using "grouping method". After that, the naive Bayesian algorithm is designed and applied for classifying gene expression patterns. In section IV we show the results of our classification methods. Finally, we present the conclusion and discussion in section V.

II. DATA ACQUISITION AND DATA CHARACTERISTICS

In this study, yeast data from an experiment in Chu et al [5] from Stanford Microarray databases were extracted from http://www-genome.stanford.edu. This microarray data contains nearly every yeast gene to be used to assay changes in gene expression during sporulation. Genes that co-express under similar experimental conditions, but different time points and dosages of a drug are of particular interest. Sporulation involves two overlapping processes, meiosis and spore morphogenesis. In meiosis, chromosomes first replicate, and then homologous chromosomes align and undergo recombination during prophase. Two consecutive nuclear divisions follow, in which, first homologous chromosomes segregate apart (meiosis I), and then sister chromates separate (meiosis II). The gene expression program of sporulation has previously been characterized as a transcriptional cascade involving seven temporal classes [5]. Fig. 1 shows the landmark events of spore formation and the corresponding temporal patterns.

There are seven time points for transferring yeast cells to a nitrogen-deficient medium to induce sporulation and mRNA samples: 0, 30 min, and 2, 5, 7, 9 and 11.5 hours. Seven microarrays are used, one for each of the seven time points. For every time point a red labeled cDNA pool was prepared. In additional, a green-labeled cDNA pool from time zero sample was prepared. Each array was probed with the green labeled sample mixed with one of the seven red labeled samples. Time zero served as a reference for all the samples. The data set contains four measurements for each time point: green signal, green background, red signal, and red background [2]. Fig. 2 gives the global pattern of gene expression during sporulation [5].

There are about 6000 genes in this microarray data set, but only 477 genes (samples) are with known class label. We use these 477 samples to build a naive Bayesian classification model, and the rest of the genes without class label can be classified based on the best model developed from the naive Bayesian classifier. Gene expression patterns from some genes of sporulation in budding yeast is given in Table I.

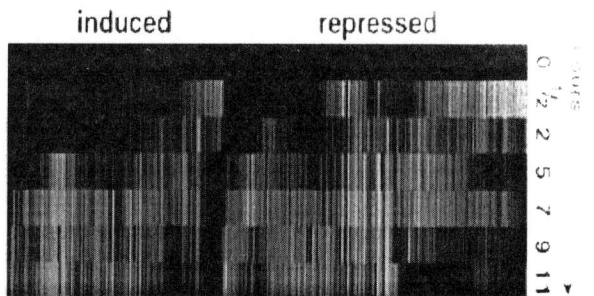

Fig. 2. The global pattern of gene expression during sporulation

III. DESIGN OF NAIVE BAYESIAN CLASSIFIER

Before we design the naive Bayesian model for a microarry data, we need to normalize the data first. Since the data set contains four measurements for each spot (green signal, green background, red signal, red background), we can transform and normalize the data by using log (background–corrected ratio). The background–corrected ratio is equal to (red signal - red background)/(green signal - green background). This transformation makes the variance stable and the data more informative [6], [7].

We invented another data preprocessing for gene expression, called "attribute grouping". This process is crucial for leaning, since it can drastically save on running time without noticeable decrease in the classification accuracy.

The "attribute grouping" divides each column (or attribute) of the measurements of gene expression into a number of groups. The number of groups can be chosen randomly. Attribute grouping is done in the following three steps:

1. Find the minimum (x_{min}) and the maximum values (x_{max}) of each column of the microarray
2. Decide the number of groups (n) we want to have in every column, then calculate Δ

$$\Delta = (x_{max} - x_{min})/n$$

3. Calculate the values of thresholds (θ_i)

$$\theta_i = x_{min} + n_i * \Delta$$

$(n_i = 1,...,n-1)$

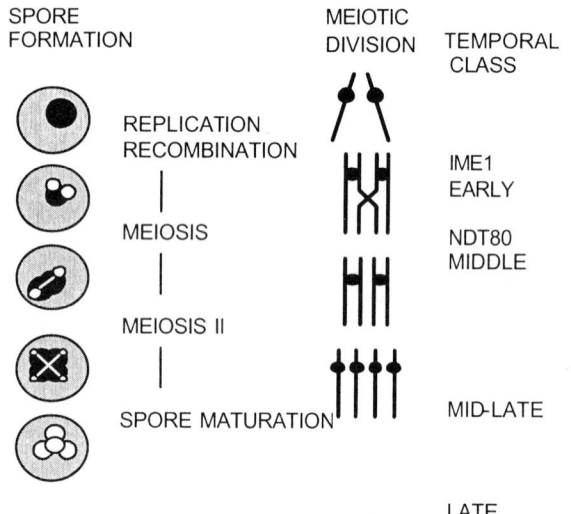

Fig.1. Landmark events of spore formation and corresponding temporal patterns

These thresholds serve as group boundaries. Any given threshold will serve as a low boundary of one group and a high boundary of another.

Now we can develop the naive Bayesian classifier for the gene expression:

$$v = \arg\max_{v_j \in V} P(v_j) \prod_{i=1}^{n} P(a_i | v_j)$$

TABLE I. SEVEN GENE EXPRESSION PATTERNS FROM SOME GENES OF SPORULATION IN BUDDING YEAST DATA

Metabolic	Early	Early II	Early -Mid	Middle	Mid-Late	Late
ACS1	ZIP1	KGD2	YBL078C	YSW1	CDC27	SPS100
PYC1	YDR374C	AGA2	QRI1	SPR28	DIT2	YKL050C
SIP4	DMC1	YPT32	PDS1	SP82	DIT1	YMR322C
CAT2	HOP1	MRD1	APC4	YLR227C		YOR391C
Y0R100C	IME2	SP O18	KNR4	ORC3		
CAR1		NAB4	STU2	YLL005C		
		YPR182W	YNL013C	YLL012W		

where v denotes the target value output by the naive Bayesian classifier. P(v_j) is the frequency with which each target value v_j occurs in the training data. a_i denotes an instance with n attributes (i=1,…,n). v_j (j=1,…,n) are classes for instances from the set of all possible classes V. $\prod_{i=1}^{n} P(a_i | v_j)$ is the product of probabilities for the individual attribute: P($a_1, a_2, …, a_n | v_j$).

The hypothesis of the naive Bayesian learning method is formed without searching, simply by counting the frequency of various data combinations within the training example. This is one interesting difference between naive Bayesian classifier and other classifiers [4].

In the yeast data set under study, the seven different time points are the seven attributes and the seven gene expression patterns are the seven target classes. We divide each attribute column into n_{th} groups. Every time, when we test a sample, first we compare the value of each attribute of the sample with the thresholds of the corresponding attribute column and check which group this value belongs to. Then we can apply the naive Bayesian classifier to find the class label for the test sample.

For example, suppose we have the following sample from our data set with seven attributes:

0.023789873, -0.034608734, 0.014058459, -0.012464913, 0.036533011, -0.043812159, 0.083176004

Our task is to predict the target value or class label (the seven classes) of this sample. First we need to calculate the probabilities of the different target values P(v_j), where v_j is one of the seven classes. This can easily be estimated based on their frequencies over the training samples. Now we will estimate the conditional probabilities, for example, using the first attribute value 0.023789873. We need to check which group this value belongs to corresponding to the same attribute column. If it, say, belongs to group 45, then we can check out the conditional probability for group 45, as follows:

P (group45 | Early I)
P (group45 | Early II)
P (group45 | Early Mid)
P (group45 | Metabolic)
P (group45 | Middle)
P (group45 | Mid Late)
P (group45 | Late)

We repeat this step until all the conditional probabilities of the remaining attribute values are estimated.

After this we calculate $\prod_{i=1}^{n} P(a_i | v_j)$, first for the class Early I. Let's suppose that the remaining six attribute values belong to group23, group60, group50, group74, group15, and group48. Therefore, we calculate
P(group45 | Early I) * P(group23 | Early I) * P(group60 | Early I) * P(group50 | Early I) * P(group74 | Early I) * P(group15 | Early I) * P(group48 | Early I)

We repeat this step for the other six classes.

After this we calculate $P(v_j) \prod_{i=1}^{n} P(a_i | v_j)$

Now we provide the probabilities of the different target values P(v_j). After this we calculate the following for the Early I class:

P(Early I) * P(group45 | Early I) * P(group23 | Early I) * P(group60 | Early I) * p(group50 | Early I) * P(group74 | Early I) * P(group15 | Early I) * P(group48 | Early I)

We repeat this step for the other six classes. Finally, we assign a class label for our sample by using

$$v = \arg\max_{v_j \in V} P(v_j) \prod_{i=1}^{n} P(a_i | v_j)$$

There are two important points to be mentioned here.

First, when we calculate the conditional probabilities, each attribute value of the sample is compared with each value in the corresponding attribute column in the data set. If we have a very large data set and many different classes, this calculation is very expensive. This is where the "attribute grouping" method can help. After we group the attribute values in each column, each attribute value of the sample is compared only with each group value in the corresponding attribute column in the data set. Since we have already computed the probability in the training phase for each group, after each attribute value is assigned to a group, the probability of that value can be estimated automatically. Using this method we can significantly save on the computational costs of time and memory. The relationship of group numbers and time units (unit=17 seconds) is shown in fig. 3.

Second, if we cannot find the same attribute value of the sample in the original training data set, how can we predict the class label for that sample? For such case, the attribute grouping method provides a viable solution. For example, we cannot find 0.023789873 in the training data set, but after we group each column into 100 groups in the training data set, we find out that 0.023789873 belong to the group 40, which has the value between 0.022889870 and 0.037685432. Therefore we can estimate the class label for this sample.

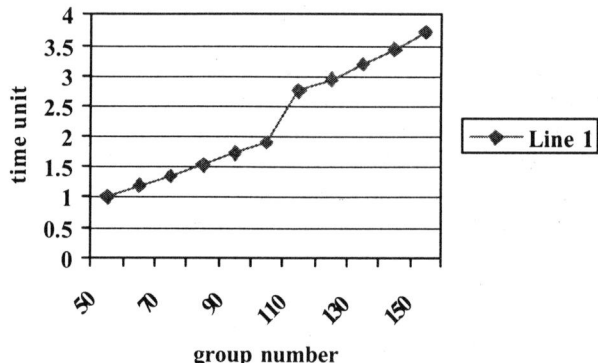

Fig. 3. The relationship between the number of groups and time units (unit=17 seconds)

IV. EXPERIMENTAL RESULTS

For implementation we used a 500 MHz Pentium III processor and the Matlab 6.1 environment. After data preprocessing, we randomly choose 25% of the data (121 samples) for testing the accuracy of the classifier and the hypothesis of changing the number of grouping attributes. The number of attribute groups to be used was ranged from 50 to 180 with an increment of 10. We also tested the trivial case with 356 groups, where each group included exactly one sample. For each number of groups we performed test ten times. With each number of groups we tested ten times. Every time we selected the 25% testing data randomly. Grouping has only been done on the training data. The average correct classification rate was 65.87% when we used 50 groups and 92.56% when we used 150 groups. No significant increase in the classification accuracy has been observed when the number of groups exceeded 150. Table 2 provides the minimum accuracy (correct classification rate), the maximum accuracy, and average accuracy for different number of groups.

Fig. 4. shows the change of the minimum, the maximum, and the average correct classification rates with the change in the number of attribute groups.

We can conclude that the more attribute groups we have, the higher the classification accuracy is. Yet, no significant increase in the classification accuracy occurs when the number of groups exceeds a certain threshold, in this case 150.

Figures 5, 6, and 7 show the testing curves for given number of groups 50, 100, and 150. x axis shows the number of the sample being used and y axis shows if a particular sample was correctly classified. y=0 means that the hypothesis matches the actual class label (sample being correctly classified).

For comparison study we have also implemented probabilistic neural networks. According to the results the Naive Bayesian classifier provided approximately 11% higher correct classification accuracy when 160 or more groups were used. Other popular methods, such as nearest neighbor, self organized map, and support vector machine were also implemented, but their performance was even lower for the given data set.

TABLE 2. CORRECT CLASSIFICATION RATES WITH NAIVE BAYESIAN FOR DIFFERENT NUMBER OF ATTRIBUTE GROUPS

Number of Groups	Minimum Accuracy	Maximum Accuracy	Average Accuracy
50	57.02%	74.38%	65.87%
60	61.16%	75.21%	69.25%
70	66.94%	76.03%	72.40%
80	71.07%	85.12%	78.59%
90	73.55%	86.78%	79.71%
100	80.99%	86.77%	84.46%
110	82.64%	90.08%	85.46%
120	80.16%	89.26%	85.79%
130	88.43%	91.74%	89.75%
140	85.94%	93.34%	89.99%
150	90.91%	95.04%	92.56%
160	90.91%	95.87%	92.65%
170	90.91%	95.87%	92.73%
180	91.74%	95.87%	92.73%
356	91.74%	96.70%	92.82%

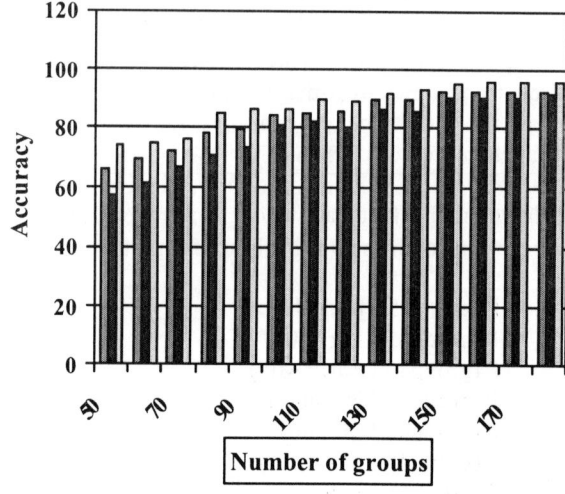

Fig. 4. Change of the minimum, the maximum, and the average correct classification rates with the change in the number of groups

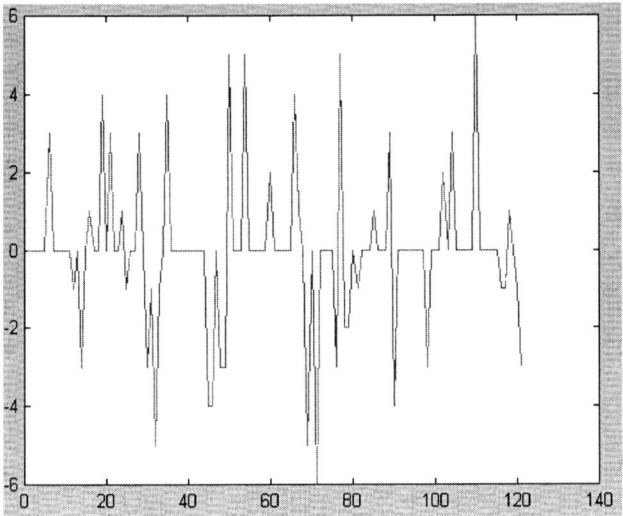

Figure 5. Testing results when the number of groups=50. x axis shows the sample being used and y axis shows if a particular sample was correctly classified. y=0 means that the hypothesis matched the actual class label

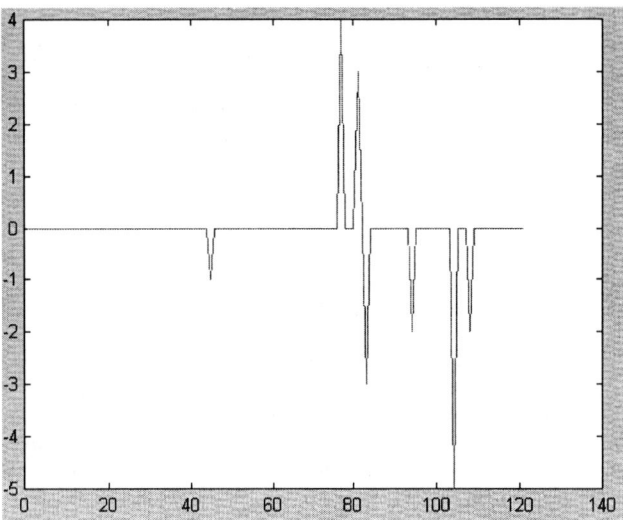

Figure 7. Testing results when the number of groups=150. x axis shows the sample being used and y axis shows if a particular sample was correctly classified. y=0 means that the hypothesis matched the actual class label

REFERENCES

[1] M. Ramoni and P. Sebastiani, "An introduction to the robust Bayesian classifier," KMi Technical Report KMi-TR-79, *Knowledge Media Institute*, March 1999.

[2] Y. Liang, E. O. George, and A. Kelemen, "Bayesian neural network for microarry data," in the proceedings of the *IEEE International Joint Conference on Neural Network*, Hawaii, pp. 193-198, 2002.

[3] J. Han and M. Kamber, *Data Mining Concepts and Techniques*, Academic Press, 2001.

[4] T. M. Mitchell, *Machine Learning*, The McGraw-Hill Companies, Inc., 1997.

[5] S. Chu, J. DeRisi, M. Eisen, J. Mulholland, D. Botstein, and P. O. Brown, "The transcriptional program of sporulation in budding yeast," *Science* 282, 699-705, 1998.

[6] M. Kerr and G. Churchill. "Bootstrapping cluster analysis: Assessing the reliability of conclusions from microarry experiments," *Proc. Natl. Acad. Sci.* USA 97:8961-8965, 2001.

[7] Y. Yang, S. Dudoit, P. Luu, and T. Speed, "Normalization for cDNA microarry data," Technical report 589, *Department of Statistics, UC-Berkeley.* T. Speed, 2000.

[8] M. L. Robert, "Parameter estimation for probabilistic document-retrieval models," *Journal of the American Society for Information Science*, 39(1), pp. 8-16, 1988.

[9] M. Ramoni and P. Sebastiani, "Learning conditional probabilities from incomplete data: an experimental comparison," in Proceedings of the *Seventh International Workshop on Artificial Intelligence and Statistics*, Morgan Kaufman, San Mateo, CA, 1999.

[10] A. Baxevanis and B. F. Ouellette, *Bioinformatics: Practical Guide to the Analysis of Genes and Proteins*, John Wiley & Sons, Inc., New York, 2001.

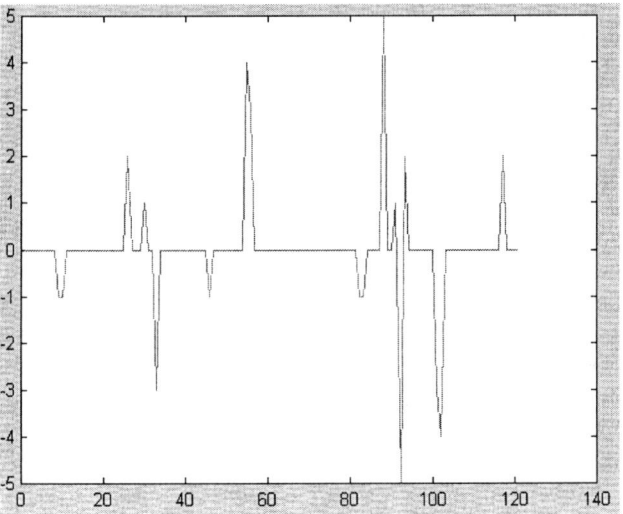

Figure 6. Testing results when the number of groups=100. x axis shows the sample being used and y axis shows if a particular sample was correctly classified. y=0 means that the hypothesis matched the actual class label

V. CONCLUSION

In this paper we propose naive Bayesian classifier to characterize the multiple gene functional temporal patterns with microarray experiments. We also invented, designed, and implemented a method, called attributes grouping, which was used in data preprocessing. Results show that with this method we can save on time and memory complexity without the loss of accuracy in the classification performance. Based on our experiment we conclude that the naive Bayesian classifier combined with the attribute grouping method can provide good classification accuracy which is comparable to other complicated classification methods.

Efficient Realization of Classification Using Modified Haar DWT

Rory Mulvaney and Dhananjay S. Phatak

Abstract— The Haar discrete wavelet transform is used as inspiration for a new simple and fast algorithm to train multiclass dyadic decision trees. A localized ordering of the training data changes a multidimensional Haar transform into the one dimensional case, and avoids cache misses. The resulting tree has very simple structure convenient for direct implementation as a fixed-depth threshold network and very fast evaluation of the classification function. The simple structure of the tree is also conducive to good compression of the function. We implement and test the learning algorithm and threshold network but without incorporating sampled interpolated-value points for improved generalization. Compression appears good in low dimensions.

I. Introduction

A. Problem Definition

A seemingly relevant and interesting, yet somewhat neglected problem is how to *efficiently* approximate with arbitrarily small error a known classification function ($\mathbb{R}^d \to S$, where S is a set of unrelated symbols) which we can query as an oracle. By "efficiently approximate," we mean having a computationally feasible method of learning a compact yet accurate approximation that we can also evaluate quickly. This basically amounts to storing the entire decision boundary surface in a possibly high dimensional space. To avoid an explosion in spatial complexity, the method needs to have good convergence properties, so that reducing the approximation error by a fraction requires as little additional storage as possible. Because of the problem definition, noise and overfitting are not concerns in the usual sense; instead, we simply desire that there are no *large contiguous regions* of error on the domain of interest. The oracle to be queried might simply be the k-nearest-neighbor or support vector machine fit of a training set. The usefulness of solving this problem is a potentially great advantage in speed of evaluation if our approximation function is fast compared to the oracle. Speed of evaluation is very important in these days of data mining, as the time-consuming search for correlations between between data might require estimates at large numbers of specified points.

This work was supported in part by NSF grants ECS-9875705 and ECS-0196362.

B. Threshold Network For Speed

To represent this approximation, it seems a fixed-depth multilayer perceptron (MLP) would offer the ultimate in speed of evaluation. The universal approximation power of single hidden layer MLPs was proven by Hecht-Nielsen in 1989 [8] using the simple observation that any one dimensional function (therefore the sine and cosine functions) may be approximated with a single hidden layer (using sigmoid or threshold transfer functions), and then a multidimensional fourier transform can be applied to extend this capability to multidimensional functions. Of course in practice, constructing a neural network for classification functions this way would require many hidden nodes, because many modes of the multidimensional fourier series may be required, and each of these modes (a sine or cosine) requires many hidden nodes (with sigmoid or threshold transfer functions) to approximate accurately.

Because of this and the fact that class values are fundamentally different from the real values approximated by a fourier transform, we turned instead to a multidimensional Haar discrete wavelet transform (DWT) [18], since it is piecewise constant and therefore much easier to represent class values using threshold nodes. (We make several modifications to the Haar DWT, including one that allows it to work with multiple class values, rather than real values.) However, whereas the multidimensional fourier transform consists of a sum of *one dimensional* fourier components (the 1-D components lie parallel to different vectors in the multidimensional frequency space), the wavelet transform consists of a sum of *multidimensional* Haar wavelet components. The net effect of all this is that 2 hidden layers are required to represent the DWT, where the output of each node in the second hidden layer basically represents the value of a Haar component. So our approximation of the function will be represented by a 2 hidden-layer threshold network.

We further show how everything after the first hidden layer of this network (first layer is required, since the inputs are not necessarily boolean) can be efficiently implemented with three levels of boolean logic (ignoring inverters). According to [6], [15], the jump from two to three levels of boolean logic can dramatically reduce the number of gates required, while little improvement is had by increasing the number of layers further. Therefore, it would be very hard to come by a faster-evaluating architecture with which to represent functions (without a large increase in gates).

In addition to the interpretation as a fixed-depth MLP or boolean logic network architecture, this Haar DWT essentially learns a forced-split "dyadic decision tree," as introduced recently in [16]. Dyadic decision trees are binary decision trees with decision nodes that always bisect their domain along a predetermined hyperplane parallel to a coordinate axis. The decision planes down any path in the tree simply cycle through the d coordinates in a forced manner. These are called *forced splits*; it is also possible to have *free splits*, where the optimal coordinate to split on can be independently chosen at any given node. In [17] a method was sketched (not very explicitly) for how to construct 2 hidden-layer MLPs (very much like the ones we construct in this paper) from an existing decision tree. They then trained the resulting MLP using gradient descent for further slight improvement in generalization. We don't deal with decision trees here, but one can actually perform the multiclass Haar DWT *directly on the nodes* of a binary decision tree to help analyze and rebalance the tree [11]; assuming the decsision nodes all represent linear boundaries, these wavelet coefficients each represent actual convex polytopic regions of space, making them more meaningful (easier to interpret) than decision nodes.

Due to their good compression and function approximation characteristics, wavelets have been used in the past to construct neural networks [1],[19], but implementing a multidimensional wavelet transform for dimensions above 2 or 3 has been seen as difficult [10] and seems to be generally avoided. Though there are many possible multidimensional Haar DWT decompositions, we have found that sorting the data into a certain order reduces the problem of performing a certain type of multidimensional Haar DWT into the trivial case of performing a one dimensional DWT on the reordered data. Thus the DWT itself is very easy to implement and fast to execute.

In this paper we simply test the generalization error of the wavelet transform on two benchmarks and note the size of the resulting threshold network. Generalization error is somewhat sub-par, but it could be improved dramatically through techniques like bagging [7] or *targeted* sampling of the k-nearest neighbor solution.

II. MULTICLASS MODIFIED HAAR DWT

We begin with a small example to demonstrate the simple operation of a one-dimensional Haar DWT. Due to space limitations, the reader can refer to [4], [18] for a more rigorous explanation of wavelets. In Figure 1, the top row is the data being transformed, and the resulting wavelet coefficients are in the bottom rows of

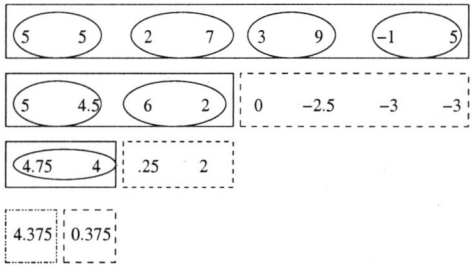

Fig. 1
HAAR DWT EXAMPLE

each column. Actually, the coefficient in the far lower-left box is not a "wavelet" coefficient, but rather the residual "scaling" coefficient. From this figure, it is very easy to understand the Haar wavelet transform. Starting at the top row, elements are paired off (indicated by the circles). The four average values of theses four pairs are placed in the second row in the left box. The "halved difference" of these four pairs are placed in the right box in the second row. These are the finest scale wavelet coefficients. The values in the left box represent an approximation of the original data (from a "low pass" filter), while values in the right box are the "details" from a "high (frequency) pass" filter. It is easy to see how to reconstruct the original data from these means and differences. This procedure is performed recursively on the left half (the low-pass coefficients) until the data has been reduced to the desired number of low-pass coefficients, in this case, the minimum, 1.

There are actually many different ways of performing a *multidimensional* wavelet transform. In a primer on wavelets [18], two methods for performing multidimensional Haar DWTs are discussed. Regarding the actual shape and form of the multidimensional wavelets, we basically use the second method, which they refer to as the "nonstandard method." The operation of this transform is simple. Figure 2 shows the two dimensional analog of low pass coefficient pairings (the circled pairs) to compute the "means and differences" in four consecutive levels of the algorithm. At each level, the algorithm simply alternates between pairing neighbors

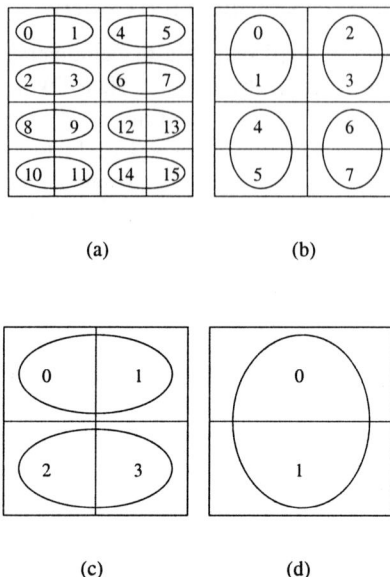

(a) (b)

(c) (d)

Fig. 2

MULTIDIMENSIONAL GROUPING PROGRESSION

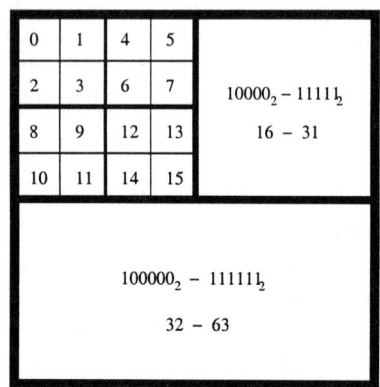

Fig. 3

SERIALIZATION OF DATA IN A TWO-DIMENSIONAL MATRIX

in the horizontal direction and pairing on the vertical direction.

In this progression of figures, we've labeled each cell with a number indicating the serialized index of each two-dimensional data point. Notice that this is not the usual row-major ordering of data that is typically used in a d-dimensional matrix. Also notice that every pairing joins cells with consecutive indices (also as it was in the one-dimensional transform in Figure 1). Thus, this 2-D transform can be more easily performed as a 1-D transform on the data sorted in this manner.

It turns out that this ordering of the data generalizes to any dimensionality, so that any d-dimensional Haar transform may be performed as a one-dimensional Haar DWT. This ordering can be simply described as the ordering induced by interleaving the bits of a point's d-dimensional coordinates into a single coordinate. For example, if x_1 represents the most significant bit of the x-coordinate, and x_n represents the least significant bit, $x_1 y_1 z_1 x_2 y_2 z_2 \ldots x_n y_n z_n$ is the merged, interleaved index for a three dimensional point.

To visualize this ordering of the data in two dimensions, refer to figure 3. The numbers in the figure represent the serialized indices of the elements in the corresponding blocks of the matrix. It has a natural block-structured recursive hierarchy that corresponds nicely with the bit pattern of the serialized index:

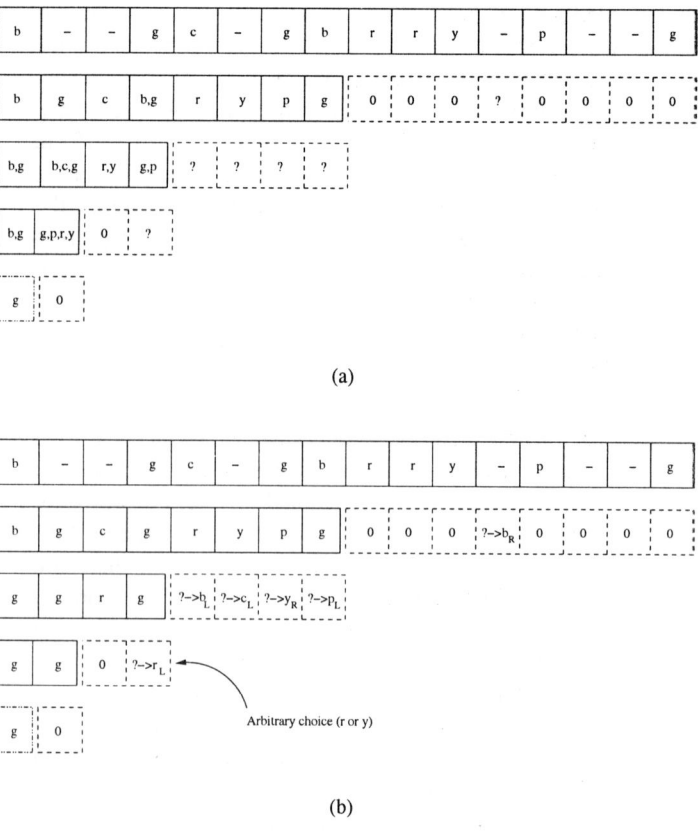

Fig. 4

MULTICLASS HAAR DWT EXAMPLE.

the bits of the serialized index tell which path to take through a binary tree whose leaves are the data elements of the matrix. In the 2-D example of the figure, the most significant bit of the index tells whether the data lies in the upper or lower half of the matrix, the second bit tells whether it lies in the right or left half of that half, and so on.

Now that the multidimensional Haar DWT has been completely specified, we describe our modifications to handle multiple class values and "unknown" regions. Figure 4 is intended as an instructive, perhaps unrealistic, example of the algorithm. This is similar to the previous example from Figure 1, except that we now have class values represented by letters (standing for the colors black, cyan, green, purple, red, and yellow) instead of real numbers, and there are also unknown regions of the function, represented by dashes. For instructive purposes we explain the algorithm in two phases. The first phase, illustrated in Figure 4(a) involves establishing "candidate sets" of low-pass coefficients. Instead of taking the mean of two low-pass coefficients to produce the low-pass coefficient at the next level, we take the intersection set of the two candidate sets, if there is an intersection. If there is no intersection, we take the union set. The dashes representing unknown regions are treated as "don't cares," so they effectively take the same value as the neighboring region. Whenever there is an intersection between the candidate sets, we also set the corresponding high-pass coefficient (recall this was the "halved-difference" in the standard Haar DWT) to zero. A high-pass coefficient corresponding to a candidate set formed as the union of two candidate sets is determined later, and represented as a '?' in the first phase figure.

In the second phase, completed in Figure 4(b), all candidate sets are narrowed to a single class value and all undetermined high-pass coefficients are also determined. Observe that the low-pass coefficients form a binary tree hierarchy (from how they were calculated) rooted at the final low-pass coefficient. Whenever there is a singleton candidate set, the candidate sets of all descendents of that node in the tree can be determined by the algorithm. If the tree is rooted by a non-singleton candidate set, the algorithm narrows the set to a single random candidate class. Once the set of a parent node has been narrowed, its two children are narrowed to the same class as the parent. It's possible that one of the children's sets doesn't contain the class of the parent. In this case, that child's class can be assigned randomly from its candidate set, and the appropriate high-pass coefficient at the next level (indicated by the arrow in Figure 4(b)) is assigned to indicate the right or left child has a different value from the parent ('L' and 'R' subscripts of the high-pass coefficients in the figure indicate whether the class applies to the left or right child). This process is repeated recursively until all coefficients in a given subtree have been uniquely determined. In [11] we show that this algorithm effectively uses dynamic programming and uses the minimum number of non-zero wavelet coefficients within the framework to capture the function at the training points (obviously there is never any training set error).

Note that neither the time or space complexity of the algorithm is affected by the number of don't-cares, since they don't actually need to be stored or ever even acknowledged by the algorithm. When the algorithm pairs off neighboring points in the serialized array, it simply needs to check their coordinates to verify that the points really are neighbors at the given resolution; otherwise, there is an implicit unknown point between them. Thus, given n original data points, only $2(n-1)$ coefficients are computed, so after the data has been sorted, the run time is linear in n. More generally, it is bounded by $O(nbk)$, where k is the number of classes and b is the total number of bits required for the coordinates of each point. One should also note that all memory accesses are **highly localized**, likely in stark contrast to other multidimensional algorithms. Thus this algorithm should encounter a minimal number of memory cycle delays, making it extremely fast.

III. CONVERSION TO FAULT-TOLERANT THRESHOLD NETWORK

A useful intuitive image is that the *non-zero* high-pass coefficients represent colored hyper-rectangular stickers which are placed on top of one another (in overruling fashion) in regions within the dyadic framework (such as those regions in Figure 2). The largest sticker corresponds to the last low-pass coefficient, and it shows through in areas where it isn't overruled by smaller stickers (higher-resolution coefficients) that "cover" it.

Now Figure 5 illustrates the architecture of the threshold network. Each node in the first hidden layer implements a hyperplane parallel to a coordinate axis, so they each require only one of the d inputs and a bias. A hashtable is used to ensure identical nodes aren't created. Each node in the second hidden layer corresponds to a non-zero high-pass coefficient, or hyper-rectangular sticker. These nodes are activated iff the input to the network is inside the region of the corresponding sticker; thus it is activated iff the input is inside all $2d$ hyperplanes that delimit the hyper-rectangular region.

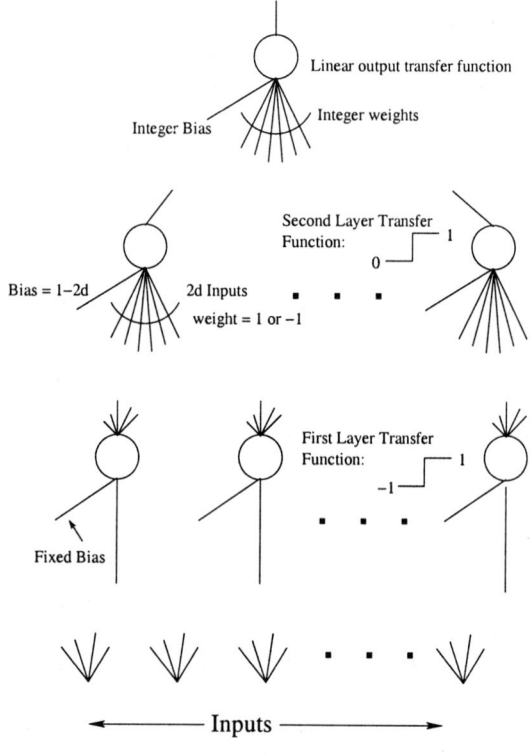

Fig. 5
ARCHITECTURE OF THE THRESHOLD NETWORK.

Output nodes output the weighted sum of their inputs and bias, so each class needs to have a numerical assignment. To understand how to set the weights to the output units, notice a general point p is inside the sticker-regions corresponding to some "signature" set $S = \{r_0, r_1, r_2, \ldots, r_k\}$ of wavelet coefficients. This set of regions always has the property that region r_i completely contains region r_{i+1}. Also note that all points whose "signature" set is equal to S are classified identically as p by the wavelet-transformed function. Let w_i represent the weight of the output connection from the node representing region r_i (w_0 represents the bias due to the final low-pass coefficient). Then given input point p, the output of the network is clearly $\sum_{i=0}^{k} w_i$. Regardless of the value of the sum $\sum_{i=0}^{k-1} w_i$, we can always set w_k so that the network outputs the correct value for point p (and all points with p's signature set). These weights can be computed efficiently in a depth-first traversal of the tree structure of the wavelet coefficients.

To use simpler *boolean* output units, it is straightforward to simply change the output layer and connections to have $\lceil \log_2 k \rceil$ boolean outputs, for k classes. All weights to the output layer would now be 1 or -1. However, now the amount of fan-in to the output nodes becomes slightly sensitive to the assignment of classes to integers. Since it's a dense coding of classes, it would seem difficult to reduce fan-in very much without trial and error, but perhaps assigning the classes with the most non-zero coefficients to the integers with the fewest bits on would help.

The original motivation of this work was to construct a fault tolerant MLP. Since all weights to the boolean output layer are 1 or -1, making the network completely fault tolerant to single faults is as simple as making two replications (for triple modular redundancy) of each subnet that feeds the output layer, as described in [13]. There it was proven the minimum number of replications required for fault tolerance is 2. Previous work [12], [14] was unable to achieve this lower bound.

IV. CONVERSION TO BOOLEAN NETWORK

Finally, we describe the simple conversion of everything after the first hidden layer of the threshold network (the inputs aren't necessarily boolean) to a AND-AND-OR boolean logic circuit of about the same size. The first layer consists of an AND gate for each non-zero wavelet coefficient. Each outputs 1 whenever the input is inside the hyper-rectangular sticker-region for its corresponding coefficient. Thinking in 2-D, there is a colored sticker at the bottom that shows through in many places. Those stickers directly on top of the bottom sticker are its "exceptions." We use a 2nd level AND gate to represent this by ANDing the bottom sticker with the NOT of each of the stickers *directly* on top of it. Now recursively treat the "exceptions to the exceptions" as if they were the bottom sticker, making 2nd level AND gates for each of them. All 2nd level AND gates, as well as some 1st level AND gates who don't have exceptions, are input to the output OR gate.

V. EXPERIMENTS

A. Benchmark Results

We applied the wavelet transform directly to the training sets of two benchmarks without any extra interpolated sampling or bagging, constructed a threshold network, and measured generalization error. The vowel benchmark [2] deals with 11-class data in a 10-dimensional space. Respective train and test sets have 528 and 462 patterns. The resulting threshold network had 73 and 132 nodes in the first and second hidden layers, and had 60.6% generalization error on the test set (this is a difficult benchmark). For comparison, [7] tabulates the performance of 17 other methods. Only

3 of of them beat nearest neighbor, which had 44% error (the best performer had 39%). The CART decision tree [7] had 56% error, and a linear perceptron tied for worst, at 67% error.

For the popular two spirals benchmark we generated 386 patterns using the code from [5]. We split this into training and test sets of 194 and 192 by taking every other pattern from each spiral. The threshold network had 36 and 57 hidden nodes in the first and second layer, and had 5.7% generalization error. Each of the 58 wavelet coefficients is a single bit and an address. Storing them in a tree format would probably require about 30 bytes or less.

B. Pen & Paper Results

Arguably, simple examples are more indicative of performance. Since decision boundaries of most practical functions are locally linear, we examined, for different linear boundaries, whether we can achieve convergence such that the error goes like $O(\frac{1}{n})$, where n is the number of wavelet coefficients (size of the approximation). This appears possible in 2 and 3 dimensions, though boundaries offset from "center" seem to require considerably more coefficients than a dyadic decision tree with "free splits."

In higher dimensions, convergence looks decidedly bad for linear function boundaries normal to the vector $(1, 1, 1, \ldots, 1)$. Error can successfully "hide in the corners" in high dimensions, apparently due to inflexibility caused by requiring the decision planes be parallel to a coordinate axis. For a decision tree architecture, this suggests allowing low precision hyperplane bisections normal to vectors whose entries are in $\{-1, 0, 1\}$.

VI. Conclusions, Speculation, and Future Work

The multiclass Haar DWT is very efficient, elegant, and simple. The coefficients have a very useful interpretation as regions of space, allowing us to easily construct fairly small, very fast-evaluating fixed depth boolean or threshold networks, and even help to balance general binary decision trees. However, despite the good reputation of wavelets for compression, it seems performance may fade quickly with increasing dimension. Better dimensionality reduction always pays off.

We think a decision tree architecture with low precision linear combination splits might help asymptotic convergence rates, though this approach has been criticized [3]. Recent advances in uniform sampling [9] may have made this strategy ultimately feasible. The resulting decision tree can still be realized as a fixed depth boolean or threshold network.

References

[1] Bhavik Bakshi, Alexandros Koulouris, and George Stephanopoulos, *Wave-nets: Novel learning techniques, and the induction of physiceally interpretable models*, SPIE Vol. 2242 Wavelet Applications, 1994, pp. 637–648.

[2] C.L. Blake and C.J. Merz, *UCI repository of machine learning databases*, http://www.ics.uci.edu/~mlearn/MLRepository.html, 1998.

[3] Leo Breiman and Jerome H. Friedman, *Tree-structured classification via generalized discriminant analysis: Comment*, Journal of the American Statistical Society (1988), no. 403, 725–727.

[4] Adhemar Bultheel, *Learning to swim in a sea of wavelets*, Bulletin of the Belgian Mathematical Society - Simon Stevin **2** (1995), 1–45.

[5] *CMU AI repository neural benchmarks*, http://www-2.cs.cmu.edu/afs/cs/project/ai-repository/ai/areas/neural/bench/cmu/bench.tgz.

[6] Debatosh Debnath and Tsutomu Sasao, *A heuristic algorithm to design AND-OR-EXOR three-level networks*, Asia and South Pacific Design Automation Conference, 1998, pp. 69–74.

[7] Trevor Hastie, Robert Tibshirani, and Jerome Friedman, *The elements of statistical learning – data mining, inference, and prediction*, Springer, 2001.

[8] Robert Hecht-Nielsen, *Theory of the backpropagation neural network*, Proceedings of International Joint Conference on Neural Networks (Washington, DC), vol. 1, 1989, pp. 593–605.

[9] Ravi Kannan, Laszlo Lovasz, and Miklos Simonovits, *Random walks and an $O^*(n^5)$ volume algorithm for convex bodies*, Random Structures and Algorithms **11** (1997), no. 1, 1–50.

[10] Tharmarajah Kugarajah and Qinghua Zhang, *Multidimensional wavelet frames*, IEEE Transactions on Neural Networks **6** (1995), 1552–1556.

[11] Rory Mulvaney and Dhananjay S. Phatak, *Efficient realization of classification in sparsely featured high dimensional input spaces using modified haar DWT*, Tech. Report TR-CS-03-21, University of Maryland, Baltimore County, January 2003.

[12] Dhananjay S. Phatak, *Fault Tolerant Artificial Neural Networks*, Proceedings of the 5th IEEE Dual Use Technologies and Applications Conference (Utica/Rome), May 1995, pp. 193 – 198.

[13] Dhananjay S. Phatak and I. Koren, *Complete and partial fault tolerance of feedforward neural nets*, IEEE Transactions on Neural Networks **6** (1995), no. 2, 446–456.

[14] Dhananjay S. Phatak and Elko Tchernev, *Synthesis of fault tolerant neural networks*, Proceedings of International Joint Conference on Neural Networks (Honolulu, Hawaii), May 2002.

[15] Tsutomu Sasao, *OR-AND-OR three-level networks*, Representations of discrete functions (Tsutomu Sasao and Masahiro Fujita, eds.), Kluwer Academic Publishers, 1996.

[16] Clayton Scott and Robert Nowak, *Dyadic classification trees via structural risk minimization*, Proceedings of Conference on Neural Information Processing Systems (Vancouver, Canada), December 2002.

[17] Ishwar K. Sethi, *Decision tree performance enhancement using an artificial neural network implementation*, Artificial Neural Networks and Statistical Pattern Recognition: Old and New Connections (Ishwar K. Sethi and Anil K. Jain, eds.), Machine Intelligence and Pattern Recognition, vol. 11, North-Holland, 1991, pp. 71 – 88.

[18] Eric J. Stollnitz, Tony D. DeRose, and David H. Salesin, *Wavelets for computer graphics: A primer, part 1*, IEEE Computer Graphics and Applications **15** (1995), no. 3, 76–84.

[19] Qinghua Zhang and Albert Benveniste, *Wavelet networks*, IEEE Transactions on Neural Networks **3** (1992), 889–898.

Predicting Intrusions with Local Linear Models

PingZhao Hu, Malcolm I. Heywood
Dalhousie University,
Faculty of Computer Science,
6050 University Avenue, Halifax, Nova Scotia. B3H 1W5

Abstract—Intrusion Detection Systems are typically deployed for real time operation, but are limited to identifying attacks once initiated. In this work we instead investigate the potential for predicting an attack before it occurs. To do so, a two-stage process is employed with a classification stage following that of a predictor. Predictors are based on the SOM and classifier on an SVM. Training and test is conducted using the 'TCP' connection features from the DARPA KDD competition data set. In spite of the simplicity of the model, the system is able to provide false positive and false negative rates of 23.8% and 7.1% respectively for one step-ahead prediction.

Index terms—Intrusion Detection Systems, Prediction, Self-Organizing Feature Map, Support Vector Machine.

I. INTRODUCTION

Intrusion Detection Systems (IDS) employ one of two general techniques, either rule-based misuse detection or anomaly detection. Rule-based misuse detection systems attempt to recognize specific behaviors that represent known forms of abuse or intrusion. On the other hand, systems for anomaly detection attempt to recognize abnormal user behavior [1]. The latter is of interest here. Specific candidate techniques of which might include, pattern templates, threatening behavior templates, traffic analysis, state-based detection and statistical methods [2]. Moreover, the norm is also to wait for an attack to be initiated and concentrate on the detection of an attack once initiated.

In this work we are interested investigating whether it is actually possible to predict attacks before they are initiated. There are naturally many contexts in which this might be attempted. Given that we are interested in testing the possibility of such an approach we utilize TCP "dump data". That is to say, *labeled* data sets are widely available in this form [3], although from an application context, session information would be more realistic. The basic objective of this work is therefore to establish the feasibility of building a one-step-ahead predictor, or $x(t + 1)$, for each of the "Basic features of an Individual TCP connection" [3]; hereafter referred to as 'TCP features'. An 'n'-step-ahead predictor, or $x(t + n)$, then being facilitated by feeding the values predicted for $x(t + 1)$ back into the input of the predictor (much like the organization of an IIR filter [4]).

The design of the one-step-ahead predictors is naturally posed as a supervised learning problem in which each TCP feature is assumed to represent a non-linear time series. Self-organizing maps (SOM) are then utilized to model this sequence [5]. Such predictive models however assume that the original data is both continuous and sampled at equal points in time. Neither condition holds true in this case as we are only interested in the order with which packets occur. We provide empirical evidence that this context provides a sufficient approximation to a continuous signal model.

The second stage is to classify the current sequence of packets as either constituting an attack or not. Given the established superiority of the Support Vector Machine (SVM) in classification roles, such a scheme is utilized here. The principle interest here lies in using the classifier to evaluate the performance of the predictor over an increasing temporal horizon. To this end the SVM is trained on samples for the current time step, $x(t)$, alone. This enables us to concentrate on the significance of the predictor.

The remainder of the paper is organized as follows. Section II provides the background and methodology of the work. Details of each learning algorithm comprising the system are detailed in Section III. Results are reported in Section IV for each component of the system and conclusions drawn in Section V.

II. METHODOLOGY

The rationale for the predictive IDS is described from the perspective of the data set and the learning algorithms, as follows.

A. Data Set

Given the preliminary nature of this work, a *labeled* IDS data set is sought in order to provide explicit feedback regarding the quality of prediction and any implications for classification accuracy. To this end the data set from the 3rd International Knowledge Discovery and Data Mining Tools Competition at KDD-99 is utilized [3]. In this work the concise training set consisting of half a million connections and a concise test set of around three hundred thousand connections is utilized. Each connection is described in terms of 41 *features*, categorized into four types: Basic TCP features; Content features; Time-based traffic features; and Host-based traffic features. We emphasize that each set of connection features are *derived* from the original TCP dump file, developed as part of a DARPA initiative, where this is

---

The second author acknowledges support through a Discovery grant from the Natural Sciences and Engineering Research Council of Canada.

unfortunately *unlabeled*. Each connection in the KDD-99 data set is labeled as either normal or attack. Moreover, attacks fall into one of 38 attack types, where there are 24 types in the training data and an additional 14 in the test data (concise test data). The attack types themselves may be categorized into one of four categories: denial-of-service (DoS); probing; unauthorized access from a remote machine; and unauthorized access to local super-user privileges. Note however, that DoS, by its nature, accounts for a greater proportion of connections than any other attack connection type; whereas attacks involving forms of unauthorized access are instances of 'content based attacks' and will therefore not be recognized by the IDS developed here.

Previous work has indicated that neural network solutions are able to provide competitive performance on the "Basic TCP features" alone [6]. Moreover, two of these features – "land" and "wrong" – do not vary across normal connections of the training set, leaving a total of 6 of the 9 different features for utilization in the IDS as follows,

- Duration, or number of seconds a connection exists;
- Protocol type, flag indicating TCP or UDP;
- Service, or type of service used by a connection;
- Flag, or 'status' of the connection;
- Destination (Source) bytes, or number of bytes transmitted by the destination (source).

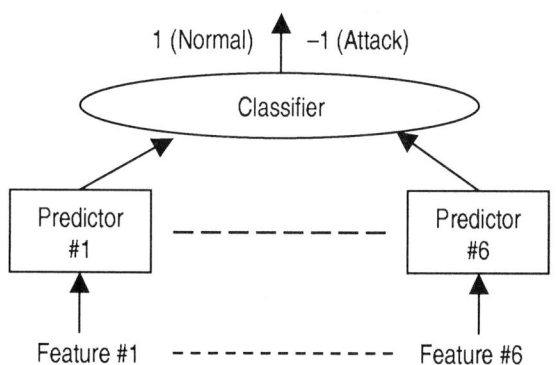

Fig. 1. Generic Two Stage Predictive IDS Architecture.

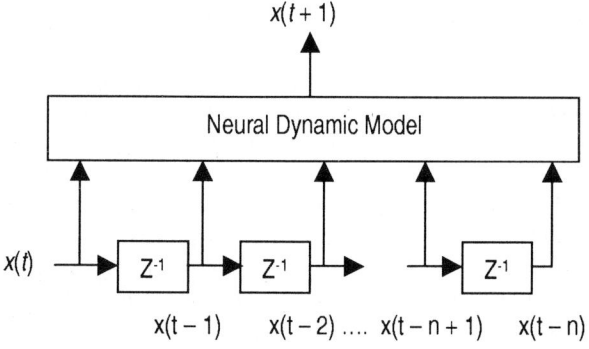

Fig. 2. Generic Neural Predictor

B. Architecture

As indicated in Section I the predictive IDS investigated here will follow a generic two-stage architecture comprising of a predictor followed by a classifier, Figure 1. This means that each of the six 'TCP features' is associated with a predictor, where each predictor is self-contained. Thus, the objective of each predictor is to estimate the next instance of that feature, Figure 2. Operation of predictor and classifier is summarized as follows.

1) Neural Predictor – SOM:

Various architectures are available for constructing neural predictive models. Examples include recurrent neural networks in which the neural network itself is responsible for all aspects of identifying the temporal model [7], reinforcement learning in which the cost function is explicitly designed to support discounting over time [8], and the augmentation of static (neural) models to provide the basis for multi-step predictors, where this is often used in the context of control problems [9]. In the case of this work additional concern is the efficiency of the learning algorithm and the throughput once trained. That is to say, a data set of half a million patterns, although larger than classically used for neural networks, is small within the IDS context. Explicitly recurrent architectures were therefore avoided. In addition, from a real-time context it would be desirable if the architecture were not highly nonlinear, but all the same able to provide predictions for nonlinear processes.

To this end, use is made of an architecture originally derived for applications in which nonlinear processes are modeled by a series of locally linear predictors [5, 10]. The basis for such models is that a time series may be embedded in a state space derived from a sequence of delayed samples of the variable under prediction. A suitable prediction made through a local approximation of the state space, Figure 2. Classically, Autoregressive models have proved very popular for this purpose [9]. However, the accuracy of such models is proportional to the complexity of the predicted feature and the size of the state space. Principe *et. al* [5, 10] observed that the state space could be approximated by a vector quantizer. This observation provided an additional benefit in that the (approximated) state space was now ordered, making the derivation of local linear models straightforward. Moreover, such a scheme also readily provides the basis for rule extraction once a suitable predictor has been identified [11]. This is the predictive model employed for this work, and is summarized as follows.

Firstly, a delay line is constructed of depth 'n', Figure 2. Note, however, that the delay line utilized in this case is modeled as a shift register. That is to say, we do not sample the target feature, x, at equally spaced intervals in time, but merely record each discrete connection as it appears. This differs from the classical approach on which the concept of a reconstruction state space is based [5, 9, 10]. Given that connection data is received at random intervals of time, the only sampling interval able to guarantee recording every connection would tend to zero. Moreover, assuming that such a sampling interval could be constructed, most of the samples would be zero, resulting in a series of impulses appearing at random points in time. This presents a second problem, because the neighborhood on which the local linear predictive model is formed is no longer smooth [5, 10]. By utilizing a shift register we are able to record each sample and avoid introducing discontinuities through sampling whenever there are no packets. Moreover, the shift register structure was previously shown to represent a suitable method for the representation of time in SOM based IDS [12]. A second implication of the shift register is that the system is a predictor of packet *sequences*, not when they will occur. Finally, in order to provide a sufficiently long temporal history on which predictions are made, but without unduly increasing the number of inputs to the quantization stage, we sample the shift register structure at every forth 'tap'. That is, if $x(k)$ represents the kth connection and $n = 12$, then the corresponding history $x(k)$ is $[x(k), x(k-4), x(k-8), x(k-12)]$. Results in Section III indicate that this appears to be a sufficiently good basis to build the predictive model.

Once the characteristics of the shift register ('reconstruction' space) are defined, the SOM is trained using the standard learning rules identified by Kohonen [13]. This provides a vector quantized description of the system dynamics for *connection* sequences, with the additional property that neighboring states correspond to neighboring SOM nodes. The third and final stage – identification of local linear predictors – follows the process determined by Principe *et al.* [5, 10]. This results in a single step-ahead predictor, where this may be fed back to the input to provide a multi-step predictor, where Section IV details the results of using such a system.

2) Classifier – SVM

The second and final stage of the simple predictive IDS is to classify each connection. To do so, each of the feature specific predictions is fed to a classification stage, Figure 1. The operation of the classifier is therefore to find the necessary decision boundaries sufficient to discriminate between attack and normal connections. This means that the classifier training process is independent of connection sequence and performed independently of the prediction stage. Specifically, a training set is formed by (uniform) random sampling of 500 normal and 500 attack connections from the training set. The classifier itself may be any standard classification architecture. To this end a Support Vector Machine (SVM) is employed [14].

III. LEARNING ALGORITHMS

Three learning algorithms are employed: one for the SOM [13], one for the local linear predictor [5, 10] and one for the SVM classification stage [14]. These are briefly summarized as follows.

A. Self-Organizing Feature Map

Kohonen's Self-Organizing Feature Map (SOM) algorithm is an unsupervised learning algorithm in which an initially 'soft' competition takes place between neurons to provide a topological arrangement between neurons at convergence [13]. The learning process is summarized as follows,
1. Assign random values to the network weights, w_{ij};
2. Present an input pattern, x, in this case a series of taps taken from the shift register providing the 'reconstruction' state space on which the SOM is to provide a suitable quantized approximation.
3. Calculate the distance between pattern, x, and each neuron weight w_j, and therefore identify the winning neuron, or

$$d = \min_j \{\|x - w_j\|\} \quad (1)$$

where $\|\cdot\|$ is the Euclidean norm and w_j is the weight vector of neuron j;
4. Adjust all weights in the neighborhood of the winning neuron, or

$$w_{ij}(t+1) = w_{ij}(t) + \eta(t)K(j,t)\{x_i(t) - w_{ij}(t)\} \quad (2)$$

where $\eta(t)$ is the learning rate at epoch t; and K(j, t) is a suitable neighborhood function, in this case of a Gaussian nature;
5. Repeat steps (2) – (4) until the convergence criteria is satisfied.

Following convergence, presentation of an input vector, x, results in a corresponding output vector, d, the Euclidian distance between each neuron and input. The neuron with the smallest distance representing the winning neuron, step (3), and defines a neighborhood of next nearest neighbors. It is this concept of a winning node and neighborhood, which is used by the local linear predictors.

B. Local Linear Predictor

On the SOM completing training, each SOM neuron, m_i, provides the basis for estimating a local linear predictor following identification of the winning SOM node, m_{i*}, or [5, 10],

$$x(k+1) = f_{i*}(x(k)) = (a_{i*})^T x(k) + b_{i*} \quad (3)$$

where $f_{i*}(\cdot)$ is the local linear model when SOM neuron m_i is the winner; and $[a_i, b_i]$ are the corresponding predictor coefficients.

Predictor coefficients are estimated over the set, M_i, of elements in the neighborhood of neuron m_i, inclusive of neuron m_i itself. Thus, given a specific winning node, m_{i*}, a local linear model is determined using the least square algorithm such that [5, 10],

$$w_{i,0} = (a_{i*})^T w_i + b_i \quad (4)$$

where $w_i = [w_{i,1}, w_{i,2}, ..., w_{i,n}]$ are the SOM weights of node i; and $w_{i,0}$ is the special case of an SOM node weight connected to the target prediction value, $x(t + 1)$ during training.

Each SOM unit, m_i, now has a corresponding linear model, $f_i(a_{i*}, b_i)$, providing the prediction for $x(k + 1)$ when the SOM node i represents the winner, $i*$. Note that this is a single pass training algorithm, independent of the data set. Thus, the most computationally expensive aspect of training the predictor is the SOM.

C. Support Vector Machine

SVMs for classification are based on two steps [14]: (1) the nonlinear transformation from input vector to some higher dimensional *feature* space, and; (2) the construction of an optimal linear hyperplane for separating the classes in the feature space. The design of a system capable of satisfying the first point is outlined by Cover's theorem for the separability of patterns. That is, the transformation is nonlinear and the dimensionality of the feature space is sufficiently high. The second point is achieved by formulating the problem in terms of the principle of structural risk minimization [14].

Space precludes the derivation of this process, so we merely state the principle results as follows. Let $\Phi(x)$ denote the nonlinear transform from input space, x, dimension m, to feature space n ($n \gg m$). The corresponding symmetric inner product kernel has the form,

$$K(x, x_i) = \Phi(x)^T \Phi(x_i) \quad (5)$$

This kernel provides for the construction of a decision surface, nonlinear in the input space, but linear in the feature space. The method of Lagrange multipliers now enables the phrasing of the construction of the SVM in terms of the following dual form. For training samples (x_i, d_i) find the Lagrange multipliers α_i maximizing,

$$Q(\alpha) = \sum_{i=1}^{P} \alpha_i - \frac{1}{2} \sum_{i=1}^{P} \sum_{j=1}^{P} \alpha_i \alpha_j d_i d_j K(x_i, x_j) \quad (6)$$

subject to:

$$\sum_{i=1}^{P} \alpha_i d_i = 0; \text{ and } 0 \leq \alpha_i \leq C \text{ for } i = 1, 2, ..., P$$

where C is a user selected parameter; x_i is input vector i; d_i is the ith desired value; and P is the number of patterns in the training set.

Given the optimum Lagrange multiplier values, the corresponding values for the (linear) weight vector w_0, connecting feature space to output space is defined by,

$$w_0 = \sum_{i=1}^{P} \alpha_{0,i} d_i \Phi(x_i) \quad (7)$$

Naturally, the choice of nonlinear Kernel, $K(x, x_i)$, has to be made *a priori*. In this work the Gaussian kernel is employed, or,

$$\exp\left(-\frac{1}{2\sigma^2} \|x - x_i\|^2\right) \quad (8)$$

IV. RESULTS

A total of three scenarios are considered: The training and testing of the predictor alone, the training and testing of the classification stage alone and finally the testing of both predictor and classification stage. In the case of the predictor, the SOM Toolbox was employed for the design of the SOM [15]. The SVM was constructed using LIBSVM [16].

A. Predictor

Parameterization of the predictor calls for the number of stages in the shift register, the location of taps (definition of inputs to predictor) and selection of SOM topology, neuron count and learning parameters. This information is summarized in Table I. Naturally, depth of the shift register will have implications for both training (overhead) and prediction (quality). That is to say, a deeper predictor will tend to improve prediction quality at the expense of training time. Given that the predictor is trained over all patterns in the concise training set (494,021 patterns), we choose to have a relatively short shift register.

TABLE I
SOM PARAMETERIZATION

Parameter	Value
Inputs (after training)	$x(t), x(t-4), x(t-8)$
Neurons	9×9
Learning rate	0.5, first epoch; 0.05 next 20 epochs
Epochs	1 + 20

As indicated in Section II.A only 6 of the 'TCP features' are utilized, where each feature is associated with an independent predictor, Figure 1. However, three features are alphanumeric: protocol type, service and flag, and are substituted with suitable numerical values, Table II; preference given to using values distributed about zero. Finally, all six features are normalized to provide zero mean at unit variance over the training set with the following transform,

$$x_i'(t) = \frac{x_i(t) - \overline{x}_i}{SD_i}$$

where $x_i(t)$ is the value of the *i*th feature at time 't'; $\overline{x}_i$ is the mean of the *i*th feature as estimated over all training set patterns; SD_i is the standard deviation of the *i*th feature as estimated over all training set patterns.

On completion of SOM training the local linear predictor associated with each SOM node is constructed, Section

III.B. Each local linear predictor, (3), is associated with a neighborhood of SOM weights over which a regression model is constructed to represent the local linear predictor for that SOM node, (4). In this case predictors are estimated over the 8 neurons surrounding each SOM node. In the case of a boundary SOM neuron, a duplicate column (row) is introduced to ensure that 8 neurons always contribute to each regression.

TABLE II
MAPPING ALPHANUMERIC TO NUMERIC

Feature	Alphanumeric	Increment	Numeric
Protocol	ICMP→UDP	1.0	$1 \to 3$
Service	whois→IRC	0.1	$-3.3 \to 3.3$
Flag	OTH → S0	0.2	$0.2 \to 1.2$
	S1 → SH	0.2	$-1.2 \to -0.4$

Table III summarizes predictor performance at look-ahead steps of 1, 2, 3 and 4 in terms of the degree of linear correlation between predicted value and actual value over the test set data. It is immediately apparent that predictions for duration, source and destination only hold for the one step-ahead case. Prediction for the other three features – protocol, flag and service – all hold relatively well. Note, this split between features predicted/ not predicted happens to correspond to the features that were originally alphanumeric/ not alphanumeric. Moreover, the features that were originally alphanumeric and given explicit numerical values do not observe a wide dynamic range. In contrast, the possible numerical range for features such as source and destination is sensitive to outliners that destroy the predictive quality of these features.

TABLE III
CORRELATION BETWEEN PREDICTED AND ACTUAL VALUES

Prediction	$x(t+1)$	$x(t+2)$	$x(t+3)$	$x(t+4)$
Protocol	0.987	0.896	0.889	0.888
Flag	0.988	0.923	0.902	0.890
Service	0.969	0.805	0.792	0.783
Duration	0.986	0.489	0.476	0.465
Source	0.997	0.000	0.000	0.000
Destination	0.991	0.007	0.009	0.007

B. Classifier

Within the context of this work, the classification stage is basically employed to provide a measure of any performance degradation associated with the predictor. To this end, the SVM is first trained and tested *independently* of the predictor. Thus any decrease in classification accuracy must be due to the predictor. An alternative, and possibly more accurate scheme, would be to train the classifier in conjunction with the predictor. This would allow the classifier to incorporate properties of the predictor in its operation.

Performance of the classifier is evaluated in terms of the false positive and detection rates, estimated as follows,

$$\text{False Positive Rate} = \frac{\text{Number of False Positives}}{\text{Total number of Normal Connections}}$$

$$\text{Detection Rate} = 1 - \frac{\text{Number of False Negatives}}{\text{Number of Attack Connections}}$$

where False Positive (Negative) Rate is the number of Normal (Attack) connections labeled as Attack (Normal).

From the summary of the SVM algorithm it is apparent that two user selected parameters are necessary, σ in (8) and C in (6). Moreover, the selection of a Gaussian kernel function, (8) was also the result of an empirical test (Linear and polynomial kernels also being evaluated). In all cases training is performed across 1,000 samples taken from the concise training set (50/ 50 split between normal and attack patterns, Section II.B) and testing is conducted across the unseen patterns from the remaining KDD concise training set (493,021 patterns). Note, no attempt is made to identify different attack types; the classification of a connection is merely as normal (+1) or attack (-1). Table IV lists training and test performance for the best-case parameter combination of $\sigma^* = 1/6$ and $C = 50$ which resulted in a total of 174 support vectors.

TABLE IV
SVM TRAINING AND TEST PERFORMANCE

Metric	Training	Test
# Normal	500	96,716
# Attack	500	396,305
FP Rate	0.4%	11.71%
Detection Rate	91.2%	99.08%

C. Predictor with Classifier

In the last case we consider the performance of the combined predictor-classifier or predictive IDS. To this end the first 100,000 connections from the 'corrected' KKD test data set is employed i.e. data as yet unseen by either predictor or classifier. This consists of 80,864 attack and 19,136 normal connections. Table V summarizes performance at look-ahead steps of 1, 2, 3 and 4 in terms of false positive and detection rates.

TABLE V
PERFORMANCE OF PREDICTIVE IDS ON TEST DATA

Prediction	FP Rate	Detection
$x(t+1)$	23.8%	92.9%
$x(t+2)$	24.2%	92.6%
$x(t+3)$	23.8%	92.4%
$x(t+4)$	26.1%	92.4%

In comparison, other research has provided results in the range of 70-98% detection rates and false positive rates in the range of 2-10% [17, 18]. However, in all cases derived, as opposed to 6 connection, features were employed, and no predictive properties were reported.

D. Discussion

Given the poor correlation between predicted and actual values for duration, source and destination, it is not surprising that the false positive rate doubled. However, we do believe that the results are encouraging enough to warrant further development of the method. In particular, different encoding schemes need to be investigated as well as the suitability of other features from the KDD data set (there are a total of 41). The depth of the shift register responsible for providing the state space representation should also be increased, and the classification stage trained in conjunction with the predictor.

V. CONCLUSION

A predictive IDS is proposed and investigated in which a simple predictor-classification architecture is used. It is shown that although the IDS context is not able to support data samples from a smoothly varying signal at equally spaced intervals in time, by utilizing a shift-register instead of a delay line, it is possible to mimic the ideal sufficiently well. Moreover, independence between the two stages enabled efficient training of each stage, where the predictor was trained across all half a million connections and the classifier only 1,000. Performance results from this initial study indicate that the method warrants further investigation.

Future work will consider the utility of alternative predictors, such as a support vector machine, and investigate the use of a deeper shift register; thus providing more input (taps) to each predictor. Such a performance evaluation would have to consider more than just classification accuracy; transparency/ complexities of the solution also represent important performance objectives. Moreover, it is also apparent from this work that sensitivity to some of the features is relatively low i.e. 'source' and 'duration' are not predicted beyond one step ahead, Table III, but FP rate only increases by 0.4-2.3%, Table V. Hence, a thorough analysis of KDD feature significance is also anticipated.

REFERENCES

[1] A.J. Hoglund, K. Hatonen, A.S. Sorvari, "A computer Host Based User Anomaly Detection System Using the Self Organizing Map", Proceedings of the International Joint Conference on Neural Networks, IEEE IJCNN 2000, Vol. 5, pp 411-416.

[2] T. Bass, "Intrusion Detection Systems and Multisensor Data Fusion", Communications of the ACM, Vol. 43, No. 4, pp 99-105, April, 2000.

[3] S. Hettich, S.D. Bay, The UCI KDD Archive. Irvine, CA: University of California, Department of Information and Computer Science, http://kdd.ics.uci.edu, 1999.

[4] R.W. Hamming, Digital Filters, Prentice-Hall, ISBN 0-13-212895-0, 1989.

[5] J.C. Principe, L. Wang, "Non-linear time series modeling with SOFM," Proceedings of the 1995 IEEE Workshop on Neural Networks for Signal Processing, pp 11-20.

[6] H.G. Kayacik, A.N. Zincir-Heywood, M.I. Heywood, "On the Capability of an SOM based Intrusion Detection System," IEEE International Joint Conference on Neural Networks, Portland, Oregon, June 20-24, 2003.

[7] P.J. Angeline, G.M. Saunders, J.B. Pollack, "An Evolutionary Algorithm that Constructs Recurrent Neural Networks," IEEE Transactions on Neural Networks, 5(1), pp 54-64, Jan. 1994.

[8] R.S. Sutton, A.G. Barto, Reinforcement learning: An Introduction, MIT Press, ISBN 0-262-19398-1, 1998.

[9] K.S. Narendra, K. Parthasarathy, "Identification and Control of Dynamical Systems using Neural Networks," IEEE Transactions on Neural Networks, 1(1), pp 4-27, 1990.

[10] J.C. Principe, L. Wang, Motter M.A., "Local Dynamic Modelling with Self-Organizing Maps and Applications to Nonlinear System Identification and Control," Proceedings of the IEEE, 86(11), pp 2240-2258, 1998.

[11] S. Mitra, S. K. Pal, "Fuzzy Self-Organization, Inferencing, and Rule Generation," IEEE Transactions on Systems, Man, and Cybernetics – Part A: Systems and Humans, 26(5), pp 608-620, 1996.

[12] P. Lichodzijewski, A.N. Zincir-Heywood, M.I. Heywood, "Host-Based Intrusion Dection Using SOMs," IEEE Joint Conference on Neural Networks, pp 1714-1719, 2002.

[13] T. Kohonen, Self-Organizing Maps, 3rd Ed., Springer-Verlag, ISBN 3-540-67921-9, 2000.

[14] V.N. Vapnik, The Nature of Statistical Learning Theory. Springer-Verlag, ISBN 0-387-98780-0, 1995.

[15] J. Vesanto, J. Himberg, E. Alhoniemi, J. Parhankangas, SOM Toolbox for Matlab 5.0, Helsinki University of Technology, Neural Networks Research Center, http://www.cis.hut.fi/projects/somtoolbox/. Retrieved December 2002.

[16] C.C. Chang., C.J. Lin, LIBSVM – A Library for Support Vector Machines. http://www.csie.ntu.edu.tw/~cjlin/libsvm/. Retrieved December 2002.

[17] E. Eskin, A. Arnold, M. Prerau, L. Portnoy, S. Stolfo, "A Geometric Framework for Unsupervised Anomaly Detection: Detecting Intrusions in Unlabeled Data," in Applications of Data Mining in Computer Security, Chapter 4, D. Barbara and S. Jajodia (editors), Kluwer, ISBN 1-4020-7054-3, 2002.

[18] W. Lee, S. Stolfo, K. Mok, "A Data Mining Framework for Building Intrusion Detection Models," Proceedings of the 1999 IEEE Symposium on Security and Privacy, pp 120-132, 1999.

A Comparison of SOM Based Document Categorization Systems

X. Luo, A. Nur Zincir-Heywood
Dalhousie University,
Faculty of Computer Science,
6050 University Avenue, Halifax, Nova Scotia. B3H 1W5

Abstract - **This paper describes the development and evaluation of two unsupervised learning mechanisms for solving the automatic document categorization problem. Both mechanisms are based on a hierarchical structure of Self-Organizing Feature Maps. Specifically, one architecture is based on the vector space model whereas the other one is based on a code-books model. Results show that the latter architecture performs better than the first as based on the quality of the returned clusters.**

I. INTRODUCTION

One of the significant tasks in document categorization systems is clustering because it offers a solution to the problems of information overload and vocabulary differences. The term information overload is used to describe the constant influx of new information [2, 3], which causes users to be overwhelmed by the subject and system knowledge required to access this information. Thus, clustering systems are used to separate a very large set of documents into groups, where grouped documents share similar content. Hence, a natural extension of such a system would be the ability to automatically provide initial document categorization in much the same way that fingerprint categorization is used to sort prints into types before the computationally expensive process of classification takes place [4]. These functions should be performed in real-time, and therefore, are of significant use to many existing on-line applications, such as document browsing, nearest neighbor search or directory structures like Yahoo [3].

A common approach among existing systems is to cluster documents based upon their word distributions, while word clustering is determined by document co-occurrence. However, the distribution of words in most real document collections can vary significantly from one document to another. Moreover, vocabulary differences mean that automatic selection and weighing of keywords in text documents may well bias the nature of the clusters found at later stages. Thus, data representations enabling accurate measurement of semantic similarities between documents would greatly facilitate such tools in terms of computational costs as well as accuracy.

In information retrieval, a typical data representation phase uses the Vector Space Model (VSM), where the frequency of occurrence of each word in each document is recorded. These values are then generally weighted using the Term Frequency (TF) multiplied by the Inverse Document Frequency (IDF), following Shannon's information theory. Note that this approach considers only term co-occurrences in documents and therefore ignoring the significance of the order in which they occur.

Thus, this work details the construction, and testing of two unsupervised clustering systems based on Self-Organizing Feature Maps (SOM) that encompass representation of word features such as word orders as well as co-occurrences. By doing so, we aim to minimize any *a priori* assumption regarding suitable word features and to discriminate higher-level concepts. Specifically, the first clustering system built is based on the VSM, which is representative of typical information retrieval approaches, and makes use of topological ordering property of SOMs. On the other hand, the second system makes use of the SOM based architecture as an encoder for data representation - by finding a smaller set of prototypes from a large input space – without using the typical information retrieval pre-processing. Our results show that the quality of clustering of the second architecture (90%) outperforms the first one (56%).

The remainder of the paper is organized as follows. Section II introduces the problem addressed by this work and makes a case for solving this problem using an entirely unsupervised learning algorithm. Section III presents the two architectures for constructing such a system. Section IV introduces the test bed on which experiments are performed, and presents the results. Finally, conclusions are drawn in section V.

II. DOCUMENT CLUSTERING WITH SELF-ORGANIZING MAPS

In this work, the aim is to investigate the potential for automating the process of document clustering as much as possible. In order to achieve this, the first step is the identification of an encoding of the original information (category) such that pertinent features (character probabilities) may be decoded most efficiently. This information is then used to measure the similarity between the characteristics of any given document to a category. Thus, the core of the approach is to automate the identification of typical category characteristics. To this end, an unsupervised learning system – Self Organizing Feature Map (SOM) – is employed to detect and visualize the characteristics of a document category.

The authors gratefully acknowledge the financial support of the Natural Sciences and Engineering Research Council of Canada for the second author's Discovery Grant.

The SOM algorithm is a vector quantization algorithm. Thus, the efficient update scheme and ability to express topological relationships of an SOM makes it very convenient for expressing relationships between different groups of documents [7]. These properties have made the SOM a popular approach for document clustering, visualization or analysis [2, 7]. The hypothesis motivating such a scheme is that similar document characteristics will be emphasized – densely populated regions of the SOM – whereas different characteristics will appear in sparse regions of the SOM [7].

On the other hand, in this work, SOMs are of particular interest not only for their topological ordering property, feature selection and density matching but also, on account of their ability to provide approximations of the input in a lower dimensional space [5]. In other words, the SOM acts as an encoder to represent a large input space by finding a smaller set of prototypes.

In this case, the SOM represented by the set of weight vectors $\{w_j\}$ in the output space – O – is to provide a good approximation of the original input space – I. To achieve this, the basic aim of the SOM algorithm is to store a large set of input vectors, $x \in I$, by finding a smaller set of prototypes, $w_j \in O$. Hence, the feature map can be considered as an Encoding-Decoding model, figure 1.

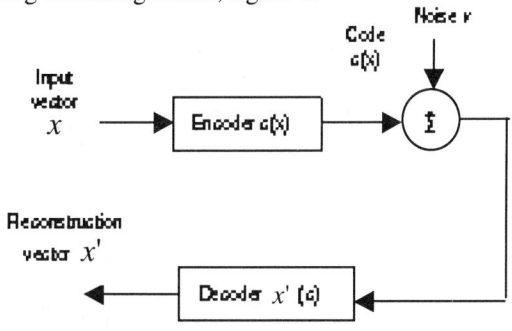

Fig.1. Encoding-Decoding Model [5]

In this model, $c(x)$ acts as an encoder of the input vector x and $x'(c)$ acts as a decoder of $c(x)$. The vector x is selected at random from a training sample, I, subject to an underlying probability density function $f_x(x)$. The optimum encoding-decoding scheme is determined by varying the functions $c(x)$ and $x'(c)$, so as to minimize the expected distortion. However, in order to overcome the local-minimum problem a signal independent noise process, v, is introduced following the encoder $c(x)$, i.e. out of category document character distributions. The noise v is associated with a fictitious communication channel between the encoder and the decoder. On the basis of this model, the best-matching neuron, $i(x)$, of the SOM algorithm corresponds to the encoder, $c(x)$; weight vector, w_j, corresponds to the reconstruction vector, $x'(c)$; and the neighborhood function, $h_{j,i(x)}$, corresponds to the probability density function, $\Pi(c-c(x))$, associated with the noise, v [5]. The details of the SOM algorithm are given in sub-section III-C.

This viewpoint forms the theoretical justification of using the SOMs as code-books, which corresponds to the motivation behind this work. As discussed in section I, the two main problems in information retrieval are information overload, i.e. large input space, and vocabulary differences, i.e. the nature of the signal. Hence, in this work, the first SOM architecture is making use of the property to map the (large) input space to a (smaller) set of prototypes independent from the signal (noise properties). On the other hand, the second architecture not only uses the above property but also aims to make use of the encoding-decoding model by building up an understanding of documents by first considering the relationships between characters, then words and finally word co-occurrences.

III. ARCHITECTURE OVERVIEW

To achieve the aforementioned objectives, the framework of figure 2 is followed, for both of the SOM architectures considered.

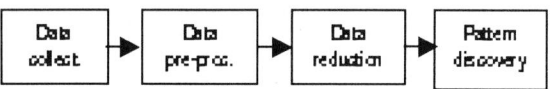

Fig.2. System flowchart

In document clustering, a typical pre-processing phase uses the Vector Space Model. There are two main parts to the vector space model: Parsing and Indexing [1, 7, 9, 10]. Parsing converts documents into a succession of words. The words are filtered using a basic Stop-List of common English words, which do not significantly contribute to discrimination between documents (such as "the", "it", etc.). A stemming algorithm is then applied to the remaining words. In the indexing part, each document is represented in the Vector Space Model where the frequency of occurrence of each word in each document is recorded. These values are then generally weighted using the Term Frequency (TF) multiplied by the Inverse Document Frequency (IDF) as per Shannon's information theory, (1). Once the set of document vectors has been created, techniques from pattern discovery are employed to form the overall classification.

$$P_{ij} = tf_{ij} \cdot log(N/df_i) \qquad (1)$$

P_{ij} – Weight of term t_j in document d_i
tf_{ij} – Frequency of term t_j in document d_i
N – Total number of documents in collection
df_i – Number of documents containing term t_j

A. Architecture-1: Emphasizing Density Matching Property

In this architecture, the objective is to form illustrative 2-D projections of distributions of items in high dimensional data spaces, such as vast document collections. With classical methods these mappings are computationally expensive [16]. Thus, the SOM as a neural network method can be employed to approximate an unlimited number of input data items by a finite set of models (neurons) [11]. In this method, relationships between documents can be viewed using spatial organizations on a 2-D grid structure.

To the best of our knowledge, the SOM method was first employed to small data sets (~100 documents) in [8, 15] and more recently to a large data set (~7 million documents) in WEBSOM project [7]. In all three cases, a vector space model is used at the pre-processing stage. Word histograms are formed as input vectors to represent documents to the SOM. Early examples had limited document vocabularies, providing for direct entry to the SOM. However, data sets met in practice require a random mapping to decouple the SOM from the size of the vocabulary space [6, 7].

In architecture-1, the classical vector space model method is utilized (1), Figure 3. Note that the random mapping method is used to reduce the dimensionality before presenting a document to the SOM.

cannot be over-emphasized. The hierarchical nature of the architecture is shown in Figure 4.

1) Input for the First-Level SOMs: The overall pre-processing process for the first-level SOM is:

- Generate vector space model to represent each document (1).
- Reduce the dimension of the vector space model for each document by random mapping (2).
- Present the new vector of each document to the SOM.

Thus, the first-level SOM is trained on the corresponding word list of documents. The assumption at this level is that similar document characteristics, i.e. words, will appear in the densely populated regions of the SOM for the patterns of words that occur in a specific document category.

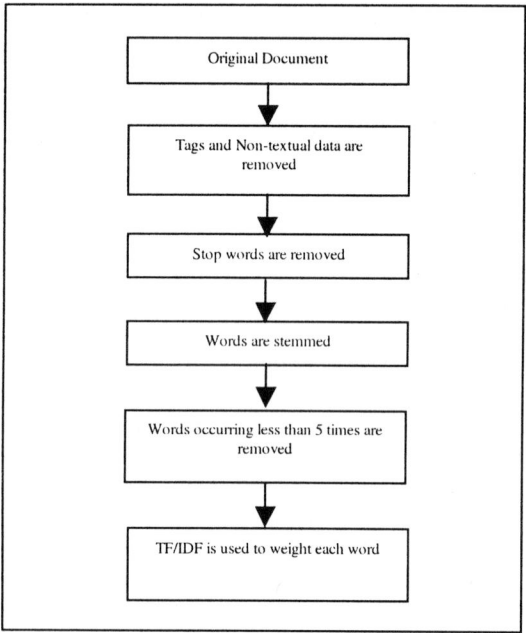

Fig.3. An overview of data pre-processing for the first architecture

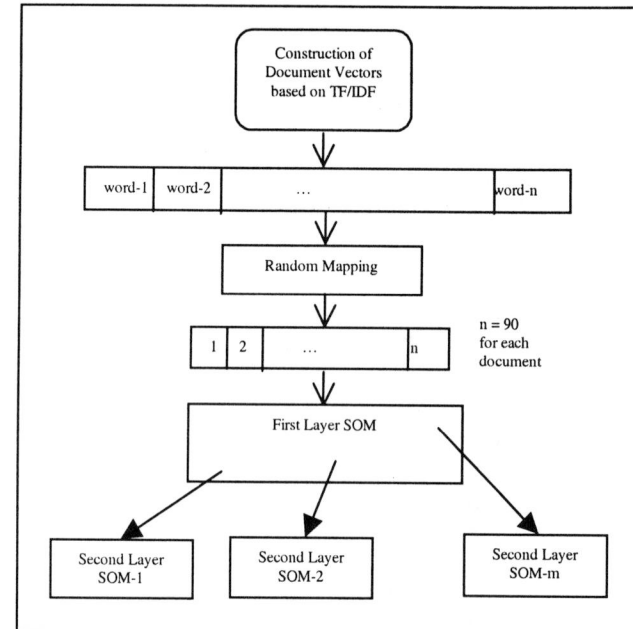

Fig.4. An overview of the first architecture

In the random mapping method [6], the original data vector is reduced by replacing, each of its dimensions by a randomly selected non-orthogonal direction. The mapping [6] is as follows:

$$x' = R x \quad (2)$$

x – The original data vector, where $x \in \mathbf{R}^N$
R – A matrix consisting of random values where the Euclidean length of each column has been normalized to unity
x' – Reduced-dimensional or quantized vector, where $x' \in \mathbf{R}^d$

Once the dimension of the input space is reduced, it is presented to a two level hierarchical SOM architecture. Hence, the significance of effective pre-processing and dimensionality reduction before presentation to the SOM

2) Input for the Second-Level SOMs: When a quantized vector representing a document is presented to a trained first-level SOM, the location of each neuron is expressed in terms of an Euclidean space with neuron topology roughly reflecting the density of the feature(s) in the document training set. However, due to the self-organizing characteristics of the map, some of the neurons may become more crowded with words (representing documents) as compared to others. Enlarging the size of the SOM solves the problem to some degree, but after a certain size the number of the crowded ones remains the same [4]. Moreover, as the size of a map increases, also the computational cost increases. Therefore, instead of increasing the size of the SOM within the level, associating additional SOMs with crowded neurons may solve the problem by a divide-and-conquer method [4]. Hence, each additional SOM network in the second-level is trained only by those samples represented by the crowded neurons in the first-level. This process is applied whenever a region in the first-level SOM was excited by more than fifty documents from 2 or more categories.

B. Architecture-2: Emphasizing Encoding-Decoding Property

In this case, the core of the approach is to automate the identification of typical category characteristics, i.e. good approximation of the input space – code-book model. Steps to achieve data pre-processing and reduction are driven by the needs of the pattern discovery component. As mentioned before, pattern discovery employs a three level hierarchical SOM architecture (characters, words, and word co-occurrences).

In this architecture, the classical parsing method (section III) is applied to remove stop words etc., after which, a different indexing scheme is used as shown in Figure 5. In this scheme, a document is summarized by its words and their frequencies (TF) in descending order, but the information theory framework is *not* used, (1). Once such a list is formed, the 15 most frequent words are retained from each document. Moreover, these words are pre-processed to provide a numerical representation for each character. An SOM may now be used to identify a suitable character encoding, then word encoding, and finally, word co-occurrence encoding. By doing so, the authors of this paper aim to minimize the amount of *a priori* knowledge required to overcome the vocabulary differences. The hierarchical nature of the architecture is shown in Figure 6.

1) Input for the First-Level SOMs: In order to train an SOM to recognize patterns in characters, the document data must be formatted in such a way as to distinguish characters and highlight the relationships between them. Characters can easily be represented by their ASCII representations. However, for simplicity, we enumerated them by the numbers 1 to 26, i.e. no differentiation between upper and lower case. The relationships between characters are represented by a character's position, or time index, in a word. For example, in the word *"news"*: *"n"* appears at time index 1, *"e"* appears at time index 2, *"w"* appears at time index 3, and *"s"* appears at time index 4. It should be noted that it is important to repeat these words as many times as they occur in the documents. In other words, for a particular document, the 15 most frequently occurring words may occur a combined total of 50 times. Therefore, a list of 50 words is formed with the words remaining in the same order as they appear in the document. The overall pre-processing process for the first-level SOM is therefore:

- Convert the word's characters to numerical representations between 1 and 26.
- Find the time indices of the characters.
- Linearly normalize the indices so that the first character in a word is represented by one, and the last by 26. Those in between are equally spaced between 1 and 26.

The indices of the characters are altered in this way so that when the list is input to an SOM, both data features (enumerated characters and indices) are spread out over a close range. The assumption at this level is that the SOM forms a code-book for the patterns in characters that occur in a specific document category.

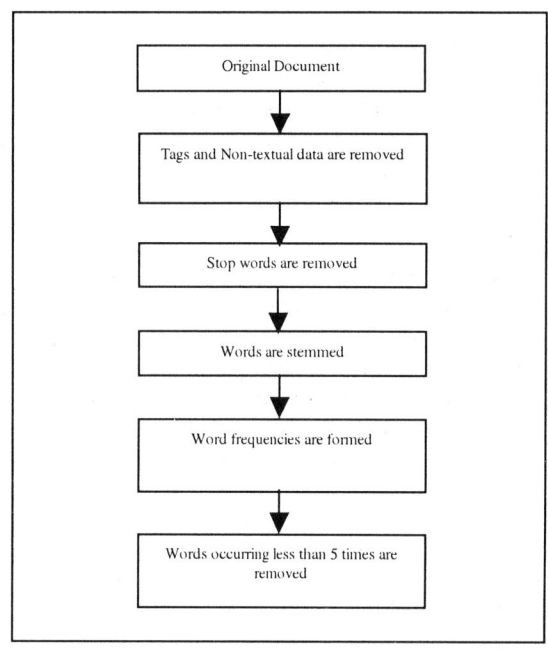

Fig.5. An overview of data pre-processing for the proposed approach

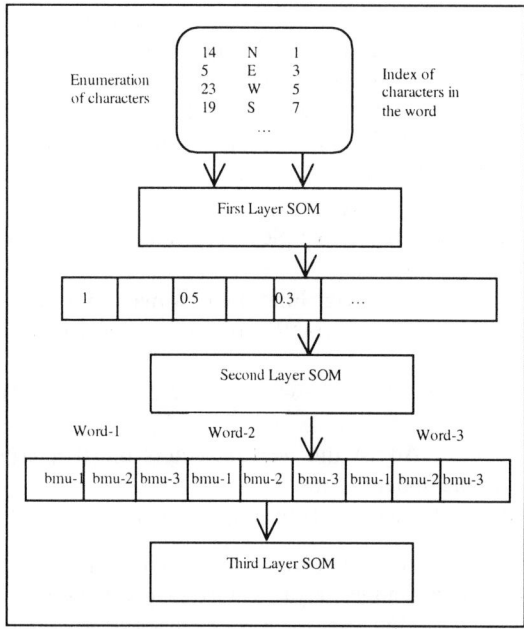

Fig.6. An overview of the second architecture

2) Input for the Second-Level SOMs: When a character and its index are run through a trained first-level SOM, the closest neurons (in the Euclidian sense), or *Best Matching Units* (BMUs), are used to represent the input space. The following inter-stage processing is therefore used for defining word level inputs to the second-level SOMs:

- For each word, k, that is input to the first-level SOM of each document,
  - Form a vector of size equal to the number of neurons (r) in the first-level SOM
  - For each character of k,
    - Observe which neurons $n_1, n_2, ..., n_r$ are affected the most (the first *3* BMUs).
    - Increment entries in the vector corresponding to the first 3 BMUs by $1/j$, $1 \leq j \leq 3$.

Hence, each vector represents a word through the sum of its characters.

3) Input for the Third-Level SOMs: In the context of this architecture, word co-occurrence is simply a group of consecutive words in a document. Thus, the third-level SOMs are used to identify such patterns in the input space. The input space of the third-level SOMs is formed in a similar manner to that in the second-level, except that the third-level input vectors are built using BMUs resulting from word vectors passed through the second-level SOMs. Furthermore, in order to form a more meaningful input space for the third-level SOMs, it should be noted that the input vectors represent consecutive words only from a single document with a sliding window of size three.

C. Training the SOMs

The algorithm responsible for the formation of the SOM involves three basic steps after initialization: sampling, similarity matching, and updating. These three steps are repeated until formation of the feature map has completed [5]. The algorithm is summarized as follows:

- Initialization: Choose random values for the initial weight vectors $w_j(0)$, $j=1,2, ...,l$, where l is the number of neurons in the map.
- Sampling: Draw a sample x from the input space with a uniform probability.
- Similarity Matching: Find the best matching neuron $i(x)$ at time step n by using the minimum distance Euclidean criterion:

$$i(x) = \arg \min_j \|x(n) - w_j\|, \quad j=1,2, ...,l \quad (3)$$

- Updating: Adjust the weight vectors of all neurons by using the update formula:

$$w_j(n+1) = w_j(n) + \eta(n) h_{j,i(x)}(n)(x(n) - w_j(n)) \quad (4)$$

- Continuation: Continue with sampling until no noticeable changes in the feature map are observed.

The sizes of the maps shown in table 1 are chosen empirically according to the observed weight changes. Hence, we considered the balance between the computational cost and the weight change in choosing the size of a map.

TABLE I
SIZES AND TRAINING TIME FOR THE MAPS

	Size of the map	Training time
Architecture-1		
Level-1	25 by 20	~38 hours
Level-2	6 by 6 – 4 by 4	~5 - ~2 minutes
Architecture-2		
Level-1	7 by 13	~ 4 hours
Level-2	8 by 8	~ 19 hours
Level-3	20 by 20	~ 25 hours

IV. PERFORMANCE EVALUATION

In this work, a subset of the Reuters-21578 document set [13] is used to evaluate the two architectures. There are a total of 12612 news stories in this collection. These stories are in English, where 9603 of them are in the training data set, and 3009 are in the test set. Moreover, among the training documents, which are labeled, approximately 333 of them have more than 3 labels, and only 25 categories have more than 50 documents. On the other hand, among the test documents, only 2733 of them are labeled, and in that set, 2526 documents belong to the 25 different categories. Hence, we selected these test cases to use for the experiments described here. Thus, our training set consists of 9603 documents, whereas the test set has 2526 documents.

Most often in information retrieval, clusters are embedded in an application and therefore evaluation takes the form of a comparison between a 'winning' labeled cluster and the class label. However, such approaches measure only the quality of the best cluster. On the other hand, the documents of the above data set belong to more than one class; hence there is no single *best cluster*, this is a multi-class multi-labeled problem. Therefore, an evaluation methodology [12] that keeps a balance between generality and goal-orientation is used to compare the performance of the two architectures. The performance measurement used is based on:

$$1 - \frac{dist(C, A)}{dist(B, A)} \quad (5)$$

A – set of correct class labels (answer key)
B – baseline clusters where each document is one cluster
C – set of clusters ('winning' clustering results)

$dist(C, A)$ – The number of operations required to transform C into A.

$dist(B, A)$ – The number of operations required to transform B into A.

In this evaluation method, it is assumed that there are correct class labels (answer keys) that define how the elements (documents) are supposed to be clustered.

Moreover, three *operations* are allowed to support construction of answer keys from 'winning' clusters.
- Merge two clusters.
- Move an element from one cluster to another
- Copy an element from one cluster to another

Hence, the performance or quality of clustering is interpreted as the percentage of savings (in terms of *operations*) from using the 'winning' clustering results to construct the answer key versus using baseline clusters to construct the answer key. In this case, we applied it as follows:

1. If a document is in a class, which is not listed in the document's label set, then we move the document to the class it belongs.
2. If a document belongs to more than one target class, then we copy the document to the remaining classes listed in its label set.

The similarity between documents and the class is computed using the cosine coefficient [14] of their outputs on the corresponding architectures. Table 2 shows the performance scores (using function 5) of both architectures for three different threshold values for their cosine coefficient functions.

TABLE II
CLUSTER QUALITY OF THE TWO ARCHITECTURES

	ARCHITECTURE-1	ARCHITECTURE-2
Threshold=0.01	56.3%	90.5%
Threshold=0.05	10.3%	62.6%
Threshold=0.1	6.7%	35.2%

V. CONCLUSION

Two systems have been developed for unsupervised clustering of document collections that encompasses pre-processing for word features as well as word co-occurrences. By doing so, the authors aim to minimize any *a priori* assumptions regarding suitable word features as well as to discriminate between higher level concepts.

Unlike earlier approaches, both systems emphasize the use of SOMs on account of their ability to provide approximations of the input in a lower dimensional space. The first architecture emphasizes a layered approach to lower the computational cost of the training of the map and employs a random mapping to decrease the dimension of the input space. Although, these techniques have been used separately in previous works [4, 7], using them together on a well know benchmarking data set (Reuter's data set) has not been previously reported.

On the other hand, the second architecture is based on a new idea where the SOM acts as an encoder to represent a large input space by finding a smaller set of prototypes. In contrast to previous methods, such a scheme significantly reduces *a priori* assumptions regarding suitable word features. Hence, code-books for automatic clustering are formed by building up an understanding of documents by first considering the relationships between characters (the first-level SOMs), then words (the second-level SOMs), and finally, word co-occurrences (the third-level SOMs).

Training and testing results for 25 document categories (as described in section 4) of the Reuters data set to utilize the above two systems have been very promising. Architecture-2 outperformed architecture-1 on this data set based on the editing distance between output clusters and the correct labels of the data set. Future work will develop a classifier, which will work in conjunction to these clustering systems and apply the technique to a wider cross-section of benchmark data sets. In addition, we are also interested in the utilization of this system to perform document categorization and as an indexing mechanism for a document database so that it does not need retraining for each new document category added.

REFERENCES

[1] Boone G., Concept features in Re:Agent, and intelligent e-mail agent, *Proceedings of the 2nd International Conference on Autonomous Agents (Agents '98)*, pages 141–148, New York, 9–13, 1998. ACM Press.

[2] Chen H., Schuffels C., Orwig R., Internet categorization and search: A self-organizing approach, *Journal of Visual Communication and Image Representation*, Vol. 7, No.1, pp. 88-102, March 1996.

[3] Freeman R., Yin H., Allinson N. M., Self-organizing maps for tree view based hierarchical document clustering, *Proceedings of the IEEE 2002 International Joint Conference on Neural Networks*.

[4] Halici, U., Ongun, G., Fingerprint classification through self-organizing feature maps modified to treat uncertainties, *Proceedings of the IEEE*, vol.84, no.10, 1996, pp. 1497-1512.

[5] Haykin S., *Neural Networks - A comprehensive foundation*, Chapter-9: Self-organizing maps, Second Edition, Prentice Hall, 1999, ISBN 0-13-273350-1.

[6] Kaski, S., Dimensionality reduction by random mapping: Fast similarity computation for clustering, *Proceedings of the IJCNN'98 Int. Joint Conf. Neural Networks*, 1998, pp. 413-418.

[7] Kohonen T., Kaski S., Lagus K., Salojrvi J., Honkela J., Paatero V., Saarela A., Self organization of a massive document collection, *IEEE Transactions on Neural Networks*, Vol.11, No.3., pp. 574-585, May 2000.

[8] Lin X., Soergel D., Marchionini G., A self-organizing semantic map for information retrieval, *Proceedings of the 14th Annu. Int. ACM/SIGIR Conf. Research and Development in Information Retrieval*, 1991, pp. 262-269.

[9] Merkl D., Exploration of document collections with self-organizing maps: A novel approach to similarity representation, *Principles of Data Mining and Knowledge Discovery*, pages 101–111, 1997.

[10] Merkl D., Lessons learned in text document classification, *Proceedings of WSOM'97, Workshop on Self-Organizing Maps*, 1997.

[11] Pal, S.K., Talwar V., Mitra, P., Web mining in soft computing framework: Relevance, state of the art and future directions, *IEEE Transactions on Neural Networks*, vol.13, no.5, 2002, pp. 1163-1177.

[12] P. Patrick, D. Lin, Document Clustering with Committees, Proceedings of SIGIR'02, pp.199-206

[13] Reuters data set, http://www.daviddlewis.com/resources/testcollections/reuters21578/

[14] Salton G., McGill M. J., Introduction to Modern Information Retrieval, McGraw Hill, 1983.

[15] Scholtes, J.C., Unsupervised learning and the information retrieval problem, *Proceedings of the IJCNN'91 Int. Joint Conf. Neural Networks*, vol.I, 1991, pp. 95-100.

[16] Sebastiani, F., Machine learning in automated text categorization, *ACM Computing Surveys*, vol.34, no.1, 2002, pp. 1-47.

[17] Vesanto J., Himberg J., Alhoniemi E., Parhankangas J., Self-organizing map in Matlab: The SOM toolbox, *Proceedings of the Matlab DSP Conference*, pages 35–40, 1999.

Neural Networks for Web Page Classification Based on Augmented PCA

Ali Selamat and Sigeru Omatu
Division of Computer and Systems Sciences, Graduate School of Engineering,
Osaka Prefecture University, Sakai, Osaka 599-8531, Japan.
Telephone: +81-722-54-9278
Fax: +81-722-57-1788
Email: aselamat@sig.cs.osakafu-u.ac.jp, omatu@cs.osakafu-u.ac.jp

Abstract— Automatic categorization is the only viable method to deal with the scaling problem of the World Wide Web (WWW). In this paper, we propose a news web page classification method (WPCM). The WPCM uses a neural network with inputs obtained by both the principal components and class profile-based features (CPBF). Each news web page is represented by the term-weighting scheme. As the number of unique words in the collection set is big, the principal component analysis (PCA) has been used to select the most relevant features for the classification. Then the final output of the PCA is augmented with the feature vectors from the class-profile which contains the most regular words in each class before feeding them to the neural networks. We have manually selected the most regular words that exist in each class and weighted them using an entropy weighting scheme. The fixed number of regular words from each class will be used as a feature vectors together with the reduced principal components from the PCA. These feature vectors are then used as the input to the neural networks for classification. The experimental evaluation demonstrates that the WPCM method provides acceptable classification accuracy with the sports news datasets.

I. INTRODUCTION

Neural networks have been widely applied by many researchers to classify the text documents with different types of feature vectors. Wermeter [1] has used the document title as the vectors to be used for a document categorization. Lam et al. [2] have used the principal component analysis (PCA) method as a feature reduction technique of the input data to the neural networks. However, if some original terms are particularly good when discriminating a class category, the discrimination power may be lost in the new vector space after using the Latent Semantic Indexing (LSI) as described by Sebastini [3].

Here, we propose a web page classification method (WPCM), which is base on the PCA and class profile-based features (CPBF). Each web page is represented by the term frequency-weighting scheme. As the dimensionality of a feature vector in the collection set is big, the PCA has been used to reduce it into a small number of principal components. Then we augment the feature vectors generated from the PCA with the feature vectors from the class-profile which contains the most regular words in each class before feeding them to the neural networks for classification. We have manually selected the most regular words that exist in each class and weighted them using an entropy weighting scheme [4]. *The CNN* [5] and *the Japan Times* [6] English sports news web pages have been used for the classification purpose. The Bayesian, TF-IDF, and WPCM methods have been used as a benchmark test for the classification accuracy. The experimental evaluation demonstrates that the proposed method provides an acceptable classification accuracy with the sports news datasets.

The organization of this paper is as follows: The news classification using the WPCM is described in Section II. The preprocessing of web pages is explained in Section III. The comparisons of web pages classification using the Bayesian, TF-IDF, and WPCM methods are discussed in Section IV. The discussions on the web pages classification results using the WPCM, Bayesian, and TF-IDF apporaches are described in Section V. In Section VI, we will conclude the classification accuracy by using the WPCM compared with other methods.

II. NEWS CLASSIFICATION USING THE WPCM

The news web pages have different characteristics where the text length for each of them is variable. Also the structures of the pages are different in the tags usage (i.e., XML, html, SGML tags, etc.). Furthermore, a huge number of distinct words exist in those pages as there is no restriction on a word usage in the news web pages discussed by Hisao et al.[7]. The high dimensionality of *the CNN* and *the Japan Times* news web pages dataset has made the classification process difficult. This is because there are many categories of news in the web news pages such as sports, weathers, politics, economy, etc. In each category there are many different classes. For example, the classes that exist in the business category are stock market, financial investment, personal finance, etc. Our approach is based on the sports news category of web pages. In order to classify the news web pages, we propose the WPCM which uses the PCA and the CPBF as the input to the neural networks. Firstly, we have used the PCA algorithm [8] to reduce the original data vectors to a small number of relevant features. Then we combine these features to the CPBF before inputting them to the neural networks for classification as shown in Fig. 1.

A. Preprocessing of Web Pages

The classification process of a news web page using the WPCM method is shown in Fig. 1. It consists of a web news retrieval process, stemming and stopping processes, a feature reduction process using our proposed method, and a web classification process using error back-propagation neural networks. The retrieving process of sports news web pages has been done by our software agent during night-time [9]. Only the latest sports news web pages category will be retrieved

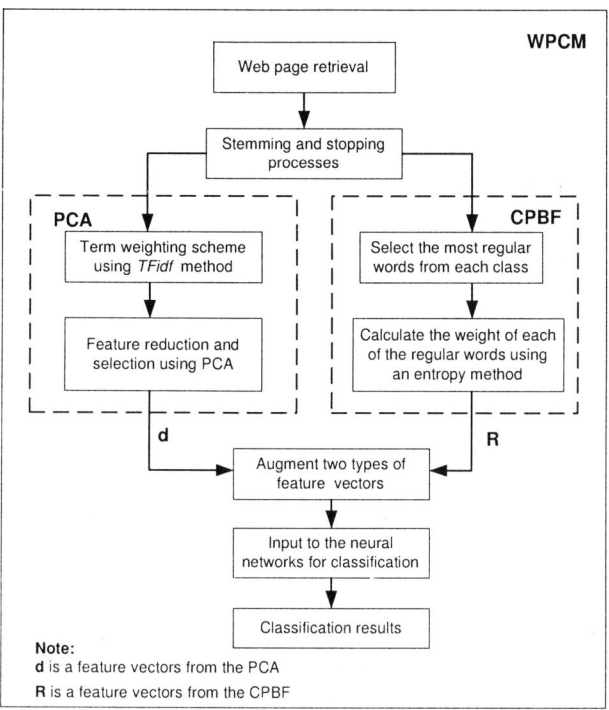

Fig. 1. The process of classification a news web page using the WPCM method.

TABLE I
THE DOCUMENT-TERM FREQUENCY DATA MATRIX AFTER THE STEMMING AND STOPPING PROCESSES.

Doc_j	TF_1	TF_2	...	TF_m
Doc_1	2	4	...	5
Doc_2	2	3	...	2
Doc_3	2	3	...	2
Doc_4	2	6	...	1
Doc_5	4	3	...	3
⋮	⋮	⋮	⋮	⋮
Doc_n	1	3	...	7

from *the CNN* and *the Japan Times* web servers from the WWW. Then these web pages will be stored in the local news database. Stopping is a process of removing the most frequent word that exists in a web page document such as 'to', 'and', 'it', etc. Removing these words will save spaces for storing document contents and reduce time taken during the search process. Stemming is a process of extracting each word from a web page document by reducing it to a possible root word. For example, the words 'compares', 'compared', and 'comparing' have similar meaning with a word 'compare'. We have used the Porter stemming algorithm [10] to select only 'compare' to be used as a root word in a web page document. After the stemming and stopping processes of the terms in each document, we will represent them as the document-term frequency matrix ($Doc_j \times TF_{jk}$) as shown in Table I. Doc_j is referring to each web page document that exists in the news database where $j = 1, \ldots, n$. Term frequency TF_{jk} is the number of how many times the distinct word w_k occurs in document Doc_j where $k = 1, \ldots, m$. The calculation of the terms weight x_{jk} of each word w_k is done by using a method that has been used by Salton [11] which is given by

$$x_{jk} = TF_{jk} \times idf_k \qquad (1)$$

where the document frequency df_k is the total number of documents in the database that contains the word w_k. The inverse document frequency $idf_k = log(\frac{n}{df_k})$ where n is the total number of documents in the database.

1) Feature reduction using the PCA: Suppose that we have A, which is a matrix with document-terms weight as below

$$\mathbf{A} = \begin{pmatrix} x_{11} & x_{12} & x_{1k} & \cdots & x_{1m} \\ x_{21} & x_{22} & x_{2k} & \cdots & x_{2m} \\ x_{31} & x_{32} & x_{3k} & \cdots & \cdots \\ \vdots & \vdots & \vdots & \ddots & \cdots \\ x_{n1} & x_{n2} & x_{nk} & \cdots & x_{nm} \end{pmatrix}$$

where x_{jk} is the terms weight that exist in the collection of documents. The definitions of j, k, m, and n have been described in the previous paragraph. There are a few steps to be followed in order to calculate the principal components of data matrix A. The mean of m variables in data matrix A will be calculated as follows

$$\overline{x}_k = \frac{1}{n}\sum_{j=1}^{n} x_{jk}. \qquad (2)$$

After that the covariance of matrix $S = \{s_{jk}\}$ is calculated. The variance, s_k^2, is given by

$$s_k^2 = \frac{1}{n}\sum_{j=1}^{n}(x_{jk} - \overline{x}_k)^2 \qquad (3)$$

where $k = 1, 2, \ldots, m$. The covariance, s_{ik}, is given by

$$s_{ik} = \frac{1}{n}\sum_{j=1}^{n}(x_{ji} - \overline{x}_i)(x_{jk} - \overline{x}_k) \qquad (4)$$

where $i = 1, \ldots, m$. Then we determine the eigenvalues and eigenvectors of the covariance matrix S which is a real symmetric positive matrix. An eigenvalue λ and a nonzero vector $\mathbf{e}$ can be found such that, $S\mathbf{e} = \lambda\mathbf{e}$ where $\mathbf{e}$ is an eigenvector of S.

In order to find a nonzero vector $\mathbf{e}$ the characteristic equation $|S - \lambda I| = 0$ must be solved. If S is an $m \times m$ matrix of full rank, m eigenvalues $(\lambda_1, \lambda_2, \ldots, \lambda_m)$ can be found. By using $(S - \lambda I)\mathbf{e} = 0$, all corresponding eigenvectors can be found. The eigenvalues and corresponding eigenvectors will be sorted so that $\lambda_1 \geq \lambda_2 \geq \ldots \geq \lambda_m$. The eigenvector matrix is represented as $\mathbf{e} = [u_1 \ u_2 \ u_3 \ u_4 \ \ldots \ u_m]$. A diagonal nonzero eigenvalue matrix is represented as

$$\mathbf{\Lambda} = \begin{pmatrix} \lambda_1 & 0 & \cdots & 0 \\ 0 & \lambda_2 & 0 & 0 \\ \vdots & \vdots & \ddots & \cdots \\ 0 & 0 & 0 & \lambda_m \end{pmatrix}.$$

In order to get the principal components of matrix S, we will perform eigenvalue decomposition which is given by

$$S = \mathbf{e}\mathbf{\Lambda}\mathbf{e^T}. \quad (5)$$

Then we select the first $d \leq m$ eigenvectors where d is the desired value, e.g., 100, 200, 400, etc. The set of principal components is represented as $Y_1 = \mathbf{e}_1^T x$, $Y_2 = \mathbf{e}_2^T x$, ..., $Y_d = \mathbf{e}_d^T x$. An $n \times d$ matrix M is represented as

$$\mathbf{M} = \begin{pmatrix} f_{11} & f_{12} & \cdots & f_{1d} \\ f_{21} & f_{22} & \cdots & f_{2d} \\ f_{31} & f_{32} & \cdots & \cdots \\ f_{41} & f_{42} & \ddots & \cdots \\ f_{n1} & f_{n2} & \cdots & f_{nd} \end{pmatrix}$$

where f_{ij} is a reduced feature vectors from the $m \times m$ original data size to $n \times d$ size.

2) Feature selection using the CPBF: For the feature selection using the class profile-based approach, we have manually identified the most regular words that exist in each category and weighted them using an entropy weighting scheme [4] before adding them to the feature vectors that have been selected from the PCA. For example, the words that exist regularly in a baseball class are 'Ichiro', 'baseball', 'league', 'baseman', etc. Then a fixed number of regular words from each class will be used as a feature vectors together with the reduced principal components from the PCA. These feature vectors are then used as the input to the neural networks for classification. The entropy weighting scheme on each term is calculated as $L_{jk} \times G_k$ where L_{jk} is the local weighting of the term k and G_k is the global weighting of the term k. The L_{jk} and G_k are given by

$$L_{jk} = \begin{cases} 1 + \log TF_{jk} & (TF_{jk} > 0) \\ 0 & (TF_{jk} = 0) \end{cases} \quad (6)$$

and

$$G_k = \frac{1 + \sum_{k=1}^{n} \frac{TF_{jk}}{F_k} \log \frac{TF_{jk}}{F_k}}{\log n} \quad (7)$$

where n is the number of documents in a collection and TF_{jk} is the term frequency of each word in Doc_j as mentioned previously. The F_k is a frequency of the term k in the entire document collection. We have selected $R = 50$ words that have the highest entropy value to be added to the first d components from the PCA as an input to the neural networks for classification.

3) Input data to the neural networks: After the preprocessing of news web pages, a vocabulary that contains all the unique words in the news database has been created. We have limited the number of unique words in the vocabulary to 1,800 as the number of distinct words is big. Each of the words in the vocabulary represents one feature vector. Each feature vector contains the document-terms weight. The high

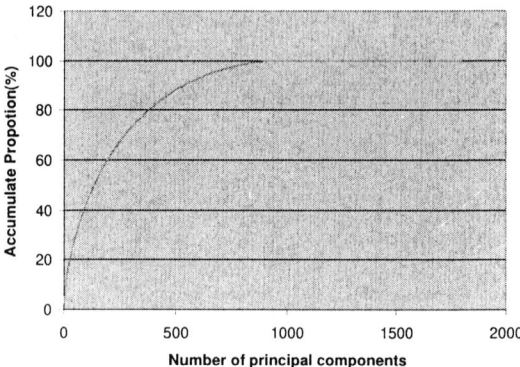

Fig. 2. Accumulated proportion of principal components generated by the PCA.

dimensionality of feature vectors to be as an input to the neural networks is not practical due to poor scalability and performance. Therefore, the PCA has been used to reduce the original feature vectors $m = 1,800$ into a small number of principal components. In our case, we have selected the value of $d = 400$ together with $R = 50$ features selected from the CPBF approach since this parameter performs better for web news classification compared to other parameters to be input to the neural networks. The loading factor graph for the accumulated proportion of eigenvalues are shown in Fig. 2. The value of d contribute 81.6% of proportions from the original feature vectors.

4) Characterization of the neural networks: The architecture of neural networks used for the classification process is shown in Fig. 3. The number of input layers (p) is 450 where principal components (d=400) and R (=50). The number of hidden layers (q) is 25. The trial and error approach has been used to find a suitable number of hidden layers that provide good classification accuracy based on the input data to the neural networks. The number of output layers (r) is 11 which is based on the number of classes in the sports news category as shown in Table II in the next page.

We have defined t as the iteration number, η is a learning rate, α is a momentum rate, θ_q is a bias on hidden unit q, θ_r is a bias on output unit r, δ_q is the generalized error through a layer q, and δ_r is the generalized error between layers q and r. The input values to the neural network are represented by $f_1, f_2, \ldots, f_{450}$. Adaptation of the weights between hidden (q) and input (p) layers is given by

$$W_{qp}(t+1) = W_{qp}(t) + \Delta W_{qp}(t+1) \quad (8)$$

where

$$\Delta W_{qp}(t+1) = \eta \delta_q O_p + \alpha \Delta W_{qp}(t) \quad (9)$$

$$\delta_q = O_q(1 - O_q) \sum_r \delta_r W_{rq}. \quad (10)$$

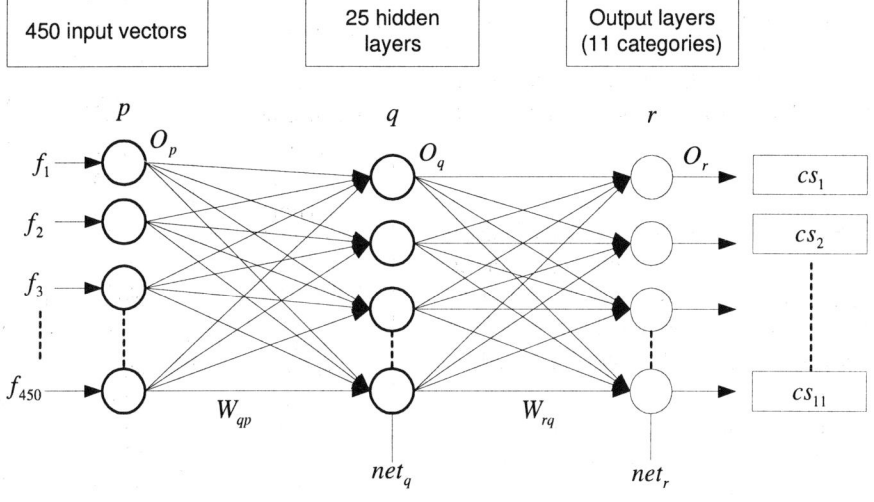

$f_{1..450}$ represents input vectors from the PCA and CPBF.

cs_a represents a class of web sports documents where $a = 1,...,11$.

Fig. 3. The feature vectors from the PCA and CPBF are fed to the neural networks for classification.

TABLE II

THE NUMBER OF TRAINING AND TESTING DOCUMENTS THAT ARE STORED IN THE NEWS DATABASE. THESE ARE THE CLASSES THAT EXIST IN SPORTS CATEGORY.

Class (cs)	Training documents (T)	Test documents
1. baseball	100	101
2. boxing	70	12
3. cycling	84	40
4. football	50	10
5. golf	100	120
6. motor-sports	50	11
7. hockey	70	20
8. rugby	50	13
9. skiing	70	26
10. swimming	70	12
11. tennis	70	17
Total	784	382

Note that the first transfer function at hidden layer (q) is given by

$$net_q = \sum_q W_{qp}O_p + \theta_q \qquad (11)$$

$$O_q = f(net_q) = 1/(1 + e^{-net_q}). \qquad (12)$$

Adaptation of the weights between output (r) and hidden (q) layers is given by

$$W_{rq}(t+1) = W_{rq}(t) + \Delta W_{rq}(t+1) \qquad (13)$$

where

$$\Delta W_{rq}(t+1) = \eta \delta_r O_q + \alpha \Delta W_{rq}(t) \qquad (14)$$

$$\delta_r = O_r(1 - O_r)(t_r - O_r). \qquad (15)$$

Then the output function at the output layer (k) is given by

$$net_r = \sum_r W_{rq}O_q + \theta_r \qquad (16)$$

$$O_r = f(net_r) = 1/(1 + e^{-net_r}). \qquad (17)$$

The error back-propagation neural networks parameters are set as in Table III.

TABLE III

THE ERROR BACK-PROPAGATION NEURAL NETWORKS PARAMETERS FOR TEST RUN1 AND RUN2.

NN Parameters	Run1	Run2
1. Learning rate (η)	0.05	0.005
2. Momentum rate (α)	0.01	0.001
3. Number of iteration (t)	1200	1000
4. Mean square error (MSE)	0.05	0.005

III. EXPERIMENTS

For the experiments, we have used a set of documents and classes as shown in Table II. There are 784 documents belonging to 1 or more classes. To select a set of documents for training, we have chosen 200 documents randomly to be a positive training set. For the negative examples, another 200 documents are selected randomly from another set of documents, which do not belong to the 11 classes set. The total number of training documents is 400 including from the negative examples and positives examples. We have used the same test as being done by Yang and Honavar [12], which includes the Bayesian and TF-IDF classifiers. Also we include the WPCM approach as a comparison to the methods that are used in order to examine the applicability of the classification system. The description of WPCM has been mentioned in Section II. The TF-IDF and Bayesian methods for the tests are described as below.

A. TF-IDF measures

TF-IDF classifier is based on the relevant feedback algorithm by Rocchio using the vector space model [13]. The algorithm represents documents as vectors so that the documents with similar contents have similar vectors. Each component of a vector corresponds to a term in the document, typically a word.

The weight of each component is calculated using the term frequency inverse document frequency weighting scheme (TF-IDF) which tries to reward words that occur many times but in few documents. To classify a new document Doc', the cosines of the prototype vectors with corresponding document vectors are calculated for each class. Doc' is assigned to the class which its document vector has the highest cosine. Further description on the TF-IDF measure is described by Joachim [14].

B. Bayesian classifier

For statistical classification, we have used a standard Bayesian classifier [14]. When using the Bayesian classifier, we have assumed that term's occurrence is independent of other terms. We want to find a class cs that gives the highest conditional probability given a document Doc'. Let $w_k^m = \{w_1, w_2, \ldots, w_m\}$ is the words representing the textual content of the document Doc' and let k denote the term number where $k = 1, \ldots, m$. The classification score is measured by

$$P(cs) = \prod_{k=1}^{m} P(w_k|cs) \quad (18)$$

where $P(cs)$ is the prior probability of a class cs, and $P(w_k|cs)$ is the likelihood of a word w_k in the class cs that is estimated on a labeled training document. A given web page document is then classified in a class that maximizes the classification score. If the scores for all the classes in the sports category are less than a given threshold, then the document is considered unclassified. The Rainbow toolkit [15] has been used for the classification of the training and test news web pages using the Bayesian and TF-IDF methods.

IV. SIMULATION RESULTS

The results of individual simulations using the Bayesian, TF-IDF, and WPCM are shown in Table IV. The accuracies using the Bayesian, TF-IDF, and WPCM are 81.00%, 83.94%, and 84.10%, respectively. Also we have found that if the number of training and test documents are low, i.e., 10-80 pages, the accuracy of classification is less than 85%. The classification accuracies of the golf, rugby, skiing, swimming, and tennis classes using the WPCM approach is better compared to the Bayesian and TF-IDF approaches, which are 95.90%, 75.26%, 89.90%, 85.90%, 96.02%, respectively, as

TABLE IV
THE PERCENTAGE OF THE NEWS WEB PAGES CLASSIFICATION ACCURACY USING THE BAYESIAN, TF-IDF, AND WPCM METHODS.

Docs. Class	Bayesian (%)	TF-IDF (%)	WPCM (%)
1. baseball	99.01	96.04	96.04
2. boxing	86.80	65.80	74.20
3. cycling	80.00	68.00	74.20
4. football	71.40	85.30	76.00
5. golf	96.67	95.00	95.90
6. hockey	80.21	85.50	78.86
7. motor sports	85.65	89.90	82.60
8. rugby	63.56	72.60	75.26
9. skiing	63.60	84.08	89.90
10. swimming	75.21	88.00	85.90
11. tennis	82.21	94.30	96.02
Average	**81.00**	**83.94**	**84.10**

shown in Table IV. The CPBF feature selection process applied in the WPCM approach is based on the highest entropy of the keywords calculated as in (6) and (7). The first 50 keywords with the highest entropy values are selected and combined with the features taken from the PCA approach. The suitability of the keywords selection belonging to the particular classes has not been carefully considered in the WPCM approach while doing the experiments as described in Section III. For example, the entropies for the keywords 'famous', 'field', 'skills', and 'manager' from the class soccer are selected although these keywords also exist in the other classes such as the basketball and baseball classes. However, identifying keywords alone are not enough. The associated weights related to each of the keywords are also important to improve the classification performance using the proposed approach as the same word may occur in different classes. This is the main reason why the classification accuracies of the boxing and cycling classes (86.80% and 80.00%) are better when using the Bayesian approach compared with the WPCM approach as shown in Table IV. Furthermore, the stemming and stopping processes are also degrading the classification performance using the WPCM approach compared with the Bayesian approach. Also, the classification accuracies of the football and hockey classes (85.30% and 85.50%) are better when using the TF-IDF approach compared with the WPCM approach as shown in Table IV. This is because the contents of training documents belong to the football and hockey classes contain many sparse keywords. A better document selection approach needs to be used for selecting the candidate documents from each class in order to increase the classification results by using the WPCM approach. The results of the experiments for the error backpropagation neural networks parameters as in Table III are shown in Figs. 4 and 5. For the momentum rate $\alpha = 0.01$, we have found that the local minima exist. But if the value of $\alpha = 0.001$ is used, we have found that the MSE is smooth. For the rest of the experiments we have used the parameter $\alpha = 0.001$ as it indicates a stable MSE value to be used for our classification process. We have also done an experiment on newsgroups datasets such as *alt.politics.people*, *alt.politics.mideast*, and *alt.politics.misc* [15] as a comparison. The results of classification using the WPCM on these datasets are shown in Table V. The average results of classifications are 87.82%. This indicates that, if the number of training datasets are more than 300 on each class, the possibility of getting a good classification performance is high. Although the WPCM approach provides an improvement of the classification results, the time taken to classify the web news pages is significantly long by using the the proposed approach compared to the other approaches.

TABLE V

THE CLASSIFICATION RESULT OF 3 NEWSGROUP DATASETS [15] USING THE WPCM METHOD.

Doc. Class	Training	Test	Result (%)
Alt.politics.people	300	1000	93.7
Alt.politics.mideast	300	1000	89.0
Alt.politics.misc	400	1000	80.8
Average	-	-	**87.82**

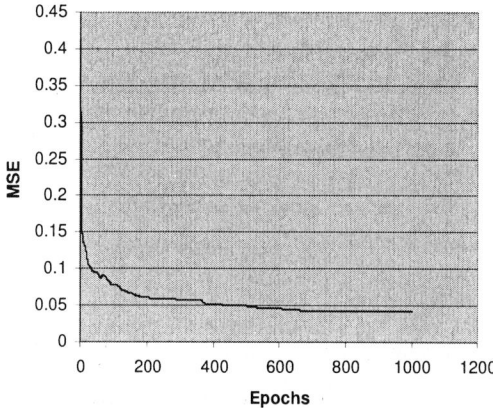

Fig. 5. The results of Run2 for MSE vs. Epochs for the news web pages classification using the neural networks (momentum rate, $\alpha = 0.001$).

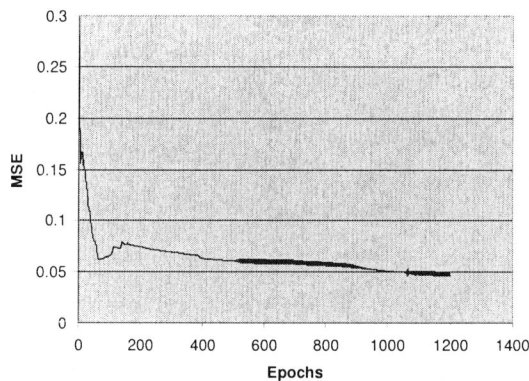

Fig. 4. The results of Run1 for MSE vs. Epochs for the news web pages classification using the neural networks (momentum rate, $\alpha = 0.01$).

V. CONCLUSIONS

We have presented a new approach of web news classification using the WPCM. In our approach, the pre-processing work needs to be done in the selection and calculation of feature vectors before the news web pages can be classified. The result is not accurate enough if the type of terms, i.e., baseball terms, football terms, etc., are not carefully chosen. The stemming process during the feature selections also affects the performance of classifications. As a conclusion, the WPCM technique has been applied to classify *the CNN* and *the Japan Times* sports news web pages. The experimental evaluation with different classification algorithms demonstrates that this method provides acceptable classification accuracy with the sports news datasets. Future works will include a web news classification using a support vector machine (SVM) with an automatic feature selection approach.

REFERENCES

[1] Stefan Wermeter, "Neural network agents for learning semantic text classification", *Information Retrieval*, Vol. 3. No. 2, pp. 87-103, 2000.

[2] Savio L.Y. Lam and Dik Lun Lee, "Feature reduction for neural network based text categorization", in *Proceedings of the 6th International Conference on Database Systems for Advanced Applications 19 - 22 April, Hsinchu, Taiwan*, 1999.

[3] Fabrizo Sebastini, "Machine learning in automated text categorization", *ACM Computing Surveys*, vol. 34, No.1, 2002.

[4] Dumais, S. T. , "Improving the retrieval of information from external sources", *Behavior Research Methods, Instruments and Computers*, Vol. 23, No. 2, pp. 229-236, 1991.

[5] The CNN web news page, (http://www.cnn.com), 2001.

[6] The Japan Times web news page, (http://www.japantimes.co.jp), 2001.

[7] Hisao Mase and Hiroshi Tsuji, "Experiments on automatic web page categorization for information retrieval system", *Journal of Information Processing, IPSJ Journal*, Feb. 2001, pp. 334-347, 2001.

[8] R. Calvo, M. Partridge, and M. Jabri, "A comparative study of principal components analysis techniques", in *Proc. Ninth Australian Conf. on Neural Networks*, Brisbane, QLD., pp. 276-281, 1998.

[9] A. Selamat, S. Omatu, H. Yanagimoto, "Information retrieval from the Internet using mobile agent search system", *International Conference of Information Technology and Multimedia 2001 (ICIMU),University Tenaga Nasional (UNITEN), Malaysia*, August 13-15, 2001.

[10] Sparck Jones, Karen, and Peter Willet, *Readings in information retrieval*, San Francisco: Morgan Kaufmann, USA, 1997.

[11] Salton & McGill, *Introduction to modern information retrieval*, New York, McGraw-Hill, USA, 1983.

[12] Yang, J., Pai, P., Honavar, V., and Miller, L. "Mobile intelligent agents for document classification and retrieval: a machine learning approach", In *Proceedings of the European Symposium on Cybernetics and Systems Research*, 1998.

[13] R. R. Korfhage, *Information storage and retrieval*, John Wiley and Sons, Inc, USA, 1997.

[14] Joachims, Thorsten, "Probabilistic analysis of the Rocchio algorithm with TFIDF for text categorization", *Proceedings of International Conference on Machine Learning (ICML)*, 1997.

[15] McCallum, Andrew Kachites, "Bow: A toolkit for statistical language modeling, text retrieval, classification and clustering", (http://www.cs.cmu.edu/~mccallum/bow) , 1996.

Neural Networks Mine for Gold at the Greyhound Racetrack

Ulf Johansson and Cecilia Sönströd
Department of Business and Informatics
University of Borås
SWEDEN
ulf.johansson@hb.se

Abstract: This paper contains a case study where neural networks are used for data mining in the gambling domain. The proposed method uses only publicly available data to train neural networks for predicting the outcome of greyhound racing. Several different betting formats are evaluated, including Win, Quinella and Exacta. The betting strategy based on the trained neural networks is as simple as possible, but still the suggested approach constantly beats the market (i.e. returns a positive result) for the harder formats. The presented technique could be used as a base for a more refined prediction tool for greyhound racing and similar domains. More generally, the paper serves as a demonstration of the power of neural networks when applied to hard and unusual data mining tasks.

I. INTRODUCTION

Data Mining is, according to Bigus [1], the efficient discovery of valuable non-apparent information from large sets of data.

When used in industry, the data sets are normally the property of the data miner, so neither the exact techniques used nor the results obtained are published.

Within the research community there are several approaches to data mining, including some from the field of Machine Learning (ML). For an extensive survey see [2].

Artificial Neural Networks (ANNs) have been applied to many different problem domains with overall good results. A survey of real-world applications can be found in [3]. ANNs have not, however, been used to a great extent on data mining problems. The main reason for this is arguably that the models learned by ANNs are opaque while the data miner would like to have a comprehensible representation to facilitate decision-making. For a discussion on this subject see e.g. [4] or [5].

Most studies involving ANNs handle problems where there is a strong but complex relationship between input and output. The powerful ANN inductively constructs a model (function) between the input and the output that captures the underlying relationship very well.

The standard way of measuring success is statistical calculations; e.g. mean square error (MSE) or correlation coefficient. Some papers also report comparisons between different ML techniques; e.g. ANNs and decision trees. The proposed approach is rarely compared to methods in actual use, and even more seldom the measurement used is economic gain.

Some domains, however, have the interesting property that different data mining methods continuously compete against each other using more or less public data. The success of one particular method must therefore be evaluated in relation to all others. Sometimes the entire process can be regarded as a zero-sum game, implying that all methods with a positive result are successful in an absolute way.

In some of these domains, the rules of the "game" are tougher than zero-sum; i.e. only a part of the stakes is returned to the players. Most bookmaker games are of this type; e.g. horseracing and greyhound racing. The exact proportion of all stakes that is returned to the gamblers differs between bookmakers and games. Typical for this kind of game is that the odds are finalized after all bets have been placed, thus guaranteeing a positive result for the bookmaker. The gamblers are really just competing for a part of the total stakes and the odds are used to determine how this part should be divided. Another key property of these games is that although chance plays a major part, most gamblers try to use historical data to predict the outcome. Enormous amounts of statistics about competing horses and greyhounds are available to the potential gambler.

This study is performed on greyhound racing with the motivation that it constitutes an interesting and demanding data mining problem, since:

- The relationship between the input variables (a greyhound's previous performance) and the output (predicted performance in the next race) is likely to be weak and/or complex.

- It is easy to evaluate success by using a natural measurement, i.e. economic gain.

- The proposed method must use only data available to all competition. A good result is therefore not due to access to more data but to a more powerful method of converting the data into information.

- To actually produce a positive result the approach must perform much better than the average gambler since the format of the game is worse than zero-sum.

A. Greyhound Racing

Greyhound racing is of course a sport for both trainers and owners (and probably for the greyhounds themselves), but is mainly viewed as a gambling object by the public.

Most races (at least in the US) have eight contending greyhounds. The length of the race differs but a common distance is 5/16 mile.

A lot of statistics about each competing greyhound is gathered in the freely available race program. It is safe to say that most gamblers use only this data when placing their bets.

The odds are continually changing during the betting process, to reflect the betting that has occurred. Only just before the race starts are the odds settled. Most gamblers will however consider the current odds when deciding how to bet.

There are several different betting formats. Some formats involve betting on more than one race; e.g. "daily double", which requires the gambler to pick the winner in two consecutive races. This paper focuses on betting options for one race only. Below is a list of some of the formats available.

- **Win**. The most obvious format. The gambler must pick the winning greyhound.

- **Place**. The gambler must pick a greyhound that finishes first or second.

- **Show**. Same as Place but the greyhound could also finish third.

- **Quinella**. The gambler picks two greyhounds and is successful if they finish first and second (regardless of order).

- **Exacta**. Same as Quinella, but now the greyhounds must finish in the order chosen by the gambler.

- **Trifecta/Superfecta**. Like Exacta but with three or four greyhounds respectively.

Very little work about machine learning approaches to greyhound racing and related domains has been published. The only article found by the authors of this paper, is Chen et al. from 1993 [6]. Many of the concepts from that article are used in this study, including the idea to use single greyhounds as input objects instead of entire races. Unfortunately Chen et al. use their test set to fix some parameters; i.e. number of epochs and hidden units. The results reported for the experiments are therefore not very significant and have little bearing on what could be expected from a fresh data set.

II. METHOD

There are several ways to model a race. In this study the technique is to use one greyhound per pattern for the neural net. During training each greyhound is classified as either winner or not winner; i.e. the desired output is 1 for a winner and 0 for a non-winner. When predicting for the betting format Win, only one greyhound from every race (the actual winner) is tagged a winner. When predicting Exacta or Quinella two greyhounds are tagged as winners.

When simulating a race, after training is complete, the greyhound with the highest winner-value in that race is the predicted winner.

A. The data set

All data is from Gulf Greyhound Park, La Marque, Texas. The chosen racetrack is one of the largest in the world and arranges races six days a week. Another reason for using this racetrack in the study is the high quantity of publicly available data.

The races used come form a period of approximately one month and all data is taken from the race programs at the website of the racetrack. For the experiments only races on the distance 5/16 miles were used. A few races with less than eight greyhounds were removed from the data set. All in all the training, validation and test sets consist of 249/100/100 races respectively.

B. Betting formats

The three "normal" betting formats: Win, Quinella and Exacta are tested. In addition two more formats: "Two-Win" and "Double-Exacta" are also evaluated.

Two-Win is simply two Win bets on two different greyhounds in the same race. Double-Exacta is two different Exacta bets (instead of one Quinella bet) on a pair of greyhounds in a single race.

C. Variables and preprocessing

There are many potential input variables listed in the race program. In general, following Chen et al, 18 input variables are selected (see Table 1).

TABLE 1
INPUT VARIABLES

#	Description	Type
1	Won races this year	%
2	Races finished 2:nd this year	%
3	Races finished 3:rd this year	%
4	Races finished 4:th this year	%
5	Won races previous year	%
6	Races finished 2:nd previous year	%
7	Races finished 3:rd previous year	%
8	Races finished 4:th previous year	%
9	Fastest time last three races	s
10	Average position out of box last three races	(1-8)
11	Average finish position last three races	(1-8)
12	Average time last three races	s
13	Average class of race last three races	(1-7)
14	Fastest time last twelve races	s
15	Average position out of box last twelve races	(1-8)
16	Average finish position last twelve races	(1-8)
17	Average time last twelve races	s
18	Average class of race last twelve races	(1-7)

To capture the fact that a race is a competition between the participants all variables have to be relative to the other greyhounds in the race. For each race and each variable the best value is set to 1 and the worst to 0. All others are proportionally normalized between the two extremes.

When training to predict winners, only greyhounds that actually won their races have a desired output value of 1; all others have a desired output of 0. When training for Exacta or Quinella the two first greyhounds have desired outputs of 1, i.e. there is no difference between the winner and the runner-up.

The odds are not included among the input variables for several reasons. First of all the final odds are only available immediately before the race starts. Second, the risk is that the network should be too eager to predict the favorite, since the correlation between the odds and the actual winner probably is high. Finally, the point of using a data mining tool in the first place is to discover "better" information than that available to the opposition. In this context the hope is to find greyhounds underrated by the competition, an edge that could be lost if the odds were included as input. We would probably win more often, but also most certainly miss the prosperous long shots.

D. *Architectures and experiment setup*

In the experiments feed-forward networks are used. The single hidden layer contains 4 hidden units. All units have the sigmoid non-linearity.

For each experiment 10 ANNs are trained and applied to the test set. The validation set is used for early stopping to avoid overtraining. The results from the 10 different nets are averaged to provide the final outcome. This is a standard technique to produce better results on unseen data, for details see [7].

To simulate a race in the test set, each competing greyhound is input to the ANN model. The model will attach a value to each greyhound, representing a relative belief in that greyhound.

There are several potential ways to use this "information"; i.e. to develop betting strategies. The most obvious is the one used here: in each race a bet is placed on the greyhound with the highest belief value attached to it. More sophisticated strategies should compare the belief values, both to other greyhound's and against the odds. Such strategies could bet on more than one greyhound (or refuse to bet at all) in a specific race. Obviously the size of the bet could also be varied.

E. *Experiments*

One experiment was conducted for each format chosen, resulting in five different experiments. For each experiment the ANN is trained on the training set and the validation set is used for early stopping to guarantee a network capable of generalization.

After training is complete the test set is traversed, race by race, to test the strategy used for the specific betting format. In each race fictional bets are placed on greyhounds according to the betting format and the strategy; see Table 2. Each experiment is repeated 20 times.

TABLE 2
BETTING FORMATS AND STRATEGIES

#	Format	Bet size	Strategy
1	Win	$2	Highest belief
2	Two-win	$2 + $2	Two highest beliefs
3	Quinella	$2	Two highest beliefs
4	Exacta	$3	Two highest beliefs. In order.
5	Double-Exacta	$3 + $3	Two highest beliefs. Both combinations.

III. RESULTS

In Table 3 below, the average results from the experiments are shown.

TABLE 3
EXPERIMENTAL RESULTS

#	Format	Correct	Net Result	%
1	Win	24,9	-$6,6	-3%
2	Two-win	34,3	-$54,2	-14%
3	Quinella	8,8	+$20,3	+10%
4	Exacta	6,1	+$114,1	+38%
5	Double-Exacta	9,1	+$39,4	+7%

For the Win format the method fails to return a positive result. It does however pick the winner one time out of four. This could be compared to random betting that would find the winner one time out of eight.

For the Two-Win format the method returns a substantial loss. It still finds the winner more often than random, though. It should be noted that the performance is much worse than for the Win format, indicating that the greyhound with the highest belief is a substantially better prediction than the greyhound with the second highest. Betting on two greyhounds does not come near doubling the correct picks.

Quinella is the first format to show a positive return. On average nine races out of 100 are correctly predicted. Random play would be right 3,5 times.

Exacta returns the best result with an amazing 38% gain. Six correctly predicted races is much better than random play (1,75).

Double-Exacta exhibits another positive result, even if it is not as good as Exacta. The same argument as for the comparison between Win and Double-Win could be applied here; i.e. the model found by the network has some precision in picking the winner, so the number of successful bets will not double when both combinations are played.

IV. CONCLUSIONS

Even if the method is kept simple the results produced stand out. It is especially interesting to note that the method performs better at the harder formats. This implies that it thrives on sometimes finding complex relationships for long shots, rather than just picking the easy favorites.

The positive outcome is a strong argument for the method since it uses only public information, also available to the opposition. The good result must therefore be credited to the neural network approach.

V. DISCUSSION AND FUTURE WORK

The data used in this study are from a specific period and racetrack. The next study should therefore use additional data (preferably from another track) to validate the results.

Another natural step is to find more sophisticated strategies. The odds should probably be included in the decision somehow. The authors do not believe, however, that the odds should be an input to the ANN.

ANNs are inherently incapable of explaining their "reasoning"; i.e. they are normally treated as black boxes. Often, however, it would be interesting to analyze the model found to identify relationships. This might be especially important for a domain where the association is weak. There are several techniques for "rule extraction" (for a survey see [8]) that could be applied on the ANNs from this study to create more transparent models. It would be interesting to compare the extracted representations to the heuristic rules used by human experts.

ACKNOWLEDGMENT

Most of the experimental work has been carried out as part of a bachelor thesis supervised by Ulf Johansson. The participating students from the Department of Business and Informatics at University of Borås were Kim Pilo and Leif Stockdale.

REFERENCES

[1] J. P. Bigus, *Data Mining with Neural Networks*, McGraw-Hill, 1996.
[2] U. Fayyad, G. Piatetsky-Shapiro, P. Smyth and R. Uthurusamy, *Advances in Knowledge Discovery and Data Mining*, AAAI Press / MIT Press, 1996.
[3] B. Widrow, D. E. Rumelhart and M. A. Lehr, "Neural networks: applications in industry, business and science," *Communication of the ACM*, Vol. 37, Issue 3, 1994, pp. 93-105.
[4] M. Craven and J. Shavlik, "Using Neural Networks for Data Mining," *Future Generation Computer Systems: special issue on Data Mining*, 1997, pp. 211-229.
[5] U. Johansson and L. Niklasson, "Neural Networks - from Prediction to Explanation," *Proc. IASTED International Conference Artificial Intelligence and Applications*, Malaga, Spain, 2002, pp. 93-98.
[6] H. Chen, P. Buntin, L. She, S. Sutjaho, C. Sommer and D. Neely, "Expert Prediction, Symbolic Learning and Neural Networks: an Experiment on Greyhound Racing, " *IEEE Intelligent Systems & their applications*, Vol 9, No 6, 1994, pp. 21-27.
[7] C. M. Bishop, *Neural Networks for Pattern Recognition*, Oxford University Press, 1995.
[8] R. Andrews, J. Diederich and A. B. Tickle, "A survey and critique of techniques for extracting rules from trained artificial neural networks," *Knowledge-Based Systems*, 8(6), 1995.

Learning Classifier Systems for Data Mining: A Comparison of XCS with Other Classifiers for the Forest Cover Data Set

A. J. Bagnall
School of Information Systems
University of East Anglia
Norwich, NR4 7TJ, England
e-mail : ajb@sys.uea.ac.uk

G. C. Cawley
School of Information Systems
University of East Anglia
Norwich, NR4 7TJ, England
e-mail : gcc@sys.uea.ac.uk

Abstract—This paper compares the performance, in terms of prediction accuracy, of a learning classifier system based on Wilson's XCS with commonly used classifiers from the fields of decision trees, neural networks and support vector machines. The experiments are performed on the Forest Cover Type database, a large data set available at the UCI KDD Archive [13]. The first objective of this paper is to highlight the potential of XCS as a data mining tool. The second objective is to provide extensive benchmarking results for experiments performed under randomised conditions for several modelling techniques. We find that C5 Decision trees perform significantly better than other techniques, and that the learning classifier system performs better or as well as three of the eight classifiers used. We discuss why C5 outperforms the other classifiers and identify ways in which XCS could be adapted to make it more suitable for data mining.

I. INTRODUCTION

Learning Classifier Systems (LCSs) are rule based classifiers, often called Genetics Based Machine Learning tools, consisting of a set of rules and procedures for performing classifications and discovering rules using genetic and nongenetic operators. A comprehensive description of LCS can be found in the literature, for example [15], [19]. Recent LCS research is described in [20], [21], [22]. Traditionally, the most common applications of LCSs have been from the domain of reinforcement learning (e.g. Markov decision problems [29]). However, the potential for LCS in supervised learning for data mining has been known for some time [16]. The rationale for believing in this potential is based in part on the following observations concerning the following characteristics of LCS:

- LCS have been shown to be capable of learning complex, non-linear classification functions that can be used to accurately predict new cases, on a variety of problem domains.
- LCS generalise over the attribute space and under ideal conditions can discover a maximally general, accurate rule set to perform classifications.
- The fact that LCS are rule based means they offer the potential for explanatory data analysis in addition to predictive modelling. In real world data mining exercises being able to explain how a technique forms classifications is often as important as accuracy, and techniques where this is difficult (such as neural networks) are often treated with suspicion in industry.
- Unlike most rule induction algorithms LCS do not discover and evaluate rules in isolation. Instead, they search the space of possible rule sets defined for a particular problem.
- In addition to being able to form complete classifications LCS can also be used for nugget discovery (the discovery of classifications for some subset of the attribute space). The degree of coverage of the attribute space required can be controlled by careful parameterisation.
- The way LCS evaluate rules and rule sets (described in Section III) make them ideal for modelling problems where the model may be changing over time, and for maintaining and updating a classification function without the requirement of retraining on all the data.

LCS are similar to Neural Networks and Support Vector Machines in the fact that the generality of models that can potentially be constructed can make them hard to parameterise properly (the similarities between LCS and NN are discussed in [27]). In order to understand how well procedures developed for generated problems such as the multiplexer and the Monk's problem work on real world data sets, a thorough examination and evaluation needs to be conducted. Recently there have been several investigations into applying LCS to machine learning and data mining classification problems [34], [2], [17], [26]. This paper continues this investigation by applying an adaptation of a recently developed LCS, Wilson's XCS [32], to a large multi-class benchmark data set available at the The UCI KDD Archive [13], the Forest Cover Type data set. The Forest Cover data set has been used in some classifier comparisons [4], [23], [10] but the work presented here is, to the best of our knowledge, the first comparative study using Neural Networks (NNs), Support Vector Machines (SVMs) and Decision Trees (DTs). The rest of this paper is structured as follows: Section II describes the data set and the experimental procedure adopted. Section III briefly describes XCS in a data mining context. Section IV outlines the NN, SVM and DT structures used in experimentation. Section V presents the results and Section VI discusses in more detail these results and suggests how XCS could be extended to improve performance.

II. FOREST COVER DATA

Experiments were performed on the Forest Cover Type data set, available from the UCI KDD Archive [13]. The classification task is to predict the forest cover type (seven classes) for 30m × 30m cells, given only cartographic data [4]. A case consists of observation of ten continuous variables and two nominal categorical variables, wilderness area designation (four types) and soil type (forty types) plus the forest type designation. The nominal categorical variables are represented by 44 binary dummy variables. The database consists of 581012 cases. This data is a representative instance of a domain of problems common in data mining and thus provides a useful benchmark for comparing classifiers. The characteristics that make it of particular interest are:

1) a large number of cases;
2) a relatively large number of attributes and classes for the response;
3) an unequal class distribution for the response classes;
4) both continuous and categorical variables.

Another feature of the data worth noting is that there are no missing values. This is often not the case in data mining problems, but this characteristic allows us to focus on the key performance issues of the classifiers compared. Unless otherwise indicated, the continuous attributes were linearly scaled to $[0, 1]$ and the nominal categorical data was represented with dummy variables.

A. Experimental Design

Previously published results for this data set have used the first 11,340 records for training data, the next 3,780 records for validation data, and last 565,892 records used for testing data. The data was rearranged so that the class frequencies are equal in the training and validation data (thus significantly reducing the number of rare classes in the testing data). Using this design, published accuracy results on the testing data include 70% using back propagation [4], 58% using Linear Discriminant Analysis [4], 71% using Support Vector Machines [23] and 73.41% using SVM modified to allow for the unrepresentative class distribution in the training data [10].

As discussed in [10], balancing the data so that the classes are equally represented in the training data by sampling the complete data set can make the final accuracy measure unrepresentative of the true model. Our goal is to provide an assessment of the accuracy performance of several classification techniques on this data, thus providing results for future classifier comparisons. Hence, the experimental procedure followed is based on that recommended in [25]. The data set was randomly split into 10 sets (thus removing the class frequency bias introduced by balancing). Each set was further split into approximately 38000 training cases and 20000 testing cases. If parameter tuning occurred it was done so on the basis of performance on the first training data set. The size of the data set means there is no need for cross validation, hence when comparing performance it seems reasonable to use a simple t-test with a Bonferroni adjustment for the number of comparisons rather than the alternative tests described in [12].

III. LEARNING CLASSIFIER SYSTEMS (LCS) AND WILSON'S ERROR BASED CLASSIFIER (XCS)

LCSs construct a rule set, and hence a classifier, through the iterated exposure to test cases. The LCS receives a single case, attempts to classify this case, then receives a reward quantifying whether the classification was correct or not. A full description of the fundamentals of "Michigan" LCS is given in [15].

LCS rules are usually of the form *if* **condition** *then* **classification**, where the condition is commonly a conjunction of logical expressions on some subset of the attributes. A rule has a set of associated parameters to estimate the quality of the rule and its suitability for use as a basis for creating new rules. The three primary components of an LCS are:

1) a production system that specifies how to construct a mapping, from the rule set, from the attribute space to either a single classification or a prediction of the suitability of some or all possible classifications;
2) a reinforcement algorithm that controls how the rule parameters are adjusted based on the reward feedback concerning the accuracy of predictions;
3) a rule discovery component that alters the rules in the rule set through (possibly genetic) operators.

The training of an LCS proceeds as follows:

- LCS is passed a single training case;
- rules whose condition match the case are formed into a match set;
- the match set is used to form a prediction array, an estimate of the reward (a value attributed to correct classification) for each possible class the case may take;
- based on the prediction array, the LCS selects a classification;
- the reinforcement algorithm receives the reward (often 1000 for a correct classification and 0 for incorrect one) and uses it to adjust the parameters of the rules in the match set advocating the selected action;
- the rule creation algorithm may, depending on some triggering procedure, create new rules by applying genetic operators of crossover and mutation to rules selected from the rule set.

It is worth noting that LCSs are usually applied to reinforcement learning problems, and as such are involved in unsupervised learning (unsupervised in the sense that it is not informed what the best classification could have been or what reward would have been received for alternative classifications).

There are many alternative implementations of LCSs (see [19] for an overview). Wilson's error based classifier, XCS, is a recently developed LCS which is designed to discover accurate, maximally general rules that form a complete classification of the attribute space. XCS was introduced in [32], and has the subject of much recent research [20], [21], [22]. A full description of the basic XCS algorithm is given in [9].

Briefly, XCS works as follows: Each rule in XCS has a prediction parameter, an estimate of the expected reward of the rule, an error parameter, an estimate of the absolute deviation of the reward around the expected value, and a fitness value, an estimate of the accuracy of the rule (an inverse function of its error) relative to other rules in the rule set matching similar attribute values and advocating the same classification.

These parameters are used to form predictions and are updated based on reward feedback. Some of the distinguishing features of XCS are that:

- XCS uses the Widrow-Hoff reinforcement learning algorithm [32] for updating rule parameters.
- XCS assesses a rules fitness (the basis for selection for the genetic algorithm) using an estimate of the classification error of a rule, rather than the expected reward. Thus in terms of creating new rules XCS treats a rule that is always wrong similarly to a rule that is always correct.
- XCS niches the genetic algorithm in a way that aims to maintain complete coverage of the attribute space for all classes.

IV. CLASSIFIER IMPLEMENTATIONS

To provide extensive benchmark results for this data set we assessed the performance of the following classifiers:

A. Classification/Decision Trees

Experiments were performed with three classification tree techniques: C5 [24], CHAID [18] and Classification and Regression Trees (CART) [5] using the Clementine package [28] for C5 and CART and KnowledgeSeeker software [1] for CHAID. The continuous attributes were not scaled for the decision trees since it would make no difference to the trees constructed.

B. Neural Networks

We used two Neural Networks to construct classifiers. The first was the NN provided by Clementine, which we denote ClemNN, with the default parameter settings. The multi-layer perceptron networks [3] have a single hidden layer containing 20 nodes.

The second NN also has a single hidden layer, initially containing 32 or 64 neurons. The output layer utilised the Softmax activation function [6], [7] with a cross-entropy error metric [14] and a standard 1-of-c encoding system. A Bayesian regularisation scheme was used to avoid overfitting, adopting a Laplace prior [31], where the usual regularisation parameters were integrated out analytically in the style of [8]. An important advantage of a Laplace prior over the more common Gaussian prior is that it sets redundant weights to exactly zero, allowing them to be pruned from the network. We call these NNs BayesNN$_{32}$ and BayesNN$_{64}$.

C. Support Vector Machines

SVMs [30] were assessed using the Java implementation of LIBSVM, an integrated software for support vector classification [11]. LibSVM implements the basic SVM algorithm of Platt [23]. The SVM we used was a standard C-Support Vector Classification using the one-against-one approach for multi-class classification in which $k(k-1)/2$ classifiers are constructed and each one trains data from two different classes. Classification is achieved by using a voting strategy for the $k(k-1)/2$ classifiers. We experimented with two kernel types: a linear kernel (LinSVM) and a radial basis function kernel (RadSVM). An adjustment was made to allow for the unbalanced class distributions.

D. XCS

A rule condition for the forest cover data combines the real valued implementation described in [33] and a standard bitstring implementation using the ternary alphabet $\{0, 1, \#\}$. A $\#$ means the rule will match this attribute whether the attribute is value 0 or 1. Wilson's real valued representation stores an interval predicate for each attribute. A rule stores two values for attribute i, $int_i = (c_i, s_i)$ and matches an input value x if and only if $c_i - s_i \leq x \leq c_i + s_i$. XCS was implemented using a maximum rule set size $N = 15,000$, a run size of 500,000 and the standard operators and parameter settings described in [33], [9].

V. RESULTS

The accuracy results for the 9 classifiers used are shown in Table I.

The first point to note is that the results fall into broad categories: less than 70% (LinSVM, CART and XCS), 70%-75% (RadSVM, CHAID and clemNN) and greater than 80% (C5 and BayesNN). Although there are significant differences within these categories, it is probably possible to experiment with parameters to improve each technique's performance within the categories. This implies there are levels of complexity in the underlying relationship between the attributes and the response, and the level of accuracy attained is determined in part by the level of complexity of model considered. This point is reinforced by the fact that the more complex model BayesNN$_{64}$ outperforms BayesNN$_{32}$.

Table I shows that C5 is the best technique for classifying this data. Using a t-test assuming unequal variance, the mean testing accuracy of C5 tests significantly higher than that of all other techniques at the 1% level (even after making a Bonferroni adjustment to allow for multiple tests). An examination of the rule sets derived from the C5 tree indicates that C5 generates approximately 2500 rules, with the majority covering less than 10 cases. Couple this with the fact that C5 is clearly overfitting the data, then the implication is that C5 is modelling almost on a case by case basis.

Restricting C5 to a minimum leaf node size of 20 cases (the default parameter in Clementine is 2) reduces the training/testing accuracy to 84% and 79% and the number of rules to 531 for data set 1. Both CHAID and CART implement stricter stopping criteria than C5, and this is probably why they perform less well. Altering CHAIDs automatic stop size from the default of 5% of the data base to 10 cases improves training/testing accuracy for data set 1 to 87.12% and 79.8%.

TABLE I
ACCURACY RESULTS FOR 10 DISJOINT DATA SETS OF THE FOREST COVER DATA

Class	Model	Train Mean	Test Mean	Test Min	Test Max	Test SD
Trees	C5	95.81%	83.71%	83.44%	83.96%	0.178
	CHAID	74.55%	72.67%	71.71%	73.57%	0.550
	CART	69.16%	68.87%	68.09%	69.3%	0.414
NN	ClemNN	75.54%	74.83%	74.1%	75.55%	0.428
	BayesNN$_{32}$	82.00%	80.32%	79.71%	80.82%	0.408
	BayesNN$_{64}$	82.97%	81.08%	80.73%	81.57%	0.278
SVM	LinSVM	69.63%	68.32%	67.35%	69.29%	0.510
	RadSVM	71.55%	70.66%	69.71%	71.3%	0.465
XCS	XCS	67.14%	66.90%	64.13%	70.88%	2.39

The Neural network results illustrate the benefits of the Bayesian regularisation, and reinforce the observation from the DT results that increasing the complexity of the model improves testing accuracy. The NN results are better than those reported in [4]. Balancing the data by duplicating training cases was found to have a detrimental performance on overall accuracy with all techniques, and this may explain the difference.

The SVMs performed worse than C5, CHAID and the NNs, but the results are broadly in line with those reported in [23], [10]. Further experimentation with the regularisation and kernel parameters would probably improve performance. For reasons discussed below, Standard XCS performed poorly.

A. Alterations to XCS

The standard implementation of XCS performed relatively poorly on the training data (see Table I). Consideration of the problem lead us to conclude that this was caused in part by the following factors:

1) The use of dummy variables means that any case will always have exactly 2 one values and 42 zero values. Using standard crossover means that offspring will often have more than 2 one values and will hence never match a case.
2) XCS deletes rules with the goal of maintaining an equal action set size for all niches. However, given the unbalanced class frequencies, this means that XCS is allocating a large proportion of its available rule space to modelling very rare classes.
3) XCS is unsupervised, hence when it performs a classification it is informed (via the passing of a reward) whether a classification was correct or not, rather than being told the correct classification. It samples possible classifications using an exploit/explore strategy (in exploit mode it chooses the classification with the highest estimate prediction, in explore mode it chooses a random classification). This means XCS is spending a large proportion of its run time attempting to gather information which is provided to other techniques in training.
4) XCS attempts to form a complete mapping from the attribute space to the class space, hence it assigns an equal proportion of its rule set to finding incorrect classifications as it does to finding correct classifications.
5) The parameter settings may be suboptimal. Problems 2, 3 and 4 outlined above could all, in theory, be overcome with a large enough rule set and a long enough run. In addition, the variability of the accuracy results relative to the other techniques may indicate that the genetic algorithm is activating too frequently or that the rule set is not large enough.

Time constraints make it unfeasible to properly assess the effect of parameter values on performance (informal experimentation suggested that increasing the rule set size to 30,000 and the run size to 1,000,000 did not significantly improve performance). Instead, we concentrated on alterations specific to data mining in general and the type of problem characterised by the Forest Cover data set. We implemented two alterations to XCS to address the first two points raised above.

1) XCS for Forest Cover Data: XCS$_2$: To stop the production of infeasible rules, crossover was altered so that it was forced to create a valid offspring. We maintain a bit string representation rather than use a categorical coding, but restrict crossover so that any child will always inherit all the binary variables for either soil type or wilderness area. Retaining a bitstring representation allows for conditions of the form (if soil type != 1 and soil type != 2) with the coding (00**). This type of condition is not easily encoded using a categorical coding.

Mutation is still allowed to change any bit, but now if it changes a bit to a one in either the soil type or wilderness area section and another bit was already set to one, it will adjust the bitstring so that the condition remains feasible.

2) XCS weighted for prior class distributions : XCS_3: In order to force XCS to concentrate on finding rules for the most frequently occurring classes, the deletion probabilities were weighted to increase the probability of deleting rules advocating the classification of the rarer classes. In addition, the GA triggering test was weighted to make the GA occur more frequently in action sets advocating the more frequent classes. XCS_3 uses the GA of XCS_2 and the class weightings.

TABLE II
RESULTS FOR XCS WITH PROBLEM SPECIFIC MODIFICATIONS

Model	Train Mean	Test Mean	Test Min	Test Max	Test SD
XCS_1	67.14%	66.90%	64.13%	70.88%	2.39
XCS_2	69.62%	69.46%	66.91%	70.53%	1.14
XCS_3	71.37%	71.15%	70.06%	72.24%	0.9379

The results for XCS_2 and XCS_3 are given in Table II. XCS_2 provides a significant improvement to XCS_1, and XCS_3 significantly outperforms XCS_2. XCS_3 is significantly better than CART and LinSVM and not significantly worse than RadSVM. XCS_3 also has lower standard deviation than the other XCS implementations, although the fact it is still higher than the standard deviation of the other classifiers is an indication that further improvement could be attained through better parameterisation.

VI. CONCLUSIONS AND FUTURE DIRECTIONS

The first objective of this paper was to provide extensive benchmarking results for the Forest Cover data set using DTs, NNs, SVMs and LCSs. It may well be possible to improve results for these techniques through experimentation with alternative parameters. For example, CHAID may perform better if dummy variables were not used, since it implements special procedures for handling nominal categorical variables (doing this gives training/testing accuracy to 76% and 74% for data set 1). However, it is clear that high accuracy requires a very complex model. The explanatory benefits of these complex models is questionable, and in many data mining problems this complexity is undesirable since it leads to considerable overfitting. C5 achieves the improvement from 75% to 85% by very low coverage leaf nodes which almost adopt a case by case classification. Techniques such as CHAID which are designed to avoid this situation are bound to underperform. When using this data to assess a classifier we would recommend three grades of performance: less than 70% is poor, 70%-75% is adequate and greater than 75% is good. Since it was not the goal of this paper to gain an understanding into the underlying relations in the data, we have not presented any confusion matrices, discussed performance on individual classes or examined rules to look for explanatory relationships.

The second objective of this paper was to assess XCS on the data set. XCS, with problem specific alterations, performs adequately. Although LCS offer real benefits to data miners in terms of ease of understanding and wide scope of applicability, further work is required to properly understand how the numerous parameters and alternative operators employed affect performance on complex, real world data sets. It is thought that more alterations could improve the accuracy on the Forest Cover data set, and may also improve XCS performance on other data mining problems. For example, the real value representation described in [33] and used here involves an interval split on an attribute, and it may be worthwhile experimenting with a binary split representation. In addition, in training XCS does not utilise all the information it could. Rather than only reinforce the selected classification, XCS could be adapted to reinforce all the rules in the match set. Initial experimentation with this supervised learning approach indicates that a re-evaluation of the parameterisation of XCS may be required. XCS attempts to construct a rule set that can evaluate all classifications, even incorrect classifications. This is often desirable but requires a large amount of resources in terms of maximum number of rules. Alterations to direct XCS to focus more on mapping correct classifications may improve performance. Finally, XCS is normally applied to problems where it is assumed a completely correct classification exists, and some of the parameters relating to assessing a rule's fitness reflect this in punishing any misclassification harshly. Further experimentation with a more controlled test problem is required to understand the effects of inherent classification error on performance.

REFERENCES

[1] Angoss. KnowledgeSeeker data mining tool. See www.angoss.com/ProdServ/AnalyticalTools.

[2] E. Bernado, X. Llora, and J. M. Garrell. XCS and GALE: A comparative study of two learning classifier systems. In Lanzi et al. [22], pages 115–132.

[3] C. M. Bishop. *Neural Networks for Pattern Recognition*. Oxford: Oxford University Press, 1995.

[4] J. A. Blackard and D. J. Dean. Comparative accuracies of artificial neural networks and discriminant analysis in predicting forest cover types from cartographic variables. *Computers and Electronics in Agriculture*, 24(3):131–151, 2000.

[5] L. Breiman, J. H. Friedman, R. A. Olshen, and C. J. Stone. *Classification and Regression Trees*. Wadsworth and Brooks, 1984.

[6] J. S. Bridle. Probabilistic interpretation of feedforward classification network outputs, with relationships to statistical pattern recognition. In F. Fogleman Soulie and J. Herault, editors, *Neurocomputing: Algorithms, Architectures and Applications*, pages 227–236. Berlin: Springer-Verlag, 1990.

[7] J. S. Bridle. Training stochastic model recognition algorithms as networks can lead to maximum mutual information estimation of parameters. In D. S. Touretzky, editor, *Advances in Neural Information Processing Systems 2*, pages 211–217. San Mateo: Morgan Kaufmann, 1990.

[8] W. L. Buntine and A. S. Weigend. Bayesian back-propagation. *Complex Systems*, 5:603–643, 1991.

[9] M. V. Butz and S. W. Wilson. An algorithmic description of XCS. In Lanzi et al. [21], pages 253–272.

[10] G. C. Cawley and N. L. C. Talbot. Manipulation of prior probabilities in support vector classification. In *Proceedings of the International Conference on Neural Networks (IJCNN-2001)*, pages 2433–2438. Washington D.C., 2001.

[11] Chih-Chung Chang and Chih-Jen Lin. *LIBSVM: a library for support vector machines*, 2001. Software available at http://www.csie.ntu.edu.tw/~cjlin/libsvm.

[12] T. G. Dietterich. Approximate statistical test for comparing supervised classification learning algorithms. *Neural Computation*, 10(7):1895–1923, 1998.

[13] S. Hettich and S. D. Bay. The UCI KDD archive. Irvine, CA: University of California, Department of Information and Computer Science, 1999. http://kdd.ics.uci.edu.

[14] G. E. Hinton. Connectionist learning procedures. *Artificial Intelligence*, 40:185–234, 1989.

[15] J. H. Holland. *Adaption in Natural and Artificial Systems*. the University of Michigan Press, 1975.

[16] J. H. Holland. Escaping brittleness: the possibilities of general purpose algorithms applied to parallel rule-based systems. In R. S. Michalski, J. G. Carbonell, and T. M. Mitchell, editors, *Machine Learning, an Artificial Intelligence Approach*, pages 593–623. Morgan Kaufmann, San Mateo, California, 1986.

[17] John H. Holmes, Dennis R. Durbin, and Flaura K. Winston. The learning classifier system: an evolutionary computation approach to knowledge discovery in epidemiologic surveillance. *Artificial Intelligence In Medicine*, 19(1):53–74, 2000.

[18] G. V. Kaas. An exploratory technique for investigating large quantities of categorical data. *Applied Statistics*, 29(2), 1980.

[19] P. L. Lanzi and R. L. Riolo. A roadmap to the last decade of learning classifier research (from 1989 to 1999). In Lanzi et al. [20], pages 33–61.

[20] Pier Luca Lanzi, Wolfgang Stolzmann, and Stewart W. Wilson, editors. *Learning Classifier Systems. From Foundations to Applications*, volume 1813 of *LNAI*, Berlin, 2000. Springer-Verlag.

[21] Pier Luca Lanzi, Wolfgang Stolzmann, and Stewart W. Wilson, editors. *Advances in Learning Classifier Systems*, volume 1996 of *LNAI*, Berlin, 2001. Springer-Verlag.

[22] Pier Luca Lanzi, Wolfgang Stolzmann, and Stewart W. Wilson, editors. *Advances in Learning Classifier Systems*, volume 2321 of *LNAI*, Berlin, 2002. Springer-Verlag.

[23] J. Platt, N. Cristianini, and J. Shawe-Taylor. Large margin DAGs for multiclass classification. In S. A. Solla, T. K. Leen, and K.-R. Muller, editors, *Advances in Neural Information Processing Systems*, volume 12, pages 547–553. MIT Press, 2000.

[24] J. R. Quinlan. *C4.5. Programs for Machine Learing*. Morgan Kaufmann, 1993.

[25] S. Salzberg. On comparing classifiers: Pitfalls to avoid and a recommended approach. *Data Mining and Knowledge Discovery*, 1(3):317–328, 1997.

[26] S. Saxon and A. Barry. XCS and the Monk's problem. In Lanzi et al. [20], pages 223–242.

[27] R. E. Smith and H. Brown Cribbs III. Is a learning classifier system a type of neural network? *Evolutionary Computation*, 2(1), 1994.

[28] SPSS. Clementine data mining tool. See http://www.spssscience.com/clementine/index.cfm.

[29] R. S. Sutton and A. G. Barto. *Reinforcement Learning: An Introduction*. MIT Press, 1998.

[30] V. Vapnik. *Statistical Learning Theory*. Wiley, 1998.

[31] P. Williams. Bayesian regularization and pruning using a laplace prior. *Neural Computation*, 7:117–143, 1995.

[32] S. W. Wilson. Classifier fitness based on accuracy. *Evolutionary Computation*, 3(2), 1995.

[33] Stewart W. Wilson. Get real! XCS with continuous-valued inputs. In Lanzi et al. [20], pages 209–222.

[34] Stewart W. Wilson. Mining oblique data with XCS. In Lanzi et al. [20], pages 158–176.

On the Capability of an SOM based Intrusion Detection System

H. Güneş Kayacık, A. Nur Zincir-Heywood, Malcolm I. Heywood
Dalhousie University,
Faculty of Computer Science,
6050 University Avenue, Halifax, Nova Scotia. B3H 1W5

Abstract—An approach to network intrusion detection is investigated, based purely on a hierarchy of Self-Organizing Feature Maps. Our principle interest is to establish just how far such an approach can be taken in practice. To do so, the KDD benchmark dataset from the International Knowledge Discovery and Data Mining Tools Competition is employed. This supplies a connection-based description of a factitious computer network in which each connection is described in terms of 41 features. Unlike previous approaches, only 6 of the most basic features are employed. The resulting system is capable of detection (false positive) rates of 89% (4.6%), where this is at least as good as the alternative data-mining approaches that require all 41 features.

Index terms—Intrusion Detection Systems, Self-Organizing Feature Map.

I. INTRODUCTION

The Internet, as well as representing a revolution in the ability to exchange and communicate information, has also provided greater opportunity for disruption and sabotage of data previously considered secure. The study of systems able to detect network borne intrusions provides many challenges. Classical network based approaches to this problem often rely on either rule-based misuse detection or anomaly detection [1]. Rule-based misuse detection systems attempt to recognize specific behaviors that represent known forms of abuse or intrusion. On the other hand, anomaly detection attempts to recognize abnormal user behavior. Both approaches have their respective advantages and disadvantages. Rule based systems typically require an exhaustive list of templates characterizing each attack instance; there is no concept of similarity to a currently listed attack instance. The anomaly detection approach will actually identify "normal" behaviors by mining the monitored behavior of each user so that "abnormal" behaviors can be characterized. Clear distinctions between normal and abnormal, however, are difficult to achieve in practice.

Given the significance of the intrusion detection problem, there have been various initiatives that attempt to quantify the current state of the art. In particular the International Knowledge Discovery and Data Mining Tools Competition [2] provided the KDD-99 data set for assessing different AI approaches to the problem. Although not without its drawbacks [3], this benchmark provides the only *labeled* dataset for comparing IDS systems, which the authors are aware of. The most recent works in this area are able to provide detection (false positive) rates in the range of 91% (8%) to 98% (10%) whilst using all 41-connection features [4, 5].

In this work, we are interested in establishing how far an approach based on a sequence of hierarchical topological maps can be taken, whilst only utilizing a sub-set of the available 41-connection features. Specifically, the work only uses the six "Basic features of an Individual TCP connection" [2]. Six Self-Organizing Feature Maps (SOM) are then built, one for each input feature. The second level of the hierarchy integrates the information from each SOM and a third layer is selectively built for second layer neurons that respond to both attack and normal connections. Neurons in the second and third layers are therefore labeled using the training set, but the training process itself is entirely unsupervised. Detection (false positive) rate of the detector on the test set varies between 89% (4.6%) to 99.7% (1.7%) depending on the KDD-99 test partition employed.

The remainder of the paper is organized as follows. Section II provides the background and methodology of the work. Details of each learning algorithm comprising the system are given in Section III. Results are reported in Section IV and Conclusions drawn in Section V.

II. METHODOLOGY

As indicated in the introduction, the basic objective of this work is to assess how far a machine learning approach may be taken which makes minimalist use of any *a priori* domain knowledge. To this end, an approach based on topological maps is employed. This assumes that given sufficient resolution in the maps, it is possible to separate normal from attack behavior. In a previous work, we established that by utilizing a shift register to embed the temporal relationship between incoming connections, described in terms of session information, a simple two layer SOM hierarchy was sufficient to distinguish between different behaviors [6]. However, the dataset used in that scheme only consisted of seven attacks. In this work, on the other hand, we thoroughly benchmark the hierarchical SOM methodology on the KDD-99 benchmark. To this end, we first describe the characteristics of the data set and then the SOM architecture utilized.

This work was supported in part by Discovery grants, of the second and third authors, from the Natural Sciences and Engineering Research Council of Canada.

1) KDD dataset:

The KDD-99 dataset is based on the 1998 DARPA initiative to provide designers of intrusion detection systems (IDS) with a benchmark on which to evaluate different methodologies [7]. To do so, a simulation is made of a factitious military network consisting of three 'target' machines running various operating systems and services. Additional three machines are then used to spoof different IP addresses, thus generating traffic between different IP addresses. Finally, there is a sniffer that records all network traffic using the TCP dump format. The total simulated period is seven weeks. Normal connections are created to profile that expected in a military network and attacks fall into one of five categories: User to Root; Remote to Local; Denial of Service; Data; and Probe. Note that User to Root and Remote to Local can represent content-based attacks, and may therefore only be detected indirectly by the type of system developed in this work (e.g. guessing passwords often manifests itself as multiple attempted login's between the same source destination pair).

In 1999 the original TCP dump files were preprocessed for utilization in the Intrusion Detection System benchmark of the International Knowledge Discovery and Data Mining Tools Competition [2]. To do so, packet information in the TCP dump file are summarized into connections. Specifically, "a connection is a sequence of TCP packets starting and ending at some well defined times, between which data flows from a source IP address to a target IP address under some well defined protocol" [8]. This process is completed using the Bro IDS [9], resulting in nine "Basic features of an Individual TCP connection" [8]; hereafter referred to as 'basic features',

- Duration of the connection;
- Protocol type, such as TCP, UDP or ICMP;
- Service type, such as FTP, HTTP, Telnet;
- Status flag, derived by Bro to describe a connection;
- Total bytes sent to destination host;
- Total bytes sent to source host;
- Whether source and destination addresses are the same or not;
- Number of wrong fragments;
- Number of urgent packets;

Note that only Protocol and Service features are not derived i.e. they are estimated immediately as opposed to after a connection has completed. Moreover, the above 'status flag' should not be confused with the TCP/IP suit flags. Finally, last three features are specific to certain attack types (no variation is observed across the normal data in the training set), hence these terms were ignored in this work.

In addition to the above nine 'basic features,' each connection is also described in terms of an additional 32 *derived* features, falling into three categories,
- *Content Features*: Domain knowledge is used to assess the payload of the original TCP packets. This includes features such as the number of failed login attempts;
- *Time-based Traffic Features*: These features are designed to capture properties that mature over a 2 second temporal window. One example of such a feature would be the number of connections to the same host over the 2 second interval;
- *Host-based Traffic Features*: Utilize a historical window estimated over the number of connections – in this case 100 – instead of time. Host based features are therefore designed to assess attacks, which span intervals longer than 2 seconds.

In this work, none of these additional features are employed.

2) Hierarchical SOM:

As in our earlier work, a hierarchical SOM architecture is employed [6]. Our basic motivation is to steadily build more abstract features as the number of SOM layers increase. That is to say, our hypothesis is that features learnt at the initial layers of a hierarchy may still be interpreted in terms of recognizable basic measured properties, whereas features at the highest level in the architecture will capture aspects synonymous with normal or attack behaviors. Specifically, three layers are employed. In the first, individual SOMs are associated with each basic TCP feature. This provides a concise summary of the interesting properties of each basic feature, as derived over a suitable temporal horizon. The second layer integrates the views provided by the first level SOMs into a single view of the problem. At this point, we use the training set labels associated with each pattern to label the respective best matching unit in the second layer. The third and final layer is built for those neurons, which win for both attack and normal behaviors. This results in third layer SOMs being associated with specific neurons in the second layer. Moreover, the hierarchical nature of the architecture means that the first layer may be trained in parallel and the third layer SOMs are only trained over a small fraction of the data set.

3) Preprocessing and Clustering

In order to build the hierarchical SOM architecture, several data normalization operations are necessary, where these are for the purposes of preprocessing and inter-layer 'quantization' of maps. Preprocessing has two basic functions, to provide a suitable representation for the initial data and support the representation of time. In the case of initial data representation, three of the basic features – Protocol type, Service type and Status flag – are alphanumeric. As the first SOM layer treats each feature independently, we merely map each instance of an alphanumeric character to sequential integer values. Numerical features – connection duration, total bytes set to destination/ source host – are used unchanged.

In the case of representing time, the standard SOM used here has no capacity to recall histories of patterns directly. However, sequence as opposed to time stamp, is the property of significance in this work [6]. A shift register of length 'l' is therefore employed in which a 'tap' is taken at a predetermined repeating interval 't' such that $l \% t = 0$, where % is the modulus operator. The first level SOMs only receive values from the shift register that correspond to tap locations. Thus, as each new connection is encountered (enters at the left), the content of each shift register location is transferred one location (to the right), with the previous item in the lth location being lost.

The requirement for 'quantization' occurs between the first and second level SOMs. Specifically, the purpose of the second level SOM is to provide an integrated view of the input feature specific SOMs developed in the first layer. There is therefore the potential for each neuron in the second layer SOM to have an input dimension defined by the total neuron count across all first layer SOM networks. This would be a brute force solution that does not scale computationally (there are half a million training set patterns). Moreover, given the topological ordering provided by the SOM, neighboring neurons will respond to similar stimuli. We therefore quantize the topology of each first layer SOM in terms of a fixed number of neurons and re-express the first layer best matching units in terms of these. This significantly reduces the dimension seen by neurons in the second layer SOM.

III. Learning Algorithms

Two learning algorithms are used to build the hierarchical SOM architecture. The first is used to train each SOM in the hierarchy [10]. The second is a clustering algorithm that is used to quantize the number of SOM neurons 'perceived' by the second layer. In the latter case the Potential Function algorithm is employed [11]. These are briefly summarized as follows.

A. Self-Organizing Feature Map

Kohonen's Self-Organizing Feature Map (SOM) algorithm is an unsupervised learning algorithm in which an initially 'soft' competition takes place between neurons to provide a topological arrangement between neurons at convergence [10]. The learning process is summarized as follows,

1. Assign random values to the network weights, w_{ij};
2. Present an input pattern, x, in this case a series of taps taken from the shift register providing the 'reconstruction' state space on which the SOM is to provide a suitable quantized approximation.
3. Calculate the distance between pattern, x, and each neuron weight w_j, and therefore identify the winning neuron, or

$$d = \min_j \{\|x - w_j\|\} \quad (1)$$

where $\|\cdot\|$ is the Euclidean norm and w_j is the weight vector of neuron j;

4. Adjust all weights in the neighborhood of the winning neuron, or

$$w_{ij}(t+1) = w_{ij}(t) + \eta(t)K(j,t)\{x_i(t) - w_{ij}(t)\} \quad (2)$$

where $\eta(t)$ is the learning rate at epoch t; and K(j, t) is a suitable neighborhood function;
5. Repeat steps (2) – (4) until the convergence criterion is satisfied.

Following convergence, presentation of an input vector, x, results in a corresponding output vector, d, the Euclidian distance between each neuron and input. The neuron with the smallest distance represents the winning or best matching neuron, step (3). The best matching neuron also defines a neighborhood of next nearest neighboring neurons. Once the maps are trained, it is this concept of a best matching node that is used to facilitate the labeling of the second and third level maps.

B. Potential Function Clustering

The Potential Function Clustering algorithm consists of four steps [11],
1. Identify the potential of each data point relative to all other data points. All data points represent candidate cluster centers;
2. Select the data point with largest potential and label as a cluster center;
3. Subtract the potential of the data point identified at step (2) from all others and remove this point from the list of candidate cluster centers;
4. Repeat on step (2) until the end criterion is satisfied.

In this application, the set of data points correspond to the set of neurons in each (first layer) SOM, where the weights of each neuron describe a neuron position in terms of the original input space. Step 1 characterizes neurons in terms of how close they are to others. A neuron with many local neighbors should have a high 'potential' as expressed by a suitable cost function, or

$$P_t(w(j)) = \sum_{i=1}^{M} \exp\left(-\alpha \|w(i) - w(j)\|^2\right)$$

where $w(j)$ is the 'j'th SOM neuron, $P_t(w(j))$ is the potential for such neuron at iteration t, M is the number of data points (in this case SOM neurons), and α is the cluster radii.

Step 2 identifies a candidate cluster center (SOM neuron) by choosing the point with largest potential $P_t(x^*)$. Step 3 removes the influence of the chosen neuron from the remaining (unselected) set of SOM neurons. That is, the remaining neurons have their respective potentials decreased by a factor proportional to the distance from the current cluster center, or

$$P_{t+1}(w(j)) = P_t(w(j)) \\ - P_t(w^*)\exp\left(-\beta \|w(i) - w(j)\|^2\right)$$

where $t + 1$ is the index of the updated potential at iteration t; w^* is the data point associated with the current cluster center, and β is the cluster radii ($\alpha < \beta$).

The result of step 3 is the labeling of a specific SOM neuron as a cluster center. Step 4 iterates the process in conjunction with some suitable stop criterion. In this case, we stop when six cluster centers are identified, where the alpha and beta values are set accordingly. That is to say, further cluster centers correspond to points with a potential value less than 10% of the first potential located. The net effect of this process is therefore that each of the six first layer SOMs are characterized in terms of 6 clusters, resulting in a total of 36 inputs to the second level SOM.

Once the 6 cluster centers are identified for each SOM, representing the 'quantized' SOM output, we normalize as follows,

$$y = \frac{1}{1 + \|w - x\|}$$

where w is the cluster center and x is the original SOM input.

The second layer SOM now receives a vector, y, of the form,

$$y = [y_{1,1}, \ldots, y_{1,6}, y_{2,1}, \ldots, y_{i,j}]$$

where i is the SOM index and j is the cluster (neuron) index.

IV. RESULTS

In all cases the SOM Toolbox and SOM-PAK were employed for the design of each SOM comprising the SOM hierarchy [12]. In the following we describe the dataset, training procedure and evaluation of the proposed architecture.

A. KDD-99 Dataset

The KDD-99 data consists of several components, Table I. As in the case of the International Knowledge Discovery and Data Mining Tools Competition, only the '10% KDD' data is employed for the purposes of training [2]. This contains 24 attack types and is essentially a more concise version of the 'Whole KDD' dataset. One side effect of this, is that it actually contains more examples of attacks than normal connections. Moreover, the attack types are not represented equally, with Denial-of-Service attack types – by the very nature of the attack type – accounting for the majority of the attack instances. However, both test sets contain an additional 14 (unseen) attacks. The so-called 'Corrected (Test)' dataset provides a dataset with a significantly different statistical distribution than either '10% KDD' or 'Corrected (Test)'.

TABLE I
BASIC CHARACTERISTICS OF THE KDD DATASET

Dataset label	Total Attack	Total Normal
10% KDD	396,744	97,277
Corrected (Test)	250,436	60,593
Whole KDD	3,925,651	972,780

B. Training

Learning parameters for the SOMs are summarized in Table II, where this process is repeated for each SOM comprising the hierarchy. In each case, training is completed in two stages, the first providing for the general organization of the SOM and the second for the fine-tuning of neurons. Table III summarizes the additional parameters utilized by the shift register and Potential Function clustering algorithm. The resulting SOM hierarchy consists of 6 SOM networks in the first layer (temporal encoding), each consisting of 6×6 grid and 20 inputs. Potential Function clustering 'quantizes' each original first layer SOM to six neurons using the process described in Section III.B, resulting in 36 inputs to the second layer SOM (responsible for integration). Once training of the second layer is complete, labeling takes place. That is, for each connection in the training set, the corresponding label is given to the best matching unit in the second layer. A count is kept for the number of normal and attack connections each best matching unit receives. Third layer SOMs are built for second layer SOM neurons that demonstrate significant counts for both attack and normal connections, Section IV.C. This results in 6 third layer SOMs being built on top of specific second layer neurons. In each case third layer SOMs consist of 20 × 20 neurons, where a larger neuron count is utilized in the third layer in order to increase the likelihood of separation between the two connection types. Moreover, only connections for which the corresponding second layer SOM is the best matching unit are used to train third layer SOMs, facilitating the use of larger SOMs without experiencing a high computational overhead. Finally, in each case, the inputs to the third level SOMs correspond to the 36-element vector of 'quantized' first layer outputs.

TABLE II
SOM TRAINING PARAMETERS

Parameter	Rough Training	Fine Tuning
Initial η	0.5	0.05
η decay scheme	$f(\text{epoch}^{-1})$	
Epoch Limit	4,000	
Neighborhood Parameters		
Initial Size	2	1
Function	Gaussian	
Relation	Hexagonal	

TABLE III
POTENTIAL FUNCTION AND SHIFT REGISTER PARAMETERS

	Potential Function (For each feature respectively)	Shift Register	
α	e-6, e-3, 2e-7, e-6, 16e-7, 0.1599015,	Length	96
β	2e-2, 2e-2, e-2, 4e-2, e-1, e-2	# Taps	20

C. Evaluation

Performance of the classifier is evaluated in terms of the false positive and detection rates, estimated as follows,

$$\text{Skipped Rate} = \frac{\text{Number of Skipped Connections}}{\text{Total number of Connections}}$$

$$\text{False Positive Rate} = \frac{\text{Number of False Positives}}{\text{Total number of Normal Connections}}$$

$$\text{Detection Rate} = 1 - \frac{\text{Number of False Negatives}}{\text{Total number of Attack Connections}}$$

Where False Positive (Negative) Rate is the number of Normal (Attack) connections labeled as Attack (Normal).

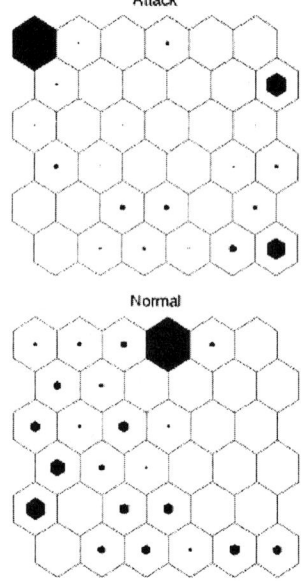

Fig. 1. Hit histogram of the second level map.

Figure 1 summarizes the count of attack and normal connections in the second level SOM; where proportionally larger counts result a greater area of the hexagon being colored. It is apparent that nodes 1, 32 and 36 account for most of the attack connections and neuron 19 most of the normal connections. It is also apparent that several neurons also respond to both normal and attack connections. To this end neurons 4, 17, 18, 23, 30 and 36 are selected for association with third level SOMs, one for each second layer neuron, where Table IV details the respective counts of normal and attack connections.

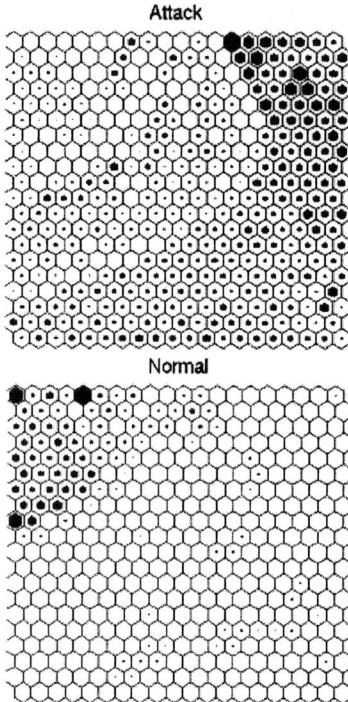

Figure 2: Third level map on top of second level map's neuron 36

On completion of training at the third level maps, a clear separation between normal and attack was achieved. Figure 2 illustrates this property for the case of neuron 36. In this case, it is clear that the normal connections all reside in the top left corner of the map, whereas the attack connections populate the remainder. Finally, the larger SOMs utilized in the third layer could result in neurons that remain unlabeled. These are listed as 'skipped' in the following analysis of test set performance.

TABLE IV
COUNT OF ATTACK AND NORMAL CONNECTIONS PER 2ND LAYER CANDIDATE NEURON

Neuron	Normal	Attack
4	2,177	2,613
17	2,051	3,151
18	1,731	1,706
23	2,304	3,204
30	2,453	5,292
36	1,688	45,440

TABLE V
TEST SET RESULTS

	Corrected (Test)		
Network level	Skipped	FP rate	Detection rate
Level 2	0 %	7.6 %	90.6 %
Level 3	0.7 %	4.6 %	89 %
	Whole KDD		
Level 3	0.06 %	1.7 %	99.7%

Table V details test set performance for the case of a two layer and three layer hierarchy on the 'Corrected (Test)'

KDD data set and the three-layer hierarchy on the 'whole KDD' test set. The superiority of the three-layer architecture is again demonstrated. Finally, performance of the two-layer and three-layer hierarchy on corrected test set for different categories is summarized in Table VI, whereas the performance on new attacks in 'Corrected Test' set is detailed in Table VII. It is readily apparent that as the hierarchical SOM approach is only utilizing 'basic features' (i.e. none of the content-based features are employed), performance on network-based attack categories (DoS, Probe) is naturally much better than that on content-based categories (U2R, R2L).

TABLE VI
PERFORMANCE OF 2 AND 3 LAYER HIERARCHY ON DIFFERENT CATEGORIES

	Normal	DoS	Probe	U2R	R2L
Level 2	92.4	96.5	72.8	22.9	11.3
Level 3	95.4	95.1	64.3	10.0	9.9

TABLE VII
DETECTION RATE OF NEW ATTACKS FOR 2-LAYER AND 3-LAYER HIERARCHY

Attack Name	Level 2	Level 3
Apache2.	90.3	90.7
httptunnel.	58.9	20.9
mailbomb.	7.8	6.8
mscan.	90.2	60.9
named.	23.5	0.0
processtable.	59.4	47.6
ps.	0.0	0.0
saint.	79.1	78.7
sendmail.	5.9	11.8
snmpgetattack.	11.5	10.3
udpstorm.	0.0	0.0
xlock.	0.0	0.0
xsnoop.	0.0	0.0
xterm.	23.1	30.8

TABLE VIII
RECENT RESULTS ON THE KDD BENCHMARK

Technique	Detection Rate	FP Rate
Data-Mining [5]	70-90%	2%
Clustering [4]	93%	10%
K-NN [4]	91%	8%
SVM [4]	98%	10%

Table VIII provides a summary of some recent results from alternative approaches trained on the KDD-99 dataset and tested using the 'Corrected (Test)' data [4, 5]. Detection rates are very similar to those reported for the SOM hierarchy constructed here. However, there are actually several additional factors with which these results need to be interpreted. Firstly, all the data mining approaches are based on all 41 features; the SOM hierarchy only utilizes 6.

Secondly, in the case of [4], figures quoted are for a mixture of specific and multiple attack types, making it difficult to determine performance over the entire dataset. Thirdly, use was also made of Host based information, thus providing an advantage when detecting content based attacks [4].

V. CONCLUSION

A hierarchical SOM approach to the IDS problem is proposed and demonstrated on the International Knowledge Discovery and Data Mining Tools Competition intrusion detection benchmark [2]. Specific attention is given to the representation of connection sequence (time) and the hierarchical development of abstractions sufficient to permit direct labeling of SOM nodes with connection type. Other than these two concepts, no additional use of *a priori* information is employed. In comparison to data mining approaches currently proposed, the approach provides competitive performance whilst utilizing a fraction of the feature set (6 of the 9 "Basic features of an Individual TCP connection" and none of the 32 additional higher-level derived features).

It is anticipated that future work will investigate the utilization of such a scheme within the context of a distributed solution to the IDS problem.

REFERENCES

[1] T. Bass, "Intrusion detection systems and multisensor data fusion," *Communications of the ACM*, 43(4), pp. 99-105, April 2000.

[2] S. Hettich, S.D. Bay, *The UCI KDD Archive*. Irvine, CA: University of California, Department of Information and Computer Science, http://kdd.ics.uci.edu, 1999.

[3] J. McHugh, "Testing intrusion detection systems: A critique of the 1998 and 1999 DARPA intrusion detection system evaluations as performed by Lincoln Laboratory," *ACM Transactions on Information and System Security*, 3(4), pp. 262-294, 2001.

[4] E. Eskin, A. Arnold, M. Prerau, L. Portnoy, S. Stolfo, "A geometric framework for unsupervised anomaly detection: Detecting intrusions in unlabeled data," in *Applications of Data Mining in Computer Security*, Chapter 4, D. Barbara and S. Jajodia (editors), Kluwer, ISBN 1-4020-7054-3, 2002.

[5] W. Lee, S. Stolfo, K. Mok, "A data mining framework for building intrusion detection models," *Proceedings of the 1999 IEEE Symposium on Security and Privacy*, pp. 120-132, 1999.

[6] Lichodzijewski P., Zincir-Heywood A.N., Heywood M.I., "Host-Based intrusion detection using Self-Organizing Maps," *IEEE International Joint Conference on Neural Networks*, pp. 1714-1719, May 12-17, 2002.

[7] *The 1998 intrusion detection off-line evaluation plan*. MIT Lincoln Lab., Information Systems Technology Group. http://www.11.mit.edu/IST/ideval/docs/1998/id98-eval-11.txt, 25 March 1998.

[8] *Knowledge discovery in databases DARPA archive*. Task Description. http://www.kdd.ics.uci.edu/databases/kddcup99/task.html

[9] *Bro user manual*, http://www.icir.org/vern/bro-manual/index.html

[10] T. Kohonen, *Self-Organizing Maps*. 3rd Ed., Springer-Verlag, ISBN 3-540-67921-9, 2000.

[11] S.L. Chiu, "Fuzzy model identification based on cluster estimation," *Journal of Intelligent and Fuzzy Systems*, 2, pp. 267-278, 1994.

[12] *Software Packages from Helsinki University of Technology*, Laboratory of Computer and Information Science Neural Networks Research Centre, http://www.cis.hut.fi/research/software.shtml

Mineral Potential Mapping using Feed-Forward Neural Networks

Andrew Skabar
School of Information Technology, Deakin University
221 Burwood Highway
Burwood, Victoria, 3125, Australia
andrews@deakin.edu.au

Abstract—**Mineral potential mapping is the process of producing a map that depicts the favorability of mineralization occurring over a specified region. The map should reflect the location of known mineral occurrences and also predict the distribution of areas of high mineral potential where little or no mining activity currently exists. Although the development of geographic information system technology and digital data manipulation techniques has enabled mineral exploration geologists to make more efficient use of resource information, many of the methods used are still inherently based on traditional techniques of map stacking in which layers of data are combined under the guidance of a mineral deposition model. This paper describes a data-driven mineral potential mapping technique based on feed-forward neural networks. Results are provided from applying the technique to gold exploration in a region of South West Victoria, Australia, using a range of geological, geophysical and geochemical input variables.**

I. INTRODUCTION

Mineral Potential Mapping is the process of combining maps containing different geoscientific data sets to produce a single map depicting areas ranked according to their potential to host deposits of a particular type [1]. The output map should reflect the location of known mineral occurrences and also predict the distribution of areas of high mineral potential where little or no mining activity currently exists. Mineral potential mapping is typically used in the early stages of mineral exploration to identify regions favorable for follow-up exploration activity.

Traditionally, the integration of geoscientific data has been performed by the exploration geologist by means of a *light table* approach, in which layers of data are combined under the guidance of a mineral deposition model. The integration of these layers is usually based on some implicit weighting scheme whereby subjectively determined weights are assigned to the different layers. One or more *targets* are then selected in areas where several favorable geological, geochemical, or geophysical features co-occur.

There are two main reasons why this traditional approach to data integration is becoming less and less adequate. Firstly, deposits are becoming harder to find. In the early days of mineral exploration, when mineral deposits at or near the surface were abundant, signatures indicating the likely presence of deposits could often be recognized from surficial geological information. For example, anomalous soil concentrations of gold or arsenic could often indicate the presence of a near-surface gold deposit. As these surface, or near surface, deposits became harder to find, attention shifted to the search for hidden deposits. Because the controlling factors for these deposits are usually subtle and ambiguous, simple visual interpretation of the data is no longer sufficient for the selection of targets. Secondly, new techniques in remote sensing and airborne geophysics are rapidly contributing to both the quantity and type of data available for exploration. As data banks get bigger and bigger, analyzing them becomes more difficult and demands the interpreter handle many variables simultaneously. Subjective judgment of the relative importance of many different layers is difficult and uncertain, and this difficulty is compounded by the fact that there is often a significant correlation between different data layers.

While the development of tools such as geographic information systems (GIS) and image processing systems have enabled mineral exploration geologists to maintain useable databases and to perform analyses that would take much more time if they were done manually, most of the methods used are still inherently based on modern analogues of traditional techniques of map stacking in which layers of data are combined under the guidance of a mineral deposition model.

Although there have been numerous applications of neural networks in the mineral-and-geosciences (ore-reserve estimation [2], land-cover classification from remote sensed data [3], discrimination of seismic signals [4], estimation of distance to ore [5], etc.) there is little published literature that directly addresses the application of neural network techniques to mineral potential mapping. Despite this, neural networks have potential in this area, because they can: (i) extract underlying patterns in a dataset, (ii) do not require pre-existing knowledge (e.g., a deposit model), (iii) do not require a statistical model for the data, (iv) can often operate at acceptable levels of accuracy when the data quality is poor or some data are missing, (v) are suitable for use on large mixed datasets, and (vi) are flexible, and can be retrained when new data become available.

This paper describes the application of neural networks to the production of mineral potential maps. Section II provides background into the field of mineral potential mapping and highlights some important differences between this domain and other spatial classification domains. Section III then describes the network structure and the training procedure required to ensure that the network output can be interpreted as a probability of mineralization. Section IV provides results of applying the technique the production of maps based on multivariate geoscientific data over the Castlemaine region of Victoria, Australia. Section V concludes the paper.

II. DATA-DRIVEN MINERAL POTENTIAL MAPPING

This section first provides background into the mineral potential mapping task. Characteristics of the domain are then compared with other spatial-based classification tasks.

A. Task Overview

In the context of GIS, mineral potential mapping can be seen as a process whereby a set of input maps, each representing a distinct geo-scientific variable, are combined using some function to produce a single map which ranks areas according to their potential to host deposits of a particular type. While the traditional *knowledge-driven* approach is to derive the mapping function on the basis of expert knowledge, *data driven* approaches attempt to discover, or *learn*, the function by measuring in some way the association between mapped predictor variables and a response map that indicates the locations of known occurrences of the sought-after mineral. The major assumption made in the data-driven approach is that the known mineral deposit occurrences constitute an adequate and unbiased sample of the true deposits in the region, and that by discovering signatures for these known deposits, other regions of high mineral potential will also be highlighted. Data-driven models are therefore most appropriate in the case of a region being sufficiently well explored such that the locations of a number of deposits of the sought after mineral are known [1]. This paper deals only with data-driven approaches.

The mineral potential mapping technique described in this paper is based on the following assumptions:

1. Deposits of the sought after mineral are distributed according to some unknown distribution;
2. The known deposits are random selections from the above distribution;
3. Geoscientific data provides clues to finding the other deposits.

The general task of inductively learning a mapping function that represents the posterior probability of mineralization can be expressed as follows:[1]

Given:

1. Background information provided by m layers of data, each of which represents the value of a distinct geoscientific variable x_i at each pixel p;
2. A subset of pixels, each of which is known from historical data to contain one or more deposits of the sought after mineral;

Find:

A function f that assigns to each pixel p in the study area a continuous value on the interval [0,1] that represents the posterior probability that pixel p contains one or more of the known deposits, given the evidence supplied by the background information.

Thus, assuming that the evidence for a pixel p is described by a vector $x = (x_1, ..., x_m)$, the objective is thus to learn a function $f: X \rightarrow [0,1]$, where $f(x)$ represents the posterior probability that p is mineralized. This task is depicted schematically in Figure 1.

In order to allow full generality, the possibility is included that the mapping function, $f(x)$, may be a composite of two or more *intermediate* functions, i.e. $f(f_1(x'), f_2(x''), ...)$ where $f_1, f_2,...$ represent intermediate mapping functions, and x', x'',... represent attribute vectors based on some subset of the m variables. In this case, the mapping produced by each of the intermediate functions $f_1, f_2,...$ will be referred to as an *evidential layer*, and may be *binary*, *multi-class*, or *continuous*. A *binary* evidential layer assigns posterior probability values to pixels on a class-based basis; that is, the input space is partitioned into two classes, and all pixels belonging to the same class will receive the same posterior probability in that evidential layer. *Multi-class* layers are a generalization of binary layers in which the number of discrete classes is greater than two. In contrast, *continuous* evidential layers do not involve any class-partitioning, but assign posterior probabilities to pixels directly. The production of binary and multi-class evidential layers is discussed in [1]. This paper deals with the more difficult problem of producing continuous-valued evidential layers.

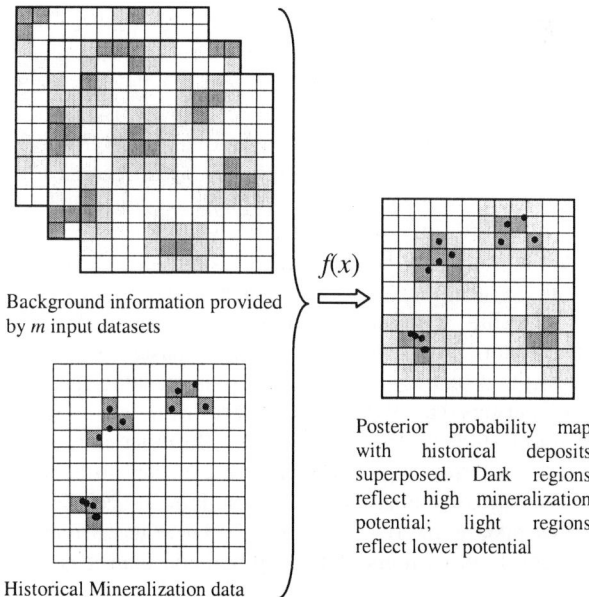

Background information provided by m input datasets

Historical Mineralization data

Posterior probability map with historical deposits superposed. Dark regions reflect high mineralization potential; light regions reflect lower potential

Fig. 1. The mineral potential mapping process. The output map should reflect the location of known mineral occurrences and also predict the distribution of areas of high mineral potential where little or no mining activity currently exists.

---

[1] It is assumed that each input layer takes the form of a *raster* image, i.e., a rectangular array of grid elements, where the intensity of each element represents the value of some geophysical variable over the physical region corresponding to the pixel.

A. Domain Characteristics

Two main factors distinguish the task of discovering evidential layers from many other inductive learning tasks: (i) the probabilistic nature of the problem domain, and (ii) the nature of the training data. To illustrate, consider first a typical classification task—land-cover classification using remote-sensed data. The problem is to classify pixels into one of several mutually exclusive land-cover classes (vegetation, desert, rock, etc.) on the basis of the pixel's radiance value in various spectral bands. This can be done by selecting a set of examples representative of each of the land-cover classes, and searching for decision boundaries in input space that minimize the classification error on these training examples. The search for decision boundaries is based on the assumption that pixels belonging to the same class will exhibit similarities in their attribute values, and the problem is to discover these patterns of similarity. Once these decision boundaries have been discovered, other pixels can then be classified depending on which side of the boundaries they fall.

While the classes in the land-cover classification domain are clear and predefined, this is not the case in the mineralization predictivity domain. The mineralization domain is inherently *probabilistic*, and we cannot speak of a pixel *belonging* to a class *mineralization_present* in the same sense in which we can say that a pixel *belongs* to class *vegetation_cover*. In the mineralization domain class-membership can only be interpreted as representing a *likelihood* of mineralization.[2]

The second major difference between these domains concerns the nature of the data to be used for training. Classification algorithms normally require that the training set consists of examples representative of each of the classes in the learning domain, and that the attribute vectors for these examples be accompanied with a *label* indicating to which class the example belongs. However, in the mineral predictivity domain, class membership is generally unknown; aside from a very few pixels which are known from historical records to contain known mineralization, all other pixels are *un*labeled.

It is also significant to note that tasks such as land-cover classification can also be performed using *unsupervised* learning algorithms, i.e., algorithms which do not require the class membership of training examples to be supplied [6]. These algorithms form *clusters* of examples based on some measure of the proximity of the examples in attribute space, and these clusters can then be identified with land-cover classes in a post-clustering operation, thus forming a classifier. Direct clustering approaches are not expected to be of much use in the mineralization prediction domain because a mineralized pixel is likely to be more similar in its attribute values to pixels in its immediate neighborhood than it is to other mineralized pixels [7]. This means that the clusters will not necessarily be good indicators of mineralization potential.

Thus, from a general inductive learning perspective, the problem of discovering mineral potential mapping functions can be characterized as one that is inherently probabilistic, and in which the training set is made up of a small number of labeled positives accompanied by a large corpus of unlabeled data. Because the search mechanism in most conventional classification and function approximation algorithms is based either directly or indirectly on some measure of the performance of the current hypothesis in classifying or approximating the training data, unmodified conventional approaches are not suitable for this task. The next section describes a neural network-based approach to solving this problem.

III. MAPPING MINERAL POTENTIAL USING NEURAL NETWORKS

The domain characteristics described in the previous section have important implications for the use of neural networks to model the mapping function. This first part of this section describes the network structure and substantiates the use of cross-entropy error for back-propagation training. The second part addresses the issue of training set selection.

Recall that the function to be learned is a function $f(\mathbf{x})$ that represents the posterior probability that a cell contains at least one deposit of the sought-after mineral. The function $f(\mathbf{x})$ can be discovered as follows. Assume the existence of a *binary* function $g(\mathbf{x})$ that represents the presence or absence of a *known* mineral deposit in a pixel p with attribute vector $\mathbf{x} = (x_1, x_2, ..., v_m)$, where x_k is the value of the kth variable for pixel p and m is the number of input variables. If pixel p contains a known deposit, then $g(\mathbf{x}) = 1$. If pixel p does not contain a known deposit, then $g(\mathbf{x}) = 0$. Now let $h(\mathbf{x})$ be a *probabilistic* function whose output is the *probability* that $g(x) = 1$. The objective is to learn the function $h: X \rightarrow [0,1]$, such that $h(\mathbf{x}) = P(g(\mathbf{x}) = 1)$.

The function $h(x)$ is to be represented by a feed-forward neural network. Because the network is required to produce only a single value for each input example, only one output unit is required. Because the output at this unit is to represent a probability, the output values should be bounded between 0 and 1, and the simplest way of arranging this is to use a sigmoidal activation function on the output node.

The function we seek to discover is the maximum likelihood function (or *maximum likelihood hypothesis*), i.e., the hypothesis h_{ML} that results in the highest probability of observing the given data D [8][9]. Suppose that an example $\mathbf{x}_i$ is drawn randomly from the training set. By the definition of $h(\mathbf{x})$, the probability that $\mathbf{x}_i$ has a target output of 1 is $h(\mathbf{x}_i)$, and the probability that is has a target output of 0 is $1 - h(\mathbf{x}_i)$. The probability of observing the correct target value, given hypothesis h, can therefore be expressed as

$$P(d_i | h, \mathbf{x}_i) = h(\mathbf{x}_i)^{d_i} (1 - h(\mathbf{x}_i))^{1-d_i} \quad (1)$$

where $\mathbf{x}_i = (x_{i1}, x_{i2}, ..., x_{im})$ is the attribute vector for pixel p_i, $h(\mathbf{x}_i)$ is the value of the hypothesis h applied to vector $\mathbf{x}_i$ and $d_i = 1$ if pixel p_i contains a known deposit, and $d_i = 0$ other-

---

[2] We could (and usually do) assign pixels to favorability classes—for the purpose of color coding output maps, for example. However, these classes are defined by selecting *ad hoc* probability thresholds and in this sense are conceptually different from land cover classes.

wise. Assuming that the examples in the training set are independent, the probability of observing the correct value for *all* the examples is given by

$$P(D \mid h) = \prod_{i=1}^{m} h(\mathbf{x}_i)^{d_i} (1 - h(\mathbf{x}_i))^{1-d_i} . \quad (2)$$

where m is the number of examples. h_{ML} is thus the function for which $P(D \mid h)$ is a maximum:

$$h_{ML} = \max_{h \in H} \prod_{i=1}^{m} h(\mathbf{x}_i)^{d_i} (1 - h(\mathbf{x}_i))^{1-d_i} . \quad (3)$$

Taking the natural logarithm, and using the fact that $\ln(h_{ML})$ is a monotonic function of h_{ML}, this can be shown to be equivalent to

$$h_{ML} = \max_{h \in H} \sum_{i=1}^{m} \{d_i \ln h(\mathbf{x}_i) + (1 - d_i) \ln(1 - h(\mathbf{x}_i))\} . \quad (4)$$

Alternatively, the maximum likelihood function can be expressed as a minimization:

$$h_{ML} = \min_{h \in H} \left[-\sum_{i=1}^{m} \{d_i \ln h(\mathbf{x}_i) + (1 - d_i) \ln(1 - h(\mathbf{x}_i))\} \right] . \quad (5)$$

The error function to be minimized (i.e., the function in square brackets in (5)) is commonly referred to as *cross-entropy* [10][11]. Alternatively, cross-entropy can be expressed as

$$E = -\sum_{i=1}^{m} \ln\left(1 - |d_i - h(\mathbf{x}_i)|\right) . \quad (6)$$

which makes the interpretation of distance between d_i and $h(\mathbf{x}_i)$ more intuitive [12].

In regard to back-propagation training of the network, it can be shown that the output node delta term for cross-entropy error reduction is $\delta_{\text{cross\_entropy}} = (d_i - h(\mathbf{x}_i))$, which differs from the delta term for quadratic error reduction which contains an additional factor $h(\mathbf{x}_i)(1 - h(\mathbf{x}_i))$ [9][13].

Up to this point, the network configuration and training scheme described are no different to that used in many binary classification tasks to which neural networks are commonly applied. However, one of the requirements of the map we wish to produce is that it represents the posterior probability of a pixel containing a known deposit. In other words, the sum of probabilities over all pixels in the map should sum to the actual number of known deposits. This has implications concerning the choice of examples used for training. To illustrate, consider a network trained using a *subset* of the pixels in the study region. Clearly, the output of the trained network will depend on the particular subset of examples (pixels) used for training. This is not necessarily a problem for the interpretation of the output values as posterior probabilities, as the outputs can be simply rescaled to sum to the number of known deposits. The problem, rather, is that the mapping function itself will be highly sensitive to the choice of training examples, especially if the number of training examples is small. This is a major problem, since we cannot be sure that a network trained using a subset of the pixels in the study region will be representative of the true posterior probability of mineralization.

To avoid this problem the network should be trained using *all* examples. Thus, rather than using the traditional approach of dividing the available data into disjoint training and test sets (and possibly also a validation set), the approach taken here is to use all pixels in the study region for training. Note however, that this does not preclude the possibility of testing the model. Rather than holding out a set of examples for testing, we hold out only the *label* of these examples. That is, we select a set of known positives (i.e., pixels known to contain an historical deposit) and assign these examples a target label of 0 rather than 1. We then test to see whether the trained network assigns a high mineralization probability to these examples.

To have outputs sum to the number of historically known deposits may at first sight appear to be at odds with the assumption that the network output represent the posterior probability of mineralization. This is because we obviously don't know the true *a priori* probability of mineralization. However, this is consistent with the assumption for data-driven mapping that the known deposits constitute an adequate and unbiased sample of the true deposits in the region, and that by discovering signatures for these known deposits, other regions of high mineral potential will be highlighted.

It was shown previously that the appropriate error reduction function for this task is cross-entropy. The use of cross-entropy error is, in fact, critical. While quadratic error reduction can often approximate the posterior probability of class membership on binary classification tasks [9], its use in the mineralization predictivity domain will lead to results that cannot be interpreted as probabilities (in fact the network output may not even approximate probabilities). The use of quadratic error reduction is justified (under maximum likelihood considerations) on problems in which the training data can be modeled by normally distributed noise added to the target function value, an assumption that usually holds when approximating continuous-valued functions (i.e., regression problems). However, in the mineralization predictivity domain target values are binary and noise follows a binomial, and not Gaussian, distribution. The problem is further compounded by the fact that there is a gross imbalance between the number of examples known to contain a historical deposit and the remaining examples (mineralization is a rare event).

We now summarize the important points from this section. Firstly, because the objective is to estimate probabilities of (binary) class membership, the appropriate error-reduction function is *cross-entropy* error, and not *quadratic* error. Secondly, because the sum of output values over the map should sum to the number of historically known deposits in the study region, it is necessary to discard the traditional approach of using separate training and test sets. Rather, all examples in the study region should be used for training.

IV. EMPIRICAL RESULTS

This section reports results from applying the technique described above to the production of mineral potential maps based on multivariate geological, magnetic and radiometric data over the Castlemaine region of Victoria, Australia. The region extends from a Northwest corner with coordinates 251,250mE, 5,895,250mN, to a Southeast corner with coordinates 258,250mE, 5,885,000mN. Input data consisted of 16 magnetic, radiometric, geochemical and geological variables made available by the Department of Natural Resources and Environment, Victoria. Based on a grid-cell resolution of 50m by 50m, the study region described above can be represented by a rectangular grid consisting of 141 cells in the horizontal direction and 206 cells vertically. The number of documented known reef gold deposits in the study area is 148. In addition, 938 other gold deposits locations have been recorded, but the historical information on these does not indicate the type of occurrence (i.e., reef or alluvial) or their significance. Additional information on Victorian geology can be found in [14] and [15]. The Castlemaine Goldfield is described in [16]. Full details of results presented here, including preprocessing input data etc., can be found in [17].

In order to test whether the output map indeed represents posterior probabilities, it useful to compare the technique with an alternative technique for estimating probabilities. For these purposes, the output map can be compared with maps produced using a non-parametric density estimation-based approach. This density estimation-based method consists in estimating the class-conditional and class unconditional probability density functions ($P(x|D)$ and $p(x)$ respectively), and combining these using Bayes' theorem. The results presented here are based on estimating density functions using the Parzen window method with Gaussian kernels [8].

Unfortunately it is not possible to adequately reproduce here in black and white the maps produced. However, it is useful to compare the two predictive models on the basis of the favorability *ranking* that they assign to pixels. A convenient means of performing such a comparison is to plot a graph of cumulative deposit frequency versus cumulative area. Such a graph can be constructed by ranking pixels according to their assigned posterior probability value, and plotting the cumulative frequency of deposits (either predicted or observed) against cumulative area as the posterior probability is increased from its minimum to its maximum value. Fig. 2(a) shows the curve produced using a neural network with a single hidden layer containing 6 units. Fig. 2(b) was produced using the Parzen window approach with a σ value of 0.2. (σ is the smoothing parameter that determines the width of the Gaussian kernel surrounding each point). As a guide to interpreting the graphs, consider the dark solid curve of Fig. 2(a), which represents prediction results for the 148 training deposits using the neural network model. It can be seen that a cumulative area value of 80% corresponds to a cumulative deposits value of approximately 25% (this is shown on the graph). This is equivalent to stating that 75% of the deposits occur in the 20% of the map depicted as being

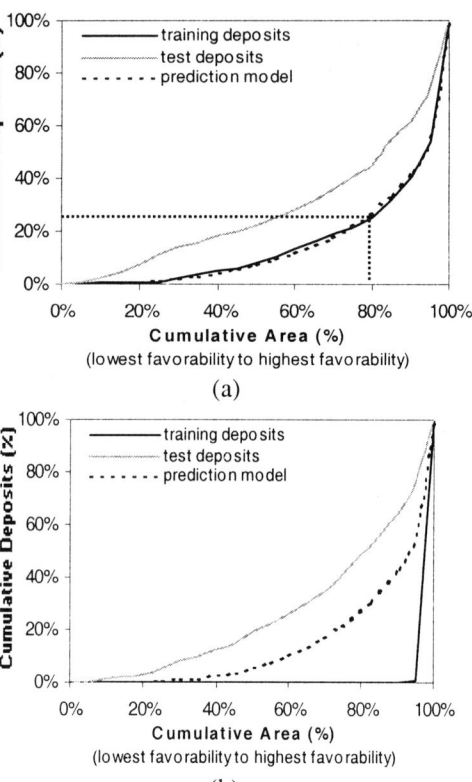

Fig. 2. Cumulative deposits versus cumulative area and cumulative deposits versus posterior probability graphs. (a) Neural network approach (6 hidden units); (b) Non-parametric density estimation approach (σ=0.2).

most favorable to host mineralization. However, of more interest is the predictive performance on the 938 holdout test deposits (represented by the grey curves), and it can be seen that both models yield similar performance in predicting these deposits. The broken curves simply represent the cumulative sum of posterior probabilities converted to a percentage, and it is useful to compare these with the grey curves. Note that some of the 938 holdout examples are alluvial, i.e., transported by water from original mineralization location. Predictive performance on test deposits would be improved significantly if the alluvial deposits were removed, however sufficient information on the type of these deposits is not available

The fact that two models provide (almost) identical prediction curves does not imply that the two maps are identical, as the curves only provide a statistical measure of predictive performance. In order to compare the actual maps, the product moment correlation coefficient, r, can be calculated. Table 1 shows the correlation between maps produced using various numbers of hidden units (for neural network models) and sigma values (for the density estimation-based method). A relatively high correlation of 0.59 occurs between a Parzen window model with σ=0.2 and neural network models with 6 and 9 hidden layer units. This suggests that the two models do indeed yield similar results, and we can be reasonably confident that these do represent mineralization probability.

TABLE 1
CORRELATION BETWEEN NETWORKS TRAINED USING CE ERROR REDUCTION AND PARZEN WINDOW MODELS

Hidden units	σ (smoothing parameter for Parzen Window model)					
	0.05	0.10	0.15	0.20	0.25	0.50
3 hlu	0.13	0.20	0.31	0.39	0.36	0.13
6 hlu	0.33	0.44	0.56	*0.59*	0.46	0.14
9 hlu	0.34	0.46	0.58	*0.59*	0.45	0.12

An obvious question arising out of these experimental results is why we should bother with neural network models at all if non-parametric density estimation-based models yield similar results. While the neural network model and the density estimation-based model will provide similar results under an appropriate choice of values for the respective parameters, the neural network approach has several advantages: (i) *Fewer free parameters to be determined subjectively*. The only free parameter requiring subjective determination in the neural network model is the number of hidden layer units. In the general case, the density estimation-based approach requires estimating a smoothing parameter for each variable; (ii) *Feature weighting*. While the density estimation-based approach implicitly assumes that all variables are equally relevant, neural networks make no such assumption; however, it cannot in general be determined how a network will react to irrelevant variables; (iii) *Better able to deal with high-dimensional input spaces*. Neural networks are more reliable than density estimation-based methods when applied to datasets containing large numbers of input variables; (iv) *Storage*. The neural network stores the mapping function; the density estimation-based method requires that all examples be stored in memory; (v) *Better able to deal with mixed data*. While density estimation-based methods can deal with mixtures of categorical and continuous-values variables (if used correctly), using mixed variables is much more straightforward with neural networks.

V. CONCLUSIONS

A technique has been presented for producing mineral potential maps using feed-forward neural networks. Results from applying the technique to a large multivariate dataset to predict gold mineralization yielded similar results to those obtained using a non-parametric density estimation-based technique. This supports the hypothesis that the network outputs do indeed represent mineralization *probabilities*. Despite the similarity of the results, the neural network approach has numerous important advantages over the alternative approach.

REFERENCES

[1] G.F. Bonham-Carter, *Geographic Information Systems for Geoscientists: Modelling with GIS*, Elsevier Science Ltd, U.K., 1994
[2] E. Clarici, D.B. Owen & S. Durucan, "Modelling and representation of spatial data using artificial neural networks", *Proceedings of the International Congress on Mine Design*, pp. 199-204, 1993.
[3] D.L. Civco, "Artificial neural networks for land-cover classification", *International Journal of Geographical Information Systems*, vol. 7, no. 2, 173-86, 1990.
[4] G. Romeo, F. Mele & A. Morelli, "Neural networks and discrimination of seismic signals", *Computers and Geosciences*, vol. 21, no. 2, pp. 279-88, 1995.
[5] D.A. Singer & R. Kouda, "Application of a feedforward neural network in the search for Kuroko deposits in the Hokoruko District, Japan", *Mathematical Geology*, vol. 28, no. 8, pp. 1017-23, 1996.
[6] B. Everitt, *Cluster Analysis*, London, Heinemann, 1980.
[7] F.P. Agterberg, *Geomathematics: Mathematical Background and Geo-Science Applications*, Elsevier Scientific Publishing Company, Amsterdam, 1974.
[8] R.O. Duda & P.E. Hart, *Pattern Recognition and Scene Analysis*, John Wiley & Sons, New York, 1973.
[9] C. Bishop, *Neural Networks for Pattern Recognition*, Oxford University Press, Oxford, 1995
[10] J.J. Hopfield, "Learning algorithms and probability distributions in feed-forward and feed-back networks", *Proceedings of the National Academy of Sciences*, vol. 84, pp. 8428-33, 1987.
[11] E.B. Baum & F. Wilczek, "Supervised learning of probability distributions by neural networks", in *Neural Information Processing Systems*, ed. D.Z. Anderson, American Inst. of Physics, New York, pp. 52-61, 1988.
[12] M. Schumacher, R. Rossner & W. Vach, "Neural networks and logistic regression: part 1", *Computational Statistics & Data Analysis*, vol. 21, pp. 661-82, 1996.
[13] T.M. Mitchell, *Machine Learning*, McGraw-Hill, New York, 1997.
[14] G.W. Cochrane, G.W. Quick & D. Spencer-Jones (eds), *Introducing Victorian Geology*, 2nd edn, Geological Society of Australia Incorporated (Victorian Division), Melbourne, Australia, 1995.
[15] I. Clark & B. Cook (eds), *Victorian Geology Excursion Guide*, Australian Academy of Science, Canberra, Australia, 1988.
[16] C.E. Willman, *Castlemaine Goldfield: Castlemaine-Chewton, Fryers Creek 1 : 10 000 Maps Geological Report*, Geological Survey Report 106, Energy and Minerals Victoria, 1995.
[17] A. Skabar, *Inductive Learning Techniques for Mineral Potential Mapping*, PhD Thesis, School of Electrical and Electronic Systems Engineering, Queensland University of Technology, Australia, 2000.

Intrusion Detection Using Radial Basis Function Network on Sequences of System Calls

Arvind Rapaka, Alexander Novokhodko, Donald Wunsch
Applied Computational Intelligence Laboratory
University of Missouri-Rolla
Department of Electrical and Computer Engineering
1870 Miner Circle
Rolla, MO 65409-0040
{anrb6b, ayn, dwunsch}@umr.edu

Abstract– Over the past few years, security has been an increasing concern, with the growth of network and technological development. An intrusion detection system is a critical component for secure information management. Unfortunately, present IDS's falls short of providing protection required for growing concern. Creation of an IDS to detect anomaly intrusions, in a timely and accurate manner, has been an elusive goal for researchers.

This paper describes a host-based IDS model, utilizing a Radial Basis Function neural network. It functions as a combined anomaly/misuse detector that helps to overcome most of the limitations in existing models. Rather than creating user profiles or behavioral characteristics, we trained our network using session data in the identification and tested experimentally on different attack/normal sessions. These results suggest that training the IDS on session data is not only effective in detecting intrusions, but also accurate and timely.

I. INTRODUCTION

As modern networks continue to grow, evaluating and detecting vulnerabilities to malicious attacks becomes more critical for e-driven-business models. Our network platforms, diverse applications, technologies and packages are growing increasingly complex. Inevitably our systems are insecure, flawed in practice and vulnerable. Given the seriousness of the problem, we need both deterrence, and termination of attacks that could prove detrimental to civilization. The security assessment problem stems from constantly changing behavior of software. Unfortunately, many of these changes happen without warning.

Therefore, we need to depend on secondary measures and tools such as IDS (Intrusion Detection System). The IDS approach to security is based on the assumption that a system will not be secure, but the violations of security policy (intrusions) can be detected by monitoring and analyzing system behavior [1].

Within the past few years, there has been steady improvement in both research and demand for effective IDS. Many research groups have proposed different methods of implementations, which proactively monitor behaviors defining the benchmark for the system. Though it is critical to profile normalcy and anomaly, it often proves detrimental to the health of the system, keeping in mind the complexity and the dynamic nature of today's computer systems.

Our results focus on generalizing the attacks for effective, fast and high detection rate with low false alarms. We first introduce the problem of creating an intrusion detection system. In section III, we review related work in intrusion detection systems. In section IV, we discuss the need and effective methods for data reduction and refinement, and our approach in data processing. In section V, we briefly discuss an implementation model, justifying the choice. Finally, we show our results obtained with the application.

II. INTRUSION DETECTION SYSTEM

Intrusion Detection Systems are normally categorized into misuse detection and anomaly detection. In *misuse detection* systems, it refers to known attacks that exploit the system. They can match the pattern on single events or multiple combinations of events. In single event pattern matching, each event is compared with a known signature in the databank. In multiple event pattern matching, it doesn't have a uniform abstract algorithm, because they do not propose the same operators to combine events. The inherent disadvantage is inability to detect an attack that is deviated or unknown to the databank. Another reproach to misuse detecting systems is their limited scope, adding attack signatures and maintaining the attack database. But low positive /negative false alarm has led to its existence [2, 3].

Anomaly detection refers to statistical knowledge about normal activity. Intrusions correspond to deviations from the normal activity of system. These anomaly detection IDS were bogged down by the difficulty in defining the normal activity because of the high variability in nominal usage. As a result, the false positive/ negative alarm rate is high, compared to misuse detection systems. However, it is more effective in detecting new attacks or deviation from the nominal usage.

Furthermore, the IDS is classified based on the data source: Network IDS (NIDS) and Host-based IDS (HIDS) systems. The NIDS watch network traffic usually from one location or network interface. Therefore, NIDS can detect probes, scans, malicious and anomalous activity across the

---

Partial support for this research from the National Science Foundation, from Sandia National Laboratories, and from the M.K. Finley Missouri endowment, is gratefully acknowledged.

whole subnetwork. It is also effective in identifying general traffic patterns for network and troubleshooting network problems. Its susceptibility to generate false alarms, as well as its inability to detect false negatives is its inherent weakness. However, HIDS technology does not have the benefits of watching the network to identify patterns like NIDS does. Instead, it watches the traces to access servers through the log data. A recommended combination of host and network intrusion detection systems, in which a NIDS is placed at the network entry point and an HIDS at critical servers, is the best way to significantly reduce risk.

Current intrusion detection systems are futile to cope with new, elegant and structured attacks, due to sever practical and theoretical limitations. These limitations have lead many researchers to apply different machine learning approaches such as neural networks [4, 5, 6, 7, 8].

We implement a neural network approach, using Radial Basis Functions, to detect novel attacks, reducing false positive and negative alarms. Our research aims at a data-driven view, to consider our system as a data analysis engine, fast and accurate enough for a real time model.

III. RELATED WORK

There are many different architectural designs for Misuse/Anomaly IDS using program and user profile behavior. Program and user profiles are built by capturing the system events under normal operational condition [1, 9, 10]. Once these profiles are created, provided they represent the nominal behavior signature, they are used to classify the deviation from the corresponding nominal behavior. Many research groups developed profile based classification for anomaly detection. Others used TCP/IP network data, collected by the network sniffer, to monitor the potential attack [10, 11].

Different techniques were proposed to classify the data based on statistical approach, machine learning, simple comparison based technique, integrity checking, data mining, state machine analysis [1, 9, 10, 11, 12, 13]. But one of the key drawbacks is their inability to generalize the anomaly from the data collection process. Hence most of the techniques suffered from the high false alarms due to low threshold for tolerance of anomalous behavior [11].

In host based systems, despite IDS being the major consumer of audit trail, it is apparent that no major operating system supports the all essential needs described above for development of IDS. Many audit data contains redundant, complex and irrelevant data, which requires vigorous screening before inputting to IDS. And also if the operating system will not provide protection to audit trails, the intruder can erase traces. A major loophole in BSM Audit Trail is inability to correlate the events; in turn the intruder would be successful in developing stealth attacks by hiding footprints. Thus we need to develop an intelligent screen activity to avoid stealth attacks. So these limitations make severe dents in the development of an effective IDS, despite elegant

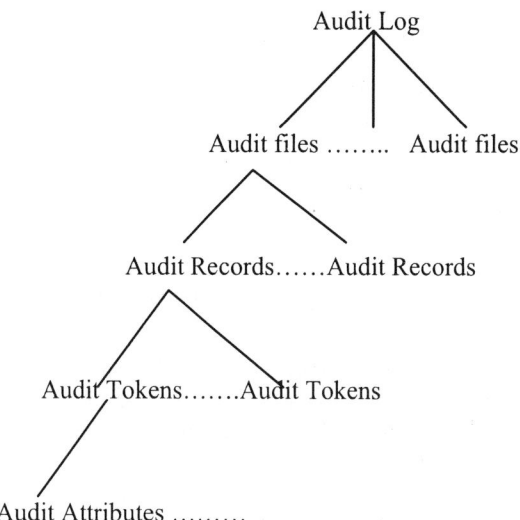

Fig. 1. Structure of Sun BSM Audit Trail

techniques for classification, and also requires effective data processing of existing audit records.

IV. DATA ANALYSIS

We have collected our BSM raw data from MIT's Lincoln Laboratory under DARPA 1998 Intrusion Detection Evaluation Program [14].

The Sun's Solaris Basic Module provides features in compliance with the TCSEC C2 trusted system rating. The BSM data include logs and events specific to users and the system.

The BSM audit trails, a binary file, include detail information about the system events attributable to a user. BSM recognizes more than 240 built-in system signals [13, 15]. In host based IDS design BSM audit trails been extensively used in both commercial and research development. "Praudit", a software tool, translates the binary BSM audit trail to readable format. Once the audit file has been translated we can parse, and can use expert knowledge to extract meaningful features and shed which do not make any difference rather consume processing time.

Audit records are described as either kernel level or user level generated records, depending on the nature of the event described in the event. The user level generated audit records are created by the applications that operate outside the kernel, unlike kernel level generated records. Each user-level and kernel-level events contain header, subject and return tokens whereas the trailer, group and sequence tokens are optional depending on the audit policy.

The event in Fig. 2 is logged when an intruder wants to execute malicious script as "root" through "ps" setuid command in UNIX model kernel. Each audit entry is encapsulated by a header and a trailer, the header line contains token id (header), the byte count (140), the version number (2), the event type (execve), the event modifier (blank), the time of the record, the milliseconds of time. The

```
Header, 140,2,execve (2),,Tue Mar 30 12:00:48
1999, +900307281 msec
Path, /usr/bin/ps
Attribute, 104555,root, sys, 8388614,22927,0
Exec…arg, 4,
Ps, -z,-u,^p^p^p^p^p^p^p^p^p^p^p^p^p^p^p^p^p^p^p^p
Subject, 2051,root,rjm,2051,rjm,1924,1816,24 5
206.222.3.297
Return, success, 0
Trailer, 140
```

Fig. 2. Raw Praudit BSM Data

event tokens, between the header and the trailer, vary depending on the event type. Next to the header is the path of the event. The attribute token consists of token id, mode, user id, group id, file system id, node id, and device. Then follows the exec_args token which contains the number of arguments. Thereafter comes the subject token consist of token id, the audit id, the effective user id, the real group id, the real user id, the process id, the session leader process group id, the terminal id containing port id, the machine id. The return token follows the subject token and consists of the token id (return), the error description (success), and the return value (0) [16, 17].

As by now, we are aware that plenty of information in the audit log is redundant and can be effectively removed without degrading the performance of IDS detection. In fact, we can improve the performance through carefully defining the inputs to the implementation model (e.g. Neural Network), which matters.

A. Audit Reduction

Audit reduction is the process of filtering irrelevant audit logs to our needs for better IDS. But all the filtering will be of no purpose if you are unable to define what constitute an intrusion? Hence, before purging the audit data we need to identify the redundant data — expert knowledge is required. Also, it requires better understanding of the implementation model, audit data, and of course intrusions.

The difficulty is not in purging data — it requires a simple file processing program. The challenge lies in providing optimal and computing efficient data to IDS, which increase the detection rate without false alarms. Thus, careful and explanatory measures are required before filtering BSM audit data introducing some determinism to an inherently nondeterministic process.

The key to filtering is to identify the trusted processes and untrusted process. In practical terms, trusted processes are those considered free of security problems. In other words, when a user command spawns a process that is trusted — and that generates only trusted sub-processes — it is sufficient to record only the audit record corresponding to the user command, and to discard all the subsequent audit records for the process. If the process generated is untrusted, we record all the audit records for the untrusted processes and the sub-processes [14]. An event that fails is assumed to be a potential attempt of failure until the completion of the transaction is recorded in chronological order.

B. Data Format

In our experiments we separate BSM data into sessions. Our model is based on generalizing differences between normal and abnormal data — very critical for high detection rate and keeping false alarms low. But it requires intensive data processing because of limitations to correlate the events by operating system data logs. Hence, during training, there is every possibility of attack washout because our training is not confined to any attack-centric or specific behavioral analysis. Processing such temporal-clustered information is another research area and would require an intensive debate.

Instead of contemplating, we went ahead with empirical analysis for different sessions with different attacks and normal data. We divided the sessions into small data chunks and let the neural network find it out what is common and what is different between the normal and abnormal data. The network would learn the attack signatures that it found on its own as well as the normal behavior patterns. Therefore, this IDS would combine both the misuse and the anomaly detection approaches.

The entire sequence of signals was stored as numbers for the corresponding system call. After that we applied a sliding window of length 15.

A sample of training data:
133 72 158 112 72 158 112 72 158 112 72 158 112 6155 2
72 158 112 72 158 112 72 158 112 72 158 112 6155 2 205
158 112 72 158 112 72 158 112 72 158 112 6155 2 205 72
112 72 158 112 72 158 112 72 158 112 6155 2 205 72 158
72 158 112 72 158 112 72 158 112 6155 2 205 72 158 112

In our experiments we selected two attacks (format and ffb) from week one and one attack (ftpwrite) from week two of 1998 BSM data, and the normal data that was immediately before and after the attacks. Sequences that appear only in the normal data were labeled as –1 ("clean"); sequences from sessions with attacks were labeled as +1 ("attack"), and sequences that appear in both types of sessions were labeled with 0 ("no detection"). After duplicates were removed we got 863 attack sequences, 3007 "clean", and 1012 "no detection" sequences. Fig. 3 shows the sequences projected onto the first two principal components. Note that while the first week attacks have a wider spread than the normal data, the attacks in the second week do not have such a spread, and cannot be linearly separated from the normal data.

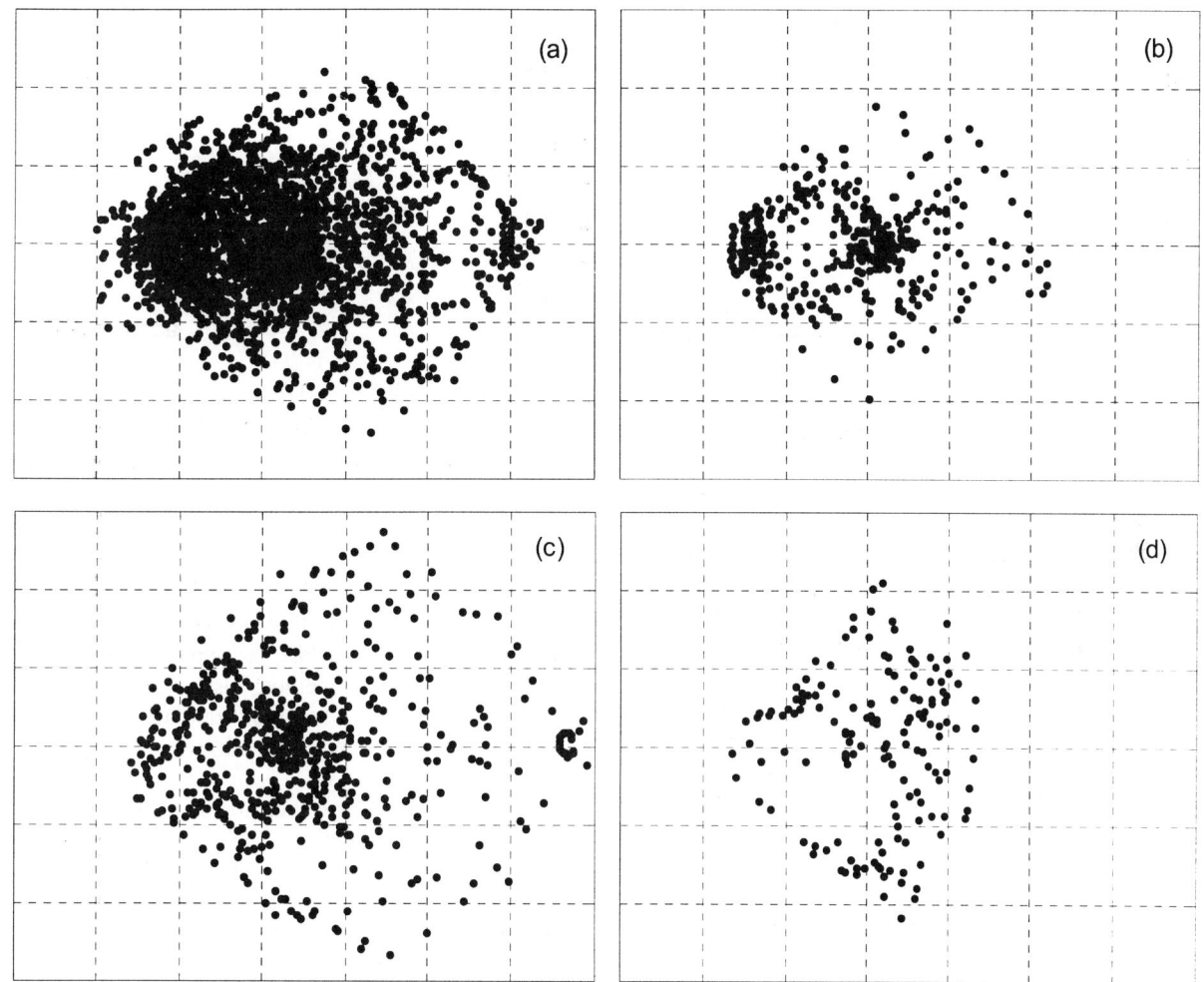

Fig. 3. System call sequences projected on the first two principal components.
(a) sequences appearing only in "clean" sessions; (b) sequences appearing in both "clean" sessions and sessions with attacks;
(c) attacks in the first week; (d) attacks in the second week.

V. NEURAL NETWORKS AS CLASSIFIERS

The ability of Artificial Neural Network to classify even if the data is complex, non-deterministic makes an effective implementation model for IDS. The sophisticated new attacks require a flexible and adaptable system that is capable to detect and generalize on the previous learning. A neural network model could potentially address such problems where unstructured data is needed to be classified. On the other hand, building neural network based IDS requires input and output data set and an appropriate architecture and training algorithm. The complexity and effectiveness is determined by the number of neurons in the network and functional relationship for interconnection. The ability of classify in response to the multifarious training data increases with the number of available neurons, where each neuron represents a computational degree of freedom available to the network.

Due to the characteristics of temporal clustered data, we have chosen a radial-basis function network [18]. The radial-basis function network involves three layers with different roles. The input layer is made up of source nodes that connect the network to its data processing unit. The output of the first-layer neurons, each of which represents the radial-basis function, is determined by the distance between the network input and the center of the basis function. The second layer applies a nonlinear transformation from the input space to the hidden space. The output layer is linear and produces a weighted sum of the outputs of the second layer.

An important feature of RBF network is that it is capable to construct local approximations to nonlinear input-output mappings. Thus, an RBF-based IDS can learn multiple local clusters of known attacks and clean data, and perform both misuse and anomaly detection at once. Given an input pattern, the network can check it against patterns it learned before, and make an educated guess as to where this input combination belongs.

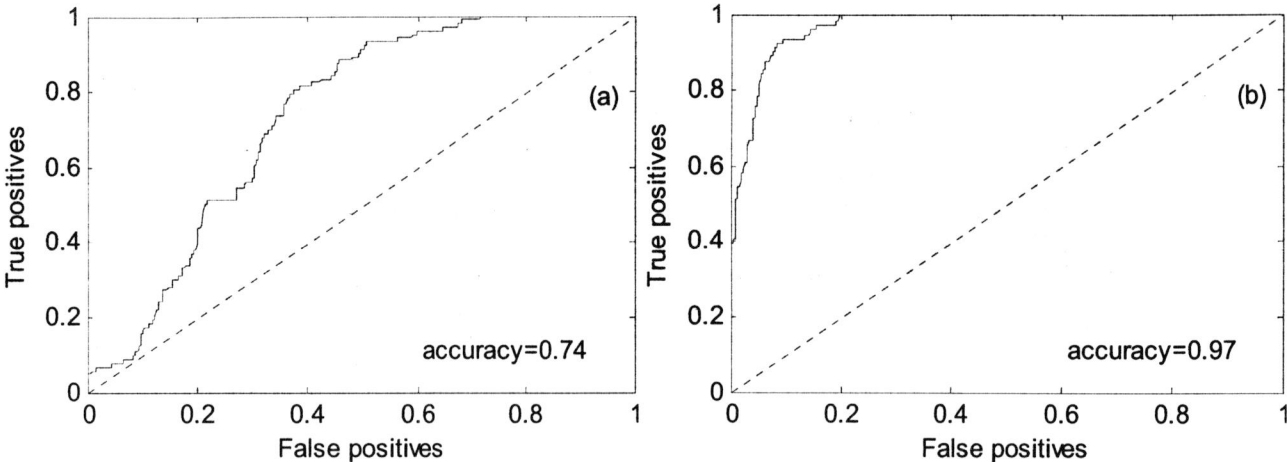

Fig. 4. Receiver operating characteristic curves for IDS trained on (a) the first week data only, and (b) the first week data and the second week "clean" data (2000 centers, spread 0.16).

To model the network we used function 'newrb' from MATLAB Neural Network toolbox [19]. This function builds the network incrementally, adding one center at a time, until the specified performance goal or number of the centers is reached. The centers are located at the positions of input vectors. Each iteration adds a center for the input with the greatest error. We trained from 32 to 2000 kernels with spreads between 0.06 and 8. The first experiment used the week one data for training and the week two data for testing; that is, the network was tested on the intrusion and clean data it had never seen. This allows to evaluate generalization and anomaly detection capabilities of the design. The ROC accuracy for different number of kernels and spreads is summarized in Table 1. An ROC curve for the best result we obtained is shown in Fig. 4(a). In the second experiment we amended the training set with the normal data from the week two; thus, in the test the network had to recognize only the unknown attack among the known normal data. As a result, the detection accuracy improved dramatically (Fig. 4(b)).

TABLE 1
ROC ACCURACY FOR DIFFERENT SPREADS AND CENTER NUMBERS

Centers	Spread									
	0.06	0.13	0.16	0.19	0.25	0.5	1	2	4	8
2000	0.69	0.73	0.74	0.73	0.72	0.64	0.55	0.51	0.54	0.50
1500	0.66	0.72	0.73	0.72	0.71	0.65	0.57	0.56	0.57	0.52
1000	0.62	0.68	0.69	0.70	0.68	0.65	0.58	0.53	0.53	0.49
500	0.59	0.68	0.67	0.67	0.65	0.67	0.58	0.49	0.50	0.45
250	0.56	0.63	0.63	0.63	0.67	0.70	0.61	0.62	0.63	0.62
125	0.55	0.63	0.62	0.65	0.65	0.68	0.68	0.68	0.70	0.70
64	0.53	0.62	0.63	0.62	0.64	0.68	0.70	0.67	0.69	0.67
32	0.53	0.63	0.63	0.60	0.67	0.64	0.65	0.64	0.65	0.62

VI. CONCLUSION

The key feature in this experiment was successful detection, using session data, to achieve high detection rate and still timely. The method, using system calls feature vectors, proved successful. Our training was not based on behavioral analysis, but rather, was to generalize the anomaly.

Due to temporally local characteristics, we have chosen RBF for our application. This prototype successfully demonstrated the capability as a data filter that highlights both anomalous intrusions and normal data on the learning patterns. Moreover, the deviations from normal behavior seem to be diagnosed quickly by our prototype. This capability is important, since our goal was to detect intrusion timely.

Experiments provide evidence that a careful audit reduction on session data would enable a high detection rate that could fit into a real time model.

The next step forward for this research would be to extend the feature vector to make IDS robust. As we are more interested in analysis of session data and results, there needs to be a thorough analysis on optimal window size. Also a hybrid network/host-based approach would be highly recommended, thereby increasing detection rate and decreasing the audit reduction processing.

ACKNOWLEDGMENT

We are thankful to Dr. Tim Draelos, Sandia National Laboratories, for helpful discussions.

REFERENCES

[1] S. A. Hofmeyr, S. Forrest, and A. Somayaji, "Intrusion detection using sequences of system calls," *Journal of Computer Security*, vol. 6, no. 3, pp. 151–180, 1998.

[2] J. Cannady, "The Application of Artificial Neural Networks to Misuse Detection: Initial Results," *Proceedings of the Recent Advances in Intrusion Detection '98 Conference (RAID'98)*, pp. 31-47, 1998.

[3] J. Cannady, "Artificial Neural Networks for Misuse Detection," *Proceedings of the 1998 National Information Systems Security Conference (NISSC'98)* October 5-8 1998. Arlington, VA, pp. 443–456, 1998.

[4] H. Debar, B. Dorizzi, "An application of a recurrent network to an intrusion detection system," *Proceedings of the 1992 IEEE International Conference on Neural Networks*, Vol. 2, pp. 478-483, 1992.

[5] J. Ryan, M. J. Lin, and R. Miikkulainen, "Intrusion detection with neural networks," *Proceedings of the 10th Advances in Neural Information Processing Systems Conference*, Denver, CO, 1998.

[6] L. Didaci, G. Giacinto, and Fabio Roli, "Ensemble Learning for Intrusion Detection in Computer Networks," *Proceedings of VIII Conference of AIIA, Siena, Italy, Sep. 10-13*, 2002. http://www-dii.ing.unisi.it/aiia2002/paper/APAUT/didaci-aiia02.pdf

[7] A. K. Ghosh and A. Schwartzbard, "A Study in Using Neural Networks for Anomaly and Misuse Detection," *Proceedings of the 8th USENIX Security Symposium*, Washington, D.C., USA, August 23–26, 1999.

[8] S. Mukkamala, G. Janoski, A. Sung, "Intrusion detection using neural networks and support vector machines," in *Proceedings of the 2002 International Joint Conference on Neural Networks, 2002, (IJCNN '02)*, vol. 2, pp. 1702 -1707, 2002.

[9] A. K. Ghosh, J. Wanken and F. Charron, "Detecting anomalous and unknown intrusions against programs," *Proceedings of the 1998 Annual Computer Security Applications Conference (ACSAC'98)*, pp. 259 –267, 1998.

[10] R. Sekar, Y. Guang, S. Verma, and T. Shanbhag, "A High-Performance Network Intrusion Detection System," in *Proceedings of the 6th ACM Conference on Computer and Communications Security*, pp. 8-17, Nov. 2-4, 1999.

[11] S. C. Lee and D. V. Heinbuch, "Training a neural-network based intrusion detector to recognize novel attacks," *Part A, IEEE Transactions on Systems, Man and Cybernetics*, Vol. 31-4, pp. 294 –299, 2001.

[12] W. Lee and S. J. Stolfo, "Data mining approaches for intrusion detection," in *Proceedings of the 7th USENIX Security Symposium (SECURITY'98)*, January 26--29, pp. 79–94, 1998.

[13] D. Endler, "Intrusion detection: Applying machine learning to Solaris audit data," Proceedings of the 1998 Annual Computer Security Applications Conference (ACSAC'98), pp. 268-279, Los Alamitos, CA, December 1998.

[14] R. K. Cunningham, R. P. Lippmann, D. J. Fried, S. L. Garfinkle, I. Graf, K. R. Kendall, S. E. Webster, D. Wyschogrod, M. A. Zissman, "Evaluating Intrusion Detection Systems without Attacking your Friends: The 1998 DARPA Intrusion Detection Evaluation", SANS 1999.

[15] *SunSHIELD Basic Security Module Guide*, Sun Microsystems, Inc., Palo Alto, 2000.

[16] K. J. Das. *"Attack development for Intrusion Detection Evaluation"*. Master Thesis, MIT, Cambridge, MA, June 2000.

[17] J. Korba, *"Windows NT Attacks for the Evaluation of Intrusion Detection Systems,"* BS/ME Thesis, MIT, 2000.

[18] S. Haykin, *Neural Networks: A Comprehensive Foundation*, 2nd ed., Upper Saddle River: Prentice Hall, 1999, pp. 256–317.

[19] H. Demuth, M. Beale, *Neural Network Toolbox User's Guide*, ver. 4, release 13, The MathWorks, Inc., Natick, MA, 2002, p. 7-7.

Application of The Method of Elastic Maps In Analysis of Genetic Texts

A. N. GORBAN
Institute of Computational
Modeling (ICM SB RAS),
Krasnoyarsk, Russia

A. Y. ZINOVYEV
Institut des Hautes Études
Scientifiques (IHES),
Bures-sur-Yvette, France

D.C. WUNSCH
University of Missouri-Rolla,
USA

Abstract - Method of elastic maps allows to construct efficiently 1D, 2D and 3D non-linear approximations to the principal manifolds with different topology (piece of plane, sphere, torus etc.) and to project data onto it. We describe the idea of the method and demonstrate its applications in analysis of genetic sequences.

I. INTRODUCTION

Numerous experimental techniques in modern molecular biology collect huge amounts of information that needs intelligent data-mining. The basic property of the information is its multidimensionality. Rather than 2-3 a typical object in database has hundreds and thousands features. Because of this the information loses it's clearness and one can't represent the data in visual form by standard visualization means – graphs and diagrams.

In this paper a technology of visual representation of data structure is described. Many interesting patterns could be discovered using visual two-dimensional (or three-dimensional) pictures of data and laying on it some additional relevant information. This data image should display cluster structures and different regularities in data.

The basic of the technology that we proposed in Gorban and Zinovyev (2001) is an original idea of *elastic net* – regular point approximation of a manifold that is embedded into multidimensional space and has minimal energy in a certain sense. This manifold is an analogue of principal surface and serves as a non-linear screen on which multidimensional data points can be projected.

Specialists in different fields can use the technology. We present an example of application of the technology in bioinformatics, where the need of visual data analysis is very necessary.

II. CONSTRUCTING ELASTIC NET

Method of elastic maps, similar to SOM (self-organizing maps), for approximation of a cloud of data points uses an ordered system of nodes which is placed in the multidimensional space.

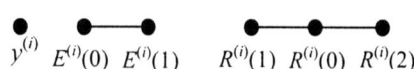

Fig 1. Node, edge and rib

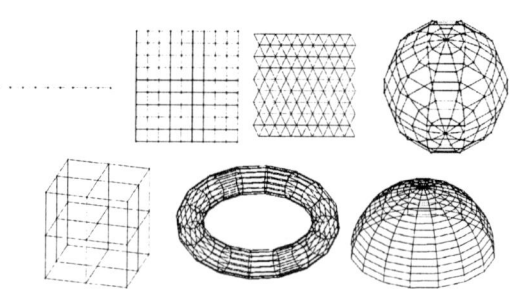

Fig 2. Elastic nets used in practice

Lets define *elastic net* as connected unordered graph $G(Y,E)$, where $Y = \{y^{(i)}, i=1..p\}$ denotes collection of graph nodes, and $\mathbf{E}=\{E^{(i)}, i=1..s\}$ is the collection of graph edges. Let's combine some of the adjacent edges in pairs $R^{(i)} = \{E^{(i)}, E^{(k)}\}$ and denote by $\mathbf{R}=\{R^{(i)}, i=1..r\}$ the collection of *elementary ribs*.

Every edge $E^{(i)}$ has the beginning node $E^{(i)}(0)$ and the end node $E^{(i)}(1)$. Elementary rib is a pair of adjacent edges. It has beginning node $R^{(i)}(1)$, end node $R^{(i)}(2)$ and the central node $R^{(i)}(0)$ (see Fig. 1).

Figure 2 illustrates some examples of the graphs practically used. The first is a simple polyline, the second is planar rectangular grid, third is planar hexagonal grid, forth – non-planar graph whose nodes are arranged on the sphere (spherical grid), then a non-planar cubical grid, torus and hemisphere. Elementary ribs at these graphs are adjacent edges that subtend a blunt angle.

Let's place nodes of the net in a multidimensional data space. This can be done in different ways, placing nodes randomly or placing nodes in a selected subspace. For example, it can be placed in the subspace spanned by first two or three principal components. In any case every node of the graph becomes a vector in R^M.

Then we define on the graph G energy function U that summarize energies of every node, edge and rib:

$$U = U^{(Y)} + U^{(E)} + U^{(R)}. \qquad (1)$$

Let's divide the whole collection of data points into subcollections (called *taxons*) $K^{(i)}$, $i = 1...p$. Each of them contains data points for which node $y^{(i)}$ is the closest one:

$$K_i = \{x^{(j)} : \|x^{(j)} - y^{(i)}\|_Y \to \min\}. \qquad (2)$$

Let's define

$$U^{(Y)} = \frac{1}{N} \sum_{i=1}^{p} \sum_{x^{(j)} \in K^{(i)}} \|x^{(j)} - y^{(i)}\|^2, \qquad (3)$$

$$U^{(E)} = \sum_{i=1}^{s} \lambda_i \|E^{(i)}(1) - E^{(i)}(0)\|^2, \qquad (4)$$

$$U^{(R)} = \sum_{i=1}^{r} \mu_i \|R^{(i)}(1) + R^{(i)}(2) - 2R^{(i)}(0)\|^2. \qquad (5)$$

Actually $U^{(Y)}$ is the average square of distance between $y^{(i)}$ and data points in $K^{(i)}$, $U^{(E)}$ is the analogue of summary energy of elastic stretching and $U^{(R)}$ is the analogue of summary energy of elastic deformation of the net. We can imagine that every node is connected by elastic bonds to the closest data points and simultaneously to the adjacent nodes (see Fig. 3).

Values λ_i and μ_j are coefficient of stretching elasticity of every edge $E^{(i)}$ and coefficient of bending elasticity of every rib $R^{(j)}$. In simple case we have

$$\lambda_1 = \lambda_2 = ... = \lambda_s = \lambda(s), \ \mu_1 = \mu_2 = ... = \mu_r = \mu(r).$$

Simplified consideration shows that, if we require that elastic energy of the net remains unchanged in case of finer net, then

$$\lambda = \lambda_0 s^{\frac{2-d}{d}}, \ \mu = \mu_0 r^{\frac{4-d}{d}} \qquad (6)$$

where d is the "dimension" of the net ($d = 1$ in the case of polyline, $d = 2$ in case of hexagonal, rectangular and spherical grids, $d = 3$ in case of cubical grid and so on).

Energy (1) is minimized to get the optimal configuration of nodes. For details of minimization procedure see Gorban et al. (2001), Gorban and Zinovyev (2001). Then the net is used as non-linear screen to visualize distribution of datapoints by projecting them onto the manifold, constructed using the net as point approximation. Then different colorings could be put onto the screen to show any function of coordinates of dataspace, for example, estimation of density of distribution (see Fig.4).

The method of constructing non-linear principal manifolds is implemented in freely distributed software ViDaExpert, working under Windows and available on the author's web page:
http://www.ihes.fr/~zinovyev/vida/vidaexpert.htm.

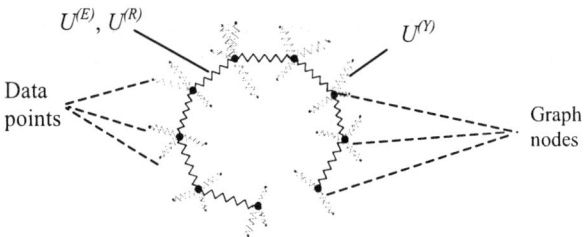

Fig. 3. Energy of elastic net

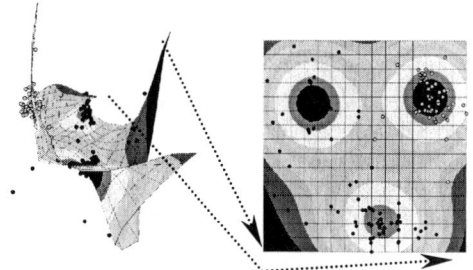

Fig.4. Visualization of distribution of datapoints, coloring by density.

III. VISUALIZATION OF TRIPLET DISTRIBUTIONS IN GENETIC TEXTS

Genetic text of DNA is a long sequence of letters (nucleotides or base pairs) A, C, G, T. Some subwords of the DNA code biological information, necessary for maintaining cell life cycle, and they are called *genes*. Areas between genes are called intergenic regions or *junk* (though it is not exactly true).

The most of working molecules in a cell are called *proteins* and they are composed from aminoacids. The information that defines the order of aminoacids in protein is coded in DNA by codons – triplets of nucleotides. If we take arbitrary window of coding sequence and divide it into successive non-overlapping triplets, starting from the first base pair in window, then this decomposition and arrangement of the real codons may not be *in phase*. We can divide the window into triplets in three ways, shifting every time on one base pair from the beginning. So we have three possible triplet distributions and one of them coincides with the real codons distribution. So the coding regions are characterized by the presence of distinguished phase.

Junk evidently has no such feature because inserting and deleting a letter in junk do not change properties of DNA considerably, thus this kind of mutations is allowed in the process of evolution. But every such mutation breaks the phase, so we can expect than the distributions of triplets in junk will be similar for all three phases.

In this section we analyze distribution of triplet frequencies in window of size W, sliding along the whole sequence.

Let us denote triplet frequency distribution by f_{ijk}, where $i,j,k \in \{A,C,G,T\}$, i.e., for example, f_{ACG} is equal to the frequency of the ACG codon in a given coding region. We have constructed datasets of triplet frequencies for several real genomes and for several model genetic sequences as follows:

1) Only the forward strands of genomes are used for triplet counting.

2) Every p positions in the sequence, we open a window $(x-W/2, x+W/2)$, of size W and centered at position x.

3) Every window, starting from the first base-pair, was divided into $W/3$ non-overlapping triplets, and the frequencies of all triplets f_{ijk} calculated.

4) The dataset consists of $N = [L/p]$ points, where L is the entire length of the sequence. Every data point $X_i = \{x_{is}\}$ corresponds to one window and has 64 coordinates, corresponding to each frequency of the sth possible triplet.

5) Then a standard procedure of centering and normalization on a unit dispersion is applied, i.e.,

$$\tilde{x}_{is} = \frac{x_{is} - m_s}{\sigma_s},$$

where $\tilde{x}_{is}$ is the value of sth coordinate of ith point after normalization, and

$m_s = \frac{1}{N} \sum_{t=1}^{N} x_{ts}$ is mean value of the sth coordinate,

$\sigma_s = \sqrt{\frac{1}{N} \sum_{t=1}^{N} (x_{ts} - m_s)^2}$ is the standard deviation of sth coordinate.

Algorithm of elastic maps was applied for these datasets. Below we present the results of visualization for *Caulobacter crescentus* complete genome (GenBank accession code is NC_002696). Parameters used are $W=300$, $p=600$.

In Fig.5a we presented distribution of data points projections on the elastic map. We made coloring by estimation of point density. One can see clearly that the distribution has 6 well-defined clusters and a sparse cloud of points between these clusters. To understand it, we used known annotation of the genome and marked by black circles points, corresponding to non-coding regions; squares and triangles corresponds to the coding regions, but in different strands of the genome (in bacterial genomes, a gene can be positioned in *forward* strand or *complementary* strand, in the last case it is red in opposite direction and consist of complementary letters G⇔C, T⇔A).

On the early stages of solving task of computational gene recognition (see, for example, Ficket, 1996), many statistics, locally defined on DNA text, were compared by means of application of the linear discrimination analysis (two classes – coding and non-coding were separated). On Fig.5b we made coloring by value of linear discriminate function. White color corresponds to the non-coding regions. One can see that linear discrimination in this case make a lot of false positive errors (many non-coding regions are predicted to be coding). More subtle analysis shows that linear discrimination is not appropriate in this case.

Figures 6a and 6b shows coloring by value of two triplet frequencies: TAA and TTA codon. It is known that many bacterial genes end with TAA stop codon and it can't be in the middle of gene. From the pictures we can understand that right bottom and top middle clusters correspond to those window, where triplet decomposition coincides with real codons, and other four clusters are windows with "shifted" phase.

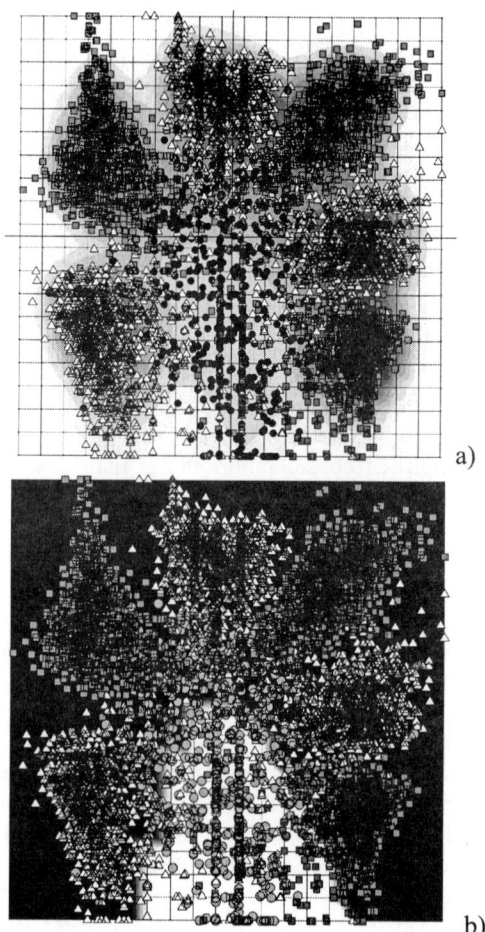

Fig. 5. Visualization of DNA triplet frequencies in sliding window.
a) point density coloring;
b) coloring by linear discrimination function

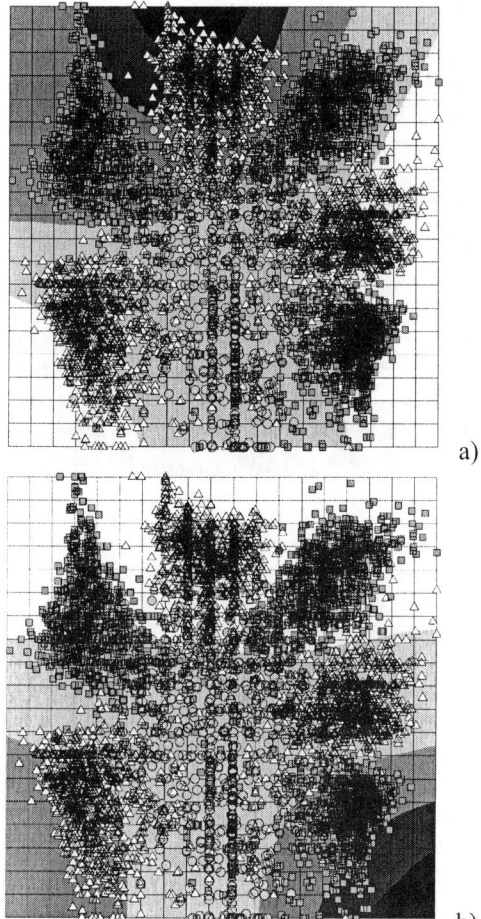

Fig. 6. Visualization of DNA triplet frequencies in sliding window.
a) coloring by TAA (stop codon) frequency;
b) coloring by TTA (complemented stop codon) frequency.

IV. CODON USAGE EXPLORATORY STUDY

As we mentioned, some parts of DNA texts encode templates, using which, all proteins in a cell are constructed. These parts are called genes. Elementary word in such a template is *codon* – three genetic letters. There is a map between all possible 64 codons and 20 aminoacids, from which proteins are constructed. In nature this is done by big biological molecule called *ribosome* – it reads sequence of codons, and link aminoacids in the order encoded by the sequence. This process is called *translation*.

Since mapping between codons and aminoacids is generative, then some aminoacids can be encoded by more then one codon. Those codons are called *synonymous* since they can be replaced in a template without change of resulting protein. Nevertheless some codons can be used in genes with much higher frequency then other their synonyms. This phenomenon is known as *codon bias*. There could be several reasons for explaining codon bias. For example, codon bias can exist because some letters of genetic text must be more frequent then others (for example, letters G and C can be very different in their frequencies then A and T).

In fast growing bacteria the codon bias is often connected with *translational efficiency* [5]. It means that not all codons are translated by ribosome with the same speed. As a result, some codons are preferred in those genes that encode proteins that must be produced at a high speed and quantity in a bacterium. For example, the ribosome itself is such a protein, cell should have many of ribosomes, and, therefore, most of ribosomal components are encoded in DNA with "fast" codons.

We are going to apply the method of elastic maps to the investigation of frequencies of codons in genes – so called *codon usage*. As in the previous section, every gene is represented as a 64-dimensional vector with components, corresponding to frequencies of all possible codons.

As our objects, we selected two very famous bacteria: **Escherichia coli** (GenBank accession code is NC_000913) and **Bacillus subtilis** (GenBank accession code is NC_000964).

Using known annotations of these genomes, we extracted all protein-coding gene sequences from these genomes. There were 4289 marked genes in Escherichia coli and 4100 in Bacillus subtilis. Tables of frequencies of codons for every gene were used to visualize codon usage for both organisms, using the elastic maps method.

On Fig.7 the codon usage of Escherichia coli is presented. Forms of the points correspond to the K-Means clustering into 4 clusters, performed in 64-dimensional space. The background coloring represents density of points. Let us call triangles as genes of class I, circles as genes of class II, squares as genes of class III, and rhombs as genes of class IV.

Comparing the picture with data known from literature on codon usage in different genomes [5-8], we can conclude that class I contains most of genes with very diverse functions. Class II contains genes that are highly expressed in a cell (present in large quantities). Class III contains genes with unusual (non-specific for a given genome) codon usage. Often these genes are suspected to be transferred from other organisms (*horizontal transfer* phenomena). Finally, genes in class IV encode proteins which are considerably different in their aminoacids composition from the rest of proteins. Namely, these proteins contain many highly hydrophobic aminoacids (like leucine and phenylalanine) and small number of hydrophilic aminoacids (like arginine and glutamate).

To demonstrate how useful the display constructed with method of elastic map could be, let us give some examples.

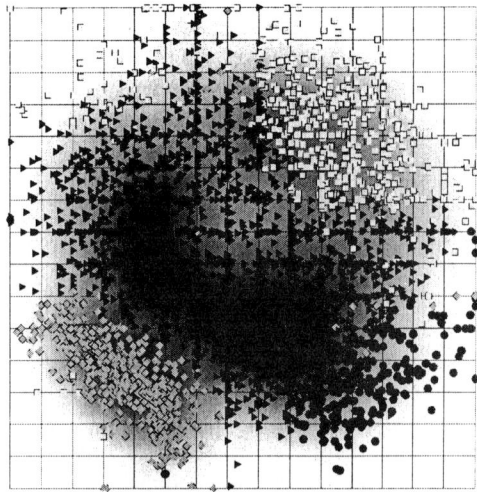

Fig. 7. Codon usage of Escherichia coli. The gray coloring shows density distribution.

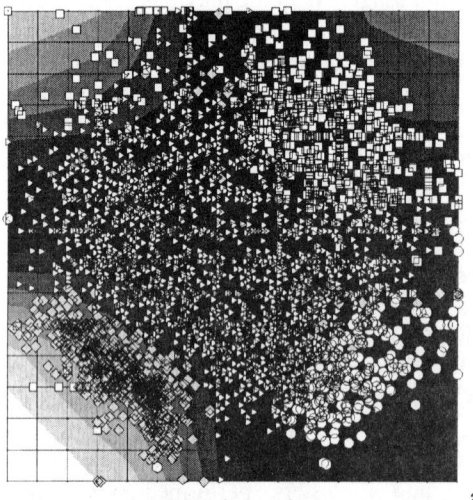

a)

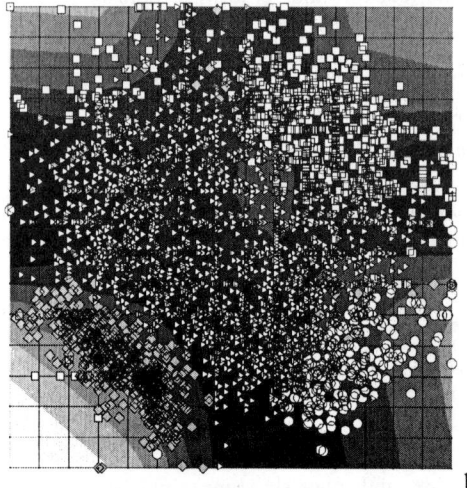

b)

Fig. 8. Codon usage of Escherichia coli. The coloring a) shows frequency of GAA codon; b) frequency of GAG codon.

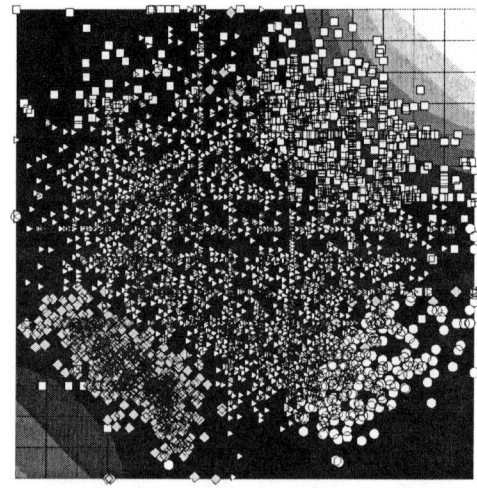

Fig. 9. Codon usage of Escherichia coli. The coloring shows GC-content of genes.

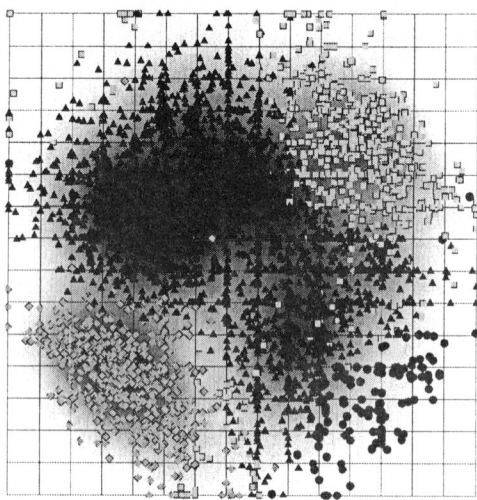

Fig. 10. Codon usage of Bacillus subtilis. The gray coloring shows density distribution.

It is known that glutamate aminoacid can be encoded in genes with two codons: GAA and GAG. Figure 8a and 8b show colorings corresponding to the frequencies of these two codons. It is clear that the class IV lacks this type of codons (as we mentioned, the class IV is glutamate-poor). Also we can conclude that part of genes in the class II uses much more GAA codons than GAG, but this is not so contrast in the genes of class I. This means that GAA codon is translationally preferred in comparison with GAG codon.

Other important characteristic of codon usage is GC-content of a gene (relative percentage of G and C letters in a gene). It is clear that GC-content is a simple linear function of codon frequencies. On Fig. 9 this function is represented. It is clear that class III of genes is very different from others in it's GC-content (it is GC-poor or AT-rich in comparison with all other classes).

Figure 10 represents visualization of codon usage of Bacillus subtilis. The pattern of codon usage in this case is very similar to E.coli bacterium. Indeed, they are both fast-growing bacteria with similar growing conditions.

V. CONCLUSION

In this paper we described the method of elastic maps for constructing representations of experimental data-tables in visual form. These representations may give insight to how data should be treated and what quantitative methods might be applied. Besides, informative pictures of data give possibility to control process of data analysis and make it more reliable.

The purpose of this method (with respect to the applications in data visualization) is to provide more informative data visualization displays that are suitable for visualizing not only data points but also informative layers of related characteristics. With increasing number of experimental datasets in such fields as molecular biology, the need in such tools will grow continuously.

As it has been demonstrated, the method allows discovering interesting patterns in large datasets, such as tables of local triplet frequencies for long genetic texts or codon usage tables.

REFERENCES

[1] Gorban A.N., Pitenko A.A., Zinov'ev A.Y., Wunsch D.C. 2001. "Visualization of any data using elastic map method." *Smart Engineering System Design*, V.11, p. 363-368.

[2] Gorban A.N., Zinovyev A.Yu. 2001. "Visualization of Data by Method of Elastic Maps and Its Applications in Genomics, Economics and Sociology." *Institut des Hautes Études Scientifiques preprint*. IHES/M/01/34, 2001 [http://www.ihes.fr/PREPRINTS/M01/Resu/resu-M01-34.html]

[3] Gorban A.N., Zinovyev A. Yu. Method of Elastic Maps and its Applications in Data Visualization and Data Modeling // International Journal of Computing Anticipatory Systems, CHAOS. 2001. V. 12. PP. 353-369.

[4] Fickett J.W. 1996. "The Gene Identification Problem: An Overview For Developers." *Computers Chem.*, Vol.20, No.1, pp.103-118.

[5] M. Gouy, Ch. Gautier. Codon usage in bacteria: correlation with gene expressivity. *Nucleic Acids Research*, 10:7055-7070, 1982.

[6] I. Moszer, E.P.C. Rocha, A.Danchin. Codon usage and lateral gene transfer in *Bacillus subtilis*. *Current Opinion in Microbiology*, 2:524-528, 1999.

[7] P.M. Sharp, E. Cowe, D.G. Higgins, D.C. Shields, K.H. Wolfe, F.Wright. Codon usage patterns in Escherichia coli, *Bacillus subtilis, Saccharomyces cerevisiae, Drosophila melanogaster and Homo sapiens:* a review of the considerable within-species diversity. Nucleic Acids Research, 16:8207-2811, 1988.

[8] C. Medigue, T. Rouxel, P. Vigier, A. Henaut, A. Danchin. Evidence for horizontal gene transfer in *Escherichia coli* speciation. *Journal of Molecular Biology*, 222:851-856, 1991.

Towards a Tactile Communication System with Dialog-based Tuning

Carsten Wilks, Thomas Schieder, and Rolf Eckmiller
Division of Neuroinformatics
Department of Computer Science
University of Bonn, Germany
{wilks, schieder, eckmiller}@nero.uni-bonn.de

Abstract—We present a tactile intelligent sensory substitution system (TIS^3) as a novel tactile communication system with dialog-based tuning. TIS^3 consists of a tactile encoder (TE) which maps desired objects or patterns (P) onto spatio-temporal stimulation patterns (P') as a parallel stream of stimulation time courses, by means of a tactile stimulator array (TS) at selected skin location to elicit tactile perceptions (P*). The human subject evaluates and compares a percept P* with a given object P as association goal. A Learning Module (LM) for dialog based TE-tuning transforms these evaluations into TE-change signals. In a first step, the application of a dialog-based TE-tuning was successfully tested using a TS version with fifteen stimulators on the lower arm for regaining the corresponding stimulation pattern P' for a given tactile reference percept P^*_{ref}. Optimization of P* was achieved in less than 100 iteration steps by means of a micro evolutionary learning algorithm (MEA).

I. INTRODUCTION

In many situations like private communication, aid for impaired or availment of visual and auditory channels by other tasks, transmission of information via the tactile channel can be advantageous [6].

In order to use the skin as a channel to transmit information which are in general not tactilely perceived, a suitable encoding, i.e. translation of the information into a tactile stimulation that evokes the appropriate perception, is essential. The problem which arises in building such an encoder [4] is that there exists no general tactile language as a basis of information coding. Besides, the information processing in the brain which leads eventually to a perception is currently not well understood.

In contrast to existing approaches TIS^3 does not use predetermined tactile patterns but it develops a set of tactile patterns with the aid of a learning module [10] [8] based on the perception of the human subject. This approach has two important advantages: The tactile patterns can be optimally adjusted a) to the tactile application and b) to the human subject.

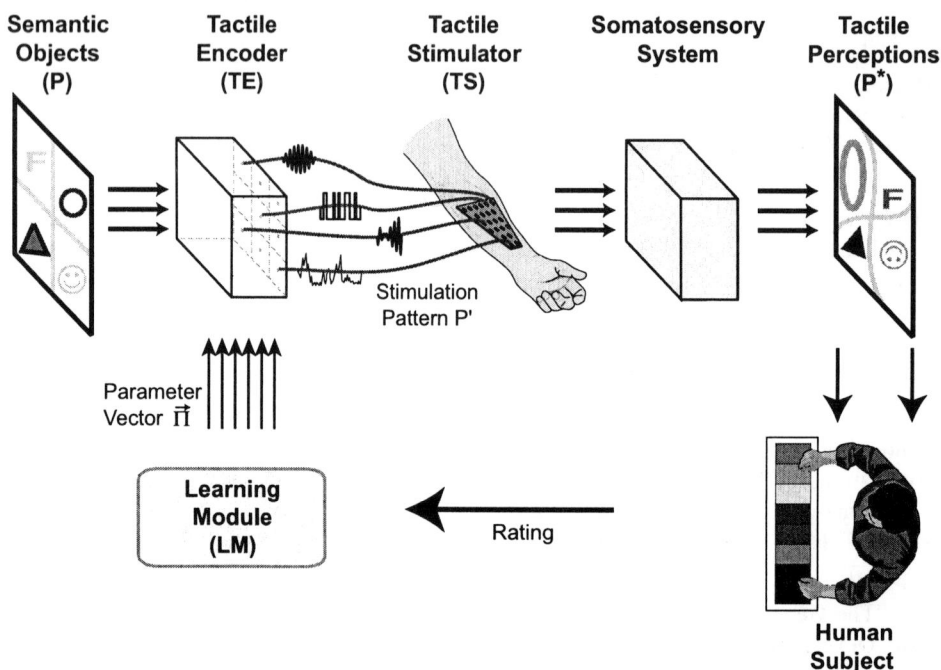

Fig. 1. *Scheme of the Tactile Intelligent Sensory Substitution System (TIS^3).* Semantic objects P are transformed by the Tactile Encoder (TE) into stimulation patterns P', thus evoking via the Tactile Stimulator (TS) tactile perceptions P* that lead eventually to an association of the semantic object P. The appropriate encoding function is learned in a perception-based dialog with a Learning Module (LM) which controls the tactile encoder via a parameter vector $\vec{\Pi}$, based on the feedback of previously rated tactile stimulations.

Our setup shown in Fig. 1 consists of a tactile encoder (TE), a tactile stimulator (TS), the human subject, and a learning module (LM).

There are two different modes of operation. Within the first mode the settings of TE are learned in a perception-based learning procedure. The second mode includes the operation in daily use. In this case the semantic objects are mapped by TE to the previously learned tactile stimulations of the first mode.

Within the first mode, the mapping of the TE is learned in an iterative process described below:

A semantic object P presented to TE should evoke a tactile perception P* that can be easily associated to P. The question is now, what is a suitable tactile perception P* to cause this association? In order to find this P* evoked by TE, LM adjusts TE by different parameter vectors $\vec{\Pi}$. Each $\vec{\Pi}$ causes the encoder to generate different temporal signals P' for TS and thus to evoke different tactile perceptions P*. The human subject has to compare these different P* with each other and with this feedback LM generates new parameter vectors $\vec{\Pi}$ for TE. This iteration is repeated until the human subject has found a suitable tactile perception P* that can be associated with the semantic object P. That way the system learns a mapping from P to P* for several objects, establishing a tactile communication system.

We implemented a first version of the tactile encoder on a DSP, which drives magneto-mechanical stimulators via a multi-channel-DAC. Furthermore we implemented a learning module with a ranking routine to be able to align and to optimize the parameters of the learning algorithm in a simulation process. With this optimized learning algorithm we examined TIS[3] in a closed loop experiment with the human subject.

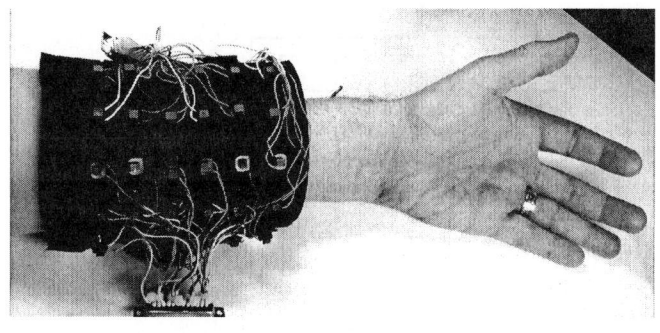

Fig. 2. Tactile arm stimulator-array, a) General position on the lower arm. b) Enlargement with electromagnetic actuators on upper side protruding tactile stimulator tips on lower side.

II. METHODS

The very challenging task of transducing semantic objects, see Fig. 1, such as alphanumerical characters or geometric objects into spatio-temporal stimulation patterns is not addressed in this paper. As a first step we investigate wether it is possible to deploy the feedback resulting from the comparison of suggested evoked perceptions P^*_{actual} with a *predetermined* evoked perception P^*_{ref} for an adaptation process in which P^*_{actual} converge to P^*_{ref}. P^*_{ref} is evoked by TE and TS based on a parameter vector $\vec{\Pi}_{ref}$. The task of LM is now to suggest different $\vec{\Pi}_{actual}$ and to minimize the difference between P^*_{ref} and P^*_{actual} in an iterative process solely based on the feedback of the human subject, i.e. based on the human's comparison of his tactile perceptions.

For a tactile application it is essential not to overstress the concentration and the patience of the human subject. This means that the number of iterations used to generate a similar perception to P^*_{ref} has to be minimized. In order to achieve this we optimized LM with the aid of simulations.

III. RESULTS

A. Tactile Arm-Stimulator (TS)

The tactile stimulator consists of magneto-mechanical vibrators, which are rectangularly arranged on a matrix (currently 5×3) at a distance of about $20\,mm$. This stimulator array is attached, for example, to the left forearm of the human subject, see Fig. 2(a). To assure the correct position of the stimulators towards the skin in regard to its curvature, the solenoids are fixed on a bended piece of foam rubber (Fig. 2(b)). Thereby the distance between the magnets stimulating the skin and the solenoids is ensured. In quiescent state the magnets impress into the skin due to the mounting on a tense membrane under the foam rubber so that the contact is guaranteed at any time.

Stimulation is possible at frequencies of 5-488 Hz, with a slide stroke of up to $0.3\,mm$. The vibrators are driven by a multi-channel-DAC with downstream power-amplifiers.

B. Tactile Encoder (TE)

In the following we briefly describe the hardware realization and afterwards the task of generating the tactile patterns.

1) Hardware design: The tactile encoder is realized on a digital signal processor (DSP TMS320C55) from Texas Instruments, operating at a clock rate of 132 MHz. A 32-channel-DAC from Analog Devices AD5532 is attached, which is controlled by the DSP via a serial port. In consideration of

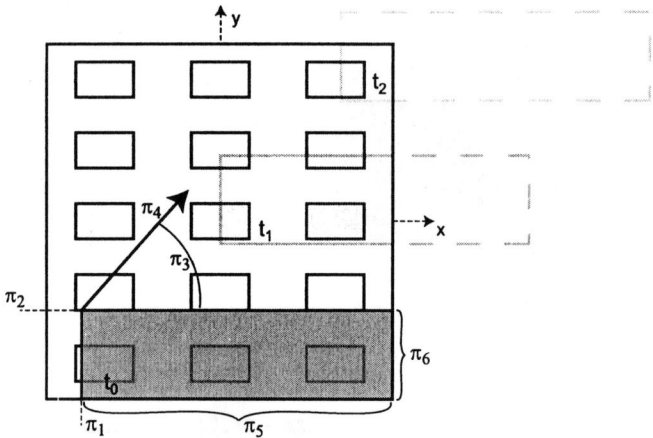
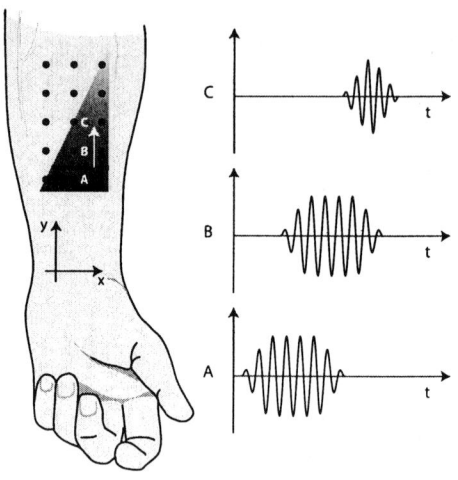

Fig. 3. *Scheme of the functionality of the simple tunable spatio-temporal signal algorithm (TSA) as a first implementation of TE function.* The rectangles uniformly covering the virtual stimulation area represent a set of function generators for tactile stimulation corresponding to an array of tactile vibrators of TS. Depending on the overlap of the moving object (MO, dark grey rectangle) with the generator areas the according stimulators are modulated.

Fig. 4. *Spatio-temporal stimulation on the forearm.* Schematic of the reference stimulation generated by TSA as depicted in Fig. 3. The sensation of this stimulation can be described as a moving bar with decreasing size. The black circles represent the locations of the stimulators. On the right side the stimulation time curves generated by TE for three stimulators A, B, C are schematically illustrated, demonstrating the amplitude modulating functionality and spatio-temporal characteristics of TSA.

the maximum speed of the serial bus of the DAC (14 MHz), the number of channels to be addressed (32), the number of bits to be transmitted (24) for updating one channel, and other limiting facts like required pauses after writing of one frame (min. 400ms), the maximum frequency of each single channel reaches about 15.7 kHz. This satisfies the requirements since the maximum frequency perceived by the skin is about 500 Hz [2].

The signals of the DAC are subsequently power-amplified so that they are able to drive the stimulators. In an analogous manner other types of stimulators may be utilized accordingly.

2) Pattern generation: In order to explore how to construct the generators suitable for producing a variety of tactile stimulations we made first experiments based on amplitude-modulated sinus-functions.

As a first step we generated stimulations by activating adjacent stimulators correlated in time to each other. By this means it is possible to generate waves or moving objects. These kinds of stimulation are easily recognized by the visual sense, and we expect it to be proper for the tactile sense [7].

On one hand the parametrization should not restrict the variety of spatio-temporal tactile stimulations. On the other hand the number of parameters should be as small as possible to reduce the time for learning.

Taking this into account we implemented a spatio-temporal Tunable Signal Algorithm (TSA) in which a moving object (MO) is characterized by a parameter vector $\vec{\Pi}$. TSA defines MO by a linear movement on a virtual 2-dimensional area (Fig. 3) and can be easily parameterized by position_x, position_y, velocity, direction, size_x, and size_y:

$$\vec{\Pi} = \begin{pmatrix} \pi_1 \\ \vdots \\ \pi_6 \end{pmatrix} = (\text{position}_x, \text{position}_y, \text{direction}, \text{velocity}, \text{size}_x, \text{size}_y)^T$$

The virtual stimulation area is uniformly covered with rectangles representing the amplitudes of the generators. If MO overlaps one of these areas, the respective stimulator is activated with a fixed frequency of 250Hz and an amplitude proportional to the overlap.

By these means the stimulators are controlled by amplitude-modulated functions with a carrier frequency which is optimally suited for the Pacinian-corpuscles of the skin. To increase the manifoldness of stimulation several MOs may be superposed.

The parameter vector $\vec{\Pi}_{\text{ref}}$ used in this paper is chosen in a way that many of the options of TSA are exploited, such as the changing of position and size of the stimulation area.

C. Learning Module (LM)

1) Learning Strategy: LM is implemented by a micro evolutionary algorithm (MEA) [5] [3] [12] with three rival populations. The populations have different mutation rates r_z and different numbers of individuals. Within our implementation each individual of MEA is represented by a parameter vector $\vec{\Pi}$. All individuals $\vec{\Pi}$ for each iteration loop (i.e. generation, numbered by t_{gen}) are rated within a ranking list. Let l_i be the place of the ranking list of the ith individual. Then the fitness of each individual is calculated by: $\text{fit}_i = 101 - 100 \cdot l_i \cdot \frac{1}{8}$.

Each population grows up autonomously for a defined number of generations (isolation time, t_{iso}). Then the populations interchange their best individual in respect to fitness (migration). The total sum of individuals of one generation is fixed to 8 while the number of individuals of each population is variable. After a defined number of generations (t_{cha}) the size of populations is changed. The population which contains the best individual in respect of fitness increases its number of individuals and the population with the worst individual decreases (resource adaption). To make sure that no population is completely deleted a maximum number of individuals (set to 6) and a minimum number of individuals (set to 1) per population are defined. The best individual of the current generation is transferred without changes to the next generation (elitist survival) [9].

A selection operator which is proportional to fitness is used (stochastic universal sampling [1]) to select two individuals per population for discrete recombination. Within the mutation task one parameter $i \in \{\pi_1 \ldots \pi_6\}$ is randomly chosen. To the current value of this parameter the random value $\sigma \cdot r_z \cdot d_i \cdot 2^{-u \cdot k_z}$ is added [11] with:

$\sigma \in \{-1, +1\}$, $u \in [0 \ldots 1]$ equally distributed,
k_z : mutation precision, d_i : domain of parameter i,
r_z : mutation rate of population z.

This procedure is repeated six times for each individual $\vec{\Pi}$. The mutation precision k_z is set in a way that the minimum value of mutation is 1.

2) Optimization of the Learning Module: To optimize the learning module many combinations of parameters of the learning algorithm (e.g. r_z, t_{iso}) have to be tested [14]. This means that a large number of iteration steps is required, making the application of an automatized ranking mandatory. We implemented a ranking routine (called *fitness oracle (FO)*) to substitute the human subject during the optimization phase. The fitness oracle computes the euclidian distance of the parameter vectors $\vec{\Pi}$ that evoke P^*_{ref} and P^*_{actual}. In order to rate a parameter set of the learning algorithm it is necessary to compute several cycles of the learning process with the same parameters, as the evolutionary algorithm is a stochastical learning process. We always computed 40 cycles to get a sufficient statistic. One cycle consists of $t_{\text{gen}} = 600$ computed generations of individuals.

3) Simulation results with Fitness Oracle: We performed a parameter sweep of the evolutionary algorithm to analyze the convergence behavior. Fig. 5 shows the typical behavior of a successful simulation: In Fig. 5a) the development of the euclidian distance of the most successful individual of each population is plotted respectively. The aim of minimizing the euclidian distance is reached within $t_{gen} = 140$ iterations. At the beginning of the iteration process ($t_{gen} < 20$) the euclidian distance of all populations decreases rapidly. This is due to the large mutation rate of population 1 and the interchange of individuals between the populations (migration). As soon as the large mutation rate becomes less successful, the number of individuals of population 1 decreases, as depicted in Fig. 5b). This demonstrates the automatically resizing populations. The euclidian distance of population 3 becomes successfully reduced with growing number of iterations ($t_{gen} > 60$), however only through the 'help' of populations 1 and 2. Since the minimal number of individuals per population is set to 1, the exploration of the parameter space is continued in a more global neighborhood by population 1 and 2 to minimize the risk of being trapped in a local minimum.

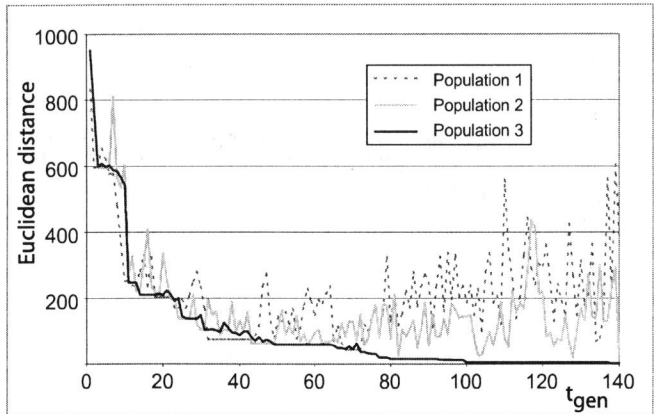

(a) Euclidian distance between reference and actual pattern vectors

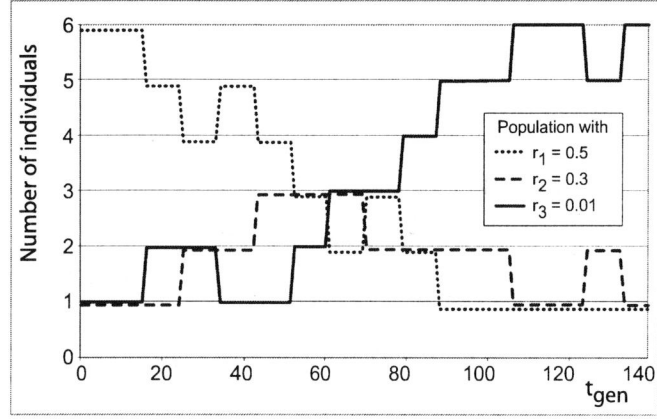

(b) Evolution of the numbers of individuals for each population

Fig. 5. *Typical curve progression of the simulation.* Fig. 5a) depicts the progression of the euclidian distance between the vector of the reference pattern $\vec{\Pi}_{ref}$ and of the best individual of each population respectively. With growing number of iterations, labelled as generation time t_{gen}, the overall best individual continuously improves its euclidian distance. As indicated in Fig. 5b), the number of individuals gradually increases in the winning population 3, while the total number of individuals of all participating and communicating populations remains constant.

D. Dialog-based tuning tests

As a first step the results of the simulation, e.g. the settings for the learning algorithm, were now used for a dialog-based tuning test of TIS[3] (see Fig. 1) including the arm stimulator-array. Within this experiment the rating of the presented patterns is solely based on the tactile perception of the human subject, comprising its inevitable fluctuations due to fatigue, minor movement of the arm, and small changes of the position of the device during the experiment.

An appreciable adaptation of perception towards the reference pattern could be obtained within less than 80 generations. This progress is reflected in a convergence of the parameter-components speed x/y and start position x/y towards the respective reference-value, as depicted in Fig. 6(a) and 6(b).

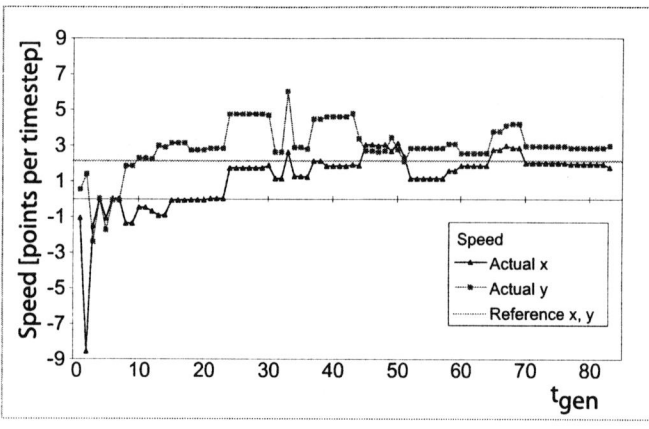

(a) Convergence of the parameters of speed

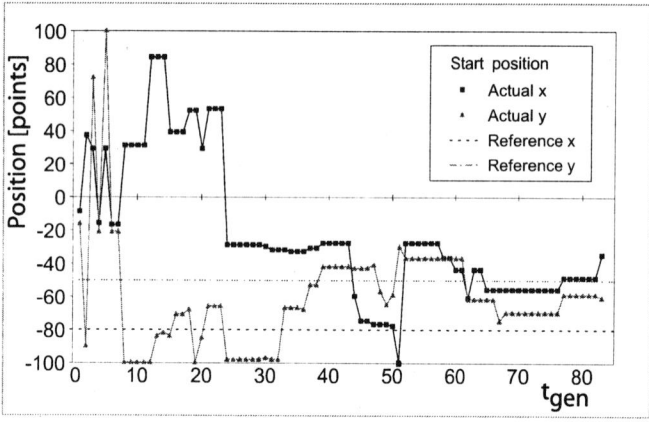

(b) Convergence of the parameters of the start position

Fig. 6. *Development of some parameters of the best individual against generation time t_{gen} for a typical closed loop experiment [13].*

IV. Discussion and Conclusion

In a first experiment the generated stimulation was successfully approximated towards a predetermined evoked perception P^*_{ref}. This indicates that it is possible to find tactile stimulations which evoke P^*_{ref}, with the learning algorithm according to the rating of perceptions of the human subject. Therewith our experimental result shows the applicability of a tactile encoder which is adjusted in a perception-based learning process.

The simulation results show the automatic resizing of populations. Thus the population with the greatest improvement automatically gets most performance. The advantage of this approach is that the algorithm adjusts itself to the learning behavior of the human subject.

In order to optimize the learning algorithm in simulation we replaced the perception-based rating of the presented stimuli by a fitness oracle, defined at a first step as the euclidian distance of $\vec{\Pi}_{ref}$ and $\vec{\Pi}_{actual}$. This simplification has the disadvantage that during the simulations the psychophysics of the tactile perception is ignored. Consequently the next step has to be to improve the fitness oracle in order to optimize the algorithm on more realistic conditions.

In the experiment within less than 100 iteration cycles the parameters of P^*_{actual} converge towards the parameters of P^*_{ref}. Otherwise, since the basis of valuation is the tactile perception and not the parameter vector, the parameters of P^*_{actual} and P^*_{ref} do not necessarily have to converge exactly to the same values, since similar perception can be evoked by different parameters. There is no unique objective function for the comparison of tactile perceptions. Hence the deployment of an adaptive System for TIS[3] seems to be the only applicable approach. Gradient based learning algorithms are not suitable because of the missing objective function.

Towards the development of a tactile language which is optimally suited for tactile perception it is necessary to develop a procedure which enables the learning of different pairs of semantic object and tactile stimulations. One approach refers to the learning of preferably distinguishable tactile patterns, which are easily discriminable and recognizable. During or after the learning process the association is defined by the user. Another approach assumes that associations from one modality can as well be addressed by another. In this case TIS[3] has to reveal this unexplored mapping by generating tactile patterns which evoke these associations.

Based on our experiment with TIS[3] we can conclude that the human tactile perceptions can be successfully communicated to a technical learning module by means of specific evolutionary algorithms.

Acknowledgment

This work has been supported by a grant ('LENI') from the German Federal Research Ministry (BMBF).

References

[1] J. E. Baker, "Reducing bias and inefficiency in the selection algorithm," in *Proceedings of the Second International Conference on Genetic Algorithms and their Application*. Hillsdale, New Jersey, USA: Lawrence Erlbaum Associates, 1987, pp. 14–21.

[2] S. J. Bolanowski, G. A. Gescheider, R. T. Verillo, and C. M. Checkosky, "Four channels mediate the mechanical aspects of touch," *J. Acoust. Soc. Am.*, vol. 84, pp. 1680–1694, Nov 1988.

[3] C. A. Coello Coello and G. Toscano Pulido, "A micro-genetic algorithm for multiobjective optimization," in *First International Conference on Evolutionary Multi-Criterion Optimization*, E. Zitzler, K. Deb, L. Thiele, C. A. C. Coello, and D. Corne, Eds. Springer-Verlag. Lecture Notes in Computer Science No. 1993, 2001, pp. 126–140.

[4] R. Eckmiller, R. Hünermann, and M. Becker, "Exploration of a dialog-based tunable retina encoder for retina implants," *Neurocomputing*, vol. 26, pp. 1005–1011, 1999.

[5] D. E. Goldberg, "Sizing populations for serial and parallel genetic algorithms," in *Proceedings of the Third International Conference on Genetic Algorithms*, J. D. Schaffer, Ed. San Mateo, California: Morgan Kaufmann Publishers, 1989, pp. 70–79.

[6] M. H. Goldstein and A. Proctor, "Tactile aids for profoundly deaf children," *J. Acoust. Soc. Am.*, vol. 77, pp. 258–265, Jan 1985.

[7] G. R. Gonzales, "Symbol recognition produced by points of tactile stimulation," *Mayo Clin. Proc.*, vol. 71, pp. 1039–1046, 1996.

[8] T. Hanne, "Global multiobjective optimization with evolutionary algorithms: Selection mechanisms and mutation control," in *Proceedings of the First International Conference on Evolutionary Multi-Criterion Optimization (EMO 2001)*, ser. Lecture Notes in Computer Science, E. Zitzler, K. Deb, L. Thiele, C. A. C. Coello, and D. Corne, Eds., vol. 1993. Berlin: Springer-Verlag, 2001, pp. 197–212.

[9] M. Laumanns, E. Zitzler, and L. Thiele, "On the effects of archiving, elitism, and density based selection in evolutionary multi-objective optimization," in *First International Conference on Evolutionary Multi-Criterion Optimization*. Springer-Verlag. Lecture Notes in Computer Science No. 1993, 2001, pp. 181–196.

[10] A. Leonhardi, W. Reissenberger, T. Schmelmer, K. Weicker, and N. Weicker, "Development of problem-specific evolutionary algorithms," in *Parallel Problem Solving from Nature – PPSN V*, A. E. Eiben, T. Bäck, M. Schoenauer, and H.-P. Schwefel, Eds. Berlin: Springer, 1998, pp. 388–397.

[11] H. Mühlenbein and D. Schlierkamp-Voosen, "Predictive models for the breeder genetic algorithm: I. continuous parameter optimization." *Evolutionary Computation*, vol. 1, pp. 25–49, 1993.

[12] C. R. Reeves, "Using genetic algorithms with small populations," in *Proceedings of the 5th International Conference on Genetic Algorithms*. San Mateo, CA: Morgan Kaufmann, 1993, pp. 92–99.

[13] T. Schieder, C. Wilks, and R. Eckmiller, "Towards a tunable tactile communication system: concept and first experiments," in *Proceedings of the 12th International Workshop on Neural Networks for Signal Processing (NNSP)*, H. Bourlard, T. Adali, B. S., L. J., and D. S., Eds., 2002, pp. 767–776.

[14] A. Simões and E. Costa, "Parametric study to enhance the genetic algorithm's performance when using transformation," in *GECCO 2002: Proceedings of the Genetic and Evolutionary Computation Conference*, W. B. Langdon, E. Cantú-Paz, K. Mathias, R. Roy, D. Davis, R. Poli, K. Balakrishnan, V. Honavar, G. Rudolph, J. Wegener, L. Bull, M. A. Potter, A. C. Schultz, J. F. Miller, E. Burke, and N. Jonoska, Eds. New York: Morgan Kaufmann Publishers, 9-13 July 2002, p. 697.

Unsupervised Similarity-Based Feature Selection Using Heuristic Hopfield Neural Networks

S. Y. M. Shi and P. N. Suganthan, *IEEE Senior Member*
School of Electrical & Electronic Engineering
Nanyang Technological University
Republic of Singapore
epnsugan@ntu.edu.sg

Abstract - An unsupervised similarity-based feature selection approach using heuristic Hopfield neural networks (UFS-HHNN) is presented. The key novel ingredient of the algorithm is to formulate the feature selection problem as a combinational optimization problem. To our best of knowledge, this is the first attempt at formulating feature selection as a combinatorial optimization problem. We map the feature selection problem to a single layered Hopfield Networks and adjust parameters. Maximum Information Compression Index (MICI), the amount of reconstruction error committed if the data is projected to a reduced dimension in the best possible way [1], is employed as a similarity measure. Simulation on eight benchmark datasets with different dimensions and size shows that feature subsets with much lower redundancy are achieved by UFS_HHNN than the recently developed unsupervised algorithm [1]. Our approach can be easily extended to supervised feature selection and feature scaling.

I. INTRODUCTION

Feature selection plays an important role in pattern classification and data mining. The problem of feature selection may be defined as follows: given a set of candidate features and a collection of data samples, select a subset that performs the best according to a specified criterion. This procedure can reduce not only the cost of processing by reducing the number of features that need to be collected, but in some cases it can also provide a better performance due to finite sample size effects [2] and elimination of redundancy. The term *feature selection* is taken to refer to algorithms that output a subset of the input feature set. More generic methods that create new features using transformations or combinations of the original features are termed feature extraction algorithms [3]. This paper is concerned primarily with the former.

Feature selection has been the focus of interest for quite some time and much work has been done [4]. There are two main approaches to feature subset selection [5]: wrapper approach [6] [7] and filtering approach. The idea of the wrapper approach is to select feature subset using the evaluation function based on the same learning algorithm that will be used for learning on the problem domain represented with the selected features [8]. It is used only in the supervised learning. While in the filtering approach, a feature subset is selected independently of the learning method that will use the selected features. Filter approach can be used in both supervised learning and unsupervised learning.

Since the interest of this paper lies with unsupervised feature selection, we briefly describe feature selection algorithms used in machine learning that are based on the filtering approaches. Almuallim and Dietterich [9] developed several feature subset selection algorithms including a simple exhaustive search and several heuristics-based algorithms. They based their feature subset evaluation function on conflicts in class value occurring when two examples have the same values for all the selected features. In the first version of the feature subset selection algorithm called FOCUS, all the feature subsets of increasing size are evaluated until a sufficient subset is encountered. The successor of that algorithm FOCUS-2 prunes the search space, thus, evaluating only promising subsets. Both algorithms assume the existence of a small set of features that forms a solution and their usage on domains with a large number of features can be computationally infeasible. Caruana and Freitag [10] developed the Relief algorithm which assigned weight to each feature and used nearest neighbor algorithm to update the weights. The Relief algorithm does not attempt to determine useful subsets of the weakly relevant features [5]. In real domains, many features may be correlated, are relevant, and will not be removed by Relief. To our best of knowledge all feature selection algorithms are sequential in nature. Our experimental results show that the combinatorial optimization approach is capable of yielding feature subset with reduced level of similarity in comparison to sequential feature selection algorithms.

Our algorithm uses the filter approach. We formulate the feature selection algorithm as a combinational optimization problem. Since Hopfield and Tank [11] has quantitatively demonstrated the computational power and speed of collective analog networks of neurons in solving optimization problems rapidly, we map the feature selection problem into a single layered Hopfield neural networks and use heuristic methods to adjust the network parameters.

From another point of view, our algorithm is a kind of similarity based method. Performance of such methods is significantly improved if feature weights are introduced, scaling their influence on calculation of similarity [12][13]. There are broadly two possible approaches [1] for measuring similarity between two random variables. One is to non-parametrically test the closeness of probability distribution of the variables. Another approach is to measure the amount of functional dependency between the variables. There are several benefits of choosing the linear dependency as feature similarity measure. Compared with two existing linear dependency measures, *Correlation Coefficient* and *Least Square Regression Error*, we employ the *maximum information compression index (MICI)* [1], which is more suitable for redundancy reduction, as the dissimilarity measure. According to [14], [15], [16], Mutual information (MI) can also be taken as similarity measure and provide better results at the cost of a higher computational complexity.

The organization of this paper is as follows: In the next section, we describe measures of similarity between a pair features. In section III, we briefly describe the principles of Hopfield networks. We present the Heuristic Hopfield Neural Network (HHNN) feature selection algorithm in Section IV. In section V, we present experimental results and comparisons with published results. The paper is concluded in Section VI with some directions for future work.

II. SIMILARITY MEASURE

In this section, we discuss some criterion for measuring similarity between two random variables, based on linear dependency between them and explain the *maximal information compression index* (MICI) as similarity measure for the feature selection.

Generally accepted, there are two possible approaches for measuring similarity between two random variables [1]. One is to non-parametrically test the closeness of probability distribution of the variables. This test is sensitive to both location and dispersion of the distributions, hence not suitable for feature selection. Another approach is to measure the amount of functional dependency between the variables [1]. There are several benefits of choosing linear dependency as a feature similarity measure: 1) the linear separability is invariant to the removal of dependent features; 2) the linear dependency measures we discuss are related to the amount of error in terms of second order statistics, in predicting one of the variables using the other.

Among the existing linear dependency measures, MICI, the smallest eigenvalue of covariance matrix of random variable pair, has many properties for feature selection not present in the similarity measure such as correlation coefficient and least square regression error. According to [1], λ_2 is defined as follows:

$$2\lambda_2(x,y) = \text{var}(x) + \text{var}(y) - \sqrt{(\text{var}(x)+\text{var}(y))^2 - 4\text{var}(x)\text{var}(y)(1-\rho(x,y)^2)} \quad (1)$$

ρ is the correlation coefficient defined as,

$$\rho(x,y) = \frac{\text{cov}(x,y)}{\sqrt{\text{var}(x)\text{var}(y)}} \quad (2)$$

MICI (λ_2) has following properties:

1. $0 \leq \lambda_2(x,y) \leq 0.5(Var(x)+Var(y))$;
2. $\lambda_2(x,y) = 0$ If and only if x and y are linearly related;
3. $\lambda_2(x,y) = \lambda_2(y,x)$ (symmetry);
4. If $u = \frac{x}{c}$ and $v = \frac{y}{d}$ for some constant a,b,c,d, then $\lambda_2(x,y) \neq \lambda_2(u,v)$;
5. λ_2 is invariant to rotation of the variables about the origin.

λ_2 possesses several desirable properties like symmetry, sensitivity to scaling, invariance to rotation. It is a property of the variable pair (x,y) reflection the amount of error committed if maximal information compression is performed by reducing the variable pair to a single variable. Hence, it is suitably used in redundancy reduction. Since the value of λ_2 is zero when the features are linearly dependent and increases as the degree of dependency decreases, we take $(1-\frac{\lambda_2}{\lambda_{2-\max}})$ as the similarity measure between features, where $\lambda_{2-\max}$ is the maximum for a given dataset.

III. OPTIMIZATION BY HOPFIELD NEURAL NETWORKS

A Hopfield neural network (HNN) is a single-layered feedback network (as shown in Figure 1) whose dynamics are governed by a system of nonlinear ordinary differential equations and by an energy function [17]. A basic artificial neuron has many inputs and weighted connections. If u_i, $i=1,2,...,n$, is defined as the network input, I_i an externally supplied input bias current to neuron, T_{ij} the weight connection from neuron i to neuron j, then the equation of motion describing the time evolution of the circuit designed by Hopfield and Tank[11] is

$$du_i/dt = -u_i/\tau + \sum_j T_{ij} \cdot V_j + I_i \quad (3)$$

$\tau = RC$
$V_j = g(u_j)$.

The energy function of the Hopfield model is defined as:

$$E = -\frac{1}{2}\sum_i\sum_j T_{ij}V_iV_j + \sum_i V_i I_i \quad (4)$$

For further details on these equations, please refer to [11].

The term energy function comes from a physical analogy to magnetic systems. A central property of the HNN is that given a starting point for the neurons, the energy of equation (4) will never increase as the states of the neurons change provided that T is a symmetric matrix with zero diagonal elements. Thus, one of the most important uses of a HNN is in solving optimization problem in which the cost function of the optimization problem is made identical to the energy function of equation (4) by properly defining the connection weights, output of neurons, and biases. Another main interest of mapping a problem into a HNN is that these models are suitable for VLSI circuit design and thus they can be implemented on hardware.

IV. HEURISTIC HOPFIELD NEURAL NETWORK BASED FEATURE SELECTION ALGORITHM

The property of the Hopfield neural network enables the network to eventually stabilize to one of the local minima of a well defined energy function, thus the Hopfield networks can be employed to generate solutions for optimization problems by minimizing an energy function. In the pioneering work by Hopfield and Tank [11], the traveling salesman problem was formulated on a highly interconnected neural network, the Hopfield network, in which the units of the network being "on" represent a certain decision made and correspond to the decision variables of the problem. Minimizing the cost function of the network is equivalent to finding the lowest cost path. The state of each neuron changes in time determined by the state of the other neurons to which it is connected. Initial states of the neurons are required to start the minimization. Subsequent iterations can be carried out using a simple local update rule. Following the ideas of the traveling salesman problem, we use a single layered HNN to solve the feature selection problem by mapping the similarity of pair of features into the cost function and the reduced feature subset size into a constraint function.

The feature selection problem can be defined as selecting a subset with N features out of the total M features in the datasets. After minimization of the energy function, feature subset with lowest redundancy and desired size will be selected.

We require a representation scheme to allow the digital output states of the neurons operating in the high-gain limit to be decoded into this list. The HNN has M neurons, and the converged HNN has N number of neurons at level "1" to indicate the N selected features. The remaining (M-N) neurons should converge to level "0".

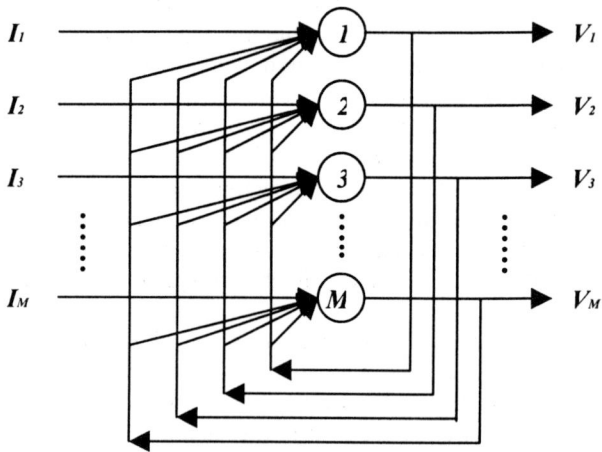

Figure 1: The Hopfield neural networks.

A Energy Function for Feature Selection

The overall redundancy when a subset with N features is selected from M features can be represented by $R(M,N) = \sum_{i=1}^{M}\sum_{j=1}^{M} D(i,j)V_iV_j$. The objective is to find the subset to minimize the overall redundancy.

To enable N neurons in the HNN to compute a solution to the problem, the network must be described by an energy function in which the lowest energy state corresponds to the best subset. This can be separated into two requirements.
1) The energy function must favor strongly stable states of the form of with N neurons 'on' and M-N neurons 'off'.
2) The summation of similarities between the selected features must favor those representing the smallest similarity.

An appropriate form for this function can be found by considering the high gain limit. In which all final normal outputs will be 0 or 1. The space over which the energy function is minimized in this limit is the 2^M corners of the M-dimensional hypercube defined by $V = 0$ or 1. The minima of the energy function:

$$E = \frac{A}{2}\sum_{i}\sum_{j \neq i} D(i,j)V_iV_j + \frac{B}{2}(\sum_{i} Vi - N)^2 \quad (5)$$

The first double sum is minimized if and only if the features with least similarity are selected. The second sum is zero if and only if there are N entries of "1" in the entire vector. Thus, the total energy of that state will be the total similarity of the N selected features, and the states with the smallest similarity will be the lowest energy state. The quadratic terms in the energy function define a connection matrix and the linear terms define input bias currents [11]. By partial differentiation, we obtain the following equations:

$$\frac{\partial E}{\partial V_i} = K \sum_{j \neq i} R(i,j) V_j + \sum_j V_j - N \qquad (6)$$

$$\frac{du_i}{dt} = -\frac{\partial E}{\partial V_i} \qquad (7)$$

K is the coefficient ratio between cost and constraint $K=A/B$
From (6) and (7) we have

$$\frac{\partial u_i}{\partial t} \cong \sum_{j \neq i} (-K \cdot R(i,j) - 1) \cdot V_j + N \qquad (8)$$

Comparing with the standard HNN energy function, the connection matrix and the input currents are

$$T_{ij} = (-K \cdot R(i,j) - 1) \cdot \delta(i,j) \qquad (9)$$

$$I_i = N \qquad (10)$$

The discrete form of iteration update of equation (6) can be written as:

$$u_i(t+1) \cong u_i(t) + (\sum_{j \neq i} T_{ij} \cdot V_j + I_i) \cdot \Delta t \qquad (11)$$

B Adapting the Constraint Parameter

The HNN is very sensitive to the adjustment of parameters. Improper parameter values often make the network to converge to invalid solutions [18]. Even if converged to valid solutions, the obtained solutions are often far from the optimal [19]. We adjust the ratio between cost and constraint weight values, $K=A/B$, using the number of increasing output values. This adjustment procedure heuristically updates K with the iteration update of equation (11). The constraint parameter update procedure is given below (while in each updating iteration):

{
Count the number of $\frac{\partial u_i}{\partial t}$ which are above 0 (N_Above_0)
   If $N\_Above\_0 > N$
       $K = K \cdot K\_Scale$
   Else if $N\_Above\_0 < N$
       $K = K / K\_Scale$
   End if
} % where K_Scale is the Scaling factor of K.

C The feature Selection Algorithm

The pseudocode of the feature selection algorithm is given below (using the variables defined below in Table 1)

Initialize the following: the Start Temperature T_ini, End Temperature T_end, the Temperature Scaling Coefficient T_Scale, K, the K Scaling Coefficient, K_Scale.

While $T >$ End Temperature
{
    For i =1 to Max_No_Iterations
    {
        Calculate the $\frac{\partial u_i(t)}{\partial t}$

        $u_i(t+1) = u_i(t) + \frac{\partial u_i}{\partial t} \cdot \Delta t$

        $V_i(t+1) = \frac{1}{1+e^{-u_i(t+1)/T}}$

        Heuristically Adjusting K
        Count the number of $\frac{\partial u_i}{\partial t}$ above 0 (N_Above_0)
        If $N\_Above\_0 > N$
            $K = K \cdot K\_Scale$
        Else if $N\_Above\_0 < N$
            $K = K / K\_Scale$
        End if
    }
    $T = T \cdot T\_Scale$
}

Table 1
: Variable and Constant Definitions and some initial values for UFS_HHNN

Coeffient	Comments	Value
T	Temperature	-
T_ini	Initial temperature value	0.5
T_end	Final temperature value	0.05
T_Scale	Adjusting Coefficient of T	0.98
K	Ratio of Cost and Constraint	-
K_Scale	Adjusting Coefficient of K	1.02
u	Input of each neuron	-
V	Output of each neuron	-
Δt	Time interval	0.05
N	Number of features to be selected	-
M	Total number of features	-

Since we have no priori knowledge of which features are the best, we want to choose the initial values of the neural input voltages u without bias in favor of any particular feature subset. According to [11], we set

$$\sum_i V_i = N \qquad (12)$$

From V we deduce $u_0(i)$ ($i=1,2,..,M$). To break the symmetry appears in magnetic phase transitions, it is therefore necessary to add some noise.

$$u_i = u_0 + \delta \cdot u_o \qquad \delta = 5\% \qquad (13)$$

D Initialization of K and Temperature

K is the ratio between constraint parameter of cost function and constraint function. From experiments, we found that the initial value affects the convergence and quality of the solution. A sensible choice might seem to use only the similarity (Cost function) to calculate the input *u*, with all *V* to 1,

$$K(0) = \max(u_i) \qquad i=1 \text{ to } M; \qquad (14)$$

There are many ways to set the initial temperature. Based on our experiments, it is appropriate to set the initial temperature to 0.5 and the final temperature to 0.05 for all datasets instead of introducing additional expressions and computations.

V. EXPERIMENT RESULTS

We tested 8 UCI benchmark datasets and compared the results with the unsupervised feature selection algorithm (UFSA, 2002) in [1], respectively. (Table 2). The feature dimensions ranges from 4 to 617 and the feature instances range from 150 to 581012. From Table 2, we can see that the HHNN feature selection algorithm selected features with much less redundancy than the UFSA.

Table 2

Datasets					Method	R(M,N)
Name	M	N	C	S		
Isolet	617	310	26	7797	UFSA	8.4479e+004
					HHNN	6.2875e+004
Mult. Features	649	325	10	2000	UFSA	1.0464e+005
					HHNN	1.0149e+005
Ionosphere	34	15	2	351	UFSA	64.5769
					HHNN	54.8495
Waveform_Noise	40	20	3	5000	UFSA	221.4996
					HHNN	170.8336
Forest	10	5	8	581012	UFSA	19.7276
					HHNN	10.5453
Cancer	9	4	2	684	UFSA	8.4436
					HHNN	5.4188
Glass	10	4	2	214	UFSA	18.4129
					HHNN	11.6046
Iris	4	2	3	150	UFSA	0.3192
					HHNN	0.0128

M: Number of features in the dataset
N: Number of features in the selected feature subset
C: Number of classes in the dataset
S: Number of samples in the dataset
UFSA: Unsupervised feature selection algorithm in [1]
HHNN: Heuristic Hopfield Neural Network based feature selection
R(M,N): The overall Redundancy of the selected feature subsets

VI. DISCUSSION AND FUTURE WORK

In this paper, we formulate the feature selection as a combinatorial optimization problem and map it onto a single layered HNN. The traditional HNN is sensitive to the adjustment of parameters. We developed a heuristic algorithm to adjust the weighting between the cost function and the constraint function. We used MICI as a measure of feature similarity. Simulations results on eight datasets of various dimensions and data sizes illustrates that feature subsets selected by UFS-HHNN has much less redundancy than by UFSA [1].

At the same time, we also find some issues that occur during the selection. For example, in small datasets such as iris, the selected features are 1 and 2. These two features contain the least similarity among all the subsets of the same size, but, they are not the most significant features for the purpose of classification. However, the proposed procedure is unsupervised and hence, the selected features may not be tuned for classification, instead would possess overall the least similarity among them.

The iterative update rule of equation (3) only guarantees convergence to one of the local minima and only for the case that the starting point is sufficiently close to the globally optimal solution, the step update rule will be a good choice. One way to avoid this dependency is to replace the update rule in equation (3) with a stochastic rule in simulated annealing. Mean field annealing (MFA) is a variant of the simulated annealing algorithm. It replaces the stochastic nature of the simulated annealing method with a set of deterministic update rules that act on the average value of the variables rather than on the variables themselves. This deterministic relaxation procedure exhibits fast convergence towards the solution for complicated optimization problems [17] [20][21], one may also consider using MFA for the feature selection. Another alternative method is the Graduate Assignment Algorithm (GAA) [22] that combines graduated non-convexity, assignment and sparsity techniques, is generally used in graph matching problems. We can also view the feature selection as a kind of matching (From the original feature space to the selected feature subset space) and apply the GAA to solve the problem.

REFERENCES

[1] P Mitra, C. A. Murthy and S K. Pal, "Unsupervised feature selection using feature similarity," *IEEE Transaction on Pattern Analysis and Machine Intelligence*, Vol. 24, pp. 1--12, April 2002.
[2] M. Kudo and J. Sklansky, "Comparison of algorithms that selects features for pattern classifiers," *Pattern Recognition*, Vol. 33, pp. 25--41, 2000
[3] A. Jain and D. Zongker, "Feature selection: evaluation, application, and small sample performance," *IEEE Transactions on Pattern Analysis and Machine Interlligence*, Vol. 19, pp. 153--158, 1997.
[4] M. Dash, H. Liu "Feature Selection for Classification" *Intelligent Data Analysis*, Vol. 1, pp. 131—156, 1997.
[5] G. H. John, R. Kohavi and K. Pfleger, " Irrelevant Features and the Subset Selection Problem," *Proceedings of the 11th International Conference on Machine Learning ICML94*, pp. 121—129, 1994.
[6] R. Kohavi and G. H. John, "Wrappers for feature subset selection," *Artificial Intelligence Journal*, Vol. 97, No. 1-2, pp. 273—324, 1997.
[7] A. L. Blum and P. Langley, "Selection of relevant features and examples in machine learning," *Artificial Intelligence Journal*, Vol. 97, No. 1-2, pp. 245—271, 1997.
[8] D. Mladenic, "Machine learning on non-homogeneous, distributed text data," Ph. D. dissertation, Univ. of Ljubljana, Ljubljana, Yugoslavia, 1998.
[9] H. Almuallin and T. G. Dietterich, "Efficient algorithms for identifying relevant features," *Proceedings of the Ninth Canadian Conference on Artificial Intelligence*, pp.38—45 Vancouver, BC: Morgan Kaufmann, 1996.
[10] R. Caruana and D. Freitag "Greedy Attribute Selection," *Proceedings of the 11th International Conference on Machine Learning ICML94*, pp. 26—28, 1994.
[11] J. J. Hopfield and D. W. Tank "'Neural' Computation of Decisions in Optimization Problems," *Biological Cybernetics*, Vol. 52, pp. 141-152, 1985.
[12] W. Duch, "A framework for similarity-based classification methods," *Intelligent Information Systems VII*, pp. 15—19, Malbork, Poland, June 1998.
[13] W. Duch and K. Grudzinski, "Search and global minimization in similarity-based methods," *International Joint Conference on Neural Networks*, paper no. 742, Washington, July 1999.
[14] N. Kwak and C. Choi, "Input feature selection for classification problems," *IEEE Transaction on Neural Networks*, Vol. 13, pp. 143--159, 2002.
[15] G. D. Tourassi, E. D. Frederick, M. K. Markey, C. E. Floyd, Jr., "Application of the mutual information criterion for feature selection in computer-aided diagnosis," *Med. Phys.*, 28(12), pp. 2394—2402, December 2001.
[16] R. Battiti, "Using mutual information for selection features in supervised neural net learning," *IEEE Transaction on Neural Networks*, Vol. 5, July 1994.
[17] C. Calderon-Macias, M. K. Sen and P. L. Stoffa, "Hopfield neural networks, and mean field annealing for seismic deconvolution and multiple attenuation," *Geophysics*, Vol. 62, No. 3, pp. 992—1002, May—June 1997.
[18] R. Wang, Z. Tang and Q. Cao, "A learning method in Hopfield neural network for combinatorial optimization problem," *Neurocomputing*, Vol. 48, pp. 1021—1024, 2002.
[19] G. V. Wilson, G. S. Pawley, "On the stability of the traveling salesman problem algorithm of Hopfield and Tank," *Biol. Cybernet.* Vol. 58 (1), pp. 63—70, 1998.
[20] D. E. Van den bout, T. K. Miller III, "Graph partitioning using annealed neural networks," *IEEE Transactions on neural networks*, Vol. 1, No. 2, pp. 192—203, June 1990.
[21] C. Peterson and B. Söderberg, "A new method for mapping optimization problems onto neural networks," *International Journal of Neural System*, Vol. 1, No. 1, pp. 3—22, 1989
[22] S. Gold and A. Rangarajan, "A graduated assignment algorithm for graph matching," *IEEE Transactions on pattern analysis and machine intelligence*, Vol. 18, No. 4, April 1996.

Bagged Ensembles of Support Vector Machines for Gene Expression Data Analysis

Giorgio Valentini
DSI, Dip. di Scienze dell' Informazione
Università degli Studi di Milano, Italy
INFM, Istituto Nazionale
di Fisica della Materia,
Email: valenti@disi.unige.it

Marco Muselli
IEIIT, Istituto di Elettronica
e di Ingegneria dell'Informazione
e delle Telecomunicazioni,
Consiglio Nazionale delle Ricerche, Italy
Email: muselli@ice.ge.cnr.it

Francesca Ruffino
DIMA, Dipartimento di Matematica
Università di Genova, Italy

Abstract—Extracting information from gene expression data is a difficult task, as these data are characterized by very high dimensional, small sized, samples and large degree of biological variability. However, a possible way of dealing with the curse of dimensionality is offered by feature selection algorithms, while variance problems arising from small samples and biological variability can be addressed through ensemble methods based on resampling techniques.

These two approaches have been combined to improve the accuracy of Support Vector Machines (SVM) in the classification of malignant tissues from DNA microarray data. To assess the accuracy and the confidence of the predictions performed proper measures have been introduced. Presented results show that bagged ensembles of SVM are more reliable and achieve equal or better classification accuracy with respect to single SVM, whereas feature selection methods can further enhance classification accuracy.

I. INTRODUCTION

DNA microarray technology provides fundamental insights into the mRNA levels of large sets of genes, offering in such a way an approximate picture of the proteins of a cell at one time [13]. The large amount of gene expression data produced requires statistical and machine learning methods to analyze and extract significant knowledge from DNA microarray experiments.

Typical problems arising from this analysis range from prediction of malignancies [15], [17] (a classification problem from a machine learning point of view) to functional discovery of new classes or subclasses of diseases [1] (an unsupervised learning problem), to the identification of groups of genes responsible or correlated with malignancies or polygenic diseases [11] (a feature selection problem).

Several supervised methods have been applied to the analysis of cDNA microarrays and high density oligonucleotide chips. These methods include decision trees, Fisher linear discriminant, Multi-Layer Perceptrons (MLP), Nearest-Neighbour classifiers, linear discriminant analysis, Parzen windows and others [5], [8], [10], [12], [14]. In particular, Support Vector Machines (SVM) have been recently applied to the analysis of DNA microarray gene expression data in order to classify functional groups of genes, normal and malignant tissues and multiple tumor types [5], [9], [17].

Other works pointed out the importance of feature selection methods to reduce the high dimensionality of the input space and to select the most relevant genes associated with specific functional classes [11].

Furthermore, ensembles of learning machines are well-suited for gene expression data analysis, as they can reduce the variance due to the low cardinality of available training sets, and the bias due to specific characteristics of the learning algorithm [7]. Indeed, in recent works, combinations of binary classifiers (one-versus-all and all-pairs) and Error Correcting Output Coding (ECOC) ensembles of MLP, as well as ensemble methods based on resampling techniques, such as bagging and boosting, have been applied to the analysis of DNA microarray data [8], [15], [17].

In this work we show that the combination of feature selection methods and bagged ensembles of SVM can enhance the accuracy and the reliability of predictions based on gene expression data.

In the next section the standard technique for training SVM with soft margin is presented together with a description of the considered method for feature selection. Then, procedure for bagging SVM is introduced examining different possible choices for the combination of classifiers. Finally, proper measures are employed to evaluate the performance of the proposed approach on two data sets available online, concerning tumor detection based on gene expression data produced by DNA microarrays.

II. SVM TRAINING AND FEATURE SELECTION

We can represent the output of a single experiment with a DNA microarray as a pair (x, y), being $x \in \mathbb{R}^d$ a vector containing the expression levels for d selected genes and $y \in \{-1, +1\}$ a binary variable determining the classification of the considered cell. As an example, $y = +1$ can be used to denote a tumoral cell and $y = -1$ for a normal cell. It is then evident that in our analysis every cell is associated with an input vector x containing the gene expression levels.

When n different experiments are performed, we obtain a collection of n pairs $\mathcal{T} = \{(x_j, y_j) : j = 1, \ldots, n\}$ (*training set*); suppose, without loss of generality, that the first n^+ pairs have $y_j = +1$, whereas the remaining $n^- = n - n^+$ possess a negative output $y_j = -1$. The target of a machine learning method is to construct from the pairs $\{(x_j, y_j)\}_{j=1}^n$ a *classifier*, i.e. a decision function $h : \mathbb{R}^d \to \{-1, +1\}$, that gives the correct classification $y = h(x)$ for every cell (determined by x).

To achieve this target, many available techniques generate a *discriminant function* $f : \mathbb{R}^d \to \mathbb{R}$ from the sample $\mathcal{T}$ at hand

and build h by employing the formula

$$h(\boldsymbol{x}) = \text{sign}(f(\boldsymbol{x})) \quad (1)$$

where the function $\text{sign}(z)$ gives as output $+1$ if $z \geq 0$ and -1 otherwise. Among these techniques, SVM [6] turn out to be a promising approach, due to their theoretical motivations and their practical efficiency. They employ the following expression for the discriminant function

$$f(\boldsymbol{x}) = b + \sum_{j=1}^{n} \alpha_j y_j K(\boldsymbol{x}_j, \boldsymbol{x}) \quad (2)$$

where the scalars α_j are obtained, in the *soft margin* version, through the solution of the following quadratic programming problem: minimize the cost function

$$W(\boldsymbol{\alpha}) = \frac{1}{2} \sum_{j=1}^{n} \sum_{k=1}^{n} \alpha_j \alpha_k y_j y_k K(\boldsymbol{x}_j, \boldsymbol{x}_k) - \sum_{j=1}^{n} \alpha_j$$

subject to the constraints

$$\sum_{j=1}^{n} \alpha_j y_j = 0, \quad 0 \leq \alpha_j \leq C \quad \text{for } j = 1, \ldots, n$$

being C a regularization parameter.

The symmetric function $K(\cdot, \cdot)$ must be chosen among the kernels of Reproducing Kernel Hilbert Spaces [16]; three possible choices are:

- Linear kernel: $K(\boldsymbol{u}, \boldsymbol{v}) = \boldsymbol{u} \cdot \boldsymbol{v}$
- Polynomial kernel: $K(\boldsymbol{u}, \boldsymbol{v}) = (\boldsymbol{u} \cdot \boldsymbol{v} + 1)^\gamma$
- Gaussian kernel: $K(\boldsymbol{u}, \boldsymbol{v}) = \exp(-\|\boldsymbol{u} - \boldsymbol{v}\|^2 / \sigma^2)$

Since the point $\boldsymbol{\alpha}$ of minimum of the quadratic programming problem can have several null components $\alpha_j = 0$, the sum in Eq. 2 receives the contribution of a subset V of patterns $\boldsymbol{x}_j$ in $\mathcal{T}$, called *support vectors*. The bias b in the SVM classifier is usually set to

$$b = \frac{1}{|V|} \sum_{\boldsymbol{x} \in V} \sum_{j=1}^{n} \alpha_j y_j K(\boldsymbol{x}_j, \boldsymbol{x})$$

where $|V|$ denotes the number of elements of the set V.

The accuracy of a classifier is affected by the dimension d of the input vector; roughly, the greater is d the lower is the probability of correctly classifying a pattern $\boldsymbol{x}$. For this reason, feature selection methods are employed to choose a subset of relevant inputs (genes) for the problem at hand, so as to reduce the number of components x_i.

A simple feature selection method, originally proposed in [10], associates with every gene expression level x_i a quantity c_i given by

$$c_i = \frac{\mu_i^+ - \mu_i^-}{\sigma_i^+ + \sigma_i^-} \quad (3)$$

where μ_i^+ and μ_i^- are the mean value of x_i across all the input patterns in $\mathcal{T}$ with positive and negative output, respectively

$$\mu_i^+ = \frac{1}{n^+} \sum_{j=1}^{n^+} x_{ji}, \quad \mu_i^- = \frac{1}{n^-} \sum_{j=n^++1}^{n} x_{ji}$$

having denoted with x_{ji} the ith component of the input vector $\boldsymbol{x}_j$. Similarly, σ_i^+ and σ_i^- are the standard deviation of x_i computed in the set of pairs with positive and negative output, respectively.

Then, the genes are ranked according to their c_i value, and the first m and the last m genes are selected, thus obtaining a set of $2m$ inputs. The main problem of this approach is the underlying independence assumption of the expression patterns of each gene: indeed it fails in detecting the role of coordinately expressed genes in carcinogenic processes. Eq. 3 can also be used to compute the weights for weighted gene voting [10], a minor variant of diagonal linear discriminant analysis [8].

III. BAGGED ENSEMBLES OF SVM

The low cardinality of the available data and the large degree of biological variability in gene expression suggest to apply variance-reduction methods, such as bagging, to these tasks.

Denote with $\{\mathcal{T}_b\}_{b=1}^{B}$ a set of B (bootstrapped) samples, whose elements are drawn with replacement from the training set $\mathcal{T}$ according to a uniform probability distribution. Let f_b be the discriminant function obtained by applying the soft-margin SVM learning algorithm on the bootstrapped sample $\mathcal{T}_b$. The corresponding decision function h_b is computed as usual through Eq. 1.

The generalization ability of classifiers h_b (*base learners*) can be improved by aggregating them through the standard formula (for two class classification problems) [3]:

$$h_{\text{st}}(\boldsymbol{x}) = \text{sign}\left(\sum_{b=1}^{B} h_b(\boldsymbol{x})\right) \quad (4)$$

In this way the decision function $h_{\text{st}}(\boldsymbol{x})$ of the bagged ensemble selects the most voted class among the B classifiers h_b.

Other choices of discriminant function for the bagged ensemble are possible, some of which lead to the above standard decision function $h_{\text{st}}(\boldsymbol{x})$ through Eq. 1. The following three expressions allow also to evaluate the quality of the classification offered by the bagged ensemble:

$$\begin{aligned}
f_{\text{avg}}(\boldsymbol{x}) &= \frac{1}{B} \sum_{b=1}^{B} f_b(\boldsymbol{x}) \\
f_{\text{win}}(\boldsymbol{x}) &= \frac{1}{|B^*|} \sum_{b \in B^*} f_b(\boldsymbol{x}) \\
f_{\text{max}}(\boldsymbol{x}) &= h_{\text{st}}(\boldsymbol{x}) \cdot \max_{b \in B^*} |f_b(\boldsymbol{x})|
\end{aligned}$$

where the set $B^* = \{b : h_b(\boldsymbol{x}) = h_{\text{st}}(\boldsymbol{x})\}$ contains the indices b of the base learners that vote for the class $h_{\text{st}}(\boldsymbol{x})$. Note that $f_{\text{avg}}(\boldsymbol{x})$ is the average of the $f_b(\boldsymbol{x})$, whereas $f_{\text{win}}(\boldsymbol{x})$ and $f_{\text{max}}(\boldsymbol{x})$ are, respectively, the average of the discriminant functions of the classifiers having indices in B^* and the signed maximum of their absolute value.

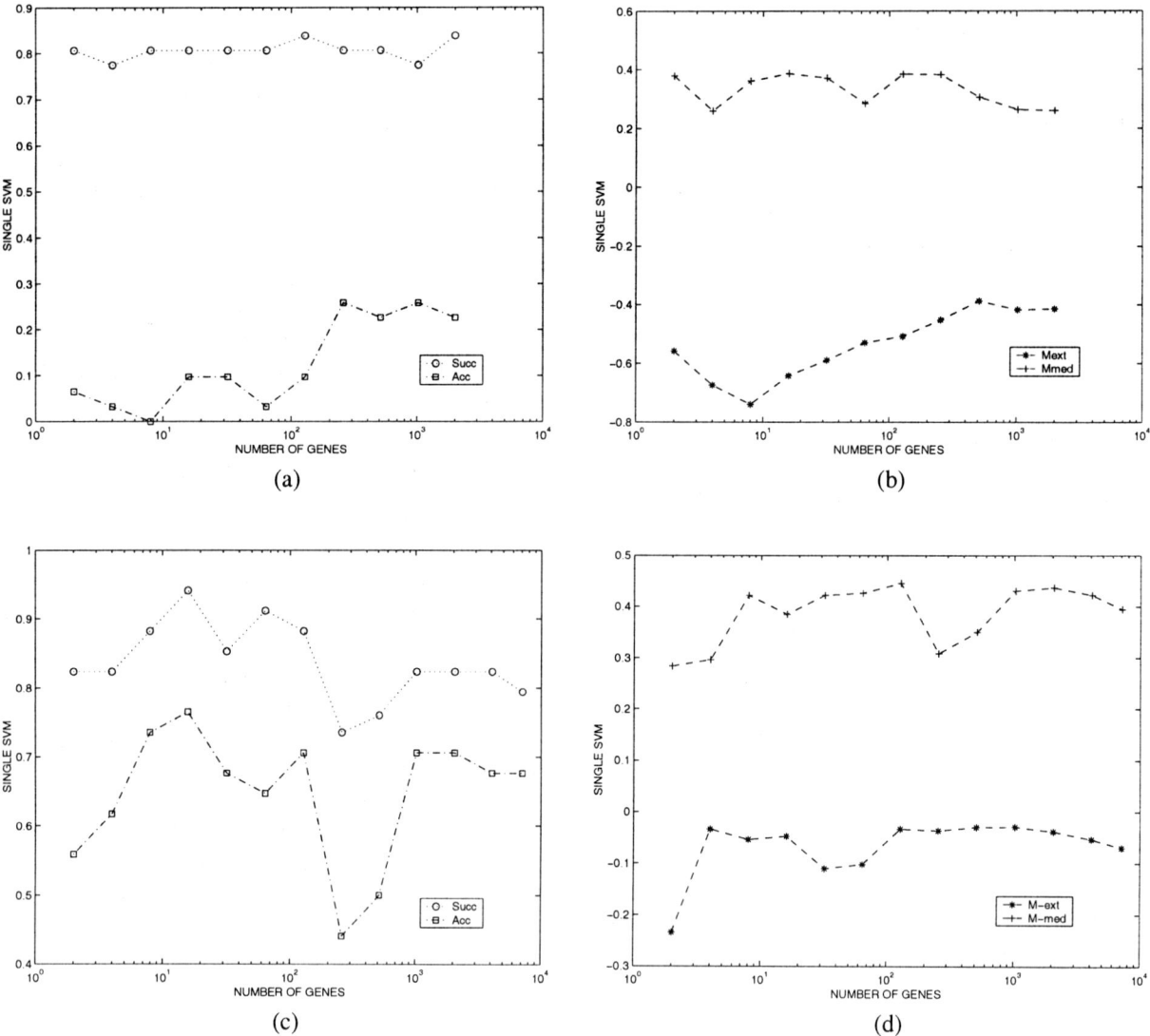

Fig. 1. Results obtained with single SVM for different numbers of selected genes. *Colon* data set: (a) Success and acceptance rate (b) Extremal and median margin. *Leukemia* data set: (c) Success and acceptance rate (d) External and median margin.

The corresponding decision functions are given by

$$h_{\text{avg}}(\boldsymbol{x}) = \text{sign}(f_{\text{avg}}(\boldsymbol{x}))$$
$$h_{\text{win}}(\boldsymbol{x}) = \text{sign}(f_{\text{win}}(\boldsymbol{x})) = h_{\text{st}}(\boldsymbol{x})$$
$$h_{\text{max}}(\boldsymbol{x}) = \text{sign}(f_{\text{max}}(\boldsymbol{x})) = h_{\text{st}}(\boldsymbol{x})$$

While $h_{\text{win}}(\boldsymbol{x})$ and $h_{\text{max}}(\boldsymbol{x})$ are equivalent to the standard choice $h_{\text{st}}(\boldsymbol{x})$, $h_{\text{avg}}(\boldsymbol{x})$ selects the class associated with the average of the discriminant functions computed by the base learners. Thus, the decision of each classifier in the ensemble is weighted via its prediction strength, measured by the value of the discriminant function f_b; on the contrary, in the decision function $h_{\text{st}}(\boldsymbol{x})$ each base learner receives the same weight.

IV. ASSESSMENT OF CLASSIFIERS QUALITY

Besides the *success rate*

$$Succ = \frac{1}{2n} \sum_{j=1}^{n} |y_j + h(\boldsymbol{x}_j)|$$

which is an estimate of the generalization error, several alternative measures can be used to assess the quality of classifiers producing a discriminant function $f(\boldsymbol{x})$. These measures can then be directly applied to evaluate the confidence of the classification performed by simple SVM and bagged ensembles of SVM.

By generalizing a definition introduced in [10], [11], a first choice is the *extremal margin* M_{ext}, defined as

$$M_{\text{ext}} = \frac{\theta^+ - \theta^-}{\max_{1 \leq j \leq n} f(\boldsymbol{x}_j) - \min_{1 \leq j \leq n} f(\boldsymbol{x}_j)} \quad (5)$$

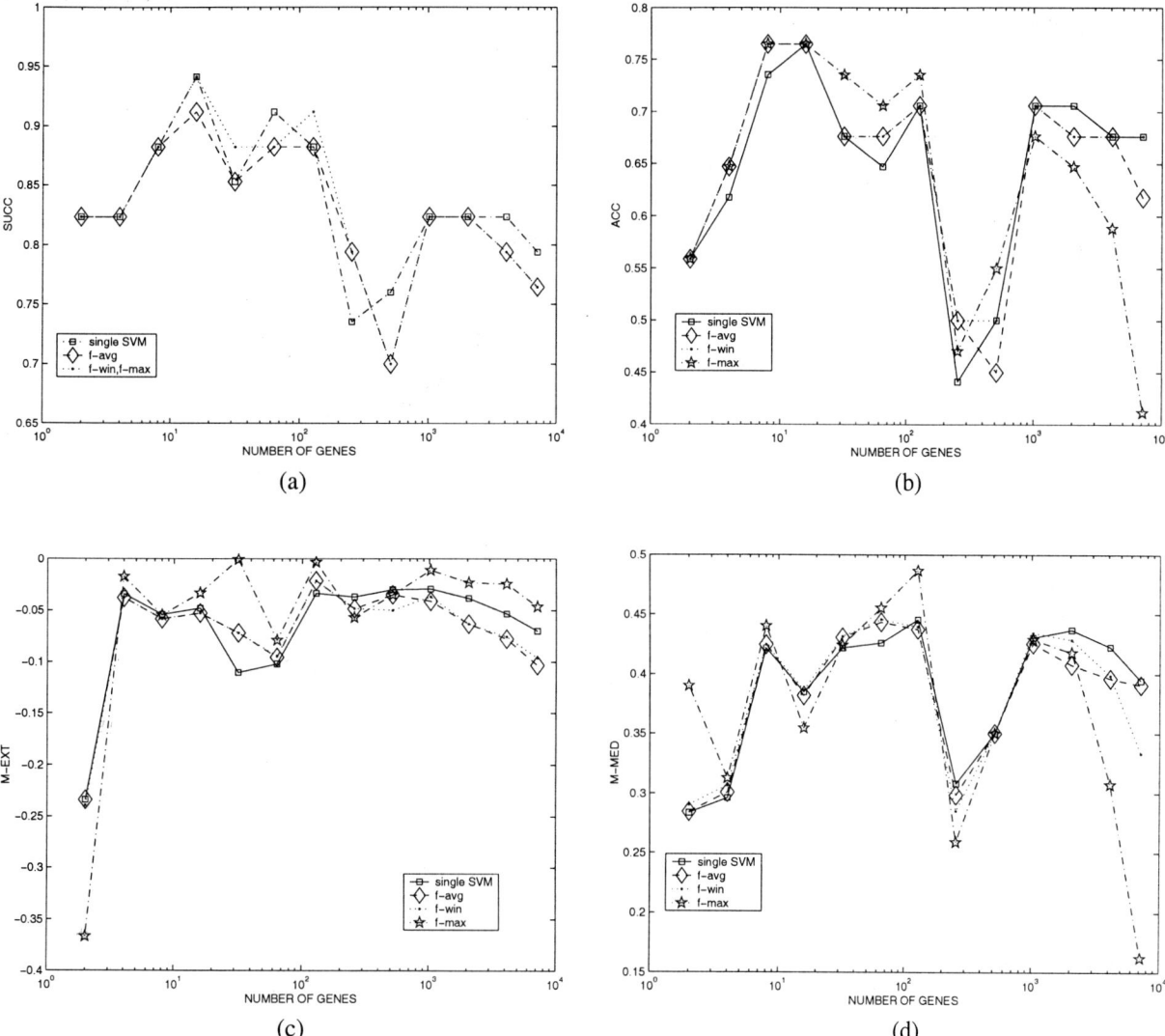

Fig. 2. Comparison of results obtained with single and bagged SVM on the *Leukemia* data set, when varying the number of selected genes: (a) Success rate (b) Acceptance rate (c) Extremal margin (d) Median margin.

where the quantities θ^+ and θ^- are given by

$$\theta^+ = \min_{1 \leq j \leq n^+} f(\boldsymbol{x}_j), \quad \theta^- = \max_{n^+ + 1 \leq j \leq n} f(\boldsymbol{x}_j)$$

It can be easily seen that the larger is the value of M_{ext}, more confident is the classifier; note that if there are no classification errors M_{ext} is positive.

An alternative measure, less sensitive to outliers, is the *median margin* M_{med}, which is defined as

$$M_{med} = \frac{\lambda^+ - \lambda^-}{\max_{1 \leq j \leq n} f(\boldsymbol{x}_j) - \min_{1 \leq j \leq n} f(\boldsymbol{x}_j)} \quad (6)$$

where λ^+ and λ^- are the median value of $f(\boldsymbol{x})$ for the positive and negative class, respectively:

$$\begin{aligned} \lambda^+ &= \min\{\lambda \in \mathbb{R} : |J_\lambda^+| \geq n^+/2\} \\ \lambda^- &= \max\{\lambda \in \mathbb{R} : |J_\lambda^-| \geq n^-/2\} \end{aligned}$$

The sets J_λ^+ (resp. J_λ^-) contain the indices j of the input patterns $\boldsymbol{x}_j$ in the training set, where the discriminant function $f(\boldsymbol{x}_j)$ is greater (resp. lower) than λ:

$$J_\lambda^+ = \{j : f(\boldsymbol{x}_j) > \lambda\}, \quad J_\lambda^- = \{j : f(\boldsymbol{x}_j) < \lambda\}$$

Finally, the *acceptance rate Acc* measures the fraction of samples that are correctly classified with high confidence. It is defined by the expression

$$Acc = \frac{|J_\theta^+| + |J_{-\theta}^-|}{n} \quad (7)$$

where $\theta = \max\{|\theta^+|, |\theta^-|\}$ is the smallest symmetric rejection zone to get zero error. It is important to remark that the acceptance rate is highly sensitive to the presence of outliers.

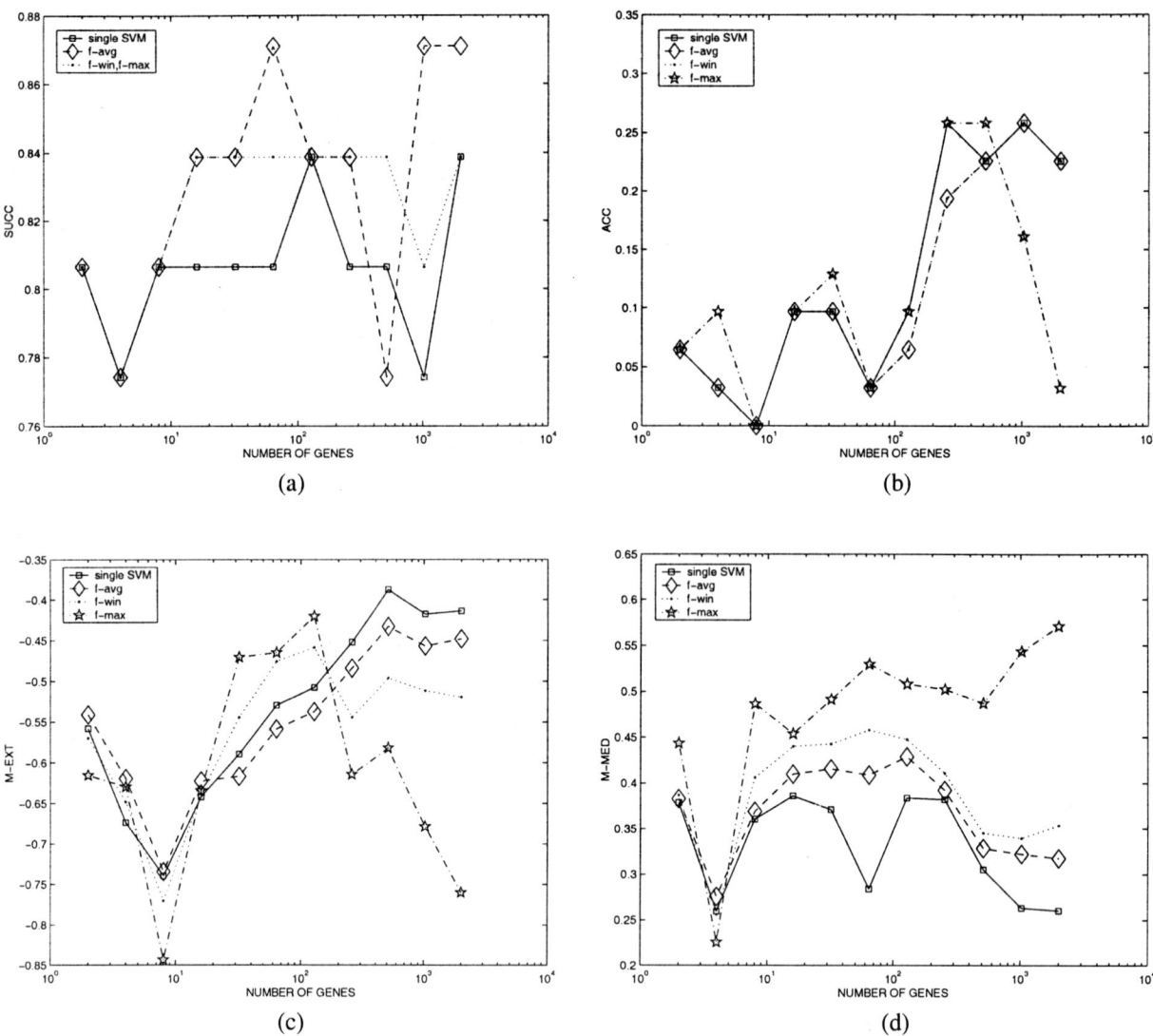

Fig. 3. Comparison of results obtained with single and bagged SVM on the *Colon* data set, when varying the number of selected genes: (a) Success rate (b) Acceptance rate (c) Extremal margin (d) Median margin.

V. NUMERICAL EXPERIMENTS

Here we present the results about the classification of DNA microarray data using the proposed techniques. We applied SVM linear classifiers to separate normal and malignant tissues with and without feature selection. Then we compare the results obtained with single and bagged SVM, using in all cases the filter method for feature selection described in Sec. II.

A. Data sets

The proposed approach has been tested on DNA microarray data available on-line.

In particular, we used the *Colon cancer* data set [2] constituted by 62 samples including 22 normal and 40 colon cancer tissues. The data matrix contains expression values of 2000 genes and has been preprocessed by taking the logarithm of all values and by normalizing feature (gene) vectors. This has been performed by subtracting the mean over all training values, by dividing by the corresponding standard deviation and finally by passing the result through a squashing arctan function to diminish the importance of outliers. The whole data set has been randomly split into a training and a test set of equal size, each one with the same proportion of normal and malignant examples.

We also compared the different classifiers on the *Leukemia* data set [10]. It is composed by two variants of leukemia, ALL and AML, for a total of 72 examples split into a training set of 38 samples and a test set of 34 examples, with 7129 different genes.

B. Results

Fig. 1 summarizes the results with single SVM, obtained by varying the number of genes selected with the filter method described in Sec. II and by using the measures for classifier assessment introduced in Sec. IV.

With the *Colon* data set, the accuracy does not change significantly when the feature selection method is applied; however, the prediction is more reliable, as attested by the higher values of Acc and M_{med} (Fig. 1a and 1b), when the number of inputs lies beyond 256.

On the contrary, we obtain the highest success rate on the *Leukemia* data set with only 16 selected genes; the corresponding acceptance rate is also significantly high (Fig. 1c). The extremal margin is negative but very close to 0, thus showing that the *Leukemia* data set is near linearly separable, with a relatively high confidence (Fig. 1d).

Fig. 2 and 3 compare the results obtained through the application of bagged ensembles of SVM (for different choice of the decision function) with those achieved by single SVM.

On the *Leukemia* data set, bagging seems not to improve the success rate, even if the predictions are more reliable, especially when a small number of selected genes is used (Fig. 2). On the contrary, bagging significantly improves the success rate scored on the *Colon* data set, both with and without feature selection (Fig. 3a).

Considering the acceptance rate, there are no significant difference between bagged SVM employing f_{avg} or f_{win} and single SVM, whereas bagged SVM adopting f_{max} achieve the highest values of Acc if the number of genes is less or equal to 512; for higher values the opposite situation occurs (Fig. 3b).

While bagged SVM (especially when f_{max} is used) show better values of the extremal margin with respect to single SVM when small numbers of genes are selected, we observe the opposite behavior if the number of considered genes is relatively large (Fig. 3c). Finally, bagged ensembles show clearly larger median margins with respect to single SVM, confirming a more overall reliability (Fig. 3d).

Summarizing, bagged ensembles seem to be more accurate and confident in predictions with respect to single SVM. The simple gene selection method adopted is effective with the *Leukemia* data set, both when single and bagged SVM are used, while the accuracy for the *Colon* data set seems to be independent of the application of feature selection.

The results obtained with single SVM are comparable to those presented in [11]; however, the application of the recursive feature elimination method allows to achieve better results than those obtained with bagged ensembles of SVM, at least for the *Leukemia* data set. Anyway, it is difficult to establish if a statistical significant difference between the two approaches exists, given the small size of the available samples.

VI. Conclusions

The results show that bagged ensembles of SVM are more reliable than single SVM in classifying DNA microarray data. Moreover they obtain an equivalent or a better accuracy in separating normal from malignant tissues, at least with *Colon* and *Leukemia* data sets. In fact, bagging is a variance reduction method which is able to improve the stability of classifiers [4], especially when the training set at hand has small size and large dimensionality, as in the present case.

Despite its simplicity, the application of the feature selection method we used in our experiments allows to achieve better value of the success rate. However, it does not take into account the interactions of the expression levels between different genes. In order to manage this effect, we plan to employ more refined gene selection methods [11], in combination with bagging, to further improve the accuracy and the reliability of the predictions based on DNA microarray data.

Acknowledgment

This work was partially funded by INFM, unità di Genova.

References

[1] A. Alizadeh et al. Distinct types of diffuse large B-cell lymphoma identified by gene expression profiling. *Nature*, 403:503–511, 2000.

[2] U. Alon et al. Broad patterns of gene expressions revealed by clustering analysis of tumor and normal colon tissues probed by oligonucleotide arrays. *PNAS*, 96:6745–6750, 1999.

[3] L. Breiman. Bagging predictors. *Machine Learning*, 24(2):123–140, 1996.

[4] L. Breiman. Arcing classifiers. *The Annals of Statistics*, 26(3):801–849, 1998.

[5] M. Brown et al. Knowledge-base analysis of microarray gene expression data by using support vector machines. *PNAS*, 97(1):262–267, 2000.

[6] C. Cortes and V. Vapnik. Support vector networks. *Machine Learning*, 20:273–297, 1995.

[7] T.G. Dietterich. Ensemble methods in machine learning. In J. Kittler and F. Roli, editors, *Multiple Classifier Systems. First International Workshop, MCS 2000, Cagliari, Italy*, volume 1857 of *Lecture Notes in Computer Science*, pages 1–15. Springer-Verlag, 2000.

[8] S. Dudoit, J. Fridlyand, and T. Speed. Comparison of discrimination methods for the classification of tumors using gene expression data. *JASA*, 97(457):77–87, 2002.

[9] T.S. Furey, N. Cristianini, N. Duffy, D. Bednarski, M. Schummer, and D. Haussler. Support vector machine classification and validation of cancer tissue samples using microarray expression data. *Bioinformatics*, 16(10):906–914, 2000.

[10] T.R. Golub et al. Molecular Classification of Cancer: Class Discovery and Class Prediction by Gene Expression Monitoring. *Science*, 286:531–537, 1999.

[11] I. Guyon, J. Weston, S. Barnhill, and V. Vapnik. Gene Selection for Cancer Classification using Support Vector Machines. *Machine Learning*, 46(1/3):389–422, 2002.

[12] J. Khan et al. Classification and diagnostic prediction of cancers using gene expression profiling and artificial neural networks. *Nature Medicine*, 7(6):673–679, 2001.

[13] D.J. Lockhart and E.A. Winzeler. Genomics, gene expression and DNA arrays. *Nature*, 405:827–836, 2000.

[14] P. Pavlidis, J. Weston, J. Cai, and W.N. Grundy. Gene functional classification from heterogenous data. In *Fifth International Conference on Computational Molecular Biology*, 2001.

[15] G. Valentini. Gene expression data analysis of human lymphoma using support vector machines and output coding ensembles. *Artificial Intelligence in Medicine*, 26(3):283–306, 2002.

[16] G Wahba. Spline models for observational data. In *SIAM*, Philadelphia, USA, 1990.

[17] C. Yeang et al. Molecular classification of multiple tumor types. In *ISMB 2001, Proceedings of the 9th International Conference on Intelligent Systems for Molecular Biology*, pages 316–322, Copenaghen, Denmark, 2001. Oxford University Press.

Improved Fuzzy Lattice Neurocomputing (FLN) for Semantic Neural Computing

Vassilis G. Kaburlasos

Technological Educational Institute of Kavala
Dept. of Industrial Informatics, Div. of Computing Systems
GR- 65404 Kavala, Greece
Email: vgkabs@teikav.edu.gr

Abstract – This work, first, shows the inherent capacity of neural net *σ-FLNMAP* for classification based on semantics and, second, it demonstrates the capacity of an ensemble of *σ-FLNMAP* voters to improve classification accuracy. The *σ-FLNMAP* neural network is presented here as a tool for function approximation. New definitions and useful properties extend coherently the applicability of *σ-FLNMAP*. An ensemble of *σ-FLNMAP* voters is treated as a statistical model whose parameters can be estimated from the training data. Noise canceling effects are discussed. Experimental results in four classification problems compare favorably with results by alternative classification methods from the literature.

I. INTRODUCTION

With the proliferation of information technologies non-numeric data appear in applications. For instance ontologies are currently in widespread use in the Semantic Web [5]. An extension of neural computing to non-numeric data domains could imply significant benefits including the capacity for massively parallel learning and generalization. Two important practical issues to be resolved include *data representation* and *data interpretation* as explained in the following.

On the one hand, by *data representation* is meant the format used to describe a single datum - usually a datum is represented as a point in the Cartesian product space $\mathbf{R}^N$, where the set $\mathbf{R}$ of real numbers is known to have emerged from the measurement process [8]; nevertheless, lately, interest has shifted to connectionist architectures which deal with structured data representations [6]. On the other hand, by *data interpretation* is meant here useful relation(s) among the data - the latter (relations) determine data *semantics*.

Neural networks, developed for application in a specific data domain, typically cannot be applied in another data domain. Hence different neural paradigms have been established for application in different data domains based on, e.g. (non) linear system theory [3], (fuzzy) logic [7], inference systems [2], etc. We believe that a critical difference among a number of neural paradigms is in the underlying data semantics. Moreover, neural networks successfully developed in a data domain are not applicable to a different data domain because the underlying data semantics differ.

This work is interested in semantics which can be expressed by a (mathematical) lattice-ordering relation between the data in a domain. It turns out that a large number of useful data domains, including vectors of real numbers, fuzzy sets, graphs, hierarchies, etc. are lattices [13], [21], [23]. Furthermore useful neural schemes, namely *Fuzzy Lattice Neurocomputing* (FLN) schemes, can be employed in a lattice data domain as explained in the work.

This article is organized as follows. Section II explains how FLN deals with semantics. Section III presents the *σ-FLNMAP* neural network for function approximation with emphasis on classification problems. Section IV proposes a technique for estimating the parameters of a statistical classification model. Section V presents experimental results in four classification problems. Finally, section VI summarizes the principal achievements and it delineates future work.

II. SEMANTICS IN FLN

This work enhances the terminology and the results in [13]. Interest here remains in *complete* lattices whose least and greatest elements are denoted, respectively, by *O* and *I*.

A basic instrument for both learning and generalization in FLN is an *inclusion measure function* σ: $\mathbf{L} \times \mathbf{L} \to [0,1]$. The latter function σ satisfies, by definition, conditions (C0) σ(x,O)=0, $x \neq O$, (C1) σ(x,x)=1, and (C2) the *Consistency Property*: $u \le w \Rightarrow \sigma(x,u) \le \sigma(x,w)$, where $u,w,x \in \mathbf{L}$. Note that σ(x,u) indicates a (fuzzy) degree of inclusion of x to u therefore symbols σ(x,u) and σ($x \le u$) are used interchangeably.

It turns out that an inclusion measure σ can be defined by a *positive valuation function v*, where a *valuation v* on a lattice $\mathbf{L}$ is a real function $v: \mathbf{L} \to \mathbf{R}$ which satisfies $v(x)+v(y) = v(x \wedge y)+v(x \vee y)$, $x,y \in \mathbf{L}$, moreover a valuation is *positive* if and only if $x < y$ implies $v(x) < v(y)$. A specific inclusion measure function is given by k($x \le u$)= $\dfrac{v(u)}{v(x \vee u)}$ [13], [14], [19], [20], [21]. A positive valuation function $v: \mathbf{L} \to \mathbf{R}$ introduces yet another useful function, namely a *metric distance* function d: $\mathbf{L} \times \mathbf{L} \to \mathbf{R}$ given by $d(x,y) = v(x \vee y) - v(x \wedge y)$. Note that lately both the inclusion measure and the distance functions have been extended in a (mathematical) "L-fuzzy" sense [15].

The following definition will eventually enhance the application of an FLN scheme.

Definition 1: The *diagonal* of an interval $[a,b] \in \tau(\mathbf{L})$, with respect to a positive valuation function v in lattice $\mathbf{L}$, is a real function $diag: \tau(\mathbf{L}) \to \mathbf{R}$ given by $diag([a,b]) = d(a,b)$, where $d: \mathbf{L} \times \mathbf{L} \to \mathbf{R}$ is a metric distance.

It follows that the inclusion measure $k(x \leq u) = \frac{v(u)}{v(x \vee u)}$ expresses the "size" of the diagonal of u in terms of the diagonal of $x \vee u$, the latter diagonal is used as the unit of the measurement. In the aforementioned sense the inclusion measure $k(x \leq u)$ introduces implicitly semantics in the computations. Moreover, semantics can be introduced explicitly by considering an ontology of semantics in a lattice. For instance, Fig.1 shows an ontology of *parent-of* relations. Note also that a tree/hierarchy implies, as well, a lattice of semantics [23].

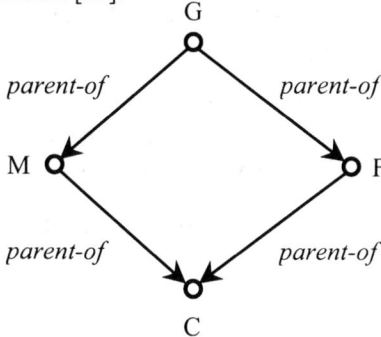

Fig.1 A lattice ontology of semantic *parent-of* relations, where 'G' stands for Grandparent, 'M', 'F' and 'C' stand for Male, Female and Child, respectively.

Since for an interval $[a,b]$ it is $a \leq b$, metric $d(x,y) = v(x \vee y) - v(x \wedge y)$ implies $diag([a,b]) = d(a,b) = v(b) - v(a)$. Note that the term *size* has been used previously [13], [14], [19] instead of term *diagonal*. The advantage of using the term *diagonal* is that it allows a convenient geometric interpretation as explained below. The following property can be shown easily.

Proposition 2: It holds $diag([a,b]) = \max_{x,y \in [a,b]} d(x,y)$.

Let $\mathbf{L}$ be a product-lattice $\mathbf{L} = \mathbf{L}_1 \times \ldots \times \mathbf{L}_N$, furthermore let $v_1, \ldots, v_N$ be positive valuation functions in *constituent lattices* $\mathbf{L}_1, \ldots, \mathbf{L}_N$, respectively. Since pair $(\mathbf{L}_i, d_i)$, $i=1,\ldots,N$, is a *metric space* with metric distance $d(x_i, y_i) = v_i(x_i \vee y_i) - v_i(x_i \wedge y_i)$, it follows that $d_p(a,b) = [d^p(x_1,y_1) + \ldots + d^p(x_N,y_N)]^{1/p}$ is a metric distance in product-lattice $\mathbf{L}$ [11]. In particular, for $\mathbf{L}_1 = \ldots = \mathbf{L}_N = \mathbf{R}$ and $v_1(x) = \ldots = v_N(x) = x$ it follows $d_p(a,b) = [|x_1-y_1|^p + \ldots + |x_N-y_N|^p]^{1/p}$. The latter distance d_p is called L_p metric. Note that the L_1 metric in $\mathbf{R}^N$ equals $d_1(a,b) = |x_1-y_1| + \ldots + |x_N-y_N|$, the latter formula also derives in product-lattice $\mathbf{R}^N$ from positive valuation function $v = v_1 + \ldots + v_N$ with $v_1(x) = \ldots = v_N(x) = x$. Note that the L_2 metric equals $d_2(a,b) = \sqrt{(x_1-y_1)^2 + \ldots (x_N-y_N)^2}$.

Positive valuation function $v = v_1 + \ldots + v_N$ can be extended to both *countably infinite* and *uncountably infinite* summation terms. First, for countably infinite summation terms, the condition for the existence of positive valuation function $v = v_1 + v_2 + \ldots$ is that the corresponding series converges. Second, for uncountably infinite summation terms, the corresponding positive valuation function is given by the (Lebesque) integral on $\mathbf{R}$. An application of the latter positive valuation function is shown in this work below.

III. THE σ-FLNMAP NEURAL NETWORK

A *family* $f = \{W_i\}_{i \in I}$ is a collection of lattice intervals $W_i \in \tau(\mathbf{L})$. Families are employed by the σ-FLN neural network for clustering described in the following.

A. *The σ-FLN Neural Network for Clustering*

0. Let f be a family $\{W_i\}_{i \in I = \{1,\ldots,M\}}$ – initially f might be empty
1. An input $X_C \in \tau(\mathbf{L})$ is presented to the initially "set" collection of lattice intervals W_i, $i \in I$ in family f.
2. While there exist "set" intervals W_i, $i \in I = \{1,\ldots,M\}$, calculate the degree of inclusion $\sigma(X_C \leq W_i)$, $i \in I$.
3. Competition among W_i's: Let W_J denote a "set" interval such that $J = \arg \max_{i \in I = \{1,\ldots M\}} \sigma(X_C \leq W_i)$.
4. Assimilation Condition: Test whether $diag(X_C \vee W_J)$ is less than a user-defined critical threshold size D_{crit}.
5. If the *assimilation condition* is satisfied, then replace W_J by $X_C \vee W_J$. Else, "reset" interval W_J.
6. If all intervals W_i, $i \in I$ have been "reset" then *memorize* input interval X_C, where *memorize* means $W_{M+1} = X_C$.

The σ-FLN neural network has been described as an enhancement of *fuzzy-ART* neural network [13], the latter is applicable solely in product-lattice $\mathbf{R}^N$, where $\mathbf{R}$ is the totally-ordered lattice of real numbers. It follows that intervals in lattice $\mathbf{R}^N$ correspond to N-dimensional hyperboxes. Note that hyperboxes have been employed effectively in applications [22] including neural network applications [7], [16].

B. *σ-FLNMAP Neural Network for Function Approximation*

The σ-FLNMAP neural network is a synergy of two σ-FLN neural networks, namely σ-FLN$_a$ and σ-FLN$_b$, coupled by a MAP field which maps lattice $\mathbf{L}$ intervals (computed in module σ-FLN$_a$) to lattice $\mathbf{M}$ intervals (computed in module σ-FLN$_b$). Hence, σ-FLNMAP is an extension of the *fuzzy-ARTMAP* neural network [4] to a lattice data domain.

In conclusion σ-*FLNMAP* learns rapidly in one-pass through the data. Since learning occurs by computing lattice intervals, any further training does not change the training data error, hence the problem of overfitting is ruled out.

The capacity of neural networks for function approximation is well established [3], [10]. The σ-*FLNMAP* neural network can be used for approximating a function $f: \tau(\mathbf{L}) \rightarrow \tau(\mathbf{M})$ based on 'n' pairs $(x_i, f(x_i))$, $i \in \{1,...,n\}$, where x_i and $f(x_i)$ are intervals in lattices $\mathbf{L}$ and $\mathbf{M}$, respectively. Note that $\mathbf{L}$ could be a product-lattice $\mathbf{L} = \mathbf{L}_1 \times ... \times \mathbf{L}_N$ involving N disparate *constituent lattices*, hence there follows the capacity of σ-*FLNMAP* for disparate data fusion [13], [19], [21].

If both $\mathbf{M} = \mathcal{M}$ above denotes a set of (category) labels and $D_{crit} = 0$ in module σ-*FLN*$_b$ then neural network σ-*FLNMAP* is used as a classifier for approximating a *category* function $g: \tau(\mathbf{L}) \rightarrow \mathcal{M}$. In this work σ-*FLNMAP* was used as a classifier.

A mapping $a \rightarrow g(a)$, effected by σ-*FLNMAP*'s MAP field, of an interval $a \in \tau(\mathbf{L})$ to a category $g(a) \in \mathcal{M}$ is interpreted as the following rule R, induced empirically from the training data

R: IF x is in interval a THEN the category of x is $g(a)$

We remark that $\sigma(x \leq a)$ could be interpreted as the degree of truth of the above rule R. Note also that $\sigma(x \leq a)$ can be interpreted as the degree of truth of the following proposition P
P: x is $g(a)$

The classification accuracy of σ-*FLNMAP* classifier depends on the order of data presentation [13]. Classification accuracy of σ-*FLNMAP* was further improved using a majority voting scheme as described in the following.

C. An Ensemble of σ-FLNMAP Classifiers

It is well known that an ensemble of classifiers can improve the classification accuracy of a single classifier. There is already a rich bibliography on the aforementioned subject, e.g. ensembles for bagging and boosting predictors [18].

An ensemble of σ-*FLNMAP* classifiers has implemented here a majority-voting scheme. A σ-*FLNMAP* in the ensemble is trained on a different random permutation of all the training data. For each random permutation a number of lattice intervals are computed. It turns out that for a sufficiently small critical diagonal size D_a an ensemble of σ-*FLNMAP* classifiers can improve the classification accuracy of any individual σ-*FLNMAP* classifier in the ensemble.

IV. Ensemble Model Parameter Estimation

An ensemble of σ-*FLNMAP* classifiers was dealt with here as a *model* with two parameters, namely the critical diagonal D_a and the number n_V of voters, the latter variables were estimated from the training data as described in the following.

Algorithm PAREST for Estimating Parameters D_a and n_V.

Consider K random partitions of the training data set R into two sets TRN_k and TST_k, such that both $TRN_k \cup TST_k = R$ and $TRN_k \cap TST_k = \emptyset$ $k=1,...,K$. Furthermore let $\mathcal{G}$ be a user-defined grid of pairs $((D_a)_i, (n_V)_j)$, where $i=1,...,I$ and $j=1,...,J$.

Steps 1 to 2 below are repeated for $k=1,...,K$.
1. For each pair $((D_a)_i, (n_V)_j)$, $i=1,...,I$ and $j=1,...,J$ in the grid $\mathcal{G}$, train an ensemble of $(n_V)_j$ σ-*FLNMAP* classifiers using the TRN_k data. Compute the *ensemble classification accuracy* $E_{k,i,j}$ as well as the *average classification accuracy* $A_{k,i,j}$ of all individual σ-*FLNMAP* classifiers in an ensemble.
2. Compute numbers $\delta_{k,i} = \frac{1}{J} \sum_{j=1}^{J} (E_{k,i,j} - A_{k,i,j})$.
Consider vector $\delta_k = (\delta_{k,1}, ..., \delta_{k,I})$.
3. Compute vector $\delta = \frac{1}{K} \sum_{k=1}^{K} \delta_k$. Let M be the index of the maximum number in vector δ. An optimal estimate for D_a is $\hat{D}_a = (D_a)_M$.
4. Use $\hat{D}_a$ and data set TRN_k, $k=1,...,K$ to train an ensemble with $(n_V)_j$, $j=1,...,J$ voters. Let n_k be the smallest number of voters which maximizes classification accuracy.
5. An optimal estimate for n_V is $\hat{n}_V = \left\lfloor \frac{1}{K} \sum_{k=1}^{K} n_k \right\rfloor$.

By *classification accuracy* above is meant the percentage of correct classifications in the testing data TST_k. Note that $\lfloor . \rfloor$ is the *floor* function which returns the largest integer smaller than its real number argument. The advantage of algorithm PAREST is that both estimates $\hat{D}_a$ and $\hat{n}_V$ are calculated optimally from the training data.

V. Experiments And Results

An ensemble of σ-*FLNMAP* classifiers has been employed in four classification problems as described in the following.

A. VOWEL Classification Problem

This data set was downloaded from the University of California Irvine (UCI) Machine Learning Repository [1].

Estimates $\hat{D}_a$ and $\hat{n}_V$ were calculated by partitioning the training data seven times into two sets TRN_k and TST_k, $k=1,...,7$. Set TRN_k, $k=1,...,7$ included the first 70.%, 68.%, 66.%, 64.%, 62.%, 60.% and 58.% of the 528 training data, whereas TST_k included in each case the remaining training data. A grid $\mathcal{G}$ of pairs (D_a, n_V) was considered for $D_a = 2, 1.99, 1.98..., 0.21, 0.20$ and $n_V = 5, 6, ..., 1000$.

For pair (TRN_k, TST_k), $k=1,...,7$ the components of vector δ_k were calculated for each value of $D_a = 2, 1.99, 1.98..., 0.21, 0.20$. A plot of the components of vector δ_1 is shown in

Fig.1(a). Vector δ is shown in Fig.1(b). The maximum of vector δ is attained at D_a=0.75. Diagonal estimate $\hat{D}_a$=0.75 was used; in conclusion the estimate $\hat{n}_V$ =442 was calculated.

Using D_a=0.75 an ensemble of n_V=442 σ-FLNMAP neural networks was trained using random permutations of the original training set of 528 10-dimensional training data vectors. Finally, the original testing set of 462 data was fed to the ensemble and a classification accuracy of 66.88% was attained.

Table I shows the classification accuracy by several classification methods. Number 104 in the first line of Table I denotes the average number of hyperboxes computed in layer F_2^a of an individual σ-FLNMAP voter in the ensemble of 442 σ-FLNMAPs; more specifically, the average number of hyperboxes has been 104.10 with standard deviation 6.20.

Note that the classification accuracy is fairly stable with respect to both parameters D_a and n_V. In particular using $\hat{D}_a$ =0.75 and any number of voters from n_V=300 to n_V=600, the average classification accuracy on the testing data set has been 66.49% with standard deviation 0.39. However, classification accuracy was more sensitive with respect to diagonal D_a for n_V=442 voters. More specifically, for D_a in the range "0.8 down to 0.7" the average classification accuracy was 65.28% with standard deviation 0.50, whereas for D_a in the range "1 down to 0.5" the average classification accuracy deteriorated to 62.57% with standard deviation 2.37.

TABLE I
CLASSSIFICATION ACCURACY BY VARIOUS METHODS IN THE VOWEL BENCHMARK CLASSIFICATION PROBLEM

Method	No. of Hidden Units	% Correct
σ-FLNMAP (442 voters)	104	67
3-D Growing Cell Structures	154	67
Gaussian ARTMAP (5 voters)	273	63
σ-FLL scheme	195	60
Gaussian ARTMAP (w/o voting)	55	59
Nearest Neighbor	-	56
Fuzzy ARTMAP (5 voters)	279	53
Fuzzy ARTMAP (w/o voting)	66	51
Multi-layer Perceptron	88	51
Radial Basis Function	88	48
Multi-layer Perceptron	22	45
Single-layer Perceptron	-	33

B. Soft Tissue Classification Problem

This classification problem demonstrates σ-FLNMAP's effective applicability outside the unit hypercube. In particular σ-FLNMAP is applied here in a complete lattice **F** of (Lebesgue) integrable functions.

Raman spectra profiles are the data used for identifying four tissue types, namely 'connective', 'muscle', 'fat' and 'skin' tissues, encountered in the Epidural Puncture [20].

Typical Raman spectrum profiles are shown in Fig.2. For soft tissue types 'connective', 'muscle', 'fat' and 'skin' there were available 6, 9, 8 and 6 Raman spectra, respectively. Each Raman spectra profile included 2100 samples defined at the same frequencies in the range 0 to 4000 wavenumber offset from the driving frequency at 633 nm whereas laser emission intensity has been less than 10000.

A Raman spectrum was treated by σ-FLNMAP as a single datum in a fuzzy lattice of integrable functions. A training data set and a testing data set were defined randomly including 16 and 13 Raman spectra profiles, respectively. The training data set was partitioned into a pair of sets (TRN_k,TST_k), k=1,...,5. A grid $\mathcal{G}$ of pairs (D_a,n_V) was considered for D_a= 0.70, 0.65, 0.60,..., 0.20 and n_V=2,3,...,30. Note that all data sets included Raman spectra profiles representative of all four tissues. Estimates $\hat{D}_a$ =0.5 and $\hat{n}_V$ =7 were calculated. An 100% classification accuracy on the corresponding testing data set of 13 Raman spectra profiles resulted in.

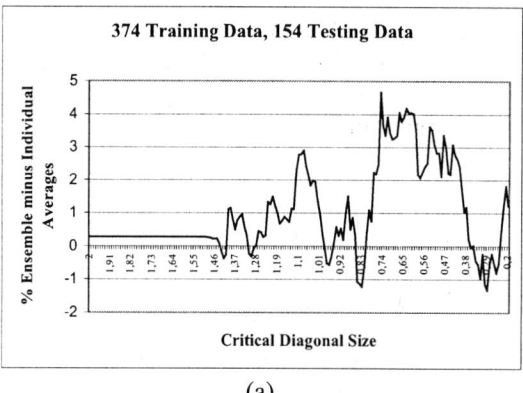

(a)

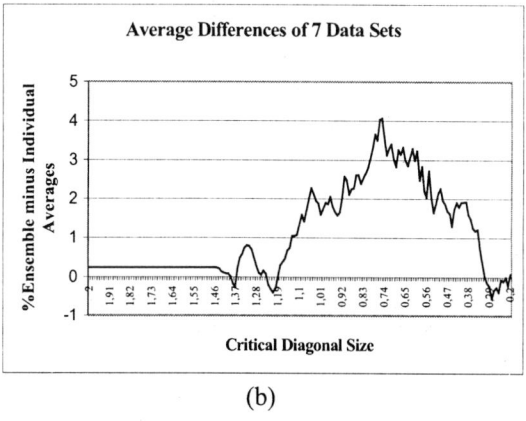

(b)

Fig. 1 (a) The components of vector δ_1 are plotted for each value of D_a= 2, 1.99, 1.98, ... , 0.2 in the VOWEL classification problem.

(b) The components of vector $\delta = \frac{1}{7}\sum_{k=1}^{7} \delta_k$ are plotted for each value D_a= 2, 1.99, 1.98,..., 0.2. The maximum is attained at D_a= 0.75, hence $\hat{D}_a$ =0.75.

C. ABALONE Classification Problem

This data set was downloaded from the University of California Irvine (UCI) Machine Learning Repository [1]. A data record in this problem includes a gender plus seven physical measurements regarding a species of marine snails, namely abalones. The ninth entry in a data record specifies one of three age groups. There exist 3133 and 1044 data records, respectively, for training and testing.

The first record entry specifies the gender of an abalone and it may obtain three values 'I', 'M' and 'F' which stand, respectively, for Infant, Male and Female. In the context of this work the lattice ontology in Fig.1 was used for representing the *parent-of* relation, where the symbol 'G' was inserted by the authors to render the corresponding constituent lattice a complete one as detailed in [20].

The training data set was partitioned into a pair of sets (TRN_k, TST_k), $k=1,...,10$. A grid $\mathcal{G}$ of pairs (D_a, n_V) was considered for D_a= 4, 3.99, 3.98,..., 0.05 and n_V=2,3,...,500. Estimates $\hat{D}_a$=4.32 and $\hat{n}_V$=36 were calculated, in conclusion a 68.29% classification accuracy resulted in on the corresponding testing data set. This classification problem has shown the potential for effective applicability of σ-FLNMAP in lattices of semantic ontologies.

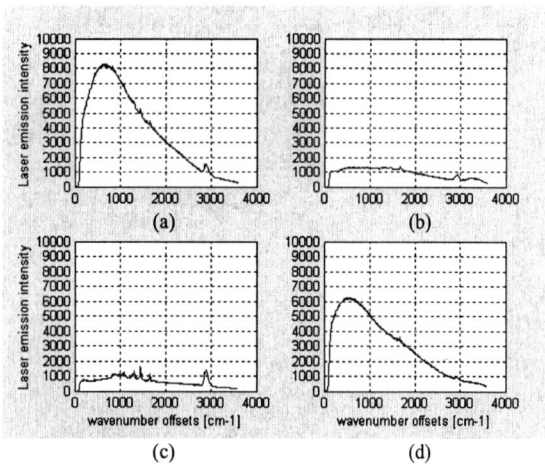

Fig. 2 Raman spectral profiles (Laser Emission Intensity vs. Wavenumber Offset) for four soft tissue types (a) Connective tissue, (b) Muscle tissue, (c) Fat tissue, and (d) Skin tissue, encountered in the Epidural Puncture surgical procedure.

TABLE II
CLASSSIFICATION ACCURACY BY VARIOUS METHODS IN THE ABALONE BENCHMARK CLASSIFICATION PROBLEM

Method	% Correct
σ-FLNMAP (36 voters)	68.29
Cascade-correlation (5 hidden nodes)	65.61
σ-FLL scheme	65.32
Back-Propagation	64.00
Nearest Neighbor (k=5)	62.46
C4.5	59.20
Linear Discriminant Analysis	32.57

The following problem was meant to compare the performance of an ensemble of σ-FLNMAP classifiers with the performance of alternative ensemble methods from the literature including bagging, arcing and boosting.

D. CLEVELAND Heart Classification Problem

This data set was downloaded from the UCI Machine Learning Repository [1]. The problem is to diagnose heart disease in a patient based on a 14-attribute vector. This benchmark consists of 303 data vectors. The severity of heart disease is indicated by an integer from 0 (no heart disease) to 4. By collapsing the classes into two, i.e. absence versus presence of heart disease, the problem becomes a 2-categories classification problem.

Because no training and testing data sets are given explicitly, a 10-fold cross validation series of 10 experiments was carried out leaving, in turn, 30 data vectors out for testing. Using an ensemble of σ-FLNMAP classifiers, as detailed in [12], the average classification accuracy error has been 9.0% as shown in Table III. The remaining entries in Table III are from [18]. We point out that in [12] there has been reported a further decrease in error down to a spectacular 5.5% using a genetically optimized ensemble of σ-FLNMAP classifiers.

TABLE III
CLASSSIFICATION ACCURACY BY VARIOUS ENSEMBLE METHODS IN THE CLEVELEND HEART CLASSIFICATION PROBLEM

Method	% Error
σ-FLNMAP with Voting	9.0
Bagging Backpropagation	17.0
Arcing Backpropagation	20.7
Boosting Backpropagation	21.1
Bagging C4.5	19.5
Arcing C4.5	21.5
Boosting C4.5	20.8

In all the experiments in this work it was observed that classification accuracy was more sensitive in parameter D_a than in parameter n_V. Furthermore, the experiments here have shown that even though a small number of voters produces, in general, better classification results, there are problems where a larger number of voters produces better classification results, e.g. in the VOWEL classification problem.

VI. DISCUSSION AND CONCLUSION

This work has demonstrated the utility of σ-FLNMAP neural network for classification based on semantics. A lattice ordering relation in the data introduced semantics.

The σ-FLNMAP neural network was presented here as an instrument for approximating a function f: **L**→**M**, where **L** and **M** are lattices. Emphasis here was on classification problems. The latter capacity could potentially be useful in developing neural models to deal with both symbols [17] and the symbol grounding problem [9] based on a fusion of disparate sensory data. New definitions and properties here extended the applicability of σ-FLNMAP to a lattice of waveforms.

Experimental results in four classification problems compared favorably with results by alternative methods from the literature [18], [20]. Apart from the improved experimental results this work has introduced additional improvements as explained in the following. The work in [20] does not employ an ensemble of classifiers, furthermore section II here has introduced a new more convenient notation; from a new perspective, the σ-FLNMAP neural network was presented here as a function approximator on a lattice data domain of semantics, moreover an ensemble of σ-FLNMAP classifiers was presented here as a model whose parameters can be estimated optimally by the new algorithm PAREST.

The classification performance of σ-FLNMAP depends the order of presenting the training data, the latter is also true for the *fuzzy-ARTMAP* neural network [4]. From statistics it is known that *bootstrap aggregating* (*bagging*) can improve a good but unstable procedure [18]. An ensemble of σ-FLNMAP classifiers was used as a statistical model whose parameters were estimated optimally from the training data and the classification accuracy was further improved. A difference with bagging, as well as with boosting, is that a σ-FLNMAP classifier in the ensemble uses a random permutation of the full training set. Even though no relevant experiments have been carried out yet, it is believed that the improved classification accuracy of an ensemble of σ-FLNMAP classifiers is mainly due to the noise canceling effects of a number of random data permutations. In other words the effects of outliers in the training data are minimized, for the data-order-dependent σ-FLNMAP, by considering jointly different permutations of the training data.

A number of important issues remain for future research. For instance, in a constituent lattice **R** of real numbers alternative positive valuations $v(x)=x$ could be used. Note that an underlying positive valuation function $v(x)$ can be regarded as an instrument for introducing non-linearities in a data domain. Moreover, optimal estimates for the model parameters in this work were calculated by exhaustive search because of the fairly small size of the parameter space; nevertheless for larger parameter spaces more efficient search techniques are needed e.g. genetic algorithms. Preliminary results in [12] using genetic algorithms have been very encouraging.

ACKNOWLEDGMENT

The Raman spectra are a courtesy of P.N. Brett, T. Parker from the Dept. of Mechanical Engineering, Univ. of Bristol, UK, and J.C.C. Day from the "Interface Analysis Centre", Bristol, UK.

REFERENCES

[1] C.L. Blake, and C.J. Merz, UCI Repository of machine learning databases, Irvine, CA: University of California, Department of Information and Computer Science, 1998. [http:// www.ics.uci.edu/ ~mlearn/ MLRepository.html].

[2] A. Browne, and R. Sun, "Connectionist inference models", *Neural Networks*, vol. 14, no. 10, pp. 1331-1355, 2001.

[3] T.P. Chen, and H. Chen, "Approximation capability to functions of several variables, nonlinear functionals, and operators by radial basis function neural networks", *IEEE Trans. Neural Networks*, vol. 6, no. 4, pp. 904-910, 1995.

[4] I. Dagher, M. Georgiopoulos, G.L. Heileman, and G. Bebis, "An ordering algorithm for pattern presentation in fuzzy ARTMAP that tends to improve generalization performance", *IEEE Trans. on Neural Networks*, vol. 10, no. 4, pp. 768-778, 1999.

[5] D. Fensel, F. van Harmelen, I. Horrocks, D.L. McGuinness, and P.F. Patel-Schneider, "OIL: An ontology infrastructure for the Semantic Web", *IEEE Intelligent Systems*, pp. 38-45, March/April 2001.

[6] P. Frasconi, M. Gori, and A. Sperduti, "Guest editors' introduction: Special section on connectionist models for learning in structured domains", *IEEE Trans. on Knowledge and Data Engineering*, vol. 13, no. 2, pp. 145-147, 2001.

[7] B. Gabrys, and A. Bargiela, "General fuzzy min-max neural network for clustering and classification", *IEEE Trans. on Neural Networks*, vol. 11, no. 3, pp. 769-783, 2000.

[8] L. Goldfarb, and S. Deshpande, "What is a symbolic measurement process ?", *Proc. IEEE Conf. on Systems, Man, and Cybernetics*, Orlando, Florida, vol. 5, pp. 4139-4145, 1997.

[9] S. Harnad, "Symbol grounding and the origin of language", in *Computationalism: New Directions*, M. Scheutz, Ed. Cambridge, MA: The MIT Press (A Bradford Book), 2002, pp. 143-158.

[10] K. Hornik, M. Stinchcombe, and H. White, "Multilayer feedforward networks are universal approximators", *Neural Networks*, vol. 2, no. 5, pp. 359-366, 1989.

[11] K. Itô, editor, *Encyclopedic Dictionary of Mathematics*, 2nd edition, the Mathematical Society of Japan, English translation Cambridge, MA: The MIT Press, 1987.

[12] Kaburlasos VG, Papadakis, SE, and Kazarlis S, "A Genetically Optimized Ensemble of σ-FLNMAP Neural Classifiers Based on Non-Parametric Probability Distributions Functions", *Proceedings of the 2003 International Joint Conference on Neural Networks (IJCNN'03)*, Portland, OR, 20-24 July 2003.

[13] V.G. Kaburlasos, and V. Petridis, "Fuzzy Lattice Neurocomputing (FLN) models", *Neural Networks*, vol. 13, no. 10, pp. 1145-1170, 2000.

[14] V.G. Kaburlasos, and V. Petridis, "Learning and decision-making in the framework of fuzzy lattices", in *New Learning Paradigms in Soft Computing*, vol. 84, L.C. Jain and J. Kacprzyk, Eds. Heidelberg, Germany: Physica-Verlag, 2002, pp. 55-96.

[15] A. Kehagias, M. Konstantinidou, "L-fuzzy valued inclusion measure, L-fuzzy similarity and L-fuzzy distance", *Fuzzy Sets and Systems*.

[16] P. Lavoie, J.-F. Crespo, and Y. Savaria, "Generalization, discrimination, and multiple categorization using adaptive resonance theory", *IEEE Trans. Neural Networks*, vol. 10, no. 4, pp. 757-767, 1999.

[17] T. Omori, A. Mochizuki, K. Mizutani and M. Nishizaki, "Emergence of symbolic behavior from brain like memory with dynamic attention", *Neural Networks*, vol. 12, no. 7-8, pp. 1157-1172, 1999.

[18] D. Opitz, and R. Maclin, "Popular Ensemble Methods: An Empirical Study", *Journal of Artificial Intelligence Research*, vol. 11, pp. 169-198, 1999.

[19] V. Petridis, and V.G. Kaburlasos, "Fuzzy Lattice Neural Network (FLNN): A hybrid model for learning", *IEEE Trans. on Neural Networks*, vol. 9, no. 5, pp. 877-890, 1998.

[20] V. Petridis, and V.G. Kaburlasos, "Learning in the Framework of Fuzzy Lattices", *IEEE Trans. on Fuzzy Systems*, vol. 7, no. 4, pp. 422-440, 1999.

[21] V. Petridis, and V.G. Kaburlasos, "Clustering and classification in structured data domains using Fuzzy Lattice Neurocomputing (FLN)", *IEEE Trans. on Knowledge and Data Engineering*, 13(2): 245-260, 2001.

[22] H. Samet, "Hierarchical representations of collections of small rectangles", *ACM Computing Surveys*, vol. 20, no. 4, pp 271-309, 1988.

[23] J.F. Sowa. *Knowledge representation*. Pacific Grove, CA: Brooks Cole Publishing Co., 2000.

A CASCADE FORM BLIND SOURCE SEPARATION CONNECTING SOURCE SEPARATION AND LINEARIZATION FOR NONLINEAR MIXTURES

Kenji Nakayama   Akihiro Hirano   Takayuki Nishiwaki

Dept. of Information Systems Eng., Faculty of Eng., Kanazawa Univ.
2-40-20, Kodatsuno, Kanazawa, 920-8667, Japan
nakayama@t.kanazawa-u.ac.jp

ABSTRACT

A network structure and its learning algorithm have been proposed for blind source separation applied to nonlinear mixtures. The network has a cascade form consists of a source separation block and a linearization block in this order. The conventional learning algorithm is employed for the separation block. A new learning algorithm is proposed for the linearization block assuming 2nd-order nonlinearity. After, source separation, the outputs include the nonlinear components for the same signal source. This nonlinearity is suppressed through the linearization block. Parameters in this block are iteratively adjusted based on a process of solving a 2nd-order equation of a single variable. Simulation results, using 2-channel speech signals and an instantaneous nonlinear mixing process, show good separation performance.

1. INTRODUCTION

Recently, many kinds of information are transmitted and processed through world wide communications. Communication terminals are used under a variety of environments. At the same time, high quality is required. For this reason, signal processing including noise cancelation, echo cancelation, equalization of transmission lines, restoration of signals have been becoming very important technology. In some cases, we do not have enough information about signal sources and interference. Furthermore, their mixing process and transmission process are not well known in advance. Under these situations, blind source separation using statistical property of the signal sources has become important.

Jutten et all proposed a blind source separation algorithm based on statistical independence and symmetrical distribution of the signal sources [1]-[8]. Two kinds of stabilization methods have been proposed for Jutten's method [9],[10]. Convolutive mixture models have been discussed [11],[12]. Convergence and separation performances are highly dependent on relation between a probability density function of the output signals and nonlinear functions, which are used in updating coefficients in a separation block. Optimum nonlinearity has been discussed [13], [14], [15], and adaptive nonlinear functions have been proposed [16], [17], [18].

In actual applications, mixing processes include nonlinearity, such as loud speakers. In this case, signal sources are mixed in a complicated manner, and are difficult to be separated. In these problems, both source separation and linearization are simultaneously required. One way to model a nonlinear mixture is a combination of a linear mixing process and a nonlinear transform in a cascade form. In a separation block, a linearization process and a linear separation process are arranged in this order. Spline nonlinear functions or spline neural networks have been applied to the linearization process [19], [20]. Furthermore, a maximum likelihood estimator has been applied [21]. However, separation performance is not enough.

In this paper, an approach is proposed, in which a linear separation process and a linearization process are arranged in this order. First, the signal sources, which include nonlinearity, are separated based on their statistical independency. In the linearization process, the nonlinear components in each signal source are suppressed through an iterative learning algorithm. Simulation using 2-channel speech signals and 2nd-order nonlinearity will be shown to confirm usefulness of the proposed method.

2. CASCADE FORM BLIND SOURCE SEPARATION

2.1. Network Structure

A proposed cascade form blind source separation (BSS) is shown in Fig.1. The nonlinear mixture model is the same as in [19], [20], [21]. First, the signal sources s_i are mixed through linear combination resulting in u_j. After that, they are transmitted through nonlinear functions F_j resulting in x_j. In the BSS block, a linear source separation process and a linearization process are arranged in this order. In the conventional methods, they are arranged in the reverse order.

In the proposed method, the number of the observations

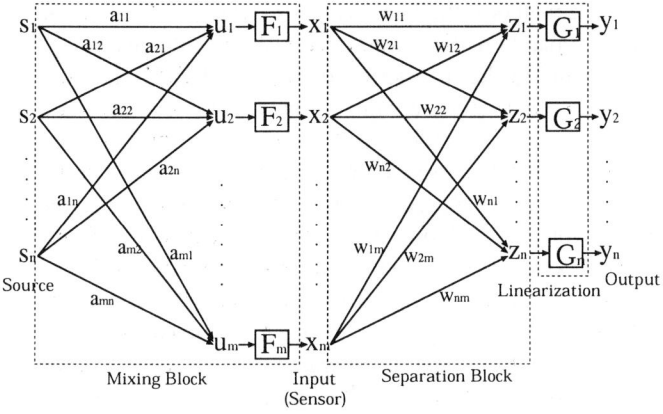

Fig. 1. Network structure of proposed cascade form BSS.

x_j are increased from that of the signa sources s_i in order to increase conditions used in cancelling the nonlinear terms in the linear separation block. For example, s_2, s_2^2 and $s_1 s_2$ are cancelled in z_1, and s_1, s_1^2 and $s_1 s_2$ are cancelled in z_2, respectively.

If linear separation is complete, its outputs z_i include only a single signal source and its nonlinear components. This nonlinearity is suppressed through the linearization block.

2.2. Example of Linear Separation and Linearization

One example is shown here. Two signal sources and 2nd-order nonlinearity are used. In this case, four observations $x_1 \sim x_4$ are required. They are expressed by

$$x_1 = a_{11}s_1 + a_{12}s_2 + a_{13}s_1^2 + a_{14}s_1 s_2 + a_{15}s_2^2 \quad (1)$$
$$x_2 = a_{21}s_1 + a_{22}s_2 + a_{23}s_1^2 + a_{24}s_1 s_2 + a_{25}s_2^2 \quad (2)$$
$$x_3 = a_{31}s_1 + a_{32}s_2 + a_{33}s_1^2 + a_{34}s_1 s_2 + a_{35}s_2^2 \quad (3)$$
$$x_4 = a_{41}s_1 + a_{42}s_2 + a_{43}s_1^2 + a_{44}s_1 s_2 + a_{45}s_2^2 \quad (4)$$

The mixing process is assumed to be linearly independent. Thus, from the above equations, the cross term $s_1 s_2$ can be cancelled, and two independent outputs z_1 and z_2 can be obtained. They still include the 2nd-order term s_1^2 and s_2^2, respectively.

$$z_1 = b_{11}s_1 + b_{12}s_1^2 \quad (5)$$
$$z_2 = b_{21}s_2 + b_{22}s_2^2 \quad (6)$$

Since z_1 and z_2 include only s_1 and s_2, respectively, they can be linearized through the following nonlinear functions.

$$y_1 = G_1(z_1) = \frac{-b_{11} \pm \sqrt{b_{11}^2 + 4b_{12}z_1}}{2b_{12}} \quad (7)$$
$$y_2 = G_2(z_2) = \frac{-b_{21} \pm \sqrt{b_{21}^2 + 4b_{22}z_2}}{2b_{22}} \quad (8)$$

Finaly, the separated and linearized signal sources are obtained.

$$y_1 = c_{11}s_1 \quad (9)$$
$$y_2 = c_{12}s_2 \quad (10)$$

c_{11} and c_{12} are some constant.

3. LEARNING ALGORITHMS

3.1. Linear Separation Block

If s_1 and s_2 are statistically independent, then $a_{11}s_1 + a_{12}s_1^2$ and $a_{21}s_2 + a_{22}s_2^2$ are also independent. They can be separated through the conventional learning algorithms for linear mixtures. So, the learning algorithm based on likelihood estimation [22], [23], [24] is employed in this paper.

$$\boldsymbol{W}(n+1) = \boldsymbol{W}(n) + \eta[\boldsymbol{\Lambda}(t) - \varphi(\boldsymbol{z}(n))\boldsymbol{z}^T(n)]\boldsymbol{W}(n) \quad (11)$$

η is a learning rate, $\boldsymbol{\Lambda}(t)$ is a diagonal matrix, and $\varphi()$ is a nonlinear function [18].

3.2. Linearization Block

Transformations in the linearization block are given by Eqs.(7) and (8). However, in real applications, the coefficients b_{ij} are not known. So, they should be adjusted through an iterative method. Equations (7) and (8) can be expressed by using two parameters as follows:

$$y_i(n) = -\frac{\alpha_i}{2} \pm \sqrt{\frac{\alpha_i^2}{4} + \frac{z_i(n)}{\beta_i}} \quad (12)$$
$$\alpha_i = \frac{b_{i1}}{b_{i2}} \quad (13)$$
$$\beta_i = \frac{1}{b_{i2}} \quad (14)$$

α_i and β_i are adjusted through an iterative method.

Error Function:

In this paper, 2nd-order nonlinearity is assumed. Thus, after the linear source separation, the outputs include 1st-order and 2nd-order terms of the signal sources. Furthermore, if we take speech and music signals into account, their average is almost zero. Therefore, the output average can be used as a cost function.

$$E_i(n) = \frac{1}{M} \sum_{l=0}^{M-1} y_i(n-l) \quad (15)$$

The gradient descent algorithm is used for adjusting the parameters.

$$\alpha_i(n) = \alpha_i(n-1) - \eta \frac{\partial E_i(n)}{\partial \alpha_i(n)} \quad (16)$$

$$\beta_i(n) = \beta_i(n-1) - \eta \frac{\partial E_i(n)}{\partial \beta_i(n)} \quad (17)$$

$$\frac{\partial E_i(n)}{\partial \alpha_i(n)} = \frac{1}{M} \sum_{l=0}^{M-1} \frac{\partial y_i(n-l)}{\partial \alpha_i(n)}$$

$$= \frac{1}{M} \sum_{l=0}^{M-1} (-\frac{1}{2} \pm \frac{\alpha_i(n)}{4}(\frac{\alpha_i^2(n)}{4}$$

$$+ \frac{1}{\beta_i(n)} z(n-l))^{-\frac{1}{2}}) \quad (18)$$

$$\frac{\partial E_i(n)}{\partial \beta_i(n)} = \frac{1}{M} \sum_{i=0}^{M-1} \frac{\partial y_i(n-l)}{\partial \beta_i(n)}$$

$$= \frac{1}{M} \sum_{l=0}^{M-1} (\mp \frac{z(n-l)}{2\beta_i^2}(\frac{\alpha_i(n)^2}{4}$$

$$+ \frac{1}{\beta_i(n)} z(n-l))^{-\frac{1}{2}}) \quad (19)$$

Porality Control

In the above update equations, there is a freedom of polarity. It should be judged which polarity should be used. For this purpose, the following conditions are introduced. These conditions do not lose generality in real applications.

1. A linear component is greater than a nonlinear component.

2. The signal source level is limited. Say, for instance $|s_i(n)| < 1$.

Under these conditions, in the linear separation output,

$$z_i(n) = b_{i1} s_i(n) + b_{i2} s_i^2 \quad (20)$$

the following inequality is always held.

$$|b_{i1} s_i(n)| > |b_{i2} s_i^2(n)| \quad (21)$$

This means the porality of $z_i(n)$ is equal to that of $b_{i1} s_i(n)$. So, except for the polarity of b_{i1}, that of the output $y_i(n)$ can be controlled so as to be the same as that of $z_i(n)$. The polarity of b_{i1} does not affect separation performance. Because in blind source separation, constant scaling inherently remains.

3.3. Combination of Both Learning Algorithms

In the proposed method, first the linear separation block is trained. After convergence, the linearization block is adjusted. This separate training is stable.

3.4. Comparison with Conventional Methods

Nonlinear BSS methods have been proposed in [19],[20],[21]. In these methods, the linearization block is used before the linear separation. However, linearization of the mixed signals including the cross terms, like $s_1 s_2$ is difficult. Furthermore, a simultaneous learning for both signal separation and linearization is unstable. In the proposed method, the linearization block is used after the linear separation. Let the mixed signals be expressed with high-order polynomial, the signal sources, including high-order components of themselves like s_i and s_i^2, can be separated through the linear separation process. In other words, s_i^2 is still independent on the $s_j, i \neq j$ components. Since the cross terms are not independent, they can be suppressed through the linear separation process. After that, the linearization in each signal source is easier than that for the mixing signals with nonlinearity.

Although the proposed method is limited to 2nd-order nonlinearity, it can be extend to 3rd-order nonlinearity. In this case, network becomes complicated. Since in a wide range of application fields, order of nonlinearity is mainly up to 3rd-order, this limitation of order does not lose generality.

4. SIMULATIONS AND DISCUSSIONS

4.1. Simulation Conditions

Two signal sources and four observations are used. The signal sources are male speech signals. The mixing matrix is

$$A = \begin{bmatrix} 1 & -2 \\ -3 & 2 \\ 2 & -1 \\ 1 & 2 \end{bmatrix}$$

The learning rate is $\eta = 0.001$. The nonlinear functions in the mixing block are

$$F_1(u) = u + 0.4u^2$$
$$F_2(u) = u + 0.2u^2$$
$$F_3(u) = u - 0.6u^2$$
$$F_4(u) = u + 0.3u^2$$

4.2. Linear Separation

The parameters w_{ji} are trained by the learning algorithm described in sec.3.1. The learning curve is shown in Fig.2. The vertical axis indicates SNR in dB, the horizontal axis is the number of update iterations. SNR is defined as follows:

$$\sigma_s^2 = \sum_{i=1}^{2} \text{power of } s_i \text{ in } z_j,$$
where s_i is dominant (22)

$$\sigma_n^2 = \sum_{j=1}^{2} \text{power of } z_j \text{ exept for } s_i,$$
where s_i is dominant (23)

$$SNR_1 = 10 \log_{10} \frac{\sigma_s^2}{\sigma_n^2} \quad (24)$$

$$\sigma_s^2 = \sum_{i=1}^{2} \text{power of } s_i \text{ and } s_i^2 \text{ in } z_j,$$
where s_i is dominant (25)

$$\sigma_n^2 = \sum_{j=1}^{2} \text{power of } z_j \text{ exept for } s_i \text{ and } s_i^2,$$
where s_i is dominant (26)

$$SNR_2 = 10 \log_{10} \frac{\sigma_s^2}{\sigma_n^2} \quad (27)$$

In this figure, both SNR_1 and SNR_2 are shown with a solid line and a dashed line, respectively. In the linear separation process, the 2nd-order components s_i^2 are not suppressed, because they are also independent components against s_j and s_j^2, $i \neq j$. So, SNR_2 has some meaning. The final

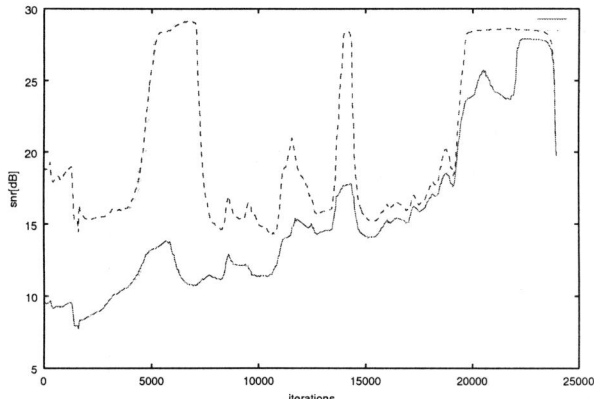

Fig. 2. Learning curve for output of linear separation block. SNR_1 and SNR_2 are shown with solid line and dashed line.

$z_1(n)$ and $z_2(n)$ are shown below.

$$z_1 = 5.28s_1 - 1.19s_2 + 6.05s_1^2 - 1.66s_1s_2 + 3.88s_2^2$$
$$z_2 = -0.21s_1 + 7.0s_2 - 0.03s_1^2 + 1.94s_1s_2 + 3.92s_2^2$$

In $z_1(n)$ and $z_2(n)$, $s_1(n)$ and $s_2(n)$ are extracted, respectively. In $z_1(n)$, $s_1(n)$ and $s_1^2(n)$ remain. On the other hand, in $z_2(n)$, $s_2(n)$ and $s_2^2(n)$ are dominant. In both outputs, the interferences, that is, s_2, s_2^2 and s_1s_2 in z_1, and s_1, s_1^2 and s_1s_2 in z_2, are reduced.

4.3. Linearization

Error valuation

In this process, separation performance is also evaluated by SNR_1 defined by Eq.(24). In the simulation, the s_i component and the other components are discriminated as follows: In the linearization block, $z_i(n)$ is linearized through

$$y_i(n) = -\frac{\alpha_i}{2} + \sqrt{\frac{\alpha_i^2}{4} + \frac{z_i(n)}{\beta_i}} \quad (28)$$

Let

$$\sqrt{\frac{\alpha_i^2}{4} + \frac{z_i(n)}{\beta_i}} = \sqrt{a_i s_i^2(n) + b_i(n) s_i(n) + c_i(n)} \quad (29)$$

Furthermore,

$$\sqrt{a_i s_i^2(n) + b_i s_i(n) + c_i(n)} = d_i s_i(n) + e_i(n) \quad (30)$$
$$a_i s_i^2(n) + b_i s_i(n) + c_i(n)$$
$$= d_i^2 s_i^2(n) + 2d_i s_i(n) e_i(n) + e_i(n)^2 \quad (31)$$

Comparing the coefficients, the following relations are obtained.

$$d_i^2 = a_i \quad (32)$$
$$2d_i e_i(n) = b_i(n) \quad (33)$$
$$e_i^2(n) = c_i(n) \quad (34)$$

a_i and $c_i(n)$ are calculated using α_i, β_i and $z_i(n)$ at each sample. SNR is evaluated by

$$SNR_1 = 10 \log \frac{p(n)}{q(n)} \quad (35)$$

$$p(n) = \frac{1}{M} \sum_{i=0}^{M-1} (y_i(n) + \frac{\alpha_i}{2} - e_i(n))^2 \quad (36)$$

$$q(n) = \frac{1}{M} \sum_{i=0}^{M-1} (-\frac{\alpha_i}{2} + e_i(n))^2 \quad (37)$$

The learning curves for both the linear separation and the linearization processes are shown in Fig.3, with a solid line and a dashed line, respectively. SNR means SNR_1. SNR after the linearization improved by $15dB$ compared with that after linear separation. Approximately, SNR_1=30dB is guaranteed, which is good separation performance.

4.4. Waveforms

Figures 4, 5 and 6 show waveforms of the speech signal sources, after the linear separation and the linearization, respectively. In Fig.4, the upper and the lower are s_1 and

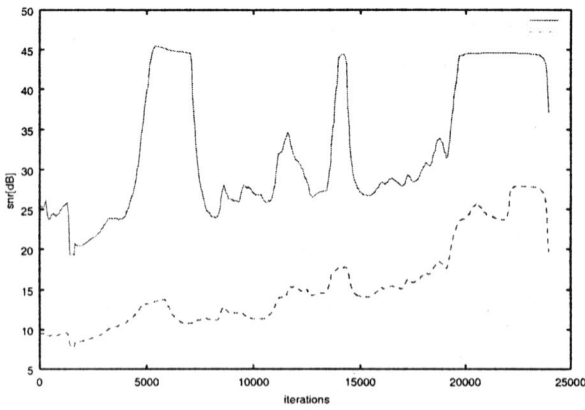

Fig. 3. Learning curve for output of both linear separation and linearization blocks with dashed line and solid line, respectively. SNR means SNR_1.

s_2, respectively. In Figs.5, 6, the upper and the lower are $z_1(n)$ and $y_1(n)$, and $z_2(n)$ and $y_2(n)$, respectively. $s_1(n)$ and $s_2(n)$ are extracted in $z_1(n)$ and $z_2(n)$, respectively. The polarity of $s_2(n)$ is reversed. The waveforms after the linear separation and the linearization are almost the same. However, SNR is slightly improved after the linearization.

5. CONCLUSIONS

In this paper, a blind source separation method has been proposed for instantaneous nonlinear mixtures. It consists of the linear separation and the linearization in a cascade form. Both blocks are separately trained. The conventional learning algorithm of linear mixtures can be used for the former block. The new learning algorithm has been proposed for the latter block. Nonlinearity in the mixture is assumed to be 2nd-order. Simulation, using two speech signals and 2nd-order nonlinearity, shows usefulness of the proposed method.

6. REFERENCES

[1] C.Jutten, J.Herault and A.Guerin, "IIN.C.A: An independent components analyzer based on an adaptive neuromimetic network", in: J.Degmongeot, T.Herve, V.Raille and C.Roche, eds., Artificial Intelligence and Cognitive Science, Manhester Univ. Press, 1988.

[2] C.Jutten and J.Herault, "Analog implementation of permanent unsupervised learning algorithm", Proc. NATO Advanced Research Workshop on Neurocomputing, Les Arcs, France, pp.145-152, Feb.27-March 3, 1989.

[3] P.Comon, "Separation of stochastic process whose linear mixtures observed", Proc. ONR- NSF-IEEE Workshop on

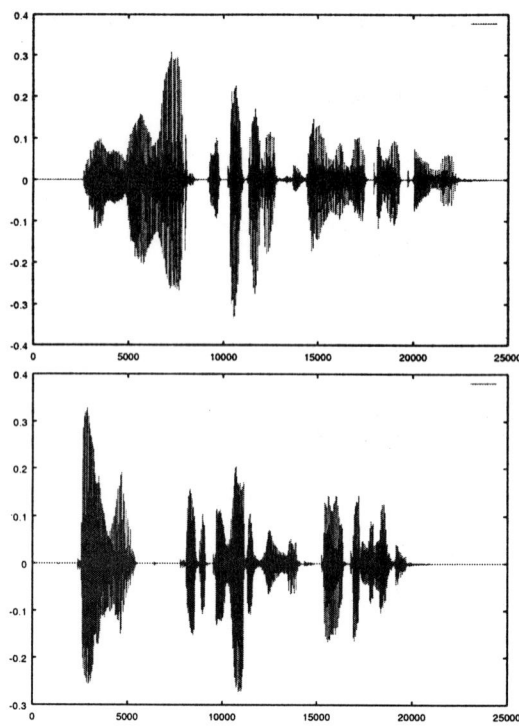

Fig. 4. Waveform of signal sources, which are male voice. Upper and lower are s_1 and s_2, respectively.

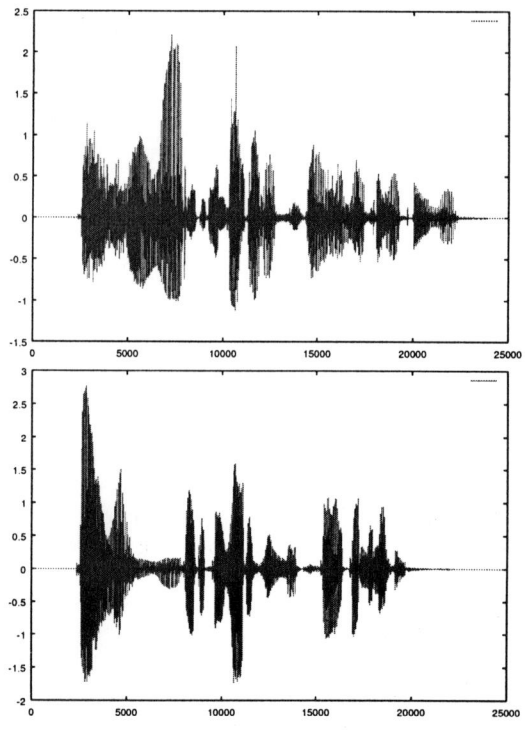

Fig. 5. Signal waveform after linear separation. Upper and lower are $z_1(n)$ and $z_2(n)$, respectively. $s_1(n)$ and $s_2(n)$ are extracted in $z_1(n)$ and $z_2(n)$, respectively.

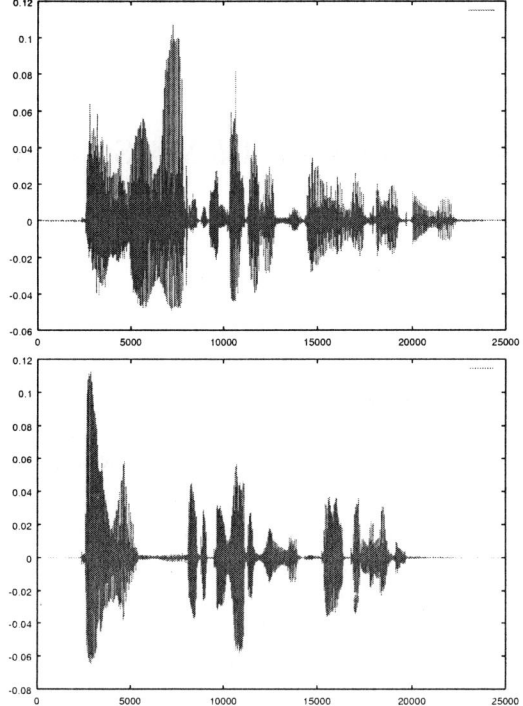

Fig. 6. Signal waveform after linearization. Upper and lower are $y_1(n)$ and $y_2(n)$, respectively. $s_1(n)$ and $s_2(n)$ are extracted in $y_1(n)$ and $y_2(n)$, respectively.

Higher Spectral Analysis Vail, pp.174-179, June 28-30, 1989.

[4] P.Comon, "Separation of sources using higher-order cumulants", SPIE Conference, Vol.1152, Advanced Algorithms and Architectures for Signal Processing IV, San Diego, pp. 170-181, August 6-11, 1989.

[5] J.F.Cardoso, "Eigen structure of the 4th order cumulant tensor with application to the blind source separation problem", ICASSP Proc. pp. 2655-1658.

[6] C.Jutten and J. Herault, "Blind separation of sources, Part I: An adaptive algorithm based on neuromimetic architecture", Signal Proc. 24, pp.1-10, 1991.

[7] P.Comon, C.Jutten and J.Herault, "Blind separation of sources, Part II: Problems statement", Signal Proc. 24, pp.11-20, 1991.

[8] E.Sorouchyari, "Blind separation of sources, Part III: Stability analysis", Signal Proc., 24, pp.21-29, 1991.

[9] K.Nakayama, A.Hirano and M.Nitta, "A constraint learning algorithm for blind source separation", Proc. IJCNN'2000, pp.24-27, July, 2000.

[10] K.Nakayama, A.Hirano and T.Sakai, "A pair-channel learning algorithm with constraints for multi-channel blind separation", Proc. IJCNN'01, July 2001.

[11] H.L.Nguyen Thi and C.Jutten, "Blind source separation for convolutive mixtures", Signal Processing, vol.45, no.2, pp.209–229, March 1995.

[12] K.Nakayama, A.Hirano and A.Horita, "A learning algorithm for convolutive blind source separation with transmission delay constraint", Proc. IJCNN'2002, pp.1287-1292, May 2002.

[13] J.F.Cardoso, "Informax and maximum likelihood for source separation", IEEE Signal Processing Letter, vol.4, no.4, pp.112-114, Apr. 1997.

[14] A.Mansour and C.Jutten, "What should we say about the kurtosis", IEEE Signal Processing Letters, vol.6, no.12, pp.321-322, Dec. 1999.

[15] H.Mathis and S.C.Douglas, "On optimal and universal nonlinearities for blind signal separation", IEEE Proc. ICASSP'01, MULT-P3.3, May 2001.

[16] L.Xu, C.C.Cheung and S.Amari, "Learned parametric mixture based ICA algorithm", Neurocomputing 22, pp.69-80, 1998.

[17] K.Nakayama, A.Hirano and T.Sakai, "An adaptive nonlinear function controlled by kurtosis for blind source separation", Proc. IJCNN'2002, pp.1234-1239, May. 2002.

[18] K.Nakayama, A.Hirano and T.Sakai, "An adaptive nonlinear function controlled by estimated output PDF for blind source separation", Proc. 4th International Symposium on Independent Copmponent Analysis and Blind Signal Separation, ICA'2003, Nara, Japan, April 2003. to be presented.

[19] M.Solazzi, F.Piazza and A.Uncini, "Nonlinear blind source separation by spline neural networks", IEEE Proc. ICASSP'2001, Salt Lake City, MULT-P3.4, May 2001.

[20] F.Milani, M.Solazzi and A.Uncini, "Blind source separation of convolutive nonlinear mixtures by flexible spline nonlinear functions", IEEE Proc. ICASSP'2002, Orlando, Florida, pp.1641-1644, May 2002.

[21] A.Koutras,"Blind separation of non-linear convolved speech mixtures", IEEE Proc. ICASSP'2002, Orlando, Florida, pp.913-916, May 2002.

[22] S.Amari, A.Cichocki and H.H.Yang, "Recurrent neural networks for blind separation of sourdes", Proc. NOLTA-95, Las Vegas, pp.37-42, 1995.

[23] A.Cichocki, S.Amari, M.Adachi, W.Kasprzak, "Self-adaptive neural networks for blind separation of sources", Proc. ISCAS'96, Atlanta, pp.157-161, 1996.

[24] S.Amari, T.Chen and A.Cichocki, "Stability analysis of learning algorithms for blind source separation", Neural Networks, vol.10, no.8, pp.1345-1351, 1997.

Natural Gradient based Blind Multi User Detection in QPSK DS-CDMA Systems

Khurram Waheed, Keyur Desai and Fathi M. Salem
Circuits, Systems and Artificial Neural network Laboratory
Michigan State University
East Lansing, MI 48824-1226

Abstract-Blind Multi User Detection (BMUD) is the process of simultaneously estimating multiple symbol sequences associated with all users in the downlink of a Code Division Multiple Access (CDMA) communication system using only the received data. We propose to apply Natural Gradient based online Blind Source Recovery (NGBSR) techniques using either the feedforward or the feedback symbol recovery structures to achieve the global task of BMUD for QPSK DS-CDMA systems. The quasi-orthogonality of the spreading codes and the inherent independence among the various transmitted user symbol sequences form the basis of the proposed BMUD methods. The application of these algorithms is justified since a slowly fading multipath CDMA environment is conveniently represented as a linear combination of convolved independent symbol sequences. The proposed structures and algorithms demonstrate promising results as compared to the conventional detection techniques comprised of matched filters (MF), RAKE, subspace LMMSE and LMMSE receivers. Illustrative simulation results compare the BER performance of the two proposed online BMUD structures to the conventional detectors.

I. INTRODUCTION

Code Division Multiple Access (CDMA) is an efficient spread spectrum technique in which multiple users share the same temporal and spectral resources [6]. In the downlink signal processing, each user is identified by a unique code, which is chosen to be "quasi-orthogonal" to the codes allotted to other users in the system. The Direct-Sequence Code-Division Multiple Access (DS-CDMA) is a promising data transmission technique capable of high data rates and immunity to channel noise. The signal energy is "spread" over a wide frequency range, which reduces the effect of fading channels. Other advantageous features include soft capacity limit, cell frequency reuse, soft handover of users etc. Wide bandwidth CDMA will be a dominant technology for the third generation (3G) wireless communication systems and forms an integral part of the UMTS/IMT-2000 and CDMA2000 standards [17].

In this paper, we apply our proposed linear BSR structures [8, 9, 14] to the case of QPSK signaling in DS-CDMA systems. As per our knowledge, this will be first such application of adaptive BSR techniques to QPSK DS-CDMA symbol recovery. QPSK is currently becoming the de-facto transmission format in CDMA/WCDMA systems. QPSK allows for more efficient utilization of the transmission medium as compared to BPSK. QPSK also provides improved synchronism between various parallel channels transmitted to the same user, e.g., the composite data and the control channels or multiple data streams etc.

Unlike the uplink communication channel, where all user codes are known and the base/controlling station possesses much higher signal processing capabilities, the downlink channel has a different set of constraints. The receiver (e.g., a mobile phone) just has the knowledge of a single self-identification code, and also has limited computational resources. The detector at the receiving end can be setup as either a single-user or a multi-user detector. While a single-user receiver basically estimates the desired signal for a desired user by modeling all the interfering users and disturbances as noise. A multi-user detector (MUD) [6] includes all the users in the signal model. This results in significant improvement [11]. However the optimal MUD [12] is computationally intensive and requires several system parameters to be known. In typical downlink signal processing, where many of the system parameters are unknown including the codes and the number of co-existing users at any instant of time, one can use the blind techniques for better estimate of the user signal [2, 8, 14, 15, 16].

In the conventional detection techniques for CDMA signals, only the second order statistics among the user codes are exploited but in most practical situations the user data symbols among themselves are independent. This is a powerful assumption, which enables one to apply the existing blind source recovery techniques to solve the detection problem in the multi user environment. Blind Source Recovery (BSR) in this context is the process of estimating the original user-specific symbol sequences independent of, and even in the absence of precise system identification [8, 9].

The received CDMA signal can be considered as a set of non-gaussian random variables generated by the linear convolutive transformation of statistically independent component variables [2, 3, 14]. This linear transformation accounts for the user codes, multiple channel paths and slowly fading channel symbol memory. Our goal is to estimate another linear transformation such that it counters, as best as possible, the effects of the first transformation resulting in the recovery of the original signals. A similar blind deconvolution approach for BPSK signals has been earlier described in [2, 3 and 14]. However, the adaptive algorithm in [2] does not represent the class of natural gradient algorithms [1, 8, 9] and fails to compare favorably to our proposed structures in [14]. Further, the proposed algorithms have competitive performance and do outperform traditional detectors such as matched filter (MF), RAKE [6, 11], linear minimum mean square (LMMSE) detectors [4, 15] and subspace LMMSE (sub LMMSE)[16] for the simulated SNR range from –10 to +20 dB.

II. DOWNLINK RECEIVER SIGNAL MODEL

We will consider a wide sense stationary slowly fading, multipath, downlink AWGN model. The received data in this case can be modeled as a multipath generalization of the model in [6] as

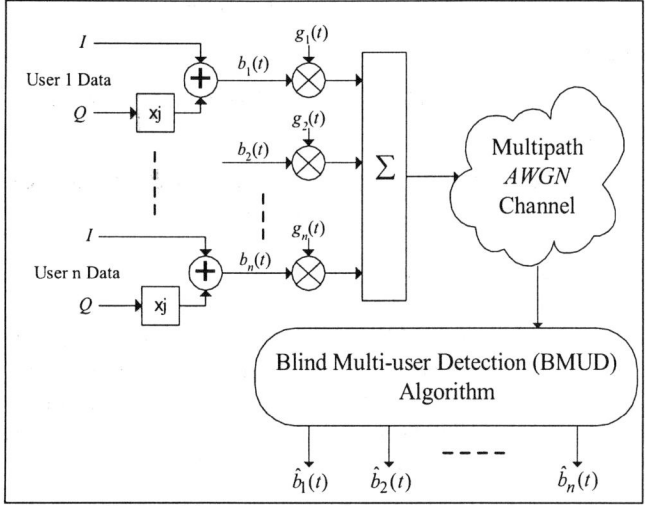

Fig. 1. Blind Multiuser Detection in a QPSK DS-CDMA system

$$r(t) = s(t) + n(t) \quad (1)$$

where

$n(t)$: represents the channel additive white gaussian noise

$s(t)$: represents the channel corrupted transmitted signal

$$s(t) = \sum_{n=1}^{N}\sum_{k=1}^{K} b_k(n)\sqrt{\varepsilon_{kn}(t)} \sum_{l=0}^{L-1} a_k(l) g_k(t - nT - \tau_l) \quad (2)$$

N : represents the total number of symbols during the observation interval

K : represents the total number of users during the observation interval

L : represents the total number of transmission paths per symbol

$b_k(n)$: represents the transmitted n^{th} QPSK symbol for the kth user.

$\varepsilon_{kn}(t)$: represents the transmitted signal energy for the nth symbol of the kth user, also used for power control

$a_k(l)$: represents the fading factor or the path attenuation co-efficients for l^{th} transmission path, and

τ_l : is the corresponding transmission delay for the lth transmission path which typically satisfies the condition that $0 \leq \tau_l \leq T$ for all users.

$g_k(t)$: represents the signature code for the kth user, generated by

$$g_k(t) = \sum_{m=0}^{M-1} \alpha_k(m) p(t - mT_c) \quad (3)$$

$\alpha_k(m); 0 \leq m \leq M-1$: is a PN code sequence for the kth user containing M chips, $\alpha_k(m) \in \{\pm 1\}$

$p(t)$: is a chipping pulse of duration T_c

T : is the total code time, given by $T = MT_c$

The model presented by (1) and (2) can be written more compactly as a linear convolutive model comprising of the synchronously received chips for the current symbol as well as the distorted and delayed versions of chips for prior transmitted $J-1$ symbols also received during the same interval. The number of symbols J in the convolutive model is given by

$$J = \left\lceil \max(\tau_l) / M \right\rceil + 1 \quad (4)$$

The convolutive model for the nth received symbol can therefore be expressed as

$$r_n(t) = \sum_{k=1}^{K} b_k(n)\sqrt{\varepsilon_{kn}} \sum_{l=0}^{L-1} a_k(l) g_k(t - nT - \tau_l) + n_n(t) + \sum_{j=1}^{J}\sum_{k=1}^{K} b_k(n-j)\sqrt{\varepsilon_{k(n-j)}} \sum_{l=0}^{L-1} a_k(l) g_k(t - (n-j)T - \tau_l) \quad (5)$$

where, for a fading channel $\sqrt{\varepsilon_{k(n-j)}} \geq \sqrt{\varepsilon_{k(n-j-1)}}; \forall j \geq 0$.

Under the condition that $\max(\tau_l) \leq M$, $J = 2$ and the convolutive model reduces to an order 2 model, where the existing symbol is corrupted by only one previously transmitted symbol, i.e.,

$$r_n = \sum_{k=1}^{K} \left[b_{kn}\sqrt{\varepsilon_{kn}} \sum_{l=0}^{L-1} a_{kl} \overline{z}_{kl} + b_{k,n-1}\sqrt{\varepsilon_{k,n-1}} \sum_{l=0}^{L-1} a_{kl} \underline{z}_{kl} \right] + n_n \quad (6)$$

where

$\overline{z}_{kl} = \begin{bmatrix} 0 & \cdots & 0 & g_k[M-\tau_l] & \cdots & g_k[1] \end{bmatrix}^T$, and

$\underline{z}_{kl} = \begin{bmatrix} g_k[M] & \cdots & g_k[M-\tau_l+1] & 0 & \cdots & 0 \end{bmatrix}^T$

and τ_l is the discretized delay satisfying the constraint $0 \leq \tau_l \leq T$.

Alternately we can represent the model in a more compact matrix-vector form as

$$r_n = H_0 b_n + H_1 b_{n-1} + n_n \qquad (7)$$

where

b_n and b_{n-1} are the K-d vectors of current and previous symbol for all the K users.

H_0 and H_1 are $M \times K$ mixing matrices given by

$$H_0 = \begin{bmatrix} H_{0,0} & H_{0,1} & \cdots & H_{0,K} \end{bmatrix}$$

$$H_1 = \begin{bmatrix} H_{1,0} & H_{1,1} & \cdots & H_{1,K} \end{bmatrix}$$

such that

$$H_{0,k} = \sqrt{\varepsilon_0} \sum_{l=0}^{L-1} a_{kl} \overline{z}_{kl} \qquad (8)$$

$$H_{1,k} = \sqrt{\varepsilon_1} \sum_{l=0}^{L-1} a_{kl} \underline{z}_{kl} \qquad (9)$$

and $\varepsilon_0 \geq \varepsilon_1 > 0$ represent the energy of the current and the previous symbol respectively at the instant of observation.

III. NATURAL GRADIENT BLIND MULTI-USER DETECTION (BMUD) ALGORITHMS

As discussed in the previous section, the received signal comprises a noise-corrupted linear mixture of delayed and convolved user symbol sequences. It is reasonable to assume that the various transmitted symbol sequences are mutually independent as they are generated by independent sources. Assuming no preamble transmission to the receiver, both the transmitted sequence and the mixing matrices in the model (7) are unknown to the user. The only known entity to the user is the self-identification code. Other available prior information is the nature of transmitted data, which is QPSK corrupted by the multipath effects and channel distortion., i.e., it falls in the class of quaternary sub-gaussian distributions. We have enough information to apply the Blind Source Recovery (BSR) algorithms for BMUD in this case [8, 9, 13, 14].

Further we assume that the DS-CDMA channel is not over-saturated and $K \leq M$. The proposed BSR algorithms do not require any pre-whitening of received data. However, in DS-CDMA systems, M is chosen to be as large as possible and in general $K < M$. Therefore, it is computationally advantageous to pre-process the data for dimension reduction to K, which is the actual number of principal independent symbol components in the received data. The process of pre-whitening will also remove the second order dependence among the received data samples and some of the additive noise [2, 3, 7]. The data pre-whitening can be achieved either online using adaptive principal component analysis (PCA) algorithms or it may be done using an algebraic PCA estimate over a large batch (say N complex samples) of received data, i.e.,

$R = \begin{bmatrix} r_1 & r_2 & \cdots & r_{N-1} & r_N \end{bmatrix}$, with the correlation matrix

$$\Lambda_C = \frac{1}{N-1} R R^H \qquad (10)$$

Then the whitening is achieved using the filtering matrix

$$W = D_s^{-1/2} V_s^H$$

where

D_s: represents the K-dim matrix of principle eigenvalues of the data correlation matrix Λ_C

V_s: represents the $K \times M$ matrix of corresponding principal eigen vectors of the data correlation matrix Λ_C, and

H: represents the Hermitian Transpose operator.

The whitened version of (7) is given by

$$r_n^w = W(H_0 b_n + H_1 b_{n-1} + n_n) \cong \overline{H}_0 b_n + \overline{H}_1 b_{n-1} \qquad (11)$$

where

r_n^w: represents the K-d received data at the nth sampling instant

$\overline{H}_0, \overline{H}_1$: represent the equivalent square K-d mixing matrices for the current and the delayed symbols.

A. Demixing Structures

The natural gradient BMUD network for such a problem can be either in the feedforward or the feedback configuration [8]. We present the update laws for both cases; further the performance of the proposed algorithms is discussed and compared with conventional user detection algorithms [2, 14].

2) Feedforward BMUD Configuration: For the feedforward configuration, the BMUD stage output is computed as

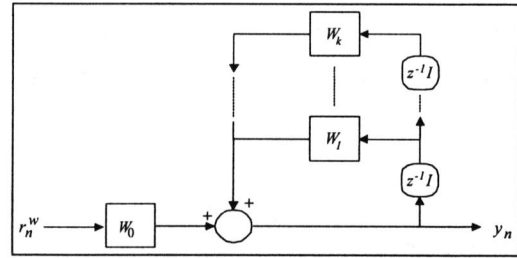

Fig. 3. Feedforward Demixing Structure

$$y_n = W_0 r_n^w + \sum_{k=1}^{K} W_k y_{n-k} \qquad (12)$$

The update laws for this feedforward structure have been derived in [1, 8, 9] and are given by

$$\Delta W_0 \propto \left(I - \varphi(y_n) y_n^H \right) W_0 \qquad (13)$$

$$\Delta W_k \propto \left(I - \varphi(y_n)y_n^H\right)W_k - \varphi(y_n)y_{n-k}^H \quad (14)$$

For initialization of the algorithm, W_0 is chosen to be either identity or dominantly diagonal, while the matrices W_k are initialized to have either small random elements or just as a matrix of zeros. Note that no matrix inversion is required for this algorithm.

1) Feedback BMUD Configuration: For the feedback configuration the output is estimated by

$$y_n = W_0^{-1}\left(r_n^w - \sum_{k=1}^{K} W_k y_{n-k}\right) \quad (15)$$

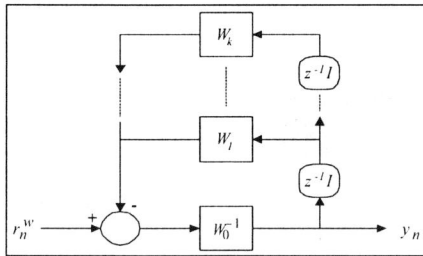

Fig. 2. Feedback Demixing Structure

The update laws for this structure using the natural gradient have been derived in [9]. The update law for the matrix W_0 is given by

$$\Delta W_0 \propto -W_0\left(I - \varphi(y_n)y_n^H\right) \quad (16)$$

While for the feedback matrices W_k, the update law is

$$\Delta W_k \propto W_0\left(\varphi(y_n)y_{n-k}^H\right) \quad (17)$$

where

$\varphi(.)$: represents an element-wise acting nonlinearity (score function) [1, 8, 9, 13]

I : represents a K-d identity matrix.

The matrices in this case are also initialized in a fashion similar to the feedforward case.

3) Conventional MUD Configurations: For the purpose of comparison, we apply the conventional user detection schemes such as the Matched Filter (MF), RAKE [6, 11], subspace Linear Minimum Mean Squared Error (sub LMMSE) [16] and the LMMSE estimators [4, 15]. The conventional estimators are computed using the following relations, respectively.

$$y_{kn,MF} = g_k^H r_n, \quad (18)$$

$$y_{kn,RAKE} = g_k^H \hat{H}^H r_n, \quad (19)$$

$$y_{kn,sub-LMMSE} = g_k^H V D^{-1} V^H r_n, \text{ and} \quad (20)$$

and

$$y_{kn,LMMSE} = g_k^H \hat{H}^H V D^{-1} V^H r_n \quad (21)$$

where

y_{kn} : represents the estimated output of the detector for the kth user at the nth instant

g_k : represents the self-identification code for the kth user

D, V: represent the eigenvalues and the corresponding eigenvectors for the estimated data auto-correlation matrix Λ_C.

The output of all the detectors (including the proposed BMUD algorithms) is then fed to a nonlinear decision element to best estimate the recovered symbol $\hat{b}_{kn}$.

$$\hat{b}_{kn} = \psi(y_{kn}) \quad (22)$$

where $\psi(.)$: represents the (nonlinear) decision operator.

IV. SIMULATION RESULTS

The adaptation for the proposed natural gradient algorithms can be done either in batch or instantaneous modes. Although the asymptotic performance of the algorithms in batch mode is slightly better than the online mode [14], however the computational cost and the data storage requirements are prohibitive for practical BMUD implementations. In this paper, we primarily focus on using online update laws for the proposed algorithms.

The BMUD performance of the proposed algorithms is compared to the performance of the conventional symbol recovery algorithms using the Bit Error rate (BER) of the recovered symbol sequences [2, 14]. The convergence criterion is set to be a threshold on the L_2 norm of the difference between consecutive updates of recovery weight matrices. As the symbol sequences are directly estimated using the proposed technique, therefore, a data preamble is used for user identification.

An alternate performance comparison can be done for the synthetic simulation cases by computing diagonalization of the absolute value of the global transfer function. The global transfer function presents the combined effect of the complex mixing and demixing transfer functions. For the order 2 transfer functions simulated, the global transfer function for the natural gradient algorithms in the z-domain are given by:

$$G(z) = G_0 + G_1 z^{-1} \quad (23)$$

where, for the *feedback* algorithm

$$G_0 = W_0^{-1}\bar{H}_0 = W_0^{-1}WH_0 \quad (24)$$

$$G_1 = W_0^{-1}\left(\bar{H}_1 - W_1\right) = W_0^{-1}\left(WH_1 - W_1\right) \quad (25)$$

and for the *feedforward* algorithm

$$G_0 = W_0\bar{H}_0 = W_0WH_0 \quad (26)$$

$$G_1 = W_0\bar{H}_1 + W_1 = W_0WH_1 + W_1 \quad (27)$$

A. Simulation Setup

For simulation, a user's composite BPSK data stream is split into quadrature components by a serial-to-parallel converter (S/P). These QPSK data stream for each user is then spread by a user's allotted signature code. The transmitted chips are generated by a summation of all the corresponding user's chips. The user's signature codes are chosen to be gold codes of length 31 (i.e., M=31) [5]. The transmitted chips arrive at the receiver after propagation through an AWGN multipath channel. The receiver is assumed to be in synchronism to the transmitter. Due to space limitations, only simulated results for 4 users (13% capacity) and 25 users (80% capacity) in the system are presented.

For the proposed BMUD algorithms, the score function is chosen as follows, see [13]

$$\varphi_i(y_i) = y_i - \left(\tanh\left(\text{Re}\{y_i\}\right) + \tanh\left(\text{Im}\{y_i\}\right)\right) \quad (28)$$

where, y_i : represents the estimated output at the ith iteration

The learning rate is initialized at 0.1 and then exponentially decayed. As the transmitted signals are QPSK, the final symbol decision is done using a sign function separately on both the real and imaginary parts of the recovered symbol.

$$\psi(y_n) = sign\left(\text{Re}\{y_n\}\right) + sign\left(\text{Im}\{y_n\}\right)i \quad (29)$$

For the sake of simulation, we assume that there are three multipaths (L=3), with delays of 0, 1 and 2 chips. The multipath channel co-efficients are assumed to be complex, i.e., they apply both scaling and rotation to the propagated signal constellation. Since $L \leq M$, the demixing network is chosen to be order 2. The channel co-efficients are assumed known for the RAKE and LMMSE detectors. Further, we also assume that the sign ambiguity for all the detection schemes can be resolved using the frame synchronous pilot bits in the composite user data streams. We now consider two cases for the multipath channel co-efficients.

1) Simulation I: Primary Path Phase Known: In this case, it is assumed that the phase of the primary path is known. Therefore the multipath attenuation co-efficient are chosen to be $a_k = \begin{bmatrix} 1 & 0.6+0.2i & 0.5+0.3i \end{bmatrix}^T$ and $a_k = a_k / \|a_k\|$. A performance comparison of all the algorithms for this simulation is shown in Fig. 4(b). It is evident that the proposed BMUD algorithm is the best of all for both lower and higher congestion of the network. For the lower congestion case, sub LMMSE and LMMSE are quite close, but at higher congestion sub LMMSE is worse as compared to even MF.

2) Simulation II: Primary Path Phase Unknown: Now it is assumed that the phase of the primary path is not known. The multipath attenuation co-efficient are chosen to be $a_k = \begin{bmatrix} 0.8+0.6i & 0.6+0.2i & 0.5+0.3i \end{bmatrix}^T$ and then normalized as before. A performance comparison of all the algorithms for this simulation is shown in Fig. 4(c). In this case, it is observed that the performance of MF and sub LMMSE is severely degraded. The BER of the proposed BMUD detectors (although more than simulation I) is still better than the LMMSE detector, which uses the perfect knowledge of the channel.

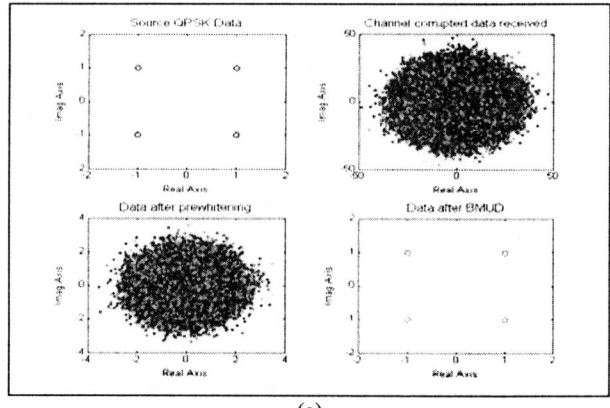

(a)

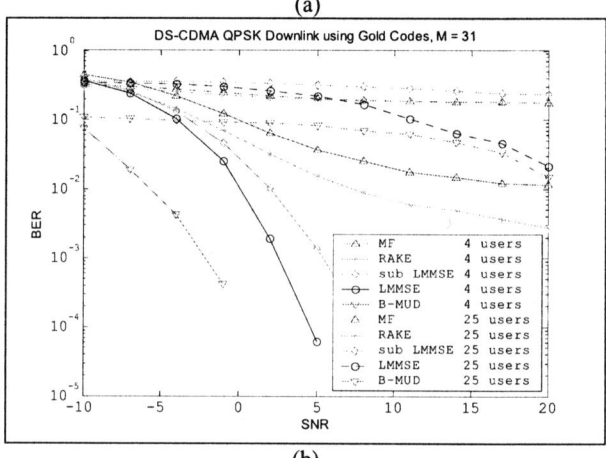

(b)

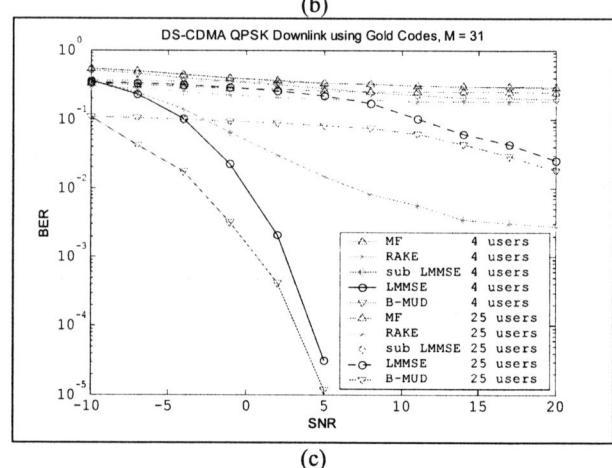

(c)

Fig. 4. BER results for QPSK DS-CDMA: (a) signal constellation after channel propagation and recovery by BMUD, Performance Comparison of Algorithms with (b) phase of reference path known, (c) phase of reference path unknown.

Notice that at poor SNR scenarios, LMMSE performance is very close to RAKE detector, but the proposed BMUD algorithms based on BSR feedforward and feedback structures exhibit one-third BER as compared both LMMSE and RAKE. Further, the BMUD algorithms maintain their performance edge even under conditions of high network congestion and lower SNR, which indicates their robustness and usefulness for DS-CDMA systems.

Fig. 5 graphically presents a typical absolute global transfer function achieved using BMUD, i.e., the convolution of the mixing environment and the demixing network transfer functions. Presented below is the $G(z)$ computed for 8 users in the network. We observe that the BMUD algorithm has identified all the users successfully. The global transfer function exhibits permutations, scaling and sign ambiguities, which are inherent in BSR solutions. In DS-CDMA, this is overcome using a data preamble/pilot for user identification.

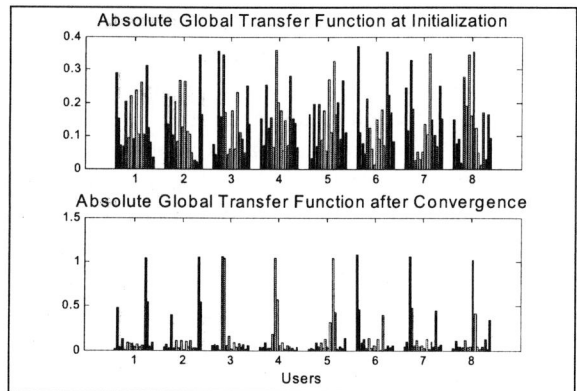

Fig. 5. Typical Absolute Global Transfer Function for $K=8$

V. CONCLUSIONS

We have introduced effective blind source recovery (BSR) algorithms in the feedforward and feedback configurations to the realm of QPSK DS-CDMA blind multi-user detection (BMUD) and recovery. The proposed algorithms outperform the conventional DS-CDMA detection techniques with significantly reduced BER even under conditions of congestion and low SNR. The instantaneous versions of the algorithms are preferred for BMUD applications as they have lesser computational complexity and smaller memory requirements. The BMUD is a promising technique as there is no need of precise synchronization required similar to the conventional techniques. The problem formulated in this paper is directly applicable to the various QPSK CDMA applications that include newer GPS enhancements, Wireless LAN: ad-hoc and ATM networks to name a few.

REFERENCES

[1] S. Amari, S.C. Douglas, A. Cichocki and H.H. Yang, "Multichannel blind deconvolution and equalization using the natural gradient," *Proc. of IEEE International Workshop on Wireless Communication*, Paris April 1997, pp. 101-104.

[2] R. Cristescu, T. Ristaniemi, J. Joutsensalo, and J. Karhunen, "Blind Separation of Convolved Mixtures for CDMA Systems", in *Proc. of the European Signal Processing Conference*, EUSIPCO2000, September 2000, Tampere, Finland

[3] R. Cristescu, T. Ristaniemi, J. Joutsensalo, and J. Karhunen, "CDMA Delay Estimation using Fast ICA Algorithm", in *Proc. of the International Symposium on Personal, Indoor and Mobile Radio Communications*, PIMRC'00, September 2000, London, UK

[4] David Gesbert, Joakim Sorelius, Arogyaswami Paulraj, "Blind multi-user MMSE detection of CDMA signals," in *ICASSP98*, (Seattle, USA), April 8-11, 1998.

[5] K.H.A. Kärkkäinen & P.A. Leppänen, "The Influence of Initial-Phases of a PN Code Set on the Performance of an Asynchronous DS-CDMA System", *Wireless Personal Communications*, vol. 3, no. 3, pp. 279-293, Jun. 2000.

[6] J. G. Proakis, *Digital Communications*, Fourth edition, McGraw-Hill, 2001

[7] T. Ristaniemi and J. Joutsensalo, "Advanced ICA-based Receivers for Block Fading DS-CDMA Channels", *Signal Processing*, vol. 82, no. 3, 2002, pp. 417-431.

[8] F. M. Salam and K. Waheed, "State-space Feedforward and Feedback Structures for Blind Source Recovery," in *3rd International Conference on Independent Component Analysis and Blind Signal Separation*, December 9-12, 2001 - San Diego, California, Page(s) 248-253

[9] F. M. Salam; G. Erten, and K. Waheed, "Blind Source Recovery: Algorithms for Static and Dynamic Environments," in *Proc. of the INNS-IEEE Int'l Joint Conference on Neural Networks*, IJCNN, July 14-19, 2001, Page(s): 902-907 vol. 2.

[10] P. Schulz-Rittich, J. Baltersee and G. Fock, "Channel Estimation for DS-CDMA with Transmit Diversity over Frequency Selective Fading Channels," in *IEEE Semiannual Vehicular Technology Conference Spring VTC2001*, May 6-9, 2002, Rhodes, Greece.

[11] S. Verdu, *Multiuser Detection*, Cambridge University Press, 1998

[12] S. Verdu, ``Minimum Probability of Error for Asynchronous Gaussian Multiple-Access Channels", IEEE Transactions on Information Theory, pp. 85-96, Jan. 1986.

[13] K. Waheed and F. M. Salem. "New Hyperbolic Models for Blind Source Recovery Score Functions," in *IEEE Int'l Symposium on Circuits & Systems 2003*, Bangkok, Thailand, in press.

[14] K. Waheed and F. M. Salem. "Blind Multi User Detection in DS-CDMA Systems using Natural Gradient based Symbol Recovery Structures," in *4th Int'l Conference on Independent Component Analysis and Blind Signal Separation*, April 1-4, 2003 - Nara, Japan, in press.

[15] S. Werner and J. Lilleberg, "Downlink Channel Decorrelation in CDMA Systems with long Codes" in *IEEE Vehicular Technology Conference, VTC'99* Spring, Houston, Texas, USA, Vol. 2, pp. 1614-1617, May 1999.

[16] X. Wang and H.V. Poor. "Blind Equalization and Multiuser Detection in Dispersive CDMA Channels", *IEEE Transactions on Communications*, vol. 46, no. 1, pp. 91 103, January 1998.

[17] Website URL: http://www.cdg.org/index.asp

The Further Discussions on Constrained Learning Algorithms[1]

De-Shuang Huang

Institute of Intelligent Machines, Chinese Academy of Sciences,
P.O.Box 1130, Hefei, Anhui 230031, China
Email: huangdeshuang@yahoo.com

Abstract-This paper revisits the constrained learning algorithm (CLA) proposed by Perantonis & Karras, and makes further analyses and discussions on the parameters with the CLA's. Specifically, we investigate the effect of removing the constrained condition of the weight change on the CLA's. It is suggested that for those problems that do not need to do precise computation, the modified CLA is a better choice. Finally, some simulation results are presented to support our claims.

I. INTRODUCTION

It is well known that the traditional error back-propagation (BP) algorithm with gradient descent type [1,2] is a very slow learning algorithm for feedforward neural networks (FNN). The drawback with slow convergence was somewhat improved by introducing the adapting learning rates [3,4] and decreasing the possibility of a premature saturation [5]. In spite of this improved convergence, these algorithms are still essentially based on the gradient descent information, thus limiting their wide applications.

To accelerate the BP algorithm, a second-order nonlinear optimizing method using Hessian information of the error cost function was proposed [6]. The shortcoming for this method, however, is that the Hessian matrix in many applications might be ill conditioning, and that the computational complexity related to the Hessian is high [6,7].

Further, to improve the convergence speed, a layer-by-layer (LBL) optimizing algorithm was proposed in which each layer of FNN's is divided into linear and nonlinear parts [8]. The weight matrix can be easily derived from the linear part by least square (LS) approach. However, when the targets for the hidden layer becomes nonlinear separable, the mean square errors (MSE) at both the hidden layer as well as the output layer can not be reduced into significantly small values. Therefore, this algorithm could not substantially improve the convergence speed either.

From the training algorithms above, it can be seen that all training algorithms have not adopted the *a priori* information from the issues, which is vital to help resolve the solutions in many applications. Obviously, the more if we obtain the *a priori* knowledge from some special problem, the easier it can be resolved. For any problems in the real world, in which there are more or less implicit knowledge, if we can incorporate the additional knowledge into the designed target function (or referred to as the error cost function in neural networks terminology), the constructed algorithm will be helped to search for the global minima along the *a priori* information direction so that the corresponding solutions will be more easily and rapidly obtained.

In 1995, Perantonis and Karras proposed a new method referred to as constrained learning algorithm (CLA), which imposes the *a priori* information from problems into the error cost function (ECF) defined at the outputs of FNN's [9]. As a result, a speedy and efficient training algorithm is derived. So far we have successfully applied this algorithm to finding the arbitrary roots of arbitrary polynomials [10,11]. In addition, we also discussed how to choose the controlling parameters with the CLA's in [12], and gave an adaptive adjustment parameter method.

This paper will further discuss if it is necessary for the CLA's to constrain the weight step-size at each iteration, then a new CLA that removes the effect of the weight change constraint is derived. To verify our claim, several experimental results are presented and compared.

II. ON THE COMMENTS ON CONSTRAINED LEARNING ALGORITHM

A. Complex Constrained Learning Algorithm

For a labeled classification or approximation problem, there are P sample pairs $\{x_k, y_k\}$ ($k = 1, 2, \cdots, P$), then, an error cost function (ECF), or error energy function (EEF) can be defined at the output of the FNN involved:

---

[1] This work was supported by NSF of China and the Grant of "Hundred Talents Program" of Chinese Academy of Sciences of China.

$$E(w) = \frac{1}{2P}\sum_{p=1}^{P}|e_p(w)|^2 = \frac{1}{2P}\sum_{p=1}^{P}(y_p - \hat{y}_p)(y_p - \hat{y}_p)^* \quad (1)$$

where w is the set of all weights in the network model, $\hat{y}_p$ denotes the actual output of the network, and $e_p(w)$ the error signal between y_p and $\hat{y}_p$.

Assume that for a special problem there are m constrained conditions (the *a priori* information), which are expressed as:

$$\Phi = [\Phi_1, \Phi_2, \cdots, \Phi_m]^T = 0 \quad (2)$$

where T denotes the transpose of a vector or matrix.

The objective of the training is how to make $E(w)$ approach to 0 under the condition of ensuring $\Phi = 0$. In other words, in mathematical terminology, the following optimizing problem is presented:

$$\begin{aligned} \text{minimize} \quad & E(w) \\ \text{subject to} \quad & \Phi = 0 \end{aligned} \quad (3)$$

In the original work by Perantonis and Karras, it considers that the ECF possibly contains many long narrow troughs, thus a constraint for updated weights is imposed in order to avoid missing the global minimum in the ECF. Consequently, the sum of square of the absolute value of the individual weight changes are confined to take a predetermined positive value $(\delta P)^2$:

$$\sum_{i=1}^{n}|dw_i|^2 = (\delta P)^2 \quad (4)$$

where dw_i denotes the change of weight w_i, δP is a constant. Therefore, the optimizing problem for the weight is renewed as:

$$\begin{aligned} \text{minimize} \quad & E(w) \\ \text{subject to} \quad & \Phi = 0 \text{ and } \sum_{i=1}^{n}|dw_i|^2 = (\delta P)^2 \end{aligned} \quad (5)$$

Hence, for this optimizing problem, according to the ECF of eqn.(1) and the two constrained relations of eqns.(2) and (4), by introducing suitable Lagrange vector and scale multipliers, V and μ, to impose the two additional constraint relations into the ECF. Considering a small change from dw_i, a new ECF including two additional constraints is defined as follows:

$$d\varepsilon = dE(w) + (\delta Q^H - d\Phi^H)V + \mu\left[(\delta P)^2 - \sum_{i=1}^{n}|dw_i|^2\right] \quad (6)$$

By expanding the terms on the right hand side of eqn (6), we easily obtain:

$$d\varepsilon = \sum_{i=1}^{n} J_i dw_i + (\delta Q^T - \sum_{i=1}^{n} dw_i F_i^T)V + \mu\left[(\delta P)^2 - \sum_{i=1}^{n}(dw_i)^2\right] \quad (7)$$

where $J_i = \partial E(w)/\partial w_i$, $F_i = [F_i^{(1)}, F_i^{(2)}, \cdots, F_i^{(m)}]^T$, $F_i^{(j)} = \frac{\partial \Phi_j}{\partial w_i}$ ($i = 1,2,\cdots,n$, $j = 1,2,\cdots,m$).

Similar to the derivation of [9], we can derive the following relation:

$$dw_i = \frac{J_i}{2\mu} - \frac{F_i^H V}{2\mu} \quad (8)$$

where

$$\mu = -\frac{1}{2}\left[\frac{I_{JJ} - I_{JF}^H I_{FF}^{-1} I_{JF}}{(\delta P)^2 - \delta Q^H I_{FF}^{-1} \delta Q}\right]^{1/2} \quad (9)$$

$$V = -2\mu I_{FF}^{-1}\delta Q + I_{FF}^{-1} I_{JF} \quad (10)$$

where $I_{JJ} = \sum_{i=1}^{n}|J_i|^2$ is a scalar, I_{JF} is a vector whose components are defined by $I_{JF}^{(j)} = \sum_{i=1}^{n} J_i F_i^{(j)}$, ($j = 1,2,\cdots,m$). Specifically, I_{FF} is a matrix, whose elements are defined by $I_{FF}^{jk} = \sum_{i=1}^{n} F_i^{(j)} F_i^{(k)}$ ($j,k = 1,2,\cdots,m$).

The above algorithm is also referred to as the original CLA (OCLA). To improve the convergence speed, literature [12] gave an adaptive adjustment method for the controlling parameter δP as follows:

$$\delta P(t) = \delta P_0 (1 - e^{-\frac{\theta_p}{t}}) \quad (11)$$

where δP_0 is the initial value for δP, which is usually chosen with a larger value; t is the time index; θ_p is the scale coefficient of time t, which is usually set as $\theta_p > 1$. The corresponding CLA is called ACLA in the following experiment.

However, the vector parameters δQ_j ($j = 1,2,\cdots,m$) are generally selected as proportional to Φ_j, i.e., $\delta Q_j = -k\Phi_j$ ($j = 1,2,\cdots,m$, $k > 0$), which ensures that the constraints Φ move towards zero at an exponential rate as the training progresses [9,10-12].

B. Modified Constrained Learning Algorithm

In fact, we have successfully applied the above ACLA to finding the roots of polynomial [10,11], it was found that, however, there are often some fluctuations around those true root values, which are caused by improperly selecting the parameter δP, or $\{\delta P_0, \theta_p\}$ with the ACLA.

From the above CLA, it can be conjured that if the

amount of the a priori information is enough, there will no local minima at the error surface. Therefore, in practical applications, if there is a significantly number of the constrained conditions available, the constraint for the weight change like eqn.(4) is not needed at all.

Hence, regardless of the weight constraint like eqn.(4), we again derive the above formulae based on the optimizing problem of eqn.(3), a new CLA, which is referred to as a modified CLA (MCLA), can be directly obtained as follows:

$$dw_i = -\eta(J_i - F_i^H V) \quad (12)$$

$$V = \eta^{-1} I_{FF}^{-1} \delta Q + I_{FF}^{-1} I_{JF} \quad (13)$$

where η ($\eta > 0$) is the learning coefficient. Obviously, there are also two free parameters $\{\eta, \delta Q\}$ in this algorithm. However, the computational complexity is considerably reduced with respect to the original CLA to some extent. Likewise, we may choose $\delta Q_j = -\zeta \Phi_j$ ($\zeta > 0$, $j = 1, 2, \cdots, m$) so that the condition $\Phi \approx 0$ can be fulfilled as soon as possible as iterating goes.

Specifically, with this MCLA, the learning coefficient η denotes the step sizes of the weight derivative change. If it is chosen as a constant in the experiment, the training will certainly become very slow. In fact, from the iterating physical process, it can be understood that at the beginning phase of iterating it should be selected as a larger value, then it would become smaller and smaller as the training progresses. Hence, similar to the controlling parameter δP with the ACLA, this learning coefficient can be selected as:

$$\eta(t) = \eta_0 (1 - e^{-\frac{\theta_\eta}{t}}) \quad (14)$$

where η_0 is the initial value for η, which is usually chosen as a larger value; t is the time index for training, θ_η is the scale coefficient of time t, which is usually set as $\theta_\eta > 1$.

Conventionally, the corresponding learning algorithm is also referred to as adaptive MCLA (AMCLA). In addition, if we derive the iterating formula directly based on the ECF of eqn.(1), the conventional BP algorithm with gradient descent type can be resulted:

$$dw_i = -\eta J_i \quad (15)$$

where η ($0 < \eta < 1$) is the learning coefficient.

Obviously, it can be seen that the above two algorithms are directly derived by just imposing the *a priori* information from the problems into the original ECF of eqn.(1). It can be shown that the CLA's consider the additional constraints of the problems involved in the iterating process and guarantee the error search to proceed along the direction of global minimum solutions. Therefore, their training speeds are significantly faster than the traditional BP algorithm.

III. EXPERIMENTAL RESULTS

To verify the effectiveness and efficiency of our approach, in this section we take two examples to conduct related experiments. The first example is about how to solve the linear simultaneous equation by constrained learning neural networks. Here, the linear relation $Ax = b$ can be regarded as the constrained conditions from the problem, which can be incorporated into the ECF and derive the corresponding CLA's. Assume that a 4-order linear simultaneous equation is considered, and the corresponding A and b can be respectively expressed as:

$$A = \begin{bmatrix} 1.7 + 3i & 1.1 - 3.1i & -0.2 + 1.3i & 2.2 - 4.2i \\ 1.1 + 2.3i & 0.1 - 1.9i & 2 - i & 0.3 - 2i \\ 2.7 + 7i & 0.2 + 0.8i & 1.3 - 3.4i & 1.2 + 3.7i \\ 6.5 + 2.9i & 7.1 + 4.7i & -1.2 + 1.3i & -2.5 + 1.2i \end{bmatrix}$$

and

$$b^T = \begin{bmatrix} -5.4 + 2.8i & 1.2 - 1.2i & -3.3 + 5.1i & -1.5 + 5.3 \end{bmatrix}$$

In addition, assume that the controlling parameters with the OCLA, the ACLA, the MCLA and the AMCLA are respectively chosen as $\{\delta P = 0.001, \eta = 0.01\}$, $\{\delta P_0 = 15.0, \eta = 0.0002, \theta_\eta = 8.0\}$, $\{\eta = 0.5, \zeta = 0.5\}$, $\{\eta = 2.0, \zeta = 2.0, \theta_\eta = 5.0\}$, and let the termination accuracies (TA) be $e_r = 10^{-8}$ for all cases. In experiment we adopt Pentium III with CPU clock of 795Mhz and RAM of 256Mb, and use Visual Fortran 90 to encode the algorithms. After the network converges, the solutions, the iterative numbers (IN), and the CPU times for the four algorithms are shown in Table 1. Moreover, the four learning error curves are depicted in Fig.1, where the logarithmic operations of the error energy values and the iterating numbers are done in order to compress their dynamic ranges and clearly see the whole curves. Here, the point to stress is that the conventional BP does not converge for this example case. From Table 1 and Fig.1, it shows that the adaptive learning algorithms are faster than the no-adaptive ones, and the modified CLA's presented in this paper are more easily to find the solutions than the previous CLA's (including the ACLA).

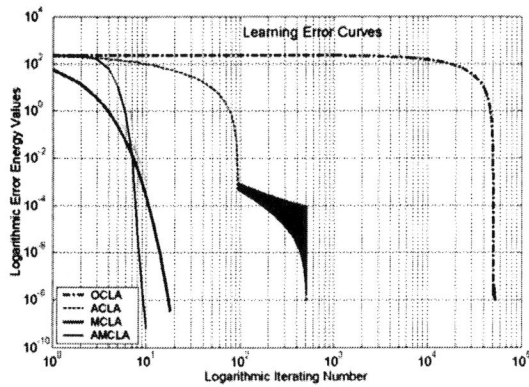

Fig. 1 The learning error curves for the 4-order linear simultaneous equation

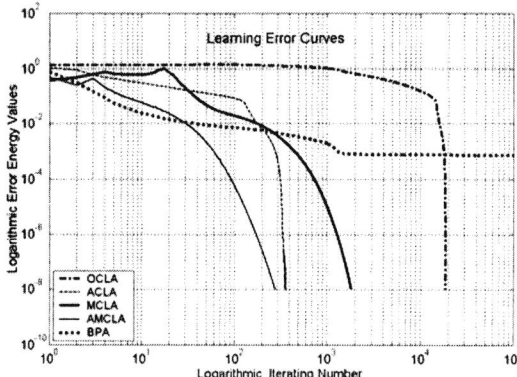

Fig. 2 The learning error curves for the 5-order polynomial

TABLE 1 THE EXPERIMENTAL RESULTS OF THE FOUR CLA'S FOR SOLVING THE 4-ORDER LINEAR SIMULTANEOUS EQUATION

Indies	x_1	x_2	x_3	x_4	IN	CPU Time (Second)
OCLA	1.270079+ 2.701037i	-0.5994370- 2.976600i	5.193102+ 0.4574763i	1.852550+ 0.1656403i	53363	9.23
ACLA	1.270089+ 2.701036i	-0.5994453- 2.976602i	5.193122+ 0.4574663i	1.852559+ 0.1656398i	516	1.46
MCLA	1.270094+ 2.701043i	-0.5994411- 2.976605i	5.193131+ 0.4574679i	1.852564+ 0.1656398i	18	0.23
AMCLA	1.270099+ 2.701050i	-0.5994378- 2.976608i	5.193141+ 0.4574684i	1.852569+ 0.1656398i	10	0.13

TABLE 2 THE EXPERIMENTAL RESULTS OF THE FOUR CLA'S AND THE BPA FOR FINDING THE ROOTS OF THE 5-ORDER POLYNOMIAL

Indices	OCLA	ACLA	MCLA	AMCLA	BPA
Root1	-1.02559- 0.98034i	-1.02565- 0.98050i	-1.02564- 0.98040i	-1.02564- 0.98047i	-1.20481- 0.84035i
Root 2	2.05954- 1.52708i	2.05913- 1.52688i	2.05941- 1.52706i	2.05940- 1.52706i	-1.33647E-02- 0.14442i
Root3	0.52741+ 7.86582E-02i	0.52744+ 7.86748E-02i	0.52737+ 7.86039E-02i	0.52755+ 7.84717E-02i	0.58306- 3.37301E-02i
Root4	0.37466+ 1.39469i	0.37474+ 1.39477i	0.37469+ 1.39469i	0.37470+ 1.39475i	0.22324+ 0.63500i
Root5	-0.53590+ 6.58961E-02i	-0.53589- 6.58810E-02i	-0.53584- 6.58390E-02i	-0.53601- 6.56837E-02i	-3.32205- 1.31861i
IN	18658	366	1839	283	100000
CPU Times (Second)	14.21	1.03	3.57	0.97	129.94

To further verify the above conclusions, we take another example of finding roots of an arbitrary polynomial to conduct the related simulations. Assume that here a 5-order polynomial $f_1(x) = x^5 - (1.4 - 1.1i)x^4 + (1.2 + 5i)x^2 + 0.2 - 1.5i$ is considered, and the controlling parameters with the

OCLA, the ACLA, the MCLA, the AMCLA and the BPA are chosen as $\{\delta P = 0.01, \eta = 0.01\}$, $\{\delta P_0 = 8.0, \eta = 0.01, \theta_p = 5.0\}$, $\{\eta = 0.1, \zeta = 0.1\}$, $\{\eta = 1.0, \zeta = 1.0, \theta_\eta = 150.0\}$, and $\eta = 0.2$, respectively. Likewise, the TA's are fixed as $e_r = 10^{-8}$ for all cases, and by the same computer to encode Visual Fortran 90 for the algorithms. We respectively use the five algorithms to train the neural network involved until it converges to the given TA's. Table 2 lists the solutions, the IN's, and the CPU times for the five algorithms, and Fig.2 shows the corresponding five learning error curves. Note that in experiment for the BPA we set a maximum number of stop iterations as 100,000 since this algorithm cannot converge to the given TA. Moreover, by comparing the BPA with the other four CLA's, it can be found that the obtained root values through the BPA are not the solutions of the polynomial due to its possibly getting in local minima.

Obviously, from Table 2 and Fig.2, it can be seen that the adaptive learning algorithms are indeed faster than the no-adaptive ones, and our proposed modified CLA's are more easily to find the solutions than the previous CLA's (including the ACLA). Furthermore, it can be also found that all CLA's are better than the BPA whether in convergent speed or in convergent accuracy.

IV. CONCLUSIONS

This paper made a further investigation and discussion on the constrained learning algorithms (CLA). Then we proposed a modified CLA, which disregards the constraint of weight change of the neural network. The important point to stress is that for some simple problems with trivial error surfaces it is not necessary to build the CLA including the weight constraint. In addition, this paper evaluated also the effects of the controlling parameters with the CLA's on the algorithms' performance. It was pointed out that whether for the original CLA's or for the modified CLA's the adaptive method for the controlling parameters is a better choice. Finally, two examples were provided to verify the effectiveness and efficiency of our approach. Future research works will include how to apply these CLA's to solving more real-world problems.

REFERENCES

[1] D.E.Rumelhart and J.L.McClelland, *Parallel Distributed Processing*. Cambridge, MA: MIT Press, 1986.

[2] D.E.Rumelhart, G.E.Hinton, and R.J.Williams, "Learning internal representations by back-propagating errors,"*Nature,* vol.323, 1986, 533-536.

[3] R.A.Jacobs, "Increased rates of convergence through learning rate adaption," *Neural Networks*, vol.1, 1988, 295-307.

[4] T.P.Vogl, J.K.Mangis, A.K.Rigler, W.T.Zink, and D.L.Alkon, "Accelerating the convergence of the back-propagation method," *Biol. Cybern.*, vol.59, 1988, 257-263.

[5] S.-H.Oh, "Improving the error backpropagation algorithm with a modified error function," *IEEE Trans. Neural Networks*, vol.8, 1997, 799-803.

[6] R.Parisi, E.D.Di Claudio, G.Orlandi, and B.D.Rao, "A generalized learning paradigm exploiting the structure of feedforward neural networks," *IEEE Trans. Neural Networks*, vol.7, 1450-1459, 1996.

[7] S.-H.Oh and S.-Y.Lee, "A new error function at hidden layers for fast training of multiplayer perceptrons," *IEEE Trans. Neural Networks*, vol.10, 1999, 960-964.

[8] G.-J.Wang and C.-C.Chen, "A fast multiplayer neural networks training algorithm based on the layer-by-layer optimizing procedures," *IEEE Trans. Neural Networks*, vol.7, 1996, 768-775.

[9] S.J.Perantonis, D.A.Karras, "An efficient constrained learning algorithm with momentum acceleration," *Neural Networks*, Vol.8, 1995, 237-249.

[10] D.S.Huang, Zheru Chi, "Neural networks with problem decomposition for finding real roots of polynomials," *2001 Int. Joint Conf. On Neural Networks (IJCNN2001),* Washington, DC, Vol. Addendum, July 15-19, 2001, 25-30.

[11] D.S.Huang, Zheru Chi, "Finding complex roots of polynomials by feedforward neural networks," *2001 Int. Joint Conf. On Neural Networks (IJCNN2001)*, Washington, DC, Vol. Addendum, July 15-19, 2001, 13-18.

[12] D.S.Huang, "Revisit to constrained learning algorithm," *The 8th inter. Conf. Neural Information Processing (ICONIP)*, Shanghai, China, vol.I, Nov. 14-18, 2001, 459-464.

Acceleration of Levenberg-Marquardt Training of Neural Networks with Variable Decay Rate

Tai-cong Chen   Da-jian Han

Department of Civil Engineering, South China University of Technology, Guangzhou, People's Republic of China, 510640

(cvchentc@scut.edu.cn   ardjhan@scut.edu.cn)

Francis T.K. Au   L.G. Tham

Department of Civil Engineering, The University of Hong Kong, Pokfulam Road, Hong Kong

(francis.au@hku.hk   hrectlg@hkucc.hku.hk)

Abstract — In the application of the standard Levenberg-Marquardt training process of neural networks, error oscillations are frequently observed and they usually aggravate on approaching the required accuracy. In this paper, a modified Levenberg-Marquardt method based on variable decay rate in each iteration is proposed in order to reduce such error oscillations. Through a certain variation of the decay rate, the time required for training of neural networks is cut down to less than half of that required in the standard Levenberg-Marquardt method. Several numerical examples are given to show the effectiveness of the proposed method.

I. Introduction

As is known, the Levenburg-Marquardt (LM) method shows the most efficient convergence during the Back Propagation (BP) training process because it acts as a compromise between the first-order optimization method (steepest-descent method) with stable but slow convergence and the second-order optimization method (Gauss-Newton method) with opposite characteristics [1].

However, when using the LM method for neural network training, several disadvantages are still observed in the numerical computations. Firstly, large memory is required for matrix operations in each iteration and the computational complexity increases with the number of weights in a quadratic manner. Researches to improve the standard LM method mostly concentrated on this issue. Memory demand and computational complexity can be greatly reduced by using techniques based on Jacobian deficiency [2], block-diagonal approximation [3] or matrix contraction [4]. Secondly, serious error oscillations during the standard LM training process frequently occur and this phenomenon even aggravates when approaching the required accuracy. As will be discussed in the following sections, such error oscillations resulting in lengthy calculations are mainly ascribed to the use of a fixed decay rate. A modified method by varying the decay rate according to a certain generally applicable rule during the training process is presented in this paper. The proposed method shows great effectiveness in convergence and reduces the amount of training work by more than half of that in the standard LM method.

II. The Levenberg-Marquardt method

In the BP algorithm, the performance index $F(\mathbf{w})$ to be minimized is defined as the sum of squared errors between the target outputs and the network's simulated outputs, namely

$$F(\mathbf{w}) = \mathbf{e}^T \mathbf{e} \qquad (1)$$

where $\mathbf{w}=[w_1, w_2,\ldots, w_N]^T$ consists of all weights of the network, $\mathbf{e}$ is the error vector comprising the errors for all the training examples.

When training with the LM method, the increment of weights $\Delta\mathbf{w}$ can be obtained as follows

$$\Delta\mathbf{w} = \left[\mathbf{J}^T\mathbf{J} + \lambda\mathbf{I}\right]^{-1}\mathbf{J}^T\mathbf{e} \qquad (2)$$

where $\mathbf{J}$ is the Jacobian matrix, λ is the training parameter which is to be updated using the decay rate β depending on the outcome. In particular, λ is multiplied by the decay rate β ($0<\beta<1$) whenever $F(\mathbf{w})$ decreases, while λ is divided by β whenever $F(\mathbf{w})$ increases in a new step.

The standard LM training process can be illustrated in

the following pseudo-codes,
1. Initialize the weights and parameter λ ($\lambda = 0.01$ is appropriate).
2. Compute the sum of squared errors over all inputs, $F(\mathbf{w})$.
3. Compute the Jacobian matrix $\mathbf{J}$.
4. Solve Equation (2) to obtain the increment of weights $\triangle \mathbf{w}$.
5. Recompute the sum of squared errors $F(\mathbf{w})$ using $\mathbf{w} + \triangle \mathbf{w}$ as the trial $\mathbf{w}$, and judge

   IF   trial $F(\mathbf{w}) < F(\mathbf{w})$ in Step 2   THEN

      $\mathbf{w} = \mathbf{w} + \triangle \mathbf{w}$

      $\lambda = \lambda \cdot \beta$ ($\beta = 0.1$)

      go back to Step 2.

   ELSE

      $\lambda = \lambda / \beta$

      go back to Step 4.

   END IF

III. Disadvantages of fixing the decay rate as $\beta = 0.1$

During the training process, the loop of Steps 2-5-2 causing a subsequently reduced value of $F(\mathbf{w})$ is called an iteration. According to Marquardt [5], a suitable strategy for decreasing $F(\mathbf{w})$ is to use a small value of λ such that the modified Gauss-Newton method would converge nicely. To achieve this, several trials of varying λ with β are carried out before deciding upon a suitable value of λ for each iteration.

In the Neural Network Toolbox of MATLAB [6], which is commonly used in neural network simulations, the default value of β is taken to be 0.1. This value is fixed during the whole training process, which is also the value recommended by Marquardt [5]. However, some disadvantages are observed in network training adopting such a strategy, as will be seen in the following numerical example.

A. Observations

A two-layer feedforward network $N_{[1 \times 5 \times 1]}$ is built to train a set of 21 input/output pairs denoted by the crosses in Fig. 1. The algorithm of the standard LM training (with $\beta = 0.1$ during the batch-mode training process) is coded in Fortran Language. Fig. 2 shows the typical training process using the standard LM method with weights initialized randomly between [-1 1], the performance of which is characterized by the variations of $F(\mathbf{w})$ and λ. As opposed to the normal practice in MATLAB of plotting the curve of $F(\mathbf{w})$ against Training Iterations, Figure 2 plots $F(\mathbf{w})$ against Training Trials, as an increased $F(\mathbf{w})$ caused by improper trial of 0.1λ results in additional computation work of solving Equation (2) and calculating $F(\mathbf{w})$.

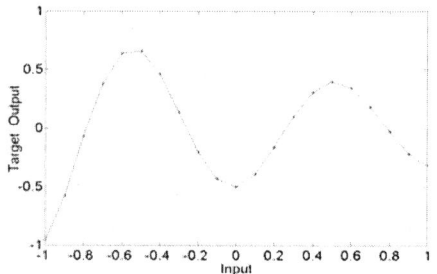

Fig. 1. Prototype of desired curve

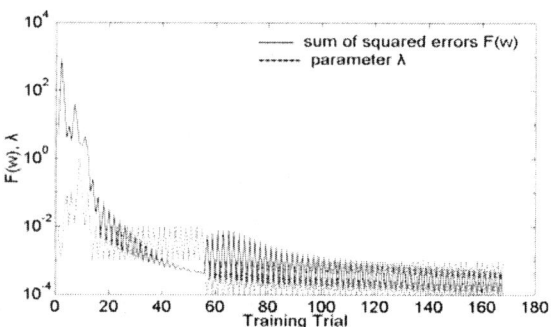

Fig. 2. Typical training process by the standard LM method

From Fig. 2, several characteristics of the training curves are observed:

1. In the curve of $F(\mathbf{w})$ against Training Trials, many error oscillations occur during the training process and this phenomenon aggravates on approaching the required accuracy. It takes only fewer than 10 oscillations (nearly 20 trials) for $F(\mathbf{w})$ to descend from the initial value of 4.4787E0 to 1E-1, while nearly 20 oscillations (nearly 40 trials) subsequently to reach 1E-3 and 50 oscillations (nearly 100 trials) eventually to reach 1E-4. Such a kind of error oscillations implies that the speed of convergence greatly slows down on approaching the required accuracy.

2. In the curve of λ against Training Trials, when

$F(\mathbf{w})$ reaches 1.0016E-1, λ takes the value of 1E-2. Then λ falls into a longtime oscillation of constant amplitude until $F(\mathbf{w})$ reaches 4.2567E-4 when λ takes the value of 1E-3. Afterwards, an even longer period of oscillation happens until $F(\mathbf{w})$ reaches the required accuracy. This kind of oscillations in λ implies that many trials in decreasing λ by multiplying $\beta = 0.1$ would not be valuable to the reduction of $F(\mathbf{w})$ but cause unexpected ascend of $F(\mathbf{w})$ and therefore waste time.

Although the exact numbers of staggered oscillations differ among different training processes due to the use of different initial weights, they all have serious problems of error oscillations before the required accuracy is reached. The main reason for this kind of error oscillations is the fixed value of the decay rate β of 0.1 during the training process.

B. Discussion

Generally, when a new reduced $F(\mathbf{w})$ is reached, an "ideal" λ is obtained and the weights are updated by adding the new increments. In the subsequent trial, the choice of a new λ is not only a choice of step direction but also a choice of step size [5]. An attempt of decreasing λ by multiplying β ($0 < \beta < 1$) can therefore be seen as a trial roughly along the Gauss-Newton direction with a step size larger than the ones determined by the former λ. In addition, having $\beta = 0.1$ means a much large scale in both aspects.

At the beginning of the training process, when $F(\mathbf{w})$ is much greater than the required accuracy, a trial with step direction close to the Gauss-Newton direction with a large step size may cause a great reduction of $F(\mathbf{w})$ which is expected in fast convergence. Repeated trials with decreasing λ by multiplying by $\beta = 0.1$ often succeed in a great reduction of $F(\mathbf{w})$, as can be seen from Fig.2. Hence, such an approach is valuable and effective at this stage.

However at the subsequent stages when $F(\mathbf{w})$ approaches the neighborhood of the minimum, the use of a small step size is as important for stable convergence as the large reduction of $F(\mathbf{w})$ at the beginning. As stable convergence is essential at this stage, adopting a step close to the Gauss-Newton direction with the corresponding step size by setting $\beta = 0.1$ is not as important. Hence at such stages, some value of β in the range of $0.1 < \beta < 1$ will be helpful for the trial of decreasing λ to obtain a relative large descend of $F(\mathbf{w})$. Actually using the value of $\beta = 0.1$ to experiment with decreasing values of λ seldom succeeds in reducing $F(\mathbf{w})$, as can be seen from Fig. 2. If an unexpected ascend of $F(\mathbf{w})$ is obtained, a redeeming trial should be made to resume λ to the former ideal one by dividing with $\beta = 0.1$. These two trials not only cause unnecessary calculations of two values of $F(\mathbf{w})$, but also obtain a small descend of $F(\mathbf{w})$ determined by the former "ideal" λ. Consequently, the speed of convergence slows down.

Similarly, the decay rate β has been tested with fixed values of 0.2, 0.3, ... 0.9 during the training process, and numerical computations show that fixing the decay rate β at any acceptable value can hardly achieve both fast descending at the beginning stages and stable convergence close to the required accuracy in one training process. In other words, β should assume different values at different stages so as to meet the relevant convergence demand for accelerating the network training.

IV. Rule of decay rate variation

In view of the above discussions, a Log-Linear function is proposed as the rule of varying β after an iteration, namely,

$$\beta = \frac{\log(F) - \log(F_{\min})}{\log(F_0) - \log(F_{\min})} \times 0.8 + 0.1 \qquad (3)$$

where F is the reduced sum of squared errors, F_0 is the first calculated $F(\mathbf{w})$ based on initialized weights and $F_{\min}$ is the required training accuracy.

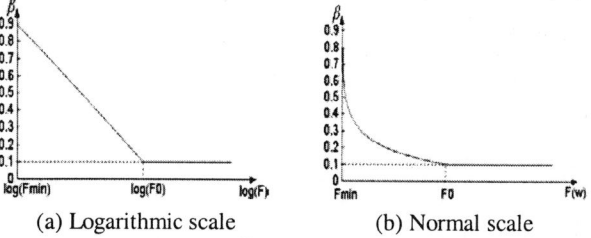

(a) Logarithmic scale   (b) Normal scale

Fig. 3. Rule of decay rate variation

When the weights are initialized with the same values used in Fig. 2, and at the same time the decay rate β is adjusted using the rule shown in Eq. (3) and Fig. 3, the speed of training is greatly accelerated. As shown in Fig. 4, the parameter λ finally reaches a minimum value of 1.677E-04 and the total number of training trials is just 44, which is much lower than the 169 trials in Fig. 2 with the fixed decay rate of $\beta = 0.1$.

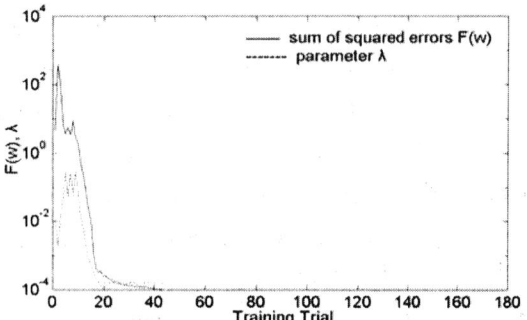

Fig. 4. Improved training process by the modified LM method

V. Case studies

Example 1: Nonlinear Curve Mapping

The objective in this test case is to learn a mapping with a training set of 21 input/output pairs denoted by the crosses in Fig. 1. A two-layer feedforward network $N_{[1 \times 5 \times 1]}$ was trained by using the standard LM method and the modified LM method. Two schemes of initializing weight are also experimented to study the performance of the new method.

TABLE I
TRAINING RESULTS FOR NONLINEAR CURVE MAPPING

	Runs	Ave. Ite.	Ave. Trials	Efficiency	Ave. Time(s)
Standard LM (I)	100	124.14	246.19	50.42%	0.15
Modified LM (I)	100	43.90	68.05	64.51%	0.05
Standard LM (II)	100	44.20	86.20	51.28%	0.06
Modified LM (II)	100	29.76	44.06	67.54%	0.03

(I) Weight initialization by random selection between [-1, 1];
(II) Weight initialization by Nguyen-Widrow method [7].
Efficiency = (Average Iterations) / (Average Trials).

The typical training curves of the standard LM method and the modified LM method using the same initialized weights are shown in Fig. 2 and Fig. 4 respectively. Table I summarizes the training results of the two methods using two different initialization cases.

Example 2: Nonlinear Static Mapping

In this example we train neural networks to approximate the surface shown in Fig. 5(a). The function describing this surface is

$$y = 0.5\sin(\pi x_1^2)\sin(2\pi x_2) \quad (4)$$

A two-layer feedforward network $N_{[2 \times 20 \times 1]}$ was trained with 451 intersection points shown in Fig. 5(a). The training results are shown in Fig. 5(b) and Table II.

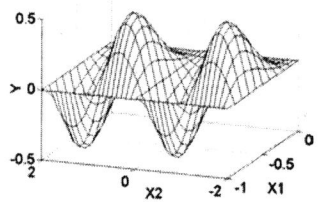

(a) Prototype of desired surface

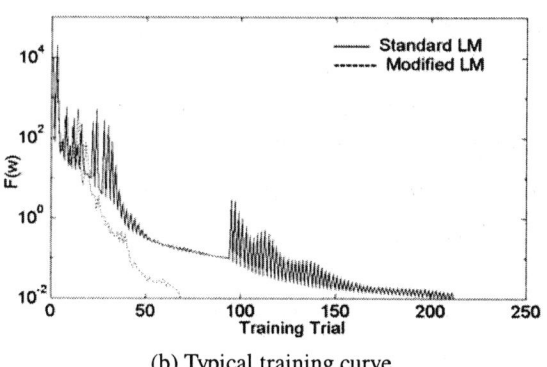

(b) Typical training curve

Fig. 5. Simulation of a 2-dimensional desired function

TABLE II
TRAINING RESULTS FOR NONLINEAR SURFACE MAPPING

	Runs	Ave. Ite.	Ave. Trials	Efficiency	Ave. Time(s)
Standard LM (I)	100	116.73	233.02	50.09%	19.35
Modified LM (I)	100	42.96	73.04	58.82%	6.85
Standard LM (II)	100	82.03	162.36	50.52%	13.45
Modified LM (II)	100	35.17	57.91	60.73%	5.46

Example 3: Five-Step Advanced Prediction

In this example we train neural networks to predict

results five steps ahead in a nonlinear dynamic process as shown in Fig. 6(a). The inputs and outputs of the system satisfy the following equation,

$$y_{(i+1)} = \frac{y_{(i)} y_{(i-1)} (y_{(i)} + 2.5)}{1 + y_{(i)}^2 + y_{(i-1)}^2} + u_{(i)} \qquad (5)$$

where,

$$u_{(i)} = \sin(2\pi i / 25) + \sin(2\pi i / 10) \qquad (6)$$

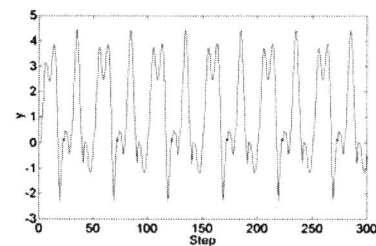

(a) Response of the nonlinear dynamic process

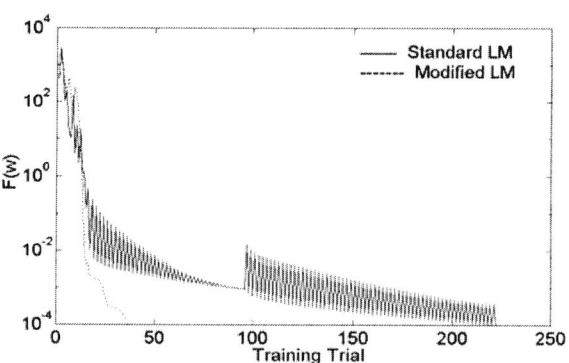

(b) Typical training curve

Fig. 6. Simulation of a five-step advanced prediction

TABLE III
TRAINING RESULTS FOR 5-STEP ADVANCED PREDICTION

	Runs	Ave. Ite.	Ave. Trials	Efficiency	Ave. Time(s)
Standard LM (I)	100	125.29	248.01	50.52%	11.41
Modified LM (I)	100	38.04	56.13	67.77%	3.32
Standard LM (II)	100	101.78	201.16	50.60%	9.98
Modified LM (II)	100	30.76	47.67	64.53%	2.98

A two-layer feedforward network $N_{[9 \times 10 \times 1]}$ was employed to predict a five-step advanced system output $y_{(i+5)}$. The 9 network inputs consist of 6 system inputs and 3 delayed outputs of the system, i.e. $(u_{(i+4)}, \ldots, u_{(i-1)}, y_{(i)}, y_{(i-1)}, y_{(i-2)})$. In all the simulations, 200 training samples were used for training the network. The training results are shown in Fig. 6(b) and Table III.

VI. Conclusions

Although the standard LM method is considered to be one of the most effective methods in training feedforward neural networks, error oscillations frequently occur during the process and the problem usually aggravates on approaching the required accuracy due to the fixed decay rate $\beta = 0.1$. As a result, the process is time-consuming because of a lot of unnecessary trials.

In the modified LM method, error oscillations are greatly reduced and therefore network training is greatly accelerated. There are three major advantages in the proposed method:

(1) The decay rate β varying from 0.1 to 0.9 with reduced $F(\mathbf{w})$ guarantees that a subsequent trial of decreasing λ would usually cause a relative large descend of $F(\mathbf{w})$, and this is valuable in the neighborhood of the minimum. As a result, training is greatly accelerated and it often involves less than half the amount of computation required in the standard LM method.

(2) Modification to the decay rate as practiced in the modified LM method is more effective in convergence than improvement in weight initialization.

(3) Training acceleration achieved by the modified LM method is not so sensitive to weight initialization condition as the standard LM method. In other words, special consideration of effective weight initialization is not essential when using the modified LM method.

In the practical application of neural networks, fast convergence in training is always desired, especially when network learning is running under a real-time mode. The method proposed in this paper can meet such requirements pretty well with little additional computation work compared with the standard LM method.

References

[1] M. T. Hagan and M. B. Menhaj, "Training feedforward

networks with the Marquardt algorithm", *IEEE Trans. on Neural Net.*, vol. 5, no. 6, pp. 989-993, 1994.

[2] G. Zhou and J. Si, "Advanced neural-network training algorithm with reduced complexity based on Jacobian deficiency", *IEEE Trans. on Neural Net.*, vol. 9, no. 3, pp. 448-453, 1998.

[3] L. W. Chan and C. C. Szeto, "Training recurrent network with block-diagonal approximated Levenberg-Marquardt algorithm", in *Proc. IJCNN*, vol. 3, pp. 1521-1526, 1999.

[4] B. M. Wilamowski, Y. Chen, and A. Malinowski, "Efficient algorithm for training neural networks with one hidden layer", in *Proc. IJCNN*, vol. 3, pp. 1725-1728, 1999.

[5] D. Marquardt, "An algorithm for least squares estimation of nonlinear parameters", *J. Soc. Ind. Appl. Math.*, pp. 431-441, 1963.

[6] H. Demuth and M. Beale, *Neural Network TOOLBOX User's Guide. For use with MATLAB*. The MathWorks Inc., 1998.

[7] D. Nguyen and B. Widrow, "Improving the learning speed of 2-layer neural networks by choosing initial values of adaptive weights", in *Proc. IJCNN*, vol. 3, pp. 21-26, 1990.

Adaptive Critic Designs and their Implementations on Different Neural Network Architectures

Jung-Wook Park[1], G. K. Venayagamoorthy[2], *Senior Member, IEEE,* and Ronald G. Harley[1], *Fellow, IEEE*

[1]School of Electrical and Computer Engineering
Georgia Institute of Technology
GA 30332-0250, U.S.A.
(e-mails: jungwookpark@ieee.org and ron.harley@ece.gatech.edu)

[2]Department of Electrical and Computer Engineering
University of Missouri-Rolla
MO 65409-0249, U.S.A.
(e-mail: gkumar@ieee.org)

Abstract – The design of nonlinear optimal neurocontrollers based on the Adaptive Critic Designs (ACDs) family of algorithms has recently attracted interest. This paper presents a summary of these algorithms, and compares their performance when implemented on two different types of artificial neural networks, namely the multilayer perceptron neural network (MLPNN) and the radial basis function neural network (RBFNN). As an example for the application of the ACDs, the control of synchronous generator on an electric power grid is considered and results are presented to compare the different ACD family members and their implementations on different neural network architectures.

I. INTRODUCTION

The adaptive critic designs (ACDs) technique, which was proposed by Werbos [1], [2], is a novel nonlinear optimization and control algorithm based on the mathematical analysis to handle the classical optimal control problem by combining concepts of *reinforcement learning* and *approximate dynamic programming* (ADP).

Use of the ACD technique based on artificial neural networks (ANNs), allows the design of an optimal adaptive nonlinear controller and has the capability of optimization over time under conditions of noise and uncertainty [3], [4]. In other words, the ACDs can be used to maximize or minimize any utility function, such as total energy error, of a system over time in a noisy nonstationary environment.

The conventional continually on-line indirect adaptive neurocontroller for generator control was described in [5], which reported that the updates/adaptation of the parameters for the neurocontroller are carried out using a gradient descent algorithm based on the error only one time step ahead. This adaptation technique is therefore short sighted. A short-term goal does not guarantee a long-term satisfactory/optimal trajectory.

To overcome the above issue and provide strong robustness for the controller, the family of ACD techniques for infinite time horizon optimal control can be seen as alternatives where the ANNs are used as tools to identify the system and implement the ACD based control algorithms [6].

Also, without the extensive computational efforts and difficult mathematical analyses required by using the dynamic programming (DP) in classical optimal control theory [7], the ACD technique provides an effective method to construct an optimal and robust feedback controller by exploiting backpropagation for the calculation of all the derivatives of user-defined target quantities [1] in order to minimize the heuristic cost-to-go approximation.

There are three representative optimization control techniques among the ACDs family. One is the heuristic dynamic programming (HDP), which approximates the heuristic cost-to-go function (**J**) *itself* by the critic network adaptation. Another is the dual heuristic programming (DHP), by which critic network performs the value iteration for *derivatives* of the heuristic cost-to-go function **J** with respect to the states of the plant. The other is the globalized dual heuristic programming (GDHP), which approximates both **J** and its derivatives by the critic network adaptation.

In the literature, there exist many ACDs based application and these have been implemented using the MLPNN for the HDP [3], [4], [6], [8]-[11], DHP [3], [4], [12], or GDHP [13] for the design of controllers. However, very few reports have appeared on implementing the HDP [14], DHP, and GDHP using the RBFNN.

In Ref. [4], the authors compared HDP and DHP based on the MLPNN. In Ref. [5], the authors compared the use of the MLPNN and RBFNN for implementing indirect adaptive control of a synchronous generator. In Ref. [6], the authors compared the HDP based on the MLPNN and RBFNN.

This paper extends the earlier works [4]-[6] by adding comparison of the performance of the DHP based on the MLPNN and RBFNN. Also, the advantages, which can be obtained through the ACDs based optimal control, are discussed with comparison of the indirect adaptive control.

II. ADAPTIVE CRITIC DESIGNS

The adaptive critic method determines optimal control laws for a system by successively adapting two neural networks, namely, an action neural network (which dispenses the control signal) and a critic neural network (which "learns" the desired performance index for some function associated with the index).

The model dependent designs for the HDP and DHP algorithms are briefly described below.

A. Heuristic Dynamic Programming (HDP)

The critic network in the HDP approximates the heuristic cost-to-go function **J** *itself* in (1).

$$\mathbf{J}(k) = \sum_{p=0}^{\infty} \gamma^p U(k+p) \quad (1)$$

where γ is the discount factor ($0 < \gamma < 1$) and U is the user-defined utility or cost function. The configuration of the critic network training (for value iteration to minimize the value of **J**) by approximate dynamic programming is shown in Fig. 1. The following error equation [3] for the training of critic network is used.

$$e_C(t) = \mathbf{J}(\Delta \hat{\mathbf{Y}}(t)) - \gamma \mathbf{J}(\Delta \hat{\mathbf{Y}}(t+1)) - U(\Delta \hat{\mathbf{Y}}(t)) \quad (2)$$

where $\Delta \hat{\mathbf{Y}}(t)$ is a vector of observables of the plant, which is the output vector from the model network (Fig. 2).

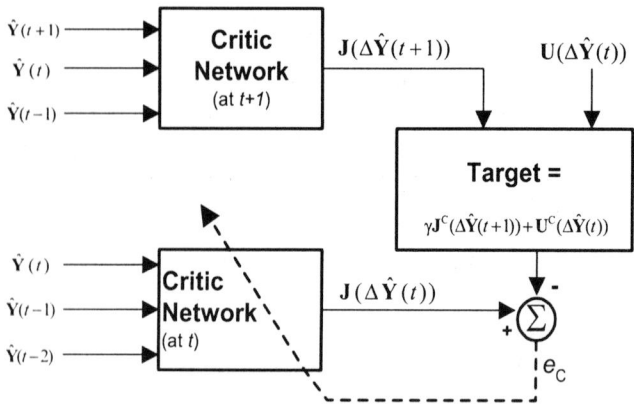

Fig. 1. Critic adaptation in HDP: The same critic network is shown for two consecutive times, $t+1$ and t. The critic's output $\mathbf{J}(\Delta \hat{\mathbf{Y}}(t+1))$ at time $t+1$ is required for the ADP to generate a target signal $\gamma \mathbf{J}(\Delta \hat{\mathbf{Y}}(t+1)) + U(\Delta \hat{\mathbf{Y}}(t))$ for training the critic network.

The input of the action network in Fig. 2 is the output vector of the plant ($\mathbf{Y}(t)$) and its time-delayed values. After minimizing **J** in (1) by the critic network, the action network is trained with the estimated output backpropagated from the critic network to obtain the converged weight for the optimal control **u***. In other words, the objective of the action network shown in Fig. 2, is to find the optimal control **u*** to minimize **J** in the immediate future, thereby optimizing the overall cost expressed as a sum of all U over the horizon of the problem in (1). This is achieved by training the action network with an error vector $\mathbf{e}_A(t)$ in (3).

$$\mathbf{e}_A(t) = \frac{\partial \mathbf{J}^c(t)}{\partial \mathbf{A}(t)} \quad (3)$$

The derivative of the cost function $\mathbf{J}(t)$ with respect to $\mathbf{A}(t)$ in (3) is obtained by backpropagating $\partial J/\partial J = 1$ (recall that the HDP approximates the function **J** itself) through the critic network and then through the pretrained model network to the action network. This gives signals $\partial J(t)/\partial \Delta \hat{\mathbf{Y}}(t)$ and $\partial J(t)/\partial \mathbf{A}(t)$ in Fig. 2 for the weights $\mathbf{W}_A(t)$ and the output vector $\mathbf{A}(t)$ of the action network. The expression for the weights' update in the action network is given in (4).

$$\Delta \mathbf{W}_A(t) = -\eta_A \cdot \mathbf{e}_A(t) \cdot \frac{\partial \mathbf{e}_A(t)}{\partial \mathbf{W}_A(t)} \quad (4)$$

where η_A is the positive learning rate.

The general training procedure for the model, critic, and action networks in the HDP is explained in [3] and [5].

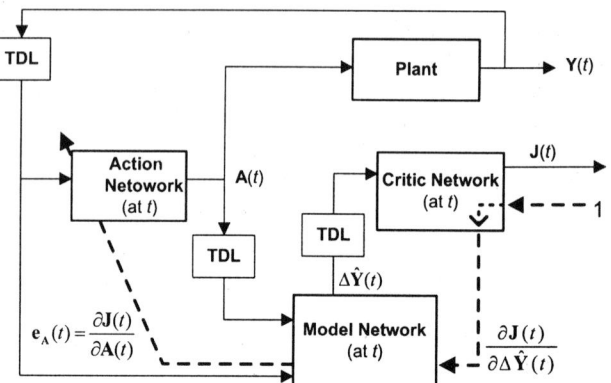

Fig. 2. The configuration for the action network adaptation in HDP.

B. Dual Heuristic Programming (DHP)

The critic network in the DHP approximates the derivatives of the heuristic cost-to-go function **J** in (1) with respect to the states of the plant. In other words, the value iteration by the critic network in the DHP is carried out with *perfect state information* of the plant, which means that the actual suboptimal path to minimize **J** is changed, and the corresponding optimal control **u*** is determined in the different optimal policy set.

The configuration for the critic network adaptation in the DHP is shown in Fig. 3. The input and output vectors of the model, action, and critic networks are the same as those in the HDP. For the critic network adaptation in the DHP, it learns to minimize the following error measure over time:

$$\|E_C\| = \sum_t \mathbf{e}_C^T(t)\mathbf{e}_C(t) \quad (5)$$

$$\mathbf{e}_C(t) = \frac{\partial \mathbf{J}[\Delta \hat{\mathbf{Y}}(t)]}{\partial \Delta \hat{\mathbf{Y}}(t)} - \gamma \frac{\partial \hat{\mathbf{J}}[\Delta \hat{\mathbf{Y}}(t+1)]}{\partial \Delta \mathbf{Y}(t)} - \frac{\partial U[\Delta \mathbf{Y}(t)]}{\partial \Delta \mathbf{Y}(t)} \quad (6)$$

After exploiting all relevant pathways of backpropagation as shown in Fig. 3, where the paths of derivatives and adaptation of the critic network are depicted by dotted and dash-dot lines, the error signal $\mathbf{e}_C(t)$ is used for training to update the weights of the critic network.

The jth component of the second term in (6) can be expressed by the output of critic network at time $t+1$, $\hat{\lambda}_i(t+1) = \partial \hat{\mathbf{J}}[\Delta \hat{\mathbf{Y}}(t+1)] / \partial \Delta \hat{\mathbf{Y}}_i(t+1)$ as follows.

$$\frac{\partial \hat{\mathbf{J}}[\Delta \hat{\mathbf{Y}}(t+1)]}{\partial \Delta \mathbf{Y}_j(t)} = \sum_{i=1}^{n} \hat{\lambda}_i(t+1) \frac{\partial \Delta \hat{\mathbf{Y}}_i(t+1)}{\partial \Delta \mathbf{Y}_j(t)} \quad (7)$$
$$+ \sum_{k=1}^{m} \sum_{i=1}^{n} \hat{\lambda}_i(t+1) \frac{\partial \Delta \hat{\mathbf{Y}}_i(t+1)}{\partial \mathbf{A}_k(t)} \frac{\partial \mathbf{A}_k(t)}{\partial \Delta \mathbf{Y}_j(t)}$$

where n and m are the numbers of outputs of the model and the action networks, respectively.

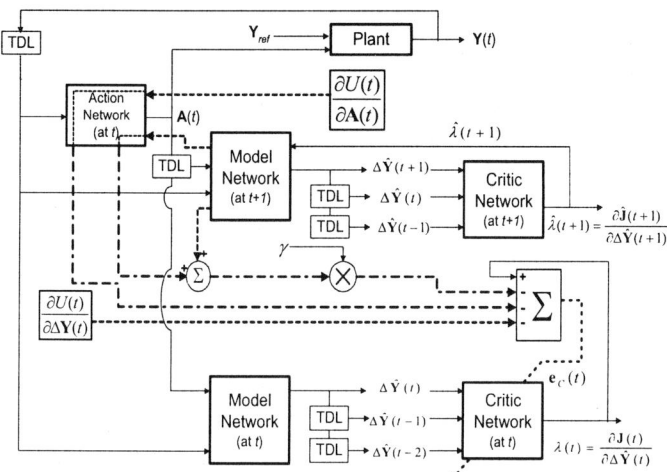

Fig. 3. Critic network adaptation in the DHP as in (8). The same critic network is shown for two consecutive times, t and $t+1$. The discount factor γ is chosen to be 0.5. Backpropagation paths are shown by dotted and dash-dot lines. The output of the critic network $\hat{\lambda}(t+1)$ is backpropagated through the model from its outputs to its inputs, yielding the first term of (6) and $\partial J(t+1)/\partial \mathbf{A}(t)$. The latter is backpropagated through the action network from its outputs to its inputs forming the second term of (6). Backpropagation of the vector $\partial U(t)/\partial \mathbf{A}(t)$ through the action results in a vector with components computed as the last term of (8). The summation of all these signals produces the error vector $\mathbf{e}_c(t)$ used for training the critic network.

By using (7), each of j components of the vector $\mathbf{e}_C(t)$ from (6) is determined by

$$\mathbf{e}_{Cj}(t) = \frac{\partial \mathbf{J}[\Delta \hat{\mathbf{Y}}(t)]}{\partial \Delta \hat{\mathbf{Y}}_j(t)} - \gamma \frac{\partial \hat{\mathbf{J}}[\Delta \hat{\mathbf{Y}}(t+1)]}{\partial \Delta \mathbf{Y}_j(t)} \quad (8)$$
$$- \frac{\partial U[\Delta \mathbf{Y}(t)]}{\partial \Delta \mathbf{Y}_j(t)} - \sum_{k=1}^{m} \frac{\partial U[\Delta \mathbf{Y}(t)]}{\partial \mathbf{A}_k(t)} \frac{\partial \mathbf{A}_k(t)}{\partial \Delta \mathbf{Y}_j(t)}$$

The adaptation of the action network in Fig. 3 is illustrated in Fig. 4, which propagates $\hat{\lambda}(t+1)$ back through the model network to the action network. The goal of this adaptation is expressed in (9) [3], and the weights of the action network are updated by (10).

$$\frac{\partial U[\Delta \mathbf{Y}(t)]}{\partial \mathbf{A}(t)} + \gamma \frac{\partial \hat{\mathbf{J}}[\Delta \hat{\mathbf{Y}}(t+1)]}{\partial \mathbf{A}(t)} = 0 \quad \forall t. \quad (9)$$

$$\Delta \mathbf{W}_A(t) = -\eta_A [\frac{\partial U[\Delta \mathbf{Y}(t)]}{\partial \mathbf{A}(t)} + \gamma \frac{\partial \hat{\mathbf{J}}[\Delta \hat{\mathbf{Y}}(t+1)]}{\partial \mathbf{A}(t)}]^T \frac{\partial \mathbf{A}(t)}{\partial \mathbf{W}_A(t)} \quad (10)$$

where η_A is a positive learning rate and $\mathbf{W}_A$ contains the weights of the DHP action network.

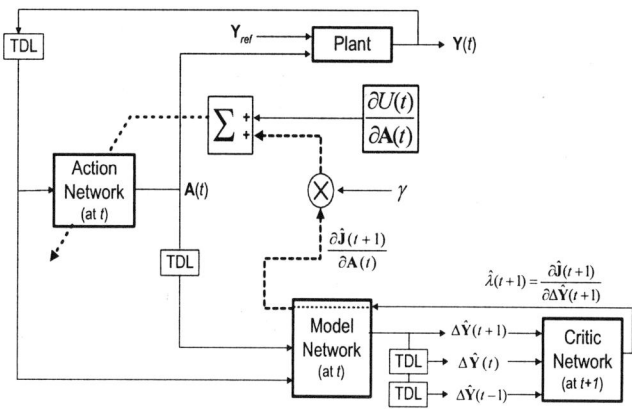

Fig. 4. Action network adaptation in the DHP: Backpropagation paths are shown by dotted lines. The output of the critic network $\hat{\lambda}(t+1)$ at time $(t+1)$ is backpropagated through the model network from its outputs to its inputs (output of the action), and the resulting vector multiplied by the discount factor ($\gamma = 0.5$) and added to $\partial U(t)/\partial \mathbf{A}(t)$. Then, an incremental adaptation of the action network is carried out by (9) and (10).

The structures and equations for the MLPNN and RBFNN used in this paper appear in [5], [6], and [16].

III. CASE STUDY: SYNCHRONOUS GENERATOR CONTROL

A. Plant Modeling

The synchronous generator, turbine, exciter and transmission system connected to an infinite bus form the plant (dotted block) in Fig. 5 that has to be controlled [5], [6].

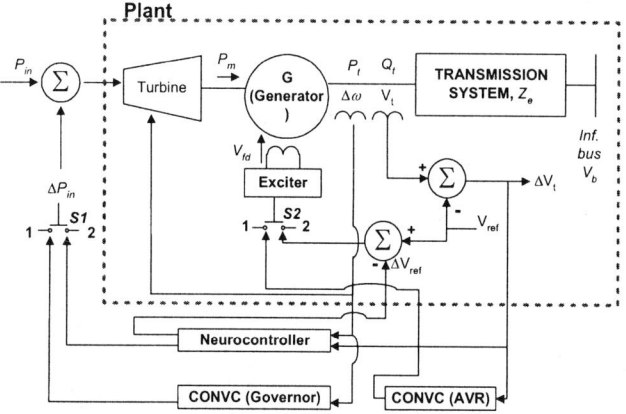

Fig. 5. Plant model used for the control of a synchronous generator connected to an infinite bus.

In the plant, P_t and Q_t are the real and reactive power at the generator terminal, respectively, Z_e is the transmission line impedance, P_m is the mechanical input power to the generator, V_{fd} is the exciter field voltage, V_b is the infinite bus voltage, $\Delta \omega$ is the speed deviation, ΔV_t is the terminal voltage deviation, V_t is the terminal voltage, ΔV_{ref} is the reference voltage deviation, V_{ref} is the reference voltage, ΔP_{in} is the input power deviation, and P_{in} is the turbine input power.

The position of the switches *S1* and *S2* in Fig. 5 determines whether the optimal neurocontroller, or the conventional controller (CONVC) consisting of governor and AVR, is controlling the plant. Block diagrams, time constants, and gains for the CONVC (AVR/exciter and turbine/governor systems) are given in [6].

B. Simulation Results

With the fixed parameters after off-line training by the same procedures (explained in [3] and [6]) for the model, critic, and action networks in the HDP and DHP, the dynamic performances of the following nonlinear optimal neurocontrollers are evaluated and compared with the CONVC.

- Neurocontrollers designed by the HDP using the MLPNN and RBFNN are called the MHDPC and RHDPC, respectively.
- Neurocontrollers designed by the DHP using the MLPNN and RBFNN are called the MDHPC and RDHPC, respectively.

The following two different types of disturbances are applied to the plant for the tests of improvement of system damping and transient stability.

- A three phase short circuit at the infinite bus in Fig. 5: At t = 0.3 s, a temporary three phase short circuit is applied at the infinite bus for 100 ms from t=0.3 s to 0.4 s for the plant operating at the steady state condition.
- ±5% step changes in the reference voltage of the exciter in Fig. 5: The synchronous generator of the plant is operating at a steady state condition. At t = 1 s, a 5% step increase (ΔV_{ref}) in the reference voltage of the exciter is applied. At t=12 s, the 5% step increase is removed, and the system returns to its initial operating point.

The results in Figs. 6 to 8 show that the optimal neurocontrollers improve the damping of low-frequency oscillations more effectively compared to the CONVC (in Fig. 6), and that the RHDPC outperforms the MHDPC for the dynamic transient response (for the new reference value), i.e. the RHDPC has a faster rising time than the MHDPC (Figs. 7 and 8). Note that the increased damping is important for generators in power system networks. From Fig. 6, it is shown that two optimal neurocontrollers (MDHPC/RDHPC) based on the DHP improve the damping of low-frequency oscillations more effectively than the MHDPC/RHDPC and the CONVC.

The results in Figs. 7 and 8 for a step change show that the DHP based neurocontrollers outperform the HDP based neurocontrollers. Also, the RDHPC has a faster rise time than the MDHPC. Especially, the performance of the MDHPC is significantly improved compared to that of the MHDPC.

Moreover, the MDHPC shows a slightly faster rise time and smaller overshoot than the RDHPC.

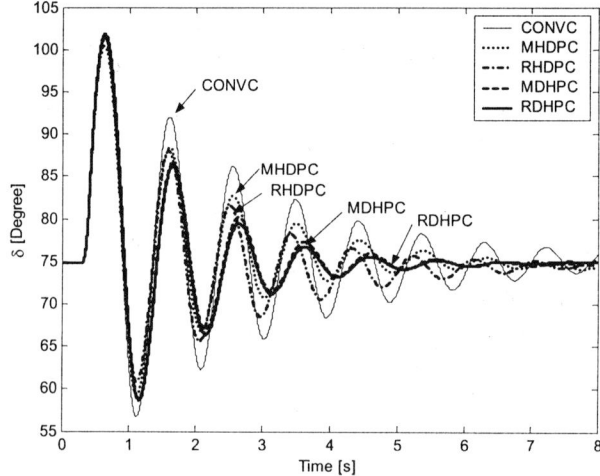

Fig. 6. Three phase short circuit test: Rotor angle.

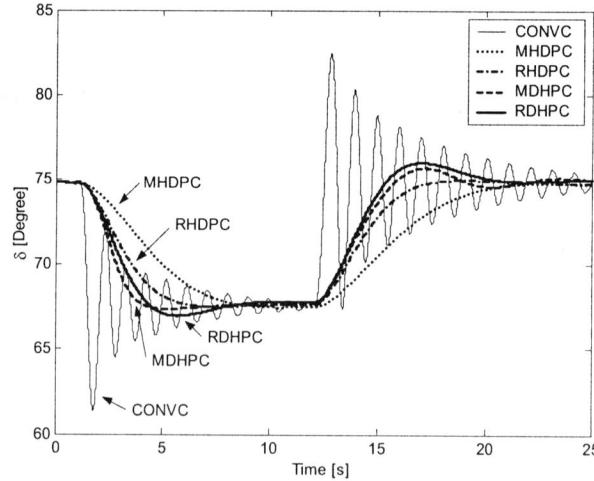

Fig. 7. ±5% Step changes in reference voltage of exciter: Rotor angle.

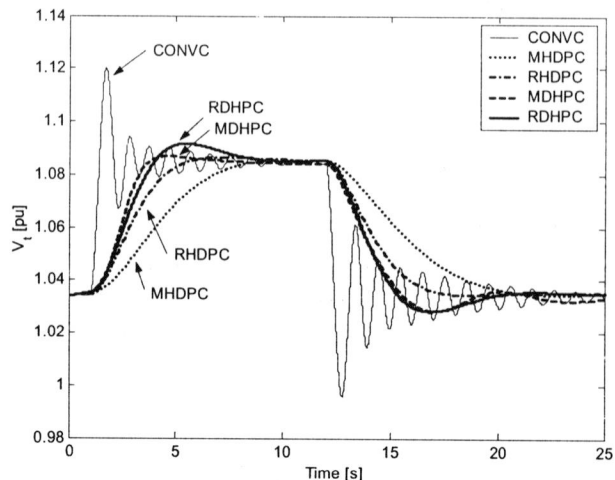

Fig. 8. ±5% Step changes in reference voltage of exciter: Terminal voltage.

C. Adaptive Critic Optimal control vs. Indirect Adaptive Control

The robustness of a controller [7], [17], [18] is judged by how well it controls a process even during uncertain changing system configurations. Therefore, the HDP and DHP techniques, which are based on the *infinite horizon optimal control* method, provide robust feedback control; this powerful dynamic control capability of adaptive critic optimal controllers has been evaluated in the previous subsection B. This robustness comes because the parameters for the critic and action networks are only trained off-line (not on-line), and remain *fixed* during real-time control.

In contrast, the model reference indirect adaptive control (MRAC) shown in [5] depends on the outputs of the desired response predictor (DRP). The response of this controller therefore varies according to the design of DRP using information from the changing system outputs.

Also, the parameters for the ANN identifier and controller in indirect adaptive control must be updated on-line at every time step in order to force the plant outputs back to the response of the DRP.

The results of the indirect adaptive control scheme [5] are compared in Figs. 9 to 11 with the responses of the MDHPC and RDHPC. In these figures, the neurocontrollers designed by the indirect adaptive control (IAC) scheme using the MLPNN and RBFNN are called the MIAC and RIAC, respectively.

From Fig. 9, the DHP neurocontrollers still have a better damping performance compared to the MIAC and RIAC in the case of a severe disturbance (three phase short circuit).

On the other hand, the results in Figs. 10 and 11 show that the MIAC is less damped and slightly oscillatory with respect to the DHP controllers. The RIAC response lies between that of the MIAC and the DHP.

Whether the ACD family of controllers or the IAC family of controllers give better results for large or small disturbances, depends on choices such as the utility function for the ACD family, and the DRP for the IAC family. The purpose of this paper is not to claim that one of these families will always perform better than the other one, but to show that the ACD has a comparable performance to the IAC, even with fixed control parameters in real-time operation.

More detailed explanations of the indirect adaptive control and the ACD based optimal control methodologies for the synchronous generator control are explained in [5] and [6], respectively.

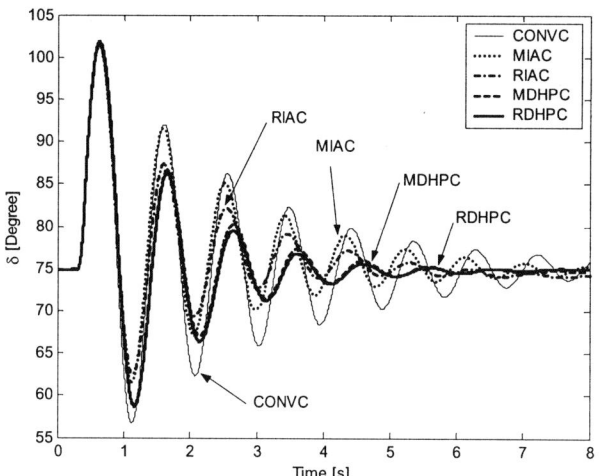

Fig. 9. Three phase short circuit test: Rotor angle.

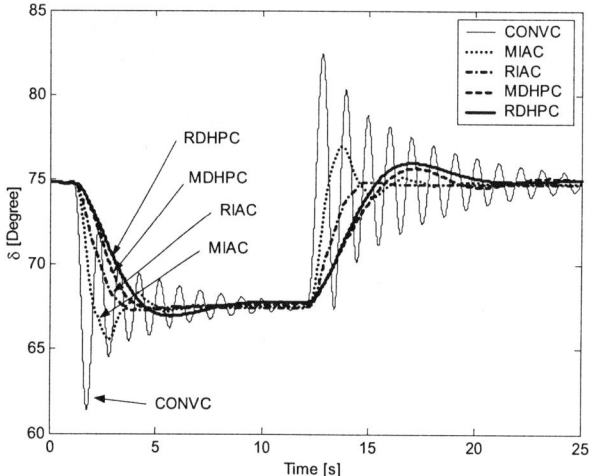

Fig. 10. ±5% Step changes in reference voltage of exciter: Rotor angle.

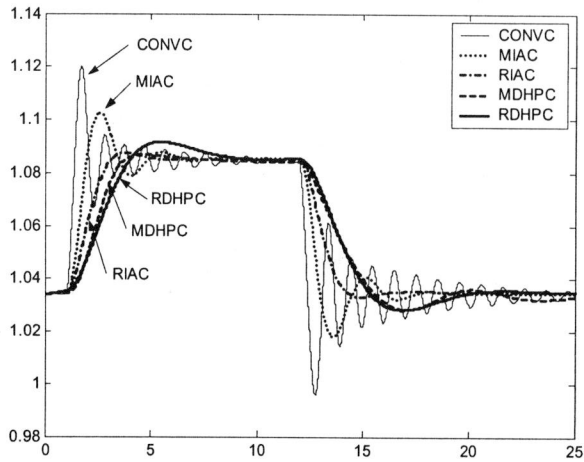

Fig. 11. ±5% Step changes in reference voltage of exciter: Terminal voltage

IV. Conclusions

This paper has presented the design of optimal neurocontrollers based on the heuristic dynamic programming (HDP) and dual heuristic programming (DHP) for the control of a synchronous generator in an electric power grid. To implement the HDP/DHP algorithm, the multilayer perceptron neural network (MLPNN) and radial basis function neural network (RBFNN) were used as function approximators. The comprehensive comparisons were carried out based on time-domain simulations to evaluate the dynamic transient and damping performances of the HDP/DHP based optimal neurocontrollers using the MLPNN/RBFNN. From the case study illustrated, the following conclusions can be drawn:

- When using the HDP, the RBFNN is preferred as function approximators for the model, critic, and action networks than the MLPNN.

- The DHP algorithm provides the effective dynamic and more robust control capability than the HDP.

- With DHP control designs, either the RBFNN or the MLPNN can be used as function approximators. However, the MLPNN is easy for hardware implementation because the RBFNN requires the feature extraction techniques to determine the centers of the RBF units, which is the most important characteristic of the RBFNN. In other words, the off-line computation to determine the centers of the RBF units must be paid the careful attention; otherwise the on-line updates for the centers of the RBF units require the highly expensive computational efforts.

Generally, the proposed neurocontrollers have *fixed parameters* for their model, action, and critic neural networks, which are trained off-line based on the infinite horizon optimal control approach. This means that there are no adaptive parameters in a real-time operation. Therefore, they provide a robust feedback with a powerful dynamic control capability under uncertain environments, and the possible instability issue associated with artificial neural networks (ANNs) based controllers can be avoided.

Investigations are continuing into more detailed treatment of different optimality conditions according to approximations for the value iteration **J** in the HDP and DHP.

Acknowledgment

Financial support by the National Science Foundation (NSF), USA under Grant No. ECS-0080764 for this research is gratefully acknowledged.

V. References

[1] W.T. Miller, R.S. Sutton, and P.J. Werbos, "Neural Networks for Control," MIT Press, Cambridge, Massachusetts, 1990, ISBN 0-262-13261-3.

[2] P. J. Werbos, "Approximate dynamic programming for real-time control and neural modeling," in *Handbook of Intelligent Control*, D. White and D. Sofge, Eds. New York: Van Nostrand Reinhold, pp.493-526, 1992.

[3] D.V. Prokhorov, and D.C. Wunsch, "Adaptive critic designs," *IEEE Trans. on Neural Networks*, Vol.8, No.5, pp. 997-1007, Sept. 1997.

[4] G.K. Venayagamoorthy, R.G. Harley, and D.C. Wunsch, "Comparison of Heuristic Dynamic Programming and Dual Heuristic Programming Adaptive Critics for Neurocontrol of a Turbogenerator," *IEEE Trans. on Neural Networks*, Vol.13, No.3, pp. 764-773, May. 2002.

[5] Jung-Wook Park, R.G. Harley, and G.K. Venayagamoorthy, "Comparison of MLP and RBF Neural Networks Using Deviation Signals for Indirect Adaptive Control of a Synchronous Generator," in *Proc. of the International Joint Conference on Neural Networks, IJCNN02*, Hawaii, pp. 919-924, May 2002.

[6] Jung-Wook Park, R.G. Harley, and G.K. Venayagamoorthy, "Adaptive Critic Based Optimal Neurocontrol for Synchronous Generator in Power System Using MLP/RBF Neural Networks," *37th IEEE IAS Annual Meeting*, Vol. 2, pp.1447-1454, October 2002. (*appear in IEEE Trans. on Industry Applications*, 2003.)

[7] Dimitri P. Bertsekas, "Dynamic Programming and Optimal Control", Athena Scientific, Belmont, Massachusetts, 2001, ISBN 1-886529-08-6.

[8] Derong Liu, Xiaoxu Xiong, and Zhang Yi, "Action-Dependent Adaptive Critic Designs," in *Proc.2001 IEEE IJCNN*, Washington DC, Vol.2, pp. 990-995, July 2001.

[9] S.N. Balakrishnan and Han Dongchen, "State-constrained agile missile control with adaptive-critic-based neural networks," *IEEE Trans. on Control System Technology*, Vol.10, No.4, pp. 481-489, July. 2002.

[10] Jennie Si and Yu-Tsung Wang, "On-Line Learning Control by Association and Reinforcement," *IEEE Trans. on Neural Networks*, Vol.12, No.2, pp. 264-276, March. 2001.

[11] Timothy Draelos, David Duggan, Michael Collins, and Donald Wunsch, "Adaptive Critic Designs for Host-Based Intrusion Detection," in *Proc. of the IJCNN02*, Hawaii, pp. 1720-1724, May 2002.

[12] G.K. Venayagamoorthy, R.G. Harley, and D.C. Wunsch, "Dual heuristic programming excitation neurocontrol for generators in a multimachine power system," *appear in IEEE Trans. on Industry Applications*, March/April. 2003.

[13] G.K. Venayagamoorthy, R.G. Harley, and D.C. Wunsch, "Adaptive Critic Based Neurocontroller for Turbogenerators with Global Dual Heuristic Programming," in *Proc.2002 IEEE PES Winter Meeting*, Singapore, Vol.1, pp. 291-294, January 2000.

[14] Chun-shin Lin, Yi-Hsun Ethan Cheng, and Hyongsuk Kim, "Radial Basis Function Networks for Adaptive Critic Learning," in *Proc.1994 IEEE WCCI IJCNN*, Orlando, Vol.2, pp. 903-906, July 1994.

[15] Jung-Wook Park, R.G. Harley, and G.K. Venayagamoorthy, "Comparison of MLP and RBF Neural Networks Using Deviation Signals for On-Line Identification of a Synchronous Generator," in *Proc.2002 IEEE PES Winter Meeting*, New York, Vol.1, pp. 274-279, January 2002.

[16] Z. Uykan, C. Guzelis, M.E. Celebi, and H.N. Koivo, "Analysis of input-output clustering for determining centers of RBFN," *IEEE Trans. on Neural Networks*, Vol.11, No.4, pp. 851-858, July 2000.

[17] W.L. Brogan, "Modern Control Theory," Prentice Hall, Englewood Cliffs, New Jersey, 1991, ISBN 0-13-589763-7.

[18] John Gregory and Cantian Kin, "Constrained Optimization in the Calculus of Variations and Optimal Control Theory," Van Nostrand Reinhold, New York, 1992, ISBN 0-442-00722-1.

Combination of On-line Clustering and Q-value Based Genetic Reinforcement Learning For Fuzzy Network Design

Chia-Feng Juang and Chun-Feng Lu*
Department of Electrical Engineering, National Chung Hsing University
Taichung, 402 Taiwan, R.O.C.

*Department of Electrical Engineering, Chung Chou Institute of Technology,
*Yuan-Lin, Chang-Hua, Taiwan, R.O.C.

Abstract- **This paper proposes a combination of on-line Clustering and Q-value based Genetic Algorithm learning scheme for Fuzzy network design (CQGAF) with reinforcements. The CQGAF fulfills GA based fuzzy network design under reinforcement learning environment where only weak reinforcement signals such as "success" and "failure" are available. In CQGAF, there are no fuzzy rules initially. They are generated automatically. The precondition part of a fuzzy network is on-line constructed by an aligned clustering-based approach. Simultaneously, the consequent part is designed by Q-value based genetic reinforcement learning. In CQGAF, evolution is performed immediately after the end of one trial in contrast to general GA where many trials are performed before evolution. The feasibility of CQGAF is demonstrated through simulations in cart-pole balancing problems with only binary reinforcement signals.**

I. INTRODUCTION

Reinforcement learning is the problem faced by a learner who must learn behavior through trial-and-error interactions with a dynamic environment. It is distinguished from supervised learning by its emphasis on learning by the individual from direct interaction with environment, without relying on exemplary supervision. In the most challenging case, a reinforcement signal may not be available at a time long after the occurrence of a sequence of actions. This leads to the temporal credit assignment problem, i.e., how to distribute reward or punishment to each individual state-action pair to adjust the chosen action and improve its performance. To solve the problem, the most popular approach is temporal difference (TD) method [1,2]. Two TD-based reinforcement learning approaches have been proposed: the Adaptive Heuristic Critic (AHC) and Q-learning. The AHC belongs to a class of adaptive critic reinforcement learning algorithm and consists of two separate networks: an action network and an evaluation network. The TD method is used to train an evaluation network that learns to predict the expected outcome of the current trial given the current state and the current decision policy of the action network. Based on the AHC, many learning approaches have been proposed [3]-[5].

In Q-learning, a Q-function is used as a predictive function that estimates the expected return from the current state and action pair [6]. Q-learning collapses the two measures used by actor/critic algorithms in AHC into one measure referred to as the Q-value. It may be considered as a compact version of the AHC, and is simpler in implementation. Some Q-learning based reinforcement learning structures for fuzzy network design have been proposed [7,8,9]. In [7], a dynamic fuzzy Q-learning is proposed for fuzzy inference system design. In this method, the consequent parts of fuzzy rules are randomly generated and the best rule set is selected based on its corresponding Q-value. The problem in this approach is that if the optimal solution is not present in the randomly generated set, then the performance may be poor. In [8], fuzzy Q-learning is applied to select the consequent action values of a fuzzy inference system. For this method, the consequent value is selected from a predefined value set which is kept unchanged during learning, and if an improper value set is assigned, then the algorithm may fail. For this problem, in CQGAF we will tune the consequent part free parameters by GA. Besides, in the aforementioned approaches, the precondition part of a fuzzy system is assigned *a priori*, here, we solve this pre-assignment problem by on-line generation of the precondition part via clustering.

GA is a stochastic search procedure based on the mechanism of natural selection. Recently, some researches on combining the advantages of GAs and TD-based reinforcement learning have been proposed [11][12]. In these studies, an additional evaluation network is incorporated into the genetic reinforcement learning process which operates only with an action network. Besides, to provide the fitness value for GA evolution, an additional accumulator is required to accumulate the time steps until failure. To ease the design, since Q-leaning is a simpler implementation than AHC, the combination of Q-learning with GA is proposed, where the learned Q-values are used as fitness values for GA evolution. Overall, the major objective of CQGAF may be viewed from two perspectives. From the perspective of fuzzy Q-learning, CQGAF provides a method, the combination of on-line clustering and GA, for automatic precondition part construction and automatic determination of the consequent parts of a fuzzy network. From the perspective of GA, CQGAF extends GA to deal with problems where only weak reinforcement signals are available, which lessens the quality and quantity of the required teaching signals.

II. ARCHITECTURE OF CQGAF

The architecture of the proposed CQGAF is shown in Fig. 1. In CQGAF, a fuzzy network acts as an agent. There are two parts in a fuzzy network, the precondition part and the consequent part. The precondition part is constructed automatically by the proposed on-line clustering approach. Simultaneously, the consequent part of this newly generated rule is designed by GA. In GA, a population of candidate consequent parts is generated. Each individual in the population encodes the consequent part of a fuzzy network and has a corresponding Q-value to evaluate the action recommended by the individual. After each trial, newly updated Q-values are used as the fitness values for GA evolution. By GA, new populations are generated. The detail function of each operation is described below.

Each rule in the fuzzy system is presented in the following form:

Rule i: IF $x_1(t)$ is A_{i1} And $\cdots$ And $x_n(t)$ is A_{in} (1)

Then $\bar{a}(t)$ is $a_i(t)$

where $x(t)$ is the input variable, $\bar{a}(t)$ is the output action variable, A is a fuzzy set, and $a(t)$ is a recommended action and is a fuzzy singleton. For fuzzy set A, a Gaussian membership function with

$$M(x) = \exp\{-(\frac{x-m}{\sigma})^2\}$$

is used, where m and σ denote the mean and width of fuzzy set A, respectively. Given an input data set $X = (x_1, x_2, \cdots, x_n)$, the firing strength $\Phi_i(X)$ of rule i is calculated by

$$\Phi_i(X) = \prod_{j=1}^{n} M_{ij} = \exp\{-\sum_{j=1}^{n} (\frac{x_j - m_{ij}}{\sigma_{ij}})^2\} \quad (2)$$

The recommended action, a_i, from each rule is a crisp value. Suppose a fuzzy system consists of r rules, then by weighted average, the output of the system is

$$\bar{a} = \frac{\sum_{i=1}^{r} \Phi_i(X) a_i}{\sum_{i=1}^{r} \Phi_i(X)} \quad (3)$$

To find the optimum consequence of each rule by GA, a population involving N individuals is created. Each individual in the population encodes the r consequent values, $a_1 \sim a_r$, in a fuzzy system. The Q-value used to predict the performance of individual i is denoted as q_i. At each time step, one over these N individuals is selected as the consequent part of a fuzzy system based on their corresponding Q-values. To accomplish the selection task, the ϵ-greedy method is used. At any time t there is at least one individual i^* whose Q-value is the largest, i.e. $q_{i^*}(t) = \max_{i=1 \sim N} q_i(t)$. We call this a greedy individual. In ϵ-greedy, the greedy individual is selected with a large probability 1-ϵ. Once in a while, with probability ϵ, an individual is randomly selected independent of the Q-values.

Suppose at time t, the individual $\hat{i}$ is selected, i.e. actions $a_1^{\hat{i}}(t) \sim a_r^{\hat{i}}(t)$ are selected for rules $1 \sim r$, respectively. Then the final output action of the fuzzy system is

$$\bar{a}(t) = \frac{\sum_{i=1}^{r} \Phi_i(X(t)) a_i^{\hat{i}}(t)}{\sum_{i=1}^{r} \Phi_i(X(t))} \quad (4)$$

The Q-value of this final output action should be a weighted average of the Q-values corresponding to the actions $a_1^{\hat{i}}(t) \sim a_r^{\hat{i}}(t)$, i.e.

$$Q(x(t), \bar{a}(t)) = \frac{\sum_{i=1}^{r} \Phi_i(X(t)) q_{\hat{i}(t)}}{\sum_{i=1}^{r} \Phi_i(X(t))} = q_{\hat{i}}(t) \quad (5)$$

From the above equation, we see that the Q-value of the system output, $Q(x(t), \bar{a}(t))$, is simply equal to $q_{\hat{i}}(t)$, the Q-value of the selected individual $\hat{i}$. This means that $q_{\hat{i}}$ simultaneously reveals both the performance of the individual and the corresponding system output action. The fuzzy system output $\bar{a}(t)$ is applied to the environment with a reward $r(t)$ received. Based on the received $r(t)$ and the estimated $q_{\hat{i}}(t)$, the Q-values of each individual are updated. The above selecting, acting, and updating process is repeatedly executed until the end of a trial, usually at the time a failure reinforcement is obtained. Then, the new Q-values of each individual are used as fitness values for the GA evolution of next generation. A new trial begins after a new population is created. The whole learning process continues to new generations until a predefined stop criterion is met.

III. LEARNING OF CQGAF

A. Aligned Clustering Algorithm

The objective of the aligned clustering algorithm is to on-line construct the precondition part of a fuzzy network. In contrast to the general grid type partition (see Fig. 2(a)), this approach provides a flexible input partition (see Fig. 2(b)) which may reduce the number of rules and eliminate the redundant fuzzy sets on each input dimension. The idea of the clustering approach is adopted. Geometrically, a rule corresponds to a cluster in the input space. For each incoming pattern $x(t)$, the firing strength can be regarded as the degree of the incoming pattern that belongs to the corresponding cluster. Based on this concept, the spatial firing strength in Eq. (2) should be used as the criterion to decide if a new fuzzy rule is generated. For each incoming data $x(t)$, find

$$I = \arg \max_{1 \le i \le r(t)} \Phi_i(X) \quad (6)$$

where $r(t)$ is the number of existing rules at time t. If $\Phi_I \le \Phi_{in}$, then a new rule is generated, where $\Phi_{in} \in (0,1)$ is a pre-specified threshold. Once a new rule is generated, the next step is to assign centers and widths of the corresponding membership functions. Here, we assign these values by

$$m_{(r(t)+1)i} = x_i(t)$$

$$\sigma_{(r(t)+1)i} = \beta \cdot \sum_{j=1}^{n} \frac{(x_j - m_{Ij})^2}{\sigma_{Ij}^2} \quad (7)$$

for $i = 1, \cdots, n$, according to the first-nearest-neighbor heuristic, where $\beta \geq 0$ decides the overlap degree between two clusters. In this paper, β is set to be 0.4. To reduce the number of fuzzy sets of each input variable and to avoid the existence of highly similar ones, we should check the similarities between the newly generated membership function and the existing ones in each input dimension. Let $M(m, \sigma)$ represent a Gaussian membership function with center m and width σ, and $E(A, B)$ the similarity measure between two fuzzy sets A and B. Detailed computation of the similarity degree $E(A, B)$ may refer to [10]. For each newly generated fuzzy rule, we have new membership functions $M(m_{new-i}, \sigma_{new-i})$ for variables $i = 1 \sim n$. Then compute

$$degree(i,t) \equiv \max_{1 \leq j \leq k_i} E[M(m_{new-i}, \sigma_{new-i}), M(m_{ji}, \sigma_{ji})]$$

where k_i is the number of existing fuzzy sets of the i th input variable. Let $\rho \in [0,1]$ be the similarity criterion assigned in advance. In this paper, ρ is set as 0.7. If $degree(i,t) \leq \rho$ then adopt this new membership function and set $k_i = k_i + 1$. Otherwise, set the new membership function as the closest one, after which an aligned clustering result occurs.

B. Learning Algorithm for Q-values

In Q-learning, an agent tries an action, $a(t)$, at a particular state, $x(t)$, evaluates its consequences in terms of the immediate reward, $r(t)$, receives and estimates the value of the state it has taken. To estimate the discounted cumulative reinforcement for taking actions from given states, an evaluation function, the Q-function, is used. The Q-function is a mapping from state-action pairs to predict return and its output for state x and action a is denoted by the Q-value, $Q(x,a)$. Based on this Q-value, at time t, the agent selects an action, $a(t)$. The action is applied to the environment, causing a state transition from $x(t)$ to $x(t+1)$, and a reward $r(t)$ is received. Then, the Q-value is updated by [6]

$$Q(x(t),a(t)) = Q(x(t),a(t)) + \alpha(r(t) + \gamma Q^*(x(t+1)) - Q(x(t),a(t)))$$
$$Q^*(x(t+1)) = \max_{b \in A(x(t+1))} Q(x(t+1),b) \quad (8)$$

where $A(x(t+1))$ is the set of possible actions in state $x(t+1)$ and α ($0 < \alpha < 1$) is the learning rate.

Every time after the fuzzy network applies an action $\overline{a}(t)$ to the environment and a reward $r(t)$ is received, learning of the Q-values is performed. As derived in Eq.(5), the estimated system Q-value, $Q(x(t), \overline{a}(t))$, is equal to $q_{\hat{i}}$ of selected individual $\hat{i}$. Then, we should update $q_{\hat{i}}$ based on the immediate reward $r(t)$ and the estimated rewards from subsequent states. Based on the Q-learning rule in Eq.(8), we can update $q_{\hat{i}}$ as

$$q_{\hat{i}}(t) = q_{\hat{i}}(t) + \alpha\left(r(t) + \gamma Q^*(x(t+1)) - q_{\hat{i}}(t)\right)$$
$$Q^*(x(t+1)) = \max_{i=1\cdots N} Q(x(t+1), \overline{a}^i) = \max_{i=1\cdots N} q_i(t) = q_{i^*}(t) \quad (9)$$

That is,

$$q_{\hat{i}}(t) = q_{\hat{i}}(t) + \alpha\left(r(t) + q_{i^*}(t) - q_{\hat{i}}\right) = q_{\hat{i}}(t) + \alpha \Delta q_{\hat{i}}(t) \quad (10)$$

where $\Delta q_{\hat{i}}(t)$ is regarded as the temporal error. In the above equation, at state $x(t)$, only the Q-value of the activating individual $\hat{i}$ is updated, and the individuals taken during the past time steps are not considered. To speed up the learning, the eligibility trace is combined with Q-learning in this paper. The eligibility trace for individual i at time t is denoted as $e_i(t)$. On each time step, the eligibility traces for all individuals are decayed by λ, and the eligibility trace for the selected individual $\hat{i}$ on the current step is increased by 1, that is

$$e_i(t) = \begin{cases} \lambda e_i(t-1), & \text{if } i \neq \hat{i} \\ \lambda e_i(t-1) + 1, & \text{if } i = \hat{i} \end{cases}$$

for $i = 1 \sim N$, where λ is a trace-decay parameter. With eligibility trace, Eq. (8) is changed to

$$q_i(t) = q_i(t) + \alpha \Delta q_i(t) e_i(t) \quad (11)$$

for all $i = 1 \sim N$. Upon receiving a reinforcement signal, the Q-values of all individuals are updated by Eq. (11). These new Q-values are then adopted as the fitness values for GA evolution after the end of each trial.

C. Q-value Based Genetic Algorithm

A GA is used to train the consequent part of a fuzzy system by using the Q-values as the fitness values. The algorithm consists of three major operators: selection, crossover, and mutation. Before going into the details of these three genetic operators, the issues of coding is discussed.

• *Coding.* Real-value encoding scheme is selected here. Suppose at time step t, there are $r(t)$ rules in a fuzzy network, then each chromosome i has the following form

$$\left|a_1^i\right|a_2^i\left|a_3^i\right|\cdots\left|a_{r(t)-2}^i\right|a_{r(t)-1}^i\left|a_{r(t)}^i\right| \quad (12)$$

where $a_1 \sim a_{r(t)}$ are floating point values in the consequent parts of rules $1 \sim r(t)$. In each chromosome, the number of genes is equal to the number of rules. Since in CQGAF the number of rules changes with time, so does the number of genes in each chromosome. When a new rule is generated, for each chromosome, a new gene is randomly generated and inserted to the rear site.

On each time step, one individual in the population is selected by ϵ-greedy method. An interpreter takes the real-value individual and uses it to set the consequent parameters in the fuzzy network. The fuzzy network then evaluates an action and forward it to the environment. With the reward from the environment, the Q-values of all individuals, not merely the selected one, are updated using Eq.(11). The above process continues until the end of a trial. The new Q-values are adopted as fitness values. With this assignment of fitness values, a new generation begins after a single trial and new populations are created by the following operations.

- *Selection.* In order to select the individuals for crossover, tournament selection is performed. In the tournament selection, two individuals in the population are selected at random, and their fitness values are compared. The individual with the highest fitness value is selected as one parent. The other parent is also selected in the same way.

- *Crossover.* The crossover probability, P_c, decides whether the two selected parents will be crossovered or reproduced directly to the next generation. A single point crossover is adopted. After selection and crossover operations, the individuals with poor performance will be replaced by the newly produced offspring.

- *Mutation.* Since real-value encoding scheme is used, a high mutation rate $P_m = 0.1$ is used. When mutation occurs, a new gene is randomly generated and replaces the original one.

IV. SIMULATIONS

In this example, CQGAF is applied to the cart-pole balancing problem. There are four state variables in the system: θ, the angle of the pole from an upright position (in degrees); $\dot{\theta}$, the angular velocity of the pole (in degrees/second); x, the horizontal position of the center of the cart (in meters); and $\dot{x}$, the velocity of the cart (in m/s). The only control action is u. The system fails either of the constraint $-12^0 \leq \theta \leq 12^0$ or $-2.4m \leq x \leq 2.4m$ is violated. The model of the system for our computer simulation is

$$\ddot{\theta} = \frac{mg \sin \theta_t - \cos \theta_t \left[u + m_p l \dot{\theta}_t^2 \sin \theta_t \right]}{\left(\frac{4}{3} \right) ml - m_p l \cos^2 \theta_t} \quad (13)$$

$$\ddot{x} = \frac{u + m_p l \left[\dot{\theta}_t^2 \sin \theta_t - \ddot{\theta}_t \cos \theta_t \right]}{m} \quad (14)$$

where $l = 0.5$ m, $m = 1.1$ kg, $m_p = 0.1$ kg, $g = 9.8$ m/s^2, and sampling interval = 0.02 (s). The goal of this control problem is to determine a sequence of forces that are applied to the cart to balance the pole upright. A control strategy is deemed successful if it can balance a pole for 120000 time steps. The control force values are allowed to be in the range [-10,10]. In designing the fuzzy controller, the four states ($\theta, \dot{\theta}, x, \dot{x}$) are fed as the controller input, and the controller output is u. The firing strength threshold $\Phi_t(X)$ is set as 0.0005. In GA, the population size N is set as 20. Initially, there are no genes in each chromosome, they are generated concurrently with the generation of a new fuzzy rule. The value of each gene is a real number randomly generated from [-10,10]. The crossover probability is $P_c = 0.5$. In ϵ-greedy selection, the parameter ϵ is set as 0.3. The parameters for Q-learning are set as $\alpha = 0.01$, $\lambda = 0.9$ and $\gamma = 0.9$. For each control trial, the initial values of ($\theta, \dot{\theta}, x, \dot{x}$) are all equal to zero. Here, the fuzzy controller is designed under the environment only with the binary reinforcement signals. That is, reward $r(t) = -1$ is received if control fails, otherwise $r(t) = 0$ is received. In this example, 50 runs are simulated, and a run ends when a successful controller is found or a failure run occurs. A failure run is said to occur if no successful fuzzy controller is found after 5,000 trials. The number of pole-balance trials is measured for each run. The average number of trials over these 50 runs is 113 and is shown in Table 1. The average number of rules is 17. One of these successful results is shown in Fig. 3. The generated rule number in this result is 6, and the numbers of fuzzy sets on $\theta, \dot{\theta}, x,$ and $\dot{x}$ are 6, 5, 4 and 5, respectively. The shapes of these fuzzy sets are shown in Fig. 4.

To verify the performance of CQGAF, other design approaches under the same environment with only binary reinforcement signals are simulated. The compared approaches include, traditional Q-learning, Fuzzy Interpolation-Based Q-Learning (FIBQL) [9], and Fuzzy Q-learning (FQL). The simulation results of these compared approaches are shown in Table 1 and interpretation of each compared approach is described below. In Q-learning, the input space on the four input variables ($x, \dot{x}, \theta, \dot{\theta}$) is quantized into $3 \times 3 \times 6 \times 3 = 162$ boxes. There are two candidate forces 10 and -10N for each box. In FIBQL, a fuzzy inference system is introduced to calculate Q-function that calculates state/action pairs, and the Q-function is updated by the use of gradient descent. In the fuzzy inference system, the number of fuzzy sets on ($x, \dot{x}, \theta, \dot{\theta}$) are 5, 3, 5, and 3, respectively. Grid type partition is adopted, so there are $5 \times 3 \times 5 \times 3 = 225$ rules in total. In FQL, the precondition part of the fuzzy system is partitioned as that FIBQL. For each rule, there are 20 candidate consequent values (actions), which are randomly generated from the region [-10,10] N.

From the simulation results in Table 1, we see that CQGAF achieves the best performance among all the aforementioned methods.

V. CONCLUSION

Reinforcement fuzzy network design by CQGAF is proposed in the paper. In CQGAF, no prepartition of the precondition part is required. Besides, the number of generated fuzzy rules is small compared to the general grid type partition. As soon as the precondition part is constructed, the consequent part is then learned by Q-value based genetic reinforcement learning. In this learning, with the assistance of Q-values we have extended GA to design fuzzy systems under reinforcement learning environments where only weak reinforcement signals are available. This lowers the quality and quantity of the required teaching signals. The results from the simulations have verified the efficiency and effectiveness of the proposed CQGAF.

ACKNOWLEDGMENT

This work was supported by the National Science Council, Taiwan, R.O.C. under Grant NSC-90-2213-E-005-033.

REFERENCES

[1] R. S. Sutton, "Learning to predict by the methods of temporal differences," *Machine Learning,* vol. 3, no. 1, pp. 9-44, 1988.
[2] R. S. Sutton and A. G. Barto, Reinforcement Learning, The MIT Press, 1998.
[3] A. G. Barto, R. S. Sutton and C. W. Anderson, "Neuron like adaptive elements that can solve difficult learning control problems," *IEEE Trans. Systems, Man and Cyber.,* vol. 13, no. 5, pp. 834-846, 1983.
[4] C. W. Anderson, "Learning to control an inverted pendulum using neural networks," *IEEE Control Systems Magazine,*, Vol. 9, pp. 31-37, 1989.
[5] H. R. Berenji and P. Khedkar, "Learning and tuning fuzzy logic controller through reinforcement," *IEEE Trans. Neural Networks,* vol.3, pp. 724-740, May, 1992.
[6] C. J. Wakins and P. Dayan, "Technical note: Q-learning," *Machine Learning,* vol. 8, pp. 279-292, 1992.
[7] P. Y. Glorennec, "Fuzzy Q-learning and dynamic fuzzy Q-learning," *Proc. of IEEE Int. Conf. on Fuzzy Systems,* Orlando, FL, vol. 1, pp. 474-479, 1994.
[8] P. Y. Glorennec and L. Jouffe, "Fuzzy Q-learning," *Proc. Of IEEE Int. Conf. On Fuzzy Systems,* pp. 659-662, 1997.
[9] T. Horiuchi, A. Fujino, O. Katai, and T. Sawaragi, "Fuzzy interporation-based Q-learning with continuous states and actions," *Proc. of IEEE Int. Conf. on Fuzzy Systems,* pp. 594-600, 1996.
[10] C.F. Juang and C.T. Lin, "An on-line self-constructing neural fuzzy inference network and its applications," *IEEE Trans. Fuzzy Systems,* Vol.6, pp. 12-32, Feb. 1998.
[11] C. K. Chiang, H. Y. Chung, and J. J. Lin, "A self-learning fuzzy logic controller using genetic algorithms with reinforcements," *IEEE Trans. Fuzzy Systems,* vol. 5, no. 3, pp. 460-467, 1997.
[12] C. T. Lin and C. P. Jou, "Controlling Chaos by GA-based reinforcement learning neural network," *IEEE Trans. Neural Networks,* vol. 10, no. 4, pp. 846-859, July, 1999.

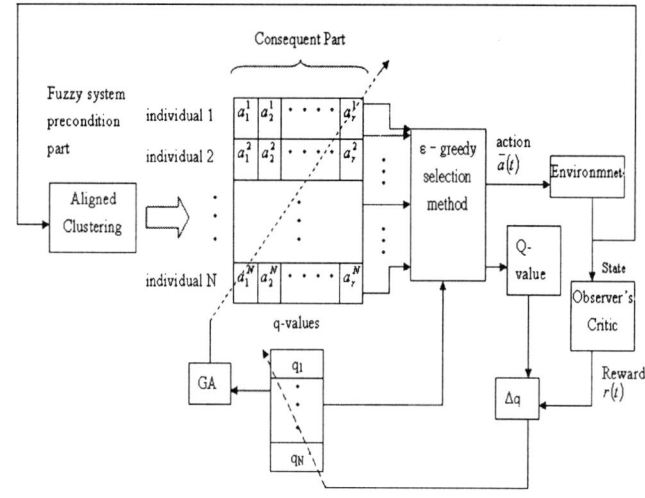

Fig. 1. Architecture of CQGAF.

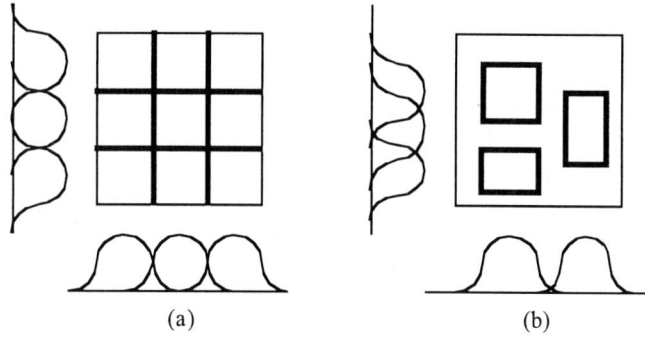

Fig.2 (a) Grid type partition. (b) Aligned clustering partition. Each grid in both figures represents a fuzzy rule.

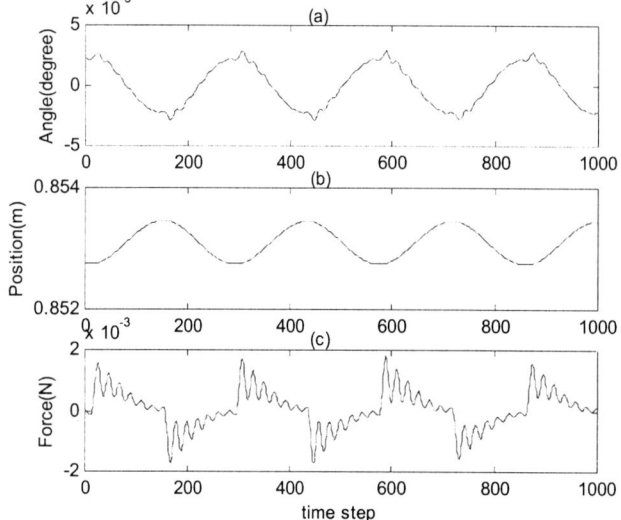

Fig. 3. Control results of the cart and pole balancing system by CQGAF. (a)Angle of the pole. (b) Position of the cart. (c) The control force.

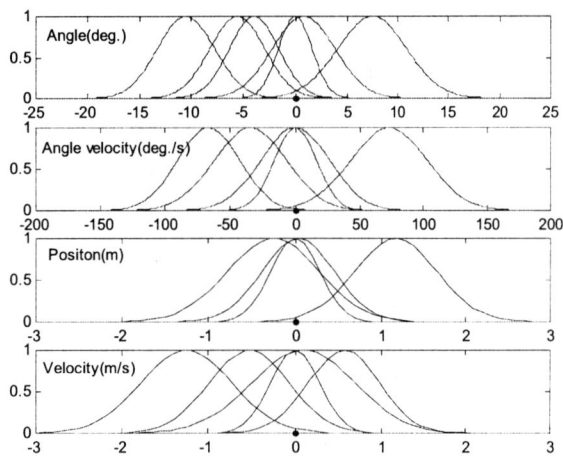

Fig. 4. The shapes of the fuzzy sets on states $\theta, \dot{\theta}, x,$ and $\dot{x}$.

Table 1. The Number Of Trials Required To Find A Successful Controller. The Numbers Are Computed Over 50 Runs For Each Method.

Methods	QL	FIBQL	FQL	CQGAF
Input space partition	162 boxes	225 rules	225 rules	Ave = 17 rules
Trials	1510	912	199	113

Approximate dynamic programming based optimal neurocontrol synthesis of a chemical reactor process using proper orthogonal decomposition

Radhakant Padhi[1] and S. N. Balakrishnan[2]
Department of Mechanical and Aerospace Engineering, and Engineering Mechanics
University of Missouri-Rolla, MO, 65409, USA

Abstract — The concept of approximate dynamic programming and adaptive critic neural network based optimal controller is extended in this study to include systems governed by partial differential equations. An optimal controller is synthesized for a dispersion type tubular chemical reactor, which is governed by two coupled nonlinear partial differential equations. It consists of three steps: First, empirical basis functions are designed using the 'Proper Orthogonal Decomposition' technique and a *low-order* lumped parameter system to represent the infinite-dimensional system is obtained by carrying out a Galerkin projection. Second, approximate dynamic programming technique is applied in a discrete time framework, followed by the use of a dual neural network structure called *adaptive critics*, to obtain optimal neurocontrollers for this system. In this structure, one set of neural networks captures the relationship between the state variables and the control, whereas the other set captures the relationship between the state and the costate variables. Third, the lumped parameter control is then mapped back to the spatial dimension using the same basis functions to result in a feedback control. Numerical results are presented that illustrate the potential of this approach. It should be noted that the procedure presented in this study can be used in synthesizing optimal controllers for a fairly general class of nonlinear distributed parameter systems.

I. INTRODUCTION

Process control problems are mostly governed by partial differential equations (PDEs) and are infinite-dimensional in nature. They are also called Distributed Parameter Systems (DPS). The DPS appear naturally in various application areas such as chemical processes, thermal processes, vibrating structures, fluid flow systems etc. They inherently have an infinite number of system modes. Since it is impossible to deal with all the modes, some sort of approximation technique is usually applied for the analysis and synthesis procedures related to DPS.

A popular DPS analysis and synthesis technique is to use orthogonal basis functions in a Galerkin procedure to first create an approximate finite-dimensional system of Ordinary Differential Equations (ODEs). This lumped parameter model model is then used for control design using various tools of lumped parameter control design. If arbitrary basis functions (*e.g.* Fourier and Chebyshev polynomials) are used in the Galerkin procedure, they can result in a high-dimensional ODE system. A better and powerful basis function design is obtained when the Proper Orthogonal Decomposition (POD) technique is used with a Galerkin approximation. In the POD technique, a set of problem-oriented basis functions is first obtained by generating a set of "snap-shot solutions" through simulations or from the actual process. Using these orthogonal basis functions in a Galerkin procedure, a low-dimensional ODE system can be developed. This technique has widely been used in recent years (*e.g.* [4, 7]).

The issue of optimal control synthesis should be addressed next. It is well known that the dynamic programming formulation offers the most comprehensive solution to nonlinear optimal control; however, a huge amount of computational and storage requirements are needed to solve the associated Hamilton-Jacobi-Bellman (HJB) equation [2], which is also known as the Bellman equation. Werbos [10] proposed a means to get around this numerical complexity by using 'approximate dynamic programming' (ADP) formulations. His methods approximate the original problem with a discrete formulation. The solution to the ADP formulation is obtained through the two-neural network adaptive critic approach. In one version of the adaptive critic approach called the dual heuristic programming (DHP) one network called the action network represents the mapping between the state variables of a dynamic system and control and the second network, called the critic, outputs the costates with the state variables as its inputs. This ADP process, through the nonlinear function approximation capabilities of neural networks, overcomes the computational complexity that plagued the dynamic programming formulation of optimal control problems. More important, this solution can be implemented on-line, since the control computation requires a few multiplications of the network weights which are trained off-line. This technique was used in [1] to solve an aircraft control problem in a domain of interest.

In this paper, this techniques of POD and approximate dynamic programming are combined, which is then applied to a more challenging *nonlinear* chemical reactor process. This dispersion type tubular chemical reactor control problem has been discussed in [3]. The authors have used Green's function to calculate optimal control. Their method for calculating the costate variables that arise in an optimal control formulation is complicated. Even though the authors have found a Greens function for the particular problem, finding an appropriate Green's function and calculating its coefficients is not an easy task in general. More important, their solution is for specific initial condition (initial state profiles) only. In other words, it is an open loop control which will severely degrade the process performance if the initial profile were different. In contrast to this, the approach presented in this paper is applicable to a large number of initial conditions (or profiles). Once the neural networks are trained to capture the relationship between state and control within a domain of interest (which is done off-line) they can be used to compute the control for "any" value of the state variables within that domain. Moreover since using a set of networks is not

---
[1] Postdoctoral Fellow
[2] Professor (Contact Person), Email: bala@umr.edu, Tel.: 1(573) 341-4675, Fax: 1(573)341-4607.

computationally intensive it can be implemented on-line. In control terminology this is a feedback solution; a feedback control is desirable because of its beneficial properties like robustness with respect to noise suppression and modeling uncertainties.

We wish to point out that we have solved the same chemical reactor optimal control problem using a different approach earlier [8]. In that approach a controller was used at every step in a finite difference scheme, which was used to discretize the spatial variable. Even though we obtained satisfactory results, there are some implementation issues. Note that one has to take a large number of node points for good finite difference approximations. However, because for each node point critic and action networks were proposed, the number of networks grows with the number of grid points and this would lead to serious problem in training of the networks. As a consequence one has to remain contented with a "coarse grid approximation". In contrast, the current approach is grid independent in the sense that lumped parameter state vector does not depend on the number of grid points assumed for the integral evaluations. Second, in the earlier technique the state (and control) values at some point in space other than the node point locations are unknown. If one wants to get value for such a location, interpolation techniques are necessary. The prediction may not be good if the grid approximation is coarse. In contrast, in the proposed methodology by definition the basis functions are supposed to be continuous functions. So values at any point in the space can theoretically be computed without resorting to any interpolation technique. This issue is of significantly less concern in our new approach, since one can have a fine-grid approximation to begin with and therefore, will result in much smaller interpolation errors.

II. SYSTEM MODEL AND OBJECTIVE

Dynamics of the chemical reactor problem considered in this research is described by the following set of partial differential equations [3]:

$$\frac{\partial v_1}{\partial t} = \frac{1}{Pe_1}\left(\frac{\partial^2 v_1}{\partial y^2}\right) - \left(\frac{\partial v_1}{\partial y}\right) + N(v_2)(1 - v_1) \quad (1a)$$

$$\frac{\partial v_2}{\partial t} = \frac{1}{Pe_2}\left(\frac{\partial^2 v_2}{\partial y^2}\right) - \left(\frac{\partial v_2}{\partial y}\right) + B N(v_2)(1 - v_1) - h(v_2 - u) \quad (1b)$$

The boundary conditions are given by

$$\left[\frac{\partial v_1}{\partial y} = Pe_1 v_1\right]_{y=0}, \left[\frac{\partial v_2}{\partial y} = Pe_2 v_2\right]_{y=0}, \left.\frac{\partial v_1}{\partial y}\right|_{y=L} = 0, \left.\frac{\partial v_2}{\partial y}\right|_{y=L} = 0 \quad (2)$$

where, v_1, v_2 are the state variables that represent concentration and temperature respectively. The control variable u represents the cooling water temperature. The terms Pe_1, Pe_2 are the *Peclet* numbers of mass and energy flows respectively. $N(v_2) = D_a \exp[v_2/(1+v_2/\varepsilon)]$, where D_a is the *Damkohler* number, ε is the activation energy, B and h are the parameters related to heat of reaction and heat transfer respectively. $y \in [0, L]$ and $t \in [t_0, t_f]$, where t_0 and t_f are initial and final times respectively. Values of different parameters describing the process are: $Pe_1 = 1$, $Pe_2 = 1$, $D_a = 1$, $\varepsilon = 20$, $B = 2$, $h = 1$, $m = 2$, $t_0 = 0$ and $L = 1$.

For convenience, we define v_{1ref} and v_{2ref} as the steady state values of v_1 and v_2 respectively while the $h(v_2 - u)$ term is omitted from the v_2 dynamics; this implies that the reactor operates with perfect insulation. Consequently, we observe that $u_{ref} = v_{2ref}$. For computing v_{1ref} and v_{2ref}, it was assumed that $\partial v_1/\partial t = \partial v_2/\partial t = 0$ (steady-state condition), in addition to $h(v_2 - u) = 0$. Then we use these conditions in (1-2) and solved the resulting two point boundary value problem (in spatial dimension) for v_{1ref} and v_{2ref}.

Defining $x_1 \triangleq (v_1 - v_{1ref})$, $x_2 \triangleq (v_2 - v_{2ref})$, we rewrite (1) as

$$\frac{\partial x_1}{\partial t} = \frac{1}{Pe_1}\left(\frac{\partial^2 x_1}{\partial y^2}\right) - \left(\frac{\partial x_1}{\partial y}\right) + f(x_1, x_2) \quad (3a)$$

$$\frac{\partial x_2}{\partial t} = \frac{1}{Pe_2}\left(\frac{\partial^2 x_2}{\partial y^2}\right) - \left(\frac{\partial x_2}{\partial y}\right) + B f(x_1, x_2) - h v \quad (3b)$$

where

$$f(x_1, x_2) \equiv N(v_{2ref} + x_2)(1 - v_{1ref} - x_1) - N(v_{2ref})(1 - v_{1ref}) \quad (3c)$$

Here $v \equiv (u - x_2)$ is the new auxiliary control variable. The objective is to find the optimal control $u(t, y)$ which ensures $\{x_1, x_2\} \to \{0, 0\}$ (*i.e.* $\{v_1, v_2\} \to \{v_{1ref}, v_{2ref}\}$) as $t \to \infty$. This objective can be met by minimizing the quadratic cost function:

$$J = \frac{1}{2} \int_0^\infty \int_0^L \left[q_1 x_1^2(t, y) + q_2 x_2^2(t, y) + r u^2(t, y) \right] dy\, dt \quad (4)$$

where $q_1, q_2 \geq 0$ and $r > 0$ are weights to be appropriately fixed by the control designer. We have used $q_1 = 5000$, $q_2 = 1$ and $r = 1$. The relatively high value of q_1 was selected mainly because our goal was to drive v_1 towards v_{1ref} as quickly as possible.

III. FINITE-DIMENSIONAL APPROXIMATION

A. Proper Orthogonal Decomposition: Design of Basis Functions

Let $\{U_i(y): 1 \leq i \leq N, 0 \leq y \leq L\}$ be a set of N snapshot solutions of the system. The goal of the POD technique is to design a set of basis functions which has the largest mean square projection on the snapshots. In other words, we try to find all such possible basis functions Φ, each of which provides a local maximum for the following figure of merit:

$$I = \frac{1}{N}\sum_{i=1}^N \left|\langle U_i, \Phi\rangle\right|^2 / \langle \Phi, \Phi\rangle = \frac{1}{N}\left[\sum_{i=1}^N \left|\int_0^L U_i \Phi\, dy\right|^2 / \int_0^L \Phi \Phi\, dy\right] \quad (5)$$

The solution approach is to seek a function $\Phi = \sum_{i=1}^N w_i U_i$, where the coefficients w_i are to be determined such that Φ maximizes I in (5). In the process we obtain N orthonormal basis functions $\Phi_i, i = 1,\ldots,N$. Depending on the energy content, this eigen spectrum is truncated to retain only $\tilde{N} \leq N$ eigen functions that will be used in the Galerkin projection. An interested reader can see [7] for detail discussions on this basis function design procedure. It may be noted, however, that the POD technique is a generalization of a familiar method known as Principal Component Analysis (PCA) [6], to continuous square integrable functions. The PCA technique is widely used as a tool in pattern recognition, image processing *etc.*

For the process control problem, the basis functions for x_1 and x_2 were designed independently. In order to determine the proper order of the system, the ratios $\sum_{j=1}^{\tilde{N}_1} \lambda_{1_j} / \sum_{j=1}^{N} \lambda_{1_j}$ and $\sum_{j=1}^{\tilde{N}_2} \lambda_{2_j} / \sum_{j=1}^{N} \lambda_{2_j}$ were plotted for different values of $\tilde{N}_1, \tilde{N}_2$ and it was observed that 99% of the ratio was accounted for by the first three eigenvalues for both the state variables. Hence, we fixed $\tilde{N}_1 = \tilde{N}_2 = 3$ and assumed that the six basis functions captured the essential characteristics contained in the snap shots with sufficient accuracy. The basis functions for state variables x_1 and x_2 in the chemical reactor control problem are shown in Figure 1.

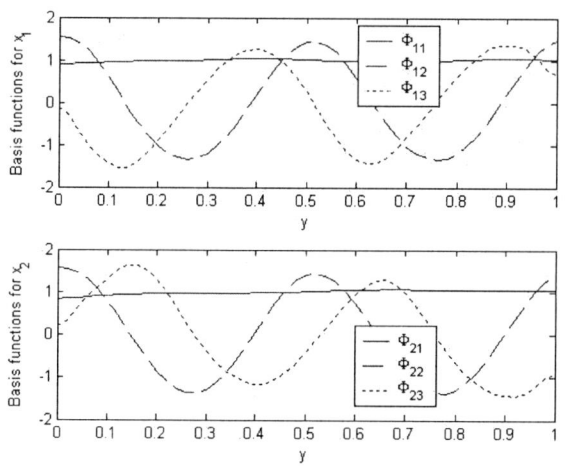

Figure 1: POD Basis functions for state variables

B. Finite-dimensional Approximation: Galerkin Projection

The state variables $x_1(t, y)$, $x_2(t, y)$ and auxiliary control variable $v(t, y)$ can be written in terms of the basis functions as

$$x_1(t, y) = \sum_{j=1}^{\tilde{N}_1} \hat{x}_{1_j}(t) \Phi_{1_j}(y), \quad x_2(t, y) = \sum_{j=1}^{\tilde{N}_2} \hat{x}_{2_j}(t) \Phi_{2_j}(y) \quad (6a)$$

$$v(t, y) = \sum_{j=1}^{\tilde{N}_1} \hat{v}_{1_j}(t) \Phi_{1_j}(y) + \sum_{j=1}^{\tilde{N}_2} \hat{v}_{2_j}(t) \Phi_{2_j}(y) \quad (6b)$$

Note that the basis functions for the state variables as well as the control are the same. This is because it is assumed in this study that the control spans a subset of the state variables as it is in a feedback form and therefore, the basis functions to represent the states are adequate to describe the control variable. Note that no mean state profiles were assumed in the expansion since our formulation is based on the state deviations.

For convenience, we define $\hat{X}_1 \triangleq [\hat{x}_1, \cdots, \hat{x}_{\tilde{N}_1}]^T$, $\hat{X}_2 \triangleq [\hat{x}_2, \cdots, \hat{x}_{\tilde{N}_2}]^T$, $\hat{V}_1 \triangleq [\hat{v}_1, \cdots, \hat{v}_{\tilde{N}_1}]^T$ and $\hat{V}_2 \triangleq [\hat{v}_2, \cdots, \hat{v}_{\tilde{N}_2}]^T$. By substituting (6a,b) in (3a), and taking the inner product with the basis function $\Phi_{1_i}, i = 1, \ldots, \tilde{N}$ and carrying out some algebra we obtain:

$$\dot{\hat{X}}_1 = \hat{A}_1 \hat{X}_1 + \hat{F}_1(\hat{X}_1, \hat{X}_2) \quad (7a)$$

where

$$\hat{A}_{1_{ij}} \triangleq -\left[\Phi_{1_i}(0) \Phi_{1_j}(0) + \frac{1}{Pe_1} \int_0^L \Phi'_{1_i} \Phi'_{1_j} dy + \int_0^L \Phi_{1_i} \Phi'_{1_j} dy \right] \quad (7b)$$

$$\hat{F}_{1_i} \triangleq \int_0^L f(x_1, x_2) \Phi_{1_i} dy$$

Similarly, by substituting (6) in (3b), and taking the inner product with the basis function $\Phi_{2_i}, i = 1, \ldots, \tilde{N}$ and carrying out some algebra we obtain:

$$\dot{\hat{X}}_2 = \hat{A}_2 \hat{X}_2 + \hat{F}_2(\hat{X}_1, \hat{X}_2) + \hat{B}_1 \hat{V}_1 + \hat{B}_2 \hat{V}_2 \quad (8a)$$

where

$$\hat{A}_{2_{ij}} \triangleq -\left[\Phi_{2_i}(0) \Phi_{2_j}(0) + \frac{1}{Pe_2} \int_0^L \Phi'_{2_i} \Phi'_{2_j} dy + \int_0^L \Phi_{2_i} \Phi'_{2_j} dy \right] \quad (8b)$$

$$\hat{F}_{2_i} \triangleq B \int_0^L f(x_1, x_2) \Phi_{2_i} dy, \quad \hat{B}_{1_{ij}} \triangleq h \int_0^L \Phi_{2_i} \Phi_{1_j}, \quad \hat{B}_2 \triangleq h I_{\tilde{N}_2}$$

It should be noted that the integrals in (7) and (8) can be computed numerically. Hence this approach is applicable for general nonlinear systems without having to first evaluate the integrals symbolically and then computing them.

By defining $\hat{X} \triangleq [\hat{X}_1^T \ \hat{X}_2^T]^T$ and $\hat{V} \triangleq [\hat{V}_1^T \ \hat{V}_2^T]^T$, we can write

$$\dot{\hat{X}} = \hat{A} \hat{X} + \hat{F}(\hat{X}) + \hat{B} \hat{V} \quad (9a)$$

where $\hat{A} \triangleq \begin{bmatrix} \hat{A}_1 & 0 \\ 0 & \hat{A}_2 \end{bmatrix}$, $\hat{B} \triangleq \begin{bmatrix} 0 & 0 \\ \hat{B}_1 & \hat{B}_2 \end{bmatrix}$ (9b)

Similarly, after carrying out some algebra we can write:

$$J = \frac{1}{2} \int_0^{t_f \to \infty} \left(\hat{X}^T \hat{Q} \hat{X} + \hat{V}^T \hat{R} \hat{V} \right) dt \quad (10a)$$

where

$$\hat{Q} \triangleq \begin{bmatrix} \hat{Q}_1 & 0 \\ 0 & \hat{Q}_2 \end{bmatrix}, \quad \hat{R} \triangleq \begin{bmatrix} \hat{R}_{11} & \hat{R}_{12} \\ \hat{R}_{21} & \hat{R}_{22} \end{bmatrix}$$

$$\hat{Q}_1 \triangleq q_1 I_{\tilde{N}_1}, \quad \hat{Q}_2 \triangleq q_2 I_{\tilde{N}_2}, \quad \hat{R}_{11} \triangleq r I_{\tilde{N}_1}, \quad \hat{R}_{22} \triangleq r I_{\tilde{N}_2} \quad (10b)$$

$$\hat{R}_{12_{ij}} \triangleq r \int_0^L \Phi_{1_i} \Phi_{2_j} dy, \quad \hat{R}_{21_{ij}} \triangleq r \int_0^L \Phi_{2_i} \Phi_{1_j} dy$$

Equations (9-10) define an analogous optimal control problem in the reduced-order lumped parameter framework. In other words, we now have a low order finite-dimensional ODE system (9) with a cost function expressed in terms of finite-dimensional state variables and control (10).

C. Domain of Interest

In the controller synthesis presented later in Section V, we choose a set of states for which the networks are to be trained. We define this set as *domain of interest*. This set has to be defined in such a way that the elements in it approximately cover the domain of states that are supposed to be encountered in actual operation of the system. For the reactor problem, we define the domain of interest as

$$S_I \equiv \left\{ \begin{Bmatrix} x_1(y) \\ x_2(y) \end{Bmatrix} : \begin{Bmatrix} \|x_1(y)\| \leq \|v_{1_{ref}}\| \\ \|x_2(y)\| \leq \|v_{2_{ref}}\| \end{Bmatrix}, \begin{Bmatrix} \|x_1'(y)\| \leq 10\|v_{1_{ref}}'\| \\ \|x_2'(y)\| \leq 10\|v_{2_{ref}}'\| \end{Bmatrix}, \begin{Bmatrix} \|x_1''(y)\| \leq 100\|v_{1_{ref}}''\| \\ \|x_2''(y)\| \leq 100\|v_{2_{ref}}''\| \end{Bmatrix} \right\} \quad (11)$$

where $x' \equiv \partial x / \partial y$, $x'' \equiv \partial^2 x / \partial y^2$ etc. We use L_2 norms. The conditions on $x_1(y)$ and $x_2(y)$ lead to "smooth" profiles. We expect that in practice the profiles representing the initial conditions will remain within S_I.

D. Generation of Initial State Profiles and Snap Shot Solutions

To generate a possible initial condition from S, first observe that Fourier series is a universal function approximator for piece-wise continuous functions and it always leads to smooth function generation. Therefore, we write

$$x_i(0, y) = a_{i_0} + \sum_{n=1}^{N} \left[a_{i_n} Cos\left(\frac{2n\pi y}{L}\right) + b_{i_n} Sin\left(\frac{2n\pi y}{L}\right) \right] \quad (12)$$

where N is chosen as a sufficiently large number (in our case, $N = 50$) and $i = 1, 2$ represent the two states. A straightforward computation then leads to

$$\|x_i(0, y)\|^2 = 2L a_{i_0}^2 + \sum_{n=1}^{N} \left(a_{i_n}^2 + b_{i_n}^2\right) L$$

$$\|x_i'(0, y)\|^2 = \sum_{n=1}^{N} \left(\frac{2n\pi}{L}\right)^2 \left(a_{i_n}^2 + b_{i_n}^2\right) L \quad (13)$$

$$\|x_i''(0, y)\|^2 = \sum_{n=1}^{N} \left(\frac{2n\pi}{L}\right)^4 \left(a_{i_n}^2 + b_{i_n}^2\right) L$$

We computed random values for the coefficients so that the conditions in (11) are satisfied. These are then used in (12) to compute state profiles which may represent possible initial conditions. Further details of this procedure are omitted for brevity. After generating an initial condition, the state solutions at random instants of time were selected to serve as snap shot solutions.

IV. APPROXIMATE DYNAMMIC PROGRAMMING

In this section, the general discussion on the optimal control of the distributed parameter systems is presented in an ADP framework.

A. Problem Description and Optimality Conditions

We consider a scalar cost function, to be minimized, of the form:

$$J = \sum_{k=1}^{N-1} \Psi_k\left(\hat{X}_k, \hat{V}_k\right) \quad (14)$$

where $\hat{X}_k$ and $\hat{V}_k$ represent the $n \times 1$ state vector and $m \times 1$ control vector respectively at time step k. N represents the number of discrete time steps. Note that when N is large, (14) represents the cost function for an infinite horizon problem. We denote the *cost function from time step k* as

$$J_k = \sum_{\tilde{k}=k}^{N-1} \Psi_{\tilde{k}}\left(\hat{X}_{\tilde{k}}, \hat{V}_{\tilde{k}}\right) \quad (15)$$

We can rewrite the cost from k in terms of the cost from ($k+1$), J_{k+1} and Ψ_k the cost to go from k to ($k+1$) (called the utility function) as $J_k = \Psi_k + J_{k+1}$. We define the costate vector $\lambda_k \equiv \partial J_k / \partial \hat{X}_k$. The necessary condition for optimality is

$$\frac{\partial J_k}{\partial \hat{V}_k} = 0 \quad (16)$$

After some algebra, we get the optimal control equation as

$$\left(\frac{\partial \Psi_k}{\partial \hat{V}_k}\right) + \left(\frac{\partial \hat{X}_{k+1}}{\partial \hat{V}_k}\right)^T \lambda_{k+1} = 0 \quad (17)$$

Similarly, after some algebra we get the costate equation on optimal path as

$$\lambda_k = \left(\frac{\partial \Psi_k}{\partial \hat{X}_k}\right) + \left(\frac{\partial \hat{X}_{k+1}}{\partial \hat{X}_k}\right)^T \lambda_{k+1} \quad (18)$$

B. Optimality Equations for Chemical Reactor Problem

We can write the state equation in a discrete form as

$$\hat{X}_{k+1} = F\left(\hat{X}_k, \hat{V}_k\right) \quad (19)$$

We notice that a discrete equivalent of the cost function weights (10a) can be written as $Q_D \equiv Q \Delta t$ and $R_D \equiv R \Delta t$. So we have

$$\Psi_k = \hat{X}_k^T Q_D \hat{X}_k + \hat{V}_k^T R_D \hat{V}_k \quad (20)$$

Using (19) and (20) in equations (17) and (18), we can write the optimal control and costate propagation equations as:

$$\hat{V}_k = -\hat{R}^{-1} \hat{B}^T \lambda_{k+1} \quad (21)$$

$$\lambda_k = G\left(\hat{X}_k, \hat{V}_k, \lambda_{k+1}\right) \quad (22)$$

We point out that explicit forms of the functions F and G depend on the type of discretization procedure. A simple way is to introduce *Euler* integration approximation [5] with a small step size in time Δt.

V. DHP WITH ADAPTIVE CRITICS

A. Neural Network Synthesis

Assuming the action networks to be optimal for t_k and critic network to be optimal for t_{k+1}, we synthesize the *critic networks* for t_k as follows (Figure 2).

1. Generate a set of $\hat{X}_k$ values from the domain of interest. For each $\hat{X}_k$, follow the steps below.
   a. Get $\hat{V}_k$ from the action networks
   b. Get $\hat{X}_{k+1}$ from the *state equation* (19)
   c. Input $\hat{X}_{k+1}$ to the trained set of critic network to get λ_{k+1}
   d. Calculate target critic λ_k^* from *costate equation* (22)
2. Train the set of critic networks with input $\hat{X}_k$ and output λ_k^* for the critic network, using all the input-output data together.

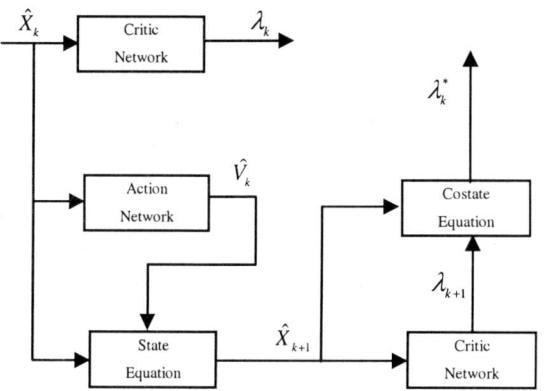

Figure 2: Schematic of critic network synthesis

Similarly assuming the critic network to be optimal for t_k, we synthesize the *action networks* for t_k as follows (Figure 3).

1. Generate a set of $\hat{X}_k$ values from the domain of interest. For each $\hat{X}_k$, follow the steps below.
   a. Get $\hat{V}_k$ from the action networks
   b. Get $\hat{X}_{k+1}$ from the *state equation* (19)
   c. Input $\hat{X}_{k+1}$ to the trained set of critic network to get λ_{k+1}
   d. Get the target optimal control $\hat{V}_k^*$ from (21)
2. Train the set of action networks with input $\hat{X}_k$ and output $\hat{V}_k^*$, using all the input-output data together.

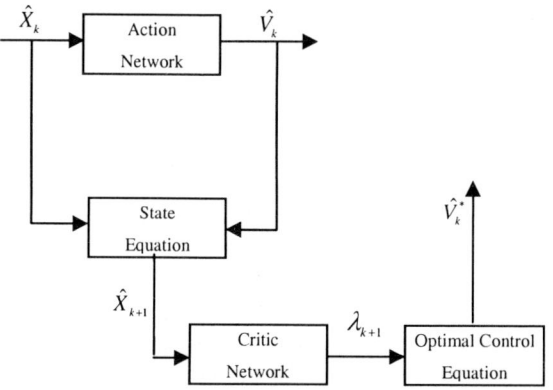

Figure 3: Schematic of action network synthesis

Once the process of action synthesis is over, we revert to the critic synthesis again and *vice-versa*. The alternate critic and action network training process is continued till no noticeable change in the output is observed in the outputs of successive training steps. This mutual convergence indicates that the action networks represent the optimal relationship between the state and control. For details on training process, the reader is referred to [1]. For more on the topic of adaptive critic (DHP) design process, the reader is referred to [10].

B. Neural Network Structures

In this study, we used six multi-layer feed forward networks of the form $\pi_{6,8,1}$ for the critics and six similar networks for the controller. Here, $\pi_{6,8,1}$ denotes a neural network with 6 neurons in the input layer to account for the six states in the reduced order system, 8 neurons in the hidden layers and 1 neuron in the output layer. Choosing separate networks for each costate and control was needed for faster convergence in this difficult nonlinear problem. We used tangent sigmoid functions for all the hidden layers and linear function for the output layer. No optimization was carried out for the 'best' neural architecture. Numerical results in Section V demonstrate that our network structures were appropriate.

C. Initialization of Neural Networks

Initialization of the network weights plays an important role in the convergence process. In order to have appropriate initial weights, we linearized (9) about $\hat{X}=0, \hat{V}=0$. We then discretized it and used standard *Linear Quadratic Regulator (LQR)* theory [2] to obtain the control and costate solutions and train the networks.

VI. NUMERICAL RESULTS

Histories of state variables and control from various simulations are presented in Figures 4-6. It should be noted that $y=0$ and $y=1$ correspond to the boundary points. The system dynamics equations for the reactor (1-2) are given in terms of normalized variables, in which time is normalized with respect to the *residence time* (*i.e.* the time for which the fluid stays within the reactor). For this reason, we have simulated the system only up to $t_f = 1$.

We picked random initial profiles of conversion and temperature and let the neuro-controller (cooling water temperature) drive the system. The resulting state variables (conversion and temperature) are plotted in Figures 4-5. It is clear that the state variables are driven towards the final profiles. Moreover, as desired, they reach the desired steady-state profiles quickly (in about 50% of the residence time). The associated control (cooling water temperature) is shown in Figure 6, which indicates that the control values are not high and the control profile is fairly smooth across the spatial dimension, a desirable characteristic for implementation.

Even though we have presented only a representative case for state and control histories, similar results were observed from a very large number of initial profiles (it was observed in every case we simulated). This indicates that the action networks, with proper training, in fact imbed optimal control solutions for a very large number of initial conditions (state profiles).

Finally, we point out that more details on some of the derivations and procedures in this paper, along with additional references, will appear in the journal version of this paper [9].

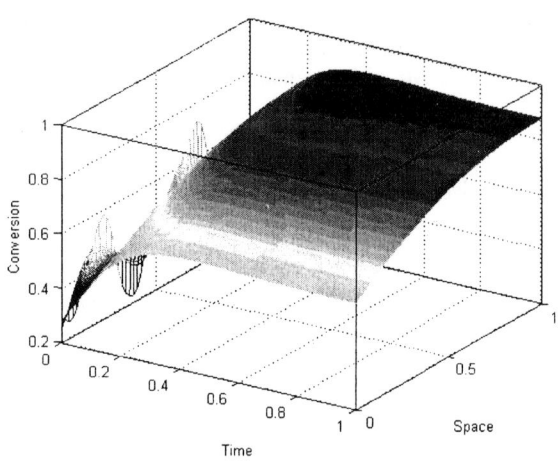

Figure 4: Development of conversion in the reactor from a random initial profile

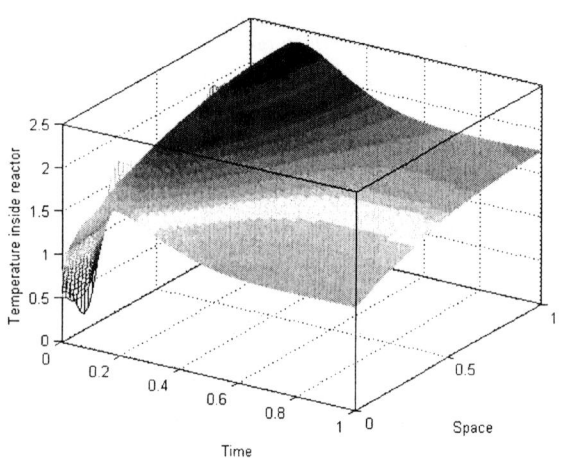

Figure 5: Temperature in the reactor for conversion as in Figure-4 from a random initial profile

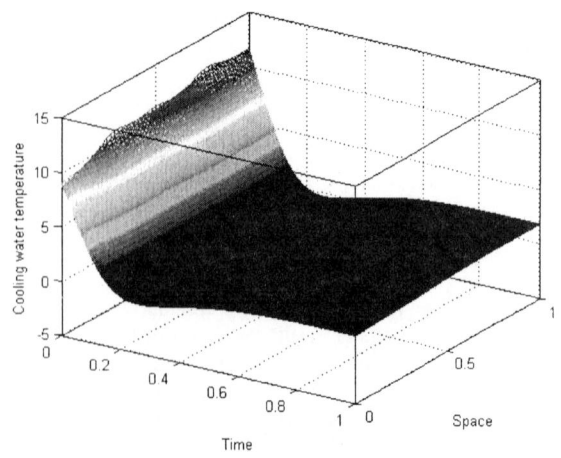

Figure 6: Cooling water temperature (control) for conversion in Figure 5 and temperature in Figure 6

VII. CONCLUSIONS

Combining the techniques of proper orthogonal decomposition and adaptive critic design, we have successfully synthesized an optimal controller for a nonlinear dispersion-type tubular reactor process. Simulation results are promising. The desired adiabatic steady state profiles are reached quickly (in about 50% of the resident time). This increases the conversion efficiency of the reactor. More important, the controller is able to drive a large number of initial state profiles in the domain of interest towards the desired profiles. For this reason the synthesized action neural network embeds the optimal control solution in a state feedback form, which is highly desired in practical implementation. The technique presented in this paper can also be viewed as a general computational tool for the optimal control of nonlinear distributed parameter systems. In other words, the procedure of synthesizing the networks remains the same. Only the relevant state, costate and optimal control equations change depending on the problem under consideration.

Acknowledgement:

This research was supported by NSF grants ECS 9976588 and ECS 0201076. The authors also express their gratitude to the anonymous reviewers, whose constructive criticisms lead to a substantial improvement of this paper.

REFERENCES

[1] Balakrishnan, S.N., & Biega, V. (1996). Adaptive-critic based neural networks for aircraft optimal control. *Journal of Guidance, Control and Dynamics, 19, 4,* 893-898.

[2] Bryson, A.E., & Ho, Y.C. (1975). Applied optimal control. *Taylor and Francis.*

[3] Choe, Y.S., & Chang, K.S. (1998). A new merging method of optimal control synthesis for distributed parameter systems. *Journal of Chemical Engineering of Japan, 31, 1,* 111-115.

[4] Christofides P.D. (2001). Nonlinear and robust control of partial differential equation systems: Methods and applications to transport-reaction processes, *Birkhauser.*

[5] Gupta, S.K. (1995). Numerical methods for engineers. *Wiley Eastern Ltd. and New Age International Ltd.*

[6] Haykin S. (1994). Neural networks, *Macmillan College Company.*

[7] Holmes, P., Lumley J.L., & Berkooz G. (1996). Turbulence, coherent structures, dynamical systems and symmetry, *Cambridge University Press.*

[8] Padhi, R., & Balakrishnan, S.N. (2001). A systematic synthesis of optimal process control with neural networks. *Proceedings of the American Control Conference, 1910-1915.*

[9] Padhi, R., & Balakrishnan, S.N., Proper orthogonal decomposition based optimal neurocontrol synthesis of a chemical reactor process using approximate dynamic programming, to appear in *Neural Networks.*

[10] Werbos, P. J. (1992). Approximate dynamic programming for real-time control and neural modeling. In White D.A., & Sofge D.A (Eds.), *Handbook of Intelligent Control, Multiscience Press.*

A Performance Comparison of TRACA - an Incremental On-line Learning Algorithm

Matthew W. Mitchell
School of Computer Science and Software Engineering
Monash University,
PO Box 197, Victoria, 3145,
Email: matt@csse.monash.edu.au

Abstract—TRACA (Temporal Reinforcement-learning and Classification Architecture) is a learning system intended for robot-navigation tasks. One problem in this area is input-generalisation. Input generalisation requires learning a small set of internal states which represent useful abstractions of the much larger set of actual states. As such, the input-generalisation problem is fundamentally similar to the classical problems of classification, concept learning and discrimination. The priorities when evaluating a system for on-line robot learning include a small number of trials, predictive accuracy and minimal parameter tuning. Other requirements are the ability to learn without predefined classes (i.e classes must be learned during training) and an efficient and adaptable representation.

This paper evaluates the performance of TRACA, a new learning algorithm, on a number of common classification tasks. The same set of parameters is used to obtain all TRACA's results, which are then compared to the results obtained by other well-known algorithms. On most tasks, TRACA's predictive accuracy is within a few percent of the best performing systems compared. Furthermore, TRACA's result is often achieved with less training experience. In a final experiment TRACA is trialled on a robot navigation task that requires discrimination of a number of discrete locations.

Keywords: Machine learning, generalisation, navigation, on-line learning

I. INTRODUCTION

TRACA is a new system designed for robot navigation tasks. Frequently, learning algorithms for such tasks assume an enumerative state representation (i.e a unique input for each possible observation in the environment) [5], [21], [20], [2]. However, it is impossible to represent the real-world using such an enumerative scheme, there are simply too many states. Consequently environmental inputs generated by sensor readings will include features (or attributes) that are irrelevant for a particular task. To cope with such a large state space learning agents must generalise - a number of states must be treated as the same or similar [15], [4], [18]. For the generalisation to be useful, the mapping of inputs to generalisations (internal states) must retain the important features of the state. This is the *input generalisation* problem which requires the correct classification of world states for success [4].

Input generalisation has been addressed specifically in relation to robot learning by the G-algorithm and U-tree among others [4], [22]. However, these algorithms have not been extensively compared to other common algorithms used for generalisation. TRACA also addresses the input generalisation problem. TRACA's intended domain of robot navigation involves many complications associated with on-line learning including noisy sensor readings and changing environments (i.e stochastic, non-stationary environments). In these environments there may be a wide variety of experiences between examples from a particular class. However, in this paper TRACA is examined primarily within the batch learning framework where a number of related examples are presented in a continual sequence.

When comparing algorithms a variety of measures can be used to assess performance [9], [13]. Given TRACA's intended problem domain the important criteria are predictive accuracy, a small number of training examples and minimal parameter tuning. Minimal parameter tuning is important if an agent is to be used to solve a variety of tasks or the developer is unfamiliar with the problem to be learned. Having a small number of training examples is necessary to reduce the risk of damage to the agent. In contrast, requiring a large number of additional training examples to achieve a small increase in predictive accuracy is generally considered not worthwhile [22].

The next section provides a description of TRACA, because of space limitations this description is at a high-level, see [25] for a more detailed description. Section III describes the experiments and the parameters used. The subsequent sections from IV to VII provide experimental results on classification tasks. Section VIII provides results on a spatial navigation task. Finally, an assessment of all results is presented in Section IX.

II. THE SYSTEM

The motivation behind TRACA's development is to implement a rule based learning system that creates default-hierarchies similar to Holland style learning classifier systems, but with more efficient reuse of useful rules and without requiring a genetic algorithm [15], [1].

TRACA is a reinforcement learning system which uses state information from the environment to determine action selection. This information is passed into the system through the *input interface*, while the decision of the system to take some action in its environment is passed out through the *effector interface*. A further input is the reinforcement learning signal indicating the agent's success or failure at achieving its goal(s) [26].

The current state of the environment is presented on the agent's environmental input interface using bit strings. For each string received, the agent is capable of selecting an action before a new input string is presented indicating the environmental state resulting from the action. In this respect TRACA is similar to Holland style Learning Classifier systems and Drescher's Schema Mechanism which also receive environmental inputs (other than reinforcement) as bit strings [16], [8].

TRACA's internal model of its environment is based on three types of nodes: *detector*, *effector* and *predictor*. Detector and effector nodes implement the interface between the agent and its environment. Predictor nodes are organised into *groups*, which are generalised internal representations of problem states. Predictor nodes and their containing groups are created as TRACA learns and represent transitions between internal states given the selection of an action.

TRACA constructs its network incrementally during learning. It begins with low-level groups representing individual bit positions in the input string. Low level groups are then probabilistically selected to create a new join group which connects two lower level groups in a logical AND construct. These AND constructs form multiple hierarchies (which represent disjunctions) with the lower-level groups acting as *subordinates* to the *superior* join groups. Once created joins can be used in turn as subordinates for other new joins, adding levels to the hierarchy. The resulting network is a default-hierarchy representation [15].

The groups created by TRACA contain nodes which represent probabilistic S-R-S (Situation-Response-Situation) rules. These rules are of the form (s_a, r_x, s_b) where s_a is an initial state, r_x is a response (action) and s_b is the state that results from taking the action r_x while in state s_a. The rules can be interpreted as:

if the current state is s_a and action r_x is taken
then the next state will be s_b with probability p

TRACA uses two types of suppression techniques implemented as message passing through the network. The first suppression technique allows the system to represent NOT using only logical AND combinations of system components. This reduces the number of possible equivalent combinations and the search space substantially. This suppression technique also acts to shift control to nodes in groups higher in the hierarchy. The second suppression technique prevents duplicates by excluding subordinates from being used in new joins. Because this can sometimes result in local minima, subordinate groups can be probabilistically excluded from the second suppression technique for a single cycle. When a group is excluded from suppression its superiors are prevented from being used in new joins.

Not all joins created are retained in the system. Initially newly created groups are in a suspended state (they do not drive system behaviour). To be retained they must demonstrate some improvement over their subordinates. Once this improvement is achieved they are set to unsuspended, however, they may still be removed later if it is revealed they are no

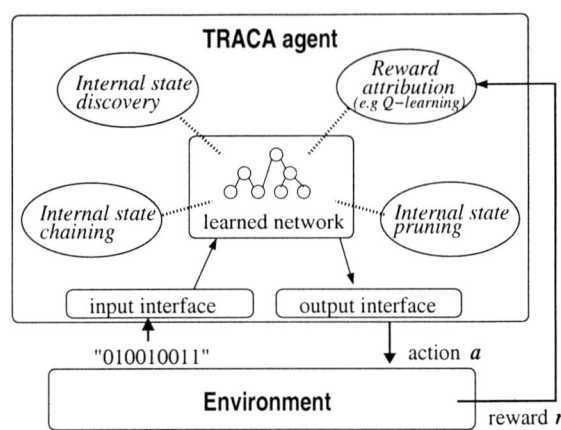

Fig. 1. An overview of TRACA.

longer useful (i.e in changing environments). Improvements are measured based on estimates of the predictive accuracy of the rules (nodes) groups contain. If a rule provides an improvement over its immediate subordinates, the group is retained, otherwise it is removed. A novel method is used to evaluate the usefulness of rules. The method involves two measures, one based on the Cox-Stuart test for trend, the other on the sign-test [7]. Since the predictive accuracy of rules is initialised to zero, the first (Cox-Stuart based) test simply measures when the value of the rule has stopped rising. The second test, which I refer to as the test for noise, measures the on-going usefulness of the rule when compared to its subordinates. It compensates for short periods where the subordinate rule may appear more useful than the superior due to either a stochastic (noisy) problem space, or the generality of the superior rule. Alternative measures for assessing internal structures used in similar learning systems include the student's t-Test [4] and the Kolmogorov-Smirnov test [22].

As TRACA is a reinforcement learning system, nodes also maintain utility estimates. These estimates are used as support for effectors to drive system behaviour. Each group sends as support only the highest positive value and lowest negative value of all nodes in the group. The value of each effector is determined as the average positive support received minus the average negative support received. The system will then select the effector with the highest value.

The different components in TRACA are depicted in Figure 1. This figure illustrates the relationship between TRACA and its environment (through the input and output interfaces) along with the mechanisms implemented within TRACA's network. The mechanisms include internal state creation (join group creation), the chaining together of successive internal states (predictor node creation), the removal (or pruning) of created groups based on statistical tests and the attribution of reinforcement values to appropriate nodes based on rewards received from the environment.

III. EXPERIMENTAL DESIGN

TRACA is trialled on a number of different classification tasks. The first three tasks are the Monks concept learning tasks from Thrun *et al* [27]. While the Monks tasks are artificial and have only six attributes they do provide a variety of challenges. Following the Monk tasks are three other tasks drawn from real-world problems. The first two tasks involve discriminating different types of irises and voters. The third task, involving a larger state space, looks at TRACA's ability to identify gene splices in DNA sequences. The final task is a navigation task that demonstrates rule chaining.

Note, that the same set of parameters is used by TRACA across all classification tasks, only the number of training epochs is varied. These parameters and the number of learning epochs were not optimised, but selected rather arbitrarily based on a small set of initial experiments. In some cases, variations to TRACA's parameters were tried and better results were achieved, occasionally these are also reported. In the standard parameter set the Cox-Stuart test and the test for noise used 10 and 20 cases respectively with a two-tailed significance of 0.05 and nodes needed to be trialled 20 times before sending returns. The exclusion rate for joins was 1 in each 20 times they were matched while the learning rate was 0.1 for all problems. 1 in 4 actions were selected randomly during training. All results are the average of 20 runs and all, apart from the Monk tasks, are cross-validated. A summary of the performance on all problems is provided following the experiments.

IV. THE MONKS CONCEPT LEARNING TASKS

The Monk problem is an artificial problem incorporating three different tasks each with its own concept. Each example has a value for each of the six attributes and is one state in the total possible space of 432 states. In the artificial domain of this problem an example represents either a friendly or unfriendly robot. The attributes are features of the robot (for example: a robot may be holding a sword, smiling and wearing a red jacket). In the different Monk tasks different combinations of features can be used to identify a robot as either friendly or unfriendly.

Each task involves presenting a subset of the possible examples to the learning agent along with – or, in TRACA's case, followed by – the information on whether the example is an instance of a friendly or unfriendly robot. From its experience with this subset of the total possible examples, the agent must try to learn how to classify the remaining examples – without being provided explicit information on the class the example belongs to. The third task includes 5% misclassifications (noise) in the training examples.

The Monk 1 and 3 tasks are in a standard disjunctive normal form. However, the combination of attributes for Monk 2 is complicated to describe in disjunctive or conjunctive normal form [27].

Experimental Methodology

The results on the Monk problems of a number of learning systems are presented in Thrun *et al* [27]. These systems were all trained on the standard set of training examples for each problem. In each case, the test set was the full set of examples. To allow comparison of results, the same training and test sets are used for TRACA as were used in Thrun *et al* [27]. For each problem the numbers of training examples are:
- Monk 1: 124.
- Monk 2: 169.
- Monk 3: 122.

After an example is presented one of two possible system actions is selected indicating TRACA's classification of the example as a member of the class or not. Once the action is selected, another input string is presented with a 0 in all bit positions except one of the last two. Of these two, the leftmost position will contain 1 if TRACA's classification was correct, otherwise, the rightmost position will contain 1. If TRACA was correct a reward of 100 is provided, otherwise the reward is -100.

Since the training sets for all runs on the Monk tasks were identical, each run was started with a different random seed. For Monk 1 TRACA was trained on the training set for 30 epochs (i.e 30 times) before testing. For Monk 2, 50 training epochs were provided before testing and for Monk 3, 40.

Results

The results presented here for comparison are the predictive accuracies of a number of other learning algorithms selected from Thrun *et al* [27]. Other results from Thrun *et al* [27] obtained by non-incremental algorithms have been excluded. The results obtained from incremental algorithms include Back-propagation neural networks with weight decay, Cascade correlation using Quickprop, ID5R, IDR5-hat and IDL. IDL and IDR5 are incremental induction algorithms for constructing decision trees. Two separate results are reported in Thrun *et al* [27] for ID5R. These are included as ID5R*a* for the results obtained by W. Van de Welde and ID5R*b* for the results gained by J. Krueziger, R Hamann, and W. Wenzel (Table I).

	Monk 1	Monk 2	Monk 3
TRACA	96.7	70.1	92.8
IDL	97.2	66.2	
ID5Ra	81.7	61.8	
ID5R-hat	90.3	65.7	
ID5Rb	79.8	69.2	95.3
Backprop. with weight decay	100.0	100.0	97.2
Cascade correlation	100.0	100.0	97.2

TABLE I
COMPARISON OF RESULTS FOR MONK PROBLEMS

TRACA's predictive accuracy was 96.7 for Monk 1, 70.1 for Monk 2 and 92.8 for Monk 3. The respective standard deviations across the 20 runs were 3.5, 2.8 and 3.7. The three rows in Table I after the first contain results obtained by W. Van de Welde. These are averaged over 10 runs for Monk 1 and 5 runs for Monk 2. He did not run experiments on Monk 3 because of the noise. However, Van de Welde's results are among the most reliable, as most of the other results compared to are from a single run. In some cases the results were obtained by the algorithm's inventor. For example, the results for Cascade-correlation were obtained by S. Fahlman [10]. His result for Monk 3 is an average of 5 runs.

For the first Monk problem, TRACA's result was up to 15 percent higher than the results for both ID5Ra and ID5Rb, and 3.3 percent lower than the two Neural Network approaches. TRACA's results for the second problem were much lower (nearly 30 percent) than the results for both Neural Networks but higher than the results for the other compared algorithms. For the third problem, due to the noise in the data, only three results are available from the compared approaches, Back-propagation, Cascade-correlation and ID5Rb. Here TRACA's result was 2.5 percent lower than the result for ID5Rb and 4.4 percent lower than the results for Back-propagation and Cascade Correlation.

Henery [14] has criticised the Monk problem for being artificial and Thrun et al [27] for including too little analysis of the results presented. Despite this criticism the Monk problem presents more of a challenge to TRACA's classification capabilities than the real-world problems trialled later in this section. W. Van de Welde mentions that the concepts in Monk 2 appear to be too difficult for decision tree based approaches. However, TRACA's poor performance seems due to the difficulties in detecting the significance of joins based on only binary combinations. Interestingly without joins (join creation is turned off) TRACA achieves 92.9 for Monk 3. For Monk 1 and Monk 2 the accuracy without joins is much lower - 72.8 and 67.0 respectively. In fact, of all the problems trialled in this paper, the Monk 1 and Monk 2 problems are the only ones on which TRACA's performance is improved by more than a few percent by using join groups. This is despite TRACA often discovering correct predictive relationships in the data.

Interestingly, TRACA can obtain an average of 75 percent with a maximum of 81 percent on Monk 2 by varying the parameters. Changes include the addition of a system operating principle which retains groups unconditionally while they have one or more unsuspended superiors, tripling the number of Cox-Stuart and sign test cases and doubling the learning epochs. The additional operating principle appeared to have no adverse effects on the other Monk tasks. In another test, performance on Monk 1 was increased by 1.7 percent to 98.4 by reducing the number of Cox-Stuart and sign test cases by half.

The following sections examine TRACA's performance on a range of classification tasks derived from real-world problems and data.

V. THE IRIS DISCRIMINATION TASK

The next task involves discriminating types of Iris based on sepal and petal length and width. There are three types of Iris; Verginica, Versicolor and Setosa, represented by four attributes in the following ranges [11]:

- Attribute 1 (A_1): values {0.2-2.5};
- Attribute 2 (A_2): values {1.0-6.9};
- Attribute 3 (A_3): values {2.0-4.4} and;
- Attribute 4 (A_4): values {4.4-7.7}.

Experimental Methodology

To represent this task for TRACA, the attribute values are coarsely placed into "buckets" of a fixed size. Intervals covered by bit positions in the respective buckets for each attribute were:

- Attribute 1 (A_1): 0.5;
- Attribute 2 (A_2): 0.1;
- Attribute 3 (A_3): 0.5; and
- Attribute 4 (A_4): 0.1.

For each attribute the first interval in the first bucket ranges from the lowest occuring value of the attribute, with the last bucket for Attribute 4 ranging from 7.4 to 7.7 inclusive.

Twenty training and test sets were randomly generated from the full data set (150 cases). Each training set contained two thirds of the data with the remaining one third in the corresponding test set. For each of the twenty runs TRACA was trained for 30 epochs on the training set. As each training set was different and in a random order, the same random seed was used for all runs. Other parameters were the same as in the previous experiments.

Results

TRACA obtained an average of 90.3 on the test sets with a standard deviation of 3.9. For comparison, the inductive learning algorithm C4 obtains 93.8 percent on this data under similar trials [17], 3.5 percent higher than TRACA's performance. On average only 5.7 unsuspended join groups (join groups driving system behaviour) were developed during learning. TRACA achieved 88.8 percent under the same conditions but without creating joins.

VI. THE VOTER DISCRIMINATION TASK

Another comparison of TRACA's discrimination and generalisation ability is on a task derived by J. Schlimmer from voting data collected about the votes of Congressmen in the U.S House of Representatives in 1984. This dataset has 435 cases with 16 attributes. Each attribute has three possible values (yes, no or unsure). Each case belongs to one of two classes, either democrat or republican.

Experimental Methodology

Twenty training and test sets were randomly generated each with two thirds of the cases in the training set and one third in the test set. As different training and test sets were used for each run, the same random seed was used. Parameters were unchanged from the previous experiment.

Results

TRACA achieves 92.7 percent on this task with a standard deviation of 2.3. An average of 53.7 unsuspended groups were created. Holte [17] reports C4 achieving 95.6 on this task – 3.1 percent higher than TRACA – which was the highest performance from a number of algorithms compared in that paper. When the same experiment was performed with the ability to create joins groups turned off, TRACA achieved an average test accuracy of 94.1, higher than its result using joins and only 1.5 percent lower than C4.

Explanation of Results

An accuracy of 95.6 percent can be achieved on the votes dataset by simply testing the value in attribute 4, *physician-fee-freeze*. This is the most accurate decision tree possible for this dataset [17], [3].

Since TRACA develops rules for each attribute, a system which has rules based on individual attributes (i.e without joins) should be capable of achieving 95.6 percent accuracy. However, TRACA has rules not only for attribute 4, but all attributes as a minimum rule set. A higher result without joins than with joins may occur if joins are incorrectly retained due to ordering effects in the data or if relationships discovered for the training set do not apply to the test set.

VII. THE DNA SPLICE TASK

This dataset includes 3186 examples each representing a window of 60 nucleotides drawn from a processed version of the Irvine Primate splice-junction database. Each nucleotide is represented by one of the symbolic values (a, c, g, t). The task is to identify whether each example represents a intron-extron boundary, an extron-intron boundary or neither. These boundaries occur in DNA sequences where superfluous DNA is removed during protein creation, the extrons are retained in this process and the introns are removed. The processing applied was the conversion of the 60 attributes into 180 binary attributes, removal of 4 spurious examples and the conversion of the symbolic class labels to numeric labels [24].

Experimental Methodology

The 20 training sets each had 2000 examples while the test sets each had 1186 examples. In each run TRACA was allowed one pass (one epoch) on the training data before being tested. Other parameters are identical to those used for the Monk, Iris and Voter tasks in Sections IV, V and VI.

Results

TRACA achieved an average of 94.9 percent classification accuracy on the test data with a standard deviation of 4.2. On average of 105.6 unsuspended join groups were created. In trials without join groups TRACA achieved an even higher result of 96.8.

In results presented in Michie *et al* [24] the best performance was for Radial Basis Functions which achieved 95.9 percent accuracy. Backpropagation Neural Networks achieved 91.2 percent accuracy and C4.5 achieved 92.4 percent accuracy.

VIII. THE NAVIGATION TASK

This task consists of a 4x4 aperiodic grid. The top left location in the grid is the goal (see Figure 2). At each timestep the agent can move in one of four directions (north, south, east and west) to one of the neighbours of its current location. The task is to learn to navigate from each non-goal location in the grid to the goal. The goal is an absorbing state, upon reaching it the agent receives a positive reward (of 100) and no further transitions are possible. For transitions other than to the goal the reward is zero. Transitions leading into the boundary leave the agent's position unchanged. Unlike the experiments

10000	10100	10010	10110
01000	01100	01010	01110
11000	11100	11010	11110
00100	00010	00110	00001

Fig. 2. The 4x4 grid and its binary inputs for each location

presented so far this task involves delayed rewards and requires chains of rules to be formed. The agent's location in the grid is presented as a binary string (see Figure 2). Distributed sensors are used so the agent is required to develop internal structures to discriminate locations in the grid. Since each location has a unique binary input there is little opportunity for generalisation.

Experimental Methodology

Learning and testing of the agent consists of a series of trials. Each trial involves placing the agent on a random (non-goal) location in the grid. Once the agent reaches the goal the trial is completed and terminates. During testing the trial may also terminate if the agent does not reach the goal within 1000 moves. During learning 1 in 3 of the agent's actions are selected randomly. The agent is allowed 50 learning trials, after which it is tested for 100 trials. If the agent does reach the goal within 1000 timesteps on every test trial, it is considered to have failed the test and is provided another 50 learning trials before being tested. This is repeated up to 5 times. If after 250 training trials the agent still has not learned the maze it is deemed to have failed. For agents which do learn the maze performance is taken as the average number of moves to reach the goal over the 100 test trials. A discount factor of 0.9 was used for Q-learning along with a learning rate of 0.2. 100 agents were tested on this problem, each with a unique random seed.

To test the ability of the agent to reuse knowledge it had gained on one task for another, the goal was moved to the diagonally opposite corner. Agents which successfully learned the maze for the first goal, were then trained again on the new task, using the learned network they had developed for the original.

A. Results

On the first goal 2 agents failed. The 98 successful agents recorded an average number of moves to goal of 3.2. An agent selecting random actions took an average of 49.8 moves to reach this goal under the same experimental conditions. The average number of unsuspended joins created during learning was 15.1 and the average number of learning trials was 112.2.

Once the goal was moved, the successful agents were trained again (retaining the networks they developed for the first goal). On testing, the average number of moves required to reach the second goal was 3.5, using an average of 18.2 unsuspended joins. The average number of learning trials for the second goal was 76.0. In summary, the second goal was learned more quickly and using only a few more additional joins than were required to achieve the first goal.

IX. Discussion

TRACA's predictive performance has been compared over six tasks using a single set of parameters. Apart from Monk 2, TRACA's predictive accuracy is no more than 4.9 percent below the best performance, and is often well above the performance of a number of other learning algorithms. It appears that the higher predictive accuracy of Neural Networks is achieved at the cost of many more training examples. For example, in the Monk 3 task, Cascade Correlation using Quickprop required 259 epochs, while TRACA's result was achieved within 40 epochs.

The small number of joins (relative to the large number of possible combinations) created by TRACA is also encouraging. The high accuracy of TRACA in many cases with zero, or small numbers of, joins is consistent with the analysis by Holte [17], who determined that many common machine learning tasks require very few rules to achieve good performance. The Monk tasks were among those which clearly required joins for successful solution.

The relative simplicity of TRACA and minimal intervention of the experimenter is important for the intended application of TRACA to, as much as possible, learn autonomously and be able to solve a diversity of problems. TRACA avoids the common requirement of Neural networks for a high level of expertise by the experimenter [24]. The fixed set of parameters consistently achieved over 90 percent on a wide range of problems. This ease of use is aided by the fact that the size and topology of TRACA's solution network is determined entirely during learning. While Cascade Correlation also allows for the automatic addition of new nodes as required, due to its batch training requirement, it is unsuitable for the on-line learning environments TRACA is intended for [10], [19].

TRACA's quick training times are most likely due to the relative independence of nodes within TRACA's network. As suggested by the experiments on the 4x4 grid problem, this may allow TRACA to avoid problems inherent in Backpropagation neural networks such as catastrophic forgetting and interference (which results in long learning times) [9], [23], [12]. Further navigation experiments are currently being completed which demonstrate that TRACA can deal with both noisy actions and sensors, and (with some additional structures) hidden-state [28], [6].

Acknowledgements

Many thanks to Ann Nicholson and David Albrecht for their constructive comments and reviews of this material. Thanks also to Selby Markham and to the anonymous reviewers.

References

[1] L.B Booker, D.E Goldberg, and J.H Holland. Classifier systems and genetic algoritihms. *Artificial Intelligence* **40**(1-3), 235–282 (September 1989).

[2] L.A Breslow. Greedy utile suffix memory for reinforcement learning with perceptually aliased states. Technical Report AIC-96-004, Navy Center For Applied Research in AI (1996).

[3] W Buntine and T Niblett. Further comparison of splitting rules for decision-tree induction. *Machine Learning* **8**(1), 75–85 (January 1992).

[4] D Chapman and L.P Kaelbling. Input generalization in delayed reinforcement learning: An algorithm and performance comparisons. In "Proceedings of the 12th International Conference on Artificial Intelligence", volume 2, pages 726–731. Morgan Kaufmann (1991).

[5] L. Chrisman. Reinforcement learning with perceptual aliasing: The perceptual distinctions approach. In "Proceedings of the 10th National Conference on Artificial Intelligence", pages 183–188. AAAI, Morgan-Kaufmann (1992).

[6] M Colombetti and M Dorigo. Training agents to perform sequential behaviour. *Adaptive Behaviour* **2**(3), 247–275 (1994).

[7] W.W Daniel. "Applied Non-parameteric Statistics". PWS-Kent, Boston, 2nd edition (1990).

[8] G.L Drescher. "Made-Up Minds: A constructivist approach to Artificial Intelligence". MIT Press (1991).

[9] S.E Fahlman. Faster-learning variations on back-propagation: An empirical study. In "Proceedings of the 1988 Connectionist Models Summer School". Morgan-Kaufmann (1988).

[10] S.E Fahlman and C Lebiere. The cascade correlation learning architecture. In "Advances in Neural Information Processing Systems 2". Morgan Kaufmann (1988).

[11] R.A Fisher. The use of multiple measurements in taxonomic problems. In "Annals of Eugenics", volume 7, pages 179–188. Cambridge University Press (1936).

[12] R.M French. Catastrophic forgetting in connectionist networks: Causes, consequences and solutions. *Trends in Cognitive Sciences* **3**(4), 128–135 (1999).

[13] R. J Henery. Classification. In D Michie, D.J Spiegelhalter, and C.C Taylor, editors, "Machine Learning, Neural and Statistical Classification", chapter 2, pages 6–16. Ellis-Horwood (1994).

[14] R. J Henery. Preview of previous empirical comparisons. In D Michie, D.J Spiegelhalter, and C.C Taylor, editors, "Machine Learning, Neural and Statistical Classification", chapter 2, pages 6–16. Ellis-Horwood (1994).

[15] J.H Holland, K.J Holyoak, R.E Nisbett, and P.A Thagard. "Induction. Processes of Inference, Learning and Discovery". The MIT Press (1986).

[16] J.J Holland. "Adaption in natural and artificial systems". University of Michigan Press (1975).

[17] R.C Holte. Very simple classification rules perform very well on most commonly used datasets. *Machine Learning* **11**, 63–91 (1993).

[18] L.P Kaelbling, L.L Littman, and A.W Moore. Reinforcement Learning: A Survey. *Journal of Artificial Intelligence Research* **4**, 237–285 (1996).

[19] L Lin. "Reinforcement Learning for Robots Using Neural Networks". PhD thesis, School of Computer Science, Carnegie Mellon University, Pittsburgh USA (1993).

[20] M.L Littman, A.R Cassandra, and L.P Kaelbling. Learning policies for partially observable environments: Scaling up. In A Preiditis and S Russel, editors, "Machine Learning: Proceedings of the 12th International Conference", pages 362–370. Morgan Kauffman (1995).

[21] A.K McCallum. Overcoming incomplete perception with utile distinction memory. In "Proceedings of the tenth international machine learning conference" (1993).

[22] A.K McCallum. "Reinforcement Learning With Selective Perception and Hidden State". PhD thesis, Department of Computer Science, University of Rochester, NY (1995).

[23] M McCloskey and N.J Cohen. Catastrophic interference in connectionist networks: The sequential learning problem. *The Psychology of Learning and Motivation* **24**, 109–164 (1989).

[24] D. Michie, D.J Spiegelhalter, and C.C Taylor, editors. "Machine Learning, Neural and Statistical Classification". Ellis Horwood (1994).

[25] M.W Mitchell. An evaluation of TRACA's generalisation performance. Technical Report 2002-197, Monash University, School of Computer Science and Software Engineering, http://www.csse.monash.edu.au/publications (2002).

[26] R.S Sutton. Reinforcement learning architectures for animats. In J Meyer and S.W Wilson, editors, "From Animals to Animats", pages 288–296. First International Conference on Simulation of Adaptive Behaviour, MIT Press (1991).

[27] S. Thrun, J. Bala, E. Bloedorn, I. Bratko, B. Cestnik, J. Cheng, K. De Jong, S. Dzeroski, S.E. Fahlman, D. Fisher, R. Hamann, K. Kaufman, S. Keller, I. Kononenko, J. Kreuziger, R.S. Michalski, T. Mitchell, P. Pachowicz, B. Roger, H. Vafaie, W. Van de Velde, W. Wenzel, J. Wnek, and J. Zhang. The MONK's problems. A performance comparison of different learning algorithms. Technical Report CMU-CS-91-197, Carnegie Mellon University (December 1991). http://www-2.cs.cmu.edu/ thrun/papers/thrun.MONK.html.

[28] S.D Whitehead and D.H Ballard. Learning to perceive and act by trial and error. *Machine Learning* **7**, 45–83 (1991).

Fast Convergence for Back-Propagation Network with Magnified Gradient Function

S. C. Ng
School of Science & Tech.
The Open University of HK
Email: scng@ouhk.edu.hk

C. C. Cheung
Dept of Comp. Eng. & Info. Tech.
City University of HK
itccc@cityu.edu.hk

S. H. Leung
Dept. of Electronic Eng.
City University of HK
eeeugshl@cityu.edu.hk

A. Luk
St. B&P Neural Investment
Pty.Ltd., Australia
neurons@attglobal.net

Abstract-This paper presents a modified back-propagation algorithm using magnified gradient function (MGFPROP), which can effectively speed up the convergence rate and improve the global convergence capability of back-propagation. The purpose of MGFPROP is to increase the convergence rate by magnifying the gradient function of the activation function. From the convergence analysis, it is shown that the new algorithm retains the gradient descent property but gives faster convergence than that of the back-propagation algorithm. Simulation results show that, in terms of the convergence rate and the percentage of global convergence, the new algorithm always outperforms the standard back-propagation algorithm and other competing techniques.

I. INTRODUCTION

Despite the general success of back-propagation in learning the neural networks, several major deficiencies are still needed to be resolved. Firstly, the original back-propagation algorithm (BP) will get trapped in local minima especially for non-linearly separable problems [13] such as the XOR problem [14]. Having trapped into local minima, BP may lead to failure in finding a global optimal solution. Secondly, the convergence rate of BP is still too slow even if learning can be achieved. Furthermore, the convergence behaviour of the back-propagation algorithm depends very much on the choices of initial values of connection weights and the parameters in the algorithm such as the learning rate and the momentum.

The main reason for the slow convergence of BP is due to the derivative of the activation function which will lead to the occurrence of premature saturation [12] of the network output units. When the actual output o_{pm} (where o_{pm} is the actual output of the *m*-th output neuron for the *p*-th pattern) is approaching to either extreme values of the sigmoidal function, that is either 0 or 1, the derivative of the activation function having the factor $o_{pm}(1-o_{pm})$ will become extremely small, and the back propagated error signal may vanish. Therefore, the output can be maximally wrong without producing a large error signal. The algorithm may then be trapped into "flat spot". Consequently, the learning process and weight adjustment of the algorithm will be very slow or even suppressed. BP usually requires tens to thousands iterations to leave the flat spots, this causes the slow convergence of the algorithm.

Different approaches had been suggested to eliminate the flat spot problem so as to accelerate the convergence speed of BP [1-7]. Among all these methods, there are basically two approaches in solving the premature saturation (or flat spot) problem. They are the modification on either the definition of system error E [1, 4], or the slope of the activation function in the weight update equation [2, 3, 7]. Although many methods had been developed to solve the premature saturation of BP, these methods did not obtain very significant improvement in both the convergence speed and global convergence capability over the standard back-propagation algorithm.

In this paper, we propose a modification on the derivative of the activation function so as to improve the convergence of the learning process by preventing the error signal drop to a very small value. The idea is to magnify the derivative term $o_{pm}(1-o_{pm})$, especially when the value of o_{pm} approaches 0 or 1, by using a power factor. In that case, the derivative of the activation function will not be too small and the convergence of the algorithm can be improved. The new algorithm is shown to have the characteristics of faster convergence rate and greater chance to escape from flat spots as compared with BP.

This paper is organized as follows. Section II introduces the basic operations of the back-propagation algorithm. Section III describes the MGFPROP algorithm. Section IV discusses the effect of normalization on the gradient term. Section V presents the convergence analysis of MGFPROP. Section VI shows the simulation results of the proposed algorithm as compared with other well-known modified BP algorithms. The conclusion is drawn in Section VII.

II. THE STANDARD BACK-PROPAGATION ALGORITHM (BP)

Consider the basic structure of a feed-forward network with a single hidden layer as shown in Figure 1. The network consists of N input nodes, K hidden nodes and M output nodes. Let o_{pm} and $\overline{o}_{pk}$ be the output of output node m and hidden node k from input pattern p, respectively. Assume

ω_{km} is the network weight for hidden node k and output node m, and $\overline{\omega}_{nk}$ is the network weight for input node n and hidden node k. Also, let x_{pn} be the input value in input node n for input pattern p, and t_{pm} be the target output value in the output node m for input pattern p. Note that the symbol Δ represents the difference between the current and the new value in the next iteration.

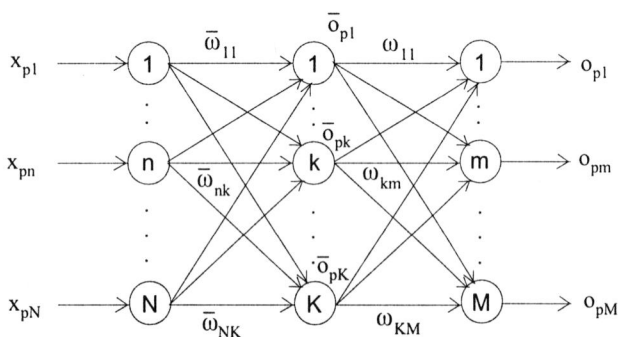

Fig. 1. Basic structure of a feedforward network

The standard back-propagation algorithm (BP) is shown below:

1. *Initialization*: Initialize all weights and refer to them as current weight $\omega_{km}(0)$ and $\overline{\omega}_{nk}(0)$. Set the learning rate μ and the momentum factor α to small positive values (e.g. 0.1). Set the error threshold E and the iteration number $i = 0$.

2. *Forward Pass*: Select the input pattern $\mathbf{x}_p = \{x_{p1}, \cdots, x_{pN}\}$ from the training set and compute $o_{pm}(i)$ and $\overline{o}_{pk}(i)$ using the followings equations:

$$o_{pm}(i) = f\left(\sum_{k=1}^{K} \omega_{km}(i)\overline{o}_{pk}(i)\right) \quad (1)$$

and $\overline{o}_{pk}(i) = f\left(\sum_{k=1}^{K} \overline{\omega}_{nk}(i) x_{pn}\right) \quad (2)$

where the activation function $f(x) = \dfrac{1}{1+e^{-x}}$.

Use the desired target $\mathbf{t}_p = \{t_{p1}, \cdots, t_{pM}\}$ associated with x_p to compute the sum of the squared system error, $E(i)$, for all input patterns as follows:

$$E(i) = \frac{1}{2}\sum_{p=1}^{P}\sum_{m=1}^{M}[t_{pm} - o_{pm}(i)]^2 \quad (3)$$

If $E(i) \le E$, then the algorithm is completed and the convergence is met; otherwise, go to step 3 (Backward Pass).

3. *Backward Pass*: Compute the changes of the weights for the next iteration $\Delta\omega_{km}(i+1)$ and $\Delta\overline{\omega}_{nk}(i+1)$ using the following equations:

$$\begin{aligned}\Delta\omega_{km}(i+1) &= -\mu\frac{\partial E(i)}{\partial \omega_{km}(i)} + \alpha\Delta\omega_{km}(i) \\ &= \mu\sum_{p=1}^{P}\delta_{pm}(i)\overline{o}_{pk}(i) + \alpha\Delta\omega_{km}(i)\end{aligned} \quad (4)$$

$$\begin{aligned}\Delta\overline{\omega}_{nk}(i+1) &= -\mu\frac{\partial E(i)}{\partial \overline{\omega}_{nk}(i)} + \alpha\Delta\overline{\omega}_{nk}(i) \\ &= \mu\sum_{p=1}^{P}\overline{\delta}_{pk}(i)x_{pn} + \alpha\Delta\overline{\omega}_{nk}(i)\end{aligned} \quad (5)$$

where $\delta_{pm}(i) = (t_{pm} - o_{pm}(i))o_{pm}(i)(1 - o_{pm}(i)) \quad (6)$

and $\overline{\delta}_{pk}(i) = \overline{o}_{pk}(i)(1 - \overline{o}_{pk}(i))\sum_{m=1}^{M}\delta_{pm}(i)\omega_{km}(i) \quad (7)$

Update the weights for the next iteration $\omega_{km}(i+1)$ and $\overline{\omega}_{nk}(i+1)$ by considering the equations

$\omega_{km}(i+1) = \omega_{km}(i) + \Delta\omega_{km}(i+1)$ and
$\overline{\omega}_{nk}(i+1) = \overline{\omega}_{nk}(i) + \Delta\overline{\omega}_{nk}(i+1)$.

Set $i = i+1$ and go to step 2 (Forward Pass).

III. THE MGFPROP ALGORITHM

The back-propagated error signals $\delta_{pm}(i)$ and $\overline{\delta}_{pk}(i)$ include the terms $o_{pm}(i)(1-o_{pm}(i))$ and $\overline{o}_{pk}(i)(1-\overline{o}_{pk}(i))$ respectively (as shown in Equation (6) and (7)). The main reason for the slow convergence of BP is due to these error signals. When the actual output $o_{pm}(i)$ or $\overline{o}_{pk}(i)$ approaches extreme values (i.e. 0 or 1), the error signals will become so small that they cannot actually reflect the true error $t_{pm} - o_{pm}(i)$. Thus, if the output diverges to the wrong value, the magnitude of $o_{pm}(i)(1-o_{pm}(i))$ or $\overline{o}_{pk}(i)(1-\overline{o}_{pk}(i))$ becomes too small. The output cannot be effectively adjusted by the error signals and the learning process or weight adjustment of the algorithm becomes very slow or even suppressed. This leads to premature saturation [12] — the "flat spot" problem, which is a phenomenon in which the error remains almost unchanged for some periods of time during learning. Moreover, even when the output approaches the target output value, the final convergence rate is hindered by the factor $o_{pm}(i)(1-o_{pm}(i))$ and $\overline{o}_{pk}(i)(1-\overline{o}_{pk}(i))$, which is the reason why the learning of BP or some modified BP algorithms is trapped into the flat spot and may not converge to the global optimal solution for some applications.

To overcome this problem, we propose to magnify the factors $o_{pm}(i)(1-o_{pm}(i))$ and $\overline{o}_{pk}(i)(1-\overline{o}_{pk}(i))$ by using a power factor $1/S$ where S is a positive real number such that $S \ge 1$, i.e. to replace $o_{pm}(i)(1-o_{pm}(i))$ and $\overline{o}_{pk}(i)(1-\overline{o}_{pk}(i))$

by $[o_{pm}(i)(1-o_{pm}(i))]^{\frac{1}{S}}$ and $[\bar{o}_{pk}(i)(1-\bar{o}_{pk}(i))]^{\frac{1}{S}}$ respectively. When compared with the standard back-propagation algorithm, the gradient term should have a larger increment when $o_{pm}(i)(1-o_{pm}(i))$ or $\bar{o}_{pk}(i)(1-\bar{o}_{pk}(i))$ approaches zero and the effect of the error term $t_{pm} - o_{pm}(i)$ will not disappear. It can be shown in convergence analysis that the new magnified gradient function will not violate the gradient-descent property of the conventional BP algorithm. Since the gradient term $o_{pm}(1-o_{pm})$ is always positive, the modified gradient term can also be kept positive to retain the gradient descent properties of BP, and the rate of change of error $E(i)$ with respect to time remains negative; i.e. the error is always decreasing (see Section V).

To show the effect of S on the derivative of the activation function $f(x)$, consider the ratio of the derivative of the activation function of the new algorithm to the original one. In BP, the activation function $f(x) = \dfrac{1}{1+e^{-x}}$ and the derivative of the activation function $f'(x) = \dfrac{e^{-x}}{(1+e^{-x})^2} = f(x)(1-f(x))$. In the new algorithm, it is magnified by using a power factor $1/S$ and thus $f'(x,S) = [f(x)(1-f(x))]^{\frac{1}{S}}$.

Now, we have

$$\frac{f'(x,S)}{f'(x)} = [f(x)(1-f(x))]^{\frac{1}{S}-1}$$

$$= \frac{e^{-x\left(\frac{1}{S}-1\right)}}{(1+e^{-x})^{2\left(\frac{1}{S}-1\right)}} = (2+e^x+e^{-x})^{1-\frac{1}{S}} \quad (8)$$

Note that $1 > 1 - \dfrac{1}{S} \geq 0$.

When $x = 0$, $\quad \dfrac{f'(x,S)}{f'(x)} = 4^{1-\frac{1}{S}} < 4 \quad (9)$

When $|x|$ is sufficiently large,

$$\frac{f'(x,S)}{f'(x)} = (2+e^x+e^{-x})^{1-\frac{1}{S}} \approx e^{|x|(1-\frac{1}{S})} \quad (10)$$

From Equation (9) and (10), the derivative is found to be scaled up a maximum of 4 times when x is very small, but it increases greatly when x is sufficiently large or when $o_{pm}(i)$ or $\bar{o}_{pk}(i)$ approaches extreme values (i.e. 0 or 1). The above effect is more significant when S increases. It shows that MGFPROP will not significantly affect the derivative when x is sufficiently small such that the convergence rate will not speed up too quickly to overshoot the error. When x is sufficiently large, the derivative increases rapidly to maintain the effect of the true error term $t_{pm} - o_{pm}(i)$ and thus the learning algorithm can escape from a "flat spot" effectively. Note that S should not be too large. If $S \to \infty$, $[o_{pm}(i)(1-o_{pm}(i))]^{\frac{1}{S}}$ and $[\bar{o}_{pk}(i)(1-\bar{o}_{pk}(i))]^{\frac{1}{S}}$ will approach unity. That means the terms $[o_{pm}(i)(1-o_{pm}(i))]^{\frac{1}{S}}$ and $[\bar{o}_{pk}(i)(1-\bar{o}_{pk}(i))]^{\frac{1}{S}}$ will be taken out from the derivative of the activation function, and hence the error signals $\delta_{pm}(i)$ and $\bar{\delta}_{pk}(i)$ will be too large, which will lead to unstable behaviour.

Based on this modification, we propose a BP algorithm with the magnified gradient function (MGFPROP). The algorithm is shown below:

1. *Initialization*: Same as BP except, additionally, we need to select a suitable value of S (a small value of S should be initially chosen for stability reasons).

2. *Forward Pass*: Same as BP.

3. *Backward Pass*: Same as BP except

$$\delta_{pm}(i) = (t_{pm} - o_{pm}(i))[o_{pm}(i)(1-o_{pm}(i))]^{\frac{1}{S}} \quad (11)$$

and $\bar{\delta}_{pk}(i) = [\bar{o}_{pk}(i)(1-\bar{o}_{pk}(i))]^{\frac{1}{S}} \sum_{m=1}^{M} \delta_{pm}(i)\omega_{km}(i) \quad (12)$

IV. Normalization

In order to further improve the performance of MGFPROP in terms of faster convergence, we consider an enhanced version of MGFPROP by taking the normalization on the gradient term of the algorithm. The idea is to normalize the error signals $\delta_{pm}(i)$ and $\bar{\delta}_{pk}(i)$ with the Fronbenius norms of $[o_{pm}(i)(1-o_{pm}(i))]^{\frac{1}{S}}$ and $[\bar{o}_{pk}(i)(1-\bar{o}_{pk}(i))]^{\frac{1}{S}}$ respectively. It is equivalent to adding the normalization factor on the learning rate μ of the algorithm. When $o_{pm}(i)$ or $\bar{o}_{pk}(i)$ approaches to 0 or 1, the above norms will be very small, and the effective learning rate will be increased. Consequently, the convergence rate for the algorithm will be greatly improved due to the use of "variable" learning rate.

The normalization factors of μ are $\left\|[o(1-o)]^{\frac{1}{S}}\right\|$ and $\left\|[\bar{o}(1-\bar{o})]^{\frac{1}{S}}\right\|$ for the output layer and the hidden layer respectively, where $\left\|[o(1-o)]^{\frac{1}{S}}\right\|$ is the Fronbenius norm of the matrix $[\mathbf{o_{pm}(1-o_{pm})}]^{\frac{1}{S}}$ for all p and m; and $\left\|[\bar{o}(1-\bar{o})]^{\frac{1}{S}}\right\|$ is the Fronbenius norm of the matrix $[\mathbf{\bar{o}_{pk}(1-\bar{o}_{pk})}]^{\frac{1}{S}}$ for all p and k.

Assume the new learning rates for upper layer and lower layer of weight updates are $\mu_{new}^{(u)}$ and $\mu_{new}^{(l)}$ respectively. The ratios of the new learning rates over original learning rate are $\mu_{new}^{(u)}/\mu = \left\|[o(1-o)]^{\frac{1}{s}}\right\|^{-1}$ and $\mu_{new}^{(l)}/\mu = \left\|[\overline{o}(1-\overline{o})]^{\frac{1}{s}}\right\|^{-1}$ for upper and lower layers respectively. The ratios will be greater than one when the outputs are located at the two "tail" regions. Hence the learning rate will be increased and the convergence speed will be accelerated when the values of $\left\|[o(1-o)]^{\frac{1}{s}}\right\|$ and $\left\|[\overline{o}(1-\overline{o})]^{\frac{1}{s}}\right\|$ are smaller than one. Therefore, the use of normalization can improve the convergence speed at flat spots and final stage of learning. In addition, the increase in effective learning rate can also help the algorithm to leak out from flat spots. In Section VI, we will show the simulation results of MGFPROP with and without the use of normalization.

V. CONVERGENCE ANALYSIS

By going through the convergence analysis of MGFPROP, the algorithm demonstrates the following convergence properties:

1. $\frac{\partial E}{\partial t} < 0$: Same as BP, the new algorithm has the gradient descent property.

2. $\left|\left(\frac{\partial E}{\partial t}\right)_{MGFPROP}\right| > \left|\left(\frac{\partial E}{\partial t}\right)_{BP}\right|$: The convergence rate of MGFPROP is faster than BP.

The complete proof of the above properties is shown below. Here, we apply the method proposed in [8] to investigate the convergence property of our proposed algorithm. Consider a feed-forward network with output $o = F(x, \omega)$, where x is the network input, ω is the vector of all adjustable weights, and F is the characteristic function of the network. Given that the sequence of training patterns $z_n = (x_n, t_n)$, where t_n is the target value of particular output, MGFPROP is trained to adjust the network weights so that the mean squared error is minimized. $E(\omega)$ is defined as the sum of squared error of the network using MGFPROP and ∇_S as the modified gradient term for MGFPROP. Then we have

$$\omega(i+1) = \omega(i) + \mu Q(z_n, \omega(i)) \quad (13)$$

where Q is a suitable function characteristics of MGFPROP. We also have

$$E(\omega) = \frac{1}{2}\sum_n [t_n - F(x_n, \omega)]^2 \quad (14)$$

$$Q(z_n, \omega) = \nabla_S F(x_n, \omega)(t_n - F(x_n, \omega)) \quad (15)$$

and $\overline{Q}(\omega) = EQ(x_n, t_n, \omega) = -\nabla_S E(\omega) \quad (16)$

where $\nabla_S E(\omega)$ is the rate of change of the training error with respect to ω for MGFPROP. Let $\nabla E(\omega)$ be the rate of change of error with respect to ω for BP, then we have:

$$\begin{aligned}\frac{\partial E}{\partial t} = \frac{\partial E(\omega)}{\partial t} &= \left(\frac{\partial E(\omega)}{\partial \omega}\right)^T \cdot \left(\frac{\partial \omega}{\partial t}\right) \\ &= [\nabla E(\omega)]^T \cdot \overline{Q}(\omega) \\ &= -[\nabla E(\omega)]^T \cdot \mathbf{A} \cdot \nabla E(\omega) < 0\end{aligned} \quad (17)$$

where $\mathbf{A}$ is a diagonal matrix with positive diagonal element $[o(1-o)]^{\frac{1}{s}-1}$. From Equation (17), it can be seen that the rate of change of error for MGFPROP is a negative term, it means that MGFPROP retains the gradient descent property. The first property is proved.

Consider the difference between the rate of change of error for MGFPROP and BP:

$$\begin{aligned}\left|\left(\frac{\partial E}{\partial t}\right)_{MGFPROP}\right| - \left|\left(\frac{\partial E}{\partial t}\right)_{BP}\right| &= [\nabla E(\omega)]^T \cdot \mathbf{A} \cdot \nabla E(\omega) - |\nabla E(\omega)|^2 \\ &= [\nabla E(\omega)]^T \cdot [\mathbf{A} - \mathbf{I}] \cdot \nabla E(\omega) \\ &> 0\end{aligned} \quad (18)$$

where $\mathbf{A}$ is a diagonal matrix with all diagonal elements $[o(1-o)]^{\frac{1}{s}-1} > 1$. From Equation (18), it can be seen that the convergence rate of MGFPROP is faster than that of BP as the rate of change of error of MGFPROP is always greater than that of BP. The second property is proved.

VI. SIMULATION RESULTS

To test the effectiveness of our new algorithm, its performance is compared with BP and other algorithms on some standard benchmark problems. A number of experiments have been conducted on different problems including the XOR, 3-bit parity, 5-bit counting problem, the regression problem and the character recognition problem to illustrate the performance of the MGFPROP algorithm. Let (N, K, M) be a network configuration with N input nodes, K hidden nodes and M output nodes respectively; then the network configuration of the above problems are (2-2-1), (3-2-1), (5,12,6), (1,6,1) and (64,20,26) respectively. Their learning rates are set as 0.5, 0.3, 0.1, 0.4 and 0.05 respectively. The momentum factor of all three problems is 0.7. For the XOR problem, the output should be unity only when the two inputs are different. For the 3-bit parity problem, the output will be set to unity when the three inputs produce an odd parity. The 5-bit counting problem, which counts the number of 1's from 5 input units, contains many local minima and thus it is a standard experiment to illustrate the performance of a learning algorithm to avoid trapping in local minima [4]. The regression problem adopted in [9] is to learn how to approximate the function $g(x) = 0.2 + 0.8(x + 0.7\sin(2\pi x))$. The character recognition problem is to recognize the inputs from an 8×8 matrix to the 26 small capital letter set of [a,...,z]. For the first three problems and the character recognition problem, the input patterns are binary (consisting of 0's and 1's). The regression problem consists of non-binary inputs, that is, the inputs are real-valued numbers. For these problems, the learning algorithm will terminate when the system errors reach 10^{-3} within 3×10^4 iterations. As all gradient based algorithms are sensitive to different starting points, we run each problem for 30 different sets of initial weights. All the results listed below are the average convergence performance of 30 runs. The initial weights are drawn at random from uniform distribution between -0.3 and 0.3. All simulations are done in Sun Ultra Sparc 5 workstations with simulation programs written in C language. The performance of various learning algorithms, including standard back-propagation (BP) [10], Quickprop [2], RPROP [6], SARPROP [11] and the MGFPROP algorithms are investigated in our simulations. From Table 1, it can be seen that the MGFPROP algorithm always converges to the global solution (having 100% of global convergence) but others cannot. Moreover, most of the cases show that the convergence rate of the MGFPROP algorithm is always faster than other fast algorithms. It can be noticed from Fig. 2 to Fig. 5 that when the value of S is set to 5, it will give quite promising results. Further increase in S will not increase the convergence speed much. Experimental results also show that the use of normalization in MGFPROP can further improve the convergence speed of the algorithm.

VII. Conclusions

This paper discusses the MGFPROP algorithm in details for improving the performance of the standard BP algorithm in terms of having faster convergence rate and better global convergence capability. The modifications on the partial derivative of the activation function will increase the back-propagated error signal, and hence improve the convergence rate of the standard back-propagation algorithm. In addition, the use of normalization on the learning rate can further increase the convergence speed. From the convergence analysis, it is found that MGFPROP reserves the properties of local convergence as that of BP. The new algorithm can speed up the convergence of BP and eliminate the flat spot problem effectively. The simulations performed indicate that the MGFPROP algorithm is considerably faster than the standard back-propagation algorithm with better global search capability. The results also show that the MGFPROP algorithm always has better performance as compared with other traditional methods.

References

[1] A. M. Franzini, "Speech recognition with back propagation," *Proceedings of the Ninth Annual Conference of the IEEE Engineering in Medicine and Biology Society*, Boston, 1987, pp. 1702–1703.

[2] S. E. Fahlman, "Fast learning variations on back-propagation: An empirical study," *Proceedings of the 1988 Connectionist Models Summer School (Pittsburgh, 1988)*, D. Touretzky, G. Hinton and T. Sejnowski, eds., p. 38–51, 1989.

[3] J. R. Chen and P. Mars, "Stepsize variation methods for accelerating the back-propagation algorithm," *Proceedings of the International Joint Conference on Neural Networks*, vol. 1, pp. 601–604, 1990.

[4] A. Van Ooyen, and B. Nienhuis, "Improving the convergence of the back-propagation algorithm," *Neural Networks*, vol. 5, pp. 465–471, 1992.

[5] Y. Lee, S. H. Oh, and M. W. Kim, "An Analysis of Premature Saturation in Back Propagation Learning," *Neural Networks*, vol. 6, pp. 719–728, 1993.

[6] M. Riedmiller and H. Braun, "A direct adaptive method for faster back-propagation learning: The RPROP Algorithm," *Proceedings of International Conference on Neural Networks*, vol. 1, p. 586–591, 1993.

[7] J. E. Vitela, and J. Reifman, "Enhanced backpropagation training algorithm for transient event identification," *Transactions of the American Nuclear Society*, vol. 69, pp. 148–149, 1993.

[8] C. M. Kuan and K. Hornik, "Convergence of Learning Algorithms with Constant Learning Rates," *IEEE Trans. on Neural Networks*, vol. 2, no. 5, p. 484–489, 1991.

[9] B. Verma, "Fast Training of Multilayer Perceptrons," *IEEE Trans on Neural Networks*, vol. 8, no. 6, p. 1314–1329, 1997.

[10] D. E. Rumelhart, G. E. Hinton and R. J. Williams, "Learning internal representations by error propagation," *Parallel Distributed Processing: Exploration in the Microstructure of Cognition*, vol. 1 MIT Press, Cambridge, Mass, 1986.

[11] N. K. Treadgold and T. D. Gedeon, "Simulated Annealing and Weight Decay in Adaptive Learning: the SARPROP Algorithm," *IEEE Trans. on Neural Networks*, vol. 9, no. 4, p. 662–668, 1998.

[12] J. E. Vitela and J. Reifman, "Premature Saturation in Backpropagation Networks: Mechanism and Necessary Conditions," *Neural Networks*, vol. 10, no. 4, p. 721–735, 1997.

[13] M. Gori, and A. Tesi, "On the problem of local minima in back-propagation," *IEEE Transactions on Pattern Analysis and Machine Intelligence*, vol. 14, no. 1, pp. 76–86, 1992.

[14] E. K. Blum, "Approximation of Boolean functions by sigmoidal networks: Part I: XOR and other two variable functions," *Neural Computation*, vol. 1, no. 4, pp. 532–540, 1989.

TABLE 1
PERFORMANCE COMPARISON AMONG DIFFERENT ALGORITHMS

Test case	5-bit counting		Regression		Character recognition	
Algorithm	Convergence rate	% of global conv.	Convergence rate	% of global conv.	Convergence rate	% of global conv.
BP	FAIL	0	4111.6	46.7	121.1	100
Quickprop	487.1	66.7	3621.7	76.7	57.0	3.3
RPROP	FAIL	0	2605.5	0	61.0	3.3
SARPROP	275.3	100	1293.6	96.7	54.9	100
MGFPROP	245.9 ($S=5$)	100	510.2 ($S=6$)	100	29.5 ($S=3$)	100

FAIL – the algorithm cannot converge to global solution after 30000 iterations

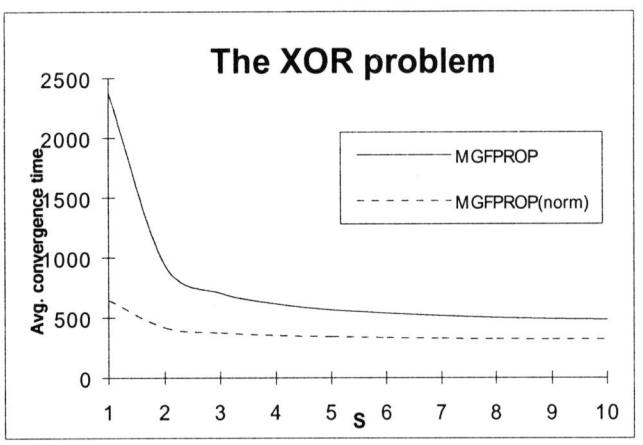

Fig. 2. The comparison of average convergence time on different values of S for the XOR problem.

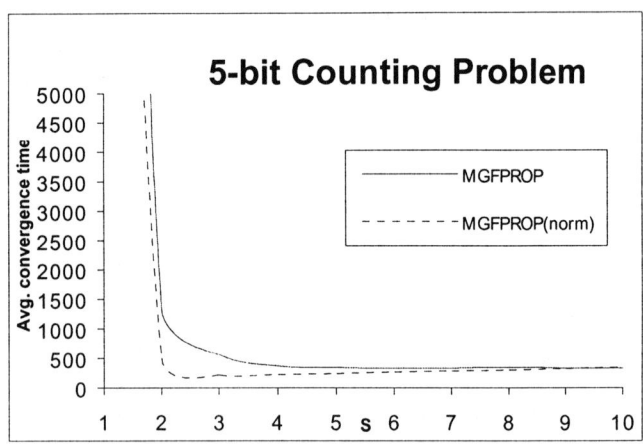

Fig. 4. The comparison of average convergence time on different values of S for the 5-bit counting problem.

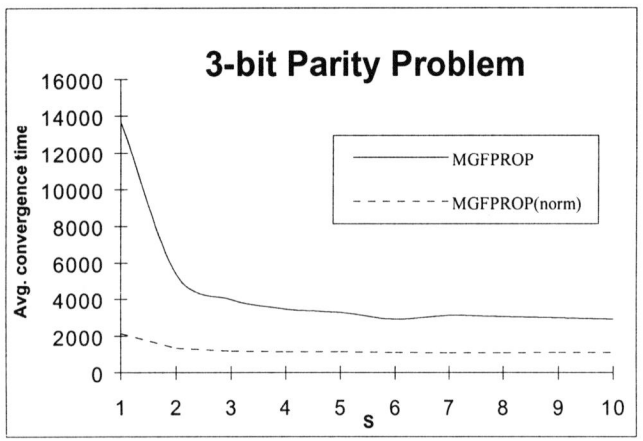

Fig. 3. The comparison of average convergence time on different values of S for the 3-bit parity problem.

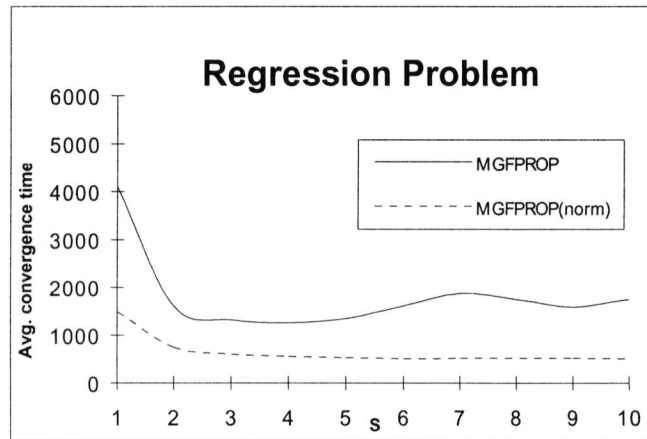

Fig. 5. The comparison of average convergence time on different values of S for the regression problem.

Competitive Reinforcement Learning in Continuous Control Tasks

Myriam Abramson
George Mason University
Fairfax, VA 22030
mabramso@gmu.edu

Peter Pachowicz
George Mason University
Department of Electronic
and Computer Engineering
Fairfax, VA 22030
ppach@gmu.edu

Harry Wechsler
George Mason University
Department of Computer Science
Fairfax, VA 22030
wechsler@cs.gmu.edu

Abstract— This paper describes a novel hybrid reinforcement learning algorithm, Sarsa Learning Vector Quantization (SLVQ), that leaves the reinforcement part intact but employs a more effective representation of the policy function using a piecewise constant function based upon "policy prototypes." The prototypes correspond to the pattern classes induced by the Voronoi tessellation generated by self-organizing methods like Learning Vector Quantization (LVQ). The determination of the optimal policy function can be now viewed as a pattern recognition problem in the sense that the assignment of an action to a point in the phase space is similar to the assignment of a pattern class to a point in phase space. The distributed LVQ representation of the policy function automatically generates a piecewise constant tessellation of the state space and yields in a major simplification of the learning task relative to the standard reinforcement learning algorithms for whom a discontinuous table look function has to be learned. The feasibility and comparative advantages of the new algorithm is shown on the cart centering and mountain car problems, two control problems of increased difficulty.

I. INTRODUCTION

Continuous control tasks typically try to influence a physical process. In simulation, they can be represented as Markov Decision Processes (MDPs) with a limited number of relevant variables. Examples of control tasks include everyday's tasks like parking a car, adjusting the temperature of the water when preparing a bath, keeping a fire burning in the fireplace, etc [5]. Control tasks require constant adjustment by the operator much like taking turns in a game where the adversary is the environment. The process is composed of a succession of *states* and moves or actions influence the next state stochastically or deterministically. Those tasks are characterized by a continuous search space, or smoothness assumption, and are different from combinatorial tasks. The smoothness assumption is the assumption that similar actions apply for situations close in input space except at some boundary conditions. The mountain car and the cart centering problems examined below are 2-dimensional control tasks varying position and velocity. Both of those problems require a long sequence of steps and the credit assignment problem is compounded by the fact that the state trajectories can contain cycles.

A task can be represented by state-action pairs where the states are real-valued variables describing the physical process at a moment in time and the action desired is typically a non-linear function of those states. It is difficult to compute an exact solution to those problems. The cart centering problem is one of the few control task problems where an exact mathematical solution is known. A solution for those problems involves computing a step function for each action which divides the input space into continuous regions. A good similarity function for those problems would therefore represent the graded correlation of a prototype vector and an input vector. Comparative experiments conducted in the cart centering problem matching randomly generated states against a table associating states and their optimal action have shown the superiority of the Euclidean distance function in this problem.

This paper is organized as follows. Section II describes the learning principles underlying LVQ as a function approximator. Section III highlights the differences between on and off policies in reinforcement learning. Section IV presents QLVQ[2] as a related algorithm and Section V describes in detail the SLVQ algorithm. Section VI applies the minimum spanning tree topology to SLVQ. Section VII describes the cart centering problem and shows SLVQ results compared to the optimal policy found by genetic programming and QLVQ. Section VIII describes the mountain car problem and shows SLVQ results compared to a tile coding approach based on discretization and QLVQ.

II. SELF-ORGANIZATION AND LVQ

Self-organization involves the ability to learn and organize (cluster) sensory information without the benefit of a teacher. Learning is driven by measures of fitness, possibly evolved over time. If the task to be learned is that of clustering, one example of such a fitness measure is that of similarity. The process of self-organization consists of iteratively modifying synaptic weights in response to sensory patterns until an optimal configuration, according to some closeness measure, eventually develops. One particular class of self-organizing systems that are of interest to us are the Self-Organizing Feature Maps (SOFM)[6], which are driven by competitive learning. In the competitive learning scheme, the output neurons of the network compete among themselves to be activated or fired, with the result that only one output neuron or one neuron per group is on at any one time. The locations of the winning neurons tend to become ordered with respect to each other in such a way that a meaningful lattice like coordinate system eventually emerges and faithfully represents the topology of the sensory input.

There are many situations where the clusters derived as a result of self-organization have to be appropriately labeled as it would be the case for information retrieval. Towards that end, one expands SOFM using a supervised learning scheme as it is the case with Learning Vector Quantization (LVQ). In the case of LVQ, the labeled clusters collection correspond to a (quantized) *codebook* of compressed pattern templates. The LVQ algorithm[6] is a supervised clustering method in which each output unit represents a particular class or category. The weight vector for an output unit is often referred to as a prototype or *codebook* vector for the class that the unit represents. It is also assumed that a set of training patterns with known class labels is provided, along with an initial distribution ("seed") of prototype vectors. After training, the neural net classifies an input vector by assigning it to the same class as the (labeled) output unit that has its weight vector closest to the input vector. After learning, the probability density function of the input is approximated by the modified set of discrete decoders or codebook vectors. The distributed representation of LVQ into codebook vectors as generalization of the input patterns significantly reduces the state space requirements and has a close correspondence to a tabular representation of state-action pairs.

III. REINFORCEMENT LEARNING POLICIES

In reinforcement learning, a learning agent interacts with its environment by taking actions and accepting input from the environment. Input from the environment constitutes the state of the environment followed by an immediate reward. State information passed to the agent summarizes all currently relevant information about the environment. In contrast to a purely reactive agent, a learning agent is endowed with an internal state that summarizes past history of its interactions with the environment. The environmental state and the internal state of the agent together are the state of the system upon which the learning agent bases its actions. An internal state enables an agent to generalize from previous experience which is missing from purely reactive architecture. The reward passed to the learning agent is a scalar reinforcement that serves to evaluate current and past actions. While interacting with the environment, the agent follows a policy to determine what actions to take. A policy is a function, denoted as π, that maps the system state to an action to be taken by the agent. Through interaction with the environment, the agent learns either a value function $V^\pi(s)$, which represent the "desirability" of a state s given a fixed policy π, or an action-value function,

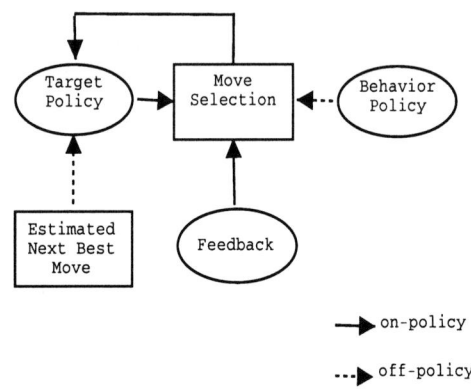

Fig. 1. On and off policies

denoted as $Q(s,a)$, which maps state s and action a to a "long-term" reward $E[\sum_{t=0}^{\infty} \gamma^t r^{t+1}]$ where $0 < \gamma \leq 1$ and r^t is the reward at time t. This form of expected long-term reward is called "discounted future" reward over an infinite horizon and has a finite value.

There are two basic ways of using experience in reinforcement learning: off-policy and on-policy[12]. They differ only by the update rule used to arrive at an optimal policy. Figure 1 illustrates the basic differences between on and off policies regarding the action selection and update step. In an on-policy, the policy being updated (target policy) affects the selection of the next move. In an off-policy, the move evaluation of the next "best" move affects the update of the current move but the move selection does not depend on the policy being updated and can come from a completely different policy (behavior policy). Both policies reflect the bootstrapping strategy of dynamic programming to update the prediction for s_t from the next prediction s_{t+1}. The off-policy, embodied in the Q-learning algorithm[13], uses the estimate of the optimal policy for update of the existing policy and consequently separates exploration from control. The on-policy, embodied in the Sarsa algorithm[9], [12], uses the current estimate of an existing non-optimal policy for refinement towards a *better* existing policy and combines exploration and control. The only guarantee to arrive at an optimal policy with Sarsa is possible only if the control policy progressively inches itself toward the optimal policy as the exploration tapers off during training[10]. On-policy RL algorithms are dependent on the exploration for the accuracy of the action values. In both policies, convergence has been proved in the discrete, tabular case if each action is selected infinitely often[14], [3]. Convergence has also been proven for TD(λ) in the linear representation case[4].

IV. QLVQ

QLVQ integrates Q-learning as an off-policy reinforcement learning algorithm with LVQ. This integration only loosely ties the two learning processes. Let $f(s)$ be the codebook vector closest to the input state s and ΔQ be the change in action value, the codebook vector is then repositioned according to the sign of ΔQ. Algorithm 1 describes this backup process.

Algorithm 1 QLVQ
- Initialize all $Q(m,a)$, the learning rates α and β, and discount factor γ
- While stopping condition is false
  1) Randomly generate state s.
  2) $m \leftarrow f(s)$
  3) Select an action a to execute.
  4) Execute action a, and let s' be the next state and r the reward received.
  5) $m' \leftarrow f(s')$
  6) Update $Q(m,a)$
     $\delta_Q \leftarrow [r + \gamma \max_b Q(m',b) - Q(m,a)]$
     $Q(m,a) \leftarrow Q(m,a) + \alpha(t)\delta_Q$
  7) $m(t+1) \leftarrow m(t) + \beta(t)[s\text{-}m(t)]$ if $\delta_Q > 0$
     $m(t+1) \leftarrow m(t) - \beta(t)[s\text{-}m(t)]$ if $\delta_Q < 0$
  8) Reduce monotonically the learning rates α and β as a function of t.
  9) Update the policy function π such that
     $\pi(m) \leftarrow \arg\max_{a \in A} Q(m,a)$

V. SARSA LEARNING VECTOR QUANTIZATION (SLVQ)

SLVQ is an adaptive heuristic critic algorithm (see Figure 2) motivated by QLVQ described above. SLVQ integrates Sarsa, an on-policy reinforcement learning algorithm, with LVQ. This integration further ties the estimation of the action value Q of a move, or Q-value, to the pattern recognition task of the situation in an adaptive fashion. This is in contrast to value function approximators which uses pattern recognition techniques to directly associate a state description to a value, e.g. the probability of success. An SLVQ codebook vector is a tuple $\{m, a, Q, \alpha\}$ where m is a weight vector, a is the associated action, Q is the action value, and α is the local learning rate.

In an off-policy control algorithm such as QLVQ, the action value of the *best* move according to the current estimate of the optimal policy is the one used. In contrast, in an on-policy control algorithm such as SLVQ, the action value of the *next* move taken a' will be used to update the state-action pair $Q(s,a)$. In addition, temporal credit assignment to previous moves, modulated by λ or *eligibility trace*[11], is not limited to a single step. The update of the weight vectors m is a function of the change in the Q-values. Let $\Delta Q(m_t, a)$ be the change in action value at time t with action a and discount factor γ. The weight vector m that matched s_t most closely then moves closer to or away from s_t accordingly:

$$m_t = \arg\max_m Similarity(s_t, m) \quad (1)$$

$$\Delta Q(m_t, a) = \alpha_m [\gamma Q(m', a') - Q(m_t, a)] \quad (2)$$

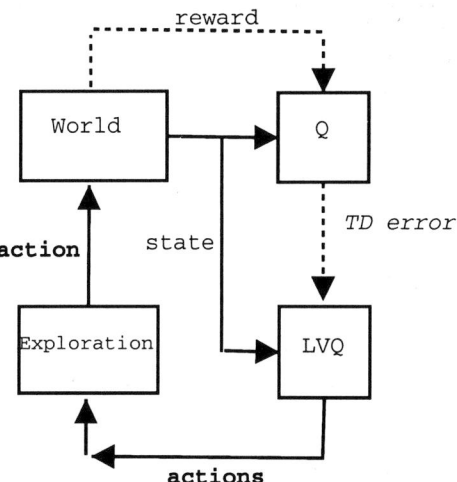

Fig. 2. SLVQ adaptive heuristic critic architecture

$$m(t+1) = m(t) + \Delta Q(m_t, a)[s_t - m_t] \quad (3)$$

The theoretical justification of using an on-policy approach with LVQ rather than an off-policy is that LVQ tries to approximate the probability distribution of its input by minimizing its distortion:

$$E = \int distance(s, m_c) p(s) ds$$

where s is the input state and m_c is the winning codebook vector. The overall error E in the codebook vectors will be minimized if $p(s)$, the sampling training distribution, corresponds to the control policy we want to optimize.

VI. SLVQ WITH MINIMUM SPANNING TREE TOPOLOGY (SLVQ-MST)

The continuous control task problem assumes that input vectors that are close from a distance point of view will be in the same neighborhood and trigger the same action except for those that lie at the boundary. It does therefore make sense for those problems to activate neurons defined by a neighborhood function or kernel to learn from the same input. Spreading the reward around makes learning converge faster and less sensitive to changes in the parameters. By doing so, a *structural* credit assignment is propagated to similar states and similar actions. The Minimal Spanning Tree (MST) algorithm defines a topology connecting the codebooks with a minimum total distance and thus defines local neighborhoods with global optimality. The SLVQ control equation where m_c is the winning codebook vector at t gets propagated to neighboring codebook vectors according to a neighborhood function h_{ci} and move label. Under SLVQ-MST, potentially all codebook vectors learn from an episode. The update equation for the neighboring codebook vectors m_j is as follows:

Algorithm 2 SLVQ-MST

Input outcome is the reward at T, the end of an episode
SLVQ (outcome,T)
    while (T>0)
        Codebook ← $\{m,a,Q,\alpha\}_T$
        δ ← r+outcome - $Q_{Codebook}$
        t ← T
        trace ←1
        Codebook.MST_PROPAGATE(δ,s_t)
        while (t>0)
            codebook ← $\{m,a,Q,\alpha\}_t$
            codebook.BACKUP($trace\delta, s_t$)
            trace ←traceλ
            t ← t -1
        T← T-1
        outcome ← $\gamma Q_{Codebook}$
BACKUP (delta, state)
    m_{t+1} ← $m_t + \alpha_t delta(state - m_t)$
    Q_{t+1} ← $Q_t + \alpha_t delta$
    decay α
MST_PROPAGATE (delta, state)
    neighbors ←neighbors($radius$)
    for   each neighbor
        h ← $Similarity$(state,neighbor)
        neighbor.BACKUP($hdelta, state$)

$$h_{ij}(t) = \begin{cases} Similarity(s_t, m_j), & if\, neighbor(i,j)\, at\, t \\ 0, & otherwise \end{cases}$$

$$\eta = \begin{cases} h_{ij}(t), & if\, same\, move \\ 0, & if\, different\, move \end{cases}$$

$$m_j(t+1) = m_j(t) + \alpha_j(t)\eta\Delta Q(m_i(t), a)[s(t) - m_j(t)] \quad (4)$$

Algorithm 2 illustrates the entire backup procedure for an episodic task. MST has been shown to fit better to certain distributions and to provide more flexibility to changes in the input distribution than a fixed spatial topology[6]. The computational time for the MST algorithm is $O(n^2)$ and might be prohibitive for large problems. Since the relative order of the codebook vectors changes slowly, the MST neighborhood reordering needs to take place only a few times. This modified SLVQ algorithm is used in the control tasks described below.

VII. THE CART CENTERING PROBLEM

In the cart centering problem the goal is to find a policy or set of rules towards a fixed point in the state space from any other point rather than finding an optimal trajectory from an initial fixed starting point as in the mountain car problem.

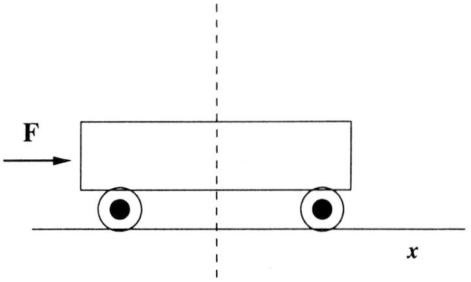

Fig. 3. Cart centering problem

A. Problem Description

The cart centering problem involves pushing a frictionless cart of mass m on a one-dimensional track until the cart becomes centered. A force of fixed magnitude F, a *bang-bang* force, is applied either to the right or to the left at each time step t. The two state variables for this system are the position x and velocity v. The object is to find an optimal policy to apply these bang-bang forces from initial random conditions until the cart becomes centered at approximately position 0.0 and velocity 0.0. Under the optimal policy, the bang-bang force is to be applied to the right if

$$-x > \frac{v^2 Sign(v)}{2|\frac{F}{m}|}$$

and to the left otherwise.

The movement of the cart is governed by the following equations:

$$a(t) = \frac{F(t)}{m}$$

$$v(t+1) = bound(v(t) + \tau a)$$

$$x(t+1) = bound(x(t) + \tau v(t))$$

where $a(t)$ is the acceleration computed by Newton's Law at time t, τ is the size of the time step (0.02 s), m the mass of the cart (2.0kg), and $|F|$, the magnitude of the force (1.0N). The control variable, left (-1.0) or right (+1.0), acts as a multiplier on the force F at time t. Positions are initialized randomly between -0.75 meters and $+0.75$ meters and velocity is initialized to 0. The bound operation enforces the range of the variables.

The optimal solution to this problem was found with genetic programming[7] where the experimental settings of this problem were taken. The payoff value was the time it took to center the cart. The optimal solution was found after 1500 evaluations of S-expressions composed of a limited function set {+,-,*,/,%,ABS,GT}.

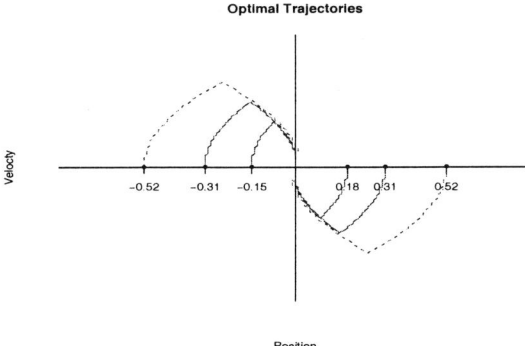

Fig. 4. Optimal trajectories

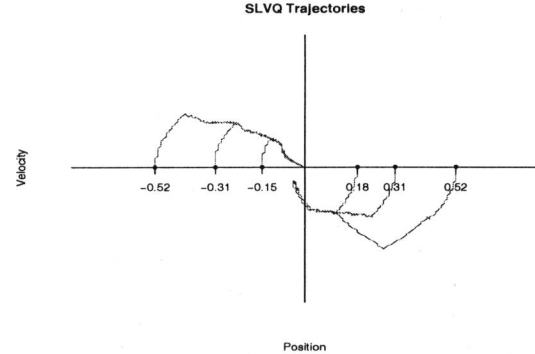

Fig. 5. SLVQ trajectories

α=1.0, λ=0.07, γ=1, $m = 200$

B. Empirical Evaluation

The optimal solution to this problem starting from different random positions and null velocity averages 76 steps in 100 trials. In our experiments, the Euclidean distance to the goal (0,0) is propagated back as a negative reward if the cart does not get approximately centered (± 0.05) within the maximum number of steps allowed (110 steps). Otherwise, +1.0 is propagated back as a positive reward. The two-dimensional codebook vectors (position and velocity) are initialized randomly within some certain distance of each other by partitioning the input space into equal 3x3 areas. The Pareto optimality of the moves along the pattern similarity and action value dimension is used for selecting the next move:

$$eval(s,a) = \frac{Similarity(s,m)Q(m,a_m)}{\sum_m Similarity(s,m)Q(m,a_m)} \quad (5)$$

where s is the current state, a the candidate action, and m the candidate codebook vector. This approach combines discrimination and the reinforcement feedback and boosts exploration at the beginning of the learning process. The learning rate α decayed monotonically. The updates were applied to the immediate neighbors in the MST topology for the first 100 episodes. SLVQ averages 77 steps in 100 trials after training for 1500 episodes over 3 runs with an average accuracy of 88% measured as the number of completed trajectories within the maximum number of steps. Figure 4 shows the trajectories given by the optimal solution for points starting at various positions and null velocity. Figure 5 shows the SLVQ trajectories for the same initial starting points. Due to finite accuracy both the computed optimal and SLVQ solutions end within an area of small uncertainty (± 0.05) around the optimum point (0,0). QLVQ takes an average of 94 steps with the same parameters and training episodes.

VIII. THE MOUNTAIN CAR PROBLEM

This control problem was first introduced as the *puck-on-the-hill* problem in [8]. A frictionless puck moves on a bumpy

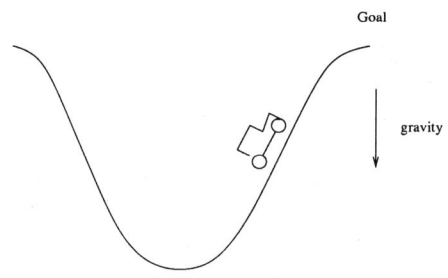

Fig. 6. The mountain car problem

surface acted on by gravity and a thruster. This problem has been reworked as the *mountain car* problem in [11] as an undiscounted task. The objective is to drive past the top of the mountain but, even at maximum thrust, the engine is not strong enough to get up the steep slope (Figure 6). The only way to solve this problem is to move *away* from the goal. This is a classic example of delayed rewards where a greedy strategy would fail.

A. Problem Description

Like the cart centering problem, this problem has two continuous state variables: the position x_t in the range $[-1.2, 0.5]$ and the velocity v_t in the range $[-0.07, 0.07]$. However, there are three possible actions: forward, backward and none, i.e. $a_t \in \{+1, -1, 0\}$. The absence of direction reduces the velocity just like when we stop accelerating before stopping. The reward is -1 on all time steps in[11] and as an exponentially decreasing function of the proximity of the goal in [8]. The position and velocity are initialized randomly at the beginning of each episode. The physics of the problem are as follows:

$$x_{t+1} = bound(x_t + v_{t+1})$$

$$v_{t+1} = bound(v_t + 0.001a_t - 0.0025cos(3x_t))$$

The bound operation enforces the range of the variables.

B. Empirical Evaluation

A solution to this problem using Sarsa and tile coding is given in [12], [11]. Tile coding discretizes a continuous input space into finer degrees of resolution with a fixed number of binary features. This encoding of the state space evolved from the state representation of CMACs[1] where the input space is mapped onto overlapping binary features which are activated depending on the size of their receptive fields. A weight representing the expected value of each tile is associated with a binary feature and the approximate value function can then be computed as a linear combination of those weights. The reward is -1 on each step and the total feedback is divided evenly among each tiles. A near optimal policy (104-109 steps) is achieved in less than 100 episodes with 9 tilings of 9x9 offsets starting at position -0.5 and velocity 0.

In our experiments with SLVQ, the relative position to the goal is propagated back as a negative reward if the car does not make it within the maximum number of steps allowed (1000 steps). Otherwise, the relative number of steps is propagated back as a positive reward since the starting position remains fixed. There is no intermediate reward/penalty and no discount. The two-dimensional codebook vectors m (position and velocity) are initialized randomly within some certain distance of each other by dividing the input space into equal 3x4 areas. The Pareto optimality of the moves was used to provide a source of exploring starts (Equation 5). The Euclidean distance determines the winning codebook vector. The learning rate α was held constant. The updates were applied to the immediate neighbors in the MST topology for the first 100 episodes. Figure 7 shows the action takens by the greedy policy with the active codebook vectors. A near optimal policy (111-119 steps) is achieved in less than 100 episodes starting at position -0.5 and velocity 0. QLVQ fails to converge in this problem with similar parameters and initialization of codebook vectors. For problems where delayed rewards is important, on-policy learning with eligibility trace has a faster performance and better convergence properties.

SLVQ learns to partition the input space into a Voronoi tesselation according to the empirical distribution of the data and the requirements of the task. It is therefore doing more than the fixed representation of tile coding by trying to learn the representation as well as the task but provides a more flexible computational approach for problems of high dimensionality. The fixed size discretization of tile coding is not desirable when different granularity is needed in different regions of the state space. It is also possible with the SLVQ approach to bias the search space with a proper initialization of the codebook vectors.

IX. Conclusions

This paper describes S(arsa)LVQ, a new hybrid RL algorithm suitable for continuous control tasks. It combines "on" policies

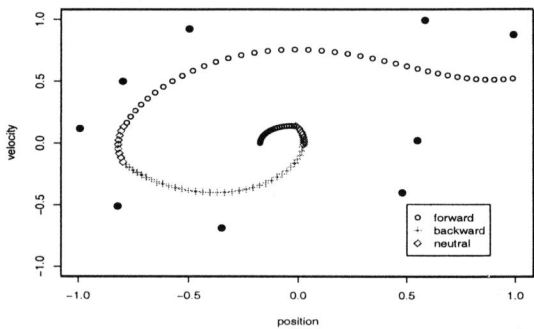

Fig. 7. SLVQ mountain car policy and relevant codebook vectors at 111 steps

$\alpha=0.1, \lambda=0.07, \gamma=1, m=12$

of the "Sarsa" type with the distributed representation of LVQ. Our experiments on two classic control problems, cart centering and mountain car, show the feasibility, usefulness and comparative advantages of our novel approach. Future work includes expanding SLVQ to further improve its ability to handle the trade-off between exploration and exploitation using heuristic search methods and leveraging from the distributed representation of the policy function.

References

[1] J.S. Albus. A theory of cerebellar function. *Mathematical Biosciences*, 10:15–61, 1971.
[2] C. Clausen, S. Gutta, and H. Wechsler. Reinforcement algorithms using functional approximation. In *16th International Joint Conference on Artificial Intelligence*, 1999.
[3] P. Dayan. The convergence of td(lambda) for general lambda. *Machine Learning*, (8):341–362, 1992.
[4] P. Dayan and T. J. Sejnowski. Td(lambda) converges with probability 1. *Machine Learning*, (14):295–301, 1994.
[5] T. L. Dean and M. P. Wellman. *Planning and Control*. Morgan Kaufman, San Mateo, CA, 1991.
[6] T. Kohonen. *Self-Organizing Maps*. Springer, 2nd edition, 1997.
[7] J. R. Koza. *Genetic Programming: on the Programming of Computers by Means of Natural Selection*. MIT Press, Cambridge, MA, 1992.
[8] A. W. Moore. Variable resolution dynamic programming: Efficiently learning action maps in multivariate real-valued state-spaces. In *Machine Learning: Proceedings of the Eighth International Workshop*, San Mateo, CA, 1991. Morgan Kaufmann.
[9] G. A. Rummery and M. Niranjan. On-line q-learning using connectionist systems. Technical report, Cambridge University Engineering Dept., 1994.
[10] S. Singh, T. Jaakkola, M. L. Littman, and Csaba Szepesvari. Convergence results for single-step on-policy reinforcement learning algorithms. *Machine Learning*, 38(3):287–308, 2000.
[11] S. P. Singh and R. S. Sutton. Reinforcement learning with replacing eligibility traces. *Machine Learning*, 22:123–158, 1996.
[12] R. S. Sutton and A. Barto. *Reinforcement Learning: an Introduction*. MIT Press, Cambridge, MA, 1998.
[13] C. Watkins. *Learning from Delayed Rewards*. PhD thesis, King's College, 1989.
[14] C. Watkins and P. Dayan. Q-learning. *Machine Learning*, (8):279–292, 1992.

A Neural Cascade Architecture for Document Retrieval

Abdelhamid Bouchachia Roland Mittermeir
University of Klagenfurt, Dept. of Informatics-Systems
Universitätsstrasse 65, A-9020 Klagenfurt, Austria
Email: {hamid, roland}@isys.uni-klu.ac.at

Abstract— This paper describes a fuzzy neural approach adopted for information retrieval. After a thematic analysis of documents that produces two conceptual sets called themes and rhemes, a fuzzy representation is derived. The fuzzy representation reflects the hierarchical nature of texts and suggests the use of type-2 fuzzy sets. It is then translated into a cascade of two neural networks. The first level in this cascade is a fuzzy associative memory network (FAM) which maps rhemes to themes and the second level consists of a fuzzy adaptive resonance theory network (Fuzzy ART) which relates themes to document categories. The approach was experimentally evaluated.

I. INTRODUCTION

Information retrieval (IR) is an instance of natural language processing. However, it is commonly known that natural language processing (NLP) is far from being a solved problem. Due to various human cognitive aspects inherent in NLP, it needs more sophisticated technologies that are able to cope with its expressive power. Information is mainly presented in the form of natural language texts. It is imprecise, ambiguous, leading to non convenience of traditional methods such as predicate logic. Technologies that focus on traditional "meaning-representation" in a rigid manner do not lend themselves the power to deal with information expressed in collection of textual NL documents. There is a real need for techniques that model information in a smooth and realistic way and that are able to cope with the uncertainty phenomena inherent in NLP. Thus, various computational intelligence (CI) (or soft computing) paradigms have recently attracted much attention of the IR community. CI [24] is generally the study of the design of intelligent agents/systems and consists of a set of coherent and symbiotic information processing techniques, namely granular computing, neurocomputing, and probabilistic computing that includes evolutionary computing. The notion of agent refers to something that acts intelligently in an environment given a set of goals. It is able to learn from experience, and makes appropriate choices. Such features are appropriate to the IR activities of searching, classifying, profiling and retrieving information. Each of these computing models has become an integrated part of the IR environment due to their ability to deal with partial truth. More interestingly, they are able to deal with the contextual meaning of information. Section II reviews the application of softcomputing techniques in the field of information retrieval. Note these computational models are not competitive, rather they are complementary leading to hybrid models.

In fact, in this paper we will describe a fuzzy neural architecture adopted in building an information retrieval system called *SyRS*. The point of departure of this work was to look for other text representations that are not statistics-based (e.g. vector space models [25]) exclusively, rather on those that take into account some cognitive aspects such as the organization of texts, and the way topics are structured in texts. Basically, the notion of the Theme-Rheme [10] which is a component of the language system, is applied. It deals with the textual meaning of texts. Based on this theory, a fuzzy representation with respect to some measures is derived after the thematic analysis of texts. The fuzzy representation is translated into a cascade of two neural networks. We approach the problem of retrieval from the angle of text categorization. This is motivated by the fact that similar documents tend to be relevant to the same query due to imprecision, incompleteness, and uncertainty that characterize user queries. If closer documents are put in the same container, the retrieval will be easier than searching along the collection.

The rest of the paper is organized as follows. Section II reviews the IR research work grounded by softcomputing techniques. Section III highlights the way documents are represented using the theme-rheme theory based on fuzzy sets. Section IV outlines the transition from fuzzy represenations to neural representations. Section V describes the SyRS's architecture. Then, the evaluation of SyRS is outlined in Section VI. Section VII concludes the paper.

II. SOFT COMPUTING FOR IR

Known for their ability to deal with different forms of uncertainty, soft computing techniques have recently gained much attention. The starting point was to fuzzify the boolean model using fuzzy sets [3], [11]. Compared with the boolean model, encouraging results raised the interest of the IR community to apply other granular computing models such as rough sets [13], [26]. More interestingly, such techniques were used to measure the strength of relation between words (fuzzy thesaurus) [19]. But the question of how to assign weights, which are assumed to be subjective, needs more attention. So far, different ideas have been implemented: using linguistic quantifiers, direct assignment by the user, and automatic statistical weight.

The second soft computing model is the connectionist paradigm which is well suited for the IR task. Neural network approaches can be successfully used in order to identify relations (that are hard for humans to identify) among documents and to keep contextual usage of words (word meanings are defined entirely by other words). Neural networks are able to perform some implicit inferences such as extending the meaning of the query. Their application is systematic [29],

[2]. All components of the IR system: documents, queries, and indexing terms are each simulated by a layer. The few systems presented had not been tested on large collections. Adding new documents or new features may be a crucial problem. However this problem is general in the framework of connectionist systems. The neural networks have been successfully used for text categorization [12]. The widely-used type of NNs are the self-organizing maps of Kohonen [14].

From another angle, the problem of information retrieval is after all a problem of representation and retrieval. If we are looking to find the best indexing features that can reflect the content of documents, then the problem is simply an optimization, which can be phrased as follows: Given a space of features and a collection of documents, find the "optimal" combination of the elements of the space enabling to capture the content of documents. The problem of retrieval can be viewed as follows: Given a population of documents, find documents that better "fit" the requirements specified in the user's query. The terms "optimal", and "fit" play a central role in Evolutionary Computing (EC). The EC model aims at finding an optimal solution of a target problem of interest. Evolutionary paradigms [8] represented by genetic algorithms (GA) have mainly been applied for finding the best representation of documents [28], finding the best combination of matching functions [22], and profiling the users [20]. Other works [9] applied GA for document clustering. Although GA are known for their optimization power, they may not converge to the appropriate solution. Furthermore, they require high computational cost. However, for setting some parameters [22], they can be successfully applied.

In addition to traditional models like probabilistic [5] and statistical [25], other paradigms such as evidential reasoning [17], logical [27], and conceptual models [7] were also applied.

Most of these models are based on uncontrolled (or free-text) indexing that aims at producing indexing features (terms) automatically. The frequency of terms is generally used as an indicator of relevance of the content to a given topic without any semantic interpretation. Despite using various techniques to reduce the number of features, the dimensionality of the feature vector is still high. Usually the vector contains some terms that are not important for the semantic content of the document. As a result to that, the retrieval performance is negatively affected. The performance of any IR-related task depends largely on the quality of the features used to represent the documents. The problem of information retrieval is foremost a problem of representation. Further research is required to accurately represent the document contents. We cannot achieve that goal simply by adopting techniques from other fields, but also by rethinking the way documents are analyzed and represented. Hence, the need to other text analysis sources that allow to focus on meaningful contents of documents. Combining such sources with soft computing in a systematic way is the best manner to deal with information retrieval taking into account all aspects related to this task.

III. FUZZY DOCUMENT REPRESENTATION

By taking advantage of the cognitive aspect inherent in the organization of texts, our aim is to find the location of important information. To satisfy this goal, we exploit the theme-rheme theory, the basis of the systemic functional theory [6]. From a structural point of view, a proposition is divided into a *topic (theme)* and a *comment (rheme)*. Halliday [10] defined **theme** as: "...a function in the clause as a message. It is what the message is concerned with, the point of departure for what the speaker is going to say." A theme identifies something known by both speaker and listener. It is the part of the sentence from which the speaker proceeds by presenting the information to be commented in the remainder of the sentence. The **rheme** is defined as the remainder of the message, where the theme is developed [10]. It introduces new information, as a comment, to further explain the topic, hence the relationship *explained by* between themes and rhemes. Daneš [6] noted that important information lies in the theme part. Writers or speakers place their concerns within the message as thematic content. Thus, the content of the rheme tends to represent the details of the theme. Details related to the thematical analysis of texts (i.e., how to find themes and rhemes) is described in [10].

Here, words or phrases are considered as semantic units. They are categorized into two sets: the set of items being explained (i.e., themes), and the set of items that represent details of themes (i.e., rhemes). We depart from the idea that an important concept is usually commented. These comments introduce details related to the topic of a given concept and represent facets of that concept leading to two questions: How much topical is a theme in the text (how strong is it explained), and how well does a rheme explain themes? To measure these strengths we introduced two measures: topicality power for the first question, and the explanatory power for the second. With r_{ij} representing the number of occurrences of concepts R_j in the explanation (rhematic part) of the topic T_i, we will have:

$$\text{Topicality power} = P_{T_i} = \sum_j r_{ij} \quad (1)$$

$$\text{Explanatory power} = P_{E_j} = \sum_i r_{ij} \quad (2)$$

The notion of *"explained by"* is actually a fuzzy association between rhemes and themes. Formally each theme is a viewed as a fuzzy set (R, h) where $h : R \longrightarrow [0, 1]$ is associated to a thematic concept (T_i) with R, the set of rhemes serving as base set (or support). The membership function h assigns a membership value h_j to each rheme j as follows:

$$h_j = \frac{\text{No. occurrences of rheme } R_j \text{ explaining } T_i}{\text{the topicality power of theme } T_i} = \frac{r_{ij}}{P_{T_i}} \quad (3)$$

A document can be identified by its set of themes which are fuzzy sets. A document can be defined as a fuzzy set (T, g) where $g : T \longrightarrow [0, 1]$ is associated to a document D with T, the set of all themes mentioned in some document kept in

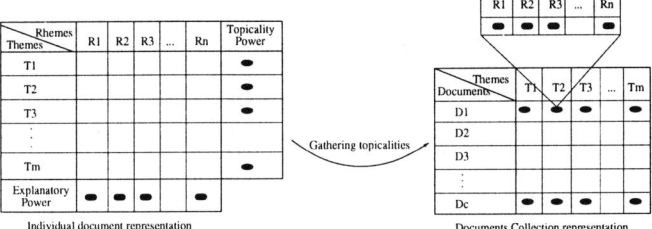

Fig. 1. Visualization of hierarchical fuzzy sets

the archive serving as base set (or support). The membership function g assigns a membership value g_i to each theme i as follows:

$$g_i = \frac{\text{the topicality of the thematic concept } T_i \text{ in } D}{\text{the thematic complexity of document } D} = \frac{P_{T_i}}{C_T} \quad (4)$$

where C_T is called the thematic complexity and reads as:

$$C_T = \sum_i P_{T_i} = \sum_i \sum_j r_{ij} \quad (5)$$

This definition tells that a document k is represented not as a simple fuzzy set but as a "complex" fuzzy set. It is a fuzzy set $D_k = \{g_1/T_1, g_2/T_2, ..., g_m/T_m,\}$ for a which a membership value g_i is a fuzzy set expressed by the membership function h_j such that $g_i = \{h_1/R_1, h_2/R_2, ..., h_n/R_n,\}$. To keep the relationship to the hierarchical nature of description representation, we refer to it as "hierarchical fuzzy sets". Figure 1 shows this notion of hierarchy more clearly.

IV. NEURAL NETWORKS FOR HIERARCHICAL FUZZY SETS IMPLEMENTATION

The simplest way to perform retrieval in this context is to use a distance which is a function of the number and weights of common features between the user's query and each document in the collection. Those documents that allow for a small distance (lower than a threshold) are retrieved. Since documents and queries are represented as fuzzy sets, it is easy to apply a similarity measure such as fuzzy equality, subsethood measure, etc. to compute the distance between a query and a document. However, the literature shows that many people have used techniques (e.g., clustering/classification) based on fuzzy sets to support text retrieval and categorization. Grouping mechanisms allow to reduce the search space, since we measure the distance only between the query and the prototype of each category. Using fuzzy sets independently has raised some critics [16], [21] stating that logic connectives based on t-norm and t-conorm operators cannot conveniently account for the prototypicality of the elements when looking for creating complex categories. Thus, we apply neural networks due to their ability to identify implicit relations among documents and to keep contextual usage of words (word meanings are defined entirely by other words). They are able to perform some implicit inferences, such as extending the meaning of the query. In the sequel, we show how the notion of "hierarchical fuzzy sets" can be implemented using a cascade of two neural networks: fuzzy associative memories (FAM) for mapping explaining concepts to explained concepts and fuzzy adaptive resonance theory (Fuzzy ART) to perform the categorization of documents using explained concepts (see Fig.2).

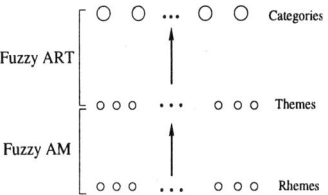

Fig. 2. The neural cascade

A. Mapping Rhemes to Themes

Dealing with semantics assumes dealing with some crucial questions such as how word meanings are related to concepts, and how word combinations are supported. Therefore, to simulate the human interpretation of words, the context of words has to be properly understood. This process allows naturally to perform a unique interpretation of a given word and thus resolves the ambiguity attached to multiple-meaning words. From this perspective neural networks are an appropriate tool. The choice of using FAMs to perform the first level of mapping in the whole process, namely the association of rhemes to themes (but also to realize "hierarchical fuzzy sets"), is motivated by the power of the FAMs in knowledge modelling. In fact, they allow to build a complex concept (theme) from fine grained pieces of knowledge (rhemes). FAMs can simulate a knowledge base as a long term memory expressed in terms of weights (matrix)(see Fig. 3). The propagation of activations along the network enables not only to determine the meaning of a given concept in given contextual conditions it also enables some implicit operations such as inference and logical connections (since weights are computed by fuzzy logic operators). If a concept is activated by a pattern, then, whenever a similar pattern is introduced, the concept is activated. Using FAMs will allow to trigger a concept with a certain degree of evidence because they map fuzzy sets to fuzzy sets [15]. The representation of the fuzzy set of rhemes R and its co-occurring fuzzy set of themes T is:

$$R : (R_1/\mu_R(R_1), R_2/\mu_R(R_2), .., R_m/\mu_R(R_m))$$
$$T : (T_1/\mu_T(T_1), T_2/\mu_T(T_2), .., T_n/\mu_T(T_n))$$

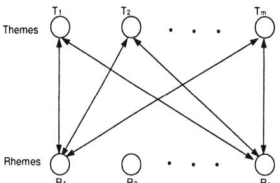

Fig. 3. Fuzzy associative memory

with μ_R and μ_T being the membership functions that map an element R_j of R and T_i of T and interpret the semantic significance of R_j for R and T_i for T. In fact, for a given document, $\mu_T(T_i)$ is the function g computed in (eq.4) and represents the averaged computed topicality power of the thematic concept T_i which is given by:

$$\mu_T(T_i) = \frac{\text{topicality power of } T_i}{\text{sum of the topicality powers}} = \frac{P_{T_i}}{\sum_i P_{T_i}} = \frac{P_{T_i}}{C_T} \quad (6)$$

$\mu_R(R_j)$ represents the averaged computed explanatory power of the rhematic concept R_j and is given by:

$$\mu_R(R_j) = \frac{\text{explanatory power of } R_j}{\text{sum of explanatory powers}} = \frac{P_{E_j}}{\sum_j P_{E_j}} \quad (7)$$

whereas the mapping from R to T plays the role of memorizing the association between both sets. The long-term memory is given by an encoding:

$$W = R^T \star T \quad (8)$$

The operation $\star$ can stand either for the fuzzy matrix composition (min-max rule) corresponding to the correlation-minimum encoding or matrix multiplication corresponding to correlation-product encoding. Note that R^T is the transposition of R. Recall of themes T and rhemes R is performed by means of Eq. 9.

$$\begin{aligned} T &= R \star W \\ R &= T \star W^T \end{aligned} \quad (9)$$

B. Mapping Themes to Categories

Retrieval efficiency can be enhanced if similar documents that can be returned in response to the same query are put in the same class. Hence, the second net in the cascade aims at document categorization using the output of the first net. In this work we are interested in unsupervised clustering techniques that rely on the principle of the degree of representativeness. In choosing the appropriate technique, one has to make a trade-off between the effectiveness (i.e. the quality of the resulting clusters), the computational efficiency, and the maintenance. The first two factors have been thoroughly studied in the literature, while the last factor is not yet well studied. Looking for models that are capable of continuously learning, adaptive resonance theory (ART) is a candidate to satisfy such a requirement. In fact, ART is able to learn additional knowledge without any risk of catastrophic forgetting, and more importantly, it is able to generate new classes as new data, sufficiently different from the previously seen data, is presented to the network. Such type of learning is known as *incremental learning* [23]. ART networks are particular with respect to this ability. It suffices to switch to the learning mode to teach the net. Given a document to classify, fuzzy ART receives, as input, a set of themes and produces, as output, the category to which the document is assigned. Fuzzy adaptive nets are able to classify patterns in overlapping categories by performing a many-to-many mapping [4], and also can be applied to perform a hierarchy by simply increasing (or decreasing) a parameter called vigilance [1]. The processing cycle of fuzzy ART, whose architecture is portrayed in Fig. 4,

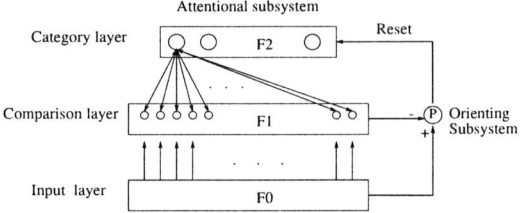

Fig. 4. Fuzzy adaptive resonance net

mainly consists of three steps: category choice, vigilance test, and resonance. During the first step, the input X representing the set of themes T is presented to the net. Then a choice function H_j is computed for each category j defined by a set of weights W_j:

$$H_j = \frac{|X \cap W_j|}{\alpha + |W_j|} \quad (10)$$

$\cap$ denotes the fuzzy AND operator and $\alpha(>0)$ is a user-defined parameter called the choice parameter. The category J with the maximum value of H_j is chosen. During the second step (i.e. the vigilance test), the similarity between W_J and the input X is compared to a parameter ρ called *vigilance*:

$$\frac{|X \cap W_J|}{|X|} \geq \rho \quad (11)$$

If the test is passed, resonance occurs and learning takes place. If not, the category J is excluded and a new category whose H_k is the largest value is chosen. Then the vigilance test is repeated until the condition is satisfied. During the last step, the weights W_J of the selected category are updated according to the rule:

$$W_J^{(new)} = \beta(X \cap W_J^{(old)}) + (1-\beta)W_J^{(old)} \quad (12)$$

C. Gluing the Two Nets

Given a document to classify, fuzzy ART receives as input a set of themes and produces as output the category to which the document is assigned. The connection between the FAM and the fuzzy ART during the learning and the recall phases has to take into account the long-term knowledge (i.e. the set of associations between themes and rhemes) stored at the level of FAM. To achieve that, the set of rhemes are presented to FAM which outputs a set of themes. Those activated themes (called `implicit` themes) will be combined with the themes that are present in the document at hand (called `explicit` themes) by means of fuzzy union (see Fig.5). We apply the fuzzy union because we are aiming at considering the items that are highly activated.

V. OVERVIEW OF THE SYSTEM

The system, built in the framework of this research and called SyRS, consists mainly of two modules (Fig. 6): the natural language processor and the neural networks. The natural language processor performs the analysis of documents (resp. the query specification). Three steps are required to do that.

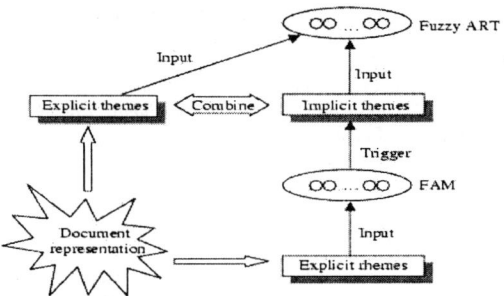

Fig. 5. Combination of explicit and implicit themes

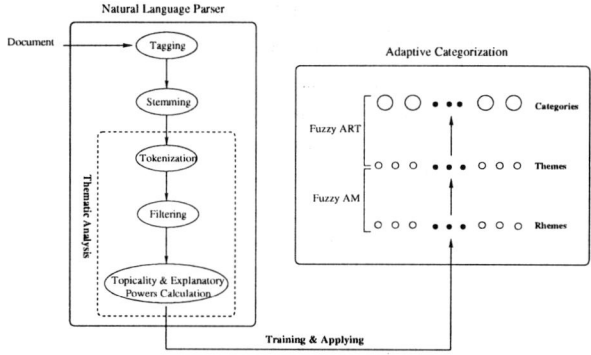

Fig. 6. Architecture of the system SyRS

First, the document is tagged by associating to each word a syntactical tag. This step aims at considering only semantically meaningful words. The second step, stemming, reduces the words to their roots. It aims at enhancing matching and reducing the size of the feature space. The third step computes the topicality and the explanatory powers by considering the list of the meaningful terms that appear as themes or rhemes in each sentence of the given document. To determine themes and rhemes. The second module in this architecture consists of the cascade of neural nets explained above. The nets are built after fixing the number of themes and rhemes extracted from a given collection of documents.

VI. EVALUATION

Given that SyRS is based on neural networks, the evaluation relies on two stages: training and testing. The former allows the classifier to learn to associate documents to categories using the features (themes and rhemes). The later is used for testing the effectiveness of the induced classifier. Each document from the testing set is fed to the classifier whose decision is compared to the human decision. The effectiveness of the classification is based on how often the human decision meets the classifier's decision using the microaveraged recall[1] (R) and precision[2] (P) [18]. We also apply a combination of recall and precision called the F-measure. It is given as:

$$F = \frac{(\beta^2 + 1)RP}{\beta^2 P + R} \quad (13)$$

The parameter β ($0 < \beta < \infty$) controls the relative weight of recall and precision (if $\beta = 1$, equal weight is assigned to R and P). Although, our main aim is to get high recall, equal importance between R and P is adopted to see the achievement of SyRS in a neutral way.

We used two data sets, namely AJPO, a collection of documents that describe software products[3], and NPL that is a collection describing electronic components. On the other hand and depending on the neural network box, two different variants of SyRS are experimented. The first variant (V1) is a simplified version using the upper-level of the architecture (fuzzy ART) only, while the second variant (V2) consists of the whole two-level architecture. The idea behind the suggestion of two variants of SyRS is to check the contribution of themes and rhemes in expressing the content of documents. The first variant relies on the fact that the explained items, i.e. the themes, are the items that bear the semantic content of documents. Hence, rhemes are neglected. In the second experiment, rhemes (i.e. explaining items), are taken into account. We expect a positive effect on the recall value because of this association.

After initial experiments aiming at finding the optimal setting of the system, particularly the value of ρ (=0.08) which controls the granularity of generated categories, we proceed to evaluate both versions V1 and V2 of SyRS. Initially, 330 documents of each collection constitute the input sample to SyRS. The training set consists of 250 randomly selected among 330 documents. The testing set consists of the remaining 80 documents. The evaluation is done by means of the effectiveness measures recall (R), precision (P), and the the F-measure (F) which represents the overall effectiveness. Table I shows the results of V1 and V2 using 80 queries. As a general remark, SyRS performs better on AJPO collection than on the NPL one. For the AJPO collection with respect to the first version of SyRS, recall is higher than that obtained with the NPL collection (a difference of 6%). The same thing can be said with respect to precision, but the difference is more important (15%). This leads to a better overall effectiveness expressed by means of the F-measure. This remark remains valid with the second version of SyRS. While, the precision for AJPO diminishes comparatively with NPL, recall, on the contrary, increases and achieves the best performance. As a conclusion, AJPO provides better performance results especially for precision, whereas the second version provides high recall values. We then attempted another experiment to test the effectiveness of SyRS with balanced classes. Let the number of queries be constant (=40), and each category of the NPL collection be represented by 10, 15, 20, and 25 documents successively. Table II shows the results obtained after training and testing SyRS. For V1, moving from a size of 10 documents for each category as learning set to 25 documents we observed an increase of 28% for recall and 27% for precision. One can admit that recall as well as precision

---
[1] R is the proportion of truly positive examples labelled positive by SyRS.
[2] P is the proportion of examples labelled positive that were truly positive.
[3] Note that SyRS was built in the framework of software retrieval.

TABLE I

EFFECTIVENESS RESULTS (IN %)

Version	Collection	R	P	F
V1	AJPO	81	73	77
V1	NPL	75	58	65
V2	AJPO	82	69	75
V2	NPL	87	57	68

TABLE II

EFFECT OF THE SIZE ON CLASSIFICATION (IN %)

Size/Cat	First version			Second version		
	R	P	F	R	P	F
10	72	37	49	79	44	57
15	87	57	69	90	50	64
20	90	62	73	100	54	70
25	100	64	78	100	51	68

increase substantially. For V2, an increase of 21% for recall and 7% for precision has been achieved. However, one can notice the contribution of integrating the FAM network in the architecture. Perfect recall is achieved earlier. Starting from size 20, recall is 100%, while in the first proposal, perfect recall is achieved only after considering 25 documents for each human determined category. Hence, our expectations about recall enhancement have been met. Furthermore, the first version allows better results with respect to precision and produces the highest overall effectiveness result expressed in terms of the F-measure with a degree of 78%. The results confirm that to consider only the thematic part of clauses for representing texts induces a loss in recall. Inferring the themes, even though they do not explicitly appear in the text, had a positive effect on recall.

VII. CONCLUSION

This paper described a hierarchical fuzzy neural architecture for document retrieval. To represent document contents, type-2 fuzzy sets were used. This representation was then carefully translated into a cascade of neural networks. The resulting architecture was then experimentally evaluated on English text. Very encouraging results were obtained. The same system is currently being evaluated on German texts.

REFERENCES

[1] G. Bartfai. An ART-based Modular Architecture for Learning Hierarchical Clusterings. *Neurocomputing*, 13:31–45, September 1996.

[2] R. Belew. Adaptive Information Retrieval: using a Connectionist Representation to Retrieve and Learn about Documents. In *Proc. of the 12th Inter. ACM SIGIR Conf. on Research and Development in Information Retrieval*, pages 11–20, Cambridge, 1989.

[3] G. Bordogna and G. Pasi. Controlling Retrieval through a User-Adaptive Representation of documents. *Inter. Journal of Approximate Reasoning*, 12:317–339, 1995.

[4] G. Carpenter, S. Grossberg, and D. Rosen. Fuzzy ART: Fast Stable Learning and Categorization of Analog Patterns by an Adaptive Resonance System. *Neural Networks*, 4(6):759, 1991.

[5] W. Croft and D. Harper. Using Probabilistic models of document retrieval without relevance information. *Journal of Documentation*, 37:285–295, 1979.

[6] F. Daneš. Functional Sentence Perspective and the Organization of the Text. In F. Daneš, editor, *Papers on Functional Sentence Perspective*, pages 106–128, Prague, 1974.

[7] N. Foo, B. Garner, A. Rao, and E. Tsui. Semantic Distance in Conceptual Graphs. In T. Nagel et al., editor, *Conceptual Structure: Current Research and Practice*. E.Horwood, 1992.

[8] D. Goldberg. *Genetic Algorithms in Search, Optimization, and Machine Learning*. Addison-Wesley, 1989.

[9] M. Gordon. User-based Document Clustering by Redescribing Subject Descriptions with a Genetic Algorithm. *Journal of the American Society for Information Science*, 42:311–322, 1991.

[10] M. Halliday. *An Introduction to Functional Grammar*. Edward Arnold, 1985.

[11] E. Herrera-Viedma. An Information Retrieval System with Ordinal Linguistic Weighted Queries Based on Two Weighting Semantic. In *Proc. of the 7th Inter. Conf. on Information Processing and Management of Uncertainty in Knowledge-Bases Systems. IPMU'2000*, volume I, pages 454–461, Madrid, 2000.

[12] T. Honkela, S. Kaski, K. Lagus, and T. Kohonen. WEBSOM: Self-organizing Maps of Document Collections. In *Proc. of the Self-Organizing Maps Workshop*, pages 310–315, Helsinki, 1997.

[13] T. Ho and K. Funakoshi. Information Retrieval Using Rough Sets. *Journal of Japanese Society for Artificial Intelligence*, 13(3):424–433, 1998.

[14] T. Kohonen. *Self-Organizing Maps*. Springer-Verlag, 1995.

[15] B. Kosko. *Neural Networks and Fuzzy Systems: a Dynamical Systems Approach to Machine Intelligence*. Prentice-Hall, 1992.

[16] G. Lakoff. *Women, Fire, and Dangerous Things: What Categories Reveal about the Mind*. University of Chicago Press, 1987.

[17] M. Lalmas. Dempster-Shafer's Theory of Evidence Applied to Structured Documents: Modelling Uncertainty. In *Proc. of the 20th Inter. ACM SIGIR Conf. on Research and Development in Information Retrieval*, pages 110–118, July 27-31 1997.

[18] D. Lewis and M. Ringuette. A comparison of Two Learning Algorithms for Text Categorization. In *Proc. of the 3rd Annual Symposium on Document Analysis and Information Retrieval*, pages 81–93, Las Vegas, 1994.

[19] S. Miyamoto. *Fuzzy sets in Information Retrieval and Cluster Analysis*. Kluwer Academic Publishers, 1990.

[20] J. Morgan and A. Kilgour. Personalising Information Retrieval using Evolutionary Modelling. In A. Moscardini and P. Smith, editors, *Proc. of PolyModel 16: Applications of Artificial Intelligence*, pages 142–149, 1996.

[21] D. Osherson and E. Smith. On the Adequacy of Prototype Theory as a Theory of concepts. *Cognition*, 9:35–58, 1981.

[22] P. Pathak, M. Gordon, and W. Fan. Effective Information Retrieval using Genetic Algorithms based Matching Functions Adaptation. In *Proc. of the 33rd Inter. Conf. on System Sciences*, Maui, Hawaii, January 4-7 2000.

[23] R. Polikar, L. Udpa, S. Udpa, and V. Honavar. Learn++: An incremental Learning Algorithm for Supervised Neural Networks. *IEEE Transactions on Systems, Man, and Cybernetics*, 31(4):497–508, 2000.

[24] D. Poole, A. Mackworth, and R. Goebel. *Computational Intelligence: A Logical Approach*. Oxford University Press, 1998.

[25] G. Salton and C. Buckley. Term Weighting Approaches in Automatic Text Retrieval. *Information Processing & Management*, 24(5):513–523, 1988.

[26] P. Srinivasan. Intelligent Information Retrieval Using Rough Set Approximations. *Information Processing and Management*, 25(4):347–361, 1989.

[27] K. van Rijsbergen. Towards an Information Logic. In *Proc. of 12th Inter. ACM SIGIR Conf. on Research and Development in Information Retrieval*, pages 77–86, 1989.

[28] D. Vrajitoru. Large Population or Many Generations for Genetic Algorithms? Implications in Information Retrieval. In F. Crestani and G. Pasi, editors, *Soft Computing in Information Retrieval, Techniques and Applications*, pages 199–222. Physica-Verlag, 2000.

[29] R. Wilkinson and P. Hingston. Using the Cosine Measure in a Neural Network for Document Retrieval. In *Proc. of 14th Inter. ACM SIGIR Conf. on Research and Development in Information Retrieval*, pages 202–210, Chicago, 1991.

A Wavelet-Based Neuro-Fuzzy System and Its Applications

Cheng-Jian Lin[*]   Cheng-Chung Chin[*]   Cheng-Ling Lee[+]

[*]Department of Computer Science and Information Engineering
Chaoyang University of Technology
168 Gifeng E. Rd., Wufeng
Taichung County, 413 Taiwan, R. O. C.
E-mail: cjlin@mail.cyut.edu.tw

[+]General Education Center
Nankai college

Abstract-This paper addresses a Wavelet-Based Neuro-Fuzzy System (WNFS) for non-linear system identification and control. The WNFS combines the traditional Takagi-Sugeno-Kang (TSK) fuzzy model and the wavelet neural network (WNN). Each fuzzy rule corresponding to a WNN consists of single-scaling wavelets. We adopt the non-orthogonal and compactly supported functions as wavelet neural network bases. The on-line structure/parameter learning algorithm is performed concurrently in the WNFS. The several simulation examples have been given to illustrate the performance and effectiveness of the proposed model.

I. INTRODUCTION

Recently, wavelets have become a very active subject in research area. Especially, wavelet neural networks (WNN) inspired by both the feedforward networks and wavelet decompositions have become a popular tool for function approximation [1]-[4]. For the WNN [4], the main problem is the selection of wavelet bases. The wavelets bases have to be selected appropriately since the choice can be critical to approximation performance. For FWN model [3], they propose a method to choose the wavelets. Step1 is selecting wavelet candidates to produce a higher size of wavelet candidates; step2 is purifying the wavelets by orthogonal least-squares (OLS) algorithm according the input training to reduce unnecessary wavelets. The off-line learning algorithm is proposed in [3].

In this paper, we propose a new type of model called a Wavelet-Based Neuro-Fuzzy System (WNFS), which consists of the traditional TSK fuzzy model and the WNN. The goal of the fuzzy model combined with WNN is to improve function approximation accurately. Each fuzzy rule corresponding to a WNN consists of single-scaling wavelets. We adopt the smooth non-orthogonal and compactly supported functions as wavelet neural network bases. The on-line structure/parameter learning algorithm is performed concurrently in the WNFS. This specification is more effective for the wavelet selection.

II. WAVELET BASES

A set of wavelet bases is a good tool to represent non-linearity. We can find these orthogonal wavelets, which are infinitely continuously differentiable. The support of these wavelets is $-\infty < x < +\infty$. Daubechies [2] presented wavelet bases, which is compactly supported but not infinitely supported. They proposed a simplest wavelet neural network, which exhibits much higher ability of generalization and much shorter time for learning, rather than a three-layered feedforward neural network. In this paper, we adopt the non-orthogonal and compactly supported functions in finitely range as wavelet bases.

The shape and position of wavelet bases are shown in Fig. 1. All the wavelet bases are allocated over the normalized range *[0,1]* on the variable space. Over-complete number of bases are adopted here, i.e., the number of bases should be 1,2,3…and M for scaling parameter $a=0, a=1 \cdots a=M$, But the orthogonal system should be set as $1, 2, 4 \cdots 2^M$. Furthermore, a+1 bases $\Phi a,0, \Phi a,1, ..., \Phi a,a$ are assigned for one scaling parameter a and $\Phi 0,0$ is assigned to be constant. The shape of bases ($a \neq 0$) is compactly supported as follows

$$\phi(x) = \begin{cases} \cos(\pi x) & (-0.5 \leq x \leq 0.5) \\ 0 & otherwise \end{cases} \quad \phi_{a,b}(x) = \phi(ax-b) \quad (1)$$

where b is defined as a shifting parameter, the maximum value of which is equal to the corresponding scaling parameter a. In general, the wavelet expansion should satisfy the admissibility condition (mean value of the wavelet function should be zero) for calculation of the wavelet coefficients. However, in this case all the coefficients (weight) might be obtained by learning process not by calculation. If the original function is reconstructed with non-orthogonal wavelet bases, then the over-complete number of bases are sufficient for it.

III. WAVELET NEURAL NETWORK

According to [1] - [4], we presented and defined the new type of wavelet neural network model, which is shown in the right-hand sides of Fig. 2, we adopted the weighted sum (linear sum) of a wavelet basis [1]. The wavelet basis is according to the number of fuzzy rules, and each wavelet basis assigned as shown in Figure 1and each linear synaptic weight is adjustable by learning.

---
*Corresponding author

Consider n inputs vectors $\{x_1, x_2 ... x_i, x_{i+1} ... x_n\} \in R^n$ and single-output $\hat{y} \in R$, respectively. An ordinary wavelet neural network model applications it is often useful to normalize the input vectors into the interval *[0,1]*, based on Section II, we calculate the $\varphi_{a.b}(x_i)$ function which input signal to fire up the interval of wavelet. Obviously, we would obtain a crisp value$\varphi_{a.b}$ as follows:

$$\varphi_{a.b} = \frac{\sum_{1}^{n} \phi_{a.b}(x_i)}{|X|} \qquad (2)$$

where |X| means the number of input dimension. The final output of the wavelet neural networks is:

$$\hat{y}_j = \sum_{i}^{k} w_i^j \varphi_{a.b}$$
$$= w_1^j \varphi_{1.1} + w_2^j \varphi_{2.1} + ... + w_k^j \varphi_{m.m} \qquad (3)$$

where $\hat{y}_j$ is the output of the local model for the *jth* rule, and the link weight w_k^j is the output action strength associated with in the *jth* rule and *kth* $\varphi_{a.b}$.

IV. THE STRUCTURE OF THE WNFS MODEL

In this section, we shall describe the structure and functions of the proposed WNFS. The Wavelet-based Neuro-Fuzzy System (WNFS) model, an idea by both the theory of TSK fuzzy model and wavelet neural network concepts.

A WNFS can be described by a set of following fuzzy rules:

R_j: IF x_1 is A_1^j and ...and x_n is A_n^j,

TFEN $\hat{y}_j = \sum_k w_k^j \phi_{a.b}$ (4)

where R_j is the *jth* rule; x_i is the *ith* input variable, respectively; $\hat{y}_j$ is the *jth* output of the local model for rule R_j; A_i^j linguistic term of the precondition part with membership function $u_{ij}^{(2)}(x_i)$.

The structure of the WNFS is shown Fig. 2 where the functions of the node in each layer are described as follows:

Layer 1: Each node in this layer is an input node, these nodes only pass the input signal to next.

Layer 2: Each node in this layer act as membership function representing the term of the respective input-linguistic variables. i.e., the membership value

$$u_{ij}^{(2)}(x_i) = \exp(-\frac{(x_i - m_{ji})^2}{\sigma_{ij}^2}) \qquad (5)$$

where m_{ij} and σ_{ij} are the mean and standard deviation, respectively, of *jth* term associated with *ith* input variable x_i.

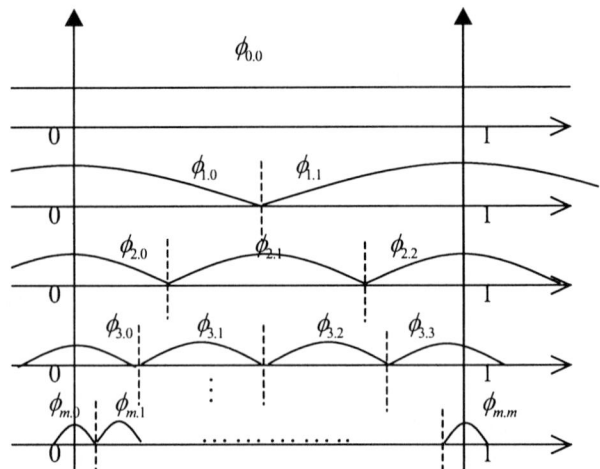

Fig. 1. Wavelet bases are over-complete and compactly supported.

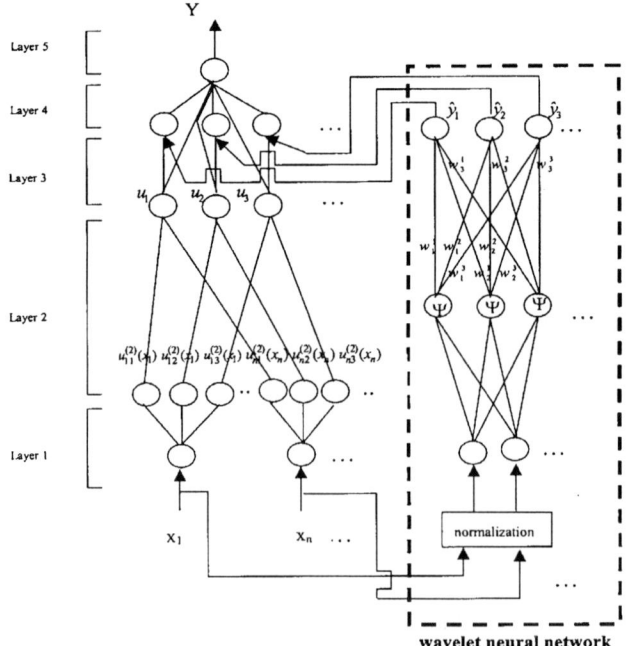

Fig. 2. Schematic diagram of WNFS.

Layer 3: Each node in this layer is a rule node representing the precondition part of one fuzzy logic rule. Therefore, each node of this layer is denoted by Π, which multiply the incoming signals from layer2 and outputs the product result, i.e. the firing strength of a rule.

For the *jth* rule node

$$u_j = u_{1j}^{(2)}(x_1) u_{2j}^{(2)}(x_2) ... u_{nj}^{(2)}(x_n) = \prod_i u_{ij}^{(2)}(x_i) \qquad (6)$$

where u_j is the output of jth rule node.

Layer 4: Each node for this layer only receives the signal, which are both u_j from upper layer and $\hat{y}_j$ from output of wavelet neural network model, finally, pass them to output layer.

Layer 5: This layer acts a deffuzzifier. We can obtain the final inferred from equation (7) and the result specifies the degree to which an input value belongs to a fuzzy set is determined in this layer. The Gaussian function as follows is adopted as the membership function:

$$Y = \frac{\sum_{j=1}^{N} \hat{y}_j u_j}{\sum_{j=1}^{N} u_j} = \frac{\sum_{j=1}^{N} (w_1^j \phi_{0.0} + w_2^j \phi_{1.0} + \ldots + w_k^j \phi_{m.m}) u_j}{\sum_{j=1}^{N} u_j} \quad (7)$$

where the link weight $\hat{y}_j$ is the output of the local model of the wavelet neural networks model for the *jth* rule, which the output action strength associated with the *jth* rule and Y is the output of the WNFS. The consequent part of one fuzzy logic rule is implicitly contained in $\hat{y}_j$ (TSK fuzzy model).

V. THE ON-LINE LEARNING ALGORITHM

In this section, we present an on-line learning scheme for the WNFS. First, a structure learning scheme is used to decide proper fuzzy partition, the membership of the rule nodes and link weight in the wavelet neural network are generated dynamically. Second, a supervised learning scheme is used to optimally adjust the membership function and link weight for the desired outputs.

The structure learning is to determine whether to perform the structure learning. Since one cluster formed in the input space corresponds to one potential fuzzy logic rule, the firing strength of a rule for each incoming data x_i can be represented as the degree that the incoming data belong to the cluster. The firing strength obtained from (8) is used as the degree measure

$$D_j = u_j \quad j = 1, \ldots, Q(t) \quad (8)$$

where $Q(t)$ is the number of existing rules at time t. According to the degree measure, the criterion of generating a new fuzzy rule for new incoming data is described as follows.

Find the maximum degree Dmax

$$D_{max} = \max_{1 \le j \le Q(t)} D_j \quad (9)$$

If $D_{max} \le \overline{D}$, then a new membership function is generated where $\overline{D} \in (0,1)$ is a pre-specified threshold that should be decayed during the learning process limiting the size of WNFS.

Next the mean and standard deviation of the new membership function and link weight are assigned with pre-specified values using heuristic or prior knowledge as follows:

$$m_i^{(new)} = x_i \quad (10)$$

$$\sigma_i^{(new)} = \sigma_i \quad (11)$$

$$w_k^{i(new)} = w_k^i \quad (12)$$

where x_i is the new incoming data σ_i and both and w_k^i are pre-specified constant.

After the network structure has been adjusted according to the current training pattern, the network enters the second learning step to adjust the parameters of the membership functions optimally with the same training pattern. The learning process involves the determination of the vector which minimize a given energy function. The gradient of the energy function with respect to the vector is computed and the vector is adjusted along the negative gradient. This method is generally referred to as the backpropagation learning rule because the gradient vector is calculated in the direction opposite to the flow of the output to each node. To describe the online parameter learning algorithm of the WNFS using the supervised gradient method, first the energy function E is defined as

$$E = \frac{1}{2}(Y - Y^d)^2 \quad (13)$$

where Y is the model output and Y^d is the desired output. Then starting at the output nodes, a backward pass is used to compute $\partial E / \partial Y$ for all parameters. The parameter learning algorithm based on backpropagation is described in the following:

Layer 5: The error to be propagated to the preceding layer is

$$\delta = -\frac{\partial E}{\partial Y} = \frac{-\partial \frac{1}{2}(Y - Y^d)^2}{\partial Y} = Y^d - Y \quad (14)$$

Layer 4: The link weight of wavelet neural network is update by

$$\Delta w_k^J = -\eta_w \frac{\partial E}{\partial w_k^J} = \left[-\eta_w \frac{\partial E}{\partial Y}\right]\left[\frac{\partial Y}{\partial w_k^J}\right] = \eta_w \delta \frac{u_i \phi_k^J(x)}{\sum_i u_J} \quad (15)$$

$$w_k^J(N+1) = w_k^J(N) + \Delta w_k^J \quad (16)$$

where factor η_w is the learning–rate parameter of the link weight and the link weights are updated according to (16), where *N* denotes the iteration number.

Layer 3: In this layer only the error term needs to be

calculated and propagated

$$-\frac{\partial E}{\partial u_j} = \left[-\frac{\partial E}{\partial Y}\right]\cdot\left[\frac{\partial Y}{\partial u_j}\right] = \delta\cdot(\hat{y}_j\sum_j u_j - \sum_j \hat{y}_j u_j)\frac{1}{(\sum_j u_j)^2} \quad (17)$$

Layer2: In this layer, the error term is computed as follows:

$$-\frac{\partial E}{\partial u_{ij}^{(2)}} = \left[-\frac{\partial E}{\partial Y}\right]\cdot\left[\frac{\partial Y}{\partial u_j}\right]\cdot\left[\frac{\partial u_j}{\partial u_{ij}^{(2)}}\right] \quad (18)$$

The updates law m_{ij} of is

$$\Delta m_{ij} = -\eta_m \frac{\partial E}{\partial m_{ij}} = [-\eta_m \frac{\partial E}{\partial u_{ij}^{(2)}}]\cdot[\frac{\partial u_{ij}^{(2)}}{\partial m_{ij}}]$$
$$= \eta_m \delta \frac{(x_i - m_{ij})}{\sigma_{ij}^2} u_j (\hat{y}_j \sum_j u_j - \sum_j u_j \hat{y}_j)\frac{1}{(\sum_j u_j)^2} \quad (19)$$

The updates law σ_{ij} of is

$$\Delta\sigma_{ij} = -\eta_\sigma \frac{\partial E}{\partial \sigma_{ij}} = [-\eta_\sigma \frac{\partial E}{\partial u_{ij}^{(2)}}]\cdot[\frac{\partial u_{ij}^{(2)}}{\partial \sigma_{ij}}]$$
$$= \eta_\sigma \delta \frac{(x_i - m_{ij})^2}{\sigma_{ij}^3} u_j (\hat{y}_j \sum_j u_j - \sum_j u_j \hat{y}_j)\frac{1}{(\sum_j u_j)^2} \quad (20)$$

where η_m and η_σ are the learning-rate parameter of the mean and the standard deviation of the Gaussian function, respectively. The mean and standard deviation of the membership functions in this layer are updated as following:

$$m_{ij}(N+1) = m_{ij}(N) + \Delta m_{ij} \quad (21)$$
$$\sigma_{ij}(N+1) = \sigma_{ij}(N) + \Delta\sigma_{ij} \quad (22)$$

The flow diagram of the learning algorithms of the WNFS is shown in Fig. 3.

VI. ILLUSTRATIVE EXAMPLES

A. Identification of the Dynamic System

In this example, the proposed WNFS model is used to identify a dynamic system. The identification model has the form:

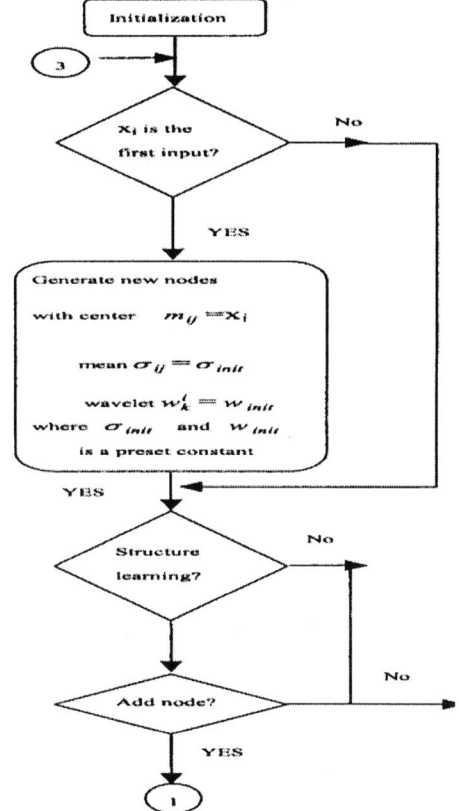
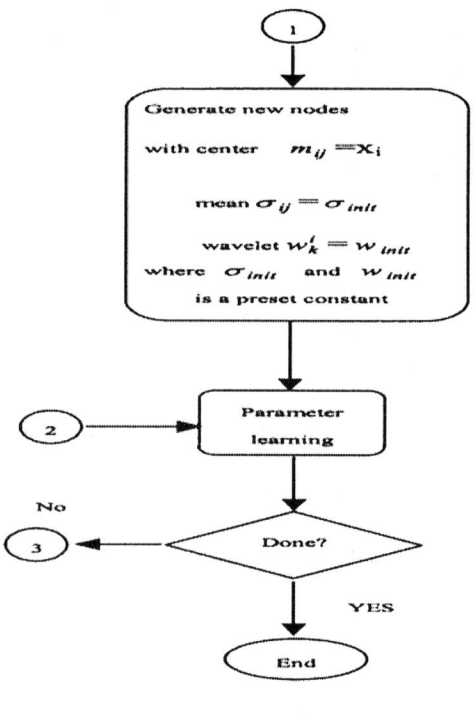

Fig.3. Flow diagram for WNFS.

$$\hat{y}(k+1) = \hat{f}[u(k), u(k+1), \ldots\ldots\ldots u(k-p+1) \\ y(k), y(k+1), \ldots\ldots\ldots y(k-q+1)]. \quad (23)$$

$$y(k+1) = \frac{y(k)}{1+y^2(k)} + u^3(k). \quad (24)$$

The output of the plant depends nonlinearly on both its past values and inputs, but the effects of the input and output values are additive. In applying the WNFS to this identification problem, the learning rate η =0.05, σ_{init}=0.25, $\overline{D}$=0.0002 are chosen, The 200 training input patterns are generated from u(k)=sin(2pk/100) and training process is continued for 300 time steps. Fig. 4, shows the root-mean-square (RMS) errors during learning. In this figure, the learning speed of the trained WNFS is quicker than the trained SCFNN [5]. After training, there are 6 rules grew dynamically for incoming training data. Fig. 5 illustrates the distribution of the training pattern and the final assignment of fuzzy rules (i.e., distribution of input membership functions) in the *[u(k),y(k)]* plain. Fig. 6, shows the outputs of the plant and the identification. In this figure, the output of the WNFS model are presented as o's while true output values are presented as *'s. The results show the good identification capability of the proposed WNFS model.

In the above simulation, the training input patterns generated from u(k)=sin(2pk/100). Now, we will adopt the training input patterns sampled randomly over $u(k) \in [-1,1]$ and $y(k) \in [-1.5,1.5]$. The initial parameters η =0.05, σ_{init}=0.6, $\overline{D}$=0.0015 are chosen. After training, there are 8 fuzzy rules grew for incoming training data. Fig. 7 shows the distribution of input training patterns and final assignment of rules. In Fig. 8, the results also show the good identification capability when the training patterns are generated randomly.

B. Prediction of the Chaotic Time Series

The Mackey-Glass chaotic time-series [6] is generated from the following delay differential equation:

$$\frac{dx(t)}{dt} = \frac{0.2x(t-\tau)}{1+x^{10}(t-\tau)} - 0.1x(t) \quad (25)$$

where τ>17. In our simulation, we choose the series with τ=30. Fig. 9 shows 1000 points of this chaotic series used to test the WNFS model. We choose nine point values in the series are used to predict the value of the next time point. The 200 points of the series from *x(500)-x(700)* are used as training data, and the final 300 points from *x(701)-x(1000)* are used as test data. The initial parameters η =0.05, σ_{init}=0.6, $\overline{D}$=0.0015 are used. After the training, there are 9 rules generated in our model. Fig. 10, shows the prediction of the chaotic time series from *x(701)-x(1000)* when 200 training data [from *x(500)-x(700)*] are used. In this figure, the output of the WNFS model are presented as o's while true output values are presented as *'s. Table I is compare the performance of our model with other existing methods that can generate fuzzy rules from numerical data automatically. The results show the good prediction capability of the WNFS model trained only by a small set of training data.

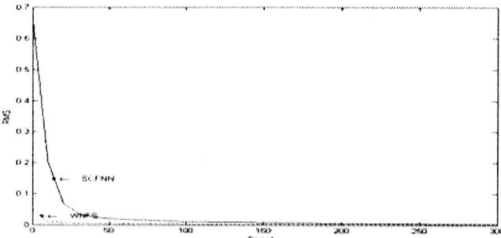

Fig. 4. Learning curve to compare WNFS with SCFNN [5] in Example A.

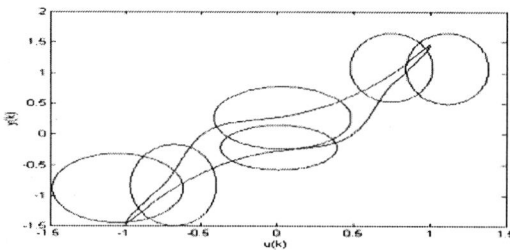

Fig. 5. The input training patterns and final assignment of rules.

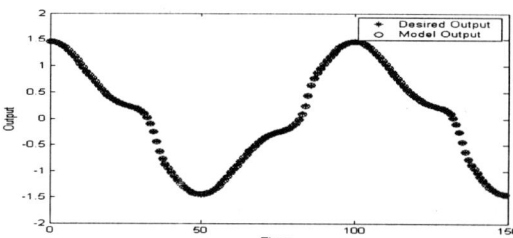

Fig. 6. The output of the plant and the identification model.

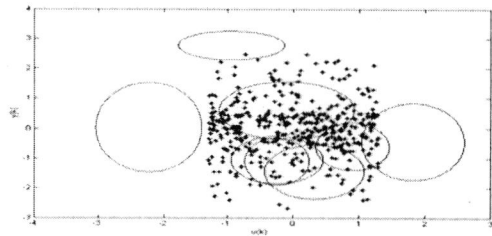

Fig. 7. The distribution of input training patterns and final assignment of rules.

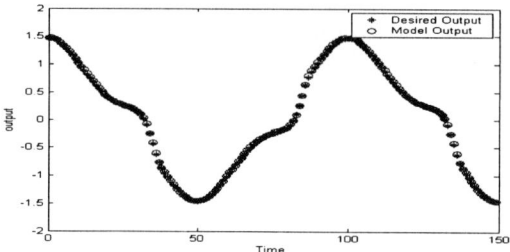

Fig. 8. The outputs of the plant and the identification model.

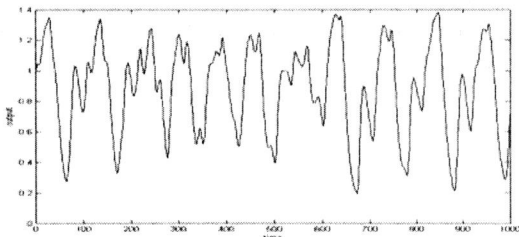

Fig. 9. The Mackey-Glass chaotic time series.

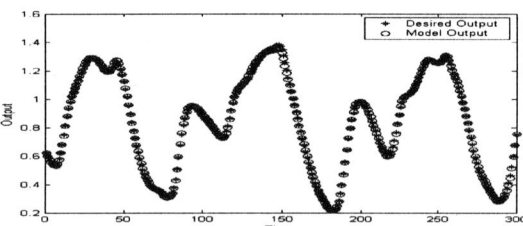

Fig. 10. Simulation results of the time-series from $x(701) - x(1000)$.

TABLE I
PERFORMANCE COMPARISON OF VARIOUS RULE GENERATION METHODS ON THE TIME-SERIES PREDICTION PROBLEM

	WNFS	FALCON-ART [6]	Wang&Mendel [7]
Rule number (200 training data)	9	22	121
RMS error	**0.002**	0.08	0.08

VII. CONCLUSION

In this paper, we proposed a new type of network called WNFS that has been introduced for function approximation from input-output observations. The presented WNFS combines fuzzy concepts with the wavelet neuron model. An on-line structure/parameter learning algorithm is proposed for constructing the fuzzy rule dynamically. The proposed parameter learning algorithm is able to adjust membership functions dynamically. The wavelet neuron model is obtained to substitute it for an ordinary neuron model such that the contribution degree of different sub-wavelet at different resolution levels can be controlled flexibly. Simulation results demonstrate that the proposed WNFS is quite effective in identification and control applications.

ACKNOWLEDGMENT

This research is supported by the National Science Council of R.O.C. under grant NSC 91-2213-E-324- 009.

REFERENCE

[1] T. Yamakawa, E. Uchino, and T. Samatsu, "Wavelet neural networks employing over-complete number of compactly supported non-orthogonal," IEEE International Conference on Neural Networks, vol. 3, 1391 –1396, 1994.

[2] I. Daubechies, "Orthonormal Bases of Compactly Supported Wavelets," Comm. Pur. Appl. Math., Vol. 41, 1998.

[3] Ho D.W.C., P. A. Zhang and J. Xu, "Fuzzy wavelet networks for function learning," IEEE Trans. on Fuzzy Systems, Vol. 9 No. 1, pp. 200 –211Feb. 2001

[4] Q. Zhang and A. Benveniste, "Wavelet networks," IEEE Trans. Neural Networks, vol. 3, pp. 889–898, Nov. 1992.

[5] F. J. Lin, C. H. Lin, and P. H. Shen, Self-Constructing Fuzzy Neural Network Speed Controller for Permanent-Magnet Synchronous Motor Drive," IEEE Trans. on Fuzzy Systems, vol. 9, No. 5, pp.751-759, 2001.

[6] C. J. Lin, and C. T. Lin, "An ART-Based Fuzzy Adaptive Learning Control Network," IEEE Trans. on Fuzzy Systems, vol. 5, No. 4, pp.477-496, Nov. 1997.

[7] L.-X. Wang and J.M. Mendel , "Generating Fuzzy Rules by Learning from Examples," IEEE Trans. on Syst., Man, and Cybern., Vol. 22, No. 6, pp. 1414-1427, Nov./Dec.1992.

Feature Extraction for Neural-Fuzzy Inference System

Chai Quek, Geok See Ng and Abdul Wahab
Intelligent System Laboratory, Nanyang Technological University,
Blk N4 #2A-32, Nanyang Avenue, Singapore 639798

Abstract-Currently, not many attempts are made to use neural-fuzzy inference system for recognizing primitive features of an input image. The objective of this paper is to propose a method of feature extraction so as the features obtained can be trained in a novel neural-fuzzy inference system called POP-CHAR. Common features of digit characters are extracted and converted into vectors. The neural-fuzzy inference system can be trained from the primitive feature vectors and produce good results. Once the fuzzy neural network is trained, it can be used to recognize digits.

I. INTRODUCTION

Raw character images without any form of pre-processing and feature extraction have been used for quite some time prior to the use of feature-based approaches. The introduction of feature extraction has been proposed by researcher [8] to improve the accuracy of the recognition. Not many works are found in using fuzzy neural system for recognizing primitive features. Hence a feature extraction is proposed in this paper for a neural-fuzzy inference system called POP-CHAR [9]. POP-CHAR can be trained from the primitive features and show its classification capability.

As of today, many neural network models have been proposed in the area of Optical Character Recognition. Neocognitron [1], back-propagation network [2], Kohonen self-organizing map [3], Hopfield network [4] and many other variants [5, 6] have been used in handwritten character recognition. However, how neural networks derive their final results is almost impossible to obtain and understand. Fuzzy logic on the other hand models human reasoning process and makes use of fuzzy membership function to derive its results [7]. However, fuzzy system lacks the learning capability like neural network. Hence combining both systems as a functional system, i.e. a neural-fuzzy system, is a solution to overcome their individual weaknesses.

II. FEATURE EXTRACTION

The binary input images have to be converted into vectors such that the POP-CHAR can process them. One simple way to convert images into numbers is to search for presence of various primitive features.

Examples of primitive features are straight lines and curves. For each feature, one or more than one templates are used. The size of the template may range from 5x5 to 9x9. In this paper, 9x9 is used. Example of a template for a long horizontal line is shown in Fig. 1. Fig. 1 shows that the 'x' characters are the actual features. The 'o' characters are close to the 'x' characters. The '.' characters are far away from the 'x' characters.

Each template is run over the entire image staring from top left corner, left to right and then top to bottom. If an 'x' character in the template sits on pixel '1' of the binary image, 1 point is added to the digit for that template. If an 'x' character in the template sits on pixel '0' of the binary image, 1 point is subtracted. The rest of the combinations of the corresponding characters are shown in Table 1.

After that, all the points in every pixel in the image for that template are summed up. If the sum is high, it indicates that it is very likely that the feature in the template is found in the digit. Otherwise, it is unlikely that the feature is found in the digit. If there are more than one template for a feature, the one with the highest sum is used. Any negative sum is set to 0. At the end of the above operations, there is a sum for each feature in each digit sample.

Fig. 1 Template of a long horizontal line

```
. . . . . . . . .
. . . . . . . . .
. . . . . . . . .
o o o o o o o o o
x x x x x x x x x
o o o o o o o o o
. . . . . . . . .
. . . . . . . . .
. . . . . . . . .
```

TABLE 1
MASKING VALUE OF THE TEMPLATE

Template Character	Binary Image	Action
X	0	Subtract 1 point
O	0	Do nothing
.	0	Add 1 point
X	1	Add 1 point
O	1	Do nothing
.	1	Subtract 1 point

Finally, only those features with high sum are selected. The primitive features used in this paper are: (1) long horizontal line; (2) long vertical line and slant line; (3) crossing of a horizontal and vertical line; (4) upward curve; (5) downward curve; (6) top right corner; (7) bottom left corner; (8) rightward curve; (9) leftward curve; and (10) 3-way junction. Fig. 2 shows examples of these features found in digits.

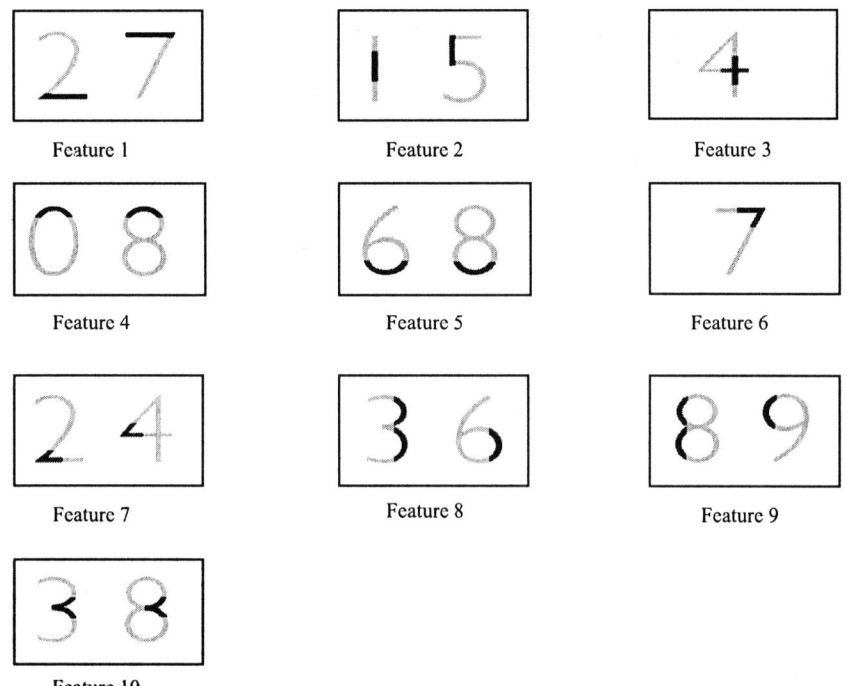

Fig. 2 Ten features found in digits

III. THE POP-CHAR

The POP-CHAR is a five-layer neural network shown in Fig. 3. Although the architecture resembles the POPFNN [9], but it requires two phases of learning while POPFNN requires additional learning phase, i.e. supervised learning. For simplicity, only the interconnections for the output y_m are shown. Each layer in POP-CHAR performs a specific fuzzy operation. The inputs and outputs of the POP-CHAR are represented as non-fuzzy vector $\mathbf{X}^T=[x_1, x_2, \ldots x_i, \ldots x_{n1}]$ and non-fuzzy vector $\mathbf{Y}^T=[y_1, y_2, \ldots y_l, \ldots y_{n5}]$ respectively. Fuzzification of the input data and defuzzification of the output data are respectively performed by the Condition and Output Linguistic layers, while the fuzzy inference is collectively performed by the Rule-based and the Consequence layers.

IV. EXPERIMENTAL RESULTS

Rigorous experiments have been conducted for the proposed system. We start with the recognition accuracy of the POP-CHAR. Then the features used are experimented to observe the behavior of POP-CHAR. In all the experiments, binary images of size 20x20 are used.

A. POP-CHAR recognition

In many applications, only a small number of samples are taken for training while large number of samples is used for recalling. Therefore, the first experiment is carried out to look for the optimal number of training samples so that the network can recognize all the digit samples.

Number of Input Linguistic nodes is 3. This is because there are three likelihoods that a feature is present in digit input, i.e. low, medium and high. The number of Output Linguistic nodes is set to 2, since there are only 2 possible outcomes for each digit. Number of training samples is varied to get the optimal performance. The results are shown in the Table 2. Each column in Table 2 shows the number of correctly classified, wrongly classified and unclassified samples for the corresponding number of training samples.

The values of each cell in Table 2 are converted to percentages and shown in Fig. 4. Fig. 4 shows that the optimal number of training samples is more than 20. Performance of this system is expected to increase further when more training samples are used. Fig. 4 shows the significant improvement of recognition accuracy when more than 10 training samples are used. The training samples are for the system to learn what are the features needed for each digit. When enough samples with enough features are learnt, the system can perform quite well. Hence it is not necessary to have large number of training samples where no features are used. Therefore, the use of proposed feature extraction for POP-CHAR in character recognition is promising.

B. Effect of feature extraction

This section discusses the effect of feature extraction on the recognition results. In this case, missing features and the number of features needed are investigated.

B.1 Effect of missing features

There are 10 features used in the feature extraction. The purpose of this experiment is to investigate how the performance of the systems will be affected if one of the features is removed. Further investigation is to find out if any digit is directly affected by the removed feature.

In the experiment, one feature is removed one at a time. That means at any one time, there are 9 features. The result is then compared with that of without removing any feature, i.e. 10 features are used. Their difference are then shown in Table 3. Each cell in Table 3 shows the differences between accuracy of without missing feature and with missing feature. A positive change means that the missing feature is not needed for recognizing the corresponding digit whereas a negative change means the missing feature is needed. Table 3 shows that by removing one feature, digits '1', '8' and '9' are affected much more than other digits.

B.2 Effect of the number of feature used

This experiment is to monitor the system performance when a feature is added one at a time to the feature vector. Table 4 shows the number of recognized digits when each feature is added. In general, Table 4 shows that the recognition accuracy improves as the number of features increases. Table 4 also shows that the performance of the digit recognition increases quickly once certain feature is added. This gives a clue that a particular feature may be significant. Percentage of change in accuracy when each feature is added is also shown in Table 5. Table 5 shows that when some features are added, the recognition accuracy improves tremendouslyn (i.e. positive change in accuracy). However, some other features might confuse the system and cause its performances to fall slightly (i.e. negative change in accuracy).

Those features that are important (i.e. those cause improvement of more than 15% in accuracy) for each digit are shown in Table 6.

V. CONCLUSION

This paper presents a method of feature extraction that is used in a neural-fuzzy system. Experimental results have shown the promising results of the proposed method. Effects of the feature extraction are investigated in this paper. The performance of the system is monitored when individual feature is removed or added. The POP-CHAR also shows what features are significant for each digit that is agreeable to the shape of the digit theoretically.

REFERENCES

[1] K. Fukushima, Neocognitron, "A hierarchical neural network capable of visual pattern recognition," *Neural Networks*, vol. 1, pp. 119-130, 1988.

[2] J. L. McClelland, D. E. Rumelhart, *Exploration in Parallel Distributed Processing*. A Bradford Book, Cambridge, Massachusetts:MIT Press, 1988.

[3] T. Kohonen, *Self-Organizing Maps*. Springer-Verlag, 1995.

[4] D. W. Tank, J. J. Hopfield, "Collective computation in neuronlike circuits," *Scientific American*, vol. 257, no. 6, pp. 62-70, December 1987.

[5] M. Revow, C. K. I. Williams, G. E. Hinton, "Using generative models for handwritten digit recognition," *IEEE Transactions on Pattern Analysis and Machine Intelligence*, vol. 18, no. 6, pp. 592-606, June 1996.

[6] S. Knerr, L. Personnaz, G. Dreyfus, "Handwritten digit recognition by neural networks with single-layer training," *IEEE Transactions on Neural Networks*, vol. 3, no. 6, pp. 962-968, November 1992.

[7] C. T. Lin, C. S. Lee, *Neural Fuzzy Systems - A Neuro-Fuzzy Synergism to Intelligent System*. Prentice Hall, 1996.

[8] G. Srikantan, S. W. Lam, S. N. Srihari, "Gradient-based contour encoding for character recognition," *Pattern Recognition*, vol. 29, no. 7, pp. 1147-1160, July 1996.

[9] H. C. Quek, R. W. Zhou, "POPFNN: A pseudo outer-product based fuzzy neural network," *Neural Networks*, vol. 9, 1996, pp. 1569-1581.

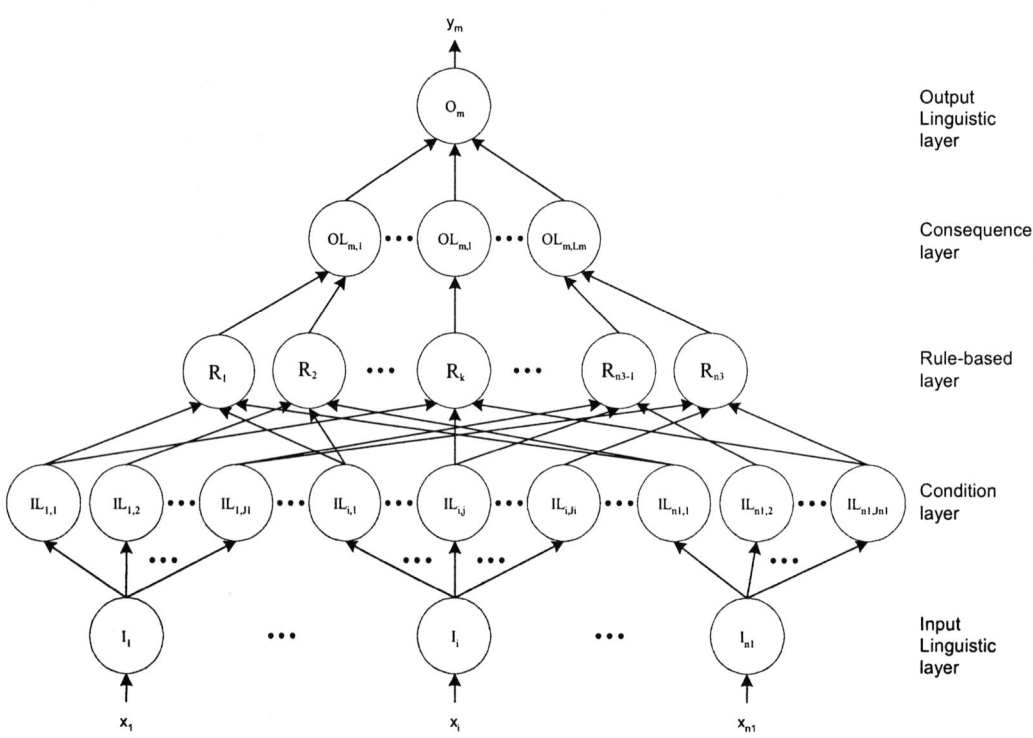

Fig.3 Architecture of POP-CHAR

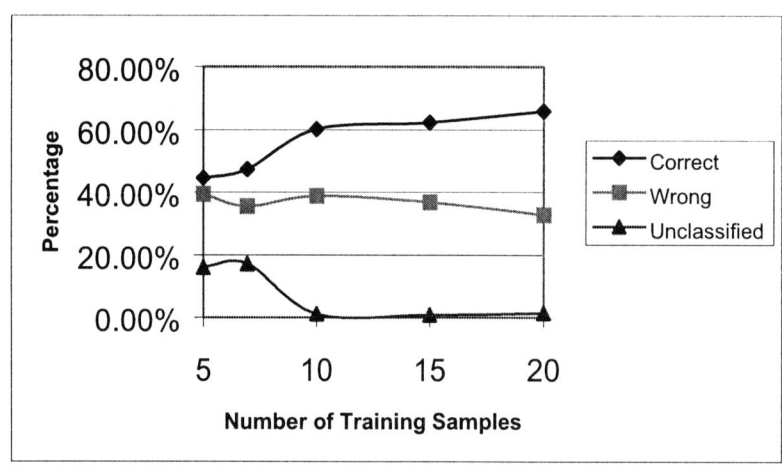

Fig. 4 Recognition results

TABLE 2
COMBINED RESULTS

	Number of training samples				
	5	7	10	15	20
Correct	161	171	217	225	238
Wrong	142	128	140	133	118
Unclassified	58	62	4	3	5

TABLE 3
ACCURACY CHANGE FOR MISSING FEATURE

Digit	Missing feature									
	1 —	2 |	3 +	4 ⌢	5 ⌣	6 ７	7 ∠	8)	9 (	10 ⊰
0	4%	8%	8%	8%	13%	8%	4%	8%	0%	8%
1	-33%	-49%	-32%	-33%	-49%	-33%	-39%	-55%	-49%	-49%
2	9%	4%	9%	4%	4%	4%	4%	9%	-5%	-5%
3	-3%	-3%	-11%	-6%	-11%	-6%	-17%	0%	-9%	-11%
4	-8%	-3%	-3%	-5%	-3%	0%	-8%	-3%	-3%	-3%
5	13%	13%	10%	0%	10%	4%	7%	13%	7%	-18%
6	0%	0%	-17%	-6%	-3%	-10%	-6%	0%	-24%	-10%
7	-10%	-10%	0%	3%	0%	-4%	-7%	0%	6%	-4%
8	-46%	-51%	-51%	-51%	-46%	-54%	-49%	-51%	-51%	-49%
9	-13%	-50%	-34%	-40%	-13%	-48%	-38%	-40%	-38%	-21%

TABLE 4
RECOGNITION RESULTS FOR DIFFERENT NUMBER OF FEATURES

Digit	Number of feature(s)									
	1	2	3	4	5	6	7	8	9	10
0	0	0	0	8	8	9	11	13	15	13
1	0	30	19	19	30	30	41	33	33	67
2	0	0	0	4	10	16	17	17	19	20
3	0	1	1	1	2	3	16	21	21	25
4	0	0	15	15	16	17	18	25	25	26
5	0	0	0	0	4	10	7	10	13	19
6	0	0	0	0	0	3	8	13	18	21
7	0	3	13	11	14	14	15	17	16	17
8	0	0	0	1	3	2	3	8	11	28
9	0	0	0	2	2	3	9	12	23	33

TABLE 5
ACCURACY CHANGE CAUSED BY INDIVIDUAL FEATURE

Digit	Feature									
	1 —	2 |	3 +	4 ⌢	5 ⌣	6 ７	7 ∠	8)	9 (	10 ⊰
0	0%	0%	0%	35%	0%	4%	9%	9%	8%	-8%
1	0%	43%	-16%	0%	16%	0%	16%	-12%	0%	49%
2	0%	0%	0%	18%	27%	28%	4%	0%	9%	5%
3	0%	3%	0%	0%	2%	3%	35%	14%	0%	11%
4	0%	0%	43%	0%	3%	3%	2%	20%	0%	3%
5	0%	0%	0%	0%	13%	18%	-9%	9%	10%	18%
6	0%	0%	0%	0%	0%	10%	18%	17%	17%	10%
7	0%	10%	33%	-6%	10%	0%	3%	7%	-4%	4%
8	0%	0%	0%	3%	6%	3%	3%	14%	8%	49%
9	0%	0%	0%	4%	0%	2%	13%	6%	23%	21%

TABLE 6
FEATURES THAT ARE IMPORTANT

Digits	Feature(s)
0	4: ⌒
1	2: |, 5: ‿, 7: ∠, 10: ⌃
2	4: ⌒, 5: ‿, 6: 7
3	7: ∠
4	3: +, 8:)
5	6: 7, 10: ⌃
6	7: ∠, 8:), 9: (
7	3: +
8	10: ⌃
9	9: (, 10: ⌃

A PID neural network controller

Yu Yongquan, Huang Ying, Zeng Bi
Institute of Computer Science and Intelligent Engineering
Guangdong University of Technology
729E.Dongfeng Rd. Guangzhou. 510080. China
Tel: +86 20 3762 6493   Fax: +86 20 3762 8481
E-mail: yyq@gdut.edu.cn

Abstract-In this paper, the new fuzzy PID controller, which is combined fuzzy controller with PID neural network (PIDNN), is proposed. Its structure is difference from the normal one. The feature of it is to use a PIDNN replace PID parameter loop in controller. And the controller is optimized by the learning processing of PIDNN. The principle of PIDNN is discussed and the learning method based on back-propagation-algorithm is given. The two processes, first and second order systems, are simulated. Results of simulating show that the fuzzy PID controller presented in this paper is a better adaptive controller for linear or nonlinear plant.

Index Terms-Fuzzy PID controller, PID neural networks, Back-propagation algorithm.

I. INTRODUCTION

Conventional proportional-integral-derivative (PID) controllers are well known and have been extensively used for industrial automation and process control for about half a century [1]. However, conventional PID controllers generally do not work well for time-delayed linear systems, nonlinear systems, complex and vague systems. Various types of modified PID controllers have been developed [2][3][4], such as self-tuning PID controllers, to overcome the shortcoming of conventional one. The fuzzy PID controllers are also designed for this purpose [5]-[9]. Fuzzy controllers have been successfully implemented for many linear and nonlinear processes, even sometimes they are proved to be more robust than conventional controllers. The natural representation of control knowledge make fuzzy controller easy to be understood. But the fuzzy controller with two inputs, error, the change rate of error, approximately behaves like a PD controller, and obviously

The authors are grateful to National Natural Science Foundation of China (60272089) and Guangdong Provincial Natural Science Foundation of China (980406) for decisive support.

there would exist steady-state error when industrial process systems are controlled by conventional fuzzy controller. It can eliminate the steady-state error of the control system to consider the integration of error in input of the fuzzy controller. Of course this can be realized by designing a fuzzy controller with three inputs, error, the change rate of error and integration of error. However, it will be hard to implement in practice because of the difficulty in constructing control rules base. First, it is not the practice for expert to observe the integration of error. Second, adding one input variable in fuzzy controller will greatly increase the number of control rules. Hence, it is the good idea to construct a fuzzy controller that possesses the fine characteristics of the PID controller by using only error or error and the change rate of error as its inputs. Fuzzy PID controllers were proposed by combining the advantage of fuzzy controllers and conventional PID controllers.

A wide variety of fuzzy PID controller have been developed [10][12][13][14][17][19], and reported that a fuzzy PID controller is proved to outperform a conventional PID controller. Stability of fuzzy PID controllers has also been analyzed and is guaranteed [8][9].

Fuzzy PID controllers can be classified into three types: the gain scheduling (GS) type [11][15][18], the direct action (DA) type [10][12][13][14][16][17][19], and a combination of GS and DA types. The majority of fuzzy PID controllers belong to the direct action type; Here the fuzzy PID controller computes the PID actions through fuzzy inference. But in the gain scheduling type controllers, fuzzy inference is need to compute the individual PID gains.

In order to improve further the performance of the transient state and the steady state of fuzzy PID controller, several optimum or near optimum solutions are developed, such as training algorithm using input/output data, genetic search algorithm [10], peak value tuning method [12] for fuzzy PID controllers. These methods regulate the parameters of membership function and the parameters of PID structures. They provide better functional properties efficiently.

In this paper, A PID neural Network (PIDNN) is and the

optimal method is given to make the performance better.

II. THE STRUCTURE AND FUNCTION OF PID NEURAL NETWORK

PID neural network is a kind of neural network that consists of P neuron, I neuron and D neuron, where P neuron possesses proportional operation function, I neuron performs integral function, D neuron carries out derivative function[20][21]. PID neural network can be used to make up PID controller that replaces traditional PID controller to control objects in the manufacturing process. PID neural network combines algorithms of PID controller with learning function of neural network, generates a kind of PID controller with learning function. In order to provide input channels for input values and feedback values, PID neural network adopts 2-3-1 topology with three layers shown in figure 1.

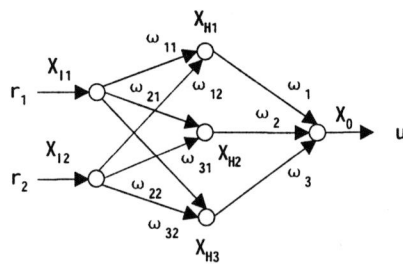

Fig.1. PID neural network

From figure 1 it can be seen that PID neural network is a forward neural network, contains two neurons X_{I1}, X_{I2} in input layer, three neurons X_{H1}, X_{H2}, X_{H3} in hidden layer, and one neuron X_0 in output layer. The input layer contains only two input nodes, its function is just to send the input signal to the neurons of hidden layer. Among the three neurons in hidden layer, X_{H1} is P neuron, X_{H2} is I neuron, X_{H3} is D neuron. The neuron of output layer is a normal neuron of forward neural network. The function of PID neural network is illuminated as follows.

To take into account the input status and output status of PID neural network at sampling time k:

1. Input Layer

$$X_{1i}(k) = r_i(k) \qquad (1)$$

Where $r_i(k)$, $i = 1, 2$, are the convergent input signals at sampling time k; $X_{1i}(k)$, $i = 1, 2$, are the output signals of neuron X_{1i} of input layer at sampling time k.

2. Hidden Layer

The hidden layer is the key layer of PID neural network, which performs PID operations. In the hidden layer X_{H1} is proportional P neuron, X_{H2} is integral I neuron, X_{H3} is derivative D neuron. Their functions will be illuminated respectively as follows:

(1) *Proportional neuron*

The input function and output function of Proportional neuron X_{H1} can be expressed with the following formulas (2),(3):

$$u_{H1}(k) = \sum_{j=1}^{2} \omega_{1j} x_{Ij}(k) \qquad (2)$$

Where ω_{1i} (i=1,2) are the weight values between X_{H1} and input layer.

$$X_{H1}(k) = \begin{cases} 1, & u_{H1}(k) > 1 \\ u_{H1}(k), & -1 \leq u_{H1}(k) \leq 1 \\ -1, & u_{H1}(k) < -1 \end{cases} \qquad (3)$$

(2) *Integral neuron*

The input function and output function of Integral neuron X_{H2} can be expressed with the following formulas (4), (5):

$$u_{H2}(k) = \sum_{j=1}^{2} \omega_{2j} x_j(k) \qquad (4)$$

Where ω_{2i} (i=1,2) are the weight values between X_{H2} and input layer.

$$X_{H2}(k) = \begin{cases} 1, & u_{H2}(k) > 1 \\ u_{H2}(k) + u_{H2}(k-1), & -1 \leq u_{H2}(k) \leq 1 \\ -1, & u_{H2}(k) < -1 \end{cases} \qquad (5)$$

(3) *Derivative neuron*

The input function and output function of Derivative neuron X_{H3} can be expressed with the following formulas (6),(7):

$$u_{H3}(k) = \sum_{j=1}^{2} \omega_{3j} x_{Ij}(k) \qquad (6)$$

Where ω_{3i} (i=1,2) are the weight values between X_{H3} and input layer.

$$X_{H3}(k) = \begin{cases} 1, & u_{H3}(k) > 1 \\ u_{H3}(k) - u_{H3}(k-1), & -1 \leq u_{H3}(k) \leq 1 \\ -1, & u_{H3}(k) < -1 \end{cases} \qquad (7)$$

3. Output Layer

Neuron X_0 is the only one neuron of output layer, its function is to converge three results of P, I, D neurons, and then to output the total control signal 2. Its input function and output function can be expressed with the following formulas (8), (9):

$$u_0(k) = \sum_{i=1}^{3} \omega_i x_{Hi}(k) \qquad (8)$$

Where ω_i (i=1,2,3) are the weight values between output layer and hidden layer.

$$X_0(k) = \begin{cases} 1, & u_0(k) > 1 \\ u_0(k), & -1 \leq u_0(k) \leq 1 \\ -1, & u_0(k) < -1 \end{cases} \qquad (9)$$

III. STRUCTURE OF FUZZY PID CONTROLLER

It is difficult to obtain control rules with the input variable sum-of-error $\sum e$, that is integral error, because the steady state value of integral n error is unknown for various control systems. So the one-input (error e) or two-inputs (error e and error change Δe) fuzzy controllers are common and conventional one in various application. It stands to reason that fuzzy PID controllers are constructed with one-input or two-inputs.

For conventional PID controllers, the output of it can be given by absolute form as follow in formula (10):

$$u_{PID}(t) = K_p e(t) + K_I T_S \sum_{i=0}^{t} e(i) + (K_D / T_S) \Delta e(t) \qquad (10)$$

Where error $e(t) = y(t) - y_d(t)$, $y(t)$ is the output response of system, $y_d(t)$ is the desired response or reference input. Error change $\Delta e(t) = e(t) - e(t-1)$. T_S is the sample period. K_p is proportional gain. K_I is integral gain, $K_I = K_p/T_I$, T_I is integral time constant. K_D is derivative gain, $K_D = K_p \cdot T_D$, T_D is derivative time constant.

In conventional PID controllers, the error terms, e(t)s in equation (10) are the numerical values. But in a fuzzy PID controller, they are expressed in a linguistic form and used to infer a fuzzy control action. The gains K_P, K_I and K_D are the digital value and stand clear from fuzzy rules. It is obvious that fuzzy controller combine with PID parameter to form fuzzy PID controller.

In any fuzzy PID controller, the error e(t) signal is the essential input for deriving any PID structure. Through the fuzzy inference the error provide the nonlinear proportional actions. It products an important difference between conventional and fuzzy PID controllers.

A one-input fuzzy PID controller is formed as shown in Fig.2. The first part in it is the fuzzy controller FC, which map the error e nonlinearly into fuzzy proportional action u_P.

The inference rule is the sentence "IF e is A_i THEN u_P is B_i".

The second part is the gains K_P, K_I and K_D which process the u_P to give the final control action u_{PID}:

$$u_{PID}(t) = K_p u_p(t) + K_I \sum_{i=0}^{t} u_p(i) + K_D [u_p(t) - u_p(t-1)] \qquad (11)$$

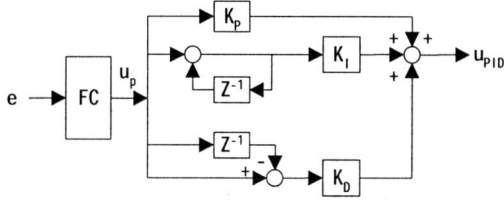

Fig. 2 The architecture of one-input one-output fuzzy PID controller

A two-inputs fuzzy PID controller is shown in Fig.3. The input signals are error e and error change Δe. In this case, a two-inputs fuzzy PID controller is formed by two-inputs fuzzy controller and K_{PD}, K_{PI} gains. The inference rule of this fuzzy controller would be "IF e is A_i and Δe is B_i THEN u_{PD} is C_i". The final control action signal can be given by formula (12):

$$u_{PID}(t) = K_{PI} \sum_{i=0}^{t} u_{PD}(i) + K_{PD} u_{PD}(t) \qquad (12)$$

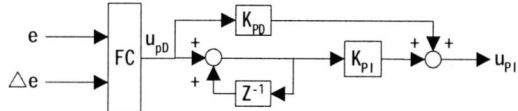

Fig.3 The architecture of two-input one-output fuzzy PID controller

The PID neural network can be used in one-input fuzzy PID controller to replace the loops of gains K_p, K_I and K_D, the new structure of fuzzy PID controller is obtained as shown in Fig.4.

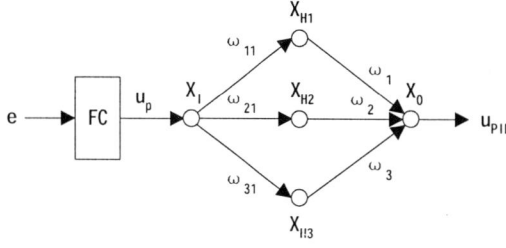

Fig. 4 One-input one-output fuzzy PID controller using PID neural network

The output of fuzzy PID controller will be produced according to the formula (13):

$$u_{PID}(t) = \omega_1 \cdot \omega_{11} x_I(t) + \omega_2 \cdot \omega_{21}[x_I(t) + x_I(t-1)]$$
$$+ \omega_3 \cdot \omega_{31}[x_I(t) - x_I(t-1)]$$
$$= \omega_1 \cdot \omega_{11} u_p(t) + \omega_2 \cdot \omega_{21} \sum_{i=0}^{t} u_p(i)$$
$$+ \omega_3 \cdot \omega_{31}[u_p(t) - u_p(t-1)] \quad (13)$$

For two-input structure, the fuzzy PID controller is shown as Fig.5, and output of u_{PID} can be written as follow:

$$u_{PID}(t) = \omega_1 \cdot \omega_{11} x_I + \omega_2 \cdot \omega_{12}[x_I(t) + x_I(t-1)]$$
$$= \omega_1 \cdot \omega_{11} u_{pD}(t) + \omega_2 \cdot \omega_{12} \sum_{i=0}^{t} u_{pD}(i) \quad (14)$$

The PID neural network is used in fuzzy PID controller because of its learning capability. The gains K_I, K_P, and K_D can be got, after to find the weight value of PID neural network through learning processing.

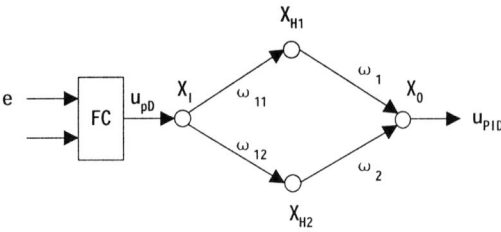

Fig. 5 Two-inputs one-output fuzzy PID controller using PID neural network

IV. BACK-PROPAGATION ALGORITHM OF PIDNN

The back-propagation algorithm of PID neural network is a analogous algorithm for conventional forward neural network. It is one of the important methods to optimize the weight value of forward neural network. The learning structure of PID neural network is shown in Fig. 6

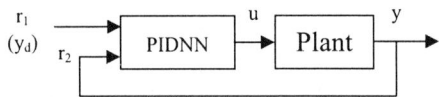

Fig.6 Learning structure of PIDNN

Consider the objective function J:

$$J = \frac{1}{2}\sum_{k=1}^{S}[y_d(k) - y(k)]^2 \quad (15)$$

Where S is the times of sample.

Suppose the learning rate is η, after learning step k, the weight value between hidden layer and output layer can be found:

$$\omega_i(k+1) = \omega_i(k) - \eta \frac{\partial J}{\partial \omega_i} \quad (16)$$

i = 1, 2, 3

The change of weight value between hidden and output layer $\partial J / \partial \omega_i$ would be solved as following:

$$\frac{\partial J}{\partial \omega_i} = \frac{\partial J}{\partial y} \cdot \frac{\partial y}{\partial x_0} \cdot \frac{\partial x_0}{\partial u_0} \cdot \frac{\partial u_0}{\partial \omega_i}$$

Due to

$$\frac{\partial J}{\partial y} = -\sum_{k=1}^{S}[y_d(k) - y(k)]$$
$$\frac{\partial y}{\partial x_0} = \frac{y(k+1) - y(k)}{x_0(k) - x_0(k-1)}$$
$$\frac{\partial x_0}{\partial u_0} = 1$$
$$\frac{\partial x_0}{\partial \omega_i} = x_i(k)$$

So that

$$\frac{\partial J}{\partial \omega_i} = -\sum_{k=1}^{S}[y_d(k) - y(k)] \cdot x_{Hi}(k) \cdot \frac{y(k+1) - y(k)}{x_0(k) - x_0(k-1)}$$
$$= -\sum_{k=1}^{S} \delta_i(k) \cdot x_{Hi}(k)$$

Where

$$\sum_{k=1}^{S} \delta_i(k) = \sum_{k=1}^{S}[y_d(k) - y(k)]\frac{y(k+1) - y(k)}{x_0(k) - x_0(k-1)}$$

The weight value between input layer and hidden layer is:

$$\omega_{ij}(k+1) = \omega_{ij(k)} - \eta \frac{\partial J}{\partial \omega_{ij}}$$

The change of weight value between input layer and hidden layer would be got as following:

$$\frac{\partial J}{\partial \omega_{ij}} = \frac{\partial J}{\partial y} \cdot \frac{\partial y}{\partial x_0} \cdot \frac{\partial x_0}{\partial x_{Hi}} \cdot \frac{\partial x_{Hi}}{\partial u_{Hi}} \cdot \frac{\partial u_{Hi}}{\partial \omega_{ij}}$$

Due to

$$\frac{\partial J}{\partial y} \cdot \frac{\partial y}{\partial x_0} = -\sum_{k=1}^{S} \delta_j(k)$$

$$\frac{\partial x_0}{\partial x_{Hi}} = \omega_i$$

$$\frac{\partial x_{Hi}}{\partial u_{Hi}} = \frac{x_{Hi}(k+1) - x_{Hi}(k)}{u_{Hi}(k) - u_{Hi}(k-1)}$$

$$\frac{\partial u_{Hi}}{\partial \omega_{ij}} = x_{Hi}(k)$$

So that

$$\frac{\partial J}{\partial \omega_{ij}} = -\sum_{k=1}^{S} \delta_i(k) \cdot \omega_i \frac{x_{Hi}(k+1) - x_{Hi}(k)}{u_{Hi}(k) - u_{Hi}(k-1)} \cdot x_{lj}(k)$$

$$= -\sum_{k=1}^{S} \delta_{ij}(k) \cdot x_{lj}(k)$$

Where

$$\delta_{ij}(k) = \delta_i(k) \cdot \omega_i \cdot \frac{x_{Hi}(k+1) - x_{Hi}(k)}{u_{Hi}(k) - u_{Hi}(k-1)}$$

The learning processing will stop when the average value of square error is smaller than the setting error value in the time of sample point S.

V. SIMULATION RESULTS

The fuzzy PID controller with PID neural network, that is proposed in this paper, is a constructed by fuzzy controller and PID neural network. The fuzzy controller part is the conventional one. But the neural network has a PID character. It is the hard work to regulate the rules in fuzzy controller. And it is difficult to improve the transient state by just changing the membership function. So the rule base in fuzzy controller is not changed, and remain its structure of condition sentence and the shape of membership functions.

In the sense of that the fuzzy PID controller need to be optimized. Thus, the rule base and the fuzzy inference map nonlinearly the input signal of fuzzy controller into output signal of it. The rule base remain and not to change. The key work to optimize the fuzzy PID controller is to choose the suitable value of PID parameters. Hence the weight value of PID neural network must be learned on account of the reason above.

The fuzzy PID controllers with PID neural network are used to simulate some control processing. The results show that these fuzzy PID controllers are more effective than conventional PID controllers and the learning of weight value make the PID parameters a optimal one. The output responses of system are much better than that of conventional PID controller.

A. First order system

The first example is the first order systems with the simple model as follow

$$G(s) = \frac{e^{-10s}}{100s + 1} \quad (17)$$

For this delay time system, according to the method of expanding response curve, the parameters are chosen as follow: sample period $T_s = 1s$, reference value r = 100, K_p = 13, K_I = 0.325, K_D = 0.008. The output response obtained is shown in Fig.1 as curve 1 for step input signal.

Curve 2 in Fig.7 also depicts the output performance of the fuzzy PID controller in which the parameters after learning are: $T_s = 1s$, r = 100, K_P = 18, K_I = 0.6, K_D = 0.034.

Curve 3 in Fig.7 shows the result of Ziegler Nichols method with K_P = 13, T_I = 5s, T_D =1.25s.

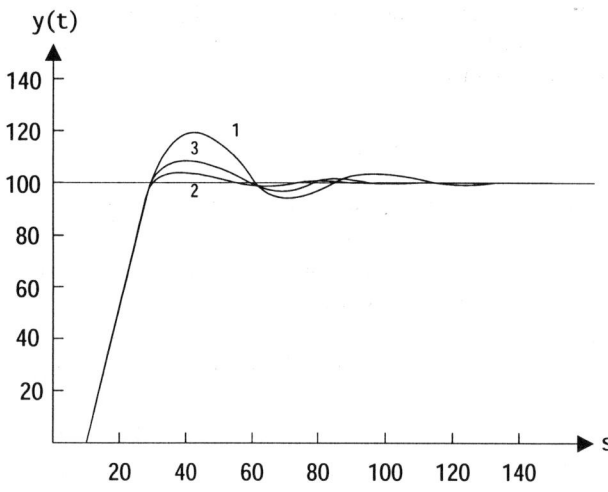

Fig. 7   The simulation result for first order system

B. Second Order System

The second example is the second order system. The model of it is obtained as following

$$G(s) = \frac{e^{-2s}}{(21s + 1)(13s + 1)} \quad (18)$$

For this process, using the method of expanding response curve, the suitable parameter of conventional PID controller are considered as: sample period T_s = 0.5s, reference value r = 10; K_p = 0.1902, K_I = 0.279, K_D = 0.26628. The curve of output response that marked curve 1 is shown in Fig 8.

For fuzzy PID controller, the output response, called curve 2, is given in the same time.

Curve 3 in Fig.8 gives the result of Ziegler-Nichols method using K_P = 0.2, T_I = 2.5s, T_D =0.625s.

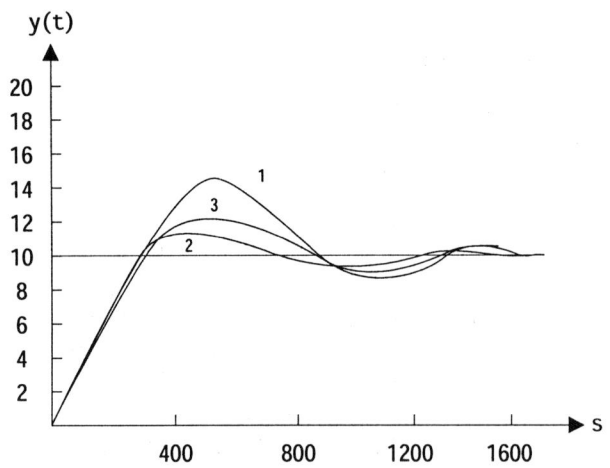

Fig. 8 The simulation result for second order process

The simulation result shows the fuzzy PID controllers have the better behave than conventional PID controller and Ziegler-Nichols controller. Own to the PID parameters of it can be learned using the PID neural network and is more suitable for the process.

VI. CONCULSION

A fuzzy PID controller with PIDNN has been proposed in this paper. It is a discrete-time version of PID controller combined fuzzy controller with PID neural network. The controller has adaptive control capability and optimized via the back-propagation algorithm. The results demonstrate that fuzzy PID controller with PIDNN has much better performance than conventional one. The controller proposed in this paper is suitable for the control of various plants, including linear or nonlinear process.

REFERENCES

[1] S. Bennett, Development of the PID controller, IEEE Contr. Syst. Mag., 13 (1993) 58~65

[2] K. J. Astrom, C. C. Hang, P. Persson, and W. K. Ho, Toward intelligent PID Control, Automatic, 28 (1992) 1~9

[3] J. H. Kim, K. K. Choi, Self-turning discrete PID Controller, IEEE Trans. Indst. Electron. 34 (2) (1987) 298~300

[4] P. Vega, C.Prada, V. Aleixander, Self-tuning predictive PID controller, IEE Proc. D 138 (3) (1991) 303~311

[5] M. Mizumoto, Realization of PID controls by fuzzy control methods, Proc. IEEE Internat. Conf. On Fuzzy Systems, San Diego, (1992) 209~715

[6] Li zheng, A practical guide to tune of proportional and integral (PI) like fuzzy controller, IEEE Int. Conf. On Fuzzy Systems, (1992) 663~640

[7] J. Carvajal, G. Chen, and H.Ogment, Fuzzy PID Controller: Design, Performance evaluation, and stability analysis, Inform. Sci., 123 (2000) 249~270

[8] G. Chen, Conventional and fuzzy PID Controllers: An overview, Int. J. Intell, Control Syst, 1(1996)235~246

[9] G.Chen and H. Ying, BIBO stability of nonlinear fuzzy PI control systems, Int. J. Intell. Control Syst, 5 (1997) 3~21

[10] K. S. Tang, K. F. Man, G. Chen and S. Kwong, An optimal fuzzy PID controller, IEEE Trans. Indust, Electron. 48 (4) (2001) 757~764

[11] R. K. Mudi and N. R. Pal, A self-tuning fuzzy PI controller, Fuzzy Sets and Systems, 115 (2000) 327~338

[12] Z. W. Woo, H. Y. Chung, and J. J. Lin, A PID type fuzzy controller with self-tuning scaling factor, Fuzzy Sets and Systems, 115 (2000) 321~326

[13] B. Hu, G. K. I. Mann and R. G. Gosine, New methodology for analytical and optimal design of fuzzy PID controller, IEEE Trans. On Fuzzy Systems, 7 (5) (1999) 521~539

[14] G. K. I. Mann, B. G. Hu, and R. G. Gosine, Analysis of direct action fuzzy PID Controller Structures, IEEE Trans, on Syst., Man, Cybern, 29 (3) (1999) 371-388

[15] Z. Y. Zhao, M. Tomizuka and S. Isaka, "Fuzzy gain scheduling of PID controllers", IEEE Trans, Syst, Man, Cybern, 23 (5) (1993) 1392-1398

[16] H.Y.Chung, B. C. Chen and J. J. Lin, A PI-type fuzzy controller with self – turning scaling factors, Fuzzy Sets and Systems, 93 (1998) 23~28

[17] W. Z. Qiao and M. Mizumoto, PID type fuzzy controller and parameters adaptive method, Fuzzy Sets and Systems 78 (1996) 23~35

[18] M. Maeda and S. Murakami, Fuzzy gain scheduling of PID controllers, Fuzzy Sets and Systems, 51 (1992) 29~40

[19] S. Z. He, S. Tan, F. L. Xu and P. Z. Wang, Fuzzy Self-tuning of PID controllers, Fuzzy Sets and Systems, 56 (1993) 37~46

[20] Shu Huailin, Analysis of PID Neural Network Multivariable Control Systems, ACTA Automatica Sinica, 25 (1) (1999) 105~111

[21] Shu Huailin, PID Newral Network Control for Complex Systems, Processdings of International Conference on Computational Intelligence for Modelling, Control and Automation CCIMCA 99'2, IOS Press, (1999) 166~171

Modular Fuzzy Hyperline Segment Neural Network

P.M.Patil, U.V. Kulkarni and T.R. Sontakke
Electronics and Computer Science & Engineering Department
SGGS College of Engineering and technology,
Vishnupuri, Nanded - 431602, (M.S.), India.
E-mail: patil_pm@rediffmail.com

ABSTRACT

This paper describes Modular Fuzzy Hyperline Segment Neural Network (MFHLSNN) with its learning algorithm, which is an extension of Fuzzy Hyperline Segment Neural Network (FHLSNN) proposed by Kulkarni and Sontakke [1]. The MFHLSNN offers higher degree of parallelism. Each module in MFHLSNN is exposed to the patterns of only one class and trained without overlap test and removal, unlike in FHSNN, leading to reduction in training time. Hence, each module captures peculiarity of only one particular class and due to decrease in training time the algorithm can be used for voluminous realistic database, where new patterns can be added on fly. The MFHLSNN is found superior than FHLSNN in terms of generalization and training time with equivalent testing time.

I. INTRODUCTION

The Fuzzy neural networks have become very popular and widely being used in the pattern recognition applications. Basically, there are two main training strategies employed by fuzzy neural networks; supervised and unsupervised learning. In supervised learning, class labels are provided with input patterns and the decision boundary between classes that minimizes misclassification is achieved. It is often referred as pattern classification problem. In unsupervised learning, training patterns are unlabeled and clusters of the patterns are formed with a suitable similarity measure, which is referred as clustering problem.

Many papers using fuzzy neural networks are reported on studies of pattern classification and clustering. Kwan and Cai [2] have proposed four-layer feed forward unsupervised fuzzy neural network (FNN). Kulkarni and Sontakke [3] have modified FNN to work under supervised environment, which is further extended, by Patil, Kulkarni and Sontakke [4] using selective aggregation operators. The modified FNN uses similarity measure and if the input pattern is similar to already learned patterns of that class then only it is accommodated by that neuron otherwise new neuron of that pattern class is constructed. Patrick Simpson [5] proposed supervised fuzzy min-max neural network (FMN) that utilizes fuzzy sets as pattern classes in which each fuzzy set is union of fuzzy set hyperboxes. Gabrys and Bargiela [6] have proposed general fuzzy min-max neural network (GFMM) for clustering and classification, which is an extension of FMN, with a fusion of supervised and unsupervised learning. Kulkarni, Sontakke and Randale [1] have proposed fuzzy hyperline segment neural network (FHLSNN) and its performance is found superior than the FMN algorithm. Patil, Dhabe, Kulkarni and Sontakke [7] have modified the membership function of FHLSNN algorithm that gives improved results. Patil, Kulkarni and Sontakke [8] have proposed general fuzzy hyperline segment neural network (GFHLSNN), which is an extension of FHLSNN with a fusion of supervised and unsupervised leaning. Doye and Sontakke [9] have proposed modular general fuzzy min-max neural network, which is used for speech recognition of Marathi language (Language spoken in the state of Maharashtra, INDIA). They have shown that the modular network has better average recognition accuracy. Patil, Kulkarni and Sontakke [10] have proposed modular fuzzy hypersphere neural network (MFHSNN), which is an extension of FHSNN [11]. The MFHSNN is found superior than FHSNN in terms of generalization and training time with equivalent testing time.

In this paper we present the MFHLSNN algorithm, which is an extension of FHLSNN and it is applied for rotation invariant handwritten character recognition. Ring and Zernike features are used as feature extraction methods. Its performance is also tested using Fisher Iris database.

This paper is organized as follows. The topology and its learning algorithm are described in section II and III, respectively. The performance comparison of MFHLSNN with FHLSNN, FMN and FNN algorithms using standard databases is presented in section IV. Finally the conclusions are stated in section V. The notations used in this paper are kept consistent with the original paper introducing FHLSNN, as far as possible for the reference and comparison purposes.

II. THE TOPOLOGY

During training phase, K modules of FHLSNN are used, if database consists of patterns of K number of classes as shown in Fig. 1, in which each module is a simple two layer feed forward neural network that grows adaptively to meet the demands of the problem.

The first layer accepts the *n*-dimensional input pattern as it consists of consists of *n* processing elements, one for each dimension of the pattern. Second layer consists of *m* processing nodes that are constructed during training. There are two

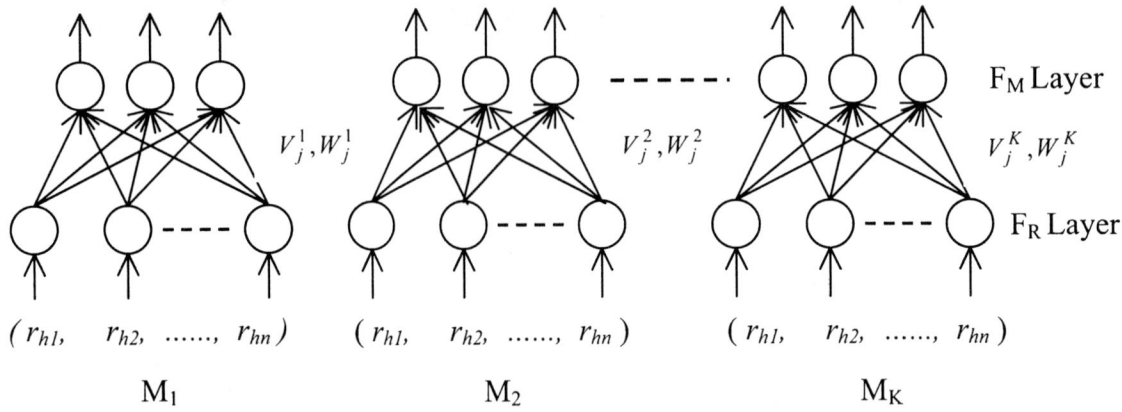

Fig.1: Modules of MFHLSNN during training phase

connections from each first to second node; one connection represents one end point for that dimension and the other connection represents another end point of that dimension, for a particular hyperline segment as shown in Fig. 2. One end point of fuzzy hyperline segment is stored in matrix V^k and the other end point is stored in matrix W^k for K modules that are present for K number of classes. Each module is trained with patterns of that class to which it represents. Hence, each module learns peculiarities of a single class.

For any k^{th} module, the weights between first and second layer represents hyperline segments (HLSs) created during learning. These HLSs are stored in matrix V^k and matrix W^k. Each row in V^k and W^k is n-dimensional vector. These two end point matrices and a fuzzy membership function, characterizes each HLS in a module. The fuzzy membership function returns values between 0 and 1. The processing performed by j^{th} fuzzy HLS node in k^{th} module, i.e. m_j^k, is shown in the Figure 2.

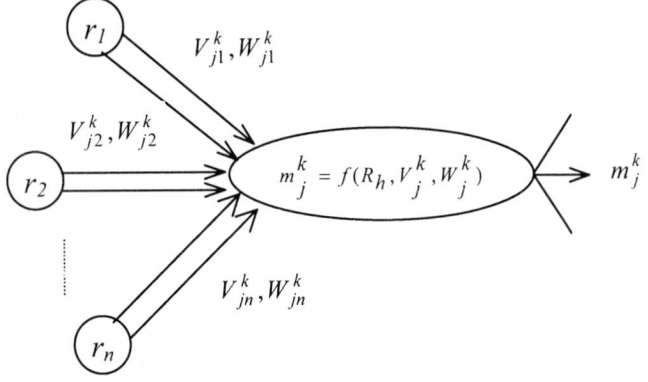

Fig.2: Implementation of Fuzzy HLS

Assuming the training set defined as $R = \{R_h \mid h = 1, 2, .., P\}$, where $R_h = (r_{h1}, r_{h2}, ..., r_{hn})$ is the hth pattern, and the end points of HLS m_j^k, are $V_j^k = (v_{j1}^k, v_{j2}^k, ..., v_{jn}^k)$ and $W_j^k = (w_{j1}^k, w_{j2}^k, ..., w_{jn}^k)$, the membership function of the jth fuzzy HLS node in k^{th} module m_j^k is defined as,

$$m_j^k(R_h, V_j^k, W_j^k) = 1 - f^3(x, \gamma_1, l), \quad (1)$$

in which $x = l_1 + l_2$ and the distances l_1, l_2 and l are defined as,

$$l_1 = \left(\sum_{i=1}^{n} (w_{ji}^k - r_{hi})^2 \right)^{1/2}, \quad (2)$$

$$l_2 = \left(\sum_{i=1}^{n} (v_{ji}^k - r_{hi})^2 \right)^{1/2}, \quad (3)$$

$$l = \left(\sum_{i=1}^{n} (w_{ji}^k - v_{ji}^k)^2 \right)^{1/2}, \quad (4)$$

and $f^3(\cdot)$ is a three-parameter ramp threshold function defined as,

$$f^3(x, \gamma_1, l) = 0 \quad \text{if } x = l \text{ otherwise}$$

$$f^3(x, \gamma_1, l) = \begin{cases} x\gamma_1 & \text{if } 0 \leq x\gamma_1 \leq 1 \\ 1 & \text{if } x\gamma_1 > 1. \end{cases}$$

The fuzzy hyperline segment membership function shown in Fig. 3 returns highest membership value equal to one if the pattern R_h falls on the hyperline segment joined by two end points V_j^k and W_j^k. The membership value is governed by the sensitivity parameter γ_1, which regulates how fast the membership value decreases when the distance between R_h and m_j^k increases. For the given input pattern R_h, m_j^k's output value is computed using (1).

After training the performance of MFHLSNN is tested using four-layer feedforward neural network architecture as shown in Fig. 4. The first two layers are constructed during training.

The third layer uses K MAX Fuzzy Neurons (FNs), one for each module. The output of kth module, n^k, is calculated as,

$$n^k = \max_{j=1}^{q^k} m_j^k \qquad \text{for } k = 1, 2, \ldots, K \qquad (5)$$

where q^k represents number of HLSs in k^{th} module created in training phase. Hence the output of third layer gives fuzzy decision and the output n^k indicates the degree of membership of the input pattern to the class k.

The fourth layer contains COMP-FNs defined as in [2]. Finally each F_C node delivers non-fuzzy output which is described as,

$$c^k = \begin{cases} 0 & \text{if } n^k < T \\ 1 & \text{if } n^k = T \end{cases} \qquad \text{for } k = 1 \text{ to } K \qquad (6)$$

where, $T = \max(n^k)$, for $k = 1$ to K

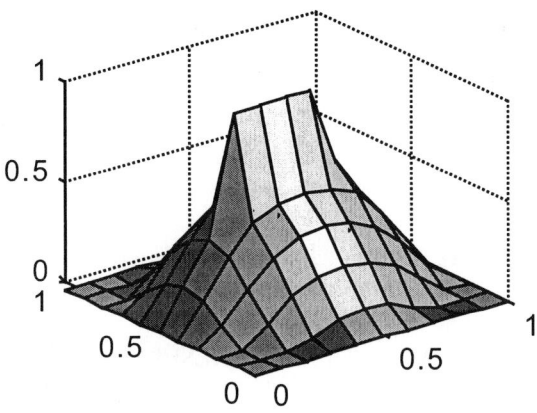

Fig.3: Plot of fuzzy hyperline segment membership function for $\gamma_1 = 1$ with end points w = [0.5 0.3] and v = [0.5 0.7]

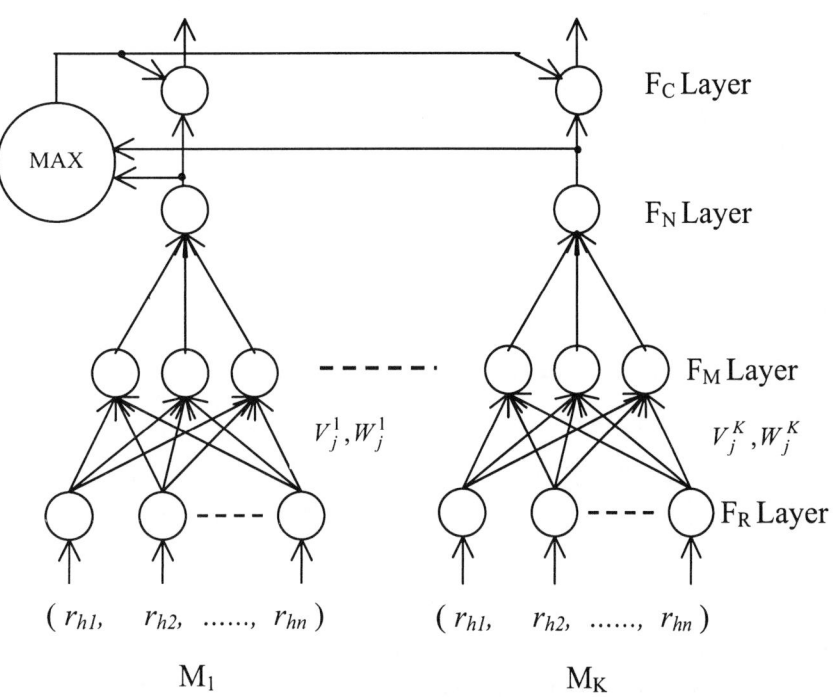

Fig.4: Architecture of MFHLSNN in testing phase

MFHLSNN LEARNING ALGORITHM

The training set R consists of a set of P ordered pairs $\{R_h, d_h\}$, where $R_h = (r_{h1}, r_{h2}, ..., r_{hn}) \in I^n$ is the hth input pattern and $d_h \in \{1, 2, ..., K\}$ is the index of one of the K classes. The learning algorithm of MFHLSNN composed of two steps.

1. Initialization: All K modules are initialized by creating a HLS in each with a first pattern belonging to the class of the module. This is a state when the network has K modules, each containing one HLS having two end points V_j^k and W_j^k equal to zero.

2. Training: Actual training begins after the initialization. An input pattern of class k is applied to k^{th} module only and fuzzy membership of the input pattern with all the HLSs within that module is calculated as described below.

In the learning process the user defined parameter θ_2 puts limit on the length of hyperline segments. The hyperline segments are extended only if the length after extension is less than or equal to θ_2. Given the hth training pair (R_h, d_h), find all the hyperline segments belonging to the class d_h. After this following four steps are carried sequentially for possible inclusion of the input pattern R_h.

Step 1: Determine whether the pattern R_h falls on any one of the hyperline segments. This can be verified by using fuzzy hyperline segment membership function described in (1). If R_h falls on any one of the hyperline segment then it is included, therefore in the training process all the remaining steps are skipped and training is continued with the next training pair.

Step 2: If the pattern R_h falls on any one of the hyperline passing through two end points of the hyperline segment, then extend the hyperline segment to include the pattern. Suppose m_j^k is that hyperline segment with end points V_j^k and W_j^k then l_1, l_2 and l are calculated using (2), (3) and (4), respectively. Where l_1 is the distance of R_h from end point W_j^k, l_2 is the distance of R_h from end point V_j^k and l is the length of hyperline segment.

2(a): If $l_1 > l_2$ then test whether the point V_j^k falls on the hyperline segment formed by the points W_j^k and R_h. This condition can be verified using (1) i.e. if $m_j^k(V_j^k, R_h, W_j^k) = 1$, then the hyperline segment is extended by replacing end point V_j^k with R_h to include R_h. Hence

$$V_j^{new} = R_h \quad \text{and} \quad W_j^{new} = W_j^k. \tag{7}$$

2(b): If $l_2 > l_1$ then test whether the point W_j^k falls on the hyperline segment formed by the points V_j^k and R_h. If $m_j^k(W_j^k, V_j^k, R_h) = 1$, hyperline segment is extended by replacing end point W_j^k with R_h to include the pattern R_h. Hence

$$W_j^{new} = R_h \quad \text{and} \quad V_j^{new} = V_j^k. \tag{8}$$

Step 3: If hyperline segment is a point then extend it to include the pattern R_h as described by (7).

Step 4: If the pattern R_h is not included by any one of the above steps then new hyperline segment is created for that class, which is described as,

$$W_{new} = R_h \quad \text{and} \quad V_{new} = R_h \tag{9}$$

IV. SIMULATION RESULTS

MFHLSNN is implemented using MATLAB 5.1 on P-III, 733MHz PC. The results obtained are compared with FNN, FMN, and FHLSNN. For comparison, same databases are used in the same sequence of data presentation. Fisher Iris data, which is well known to the pattern recognition community, is used in the experimentation, and collected from the machine-learning databases [12]. This database contains 150 patterns of 3 classes. Each class has 50 instances. Each class refers to a type of Iris plant. One class is linearly separable from other two but the latter are not linearly separable from each other. Pattern classes are Iris-Setosa, Iris-Versicolor and Iris-Virginica. Feature vector is 4-dimensional excluding class label.

	Set-I	Set-II	θ_2	HLS
FHLSNN	96	100	0.95	66
FHLSNN	100	90.66	0.8	40
MFHLSNN	96	100	0.05	69
MFHLSNN	100	94.66	0.05	70

Table 1. Percentage recognition rates with Fisher Iris database.

For recognition purpose set I, and II are prepared from Fisher Iris database by randomly selecting 75 patterns in each set. When MFHLSNN is trained with $\theta_2 = 0.05$ with set II it has created 69 HLSs and recognized 72 patterns in set I. When it is trained with $\theta_2 = 0.05$ for set I it has created 70 HLSs and recognized 71 patterns from set II. When FHLSNN is trained with $\theta_2 = 0.95$ with set II it has created 66 HLSs and recognized 72 patterns in set I. When it is trained with $\theta_2 = 0.8$ for set I it has created 40 HLSs and recognized 68 patterns from set II. This is shown in Table 1. From Table 1 it is clear that the MFHLSNN gives better recognition rate.

	Set-1	Set-2	Set-3	Set-4	Avg.	HBs/HSs /FNs/HLSs
FNN	100	25.6	20.8	13.9	40.075	989
MFNN	100	27.9	20.1	15.4	40.85	976
FMN	100	51.9	28.7	21.5	50.525	957
FHSNN	100	53.5	29.3	24.2	51.75	997
MFHSNN	100	56.05	29.5	24.5	52.51	997
FHLSNN	100	53.5	29.5	24.5	51.875	913
MFHLSNN	100	56.69	29.1	24.2	53.25	869

Table 2. Percentage recognition rates with Zernike features

The performance of MFHLSNN algorithm is also verified for rotation invariant handwritten character recognition and compared with FNN, FMN and FHLSNN algorithms. The handwritten characters can be in arbitrary location, scale and orientation. Ten numerals from two hundred writers are scanned and stored in BMP format. The linear moment normalization discussed by Perantonis and Lisboa [13] is used to normalize characters to get translation and scale invariance. After normalization the rotation invariant ring features defined as in [14] are extracted from the normalized characters by setting ring width to two. These feature vectors are scaled within the range [0,1]. Therefore, the pattern space with 16 ring features is a 16-dimensional unit cube. The Zernike features up to order five defined in [15] are also extracted and then scaled within the range [0,1] along each dimension. Pattern space with Zernike features is 16-dimensional unit cube because; selected features start from second order moments. Hence, the database of handwritten characters consists of two thousand characters. Details of four data sets prepared from this database and used in the experiments are given below.

Set-1 is unrotated training set, i.e. original training set consisting of one thousand training patterns, which is reused to verify the recognition. Set-2 is rotated training set extracted from set 1, i.e. each sample of set-2 is a rotated version of sample in set 1 with an angle of 15^0. Set 3 is unrotated testing set consisting of remaining one thousand patterns in the database that is used to evaluate generality. Set-4 is rotated testing set extracted from set-3, i.e. each sample of set-4 is a rotated version of sample in set-3, with an angle of 15^0.

The results obtained with Zernike features are tabulated in Table 2. The MFHLSNN algorithm created 869 hyperline segments (HLSs) when trained with $\theta_2 = 0.058$. It is observed that the recognition rates of MFHLSNN are better for even less number of HLSs, as shown in Table 2.

When the MFHLSNN algorithm is trained with ring features, its performance is listed in Table 3. The MFHLSNN algorithm gives better recognition rates for all the sets as compared to other algorithms. The comparison of Table 2 and Table 3 shows that recognition rates with ring features are superior than Zernike features.

	Set-1	Set-2	Set-3	Set-4	Avg.	HBs/HSs/FNs/HLSs
FNN	100	78.7	33.1	29.6	60.35	971
MFNN	100	81.1	34.1	29.9	61.2	963
FMN	100	99.3	47.3	45.5	73.025	851
FHSNN	100	99.3	45.6	44.5	72.35	934
MFHSNN	100	99.7	45.9	44.8	72.65	995
FHLSNN	100	99.7	45.8	44.7	72.55	801
MFHLSNN	100	99.7	45.8	44.4	72.48	888

Table 3. Percentage recognition rates with Ring features

The timing analysis using ring features is listed in Table 4 along with the neurons in output layer, HBs, HSs and HLSs created by FNN, MFNN, FMN, MFMN, FHSNN, MFHSNN, FHLSNN and MFHLSNN algorithms, respectively, to get 100% recognition rate for set 1.

	Training time (sec)	Recall time / pattern (sec)	HBs/HSs/FNs/HLSs
FNN	1228.5	1.4252	992
MFNN	702.61	1.3848	963
FMN	435.45	1.4986	851
MFHSNN	200.32	0.384	995
FHLSNN	42.461	0.593	801
MFHLSNN	88.45	0.493	868

Table 4. Timing analysis

V. CONCLUSIONS

The MFHLSNN has ability to learn the patterns faster than FNN, FMN, MFMN and FHLSNN because it creates/expands HSs without any overlap test and its removal, which is a substantial overhead in the FMN and FHSNN algorithms. Recognition rates with ring features are superior than Zernike features. The MFHLSNN algorithm gives better recognition rates for all the sets as compared to other algorithms. Thus it can be used in voluminous realistic database recognition purposes where less training time is the prime demand.

REFERENCES

[1] U. V. Kulkarni, T. R. Sontakke, and G. D. Randale, "Fuzzy hyperline segment neural network for rotation invariant handwritten character recognition," in Proc. Joint Int. Conference on Neural Networks, Washington DC, USA, (IEEE: INNS: IJCNN 2001), Vol. 4, pp. 2918-2923, July 2001.

[2] H.K. Kwan and Yaling Cai, "A fuzzy neural network and its applications to pattern recognition," IEEE Trans. on fuzzy systems, Vol. 2, No. 3, pp. 185-192, 1994.

[3] U.V. Kulkarni and T.R. Sontakke, "Modified fuzzy neural network classifier for pattern recognition," All India seminar on recent trends in computer communication networks (CCN 2001), I.I.T. Roorkee, pp. 69-75, 2001.

[4] P.M. Patil, U.V. Kulkarni and T.R. Sontakke, "Performance evaluation of Fuzzy Neural Network with various aggregation operators," accepted in 9th International Conference on Neural Information Processing, ICONIP'02, to be held in November 2002 at Singapore.

[5] P.K. Simpson, "Fuzzy min-max neural networks-part1: classification," IEEE Trans. neural networks, Vol. 3, No. 5, pp. 776-786, 1992.

[6] Bogdan Gabrys and Andrzej Bargiela, "General fuzzy min-max neural network for clustering and classification," IEEE Trans. on neural networks, Vol. 11 No.3, May 2000.

[7] P.M. Patil, P.S. Dhabe, U.V. Kulkarni and T.R. Sontakke, "Recognition of Handwritten Characters using Modified Fuzzy Hyperline Segment Neural Network," accepted for oral presentation in the IEEE International Conference on Fuzzy Systems, FUZZ-IEEE2003, to be held in May 2003 at Marriott Pavilion Downtown Hotel, St. Louis, MO.

[8] P.M. Patil, U.V. Kulkarni and T.R. Sontakke, "General Fuzzy Hyperline Segment Neural Network," in Proc. of IEEE SMC02, Hammamet, Tunisia, October 2002.

[9] Dharmpal Doye and Trimbak Sontakke, "Speech Recognition using modular General Fuzzy Min-Max Neural Network," Journal of IETE,

[10] P.M. Patil, U.V. Kulkarni and T.R. Sontakke, "Rotation Invariant Handwritten Character Recognition using Modular Fuzzy Hypersphere Neural Network," accepted for oral presentation in the IEEE International Conference on Fuzzy Systems, FUZZ-IEEE2003, to be held in May 2003 at Marriott Pavilion Downtown Hotel, St. Louis, MO.

[11] U. V. Kulkarni and T. R. Sontakke, "Fuzzy hypersphere neural network classifier," accepted for publication *in 10th int. IEEE Conference on Fuzzy Systems* to be held at University of Melbourne, Australia, December 2001.

[12] C. Blake, E. Keogh, and C. J. Merz. (1998) UCI repository of machine learning databases, Univ. California, Irvine.
http://www.ics.uci.edu/\~mlearn/MLRepository.html

[13] S.J. Perantonis and P.J.G. Lisboa, "Translation, rotation and scale invariant pattern recognition by high-order neural networks and moment classifiers," IEEE Trans. neural networks, Vol. 3, No. 2, pp. 241-251, 1992.

[14] Hung-Pin Chiu and Din-Chang Tseng, "Invariant handwritten Chinese character recognition using fuzzy min-max neural networks," Pattern recog. letters, Vol. 18, pp. 481-491, 1997.

[15] Khotanzad and J.H. Lu, "Classification of invariant image representations using a neural network," IEEE Trans. ASSP, Vol. 38, No. 6, pp. 1028-1038, 1990.

Multivariate Time Series Model Discovery with Similarity-Based Neuro-Fuzzy Networks and Genetic Algorithms

Julio J. Valdés
National Research Council Canada
Institute for Information Technology
1200 Montreal Road, Ottawa ON K1A 0R6
Canada

Email: julio.valdes@nrc.ca

Alan J. Barton
National Research Council Canada
Institute for Information Technology
1200 Montreal Road, Ottawa ON K1A 0R6
Canada

Email: alan.barton@nrc.ca

Abstract—This paper studies the properties of a hybrid technique for model discovery in multivariate time series, using similarity based hybrid neuro-fuzzy neural networks and genetic algorithms. This method discovers *dependency patterns* relating future values of a target series with past values of all examined series, and also constructs a prediction function. It accepts a mixture of numeric and non-numeric variables, fuzzy information, and missing values. Experiments were made with a real multivariate time series for studying the model discovery ability and the influence of missing values. Results show that the method is very robust, discovers relevant interdependencies, gives accurate predictions and is tolerant to considerable proportions of missing information.

I. INTRODUCTION

Multivariate time-varying processes occur in many domains and their importance is increasing with the developments in sensor technologies and advanced monitoring systems. Processes of this kind involve many variables changing simultaneously with time. In general, these processes are heterogeneous in nature, consisting of numeric and non-numeric quantities, typically with missing values (i.e. gaps in the observations occur due to sensor saturation, malfunctioning, etc.), which do not necessarily distribute in the same way in the different observed variables. Also, measurements and observations are obtained with different degrees of precision and indetermination (e.g. data may be fuzzy). One of the most important data mining and knowledge discovery tasks in the study of time dependent information is finding *interesting dependencies* between past and future values of the observed variables (i.e. *dependency patterns* or *models*). Another goal is to find suitable prediction estimators for forecasting purposes. The use of classical methods is limited by different factors. Some factors are related to the underlying assumptions about the data concerning type, volume, homogeneity, complexity, precision, the curse of dimensionality, etc. In many cases these methods are based on assumptions which don't hold or are unpractical to verify. From a soft-computing approach to solving this problem, neural networks have been applied extensively for time series and signal analysis, however, the multivariate case is less frequently studied. A technique for model discovery and prediction in multivariate time series was introduced recently in [6]. That method accepts heterogeneous, large series with different degrees of imprecision (possibly with missing data) and uses hybrid networks mixing different neuron models (similarity-based and classical). These networks operate in a neuro-fuzzy mode. Preliminary applications showed interesting behavior with respect to speed, performance and sensitivity to detect internal dependencies. This paper studies the behavior of this kind of network in a strongly multivariate time series modeling and forecasting problem. The paper also shows the network's robustness w.r.t. increased presence of missing values in the time series, and choice of algorithm parameters.

II. METHOD OUTLINE

The objective is to extract plausible *dependency models* in heterogeneous multivariate time varying processes, expressing the relationship between future values of a previously selected time series (the target), and the entire set of series. Heterogeneity means the presence of ratio, interval, ordinal or nominal scales, and fuzzy magnitudes. Moreover, the series may contain missing values. The first step is to set a conceptual class of functional models and in this case a generalized non-linear auto-regressive (AR) model was used (1) (other classes of functional models are also possible),

$$S_T(t) = \mathbf{F} \begin{pmatrix} S_1(t-\tau_{1,1}), \cdots, S_1(t-\tau_{1,p_1}), \\ S_2(t-\tau_{2,1}), \cdots, S_2(t-\tau_{2,p_2}), \\ \cdots \\ S_n(t-\tau_{n,1}), \cdots, S_n(t-\tau_{n,p_n}) \end{pmatrix} \quad (1)$$

where $S_T(t)$ is the target signal at time t, S_i is the i-th time series, n is the total number of signals, p_i is the number of time lag terms from signal i influencing $S_T(t)$, $\tau_{i,k}$ is the k-th lag term corresponding to signal i ($k \in [1, p_i]$), and $\mathbf{F}$ is the unknown function describing the process. The second step in the proposed method, is the simultaneous determination of: *i)* the number of required lags for each series, *ii)* the particular lags within each one carrying the dependency information, and *iii)* the prediction function. A natural requirement on function F is the property of minimizing a suitable prediction error. This is approached with a soft computing precedure based on: (a) exploration of a subset of the entire *model space* with a genetic algorithm, and (b) use of a similarity-based neuro-fuzzy system representation for the unknown prediction function.

Evolving neuro-fuzzy networks with genetic algorithms has been done for a long time, but only for training purposes and in the context of a *single* network. The situation here is very different: it involves the construction and evaluation of *thousands* or even *millions* of networks, since the search in the space of dependency models is equivalent to the search in the space of networks. Thus, the use of conventional architectures and training procedures becomes prohibitive. Other difficulties with classical approaches include finding the number of hidden layers and their composition, using mixed numeric, non-numeric, fuzzy and missing values, etc. The present approach is based on the heterogeneous neuron model [5], [1], [7], which considers a neuron as a general mapping between heterogeneous multidimensional spaces $h : \hat{\mathcal{H}} \times \hat{\mathcal{H}} \to \mathcal{Y}$, where $\mathcal{Y}$ is an abstract set. If $\overleftarrow{x}, \overleftarrow{w} \in \hat{\mathcal{H}}$ (the input and the neuron weights respectively) and $y \in \mathcal{Y}$, then $y = h(\overleftarrow{x}, \overleftarrow{w})$.

In the *similarity-based* h-neuron model, the aggregation function is given by a *similarity function* $s(x, w)$ between the input and the neuron weights (vectors from a heterogeneous space), whereas the activation is a non-linear function. For the h-neuron used in the experiments, the chosen aggregation is a similarity function constructed by non-linearly transforming a distance function (allowing missing values), and the chosen activation function is the identity. Several distance functions were used in the experiments (see section III). This neuron maps a n-dimensional heterogeneous space onto the extended [0,1] real interval in such a way that the output expresses the degree of similarity between the input pattern and neuron weights $s : (\hat{\mathcal{H}} \times \hat{\mathcal{H}}) \to [0, 1] \cup \{X\}$, where X is the symbol denoting the missing value. A hybrid network layout using heterogeneous neurons in the hidden layer and classical neurons in the output layer is suitable for the purpose of model mining. In the particular case of multivariate heterogeneous time series, where a single time series is targeted for prediction based on the entire signal set, a suitable network architecture is shown in (Fig-1).

Network operation is as follows: Each neuron in the hidden layer computes its similarity with the input vector and the k-best responses are retained (k is a pre-set number of h-neurons to select). They represent the fuzzy memberships of the inputs w.r.t. the classes defined by the hidden layer neurons. Neurons in the output layer compute a normalized linear combination of the expected target values used as neuron weights (W_i), with the k-similarities coming from the hidden layer.

$$output = (1/\Theta) \sum_{i \in \mathcal{K}} h_i W_i, \quad \Theta = \sum_{i \in \mathcal{K}} h_i \quad (2)$$

where $\mathcal{K}$ is the set of k-best h-neurons of the hidden layer and h_i is the similarity of the i-best h-neuron w.r.t the input vector, representing a fuzzy estimate for the predicted value.

Assuming that a similarity function $\mathcal{S}$ has been chosen and that the target is a single time series, this *case-based* neuro-fuzzy network is built and trained as follows: Define a similarity threshold $T \in [0, 1]$ and extract the subset

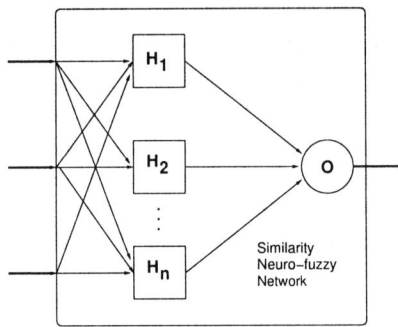

Fig. 1. Neuro-fuzzy network composed by h-neurons in the hidden layer and one classical neuron in the output layer.

$\mathcal{L}$ of the set of input patterns Ω ($\mathcal{L} \subseteq \Omega$) such that for every input pattern $x \in \Omega$, there exist a $l \in \mathcal{L}$ such that $\mathcal{S}(x, l) \geq T$. The hidden layer is constructed by using the elements of $\mathcal{L}$ as h-neurons, while the output layer is built by using the corresponding target outputs as the weights of the neuron(s). This training procedure is *very* fast and allows for the rapid construction and testing of many networks, as training complexity is $O(n^2)$ (In the case of $T = 1$, training is exactly $\Omega(n)=O(n)$).

A parallel implementation following a master-slave approach was made using LAM/MPI [3] and the GaLib [8]. The slaves construct and evaluate individual neuro-fuzzy networks based on models received from the master, which controls the genetic algorithm process at the population level. The system architecture is shown in Fig-2.

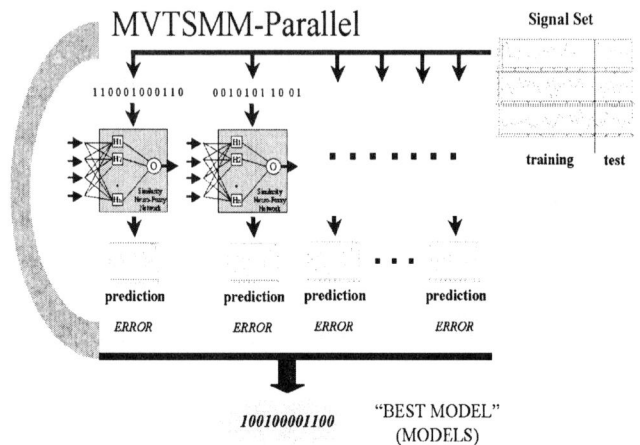

Fig. 2. Multivariate Time Series Model Miner System Architecture. The arc is the parallel genetic algorithm evolving populations of similarity-based networks. They represent different dependency patterns which are generated and evaluated during the search in the space of multivariate time series models.

The system's behavior is controlled by three classes of factors related to: *i)* the neuro-fuzzy network, *ii)* the genetic algorithm, and *iii)* the parallel implementation. Related to *(i)* are the specific similarity function modeling the neuron's computation (Sf), the number of responsive neurons in the hidden layer (Rn) representing the number of terms used to compute (2), the similarity threshold (St) determining the hidden layer composition, the maximun lag depth (Ld), and the relative percentage of the training set vs test set (Rp) when learning the prediction function for a given time series dependency model. In all experiments St was kept fixed and equal to 1.

The process of model search is performed by the genetic algorithm. Binary chromosomes coding model components as given by (1) were used with single and double point crossover operators and standard bit-reversal mutation. Selection was kept constant (roulette wheel method) and complete population replacement with elitism were used. In *(ii)* the influence of the number of generations (Ng), and the crossover operator were investigated. Population size P_s controls the richness of the "genetic pool" used in the evolutionary process. In these experiments it was fixed at 50. As for *(iii)* the number of physical nodes was fixed at three (dual CPUs), and the number of slaves fixed at 15 in all runs.

III. EXPERIMENTAL SETUP

A multivariate time series data set consisting of 10 series with 1140 observations of average monthly temperatures from different sites in the Washington State (USA) was chosen. They were recorded during the period 1895-1989 [4], and compiled by the National Oceanic and Atmospheric Administration (USA). Originally this data had no missing values and is shown in Fig-3. The West Olympic Coastal drainage region (the top series) was chosen as the target for a model mining study. No preprocessing was applied to the time series. This is not the usual way to analyze time series data, but by eliminating additional effects, the properties of the proposed procedure, in terms of approximation capacity and robustness, are better exposed.

With the purpose of investigating the behavior of the hybrid heterogeneous network, three new sets of time series were constructed by introducing 25%, 50% and 75% of uniformly distributed missing values into all 10 original series. The introduction of the missing values was done in a "signal-wise" manner. Each series was divided evenly into a training set and a test set. The training set for each signal contains the same precentage of introduced missing values, while the test sets were left intact. In this way, all signals contain exactly the same amount of missing values, as defined by the corresponding preset percentage. These training set variants were used by the evolutionary algorithm to explore the model space. The reported error measure is, in all cases, the *root mean squared error* (RMS error) computed by applying the trained networks to the test set.

The similarity functions were constructed from versions of the Euclidean, Clark and Canberra distance functions [2], and account for missing values. Given two vectors $\overleftarrow{x} = <x_1, \cdots, x_n>$, $\overleftarrow{y} = <y_1, \cdots, y_n> \in \mathbb{R}^n$, defined by a set of variables (i.e. attributes) $A = A_1, \cdots, A_n$, let $A_c \subseteq A$ be the subset of attributes s.t. $x_i \neq \mathtt{X}$ and $y_i \neq \mathtt{X}$. Then the corresponding distance functions are given in Table-I. Note that they are normalized distances and therefore, are

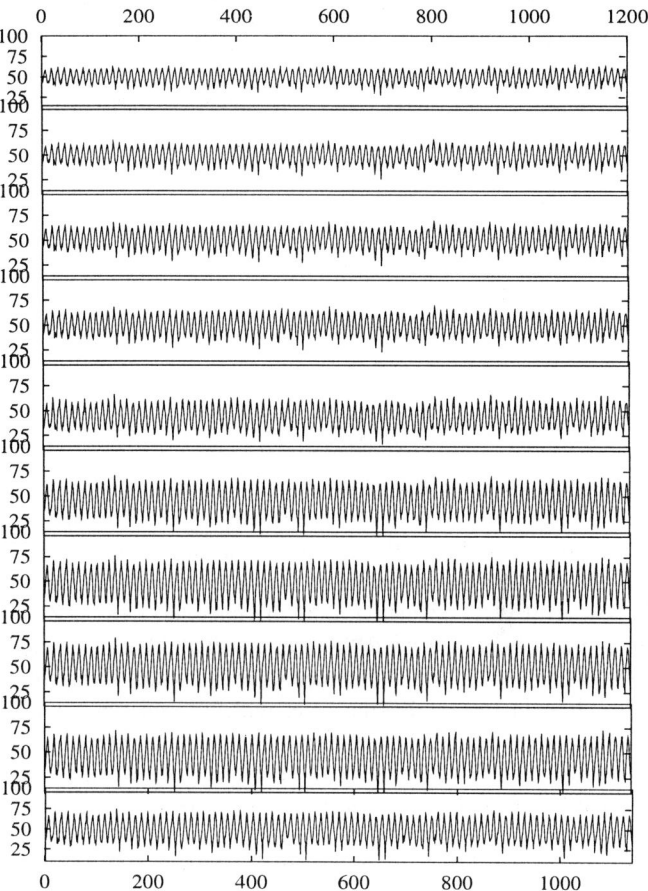

Fig. 3. Temperature data from 10 Washington State sites (Farenheit). See text for details.

independent of the number of attributes, and that *no imputation* of missing values to the data set is performed.

Name	Distance
Euclidean	$\frac{\sum_{A_c} (x_i - y_i)^2}{card(A_c)}$
Clark	$\frac{\sum_{A_c} \frac{(x_i - y_i)^2}{(x_i + y_i)^2}}{card(A_c)}$
Canberra	$\frac{\sum_{A_c} \frac{|x_i - y_i|}{(x_i + y_i)}}{card(A_c)}$

TABLE I

EUCLIDEAN, CLARK, AND CANBERRA MODIFIED DISTANCES

A total of 288 experiments were made varying the two classes of controlling factors and their corresponding parameters. In fact, 72 experiments were performed for each of the 4 missing value data set variants ($[0\% - 75\%]$). See Table-II.

The experiments were conducted on a Beowulf cluster consisting of three dual Xeon processor units operating at 2 Ghz frequency, each with 1Gb RAM. The cluster operates with 100 Mbit Ethernet connections. The operating system is Red Hat Linux 7.2 running LAM-MPI version 6.5.4/MPI 2, C++/ROMIO.

Factors	Parameter	Values
(i)	Sf	$(1/(1+d))$
	Rn	$<1, 3, 5, 7, 13, 20>$
	Ld	$<5, 10, 20, 30, 50>$
	Rp	$<50\%>$
(ii)	Ng	$<2, 10, 100>$
	Ps	$<50>$
	Cp	$<0.6>$
	Mp	$<0.01>$
	Ct	$<single, double>$

TABLE II

EXPERIMENTAL PARAMETERS. IN *(i)* d STANDS FOR EUCLIDEAN, CLARK, OR CANBERRA NORMALIZED DISTANCES.

IV. RESULTS

The distribution of the RMS error for all data sets ([0% − 75%] of missing data) is shown in Fig-4. All distributions are highly skewed towards the lower end of the RMS error measure. For the present analysis the range corresponding to the best error was considered to be the interval $[2.167 − 2.3]$. Due to the skewness of the RMS error distribution, the selected range comprises 75% of all the models found with 0% missing values. It is interesting that the series with 75% missing values still have more than 25% of their models with error in this lower end. The Q1-Q3 interquartile range (between the first and third quartiles) gets broader as would be expected since the information content in the series decreases. However it does it very slowly up until 75%, when it abruptly increases. Remarkably, the absolute minimum errors are almost constant, even considering the extreme 75% case. Thus, the algorithm exhibits a very robust behavior and a capacity to retrieve good models in this data set, even though it contains scarce information.

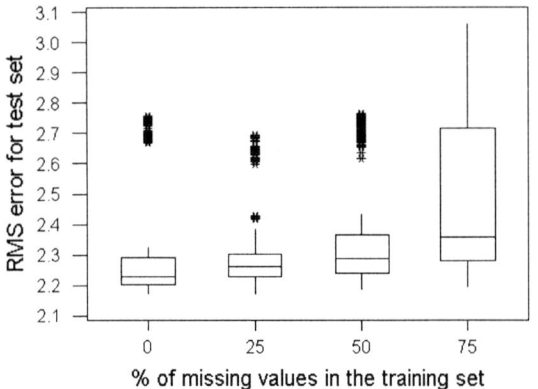

Fig. 4. Boxplots showing the main distribution parameters of the RMS Error for the different percentages of missing values for all experiments. Stars represent outlying elements in the tail of the distribution.

A. Influence of neuro-fuzzy network parameters

The neuro-fuzzy network relies on the responses of the heterogeneous neurons in the hidden layer which happen to be similarity-based units. Similarity functions are known to be sensitive to data structure, which in turn, is influenced by data dilution. The relations between the combination of percentage of missing values and the different similarity functions are shown in Fig-5 as boxplots of their corresponding error distributions.

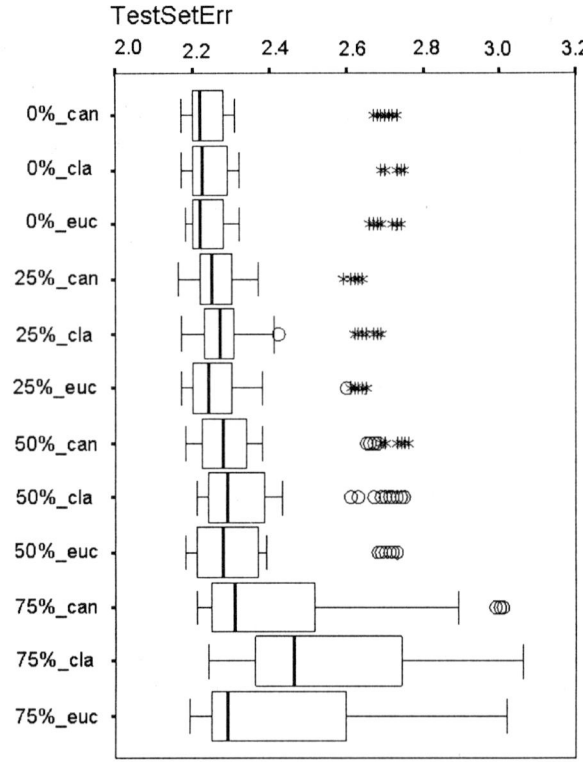

Fig. 5. Boxplots showing the main distribution parameters of the RMS Error for the different percentages of missing values and similarity measures for all experiments. Stars represent outlying elements in the tail of the distribution.

The different similarity measures don't appear to exert a large influence on the RMS error for most of the missing value variants, with the exception of 75%. Overall, errors for all cases except this last one, are within a relatively narrow band at the lower end. In the range [0% − 50%] there are no within variant pairwise differences between similarities. In the 75% case the similarity function based on Clark's distance clearly under performs and actually is responsible for the increase of the interquartile range in the overall (see Fig-4). It is also interesting to observe that with the exception of this last case, models with good prediction errors can be found with any choice of distance measure for all missing data set variants. Within the set of selected similarities, none of them performs significantly better than the others. In the context of this kind of data, the similarity function was not influential w.r.t the quality of the models discovered.

The number of responsive neurons (R_n) is an important parameter controlling the neuro-fuzzy network output. It determines the number of terms used in computing the fuzzy interpolation (2). The dependency of the RMS error with the number of responsive neurons (R_n) and the percentage of missing values is shown in Fig-6. In the specific case when $R_n = 1$ (representing the "winner take all" strategy), errors are systematically several times higher than those obtained from other larger choices of R_n, for all missing value variants. In general, in order to achieve a good fuzzy estimate for the predicted output, comparatively few terms (small R_n) are required in (2).

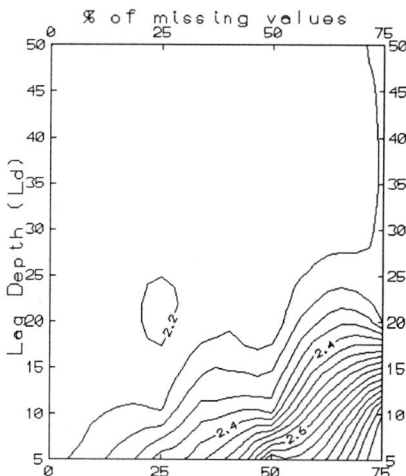

Fig. 7. Dependency of the RMS Error with the percent of missing values and the Lag Depth (L_d).

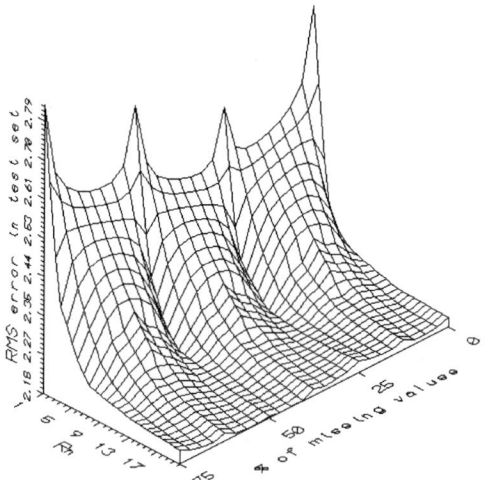

Fig. 6. Dependency of the mean RMS errors with the percentage of missing values and the number of responsive neurons (R_n).

The maximum lag (L_d) parameter defines the size of the search space of models by imposing an upper bound in the number of lag terms available for model construction. A value too small may preclude the discovery of good models if the memory of the process is large, whereas a value too large will increase unnecessarily the search space (it does it exponentially), thus decreasing the chances of discovery by "diluting" the good models. Moreover, it introduces noise in the search process. The behavior of L_d for the cases of [0% − 75%] missing values is shown in Fig-7

Clearly, when information is complete (0%), maximum lag depth has no influence on the error level. Therefore, small L_d values lead to compact, short-memory models. When data is severely affected by missing information larger L_d values (medium-memory models) are necessary in order to obtain comparable error levels. As missing values increases, the required lag depth increases and it does it linearly with a highly significant correlation coefficient (0.977). Moreover, the model mining procedure proved that looking deeper into the past of the process, does not necessarily improve the explanation of the target series, as shown by the large plateau in the investigated ranges of missing values and lag depths.

B. Influence of genetic algorithm parameters

Most of the parameters controlling the behavior of the genetic algorithm responsible for the evolutionary process of model discovery were kept fixed. However, a few experiments varying the number of generations (N_g) and crossover type (C_t) were performed. The behavior of the number of generations of the genetic algorithm (N_g) is shown in Table-III.

N_g	0% miss	25% miss	50% miss	75% miss
2	2.3013	2.2987	2.3020	2.3870
10	2.2842	2.2832	2.2849	2.2875
100	2.2374	2.2146	2.2296	2.2510

TABLE III
DISTRIBUTION OF $\overline{RMSerror}$ W.R.T. THE NUMBER OF GENERATIONS.

Clearly, the experiments show that it is enough to let the system evolve a medium-to-small number of generations in order to discover accurate models. Since a small number of generations are required, appropriate models can be found quickly. For a fixed N_g, doesn't affect the average error substantially, another indication of the robustness of the neuro-fuzzy network.

Single and double point crossover operators were used and their relation with the percentage of missing values and the $\overline{RMSerror}$ is shown in the boxplots of Fig-8.

The interquartile ranges up until 50% missing value are comparable. However, there seems to be a slight advantage for choosing double point over single point. This is demonstrated most clearly in the 75% case. Again, the overall minimum for each of the combinations is comparable. That is, model quality is not affected by the particular crossover operator.

C. Prediction Example

The performance of the overall best model found for the test set is shown in Fig-9. In the model, all 10 signals are contributing with different lag terms to the prediction of the target series. This best selected model is not significantly different from the top 20 models in terms of RMS error and further 65% of these models contained complete information. The other 35% contain 25% missing values.

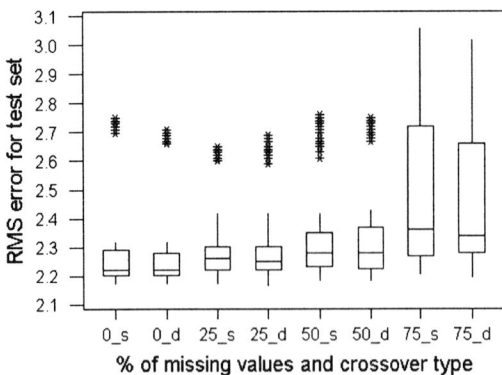

Fig. 8. Dependency of the RMS Error with the percent of missing values and the Crossover Type (C_t).

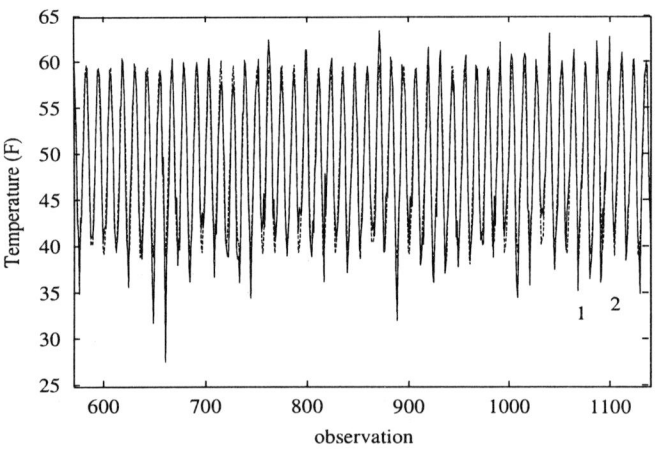

Fig. 9. Behavior of the overall best model found for the target series (West Olympic Coastal) in the test set. RMS error = 2.167 (1: observed, 2: predicted).

V. CONCLUSIONS

The results obtained show that the method studied here is robust, effective, and able to discover accurate models in a consistent way. Taking into account the astronomical size of the search space for the experiments performed, it is remarkable that the exploration of the extremely small fraction covered by the chosen parameters lead to extremely simple and very accurate models, even with 75% missing data. These features make this method appropriate for the study of poorly known or unknown processes for data of this kind. The experiments proved that there is an optimal combination of neuro-fuzzy and genetic algorithm parameters which maximizes the chances of discovering good models. Moreover, it is clear that the construction of a fuzzy estimate of the predicted signal based on more than one responsive neuron in the heterogeneous layer is decisive in obtaining good predictions. Clearly, these results are conditioned to multivariate data of the kind used in this paper and no claims are made outside of this context. Further studies must be carried out with multivariate series data coming from different processes in order to study the properties of the model mining technique proposed and determine the conditions of its optimal use.

ACKNOWLEDGMENT

The authors would like to thank Robyn Paul from the University of Waterloo for her assistance during the final stages of this research.

REFERENCES

[1] Belanche, Ll. : Heterogeneous neural networks: Theory and applications. PhD Thesis, Department of Languages and Informatic Systems, Polytechnic University of Catalonia, Barcelona, Spain, July, (2000)
[2] Chandon, J.L., Pinson, S. : *Analyse Typologique. Thorie et Applications.* Masson, Paris, (1981)
[3] : *MPI Primer/ Developing with LAM.* Ohio Supercomputer Center. The Ohio State University, (1996)
[4] Masters, T. : *Neural, Novel & Hybrid Algorithms for Time Series Prediction.* John Wiley & Sons, (1995)
[5] Valdés, J.J., García, R. : A model for heterogeneous neurons and its use in configuring neural networks for classification problems. *Proc. IWANN'97, Int. Conf. On Artificial and Natural Neural Networks.* Lecture Notes in Computer Science **1240**, Springer Verlag, (1997), 237–246
[6] Valdés, J.J. : Time Series Models Discovery with Similarity-Based Neuro-Fuzzy Networks and Evolutionary Algorithms. *IEEE World Conference on Computational Intelligence* WCCI'2002, Hawaii, USA, 2002.
[7] Valdés, J.J. : Similarity-based heterogeneous neurons in the context of general observational models. *Neural Network World*, **12** (5), (2002), 499–508.
[8] Wall, T. : *GaLib: A C++ Library of Genetic Algorithm Components.* Mechanical Engineering Dept. MIT (http://lancet.mit.edu/ga/), (1996)

Adaptive Fuzzy-Neural Control for Uncertain Time-Delayed Systems

Wen-Shyong Yu
Department of Electrical Engineering, Tatung University,
40 Chung-Shan North Rd. 3rd. Sec., Taipei, Taiwan 10451 Taiwan
E-mail: wsyu@ctr1.ee.ttu.edu.tw

Abstract—In this paper, a novel adaptive fuzzy-neural control (AFNC) scheme for uncertain dynamical systems is proposed to suppress the effects caused by multiple time-delayed state uncertainties, unmodeled dynamics, and disturbances. Each delayed uncertainty is assumed to be bounded by an unknown gain. A reference model with the desired amplitude and phase properties is given to construct an error model. A fuzzy-neural (FN) system is used to represent the unknown controlled system from the strategic manipulation of the model following tracking errors. The proposed AFNC scheme uses two on-line estimations, which allows for the inclusion of identifying the gains of the delayed state uncertainties and training the weights of the FN system simultaneously. Stability and robustness of the AFNC scheme is analyzed in Lyapunov sense. It is shown that the proposed control scheme can guarantee parameter estimation convergence and stability robustness of the closed-loop system. The performance of the proposed scheme is evaluated through the simulation results. Simulations are given to show the validity and confirm the performance of the proposed scheme.

I. INTRODUCTION

Most plants in the industry are multivariable multi-input/multi-output (MIMO) systems with unknown but bounded uncertainties (e.g., parametric uncertainties and delayed state uncertainties, etc.) and most of them usually are operated based on human knowledge and expertise. Thus, they post additional difficulties to the control theory of general single-input single-output (SISO) system and the design of their controllers. In order to overcome these kinds of difficulties in the design of a controller, various schemes have been developed in the last decades, among which a successful approach is fuzzy logic control with tuning capability in neural weights. Recently, adaptive fuzzy-neural control has attracted increasing attention, essentially because it can provide a powerful learning technique for complex unknown plants to perform complex tasks in highly nonlinear dynamical environment [1], and can have available quantitative knowledge from repetitive adjustment of the system with better performance than those of fuzzy controls with constant rule bases [2]–[7]. Since design techniques for dynamical systems are closely related to their stability, robustness, and performance properties, this technique including the adaptation capability provides good results to the trajectory tracking problem with good-fitting data by using a small amount of the fuzzy inference mechanisms. However, the inference rules of the FLC will typically contain a number of subjectively as well as empirically determined parameters, and in most cases the nonlinearities existing in the dynamical system are not known *a priori*. When the controlled systems are with unknown parametric uncertainties and load disturbances, their design method can not guarantee stability of the closed-loop control system. In some of the above applications, fuzzy logic control by updating the fuzzy basis function is used in constructing a set of rules to obtain the fuzzy control parameters. But, they can not achieve the tracking control purpose. Furthermore, systems with unknown delayed states are often encountered in practice, such as economic, chemical processes, and hydraulic systems. Besides, systems unavoidably have some uncertain parameters and external disturbances resulting from measurement errors, linearization approximations, modeling errors, and so on. For this reason, the robust stabilization of uncertain dynamical systems with delayed states has received considerable attention over the years (see, e.g., [8]–[13], and the references therein). For dynamical systems with delayed state uncertainties, where the system state vector is available, the norm bounds of the delayed state uncertainties is generally supposed to be known, and such a bound is employed either to construct some types of stabilizing state feedback controllers [8]. However, they are all based on the assumption that the bounds of the delayed state uncertainties are exactly known. Recently, Cao and Frank [9] and Lee *et al.* [10] utilize the T-S model with delays for modeling the nonlinear time-delay systems and construct the stability condition which is independent of the delays, where the delayed dependent stability conditions are given by Yi and Heng [11]. The former design the state feedback gain and observer gain of the fuzzy model by solving a set of coupled linear matrix inequalities, and the later design the output feedback controller based on H^∞ and linear matrix inequality. Although, they all assume that the delays of the system are bounded and are not known *a priori*, the results are conservative. When researchers deal with the problem of dynamical systems with delayed state uncertainties, where the system state vector is available, the parameters of the physical plant are generally supposed to be known [12], which is impractical in real applications. On the other hand, when they treat the plant with unknown parameters, the problem of delayed state uncertainties is not considered, instead, it focuses on the plants with known structures but unknown parameters which are dependent on known variables. The key assumptions is that the bounds on norm of the delayed state uncertainties are available for design. However, due to the complexity of the structure on uncertainties, delayed uncertainty bounds may not be easily obtained.

To relax the assumption as well as attenuate the effects caused by unmodeled dynamics and disturbances, we adopt the AFNC scheme in this paper for MIMO uncertain dynamical systems. Each delayed uncertainty is assumed to be bounded by an unknown gain. A reference model with the desired amplitude and phase properties is given to construct an error model. A FN system is used to represent the unknown controlled system with the desired accuracy to any degree from the strategic manipulation of the model following tracking errors. The AFNC scheme uses two on-line estimations simultaneously for achieving the model following purpose, which allows for the inclusion of identifying the gains of the delayed state uncertainties and training the weights in the FN system. The parameters of the plant model are updated using dynamical adaptation weights and fuzzy inference rules of the FN system, which provides fast parameters update and hence for fast convergence of the tracking errors. The stability and robustness properties of the proposed AFNC scheme are established in the Lyapunov theory framework. The results demonstrate the feasibility of the proposed control scheme, which can guarantee parameter estimation convergence and stability robustness of the closed-loop system with the model following tracking errors approaching zero if there are no disturbances and uncertainties and converging to the neighborhood of zero for all realizations of uncertainties and disturbances. The performance is evaluated by simulation studies. The simulation results demonstrate the computational simplicity, tracking performance and robustness by the proposed control scheme.

II. Problem Formulation

Consider the dynamical equation of an n-link robotic manipulator described by the following nonlinear differential equation with multiple delayed state uncertainties and external disturbances:

$$\mathbf{H}(\mathbf{q})\ddot{\mathbf{q}}(t)+\mathbf{C}'(\mathbf{q},\dot{\mathbf{q}})\dot{\mathbf{q}}(t)+\mathbf{g}'(\mathbf{q})=\boldsymbol{\tau}(t)+\boldsymbol{\zeta}'(t) \quad (1)$$

where $\mathbf{H}(\mathbf{q})$ is the $n \times n$ symmetric positive definite inertial matrix, $\mathbf{C}'(\mathbf{q},\dot{\mathbf{q}})\dot{\mathbf{q}}$ is the $n \times 1$ vector of coupled Coriolis and Centripetal torques, $\mathbf{g}'(\mathbf{q})$ is the $n \times 1$ vector of gravitational torques, $\boldsymbol{\tau}$ is the $n \times 1$ vector of joint torques, $\mathbf{q}$ is the $n \times 1$ vector of the joint displacement, and $\ddot{\mathbf{q}}$ and $\dot{\mathbf{q}}$ are the $n \times 1$ vectors of the joint acceleration and velocity terms, respectively. Furthermore, $\boldsymbol{\zeta}'(t) \in \mathbb{R}^n$ is the external disturbance and is assumed to be bounded, i.e., $\|\boldsymbol{\zeta}(t)\| \leq \gamma$, where γ is a known constant parameter. It is assumed that vectors $\dot{\mathbf{q}}, \mathbf{q}$ are measurable. The followings are the properties of the robotic dynamics:

P1: The inertia matrix $\mathbf{H}(\mathbf{q})$ is bounded by $c_1\mathbf{I} \leq \mathbf{H}(\mathbf{q}) \leq c_2\mathbf{I}$, where c_1, c_2 are positive known constants.
P2: The matrix $\dot{\mathbf{H}}(\mathbf{q}) - 2\mathbf{C}'(\mathbf{q},\dot{\mathbf{q}})$ is skew-symmetric.
P3: $\mathbf{C}'(\mathbf{q},\dot{\mathbf{q}})$ is bounded in $\mathbf{q}$ and linear in $\dot{\mathbf{q}}$.

Since each link transmitting the energy or the moment to the following links will have some delayed behavior due to inertia effect, the states with delayed uncertainties are unavoidable and should be included in the dynamical system. Therefore, the equation of the manipulator can be modified as

$$\ddot{\mathbf{q}}(t)+\mathbf{C}(\mathbf{q},\dot{\mathbf{q}})\dot{\mathbf{q}}(t)+\mathbf{g}(\mathbf{q})=\mathbf{B}(\mathbf{q})\boldsymbol{\tau}(t)+\sum_{j=1}^{r}\mathbf{d}_j(\bar{\mathbf{q}}(t-h_j))+\boldsymbol{\zeta}(t) \quad (2)$$

where $\mathbf{C}(\mathbf{q},\dot{\mathbf{q}}) = \mathbf{H}(\mathbf{q})^{-1}\mathbf{C}'(\mathbf{q},\dot{\mathbf{q}})$, $\mathbf{g}(\mathbf{q}) = \mathbf{H}(\mathbf{q})^{-1}\mathbf{g}'(\mathbf{q})$, $\mathbf{B}(\mathbf{q}) = \mathbf{H}(\mathbf{q})^{-1}$, and $\boldsymbol{\zeta}(t) = \mathbf{H}(\mathbf{q})^{-1}\boldsymbol{\zeta}'(t)$. Further, $\bar{\mathbf{q}} = [\dot{\mathbf{q}}^\top \mathbf{q}^\top]^\top$ and $\mathbf{d}_j(\cdot): \mathbb{R}^{2n} \to \mathbb{R}^n$, $j = 1, 2, \cdots, r$, are nonlinear continuous vector-valued functions which represent the delayed state uncertainties for the system and are assumed to satisfy $\|\mathbf{d}_j(\bar{\mathbf{q}}(t-h_j))\| \leq \beta_j \|\bar{\mathbf{q}}(t-h_j)\|$, where β_j's, $j = 1, 2, \ldots, r$, are unknown but positive constants, and $\|\cdot\|$ the Euclidean norm. To simplify the notation the argument t is in many cases dropped out. For convenience, we define

$$\vartheta_j := \beta_j^2, \quad j = 1, 2, \cdots, r. \quad (3)$$

Hence, ϑ_j is obviously an unknown positive constant. Let $\boldsymbol{\vartheta} = [\vartheta_1 \vartheta_2 \cdots \vartheta_r]^\top$. Define $\hat{\boldsymbol{\vartheta}}$ as the estimate of the unknown bound $\boldsymbol{\vartheta}$ and the error gain of the delayed state uncertainties as $\tilde{\boldsymbol{\vartheta}} := \hat{\boldsymbol{\vartheta}} - \boldsymbol{\vartheta}$.

As for the dynamical system (2), it can be parameterized as follows:

$$\begin{bmatrix}\ddot{q}_1\\\ddot{q}_2\\\vdots\\\ddot{q}_n\end{bmatrix}+\begin{bmatrix}a_1 & a_2 & \cdots & a_n\\a_{2n+1} & a_{2n+2} & \cdots & a_{3n}\\\vdots & \vdots & & \vdots\\a_{2n^2-2n+1} & a_{2n^2-2n+2} & \cdots & a_{2n^2-n}\end{bmatrix}\begin{bmatrix}\dot{q}_1\\\dot{q}_2\\\vdots\\\dot{q}_n\end{bmatrix}$$
$$+\begin{bmatrix}a_{n+1} & a_{n+2} & \cdots & a_{2n}\\a_{3n+1} & a_{3n+2} & \cdots & a_{4n}\\\vdots & \vdots & & \vdots\\a_{2n^2-n+1} & a_{2n^2-n+2} & \cdots & a_{2n^2}\end{bmatrix}\begin{bmatrix}q_1\\q_2\\\vdots\\q_n\end{bmatrix}=\hat{\mathbf{B}}\begin{bmatrix}\tau_1\\\tau_2\\\vdots\\\tau_n\end{bmatrix}$$
$$+\sum_{j=1}^{r}\mathbf{d}_j(\bar{\mathbf{q}}(t-h_j))+\boldsymbol{\zeta}(t) \quad (4)$$

where $\hat{\mathbf{B}} = \frac{1}{\sqrt{c_1 c_2}}\mathbf{I}$. Let $\mathbf{a} = [a_1\ a_2\cdots a_n\ a_{n+1}\cdots a_{2n}\ a_{2n+1}\cdots a_{3n}\cdots a_{2n^2-n+1}\ a_{2n^2-n+2}\cdots a_{2n^2}]^\top$ be the unknown plant parameter vector.

The reference model for the plant to follow is an linear time invariant system with a piecewise continuous and uniformly bounded input $\mathbf{r}_m$, and output $\mathbf{q}_m$, related by

$$\ddot{\mathbf{q}}_m + \mathbf{M}_1\dot{\mathbf{q}}_m + \mathbf{M}_0\mathbf{q}_m = \mathbf{r}_m. \quad (5)$$

Rewrite (4) as the following form:

$$\ddot{\mathbf{q}} + \mathbf{V}\mathbf{a} = \hat{\mathbf{B}}\boldsymbol{\tau} + \sum_{j=1}^{r}\mathbf{d}_j(\bar{\mathbf{q}}(t-h_j)) + \boldsymbol{\zeta} \quad (6)$$

where

$$\mathbf{V} = \begin{bmatrix}\bar{\mathbf{q}}^\top & \mathbf{0}\\\mathbf{0} & \bar{\mathbf{q}}^\top\end{bmatrix}_{2\times(4n)}. \quad (7)$$

Let $\mathbf{e} := \mathbf{q} - \mathbf{q}_m$ denote the tracking error. In order to design a stable adaptive fuzzy controller, we first select a set of parameter matrices $\mathbf{F}_1, \mathbf{F}_0$ such that the error matrix polynomial $\mathbf{e}^h + \mathbf{F}_1\dot{\mathbf{e}} + \mathbf{F}_0\mathbf{e}$ is a Hurwitz polynomial. Then, define $\mathbf{z}$ as

$$\mathbf{z} := \ddot{\mathbf{q}}_m - \mathbf{F}_1\dot{\mathbf{e}} - \mathbf{F}_0\mathbf{e}. \quad (8)$$

Adding $-\mathbf{z}$ to both side of (6), we have

$$\ddot{\mathbf{q}} - \mathbf{z} = \hat{\mathbf{B}}\boldsymbol{\tau} - \mathbf{z} - \mathbf{V}\mathbf{a} + \sum_{j=1}^{r}\mathbf{d}_j(\bar{\mathbf{q}}(t-h_j)) + \boldsymbol{\zeta}. \quad (9)$$

Substituting (8) in (9), we can obtain

$$\ddot{\mathbf{e}} + \mathbf{F}_1\dot{\mathbf{e}} + \mathbf{F}_0\mathbf{e} = \hat{\mathbf{B}}\boldsymbol{\tau} - \mathbf{z} - \mathbf{V}\mathbf{a} + \sum_{j=1}^{r}\mathbf{d}_j(\bar{\mathbf{q}}(t-h_j)) + \boldsymbol{\zeta} \quad (10)$$

which leads to the following matrix form:

$$\dot{\bar{\mathbf{e}}} = \boldsymbol{\Phi}\bar{\mathbf{e}} + \mathbf{B}\left(\hat{\mathbf{B}}\boldsymbol{\tau} - \mathbf{z} - \mathbf{V}\mathbf{a} + \sum_{j=1}^{r}\mathbf{d}_j(\bar{\mathbf{q}}(t-h_j)) + \boldsymbol{\zeta}\right) \quad (11)$$

where $\bar{\mathbf{e}} = [\mathbf{e}^\top\ \dot{\mathbf{e}}^\top]^\top$ and

$$\boldsymbol{\Phi} = \begin{bmatrix}\mathbf{0}_{(n)} & \mathbf{I}_{(n)}\\-\mathbf{F}_0 & -\mathbf{F}_1\end{bmatrix}_{2n\times 2n}, \quad \mathbf{B} = \begin{bmatrix}\mathbf{0}_{(n)}\\\mathbf{I}_{(n)}\end{bmatrix}_{2n\times n}$$

for which $\mathbf{I}_{(n)}$ is an $n \times n$ identity matrix and $\mathbf{0}_{(n)}$ an $n \times n$ zero matrix.

The purpose of the paper is to synthesize an AFNC scheme so that all signals in the overall system are bounded and $\mathbf{q}$ tracks a desired reference output $\mathbf{q}_m$ in (5) in the presence of the unknown uncertain parameters, the unknown delayed state uncertainties, and the external disturbances.

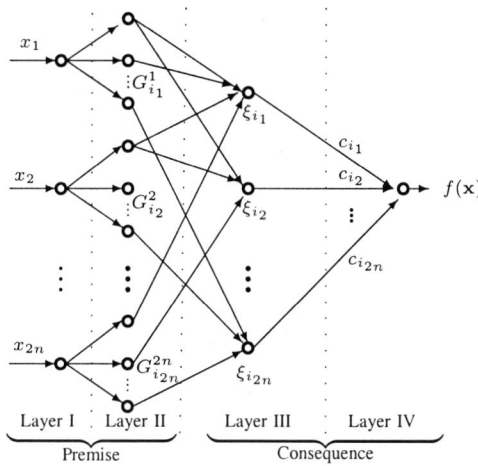

Fig. 1. Configuration of a FN system.

III. ADAPTIVE CONTROL WITH FN SYSTEM

Let $\mathbf{x} = [x_1\ x_2\ \cdots\ x_n\ x_{n+1}\ \cdots\ x_{2n}]^\top = [\dot{\mathbf{q}}^\top\ \mathbf{q}^\top]^\top$. As shown in Fig. 1, the FN system is characterized by fuzzy **IF-THEN** rules and a fuzzy inference engine. The fuzzy inference engine uses the fuzzy **IF-THEN** rules to perform a mapping from an input linguistic vector $\mathbf{x}$ to an output linguistic variable $f(\mathbf{x}) \in \mathbb{R}$. The Gaussian membership functions with equal-width intervals of the means are thus proposed to eliminate the sharp boundary and is defined as

$$\mu_k(\mathbf{x}) = exp(-\frac{x_k - \bar{x}_k}{2\sigma_k}), \quad k = 1, 2, \ldots, 2n \quad (12)$$

where $\bar{x}_k$ and σ_k are the mean and variance of the kth Gaussian membership function $\mu_k(\mathbf{x})$, respectively. Since a MIMO fuzzy system can always be approximated by a group of multi-input single-output (MISO) fuzzy systems, we assume that the fuzzy systems are MISO systems consists of $N = \Pi_{k=1}^{2n} N_k$ rules in the following form:

$R_{i_1,i_2,\cdots,i_{2n}}$: **IF** x_1 is $G_{i_1}^1$ **AND** x_2 is $G_{i_2}^2$ **AND** $\cdots$ **AND** x_n is $G_{i_n}^n$ **AND** x_{n+1} is $G_{i_{n+1}}^{n+1}$ **AND** $\cdots$ **AND** x_{2n} is $G_{i_{2n}}^{2n}$ **THEN** $f(\mathbf{x})$ is $C_{i_1,i_2,\cdots,i_{2n}}$,
$i_1 = 1, \ldots, N_1, i_2 = 1, \ldots, N_2, \cdots, i_{2n} = 1, \ldots, N_{2n}$

where x_k's, $k = 1, 2, \ldots, 2n$, and $f(\mathbf{x})$ denote the linguistic variables associated with the inputs and output of the fuzzy system. $G_{i_k}^k$ and $C_{i_1 i_2 \cdots i_{2n}}$ are linguistic values of linguistic variables $\mathbf{x}$ and f in the universes of discourse $U \subset \mathbb{R}^{2n}$ and $V \subset \mathbb{R}$, respectively, $k = 1, 2, \ldots, 2n$.

By using a singleton fuzzier, product inference, center-average defuzzier and Gaussian membership functions, output $f(\mathbf{x})$ from the FN system can be expressed as

$$f(\mathbf{x}) = \sum_{i_1=1}^{N_1} \cdots \sum_{i_{2n}=1}^{N_{2n}} \frac{\prod_{k=1}^{2n} \mu_{k i_k}(x_k)}{\sum_{i_1=1}^{N_1} \cdots \sum_{i_{2n}=1}^{N_{2n}} \prod_{k=1}^{2n} \mu_{k i_k}(x_k)} c_{i_1 i_2 \cdots i_{2n}}$$
$$= \sum_{i_1=1}^{N_1} \cdots \sum_{i_{2n}=1}^{N_{2n}} \xi_{i_1 i_2 \cdots i_{2n}}(\mathbf{x}) c_{i_1 i_2 \cdots i_{2n}} \quad (13)$$

where $c_{i_1 i_2 \cdots i_{2n}}$ is the center of the i_kth fuzzy set and is the point at which $\mu_{k i_k}$ is maximum or equal to 1, and the following nonlinear mapping of a neural network:

$$\xi_{i_1 i_2 \cdots i_{2n}}(\mathbf{x}) = \frac{\prod_{k=1}^{2n} \mu_{k i_k}(x_k)}{\sum_{i_1=1}^{N_1} \cdots \sum_{i_{2n}=1}^{N_{2n}} \prod_{k=1}^{2n} \mu_{k i_k}(x_k)} \quad (14)$$

for $i_k = 1, 2, \ldots, N_k$, $k = 1, 2, \ldots, 2n$. Because $\sum_{i_1=1}^{N_1} \cdots \sum_{i_{2n}=1}^{N_{2n}} \xi_{i_1 i_2 \cdots i_{2n}}(\mathbf{x}) = 1$, $\xi_{i_1 i_2 \cdots i_{2n}}(\mathbf{x})$ can be viewed as a weighting function. For each point $\mathbf{x}$, $\xi_{i_1 i_2 \cdots i_{2n}}(\mathbf{x})$ is the weighting for the $(i_1 i_2 \cdots i_{2n})$th fuzzy rule. Hence, these fuzzy inferences can be described in the form of a linear equivalent neural network:

$$\mathbf{a} = \Xi \mathbf{c} \quad (15)$$

where $c_{i_1 i_2 \cdots i_{2n}}$'s are free (adjustable) parameters and $\Xi = diag\{\boldsymbol{\xi}^\top, \boldsymbol{\xi}^\top, \cdots, \boldsymbol{\xi}^\top\}$ with dimension $(4n) \times (N4n)$ for which $\boldsymbol{\xi} = [\xi_{11\cdots 1}\ \xi_{11\cdots 2}\ \cdots\ \xi_{11\cdots N_{2n}}\ \cdots\ \xi_{N_1 N_2 \cdots 1}\ \cdots\ \xi_{N_1 N_2 \cdots N_{2n}}]^\top$ is an $N \times 1$ fuzzy basis function vector and $\xi_{i_1 i_2 \cdots i_{2n}}$'s are defined in (14), and $\mathbf{c} = [\mathbf{c}_1\ \mathbf{c}_2 \cdots \mathbf{c}_{4n}]^\top$ for which $\mathbf{c}_\ell = [c_{11\cdots 1\ell}\ c_{11\cdots 2\ell}\ \cdots\ c_{11\cdots N_{2n}\ell}\ \cdots\ c_{N_1 N_2 \cdots 1\ell}\ \cdots\ c_{N_1 N_2 \cdots N_{2n}\ell}]^\top$, $\ell = 1, 2, \ldots, 4n$.

Note from (13) and (15) that the hidden relation to be linear in the sense that the unknown parameter vector $\mathbf{a}$ depends only on the coefficients in the fuzzy sets and the coefficients in the linear combination of the FN system. For control, FN is used as a model of nonlinear system or human expertise. It is capable of approximating a wide variety of nonlinear systems as proved in [14]. Based on the universal approximation theorem, that above FN system in the form of (15) is capable of uniformly approximating any nonlinear function over Z to any degree of accuracy if Z is compact.

Because the time-varying parameters of the controlled plant represented as the parameter vector $\mathbf{a}$ are absorbed partly into the FN system, $\mathbf{a}$ can be obtained more accurately by further estimating the unknown but constant weight vector $\mathbf{c}$ according the tracking error and the coefficients of the FN system. Let $\hat{\mathbf{a}} = \Xi \hat{\mathbf{c}}$ be the estimate of $\mathbf{a}$ due to $\hat{\mathbf{c}}$ and $\tilde{\mathbf{c}} := \hat{\mathbf{c}} - \mathbf{c}$ the error vector. Then, the certainty equivalent controller τ can be defined as

$$\tau = \hat{\mathbf{B}}^{-1}\left(\mathbf{z} + \mathbf{V}\hat{\mathbf{a}} - \frac{1}{2}\eta^\top \hat{\vartheta}\mathbf{B}^\top \mathbf{P}\bar{\mathbf{e}} - \frac{1}{2}\frac{1}{\rho^2}\mathbf{B}^\top \mathbf{P}\bar{\mathbf{e}}\right)$$
$$= \hat{\mathbf{B}}^{-1}\left(\mathbf{z} + \mathbf{W}\hat{\mathbf{c}} - \frac{1}{2}\eta^\top \hat{\vartheta}\mathbf{B}^\top \mathbf{P}\bar{\mathbf{e}} - \frac{1}{2}\frac{1}{\rho^2}\mathbf{B}^\top \mathbf{P}\bar{\mathbf{e}}\right) \quad (16)$$

where $\mathbf{W} = \mathbf{V}\Xi$, ρ is any positive constant, and $\mathbf{P}$ is a symmetric positive definite matrix satisfying the following matrix Riccati equation:

$$\mathbf{\Phi}^\top \mathbf{P} + \mathbf{P}\mathbf{\Phi} = -\mathbf{Q}, \quad (17)$$

for which $\mathbf{Q} = \mathbf{Q}^\top$ is a symmetric positive definite matrix. Furthermore, $\boldsymbol{\eta} := [\nu_1^{-1}\ \nu_2^{-1} \cdots \nu_r^{-1}]^\top$, where ν_j's, $j = 1, 2, \ldots, r$, are positive constants satisfying the following equation:

$$\tilde{\mathbf{Q}} := \mathbf{Q} - 2\sum_{j=1}^{r} \nu_j \mathbf{I}_{2n} > 0. \quad (18)$$

Substituting (16) into (11) leads to the following

$$\dot{\bar{\mathbf{e}}} = \left(\mathbf{\Phi} - \frac{1}{2}\eta^\top \hat{\vartheta}\mathbf{B}\mathbf{B}^\top \mathbf{P} - \frac{1}{2\rho^2}\mathbf{B}\mathbf{B}^\top \mathbf{P}\right)\bar{\mathbf{e}}$$
$$+ \mathbf{B}\left(\mathbf{W}\tilde{\mathbf{c}} + \sum_{j=1}^{r} \mathbf{d}_j(\bar{\mathbf{q}}(t - h_j)) + \boldsymbol{\zeta}\right). \quad (19)$$

Theorem 1: Consider the system in (2) or (4). The adaptive control law for the system is given in (16) in which the weight vector and the gain vector of delayed state uncertainties by (21) are updated by

$$\dot{\mathbf{c}} = \dot{\tilde{\mathbf{c}}} = -\mathbf{P}_1\left(\mathbf{\Xi}^\top\mathbf{V}^\top\mathbf{B}^\top\mathbf{P}\bar{\mathbf{e}} + \mathbf{W}^\top\mathbf{W}\tilde{\mathbf{c}}\right) \quad (20)$$

$$\dot{\hat{\vartheta}} = -\Gamma\mathbf{S}\hat{\vartheta} + \frac{1}{2}\Gamma\eta\left\|\mathbf{B}^\top\mathbf{P}\bar{\mathbf{e}}\right\|^2$$

$$= -\Gamma\mathbf{S}\tilde{\vartheta} + \frac{1}{2}\Gamma\eta\left\|\mathbf{B}^\top\mathbf{P}\bar{\mathbf{e}}\right\|^2 - \Gamma\mathbf{S}\vartheta \quad (21)$$

respectively, where $\mathbf{S}$ is any positive definite matrix and $\mathbf{P}_1$ is defined as

$$\mathbf{P}_1(t) = \left(\int_{0^+}^{t}\exp\left(-\int_{s}^{t}\alpha(r)dr\right)\mathbf{W}^\top(s)\mathbf{W}(s)ds\right)^{-1} \quad (22)$$

where

$$\alpha(t) = \alpha_0\left(1 - \frac{\|\mathbf{P}_1\|}{k_0}\right) \quad (23)$$

for which α_0 and k_0 are constants. Then the tracking error $\mathbf{e}(t)$ defined by (10) would approach zero if there are no disturbances and uncertainties, and converge to the neighborhood of zero for all realizations of uncertainties and disturbances.

Proof: Choose the Lyapunov-Krasovskii functional candidate as

$$V(\bar{\mathbf{e}}, \tilde{\mathbf{c}}, \tilde{\vartheta}) = \bar{\mathbf{e}}^\top\mathbf{P}\bar{\mathbf{e}} + \tilde{\mathbf{c}}^\top\mathbf{P}_1^{-1}\tilde{\mathbf{c}} + \tilde{\vartheta}^\top\Gamma^{-1}\tilde{\vartheta}$$

$$+ 2\sum_{j=1}^{r}\nu_j\int_{t-h_j}^{t}\bar{\mathbf{e}}^\top(\tau)\bar{\mathbf{e}}(\tau)d\tau \quad (24)$$

Taking the derivative of V in (24) and using (19) and (22), we have

$$\dot{V} \leq -\lambda_{min}(\tilde{\mathbf{Q}})\|\bar{\mathbf{e}}\|^2 - \lambda_{min}(\mathbf{W}^\top\mathbf{W})\|\tilde{\mathbf{c}}\|^2$$
$$-\lambda_{min}(\mathbf{P}_1^{-1})|\alpha|\|\tilde{\mathbf{c}}\|^2 - \lambda_{min}(\mathbf{S})\|\tilde{\vartheta}\|^2 + \bar{\epsilon} \quad (25)$$

where $\bar{\epsilon} = 2\sum_{j=1}^{r}\nu_j\|\bar{\mathbf{q}}_m(t-h_j)\|^2 + \lambda_{min}^{-1}(\mathbf{S})\lambda_{max}^2(\mathbf{S})\|\vartheta\|^2 + \rho^2\gamma^2$. In light of Lyapunov stability theory to the retarded functional differential equation [15], [16], it can be concluded from (25) that for any $t \geq t_0$, $\bar{\mathbf{e}}(t)$, $\tilde{\mathbf{c}}(t)$, and $\tilde{\vartheta}(t)$ are uniformly bounded in the presence of the delayed state uncertainties $\mathbf{d}_j(\bar{\mathbf{q}})$, $j = 1, 2, \ldots, r$, and the external disturbance ζ. ∎

IV. DESIGN EXAMPLE

In this section, we consider a gyroscopic system with single actuating input which is similar to that of [17] with some slight difference on the assumptions that the gimbals are rigid but with a little unbalanced bodies and the conservation of the angular momentum constants are not zero. The inertia of the system is concentrated in the rotor, with J as the radial moment of the inertia and I the axial moment of inertia. This system is acted upon by a single torque input $\tau(t)$ applied along the x-axis. From the Newton's law, the equations of motion for the gyroscopic system are shown as follows:

$$J\ddot{\theta}(t) = \tau(t) + J\dot{\beta}^2(t-h)\sin(\theta(t-h))\cos(\theta(t-h))$$
$$- E_2\dot{\beta}(t-h)\sin(\theta(t-h)) + \zeta(t) \quad (26)$$

$$J\dot{\beta}(t)\sin^2(\theta(t)) + E_2\cos(\theta(t)) = E_1 \quad (27)$$

$$I(\dot{\psi}(t) + \dot{\beta}(t)\cos(\theta(t))) = E_2 \quad (28)$$

where E_1, E_2 are conservation of the angular momentum constants, h is the delay time for the rate of change, $\dot{\beta}$, due to the inertias of the radial and axial moments, and ζ is the bounded disturbance caused by the unbalanced effects. Without loss of generality, counterclockwise and clockwise rotations are defined as positive and negative, respectively.

There are three outputs θ, β, and ψ in this gyroscopic system. From (27) and (28), we have

$$\dot{\beta} + \frac{E_2\cos(\theta) - E_1}{J\sin^2(\theta)} = 0 \quad (29)$$

$$\dot{\psi} + \frac{E_1\cos(\theta) - E_2\cos^2(\theta)}{IJ\sin^2(\theta)} = \frac{E_2}{I} \quad (30)$$

Hence, the rate changes of β, $\dot{\beta}$, and of ψ, $\dot{\psi}$, can be seen as in function of θ. From (4) and (26)–(28), since $n = 2$ for θ and $n = 1$ for ψ, we can express the plant model as follows:

$$\ddot{\theta} + a_1\dot{\theta} + a_2\theta + a_3\psi = \tau + d(\theta(t-h), \dot{\beta}(t-h)) + \zeta \quad (31)$$

where a_i, $i = 1, 2, 3$, are unknown parameters to be estimated.

Step 1: A gyroscope having the following parameters is chosen for this simulation: the inertias are taken as $I = 2$ and $J = 1$, the delay time as $h = 0.01$ sec., and the angular momentum constants as $E_1 = E_2 = 1$ since (27) and (28) satisfy the conservation laws of the angular momentum. Let the reference model be specified as:

$$\ddot{\theta}_m + 96\dot{\theta}_m + 3072\theta_m + 32768\psi_m = r_m \quad (32)$$

where $r_m = 32768$ for unit step tracking. Further, from (8), the parameter matrix $\mathbf{F}_0$ is specified as:

$$\mathbf{F}_0 = \begin{bmatrix} 1024 & 64 & 0 \\ -1 & 0 & 0 \\ 0 & 0 & 1 \end{bmatrix}. \quad (33)$$

Therefore, we have $\mathbf{\Phi} = \mathbf{F}_0$. From (17) for $\mathbf{Q} = \mathbf{I}_{3\times 3}$, we have

$$\mathbf{P} = \begin{bmatrix} 2054.1 & 192.1 & 0.0000 \\ 192.1 & 24 & 0.1 \\ 0.0000 & 0.1 & 0.0000 \end{bmatrix}. \quad (34)$$

Step 2: Set $\mathbf{S} = 0.5$, $\Gamma = 2$, $\eta = 1$, and $\nu = 0.25$. In practice, friction and mass unbalance are inevitable for the gyro and will cause disturbance torques on the gimbals when the body is accelerating and rotating. Therefore, the sinusoidal disturbances are used to simulate these imperfections. It is desired that an AFNC scheme is described so that all signals in the overall system are bounded, and to keep ψ nonrotating and consequently maintain the same direction in inertia space as the desired direction ψ_m provided by a given linear reference model (32) in the presence of the unknown uncertain parameters, the unknown delayed state uncertainties, and the external disturbances.

Step 3: Since the amount of overlap with the fuzzy sets affects the efficiency of the FN system, the fuzzy membership functions for $\mathbf{x} = [x_1\ x_2\ x_3]^\top = [\dot{\theta}\ \theta\ \psi]^\top$ are chosen carefully as follows:

$$\mu_{11}(\psi) = \begin{cases} 1 & ,\psi < 0.9 \\ exp\left(-\frac{(\psi-0.9)^2}{2(0.03)^2}\right) & ,\psi \geq 0.9 \end{cases} \quad (35)$$

$$\mu_{15}(\psi) = \begin{cases} 1 & ,\psi > 1.1 \\ exp\left(-\frac{(\psi-1.1)^2}{2(0.03)^2}\right) & ,\psi \leq 1.1 \end{cases} \quad (36)$$

$$\mu_{12}(\psi) = exp\left(-\frac{(\psi-0.95)^2}{2(0.03)^2}\right), \mu_{13}(\psi) = exp\left(-\frac{(\psi-1)^2}{2(0.03)^2}\right), \quad (37)$$

$$\mu_{14}(\psi) = exp\left(-\frac{(\psi-1.05)^2}{2(0.03)^2}\right), \quad (38)$$

$$\mu_{21}(\theta) = \begin{cases} 1 & ,\theta < -0.1 \\ exp\left(-\frac{(\theta+0.1)^2}{2(0.03)^2}\right) & ,\theta \geq -0.1 \end{cases}, \quad (39)$$

$$\mu_{25}(\theta) = \begin{cases} 1 & ,\theta > 0.1 \\ exp\left(-\frac{(\theta-0.1)^2}{2(0.03)^2}\right) & ,\theta \leq 0.1 \end{cases}, \quad (40)$$

$$\mu_{22}(\theta) = exp\left(-\frac{(\theta+0.05)^2}{2(0.03)^2}\right), \mu_{23}(\theta) = exp\left(-\frac{(\theta)^2}{2(0.03)^2}\right), \quad (41)$$

$$\mu_{24}(\theta) = exp\left(-\frac{(\theta-0.05)^2}{2(0.03)^2}\right), \quad (42)$$

$$\mu_{31}(\dot{\theta}) = \begin{cases} 1 & ,\dot{\theta} < -0.1 \\ exp\left(-\frac{(\dot{\theta}+0.1)^2}{2(0.03)^2}\right) & ,\dot{\theta} \geq -0.1 \end{cases}, \quad (43)$$

$$\mu_{35}(\dot{\theta}) = \begin{cases} 1 & ,\dot{\theta} > 0.1 \\ exp\left(-\frac{(\dot{\theta}-0.1)^2}{2(0.03)^2}\right) & ,\dot{\theta} \leq 0.1 \end{cases}, \quad (44)$$

$$\mu_{32}(\dot{\theta}) = exp\left(-\frac{(\dot{\theta}+0.05)^2}{2(0.03)^2}\right), \mu_{33}(\dot{\theta}) = exp\left(-\frac{(\dot{\theta})^2}{2(0.03)^2}\right), \quad (45)$$

$$\mu_{34}(\dot{\theta}) = exp\left(-\frac{(\dot{\theta}-0.05)^2}{2(0.03)^2}\right). \quad (46)$$

As we will see from (26)–(28), there is a corresponding influence from the ψ gimbal on the θ gimbal. So, rules (35)–(42) are constructed when the present positions of θ and ψ are cross coupling very much and far away from the set point. Therefore, it requires a large drive output to tune the shaft to the set point quickly. In addition, rules (37), (38), (41), and (42) implement the condition when the error starts to decrease and the FBFE's are approaching the neighborhood of the true parameters, and the set point is very nearly reached. Thus, a small drive output is given. Because of the inertia of the gyero, it is necessary to stop the drive at this instant to keep the overshoot at a minimum. However, rules (43)–(46) deal with the condition when overshoot does occur. A small reverse drive signal is given to bring the shafts to its set point. The rule of (43) implies the reverse condition of the left. We now establish the center-average formulation for fuzzy logic inference rules.

Step 4: From (7), we have

$$\mathbf{V} = \begin{bmatrix} \dot{\theta} & \theta & \psi & 0 & 0 & 0 & 0 \\ 0 & 0 & 0 & 0 & \dot{\theta} & \theta & \psi \end{bmatrix} \quad (47)$$

To simplify the statement of a rule, and to take into account as well the associated membership functions (36)–(46), we have the following: Let

$$\xi_{i_1 i_2 i_3} = \frac{\Pi_{k=1}^3 \mu_{k i_k}}{\sum_{i_1=1}^5 \sum_{i_2=1}^5 \sum_{i_3=1}^5 \Pi_{k=1}^3 \mu_{k i_k}}, \quad i_k = 1,2,3,4,5, \ k = 1,2,3$$

for which $\boldsymbol{\xi} = [\underbrace{\xi_{111}\ \xi_{112}\ \xi_{113}\ \xi_{114}\ \xi_{115}\ \cdots\ \xi_{551}\ \xi_{552}\ \xi_{553}\ \xi_{554}\ \xi_{555}}_{125}]^\top$.

Therefore,

$$\boldsymbol{\Xi} = \begin{bmatrix} \boldsymbol{\xi}^\top & & \mathbf{0} \\ & \boldsymbol{\xi}^\top & \\ \mathbf{0} & & \boldsymbol{\xi}^\top \end{bmatrix}_{3\times 375} \quad (48)$$

Step 5: Update the estimates of the vectors $\hat{\mathbf{c}}$ and $\hat{\boldsymbol{\vartheta}}$ and obtain the weighting matrix $\mathbf{P}_1$ from (20), (21), and (22), respectively, where $\mathbf{P}_1(0)^{-1} = \mathbf{I}_{375\times 375}$, $\hat{\mathbf{c}}(0) = [\underbrace{10\ 10\ \cdots\ 10}_{375}]^\top$, and $\hat{\boldsymbol{\vartheta}}(0) = 0$. Therefore, each element of the vector $\hat{\mathbf{a}} = [\hat{a}_1\ \hat{a}_2\ \hat{a}_3]^\top$ can be expressed as

$$\hat{a}_\ell = \sum_{i_1=1}^5 \sum_{i_2=1}^5 \sum_{i_3=1}^5 \xi_{i_1 i_2 i_3} \hat{c}_{i_1 i_2 i_3 \ell}, \quad \ell = 1,2,3. \quad (49)$$

Step 6: Let $\hat{\mathbf{B}} = \mathbf{I}$ and we can obtain the adaptive controller from (16) as follows:

$$\boldsymbol{\tau} = \ddot{\mathbf{q}}_m - \mathbf{F}_1 \dot{\mathbf{e}} - \mathbf{F}_0 \mathbf{e} + \mathbf{W}\hat{\mathbf{c}} - \frac{1}{2}\boldsymbol{\eta}^\top \hat{\boldsymbol{\vartheta}} \mathbf{B}^\top \mathbf{P}\bar{\mathbf{e}} - \frac{1}{2}\frac{1}{\rho^2}\mathbf{B}^\top \mathbf{P}\bar{\mathbf{e}}. \quad (50)$$

Then, it is used recursively for stabilizing the gyroscopic system.

Figs. 2 shows the simulation results. From figures (a) and (b) in Figs. 2 with disturbance $5\sin(20t)$, the model following purpose can be achieved effectively and the steady state tracking errors are 1.95% ($\alpha_0 = 1$, $k_0 = 1$, and $\rho = 10$) of the magnitude of the reference model output, respectively. It is seen from Fig. 2, the time-varying disturbances are absorbed partly into the FN system and the estimates can be obtained more accurately and a higher control torque is used to achieve an excellent tracking performance. The responses of the estimates of the plant model and delayed state uncertainties for the uncertain plant converge and do not drift to infinity due to strong compensation of the estimation algorithms for the weights of the neural network and the gains of the delayed state uncertainties (see figures (f) and (g) of the Figs. 2). The proposed AFNC scheme derived from these estimates iteratively for achieving model following purpose has the ability to stabilize the controlled plant and has better performance than that without using the FN system. In other words, the use of the FN system with adaptation weights can indeed improve the performance of the closed-loop system (see Figs. 2 (a), (b), and (h)). The main reason of the result is that the only use of updating law for delayed state uncertainties can't achieve an excellent model following result as the system is subject to the controlled plant with plant uncertainties and disturbances. This is one of the important motivation for the study. The results reveal that the proposed AFNC scheme indeed improves the system performances including convergence of the estimations and tracking errors, the smoothness of the control inputs, and easy selection of the parameters of the estimations. It seems that the robustness of the proposed control scheme is excellent. In summary, the control input is bounded, and the estimations of the FN system and the gain of the delayed state uncertainty will gradually approach a steady state in which the plant follows the reference model with faster rising time, little oscillations and tracking errors, and has a rather good dynamical performance.

V. Conclusion

In this paper, an AFNC scheme for uncertain time-delayed systems has been developed based on the general idea that appropriate estimation of the adaptation process should provide a satisfactory basis for the control. Nonideal effects such as system with unknown parameters and nonlinearities and multiple delayed state uncertainties are considered from practical point of view. The considered delayed state uncertainties are assumed to be bounded by some unknown gains. As well, a FN system is used to represent the unknown controlled system according to the Stone Weierstrass theorem. A reference model with the desired amplitude and phase properties is given to construct an error model. The AFNC scheme uses two on-line estimations operating simultaneously, which allows for the inclusion of identifying the gains of the delayed state uncertainties and training the weights of the FN system simultaneously. It is shown that, in the sense of Lyapunov type stability, the proposed control scheme not only can guarantee estimation convergence and stability robustness of the closed-loop system with the tracking errors approaching zero if there are no disturbances and uncertainties and converging to the neighborhood of zero for all realizations of uncertainties and disturbances, but also can achieve the model following tracking purpose. Furthermore, the constraint demanding prior knowledge on upper bounds of the delayed state uncertainties is removed through the design algorithm of the proposed scheme. As demonstrated in the illustrated example, the AFNC scheme proposed in this paper can achieve a better model following tracking performance over that without using FN system with adaptation weights.

ACKNOWLEDGMENT

This work is supported by Tatung University, Taipei, Taiwan, R.O.C. under project B91-E02-018.

REFERENCES

[1] S. Haykin, *Neural Networks*, Ottawa, ON, Canada: Maxwell Macmillan, 1994.
[2] F.-J. Lin, K.-K. Shyu, and R.-J. Wai,"Recurrent-fuzzy-neural-network sliding-mode controlled motor-toggle servomechanism," *IEEE/ASME Transactions on Mechatronics*, Vol. 6 (4), pp. 453-466, Dec. 2001.
[3] F. Cuesta, F. Gordillo, J. Aracil, and A. Ollero,"Stability analysis of nonlinear multivariable Takagi-Sugeno fuzzy control systems," *IEEE Trans. Fuzzy Systems*, Vol. 7, pp. 508-520, Oct. 1999.
[4] W.-S. Yu and C.-J. Sun," Fuzzy model based adaptive control for a class of nonlinear systems," *IEEE Trans. Fuzzy Systems*, VOL. 9, NO. 3, pp. 413-425, June 2001.
[5] N. Golea, A. Golea, and K. Benmahammed,"Fuzzy model reference adaptive control," *IEEE Trans. Fuzzy Systems*, Vol. 10, pp. 436-444, Aug. 2002.
[6] R. Ordonez and K.M. Passino,"Stable multi-input multi-output adaptive fuzzy/neural control," *IEEE Trans. Fuzzy Systems*, Vol. 7, pp. 345-353, June 1999.
[7] S. Tong, J. Tong, and T. Wang,"Fuzzy adaptive control of multivariable nonlinear systems," *Fuzzy Sets and Systems*, Vol. 111, pp. 153-167, 2000.
[8] E. Cheres, S. Gutman, Z. Palmor, "Stabilization of uncertain dynamic systems including state delay," *IEEE Trans. Automat. Contr.*, vol. 34, pp. 1199-1203, 1989.
[9] Y.-Y. Cao and P.M. Frank, "Analysis and synthesis of nonlinear time-delay systems via fuzzy control approach," *IEEE Trans. Fuzzy Systems*, VOL. 8, NO. 2, pp. 200-211, 2000.
[10] K.R. Lee, J.H. Kim, E.T. Jeung, and H.B. Park, "Output feedback robust H^∞ control of uncertain fuzzy dynamic systems with time-varying delay," *IEEE Trans. Fuzzy Systems*, VOL. 8, NO. 6, pp. 657-664, 2000.
[11] Z. Yi and P.A. Heng, "Stability of fuzzy control systems with bounded uncertain delays," *IEEE Trans. Fuzzy Systems*, VOL. 10, NO. 1, pp. 92-97, 2002.
[12] H. Wu, "Adaptive stabilizing state feedback controllers of Uncertain dynamical systems with multiple time delays," *IEEE Trans. Automat. Contr.*, vol. 45, no 9, pp.1697-1701, Sept. 2000.
[13] M.S. Mahmoud, M. Zribi, and Y.C. Soh,"Exponential stabilization of state-delay systems," *IEE Proceedings Control Theory Appli.*, Vol. 146, No. 2, pp. 131-136, March 1999.
[14] X.-J. Zeng and M.G. Singh,"Approximation theory of fuzzy systems–MIMO case," *IEEE Trans. Fuzzy Systems*, VOL. 3, NO. 2, pp. 219-235, May 1995.
[15] J.K. Hale and S.M.V. Lunel, *Introduction to Functional Differential Equations*. New York: Springer-Verlag, 1993.
[16] V.B. Kolmanovskii and V.R. Nosov, *Stability of Functional Differential Equations*, London, U.K.: Academic, 1986.
[17] A.M. Ferreira and S.K. Agrawal,"Planning and optimization of dynamic systems via decomposition and partial feedback linearization," *Proceedings of the 38th Conference on Decision & Control*, Phonex, Arizona USA, pp.740-745, December 1999.

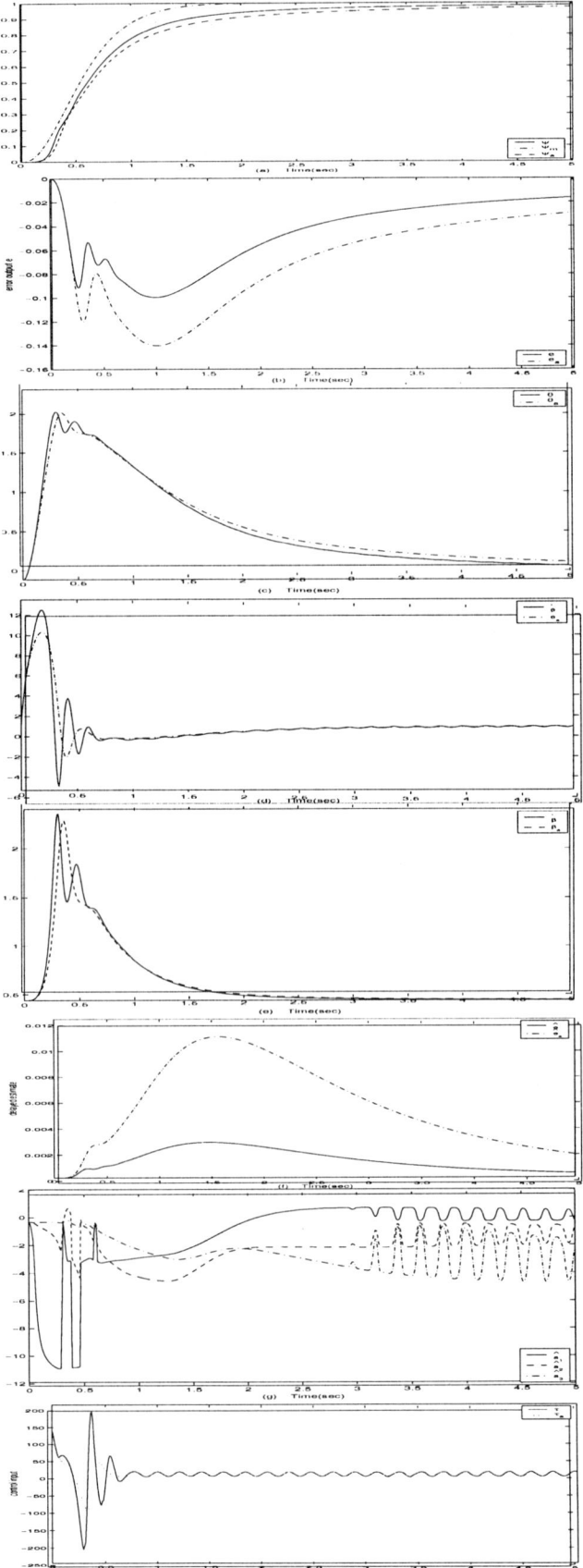

Fig. 2. Step responses of the gyroscopic system with disturbance $5\sin(20t)$ for $\lambda_0 = 1$, $\rho = 10$, and $k_0 = 1$, where the subscript a denotes the responses without using the FN system.

Three Improved Fuzzy Lattice Neurocomputing (FLN) Classifiers

Al Cripps[a], N. Nguyen[b], and V.G. Kaburlasos[c]

[a] Department of Computer Science <acripps@mtsu.edu>   [b] Department of Economics and Finance
Middle Tennessee State University, Murfreesboro, TN 37132, USA

[c] Department of Industrial Informatics, Division of Computing Systems
Technological Educational Institute of Kavala, GR 65404, Greece

Abstract—Three novel fuzzy lattice neurocomputing (FLN) classifiers, namely *FLN first fit* (*FLNff*), *FLN ordered tightest fit* (*FLNotf*), and *FLN selective fit* (*FLNsf*), are introduced in this work. Learning is incremental, memory-based, data order dependent, and polynomial $\mathcal{O}(n^3)$ where n is the number of the training data. Convenient geometric interpretations on the plane illustrate the mechanics of the aforementioned FLN classifiers whose capacity is demonstrated in three benchmark classification problems. The classification results compare favorably with the results by alternative classification methods from the literature. In addition, an FLN classifier can both induce rules from the data and it can deal with numeric and/or nominal data including missing attribute values. An important experimental outcome of this work is that the computation of "smaller than maximal" lattice intervals can increase considerably the capacity for generalization.

I. INTRODUCTION

Fuzzy lattice neurocomputing (FLN) emerged from an application of fuzzy adaptive resonance theory (*fuzzy-ART*) neural network to medical diagnosis problems in [8] where lattice-ordered N-dimensional hyperboxes were computed in R^N. Later work extended the capacity of FLN to the Cartesian product $\mathbf{L} = \mathbf{L}_1 \times \ldots \times \mathbf{L}_N$ of N *constituent lattices* $\mathbf{L}_1,\ldots,\mathbf{L}_N$ [9], [14]. A practical advantage of a product-lattice $\mathbf{L}$ data domain is that disparate types of data, e.g. vectors of numbers, fuzzy sets, symbols, graphs, etc., can be dealt with in applications [10], [11], [15].

This work builds on a previous work on FLN [10] and it introduces three improved FLN classifiers, namely *FLN first fit* (*FLNff*), *FLN ordered tightest fit* (*FLNotf*), and *FLN selective fit* (*FLNsf*). In a series of experiments the aforementioned neural networks demonstrate comparatively good results in three benchmark data classification problems.

Learning and generalization are based here on lattice intervals computed from the training data. It follows that lattice intervals in the product-lattice R^N, where R is the totally-ordered lattice of real numbers, correspond to conventional N-dimensional hyperboxes. Note that several neural networks in the literature including ART, Min-Max neural networks and variations [4], [5], [6], [7], [16] compute hyperboxes in R^N.

The layout of this paper is as follows. Section II delineates the theoretical background. Section III introduces three novel FLN classifiers. Section IV illustrates convenient geometric interpretations on the plane. Section V presents comparatively classification results in three benchmark data classification problems. Finally, section VI summarizes the contribution of this work and it delineates future work.

II. THEORETICAL BACKGROUND

The lattice theoretic notation introduced in [10] is employed here. More specifically, let $\tau(\mathbf{L})$ denote the set of lattice $\mathbf{L}$ intervals, moreover let $a(\mathbf{L})$ denote the set of *atoms* in a lattice $\mathbf{L}$, that is set $a(\mathbf{L})$ includes all trivial intervals (singletons); it follows $a(\mathbf{L}) \subset \tau(\mathbf{L})$. Furthermore, a category function $g: a(\mathbf{L}) \to \mathcal{M}$ is employed, where $\mathcal{M}$ is a finite set of category labels.

The training data here include pairs $(a_i, g(a_i))$, $i=1,\ldots,n$ where a_i is an atom in $a(\mathbf{L})$ and $g(a_i)$ is the corresponding category label. The labeled training data are used to compute *fits*. A *fit* T is computed as the lattice-join of training data in the same category such that no training data "contradict" T, the latter means that no training data from a different category are included in T. A fit T is called *tightest* when the lattice-join with a training datum in the same category (and not already in T) causes a contradiction. Examples of (*tightest*) *fits* are shown below in Fig.2, on the plane.

Generalization by an FLN classifier in the context of this work was effected based on an *inclusion measure* function whose definition is shown in the following.

Definition 1: Let $\mathbf{L}$ be a complete lattice with least and greatest elements O and I, respectively. An *inclusion measure* σ is a map $\sigma: \mathbf{L} \times \mathbf{L} \to [0,1]$, which satisfies the following conditions for $u,w,x \in \mathbf{L}$.

(C0) $\sigma(x,O) = 0$, $x \neq O$,
(C1) $\sigma(x,x) = 1$,
(C2) $u < w \Rightarrow \sigma(w,u) < 1$, and
(C3) $u \leq w \Rightarrow \sigma(x,u) \leq \sigma(x,w)$ - *Consistency Property*

We remark that $\sigma(x,u)$ denotes the degree of inclusion of lattice element x to lattice element u, hence symbols $\sigma(x,u)$ and $\sigma(x \le u)$ are used interchangeably. Note that initial definitions of inclusion measure σ did not include condition (C2) above. Condition (C2) was inserted later in order to exclude trivial *inclusion measure functions* of limited practical value.

A *valuation* v on a lattice **L** is a real function $v: \mathbf{L} \to \mathbf{R}$ which satisfies $v(x)+v(y) = v(x \wedge y)+v(x \vee y)$, $x,y \in \mathbf{L}$. A valuation is *monotone* if and only if $x \le y$ implies $v(x) \le v(y)$, and *positive* if and only if $x < y$ implies $v(x) < v(y)$. Given a positive valuation function in a lattice **L** it can be shown that function $\sigma(u \le w) = \dfrac{v(w)}{v(u \vee w)}$ implies an inclusion measure in $\mathbf{L} \times \mathbf{L}$ [10].

III. THREE NOVEL FLN CLASSIFIERS

This section introduces three novel FLN classifiers implementable in one neural architecture.

A. The Basic Neural Architecture

The basic, three-layer neural architecture used in this work is shown in Fig.1. A node in a layer, denoted by a rectangle, is a σ-*FLN* neural network [10]. Two consecutive layers are fully interconnected. There are no interconnections between non-consecutive layers. The nodes in layers F_d and F_f are drawn in solid lines and they constitute the system's long-term memory. The nodes in layer F_h are drawn in dotted lines and they constitute the system's short-term memory.

Layer F_d stores one-by-one all the incoming training data; layer F_f keeps the ever-updated *fits*; layer F_h is active only during learning and it computes intermediate lattice intervals. A double link is used for 'conducting' both an interval and the corresponding category index from one σ-*FLN* to another. A single link from the Hypothesis Testing Layer to the Training Data Layer is used for transmitting a 'binary acknowledgement' signal. For further details the reader may refer to [10].

The training phase of the three FLN classifiers is described algorithmically in the following.

B. The Training Phase of Classifier FLNff (FLN first fit)

Step 1: (Initialization) Mark all the training data as "unused".

Step 2. Let a be the next "unused" training datum. Mark a as "used". Consider trivial interval I which contains only the training datum a.

Step 3. For the next "unused" training datum x with $g(x) = g(a)$ compute $I \vee x$.

Step 4. If there is a training datum z such that $g(z) \ne g(a)$ and datum z is inside interval $I \vee x$, symbolically $\sigma(z \le I \vee x) = 1$, then contradictory datum z implies that interval $I \vee x$ cannot be a fit.

Step 5. Otherwise, if there is no contradictory datum z, then mark x as "used" then replace interval I by interval $I \vee x$.

Step 6. Repeat Steps 3, 4 and 5, in turn, for each "unused" datum.

Step 7. Repeat Steps 2, 3, 4, 5 and 6, in turn, for each "unused" datum.

Fits/Rules Layer F_f
(Long Term Memory)

Hypothesis Testing Layer F_h
(Short Term Memory)

Training Data Layer F_d
(Long Term Memory)

Input Buffer

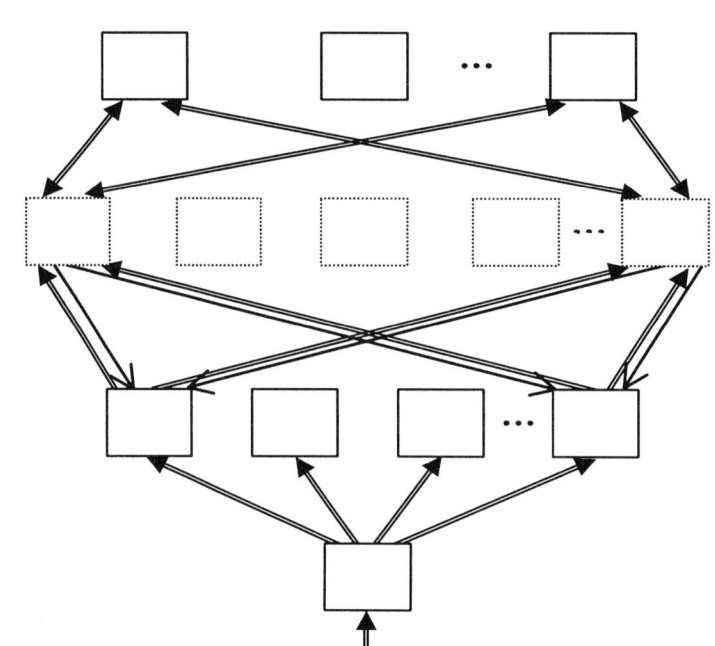

Fig. 1   The basic three layer neural architecture for implementing any of the three novel FLN classifiers introduced in this work. A node, denoted by a rectangle, is a σ-*FLN* neural network.

C. The Training Phase of FLNotf (FLN ordered tightest fit)

Steps 1 – 6, are the same as for classifier *FLNff* above.

Step 7. Repeat Steps 3, 4, 5, and 6, in turn, for each "used" datum outside interval *I*.

Step 8. Repeat Steps 2, 3, 4, 5, 6, and 7, in turn, for each "unused" datum.

D. The Training Phase of FLNsf (FLN selective fit)

Steps 1 – 6, are the same as for classifier *FLNff* above.

Step 7. Repeat Steps 3, 4, 5, and 6 with "used" data *x* outside interval *I* such that the corners of interval $I \vee x$ reside either in interval *I* or in the interval which contains *x*.

Step 8. Repeat Steps 2, 3, 4, 5, 6, and 7, in turn, for each "unused" datum.

We remark that each of the above algorithms induces a *fit* from the training data. Based upon the benchmark results below, a *fit* computed by any of the algorithms above is smaller than a *tightest fit*. Furthermore, the procedure of computing join-intervals is incremental, memory-based, data order dependent, and polynomial $\mathcal{O}(n^3)$ where *n* is the number of the training data. For algorithm *FLNsf* note that previously "used" data *x* are employed only if join-interval $I \vee x$ corners meet certain containment criteria. Also, the difference between algorithms *FLNsf* and *FLNotf* is that *FLNsf* requires all join-interval $I \vee x$ corners to reside either in join-interval *I* or in the join-interval which contains *x*, whereas *FLNotf* poses no restrictions whatsoever regarding the corners of join-interval $I \vee x$. Finally note that both algorithms *FLNff* and *FLNsf* are restricted forms of algorithm *FLNotf*.

E. The Testing Phase

The testing phase for all aforementioned FLN classifiers is the same based on inclusion measure function σ. Consequently, a testing datum *x* is classified to the category whose label is attached to the interval in which *x* is included the most.

IV. GEOMETRIC INTERPRETATIONS

This section illustrates on the plane the mechanics of the three FLN classifiers introduced in the previous section. For comparison, the mechanics of classifier *FLNtf* [10] are also illustrated. Fig.2(a) shows the order of presenting the training data which belong in two categories. Fig.2(b), Fig.2(c), Fig.2(d) and Fig.2(e) demonstrate the differences between algorithms *FLNff*, *FLNotf*, *FLNsf* and *FLNtf*, respectively. Note that the rectangles (fits) in Fig.2(e) are *maximal* in the sense that no datum from the same category can be included in any rectangle (fit) without also including a datum from another category, i.e. a contradiction, whereas the rectangles (fits) shown in Fig.2(b), Fig.2(c) and Fig.2(d) are smaller than maximal.

The above geometric illustrations clearly imply that the order of presenting the training data is important in all of the aforementioned FLN classifiers, but the *FLNtf* classifier. For the latter it is known that any order of presenting the training data results in the same hyperboxes [10]. Furthermore note that a hyperbox can be interpreted as a "rule for classification" induced from the training data.

V. EXPERIMENTS AND RESULTS

The learning capacity of *FLNff*, *FLNotf*, and *FLNsf* is demonstrated in this section comparatively with the results by alternative classification methods from the literature. Three benchmark classification problems were employed from the UCI repository of machine learning data sets [3]. A large number of experimental results have been produced. Here are shown only a few selected results.

The data sets below involve numeric and/or nominal data of various sizes including missing attribute values. A missing attribute value was dealt with by replacing it with the least element in the corresponding constituent lattice as explained in [10]. The lattices involved include the unit-hypercube, a probability space, and a Boolean algebra. A data vector was represented in lattice $\mathbb{R}^N$, furthermore positive valuation function $v = v_1 + \ldots + v_N$ was employed. Note also that *complement coding* was used to represent a data vector, in particular instead of $(x_1, \ldots, x_N)$ vector $(1-x_1, x_1, \ldots, 1-x_N, x_N)$ was used instead, as detailed in [10].

A. CLEVELAND's HEART Benchmark

The problem is to diagnose heart disease in a patient from a 14-attribute vector. This benchmark consists of 303 data vectors. The severity of heart disease is indicated by an integer ranging from 0 (no heart disease) to 4. By collapsing the classes into two, i.e. absence versus presence of heart disease, the problem becomes a '2-category problem' as opposed to the original '5-category problem'.

Because no training and testing data sets are given explicitly, a "keep-250-in" series of 100 experiments was carried out such that in each experiment 250 randomly selected data were used for training and the remaining 53 data were left out for testing.

Table I shows published results using different classification methods in the '2-category problem'. Furthermore, Table II shows results in both the '2-category problem' and the '5-category problem' using various FLN classifiers. In the latter Table both the average and the corresponding standard deviation are shown for both the classification accuracy and the number of rules in a series of experiments. Note that the same 100 randomly generated data sets were used in both the '2-category' and the '5-category' problems.

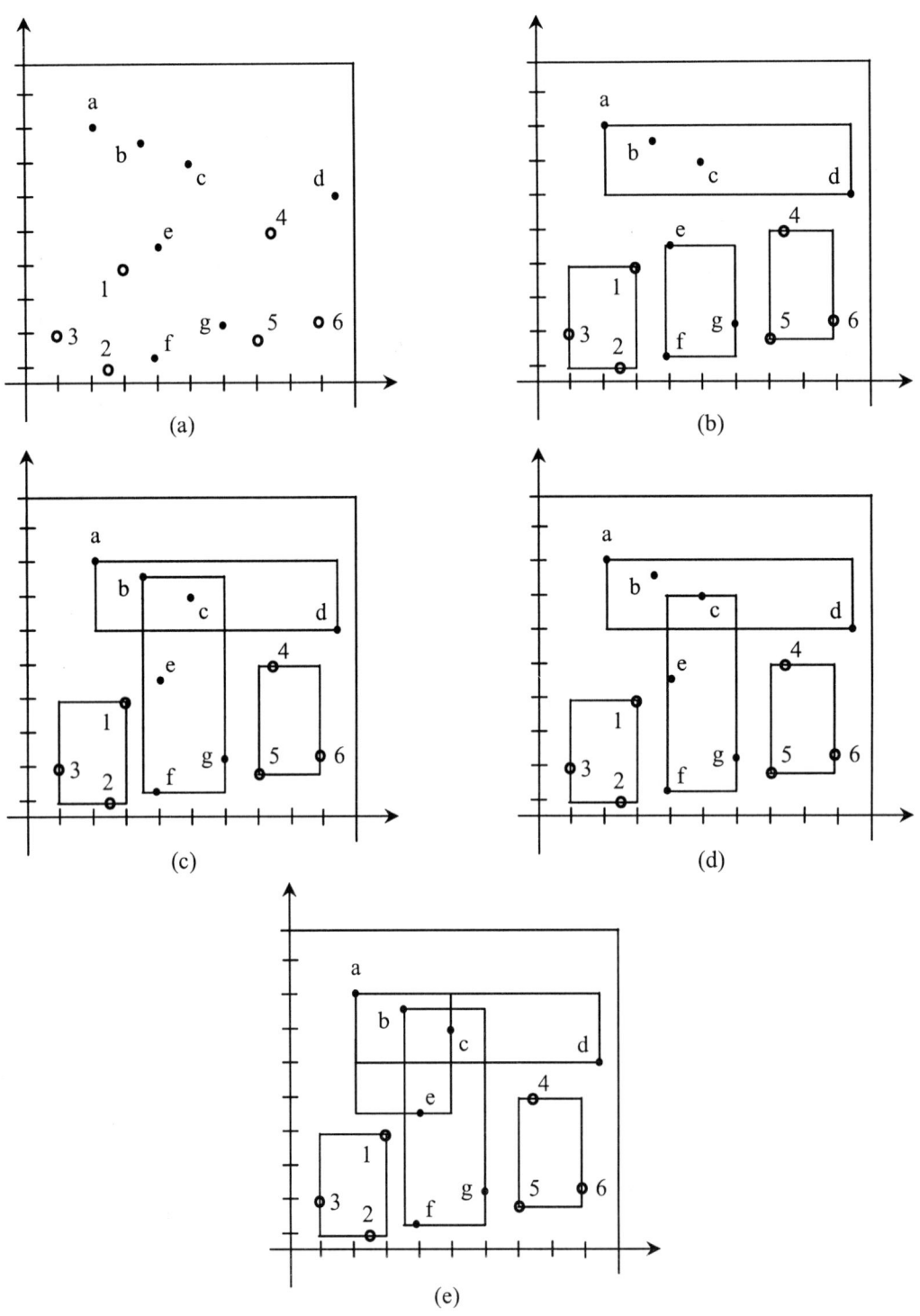

Fig. 2 (a) Thirteen training data are presented in the order a, b, c, d, e, f, g (category "•") followed by 1, 2, 3, 4, 5, 6 (category "o").
(b) Algorithm *FLNff* computes two *fits* for category "o", i.e. 1∨2∨3 and 4∨5∨6, and another two *fits* for category "•", i.e. a∨b∨c∨d and e∨f∨g.
(c) Algorithm *FLNotf* computes two *fits* for category "o", i.e. 1∨2∨3 and 4∨5∨6, and another two *fits* for category "•", i.e. a∨b∨c∨d and b∨c∨e∨f∨g.
(d) Algorithm *FLNsf* computes two *fits* for category "o", i.e. 1∨2∨3 and 4∨5∨6, and another two *fits* for category "•", i.e. a∨b∨c∨d and c∨e∨f∨g.
(e) Algorithm *FLNtf* computes two *fits* for category "o", i.e. 1∨2∨3 and 4∨5∨6, and three *fits* for category "•", i.e. a∨b∨c∨d, b∨c∨e∨f∨g and a∨b∨c∨e.

TABLE I
PERFORMANCE OF VARIOUS METHODS FROM THE LITERATURE IN CLASSIFYING CLEVELAND'S 2-CATEGORIES BENCHMARK HEART PROBLEM

Pattern classification method	Classification accuracy (%)
Probability analysis	79
Conceptual clustering (CLASSIT)	78.9
ARTMAP-IC (10 voters)	78
FLNtf (Keep-250-in, 100 experiments)	77.88
Discriminant analysis	77
Instance based prediction (NTgrowth)	77
Instance based prediction (C4)	74.8
Fuzzy ARTMAP (10 voters)	74
KNN (10 neighbors)	67

TABLE II
CLASSIFICATION ACCURACY OF *FLNtf*, *FLNff*, *FLNotf*, AND *FLNsf* IN THE CLEVELAND'S BENCHMARK HEART PROBLEM

Performance of various FLN classifiers		Statistics of % classification accuracy		Statistics of the number of rules	
		Average	Std deviation	Average	Std deviation
2-Categories Problem	*FLNotf*	89.51	3.60	34.79	6.58
	FLNsf	89.51	3.60	34.80	7.12
	FLNff	89.13	3.92	34.71	7.22
	FLNtf	77.88	4.58	53.80	4.58
5-Categories Problem	*FLNff*	66.74	4.96	53.47	10.3
	FLNotf	66.60	5.52	51.18	11.0
	FLNsf	66.49	5.59	49.47	9.8
	FLNtf	56.74	7.23	86.81	4.67

Table III below shows two hyperboxes computed in this problem. In particular, the corresponding intervals are shown in each constituent lattice. A hyperbox can be interpreted as a rule, e.g. the first line in Table III is interpreted as "IF $x_1 \in [49,77]$ and $x_2 \in [0,1]$ and $x_3 \in [2,4]$ and $x_4 \in [114,160]$ and $x_5 \in [149,318]$ and $x_6 \in [0,1]$ and $x_7 \in [0,2]$ and $x_8 \in [106,162]$ and $x_9 \in [0,1]$ and $x_{10} \in [0,4.4]$ and $x_{11} \in [1,3]$ and $x_{12} \in [3,3]$ and $x_{13} \in [3,6]$ THEN class is 1, i.e., presence of heart disease". In general, due to the inclusion measure function $\sigma(u \leq w) = \dfrac{v(w)}{v(u \vee w)}$, a datum $x = (x_1, \ldots, x_{13})$ can always be assigned to a category even if x is outside all hyperboxes.

The three FLN classifiers introduced in this work have demonstrated superior classification performance in this problem. The clear improvement over *FLNtf* is attributed to the computation of *fits* smaller than *tightest fits*. Table II also shows that classifiers *FLNff*, *FLNotf* and *FLNsf* also produce a clearly smaller number of rules than *FLNtf*. Finally, note that the induction of rules from the training data is considered a significant advantage of an FLN classifier over alternative neural networks, e.g. the backpropagation neural network.

B. CYLINDER BANDS Benchmark

The Cylinder Bands benchmark data set consists of 540 data records including 20 numeric plus 20 nominal attributes per data record. The 'class' attribute is among the nominal data and it specifies one of two classes, 'band' and 'noband.' No training set is given explicitly for the benchmark data set.

The Cylinder Bands benchmark data set has been partitioned into a training/testing pair of data sets in the same six different ways as in [10]. Table IV reports results by various FLN classifiers for the "sixth" training/testing pair of data sets obtained by selecting the first and second data record of every three data for training and leaving the third data record out for testing. Note that the aforementioned "sixth" partition included 360 data records in the training data set, i.e. 148 and 212 records for the 'band' and the 'noband' classes, respectively, moreover the testing data set included 180 records, i.e. 80 and 100 records for the 'band' and the 'noband' classes, respectively. The results in Table IV imply that the computation of *fits* smaller than *tightest fits* clearly improves the capacity for generalization.

C. FOREST COVERTYPE Benchmark

The Forest Cover Type data set contains 581,012 data records of which 11,340 records are given for training, 3780 are given for validation, and 565,892 data records are given for testing. This data set involves, jointly, 12 numeric and nominal attributes per data record. A data record stems from a 30 x 30 m^2 plot in the Roosevelt National Forest of northern Colorado. The first 10 attributes are numeric cartographic variables which specify the location of the 30 x 30 m^2 plot in the forest, whereas the last two attributes are Boolean strings of zeros and ones and specify both the corresponding wilderness area and soil type. The 'class' of a data record is denoted by an integer between 1 and 7, that is there exist seven underlying classes which specify the forest cover type. There are no missing attribute values.

TABLE III
RULES/HYPERBOXES COMPUTED BY AN FLN CLASSIFIER IN THE CLEVELAND'S 2-CATEGORIES BENCHMARK HEART PROBLEM

Rule	x_1	x_2	x_3	x_4	x_5	x_6	x_7	x_8	x_9	x_{10}	x_{11}	x_{12}	x_{13}	class
1	[49,77]	[0,1]	[2,4]	[114,160]	[149,318]	[0,1]	[0,2]	[106,162]	[0,1]	[0,4.4]	[1,3]	[3,3]	[3,6]	1
2	[56,64]	[0,1]	[3,4]	[124,140]	[197,335]	[0,1]	[0,2]	[136,158]	[0,1]	[0,1.2]	[1,2]	[0,1]	[3,3]	0

TABLE IV
THE CLASSIFICATION ACCURACY IN THE CYLINDER BANDS BENCHMARK OF VARIOUS FLN CLASSIFIERS. THE LAST COLUMN SHOWS THE NUMBER OF RULES INDUCED IN THE TRAINING DATA

Various FLN classifiers	% classification accuracy	Testing misclassifications (band + noband)	No. of rules
FLNotf	85.56	17 + 9 = 26	11
FLNff	80.56	27 + 8 = 35	10
FLNsf	80.56	27 + 8 = 35	10
FLNtf	78.88	29 + 9 = 38	10

Table V summarizes the classification results by backpropagation, linear discriminant analysis [2] and *FLNtf* [10], as well as by *FLNff*, *FLNotf*, and *FLNsf*. The results in Table V confirm again that the computation of *fits* smaller than *tightest fits* clearly improves the capacity for generalization. In addition, all three *FLNff*, *FLNotf*, and *FLNsf* have resulted in considerably fewer rules than *FLNtf*. Number 6600 (within parentheses) in the first line of Table V indicates the total number of connection weights in the corresponding backpropagation neural network.

TABLE V
PERFORMANCE OF VARIOUS METHODS IN CLASSIFYING THE FOREST COVERTYPE BENCHMARK

Pattern classification method	Classification accuracy (%)	No. of rules
Backpropagation	70	(6600)
FLNff	68.25	654
FLNotf	66.13	516
FLNsf	66.10	503
FLNtf	62.58	3684
Linear discriminant analysis	58	-

VI. DISCUSSION AND CONCLUSION

Three improved fuzzy lattice neurocomputing (FLN) classifiers, namely *FLNff*, *FLNotf* and *FLNsf* were introduced in this work. Application in three benchmark classification problems compared favorably with alternative classification methods from the literature. The mechanics of learning have been illustrated geometrically on the plane. Apart from the good classification results, an additional advantage of the aforementioned three FLN classifiers has been a set of meaningful rules for classification induced from the training data.

This work has built upon a previous work in FLN [10]. An improvement was shown here regarding the computation of *fits*, the latter are join-intervals in a lattice. Note that in product-lattice $\mathbf{R}^N$, in particular, a join-interval corresponds to an N-dimensional hyperbox. The experiments in this work have demonstrated that *fits* smaller than *tightest fits* improve the capacity for generalization. The three classifiers introduced here are, basically, memory-based classifiers [1], [13], they compute "off line" lattice join-intervals and, furthermore, the corresponding classification accuracy depends on the order of presenting the training data.

Lately it has been shown that the data order dependency of an individual FLN classifier can be capitalized on for improving the classification accuracy based on an ensemble of FLN voters [12]. Moreover it has been shown in [12] that an employment of a different positive valuation function than $v(x) = x$ in a constituent lattice can further improve classification accuracy. Future plans include both the design of ensembles of FLN classifiers, where an individual classifier is trained on a different permutation of the training data, and the employment of different positive valuation functions than $v(x) = x$ in a constituent lattice.

REFERENCES

[1] D.W. Aha, D.F. Kibler, and M.K. Albert, "Instance-Based Learning Algorithms", *Machine Learning*, vol. 6, pp. 37-66, 1991.

[2] J.A. Blackard, and D.J. Dean, "Comparative accuracies of artificial neural networks and discriminant analysis in predicting forest cover types from cartographic variables", *Computers and Electronics in Agriculture*, vol. 24, no. 3, pp. 131-151, 2000.

[3] C.L. Blake, and C.J. Merz, UCI Repository of machine learning databases, Irvine, CA: University of California, Department of Information and Computer Science, 1998. [http:// www.ics.uci.edu/ ~mlearn/ MLRepository.html].

[4] G.A. Carpenter, S. Grossberg, and D. Rosen, "Fuzzy ART: Fast stable learning and categorization of analog patterns by an adaptive resonance system", *Neural Networks*, vol. 4, pp. 759-771, 1991.

[5] G.A. Carpenter, S. Grossberg, N. Markuzon, J.H. Reynolds, and D.B. Rosen, "Fuzzy ARTMAP: a neural network architecture for incremental supervised learning of analog multidimensional maps", *IEEE Trans. on Neural Networks*, vol. 3, no. 5, pp. 698-713, 1992.

[6] I. Dagher, M. Georgiopoulos, G.L. Heileman, and G. Bebis, "An ordering algorithm for pattern presentation in fuzzy ARTMAP that tends to improve generalization performance", *IEEE Trans. on Neural Networks*, vol. 10, no. 4, pp. 768-778, 1999.

[7] B. Gabrys, and A. Bargiela, "General fuzzy min-max neural network for clustering and classification", *IEEE Trans. on Neural Networks*, vol. 11, no. 3, pp. 769-783, 2000.

[8] V.G. Kaburlasos. *Adaptive resonance theory with supervised learning and large database applications*. PhD dissertation. Department of Electrical Engineering, University of Nevada, Reno, 1992.

[9] V.G. Kaburlasos, and V. Petridis "Fuzzy Lattice Neurocomputing (FLN) : A novel connectionist scheme for versatile learning and decision making by clustering", *International Journal of Computers and Their Applications*, vol. 4, no. 3, pp. 31-43, 1997.

[10] V.G. Kaburlasos, and V. Petridis, "Fuzzy Lattice Neurocomputing (FLN) models", *Neural Networks*, vol. 13, no. 10, pp. 1145-1170, 2000.

[11] V.G. Kaburlasos, and V. Petridis, "Learning and decision-making in the framework of fuzzy lattices", in *New Learning Paradigms in Soft Computing*, vol. 84, L.C. Jain and J. Kacprzyk, Eds. Heidelberg, Germany: Physica-Verlag, 2002, pp. 55-96.

[12] V.G. Kaburlasos, and S. Kazarlis, "σ-FLNMAP with Voting (σFLNMAPwV): A genetically optimized ensemble of classifiers with the capacity to deal with partially-ordered, disparate types of data. Application to financial problems", *Proc. 4th Intl. Conf. on Technology & Automation*, pp. 276-281, Thessaloniki, Greece, 5-6 October 2002.

[13] J. Kolodner, *Case-Based Reasoning*. San Mateo, CA: Morgan Kaufmann Publishers, 1993.

[14] V. Petridis, and V.G. Kaburlasos, "Fuzzy Lattice Neural Network (FLNN): A hybrid model for learning", *IEEE Trans. on Neural Networks*, vol. 9, no. 5, pp. 877-890, 1998.

[15] V. Petridis, and V.G. Kaburlasos, "Clustering and classification in structured data domains using Fuzzy Lattice Neurocomputing (FLN)," *IEEE Trans on Knowledge and Data Engineering*, vol. 13, no. 2, pp. 245 - 260, 2001.

[16] P.K. Simpson, "Fuzzy Min-Max neural networks - Part2: clustering", *IEEE Trans. on Fuzzy Systems*, vol. 1, no. 1, pp. 32-45, 1993.

PARAMETER SENSITIVITIES OF A NEURO-BASED ADAPTIVE CONTROLLER WITH GUARANTEED STABILITY

M. B. Menhaj[*] and Swakshar Ray

School of Electrical and Computer Engineering
Department of Computer Science
Oklahoma State University, MSCS 219
Stillwater, OK-74078-5032, USA
Fax: 405-744-9097
Tel. 405-744-2283

menhaj@cs.okstate.edu

ABSTRACT

This paper provides a detailed analysis and study on the parameter sensitivities and domain of attraction of the novel neuro-based adaptive controller based on the previously published paper [1,2]. The special learning algorithm similar to back propagation provides better stability and wide domain of attraction for the controller provided that the neural network parameters are chosen carefully. The controller acts as a direct adaptive controller and the weight and bias matrices are updated online without any prior offline training. It is easy to implement in real time due to less complexity in terms of absence of several neural networks and robustifying terms. This paper reveals the domain of attraction based on different parameter values and the sensitivities of the error surface with respect to designed parameters. We have tested the controller on a two link robot arm system and extensive simulation results show the dependence and effectiveness of the controller with respect to parameters of the designed neural network. This gives a better insight of the controller that has been investigated with systems of the form $\dot{x} = f(x) + u + w$ and $\dot{x} = f(x) + g(x)u(t) + w$. The theoretical proof on the stability of the closed loop nonlinear systems with the adaptive controller has been investigated in detail in this paper. The paper also summarizes the potential advantages, disadvantages, prospective developments and real life applicability of the controller scheme at the end.

1. INTRODUCTION

Although there are many different ways to use neural networks(NN) for controlling a dynamic system but the main issue still remains that whether the NN is trained with sufficient data to control the system over a larger domain. So, the responsibilities lie on the designer to use the learning rules such that NN can control the system over greater regions and maintain stability while dealing with the dynamic behavior. In a classical control, the nonlinear system should be known to design a controller with output feedback linearization or similar type of technique. In contrast, neural networks can be used for any system with unknown dynamics using a proper set of input and output data pairs collected from the system during operation. So the neuro-controller should be carefully designed to be stable and bounded within the operating region and to use the well driven classical control theory, we need to impose certain constraints on the parameters as well as on the system itself.

In 1990's some achievements on stability of neuro-controllers have been reported. Tzirkel-Hancock et al. [14] designed a direct neuro-controller scheme for a special class of minimum phase nonlinear systems through input/output linearization and state feedback control mechanism in which instead of employing the Lie-derivatives the neural network approximations are used. The design of neuro-controllers along with its stability and convergence analysis have been continued by Chen et al. [7][8][9], Lewis et al. [10][11], Sadegh [13]...

For real time use of neural network controllers as intelligent systems, two main factors are important, 1) it has to be easy to implement and 2) the response time has to be fast as delays will cause the controller lagging behind the plant; this in turn might cause stability problems. Several radial basis neural networks have been dealt with in the literature [15],[16],[17], but MLP neural networks have some advantages over radial basis networks in certain situations. As it is much difficult to prove theoretically the stability of MLP neural networks, these networks have been studied less. In this paper, we consider a special type of MLP neural networks with a single hidden layer, a pre-processing block and a linear output layer which uses a special type of BP-like learning rules to adjust parameters in the neural network. The controller is basically a direct adaptive controller which does not need any pre-learning and furthermore the training is done online while controlling the plant in accordance with desired trajectories given by some reference model. It is assumed that all the state of the plant is available for measurement and the linear reference model is chosen by the designer. No additional controller is required. Stability analysis shows both tracking error and

---
[*] He is also with Department of Electrical Engineering, AmirKabir University, Tehran.

neural network weights remain bounded if the plant disturbed by a bounded disturbance input signal. Parameter sensitivities, tested by simulations verifies the theoretical study of the Lyapunov Based stability analysis.

The rest of the paper is organized as follows. Section 2 presents the neuro-based adaptive controller. The performance of the controller is illustrated by some simulation examples along with some discussion on results in section 3. Section 4 gives a detail stability analysis and finally section 5 concludes the paper.

2. THE PROPOSED NEURO-ADAPTIVE CONTROLLER

2.1 General Problem Statement

This paper addresses the model following control problem for a special class of dynamical systems with the following dynamical equation:

$$\underline{\dot{x}}(t) = \underline{f}(\underline{x}) + \underline{u}(t) + \underline{w}(t) \tag{1}$$

where, $\underline{f}: \mathbb{R}^n \to \mathbb{R}^n$ is an unknown smooth non-linear function, $\underline{u}$ and $\underline{w}$, which represents the model uncertainties and state noise, are the system's control and disturbance signal vectors, respectively. It is assumed that states are available and the additive disturbance $\underline{w}$ is bounded. Though during the simulation we see that the controller is also capable to control class of dynamical systems $\underline{\dot{x}} = \underline{f}(\underline{x}) + g(\underline{x})\underline{u} + \underline{w}(t)$.

The objective is to design a neuro-adaptive controller so that the plant (1) follows asymptotically a desired trajectory given by the following reference model:

$$\underline{\dot{x}}_d = A_d \underline{x}_d + B_d \underline{r}(t) \tag{2}$$

In the above, the matrix A_d is asymptotically stable.

Figure 1 represents the overall closed loop neuro-control system. The control signal is defined as:

$$u = A_d \underline{x}_d + \underline{u}_{NN}(\underline{x}, W_1, b_1, W_2, b_2) + B_d \underline{r}(t) \tag{3}$$

where

$$\underline{u}_{NN}(\underline{x}, W_1, b_1, W_2, b_2) = W_2 f_1(W_1 f_0(W_0 \underline{x}) + b_1) + b_2,$$

W_1, W_2, b_1, b_2 are tunable weight matrices and biases of the multilayer perceptron neural network, and f_0, f_1 are any nonlinear smooth squashing functions (i.e., sigmoidal type functions).; that is

$$\underline{f}_1(y) = [f_1(y_1)...f_1(y_n)]^T; \underline{y} \in \mathbb{R}^n$$
$$|f_1(z)| < 1, \forall z \in R$$

Note that the first layer represents a preprocessing block.

Universal approximation property of MLP neural network assures the existence of weight and bias matrices W_1, W_2, b_1, b_2 so that

$$\left| \underbrace{\underline{f}(\underline{x}) + \underline{u}_{NN}(\underline{x}, W_1, b_1, W_2, b_2)}_{\varepsilon(\underline{x})} \right| < \bar{\varepsilon}, \forall \underline{x} \in B \subset R^n$$

with $\|W\| \equiv Trace(W^T W) \leq \overline{W}$. Now the tracking signal error will be $\underline{e} = \underline{x} - \underline{x}_d$, $\underline{\dot{e}} = A_d \underline{e} + \underbrace{(\underline{u}_{NN} - \underline{u}^*_{NN})}_{\tilde{u}_{NN}} + \underbrace{\underline{u}^*_{NN} + \underline{f}(\underline{x})}_{\varepsilon(\underline{x})} + \underline{w}$

(4)

$\tilde{W} = W_i - W^*_i, i = 1, 2, \ldots$. In this context note that the neural network control signal $\underline{u}_{NN}$ is approximating $-f(x)$.

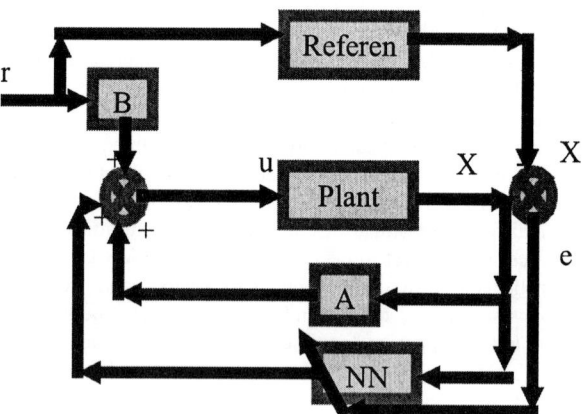

Figure 1. A Block Diagram Representation of the MLP Based Closed-loop Control System.

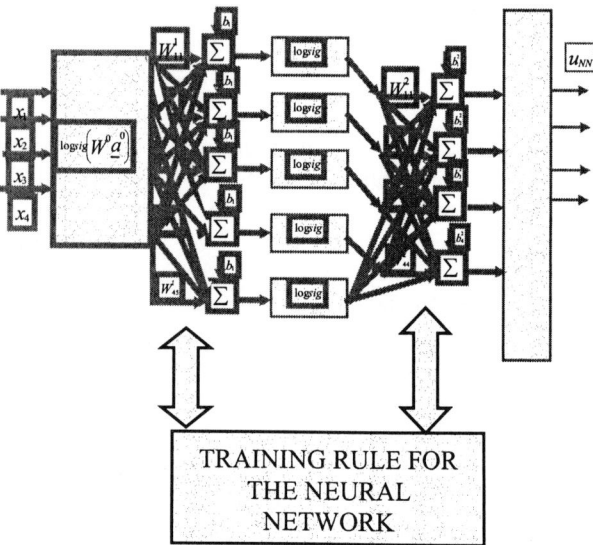

Figure 2: An MLP Based Neural Network Diagram

2.2 Learning Rule for Parameter Adaptation

From (3) and Figure 1, one may easily notice that the control system is nothing but a direct adaptive control with parameters $W_1, W_2, \underline{b}_1$ and $\underline{b}_2$. The following BP-like learning rules are proposed for adjusting the parameters of the controller

$$\dot{W}_1 = -\Gamma_1 \gamma\, W_1 - \frac{1}{1+|e|\|W_2\|}\Gamma_1 \dot{F}_1^T(n_1) W_2 P e \underline{f}_0^T(x)$$

$$\dot{b}_1 = -\Gamma_1 \gamma\, b_1 - \frac{1}{1+|e|\|W_2\|}\Gamma_1 \dot{F}_1(n_1) W_2 P \underline{e} \qquad (5)$$

$$\dot{W}_2 = -\Gamma_2 \gamma\, W_2 - \Gamma_2 P e \underline{f}_{-1}^T(x)$$

$$\dot{b}_2 = -\Gamma_2 \gamma\, b_2 - \Gamma_2 P \underline{e}$$

where the matrices Γ_i are positive definite, $\gamma_i > 0$, the positive definite matrix P is the solution of the Lyapunov equation $A_d^T P + P A_d + Q = 0$ for an arbitrary positive definite matrix Q to be selected by the designer and

$\dot{F}(y) = [\dot{f}(y_1) \ldots \dot{f}(y_n)]^T, y \in R^n$ and $\|\dot{F}(y)\| \le 1$ as $\|\dot{f}(y)\| < 1, y \in R^n$

3. SIMULATION RESULTS

Earlier papers[1,2] provided simulation results in details for some nonlinear systems including single and two link robot arm system using the new neuro-adaptive controller (bias terms ignored). In this paper, we will provide tests on a two link robot arm system from paper [1] with the neuro-adaptive controller proposed in section 2.1 and 2.2. The unstable nonlinear system for two link robot arm is shown below:

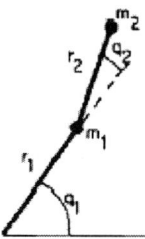

Figure 3.   Two Link Robot Arm

The parameters for the robot are chosen as follows:

$r_1 = 1m, r_2 = 0.8m$

$m_1 = 0.5 kg, m_2 = 6.25 kg$

$J1 = J2 = 5 kg - m$

$g = 9.8 m/s^2$

The neuro-based adaptive controller was designed with the following parameters:

$\Gamma_1 = \Gamma_2 = 200 * I$, $\gamma = 0.2$, Q=200*I, reference signal is

r=[10(sin2t+sin4t);10(cos6t+cos8t)]

$$A_d = \begin{bmatrix} 0 & 0 & 1 & 0 \\ 0 & 0 & 0 & 1 \\ -10 & 0 & -20 & 0 \\ 0 & -10 & 0 & -30 \end{bmatrix}, \underline{x}(0)=[-3;3;0;0], x_{d0}=[0;0;0;0]$$

No of neurons used in the hidden layer is 5. Figure 4.a shows how well the plant can follow the reference trajectory (angular positions) and figure 4.b presents the output of the controller which is reasonable considering the dynamic behavior of the plant.

Next we considered a variable load and changed its value from 6.25 kgs to 10 kgs. Figure 5. shows the simulation results. The response of the neuro controller is still satisfactory. In figure 6, we can see the effect of the value of Q on the tracking error. A higher Q yields smaller tracking error. Figure 7 shows the effect of Γ_1 and Γ_2 on the tracking error. A higher Γ_1, Γ_2 gives a better tracking. We have also done extensive simulations to show the effect of eigenvalues of the reference model and different values of Q on the tracking error. The error signals depicted in figures 8 and 9 are the norm of the tracking error vector. Figure 10 shows the stable region as shaded area w.r.t different values of Q, $\Gamma_1 = \Gamma_2 = \Gamma$ and it verifies the validity of inequality (12). All the simulations show the remarkable performance of the proposed controller. The theoretical foundation for the simulation results will be given in the next section.

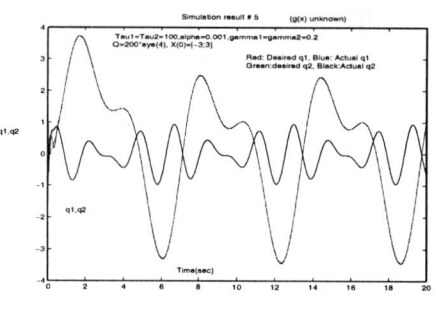

(a) State Trajectories

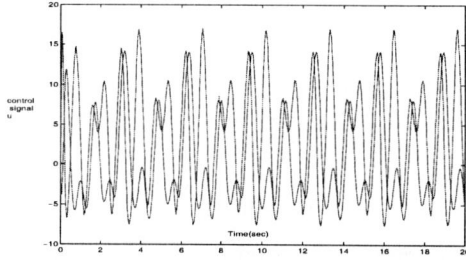

(b) Control signal

Figure 4 Performance of the neuro-based adaptive controller for the two link robot arm system

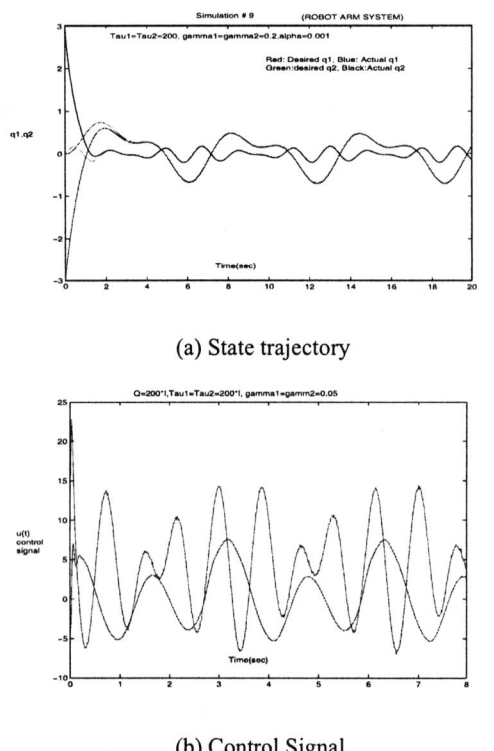

(a) State trajectory

(b) Control Signal

Figure 5. Close loop Response for the two link robot arm problem

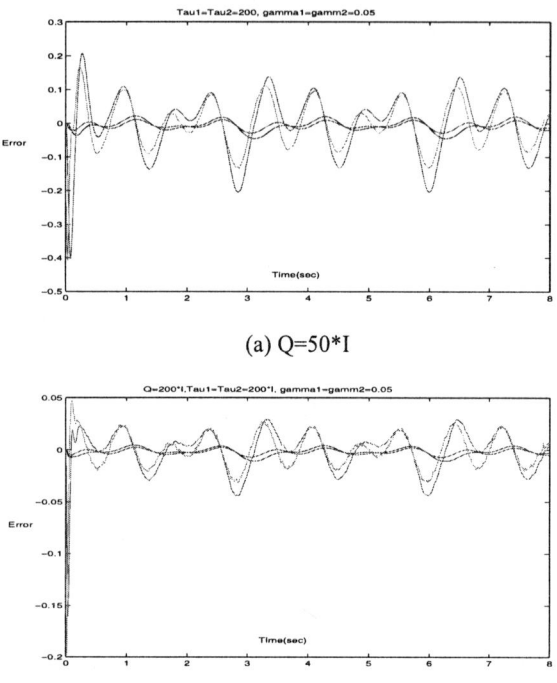

(a) Q=50*I

(b) Q=200*I

Figure 6 Tracking Error trajectories for different Q

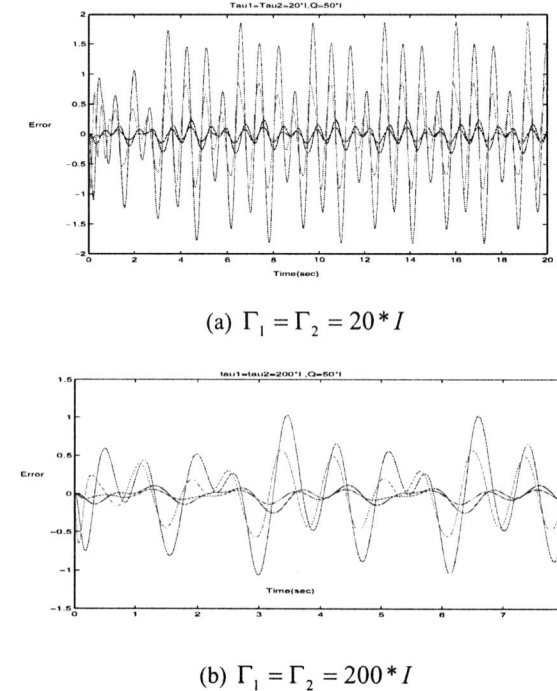

(a) $\Gamma_1 = \Gamma_2 = 20*I$

(b) $\Gamma_1 = \Gamma_2 = 200*I$

Figure 7 Error Trajectories with different $\Gamma_1 = \Gamma_2$

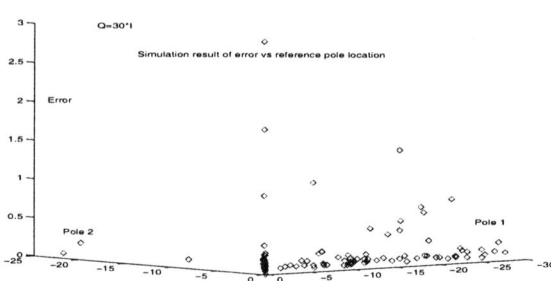

(a) Reference model Poles Vs Error (x, y axis= poles, z axis=error)

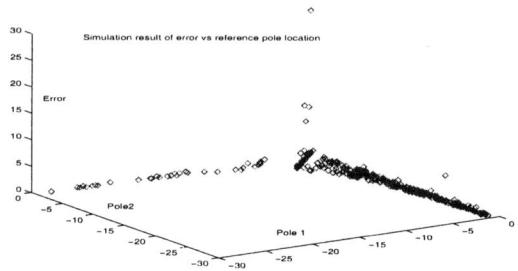

(b) Reference model poles vs Error

Figure 8 Effect of Eigenvalues of the reference model on Closed-loop Control System

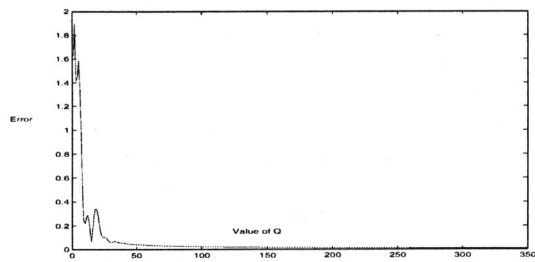

Figure 9 Effect of Q on the Tracking Error

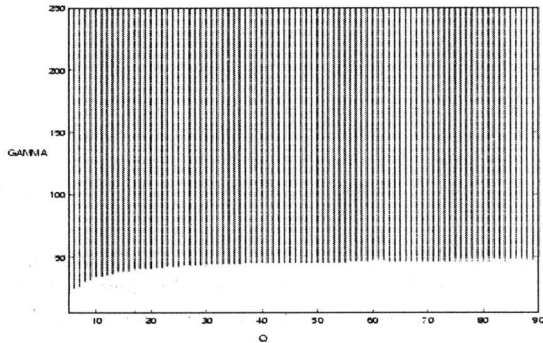

Figure 10 Stability region as a function of Q and Γ.

4. PARAMETER SENSITIVITY AND STABILITY STUDY

To investigate the stability of the neuro-based adaptive controller proposed in this paper, we used Lyapunov's stability criteria. The Lyapunov function was chosen as:

$$V = e^T Pe + Trace\left(W_1^T \Gamma_1^{-1} W_1 + W_2^T \Gamma_2^{-1} W_2 + b_1^T \Gamma_1^{-1} b_1 + b_2^T \Gamma_2^{-1} b_2\right)$$
$$= V_e + V_{W_1} + V_{W_2} + V_{b_1} + V_{b_2} \qquad (7)$$

Now, taking the derivative w.r.t time, we can write:

$$\dot{V} = \dot{e}^T Pe + e^T P\dot{e} + \frac{d}{dt}\left[Trace\left(W_1^T \Gamma_1^{-1} W_1 + W_2^T \Gamma_2^{-1} W_2 + b_1^T \Gamma_1^{-1} b_1 + b_2^T \Gamma_2^{-1} b_2\right)\right]$$
$$= \dot{V}_e + \dot{V}_{W_1} + \dot{V}_{W_2} + \dot{V}_{b_1} + \dot{V}_{b_2} \qquad (8)$$

Now, the 1st term can be extended as

$$\begin{aligned}\dot{V}_e &= \dot{e}^T Pe + e^T P\dot{e} \\ &= (A_d e)^T Pe + (\varepsilon^T + w^T)Pe + e^T P(A_d e) + e^T P(\varepsilon + w) \\ &= e^T\left(A_d^T P + PA_d\right)e + (\varepsilon^T + w^T)Pe + e^T P(\varepsilon + w) \\ &= -e^T Qe + (\varepsilon^T + w^T)Pe + e^T P(\varepsilon + w) \\ &\leq -\lambda_{\min}(Q)\|e\|^2 + 2(\overline{\varepsilon} + \overline{w})\|P\|\|e\|\end{aligned} \qquad (9)$$

and the 2nd term can be bounded as follows:

$$\dot{V}_{W_1} = Tr\left(\widetilde{W}_1^T \Gamma_1^{-1} \widetilde{W}_1 + \widetilde{W}_1^T \Gamma_1^{-1} \widetilde{W}_1\right)$$
$$= \dot{V}_{W_{11}} + \dot{V}_{W_{12}}$$
$$\dot{V}_{W_{11}} = -\gamma Tr\left(\widetilde{W}_1^T \Gamma_1 \Gamma_1^{-1} \widetilde{W}_1\right) - \gamma Tr\left(\frac{1}{1+\|e\|\|W_2\|} f^0(\underline{x}) e^T P\dot{F}(y) W_2 \Gamma_1 \Gamma_1^{-1} \widetilde{W}_1\right)$$
$$= -\gamma Tr\left(W_1^T W_1\right) + \gamma Tr\left(W_1^T W^*_1\right) - \frac{1}{1+\|e\|\|W_2\|} Tr\left(f^0(\underline{x}) e^T P\dot{F}(y) W_2 W_1\right)$$
$$+ \frac{1}{1+\|e\|\|W_2\|} Tr\left(f^0(\underline{x}) e^T P\dot{F}(y) W_2 W^*_1\right)$$
$$\leq -\gamma\|W_1^T W_1\| + \gamma n\|W_1^T W^*_1\| - \frac{1}{1+\|e\|\|W_2\|}\|f^0(\underline{x}) e^T P\dot{F}(y) W_2 W_1\|$$
$$+ \frac{n}{1+\|e\|\|W_2\|}\|f^0(\underline{x}) e^T P\dot{F}(y) W_2 W^*_1\|$$
$$\Rightarrow \dot{V}_{W_{11}} \leq \gamma n\overline{W}^2 + \frac{n\overline{W}^2}{1+\|e\|\|W_2\|}\|P\|\|e\| \qquad (10)$$
$$\leq \gamma n\overline{W}^2 + n\overline{W}^2\|P\|\|e\| \quad as, \|f^0(\underline{x})\|<1 \text{ and } \|\dot{F}(y)\|\leq 1$$

We can get the bound for other terms in the similar way. Due to space constraint all the detailed analysis could not be shown here. So we can write,

$$\begin{aligned}\dot{V}_e &\leq -\lambda_{\min}(Q)\|e\|^2 + 2(\overline{\varepsilon}+\overline{w})\|P\|\|e\| \\ \dot{V}_{W_1} &\leq 2\gamma n\overline{W}^2 + 2n\overline{W}\|P\|\|e\| \\ \dot{V}_{W_2} &\leq 2\gamma n\overline{W}^2 + 2n\overline{W}\|P\|\|e\| \\ \dot{V}_{b_1} &\leq 2\gamma n\overline{b}^2 + 2n\overline{b}\|P\|\|e\| \\ \dot{V}_{b_2} &\leq 2\gamma n\overline{b}^2 + 2n\overline{b}\|P\|\|e\|\end{aligned} \qquad (11)$$

Finally, $\dot{V} \leq -\lambda_{\min}(Q)\|e\|^2 + 2(\overline{\varepsilon}+\overline{w})\|P\|\|e\| + 2\gamma n\overline{W}^2 + 2n\overline{W}\|P\|\|e\| +$
$\qquad 2\gamma n\overline{W}^2 + 2n\overline{W}\|P\|\|e\| + 2\gamma n\overline{b}^2 + 2n\overline{b}\|P\|\|e\| + 2\gamma n\overline{b}^2 + 2n\overline{b}\|P\|\|e\|$

$$\Rightarrow \dot{V} \leq -\lambda_{\min}(Q)\|e\|^2 + 2(\overline{\varepsilon}+\overline{w})\|P\|\|e\| + 4\gamma n\overline{W}^2 + 4n\overline{W}\|P\|\|e\| \qquad (12)$$
$$\qquad + 4\gamma n\overline{b}^2 + 4n\overline{b}\|P\|\|e\|$$

$$\Rightarrow \dot{V} \leq \underbrace{-\lambda_{\min}(Q)\|e\|^2}_{1st} + \underbrace{\left[2(\overline{\varepsilon}+\overline{w})+4n\overline{W}+4n\overline{b}\right]\|P\|\|e\|}_{2nd} + \underbrace{\left[4\gamma n\overline{W}^2 + 4\gamma n\overline{b}^2\right]}_{3rd}$$

It is obvious from the final expressions (12) that the Lyapunov stability will be valid under certain boundary space for controller parameters such as $Q, A_d, \Gamma_1, \Gamma_2, \gamma$. The controller is very stable with respect to initial error if controller parameters are chosen properly, though more energy will be required for the control signal if the initial error is too high. The Lyapunov stability of the composite system mainly depends on the proper selection of these parameters. From the expression (12), we can see that a large Q will make the 1st term in the expression more negative while γ should be selected as small as possible to make the positive 3rd term small. Also the positive 2nd term, which depends on P, needs to be small so that the right hand side of (12) is negative; this will guaranty asymptotic stability even with a large initial error. As selection of the reference model will yield P matrix, we can see that the minimum eigenvalue for A_d should be high enough to make norm (P) small i.e. the poles of the reference model ought to be selected as far from the imaginary axis as possible. Figure 10 gives a better insight of the fact that if we increase Q the lower envelop of the stable region w.r.t Γ becomes exponential. As all these parameters are designer's choices and can be controlled depending on the energy constraint on control signal generation, the proposed MLP based adaptive controller can be stable, fast and easy to implement.

5. SUMMARY

This paper presented a neuro-based adaptive controller for a special class of dynamical systems. The control scheme can be viewed as a direct adaptive controller. No off-line training phase for neural network is required. A BP-like learning rule adjusts the weights of the MLP-based NN and keeps them as well as the tracking error ultimately bounded, starting from any initial value in some compact bounded set in $\mathbb{R}^n$. The stability analysis of the neuro-control system and the parameter sensitivities of the proposed MLP based controller have been discussed in detail. Considering real time application, the proposed controller is fast, reliable and easy to implement which certainly gives it an edge over other complex adaptive controller. More study on the proposed controller and its application in different real life systems is going on and will be published in future.

REFERENCES:

1. *Menhaj, M.B.; Rouhani, M.;* "A novel neuro-based model reference adaptive control for a two link robot arm" ,Neural Networks, 2002. IJCNN '02. Proceedings of the 2002 International Joint Conference on , Volume:1,2002,Page(s): 47 -52

2. *Menhaj, M.B.; Rouhani, M.;* "A neuro-controller with guranteed stability", Presented on IEEE Midwest Conference, 2002

3. *Wang, Q.; Broome, D.R.;* "A novel neural adaptive controller for robots" ,Control, 1994. Control '94. Volume 1., International Conference on , 21-24 Mar 1994 Page(s): 486 -491 vol.1

4. *Meyne, Ph.; Houkari, M.; Barret, C.; Martinez, J.M.; Garassino, A.; Tormo, P.;* "A neural adaptive controller", Systems, Man and Cybernetics, 1993. 'Systems Engineering in the Service of Humans', Conference Proceedings., International Conference on , 17-20 Oct 1993 Page(s): 80 -84 vol.4

5. Jeffrey T. Spooner, Manfredi Maggiore, Raul Ordonez and Kevin M. Passino; "Stable Adaptive Control and Estimation for Nonlinear Systems", A John Willey and sons, Inc Publication.,2002.

6. *Hagan, M.T.; Menhaj, M.B.;* "Training feedforward networks with the Marquardt algorithm",Neural Networks, IEEE Transactions on , Volume: 5 Issue: 6 , Nov 1994 Page(s): 989 -993

7. *Tzirkel-Hancock E., and Fallside F.* "A Stability Based Neural Network Control Method for a Class of Non-Linear Systems". *IEEE Inter. Joint Conf. on N.N.*, 2, pages 1047-1052, 1991.

8. Chen F-C., and Khalil H. K. "Adaptive Control of Nonlinear Systems Using Neural Networks". *Int. J. Control*, **55**, 1299-1317, 1992.

9. Chen F-C, and Liu C-C. "Adaptively Controlling Nonlinear Continuous-Time Systems Using Neural Networks". *IEEE Trans.on AC,* 39(6), 1306-1310, 1994.

10. Chen F-C., and Khalil H. K. "Adaptive Control of a Class Of Nonlinear Discrete-Time Systems Using Neural Networks". *IEEE Trans. on AC,* 40(5), 791-801, 1995.

11. Lewis F. L., Yesildirek A., and Liu K. "Neural Net Robot Controller with Guaranteed Stability". 3rd *Inter. Conf. on Indus. Fuzz. Cont.*, pages 103-108, 1993.

12. Lewis F. L., Liu K., and Yesildirek A. "Multilayer Neural Net Robot Controller With Guaranteed Tracking Performance". *IEEE Trans. on Neural Networks*, 6(3), 703-715, 1995.

13. Sadegh N. "A Perceptron Network For Functional Identification and Control of Nonlinear Systems". *IEEE Trans. on Neural Networks,* 4(6), 982-988, 1993.

14. Tzirkel-Hancock E., and Fallside F. "A Stability Based Neural Network Control Method for a Class of Non-Linear Systems". *IEEE Inter. Joint Conf. on N.N.*, 2, pages 1047-1052, 1991.

15. Sanchez, E.N.; Vega, V.; "Stability of neurofuzzy controllers",American Control Conference, 1995. Proceedings of the , Volume: 6 , 21-23 Jun 1995 Page(s): 4251 -4252 vol.6

16. Meyer-Base, A.; Watzel, R.; "Relevant features selection with radial basis neural networks",Neural Networks, 1995. Proceedings., IEEE International Conference on , Volume: 2 , Nov/Dec 1995 Page(s): 963 -967 vol.2

17. Karayiannis, N.B.; Weiqun Mi; "Growing radial basis neural networks", Neural Networks,1997., International Conference on , Volume: 3 , 9-12 Jun 1997 Page(s): 1406 -1411 vol.3

A COMPARATIVE STUDY OF THE CATEGORY CHOICE OF THE FUZZY ART WITH THE L-1 NORM

Issam Dagher
University of Balamand. Department of Electrical and Computer Engineering.
dagheri@balamand.edu.lb

Abstract- In this paper, a comparative study of the category choice of the Fuzzy ART with the L-1 norm is presented. It is shown that the category choice can be replaced by a distance measure related to the L-1 norm. This distance measure will have the following advantages over the category choice of the Fuzzy ART network:
1. No need for augmenting the dimensions of the input patterns. The distance measure will operate directly on the input patterns without the need for doing complement coding.
2. No need for normalizing the input patterns. The input patterns need not to be in the interval [0,1].

I. INTRODUCTION

Clustering is the process of separating the elements of some universal set and groups them according to some similarity measure [8,9]. Each cluster contains elements which are similar to each other and dissimilar to the elements of another cluster. Fuzzy ART [1, 2, 6, 7] is a clustering algorithm that operates on analog elements. Similarity of the elements is based on the category choice function Tj(I). Each element is assigned to the category that maximizes Tj(I) while satisfying the vigilance criterion:

$$\frac{|I \wedge W_j|}{|I|} \geq \rho \; ; \; 0 \leq \rho \leq 1 \qquad (1)$$

If the node j does not satisfy the vigilance criterion, it will be reset and the search is repeated until a satisfactory category k is found. Learning occurs using the following formula:

$$W_k = \beta(I \wedge W_k) + (1-\beta)W_k \qquad (2)$$

In this paper, β is taken to be one (fast learning) and the learning parameter α is taken to be very small value $\cong 0$. Properties of learning for big values of α were developed in [5]
The effect of the order of pattern presentation is discussed in [3, 4] .

II. ART CATEGORY CHOICE

The category choice of the ART networks is given by the following formula:

$$T_j(I) = \frac{|I \wedge W_j|}{\alpha + |W_j|} \qquad (3)$$

Where:
1. the learning parameter α is a very small number
$$T_j(I) \approx \frac{|I \wedge W_j|}{|W_j|}$$

2. I is the input pattern which have been preprocessed as follows:
- **Normalization.** For example: $I = \frac{I}{I_{\max}}$ (every component of I $\in$ [0,1]).
- **Complement coding.** Augmenting the M-dimensional vector I to 2M- dimensional vector I=(I1,I2,…,IM,1-I1,1-I2,…,1-IM) .

3. Wj represents the 2M-dimensional hyper rectangle. It is shown in Fig. 1 and it can be written in the following form:

$$W_j = (I1 \wedge I2, (I1 \vee I2)^c) \qquad (4)$$
where
$$I1 \wedge I2 = \min(I1, I2) \qquad (5)$$
$$I1 \vee I2 = \max(I1, I2) \qquad (6)$$
$$I^C = 1 - I \qquad (7)$$

From Fig. 1 (M=2), W_j can be written as:

$$W_j = (I_{11}, I_{12}, 1 - I_{21}, 1 - I_{22}) \qquad (8)$$

The category choice equation can be interpreted for the following 3 cases:

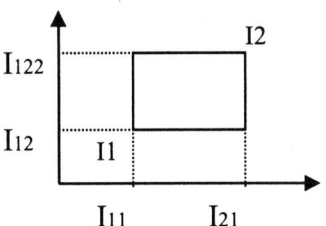

Fig. 1. A weight vector with endpoints I1 and I2.

Case1: No complement coding

In this case, the input vector and the weight vector are M-dimensional vectors. It can be seen from Fig. 2 (M=2) that:

$$I \wedge W_j = J = (I_{21}, I_2) \qquad (9)$$

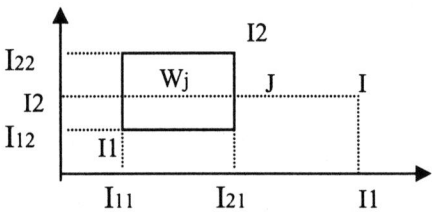

Fig. 2. Representation of I ∧ Wj by J

The category choice Tj(I) represents a ratio of areas as shown in Fig. 3.

$$T_j(I) = \frac{|I \wedge W_j|}{|W_j|} = \frac{A2}{A1} \qquad (10)$$

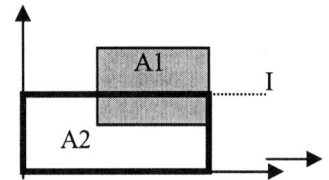

Fig. 3. Representation of the category choice when no complement coding is used.

The problem with using this category choice is even when I moves away from the rectangle as shown in Fig. 3, the category choice will remain the same. A better approach in this case is to use the L-1 norm which is defined as follows:

$$T_j(I) = d(I, W_j) = \sum_{i=1}^{M} |I_i - W_j^*| \qquad (11)$$

Where W_j^* is the closest point to I on the rectangle. For example, W_j^* is shown in Figure 4 and it can be proven as follows:

$I_i \succ J_i$ for any $J_i \in W_j$
$\Rightarrow d(I, W_j)$ is minimum when J_i is maximum $\Rightarrow$
$J_i = W_j^*$.

Using the L-1 norm, the category choice will increase if I will move away from the rectangle.

Case2: With complement coding

In this case, the input vector and the weight vector are 2M-dimensional vectors. In Fig. 2, the input vectors I and Wj are represented as follows:

$$I = (I_1, I_2, 1-I_1, 1-I_2) \qquad (12)$$

$$W_j = (I_{11}, I_{12}, 1-I_{21}, 1-I_{22}) \qquad (13)$$

$$I \wedge W_j = (I_{11}, I_{12}, 1-I_1, 1-I_{22}) \qquad (14)$$

$$|W_j| = I_{11} + I_{12} + 1 - I_{21} + 1 - I_{22} \qquad (15)$$

$$|I \wedge W_j| = I_{11} + I_{12} + 1 - I_1 + 1 - I_{22} \qquad (16)$$

$$T_j(I) = \frac{I_{11} + I_{12} + 1 - I_1 + 1 - I_{22}}{I_{11} + I_{12} + 1 - I_{21} + 1 - I_{22}} \qquad (17)$$

|Wj| can be represented by Fig. 5.

|I∧Wj| is represented by Fig. 6.

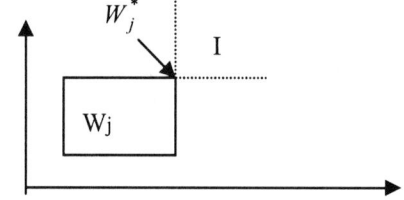

Fig. 4. The closest point to I using the L1-norm.

The category choice Tj(I) can be represented by how much the rectangles (I1,1,I22,1) and (I21,1,I22,1) in Fig. 6 are overlapped. As I moves away from Wj, the rectangle (I1,1,I22,1) will decrease its size and Tj(I) is going to be decreased and vice versa. Tj(I) can proven to be equivalent to the L-1 norm as follows: Any 2 points I and J with same L-1 norm with respect to the rectangle Wj will have the same values of Tj(I). For example, given the configuration shown in Fig. 7.

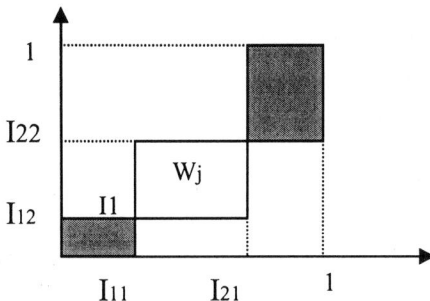

Fig. 5. Representation of |Wj| by the gray rectangles.

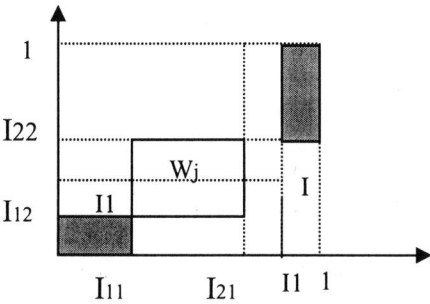

Fig. 6. Representation of |I ∧ Wj| by the gray rectangles.

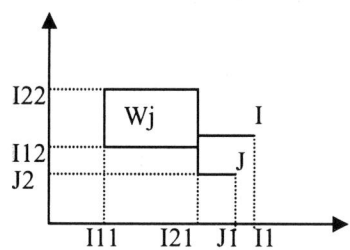

Fig. 7. I and J have the same L-1 norm with respect to Wj

$$d(I, W_j) = I_1 - I_{21} \tag{18}$$
$$d(J, W_j) = J_1 - I_{21} + I_{12} - J_2 \tag{19}$$
$$T_j(I) = \frac{I_{11} + I_{12} + 1 - I_1 + 1 - I_{22}}{I_{11} + I_{12} + 1 - I_{21} + 1 - I_{22}} \tag{20}$$
$$T_j(J) = \frac{I_{11} + J_2 + 1 - J_1 + 1 - I_{22}}{I_{11} + I_{12} + 1 - I_{21} + 1 - I_{22}} \tag{21}$$
$$T_j(I) = T_j(j) \Leftrightarrow d(I, W_j) = d(J, W_j) \tag{22}$$

This proof can be generalized to include the position of any 2 points with respect to the rectangle Wj.

Case3: More than one rectangle and with complement coding.

In this case, the category choice does not depend only on the position of the point with respect to each rectangle but also to the size of the rectangle. The L-1 norm is equivalent to Tj(I) when the rectangles are of equal sizes. For example consider the 2 1-dimensional rectangles W1=(I1,1-I2), W2=(J1,1-J2) and the point I=(I,1-I). This is shown in Fig. 8.

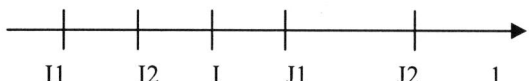

Fig. 8. Representation of 2 1-dimensional rectangles.

Given that I is of equal L-1 norm to W1 and W2

$$I = \frac{J_1 + I_2}{2} \tag{23}$$

The category choices of I with respect to W1 and W2 are given by:

$$T_1(I) = \frac{I_1 + 1 - I}{I_1 + 1 - I_2} \tag{24}$$
$$T_2(I) = \frac{I + 1 - J_2}{J_1 + 1 - J_2} \tag{25}$$
$$T_1(I) = T_2(I) \Leftrightarrow J_2 - J_1 = I_2 - I_1 \tag{26}$$

Fig. 9 shows the results of applying the category choice Tj(I) (bottom line) and the L-1 norm (upper line) for 2 rectangles :W1:(I1=0,I2=0.4) and W2(J1=0.9,J2=1). The (o) represents that W1 is the winner and the (x) represents that W2 is the winner.

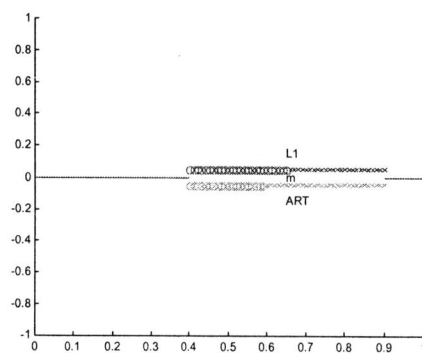

Fig. 9. ART and L-1 results.

Fig. 9 shows that for the Fuzzy ART some data (for example I=0.6) which is closer to W1 than to W2 is assigned for class2. This is due to the effect of the size of the rectangles. This effect can be introduced in the L-1 norm in order to have the following modified L-1 distance measure:

$$dn(I, W_j) = d(I, W_j) |R_j|^p \tag{27}$$

Where:

$d(I, W_j)$ is the L-1 norm

$|R_j|$ is the size of rectangle Wj

$0 \leq p \leq 1$

Fig. 10 shows the effect of using this modified distance measure for p=0.3. The same results were obtained.

III. FUZZY ART WITH MODIFIED L-1 NORM

The weight vector consists of the coordinates of the endpoints of each rectangle. For example in Fig. 11, the weight is represented by Wj=(Wj1,Wj2,Wj3,Wj4).
No complement coding or normalization is needed.
The category choice function is the modified L-1 norm (Equation (27)) where the L-1 norm formula is implemented using the following formula:

$$T_j(I) = \sum_{i=1}^{M} (\text{sgn}((W_{j,k} - I_i)(W_{j,k+1} - I_i)))(\wedge(|W_{j,k} - I_i|, |W_{j,k+1} - I_i|))$$
$$k = 2i - 1 \tag{28}$$

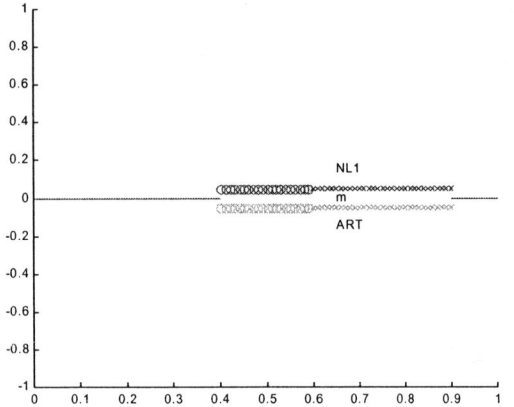

Fig. 10. Fuzzy ART and the modified L-1 norm results.

Where

$$\text{sgn}(x) = \begin{cases} 1 & x > 0 \\ 0 & x \leq 0 \end{cases} \tag{29}$$

$$\wedge(a,b) = \min(a,b) \tag{30}$$

Equation (28) can be shown when M=2. It becomes:

$$T_j(I) = \text{sgn}((W_{j1} - I_1)(W_{j2} - I_1))(\wedge(|W_{j1} - I_1|, |W_{j2} - I_1|))$$
$$+ \text{sgn}((W_{j3} - I_2)(W_{j4} - I_2))(\wedge(|W_{j3} - I_2|, |W_{j2} - I_2|))$$

Looking at Fig. 11:

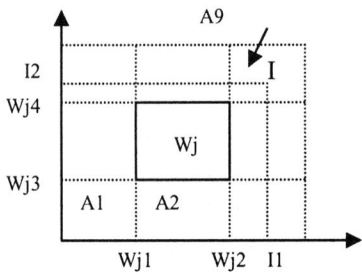

Fig. 11. Position of the input pattern I with respect to the rectangle Wj.

The input pattern I can be in any of the 9 areas A1 to A9 with respect to the rectangle Wj including the area A5 where I is inside the rectangle.

For example if I is in A9 (Fig. 11), the Hamming distance from I to Wj is:

$$d(I, W_j) = |W_{j2} - I_1| + |W_{j4} - I_2| \tag{31}$$

If we apply Equation (28):

$$\text{sgn}((W_{j1} - I_1)(W_{j2} - I_1)) = 1$$
$$\text{sgn}((W_{j3} - I_2)(W_{j4} - I_2)) = 1$$
$$\wedge(|W_{j1} - I_1|, |W_{j2} - I_1|) = |W_{j2} - I_1|$$
$$\wedge(|W_{j3} - I_2|, |W_{j4} - I_2|) = |W_{j4} - I_2|$$
$$\Rightarrow T_j(I) = d(I, W_j)$$

If I is in A2, the Hamming distance from I to Wj is:

$$d(I, W_j) = |W_{j3} - I_2| \tag{32}$$

If we apply Equation (28):

$$\text{sgn}((W_{j1}-I_1)(W_{j2}-I_1)) = 0$$
$$\text{sgn}((W_{j3}-I_2)(W_{j4}-I_2)) = 1$$
$$\wedge(|W_{j3}-I_2|,|W_{j4}-I_2|) = |W_{j3}-I_2|$$
$$\Rightarrow T_j(I) = d(I,W_j)$$

We can prove the validity of Equation (28) for all the other areas including the case where the input is inside the rectangle (area A5) where the category choice becomes zero.

The weight update formulas are the following:

$$W_{jknew} = \wedge(W_{jk}\wedge I_k, W_{jk+1}\wedge I_k, W_{jk}\vee I_k, W_{jk+1}\vee I_k) \quad (33)$$
$$W_{jk+1new} = \vee(W_{jk}\wedge I_k, W_{jk+1}\wedge I_k, W_{jk}\vee I_k, W_{jk+1}\vee I_k) \quad (34)$$
$$k = 1,3,5,....,2M-1$$

$$\vee(a,b,c,d) = \max(a,b,c,d) \quad (35)$$

The vigilance criterion is given by:

$$\begin{cases} |W|_{new} \leq \rho & \text{resonance} \\ |W|_{new} > \rho & \text{reset} \end{cases} \quad (36)$$

For example, looking at Fig. 12 and applying Equations (33) and (34) the new rectangle is shown in Fig. 13.

$$W_{j1}\wedge I_1 = W_{j1}, W_{j2}\wedge I_1 = W_{j2}$$
$$W_{j1}\vee I_1 = I_1, W_{j2}\vee I_1 = I_1$$
$$W_{j3}\wedge I_2 = I_2, W_{j4}\wedge I_2 = I_2$$
$$W_{j3}\vee I_2 = W_{j3}, W_{j4}\vee I_2 = W_{j4}$$
$$\Rightarrow W_{j1new} = \wedge(W_{j1},W_{j2}) = W_{j1}$$
$$W_{j2new} = \vee(I_1,I_1) = I_1$$
$$W_{j3new} = \wedge(I_2,I_2) = I_2$$
$$W_{j4new} = \vee(W_{j3},W_{j4}) = W_{j4}$$

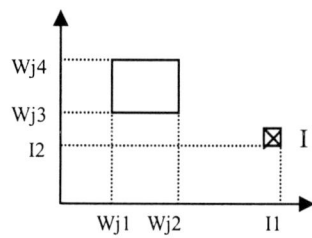

Fig. 12. Example of the weight update formula

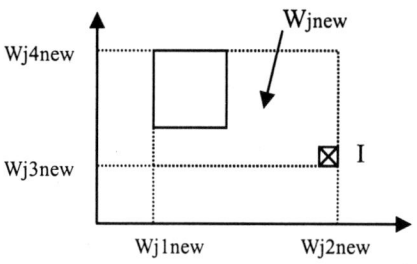

Fig. 13. Representation of the new size rectangle.

IV. SIMULATION RESULTS

The data (0,0),(1,1),(3,3),(4,4),(5,5),(6,6) are submitted to the modified network without any preprocessing stage and the following results were obtained for $\rho=0,5,10,15$. Six rectangles were formed for $\rho=0$; 3 rectangles for $\rho=5$; 2 rectangles for $\rho=10$; and 1 rectangle for $\rho=15$.

V. CONCLUSIONS

In this paper, the relationship between the category choice of the Fuzzy ART and the L-1 norm is presented. It was shown that the category choice $T_j(I)$ and the L-1 norm are equivalent for one rectangle. For more than one rectangle, the category choice can be replaced by a modified L-1 norm taking into account the size of each rectangle. Fuzzy ART requires 2 preprocessing stages: complement coding and normalization of the input patterns. These 2 stages can be eliminated using the modified version of the L-1 norm presented in this paper.

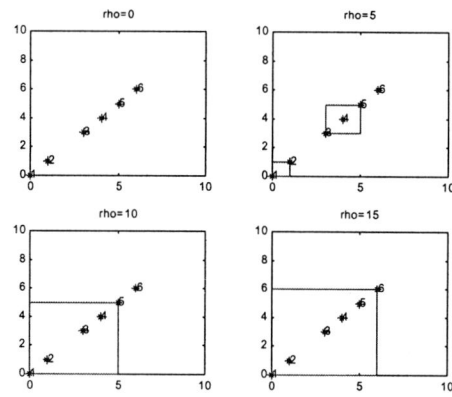

Fig. 14. Clustering non-normalized data with the modified L-1 norm.

REFERENCES

[1] Carpenter G.A., Grossberg S., and Rosen D.B. Fuzzy ART: Fast stable learning and categorization of analog

patterns by an adaptive resonance system, *Neural Networks*, 1992, pp. 4, 759-771.

[2] Carpenter G.A., and Gjaja M.N. (1994): Fuzzy ART choice functions. *Proceedings of the world congress on Neural Networks,* pp. 1713-1722, San Diego, CA.

[3] Dagher I., Georgiopoulos M., Heileman G.L, and Bebis G. An Ordering Algorithm for Pattern presentation in Fuzzy ARTMAP that tends to improve generalization performance. *IEEE Transactions on Neural Networks, 1999,* pp. 768-778.

[4] Dagher I., Georgiopoulos M., Heileman G.L, and Bebis G., ``Fuzzy ARTVar: An improved Fuzzy ARTMAP algorithm, IJCNN-98, Vol. 3, pp. 1688-1693 Alaska, AK, 1998.

[5] M. Georgiopoulos, I. Dagher, G. L. Heileman, and G. Bebis, ``Properties of learning of a Fuzzy ART Variant, "Neural Networks; Vol. 12, No 6, July 1999, pp. 837-850.

[6] Grossberg S. (1976). Adaptive pattern recognition and universal recoding II: Feedback, expectation, olfaction, and illusions. *Biological Cybernetics*, 4(1), pp. 9-20.

[7] Huang J., Georgiopoulos M., and Hielman G.L. (1995). Fuzzy ART properties. *Neural Networks*, 8(2):203-213.

[8] Park D., and Dagher I. (1994): Gradient Based Fuzzy C-means Algorithm. *IEEE International Conference on Neural Networks.* Pages1626-1631, Orlando, FL

[9] Simpson P.K. (1992): Fuzzy min-max neural networks-Part2:Clustering. *IEEE Transactions on Fuzzy Systems*, pp. 32-45

Fuzzy ARTMAP with Relevance Factor

Răzvan Andonie
Department of Electronics and Computers
Transylvania University of Braşov
Email: andonie@deltanet.ro

Lucian Sasu
Department of Computer Science
Transylvania University of Braşov
Email: lmsasu@unitbv.ro

Valeriu Beiu
School of EE and CS
Washington State University, Pullman
Email: vbeiu@eecs.wsu.edu

Abstract— An incremental, nonparametric probability estimation procedure using a variation of the Fuzzy ARTMAP (FAM) neural network is introduced. The resulted network, called Fuzzy ARTMAP with Relevance factor (FAMR), uses a relevance factor assigned to each sample pair, proportional to the importance of the respective pair during the learning phase. Experimental results have shown that FAMR favorably compares with FAM and Probabilistic FAM (PFAM, defined in [1], [2]), both as a classifier and as a probability estimator.

I. INTRODUCTION

When designing and implementing data mining applications for large data sets, we face processing time and memory space problems. In this case, incremental learning is a very attractive feature. According to [3], we define an *incremental learning* algorithm as one that meets the following criteria:

1) It should be able to learn additional information from new data.
2) It should not require access to the original data, used to train the existing system.
3) It should preserve previously acquired knowledge.
4) It should be able to accommodate new data categories that may be introduced with new data.

The fundamental issue in incremental learning is: how can a learning system adapt to new information without corrupting or forgetting previously learned information – the so-called *stability-plasticity* dilemma addressed by Carpenter and Grossberg [4].

In the context of supervised training, incremental learning means learning each input-output sample pair, without keeping it for subsequent processing.

The topic addressed in this paper is the development of a supervised incremental learning algorithm satisfying all of the above-mentioned criteria. Very few algorithms perfectly fit into this description of incremental learning. The FAM family of neural networks, having the roots in Carpenter, Grossberg, Markuzon, Reynolds, and Rosen's seminal paper [5] is the best known example. A more recent neural network having this strong property is described by Polikar, Udpa, Udpa, and Honovar [3].

Many pattern recognition applications require an estimate of the *posterior* probability $P(C|\mathbf{a})$, where C is a class index and $\mathbf{a}$ is an input pattern. This task also allows classification because one can select the class C with the maximum conditional probability.

The present paper only deals with the posterior probability estimation from data samples in supervised incremental learning systems based on FAM architectures. Such procedures have been developed by Carpenter, Grossberg, and Reynolds [6], and Marriott and Harrison [7].

Lim and Harrison's PFAM [1], [2] is a hybrid FAM + Probabilistic Neural Network (PNN, see [8]) classifier with incremental probability estimation capabilities. It uses the PNN's ability to incrementally construct an approximation of the probability density functions (pdf) and it also uses the code compression feature of FAM. Instead of considering every sample pattern in estimating pdf, the clustering property of FAM is used to obtain the centroid of each cluster. The pdf approximation is made based on these centroids only.

This paper introduces a variation of the probability estimation phase of FAM and identifies the resulted network as FAMR to distinguish it from the original architecture. FAMR is an incremental learning system for general classification and nonparametric estimation of the probability that an input belongs to a given class. The architecture of the network is able to incrementally 'grow' and to sequentially accommodate input-output sample pairs. Each training pair has a *relevance factor* assigned to it. This factor is proportional to the importance of the respective pair in the learning process. Using a relevance factor adds more flexibility to the training phase, allowing ranking of sample pairs according to the confidence we have in the information source. The training sequence may include sample pairs from sources with different levels of noise.

Experimental results have demonstrated that FAMR favorably compares with FAM and PFAM, both as a classifier and as a probability estimator.

In Section II, we briefly discuss how the FAM architecture was used for probability estimation. Section III introduces our modification of the FAM algorithm. In Section IV we present the experimental results comparing the FAMR model to FAM and PFAM. Section V concludes with some closing remarks.

II. FAM AS AN INCREMENTAL PROBABILITY ESTIMATOR

Carpenter, Grossberg, and Reynolds' FAM [6] can estimate posterior probabilities via formation and associations between intermediate categories. We present here only the necessary details.

FAM includes a pair of ART modules (ART_a and ART_b) that create stable recognition categories in response to arbitrary sequences of input patterns. These modules are linked by an inter-ART module called Mapfield whose purpose is to determine whether the correct mapping has been established from inputs to outputs or not. The ART_a and ART_b vigilance parameters ρ_a, respectively ρ_b, control the matching mechanism inside the modules.

During learning, FAM updates its Mapfield weights to estimate the probability that an input belongs to a given output class: the strength of the weight projecting from the selected ART_a category to the correct ART_b category is increased, while the strength of the weights to other ART_b categories are decreased. A Mapfield vigilance parameter ρ_{ab} calibrates the degree of predictive mismatch, necessary to trigger the search for a different ART_a category. If the weight projecting from the active ART_a category through the Mapfield to the active ART_b category is smaller than ρ_{ab} (vigilance test), then the system responds to the unexpected outcome through the so-called *match tracking*, that triggers an ART_a search for a new input category.

Once an ART_a category J is chosen, whose prediction of the correct ART_b category is strong enough, match tracking is disengaged, and the network is said to be in a resonance state. In this case, Mapfield learns by updating the weights of associations between ART_a and ART_b categories. According to this updating scheme, weight w_{jk}^{ab} is a non-decreasing function of the frequency of associations between the jth ART_a category and the kth ART_b category during the training phase.

This last feature is made more explicit in PROBART [7], where Mapfield weight w_{jk}^{ab} is exactly the frequency of associations between the jth ART_a category and the kth ART_b category. Therefore, $w_{jk}^{ab}/|\mathbf{w}_j^{ab}|$ is the empirical estimate of the posterior probability $P(k|j)$ that ART_a category j is associated to ART_b category k.

III. THE FAMR ALGORITHM

A. A probability estimation procedure

A stochastic approximation procedure described in [9] is introduced and new theoretical results are developed. Let us consider a sequence of independent experiments according to the finite probability distribution $P(a_1),\ldots,P(a_n)$, where $P(a_i) \geq 0$ is the probability of outcome a_i, $\sum_{i=1}^n P(a_i) = 1$. These *objective probabilities* are not known and will be estimated at each step based on the previous observations. A criterion for a qualitative differentiation of the experiments is represented by the relevance associated to each experiment. The *relevance* q_t is a real positive finite number directly proportional to the importance of the experiment considered at step t ($t = 1, 2, \ldots$). This number may be either of objective or subjective nature.

The following estimation procedure makes use of both the results and the relevances of the present, and previous experiments.

The *subjective probability* of outcome a_i ($i = 1, \ldots, n$) at step t ($t = 1, 2, \ldots$) is given by:

$$w_t(a_i) = \frac{\left(q_0 w_0(a_i) + \sum_{s=1}^t q_s \delta_s(a_i)\right)}{Q_t} \quad (1)$$

where: if at step t we get outcome a_j, $\delta_t(a_j) = 1$ and $\delta_t(a_i) = 0$ for $j \neq i$; $w_0(a_i) \geq 0$ is the initial subjective probability, $\sum_{i=1}^n w_0(a_i) = 1$; $q_0 \geq 0$ is the initial relevance, and $Q_t = \sum_{s=0}^t q_s$.

At each step t ($t = 0, 1, \ldots$) we have a probability vector with $w_t(a_i) \geq 0$ ($i = 1, \ldots, n$), $\sum_{i=1}^n w_t(a_i) = 1$.

Relation (1) can be rewritten in a recursive form:

$$w_t(a_i) = w_{t-1}(a_i) + A_t(\delta_t(a_i) - w_{t-1}(a_i)) \quad (2)$$

where $A_t = q_t/Q_t$ ($t = 1, 2, \ldots$). The following result is from [9]:

Theorem 1: $w_t(a_i) \xrightarrow{t} P(a_i)$ in probability iff $Q_t \xrightarrow{t} \infty$.

Consequently, $w_t(a_i)$ is a correct biased estimator of $P(a_i)$ iff $Q_t \to \infty$. Further analysis of the estimate can be made if we compute the mean square error:

$$\alpha_t(a_i) = (1 - A_t)^2 \alpha_{t-1}(a_i) + P(a_i)(1 - P(a_i)) A_t^2 \quad (3)$$

where $\alpha_t(a_i) = E(w_t(a_i) - P(a_i))^2$. This expression gives us the possibility of evaluating the rate of convergence.

For some additional conditions imposed to q_t, the direct result can be strengthened:

Theorem 2: If $q_0 \in [0, b]$, $q_t \in [a, b]$ ($t = 1, 2, \ldots$), for two real values $0 < a \leq b < \infty$, then $w_t(a_i) \xrightarrow{t} P(a_i)$ with probability one.

Sketch of proof: Equation (2) can be rewritten as a Robbins–Monroe process. The proof is based on the Stochastic Approximation Theorem.

In practice, the above restriction imposed to q_t does not restrict our estimation procedure. The meaning of the conditions in the previous theorems is: an observer who intends to learn objective probabilities from examples has to have sufficient confidence in the results of the experiences.

Let $w_t^{(n)}(a_i)$ be the subjective probabilities at step t ($t = 1, 2, \ldots$), for n possible outcomes. What is happening if at some step we get a new outcome, a_{n+1}? Assuming we have $w_0^{(n)}(a_i) = 1/n$ ($i = 1, \ldots, n$), then the new subjective probabilities $w_t^{(n+1)}(a_i)$ for $n+1$ possible outcomes may be obtained by the following relations:

$$\begin{aligned} w_t^{(n+1)}(a_{n+1}) &= q_0/(n+1)Q_t \\ w_t^{(n+1)}(a_i) &= w_t^{(n)}(a_i) - w_t^{(n+1)}(a_{n+1})/n, \; i = 1, 2, \ldots, n \end{aligned} \quad (4)$$

Relations (4) will be used in the dynamic allocation of ART_b categories (*Step 2* in Algorithm 1.)

B. The FAM modification

A modification of the FAM, named FAMR, that enhances the probability estimation ability of FAM is presented.

Mapfield weight w_{jk}^{ab} can be considered an estimate of the posterior probability $P(k|j)$. This enables us to use formula (2) to update the weights w_{jk}^{ab}:

$$w_{Jk}^{ab(new)} = \begin{cases} w_{jk}^{ab(old)} & \text{if } j \neq J \\ w_{JK}^{ab(old)} + A_t(1 - w_{JK}^{ab(old)}) & \\ w_{Jk}^{ab(old)}(1 - A_t) & \text{if } k \neq K \end{cases} \quad (5)$$

Is w_{jk}^{ab} a good estimate of $P(I_\mathbf{b}|I_\mathbf{a})$, where $I_\mathbf{a}$ and $I_\mathbf{b}$ are intervals based around input pattern **a** and output pattern **b**, respectively? As depicted by Marriott and Harrison the feedback via match tracking alters this estimation [7]. One way to avoid this problem is to eliminate match tracking. This approach is used in PROBART and ensures that a given input to ART_a will always select the same category. Meanwhile, eliminating match tracking allows for one-to-many mapping between ART_a and ART_b categories, which may be important in situations where more than one action result from a single input [7].

If the conditions in Theorem 2 are fulfilled and match tracking is not used, then for each ART_a category j ($j = 1, \ldots, N_a$) and each ART_b category k ($k = 1, \ldots, N_b$) we have:

$$w_{jk}^{ab} \to P(k|j) \text{ with probability one.} \quad (6)$$

Match tracking can be avoided by setting $\rho_{ab} = 0$. Eliminating match tracking is not always convenient, because match tracking controls category proliferation in ART_a. On the other hand, one could hardly say anything about this probability approximation in the presence of match tracking, since in this case w_{jk}^{ab} is not necessarily a good estimate of the posterior probability with respect to the already processed data. A smaller value for ρ_{ab} results in a better approximation. For $\rho_{ab} = 0$ the approximation is statistically correct. However, in our experiments, match tracking has not significantly altered probability estimation.

Let **Q** be the vector $[Q_1 \ldots Q_{N_a}]$. N_a and N_b are the number of categories in ART_a and ART_b, initialized to 0, respectively. For incremental learning of one training pair, the new procedure in Mapfield is given in Algorithm 1.

Since we initialize the weights w_{jk}^{ab} with $1/N_b$ and not with 1, we have to modify the vigilance test. The new test is:

$$N_b\, w_{JK}^{ab} \geq \rho_{ab} \quad (7)$$

The rest of the FAM mechanism remains unchanged. The resulted algorithm will be called FAMR (Fuzzy Artmap with Relevance factor.) In [10], we have introduced a probability estimator based on a restricted FAMR version, where estimated probabilities are strictly positive.

For $\rho_{ab} = 0$ (no match tracking), $q_0 = 0$, $q_t = q$, $0 < q < \infty$ ($t = 1, 2, \ldots$), probability estimate w_{jk}^{ab} is exactly the empirical estimate of the posterior probability $P(k|j)$. This can be observed from the nonrecursive formula (1). Therefore, PROBART is a particular case of FAMR.

In our experiments, since we have used relatively large training sets, the influence of the initial values (probabilities and relevance) was insignificant. We have set $q_0 = 1$ for all experiments. The initial probabilities in Algorithm 1 are equal. Generally, the initial values can influence the stability of the system (i.e., how fast it learns), especially for the first iterations.

Step 1. Accept vector pair (**a**, **b**) with relevance factor q.
Step 2. If necessary, create category K in ART_b:
 $N_b = N_b + 1$
 $K = N_b$
 if $N_b > 1$ **then**
  $w_{jK}^{ab} = \frac{q_0}{N_b Q_j}$ for $j = 1, \ldots, N_a$
  {append new component to $\mathbf{w}_j^{ab}$}
  $w_{jk}^{ab} = w_{jk}^{ab} - \frac{w_{jK}^{ab}}{N_b - 1}$ for $k = 1, \ldots, K-1$,
  $j = 1, \ldots N_a$ {normalize}
 endif
Step 3. If necessary, create category J in ART_a:
 $N_a = N_a + 1$
 $J = N_a$
 $Q_J = q_0$ {append new component to **Q**}
 $w_{Jk}^{ab} = 1/N_b$ for $k = 1, \ldots, N_b$
 {append new line to $\mathbf{w}^{ab}$}
Step 4. J, K are winners or new added nodes.
 if vigilance test (7) is passed **then**
  {learn in Mapfield}
  $Q_J = Q_J + q$
  $w_{JK}^{ab} = w_{JK}^{ab} + \frac{q}{Q_J}(1 - w_{JK}^{ab})$
  $w_{Jk}^{ab} = w_{Jk}^{ab}\left(1 - \frac{q}{Q_J}\right)$ for $k = 1, \ldots, N_b$, $k \neq K$
 else
  perform match tracking and restart from step 3
 endif

Algorithm 1: **One iteration in the new Mapfield algorithm**

C. Application areas of the relevance factor

Ranking the importance of training examples in neural computing has been considered by several authors. Gallant uses an importance factor attached to each training sample [11]. Proportional to the importance factor, additional duplicates of each training sample are created.

In FAMR, using a relevance factor is not equivalent to repeatedly present a training sample to the system: the variation of w_{JK}^{ab} values is finer than in the case of repeating the presentation of the training pair, since the relevance factor can be a real value. Second, learning is faster, because we can learn in one step instead of repeatedly learning the same pair.

How to assign a relevance factor to a training sample? An answer could reside in ranking the sample pairs according to the (subjective) confidence we have in the information source. Two application areas are considered for such learning systems with relevance factor:

1. When training neural networks with noisy data, a relevance factor could be assigned to each learning pattern, inversely proportional to the noise. Let us suppose that we have a training sequence consisting of two sample pairs: ($\mathbf{a}_1 = 0.1, class\_index(\mathbf{a}_1) = 1$) with $q_1 = 1$, and ($\mathbf{a}_2 = 0.3, class\_index(\mathbf{a}_2) = 2$) with $q_2 = 1$. We assume that $class\_index(\mathbf{a}_1)$ is a correct association, whereas $class\_index(\mathbf{a}_2)$ is a noisy association (that should be 1.) After two iterations in the FAMR algorithm, assuming that

only one ART_a category is generated, the new probability vector will be

$$\mathbf{w}_1^{ab} = [0.5 \; 0.5] \quad (8)$$

If we perform FAMR training with $q_1 = 2$ and $q_2 = 1$ (the first pair is more relevant than the second one), we obtain:

$$\mathbf{w}_1^{ab} = [0.62 \; 0.37] \quad (9)$$

Let us classify pattern $\mathbf{a}_2$. The second trained network makes a better prediction, indicating class 1 with the highest probability. In this example, the relevance factor acts as a noise filter.

2. Training pairs are usually randomly selected. However, it seems reasonable to expect that if correctly classified examples are chosen near the decision boundaries then the classifier will learn the boundaries better. This conjecture has not been significantly explored, most probably because the true boundaries are usually unknown at the beginning of the training. Assuming we can generate points close to the boundary, we could assign a relative higher relevance factor to this samples. There are experimental results reported [12] showing that choosing examples from the boundary area does not necessarily lead to better classification performances. That remains an open area for further investigation.

IV. Experiments and Results

A suite of experiments were performed to test the FAMR's ability for probability estimation and classification, compared to FAM and PFAM. The classification was made based on the probability estimation by hard-decision: an input pattern belongs to the category with maximum posterior probability. The performance of the probability estimator was quantified by an average Brier score. The Brier score measures the quality of the probability estimation by comparing it to the real conditional probability [6]. The score $u(q, p)$ is a function of the estimated probability q and the true probability p:

$$u(q, p) = 1 - (q - p)^2 \quad (10)$$

We have used only incremental learning, though the network is able to improve its performance using off-line processing, when the training set is reprocessed, or using Multiple Classifier Systems. Unless otherwise specified, the used relevance factor was 1. In the prediction phase, we took $\rho_a = 0$; thus, any input pattern is assigned to an ART_a category and subsequently to an output class.

A. Circle-in-the-square

This problem requires a system to identify which points of a square lie inside and which lie outside a circle whose area equals half that of the square. Patterns were generated inside the square using an uniform distribution for each coordinate. The points were classified according to their position relative to the circle, whose center coincides with the center of the square. Thus we have two classes of points: points located inside the circle and points located outside the circle. For computing the Brier score, 1000000 evenly spaced points were generated inside the square.

TABLE I

Circle-in-the-square: Average values of ART_a categories number and test set recognition rate for FAMR compared to results from [5]. The FAMR results represent average values for 5 different training sets.

Train size	ART_a categories number		Test set recognition rate (%)	
	FAMR	Carpenter [5]	FAMR	Carpenter [5]
1000	18.2	21	93.0	92.5
10000	45.2	50	96.8	96.7
100000	111.6	121	98.1	98.0

The training sets contained 1000, 10000, and 100000 patterns. The test set consisted of 100000 patterns in each case. For each training set size, five different training sets were generated and the average Brier score was computed at the end of every training phase. The number of ART_a categories was at most as large as reported in [5], but the performance was superior. The results for the three training sets are presented in Table I. As expected, the test set recognition rate and the Brier score increased with the number of training patterns from an average value of 93.0% and 0.9327 (for 1000 training patterns) to 98.1% and 0.9810, respectively (for 100000 training patterns.)

B. Noisy circle-in-the-square

We used a modified version of the circle-in-the-square problem in order to test the effectiveness of the relevance factor. We considered three data sources (called A, B, C), each of them producing the same number of training samples. Each source has an associated probability (p_A, p_B, and p_C, respectively) of producing wrong associations. We took $(p_A, p_B, p_C) = (0, 0.2, 0.35)$. First, the relevance factor q_t was set to 1, for each information source. The average Brier score obtained for 6 different data sets was 0.89568. Subsequently, we considered different relevance factors, in accordance to the noise level of the three sources: $(q_A, q_B, q_C) = (100, 10, 1)$, where q_X is the relevance factor associated with the data source X. The average Brier score obtained for the 6 different data sets was 0.91896, higher than the previous case (Table II.) The total number of training patterns was 10000 for each experiment, and the Brier score was computed for 10000 points evenly distributed inside the square.

Correlating the relevance factors to the degree of confidence in each data source resulted in higher performances for the system. The relatively small value of the average Brier score is explained by the presence of noise.

In order to prove the advantage of taking into account supplementary data sources, though these sources were noisy, we developed another experiment. This experiment proved more relevant when the number of available correct training samples was relatively small. First, we have generated 1000 associations using three data sources (A, B, C), each with the same probability of producing training patterns, $(p_A, p_B, p_C) = (0, 0.2, 0.35)$, and $(q_A, q_B, q_C) = (100, 10, 1)$. The average Brier score for different training sets was 0.88370

TABLE II

AVERAGE BRIER SCORE FOR NOISY CIRCLE–IN–THE–SQUARE ASSOCIATIONS. $(p_A, p_B, p_C) = (0, 0.2, 0.35)$, WHERE p_X IS THE PROBABILITY THAT DATA SOURCE X GIVES WRONG ASSOCIATIONS. q_X IS THE RELEVANCE FACTOR ASSOCIATED WITH DATA SOURCE X.

Test	Average Brier score	
no.	$(q_A, q_B, q_C) = (100, 10, 1)$	$(q_A, q_B, q_C) = (1, 1, 1)$
1	0.92164	0.89810
2	0.91672	0.89251
3	0.93540	0.90876
4	0.91018	0.88908
5	0.91298	0.89215
6	0.91682	0.89346
Average	0.91896	0.89568

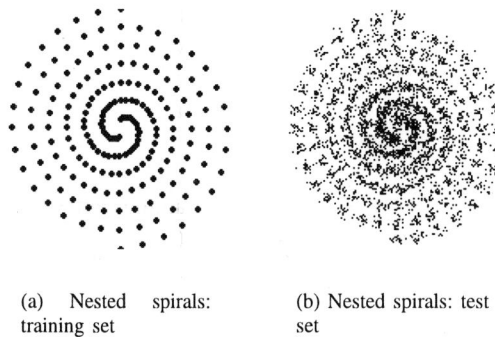

(a) Nested spirals: training set

(b) Nested spirals: test set

Fig. 1. Two nested spirals

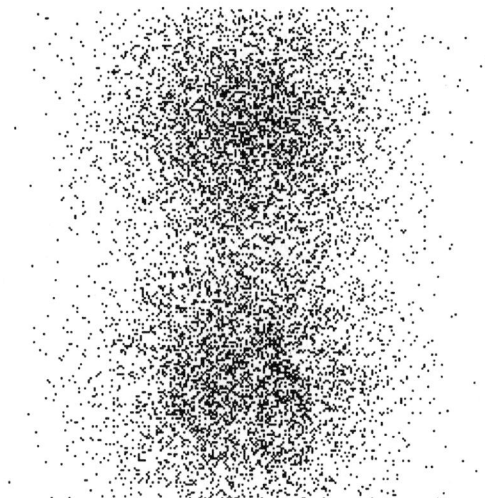

Fig. 2. Two bidimensional overlapping Gaussian distributions.

for 1000 training patterns, above 0.88033, the value obtained when using only the 1000/3 correct samples from source A to train the FAMR.

C. Learning to tell two spirals apart

The two spirals [13] make three complete turns in the plane, totaling 194 points (the training set.) For the test set, we added Gaussian noise centered in each point, with standard deviation 0.1. The train and the test set are represented in Fig. 1(a) and Fig. 1(b), respectively.

Each Gaussian cluster contains 20 points giving a total number of 3880 test patterns. The number of ART_a categories is 82, and the test set recognition rate has an average value of 94.55% (using five differents test sets), while the clusters are fairly close. As justified in [6], the Brier score is an underestimate of FAMR performance because it does not reflect the network's ability of recomposing the complex underlying geometrical shape.

D. Two Gaussians

This test [6] consists of estimating the posterior probability of input patterns from two normally distributed overlapping classes (Fig. 2.) The input points are located inside the unit square and they are drawn from two Gaussian distributions centered in $\mu_1 = (0.5, 0.75)$ and $\mu_2 = (0.5, 0.25)$, with covariance matrix

$$\Sigma = \begin{pmatrix} 0.15^2 & 0 \\ 0 & 0.15^2 \end{pmatrix} \qquad (11)$$

Using the FAM architecture [6], the authors reported an average Brier score of 0.984 using 1000 training patterns. The average number of ART_a categories is reported to be 8. For a Maxnode strategy, the system evolved to 20 categories and a Brier score of 0.979.

We trained the FAMR for this benchmark. The initial value for ρ_a was set to 0.7 and ρ_{ab} was set to 0. First, we used a constant relevance factor 1, and obtained the average Brier score 0.894, and an average number of 6.85 ART_a categories. It would be unfair to compare directly our results to the results in [6] since, in our experiments, the training set was processed on-line. In [6], the order dependence problem was alleviated by retraining the system on different permutations of the training set.

Second, we chose a relevance factor inversely proportional to the distance between the pattern and the line bisecting the segment of the two Gaussian centers. This way, we payed more attention to training patterns with high classification uncertainty from the overlapping area of the classes. The main idea is how to make use of additional knowledge (the Gaussian centers) in the learning phase. We did not obtained a significant improvement and we believe that a deeper investigation is necessary here. This problem is interesting because it is connected to learning in hybrid systems, where explicit rules are mixed with learning from examples.

E. Landsat satellite images

This part of the experiments was concerned with classification of Landsat satellite images as used in Statlog project [14]. The dataset can be obtained from UCI Repository of Machine Learning Databases and Domain Theories [15] and consists of subsections of a scene drawn from the original satellite images. The measurements comprise the intensities of four spectral bands from the same scene. Given these values, the purpose is to predict the target output of a pixel as belonging to one of the six classes. This is a challenging benchmark problem because of the noisy images. Each input pattern has 36 integer

TABLE III
PERFORMANCE FOR THE LANDSAT DATA. THE FAM RESULTS ARE THOSE REPORTED IN [17] AND THE PFAM RESULTS ARE FROM [16]. THE PFAM RESULTS ARE OBTAINED ON MULTIPLE NETWORKS.

Algorithm		$\overline{\rho}_a = 0.0$	$\overline{\rho}_a = 0.9$
FAM	Test set recognition rate(%)	83.0	89.0
	No. of ART_a Categories	89	704
PFAM	Test set recognition rate (%)	81.4	89.0
	No. of ART_a Categories	87	518
FAMR	Test set recognition rate (%)	81.45	87.5
	No. of ART_a Categories	40	340

value attributes. The training set contains 4435 samples and the test file has 2000 samples.

Lim and Harrison [16] used this dataset to compare PFAM's performance to that from [17]. In their off-line experiments training patterns were randomized to produce different ordering sets. Each set was used to train a different PFAM network. In the prediction mode, the results were averaged across five individual networks.

In order to test the FAMR's incremental learning ability, we did not use different orderings of the training set as in [16] and the original data was trained on a single network. Thus, we did not eliminate the order–dependency.

For values of $\overline{\rho}_a$ ($\overline{\rho}_a$ is the initial value for ρ_a) close to the ones used in [16], [17], the results (test set recognition rate, number of ART_a categories) are reported in Table III.

The results are rather good, compared to those from [16], taking into consideration that the decision of only one system was used. For instance, for $\overline{\rho}_a = 0$, the test set recognition rate was close to the one reported in [16], but for a smaller number of ART_a categories, and also for an incremental (not off-line) training.

The trade-off between a high recognition rate and a small number of ART_a categories is generally better in the case of FAMR than in the case of FAM and PFAM.

V. CONCLUSIONS AND FUTURE WORK

The Mapfield algorithm developed here expands the range of FAM applications by allowing us assignation of a relevance factor to each training pair. The FAMR probability estimation is computationally simple and converges with probability one to the posterior probability. When the initial relevance is zero and all other relevances are constant, FAMR is equivalent to PROBART.

Compared to the FAM probability estimator, FAMR shows similar or better performances with respect to the Brier score, test set recognition rate, and number of generated nodes. As a classifier, FAMR favorably compares with PFAM. The true benefits of using FAMR may come from using a relevance factor assigned to the training samples, improving the quality of the results, especially for probability estimation.

Usage of the mean square error (3) allows us to evaluate the rate of convergence. Choosing an adequate variable relevance factor can result in a faster convergence and a better performance of the network. This is left for further research work.

REFERENCES

[1] C. P. Lim and R. F. Harrison, "An incremental adaptive network for on-line supervized learning and probability estimation," *Neural Networks*, vol. 10, no. 5, pp. 925–939, 1997.
[2] ——, "ART-Based Autonomous Learning Systems: Part I - Architectures and Algorithms," in *Innovations in ART Neural Networks*, L. C. Jain, B. Lazzerini, and U. Halici, Eds. Springer, 2000.
[3] R. Polikar, L. Udpa, S. S. Udpa, and V. Honovar, "Learn++: An incremental learning algorithm for supervised neural networks," *IEEE Transactions on Systems, Man, and Cybernetics–PartC*, vol. 31, no. 4, pp. 497–508, 2001.
[4] G. A. Carpenter and S. Grossberg, "The ART of adaptive pattern recognition by a self-organizing neural network," *IEEE Computer*, vol. 21, no. 3, pp. 77–88, 1988.
[5] G. Carpenter, S. Grossberg, N. Markuzon, J. Reynolds, and D. Rosen, "Fuzzy ARTMAP: A neural network architecture for incremental supervised learning of analog multidimensional maps," *IEEE Transactions on Neural Networks*, vol. 3, no. 5, pp. 698–713, 1992.
[6] G. Carpenter, S.Grossberg, and J. Reynolds, "A fuzzy ARTMAP nonparametric probability estimator for nonstationary pattern recognition problems," *IEEE Transactions on Neural Networks*, vol. 6, no. 6, pp. 1330–1336, 1995.
[7] S. Marriott and R. F. Harrison, "A modified fuzzy ARTMAP architecture for the approximation of noisy mappings," *Neural Networks*, vol. 8, no. 4, pp. 619–641, 1995.
[8] D. Specht, "Probabilistic Neural Networks," *Neural Networks*, vol. 3, pp. 109–118, 1990.
[9] R. Andonie, "A converse H-theorem for inductive processes," *Computers and Artificial Intelligence*, vol. 9, pp. 159–167, 1990.
[10] R. Andonie and L. Sasu, "A Fuzzy ARTMAP Probability Estimator with Relevance Factor," in *Proceedings of the 11th European Symposium on Artificial Neural Networks (ESANN 2003)*, April 23-25, Bruges, Belgium, 2003.
[11] S. Gallant, *Neural Network Learning and Expert Systems*. MIT Press, 1994.
[12] V. Ciesielski, "Boundary points do not improve the accuracy of neural net classifiers," in *Proceedings of the Eights Australian Joint Conference on Artificial Intelligence*, Canberra, 1995, pp. 163–170.
[13] K. Lang and M. Witbrock, "Learning to tell two spirals appart," in *Proceedings 1988 Connectionist Models Summer School*, 1989, pp. 52–59.
[14] D. Michie, D. J. Spiegelhalter, and C. C. Taylor, *Machine Learning, Neural and Statistical Classification*. Oxford Press, 1994.
[15] K. Blacke, E. Keogh, and C. J. Merz. (1998) UCI Repository of Machine Learning Databases. [Online]. Available: http://www.ics.uci.edu/~learn/mlrepository.html
[16] C. P. Lim and R. F. Harrison, "ART-Based Autonomous Learning Systems: Part II - Applications," in *Innovations in ART Neural Networks*, L. C. Jain, B. Lazzerini, and U. Halici, Eds. Springer, 2000.
[17] R. Y. Asfour, "Fuzzy ARTMAP: Neural Networks for Multisensor Fusion and Classification," Ph.D. dissertation, Boston University, 1995.

From Categorical Semantics to Neural Network Design

Michael J. Healy
University of New Mexico and
University of Washington
13544 23rd Place NE
Seattle, WA 98125, USA
mjhealy@u.washington.edu

Thomas P. Caudell, Yunhai Xiao
University of New Mexico
Department of Electrical and
Computer Engineering
Albuquerque, New Mexico 87131, USA
tpc,yhxiao@eece.unm.edu

Abstract - We introduce a new architecture designed by applying a recently-developed mathematical model of neural network semantics using category theory. The new design has multiple subnetworks associated with different sensors and association regions. The subnetworks form individual, hierarchical representations of a body of knowledge. Subnetwork interconnections adapt to link the individual concept representations appropriately and provide knowledge coherence, representing a single knowledge heirarchy across the multi-sensor network.

I INTRODUCTION

Some researchers have been investigating the capabilities of neural networks in terms of their ability to acquire and use knowledge [1, 2, 3, 4, 5]. We have been developing a mathematical semantic model to achieve a high level of rigor in analyzing the acquisition and representation of knowledge by neural networks[6, 7, 8]. Category theory is the principal mathematical discipline applied in the model. Here, we describe its application to the design of a neural network architecture for knowledge acquisition from input data examples processed through two or more sensors. We begin with an introduction to categorical semantic modeling, then discuss the modeling specific to the architecture's design. The design serves as an example application of the semantic model and provides an experimental device for further research.

II CATEGORICAL SEMANTICS

There are many introductions to category theory, examples being[9] and [6]. A category has objects, which are examples of some type of mathematically-definable structure, and morphisms, which are relationships between pairs of objects that express some aspect of that type of structure, together with a law of composition by which properly-aligned pairs of morphisms can be combined to calculate other morphisms. A morphism directed from object a (its domain) to object b (its codomain) is denoted $f: a \longrightarrow b$. The composition for an aligned pair $f: a \longrightarrow b$ and $g: b \longrightarrow c$ (meeting head to tail at an object b) in a category is a morphism from a to c, written $g \circ f: a \longrightarrow c$. Composition is associative, $h \circ (g \circ f) = (h \circ g) \circ f$, and each object a has an *identity morphism* $\text{id}_a: a \longrightarrow a$ such that for any $f: a \longrightarrow b$ and $g: c \longrightarrow a$, $\text{id}_a \circ g = g$ and $f \circ \text{id}_a = f$. The ability to form compositions of morphisms makes it possible to formulate and solve equations involving them.

A diagram in a category $\mathcal{C}$ appears as a figure containing some of the objects and morphisms of $\mathcal{C}$. A commutative (or commuting) diagram is one with the property that for any two paths through the diagram morphisms between a pair of diagram objects a and b, if at least one of the paths contains two or more morphisms, then the composition of the morphisms along either path yields one and the same result morphism. A colimit for a diagram is an object (the colimit object) and a collection of morphisms that extends the diagram to a commutative diagram with minimal added information[6]. Colimits are used extensively to represent the learning of new concepts by a neural network based upon the merging of pre-existing concepts, beginning with the simple concepts about stimuli represented by the input nodes. Here, we shall restrict colimits to the simplest kind, coproducts, which are the colimits of discrete diagrams (diagrams consisting only of objects, with no morphisms). As an example, consider a discrete diagram containing two objects a and b. A coproduct for this diagram consists of a coproduct object $a + b$ and two morphisms $i_1: a \longrightarrow a + b$ and $i_2: b \longrightarrow a + b$ called the injections of the coproduct. A coproduct object for a and b in the category of sets and functions is a disjoint union, the coproduct morphisms being the injection functions of a and b separately into $a + b$.

Structure-preserving mappings between categories, called functors, are basic to category theory. A functor $\mathbf{F}: \mathcal{C} \longrightarrow \mathcal{D}$ from a category $\mathcal{C}$ to a category $\mathcal{D}$ maps the objects a, b and morphisms $f: a \longrightarrow b$ of $\mathcal{C}$ to unique images $\mathbf{F}(a), \mathbf{F}(b)$ and $\mathbf{F}(f): \mathbf{F}(a) \longrightarrow \mathbf{F}(b)$ in $\mathcal{D}$. A functor $\mathbf{F}$ is structure-preserving by virtue of two properties it has with respect to the compositions in $\mathcal{C}$

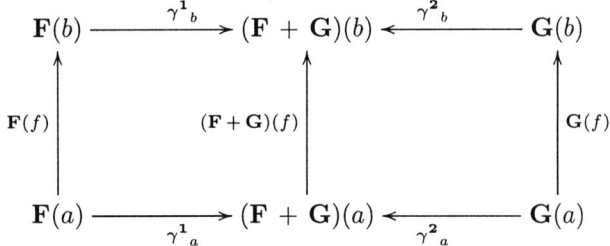

Figure 1: **A coproduct in $\mathcal{D}^\mathcal{C}$ "pastes together" commutative squares along the morphism images of the coproduct functor.**

and $\mathcal{D}$: $\mathbf{F}(g \circ_\mathcal{C} f) = \mathbf{F}(g) \circ_\mathcal{D} \mathbf{F}(f)$ (where g is a morphism with domain b, so $g \circ_\mathcal{C} f$ is defined in $\mathcal{C}$) and $\mathbf{F}(\mathrm{id}_a) = \mathrm{id}_{\mathbf{F}(a)}$. Functors can be many-to-one on either or both objects and morphisms; for two objects a and b, for example, it can be that $\mathbf{F}(a) = \mathbf{F}(b)$. Because of its significance in architecture design[7, 8], we refer to this "merging of objects and morphisms" as *compression*.

A natural transformation $\gamma: \mathbf{F} \longrightarrow \mathbf{G}$ between functors $\mathbf{F}, \mathbf{G}: \mathcal{C} \longrightarrow \mathcal{D}$ consists of $\mathcal{D}$-morphisms γ_a, one for each object a of $\mathcal{C}$, such that for each morphism $f: a \longrightarrow b$ of $\mathcal{C}$, $\mathbf{G}(f) \circ \gamma_a = \gamma_b \circ \mathbf{F}(f)$. The square-shaped commutative diagrams for two natural transformations $\gamma^1, \gamma^2: \mathbf{F}, \mathbf{G} \longrightarrow (\mathbf{F} + \mathbf{G})$ evaluated at two objects a and b and a morphism $f: a \longrightarrow b$ are shown in Fig. 1. This figure also illustrates the notion of a coproduct for two functors $\mathbf{F}$ and $\mathbf{G}$. Given categories $\mathcal{C}$ and $\mathcal{D}$, there is a category $\mathcal{D}^\mathcal{C}$ whose objects are the functors $\mathbf{F}: \mathcal{C} \longrightarrow \mathcal{D}$ and whose morphisms are the natural transformations, such as γ^1, γ^2. A coproduct functor $\mathbf{F} + \mathbf{G}$ for two functors $\mathbf{F}, \mathbf{G}$ in $\mathcal{D}^\mathcal{C}$ (provided the required injection morphisms exist) is one that compresses a pair of objects or of morphisms from $\mathcal{C}$ if and only if the pair is compressed by both $\mathbf{F}$ and $\mathbf{G}$. The coproduct has the effect of "pasting together" the corresponding commutative squares of the natural transformation injections as shown in Fig. 1.

The semantic model begins with a category we call **Concept**; its objects are concepts (expressed as theories in a formal logic) and its morphisms are relations that show how one concept is used in another (actually theory morphisms, which map the sorts and formulas in one theory into another so that the algebraic strcuture of logic is preserved and axioms map to axioms or theorems). This is our mathematical representation of the hierarchical structure of knowledge, and is meant include everything a neural network will ever learn.

For each neural network architecture, we define another category, which we shall call **Neural** here. The objects of **Neural** are intervals on the real line, serving as the quanta in a quantized representation of the output levels of the nodes. In the initial categorically-derived architecture presented here, the nodes can be considered as binary. Hence, for each node p_i ($0 \leq i \leq n$), where there are n nodes, we need consider only two objects, $(p_i, \eta_{i,1}), (p_i, \eta_{i,2})$, where $\eta_{i,1} = \{x \mid -\infty < x \leq 0\}$, $\eta_{i,2} = \{x \mid 0 < x < +\infty\}$. For brevity, we omit a detailed description of neural morphisms, which are somewhat complex. Briefly, a morphism from (p_i, η) to (p_j, η') (where η, η' are arbitrary intervals) consists of (1) a set of weights for the network and (2) a bundle of connection paths (each path having possibly more than one intermediate node, i.e., multiple connections) satisfying the following conditions: (a) the paths all originate at p_i and terminate at p_j; (b) they are all activated by the same set of network inputs for any weight vector in the set so that p_i, p_j emit outputs in the intervals η, η', respectively, and all intermediate path nodes of the paths in the bundle emit outputs in specified intervals (see[6]; for simplicity, we have substituted inputs for node activation state sequences).

An algorithm for the colimit construction in **Concept** [6] enables the calculation of complex concepts via the colimits of diagrams involving simpler concepts and morphisms. Functors in the category **Neural**$^\mathbf{Concept}$ preserve the colimit construction, in part because functors preserve diagram commutativity. A given functor $\mathbf{M}_A:$ **Concept** $\longrightarrow$ **Neural**, therefore, effectively transports the structure of all possible knowledge— represented by the concept category—into the categorical architecture representation. The colimit construction also indicates how concepts are formed through adaptation. Of necessity, $\mathbf{M}_A$ entails a large amount of compression; in fact, it represents a single state of learning in the network, with all other knowledge compressed. Many such functors are required to represent many stages of learning.

Of particular interest to us are networks having several subnetwork regions, each providing network computations associated with a sensor or an actuator or performing some other function, such as serving as an association region for two or more sensor regions. Correspondingly, we use several functors from **Neural**$^\mathbf{Concept}$ to represent a given state of learning, where each functor models the existing knowledge representation within a region. Our goal is to blend the individual, regional knowledge representations to achieve a single working knowledge representation. We call this knowledge coherence, which we model as a system of natural transformations connecting the region functors.

To see how we apply this in analyzing existing neural network designs, consider some of the ART mapping networks (for example, as analysed in a rule-base analysis in [3]). These couple separate, unsupervised ART networks (sometimes with an intermediate "mapping field" subnetwork) to provide supervised ART systems. We have shown[7] that each ART network has solely coproduct formation as a means of learning complex concepts in terms of the simple concepts represented by its input nodes. This stems from the lack of connections within the input (F_0) and matching (F_1) layers. The more general colimits required to capture knowledge representation are missing. Also, there are no nodes available for compression of yet more complex (or less complex) concepts, or input concepts not represented by the present input layer. The effect is to limit the concept hierarchy representation to a functor image fragment containing at most coproducts over a single layer. Further, the interconnections between ART networks required for commutative squares are not present, so any natural transformations would be only partially represented[7].

On the positive side, ART networks have important advantages for a study of knowledge representation. The explicit learning procedure and the presence of feedback (top-down) connections facilitates the identification of intervals η of the F_2 nodes as coproduct objects: The bottom-up connections to a previously-committed F_2 node that have nonzero weights are the connection paths of the coproduct injection morphisms. Using an ART 1 network as an example[10], the coproduct objects are the previously-mentioned intervals η_2 of the committed F_2 nodes. Suppose that the template of a winner-take-all node in the F_2 competition to represent an input pattern is a subset template of "sufficient size" (see [10]; "subset" means that each nonzero template connection weight corresponds to a nonzero input pattern value, and "sufficient size" means that there are "enough" template nonzeros). The top-down, unit-weight template connections then ensure the activation in their η_2 intervals of exactly the F_1 nodes in the discrete diagram upon which the currently-expressed coproduct is based, thus ensuring the continued activation of the coproduct morphism connections. This largely describes the semantics of resonance in a typical ART network.

The interconnects between F_2 layers of the separate ART networks is suggestive of natural transformation components corresponding to the concepts represented by the F_2 η_2 intervals. What is missing are the components corresponding to the concepts at the F_0 (or, equivalently, the F_1) level. We decided to exploit the properties of network templates and interconnections by using ART networks as a point of departure in developing new architectures more compatible with knowledge representation and coherence.

III A CATEGORICALLY-MOTIVATED DESIGN

We have given a very brief example of applying the categorical semantic theory using ART mapping networks. The example emphasized binary nodes for simplicity, us-

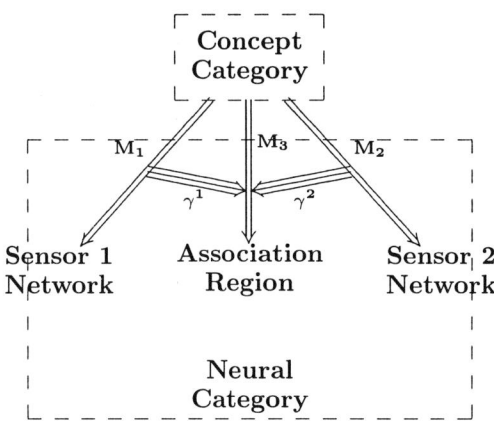

Figure 2: Functors map the hierarchy of a concept category to multiple regions. Natural transformations represent coherent interconnections between hierarchy representations.

ing the binary intervals η_2. Our other example, the proposed categorical neural architecture that is the subject of this paper, will be described next. Although this initial architecture is designed to operate in a binary fashion, we use the more general notation η for arbitrary intervals for simplicity and also to emphasize that the semantic model applies to other than binary-node networks.

Fig. 2 shows the overall scheme for an architecture that represents and coherently fuses the information from two sensors according to our theory. There are three regions, two receiving input from sensors and the third, an association region, receiving input from the other two regions. In terms of the semantic model, the architecture is represented by the category **Neural** and the sensor regions are represented by the images of the functors $\mathbf{M}_1$ and $\mathbf{M}_2$. The association region is represented by the image of $\mathbf{M}_3$. Two natural transformations $\gamma^i : \mathbf{M}_i \longrightarrow \mathbf{M}_3$ ($i \in \{1, 2\}$) are coproduct morphisms for the discrete diagram containing $\mathbf{M}_1, \mathbf{M}_2$ in $\mathbf{Neural^{Concept}}$, and $\mathbf{M}_3$ is the corresponding colimit object, $\mathbf{M}_3 = \mathbf{M}_1 + \mathbf{M}_2$. Fig. 3 shows an initial architecture designed in accordance with this scheme and using properties of ART networks where these can be exploited. We call the sensor regions *primaries* and denote these by $\mathbf{P}_1$ and $\mathbf{P}_2$, corresponding to the functors $\mathbf{M}_1$ and $\mathbf{M}_2$. We call the region corresponding to $\mathbf{M}_3$ an *associator*, which we will denote by $\mathbf{A}$. Adaptive connections are indicated by arrows ending in bullets and non-adaptive connections have standard arrowheads. Connection polarity is indicated by + (excitatory), - (inhibitory), or R (a bundle of non-phasic reset connections).

An immediate problem occurs in implementing the scheme of Fig. 2 as a multi-sensor architecture. Let us suppose that the two sensors are logically independent. For example, let $\mathbf{P}_1$ be coupled to a visual sensor, with its F_0 layer representing concepts describing visual prim-

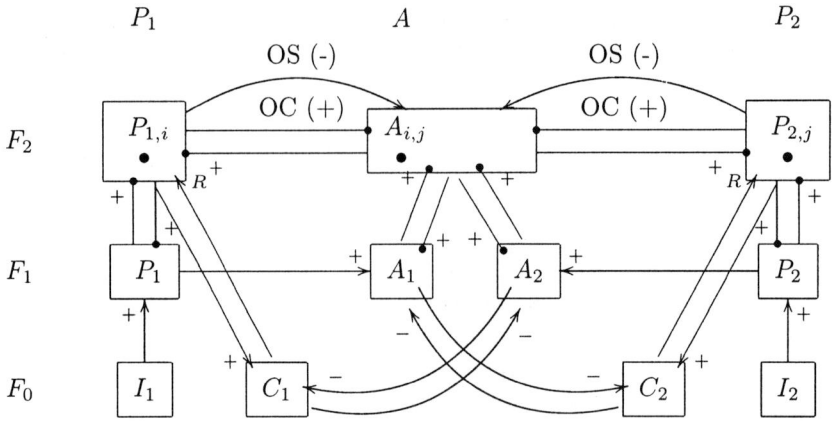

Figure 3: A schematic for NR 1.3, an architecture design based upon three objects (functors) P_1, A and P_2 and two morphisms (natural transformations) $\gamma^1: P_1 \longrightarrow A$ and $\gamma^2: P_2 \longrightarrow A$ in the functor category **Neural**^{Concept}.

itives of some kind, and let the F_0 nodes at $\mathbf{P}_2$ represent tactile information provided by an array of pressure sensors. Then, since the two kinds of sensor primitives convey entirely different kinds of information, each subnetwork must omit the input concepts associated with the other subnetwork's sensor. However, our semantic model requires that each functor map the entire knowledge space of **Concept** into its subnetwork region, including all of the concepts that describe both kinds of sensor primitives. To satisfy these competing requirements, there must be **Neural** objects and morphisms available to represent the functorial compression of sensor primitives for each subnetwork within the other subnetwork. We choose to represent these as a sort of auxiliary F_1 node, because it is at F_1 that the discrete diagrams form via bottom-up/top-down matching (ART-based, although the gain control subsystem is not shown). We include one of these compression nodes in each subnetwork to serve as the target for the functor images of the missing sensor primitives. They are labelled C_1 (for $\mathbf{P}_1$) and C_2 (for $\mathbf{P}_2$) in Fig. 3. The coproduct functor $\mathbf{M}_3$, on the other hand, fully represents the non-compressed knowledge represented by $\mathbf{M}_1$ and $\mathbf{M}_2$. Therefore, region $\mathbf{A}$ has two F_1 layers whose nodes receive inputs from their corresponding F_1 nodes in $\mathbf{P}_1$ and $\mathbf{P}_2$, respectively. We use the term "proxies" for the two F_1 layers in $\mathbf{A}$; however, their bottom-up/top-down connections with the $\mathbf{A}$ F_2 layer operate independently of $\mathbf{P}_1$ and $\mathbf{P}_2$.

We connect each compression node to the proxy of the opposite subnetwork's F_1 layer as shown. There are pairs of connection paths emanating from the F_1 nodes of $\mathbf{P}_1$ and $\mathbf{P}_2$ to the appropriate $\mathbf{A}$ F_2 nodes. These form the commutative squares of the two natural transformations $\gamma^1: \mathbf{M}_1 \longrightarrow \mathbf{M}_3$ and $\gamma^2: \mathbf{M}_2 \longrightarrow \mathbf{M}_3$. For example, let S be an object in **Concept** that descibes a sensor primitive via the functor $\mathbf{M}_1$, so that for some $\mathbf{P}_1$ F_1 node $F^1_{1,k}$ and an appropriate interval η, $(F^1_{1,k}, \eta) = \mathbf{M}_1(S)$. To simplify notation, we shall simply use the functorial representation, in the present case $\mathbf{M}_1(S)$. Proceeding, let S be represented in the $\mathbf{A}$ subnetwork's $\mathbf{P}_1$ F_1-proxy layer via the functor $\mathbf{M}_3$ as $\mathbf{M}_3(S)$. This yields two F_1 representations of S, connected across subnetworks by a $\mathbf{P}_1$ F_1 to $\mathbf{A}$ F_1 connection that represents the natural transformation component $\gamma^1(S): \mathbf{M}_1(S) \longrightarrow \mathbf{M}_3(S)$. Let T be a coproduct concept with a coproduct injection morphism $m: S \longrightarrow T$, and let T be represented in the $\mathbf{P}_1$ and $\mathbf{A}$ F_2 layers by $\mathbf{M}_1(T)$ and $\mathbf{M}_3(T)$, respectively. Then, there are two connection paths from $\mathbf{M}_1(S)$ to $\mathbf{M}_3(T)$ forming the sides of a commutative square, as follows. One path consists of two connections: a $\mathbf{P}_1$ F_1 to $\mathbf{P}_1$ F_2 connection, the coproduct morphism image $\mathbf{M}_1(m): \mathbf{M}_1(S) \longrightarrow \mathbf{M}_1(T)$, followed by the $\mathbf{P}_1$ F_2 to $\mathbf{A}$ F_2 connection for the γ^1 component $\gamma^1(T): \mathbf{M}_1(T) \longrightarrow \mathbf{M}_3(T)$, yielding the composition morphism $\gamma^1(T) \circ \mathbf{M}_1(m): \mathbf{M}_1(S) \longrightarrow \mathbf{M}_3(T)$. The second path consists of two connections: a $\mathbf{P}_1$ F_1 to $\mathbf{A}$ F_1 connection for the γ^1 component $\gamma^1(S): \mathbf{M}_1(S) \longrightarrow \mathbf{M}_3(S)$, followed by an $\mathbf{A}$ F_1 to $\mathbf{A}$ F_2 connection, the coproduct morphism image $\mathbf{M}_3(m): \mathbf{M}_3(S) \longrightarrow \mathbf{M}_3(T)$, yielding the composition morphism $\mathbf{M}_3(m) \circ \gamma^1(S): \mathbf{M}_1(S) \longrightarrow \mathbf{M}_3(T)$. The composition morphisms are the same morphism, $\gamma^1(T) \circ \mathbf{M}_1(m) = \mathbf{M}_3(m) \circ \gamma^1(S)$, hence, in the architecture, the two connection paths must represent the same **Neural** morphism. In other words, the square whose sides are the four factors in the two compositions is commutative. Thus, the relationship between the primary sensor primitive concept representation $\mathbf{M}_1(S)$ and the associator colimit concept representation $\mathbf{M}_3(T)$, where concept T includes concept S as one of its parts, is independent of the path that expresses the relationship across the primary $\mathbf{P}_1$ and the associator $\mathbf{A}$. This is the basis for knowledge coherence and is one of the theoretical considerations that help determine the operational rules for the architecture.

Joined to the preceding commutative square is one for the natural transformation $\gamma^2 : \mathbf{M}_2 \longrightarrow \mathbf{M}_3$. In the latter, we obtain two connection paths from $\mathbf{M}_2(S)$ to $\mathbf{M}_3(T)$; however, there is no $\mathbf{P}_2$ F_1 node representing S, but instead the compression node C_2. Defining the appropriate functor images and natural transformation components as before, but this time using C_2 instead of a $\mathbf{P}_2$ F_1 node (but using again the same $\mathbf{A}$ F_1 node from the proxy layer for $\mathbf{P}_1$ F_1), we obtain the commutative square associated with the equality $\gamma^2(T) \circ \mathbf{M}_2(m) = \mathbf{M}_3(m) \circ \gamma^2(S)$. The fact that the two commutative squares are "pasted together" along $\mathbf{M}_3(m) : \mathbf{M}_3(S) \longrightarrow \mathbf{M}_3(T)$ implies that in the operational architecture, all four connection paths must become activated for the same inputs. The details of operation must be defined to be consistent with this.

IV DISCUSSION OF OPERATION

There is not space here to describe the operational flow of the new architecture in full, but we can point out a few guiding principles. First, the fact that the architecture is to implement coproducts, functors and natural transformations and, in particular, coproducts in **Neural**^{**Concept**}, serves as a basis for the algorithm for the activation and connection-weight modifications. Thus, the appropriate commutative square diagrams must be activated connecting the $\mathbf{P}_1$ and $\mathbf{P}_2$ F_1 and compression nodes to the currently-active $\mathbf{A}$ F_2 coproduct node. This operational consideration is a realization of a theoretical implication of the semantic model: The fusion of information from multiple sensors is a consequence of knowledge coherence, fully expressed as the calculation of colimits at two levels. First, colimits in **Concept** are mapped to their neural representations by functors, which preserve the commutativity of diagrams. Second, natural transformations representing interconnects to an association region in a neural network define the latter as a coproduct of functors; in the presented architecture, this results in the appropriate "pasting together" of the commutative squares some of whose sides are the colimit (in this case, coproduct) morphism images for the functors.

More operational detail is provided by the desire to stay as close as possible to ART network design. The F_2 choice and template modification operations within each subnetwork proceed according to the ART gain control and connectionist adaptation mechanisms. For example, **Neural** morphisms such as $\mathbf{M}_1(m) : \mathbf{M}_1(S) \longrightarrow \mathbf{M}_1(T)$ and $\mathbf{M}_3(m) : \mathbf{M}_3(S) \longrightarrow \mathbf{M}_3(T)$ in the illustration of commutative squares for $\gamma^1 : \mathbf{M}_1 \longrightarrow \mathbf{M}_3$ are implemented as bottom-up connections, but the latter are assisted in this role by their corresponding top-down template connections, which ensure their activation during the appropriate periods.

The principle of connections not directly involved in a morphism supporting those that are in their role is extended throughout the new architecture. For example, the morphism $\gamma^1(T) : \mathbf{M}_1(T) \longrightarrow \mathbf{M}_3(T)$ is implemented as a $\mathbf{P}_1$-F_2-to-$\mathbf{A}$-F_2 connection (an on-center (OC) connection in Fig. 3), but the latter receives support in that role from its attendant F_2-to-F_2 off-surround (OS) connections to the rest of the $\mathbf{A}$ F_2 layer and also from a reciprocal connection with which it is paired. Thus, coproduct nodes in $\mathbf{P}_i$ and $\mathbf{A}$ ($i = 1, 2$) that represent the same coproduct concept form mutually-supportive pairs. Sustained activation of a chosen $\mathbf{P}_1$ F_2 node, for example, depends upon this, for its support from its own template weakens during the time the input it is representing is presented to the network.

The $\mathbf{P}_2$-to-$\mathbf{A}$ commutative square that shares a side with the previously-described $\mathbf{P}_1$-F_1-to-$\mathbf{A}$-F_2 square has the $\mathbf{P}_2$ compression node C_2 in the role of the third representation of concept S, $\mathbf{M}_2(S)$, and its connections to/from the $\mathbf{P}_1$ F_1 proxy in $\mathbf{A}$ are inhibitory. To examine the effect this has in a typical operational scenario, let us assume that for the current episode of presentation of input patterns to the $\mathbf{P}_1$ and $\mathbf{P}_2$ F_0 layers, $\mathbf{P}_1$ was the first to reach its candidate for its F_2 choice, a node representing the functor image $\mathbf{M}_1(T)$ of a concept T. Suppose that, next, a node representing the image $\mathbf{M}_2(T')$ of a concept T' becomes activated. This causes the activation of C_2 (see the appropriate top-down connection in Fig. 3), which then acts to suppress the $\mathbf{P}_1$ F_1 proxy layer in $\mathbf{A}$; but $\mathbf{M}_1(T)$ has already provided excitation to C_1, which acts in a similar manner to suppress the $\mathbf{P}_2$ F_1 proxy. Under an ART-like "2/3 Rule" operating in $\mathbf{A}$, the proxies can only sustain their activities if the nodes representing $\mathbf{M}_3(T')$ and $\mathbf{M}_3(T)$ can provide the top-down excitatory stimulation through the proxy template connections. However, if $\mathbf{M}_3(T') \neq \mathbf{M}_3(T)$, then two distinct $\mathbf{A}$ F_2 nodes will be competing for activation as winner-take-all nodes. This results in their mutual suppression through the OS inhibitory connections from $\mathbf{P}_1$ and $\mathbf{P}_2$, resulting in loss of top-down support to their proxies. The final result is a loss of activity in the node representing $\mathbf{M}_1(T)$, for its support from its template has weakened with the passage of time, as mentioned before (in the current architectural design, $\mathbf{M}_2(T)$, having reached its choice later, has support from its "fresh" nonzero template bottom-up connections, hence, remains near full activation). The weakened state of the $\mathbf{M}_1(T)$ node allows the reset connection from C_1 to the $\mathbf{P}_1$ F_2 layer to have its full effect (C_1, like $\mathbf{P}_2$, lags behind $\mathbf{P}_1$ F_1 and F_2 in its cycle of activation). This results in the stimulation of the F_2 competitors for $\mathbf{M}_1(T)$, which then compete to choose a new winner. Thus, the functor coproduct is enforced by rejecting the choice of the primary subnetwork that made the original prediction.

If, on the other hand, $\mathbf{M}_3(T') = \mathbf{M}_3(T)$, then the primary subnetwork predictions are consistent and the entire network is said to be in resonance. The proper associations between concept representatives have been established and enforced at both the F_1 and F_2 levels across all three subnetworks. Thus, resonance as here described corresponds to coherence at both concept levels. That is, a concept representation at F_1 in both primaries is related to a single associator F_2 representation through a morphism representation, a bundle of connections representing a commutative square. The two commutative squares express the notion that the primary-to-associator subconcept-to-concept relationships are independent of path, hence, are expressed without ambiguity.

This architecture is currently in preliminary testing for a series of experiments that will follow. Experience gained with it so far has led to some design refinements. The refinements are not completely determined by expediency: When a difficulty arises, it leads us to consider the semantic model, and to ask if we are being fully consistent with it and to what extent does it determine the architectural details.

V CONCLUSION

We have derived novel architecture design principles from a semantic model for neural networks based upon category theory. We have given two examples to illustrate the use of this model: Its application to understanding the semantics of ART networks, and the design of a multi-region, multi-sensor neural network capable of coherent knowledge representation based upon the new design principles. In the new design, nodes and connections are explicitly organized to implement coproducts, functors and natural transformations. Experimentation with the new architecture is under way.

There are still details implied by the semantic model that are missing in the new architecture introduced here. First, as in ART, the colimits represented in each subnetwork are only two-layer coproducts. Second, the compression nodes and morphisms for the infinite variety of concepts not representable in any of the three subnetworks are missing, with the sole exception of the compression nodes for the alternate sensor in each sensor subnetwork. Nevertheless, the architecture described here has filled in some of the semantic detail. It is a start at fully realizing the semantic model in architectural design.

References

[1] R. Andrews, J. Diederich and A. B. Tickle, "Survey and critique of techniques for extracting rules from trained artificial neural networks", *Knowledge-Based Systems*, vol. 8, no. 6, 373-389, 1995.

[2] M. W. Craven and J. W. Shavlik, "Learning symbolic rules using artificial neural networks", *Proceedings of the 10th International Machine Learning Conference*, Amherst, MA. San Mateo, CA:Morgan Kaufmann, 1993, pp. 73-80.

[3] M. J. Healy and T. P. Caudell, "Acquiring rule sets as a product of learning in a logical neural architecture", *IEEE Transactions on Neural Networks*, vol. 8, no. 3, pp. 461-475, 1997.

[4] N. K. Kasabov, "Adaptable neuro production systems", *Neurocomputing*, vol. 13, pp. 95-117, 1996.

[5] G. Pinkas, "Reasoning, nonmonotonicity and learning in connectionist networks that capture propositional knowledge", *Artificial Intelligence* vol. 77, pp. 203-247, 1995.

[6] M. J. Healy, "Category theory applied to neural modeling and graphical representations", in *Proceedings of the International Joint Conference on Neural Networks (IJCNN 2000)*, July 24-27, Como, Italy, IEEE CS Press, vol. III, 2000, pp. 35-40.

[7] M. J. Healy and T. P. Caudell, "A categorical semantic analysis of ART architectures", *IJCNN'01:International Joint Conference on Neural Networks*, Washington, DC. IEEE Press. vol. 1, 2001, pp. 38-43.

[8] M. J. Healy and T. P. Caudell, "Aphasic compressed representations: a functorial semantic design principle for coupled ART networks", *IJCNN'02:International Joint Conference on Neural Networks*, Honolulu, Hawaii. CD-ROM Proceedings. The Printing House, Inc.:Stoughton, WI, 2002, P. 2656.

[9] B. C. Pierce, *Basic Category Theory for Computer Scientists*, MIT Press, 1991.

[10] G. A. Carpenter and S. Grossberg, "A Massively Parallel Architecture for a Self-Organizing Neural Pattern Recognition Machine", *Computer Vision, Graphics, and Image Processing*, vol. 37, pp. 54-115, 1987.

Universal Approximation With Fuzzy ART and Fuzzy ARTMAP

Stephen J. Verzi
Computer Science Department, University of New Mexico
Albuquerque, NM 87131, USA
verzi@eece.unm.edu
and
Gregory L. Heileman
Department of Electrical & Computer Engineering, University of New Mexico
Albuquerque, NM 87131, USA
heileman@eece.unm.edu
and
Michael Georgiopoulos
School of Electrical Engineering and Computer Science, University of Central Florida
Orlando, FL 32816, USA
michaelg@mail.ucf.edu
and
Georgios C. Anagnostopoulos
Department of Electrical & Computer Engineering, Florida Institute of Technology
Melbourne, FL 32901, USA
georgio@fit.edu

Abstract

A measure of success for any learning algorithm is how useful it is in a variety of learning situations. Those learning algorithms that support universal function approximation can theoretically be applied to a very large and interesting class of learning problems. Many kinds of neural network architectures have already been shown to support universal approximation. In this paper, we will provide a proof to show that Fuzzy ART augmented with a single layer of perceptrons is a universal approximator. Moreover, the Fuzzy ARTMAP neural network architecture, by itself, will be shown to be a universal approximator.

Keywords: Adaptive Resonance Theory, Machine Learning, Neural Networks, Universal Function Approximation.

I. INTRODUCTION

In the late 1980's and early 1990's, important theoretical results were proved that showed certain classes of learning algorithms capable of universal function approximation. Early on it was shown that combinations of sigmoid functions could be used to support universal function approximation [1]. This result was important since a standard neural network perceptron computes a sigmoid function. Then multi-layered feedforward neural networks with either sigmoid or Gaussian kernel functions were shown to be universal approximators [2], [3], [4]. Also, radial basis function neural networks were proved to be capable of universal function approximation [5]. Very recently a hybrid ART-based neural network has been shown to be a universal approximator [6].

In this paper we will show that Fuzzy ART with only an extra layer of perceptrons can support universal approximation. More importantly, the Fuzzy ARTMAP neural network by itself can perform universal approximation. The result showing Fuzzy ART to be a universal approximator is an important fact in establishing the utility of ART-based neural network architectures as viable learning techniques. A learning algorithm which is known to be a universal approximator can be applied to a large class of interesting problems with the confidence that a solution is at least theoretically available.

Before presenting our main results, we will describe the Fuzzy ART and Fuzzy ARTMAP neural network architectures. Then we will present a proof showing how a Fuzzy ART neural network extended with a layer of perceptrons can be used to support universal function approximation. Next we will show how Fuzzy ARTMAP by itself can support this same capability. Finally, we will discuss the utility of Fuzzy ART, the curse of dimensionality and practical learning algorithms.

II. FUZZY ART AND FUZZY ARTMAP

Fuzzy ARTMAP is a neural network architecture designed to learn a mapping between example instances and their associated labels [7]. These training examples are denoted (x, y), where $x \in [0,1]^m$ is an example data instance, and $y \in [0, \infty)^d$ is its corresponding d-dimensional label. Fuzzy ARTMAP is composed of two Fuzzy ART neural network modules connected through a MAP field, as shown in Fig. 1.

During training, the pair (x, y) is preprocessed to form the pair $((x\ x^c), (y\ y^c))$ which is then presented to the neural network. The instance x is presented to the A-side Fuzzy ART module (ART^A) and label y is presented to the B-side Fuzzy ART module (ART^B) in Fig. 1. Fuzzy ARTMAP performs supervised learning by enforcing that the A-side F_2 node which learns x will only be associated with a single B-side F_2 which learns y.

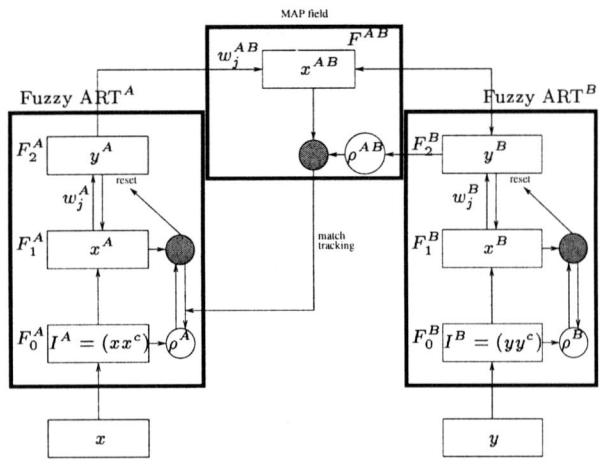

Fig. 1. The Fuzzy ARTMAP Architecture.

A. Fuzzy ART

The Fuzzy ART neural network architecture was designed to conduct unsupervised learning, or clustering, on real-valued data [8]. Clustering is the process of grouping similar data points into *cluster groups*, *clusters* or *categories*. The measure of similarity among data points for Fuzzy ART will be specified in detail below. In this section, we will describe the structure of the Fuzzy ART neural network architecture, followed by a detailed look at its clustering algorithm.

Fuzzy ART Input Data. The Fuzzy ART neural network architecture, with complement coding, assumes that the input data used to train it is normalized to fit within the unit hypercube. Thus, an input data point, x, is a m-dimensional vector of values each of which lies between zero and one, inclusive (i.e., $x_i \in [0,1], i = 1, 2, \ldots, m$). The dimension, m, is constant for a particular learning problem. The complement of an input vector, x, is now well defined as $x_i^c = 1 - x_i, i = 1, 2, \ldots, m$.

Fuzzy ART Structure. Fuzzy ART is structured into three layers of interacting nodes, labeled F_0, F_1 and F_2, where the output of F_0 is connected to F_1, and F_1 and F_2 are mutually interconnected, as shown in Fig. 1. At F_0, a m-length input vector from the environment is complement coded and passed on to F_1. The process of *complement coding* a pattern vector, x, produces a new vector $I = (x, x^c)$, where x^c is the complement of x defined previously.

There are $2m$ nodes in layer F_1, and $N \geq 1$ nodes in layer F_2. Each node in the F_2 layer is fully connected, by a weighted link, w_j in Fig. 1, to each node in the F_1 layer.[1] The number of nodes in the F_2 layer is allowed to grow as necessary during learning. An F_2 layer node that has learned at least one data point is called *commit-

---

[1] Actually, there are bottom-up and top-down weights connecting the nodes in the F_1 layer to the nodes in the F_2 layer. In this paper, the top-down weights representing the cluster template are the only weights of interest, and so these weight will be referred to as w_j.

ted. A Fuzzy ART neural network module always has one uncommitted node in the F_2 layer available for training, along with $N - 1$ committed nodes. When the uncommitted node learns its first data point, a new uncommitted node then becomes available, and N is increased by one. Each committed F_2 node and its associated weights, w_j represents a separate category of input data, also called a category *template*.

The output vector, y, from a Fuzzy ART network consists of boolean values signifying those F_2 nodes which are active. Thus

$$y_j = \begin{cases} 1, & \text{if } F_2 \text{ node } j \text{ is active} \\ 0, & \text{otherwise} \end{cases} \quad (1)$$

where $1 \leq j \leq N$. Note that the uncommitted node, N, is available in (1). The operation of Fuzzy ART ensures that only a single F_2 node is active for a given pattern. We will see this in more detail in the algorithmic description presented next.

Fuzzy ART Algorithm. The Fuzzy ART algorithm described here is a combination of work presented by Carpenter and Moore, however, the symbols used will reflect those used throughout the rest of this paper for consistency [8], [9]. For a given input data point, the Fuzzy ART learning algorithm has three stages. First, the input is complement coded. Then the "best" matching F_2 node is found for the complement coded input data. Note that the F_2 node found might be the uncommitted node, and initially, a Fuzzy ART neural network architecture has only the single uncommitted node available for learning. Finally, the best matching F_2 node found is allowed to learn the new data point. Given a complement coded input vector, I, the similarity measure at node j of the F_2 layer, called $T_j(I)$, is computed as a weighted sum of I and the weights w_j, shown in (2). Note that these weights connect the F_1 layer nodes to node j in the F_2 layer.

The mathematical formula used by Fuzzy ART to find the best matching category template during cluster formation is

$$J = \arg\max_{0 \leq j \leq N} T_j(I), \quad (2)$$

where

$$T_j(I) = \begin{cases} \frac{|I \wedge w_j|}{\alpha + |w_j|}, & \text{if } \frac{|I \wedge w_j|}{|I|} \geq \rho \\ 0, & \text{otherwise}. \end{cases} \quad (3)$$

The parameter α, called the choice parameter, is usually a small positive quantity, $\wedge$ is the element-wise vector *min* operator, and $|\cdot|$ is the L_1-norm of a vector. The best matching F_2 node from the choice competition, J, must satisfy the vigilance criterion

$$\frac{|I \wedge w_J|}{|I|} \geq \rho. \quad (4)$$

The vigilance parameter, ρ in (4), is a user-supplied input between zero and one. Note that at least one F_2 node, the uncommitted node, will always satisfy the vigilance criterion. The maximum choice F_2 template node satisfying the vigilance criterion is allowed to learn the input vector, a condition called *resonance*. Ties between F_2 nodes with the same choice value are broken by assigning an index to all F_2 nodes, and choosing the node with the lowest index value in a tie. The index values are assigned when F_2 nodes are committed.

Initially all template weights w_j are set to one, and learning proceeds as follows

$$w_J^{(new)} = \beta(I \wedge w_J^{(old)}) + (1-\beta)w_J^{(old)}, \quad (5)$$

where β is the learning parameter. In this paper we use $\beta = 1$, which is a special case called *fast learning*. Note that learning only occurs at the winning F_2 node, J, during resonance. An important feature of Fuzzy ART is that the F_2 layer grows as needed for a particular problem.

Fuzzy ART F_2 Node Category Template. The Fuzzy ART neural network module accepts a vector of values as input, but it also produces a vector of values as output. A committed Fuzzy ART F_2 node j has a weight vector defined as $w_j = x_1 \wedge x_2 \wedge \ldots \wedge x_n$, where F_2 node j has learned all of the input data points in $X = \{x_1, x_2, \ldots, x_n\}$. Because of complement coding, w_j defines the minimum hyperbox containing the data points in X. The vigilance criterion ensures that $|w_j| \geq \rho$.

$$|w_j| = \sum_{i=1}^{2m} w_{ji} = \sum_{i=1}^{2m} \min_{k=1}^{n} x_{ki} \geq \rho \quad (6)$$

Thus, $w_j = (pq^c)$ where $p_k = \min_{i \in \{1,2,\ldots,n\}} x_{ik}$ and $q_k = \max_{i \in \{1,2,\ldots,n\}} x_{ik}$. The axis-parallel hyper-rectangle for w_j has a minimum point at p and a maximum point at q. The first m points from w_j are the "lower left" corner, and the second m points are the complement of the "upper right" corner of the hyperbox defined by the F_2 node j. The vigilance parameter, ρ, can be used to control the granularity of clusters covering the problem space. A larger ρ value will force Fuzzy ART to create smaller clusters, necessitating more clusters to cover a larger problem space. A smaller ρ value will allow Fuzzy ART to create larger clusters, meaning fewer clusters are needed to cover a problem space.

B. Fuzzy ARTMAP

The Fuzzy ARTMAP architecture shown in Fig. 1 consists of two Fuzzy ART modules connected by a MAP field. The ART^A module is given pattern data and the ART^B module is given label data for a given supervised learning task. The MAP field links data cluster templates (A-side) with label cluster templates (B-side). Supervised learning is performed in Fuzzy ARTMAP by ensuring that each ART^A template is linked with only one ART^B template. Thus, a many-to-one association from pattern to label templates is formed in the Fuzzy ARTMAP MAP field.

The Fuzzy ARTMAP MAP field weights, w_{jk}^{AB}, are used to control associations between A-side F_2 nodes and B-side F_2 nodes. An uncommitted A-side F_2 node, j, has the following initial weight values

$$w_{jk}^{AB} = 1, \ \forall k, \ 0 \leq k \leq N^B, \quad (7)$$

meaning that j is not currently associated with any B-side F_2 node (there are N^B B-side F_2 nodes), and in fact it is available for future learning. An uncommitted A-side F_2 node j becomes committed with B-side F_2 node K through the following weight assignments

$$w_{jK}^{AB} = 1 \text{ and } w_{jk}^{AB} = 0, \ \forall k \neq K, \quad (8)$$

thus A-side F_2 node, j, is exclusively and permanently linked with B-side F_2 node, K.

The Fuzzy ARTMAP architecture ensures the many-to-one mapping through the use of a match tracking lateral reset, as shown in Fig. 1. The lateral reset is used in Fuzzy ARTMAP to ensure that each training pattern resonates with an A-side F_2 node associated with a B-side F_2 node that is consistent with the pattern's label. After a bounded number of epochs, Fuzzy ARTMAP is guaranteed to reach a steady state [10]. Note that during testing it is possible for a test pattern, never seen before, to choose the uncommitted node. In this case no B-side label prediction is possible.

III. Main Results

In this chapter, we will present a proof showing the universal approximation capabilities of the Fuzzy ART neural network. Actually, these results will apply to a modified Fuzzy ART network. It will also be shown that the Fuzzy ARTMAP network can be used without further modification to perform universal approximation.

In order to show that the Fuzzy ART F_2 node is capable of universal approximation, it will be necessary to show that the Fuzzy ART neural network architecture is capable of computing any member of a sequence of functions, $S = \bigcup s_n(x)$ which are dense in $L^p(\Re^m)$. Actually, Fuzzy ART with complement coding operates in the unit hypersquare, thus the space of interest is $L^p([0,1]^m)$ where $[0,1]^m \subset \Re^m$. Saying that $s_n(x)$ is dense in $L^p([0,1]^m)$ where $1 \leq p < \infty$ is equivalent to saying that for every $f \in L^p([0,1]^m)$ and every $\epsilon > 0$, there exists $\phi \in S$ such that $\|f - \phi\|_p \leq \epsilon$. If we have $S \subset L^p([0,1]^m)$ and our modified Fuzzy ART architecture can be shown to compute any member of S, then we will have shown that this neural network is capable of universal function approximation in $L^p([0,1]^m)$.

Fuzzy ART F_2 nodes conduct data clustering similar to the internal layer nodes of a radial basis function (RBF) neural network [5]. By itself then, the Fuzzy ART module cannot be expected to perform function approximation, but by adding an output layer of perceptron nodes, this approximation can be achieved. The internal layer of an

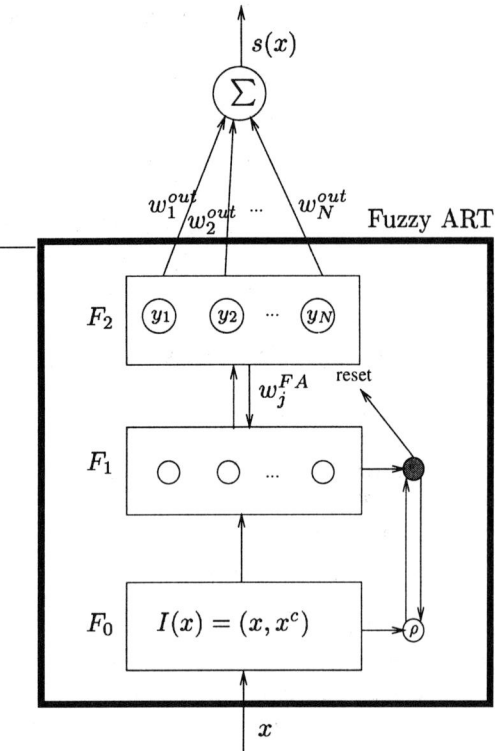

Fig. 2. Modified Fuzzy ART for Universal Approximation.

RBF neural network is connected to an output layer of nodes to perform approximation in a similar manner, see Figure 1 in [5]. In Fig. 2, the Fuzzy ART neural network module is connected to an output layer perceptron. Universal approximation for the Fuzzy ART will apply to an m-dimensional input space, but for simplicity in this paper, only a single input dimension will be considered. Also, the approximation output will, in general, fit multi-dimensional output, but for simplicity, only a single output dimension will be considered, and thus, only a single output layer perceptron is used, as shown in Fig. 2.

There are several steps necessary to prove the universal approximation capabilities of the Fuzzy ART F_2 node. Given a measurable function $f \geq 0$, the first task will be to determine a sequence of functions which will be used to approach f from below. This sequence of functions will rely upon partitioning of the domain of f into disjoint sets. Next, the Fuzzy ART F_2 node will be shown to be capable of computing the indicator function for an arbitrary member of these disjoint sets. It is this indicator function that will actually be used in the sequence of functions that we are interested in. Finally, these results will be pulled together with the construction and specification of the modified Fuzzy ART neural network architecture, shown in Fig. 2, for computing the sequence of functions for approximating f, and this sequence of functions will be shown to be dense in $L^p([0,1]^m)$.

Given a measurable function $f \in L^p([0,1]^m)$, $f \geq 0$ and $\epsilon > 0$, Consider the following sequence of functions

for $n = 1, 2, 3, \cdots$

$$s_n(x) = \sum_{j=1}^{2^n} C_{n,j} \chi_{D_{n,j}}(x) \qquad (9)$$

$$D_{n,j} = \left[\frac{j-1}{2^n}, \frac{j}{2^n}\right), \quad 1 \leq j < 2^n$$

$$D_{n,2^n} = \left[\frac{2^n-1}{2^n}, 1\right],$$

where the coefficients $C_{n,j}$ are determined using f and the diadic sets $D_{n,j} \subset [0,1]$. Diadic sets, also called diadic intervals, boxes or cubes are members of $\Omega = \Omega_1 \cup \Omega_2 \cup \Omega_3 \cup \cdots$, where Ω_n is defined as the collection of all 2^{-n} boxes with corners at P_n, and P_n is the set of all $x \in \Re^m$ whose coordinates are integer multiples of 2^{-n} [11]. Thus, $D_{n,j} \in \Omega_n$. Ω's density in $\Re^m$ and its capacity to cover (measurable) sets is exploited by the sequence of functions defined in (10) [11], [12]. Later it will be shown that $s_n(x) \leq f(x)$ for all x except for a set of measure less than ϵ. Note that $s_n(x)$ are simple functions if the coefficients take on a finite number of values, and this will be shown below. Thus $s_n(x) \in L^p([0,1]^m)$.

Next, it will be shown that the modified Fuzzy ART neural network architecture in Fig. 2 can be configured such that it computes $s_n(x)$ in (10). The first step is to show that F_2 nodes in Fig. 2 can compute the indicator functions of $D_{n,j}$ from (10) with proper network quantities including weights, indexes and vigilance values).

Lemma 1: The Fuzzy ART F_2 node can compute the indicator function for $D_{n,j} \in \Omega_n$.

Proof. Given $D_{n,j}$, the network quantities for a Fuzzy ART F_2 node will be determined so that it computes $\chi_{D_{n,j}}(x)$. A Fuzzy ART F_2 node has three quantities that need to be determined, w_j^{FA}, ρ and the node index V_j. The minimum point in $D_{n,j}$ is $\frac{j-1}{2^n}$ and the minimum point not in $D_{n,j}$ is $\frac{j-1}{2^n} + 2^{-n} = \frac{j}{2^n}$. Therefore, the weights become

$$w_j^{FA} = \left(\frac{j-1}{2^n} \left(\frac{j}{2^n}\right)^c\right) \qquad (10)$$

The function computed by the Fuzzy ART F_2 node j is

$$y_j(x) = \begin{cases} 1 & \text{if } j = \arg\max_{1 \leq i \leq N} T_i(I(x)) \\ 0 & \text{otherwise} \end{cases} \qquad (11)$$

$$I(x) = (x \ x^c)$$

$$T_j(I) = \begin{cases} \frac{\|w_j^{FA} \wedge I\|_1}{\|w_j^{FA}\|_1 + \alpha} & \text{if } \frac{\|w_j^{FA} \wedge I\|_1}{\|I\|_1} \geq \rho \\ 0 & \text{otherwise} \end{cases}$$

where $I(x)$ is the complement coded value for x and α is a small positive number. Note that because of complement coding $\|I(x)\|_1 = 1$, $\forall x$ (in general this will be m, but here $m = 1$). The vigilance parameter will have the following value

$$\rho = \frac{\|w_j^{FA}\|_1}{m} = \|w_j^{FA}\|_1 \qquad (12)$$

Thus, $y_j(x)$ will only be 1 if $x \in \left[\frac{i-1}{2^n}, \frac{j}{2^n}\right]$. And so the Fuzzy ART F_2 node j computes the indicator function for the closed interval $\left[\frac{j-1}{2^n}, \frac{j}{2^n}\right]$ and F_2 node $j+1$ will compute the indicator function for $\left[\frac{j}{2^n}, \frac{j+1}{2^n}\right]$. Note that these two overlap at $\frac{j}{2^n}$. In Fuzzy ART ties between competing F_2 nodes are broken by assigning an index value to the competing F_2 nodes and choosing the F_2 node with the lowest index. The index values, V_j, for the modified Fuzzy ART F_2 nodes become $V_j = 2^n - j + 1$. Thus, $y_j(x) = \chi_{\left[\frac{j-1}{2^n}, \frac{j}{2^n}\right)}(x)$ for $1 \leq j < 2^n$, and $y_{2^n}(I(x)) = \chi_{\left[\frac{2^n-1}{2^n}, 1\right]}(x)$. Therefore, the Fuzzy ART F_2 nodes constructed as described above compute the disjoint intervals $D_{n,j}$ for $1 \leq j \leq 2^n$ from (10). $\Diamond$

Before proceeding with the construction of the modified Fuzzy ART network, the coefficients $C_{n,j}$ from (10) will be specified. Here is the complete specification of the sequence of functions $s_n(x)$ including the coefficients

$$s_n(x) = \sum_{j=1}^{2^n} C_{n,j} \chi_{D_{n,j}}(x) \tag{13}$$

$$C_{n,j} = \frac{A_{n,j} - 1}{2^n}$$

$$A_{n,j} = \min_{i \in B_{n,j}}(i)$$

$$B_{n,j} = \left\{ i : \mu(E_{n,i} \cap D_{n,j}) \geq \frac{\epsilon}{2^n} \right\},$$
$$1 \leq i \leq n2^n + 1$$

$$D_{n,j} = \left[\frac{j-1}{2^n}, \frac{j}{2^n}\right), \quad 1 \leq j < 2^n$$

$$D_{n,2^n} = \left[\frac{2^n-1}{2^n}, 1\right],$$

$$E_{n,i} = f^{-1}\left(\left[\frac{i-1}{2^n}, \frac{i}{2^n}\right)\right), \quad 1 \leq i \leq n2^n$$

$$E_{n,n2^n+1} = f^{-1}([n, \infty)).$$

Note that $E_{n,i}$ are the pre-images of the Lebesgue intervals of f [11]. The index values in $B_{n,j}$ refer to those $E_{n,i}$ which intersect with $D_{n,j}$ with measure greater than or equal to $\frac{\epsilon}{2^n}$. Therefore, $C_{n,j} \leq f(x)$ for all $x \in D_{n,j}$ except for a set of measure $< \frac{\epsilon}{2^n}$. Note that there are 2^n diadic sets $D_{n,j}$. And so, $s_n(x) \leq f(x)$ for all x except for a set of measure ϵ.

Now the final result can be shown.

Theorem 1: The modified Fuzzy ART neural network, shown in Fig. 2, can be used to universally approximate any measurable function in $L^p([0,1])$.

Proof. Given $1 \leq p < \infty$ and $f \in L^p([0,1])$, $f \geq 0$, a series of functions, s_n, computable by the modified Fuzzy ART neural network in Fig. 2, will be determined such that these functions approximate f in the limit, and it will be shown that s_n is dense in $L^p([0,1])$. The Fuzzy ART neural network shown in Fig. 2 with parameters determined in (10) and (12) computes the following function

for the $N = 2^n$ F_2 nodes

$$s_n(x) = \sum_{j=1}^{N} w_{n,j}^{out} \cdot y_{n,j}(x) \tag{14}$$

$$y_{n,j}(x) = \begin{cases} 1 & \text{if } j = \arg\min_{k \in J_n} V_k \\ 0 & \text{otherwise} \end{cases}$$

$$J_n = \left\{ i : i = \arg\max_{1 \leq j \leq N} T_{n,j}(I(x)) \right\}$$

$$T_{n,j}(I) = \begin{cases} \frac{\|w_{n,j}^{FA} \wedge I\|_1}{\|w_{n,j}^{FA}\|_1 + \alpha} & \text{if } \frac{\|w_{n,j}^{FA} \wedge I\|_1}{\|I\|_1} \geq \rho \\ 0 & \text{otherwise} \end{cases}$$

Given the results from Lemma 1, these equations can be reduced to

$$s_n(x) = \sum_{j=1}^{N} w_{n,j}^{out} \cdot \chi_{D_{n,j}}(x) \tag{15}$$

$$D_{n,j} = \left[\frac{j-1}{2^n}, \frac{j}{2^n}\right), \quad 1 \leq j < 2^n$$

$$D_{n,2^n} = \left[\frac{2^n-1}{2^n}, 1\right]$$

The final step is to determine the values for $w_{n,j}^{out}$, which can be set as

$$w_{n,j}^{out} = C_{n,j} \tag{16}$$

where $C_{n,j}$ is defined in (14).

Since $|f(x) - s_n(x)|^p \leq f^p$, Lebesgue's dominated convergence theorem implies $\|f(x) - s_n(x)\|^p \to 0$ as $n \to \infty$ [11]. Our modified Fuzzy ART neural network computes the function in (14). Since $0 \leq s_n \leq f$, then $s_n \in L^p([0,1]^m)$. Thus, f is in the L^p-closure of s_n. $\Diamond$

We have implemented a very simple, proof of concept, version of the modified Fuzzy ART architecture in MATLAB™, as shown in Fig 3. The modified Fuzzy

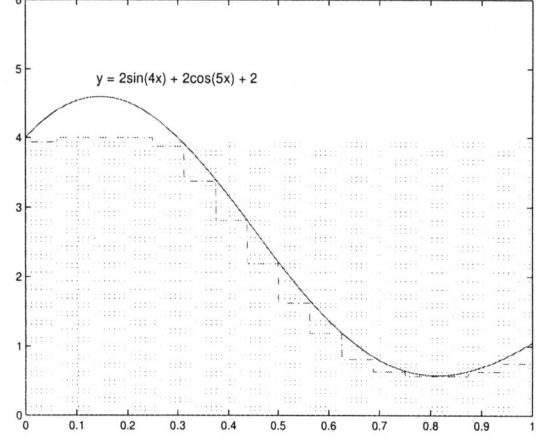

Fig. 3. Modified Fuzzy ART with $n = 4$.

ART architecture is capable of representing any measurable function in $L^p([0,1])$ with an arbitrarily large number of F_2 nodes. Note that for each n in the sequence defined above, a separate Fuzzy ART network is needed since there is only a single vigilance parameter ρ. Fuzzy ART F_2 nodes, in a single network, can represent any $D_{n,j} \in \Omega_n$.

A. Universal Approximation With Fuzzy ARTMAP

It is a very simple extension to use Fuzzy ARTMAP, by itself, instead of the modified Fuzzy ART neural network to perform universal approximation. With Fuzzy ARTMAP, we need to construct the A-side Fuzzy ART module, the B-side Fuzzy ART module and the MAP field. The A-side Fuzzy ART module will be constructed precisely as described in the previous section, however, instead of using the extra layer of perceptron nodes with their association weights, we use the Fuzzy ARTMAP MAP field and the B-side category templates. There will be one B-side template for each of the Lebesgue intervals, $E_{n,i}$ in (14). The value of the B-side template weight will be exactly the same as the coefficients used in the modified Fuzzy ART network, $C_{n,j}$ in (14). Note that there will be no complement coding in the B-side Fuzzy ART module. Next, the MAP field will be used to compute the minimum intersection between the diadic cube that A-side node J computes and the pre-images of all B-side nodes $1 \le k \le N^B$, $A_{n,j}$ in (14). Therefore, $w_{jk}^{AB} = 1$ if $A_{n,j} = k$, otherwise $w_{jk}^{AB} = 0$. Because each $A_{n,j}$ is unique, then the constructed MAP field will conform to Fuzzy ARTMAP learning in that each A-side F_2 node is associated with only a single B-side F_2 node. Thus, given input x, the value output by this Fuzzy ARTMAP network will be $C_{n,j}$ where $x \in D_{n,j}$.

IV. CONCLUDING REMARKS

An example of an ART-based neural network architecture that can perform such universal approximation described above is BARTMAP-SRM [13]. BARTMAP-SRM operates using the diadic hyperboxes described previously. The network is initiated using the unit hyperbox, which is subsequently split in half across each dimension creating 2^m new squares for an m-dimensional input learning space. Note that BARTMAP-SRM as well as the network constructions described in our main results above both suffer from the curse of dimensionality [14]. This means that for an m-dimensional input space, an exponentially large number of internal layer F_2 nodes may be required to reach a final solution. BARTMAP-SRM was not designed as a practical solution for high dimension input problems but rather as a theoretical construct for demonstrating the universal approximation capabilities. Another modification to Fuzzy ART, called Boosted ART has been shown to represent the same data space with exponentially fewer F_2 nodes, with respect to the input dimension m [15]. It is hoped that Boosted ART can be used in high dimension input spaces to help address the curse of dimensionality.

In this paper we have shown that Fuzzy ART augmented with a single layer of perceptron nodes can support universal function approximation. Furthermore, we have demonstrated that Fuzzy ARTMAP, by itself is a universal approximator. These results establish both of these neural network architectures as viable learning techniques on a large class of learning problems. These results continue to suffer from the curse of dimensionality, as do other universal approximation results. Our future research continues to expand upon these results in designing practical ART-based neural network architectures for conducting learning.

ACKNOWLEDGMENT

The authors from the University of Central Florida acknowledge the partial support from NSF through a CRCD grant number 0203446 entitled "Machine Learning Advances for Engineering Education".

REFERENCES

[1] G. Cybenko, "Approximation by superpositions of a sigmoidal function," *Mathematical Journal of Control, Signals, and Systemics*, vol. 2, pp. 303–314, 1989.

[2] K. Funahashi, "On the approximate realization of continuous mappings by neural networks," *Neural Networks*, vol. 2, pp. 183–192, 1989.

[3] K. M. Hornik, M. Stinchcombe, and H. White, "Multllayer feedforward networks are universal approximators," *Neural Networks*, vol. 2, pp. 359–366, 1989.

[4] E. J. Hartman, J. D. Keeler, and J. M. Kowalski, "Layered neural networks with gaussian hidden units as universal approsimators," *Neural Computation*, vol. 2, pp. 210–215, 1990.

[5] J. Park and I. W. Sandberg, "Universal approximation using radial-basis-function networks," *Neural Computation*, vol. 3, pp. 245–257, 1991.

[6] L. Martí, A. Policriti, and L. García, "AppART: An ART hybrid stable learning neural network for universal function approximation," in *Hybrid Information Systems*, A. Abraham and M. Koeppen, Eds., Heidelberg, Jul 2002, pp. 92–120, Physica Verlag.

[7] G. A. Carpenter, S. Grossberg, N. Markuzon, J. H. Reynolds, and D. B. Rosen, "Fuzzy ARTMAP: A neural network architecture for incremental supervised learning of analog multidimensional maps," *IEEE Transactions on Neural Networks*, vol. 3, no. 5, pp. 698–713, 1992.

[8] G. A. Carpenter, S. Grossberg, and D. B. Rosen, "Fuzzy ART: Fast stable learning and categorization of analog patterns by an adaptive resonance system," *Neural Networks*, vol. 4, no. 5, pp. 759–771, 1991.

[9] B. Moore, "ART 1 and pattern clustering," in *Proceedings of the 1988 Connectionist Summer School*. 1988, pp. 174–185, Morgan Kaufmann.

[10] M. Georgiopoulos, J. Huang, and G. L. Heileman, "Properties of learning in ARTMAP," *Neural Networks*, vol. 7, no. 3, pp. 495–506, 1994.

[11] W. Rudin, *Real and Complex Analysis*, McGraw-Hill, New York, second edition, 1974.

[12] E. DiBenedetto, *Real Analysis*, Birkhäuser, Boston, 2001.

[13] S. J. Verzi, G. L. Heileman, M. Georgiopoulos, and G. C. Anagnostopoulos, "Off-line structural risk minimization and BARTMAP-S," in *Proceedings of the International Joint Conference on Neural Networks*, 2002.

[14] H. White, *Artificial Neural Networks: Approximation and Learning Theory*, Blackwell, Cambridge MA, 1992.

[15] S. J. Verzi, *Boosted ART and Boosted ARTMAP: Extensions of Fuzzy ART and Fuzzy ARTMAP*, Ph.D. thesis, University of New Mexico, Albuquerque, New Mexico, 2002.

Perceptron Learning in the Domain of Graphs

Brijnesh J. Jain and Fritz Wysotzki
Dept. of Electrical Engineering and Computer Science
Technical University of Berlin, Germany
E-mail: {bjj,wysotzki}@cs.tu-berlin.de

Abstract— We develop a new mathematical framework, which embeds weighted graphs into quasi metric spaces. This concept establishes a theoretical basis to apply neural learning machines for structured data. To exemplarily illustrate the applicability of metric graph spaces, we propose and analyze a perceptron learning algorithm for graphs in its primal and dual form.

I. INTRODUCTION

Assume that we are given a training sample

$$\mathcal{Z} = \{(\boldsymbol{x}_1, y_1), \ldots, (\boldsymbol{x}_M, y_M)\}$$

consisting of a set of training data

$$\mathcal{X} = \{\boldsymbol{x}_1, \ldots, \boldsymbol{x}_M\} \subseteq \mathbb{R}^n$$

together with corresponding labels

$$\mathcal{Y} = \{y_1, \ldots, y_M\} \subseteq \{-1, +1\}.$$

The basic *classification learning task* is to find a decision function $h : \mathbb{R}^n \to \{-1, +1\}$ that 'accurately' predicts the labels of the training data as well as of unseen data points. Since Fisher's linear discriminant [5] numerous classification algorithms have been developed [1], [4], [14]. Rosenblatt's perceptron is possibly the simplest learning procedure for the classification of a set of linearly separable patterns. Basically, the perceptron consists of a single neuron with adjustable synaptic weight vector $\boldsymbol{w}_t \in \mathbb{R}^n$ and bias b_t. The algorithm to adjust the weights and the bias is *mistake driven* because only the occurrence of a classification error leads to an update of $\boldsymbol{w}_t$ and b_t.

A limitation not only of the perceptron learning (PL) algorithm, but also in the field of neural learning machines is the representation of data in terms of fixed-length real-valued feature vectors. Many important problems, however, do not admit such a vector representation easily [10]. Problems of this kind include the analysis of complex visual scenes [2], [3], the classification of organic molecules [16] and of positions in the game of Go [12], and many tasks related to language processing and understanding. In all of those problems the data under considerations are structured data, which are more adequately represented by graphs [8], [9].

Neural Networks for processing data structures have been proposed in [6], [11], [15], [17]. These approaches have in common that they combine symbolic and subsymbolic components by means of an adaptive encoding and decoding scheme between structured data and real valued vectors of fixed length. Usually, the coding is performed by a recursive neural network where the recursion corresponds to the recursive structure of the data. Due to its recursive architecture this approach is confined to quasi linear structures like term structures, trees or directed acyclic graphs.

In this paper we develop the fundamental concept of *metric graph spaces*, which enables the processing of arbitrary graphs by neural learning machines in a natural way. A metric graph space combines graph theoretical properties with properties of inner product vector spaces. A metric graph space is a quasi metric space in the sense that it is in fact not a vector space but has similar properties like a metric vector space.

To demonstrate the applicability of the proposed concept in the field of neural networks we propose and analyze an algorithm for perceptron learning for structures PLS in a primal and dual form. The basic procedure of PLS adapts the principal constituents of the classical PL algorithm: The adjustable weights W_t of a perceptron form a weighted graph. Given an input graph X the perceptron fires, if the *Schur-Hadamard inner product* of W_t and X exceeds a threshold (bias) $-b_t$. The Schur-Hadamard inner product of graphs is a concept similar to an inner product of vectors.

The rest of this paper is organized as follows: Section 2 introduces graph theoretic concepts and further terminologies used throughout this paper. Section 3 develops the theory of metric graphs spaces. Section 4 proposes two PLS algorithms. Finally, Section 5 concludes this contribution.

II. TERMINOLOGY AND NOTATIONS

Basic Notations

By $\mathbb{R}$ we denote the set of real numbers and by $\mathbb{R}_+$ the subset of all non-negative real numbers. Vectors $\boldsymbol{x} \in \mathbb{R}^n$ are denoted by bold faced lower case letters and $n \times m$ real valued matrices X are denoted by upper case letters. We write $\boldsymbol{x}^t$ and X^t for the transpose of a vector $\boldsymbol{x}$ and a matrix X, respectively. The set of all real valued $n \times n$-matrices is denoted by $\mathbb{R}[n]$. A *zero matrix* $0_{n,m}$ with n rows and m columns is a matrix with all its entries zero.

Graph Theory and Permutation Groups

For purpose of clarity and simplicity we consider weighted graphs only. Extension to the more general case of colored graphs is straightforward, but requires tedious and necessary technical preparations as defining the addition, subtraction, and the scalar multiplication on symbolic colors.

A *weighted graph* is a pair $X = (V, \mu)$ consisting of a finite set $V \neq \emptyset$ of *vertices* and a mapping $\mu : V^2 \to \mathbb{R}$ assigning each pair $(i, j) \in V^2$ a real valued scalar. The elements of V are the *vertices* of the graph X, and the pairs $(i, j) \in V^2$

of distinct vertices $i \neq j$ with positive weight $\mu((i,j)) > 0$ are its *edges*. The vertex set of a graph X is referred to as $V(X)$, its edge set as $E(X)$, and its real valued mapping as μ_X. By $\mathbb{G}$ we denote the set of weighted graphs. Note that the definition of weighted graphs comprises graphs with negative weights.

The number of vertices of a graph X is its *order*, written as $|X|$. We use a *labeling* of the vertex set V in order to deal with it conveniently. A labeling of $V(X)$ is a bijection

$$l : V(X) \to \{1, \ldots, |X|\},$$

which identifies each element of $V(X)$ with a certain number between 1 and $|X|$. The *adjacency matrix* of a graph X with n vertices is a matrix $A(X) = (x_{ij}) \in \mathbb{R}[n]$ with entries $x_{ij} = \mu_X(i,j)$.

Let X and Y be two graphs. We call X and Y *isomorphic*, and write $X \simeq Y$, if there exists a bijection $\phi : V(X) \to V(Y)$, $i \mapsto i^\phi$ with $\mu_X((i,j)) = \mu_Y((i^\phi, j^\phi))$. Such a map ϕ is called *isomorphism*; if $X = Y$, it is called an *automorphism*.

A *permutation* acting on X is a bijection $\pi : V(X) \to V(X)$ from V onto itself. The image graph of a permutation π acting on X is denoted by X^π. The set $\mathcal{S}_X$ of all permutations acting on X is called the *symmetric group* of X. A permutation π acting on X corresponds to a relabeling of X and thus yields a reordering of its adjacency matrix. In general we have $A(X) \neq A(X^\pi)$. Equality $A(X) = A(X^\pi)$ holds if and only if $\pi \in \mathcal{S}_X$ is an automorphism of X. Let $|X| = n$. Since we assume a labeling $V(X) = \{1, \ldots, n\}$, we simply write $\mathcal{S}_n$ instead of $\mathcal{S}_X$.

III. METRIC GRAPH SPACES

A. The Graph Space of order n

In order to facilitate arithmetic operations on graphs by means of their adjacency matrices we align graphs of different order to graphs of equal order as follows: For any $n \geq 1$ the graph space $\mathbb{G}^n$ consists of all graphs $X \in \mathbb{G}$ of order $|X| \leq n$. Graphs $X \in \mathbb{G}$ of order $|X| = p < n$ are aligned to a graph $X' \in \mathbb{G}^n$ by inserting $q = n - p$ vertices of weight zero such that the adjacency matrix $A(X') \in \mathbb{R}[n]$ of X' is of the form

$$A(X') = \begin{pmatrix} A(X) & 0_{p,q} \\ 0_{q,p} & 0_{q,q} \end{pmatrix}$$

where $A(X)$ is the adjacency matrix of X, $0_{p,q}$, $0_{q,p}$, and $0_{q,q}$ are padding zero matrices.

Next we define addition and scalar multiplication of graphs in $\mathbb{G}^n$. Let $X, Y \in \mathbb{G}^n$ be graphs, and $\lambda \in \mathbb{R}$ a scalar. Then

$$\begin{aligned} X + Y &:= A(X) + A(Y) \\ \lambda \cdot X &:= \lambda \cdot A(X) \end{aligned}$$

Addition and scalar multiplication of graphs are the usual componentwise addition and scalar multiplication of their adjacency matrices.

The set $\mathbb{G}^n$ together with the binary operations $+ : \mathbb{G}^n \times \mathbb{G}^n \to \mathbb{G}^n$ and $\cdot : \mathbb{G}^n \times \mathbb{G}^n \to \mathbb{R}$ is a vector space. The vector space $\mathbb{G}^n$ has the objectionable property, that in general $X + Y \neq X' + Y$ for isomorphic graphs $X \simeq X'$.

B. Inner Product Graph Spaces

Fundamental for the following considerations and derivations is the *Schur-Hadamard inner product* of pairs of graphs in $\mathbb{G}^n$. The concept of a Schur-Hadamard inner product of graphs is the counterpart of the concept of an inner product defined on vector spaces.

Let $A, B \in \mathbb{R}[n]$. The *Schur-Hadamard inner product of matrices* A and B is defined by

$$\langle A, B \rangle = \langle \text{vec}(A), \text{vec}(B) \rangle.$$

where $vec(A)$ and $vec(B)$ are the n^2 dimensional vectors obtained by concatenating the rows of A and B, respectively.

Similarly, we define a norm on $\mathbb{R}[n]$. Let $\|.\|$ be a norm on $\mathbb{R}^{n^2}$. Obviously,

$$\|.\| : \mathbb{R}[n] \to \mathbb{R}, \quad A \mapsto \|\text{vec}(A)\|$$

is a norm on $\mathbb{R}[n]$.

Definition III.1 (Schur-Hadamard inner product on $\mathbb{G}^n$)
Let

$$\langle\,,\,\rangle : \mathbb{R}^{n^2} \times \mathbb{R}^{n^2} \to \mathbb{R}$$

be an inner product. We call the mapping

$$\sigma : \mathbb{G}^n \times \mathbb{G}^n \to \mathbb{R}, \quad (X,Y) \mapsto \max_{\pi \in \mathcal{S}_n} \langle A(X^\pi), A(Y) \rangle$$

Schur-Hadamard inner product of graphs induced by $\langle\,,\,\rangle$.

Of special interest are permutations $\pi \in \mathcal{S}_n$, which maximize the inner product $\langle A(X^\pi), A(Y) \rangle$. We call a permutation $\pi \in \mathcal{S}_n$ with $\sigma(X,Y) = \langle A(X^\pi), A(Y) \rangle$ *embedding* from X into Y. By $\mathcal{I}(Y,X)$ we denote the set of all embeddings from X into Y.

The following result lists some properties of the Schur-Hadamard inner product, which will be used implicitly throughout this section.

Proposition III.1 *Let $\langle\,,\,\rangle$ be a inner product on $\mathbb{R}^{n^2}$. Then for all $X, Y, Z \in \mathbb{G}^n$ the Schur-Hadamard inner product σ induced by $\langle\,,\,\rangle$ satisfies the following properties*

SH 1. $\sigma(X,X) = \langle A(X), A(X) \rangle \geq 0$
SH 2. $\sigma(X,X) = 0 \Leftrightarrow A(X) = 0_{n,n}$
SH 3. $\sigma(X,Y) = \sigma(Y,X)$
SH 4. $\sigma(\lambda \cdot X, Y) = \lambda \cdot \sigma(X,Y)$ for all $\lambda \in \mathbb{R}_+$
SH 5. $\sigma(X + Y, Z) \leq \sigma(X,Z) + \sigma(Y,Z)$

Proof: (SH 1): Let $\pi \in \mathcal{I}(X,X)$ be an embedding. Then

$$\begin{aligned} \sigma(X,X) &= \langle A(X^\pi), A(X) \rangle \\ &= \|A(X^\pi)\| \cdot \|A(X)\| \cdot \cos\alpha \\ &= \langle A(X), A(X) \rangle \cdot \cos\alpha \\ &\leq \langle A(X), A(X) \rangle \end{aligned}$$

where α is the angle between $vec(A(X^\pi))$ and $vec(A(X))$. The equation in the third line follows from $\|A(X)\| = \|A(X^\pi)\|$ for all $\pi \in \mathcal{S}_n$. Since π is an embedding, we have $\langle A(X^\pi), A(X) \rangle \geq \langle A(X), A(X) \rangle$. Combining both inequalities yields $\sigma(X,X) =$

$\langle A(X), A(X) \rangle$. This together with $\langle A(X), A(X) \rangle \geq 0$ proves property (SH 1).

(SH 2): Follows directly from the positive definiteness of $\langle \, , \, \rangle$.

(SH 3): Assume that $\pi \in \mathcal{I}(X, Y)$ is an embedding from X into Y. Then by definition of the Schur-Hadamard-inner product induced by $\langle \, , \, \rangle$ we have

$$\sigma(X, Y) = \langle A(X^\pi), A(Y) \rangle$$

Since $\pi \in \mathcal{S}_n$ there exists a permutation matrix $P \in \mathbb{R}[n^2]$, such that

$$A(X^\pi) = P^t A(X) P$$

Permutation matrices are orthogonal and preserve length. Repeated application of the properties of an orthogonal matrix yields

$$\begin{aligned}
\sigma(X, Y) &= \langle P^t A(X) P, A(Y) \rangle \\
&= \langle P(P^t A(X) P), P A(Y) \rangle \\
&= \langle (A(X) P) P^t, (P A(Y)) P^t \rangle \\
&= \langle A(X), P A(Y) P^t \rangle = \langle P A(Y) P^t, A(X) \rangle
\end{aligned}$$

where the last equation follows from the symmetry of the inner product. From $P A(Y) P^t = A(Y^\phi)$ with $\phi = \pi^{-1} \in \mathcal{S}_n$ follows that $\sigma(X, Y) \leq \sigma(Y, X)$. A similar argumentation shows $\sigma(Y, X) \leq \sigma(X, Y)$. Combining both inequalities yields property (SH 3).

(SH 4): Let $\pi \in \mathcal{I}(X, Y)$ be an embedding and $\lambda \in \mathbb{R}_+$. It is sufficient to show that $\pi \in \mathcal{I}(\lambda \cdot X, Y)$. Since $\pi \in \mathcal{I}(X, Y)$ is an embedding, it maximizes the Schur-Hadamard inner product of adjacency matrices

$$\langle A(X^\pi), A(Y) \rangle = \max_{\phi \in \mathcal{S}_n} \langle A(X^\phi), A(Y) \rangle.$$

From $\lambda \geq 0$ and

$$\lambda \cdot \max_{\phi \in \mathcal{S}_n} \langle A(X^\phi), A(Y) \rangle = \max_{\phi \in \mathcal{S}_n} \langle \lambda \cdot A(X^\phi), A(Y) \rangle$$

follows $\pi \in \mathcal{I}(\lambda \cdot X, Y)$.

(SH 5): Let $\pi \in \mathcal{I}(X+Y, Z)$, $\phi \in \mathcal{I}(X, Z)$, and $\psi \in \mathcal{I}(Y, Z)$ be embeddings into Z. Then

$$\begin{aligned}
\sigma(X+Y, Z) &= \langle A((X+Y)^\pi), A(Z) \rangle \\
&= \langle A(X^\pi) + A(Y^\pi), A(Z) \rangle \\
&= \langle A(X^\pi), A(Z) \rangle + \langle A(Y^\pi), A(Z) \rangle \\
&\leq \langle A(X^\phi), A(Z) \rangle + \langle A(Y^\psi), A(Z) \rangle \\
&= \sigma(X, Z) + \sigma(Y, Z).
\end{aligned}$$

$\square$

C. Normed Graph Spaces

A *norm* on $\mathbb{G}^n$ is a function $N : \mathbb{G}^n \to \mathbb{R}$ with

N 1. $N(\lambda \cdot X) = |\lambda| \cdot \|X\|$
N 2. $N(X+Y) \leq N(X) + N(Y)$
N 3. $N(X) = 0 \Rightarrow A(X) = 0_{n,n}$

for all $X, Y \in \mathbb{G}^n$, and $\lambda \in \mathbb{R}$. A graph space equipped with a norm is called *normed graph space*. The Schur-Hadamard inner product gives rise to the *Euclidean norm*

$$\|X\| = \sqrt{\sigma(X, X)}.$$

According to property (SH 1) the Euclidean norm of X can simply be computed by taking the square root of the Schur-Hadamard inner product of its adjacency matrix $A(X)$.

Theorem III.1 shows that the Euclidean norm $\|\ \|$ is indeed a norm on $\mathbb{G}^n$.

Theorem III.1 *The function*

$$\|\ \| : \mathbb{G}^n \to \mathbb{R}, \quad X \mapsto \|X\|$$

defines a norm on $\mathbb{G}^n$.

Proof: We have

$$\|\lambda \cdot X\|^2 = \langle \lambda \cdot A(X), \lambda \cdot A(X) \rangle = \lambda^2 \cdot \|X\|^2.$$

Taking the square root of each side proves property (N 1). To show (N 2) we prove $\|X+Y\|^2 \leq \left(\|X\| + \|Y\|\right)^2$.

Since the Schur-Hadamard inner product $\langle \, , \, \rangle$ of matrices is bilinear, we find

$$\begin{aligned}
\|X+Y\|^2 &= \langle A(X) + A(Y), A(X) + A(Y) \rangle \\
&= \|A(X)\|^2 + 2 \cdot \langle A(X), A(Y) \rangle + \|A(Y)\|^2 \\
&\leq \|A(X)\|^2 + 2 \cdot |\langle A(X), A(Y) \rangle| + \|A(Y)\|^2.
\end{aligned}$$

Hence, by the *Cauchy-Schwarz inequality*,

$$\begin{aligned}
\|X+Y\|^2 &\leq \|A(X)\|^2 + 2 \cdot \|A(X)\| \cdot \|A(Y)\| + \|A(Y)\|^2 \\
&= \left(\|A(X)\| + \|A(Y)\|\right)^2 = \left(\|X\| + \|Y\|\right)^2.
\end{aligned}$$

Taking the square root of each side yields property (N 2). Finally, property (N 3) follows from (SH 1).

$\square$

IV. Vector Space of Abstract Graphs

The notion of vector spaces of abstract graphs is motivated from a suitable formulation of the dual form of perceptron learning for graphs. Let $X \in \mathbb{G}^n$ be a graph. The set

$$\hat{X} = \{Y \mid X \simeq Y\}$$

is called the *isomorphism class* of X. Any representative X of $\hat{X}$ is an *abstract graph*. By

$$\hat{\mathbb{G}}^n = \{\hat{X} \mid X \in \mathbb{G}^n\}$$

we denote the *set of abstract graphs* of order n. Next we introduce the one dimensional vector space $(\mathcal{L}(\hat{X}), +, \cdot)$ generated by an abstract graph $\hat{X}$. The set

$$\mathcal{L}(\hat{X}) = \{\hat{Y} \in \hat{\mathbb{G}}^n \mid Y \simeq \lambda \cdot X, \lambda \in \mathbb{R}\}$$

is the *line of abstract graphs* in direction of $\hat{X}$. Addition and scalar multiplication are defined as follows:

$$+ : \mathcal{L}(\hat{X}) \times \mathcal{L}(\hat{X}) \to \mathcal{L}(\hat{X}), \quad \hat{Y} + \hat{Z} = \widehat{(\lambda_Y + \lambda_Z) \cdot X}$$
$$\cdot : \mathbb{R} \times \mathcal{L}(\hat{X}) \to \mathcal{L}(\hat{X}), \quad \lambda \cdot \hat{Y} = \widehat{\lambda \cdot Y}$$

where $\lambda_Y, \lambda_Z \in \mathbb{R}$ with $Y \simeq \lambda_Y \cdot X$ and $Z \simeq \lambda_Z \cdot X$.

It is easy to verify that addition and scalar multiplication are well-defined and that $\mathcal{L}(\hat{X})$ is a vector space over $\mathbb{R}$. We observe merely that the zero element of $\mathcal{L}(\hat{X})$ is the abstract zero graph $\hat{0} = 0 \cdot \hat{X}$ with adjacency matrix $A(0) = 0_{n,n}$.

Let $\mathcal{L} = \left(\mathcal{L}(\hat{X}_1), \ldots, \mathcal{L}(\hat{X}_M)\right)$ be an M-tuple of lines of abstract graphs. The sum of $\mathcal{L}$ is the vector space

$$\sum_{i=1}^{M} \mathcal{L}(\hat{X}_i) = \{\lambda_1 \hat{X}_1 + \cdots + \lambda_M \hat{X}_M \mid \lambda_1, \ldots, \lambda_M \in \mathbb{R}\}$$

consisting of all linear combinations of elements of $\mathcal{L}(\hat{X}_i)$.

Remark IV.1 Let $\mathcal{L} = \big(\mathcal{L}(\hat{X}_1), \mathcal{L}(\hat{X}_2)\big)$ be a tuple of lines and let $\hat{Y}_1 \in \mathcal{L}(\hat{X}_1)$ and $\hat{Y}_2 \in \mathcal{L}(\hat{X}_2)$ be abstract graphs lying on the lines $\mathcal{L}(\hat{X}_1)$ and $\mathcal{L}(\hat{X}_2)$, respectively. Two cases can occur:
1) $\mathcal{L}(\hat{X}_1) \neq \mathcal{L}(\hat{X}_2)$: Then the sum of $\mathcal{L}$ is equal to the direct sum
$$\mathcal{L}(\hat{X}_1) + \mathcal{L}(\hat{X}_2) = \mathcal{L}(\hat{X}_1) \oplus \mathcal{L}(\hat{X}_2)$$
with $\hat{Y}_1 + \hat{Y}_2 = \hat{Y}_1 \oplus \hat{Y}_2$.
2) $\mathcal{L}(\hat{X}_1) = \mathcal{L}(\hat{X}_2)$: Then we have
$$\mathcal{L}(\hat{X}_1) + \mathcal{L}(\hat{X}_2) = \mathcal{L}(\hat{X}_1) = \mathcal{L}(\hat{X}_2)$$
where $\hat{Y}_1 + \hat{Y}_2$ is the usual addition as defined for elements of the same line.

The *vector space of abstract graphs*
$$\mathcal{G}^n = \sum_{\hat{X} \in \hat{G}^n} \mathcal{L}(\hat{X})$$
consists of all finite linear combinations of abstract graphs. From linear algebra we know that the sum of infinitely many vector spaces is also a vector space. Note that the sum $\sum_i V_i$ of vector spaces V_i is also referred to as the vector space generated by the union of all V_i.

Let $\mathcal{X} = \{X_1, \ldots, X_M\} \subseteq \mathcal{G}^n$ be a finite subset of abstract graphs. By
$$\mathcal{G}^n_{\mathcal{X}} = \sum_{i=1}^M \mathcal{L}(\hat{X}_i)$$
we denote the subspace $\mathcal{G}^n_{\mathcal{X}}$ of $\mathcal{G}^n$ generated by $\mathcal{X}$. We equip the subspace $\mathcal{G}^n_{\mathcal{X}}$ with the $\mathcal{X}$-Schur-Hadamard inner product of abstract graphs as follows:

Definition IV.1 (Schur-Hadamard inner product on $\mathcal{G}^n_{\mathcal{X}}$)
Let σ be the Schur-Hadamard inner product of graphs induced by an inner product $\langle\ ,\ \rangle$ on $\mathbb{R}^{n^2}$. We call the mapping $\hat{\sigma}_{\mathcal{X}} : \mathcal{G}^n_{\mathcal{X}} \times \mathcal{G}^n_{\mathcal{X}} \to \mathbb{R}$ with
$$\left\langle \sum_{i=1}^M \lambda_i \hat{X}_i, \sum_{j=1}^M \mu_j \hat{X}_j \right\rangle = \sum_{i,j} \lambda_i \mu_j \sigma(X_i, X_j)$$
$\mathcal{X}$-Schur-Hadamard inner product of abstract graphs induced by $\langle\ ,\ \rangle$.

The $\mathcal{X}$-Schur-Hadamard inner product is an inner product on $\mathcal{G}^n_{\mathcal{X}}$ and it is obvious how to define $\mathcal{G}^n_{\mathcal{X}}$ as an Euclidean space.

V. Perceptron Learning for Graphs

Let $\mathcal{X} = \{X_1, \ldots, X_M\} \subseteq \mathbb{G}^n$ be a set of training graphs together with corresponding labels $\mathcal{Y} = \{y_1, \ldots, y_M\} \subseteq \{-1, +1\}$. By $\mathcal{Z} = \{(X, y_i) : 1 \leq i \leq M\} \subset \mathcal{X} \times \mathcal{Y}$ we denote the set of training examples. The goal is to find a decision function
$$h : \mathbb{G}^n \to \{-1, +1\}$$
that 'accurately' predicts the labels of unseen data (X, y).

This section introduces a primal and dual form of perceptron learning (PLS-I and PLS-II, resp.) for finding a decision function of the form
$$h : \mathbb{G}^n \to \{-1, +1\}, \quad X \mapsto sgn\big(f(W, X) + b\big)$$
where sgn is the sign function.

A. Primal Form of Perceptron Learning for Structures

Like Rosenblatt's perceptron the PLS-I algorithm is an *online* and *mistake-driven* procedure, which starts with an initial weight graph $W_0 \in \mathbb{G}^n$ and updates it each time a training example is misclassified by the current weight graph. The PLS-I algorithm also referred to as the *primal form of perceptron learning for graphs* is shown in Figure 1.

PRIMAL FORM OF PERCEPTRON LEARNING:
Let $\mathcal{Z}$ be a training sample.
1) **Initialization:** Set $W \leftarrow 0_{n,n}$ and $b \leftarrow 0$.
2) **repeat**
   for $i = 1$ to M
   if $y_i\big(\sigma(W, X_i) + b\big) \leq 0$ then
   $\quad W \leftarrow W + y_i \cdot X_i$
   $\quad b \leftarrow b + y_i$
   until all $z \in \mathcal{Z}$ are classified correctly.
3) **return** (W, b).

Fig. 1. Outline of the PLS-I algorithm.

A training example $z = (X, y) \in \mathcal{Z}$ is misclassified, if the Schur-Hadamard inner product of the weight graph W_t after t updates and the current input graph X does not exceed the bias $-b_t$
$$\sigma(W_t, X) + b_t \leq 0.$$

To adjust W_t the algorithm first chooses an embedding $\pi(t) \in \mathcal{I}(X, W_t)$ from X into the current weight graph W_t. Then the algorithm operates on the adjacency matrices $A\big(X^{\pi(t)}\big)$ and $A(W_t)$ to apply the same update rule as in the case of perceptron learning for feature vectors.

To theoretically analyze the behavior of PLS-I we assume that there exists a solution that classifies the training sample $\mathcal{Z}$ correctly. In this case $\mathcal{Z}$ is said to be *separable*.

Definition V.1 (Separability) *A training sample $\mathcal{Z}$ is said to be* separable, *if there exists a solution graph $W^* \in \mathbb{G}^n$ with*
$$y = sgn\big(\sigma(W^*, X) + b\big)$$
for all training examples $(X, y) \in \mathcal{Z}$. We call $\mathcal{Z}$ uniformly separable, *if there exists a graph $W^* \in \mathbb{G}^n$ such that*
$$y = sgn\big(\langle A(W^*), A(X^\pi)\rangle + b\big)$$
for all $(X, y) \in \mathcal{Z}$ and for all $\pi \in \mathcal{S}_n$.

Assume that $\mathcal{Z}$ is a separable training sample. Since

$$\sigma(W_{t+1}, X) + b_{t+1} = \sigma(W_t + X, X) + b_t + 1$$
$$= \sigma(W_t, X) + \|X\|^2 + b_t + 1$$
$$\geq \sigma(W_t, X) + b_t$$

the update rule moves the weight graph and the bias in a 'good' direction. But in contrast to the inner product of feature vectors, the Schur-Hadamard inner product does not satisfy the bilinearity property. Furthermore, the particular choice of $\pi(t) \in \mathcal{I}(X, W_t)$ is not unique. For these reasons we assume that the sequence of weight vectors does not converge to a solution in general.

If we assume that $\mathcal{Z}$ is uniformly separable, then the perceptron convergence Theorem holds.

Theorem V.1 (Convergence Theorem for PLS-I) *Let $\mathcal{Z}$ be a uniformly separable training set. Then the primal form of the perceptron algorithm on $\mathcal{Z}$ converges to a solution graph W after a finite number of update steps.*

Proof: Let $\mathcal{X}' = \{y_1 \cdot X_1, \ldots, y_M \cdot X_M\}$ be a normalization of $\mathcal{X}$ to simplify the treatment. To simplify the analysis assume that $X \in \mathcal{X}'$ is extended by a non-permutable and isolated vertex of constant weight 1. Similarly we extend the weight graph W_t by a a non-permutable and isolated vertex of adjustable weight b_t. This commonly used technique absorbs the bias into the graphs.

Since $\mathcal{Z}$ is uniformly separable, there exists a solution graph W^* with $\langle A(W^*), A(X^\pi) \rangle > 0$ for all $X \in \mathcal{X}'$ and for all $\pi \in S_n$. Without loss of generality we assume $\|W^*\| = 1$. Let $\lambda > 0$ be a positive scale factor. From the update rule follows

$$W_{t+1} - \lambda W^* = W_t + \tilde{X}_t - \lambda W^* = (W_t - \lambda W^*) + \tilde{X}_t$$

where $\tilde{X}_t = X_t^{\pi(t)} \in \mathcal{X}'$ with $\pi(t) \in \mathcal{I}(X_t, W_t)$. Therefore,

$$\|W_{t+1} - \lambda W^*\|^2 = \|W_t - \lambda W^*\|^2 + \|X_t\|^2$$
$$+ 2 \cdot \langle A(W_t) - \lambda A(W^*), A(\tilde{X}_t) \rangle.$$

Since X_t was misclassified, $\sigma(W_t, X_t) = \langle A(W_t), A(\tilde{X}_t) \rangle < 0$, and thus

$$\|W_{t+1} - \lambda W^*\|^2 \leq \|W_t - \lambda W^*\|^2 + \|X_t\|^2$$
$$- 2\lambda \cdot \langle A(W^*), A(\tilde{X}_t) \rangle.$$

By assumption $\langle A(W^*), A(\tilde{X}_t) \rangle > 0$. Let

$$R = \max_{1 \leq i \leq M} \|X_i\|$$
$$\gamma = \min_{1 \leq i \leq M} \langle A(W^*), A(\tilde{X}_i) \rangle$$
$$\lambda = \frac{R^2}{\gamma}.$$

Then by induction we obtain

$$\|W_{t+1} - \lambda W^*\|^2 \leq \|W_t - \lambda W^*\|^2 - R^2$$
$$\leq \|W_1 - \lambda W^*\|^2 - t \cdot R^2$$
$$= \lambda^2 - t \cdot R^2.$$

Since the squared distance $\|W_{t+1} - \lambda W^*\|^2 \geq 0$, it follows that t is bounded by

$$t \leq \frac{\lambda}{R^2} = \left(\frac{R}{\gamma}\right)^2.$$

□

B. Dual Form of Perceptron Learning for Structures

The dual form implicitly operates on abstract weight graphs $\hat{W} \in \mathcal{G}_{\mathcal{X}}^n$. Figure 2 outlines the PLS-II algorithm.

DUAL FORM OF PERCEPTRON LEARNING:
Let $\mathcal{Z}$ be a training sample.
1) **Initialization:** Set $\boldsymbol{\alpha} \leftarrow \mathbf{0}$ and $b \leftarrow 0$.
2) **repeat**
    for $i = 1$ to M
       if $y_i \left(\sum_j \alpha_j y_j \sigma(X_i, X_j) \right) \leq 0$ then
           $\alpha_i \leftarrow \alpha_i + 1$
           $b \leftarrow b + y_i$
    until all $z \in \mathcal{Z}$ are classified correctly.
3) **return** $(\boldsymbol{\alpha}, b)$.

Fig. 2. Outline of dual perceptron learning for graphs.

The weight space $\mathcal{G}_{\mathcal{X}}^n$ of the PLS-II algorithm is determined by the set $\mathcal{X}$. The PLS-II algorithm starts with an initial abstract weight graph $\hat{W} = \hat{0}_{n,n} \in \mathcal{G}_{\mathcal{X}}^n$. During learning PLS-II adds misclassified positive training examples or subtracts misclassified negative ones to $\hat{W}$. So the final hypothesis will be a linear combination of the training graphs

$$\hat{W} = \sum_{i=1}^{M} \alpha_i y_i \hat{X}_i \in \mathcal{G}_{\mathcal{X}}^n.$$

To analyze the convergence behavior of PLS-II we consider the case of a *linearly separable* training sample $\mathcal{Z}$.

Definition V.2 (Linear Separability) *A training sample $\mathcal{Z}$ is said to be* linearly separable, *if there exists a pair $(\boldsymbol{\alpha}, b) \in \mathbb{R}^{n+1}$ with*

$$h(X) = sgn\left(\sum_{j=1}^{M} \alpha_j y_j \sigma(X_j, X) + b\right) = y$$

for all training examples $(X, y) \in \mathcal{Z}$.

Proposition V.1 states that separability in the sense of Def. V.1 implies linear separability in the sense of Def. V.2.

Proposition V.1 *Let $\mathcal{Z}$ be a training sample. Then*

$$\mathcal{Z} \text{ separable} \Rightarrow \mathcal{Z} \text{ linearly separable}.$$

Proof: Let $\mathcal{X}' = \{y_1 \cdot X_1, \ldots, y_M \cdot X_M\}$ be the normalization of $\mathcal{X}$ as in the proof of Theorem V.1. If $\mathcal{Z}$ is separable, then there exists a solution $W^* \in \mathbb{G}^n$ with $\sigma(W^*, X) + b > 0$ for all $X \in \mathcal{X}'$. Then $\hat{W}^* \in \mathcal{G}^n$ is an abstract graph. With $\mathcal{X}'' = \mathcal{X}' \cup \{\hat{W}^*\}$ we have $\hat{\sigma}_{\mathcal{X}''}(\hat{W}^*, \hat{X}) = \sigma(W^*, X) > 0$ for all $X \in \mathcal{X}'$. With a similar argumentation as in the proof of Theorem V.1 we can show that the sequence of weight graphs

$$\hat{W}_t = \sum_{i=1}^{M} \alpha_i(t) X_i \in \mathcal{G}_{\mathcal{X}'}^n$$

converges to a solution within $\mathcal{G}_{\mathcal{X}'}^n \subseteq \mathcal{G}_{\mathcal{X}''}^n$, provided that W^* is a solution in the larger subspace $\mathcal{G}_{\mathcal{X}''}^n$. Thus $\mathcal{Z}$ is linearly separable.

□

The following result shows that if the training sample $\mathcal{Z}$ is linearly separable, then the PLS-II algorithm converges after a finite number of updates.

Theorem V.2 (Convergence Theorem for PLS-II) *Let $\mathcal{Z}$ be a separable training set. Then the perceptron algorithm on $\mathcal{Z}$ converges to a solution (α, b) after a finite number of update steps.*

Proof: Let
$$V = \sum_{i=1}^{M} \alpha_i y_i \hat{X}_i \quad \text{and} \quad W_{t+1} = \sum_{i=1}^{M} \alpha_i(t+1) y_i \hat{X}_i$$
be the abstract solution graph and the abstract weight graph, respectively. Since $\mathcal{G}_\mathcal{X}^n$ together with its $\mathcal{X}$-Schur-Hadamard inner product $\hat{\sigma}_\mathcal{X}$ is an inner product vector space, the proof follows the same argumentation as in [13] for real valued feature vectors. □

C. Discussion

So far we have not mentioned how we can determine an embedding π form one graph X to another graph Y in order to compute the Schur-Hadamard inner product and to apply the update rule of the PLS-I algorithm. The problem of finding an embedding belongs to the class of *graph matching problems*. In its most general form the graph matching problem is the problem of finding the best partial mapping between two graphs where the quality of the mapping is estimated in terms of a problem dependent objective function. Since the graph matching problem is NP complete [7], exact algorithms, which guarantee an optimal solution are useless in a practical setting for all but the smallest graphs. In the context of linear classifiers for graphs like the perceptron it is reasonable to apply heuristics, which approximately solve the graph matching problem within an acceptable amount of time.

From the perspective of learning and from the theoretical point of view the PLS-II is more attractive than PLS-I for two reasons: Firstly, during learning PLS-II requires at most $M(M-1)/2$ computations of the Schur-Hadamard inner product. This number is independent from the number of epochs with which PLS-II cycles through the training sample. The number of graph matchings performed by PLS-I is proportional to the number of training examples presented during learning. Secondly, in the case of separable training data PLS-II guarantees convergence to a solution.

From a practical point of view one might prefer to apply PLS-I. To assign an unseen graph X to one of the labels $y = -1$ or $y = +1$, the primal form requires a single computation of the Schur-Hadamard inner product. The dual form PLS-II again performs at most $M(M-1)/2$ computations of the Schur-Hadamard inner product, since it is not clear how to map an abstract solution graph $\hat{W}^* \in \mathcal{G}_\mathcal{X}^n$ to a solution graph $W^* \in \mathbb{G}^n$. Thus the dual form might be intractable as a classifier in a practical setting.

VI. CONCLUSION

In this paper we have developed the theory of metric graph spaces. To illustrate the benefit of metric graph spaces within the field of neural learning machines, we exemplary proposed a perceptron learning algorithm for structures in a primal and dual form. Given a separable training sample, PLS-II converges to a solution after finite updates of the abstract weight graph. The same holds under some assumptions for PLS-I.

Future work comprises an experimental study of PLS-I and application of metric graph spaces to more complex supervised and unsupervised neural learning machines, like Backpropagation, Radial Basis Functions, Competitive Learning with Self-Organizing Maps, etc. From a theoretical point of view the fundamental questions at issue are the explicit formulation of a gradient descent procedure for graphs and the construction of a suitable mapping from $\mathcal{G}_\mathcal{X}^n$ into $\mathbb{G}^n$, which transforms an abstract solution graph $\hat{W}^*$ to a solution graph W^*.

REFERENCES

[1] C.M. Bishop. *Neural Networks for Pattern Recognition*. Clarendon Press, Oxford, 1995.
[2] H. Bunke. Recent developments in graph matching. In *Proceedings of the 15th International Conference on Pattern Recognition*, volume 2, pages 117–124, Barcelona, Spain, 2000.
[3] H. Bunke. Recent advances in structural pattern recognition with applications to visual form analysis. In C. Arcelli, L. Cordella, and G. Sanniti di Baja, editors, *Visual Form 2001*, LNCS 2059, pages 11–23. Springer Verlag, 2001.
[4] R.O. Duda and P.E. Hart. *Pattern classification and scene analysis*. John Wiley & Sons, Inc., 1973.
[5] R.A. Fisher. The use of multiple measurements in taxonomic problems. *Annual Eugenics*, 7:179–188, 1936.
[6] P. Frasconi, M. Gori, and A. Sperduti. A general framework for adaptive processing of data structures. *IEEE Transactions on Neural Networks*, 9(5):768–786, 1998.
[7] M. Garey and D. Johnson. *Computers and Intractability: A Guide to the Theory of NP-Completeness*. W.H. Freeman and Company, New York, 1979.
[8] P. Geibel and F. Wysotzki. Learning relational concepts with decision trees. In L. Saitta, editor, *Machine Learning: Proceedings of the 13th International Conference*, pages 166–174. Kaufmann Publishers, San Fransisco, 1996.
[9] P. Geibel and F. Wysotzki. Relational learning with decision trees. In W. Wahlster, editor, *Proceedings of the 12th European Conference on Artificial Intelligence*, pages 428–432. John Wiley and Sons, Ltd., 1996.
[10] L. Goldfarb, J. Abela, V. C. Bhavsar, and V. N. Kamat. Can a vector space based learning model discover inductive class generalization in a symbolic environment? *Pattern Recognition Letters*, 16:719–726, 1995.
[11] C. Goller and A. Küchler. Learning task-dependent distributed representations by backpropagation through structure. In *Proceedings of the IEEE Conference on Neural Networks*, pages 347–352, 1996.
[12] T. Graepel, M. Goutrié, M. Krüger, and R. Herbrich. Learning on graphs in the game of go. In *Proceedings of the International Conference on Neural Networks*, LNCS 2130, pages 347–352. Springer-Verlag, 2001.
[13] S. Haykin. *Neural Networks*. Prentice Hall, Inc., 2nd edition, 1999.
[14] R. Herbrich. *Learning Kernel Classifiers*. The MIT Press, Cambridge, MA, 2002.
[15] J.B. Pollack. Recursive distributed representations. *Artificial Intelligence*, 46(1-2):77–106, 1990.
[16] K. Schädler and F. Wysotzki. Comparing structures using a Hopfield-style neural network. *Applied Intelligence*, 11:15–30, 1999.
[17] A. Sperduti and A. Starita. Supervised neural networks for the classification of structures. *IEEE Transactions on Neural Networks*, 8(3):714–735, 1997.

A Novel Approach for training small-sized Multi-Layer Perceptrons

Deepak P. Chermakani, IEEE Student Member
School of Electrical and Electronic Engineering
Nanyang Technological University, Singapore
Email: deepak_pc@ieee.org

Abstract— I present a novel approach tailored for training small-sized Multi-Layer Perceptrons. My approach updates a single randomly chosen weight with a stable second-order update rule, at each epoch. I discuss the analytical proof of stability and convergence at local minima. My paper identifies the situations when my approach is better than back-propagation for learning. Based on the experiments conducted, I show four important results: - Firstly, my approach outperforms back-propagation when the network size is very small. Secondly, with slightly larger sized networks, though back-propagation tends to beat my approach when the perceptron activation function slope is low, my approach reaches better minima when the activation function slope is high. Thirdly, my approach normally reduces error when all the initial weights are equal, which is when back-propagation performs poorly. Fourthly, my approach tends to avoid premature saturation, during the early stages of learning, due to poorly initialized weights.

I. INTRODUCTION

Multi-Layer Perceptron (MLP) learning is essentially a function minimization problem in which learning is achieved through the iterative update of weights, so as to minimize the error function (E). E usually represents the summation, of the squared differences between the desired outputs and the actual outputs of the MLP, over the entire training set [1][2].

The back-propagation (BP) learning algorithm of Rumelhart et al [3] for MLPs, iteratively updates the entire weight vector of the MLP using a small constant learning rate, at each epoch, until E converges.

I present a novel learning algorithm tailored for small-sized MLPs using the solutions I give to overcome two drawbacks of BP, namely:

A. Poor performance with equal initial weights

Models of learning networks will be highly beneficial if they suggest mechanisms of learning in biological systems [4]. It has been experimentally recorded that, many times, the variance of the synaptic weights of neighboring biological neurons, before training, is zero, which is not so after training [4]. When BP is used to train an MLP with equal initial weights, there is a perfect symmetry of the back-propagated errors [5][6]. This prevents adjacent weights from differentiating themselves from each other [6] and causes learning to fail. To the best of my knowledge, my paper is the first to address a solution to this issue for MLPs.

Many researchers have studied how to initialize weights in the MLP, but frustrating problems still remain [7-13].

BP still suffers from premature saturation, due to which the error stays almost constant for some time during the early stages of learning, due to poorly initialized weights [11][14]. Randomization of initial weights can also get them stuck in deep local minima [12], and extracting them out can become very tough [10][13]. Further, optimal initialization of weights is problem-dependent [7][15], and though a large number of techniques have been suggested for initialization, no single technique has been universally accepted [12].

My argument is that, when there is no universally accepted technique for initializing weights, it will be help to develop MLP learning algorithms that perform as normally, with equal initial weights, as with randomized initial weights. The algorithms can then be less dependent on initialization techniques and biologically more satisfying.

B. Difficulty of learning when the perceptron activation function slope is high

The advantage of training networks with discrete activation functions is that the networks are immune to noise and capture only the main features in the training set [16][17]. It is natural to conclude that it would be preferable to train a network with a high, and not a low, value of the MLP's activation function slope, beta (β), right from the onset of training. This is true, especially when the training set is large, increasing the likelihood for it to contain noise.

Fig. 1 describes the effect of β on the error function. A low value of β produces a smooth error function, as a result of which learning is very easy. As β increases, gradient contrasts begin to grow sharper. Therefore, a high learning rate chosen to cause rapid descent over flatter regions causes overshoots on steep slopes, while a smaller learning rate chosen for steady descent on steep slopes, is too slow over flatter regions. Learning, with BP, thus becomes difficult [2].

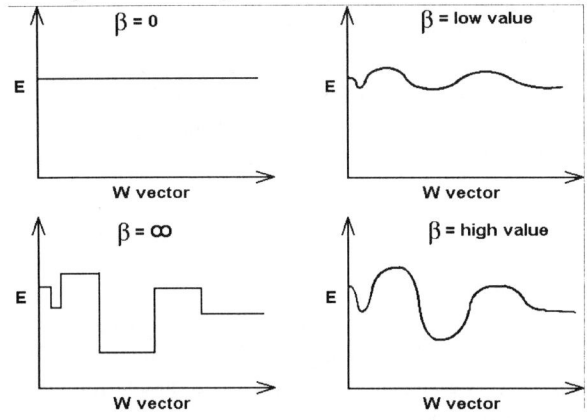

Fig. 1. Effect of β on the error function

A number of variants of gradient descent have been suggested to train networks with discrete activation functions [16]. Various techniques have been suggested in the literature to train networks by increasing β iteratively during training [18][19]. However, I haven't come across any technique catered to train networks with a steep activation function slope (which is still continuous, not discrete), right from the onset of training, so as to dispel noise in the training set.

II. THE NEW APPROACH

A. Solutions I give for the two discussed drawbacks of BP

To solve the problem of starting out with equal initial weights, I decide to update a randomly chosen partial weight vector, at each epoch. This will help break the initial symmetry of the back-propagated errors.

To reduce the difficulty of learning with high β, I decide to use a different weight update rule. Instead of updating the weight by a small multiple of the derivative, I perform updates by a small multiple of the sign of the derivative, i.e. by small amounts, d, depending on the error gradient.

The weight update rule now becomes:

$$\Delta w = -\frac{d * (\partial E / \partial w)}{abs(\partial E / \partial w)} \quad (1)$$

where 'abs' represents the absolute value function.

However, using (1) as the update rule will cause oscillations when the minimum is near. Some non-negative term, σ, which is large near the minimum, and small far away from it, has to be added to the denominator of (1). To obtain σ, I decide to look at the higher derivatives of the valley [20] in the MLP learning surface, since the valley is where the minimum lies.

First, I define a valley as a stretch, which must consist of exactly one area surrounding the minimum where the second derivative is continuously positive, and which cannot consist of more than two areas where the second derivative is continuously negative.

Based on the above definition of a valley, I divide the most generic valley into three regions (Fig. 2):
a) Region 3, representing the two areas where the second derivative is continuously negative.
b) Region 2, representing the two thin areas where the second derivative is continuously positive, but still close to zero.
c) Region 1, representing the area surrounding the minimum where the second derivative is continuously positive & high.

The discrete sigmoid function of the second derivative has a value of one in Regions 1 and 2, and is equal to zero in Region 3, of the generic valley. If this function were multiplied by the second derivative, the resulting expression would be equal to zero in Region 3, slightly greater than zero in Region 2, and have a high positive value in Region 1. Therefore, this expression is a very good choice for the term σ, to be used in (1).

Therefore,

$$\sigma = \frac{(\partial^2 E / \partial w^2)}{1 + \exp(-\lambda * \partial^2 E / \partial w^2)}$$

where λ is a very large positive number (2)

The weight update rule thus becomes:

$$\Delta w = -\frac{d * (\partial E / \partial w)}{\sigma + abs(\partial E / \partial w)} \quad (3)$$

I modify equation (3) to (4) so that the weight update becomes a slower version of Newton's step in Region 1, near the minimum, as the first derivative approaches zero.

Thus, the final weight update rule is:

$$\Delta w = -\frac{(\partial E / \partial w)}{\sigma + \dfrac{abs(\partial E / \partial w)}{d}} \quad (4)$$

The problem of starting out with equal initial weights is solved by updating a randomly chosen partial weight vector, at each epoch. However, updating more than a single weight with a complicated second order equation like (4) will call for, a computationally costly, use and inversion of NxN Hessian matrices [21]. Further, when ill-conditioned, these matrix inversions can fail [22]. To avoid these problems, I restrict the number of weights updated, at each epoch, to one.

Besides, I felt it would be very interesting to explore & present the situations when a learning approach (**which updates a single randomly chosen weight with a second order update rule, at each epoch**) would perform better than back-propagation (**which updates the entire weight vector with a first order update rule, at each epoch**).

This interest of mine, along with my desire to avoid matrix inversions, leads me to a novel training algorithm tailored for small-sized MLPs, shown below.

B. The "single update per epoch" (SUPE) training algorithm

Step 1: Start with equal or randomized values of initial weights
Step 2: Randomly choose any single weight w_{JI} from the MLP
Step 3: Run though entire training set once to obtain $E, \dfrac{\partial E}{\partial w_{JI}}$ and $\dfrac{\partial^2 E}{\partial w_{JI}^2}$; storing these in variables E_{NOW}, $D1$ and $D2$ respectively
Step 4: Set variable $ROW = \dfrac{D2}{1 + \exp(-\lambda * D2)}$
Step 5: Set variable $UPDATE = -\dfrac{D1}{ROW + \dfrac{abs(D1)}{d}}$
Step 6: Set $w_{JI} = w_{JI} + UPDATE$
Step 7: Go back to Step 2 if $E_{NOW} > E_{STOP}$

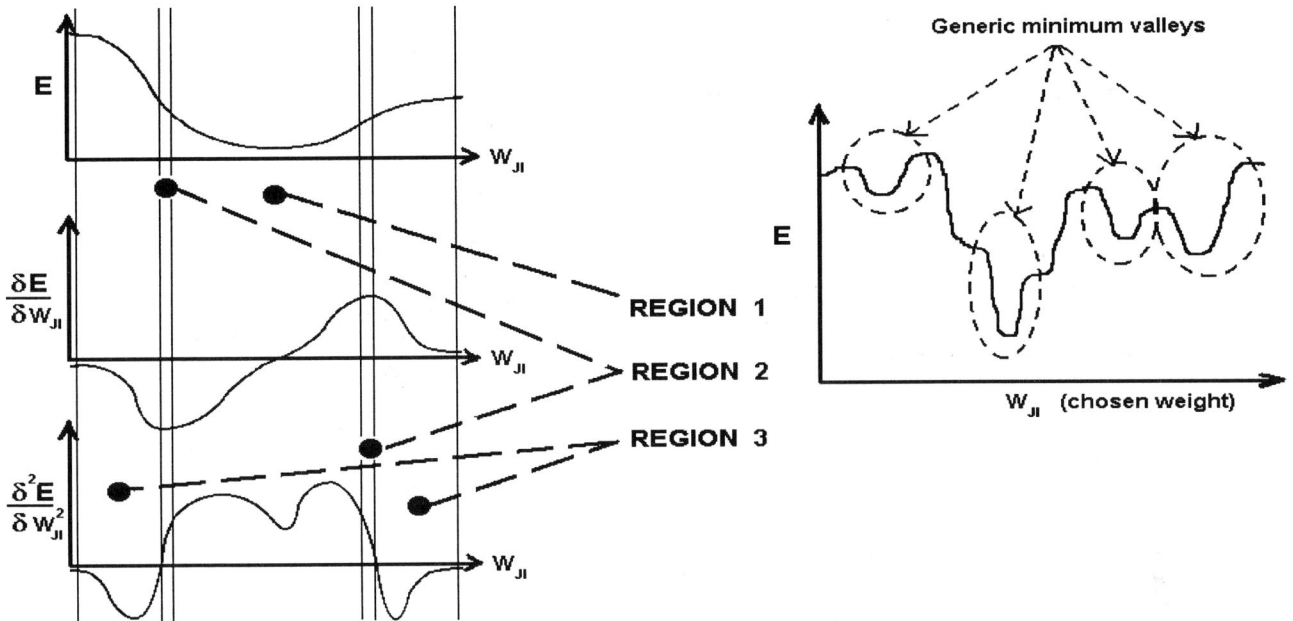

Fig. 2. The three regions of a generic valley

C. Analytical Proof of Convergence at local minima if d is small & Stability of the update rule of SUPE

I give SUPE's analytical proof of convergence at local minima using the following six points:

i) The weight update rule is essentially a form of gradient descent, since the denominator in (4) is always positive.
ii) The magnitude of the chosen weight's update, at any epoch, is limited to d, because σ always ≥ 0.
iii) At any epoch, SUPE tends to shift the chosen weight by gradient descent, either into the nearest valley, or if already inside a valley, then through Regions 3 and 2 to Region 1 of the valley.
iv) Inside the valley: - In Region 3, σ is zero, so the magnitude of the chosen weight's update becomes d. In Region 2, σ is a positive quantity close to zero, so the magnitude of the chosen weight's update becomes a quantity slightly less than d. At the outskirts of Region 1, the first derivative has a high absolute value and the second derivative is positive, so the chosen weight's update becomes a slower version of Newton's step, shown below in (5).

$$\Delta w_{JI} = -\frac{\partial E / \partial w_{JI}}{\partial^2 E / \partial w_{JI}^2} \qquad (5)$$

Near the minimum in Region 1, the first derivative approaches zero, so the chosen weight's update becomes a more exact version of Newton's step.
v) The Newton's trust region is the region surrounding the minimum, where Newton's step never overshoots the minimum, but guarantees convergence [23].
vi) It may thus be concluded, with certainty, that E will decrease after each epoch, irrespective of the weight chosen for update, if d is lesser than the length of the trust region of the chosen weight's nearest valley.

The stability of the update rule of SUPE is due to the automatic limit, $\pm d$, imposed on the chosen weight's update, at any epoch. This stability is absent in BP and most learning paradigms which need extra externally imposed limits to cap their weight updates, during unstable learning conditions.

III. EXPERIMENTS

I used only three layered networks, because of their robust computational abilities [24], to explore the situations when SUPE is better than BP for MLP training. The hidden layer and the output layer neurons used bipolar and unipolar sigmoid activation functions respectively. Only batch mode presentation of the training set was used. For SUPE, I chose d between 0.01 and 1, and for BP, I chose the learning rate between 0.01 and 100, systematically, for best convergence. I experimented with **two types of small-sized networks**:

*A. Two-input **XOR** problem with 4 training patterns*
Two hidden units were used. This network with 6 weights represents a **very small-sized MLP**.

*B. Three-input function approximation (**FA**) with 200 training patterns:* - Y = (exp(u1) + u1*u2*cos(u1*u2) + u1*u3) / 10
where u1, u2, and u3 were determined on the value of a randomly chosen number, T, equally distributed between 0 and 1, according to the following rules:
u1 = T
u2 = 8*T-2   if T<0.5   ; u2 = -8*T+6 otherwise
u3 = -1   if 0.25<T or T>0.75 ; u3 = 1   otherwise
Nine hidden units were used. This network with 36 weights represents a **slightly larger-sized MLP**.

IV. RESULTS: - COMPARISON OF BP and SUPE

A. With Equal initial weights of unit values (Figs. 3 and 4)

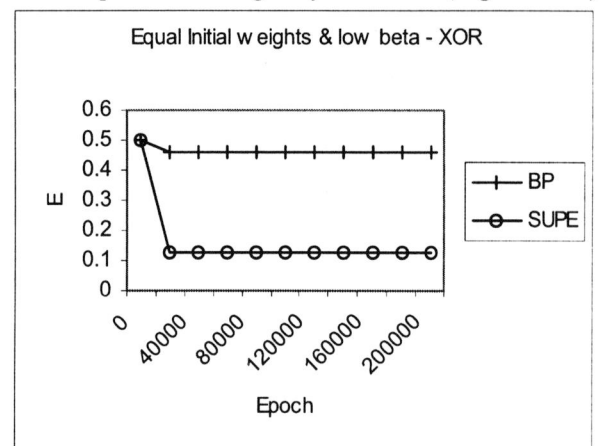

Fig. 3. SUPE normally reduces error for the very small-sized MLP

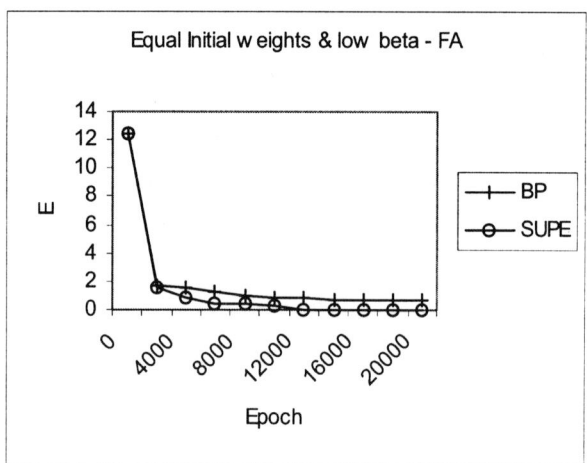

Fig. 4. SUPE normally reduces error for the larger-sized MLP

B. Effect of β, with random initial weights between 0 and 1
B. i. When β=0.2, a low value (Figs. 5 and 6)

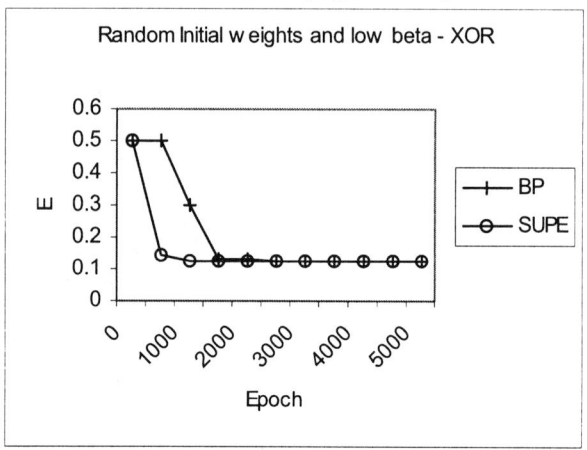

Fig. 5. SUPE outperforms BP for the very small-sized MLP

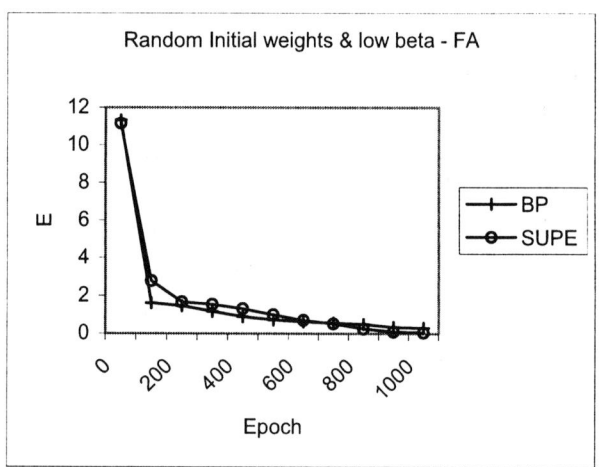

Fig. 6. BP tends to beat SUPE for the larger-sized MLP

B. ii. When β has a high value (Figs. 7 and 8)

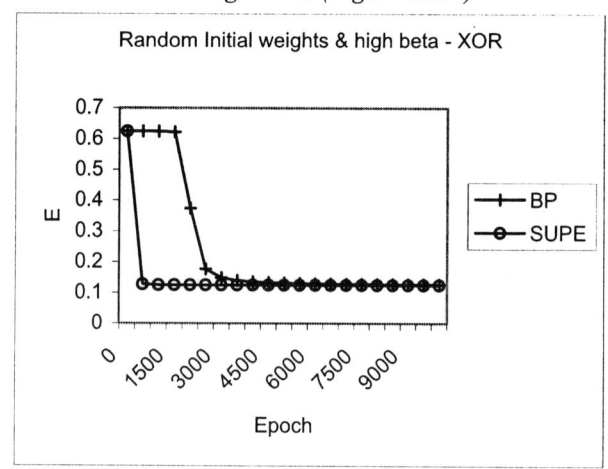

Fig. 7. SUPE outperforms BP faster when β=10 compared to when β=0.2, for the very small-sized MLP

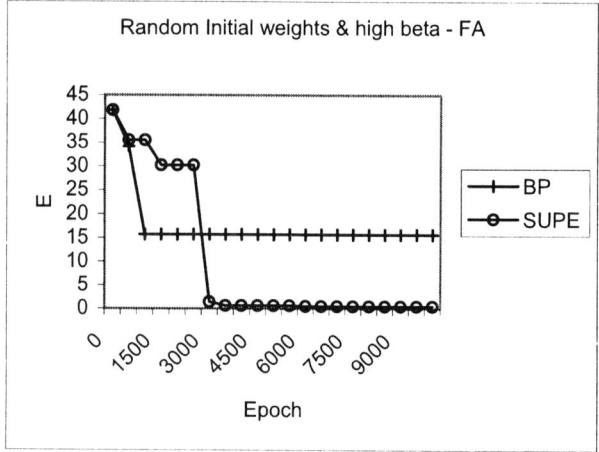

Fig. 8. BP reaches only a poor minimum when β=50, for the larger-sized MLP

C. Simulation to confirm SUPE's tendency to avoid premature saturation at the early stage of training (Fig. 9)

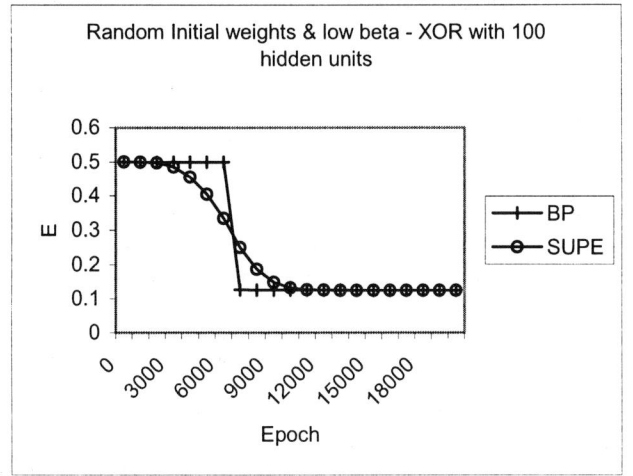

Fig. 9. Two-input XOR with 100 hidden units, initial weights variance=0.1, and β=0.5

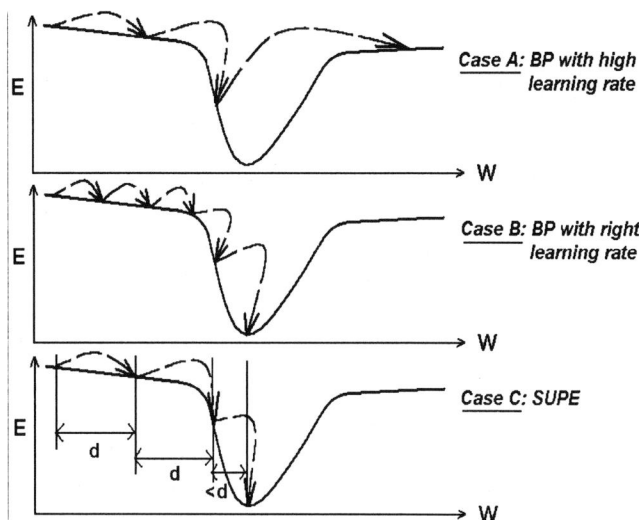

Fig. 10. Illustration of why SUPE beats BP when β is high

V. DISCUSSION OF RESULTS

A. Discussion on simulations when initial weights were equal

When BP is used to train an MLP with equal initial weights, there is a perfect symmetry of the back-propagated errors [5][6]. This prevents adjacent weights from differentiating themselves from each other [6] and causes only poor minima to be reached (Figs. 3 and 4). Updating one randomly chosen weight of the MLP, at each epoch, ensures that this initial symmetry is broken. SUPE is thus able to normally reduce error.

B. Discussion on simulations to study the effect of β

I make an interesting conclusion from the simulations in which the MLP has very few weights like in the XOR problem (Figs. 5 and 7) → SUPE is much better than BP when the number of weights in the MLP is very small, irrespective of whether β is high or low. When β is large, SUPE outperforms BP much faster for the very small-sized MLP (Fig. 7) than when β is small (Fig. 5).

Fig. 6 shows that when the number of weights in the MLP is larger, BP would tend to beat SUPE under easy learning conditions i.e. when β is small. This result is expected because BP updates all the weights, unlike SUPE, which updates a single weight, at each epoch. But, when β=50 for the larger-sized MLP, BP manages to reach only a poor minimum (Fig. 8), whereas SUPE normally reduces error.

Fig. 10 gives a proposed explanation of why SUPE outperforms BP when β is high. Case A shows how BP causes overshoot on the steep slope when a learning rate is chosen to cause rapid descent over the flatter region. Case B shows that the right learning rate for BP, chosen for steady descent on the steep slope is too slow over the flatter region. Finally, Case C shows how SUPE steadily updates the weight by fixed amounts of *d*, and gradually decreases this amount as the minimum approaches, thereby reducing error in a lesser number of steps than BP.

C. Discussion of SUPE's tendency to avoid premature saturation during the early stages of training

The study on premature saturation indicates that this phenomenon usually occurs during the early stages of training, due to poorly initialized weights [14]. Also, one of its causes while using BP is the combination and interference of several components of the weight update vector [14]. Updating the weights simultaneously at each epoch, using BP, does produce highly non-linear interference among the changing weights [25].

SUPE updates weights one-by-one, so there is no interference among the changing weights. Error is reduced steadily with every update (which is very clear from SUPE's smooth curve in Fig. 9), as discussed earlier under the analytical proof of convergence of SUPE. This possibly explains why SUPE tends to avoid premature saturation during the early stages of training (Figs. 5, 7 and 9).

D. Note on the computational complexity involved in SUPE

I note that BP takes roughly two-thirds the computation time that SUPE takes to complete an epoch for XOR (4 training patterns), and BP's superiority in this increases with the size of the training set. This is mainly because SUPE calculates the time-costly second partial derivative of the chosen weight, as it runs through the training set.

For larger-sized MLPs, SUPE is likely to be vastly outperformed by standard second-order algorithms (which update the entire weight vector with second-order update rules, at each epoch). However, very small-sized MLP training might show different results in terms of computation time, because SUPE does not invert Hessian matrices. The absence of Hessian matrix inversions also reduces SUPE's computer memory requirements.

VI. Future Work for SUPE

Though SUPE is tailored for training small-sized MLPs, it can be still used for training very large-sized MLPs. I propose a logical approach for doing so, for future work.

First, the large-sized MLP's training set may be divided into several smaller sets using a similarity criterion, in which, similar training patterns are grouped within the same small set. Next, the large-sized MLP may also be broken into several small-sized MLPs, simultaneously assigning a small training set for each small-sized MLP. After the division process is complete, SUPE may be used to parallely train these small-sized MLPs, using their respective training sets.

Once training is complete, the various small-sized MLPs may be logically inter-connected based on a relation-ship among the geometric centres of their respective training sets.

VII. Conclusion

In this paper, I presented a novel approach called SUPE tailored for training small-sized MLPs. My approach updates a single randomly chosen weight using a stable second order update rule, at each epoch. Based on the small-sized MLP training experiments conducted, I made the following conclusions while comparing SUPE and BP:

i) SUPE outperforms BP for very small-sized networks.
ii) BP beats SUPE in larger-sized networks, when β is small.
iii) Even for larger-sized networks, SUPE reaches better minima than BP, as β increases. A network captures only the main features in a large training set when β is high.
iv) SUPE has a stable, matrix-free update rule and does not need extra, externally imposed limits on its weight update.
v) When the initial weights are equal, BP performs poorly. But, SUPE normally reduces error. If a learning algorithm performs as normally, with equal initial weights, as with randomized initial weights, it can be less dependent on initialization techniques and biologically more satisfying.
vi) SUPE tends to avoid premature saturation due to poorly initialized weights, during the early stages of learning.

Acknowledgment

I greatly thank Dr. Meng Hiot Lim and his student Amit Agarwal for their precious time and useful improvements suggested to my paper. I also thank Dr. Jagath C. Rajapakse for the enlightening discussions held and time spent with him.

References

[1] Mizutani E. and S. E. Dreyfus, "MLP's Hidden Node Saturations and insensitivity to initial weights in two classification benchmark problems: parity and two spirals", IEEE IJCNN 2002, page 2831.
[2] Marco Budinich, "Some Notes on Perceptron Learning", IEEE ICNN 1993, pp 371-376.
[3] D. E. Rumelhart, G. Hinton and R. Williams, "Learning Internal Representations by Error propagation", Parallel Distributed Processing, Vol I, Cambridge, MIT Press.
[4] Christopher Miall, "The diversity of Neuronal Properties", The Computing Neuron, 1989, pp 11-20.
[5] Gang Li, Hussein Alnuweiri and Yuejian Wu, "Acceleration of Back Propagation through initial weight pre-training with Delta Rule", IEEE IJCNN 1993, page 582.
[6] DE Rumelhart, JL McClelland and the PDP Research Group, "Explorations in the Microstructure of Cognition", Parallel Distributed Processing, Vol. 1: Foundations, Cambridge MA, MIT Press, 1986.
[7] George Thimm and Emile Fiesler, "High-Order and Multilayer Perceptron Initialization", IEEE Transactions on Neural Networks, 1997, Vol 8, No. 2, pp 349-359.
[8] Manic M; Wilamowski B, "Robust algorithm for Neural Network training", IEEE IJCNN 2002, page 1528.
[9] Shi Zong and Vladimir Cherkassky, "Factors Controlling Generalization Ability of MLPs", IEEE IJCNN 1999, page 625.
[10] Leandro Nunes De Castro, Eduardo Masato Iyoda, Fernando J.V Zuben, R. Gudwin, "Feedforward Neural Network Initialization: an evolutionary approach", IEEE IJCNN 1998, page 43.
[11] Youngjik Lee, Sang-Hoon Oh, Myung Won Kim, "Effect of initial weights on Premature saturation in Back Propagation learning", IEEE IJCNN 1991, page 765.
[12] Zvi Boger, "Who is afraid of the big bad ANN?", IEEE IJCNN 2002, page 2000.
[13] Osowski, "New Approach to selection of initial weights in neural function approximation", IEEE IJCNN 1993, page 313.
[14] Vitela J.E., Reifman J., "The causes of premature saturation with back-propagation training", IEEE World Congress on Computational Intelligence 1994, page 1450.
[15] HL Najafi, Muhammed Nasiruddin, Tariq Samad, "Effect of initial weights on Back-Propagation and its variations", IEEE International Conference on Man and Cybernetics, 1989, page 218.
[16] Plagianakos VP, Magaolas GD, Nousis, Vrahatis MN, "Training Multi-layer networks with discrete activation functions", IEEE IJCNN 2001, page 2805.
[17] Plagianakos VP, Vrahatis MN, "Training neural networks with threshold activation functions and constrained integer weights", IEEE IJCNN 2000, page 161.
[18] Trentin E, "Activation functions with learnable amplitude", IEEE IJCNN 1999, page 1794.
[19] EM Corwin, AM Logar and WJB Oldham, "An iterative method for training multi-layer networks with threshold functions", IEEE Transactions on Neural Networks, Vol 5, 1994, pp 507-508.
[20] S.J. Huang, S.N. Koh, H.K Tang, "Training Algorithm based on Newton's method with dynamic error control", IEEE IJCNN 1992, page 904.
[21] Laszlo Erdos and Alfred D. Andrew, "Note on the Hessian and the Second Derivative Test", Georgia Tech School of Mathematics, Calculus III for Computer Science, August 2000, page 3.
[22] Lloyd G. Alfred, "Supervised Learning Techniques for back-propagation", IEEE IJCNN 1990, Vol 1, page 721.
[23] L.T. Biegler, "Optimization", Carnegie Mellon University, 2000, page 15.
[24] Hecht Nielson, R., "Theory of the back-propagation neural network", IEEE IJCNN 1989.
[25] Tomas Hrycej, "A modular architecture for efficient learning", IEEE IJCNN 1990, page 560.

Accurate Initialization of Neural Network Weights by Backpropagation of the Desired Response

Deniz Erdogmus[1], Oscar Fontenla-Romero[2], Jose C. Principe[1],
Amparo Alonso-Betanzos[2], Enrique Castillo[3], Robert Jenssen[1]

[1] Electrical Engineering Department, University of Florida, Gainesville, FL 32611, USA
[2] Department of Computer Science, University of A Coruña, 15071 A Coruña, Spain
[3] Department of Applied Mathematics, University of Cantabria, 39005, Santander, Spain

Abstract – Proper initialization of neural networks is critical for a successful training of its weights. Many methods have been proposed to achieve this, including heuristic least squares approaches. In this paper, inspired by these previous attempts to train (or initialize) neural networks, we formulate a mathematically sound algorithm based on backpropagating the desired output through the layers of a multilayer perceptron. The approach is accurate up to local first order approximations of the nonlinearities. It is shown to provide successful weight initialization for many data sets by Monte Carlo experiments.

I. INTRODUCTION

Due to the nonlinear nature of neural networks, training requires the use of numerical nonlinear optimization techniques. Practically feasible training algorithms are usually susceptible to local optima and might require parameter fine-tuning. There are various approaches undertaken to find the optimal weights of a neural network. These include first- and second-order descent techniques, which are mainly variants of gradient [1], natural gradient [2], and Newton [3] optimization methods. Although higher order search techniques could speed up convergence at the cost of complexity, they are still vulnerable to local minima. Global search procedures, such as random perturbations [4], genetic algorithms [5], and simulated annealing [6] are not feasible for practical applications due to time constraints. Alternative approaches to help multilayer perceptrons (MLP) learn faster and better include *statistically proper* weight initialization [7,8], and approximate optimization through heuristic least squares application [9, 10]. Although there are many other references to list, we cannot go into such a detailed review of the state-of-the-art in MLP initialization and training, mainly due to the limited space available.

As mentioned, approximate least squares solutions have been previously proposed to initialize or train MLPs. However, these methods mostly relied on minimizing the mean square error (MSE) between the signal of an output neuron before the output nonlinearity and a modified desired output, which is exactly the actual desired output passed through the inverse of the nonlinearity. This approach, unfortunately does not consider the scaling effects of the nonlinearity slope on the propagation of the MSE through the nonlinearity. Nevertheless, they provided the invaluable inspiration for the work presented in this paper, which takes into account the effect of weights and nonlinearities on the propagation of MSE through the network. Specifically, we present an algorithm, which we named *backpropagation of the desired response* that can initialize the weights of an MLP to a point with very small MSE. This algorithm is an approximation of the nonlinear least squares problem with linear least squares and is accurate up to the first-order term in the Taylor series expansion. We considered including higher order terms in the expansion, but then the utility of linear least squares method is not possible.

In this paper, we first present two theoretical results that form the basis for the backpropagation of the desired response algorithm. Then, we provide the algorithm and demonstrate its performance with Monte Carlo experiments.

II. THEORETICAL RESULTS

Notice that in the L-layer MLP architecture shown in Fig. 1 there are two parts that need to be investigated to achieve successful backpropagation of the desired output through the layers: linear weight matrix and neuron nonlinearity. For our algorithm, we require this nonlinearity to be invertible at every point in its range. We use the following notation to designate signals: the output of the lth layer is $\mathbf{z}^l$ and $\mathbf{y}^l$ before and after the nonlinearity. The weight matrix and the bias vector of this layer are $\mathbf{W}^l$ and $\mathbf{b}^l$, respectively. The input vector is $\mathbf{x}$. The number of neurons in a layer is denoted by n_l and n_0 is the number of inputs. The training set consisting of N input-desired pairs is given in the form $(\mathbf{x}_t, \mathbf{d}_t^L)$. The backpropagated desired output for the lth layer is denoted by $\mathbf{d}^l$ at the output of the nonlinearity and $\overline{\mathbf{d}}^l$ at the input of the nonlinearity.

A. Backpropagating Through a Nonlinearity

Consider a single-layer nonlinear network for which the output is obtained from $\mathbf{z} = \mathbf{W}\mathbf{x} + \mathbf{b}$ and $\mathbf{y} = \mathbf{f}(\mathbf{z})$, where $\mathbf{f}(.)$ is a vector-valued nonlinear function, invertible on its range. Assume that the objective is to minimize a weighted MSE cost function defined on the error between $\mathbf{y}$ and $\mathbf{d}$. Let $\mathbf{H}$ be

---

This work is partially supported by NSF grant ECS-9900394 and the Xunta de Galicia project PGIDT-01PXI10503PR.

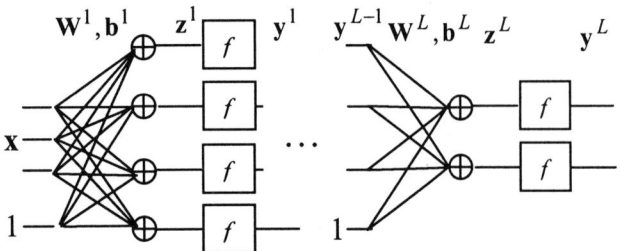

Fig. 1. MLP structure and variables

the weighting matrix. Then Lemma 1 describes the backpropagation of **d** through **f**(.).

Lemma 1. Let $\mathbf{d}, \mathbf{y}, \mathbf{z}, \overline{\mathbf{d}} \in \Re^n$ be the desired and actual outputs, $\mathbf{W} \in \Re^{n \times m}$ and $\mathbf{b} \in \Re^{n \times 1}$ be the weight matrix and the bias vector, and $\mathbf{f}, \mathbf{f}^{-1}, \mathbf{f}': \Re^n \to \Re^n$ be the nonlinearity, its inverse and its derivative. Then the following equivalence between two optimization problems is accurate up to the first order of Taylor series expansion.

$$\min_{\mathbf{W},\mathbf{b}} E[(\mathbf{d}-\mathbf{y})^T \mathbf{H}(\mathbf{d}-\mathbf{y})] \equiv \min_{\mathbf{W},\mathbf{b}} E[(\mathbf{f}'(\overline{\mathbf{d}}).*\overline{\boldsymbol{\varepsilon}})^T \mathbf{H}(\mathbf{f}'(\overline{\mathbf{d}}).*\overline{\boldsymbol{\varepsilon}})] \quad (1)$$

where '.*' denotes element-wise vector product, $\overline{\mathbf{d}} = \mathbf{f}^{-1}(\mathbf{d})$, and $\overline{\boldsymbol{\varepsilon}} = \overline{\mathbf{d}} - \mathbf{z}$.

Proof. Recall that $\mathbf{y} = \mathbf{f}(\mathbf{z})$ and $\mathbf{d} = \mathbf{f}(\overline{\mathbf{d}})$. Substituting the first-order expansion $\mathbf{f}(\mathbf{z}) = \mathbf{f}(\overline{\mathbf{d}} - \overline{\boldsymbol{\varepsilon}}) \approx \mathbf{f}(\overline{\mathbf{d}}) - \mathbf{f}'(\overline{\mathbf{d}}).*\overline{\boldsymbol{\varepsilon}}$, we obtain the result. Due to space restrictions, we do not present this proof in detail. □

According to this lemma, when backpropagating the desired response through a nonlinearity, the sensitivity of the output error with respect to the slope of the nonlinearity at the operating point should be taken into consideration. Simply minimizing the MSE between the modified desired $\overline{\mathbf{d}}$ and **z** is not equivalent to minimizing the MSE between the **d** and **y**. Note that if $\text{var}(\|\overline{\mathbf{d}}\|)$ is also small, then since the operating point of the nonlinearity is almost fixed for all samples, the $\mathbf{f}'$ terms become redundant. Previous applications of least squares to MLPs did not consider the variance of **d** and the correction scale factor based on the derivative of the nonlinearity at the operating point.

B. Backpropagating Through Linear Weight Layer

Consider a linear network given by $\mathbf{z} = \mathbf{W}\mathbf{x} + \mathbf{b}$ and let $\overline{\mathbf{d}}$ be the desired output. In this scheme, we assume that the weights **W** and **b** are fixed already. The objective is to find the best input vector **x** that minimizes the output MSE. In the MLP context, the input vector will correspond to the output of the nonlinearity of the preceding layer. The result regarding the optimization of **x** in this situation is summarized in the following lemma.

Lemma 2. Let $\mathbf{d}, \mathbf{x} \in \Re^m$, $\overline{\mathbf{d}}, \mathbf{z} \in \Re^n$ be the desired signals and the corresponding output signals, $\mathbf{W} \in \Re^{n \times m}$ and $\mathbf{b} \in \Re^{n \times 1}$ be fixed weights. Then the following equivalence between the optimization problems holds.

$$\min_{\mathbf{x} \in D \subset \Re^{m \times 1}} E[(\overline{\mathbf{d}}-\mathbf{z})^T \mathbf{H}(\overline{\mathbf{d}}-\mathbf{z})]$$
$$\equiv \min_{\mathbf{x} \in D \subset \Re^{m \times 1}} E[(\mathbf{d}-\mathbf{x})^T \mathbf{W}^T \mathbf{H} \mathbf{W}(\mathbf{d}-\mathbf{x})] \quad (2)$$

where D is the set of allowed input values. In the MLP context, this set is determined by the output range of the nonlinearities in the network.

Proof. The proof of this result is very similar to the derivation of the least squares solution for a vector from an overdetermined (or underdetermined) system of linear equations. Due to space restrictions, we do not present this proof in detail. □

In the application of this lemma, two situations may occur: if $n \geq m$, then $\mathbf{d} = (\mathbf{W}^T \mathbf{H} \mathbf{W})^{-1} \mathbf{W}^T \mathbf{H}(\overline{\mathbf{d}} - \mathbf{b})$; if $n < m$ then the desired input **d** can be determined using QR factorization as the minimum norm solution to the underdetermined linear system of equations $\mathbf{W}\mathbf{d} + \mathbf{b} = \overline{\mathbf{d}}$ [11].

In both cases, in an MLP setting, given a desired signal $\overline{\mathbf{d}}^l$ for $\mathbf{z}^l$, we can determine $\mathbf{d}^{l-1}$ as the desired output for the preceding layer. output (after the nonlinearity) of the previous layer. The latter can then be backpropagated through the nonlinearity of layer l-1 as described in Lemma 1.

III. OPTIMIZING THE WEIGHTS USING LEAST SQUARES

Once the desired output is backpropagated through the layers, the weights of each layer can be optimized (approximately) using linear least squares. The following problem treats the optimization of the weights taking the two lemmas of the previous section into account.

Problem 1. Given a linear layer $\mathbf{z} = \mathbf{W}\mathbf{x} + \mathbf{b}$ with $\mathbf{W} \in \Re^{n \times m}$ and $\mathbf{b} \in \Re^{n \times 1}$, the training data in the form of pairs, i.e., $(\mathbf{x}_s, \overline{\mathbf{d}}_s)$ $s = 1, \ldots, N$, and a matrix **G** as the weighting matrix for least squares. Define the error for every sample of the training data for each output of the network as

$$\overline{\varepsilon}_{js} = \overline{\mathbf{d}}_{js} - \mathbf{z}_{js} \quad j=1,\ldots,n \;,\; s=1,\ldots,N \quad (3)$$

where the outputs are evaluated using

$$\mathbf{z}_{js} = \mathbf{b}_j + \sum_{i=1}^{N} \mathbf{W}_{ji} \mathbf{x}_{is} \;,\; j=1,\ldots,n \;,\; s=1,\ldots,N \quad (4)$$

with $\mathbf{x}_{is}$ denoting the ith entry of the input sample $\mathbf{x}_s$. The optimal weights for this layer of the MLP under consideration, according to the arguments in Lemmas 1 and 2 become the solution to the following minimization problem.

$$\min_{\mathbf{W},\mathbf{b}} J = \frac{1}{N} \sum_{s=1}^{N} \sum_{i=1}^{n} \sum_{j=1}^{n} \mathbf{G}_{ij} f'(\overline{\mathbf{d}}_{is}) f'(\overline{\mathbf{d}}_{js}) \overline{\varepsilon}_{is} \overline{\varepsilon}_{js} \quad (5)$$

Solution. The minimization problem in (5) is quadratic in the weights, therefore, taking the gradient and equating to zero yields a system of linear equations. These equations are easily found to be ($l = 1,...,m$, $k = 1,...,n$)

$$\sum_{i=1}^{n} b_i \gamma_{ik} \left[\sum_{s=1}^{N} f'(\bar{d}_{ks}) f'(\bar{d}_{is}) x_{ls} \right]$$
$$+ \sum_{p=1}^{m} \sum_{i=1}^{n} w_{ip} \gamma_{ik} \left[\sum_{s=1}^{N} f'(\bar{d}_{ks}) f'(\bar{d}_{is}) x_{ls} x_{ps} \right]$$
$$= \sum_{i=1}^{n} \gamma_{ik} \left[\sum_{s=1}^{N} f'(\bar{d}_{ks}) f'(\bar{d}_{is}) x_{ls} d_{is} \right]$$
$$\sum_{i=1}^{n} b_i \gamma_{ik} \left[\sum_{s=1}^{N} f'(\bar{d}_{ks}) f'(\bar{d}_{is}) \right] \quad (6)$$
$$+ \sum_{p=1}^{m} \sum_{i=1}^{n} w_{ip} \gamma_{ik} \left[\sum_{s=1}^{N} f'(\bar{d}_{ks}) f'(\bar{d}_{is}) x_{ps} \right]$$
$$= \sum_{i=1}^{n} \gamma_{ik} \left[\sum_{s=1}^{N} f'(\bar{d}_{ks}) f'(\bar{d}_{is}) d_{is} \right]$$

The unknowns in this square system with $n \cdot m + n$ equations of (6) are the entries of $\mathbf{W}$ and $\mathbf{b}$. This system of equations can easily be solved using a variety of computationally efficient approaches. The weight matrix $\mathbf{G}$ allows one to take into account the magnifying effect of the succeeding layers on the error of the specific layer. The derivatives of the nonlinearity, however, introduce the effect of the nonlinear layers on the propagation of the MSE through the layers.

IV. Optimization Algorithm for an MLP

The individual steps described in the preceding sections can be brought together to initialize the weights of an arbitrary size MLP in a very accurate fashion. In this section, we will consider the single hidden layer MLP case for simplicity. However, the described algorithm can easily be generalized to larger MLP topologies.

Initialization. Given training data in the form $(\mathbf{x}_s, \mathbf{d}_s^2)$, $s = 1,...,N$. Initialize the weights $\mathbf{W}^1$, $\mathbf{W}^2$, $\mathbf{b}^1$, $\mathbf{b}^2$ randomly. The superscripts '1' and '2' denote layer. Evaluate network outputs and store $\mathbf{z}_s^1$, $\mathbf{y}_s^1$, $\mathbf{z}_s^2$, $\mathbf{y}_s^2$ corresponding to $\mathbf{x}_s$. Set J_{opt} to the MSE between $\mathbf{y}_s^2$ and $\mathbf{d}_s^2$. Set $\mathbf{W}_{opt}^1 = \mathbf{W}^1$, $\mathbf{b}_{opt}^1 = \mathbf{b}^1$, $\mathbf{W}_{opt}^2 = \mathbf{W}^2$, $\mathbf{b}_{opt}^2 = \mathbf{b}^2$.

Step 1. Compute $\bar{\mathbf{d}}_s^2 = f^{-1}(\mathbf{d}_s^2)$, $\forall s$.

Step 2. Compute $\mathbf{d}_s^1 = \left(\mathbf{W}^{2T}\mathbf{W}^2\right)^{-1}\mathbf{W}^{2T}(\bar{\mathbf{d}}_s^2 - \mathbf{b}^2)$ (if overdetermined) or the minimum norm solution.

Step 3. Compute $\bar{\mathbf{d}}_s^1 = f^{-1}(\mathbf{d}_s^1)$, $\forall s$.

Step 4. Optimize $\mathbf{W}^1$ and $\mathbf{b}^1$ using (6). Since this is the first layer, the input $\mathbf{x}$ is the actual input of the MLP. The desired output is $\bar{\mathbf{d}}_s^1$. Optionally use $\mathbf{G} = \mathbf{W}^{2T}\mathbf{W}^2$ or $\mathbf{G} = \mathbf{I}$ (experimentally the latter gives better results).

Step 5. Evaluate $\mathbf{z}_s^1$, $\mathbf{y}_s^1$ using the new weights.

Step 6. Optimize $\mathbf{W}^2$ and $\mathbf{b}^2$ using (6). Since this is the second layer, the input $\mathbf{x}$ is the output of the previous layer, $\mathbf{y}_s^1$. The desired output is $\bar{\mathbf{d}}_s^2$.

Step 7. Evaluate $\mathbf{z}_s^2$, $\mathbf{y}_s^2$ using the new weights.

Step 8. Evaluate the new MSE and if $J < J_{opt}$, set $\mathbf{W}_{opt}^1 = \mathbf{W}^1$, $\mathbf{b}_{opt}^1 = \mathbf{b}^1$, $\mathbf{W}_{opt}^{21} = \mathbf{W}^2$, $\mathbf{b}_{opt}^2 = \mathbf{b}^2$.

Step 9. Go back to *Step 2* or stop.

The algorithm above backpropagates the desired signal to the first layer and then optimizes the weights of the layers sweeping them from the first to the last. Alternatively, first the last layer weights may be optimized, then the desired signal can be backpropagated through that layer using the optimized values of the weights, and so on. Thus, in this alternative algorithm, the layers are optimized sweeping them from the last to the first. Simulations with the latter yield results similar to those obtained by the presented algorithm.

The algorithm is iterated a number of times (two to five). The weight values that correspond to the smallest MSE error are assigned as initial conditions to a standard backpropagation or some other optimization algorithm. Although determining the optimal weights requires using this hybrid approach, since the least squares approach yields approximate optimization, for some applications, the least squares initialization solution for the weights might yield satisfactory results. The loss in MSE, in the latter situation, is compensated for by the fast determination of these suboptimal solutions.

V. Case Studies

In this section, we present the results of Monte Carlo initialization and training experiments performed using the procedure described in the preceding sections. In these experiments, we used three data sets: the laser time-series [12], the Dow Jones Closing Index [12], and realistic engine manifold pressure-temperature dynamics data [13]. The first two data sets will be utilized in the single-step prediction framework, whereas, the last one will be considered as a nonlinear system identification problem. In this system identification problem, the input is the throttle angle that controls the amount of air flowing into the manifold. The system states are the internal manifold temperature and pressure.

For these three data sets, we have employed the following networks respectively: TDNN(3,11,1) for the laser data, TDNN(5,7,1) for the Dow Jones data, and MLP(4,5,1)

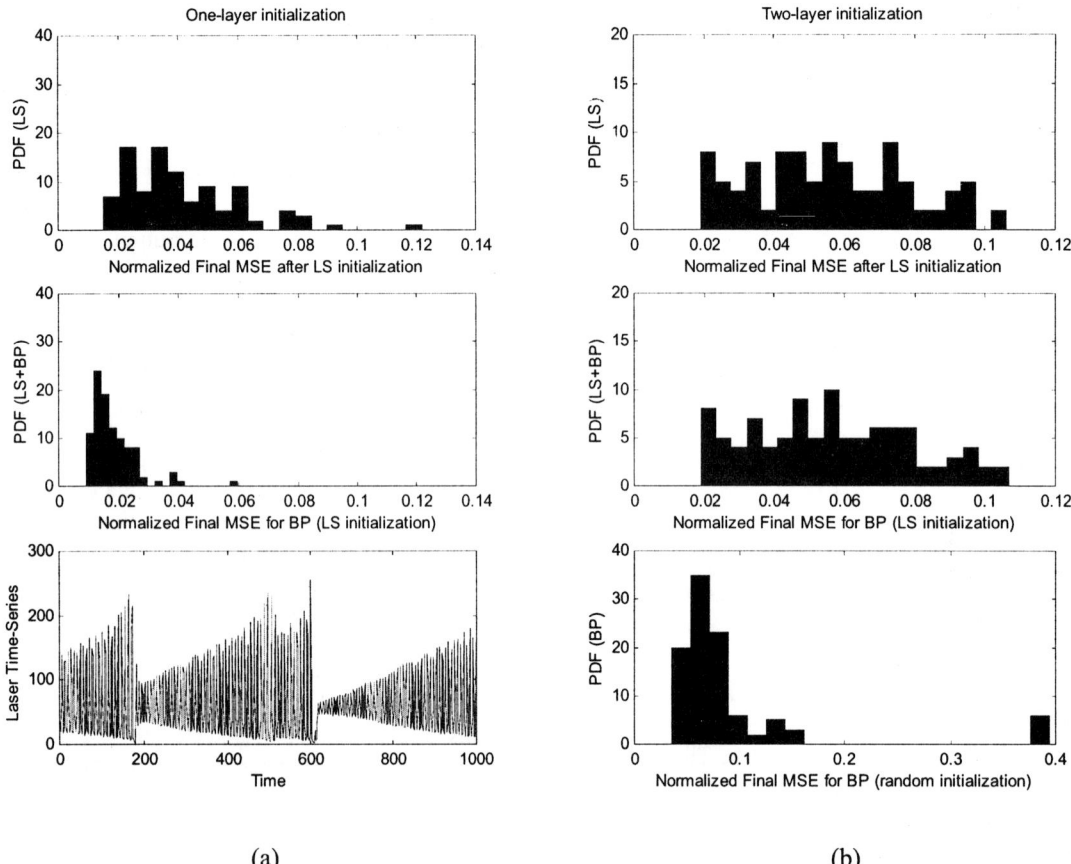

Figure 2. Histograms of final MSE values for the laser-series.

for system identification. In this notation, the first value denotes the number of inputs, the second value denotes the number of processing elements (PE) in the hidden layer and the last value denotes the number of outputs of the MLP-type neural network. In the system identification example, the four inputs of the MLP are the current and the previous values of the input and the output (manifold pressure) of the system. In all examples, PEs have sigmoid nonlinearities (*arctan*).

A total of five different approaches are taken in the training of all networks in all three examples. These are listed below and in the rest of the paper they will be addressed by the designated letter codes.

- Backpropagation with random initial weights (BP).
- Initialize second layer only using Steps 5-7 of the least squares algorithm (LS1). Iterate once.
- Initialize both layers using the least squares algorithm in its entirety (LS2). Iterate three times.
- Use LS1 to initialize second layer and run BP starting with random weights for first layer and LS1-initialized weights for second layer (LS1+BP).
- Use LS2 to initialize all the weights and run BP starting with LS2-initialized weights (LS2+BP).

For the three data sets, we have iterated BP for 1000, 2000, and 200 epochs, respectively. In contrast, for LS+BP approaches, the BP step was iterated 250, 500, and 50 epochs only. For all backpropagation updates, MATLAB®'s Neural Network Toolbox was utilized. The numbers of epochs mentioned above that are required for convergence was determined experimentally beforehand.

The results for laser time series prediction are summarized in the histograms given in Fig. 2. In the 100 Monte Carlo experiments, LS1 and LS2 initialization schemes achieved low normalized MSE levels as seen in subfigures a1 and b1 (MSE is normalized by dividing with the power of the desired signal). Further training with backpropagation resulted in an improvement in MSE in the LS1+BP approach, but it did not change MSE much in LS2+BP (see a2 and b2). Training with BP, on the other hand, in general resulted in higher MSE values either due to slow convergence or local minima. Notice that the least squares algorithm has a much smaller computational complexity compared to backpropagation, yet it still achieves very small MSE levels.

The results of the Dow Jones series prediction are summarized in Fig. 3. Similarly, LS1 and LS2 initialization schemes achieved very small MSE levels and further training with backpropagation (LS+BP) did not improve MSE significantly. At the end of the preset number of iterations,

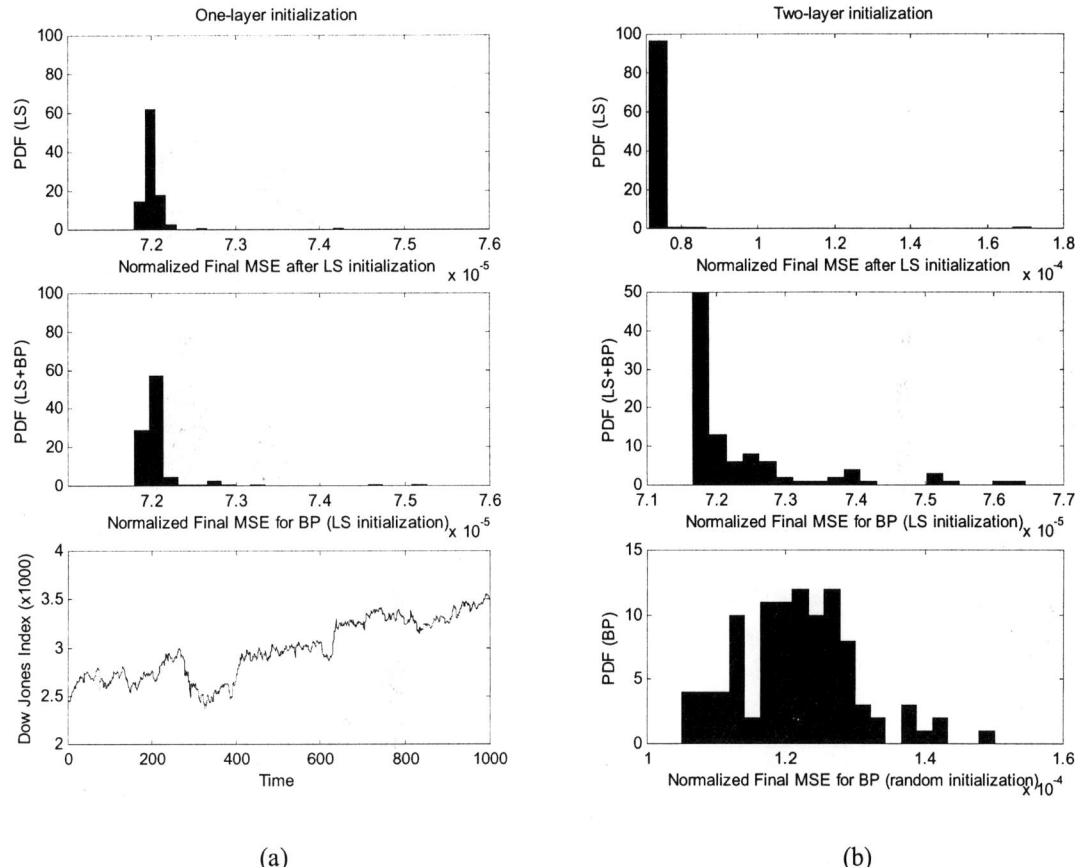

Figure 3. Histograms of final MSE values for the Dow-Jones-series.

the MSE levels of BP were much larger than those obtained with methods that used LS initialization.

We have seen the advantage of using LS1 and LS2 initialization in MLP training in the first two examples. Performance-wise, we did not observe great differences between these two LS approaches, however. In this last example, we see a possible benefit of using LS2 over LS1. The results of the engine-dynamics-identification example are shown in Fig. 4. Notice that LS1 achieves an MSE around 5×10^{-2} (subfigure a1), while LS2 yields an MSE on the order of 10^{-5} (subfigure b1). In both cases, further training using backpropagation does not improve MSE significantly. The BP approach was trapped in the same local minimum as LS1.

VI. CONCLUSIONS

The training speed and accuracy of neural networks can be improved drastically by proper initialization of the weights before a conventional nonlinear optimization tool is employed. In this paper, we have investigated a previously studied initialization scheme, namely least squares, in a mathematically rigorous manner. Previous work using this methodology often ignored the effect of the network nonlinearities on the propagation of the MSE through the layers of the network. Based on the theoretical results that are presented here, we have determined an algorithm to accurately initialize the weights of an MLP to a suboptimal solution, which yields a very small MSE. This algorithm is named as *backpropagation of the desired response*, due to the procedure actually prescribing how to propagate the desired output to the internal layers of the MLP. Then each layer of weights can be (almost) optimally trained by solving a linear system of equations, which correspond to finding the linear least squares solution for this layer of weights.

Although we have focused on the initialization aspect of this least squares algorithm, in many practical problems, such as real-time adaptive control using neural network models and controllers, the solutions offered by the proposed algorithm could be sufficiently accurate. This was demonstrated by a nonlinear system identification problem example, in which an MLP was trained to approximate a realistic engine manifold model accurately.

REFERENCES

[1] D.E. Rumelhart, G.E. Hinton, R.J. Williams, "Learning Representations of Back-Propagation Errors," Nature, vol. 323, pp.533-536, 1986.

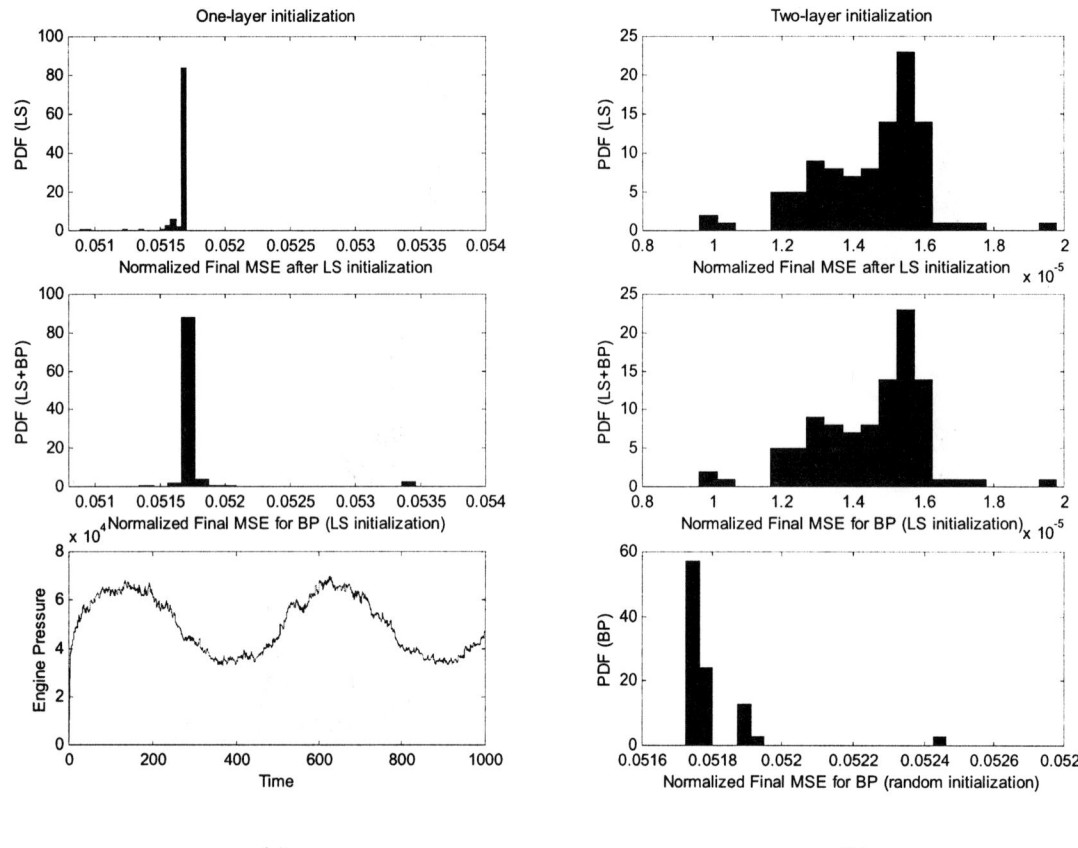

Figure 4. Histograms of final MSE values for engine-dynamics-identification.

[2] S. Amari, "Natural Gradient Works Efficiently in Learning," Neural Computation, vol.10, pp.251-276, 1998.

[3] C.M. Bishop, "Exact Calculation of the Hessian Matrix for the Multilayer Perceptron," Neural Computation, vol. 4, no. 4, pp.494-501, 1992.

[4] M.A. Styblinski, T.S. Tang, "Experiments in Nonconvex Optimization: Stochastic Approximation with function Smoothing and Simulated Annealing," Neural Networks, vol. 3, pp.467-483, 1990.

[5] S. Bengio, Y. Bengio, J. Cloutier, "Use of Genetic Programming for the Search of a New Learning Rule for Neural Networks," Proceedings of the First IEEE World Congress on Computational Intelligence and Evolutionary Computation, pp.324-327, 1994.

[6] V.W. Porto, D.B. Fogel, "Alternative Neural Network Training Methods [Active Sonar Processing]," IEEE Expert, vol. 10, no. 3, pp. 16-22, 1995.

[7] D. Nguyen, B. Widrow, "Improving the Learning Speed of 2-layer Neural Networks by Choosing Initial Values of the Adaptive Weights," Proceedings of International Joint Conference on Neural Networks, vol. 3, pp.21-26, 1990.

[8] G.P. Drago, S. Ridella, "Statistically Controlled Activation Weight Initialization (SCAWI)," IEEE Transactions on Neural Networks, vol. 3, pp. 899-905, 1992.

[9] Y.F. Yam, T.W.S. Chow, "A New Method in Determining the Initial Weights of Feedforward Neural Networks," Neurocomputing, vol. 16, no. 1, pp.23-32, 1997.

[10] F. Biegler-Konig, F. Barnmann, "A Learning Algorithm for Multilayered Neural Networks Based on Linear Least Squares Problems," Neural Networks, vol. 6, pp. 127-131, 1993.

[11] G. Golub, C.V. Loan, *Matrix Computation*, John Hopkins University Press, Baltimore, MD, 1993.

[12] http://www.kernel-machines.org/

[13] J.D. Powell, N.P. Fekete, C-F. Chang, "Observer-Based Air-Fuel Ratio Control," IEEE Control Systems Magazine, vol. 18, no. 5, pp. 72-83, Oct. 1998.

NEW LEARNING FACTOR AND TESTING METHODS FOR CONJUGATE GRADIENT TRAINING ALGORITHM

Tae Kim[1], Michael T. Manry[1], and Javier Maldonado[2]
[1]Department of Electrical Engineering
University of Texas at Arlington
Email; tkim@ieee.org, manry@uta.edu
[2]Chihuahua Institute of Technology, Av. Tecnológico 2909, Chihuahua, Chih., México, 31310

ABSTRACT

The conjugate gradient method has advantages over backpropagation in the training of artificial neural networks. Unlike previous investigators who have obtained learning factors using computationally expensive iterative line searches, we obtain the optimal learning factor in one step. We validate the learning factor with several tests, and analyze the input bias problem. Examples confirm the usefulness of improved conjugate gradient.

1. INTRODUCTION

Many people have used conjugate gradient (CG) artificial neural network (ANN) training because of its advantages as a second-order optimization method. They applied it to applications such as temporal differences learning, [11] image processing, [12, 16] optimal modeling, [13], agricultural prediction, [14] and power system control [15]. In CG, accurate calculation of the learning factor is critical for the conjugacy of direction vectors, and conjugacy is critical for finding the error function minimum [2, 3].

The learning factor, which exactly minimizes the error function in a given iteration, is the optimal learning factor (OLF). Investigators have used the line search technique [7 – 10] and other methods [17, 18] to obtain approximate OLFs. Unfortunately, these methods are computationally expensive, and it is not clear when the learning factors produced are accurate.

In this paper, we find a closed form expression for the OLF in the multilayer perceptron (MLP) and methods for validating it. In section 2, we review the structure and notation used in this paper. A brief summary of the CG algorithm is given in section 3. A Taylor series expansion of the error function is used to develop our OLF approach in section 4. Tests for validating OLF methods are developed in section 5. Examples illustrating the tests are also given.

2. STRUCTURE AND NOTATION

In this section, we discuss the structure and notation of the three layered MLP used for our research. In Fig. 2.1, the MLP is shown. The subscript p denotes the pattern number in the training data. Thus x_{pi} represents the ith input element of the pth training patterns, where $1 \leq i \leq N$. x_{pN+1} which has a value of 1 allows weights to replace thresholds in the hidden and output layer.

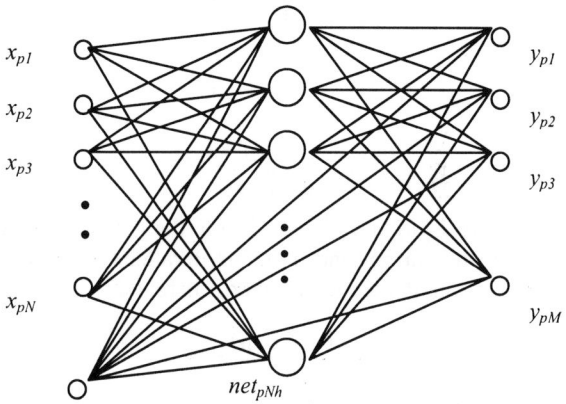

Figure 2.1. Multilayer Perceptron Structure

N, N_h, and M are the numbers of input, hidden, and output nodes respectively. y_{pk} denotes the output of the kth node in the output layer, and net_{pj} denotes the jth hidden node net function, all for the pth training pattern.

Except for the input nodes, multiple weighted terms are input to nodes. These combined terms, called net functions, are expressed in Eq.s (2.1) and (2.2). Here, $w(j,i)$ represents the weight connecting the ith input unit to the jth hidden unit and $w_o(k,i)$ is the weight connecting the ith input to the kth output unit and $w_{oh}(k,j)$ connects the jth hidden unit to the kth output unit. $w(j,N+1)$ represents the threshold to the jth hidden unit and $w_o(k,N+1)$ represents the threshold to the kth output unit. For the hidden units and output units respectively,

$$net_{pj} = \sum_{i=1}^{N+1} w(j,i) \cdot x_{pi} \quad (2.1)$$

$$y_{pk} = \sum_{i=1}^{N+1} w_o(k,i) \cdot x_{pi} + \sum_{J=1}^{N_h} w_{oh}(k,j) \cdot f(net_{pj}) \quad (2.2)$$

Nodes other than hidden ones have linear activation functions. The sigmoid function is used in hidden units. Outputs are calculated using inputs, hidden unit outputs and thresholds. Thus the number of contributions is $N+N_h+1$. Since output nodes don't have activation functions, it is not necessary to express y_{pk} using the *net* symbol.

3. CONJUGATE GRADIENT TRAINING

CG is an unconstrained optimization technique used to minimize the nonnegative error function $E(\mathbf{w})$ of an ANN with respect to $\mathbf{w}$ which represents all the networks weights and thresholds [1, 2]. Let N_w be the number of elements in the weight vector $\mathbf{w}$. In CG, we use the gradient vector $\mathbf{g} = (g_1, g_2, ..., g_{Nw})'$ which is $\mathbf{g} = \partial E / \partial \mathbf{w}$ and the direction vector $\mathbf{p} = (p_1, p_2, ..., p_{Nw})'$ to obtain the weights for the ANN. In the first iteration, $\mathbf{p}$ equals $-\mathbf{g}$. Then for next N_w-1 iterations, $\mathbf{p}$ is found as

$$\mathbf{p} \leftarrow -\mathbf{g} + B_1 \cdot \mathbf{p} \quad (3.1)$$

where

$$B_1 = \frac{E_g(i_t)}{E_g(i_t - 1)} \quad (3.2)$$

and where $E_g(i_t)$ and $E_g(i_t-1)$ denote the gradient vectors' energies in the current and previous iterations respectively. In each iteration, the learning factor Z is found by solving

$$\frac{dE(\mathbf{w} + Z \cdot \mathbf{p})}{dZ} = 0 \quad (3.3)$$

for Z_{OLF}. Then the weights are updated as

$$w \leftarrow w + Z_{OLF} \cdot p \quad (3.4)$$

4. OPTIMAL LEARNING FACTOR FOR CG

There are many ways to obtain the learning factor Z_{OLF}. A common one is to use the line search method. Using a Taylor series expansion of $E(\mathbf{w}+Z\cdot\mathbf{p})$, a third degree expansion of $E(Z)$ is

$$E(\mathbf{w} + Z \cdot \mathbf{p}) \cong A_0 + A_1 \cdot Z + A_2 \cdot Z^2 + A_3 \cdot Z^3 \quad (4.1)$$

where

$$A_j = \frac{1}{j!} \cdot \frac{\partial^j E}{\partial Z^j}\bigg|_{Z=0} \quad (4.2)$$

Depending on whether the second degree or the third degree approximations of the error are used, Z_{OLF} can be obtained using Eq. (3.3) either as

$$Z_{OLF} = \frac{-A_1}{2 \cdot A_2} \quad (4.3)$$

or

$$Z_{OLF} = \frac{-A_2 \pm \sqrt{A_2^2 - 3 \cdot A_1 \cdot A_3}}{3 \cdot A_3} \quad (4.4)$$

Two possible solutions are available from Eq. (4.4). From the second derivative test, $\partial^2 E(Z) / \partial Z^2$ should be greater than zero when $E(Z)$ is at the local minimum. The second derivative of $E(Z)$ at Z_s, which are the solution points of Eq. (3.3) is expressed as

$$\frac{\partial^2 E}{\partial Z^2}\bigg|_{Z=Z_s} \cong 2A_2 + 6A_3 \cdot Z = \pm 2\sqrt{A_2^2 - 2 \cdot A_1 \cdot A_3} \quad (4.5)$$

Since only the positive part of Eq. (4.5) can be used, the resulting solution for optimal Z is

$$Z_{OLF} = \frac{-A_2 + \sqrt{A_2^2 - 3 \cdot A_1 \cdot A_3}}{3 \cdot A_3} \quad (4.6)$$

Whenever the argument of the square root in Eq. (4.6) is negative, we use the solution from Eq. (4.3). Since the correctly obtained direction vector should point toward the trough of the error function, the optimal learning factor should be greater than zero. When the solution from either Eq.s (4.3) or (4.6) turns out to be negative, we use $-g$ as a new direction vector and obtain the optimal learning factor again from Eq.s (4.3) or (4.6). The optimal learning factor of Eq. (4.6) is more accurate but it is computationally more expensive.

Traditional line search or curve fitting methods start with a user given step size ε and look for three points Z_n, Z_{n+1}, and Z_{n+2} defined as

$$E(Z_n) = E(W + n \cdot \varepsilon \cdot P) \quad (4.7)$$

which satisfy

$$E(Z_n) \geq E(Z_{n+1}) \text{ and } E(Z_{n+2}) \geq E(Z_{n+1}) \quad (4.8)$$

Then a parabolic function is fit through the points Z_n, Z_{n+1}, and Z_{n+2} and the minimum Z_{n+4} of the parabolic function is obtained. Among the points Z_n, Z_{n+1}, Z_{n+2}, and Z_{n+4}, a new set of three points satisfying Eq. (4.8) is found. From the new set, a second and subsequent parabolic fits are performed. This process is continued until a point close to the minimum of $E(Z)$ is found [1, 2].

From Eq. (4.7) and (4.8), we see that our Taylor's Series approach has two advantages. First, it requires only one pass through the training data, in contrast to the curve fitting approach, which requires many passes. Second, our approach doesn't require a step size ε to be chosen.

In order to obtain the optimal learning factor Z_{OLF}, the error function needs to be expressed in terms of all the weights, weights change vector elements, and the learning factor Z as in the following. These extended forms are used for the derivation of Z_{OLF}. Let $e(j,i)$ denote the change in weight $w(j,i)$. Similarly, $e_o(k,i)$ denotes the change in weight $w_o(k,i)$, Net_{pj} the change in net_{pj}, $e_{oh}(k,j)$ the change in weight $w_{oh}(k,j)$, and f represents the activation function.

The error function E may be written in terms of the learning factor as

$$E(Z) = \frac{1}{N_v} \sum_{p=1}^{N_v} \sum_{k=1}^{M} \left[t_{pk} - y_{pk}\right]^2 \quad (4.9)$$

$$y_{pk} = \sum_{i=1}^{N+1} \left[w_o(k,i) + Z \cdot e_o(k,i)\right] \cdot x_{pi}$$

$$+\sum_{j=1}^{N_h}\left[w_{oh}(k,j)+Z\cdot e_{oh}(k,j)\right]\cdot f\left(net_{pj}+Z\cdot Net_{pj}\right) \quad (4.10)$$

where

$$net_{pj}=\sum_{i=1}^{N+1}w(j,i)\cdot x_{pi}$$
$$Net_{pj}=\sum_{i=1}^{N+1}e(j,i)\cdot x_{pi} \quad (4.11)$$

Utilizing either Eq. (4.3) or (4.6), we can obtain Z_{OLF}. Further details in the calculations of coefficients A_j are given in the Appendix.

5. LEARNING FACTOR TESTS

Several problems can lead to the failure of Eq. (3.3) to be true. First, the approximation in Eq. (4.1) can be false. Second, there can be round off errors in calculating the coefficients of Eq. (4.1). Third, the derivations of these coefficients can be in error. The following tests can be utilized to validate the learning factor:

ORTHOGONALITY TEST

In CG, the gradient vector g must be orthogonal to the previous direction vector **p** when we use the optimal learning factor. Thus the cosine of the angle θ between **p** and **g**, should be near zero when we use the good OLF. The cosine of θ is expressed as:

$$\cos\theta=\frac{\mathbf{p}\cdot\mathbf{g}}{|\mathbf{p}|\cdot|\mathbf{g}|}=\frac{\sum_{i=1}^{N_w}p_i\cdot g_i}{\sqrt{\sum_{i=1}^{N_w}p_i^2}\cdot\sqrt{\sum_{i=1}^{N_w}g_i^2}} \quad (5.1)$$

In Fig. (5.1), we plot cos θ when **p** is obtained using our OLF. The training data RV400.tra consists of 400 random patterns having 8 inputs and 1 output. The MLP has 4 hidden units. We see that cos θ is confined to less than 0.015.

ERROR PREDICTION TEST

Using Eq. (4.1) in section 4, we can predict the error after the weight update. If the predicted error and the actual error significantly disagree, we see that the OLF is in error. E_{pre} represents the predicted error. For the second degree and third degree series respectively,

$$E_{pre}=A_0+A_1\cdot Z_{OLF}+A_2\cdot Z_{OLF}^2$$
$$E_{pre}=A_0+A_1\cdot Z_{OLF}+A_2\cdot Z_{OLF}^2+A_3\cdot Z_{OLF}^3$$
$$(5.2)$$

where A_j is expressed in Eq. (4.2). Let the relative error R_e be defined as

$$R_e=\frac{|E_{pre}-E|}{|E|} \quad (5.3)$$

Good OLFs corresponds to $R_e\leq 0.01$. In the following, we ran CG for a network having 8 inputs, 4 hidden units, and 1 output. The training data RV400.tra again consisted of 400 random patterns. We see that R_e is less than 2.5E-03.

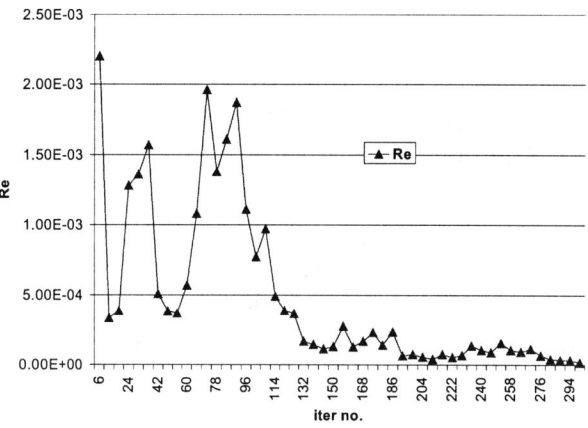

Figure 5.2. Relative error for CG training on RV400.tra.

DOUBLE LEARNING FACTOR TEST

When $E(Z)$ is approximated quadratically, the error E at twice the value of the OLF is very close to the error before the update. Quadratic approximation of $E(Z)$ is illustrated in Fig. 5.3.

From Fig. 5.3, we see why $E(0)\approx E(2\cdot Z_{OLF})$. When the quadratic approximation of the error is correct, the training error should remain constant when we use $2\cdot Z_{OLF}$ as a learning factor. When we use Z_{OLF} as a learning factor the error should decrease.

In Fig. 5.4, we show the actual running of CG on the network and training data used in tests 1 and 2. As predicted, we see that the training error remains fairly

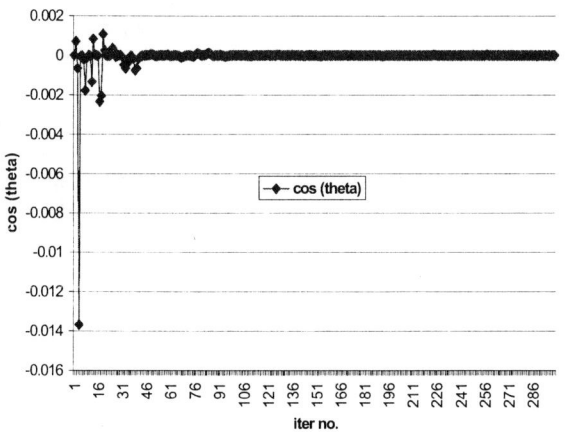

Figure 5.1. cos(θ) values for CG training on RV400.tra.

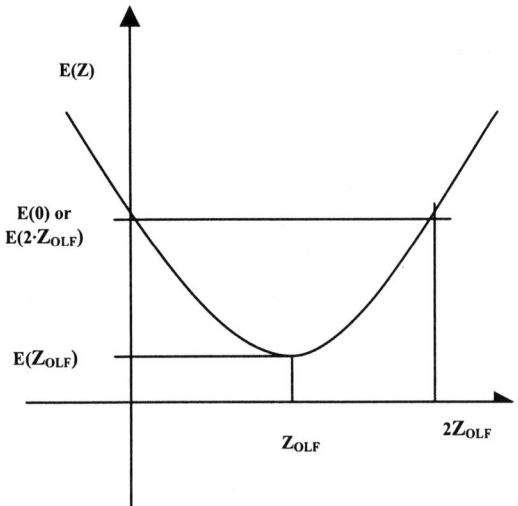

Figure 5.3. Quadratic approximation of the error function in terms of the learning factor

constant when we use $2 \cdot Z_{OLF}$ as a learning factor. When we use Z_{OLF} as a learning factor, the error is successfully decreased.

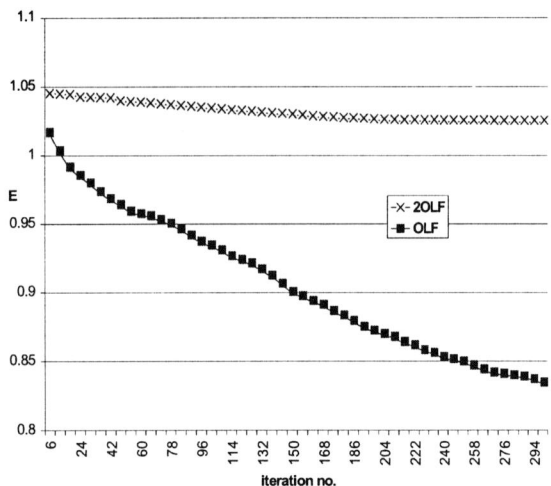

Figure 5.4. Double learning factor test applied to real data

Using the above three learning factor tests, we found out that our OLF works fine. We can apply these learning factor testing methods to other learning factor methods [7 – 10, 17, 18] to see how good their learning factors are.

6. THE INPUT BIAS PROBLEM.

It is desirable that MLP training algorithms be invariant to input biases. In this section, however, we show that gradient based training algorithms, including CG, are sensitive to input biases.

Assume that biased and unbiased training data sets $\{x_p, t_p\}$ and $\{z_p, t_p\}$ respectively are available, where

$$x_p = z_p + m \quad (6.1)$$

Here, the N - dimensional mean vector m is approximately

$$m = \frac{1}{N_v} \sum_{p=1}^{N_v} x_p \quad (6.2)$$

Assume that the initial neural nets for the two sets have identical weights. Also assume that hidden layer and output layer thresholds are adjusted so that the networks have identical hidden layer net function and output values for all patterns. During training, the two neural nets have output and hidden unit delta functions calculated as [2]

$$\delta_{po}(k) = 2 \cdot (t_{pk} - y_{pk}) \quad (6.3)$$

$$\delta_{ph}(j) = O_j \cdot (1 - O_j) \cdot \sum_{k=1}^{M} \delta_{po}(k) \cdot w_o(k, N + j + 1) \quad (6.4)$$

These delta functions are the same for both networks. From Eq. (6.1) the input to hidden weight gradients for the unbiased and biased cases are respectively:

$$\frac{-\partial E_p}{\partial w(j,i)} = \delta_{ph}(j) \cdot z_{pi} \quad (6.6)$$

$$\frac{-\partial E_p}{\partial w(j,i)_b} = \delta_{ph}(j) \cdot (z_{pi} + m_i) = \frac{-\partial E_p}{\partial w(j,i)} + \delta_{ph}(j) \cdot m_i \quad (6.7)$$

The input to output gradients for unbiased and biased data are respectively:

$$\frac{-\partial E_p}{\partial w_o(k,i)} = \delta_{po}(k) \cdot z_{pi} \quad (6.8)$$

$$\frac{-\partial E_p}{\partial w_o(k,i)_b} = \delta_{po}(k) \cdot (z_{pi} + m_i) = \frac{-\partial E_p}{\partial w_o(k,i)} + \delta_{po}(k) \cdot m_i \quad (6.9)$$

Lastly, hidden to output gradients for unbiased and biased data are both equal to

$$\frac{-\partial E_p}{\partial w_o(k,j)} = \delta_{po}(k) \cdot O_j \quad (6.10)$$

From equations (6.6–6.10), we observe that some gradient vector elements are dependent upon the input bias vector m. Therefore, the gradient vectors for the two initial networks are not proportional to each other, and the weight vectors for the networks diverge during training. Thus the performance of CG is dependent on input biases. We presume that good algorithms perform identically on both unbiased and biased data.

As an example, we apply CG to an MLP with structure 8-36-1, where the training data is unbiased and biased data. We see that the training error reaches a small value for the unbiased data but remains large for the biased data, even after many iterations. CG consistently performs poorly in the presence of input biases.

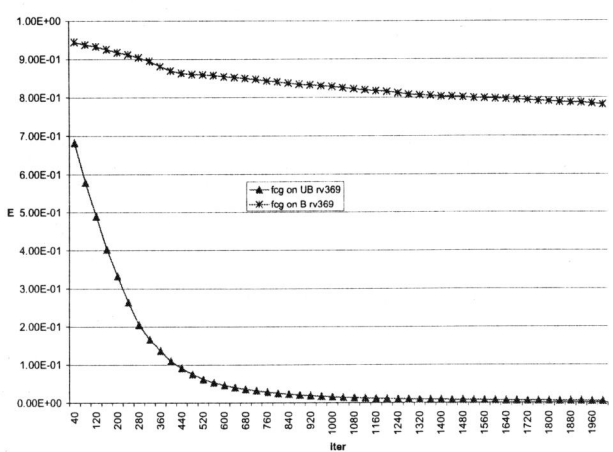

Figure 6.1. CG applied to biased and unbiased random data

7. CONCLUSIONS

A new one-pass algorithm was developed for calculating CG optimal learning factors. Tests were developed and demonstrated for validating OLFs. An analysis has shown that gradient-based training algorithms are sensitive to input biases. Better training was demonstrated after biases were removed.

8. ACKNOWLEDGEMENT

This work was supported by the Advanced Technology Program of the state of Texas Under grant number 003656-0129-2001

9. REFERENCES

[1] Fletcher, R.; *Practical Methods of Optimization*, second edition, New York: Wiley, 1987

[2] S. Haykin, *Neural Networks-A comprehensive foundation*, Prentice-Hall, Inc., NJ, 1999.

[3] M.T. Manry, M.S. Dawson, A.K. Fung, S.J. Apollo, L.S. Allen, W.D. Lyle, and W. Gong, "Fast Training of Neural Networks for Remote Sensing," *Remote Sensing Reviews*, 1994, vol. 9, pp. 77-96

[4] K. Hornik, M. Stinchcombe, and H. White, "Multilayer feedforward networks are universal approximators," *Neural Networks* vol. 2, no. 5, pp. 359-366, 1989.

[5] K. Hornik, M. Stinchcombe, and H. White, "Universal approximation of an unknown mapping and its derivatives using multilayer feedforward networks," *Neural Networks* vol. 3, no. 5, pp. 551-560, 1990.

[6] G. Cybenko, "Approximation by Superpositions of a Sigmoidal Function," *Mathematics of Control, Signals, and Systems*, vol. 2, no. 4, pp. 303-314, 1989

[7] Fitch, J.P.; Lehman, S.K.; Dowla, F.U.; Lu, S.Y.; Johansson, E.M.; Goodman, D.M., "Ship wake-detection procedure using conjugate gradient trained artificial neural networks," *Geoscience and Remote Sensing,* IEEE Transactions on, vol. 29 Issue: 5, Sept. 1991 pp. 718-726.

[8] Johansson, E. M., Dowla, F.U.; Goodman, D.M., "Backpropagation learning for multilayer feed-forward neural networks using the conjugate gradient method," *International Journal of Neural Systems*, vol.2, no.4 1991 pp. 291-301.

[9] Charalambous, C., "Conjugate gradient algorithm for efficient training of artificial neural networks," *Circuits, Devices and Systems, IEE Proceedings G*, Volume: 139 Issue: 3, June 1992 pp. 301–310

[10] Barnard, E., "Optimization for training neural nets," *Neural Networks, IEEE Transactions on*, Volume: 3 Issue: 2, March 1992 pp 232–240

[11] Falas, T.; Stafylopatis, A.-G., "Temporal differences learning with the conjugate gradient algorithm," *Neural Networks, 2001. Proceedings. IJCNN '01. International Joint Conference on*, 2001 pp. 171-176 vol.1

[12] Yap, K.-H.; Guan, L., "A recursive soft-decision PSF and neural network approach to adaptive blind image regularization,"*Image Processing, Proceedings. 2000 International Conference on*, pp. 813-816 vol.3

[13] Campello, R.J.G.B.; Amaral, W.C., "Optimization of hierarchical neural fuzzy models," *Neural Networks,. IJCNN 2000, Proceedings of the IEEE-INNS-ENNS International Joint Conference on*, pp. 8-13 vol.5

[14] Serele, C.Z.; Gwyn, Q.H.J.; Boisvert, J.B.; Pattey, E.; McLaughlin, N.; Daoust, G., " Corn yield prediction with artificial neural network trained using airborne remote sensing and topographic data," *Proceedings. IGARSS 2000. IEEE International , Volume: 1* ,pp. 384 -386

[15] Lizi Zhang; Jinping Kang; Xianshu Lin; Yinghui Xu, " Application of neural networks trained with an improved conjugate gradient algorithm to the turbine fast valving control," *Proceedings. PowerCon 2000. International Conference on* , pp.1679 -1682 vol.3

[16] Kim-Hui Yap; Ling Guan, "A recursive approach to joint image restoration and compensated blur identification," *Neural Networks for Signal Processing X, 2000. Proceedings of the 2000 IEEE Signal Processing Society Workshop*, pp. 567 -575 vol.2

[17] Jiang Minghu; Zhu Xiaoyan; Yuan Baozong; Tang Xiaofang; Lin Biqin; Ruan Qiuqi; Jiang Mingyan, "A fast hybrid algorithm of global optimization for feedforward neural networks," *WCCC-ICSP 2000. 5th International Conference on*, Vol. 3, pp. 1609 –1612

[18] Moller, M.F., "A scaled conjugate gradient algorithm for fast supervised learning," *Neural Networks* 1993 Vol. 6 pp 525-533

[19] Kim, T., "Development and Evaluation of multiplayer perceptron training algorithms," *dissertation*, University of Texas at Arlington 2001

10. APPENDIX

The expression of the error function and its derivatives in terms of all the weights, weights change vector elements, and the OLF is as follows:

$$y_{pk} = \sum_{i=1}^{N+1} \left(w_o(k,i) + Z \cdot e_o(k,i)\right) \cdot x_{pi}$$
$$+ \sum_{j=1}^{N_h} \left[w_{oh}(k,j) + Z \cdot e_{oh}(k,j)\right] \cdot f\left(net_{pj} + Z \cdot Net_{pj}\right) \quad (A.1)$$

$$\frac{\partial y_{pk}}{\partial Z} = \sum_{i=1}^{N+1} e_o(k,i) \cdot x_{pi} + \sum_{j=1}^{N_h} \{e_{oh}(k,j) \cdot f\left(net_{pj} + Z \cdot Net_{pj}\right)$$
$$+ \left[w_{oh}(k,j) + Z \cdot e_{oh}(k,j)\right] \cdot f \cdot (1-f) \cdot Net_{pj}\} \quad (A.2)$$

where
$$f = f\left(net_{pj} + Z \cdot Net_{pj}\right) \quad (A.3)$$
$$f_0 = f\left(net_{pj}\right) \quad (A.4)$$

$$\frac{\partial^2 y_{pk}}{\partial Z^2} = \sum_{j=1}^{N_h} Net_{pj} \cdot f \cdot (1-f) \cdot$$
$$\{2 \cdot e_{oh}(k,j) + Net_{pj} \cdot (1-2f) \cdot \left[w_{oh}(k,j) + Z \cdot e_{oh}(k,j)\right]\} \quad (A.5)$$

Let
$$X_1 = \{2 \cdot e_{oh}(k,j) + Net_{pj} \cdot (1-2f) \cdot \left[w_{oh}(k,j) + Z \cdot e_{oh}(k,j)\right]\}$$

And $X_2 = \left[w_{oh}(k,j) + Z \cdot e_{oh}(k,j)\right]$

Then,
$$\frac{\partial^3 y_{pk}}{\partial Z^3} = \sum_{j=1}^{N_h} Net_{pj}^2 \cdot f \cdot (1-f) \cdot$$
$$\{(1-2f) \cdot X_1 + \{Net_{pj} \cdot X_2 \cdot (-2f) \cdot (1-f)$$
$$+ (1-2f) \cdot e_{oh}(k,j)\}\} \quad (A.6)$$

$$\frac{\partial y_{pk}}{\partial Z}\bigg|_{Z=0} = \sum_{i=1}^{N+1} e_o(k,i) \cdot x_{pi} +$$
$$\sum_{j=1}^{N_h} f_0 \cdot \{e_{oh}(k,j) + w_{oh}(k,j) \cdot (1-f_0) \cdot Net_{pj}\} \quad (A.7)$$

$$\frac{\partial^2 y_{pk}}{\partial Z^2}\bigg|_{Z=0} = \sum_{j=1}^{N_h} Net_{pj} \cdot f_0 \cdot (1-f_0) \cdot$$
$$\{2 \cdot e_{oh}(k,j) + w_{oh}(k,j) \cdot Net_{pj} \cdot (1-2f_0)\} \quad (A.8)$$

$$\frac{\partial^3 y_{pk}}{\partial Z^3}\bigg|_{Z=0} = \sum_{j=1}^{N_h} Net_{pj}^2 \cdot f_0 \cdot (1-f_0) \cdot$$
$$[(1-2f_0) \cdot \{2 \cdot e_{oh}(k,j) + w_{oh}(k,j) \cdot Net_{pj} \cdot (1-2f_0)\}$$
$$+ Net_{pj} \cdot (-2f_0) \cdot (1-f_0) \cdot w_{oh}(k,j)$$
$$+ (1-2f_0) \cdot e_{oh}(k,j)] \quad (A.9)$$

Now,
$$\frac{\partial E}{\partial Z} = \frac{2}{N_v} \sum_{p=1}^{N_v} \sum_{k=1}^{M} \left[t_{pk} - y_{pk}\right] \cdot \left(-\frac{\partial y_{pk}}{\partial Z}\right) \quad (A.10)$$

$$\frac{\partial^2 E}{\partial Z^2} = \frac{2}{N_v} \sum_{p=1}^{N_v} \sum_{k=1}^{M} \left[\left(\frac{\partial y_{pk}}{\partial Z}\right)^2 - \left[t_{pk} - y_{pk}\right] \cdot \frac{\partial^2 y_{pk}}{\partial Z^2}\right] \quad (A.11)$$

$$\frac{\partial^3 E}{\partial Z^3} = \frac{2}{N_v} \sum_{p=1}^{N_v} \sum_{k=1}^{M} \left[3 \cdot \left(\frac{\partial y_{pk}}{\partial Z}\right) \cdot \left(\frac{\partial^2 y_{pk}}{\partial Z^2}\right) - \left[t_{pk} - y_{pk}\right] \cdot \frac{\partial^3 y_{pk}}{\partial Z^3}\right] \quad (A.12)$$

From equations (4.3), (A.7), (A.8), (A.10), and (A.11), we can get second degree learning factor Z. Also from equations (4.5), (A.7), (A.8), (A.9), (A.10), (A.11), and (A.12), we obtain the third degree learning factor. In order to obtain Z, only one pass through the training data is required.

We note here that A_1 can be obtained using the chain rule, the gradient **g**, and the weight change vector **p** as follows. This formula uses the already obtained **g** and **p** to save time for obtaining A_1.

$$A_1 = \frac{\partial E}{\partial Z}\bigg|_{Z=0} = \frac{\partial E}{\partial \mathbf{w}}\bigg|_{Z=0} \cdot \mathbf{p} = \mathbf{g} \cdot \mathbf{p} \quad (A.13)$$

On Variable Sizes and Sigmoid Activation Functions of Multilayer Perceptrons

Gao Daqi, Liu Hua, Li Changwu

Department of Computer, East China University of Science & Technology
State Key Laboratory of Bioreactor Engineering, ECUST
Shanghai 200237, China

Abstract-This paper studies the influences of variable scales and sigmoid activation functions on the performances of multilayer perceptrons. Generally speaking, it is not certainly suitable to normalize the input data or make the sizes of input variables in the range of [0.0, 1.0]. The viewpoint is explained in details according to the theory of support vector machine (SVM). The convergence and generalization abilities of multilayer perceptrons can be evidently improved by means of the following three methods: (A). Enlarge the sizes of the variable components in the range of [0.0, 3.0]. (B). Change the standard sigmoid activation function $f(x)=(1+\exp(-x))^{-1}$ into $f(x)=3(1+\exp(-x/3))^{-1}$. (C). Introduce the sum-of-squares weight term W^TW into the error functions. The classification experiment shows that more than a learning round should be done and the perceptron with the best good generalization performance be held back.

I. Introduction

Multilayer perceptrons take the back-propagation (BP) algorithm [1, 2], sometimes called gradient or steepest descent method, as their main learning algorithm. Some of their major drawbacks are overlong learning time, poor convergence and generalization abilities. In other words, its performances are not so superior as expected. Generally speaking, there are three approaches to solve these problems such as higher-speed computers, faster learning algorithms, and optimal structures and activation functions. The last one often plays a decisive role.

A lot of methods have been presented for improving the *BP* algorithm itself. Besides adding the momentum term in the weight updating formulas [2, 3, 4], the following methods have been proposed: (A). The learning factor η changes with the number of iterations [5] and the sizes of errors [6] as well as the directions of gradients [7, 8]. (B). An updated weight is immediately used to calculate the new error and adjust the other ones [9], (C). Weights are updated layer by layer [10, 11], etc. However, most of the above methods are empirical and devoid of generalizations.

The structures are one of the important factors that influence the performances of networks. It is a natural hope to employ as small structures as possible. Not only is a small network able to have faster learning speeds, but also it cuts down the hardware complexity. Unfortunately, till now the structures of multilayer feedforward perceptrons are mainly determined by experiences and there hasn't been a valid formula that is suitable for different situations [12].

The types of activation functions have very important influences on the networks' learning speeds, classification and nonlinear mapping accuracy. The relationship between the output $f(x)$ and the input x of the standard sigmoid activation function is

$$f(x) = (1+\exp(-x))^{-1} \qquad (1)$$

Its general form [13] may be written as

$$f(x) = \gamma(1+\exp(-\beta x))^{-1} \qquad (2)$$

where γ is the strength parameter, which limits the output values in the range $(0, \gamma)$, and β is the gain factor, which controls the steepness (or slope) of a sigmoid activation function. When γ is finite and $\beta \to +\infty$, (2) is known as the threshold activation function. When γ is finite and $\beta \to 0+$, (2) is named the ramp (linear) activation function. One of the characteristics of sigmoid activation functions is that the change of $f(x)$ will be very small after x goes beyond a certain range, or the first-order derivative of $f(x)$ becomes close to zero when a saturated or cut-off phenomenon emerges. In that case, the sum-of-squares error $E(t)$ hardly changes, so do the weights. At the moment, the network either falls into a local minimum point or is situated at a saddle point or a platform. Some existing methods to solve those problems are as follows: (I). The weights linked with such a node that is in a saturated or cut-off state are re-initiated [7], (II). γ and β are both self-adapted [14, 15], (III). Activation functions are locally linearized [10, 11], etc. One of the main defects of those methods is excess calculating workload. Therefore, Ref. [16] proposed to replace cubic-spline-type activation functions with sigmoid activation functions in order to speed up the learning process. In addition, by approximating the weights with the second order Taylor expansion may improve learning speed and accuracy for some small networks [17], but is considered inappropriate for large networks because calculating workload rapidly increases. The selection of activation functions depends upon practical applications, so diverse non-linear activation functions are presented [18, 19].

This paper analyses the characteristics of a class of sigmoid activation functions, studies the influences of absolute scales of variables on learning speeds and recognition percentage, presents the way how to select suitable activation functions. Finally an example is given to illustrate the validity of the above methods. The conclusions are easily generalized to multilayer feedforward perceptrons.

II. The Generally Optimal Separating Hyperplanes

---

* This work is supported by the National Science Foundation of China (NSFC) under Grant No. 60275017 and the Key Science and Technology Development Foundation of Shanghai, China, under Grant No. 025115028.

Seeking for a separating hyperplane to make the samples in the same class as close and those in the different categories as far as possible is the basic thought of the Fisher's decision method. The support vector machine (SVM) is a new statistic learning theory [20-22] that has sprung up in the last decade or so. Its basic purpose is to make the separate margin 2δ as big as possible in order to make the difference $\phi(N/v)$ between the expected risk $R(w)$ and the empirical risk $R_{emp}(w)$ as small as possible. In other words, with limited learning samples, the main aim of the SVM is to make a learning machine have as high learning accuracy as possible (equal to minimize $R_{emp}(w)$) and as good generalization performances as possible.

Taking two linear separable categories for an example, an optimal separate hyperplane is one that divides all the patterns in the training set correctly and makes the margin between the two classes as wide as possible, as shown in Fig. 1. Let the pth learning sample pair in the training set be (x_p, t_p), $p=1, 2, ..., N$, where $x_p \in R^m$ is the pth input pattern, $t_p \in \{0,1\}$ the class tag. For purposes of analysis, let $t_p \in \{-1, 1\}$. The m-dimensional linear separable hyperplane is written as

$$H: w^T x + \theta = 0 \tag{3}$$

where $w \in R^m$ is a weight vector and θ a threshold. Let the sample x^* that is the nearest to the optimal separate hyperplane H satisfy $|w^T x^* + \theta| = \delta$, and $\delta/\|w\|$ the smallest equivalent divided margin, the following relationship holds water for the pattern x_p

$$|w^T x_p + \theta| / \|w\| \geq \delta / \|w\| \tag{4}$$

Evidently, to make the separate margin as big as possible is equivalent to let δ as large or $\|w\|$ as small as possible. If a separate hyperplane is required to label all the samples correctly, we have

$$t_p(w^T x_p + \theta) - \delta \geq 0 \qquad p=1,2,\cdots,N \tag{5}$$

Therefore, the Lagrange function is defined as

$$L(w,\theta,\lambda) = \frac{1}{2}w^T w - \sum_{p=1}^{N} \lambda_p \left[t_p(w^T x_p + \theta) - \delta \right] \tag{6}$$

where λ_p is a Lagrange multiplier. The Lagrangian formula has to be minimized with respect to w and θ. Let the first-order derivatives of (6) with respect to w and θ be zero, we obtain

$$w = \sum_{p=1}^{N} \lambda_p t_p x_p \tag{7a}$$

$$\sum_{p=1}^{N} \lambda_p t_p = 0 \tag{7b}$$

According to the Kuhn-Tucker conditions, $\lambda_p \geq 0$, and λ_p ought to satisfy the following restraint

$$\lambda_p [t_p(w^T x_p + \theta) - \delta] = 0 \tag{8}$$

The vectors that make $t_p(w^T x_p^* + \theta) - \delta = 0$ are called the support ones (SVs), where $\lambda_p \neq 0$, and for the other vectors $\lambda_p = 0$. Substituting (7) into (8) and rearranging, we have

$$Q(\lambda) = \delta \sum_{p=1}^{N} \lambda_p - \frac{1}{2} \sum_{p,q=1}^{N} \lambda_p \lambda_q t_p t_q (x_p, x_q) \tag{9}$$

Here 1/2 is a coefficient specifically added for the sake of convenient analysis. Seeking λ_p^* so as to maximize $Q(\lambda^*)$, hence, the weight vectors for the optimal separate hyperplane are given by

$$w^* = \sum_{support\ vector} \lambda_p^* t_p x_p^* \tag{10}$$

It is obvious that the optimal separate hyperplane is determined by only a few patterns of the training set, called the support vectors. When the samples are linearly non-separable, (5) may be rewritten as

$$t_p(w^T x_p + \theta) - \delta + \xi_p \geq 0 \tag{11}$$

where $\xi_p \geq 0$. $\|w\|^2 + C\Sigma\xi_p$ should be minimized (C is a constant). Minimizing $\|w\|^2$ is to minimize the VC dimension or maximize δ, and minimizing $C\Sigma\xi_p$ is equivalent to lessen $R_{emp}(w)$[26, 27, 28]. If one substitutes (x_p, x_q) with $K(x_p, x_q)$, he gets a general SVM, and the optimal separate hyperplane is called the generally separating hyperplane. Here, $K(x_p, x_q)$ either is the polynomial function of inner product (x_p, x_q) or a Gaussian or Sigmoid function. From the SVM theory, we get such an important conclusion that the generally optimal separate hyperplane may be obtained by the following two ways: (A) suitably enlarges the variable scales, (B) minimizes the sum-of-squares weights.

III. INFLUENCES OF VARIABLE SCALES AND ACTIVATION FUNCTIONS ON THE PERFORMANCES OF MULTILAYER FEEDFORWARD PERCEPTRONS

A. A feedforward single-hidden-layer network and the back-propagation algorithm

Fig. 2 is a feedforward single-hidden-layer network, in which the number of input and hidden and output nodes are m, s and n respectively, and the activation functions of hidden and output nodes Sigmoidal. Suppose the weight vector between all input nodes and hidden node h at the kth iteration step is $w_h(k)=(w_{h1}(k),...,w_{hi}(k),...,w_{hm}(k))^T \in R^m$, for the pth input pattern $x_p \in R^m$, the total input value of node h is given by

$$\phi(x_p, w_h(k), \theta_h(k)) = w_h^T(k) x_p + \theta_h(k) = \sum_{i=0}^{m} w_{hi}(k) x_{pi} \tag{12}$$

Here $x_{p0}=+1$, $w_{h0}(k)=\theta_h(k)$ is the threshold. It is evident that $\phi(x_p, w_h(k), \theta_h(k))$ is a linear combination of x_p. That is the

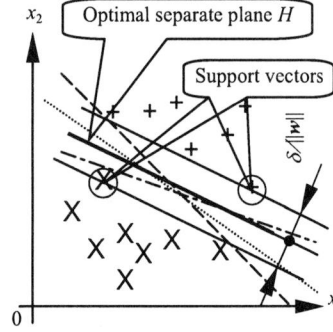

Fig.1. Diagram of optimal separate plane

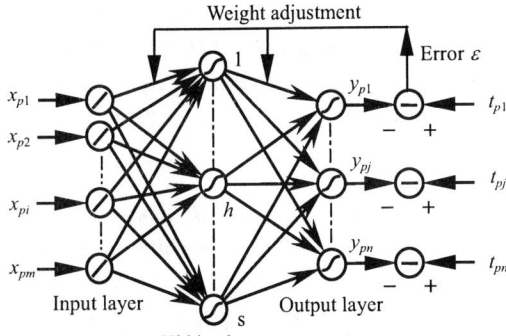

Fig.2. A feedforward single-hidden-layer perceptron

reason why a general multilayer feedforward neural network is sometimes called a linear basis function (LBF) network. The actual output of node h is

$$z_{ph}(k) = f(\mathbf{w}_h^T(k)\mathbf{x}_p + \theta_h(k)) \tag{13}$$

By similar reasoning, the weight vector between all the hidden nodes and the output unit j is $\mathbf{w}_j(k)=(w_{j1}(k),\ldots,w_{jh}(k),\ldots,w_{js}(k))^T \in R^s$. To the pth pattern, the actual output of node j is

$$y_{pj}(k) = f(\mathbf{w}_j^T(k)\mathbf{z}_p(k) + \theta_j(k)) \tag{14}$$

where $\mathbf{z}_p(k)=(z_{p1}(k),\ldots,z_{ph}(k),\ldots,z_{ps}(k))^T \in R^s$ is the pth actual output vector in the hidden layer. Therefore the sum-of-squares error of the network is written as

$$E(k) = \frac{1}{2}\sum_{p=1}^{N}\sum_{j=1}^{n}(t_{pj}-y_{pj}(k))^2 \tag{15}$$

Generally, the batch learning mode is adopted. If the activation functions are given by (1), the gradient components of weights may be obtained by the chain derivation rule. So the gradient component between hidden node h and output unit j is in the following form

$$\frac{\partial E(k)}{\partial w_{jh}(k)} = -\sum_{p=1}^{N}\left((t_{pj}-y_{pj}(k))z_{ph}(k)y_{pj}(k)(1-y_{pj}(k))\right) \tag{16}$$

and the gradient component between input unit i and hidden node h is

$$\frac{\partial E}{\partial w_{hi}} = -\sum_{p=1}^{N}\sum_{j=1}^{n}(t_{pj}-y_{pj})w_{jh}y_{pj}(1-y_{pj})z_{ph}(1-z_{ph})x_{pi} \tag{17}$$

The gradient components of thresholds are in the same form as the above two formulas, omitted here. The uniformly updating formula of weights and thresholds is

$$w(k+1) = w(k) - \eta\,\partial E(k)/\partial w(k) + \alpha(w(k)-w(k-1)) \tag{18}$$

where k is the iteration step, η the learning rate and α the momentum factor. The third term on the right-hand side of (18) is the dynamic one. If $E(k)>\varepsilon^*$, we repeatedly use the BP algorithm to adjust the weights until $E(k)\leq\varepsilon^*$ or the preset number of iterations is reached.

B. Influence of variable sizes on the performances of networks

Let us analysis the relationship between hidden node h and all the input units. Suppose the pth component of the sample $\mathbf{x}_p$ is x_{pi}, the equivalent directed distance is

$$\phi(\mathbf{w}_h,\mathbf{x}_p,\theta_h) = \mathbf{w}_h^T\mathbf{x}_p + \theta_h$$
$$= w_{h1}x_{p1}+\cdots+w_{hi}x_{pi}+\cdots+w_{hm}x_{pm}+\theta_h \tag{19}$$

The relationship between $\phi(\mathbf{w}_h,\mathbf{x}_p,\theta_h)$ and x_{pi} is linear. The bigger the absolute value $|x_{pi}|$, the bigger the absolute value $|\phi(\mathbf{w}_h,\mathbf{x}_p,\theta_h)|$. If all the variable scales of patterns in the training set are enlarged ρ times, the separate margin expands ρ times, too. The separate hyperplanes decided in this way have the best generalization capacity according to the Fisher's decision rule and the SVM theory.

The so-called error back-propagation algorithm is, in fact, that the adjustment size $\Delta w(k)$ of a weight is equal to its negative gradient $-\partial E(k)/\partial w(k)$ multiplied by a step length factor η. On the premises that a network is not caught into local points or doesn't oscillate, a larger value of $-\partial E(k)/\partial w(k)$ is favorable as for convergent rate improvements. To proceed further, (19) is simplified as

$$\phi(\omega,\xi,\vartheta) = \omega\xi + \vartheta \tag{20}$$

where $\omega=w_{hi}$, $\xi=x_{pi}$, $\vartheta=w_{h1}x_{p1}+\ldots+w_{h,i-1}x_{p,i-1}+w_{h,i+1}x_{p,i+1}+\ldots+w_{hm}x_{pm}+\theta_h$. Thus, to the standard sigmoid activation function shown in (1), (13) and (14) may be uniformly written as

$$z(\omega,\xi,\vartheta) = f(\omega,\xi,\vartheta) = (1+\exp(-\omega\xi-\vartheta))^{-1} \tag{21}$$

According to (21), the first derivative with relation to ω is

$$\partial f(\omega,\xi,\vartheta)/\partial\omega = \xi\exp(-\omega\xi-\vartheta)/(1+\exp(-\omega\xi-\vartheta))^{-2} \tag{22}$$

Equation (22) shows that $\partial f(\omega,\xi,\vartheta)/\partial\omega$ has a certain proportional relationship with ξ to some extent. Because of $\partial f(-\omega,-\xi,\vartheta)/\partial\omega = -\partial f(\omega,\xi,\vartheta)/\partial\omega$, it is enough to inspect $\xi>0$ only. Fig. 3 illustrates the relationship between $\partial f(\omega,\xi,\vartheta)/\partial\omega$ and the variables ω, ξ and ϑ for the standard sigmoid activation function. It is quite clear that the notably changing ranges of $\partial f(\omega,\xi,\vartheta)/\partial\omega$ are comparatively wide near $\xi=1.0$ and very small while $\xi>3.0$. And furthermore, if the absolute magnitude $|\xi|$ is tiny, the value $|\partial f(\omega,\xi,\vartheta)/\partial\omega|$ is very small, too. In other words, in order to enhance the learning speeds, $|\xi|$ ought not to be too large or too small. The characteristics of the standard sigmoid activation function are not in agreement

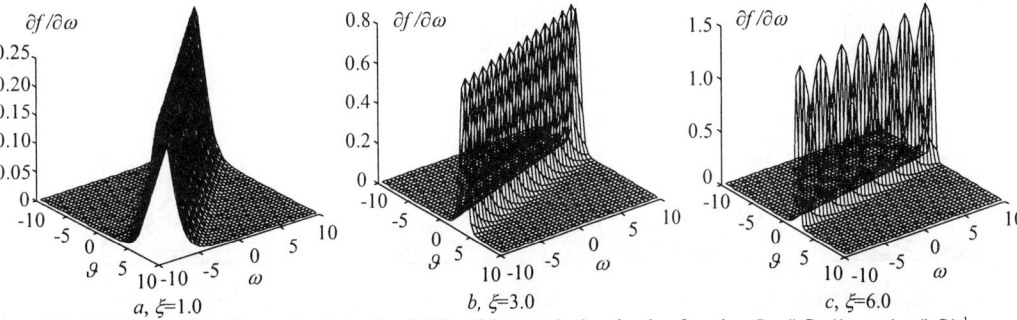

Fig.3. Changes of the first-order derivative $\partial f/\partial\omega$ of the standard activation function $f(\omega,\xi,\vartheta)=(1+\exp(-\omega\xi-\vartheta))^{-1}$

with the Fisher's decision rule and the SVM theory.

C. Influence of activation functions on the performances of networks

One of the main defects of the standard sigmoid activation function is that its effectively adjustable range is not wide enough. A big variable scale or weight or threshold will make the function quickly reach its saturate or cut-off states. As a matter of fact, not only ought the activation functions in multilayer feedforward networks to be continuous and bounded and differentiable everywhere, but also their first-order derivatives have as widely changing ranges as possible according to the SVM theory. Only in this way can the networks have faster learning speeds and better generalization. For easier analysis, (16) and (17) are rewritten as

$$\frac{\partial E(k)}{\partial w_{jh}(k)} = -\sum_{p=1}^{N}\left((t_{pj}-y_{pj}(k))\frac{\partial y_{pj}(k)}{\partial w_{jh}(k)} \right) \quad (23)$$

$$\frac{\partial E(k)}{\partial w_{hi}(k)} = -\sum_{p=1}^{N}\sum_{j=1}^{n}\left((t_{pj}-y_{pj}(k))\frac{\partial y_{pj}(k)}{\partial z_{ph}(k)}\frac{\partial z_{ph}(k)}{\partial w_{hi}(k)} \right) \quad (24)$$

If the total input of a node is simplified as (20) and the kind of activation functions expressed in (2) is adopted, the three first-order derivatives $\partial y_{pj}(k)/\partial w_{jh}(k)$, $\partial y_{pj}(k)/\partial z_{ph}(k)$ and $\partial z_{ph}(k)/\partial w_{hi}(k)$ in (23) and (24) have the same forms, or

$$\frac{\partial f(\omega,\xi,\vartheta)}{\partial \omega} = \frac{\gamma\beta\xi\exp(-\beta(\omega\xi+\vartheta))}{(1+\exp(-\beta(\omega\xi+\vartheta)))^{-2}}$$
$$= \beta\xi f(\omega,\xi,\vartheta)(1-f(\omega,\xi,\vartheta)/\gamma) \quad (25)$$

When $\gamma=\beta=1.0$, (25) is exactly the same as (22). Because $\partial f(-\omega,\xi,\vartheta)/\partial\omega = -\partial f(\omega,\xi,\vartheta)/\partial\omega$, it is enough to only analyze the situation $\xi>0$. Fig. 4 gives the curves of the first-order derivatives of different sigmoid activation functions expressed by (2) with the different sizes of γ and β. Among them the unlabeled is that of the standard activation function. It is evident that the curve of the first-order derivative with $\gamma=3.0$ and $\beta=1/3$ has the widest adjustable range compared with the others. The right-hand sides of (23) and (24) are, in fact, the results of multiplying each difference $\Delta E_{pj}(k)=t_{pj}-y_{pj}(k)$ between a target and a real output either with one or two first-order derivatives and then sum them up. If let $|\partial f(\omega,\xi,\vartheta)/\partial\omega| \leq 0.001$, under the condition of $\xi=1.0$, for the standard sigmoid activation function, $|\omega\xi+\vartheta|\leq 6.906$ and for the activation function $f(\omega,\xi,\vartheta)=3(1+\exp(-(\omega\xi+\vartheta)/3))^{-1}$, $|\omega\xi+\vartheta|\leq 20.717$. With the help of the complete differential equation, we have

$$\Delta E(k) = \sum_{j=1}^{n}\sum_{h=0}^{s}\frac{\partial E(k)}{\partial w_{jh}(k)}\Delta w_{jh}(k) + \sum_{h=1}^{s}\sum_{i=0}^{m}\frac{\partial E(k)}{\partial w_{hi}(k)}\Delta w_{hi}(k) \quad (26)$$

Because of $|t_{pj}-y_{pj}(k)|\leq 1$, let all $|\partial f(\omega,\xi,\vartheta)/\partial\omega|\leq 0.001$ and $\Delta\omega(k)=0.05$, according to (23) and (24), one obtains $|\partial E(k)/\partial w_{jh}(k)|\leq 0.001 N$ and $|\partial E(k)/\partial w_{hi}(k)|\leq 0.000001 nN$. Therefore

$$|\Delta E(k)| \leq 0.00005n(s+1)N + 0.00000005ns(m+1)N \quad (27)$$

This is a very conservative estimation. The reason is that for quite some part of patterns the network is already able to do correct classification and fitting when the sum-of-squares error is slow in descent. According to (27), the maximum error descent magnitude is approximately directly proportional to N, n and s. For example, to the two-dimensional XOR problem, $N=4$, $m=s=2$ and $n=1$, $|\Delta E(k)|\leq 0.0006$. If all the absolute values of first-order partial derivatives are infinitesimal, naturally the corresponding gradient components are very small. As a result, the sum-of-squares error will be quite slow in descent. In other words, the learning time of networks will be quite long. Also, we note that the evidently changing range of the first-order derivative for the hyperbolic tangent activation function $tanh(x)$ is very narrow. And based on that, one can foresee that the kind of networks with $tanh(x)$ will not have faster learning speeds than that of the others shown in Fig. 4. That is one of the main causes why $tanh(x)$ are not so widely used. Fig. 5 gives the changing trend of the ratio ρ between the first-order partial derivatives of all the activation functions and that of the standard one. Fig. 5 says that the ratio $\rho=(3(1+\exp(-x/3))^{-1})'/((1+\exp(-x))^{-1})'$ is 732.6 when $x=\pm 10$. The changing situation of first-order partial derivatives of $f(x)=3(1+\exp(-x/3))^{-1}$ is shown in Fig. 6. Compared with Fig. 3, it is very obvious that $f(x)=3(1+\exp(-x/3))^{-1}$ has more widely adjustable range than $f(x)=(1+\exp(-x))^{-1}$ does. One can predict that the former has faster convergent rate than the latter does. Through the above analyses, we still get such a conclusion that if the variable scale ξ or the strength factor γ enlarges, the gain β ought to lessen appropriately, otherwise the observable changing range of the first-order derivative will be narrow. For example, under the condition $\gamma=3.0$, when $\beta=1/3$, $2/3$ and 1.0 respectively, the visible changing ranges of first-order derivatives of the activation functions become narrow in sequence. Therefore, not only ought a superior activation function to be continuous and bounded, but also its first-order partial derivatives ought to have as widely evidently changing ranges as possible.

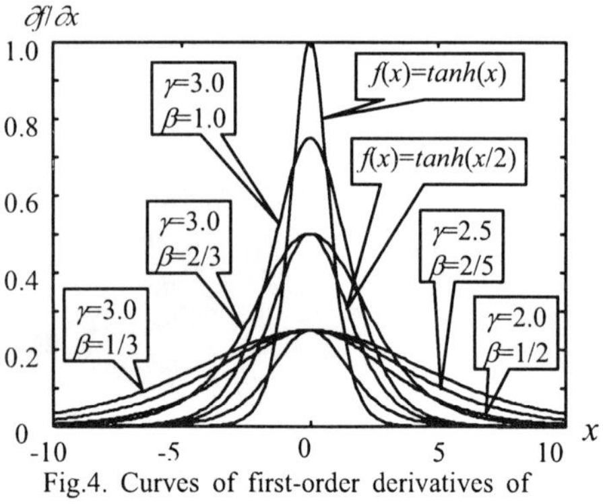

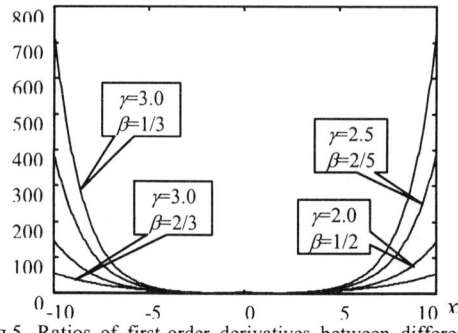

Fig.4. Curves of first-order derivatives of various activation functions

Fig.5. Ratios of first-order derivatives between different activation functions and the standard one

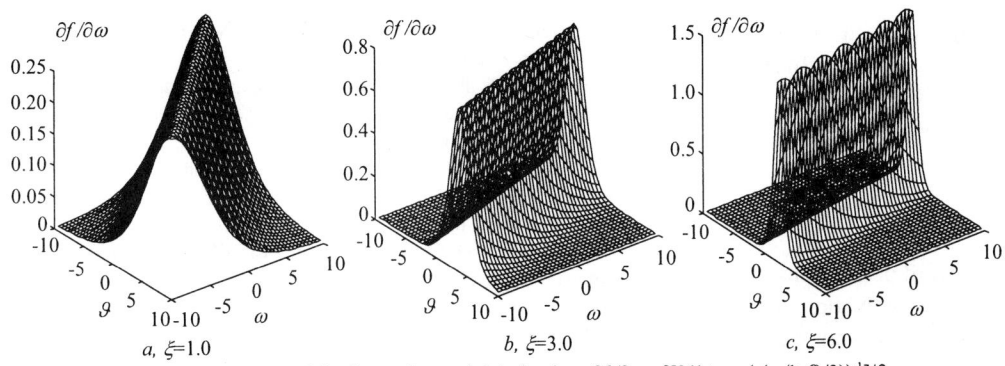

Fig.6. Changes of the first-order partial derivatives $\partial f/\partial \omega = \partial[3(1+\exp(-(\omega\xi+\vartheta)/3))^{-1}]/\partial \omega$

a, $\xi=1.0$ b, $\xi=3.0$ c, $\xi=6.0$

IV. A APPLICATION–SONAR TARGET RECOGNITION

According to the Fisher's discriminant rule and the SVM theory, (15) is rewritten as

$$E(k) = \frac{1}{2}\sum_{p=1}^{N}\sum_{j=1}^{n}(t_{pj}-y_{pj}(k))^2 + \frac{\mu}{2}\sum_{j=1}^{n}\sum_{h=0}^{s}w_{jh}^2(k) + \frac{\mu}{2}\sum_{h=1}^{s}\sum_{i=0}^{m}w_{hi}^2(k) \qquad (28)$$

where μ is the weight restraint factor. In fact, (28) is a generalization of the non-linear inequality constraint optimization methods. In that circumstance, (16), (17), (23) and (24) ought to be changed and are omitted here.

6 kinds of feedforward single-hidden-layer networks are used. And their structures are all the same. In order to contrast their performances on a uniform standard, all the errors taken to compare are given by (15), in fact, the error $\varepsilon=\sqrt{E(k)/nN}$. In other words, Networks 4 and 6 take the first term of the right-hand side of (28) to compare with the others. Naturally, the target output values of Networks 5 and 6 are enlarged 3 times, so do their real error ε and permissible one ε^* accordingly.

Since the first used in 1988 [23, 24], Sonar target recognition has been widely employed to evaluate the performances of various classification methods. There are a metal cylinder and a roughly cylindrical rock in the sea, which are similar in shape, to be discriminated through the sonar signals bounced off them, so the number of classes $n=2$. 60 attributes are picked from the reflecting sonar signals, or the number of dimensions of input patterns $m=60$. Measuring 208 times in different directions and angles, among them 104 patterns are selected to form the training set, and the others the test set. Let all the structures of networks be $60\times 8\times 2$, the momentum factors $\alpha=0.075$, the weight restraint parameters $\mu=0.005$, and the permissible errors $\varepsilon^*=0.01$. If a network converges into ε^*, it will reach a recognition rate of 100% for the training set. The results are assembled on Table I. According to the table, we can get the following conclusions: (I). Though the learning rate η is the smallest, the convergent times of Network 1 are still the least. (II). After enlarging the sizes of variable to a certain extent, the networks adopting $tanh(x)$ and $tanh(x/2)$ as activation functions have slow learning speeds and few convergent times. Because $tanh(x)$ and $tanh(x/2)$ have much narrower adjustable ranges of the first-order derivatives than the others do, Networks 1 and 2 quite quickly fall into the regions that the values of the first-order derivatives are very small. (III). By adequately enlarging the variable scales and selecting suitable γ and β and introducing the term W^TW into the error expression, not only are the learning of networks speeded up, but also the classification correction rates are improved in evidence.

It ought to be made clear that the probability for the networks to obtain their best results enumerated in Table I is only about 15%. The experimental results also show that Network 6 can even reach a classification correction rate of 99/104=95.19% for the test set, albeit with a probability of only about 2%. In other words, in 100 leaning rounds from different initial points, Network 6 makes the best result for about 2 times. Five other networks are not able to reach such a recognizing accuracy no matter how many learning rounds they carry out. This kind of phenomenon verities the above theoretical analysis. The optimal separate hyperplanes based on the training set are not always the optimal for the test set. Not only that, the generalization performances of multilayer perceptrons are of great relationship with the initial weights yet. Using the standard feedforward single-hidden-layer networks with 0, 2, 3, 6, 12, 24 hidden nodes in turn, Ref. [24] obtained a best classification correction rate of 90.38%; and

TABLE I
RESULTS OF THE NETWORKS WITH DIFFERENT ACTIVATION FUNCTION FOR THE SONAR DATA

Network No.	1		2		3		4		5		6	
Activation function	$tanh(x)$		$tanh(x/2)$		$(1+\exp(-x))^{-1}$		$(1+\exp(-x))^{-1}$		$3(1+\exp(-x/3))^{-1}$		$3(1+\exp(-x/3))^{-1}$	
Error formula	(15)		(15)		(15)		(28)		(15)		(28)	
Learning rate η	0.02	0.01	0.04	0.01	0.04	0.04	0.04	0.04	0.04	0.04	0.04	0.04
Range of variables	0~1.0	0~3.0	0~1.0	0~3.0	0~1.0	0~3.0	0~1.0	0~3.0	0~1.0	0~3.0	0~1.0	0~3.0
Iteration steps	5194	21507	7748	15657	19873	15592	2059	2122	5539	3313	1863	1460
Learning time (s)	26.20	107.03	38.79	3.132	99.06	71.15	10.39	10.71	27.57	16.80	9.44	7.51
Number of convergence	8	2	9	6	10	10	10	7	10	10	10	10
Average recog. rate(%)	85.94	85.58	85.15	85.15	89.81	87.59	87.69	87.91	88.56	88.25	88.27	90.86
Best recognition rate(%)	89.42	89.42	88.46	89.42	90.38	91.35	89.42	89.42	91.35	90.38	90.38	93.27
Max. abs. value of weights	3.48	4.36	7.37	6.56	8.82	7.71	14.38	11.76	15.59	14.67	18.79	11.82

with a *k*-nearest-neighbor (*K-NN*) classifier, it only reached that of 82.7%. By a radial-basis-function (RBF) network with different numbers and widths of RBFs, Ref. [25] only achieves a recognition result of 78.85%. Obviously the presented method is quite effective.

V. CONCLUSIONS

The abilities of multilayer feedforward perceptrons closely depend on the variable scales, the types of activation functions, the structures, as well as the learning rate and the weight restraint factor, the initial weights, etc. This paper studies the characteristics of a few sigmoid activation functions, presents the methods of selecting suitable activation functions, and modifies the sum-of-squares error formula. An application example shows that the proposed method is able to effectively increase the learning speeds of networks and improve their classification accuracy.

REFERENCES

[1] R. P. Lippmann. "An introduction to computing with neural nets," *IEEE ASSP magazine*, Vol. 4, pp. 4-22, 1987.

[2] D. E. Rumelhart, J. L. McClelland. Parallel distributed processing. *Cambridge, MA: MIT Press*, 1986.

[3] C. M. Bishop. Neural networks for pattern recognition. *Clarendon Press, Oxford*, 1998.

[4] V. V. Phansalkar, P. S. Sastry. "Analysis of the back-propagation algorithm with momentum," *IEEE Transactions on Neural Networks*, Vol. 5, pp. 505-507, 1994.

[5] E. Corwin, A. Logar, W. Oldham. "An iterative method for training multilayer networks with threshold functions," *IEEE Transactions on Neural Networks*, Vol. 5, pp. 507-508,1994.

[6] G. D. Magoulas, M. N. Varhatis, G. S. Androulakis. "Effective backpropagation training with variable stepsize," *Neural Networks*, Vol. 10, pp. 69-82, 1997.

[7] F. Stager, M. Agarwal. "Three methods to speed up the training of feedforward and feedback perceptrons," *Neural Networks*, Vol. 10, pp. 1435-1443, 1997.

[8] A. G. Parlos, F. Fernandez, A. F. Atiya, et al. "An accelerated learning algorithm for multilayer perceptron networks," *IEEE Transactions on Neural Networks*, Vol. 5, pp. 493-497, 1994.

[9] R. D. Leone, R. Capparuccia, E. Merelli. "A successive overrelaxative backpropagation algorithm for neural-network training," *IEEE Transactions on Neural Networks*, Vol. 9, pp. 381-387, 1998.

[10] S. Ergezinger, E. Thomsen. "An accelerated learning algorithm for multilayer perceptrons: optimization layer by layer," *IEEE Transactions on Neural Networks*, Vol. 6, pp. 31-42, 1995.

[11] N. S. Rubanov. "The layer-wise method and the backpropagation hybrid approach to learning a feedforward neural network," *IEEE Transactions on Neural Networks*, Vol. 11, pp. 295-305, 2000.

[12] D. C. Psichogios, L. H. Ungar. "SVD-NET: an algorithm that automatically selects network structure," *IEEE Transactions on Neural Networks*, Vol. 5, pp. 513-515, 1994.

[13] G. Thimm, P. Moerland, E. Fiesler. "The interchangeability of learning rate and gain in backpropagation neural networks," *Neural Computation*, Vol. 8, pp. 451-460, 1996.

[14] C.-T. Chen, W.-D. Chang. "A feedforward neural network with function shape autotuning," *Neural Networks*, Vol. 9, pp. 627-641, 1996.

[15] D. Christian, M. John. "Note on learning rate schedules for stochastic optimization," *Neural Information Processing Systems, Lippmann R P, et al (ED)*, pp. 832-838, 1991.

[16] S. Guarnieri, F. Piazza, A. Uncini. "Multilayer feedforward networks with adaptive spline activation function," *IEEE Transactions on Neural Networks*, Vol. 10, pp. 672-684, 1999.

[17] W. L. Buntine, A. S. Weigend. "Computing second derivatives in feedforward neural networks: a review," *IEEE Transactions on Neural Networks*, Vol. 5, pp. 480-488, 1994.

[18] G.-B. Huang, Y.-Q. Chen, H. A. Babri. "Classification ability of single hidden layer feedforward neural networks," *IEEE Transactions on Neural Networks*, Vol. 11, pp. 799-801, 2000.

[19] G.-B. Huang, H. A. Babri. "Upper bounds on the number of hidden neurons in feedforward networks with arbitrary bounded nonlinear activation function," *IEEE Transactions on Neural Networks*, Vol. 9, pp. 224-228, 1998.

[20] V. N. Vapnik. "An overview of statistical learning theory," *IEEE Transactions on Neural Networks*, Vol. 10, pp. 988-999, 1999.

[21] M. Lehtokangas. "Modified cascade-correlation learning for classification," *IEEE Transactions on Neural Networks*, Vol. 11, pp. 795-798, 2000.

[22] J. A. Suykens, J. Vandewalle. "Training multilayer perceptron classifiers based on a modified support vector method," *IEEE Transactions on Neural Networks*, Vol. 10, pp. 907-911, 1999.

[23] ftp://ftp.ics.uci.edu/pub/mechine-learning-databases or http://www.ics.uci.edu/-mlearn.

[24] R. P. Gormann, T. J. Sejnowski. "Analysis of hidden units in a layered network trained to classify sonar targets," *Neural Networks*, Vol. 1, pp. 75-89, 1988.

[25] A. Roy, S. Govil, P. Miranda. "An algorithm to generate radial basis function (RBF)-like nets for classification problems," *Neural Networks*, Vol. 8, pp. 179-201, 1995.

[26] G. Dundar, K. Rose. "The effects of quantization on multilayer neural networks," *IEEE Transactions on Neural Networks*, Vol. 6, pp. 1445-1451, 1995.

[27] D. Anguita, S. Ridella, S. Rovetta. "Worst case analysis of weight inaccuracy effects in multi perceptrons," *IEEE Transactions on Neural Networks*, Vol. 10, pp. 415-419, 1999.

[28] A. Menon, K. Mehrotra, C. K. Mohan, et al. "Characterization of a class of sigmoid functions with applications to neural networks," *Neural Networks*, Vol. 9, pp. 819-835, 1996.

[29] N. B. Karayiannis. "Reformulated radial basis neural networks trained by gradient descent," *IEEE Transactions on Neural Networks*, Vol. 10, pp. 1121-1138, 1999.

[30] S. E. Fahlman. "Faster-learning variations on back-propagation: an empirical study," *Proc. 1988 Connectionist Model Summer School, Carnegie Mellon University*, pp. 38-51, 1989.

[31] D. Nguyen, B. Widrow. "Improving the learning speed of 2-layer neural networks by choosing initial values of adaptive weights," *Proc. IJCNN*, Vol. 3, pp. 21-26, 1990.

[32] D. S. Yueng, X. Sun. "Using function approximation to analyze the sensitivity of MLP with antisymmetric squashing activation," *IEEE Transactions on Neural Networks*, Vol. 13(1), pp. 34-44, 2002.

[33] N. Kwak, C. H. Choi. "Input feature selection for classification problems," *IEEE Transactions on Neural Networks*, Vol. 13(1), pp. 143-159, 2002.

[34] J. P. Marten, N. Weymaere. "An equalized error backpropagation algorithm for the on-line training multilayer perceptrons," *IEEE Transactions on Neural Networks*, Vol. 13(3), pp. 532-541, 2002.

[35] J. Sima. "Training a sigmoidal neuron is hard," *Neural Computation*, Vol. 14(11), pp.2709-2728, 2002.

[36] A. Alessandri, M. Sanguineti, M. Maggiore. "Optimization-based learning with bounded error for feedforward neural networks," *IEEE Transactions on Neural Networks*, Vol. 13(2), pp. 261-273, 2002.

Improved Neural Network Training Using Redundant Structure

Yingjie Yang
Centre for Computational
Intelligence
School of Computing
De Montfort University
The Gateway, Leicester
LE1 9BH, UK

Chris Hinde
Department of Computer Science
Loughborough University
Loughborough
Leics.
LE11 3TU
UK

David Gillingwater
Department of Civil and
Building Engineering
Loughborough University
Loughborough
Leics.
LE11 3TU, UK

Abstract: It is a common understanding in neural network research and applications that a network with fewer redundant nodes is more reliable. This paper argues that a redundant network structure approach improves the learning process of neural networks. This redundant structure is shown to be free from extra parameters and hence does not introduce additional uncertainty. Using a small partition problem, the training results of standard BP networks are compared with those networks with a redundant structure. The comparison shows that a redundant structure does not necessarily always have a negative effect, and as a result it is possible to help a neural network obtain better performance.

I. INTRODUCTION

One of the difficulties in establishing a Neural Network (NN) is the determination of its structure. It is a common understanding that only the simplest network structure can give the best solution. Therefore, various network pruning technologies have been developed [1-8]. However, one of the key features in neural networks is that they perform complicated analyses or mapping by means of a combination of huge amounts of simple neurons [9]. The real biological world does not necessarily rely on strict mathematics or pruning technology to run their activities, but they do display such an array of functionality that scientific analysis may never be able to explain it adequately. The 'compound eye' of an insect [10] is just one of these: in addition to its ability to accommodate overlapping inputs, it involves many other different mechanisms which makes it impossible to simulate with only a simple structure. This fact does not exclude the notion that simple overlapped inputs may contribute to its power.

Bearing this in mind, a simple approach to making use of overlapped or redundant inputs to improve the training results of NN is put forward here. This method employs multiple input nodes for the same input parameter in the network structure and simulates their influences in the compound eye of insects [11] by a random initialisation of their connecting weights. Unlike redundant hidden nodes, overlapped inputs do not produce more dimensions in the solution space and hence do not involve new uncertainties. In principle, we prove that the proposed overlapped input structure could be replaced exactly by an equivalent ordinary neural network structure. However, the difficulty in initialising the connecting weights between different nodes makes it difficult for an ordinary network to find the same ideal solution. With the increase of the number of the overlapped input nodes in the input layer, the mean of the distribution of the ideal connecting weights approaches zero, and hence a random initialisation around zero would appear to be suitable for the proposed simple structure. This does not apply in traditional neural networks as an initial value of zero would inhibit any learning in the network. Therefore, the proposed method has a better chance to find the ideal solution with the same available training data than the traditional one. Because of the different initialisation of the connecting weights, the same input from different input nodes may have different influences on the training operation. This difference may reduce with the training process, but it would not disappear completely. Therefore, the node for the same input may "see" different "pictures" and reflects the position effects of the compound eye of insects.

In conclusion, a simple partition example is illustrated to show the efficiency of the proposed method. The details neglected by traditional networks are revealed clearly using the proposed networks. This shows that a simple overlapped input does improve the training of the neural networks.

II. COMPOUND EYE AND REDUNDANT STRUCTURE

It is well known that insects are very sensitive to objects moving around them. Research shows that *Drosophila*, the fruit fly, has a reiterated pattern of 800 ommatidia in its compound eye [10], and the lacewing *Mallada basalis* (Walker) has approximately 600 ommatidia [11]. There is a lens in every ommatidium and hence the compound eye is composed of a large number of lenses. Instead of one lens they see through spheres with many lenses. Each lens of the compound eye catches its own image. The more lenses the compound eye bears, the higher the resolution of the image. The two large spherical eyes of a fly give an almost complete 360 degree vision.

The mechanisms of the compound eye are very complicated and still being analysed although some have been recognised. For example, a well-focused clear zone diurnal eye of the Skipper butterfly is illustrated in Figure 1[12]. The parallel rays falling on the eye pass through many facets to converge on a small region of the receptor layer.

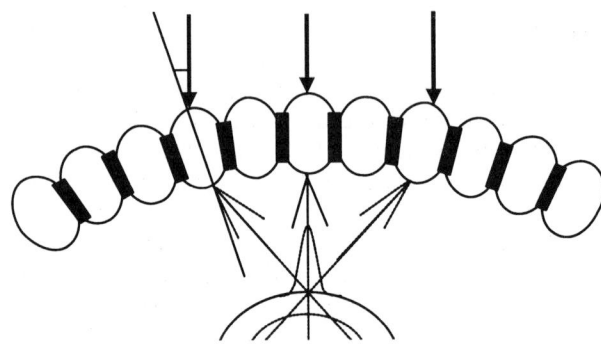

Fig. 1 A well-focused clear zone eye

The individual ommatidium of the insect's compound eye possesses only a few photoreceptors. For example, there are 8 photoreceptors in the adult *Drosophila* ommatidium [13]. Obviously, the single ommatidium cannot catch very much information about its view. However, a large number of them makes the insect very sensitive to its visual environment. It proves that the combination of the large number of ommatidia improves dramatically the function of the insect eye. There are some differences between the images captured by different ommatidia from different angles; however, the main image taken by these ommatidia are similar to each other in that they come from the same picture. In another words, there is some kind of redundant structure in the compound eye of insects, and that structure contributes to the combination of the final image.

Inspired by the compound eye of insects, we constitute a redundant structure for neural networks, as shown in Figure 2. Figure 2 illustrates the structure of a NN with redundant inputs and an ordinary NN. A, B and C are the attributes of the observed object, and they serve as the inputs of the neural network. For the ordinary one, there are only three input nodes in this case: A, B and C. There are 9 nodes in the input layer of the redundant one for the same object here, and it corresponds to three lenses in the compound eye. The first three input nodes act as one "lens", the second three nodes as another lens, and so do the other three nodes in the input layer of the NN with redundant inputs. In this way, the redundant NN could "see" three similar "images" for the same sample data at the same time, just like the insect's

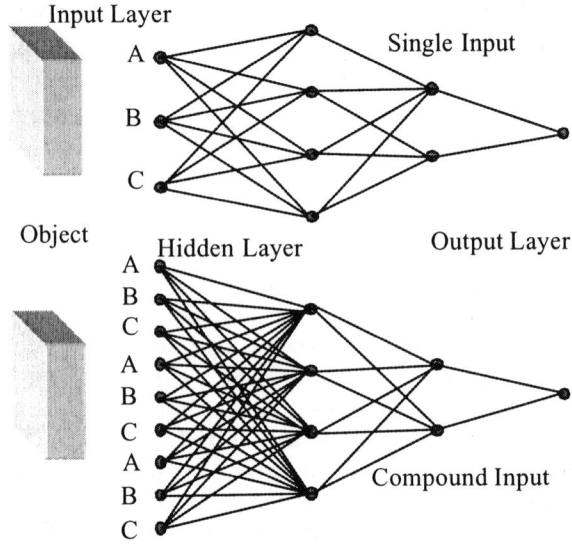

Fig. 2 Redundant input NN and ordinary NN

mosaic image from its compound eye. In this way, the input "image" is multiplied as a number of similar "images" from a series of input "lenses", and their messages are projected to the hidden layer to combine into a single "picture". Due to the random initialisation of the connecting weights, it is acknowledged that the different "lens" would "see" a different "image". This difference could be reduced with the learning operation, but it is difficult to remove completely statistically. Thus to some extent this mechanism simulates the operation of the compound eye of an insect.

III. PROPERTIES OF THE REDUNDANT STRUCTURE

According to Figure 2, it is obvious that the structure of the hidden layers and the output layer of the two different kinds of structure are exactly the same structure: they have the same number of nodes and connecting weights. The only difference comes from the input layer and their connecting weights with the first hidden layer. In principle, there should be an equivalent ordinary network structure to the redundant one.

Considering a network with n input factors, suppose there are k input sets in its corresponding redundant network, W_{ij} as the connecting weight between input factor i and node j in the first hidden layer, V_i denotes the value in input node i, then the receipt of the hidden node j in the redundant network is:

$$V_{ij} = \sum_{i=1}^{n*k} W_{ij} V_i + \sigma_j \quad (1)$$

Change the order of the input factors so that all the first n input nodes are from factor 1, and the second n input nodes from factor 2, and so on. Then we have

$$V_{ij} = \sum_{i=1}^{n*k} W_{ij} V_i + \sigma_j$$
$$= v_1 \sum_{i=1}^{k} w_{ij} + v_2 \sum_{i=k+1}^{2k} w_{ij} + \ldots + v_k \sum_{i=(n-1)*k+1}^{i=n*k} w_{ij} + \sigma_j$$
$$= \sum_{s=1}^{n} w'_{sj} v_s + \sigma_j \quad (2)$$

Here, w_{ij} means the connection between input node i and the hidden node j after the changing of the order for input nodes. v_s represents the value of input factor s. w'_{sj} is the connecting weight between input s and hidden node j in the equivalent ordinary network.

$$w'_{sj} = \sum_{i=(s-1)*k+1}^{s*k} w_{ij} \quad (3)$$

According to Equations (2) and (3), the compound input ANN can be converted exactly into an equivalent ordinary one. Therefore, it does not introduce any new parameters, thus does not bring new uncertainties to the network. This is very different from a pure increment of the hidden nodes where new uncertainties are inevitable.

Suppose that a global minimum point in the error space requires the connecting weight between input factor m and node n in the first hidden layer to be W'_{mn} in the ordinary NN, and w'_{in} (i=1, 2, …,k) for the compound input, where k means the number of the sub networks. Then

$$W'_{mn} = \sum_{i=1}^{k} w'_{in} \quad (4)$$

Suppose the initialised value of W'_{mn} is W_{mn}, and w_{in} for w'_{in}. Considering the random feature of W_{mn} and w_{in}, thus

$$E(w_{in}) = E(W_{mn}) = 0 \quad (5)$$

and

$$\lim_{k \to \infty} \sum_{i=1}^{k} w_{in} = 0 \quad (6)$$

Therefore, the increment of the number of nodes for the same input factor does not increase the initial weight of its corresponding traditional NN.

According to the Jaynes' Maximum Entropy Principle [14], we should assume that $w_{in} = \dfrac{W_{mn}}{k}$ when we do not know the value of every w_{in}. It is clear that

$$\lim_{k \to \infty} w_{in} = \lim_{k \to \infty} \frac{W_{mn}}{k} = 0 \quad (7)$$

Therefore, a large number of sub networks in the redundant input NN would move the start point towards the true global minimum in the error space under the condition of a small value initialisation within [-1,1]. The true global minimum in the error space is a precondition for NN to give a reliable solution to its mapping. The random initialisation of weights within the neighbourhood of 0 is more reasonable for a redundant input NN than an ordinary one.

IV. APPLICATION EXAMPLE

To demonstrate the performance of the redundant NN, a simple example for partition is illustrated here in Figure 3. Points in Figure 3 belong to two different parts. The input factors of the network are the coordinates of the points, and

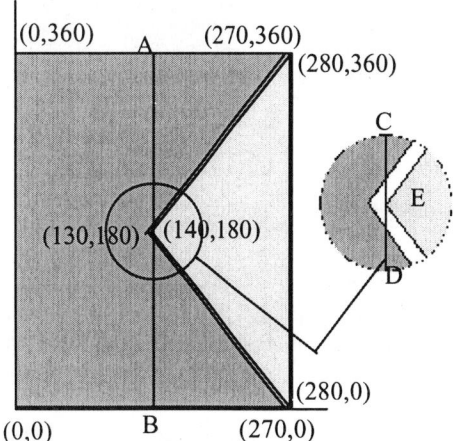

Fig. 3 The partition problem

the output is 0 for points located to the left and 1 for the right. This simple problem shows the difference between the networks trained with simple inputs and redundant inputs under conditions of the same random initialisation operation. The training points include the vertex of the two parts and some inside points produced randomly.

After some trials, the minimum requirement for the number of hidden nodes is 2 (one hidden layer). Two networks are established: each with two hidden nodes, the redundant input network with 30 sets of inputs. With exactly the same initial hidden layer and output layer as well as their connections, two networks for the same application are established under the same error limit. Their different outputs are compared in Figure 4. The status of points in the whole area in Figure 4 is calculated with the redundant input and ordinary one. Figure 4(a) is produced by the redundant input network, and 4(b) by the ordinary one. It is obvious that the redundant one gives a better resolution than the ordinary. The detail in the central area has a higher resolution. The ordinary NN is less accurate: its centre boundary is estimated as an arch which is different from Figure 3. The arch in the ordinary NN produces information that does not exist in the training set. This is not the best of solutions according to Jaynes' Maximum Entropy Principle [14].

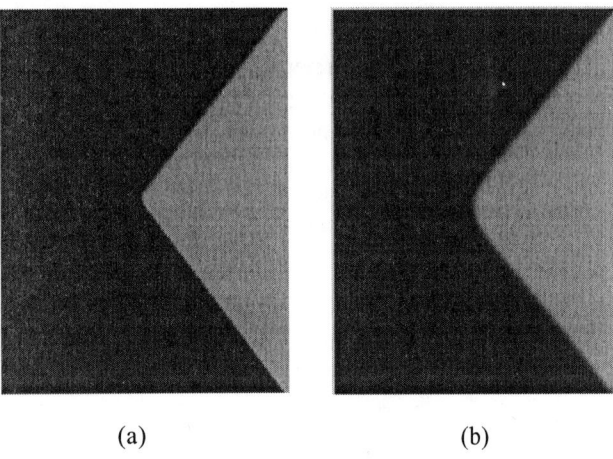

(a)　　　　　　　　(b)

Fig. 4 The results of compound and standard input

To test the reliability of this difference, the initial connection weights are updated with random initialization and the same experiment is repeated. In the end, all converged networks give similar differences between the two kinds of networks. However, our experiment shows also that convergence is difficult with a minimum number of hidden layer nodes: both structures have over 95% of failures (not convergent in the end). The compound (redundant) one takes much longer. In a real world application, the optimum hidden node number is difficult to know in advance, and it is more likely that the neural network is initialised with a structure involving some extra hidden nodes. Therefore, a series of experiments for redundant hidden nodes are carried out to test their influence on neural network learning. The results demonstrate that, in addition to the improvement in the solution compared with the network with ideal network structure, a redundant structure shows also a robust feature for the possible false solution introduced by extra hidden nodes.

Figure 5 shows the results of this experiment for acceptable and false mapping rates which change with respect to different network size. Here, by size we mean the number of hidden nodes in the hidden layer for the ordinary network and the number of the sub input sets in redundant networks with 3 hidden nodes in the hidden layer. Figure 5(a) shows the result for ordinary networks and Figure 5(b) gives the performance of redundant input networks.

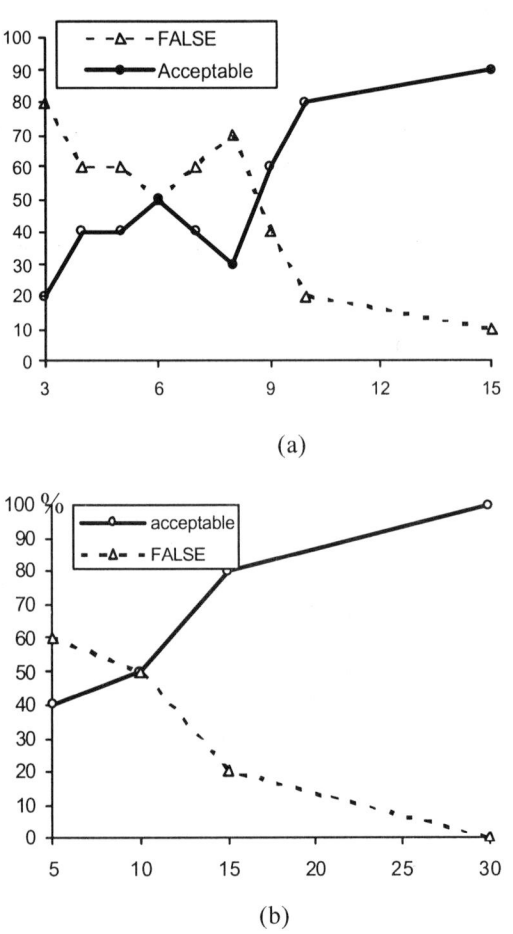

Fig. 5 The rate (%) of acceptable and false mapping vs. network size
a—ordinary network; b—redundant input

The common perception is that a neural network of small size is more reliable. However, it is true only for the minimum size which is less likely to learn the idiosyncrasies or noise in the training data [15] - although it may exhibit serious convergence problems as stated before. The example here shows that the small size with extra hidden nodes would have a high probability to give a false mapping, as demonstrated in Figure 5(a). This result is caused by the poor initialization of the weights. With the increase of the hidden nodes, the ideal distribution of the initalised weights approaches 0 (Equation 7) and hence the starting position for the learning is improved.

The redundant hidden nodes are sometimes inevitable for a complicated application due to our ignorance of the "black box" structure of NN. Figure 5(a) demonstrates that an ordinary network with 3 hidden nodes for this problem is highly likely (80%:20%) to introduce false solutions. Because of this, all the experiments in Figure 5(b) are based on 3 hidden nodes to test its robustness. Figure 5(b) shows that the increment of a redundant input network has a similar function like hidden nodes in reducing possible false solutions. However, as illustrated by Equation 3, the redundant input network has a crucial difference from the pure extra hidden nodes: it does not introduce any new parameter to the network. Hence it keeps the generality of the trained network.

VI. CONCLUSIONS

Redundant structure does not always have negative effects with regard to the training of neural networks. It could play a significant role in improving the network performance under certain conditions. The redundant structure proposed here does not introduce new uncertainties into the network, but it reduces the possibility of false mappings and improves mapping quality. The method proposed is novel although simple, it does bring new problems like longer training times, but it provides a prospective direction for the improvement of neural network training operations, especially for hardware realisation.

REFERENCES

[1] MC.Mozer & P. Smolensky. Skeletonization: A technique for trimming the fat from a network via relevance assessment. Advances in Neural Information Processing. 1. D. S. Touretzky, Ed.. Denver, pp 107-115, 1988.

[2] R Reed. Pruning algorithms - a survey. *IEEE Transactions on Neural Netwroks*, 4(5):740–747, September 1991.

[3] B Hassibi and D Stork. Second order derivatives for pruning: optimal brain surgeon. In *Advances in Neural Information Processing Systems*, volume 5, pages 164–171, 1993.

[4] M. Hagiwara, Removal of hidden units and weights for back propagation networks. In: *Proc. IJCNN*, Nagoya, Japan, Vol.1. -pp. 351-354, 1993.

[5] D. Stork & B. Hassibi. Second order derivatives for network pruning: Optimal Brain Surgeon. in Advances in Neural Information Processing Systems. (NIPS) 5, pages 164--171, T. J. Sejnowski G. E. Hinton and D. S. Touretzky, editors, San Mateo, Morgan Kaufmann Publishers Inc. 1993.

[6] J Mao, K Mohiuddin, and A Jain. Parsimonious network design and feature selection through node pruning. In *12th International Conference on Pattern Recognition*, pages 622–624, 1994.

[7] N. Majima, A. Watanabe, A. Yoshimura, T. Nagano. A new criterion "Effectiveness Factor" for pruning hidden units. In: *Proc. ICNN*, Seoul, Korea. - Vol.1. - pp.382-385, 1994.

[8] R Setiono. A penalty function approach for pruning feed-forward neural networks. *Neural Computation*, 9:185–204, 1997.

[9] RH. Nielsen, Neurocomputing, Addison-Wesley Publishing Company, 433pp, 1990.

[10] JM. Karpilow, AC. Pimentel, HK. Shamloula & TR. Venkatesh, Neuronal development in the Drosophila compound eye: Photoreceptor cells R1, R6, and R7 fail to differentiate in the retina aberrant in pattern (rap) mutant, *Journal of Neurobiology*, (31)2: 149-165, 1996.

[11] IF. Yang, JT. Lin & CY. Wu. Fine structure of the compound eye of Mallada basalis (Neuroptera: Chrysopidae). *Annals of the Entomological Society of America*, (91)1:113-121, 1998.

[12] GA. Horridge. Optical mechanisms of clear-zone eyes, The compound eye and vision of insects, pp. 255-298, Oxford: Clarendon Press, 1975.

[13] T. Wolff & DF. Ready. Pattern formation in the Drosophila retina. In: The Development of Drosophila melanogaster. Cold Spring Harbor Laboratory Press. Vol. 2 Pp. 1277-1325, 1993.

[14] JN. Kapur & HK. Kesavan, Jaynes' Maximum Entropy Principle, *Entropy optimisation principles with applications*, pp. 23-76, San Diego, Academic Press, 1992.

[15] S. Haykin. Neural Networks: A Comprehensive Foundation, Prentice Hall, New Jersey, 842.pp, 1999.

An Efficient Learning Algorithm with Second-Order Convergence for Multilayer Neural Networks

Hiroshi NINOMIYA[*1], Chikahiro TOMITA[*2] and Hideki ASAI[*2]

[*1] *Shonan Institute of Technology*
Faculty of Engineering, Department of Information Science
1-1-25, Tsujido-Nishikaigan, Fujisawa, 251-8511, Japan
Tel:+81-466-30-0218, Fax:+81-466-34-5932
e-mail:ninomiya@info.shonan-it.ac.jp
[*2] *Shizuoka University*
Faculty of Engineering, Department of Systems Engineering
3-5-1, Johoku, Hamamatsu, 432-8561, Japan
Tel:+81-53-478-1237, Fax:+81-53-478-1269
e-mail:hideasai@sys.eng.shizuoka.ac.jp

Abstract-**This paper describes an efficient second-order algorithm for learning of the multilayer neural networks with widely and stable convergent properties. First, the algorithm based on iterative formula of the steepest descent method, which is "implicitly" employed, is introduced. We show the equivalent property between the Gauss-Newton(GN) method and the "implicit" steepest descent(ISD) method. This means that ISD method satisfy the desired targets by simultaneously combining the merits of the GN and SD techniques in order to enhance the very good properties of SD method. Next, we propose very powerful algorithm for learning multilayer feedforward neural networks, called "implicit" steepest descent with momentum(ISDM) method and show the analogy with the trapezoidal formula in the field of numerical analysis. Finally, the proposed algorithms are compared with GN method for training multilayer neural networks through the computer simulations.**

I. INTRODUCTION

Since the back-propagation(BP) algorithm[1] which was based on an iterative gradient algorithm to minimize the mean-squared error between the desired outputs and the actual outputs for a particular inputs to the net, was proposed many years ago, it has been successfully applied to many areas of science and engineering. In addition to BP algorithm, various learning rules have been proposed for training of various types of neural networks[2]-[4]. In developing training algorithm for artificial neural networks, optimization algorithm has played an important role. Indeed, the realization that the training of multilayer feedforward networks can be considered as an unconstrained optimization problem has led to the introduction of a plethora of first- and second-order algorithm in the neural networks literature[5]. In the former case, the representative algorithm is based on the standard steepest descent iteration of the form employed in the back-propagation algorithm. The steepest descent(SD) method works fine for very simple models, but requires an extremely long time for convergence. Gauss-Newton(GN) method is generally-cited as a representative second-order technique. It is well-known that GN method has quadratic convergent property for the initial guess suitably close to the solution, but it dose not have widely convergent property compared with the steepest descent method. For the above problems, the typical algorithm is Levenberg-Marquardt(LM) method[6]-[8] which combines the excellent local convergent properties of GN method near a minimum with the consistent error decrease provided by gradient descent far away from a solution.

In this paper, we concentrate on the development of optimization methods that can lead to powerful second-order algorithm for the training of the multilayer neural networks. First, we describe the training algorithm that is based on iterations of the form "implicitly" employed in the steepest descent method[9][10] and show that Gauss-Newton method is in a class with this implicit method. Therefore this method has both properties of SD and GN methods, that is, widely and quadratic convergent properties. We refer to this method as "implicit" steepest descent(ISD) method.

Although most of neural networks training are actually realized by using steepest descent schemes such as well-known backpropagation(BP) method, a standard BP is not only slow but also easy to be stuck at a local minimum which often results in a poorly trained network. One way to increase the reliability of BP is to decrease its sensitivity to small details in the error surface. This can be done by introducing a momentum term in BP algorithm, which allows a network to respond not only to the local gradient, but also recent trends in the error surface. The momentum term actually inserts second-order information in the training process and provides iterations. From the above discussion, it should be obvious that an analogous methodology for including a momentum term in "implicit" steepest descent scheme would be highly beneficial for dealing with the inability of second-order methods (and consequently of ISD) to escape from local minima. Therefore this methodology greatly improves the reliability of ISD algorithm. We propose very powerful training algorithm for training multilayer feedforward neural networks, called "implicit" steepest descent with momentum(ISDM) method. Furthermore we show the analogy with trapezoidal formula[11] for a numerical integration in the field of numerical analysis.

Finally, the implicit algorithms are compared with GN method for training multilayer neural networks. It is shown that the method proposed here has widely and stable convergent properties through the computer simulations. As a result, it is confirmed that our algorithm is efficient and practical for the learning of the multilayer neural networks.

II. IMPLICIT STEEPEST DESCENT(ISD) METHOD

The input-output characteristics of a feedfoward multilayer neural network which consists of an input layer of neurons, an arbitrary number of hidden layers and an output layer, all neurons with sigmoid activation functions, $g(x) = 1/(1+\exp(-x))$, is defined as

$$\mathbf{O}_p = f_{NN}(\mathbf{x}_p, \mathbf{w}), \quad (1)$$

where $\mathbf{O}_p$, $\mathbf{x}_p$ and $\mathbf{w}$ are the output vector of the output layer's neurons for *p-th* input, the *p-th* input vector and the weight vector, respectively. Let $\mathbf{T}_p$ be the *p-th* desired vector, the residual vector $\mathbf{r}_p$ is given by

$$\mathbf{r}_p(\mathbf{w}) = \mathbf{T}_p - \mathbf{O}_p. \quad (2)$$

In general, the optimization problem associated with (2) can be formulated as follows. Find the solutions of $\mathbf{r}_p = \mathbf{0}$ for $\mathbf{w}$ that minimizes the cost function $E(\mathbf{w})$,

$$E(\mathbf{w}) = \frac{1}{2}\sum_p \|\mathbf{T}_p - \mathbf{O}_p\|^2 = \frac{1}{2}\sum_p \|\mathbf{r}_p\|^2. \quad (3)$$

Since the steepest descent

$$\frac{\partial E}{\partial \mathbf{w}} = \sum_p \mathbf{J}_p^T(\mathbf{w})\mathbf{r}_p(\mathbf{w}), \quad (4)$$

the standard steepest descent iteration formula at *t-th* step is given by

$$\mathbf{w}_{t+1} = \mathbf{w}_t - \alpha \sum_p \mathbf{J}_p^T(\mathbf{w}_t)\mathbf{r}_p(\mathbf{w}_t), \quad (5)$$

where $\mathbf{J}_p(\mathbf{w})$ is the Jacobian matrix of first derivatives of the residual vector $\mathbf{r}_p$ and T stands for transposition. The learning coefficient is denoted by α. This equation (5) is regarded as the explicit iteration formula. Here, we suggest the following "implicit" formula,

$$\mathbf{w}_{t+1} = \mathbf{w}_t - \alpha \sum_p \mathbf{J}_p^T(\mathbf{w}_{t+1})\mathbf{r}_p(\mathbf{w}_{t+1}) \text{ for } \mathbf{w}_{t+1}. \quad (6)$$

This is the nonlinear algebraic equation,

$$\mathbf{F}(\mathbf{w}_{t+1}) = \mathbf{w}_{t+1} - \mathbf{w}_t + \alpha \sum_p \mathbf{J}_p^T(\mathbf{w}_{t+1})\mathbf{r}_p(\mathbf{w}_{t+1}) = \mathbf{0}, \quad (7)$$

for the unknown vector $\mathbf{w}_{t+1}$. In this research, Newton-Raphson(NR) method is applied to the above equation. The *n-th* iterative formula of NR method is given by

$$\frac{\partial \mathbf{F}((\mathbf{w}_{t+1})^n)}{\partial (\mathbf{w}_{t+1})^n} \Delta \mathbf{w} = -\mathbf{F}((\mathbf{w}_{t+1})^n), \quad (8)$$

where $\Delta \mathbf{w} = (\mathbf{w}_{t+1})^{n+1} - (\mathbf{w}_{t+1})^n$. When NR method of (8) is applied to (7), second derivatives of $\mathbf{r}_p(\mathbf{w}_{t+1})$ occur because the gradient of (4) already has dependence on $\partial \mathbf{r}_p(\mathbf{w}_{t+1})/\partial \mathbf{w}_{t+1}$. The second derivative term can be dismissed when it is small enough to be negligible compared to the term involving the first derivative within each ISD step in which the learning rate α is suitably selected. Therefore, in this research the second derivative terms tend to cancel out. From (7) and (8), the iterative formula by NR method is derived as

$$\left\{\mathbf{I} + \alpha \sum_p \mathbf{J}_p^T((\mathbf{w}_{t+1})^n)\mathbf{J}_p((\mathbf{w}_{t+1})^n)\right\}\Delta \mathbf{w} = \\ -\left\{(\mathbf{w}_{t+1})^n - \mathbf{w}_t + \alpha \sum_p \mathbf{J}_p^T((\mathbf{w}_{t+1})^n)\mathbf{r}_p((\mathbf{w}_{t+1})^n)\right\}, \quad (9)$$

where $\mathbf{I}$ denotes the unit matrix. Here, the initial value of each NR method is given by the value of preceding ISD iteration, that is,

$$(\mathbf{w}_{t+1})^0 = \mathbf{w}_t. \quad (10)$$

In this method NR iterations of (9) are performed on each ISD iteration stage of (6). Then we call the above method "ISD-NR" method. The algorithm of ISD-NR method is illustrated in Fig.1.

```
Program of ISD-NR method:
  while( ε_ISD < δ_ISD ){
    iterate (6) for t;
    while( ε_NR < δ_NR ){
      iterate (9) for n;
      solve (9) for Δw;
      δ_NR = ‖Δw‖² ;
    }
    δ_ISD = ‖w_{t+1} − w_t‖² ;
  }
```

Fig.1. Algorithm based on ISD-NR method(ε_{ISD} and ε_{NR} are positive small values).

Note that, if NR iterations are restricted to one step, (9) is transformed into

$$\left\{\frac{1}{\alpha}\mathbf{I} + \sum_p \mathbf{J}_p^T(\mathbf{w}_t)\mathbf{J}_p(\mathbf{w}_t)\right\}\Delta\mathbf{w} = -\sum_p \mathbf{J}_p^T(\mathbf{w}_t)\mathbf{r}_p(\mathbf{w}_t), \quad (11)$$

by substituting (10) for (9). Then the update formula becomes the Gauss-Newton(GN) method. This means that GN method is in a class with ISD method. Therefore, it is expected that ISD method has both properties of SD and GN methods, that is, widely and quadratic convergent properties.

III. ISDM METHOD

In the above section, the nonlinear algebraic equation of (7) is solved by Newton-Raphson(NR) method. It is well known that NR method can achieve the quadratic convergence, however, far away from the solution, the convergence rates become slow. This problem results from the fact that the large value is selected as the learning rate α in the "implicit" formula of (6), because of the rapid and stable convergences. For this problem, the algorithm based on "implicit" steepest descent including the momentum term, is proposed. We refer to this method as "implicit" steepest descent with momentum(ISDM) method. The iterative formula of ISDM method is given by

$$\begin{aligned}\mathbf{w}_{t+1} &= \mathbf{w}_t - \alpha \sum_p \mathbf{J}_p^T(\mathbf{w}_{t+1})\mathbf{r}_p(\mathbf{w}_{t+1}) + m(\mathbf{w}_t - \mathbf{w}_{t-1})\\ &= \mathbf{w}_t - \alpha \sum_p \mathbf{J}_p^T(\mathbf{w}_{t+1})\mathbf{r}_p(\mathbf{w}_{t+1}) + m\left(-\alpha \sum_p \mathbf{J}_p^T(\mathbf{w}_t)\mathbf{r}_p(\mathbf{w}_t)\right)\end{aligned}$$
(12)

where m is the momentum coefficient. Effectiveness of ISDM method is evaluated as follows. Here, replace α and m with $\alpha'/2$ and 1, respectively. Due to these replacements, (12) is rewritten by

$$\mathbf{w}_{t+1} = \mathbf{w}_t - \frac{1}{2}\left\{\alpha'\sum_p \mathbf{J}_p^T(\mathbf{w}_{t+1})\mathbf{r}_p(\mathbf{w}_{t+1}) + \alpha'\sum_p \mathbf{J}_p^T(\mathbf{w}_t)\mathbf{r}_p(\mathbf{w}_t)\right\}.$$
(13)

This equation is equivalent to the trapezoidal formula which is a numerical integration used for solving the ordinary differential equation. In the same way, (6) can be regarded as the equivalent of the backward euler method. It is well known that the trapezoidal formula is an example of a second-order approximation method. On the contrary the backward euler formula is an example of the first-order approximation method. This means that (12) is more accurate approximation compared with (6) from the viewpoint of the numerical analysis. The validity of the proposed method is shown in the above discussion. The final formula for ISDM method is derived as

$$\left\{\mathbf{I} + \alpha\sum_p \mathbf{J}_p^T((\mathbf{w}_{t+1})^n)\mathbf{J}_p((\mathbf{w}_{t+1})^n)\right\}\Delta\mathbf{w} = \\ -\left\{(\mathbf{w}_{t+1})^n - \mathbf{w}_t + \alpha\sum_p \mathbf{J}_p^T((\mathbf{w}_{t+1})^n)\mathbf{r}_p((\mathbf{w}_{t+1})^n) + m\alpha\sum_p \mathbf{J}_p^T(\mathbf{w}_t)\mathbf{r}_p(\mathbf{w}_t)\right\},$$
(14)

where NR method is utilized for solving the nonlinear algebraic equation as follows,

$$\mathbf{w}_{t+1} - \mathbf{w}_t + \alpha\sum_p \mathbf{J}_p^T(\mathbf{w}_{t+1})\mathbf{r}_p(\mathbf{w}_{t+1}) + m\alpha\sum_p \mathbf{J}_p^T(\mathbf{w}_t)\mathbf{r}_p(\mathbf{w}_t) = \mathbf{0}.$$
(15)

The algorithm according to (14) is shown in Fig.2. In the same way as ISD method, NR iterations of (9) are carried out within one ISDM iteration stage. Therefore, this method is referred to as "ISDM-NR" method.

```
Program of ISDM-NR method:
  while( ε_ISDM < δ_ISDM ){
    iterate (12) for t;
    while( ε_NR < δ_NR ){
      iterate (14) for n;
      solve (14) for Δw;
      δ_NR = ||Δw||² ;
    }
    δ_ISDM = ||w_{t+1} - w_t||² ;
  }
```

Fig.2. Algorithm based on ISDM method(ε_{ISDM} and ε_{NR} are positive small values).

IV. SIMULATION RESULTS

In this section, computer simulations are demonstrated in order to test the validity of the proposed algorithm for standard multilayer networks with sigmoid activation functions. Simulations were carried out for 3-, 4- and 5-bit parity problems. The performance of the proposed algorithm was compared to the performances of GN, ISD-NR and ISDM-NR methods. In all instances, 1000 simulation runs were performed with initial weights, which are random numbers uniformly distributed in [-1.0, +1.0]. Each training trial for all algorithms was conducted with the same randomly initialized weights, because the convergent property of each method is compared. The maximum iteration counts were set to 1000, 3000 and 5000 for 3-, 4- and 5-bit parity problems, respectively. It is well known that parity problems are difficult tasks for feedforward networks especially as the order of the problem increases. Some learning coefficients were used for all methods. Fig.3 shows the results of training a 3-3-1, which is three inputs, one hidden layer with three neurons and one output node network on the 3-bit parity problem. From Fig.3, it was confirmed that all methods had same success rates, when the learning coefficients, α were small values. On the contrary, for the fast convergence, it is expected that α is large. It was shown that ISDM-NR method was almost equivalent to ISD-NR method and superior to GN method from the viewpoint of convergence speed. Results for 4-bit parity problem are presented in Fig.4. The network for training is 4-4-1. Fig.5 illustrates the simulation results for 5-bit parity problem. The network is composed of five input neurons, one hidden layer with five nodes and one output neuron. From Fig.4 and 5, it is confirmed that two implicit methods, that is ISD-NR and ISDM-NR methods, greatly improve the convergence rates compared with GN method, when the learning coefficients are large values for the fast convergence. As a result we have found that the implicit steepest descent method is superior to the conventional second-order method, that is GN method, from the viewpoint of widely and fast convergent properties.

V. Conclusion

In this paper we have described the efficient second-order algorithm for training of the multilayer neural networks with widely and stable convergent properties. First, the algorithm based on iterative formula of the steepest descent method which is "implicitly" employed, has been introduced. We have shown that this "implicit" method satisfy the desired targets by simultaneously combining the merits of the GN and SD techniques in order to enhance the very good properties of SD method. Next, we have proposed very powerful second-order training algorithm, for training multilayer feedforward neural networks, called "implicit" steepest descent with momentum(ISDM) method and shown the analogy with trapezoidal method in the field of numerical analysis. Finally, the computer simulations have been conducted in order to test the validity of the proposed algorithm for standard multilayer networks. The proposed algorithm was able to solve several parity problems with high success rates compared of other second-order training algorithms. As a result, it has been confirmed that our algorithm is efficient and practical for the learning of the multilayer neural networks.

References

[1] D. E. Rumelhart, G. E. Hinton and R. J. Williams: "Learning representations by back-propagation errors", *NATURE*, vol.323, 9, pp.533-536, Oct., 1986.

[2] S. Haykin: "Neural Networks –A Comprehensive Foundation- 2nd ed.", Prentice Hall, 1999.

[3] H. Ninomiya and N. Kinoshita: "A New learning Algorithm without Explicit Error Back-Propagation", *ProcIEEE&INNS/IJCNN'99*, July, 1999.

[4] H. Ninomiya and A. Sasaki: "3-Layer Recurrent Neural Networks and their Supervised Learning Algorithm", *Proc.IEEE&INNS/IJCNN'01*, July, 2001.

[5] R. Battiti: "First and second-order methods for learning: Between steepest descent and Newton's method", *Neural Computa.*, vol.4, no.2, pp.141-166, 1992.

[6] K. Levenberg: "A method for the solution of certain problems in least squares", *Quart. Appl. Math.*, vol.5, pp.164-168, 1944.

[7] D. Marquardt: "An algorithm for least squares estimation of nonlinear parameters", *SIAM J. Appl. Math.*, vol.11, pp.431-441, 1963.

[8] M. T. Hagan and M. Menhaj: "Training feedforward networks with the Marquardt algorithm", *IEEE Trans. Neural Networks*, vol.5, pp.989-993, Nov., 1994.

[9] H. Asai: "Implicit Steepest Descent Method and its Analogy with Charge-Up Method based on virtual Capacitors in Network Analysis", *Proc. IEEE/ISCAS'88*, pp.1115-1118, 1988.

[10] H. Asai: "Equivalent Property between Network Analysis Using Virtual Capacitors and Steepest Descent Method", Trans. IEICE(A), vol.J71-A, no.5, pp.1132-1138, May, 1998(in Japanese).

[11] W. J. McCalla: "Fundamentals of Computer-Aided Circuit Simulation", Boston, MA, *Kluwer Academic Publishers*, 1988.

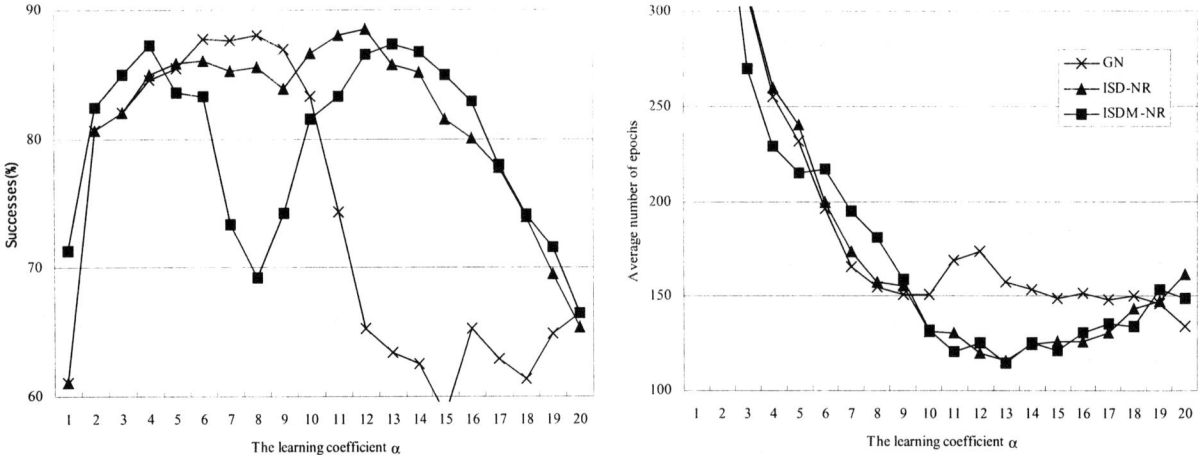

Fig.3. Results in terms of success rates and number of epochs for 3-bit parity problem ($m = 0.1$).

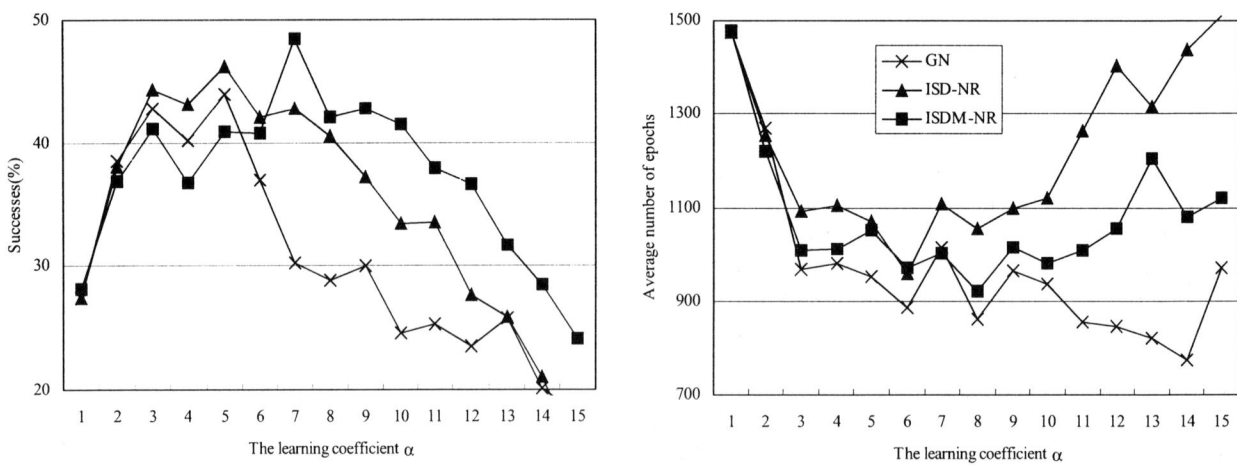

Fig.4. Results in terms of success rates and number of epochs for 4-bit parity problem ($m = 0.1$).

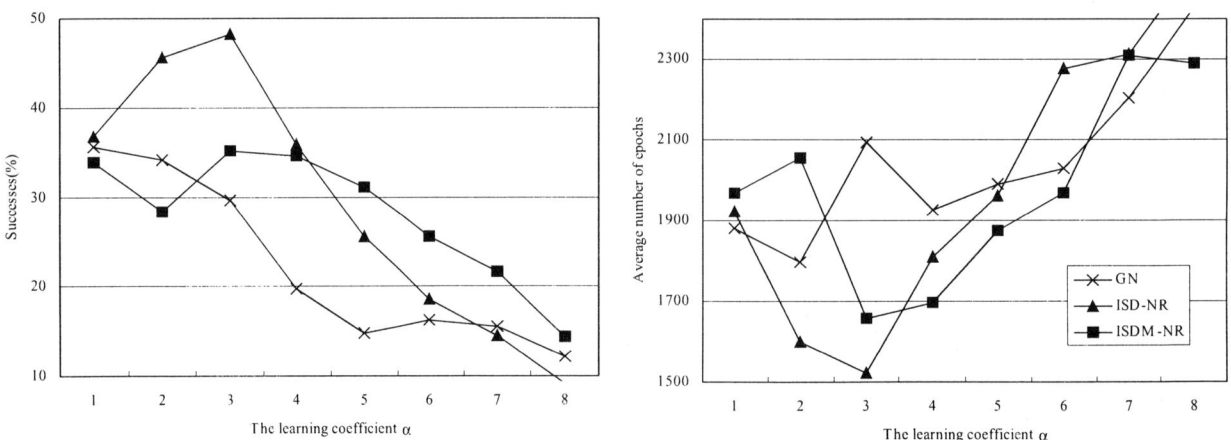

Fig.5. Results in terms of success rates and number of epochs for 5-bit parity problem ($m = 0.1$).

A Novel Min-Max Feature Value Based Neural Architecture And Learning Algorithm For Classification of Microcalcifications

Brijesh Verma
School of Information Technology
Griffith University, Australia
b.verma@griffith.edu.au

Rinku Panchal
School of Information Technology
Griffith University, Australia
rinkoopanchal@yahoo.com

Kuldeep Kumar
School of Information Technology
Bond University, Australia
kuldeep_kumar@bond.edu.au

Abstract

The paper proposes a novel min-max feature value based neural architecture and learning algorithm for classification of microcalcification patterns in digital mammograms. The neural architecture has a single hidden layer and it has a fixed number of hidden units and outputs. One class is represented by three hidden units and an output. The suspicious areas represented by chain code, are extracted from digital mammograms. The feature values are extracted for benign and malignant microcalcifications. A set of min, average and max values for every input feature is defined and assigned to the weights between input and hidden layer. The weights of the output layer are calculated using least squares methods or assigned in such a way that it maximizes the output value for only one class. Many experiments were conducted on a benchmark database of digital mammograms and comparative results are included in this paper.

1 Introduction

Breast Cancer is a leading cause of non-preventable cancer deaths among women, with 1 in 11 women developing this disease during their lifetime[1]. Early detection and diagnosis of breast cancer gives good chance of survival. While late detection and diagnosis often leads patient to unrecoverable stage of cancer ending in casualty. Digital Mammography currently offers the best control strategy for early detection of breast cancer. However, it is very difficult to distinguish benign and malignant microcalcification in digital mammogram. Sometimes microcalcification are very small and random in appearance. It makes very hard for doctor to detect and diagnose them. Recent revolution/development in image processing techniques, make microcalcification detection easy, however classification of malignant and benign microcalcifications is still very challenging and difficult problem for radiologists. In last two decades, many papers have been published with novel techniques [1-14] to improve the detection and classification of benign and malignant microcalcifications. Researchers have proposed and investigated both traditional as well as intelligent techniques such as nearest neighbor, bayes rule, neural networks, etc. Some of the existing techniques are reviewed below.

Mascio et al [2] developed a microcalcification detection technique, which operates on original digitised mammograms by combining morphological image processing with arithmetic processing. Yoshida et al [3] used wavelet transform for their CAD application. They employed *Least Asymmetric Daubechies'* wavelets in conjunction with different image processing techniques to detect microcalcifications. The technique is very effective in separating microcalcification from normal background tissue and they achieved a detection rate of approximately 90%. Zheang et al [4] used a Multistage Neural Network. In proposed network architecture the first stage called as the "detailed network" where all pixel values of an original image is used as its input, while the second is known as a "feature network". Feature network used backpropagation learning algorithm and extracted features with output for detailed network set as an input. Qain et al [5] used Multichannel (M = 4) Wavelet Transform for segmentation and feature extraction purposes. They used M-channel (M = 4) Wavelet analysis in three ways: with a polyphase quadrature mirror filter (QMF) structure, with a tree structure, and with a lattice structure. Barman et al [6] used a low-pass filter to detect microcalcification by analysing digital mammogram. Woods et al [7, 8] used backpropagtion algorithm and reported that a long training time was required for neural network training. It was difficult to determine the learning rate by which the weights were changed and updated. A learning rate that was too small needed more time to converge on a solution while a large learning rate jumped over the solution, this did not let to network learn properly resulting with poor classification rate. Chitre et al [9] used backpropagation neural network for image structure microcalcification classification and compared results with statistical classifiers. Though results were not promising but

---

[1] NSW Breast Cancer Institute, NSW, Australia
This research was funded by Griffith University Research Development (GURD) grant.

they were better than the statistical classifiers. Verma et al [11] investigated two neural network based techniques such as an error backpropagation (EBP) and a direct solution method (DSM). Zakos et al [12] proposed and investigated a neuro-fuzzy technique of detecting and classifying microcalcification patterns in Digital Mammogram. They have investigated 10 standard features and 4 modified features. Main idea behind the modified feature was to exploit characteristic of area more efficiently. They achieved promising results with the use of modified features. Normal features were – *{skew, number of pixels, histogram, standard deviation}*, Modified features were – *{entropy, number of pixels, histogram, standard deviation}* which produced good results.

As it can be seen from literature review above, that a lot of research has been conducted with promising results especially neural based intelligent techniques. Radiologists (at least from our local hospital) are very impressed with classification rates such as 88% on Nigmegan database, however they have reservations in using such a technique because it doesn't give any reason why it is classifying a particular area into benign or malignant. Other problems are inconsistency with classification rates, variable neural architecture, long training, etc. This paper proposes a novel architecture and a weight adjustment algorithm based on set of min, average and max values extracted from feature values which will be able to avoid a number of problems discussed above with current techniques. There are a number of advantages of our novel approach over the existing approaches. Some of them are as follows:

1. The architecture especially the #of hidden units is fixed therefore there will be no searching of a proper architecture using a very inefficient time consuming methods such as a trial and error based method.
2. The learning is based on a set of <min, max> values therefore it is possible to explain the reason for any output (benign, malignant, rubbish) provided by the network.
3. There is a simple rule based weight adjustment without any iterative time consuming learning process, therefore the learning process will be very fast and guaranteed.

The remainder of the paper is broken down into 4 sections. Section 2 describes the proposed approach, Section 3 provides experimental results and analysis, and a conclusion is drawn in Section 4.

2 Proposed Approach
2.1 An Overview of the Proposed Approach
The proposed approach first extracts the suspicious area from the image (digital mammogram) using the *chain code* already annotated (provided by radiologists) in the database. Features are then extracted from this area and most significant features are fed to the neural network for classification into benign, malignant and rubbish. A novel *learning algorithm* is proposed in this paper to train the classifier. An overview of the proposed approach is presented below in Figure 1.

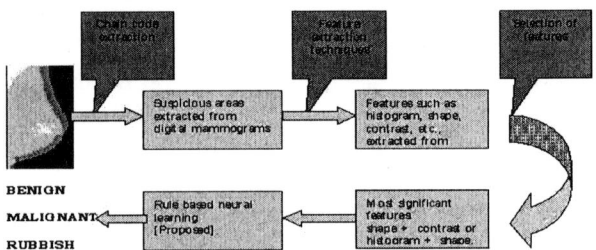

Figure 1. An Overview of Proposed Technique

The proposed approach contains the following stages: Mammographic database, Area extraction, Feature extraction, Selection of most significant features, Classification of features into benign/malignant/rubbish (Neural Network).

Stage 1: Mammographic database
The benchmark database (DDSM) of digital mammograms from the University of South Florida is currently being used. Previously, the database from the University of Nijmegen (The Netherlands), was used. All images (mammograms) were/are in raw format and were of size 2048x2048. They used 12 bits (2 bytes) per pixel of grey-level information.

Stages 2-3: Area extraction/Feature extraction
The suspicious areas are extracted as described in Section 3 from every mammogram using a chain code supplied with digital mammograms. The features such as average histogram, average grey level, energy, modified energy, entropy, modified entropy, number of pixels, standard deviation, modified standard deviation, skew, modified skew, average boundary grey level, difference and contrast were investigated. The formulae for entropy, energy, skew, and standard deviation were modified so that the iterations started with the first pixel of the pattern and ended at the final pixel. Traditionally, the formulae for these features have iterations starting with the lowest grey level and ranging to the highest grey level. This modification was done in an attempt to achieve a better classification rate than its traditional version. All 14 features are described below in detail. The following symbols are used in feature extraction formulae (1)-(12).

T	is the total number of pixels,
g	is an index value of image **I**,
K	is the total number of grey levels (i.e 4096),
j	is the grey level value (i.e. 0-4095),
I(g)	is the grey level value of pixel **g** in image **I**,

N(j) is the number of pixels with grey level **j** in image **I**,
P(I(g)) is the probability of grey level value **I(g)** occurring in image **I**,
P(j) is the probability of grey level value **j** occurring in image **I**

Number of Pixels
Number of pixels is a count of the pixels in the microcalcification area. It gives an indication of the size of area.

Average Histogram
A histogram value gives an indication of the grey-level distribution for the mammogram. First generating the histogram for microcalcification and then calculating the average frequency across all grey-level intervals calculate average histogram.

$$Average\ Histogram = \frac{1}{k}\sum_{j=0}^{k-1} N(j)/T \quad (1)$$

Average Grey Level
Average grey level gives an indication of the grey level value associated with the entire microcalcification area.

$$Average\ Grey = \frac{1}{T}\sum_{g=0}^{T-1} I(g) \quad (2)$$

Energy and Modified Energy
Energy gives an indication of how the grey levels are distributed. If the energy value is high there is high grey level values. If energy value is low than there is low grey level values.

$$Energy = \sum_{j=0}^{k-1} [P(j)]^2 \quad (3)$$

$$Modified\ Energy = \sum_{g=0}^{T-1} [P(I(g))]^2 \quad (4)$$

Entropy and Modified Entropy
Entropy provides a measure of non-uniformity. As the pixel values in the image are distributed among more grey levels, the entropy increases.

$$Entropy = -\sum_{j=0}^{k-1} P(j)\log_2[P(j)] \quad (5)$$

$$Modified\ Entropy = -\sum_{g=0}^{T-1} P(g)\log_2[P(I(g))] \quad (6)$$

Standard Deviation and Modified Standard Deviation
Standard deviation is the spread of the data in the area.

$$Standard\ Deviation\ (\sigma) = \sqrt{\sum_{g=0}^{T-1}(j-AvgGrey)^2 P(j)} \quad (7)$$

$$Modified\ Standard\ Deviation\ (\sigma) = \sqrt{\sum_{g=0}^{T-1}(I(g)-AvgGrey)^2 P(I(g))} \quad (8)$$

Skew and Modified Skew
Skew is a measure of the asymmetry about the mean grey level.

$$Skew = \frac{1}{\sigma_j^3}\sum_{j=0}^{k-1}(j-AvgGrey)^3 P(j) \quad (9)$$

$$Modified\ Skew = \frac{1}{\sigma_g^3}\sum_{g=0}^{T-1}(I(g)-AvgGrey)^3 P(I(g)) \quad (10)$$

Average Boundary Grey
The average boundary grey is the average grey level value around the outside of the microcalcification. Define some width of strip around microcalcification area, and calculate average grey level value of that strip.

Difference
Difference gives an indication of the change of intensity across the boundary of the microcalcification.

$$Difference = Average\ Grey - Average\ Boundary\ Grey \quad (11)$$

Contrast
Contrast gives an indication of how sharp the microcalcification structural features are.

$$Contrast = \frac{Difference}{AvgGrey + AvgBoundryGrey} \quad (12)$$

Stage 4: Selection of most significant features
Initially, we determine the ranking of single features from best to worst by using each feature as a single input to the neural network. After this is completed, a combination of features is tested and a best feature or a combination of features is determined.

First feature vector [10 features]: average histogram, average grey level, number of pixels, average boundary grey, difference, contrast, energy, entropy, standard deviation and skew.

Second feature vector [14 features]: average histogram, average grey level, number of pixels, average boundary grey, difference, contrast, modified energy, modified entropy, modified standard deviation and modified skew.

The most significant feature or combination of features are selected based on neural network classification. It is done as follows. We start with a single feature by feeding it to the neural network and analysing the classification rate. If it is increased or unchanged by adding a particular feature then we include this feature to the input vector. Otherwise we remove this feature and add another feature to the existing input vector and repeat the whole process again. In our other research project, an evolutionary approach is being investigated to find the most significant feature.

Stage 5: Classification of features into benign/malignant/rubbish

A novel learning architecture described in the next Section (2.2) is used for classification of features into benign/malignant/rubbish.

2.2 Novel Learning Algorithm
2.2.1 Neural Architecture

A novel neural architecture is proposed which is shown below in Figure 2. It has inputs, outputs and a fixed number of hidden units. There are 3 hidden neurons for each class. The number of input and output nodes must be equal to the number of features and number of classes respectively. Possible input feature vector values include one feature or combination of features described in the previous section.

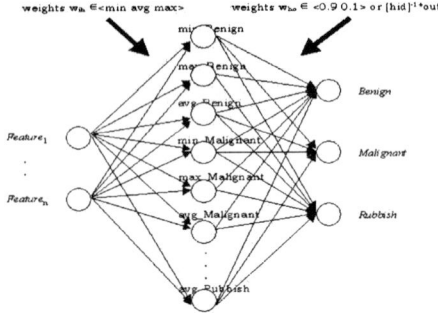

Figure 2. Proposed Neural Architecture

There are two novel things introduced in the above architecture, first that it has a fixed number of hidden units in the hidden layer. The total number of hidden units depends on the total number of classes. The *hidden unit* represents the part of (lower, middle or upper boundary) class. Depending on the input feature value (s), one of the hidden units will be fired by minimising/maximising the hidden neuron output, which will have influence in firing output layer neuron by maximising one of the outputs of the neural network. The second novel thing is that in the output layer, the *rubbish neuron* represents the areas, which don't contain benign and malignant microcalcifications. This is useful when radiologist select random areas on digital mammograms. The system should be able to provide suggestions even for random non-microcalcification areas.

2.2.2 Stepwise Learning Algorithm

Step 1: Calculate Min, Max and Average values of every input feature for all classes

Step 2: Initialise network architecture
#of inputs = #of features
#of outputs = #of classes + an extra class for rubbish
#hidden units = 3*#of classes (min, max, avg for ben/mal/rubbish)
#activation function = Gaussian type function

Step 3: Assign values to weights between input and hidden layer
$W_{ih}[i][j]$ = {min, max, average} value$_{ik}$, Where k is the class {ben/mal/rub}

Step 4: Calculate the output of the hidden layer
Out {benign, malignant, rubbish} = $e^{-||(wih-feature)*who||}$

Step 5: Calculate the weights between hidden and output layer
$W_{ho}[i][k]$ = {0.9/0.1},
Where, i is the hidden unit class {3 classes for each} and k is the output class
or $W_{ho}[i][k]$ = HID^{-1} * OUT {using least squares method}

3 Experimental Results And Analysis
3.1 Database (Digital Mammograms) Preparation

Digital mammogram database "DDSM" is taken from the university of South Florida. This is a benchmark database, available free of cost. It can be downloaded from the following web site http://marathon.csee.usf.edu/Mammography/

DDSM has four cases for each patient. Each case contains four mammograms from a screening exam. Each case consist of three files as follows:

> *".ics" file,* this file provides information about a case as a whole. Including other relevant information, it provides the size of each image file, number of bits per pixel, and the scanning resolution (in microns).

> *".OVERLAY" file,* this file gives *no of abnormalities* a particular digital mammogram has and the most important, it gives *starting position (x, y coordinates) for suspicious area with chain code value* that is very important for area extraction.

> *".LJPEG" file,* this file contains a *compressed digital mammogram*. The images were scanned on a HOWTEK 960 digitizer with a sample rate of 43.5 microns at 12 bits per pixel. The images were preprocessed to crop out much of the image that did not contain breast tissues. Each image was compressed using truly loss less compression algorithm. Software is also available for decompression. Once uncompressed, each image file contains only raw pixel values (0~4095).

3.2 Area Resizing and Extraction

Once digital mammogram is uncompressed, then suspicious area is resized and extracted. Suspicious area is already marked in all digital mammograms of DDSM by three expert radiologists. Starting position of suspicious area and a chain code for area extraction is available from ".OVERLAY" file. With the help of chain code we find the exact width and length of each suspicious area from each mammogram. The suspicious areas from different mammograms are different in size. To make all the suspicious area of same size, we need average size of each width and length. Using chain code values we define the boundary of area, by defining upper most side, lower most side, left outer side and right outer side of area. With the help of boundary, we define width and length of area. Using the length and width of all suspicious areas from all mammograms, we calculate the average width and average length. Finally we extract the 14 features as described in Section 2. Sample feature values for modified features are shown below in Table 1.

3.3 Feature Extraction Results

Table 1. Feature Values for 4 Modified Features

Malignant	Benign	mod No of Pixels	mod Histogram	mod Entropy	mod Stand Dev
0.9	0.1	0.09239	0.09239	0.107923	0.131301
0.9	0.1	0.16983	0.16983	0.121968	0.206651
0.9	0.1	0.094304	0.094304	0.121569	0.084525
0.9	0.1	0.06046	0.06046	0.117162	0.059979
0.9	0.1	0.057288	0.057288	0.123136	0.047323
0.9	0.1	0.376842	0.376842	0.388009	0.214423
0.9	0.1	0.099289	0.099289	0.102017	0.117806
0.9	0.1	0.180932	0.180932	0.215848	0.129321
0.1	0.9	0.031011	0.031011	0.090777	0.03305
0.1	0.9	0.032935	0.032935	0.050893	0.045669
0.1	0.9	0.039426	0.039426	0.062295	0.047891
0.1	0.9	0.067667	0.067667	0.089175	0.070222
0.1	0.9	0.000436	0.000436	0.001854	0.002644
0.1	0.9	0.01711	0.01711	0.039887	0.02785
0.1	0.9	0.082332	0.082332	0.081155	0.218348
0.1	0.9	0.008716	0.008716	0.011071	0.034072
0.1	0.9	0.016763	0.016763	0.015076	0.069995

Min-Avg-Max Values

The min, max and average values have been extracted for every feature. It is not easy to always find a clear boundary, so if there is a conflicting value, it is removed. For example, min, max and average values for the mod Entropy features can be described as follows:

Benign microcalcification:
    <min, max> = <0.001854, 0.090777>
    <avg>=0.0491
Malignant microcalcification
    <min, max> = <0.102017, 0.388009>
    <avg>=0.151

3.5 Feature Selection Results -Best 4 Features

The top four features from many initially tested experiments are shown in Table 2. The genetic selection of best features is still in progress. The results shown in Table 2 were obtained from experiments conducted on neural network based selection without using genetic algorithm.

Table 2 Ranking of normal and modified features

Ranking	Features	
	Normal	Modified
1	Skew	Entropy
2	Number of pixels	Number of pixels
3	Histogram	Histogram
4	Standard Deviation	Standard Deviation

3.6 Classification Results

We have implemented our proposed novel neural learning approach and MLP based approach and we have tested them using just one feature, which was mod Entropy. The preliminary experiments are listed below in Tables 3 and 4.

Table 3. Classification rates for benign & malignant using proposed algorithm

#	# Hidden Units (fixed size)	# Iterations (no iteration)	Classification Rate [%]	
			Training Set	Test Set
1	6	0	100	81.80

Table 4. Classification rates for benign & malignant using EBP-MLP

#	# Hidden Units	# Iterations	Classification Rate [%]	
			Training Set	Test Set
1	8	20000	88.90	63.60
2	12	20000	100	81.80
3	12	50000	84.40	54.50

As it can be seen above in Tables 3 and 4, the classification rate on training and testing data sets for both techniques, is the same. However, first thing is to note that the proposed approach needs to be run only once because there is no problem in finding the number of iterations or hidden units, etc as in our traditional neural network based technique such as an error back propagation algorithm based MLP. The second most important thing is to note that our proposed approach can provide a reason for misclassification and an exact rule can be extracted. The third and final thing is to note that the classification rate on test set for both techniques is not very high. During the analysis of misclassification, we found that the reason of misclassification is incorrect (conflicting) feature value. Some miss-classified classes in test set have the following feature values: 0.06 - malignant, 0.1 - benign, etc. As you can see above that the value 0.06 is labeled as malignant and 0.1 as benign in our test set, which is incorrect based on our min-max values. The results so far are in favor of the proposed approach.

4 Conclusions

We have proposed and investigated a novel min-max feature value based neural architecture and learning algorithm for classification of microcalcification patterns. The proposed approach was implemented in C/C+ on UNIX platform and many experiments were conducted. The preliminary experiments are very promising. As discussed in previous section and shown in Tables 1-4, our proposed approach has many advantages over traditional EBP-MLP based approach. The most important advantages are (1) it can provide the reason for misclassification or correct classification, which is very important in convincing radiologists (2) it is very quick, there are no unsuccessful training, trial & error based training to find hidden units, iterations, best classifications, etc. We are currently investigating and testing our approach with other features, combination of features, etc. and we will be able to include more results and a detailed analysis in our next paper.

References

1. Karessemeijer N., Computer-Assisted Reading of Mammograms, European Radiology, 1997, vol. 7, pp. 743-748.
2. Mascio L. N., Hernandz J. M. and Logan C. M., Automated Analysis for Microclacifications in High Resolution Digital Mammograms, can be found at http://canopus.llnl.gov/docum,documents/ imaging/jmhspie93.html ..
3. Yoshida H., Doi K. and Nishikawa R. M., Application of The Wavelet Transform To Automated Detection of Clustered Microclacifications In Digital Mammogram., 1994, Academic Reports of Tokyo Institute of Polytechnics, vol.16, pp.24-37.
4. Zheng B., Qian W. and Clarke L. P., Multistage Neural Network for Pattern Recognition in Mammogram Screnning, IEEE International Conference on Neural Networks (ICNN), 1994, pp. 3437-3447.
5. Qian W. and Xuejun S., Digital mammography: Wavelet Transform and Kalman-Filtering Neural Network in Mass Segmentation And Detection, IEEE Joint International Conference on Neural Networks (IJCNN), 2001, pp. 234-239.
6. Barman H., Granlund G. and Haglund L., Feature Extraction for Computer-Aided Analysis of Mammograms in state in *The Art of Digital Monographic Image Analysis*, World Scientific Publishing, 1994, vol. 7, no 6, pp. 128-147.
7. Woods K., Doss C. C. and Bowyer K. W., Comparative Evaluation of Pattern Recognition Technique for Detection of Microclacifications in Mammography, International Journal of Pattern Recognition and Artificial Intelligence, 1993, vol. 7, no. 6, 1417-1436.
8. Woods K., Automated Image Analysis techniques for Digital Mammography, PhD Thesis, University of South Florida, 1994.
9. Chitre Y., Dhawan A. P. and Moskowitz M., Artifical Neural Network Based Classification if Mammographic Microclacifications using Image Structre Features, International Journal of Pattern Recognition and Artificial Intelligence, 1993, vol. 7, no 6, pp.1377-1401
10. Shen L., and Rangayyan R. M., Detection and Classification of Mammograhic Classifications, International Journal of Pattern Recognition and Artificial Intelligence 1993, vol. 7, no 6, pp.1403-1416.
11. Verma B.K., Comparative Evaluation of Two Neural Network based Techniques for Classification of Microcalcifications in Digital Mammograms, Knowledge and Information Systems: An International Journal, Springer-Verlag, 1999, vol. 1, no. 1, pp. 107-117.
12. Zakos J., A Computer-Aided Diagnosis System For Digital Mammograms using Computational Intelligence Techniques, 1998, pp.1-110, Honours Thesis, Griffith University, Australia.
13. Sutton M., Bezdek J., Neumann R., and Goar B., Enhancement and Analysis of Digital Mammograms Using Fuzzy Models, SPIE Proceedings 3240 on Exploiting New Image Sources and Sensors, 1997, pp. 345-352.
14. Solka J. and Poston W., The Detection of Micro-Calcification in Mammographic Images Using High Dimensional Features, Seventh Annual IEEE Symposium on Computer-Based Medical Systems, 1993, pp. 139-145.

Robust Optimization in Support Vector Machine Training with Bounded Errors

Theodore B. Trafalis and Samir A. Alwazzi
Laboratory of Optimization and Intelligent Systems
School of Industrial Engineering
University of Oklahoma
202 West Boyd, Room 124
Norman, OK 73019
ttrafalis@ou.edu, al7941@msn.com

Abstract-In this paper, we investigate the stability of the linear programming Support Vector Machine (LP-SVM) solution under bounded perturbations of the input data using a robust optimization model. Preliminary experimental results are presented for toy and real world data.

Keywords: Robust Optimization, Kernel Methods, Support Vector Machines, Semidefinite Programming.

I. INTRODUCTION

Estimation of parameters in the presence of data uncertainties is a problem of significant practical importance and many estimators have been proposed in the optimization and statistics literature with the objective of handling modeling errors and measurement noise. Uncertainty is due to data collection, soft constraints (partial knowledge), model reduction (approximate modeling) and uncertainty about future (e.g. in finance).

Several optimization criteria have been used like linear least–squares [4], regularized least-squares [5], ridge regression [5,7] total least squares [3,4,5,6] and robust estimation [8]. Those formulations allow incorporation of a priori information about the unknown parameters of the problem. More recently, robust optimization techniques have been investigated by several authors [1,2,9]. These techniques are more meaningful in formulations with prior bounds on the size of the uncertainties on the data. Specifically, we consider the case where we have data with bounded errors. The solutions coming from robust optimization models are more stable and more appropriate for this kind of uncertainty. Our objective is to investigate the stability of the LP-SVM solution under bounded perturbations of the input data.

When operation researchers try to construct a model of a real-world system, they always find incomplete, noisy or uncertain data. On the other hand, in the world of mathematical programming, it is assumed that the model is deterministic something that does not hold generally in the real world. It has been found that large error bounds arise when one solves mean value problems [10]. An approach to incorporate uncertainty in traditional mathematical programming is to use stochastic programming [11].

Alternatively, sensitivity analysis can be employed to observe data uncertainty on the model's construction or recommendations [11]. Thus, and under these legitimate pressures, creating model formulations that, by design, will lead to solutions, which are less sensitive to the model data than the usual existing methods, becomes a necessity. The sensitivity of a solution to changes in the input data is measured, but it offers no tool by which this sensitivity can be controlled. In contradistinction, robust optimization incorporates [2] uncertainty in the problem design itself, using novel mathematical programming formulations [1,2] and thereby generating solutions, which are less sensitive to realizations of the model data.

This paper is organized as follows. In section 2 we discuss the fundamentals of SVM classification. In section 3 SVM classifications with linear separation and bounded errors in the input data is formulated as a second order conic quadratic programming problem. Section 4 discusses the idea of kernelization applied to LP-SVM classification with nonlinear separation and bounded errors of the data in the feature space. Computational results are provided in section 5. Finally section 6 concludes the paper.

II. FUNDAMENTALS OF SUPPORT VECTOR MACHINE CLASSIFICATION

The Support Vector Machine (SVM) algorithm developed by Vapnik [12,13] is based on statistical learning theory. The initial formulation of the problem of optimal separation of two classes of data points consists on finding the hyperplane that separates the two sets in such a way that the distance between it (optimal hyperplane) and the nearest point of each of the data set is maximum. This distance is known as the margin. The hyperplane that divides these two classes with maximum margin is called the optimal separating hyperplane. More specifically a separating hyperplane in canonical form must satisfy the following constraints,

$$y_i[(w \cdot x_i) + b] \geq 1, \quad i = 1,\ldots,l, \quad (2.1)$$

where $\{(x_1,y_1)\ldots(x_l,y_l)\}$ are given training data, with $x_i \in \mathbb{R}^d$ and $y_i = \pm 1$. Note that, the dot product between vectors w, x is denoted either as w·x or <w,x>.

The optimal hyperplane can be obtained by maximizing the margin $\rho(w, b) = \dfrac{2}{\|w\|}$ subject to the constraints of equation (2.1). Therefore the hyperplane that minimizes the norm $\|w\|$ will be the optimal hyperplane. SVM formulations based on a general L_p norm can be found in

[14]. If one uses the L_∞ norm to measure the distance between the training points and the separating hyperplane, the problem can then be formulated as a linear optimization problem. We consider the following two cases:

A. Linearly Separable Case

It can be shown that the margin in this case is as follows

$$\rho(w,b) = \frac{2}{\sum_j |w_j|} \quad j=1,\ldots,d. \quad (2.2)$$

Therefore, we need to solve the following optimization problem:

$$\min_{w,b} \sum_j |w_j| \quad (2.3)$$

s.t. $y_i[(w \cdot x_i) + b] \geq 1, \quad i=1,\ldots,l.$

B. Linearly Non-separable Case

In this case, by introducing slack variables z_i for possible infeasibilities, we have the following optimization problem:

$$\min_{w,b,z} \|w\|_1 + C \sum_{i=1}^{l} z_i \quad (2.4)$$

s.t. $y_i(x_i \cdot w + b) + z_i \geq 1$
$z_i \geq 0 \quad i=1,\ldots,l,$

where the parameter C is the tradeoff between minimizing the training set error and maximizing the margin and $\|w\|_1$ is the L_1 norm of the vector w. Now the problem can be formulated directly in the kernel or feature space to create nonlinear discriminants. This can be accomplished through a feature map φ. Next, we provide the necessary definitions for the feature space and kernel functions.

Definition 1 (Features and Feature Space)

A function $\varphi_i : \mathbb{R}^d \to R$ that maps each point x in $\mathbb{R}^d$ to a real value $\varphi_i(x)$ is called a **feature**. Combining n features $\varphi_1, \varphi_2,\ldots, \varphi_n$ results in a feature map $\varphi: \mathbb{R}^d \to H$ and the space H is called a feature space.

In order to avoid an unnecessarily complicated notation, we will abbreviate φ(x) by **x** for the rest of the paper. The vector **x** in H is also called the representation of x in $\mathbb{R}^d$

Definition 2

Suppose we are given a feature map $\varphi: \mathbb{R}^d \to H$. The kernel is the inner product function
K: $\mathbb{R}^d \times \mathbb{R}^d \to \mathbb{R}$ in H, i.e for all x_i, x_j, in $\mathbb{R}^d$,
K(x_i, x_j) = < φ(x_i), φ(x_j)> = < $\mathbf{x_i}, \mathbf{x_j}$ >.

Definition 3 (Kernel Matrix)

Given a kernel K: $\mathbb{R}^d \times \mathbb{R}^d \to \mathbb{R}$ and a set of l points $x_1,\ldots,x_l$ in $\mathbb{R}^d$, we call the $l \times l$ matrix with, K_{ij} = < φ(x_i), φ(x_j)> = < $\mathbf{x_i}, \mathbf{x_j}$ >, the kernel matrix of k at $x_1,\ldots,x_l$.

Note that, since $w = \sum_{i=1}^{l} y_i \alpha_i x_i$ in the feature space problem (2.4) can be expressed as follows:

$$\min_{\alpha,b,z} \|\alpha\|_1 + C \sum_{i=1}^{l} z_i$$

S.t
$$y_i \left(\sum_{j=1}^{l} y_j \alpha_j k(x_i, x_j) + b \right) + z_i \geq 1 \quad (2.5)$$

$z_i \geq 0, \alpha_i \geq 0, i=1,\ldots,l, j=1,\ldots,l.$

Then the discriminant function [15] can be written as,

f(x) = sign $\left(\sum_i y_i \alpha_i k(x,x_i) + b \right)$, where, sign(z) = $\begin{cases} +1 & \text{if } z \geq 0 \\ -1 & \text{otherwise} \end{cases}$.

III. SUPPORT VECTOR MACHINE CLASSIFICATION WITH BOUNDED ERRORS IN INPUT DATA

In this section we consider the LP-SVM formulation with bounded errors in the input data. Let us consider a set of given training data $\{(x_1,y_1)\ldots(x_l,y_l)\}$, where l represents the number of samples or the training set size, where $x_i \in \mathfrak{R}^d$ and $y_i = \pm 1$. The LP-SVM formulation with precise data can be expressed as in (2.4). Next, we consider a bounded perturbation of the input data. More specifically, let $x_i = \widetilde{x}_i + u_i$, such that $\|u_i\| \leq \sqrt{\eta}$, where u_i is the perturbation, $\widetilde{x}_i$ is the center of the uncertainty sphere and $\sqrt{\eta}$ refers to the radius of the uncertainty sphere. Therefore, the constraints of (2.4) can be written as follows:

$y_i(\langle w, \widetilde{x}_i + u_i \rangle + b) + z_i \geq 1 \quad \Leftrightarrow$
$y_i(\langle w, \widetilde{x}_i \rangle + \langle w, u_i \rangle + b) + z_i \geq 1 \quad \Leftrightarrow$
$y_i \langle w, \widetilde{x}_i \rangle + y_i \langle w, u_i \rangle + y_i b + z_i \geq 1 \quad (3.1)$
$z_i \geq 0, i=1,\ldots,l, \forall u_i$ such that $\|u_i\| \leq \sqrt{\eta}$.

Our objective is to find a feasible solution of (3.1) for every realization of the bounded perturbation u_i. This can be characterized as a robust feasible solution of (3.1), [2]. Note that w is robust feasible if and only if for every i=1,…,l we have:

$$\min_{\|u_i\| \leq \sqrt{\eta}} y_i \langle w, \widetilde{x}_i \rangle + y_i \langle w, u_i \rangle + y_i b + z_i \geq 1.$$

Therefore, we need to minimize the dot product of w and u_i subject to $\|u_i\| \le \sqrt{\eta}$. Thus, we need to solve the following problem:
$$\min \langle w, u_i \rangle$$
$$\text{st} \quad \|u_i\| \le \sqrt{\eta}.$$

Using Cauchy's Schwarz inequality the minimum of $\langle w, u_i \rangle$ is equal to $-\sqrt{\eta}\|w\|$. By substituting this minimum in (3.1) we have:
$$y_i \langle w, \tilde{x}_i \rangle - y_i \sqrt{\eta}\|w\| + y_i b + z_i \ge 1 \quad (3.2)$$
$$z_i \ge 0, i = 1,...,l.$$

Therefore, we need to solve the following robust formulation of problem (2.4): $\min_{w,b,z} \|w\|_1 + C \sum_{i=1}^{l} z_i$

s.t.
$$y_i \langle w, \tilde{x}_i \rangle - y_i \sqrt{\eta}\|w\| + y_i b + z_i \ge 1 \quad (3.3)$$
$$z_i \ge 0, i = 1,...,l.$$

The above problem is a second order cone-programming problem [9]. Next, we discuss the case where the data have bounded perturbations in the feature space.

IV. KERNELIZATION

In the previous section, we have introduced hyperplanes as linear functions in the input space. In this section, we will extend these ideas to the non-linear case. Noting that,
$$w = \sum_{i=1}^{l} y_i \alpha_i x_i, \text{ where } \alpha_i \ge 0 \text{ and by}$$
defining $y_i y_j \langle x_i, x_j \rangle = \tilde{k}(x_i, x_j)$, we have:
$$\|w\|^2 = \sum_{i=1}^{l} \sum_{j=1}^{l} \alpha_i \alpha_j \tilde{k}(x_i, x_j) = \alpha^t \tilde{k} \alpha \Leftrightarrow$$
$$\|w\| = \sqrt{\alpha^t \tilde{k} \alpha}.$$

By considering the above substitutions in (3.3), the robust formulation of (2.4) will be as follows:
$$\min \sum_{i=1}^{l} \alpha_i + C \sum_{i=1}^{l} z_i \quad (4.1)$$

s.t. $-\sqrt{\eta} y_i \sqrt{\alpha^t \tilde{k} \alpha} + y_i \sum_{j=1}^{l} y_j \alpha_j \left[k(\tilde{x}_j, \tilde{x}_i) - \sqrt{\eta}\|\tilde{x}_j\| \right]$
$+ y_i b + z_i \ge 1$
$z_i \ge 0, \alpha_i \ge 0 \quad i=1,...,l$, where $\|\tilde{x}_j\| = \sqrt{k(x_j, x_j)}$.

Now we can find the discriminant function for the optimal hyperplane to be:

$$f(x,\alpha,b,u) = \sum_{i=1}^{l} y_i \alpha_i \langle x_i, x \rangle + b = \sum_{i=1}^{l} y_i \alpha_i \langle \tilde{x}_i + u_i, x \rangle + b$$
$$= \sum_{i=1}^{l} (y_i \alpha_i \langle \tilde{x}_i, x \rangle + \sum y_i \alpha_i \langle u_i, x \rangle) + b$$
$$= \sum_{i=1}^{l} y_i \alpha_i \langle \tilde{x}_i, x \rangle + \sum_{i=1}^{l} y_i \alpha_i \langle u_i, x \rangle + b$$

Considering the worst case, we replace $\langle u_i, x \rangle$ by its minimum value $-\sqrt{\eta}\|x\|$. Therefore, by denoting the robust discriminant function by $\hat{f}(x,\alpha,b)$ we have:
$$\hat{f}(x,\alpha,b) = \sum_{i=1}^{l} (y_i \alpha_i k(\tilde{x}_i, x) - y_i \alpha_i \sqrt{\eta}\|x\|) + b \text{ or}$$
equivalently,
$$\hat{f}(x,\alpha,b) = \sum_{i=1}^{l} y_i \alpha_i k(\tilde{x}_i, x) - \sqrt{\eta}\|x\| \sum_{i=1}^{l} y_i \alpha_i + b \quad (4.2)$$

In the following nonlinear separable XOR problem we will illustrate the above approach by using a polynomial kernel of degree 2 ($k_{ij} = [(x_i \cdot x_j)+1]^2$). In figures (1, 2 and 3) we show the resulting discriminant functions in the input space for different values of the uncertainty parameter η.

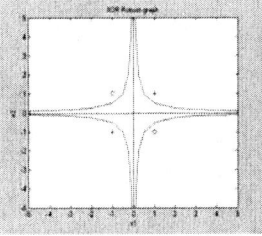 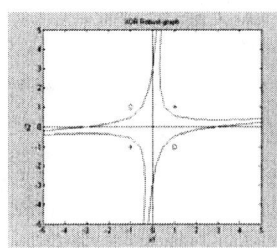

Fig 1. XOR with eita = 0.   Fig 2. XOR with eita = 0.4.

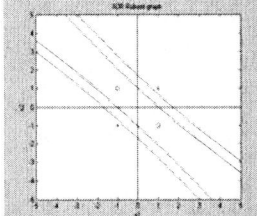

Fig 3. XOR with eita = 1.06 (No Separation).

V. COMPUTATIONAL RESULTS

All experiments have been conducted in MATLAB. We used a 2.4 GHZ Intel processor, Dell workstation-computer with 2 GB RAM and running Microsoft windows 2000 professional version with service pack 2 installed. The XOR problem shows the mechanics of the SVM calculations for the non-linear separable case. Figures 1, 2, and 3 show how the optimal separating hypersurface changes with changes in the parameter eita. When eita equals to 1.06, no separation was possible. The two blue circles in figure 3 should be outside the two blue lines. Therefore, if one provides a specific value of *u*, then estimation can be made of the changes that will occur to the SVM solution.

A. Echocardiogram Classification Application Description and Analysis

Each exemplar contains information collected from patients who have had a recent heart attack. The problem is to determine if the patient will survive for 1 year following their heart attack [16]. We used 60 data points, 40 points as training points and 20 as testing. We observed that there were no big changes in the values of the mean square testing error (mse), when we used different values of η. This advocates for the robustness (stability) of the proposed model. Results can be seen in Table 1.

TABLE 1. RESULTS FOR THE ECHOCARDIOGRAM

Trade off C	Un-certainty Eita (η)	Training Error %	# of Training points misclassified	Testing Error %	# of Testing Points misclassified
1000	0	10	4	20	4
1000	0.03	10	4	25	5
8500	0.05	12.5	5	20	4
8500	0.07	12.5	5	25	5
8500	0.09	7.5	3	25	5

B. Breast cancer Classification Application Description and Analysis

In this problem we try to classify breast cancer data [16] using 9 attributes. We used 100 data points, 60 points for training and 40 for testing. We observed stability of the method, that is, no big changes in the values of the mean square testing error (mse) occurred with changes of the values of parameter η. What we want to show here is that the number of misclassified testing points are continuously changing with respect to continuous changes of the uncertainty parameter eita. Therefore, we can obtain estimations of the changes of the LP-SVM solutions when we are dealing with given uncertain data. Results can be seen in Table 2.

TABLE 2. RESULTS FOR THE BREAST CANCER CLASSIFICATION APPLICATION

Trade off C	Un-Certainty Eita η	Training Error %	# of Training points misclassified	Testing Error %	# of Testing points misclassified
1000	0	0	0	5	2
1000	0.01	0	0	5	2
1000	0.02	0	0	5	2
1000	0.05	0	0	5	2

V. CONCLUSIONS
VI.

The contribution of this paper was to investigate the robustness and stability of the SVM classification model under bounded perturbations of the input data in the feature space. Preliminary experimentations in synthetic and real world data has shown that the SVM model is stable under bounded perturbations of the data in the feature space.

ACKNOWLEDGMENTS

The present work has been partially supported by the NSF grants ECS-9978813 and ECS-0099378.

REFERENCES

[1] A. Ben-Tal, and A. Nemirovski, "Robust solutions to uncertain linear programs via convex programming," *Operations Research Letters*, vol.25:1, pp.1-17, 1996.

[2] A. Ben-Tal and A. Nemirovski, "Robust convex optimization," *Mathematics of Operations Research*, vol.23:4, pp. 769-805, 1998.

[3] G.H. Golub, "Some modified matrix eigenvalue problems," *SIAM Rev.*, 15, pp.318-344, 1973.

[4] G.H. Golub and C.F. Van Loan, "An analysis of the total least squares problem," *SIAM J. Numer. Anal.*, 17, pp.883-893, 1980.

[5] G.H. Golub and C.F. Van Loan, *Matrix Computations*, 3rd ed., Baltimore, MD, The Johns Hopkins University Press, 1997.

[6] S.V. Huffel and J. Vandewalle, *The Total Least Squares Problem: Computational Aspects and Analysis*, Philadelphia, PA, SIAM, 1991.

[7] C.L. Lawson and R.J. Hanson, *Solving Least-Squares Problems*, Philadelphia, PA, SIAM, 1995.

[8] L.E. Ghaoui L. and H. Lebret, "Robust solutions to least- square problems with uncertain data," *SIAM J.Matrix Anal. Appl.*, 18, pp. 1035-1064, 1997.

[9] S. Boyd, M.S.Lobo, and L. Vandenberghe, "Applications of second-order cone programming," *Linear Algebra and its Applications*, vol.284, pp. 193-226, 1998.

[10] J.R. Birge, "The value of the statistic solution in stochastic linear programs with fixed resources," *Math. Programming*, vol.24, pp. 314-325, 1982.

[11] J.M. Mulvey, R.J. Vanderbei, and S.A. Zenios, "Robust optimization of large- scale systems," *Operations Research*, vol.43:2, pp. 264-281, 1995.

[12] V. Vapnik, *The Nature of Statistical Learning Theory*, Springer Verlag, 1995.

[13] V. Vapnik, *Statistical Learning Theory*, Wiley, 1998.

[14] O.L. Mangasarian, "Minimum- support solutions of polyhedral concave programs," *Optimization*, vol. 45, pp. 149-162, 1999.

[15] K.P Bennett and C. Campbell, "Support vector machines: hype or hallelujah?" *SIGKDD Explorations*, 2:2, pp.1-6, 2000.

[16] UCI Machine Learning Data base ftp. ics. uci. edu /pub/machine-learning databases.

A Kernel Fuzzy Classifier with Ellipsoidal Regions

Kenichi Kaieda
Graduate School of Science and Technology
Kobe University
Email: kaieda@frenchblue.scitec.kobe-u.ac.jp

Shigeo Abe
Graduate School of Science and Technology
Kobe University
Email: abe@eedept.kobe-u.ac.jp

Abstract— In this paper, we discuss a kernel version of fuzzy classifiers with ellipsoidal regions to improve generalization ability. First, we map the input space into the implicit feature space induced by a kernel function. Then we generate a fuzzy rules in the feature space and tune the slopes of membership functions successively until there is no improvement in the recognition rate of the training data.

We evaluate our method using numeral and hiragana data of vehicle license plates, and blood cell data. Except for the numeral data, the generalization ability is improved against that of the conventional fuzzy classifier with ellipsoidal regions, and is comparable to that of support vector machines.

I. INTRODUCTION

Support vector machines developed by Vapnik are known to be a powerful tool for generating pattern recognition systems with high generalization ability [1]. SVMs first map the input space into a high dimensional feature space and find the optimal hyperplane that maximizes a margin between two classes. Inspired by the success of SVMs, many conventional techniques, mostly linear techniques, are reformulated in the feature space to improve generalization ability. These techniques, are called kernel-based methods. Kernel least squares [2] and kernel principal component analysis (KPCA) [3] are examples of kernel-based methods.

In this paper, we discuss a kernel fuzzy classifier with ellipsoidal regions in an implicit feature space. Namely, we map the input space into a high dimensional feature space and generate a fuzzy classifier with ellipsoidal regions in that space. To do so, we need to calculate the Mahalanobis distance in the feature space, called kernel Mahalanobis distance. But if the dimension of the feature space is infinite, we cannot calculate it directly. To avoid this problem, we use a kernel method, discussed in [2], in which the kernel Mahalanobis distance is calculated without explicitly treating variables in the feature space.

In calculating the kernel Mahalanobis distance, we need to calculate a pseudo-inverse by the singular value decomposition. But according to our computer experiments, we find that if the number of training data is small, the generalization ability of the kernel-based classifier is lower than that of the conventional classifier. This is because all components with small singular values are neglected. So we propose a new method in which all components are taken into consideration, when we calculate a pseudo-inverse.

In the conventional method, we first divide training data belonging to a class into several clusters [4], [5]. But by the kernel-based method, clustering is not necessary. Thus,
we define a fuzzy rule for each class calculating the center and covariance matrix in the feature space. We then tune fuzzy rules so that the recognition rate of the training data is improved in the similar way discussed in [4], [5].

In Section II we describe a classifier architecture, and in Section III we discuss how to calculate the kernel Mahalanobis distance without treating the feature variables. Then in Section IV, we propose a method for calculating a pseudo-inverse so that the generalization ability is improved and in Section V we discuss a fuzzy rule tuning. In Section VI, we evaluate our methods using some benchmark data sets.

II. CLASSIFIER ARCHITECTURE

We discuss a kernel fuzzy classifier with ellipsoidal region in a feature space, which is mapped by a non-linear mapping function. Here we consider classification of the m-dimensional input vector x into n classes. For each class we define the following fuzzy rule:

$$R_i: \text{if } \phi(x) \text{ is } \phi(\mu_i) \; x \text{ belongs to class } i, \quad (1)$$

where ϕ is the nonlinear mapping function that maps x into the l-dimensional feature space and $\phi(\mu_i)$ is the center of class i in the feature space. We define a membership function $m_i(\phi(x))$ ($i \in 1, \cdots, n$) for input datum x by

$$m_i(\phi(x)) = \exp(-h_i^2(\phi(x))), \quad (2)$$

$$h_i^2(\phi(x)) = \frac{\delta_i^2(\phi(x))}{\alpha_i}, \quad (3)$$

$$\delta_i^2(\phi(x)) = [\phi(x) - \phi(\mu_i)]^T \phi_{C_i}^{-1} [\phi(x) - \phi(\mu_i)], \quad (4)$$

where $\delta_i(\phi(x))$: the kernel Mahalanobis distance between x and μ_i; $h_i(\phi(x))$: tuned distance; α_i: tuning parameter for class i; ϕ_{C_i}: the covariance matrix for class i in the feature space.

We calculate a membership function of input datum x for each class. If the degree of membership for class j is maximum, the input datum is classified into class j. This is equivalent to finding the minimum Mahalanobis distance when α_i in (3) is equal to 1. Function (2) makes the output range of (2) lie in [0,1], and if $m_j(\phi(x))$ is equal to 1, the input vector x corresponds to the center of class j, $\phi(\mu_j)$. We tune the membership function using α_i in (3). This tuning method is described in Section V.

III. KERNEL MAHALANOBIS DISTANCE

To calculate the kernel Mahalanobis distance given by (4) without explicitly treating the variables in the feature space, we use the kernel method. Namely, we transform (4) so that only the dot products $\phi(x)^T\phi(x)$ appear in (4) [2].

The covariance matrix in the feature space is expressed in a matrix form as follows:

$$\begin{aligned}\phi_{C_i} &= \frac{1}{M_i}\sum_{j=1}^{M_i}(\phi(x_{ij})-\phi(\mu_i))(\phi(x_{ij})-\phi(\mu_i))^T \\ &= \phi^T(X_i)\left(\frac{1}{M_i}(I_{M_i}-\mathbf{1}_{M_i})\right)\phi(X_i),\end{aligned} \quad (5)$$

where $x_{ij} = [x_{ij1}\cdots x_{ijm}]^T$ is the jth training data for class i, M_i is the number of training data for class i, I_{M_i} is the $M_i \times M_i$ dimensional unit matrix, $\mathbf{1}_{M_i}$ is the $M_i \times M_i$ dimensional matrix with all component equal to $1/M_i$, and $\phi(X_i)$ is an $M_i \times l$ matrix:

$$\phi(X_i) = \begin{bmatrix}\phi^T(x_{i1})\\ \vdots \\ \phi^T(x_{iM_i})\end{bmatrix}. \quad (6)$$

Since $I_{M_i}-\mathbf{1}_{M_i}$ is a symmetric positive semi-definite matrix, we can define the square root of the matrix, Z_i:

$$Z_i = \left(\frac{1}{M_i}(I_{M_i}-\mathbf{1}_{M_i})\right)^{\frac{1}{2}}. \quad (7)$$

Substituting (7) into (5) we obtain

$$\phi_{C_i} = \phi^T(X_i)Z_i^2\phi(X_i). \quad (8)$$

Substituting the above equation into (4) gives

$$\begin{aligned}\delta_i^2(\phi(x)) &= [\phi(x)-\phi(\mu_i)]^T[\phi^T(X_i)Z_i^2\phi(X_i)]^{-1}\\ &\quad \times[\phi(x)-\phi(\mu_i)].\end{aligned} \quad (9)$$

Now the following equation is valid for any integer number n and symmetric matrix A and any vectors t and u:

$$\begin{aligned}&t^T(X^TAX)^n u \\ &= t^TX^T(A^{\frac{1}{2}}(A^{\frac{1}{2}}KA^{\frac{1}{2}})^{n-1}A^{\frac{1}{2}})Xu,\end{aligned} \quad (10)$$

where $K = XX^T$. If n is negative, it means pseudo-inverse. We calculate a pseudo-inverse using the singular value decomposition. It will be discussed in the next section.

Here since Z_i^2 of (9) is a symmetric matrix, we can apply (10) to (9):

$$\begin{aligned}\delta_i^2(\phi(x)) &= [\phi(X_i)\phi(x)-\phi(X_i)\phi(\mu_i)]^T\\ &\quad \times[Z_i(Z_i\phi(X_i)\phi^T(X_i)Z_i)^{-2}Z_i]\\ &\quad \times[\phi(X_i)\phi(x)-\phi(X_i)\phi(\mu_i)].\end{aligned} \quad (11)$$

Since the above equation consists of only dot products in the feature space, we can replace them with kernel functions:

$$K(x,y) = \phi(x)^T\phi(y). \quad (12)$$

The kernel functions that we use in the following study are:
1) Dot product kernels

$$K(x,y) = x^Ty, \quad (13)$$

2) Polynomial kernels

$$K(x,y) = (1+x^Ty)^d, \quad (14)$$

where d is a positive integer,
3) RBF kernels

$$K(x,y) = \exp(-\gamma\|x-y\|^2), \quad (15)$$

where γ is a positive parameter.

Using (12), we can rewrite the dot products in (11) as follows:

$$\begin{aligned}\phi(X_i)\phi(x) &= \begin{bmatrix}\phi^T(x_{i1})\phi(x)\\ \vdots\\ \phi^T(x_{iM_i})\phi(x)\end{bmatrix}\\ &= \begin{bmatrix}K(x_{i1},x)\\ \vdots\\ K(x_{iM_i},x)\end{bmatrix} = K(X_i,x),\end{aligned} \quad (16)$$

$$\phi(X_i)\phi(\mu_i) = K(X_i,\mu_i), \quad (17)$$

$$\begin{aligned}\phi(X_i)\phi^T(X_i) &= \begin{bmatrix}\phi^T(x_{i1})\\ \vdots\\ \phi^T(x_{iM_i})\end{bmatrix}\begin{bmatrix}\phi(x_{i1}) & \cdots & \phi(x_{iM_i})\end{bmatrix}\\ &= \begin{bmatrix}K(x_{i1},x_{i1}) & \cdots & K(x_{i1},x_{iM_i})\\ \vdots & \ddots & \vdots\\ K(x_{iM_i},x_{i1}) & \cdots & K(x_{iM_i},x_{iM_i})\end{bmatrix}\\ &= K(X_i,X_i^T).\end{aligned} \quad (18)$$

Substituting (16), (17), and (18) into (11), we obtain

$$\begin{aligned}\delta_i^2(\phi(x)) &= [K(X_i,x)-K(X_i,\mu_i)]^T\\ &\quad \times[Z_i(Z_iK(X_i,X_i^T)Z_i)^{-2}Z_i]\\ &\quad \times[K(X_i,x)-K(X_i,\mu_i)].\end{aligned} \quad (19)$$

Using (19) we can calculate the kernel Mahalanobis distance without treating variables in the feature space.

IV. SINGULAR VALUE DECOMPOSITION

In (19), $(Z_iK(X_i,X_i^T)Z_i)^{-2}$ needs to be calculated by the singular value decomposition. In this section, we discuss the singular value decomposition and its variant to improve generalization ability when the number of data is small.

Any matrix A is decomposed into $A = S\Lambda U^T$ by the singular value decomposition, where S and U are orthogonal matrices ($SS^T = I, UU^T = I$, where I is a unit matrix) and Λ is a diagonal matrix. If A is an $m \times m$ positive semi-definite matrix, the singular value decomposition is equivalent to the diagonalization of the matrix. Namely, S, Λ, U are $m \times m$ square matrices and $S = U$. Since $Z_iK(X_i,X_i^T)Z_i$ is a symmetric, positive semi-definite matrix, in the following discussion we assume that A is symmetric and positive semi-definite.

If A is positive definite, the inverse of A is expressed as follows:

$$\begin{aligned} A^{-1} = (U\Lambda U^T)^{-1} &= (U^T)^{-1}\Lambda^{-1}U^{-1} \\ &= U\Lambda^{-1}U^T \end{aligned} \quad (20)$$

Assume that A is positive semi-definite with rank r ($m > r$). In this case the pseudo-inverse of A, A^+, is used. In the following we discuss two methods to calculate a pseudo-inverse: the conventional and proposed methods.

A. Conventional Method

Since $m > r$ holds, the $(r+1)$st to mth diagonal elements of Λ are zero. In the conventional pseudo-inverse, if a diagonal element λ_i is larger than or equal to ϵ, where ϵ is a predefined threshold, we set $1/\lambda_i$ to the ith element of Λ^+. But if it is smaller, we set 0.

B. Proposed Method

According to our computer experiments, if the number of training data was small, the generalization ability of the kernel classifier was inferior to that of the conventional classifier. This situation occurred when the covariance matrix in the input space is singular as will be shown in Section VI. In the conventional method, if a diagonal element is smaller than ϵ, the associated diagonal element of the pseudo-inverse is set to 0. It means that all components with small singular values are neglected. Namely, the subspace corresponding to the zero diagonal elements is neglected. This leads to decreasing the generalization ability. To avoid this we set $1/\epsilon$ instead of 0. Namely we calculate the pseudo-inverse as follows:

$$\begin{aligned} A^+ &= U\Lambda^+ S^T \\ &= U \begin{bmatrix} \lambda_1^{-1} & & & & & \\ & \ddots & & & & \\ & & \lambda_r^{-1} & & & \\ & & & \frac{1}{\epsilon} & & \\ & & & & \ddots & \\ & & & & & \frac{1}{\epsilon} \end{bmatrix} S^T. \end{aligned} \quad (21)$$

V. FUZZY RULE TUNING

A. Concept

The conventional fuzzy classifier with ellipsoidal regions is generated in the input space. And in the conventional fuzzy classifier, slopes of membership functions are tuned until there is no improvement in the recognition rate [4]. For the kernel fuzzy classifier with ellipsoidal regions, since we can calculate the kernel Mahalanobis distance using (19), the tuning algorithm in the input space can be readily expanded to the feature space. In this section we explain the tuning algorithm.

For example, when tuning parameter α_i in (3) is increased, the slope of $m_i(\phi(\boldsymbol{x}))$ decreases, and at the same time the degree of $m_i(\phi(\boldsymbol{x}))$ increases. This may lead to correct classification of the data which were misclassified before tuning, while some data which were correctly classified may be misclassified. Here we allow the data which were classified correctly before tuning to be misclassified as long as the overall recognition rate of the training data is improved. We divide the training data into the following four cases:

Case 1. Input $\boldsymbol{x}$ is correctly classified into class i.
Case 2. Input $\boldsymbol{x}$ is correctly classified into a class other than class i.
Case 3. Input $\boldsymbol{x}$, which belongs to class i, is misclassified into another class.
Case 4. Input $\boldsymbol{x}$, which belongs to a class other than i, is misclassified into class i.

We define X_i ($i = 1, \cdots, 4$) as a data set in Case i.

B. Lower and Upper Bound of α_i

Here we consider the training data for Case 1. Before tuning, the input datum $\boldsymbol{x}$ is correctly classified into class i. While maintaining the correct classification of $\boldsymbol{x}$, we can change α_i until the dotted curve in Fig. 1. In other words, so long as the following equation is satisfied:

$$\frac{\delta_i^2(\phi(\boldsymbol{x}))}{\min_{j \neq i} h_j^2(\phi(\boldsymbol{x}))} < L_i(\phi(\boldsymbol{x})), \quad (22)$$

where $L_i(\phi(\boldsymbol{x}))$ is defined as the lower bound of α_i to maintain correct classification of $\boldsymbol{x}$. Next, we calculate the

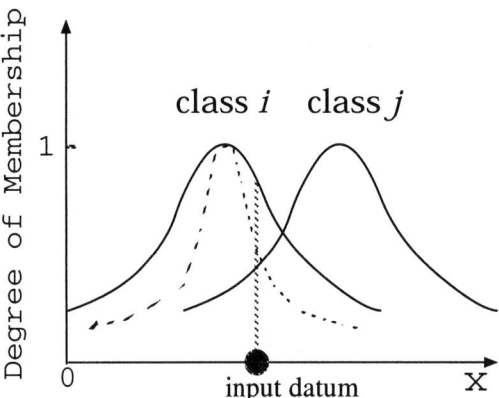

Fig. 1. Lower Bound of α_i. We can change α_i until a dotted curve to maintain correct classification.

lower bounds for all data in Case 1, and the maximum lower bound among them is defined as follows:

$$L_i(1) = \max_{\boldsymbol{x} \in X_1} L_i(\phi(\boldsymbol{x})), \quad (23)$$

where $L_i(1)$ is the lower bound that does not lead to any misclassification.

In general $L_i(l)$ which allow $l-1$ correctly classified data to be misclassified is defined as follows:

$$L_i(l) = \max_{\boldsymbol{x} \in X_1, L_i(\phi(\boldsymbol{x})) \neq L_i(1), \cdots, L_i(l-1)} L_i(\phi(\boldsymbol{x})). \quad (24)$$

Next, we consider the training data in Case 2. In a similar way we can define $U_i(\phi(\boldsymbol{x}))$ as the upper bound of α_i to maintain correct classification of $\boldsymbol{x}$:

$$\frac{\delta_i^2(\phi(\boldsymbol{x}))}{h_j^2(\phi(\boldsymbol{x}))} > U_i(\phi(\boldsymbol{x})). \qquad (25)$$

Then we calculate the upper bounds for all data in Case 2.

In general, we define the upper bound of α_i, $U_i(l)$, that allows $l-1$ correctly classified data to be misclassified as follows:

$$U_i(l) = \min_{\boldsymbol{x} \in X_2, U_i(\phi(\boldsymbol{x})) \neq U_i(1),\cdots,U_i(l-1)} U_i(\phi(\boldsymbol{x})). \qquad (26)$$

C. Maximizing Margins

In SVM training, the optimal hyperplane is determined so that the margin between two classes is maximized. Thus the optimal hyperplane is determined uniquely and it has the highest generalization ability. But in fuzzy rule tuning, since we move the boundary to resolve overlaps between classes, the boundary is not changed when classes do not overlap. This means that we do not consider margins among classes. Therefore, when the number of training data is small, the generalization ability may be worsened compared to SVMs. To improve the generalization ability in such a situation, we maximize margins among classes in the same way as discussed in [6]. In training if we set α_i in $[L_i(1), U_i(1)]$, it does not cause any new misclassification. Thus to maximize margins we set α_i in the middle point of $[L_i(1), U_i(1)]$ (see Fig. 2).

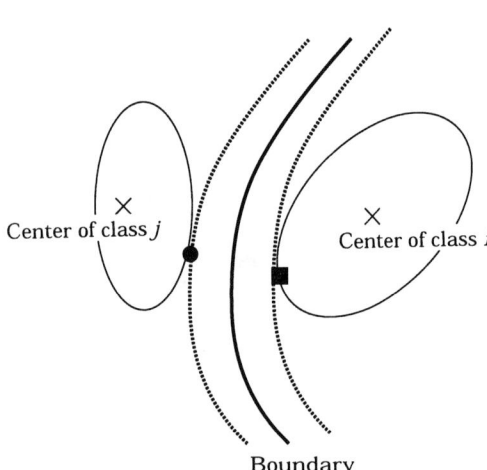

Fig. 2. Maximizing Margin between Class i and Class j

D. Bounds to Resolve Misclassification

In this section we check whether the misclassified data can be correctly classified by changing α_i.

First, we consider the training data for Case 3. Thus, input $\boldsymbol{x}$ which belongs to class i is misclassified into another class (e.g., class j ($j \neq i$)). If the following equation is satisfied, input $\boldsymbol{x}$ is correctly classified:

$$\frac{\delta_i^2(\phi(\boldsymbol{x}))}{\alpha_i} < h_j^2(\phi(\boldsymbol{x})). \qquad (27)$$

We define $V_i(\phi(\boldsymbol{x}))$ as the lower bound of α_i to resolve misclassification of input $\boldsymbol{x}$:

$$V_i(\phi(\boldsymbol{x})) = \frac{\delta_i^2(\phi(\boldsymbol{x}))}{h_j^2(\phi(\boldsymbol{x}))} < \alpha_i. \qquad (28)$$

We define Inc(l) as the number of the misclassified data that are correctly classified if we set the value of α_i in $[U_i(l-1), U_i(l))$. When $V_i(\phi(\boldsymbol{x}))$ is in the range of $(\alpha_i, U_i(l))$, Inc(l) is increased by one. Here we define $\beta_i(l)$ as follows:

$$\beta_i(l) = \max_{V_i(\phi(\boldsymbol{x})) < U_i(l)} V_i(\phi(\boldsymbol{x})). \qquad (29)$$

If α_i is set to be larger than $\max(\beta_i(l), U_i(l-1))$, Inc($l$) misclassified data are correctly classified. But on the other hand, $l-1$ correctly classified data are misclassified (see Fig. 3).

Next we consider the training data for Case 4. Thus input $\boldsymbol{x}$ which belongs to another class (e.g., class j ($j \neq i$)) is misclassified into class i. Here the tuned distance for class j need to be the second minimum among n classes. Otherwise we may not classify $\boldsymbol{x}$ correctly by changing α_i. Then the datum $\boldsymbol{x}$ is classified correctly if the following equation is satisfied:

$$\alpha_i < \frac{\delta_i^2(\phi(\boldsymbol{x}))}{h_j^2(\phi(\boldsymbol{x}))} = K_i(\phi(\boldsymbol{x})), \qquad (30)$$

where $K_i(\phi(\boldsymbol{x}))$ is an upper bound of α_i to make misclassification of $\boldsymbol{x}$ be correctly classified. We define Dec(l) as the number of the misclassified data that are correctly classified if we set the value of α_i in $(L_i(l), L_i(l-1)]$. When $K_i(\phi(\boldsymbol{x}))$ is in the range of $[L_i(l), \alpha_i]$, Dec(l) is increased by one. Here we define $\gamma_i(l)$ as follows:

$$\gamma_i(l) = \min_{K_i(\phi(\boldsymbol{x})) > L_i(l)} K_i(\phi(\boldsymbol{x})). \qquad (31)$$

If α_i is set to be smaller than $\min(\gamma_i(l), L_i(l-1))$, Dec($l$) misclassified data are correctly classified, and $l-1$ correctly classified data are misclassified.

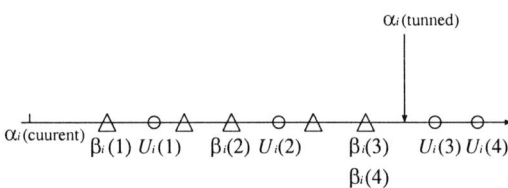

Fig. 3. Tuning Example. Circles denote the correctly classified data and triangles denote the misclassified data before tuning. For example if we set α_i between $\beta_i(3)$ and $U_i(3)$, five misclassified data become correctly classified, but two correctly classified data are misclassified.

E. Modification of α_i

For Inc(l) ($l = 1, \cdots, l_M$), where l_M is a positive integer, we find the l that satisfies the following equation:

$$\max_l (\text{Inc}(l) - l + 1). \tag{32}$$

Similarly, for Dec(l) ($l = 1, \cdots, l_M$) we find the l that satisfies the following equation:

$$\max_l (\text{Dec}(l) - l + 1). \tag{33}$$

If the above equations are satisfied for plural l, we select the smallest l. First we consider the case where (32) is larger or equal to (33). If we set α_i larger than $\beta_i(l)$ in the range of $(\alpha_i, U_i(l))$, the net increase of the correctly classified data is inc(l) $- l + 1$. So we set α_i in the range of $[\beta_i(l), U_i(l)]$ as following:

$$\alpha_i = \beta_i(l) + \eta(U_i(l) - \beta_i(l)), \tag{34}$$

where $0 < \eta < 1$.

Next, we consider the case where (32) is smaller than (33). If we set α_i smaller than $\gamma_i(l)$ in the range of $(L_i(l), \alpha_i)$, the net increase of the correctly classified data is Dec(l) $- l + 1$. So we set α_i in the range of $[L_i(l), \gamma_i(l))$ as follows:

$$\alpha_i = \gamma_i(l) - \eta(\gamma_i(l) - L_i(l)). \tag{35}$$

Here the recognition rate of test data does not depend on the value of η. So we could change η freely, but in the experiment in Section VI we set $\eta = 0.1$.

F. Tuning Procedure

According to above discussion, we change tuning parameter α_i as follows:

1) We set a positive number to parameter l_M, where $l_M - 1$ is the maximum number of misclassification allowed for tuning α_i, and set a value in (0,1) to η of (34) and (35). At first we set $\alpha_i (i \in (1, \cdots, n))$ to 1.
2) Next, we change α_i from ($i = 1$) to ($i = n$) so that the margins are maximized, which is to say we set $\alpha_i = \frac{1}{2}(L_i(1) + U_i(1))$.
3) After maximizing margins, for $\alpha_i (i = 1, \cdots, n)$ calculate $L_i(l), U_i(l)$, Inc(l), Dec(l), $\beta_i(l)$ and $\gamma_i(l)$ for $l = 1, \cdots, l_M$. Find l that maximize (32) or (33) and change α_i using (34) or (35). Then we iterate the procedure of Step 3) until there is no improvement in the recognition rate of the training data.

VI. PERFORMANCE EVALUATION

We evaluate our method using blood cell data [7], numeral data, and hiragana data [8], listed in Table I. We use a Pentium III 1GHz PC to evaluate our method.

In the following tables, $l_M - 1$ is the maximum number of misclassification allowed for tuning. We change the number of l_M in $\{1, 2, \ldots, 10\}$ and we list the highest recognition rate for each kernel. In each table, the numeral of the bracket shows the recognition rate of the training data. By way of comparison, we also list the result of support vector machines. In the bottom

TABLE I
BENCHMARK DATA SPECIFICATION

Data	Inputs	Classes	Train	Test
Blood cell	13	12	3097	3100
Numeral	12	10	810	820
Hiragana-13	13	38	8375	8356

row, "Initial" shows the result of the support vector machine, and "Final" shows that of fuzzy support vector machine [9].

In the following tables, "Type 1" and "Type 2" denote that the conventional method and the proposed method in Section V are used for calculating the pseudo-inverse of $Z_i K(X_i, X_i^T) Z_i$, respectively.

Type 1 is useful when the covariance matrix in the input space is not singular (the blood cell and hiragana data) and Type 2 is useful for the numeral data. To show the difference between Type 1 and Type 2, in the following, we include the results of the both types for the blood cell and numeral data.

In theory the kernel fuzzy classifier with dot product kernels is equivalent to the conventional fuzzy classifier. For the blood cell and hiragana data, the results for dot product kernels are the same as those of the conventional fuzzy classifier with ellipsoidal regions, in which symmetric Cholesky factorization is used [4].

But for the numeral data, since the covariance matrix in the input space is singular, there is much difference between the result of Type 1 and that of the conventional fuzzy classifier. Thus by way of comparison for numeral data, we list the result of conventional fuzzy classifier in which kernel method is not used.

A. Blood Cell Data

Blood cell classification involves classifying optically screened white blood cells into 12 classes using 13 features. This is a very difficult problem; class boundaries for some classes are ambiguous because the classes are defined according to the growth stages of white blood cells.

TABLE II
PERFORMANCE FOR BLOOD CELL DATA (TYPE 1) ($\epsilon = 10^{-8}$)

Kernel	l_M	Initial[%]	Final[%]
Dot	10	87.42(92.70)	91.32(95.35)
$d = 2$	1	92.65(98.77)	92.84(98.97)
$d = 3$	1	92.48(99.61)	92.58(99.77)
$\gamma = 0.1$	1	91.65(96.51)	91.87(97.13)
SVM($d = 3$)	—	89.03(96.19)	93.26(98.22)

Table II shows the performance for the blood cell data when Type 1 is used. From the table, the recognition rate of the kernel fuzzy classifier with $d = 2, 3$ or $\gamma = 0.1$ is better than that of the conventional fuzzy classifier (Dot). But the result of our method is a little lower than that of the fuzzy support vector machine.

In the feature space overfitting occurs if we allow misclassification in tuning. Therefore, we set $l_M = 1$. The effect of tuning is small compared to the conventional fuzzy classifier.

TABLE III
PERFORMANCE FOR BLOOD CELL DATA (TYPE 2) ($\epsilon = 10^{-8}$)

Kernel	l_M	Initial[%]	Final[%]
Dot	10	87.45(92.64)	91.32(95.41)
$d = 2$	1	92.45(98.97)	92.52(99.19)
$d = 3$	1	92.39(99.81)	92.32(99.84)
$\gamma = 0.1$	1	92.00(97.26)	91.81(97.68)

Table III shows performance for the blood cell data when Type 2 is used. Comparing Tables II and III, there is not much difference between Type 1 and Type 2. It means that if the covariance matrix in the input space is not singular, we can obtain enough performance with the conventional method. But although the differences are small, we must notice that the recognition rates of the training data for Type 2 are always better than those for Type 1.

B. Numeral data

The numeral data were collected to identify Japanese license plates of running cars, which include numerals, hiragana, and kanji characters. The original image taken from a TV camera was preprocessed and each numeral was transformed into 12 features such as the number of holes and the curvature of a numeral at some point.

TABLE IV
PERFORMANCE FOR NUMERAL DATA (TYPE 2) ($\epsilon = 10^{-8}$)

Kernel	l_M	Initial[%]	Final[%]
—	10	99.39(99.63)	99.88(100)
Dot	10	98.54(97.28)	98.78(98.52)
$\gamma = 0.1$	10	98.41(100)	98.05(100)
$\gamma = 0.01$	10	99.15(99.51)	99.27(100)
SVM	—	99.76(100)	100(100)

Table IV shows the results when Type 2 is used. In the table, the first row shows the result of the conventional fuzzy classifier, which is generated in the input space [4]. The recognition rates by the kernel fuzzy classifier with dot product kernels are inferior to those of the conventional fuzzy classifier. This may be caused by the singularity of the covariance matrix in the input space. Using RBF kernels with $\gamma = 0.01$, the recognition rates are improved but still lower than those of the support vector machines and the conventional fuzzy classifier.

TABLE V
PERFORMANCE FOR NUMERAL DATA (TYPE 1) ($\epsilon = 10^{-8}$)

Kernel	l_M	Initial[%]	Final[%]
Dot	10	88.78(90.00)	88.90(91.11)
$\gamma = 0.1$	10	98.17(100)	98.05(100)
$\gamma = 0.01$	10	97.93(98.89)	98.90(100)

Table V shows the results when Type 1 is used. Comparing Tables IV and V, the recognition rates of Type 1 are lower especially for dot product kernels.

C. Hiragana Data

Hiragana-13 data were generated by calculating the 13 central moments for the original 7 × 15-pixel images of hiragana characters in the Japanese license plates.

TABLE VI
PERFORMANCE FOR HIRAGANA-13 DATA (TYPE 1)($\epsilon = 10^{-8}$)

Kernel	l_M	Initial[%]	Final[%]
Dot	10	98.36(99.84)	99.25(99.99)
$d = 2$	10	99.39(99.98)	99.22(100)
$\gamma = 0.1$	10	99.86(99.99)	99.82(100)
SVM	—	99.37(100)	99.58(100)

Table VI shows the results for hiragana data using Type 1. The recognition rates of the kernel fuzzy classifier with $d = 2$ or $\gamma = 0.1$ are better than those of the conventional fuzzy classifier (Dot) when membership functions are not tuned. When membership functions are tuned, overfitting occurred and the recognition rates of the test data decreased. The best recognition rate of the kernel fuzzy classifier is better than that of the support vector machines.

VII. CONCLUSIONS

In this paper we proposed a kernel fuzzy classifier with ellipsoidal regions, in which the input space is mapped into a high dimensional feature space and a fuzzy classifier is generated in the feature space. And we demonstrated the validity of our classifier using numeral, blood cell, and hiragana data sets. Except for numeral data, the generalization ability of our classifier was better than that of a conventional fuzzy classifier and especially for the blood cell data, improvement was significant. In addition, the generalization ability of our classifier is comparable to that of support vector machines.

REFERENCES

[1] V. Vapnik, "*Statistical Learning Theory,*" John Wiley & Sons, 1998.
[2] A. Ruiz and P. E. López-de-Teruel, "Nonlinear Kernel-Based Statistical Pattern Analysis," *IEEE Transactions on Neural Networks*, Vol. 12, No. 1. pp. 16–32, January 2001.
[3] B. Schölkopf, A. Smola, and K. Robert Müller, "Nonlinear Component Analysis as a Kernel Eigenvalue Problem," *Neural Computation*, Vol. 10, pp. 1299–1319, 1998.
[4] S. Abe and R. Thawonmas, "A Fuzzy Classifier with Ellipsoidal Regions," *IEEE Transactions on Fuzzy Systems*, Vol. 5, No. 3, pp. 358–368, August 1997.
[5] S. Abe, "*Pattern Classification, Neuro-fuzzy Method and Their Comparison,*" Springer-Verlag, London, 2001.
[6] S. Abe and K. Sakaguchi, "Generalization Improvement of a Fuzzy Classifier with Ellipsoidal Regions," *Proc. 10th IEEE International Conference on Fuzzy Systems (FUZZ - IEEE 2001)*, pp. 207–210, Melbourne, Australia, December 2001.
[7] A. Hashizume, J. Motoike, and R. Yabe, "Fully Automated Blood Cell Differential System and Its Application," *Proc. IUPAC 3rd International Congress on Automation and New Technology in the Clinical Laboratory*, pp. 297–302, Kobe, Japan, 1988.
[8] H. Takenaga et al., "Input Layer Optimization of Neural Networks by Sensitivity Analysis and Its Application to Recognition of Numerals," *Electrical Engineering in Japan*, Vol. 111, No. 4, pp. 130–138, 1991.
[9] T. Inoue and S. Abe, "Fuzzy Support Vector Machines for Pattern Classification," *Proc. IJCNN'01*, pp. 1449–1454, 2001.

A Role of Total Margin in Support Vector Machines

Min Yoon
Department of Applied Statistics
Yonsei University
Seoul, South Korea 120-749
Email: myoon@base.yonsei.ac.kr

Yeboon Yun
Department of Reliability-based
Information System Engineering
Kagawa University
Takamatsu, Japan 761-0369
Email: yun@eng.kagawa-u.ac.jp

Hirotaka Nakayama
Department of Information Science
and Systems Engineering
Konan University
Kobe, Japan 658-8501
nakayama@konan-u.ac.jp

Abstract—The support vector algorithm has paid attention on maximizing the shortest distance between sample points and discrimination hyperplane. This paper suggests the total margin algorithm which considers the distance between all data points and the separating hyperplane. The method extends existing support vector machine algorithms. In addition, the method improves the generalization error bound. Numerical studies show that the total margin algorithm provides good performance, comparing with the previous methods.

I. INTRODUCTION

Support Vector Machines (SVMs) [7], [19], [20] have been gaining much popularity in machine learning due to many attractive features and promising practical performance. One of the main ideas of SVM is based on linear classifier with maximal margin which can be obtained by maximizing the minimum distance from sample points to separating hyperplane.

Consider a training data set denoted by $S = ((x_1, y_1), \ldots, (x_\ell, y_\ell)) \in (X \times \{-1, 1\})^\ell$, where X is the input space. Each data is supposed to be classified by the sign of a linear function $f(x) = \langle w \cdot x \rangle + w_0$.

A conventional maximal margin (hard margin) algorithm can be formulated by

$$\begin{aligned}
& \underset{w, w_0}{\text{minimize}} && \langle w \cdot w \rangle \\
& \text{subject to} && y_i(\langle w, x_i \rangle + w_0) \geq 1, \ i = 1, \ldots, \ell.
\end{aligned}$$

The resulting optimal separating hyperplane maximizes the minimal distance from sample points.

In practice, if data are contaminated by noise, then a perfectly separating hyperplane may not exist. In order to overcome this difficulty, slack variables are introduced in order to relax the measure of margin for data points. The soft margin algorithm can be formulated as follows:

$$\begin{aligned}
& \underset{w, w_0, \xi^-}{\text{minimize}} && \langle w \cdot w \rangle + C \sum_{i=1}^{\ell} \xi_i^- \\
& \text{subject to} && y_i(\langle w, x_i \rangle + w_0) \geq 1 - \xi_i^-, \\
& && \xi_i^- \geq 0, \ i = 1, \ldots, \ell,
\end{aligned}$$

where C is a weight parameter for slack variables.

In this paper, we define the surplus variable as a measure of margin which is defined by the distance between data points and the separating hyperplane. We propose the total margin algorithm which considers totally both the deviation of misclassified data and the deviation of correctly classified data(i.e., surplus variable). The total margin means the sum of distances between data points and the separating hyperplane. We prove that generalization error bound for the total margin can be reduced by minimizing slack variables and maximizing surplus variables. Finally, we compare the total margin algorithm with conventional soft margin algorithms through numerical examples.

II. GENERALIZATION ERROR BOUND USING TOTAL MARGIN BOUND

To begin with, we recall briefly several important background results. Consider a training data set denoted by $S = ((x_1, y_1), \ldots, (x_\ell, y_\ell)) \in (X \times \{-1, 1\})^\ell$, where X is the input space. We introduce the *margin*, which serves as measure of classifiers and means the distance between sample points and classification function.

Definition 1: Consider using a class $\mathcal{F}$ of real-valued functions on an input space X for classification by thresholding at 0. The *margin* of an example $(x_i, y_i) \in X \times \{-1, 1\}$ with respect to a function $f \in \mathcal{F}$ to be the quantity is defined by

$$\gamma_i = y_i f(x_i).$$

Standard(hard margin) SVMs try to maximize the minimum of margins γ_i ($i = 1, \ldots \ell$). On the other hand, in order to make the classification robust against noise, soft margin algorithms have been developed by introducing slack variables. The following Definition 2 and Theorem 2.1 are their main concept and a part of results [16].

Definition 2 (Slack Variable): Consider using a class $\mathcal{F}$ of real-valued functions on an input space X for classification by thresholding at 0. For a function $f \in \mathcal{F}$ and the target margin γ, the *margin slack variable* of an example $(x_i, y_i) \in X \times \{-1, 1\}$ is given by the quantity

$$\xi^-((x_i, y_i), f, \gamma) = \xi_i^- = \max(0, \gamma - y_i f(x_i)).$$

The *margin slack vector* $\boldsymbol{\xi}^-(S, f, \gamma)$ of a training set S with respect to a function f and the target margin γ represents the vector of margin slack variables

$$\boldsymbol{\xi}^- = \boldsymbol{\xi}^-(S, f, \gamma) = (\xi_1^-, \xi_2^-, \ldots, \xi_\ell^-).$$

As seen in Figure 1, ξ_i^- represents how much f fails to reach the target margin γ on the point (x_i, y_i). The following

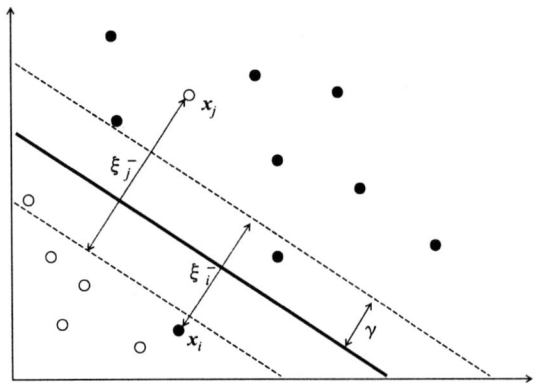

Fig. 1. slack variables

theorem shows generalization error bound of soft margin algorithm.

Theorem 2.1: [16] Fix $\Delta > 0$. Consider a fixed but unknown probability distribution on the space $X \times \{-1, 1\}$ with support in the ball of radius R about the origin in X. Then with probability $1 - \delta$ over randomly drawn training sets S of size ℓ, for any target margin $\gamma > 0$ the generalization of a linear classifier u on X with $\|u\| = 1$, thresholded at 0 is bounded by

$$\varepsilon(\ell, d, \delta) = \frac{2}{\ell}\left(d\log_2\left(\frac{8e\ell}{d}\right)\log_2(32\ell) + \log_2\left(\frac{8\ell}{\delta}\right)\right),$$

where

$$d = \left\lfloor \frac{64.5(R^2 + \Delta^2)(1 + \|\boldsymbol{\xi}^-\|_2^2/\Delta^2)}{\gamma^2} \right\rfloor$$

provided $\ell \geq 2/\varepsilon$, $d \leq e\ell$ and there is no discrete probability on misclassified training points.

The soft margin procedure aims at extending hard margin algorithms to noisy cases by permitting a slight sacrifice of accuracy, that is, introducing slack variable. Therefore, we newly introduce "*surplus variable*". Conceptually, surplus variable is in effect an opposite idea of slack variable. Whereas slack variable is a measurement of the misclassified data point, surplus variable is a measurement of the correctly classified data point.

Definition 3 (Surplus Variable): For a real-valued classification function f on X, the *margin surplus variable* of an example $(\boldsymbol{x}_i, y_i) \in X \times \{-1, 1\}$ with respect to a function $f \in \mathcal{F}$, where $\mathcal{F}$ is a class of real-valued functions, and a target margin γ is given by

$$\xi_i^+ := \xi^+((\boldsymbol{x}_i, y_i), f, \gamma) = \max\{0, y_i f(\boldsymbol{x}_i) - \gamma\}.$$

We denote the *margin surplus vector* $\boldsymbol{\xi}^+(S, f, \gamma)$ of a training set S with respect to a function f and target margin γ by

$$\boldsymbol{\xi}^+ := \boldsymbol{\xi}^+(S, f, \gamma) = (\xi_1^+, \xi_2^+, \ldots, \xi_\ell^+).$$

Letting

$$\frac{1}{\boldsymbol{\xi}^+ + \mathbf{1}} := \left(\frac{1}{\xi_1^+ + 1}, \frac{1}{\xi_2^+ + 1}, \cdots, \frac{1}{\xi_\ell^+ + 1}\right),$$

we define the 2-norm of $\boldsymbol{\xi}^+$ as follows

$$\left\|\frac{1}{\boldsymbol{\xi}^+ + \mathbf{1}}\right\|_2 := \sqrt{\sum_{(\boldsymbol{x}_i, y_i) \in S}\left(\frac{1}{\xi^+((\boldsymbol{x}_i, y_i), f, \gamma) + 1}\right)^2}.$$

In order to obtain the error bound introducing slack and surplus variables, we first summarize the following definitions from [16]. Let X be the input space and define the following inner product space derived from X.

Definition 4: Let $L(X)$ be the set of real-valued functions f on X with countable support $\mathrm{supp}(f)$, that is, functions in $L(X)$ are non-zero for only countably many points. Consider two norms, the 2-norm $\|f\|_2$ is defined by

$$\|f\|_2^2 = \sum_{\boldsymbol{x} \in \mathrm{supp}(f)} f(\boldsymbol{x})^2 < \infty,$$

while the 1-norm is given by

$$\|f\|_1 = \sum_{\boldsymbol{x} \in \mathrm{supp}(f)} |f(\boldsymbol{x})| < \infty.$$

We define the inner product of two functions $f, g \in L(X)$, by

$$\langle f \cdot g \rangle = \sum_{\boldsymbol{x} \in \mathrm{supp}(f)} f(\boldsymbol{x})g(\boldsymbol{x}).$$

Obviously, the space is closed under addition and multiplication by scalars.

Definition 5: For any fixed $\Delta > 0$ we define an embedding of X into the inner product space $X \times L(X)$ as follows.

$$\tau_\Delta : \boldsymbol{x} \mapsto X_\Delta = (\boldsymbol{x}, \Delta\delta_{\boldsymbol{x}}),$$

where $\delta_{\boldsymbol{x}} \in L(X)$ is defined by

$$\delta_{\boldsymbol{x}}(\boldsymbol{z}) = \begin{cases} 1, & \text{if } \boldsymbol{x} = \boldsymbol{z} \\ 0, & \text{otherwise.} \end{cases}$$

In a similar way to Shawe-Taylor and Cristianini [16], given a real-valued function f and a training data set S, we construct an auxiliary function $g_f \in L(X)$, which will ensure that (f, g_f) achieves a target margin γ on S as follows:

$$g_f = \frac{1}{\Delta}\sum_{(\boldsymbol{x}, y) \in S} y \frac{\xi^-((\boldsymbol{x}, y), f, \gamma)}{\xi^+((\boldsymbol{x}, y), f, \gamma) + 1}\delta_{\boldsymbol{x}}.$$

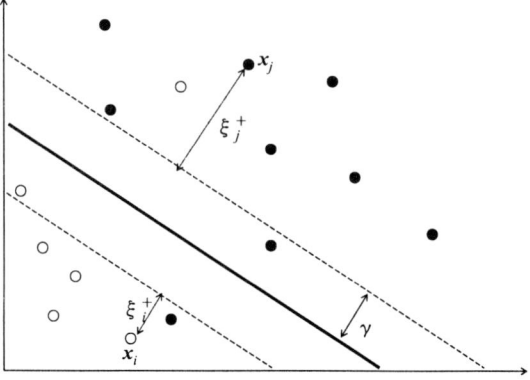

Fig. 2. surplus variables

For the above auxiliary function, we can get the following lemma 2.2.

Lemma 2.2: For any training set S, real-valued function f and margin γ, the function (f, g_f) satisfies the properties as following.
1) $m((f, g_f), \tau_\Delta(S)) \geq \gamma$
2) For $(x, y) \notin S$, $(f, g_f)(\tau_\Delta(x), y) = f(x)$

Proof: 1. If we consider the margin of the function (f, g_f) applied to a training point $(\tau_\Delta(x), y) \in \tau_\Delta(S)$, we have

$$y(f, g_f)\tau_\Delta(x) = yf(x) + \frac{y}{\Delta} \sum_{(x', y') \in S} y' \frac{\xi^-((x', y'), f, \gamma)}{\xi^+((x', y'), f, \gamma) + 1} \langle \delta_{x'}, \Delta \delta_x \rangle$$

$$= yf(x) + \frac{\xi^-((x, y), f, \gamma)}{\xi^+((x, y), f, \gamma) + 1}$$

$$\geq \gamma,$$

because if (x, y) is correctly classified, then

$$yf(x) \geq \gamma, \quad \xi^-((x, y), f, \gamma) = 0,$$
$$\text{and} \quad \xi^+((x, y), f, \gamma) = yf(x) - \gamma \geq 0$$

and otherwise, i.e., (x, y) is misclassified, then

$$yf(x) < \gamma, \quad \xi^+((x, y), f, \gamma) = 0,$$
$$\text{and} \quad \xi^-((x, y), f, \gamma) = \gamma - yf(x) > 0,$$

from the definitions 1, 2 and 3. Therefore the property 1 holds.

2. If we apply the function (f, g_f) to a point $(\tau_\Delta(x), y) \notin \tau_\Delta(S)$, we observe that for $(x', y') \in S$ and $\langle \delta_{x'} \cdot \delta_x \rangle = 0$,

$$\langle g_f \cdot \delta_x \rangle = \sum_{(x', y') \in S} y' \frac{\xi^-((x', y'), f, \gamma)}{\xi^+((x', y'), f, \gamma) + 1} \langle \delta_{x'}, \delta_x \rangle$$

$$= 0.$$

Hence, the second property of this lemma that shows a point x not in the training set performance of (f, g_f) exactly matches the original function. That is,

$$(f, g_f)\tau_\Delta(x) = f(x). \blacksquare$$

Finally, the generalization error bound with surplus and slack variables is given by the following theorem, which is an extended version of Shawe-Taylor and Cristianini [16].

Theorem 2.3: Fix $\Delta > 0$. Consider a fixed but unknown probability distribution on the space $X \times \{-1, 1\}$ with support in the ball of radius R about the origin X. Then with probability $1 - \delta$ over randomly drawn training sets S of size ℓ for all $\gamma > 0$ the generalization of a linear classifier $\mathbf{u}$ on X with $\|\mathbf{u}\| = 1$, thresholded at 0 is bounded by

$$\varepsilon(\ell, d, \delta) = \frac{2}{\ell} \left(d \log_2 \left(\frac{8e\ell}{d} \right) \log_2(32\ell) + \log_2 \left(\frac{8\ell}{\delta} \right) \right),$$

where

$$d = \left\lfloor \frac{64.5(R^2 + \Delta^2)\left(1 + \|\boldsymbol{\xi}^-\|_2^2 \left\|\frac{1}{\boldsymbol{\xi}^+ + 1}\right\|_2^2 \frac{1}{\Delta^2}\right)}{\gamma^2} \right\rfloor$$

provided $\ell \geq 2/\varepsilon$, $d \leq e\ell$ and there is no discrete probability on misclassified training points.

Proof: Consider fixed mapping τ_Δ and the augmented linear function over $X \times L(X)$,

$$\mathbf{u}' = (\mathbf{u}, g_\mathbf{u}).$$

By the first property of Lemma 2.2, $\mathbf{u}'$ has target margin γ on $\tau_\Delta(S)$. That is,

$$m(\mathbf{u}', \tau_\Delta(S)) \geq \gamma,$$

while its action on new examples matches that of $\mathbf{u}$.

Additionally, since $\mathbf{u}'$ is a linear function on the space $X \times L(X)$, we can form the function

$$\hat{\mathbf{u}} = \frac{\mathbf{u}'}{\|\mathbf{u}'\|}.$$

Then $\hat{\mathbf{u}}$ has norm 1, and satisfies

$$m(\hat{\mathbf{u}}, \tau_\Delta(S)) = m\left(\frac{\mathbf{u}'}{\|\mathbf{u}'\|}, \tau_\Delta(S)\right)$$

$$\geq \frac{\gamma}{\|\mathbf{u}'\|} = \frac{\gamma}{\|(\mathbf{u}, g_\mathbf{u})\|}$$

$$= \frac{\gamma}{\sqrt{\|\mathbf{u}\|^2 + \sum_{(x_i, y_i) \in S} \left(\frac{\xi^-((x_i, y_i), f, \gamma)}{\xi^+((x_i, y_i), f, \gamma) + 1}\right)^2 \frac{1}{\Delta^2}}}$$

$$\geq \frac{\gamma}{\sqrt{1 + \|\boldsymbol{\xi}^-\|_2^2 \left\|\frac{1}{\boldsymbol{\xi}^+ + 1}\right\|_2^2 \frac{1}{\Delta^2}}},$$

and also mimics the classification of $\mathbf{u}$ for $(x, y) \notin S$.

Note that the support for the distribution of $\tau_\Delta(x)$ is contained within a ball of radius

$$\sqrt{R^2 + \Delta^2},$$

because $\tau_\Delta : x \mapsto (x, \Delta \delta_x)$.

Therefore, we can apply corollary in [8] and Theorem 5 provided that there are non misclassified training points with discrete probability. Note that the support for the distribution of $\tau_\Delta(x)$ is contained within a ball of radius $\sqrt{R^2 + \Delta^2}$. The theorem follows. $\blacksquare$

As shown in Theorem 2.3, $\varepsilon(\ell, d, \delta)$ is monotonically increasing with respect to d for fixed ℓ and δ. Besides, d depends on a target margin and the amount of the slack variables and the surplus variables. Finally, the generalization error is given in terms of a norm of the slack variables and the surplus variables, which implies that the quantity of $\|\boldsymbol{\xi}^-\|_2$ and $\left\|\frac{1}{\boldsymbol{\xi}^+ + 1}\right\|_2$ should be minimized in order to reduce the generalization error.

III. Total Margin Algorithm

A. formulation

In order to minimize the slack vector and to maximize the surplus variable vector, we formulate the following optimization problem (T):

$$\min_{w,w_0,\xi^-,\xi^+} \quad \langle w \cdot w \rangle + C_1 \sum_{i=1}^{\ell} \xi_i^- - C_2 \sum_{i=1}^{\ell} \xi_i^+ \quad (T)$$

$$\text{subject to} \quad y_i(\langle w \cdot x_i \rangle + w_0) \geq 1 - \xi_i^- + \xi_i^+,$$
$$\xi_i^- \geq 0, \ \xi_i^+ \geq 0, \ i=1,\ldots,\ell,$$

where C_1 and C_2 are chosen in such a way that $C_1 > C_2$.

Note $C_1 > C_2$ that ensures that at least one of ξ_i^- and ξ_i^+ becomes zero. First, we investigate the dual to the primal problem (T) making the total margin algorithm. The Lagrangian function for the problem (T) is

$$L(w, w_0, \xi^-, \xi^+, \alpha, \beta, \gamma)$$
$$= \frac{1}{2}\langle w \cdot w \rangle + C_1 \sum_{i=1}^{\ell} \xi_i^- - C_2 \sum_{i=1}^{\ell} \xi_i^+$$
$$- \sum_{i=1}^{\ell} \alpha_i \left[y_i(\langle w \cdot x_i \rangle + w_0) - 1 + \xi_i^- - \xi_i^+ \right]$$
$$- \sum_{i=1}^{\ell} \beta_i \xi_i^- - \sum_{i=1}^{\ell} \gamma_i \xi_i^+,$$

where $\alpha_i \geq 0$, $\beta_i \geq 0$ and $\gamma_i \geq 0$.

To derive the dual problem to the problem (T), differentiating the Lagrangian function with respect to w, w_0, ξ^- and ξ^+ yields the following conditions:

$$\frac{\partial L(w,w_0,\xi^-,\xi^+,\alpha,\beta,\gamma)}{\partial w} = w - \sum_{i=1}^{\ell} \alpha_i y_i x_i = \mathbf{0},$$

$$\frac{\partial L(w,w_0,\xi^-,\xi^+,\alpha,\beta,\gamma)}{\partial \xi_i^-} = C_1 - \alpha_i - \beta_i = 0,$$

$$\frac{\partial L(w,w_0,\xi^-,\xi^+,\alpha,\beta,\gamma)}{\partial \xi_i^+} = -C_2 + \alpha_i - \gamma_i = 0,$$

$$\frac{\partial L(w,w_0,\xi^-,\xi^+,\alpha,\beta,\gamma)}{\partial w_0} = \sum_{i=1}^{\ell} \alpha_i y_i = 0.$$

Substituting the above stationary conditions into the Lagrangian function L and using kernel representation, we obtain the following dual optimization problem:

$$\max_{\alpha} \quad \sum_{i=1}^{\ell} \alpha_i - \frac{1}{2} \sum_{i,j=1}^{\ell} y_i y_j \alpha_i \alpha_j K(x_i, x_j) \quad (T_D)$$

$$\text{subject to} \quad \sum_{i=1}^{\ell} y_i \alpha_i = 0,$$
$$C_2 \leq \alpha_i \leq C_1, \ i=1,\ldots,\ell,$$

where $K(x_i, x_j) = \langle \Phi(x_i) \cdot \Phi(x_j) \rangle$, Φ is a map from the original input space into a high dimensional feature space.

As typical kernel functions, there are Gaussian function and p-dimensional polynomial function:

$$K(x,y) = \exp\left(-\frac{\|x-y\|^2}{\sigma^2}\right),$$

$$K(x,y) = (\langle x \cdot y \rangle + 1)^p.$$

Later, Gaussian function will be used as kernel in our numerical studies of this paper.

Now, we compute a bias w_0. Let α^* be the optimal solution to the problem (T_D). Let n_+ be the number of x_j with $C_2 < \alpha_j^* < C_1$ and $y_j = +1$, and let n_- be the number of x_j with $C_2 < \alpha_j^* < C_1$ and $y_j = -1$, respectively. From the Karush-Kuhn-Tucker complementarity conditions, if $C_2 < \alpha_i^* < C_1$, then $\beta_i > 0$ and $\gamma_i > 0$. This implies that $\xi_i^- = \xi_i^+ = 0$. Then,

$$w_0^* = \frac{1}{n_+ + n_-}\left((n_+ - n_-) - \sum_{j=1}^{n_+ + n_-}\sum_{i=1}^{\ell} y_j \alpha_i^* K(x_i, x_j)\right).$$

Of course, we let $w_0 = 0$ if $n_+ = n_- = 0$.

In the next section, we compare the soft margin algorithm and the total margin algorithm for several values of C_1 and C_2. In terms of kernel, the dual 1-norm soft margin algorithm (S_D) is used to the primal problem (S) introduced in Section 1:

$$\max_{\alpha} \quad \sum_{i=1}^{\ell}\alpha_i - \frac{1}{2}\sum_{i,j=1}^{\ell} y_i y_j \alpha_i \alpha_j K(x_i, x_j) \quad (S_D)$$

$$\text{subject to} \quad \sum_{i=1}^{\ell} y_i \alpha_i = 0,$$
$$0 \leq \alpha_i \leq C, \ i=1,\ldots,\ell.$$

B. Numerical Example

In this subsection, we provide results of our numerical studies, and compare the existing soft margin algorithm with the total margin algorithm. We adopt 'train-and-test' method which usually used classification problem. Here, we perform the data using the Gaussian kernel with $\sigma = 1.0$ case in the several penalty parameters.

The first data set is the liver-disorders data set from BUPA Medical Research Ltd. The data set includes 11 numeric valued independent variables and 345 instance with only male patients. The second data set is Cleveland heart disease database and the source is Cleveland Clinic Foundation. The heart disease database includes 13 numeric valued independent variables and 303 observations. In order to simulation, the training set is composed by 70%, the remaining 30% are used for testing purposes each data sets. After performing 100 times of the process, two models are compared misclassification rate. The result tables are shown as following:

In our numerical studies, the existing soft margin algorithm and the newly proposed total margin algorithm are examined using value of misclassification rate. It is shown that results of

TABLE I

THE COMPARISON WITH MISCLASSIFICATION RATE BETWEEN SOFT MARGIN AND TOTAL MARGIN FOR GAUSSIAN KERNEL WITH LIVER-DISORDER DATA

	Gaussian kernel		
	Soft Margin	Total margin	
$C_1 = 1.0$	34.62	$C_2 = 0.05$	34.19
		$C_2 = 0.10$	**33.87**
		$C_2 = 0.50$	34.40
$C_1 = 5.0$	36.54	$C_2 = 0.10$	36.43
		$C_2 = 0.50$	35.36
		$C_2 = 1.00$	**34.40**
$C_1 = 10$	36.32	$C_2 = 0.10$	36.22
		$C_2 = 0.50$	36.00
		$C_2 = 1.00$	**34.94**

TABLE II

THE COMPARISON WITH MISCLASSIFICATION RATE BETWEEN SOFT MARGIN AND TOTAL MARGIN FOR GAUSSIAN KERNEL WITH CLEVELAND HEART-DISEASE DATA

	Gaussian kernel		
	Soft Margin	Total margin	
$C_1 = 1.0$	20.00	$C_2 = 0.05$	20.00
		$C_2 = 0.10$	19.56
		$C_2 = 0.50$	**19.23**
$C_1 = 5.0$	21.21	$C_2 = 0.10$	21.10
		$C_2 = 0.50$	**20.22**
		$C_2 = 1.00$	20.99
$C_1 = 10$	21.32	$C_2 = 0.10$	21.32
		$C_2 = 0.50$	**19.87**
		$C_2 = 1.00$	21.10

the total margin algorithm obtained lower values of misclassification rate mostly. Tables are indicated that the total margin algorithm is improved than soft margin classifier model in testing set.

From this simulation, we can find newly proposed method is improved the classification rate for the existing soft margin classifier. Therefore, we were able to find that the total margin algorithm is more effective than the soft margin algorithm.

IV. CONCLUSION

In this paper, we have proposed the total margin algorithm which considers the distance between all data points and separating hyperplane. And we have illustrated and proven a generalization error bound of the total margin algorithm for linear classifiers. The novelty with this approach is to be considered not only slack variables of the soft margin but also surplus variables of the total margin simultaneously. By using this technique we are able to improve the existing soft margin algorithm. This method has extended the existing support vector machine algorithms.

In the numerical studies, when the soft margin algorithm and the total margin algorithm are compared in a variety values of C_1 and C_2, generally the total margin algorithm was found to be good performance to the soft margin algorithm. We also found that the generalization error bound for the total margin can be reduced by minimizing slack variables and maximizing surplus variables.

Therefore, it is expected that the total margin algorithm can be more effective than the soft margin algorithm by the controlling slack and surplus variables.

REFERENCES

[1] N. Alon, S. Ben-David, N. Cesa-Bianchi, and D. Haussler, Scale-Sensitive Dimensions, Uniform Convergence, and Learnability *Journal of the ACM*, **44**, 615-631, 1997.
[2] M. Anthony, Probabilistic Analysis of Learning for Artificial Neural Networks: The PAC Model and its Variants, *Neural Computing Surveys*, **1**, 1-47, 1997.
[3] P. Bartlett and J. Shawe-Taylor, Generalization performance of Support Vector Machines an Other Pattern Classifiers, In Schölkopf, B., Burges, C. J. C., and Smola, A. J. editors, *Advances in Kernel Methods - Support Vector Learning*, 43-54, MIT Press, 1999.
[4] D.P. Bertsekas, *Nonlinear Programming* Belmont, MA, Athena Scientific, 1995.
[5] A. Blumer, A. Ehrenfeucht, D. Haussler, and M.K. Warmuth, Learnability and the Vapnik-Chervonenkis Dimension. *Journal of the ACM*, **36**, 929-965, 1989.
[6] V. Cherkassky, and F. Mulier, *Learning from Data Concepts, Theory, and Methods*. John Wiley & Sons, INC., New York, (1998).
[7] C. Cortes, *Prediction of Generalization Ability in Learning Systems*, PhD Thesis, University of Rochester,(1995).
[8] N. Cristianini and J. Shawe-Taylor, *An Introduction to Support Vector Machines and Other Kernel-based Learning Methods*, Cambridge University Press, 2000.
[9] Y. Freund, and R.E. Schapire, Large margin classification using the perceptron algorithm, In Shavlik, J. editor *Machine Learning: Proceedings of the Fifteenth International Conference*, Morgan Kaufmann, (1998).
[10] L. Gurvits, A Note on a Scale-Sensitive Dimension of Linear Bounded Functionals in Banach Spaces, In *Proceedings of Algorithmic LearningTheory*, ALT-97,(1997).
[11] M.J. Kearns, and U.V. Vazirani, *An Introduction to Computational Learning Theory*, MIT Press,(1995).
[12] A.B. Novikoff, On the Convergence Proofs on Perceptrons, In *Symposium on the Mathematical Theory of Automata*, **12**, 615-622, Polytechnic Institute of Brooklyn, (1962).
[13] B.D. Ripley, *Pattern Recognition and NeuralNetworks*, Cambridge University Press, 1996.
[14] R. Schapire, Y. Freund, P. Bartlett, and W. Sun Lee, Boosting the Margin: A New Explanation for the Effectiveness of Voting methods, *Annals Statistics*, **26**, 1651-1686, 1998.
[15] J. Shawe-Taylor, P.L. Bartlett, R.C. Williamson, and M. Anthony, Structural Risk Minimization over Data-Dependent Hierarchies, *IEEE Transactions on Information Theory*, **44**, 1926-1940, 1998.
[16] J. Shawe-Taylor and N. Cristianini, On the Generalisation of Soft Margin Algorithms, *NeuroCOLT2 Technical Report Series*, 2000.
[17] L.G. Valiant, A Theory of the Learnable, *Communications of the Association for Computing Machinery*, **27**, 1134-1142, 1984.
[18] V.N. Vapnik, *Estimation of Dependences Based on Empirical Data [in Russian].*, Moscow, Nauka,(English translation: Springer Verlag, New York, 1982), 1979.
[19] V.N. Vapnik, *Statistical Learning Theory* John Wiley & Sons, New York, 1998.
[20] V.N. Vapnik, *The Nature of Statistical Learning Theory.(2nd ed.)*, Springer Verlag, New York, 1999.
[21] V.N. Vapnik, and A.Y. Chervonenkis, A Note on One Class of Perceptrons, *Automation and Remote Control*, **25**, 1964.
[22] V.N. Vapnik, and A.Y. Chervonenkis, Uniform Convergence of the Frequencies of Occurence of Events to their Probabilities, *Dokl. Akad. Nauk. SSSR*, **181**, 915-918, 1968

Comparison of L1 and L2 Support Vector Machines

Yoshiaki Koshiba
Graduate School of Science and Technology
Kobe University
Rokkodai, Nada, Kobe, Japan
Email: koshiba@chevrolet.eedept.kobe-u.ac.jp

Shigeo Abe
Graduate School of Science and Technology
Kobe University
Rokkodai, Nada, Kobe, Japan
Email: abe@eedept.kobe-u.ac.jp

Abstract— In this paper, we compare L1 and L2 support vector machines from the standpoint of training time and the generalization ability. The generalization ability for seven benchmark data sets are almost the same but training time of L1-SVMs is usually shorter than that of L2-SVMs. We also compare the effect of the approximate KKT (Karush-Kuhn-Tucker) conditions using the bias term and the exact KKT conditions. According to the computer experiments, since the approximate KKT conditions give a conservative estimate of violating variables, training time using the approximate KKT conditions is usually shorter.

I. INTRODUCTION

Support vector machines [1], [2], are widely used for pattern classification problems. The advantages of SVMs over conventional methods are high generalization ability especially when the number of training data is small, adaptability to various classification problems by changing kernel functions, and global optimal solution obtained by quadratic programming.

Support vector machines with linear sum of slack variables, which are commonly used, are called L1-SVMs, and SVMs with the square sum of slack variables are called L2-SVMs. Characteristics of both L1- and L2-SVMs have been studied analytically [3], [4], [5], [6], [7]. For instance, dependence of the solutions on the margin parameter C [3] and non-uniqueness of solutions [6], [7] are studied.

A support vector machine is trained by solving the associated dual problem by the quadratic programming technique. But since the number of variables is the number of training data, training time becomes very long for the large number of training data. To overcome this problem, the decomposition technique [9], [10] is usually used. The training is continued until the solution satisfies the Karush-Kuhn-Tucker (KKT) complementarity condition. But since the KKT condition includes a primal variable, detection of the variables that violate the KKT condition is inexact during training. To overcome this problem, in [11], the exact KKT condition is derived for the SMO (Sequential Minimal Optimization) technique.

In this paper, first we extend the exact KKT condition for the SMO to general training of L1- and L2-SVMs. Then by computer experiments, we compare L1- and L2-SVMs from the standpoint of training time and the generalization ability. Since the Hessian matrix of L2-SVMs is positive definite, the associated optimization problem is considered to be more computationally stable than that of L1-SVMs. Using some benchmark data sets, we show that this does not hold for most cases. Then, we compare the training time using the approximate and exact KKT conditions.

This paper is organized as follows. In Section II, we explain L1-SVMs and L2-SVMs. In Section III, we discuss the approximate and exact KKT conditions. Then, in Section IV, we discuss training of SVMs by decomposition techniques, and in Section V, we compare performance of L1- and L2-SVMs by computer simulations.

II. SUPPORT VECTOR MACHINES

In this section, we describe the theory of L1-SVMs and L2-SVMs for two-class problems.

A. L1 Support Vector Machines

Let training datum be $\mathbf{x}_i$ ($i = 1, ..., M$) and its label be $y_i = 1$ if $\mathbf{x}_i$ belongs to Class 1, and $y_i = -1$ if Class 2. In SVMs, to enhance linear separability, the input space is mapped into a high dimensional feature space using the mapping function $\mathbf{g}(\mathbf{x})$.

To obtain the optimal separating hyperplane of the L1-SVM in the feature space, we consider the following optimization problem:

$$\begin{aligned}\text{minimize} \quad & \frac{1}{2} \| \mathbf{w} \|^2 + C \sum_{i=1}^{M} \xi_i, \\ \text{subject to} \quad & y_i(\mathbf{w}^t \mathbf{g}(\mathbf{x}_i) + b) \geq 1 - \xi_i, \\ \text{for} \quad & i = 1, ..., M, \end{aligned} \quad (1)$$

where $\mathbf{w}$ is a weight vector, C is the margin parameter that determines the tradeoff between the maximization of the margin and the minimization of the classification error, ξ_i ($i = 1, ..., M$) are the nonnegative slack variables and b is a bias term. Introducing the Lagrange multipliers α_i, we obtain the following dual problem:

maximize

$$Q(\alpha) = \sum_{i=1}^{M} \alpha_i - \frac{1}{2} \sum_{i,j=1}^{M} \alpha_i \alpha_j y_i y_j \mathbf{g}(\mathbf{x}_i)^t \mathbf{g}(\mathbf{x}_j),$$

$$\text{subject to} \quad \sum_{i=1}^{M} y_i \alpha_i = 0, \quad 0 \le \alpha_i \le C. \tag{2}$$

We use the mapping function that satisfies

$$H(\mathbf{x}, \mathbf{x}') = \mathbf{g}(\mathbf{x})^t \mathbf{g}(\mathbf{x}'), \tag{3}$$

where $H(\mathbf{x}, \mathbf{x}')$ is a kernel function. By this selection, we need not treat the variables in the feature space explicitly.

Solving the above dual problem, we obtain the decision function:

$$D(\mathbf{x}) = \sum_{i=1}^{M} \alpha_i^* y_i H(\mathbf{x}_i, \mathbf{x}) + b^*, \tag{4}$$

where an asterisk denotes the optimal solution.

B. L2 Support Vector Machines

L2-SVMs use the square sum of the slack variables ξ_i in the objective function instead of the linear sum of the slack variables. Thus we consider optimization problem as follows:

$$\begin{aligned}
\text{minimize} \quad & \frac{1}{2}\|\mathbf{w}\|^2 + \frac{C}{2}\sum_{i=1}^{M}\xi_i^2, \\
\text{subject to} \quad & y_i(\mathbf{w}^t \mathbf{x}_i + b) \ge 1 - \xi_i, \\
\text{for} \quad & i = 1, ..., M.
\end{aligned} \tag{5}$$

Introducing the Lagrange multipliers α_i, we obtain the dual problem:

maximize

$$Q(\alpha) = \sum_{i=1}^{M}\alpha_i - \frac{1}{2}\sum_{i,j=1}^{M} y_i y_j \alpha_i \alpha_j \Big(H(\mathbf{x}_i, \mathbf{x}_j) + \frac{\delta_{ij}}{C}\Big) \tag{6}$$

subject to

$$\sum_{i=1}^{M} y_i \alpha_i = 0, \quad \alpha_i \ge 0 \quad \text{for} \quad i = 1, ..., M, \tag{7}$$

where δ_{ij} is Kronecker's delta function, in which $\delta_{ij} = 1$ for $i = j$ and 0, otherwise. Since $1/C$ is added to the diagonal elements of the Hessian matrix H, the matrix becomes positive define. Therefore, the associated optimization problem is more computationally stable than the L1-SVMs, in which the Hessian matrix is positive semi-definite [7].

III. STOPPING CRITERIA

In this section, we describe the stopping criteria of L1 and L2 dual problems. Since the optimal solution must satisfy Karush-Kuhn-Tucker (KKT) complementarity condition, during training we check the condition, and if all training data satisfy the condition, we terminate training. But since the KKT condition of the dual problem includes the primal variable, the detection of violation becomes inexact. Thus the exact KKT condition is derived for the SMO (Sequential Minimal Optimization) technique [11]. In the following we discuss the approximate method and the exact method, which is an extension of [11].

A. Approximate KKT Conditions

In L1-SVMs, the KKT condition is given by

$$\alpha_i^*(y_i(\mathbf{w}^{*t}\mathbf{x}_i + b^*) - 1 + \xi_i^*) = 0, \tag{8}$$
$$b_i^* \xi_i^* = (C - \alpha_i^*)\xi_i^* = 0. \tag{9}$$

Thus, there are three cases as follows:

1) $\alpha_i^* = 0$. Then $\xi_i^* = 0$. Therefore, $\mathbf{x}_i$ is correctly classified.
2) $0 < \alpha_i^* < C$. Then $y_i(\mathbf{w}^{*t}\mathbf{x}_i + b^*) - 1 + \xi_i^* = 0$ and $\xi_i^* = 0$. Thus, $y_i(\mathbf{w}^* \mathbf{x}_i + b^*) = 1$ and $\mathbf{x}_i$ is a support vector.
3) $\alpha_i^* = C$. Then $y_i(\mathbf{w}^{*t}\mathbf{x}_i + b^*) - 1 + \xi_i^* = 0$ and $\xi_i^* \ge 0$. Therefore $\mathbf{x}_i$ is a bounded support vector and if $0 \le \xi_i^* < 1$, $\mathbf{x}_i$ is correctly classified, and if $\xi_i^* \ge 1$, $\mathbf{x}_i$ is misclassified.

While, in L2-SVMs, the KKT condition is given by

$$y_i\Bigg(\sum_{j=1}^{M}\alpha_j^* y_j \Big(H(\mathbf{x}_j, \mathbf{x}_i) + \frac{\delta_{ij}}{C}\Big) + b^*\Bigg) - 1 = 0. \tag{10}$$

In the above KKT conditions, since b, which is calculated exactly only after the optimal solution is obtained, is included, the violation check becomes inexact.

B. Exact KKT Conditions

To derive the exact KKT condition [11], we redefine the dual objective function of the L1-SVM given by (6) and (7), introducing the Lagrange multipliers δ_i, μ_i, and β:

$$\begin{aligned}
Q(\alpha, \delta, \mu, \beta) = & \sum_{i=1}^{M}\alpha_i - \frac{1}{2}\sum_{i,j=1}^{M}\alpha_i\alpha_j y_i y_j H(\mathbf{x}_i, \mathbf{x}_j) \\
& + \sum_{i=1}^{M}\delta_i\alpha_i - \sum_{i=1}^{M}\mu_i(\alpha_i - C) \\
& + \beta\sum_{i=1}^{M}\alpha_i y_i.
\end{aligned} \tag{11}$$

Thus, we obtain the KKT conditions as follows.

$$\frac{\partial Q}{\partial \alpha_i} = (F_i + \beta)y_i + \delta_i - \mu_i = 0, \tag{12}$$
$$\delta_i \alpha_i = 0, \quad \delta_i \ge 0, \tag{13}$$
$$\mu_i(\alpha_i - C) = 0, \quad \mu_i \ge 0, \quad \text{for} \quad i = 1, ..., M, \tag{14}$$

where
$$F_i = y_i - \sum_{j=1}^{M} y_j \alpha_j H(\mathbf{x}_i, \mathbf{x}_j). \quad (15)$$

These KKT conditions are reduced to the three cases as follows:

1) For $\alpha_i = 0$,
$$(F_i + \beta)y_i \leq 0. \quad (16)$$

2) For $0 < \alpha_i < C$,
$$(F_i + \beta)y_i = 0. \quad (17)$$

3) For $\alpha_i = C$,
$$(F_i + \beta)y_i \geq 0. \quad (18)$$

These three equations are further simplified to the following two cases.

1) For $i \in I_{up}$,
$$(F_i + \beta) \leq 0, \quad (19)$$

where
$$\begin{aligned}
I_{up} &= I_0 \cup I_1 \cup I_2, \\
I_0 &= \{i | 0 < \alpha_i < C\}, \\
I_1 &= \{i | y_i = 1, \alpha_i = 0\}, \\
I_2 &= \{i | y_i = -1, \alpha_i = C\}. \quad (20)
\end{aligned}$$

2) For $i \in I_{down}$
$$(F_i + \beta) \geq 0, \quad (21)$$

where
$$\begin{aligned}
I_{down} &= I_0 \cup I_3 \cup I_4, \\
I_3 &= \{i | y_i = 1, \alpha_i = C\}, \\
I_4 &= \{i | y_i = -1, \alpha_i = 0\}. \quad (22)
\end{aligned}$$

If for any $i \in I_{up}$ and $j \in I_{down}$ there exists β that satisfies
$$-F_j \leq \beta \leq -F_i, \quad (23)$$

the KKT conditions for the dual problem are satisfied. We define
$$F_{max} = \max_{j \in I_{down}} -F_j, \quad F_{min} = \min_{i \in I_{up}} -F_i. \quad (24)$$

Then, since I_0 is included in both I_{up} and I_{down}, (23) is equivalent to
$$F_{max} = F_{min} = \beta. \quad (25)$$

If this equation is satisfied, the solution is optimal. Therefore, we can use this as a stopping criterion for training. We loose (25) to soften a computational burden as follows,
$$F_{min} \geq F_{max} - \tau, \quad (26)$$

where τ is a positive tolerance parameter. Introducing parameter τ, let the τ-violating set V_{KKT} be

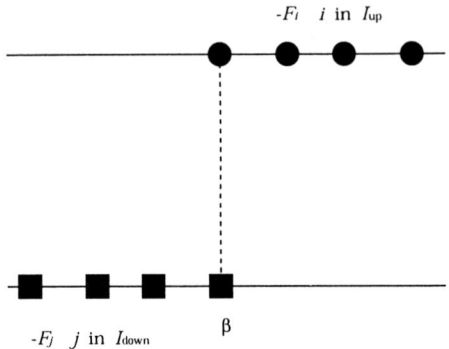

Fig. 1. KKT Conditions Satisfied

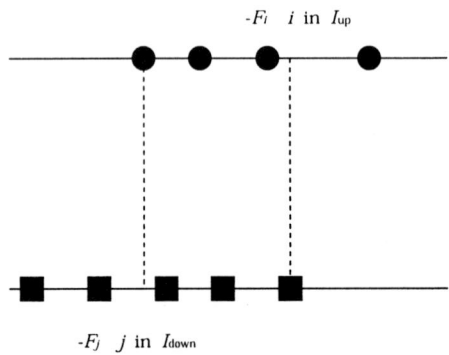

Fig. 2. KKT Conditions Violated

$$\begin{aligned}
V_{KKT} = \{\mathbf{x}_i | F_{min} + \tau < -F_i \text{ for } i \in I_{down}, \\
F_{max} - \tau > -F_i \text{ for } i \in I_{up}\}. \quad (27)
\end{aligned}$$

Fig. 1 shows a case where the KKT conditions are satisfied. The filled circles show $-F_i$ ($i \in I_{up}$) and the filled rectangles show $-F_j$ ($j \in I_{down}$). Fig. 2 shows a case where the KKT conditions are not satisfied. The data between the two dotted lines including the data on the lines violate the KKT conditions.

For L2-SVMs instead of (15), the following equation is obtained:
$$F_i = y_i - \sum_{j=1}^{M} y_j \alpha_j (H(\mathbf{x}_i, \mathbf{x}_j) + \delta_{ij}/C). \quad (28)$$

And furthermore, I_{up} and I_{down} are defined by
$$I_{up} = I_0 \cup I_1, \quad I_{down} = I_0 \cup I_4. \quad (29)$$

The other calculation is similar to those of L1-SVMs.

IV. DECOMPOSITION TECHNIQUE

Since the number of variables of the dual problem is the number of training data, it becomes difficult to solve the problem for a large number of training data. To overcome this problem decomposition techniques are used [9], [10]. Here, we use variable size chunking discussed in [9]. We divided the training data into the working set W and the fixed set B.

We solve the subproblem for α_i associated with the data in W, fixing the variables associated with the data in B. After the solution of the subprogram is obtained, we delete the variables with non-zero α_i, from W, that satisfy the KKT condition and add F points from B, where F is a fixed integer, that do not satisfy the KKT condition. Then we solve the subproblem. We iterate this procedure until V_{KKT} is empty.

For the approximate KKT condition, we randomly select F points that violate the KKT condition. For the exact KKT condition, first we sort the sets I_{up} and I_{down} in the descending order of KKT violations. Then we alternately select F points from the top of I_{up} and I_{down}.

V. Simulation Experiments

We evaluated the performance of L1-SVMs and L2-SVMs using the iris data [12], [13], the numeral data [14], the thyroid data [15], the blood cell data [16], and hiragana data [17]. Specifications of these data are shown in TABLE I; the numbers of inputs, classes, training data, and test data. Since these benchmark data sets are multiclass problems, we used one-against-all fuzzy SVMs [8] to resolve unclassifiable regions. We set $\tau = 0.01$ for the exact KKT condition. We use the following dot product and polynomial kernels:

Dot product kernels : $\quad H(\mathbf{x}, \mathbf{x}') = \mathbf{x}^t \mathbf{x}',\quad$ (30)

Polynomial kernels : $\quad H(\mathbf{x}, \mathbf{x}') = (\mathbf{x}^t \mathbf{x}' + 1)^d.\quad$ (31)

TABLE I
BENCHMARK DATA SPECIFICATION

Data	Inputs	Classes	Training data	Test data
Iris	4	3	75	75
Numeral	12	10	810	820
Thyroid	21	3	3772	3428
Blood cell	13	12	3097	3100
Hiragana-50	50	39	4610	4610
Hiragana-105	105	38	8375	8356
Hiragana-13	13	38	8375	8356

For dot product kernels, the maximum rank of the Hessian matrix for L1-SVMs is the number of input variables plus 1 [7]. Thus, if the working set size exceeds this value, the Hessian matrix for L1-SVMs is positive semi-definite. But the Hessian matrix for L2-SVMs is always positive definite. Thus, for dot product kernels, training of L2-SVMs should be faster than that of L1-SVMs.

The dual problem was solved by combining the primal-dual interior-point method [18] with the variable chunking technique. We ran the c program on a Pentium III 1 GHz PC.

TABLE II shows the results of L1-SVMs and L2-SVMs using the approximate KKT condition. Here, we set $F = 50$. Namely, we added 50 data after the subproblem was solved. From the table, except for the thyroid data, training of the L2-SVM with dot product kernels is slower than that of the L1-SVM with dot product kernels. And for polynomial kernels, in most cases, training of the L1-SVM is faster.

The recognition rates of the test data by the L2-SVM are higher than those by the L1-SVM for 12 cases out of 26. But those by the L1-SVM are higher for 6 cases. Thus the L2-SVM performed better than the L1-SVM, but the difference of the recognition rate is small.

TABLE III shows the results when the exact KKT condition was used. Similar to the approximate KKT condition, in most cases, training time of L1-SVM is shorter than that of the L2-SVM. The recognition rates of the test data by the L2-SVM tend to be better than those by the L1-SVM, but the difference of the recognition rate is small.

Comparing TABLES II and III, training time by the exact KKT condition was not always shorter than that by the approximate KKT condition. But the exact KKT condition for L1-SVMs with dot product kernels performed better than the approximate KKT condition for the thyroid, blood cell, and hiragana-13 data.

To investigate why the exact KKT condition is not always better than the approximate KKT condition, we study the case for the blood cell data with $d = 3$. Fig. 3 shows training time of the approximate and exact KKT conditions for the change of F, namely the number of variables added to the working set W. For the approximate KKT condition, training time decreases as the number of variables added to the working set is increased. But for the exact KKT condition, the shortest training time is around $F = 25$. By this characteristics the selection of the optimum F is difficult for the exact KKT condition.

Fig. 4 shows the working set sizes of the approximate and exact KKT conditions against the number of iterations, when Class 2 is separated from the remaining classes. From the figure, the working set size of the exact KKT condition is larger than that of the approximate KKT condition after the second iteration. This means that the approximate KKT condition estimates the violating variables conservatively. Thus, with the smaller working set size, training by the approximate KKT condition is faster.

VI. Conclusions

In this paper, we evaluated training time and the generalization ability of L1-SVMs and L2-SVMs. As a result of the experiment, training of L2-SVMs was not always faster than that of L1-SVMs, and the difference of the generalization abilities between the two is small. Further, we compared the training time using the exact KKT condition and the approximate KKT conditions, and showed that training by

TABLE II
PERFORMANCE OF L1-SVM AND L2-SVM USING THE APPROXIMATE KKT CONDITION

Data	Kernel	L1-SVM (%)	Time (s)	L2-SVM (%)	Time (s)
Iris (C=5000)	Dot	96.00 (97.33)	**0.06**	**97.33** (98.67)	0.07
	$d=2$	94.67 (100)	0.03	94.67 (100)	0.03
	$d=3$	94.67 (100)	0.03	94.67 (100)	0.03
Numeral (C=2000)	Dot	99.27 (100)	**0.89**	**99.39** (100)	1.15
	$d=2$	99.39 (100)	**0.87**	99.39 (100)	1.11
	$d=3$	99.51 (100)	**0.88**	99.51 (100)	1.10
	$d=4$	99.51 (100)	**0.94**	99.51 (100)	1.15
Thyroid (C=10000)	Dot	**95.82** (96.58)	12234	94.22 (94.67)	**3880**
	$d=2$	**97.14** (98.75)	2951	96.47 (98.38)	**888**
	$d=3$	**97.49** (99.31)	59	97.26 (99.10)	326
	$d=4$	**97.43** (99.34)	38	97.35 (99.23)	152
Blood cell (C=2000)	Dot	87.23 (91.02)	**925**	**87.87** (90.64)	1094
	$d=2$	92.97 (96.67)	35	**93.48** (97.05)	76
	$d=3$	93.19 (98.22)	34	**93.71** (98.55)	57
	$d=4$	92.68 (98.93)	32	**93.42** (99.00)	47
Hiragana-50 (C=5000)	Dot	93.95 (97.81)	**302**	**94.12** (98.48)	474
	$d=2$	99.24 (100)	**191**	99.24 (100)	233
	$d=3$	**99.31** (100)	**205**	99.26 (100)	234
	$d=4$	**99.33** (100)	**195**	99.28 (100)	255
Hiragana-105 (C=2000)	Dot	97.03 (97.50)	**1951**	**97.45** (98.08)	4424
	$d=2$	100 (100)	**903**	100 (100)	1066
	$d=3$	100 (100)	**964**	100 (100)	1102
Hiragana-13 (C=1000)	Dot	91.92 (93.77)	**1094**	**96.47** (97.41)	1518
	$d=2$	98.56 (98.96)	1205	**98.72** (99.26)	**948**
	$d=3$	98.74 (99.12)	**586**	**98.84** (99.26)	998
	$d=4$	98.71 (99.04)	**724**	**98.77** (99.13)	1164

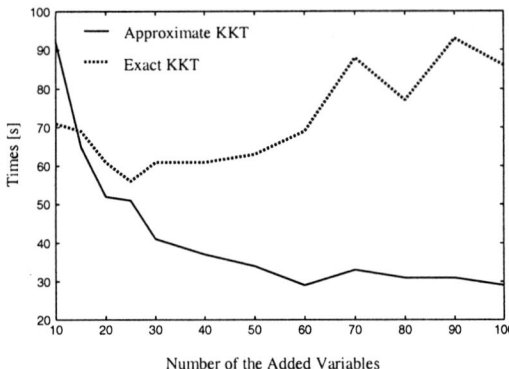

Fig. 3. Relationship between the Number of Variables Added and Training Time

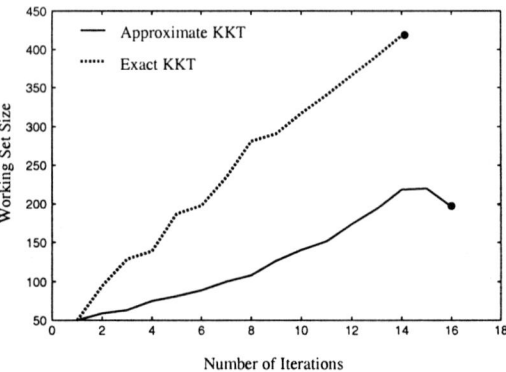

Fig. 4. Relationship between the Working Set Size and Number of Iterations

TABLE III
PERFORMANCE OF L1-SVM AND L2-SVM USING THE EXACT KKT CONDITION

Data	Kernel	L1-SVM (%)	Time (s)	L2-SVM (%)	Time (s)
Iris (C=5000)	Dot	96.00 (97.33)	0.08	**97.33** (98.67)	0.08
	$d=2$	94.67 (100)	**0.03**	94.67 (100)	0.05
	$d=3$	94.67 (100)	**0.03**	94.67 (100)	0.05
Numeral (C=2000)	Dot	99.27 (100)	**1.38**	**99.39** (100)	1.68
	$d=2$	99.39 (100)	**1.44**	99.39 (100)	2.10
	$d=3$	99.51 (100)	**1.69**	99.51 (100)	2.33
	$d=4$	99.51 (100)	**1.75**	99.51 (100)	2.27
Thyroid (C=10000)	Dot	**95.74** (97.24)	154	94.19 (94.67)	48200
	$d=2$	**97.14** (98.81)	113	96.44 (98.33)	1529
	$d=3$	**97.52** (99.26)	106	97.08 (99.07)	309
	$d=4$	**97.46** (99.31)	73	97.32 (99.23)	122
Blood cell (C=2000)	Dot	87.89 (91.51)	**272**	**88.45** (91.12)	3270
	$d=2$	93.00 (96.74)	80	**93.48** (97.06)	91
	$d=3$	93.26 (98.22)	63	**93.71** (98.55)	64
	$d=4$	92.65 (98.93)	51	**93.42** (99.00)	63
Hiragana-50 (C=5000)	Dot	93.99 (97.81)	**314**	**94.12** (98.46)	539
	$d=2$	99.24 (100)	**203**	99.24 (100)	224
	$d=3$	**99.31** (100)	**208**	99.26 (100)	233
	$d=4$	**99.33** (100)	**213**	99.28 (100)	240
Hiragana-105 (C=2000)	Dot	97.04 (97.55)	**2112**	**97.47** (98.10)	4353
	$d=2$	100 (100)	**868**	100 (100)	961
	$d=3$	100 (100)	**868**	100 (100)	979
Hiragana-13 (C=1000)	Dot	94.57 (95.68)	**798**	**96.72** (97.39)	1900
	$d=2$	98.50 (98.93)	687	**98.73** (99.24)	1045
	$d=3$	98.72 (99.08)	**708**	**98.86** (99.27)	1005
	$d=4$	98.70 (99.01)	**776**	**98.78** (99.13)	1213

the exact KKT condition was not always faster than by the approximate KKT condition.

REFERENCES

[1] V. Vapnik, *Statistical Learning Theory*, John Wiley & Sons, 1998.
[2] V. Cherkassky and F. Mulier, *Learning from Data: Concepts, Theory, and Methods*, John Wiley & Sons, 1998.
[3] M. Pontil and A. Verri, "Properties of Support Vector Machines," *Neural Computation*, Vol. 10, No. 4, pp. 955–974, 1998.
[4] R. Rifkin, M. Pontil, and A. Verri, "A Note on Support Vector Machine Degeneracy," *Proc. 10th International Conference on Algorithmic Learning Theory, (ALT'99). (Lecture Notes in Artificial Intelligence Vol.1720)*, pp. 252–263, 1999.
[5] R. Fernández, "Behavior of the Weights of a Support Vector Machine as a Function of the Regularization Parameter C," *Proc. 8th International Conference on Artificial Neural Networks (ICANN'98)*, Vol. 2, pp. 917–922, 1998.
[6] C. J. C. Burges and D. J. Crisp, "Uniqueness of the SVM Solution," In S. A. Solla, T. K. Leen, and K.-R. Müller, editors, *Advances in Neural Information Processing Systems 12*, pp. 223–229, MIT Press, 2000.
[7] S. Abe, "Analysis of Support Vector Machines," *Neural Networks for Signal Processing XII—Proc. 2002 IEEE Signal Processing Society Workshop*, pp. 89–98, 2002.
[8] T. Inoue and S. Abe, "Fuzzy Support Vector Machines for Pattern Classification," *Proc. IJCNN'01*, pp. 1449–1454, 2001.
[9] C. Saunders, M. O. Stitson, J. Weston, L. Bottou, B. Schölkopf, and A. Smola, "Support Vector Machine Reference Manual," Technical Report CSD-TR-98-03, Royal Holloway, University of London, London, 1998.
[10] E. Osuna, R. Freund, and F. Girosi, "An Improved Training Algorithm for Support Vector Machines," *Neural Networks for Signal Processing VII—Proceedings of the 1997 IEEE Signal Processing Society Workshop*, pp. 276–285, 1997.

[11] S. S. Keerthi and E. G. Gilbert, "Convergence of a Generalized SMO Algorithm for SVM Classifier Design," *Machine Learning*, Vol. 13, pp. 637–649, 2001.

[12] R. A. Fisher, "The Use of Multiple Measurements in Taxonomic Problems," *Annals of Eugenics*, Vol. 7, pp. 179–188, 1936.

[13] J. C. Bezdek et al., "Will the Real Iris Data Please Stand up?" *IEEE Transactions on Fuzzy Systems*, Vol. 7, No. 3, pp. 368–369, 1999.

[14] H. Takenaga et al., "Input Layer Optimization of Neural Networks by Sensitivity Analysis and Its Application to Recognition of Numerals," *Electrical Engineering in Japan*, Vol. 111, No. 4, pp. 130–138, 1991.

[15] S. M. Weiss and I. Kapouleas, "An Empirical Comparison of Pattern Recognition, Neural Nets, and Machine Learning Classification Methods," *Proc. IJCAI-99, Workshop ML3*, pp. 55–60, 1999.

[16] A. Hashizume, J. Motoike, and R. Yabe, "Fully Automated Blood Cell Differential System and Its Application," *Proc. IUPAC 3rd International Congress on Automation and New Technology in the Clinical Laboratory*, pp. 297–302, Kobe, Japan, 1988.

[17] S. Abe, *Pattern Classification, Neuro-fuzzy Methods and Their Comparison*, Springer-Verlag, London, 2001.

[18] R. J. Vanderbei, "LOQO: An Interior Point Code for Quadratic Programming," Technical Report SOR-94-15, Princeton University, 1998.

Fast linear stationary methods for Automatically Biased Support Vector Machines

D. Lai*, M. Palaniswami+, N. Mani*
*Dept. of Electrical and Computer Systems Engineering
Monash University, Clayton, Vic. 3168, Australia.
+Dept. of Electrical and Electronic Engineering
The University of Melbounre, Vic. 3010, Australia.

Abstract: We present a new training algorithm, which is capable of providing fast training for a new automatically biased SVM. We compare our agorithm to the well-known Sequential Minimal Optimization (SMO) algorithm. We then show that this method allows for the application of acceleration methods which further increases the rates of convergence.

A. INTRODUCTION

In recent years, machine learning has gained increasing attention. Support Vector Machines [5] is a relatively new supervised machine learning formulation. The difference between Support Vector Machines and existing machine learning methods such as Neural Networks (NN) is that instead of working on the traditional Empirical Risk Minimization (ERM) principle, it performs Structural Risk Minimization (SRM). Since, the introduction of SVMs many researchers have applied it to non-linear problems with remarkable results. The formulation is well understood, but practical use for online implementations has not been widespread due to excessive training times. The optimization speed scales with the size of the dataset. Several optimisation techniques have been employed which include methods such as gradient ascent/decent methods[1], Sequential Minimal Optimization(SMO) [6], Successive Over Relaxation(SOR) [7] and so on. Faster optimisation methods suffer from less than optimal solutions and more elegant methods require increased code complexity.

In this paper, we extend our recently proposed automatically biased SVM formulation (ASVM)[8], which eliminates the need to enforce the equality constraint at each step. The formulation allows for a simple matrix representation of the optimization problem. We then employ a modified linear stationary method known as the Jacobi Method. We show how the optimisation speed can be further increased by correctly applying acceleration methods such as the extrapolation method. This paper is divided into the following sections; section B will describe the pattern recognition SVM formulation and the ASVM variant, section C will describe our iterative method and the remaining sections will be left for our experimental results and discussion.

B. SUPPORT VECTOR MACHINE FORMULATION

We describe briefly the standard support vector machine formulation[1] for pattern recognition. We define our training set as

$$\mathbf{D} = \{(\mathbf{x}_1, y_1), (\mathbf{x}_2, y_2)...(\mathbf{x}_s, y_s)\}$$
$$\mathbf{x}_i \in \mathbb{R}^N$$
$$y_i = \{1, -1\}$$
(1.1)

If our training set is not linearly separable, as is the case in most real life applications, we define a non-linear mapping from input space to some higher dimensional feature space, denoted by $\varphi : \Re^N \rightarrow \Re^M$, so that the points in feature space map via, $\mathbf{x}_F : \mathbf{x} \rightarrow \varphi(\mathbf{x})$. In the normal, SVM problem, we then construct a linear discriminant function in feature space so that,

$$f(\mathbf{x}) = \mathbf{w}^T \varphi(\mathbf{x}) + b$$
$$f(\mathbf{x}) > 0 \quad \forall \quad i : y_i = +1$$
$$f(\mathbf{x}) < 0 \quad \forall \quad i : y_i = -1$$
(1.2)

The hyperplane that separates the two classes is the decision surface defined by,

$$\mathbf{w}^T \varphi(\mathbf{x}) + b = 0$$
(1.3)

It turns out that only the points closest to the hyperplane are important, and these points are referred to as Support Vectors. The distance from the hyperplane to a support vector is $\frac{1}{\|\mathbf{w}\|}$ and the distance between the support vectors of one class to the other class is simply $\frac{2}{\|\mathbf{w}\|}$. The task is then to derive the best possible hyperplane which has the maximum possible margin between the classes. The problem is reduced to,

$$\min \tfrac{1}{2} \mathbf{w}^T \mathbf{w}$$
$$\text{subject to: } y_i(\mathbf{w}^T \mathbf{x} + b) \geq 1 \quad \forall i$$
(1.4)

When the separation in feature space is not perfect, we introduce non-negative slack variables, ξ to relax the inequality constraint. We also introduce a new term to the cost function to penalise for misclassification of training points giving us the SVM primal problem,

$$\min \; \tfrac{1}{2} \mathbf{w}^T \mathbf{w} + C\mathbf{1}^T \xi_i$$
$$\text{subject to: } y_i(\mathbf{w}^T \mathbf{x} + b) \geq 1 - \xi_i \quad \forall I \quad (1.5)$$
$$\xi \geq \mathbf{0}$$

The primal problem offers a dual representation, which is found by differentiating the primal Lagrange form and maximizing the dual form,

$$\max_{\alpha} \; L(\alpha) = \mathbf{1}^T \alpha - \tfrac{1}{2} \alpha^T \mathbf{G} \alpha \quad (1.6)$$

subject to the conditions known as the Karush-Kuhn-Tucker (KKT) conditions.

$$0 \leq \alpha \leq \mathbf{1}^T C$$
$$\alpha^T \mathbf{y} = 0 \quad (1.7)$$

where

$$\mathbf{G} \in \mathfrak{R}^{S \times S}$$
$$G_{ij} = y_i y_j \varphi(\mathbf{x}_i)^T \varphi(\mathbf{x}_j)$$

By Mercer's Theorem[2], we can replace the dot product with a kernel function,

$$K(\mathbf{x}_i, \mathbf{x}_j) = \varphi(\mathbf{x}_i)^T \varphi(\mathbf{x}_j) \quad (1.8)$$

The decision function can then be written in terms of the kernel as,

$$f(\mathbf{y}) = \sum_{i=1} \alpha_i y_i K(\mathbf{x}_i, \mathbf{y}) + b \quad (1.9)$$

1) Automatically Biased Support Vector Machines

We can define an augmented feature space by defining an augmented feature mapping $\varphi_A : \mathfrak{R}^N \to \mathfrak{R}^{M+1}$, where $\varphi_A = \{\varphi_j : \mathfrak{R}^N \to \mathfrak{R}^{M+1} | 0 \leq j \leq M\}$. The augmented feature space is identical to the feature space defined previously with the restriction that $\varphi_0 = \beta$. Then, we can define a similar decision surface as,

$$f(\mathbf{x}) = \mathbf{w}_A^T \varphi(\mathbf{x})$$
$$f(\mathbf{x}) > 0 \quad \forall \; i : y_i = +1$$
$$f(\mathbf{x}) < 0 \quad \forall \; i : y_i = -1 \quad (1.10)$$

defined by :
$$\mathbf{w}_A^T \varphi(\mathbf{x}) = 0 \quad (1.11)$$

by setting :
$$\mathbf{w}_A = \begin{bmatrix} b \\ \beta \\ \mathbf{w} \end{bmatrix} \quad (1.12)$$

The primal problem is then simply,

$$\min \; \tfrac{1}{2} \mathbf{w}_A^T \mathbf{w}_A + C\mathbf{1}^T \xi_i$$
$$\text{subject to: } y_i(\mathbf{w}_A^T \mathbf{x}) \geq 1 - \xi_i \quad \forall i \quad (1.13)$$
$$\xi \geq \mathbf{0}$$

It was then shown that dual of this form could be written in the form of the augmented kernel function, $K_A(\mathbf{x}_i, \mathbf{x}_j)$ where

$$K_A(\mathbf{x}_i, \mathbf{x}_j) = \varphi(\mathbf{x}_i)^T \varphi(\mathbf{x}_j) + \beta^2$$
$$= K(\mathbf{x}_i, \mathbf{x}_j) + \beta^2 \quad (1.14)$$

and the resulting decision surface:

$$f(\mathbf{x}) = \sum_{i=1}^{S} \alpha_i y_i K_A(\mathbf{x}_i, \mathbf{y}) \quad (1.15)$$

In (1.15), we can see that the bias term, b in (1.9) has been incoporated into the kernel function and does not require to be computed seperately as suggested by [1][2][6][7]. We note here that work in [7] is a special case of our model with $\beta^2 = 1$. Optimization of our form will automatically bias the hyperplane in feature space and avoids the unneccessary extra computation for the threshold.

We note that for the given training set, $\mathbf{D}$ the maximization of the dual Lagrange form is implicitly formulated in equation (1.15) and the problem is then to find the α vector such that for each training example the following is satisfied within a tolerance δ,

$$y_i f(\mathbf{x}) - y_i \leq \delta \quad (1.16)$$

subject also to the stationary Karush-Kuhn-Tucker (KKT) conditions at optimality of,

$$0 \leq \alpha \leq \mathbf{1}^T C$$

We note that the ASVM form does not require enforcing the equality constraint (1.7), and indeed, this allows us to then rewrite (1.16) for S training examples;

$$\mathbf{Hu} = \mathbf{Y} \quad (1.17)$$

where
$$\mathbf{H} = \{K_A(\mathbf{x}_i, \mathbf{x}_j)\}_{i,j=1..s}$$
$$\mathbf{u} = \{u_1, u_2, \ldots, u_s\} = \{\alpha_1, \alpha_2, \ldots, \alpha_s\}$$
$$\mathbf{Y} = \{y_1, y_2, \ldots, y_s\}$$

The tolerance term δ is enforced in the training phase when considering whether a particular example satifies the model being optimized. We will show next how this form is suitable for application of our iterative method, with the addition of enforcing at each step:

$$u_i^{t+1} = \begin{cases} C & \text{if } u_i^{t+1} > C \\ u_i^{t+1} & \text{if } 0 < u_i^{t+1} < C \\ 0 & \text{if } u_i^{t+1} < 0 \end{cases}$$

We point out that the optimal solution will be in the form of (1.15) and it is a trivial matter to obtain (1.9) by substitution. However, this is not needed if a sufficiently large β^2 is chosen as shown in [8].

C. ITERATIVE STATIONARY METHODS OF FIRST DEGREE

The basic iterative linear stationary method of first degree is applicable to a system of q linear equations written in the following matrix form,

$$\mathbf{Hu} = \mathbf{F} \quad (1.18)$$

where H is a $q \times q$ matrix, $\mathbf{u}$ is a vector of scalars $\mathbf{u}=\{u_1, u_2 \ldots u_q\}$ and $\mathbf{F}$ is a vector containing scalars or commonly known boundary values. We note here that this form is identical to (1.17) and hence allows us to apply it directly to solve the SVM optimization problem. Then, the specific updates can be written in the following form,

$$\mathbf{u}^{t+1} = \mathbf{Bu}^t + \mathbf{k} \quad (1.19)$$

Theorem 1: *There exists a solution, $\mathbf{u}^*$ to the related system of real equations expressed as,*

$$(\mathbf{I} - \mathbf{B})\mathbf{u} = \mathbf{k}$$

if and only if it is unique to $\mathbf{u}^* = \mathbf{H}^{-1}\mathbf{F}$

Proof: Let $\mathbf{B} = \mathbf{I} - \mathbf{Q}^{-1}\mathbf{H}$ and $\mathbf{k} = \mathbf{Q}^{-1}\mathbf{F}$ where Q is some non-singular matrix, then substituting into the equation above, we get

$$(\mathbf{I} - (\mathbf{I} - \mathbf{Q}^{-1}\mathbf{H}))\mathbf{u} = \mathbf{Q}^{-1}\mathbf{F}$$
$$\mathbf{u} = \mathbf{H}^{-1}\mathbf{F}$$

If both $\mathbf{H}$ and $\mathbf{F}$ are real then it is simple to see that $\mathbf{u}$ must also be real and unique.

The Modified Jacobi Method

We utilize the basic Jacobi method[3] to demonstrate its effectiveness in obtaining a fast solution for the Support Vector Machine problem. This technique is a matrix splitting method. The method is applicable to a system of equations partioned in the following form,

$$\begin{pmatrix} H_{11} & \cdots & H_{1q} \\ \vdots & \ddots & \vdots \\ H_{q1} & \cdots & H_{qq} \end{pmatrix} \begin{pmatrix} u_1 \\ \vdots \\ u_q \end{pmatrix} = \begin{pmatrix} F_1 \\ \vdots \\ F_q \end{pmatrix} \quad (1.20)$$

where $H_{ij} = n_i \times n_j$ submatrix and

$$\sum_{i=1}^{q} n_i = q$$

For our SVM problem, we choose $H_{ij} = 1 \times 1$ matrix or a scalar value. This is sometimes referred to as the Jacobi *point* form. The matrix H can then be expressed as a sum,

$$\mathbf{H} = \mathbf{D} + \mathbf{L} + \mathbf{L}^T \quad (1.21)$$

Where $\mathbf{D}$ is a diagonal matrix containing the diagonal elements of $\mathbf{H}$ and $\mathbf{L}$ is a strictly lower triangle matrix containing the lower elements of $\mathbf{H}$.

Then

$$D = \begin{pmatrix} H_{11} & 0 & \cdots & 0 \\ 0 & \ddots & & \vdots \\ \vdots & & \ddots & \vdots \\ 0 & \cdots & \cdots & H_{qq} \end{pmatrix}$$

$$L = \begin{pmatrix} 0 & 0 & \cdots & 0 \\ H_{21} & \ddots & & \vdots \\ \vdots & & \ddots & \vdots \\ H_{q1} & \cdots & H_{qq-1} & 0 \end{pmatrix}$$

The iterates of the Jacobi Method are then given by the following update rule[3]

$$H_{i,i} u_i^{(t+1)} = -\sum_{j=1, j \neq i}^{q} H_{i,j} u_j^{(t)} + F_i \quad i = 1 \ldots q \quad (1.22)$$

This can be rewritten in matrix form as

$$\mathbf{D} \mathbf{u}^{t+1} = -(\mathbf{L} + \mathbf{L}^T)\mathbf{u}^t + \mathbf{F}$$
$$\mathbf{u}^{t+1} = -\mathbf{D}^{-1}(\mathbf{L} + \mathbf{L}^T)\mathbf{u}^t + \mathbf{D}^{-1}\mathbf{F}$$

where

$$\mathbf{B} = -\mathbf{D}^{-1}(\mathbf{L} + \mathbf{L}^T)$$
$$= (\mathbf{I} - \mathbf{D}^{-1}\mathbf{H})$$
$$\mathbf{k} = \mathbf{D}^{-1}\mathbf{F} \quad (1.23)$$

For a single update, we can write (1.23) as

$$u_i^{t+1} = \sum_{j=1}^{q} B_{ij} u_j^t + k_i \quad (1.24)$$

However, we propose a modification to this by using every new update of u_i^{t+1} immediately after it is computed to give an overall faster increase in the objective.

$$u_i^{t+1} = \sum_{j=1}^{i-1} B_{ij} u_j^{t+1} + \sum_{j=i}^{q} B_{ij} u_j^t + k_i \quad (1.25)$$

Extrapolation method

It is possible to further increase the speed of convergence by using an extrapolation technique, which is convergent whenever the basic method (1.19) is symmetrizable.

Definition 1: The basic method (1.19) is symmetrizable if for some non-singular matrix $\mathbf{A}$, the matrix $\mathbf{A}(\mathbf{I}-\mathbf{B})\mathbf{A}^{-1}$ is symmetric and positive definite[3]. Otherwise the method is non-symmetrizable.

We will state the following theorem without proof [3],

Theorem 2: If the basic method is symmetrizable then, a) the largest eigenvalue of $\mathbf{B}$, $\varpi(\mathbf{B})$ is less than unity, b) the eigenvalues of $\mathbf{B}$ are real, c) the set of eigenvectors of $\mathbf{B}$ forms a basis of $\mathbf{B}$.

The extrapolation method is then defined by

$$u^{t+1} = \gamma(\mathbf{B}u^t + \mathbf{k}) + (1-\gamma)u^t$$
$$= \mathbf{B}_{[\gamma]} u^t + \gamma \mathbf{k} \qquad (1.26)$$

For a single iterate this can be expanded and written as,

$$u_i^{t+1} = \gamma\left(\sum_{j=1}^{t-1} B_{ij} u_j^{t+1} + \sum_{j=t}^{q} B_{ij} u_j^t + k_i - u_i^t\right) + u_i^t \qquad \forall i=1...q \qquad (1.27)$$

The factor γ is referred to as the *extrapolation factor* and the optimum value[3] is given by

$$\gamma^* = \frac{2}{(2 - \lambda_{max}(\mathbf{B}) - \lambda_{min}(\mathbf{B}))}$$

where $\lambda(\mathbf{B})$ = eigenvalue of $\mathbf{B}$

The eigenvalues of $\mathbf{B}$ are usually unknown prior, however we propose using estimated eigenvalues instead. This would not give the optimal performance of the method but an estimated optimal performance where the subscript E refers to estimated values. Then we have as before,

$$\gamma_E = \frac{2}{(2 - \lambda'_{max}(\mathbf{B}) - \lambda'_{min}(\mathbf{B}))} \qquad (1.28)$$

where $\lambda'(\mathbf{B})$ = estimated eigenvalue of $\mathbf{B}$

It is easy to see from (1.28), that γ_E is constrained to lie in the interval $1 < \gamma_E < 2$ due to Theorem 2a.

Consistency and Convergence

The iterative method is said to be *completely consistent*, if the solution, $\mathbf{u}^*$ of (1.19) is also the solution for (1.18). This implies that for a sequence of iterates, $\{u^{(t)}\}=u^*$ for some t and $u^{t+1}=u^{t+2}=...u^*$ or the final solution u^* is static and does not change further.

The method is convergent, if the sequence of iterates $u^{(1)}$, $u^{(2)}$ .. converges to u^*. A necessary and sufficient condition of convergence [3] is that

$$\mathbf{S}(B) < 1 \qquad (1.29)$$

where $\mathbf{S}(B)$ is the spectral radius of the $q \times q$ matrix $\mathbf{B}$ and is defined as,

$$\mathbf{S}(B) = \max_{1 \leq i \leq q} |\lambda_i| \qquad (1.30)$$

D. EXPERIMENTAL RESULTS

We implemented our method and the SMO pseudocode[6] on Matlab 5.0 and ran it on a series of datasets. The experiments were designed to demonstrate the speed of our iterative algorithm and the effectiveness of the extrapolation method. All our experiments are done on a Pentium 4, 1.6Ghz machine with 256MB RAM. We ran the first two experiments using a standard Gaussian kernel with $\sigma=10$ and $C=1$ on the UCI datasets[10]. The detailed results on the number of non-bound Support Vectors and bound Support Vectors are reported in [8].

Experiment 1: Sorting and non-sorting of Support Vectors

We note that in J. Platt's algorithm, the sweep through Support Vectors is done randomly. In Mangasarian's work[7], the support vectors are sorted according to magnitude before sweeping through them in descending order. However, we hypothesize that this is still some random form of sweeping through the Support Vectors. Instead, at each pass through the data points or Support Vectors, we compute the magnitude of change, ε_i for each new α_i,

$$\varepsilon_i(n+1) = |\alpha_i^{n+1} - \alpha_i^n| \qquad i \in SV$$

We then sort the Support Vectors in decending order of the magnitudes of ε_i, so that on the next pass, the Support Vector with the largest ε_i is updated first. The intuition for doing this comes from viewing the optimisation process as adjusting the position of the hyperplane in feature space by gradually adjusting the values of α_i. Large ε values show that the particular alpha value is still loosely bounded and not within the optimal region, while small ε show alphas that lie close to their optimal values. So adjusting the loose alphas first would allow for quicker adjustment of the position of the hyperplane without altering the alpha values that are already close to optimality.

We ran our algorithm on the UCI adult dataset 1 which contains 1605 training examples. We use $\beta^2=1$ and $\delta=10^{-3}$ for all experiments. The experiments are done to compare between no sorting, sorting according to magnitude of Support Vectors (sorting 1), sorting according to our proposed method, (sorting 2) and the extrapolated method. The results are presented in Fig 1.1.

Experiment II : Comparison of basic method and acceleration with extrapolation

We next applied the extrapolation method to the basic iterative method. We investigate the effect of choosing an estimate of the extrapolation factor, γ by varying the range of γ through a series of evenly spaced values. For $\gamma=1$, we find from (1.27) that the extrapolation method reduces to the basic iterative method of (1.25). We ran the experiment on the first adult dataset, UCI 1, using $\beta=1$ and $\beta=100$ for tolerance levels, $\delta=10^{-2}$ and $\delta=10^{-3}$. Results are presented in Fig 1.2 and Fig 1.3.

Experiment III: Comparison against SMO using a real time image recognition application.

We applied both algorithms to a practical image recognition problem that is electronic monitoring of fishways. The complete experimental setup is found in [9]. For comparison, we ran SMO and our algorithm using $\delta=10^{-3}$.

We obtained a flop count and real computation times for comparison. We used 5-fold cross validation in all cases to investigate the generalization capabilities. The kernel matrix was cached for both algorithms since there was enough

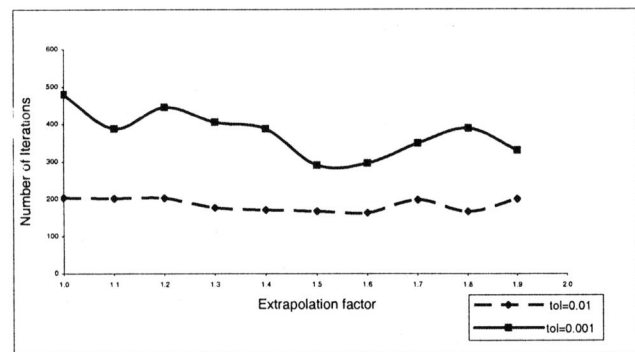

Fig 1.2: Extrapolation on UCI 1 with $\beta^2=1$

memory available. We ran experiments on various kernels however due to space constraints we present results from experiments done on a Gaussian kernel with a kernel width of 10.

E. DISCUSSION

We also demonstrate the validity of our hypothesis when sorting the Support Vectors according to the magnitudes of change. A significant increase in performance is observed when sorting the Support Vectors according to our method then compared to non-sorting. Against Mangasarian's method, we record a 15% increase in optimization speed for the basic iterative method when sorting using our proposed method. Performance increases further with the use of extrapolation.

Fig. 1.2 and Fig 1.3 demonstrates that extrapolation can effectively increase in the rates of convergence. In this paper we only demonstrate the capabilities of the extrapolation method, and we note that if we are to use them effectively, we should try to obtain good eigenvalues estimates to give optimal performance. The true eigenvalues could be obtained using decomposition methods but, they will require additional computational complexity. We are looking into

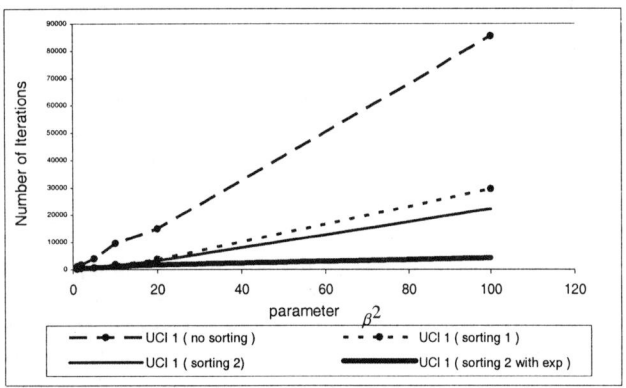

Fig 1.1 : Optimization speed for sorting and no sorting over a range of β^2 for UCI dataset 1.

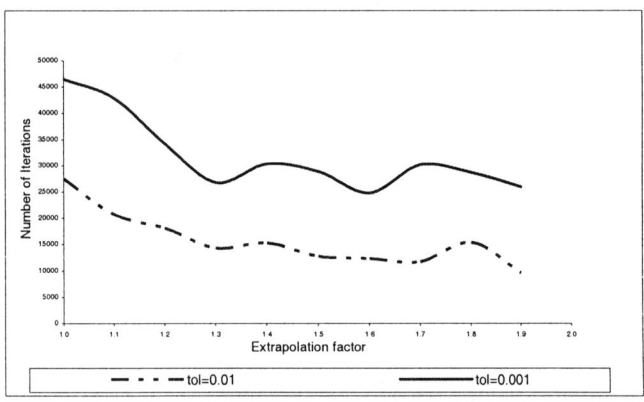

Fig. 1.3 : Extrapolation on UCI 1 with $\beta^2=100$

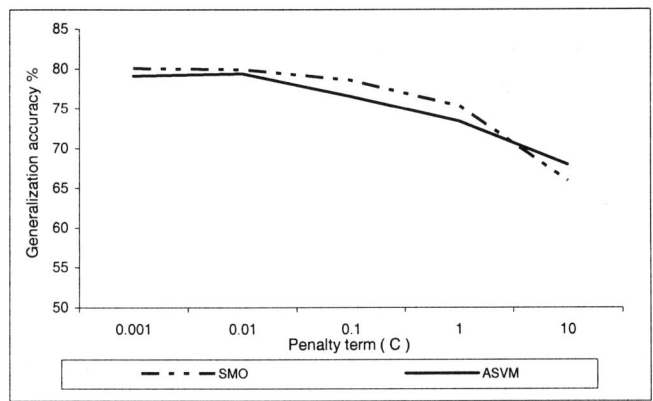

Fig 1.4: Generalization on a Gaussian kernel with $\sigma = 10$

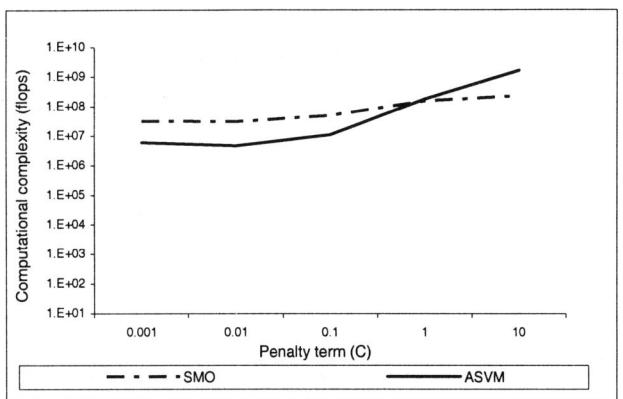

Fig 1.6: Computational complexity i on a Gaussian kernel with $\sigma = 10$

adaptive methods to adjust the extrapolation factor since the extrapolation method gives us an increase of almost an order of magnitude in performance compared to just the basic method.

We also show from Fig 1.5 that our algorithm is capable of achieving a much faster optimization compared to SMO. For small values of C, we found that our algorithm was more efficient than SMO, requiring lesser floating point operations (flops). However, we observed that the our method became less efficient at higher values of C. This is of little concern since at higher values of C, the trained SVM's generalization capabilities (see Fig 1.4) become unacceptable and we would not be using those values. Thus in the acceptable region, we have demonstrated that our algorithm is much faster and more computationally efficient than the SMO.

F. CONCLUSION

In this paper, we have presented a new training algorithm for the Automatically biased Support Vector Machine formulation based on iterative stationary methods of first degree. The iterative method is simple to use and can be extended further with use of acceleration methods such as the extrapolation method. We also demonstrate that our method of sorting the support vectors to be updated gives significant increase in performance compared to previous methods. We show that the ASVM model possesses comparable generalization capabilities to the standard SVM model. Future work will concentrate on application of polynomial acceleration techniques, adapative estimation of the extrapolation factor and incremental models to further increase optimization speed.

ACKNOWLEDGMENT

The authors would like to acknowledge the support of the Australian Research and Discovery grant and the Centre for Networked Decision and Sensor Systems. We also would like to thank A. Shilton for his useful comments.

REFERENCES

[1] N. Cristianini and J. Shawe-Taylor, *An Introduction to Support Vector Machines (and other kernel-based learning methods)*, Cambridge University Press 2000 ISBN: 0 521 78019 5

[2] C. Burges. A tutorial on support vector machines for pattern recognition. Data Mining and Knowledge Discovery, 2(2): 11-167, 1998.

[3] Louis A. Hageman, David M. Young, Applied Iterative Methods, Academic Press 1981

[4] Philip E. Gill, Walter Murray and Margaret H. Wright, Practical Optimization, Academic Press 1981

[5] Vladimir N. Vapnik, The nature of statistical learning, Springer-Verlag New York, 1995.

[6] J. Platt, *Fast Training of Support Vector Machines using Sequential Minimal Optimization*, in Advances in Kernel Methods - Support Vector Learning, B. Schölkopf, C. Burges, and A. Smola, eds., MIT Press, (1998).

[7] Mangasarian, O.L.; Musicant, D.R., Successive overrelaxation for support vector machines Neural Networks, IEEE Transactions on , Volume: 10 Issue: 5 , Sept. 1999

[8] M. Palaniswami, D. Lai , A.Shilton, Automatically Biased Support Vector Machines for electronic monitoring of fishways, Technical Report CENDS 2002/12-1 University of Melbourne .

[9] B. Owen, M. Palaniswami and J. Harris, Automated Monitoring of Fishways, in Proc. of 3rd IEEE International Conference on Intelligent Processing Systems, ICIPS, pp. 238-242, Gold Coast, Australia, August 1998.

[10] Blake, C.L. & Merz, C.J. (1998). UCI Repository of machine learning databases Irvine, CA: University of California, Department of Information and Computer Science. [http://www.ics.uci.edu/~mlearn/MLRepository.html].

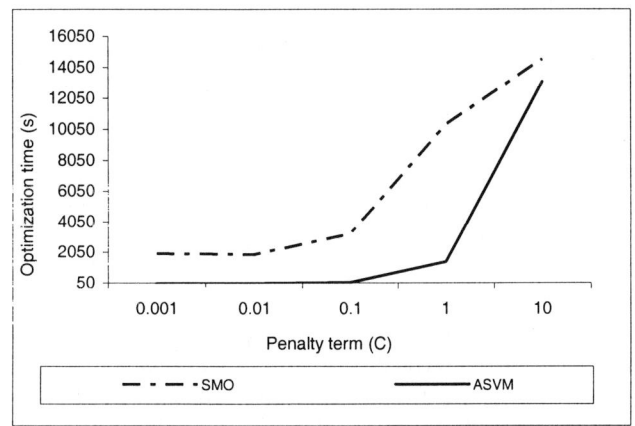

Fig 1.5:Optimization time(s) on a Gaussian kernel with $\sigma = 10$

Identification of Chaotic Process Systems with Least Squares Support Vector Machines

G.T. Jemwa and C. Aldrich[‡]

Department of Chemical Engineering, University of Stellenbosch
Private Bag X1, Matieland 7602, South Africa, [‡]E-mail: CA1@sun.ac.za

Abstract – We investigate the nonlinear identification of chaotic process systems with least squares support vector machines, based on a case study of a parallel cubic autocatalytic reaction. State space reconstruction techniques are used to obtain a low-dimensional representation of the system in a different, but equivalent coordinate system. The performance of the support vector machine models are compared to corresponding models obtained when using multilayer perceptron neural networks, which are known to model chaotic dynamical systems well.

I. INTRODUCTION

Many chemical reactive systems exhibit complex, nonlinear deterministic behaviour. Mathematical descriptions of these systems are invariably difficult and, hence numerical or empirical representations are usually sought for use in advanced model-based control strategies. The success of these strategies depends crucially on the accuracy with which relationships between the input and output state vectors can be identified and their implementation represents a major cost factor in the overall development of these control systems. To complicate matters, the engineer often has no access to the underlying state variables, except through measurements obtained from the physical system. Fortunately, it has been established that in principle, for systems whose asymptotic dynamical behaviour collapses onto a low-dimensional attractor, a one-to-one correspondence can be found that preserves differential information between the true states of the system and delay-coordinate vectors [1,2]. This is particularly important in situations where there is no knowledge of the underlying state variables and their relationships.

Different classes of functions can be used to define empirical equations of motion for such low-dimensional deterministic systems. Most of these approaches are based on the empirical risk minimization (ERM) principle, where the best model is found by optimizing its performance on a training data set. These model classes include multilayer perceptron and radial basis function neural networks, multivariate adaptive regression splines, projection pursuit regression, etc. However, the ERM principle does not guarantee that models such as these will be able to correctly predict future outputs given future inputs.

A relatively new learning paradigm, support vector machine (SVM) learning, is based on minimizing the probability of incorrectly predicting yet-to-be-seen future outputs for a fixed, but unknown probability distribution of the data – the structural risk minimization (SRM) principle. This approach has proved successful in instances where other model classes have failed.

In this paper we investigate the use of a variant of the standard SVM regression technique to identify a chemical process system exhibiting chaotic dynamics, with state space reconstruction based on single and multiple time series measurements from the system.

II. STATE SPACE RECONSTRUCTION

A. Scalar Embedding.

The embedding theorems [1,2] guarantee that given observations of a variable related to a physical system, it is possible to reconstruct a state space equivalent to the (possibly unknown) underlying state space, except for a smooth coordinate change using. For example, with the method of delay coordinates one constructs a vector space using time lagged values of the observed time series, that is,

$$\mathbf{x}(t) = \left(s(t), s(t-T_1), s(t-2T_2), \ldots, s(t-(m-1)T_{m-1})\right), \quad (1)$$

where $s(t)$ is the observed time series for $t = 1, 2, \ldots N$; T_i are the time delays between successive components in the reconstructed vector $\mathbf{x}(t)$, and m is the embedding dimension. A delay T_i is chosen such that successive coordinates are independent and the attractor is completely unfolded (for one-to-one correspondence) in the reconstructed space. If the same T_i is defined between components, we refer to the reconstruction as *uniform* embedding. Different heuristic criteria exist for selecting T_i (uniform) and m, of which Shannon's average mutual information and the lag index corresponding to the first minimum of the autocorrelation function are criteria that are widely used [3].

A uniform delay approximately captures dynamics at a single dominant periodicity or recurrence time. This risks loss of dynamical information occurring at other time scales in systems without a dominant recurrence time [4]. In this case, the problem can be obviated by *non-uniform* embedding of the observations. Here, the time delays between successive components are not equal, i.e. $T_i \neq T_j, j \neq i$. Such a time delay or lag vector $\{T_i\}$ can be found by optimizing it according to some criterion within a modelling context, which also determines the dimensionality of the embedding. Although this approach can improve the performance of nonlinear models, the resulting coordinates may not be independent, as would be required of a true state space representation.

B. Multivariate Embedding

A reconstruction based on a scalar time series may be unable to capture the dynamics of the system completely, if it is not related to some original state variables [5]. Furthermore, measurement errors invariably amplify the uncertainty in the reconstructed attractor. It may then be advantageous to exploit correlation information in simultaneously measured variables. The multidimensional reconstructed matrix is simply a combination of the individual time series embeddings, possibly optimised with respect to some property or dimensionality reduction method [6].

III. NONLINEAR SYSTEM IDENTIFICATION USING TIME SERIES OBSERVATIONS

State space parameterization is often used in the identification of system dynamics from observed time series. System identification for linear systems is now well established [7], but for nonlinear systems the problem is not well-defined. Discrete nonlinear dynamical systems can be represented by a state equation in terms of the state variables

$$\mathbf{x}_{t+1} = \mathbf{f}(\mathbf{x}_t, \mathbf{u}_t, \theta) \qquad (2)$$

where $\mathbf{x}_t$ is the state vector at time t, $\mathbf{u}_t$ the input vector of independent variables at time t, $\mathbf{f}$ the function or map defining the temporal evolution of the system, and θ a finite-dimensional parameterization vector. The output vector of the dependent variables of the system is defined by

$$\mathbf{y}_t = \mathbf{g}[\mathbf{x}_t, \mathbf{u}_t, \eta] \qquad (3)$$

where $\mathbf{g}$ is a nonlinear function that projects $[\mathbf{x}_t, \mathbf{u}_t]$ onto the output vector $\mathbf{y}_t$.

The nonlinear system identification problem using a state space model representation is then comprized of two parts.

1) First, the *regression vector* $\mathbf{x}_t$ is reconstructed using the approach mentioned in section II. Using the ideas of Eckmann and Ruelle [8] of examining the delay coordinates of a point and the next time point occurring one sampling time step later, a training data set $[\mathbf{x}_t, \mathbf{y}_{t+1}]$ is constructed, and

2) Second, an approximation of the nonlinear mapping $\mathbf{g} \circ \mathbf{f}$ has to be found, so that

$$f : \mathbf{x}_t \to \mathbf{y}_{t+1}. \qquad (4)$$

A. Approximating the Nonlinear Mapping f

In the estimation of a regression function, the objective is to select the optimal function $f(\mathbf{x}, \alpha_0)$ from a set of real functions $f(\mathbf{x}, \alpha)$, $\alpha \in \Lambda$ according to some criterion. Model selection is done using a training data set of N independent and identically distributed observations generated according to an unknown joint probability distribution function

$$P(\mathbf{x}, y) = P(\mathbf{x})P(y | \mathbf{x}), \quad \{\mathbf{x}_i \in \Re^n, y_i \in \Re\}_{i=1}^N, \qquad (5)$$

The best approximation minimizes the risk functional

$$R(\alpha) = \int \ell(y, f(\mathbf{x}, \alpha)) dP(\mathbf{x}, y), \qquad (6)$$

where $\ell(\cdot, \cdot)$ is a loss function depending on the response of the learning machine or model relative to the observed response. However, since $P(\mathbf{x},y)$ is generally unknown, an induction principle (ERM) is typically used in which the expected risk functional is replaced by the empirical risk functional,

$$R_{emp}(\alpha) = \frac{1}{N} \sum_{i=1}^{N} \ell(\mathbf{x}, y), \qquad (7)$$

which is constructed from the training data [9,10].

Traditional regression approaches, such as neural networks and polynomial fits, seek a function f that minimizes the least squares function,

$$\ell(\mathbf{x}, y) = (y - f(\mathbf{x}, \alpha))^2 \qquad (8)$$

of the differences between the observed targets and model outputs. Unfortunately, minimizing the training error in (8) does not imply a small risk functional (6). The limitation of this approach is that the *capacity* of the learning machine is not optimized. Therefore, the selected function may not generalize well with regard to unseen data.

An alternative approach is support vector learning, which is founded in statistical learning or Vapnik-Chervonenkis (VC) theory [9,10]. VC theory restricts the family of functions f so that the optimal function has a capacity suitable for the size of the training data. The framework provides for bounds on the test error, which depend on both the empirical risk (7) and the capacity of the family of functions, i.e.

$$R(\alpha) = R_{emp} + R_{cap}. \qquad (9)$$

Various capacity concepts have been formulated, which include the VC dimension, annealed VC entropy, and the Growth function [10]. Of these, the VC dimension is the easiest to evaluate and, therefore commonly used.

In this study, a variation of support vector machines was used in the identification problem. For purposes of comparison, multilayer perceptron neural networks were used as a benchmark. The theoretical framework underpinning both model classes is described below, but since support vector learning is relatively new, it is described in more detail than the multilayer perceptron neural network.

B. Feed-forward Multilayer Perceptrons

Feed-forward multilayer perceptrons (MLPs) are a subset of a class of strong functional approximators called neural networks. A neural network is a massive parallel distributed structure consisting of interconnected structural units called nodes or neurons [11]. In the case of an MLP, the network structure consists of an input layer, one or more hidden layers of computational nodes, and an output layer of computational nodes. Hidden and output layers usually also contain bias nodes. MLPs learn the relationship between inputs and outputs by using an error back-propagation algorithm to adjust the interconnection strengths or weights (model parameters) linking the nodes. A smooth nonlinearity is introduced by means of appropriate basis functions in the nodes of the computational layers, the most common of which are sigmoidal functions:

$$\phi(\mathbf{x}) = 1/(1+e^{-x}) \tag{10}$$

$$\phi(\mathbf{x}) = (1-e^{-x})/(1+e^{-x}). \tag{11}$$

An optimal model structure is obtained as a compromise between the model accuracy and model complexity to prevent the network from learning patterns in the data attributable to noise.

C. Vapnik's Standard ε-SVM

Vapnik's ε-loss function [9,10,12] seeks a regression model that has at most a deviation of ε from the observed response variables y_i, and is as flat as possible, i.e. $|f(\mathbf{x}_i) - y_i| \le \varepsilon$, for $i = 1, 2, \ldots N$. Hence, errors are considered insignificant, as long as they are less than ε. This could be attributed to round-off errors in a digital measuring instrument, for example. In the case of linear functions, and assuming that the input space $\mathbf{x}$ is defined in a Hilbert space, the regression model is given by

$$f(x) = \langle \mathbf{w}, \mathbf{x} \rangle + b, \quad \mathbf{w}, \mathbf{x} \in \Re^n, b \in \Re \tag{12}$$

where $\langle \cdot, \cdot \rangle$ is the dot product in input space function. Flatness requires that $\mathbf{w}$ be as small as possible. One criterion for ensuring flatness is to minimize $\|\mathbf{w}\|_p^2$, where $\|(\cdot)\|_p$ is the ℓ_p-norm. In the following, the ℓ_2-norm will be assumed and, hence, the subscript will be omitted forthwith. Formulating the problem as a convex optimization problem gives

$$\min \quad \tfrac{1}{2}\|\mathbf{w}\|^2 \tag{13}$$

$$\text{subject to} \quad \begin{cases} y_i - (\langle \mathbf{w}, \mathbf{x}_i \rangle + b) \le \varepsilon \\ (\langle \mathbf{w}, \mathbf{x}_i \rangle + b) - y_i \le \varepsilon \end{cases} \tag{14}$$

The above constitutes a quadratic programming problem, assuming such a function exists. To allow for otherwise infeasible constraints of the optimization problem in (13,14), one introduces slack variables ξ_i, ξ_i^*, which leads to a reformulation of the problem as [12]

$$\min \quad \tfrac{1}{2}\|\mathbf{w}\|^2 + C\sum_{i=1}^{N}(\xi_i + \xi_i^*) \tag{15}$$

$$\text{subject to} \quad \begin{cases} y_i - (\langle \mathbf{w}, \mathbf{x}_i \rangle + b) \le \varepsilon + \xi_i \\ (\langle \mathbf{w}, \mathbf{x}_i \rangle + b) - y_i \le \varepsilon + \xi_i^* \\ \xi_i, \xi_i^* \ge 0 \end{cases} \tag{16}$$

The parameter C is a regularization parameter and determines the trade-off between the flatness of f and the degree to which deviations larger than ε are tolerated. The expression (16) corresponds to the so-called ε-insensitive loss function $|y - f(\mathbf{x})|_\varepsilon$ described by [9,10,12], i.e.

$$|y - f(\mathbf{x})|_\varepsilon = \begin{cases} 0 & \text{if } |y - f(\mathbf{x})| \le 0, \\ |y - f(\mathbf{x})| - \varepsilon & \text{otherwise.} \end{cases} \tag{17}$$

D. Least Squares Support Vector Regression

In least squares support vector regression [14], the ε-insensitive formulation is modified so that one solves a linear system, instead of a quadratic programming problem. This is achieved by introducing a squared error term and equality constraints in Vapnik's standard SVM problem (15,16). Thus, the least-squares optimization formulation is

$$\min_{\mathbf{w},e} \quad \zeta(\mathbf{w},e) = \tfrac{1}{2}\langle \mathbf{w}, \mathbf{w}\rangle + \gamma \tfrac{1}{2}\sum_{k=1}^{N} e_k^2 \tag{18}$$

$$\text{subject to} \quad y_k = \langle \mathbf{w}, \mathbf{x}_k \rangle + b + e_k, \quad k = 1,\ldots,N. \tag{19}$$

The solution to (18,19) is obtained by constructing the Lagrange function [14]

$$\Im(\mathbf{w},b,e;\alpha) = \zeta(\mathbf{w},e) - \sum_{k=1}^{N} \alpha_k \{\langle \mathbf{w}, \mathbf{x}_k \rangle + b + e_k - y_k\} \tag{20}$$

where α_k are the Lagrange multipliers. From conditions of optimality it can be shown that the LSSVM model solution function is given by

$$y(x) = \sum_{k=1}^{N} \alpha_k \langle \mathbf{x}, \mathbf{x}_k \rangle + b \tag{21}$$

where α_k, b are solutions to a set of linear equations.

E. Nonlinear Function Estimation using SVMs – Kernel Representation

In the preceding support vector machine formulations, it has been assumed that a linear function f has to be found. An extension to nonlinear function estimation is made possible by a mapping of the input space $\aleph$ to a *feature* space Γ, that is, $\Phi: \aleph \to \Gamma$, where Φ is the mapping function. The learning problem is then defined as

$$f(x) = \langle \mathbf{w}, \Phi(\mathbf{x}) \rangle + b, \quad \mathbf{w}, \mathbf{x} \in \Gamma, b \in \Re. \tag{22}$$

Essentially, one replaces the occurrences of **x** in the above linear SVM formulations with $\Phi(\mathbf{x})$ to obtain the corresponding nonlinear formulation.

However, the feature map representation introduces some complications. For example, since the feature space is invariably high-dimensional, computational cost increases with the number of features. It is also not clear what appropriate features would be in the absence of domain information. Also, the question remains of how to enforce the "flatness" requirement in the feature space, which corresponds to f defined in the input space. Fortunately, for certain feature spaces and corresponding mappings the dot product can be computed effectively using a kernel representation [9,10], that is

$$k(\mathbf{x}, \mathbf{x}) = \langle \Phi(\mathbf{x}), \Phi(\mathbf{x}) \rangle, \tag{23}$$

where k is an appropriately chosen kernel.

Several possibilities are available for kernel functions. For conditions necessary for a function to be a valid kernel see [9,10]. In the following case study, Gaussian radial basis functions are used,

$$k(\mathbf{x}, \mathbf{y}) = \exp\left\{ \frac{-\|\mathbf{x} - \mathbf{y}\|^2}{\sigma^2} \right\} \tag{24}$$

IV. Case Study: An Autocatalytic Reaction System

A. Process Description

Parallel cubic autocatalytic reactions occurring in an isothermal reactor have been described by [14]

$$A + 2B \to 3B \quad -r_A = k_1[A][B]^2 \tag{25}$$
$$D + 2B \to 3B \quad -r_D = k_2[D][B]^2 \tag{26}$$
$$B \to C \quad r_C = k_3[B] \tag{27}$$

where A, B, C and D are reacting species, [i] is the concentration of species i, r_i is the rate of reaction with respect to species i and k is a reaction constant. Defining dimensionless concentrations X, Y and Z for species A, D and B respectively, it can be shown that the model equations describing the system are given by

$$\frac{dX}{d\tau} = 1 - X - Da_X XZ^2 \tag{28}$$

$$\frac{dY}{d\tau} = \beta - Y - Da_Y YZ^2 \tag{29}$$

$$\frac{dZ}{d\tau} = 1 - (1 + Da_Z)Z + \alpha(Da_X XZ^2 + Da_Y YZ^2) \tag{30}$$

where $\alpha = [A]_f/[B]_f$, and $\beta = [C]_f/[A]_f$ are ratios of species in the feed; τ is the dimensionless time and Da_i the Damköhler number for species i. The system was shown to behave chaotically for $\alpha = 1.5$, $\beta = 2.81$, $Da_X = 18\,000$, $Da_Y = 400$ and $Da_Z = 80$ [14].

Using initial random conditions and an integration time step of 0.01, time series consisting of 15 000 observations were generated by numerically solving the system (17-18) using a fifth-order Runge-Kutta ODE solver. The data were *resampled* at time intervals of 10, 20 and 25 time steps for further analysis. Furthermore, we generated other time signals from these by adding normally distributed noise for different percentages of the standard deviations of individual channels, viz. 1, 5, 10, and 20%.

B. Determining Embedding Parameters

In the case of uniform embedding, the time delay and embedding dimension for each of the differently sampled time signals were determined using the method of mutual information and the false nearest neighbours algorithm [3], while a reduced autoregressive modelling scheme [4] was used to determine the embedding lag vectors for each of the observed channels. Tables I and II show the results obtained.

The addition of noise had a negligible effect on the time delay, hence the use of a unitary time delay value in all cases, previously determined using the lower index of the decay of the autocorrelation and Shannon's average mutual information criterion. We attribute this to the low resampling rate used, which resulted in rapid decorrelation of the observations.

TABLE I
UNIFORM EMBEDDING PARAMETERS

Sampling Interval	X		Y		Z	
	m	T	m	T	m	T
10	5	1	7	1	7	1
20	6	1	4	1	7	1
25	6	1	5	1	6	1

TABLE II
NON-UNIFORM EMBEDDING PARAMETERS

Sampling Interval	X	Y	Z
	lag vector	lag vector	lag vector
10	1 4 6 11 1 15 8 2	0 4 2 1 14 7 15 8 9 3	1 4 2 6 8 11
20	7 3 4 1	0 2 1 7	7 3 4 1
25	0 5 4 3	0 4 1 5	0 5 4 3

C. Predictive Modelling

As mentioned earlier, least squares support vector machines (LSSVM) and MLPs were used as model structures. In each case the first 2/3 of the resampled data points were used for training and validation, while the remainder was used for model verification. Note that because of different resampling time intervals the lengths of the different training and test data sets differed.

Model parameterization is not a simple matter. A good model must be able to minimize the discrepancies between model and actual output, while simultaneously retaining good generalization capability, i.e. it must capture the dynamics of the system without explaining variations introduced by random inputs. Various criteria are available to ensure that the best model is selected. In the case of MLP neural networks, a simple Schwarz Information Criterion (*SIC*) was used. In standard SVM learning, the complexity of the model is dependent on the size of the training data set. In fact, often only a few of the training data points are required to describe the model. However, sparseness is lost when one uses LSSVMs [15]. Nevertheless, it is still possible to define a sparse structure by choosing those support vectors that contribute most to the model without affecting the performance of the resulting model. As a result, it was not necessary to define a sparse LSSVM model in this investigation.

Using the *SIC* criterion, an optimal MLP structure with 18 nodes in the hidden layer was selected. An optimal weight matrix was determined by 10-fold cross-validation, whereby the input-output pairs of the training data set were randomly permuted and divided into 10 subsets of similar size. In the *k*-th ($k = 1, 2, \ldots 10$) iteration the *k*-th subset was used to validate the model trained on the other subsets. The model structure with the least mean square error was chosen.

The alpha and kernel parameters of the LSSVM were determined by grid-search numerical optimization.

V. RESULTS AND DISCUSSION

A. Relative Performance of the LSSVM and MLP Model Classes.

Tables III and V show the one-step-ahead root mean square error (RMSE) and regression coefficient (R^2) results obtained from the empirical modelling of simulated data from the cubic autocatalytic system. In all cases it is clear that the LSSVM models performed significantly better than the corresponding MLP models. In fact, analysis of the RMSE and R^2 values indicated that in some cases a simple model that assumes an average of the past values performed better than some of the MLP nonlinear models. However, the nonlinear nature of the process is evident from the outstanding results obtained using LSSVMs. Not surprisingly, increasing noise levels and sampling intervals reduced the predictive (RMSE) and generalization (R^2) performance of the models. This is attributable to the loss of certainty introduced by noise and loss of information between successive values separated by wider time intervals.

B. Uniform and Non-uniform Embedding

In all cases the uniform embedding strategy based on the method of delay coordinates gave better results than the non-uniform embedding strategy. Tables III and IV are comparisons of results obtained by employing the two approaches. In both cases the tables show similar trends with respect to increasing noise levels and variation of the sampling time. However, the values obtained with the non-uniform embedding are higher than corresponding values obtained with the uniform embedding.

TABLE III
MODELING RESULTS USING LSSVMs – UNIFORM EMBEDDING

Noise level %STD$_{data}$	Sampling Interval					
	10		20		25	
	RMSE	R^2	RMSE	R^2	RMSE	R^2
0	0.0001	1.0000	0.0017	0.9845	0.0053	0.8615
1	0.0004	1.0000	0.0019	0.9805	0.0057	0.8494
5	0.0015	0.9941	0.0034	0.9378	0.0060	0.8252
10	0.0027	0.9603	0.0048	0.8755	0.0065	0.7828
20	0.0052	0.8605	0.0075	0.8367	0.0088	0.6233

TABLE IV
MODELING RESULTS USING LSSVMs – NON-UNIFORM EMBEDDING

Noise level %STD$_{data}$	Sampling Interval					
	10		20		25	
	RMSE	R^2	RMSE	R^2	RMSE	R^2
0	0.0025	0.9669	0.0066	0.7717	0.0064	0.7875
1	0.0025	0.9679	0.0064	0.7798	0.0077	0.7280
5	0.0036	0.9310	0.0075	0.7013	0.0077	0.7027
10	0.0049	0.8688	0.0087	0.6030	0.0079	0.6760
20	0.0077	0.6908	0.0105	0.4190	0.0098	0.5250

This is in contrast with results obtained in our earlier research [16], where it was observed that non-uniform embedding led to better models.

These differences can probably be explained by the larger sampling times used in the present study. Specifically, it may not be advisable to use a non-uniform embedding strategy, if a time delay of unity is found using either the average mutual information or linear autocorrelation methods.

TABLE V
MODELING RESULTS USING MLPs – UNIFORM EMBEDDING

Noise level %STD$_{data}$	Sampling Interval					
	10		20		25	
	RMSE	R^2	RMSE	R^2	RMSE	R^2
0	0.0167	0.1782	0.0463	0.0217	0.0243	0.1625
1	0.0236	0.0292	0.0205	0.0258	0.0226	0.0000
5	0.0212	0.0017	0.0228	0.0768	0.0176	0.0344
10	0.0220	0.0761	0.0206	0.0638	0.0177	0.0397
20	0.0522	0.0055	0.0229	0.0211	0.0458	0.2624

TABLE VI
UNIVARIATE VERSUS MULTIVARIATE EMBEDDING – PREDICTIVE MODELLING RESULTS USING LSSVMs FOR $T = 10, \sigma = 5\%$ STD$_{data}$

Variable(s)	UNIFORM		NON-UNIFORM	
	RMSE	R2	RMSE	R2
X	0.0015	0.9941	0.0036	0.9310
XY	0.0009	0.9952	0.0020	0.9781
XZ	0.0010	0.9950	0.0025	0.9657

C. Univariate Versus Multivariate Embedding

Table VI shows typical results obtained in the comparison of univariate and multivariate embedding strategies. As expected, the inclusion of simultaneously measured signals in the reconstruction of the attractor improved the performance of the resulting models. However, the flow of information was different, depending on the choice of the measured observables used in the embedding. In the case shown, the flow of information from the Y variable was substantially higher than from the Z variable. Hence, xy-embeddings gave better models than xz-embeddings, although both were significantly better than the use of a single observable in the reconstruction of the time series.

D. Effect of Random Permutation of Training Data in the Performance of the MLP Models.

As discussed earlier, the MLP models gave poor models. We further investigated the use of the same data during training of the models, but without random permutation. Table VII shows some of the results obtained for T = 10 and σ = {0, 20}%.

In this case the MLP models were of similar quality to the LSSVM models derived earlier, since they could exploit the information associated with the autocorrelation structure of successive input-output vectors, rather than capturing the actual dynamic relationship between the vectors.

TABLE VII
MODELLING USING MLP NETWORKS WITHOUT RANDOM PERMUTATION OF TRAINING INPUT-OUTPUT PAIRS

Embedding Strategy	Variables	Noise Level %STDdata			
		0		20	
		RMSE	R^2	RMSE	R^2
Uniform	X	0.0004	0.9992	0.0053	0.8521
	XY	0.0000	1.0000	0.0042	0.9089
	XZ	0.0001	1.0000	0.0042	0.9079
Non-Uniform	X	0.0044	0.8955	0.0086	0.6114
	XY	0.0021	0.9751	0.0061	0.8016
	XZ	0.0024	0.9685	0.0077	0.6880

VI. CONCLUSIONS

We observed that LSSVM models were markedly better than MLP models when the training data were randomly permuted before parameterization of the chosen model structures. However, MLP models of similar quality were obtained when the correlational structure of the input-output vector pairs were retained.

Likewise, uniform embedding in the state space reconstruction yielded better models compared to the use of non-uniform embedding strategies. This was attributed to the poor autocorrelational structure in the data, that is, the data were undersampled, since other studies have indicated contrasting results. Multivariate embedding is potentially superior to univariate embedding as a first step in the development of predictive models, but not necessarily for other analyses dependent on a reliable state space representation, as the independence of the channels may be compromised by this approach.

REFERENCES

[1] F. Takens, "Detecting strange attractors in turbulence," in Dynamical Systems and Turbulence, D.A. Rand and L.S. Young, Eds Springer-Verlag, Berlin, pp. 366-381, 1981.
[2] T. Sauer, J.A. Yorke, and M. Casdagli, "Embedology", J. Stat. Phys, vol. 65, nos. 3/4, pp. 579-616, 1991.
[3] H. Kantz and T. Schreiber, Nonlinear Time Series Analysis, Cambridge University Press, Cambridge, 1997.
[4] K Judd, M. Small, and A.I. Mees, "Achieving good nonlinear models: Keep it simple, vary the embedding and get the dynamics right," in Nonlinear Dynamics and Statistics, A.I. Mees, Ed. Boston: Birkhauser, 2001, pp. 65-80.
[5] L. Cao, A. Mees, and K. Judd, "Dynamics from multivariate time series," Physica D., vol 121, pp. 75-88, 1998.
[6] J.P. Barnard, C. Aldrich, and M., Gerber, "Embedding of multidimensional time-dependent observations , Phys. Rev., E., vol. 64, no. 4, pp. 1-4. 2001.
[7] L. Ljung, System Identification, Prentice Hall, New Jersey, 1987.
[8] J.P. Eckmann and D. Ruelle, "Ergodic theory of chaos and strange attractors," Rev. Mod. Phys., vol 57, no. 3, pp. 617-656, 1985.
[9] N. Cristianni and J. Shawe-Taylor, An Introduction to Support Vector Machines, Cambridge University Press, 2000.
[10] B. Scholkopf and A.J. Smola, Learning with kernels: support vector machines, regularization, optimization, and beyond, MIT Press, Massachusetts, 2002.
[11] S. Haykin, Neural Networks – A Comprehensive Foundation, Macmillan College Publishing, New Jersey, 1994.
[12] C. Cortes and V.N. Vapnik, "Support vector networks," Machine Learning, vol. 20, pp. 273- 297, 1995.
[13] J.A.K. Suykens, "Nonlinear modelling and support vector machines," IEEE Instrumentation and Measurement Technology Conference, Budapest, Hungary, May 21-23, 2001.
[14] D.T. Lynch, "Chaotic behaviour of reaction systems: mixed cubic and quadratic autocatalysis," Chem. Eng. Sci., vol. 47, no. 17/18, pp. 4435-4444, 1992.
[15] J.A.K. Suykens, J. De Brabanter, L. Lucas, and J. Vandewalle, "Weighted least squares support vector machines: robustness and sparse approximation," Internal Report 00-37, ESAT-SISTA, K.U. Lueven, 2000.
[16] G.T. Jemwa, Multivariate Nonlinear Time Series Analysis of Dynamic Process Systems, M.Sc. Eng. Thesis, University of Stellenbosch, Stellenbosch, South Africa, 2003.

SVM learning with fixed–point math

Davide Anguita
University of Genova
DIBE
Via all'Opera Pia, 11a
16145 Genova, Italy
Email: anguita@dibe.unige.it

Andrea Boni
University of Trento
DIT
Via Sommarive 14
38050 Povo (Trento), Italy
Email: aboni@ing.unitn.it

Sandro Ridella
University of Genova
DIBE
Via all'Opera Pia, 11a
16145 Genova, Italy
Email: ridella@dibe.unige.it

Abstract—We present in this paper an algorithm for Support Vector Machine (SVM) learning, which can be implemented using fixed–point math. The advantages of the fixed–point representation, respect to the more common floating–point one, allows us to address digital VLSI implementations of SVM. In particular, simple algorithms and simple architectures can be exploited for targeting programmable devices like Field Programmable Gate Arrays (FPGAs), which are the basis of many embedded systems. This paper focuses on the SVM learning algorithm: for the complete version of this work, including an actual FPGA realization, we refer the reader to [1]

I. INTRODUCTION

After the first studies in the early '90s, the FPGAs–based technology is greatly emerging as an efficient approach to build embedded evolvable and adaptable systems, coarse–grain reconfigurable (sub)systems and are very useful in System on Chip (SoC) development [2]. The popularity of FPGA technology is mainly due to its versatile nature that permits reprogrammability, fast development time and reduced efforts with respect to full-custom VLSI design. Furthermore, the advances in the microelectronics process technology allow the design of FPGA–based digital systems having performances very close to the one obtained by a manually full–custom layout, thus allowing the building of efficient neural processor chips [3].

The hardware implementation of neural networks has recently attracted new interest from the neurocomputing community despite the skepticism generated by the devices of the first generation, which appeared during the '80s (see, for example, [4] for a survey of these solutions).

We are interested in hardware implementation of algorithms which are inspired by the neurocomputing framework but not necessarily justified form a biological point of view. Our main target is the design of dedicated analog or digital hardware, with improved characteristics (e.g. performance, silicon area, power consumption, etc.) respect to a software implementation on a general–purpose microprocessor, which can be exploited in all the applications where special–purpose VLSI technologies can be preferable [5].

Here we discuss a simple algorithm for Support Vector Machine (SVM) learning that can be easily implemented in digital hardware and is quite robust to fixed–point math imprecisions. The algorithm is tested on a telecommunication application, where embedded VLSI systems are widely used. The full version of this paper will appear in [1].

In the following section we revise briefly the SVM. Section III addresses our proposal when targeting digital solutions, and Section IV shows some experimental results.

II. THE SUPPORT VECTOR MACHINE

From a mathematical point of view, the key issue in SVM learning is to find a classification function $\hat{\Phi}: X \to Y$ that approximates the unknown Φ, on the basis of the set of measures $\{x_i, y_i\}_{i=1}^m$, where $x_i \in X \subseteq \Re^l$ is an input pattern, and $y_i \in Y = \{-1, +1\}$ the corresponding target.

The SVM finds the hyperplane with the maximal distance (margin) from the two classes To allow for nonlinear classification functions, the training points are mapped from the input space X to a *feature space* $Z \subseteq \Re^L$, with $L \gg l$, through a nonlinear mapping $\varphi: X \to Z$. Then, the function $\hat{\Phi}$ is given by:

$$\hat{\Phi}(x) = w \cdot \varphi(x) + b \quad (1)$$

where w is the normal vector of the separating hyperplane. The main advantage of this formulation is that, by using clever mathematical properties of nonlinear mappings, SVMs avoid to explicitly work in the feature space, so that the advantages of the linear approach are retained even though a nonlinear separating function is found (see [6], [7], [8] for more details)

Formally, this description leads to a constrained quadratic optimization problem (CQP), by requiring to find:

$$\min_{w,b} \left[\frac{1}{2} \|w\|^2 + C \sum_{i=1}^m \xi_i \right] \quad (2)$$

subject to

$$y_i (w \cdot \varphi(x_i) + b) \geq 1 - \xi_i, \quad \forall i = 1, \ldots, m \quad (3)$$

This is usually referred as the *Primal* ($\mathcal{P}$) CQP.

The above $\mathcal{P}$–CQP is usually rewritten in dual form ($\mathcal{D}$), by using the Lagrange multiplier theory [6]:

$$\begin{array}{l} \min_{\alpha} \left[\alpha^T Q \alpha - r^T \alpha \right] \\ 0 \leq \alpha \leq C \\ \alpha^T y = 0 \end{array} \quad (4)$$

where $q_{ij} = y_i y_j k(x_i, x_j)$ and r is a vector of all ones. The kernel function $k(x_i, x_j)$ embeds implicitly the nonlinear mapping

$$k(x_i, x_j) = \varphi(x_i) \cdot \varphi(x_j) \quad (5)$$

if it fullfills some mathematical properties [6]. Since the seminal works on kernel functions, many kernels of the form given by Eq. (5) have been suggested:

$$k(x_i, x_j) = x_i \cdot x_j$$
$$k(x_i, x_j) = e^{-\frac{\|x_i - x_j\|^2}{2\sigma^2}} \quad (6)$$
$$k(x_i, x_j) = (1 + x_i \cdot x_j)^p$$

As a final remark, note that the threshold b does not appear in the dual formulation, but it can be found by using the Karush–Kuhn–Tucker (KKT) conditions at optimality [17], [18]. It is important to note, however, that the presence of the threshold b in the ($\mathcal{P}$) CQP gives rise to the equality constraint in the ($\mathcal{D}$) CQP. This is a severe inconvenience for digital hardware implementations, because the equality constraint is more difficult to fullfill, when using low–precision fixed–point math, than the inequality ones, which can be simply implemented by saturating the values of the involved variables.

III. Algorithm and Hardware implementation

Optimization problems like $\mathcal{D}$–CQP have been deeply studied by researchers, and several methods have been proposed for their resolution. Among others, methods that can be easily implemented in hardware (which we call *VLSI–friendly*) are particularly appealing. Many of them approach the problem by mapping it on a dynamical system described by a differential equation:

$$\dot{\nu} = F_A(\nu) \quad (7)$$

with $\nu^T = [\alpha^T, b]$, and whose stable point, for $t \to \infty$, coincides with the solution of the optimization problem.

Equation (7) can be seen as a recurrent neural network and, from an electronic point of view, can be implemented, on analog hardware, with simple electronic devices [9], [10].

A digital architecture can be targeted in a similar way by defining a recurrent relation of the form:

$$\nu^{k+1} = F_D(\nu^k) \quad (8)$$

which can be derived from the previous one by using, for example the Euler's method for integration.

Recently, a useful convergence result has been presented for a network that solves a CQP with inequality constraints [11], [12]. As showed in [13], this algorithm (Digital SVM or DSVM) can be applied effectively to SVM learning when a Gaussian kernel is chosen. The underlying idea is to exploit the fact that a Gaussian kernel maps the data to an infinite feature space, so the effect of removing one of the parameters of the SVM from the learning process can be neglegible. In particular, if we let $b = 0$, we force the separating hyperplane to pass through the origin in the feature space and the equality constraint disappears from the dual formulation of the CQP. The core of DSVM is very simple:

$$z^k = \alpha^k + \eta g \quad (9)$$
$$\alpha^{k+1} = \max(0, \min(z^k, C)) \quad (10)$$

where $g = -Q\alpha + r$. The convergence of the above recurrent relation is guaranteed, provided that $\eta \leq 2/m$.

Even if several experiments on real–world data sets have demonstrated the effectiveness of this method, it is greatly penalized by two facts: the generalization of a SVM with a constant threshold does not fit the usual theoretical framework, and it is not easily applicable to other kernels (e.g. the linear one).

Here, we suggest a new approach, which allows the use of the DSVM algorithm and the computation of the threshold as well. This result is based on a recent work on parametric optimization [14]: the main idea is to design a learning algorithm composed by two parts working iteratively. The first part addresses the resolution of a CQP with fixed b, whereas the second one implements a procedure for updating the value of b itself, in order to reach iteratively the optimal threshold value b^*.

If we consider the $\mathcal{P}$ problem of SVM learning, it is easy to deduce that, whenever the threshold b is considered as an a–priori known parameter, then the dual formulation becomes:

$$\min_{\alpha} \left[\tfrac{1}{2} \alpha^T Q \alpha - \tilde{r}^T \alpha \right]$$
$$0 \leq \alpha \leq C \quad (11)$$

where $\tilde{r} = (r - yb)$.

Such a problem can be solved by a slightly modified version of DSVM, listed in table I. Given the input kernel matrix Q, a threshold b, and a starting value α^0, the algorithm solves the CQP of (11) by providing an intermediate solution α'.

As our aim is to solve the CQP with the equality constraint, it is possible to deduce, from the term $s = \text{sgn}(y^T \alpha')$, the range of variation of b^*. In fact, if $s < 0$ then the optimal value of the threshold is $b^* < b$, otherwise, if $s > 0$ then $b^* > b$ [14]. A simple iterative procedure can be consequently derived for finding b^*.

Our proposal, called *FIxed b Svm* (Fibs), is listed in Table II. Obviously, it has been designed with the goal of an implementation on a digital architecture, but, as will be clear subsequently, it can be implemented on a general–purpose floating–point platform as well.

Its functionality is based on the search of a range of values $[b_{low}, b_{up}]$ to which the threshold b^* belongs. Then, at each step, it proceeds according to a simple bisection process by finding a tentative value $b = (b_{low} + b_{up})/2$, and by updating b_{low} and b_{up} on the basis of the value of s. It terminates when the range $[b_{low}, b_{up}]$ is reached with a given tolerance ε_b. Note that, when the algorithm starts, both b_{low} and b_{up} are not known, therefore a first search of the feasible range must be performed. We found experimentally that $b_{low} = -1$ and $b_{up} = 1$ are good starting choices. As soon as the the starting range is found, the described bisection process begins.

IV. Experimental results

In order to test the proposed algorithm and the corresponding digital architecture, we chose several data sets from a telecomunication problem, recently used for the application of SVMs to channel equalization purposes. The fixed–point version of the algorithm is mapped on a Xilinx Virtex–II FPGA [1], [19], while the floating–point version is simulated on a conventional computer and compared also with the well–known SMO algorithm [15], [16], [18] for SVM learning.

The channel equalization problem is a typical application where a special–purpose device can be effectively used, on the receiver side, in order to estimate one among two symbols $u_n \in \{\pm 1\}$, of an indipendent sequence emitted from a given source. All the unknown non–linear effects of the involved components (transmitter, channel and receiver) are modelled as FIR filters, plus a Gaussian distributed noise e with zero mean and variance σ_e^2:

$$\begin{aligned} \tilde{x}(n) &= \sum_{k=0}^{N} h_k u(n-k) \\ \hat{x}(n) &= \sum_{p=1}^{P} c_p \tilde{x}^p(n) \\ x(n) &= \hat{x}(n) + e(n) \end{aligned} \quad (12)$$

The classical theory, tackles this problem by finding an optimal classifier (the Bayesian maximum likelihood detector), which provides an estimate $\hat{u}(n-D)$ of $y_n = u(n-D)$ through the observation of an l–dimensional vector $\boldsymbol{x}_n = [x(n), x(n-1), \ldots, x(n-l+1)]^T$. Whereas these methods require the knowledge of the symbols probability, and the analitic structure of the model, neural network–based approaches have been successfully applied [20], [21] to systems where such information is not known.

In practice, a classifier is selected on the basis of m previous samples, having the following structure:

$$\{(\boldsymbol{x}_{n-i}, u(n-D-i))\}_{i=0}^{m-1} \quad (13)$$

Here we consider two different nonlinear models of the channel, that, substantially, differ for the delay D:

- **Model 1**: $D = 2$;
- **Model 2**: $D = 0$.

Furthermore, as our aim is to test the behavior of the algorithm, we consider different number of training patterns. In particular, we choose $m^a = 500$, as in [21], and $m^b = 32$: this last choice guarantees a good trade off between the final generalization ability of the learned model and its device utilization. We call Model 1a, 1b, 2a, 2b, the corresponding distributions. Finally, in order to estimate the generalization error of the obtained SVM, we use a separate test set composed by $m_t^a = 2400$ and $m_t^b = 2900$ samples respectively.

With reference to equation (12) we consider the following channel:

$$\begin{aligned} \hat{x}(n) &= \tilde{x}(n) - 0.9\tilde{x}^3(x) \\ \tilde{x}(n) &= u(n) + \tfrac{1}{2}u(n-1) \end{aligned} \quad (14)$$

that assumes an ISI equal to 2. We choose $l = 2$ and $\sigma_e^2 = 0.2$. Figures 1–2 show the distribution of data obtained by (14) with the given parameters.

When designing a digital architecture one of the most important aspects that must be considered is the length of the word that represents the information inside the design. This parameter has a crucial role because it influences both the length of the registers and, as a consequence, the device utilization and the performance of the digital learning system.

When we faced the design of Fibs and the design of the corresponding architecture in particular, we needed to understand: 1) its behaviour when using a floating–point math with respect to standard SVM learning algorithms, like the SMO; 2) its behaviour when using a fixed–point math, and, finally 3) the required number of bits. To obtain these answers, we designed several experiments, at first on the linear–sonar, and then on models 1a,1b,2a,2b.

The results of our experiments are reported in Table III–VI. In these tables we report, for every kind of architecture, the number of support vectors (nsv), the threshold (b), the value of the quantity $\boldsymbol{y}^T\boldsymbol{\alpha}'$ (eq.), the number of training errors (TR) and finally the number of test errrors (TS). As expected, the floating–point version (FP) of our algorithm obtains good results with respect to the SMO algorithm. Note that we used a RBF–SVM with $\sigma^2 = 0.5$ for both models and $C = 0.05$ (for Model 1a), $C = 0.9$ (for Model 1b), $C = 0.2$ (for Model 2a) and $C = 0.8$ (for Model 2b).

The results of the fixed–point experiments are reported in the second part of the table, where, with the notation $xx - yy - zz$, we intend the number of bits used to code each $\tilde{q}_{ij}$ (xx), the number of bits used to code the integer (yy), and the fractional part (zz) of each α_i and b. From the observation of the results three main important properties emerge: 1) Fibs requires a relatively low number of bits, especially to code the kernel matrix; 2) the accuracy obtained on th equality constraint is not very critical, but, above all, 3) the quantization effect of the kernel matrix is a benefit for the generalization capability.

To complete our preliminary analysis, we compared our results with the ones reported in [21]. The results of our algorithm outperform the ones reported there, obtained with polynomial kernels, even by using only 32 samples. In fact, whereas [21] reaches an accuracy of 4.2% on the test of Model 1a, we reached 3.6% with Model 1a and 4.2% with Model 1b. Similar results are obtained with Model 2: case 2a improves on [21] with an accuracy of 16%; case 2b, instead, is worse, as we measured an accuracy of 23.5%.

In order to study the main properties of our design, such as the device utilization, we performed several experiments, at first by chosing a small number of patterns ($m = 8$), and then by chosing a more realistic size, that is $m = 32$, discussed also, from the generalization point of view, in the previous section. By using a VHDL description, we could parametrize our design and change the size from $m = 8$ to $m = 32$ without any particular effort, thus allowing an efficient study of the implementation properties for different training set sizes.

The functional simulations are summarized in Figure 3. In particular, it shows the convergence of the threshold b towards the optimum for different number of clock cycles, in both $m = 8$ (A) and $m = 32$ (B) cases. Each learning phase terminates after 14,000 (A) and 140,000 (B) cycles, whilst each loading phase terminates after 290 (A) and 4226 (B) cycles. Figures 3–

A–B indicate that a feasible b can be reached quite soon during learning: this suggests an acceptable rate of classification can be obtained well before the end of the learning process. In order to validate this assertion, we measured the percentage of test error during learning. Figure 3–C shows the value of test errors for different clock cycles for $m = 32$. As one can easily verify, after only 90,000 clock cycles (50,000 before the termination of the learning), the obtained performances are quite stable around the value obtained at the end of the algorithm.

V. CONCLUSIONS

We have presented a learning algorithm for SVM that can be easily implemented in digital hardware and allows the use of low–precision fixed–point math. More details on the analysis of quantization errors and the actual FPGA implementation will be presented in an upcoming work [1].

REFERENCES

[1] D. Anguita, A. Boni, S. Ridella, "A Digital Architecture for Support Vector Machines: theory, algorithm and FPGA implementation", *IEEE Trans. on Neural Networks – Special Issue on Hardware Implementations*, in press.

[2] M. Glesner, P. Zipf, and M. Renovell (eds.), Field–Programmable Logic and Application: Reconfigurable Computing is Going Mainstream, Proc. of the 12th International Conference on Field-Programmable Logic and Applications, Montpellier, France, September 2002.

[3] S. McBader, L. Clementel, A. Sartori, A. Boni and P. Lee, *SoftTotem: an FPGA Implementation of the Totem Parallel Processor*, Proc. of 12th International Conference on Field Programmable Logic and Application, France, 2002.

[4] C.S. Lindsey, "Neural Networks in Hardware: Architectures, Products and Applications", Royal Inst. of Technology on line lectures, Stockolm, Sweden, March 1998.

[5] U. Rückert, "ULSI Architectures for Artificial Neural Networks", *IEEE Micro*, May–June 2002, pp. 10–19.

[6] V. Vapnik, *Statistical Learning Theory*, Wiley, 1998.

[7] N. Cristianini, J. Shawe–Taylor, *An Introduction to Support Vector Machines*, Cambridge University Press, 2000.

[8] B. Schölkopf, A. Smola, *Learning with Kernels*, The MIT Press, 2002.

[9] D. Anguita, S. Ridella, S. Rovetta, "Circuital Implementation of Support Vector Machines", *Electronics Letters*, Vol. 34, No. 16, 1998, pp. 1596–1597.

[10] D. Anguita, A. Boni, "Improved Neural Network for SVM learning", *IEEE Trans. on Neural Networks*, Vol. 13, No. 5, Sept. 2002, pp. 1243–1244.

[11] M.J. Perez–Ilzarbe, "Convergence Analysis of a Discrete–time Recurrent Neural Network to Perform Quadratic Real Optimization With Bound Constraints", *IEEE Trans. on Neural Networks*, Vol. 9, No. 6, 1998, pp. 1344–1351.

[12] S. Hu, J.Wang, "Global Stability of a Class of Discrete-Time Recurrent Neural Networks", *IEEE Trans. on Circuits and Systems-I*, Vol. 49, No. 8, 2002, pp. 1104–1117.

[13] D. Anguita, A. Boni, S. Ridella, "Learning Algorithm for Nonlinear Support Vector Machines Suited for Digital VLSI", *Electronics Letters*, Vol. 35, No. 16, 1999.

[14] S. Fine, K. Scheinberg, "Incremental Learning and Selective Sampling via Parametric Optimization Framework for SVM", in T.G. Dietterich, S. Becker, and Z. Ghahramani (eds.), *Advances in Neural Information Processing Systems 14*, The MIT Press, 2002.

[15] J. Platt, "Fast Training of Support Vector Machines Using Sequential Minimal Optimization", in B. Schölkopf, C. Burges, and A. Smola (eds.) *Advances in Kernel Methods – Support Vector Learning*, The MIT Press, 1999.

[16] S.S. Keerthi, E.G. Gilbert, "Convergence of a Generalized SMO Algorithm for SVM Classifier Design", *Machine Learning*, Vol. 46, 2002, pp. 351–360.

[17] P. Laskov, "Feasible Direction Decomposition Algorithms for Training Support Vector Machines", *Machine Learning*, Vol. 46, 2002, pp. 315–350.

[18] C.-J. Lin, "Asymptotic Convergence of an SMO Algorithm Without Any Assumption", *IEEE Trans. on Neural Networks*, Vol. 13, No. 1, Jan. 2002, pp. 248–250.

[19] *Virtex II Platform FPGA Handbook* (ver. 1.3), http://www.xilinx.com/products/virtex/handbook/.

[20] S. Chen, G.J. Gibson, C.F.N. Cowan, P.M. Grant, "Adaptive Equalization of Finite Nonlinear Channels Using Multilayer Perceptrons", *Signal Processing*, Vol. 20, No. 2, 1990, pp. 107–119.

[21] D.J. Sebald, J.A. Bucklew, "Support Vector Machine Techniques for Nonlinear Equalization", *IEEE Trans. on Signal Processing*, Vol. 48, No. 11, 2000, pp. 3217–3226.

TABLE I

ALGORITHM 1: DSVM WITH FIXED BIAS.

Step	Description
1.	input: $Q, b, \boldsymbol{\alpha}^0$;
2.	set $\tilde{\boldsymbol{r}} = (\boldsymbol{r} - \boldsymbol{y}b)$; $\quad \eta = \dfrac{2}{m \max\limits_{i,j}(q_{ij})}$
3.	set endrun=false; $\quad k=0$
4.	while not endrun do
5.	$\quad \boldsymbol{g} = \left(-Q\boldsymbol{\alpha}^k + \tilde{\boldsymbol{r}}\right)$
6.	$\quad \boldsymbol{z}^{k+1} = \boldsymbol{\alpha}^k + \eta \boldsymbol{g}$
7.	$\quad \alpha_i^{k+1} = \max\left(0, \min\left(z_i^{k+1}, C\right)\right), \forall i = 1, \ldots, m$
8.	$\quad$ if $\forall i \left(\alpha_i^{k+1} - \alpha_i^k\right) \leq \varepsilon$ then
8.	$\quad\quad$ endrun=true
10.	$\quad$ else k=k+1
11.	enddo
12.	output: $\boldsymbol{\alpha}' = \boldsymbol{\alpha}^{k+1}$

TABLE II

ALGORITHM 2: FIBS.

Step	Description
1.	$b_{low} = b = -1;\quad \boldsymbol{\alpha}^0 = 0;\quad b_{up} = +1;\quad$ endFibs=false
2.	$\boldsymbol{\alpha}' = \mathcal{A}_b(Q, b, \boldsymbol{\alpha}^0);\quad s = \text{sgn}\left(\boldsymbol{y}^T\boldsymbol{\alpha}'\right);\quad \boldsymbol{\alpha}^0 = \boldsymbol{\alpha}'$
3.	if $s < 0$ then
4.	$\quad$ while $s < 0$ do
5.	$\quad\quad b_{up} = b;\quad b = 2b;\quad b_{low} = 2b_{low}$
6.	$\quad\quad \boldsymbol{\alpha}' = \mathcal{A}_b(Q, b, \boldsymbol{\alpha}^0);\quad s = \text{sgn}\left(\boldsymbol{y}^T\boldsymbol{\alpha}'\right);\quad \boldsymbol{\alpha}^0 = \boldsymbol{\alpha}'$
7.	$\quad$ enddo
8.	else if $s > 0$ then
9.	$\quad b = b_{up}$
10.	$\quad \boldsymbol{\alpha}' = \mathcal{A}_b(Q, b, \boldsymbol{\alpha}^0);\quad s = \text{sgn}\left(\boldsymbol{y}^T\boldsymbol{\alpha}'\right);\quad \boldsymbol{\alpha}^0 = \boldsymbol{\alpha}'$
11.	$\quad$ if $s > 0$ then
12.	$\quad\quad$ while $s > 0$ do
13.	$\quad\quad\quad b_{low} = b;\quad b = 2b;\quad b_{up} = 2b_{up}$
14.	$\quad\quad\quad \boldsymbol{\alpha}' = \mathcal{A}_b(Q, b, \boldsymbol{\alpha}^0);\quad s = \text{sgn}\left(\boldsymbol{y}^T\boldsymbol{\alpha}'\right);\quad \boldsymbol{\alpha}^0 = \boldsymbol{\alpha}'$
15.	$\quad\quad$ enddo
16.	$\quad$ else endFibs = true
17.	while not endFibs do
18.	$\quad b = (b_{low} + b_{up})/2$
19.	$\quad \boldsymbol{\alpha}' = \mathcal{A}_b(Q, b, \boldsymbol{\alpha}^0);\quad s = \text{sgn}\left(\boldsymbol{y}^T\boldsymbol{\alpha}'\right);\quad \boldsymbol{\alpha}^0 = \boldsymbol{\alpha}'$
20.	$\quad$ if $s = 0$ or $(b_{low} - b_{up}) \leq \varepsilon_b$ then endFibs=true
21.	$\quad$ else if $s < 0$ then $b_{up} = b$
22.	$\quad$ else $b_{low} = b$
23.	enddo

TABLE III
FLOATING AND FIXED–POINT EXPERIMENTS FOR MODEL 1A ($\sigma^2 = 0.5$; $C = 0.05$).

	nsv	b	eq.	TR	TS
FP(SMO)	271	1.3E-16	1.32E-16	17	88
FP(FIBS)	271	4.29E-2	-2.17E-4	17	88
16–3–8	500	1.17E-2	-3.9E-3	19	90
16–3–13	282	4.45E-2	-6.1E-5	18	89
12–3–8	500	1.17E-2	-3.9E-3	19	90
12–3–13	282	4.45E-2	2.4E-4	18	89
8–3–8	500	1.17E-2	0.0	19	91
8–3–13	282	4.41E-2	1.2E-4	18	88
4–3–8	500	1.17E-2	-1.56E-2	18	88
4–3–13	279	1.17E-2	6.1E-5	18	88

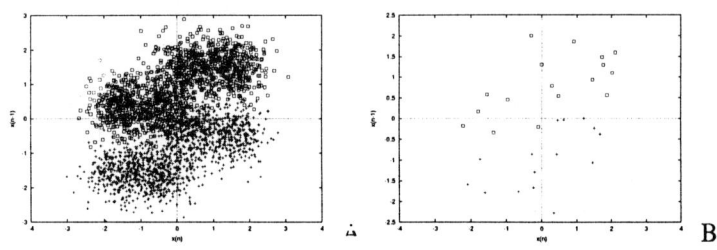

Fig. 1. Distribution of data for Models 1a (A) and 1b (B) ($D = 2, \sigma_e^2 = 0.2$, $m = 500$ (A), $m = 32$ (B)).

TABLE IV
FLOATING AND FIXED–POINT EXPERIMENTS FOR MODEL 1B ($\sigma^2 = 0.5$; $C = 0.9$).

	nsv	b	eq.	TR	TS
FP(SMO)	23	-7.37E-2	-6.9E-18	1	122
FP(FIBS)	23	-7.37E-2	-9.16E-5	1	122
16–3–8	23	-7.4E-2	-1.95E-2	1	124
16–3–13	23	-7.36E-2	0.0	1	122
12–3–8	23	-7.4E-2	-1.56E-2	1	124
12–3–13	23	-7.35E-2	-4.8E-4	1	122
8–3–8	23	-8.2E-2	1.95E-2	1	125
8–3–13	23	-7.54E-2	3.6E-4	1	121
6–3–8	23	-6.6E-2	1.95E-2	1	120
6–3–13	23	-6.12E-2	-3.6E-4	1	118

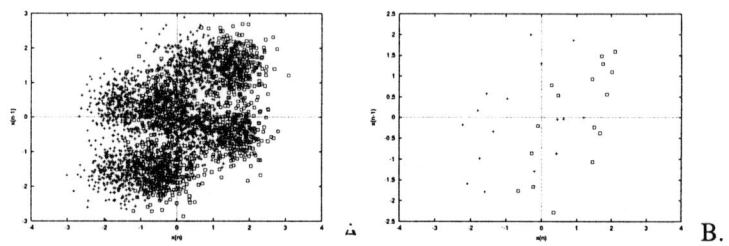

Fig. 2. Distribution of data for Models 2a (A) and 2b (B) ($D = 0$, $\sigma_e^2 = 0.2$, $m = 500$ (A), $m = 32$ (B)).

TABLE V
FLOATING AND FIXED–POINT EXPERIMENTS FOR MODEL 2A ($\sigma^2 = 0.5$; $C = 0.2$).

	nsv	b	eq.	TR	TS
FP(SMO)	324	6.01E-2	0.0	80	386
FP(FIBS)	324	6.01E-2	-3.6E-4	80	386
16–3–8	500	4.3E-2	-7.8E-3	80	386
16–3–13	327	5.69E-2	1.83E-4	80	385
12–3–8	500	4.3E-2	-7.8E-3	80	387
12–3–13	327	5.6E-2	3.6E-4	80	385
8–3–8	500	4.3E-2	-7.8E-3	81	387
8–3–13	329	5.56E-2	-4.2E-4	79	383
6–3–8	500	4.3E-2	3.52E-2	79	392
6–3–13	328	5.76E-2	-3.05E-2	83	388

TABLE VI
FLOATING AND FIXED–POINT EXPERIMENTS FOR MODEL 2B ($\sigma^2 = 0.5$; $C = 0.8$).

	nsv	b	eq.	TR	TS
FP(SMO)	28	2.05E-2	0.0	3	683
FP(FIBS)	28	2.06E-2	-1.2E-4	3	683
16–3–8	29	2.73E-2	-1.17E-2	3	691
16–3–13	28	2.07E-2	-1.2E-4	3	685
12–3–8	29	2.7E-2	.1.17E-2	3	692
12–3–13	28	2.09E-2	-3.6E-4	3	685
8–3–8	29	2.7E-2	-2.34E-2	3	692
8–3–13	28	1.97E-2	-3.05E-4	3	688
4–3–8	28	2.73E-2	-7.8E-3	5	685
4–3–13	28	3.46E-2	-3.6E-4	3	680

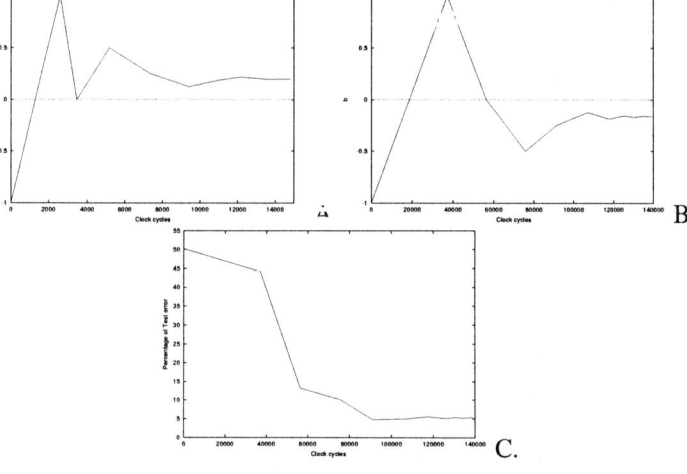

Fig. 3. Convergence of b for $m = 8$(A) and $m=32$(B); and percentage of test errors during learning for $m = 32$(C).

Optimizing Support Vector Regression Hyperparameters Based on Cross-Validation

Kentaro Ito, Ryohei Nakano

Nagoya Institute of Technology
Gokiso-cho, Showa-ku, Nagoya 466-8555, Japan
Email: {kntritoh,nakano}@ics.nitech.ac.jp

Abstract—This paper proposes a method to optimize hyperparameters for Support Vector (SV) regression so that the cross-validation error is minimized. The performance of SV regression depends on its hyperparameters such as ε (the thickness of a tube), C (a penalty factor), σ (kernel function parameter), and so on. This paper employs the procedure of cross-validation to optimize these hyperparameters together with training the corresponding SV regression models; thus, the learning is performed by using a coordinate descent method. Since an error surface produced by the usual ε-insensitive l_1 loss is not smooth, not suitable for our approach, we introduce the ε-insensitive l_2 loss. The experiments show the l_2 loss produces very smooth error surfaces and our coordinate descent nicely works, reaching the model whose validation performance is globally optimal.

I. INTRODUCTION

Although Support Vector (SV) machines were first developed for pattern recognition, they can be applied to regression [6], [5]. SV regression is expected to inherit the good SV characteristic that it generalizes well to unseen data.

The performance of SV regression depends on its hyperparameters. This paper focuses on the following three hyperparameters. The first is the thickness ε of a tube. SV regression uses the ε-insensitive loss function which does not penalize errors below some $\varepsilon (\geq 0)$. The second is a penalty factor C which penalizes any deviation beyond the ε-tube. The multiplying factor can be considered as a penalty factor used in the regularization of neural networks. The third is a kernel function parameter; here, the Gaussian basis function is considered, so the third hyperparameter is σ.

To optimize the hyperparameters we need validation data, and to train SV regression under the hyperparameters we need training data. Often the size of data is severely limited, so we employ *cross-validation* [7]. Then the hyperparameters are optimized so that the cross-validation error is minimized. This *MCV (Minimum Cross-Validation)* method worked nicely in the regularization of neural networks to learn a distinct penalty factor for each weight, called the MCV regularizer [3]. Since the MCV method is general enough, it can be applied here.

In our early experiments, we used the usual SV regression, and found a validation error surface far from smooth, full of sharp edges. Such a landscape is not suited to any gradient search. We have tried the ε-insensitive l_2 loss, which turns out to produce very smooth surfaces. The surface produced by the l_2 loss looks like being generated by smoothing the l_1 surface. At least in our experiments, employing the l_2 loss instead of the l_1 loss hardly affects the generalization performance.

The problem of automatically tuning kernel parameters for SV machines was addressed in [1]. The adjustment of a tube was investigated in the context of ν-SV regression [4]. A derivative-free optimization method called pattern search was tried for automatic model selection of SV regression [2].

Section 2 briefly explains SV regression, how the hyperparameters influence the performance, and the MCV method. Section 3 shows how the MCV method is applied to SV regression. Section 4 compares an error surface produced by the l_1 and l_2 losses, how our method automatically finds the optimum, and evaluates the solution quality and the complexity of the proposed method.

II. BACKGROUND

A. Support Vector Regression

Suppose we are given data $D: \{(\boldsymbol{x}^\mu, y^\mu), \mu = 1, \cdots, N\}$. We begin with the linear SV regression.

$$y(\boldsymbol{x}) = \langle \boldsymbol{w}, \boldsymbol{x} \rangle + b \quad (1)$$

Here $\langle, \rangle$ denotes the dot product. The target function to minimize can be defined as follows, where the coefficient C denotes a penalty factor.

$$\frac{1}{2}\|\boldsymbol{w}\|^2 + C \sum_{\mu=1}^{N} |y^\mu - y(\boldsymbol{x}^\mu)|_\varepsilon \quad (2)$$

The first term seeks a small $\|\boldsymbol{w}\|^2$, which means seeking as flat a line as possible. The second term is the ε-insensitive penalty, where $|\cdot|_\varepsilon$ denotes the ε-insensitive loss function. In most cases the following ε-insensitive l_1 loss function has been used [6], but it generates an error surface far from smooth.

$$|y^\mu - y(\boldsymbol{x}^\mu)|_\varepsilon = \max\{0, |y^\mu - y(\boldsymbol{x}^\mu)| - \varepsilon\} \quad (3)$$

Thus, this paper employs the following ε-insensitive l_2 loss function.

$$|y^\mu - y(\boldsymbol{x}^\mu)|_\varepsilon = \begin{cases} 0 & \text{if } |y^\mu - y(\boldsymbol{x}^\mu)| < \varepsilon \\ \frac{1}{2}(|y^\mu - y(\boldsymbol{x}^\mu)| - \varepsilon)^2 & \text{otherwise} \end{cases} \quad (4)$$

Then our optimization problem can be formalized as follows. Slack variables $\xi^\mu, \xi^{*\mu}$ denote deviations from the ε-tube.

$$\text{minimize} \quad \frac{1}{2}\|\boldsymbol{w}\|^2 + \frac{C}{2}\sum_{\mu=1}^{N}\left((\xi^\mu)^2 + (\xi^{*\mu})^2\right)$$

$$\text{subject to} \begin{cases} y^\mu - \langle \boldsymbol{w}, \boldsymbol{x} \rangle - b & \leq \varepsilon + \xi^\mu \\ \langle \boldsymbol{w}, \boldsymbol{x} \rangle + b - y^\mu & \leq \varepsilon + \xi^{*\mu} \\ \xi^\mu, \xi^{*\mu} & \geq 0 \end{cases} \quad (5)$$

To make the above model nonlinear, consider a mapping Φ from the input space into some feature space. The dot product in the feature space can be expressed as a kernel function $K(x_1, x_2) = \langle \Phi(x_1), \Phi(x_2) \rangle$. Then we have the following dual nonlinear (quadratic programming) problem. Here $\alpha^\mu, \alpha^{*\mu}$ are Lagrange multipliers.

maximize
$$W = -\frac{1}{2}\sum_{\mu=1}^{N}\sum_{\mu'=1}^{N}(\alpha^\mu - \alpha^{*\mu})(\alpha^{\mu'} - \alpha^{*\mu'})K(x^\mu, x^{\mu'})$$
$$-\varepsilon\sum_{\mu=1}^{N}(\alpha^\mu + \alpha^{*\mu}) + \sum_{\mu=1}^{N}y^\mu(\alpha^\mu - \alpha^{*\mu})$$
$$-\frac{1}{2C}\sum_{\mu=1}^{N}\left((\alpha^\mu)^2 + (\alpha^{*\mu})^2\right)$$

subject to
$$\begin{cases} \sum_{\mu=1}^{N}(\alpha^{*\mu} - \alpha^\mu) = 0 \\ \alpha^\mu, \alpha^{*\mu} \in [0, \infty) \end{cases} \quad (6)$$

Then we have the following nonlinear SV regression function.
$$y(x|\theta) = \sum_{\mu=1}^{N}(\alpha^\mu - \alpha^{*\mu})K(x^\mu, x) + b \quad (7)$$

Here $\theta = (\alpha^T, \alpha^{*T})^T$ denotes a parameter vector of SV regression. As for b, we use the least-square estimate given below.
$$b = \frac{1}{N}\sum_{\mu=1}^{N}\left(y^\mu - \sum_{\mu'=1}^{N}(\alpha^{\mu'} - \alpha^{*\mu'})K(x^\mu, x^{\mu'})\right) \quad (8)$$

As a kernel function, we use the Gaussian basis function.
$$K(x^\mu, x^{\mu'}) = \exp\left(-\frac{\|x^\mu - x^{\mu'}\|^2}{2\sigma^2}\right) \quad (9)$$

B. Hyperparameters of SVR

Now let's have a look around on the tendency how the performance of SV regression depends on the hyperparameters: C, ε, and σ. Figure 1 exemplifies how these three hyperparameters have a serious influence on the performance of SV regression. A plus symbol enclosed with a circle indicates a Support Vector. A fine curve shows the true function. A heavy curve indicates the center of the ε-tube, and dotted curves are the boundaries of the tube.

Figure 1(a) shows the influence of C; for a very small C, a penalty gets negligible and SV regression gets flat, while for a large C a penalty gets more important and SV regression tries to fit the data. Figure 1(b) shows the influence of ε; since a very thin ε-tube does not have enough margin to include data points, SV regression function tries to fit the data, but a thick ε-tube has enough margin, having a tendency to get flat. Figure 1(c) shows the influence of σ; a very small σ means the kernel is more localized, thus, SV regression has a tendency to overfit, while a large σ makes the ε-tube less flexible.

As is observed above, since these three hyperparameters have a serious influence on the performance of SV regression,

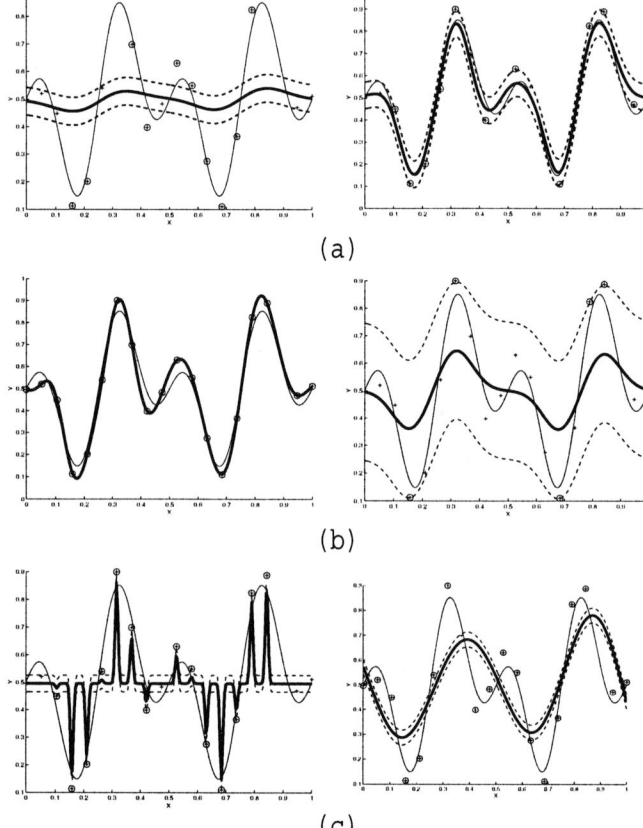

Fig. 1. Influence of the Hyperparameters on SV Regression, (a) left: small $C(= 0.01)$ and right: large $C(= 10^6)$, (b) left: small $\varepsilon(= 0.0)$ and right: large $\varepsilon(= 0.25)$, and (c) left: small $\sigma(= 0.005)$ and right: large $\sigma(= 0.2)$.

the optimization of the hyperparameters is indispensable to obtain high generalization.

C. MCV Method

Our goal is to find the SV regression model having the best generalization. Given a set of hyperparameters, each SV regression is determined by using training data D. To achieve our goal, we have to find the best set of hyperparameters, and for this purpose we need validation data V, independent of D. Often the size of data is severely limited; thus, we employ the procedure of *cross-validation* [7].

The procedure of cross-validation divides given data D at random into S distinct segments $\{G_s, s = 1, \cdots, S\}$, and uses $S - 1$ segments for training, and uses the remaining one for the test. This process is repeated S times by changing the remaining segment, and the generalization performance is evaluated by using the following MSE (mean squared error) over all test results.

$$MSE_{CV} = \frac{1}{N}\sum_{s=1}^{S}\sum_{\mu \in G_s}(y^\mu - y(x^\mu|\widehat{\theta}_s))^2. \quad (10)$$

Here G_s denotes the s-th segment for the test, and $\widehat{\theta}_s$ denotes the optimal parameter vector obtained by using $D - G_s$ for training. The extreme case of $S = N$ is known as the *leave-one-out (LOO)* method, often used for a small size of data.

$$MSE_{LOO} = \frac{1}{N} \sum_{\mu=1}^{N} (y^\mu - y(\bm{x}^\mu|\widehat{\bm{\theta}}_\mu))^2 \quad (11)$$

Here $\widehat{\bm{\theta}}_\mu$ denotes the optimal parameter vector obtained by using $D - \{(\bm{x}^\mu, y^\mu)\}$ for training.

By using cross-validation, the hyperparameters are optimized so that the cross-validation error MSE_{CV} is minimized. This MCV (Minimum Cross-Validation) idea worked nicely in the regularization of neural networks to learn a distinct penalty factor for each weight, called the *MCV regularizer* [3]. The procedure used in the MCV regularizer can be generalized as the following method.

The general **MCV method** is outlined below. Let $\bm{\lambda}$ be a hyperparameter vector, and a target function for optimizing $\bm{\lambda}$ is MSE_{CV}. Let $\bm{\theta}$ and $J(\bm{\theta}|\bm{\lambda})$ be a parameter vector of a model and a target function used to train $\bm{\theta}$ under the given hyperparameters $\bm{\lambda}$ respectively. The MCV method employs the coordinate descent; that is, it iterates the following two steps until convergence:

step 1: Given $\bm{\lambda}$, optimize $\{\bm{\theta}_s, s = 1, \cdots, S\}$.
step 2: Given $\{\bm{\theta}_s, s = 1, \cdots, S\}$, improve $\bm{\lambda}$.

In step 2, since $\{\bm{\theta}_s\}$ depends on $\bm{\lambda}$, we should not optimize $\bm{\lambda}$ with $\{\bm{\theta}_s\}$ fixed; instead, we just improve $\bm{\lambda}$. Here we assume we have some learning algorithm to perform step 1. Thus, below we consider how to perform step 2. To perform step 2, the following gradient will suffice.

$$\frac{\partial MSE_{CV}}{\partial \bm{\lambda}^T} = -\frac{2}{N} \sum_{s=1}^{S} \sum_{\mu \in G_s} (y^\mu - y(\bm{x}^\mu|\widehat{\bm{\theta}}_s)) \frac{\partial y(\bm{x}^\mu|\widehat{\bm{\theta}}_s)}{\partial \bm{\lambda}^T} \quad (12)$$

Then we need the gradient of y in respect of $\bm{\lambda}$.

$$\frac{\partial y(\bm{x}^\mu|\widehat{\bm{\theta}}_s)}{\partial \bm{\lambda}^T} = \frac{\partial y(\bm{x}^\mu|\widehat{\bm{\theta}}_s)}{\partial \bm{\theta}_s^T} \frac{\partial \widehat{\bm{\theta}}_s}{\partial \bm{\lambda}^T} \quad (13)$$

The remaining problem is to compute the gradient $\frac{\partial \widehat{\bm{\theta}}_s}{\partial \bm{\lambda}^T}$. The optimal $\widehat{\bm{\theta}}_s$ satisfies the following

$$\frac{\partial J(\widehat{\bm{\theta}}_s|\bm{\lambda})}{\partial \bm{\theta}_s} = 0 \equiv \bm{f}(\widehat{\bm{\theta}}_s, \bm{\lambda}). \quad (14)$$

By differentiating this equation in respect of $\bm{\lambda}$, we obtain

$$0 = \frac{\partial^+ \bm{f}}{\partial \bm{\lambda}^T} = \frac{\partial \bm{f}}{\partial \widehat{\bm{\theta}}_s^T} \frac{\partial \widehat{\bm{\theta}}_s}{\partial \bm{\lambda}^T} + \frac{\partial \bm{f}}{\partial \bm{\lambda}^T}. \quad (15)$$

This gives us the following gradient we wanted.

$$\frac{\partial \widehat{\bm{\theta}}_s}{\partial \bm{\lambda}^T} = -\left(\frac{\partial \bm{f}}{\partial \widehat{\bm{\theta}}_s^T}\right)^{-1} \frac{\partial \bm{f}}{\partial \bm{\lambda}^T} \quad (16)$$

III. MCV-SVR Method

This section shows how the MCV method can be straightforwardly applied to the optimization of hyperparameters of SV regression. The method is called the **MCV-SVR method**. We assume the leave-one-out (LOO) is used here as cross-validation. Note that the parameters of SV regression in the context of the MCV are $\Theta = \{\bm{\alpha}_\nu, \bm{\alpha}_\nu^*, \nu = 1, \cdots, N\}$. The MCV-SVR method iterates the following two steps until convergence:

step 1: Given C, ε, and σ, optimize Θ.
step 2: Given Θ, improve C, ε, and σ.

Since we have a learning algorithm to perform step 1, below we consider only step 2. SV regression can be written as below.

$$y(\bm{x}^\nu|\bm{\theta}_\nu) = \sum_{\mu \notin \nu} (\alpha_\nu^\mu - \alpha_\nu^{*\mu}) K(\bm{x}^\mu, \bm{x}^\nu) + b_\nu \quad (17)$$

$$b_\nu = \frac{1}{N-1} \sum_{\mu \notin \nu} \left(y_\mu - \sum_{\mu' \notin \nu} (\alpha_\nu^{\mu'} - \alpha_\nu^{*\mu'}) K(\bm{x}^\mu, \bm{x}^{\mu'}) \right) \quad (18)$$

To perform step 2, the following gradient will suffice.

$$\frac{\partial MSE_{LOO}}{\partial C} = -\frac{2}{N} \sum_{\nu=1}^{N} (y^\nu - y(\bm{x}^\nu|\bm{\theta}_\nu)) \frac{\partial^+ y(\bm{x}^\nu|\bm{\theta}_\nu)}{\partial C} \quad (19)$$

$$\frac{\partial MSE_{LOO}}{\partial \varepsilon} = -\frac{2}{N} \sum_{\nu=1}^{N} (y^\nu - y(\bm{x}^\nu|\bm{\theta}_\nu)) \frac{\partial^+ y(\bm{x}^\nu|\bm{\theta}_\nu)}{\partial \varepsilon} \quad (20)$$

$$\frac{\partial MSE_{LOO}}{\partial \sigma} = -\frac{2}{N} \sum_{\nu=1}^{N} (y^\nu - y(\bm{x}^\nu|\bm{\theta}_\nu)) \frac{\partial^+ y(\bm{x}^\nu|\bm{\theta}_\nu)}{\partial \sigma} \quad (21)$$

Then we need the gradient of y in respect of C, ε, and σ.

$$\frac{\partial^+ y(\bm{x}^\nu|\bm{\theta}_\nu)}{\partial C} = \frac{\partial^+ y}{\partial \bm{\alpha}_\nu^T} \frac{\partial \bm{\alpha}_\nu}{\partial C} + \frac{\partial^+ y}{\partial \bm{\alpha}_\nu^{*T}} \frac{\partial \bm{\alpha}_\nu^*}{\partial C} + \frac{\partial y}{\partial C} \quad (22)$$

$$\frac{\partial^+ y(\bm{x}^\nu|\bm{\theta}_\nu)}{\partial \varepsilon} = \frac{\partial^+ y}{\partial \bm{\alpha}_\nu^T} \frac{\partial \bm{\alpha}_\nu}{\partial \varepsilon} + \frac{\partial^+ y}{\partial \bm{\alpha}_\nu^{*T}} \frac{\partial \bm{\alpha}_\nu^*}{\partial \varepsilon} + \frac{\partial y}{\partial \varepsilon} \quad (23)$$

$$\frac{\partial^+ y(\bm{x}^\nu|\bm{\theta}_\nu)}{\partial \sigma} = \frac{\partial^+ y}{\partial \bm{\alpha}_\nu^T} \frac{\partial \bm{\alpha}_\nu}{\partial \sigma} + \frac{\partial^+ y}{\partial \bm{\alpha}_\nu^{*T}} \frac{\partial \bm{\alpha}_\nu^*}{\partial \sigma} + \frac{\partial y}{\partial \sigma} \quad (24)$$

Parameters $\bm{\theta}_\nu = (\bm{\alpha}_\nu^T, \bm{\alpha}_\nu^{*T})^T$ have to minimize the following under the training data $D - \{(\bm{x}^\nu, y^\nu)\}$.

$$J = W_\nu - \kappa_\nu \sum_{\mu \notin \nu} (\alpha_\nu^\mu - \alpha_\nu^{*\mu}) - \sum_{\mu \notin \nu} \left(\lambda_\nu^\mu \alpha_\nu^\mu + \lambda_\nu^{*\mu} \alpha_\nu^{*\mu} \right) \quad (25)$$

Here $\kappa_\nu, \lambda_\nu^\mu, \lambda_\nu^{*\mu}$ are Lagrange multipliers. That is, the optimal $\widehat{\bm{\theta}}_\nu$ satisfies the following.

$$\frac{\partial J}{\partial \bm{\alpha}_\nu} = 0, \quad \frac{\partial J}{\partial \bm{\alpha}_\nu^*} = 0, \quad \frac{\partial J}{\partial \kappa_\nu} = 0 \quad (26)$$

More specifically we have

$$\frac{\partial J}{\partial \alpha_\nu^\mu} = \sum_{\mu' \notin \nu}(\alpha_\nu^{\mu'} - \alpha_\nu^{*\mu'})K(\boldsymbol{x}^\mu, \boldsymbol{x}^{\mu'}) + \varepsilon - y^\mu$$
$$+ \frac{\alpha_\nu^\mu}{C} - \kappa_\nu - \lambda_\nu^\mu = 0 \quad (27)$$

$$\frac{\partial J}{\partial \alpha_\nu^{*\mu}} = -\sum_{\mu' \notin \nu}(\alpha_\nu^{\mu'} - \alpha_\nu^{*\mu'})K(\boldsymbol{x}^\mu, \boldsymbol{x}^{\mu'}) + \varepsilon + y^\mu$$
$$+ \frac{\alpha_\nu^{*\mu}}{C} + \kappa_\nu - \lambda_\nu^{*\mu} = 0 \quad (28)$$

From the KKT conditions, we obtain the following.

$$f_\nu^\mu \equiv \left[\sum_{\mu' \notin \nu}(\alpha_\nu^{\mu'} - \alpha_\nu^{*\mu'})K(\boldsymbol{x}^\mu, \boldsymbol{x}^{\mu'}) + \varepsilon - y^\mu \right.$$
$$\left. + \frac{\alpha_\nu^\mu}{C} - \kappa_\nu\right] \cdot \alpha_\nu^\mu = 0 \quad (29)$$

$$f_\nu^{*\mu} \equiv \left[\sum_{\mu' \notin \nu}(\alpha_\nu^{\mu'} - \alpha_\nu^{*\mu'})K(\boldsymbol{x}^\mu, \boldsymbol{x}^{\mu'}) - \varepsilon - y^\mu \right.$$
$$\left. - \frac{\alpha_\nu^{*\mu}}{C} - \kappa_\nu\right] \cdot \alpha_\nu^{*\mu} = 0 \quad (30)$$

By differentiating the above equations in respect of C, ε, and σ, we obtain

$$0 = \frac{\partial^+ \boldsymbol{f}_\nu}{\partial C} = \frac{\partial \boldsymbol{f}_\nu}{\partial \widehat{\boldsymbol{\alpha}}_\nu^T}\frac{\partial \widehat{\boldsymbol{\alpha}}_\nu}{\partial C} + \frac{\partial \boldsymbol{f}_\nu}{\partial \widehat{\boldsymbol{\alpha}}_\nu^{*T}}\frac{\partial \widehat{\boldsymbol{\alpha}}_\nu^*}{\partial C} + \frac{\partial \boldsymbol{f}_\nu}{\partial C} \quad (31)$$

$$0 = \frac{\partial^+ \boldsymbol{f}_\nu^*}{\partial C} = \frac{\partial \boldsymbol{f}_\nu^*}{\partial \widehat{\boldsymbol{\alpha}}_\nu^T}\frac{\partial \widehat{\boldsymbol{\alpha}}_\nu}{\partial C} + \frac{\partial \boldsymbol{f}_\nu^*}{\partial \widehat{\boldsymbol{\alpha}}_\nu^{*T}}\frac{\partial \widehat{\boldsymbol{\alpha}}_\nu^*}{\partial C} + \frac{\partial \boldsymbol{f}_\nu^*}{\partial C} \quad (32)$$

$$0 = \frac{\partial^+ \boldsymbol{f}_\nu}{\partial \varepsilon} = \frac{\partial \boldsymbol{f}_\nu}{\partial \widehat{\boldsymbol{\alpha}}_\nu^T}\frac{\partial \widehat{\boldsymbol{\alpha}}_\nu}{\partial \varepsilon} + \frac{\partial \boldsymbol{f}_\nu}{\partial \widehat{\boldsymbol{\alpha}}_\nu^{*T}}\frac{\partial \widehat{\boldsymbol{\alpha}}_\nu^*}{\partial \varepsilon} + \frac{\partial \boldsymbol{f}_\nu}{\partial \varepsilon} \quad (33)$$

$$0 = \frac{\partial^+ \boldsymbol{f}_\nu^*}{\partial \varepsilon} = \frac{\partial \boldsymbol{f}_\nu^*}{\partial \widehat{\boldsymbol{\alpha}}_\nu^T}\frac{\partial \widehat{\boldsymbol{\alpha}}_\nu}{\partial \varepsilon} + \frac{\partial \boldsymbol{f}_\nu^*}{\partial \widehat{\boldsymbol{\alpha}}_\nu^{*T}}\frac{\partial \widehat{\boldsymbol{\alpha}}_\nu^*}{\partial \varepsilon} + \frac{\partial \boldsymbol{f}_\nu^*}{\partial \varepsilon} \quad (34)$$

$$0 = \frac{\partial^+ \boldsymbol{f}_\nu}{\partial \sigma} = \frac{\partial \boldsymbol{f}_\nu}{\partial \widehat{\boldsymbol{\alpha}}_\nu^T}\frac{\partial \widehat{\boldsymbol{\alpha}}_\nu}{\partial \sigma} + \frac{\partial \boldsymbol{f}_\nu}{\partial \widehat{\boldsymbol{\alpha}}_\nu^{*T}}\frac{\partial \widehat{\boldsymbol{\alpha}}_\nu^*}{\partial \sigma} + \frac{\partial \boldsymbol{f}_\nu}{\partial \sigma} \quad (35)$$

$$0 = \frac{\partial^+ \boldsymbol{f}_\nu^*}{\partial \sigma} = \frac{\partial \boldsymbol{f}_\nu^*}{\partial \widehat{\boldsymbol{\alpha}}_\nu^T}\frac{\partial \widehat{\boldsymbol{\alpha}}_\nu}{\partial \sigma} + \frac{\partial \boldsymbol{f}_\nu^*}{\partial \widehat{\boldsymbol{\alpha}}_\nu^{*T}}\frac{\partial \widehat{\boldsymbol{\alpha}}_\nu^*}{\partial \sigma} + \frac{\partial \boldsymbol{f}_\nu^*}{\partial \sigma} \quad (36)$$

These are quite similar equations and can be rewritten as follows.

$$Z \cdot \boldsymbol{p}_C = -\boldsymbol{q}_C, \quad Z \cdot \boldsymbol{p}_\varepsilon = -\boldsymbol{q}_\varepsilon, \quad Z \cdot \boldsymbol{p}_\sigma = -\boldsymbol{q}_\sigma \quad (37)$$

Here

$$Z = \begin{bmatrix} \frac{\partial \boldsymbol{f}_\nu}{\partial \widehat{\boldsymbol{\alpha}}_\nu^T} & \frac{\partial \boldsymbol{f}_\nu}{\partial \widehat{\boldsymbol{\alpha}}_\nu^{*T}} \\ \frac{\partial \boldsymbol{f}_\nu^*}{\partial \widehat{\boldsymbol{\alpha}}_\nu^T} & \frac{\partial \boldsymbol{f}_\nu^*}{\partial \widehat{\boldsymbol{\alpha}}_\nu^{*T}} \end{bmatrix} \quad (38)$$

$$\boldsymbol{p}_C = \begin{bmatrix} \frac{\partial \widehat{\boldsymbol{\alpha}}_\nu}{\partial C} \\ \frac{\partial \widehat{\boldsymbol{\alpha}}_\nu^*}{\partial C} \end{bmatrix}, \quad \boldsymbol{p}_\varepsilon = \begin{bmatrix} \frac{\partial \widehat{\boldsymbol{\alpha}}_\nu}{\partial \varepsilon} \\ \frac{\partial \widehat{\boldsymbol{\alpha}}_\nu^*}{\partial \varepsilon} \end{bmatrix}, \quad \boldsymbol{p}_\sigma = \begin{bmatrix} \frac{\partial \widehat{\boldsymbol{\alpha}}_\nu}{\partial \sigma} \\ \frac{\partial \widehat{\boldsymbol{\alpha}}_\nu^*}{\partial \sigma} \end{bmatrix} \quad (39)$$

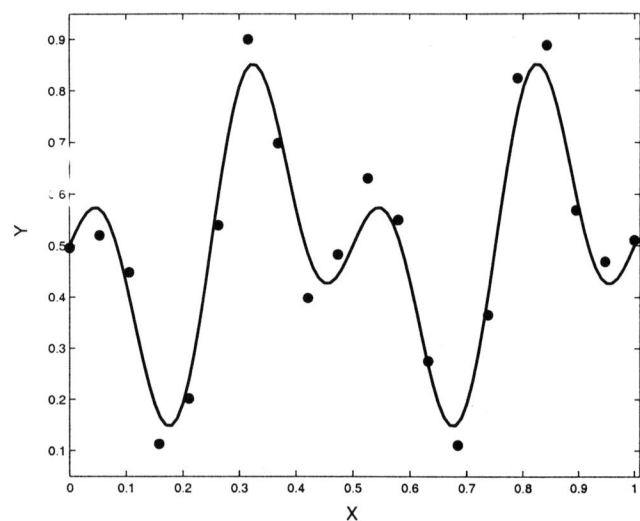

Fig. 2. True Function $0.5 + 0.4\sin(2\pi x)\cos(6\pi x)$ and the Samples

$$\boldsymbol{q}_C = \begin{bmatrix} \frac{\partial \boldsymbol{f}_\nu}{\partial C} \\ \frac{\partial \boldsymbol{f}_\nu^*}{\partial C} \end{bmatrix}, \quad \boldsymbol{q}_\varepsilon = \begin{bmatrix} \frac{\partial \boldsymbol{f}_\nu}{\partial \varepsilon} \\ \frac{\partial \boldsymbol{f}_\nu^*}{\partial \varepsilon} \end{bmatrix}, \quad \boldsymbol{q}_\sigma = \begin{bmatrix} \frac{\partial \boldsymbol{f}_\nu}{\partial \sigma} \\ \frac{\partial \boldsymbol{f}_\nu^*}{\partial \sigma} \end{bmatrix} \quad (40)$$

Thus, we have the following gradient we wanted.

$$\boldsymbol{p}_C = -Z^{-1} \cdot \boldsymbol{q}_C \quad (41)$$

$$\boldsymbol{p}_\varepsilon = -Z^{-1} \cdot \boldsymbol{q}_\varepsilon \quad (42)$$

$$\boldsymbol{p}_\sigma = -Z^{-1} \cdot \boldsymbol{q}_\sigma \quad (43)$$

IV. EXPERIMENTS

To evaluate the ε-insensitive l_2 loss and our MCV-SVR method, we used the following function.

$$y(x) = 0.5 + 0.4\sin(2\pi x)\cos(6\pi x) \quad (44)$$

Twenty samples are generated based on the above function, and Gaussian noise with a mean of 0 and a standard deviation of 0.05 is added to each sample. Figure 2 shows the true function and the samples. We used Matlab Optimization Toolbox to solve the quadratic programming problems and used Dell Precision 530 (2GHz) PCs.

A. Comparison Between ε-insensitive Loss Functions

The ε-insensitive l_2 loss was compared with the l_1 loss. Since any descent method does not work for the l_1 loss, we used an exhaustive method by dividing each value range of hyperparameters. To get a three-dimensional landscape, one hyperparameter was fixed at a certain value, and each of two others was divided into 100 values, thus total 10,000 grids were examined.

Figures 3 and 4 show the landscapes of MSE_{LOO} based on the l_1 and l_2 losses respectively for $C = 500$. We can see the following. First, the landscape based on the l_1 loss is not smooth, while the l_2 loss produces a very smooth landscape.

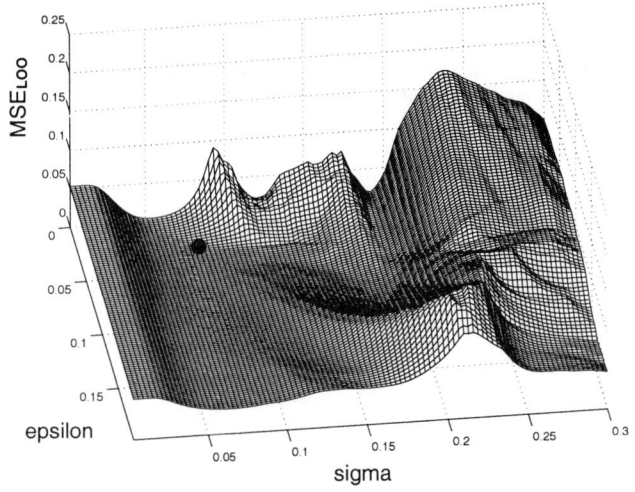

Fig. 3. Landscape of MSE_{LOO} based on ε-insensitive l_1 Loss ($C = 500$)

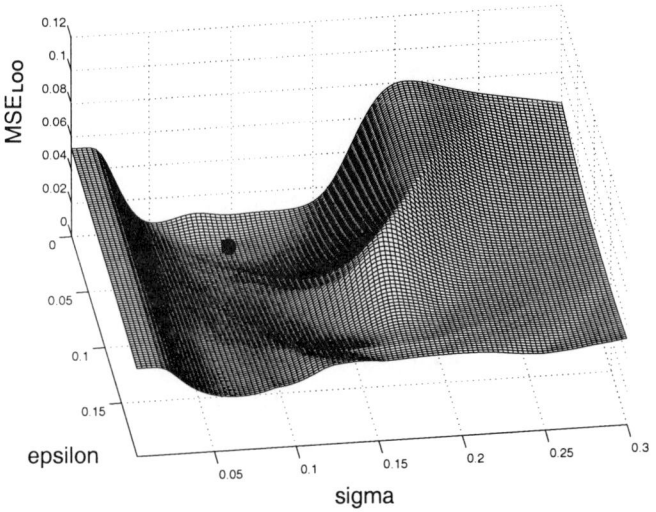

Fig. 4. Landscape of MSE_{LOO} based on ε-insensitive l_2 Loss ($C = 500$)

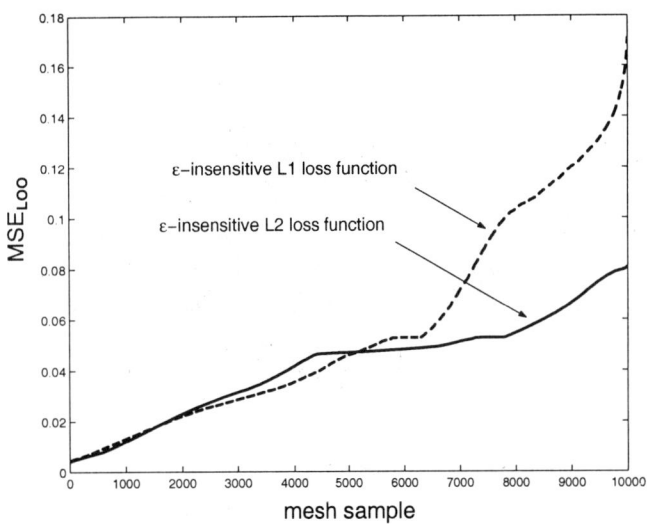

Fig. 5. Distribution of MSE_{LOO} based on l_1 and l_2 Loss

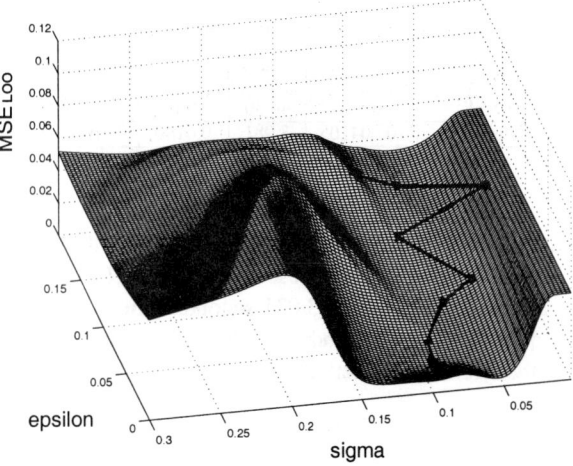

Fig. 6. Optimization Process by the MCV-SVR Method ($C = 500$)

Second, these two landscapes are rather similar when we see them from the global viewpoint. Third, each minimal point marked by a black circle is located at much the same place. These can be seen at other comparisons.

Figure 5 compares the distributions of MSE_{LOO} based on the l_1 and l_2 losses. The values of MSE_{LOO} are sorted each in the ascending order. We can see that both losses generate much the same minimal MSE_{LOO} values, which rationalizes using the l_2 loss instead of the l_1 loss.

B. Performance of the MCV-SVR Method

The MCV-SVR method worked nicely in the three-dimensional hyperparameter space. To observe the optimization process, one hyperparameter was fixed at some value and let the method run. Figures 6 and 7 show the optimization process for $C = 500$ and $\varepsilon = 0.02$ respectively. We can see the MCV-SVR method ran toward the minimal point.

The solution quality of the MCV-SVR method was compared with that of the exhaustive method. Since the landscape seems to have several local optima, we tried the MCV-SVR method 27 times by changing initial values. The initial values are generated by the combination of $C = 10, 10^4, 10^7$, $\varepsilon = 0.001, 0.01, 0.15$, and $\sigma = 0.01, 0.05, 0.15$. As for the exhaustive method, each range was divided into 30 values, thus total $30^3 = 27,000$ grids were examined. The ranges examined were as follows: $C = [10^{0.2}, 10^6]$, $\varepsilon = [0.0, 0.203]$, and $\sigma = [0.01, 0.3]$.

Table I compares the solution quality MSE_{LOO}. The MCV-SVR method slightly exceeds the exhaustive method since the latter can evaluates only at grid points. As for the optimal σ, two values are much the same, but as for the optimal C, two values are quite different, which indicates C has the large optimal range for the present data.

The complexity of the MCV-SVR method was also com-

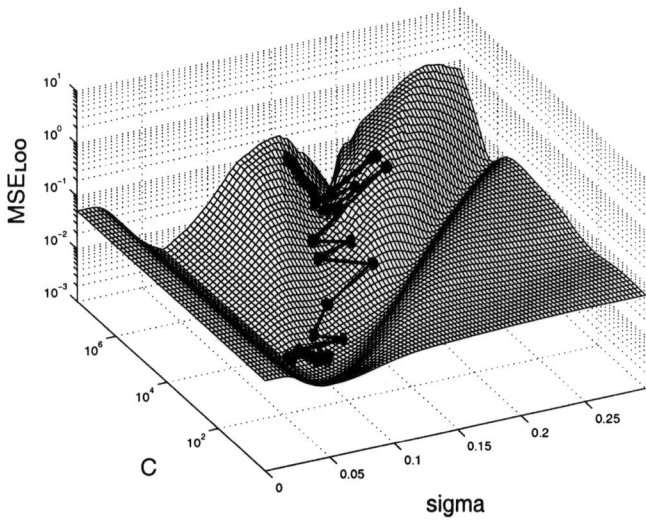

Fig. 7. Optimization Process by the MCV-SVR Method ($\varepsilon = 0.02$)

TABLE I
OPTIMAL HYPERPARAMETERS OBTAINED

method	MSE_{LOO}	C	ε	σ
MCV-SVR	0.004097	46.80	0.0052	0.0794
Exhaustive	0.004105	3.981	0.0140	0.0800

pared with that of the exhaustive method. The MCV-SVR method repeated the coordinate descent cycle 23.6 (= 637/27) times on average, and required 3,031 seconds. The exhaustive method required 114,693 seconds, which is 37.8 times as large as that of the MCV-SVR method.

V. CONCLUSION

This paper proposed a method called the MCV-SVR to optimize the hyperparameters such as C, ε, and σ for SV regression. The method applies the general MCV method to SV regression. Since the ε-insensitive l_1 loss is not suitable for our approach, we introduce the l_2 loss. The experiments showed the l_2 loss produced very smooth error surfaces, the MCV-SVR nicely worked, and the performance of the MCV-SVR exceeded that of the exhaustive method in respect of the solution quality and the complexity. In the future, we plan to enhance and evaluate the MCV-SVR by using larger datasets.

REFERENCES

[1] O. Chapelle, V. Vapnik, O. Bousquet and S. Mukherjee. Choosing multiple parameters for support vector machines. Machine Learning, Vol.46, pp.131–159, 2002.
[2] M. Momma and K. P. Bennett. A pattern search method for model selection of support vector regression. Proc. of SIAM conference on Data Mining, 2002.
[3] K. Saito and R. Nakano. Discovery of relevant weights by minimizing cross-validation error. Proc. of PAKDD conference, LNAI 1805, pp.372–375, 2000.
[4] B. Scholkopf, P. Bartlett, A. J. Smola and R. Williamson. Shrinking the tube: a new support vector regression algorithm. Advances in Neural Information Processing Systems 11, pp.330–336, 1999.
[5] B. Scholkopf and A. J. Smola. Learning with kernels. MIT Press, 2002.
[6] A. J. Smola and B. Scholkopf. A Tutorial on support vector regression. NeuroCOLT2, NC2-TR-1998-030, 1998.
[7] M. Stone. Cross-validatory choice and assessment of statistical predictions. Journal of the Royal Statistical Society B, Vol.64, pp.111–147, 1974.

Design of Support Vector Machine by Adaptive Aggregation

Oscar Chacon(IEEE member), Igor Litvintchev, Ada Alvarez, Ernesto Vazquez(IEEE member)
Graduate Program of Systems Engineering
Graduate Program of Electrical Engineering
Universidad Autonoma de Nuevo Leon
Apdo. Postal 34F Cd. Universitaria
San Nicolás de los Garza, Nuevo León 66450, MEXICO
ochacon@yalma.fime.uanl.mx

Abstract— This article provides a new algorithm to solve the design of classification machine, for linearly separable sets, based in support vectors. For large scale binary classification, an adaptive aggregation (AAM) procedure is executed so that the size of possible support vectors decrease, in each iteration, until convergence to maximum separation margin is achieved.

I. Introduction

Support Vector Machines (**SVM**) are a type of classifier that have attracted attention due to the novelty of the concepts that they bring to pattern recognition, data modelling and regression excellent results in practical problems. The foundations of **SVM** have been developed by Vapnik, Chervonenkis and others [1], [2], [3] as a result of Statistical Learning Theory. A comprehensive tutorial on **SVM** classifiers has been published by Burgues [4] and by Smola and Schölkopf [5] on **SVM** regression.

There are applications where the precision of the solution is not required but the computing time is. The patterns are either support vectors (dual solutions are different of zero and sometimes constrained to an upper level - *soft margin*) or not a support vectors at all (dual solutions equal to zero). In any of these cases it is possible to solve the problem of maximum separation margin iteratively reducing the pattern training set by aggregation techniques, determining the suboptimal separation hyperplane and identifying the pattern subset that improves the separation margin. In this paper we approach the optimal classifier based on **SVM** through an adaptive aggregation of the pattern set.

The paper is organized as follows: Section II presents the maximum separation margin problem and the soft margin case. In Section III, the aggregation problem and the dual solution are described. In Section IV the Frank-Wolfe method is presented as the subset selection approach and a new adaptive aggregation weight method is discussed. Section V discuss the results of an experimental study using generated data and the conclusion is in Section VI.

II. Solution of the maximum separation margin problem

The statistic learning theory, under the support vector context, has as main learning goal to find a canonic optimal hyperplane: the hyperplane with maximum separation margin between the classes.

In the learning process for a binary classification of data set $\mathcal{X} = \{(x_1, y_1), \ldots, (x_N, y_N)\}, x_i \in \mathcal{R}^n$, $y \in \{1, -1\}$, the minimum structural risk condition establish the construction of separating hyperplane $H_0 = \{x | w^t x + b = 0\}$ such that :

$$w^t x_i + b \geq 1, \quad y_i = 1, \quad i \in I_+ \quad (1)$$
$$w^t x_i + b \leq -1, \quad y_i = -1, \quad i \in I_- \quad (2)$$
$$I = \{1, \ldots, N\}, \quad I_+ \bigcup I_- = I, \quad N = N_+ + N_- \quad (3)$$

If furthermore the hyperplane H_0 has the same separation distance $M = \frac{1}{\|w\|_2}$ to the support hyperplane $H_1 = \{x | w^t x + b = 1\}$ of group $\mathcal{X}_+ = \{x_i \in \mathcal{X} | i \in I_+\}$ and to the support hyperplane $H_{-1} = \{x | w^t x + b = -1\}$ of group $\mathcal{X}_- = \{x_i \in \mathcal{X} | i \in I_-\}$, then the solution of problem :

$$f^* = \min_{w,b} \frac{1}{2} w^t w$$
subject to $\quad$ (4)
$$y_i (w^t x + b) \geq 1, \quad i \in I_+$$
$$y_i (w^t x + b) \geq 1, \quad i \in I_-$$

determines the parameters $\bar{w}$ and $\bar{b}$ for the linear classifier $\bar{w}^t x + \bar{b}$ with the maximum separation margin $M^* = \frac{2}{\|w\|_2}$. For the dual problem of (4):

$$L(\alpha^*) = \max_\alpha \sum_{i=1}^N \alpha_i - \frac{1}{2} \sum_{i=1}^N \sum_{j=1}^N \alpha_i \alpha_j y_i y_j x_i^t x_j$$
subject to: $\quad$ (5)
$$\sum_{i=1}^N y_i \alpha_i = 0$$
$$\alpha_i \geq 0$$

the optimal solution gives values $\alpha_{*i} \neq 0$ corresponding to *support vectors* $x_{+i} \in \mathcal{X}_+$ and $x_{-i} \in \mathcal{X}_-$ that fulfill the condition $\bar{w}^t x_{+i} + \bar{b} = 1$ and $\bar{w}^t x_{-i} + \bar{b} = -1$ respectively.

The authors would like to acknowledge *Consejo Nacional de Ciencia y Tecnologia* and *Universidad Autonoma de Nuevo Leon* by the support provided to this research through the projects 38870-A and CA762-02 respectively.

The parameters values $\bar{w}$ and $\bar{b}$ are determined as follow:

$$\bar{w} = \sum_{i=1}^{N} \alpha_i y_i x_i, \quad \alpha_i \neq 0 \qquad (6)$$

$$\bar{b} = \frac{1}{N_{vs}} \left(\sum_{k=1}^{N_{vs}} \left(\frac{1}{y_{\phi(k)}} - x_{\phi(k)}^t \hat{w} \right) \right) \qquad (7)$$

where $\phi(k)$ is the index of a support vector and N_{vs} is the number of support vectors.

The maximum separation margin M is then

$$M = \frac{2}{\|\bar{w}\|} \qquad (8)$$

The existence of outliers (training data whose removal cause a large increase in the separation margin) can slower or avoid the convergency of the algorithm designed to solve this problem. Cortes and Vapnik [6] introduced the slack variables

$$\xi_{+i} \geq 0 \quad \text{when} \quad i \in I_+ \quad \text{and} \quad \xi_{+i} \geq 0 \quad \text{when} \quad i \in I_- \qquad (9)$$

to construct the relaxed constraints

$$y_{+i}\left(w^t x_{+i} + b\right) \geq 1 - \xi_{+i} \qquad (10)$$
$$y_{-i}\left(w^t x_{-i} + b\right) \geq 1 - \xi_{-i}$$

and therefore allow the possibility that training data violate restrictions (4). To avoid large values of ξ_i (trivial case), it is necessary to penalize them in the objective function given as a result the problem named *soft margin SVM* as follow:

$$f^* = \min_{w,b} \frac{1}{2} w^t w + \frac{C}{N} \sum (\xi_{+i}^2 + \xi_{-i}^2)$$

$$\text{subject to} \qquad (11)$$

$$y_{+i}\left(w^t x_{+i} + b\right) \geq 1 - \xi_{+i}$$
$$y_{-i}\left(w^t x_{-i} + b\right) \geq 1 - \xi_{-i} \qquad (12)$$
$$\xi_{+i} \geq 0, \quad \xi_{-i} \geq 0 \qquad (13)$$

being C a positive constant determining the trade off between minimizing the training error and maximizing the separation margin. The optimal solution are the same given in (6) and (7) but with upper bound on dual variables $0 \leq \alpha_{*i} \leq C$.

III. THE AGGREGATED PROBLEM

Each of the data subsets $\mathcal{X}_+$ y $\mathcal{X}_-$ ($\mathcal{X}_+ \bigcup \mathcal{X}_- = \mathcal{X}$) can be aggregated as a convex combination of their elements given as a consecuence the prototypes $\hat{x}_+$ y $\hat{x}_-$ respectively; that is:

$$\hat{x}_+ = \sum_{i=1}^{N_+} \beta_{+i} x_i, \quad \sum_{i=1}^{N_+} \beta_{+i} = 1, \quad \beta_{+i} \geq 0 \qquad (14)$$

$$\hat{x}_- = \sum_{i=1}^{N_-} \beta_{-i} x_i, \quad \sum_{i=1}^{N_-} \beta_{-i} = 1, \quad \beta_{-i} \geq 0 \qquad (15)$$

The data aggregation transforms the primal problem (4) into the problem:

$$\theta(\beta_+, \beta_-) = \min_{\beta_+, \beta_-} \frac{1}{2} w^t w$$

$$\text{subject to} \qquad (16)$$

$$w^t \hat{x}_+ + b \geq 1$$
$$w^t \hat{x}_- + b \leq -1$$

We observe that the aggregated problem is related with the primal problem as $f^* \geq \theta$, where $f^* = \min_\beta \theta(\beta)$, $\beta = [\beta_+ \beta_-]^t$. To determine the effect of parameters β_+ and β_- in (16) solution, lets construct the aggregated lagrangian problem:

$$\mathcal{L}(\hat{\alpha}_+, \hat{\alpha}_-, \beta_+, \beta_-) = \frac{1}{2} w^t w$$
$$+ \hat{\alpha}_+ \left[1 - w^t \sum \beta_{+i} x_{+i} - b \right] \qquad (17)$$
$$- \hat{\alpha}_- \left[1 + w^t \sum \beta_{-i} x_{-i} + b \right]$$

furthermore, the equivalent lagrangian aggregated problem to (16) becomes:

$$\min \mathcal{L}(\hat{\alpha}_+, \hat{\alpha}_-, \beta_+, \beta_-) \qquad (18)$$

subject to

$$\beta_+ \in \Omega_+ = \left\{ \beta_+ | \sum_{i=1}^{N_+} \beta_{+i} = 1, \quad \beta_{+i} \geq 0 \right\} \qquad (19)$$

$$\beta_- \in \Omega_- = \left\{ \beta_- | \sum_{i=1}^{N_-} \beta_{-i} = 1, \quad \beta_{-i} \geq 0 \right\} \qquad (20)$$

A. The Aggregated Dual Problem Solution

Given the aggregated relations (14) and (15), the dual problem (5) is described as:

$$\mathcal{L}(\alpha^*) = \max_\alpha [\hat{\alpha}_+ + \hat{\alpha}_- - \frac{1}{2} [\hat{\alpha}_+^2 \hat{x}_+^t \hat{x}_+ \qquad (21)$$
$$- \hat{\alpha}_+ \hat{\alpha}_- \hat{x}_+^t \hat{x}_- - \hat{\alpha}_- \hat{\alpha}_+ \hat{x}_-^t \hat{x}_+ + \hat{\alpha}_-^2 \hat{x}_-^t \hat{x}_-]]$$

subject to:
$$\hat{\alpha}_+ - \hat{\alpha}_- = 0 \qquad (22)$$
$$\hat{\alpha}_+, \hat{\alpha}_- \geq 0$$

Condition (22) establish the equality $\hat{\alpha}_+ = \hat{\alpha}_- = \hat{\alpha}$ given the optimal solution of the dual aggregated problem (21) as:

$$\hat{\alpha} = \frac{2}{\|\hat{x}_+ - \hat{x}_-\|^2} \qquad (23)$$

As the aggregated problem considers only two points (the aggregated classes $\hat{x}_+$ and $\hat{x}_-$), these correspond to the support vectors and therefore the parameters $\bar{w}$ and $\bar{b}$ can be evaluated through equations (6) and (7) respectively with the appropriated considerations, given the following relations:

$$\bar{w} = 2\frac{\hat{x}_+ - \hat{x}_-}{\|\hat{x}_+ - \hat{x}_-\|^2} \quad (24)$$

$$\bar{b} = -\frac{\|\hat{x}_+\|^2 - \|\hat{x}_-\|^2}{\|\hat{x}_+ - \hat{x}_-\|^2} \quad (25)$$

These parameters correspond to the approximation of the hyperplane with maximum margin of separation, using the aggregated problem for an arbitrary weights of aggregations β_+ and β_-

IV. THE FRANK WOLFE CONDITIONAL GRADIENT METHOD

With the information given in the previous section we can find the variations of the lagrangian (17) with respect to the aggregation weights β_{+i} and β_{-i} and determine a factible search direction that solves problem (18) subject to restrictions (19) and (20). This kind of problems can be solve easily through the Frank-Wolfe Conditional Gradient Method [7].

A. Standard Conditions

Problem (18) is characterized as an objective function continuous and differentiable with respect to β_+ and β_-. It is clear that the factibility regions (19) and (20) are not empty, close convex sets. These kind of problems can be solved using any *Factible Directions Algorithms*.

The Factible Directions Algorithms use an initial factible point β_+^0 and β_-^0 generating a sequence of factible points $\{\beta_+^k\}$ and $\{\beta_-^k\}$ according to the recurrent relation:

$$\beta_+^{k+1} = \beta_+^k + \delta_+^k d_+^k \quad (26)$$
$$\beta_-^{k+1} = \beta_-^k + \delta_-^k d_-^k \quad (27)$$

If β_+^k or β_-^k are not stationary, d_+^k and d_-^k are descent factible directions

$$\nabla^t \mathcal{L}(\beta_+^k) d_+^k < 0 \quad (28)$$
$$\nabla^t \mathcal{L}(\beta_-^k) d_-^k < 0 \quad (29)$$

and the step lengths δ_+^k and δ_-^k are selected to preserve no negativity such that

$$\beta_+^{k+1} = \beta_+^k + \delta_+^k d_+^k \in \Omega_+$$
$$\beta_-^{k+1} = \beta_-^k + \delta_-^k d_-^k \in \Omega_-$$

On the contrary, if β_+^k and β_-^k are stationary the algorithm ends.

When the factibility region is a convex set, as this is the case for Ω_+ and Ω_-, the directions d_+^k in the point β_+^k and d_-^k in the point β_-^k can be represented as:

$$d_+^k = \gamma(\bar{\beta}_+^k - \beta_+^k), \quad \gamma > 0$$
$$d_-^k = \gamma(\bar{\beta}_-^k - \beta_-^k), \quad \gamma > 0$$

where $\bar{\beta}_+^k$ and $\bar{\beta}_-^k$ are some factible points different from β_+^k and β_-^k respectively. The most practical way to generate a factible direction $\bar{\beta}_+^k - \beta_+^k$ that satisfy the descendent condition (28) and be acceptable by recurrent formula (26) is to solve the optimization problem

$$\min \nabla^t \mathcal{L}(\beta_+^k)(\beta_+ - \beta_+^k) \quad (30)$$
subject to
$$\beta_+ \in \Omega_+$$

In the same way, for factible direction $\bar{\beta}_-^k - \beta_-^k$ is the solution to problem

$$\min \nabla^t \mathcal{L}(\beta_-^k)(\beta_- - \beta_-^k) \quad (31)$$
subject to
$$\beta_- \in \Omega_-$$

The corresponding solutions for $\bar{\beta}_+^k$ and $\bar{\beta}_-^k$ are

$$\bar{\beta}_+^k = \arg \min_{\beta_+ \in \Omega_+} \nabla^t \mathcal{L}(\beta_+^k)(\beta_+ - \beta_+^k) \quad (32)$$

$$\bar{\beta}_-^k = \arg \min_{\beta_- \in \Omega_-} \nabla^t \mathcal{L}(\beta_-^k)(\beta_- - \beta_-^k) \quad (33)$$

As we can see Ω_+ and Ω_- are compacts, therefore the subproblems (30) and (31) have solutions and generate descent factible directions. This factible directions search method is named *conditional gradient method* or *Frank-Wolfe method*

B. The Aggregation Problem solution by the Conditional Gradients Method

The solutions (32) and (33) are simple to determine (for this case) and correspond to solutions where all the aggregation weights are zero except one (lets say the jth and k^{th} aggregation weights of class $\mathcal{X}_+$ and $\mathcal{X}_-$ respectively), taking values of 1; for this β_{+j} and β_{-k} values correspond the minimum partial derivatives; that is,

$$j = \arg \min_{i=1,\ldots,N_+} \frac{\partial \mathcal{L}(\beta_+^k, \beta_-^k)}{\partial \beta_{+i}} \quad (34)$$

$$k = \arg \min_{i=1,\ldots,N_-} \frac{\partial \mathcal{L}(\beta_+^k, \beta_-^k)}{\partial \beta_{-i}} \quad (35)$$

C. The Adaptive Aggregation: A Relaxed Conditional Gradient

For problems (30) and (31) with relaxed conditions, the objective functions and the realization conditions will be given by:

$$\Delta_{\beta_*} \mathcal{L} = \sum_{i=1}^{n_*} \frac{\partial \mathcal{L}}{\partial \beta_{*i}} s_{*i} \quad (36)$$

where $\quad s_{*i} = \beta_{*i}^{(k+1)} - \beta_{*i}^{(k)} \quad (37)$

$$\beta_{*i}^{(k+1)} = 0 \quad \text{if} \quad \frac{\partial \mathcal{L}}{\partial \beta_{*i}} > 0 \quad (38)$$

$$\sum_{i=1}^{n} s_{*i} = 0 \quad (39)$$

Keeping constant w, b and α, the gradients of $\mathcal{L}$ (17), with respect to β_{+i} and β_{-i} are:

$$\frac{\partial \mathcal{L}}{\partial \beta_{+i}} = \hat{\alpha}_+ \left[1 - w^t x_{+i} - b \right] \quad (40)$$

$$\frac{\partial \mathcal{L}}{\partial \beta_{-i}} = \hat{\alpha}_- \left[1 + w^t x_{-i} + b \right] \quad (41)$$

If $\frac{\partial \mathcal{L}}{\partial \beta_{*i}} \geq 0$, $\forall i$ and $\beta_{*j} = 1$ for $j = arg\ min \left\{ \frac{\partial \mathcal{L}}{\partial \beta_{*i}} \right\}$, the actual aggregation weights are stationary respect to the maximization of the objective function (17).
If stationary condition is not achieved, a descent ordering of $\frac{\partial \mathcal{L}}{\partial \beta_{*i}} < 0$ can be done generating the new vector $\nabla_{\beta_*} \mathcal{L} = \left\{ \frac{\partial \mathcal{L}}{\partial \beta_{*k(1)}}, \ldots, \frac{\partial \mathcal{L}}{\partial \beta_{*k(n)}} \right\}$. With this gradient ordering and the associated aggregation weights $\beta_{*k(j)}$, it is possible to establish a convex ($\sum \beta_{*i}^{(k)} = 1$, $\sum \beta_{*i}^{(k+1)} = 1$) strategy of these aggregation weights.
For a fix percent ρ of the variation range $\left(\frac{\partial \mathcal{L}}{\partial \beta_{*k(1)}} - \frac{\partial \mathcal{L}}{\partial \beta_{*k(n)}} \right)$, the aggregation weights that reduce their values to zero will be those whose index $k(j)$ fulfill the following condition :

$$\left\{ \frac{\partial \mathcal{L}}{\partial \beta_{*k(j)}} \mid \frac{\partial \mathcal{L}}{\partial \beta_{*k(j)}} > \frac{\partial \mathcal{L}}{\partial \beta_{*k(1)}} + \rho \left(\frac{\partial \mathcal{L}}{\partial \beta_{*k(n)}} - \frac{\partial \mathcal{L}}{\partial \beta_{*k(1)}} \right) \right\} \quad (42)$$

On the other hand, the aggregation weights that increase their values will be those whose index $k(j)$ fulfill the relation:

$$\left\{ \frac{\partial \mathcal{L}}{\partial \beta_{*k(j)}} \mid \frac{\partial \mathcal{L}}{\partial \beta_{*k(j)}} \leq \frac{\partial \mathcal{L}}{\partial \beta_{*k(1)}} + \rho \left(\frac{\partial \mathcal{L}}{\partial \beta_{*k(n)}} - \frac{\partial \mathcal{L}}{\partial \beta_{*k(1)}} \right) \right\} \quad (43)$$

Observe that $\rho = 1$ represents a greedy solution and only the aggregation weight $\beta_{*k(n)}$ takes the value of 1 and zero the others; this is the solution (34,35) corresponding to the standard conditions. For $\rho = 1$ the solution is related with problems where the initial aggregation weights are known. On the contrary, for those problem where information is not available and the initial weights are fixed randomly, it is necessary to search for new weights with a not so aggressive convex strategy .
For $0 < \rho < 1$, a convex strategy solution for new aggregation weights β_{*r}^{k+1} can be:

1) $\beta_{*r}^{k+1} = 0 \quad \text{para} \quad r = k(1), \ldots, k(j-1) \quad (44)$

2) $\beta_{*r}^{k+1} = \beta_{*r}^k + \frac{\frac{\partial \mathcal{L}}{\partial \beta_{*r}}}{\sum_{r=k(j)}^{k(n)} \frac{\partial \mathcal{L}}{\partial \beta_{*r}}} \sum_{t=1}^{t=j-1} \beta_{*k(t)}^k \quad (45)$

for $r = k(j), \ldots, k(n)$

Let us analyze the results when assigning in these fashion the weights β_*^{k+1}. Let us define the following terms:

$$\mathbf{t} = \left\{ i \mid \frac{\partial \mathcal{L}}{\partial \beta_{*i}} \geq 0 \right\} \quad (46)$$

$$\mathbf{r} = \left\{ i \mid \frac{\partial \mathcal{L}}{\partial \beta_{*i}} < 0 \right\} \quad (47)$$

$$\beta_*^k = \begin{bmatrix} \beta_{*t}^k \\ \beta_{*r}^k \end{bmatrix} \quad (48)$$

$$\delta_r = \left(\sum_{i \in t} \beta_{*i}^k \right) \left[\frac{\frac{\partial \mathcal{L}}{\partial \beta_{*i}}}{\sum \frac{\partial \mathcal{L}}{\partial \beta_{*i}}} \right]_{i \in r} \quad (49)$$

Now in matrix notation, equations (44) and (45) are described as:

$$\beta_*^{k+1} = \begin{bmatrix} \beta_{*t}^k \\ \beta_{*r}^k \end{bmatrix} + \begin{bmatrix} -\beta_{*t}^k \\ \delta_r \end{bmatrix} \quad (50)$$

If $s_*^k = \beta_*^{k+1} - \beta_*^k$ it is observed that the vector product

$$\nabla^T \mathcal{L}(\beta_*^k) s_*^k = \begin{bmatrix} \nabla_{\beta_t} \mathcal{L} \\ \nabla_{\beta_r} \mathcal{L} \end{bmatrix}^T \begin{bmatrix} -\beta_{*t}^k \\ \delta_r \end{bmatrix} \quad (51)$$

is a negative value, therefore the way that values β_*^{k+1} are assigned (44, 45 or 50) assure that s_*^k be a descendent factible direction.
The procedure used to apply this method is as follow:

```
procedure adaptive aggregation(X_+, X_-, C)
1 Set stop criteria:  maxiter;
2 Initialize aggregation weights β_+, β_- and
determine data prototypes x̂_+ and x̂_- by equations
(14) and (15);
3 Determine w̄ and b̄ by equations (24) and (25);
4 while card (∇_β+ L < 0) > 0 ∧ card (∇_β+ L < 0) > 0
do
5 Choose a ρ value and define subindex k(j) by
relations (42) and (43);
6 Update aggregation weights by equations (44)
and (45);
7 Determine w̄ and b̄ by equations (24) and (25);
8 end while;
end adaptive aggregation;
```

V. Applications

A set of 500 numerical experiments were carried out based on $\mathcal{R}^2$ synthetic data, consisting in a pair of data sets $(\mathcal{X}_+, \mathcal{X}_-)$ lineally separable, with 50 elements each one, for each experiment. A typical initial data set is shown in Fig. 1.(a) with magenta ($\mathcal{X}_+$) and cyan ($\mathcal{X}_-$) colors.
In all figures the red line is the graphics of classifier $H_0 = \{ x | w^t x + b = 0 \}$ determined solving problem (5). The blue line is the graphics of classifier approach $\bar{H}_0 = \{ x | \bar{w}^t x + \bar{b} = 0 \}$ determined by the **AAM**. The green lines are the graphics of hyperplane $\bar{H}_{+1} = \{ x | \bar{w}^t x + \bar{b} = 1 \}$ related with set $\mathcal{X}_+$ (magenta) and hyperplane $\bar{H}_{-1} = \{ x | \bar{w}^t x + \bar{b} = -1 \}$ related with set $\mathcal{X}_-$

TABLE I
CPU RUN TIME (S)

Method	90% data	10% data
Quadratic Programming	[4.974, 6.149]	[6.149, 8.853]
Adaptive Aggregation	[0.00, 0.03]	[0.03, 0.10]

(cyan). The hyperplanes $\bar{H}_1$ and $\bar{H}_{-1}$ are parallels to $\bar{H}_0$ and go through prototypes $\hat{x}_+$ and $\hat{x}_-$ respectively. In step 5 of the Adaptive Agregation procedure, the $k(j)$ indexes are determined by relation (42) and related data are assigned an aggregation weight value of zero; these data are marked by color blue in both sets ($\mathcal{X}_+$, magenta) and ($\mathcal{X}_-$, cyan) as shown in Fig. 1.(b).

The others $k(j)$ index, determined by relation (43), are used to assign to related data a new aggregation weight value (step 6) through equation (45). The procedure continue as shown in Fig. 1.(b)-Fig. 1.(f) until connvergence is reached. Observe that hyperplane $\bar{H}_0$ change orientation until it approach H_0 when the procedure converge. Each experiment was solve by the **AAM** using a computational algorithm designed in MatLab and by a computer program [8] based in the solution of dual problem 5 . Two relations were used to analyse the results:

1. Projection *proj* of the separation hyperplane gradients of both computational programs. If it is assigned w_o and $\hat{w}$ (the adaptive aggregation result) as the corresponding gradients, then *proj* is evaluated as

$$proj = \frac{w_o^T \hat{w}}{\|w_o\| \|\hat{w}\|}$$

The minimum projection in these experiments is 0.8746 and only 5% of them result with $proj <= 0.93$

2. Ratio RMS of the separation margins $ms_o = \frac{2}{w_o^T w_o}$ and $\hat{ms} = \frac{2}{\hat{w}^T \hat{w}}$. This ratio $RMS = \frac{ms_o}{\hat{ms}}$ gets its maximum value of 1.5445 and 8 out of 500 take values $RMS > 1.3$.

The CPU run time for all the 500 experiments, in both approach, were registered giving in Table I the intervals for the 90% and 10% of data in ascending order. These results show that the process time by **AAM** is less than the standard one using quadratic programming.

VI. CONCLUSIONS

When run-time speed is an issue in design of classifiers, the **SVM** method is inferior to adaptive aggregation method. On the other hand, as shown in the application, the adaptive aggregation method do not always give correct answer because it does not take in account the dual variables α, instead works with aggregation weights β that identify a pattern prototype from a subset containing the support vectors. The prototypes and not the support vector determine the separation hyperplane characteristics ($\bar{w}, \bar{b}$). A simple solution in the last stage of the **AAM** is to switch to the **SVM** to solve these reduced subset in obviously lesser time that the original problem.

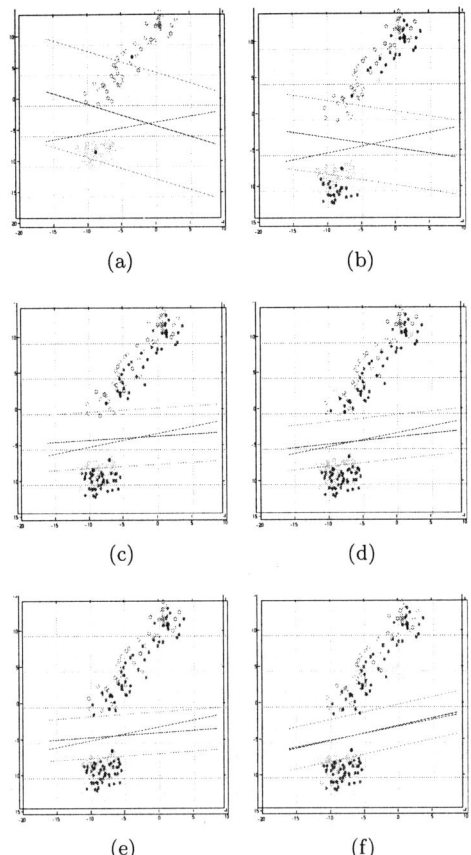

Fig. 1. Sequence of subset by aggregation.

The extension off **AAM** for *soft margin* problems (existence of outliers) presents a new problem when giving the adequate aggregation weights for those patterns that are misclassified during the adaptive aggregation process. A reformulation of the **AAM** must be done for classification of non linear separable sets.

REFERENCES

[1] V. N. Vapnik and A. Chervonenkis, *Theory of Pattern Recognition [in Russian]*, Nauka, Moscow, 1974.
[2] V. N. Vapnik, *Estimation of Dependences Based on Empirical Data*, Springer-Verlag, Berlin, 1982.
[3] V. N. Vapnik, *Statistical Learning Theory*, John Wiley & Sons, N. Y., 1998.
[4] C.J.C. Burges, *A Tutorial on Support Vector Machines for Pattern Recognition*, Knowledge Discovery and Data Mining, 1998.
[5] A. J. Smola and B. Schölkopf , *A Tutorial on Support Vector Regression*, NeuroCOLT2 Technical Report Series, NC2-TR-1998-030. http://www.neurocolt.com
[6] C. Cortes and V. Vapnik, *A Support vector networks*, Machine Learning, V. 20, pp. 273-297, 1995
[7] D. P. Bertsekas, *Nonlinear programming*, Athena Scientific, 2nd. Edition 1999
[8] Steve Gunn, http://www.isis.ecs.soton.ac.uk/seminars, /1997/SteveGunn.htm

SMO Algorithm for Least Squares SVM

S.S. Keerthi
Dept. of Mechanical Engineering
National University of Singapore
Singapore 117576
Email: mpessk@guppy.mpe.nus.edu.sg

S.K. Shevade
Dept. of Computer Science and Automation
Indian Institute of Science
Bangalore, India
Email: shirish@csa.iisc.ernet.in

Abstract— This paper extends the well-known SMO algorithm of Support Vector Machines (SVMs) to Least Squares SVM formulation. The algorithm is asymptotically convergent. It is also extremely easy to implement. Computational experiments show that the algorithm is fast and scales efficiently (quadratically) as a function of the number of examples.

I. Introduction

This paper concerns least squares formulation of SVMs. This formulation, which provides interesting and useful alternative to SVM, has been proposed both for regression as well as classification. Saunders et al. (1998) proposed the kernel version of ridge regression and empirically demonstrated its usefulness. Suykens and Vandewalle (1999) gave an interesting and useful extension of the idea to classification and called their method as Least Squares SVM (LS-SVM). A careful empirical study by Van Gestel et al. (2000) has shown that LS-SVM is comparable to SVM in terms of generalization performance. Recently Van Gestel et al. (2002) have also established the equivalence of LS-SVM with a particular form of regularized Kernel Fisher Discriminant (KFD) method (Mika et al. 2001).

While SVMs are characterized by convex quadratic programming problems involving inequality constraints, kernel ridge regression and LS-SVMs on the other hand, are formulated using equality constraints only. Hence, their solution is obtained by solving a system of linear equations (of the order of the number of training examples) involving the dense kernel matrix. To tackle large scale problems, Suykens et al (1999) and Van Gestel et al. (2000) effectively employed the conjugate-gradient method. In this paper we propose a new iterative algorithm for these problems. It is based on the solution of the Wolfe dual problem using ideas similar to those of the SMO (Sequential Minimal Optimization) algorithm for SVMs (Platt, 1998, Keerthi et al., 2001). The algorithm is extremely easy to implement and scales efficiently (quadratically) as a function of the number of examples. The scaling is much better than that of the CG algorithm.

The paper is organized as follows. In section II we formulate the problem and develop the Wolfe dual. Optimality conditions for the dual are derived in section III. A useful condition for terminating numerical algorithms solving the least squares formulations is also given. These conditions form the basis for the SMO algorithm developed in section IV. Computational experiments describing the effectiveness of the algorithm are given in section V. Section VI concludes the paper.

II. Problem Formulation

Throughout we will use x to denote the input vector of the classification/regression problem and z to denote the feature space vector which is related to x by the transformation, $z = \varphi(x)$. As in all kernel designs, we do not assume φ to be known; all computations will be done using only the kernel function,

$$k(x, \hat{x}) = \varphi(x) \cdot \varphi(\hat{x}) \qquad (2.1)$$

where "$\cdot$" denotes inner product in the z space. Let $\{(x_i, y_i)\}_{i=1}^m$ denote the training set, where x_i is the i-th input pattern and y_i is the corresponding target value. For classification problems (two classes) y_i takes only two possible values (say, 1 if x_i is in class 1 and -1 if x_i is in class 2) while, for regression y_i takes any real value. Let $z_i = \varphi(x_i)$. In kernel ridge regression[1] and classification by LS-SVMs the following optimization problem is solved:

$$\begin{aligned} \min E &= \tfrac{1}{2}\|w\|^2 + \tfrac{C}{2}\sum_i \xi_i^2 \\ \text{s.t.} \quad & y_i - (w \cdot z_i - b) = \xi_i \;\; \forall i \end{aligned} \qquad (2.2)$$

Define:

$$\tilde{w} = \begin{pmatrix} w \\ \sqrt{C}\xi \end{pmatrix}; \quad \tilde{z}_i = \begin{pmatrix} z_i \\ \frac{1}{\sqrt{C}}e_i \end{pmatrix} \;\; \forall i \qquad (2.3)$$

where ξ is a m dimensional vector containing the ξ_i's and, for every i, e_i is the m dimensional vector in which the i-th component is 1 and all other components are 0. Define $\tilde{k}(x_i, x_j) = \tilde{z}_i \cdot \tilde{z}_j$. By (2.1) and (2.3),

$$\tilde{k}(x_i, x_j) = k(x_i, x_j) + \frac{1}{C}\delta_{ij} \qquad (2.4)$$

where $\delta_{ij} = 1$ if $i = j$ and 0 otherwise. It is easy to see that (2.2) transforms to

$$\min E = \frac{1}{2}\|\tilde{w}\|^2 \;\; \text{s.t.} \; y_i - (\tilde{w} \cdot \tilde{z}_i - b) = 0 \; \forall i \qquad (2.5)$$

The Lagrangian for this problem is:

$$L = \frac{1}{2}\|\tilde{w}\|^2 + \sum_i \alpha_i [y_i - (\tilde{w} \cdot \tilde{z}_i - b)] \qquad (2.6)$$

The KKT optimality conditions are given by:

$$\nabla_{\tilde{w}} L = \tilde{w} - \sum_i \alpha_i \tilde{z}_i = 0 \qquad (2.7)$$

[1]Saunders et al. (1998) leave out b from their formulation. This actually leads to a simpler problem.

$$\frac{\partial L}{\partial b} = \sum_i \alpha_i = 0 \qquad (2.8)$$

Note that, because (2.5) has only equality constraints, the α_i's are not constrained to be non-negative. Using (2.7) $\tilde{w}$ can be expressed as a function of the α_i's:

$$\tilde{w}(\alpha) = \sum_i \alpha_i \tilde{z}_i \qquad (2.9)$$

Let us now apply Wolfe duality theory to (2.5). The Wolfe dual corresponds to the maximization of L subject to (2.7) and (2.8), with $\tilde{w}$, b and α_i's as variables. Using (2.8) and (2.9) we can simplify the Wolfe dual as

$$\max f(\alpha) = -\frac{1}{2}\|\tilde{w}(\alpha)\|^2 + \sum_i \alpha_i y_i \quad \text{s.t.} \quad \sum_i \alpha_i = 0 \qquad (2.10)$$

Note that $\|\tilde{w}\|^2 = \sum_i \sum_j \alpha_i \alpha_j \tilde{k}(x_i, x_j)$. Hence (2.10) is a simple convex quadratic programming problem involving a single equality constraint and no nonnegativity constraints. Once the α_i's are obtained by solving (2.10), the primal variables, w and ξ_i's can be determined using (2.9) and (2.3). The determination of b will be addressed in the next section.

III. OPTIMALITY CONDITIONS FOR DUAL

To derive proper stopping conditions for algorithms which solve the dual and also determine the threshold parameter b, it is important to write down the optimality conditions for the dual. The Lagrangian for (2.10) is:

$$\bar{L} = -\frac{1}{2}\|\tilde{w}(\alpha)\|^2 + \sum_i \alpha_i y_i + \beta \sum_i \alpha_i \qquad (3.1)$$

Define

$$F_i = -\frac{\partial f}{\partial \alpha_i} = \tilde{w}(\alpha) \cdot \tilde{z}_i - y_i = \sum_j \alpha_j \tilde{k}(x_i, x_j) - y_i \qquad (3.2)$$

where f is defined in (2.10). The KKT conditions for the dual problem are:

$$\frac{\partial \bar{L}}{\partial \alpha_i} = (\beta - F_i) = 0 \ \forall \ i \qquad (3.3)$$

Define:

$$\begin{array}{ll} b_{\text{up}} = \max_i F_i \,; & i\_up = \arg\max_i F_i \,; \\ b_{\text{low}} = \min_i F_i \,; & i\_low = \arg\min_i F_i. \end{array} \qquad (3.4)$$

Then optimality conditions will hold at a given α iff

$$b_{\text{low}} = b_{\text{up}} \qquad (3.5)$$

In the above, note that F_i, b_{up}, i_up, b_{low} and i_low are all functions of α. The functional dependancies have not been put down to avoid notational clutter.

Using (3.3), (3.2) and (2.5), it is easy to see the close relationship between the threshold parameter b in the primal problem and the multiplier, β. In particular, at optimality, β and b are identical. Therefore, in the rest of the paper β and b will denote one and the same quantity.

We will say that an index pair (i, j) defines a *violation* at α if

$$F_i \neq F_j \qquad (3.6)$$

Thus, optimality conditions will hold at α iff there does not exist any index pair (i, j) that defines a violation.

Suppose (i, j) satisfies (3.6) at some α. Then it is possible to achieve an increase in f (while maintaining the equality constraint, $\sum \alpha_k = 0$) by adjusting α_i and α_j only. To see this, let us define the following:

$$\begin{array}{rcl} \tilde{\alpha}_i(t) & = & \alpha_i - t \,; \\ \tilde{\alpha}_j(t) & = & \alpha_j + t \,; \\ \tilde{\alpha}_k(t) & = & \alpha_k \ \forall k \neq i, j, \end{array} \qquad (3.7)$$

and

$$\phi(t) = f(\tilde{\alpha}(t)) \qquad (3.8)$$

Then it is easy to verify that

$$\phi'(t) = F_i - F_j \qquad (3.9)$$

where F_i and F_j are evaluated at $\tilde{\alpha}(t)$. Since, by (3.6), $F_i - F_j \neq 0$ at $t = 0$, an increase in ϕ is possible by choosing t suitably away from 0.

Since, in numerical solution, it takes too much computing time to compute the exact optimal solution, there is a need to define approximate stopping conditions that guarantee a specified closeness to the solution of the primal problem, (2.2). We consider a stopping condition based on duality gaps. This has been used effectively by Smola and Schölkopf (1998) in SVM regression.

Suppose α is any vector that satisfies $\sum_i \alpha_i = 0$, b is any real number, $w = \sum_i \alpha_i z_i$ and

$$\xi_i = y_i - (w \cdot z_i - b) = b + \frac{\alpha_i}{C} - F_i \qquad (3.10)$$

where F_i is as defined by (3.2). Note that (w, b, ξ) satisfies the constraints of the primal, (2.2) and α satisfies the constraints of the dual, (2.10). Let: E denote the primal cost corresponding to (w, b, ξ); $E^\star$ be the optimal primal cost of (2.2); f denote the dual objective function value given by α; and $f^\star$ be the optimal dual objective function value. By Wolfe duality (Fletcher, 1987) we have:

$$E \geq E^\star = f^\star \geq f \qquad (3.11)$$

Eventhough $E^\star (= f^\star)$ is unknown, (3.11) allows us to obtain guaranteed bounds using duality gap (a computable quantity) defined by

$$Dgap = E - f = \sum_i [\alpha_i(F_i - \frac{\alpha_i}{2C}) + \frac{C}{2}\xi_i^2] \qquad (3.12)$$

$Dgap$ is a nonnegative quantity that becomes zero iff optimality is reached. Thus, if $\{\alpha^r\}$ is a sequence that converges to $\alpha^\star$, the solution of (2.10), then the continuity of the $Dgap$ function implies that $\{Dgap^r\}$ goes to zero, where $Dgap^r$ is the value of $Dgap$ for α^r. Also, for any non-trivial problem, $E^\star = f^\star > 0$. Thus, it is appropriate to choose $\epsilon > 0$ and use the stopping criterion,

$$Dgap \leq \epsilon f \qquad (3.13)$$

More importantly, if (3.13) is satisfied, then we can obtain a guaranteed bound for the primal problem using (3.11):

$$E - E^\star \leq Dgap \leq \epsilon f \leq \epsilon E \quad (3.14)$$

Thus, if $\epsilon = 10^{-p}$ and (3.13) is satisfied, then the closeness of E to $E^\star$ has more than p decimal digits of accuracy. These ideas are used in interior point methods of linear programming (Vanderbei, 1994) and have also been employed in SVMs (Smola and Schölkopf, 1998).

In our implementation of the SMO algorithm derived in the next section, we employ (3.13) as the stopping criterion.

At a given α, we need a method for determining a good value of b for use in the above calculations as well as for use in the classifier function defined by

$$o(x) = w \cdot \varphi(x) - b = \sum_i \alpha_i k(x, x_i) - b \quad (3.15)$$

One possibility is to take

$$b = \frac{b_{\text{low}} + b_{\text{up}}}{2} \quad (3.16)$$

where b_{up} and b_{low} are as defined in (3.4). An alternative method is to choose b to minimize $Dgap$ after fixing w at $w(\alpha)$. This is equivalent to minimizing $\sum_i \xi_i^2$, which can be done in closed form to get

$$b = \frac{1}{m} \sum_i (F_i - \frac{\alpha_i}{C}) \quad (3.17)$$

IV. SMO Algorithm

In this section we give the SMO algorithm for solving (2.10). A basic step consists of starting with a point α and optimizing only two variables α_i and α_j to form the new point α_{new}. Consider (3.7) and (3.8). Given (3.9), the natural choice is $i = i\_up$ and $j = i\_low$ so as to make $|\phi'(0)|$ as large as possible. Using the notations of section III, we can write the optimization problem and the resulting solution as

$$t^\star = \arg\max_t \phi(t) \quad \text{and} \quad \alpha_{\text{new}} = \tilde{\alpha}(t^\star) \quad (4.1)$$

The function $\phi(t)$ is a simple quadratic function of t:

$$\phi(t) = \phi(0) + t\phi'(0) + \frac{t^2}{2}\phi''(0) \quad (4.2)$$

where ϕ' is given by (3.9) and

$$\phi''(0) = \eta = 2\tilde{k}(x_i, x_j) - \tilde{k}(x_i, x_i) - \tilde{k}(x_j, x_j) \quad (4.3)$$

Thus (4.1) can be easily solved in closed form:

$$t^\star = -\frac{\phi'(0)}{\phi''(0)} = -\frac{F_i - F_j}{\eta} \quad (4.4)$$

The SMO algorithm can now be described. It is very much along the lines of the simplified version of the SMO algorithm for SVMs given by Chang and Lin (2001).

SMO Algorithm for (2.10).
1) Choose any α^0 and set $r = 0$.
2) If α^r satisfies (3.5), stop. If not, set $\alpha = \alpha^r$, choose $i = i\_up$, $j = i\_low$ and solve (4.1).
3) Let $\alpha^{r+1} = \alpha_{\text{new}}$, $r := r + 1$ and go back to step 2.

Convergence of this algorithm can be shown (Keerthi and Shevade, 2002). The implementation of the SMO algorithm is extremely simple. The details and the pseudocode can be found in (Keerthi and Shevade, 2002).

For efficiency, a cache is maintained for all F_i's. At each basic step, when only two indices, say $i1$ and $i2$ change their values from α_{i1}^{old} and α_{i2}^{old} to α_{i1}^{new} and α_{i2}^{new}, the F_i's can be updated as

$$\begin{aligned} F_i^{new} &= F_i^{old} + (\alpha_{i1}^{new} - \alpha_{i1}^{old})\tilde{k}(x_{i1}, x_i) \\ &\quad + (\alpha_{i2}^{new} - \alpha_{i2}^{old})\tilde{k}(x_{i2}, x_i) \; \forall \; i \end{aligned} \quad (4.5)$$

Putting (4.4) in (4.2) and simplifying, we get

$$f(\alpha^{r+1}) - f(\alpha^r) = \phi(t^\star) - \phi(0) = -\frac{(t^\star)^2}{2}\eta \quad (4.6)$$

The updating of the dual objective function can be written, using (4.4) and (4.6) as

$$f^{new} = f^{old} - \frac{\eta}{2}(t^\star)^2 \quad (4.7)$$

where $t^\star = (\alpha_{i2}^{new} - \alpha_{i2}^{old}) = (\alpha_{i1}^{old} - \alpha_{i1}^{new})$.

The algorithm can be initialized with $\alpha = 0$. For this choice, $F_i = -y_i$ for all i and $f(\alpha) = 0$. When the regularization parameter C is tuned (say, using k-fold cross validation) we usually come across a situation in which the solution of (2.10) is available for some C and (2.10) needs to be solved again for δC where $\delta > 0$. In such a situation we can do *alpha seeding* (DeCoste and Wagstaff, 2000), i.e., utilize the solution at C to initialize the variables for solving the problem at δC. We give below the details.

Suppose α is the solution at C and, f, $F_i \; \forall \; i$ are available. Then, to start the algorithm for δC, we can use the same α. For this choice, the F_i for δC can be initialized using

$$F_i := F_i - \frac{(\delta - 1)\alpha_i}{\delta C} \; \forall i \quad (4.8)$$

After the F_i are computed, f can be obtained using

$$f = \frac{1}{2} \sum_i \alpha_i (y_i - F_i) \quad (4.9)$$

An alternative is to initialize with $\delta\alpha$ for solving the problem at δC. Update formulas similar to (4.8) and (4.9) can be derived for this case too. Both the above initializations work effectively and give similar performance.

V. Numerical Experiments on Classification Problems

The SMO and CG methods were implemented in Fortran and executed on a Pentium IV 1.5 GHz machine running on Windows platform. For fair comparison of the two methods, the implementation of the CG method was modified and the full details are given in (Keerthi and Shevade, 2002). The Gaussian kernel $k(x, \bar{x}) = \exp(-\frac{\|x - \bar{x}\|^2}{2\sigma^2})$ was used. For both methods we used the termination criterion in (3.13) with $\epsilon = 10^{-6}$.

We empirically compared the two methods in terms of computational cost. This cost is measured using the number of kernel evaluations since the bulk of the effort in both the algorithms resides in computing kernels. Four benchmark datasets were used for this purpose: Banana, Image, Splice and Waveform. Detailed information about these datasets can be found at the site: *http://ida.first.gmd.de/~raetsch/data/benchmarks.htm*. For each dataset, we fixed σ at a suitable value which gives good generalization performance and varied C over a wide range.

In the first experiment we tried the following nine C values: 10^i, $i = -4, -3, \ldots, 3, 4$. For each C, the methods were initialized with $\alpha = 0$. The computational costs associated with the four datasets are given in Table I as functions of C.

In the second experiment we tested the effect of alpha seeding on the computational cost. C was sequentially varied from 2^{-10} till 2^{10} in multiples of 2. Thus there were twenty one C values. For $C = 2^{-10}$ the methods were initialized with $\alpha = 0$. For all other C values alpha seeding was used.[2] The computational costs associated with the four datasets are given in Table II as functions of C.

For the SMO algorithm the increase in cost at large C values is sharp. See, for instance, the growth in cost of SMO after $C = 10^2$ for Banana and Image datasets. In the case of Image dataset, while SMO was doing quite better than CG at low and medium C values, it became very expensive at large C values. In most practical problems, the optimal value of C where best generalization occurs (say, the value at which the k-fold cross validation error is smallest) is usually not high. For instance, in the case of Image dataset, 5-fold cross validation error was smallest around $C = 24.16$. Thus, when searching for the optimal C, if large C values can be carefully avoided, then the SMO algorithm will work very efficiently. It is also worth noting that, for both SMO and CG methods, the effectiveness of the alpha seeding diminishes at large C values. Since large C values correspond to large costs for both methods, such values should be avoided (unless really needed) in the C tuning procedure to maintain efficiency.

On the Image and Splice datasets SMO was quite faster than CG at the middle C values. Since the 'optimal' C usually occurs in this range, this is an advantage in favor of the SMO method. On the Banana and Waveform datasets the difference between the two methods was not much in this range of C values. When C is tuned using cross validation, we usually start with a low C value, say 2^{-10}, increase C in steps (say in multiples of 2) and stop when the cross validation error clearly shows no further decrease. We compared the CG and the SMO methods with respect to the total cost associated with this process. To do this, we used the same four datasets of Table II, while also fixing σ^2 at the values given in that table. Five fold cross validation was employed. Table III gives the ratio of the coputational efforts associated with the two

[2] In section IV we mentioned two alpha seedings: (a) set α to the optimal α of the previous C value; and (b) set α to δ times the optimal α of the previous C value. Our experiment showed that both initializations give nearly the same cost.

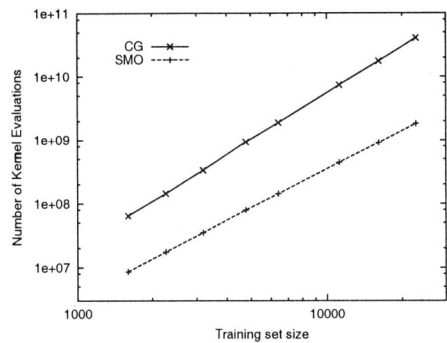

Fig. 1. Variation of computational cost with training set size for Adult dataset.

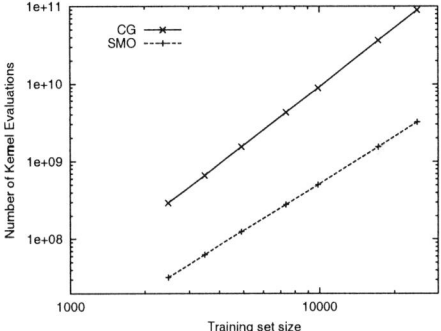

Fig. 2. Variation of computational cost with training set size for Web dataset.

methods. The SMO method is clearly faster in all cases. So the SMO algorithm proposed in this paper can be viewed as an excellent alternative method for solving LS-SVMs.

To see how the SMO algorithm for LS-SVM scales to large size problems, we did a scaling experiment on the Adult and Web datasets by gradually increasing the training set size in eight steps and observing the training cost. These datasets are available from Platt's SMO page:
http://www.research.microsoft.com/~jplatt/smo.html. The Adult dataset was trained with $C = 1.0$ and $\sigma^2 = 10$ while the Web dataset was trained with $C = 5.0$ and $\sigma^2 = 10$. Figures 1 and 2 give plots of the computational costs of the two algorithms as functions of the problem size. The SMO algorithm for LS-SVM scales well on both the datasets, with scaling exponents of 2.017 and 2.006 respectively for the Adult and Web datasets. For the CG algorithm the corresponding scaling exponents were 2.385 and 2.496. This is due to the fact that the number of conjugate gradient iterations needed to achieve (3.13) slowly rises as the number of examples increases. The above results indicate that the SMO algorithm is better suited for large problems.

Next we briefly compared the generalization performance of SVM and LS-SVM. Five-fold cross validation was used to tune the hyperparameters involved in the problem formulations (that is, C and σ) and the test set error was obtained using the optimal hyperparameter values for each of the formulations. The search for optimal hyperparameters was done on a 20×20

TABLE I

COMPUTATIONAL COSTS FOR SMO AND CG ALGORITHMS ($\alpha = 0$ INITIALIZATION). EACH UNIT CORRESPONDS TO 10^6 KERNEL EVALUATIONS.

$\log_{10} C$	Banana $\sigma^2 = 1.8221$		Image $\sigma^2 = 2.7183$		Splice $\sigma^2 = 29.9641$		Waveform $\sigma^2 = 24.5325$	
	SMO	CG	SMO	CG	SMO	CG	SMO	CG
-4	0.90	0.32	9.30	3.38	4.73	1.00	0.93	0.32
-3	0.83	0.48	7.48	5.07	4.35	2.00	0.91	0.48
-2	0.53	0.64	5.17	8.05	2.94	3.00	0.52	0.64
-1	0.50	1.28	4.84	20.28	3.13	6.00	0.42	1.12
0	0.70	2.24	7.05	49.01	3.07	13.00	0.54	2.40
1	3.53	4.00	33.65	131.82	5.33	30.00	2.39	5.76
2	31.58	7.84	254.13	410.67	11.45	65.00	10.51	14.56
3	320.42	14.40	1908.62	1275.95	29.88	89.00	21.62	23.36
4	3317.90	32.32	11825.40	4096.56	99.90	109.00	28.33	27.36

TABLE II

COMPUTATIONAL COSTS FOR SMO AND CG ALGORITHMS WITH ALPHA SEEDING. EACH UNIT CORRESPONDS TO 10^6 KERNEL EVALUATIONS.

$\log_2 C$	Banana $\sigma^2 = 1.8221$		Image $\sigma^2 = 2.7183$		Splice $\sigma^2 = 29.9641$		Waveform $\sigma^2 = 24.5325$	
	SMO	CG	SMO	CG	SMO	CG	SMO	CG
-10	0.83	0.48	7.44	5.07	4.37	2.00	0.91	0.48
-9	0.62	0.32	6.15	3.38	3.50	1.00	0.78	0.32
-8	0.47	0.32	5.54	5.07	3.34	2.00	0.70	0.32
-7	0.51	0.48	4.56	5.07	2.92	2.00	0.50	0.48
-6	0.44	0.64	4.69	6.76	2.96	3.00	0.39	0.48
-5	0.44	0.80	4.09	10.14	2.75	3.00	0.40	0.64
-4	0.42	0.96	3.98	13.52	2.56	4.00	0.42	0.80
-3	0.42	1.12	3.79	18.59	2.70	5.00	0.37	0.96
-2	0.43	1.28	3.82	21.97	2.40	6.00	0.38	1.12
-1	0.45	1.60	4.38	28.73	2.32	8.00	0.39	1.44
0	0.60	2.08	5.83	38.87	2.43	10.00	0.49	1.92
1	0.90	2.24	8.71	54.08	2.74	14.00	0.73	2.56
2	1.47	2.88	13.95	72.67	3.19	17.00	1.09	3.68
3	2.61	3.04	24.16	98.02	3.62	23.00	1.82	4.96
4	4.84	4.00	43.70	138.58	3.91	32.00	2.99	6.40
5	9.31	5.12	81.07	197.73	4.09	37.00	4.70	8.96
6	18.42	5.44	149.06	265.33	4.04	52.00	7.09	11.84
7	36.56	7.04	278.62	378.56	4.17	65.00	9.92	14.72
8	72.40	8.64	518.92	549.25	4.18	73.00	12.78	17.44
9	146.95	9.76	955.57	763.88	4.04	82.00	14.91	20.64
10	297.37	12.16	1717.04	1098.50	3.77	88.00	15.83	23.36

TABLE III

RATIO OF THE CROSS VALIDATION COST OF CG AND THE CROSS VALIDATION COST OF SMO ALGORITHM.

Banana ($\sigma^2 = 1.8221$)	Image ($\sigma^2 = 2.7183$)	Splice ($\sigma^2 = 29.9641$)	Waveform ($\sigma^2 = 24.5325$)
1.89	2.62	5.77	1.34

TABLE IV
GENERALIZATION PERFORMANCES OF LS-SVM AND SVM ON FOUR BENCHMARK DATASETS.

Dataset	LS-SVM	SVM
Banana	.1161	.1180
Image	.0208	.0228
Splice	.1012	.0989
Waveform	.1089	.1076

uniform grid in the $(\log C, \log \sigma)$ space. The fraction of test set errors (TErr) are given in Table IV. It is clear that the generalization capabilities of both methods are comparable. This observation is consistent with that made by Van Gestel et al. (2000).

VI. CONCLUSION

In this paper we have given a new algorithm for least squares formulation of SVM (LS-SVM and kernel ridge regression) and discussed implementation aspects. The algorithm is robust in the sense that on the many complex datasets we have tried there was not even a single case of failure. It is also fast and scales well to large size problems. It provides a better alternative to the conjugate gradient algorithm developed by Hamers et al. (2001), especially for large problems.

References

Chang, C.C., and Lin, C.J. (2001). *LIBSVM: A library for support vector machines,* Dept. of Computer Science and Information Engineering, National Taiwan University, Taipei, Taiwan.

DeCoste, D., and Wagstaff, K. (2000). *Alpha seeding for support vector machines,* International Conference on Knowledge Discovery & Data Mining (KDD-2000).

Fletcher, R. (1987). *Practical Methods of Optimization.* John Wiley and Sons, 2nd Edition.

Hamers, B., Suykens, J., and De Moor, B. (2001). *A comparison of iterative methods for least squares support vector machine classifiers,* Internal Report 01-110, ESAT-SISTA, K.U.Leuven (Leuven, Belgium).

Keerthi, S.S., Shevade, S.K., Bhattacharyya, C., and Murthy, K.R.K. (2001). *Improvements to Platt's SMO algorithm for SVM design,* Neural Computation, vol. 13, pp.637-649.

Keerthi, S.S., and Shevade, S.K. (2002). *SMO Algorithm for Least Squares SVM Formulations,* Technical Report CD-02-08, Control Division, Dept. of Mechanical Engineering, National University of Singapore, Singapore. Available at: *http://guppy.mpe.nus.edu.sg/~mpessk/papers/lssvm_smo.ps.gz*

Mika, S., Rätsch, G., and Müller, K.R. (2001). *A mathematical programming approach to the kernel Fisher algorithm,* In T.K. Leen, T.G. Dietterich, and V. Tresp, editors, Advances in Neural Information Processing Systems 13, pp.591-597, MIT Press.

Platt, J. (1998). *Sequential minimal optimization: A fast algorithm for training support vector machines,* Technical Report MSR-TR-98-14, Microsoft Research, Redmond.

Saunders, C., Gammerman, A., and Vovk, V. (1998). *Ridge regression learning algorithm in dual variables,* Proceedings of the 15th International Conference on Machine Learning ICML-98, Madison, WI, USA.

Smola, A., and Schölkopf, B. (1998) *A tutorial on support vector regression,* NeuroColt2 Technical Report NC2-TR-1998-030, ESPRIT Working Group in Neural and Computational Learning II.

Suykens, J., and Vandewalle, J. (1999). *Least squares support vector machine classifiers,* Neural Processing Letters, vol. 9, no. 3, June 1999, pp. 293-300.

Suykens, J., Lukas, L., Van Dooren, P., De Moor, B., and Vandewalle, J., (1999). *Least squares support vector machine classifiers: a large scale algorithm,* in Proc. of the European Conference on Circuit Theory and Design (ECCTD'99), Stresa, Italy, Sep. 1999, pp. 839-842.

Vanderbei, R.J. (1994). *LOQO: An Interior Point Code for Quadratic Programming,* Technical Report SOR-94-15, Statistics and Operations Research, Princeton University, NJ, USA.

Van Gestel, T., Suykens, J., Baesens, B., Viaene, S., Vanthienen, J., Dedene, G., De Moor, B., and Vandewalle, J. (2000). *Benchmarking least squares support vector machine classifiers,* Internal Report 00-37, ESAT-SISTA, K.U.Leuven (Leuven, Belgium), 2000.

Van Gestel, T., Suykens, J., Lanckriet, G., Lambrechts, A., De Moor, B., and Vandewalle, J. (2002). *A Bayesian framework for least squares support vector machine classifiers,* Neural Computation.

Power System Security Evaluation Using ANN: Feature Selection Using Divergence

K. R. Niazi
Reader in Elect. Engg.
Malaviya National Inst. Of Tech.
Jaipur, India 302017

C. M. Arora
Professor in Elect. Engg.
Malaviya National Inst. Of Tech.
Jaipur, India 302017

S. L. Surana
Prof. in Elect. Engg. &Principal
S. K. Inst. Of.Tech.
Jaipur, India 302017

Abstract- **This paper presents an Artificial Neural Network (ANN) based method for on-line security evaluation of power systems. One of the important considerations in applying ANN is feature selection. A new divergence based feature selection algorithm has been proposed and investigated. The method has been applied on an IEEE test system and the results demonstrate the suitability of the proposed method for on-line security evaluation of power systems even under changing topological conditions.**

I. INTRODUCTION

Security evaluation is a major concern in the real time operation of modern power systems. The present trend towards deregulation has forced modern electric utilities to operate their systems under stressed operating conditions closer to their security limits. Under such fragile conditions, any disturbance could endanger system security and may lead to system collapse. Therefore, there is a pressing need to develop fast on-line security monitoring method which could analyze the level of security and forewarn the system operators to take necessary preventive actions in case need arises.

A complete answer about power system security requires evaluation of transient stability of power systems following some plausible contingencies. Several methods for fast transient stability evaluation have been proposed in the past by adopting namely direct methods, pattern recognition (PR) technique, Decision Tree (DT) methods and Artificial Neural Network(ANN) approach [1-6].

Direct methods aim to circumvent computational drawback of classical method by avoiding the exploration of post disturbance phase. Direct methods in the form of Transient Energy Function (TEF) have been successfully used for dynamic security assessment purposes [1,2]. However, this approach is applicable under simplified modelling assumptions. The determination of TEF is a cumbersome task, specially for modern power systems which are large and complex.

PR approach despite its appealing principle does not offer satisfactory transient security evaluation tool [3]. The main drawback of PR approach is that it requires generation of a quadratic or higher order security classifier, which is a function of the potential features (variables) of the power system. As the size of power system grows, the number of classifier parameters becomes very large and may make the classifier unreliable unless a prohibitively large learning set is considered [4].

DT approach falls in the broader category of PR approach. Conceptually the two approaches proceed in a similar manner viz., on the basis of information gathered in off-line phase, they aim at building on-line classifier [4]. The DT approach pursues much broader objective than mere classification. However DT approach suffers from the same drawback as the classical PR approach, that is, as the size of power system grows, complexity of DT classifier becomes very high which requires a prohibitively large training set.

The ANNs have shown a great promise as a means of predicting security of large electric power systems [5,6]. The research paper of Fidalgo, Miranda and Lapes [7] highlights the superiority of ANN approach over PR and DT approaches for predicting dynamic security of power systems. This paper presents an ANN based method for on-line security evaluation of power systems. One of the important consideration in applying neural networks to power system security evaluation is the proper selection of training features among a large number of features that may characterize a given power system. Many feature selection criteria are available in the literature such as feature selection through entropy minimization, function expansion, f-value maximization, divergence maximization etc. The basic problem encountered in all feature selection algorithms is searching an optimal combination of features among a large number of possible solutions. Recently Jensen, Sharkawi and Marks [5] proposed a fisher discrimination function based back track feature selection algorithm to find an optimal subset of neural network training feature for power system security assessment purposes. However, the problem with this feature selection algorithm is that it works well with linearly separable classes because fisher discrimination function basically seeks to find an optimal linear discrimination function for separating the two classes. How well this algorithm will perform on non-linearly separable classes is not established. Power system security evaluation is a complex non-linear problem, which may not have linear seperability between secure and insecure classes. Moreover the proposed back-track algorithm requires to pre define an optimal number of features to search for, which seems to be a difficult task. The present paper attempts to investigate the concept of divergence coupled with a backward sequential algorithm to find an optimal number and optimal combination of neural network training features.

The organization of this paper is as follows. In Section II the ANN methodology is described and a divergence based feature selection algorithm is presented. In section III, the method has been applied and tested for its applicability and effectiveness on the IEEE 57-bus power system. Finally conclusions are presented in sections IV.

II. THE ANN METHODOLOGY

The proposed method uses ANN as a classifier, which classifies the operating state of a power system into secure and insecure classes under a predefined set of contingency. The ANN classifier is trained using an off-line data set, which is generated by most accurate power system solution methodology. The trained network is then, used for on-line security evaluation propose. The complete description of the ANN methodology is not within the scope of this paper. Nevertheless, it is important to discuss the basic design procedure, which involves the following steps.

(1) Feature selection.
(2) Data set generation for training
(3) Architecture of ANN model and its training algorithm.
(4) Performance evaluation.

Feature selection is a process of selecting a small subset of features from a large number of features (variables) that may characterize a given power system. It involves dimensionality reduction to identify most significant and useful subset of features that carries sufficient discriminating properties to perform the given classification task most accurately. If too small feature subset is used to train the network, the neural network may not acquire the desired discriminating properties or may fail to converge even during training phase. If the size of feature subset is too large, it may require a prohibitively large size of training set beside taking large training time. In fact the curse of dimensionality states that as a rule of thumb, the required cardinality of the training set for accurate training increases exponentially with the input dimension (training features) [5]. Mansour, Vaahedi and Sharkawi observed in a study on B.C.Hydro and Hydro Cubec for dynamic contingency screening that accuracy of ANN classifier increased when the number of neural training features were reduced [8]. Therefore as regards to ANN, feature selection is a process to identify an optimal combination of features which contributes most to the discriminating ability of the network and discard the rest.

In the present method feature selection is carried out in two stages. In the first stage, an initial feature set is selected which is based on the knowledge of power system and objective of the problem to be solved. Initial feature set is a general set of features, which is independent of data set used for training. The idea behind the first stage of feature selection is to eliminate the insensitive features apriori so as to avoid exhaustive search of second stage of feature selection algorithm. The initial feature set should have the following properties [7]:

1. The feature set should adequately characterize an operating state of a power system from security point of view. At the same time it should be small enough to avoid unnecessary computation.
2. Features in the feature set should be independent.
3. Features should be monitorable and controllable so that control action may be exercised, if need be.
4. As far as possible, features should be independent of network topology.

C.M. Arora and Surana [9,10] have derived that if power system is not optimally dispatched, the feature set consisting of pre-disturbance real and reactive power generations and real and reactive power demands at each system bus carry sufficient information about system security. Under certain justified assumptions, the generator currents and load currents can be expressed as a function of generator currents. The generator currents are directly related to the real and reactive powers of the generators. Therefore, the real power and reactive power demands can be expressed as a function of real and reactive powers of generators. Thus, an attribute set (feature set) consisting of only real and reactive power generations is capable of providing sufficient discriminating information about the class of system security (secure or insecure). This fact is also supported by the outcome of the research paper [5]. Therefore, the proposed initial feature set consists of pre-disturbance real and reactive power generation of each generator.

The second stage of feature selection makes use of the concept of divergence, which is calculated using the training set and therefore final feature subset is specific to the power system and contingency set considered.

Divergence is a measure of dissimilarly between two classes and therefore, it can be used in feature ranking and feature selection. The divergence J_{ij} between two classes, say i and j, can be expressed as [11]

$$J_{ij} = \frac{1}{2} t_r \left[(C_i - C_j)(C_j^{-1} - C_i^{-1}) \right] + \frac{1}{2} t_r \left[(C_i^{-1} + C_j^{-1})(m_i - m_j)(m_i - m_j)^t \right]$$

(1)

Where,

t_r = trace of a matrix and is equal to sum of its Eigen values,

C_i = covariance matrix of class i of size [n×n],

C_j = covariance matrix of class j of size [n×n],

m_i = mean vector of class i of size [n × 1],

m_j = mean vector of class j of size [n × 1]

$(m_i-m_j)^t$ = transpose of (m_i-m_j) and

n = number of features.

Since divergence is a measure of dissimilarity between two classes, the features, which give large divergence, are more important. Any feature that makes the least contribution to the total divergence may be discarded.

There are many ways to search for the best feature subset using the concept of divergence such as back track method, forward sequential method, backward sequential method etc. The proposed feature selection algorithm makes use of the divergence in backward sequential manner. The backward sequential search guarantees the optimal solution if the criterion function satisfies the monotonicity condition. The monotonicity condition requires that values of the criterion function be non-decreasing when additional features are added. The divergence satisfies the condition of monotonicity [11]. The advantage of using backward sequential method is that feature selection process can be stopped at any stage, if it is found that further reduction in the size of feature subset is significantly affecting the discriminating properties of feature subset. Though the backward sequential method is computationally more demanding but since feature selection is carried out in off-line phase it does not affect the on-line classification time of the ANN classifier. The feature selection method, in brief, proceeds as follows:

Determine the divergence J_{ij} (n) of initial feature subset. Now selectively remove one feature at a time till all the features are considered and determine the divergences corresponding to all the n subset of (n-1) features. The feature that results in the smallest decrease in the divergence, at each iteration, is then removed. This process is then repeated for remaining features.

The size of feature subset is an important ANN design consideration. So far, in the literature, the size of feature set has been chosen using heuristics or trial and error method. However to solve this problem in a systematic manner it is proposed to define and use two terms namely "maximum permissible percentage change in divergence", ΔJ_{max} and "minimum number of features required by the classifier", n_{min}. The parameter, ΔJ_{max} is a measure of maximum permissible reduction in the discriminating properties of the feature subset, whereas the parameter n_{min} is the minimum size of feature subset required by the ANN classifier.

Thus, at any intermediate stage of feature selection, if it is found that further reduction in dimensionality is causing a decrease in divergence more than ΔJ_{max}, then the process of feature selection is stopped. Thus, this parameter helps to find the optimal number of training features. The detailed feature selection algorithm is as follows:

1. Read the data of initial feature subset and assume suitable values of ΔJ_{max}, n_{min}.
2. Find the divergence $J_{ij}(n)$ of feature subset a(n) having n number of features.
3. Remove one feature, at a time, from the feature subset a(n) to form n feature subsets having (n-1) features and determine the corresponding divergences J_{ij}^k (n-1), k= 1, 2, ... n.
4. Determine the decrease in divergence due to each individual feature i.e

$$\Delta J_{ij}^k(n) = J_{ij}(n) - J_{ij}^k(n-1)$$

For k = 1, 2, ... n
Where n is the size of current feature subset

5. if $\Delta J_{ij}^k(n) \geq \Delta J_{max}$ for all k = 1, 2, ... n,

go to step 7
else remove the feature which is causing minimum change in divergence i.e.

$$\Delta J_{ij}^k(n)_{min}$$

6. Set n = n –1

If n = n_{min}, then go to step 7
else go to step 2

7. Output the desired feature subset a(n).

The second step in the design of ANN classifier is data set generation for network training. The primary objective of data set generation is to obtain a sufficiently rich data base containing plausible operating states of the power system. To generate a data set, initially a large number of load samples are randomly generated in the typical range of 50 to 150 percent of their base case values. For each load sample (load combination) optimal power flow (OPF) study is performed to obtain steady operating state. A disturbance (fault), from a predefined set of contingency, is simulated for a specified duration of time. Using dynamic stability studies, load angle trajectories of all generators are computed and plotted over a period long enough to ascertain system stability under the specified disturbance. Similarly for each of the disturbances from the contingency set dynamic simulation is performed to ascertain system stability under the corresponding disturbance. For carrying out dynamic simulation, numerical integration technique is used as it has the flexibility to include all kinds of modelling sophistication and thus is able to provide desired degree of accuracy. If a steady state operating point is found to be stable, for all disturbances of the contingency set, the operating state is assigned "secure (0)" class label else it is assigned "insecure (1)" class label.

Thus for each operating state a labeled pattern is formed which contains the values of selected features along with its associated security class label. During data set generation some operating states are also generated in the neighbourhood of optimal dispatch to ensure inclusion of all realistic operating states. Some frequent topological changes may also be considered during data generation. The data set is then, normalized to suit the requirement of the ANN training. The whole data set is suitably divided into training set and test set for training and performance evaluation purposes.

The ANN model selected for on-line security evaluation is a Multi-Layer Perceptron (MLP) as shown in Fig. 1. It consists of an output layer with one neuron specifying the security class. The number of inputs to the network is equal to the number of training features. The number of hidden layers is one or more. The network is trained using Resilient error back propagation algorithm commonly abbreviated as RPROP [12,13]. It is an adaptive weight learning algorithm, which adapt the weight step based on the local gradient information. In this algorithm the sign of partial derivative of performance function with respect to the weight is used only to determine the direction of weight update. The magnitude of partial derivative has no effect on the weight update unlike other common adaptive learning algorithms. This overcomes the problem of slow convergence due to unforeseeable behaviour of the value of partial derivative. The size of weight update is determined by a separate update value. The complete description of RPROP is given in [12]. Due to its very nature of weight update the Resilient back propagation algorithm converges much faster than the conventional error back propagation algorithm and is not very sensitive to the settings of training parameters.

During the training, the network performance is closely monitored to prevent network memorization. The trained network is tested for its performance on a test set of unseen patterns.

III. SIMULATION AND RESULTS

To investigate the effectiveness of the proposed method a study was performed on IEEE - 57 bus system. The system consists of 7 generators, 57 buses, 67 transmission lines, 18 transformers and 42 loads. The diagram of the system is given in [14] and the data were taken from [14, 15].

It is assumed that contingency set contains only one disturbance, which is a 3-phase fault on the 400kV transmission line connecting buses 8 and 9, near bus 9. Duration of the disturbance is assumed to be 210 ms, which is cleared by opening the line at both the ends. By varying the loads randomly between 50% to 150% of their base case values two sets of data have been generated. The first data set consists of 1000 operating states with fixed system topology. Second data set consisting of 2200 operating states is generated under 12 different topological conditions.

The changes in topology are spread through out the system and include removal of single 400kV transmission lines 2, 5, 14, 15, 19 and 28 one at a time, simultaneous removal of a set of three transmission lines at a time such as (2, 5, 14), (15, 19, 28) etc. The second data set is then shuffled several times to thoroughly mix the data of different topology. The application of proposed feature selection algorithm on the fixed system topology data gave an optimal feature set consisting of PG_1, QG_5 and QG_7. While multiple topology data set gave an optimal feature subset which consists of PG_1 and QG_5.

Using the data set and feature subset of fixed system topology, an MLP has been trained using Resilient back propagation algorithm. The neural architecture used in this study consists of three layers with 20 neurons in the first hidden layer, 10 neurons in the second hidden layer and one neuron in the output layer specifying the security class.

Three training and testing runs have been performed for the network and their results are shown in Table 1. Similarly a second neural network has been trained using multiple topology data and features. The test results for three training runs are shown in Table 2. The high accuracy rate of the test results shown in Table 1 and Table 2 highlights the effectiveness of the method for predicting security of power systems using a small subset of power system variables.

Modern power systems are prone to frequent changes in system topology due to many factors such as maintenance, repair etc. Therefore, special care needs to be taken to minimize the effect of topology changes on the performance of the neural network. One approach to deal with this problem is to train different neural networks for each possible system topology and to use the specific network that reflects

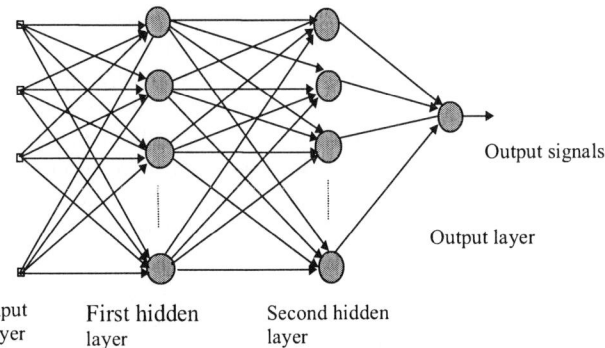

Fig. 1 Architecture of a MLP with two hidden layers

the current topology of the system. This approach is only practical when there are a few possible changes in system topology.

Another approach is to choose training features that are independent of changes in system topology. This allows a single neural network to tackle security assessment problem of the power system under varying system topology. This also allows the single network to predict security of the power system under unexpected topological changes.

The proposed feature selection algorithm when applied on a data set containing examples of as many different topologies as possible, gives features which are independent of changes in system topology and at the same time, which carries sufficient discriminating properties about system security. To investigate this capability of proposed feature selection algorithm, two more neural networks have been trained using the same fixed topology data. However the first neural network is trained using features selected from fixed topology data i.e., P_{G1}, Q_{G5} and Q_{G7} while the second neural network is trained using features selected from multiple topology data i.e., P_{G1} and Q_{G5}. The trained networks have been tested on the same data set of multiple system topology. The test results of the two networks are shown in Table 3.

It can be seen from this table that neural network trained with features selected from multiple topology data gives an accuracy rate of nearly 98.6% which is much better than the one obtained by the network trained using features selected from fixed topology data. This is a remarkable result considering the facts that both neural networks were trained by the same single topology data and tested on the same multiple topology data. The test results highlight the importance of selecting features, which are independent of changes in power system topology. This result also indicates that the feature Q_{G7} is not independent of topological changes in the power systems as because of this feature only there is decrease in accuracy under varying topological conditions. Thus, the test results demonstrate the capability of the proposed feature selection algorithm to select an optimal subset of training features, which are independent of topological changes.

TABLE 1

RESULT OF FIXED TOPOLOGY DATA

S.No	Network Architecture used h1-h2-h3-0 or h1-h2-0	Percentage Error on training set (500)	Percentage Error on test set (500)
1	20-10-1	1.2	1.2
2	20-10-1	1	1.6
3	20-10-1	1	1.2
	Average	1.06	1.33

TABLE 2

RESULTS OF MULTIPLE TOPOLOGY DATA

S.No	Network Architecture Used h1-h2-h3-0 or h1-h2-0	Percentage Error on training set (1000)	Percentage Error on test set (1200)
1	20-10-1	2	1.53
2	20-10-1	1.57	1.4
3	20-10-1	2.14	1.46
	Average	1.90	1.46

TABLE 3

EFFECT OF TOPOLOGY ON THE PERFORMANCE OF ANN CLASSIFIER

S. No.	Feature selected from single topology data (P_{G1}, Q_{G5}, Q_{G7}) Error in Percent on		Feature selected from multiple topology data (P_{G1}, Q_{G5}) Error in Percent on	
	Training set(1000)	Test set (2200)	Training set (1000)	Test set (2200)
1.	0.8	2.86	1.1	1.363
2.	0.9	3.27	1.3	1.409
3.	1.0	3.63	1.2	1.409
Average	0.9	3.253	1.2	1.393

IV. CONCLUSION

Artificial neural network based method for on-line security evaluation of power systems is presented. A divergence based backward sequential algorithm is proposed to select an optimal set of neural training feature. The proposed method has been applied on the IEEE 57-bus system under different operating conditions and the test results are promising giving an accuracy rate of nearly 99 %. The test results highlight the importance of selecting features, which are independent of changes in power system topology. The test results also show that the proposed feature selection algorithm can be effectively used to select features, which are independent of changes in system topology. The neural network trained using such features works well even under unexpected change in topology. Thus, it relives the burden of designing a separate neural network classifier for each possible system topology and minimizes the need to keep abreast with every possible change in system topology.

REFERENCES

[1] Ebrahim Vaahedi, Y. Mansour, E.K. Tse, "A General purpose method for on-line dynamic security assessment", *IEEE Trans. on Power Systems,* Vol. 13, No. 1, Feb. 1998, pp. 243-250.

[2] M.J. Laufenferg, M.A. Pai, "A new approach to dynamic security assessment using trejectory sensitivities", *IEEE Trans. on Power Systems*, Vol. 13, No. 3, Aug., 1998, pp. 953-958.

[3] L. Wehenkal, Th. Van Cutsem, M. Ribbens-Pavella, "Inductive inference applied to on-line transient stability assessment of electric power systems", *Automatica*, Vol. 25, No. 3, 1989, pp. 445-451.

[4] L. Wehenkal, Th. Van Custsem, M. Ribbens-Pavella, "An artificial intelligence frame work for on-line transient stability assessment of power systems", *IEEE Trans. on Power Systems*, Vol. 4, No. 2, May 1989, pp. 789-800.

[5] C.A. Jensen, M.A. El-Sharkawi, R.J. Marks II, "Power systems security assessment using neural networks: Feature selection using Fisher discrimination", *IEEE Trans. on Power Systems*, Vol. 16, No. 4, Nov., 2001, pp. 757-763.

[6] K. Santi Swarup, P. Britto Corthis, "ANN approach assesses system security", *IEEE Computer Applications in Power*, July 2002 pp. 31-38.

[7] J.N. Fidalgo, V. Miranda, J.A. P. Lapes, "Neural networks applied to preventive control measures for the dynamic security of isolated power systems with renewables", *IEEE Trans. on Power Systems* Vol. 11, No. 4, Nov., 1996, pp. 1811-1816.

[8] Y. Mansour, E. Vaahedi, M.A. El-Sharkawi, "Large scale dynamic security screening and ranking using neural networks", *IEEE Trans. on Power Systems* Vol. 12, No. 2, May 1997, pp. 954-960.

[9] C.M. Arora, "On-line transient security evaluation using pattern recognition technique", Ph.D. Thesis, Deptt. of Elect. Engg., JNV Univ., Jodhpur, India, 1991.

[10] C. M. Arora, S. L. Surana, "Transient security evaluation and preventive control of power systems using PR techniques", IE(I) Journal-EL, Vol. 76, Feb/March 1996, pp199-203.

[11] J.T. Tau, R.C. Ganzalez, "*Pattern recognition principles*", Addison-Wesley, 1994.

[12] M. Riedmiller, H. Braun, " A direct adoptive method for faster backpropagation learning : The RPROP algorithm", IEEE Int. Conf. On Neural Networks, 1993, Vol. 1, pp. 586-589.

[13] H. Demuth, M. Beale, "Neural network tool box for use with MATLAB", User's Guide, Version 4, The Math works Inc, 2001.

[14] http://www.ee.washington.edu/research/pstca.

[15] http://www.pserc.cornell.edu/matpower.

Evaluation of Cosine Radial Basis Function Neural Networks on Electric Power Load Forecasting

Nicolaos B. Karayiannis, Mahesh Balasubramanian
Dept. of Electrical and Computer Engineering
N308 Engineering Building 1
University of Houston
Houston, Texas 77204-4005, USA.

Heidar A. Malki
Engineering Technology Dept.
312 Technology Building
University of Houston
Houston, Texas 77204-4022, USA.

Abstract-This paper presents the results of a study aimed at the development of a system for short-term electric power load forecasting. This was attempted by training feedforward neural networks (FFNNs) and cosine radial basis function (RBF) neural networks to predict future power demand based on past power load data and weather conditions. This comparison indicates that both neural network models exhibit comparable performance when tested on the training data but cosine RBF neural networks generalize better since they outperform considerably FFNNs on the testing data.

I. INTRODUCTION

Radial basis function (RBF) neural networks are function approximation models that can be trained by examples to implement a desired input-output mapping [2], [6]. Under certain mild conditions on the radial basis functions, RBF neural networks are capable of approximating arbitrarily well any function. The performance of an RBF neural network depends on the number and centers of the radial basis functions, their shapes, and the method used for learning the input-output mapping [14]. Broomhead and Lowe [3] suggested that the centers of the radial basis functions can either be distributed uniformly within the region of the input space for which there is data, or chosen to be a subset of the training vectors by analogy with strict interpolation. Moody and Darken [20] proposed a hybrid learning process for training RBF neural networks with Gaussian radial basis functions, which employs a supervised scheme for updating the output weights, i.e., the weights that connect the radial basis functions with the output units, and an unsupervised clustering algorithm for determining the centers of the radial basis functions. The centers of the radial basis functions are often determined by the k-means (or c-means) clustering algorithm [14]. Poggio and Girosi [24] proposed a supervised approach for training RBF neural networks with Gaussian radial basis functions, which updates the radial basis function centers together with the output weights. Chen et al. [5] proposed a learning procedure for RBF neural networks based on the orthogonal least squares (OLS) method, which is used as a forward regression procedure to select a suitable set of radial basis function centers. Cha and Kassam [4] proposed a stochastic gradient training algorithm for RBF neural networks with Gaussian radial basis functions, which uses gradient descent to update all their free parameters (radial basis function centers, widths of the Gaussian radial basis functions, and output weights).

The training of RBF neural networks using gradient descent offers a solution to the tradeoff between performance and training speed and can make RBF neural networks serious competitors to feedforward neural networks (FFNNs) with sigmoid hidden units [8]-[13], [15]. The convergence of gradient descent learning and the performance of the trained RBF neural networks are both affected rather strongly by the choice of radial basis functions. The search for admissible radial basis functions other than the Gaussian function motivated the development of an axiomatic approach for constructing reformulated RBF neural networks suitable for gradient descent learning [8]-[13], [15]. This approach reduces the development of reformulated RBF models to the selection of admissible generator functions that determine the form of the radial basis functions.

This paper presents the results of a study aimed at short-term electric power load forecasting by relying on neural network models. In this study, FFNN and cosine RBF models were trained using actual power load data to predict the electric power load for the next day based on past load data and the weather conditions. This study focused on the performance of the neural network models trained to forecast power load for the next day.

II. COSINE RBF NEURAL NETWORKS

Consider the $\mathbb{R}^n \to \mathbb{R}^{n_o}$ mapping implemented by the model

$$\hat{y}_i = f\left(w_{i0} + \sum_{j=1}^{c} w_{ij} g_j\left(\|\mathbf{x} - \mathbf{v}_j\|^2\right)\right), 1 \leq i \leq n_o, \quad (1)$$

where $f(\cdot)$ is a non-decreasing, continuous and differentiable everywhere function. The model (1) describes an RBF neural network with inputs from $\mathbb{R}^n$, c radial basis functions, and n_o output units if $g_j(x^2) = \phi_j(x)$, and $\{\phi_j(x)\}$ are radial basis functions. In such a case, the response of the RBF neural network to the input vector $\mathbf{x}_k$ is

$\hat{y}_{i,k} = f\left(\sum_{j=0}^{c} w_{ij} h_{j,k}\right)$, where w_{ij} is the weight connecting the ith output unit with the jth radial basis function, $h_{0,k} = 1, \forall k$, and $h_{j,k}$ represents the response of the radial basis function centered at the prototype $\mathbf{v}_j$ to the input vector $\mathbf{x}_k$, that is, $h_{j,k} = g_j\left(\|\mathbf{x}_k - \mathbf{v}_j\|^2\right), 1 \le j \le c$.

A. Reformulated RBF Neural Networks

Reformulated RBF neural networks were developed to facilitate the training of RBF models by learning algorithms based on gradient descent [8]-[13], [15]. This was attempted by including the centers of the radial basis functions in the adjustable model parameters and searching for radial basis functions that improve the effectiveness of gradient descent learning. The search for admissible radial basis functions can be simplified by considering basis functions of the form $\phi_j(x) = g_j(x^2)$, with $g_j(x)$ defined in terms of a generator function $g_{j0}(x)$ as $g_j(x) = \left(g_{j0}(x)\right)^{1/(1-m)}$, $m \ne 1$. If $m > 1$, the exponential generator functions $g_{j0}(x) = \exp(\beta_j x)$, $\beta_j > 0$, correspond to $g_j(x) = \exp(\beta_j x/(1-m))$, which lead to Gaussian radial basis functions $\phi_j(x) = g_j(x^2) = \exp(-x^2/\sigma_j^2)$, with $\sigma_j^2 = (m-1)/\beta_j$. Linear generator functions $g_{j0}(x) = a_j x + b_j$, $a_j > 0$, $b_j \ge 0$, produce radial basis functions of the form $\phi_j(x) = g_j(x^2) = \left(a_j x^2 + b_j\right)^{1/(1-m)}$, with $m > 1$. A useful generator function for practical applications can be obtained from $g_{j0}(x) = a_j x + b_j$ by selecting $b_j = 1$ and $a_j = \delta_j > 0$ [12], [13], [15].

B. Cosine Radial Basis Functions

Consider the linear generator function $g_{j0}(x) = 1 + \delta_j x$, $0 < \delta_j < \infty$. If $m = 3$, then $g_{j0}(x) = (1+\delta_j x)^{-\frac{1}{2}}$. If $\delta_j = 1/a_j^2$, with $a_j \ne 0$, then

$$g_j(x) = \frac{a_j}{\left(x + a_j^2\right)^{\frac{1}{2}}}. \quad (2)$$

The corresponding radial basis function $\phi_j(x) = g_j(x^2)$ can be obtained from (2) as

$$\phi_j(x) = \frac{a_j}{\left(x^2 + a_j^2\right)^{\frac{1}{2}}}. \quad (3)$$

The response $h_{j,k} = g_j\left(\|\mathbf{x}_k - \mathbf{v}_j\|^2\right)$ of the radial basis function centered at the prototype $\mathbf{v}_j$ to the input $\mathbf{x}_k$ can be obtained according to (2) as

$$h_{j,k} = \frac{a_j}{\left(\|\mathbf{x}_k - \mathbf{v}_j\|^2 + a_j^2\right)^{\frac{1}{2}}}. \quad (4)$$

Let $\mathbf{x}_k = \left[x_{1,k}, x_{2,k}, \cdots, x_{n,k}\right]^T \in \mathbb{R}^n$ be a training vector and $\mathbf{v}_j = \left[v_{1,j}, v_{2,j}, \cdots, v_{n,j}\right]^T \in \mathbb{R}^n$ be a prototype. Define a new vector $\mathbf{x}_k' \in \mathbb{R}^{n+1}$ obtained by augmenting as $\mathbf{x}_k$ as $\mathbf{x}_k' = \left[\mathbf{x}_k^T, 0\right]^T = \left[x_{1,k}, x_{2,k}, \cdots, x_{n,k}, 0\right]^T \in \mathbb{R}^{n+1}$. Augmenting the prototype $\mathbf{v}_j$ in a similar manner gives $\mathbf{v}_j' = \left[\mathbf{v}_j^T, 0\right]^T = \left[v_{1,j}, v_{2,j}, \cdots, v_{n,j}, 0\right]^T \in \mathbb{R}^{n+1}$. Let $\mathbf{p}_j$ be a vector obtained by augmenting the prototype $\mathbf{v}_j$ as $\mathbf{p}_j = \left[\mathbf{v}_j^T, a_j\right]^T = \left[v_{1,j}, v_{2,j}, \cdots, v_{n,j}, a_j\right]^T \in \mathbb{R}^{n+1}$ with $a_j \in \mathbb{R} - \{0\}$. For $n = 2$, $\mathbf{x}_k \in \mathbb{R}^2$ and $\mathbf{v}_j \in \mathbb{R}^2$ lie in a plane. The vectors $\mathbf{x}_k'$ and $\mathbf{v}_j'$ obtained by augmenting $\mathbf{x}_k$ and $\mathbf{v}_j$ respectively, are defined in $\mathbb{R}^3$. For $a_j \ne 0$, $\mathbf{p}_j$ defines a vector $\mathbf{v}_j' - \mathbf{p}_j$ which is orthogonal to the plane that contains $\mathbf{x}_k \in \mathbb{R}^2$ and $\mathbf{v}_j \in \mathbb{R}^2$ (see Fig. 1). Using the definitions of $\mathbf{p}_j, \mathbf{v}_j'$, and $\mathbf{x}_k'$, $\|\mathbf{x}_k - \mathbf{v}_j\|^2 + a_j^2 = \|\mathbf{x}_k' - \mathbf{p}_j\|^2$ and the response $h_{j,k}$ defined in (4) can be written as

$$h_{j,k} = \frac{a_j}{\|\mathbf{x}_k' - \mathbf{p}_j\|}. \quad (5)$$

For $\mathbf{x}_k, \mathbf{v}_j \in \mathbb{R}^2$, Fig. 1 indicates that $\|\mathbf{v}_j' - \mathbf{x}_k'\| = \|\mathbf{v}_j - \mathbf{x}_k\|$ and $\|\mathbf{v}_j' - \mathbf{p}_j\| = a_j$ are the lengths of the legs of a right triangle, $\|\mathbf{x}_j' - \mathbf{p}_j\|$ is the length of its hypotenuse, and

$$h_{j,k} = \cos(\theta_{jk}), \quad (6)$$

where θ_{jk} is the angle between $\mathbf{v}_j' - \mathbf{p}_j$ and $\mathbf{x}_k' - \mathbf{p}_j$. In general, the response of a radial basis function centered at the prototype $\mathbf{v}_j$ to an input vector $\mathbf{x}_k$ measures the similarity between this input vector and the prototype $\mathbf{v}_j$. The similarity between $\mathbf{v}_j$ and $\mathbf{x}_k$ is measured in this case by using $\mathbf{p}_j$ as a reference for computing the cosine of the angle θ_{jk} between $\mathbf{v}_j' - \mathbf{p}_j$ and $\mathbf{x}_k' - \mathbf{p}_j$.

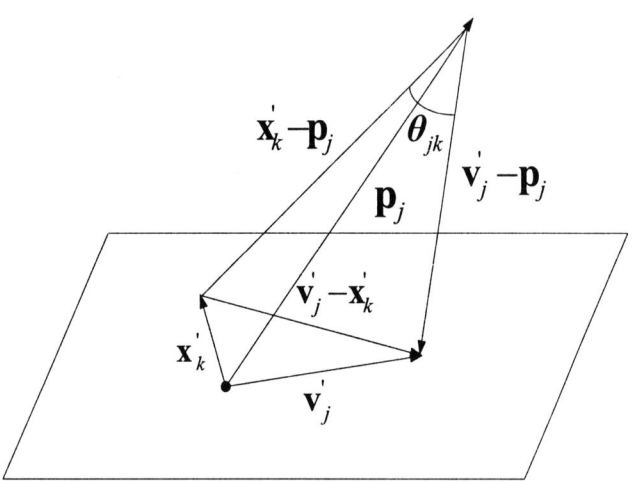

Fig. 1: Geometric interpretation of cosine radial basis functions for $\mathbf{x}_k \in \mathbb{R}^2$ and $\mathbf{v}_j \in \mathbb{R}^2$.

C. Training Cosine RBF Neural Networks

RBF neural networks can be trained to map $\mathbf{x}_k \in \mathbb{R}^n$ into $\mathbf{y}_k = \left[y_{1,k}, y_{2,k}, \cdots, y_{n_o,k} \right]^T \in \mathbb{R}^{n_o}$, where the vector pairs $(\mathbf{x}_k, \mathbf{y}_k), 1 \le k \le M$, form the training set. If $\mathbf{x}_k \in \mathbb{R}^n$ is the input to an RBF neural network, its output is $\hat{\mathbf{y}}_k = \left[\hat{y}_{1,k}, \hat{y}_{2,k}, \cdots, \hat{y}_{n_o,k} \right]^T$, where $\hat{y}_{i,k} = f(\bar{y}_{i,k}) = f(\mathbf{w}_i^T \mathbf{h}_k)$, $\mathbf{h}_k = \left[h_{0,k}, h_{1,k}, \cdots, h_{c,k} \right]^T$, $h_{0,k} = 1$, $h_{j,k} = g_j \left(\| \mathbf{x}_k - \mathbf{v}_j \|^2 \right)$, $1 \le j \le c$, and $\mathbf{w}_i = [w_{i0}, w_{i1}, \cdots, w_{ic}]^T$

Cosine RBF neural networks can be trained by batch learning algorithms, developed by using gradient descent to minimize [10]

$$E = \frac{1}{2} \sum_{k=1}^{M} \sum_{i=1}^{n_o} \left(y_{i,k} - \hat{y}_{i,k} \right)^2. \quad (8)$$

Cosine RBF neural networks can also be trained "on-line" by sequential learning algorithms, which can be developed by using gradient descent to minimize [10]

$$E_k = \frac{1}{2} \sum_{i=1}^{n_o} \left(y_{i,k} - \hat{y}_{i,k} \right)^2, \quad (9)$$

for $k = 1, 2, \cdots, M$. After an example $(\mathbf{x}_k, \mathbf{y}_k), 1 \le k \le M$, is presented to the RBF neural network, the new estimate $\mathbf{w}_{i,k}$ of each weight vector $\mathbf{w}_i, 1 \le i \le n_o$, is obtained by incrementing its current estimate $\mathbf{w}_{i,k-1}$ by the amount $\Delta \mathbf{w}_{i,k} = -\alpha \nabla_{\mathbf{w}_i} E_k$ as

$$\mathbf{w}_{i,k} = \mathbf{w}_{i,k-1} + \alpha \, \varepsilon_{i,k}^o \, \mathbf{h}_k, \quad (10)$$

where α is the learning rate and $\varepsilon_{i,k}^o = f'(\bar{y}_{i,k})(y_{i,k} - \hat{y}_{i,k})$ is the output unit error. Following the update of all the weight vectors $\mathbf{w}_i, 1 \le i \le n_o$, the new estimate $\mathbf{v}_{j,k}$ of each prototype $\mathbf{v}_j, 1 \le j \le c$, can be obtained by incrementing its current estimate $\mathbf{v}_{j,k-1}$ by the amount $\Delta \mathbf{v}_{j,k} = -\alpha \nabla_{\mathbf{v}_j} E_k$ as

$$\mathbf{v}_{j,k} = \mathbf{v}_{j,k-1} + \alpha \, \varepsilon_{j,k}^h \left(\mathbf{x}_k - \mathbf{v}_{j,k-1} \right), \quad (11)$$

where α is the learning rate and $\varepsilon_{j,k}^h$ is the hidden unit error, defined as

$$\varepsilon_{j,k}^h = \left(h_{j,k}^3 \big/ a_j^2 \right) \sum_{i=1}^{n_o} \varepsilon_{i,k}^o w_{ij}. \quad (12)$$

Finally the new estimate $a_{j,k}$ of each $a_j, 1 \le j \le c$, can be obtained by incrementing its current estimate $a_{j,k-1}$ by the amount $\Delta a_{j,k} = -\eta \, \partial E_k / \partial a_j$ as

$$a_{j,k} = a_{j,k-1} + \eta \, a_{j,k-1} \left[\left(1 - h_{j,k}^2 \right) \big/ h_{j,k}^2 \right] \varepsilon_{j,k}^h. \quad (13)$$

where η is the learning rate. An adaptation cycle is completed in this case after the sequential presentation to the RBF neural network of all the examples included in the training set.

III. ELECTRIC POWER LOAD FORECASTING

Accurate power load forecasting is of great importance to utility companies for: 1) the economic dispatching of generation units, 2) power interchange with other utilities, and 3) production scheduling that can result in cost savings to consumers. In addition, reliable power load forecasting reduces energy consumption and decreases environmental pollution.

Electric power load forecasting was one of the earliest applications of neural networks [7], [22], [23]. The existing power load forecasting systems vary considerably in terms of their performance and design sophistication. Most, if not all, of the existing power load forecasting systems relied on FFNNs trained by gradient descent [1], [7], [16]-[19], [21]-[23]. The study outlined in this paper was an attempt to perform power load forecasting based on a different neural network model. Thus, the results of this study can be used to explore the potential of improving the prediction accuracy of power load forecasting systems by focusing on the neural network models employed. On the other hand, forecasting power load based on actual data is a challenging real-world problem that provides a reliable basis for comparing cosine RBF neural networks and FFNNs in terms of their capacity for function approximation and their ability to generalize.

Power load forecasting depends on several factors such as temperature, seasonal changes, heat waves, cold fronts and holidays. The data selected for use in this project involved measurements acquired during the course of at least one calendar year in order to include seasonal changes, cold fronts, and heat waves. The following factors play an important role in short-term power load forecasting:

1) <u>Temperature</u>: There is a strong link between the temperature and the amount of power consumed.

The power consumed increases due to air-conditioning when the temperature increases; power consumption also increases due to heating when the temperature decreases.
2) Time: Daily power load forecasting is influenced by the day of the week. As an example, weekdays from Monday to Friday are expected to have different power load patterns from Saturdays and Sundays.

The development of a system for daily power load forecasting relied on the hypothesis that the demand for power at a certain day of the week relates to the history of demand during previous days and measurements recorded for the same day during previous weeks. It was also hypothesized that the daily demand for electric power is affected by the weather conditions and the temperature profile along the power distribution network. Thus, neural networks were trained to forecast power load for a certain day based on: 1) the power load measurements from previous days, and 2) the weather conditions during these days, including the temperature and humidity. The inputs used to forecast power load for the next day are listed below:
1) The average temperature of the previous week (input 1).
2) The average temperature of the previous two days (input 2).
3) The average temperature of the previous day (input 3).
4) The average humidity of the previous week (input 4).
5) The average humidity of the previous two days (input 5).
6) The average humidity of the previous day (input 6).
7) The average power load of the previous week (input 7).
8) The average power load of the previous two days (input 8).
9) The average power load of the previous day (input 9).
10) A single-digit binary code distinguishing weekdays from weekends (input 10). The input 10 was 0 for any weekday from Monday to Friday and 1 for Saturday and Sunday.
11) A seven-digit binary code for the day of the week (inputs 11 to 17). The input corresponding to a certain day was 1 and the others were 0. Monday was considered to be the first day (input 11) and Sunday was considered to be the last day (input 17).

The neural networks were trained using these inputs to predict the absolute value of the power load for the next day. The same inputs were used in this study to train the neural networks to predict the difference between the power load in the next day and that of the previous day. The clear advantage of such a strategy was revealed by the experiments, which indicated that predicting power load differences between successive days leads to lower prediction errors. This can be attributed to the fact that the power load differences between successive days typically span a shorter range of values than the absolute power load values. Let P_{n-1} be the power load at day $n-1$, P_n be the power load at day n, and let $\Delta P_n = P_n - P_{n-1}$. The output of the network was the difference of the power load $\Delta \overline{P}_n$. The power load demand at day n was obtained by adding $\Delta \overline{P}_n$ to the previous day load P_{n-1}.

IV. EXPERIMENTAL RESULTS

This section presents the results produced by FFNNs and cosine RBF neural networks trained to predict the differences between the power load in the next day and that of the previous day. All neural networks were trained to forecast power load using temperature, humidity, and power load measurements recorded daily over a period of two years in Berkeley, California. The trained neural networks were tested on the data recorded during a year different from those that produced the training data. The temperature was normalized by dividing the temperature averages by the maximum temperature value over an entire year. The same scheme was also employed to normalize the humidity and the power load data. Power load forecasting was performed by training FFNNs with one layer of hidden units, and a single linear output unit. The number of hidden units varied in the experiments from 4 to 15. The FFNNs were trained by the error back propagation algorithm, which relies on gradient descent, with a learning rate value of 0.01 [2], [6]. Power load forecasting was also performed by training cosine RBF models with a linear output unit. The number of radial basis functions varied from 4 to 12. The cosine RBF neural networks were trained by the gradient descent algorithm outlined in this paper. The learning rate used to update the output weights and the prototypes was $\alpha = 0.01$, while the learning rate η used to update the reference distances $\{a_j\}$ was $\eta = \alpha/10$. The centers of the radial basis functions were initialized by generating randomly a set of c prototypes over the range of the training vectors in the input space. The output weights were also initialized randomly. The training of all neural networks tested was terminated if the total error increased considerably after five consecutive adaptation cycles. If this never occurred, the training of all neural networks was terminated after 500 adaptation cycles.

Fig. 2 shows the prediction error produced by the trained FFNN with 10 hidden units on training data. The same information is shown in Fig. 3 for the cosine RBF neural network with 7 radial basis functions. Both neural networks predicted power load with comparable accuracy but the FFNN outperformed slightly the cosine RBF neural network, as indicated by the mean square error (MSE) values computed on the training data.

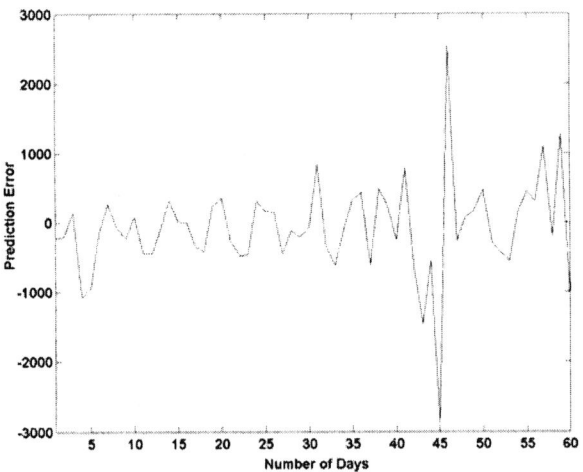

Fig.2. Prediction error (in MWatts) produced by an FFNN on training data recorded from April 10, 1999 to June 9, 1999 (MSE = 3.0120×10^7).

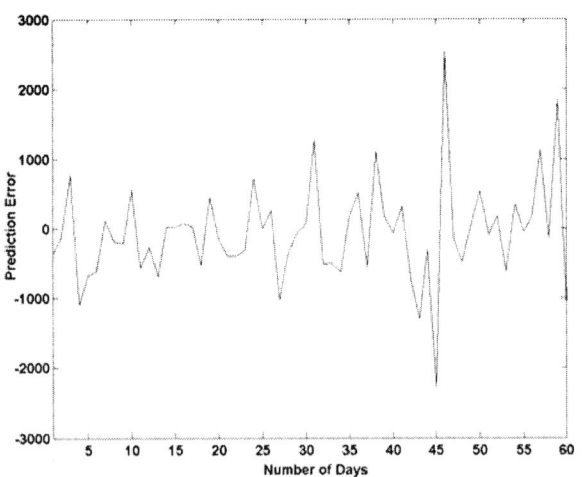

Fig. 3. Prediction error (in MWatts) produced by a cosine RBF neural network on training data recorded from April 10, 1999 to June 9, 1999 (MSE = 3.2296×10^7).

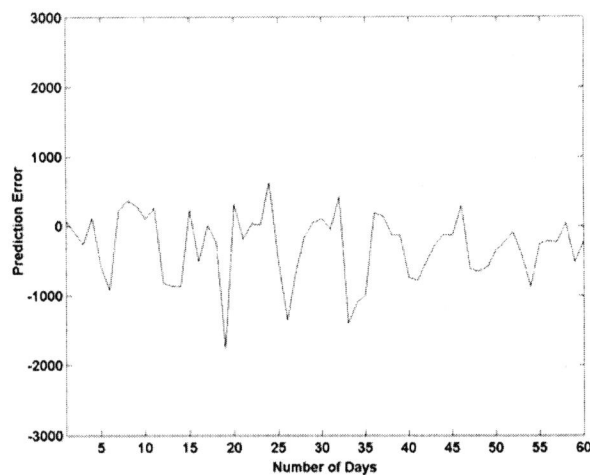

Fig. 4. Prediction error (in MWatts) produced by an FFNN on testing data recorded from January 25, 2001 to March 26, 2001 (MSE= 2.0034×10^7).

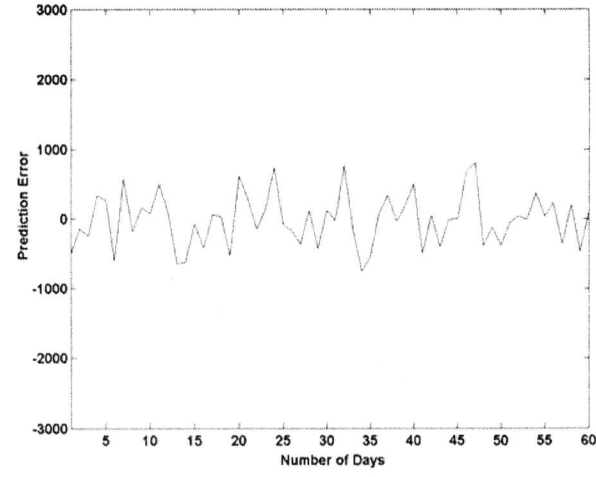

Fig. 5. Prediction error (in MWatts) produced by a cosine RBF neural network on testing data recorded from January 25, 2001 to March 26, 2001 (MSE = 8.6792×10^6).

The performance differences between the neural networks trained in the experiments can be seen in Figs. 4 and 5, which show the prediction error produced on testing data by the trained FFNN with 10 hidden units and the cosine RBF neural network with 7 radial basis functions, respectively. According to Figs. 4 and 5, the prediction error produced by the cosine RBF neural network was smaller than that produced on the same data by the trained FFNN. These performance differences were also quantified by computing the MSE values produced by the trained neural networks on the testing data over the period of two months shown in Figs. 4 and 5.

V. CONCLUSIONS

This study evaluated the performance of FFNNs and cosine RBF neural networks trained to forecast power load based on past load data and weather conditions. This experimental study indicated that cosine RBF neural networks achieved comparable performance with FFNNs on the training set. Nevertheless, the trained cosine RBF neural networks performed considerably better than FFNNs on the testing set. Since the performance of trained neural networks on the testing set relates to their generalization ability, trained cosine

RBF neural networks generalized better than FFNNs in this particular application. This is a significant outcome regarding the true potential of RBF models. It is generally believed that conventional RBF neural networks can be trained faster than FFNNs but they are inferior to FFNNs in terms of their generalization ability. The outcome of this experimental study reinforces the conclusions of earlier studies, which indicated that the inferior generalization ability of conventional RBF neural networks can only be attributed to their training by hybrid learning schemes that rely on unsupervised clustering procedures to determine the centers of the radial basis functions [10], [12], [15]. These centers are often kept fixed during the updates of the output weights by a supervised learning scheme. It seems that this counterintuitive learning strategy was actually forced by the construction of conventional RBF models by Gaussian radial basis functions, which prevented the training of such models by fully supervised algorithms based on gradient descent. In fact, the outcome of this study reveals the significance of the methodology proposed for constructing reformulated RBF neural networks that can be trained by gradient descent. The improved performance of the trained cosine RBF neural networks can be attributed to the properties of these models and, in particular, to the sensitivity properties of cosine radial basis functions that were also revealed by the analysis reported in [15]. Finally, it must be emphasized here that FFNNs and cosine RBF neural networks were trained in this application by sequential supervised learning algorithms based on gradient descent. Not surprisingly, the experiments indicated that the computational effort associated with the training of FFNNs and cosine RBF neural networks was comparable.

ACKNOWLEDGMENTS

This project was supported in part by a University of Houston GEAR Grant number 1-116397.

REFERENCES

[1] G. Bakirtzis, V. Petridis, S.J. Klartzis, M.C. Alexiadis, and A.H. Maissis "A neural network short term load forecasting model for the Greek power system," *IEEE Trans. on Power System*, vol. 11, no. 2, pp. 858 - 863, 1996.

[2] C. M. Bishop, *Neural Networks for Pattern Recognition*, Oxford University Press, Oxford, 1995.

[3] D. S. Broomhead and D. Lowe, "Multivariable functional interpolation and adaptive networks," *Complex Systems*, vol. 2, pp. 321 - 355, 1988.

[4] I. Cha and S. A. Kassam, "Interference cancellation using radial basis function networks," *Signal Processing*, vol. 47, pp. 247 - 268, 1995.

[5] S. Chen, C. F. N. Cowan, and P. M. Grant, "Orthogonal least squares learning algorithm for radial basis function networks," *IEEE Trans. on Neural Networks*, vol. 2, no. 2, pp. 302 - 309, 1991.

[6] S. Haykin, *Neural Networks: A Comprehensive Foundation*, Prentice Hall, Upper Saddle River, NJ, 1999.

[7] K. Ho, Y. Hsu, and C. Yang, "Short term load forecasting using a multi-layer neural network with an adaptive learning algorithm," *IEEE Trans. on Power Systems*, vol. 7, no. 1, pp.141 - 149, 1992.

[8] N. B. Karayiannis, "Gradient descent learning of radial basis neural networks," *Proceedings of 1997 IEEE International Conference on Neural Networks, Vol. 3*, Houston, TX, June 9-12, 1997, pp. 1815 - 1820.

[9] N. B. Karayiannis, "Learning algorithms for reformulated radial basis neural networks," *Proceedings of 1998 International Joint Conference on Neural Networks*, Anchorage, AK, 1998, pp. 2230 - 2235.

[10] N. B. Karayiannis, "Reformulated radial basis neural networks trained by gradient descent," *IEEE Trans. on Neural Networks*, vol. 10, no. 3, pp. 657 - 671, 1999.

[11] N. B. Karayiannis, "Reformulating learning vector quantization and radial basis neural networks," *Fundamenta Informaticae*, vol. 37, pp. 137 - 175, 1999.

[12] N. B. Karayiannis, "New developments in the theory and training of reformulated radial basis neural networks," *Proceedings of 2000 International Joint Conference on Neural Networks*, vol. 3, Como, Italy, July 24 - 27, 2000, pp. 614 - 619.

[13] N. B. Karayiannis and S. Behnke, "New radial basis neural networks and their application in a large-scale handwritten digit recognition problem," in *Recent Advances in Artificial Neural Networks: Design and Applications*, L. C. Jain and A. M. Fanelli, Eds, CRC Press, Boca Raton, FL, pp. 39 - 94, 2000.

[14] N. B. Karayiannis and W. Mi, "Growing radial basis neural networks: Merging supervised and unsupervised learning with network growth techniques," *IEEE Trans. on Neural Networks*, vol. 8, no. 6, pp. 1492 - 1506, 1997.

[15] N. B. Karayiannis and M. M. Randolph-Gips, "On the construction and training of reformulated radial basis function neural networks," *IEEE Trans. on Neural Networks*, under review.

[16] A. Khotanzad, R. Afkhami-Rohani, T. L. Lu, M. H. Davis, A. Abaye, and D. J. Maratukulam, "ANNSTLF- A neural network-based electric load forecasting system," *IEEE Trans. on Neural Networks*, vol. 8, no. 4, pp. 835 - 846, 1997.

[17] A. Khotanzad, R. Afkhami-Rohani, and D. Maratukulam, "ANNSTLF- A neural network short-term load forecaster – generation three," *IEEE Trans. on Power Systems*, vol. 13, no. 4, pp. 1413 - 1422, 1998.

[18] A. Khotanzad, M. H. Davis, A. Abaye, and D. J. Martukulam, "An artificial neural network hourly temperature forecaster with applications in load forecasting," *IEEE Trans. on Power Systems*, vol. 11, no. 2, pp. 870 - 876, 1996.

[19] N. Lu, N. T. Wu, and S. Vemuri, "Neural network based short term load forecasting," *IEEE Trans. on Power Systems*, vol. 8, no. 1, pp. 336 - 342, 1993.

[20] J. E. Moody and C. J. Darken, "Fast learning in networks of locally-tuned processing units," *Neural Computation*, vol. 1, pp. 281 - 294, 1989.

[21] A. D. Papalexopoulos, S. Hao, and T. M. Peng, "An implementation of a neural network based load forecasting model for the EMS," *IEEE Trans. on Power Systems*, vol. 9, no. 4, pp. 1956 - 1962, 1994.

[22] D. C. Park, M. A. El-Sharkawi, R. J. Marks II, L. E. Atlas, and M. J. Damborg, "Electric load forecasting using an artificial neural network," *IEEE Trans. on Power Systems*, vol. 6, no. 2, pp.442- 449, 1991.

[23] T. M. Peng, N. F. Hubele, and G. G. Karady, "Advancement in the application of neural networks for short-term load forecasting," *IEEE Trans. on Power Systems*, vol. 8, no. 3, pp. 1195 - 1202, 1993.

[24] T. Poggio and F. Girosi, "Regularization algorithms for learning that are equivalent to multilayer networks," *Science*, vol. 247, pp. 978--982, 1990.

Direct Torque Control of Induction Motors by Use of the GMR Neural Network

Giansalvo Cirrincione
Department of Electrical Engineering
University of Picardie-Jules Verne
33, rue Saint Leu
80039 Amiens - France
exin@u-picardie.fr

Maurizio Cirrincione
I.S.S.I.A.-C.N.R. Section of Palermo (former CE.RI.S.E.P.)
(Institute on Intelligent Systems for the Automation)
Viale delle Scienze snc,
90128 Palermo - Italy
nimzo@cerisep.pa.cnr.it

Chuan Lu
Katholieke Universiteit Leuven
Departement Elektrotechniek (ESAT)
Afd. ESAT SCD (SISTA), Kasteelpark Arenberg 10, B-3001
Heverlee,Leuven-Belgium
chuan.lu@esat.kuleuven.ac.be

Marcello Pucci
I.S.S.I.A.-C.N.R. Section of Palermo (former CE.RI.S.E.P.)
(Institute on Intelligent Systems for the Automation)
Viale delle Scienze snc,
90128 Palermo - Italy
pucci@cerisep.pa.cnr.it

Abstract— **This paper deals with the application of the General Mapping Regressor (GMR) neural network to the direct torque control DTC of an induction motor. In particular it shows that the GMR neural network is able to correctly learn the classical DTC, as well as any other more involved control strategy. A suitable test bench has been set up in order to verify the performance of the neural controller.**

Keywords—Induction machines, electrical drives, direct torque control, neural networks.

I. INTRODUCTION

Modern control strategies of electrical drives generally involve the choice of a reference voltage to be generated by the power converter on the basis of the desired flux and torque of the motor. Accordingly several control strategies can be come up with e.g. the scalar control, the field oriented control (FOC) [1][2][3], the direct torque control (DTC) [2][3][4][5] or other control algorithms aimed to minimise the torque ripple or the losses of the drive or its conducted emissions (EMC = Electro-Magnetic Compatibility). In general this implies, on the basis of the working conditions of the drive, the proper choice of commands to be given to the power devices of the converter. This choice is essentially a pattern recognition problem where the input space is generally made up of the values of actual fluxes and torques. From this standpoint the property of neural networks to solve for pattern recognition problems and function approximation problems can be successfully employed in carrying out the control strategy. This paper deals with the application of GMR (Generalised Mapping Regressor) [6][7][8] neural network to the control of high performance electrical drive with induction motor. In particular a classical DTC control strategy has been learnt by the GMR network and then the performance of the neural controller has been verified both in numerical simulations and experimentally by means of a properly devised test bench. In [9][10][11] the DTC has also been used with "feed-forward neural networks" in order to substitute for the "optimal switching table". As this is simply a pattern recognition problem, the GMR has been attempted to be used to show also its suitability for such task. Differently from most of the above previous papers, an experimental test bench has been set up and then the good working of the GMR has been experimentally verified.

Section II briefly describes the fundamentals of the GMR neural network. Section III summarises the classical DTC. Section IV shows how the GMR has been applied to the DTC. Section V describes the test bench suitably set up for the experimental verification. Section VI shows and discusses the simulation and experimental results.

Research of C.L. is supported by FWO: G.0407.02,KU Leuven: GOA-Mefisto 666 and DWCT. IUAP V-22.
Research of M.C. and M.P. has been funded by CNR.

II. BRIEF DESCRIPTION OF THE GMR NEURAL NETWORK

GMR, whose architecture is shown in fig. 1, is an incremental self organizing (first layer weights) neural network with chains (second layer weights) among neurons. It transforms the mapping problem in a pattern recognition problem by working in the augmented space whose vectors are created by attaching to the input vector the corresponding output vector. Hence, the input in Fig. 1 is one of these augmented vectors. In this space, the mapping branches become clusters which have to be identified by the GMR linking phase. If, from one side, working in an augmented space is more difficult because of the curse of dimensionality, from the other side it allows to input each possible choice of vector components (reduced space) to the trained network in order to obtain, as output, the remaining components (recall phase): one of the advantages is the possibility to model both the mapping and its inverse. If the mapping is multivalued, GMR can output all values, also specifying to which mapping branch they belong. It is also able to output infinite solutions (as discretized equilevel hypersurfaces).

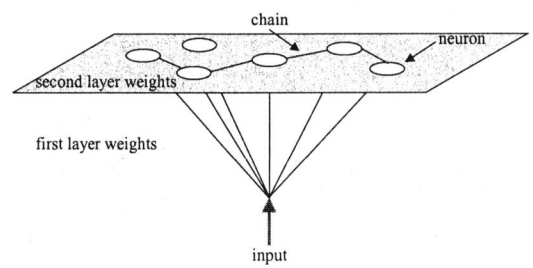

Fig. 1: GMR architecture

The algorithm is here briefly described, in a qualitative way (it is detailed in [8]). It is composed of four phases : training, linking, merging and recall. The training is incremental, competitive and self organizing. The algorithm EXIN SNN [6] is used : it recovers the augmented space by either creating neurons or adapting their weights according to the novelty of the input data. This novelty is quantified by a threshold, called vigilance threshold, which determines the resolution of the modelling. The neurons created after the first epochs (presentations of the whole training set, TS, to the network) are called object neurons (coarse quantization); then, data are labelled according to the nearest (in modulus) object neuron (object). In the next epochs (fine quantization) as many EXIN SNN's as objects are trained, by using data with the same label as TS's (multiresolution approach). A pool of neurons (final neurons) is found. Once trained, all data are relabelled according to the nearest final neuron. All data labelled according to the same neuron are defined as the neuron domain. For each domain, the principal direction (domain PD) of data is determined by using a neural approach for Principal Component Analysis [8]. In the linking phase, a link between two neurons is found at the presentation of each TS data in this way: the nearest (winning) neuron is linked to the neuron whose PD is the most similar to the winner's PD. A geometrical additional rule prevents from linking too far neurons. In the merging phase it is checked if different objects are linked: if the case, these objects are merged. The recall phase, which is explained in [8] replaces the neurons in the reduced space with Gaussians representing the domain. Their parameters are estimated by maximum likelihood. Simple tests and a Gaussian kernel interpolation determine all the possible outputs of the network. As a consequence of linking and merging, the corresponding mapping branches are also output.

III. THE DIRECT TORQUE CONTROL (DTC)

Nowadays in induction motor drives, along with field oriented controlled systems (FOC), the instantaneous torque control can be carried out by the use of direct torque control (DTC). This technique permits the direct and independent control of both electromagnetic torque and the flux linkage by selecting the optimum inverter switching modes so that the torque reference and the flux reference are tracked by the application of suitable stator voltages [2][3][4]. The implementation of the direct torque control, in order to perform the decoupling between the torque and flux control, requires information on the magnitude of the stator flux linkage space vector and on its angle with respect to the stationary reference frame. In classical DTC the knowledge of the sector in which the stator flux linkage lies is necessary while its exact angular position is not required. Even if the stator flux linkage can be directly measured, it is usually computed by a suitable flux model, which is based on the mathematical model of the motor. Any flux model requires, at each instant, the measurements of some stator quantities (stator voltages and currents) and the knowledge of some electrical parameters of the machine. In the following Fig.2 the classical DTC scheme with an induction machine is shown. The block "inverter optimal switching table" operates the generation of the stator voltage space vector, with a suitable choice of the switching pattern of the inverter, on the basis of the knowledge of the sector (supplied by the stator flux model block) in which the stator flux lies, and of the amplitudes of the stator flux and the torque.

In this scheme the closed loop control both of stator flux and rotor speed is performed. Speed control is performed by a PI controller whose output is the torque reference t^*_e. Flux and torque control is performed by hysteresis comparators whose bands are suitably chosen in order to reduce the flux and torque ripple. The flux model employed is based on the stator equations of the machine. The electromagnetic torque is estimated by the estimated stator flux components and the stator current components.

The employed control strategy is that shown in Tab. 1, where are shown the voltage space vectors to be applied when the stator flux linkage lies in the kth the sector.

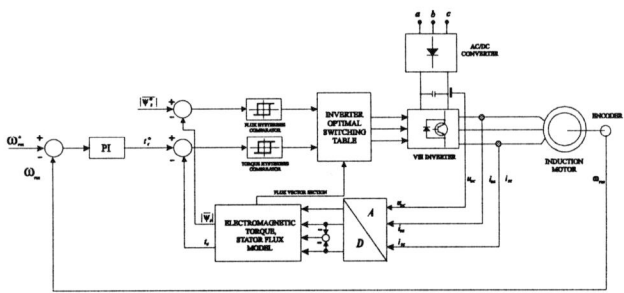

Fig.2: Block diagram of the classical DTC

TABLE I. ADOPTED CONTROL STRATEGY

	$t_e \Uparrow$ | $\psi_s \Uparrow$	$t_e \Uparrow$ | $\psi_s \Downarrow$	$t_e \Downarrow$ | $\psi_s \Uparrow$	$t_e \Downarrow$ | $\psi_s \Downarrow$
Control strategy	u_{k+1}	u_{k+2}	u_{k-1}	u_{k-2}

This control strategy has been chosen as it permits the best dynamic performance even in the breaking phase. The adopted sampling frequency of the control system is 10 kHz.

IV. THE GMR BASED DTC

As described in the introduction the target of this paper is to prove the suitability of the GMR neural network in applications to the control of induction motors. In general any control strategy which involves a pattern recognition problem can be implemented by a proper neural network as for example the GMR. In particular it is possible to implement any particular control strategy in dependence on predefined targets. In the case presented in this paper the DTC control strategy shown on Table I has been implemented. A GMR neural network has been devised having as inputs the torque error, the stator flux linkage error and the sector in which it lies, and as output the voltage space vector to be generated by the inverter. The GMR then replaces the "inverter optimal switching table" block of Fig. 2 as well as the hysteresis comparators, thus resulting in an easy implementation (Fig.3). However any other more involved control algorithm can be likewise implemented, e.g. predictive control, ripple torque minimisation, optimal efficiency algorithms, field oriented control, adaptive inverse control.

V. DESCRIPTION OF THE TEST BENCH

The DTC algorithm has been tested in simulation and experimentally. A test bench has been built for this purpose. The test bench consists of [12]:

- A three-phase induction motor with rated values shown in Table II;
- An electronic power converter (three-phase diode rectifier and VSI composed of 3 IGBT modules without any control system) of rated power 7.5 kVA.
- An electronic card with voltage sensors (model LEM LV 25-P) and current sensors (model LEM LA 55-P) for monitoring the instantaneous values of the stator phase voltages and currents;
- A voltage sensor (Model LEM CV3-1000) for monitoring the instantaneous value of the DC link voltage;
- An electronic card with analog 4th order low-pass Bessel filters and cut-off frequency of 800 Hz;
- An incremental encoder (model RS 256-499, 2500 pulses per round);
- A dSPACE card (model DS1103) with a floating-point DSP.

Special care has been taken for the signal processing of the signals because anti-aliasing filters, low-pass filters and differentiators are necessary.

TABLE II. PARAMETERS OF THE INDUCTION MOTOR

Rated power P_{rated} [kW]	2.2
Rated voltage U_{rated} [V]	220
Rated frequency f_{rated} [Hz]	50
Pole-pairs	2
Stator resistance R_s [Ω]	3.88
Stator inductance L_s [mH]	252
Rotor resistance R_r [Ω]	1.87
Rotor inductance L_r [mH]	252
3-phase magnetizing inductance L_m [mH]	236
Moment of inertia J [Kg·m^2]	0.0266

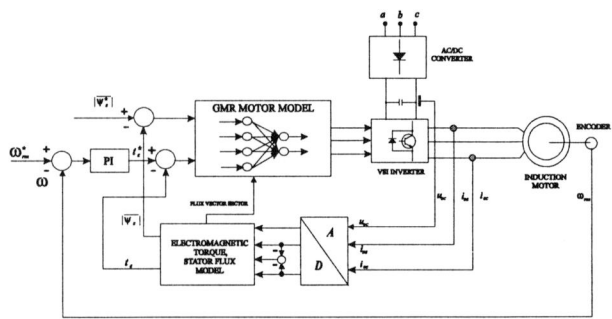

Fig. 3: GMR based DTC scheme

VI. SIMULATION AND EXPERIMENTAL RESULTS

The GMR based algorithm has been verified both in simulation and in experimentation by means of the test bench described in section V. Simulations have been performed by the Matlab®-Simulink® software, while in the experimental test the Dspace 1103 DSP (Digital Signal Processor) board has been programmed in the Matlab®–Simulink®-Real-Time-Workshop® environment.

The training set to give to the GMR has been chosen in order to comply with the "persistent excitation" theorem, which means that the frequency spectrum of the data should be as informative as possible both in frequency and in magnitude. In particular the network has as its inputs the difference between the desired value of the torque and estimated one, the difference between the actual amplitude of the stator flux and its reference, and the sector in which the stator flux linkage lies (discrete value ranging from 1 to 6). The output of the network is the voltage space vector to be generated (discrete value ranging from 1 to 6), which is directly linked to the switching pattern of the power devices of the inverter. More specifically the training set which has been used in experimentation is the one shown in Fig.4. The reference speed consists of negative and positive steps ranging from –150 rad/s to 150 rad/s. For each speed a load ranging from the rated load (± 10 Nm) to no-load has been given. The flux has been set to the rated value 0.8 Vs. Fig. 5 shows the corresponding torque as obtained by the test bench. By giving these references of speed and load to the drive, the corresponding data of the flux error, the sector in which the stator flux linkage lies, the torque error and the corresponding generated voltage space vector have been obtained. By choosing this last variable as the target and the other three variables as the three inputs, a collection of input/output data for the GMR has been obtained. The three input variables have been rescaled into [-1,1] before training and testing, while the output variable voltage vector still keeps the original scale value from 1 to 6. The 60% of these data have been picked up randomly to create the training set while the rest has been used as a test set. Fig. 6 shows the 3-dimensional input space of all the data of the training set. Fig. 7 shows the corresponding plot of the data of the test set. The GMR has been then trained with the following parameters: vigilance threshold of the coarse quantization = 0.3, vigilance threshold of the fine quantization = 0.02. The object neurons obtained are 130 and the pool of neurons after the fine quantization is composed of 1026 neurons. By using a merging threshold of one the objects are reduced to 75 as shown in Fig. 8. The GMR gives good results in the recall phase as shown in Fig. 9 where the data are well represented by the different branches. The GMR network can provide multiple solutions given the input data. 20 % of the output given by GMR are multi-valued, mostly 2-valued, which is also a character of the training set. Thus the GMR response is judged correct if the output voltage values given by the GMR network have included the target value. In this case an accuracy of 85% is achieved. Here no interpolation is used in the GMR recall phase: only the weights of the closest neurons to the input are considered.

Though in this case the accuracy on the training set is still as high as 90%, the accuracy however on the test set goes down to 76%. This is obviously due to the wealth of information of the training set, but also to the fact that no interpolation has been used to speed up the algorithm. Future work will deal with the accuracy of the results. Fig. 10 shows the error on the output as obtained with the whole training set. Fig.11 shows the linking between neurons made by the GMR, with threshold 1, in the subspace obtained by using the three first principal component vectors obtained on the test set: here the linking within each cluster is apparent.

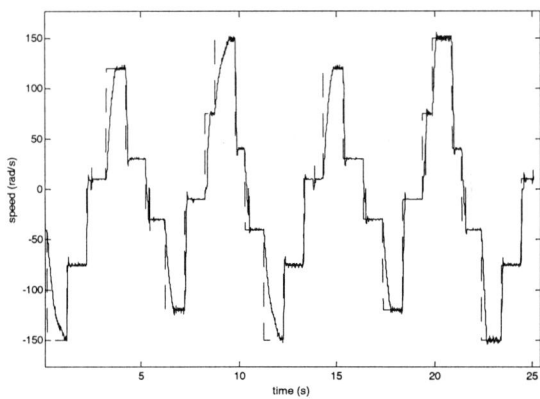

Fig 4: Reference and measured speed during the training phase (experiment)

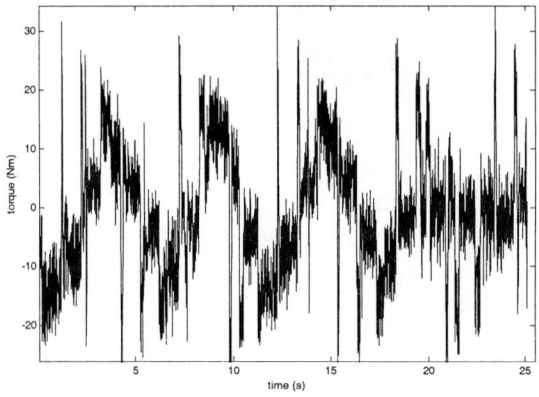

Fig 5: Electromagnetic torque during the training phase (experiment)

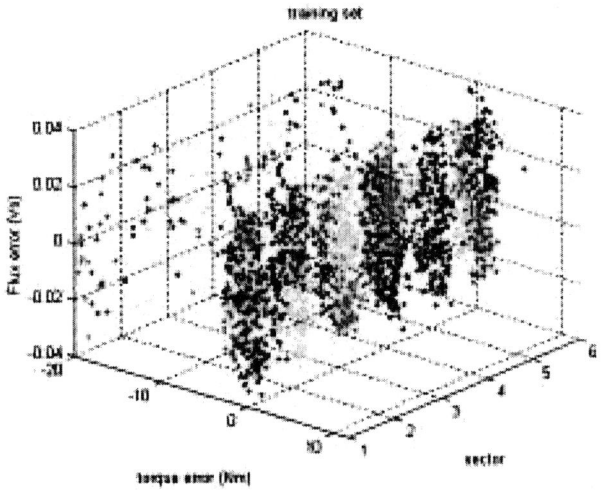

Fig 6: Input space of the training set

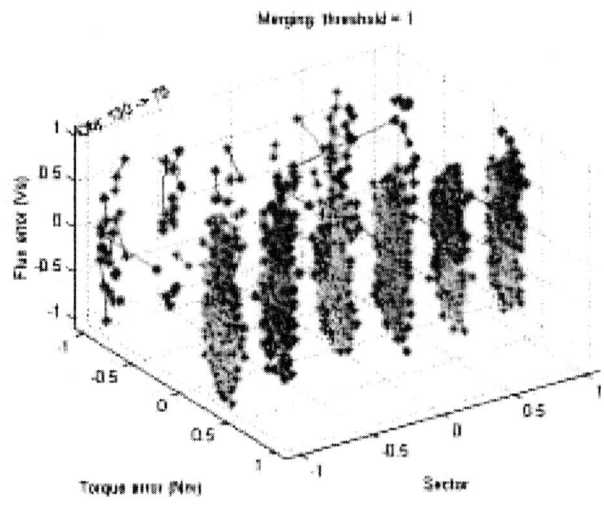

Fig 8: Input space after merging

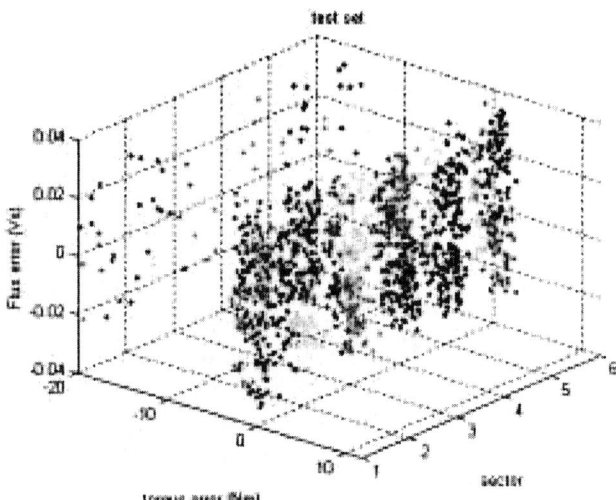

Fig 7: Input space of the test set

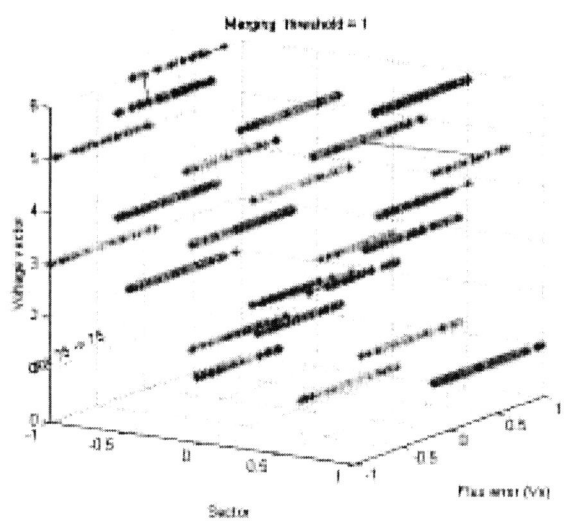

Fig 9: GMR mapping

VII. CONCLUSIONS

In this paper an application of the GMR to the control of an electrical drive with an induction motor has been presented. More specifically a particular strategy of the direct torque control has been taught to the GMR and the goodness of its learning capability has been verified by using experimental data obtained on a purposely developed test bench. The results show that this novel neural network gives at least the same results as those obtained in literature with other neural networks; but whereas those works aimed at solving an error minimisation problem by using well known feedforward neural networks, this work instead, considering that the task to be accomplished is the learning of a simple look-up table, exploits the pattern recognition capability of the GMR.

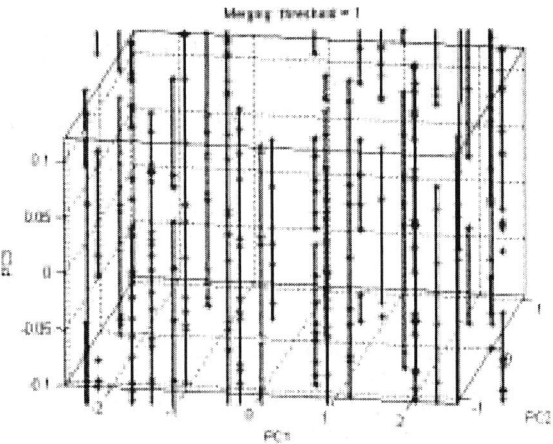

Fig.11 Linking of GMR on the test set in the principal component space

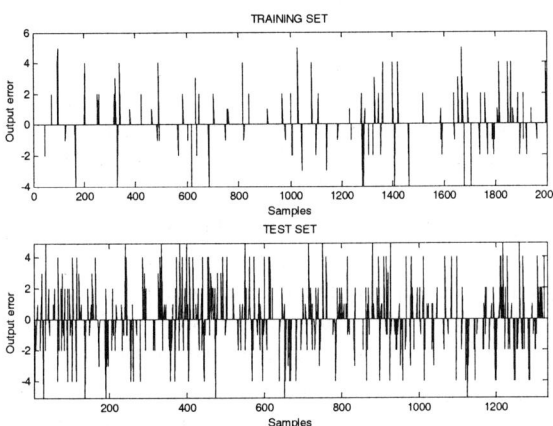

Fig. 10: Training and test set: output error between the output voltage vector with classical DTC and the GMR DTC

On the other hand the linking ability of the GMR as well as its potentiality in learning the inversion of relationships opens up also the possibility that it can be used also for more complex input-output control functions, e.g. adaptive inverse control, maximisation of efficiency, minimisation of torque ripple,. With this last regard the GMR can be used to control the duty-ratio of the power converter, which is a nonlinear function of the electromagnetic torque error, stator flux-linkage error and the position of the stator flux-linkage space vector. This nonlinear function can be easily implemented by GMR, which can determine the duty ratio during every switching cycle by proper recognition of the input space clusters so that the torque ripple can be minimised. Current work is on progress about all these last topics.

REFERENCES

[1] W. Leonhard, "Control of electrical drives", Springer, 1996.

[2] P. Vas, "Sensorless Vector and Direct Torque Control", Cambridge University Press, 1998.

[3] P. Vas, "Artificial-Intelligence-Based Electrical Machines and Drives", Cambridge University Press, 1999.

[4] Takahashi, Noguchi, "A new quick response and high-efficiency control strategy of an induction motor", IEEE Transactions on Industry Applications, 1986, 22.

[5] Depenbrock, "Direct self-control (DSC) of inverter fed induction machine", IEEE Transactions on Power Electronics, 1988, 3.

[6] G. Cirrincione, "Neural structure from motion", Ph.D. Thesis, LIS INPG, Grenoble, France, 1998.

[7] Chuan Lu, "The Generalised Mapping Regressor (GMR) Neural Network for Inverse Discontinuous Problems", Master of Artificial Intelligence Thesis, Katholieke Universiteit Leuven, Belgium, 2000.

[8] G. Cirrincione, M. Cirrincione, C. Lu, S. Van Huffel, "A Novel Neural Approach to Inverse Problems with Discontinuities (the GMR Neural Network)", accepterd in IEEE IJCNN 03.

[9] M. P. Kazmierkowski, "Control Strategies for PWM Rectifier/Inverter fed Induction Motors", IEEE ISIE 2000, vol. 1.

[10] L. A. Cabrera, M. E. Elbuluk, D. S. Zinger, "Learning Techniques to Train Neural Networks for Inverter-Fed Induction Machines Using Direct Torque Control", IEEE Transactions on Power Electronics, vol. 12, no.5, September 1997.

[11] C. Z. Cao, H. P. Li, "An Application of Fuzzy-Inference-Based Neural Network in DTC System of Induction Motor", 1st International Conference on Machine Learning and Cybernetics, Beijing, 4-5 November 2002.

[12] M. Pucci, Novel Numerical Techniques for the Identification of Induction Motors for the Control of AC Drives: Simulations and Experimental Implementations (in Italian), PhD Thesis, University of Palermo (Italy), January 2001.

ACKNOWLEDGMENT

All sections have been equally and jointly developed by the authors.

Neuro-Hybrid Genetic Algorithm Based Economic Dispatch for Utility System

N. Kumarappan, *Student Member, IEEE,* and M. R. Mohan

Abstract-A neuro hybrid Genetic Algorithm (GA) is used to solve an economic dispatch problem. The algorithm has been proposed for minimum cost of operating units. Here Real Coded GA is used for global search and fine tunings are done by Tabu Search (TS) to direct the search towards the optimal region and local optimization. The Fast Decoupled Load Flow (FDLF) is conducted to find the losses by substituting the generation values to the respective PV buses. Then the loss is participated among all generating units using participation factor method. Applying the results again to the load flow checks the voltage limit violation. Artificial Neural Network (ANN) is applied to the Hybrid GA. The algorithm is tested on IEEE 6-bus system and 66-bus utility system. It is observed that the proposed algorithm is optimal, reliable and fast.

Index Terms—Economic Dispatch, FDLF, Hybrid GA, Neuro Hybrid GA, Real Coded GA, Tabu Search.

I INTRODUCTION

The lambda-iteration method [1] has been applied in many software packages and used due to its ease of implementation.

An expression for the transmission loss derived by Krichmayer [2] uses krons matrix transformation technique for power network. Here system loss is expressed in terms of loss-coefficients, the derivation of which was based on the assumption that, all load current maintain a constant ratio to the total current, the voltage at every source bus remains constant in magnitude, power factor at each source remains constant, voltage phase angles at source buses remains constant.

Elgerd [3] suggested a method for real power optimal load dispatch in which Incremental Transmission Loss (ITL) for the generator buses are calculated directly using the Jocabian matrix of the load flow analysis and the ITL for the slack bus is taken as zero.

Hyunchul Kim et al [4] describe the method of solving a large-scale long-term thermal unit maintenance-scheduling problem. In the solution algorithm simulated Annealing (SA), GA and the TS are co-operatively used. The solution algorithm shows a reasonable combination of local search and global search.

N. Kumarappan and M. R. Mohan are with the School of Electrical and Electronics Engineering, Anna University, Chennai-600 025, India (e-mail: kumarappan_n@yahoo.com).

X.Lei et al [5] presents an economic dispatch algorithm based on the GA for the determination of the global or quasi-global optimum dispatch solution under consideration of transmission losses. The algorithm is implemented in the binary searched space. Transmission loss is calculated using loss co-efficient.

Pathom Attaviriyanupap et al [6] presents a hybrid EP and SQP for dynamic economic dispatch with non-smooth fuel cost function. In this method a simple EP is applied as a base level search and a local search SQP is used as a fine-tuning, transmission loss is neglected.

The calculation of loss by B_{mn} method [2],[5] is approximate and the coefficients are calculated for some average operating condition and the major system changes require recalculation of the coefficients. In this paper transmission loss is computed using the FDLF, which gives actual transmission loss.

The proposed method is to develop an efficient and reliable algorithm to solve the economic dispatch problem using hybrid GA, which integrates the features of GA and TS. Since GA is capable of identifying the performance region at an affordable time with real coding. TS is used to perform local search and to do fine tuning to obtain the exact local optimum. Here ANN is applied to hybrid GA using back propagation algorithm. It gives fast results and the number of function evolution is reduced.

II. PROBLEM FORMULATION

The achievement of economic dispatch in power system operation consists of minimizing the operating costs depending on demand and subjected to certain constraints i.e. how to allocate the required load demand among the available generation units.

$$\text{Minimize} \quad F = \sum_{i=1}^{n} f_i(P_i) \quad (1)$$

$$\text{Subject to:} \quad \sum_{i=1}^{n} P_i = P_D + P_{loss} \quad (2)$$

$$P_{i\min} \leq P_i \leq P_{i\max}, \quad I = 1,2,3,\ldots n \quad (3)$$

where

n is number of generating units

P_D : total system demand (MW)
P_i : power generated by i^{th} unit (MW)
$f_i(P_i)$: operating cost of unit I
P_{loss} : total transmission loss (MW)
$P_{i\,max}$: maximum power output of the ith unit (MW)
$P_{i\,min}$: minimum power output of the ith unit (MW)

Fuel cost function of each unit

$$f_i(P_i) = a_i P_i^2 + b_i P_i + c_i \quad \text{Rs/hr} \tag{4}$$

where

a_i, b_i, c_i are cost coefficients of the ith generating units.

III. DEVELOPMENT OF THE TECHNIQUE

Genetic algorithms are, by far, the most popular form of evolutionary algorithms. They derive their behavior from a metaphor of the mechanism of evolution in nature and, in essence, consist of a population of chromosomes transformed by three genetic operators: selection, crossover and mutation. Each chromosome represents a possible solution to the problem being optimized and each chromosome represents a value or some variable of the problem. These solutions are classified by an evaluation function, giving better values or fitness, to better solutions. Each solution must be evaluated by the fitness function to produce a value. The pair (chromosome, fitness) represents an individual.

Michaelewicz [7] indicates that for real valued numerical optimization problems, floating-point representations outperform binary representation because they are more consistent, more precise and lead to faster execution. Also, for most applications of GA to constrained optimization problems, the real coding technique is used to represent a solution to a given problem. Hence, real coded GA is considered in this paper.

A. Real Coded GA

As all the independent variables are continuous floating-point numbers, it has been found suitable to encode the independent variables as chromosome of floating point numbers [7], [8]. In the floating-point implementation each chromosome was coded as vector of floating point numbers of the same length as the solution vector. The precision of such an approach depends on underlying machine, but is generally much better than that of binary representation. Of course, introducing more bits can always extend the binary representation, but this considerably slows down the algorithm. Parents are initialized by selecting a random number in the range (0,1) for each element of the chromosome. Each chromosome, $x_i = 1,2\ldots n_p$, in the population is converted into a form appropriate for evaluation (actual problem variables x_d) and then is assigned a fitness value, according to the objective function equation (4). Moreover, the lower and upper bound inequality condition has been embedded in the coding itself by the elements of chromosomes in the range (0,1) using following encoding scheme:

$$x_d = x' + (x'' - x')x \tag{5}$$

where x' and x'' are lower and upper bound respectively, on problem variables, x_d the actual solution vector and x is the normalized solution vector. Then GA operators (selection, crossover and mutation) are applied for several generations until one of the individuals of the population coverage to an optimal value or the required maximum numbers of generations are reached. In recent years, following genetic operators are normally used in real coded GA [7], [8].

1) Arithmetic Crossover

The basic concept of this kind of operator is borrowed from the convex set theory [8]. Simple arithmetic operators are defined as the combination of two vectors (chromosomes) as follows:

$$\begin{aligned} x' &= \alpha x + (1-\alpha)y \\ x'' &= (1-\alpha)x + \alpha y \end{aligned} \tag{6}$$

Where α is a uniformly distributed random variable between 0 and 1.

2) Dynamic Mutation

Michaelewicz [7] proposed that this mutation operator is also called non-uniform mutation. It is designed for fine tuning capabilities aimed at achieving high precision. For a given parent x, if the element x_k of it is selected for mutation, the resulting offspring is $x' = (x_1, \ldots, x_k', \ldots x_n)$, where, x_k' is randomly selected from following two possible choices:

$$\begin{aligned} x_k' &= x_k + \Delta(t, x_k^U - x_k) \quad \text{or} \\ x_k' &= x_k - \Delta(t, x_k - x_k^L) \end{aligned} \tag{7}$$

The function $\Delta(t,y)$ returns a value in the range $(0,y)$ such that the value of $\Delta(t,y)$ approaches 0 as t increases. This property causes the operator initially to search the space uniformly (when t is small) and locally at later stages. The function $\Delta(t,y)$ is given as follows:

$$\Delta(t, y) = yr(1 - t/T)^d \tag{8}$$

where, r is a random number from (0,1), T the maximal generation number and d is a parameter determining the degree of non-uniformity.

B. Hybrid GA

In this paper new hybrid real coded GA based technique has been used to solve the economic dispatch problem. This algorithm integrates main features of GA and TS. The proposed algorithm is very much useful when addressing heavily constrained optimization problems in terms of solution accuracy and computation time. It can out-perform conventional GAs. The proposed neuro hybrid GA is developed in such a way that a simple real coded GA is acting as base level search, which makes a quick decision to direct the search towards the optimal region and local optimization. The fine tuning are done by TS.

1) Tabu Search

The basic concept of TS as described by Glover [9] is "a metaheuristic super imposed on another heuristic ". The overall approach is to avoid entertainment in cycles by forbidding or penalizing moves, which takes the solution, in the next iteration, to points in the solution space previously visited (hence "Tabu"). The TS method operates in this way with the exception that new course are not chosen randomly. Instead the TS proceeds according to the supposition that there is no point in accepting the new (poor) solution unless it is to avoid a path already investigated. This ensures that new regions of problem solution space will be investigated with the goal of avoiding local minima and ultimately finding the desired solution. The TS begins by marching to a local minima to avoid retracing the steps used, the method records recent moves in one or more Tabu lists. The original intent of the list has not prevented a previous move from being repeated but rather to insure it was not reversed. The Tabu lists are historical in nature and from the TS memory. The roll of the memory can change as the algorithm proceeds. At initialization the goal is to make a coarse examination of the solution space, known as diversification, but as candidate locations are identified then the search is more focused to produce local optimal solutions in a process of 'intensification'. In many cases the differences between the various implementations of the Tabu method have to do with the size, variability and adoptability of the Tabu memory to a particular problem domain (Fig. 1).

2) Implementation of TS in GA

The TS has traditionally being used on combination optimization problems. Local search employs the idea that a given solutions may be improved by making small changes. Those solution S obtained by modifying solution S are called neighbors of S. The local search algorithm starts with some initial solution and moves from neighbor to neighbor as long as possible while decreasing the objective function value. The main problem with this strategy is to escape from local minima where the search cannot find any further neighborhood solution that decreases the objective function value. Different strategies have been proposed to solve this problem. One of the most efficient strategies is TS. It allows the search to explore the solutions that do not decreases the objective function value, only in those cases where these solutions are not forbidden. This is usually obtained by keeping track of the last solutions in term of the action used to transform one solution to the next. When an action is performed it is considered Tabu for next T iterations, where T is the Tabu status length. A solution is forbidden if it is obtained by applying Tabu action to the current solution (Fig. 2).

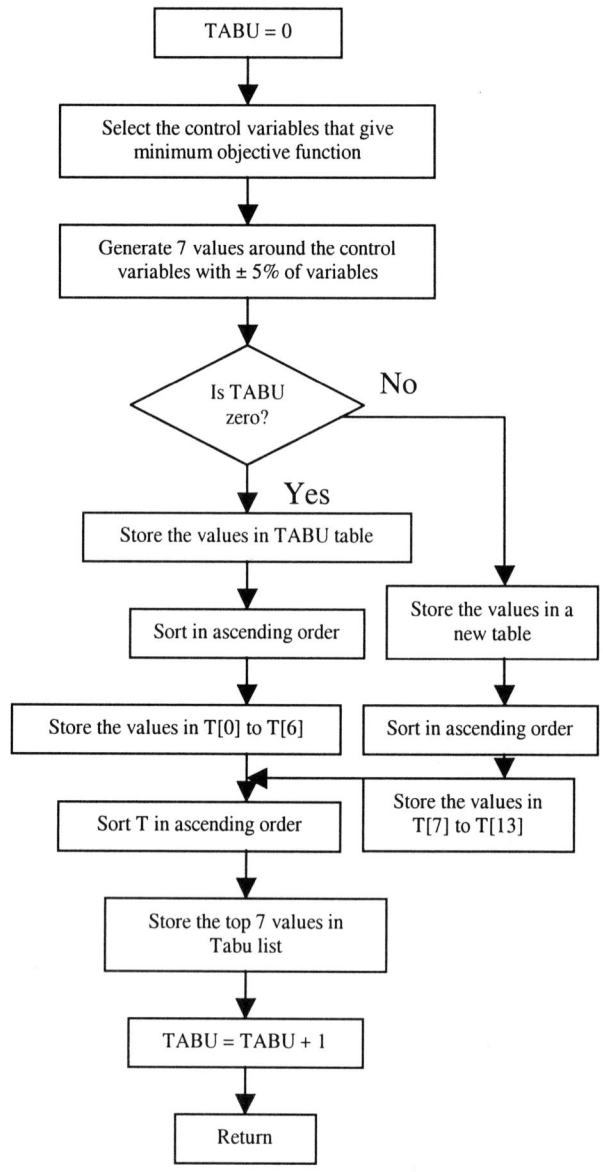

Fig. 1 Tabu search part of the hybrid GA algorithm

C. *Participation Factor Method*

The transmission power loss (PL) is computed from load flow analysis and is distributed optimally to the thermal plants [10]. The participation factor of the kth thermal plant is (PF_k) calculated as

$$PF_k = \frac{(1/R_k^*)}{\sum_{m=1}^{N}(1/R_m^*)} \quad (9)$$

where m = 1,2...N

The thermal generation is updated as

$$P_k = P_k^0 + PF_k \cdot PL \quad (10)$$

where

P_k : Generation of the kth thermal plant

P_k^0: Generation of the kth thermal plant (losses neglected)

R_k'': Second derivative of cost function of the kth thermal plant

R_m'': Second derivative of cost function of the mth thermal plant

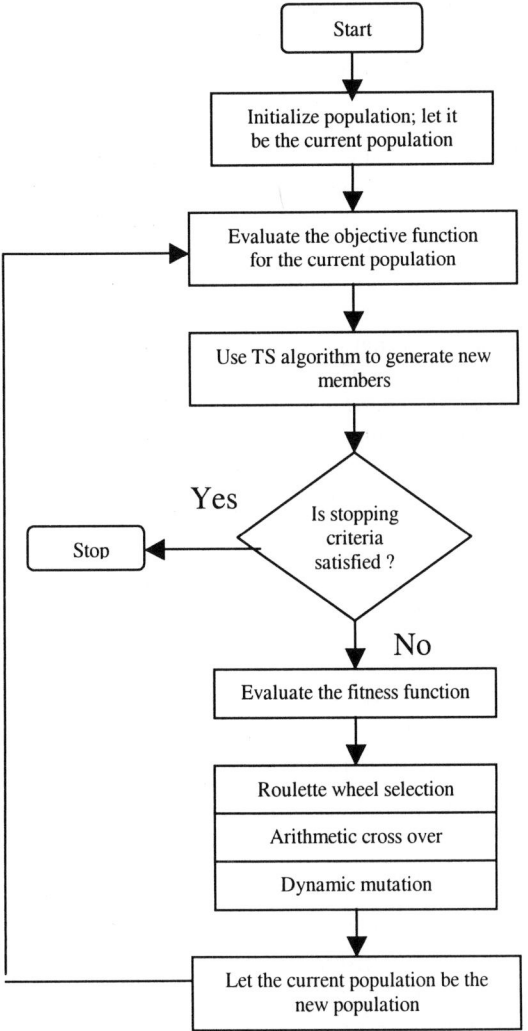

Fig. 2 Flow chart for the proposed hybrid GA

D. Artificial Neural Network

Artificial Neural Network [11] can be divided into those trained with and without supervision. In unsupervised learning, the desired outputs for input patterns are not specified. In supervised learning, the desired outputs for each input set provided to the network are set on the basis of the detailed error information obtained from the input - output sets supplied to the network. For determination of economic and emission dispatches of thermal units a neural network of supervised learning is needed. This is because of this problem the output for each input in the training set is known in advance by the application of conventional method described earlier. The multi-layer feed forward network is employed for supervised learning in this paper.

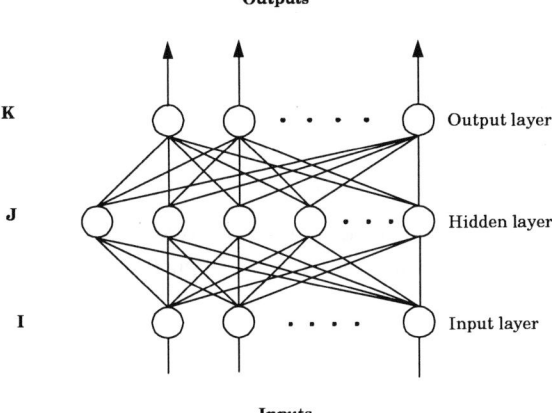

Fig. 3 A schematic multi-layer feed forward network

As shown in Fig.3 the neural network consists of a number of nodes or neurons connected by weighted links. The neurons are divided into several layers; the input layer, the output layer and some hidden layers in between. The nodes in the input layer take the input signal and the nodes in the output layer provide the desired output signal. It should be noted that only the neurons in the hidden layer and the output layer, which perform activation function, are called ordinary neurons. It should also be noted that in the feed forward network, signals could only be propagated from the input layer to the hidden layers and from the hidden layer to the output node.

For each neuron in the input layer the neuron output is the same as the neuron input. For any neuron k in the output layer or the hidden layer, the neuron input is given by

$$net_k = \sum_k w_{kj} O_j \qquad (11)$$

where j is a neuron in the proceeding layer, O_j output of neuron j and w_{kj} the connection weight from neuron j to neuron k. The output of neuron k is give by

$$O_k = \frac{1}{1+\exp-(net_k + \theta_k)} = f_k(net_k, \theta_k) \qquad (12)$$

where net_k is the input to neuron k and θ_k is a bias threshold.

In the learning process (back propagation algorithm), O_k is regarded as a modified connection weight between neuron k and a fictitious neuron in the proceeding layer whose output always remains at unity.

The connection weights of the feed forward network from the P input-output patterns in the training sets are divided from the generalized delta rule. The algorithm begins with assigning a set of random numbers in the connection weight. When a pattern P with target output vector $t_p = [tp_1, tp_2 ... tp_m]^T$

is presented the connection weights can be updated, using the following equations

$$\Delta W_{kj}(P) = \eta \delta_{pk} O_{pk} + \alpha \Delta w_{kj}(P-1) \quad (13)$$

where for output neurons

$$\delta_{pk} = (t_{pk} - O_{pk}) O_{pk} (1-O_{pk}) \quad (14)$$

and for other neurons

$$\delta_{pj} = (\Sigma \delta_{pk} w_{kj}) O_{pj} (1-O_{pj}) \quad (15)$$

These equations have been derived based on the criterion of minimizing the error function (sum of squared errors).

$$E_p = 1/2 \sum_{k=1}^{M} (t_{pk} - O_{pk})^2 \quad (16)$$

where M is the number of output neurons.

E. Proposed Method

The power dispatch problem is solved using hybrid GA without losses (Fig. 2) and the resulting solution is taken as initial value (generations) for FDLF to compute losses. These computed losses are distributed to the thermal plants using participation factor method [10]. The obtained results are optimal because the previous schedule without losses were already optimal. Voltage and capacity violations are checked from FDLF results. If there is no violation the obtained results are feasible and optimal. Apply back propagation ANN training algorithm [11] to the final results. Training data are generated from the hybrid GA based economic dispatch. The main advantage of the ANN application is its flexibility i.e. the number and the range of input-output variable can be expanded very easily by providing the network with the necessary input – output training set. Hence, several practical constraints to be considered for such economic loading problem can be incorporated in the network as the additional input variables.

1) *Algorithmic Steps*
   a. Compute P_i using hybrid GA
   b. Conduct FDLF analysis and find transmission losses by substituting generation values to the respective PV buses.
   c. Distribute the losses among all the generators using participation factor method.
   d. Check the voltage limit violation by applying the results again to FDLF.
   e. Apply ANN to the final set of results.

IV TEST RESULTS

The proposed neuro hybrid GA approach was numerically tested on two test cases of economic dispatch problem. The test system in case 1 is IEEE 6-bus system and case II is 66-bus utility system. Computer program in implementing the solution method has been written in C++ language on a Pentium III, 933 MHz personal computers.

Table I shows hybrid GA results. Here, population size = 20, generation = 50, probability of crossover = 0.8, probability of mutation = 0.3, α in arithmetic crossover = 0.3, order of non-linearity d in dynamic mutation = 4, TS list size is selected as 7.

Table III shows the results of neuro hybrid GA, ANN has been considered with one neuron in the input layer i.e. for power demand, five output neurons in the output layer, three neurons are for power dispatch, one for power loss and one for fuel cost. The results obtained for the value of η = 0.73 and α = 0.88.The percentage of error is almost nil.

Table II shows the results of hybrid GA for 66-bus utility system.

Table IV shows the results of neuro hybrid GA for 66-bus utility system. ANN has been considered with one input neuron in the input layer i.e. for the power demand, six output neurons in the output layer, four neurons are for power dispatch, one neuron for power loss and one neuron for fuel cost. The results obtained for the value of η = 0.71, α = 0.9 and n = 5.It is observed that the percentage of error is in the acceptable level (0.37% to 0.6%).

Execution time for neuro hybrid GA is faster and the number of function evaluation is reduced. Convergence characteristics of neuro hybrid GA are superior.

TABLE I
HYBRID GA POWER DISPATCH WITH LOSSES FOR IEEE SIX BUS SYSTEM

P_D (MW)	P1 (MW)	P2 (MW)	P4 (MW)	PL (MW)	F_T ($/hr)
55	35.5016	15.7405	6.2361	2.4782	135.090
65	44.1674	18.18.92	6.4115	3.7683	170.459
67.5	45.4122	18.9930	7.0789	3.9842	179.589

TABLE II
HYBRID GA POWER DISPATCH WITH LOSSES FOR 66-BUS UTILITY SYSTEM

P_D (MW)	P22 (MW)	P37 (MW)	P32 (MW)	P7 (MW)	PL MW	F_T (Rs/hr)
1000	394.40	127.85	249.68	256.92	29.04	431311
1100	439.47	129.54	283.01	283.29	33.31	525718
1195	491.49	131.54	303.66	310.13	37.70	624572

TABLE III
NEURO-HYBRID GA POWER DISPATCH WITH LOSSES FOR IEEE SIX-BUS SYSTEM

P_D (MW)	P1 (MW)	P2 (MW)	P4 (MW)	PL (MW)	F_T ($/hr)
55	35.50	15.74	6.20	2.480	135.11
65	44.09	18.21	6.44	3.733	170.13
67.5	45.28	18.91	7.05	3.965	178.781

TABLE IV
NEURO-HYBRID GA POWER DISPATCH WITH LOSSES FOR 66-BUS UTILITY SYSTEM

P_D (MW)	P22 (MW)	P37 (MW)	P32 (MW)	P7 (MW)	PL MW	F_T (Rs/hr)
1000	392.97	127.78	251.72	256.57	28.98	429725
1100	444.20	129.60	282.20	284.04	33.40	528763
1195	489.60	131.47	302.66	309.10	37.53	620829

V. CONCLUSION

In this paper the economic dispatch problem is solved by using neuro hybrid GA method to minimize the fuel cost for a given load condition. In this problem real coded GA is used as base search and TS is used as local search. The neuro hybrid GA is applied to IEEE 6-bus system and 66–bus utility system for economic dispatch problem. Neuro hybrid GA converges soon. Memory savings is also found to be very less. Results using proposed method shows superiority of the solution. Also the consistency of results obtained shows high reliability.

The calculation of losses by B_{mn} is approximate. The coefficients are calculated for some average operating conditions and the major system change require recalculation of the coefficients. So FDLF method is used for computing the loss, which gives the accurate results. The results obtained prove that the proposed method is effective. In both the case studies there is no voltage limit violation.

The principle advantage of ANN lies in its flexibility. Simply providing necessary additional input- output training sets can expand the numbers and the range of input-output variable. In these cases the saving in computational time will be significant and number of function evaluation is reduced. Use of hybrid GA along with ANN based method made the algorithm fast enough for large-scale utility system.

VI. REFERENCES

[1] Allen J Wood and Bruce F Wollenberg, *Power Generation, Operation and Control*, New York: John Wiley and Sons, 1984.
[2] L.K.Krichmayer, *Economic Operation of Power System*, New York: Wiley, 1958.
[3] O.I.Elgerd, *Electric Energy Systems Theory – An Introduction*, New York: McGraw – Hill, 1971.
[4] Hyunchul Kim, Yasuhiro Hayashi and Koichi Nara, "An algorithm for thermal unit maintenance scheduling through combined use of GA SA and TS", *IEEE transactions on power systems*, vol.12, no. 1, pp. 329-335,1997.
[5] X.Lei, E.Lerch and D.Povh, "Genetic algorithm solution to economic dispatch problems", *ETEP*, vol. 9, no. 6, pp. 347-353, 1999.
[6] Pathom Attaviriyanupap, Hiroyuki Kita, Eiichi Tanaka and Jun Hasegawa, "A Hybrid EP and SQP for dynamic economic dispatch with non-smooth fuel cost function", *IEEE transactions on power systems*, vol. 17, no. 2, pp. 411-416, 2002.
[7] Z.Michaelwicz, *Genetic Algorithms + Data Structures =Evolutionary Programs*, Springer, 1996.
[8] M Gen and R Cheng, *Genetic Algorithms and Engineering Designs*, John Wiley and Sons, Inc, 1997.
[9] F. Glover, "Tabu Search-Part 1", *ORSA Journal on Computing*, vol. 1, no.3, pp. 190-206, 1989.
[10] G. Baskar, N. Kumarappan and M.R. Mohan, "Optimal Dispatch Using Improved Lambda Based Genetic Algorithm Suitable For Utility System", Accepted for publication, *Electric Power Component and Systems*, vol. 31, no.7, 2003.
[11] N.Kumarappan, M.R.Mohan and S.Murugappan, "ANN approach applied to combined economic and emission dispatch for large-scale system", *IJCNN'02*, vol. 1, pp.323-327, 2002.

VII. BIOGRAPHIES

N. Kumarappan (S' 2001) was born in Puduvayal, Tamilnadu, India, on November 27, 1961. He graduated from Madurai Kamaraj University and studied at Annamalai University, India.

He has been with the Department of Electrical Engineering, Annamalai University, India. His research interests include power system optimization, power system operation and control and artificial intelligence techniques.

He is the life member of Institution of Engineer's, (India) and Indian Society of Technical Education. He is the student member of the IEEE (USA) and IEE (UK).

M. R. Mohan was born in Madurai, Tamilnadu, India, on July 11, 1950. He graduated from Thiagarajar College of Engineering, Madurai, India. He obtained his Doctoral degree from Anna University, Chennai, India.

His employment experience as is at A.C. College of Engineering and Technology, Tamilnadu, India and at Anna University, India. His field of interest is power system optimization, operation and control and power system modeling.

He is student counselor, IEE of UK at Chennai Chapter, Charted Engineer and Member of IEE.

Self-Organizing Neural-Based Fuzzy Controller for Transient Stability of Multimachine Power Systems Using Flywheel Battery

M. H. Wang, *Member, IEEE*   C. P. Hung

Department of Electrical Engineering, National Chin-Yi Institute of Technology,
35, 215 Lane, Sec. 1, Chung Shan Road, Taiping, Taichung, Taiwan, ROC.

Abstract—In this paper, a self-organizing fuzzy neural network controller (SOFNC) is design for high-speed flywheel energy storage system (FESS) to improve the transient stability and increase transfer capability of power systems. The main feature over traditional control approach lies in the model-free description of control system and parallel computing capability. Simulation results in Taiwan power system (Taipower) show that the FESS with the proposed controller has produced significant improvement in the power system performance.

I. INTRODUCTION

Transient stability is one of the most important investigations in power systems. Power companies usually operate power systems close to their thermal and stability limits. But following sudden and large disturbances, a power system may lose stability in the first swing, if it is not equipped with proper transient control devices. In the past, much research interest has been directed towards the enhancement of the transient stability of power systems, ranging from theoretical studies to advanced control devices. Recently, many researchers have employed various Flexible AC Transmission Systems (FACTS) devices, such as braking resistors, thyristor controlled series compensators, thyristor controlled phase angle shifters, unified power flow controllers, and superconducting magnetic energy storage (SMES) [1-4]. Theses devices have been shown to help to reduce the flows in heavily loaded lines and improve stability of power systems.

Recently, FESS has become the most popular energy storage devices due to advances in power electronics, materials, and magnetic bearings [5]. The advantages of FESS versus traditional batteries and SMES are higher power density, no hazardous chemicals, ease of checking the charge, insensitivity to environmental conditions and long life [5-11]. Modern FESS have been designed for a variety of applications, their capability to store energy is approximately 1-500MJ and the peak power ranges from kilowatts to gigawatts, with the higher powers aimed at pulsed-power application [5]. Today, the power electronic devices and control systems enable the FESS to respond to system disturbances within a few electrical cycles. Therefore, the FESS will be most popular in power system control.

Due to the advantages of FESS, this paper proposes using a FESS with a self-organizing neural fuzzy controller to enhance the transient stability of multimachine power systems. The proposed controller integrates the ideas of the fuzzy logic control and neural network structure into an intelligent control system. In this NN structure, the input and output nodes represent the input speed and acceleration states, and output control signal, respectively, and the nodes in the hidden layers function as membership functions and fuzzy control rules. Initially, we set up the controller with a set of coarse fuzzy control rules that are based on a simple engineering knowledge concerning the controlled machine. Then, the fuzzy control rules and input/output fuzzy membership functions can be optimally tuned by the backpropagation learning algorithm according to the control credit that is evaluated by a performance index table (PIT). For the robustness considered, a multilayer neural network is used to learn the relation of operation conditions and optimally parameters of the controller. A Taipower tested data is selected for computer simulation to demonstrate the effectiveness of the proposed methodology.

II. PROBLEM FORMULATION

Basically, the model of a FESS transient control system is a nonlinear dynamic equation in multimachine power systems. An n-machine power system model including the effects of field flux decay, damper windings, the automatic voltage regulator rotating (AVR), and the exciter concerning a center of inertia (COI) rotating reference frame is given below [4]:

$$\dot{\theta}_i = \widetilde{\omega}_i \qquad (1)$$

$$\dot{\widetilde{\omega}}_i = \frac{1}{M_i}(P_{mi} - P_{ei} - P_{fbi}) - \frac{1}{M_T}P_{COI} \qquad (2)$$

$$\dot{E}'_{qi} = \frac{1}{T'_{doi}}(E_{fdi} - E'_{qi}) + \frac{I_{di}}{T'_{doi}}(X_{di} - X'_{di}) \qquad (3)$$

$$\dot{E}'_{di} = -\frac{1}{T'_{qoi}}E'_{di} - \frac{1}{T'_{qoi}}(X_{qi} - X'_{qi})I_{qi} \qquad (4)$$

$$\dot{V}_{ri} = \frac{K_{ai}}{T_{ai}}V_{ei} - \frac{1}{T_{ai}}V_{ri} \qquad (5)$$

$$\dot{V}_{fi} = \frac{K_{fi}}{T_{fi}T_{ei}}[V_{rli} - (S_{ei} + K_{ei})E_{fdi}] - \frac{1}{T_{fi}}V_{fi} \quad (6)$$

$$\dot{E}_{fdi} = \frac{1}{T_{ei}}V_{rli} - \frac{E_{fdi}}{T_{ei}}(S_{ei} + K_{ei}) \quad (7)$$

$$\dot{E}_{fessi} = P_{fbi} \quad (8)$$

$$\text{for } i=1,2,...,n$$

Although the system model is a simple one, it suffices to demonstrate the effectiveness of the proposed controller due to the model-free nature of the fuzzy neural network control schemes. In (2), the term P_{fb} represents additive real power control of the FESS for the i-the generator, which is determined by the proposed controller depending on the state of the generator. Fig. 1 shows the schematic structure of transient stability control using FESS that includes a flywheel, a motor-generator set, and control electronics with a controller for connection to an electric power system. The energy stored in a rotating mass can be found from:

$$E_{fess} = \frac{1}{2}J\omega^2 \quad (9)$$

The amount of energy storage increases linearly with the moment of inertia J, and increases with the square of the rotational velocity ω. Due to free from depth-of-discharge effects, FESS can accept and deliver large amounts of energy in a very short time [5,9], which is a very helpful characteristic for transient stability control of power systems.

III. THE PROPOSED CONTROL SYSTEM

Because of the nonlinear natures in the transient stability control, a self-organizing neural fuzzy controller is presented for FESS. The proposed methodology is to design self-organizing fuzzy systems that have capability to create the control strategy by learning. The structure of the proposed SONFC is a combination of both the neural network and self-organizing fuzzy control techniques. The fuzzy method proves a structural control framework to express the input/output relationship of the neural network that can embed the salient features of computation power and learning capability into the fuzzy controller.

A. Structure of the overall control system

The overall structure of the proposed SONFC system is shown in Fig. 2. It consists of: (i) a neural fuzzy control (NFC) to control the plant, (ii) a performance index table (PIT) as an instructor for learning the control strategy, (iii) three scaling factors GS, GA, and GU to adjust the input/output values of the controller into proper ranges, which are set at 1, 0.01, and 1, (iv) a multilayer neural network (MNN) to learn the relations of operation conditions and optimal control parameters, and (v) a limiter to constrain the control action within admissible limits. In this work, the shaft speed and acceleration of the generator at each sample time are chosen to be input signals of the controller. The target controller output P'_{fb} is the absorbed power of FESS. The actual control signal P_{fb} can be obtained through the limiter block to satisfy practical constraints.

To implement the proposed controller, the overall operation algorithm is shown as follows:

Step 1: Set the admissible operation range of power system,

Step 2: Give a minimum operation point P_{eo},

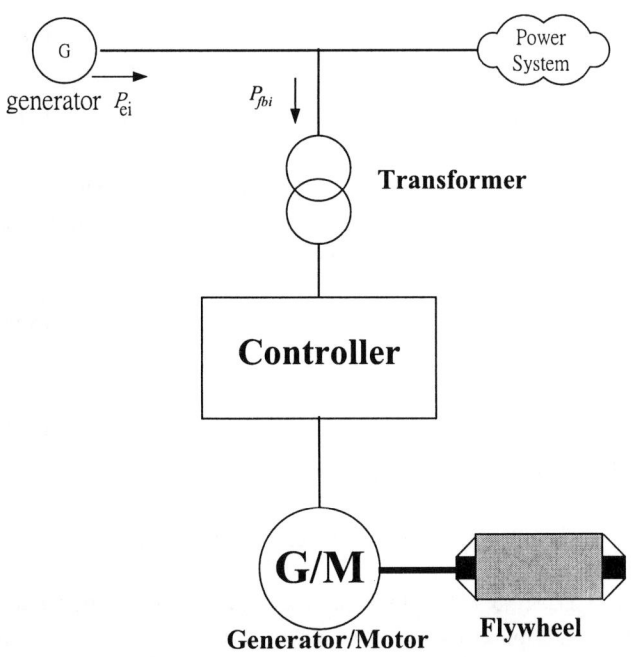

Fig. 1. The schematic structure of the FESS.

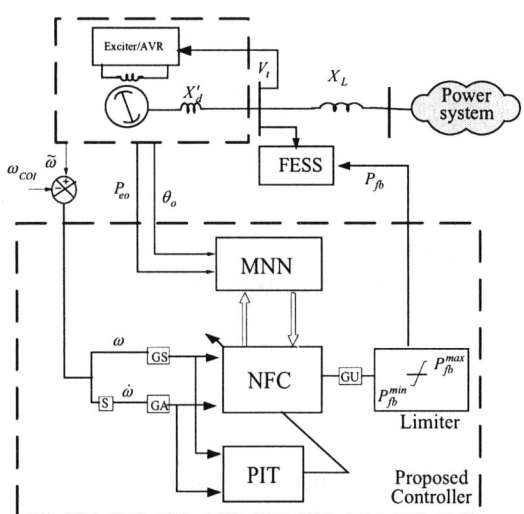

Fig. 2. Schematic structure of the proposed control system.

Step 3: Calculate the operation point of the power system,

Step 4: Set up the controller with a set of coarse fuzzy control rules,

Step 5: Tune the parameters of NFC by a backpropagation learning algorithm according to of performance index table (PIT),

Step 6: Go to step 7, if the performance index per epochs is less than a preset value, otherwise go to step 5,

Step 7: Save the optimal parameters of NFC,

Step 8: Set $P_{eo} = P_{eo} + 0.05$ (pu),

Step 9: Go to step 10, if the P_{eo} is larger than the maximum operation point; otherwise go to step 3,

Step 10: Learn the relations of operation conditions and optimal parameters of the controller by MNN,

Step 11: Terminate the learning process, when the mean square error of the MNN is reduced to a preset value. Then, use the trained controller directly to control the power system.

B. Topology of the neural fuzzy controller

The topology of the proposed NFC, as shown in Fig. 3, is a five-layer neural network-based fuzzy controller. Since two input variables and one output variable are employed in the present work, there are two nodes in layer 1 and one node in layer 5. The nodes in layers 2 and 4 are term nodes that act as membership functions to express the input/output fuzzy linguistic variables. A bell-shaped function is adopted to represent the membership function, in which the mean value and the variance will be adapted through the learning process. The fuzzy set defined for input/output variables are positive big (PB), positive medium (PM), positive small (PS), zero (ZE), negative medium (NM), and negative big (NB), which are numbered in descending order in the term nodes. Hence, 14 nodes and 7 nodes are included in layers 2 and 4, respectively, to indicate the input/output linguistic variables. Nodes in layer 3 represent the fuzzy control rule, and there are 49 nodes in layer 3 to form a fuzzy rule base for two linguistic input variables. The links of layers 3 and 4 define the preconditions and the consequences of the rule nodes, respectively. There are two fixed links from the input term nodes for each rule node. Layer 4 links encircled in dotted line is adjusted in response to varying control situations. The links of layers 2 and 5 remain fixed between the input/output nodes and their corresponding term nodes. In short, the proposed controller can adjust the fuzzy control rules and their membership functions by modifying layer 4 links and the parameters of the membership functions for each node in layers 2 and 4. As a convenience in notation, the following symbols are used to describe the functions of the nodes in each of the five layers:

NET_i^{Lj} : the net input value of the i-th node in layer j,

O_i^{Lj} : the output value of the i-th nodes in layer j,

m_i^{Lj}, σ_i^{Lj} : the mean and variance of the bell-shaped activation function of the i-th mode in layer j,

W_{ij} : the link that connects the output of the j-th node in layer 3 with the input to the i-th node in layer 4.

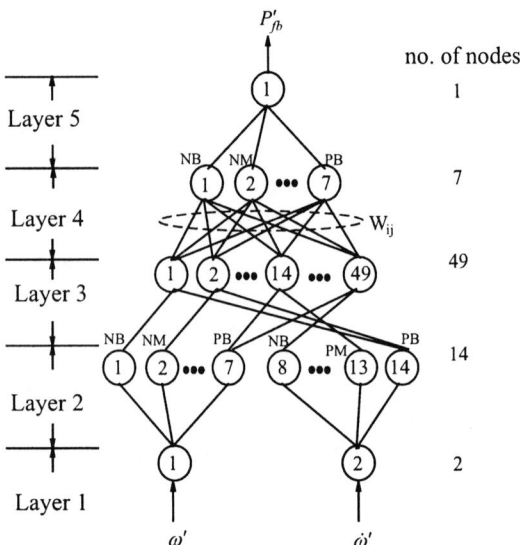

Fig. 3. Topology of the proposed NFC.

The schematic structure of each layer of NFC is shown as follows:

Layer 1: The nodes of this layer directly transmit input signals to the next layer. That is

$$O_1^{L1} = \omega' \qquad (10)$$

$$O_2^{L1} = \dot{\omega}' \qquad (11)$$

Layer 2 : The nodes of this layer act as membership functions to express the terms of input linguistic variables. For a bell-shaped function, they are:

$$NET_i^{L2} = \begin{cases} O_1^{L1} & , for\ i = 1,2,...,7 \\ O_2^{L1} & , for\ i = 8,9,...,14 \end{cases} \qquad (12)$$

$$O_i^{L2} = e^{-\left[\frac{NET_i^{L2} - m_i^{L2}}{\sigma_i^{L2}}\right]^2}, for\ i = 1,2,...,14 \qquad (13)$$

The link weights in this layer are set to unity.

Layer 3 : The links in the layer are used to perform preconditioned matching of fuzzy rules. Each node has two input values from layer 2. If the correlation-minimum inference procedure is used here to determine the firing strengths of each rule, then the output of nodes in the layer is determined by the fuzzy AND operation. Thus, the functions of the layer are given below [12]:

$$NET_i^{L3} = min(O_j^{L2}, O_k^{L2}), \quad i = 7(j-1) + (k-7) \quad (14)$$

$$O_i^{L3} = NET_i^{L3}, \quad i=1,2,...,49; j=1,2,...,7; k=8,9,...,14 \quad (15)$$

The link weights in this layer are also set to unity.

Layer 4: Each node in the layer performs the fuzzy OR operation to integrate the fired rules leading to the same output linguistic variable. For example, the weight of rule 4 that connects rule node 4 to the output term node " PB" is set at unity. Except for the weights predetermined from the initial rules, the rest of layer 4 links are all set to zero initially. Based on the simulation resul, starting with the good initial fuzzy control rules provides much faster convergence in the learning phase. The functions of this layer are expressed as follows:

$$NET_i^{L4} = \sum_{j=1}^{49} W_{ij} O_j^{L3} \quad (16)$$

$$O_i^{L4} = min(1, NET_i^{L4}), \text{ for } i=1,2,7. \quad (17)$$

The link weight W_{ij} in this layer indicates the probability of the j-th rule with the i-th linguistic output.

Layer 5 : The output node in this layer together with layer 5 links act as a defuzzifier of the NFC. The defuzzification aims at producing a nonfuzzy control action that best represents the possibility distribution of an inferred fuzzy control action. The center of area defuzzification scheme can be simulated by:

$$NET_I^{L5} = \sum_{j=1}^{7} m_j^{L4} \sigma_j^{L4} O_j^{L4} \quad (18)$$

$$O_I^{L5} = P'_{fb} = \frac{NET_I^{L5}}{\sum_{j=1}^{7} \sigma_j^{L4} O_j^{L4}} \quad (19)$$

Where m and σ can be viewed as the center and the width of the membership function. Hence the link weight in this layer is $m_j^{L4} \sigma_j^{L4}$.

C. *Learning algorithm of the proposed controller*

There are learning and operation phases to implement the proposed control system. Based on simple engineering knowledge concerning the controlled machine, we set up the controller with a set of coarse fuzzy control rules. Then, the parameters of the NFC are tuned to achieve good control performance. For this purpose, a performance index table (PIT) and its related lookup table as shown in Fig. 4 are developed. The performance of the controller in each learning step is evaluated by the performance index table (PIT), from which a credit is assigned according to the deviation of the control response from the desired response. It should be noted that the PIT is developed based on the control objective. The zero elements in the look up table are in the desired response regions, and the other regions indicate where the corrective control needs to be taken. The membership functions and fuzzy rules of the NFC could be adapted on-line by the credit value using a supervised learning mechanism. For the k-th learning step, the required change $\Delta P'_{fb}(k)$ of the NFC can be defined as

$$\Delta P'_{fb}(k) = \lambda \times PI[\omega'(k), \dot{\omega}'(k)] \quad (20)$$

Where $PI[.]$ represents lookup values in the PIT, and λ is a learning constant, which is set at 0.005 in this study. Hence the desired control action $P'^d_{fb}(k)$ of the NFC can be obtained by

$$P'^d_{fb}(k) = P'_{fb}(k) + \Delta P'_{fb}(k) \quad (21)$$

		Speed						
		-3.	-2.	-1.	0.	1.	2.	3.
Acceleration	0.6	0.	0.3	0.3	0.6	0.6	1.	1.
	0.4	-0.3	0.	0.3	0.3	0.6	1.	1.
	0.2	-0.3	-0.3	0.	0.3	0.3	0.6	0.6
	0.	-0.6	-0.3	-0.3	0.	0.3	0.3	0.6
	-0.2	-0.6	-0.6	-0.3	-0.3	0.	0.3	0.3
	-0.4	-1.	-1.	-0.6	-0.3	-0.3	0.	0.3
	-0.6	-1.	-1.	-0.6	-0.6	-0.3	-0.3	0.

Fig. 4. Look up table of performance index.

The optimal parameters of membership functions and fuzzy rules can be found by gradient descent search techniques. The error or energy function of the control system can be defined

$$E = \frac{1}{2}\left(P'^d_{fb}(k) - P'_{fb}(k)\right)^2 \quad (22)$$

From (21) and (22), the minimization of the error function E results in guiding the controlled plant into the desired response regions where the error function reaches a local minimum. Then, the generalized delta-learning rule can be used to solve the training task of the NFC to achieve the energy minimization. In standard notation, the generalized delta-learning rule can be expressed as [4]:

$$y_i(k+1) = y_i(k) + \eta(-\frac{\partial E}{\partial X_i}) + \alpha \Delta y_i(k) \quad (23)$$

Where y_i is the parameter to be updated, and η and α are the learning rate and the gain of the momentum term, which are set to 0.1 and 0.9, respectively.

IV. SIMULATION AND DISCUSSION

A. Test condition

The 345kV transmission system network of Taipower system is shown as Fig. 5. The system has four main load areas, North, Center, South, and East. There will be, totally, three 345kV double circuit corridors from south to north in Taipower in 2002. The peak demand on the Taipower system has reached 26,296 MW in 2001 and the annual growth rate of peak demand is 1.7%. This system consists of 6 nuclear units, 57 thermal units and 19 hydro units, including 10 pumped-storage units. There are 2 nuclear plants in the north and 1 nuclear plant in the south; the 2nd nuclear plant is the biggest nuclear plant in Taiwan. To test the proposed methodology, the main disturbance is a three-phase short circuit fault with various clearing times in the generator bus of the 2nd nuclear plant. Unless otherwise stated, the controller is installed only on generator #2 of the 2nd nuclear plant with the others uncontrolled in the test cases. The lower limit and upper limit of the FESS power are set between –0.5 pu and 0.5 pu, respectively. To evaluate the performance of the proposed controller a quadratic performance index J is defined below:

$$J = \sum_{k=1}^{200} \omega_i^2(k) \quad (24)$$

In (24), the sampling time of system measurements is set at 0.01s, thus there are a total 200 training patterns in each learning process.

B. Test results

To show the learning capability of the proposed controller, consider a particular three-phase fault at generator #2 of 2nd nuclear plant with the fault cleared at 0.28 s. Fig.6 shows the curve of the performance index with respect to the number of learning epochs. It indicates that only 35 epochs are required to reach convergency. The fast learning time is due to the fact that the priori knowledge of the controller is incorporated into the training process. Fig. 7 and 8 show the dynamic responses of the controlled generator between 1 and 40 epochs of learning. Results obtained apparently show that the control performance can be significantly improved through the learning process. Fig. 9 shows the absorbed power and energy of FESS, the maximum power of the FESS is set in about 458MW (or 0.5 pu). It is clear that the transient energy of the power system has been stored in the FESS; it will be most useful for power flow control when the power system recovers its stability.

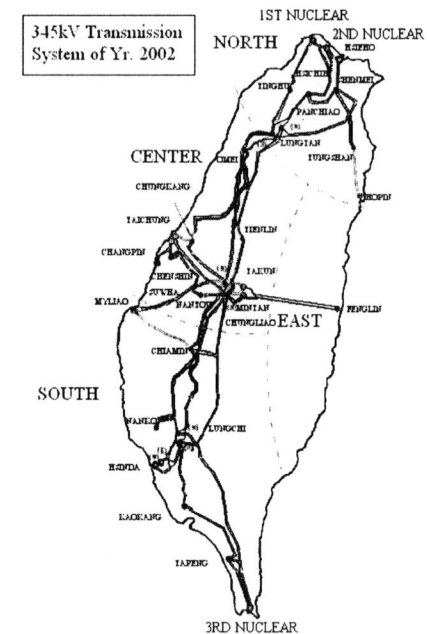

Fig. 5. Taipower 345kV transmission system network [1].

To test the effect of the proposed controller with FESS, the critical clearing time (CCT) with different capabilities of FESS was carried out in Fig. 10. The test results show that the FESS is the most effective method for the improvement of transient stability. It could be used to enhance the CCT of Taiwan power system. Although the system model is a simple one, it suffices to demonstrate the effectiveness of the presented control method for FESS due to the model-free nature of the fuzzy neural network controller.

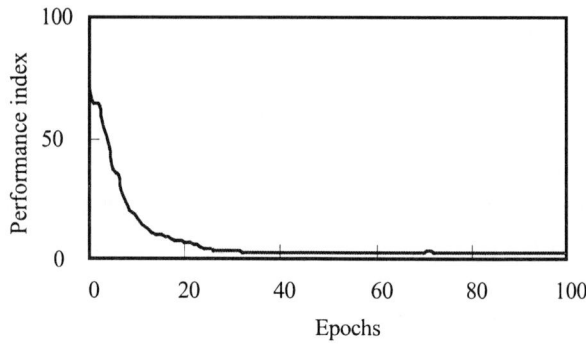

Fig. 6. Learning curve of the proposed controller.

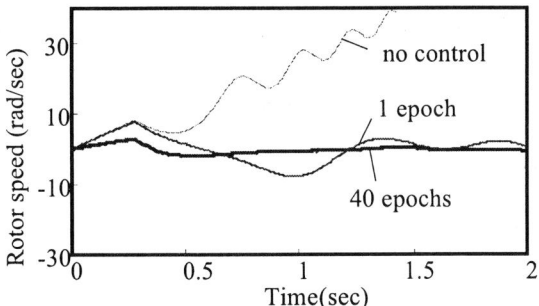

Fig. 7. The dynamic responses of generator #2 in the 2nd nuclear plant.

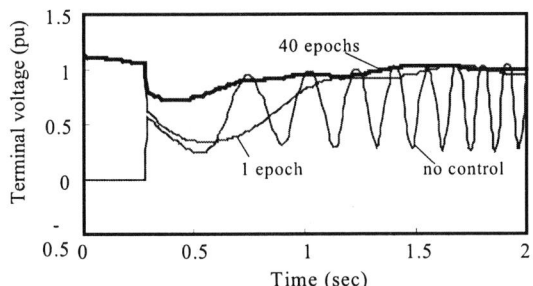

Fig. 8. Terminal voltage responses of generator #2 in the 2nd nuclear plant.

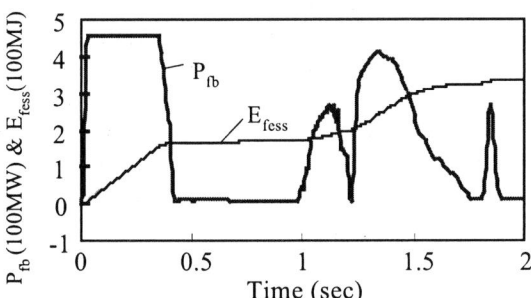

Fig. 9. The absorbed power and energy of FESS.

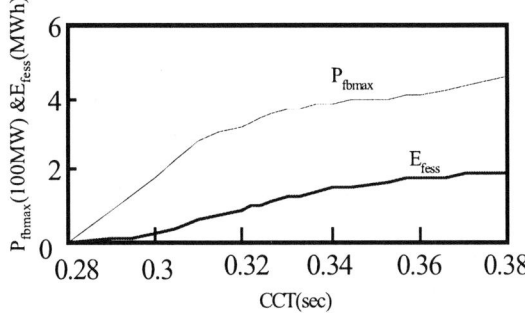

Fig. 10. The capability of FESS with different CCT.

V. Conclusions

The FESS has been shown as one of the most potential devices for transient stability control of power systems, because the FESS can accept and deliver large amounts of energy in a very short time. Due to nonlinear model in this control problem, this paper has designed an efficient self-organizing neural fuzzy controller to enhance the transient stability of multi-machine power system. The controlled parameter of proposed controller can optimally tune from training examples by the learning algorithm. To illustrate the performance of the proposed method, a series time simulation is also conducted on Taipower system with rather encouraging results.

Acknowledgments

The authors are greatly indebted to the engineers of the Taiwan Power Company for their providing the valuable field test data. We also gratefully acknowledge the financial support of the National Science Council, Taiwan, R.O.C., (Project No: 91-2815-C-167-005-E).

References

[1] C. M. Lin, C. H. Chiang, C. M. Lin, T. C. Huang, and S. G. Jalali, "Feasibility studies of FACTs application in the Taiwan Power Company 345 kV Transmission System," *The 22nd Symposium on Electrical Power Engineering*, 2001.

[2] N. G. Hingorani, "High Power Electronics and Flexible AC Transmission Systems," *IEEE Power Engineering Review*, pp.3-4, July 1998.

[3] E. V. Larsen, J. J. Sanchez-Gaseca, and J. H. Chow, "Concept for Design of FACTS Controller to Damp Power System Swing," *IEEE Trans. Power Systems*, Vol.10, No.2, pp948-956, 1995.

[4] H. C. Chang and M. H. Wang, "Neural Network-Based Self-Organizing Fuzzy Controller for Transient Stability of Multimachine Power Systems," *IEEE Trans. on Energy Conversions*, Vol. 10, No. 2. pp. 339-346, June 1995

[5] R. Hebner, J. Beno, and A. Walls, "Flywheel Batteries Come Around Again, " *IEEE Spectrum*, pp.46-51, April 2002.

[6] H. J. Borneman and M. Sander, "Conceptual System Design of a 5 MWh/100MW Superconducting Flywheel Energy Storage Plant for Power Utility Applications, " *IEEE Trans. Applied Superconductivity*, Vol. 7, No. 2, pp. 398-401, June 1997.

[7] R. S. Weissbach, G. G. Karady and R. G. Farmer, "Dynamic Voltage Compensation on Distribution Feeders Using Flywheel Energy Storage, " *IEEE Trans. on Power Delivery*, Vol. 14, No. 2, April 1999.

[8] H. Akagi, and H. Sato, " Control and Performance of a Doubly-Fed Induction Machine Intended for a Flywheel Energy Storage System," *IEEE Trans. on Power Electronics*, Vol. 17, No. 1, January 2002.

[9] R. Cardenas, and R. Pena, G. Asher, and J. Clare," Control Strategies for Enhanced Power Smoothing in Wind Energy systems using a Flywheel Driven by a Vector-Controlled Induction Machine, " *IEEE Trans. on Industrial Electronics*, Vol. 48, No. 3, pp. 625-635, June 2001.

[10] D. E. Hampton, C. E. Tindall, J. M. McArdle, "Emergency Control of Power System Frequency Using Flywheel Energy Injection, " *IEE International Conference on Advances in Power System Control, Operation and management*, pp. 662-667, Nov. 1991.

[11] M. Komori and N. Akinaga, " A Prototype of Flywheel Energy Storage System Suppressed by Hybrid Magnetic bearings with H^∞ Controller, " *IEEE Trans. on Applied Superconductivity*, Vol. 11, No. 1, pp. 1733-1736, March 2001.

[12] T. J. Ross, *Fuzzy Logic with Engineering Applications*, Mcgraw-Hill, Inc., 2000.

Neural Systems for Solving the Inverse Problem of Recovering the Primary Signal Waveform in Potential Transformers

Nikola Kasabov[1] *Senior Member IEEE*, Gancho Venkov[2] and Stefan Minchev[3] *Student Member, IEEE*

[1] Knowledge Engineering and Discovery Research Institute
Auckland University of Technology
Private Bag 92006, Auckland 1020, New Zealand
Emails: nkasabov@aut.ac.nz; qsong@aut.ac.nz

[2]Technical University of Sofia, Bulgaria

Abstract—The inverse problem of recovering the potential transformer primary signal waveform using secondary signal waveform and information about the secondary load is solved here via two inverse neural network models. The first model uses two recurrent neural networks trained in an off-line mode. The second model is designed with the use a Dynamic Evolving Neural-Fuzzy Interface System (DENFIS) and suited for on-line application and integration into existing protection algorithms as a parallel module. It has the ability of learning and adjusting its structure in an on-line mode to reflect changes in the environment. The model is suited for real time applications and improvement of protection relay operation. The two models perform better than any existing and published models so far and are useful not only for the reconstruction of the primary signal, but for predicting the signal waveform for some time steps ahead and thus for estimating the drifts in the incoming signals and events.

I. INTRODUCTION

The growing of power system complexity and size leads to an increased importance of protective relays. An accurate reproduction of the real signals from the power system is needed. Iron-core measurement transformers are not ideal, because of the non-linearity of their excitation characteristics and their ability to retain large flux levels in their cores, known as remanent flux. The distorted waveforms can introduce large uncertainties, leading to delays or malfunction in relay tripping It is important to investigate the deformation of the real signals, caused by the transformers, and to recover the primary signals using the secondary ones.

Electric power systems are subjected to many types of disturbances that result in electrical transients due to faults or routine switching operations. During the first few cycles following a power system fault, high-speed protective relays are expected to make a correct decision as to the presence and location of the fault in order to preserve system stability and to minimize the extent of equipment damage. The dynamic performance of the protective relays depends to the large extent on the signals produced by the potential transformers (PT) and the current transformer (CT). Power system faults or other transients can cause saturation in the PT and CT, leading to distortion of their signals. The PT and CT transient errors can have a major impact on the security of the protective relays and can cause relay protection misoperations; unacceptably delayed operations or failures to operate.

Additional algorithms for prediction of PT primary signal for a few time samples ahead can increase the operational speed and reliability of the existing protection algorithms that would result in an improved decision-making and an increased overall performance of the relay protection.

There are several methods used so far to achieve the above goal. The methods of neural networks (NN), fuzzy systems (FS) and knowledge engineering have been used extensively for solving prediction and control problems across areas of applications [1]. NN-based predictors have been developed for systems, governed by linear models [2]. A recurrent NN predictor of power transformer magnetizing current, using terminal voltages as input values is realized in [3]. In [4] a reconstruction of primary current waveform for partially saturated CT is suggested via logical block and 3-layered time-delay feed-forward NN (FNN). The use of FNN for CT saturation correction is considered in [5]. The CT is modelled in inverse direction by the FNN. In [6] and [7] the reproduction of CT primary current is considered, assuming steady state conditions for the magnetic flux and without remanent flux.

Despite of the successful applications of the above systems, there is a need for on-line learning and adaptive prediction techniques. One paradigm introduced for this purpose is called evolving connectionist systems (ECOS) [8]. ECOS evolve their structure and functionality through on-line, incremental, life-long learning from incoming data, thus being able to better predict future events. For the purpose of improving the relay protection performance we are introducing here the use of Dynamic Neuro-Fuzzy Inference Systems DENFIS [9], which is a specific prediction technique from the class of ECOS [8]. DENFIS is used here not only for the prediction and the recovery of the power system real current and voltage signals, but also for the prediction of future events. For initial training of the predictors, classical PT model is built first. Then the DENFIS predictor is used for on-line, real time learning and prediction.

This paper is organized as follows: Section II presents the mathematical modelling of PT and its classical description as a non-linear dynamic system with hysteresis. Section III refers to the design of inverse model via two recurrent neural networks in a series. Simulation results that prove its adequate behaviour are shown. Section IV introduces a novel method for the design of neural-fuzzy predictors with the use of DENFIS. Verification test and simulation results are applied.

II. MATHEMATICAL DESCRIPTION OF POTENTIAL TRANSFORMERS

In this section a classical non-linear PT model with hysteresis is built for the purpose of generating training sequences that are used for the training the neural systems. The model is realized in MATLAB. The PT equivalent circuit is shown on fig. 1.

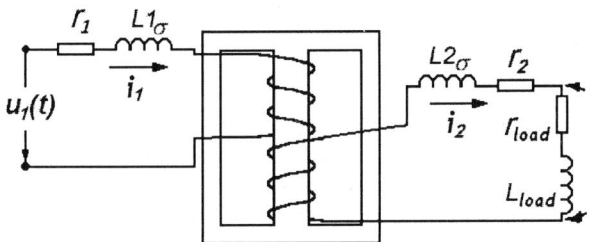

Fig. 1. Equivalent circuit of a single phase PT.

As a non-linear system with hysteresis, a 1-phase, 2-winding PT can be described mathematically via non-linear system of differential-algebraic equations [10]:

$$\dot{\varphi}_1(t) = -\frac{r_1(G_{\mu e} + L_{2\sigma} + L_{load})}{D}\varphi_1(t) + \frac{r_1 G_{\mu e}}{D}\varphi_2(t) + u_1(t)$$
$$\dot{\varphi}_2(t) = \frac{(r_2 + r_{load})G_{\mu e}}{D}\varphi_1(t) - \frac{(r_1 + r_{load})(G_{\mu e} + L_{2\sigma} + L_{load})}{D}\varphi_2(t)$$
(1)

where $D = G_{\mu e}(L_{1\sigma} + L_{2\sigma} + L_{load}) + L_{1\sigma}(L_{2\sigma} + L_{load})$

and

$$G_{\mu e} = \frac{s_e}{l_e}\mu_{DYN}(B) = \frac{s_e}{l_e}f\left(\frac{G_{\mu e}((L_{2\sigma} + L_{load})\varphi_1 + L_{1\sigma}\varphi_2)}{D}\right)$$
(2)

The supplying voltage $u_1(t)$ is the excitation signal; $u_2(t)$ is the secondary voltage; Ψ_1 and Ψ_2 are flux linkages; r_1, r_2, $L_{1\sigma}$, $L_{2\sigma}$ are parameters of the windings; B is magnetic flux density; $G_{\mu e}$ is the equivalent permeance of the magnetic core; s_e and l_e are geometrical parameters of the core; r_{load} and L_{load} are load resistance and inductance. The auxiliary variables $\varphi_1(t) = L_{1\sigma}i_1(t) + \Psi_1(t)$ and $\varphi_2(t) = (L_{2\sigma} + L_{load})i_2(t) + \Psi_2(t)$ are introduced. The secondary voltage is calculated from:

$$u_2(t) = r_{load}\left(-\frac{G_{\mu e}}{D}\varphi_1(t) + \frac{(G_{\mu e} + L_{1\sigma})}{D}\varphi_2(t)\right) + $$
$$+ L_{load}\left(-\frac{G_{\mu e}}{D}\frac{d\varphi_1(t)}{dt} + \frac{(G_{\mu e} + L_{1\sigma})}{D}\frac{d\varphi_2(t)}{dt}\right)$$
(3)

The non-linear implicit relation (2) is given as data set $\mu_{DYN} = f(B)$ and shown on fig. 2. According to [11] eddy current and hysteresis losses are combined into one core loss term, which is accounted for by a voltage-dependent resistance additional load $r_{2h} = r_{2h}(u_2(t))$ on the PT secondary. This explicit relation is shown on fig. 3.

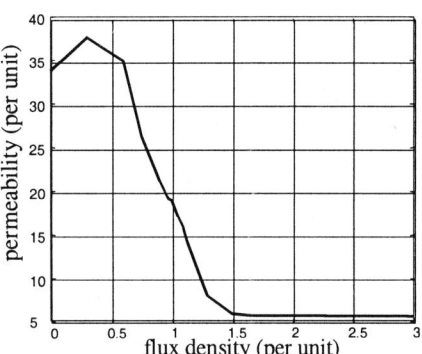

Fig. 2. The relation $\mu_{DYN} = f(B)$.

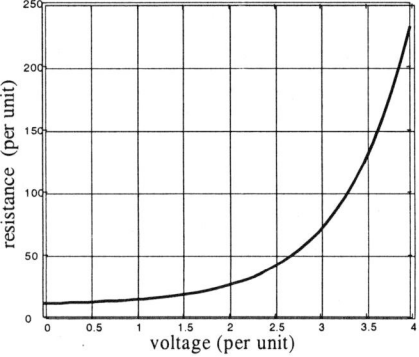

Fig. 3. The relation $r_{2h} = r_{2h}(u_2(t))$.

The classical PT model based on (1), (2), (3) and also based on the non-linear relations $\mu_{DYN} = f(B)$ and $r_{2h} = r_{2h}(u_2(t))$ is constructed for generation of training samples. Certain PT parameter values are chosen as follows: $U_1 = 220V$; $U_2 = 2200V$; $I_1 = 2A$; $I_2 = 1A$ and the model parameter values are: $r_1 = 2.991\Omega$; $r_2 = 121.99\Omega$; $L_{1\sigma} = 0.051mH$; $L_{2\sigma} = 2.45mH$; $r_{load} = 20k\Omega$; $L_{load} = 1.27H$.

III. INVERSE MODEL FOR RECOVERING PRIMARY SIGNAL WAVEFORM BASED ON RECURRENT NEURAL NETWORKS

The idea for construction of recurrent neural network (RNN) using FNN and feedbacks from its outputs to the inputs is presented in [12]. For the training phase the input to a FNN includes the excitation signal and the past values of the classical model output. We assume that after a suitable training the FNN gives a good representation of the original dynamic system. For the subsequent post-training purposes the FNN output itself (and its delayed values) can be fed back and used as a part of the NN input. In this way the initial FNN can be upgraded to time-delayed RNN and can be used independently of the original system.

The algorithm for construction of PT neural based inverse model has two steps. In the first step simulations with various excitations - supplying voltages $u_1(t)$ and different load parameters (r_{load}, L_{load}) have been conducted and the corresponding classical model responses $\Phi(t)$ and $u_2(t)$ have been recorded. The excitations $u_1(t)$ are constructed for thorough characterization of the considered dynamic system. They are composed of sine waves (with fundamental frequency 50 Hz and different magnitudes from 1 to 1000V) and random noise with normal distribution. The sample time is $3.125 \times 10^{-4} s$ or 64 points pre fundamental frequency cycle (0.02s). Furthermore, to cover more of the real secondary loads the simulations were performed with varying r_{load} and L_{load} and a sample time of 0.1s. The limits for the load resistance and inductance are $r_{2load} \in [0.5;5000]\Omega$ and $L_{load} \in [0.01;10]H$. The excitations, the load variations and the corresponding classical model responses are used for construction of training sequences.

In the second step the two RNNs – NN1 and NN2 are trained independently, using standard backpropagation training technique, available in MATLAB. NN1 is for approximation of magnetic flux $\Phi(t)$ waveform. It has two hidden layers with neurons (10-10) having tansig activation functions. The output layer has one linear neuron. After the training error is driven to sufficiently small value (less than 1.0×10^{-8}) the training process is stopped. The parameters of the FNN are fixed and after inclusion of the feedback connections and buffers for 3 past values the training is finished. The second RNN- NN2 is for approximation of the primary voltage $u_1(t)$ waveform. It has two non-linear layers (17-12) with tansig activation functions and one linear output neuron. NN2 is constructed and trained in the same way like NN1. Then the two RNN are combined to work in series (fig.4) and they form a complex neural system for modeling of the PT inverse dynamics.

The designed neural system was tested thoroughly with wide range of signals and loads, different from those, used in the training samples. The neural inverse model approximates the classical model results with acceptable accuracy (less than 5%). We found that the neural system has not only learned the training samples, but also exhibited a good capability for generalization beyond the training data.

To show the capabilities of the presented inverse model we have used an extreme case (not included in the training samples), the transformer load changes rapidly while the dynamics in the secondary voltage is considerable. This is a demonstration of the high non-linear inverse dynamics of the physical object, as it is driven to saturation levels.

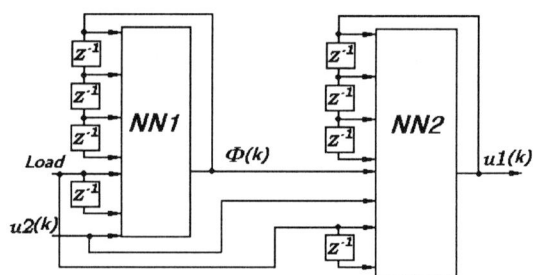

Fig. 4. Potential transformer inverse model architecture.

The PT inverse model, realized by means of RNN structures is described by:

$$\Phi(k) = \gamma \begin{pmatrix} \Phi(k-1), \Phi(k-2), \Phi(k-3), u_1(k), \ldots \\ \ldots r_{load}(k), r_{load}(k-1), L_{load}(k), L_{load}(k-1) \end{pmatrix}$$

$$u_2(k) = \delta \begin{pmatrix} u_1(k), \Phi(k), u_2(k-1), u_2(k-2), u_2(k-3), \ldots \\ \ldots r_{load}(k), r_{load}(k-1), L_{load}(k), L_{load}(k-1) \end{pmatrix}$$

(4)

where $\gamma(\bullet)$ and $\delta(\bullet)$ are non-linear functions.

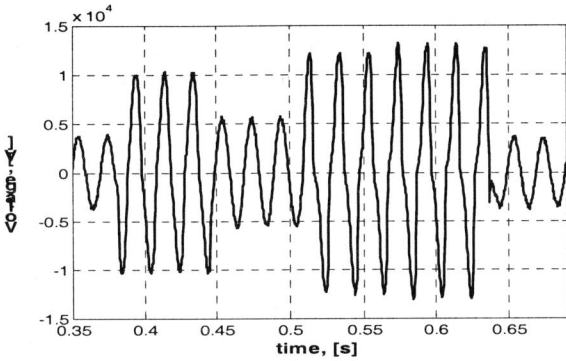

Fig. 5. Secondary voltage $u_2(t)$ the input signal to the neural model.

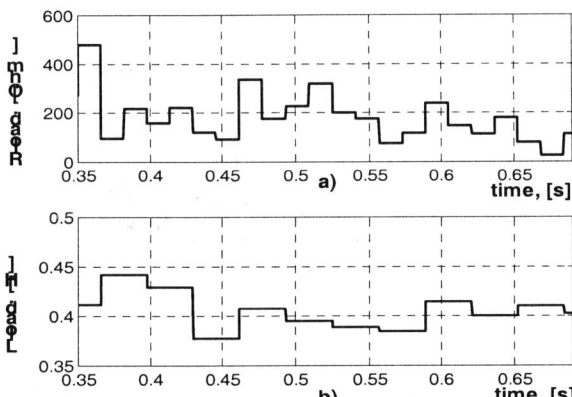

Fig. 6. Secondary load variations during the simulation test: a) load resistance r_{load}; b) load inductance L_{load}.

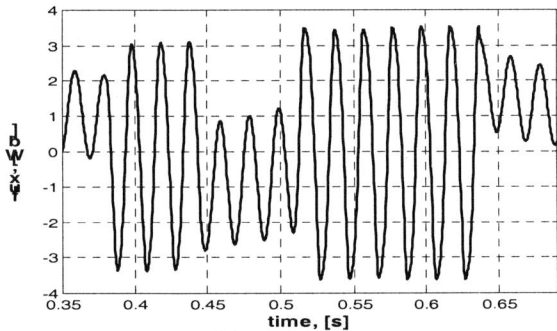

Fig. 7. Magnetic flux $\Phi(t)$ obtained from the neural model.

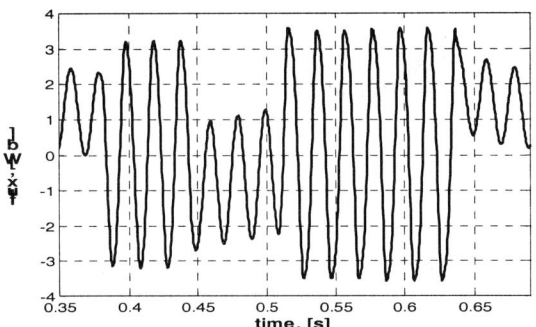

Fig. 8. Magnetic flux $\Phi(t)$ obtained from the neural model.

A simulation test results are presented on fig.5 – fig.12. The input signal $u_2(t)$ is shown on fig.5 and the load variations are on fig. 6. The result from NN1 (fig.7) is approximation of the magnetic flux waveform and is in good agreement with the classical model dynamic trajectory, shown on fig.8. The reconstructed primary voltage waveform $u_1(t)$, obtained from the inverse neural model is on fig.9 and the corresponding signal concerned with the classical model is on fig.10. The errors of the neural system versus the classical model reactions are depicted on fig. 11.

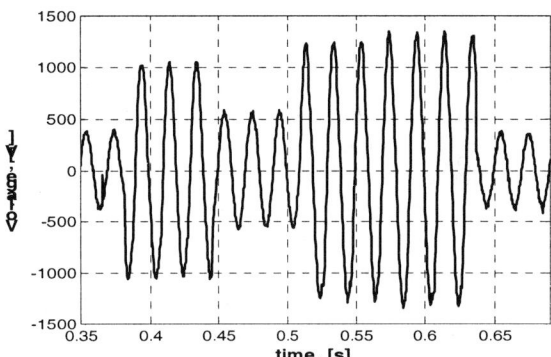

Fig. 9. Primary voltage $u_1(t)$ obtained from the neural model.

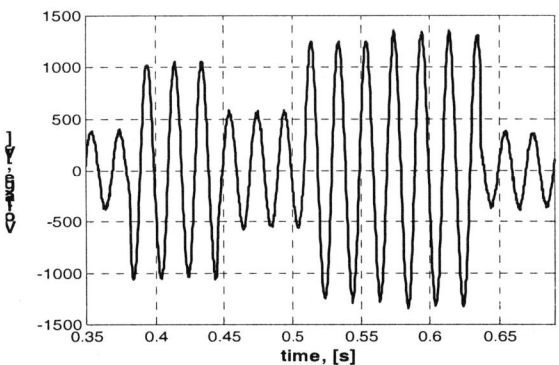

Fig. 10. Primary voltage $u_1(t)$ obtained from the classical model.

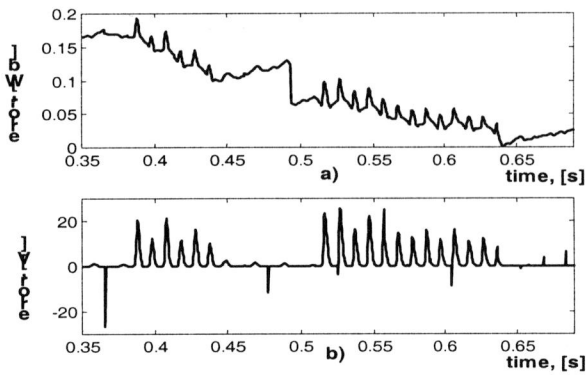

Fig. 11. The errors: a) in approximation of the magnetic flux; b) in approximation of the primary voltage.

IV. Primary Voltage Predictor Via DENFIS Modelling

A. DENFIS: Dynamic Evolving Neural-Fuzzy Interface System

DENFIS belongs to the paradigm of the evolving connectionist systems (ECOS) [8]. DENFIS evolve through incremental learning and accommodate new input data through local element tuning [9]. New fuzzy rules are created and updated during the operation of the system. A new evolving clustering method is employed in DENFIS. At each time step, depending on the position of the input vector in the input space, the DENFIS output is calculated through a fuzzy interface system, based on m-most activated fuzzy rules, which are dynamically chosen from a fuzzy rule set. Papers and software written in MATLAB of several ECOS models that include DENFIS, can be found in [8] and also downloaded from www.kedri.info (the book ref. [8] entry) or from (www.spinger.de -> the book ref. [8] entry).

B. Problem Definition

The diagram for prediction of PT input signal is shown on Fig. 12. The input value $x(k)$ is the primary signal at instant k. After sampling the secondary signal $y(k)$ together with information about the load are fed to the predictor. The aim is to predict the primary signal value $x(k+1)$ for some time sample ahead in the future and thus to predict possible drifts in the real power system voltages.

The construction algorithm has two steps. In the first step simulation with various signals - supplying voltages and different load conditions have been performed with the classical PT model. The input signal waveforms, the load variations and the corresponding secondary signal waveforms are recorded and used for construction of training sequences. The chosen sample time is 1.0×10^{-3} s. In the second step the DENFIS model is trained as an initial training and initial adjustment of its structure, as it will further adapt to new data in an on-line mode.

C. Simulation Results

The constructed DENFIS based predictor for primary voltage was tested with wide range of excitation signals and load conditions to prove its validity. To demonstrate its adequate operation, simulation results are shown below. Fig. 13 shows the desired and the predicted over time values of the PT primary voltage with the use of a DENFIS operating in an on-line learning mode. The prediction error is much lower that the error produced by other prediction models so far.

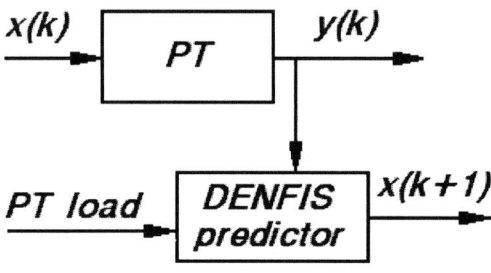

Fig. 12. Block diagrams for construction of PT primary signal predictor.

The designed predictor for estimation of PT primary voltage $u_1(t)$ waveform or power system real voltage, constructed according the diagram from Fig. 12 is suited for on-line operation. The testing results (fig. 13) show good coincidence of the two time series data with acceptable differences. The time series values are scaled with the primary voltage rated value ($220V$).

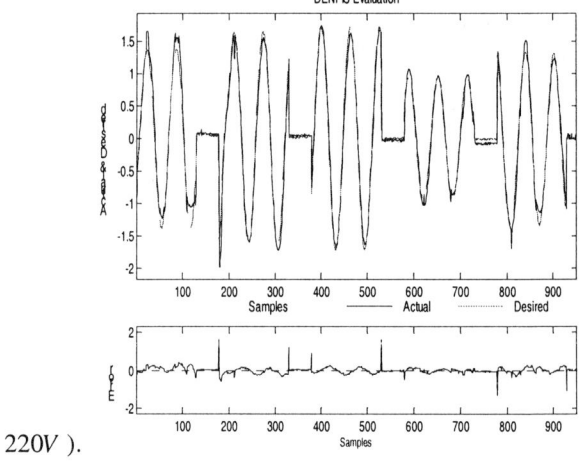

Fig. 13. PT primary voltage predictor results from verification test.

V. Conclusion

It is well known (see [6], [7]) that an accurate estimation of the primary signal waveform using the measured secondary signal waveform can not be achieved in real time using conventional modeling methods, because of the complexity in modeling of transformers magnetic systems. The first NN inverse model based on two recurrent NN is trained in an off-line learning mode and has a great computational power and is suited for real-time application. The results show that one high non-linear dynamic system with hysteresis can be modelled successfully with NN system. The inverse PT neural model is adopted for being integrated into the existing digital protection ralays algorithms as a parallel function. The incorporation of the proposed routine in digital protective relaying algorithms provides much more accurate estimate of the real primary signal waveform than the usually achieved with using the PTs nominal ratio. The added element of artificial intelligence improves the protection relays reliability and increases the operational speed. The first model, based on RNN is difficult to train on new data in an on-line mode as it operates in a working environment.

The complexity and dynamics of power system transients require sophisticated methods and tools for building on-line adaptive intelligent systems for an improved relay protection operation. They should be able to adapt as they operate, and to refine their algorithms with possible environmental changes.

The second model in this paper is an application of a new fuzzy interface system, DENFIS for the design of an on-line primary voltage value predictor for relay protection purposes. It is suited for real time applications.

The two models perform better than any existing and published models so far and are useful not only for the reconstruction of the primary signal, but for predicting the signal waveform for some time steps ahead and thus for estimating the drifts in the incoming signals and events.

The analysis of the results indicates clearly the advantages of DENFIS when used for on-line applications for predicting input-output signals of high non-linear dynamic systems with hysteresis.

The ECOS [8] are not only adaptive learning systems, but also knowledge-based systems as they allow for rules to be extracted from a trained system. These rules can be further analyzed for a better understanding of the relation between environmental changes and power security protection.

Acknowledgement

The work is supported through funding from the Technical University in Sofia, Bulgaria and from the Foundation for Research, Science and Technology of New Zealand (NERF grant AUT02/001). We would like to acknowledge Dr. Qun Song, Mrs Joyce D'Mello and Peter Hwang from the Knowledge Engineering and Discovery Research Institute (KEDRI) for their assistance.

References

[1] N. Kasabov, *Foundations of neural networks, fuzzy systems and knowledge engineering,* The MIT Press, 1996.
[2] C. Alippi and V. Piuri, "Experimental neural networks for prediction and identification," *IEEE Trans. on Instrumentation and Measurement,* vol. 45, no. 2, pp. 670-676, 1996.
[3] I. Kamwa, et al, "Recurrent neural networks for phasor detection and adaptive identification in power system control and protection," *IEEE Trans. on Instrumentation and Measurement,* vol. 45, no. 2, pp. 657-663, 1996.
[4] J. Pihler, B. Grcar, D. Dolinar, K. Elissa, "Improved operation of power transformer protection using artificial neural networks," *IEEE Trans. on Power Delivery,* vol. 12, no. 3, pp. 1128-1136, 1997.
[5] D. C. Yu, J. C. Cummins, Z. Wang, H-J. Yoon, L. A. Kojovic, "Correction of current transformer distorted secondary currents due to saturation using artificial neural networks," *IEEE Trans. on Power Delivery,* vol. 16, no. 1, pp. 189-194, 2001.
[6] N. Locci and C. Muscas, "Hysteresis and eddy currents compensation in current transformers," *IEEE Trans. on Power Delivery,* vol. 16, no. 2, pp. 154-159, 2001.
[7] Y. C. Kang et al, "An algorithm for compensating secondary current of current transformers," *IEEE Trans. on Power Delivery,* vol. 12, no. 1, pp. 116-122, 1997.
[8] N. Kasabov, *Evolving connectionist systems: Methods and Applications in Bioinformatics, Brain Study and Intelligent Machines,* Springer Verlag, London-New York, 2002.
[9] N. Kasabov, Q. Song, "DENFIS: Dynamic evolving neural-fuzzy interface system and its application for time-series prediction," *IEEE Trans. on Fuzzy Systems,* vol. 10, no. 1, pp. 144-154, 2002.
[10] S. Minchev, "A potential transformer digital model and parameters calculation via optimization procedures," *Proc. of the XVII Int.Conf. Applications of Mathematics in Engineering and Economy, Sozopol, Bulgaria,* pp. 485-496, 2001.
[11] X. S. Chen, P. Neudorfer, "Digital model of three phase five-legged transformer," *IEE Proceedings C,* vol. 139, no. 4, pp. 351-358, 1992.
[12] K. Hunt, D. Sbarbaro, R. Zbikowski and P. Gawthrop, "Neural networks for control systems – a survey," *Automatica,* vol. 28, no. 6, pp. 1083-1112, 1992.

Recognition System for EMG Signals by using Non-negative Matrix Factorization

Yuuki Yazama
Dept. of Information Science & Intelligent Systems,
Faculty of Engineering, University of Tokushima
`rabbit@is.tokushima-u.ac.jp`

Yasue Mitsukura
Dept. of Information Science & Intelligent Systems,
Faculty of Engineering, University of Tokushima
`mitsu@is.tokushima-u.ac.jp`

Minoru Fukumi
Dept. of Information Science & Intelligent Systems,
Faculty of Engineering, University of Tokushima
`fukumi@is.tokushima-u.ac.jp`

Norio Akamatsu
Dept. of Information Science & Intelligent Systems,
Faculty of Engineering, University of Tokushima
`akamatsu@is.tokushima-u.ac.jp`

Abstract

IIn this paper, the feature vector of a few dimension for the electromyograph (EMG) recognition systems is extracted. We aim at the construction of the comprehensive operation equipment to which the operation used frequently was summarized. Important frequency bands of EMG signals are selected by using a genetic algorithm. The EMG signals are a kind of the living organism signal. The EMG signals based on 7 operations at a wrist are measured and recognized. We perform a recognition experiment of EMG signals by neural network using the selected frequency band. We show the effectiveness of this method by means of computer simulations.

1 Introduction

Electromyograph (EMG) is an electrical recording of muscle activity which is measured from the surface of the skin. It is possible to perform control of a manipulator or prosthetic hand by utilizing EMG as an incoming signal. A facial expression and gesture is used as a natural interface of man, and a machine and a computer. But systems using EMG which can be used as interface more easily have studied since 1960s. The myoelectric upper limb prosthesis using EMG has a significant role in the field of rehabilitation medicine or welfare as an equipment which realizes natural motions as man's hand by engineering progress. Furthermore personal digital assistant (PDA) apparatuses, for example cellular phone, have spread quickly. The portability of the PDA, miniaturization and weight saving are developing the technology of the PDA and radio-communications standards, such as bluetooth. If we use this technology, we can access to various apparatus by using one operation apparatus to which the operation used frequently is collected. Then, it is thought that a wristwatch-type or a ring-type are desirable as for comprehensive operation equipment by EMG signal. In addition, a feature vector in a few dimension is necessary in order to aim at reduction of learning cost and improvement of recognition accuracy. A neural network (NN) which has on-line type separation capability is useful for classification of EMG patterns [?],[?]. In this paper, important frequency bands of EMG signals are selected by using a genetic algorithm (GA) and the EMG signals based on 7 operations at a wrist are recognized by using a back-propagation trained network. We carry out the experiments with combination of GA and NN and show the effectiveness of the present approach.

2 Classification of EMG Patterns at a Wrist

We focused on 7 operations which are considered as a basic wrist motion type, neutral, top, bottom, left, right, outward rotation and inward rotation. The EMG patterns are recorded under the wrist motion. These operations are thought as standard motions and reflect a subject's simple operation.

Data extraction is preformed for three male subjects and 30 sets are measured, each of which is composed of 7 operations. The EMG signals are measured by a surface electrode. Moreover, the surface electrode of dry type (electrolysis cream was not used) is adopted because of a subject's displeasure and a practical application as PDA operation machines. The EMG pattern which is amplified electrically the feeble signal emitted from a living body, and is obtained as time series data. 4 electrodes are placed around the wrist (see Figure 2). The EMG patterns (see Figure 2) are measured under sampling frequencies of 20.48kHz and for 2.048 seconds for all electrodes.

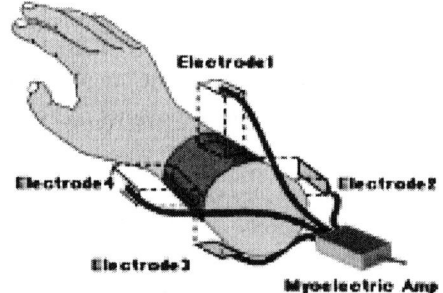

Figure 2 : Wrist with 4 electrode

The Fast Fourier Transform (FFT) is used for the time series data of the EMG patterns. The feature vector is generated as frequency distribution of the EMG pattern.The normalization is performed to 4ch signals at the maxinum of a power spectrum of the signal of 4ch, and The frequency band to be used is from 40Hz to

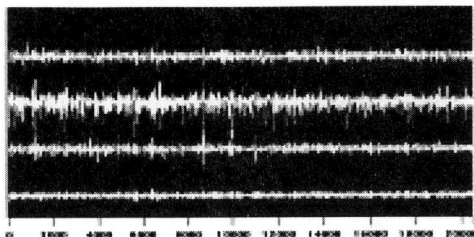

Figure 2 : Row EMG pattern

1000Hz. Frequency bands are selected by using a GA, and then NN performs learning and recognition by using only the selected frequency band.

3 Selection of an Important Frequency Band

Data mining is intellectual discovery which extracts effective information from huge information. Intellectual discovery is regularity with validity, freshness, or the understanding possibility, and the pattern of a relation. It is effective to extract important information from many information also not only in pattern recognition but in composition of a system.

3.1 Genetic Algorithm

Genetic Algorithm is the method of having considered evolutionary process. It is one of optimization techniques which calculate the better solution, changing two or more solutions hereditarily. Research which grasps the correlation of two or more objects using a genetic GA is done [7]. This research can use the method of pattern recognition on the Euclid space by the map to the Euclid space. And the analysis of the object from the new starting point is attained.It proposes extracting the information which takes in this method and is characteristic using a GA from many information acquired.

The unnecessary feature can be included in the feature vector(frequency band) generated from the EMG pattern. Then, the required attributes in the frequency band is chosen by using a genetic algorithm. The chromsome used for GA is based on binary coding. The frequency band corresponding to a code "0" is not used, but the frequency band corresponding to a code "1" is uesd. The selection of the genetic operator is Roulette wheel selection and elite preservation strategy and one-point crossover are adopted.

3.2 Fitness Function

The fitness function is a index which shows how the each chromsome adapt to the environment. To improve the level of pattern accuracy, it is thought that the case where the distance in a class is near and where the distance between classes is far is desirable. Then, the fitness function is given by the formula in consideration of distance calculation of a class. The fitness value is obtained from the product of two evaluations shown below,

- Total of the change in a class.
- Total of the distance between classes by the representation vector using the selected frequency.

We use the normalized spectrum, $x = (x^1, x^2, ..., x^p)$, as the EGM signal feature. Evaluation of change in a class to the chromsome i is a pattern of operation j, and was defined as follow:

$$S_i = \alpha * \sum_{j}^{p} \sum_{h}^{n} (s_{ij}^h)^{-1} / g_i,$$

where h is the sensor number, g_i is the number of selected frequency bannds and s_{ij}^h is each sensor and change in the class for every pattern:

$$s_{ij}^h = \sum_{k}^{n_i} \sum_{t}^{m} (x_{kt}^{jh} - \bar{x}_k^{jh})^2 / \bar{x}_k^{jh},$$

where $k = (1, ..., n_i)$ is selected frequency bands and the number of selected frequency band every chromsome, and $\bar{x}_k^j$ is the average value of the power supectrum obtained by each sensor j and the frequency band. S_i is set up that such a high value that the change in a class is small can be acquired.

In order to define the distance between classes, it is calculated the vector representing the class:

$$V_{ij} = \sqrt{\sum_{h} \sum_{k}^{n_i} (\bar{x}_k^{jh})^2}.$$

Total of the distance between classes is computed by the vector representing the class obtained:

$$L_i = \beta * \sum_{k1}^{n_i} \sum_{k2}^{n_i} (V_{ik1} - V_{ik2})^2 / g_i.$$

The fitness value to each chromsome is calculated based on these distance, which is between the classes and in class:

$$F_i = S_i * L_i.$$

α and β are weight parameter, α is set up by 10.0 and $beta$ is set up by 0.01. The fitness value is calculated by using only the obtained data. Then, the important frequency band can be specified from the feature which original data have independent of the recognition accuracy.

3.3 Neural Network

Because of a muscular quantity and a difference in transfer characteristic to the skin, the living body signal has a large individual difference. In this research, a back-propagation trained network is used, which can obtain a nonlinear map by learning. It can be seen that NN is suitable for modeling feature like the living body signal with nonliear property. NN has a three-layered structure. The number of input layer units depending on the number of genes chosen by GA is variable from the maximum number of genes to 1. The number of hidden layer units is 10 and the number of output layer units is 7 corresponding to the number of EMG patterns.

4 Computer Simulation

The computer simulations are perfomed using the data obtained from 3 subjects. Selection of the important frequency band is performed by using GA. The parameters of GA in this simulation are shown in Table 4.

Table 4 : The parameters of GA

The number of generations	50
The number of chromsomes	50
The length of chromsome	25
The rate of elite	0.08
The probability of cossover	0.6
The probability of mutation	0.05

4.1 Selection of the Important Frequency Band

Extraction of the important frequency band is perform 10 simulations and by extracting the chromsome of highest evaluation from each generation without overlapping. The recognition experiment by using NN is conducted by the chromsome extracted 100 chromsome in order of the high evaluation out of the extracted chromsome. The chromsome with 80% or more of recognition accuracy of the highest recognition obtained from the recognition experiment is extracted, and the chromsome which can be performing 60% or more of data deletion is extracted (see figure 4.1).

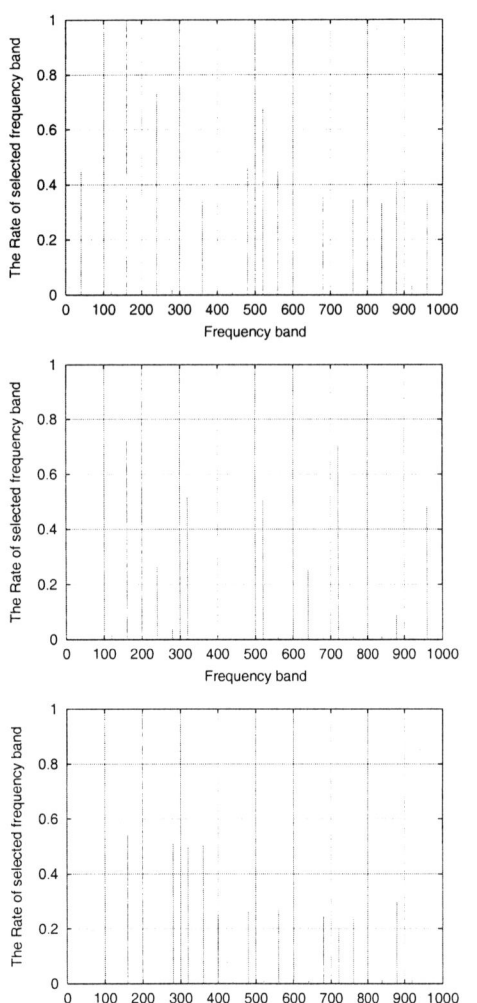

Figure 4.1 : The rate of the selected genes, the selected important frequency band, by three subjects

It being able to say in common for three subjects that about 200Hz is most often chosen as an important frequency band. About 200Hz is considered to be an important frequency band by this result.

The extracted band exceeding 5 rates of frequency band chosen in the result from each three subjects select(see Figure 4.1) is 160, 200, 240, 280, 320, 360, 520, 600 and 720Hz. The normalized power spectrum which is obtained from electrode2 at the time of 7operation is shown in Figure 4.1. The meaning of a sign is in the state in which "N" lengthened the wrist. "T" is upwards movement, "U" as downward movement, "R" as bent on the right, "L" as bent on the left, "RI" as moved inward rotation and "RO" as moved outward rotation. It is shown visually that the range which has abig value is to about 700Hz. It is thought that extraction of the frequency band considered that each feature has probably appeared has been performed.

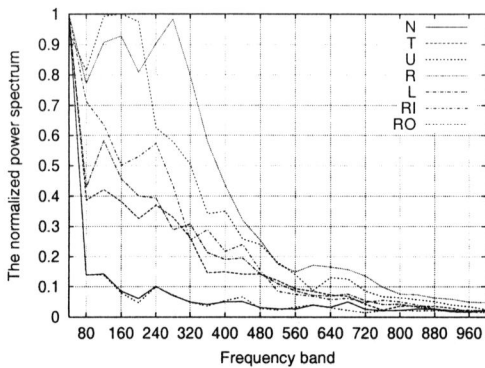

Figure 4.1 : The normalized power spectrum measured from electrode2(see Figure 2)

4.2 Summary of Result

The recognition experiment is agein conducted to three subjects using from 160Hz to 360Hz considered to be selected most, and 520Hz which selected in two subjects. The recognition experiment is performed NN. The number of input layer units is 28, the number of hidden layer units is 10 and the number of output layer units is 7. The result of simulation is shown average recognition accuracy by 30 simulation of NN using the selected frequency band. In addition , the comparison simulation of NN using the frequency band from 40Hz to 1000Hz is also shown. The result is shown in Table 4.2.

In each people, improvement in about 5 to 10% of rate of recognition is found. The number of used frequency bands can also be performing deletion 72%. It is thought that many information which causes incorrect recognition from the rate of data deletion is included. However, the important frequency band obtained by GA is not stable with an individual. It is thought that the signal which gained for the feature which appears in the living body signal by the individual, or the strong nonlinear nature which it has is not stable. However, since it is thought that it is almost the same even if man's structure is the different subject, the frequency band around 200Hz is chosen from the subject. Even if it is a different subject, it is considered also among different subjects for main frequency bands to be the same.We want to specify the frequency band stabilized even if the subject was different.

Table 2 : Recognition acurracy

The stage of "subject" is the result of being obtained using this method. "*" is the result of being obtained from the recognition experiment using the power spectrum from 40Hz to 1000Hz obtained from the subject with the same number.

	N	T	U	R
Subject1	65.1	50.8	88.8	63.0
*1	47.5	40.5	81.5	68.6
Subject2	74.1	59.6	90.3	78.0
*2	83.3	53.6	91.5	69.3
Subject3	91.8	70.6	71.5	89.3
*3	89.1	52.5	62.5	77.1
	L	RI	RO	Total
Subject1	90.3	73.8	56.0	69.7
*1	81.1	69.1	50.3	62.6
Subject2	77.8	68.0	62.0	72.8
*2	66.6	63.0	44.5	67.4
Subject3	96.1	82.5	83.3	83.6
*3	89.0	68.0	69.5	72.5

5 Conclusion

In the present work, Selection of the characteristic frequency band of the EMG signal is performed in consideration of the distance in the class and between classes by using GA. The recognition experiment by using NN is conducted using the selected frequency band, which appeared the good feature by GA. Furthermore, the important frequency band by the recognition accuracy and the rate of data deletion is extracted. In order to try the flexible feature extraction, the same frequency band toward three subjects is chosen in consideration of the amount of the feature obtained from three subjects. And the improvement of about 5% to 10% in the average recognition accuracy is attained. In addition, it is able to be performed 72% of data deletion.

As future work, we will extract the features which is based on selection of the same important frequency band by the different subject, and the correlation of the signal acquired from the EMG signal of 4ch(es). We wants to perform the emphasis and noise removal of a spectrum in which the feature of the signal acquired by extracting the correlation of the EMG signal of 4ch(es) appears. As for emphasis and noise removal of the spectrum, we consider that these are possible by mapping the EMG signal to another space.

In addition, improvement in the recognition accuracy is due to be aimed at by generating the more effective feature vector and conducting a recognition experiment using the generated feature vector.

References

[1] D.Nishikawa, W Yu, H.Yokoi and Y.Kakazu. n-Line Learning Method for EMG Prosthetic Hand Controlling. *IEICE*, D-II Vol J82, No.9, pp.1510-1519, in japanese, September 1999.

[2] D.Nishikawa, H.Yokoi, and Y.Kakazu. Design of motion-recognizer using electoromyogram. In *Robotics and Mechatronics Division*, in japanese, June 1998.

[3] D.Nishikawa, W Yu, H.Yokoi, and Y.Kakazu. On-Line Supervising Mechanism for Learning Data in Surface Electromyogram Motion Classifiers. In *IEICE*, D-II Vol J84, No.12, pp.2634-2643, December 2001.

[4] M.Vuskovic, and S.Du. Classification of Prehensile EMG Patterns With Simplified Fuzzy ARTMAP Networks. *JIJCNN*, Honolulu, Hawaii, May 2002.

[5] Wenwei Yu, Hiroshi Yokoi, Yukinori Kakazu, and Daisuke Nishikawa. Electromyographic(EMG) Pattern Recognition by Reinforcement Learning Method for Prosthetic Arm Control. *Complex System Engineering Dept.*, Hokkaido University, SAPPORO in Japanese.

[6] Yuuki Yazama, Yasue Mitsukura, Fukumi Minoru and Norio Akamatsu. Feature Analysis for EMG signals by Using an Evolutionary Method. *SICE System Integration Division Annual Conference.*, Kobe, in Japanese, December 2002.

[7] Shin'ichiro Omachi, Hiroko Yokoyama and Hirotomo Aso. Subject Arrangement in the Euclidean Space Using Geneteic Algorithm. *IEICE.*, D-II Vol.J82-D-II, No.12, pp.2195-2202, December 1999.

Human Head Detection Using Multi-modal Object Features

Yun Luo   Yi Lu Murphey
Department of Electrical and Computer Engineering
The University of Michigan-Dearborn
Dearborn, MI 48128-1491, U.S.A.

Farid Khairallah
Advanced Safety Systems
TRW Automotive
Farmington Hills, MI 48335-2642, U.S.A.

Abstract - **This paper describes a neural network system that automatically detects whether a human head exists in a given image. We focus our research in the first two levels of head detections. At the first level, it extracts candidates of a head using range information, motion clue and 3D spherical shape. At the second level, the system uses multiple visual modalities including gray scale value distribution, shape, motion and range information obtained using a stereo vision system to represent head features. A neural network classifier is used to evaluate the effectiveness of various object features for generating and representing human head. The system is validated on a large collection of images taken from a stereo camera system mounted inside a vehicle. Our experiments show the presented system has an accurate rate over 96%.**

I. Introduction

Extensive research work has been done to develop intelligent vision systems that can autonomously interact with humans in the surrounding environment and can provide maximum safety protection. The presence and location of the human head are the most critical parameters in many of such applications[1,2,4,6,11]. Robust head detection and tracking is a challenging task.

The main difficulties in head detection are caused by the amount of variation in the visual appearance such as scale, location, orientation, background and pose of the head. In addition, occlusion and lighting conditions make the head detection even more difficult in many applications. A robust head detection system must cope with both the variation within the head category and with the diversity of other object categories that could appear in the scene.

Most traditional head detection algorithms use exhaustive search for head detection or build a coarse-to-fine grid to gradually search the location of the head which could be computationally prohibitive or less accurate[1,2]. In this paper, we presented a head detection system that achieves robust performance through the integration of multiple visual modalities including gray scale, shape, motion and the range information provided by a stereo vision system. A neural network system is trained to detect a head location in an image using these visual features. Fig. 1 illustrates the framework of the proposed head detection. The first major step of computation is to generate head candidate images. The head candidates are generated from range images combined with motion features and 3D spherical shape. The head detection results including head location and confidence value generated from the previous image frame are used to eliminate head candidates of the current image frame.

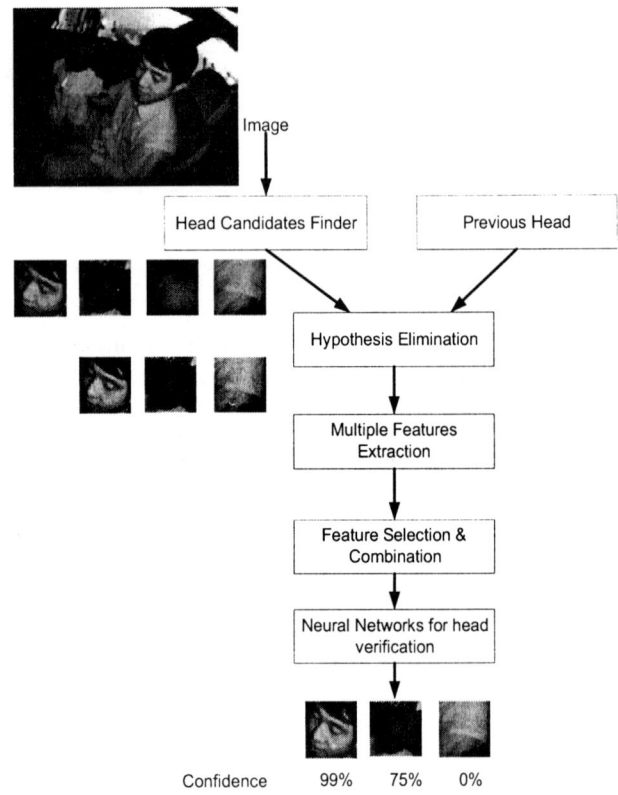

Fig. 1. A system for head detection

Constraints generated from assumptions such as the head moving trajectory is smooth and heads in consecutive frames have high consistency (appearance, orientation, etc). We incorporate head shape descriptors, gray scale grid features, relative head location, and head movements into a feature vector to represent a head. A neural network classifier is trained on the feature vectors to detect true head images. The following sections describe the computational details involved in the head candidate image generation and head feature extraction and representation.

II. Generating Head Candidates

Our research explores the range features for generating head candidates. Most previous solutions to head detection are based on intensity images and as a result, suffer from the problems including sensitivity to background clutter and lighting variations. Real-time stereo systems have recently made good advances. These stereo vision system are well-calibrated, and affordable for low cost system[4,5,10]. Fig. 2

illustrates the computational steps for generating head candidates using a range image provided by a stereo vision system.

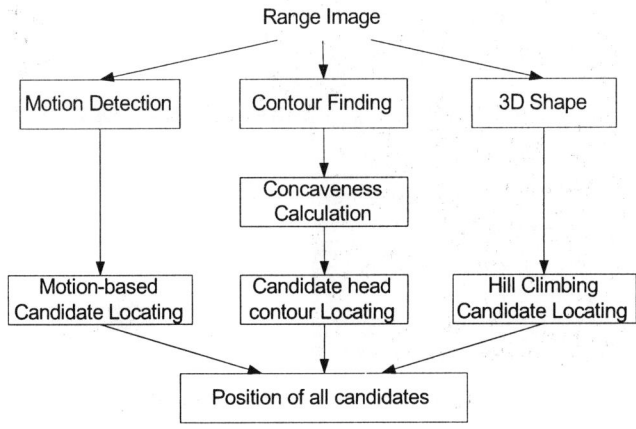

Fig. 2. Flowchart of head candidate generation

Three types of approaches are investigate: concave points finding along a body contour, 3D head shape finding using Hill climbing and locating strong moving pixels.

We first apply the Otsu algorithm[9] to a range image to obtain a binary image with the assumption that the person of interest is close to the camera system. Then we extract the large connected components in the binary image as the possible human bodies. For each selected component, we calculate three types of features: turning points on body contour, spherical matching and motion.

Turning points are calculated by finding concave points along a body contour. The concaveness of each contour pixel is measured by a circle centered at the pixel. A pixel has higher concaveness if the circle covers more on-pixels as shown in Fig. 3. Let the radius of the circle be r. We place the center of the circle to every contour point (x, y) and the concaveness of pixel (x,y) is calculated as follows:

$$\text{Concaveness}(x, y) = \sum_{i,j,(i^2+j^2) \leq r^2} I(x+i, y+j)) / \pi r^2$$

where I(x, y) is a binary image with on pixel equal to 1 and background pixel equal to 0. The points with the large concaveness values represent the possible turning points on a body contour. Fig. 3 shows four contour points, among which three are concave and one is convex point. The concaveness for each of these four points is 0.767, 0.375, 0.79, 0.901, starting from the bottom right side going counter clock wise. A head candidate is obtained by the following procedure. For each pair of consecutive turning points, an ellipse fitting is performed. If a contour segment that connects the two consecutive turning points has a high fitting to an ellipse, it is considered a head candidate. Fig. 4 illustrates the four head contour candidates obtained by this procedure. The contour segment from point 5 to point 1 in Fig. 4 fitted poorly to an ellipse, therefore it is not considered as a head candidate.

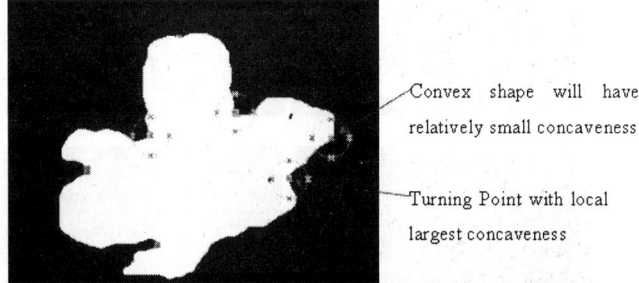

Fig. 3. Concaveness calculation and head candidates

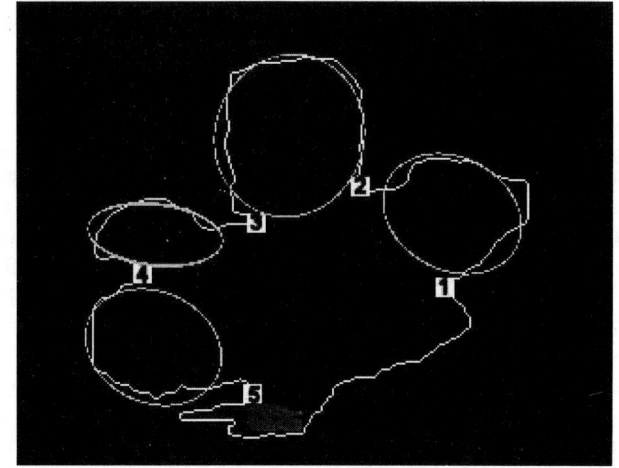

Fig. 4. Illustration of ellipse fitting to head contour candidates

The second type of visual cue used in head candidate finding is to use the 3D information provided by the depth map.

We used a Hill climbing algorithm to find all areas that have local maxima. For a pixel (x, y) in a range image, we compare its depth value with its neighbors. If its neighbors have higher values which means closer range, we move to the point that has the closest range. This process continues until we find a pixel that has the disparity value larger than any of its neighbors. The neighborhood of a pixel is defined by a circle.

In Fig. 5, (a) to (d) are the example of the 3D shape based head contour locating algorithm. (a) is the original image taken from a lab, (b) is the range image after background subtraction, (c) shows the contour and the turning points superimposed on the range image and (d) shows all the locations marked by crosses that has the local maxima found by the hill climbing. We can tell from (d), the soccer ball, the fake head and the knee all have similar spherical shape as the true head.

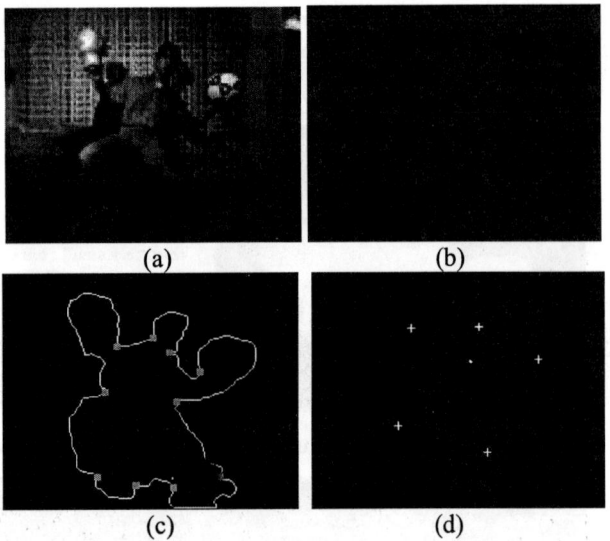

Fig. 5. Head Candidates finding using depth feature

The third type feature used in locating head candidates is motion. In many object recognition applications, the objects of interest are moving, whereas the background is static or stabilized. Although in general motion feature alone is not enough to detect human body, it can be a very useful supporting feature to recognize the presence of a person if he or she is moving. We use global and local motion analysis to extract motion features.

In global Motion Analysis, we subtract every two adjacent image frames and calculate the number of all moving pixels. The difference image from two consecutive frames in a video sequence removes noise such as range information drop out and disparity calculation mismatch, therefore it is a good indication of whether there is a moving object in the image. We calculate the vertical and horizontal projections of the difference image to locate concentrations of moving pixels. The concentrated moving pixels usually correspond to fast moving objects such as the moving head or hand. Our algorithm searches for peaks in horizontal and vertical projections. We choose the location (x,y) that corresponds to the peaks from the horizontal projection and the top peak from the vertical projection.

Fig. 6 is the example of the motion analysis. The top two images are the disparity image (left) and the difference image (right). The bottom two images are the gray scale image(left) and the vertical and horizontal projection of the difference image. The head candidate location is marked by a cross.

III. Head Feature Extraction and Representation

For head detection, we use a neural network to classify the true head from the false head in the head candidate pool. In order to make a neural network system effective, it is extremely important to find features that can best discriminate heads from other objects.

Fig. 6. Moving candidate locating

We investigated the following features, head shape descriptors, grid features of both gray and disparity images, relative head location, and head movements.

We use ellipse to describe head shapes. There are several advantages of using ellipse to fit the head[6]: 1) The shape of human head is more like an ellipse than other shapes and the ellipse shape can be easily represented by 5 parameters (the center coordinates (x,y), the major/minor axis (a, b) and orientation (θ); 2) The position (center) of the ellipse is more robust to contour; 3) From these 5 parameters of the ellipse, we can obtain the size of the ellipse which represents the size of the head, and the orientation of the ellipse, which is defined as the orientation of the head.

There are a number of different methods that can be used to calculate ellipse features[7, 8]. We used the second order central moments method and the mathematical equations are as follows:

$$\theta = \frac{1}{2}\tan^{-1}(\frac{2\mu_{1,1}}{\mu_{0,2}-\mu_{2,0}}), a = \sqrt[4]{\frac{4\sqrt{\mu_{2,0}^3}}{\pi\sqrt{\mu_{0,2}}}}, b = \sqrt[4]{\frac{4\sqrt{\mu_{0,2}^3}}{\pi\sqrt{\mu_{2,0}}}}.$$

Based on these parameters, we can calculate the following ellipse features

1) Length of major axis: a
2) Length of minor axis: b
3) Orientation of the major axis of the ellipse: θ
4) Ratio of Minor axis by Major axis: r
5) Length of head contour: $perimeter$
6) Size of the head: $area$
7) $Arperat = \dfrac{\sqrt{area}}{perimeter}$

The second type of features are statistic features extracted from gray and disparity images using a grid structure as shown in Fig. 7.

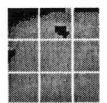

Fig. 7. **Grids of intensity and range image**

The following statistic features are extracted from each grid area:

1) Average Intensity: $\bar{I} = \frac{\sum_{i=1}^{n} I_i}{n}$

2) Variance of average gray scale: $\sigma = \sqrt{\frac{\sum_{i=1}^{n}(I_i - \bar{I})^2}{n-1}}$

3) Coarseness: $Co = \sum_{(x,y) \in \text{Region}} C(x,y)$

The coarseness is used to represent the texture. For the intensity space $I(x, y)$, we define the coarseness space: $C(x, y) = 1$ if $C(x, y)$ is a local intensity extrema, $C(x, y) = 0$ otherwise.

The relative head location is measured by the length and orientation of the head-body vector that connects the centroid of the body contour and the centroid of the head candidate contour. The head-body vector gives clue of what the person's stance appears to be. For example, the vector can measure whether a person can stand straight, lie down, but not possible stay upside down. If the head-body vector indicates that the head is far below the body position, we can eliminate this candidate.

Motion vector, (d, θ) or (dx, dy) of the head is used to represent the head moving patterns. Head movement usually follows certain patterns such as a smooth and continuous trajectory from consecutive frames. Therefore, we can predict the head location based on its previous head movement. Fig. 8 shows a typical sequence of images containing head movement, and the trajectory of movement. The trajectory of the head starts from darker pixel and ends at the lighter pixel. From the track of the head movement, we can see, the movement is smooth. And the movements near the two extreme conditions (leaning forward and backward) tend to be slower. Based on this analysis, we developed the following procedure to calculate head trace features.

We assume there are n candidates in the current frame t. For each candidate i, i = 1...n we have: (x_i^t, y_i^t) : x-y coordinates of the head candidate, and dx_i^t, dy_i^t : $dx_i^t = x_i^t - x_i^{t-1}$; $dy_i^t = y_i^t - y_i^{t-1}$. The x and y direction movement from the previous head to the current candidate are represented by $dx^{(t-1)}, dy^{(t-1)}, dx^{(t-2)}, dy^{(t-2)}$, etc.(see Fig. 9). Six dimensional head trace features are extracted, $M\_V = \{x_i^t, y_i^t, dx_i^t, dy_i^t, dx^{(t-1)}, dy^{(t-1)}\}$, to represent the head candidate moving patterns.

These trace features tell us the current and previous location of the candidate head and the information of how far the candidate head has moved.

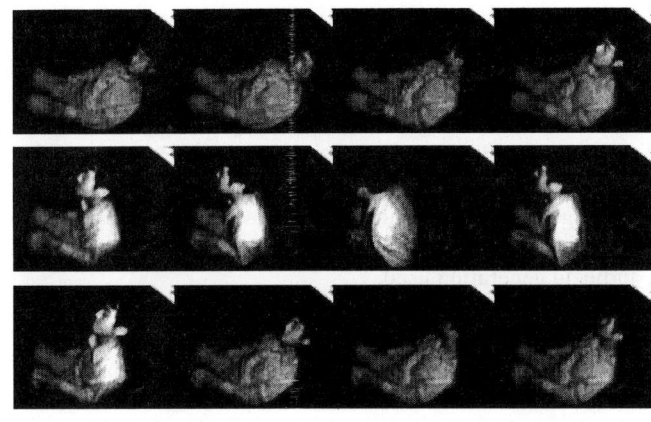

Fig. 8. **Moving sequence**

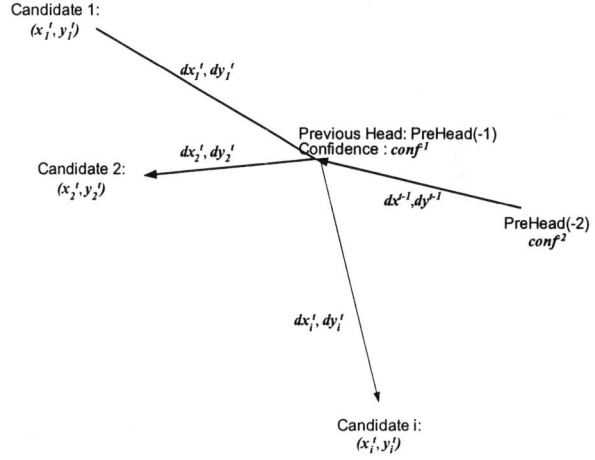

Fig. 9. **Illustration of head trace features**

IV. Experiments Results

A neural network classifier with a hidden layer of 30 nodes is trained in advance from the manually marked true head and falsely detected candidates. We use the neural network classifier to evaluate the multi-modal image features on a blind lab image dataset as well as a large set of images captured inside a vehicle.

Two sets of data have been used to test the multiple paths of head candidates generation algorithms described in section 2. The results are presented in Table 1 and 2. In Table 1, Image data set 1 contains 301 images taken under the lab environment. Different objects such as a soccer ball and a fake head which have similar 3D shape were used to analyze the effectiveness of our spherical shape algorithm. Different positions and stance have been tested for our contour-based candidates locating algorithms. When there is strong movement, (strong enough for moving pixel histogram analysis and moving object locating), the motion based candidates locating algorithm was used to find the moving candidates too. The combination of all the candidates gave us a manageable size of candidate pool and 96 percent of the true head was correctly detected when all three algorithms of candidate generation used.

Image data set 2 presented in Table 2 was taken inside a vehicle under controlled environment to test the two head candidate generation algorithms, spherical shape based and contour based. Our results show that the candidate generation algorithms give better results when they are combined.

Fig. 10 shows the detailed features used in the head detection neural network. Table 3 shows the experiment result of different combinations of the object features presented in section 3. The neural network classifier was trained using the image data set 2 described above. The results presented in Table 3 were obtained from a blind test data taken inside a vehicle at a rate of 30 Hz. The test data set contains about 200 frames.

The system is running at 30 Hz or higher using a Pentium 3/ 866 MHz PC with the resolution of 320*240 pixels. From the experiments result we can tell the performance of the combination of multi-modal features worked very well. In particular the combination of visual, trace, motion and relative location features give significantly improved performance.

V. Conclusion

In this paper we presented a head detection neural network system that uses multiple modal of image features for finding and representing human head. These features are the statistical features extracted from gray scale and disparity images, 3D spherical shape extracted from range image; concaveness of body contour, motion, ellipse fitting and trace features. Our experiments show that the combination of these features can give extremely promising results.

VI. Reference

[1] Essa I, Basu S, Darrell T, Pentland A, Modeling, tracking and interactive animation of faces and head using input from video. Proceedings of Computer Animation, Geneva, June, pp68-79

[2] Ming-Hsuan Yang; Kriegman, D.J.; Ahuja, N., Detecting faces in images: a survey, Pattern Analysis and Machine Intelligence, IEEE Transactions on , Volume: 24 Issue: 1 , Jan. 2002, Page(s): 34 -58

[3] Chellappa, R.; Wilson, C.L.; Sirohey, S., Human and machine recognition of faces: a survey, Proceedings of the IEEE , Volume: 83 Issue: 5 , May 1995 , Page(s): 705 -741

[4] Russakoff, D.; Herman, M., Head tracking using stereo, Applications of Computer Vision, 2000, Fifth IEEE Workshop on. , 2000, Page(s): 254 - 260

[5] Zhao, L.; Thorpe, E., Stereo- and neural network-based pedestrian detection, Intelligent Transportation Systems, IEEE Transactions on , Volume: 1, Issue: 3 , Sept. 2000, Page(s): 148 -154

[6] Birchfield, S., An elliptical head tracker, Signals, Systems & Computers, 1997. Conference Record of the Thirty-First Asilomar Conference on , Volume: 2 , 1997 Page(s): 1710 -1714 vol.2

[7] Fitzgibbon, A.; Pilu, M.; Fisher,R.B., Direct least square fitting of ellipses, Pattern Analysis and Machine Intelligence, IEEE Transactions on ,Volume: 21 Issue: 5 , May 1999, Page(s): 476 -480

[8] A. Kavianpour, N. Bagherzadeh, S. Shoari, Finding Elliptical Shapes in an Image using a Pyramid Architecture, Computers & Electrical Engineering, Vol 21, N1:69-75, January 1995

[9] Nobuyuki Otsu, "A Threshold Selection Method from Gray-Level Histograms," IEEE Transactions on Systems, Man, and Cybernetics, Vol. 9, No.1, pp. 62-66, 1979

[10] K. Konolige, "Small Vision Systems: Hardware and Implementation," in *Proceedings of* Eighth International Symposium on Robotics Research, Hayama, Japan, October, 1997.

[11] Yun Luo, "Object Classification, Detection and Tracking," Master's Thesis, Department of Electrical and Computer Engineering, University of Michigan-Dearborn, 2002.

Table 1. Head candidates locating experiment 1

Candidates Generation Algorithm	Image Data Set 1: Lab Images. Image number: 301			
	Candidates Size	Candidates per image	True head picked	True head detected among candidates
Spherical shape (top 4 candidates)	1204	4.0	234	77.8%
Spherical shape (top 8 candidates)	2408	8.0	269	89.4%
Contour-based	542	1.8	247	82.1%
Motion based	251	0.8	104	34.6%
Combine three methods above	3134	10.4	289	96.0%

Table 2. Head candidates locating experiment 2

Image Data Set 2: Passenger inside vehicle. Image number: 5279				
Candidates Generation Algorithm	Candidates Size	Candidates per image	True head picked	True head detected Correctness
Spherical shape	19004	3.6	5045	95.2%
Contour-based	11614	2.2	4909	93.0%
Combine two methods above	30618	5.8	5108	96.8%

Table 3. Candidates verification by different features combination

Features Combination	Visual Features 37 dim	Trace Features 6 dim	Shape Features 7 dim	Mutual Position Features 2 dim	Combined feature dimension	Performance
1	X				37	90%
2		X			6	87%
3			X		7	47%
4	X			X	39	91%
5	X	X	X		50	98%
6	X	X	X	X	52	98%

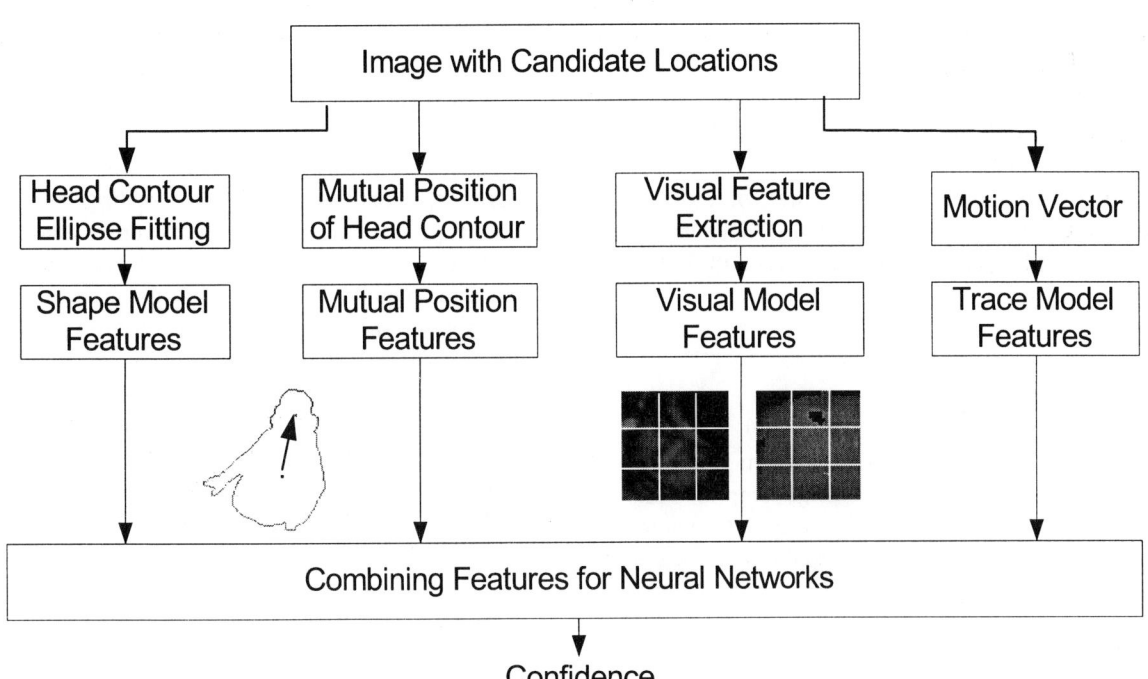

Fig. 10. Multi-modal feature representation for a head detection neural network

Local Voting Networks for Human Face Recognition

Metin Artiklar
Electronics and Engineering Department
Fatih University
Istanbul, Turkey

martiklar@fatih.edu.tr

Xiaoyan Mu and Mohamad H. Hassoun
Department of Electrical and Computer Engineering
Wayne State University
Detroit, MI 48202

hassoun@brain.eng.wayne.edu

Paul Watta
Department of Electrical and Computer Engineering
University of Michigan-Dearborn
Detroit, MI 48128

watta@umich.edu

Abstract

We investigate a template matching-based classifier system which uses local distance computations and a voting scheme. The proposed system has a mechanism to reject unknown patterns, and provides invariance to small amounts of translation. Experimental results are presented for 3 different types of face recognition problems: *classification experiments* where we measure the ability of the system to identify known individuals; *false positive experiments* where we measure the ability of the system to reject images of unknown individuals; and *temporal experiments*, where we measure the ability of the system to recognize images of known individuals taken over a period of time (6 months). The results show that the proposed system performs well on all 3 of these problems.

1. Introduction

The automated face recognition problem is formulated as follows [1]. We are given a set of image samples of known individuals: **DB**. The task is to design a fully automated recognition system such that for any input image, the system does one of the following:

1. Identify the input with one of the known individuals, or

2. Reject the input as not known to the system.

Rejections can arise either because the input image is not a face, or else it is a face of an individual who is not in the database. Of course, the trick is to reliably recognize known individuals (that is, achieve a high correct classification rate) and reject all unknown individuals (that is, achieve a low false positive rate).

A block diagram of a typical template matching-based face recognition system is shown in Figure 1. The *preprocessor* is responsible for extracting the face portion of the image (from, conceivably, a much larger image containing background and clutter, etc.) and normalizing the image to a standard position, scale, etc. After segmenting and normalizing the face, typically some *feature extraction* is applied to the pixel data in order to reduce the dimensionality and/or provide some invariance to common distortions, such as translation, scaling, and rotation. Common types of feature extraction methods include eigenfaces [2], Fisherfaces, [3], and wavelets [4]. Once chosen, the methods of preprocessing and feature extraction are applied to all images in **DB** to create a *memory set* or *database* **DB-M**. Hence for each image in **DB**, **DB-M** contains the corresponding feature vector. Of course, the preprocessing and feature extraction needed to construct **DB-M** can be done in advance, and hence is an off-line computation. We will assume that **DB-M** contains multiple samples of each known individual. If there are M known individuals and K samples per individual, then

$$\mathbf{DB\text{-}M} = \{\mathbf{x}_{mk} : m = 1, 2, ..., M; k = 1, 2, ..., K\}$$

Once the feature extraction method is chosen and the database **DB-M** is constructed, a classifier system is needed to map the input image to the proper output. In this paper, we focus on template matching-based classifiers. In this case, the classifier has two main computational steps: a *matching* stage and a *decision* stage. Of course before matching can be done, we must apply the preprocessing and feature extraction to the input image (typically, the same processing that was applied to the memory set). The matching stage involves comparing the input feature vector to each of the stored feature vectors in **DB-M**. Finally, the decision stage examines the results of the matching stage and either identifies the input with a known individual, or else rejects the input.

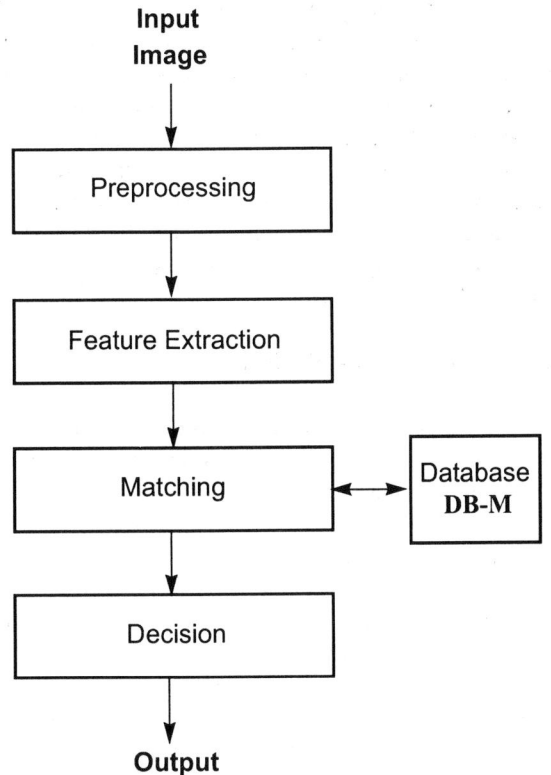

Figure 1. Main computational stages of a face recognition system.

Note that since we require the system to reject unknown individuals, the decision network must necessarily be more sophisticated than a simple min select, as used by the classical nearest neighbor algorithm (which just identifies the input with the best matching database pattern). In order to determine whether a pattern should be identified or rejected, the decision algorithm typically uses some type of *threshold*. If the best matching distance is lower than the chosen threshold, then the input is classified; otherwise it is rejected. In Section 2, we will devise a training method for computing suitable thresholds.

Even though many sophisticated neural net-based classifiers and associative memory models have been developed in the last few decades, there are several reasons why this simple type of template matching approach is so often used in practical systems. First, template matching systems typically require far less training than neural net-based approaches. Second, template matching systems are much easier to maintain. Individuals can be added to or deleted from the system by simply adding or deleting the corresponding image samples from the database. Some neural network approaches require complete retraining, even when adding or deleting a single individual.

On the other hand, there are several disadvantages associated with template matching. First, in the case of large databases, since the input has to be compared to each prototype, the system may operate too slowly. Second, template matching is sensitive to common types of distortions, such as shift, rotation, and scaling.

To address these disadvantages, a template matching-based system was devised which uses local distance measures and a voting mechanism [5, 6]. This algorithm can be called *local matching and voting network* (LMVN) and combines the parallel and distributed processing (PDP) paradigm of neural networks with the flexibility and practical advantages of template matching.

2. Review of the Local Matching and Voting Network

To address the speed problem associated with template matching systems, local distance computations are introduced which can be performed independently and hence in parallel [5]. This type of parallel and distributed processing approach is well suited for VLSI hardware implementation and fine-grained processor arrays. In addition, the proposed system offers tolerance to small amounts of image shift by allowing each window to be optimally positioned in its surrounding neighborhood.

2.1 Local Distance Calculations

To localize the distance computation, we partition both the input image **x** and the database images $\mathbf{x}_{mk}$ using non-overlapping windows, as shown in Figure 2. Matching is then determined locally between corresponding windows. For example, consider the highlighted window of the input image in Figure 2. We compute the city-block distance between this window and the corresponding windows of the database images (also highlighted). The local window determines the database image which gives the smallest distance, and casts a vote for that image. We repeat this process for all the local windows and keep track of all the votes v_{mk} received by each image in the database.

Once the local voting is done, we determine how many votes were cast for each individual by summing among all the image samples for that individual:

$$v_m = \sum_{k=1}^{K} v_{mk} \quad (1)$$

Note that, depending on the type of image samples used, we may not want to include all of the samples in the sum in (1). Rather, we can select just a portion of the samples to use. For example, for the simulations presented in Section 4, we store 4 image samples per person in the database. But when computing the vote sum, we only include the best 3 matching prototype images and not all 4. The number of prototypes to include can easily be determined by running trial simulations [6].

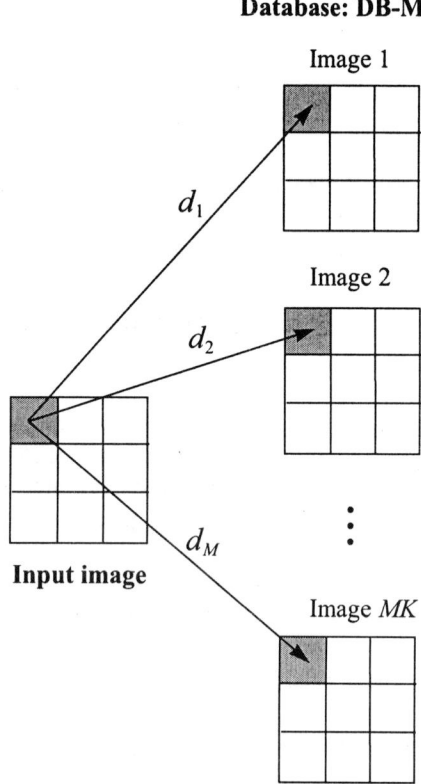

Figure 2. Schematic diagram of the voting process. Each window computes local distances and then casts a vote for the best matching image in the database.

Note that this voting network was studied both theoretically and experimentally for memory sets consisting of random binary images [5, 6]. It was found that local window size had a profound effect on system performance. In particular, it was found that the system performed best for very small and very large window sizes. In this paper, we consider the case of grayscale face images.

2.2 Optimizing Window Position for Shift Invariance

As mentioned above, template matching is sensitive to image shift. In order to provide robustness to small amounts of shift, we propose the following technique to optimize the position of the local windows during the matching process. The shift process is applied when computing the (local) distance between an input window and a database window.

First, the distance between the input window and the corresponding database window is computed and recorded. Then, we shift the input window by 1 pixel in 4 directions: north, south, east, and west and measure the resulting distance with the prototype. If the smallest of these 4 distances is smaller than the recorded distance, then we move the input window in that direction and repeat the process. The process terminates when none of the 4 distances yield a smaller value than the best recorded distance. In addition, the process terminates when a maximum number of shifts have occurred. In the experiments reported here, a maximum of 5 steps are used. A more detailed explanation of the shifting method can be found in [7].

2.3 Threshold Calculation

As mentioned above, in order for the system to determine whether to classify or reject an input, suitable thresholds are needed. In the case of the voting network, we determine closeness of match between the input and the database individuals according to number of votes received. Hence the threshold will be used to determine if the best matching individual received a sufficiently large number of votes in order to make an identification.

Unlike a typical nearest neighbor-based system where a separate threshold is needed for each individual in the database, the voting network requires only a single threshold. The threshold T is used in the following way. From the ordered list of best matching prototypes, we select the individual who received the most votes; call this individual i^*. We compare v_{i^*} to the threshold T. If v_{i^*} exceeds T, then we identify the input as individual i^*; otherwise, we reject it [6].

Now how does one determine the value of the threshold T? We propose that T be computed so as to ensure good performance on the classification task, as well as the rejection task. Hence, for the training phase, we construct a training set **TS** which contains two parts: **TS-C** (for classification training set) and **TS-FP** (for false positive training set). **TS-C** contains additional image samples of each individual in the database and is used to determine how many votes known individuals are likely to receive (addresses the correct classification ability). **TS-FP** contains image samples of unknown individuals and is used to determine how many votes strangers are likely to receive (addresses the performance on false positive experiments).

In the training phase, we store all of the desired prototypes in **DB-M**. Then for each image in **TS-C**, we perform the voting template matching process as outlined above (complete with the window alignment procedure). Since this is a training phase, we know the true identity of each image in **TS-C**. Hence we record the number of votes received by the true person. Similarly, for each image in **TS-FP**, we record the number of votes received by the samples of the best-matching database individual.

Figure 3 shows the average number of votes received by the best matching image samples in **DB-M** when the input is a known person (circle on top) and a stranger (circle on bottom). The standard deviation is also shown. For example, consider the results for the 1st best match case. This result says that when the input is a sample of, say, known individual i^*, the best matching image sample of i^* in **DB-M** receives (on average) 19.1 votes with standard deviation 7.0. However, when the input is a stranger (in **TS-FP**), the average number of votes received by the best matching image is 3.2 with standard deviation 1.2.

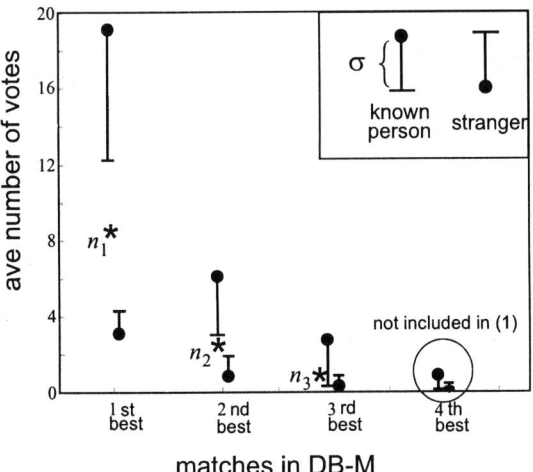

Figure 3. Average number of votes received by the best matching images in **DB-M** when the input is a known person (circle on top) and unknown person (circle on bottom). The standard deviation is indicated by the length of the attached line.

In order to find a threshold, we look for separation between the average vote values of known people and strangers. For the first 2 samples, there is clear separation in mean, and separation even if the standard deviation is taken into account. For the 3rd sample, the separation starts to disappear. However, there is such a large separation in mean (2.7 for known people and 0.3 for strangers) that we also include the 3rd sample in the sum. We don't include the 4th sample in the sum (see Eq. 1) because there is very little separation in mean.

Finally, the threshold is determined from Figure 3 by summing the average number of votes in the middle of each separation area (indicated on the graph by n_1, n_2, and n_3): $T = n_1 + n_2 + n_3$. Note that, in general, the threshold is a function of the given database $T = T(\mathbf{DB\text{-}M})$. However, at least for the relatively well-behaved CNNL database (described later) we found that T is only a function of the number of people included: $T = T(M)$. For example, if we start with a gallery of 1000 individuals and randomly choose 500 individuals to comprise **DB-M**, then a threshold of $T = 10$ will result, no matter which 500 individuals are chosen. Also, T changes relatively slowly as M increases. For example, for $M = 200$, $T = 11$, while for $M = 1000$, $T = 9$.

3. Weighted Voting

In the voting method outlined above, if we neglect the unlikely case of a tie in the distance calculation, then a local window casts only a single vote for the best matching image. All other images don't receive any votes. The idea here is that the correct person may not be first on the list, but may be second or third. We propose a weighted or fuzzy-type of voting whereby the vote is not cast as a 0-1 binary decision; rather, the vote is cast as a real number in the interval [0, 1].

To determine the proper weight of the vote, we construct a graph like the one in Figure 4.

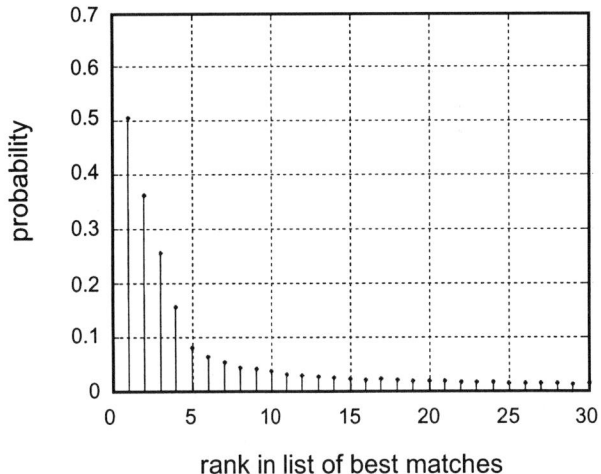

Figure 4. Probability that the correct person appears 1st, 2nd, 3rd, etc. on the list of best matching images.

This Figure shows (for each local window) the probability that the correct person is in position i on the (sorted) list of best-matching images. Note that the experiment is run one window at a time and then the results over all the windows are averaged. Consider the result for the best matching image (rank 1). Here we see a surprising result: Each window votes for the correct person only 50% of the time! But even though the local decisions are so unreliable, the overall system can achieve a very high correct classification rate. How? Well, it's due to the voting mechanism itself. The local windows will choose the correct person 50% of the time. However, the other 50% of the time, the votes are split among several different alternate candidates. When the votes are tallied, the correct person ends up with the most votes.

The weighted voting scheme is based on giving each candidate image a vote weighted by the probabilities given in Figure 4. So instead of the best matching image getting a vote of 1, it now gets a vote of 0.5. The second best matching image gets a vote of 0.36, and so on. We will compare the performance of this weighted voting scheme to the basic voting model.

4. Testing Methodology

4.1 Performance Evaluation

In this paper, we use a rigorous testing methodology to study the performance of the voting network. We will assess system performance by performing 3 different types of experiments:

1. **Correct classification experiments**. Measure the ability of the system to correctly identify known individuals. There are 3 important measures to consider here: percent correct, percent rejected, and percent misclassified. Of course since these quantities sum to 100%, only two need to be reported. We will report percent rejected and percent misclassified.

2. **False positive experiments**. Measure the ability of the system to reject individuals who are not part of the database. Here the measure of merit is the number of false positive matches (i.e., incorrectly identified as a known individual).

3. **Temporal experiments**. Measure the ability of the system to correctly classify individuals over time. In many of the publicly available face databases, the database images and the test images of each person are collected on the same day. However, in a practical setting, the database samples will nearly always be collected on a different day from the input image. Unfortunately, there are surprisingly few studies in which these type of experiments are considered.

From previous work, we have found that it is not terribly difficult to design systems that perform well on one of the above problems. But designing a system to perform well on all three problems simultaneously is quite a challenge. Unfortunately, many face recognition algorithm designs reported in the literature just report performance on the correct classification experiments. However, it is clear that a practical system must have good performance on all 3 types of problems [1].

4.2 The Database of Face Images

The CNNL face database used for the experiments reported here was collected at Wayne State University and contains 1400 different people and 10 samples of each person: 6 showing a blank facial expression, 1 with a smile, 1 with an angry expression, 1 with a look of surprise, and one with an arbitrary facial expression, where the subject tries to fool the system. A few sample images are shown in Figure 5. A detailed discussion of the construction of the face database can be found in [8]. For a few selected individuals, additional images were captured periodically over 6 months. These images will form the temporal test set.

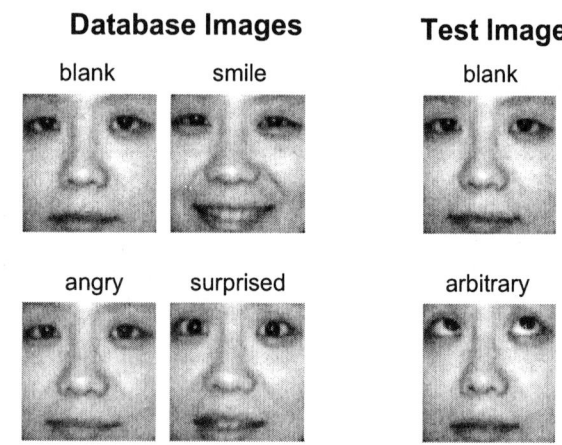

Figure 5. Samples of the database and test images.

We will partition the CNNL database in the following way. The database of stored prototypes **DB-M** will contain 1000 people and 4 image samples for each person: a blank, smile, angry, and surprised image. The training set **TS-C** will contain 4 blank images per person; **TS-FP** will contain 200 people (not in **DB-M**) and all 10 samples for each person (hence 2000 images total). The correct classification test set will contain 2 samples per person: a blank expression and the arbitrary expression. The false positive test set will contain 200 people (not in **DB-M** and not in **TS-FP**) and all 10 samples per person (hence 2000 images).

5. Results

The results of the correct classification experiments are shown in Table 1. We see that the results on the blank test images are very reliable, with 100% correct classification at less than 3% rejection. As expected, since the arbitrary test image is a much harder test set, the number of rejections are much higher. Here we have 100% correct classification with less than 23% rejection.

The results of the false positive experiments are also shown in Table 1. Both the basic voting network and the weighted voting network achieve less than 1% false positive matches.

Finally, for the temporal database, images of 3 individuals in **DB-M** were captured periodically over a period of 6 months (about 30 different sessions for each person and 10 samples taken each time). The classification results on this database are: 100% correct classification (0% misclassification) with 9% rejection for the basic voting method and 5.7% rejection for the weighted voting method. The high rejection rate here is indicative of the difficulty of the temporal classification problem [9].

Test Set	Basic Voting (%)		Weighted Voting (%)	
	Reject	Misclass.	Reject	Misclass.
Classification blank expression	1.1	0	0.8	0
Classification arbitrary Expression	26.7	0	22.0	0
False Positive	-	0.5	-	0.7
Temporal	9.0	0	5.7	0

Table 1. False positive performance for the voting network. The results are reported as %Rejection and %Misclassification.

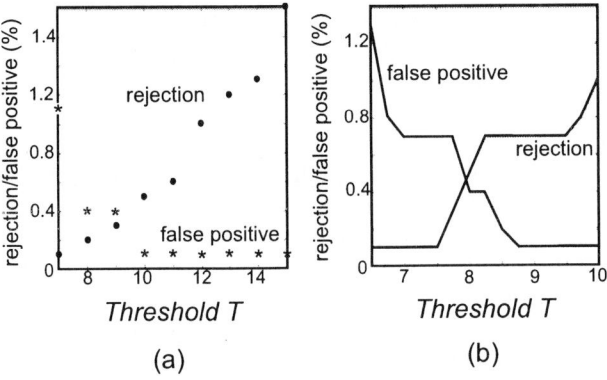

Figure 6. The false positive and reject rates for (a) the basic voting method and (b) weighted voting.

As with most practical systems, there is no one optimal solution or operating point. In the case of the proposed voting network, system performance is determined by the value of the threshold. Figure 6 shows how the performance of the system varies as a function of the threshold T. Notice that the threshold plot is discrete for the standard voting and continuous for the weighted voting. Although both voting methods perform nearly equally well, the weighted voting offers more flexibility in that there are more operating points to choose from (continuous choice of T rather than discrete).

References

1. Chellappa, R., Wilson, C., and Sirohey, S. (1995). "Human and Machine Recognition of Faces: A Survey," *Proceedings of the IEEE*, **83**(5), 705-740.

2. Turk, M., and Pentland, A. (1991). "Eigenfaces for Recognition," *J. Cognitive Neuroscience*, **3**(1), 71-86.

3. Belhumeur, P., Hespanha, J., and Kreigman, D. (1997). "Eigenfaces vs. Fisherfaces: Recognition using Class Specific Linear Projection," *IEEE Transactions on Pattern Analysis and Machine Intelligence*, **19**(7), 711-720.

4. Duc, B. and Fischer, S. (1999). "Face Authentication with Gabor Information on Deformable Graphs," *IEEE Transactions on Image Processing*, **8**(4), 504-516.

5. Ikeda, N., Watta, P., Artiklar, M, and Hassoun, M., (2001). "A Two-level Hamming Network for High Performance Associative Memory," *Neural Networks*, **14**, 1189-1200.

6. Artiklar, M. (2002). *Capacity Analysis of Voting Networks with Application to Human Face Recognition*, Ph D. Thesis, Dept. Electrical and Computer Engineering, Wayne State Univbersaity, Detroit, MI.

7. Artiklar, M., Hassoun, M., and Watta, P. (1999). "Application of a Postprocessing Algorithm for Improved Human Face Recognition," *Proceedings of the IEEE International Conference on Neural Networks*, IJCNN-1999, July 10-16, 1999, Washington, DC., Paper #JCNN 2166.

8. Watta, P., Artiklar, M., Masadeh, A., and Hassoun, M. H. (2000). "Construction and Analysis of a Database of Face Images which Requires Minimal Preprocessing," *Proceedings of the IASTED Conference on Modeling and Simulation MS'2000*, May 15-17, 2000, Pittsburg Pennsylvania, .

9. Phillips, P., Moon, H., Rizvi, S., and Rauss, P. (2000). "The FERET Evaluation Methodology for Face-Recognition Algorithms," *IEEE Transactions on Pattern Analysis and Machine Intelligence*, **22**(10), 1090-1104.

Application of Four-layer Neural Network on Information Extraction

Min Han, Lei Cheng and Hua Meng

School of Electronic and Information Engineering

Dalian University of Technology

Dalian, 116023, China

E-mail: minhan@dlut.edu.cn

Abstract-This paper applies neural network to extract marsh information. An adaptive back-propagation algorithm based on a robust error function is introduced to build a four-layer neural network, and it is used to classify Thematic Mapper (TM) image of Zhalong Wetland in China and then extract marsh information. Comparing marsh information extraction results of the four-layer neural network with three-layer neural network and the maximum likelihood classifier, conclusion can be drawn as follows: the structure of the four-layer neural network and the adaptive back-propagation algorithm based on the robust error function is effective to extract marsh information. The four-layer neural network adopted in this paper succeeded in building the complex model of TM image, and it avoided the problem of great storage of remotely sensed data, and the adaptive back-propagation algorithm speeded up the descending of error. Above all, the four-layer neural network is superior to the three-layer neural network and the maximum likelihood classifier in the accuracy of the total classification and marsh information extraction.

Index Terms- Remote sensing, Neural network, Information extraction, Marsh

I. INTRODUCTION

Remotely sensed images distinguish different landform mainly through the different brightness of pixels. Different brightness of pixels shows the different information of spectrum. According to this, classifying the land cover to categories and then extracting needed category is an important application of the remotely sensed images. Traditionally, the ways to classify the land cover are based on the Bayesian classifier. It is well known that the Bayesian classifier is theoretically optimal if the assumptions about the probability density functions (PDF's) are correct. Poor performance may be obtained if the true PDF's are different from those assumed by the model (Heermann and Khazenie, 1992). The need to have a specific probabilistic model is a major limitation of the Bayesian approach. Maximum likelihood classification is based on the Bayesian classifier. It has the minimum value of classification error probability. We assume all kinds of targets on the ground submit to normal distribution when we conduct the statistic classification of image. According to this assumption, a distribution of a response pattern can be completely presented by the mean vector and variance. The statistic probability of some pixel belonging to each category can be computed through these parameters.

Artificial neural network has been greatly applied in the field of classification and information extraction of remotely sensed image, especially back-propagation neural network classifier. Back-propagation neural network has succeeded in realizing the supervised classification of remotely sensed image (Kanellopoulos and Wilkinson 1997, Li 1998). Yang and Zhou (2001) presented a classification method based on knowledge. Compared with traditional method, neural network does not need the probability pattern but becomes a classifier by its adaptive learning ability. It starts with an inherently parallel processing, adaptive learning and nonlinear technique. The problems solved by neural network usually focus on the small data sets less than 200 patterns. However, remotely sensed image has great training data sets usually more than 1000. Therefore, we should select the network structure and learning algorithm carefully when we use neural network to classify the remotely sensed image and extract needed category, so that neural network can solve the problems more efficiently and precisely.

Multilayer feed-forward neural networks realize the complex nonlinear mapping. Single-hidden-layer structure can solve most classification and information extraction problems, but if samples are comparatively complex, that is, they are highly in discretization, two-hidden-layer neural network can be adopted (Zhang 1999). The general back-propagation has some disadvantages, such as long-time training and difficulty of converge etc. Bruzzone and Serpico (1997) presented a technique—training for two steps—to accelerate the training time. Du et al. (1998) introduced Conjugate gradient with line search (CGL) to optimize the learning rate. In this paper, the model of remotely sensed image is built with a four-layer feed-forward neural network, and an adaptive back-propagation algorithm based on a robust error function is introduced to avoid the problem of long-time training and difficulty of convergence. Comparing the four-layer neural network with the three-layer neural network and the maximum likelihood method through the analysis of classification process and marsh information extraction results, conclusion can be drawn that the four-layer neural network is able to perform best in the accuracy of the marsh information extraction.

II. ALGORITHM DESCRIPTION OF BP NEURAL NETWORK

Land cover classification of remotely sensed image should be done before marsh information extraction. The main idea of remotely sensed image classification using neural network is to make the feature of the image as the input signals, to train the neural network following some rule, then to classify output signals. In this paper, a four-layer neural network with two-hidden-layer is used to build the model of remotely sensed data. In figure 1 the structure of the four-layer neural network is shown.

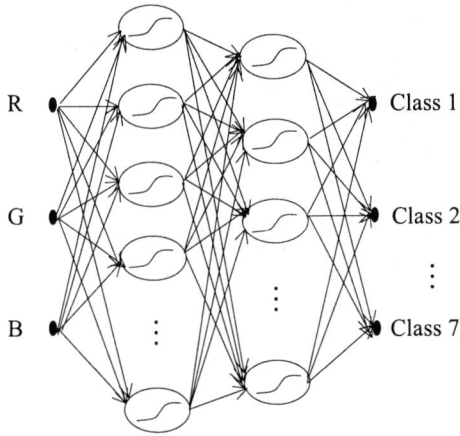

Fig.1. Structure of four-layer feed-forward neural network

In all kinds of algorithms of neural network, the back-propagation algorithm has gained nearly full development. However, it still has several limitations, for example, it easily falls into local minimum, cannot acquire the global optimum solution, its convergence rate is slow and so on. It is difficult to determine the learning rate, but the learning rate is the key to influence the efficiency of the back-propagation learning algorithm (Zhou et al. 2001, Wang et al. 2001). In normal back-propagation learning algorithm, the value of learning rate is constant. However, the optimum learning rate should be adjusted on line; training process is done under the direction of summed squared error function and reaches the minimum through the weight adjustment. This kind of error function is sensitive to the great error (Xia and Bian 1998). In this paper, a robust error function is adopted to train the neural network, and an adaptive back-propagation algorithm, which is later proved to suit to classify the TM image of Zhalong wetland in China, is introduced to adjust the learning rate on line. The principle of the learning algorithm is introduced as following:

Firstly, define the new robust error function $\varphi(\varepsilon)$ under the following conditions ($\varepsilon = d_j(k) - y_j(k)$ is called the remain error):

(a) $\varphi(\varepsilon) = 0$, when $\varepsilon = 0$;

(b) $\varphi(\varepsilon)$ is continuous everywhere;

(c) $\varphi(\varepsilon)$ is symmetrical;

(d) $\Phi(\varepsilon) = \dfrac{\partial \varphi(\varepsilon)}{\partial \varepsilon} \geq 0$, when $\varepsilon \geq 0$;

(e) $\lim_{\varepsilon \to \infty} \Phi(\varepsilon) = 0$.

Typically, $\varphi(\varepsilon)$ can be selected as:

$$\varphi(\varepsilon) = \frac{\varepsilon^2}{b + a\varepsilon^2} \quad (1)$$

Then

$$\Phi(\varepsilon) = \frac{\partial \varphi(\varepsilon)}{\partial \varepsilon} = \frac{2b\varepsilon}{(b + a\varepsilon^2)^2} \quad (2)$$

The parameter a, b in equation should be selected according to the actual need. In this paper, we selected $a=1$, $b=2$.

From the above equation, we can see that $\Phi(\varepsilon)$ is changing normally when ε is small. However, the increasing speed of $\Phi(\varepsilon)$ drops when ε is bigger, this leads to depress the influence of great error. Therefore, $\varphi(\varepsilon)$ is a robust function. When $a=0$, $b=1$, we have $\Phi(\varepsilon) = \varepsilon^2$, which is the error energy function in normal back-propagation learning algorithm.

Suppose the number of samples is P. Input a sample whose serial number is k, then the algorithm flow can be described as follows:

Step 1) Forward-propagation process, The relation is

$$y_j^l(k) = f(\sum_i \omega_{ji}^l(k) y_i^{l-1}(k) - \theta_j^l) \quad (3)$$

where $y_j^l(k)$ is the output of the j-th unit of the l-th layer. $\omega_{ji}^l(k)$ is the weight connecting i-th unit of the $(l-1)$-th layer and j-th unit of the l-th layer. θ_j^l is threshold value of the j-th unit of the l-th layer. $f(\cdot)$ is the active function. The active function of the hidden layer is nonlinear function usually, such as a sigmoid function and a hyperbolic function.

Step 2) Back-propagation process. It is also the adjustment process of the weight. The relation is:

$$\omega_{ji}^l(k+1) = \omega_{ji}^l(k) + \mu(k) \cdot \Delta\omega_{ji}^l(k) \quad (4)$$

where μ is the adaptive learning rate, $\Delta\omega_{ji}^l(k)$ is the adjusted value of the weight. It can be carried out through the gradient descent algorithm.

$$\Delta \omega_{ji}^l(k) = \delta_j^l(k) \cdot y_i^{l-1}(k) \quad (5)$$

For output units, we have
$$\delta_j(k+1) = y_j(k)[1-y_j(k)]\Phi(\varepsilon_j) \quad (6)$$

For hidden units, we have
$$\delta_j^l(k+1) = y_j^l(k)[1-y_j^l(k)] \cdot \sum_q \delta_q^{l+1}(k)\omega_{qj}^{l+1}(k) \quad (7)$$

Train the neural network by inputing the neural network input-output samples. When P samples have been input, compute the total squared error E, which can be defined as
$$E = \frac{1}{2P}\sum_{k=1}^P \sum_{j=1}^m \varphi(\varepsilon_j(k)) \quad (8)$$

Step 3) Input P samples again and compare the total error acquired in two epochs. Suppose k is the serial number of circulation. The comparative results could be divided to three situation:

(1). If $E_k < E_{k-1}$, that is the error is descending, learning direction is right, learning rate μ can be increased as follows:
$$\mu'_{k+1} = \beta \cdot \mu_k \quad (\beta \geq 1) \quad (9)$$
If $\mu'_{k+1} > \mu_{max}$, $\mu_{k+1} = \mu_{max}$, otherwise $\mu_{k+1} = \mu'_{k+1}$.

(2). If $E_k > E_{k-1}$, it shows that learning step length is too long, then
$$\mu'_{k+1} = \alpha \cdot \mu_k \quad (\alpha < 1) \quad (10)$$
If $\mu'_{k+1} < \mu_{min}$, $\mu_{k+1} = \mu_{min}$, otherwise $\mu_{k+1} = \mu'_{k+1}$.

(3). If $E_k > \lambda E_{k-1}$ ($\lambda > 1$), make k-th learning result unused, decrease the learning rate and train the neural network again.

In a word, TM image model of Zhalong wetland is established by four-layer feed-forward neural network; training process is done under direction of a robust error function and weight value is adjusted by the adaptive back-propagation algorithm.

III. MARSH INFORMATION EXTRACTION OF ZHALONG WETLAND USING NEURAL NETWORK

In this paper, a four-layer feed-forward neural network is adopted to classify the TM image model of Zhalong wetland and then extract marsh information. The information extraction results are compared with three-layer feed-forward neural network and the maximum likelihood classifier.

A. Research area and its data

Our research area, that is named Zhalong protected district, lies in the the lower reaches of Wuyuer river in the west of Heilongjiang province in China. Its geographic coordinate is 46°52'~ 47°32'N and 123°47'~124°37'E. Zhalong protected district is an upcountry wetland and ecosystem which is mostly covered by reed marsh, and it is the most complete, original and broad wetland ecosystem in the north of China compared to area of the same latitude. It has been listed in the international important wetland contents. Therefore, it is important to monitor the marsh change. Marsh information extraction from the remotely sensed image is an effective way to acquire the situation of the marsh.

The data we used for land cover classification and information extraction is half of a Landsat TM scene of the surroudings of Zhalong wetland. Date of TM image of Zhalong wetland acquisition is October 5, 2001.

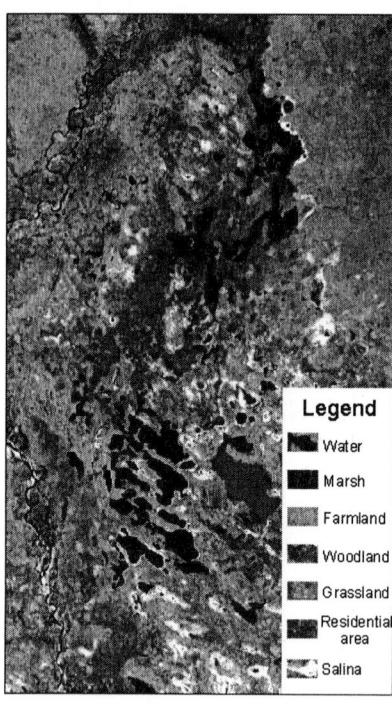

Fig. 2. Bands 4,3,2 composite image

The TM scene contains seven bands. In this research, we use combination of TM band 4, 3 and 2 to create a false color composite as seen in figure 2, which is suitable for land cover classification. The image was interpreted by comprehensive analysis and compared with map of land use and ability of visual interpreters. Then seven classes were confirmed in the region of TM image, which include water, marsh, farmland, woodland, grassland, residential area and salina.

B. Build the neural network model

1) Select the training and testing data

According to the results of visual interpreter, we select 1500 pixels from the false color composite to train the network and 700 pixels to test the network. The maximum likelyhood classifier adopted the same samples. Table 1 shows the sample examples of every class in training sets and the numbers of every class samples, where TM4, TM3 and TM2 respectively presents the sample value of TM band 4, 3 and 2.

Before classification of remotely sensed image using neural network classifier, the samples should be changed into the region of [0,1]. In this way, the supersaturated phenomenon could be avoided.

TABLE 1
SAMPLE EXAMPLES OF TRAINING SETS

class \ band	TM4	TM3	TM2	number
water	18	63	93	400
marsh	112	97	99	200
farmland	195	190	162	200
woodland	147	67	92	100
grassland	73	90	106	300
residential area	85	133	140	200
salina	215	255	253	100

2) Confirm the parameter of input and output units of the network

The number of input units is three according to RGB color, and the number of output units is seven according to the number of categories. Each output unit presents a kind of category. The output vector can be described as follows: (0.9,0.1,0.1,0.1,0.1,0.1,0.1),(0.1,0.9,0.1,0.1,0.1,0.1,0.1), ⋯ , (0.1,0.1,0.1,0.1,0.1,0.1,0.9). An input pattern will be divided to i-th category if it has the highest output value in i-th unit.

The number of hidden layers and the number of hidden units are obtained by experiments. In the experiments, we found out that single hidden layer network structure cannot get the needed accuracy. When we adopted the two hidden layer network structure, we found out that the number of first hidden layer should be at least twice the number of input layer units. The number of second hidden layer should at least be the larger one of the input units and the output units. If we increase the number of the hidden layer units, accuracy can be improved, but it needs more learning time.

Parameters of the neural network can be obtained by such method. The result is, the number of the input units is three; the number of the hidden layer is two; the number of first hidden layer units is eight; the number of second hidden layer units is seven; the number of the output units is seven; the initial learning rate is 0.1; the initial weight and threshold value is random numbers. The structure of the neural network is shown in figure 1.

3) Compare the classification and extraction results of neural network and maximum likelihood classifier

The classification process of neural network is mainly realized by two steps. The first step is to train the network according to the samples; the second step is to classify the whole remotely sensed data using learning results.

Firstly, we should input the training data into the model of the neural network and train the neural network. The four-layer neural network adopts the adaptive back-propagation learning algorithm introduced in this paper and the three-layer neural network adopts normal back-propagation learning algorithm. The learning error curve of the three-layer neural network and the four-layer neural network are shown in figure 3, where error is computed by summed squared error function. We can see the error of four layer neural network falls faster than the three layer neural network, and the convergence error is also lowest than the three layer neural network. Therefore, the two hidden layer structure can reach more accurate degree compared with the single layer structure. At the same time we found out that the error function would not be convergent in simulation if we didn't adopt the adaptive learning algorithm. It was noticeable that the robust error function makes the training time shorter comparing with normal summed squared error function.

The error matrix can be obtained from the classification results of test samples. The classification error matrices of four-layer neural network, three-layer neural network and maximum likelihood method are respectively shown in table 2, table 3 and table 4. From the three tables, we can see that the four-layer neural network can get best classification results. Three-layer neural network mistook other classes of land cover as marsh and maximum likelihood classifier had weak ability to judge the grassland and residential area.

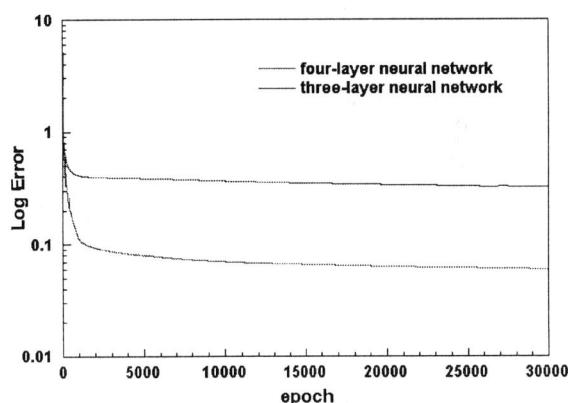

Fig.3. Learning error curve of four-layer and three-layer neural network

Classification accuracy calculations on pixels are based on the error matrix. Accuracy of each class can be calculated by the error matrix showed in table 2, table 3 and table 4. As seen in table 5, four-layer neural network can obtain highest accuracy of each class.

In most cases, the integrated classification accuracy reflects the total effect of classification. The integrated classification accuracy is average classifier accuracy. The integrated classification accuracy of four-layer neural network, three-layer neural network and maximum likelihood classifier is respectively 97.29%, 92.43% and 89.43%. It shows that the classification result of four-layer neural network is better than three-layer neural network and maximum likelihood classifier in integrated accuracy, which presents that the four-layer neural network adopted in this paper is more suitable to build complicated model of TM image.

After the classification of the whole remotely sensed image using trained neural network and maximum likelihood classifier, the result images of marsh information extraction are obtained and shown in figure 4 (a), (b) and (c). Since the four-layer neural network can get highest accuracy of each category (including marsh), the accuracy of marsh information extraction is highest.

TABLE 2
THE ERROR MATRIX OF FOUR-LAYER NEURAL NETWORK CLASSIFICATION

practice \ class	water	marsh	farmland	woodland	grassland	residential area	salina	total
water	99	0	0	0	0	2	0	101
marsh	0	98	0	2	0	0	0	100
farmland	0	1	100	2	0	0	0	103
woodland	0	0	0	96	0	0	0	96
grassland	0	1	0	0	93	3	0	97
residential area	1	0	0	0	7	95	0	103
salina	0	0	0	0	0	0	100	100
total	100	100	100	100	100	100	100	700

TABLE 3
THE ERROR MATRIX OF THREE-LAYER NEURAL NETWORK CLASSIFICATION

practice \ class	water	marsh	farmland	woodland	grassland	residential area	salina	total
water	97	2	0	0	0	2	0	101
marsh	1	83	0	0	7	0	0	91
farmland	0	5	87	1	1	0	0	94
woodland	0	0	0	94	0	0	0	94
grassland	0	10	13	5	92	4	0	124
residential area	2	0	0	0	0	94	0	96
salina	0	0	0	0	0	0	100	100
total	100	100	100	100	100	100	100	700

TABLE 4
THE ERROR MATRIX OF MAXIMUM LIKELIHOOD CLASSIFICATION

practice \ class	water	marsh	farmland	woodland	grassland	residential area	salina	total
water	87	0	0	0	0	4	0	91
marsh	6	95	4	2	22	0	0	129
farmland	0	2	95	0	4	0	0	101
woodland	0	0	0	96	0	0	0	96
grassland	0	3	1	2	66	9	0	81
residential area	7	0	0	0	8	87	0	102
salina	0	0	0	0	0	0	100	100
total	100	100	100	100	100	100	100	700

TABLE 5
ACCURACY OF THE THREE METHODS

method \ class	water	marsh	farmland	woodland	grassland	residential area	salina	average accuracy
four-layer neural network	99.00%	98.00%	100.00%	96.00%	93.00%	95.00%	100.00%	97.29%
three-layer neural network	97.00%	83.00%	87.00%	94.00%	92.00%	94.00%	100.00%	92.43%
maximum likelihood	87.00%	95.00%	95.00%	96.00%	66.00%	87.00%	100.00%	89.43%

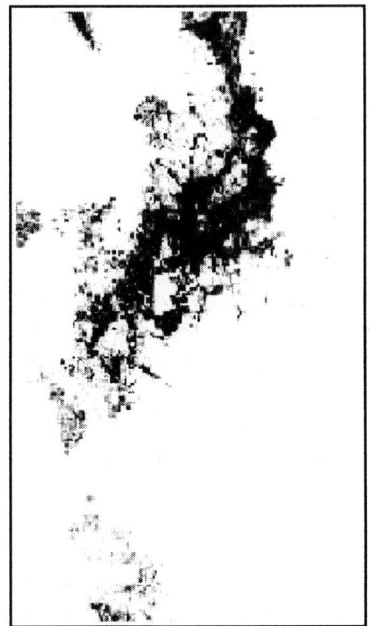 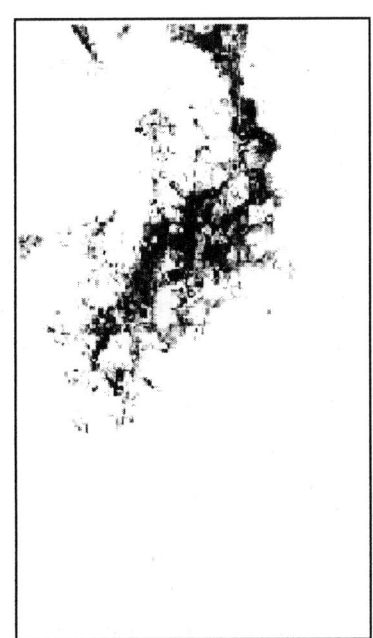 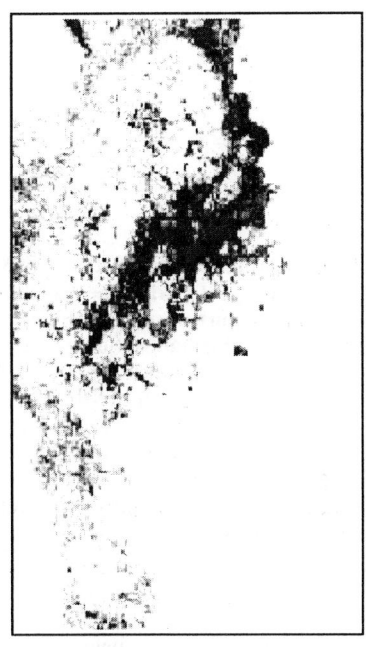

(a) Marsh information extraction with four-layer neural network

(b) Marsh information extraction with three-layer neural network

(c) Marsh information extraction with maximum likelihood classifier

Fig.4. Marsh information extraction results with three methods

IV. CONCLUSION

The four-layer neural network and the adaptive back-propagation algorithm based on the robust error function appear to be feasible to classify the TM image of Zhalong wetland and extract marsh information. Compared to three-layer neural network, four-layer neural network could avoid the burden of large storage; Compared to the traditional maximum likelihood classifier, neural network needs not to assume the model of probability but acquires weight value through learning ability then becomes a classifier. Therefore, it avoided the error made by the imprecise probability model. From the simulation results, mistaken and lack classification phenomena of four-layer neural network decreased greatly. Therefore, the classification and information extraction accuracy of four-layer neural network is superior to three-layer neural network and the maximum likelihood classifier; the adaptive back-propagation learning algorithm based on the error robust function avoids the divergence of error function, decreases the general error to a smaller degree and accelerates the learning rate. These lead the marsh information extraction to be conducted successfully. Other neural network structure and algorithm should be taken to try to improve the information extraction accuracy.

ACKNOWLEDGEMENTS

This research is supported by the project (50139020) of the National Natural Science Foundation of China. All of these supports are appreciated.

REFERENCES

[1] Philip D. Heermann and Nahid Khazenie. (1992). Classification of multispectral remote sensing data using a back-propagation neural network. IEEE Transactions On Geoscience and Remote Sensing, 30, (1), 81-88.

[2] I.Kanellopoulos. (1997). G.Wilkinson. Strategies and best practice for neural network image classification. Remote Sensing, 18(4), 711-725.

[3] Li Zuoyong. (1998). Supervised classification of multispectral remote sensing image using B-P neural network. J. Infrared Millim. Waves, 17(2), 153-156.

[4] Yang Cunjian and Zhou Chenghu. (2001). Investigation on classification of remote sensing image on the basis of knowledge. Geography and Territorial Research, 17(1), 72-77.

[5] Zhang Jianbao. (1999). Construction of a neural network on remote sensing image classification. Journal of Image and Graphics, 4 (A), (10), 831-834.

[6] L.Bruzzone, S.B.Serpico. (1997). Classification of imbalanced remote-sensing data by neural networks. Pattern Recognition Letters, 18, 1323-1328.

[7] Du Huiqian, Mei Wenbo, and Li Desheng. (1998). Classification of remote sensing images using BP neural network with dynamic learning rate. Journal of Beijing Institute of Technology, 18(4), 485-488.

[8] Zhou Chenghu, Luo Jiancheng, Yang Xiaomei, Yang Cunjian and Liu Qingsheng. (2001). Geography Understanding and Analysis of Remotely Sensed Image (pp. 229-239). Beijing: Science Press,.

[9] Wang Yaonan, Li shutao and Mao Jianxu. (2001). Image Processing and Recognition with Computer (pp.197-205). Beijing: Higher Education Press,.

[10] Xia Guoqing and Bian Xinqian. (1998). BP algorithm based on robust error function. Journal of Harbin Engineering University, 19(3), 33-37.

Submodular Neural Network is better than Modular Neural Network and Support Vector Machines for Personal Verification

Takashi Nagano, Makoto Hirahara and Hideo Eguchi
Faculty of Engineering, Hosei University
3-7-2 Kajinocho Koganei-shi, Tokyo 184-8584, Japan
Email: nagano@k.hosei.ac.jp

Abstract— A sub-modular neural network (SMNN) proposed a few years ago is compared with the usual modular neural network (MNN) and support vector machines (SVM) in terms of pattern recognition performance. Some computer simulation results showed that SMNN was much superior to MNN and SVM as for rejection rates of patterns in unlearned classes under the condition that they gave almost the same recognition rates for patterns in learned classes. These results strongly suggest that SMNN is more suitable for personal verification systems than the other two as such systems require high rejection rate for patterns in unlearned classes.

I. INTRODUCTION

Neural network techniques have been recognized to be one of the most useful methods for pattern recognition problems. Among them, modular neural networks [1–3] and support vector machines [4] are thought to have good performances for multi-class pattern recognition. In order to use these techniques for the purpose, a given problem has to be divided into smaller and simpler subproblems. The usual way to do this is to divide a K-class problem into K subproblems each of which classifies each corresponding class from all the other $K-1$ classes. This way of division, however, sometimes causes the reduction of recognition rate because subproblems themselves are still complex when the original problem is large-scaled and very complex. Recently a useful technique was proposed to give a solution to this problem [5]. Hereafter we call this technique the submodular neural network (SMNN). It divides each subproblem into smaller mini-problems and integrates solutions of these mini-problems to get the solution of the subproblem. In an extreme case a subproblem is divided into $K-1$ mini-problems each of which classifies the class corresponding to the subproblem from one of the other classes. So, this way of division requires $K(K-1)/2$ classifiers for a K-class problem. The submodular neural network was shown to have better performance in training speed and learning accuracy.

We applied this technique to personal verification using biometric cues, and compared its performance with those of the usual modular neural network (MNN) and support vector machines (SVM). The results are shown in the following sections that SMNN has much superior performance to MNN and SVM in rejecting patterns of unlearned classes. As the rejection of unlearned classes is the most important point in personal verification systems, SMNN is thought to be very appropriate for such systems.

II. RECOGNITION TECHNIQUES

Three neural network techniques for pattern recognition used in this paper are briefly described in this section. The two of these, MNN and SVM, are well-known techniques. SMNN is a kind of MNN, but is composed of more modules with simpler structure than MNN. We compare experimentally the performance of three distinct recognition systems using the three techniques.

A. MNN

The structure of MNN is shown in Fig.1. It has the same number of modules as that of classes. Inputs are fed in parallel to all the modules. Each module classifies its corresponding class from all the other classes. These modules can generally be any two-category classifier. In our case each module is a three layered neural network with one output unit. The usual back-propagation algorithm is used to train each module. The modular neural network has been shown to have better recognition performance than the usual layered neural network in which each neuron in a layer is connected to all the neurons in the succeeding layer [3].

B. SMNN

SMNN is an improved version of MNN. A task of each module in this case is decomposed into smaller subtasks. A subtask is to classify the corresponding class of a module from some (not all) of the other classes. Each submodule solves its corresponding subtask. It is trained to give output 1 to the corresponding class and 0 to all the other classes to be trained. Each module in SMNN is composed of the same number of submodules as that of the subtasks. The output of a module is given by the minimum value of all the submodules in the module. SMNN was shown to have better performance in training speed and learning accuracy than MNN [5].

An extreme case of decomposition of a task of a module is that each subtask is to classify the class corresponding to the module from only one of the other classes as is shown in Fig.2. So, this way of decomposition requires $K(K-1)/2$ classifiers for a K-class problem. In this paper we used this decomposition. Each submodule is a three layered neural network of smaller scale in our case.

C. SVM

SVM is a kind of linear classifier that classifies input patterns $x = (x_1, \cdots, x_n)^T$ into two classes according to

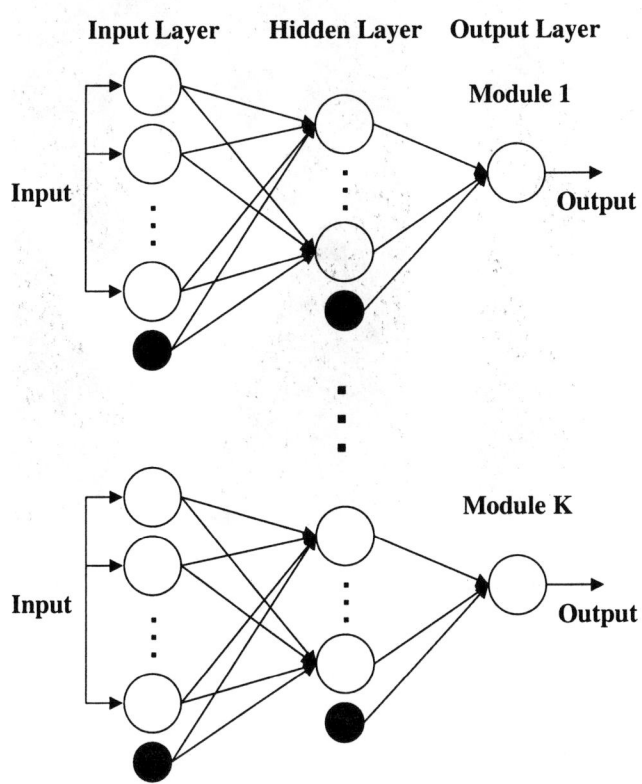

Fig. 1. Structure of MNN. K is the number of classes. An input vector is in parallel fed to K modules.

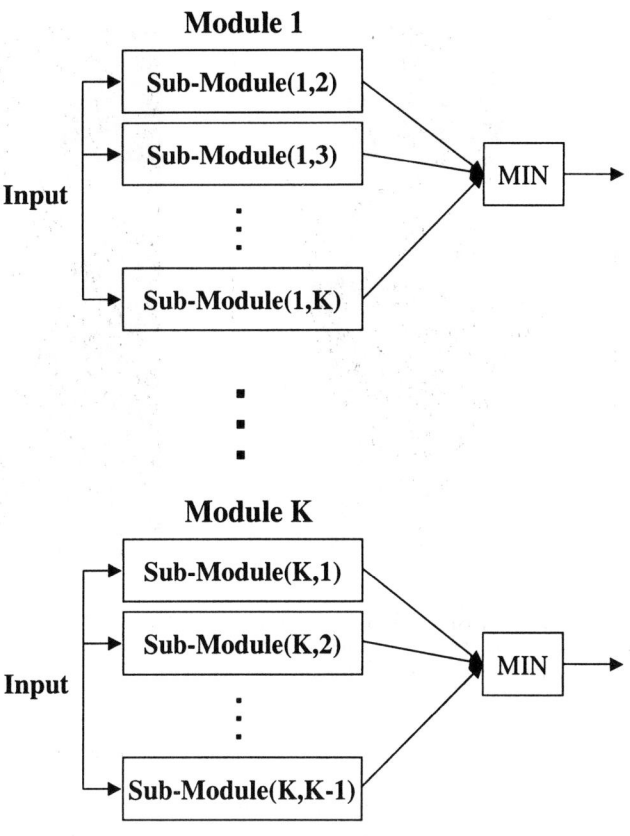

Fig. 2. Structure of SMNN.

the linear discriminant function $f(x) = w \cdot x + b$, where w is a parameter vector called "weight vector", and b is a parameter called "bias". In SVM w is determined so as to maximize the distances from the decision hyperplane to the patterns in the two classes which are nearest to the hyperplane assuming that the two classes are linearly separable. This assumption is not realistic because most practical problems are not linearly separable. To solve this problem, the original patterns x are mapped into a higher order space by using a nonlinear mapping function $\phi(\cdot)$. It is assumed that the inner product of any two patterns in the higher order space $\phi(x) \cdot \phi(x')$ is given by a kernel function $K(x, x')$. Then it is known that the discriminant function satisfying the above condition is given by

$$f(\phi(x)) = \sum a_i d_i K(x, x_i) + b$$

, where d_i is the target value of x_i, and a_i is a parameter value determined by a learning algorithm. Note that we don't have to know the exact form of $\phi(\cdot)$ describing the linear discriminant function in the higher order space. Polynomial kernel function and Gaussian kernel function defined in the following equations are used in this paper.

$$K(x, x') = (x \cdot x' + 1)^p \quad (1)$$
$$K(x, x') = \exp(-\|x - x'\|^2 / \sigma^2) \quad (2)$$

, where p and σ are some positive constants.

In this paper we use one SVM to classify a class corresponding to it from all the other class. This means that we use K SVMs for a K-class problem. So, SVM system is also a kind of modular systems. The difference between MNN and SVM is that they use different classifiers as a module.

III. INPUT PATTERNS

We use handshape as a biometric cue for personal verification. It is thought to be one of the useful physical characteristics [7], [8]. Images of right hands were taken by using an image scanner (716x573 pixels, 256 gray levels and 75dpi). As shown in Fig.3, the top and the left side of the middle finger were fitted to the guide bars, and five fingers were separated freely each other when a user put the right hand on the scanner. No other positional restrictions were imposed. An original hand image was segmented from its background with an appropriate threshold [9]. 11 feature points P1,P2,$\cdots$,P11 (see Fig.4 and Table 1) were extracted from it with a simple algorithm. 19 features shown in Fig.5 were selected based on the results of statistical analysis on 1920 images of 40 persons (48 images/person). 18 features were line segments connecting two feature points and the rest one was the area of the white part in the segmented hand image in Fig.5. So, each input pattern was composed by using some or all of these feature values.

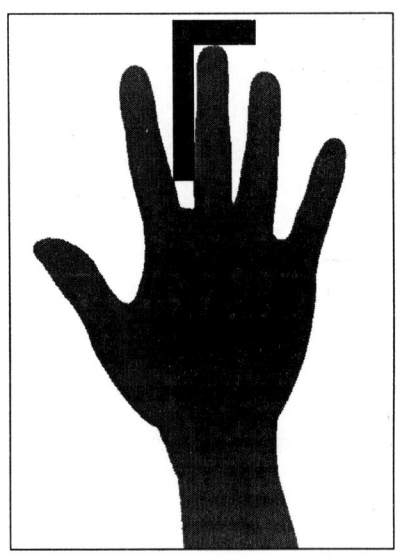 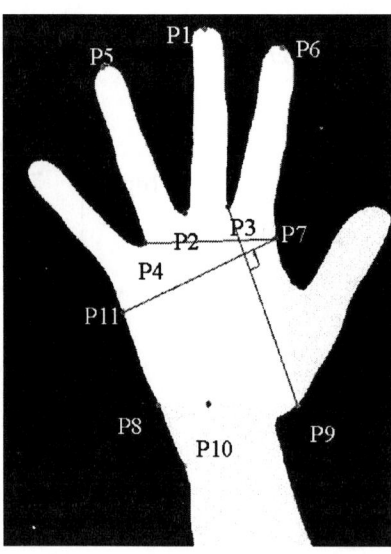 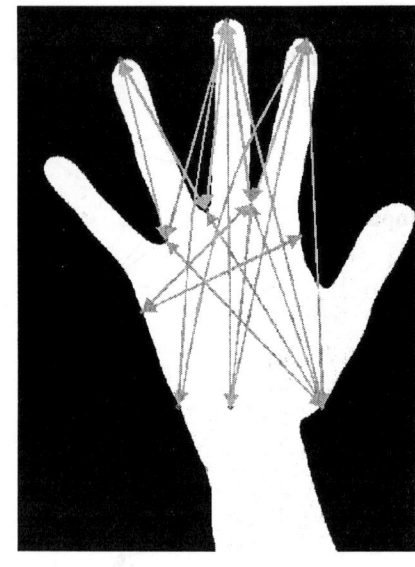

Fig. 3. How to put the right hand on a scanner. Black angle on the top of the square is guide bars to fix the position of the middle finger.

Fig. 4. 11 feature points to define features of handshape.

Fig. 5. 19 features used in experiments.

TABLE I
DEFINITION OF 11 FEATURE POINTS

P1	Top of the middle finger.
P2	Bottom of the trough between the middle finger and the third finger.
P3	Bottom of the trough between the index finger and the middle finger.
P4	Bottom of the trough between the third finger and the little finger.
P5	Top of the third finger.
P6	Top of the index finger.
P7	Cross point of the left outline of the palm and the bottom horizontal line crossing P4.
P8	Cross point of the left outline of the palm and the bottom horizontal line of the hand part. The bottom horizontal line is defined by the vertical position at which the horizontal width of hand image is equal to 0.9×(length of the middle finger) around the wrist.
P9	Cross point of the right outline of the palm and the bottom horizontal line of the hand part.
P10	Cross point of the vertical line crossing P1 and the horizontal line connecting P8 and P9.
P11	Cross point of the left outline of the palm and the line crossing P7 which is orthogonal to the line connecting P3 and P9.

IV. Verification Experiments

In our experiments, 2880 patterns of 60 persons (48 patterns/person) were used in order to examine the performance of the three recognition techniques. 800 patterns of 40 persons (20patterns/person) were used to train the three systems. So, our identification systems have 40 registrants. The rest patterns of the registrants (28 patterns/person) were used for test. 960 patterns of non-registrants (48 patterns/person) were used to check how well the three systems rejected input patterns other than those of the registrants.

A. Criteria for Verification

An input pattern with the name of a registrant (class) is given to the module corresponding to the registrant. In MNN and SMNN the pattern is accepted as that of the registrant if its output exceeds a certain threshold. It is rejected if it does not exceed the threshold. In SVM an input pattern is accepted as a correct one if its output of SVM is positive and rejected as a wrong one if its output is zero or negative.

B. Results

We tried five cases of the numbers of features: 15,16,17,18 and 19. The five cases gave similar performances. So, we describe only the results on the case of 15 features in the following. These features were selected from all the features of handshape according to the ratio of between-class variance to within-class variance. We assumed that a feature with a larger ratio was a better one.

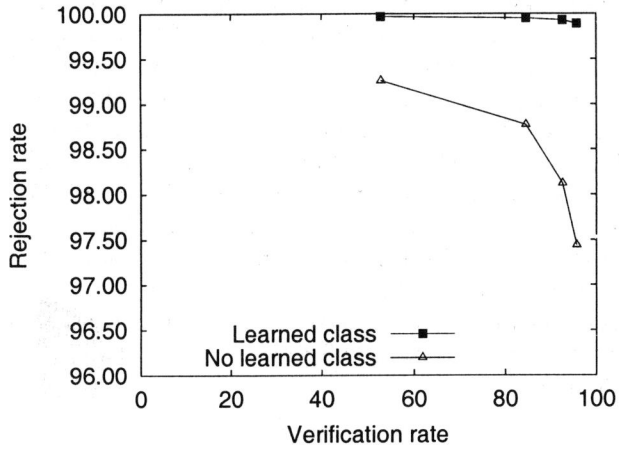

Fig. 6. Relation between verification rate and rejection rate in the case of MNN.

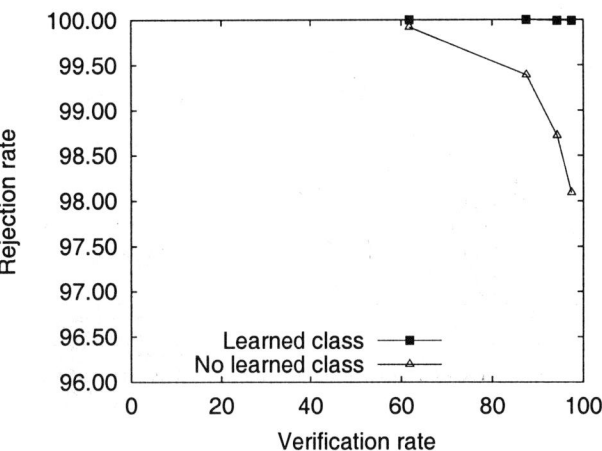

Fig. 7. Relation between verification rate and rejection rate in the case of SMNN.

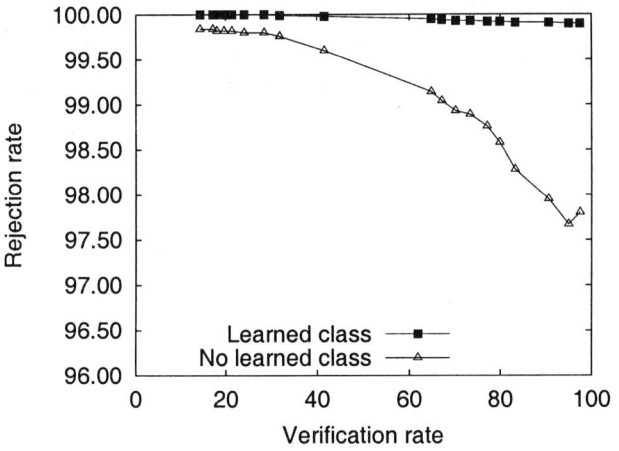

Fig. 8. Relation between verification rate and rejection rate in the case of SVM using the Gaussian kernel function.

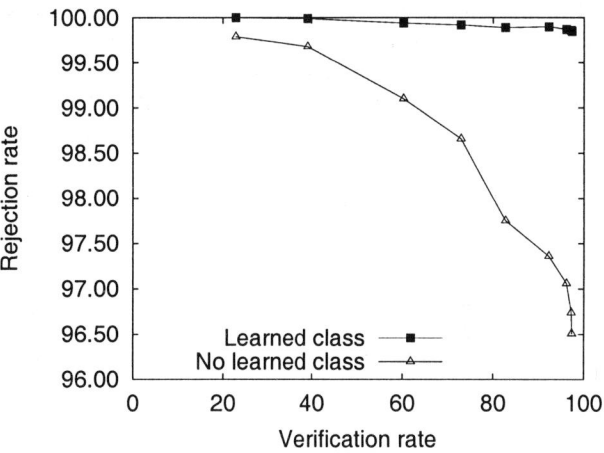

Fig. 9. Relation between verification rate and rejection rate in the case of SVM using the polynomial kernel function.

The number of hidden units of a module in MNN was 7. These numbers were determined by trial and error. Results in the case of MNN were shown in Fig.6. High rejection rates were obtained for test patterns of the learned classes. Rejection of a test pattern of a learned class means that the test pattern is fed to the system with false names of registrants. However, rejection rates for the unlearned classes were relatively lower than those for the learned classes.

All the numbers of hidden units of submodules in SMNN were 4. These numbers were also determined by trial and error. Results in the case of SMNN were shown in Fig.7. Much better performance was obtained both for test patterns of the learned classes and for those of the unlearned classes. Almost 100% rejection rates were attained for both of them at the verification rate of about 60% for test patterns of the learned classes.

In the case of SVM we tried the two kernel functions given in eqs.(1) and (2). Results for the Gaussian kernel function are shown in Fig.8. Eighteen values of the parameter σ^2 between $[0.1, 10.0]$ were tried. A smaller σ^2 gives a higher rejection rate and a lower verification rate. Results of the polynomial kernel function are shown in Fig.9. Nine values of the parameter p between $[2.0, 10.0]$ were tried. Both of the results show that SVMs gave similar performance to that of MNN that was inferior to the performance of SMNN.

V. Discussion

We showed experimentally that SMNN was much superior to MNN and SVM. In this paper this was shown only in the case of personal verification using handshape. We obtained an another result supporting this finding by using palm print in the case of SMNN vs. MNN. We are now doing experiments in the case of SMNN vs. SVM. Similar results are expected because SVM is a kind of three layered neural networks and results in the case of handshape show that they gave similar

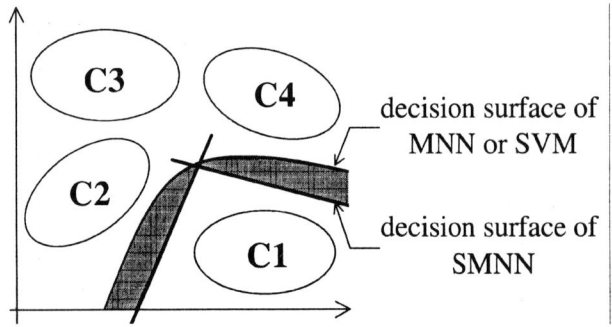

Fig. 10. Difference of a decision surface of SMNN from those of MNN and SVM.

performance. The point is how we explain this superiority of SMNN. The main reason for this superiority is, we think, the difference in the form of decision surface. Two pattern distributions to be classified are separated by a smoothly curved surface in MNN and SVM. This will sometimes cause misclassification of test patterns because requirement of smoothness might disturb the decision surface to be located at the middle of the two pattern distributions in the 'original' pattern space as is illustrated in Fig.10. SMNN, on the other hand, separates two pattern distributions by a decision surface composed of segments of simpler (e.g. linear) surfaces. Each decision surface segment classifies a class from one of the other classes. This classification is much easier than the classification of a class from all the other classes by one decision surface, which is required for MNN and SVM. So, a decision surface segment in SMNN will have more possibility to locate in the middle of two distributions corresponding two classes.

Other advantages of SMNN over MNN and SVM are simple structure and fast learning. Submodules in SMNN are neural networks with smaller scale. So, it is easier for us to determine actual values of parameters, e.g. the number of hidden units, learning coefficient etc. Learning speed is much faster in SMNN than in MNN and SVM as each task assigned to each submodule is much simpler. In the cases of MNN and SVM more time is needed to determine parameter values such as the number of hidden units and learning coefficient in MNN and σ^2 and p in SVM.

Consequently it can be said that SMNN is a very useful neural network for pattern recognition especially for personal verification.

References

[1] C.H. Chen and G.H. You, "Class-sensitive neural network," Neural Parallel Scie. Compt., vol.1, no.1, pp.93-96, 1993.
[2] R. Anand, K.G. Mehrotra, C.K. Mohan and S. Ranka, "Efficient classification for multi-class problems using modular neural networks," IEEE Trans. Neural Networks, vol.6, pp.117-124, 1995.
[3] S. Ishihara and T. Nagano, "Text-independent speaker recognition utilizing neural network techniques," Tech. Rep. IEICE vol. NC93-121, pp.71-77, 1994 (in Japanese)
[4] V.N. Vapnik, Statistical Learning Theory, John Wiley & Sons, Inc. 1998.
[5] B.G. Lu and M. Ito, "Task decomposition and module combination based on Class relations: A modular neural network for pattern recognition," IEEE Trans. Neural Networks, vol.10, no. 5, 1999.
[6] S. Ishihara and T. Nagano, "How to use a layered neural network depends on the number of classes," Proc. of EUFIT'98(Aachen, Germany), vol.1, pp.255-259, 1998.
[7] T. Nagano and Y. Hirai, "Personal verification with palm print and hand shape by utilizing neural network techniques," Proc. of Int. ICSC/IFAC Symposium on Neural Computation, pp.398-404, 1998.
[8] T. Nagano, S. Ishihara and H. Eguchi, "Hand shape has sufficient information for personal verification," Proc. of EUFIT'99(Aachen, Germany), pp.271, 1999.
[9] H.Eguchi, M. Hirahara and T. Nagano, "Personal verification system using handshape," Tech. Rep. IEICE vol. NC2000-126, pp.173-78, 2001 (in Japanese)

A New Class of Convolutional Neural Networks (SICoNNets) and their Application to Face Detection

F.H.C Tivive and A. Bouzerdoum

Edith Cowan University
School of Engineering and Mathematics
100 Joondalup Drive, Joondalup WA 6027
Perth AUSTRALIA
Tel: +61 (8) 9400-5874, Fax: +61 (8) 9400-5811
Email: [f.tivive@ecu.edu.au], [a.bouzerdoum@ieee.org]

Abstract – Artificial neural networks (ANNs), evolved from biological insights, have equipped computers with the capacity to actually learn from examples using real world data. With this remarkable ability, ANNs are able to extract patterns and detect trends that are too complex to be noticed or perceived by either humans or classical computer techniques. Nevertheless, as the amount of data to be processed increases significantly there is a demand for developing other types of artificial neural networks to perform complex pattern recognition tasks. In this article, a new class of convolutional neural networks, namely *shunting inhibitory convolutional neural networks* (SICoNNets), is introduced, and a training algorithm is developed using supervised learning based on *resilient backpropagation with momentum*. Three different network topologies, ranging from fully-connected to partially-connected, are implemented and trained to discriminate between face and non-face patterns. All three architectures achieve more than 96% correct face classification; the best architecture achieves 97.6% correct face classification at a false alarm rate of 3.4%.

I. INTRODUCTION

Neural networks are considered as one of the promises for computing in the future; they offer computers an ability to perform tasks outside the scope of traditional microprocessors. However, there is a need to develop new class of neural networks that can accommodate large amounts of data. Generally, vision and visual pattern recognition problems are multi-dimensional and highly correlated; conventional artificial neural networks have difficulty coping with this type of problems. Fukushima, inspired by mammalian visual processing abilities, developed the *Necognitron*, as an attempt to model the mechanism of visual pattern recognition [1]. The Neocognitron may be considered as the first realisation of *convolutional* neural networks. This type of networks represents a novel two-dimensional class of image processing algorithms, based on some fundamental principles of mammalian visual processing.

Another version of convolutional neural networks, known as LeNet-5, was proposed by LeCun et al. [2], and was used as a character recognizer. The network is based on three architectural ideas: local receptive fields, weight-sharing and spatial sub-sampling, to ensure some degree of invariance to local distortion or translation of the input patterns. Even though numerous studies have been carried out to demonstrate the usefulness of such neural networks, the topologies of these networks are still quite complicated, and very few training methods have been developed for such networks.

In this article, a new class of convolutional neural networks, based on the physiologically plausible mechanism of shunting inhibitory, is presented. To investigate its efficiency and learning capability, a training algorithm is developed using a supervised learning technique. The proposed architecture was tested by training the new network to discriminate between face and nonface patterns. In the next section, detailed descriptions of the network architecture and its basic building block, the shunting neuron, are given. Section III describes the network training methodology. Experimental results on face/nonface discrimination are presented in Section IV. Finally, concluding remarks are presented in Section V.

II. SHUNTING INHIBITORY CONVOLUTIONAL NEURAL NETWORKS

A. Network architecture

The architecture of the proposed neural network shares some similarities with LeNet-5 [3], such as the use of local receptive fields, weight-sharing and sub-sampling. The input layer is a matrix of any size, as long as it has a square shape. Each hidden layer consists of one or more planes (also called feature maps), and each plane is made up of a two-dimensional lattice of shunting inhibitory neurons. Each shunting neuron in a feature map shares the same $N \times N$ set of incoming weights, where N is an odd integer. The set of weights of each neuron are connected to a unique square region in the input image. This $N \times N$ set of weights, which is called the receptive field, can be viewed as a convolution filter or template. Each feature map has one receptive field, and all feature maps in the network use the same size of receptive field. Sub-sampling within the convolutional layer is done at the input level by shifting the centre of the receptive field of a neighbouring neuron in a feature map by two neurons, horizontally and vertically, in the input image (see Fig. 1 (a)).

Three connection schemes, fully-connected, semi-connected and binary-connected, have been developed to connect each feature map in a feed forward topology. In a fully-connected network, each feature map in a particular layer is fully linked to all feature maps in the next layer, and within each layer the number of feature maps is arbitrary. In semi-connected and binary-connected networks, each layer has a limited number of feature maps equals to $2^{\text{index-of-the-layer}}$; that is, layer one has two feature maps, layer two has four feature maps, and so on. In the binary-connection strategy, the input layer is connected to two feature maps in the first hidden layer, and each feature map within that layer is also linked to two feature maps in the next layer, forming a binary tree as shown in Fig. 1(b). In the semi-connected connection scheme a feature map in a layer can either have one-to-one or one-to-many links with the feature maps in the preceding layer. For example, if the feature maps are labelled A, B, C, D, etc., then in layer two feature map A is only linked with feature map A in layer one, feature maps B or C have connections with both feature maps A and B in the preceding layer, and the last feature map D is only connected to the feature map B, as shown in Table 1. In the third column of the table, the indices of the feature maps in layer one are shifted one row downward, and this continues until the last feature map in layer one is in the same row as the last feature map in layer two. The same methodology is applied to connect to higher layer. One constraint of this architecture is that the number of layers depends on the size of the input.

Table 1: Links between feature maps in layer one with those in layer two.

Feature maps in layer 2	Feature maps in layer 1		
A	A		
B	B	A	
C		B	A
D			B

The output layer of the network is a set of linear or sigmoid neurons (perceptrons). The inputs to the output layer are the local averages of 2×2 non-overlapping regions from all feature maps in the last hidden layer, i.e., each 2×2 region in a feature map provides one input signal to the output layer. The weighted sum of these locally averaged signals is passed through an appropriate activation function to generate the output. This combination of shunting inhibitory neurons with perceptrons in a feedforward convolutional neural network architecture is hereafter called the *Shunting Inhibitory Convolutional Neural Network,* or SICoNNet for short.

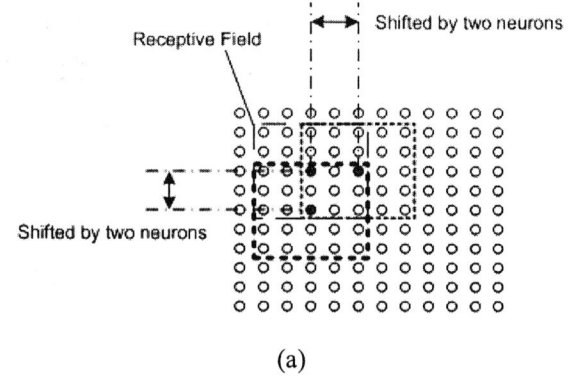

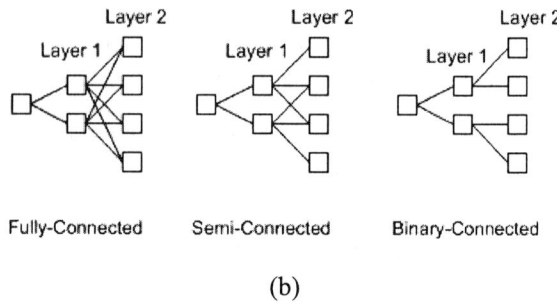

Fig. 1. (a) The position of the receptive field in the input image. (b) The three connection strategies of SICoNNet.

B. Shunting Inhibitory Neuron

The shunting inhibitory neuron is a biologically inspired neuron based on a non-linear mechanism called shunting inhibition. This neuron has been used to construct cellular neural network that have been applied to various vision and image processing tasks [4]. In classification and function approximation, the shunting inhibitory neuron has been used in a feed forward network that can be trained to perform classification and regression tasks [5, 6]. The stability of these shunting inhibitory networks has been investigated in [4] and [7]. The activity of a shunting neuron is described by a nonlinear differential equation of the form.

$$\frac{dz_i}{dt} = I_i - a_i z_i - f\left(\sum_{j=1} w_{ij} z_j\right) z_i + b_i \qquad (1)$$

where z_i is the activity of the ith neuron, I_i is the external input, a_i is the passive decay rate, w_{ij} is the connection weight from the jth neuron to the ith neuron, b_i is a constant bias, and f is a positive non-decreasing activation function. Equation (1) describes a recurrent shunting inhibitory neural network [4]. In a feedforward shunting inhibitory neural network, the feedback signal z_j is replaced by the input signal I_j. Instead of attempting to solve a set of nonlinear ordinary differential equations, the steady state solution of the feedforward network was used in [5] and [6] as the response of a static shunting neuron. Therefore, the output of a static shunting neuron is given by

$$z_i = \frac{I_i + b_i}{a_i + f\left(\sum_{j=1}^n w_{ij} I_j\right)} \quad (2)$$

The proposed SICoNNet architecture uses an extended version of (2), by including extra trainable parameters in the numerator as well as in the denominator. Hence, the formula to compute the output of a feature map is modified as follows:

$$Z_{L,k}(i,j) = \frac{g_L\left(\sum_{v=1}^{S_{L-1}} \left[rot\{C_{L,k}\} * Z_{L-1,v}\right]_{(2i)(2j)} + b_{L,k}(i,j)\right)}{a_{L,k}(i,j) + f_L\left(\sum_{v=1}^{S_{L-1}} \left[rot\{D_{L,k}\} * Z_{L-1,v}\right]_{(2i)(2j)} + d_{L,k}(i,j)\right)} \quad (3)$$

where $Z_{L,k}$ is the two dimensional output of the kth feature map in the Lth layer. S_{L-1} is the number of feature maps in the $(L-1)^{th}$ layer; f_L and g_L are the activation function in the Lth layer; $a_{L,k}$ is the passive decay rate for the kth feature map in the Lth layer; $b_{L,k}$ and $d_{L,k}$ are the biases; $C_{L,k}$ and $D_{L,k}$ are the set of weights for the kth feature map in the Lth layer, and * is the convolution operator. The function, $rot\{\ \}$, rotates the convolution mask by 180 degrees before performing convolution. In a feature map, each shunting neuron has its own bias and passive decay rate. However, it was found that constraining the passive decay rate and the bias parameters to be the same throughout the feature map can speed up training convergence for some problems.

At the output layer, the activation of the output neurons is given by

$$y = h\left(\sum_v w_v z_v + b\right) \quad (4)$$

where h is the activation function (a linear or sigmoid function), w_v's are the connection weights, and b is a bias.

III. TRAINING METHOLOGY

The beauty of training using error backpropagation algorithm is that it is a systematic, step-by-step procedure that can be applied independent of the topology of the network and the input dimensionality. Larger and more complex networks may require more training time, but error backpropagation is still fully capable of training them. To increase the convergence speed and training stability, *resilient backpropagation with momentum* [8] has been implemented in the experiments presented herein.

The basic building block of error *backpropagation* algorithm is to derive the backpropagated error signal, or error sensitivity, in each layer. Assuming the error function to be the squared error, the network to have N layers (including the output layer), and the output layer to consist of one neuron, then for each input pattern we have the error given by

$$E = \frac{1}{2}e^2 = \frac{1}{2}(y - t)^2 \quad (5)$$

where t is the target output, y is the actual network output, and e is the error. The error sensitivity at the output is

$$\delta_N = \frac{\partial E}{\partial y} = y - t \quad (6)$$

At the first layer preceding the output layer, the error sensitivities are given by

$$\delta_{N-1,i} = \sum_{j=1}^{S_N} \delta_{N,j} h'\left(\sum_{v=1}^{S_{N-1}} w_{N,jv} z_{N-1,v} + b_{N,j}\right) w_{N,ji} \quad (7)$$

for $i = 1$ to S_{N-1}. Where $w_{N,jv}$ is the synaptic weight from the vth neuron in the $(N-1)^{th}$ layer to the jth neuron in the Nth layer, and S_{N-1} is the number of neurons in the $(N-1)^{th}$ layer. The prime on f signifies differentiation with respect to the argument.

As the $(N-1)^{th}$ layer is made up of feature maps, the computed error sensitivities $\delta_{N-1,i}$ have to be rearranged into a matrix form, duplicating each error sensitivity four, as shown in Fig. 2 below.

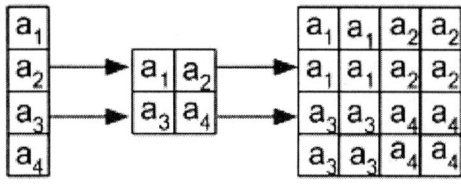

Fig. 2. Arrangement of error sensitivities into a matrix.

For other layers $L < N - 1$, the error sensitivities for the rth feature map at (i, j) is computed as

$$\delta_{L,r}(i,j) = \sum_{k=1}^{S_{L+1}} \left[C_{L+1,k} * A_{L+1,k}\right]_{(i,j)} - \left[D_{L+1,k} * B_{L+1,k}\right]_{(i,j)} \quad (8)$$

where

$$A_{L+1,k}(i,j) = \frac{g'_{L+1,k}\left(Y_{L+1,k}(i,j)\right)\delta_{L+1,k}(i,j)}{a_{L+1,k}(i,j) + f_{L+1}\left(X_{L+1,k}(i,j)\right)} \quad (9)$$

2159

$$B_{L+1,k}(i,j) = \frac{f'_{L+1}\left(X_{L+1,k}(i,j)\right)\delta_{L+1,k}(i,j)Z_{L+1,k}(i,j)}{a_{L+1,k}(i,j) + f_{L+1}\left(X_{L+1,k}(i,j)\right)} \quad (10)$$

and

$$Y_{L+1,k}(i,j) = \sum_{v=1}^{S_L}\left[rot\{C_{L+1,k}\} * Z_{L,v}\right]_{(2i)(2j)} + b_{L+1,k}(i,j) \quad (11)$$

$$X_{L+1,k}(i,j) = \sum_{v=1}^{S_L}\left[rot\{D_{L+1,k}\} * Z_{L,v}\right]_{(2i)(2j)} + d_{L+1,k}(i,j) \quad (12)$$

The expressions $A_{L+1,k}$ and $B_{L+1,k}$ have to be up-sampled by two before convolving with the corresponding set of weights, and this is done by adding odd columns and rows that contain zeros.

Once the error sensitivities have been calculated, the gradient of E with respect to a parameter, P, is obtained by applying the chain rule of differentiation.

$$\frac{\partial E}{\partial P} = \frac{\partial E}{\partial Z}\frac{\partial Z}{\partial P} = \delta\frac{\partial Z}{\partial P} \quad (13)$$

where δ is the error sensitivity.

IV. EXPERIMENTAL RESULTS

To evaluate the proposed network, a face discrimination task has been chosen. The fundamental reason for selecting this specific problem is that human face detection is becoming a very important research topic because of its wide range of applications, such as security access control, model-based video coding or content-based video indexing, and advance human/computer interactions [9]. A two-hidden-layer network with a receptive field of size 5×5 and a perceptron at the output has been used, see Fig. 3. The input pattern is an image of size 20×20. This particular window size is the smallest window that one can use without losing critical information, and most of the network-based approaches in the literature [10, 11] use this window size too. The first hidden layer of the network has two feature maps of size 10×10, and the second hidden layer has four feature maps of size 5×5.

A database of face and non-face patterns has been built by manually cropping 1000 faces and non-face images. The database is divided into two sets; one set is for training the network and the other set is for testing it. Hence, five hundred face and non-face patterns are used as the training set, and the remaining face and non-face patterns are considered to be the test set. These face patterns are frontal view with various facial expressions, and some of them have some facial features such as beard, moustache or even glasses. Samples of face and nonface patterns are shown in figure 4. The images in the database are converted into gray scale images and normalised between zero and one before they are fed to the network. The activation function of the output neuron is the *linear* function, and the desired outputs were +1 and -1. Therefore, initially a threshold value of zero is used to separate the two classes. Table 2 summarizes the classification rates for the three connection strategies. With a binary-connected scheme, the neural network has achieved a face and non-face classification accuracy of almost 96.1%. Due to weight sharing and sub-sampling, the network has only 1237 trainable parameters.

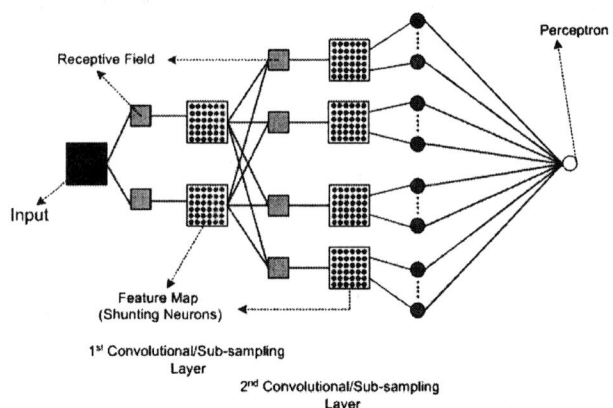

Fig. 3. A 2 hidden layer SICoNNet Network.

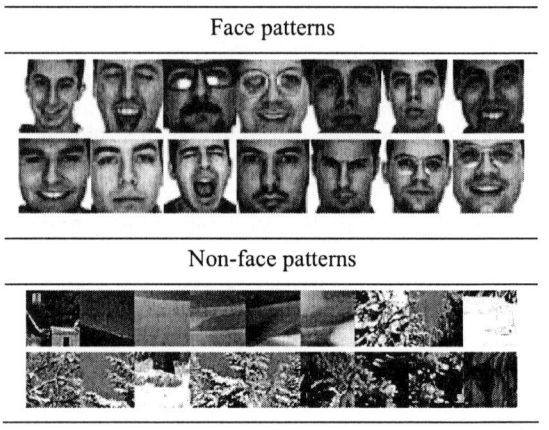

Fig. 4. Sample patterns from training and test sets.

However, changing the threshold value can improve the correct face detection rate, albeit at the expense of increasing the false alarm rate. For face detection applications, a higher face detection rate may be required to detect as many faces as possible. Table 3 presents the correct classification rates of face and nonface patterns using a threshold of -0.2. Clearly the correct classification rates have been significantly improved without too much compromising the false alarm rate. Both the binary- and semi-connected topologies achieve more than 96% correct face classification at around 3% false alarm rate. These two connection strategies have similar performances.

Table 2. Classification rates for face and non-face patterns using a threshold value of 0.

Connection scheme	Correct face classification rate	Correct nonface classification rate	Total classification accuracy
Fully-connected	85.0 %	97.6 %	91.3 %
Semi-connected	90.8 %	99.2 %	95.0 %
Binary-connected	94.0 %	98.2 %	96.1 %

Table 3. Classification rates for face and non-face patterns using a threshold value of -0.2.

Connection scheme	Correct face classification rate	Correct non-face classification rate	Total classification accuracy
Fully-connected	93.8 %	95.6 %	94.7 %
Semi-connected	96.6 %	97.0 %	96.8 %
Binary-connected	96.6 %	96.8 %	96.7 %

Table 4. Classification rates for face and non-face patterns for the three network topologies at their optimal thresholds

Connection scheme	Optimal threshold	Correct face classification rate	Correct non-face classification rate	Total classification accuracy
Fully-connected	-0.27	96.2 %	94.2 %	95.2 %
Semi-connected	-0.24	97.6 %	96.6 %	97.1 %
Binary-connected	-0.25	97.8 %	96.0 %	96.9 %

Furthermore, for each network the optimum threshold was derived as the threshold which results in the smallest total misclassification error. Table 4 presents the optimum thresholds and the corresponding classification rates for each network topology. At the optimal thresholds, all three network topologies exceed 95% total classification accuracy. However, Table 4 clearly indicates that the semi-connected and binary-connected schemes perform slightly better than the fully-connected topology. Both of them have the same amount of trainable parameters, but the only difference is the amount of connections. For instance, the binary-connected scheme has 15937 connections whereas the semi-connected scheme has 18587.

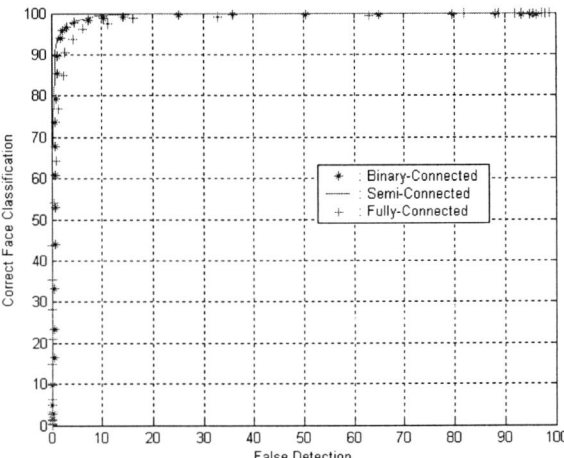

Fig. 5. Correct face detection rate versus false alarm rate for the three connection schemes.

Figure 5 presents the *receiver operating characteristic* (ROC) curves for the three connection strategies. It is clear that the performances of the binary-connected and semi-connected topologies are very close to each other, but they are only slightly better than the fully-connected topology. The reason for the slight degradation in performance of the fully-connected network is that it has too many parameters for this task, and hence it is a slightly harder to train compared to the other two topologies.

V. CONCLUSION

In this paper we presented a new class of convolutional neural networks, known as shunting inhibitory convolutional neural networks, and in short referred as SICoNNets. The architecture of the network is a feed forward topology, which combines the shunting inhibitory neurons in the hidden layers and the perceptron neurons in the output layer. Three types of connection schemes have been studied: fully-connected, semi-connected and binary-connected. Using supervised learning, training algorithms have been developed for the three topologies and evaluated on the face detection problem. All network topologies performed well in that they all achieved over 95% total classification accuracy with the best topology achieving 97.1% total classification accuracy; this has been achieved using a three layer network only. Compared with other network architectures [2, 12], the presented network structure is less complex and requires fewer trainable parameters.

References

[1] K. Fukushima, S. Miyake, and T. Ito, "Neocognitron: a neural network model for a mechanism of visual pattern recognition," *IEEE Transactions on Systems, Man, and Cybernetics*, vol. 13, pp. 826-834, 1983.

[2] Y. LeCun, L. Bottou, Y. Bengio, and P. Haffner, "Gradient-based learning applied to document recognition," *Proc. of the IEEE*, vol. 86, no. 11, pp. 2278-2324, 1998.

[3] Y. LeCun and Y. Bengio, "Convolutional networks for images, speech, and time-series," in *The Handbook of Brain Science and Neural Networks*, M. Arbib, Ed.: Cambridge, pp. 255-258, 1995.

[4] A. Bouzerdoum and R. B. Pinter, "Shunting inhibitory cellular neural networks: derivation and stability analysis," *IEEE Transactions on Circuits and Systems I: Fundamental Theory and Applications*, vol. 40, pp. 215-221, 1993.

[5] A. Bouzerdoum, "A new class of high-order neural networks with nonlinear decision boundaries," *Proc. of the Sixth International Conference on Neural Information Processing*, vol. 3, pp. 1004-1009, 1999.

[6] G. Arulampalam and A. Bouzerdoum, "Application of shunting inhibitory artificial neural networks to medical diagnosis," *Proc. seventh Australian and New Zealand Intelligent Information Systems Conf.*, pp. 89-94, 2001.

[7] A. Bouzerdoum, "Convergence of symmetric shunting competitive neural networks," in *Complex Systems: From Biology to Computation*, D. Green and T. Bossomaiser, Eds.: IOS Press, pp. 301-312, 1992.

[8] M. Riedmiller and H. Braun, "RPROP — A fast adaptive learning algorithm," *Proc. of the 1992 International Symposium on Computer and Information Sciences*, pp. 279-285, 1992.

[9] C. Garcia and M. Delakis, "A neural architecture for fast and robust face detection," *Sixteenth International Conference on Pattern Recognition (ICPR'02)*, vol. 2, pp. 20044-20048, 2002.

[10] H. Rowley, S. Baluja, and T. Kanade, "Neural network-based face detection," *IEEE Transactions on Pattern Analysis and Machine Intelligence*, vol. 20, no. 4, pp. 1019-1031, 1997.

[11] E. Osuna, R. Freund, and F. Girosi, "Training support vector machines: an application to face detection," *Proc. of the IEEE Computer Society Conference on Computer Vision and Pattern Recognition*, pp. 130-136, 1997.

[12] D. R. Lovell, T. Downs, and A. C. Tsoi, "An evaluation of the neocognitron," *IEEE Transactions on Neural Networks*, vol. 8, no. 5, pp. 1090-1105, 1997.

Permutative coding technique for handwritten digit recognition system

E. Kussul, T. Baidyk
Center of Applied Science and Technological Development,
UNAM (National Autonomous University of Mexico),
Cd. Universitaria, A.P. 70-186, C.P. 04510,
Mexico, D.F.
ekussul@servidor.unam.mx
tbaidyk@aleph.cinstrum.unam.mx
Tel.: (52) 5622-86-02 ext.116
Fax: (52) 5550-06-54

Abstract – **The new neural classifier for the handwritten digit recognition is proposed. The classifier is based on the Permutative Coding technique. This coding technique is derived from the associative-projective neural networks developed in the 80th-90th. The classifier performance was tested on the MNIST database. The error rate of 0.54 % was obtained.**

I. Introduction

The handwritten digit recognition could be used for automatic reading of the bank checks, the custom declarations, the post addresses, and other documents. Many efforts were done to improve the performance of such systems. To test the performance of handwritten digit recognition systems some public available databases are used. Among them the MNIST database has the following advantages: it contains large number of samples in training- and test sets, all the images are centered and transformed to grey scale. Many recognition systems were tested on this database and the obtained results are available in the literature [1] - [3], [5]-[7]. Some systems showed good results. The best result in [1] is 70 errors from 10 000 samples. They used the convolution neural network LeNet-4. In 2001 Belongie [5] reported the result of 63 errors. His system is based on the shape matching method [6]. In 2001 we developed the neural classifier LIRA that showed 79 errors [7]. In 2002 we improved LIRA [8] and repeated the Belongie's result of 63 errors. The latest version of the classifier LIRA gave the result of 58 errors (is preparing for publication). Cheng-Lin Liu et al. in 2002 made the investigations of the handwritten digit recognition combining the eight methods of feature extraction with seven classifiers. They obtained 56 results for each tested database including the MNIST database. The best result obtained on the MNIST database was 42 errors [9].

In this article we describe the new method of handwritten digit recognition based on Permutative Coding Neural Classifier (PCNC) that shows the result of 54 errors as a mean value of 7 trials. The best result of this method is 49 errors. To our knowledge it is the second result on the MNIST database.

II. Permutative Coding Neural Classifier

The principles of the proposed method we worked out on the base of the associative-projective neural networks (APNN) [10], [11]. We are developing the APNN since 80th. We use the APNN paradigm as generic structure for different applications such as random threshold classifier (RTC) [12], [13] random subspace neural classifier, LIRA [7], [8] and PCNC.

In this article we propose new algorithm, which outperforms the predecessors due to new elements (feature extractor and encoder) included into its structure.

A. PCNC structure

The PCNC structure is presented in Fig.1.

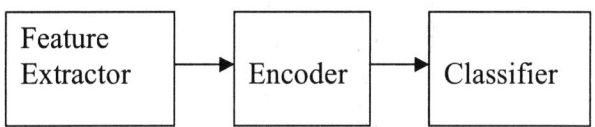

Fig.1. Structure of Permutative Coding Neural Classifier

The handwritten digit image is input to the feature extractor. The extracted features are applied to the encoder input. The encoder produces the output binary vector of large dimension, which is presented to the one-layer neural classifier input.

B. Feature extractor

In Fig. 2, *a* an example of the digit "0" transformed to grey scale is shown. The feature extractor begins the work with the selection of the specific points in the image. In principle various methods of the specific points selection could be proposed. For example, the contour points could be selected as the specific points. In this work we selected the specific points P_{ij}, which have the brightness b_{ij} higher than the predetermined threshold B. These points correspond to the black area in Fig. 2, *b*.

Each specific point is located within a rectangle of $h \bullet w$ size (Fig.3). Multiple features are extracted from the image in the rectangle. The p positive and the n negative points determine each feature. These points are randomly distributed in the rectangle. Each point P_{rs} has the threshold T_{rs} that is randomly selected from the range:

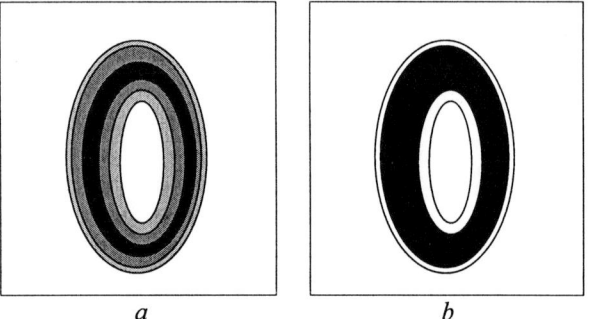

Fig.2. Grey scale image of "0".

$$T_{min} \leq T_{rs} \leq T_{max} \quad (1)$$

The positive point is "active" if it has brightness:
$$b_{rs} \geq T_{rs} \quad (2)$$

The negative point is "active" if it has brightness:
$$b_{rs} \leq T_{rs}. \quad (3)$$

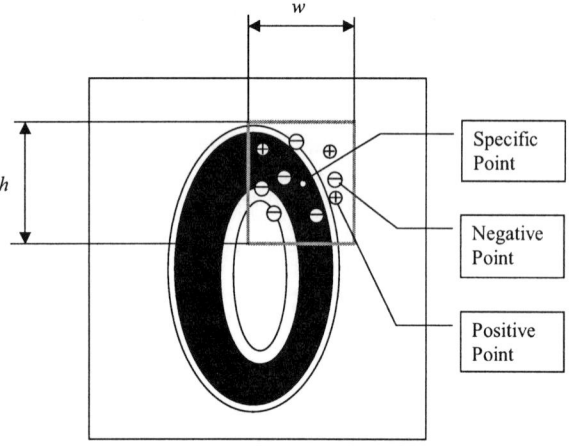

Fig.3. Specific points selected by the feature extractor (black area)

The feature under investigation is present in the rectangle if all its positive and negative points are active.

We used different features F_i ($i = 1, ..., S$). In final experiments we worked with $S = 6400$; $p = 3$; $n = 6$; $h = w = 11$; $T_{min} = 1$; $T_{max} = 254$; $B = 127$. The feature extractor examines all S features for each specific point in the handwritten digit image.

In the MNIST database the images have dimensions 28x28 pixels. For the feature extractor we expanded the images to $h/2$ at the top and down sides and to $w/2$ at the left and right sides. All extracted features are transferred to the encoder.

C. Encoder

The encoder transforms the extracted features to the binary vector:
$$V = \{v_i\} \ (i = 1, ..., N),$$
where $v_i = 0$ or 1. For each extracted feature F_k the encoder creates an auxiliary binary vector:
$$U = \{u_i\} \ (i = 1, ..., N),$$
where $u_i = 0$ or 1. This vector contains K 1's, where $K \ll N$. In our experiments $K = 16$, $N = 128\,000$. A special random procedure is used to obtain the positions of ones in the vector U for each feature F_k. This procedure generates the list of the positions of ones for each feature and saves all these lists in the memory. The vector U_k we term "mask" of the feature F_k.

In the next stage of encoding process it is necessary to transform the auxiliary vector U to the new vector U^* which corresponds to the feature location in the image. This transformation is made with permutations of the vector U components (Fig. 4). The number of permutations depends on the feature location on the image. The permutations in horizontal (X) (Fig.4, a) and vertical (Y) (Fig.4, b) directions are different permutations.

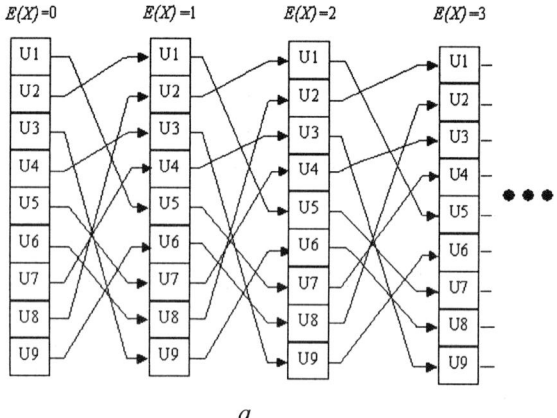

a

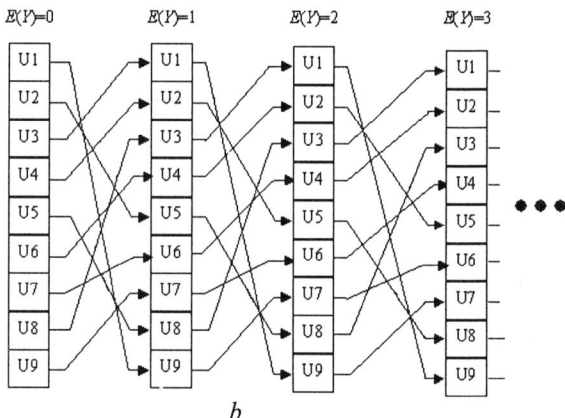

b

Fig. 4. Permutation pattern.

The problem is to obtain such binary codes of the features that are strongly correlated if the distance between the feature locations is small and are weakly correlated or not correlated if the distance is large. For example, if the feature F_k is extracted at the top point of the handwritten digit and the same feature is extracted at the down point of the digit they must be coded by different binary vectors U^*_{k1} and U^*_{k2} which has weak correlation or has no correlation at all. If the same features are extracted at the neighbor points they must be coded with almost the same vectors U^*_{k3} and U^*_{k4}. This property permits to make the recognition system insensible to the small displacements of the digits in the image.

To code the feature F_k location in the image it is necessary to select the correlation distance D_c. Let the same feature F_k be detected in two different points P_1 and P_2. If the distance d between them $d < D_c$, the corresponding codes will be correlated. If the distance $d > D_c$ the codes will be not correlated. To obtain this property we have to calculate the following values:

$$X = j / D_c,$$
$$E(X) = (int)X, \qquad (4)$$
$$R(X) = j - E(X) \cdot D_c,$$

$$Y = i / D_c,$$
$$E(Y) = (int)Y, \qquad (5)$$
$$R(Y) = i - E(Y) \cdot D_c,$$

$$P_x = \frac{R(X) \cdot N}{D_c}, \qquad (6)$$

$$P_y = \frac{R(Y) \cdot N}{D_c}, \qquad (7)$$

where $E(X)$ is the integer part of X; $R(X)$ is the fraction part of X; i – the vertical coordinate of the detected feature; j – the horizontal coordinate of the detected feature.

The mask of the feature F_k is considered as a code of this feature located at the left top corner of the image. To shift the feature location in the horizontal direction it is necessary to make the permutations $E(X)$ times and to make an additional permutation for P_x components of the vector. After that it is necessary to shift the code to the vertical direction making the permutations $E(Y)$ times and an additional permutation for P_y components.

Let the feature F_k be detected at the point $j = 11$ and $I = 21$; $D_c = 8$; $N = 9$. In this case $E(X) = 1$; $E(Y) = 2$; $P_x = 3$; $P_y = 6$. In Fig.5, a, b all components that have to be permutated are shown as grey.

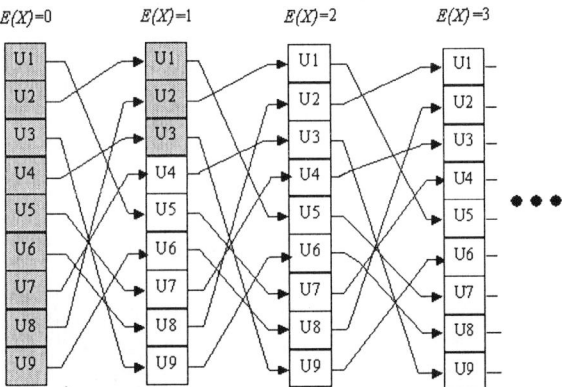

Fig5, a. An example of X permutations.

To make the permutations of the k-th component of the vector U it is necessary to select the k-th cell in the first column in Fig.5, a and then to follow the arrows until the first white cell appears. This white cell corresponds to the new position of the selected component. This position is necessary to select in the first column of Fig. 5, b and to follow the arrows until the first white cell appears. This white cell corresponds to the final position of the selected component. For example, trajectory of component U_3 will be (Fig.5 a, b):
$U_3 \rightarrow U_9 \rightarrow U_7 \rightarrow U_6 \rightarrow U_4$.

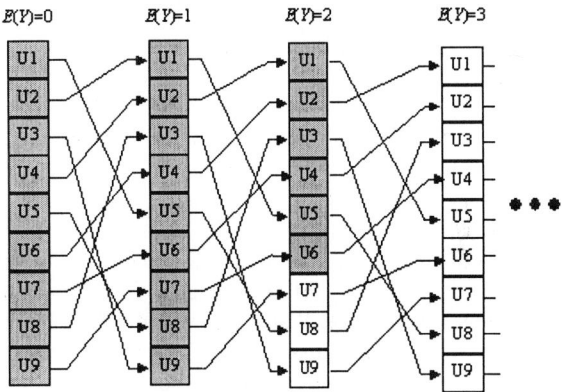

Fig. 5, b. An example of Y permutations.

The permutations of all components are shown in Fig.6.

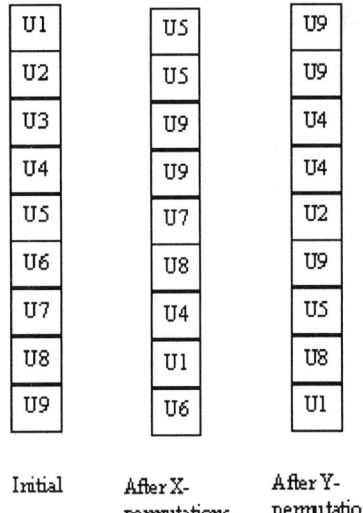

Fig. 6. The results of X and Y permutations.

Let us consider the properties of described permutations. Let the feature F_k be detected in two locations $P_1(i_1, j_1)$ and $P_2(i_2, j_2)$. Let $dx = |j_2 - j_1|$; $dy = |i_2 - i_1|$. The feature mask corresponds to the vector U. After the X permutations the vectors U_1 and U_2 will be different. Let the difference of the number of 1-th in the vectors be Δn. It could be shown that the mean value of Δn could be calculated with the approximate equation:

$$\Delta n \approx \frac{K}{D_c} dx. \quad (8)$$

After the Y permutations the vectors U_1^* and U_2^* will have difference which could be estimated as:

$$\overline{\Delta n} \approx K\left(1 - \left(1 - \frac{dx}{D_c}\right)\left(1 - \frac{dy}{D_c}\right)\right), \quad (9)$$

$1 > \overline{\Delta n} > 0$.

Thus the vectors U_1^* and U_2^* are correlated only if $dx < D_c$ and $dy < D_c$. The correlation increases if dx and dy are decreasing.

It could be seen in Fig. 6 that different components of the vector U could be placed in the same cell after the accomplished permutations. For example, after the X permutations the components U_1 and U_2 are allocated in the cells U_5; U_3 and U_4 - in the cell U_9. Such events are undesirable. The probability of such events decreases with increasing of the vector size N and the relation N/K. In our experiments $N = 128\,000$ and $K = 16$. In this case the probability of the described event could be estimated as 0.01 or less.

The code vector V is composed from all code vectors U_r^* of the detected features:

$$v_i = \bigvee_r u_{ri}^* \quad (10)$$

where v_i is the i-component of the vector V, u_{ri}^* is the i-component of the vector U_r^* which corresponds to the detected feature F_r, $\bigvee_r$ is the sign of disjunction.

This coding process produces almost independent representations of all features because we use independent random numbers for the feature mask generation. The weak influence of one feature to other appears only from the absorption of 1'th in disjunction (Equation 10).

To recognize the handwritten digits it is necessary to use feature combinations. For example, "the feature F_a is present in the image, but the feature F_b is absent". To take into account such feature combinations the Context Dependent Thinning (CDT) was proposed [14]. CDT was developed on the base of vector normalization procedure [15]. There are different procedures of CDT implementation. Here we use the following procedure. The new permutation pattern (Fig. 7), which is independent on the X and Y permutations, is generated. After that we test each component v_i of the vector V. If $v_i = 0$, nothing to be done. If $v_i = 1$, we consider the trajectory of this component during permutations (according to arrows). If this trajectory contains at least one "1", the value of v_i is converted to 0. For example, in Fig.7 the trajectory of the v_3 component is $v_4 \rightarrow v_8 \rightarrow v_7$. If v_4 or v_8 or v_7 equals 1 we put $v_3 = 0$. The number of the permutations Q in CDT is the parameter of the recognition system. In our experiments we used $Q = 5$. After the realization of CDT the binary vector V is prepared for the neural classifier.

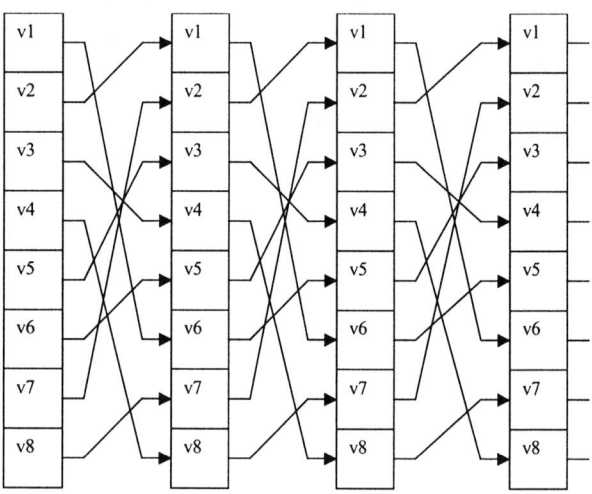

Fig.7. Permutation pattern for Context Dependent Thinning.

D. Neural Classifier

Earlier we have described the handwritten digit recognition system based on Rosenblatt perceptron [7], [8]. One-layer perceptron has very good convergence but it demands the linear separability of the classes in the parametric space. To obtain the linear separability it is necessary to transform initial parametric space presented by pixel brightness to the parametric space of larger dimension. In our case the feature extractor in the encoder transforms initial 784-D space into 128 000-D space represented by binary code vector V. This procedure improves the linear separability.

The LIRA classifier structure is presented in Fig. 8.

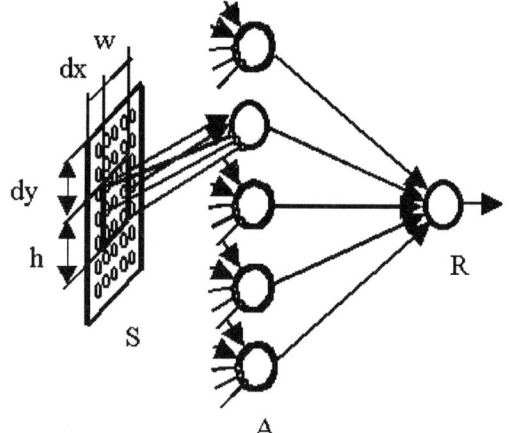

Fig.8. Neural classifier LIRA.

In this recognition system the associative neuron layer A is connected with the sensor layer S with the randomly selected, no trainable connections. The set of these connections could be considered as a feature extractor. Here we propose the new recognition system, which contains the feature extractor and the encoder instead of the mentioned connection set (Fig.9). The neural layers A and R are the same as in the previous recognition system. The training rules for connections between the layers A and R also are the same [8].

It is known [3] that the performance of the recognition systems could be improved due to the distortions of the input image during the training process. In [8] we had shown that the further improvement could be obtained if the distortions are used not only in the training process but in the recognition process too.

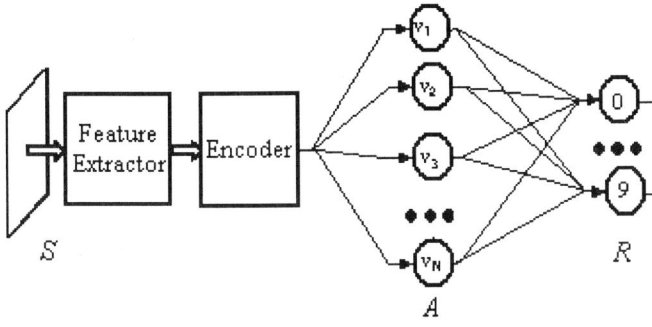

Fig.9. Permutative Coding Neural Classifier.

Our new recognition system is not sensible to the small displacements of the object in the image. Therefore we used only skewing as image distortion. In our experiments we used 3 skewings (11.3°, 18.5°, 26.5°) to the left side and 3 skewings of the same angles to the right side. Thus the total number of the distortions in the training process was 6. In the recognition process we tested 3 variants of the system: without distortions, with 2 distortions and 4 distortions.

III. Results obtained on the MNIST database

The MNIST database contains 60 000 samples in the training set and 10 000 samples in the test set. In our experiments we used the total number of the samples of the both sets. The results of these experiments are presented in Table 1. The values presented in this Table correspond to the number of errors in the recognition of 10 000 test samples. The proposed recognition system includes the feature extractor and the encoder having random structure. The recognition results depend on these random structures. To obtain reliable data we made seven experiments with different structures. Each row in the Table 1 corresponds to one of these experiments. The first column of the Table enumerates the experiments. The second column contains the results obtained without image distortions in the recognition process. The third column contains results with two image distortions and the fourth column contains the results with four image distortions.

TABLE 1.
RECOGNITION RESULTS

Trials	Recognition Error Number		
	Without recognition distortions	2 recognition distortions	4 recognition distortions
1	58	56	50
2	62	53	52
3	61	54	54
4	64	56	55
5	59	49	53
6	62	56	56
7	68	59	55
Mean value	62	54.7	53.6

Unrecognized digits of the best experiment are presented in Fig.10.

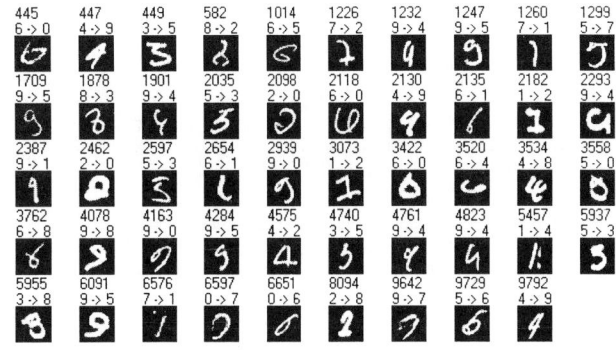

Fig. 10. An example of unrecognized handwritten digits.

IV. Discussion

It was shown [7], [8] that large-scale classifiers having more than 100000 neurons in the associative layer demonstrate the high performance in the hand-written digit recognition task. The main drawback of a perceptron-like classifier (for example, LIRA) is the sensitivity to the object displacements in the image. In this work we propose other version of the large-scale neural classifier, which is insensitive to the small displacements of the objects. The best result of this classifier on the MNIST database is 49 errors (Fig.10). The main drawback of this classifier is its sensitivity to the object rotation and scale change. For this reason it is necessary to use the image distortions during the training and the recognition processes. The usage of the image distortions increases the training and the recognition time. In our experiments the training time was 50 hours on Pentium 500 MHz. The recognition time was 3.5 hours for 10 000 images.

To decrease the training and the recognition time it is necessary to develop the mask generation methods, which permit to decrease the sensitivity to rotation and scale change of the object in the image. This work will be made in the future.

V. Conclusions

The new neural classifier for hand-written digit recognition was developed. The classifier is based on the permutation coding technique. This technique decreases the sensitivity to the object displacements in the image. Tests of the classifier on the MNIST database show very good recognition rate (mean value of 54 errors from 10000 samples). In the future the recognition methods, which are insensitive to the object rotation and scale change, would be developed.

Acknowledgment

This work was funded by the Projects CONACYT 33944-U, MEC 0204, NSF-CONACYT39395A, PAPIIT IN 112102.

Reference

[1] L.Bottou, C. Cortes, J. Denker, H. Drucker, L. Guyon, L. Jackel, J. LeCun, U. Muller, E. Sackinger, P. Simard, V. Vapnik, Comparison of Classifier Methods: a Case Study in Handwritten Digit Recognition", *Proc. of 12th IAPR Intern. Conf. on Pattern Recognition,* 1994, V. 2, 77-82.

[2] http://www.research.att.com/~yann/ocr/mnist/index.html

[3] LeCun Y, Bottou L, Bengio Y, Haffner P, Gradient-based Learning Applied to Document Recognition, *Proceedings of the IEEE*, V 86, N 11 (1998) 2278-2344.

[4] Hoque M S, Fairhurst M C, A Moving Window Classifier for Off-line Character Recognition, *Proceedings of the 7-th International Workshop on Frontiers in Handwriting Recognition* (2000) 595-600.

[5] Belongie S, Malik J, Puzicha J, Matching Shapes, *Proceedings of the 8-th IEEE International Conference on Computer Vision ICCV*, V.1 (2001) 454-461.

[6] Belongie S, Malik J, Puzicha J, Shape Matching and Object Recognition Using Shape Contexts, *IEEE Transactions on Pattern Analysis and Machine Intelligence*, V. 24, No 4 (2002) 509-522.

[7] Kussul E., Baidyk T., Kasatkina L., Lukovich V. Rosenblatt Perceptrons for Handwritten Digit Recognition. *Proceedings of International Joint Conference on Neural Networks "IJCNN'01"*. Washington, USA, July 15-19 2001, 1516-1520.

[8] E. Kussul, T. Baidyk, Improved Method of Handwritten Digit Recognition Tested on MNIST Database, *Proceedings of the 15-th Intern Conf. on Vision Interface,* Calgary, Canada, 2002, 192-197.

[9] Cheng-Lin Liu, Nakashima K., Sako, H., Fujisawa H. Handwritten Digit Recognition Using State-of-the-art Techniques, *Proceedings of the 8-th International Workshop on Frontiers in Handwritten Recognition*, Ontario, Canada, August 2002, 320-325.

[10] Kussul E.M., Rachkovskij D.A., Baidyk T.N. On image texture recognition by associative-projective neurocomputer. *Proc. of the ANNIE'91 conference.* "Intelligent engineering systems through artificial neural networks", ed. by C.H.Dagli, S. Kumara and Y.C.Shin, ASME Press, 1991. - P.453-458.

[11] Kussul E.M., Rachkovskij D.A., Baidyk T.N. Associative-projective neural networks: architecture, implementation, applications. *Proc. of Fourth Intern. Conf. "Neural Networks & their Applications"*, Nimes, France, Nov.4-8,1991. - EC2 Publishing - P.463-476.

[12] E. Kussul, T. Baidyk, Neural Random Threshold Classifier in OCR Application", *Proc. of the Second All-Ukrainian Intern. Conf.*, Kiev, Ukraine, 1994, 154-157.

[13] E.Kussul., T. Baidyk, V. Lukovitch, D. Rachkovskij, Adaptive high performance classifier based on random threshold neurons, in R. Trappl (Ed.) *Cybernetics and Systems'94* (Singapore: World Scientific Publishing Co. Pte. Ltd., 1994) 1687-1695.

[14] Rachkovskij D., Kussul E. Binding and Normalization of Binary Sparse Distributed Representations by Context-Depending Thinning. Neural Computation **13,** 2001, 411-452.

[15] Artikutsa S., Baidyk T., Kussul E., Rachkovskij D. Texture recognition with the neurocomputer. *Preprint 91-8 of Institute of Cybernetics*, Ukraine, 1991, 20 (in Russian).

3D Face Recognition by Profile and Surface Matching

Gang Pan, Yijun Wu, Zhaohui Wu and Wenyao Liu
Department of Computer Science and Engineering
Zhejiang University, Hangzhou, 310027, P.R.China
{gpan,wzh}@cs.zju.edu.cn

Abstract— In this paper, we presented an approach for automatic face verification from range data. The method consists of profile and surface matching. The profile is extracted on the basis of symmetry of human face, and a global profile matching method based on k-th Hausdorff distance is used to align and compare profiles, without detection of fiducial points that is often unreliable. For each individual, a statistical model of facial surface is built to represent the distinct discriminative capability of the different parts in the facial surface. Then the model is incorporated into a weighted distance function to measure similarity of surfaces. Finally two experts are combined to give a decision. The comparable experimental results are obtained on a database with 180 pieces of range data of 30 individuals.

I. Introduction

The automatic face recognition based on 2D image processing has been actively researched in recent years, and various techniques have been presented [?], [?]. Although great strides have been made during the past three decades, the task of robust face recognition is still difficult. Current methods work very well under conditions similar to those of the training images. However, either of the illumination variation and pose change may cause serious performance degradation for most existing systems.

Recent advances in modelling and digitizing techniques have made the acquisition of 3D human face data much easier. The 3D data have the potential to overcome these problems, whose advantage is the explicit representation of 3D shape. For a applied point of view, an economical and accurate 3D face recognition system is preferred, whereas the data acquired by an economical fully automatic 3D acquisition system are often the limited quality of range data that contain inaccurate and noisy data. 3D face verification method tolerant to relatively coarse range data is highly encouraged. Also, for optimal performance, a system should incorporate as many observations as are available, and extract as many informative cues as possible. Therefore, the recognition approach using facial surface and profile cues from range data is likely to be quite feasible.

In this work, we proposed an automatic 3D face verification method based on surface and profile matching. It can work well with a low-resolution facial range data (only nearly 3000 points) and can compare two models in about 10 seconds. After facial range data registration with ICP, the correspondences are computed by nearest neighbor rule. Prior to online recognition, with the correspondences, a statistical model of facial surface is built for each individual to represent the discriminative capability of each point. Then the similarity of facial surface is defined as a weighted distance function whose weights are determined by the statistical model. Meanwhile, the facial profile is extracted by detecting the symmetry plane of the range data. And a global profile matching method based on k-th Hausdorff distance as similarity measure is employed to align profiles, without detection of fiducial points which is often unreliable. Finally two experts are combined to give a decision. The experiments are carried out on a database with 180 pieces of range data of 30 individuals, and the competitive results are obtained.

In the following section we will review some of the previous work related to face recognition from range data and from facial profile. Section ?? presents the surface-based method and section ?? gives the profile-based method. The experimental results are reported in section ?? and conclusions are drawn in section ??.

II. Previous work

The activities to exploit the additional information in 3D data to improve the accuracy and robustness of face recognition system are still weakly addressed. Only a few work on the use of 3D data have been reported. Several studies concentrated on curvature analysis[?], [?], [?], [?]. Gordon [?], [?] presented a template-based recognition system involving descriptors based on curvature calculations from range image data. The sensed surface regions are classified as convex, concave and saddle by calculating the minimum and maximum normal curvatures. Then locations of nose, eyes, mouth and other features are determined, which are used for depth template comparison. Lee et al [?] proposed a method to detect corresponding regions in two range images by graph matching based on extended Gaussian image. An approach to label the components of human faces is proposed by Yacoob et al [?]. Its preprocessing stage employs a multistage diffusion process to identify convexity and concavity points. These points are grouped into components. Qualitative reasoning about possible interpretations of the components is performed, followed by consistency of hypothesized interpretations. However, because they are all involved in computing curvatures, each of these techniques requires high quality of the range data, otherwise the computation of curvature will be inaccurate and unreliable. Recently Chua et al [?] describes a technique based on point signature - a representation for free-form surfaces. The rigid parts of the face of one person are extracted to deal with different facial expressions. Beumier et al [?] proposed two 3D comparison methods respectively based on surface matching and profiles matching. Blanz [?] utilized a 3D morphable model [?] to tackle variation of pose and illumination in face recognition, in which the input is 2D face images. However, the shape and texture fitting procedure is hugely time-consuming of about 40 minutes on Pentium III, 800MHz.

For recognition using facial profile, many methods have been done. Most of previous work is based on fiducial points extracted. [?], [?], [?], [?] extracted fiducial marks from the profile by heuristic rules, and a set of features was detected in terms of the positions of these fiducials. The distance between the features of a test profile's fiducial points and that of the model's fiducial points was calculated. Harmon et al. [?] manually drew the outlines from profile photos of 256 males. Nine fiducial points were selected. A set of 11 features was derived from these fiducial points. After aligning the two profiles to be matched by two selected fiducial marks, the matching was achieved by measuring the Euclidean distance of the feature vectors derived from the outlines. Wu et al. [?] developed a face profile recognition procedure based on 24 fiducial points. The outline curves were automatically obtained instead of by an artist's drawing. Then, they used a B-spline to extract turning points on the outline curve. Subsequently, six interesting points and 24 features were derived from these points. A database of 18 oriental faces was used to test the performance of their approach. The stored features were obtained in a training process that used three profiles per person. Out of the 18 test images, 17 were reported correctly recognized. Yu et.al [?] used a tuning method to get more precise position of the fiducial points. They define a number of small steps around the determined positions of the fiducial points. For each combination of the new positions of the fiducial points, the matching was performed,and the one with the best matching score is chosen. Recently an attributed string matching method for profile recognition is proposed to tackle the inconsistency problem of feature point detection, in which a quadratic penalty function is proposed to prohibit large angle changes and over-merging [?].

III. FACIAL SURFACE MATCHING

A. Facial data registration

An object recognition system generally makes up of two key parts: data registration and data comparison. The accuracy of registration will greatly impact on the result of following comparison. Although Blanz[?] gave a nice solution to registration of 3D facial data, high time-cost made it hard to be incorporated into a practical recognition system. Here we use the popular approach of the Iterated Closest Point (ICP) [?]. ICP is attractive because of its simplicity and its performance. It works well on the range data from $3D\_RMA$, a database of facial range data,which is a part of M2VTS project.

Given two sets of facial range data, probe data $S = \{s_1, \cdots, s_n\}$ and gallery data $M = \{m_1, \cdots, m_k\}$, the task of 3D registration is to find the transformation (translation, rotation and scaling) which will optimally align the regions of S with those of M. The transformation T_{3d} include a rotation about the axes X, Y, Z of angles ϕ, γ and θ, a scaling factor f for tuning the data acquisition error and a translation t_{3d}. So the result of this transformation of 3D point s_i is

$$T_{3d}(s_i) = fR_\phi R_\gamma R_\theta s_i + t_{3d} \quad (1)$$

Alignment is measured by an error function $\epsilon^2(|x|)$, and a typical choice is to define

$$\epsilon^2(|x|) = \|x\|^2 = \|T_{3d}(s_i) - m_{\psi(i)}\| \quad (2)$$

where $m_{\psi(i)}$ is the corresponding model point for s_i. Thus, the estimate of the optimal registration is given by minimizing the error:

$$\begin{aligned}\widehat{T}_{3d} &= \underset{T_{3d}}{argmin} \sum_i \|T_{3d}(s_i) - m_{\psi(i)}\| \\ &= \underset{T_{3d}}{argmin} \sum_i \|fR_\phi R_\gamma R_\theta s_i + t_{3d} - m_{\psi(i)}\| \quad (3)\end{aligned}$$

If there were no scaling factor f, Equ. ?? would be a linear least-square problem and could been solved analytically [?]. But the scaling factor f introduced made it become a nonlinear least-square problem. In fact, we solve this nonlinear numerical problem using the Levenberg-Marquardt method[?], which is particularly suited to functions such as $\epsilon^2(|x|)$ that are expressed as a sum of squared residuals. Alternative procedures such as conjugate gradients or even a pure Gauss-Newton algorithm could be used.

To speed up the LM-ICP registration procedure, an appropriate initial position is necessary. In our system, the following steps are performed before LM-ICP registration, in which *a priori* knowledge of the human face and facial features is exploited.

1) A plane is fitted to probe S,and frontal view and back view are detected on the basis of point distribution on both sides of the plane.
2) Find the location of nose tip, then approximately detect the chin and cheeks, and estimate the width and height of face by the location of chin and cheek.
3) Translate, rotate and scale S according to the parameters obtained from step 1-2.

When computing the correspondences of models, we reject the worst 10% of pairs based on point-to-point distance. The purpose is to eliminate outliers which may have a large effect when performing least-squares minimization.

B. The statistical model for discrimination

In surface-based face recognition, the different facial surface regions have different amounts of importance and have different discriminative distribution for classification. Nevertheless, it is not explicit,even these regions are different over each individual, thus hard to define the discriminative distributions of each part heuristically.

For this reason, we build a statistical model for each subject to describe the different discrimination of each point. After the registration by ICP, the correspondences between each pair of model are available. Given models (or range data) $A_0 = \{a_{0k}, k = 1, \cdots, N_a\}$, $\{A_i = \{a_{ik}\}, i = 1, \cdots, m\}$ labelled subject A, and models $\{B_j = \{b_{jk}\}, j = 1, \cdots, n\}$

labelled non-subject A, we assume that $\{A_i\}$ and $\{B_j\}$ have be registered by A_0 where each point a_{ik} or b_{jk} corresponds to the point a_{0k} with the same index. We define the *within-class scatter matrix* S_w and *between-class scatter matrix* S_b for each point in A_0:

$$S_w(a_{0k}) = \frac{1}{m+1}\sum_{i=0}^{m}(a_{ik}-m_{1k})(a_{ik}-m_{1k})^T \quad (4)$$

$$S_b(a_{0k}) = (m_{1k}-m_{2k})(m_{1k}-m_{2k})^T \quad (5)$$

Where m_{1k} is the mean given by

$$m_{1k} = \frac{1}{m+1}\sum_{i=0}^{m} a_{ik} \quad (6)$$

$$m_{2k} = \frac{1}{n}\sum_{j=1}^{n} b_{jk} \quad (7)$$

Thus, the discriminative model for A_0 is defined as follows

$$DModel(A_0) = \{(\alpha_k, \beta_k), k=1,\cdots,N_a\} \quad (8)$$

Where α_k and β_k is given by

$$\alpha_k = |S_w|, \quad \beta_k = |S_b| \quad (9)$$

Represented by within-class scatter and between-class scatter respectively, α_k and β_k together describe the discriminative capability of point a_{0k}. Its idea is similar to Fisher's linear discriminant.

C. Similarity measure

Given two pieces of range data $A = \{a_i\}$, $B = \{b_i\}$ where each point b_j corresponds to the point a_j with the same index, and the statistical discriminative model of $DModel(A) = \{(\alpha_k,\beta_k)\}$. The weighted distance is defined as follows, to measure the similarity measure of A and B:

$$Sim(A,B) = \frac{1}{N_a}\sum_{i}\frac{\alpha_i}{\beta_i}\min_{b\in B}\|a_i - b\| \quad (10)$$

Note that the worst 10% of pairs are rejected based on point-to-point distance when computing the correspondences.

IV. FACIAL PROFILE MATCHING

As described in Sec. 1, most existing methods for profile recognition are based on fiducial points, which involved in inconsistency problem of feature point detection. One solution to this issue is to match the whole profile without detection of fiducial points. In this section we present a robust symmetry plane detection method to extract profile and a global matching approach to align and compare two profiles.

A. Extracting Profile from Range Data

Given range data for facial profile recognition, we should first extract the profile from range data or detect the symmetry plane. Cartoux et al [?] proposed an approach which extracts the profile by looking for the vertical symmetry axis of Gaussian curvature values of the facial surface. However computation of Gaussian curvature needs sufficiently accurate

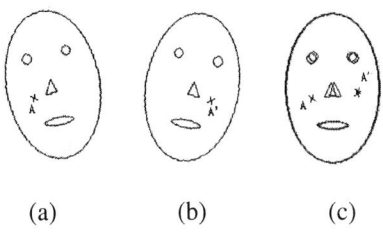

(a)   (b)   (c)

Fig. 1. Finding symmetry plane with alignment. (a) The original facial surface, (b) The mirrored facial surface with respect to an initial symmetry plane, (c) Alignment of both surfaces.

range data. Here we present an effective approach based on alignment, which is not involved in curvature and can robustly extract the symmetry plane from symmetrical object.

Assume that the 3D facial surface is symmetrical and continuous. After setting the facial surface an initial but inaccurate symmetry plane, its mirrored surface can be easily obtained, as shown in Fig. ??, where point A' in Fig. ??(b) is symmetrical to point A in Fig. ??(a) with respect to the initial symmetry plane. Once we align the two surface accurately, segment AA' must be vertical to the true symmetry plane and its central point must lie on the true symmetry plane. That is the segment AA' determines the true symmetry plane.

The true symmetry plane can be written as

$$\vec{n}\cdot\vec{x} + k = 0 \quad (11)$$

where $\vec{n}$ is the normal vector of the plane and k is a constant. After alignment of two surfaces, for point A denoted by $\vec{a}(a_x, a_y, a_z)$ and point A' denoted by $\vec{a}'(a'_x, a'_y, a'_z)$, the symmetry plane can be obtained by solve:

$$\begin{cases} \vec{n} = (\vec{a}-\vec{a}')/(\|\vec{a}-\vec{a}'\|) \\ \vec{n}\cdot(\vec{a}+\vec{a}')/2 + k = 0 \end{cases} \quad (12)$$

Considering error from range data acquisition and non-exact-symmetry of facial surface, in addition, for robustness purpose, actually we solve Eq. ?? for each point in facial surface and then perform least-mean-square method for final solution.

The algorithm we have used for alignment in our system is a variant of ICP. In this case, the scaling factor does not exist, which is different from the alignment for surface matching. For our needs, we are interested in an algorithm that offers the highest possible performance. After some experimentation, we employ a scheme similar to [?], which can complete alignment in one second.

Some results are shown in Fig. ??. The sample in the first row is seriously incomplete around eye regions. The second row is a sample whose data on the right side obviously less than that on the left side. The third row shows a sample with depth rotation. However, in these cases, symmetry planes all are detected correctly.

B. Similarity Metric

To be tolerant towards the noise and lack of features, the function measuring the difference between two profiles

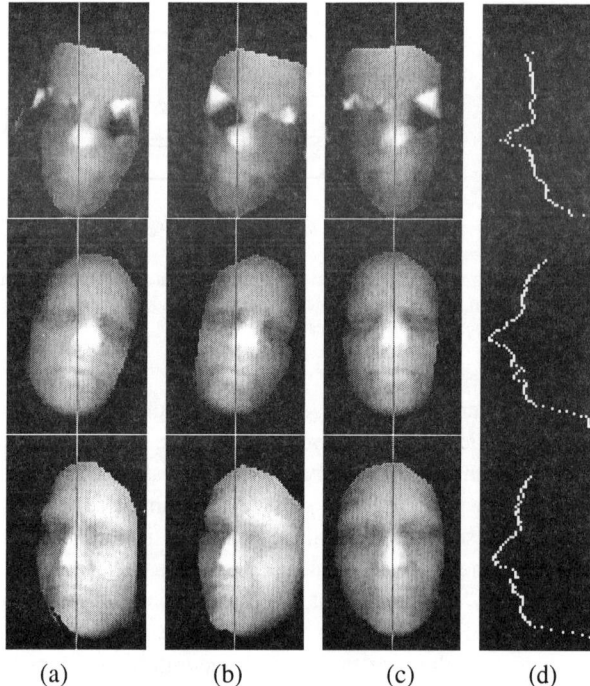

(a) (b) (c) (d)

Fig. 2. Profile extracting with symmetry plane detection. (a) the test model after triangle-based linear interpolation of the original range data, and its initial symmetry plane denoted by a gray line, (b) the mirrored model after aligning, (c) the symmetry plane detected, (d) the profile extracted.

should be robust enough. It should be insensitive to the small difference and mainly measure a the global difference between the profiles.

Hausdorff distance is a function measuring the distance between two point sets [?]. Regarding the profile as a point set, Hausdorff distance between the profiles gives a measure of the difference between two profiles.

Given two sets of points $A = \{a_1, ..., a_m\}$ and $B = \{b_1, ..., b_n\}$, the hausdorff distance is defined as

$$H(A, B) = \max(h(A, B), h(B, A)) \quad (13)$$

where

$$h(A, B) = \max_{a \in A} \min_{b \in B} \|a - b\| \quad (14)$$

But the Hausdorff distance is very sensitive to even a single "outlying" point of A or B. Thus rather than $H(A, B)$, we use a generalization of the Hausdorff distance, which is insensitive to small perturbations of the point sets and allows for small positional errors in point sets:

$$h_k(A, B) = kth \min_{a \in A} \min_{b \in B} \|a - b\| \quad (15)$$

where kth denotes the k-th ranked value (or equivalently the percentile of m values). If user specifies the fraction f, $0 \leq f \leq 1$, k can be determined by $k = \lfloor fm \rfloor$.

In terms of set containment, $h_k(A, B) \leq \delta$ if and only if there is some $A_k \subseteq A$ such that $A_k \subseteq B'$, where A_k contains k points of A. Thus we can think of $h_k(A, B)$ as partitioning A into two sets, A_k which is "close to" (within δ of) B and

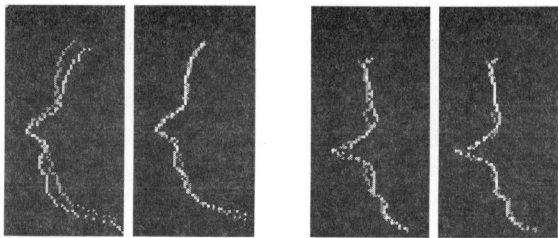

Fig. 3. Profiles at the initial position and the matching result.

the "outliers" $A - A_k$. This is in practice an important aspect of the generalized Hausdorff measure: it separately accounts for perturbations (by distance δ) and for outliers (by the rank k).

C. Matching by Optimization

For alignment of profiles, the dimension of transformation space is 3, they are rotation angle θ and translation vector (t_x, t_y). After collecting the parameters into a parameter vector $\vec{a} = (\theta, t_x, t_y)$, given a point x in a profile, the transformation is:

$$\begin{aligned} T_{2d}(\vec{a}; x) &= T(\theta, t_x, t_y; x) \\ &= \begin{pmatrix} \cos\theta & \sin\theta \\ -\sin\theta & \cos\theta \end{pmatrix} x + \begin{pmatrix} t_x \\ t_y \end{pmatrix} \end{aligned} \quad (16)$$

Thus, the alignment of profile $L_1 = p_i$ by $L_0 = q_j$ can be formalized as:

$$\underset{\vec{a}}{argmin}\, H_{lk}(L_0, T_{2d}(\vec{a}; L_1)) \quad (17)$$

As a wide variation of profiles and the characteristic of Hausdorff distance, many local minimums occur in the state space, with the result that many conventional optimization methods like Newton algorithm usually can not converge at the global minimum of the function. Here we use the simulated annealing method [?] to solve this optimization problem.

A good choice of the initial parameter can reduce notably the number of iterations needed for the convergence of the simulated annealing. We used a line to fit the profile curve, followed by rotation and translation of the profiles so that the two lines and their centroid overlapped each other. Figure ?? demonstrates the profiles at the initial position and the final position converged.

V. EXPERIMENTS

Our experiments use the facial range data from $3D\_RMA$ database, which is a part of M2VTS project. The range data were obtained by a 3D acquisition system based on structured light, in xyz form. There are about 3000 points in a model. It consists of four parts ($DBs1m, DBs2m, DBs1a, DBs2a$) that were built up from two sessions taken in different time separated by several months. See [?] for more details. In each part a person has exactly three shots with different orientation of head: straight forward, left or right, upward or downward, and some people smiled in some shots. Since spectacles, beards and moustaches may be present, some facial features are often incomplete, like nose, eye. Figure **??** shows two examples, two views for each.

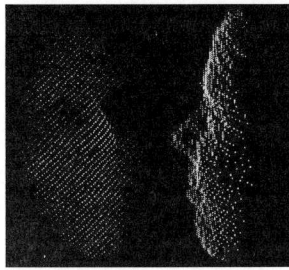 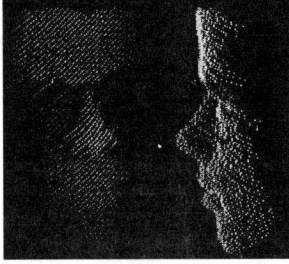

Fig. 4. Two sample models from $3D\_RMA$, two views for each model.

The proposed system is implemented on the Pentium IV 2.0GHz. The percentile of k-th Hausdorff distance is set to 0.8. It takes about 7 seconds to compare two facial surfaces, including registration and calculation of similarity, and about 2 seconds to match two profiles.

Profile matching results on six databases are shown in Table **??**. For test on database $DBs1m$, each shot of each person (30 models totally) is selected in the gallery database once, and the two shots remained act as the probe data. The other databases are dealt in the same way. ROC curve is shown in Fig. **??**. The best EER performance, tested for $DBs1m$, reaches 2.22%.

Surface matching results on three databases are shown in 3rd row of Table **??**. The best EER performance is 3.33% obtained on $DBs1m$. we also implemented the verification approach based on eigenface, which is composed of three consecutive parts: the proposed facial data registration, conversion of 3D data into 2D facial depth image based on triangle-based linear interpolation, and final verification in the facial image eigenspace [**?**]. EER by eigenface method is shown in 2rd row of Table **??**. Although it is outperformed by the approach with ours method, its performance is similar to the one of method by [**?**].

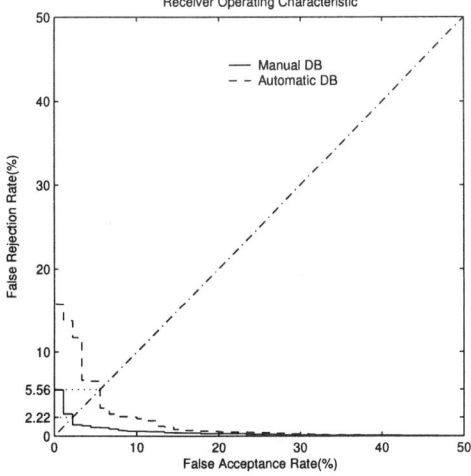

Fig. 5. ROC curves of profile matching for $DBs1m$ and $DBs1a$(30 persons).

The main motivation of the profile analysis is to access additional information in range data to be combined with the surface analysis in order to improve the recognition performance and robustness of the system. In the experiments, we make simply the fusion of the two experts by MAX rule. The result is demonstrated in Table **??**. EER is obviously decreased after fusion. It also shows that the compensation information between surface and profile exists.

VI. CONCLUSIONS

This paper described a novel approach for full automatic face verification from range data. Our system combines facial surface and profile recognition methods. To deal with discriminative ability of different regions in facial surface, a statistical discriminative model is presented for surface-based recognition. A robust symmetry plane detection method is proposed for profile extracting. We also introduced the k-th Hausdorff distance into the profile recognition to discard the detection of feature points in the profile. The experiments on the $3D\_RMA$ database show that the proposed approach can work well with the limited quality of facial range data, and also can deal with variation of pose and some changes of expression. Therefore a system based on our method is considerably practical. The fusion result gave a experimental proof for the presence of compensation information between surface and profile.

Despite variant of head pose, the viewpoint is more easily recovered in range data rather than in 2D images. Moreover, lighting condition has no effect on the range data. These two issues, which are serious in image-based face recognition, however, do not influence range data. Face recognition from range data is promising.

In the future work, experiments on a larger database are expected. It is also necessary to characterize the noise in range data produced by different 3D acquisition system like laser range scanners and photometric stereo techniques and the effect the noise has on the face recognition algorithms. And robustness of the 3D algorithms to facial expression will be addressed.

ACKNOWLEDGMENTS

The authors would like to thank Natural Science Foundation of P.R.China(No.60273059), National 863 High-Tech Programme (No.2001AA4180) and Zhejiang Provincial Natural Science Foundation for Young Outstanding Scientist of P.R.China(No.RC01058) for their financial supports. The authors would also like to thank Signal and Image Center at Royal Military Academy of Belgium for their database $3D\_RMA$.

REFERENCES

[1] Rama Chellappa, C.L.Wilson, and S.Sirohey. Human and machine recognition of faces: A survey. *Proceedings of the IEEE*, 83(5):705–740, 1995.
[2] Wenyi Zhao and Rama Chellappa. Image based face recognition: Issues and methods. In B.Javidi and Mercel Dekker, editors, *Image Recognition and Classification*, pages 375–402. 2002.

TABLE I

EQUAL ERROR RATES (EER) ON SIX DATABASES, EACH DATABASE HAS 30 INDIVIDUALS.

Database	$DBs1m$	$DBs2m$	$DBs1m+s2m$	$DBs1a$	$DBs2a$	$DBs1a+s2a$
Eigenface on 2D depth image (60 PCs) [?]	5.56%	6.67%	7.78%	-	-	-
Surface matching by ours	3.33%	5.56%	6.67%	-	-	-
Curvature matching	11.11%	12.22%	15.56%	14.44%	15.56%	19.94%
Profile matching by ours	2.22%	4.44%	6.67%	5.56%	7.78%	8.89%
Fusion of profile and surface	1.11%	2.22%	4.44%	-	-	-

[3] G. G. Gordon. Face recognition based on depth maps and surface curvature. In *Geometric Methods in Computer Vision, SPIE Proceedings*, volume 1570, pages 234–247, 1991.

[4] G. G. Gordon. Face recognition based on depth and curvature features. In *Proc. IEEE Computer Society Conference on Computer Vision and Pattern Recognition*, pages 808–810, June 1992.

[5] J. C. Lee and E. Milios. Matching range images of human faces. In *Proc. IEEE International Conference on Computer Vision*, pages 722–726, 1990.

[6] Y. Yacoob and L. S. Davis. Labeling of human face components from range data. *CVGIP: Image Understanding*, 60(2):168–178, September 1994.

[7] C. S. Chua, F. Han, and Y. K. Ho. 3d human face recognition using point signature. In *Proc. IEEE International Conference on Automatic Face and Gesture Recognition*, pages 233–238, March 2000.

[8] C. Beumier and M. Acheroy. Automatic 3d face authentication. *Image and Vision Computing*, 18(4):315–321, 2000.

[9] Volker Blanz, Sami Romdhani, and Thomas Vetter. Face identification across different poses and illumination with a 3d morphable model. In *Proc. IEEE International Conference on Automatic Face and Gesture Recognition*, pages 202–207, 2002.

[10] Volker Blanz and Thomas Vetter. A morphable model for the synthesis of 3d faces. In *Computer Graphics Proceedings SIGGRAPH'99*, pages 187–194, 1999.

[11] L. D. Harmon, M. K. Khan, R. Larsch, and P.F. Raming. Machine identification of human faces. *Pattern Recognition*, 13:97–110, 1981.

[12] C.J. Wu and J.S. Huang. Human face profile recognition by computer. *Pattern Recognition*, 23:255–259, 1990.

[13] K. Yu, X. Y. Jiang, and H. Bunke. Robust facial profile recognition. In *Proc. IEEE Int. Conf. on Image Processing*, volume 3, pages 491–494, 1996.

[14] L. D. Harmon and W. F. Hunt. Automatic recognition of human face profiles. *Computer Graphics Image Process*, 6, 1977.

[15] Yongsheng Gao and Maylor K.H. Leung. Human face profile recognition using attributed string. *Pattern Recognition*, 35:353–360, 2002.

[16] Neil D. Mckay Paul J. Best. A method for registration of 3-d shapes. *IEEE Transactions on Pattern Analysis and Machine Intelligence*, 14(2):239–256, 1992.

[17] D. W. Marquardt. An algorithm for least-squares estimation of nonlinear parameters. *J. Soc. Indust. Appl. Math.*, 11(2):431–441, 1963.

[18] J.Y. Cartoux, J.T.Lapreste, and M.Richetin. Face authentification or recognition by profile extraction from range images. In *Workshop on Interpretation of 3D Scenes*, pages 194–199, Nov. 1989.

[19] Szymon Rusinkiewicz, Olaf Hall-Holt, and Marc Levoy. Real-time 3d model acquisition. In *SIGGRAPH 2002 Proceedings*, pages 438–446, July 2002.

[20] D. P. Huttenlocher, G. A. Klanderman, and W. J. Rucklidge. Comparing images using the hausdorff distance. *IEEE Transactions on Pattern Analysis and Machine Intelligence*, 15(9):850–863, September 1993.

[21] William L. Goffe. Global optimization of statistical functions simulated annealing. *Journal of Econometrics*, 60:65–99, 1994.

[22] Matthew Turk and Alex Pentland. Eigenfaces for recognition. *Journal of Cognitive Neuroscience*, 3(1):71–86, 1991.

Various Decomposition Methods Applied to Face Recognition

Jaepil Ko, Eunju Kim and Hyeran Byun

Dept. of Computer Science, Yonsei Univ.

134, Shinchon-dong Sudaemoon-ku, Seoul 120-749, Korea

Abstract—Face recognition has mainly focused on face representation, so a simple classifier is frequently used. For a robust system, it is common to construct a multiclass classifier by combining outputs of several binary ones. In this paper, we overviews basic decomposition and decoding schemes and propose new methods then give empirical results of recognition performance on the ORL face dataset.

I. INTRODUCTION

Face recognition is one of the active research areas in computer vision and pattern recognition. Most researches on face recognition have focused on representation of face appearances rather than the classifiers. So it is frequently used a simple classifier such as *K*-NN after representing appearance of face image. *K*-NN is one of the lazy learners that does not need learning phase, so it is appropriate for applications which are not fixed in the number of classes like face recognition. For a robust system, it is desirable to adopt eager learning algorithm. It has been studied to decompose complex multiclass problem into a set of binary problems and then reconstruct the output of binary classifiers for each binary problem. The performance of decomposition methods depends on accuracy of base binary classifiers. Support vector machine (SVM) which is recently proposed by Vapnik [1] is well suited for a base learner and has been adopted as a classifier in face recognition [2,3,4]. The basic decomposition schemes are one-per-class (OPC) and pairwise coupling (PWC) [5] and their general form is error correcting output code (ECOC) [6]. OPC separates one class from all other classes and PWC separates only two classes for each possible pair of classes. ECOC consists of several dichotomizers with class redundancy to get robustness in case some dichotomizers fail. Correcting classifier (CC) is introduced for improving PWC in [7].

In this paper, we overview various decomposition schemes and propose new decomposition schemes based on OPC and we also propose decoding schemes to handle habitual outputs and complex dichotomy problem, then examine their properness for face recognition through the experiments on the ORL face dataset.

This paper is organized as follows. We describe SVM in Section II. In Section III, we overview basic decomposition schemes, and we introduce various decomposition schemes in Section IV. In Section V, we present two decoding schemes.

The experimental results and discussion are given in Section VI. Finally, we have conclusions in Section VII.

II. SUPPORT VECTOR MACHINES

SVM is a binary classifier based on the structural risk minimization [1]. SVM finds a linear classifier $f: \mathbf{R}^d \to \mathbf{R}$ of the form $f(x) = <\mathbf{w} \cdot \mathbf{x}> + b$ that minimizes the objective function for penalty parameter C, subject to the linear constraints with n training examples, $\{\mathbf{x}_i, y_i\}^n, \mathbf{x}_i \in \mathbf{R}^d, y_i \in \{-1,1\}$, where y_i is the class label.

$$\frac{1}{2}\|\mathbf{w}\|_2^2 + C\sum_{i=1}^n \xi_i \quad (1)$$
$$y_i((x_i \cdot \mathbf{w}) + b) \geq 1 - \xi_i, \ \xi_i \geq 0$$

$f(\mathbf{x})$ is a function that maximizes the *margin* which is the distance from $\mathbf{x}$ to the hyperplane that separating classes. The margin of an example $(\mathbf{x}, y)$ with respect to f is defined as $y \cdot f(\mathbf{x})$ [8]. The parameter C gives the trade-off between margin maximization and training error minimization. SVM can be applied to nonlinear separation as a linear machine in a high dimensional feature space using kernel function. Linear SVM can be rewritten as follows:

$$f(\mathbf{x}) = \sum_{i=1}^n \alpha_i y_i \mathbf{x}_i^T \mathbf{x} + b \quad (2)$$
$$\mathbf{w} = \sum_i^n \alpha_i y_i \mathbf{x}_i$$

where α_i is coefficient weight. In feature space with nonlinear mapping $\Phi: \mathbf{R}^d \to \mathbf{R}^D$, $f(\mathbf{x}) = \sum_{i=1}^n \alpha_i y_i \Phi(\mathbf{x}_i)^T \Phi(\mathbf{x}) + b$ and kernel function $K: \mathbf{R}^d \times \mathbf{R}^d \to \mathbf{R}$, $K(\mathbf{x}, \mathbf{z})$ can be replaced as $\Phi(\mathbf{x})^T \Phi(\mathbf{z})$ avoiding mapping Φ. Three common types of kernels are polynomial function, radial-basis function and two-layer perceptron.

In decomposition methods for multiclass problem, the principal merits of SVM are presented in [9] as follows. First, SVM learning algorithms generate dichotomizers that can adapt to the complexity of the problem, selecting a number of support vectors proportional to the problem complexity when dichotomies induced by decomposition methods can induce two-class classification problem with different level of complexity, and Second, SVM can perform accurate nonlinear separation of two classes in the input space using kernel function.

III. BASIC DECOMPOSITION SCHEMES

A. Fundamentals

Learning machines implementing decomposition methods are composed of two parts; one is decomposition (encoding) and the other is reconstruction (decoding) [10].

In decomposition step, we generate decomposition matrix $D \in \{-1, 0, +1\}^{L \times K}$ that specify K classes to train L dichotomizers, $f_1, \ldots, f_L$. The dichotomizer f_l is trained according to row $D(l, \cdot)$. If $D(l,k) = +1$, all examples of class k are positive and if $D(l,k) = -1$, all examples of class k are negative, and if $D(l,k) = 0$ none of the examples of class k participates in training of f_l [11]. The columns of D are called *codewords* [12].

In reconstruction step, a simple nearest-neighbor rule is commonly used. The class output is selected that maximizes the some similarity measure $s : \mathbf{R}^L \times \{-1,0,1\}^L \to [-\infty, \infty]$, between $f(\mathbf{x})$ and column $D(\cdot, k)$ [12].

$$class\_output = \arg\max_k s(f(\mathbf{x}), D(\cdot, k)) \quad (3)$$

When the similarity measure is defined based on *margin*, the method is called *margin decoding*

$$s(f(\mathbf{x}), D(\cdot, k)) = \sum_l f_l(\mathbf{x}) D(l, k) \quad (4)$$

When classifier outputs hard decision, $h(\mathbf{x}) \in \{-1,1\}$, the method is called *hamming decoding*.

$$s_H(h(\mathbf{x}), D(\cdot, k)) = 0.5 \times \sum_l (1 + h_l(\mathbf{x}) D(l, k)) \quad (5)$$

Theoretical and experimental results indicate that *margin decoding* is better than *hamming decoding* [9].
Unlike margin decoding, hamming decoding depends heavily on hamming distance among codewords. When the minimum hamming distance between codewords is Δ, the maximal number of error that can be corrected in an ECOC is $\lfloor \Delta - 1 \rfloor / 2$ [6].

Some other decoding schemes such as max-win, tree-structure based [3,13] and voting based [16] decoding are also used.

B. One Per Class (OPC)

Each dichotomizer f_i has to separate a single class from all the others. Therefore, if we have K classes, we need K dichotomizers. In reconstruction step, *max-win* decoding is commonly used for this scheme, i.e., a new input $\mathbf{x}$ can be classified as j such that f_j gives the highest value as we use similarity measure. In real applications, the decomposition of a polychotomy gives rise to complex dichotomies and we need in turn complex dichotomizers [12]. One of the merits of OPC is to train all the classes at once and it can be benefit when training sample is small for each class like face recognition, however it can give complex dichotomies because it groups various classes into one, so it needs an accurate classifier such as SVM and the performance of OPC depends heavily on the performance of base classifiers.

C. Pairwise Coupling (PWC)

Each dichotomizer f_{ij} is to separate a class i from a class j for each possible pair of classes therefore a dichotomizer is trained on the samples related to the two classes only. This can be a merit in that simpler dichotomy can be made. This can be a demerit when we consider decoding procedure. If an input $\mathbf{x}$ that belongs neither to class i nor to class j is fed into f_{ij}, nonsense output can come out [7]. As the number of classes increases, the performance becomes lowered by the nonsense outputs. To improve the performance, it needs to decode relative classifiers only. The number of dichotomizer is $_K C_2 = K(K-1)/2$ and hamming decoding is frequently used. To reduce decoding time, *tree-structured* decoding is applied in [3].

D. Correcting Classifier (CC)

Correcting classifier is proposed in [7] to handle the problem of nonsense outputs of PWC. Each dichotomizer f_{ij} is to separate two classes i and j from the other classes for each possible pair of classes, so the number of dichotomizer is the same as PWC. The performance of this method shows significant improvement than OPC or PWC in their experiments. This is because of its error correcting ability based on large hamming distance, $\Delta = 2(K-2)$. The disadvantage is that all the data is used for the training of each dichotomizer, as a result it needs a considerable amount of total training time.

$$\begin{bmatrix} +1 & -1 & -1 & -1 \\ -1 & +1 & -1 & -1 \\ -1 & -1 & +1 & -1 \\ -1 & -1 & -1 & +1 \end{bmatrix} \quad \begin{bmatrix} +1 & -1 & 0 & 0 \\ +1 & 0 & -1 & 0 \\ +1 & 0 & 0 & -1 \\ 0 & +1 & -1 & 0 \\ 0 & +1 & 0 & -1 \\ 0 & 0 & +1 & -1 \end{bmatrix} \quad \begin{bmatrix} +1 & +1 & -1 & -1 \\ +1 & -1 & +1 & -1 \\ +1 & -1 & -1 & +1 \\ -1 & +1 & +1 & -1 \\ -1 & +1 & -1 & +1 \\ -1 & -1 & +1 & +1 \end{bmatrix}$$

(a) OPC (b) PWC (c) CC

Fig. 1 Decomposition matrix of OPC, PWC and CC schemes for $K = 4$

IV. Various Decomposition Schemes Based on OPC

When the dimension of feature vector is high and the number of samples is not enough, it is better to learn all the classes at a time. In this case, we can consider the various decomposition schemes based on OPC, however OPC with hamming decoding does not have error correcting ability. So, we should introduce additional machines to endow it with an error correcting ability. In this section, we present variants of OPC with the additional machines. Usually, OPC generates complex dichotomy, so to deal with such a complex dichotomy, we adopt SVM, which can deal it by kernel trick, as a base learner.

A. Tree-based Decomposition

In tree-based decomposition, we construct binary decomposition tree by dividing classes into two equal parts. The classes of a parent node are distributed to its child nodes in a crossing manner. Fig. 2 shows the example of the generated decomposition tree on 8 classes. After the decomposition tree is generated, each node except for the root node makes one row in decomposition matrix by assigning positive value for classes it has and negative value for the other classes in the sibling nodes. The root node gives positive value for the half of the whole classes and negative value for the rest half. When the number of classes is K, $2\times(K-1)$ machines are generated. In this method, the number of positive valued classes is different among nodes. Therefore, it is desirable to introduce weights into the decoding process to reflect the difference.

B. N-Shift Decomposition

In this method, we first decide the number of positive classes N, and then form first row of decomposition matrix by setting N elements from left positive and the remains negative. The rest of rows are easily constructed by right-shifting the elements of the preceding row. Finally, OPC decomposition matrix is added to it. When the number of classes is K, $2\times K$ machines are generated by this decomposition method. Fig. 3 shows two examples of generated decomposition matrix having different N values, 2 and 3 respectively when K is 4.

$$\begin{bmatrix} +1 & +1 & -1 & -1 \\ -1 & +1 & +1 & -1 \\ -1 & -1 & +1 & +1 \\ +1 & -1 & -1 & +1 \\ & + & & \\ & OPC & & \end{bmatrix} \quad \begin{bmatrix} +1 & +1 & +1 & -1 \\ -1 & +1 & +1 & +1 \\ +1 & -1 & +1 & +1 \\ +1 & +1 & -1 & +1 \\ & + & & \\ & OPC & & \end{bmatrix}$$

(a) $N=2$ \qquad\qquad (b) $N=3$

Fig. 3 Decomposition matrix of *2*-Shift and *3*-Shift when $K=4$

C. N-Division Decomposition

In OPC, decomposition is done by separating one positive class from the other negative classes. Because various classes belong to the negative part, the dichotomy generated from this decomposition is apt to be complex. To reduce the complexity of the negative part, N-division decomposition method divides it into N sub parts and has N machines that are learned from corresponding N sub parts. If the number of given classes is K, and we choose K for N, the number of machine generated from this N division condition will be the same to that of PWC. In this method, we can make the decomposition varied from OPC to PWC by controlling the value of N. As N is decreased, the decomposition becomes similar to OPC. If N is growing, it becomes similar to PWC. It is a kind of generalized form of OPC and PWC. With this decomposition concept, we can control the level of decomposition, considering the characteristics of a given problem. Actually, OPC suffers from the problem complexity for which a machine responds and PWC has a problem of nonsense output. In this method, N is a trade-off between the problem complexity and the risk of nonsense outputs. When the number of classes is K, $N\times K$ machines are generated by this decomposition method. Fig. 4

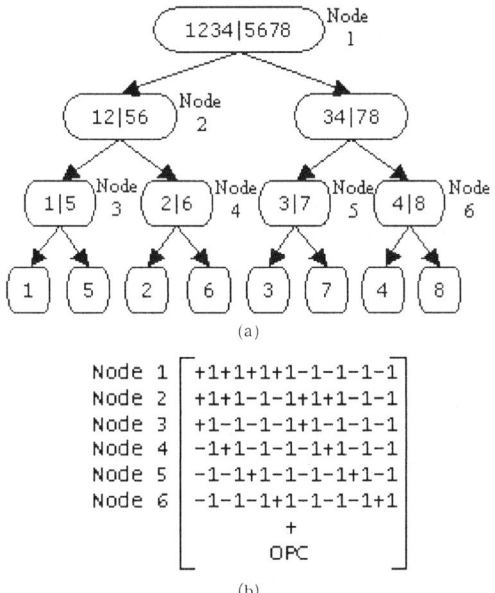

$$\begin{array}{c} \text{Node 1} \\ \text{Node 2} \\ \text{Node 3} \\ \text{Node 4} \\ \text{Node 5} \\ \text{Node 6} \end{array} \begin{bmatrix} +1+1+1+1-1-1-1-1 \\ +1+1-1-1+1+1-1-1 \\ +1-1-1-1+1-1-1-1 \\ -1+1-1-1-1+1-1-1 \\ -1-1+1-1-1-1+1-1 \\ -1-1-1+1-1-1-1+1 \\ + \\ OPC \end{bmatrix}$$

(b)

Fig. 2 Decomposition matrix of Tree scheme for $K=8$, (a) tree-structure on 8 classes. (b) Its decomposition matrix

$$\begin{array}{c} C1 \\ C1 \\ C2 \\ C2 \\ C3 \\ C3 \\ C4 \\ C4 \\ C5 \\ C5 \end{array} \begin{bmatrix} +1 & -1 & -1 & 0 & 0 \\ +1 & 0 & 0 & -1 & -1 \\ -1 & +1 & -1 & 0 & 0 \\ 0 & +1 & 0 & -1 & -1 \\ -1 & -1 & +1 & 0 & 0 \\ 0 & 0 & +1 & -1 & -1 \\ -1 & -1 & 0 & +1 & 0 \\ 0 & 0 & -1 & +1 & -1 \\ -1 & -1 & 0 & 0 & +1 \\ 0 & 0 & -1 & -1 & +1 \end{bmatrix}$$

Fig. 4. Decomposition matrix of *2*-Division for $K=5$, Cn means that class n is the positive class in that machine

shows the decomposition matrix when K is 5 and N is 2.

In decoding process, similarity is not calculated for every machine as in (4), but for the machines with same positive classes as follows:

$$s(f(\mathbf{x}), D(\cdot,k)) = \sum_{l \in C_k} f_l(\mathbf{x}) D(l,k) \quad (6)$$

where, C_k denotes the set of machines having kth class as one of its positive classes.

V. RELATIVE DISTANCE DECODING AND WEIGHTED DECODING

We propose two decoding methods, called *relative distance decoding* and *weighted decoding*. Those two decoding method are invented to deal with habitual outputs problem and complex dichotomizer problem respectively.

A. Relative Distance Decoding

Habitual output problem is about biased outputs for classes of a machine. Since the machine has different scale outputs for the two classes so the same outputs should be understood differently. For an example, we can imagine that for samples belonging to the class i, the machine habitually generates 0.8 and for samples belonging to class j, 0.5. The habit, generating uneven outputs for classes, is formed during the learning process. To deal with the problem, we introduce average template. Average template is constructed by calculating average of outputs from every base machine. The formulation is as follows:

$$D'(i,j) = \left(\sum_{\mathbf{x} \in C_j} f_i(\mathbf{x})\right) / |C_j| \quad (7)$$

where $|C_j|$ means the number of samples belonging to the class j. The following equation calculates the similarity between given input and a considered class by relative distance.

$$rd(f(x), D'(\cdot,k)) = 1/(1 + \exp(Ad + B))$$
$$d = \sum_l \|f_l(\mathbf{x}) - D'(l,k)\|_2 \quad (8)$$

A and B are constants of exponential function and they can be usually fixed through experiment. By the way of described above, we can consider the difference of habitual outputs of base machines and adjust the final decision to those relative differences. We call this method a *relative distance decoding*.

B. Weighted Decoding

As the number of positive classes increases, the complexity of dichotomy increases accordingly. To deduce the complexity of such a dichotomy, we introduce weighting into the decoding process. The weight for learner l, w_l, is calculated as follows:

$$L(D(l,k)) = \begin{cases} 1 & if\ D(l,k) > 0 \\ 0 & else \end{cases}$$
$$w_l = 1 / \sum_k L(D(l,k)) \quad (9)$$

where, $L(D(l,k))$ is a function for discerning positive classes from negative classes.

VI. EMPIRICAL RESULTS AND DISCUSSION

A. Face Database

We demonstrate our method on face images from ORL dataset. There are 10 different images for 40 individuals. Each image for one person differs from each other in lighting, facial expression and pose. The preprocessing for experiments was carried out as follows. First, to fix the problems of rotation, scaling, and translation, the preprocessing procedure was performed based on manually localized eye positions. Then we applied histogram equalization to flatten the distribution of image intensity values. Fig. 5 shows examples of the normalized face images whose dimension is 1024.

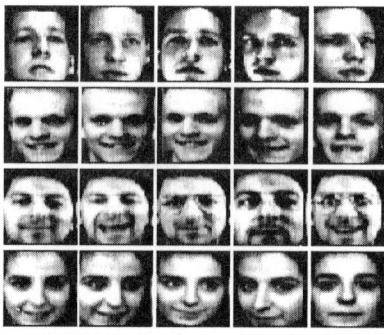

Fig. 5 Some normalized face images in the ORL face images

Secondly, we performed PCA to transform input space into face space. We varied the dimension of face space by changing the number of eigenvectors, and obtained the highest recognition rate at 48-dimension with a PCA-based algorithm. The outputs of PCA that was an input of SVM were shifted using the mean and scaled by their standard deviation. We used SMOBR[16] SVM with RBF kernels and C. In this experiment, we use the first five images of each person for training and the remaining five for testing. The number of samples for training and testing is both 200 respectively and the dimension of one sample is 48. The dataset, on which we test various decomposition schemes, has relatively small number of samples for its high dimensional feature space.

B. Performance Comparison

We evaluated various decomposition schemes on the ORL face dataset and compared the their recognition results. Table

TABLE I
DECODING SCHEMES

Symbol	Meaning
hm	Hamming decoding
mg	Margin decoding
rd	Relative distance decoding
whm	Hamming decoding with weighting
wmg	Margin decoding with weighting
wrd	Relative distance decoding with weighting
d-hm	Hamming decoding in N-Division scheme
d-mg	Margin decoding in N-Division scheme

I shows the decoding methods we tried. In Table II and III, the recognition rate of each decomposition schemes is presented. For those results, we calculated the recognition rates, varying C from 1 to 10 and dispersion from 0.2 to 1.2 and chose the best recognition rate among them.

From the Table II, in case of hamming decoding, the recognition rate increase with the number of machines. However, in case of margin decoding, the number of machines are less concerned in the recognition rate. N-Shift and Tree have almost the same number of machines, but their recognition rate with margin decoding is considerably different.

The main difference between OPC and PWC is the number of classes that are concerned in training. In OPC, all the classes are trained for one machine, on the other hand just two classes are trained for one machine in PWC.

When we compare the two methods, in case of hamming decoding, PWC shows significantly better performance than OPC, but in case of margin decoding, OPC shows better performance. Overall OPC with margin decoding shows slightly better performance than PWC with hamming decoding. We can infer that because the number of training face image of one person is small so, the performance of OPC training all the classes at a time is better than that of PWC.

Each machine in OPC and CC trains all the classes at a time. In this case, CC shows significantly better performance than OPC in hamming decoding like PWC due to its large number

TABLE II
RECOGNITION RATE I

Method (# of SVM)	hm	mg	rd	whm	wmg	wrd
OPC(40)	0.690	0.920	**0.930**	-	-	-
PWC(780)	**0.910**	0.885	0.885	-	-	-
CC(780)	0.895	**0.925**	**0.930**	-	-	-
2-Shift(80)	0.735	0.900	**0.930**	0.735	0.910	0.930
3-Shift(80)	0.735	0.890	0.900	0.715	0.925	**0.940**
Tree(78)	0.735	0.840	0.855	**0.750**	0.910	0.930

TABLE III
RECOGNITION RATE II

Method (# of SVM)	hm	mg	rd	d-hm	d-mg
2-Division(80)	0.745	**0.890**	**0.925**	0.745	**0.935**
3-Division(120)	0.795	0.885	**0.925**	0.795	0.925
5-Division(200)	0.865	0.845	0.910	0.860	0.915
10-Division(400)	**0.895**	0.880	0.905	**0.890**	0.910

of machines, however when it comes to margin decoding, the performance of the two is almost the same regardless of quite different number of machines. From the result, when we have small number of samples like face images, OPC-like methods at the point of training all the classes at a time can be a good choice, but we think that it is unnecessary to make too much machines like CC method.

In case of Tree and N-Shift that is OPC-like methods but they have small number of machines than CC, they have almost the same machines and result in the same recognition rate with hamming decoding however, with margin decoding, Tree method shows poor recognition rate than N-Shift. Tree method has machines from more complex dichotomies relative to N-Shift because dichotomies in Tree consist of large number of classes in supper classes. We can think that overall performance of Tree becomes poor because of its complex dichotomies. This inference can be supported by the fact that 3-Shift does not show better recognition rate than 2-Shift.

In the methods including machines from complex dichotomies, the performance of margin decoding is decreased. To overcome this property, we suggested weighted decoding. With the weighted margin decoding, we can show almost the same performance to OPC with 2-Shit, 3-Shift, and Tree.

In case of applying relative distance decoding, OPC, CC and 2-Shift, show recognition rate of 93%. Tree that is trained too complex dichotomies does not show the same recognition with the relative decoding, however with adding weighted decoding, it can also achieve the same recognition rate

Table III shows the performance of N-Division scheme. As N increases, both the number of machines and performance of hamming decoding also increase, however the performance of margin decoding is decreased. It means that nonsense outputs of unrelated machines strongly affect the overall performance when the number of samples is small while the number of classes is large like the ORL face dataset. Therefore, we can conclude that OPC is more suitable decomposition scheme than PWC in this case. On the other hand, some literature report that PWC is better than OPC on some datasets of UCI repository in which the number of classes is small and/or the number of samples is sufficiently large.

As N increases, the performance of margin decoding

becomes low and in case of $N=2$, the performance is lower than OPC. However, the proposed decoding scheme for N-Division, d-mg, shows almost the same performance to the other OPC-based methods. 2-Division with d-mg shows slightly better performance than OPC.

VII. CONCLUSION

In this paper we overview basic decomposition schemes for multiclass problem. We introduced various decomposition schemes based on OPC and proposed decoding scheme s suitable for the proposed decomposition schemes. Especially, we designed N-Division scheme that is a kind of generalized form of OPC and PWC, in which N is a tradeoff between the problem complexity and the risk of nonsense outputs. By controlling N, we can expect better performance than OPC or PWC.

From the experiment on the ORL face dataset, we showed that the performance of margin decoding does not strongly depend on the hamming distance of decomposition matrix. In case of the application in which the number of classes is large and the number of samples is small like face recognition, we also showed that OPC-like methods are more suitable than PWC from the experiment of N-Division scheme.

REFERENCES

[1] V.N. Vapnik, "Statistical Learning Theory", John Wiley & Sons, New York, 1998
[2] P.J. Phillips, "Support vector machines applied to face recognition", Advanced in Neural Information Processing System II, MIT Press, pp. 803-809, 1998
[3] G.Guo, S.Z. Li, and K.L. Chan, "Support vector machines for face recognition", Image and Vision Computing, Vol. 19, pp.631-638, 2001
[4] B.Heisele, P.Ho, and T. Poggio, "Face recognition with support vector machines: Global versus Component-based Approach", Proc. of IEEE ICCV, pp.688-694, 2001
[5] T. Hastie and R. Tibshirani, "Classification by Pairwise Coupling", Advances in Neural Information Processing Systems, Vol. 10, MIT Press, 1998
[6] T.G. Dietterich and G. Bakiri, "Solving Multiclass Learning Problems via Error-Correcting Output Codes", Journal of Artificial Intelligence Research, Vol. 2, pp. 263-286, 1995
[7] M. Moreira and E. Mayoraz, "Improved Pairwise Coupling Classification with Correcting Classifiers", Proc. of ECML, pp.160-171, 1998
[8] L. Hansen and P. Salamon, "Neural network ensembles", IEEE Trans. on PAMI, Vol.12, pp.993-1001, 1990
[9] E.L. Allwein, R.E. Schapire and Y. Singer, "Reducing Multiclass to Binary: A Unifying Approach for Margin Classifiers", Proc. of ICML, pp. 9-16, 2000
[10] G. Valentini, "Upper bounds on the training error of ECOC-SVM ensembles", Technical Report TR-00-17, DISI - Dipartimento di Informatica e Scienze dell' Informazione - Universita di Genova, 2000.
[11] F. Masulli and G. Valentini, "Comparing Decomposition Methods for Classification", Proc. of International Conference on Knowledge-based Intelligent Engineering Systems & Allied Technologies, Vol. 2, pp.788-791, 2000
[12] A.Klautau, N.Jevtic and A. Orlisky, "Combined Binary Classifiers with Applications to Speech Recognition", Proc. of ICSLP, pp. 2469-2472, 2002
[13] E. Alpaydm and E. Mayoraz, "Learning Error-Correcting Output Codes from Data", Proc. of ICANN, 1999
[14] J. Platt, N. Cristianini and J.S. Taylor, "Large margin DAGs for multiclass classification", In Advances in Neural Information Processing Systems, Vol. 12, pp.547-553, MIT Press, 2000
[15] J.H. Friedman, "Another Approach to Polychotomous Classification", Technical Report, Department of Statistics, Stanford University, 1996
[16] SMOBR: http://www.cpdee.ufmg.br/~barros/

Feature Selection Forcing Overtraining May Help to Improve Performance

Enrique Romero
Llenguatges i Sistemes Informàtics
Universitat Politècnica de Catalunya
eromero@lsi.upc.es

Josep M. Sopena
Lab. Neurocomputació
Universitat de Barcelona
jsopena@psi.ub.es

Gorka Navarrete
Lab. Neurocomputació
Universitat de Barcelona
gnavarga7@psi.ub.edu

René Alquézar
Llenguatges i Sistemes Informàtics
Universitat Politècnica de Catalunya
alquezar@lsi.upc.es

Abstract—One of the main drawbacks of Machine Learning systems is the negative effect caused by overtraining. If the points in the dataset are perfectly fitted, the generalization performance is usually bad. We propose to take profit of overtraining, together with Feature Selection, to improve the performance of a learning system. The main idea lies in the hypothesis that when the dataset is as fitted as possible, the system is forced to use all the available variables as much as possible. Noisy and useless variables can be detected if generalization improves when the system is not allowed to use them. Forcing overtraining, noisy and useless variables should be more outstanding. In order to test this hypothesis, we performed several Feature Selection experiments using Feed-forward Neural Networks. The particular Feature Selection procedure used was *Sequential Backward Selection*. Experimental results with several real-world problems suggest that our hypothesis seems to be well-founded. Ironically, forcing overtraining may help to achieve good performance.

I. INTRODUCTION

Suppose that someone wants to apply a Machine Learning (ML) technique to a certain problem. There exist many situations where one does not have *a priori* neither a model that could describe the phenomenon nor the knowledge of which variables are adequate to describe it. This is very common in Medicine or Psychology, for example. The expert may have several intuitions about the variables related to the problem, but by no means has neither the security that those are all the features needed to explain the phenomenon nor the confidence that all the features are useful. When important variables are missing, the problem cannot be solved. If some variables are useless, solutions that use them will probably have important performance problems. In addition, the number of available examples is usually small and they may be noisy or incomplete. In this situation, a Feature Selection (FS) procedure may be a very useful tool to select a good subset of variables. In addition of reducing the input dimension, FS may lead to a marked improvement in the performance of a ML system [5]. A justification for this assertion comes from the Bias/Variance decomposition [3], which suggests that the optimal performance is obtained when a tradeoff between the quality of the approximation to the training set and the variance of the solution is achieved. When too many variables are present the system can (surely) approximate very well the training set, but it is (probably) too complex, increasing the variance term. As far as the variables are eliminated, the complexity of the system is reduced (together with its capacity of approximation).

We will focus our work in classification tasks. In this paper we propose the use of Feed-forward Neural Networks (FNNs) to perform FS within the *wrapper* approach [6]. In particular, the *Sequential Backward Selection* (SBS) procedure was applied in our experiments (see Section II for a brief description of SBS and the wrapper approach). Our main motivation to use the SBS method was the expectation that it could be possible to identify noisy and useless variables as the features deleted in the first steps of the SBS procedure, while maintaining all the possible interactions among the initial set of variables. The *Sequential Forward Selection* (SFS) procedure, for example, does not satisfy this property. Ideally, there would exist an optimal point where the addition or elimination of any variable would lead to a worse performance.

In order to encourage the SBS procedure to eliminate noisy and useless variables in the first steps, we propose to fit the data as much as possible (that is, forcing overtraining). In theory, generalization improves when the system does not use noisy and useless variables. Our hypothesis is that this effect will be more evident if we try to fit the training set as much as possible (that is, when overtraining is highly present), since in this situation the variables in the system are forced to be as used as possible. Therefore, forcing overtraining, together with FS, may help to achieve good performance. This idea may be valid for both linear and non-linear classifiers.

The main motivation to use FNNs was their well-known universal approximation capability [7]. Using FNNs it is possible to fit enough the data to test our hypothesis.

After the selected variables are discarded, a different approach to the problem can be performed. In spite of the fact that the negative effect of overtraining may still be present, we expect that it will probably be lower. A standard technique that tries to control the overtraining (early stopping, for example) is expected to obtain better results with this reduced number of variables. We tested our proposal with several real-world problems. Experimental results suggest that our hypothesis seems to be well-founded.

The rest of the paper is organized as follows. In Section II, the FS problem is briefly described. The main ideas are explained in Section III. An algorithmic description of the proposed scheme is given in Section IV. The experimental work is presented in Section V. Finally, some conclusions and future work are drawn in Section VI.

II. FEATURE SELECTION

The problem of FS can be defined as follows [8]: given a set of N_f candidate features, select a subset that performs the best under some evaluation criterion. From a computational point of view, the previous definition of FS leads to solve a search problem in a space of 2^{N_f} elements. In order to obtain a solution, we need to specify two components: the feature subset evaluation criterion and the procedure for searching through candidate subsets of features. Many different evaluation criteria have appeared in the literature, based on different measures, such as distance, information, consistency, dependence or accuracy, among others [8]. Concerning the search procedure there also exists a wide range of methods to avoid the computationally prohibitive (in the general case) exhaustive search. Some of them determine the optimal feature subset under certain assumptions, such as the *Branch and Bound* algorithm, which needs monotonicity of the evaluation criterion. Other methods seek for a suboptimal solution heuristically. Rather well-known methods of this type are the sequential ones, where features are deleted from (or added to) the partial solution at every step. The simplest ones are the SBS and the SFS procedures. SBS is a top-down process. Starting from the complete set of available features, one feature is deleted at every step of the algorithm, chosen on the basis of which of the available candidates gives rise (when deleted) to the best value of the selection criterion. SFS is a bottom-up process. The procedure begins by considering each of the variables individually and selecting the one which gives the best value for the selection criterion. At every step, the feature which gives rise (when added) to the best value of the selection criterion is added to the set. It is expected that performance may improve as far as features are deleted (added), but at some point the elimination (inclusion) of further features results in performance degradation [5].

Specially important is the wrapper approach (see, for example, [6]), where the feature subset selection is done using an induction algorithm as a black box (that is, no knowledge of the algorithm is needed, just the interface). The feature subset evaluation criterion is the accuracy of the induced classifiers (which is not necessarily monotone).

III. OVERTRAINING, FNNs AND SBS

One of the main drawbacks of ML frameworks in general is the poor generalization behaviour as a consequence of overtraining. If the points in the training set are perfectly fitted, the generalization performance is usually bad, specially in real-world problems. As previously said, in addition to the possible lack of information (including both missing values and missing variables), features in real-world datasets may be noisy or useless for the problem at hand. *A priori*, when many variables are present, there may be many different solutions capable of approximating the same training set. But only a few number of these solutions will lead to good generalization.

There is no reason to think that a good one will be selected by our inducer. If the system gives some importance to noisy or useless variables in order to approximate the dataset, it will use this information for new data, probably leading to poor generalization even if we try to control the overtraining. The problem is that the relevance of the variables is not known a priori. Imagine that we have collected a database where we have a useless variable, say the color of the eyes, to predict a heart disease. Unfortunalely, there is no reason to think that this variable will not be used in the training procedure to approximate the dataset. Therefore, generalization will probably be poor, even if we try to control the overtraining. The existence of many solutions consistent with the data contribute to high variance in the Bias/Variance decomposition [3]. This behaviour is more probable to happen when only a small number of examples is available.

In this context, it may be convenient to use an FS procedure. Suppose that the system uses a (very) noisy or useless variable to approximate the dataset (the color of the eyes to predict a heart disease). Without this variable, generalization should improve (or, at least, should not worsen). Our hypothesis is that this effect will be more evident if we try to fit the training set as much as possible, that is, when overtraining is highly present. An intuitive justification of this statement could be the fact that, if we try to adjust perfectly the dataset, we are forcing all the variables to be as used as possible in the resulting solution. In this situation, noisy and useless variables should emerge more clearly if generalization improves when the system is not allowed to use them. Ironically, we want to improve generalization forcing overtraining. This reasoning may be valid for both linear and non-linear classifiers.

We conjecture that this idea will allow to detect useless and (very) noisy variables for the problem at hand. After these variables have been discarded, a different approach to the problem can be performed, since we can consider (of course, with a certain probability of error) that all the remaining variables are quite useful. It does not necessarily imply that the system will not present the negative effect of the overtraining with the selected variables, but it will probably be lower. A standard technique that tries to control the overtraining (early stopping, for example) is expected to obtain better results with this reduced number of variables.

Since the evaluation criterion is the performance of the system, we decided to use a wrapper approach in order to select the resulting feature subset. Therefore, we only needed to specify the induction algorithm and the search procedure. In order to fit the dataset as much as possible, we decided to use FNNs. As it is well-known, FNNs have been shown to be universal approximators [7]. Thus, they are an appropiate induction framework to fit the data as required. Among all the existing FS techniques, we decided to use a standard SBS procedure, so that it could be possible to identify noisy and useless variables as the features deleted in the first steps of the SBS procedure, while maintaining all the possible interactions among the initial set of variables (standard SFS, for example, does not satisfy this property).

Algorithm
  Let V_1 the full set of N_f features
  for $N = 1$ **up to** $N_f - 1$ **do**
    for each $v \in V_N$ **do**
      Set $V = V_N - \{v\}$
      Train the network with V and keep its generalization performance. The network is overtrained, trying to fit the data as much as possible.
    end for
    Set $V_{N+1} = V_N - \{v^*\}$ where v^* corresponds to the worst performance of the network in the previous loop
  end for
  Return V_{N^*} where N^* corresponds to the best performance of the network in the previous loop
end Algorithm

Fig. 1. The SBS procedure with FNNs forcing overtraining at every step.

Dataset	#Var.	#Cla.	#Exa.	Missing	Source
Australian Credit	14	2	690	yes	UCI/Statlog
Ionosphere	33	2	351	no	UCI/Statlog
Sonar	60	2	208	no	UCI/Statlog
Hepatitis	19	2	155	yes	UCI/Statlog
Cleveland Heart	13	2	303	yes	Statlog
Statlog Heart	13	2	270	no	Statlog
Bupa Liver	6	2	345	no	UCI
Lung Cancer	56	3	32	yes	UCI
IIM Dataset	25	2	62	no	New

TABLE I

DESCRIPTION OF THE DATASETS. THE COLUMN '#VAR.' INDICATES THE NUMBER OF VARIABLES, THE COLUMN '#CLA.' THE NUMBER OF CLASSES, AND THE COLUMN '#EXA.' SHOWS THE NUMBER OF EXAMPLES.

IV. ALGORITHM

The proposed SBS procedure with FNNs forcing overtraining can be seen in Figure 1. It works roughly as follows. First, the parameters of the network are adjusted so as to achieve a low value of the total squared error in a reasonable number of epochs N_e. Then, the SBS procedure starts. For every variable, we train the network N_e epochs without this variable, so that the training set is "as approximated as possible" with the selected parameters. The variable such that, when deleted, gives rise to the best generalization performance, is permanently removed. This loop is repeated until only one variable remains. Typically, it is expected that performance will improve until some point where the elimination of further features results in performance degradation. This is the subset of features returned by the algorithm.

V. EXPERIMENTS

We now present the experiments performed in order to test the hypothesis presented in Section III.

A. Datasets description

1) UCI and Statlog Benchmarks: We selected several datasets from two well-known ML repositories: UCI [2] and Statlog [9]. A wide variety of problems is represented by these benchmarks, as can be seen in Table I. When the range of inputs was not normalized, we performed a linear scale transformation in $[0, 1]$. For real-valued variables, missing values were substituted by the average within the class. For discrete ones, they were substituted by the most frequent value in the class.

2) IIM Dataset: We had the opportunity to work on a real-world problem of medical diagnosis. The dataset contained the data of 62 patients suffering from Idiopathic Inflamatory Myopathies (IIMs). IIMs, specially dermatomyositis, are associated with an increased risk of cancer. Evaluation of patients for the presence of an occult malignancy is worrisome, deserves time consumption and patients are often subjected to extensive invasive investigations. Although some factors as age, sex, refractory or recurrent disease and some types of myositis specific antibodies (such as antisynthetase or anti-Mi-2) have been proposed to be related to the risk of cancer in IIM patients, conclusive studies are lacking [4].

On average, the 62 patients diagnosed of IIM in our study were followed up for 8 years in the Hospital de la Vall d'Hebron, Barcelona. The diagnosis of inflamatory myopathy was based on a strict clinical definition and histologic criteria. The input consisted of 25 variables containing clinical and laboratory data. Fortunately, there was no missing value and the values of the variables had (presumably) little noise. The target was the presence or absence of cancer. All the malignancies were registered and pathologically confirmed in the hospital. The number of patients diagnosed of cancer was 11. This low number of examples in our dataset is due to the fact that IIMs are extremely rare diseases.

Neither the noise in the data nor the absence of information were seen as severe drawbacks in the IIM dataset. In contrast, the existence of useless variables was considered our outstanding problem. As explained previously, the reason is that many of the variables were gathered without knowing exactly their importance (although guessing that they could help to give an insight of the problem). Real-valued variables were normalized with mean 0 and variance 1, whereas discrete ones were codified in a unary 1-of-C scheme. In this problem the two classes are clearly unbalanced. It was considered a major error to predict absence of cancer when this was not the case. Therefore, the sum-of-squares error function was modified to assign equal importance to every class, as in [10].

B. Experimental Setting

The training of the networks was performed with standard Back-propagation (BP) [12] in pattern learning mode (weights are modified after the presentation of each example). We used both linear and non-linear FNNs. For non-linear FNNs, and in order to reduce the computational cost, we decided to use Multi-layer Perceptrons (MLPs) with one hidden layer of units, with the sine as the activation function in the hidden layer and

Benchmark	Lin (All)	Sin (All)	Lin (SBS)	Sin (SBS)
Australian Credit	85.9%	86.0%	87.4% (8)	87.2% (7)
Ionosphere	86.9%	89.5%	92.4% (11)	92.6% (11)
Sonar	77.4%	86.1%	90.6% (25)	91.6% (20)
Hepatitis	85.3%	76.0%	92.3% (3)	94.0% (6)
Cleveland Heart	83.4%	80.7%	83.8% (5)	82.5% (3)
Statlog Heart	83.3%	81.3%	85.2% (4)	84.5% (3)
Bupa Liver	68.3%	72.4%	69.1% (4)	71.8% (4)
Lung Cancer	46.9%	36.3%	87.5% (14)	87.5% (9)
IIM Dataset	73.6%	74.5%	93.2% (12)	94.2% (9)

TABLE III

GENERALIZATION RESULTS BEFORE AND AFTER THE APPLICATION OF THE SBS PROCEDURE, EXPRESSED AS THE AVERAGE OF 5 RUNS OF A CROSS-VALIDATION PROCEDURE. THE NUMBER OF SELECTED VARIABLES IS INDICATED BETWEEN BRACKETS.

Dataset	#Hidd.	Weights Range	Epochs
Australian Credit	20	[-1.0,+1.0]	1000
Ionosphere	10	[-0.5,+0.5]	300
Sonar	35	[-1.0,+1.0]	300
Hepatitis	15	[-2.5,+2.5]	500
Cleveland Heart	20	[-1.0,+1.0]	500
Statlog Heart	20	[-0.5,+0.5]	600
Bupa Liver	20	[-2.0,+2.0]	1500
Lung Cancer	20	[-1.0,+1.0]	100
IIM Dataset	15	[-0.5,+0.5]	150

TABLE II

DESCRIPTION OF THE PARAMETERS OF THE SINUSOIDAL ARCHITECTURES.

the hyperbolic tangent in the output layer, as in [13]. Units in the hidden layer had no bias, and the momentum term was set to 0. For every dataset, the number of hidden units, the initial range of weights in the hidden layer and the number of epochs trained can be seen in Table II. The learning rates were adjusted for every particular dataset to fit the data as much as possible.

C. Results

The generalization results for every dataset can be seen in Table III as the average of 5 runs of a cross-validation procedure. For the Lung Cancer and the IIM datasets a leave-one-out method was applied, whereas the rest of the datasets were tested with a 10-fold cross-validation.

For every dataset, the following experiments were performed. First, an early stopping procedure was run with the whole set of variables. These results can be seen in the columns 'Lin (All)' for linear networks and 'Sin (All)' for sinusoidal ones. Second, SBS was applied to every dataset (both for linear and sinusoidal FNNs), as explained in Section III and Section IV. The results with the set of variables selected by SBS are shown in the columns 'Lin (SBS)' for linear networks and 'Sin (SBS)' for sinusoidal ones. The number of selected variables is indicated between brackets in the same columns.

To the best of our knowledge, the results obtained for UCI and Statlog datasets are as good as most of previous published results for FS procedures with these benchmarks. For the IIM dataset, the results are also excellent. In order to have only a brief reference, the best results and the results of BP in [9] (when cross-validation tests were available) are included in Table IV. Although these results are probably out of date, they were performed with the same methodology than ours. It should also be noted that all our results are obtained with MLPs trained with BP, although there may be problems better suited for other kind of classifiers or learning methods. In [9] some of the datasets were tested with more than 20 different methods, and the results of BP were far from the best, as can be seen in Table IV. It is not clear, however, whether a FS procedure has been applied in the results shown in [9] or not.

Benchmark	Best (Statlog)	BP (Statlog)
Australian Credit	86.9%	84.6%
Sonar	87.5%	84.7%
Hepatitis	92.9%	82.1%
Cleveland Heart	85.1%	81.3%
Statlog Heart	83.6%	65.6%

TABLE IV

STATLOG RESULTS [9] FOR THE DATASETS WHERE CROSS-VALIDATION TESTS WERE AVAILABLE.

Anyway, the important point is the fact that there has been, on average, a great improvement after the FS procedure has been applied, leading to a very good performance. In our opinion, this means that the system has eliminated noisy and useless variables. Specially remarkable is the behaviour of linear networks, which are able to obtain very good results, although usually with more variables than non-linear networks. This supports the independence of our hypothesis from a particular learning model.

Figure 2 shows, for every dataset, how varies the percentage of correct examples in the training and test set with respect to the number of eliminated variables in the SBS procedure. Basically, two kinds of behaviour can be observed. There exist

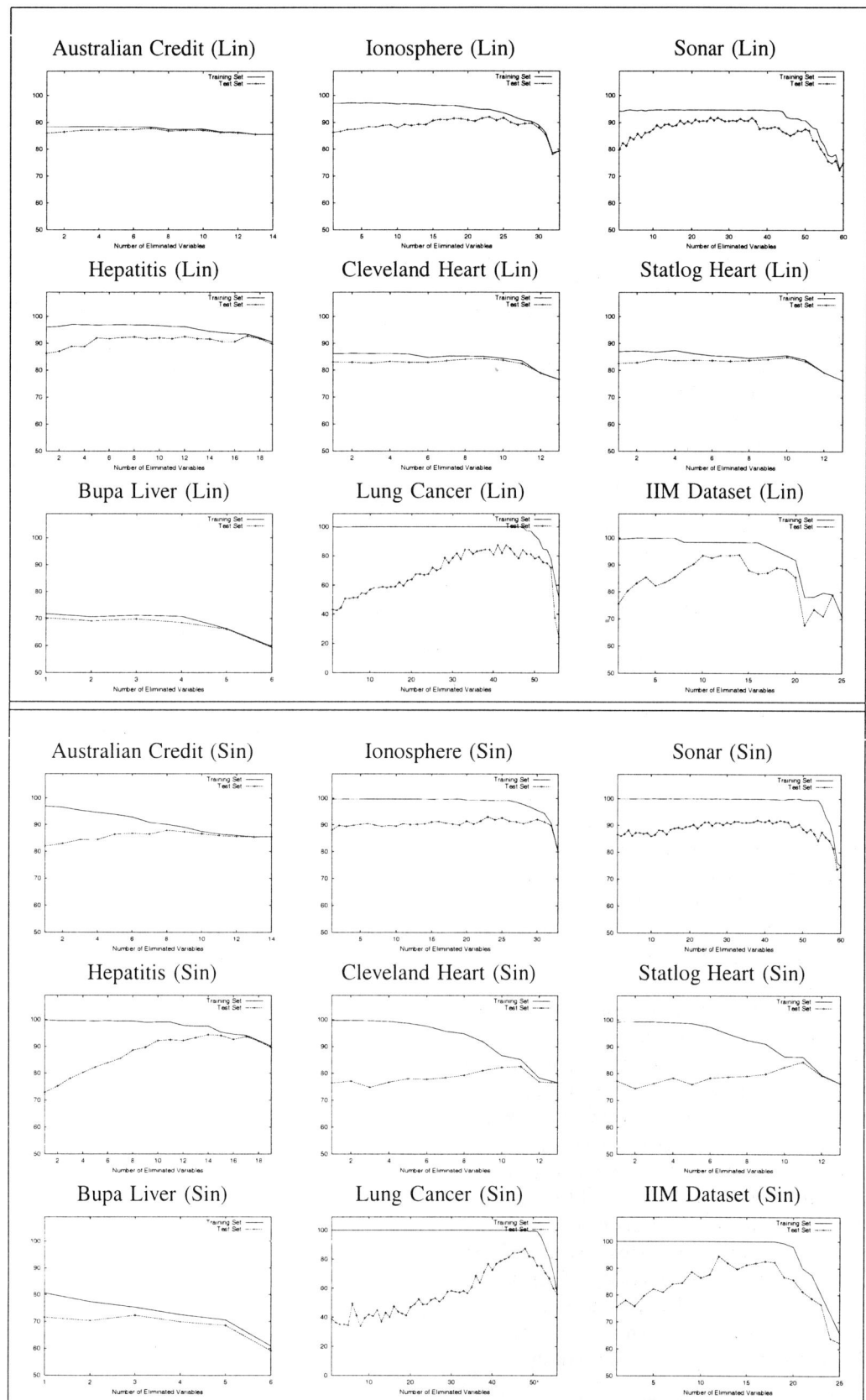

Fig. 2. Percentage of correct examples in the training and test set with respect to the number of eliminated variables in the SBS procedure for linear (top) and sinusiodal (bottom) FNNs.

problems where the performance hardly improves. The Bupa Liver dataset is probably the most representative example of this type. On the other hand, there exist datasets where the curve of performance has a more desired behaviour, as the Lung Cancer or Hepatitis datasets: test error usually improves as far as variables are being eliminated, up to a point where starts to degenerate. It is interesting to note that these two datasets are very different with respect to the number of examples and variables.

There is a surprising coincidence when comparing linear and non-linear networks in Figure 2. The respective test curve shapes are very similar for the same problem. This fact could also may be indicating that the method is quite independent of the particular learning system used.

For some problems (Bupa Liver or Australian Credit, for example), it could be possible that important variables are lacking, since the system fails to approximate the training set from the first steps of the SBS procedure.

VI. CONCLUSIONS AND FUTURE WORK

In this paper it is experimentally shown how overtraining can be used, together with FS, to improve generalization performance in many cases. The idea lies in the hypothesis that when overtraining is present, the variables are forced to have too much importance in the resulting solution. In this situation, the effect of noisy and useless variables should be more evident. The proposed methodology is based on perform FS forcing overtraining, so that it can be easier to detect noisy and useless variables. In our experiments, we used FNNs to perform SBS within the wrapper approach.

There exist several issues that can be improved. For example, the parameters (number of hidden units, learning rates, etc) of the network should be readjusted after the elimination of every variable in the SBS procedure. Although it is expected that the new parameters should be quite similar to the previous ones, they may not be necessarily equal. In this sense, an automatic selection of the parameters would be desirable [11]. A different training algorithm may also be used in order to reduce the computational cost. Larger datasets with a larger number of variables could need a different treatment.

More experiments are needed to confirm the hypothesis. For example, suppose that we select the variable to eliminate in the SBS procedure performing early stopping instead of forcing overtraining. According to our hypothesis, our method would detect noisy and useless variables better than this approach.

In addition, there exist several issues that can be modified. Although we have used FNNs in our experiments, we think that our hypothesis is independent of a particular learning model. The only requirement is the capacity of fitting the training set. In a similar way, other FS procedures, instead of SBS, could be used, such as hybrid or bidirectional methods applying SBS and SFS alternatively or simultaneously.

ACKNOWLEDGMENT

This work was supported by Consejo Interministerial de Ciencia y Tecnología (CICYT), under project DPI2002-03225.

REFERENCES

[1] Bishop, C.M. (1995). *Neural Networks for Pattern Recognition*. Oxford University Press Inc., NY.
[2] Blake, C.L. and Mertz, C.J. (1998). UCI Repository of Machine Learning Databases. University of California, Irvine, Department of Information and Computer Science. http://www.ics.uci.edu/~mlearn/MLRepository.html.
[3] Geman, S., Bienenstock, E. and Doursat, R. (1992). Neural Networks and the Bias/Variance Dilemma. *Neural Computation* 4, 1-58.
[4] Hill, C.L, Zhang, Y., Sigurgeirsson, B., Pukkala, E., Mellemkjaer, L., Airio, A., Evans S.R. and Felson, D.T. (2001). Frequency of Specific Cancer Types in Dermatomyositis and Polymyositis: A Population-based Study. *Lancet* 357, 96-100.
[5] Kittler, J. (1986). Feature Selection and Extraction. In *Handbook of Pattern Recognition and Image Processing*, Academic Press, New York, 59-83
[6] Kohavi, R. and John, G.H. (1997). Wrappers for Feature Subset Selection. *Artificial Intelligence* 97 (1-2), 273-324.
[7] Leshno, M., Lin, V.Y., Pinkus, A. and Schocken, S. (1993). Multilayer Feedforward Networks With a Nonpolynomial Activation Function Can Approximate Any Function. *Neural Networks* 6, 861-867.
[8] Liu, H. and Motoda, H. (1998). *Feature Selection for Knowledge Discovery and Data Mining*. Kluwer Academic Publishers.
[9] Michie, D., Spiegelhalter, D.J. and Taylor, C.C. (1994). Machine Learning, Neural and Statistical Classification. Ellin Horwood. Results available at http://www.phys.uni.torun.pl/kmk/projects/datasets-stat.html.
[10] Parikh, C.R, Pont, M.J. and Jones, B. (1999). Improving the Performance of Multi-layer Perceptrons when Limited Training Data are Available for Some Classes. *9th International Conference on Artificial Neural Networks*, 227-232.
[11] Romero, E. and Alquézar, R. (2002). A New Incremental Method for Function Approximation using Feed-forward Neural Networks. *International Joint Conference on Neural Networks*, vol 2, 1968-1973.
[12] Rumelhart, D.E., Hinton, G.E. and Williams, R.J. (1986). *Parallel Distributed Processing*, Vol 1. MIT Press.
[13] Sopena, J.M., Romero, E. and Alquézar, R. (1999). Neural Networks with Periodic and Monotonic Activation Functions: A Comparative Study in Classification Problems. *9th International Conference on Artificial Neural Networks*, 323-328.

Pattern recognition device using scalar vector graphics

Rex Sandwith
rex@livingdatabase.com

Abstract

Scalar vector graphics (SVG), an Extensible Markup Language (XML) based graphical language can be used to recognized patterns in categorized binary strings. We show how binary trees can be constructed where the hierarchical structure of the SVG file is a mirror of the hierarchical structure of the tree. We also show that this binary SVG structure can model a neuron by a applying a temporal signal to the leaves and summing the values of attributes of adjacent nodes. We present this as a framework, which can represent the geometric properties of the neuron while simultaneously defining valid logical paths for signal transmission. Because SVG is an XML based technology it is an excellent medium for representing tree based structures and processes. Additionally, the line and color properties of SVG provide an excellent way to view the state of a network at any given time.

1. Introduction

Decision trees have been used to classify a pattern based on a sequence of questions (Duda 2000). We present a method here where this sequential questioning is mapped onto an XML file that can be rendered as a vector drawing. A memory of the navigation is stored in the XML file using attributes. This memory allows for temporal summation of data. All parameters of the pattern are stored in the XML file during navigation.

These XML structure may also be suitable for compartmentalized modeling of the Neuron. The branching structure of the neuron has been modeled as a binary tree (Pelt 1983). The modeling of the neuron by segmentation has been studied by (McGee 1997). The process we discuss here would allow the electrical properties of the neuron to be stored in the XML structure itself and not in a separate text file.

This paper outlines the requirements, restrictions, and methods for using SVG in pattern recognition problems. This paper will discuss the basics of XML and SVG, create a simple binary decision tree using SVG, discuss color and line width modifications, and explain how a string of binary numbers can be used to navigate the SVG structure. Then, two applications showing how these structures can be applied to pattern recognition problems are shown. The first shows how the SVG structure can be dominated by a category after training with categorized data and then how to predict the category of an uncategorized string. In the second, the SVG structure is used to simulate the summation of states flowing down a binary tree.

Most of the images in this paper are produced from various programs written in Visual Basic.net. These programs navigate and modify the attributes and nodes of an XML file in an ordered fashion. The key here to note is that the structure of the XML file defines acceptable logical paths and that this file can be rendered in a web browser at any point in time to view the state of the network.

2. Extensible Markup Language (XML)

Extensible Markup Language (XML) is a simple, very flexible text format derived from SGML (ISO 8879). XML is a useful way to describe information. The XML structure can be viewed in terms of a tree structure. Here is a sample XML file.

```
<?xml version="1.0" standalone="no" ?>
<root>
  <child b="2">
  </child>
</root>
```

The first line in the document - the XML declaration - defines the XML version and the character encoding used in the document. The next line, <root>, describes the root element of the document. The next element, <child>, is nested in the root. Each opening element must have a closing element. For example </root> closes the <root> element. This file also contains the attribute "b" which has a value 2. Attribute values must always be enclosed in quotes, but either single or double quotes can be used. All XML documents must be well formed. The nesting feature of XML makes it a natural choice for decision tree pattern recognition problems.

3. Scalar Vector Graphics (SVG)

SVG is a language for describing two-dimensional vector and mixed vector/raster graphics in XML. The specification can be found at http://www.w3.org/TR/SVG. SVG is generally viewed in a web browser that has the Adobe SVG viewer plug in installed. The plug in can be found at http://www.adobe.com/SVG/main.html

We use several key features of SVG: the 'g', 'transform', 'line', and 'style' elements. The g element is a container element for grouping together related graphics elements. A 'g' element can contain other 'g' elements nested within it, to an arbitrary depth. The 'transform' attribute transform user space coordinates and lengths on sibling attributes on the given element and all of its descendants. The 'line' element is a graphics element that is defined by some combination of straight lines and curves.

The 'style' attribute contains a 'stroke' property that paints along the outline of the given graphical element.

4. Construct a simple tree

First we will show some of the basics of SVG and how we can use lines and transforms to generate networks that can be traversed in a binary fashion. The grid spacing is 50 units in the x and y direction for all figures with grids.

To start we will first generate a line 20 units long along the x axis, see figure 1. The SVG structure for this image is shown below. The text "<svg width="500" height="500">" specifies the working space for the document.

```
<?xml version="1.0" standalone="no"?>
<svg width="500" height="500">
        <line x2="20" style="stroke:rgb(0,0,0);stroke-width:4"/>
</svg>
```

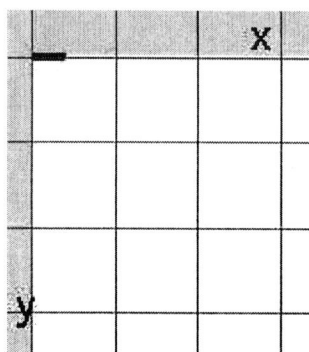

Figure 1, 20 unit length line.

Looking at the above file-listing note the "x2" and "style" attributes. All lines can be generated from a line on the x-axis using rotation and transforms. For our purposes all lines are specified by an "x2" attribute, the x1, y1, and y2 coordinate for the line are implied to be zero. The stroke is defined by a red, green, blue '(rgb)' value and a 'width' value in the 'style' attribute. In this case the line color is black (0,0,0) and the line width is 4.

The next step is to rotate the line 90 degrees. This is done by nesting the <line> element in a <g> element. A transform attribute is added to the <g> element to perform the rotation, see figure 2. The SVG structure for this image is shown below.

```
<?xml version="1.0" standalone="no"?>
<svg width="500" height="500">
        <g transform="rotate(-90)">
            <line x2="20" style="stroke:rgb(0,0,0);stroke-width:4"/>
        </g>
</svg>
```

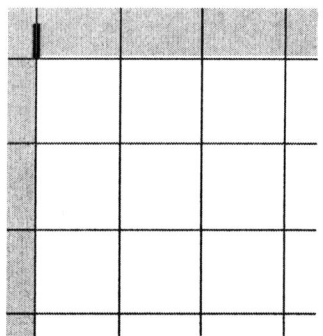

Figure 2, rotate the line 90 degrees

Next, we translate the line down 150 units and to the right 200 units. This is done by adding a translate property to the transform attribute, see figure 3. The SVG structure for this image is shown below.

```
<?xml version="1.0" standalone="no"?>
<svg width="500" height="500">
    <g transform="translate(100 150) rotate(-90)">
        <line x2="20" style="stroke:rgb(0,0,0);stroke-width:4"/>
    </g>
</svg>
```

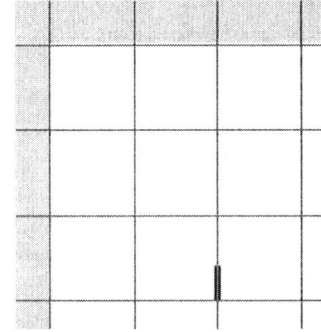

Figure 3, showing translation of line

Next we add a 50 unit long line, rotated 10 degrees relative to the 20 unit line, to the end of the 20 unit long line. This is done by nesting a <g> element with a nested <line> element in the first <g> element, see figure 4. The SVG file listing for this image is shown below.

```
<?xml version="1.0" standalone="no"?>
<svg width="500" height="500">
    <g transform="translate(100 150) rotate(-90)">
        <line x2="20" style="stroke:rgb(0,0,0);stroke-width:4"/>
        <g transform="translate(20 0) rotate(10)">
            <line x2="50" style="stroke:rgb(0,0,0);stroke-width:2"/>
        </g>
    </g>
</svg>
```

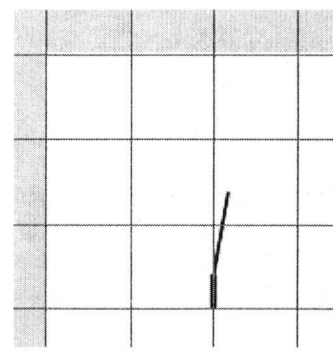

Figure 4, adding the 50 unit long line.

The 50 unit line shows up in the correct location because it receives the transformation from the first 'g' element plus the transformation from the second 'g' element.

We repeat this process and add a 40 unit long line, rotated 30 degrees relative to the 20 unit line, to end of the 20 unit long line, see figure 5. The SVG structure for this image is shown below.

```
<?xml version="1.0" standalone="no"?>
<svg width="500" height="500">
    <g transform="translate(100 150) rotate(-90)">
        <line x2="20" style="stroke:rgb(0,0,0);stroke-width:4"/>
        <g transform="translate(20 0) rotate(10)">
            <line x2="50" style="stroke:rgb(0,0,0);stroke-width:2"/>
        </g>
        <g transform="translate(20 0) rotate(-30)">
            <line x2="40" style="stroke:rgb(0,0,0);stroke-width:2"/>
        </g>
    </g>
</svg>
```

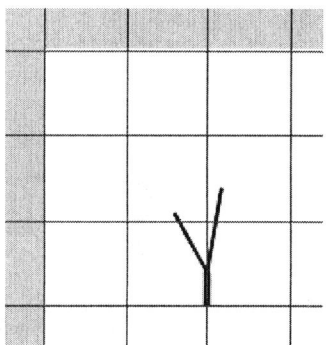

Figure 5, adding the 40-unit line

Note that the transformations applied to the 50 and 40 unit lines do not affect each other because they are siblings.

Adding four more lines gives us our final sample tree, figure 6.

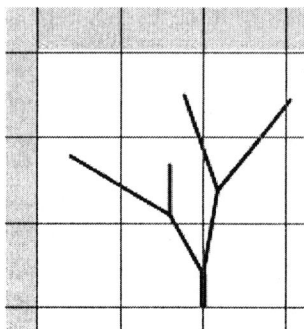

Figure 6, our final tree sample

5. Color and line width modification

The color and line width are used to show the state of the network. Making the following modifications to the 40 and 50 unit lines in the figure 5 demonstrate this;

<line x2="50" style="stroke:rgb(128,128,128);stroke-width:3" darkgrey="3"/>

<line x2="40" style="stroke:rgb(192,192,192);stroke-width:3" lightgrey="3"/>

When the SVG file is rendered we get the image in figure 7.

Figure 7, SVG showing modification to color and width.

The line on the right is colored dark gray (128,128,128) and a "darkgray" attribute with a value of "3" has been added. The line on the left has been colored light gray and a "lightgray" attribute with a value of "3" has been added. This demonstrates how we can color the line based on the value of an attribute. Also note that the value of the line width can be modified based on the magnitude of the attribute.

6. From Xpath to binary

How do we relate binary numbers to lines in the SVG file? We do this by using Xpath statements. XPath is a language for addressing parts of an XML document and has been endorsed by the W3C, the specification can be found at http://www.w3.org/TR/xpath. XPath models an XML document as a tree of nodes. You can walk down the tree using the node name combined with a forward slash "/" character. Because the SVG file is XML we can use the Xpath syntax to select the right and left lines in figure 5.

The Xpath statements and their binary equivalents is shown below.

Line	Xpath	binary
50	svg/g/g[1]/line	0
40	svg/g/g[2]/line	1

By default a 'g' with no bracket in the Xpath statement will select the first child 'g' element of the parent node. If brackets "[ ]" follow the 'g' element then the 'g' element specified by the number in the brackets will be selected. You can follow this by looking at the file structure for figure 5. In our case any 'g' element will only have 0 or 2 child 'g' elements. This allows us to equate a binary "0" to "g[1]" and a binary "1" to "g[2]".

7. Pattern recognition with a single tree

If we have data that can be represented as a series of yes/no questions and separated into two categories we can use our SVG file to recognize patterns in the data. For example lets say we have the following 18 sets of binary strings separated into two categories.

Binary string	category
01 00 01 01 00 01 10 01 01	dark gray
10 01 11 11 10 11 10 10 10	light gray

We can convert these binary strings into their corresponding Xpath statements

Binary	Xpath
01	svg/g/g[1]/g[2]/line
00	svg/g/g[1]/g[1]line
11	svg/g/g[2]/g[2]/line
10	svg/g/g[2]/g[1]line

To train our sample tree, figure 6, we first add a "darkgray" and "lightgray" attribute to the each of the lines in the SVG file. for example the 50 unit line is modified as follows;

```
<line x2="50" style="stroke:rgb(0,0,0);stroke-width:2"
darkgray="0" lightgray="0" />
```

We can now apply the Xpath statements to the SVG file and modify the appropriate attribute depending on the category. We also set the color to the dominant category and the width to the difference between the attribute values. After training the network with the data we get the image in figure 8.

Figure 8, figure 6 after training

The two lines that specify where the categories dominate are shown below.

```
<line x2="50"
style="fill:none;stroke:rgb(128,128,128);stroke-width:7"
darkgray="8" lightgray="1" />

<line x2="40"
style="fill:none;stroke:rgb(192,192,192);stroke-width:7"
darkgray="1" lightgray="8" />
```

Once the tree has been sufficiently trained we attempt to predict the category of an uncategorized string. For example if we are given the binary string 01 and asked to predict which category it belonged to we would apply the binary string to the fully trained tree and notice that it would pass through the right branch of figure 8. We would then categorize it as belonging to dark gray.

The advantage of using this system is that domination can be seen visually. The following image, figure 9, show a much more complicated network but it is still easy to spot the dominant path.

Figure 9, a more complicated tree

This navigation process can be extended to a collection of trees by adding appropriate linking attributes to the leafs and roots of additional trees.

8. Neural network and summation engine

Representation of the neuron by modeling different segments of the neuron as separate compartments has been discussed in the literature (McGee 1997) and (Lytton 2002). A good review of the geometric modeling of the neuron is given by (Deschutter 2001). NEURON http://www.neuron.yale.edu/ and GENESIS http://www.genesis-sim.org/GENESIS/ are software programs that use compartmentalization to model the neuron. Using SVG to model the neuron has many advantages. After a neuron has been accurately geometrically modeled using SVG, attributes can be added to the line elements that could be used to model the electrical properties of the cell. We will not attempt to model the electrical properties of the neuron here but instead present a method of how the SVG structure can be used to simulate the summation of states flowing down a binary tree structure. We present this as a framework, which can represent the geometric properties of the neuron while simultaneously defining valid logical paths for signal transmission.

By modeling the neuron as a series of compartments different parts of the neuron can be performing different tasks at the same time. Each individual compartment will have a single state.

For this example we use the SVG file we generated in figure 6. We modify the SVG file slightly by adding an "id" attribute to the leaf nodes and a "state" attribute to all the line nodes. For example the right leaf node on figure 6 would be modified as follows;

```
<line x2="70" style=" stroke:rgb(0,0,0);stroke-width:2" id="3" state="0" />
```

If we use the SVG to model the neuron lines 0,1,2,3 are the dendrites and line 6 is the axon, see figure 10.

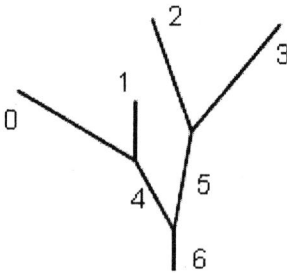

Figure 10, modeling a neuron

To demonstrate the concept the state attribute in lines 0,1,2,3 are updated with the values in table 1 at each time step. At each time step the state attribute of the node that has children will receive the sum of the states of its children. In this way the states are summed as they flow into the root node. See table 1 below where data is shown for 5 time steps.

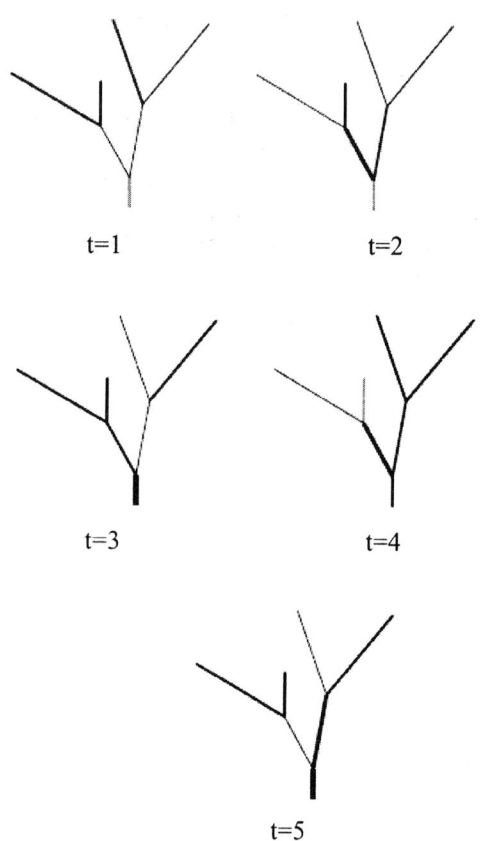

Figure 11, state of tree at different times

We can link the output from one tree (root) to the input of another (leaf). In this way we can create very complex summation networks.

	Time				
	1	2	3	4	5
line	state				
0	1	0	1	0	1
1	1	1	1	0	1
2	1	0	0	1	0
3	0	0	1	1	1
4	0	2	1	2	0
5	0	1	0	1	2
6	0	0	3	1	3

Table 1, state values vs time

In the figure 11 below we assign the line thickness the value of the state attribute. In this way we can graphically see the movement and summation of the signal in the tree.

References

[1] Richard Duda, pg 395-551, Pattern Classification, Wiley-Interscience; 2nd edition (October 2000)

[2] Verwer R W H, J Van Pelt, 1983, "A new method for the Topological Analysis of Neuronal Tree Structures." J Neurosci Meth, 8, 335-351.

[3] William Lytton, From Computer to Brain, Foundations of Computational Neuroscience, 2002, Springer

[4] Erik Deschutter, Computaton Neuroscience, CRC press, 2001, pg 183

[5] Y Cai, E Walsh, J McGee, "A simple program for simulating the response of neurons with arbitrary structure and active dendritic trees", Journal of Neuroscience Methods, 74 (1997) 27-35

A Novel Electromyography (EMG) Based Classification Approach for Arabic Handwriting

Azzedine Lansari, Faouzi Bouslama, Mohammed Khasawneh, Akram Al-Rawi

College of Information Systems, Zayed University
P.O.Box 4783, Abu Dhabi, UAE
E-mail: *azzedine.lansari@zu.ac.ae*.

Abstract- **In this paper, a novel classification approach for handwritten Arabic characters is proposed. Features for classification are extracted from electromygraphic (EMG) signals detected on two forearm muscles. Noise cancellations in conjunction with a process parameter estimator for feature identification are proposed. Neural networks using a potentially damped least mean squared algorithm is used at the classification stage. The proposed new classification technique is used on handwritten Arabic characters.**

I. INTRODUCTION

The study of human handwriting movements is of a great interest to mankind. It leads to an understanding of the properties of the biological system that generates the human handwriting movements. Handwriting may be used to characterize people and the study of hand movements can be used to detect neurological disorders.

The muscles in the hand receive the driving signals from the nervous system and move the hand to generate any desired shapes and characters. The human hand performs a supervised learning action where the desired movement trajectory is known but not the motor command. The goal of the movement is to move the hand to draw an exact image. With the identification of a dynamic system that exhibits similar characteristics as the biological one, it is possible to study the handwriting movements, identify their driving (motor) signals and try to reproduce the handwriting motion.

Several modeling techniques were used to derive the motor signals and simulate the handwriting process [1], [2], [3], [4], [5]. Although these models succeeded in synthesizing the control pulses that drive the muscles, they are a rather simplified representation of the real physical model of the hand-muscle system.

In this paper, we propose a new classification technique for handwritten Arabic characters. EMG signals are used in the identification of human hand movements. We study these motor signals and show how they can be used to characterize the handwriting process. We apply the results to the generation of handwritten Arabic letters. We propose a new gradient-based adaptive learning algorithm, which is used to improve the performance of a neural network used as a classifier. We present the basic idea and show how classification can be performed. The trained neural network is then used to identify characters stemming specifically from a particular user.

The paper is organized as follows: Section II gives an analysis of the human forearm muscles and the handwriting system; section III shows the experimental set up; section IV explains the proposed feature extraction and classification approach; section V is the conclusion.

II. ANALYSIS OF THE HUMAN FOREARM MUSCLES

Any movement of the hand involves the use of a combination of several muscles of the forearm. There are two muscle groups that are involved in this process the flexors and the extensors. Flexors are muscles that bring a body part close in. Extensors are muscles that move a body part further out. The flexors and extensors that generate the movements of the hand and fingers are located in the forearm. The flexors are on the inside of the forearm and the extensors are on the outside or the back of the forearm. Figure 1 shows the forearm muscles involved in the horizontal movements of the hand.

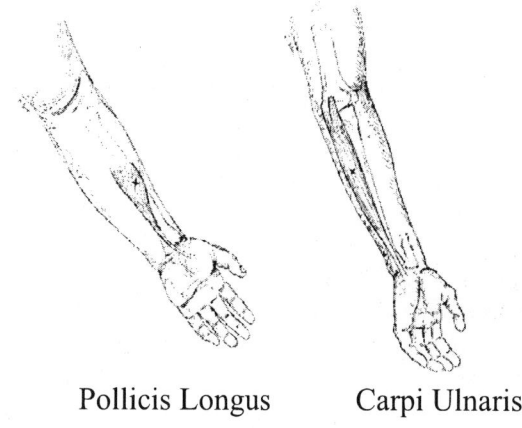

Fig.1. Flexion and extension muscles for horizontal movements

The handwriting process involves planar movements of the hand. For the execution of the horizontal movements in a plane, the following muscles perform the activity: the extension muscle or Carpi Ulnaris, and the abduction muscle or Pollicis Longus. The vertical movements are the results of the efforts provided by the following muscles: the flexion muscle or Digitorum Superficialis and the extension muscle or Digitorum Communis.

All of these muscles play a major role in the handwriting process. It is difficult to analyze the hand movements based on all of these muscles. For simplification purposes, the hand motion is formulated at the wrist joint. The movements at the wrist joint are those derived from the forearm and the hand. They can be decomposed into either an extension or a contraction of the arm or an abduction of the hand and the fingers. During the handwriting process the hand movements are complicated and cannot be easily interpreted. However, if the hand movements are represented by two principal and independent components, and if the wrist joint is assumed fixed, then a simplified model can be derived to interpret the hand movements.

III. EXPERIMENTAL SETUP

Figure 2 show the experimental setup used in the handwriting process and signal measurements. An object is drawn on a graphic tablet using a special pen that emits the coordinates of the plotted points at a constant frequency. The graphic tablet has a dimension of 12800 by 9600 with a resolution of 2540 lines per inch. An object is represented by a sequence of points separated by signs indicating when the pen has been lifted from the tablet surface. While the shapes of objects are drawn on the tablet, an electromyographic (EMG) device, a TEAC DR-C2 signal recorder, is used to detect and record the EMG signals.

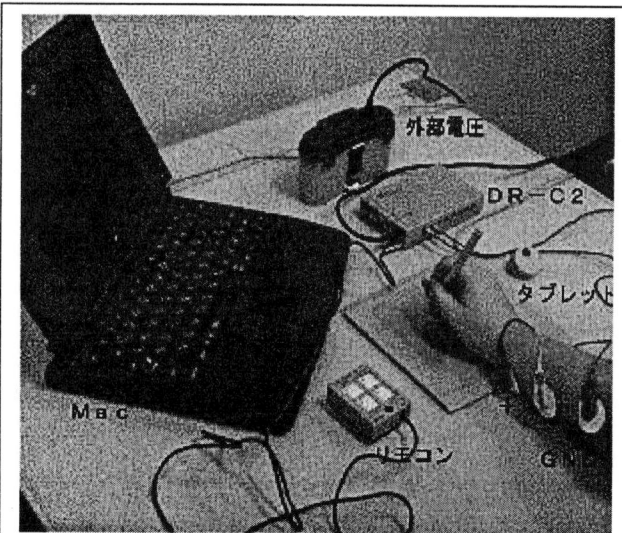

Fig.2. Experimental setup

The muscles to be studied are fairly large in size and are located just under the forearm skin. We have selected two forearm muscles having a well-defined response and are relatively isolated from other muscles. One muscle was selected in the middle of the front forearm and the other one on the back of the forearm. We use the surface type of electrodes having small silver discs at their ends. The electrodes are used in pairs with a common ground where the positive and negative electrodes are placed about 2 [cm] apart. Recording electrodes are placed over the belly of the muscle to be studied. The recorded signals, electrical changes, are amplified where the maximum voltage is set to 500 [mV] and the signals are sampled at the rate of 2000 pulses per second. An aluminum sheet of foil covers the subject's hand and the electrodes to minimize the effects of noise and surrounding disturbances.

The goal of the experiment is to collect EMG signals generated by a number of subjects, as they write the whole set consisting of 28 isolated Arabic characters, to form an ensemble. The subjects write the letters at a regular writing speed while fixing their wrist and only moving their hand. Figure 3 shows an example of an isolated character, the letter ع AYN, and the recorded EMG signals.

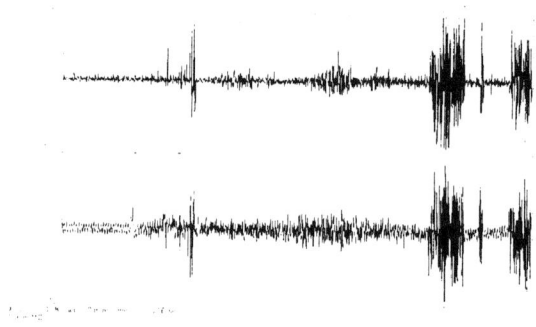

Fig.3. The EMG signals of the letter AYN (ع)

IV. FEATURE EXTRACTION EXPERIMENT USING LINEAR PREDICTION

The recorded EMG signals are very noisy. This is due to ambient noise emanating from many sources such as the inherently accompanying noise, surrounding electrical frequency sources, as well as fluorescent type lighting. Noise is also generated within the human body itself, which includes the high frequency components of the heartbeats.

In order to tackle the noise issue, a noise cancellation configuration is used in conjunction with process parameter estimation (feature identification). The process parameter estimation is based on a novel adaptive algorithm, the potentially damped least mean squares algorithm (PDLMS), described by the following recursion:

$W_N(n+1) = (1 + K(n))W_N(n) + 2\mu e(n)X_N(n)$

Where K(n) is given by the following expression, as proposed in [8]:

$K(n) = r \exp\{-v/e^2(n)\}[e^2(n) - \varepsilon_{min}]$

This algorithm was shown to achieve a much faster convergence than its predecessor, the LMS, at a modest computational cost increase of N+3. This algorithm was successfully applied to a range of biomedical signals and did prove its validity at cleaning up signals from accompanying noise.

In the EMG records, except for the starting part, with no muscle activity, and the noisy ending part, we observed the presence of three regions corresponding to the activation of the forearm muscles. From these results, we noticed that the chosen muscles exhibited the same number of major peaks. In other words, they are related to a similar type of motion of the hand. As for the Arabic letter AYN (ع), we can characterize it by the presence of a three major activation regions related to the muscles involved.

We conducted feature detection tests on other Arabic samples. We have observed major activity regions related to the features of other Arabic characters as was explained in [7]. We concluded that the chosen muscles reflected the movements of the hand in the vertical direction in the plane.

Figure 4 shows the block diagram for the proposed classification scheme. EMG signals, representing the various Arabic handwritten letters, are passed thru a linear predictor/noise canceller combo to both clean up the ambient noise, and to identify the features for each of the Arabic alphabets. For simplicity, we have confined our study to non-diacritic Arabic characters, which do not require a third dimension.

Identification of the extracted features for the various alphabets is accomplished as the varying weight vectors reach their steady state values, a^*_N, as n goes to ∞. The converged weight vectors, $\{a^*_N\}$, are then stored in a database, to be used at some later stage to train a neural network using the PDLMS algorithm. This algorithm is used because of its faster convergence rate compared with that of the LMS. Figure 5 shows a comparison between the LMS and the PDLMS algorithm convergence rates [8].

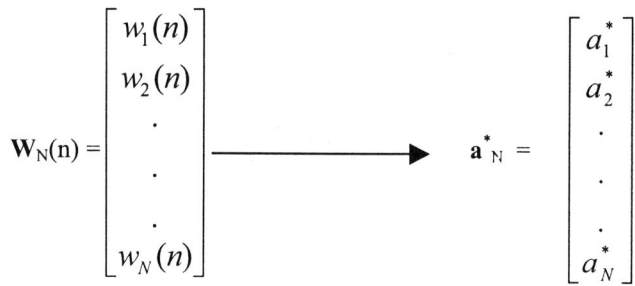

V. CONCLUSIONS

We have proposed a novel classification approach for handwritten Arabic characters. It is based on electromygraphic signals recorded on the muscles of the forearm that are responsible for the planar movements of the hand. We used an adaptive noise cancellation technique in conjunction with a process parameter estimator for feature identification, using the PDLMS algorithm. For classification purposes, we used the same algorithm to train a neural network for recognizing Arabic characters. This approach was shown to effectively extract the key features and properly classify the Arabic handwriting system.

REFERENCES

[1] D. van der Gon and J. Thuring, "A handwriting simulator," Phys. Med. Biol., 6, pp. 407-414, 1962.
[2] J. MacDonald, "Experimental studies of handwriting signals," Tech. Report 443, MIT, 1966.
[3] M. Yasuhara, "Experimental studies of handwriting process, " Report Univ. Electro-Comm., Tokyo, 25-2 (Sci. & Tech. Sect.), pp. 233-254, 1975.
[4] S. Edelman and T. Flash, "A model of handwriting," Biological Cybernetics 5, pp. 25-36, 1987.
[5] F. Bouslama, V. Kalanovic, and M. Benrejeb, "Identification of dynamic models for handwriting process: Application to character recognition," Proc. of Tunisian Interdisciplinary Workshop on Science and Society-TIWSS'99, Tokyo, Japan, pp. 13-15, 1999.
[6] M. Kawato, "Computational schemes and neural network models for formation and control of multi-joint arm trajectory, " In W. T. Miller, R .S. Sutton and P. J. Werbos (Eds) Neural Network for Control, MIT Press, 1990.
[7] F. Bouslama, and M. Benrejeb, "Exploring the human handwriting process," Int. Journal of Applied Math & Comput. Sci., vol. 10, No. 4, pp. 877-904, 2000.
[8] T. F. Haddad, and M. A. Khasawneh, "A New forced LMS-based adaptive algorithm utilizing the principle of potential energy, " Journal of the Franklin Institute 337, pp. 515-542, 2000.

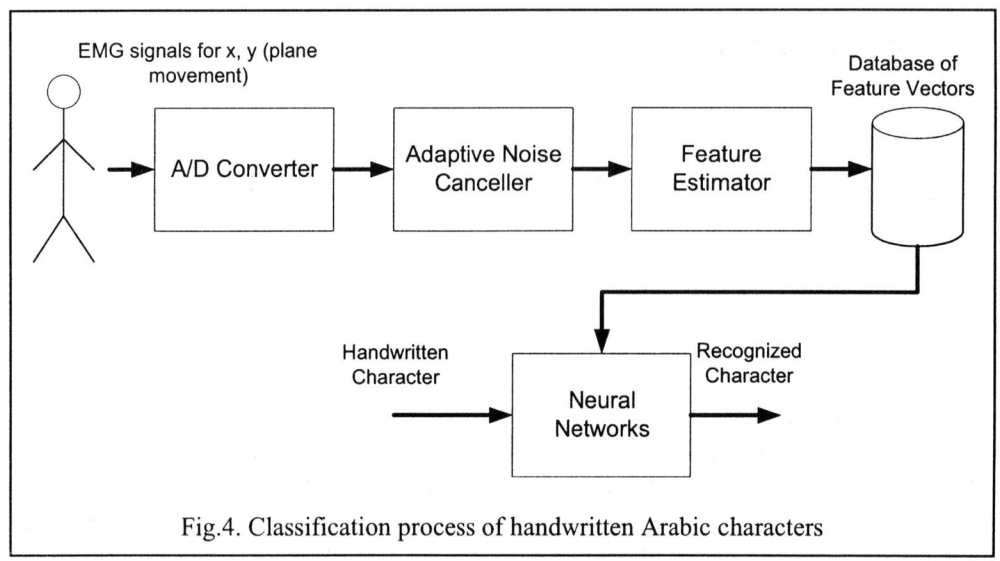

Fig.4. Classification process of handwritten Arabic characters

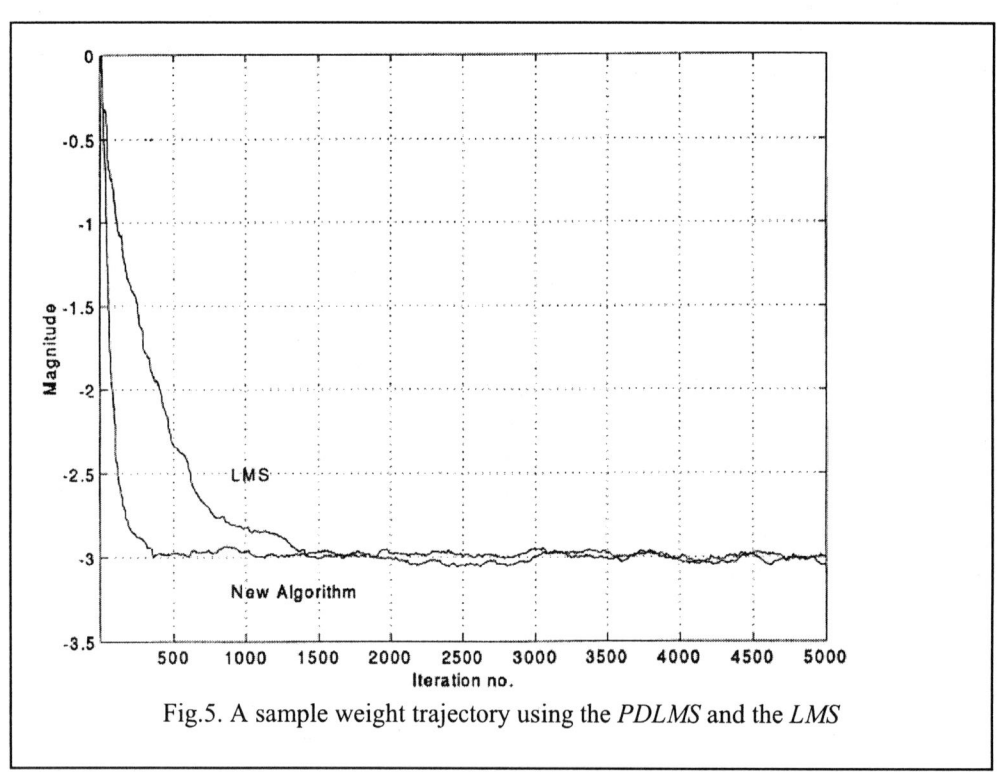

Fig.5. A sample weight trajectory using the *PDLMS* and the *LMS*

An Adaptive Sparse Distributed Memory

J. L. Aguilar

CEMISID. Dpto. de Computación.
Facultad de Ingeniería. Universidad de los Andes.
Av. Tulio Febres. 5101. Mérida, Edo. Mérida-Venezuela
Telf: (58.74)440002 Fax:(58.74)402872
email: aguilar@ing.ula.ve

Abstract. Sparse Distributed Memory is a content addressable, associative memory technique which relies on close memory items tending to be clustered together, with some abstraction and blurring of details. This paper discusses the limitations of the original model. Then, we propose a method which improve Sparse Distributed Memory efficiency through an adaptive threshold. The results obtained are good and promising.

I. INTRODUCTION

The Sparse Distributed Memory (SDM) was developed by Pentti Kanerva [4], and it may be regarded either as an extension of a classical or as a special type of three layer feedforward neural network. We can simulate some of the human cognitive capabilities because it work in a similar way of the human memory (associative memory recognition, etc.). SDM implements transformation from logical space to physical space using distributed data storing. A value corresponding to a logical address is stored into many physical addresses. This way of storing is robust and not deterministic. In, general, the main properties are [4]: a physical address can keep several logical addresses, the memory capabilities are large, a memory cell is not addressed directly, and if logical addresses are partially damaged, we can get correct output data.

The SDM standard uses a fix threshold to active the memory cell [1, 2, 5]. That simplifies the system but gives poor results because some of the memory cells can't be reusable due to that a fix threshold only allow recovery the information previously learn. That limits the capabilities and fault tolerance of the system and some information storing can't be recovery (specifically, when the number of information store is large). In this paper we propose an adaptive threshold to solve this problem. We present some experiments with results, which are promising.

II. SPARSE DISTRIBUTED MEMORY

SDM is a model proposed by Karneva that can work as an auto-associative memory technique where the contents and the addresses are from the same space and used alternatively [4]. The inner workings of SDM rely on large binary spaces. The dimension of the space determines how rich is each word. Another important factor is how many actual memory locations are there in the space. In general, when we use a SDM, the features are represented as one or more bits. Groups of features are concatenated to form a word which becomes a candidate for writing into SDM. When writing copy of this binary string is placed in all close enough hard locations. When reading, a close enough cue would reach all close enough hard locations and get some sort of aggregate or average out of them. Reading is not always successful. Depending on the cue and the previously written information, among other factors, convergence or divergence during a reading may occur. If convergence occurs, the pooled word will be the closest match of the input reading cue. On the other hand, when divergence occurs, there is not relation-in general-between the input cue and what is retrieved from memory. The main aspects of SDM are [1, 2, 3, 4]:

- The SDM calculates Hamming distances between the reference address and each location address. For each distance, which is less or equal to a given radius, the corresponding location is selected.
- The memory is represented by n*m counters (where n is number of locations and m is the input data length) instead of single-bit storage elements.
- Writing to the memory, instead of overwriting, is as follows:
    - If the i-bit of the input data is 1, the corresponding counters (counters in the selected locations (rows) and in the i-th columns) are incremented
    - If the i-bit of the input data is 0, the corresponding counters are decreased
- Reading (or recall) from the memory is similar:

- The contents of the selected locations are summed columnwise.
- Each sum is thresholded. If the sum is greater that or equal to the threshold value, the corresponding output bit is set to 1, in the opposite case it is cleared.

Some of the limitations of the SDM are [2, 3, 5]:

> The addresses and the data vector must be coded in a binary alphabet. Because a lot of real problems using a different alphabet, we need a system to translate the pattern of real problems in a code to be used for the SDM.

> The standard model uses an uniform distribution at the level of the input addresses. In the reality, the input vectors are grouped in a set distributed in a large multidimensional space. For that, if the addresses are choose randomly like is proposed by Karneva, a large number of cells maybe can't activate and other ones would be activate a lot of time.

> If we save a lot of data in a SDM, we can overlap a lot of information. In this case the results of the output vector will be incorrect. Only, if we store several time the same information, the probability to recovery a correct information that we have stored can increase. The reason is because the standard SDM use a fix threshold to activate the cells. That gives poor performances. For this last case is that we propose our approach.

III. OUR ADAPTIVE THRESHOLD APPROACH

The standard SDM has been modified in order to use an adaptive threshold. That is, the decodification of the addresses is not fixed, and the threshold is modified according to the results of the recognition phase of previous learned patterns. If the recognition rate is bigger than 95% that means that the threshold must continue fix, otherwise we must decrease or increase the threshold according to the quality of the recognition of previous learned patterns and the number of input patterns. Once modified the threshold, the SDM relearns the set of pattern with the new threshold. In this way, we can filter the information and introduce them in the SDM in the correct places. The threshold will be modified according to the next conditions:

1. If the recognition rate (Tr) is bigger than 95% then:

$$\text{threshold}(t) = \text{threshold}(t-1) \qquad (1)$$

For this case, the threshold is not modified for the recognition phase.

2. If the recognition rate (Tr) is smaller than 95% and the data quantity stored is smaller than (number of memory cells/2) then:

$$\text{threshold}(t) = \text{threshold}(t-1) - (100 - Tr) * \bullet \qquad (2)$$

- Where Tr is the recognition rate, which is calculated during the recognition phase as the average recognition rate:

$$Tr = \sum_{i=1}^{N} Tr(i)/N$$

- $\bullet$: is the learning rate ($0 \leq \bullet \leq 1$). In our experiment we have used $\bullet = 0.1$ because with it we have obtained the best results, see [2] for more details.
- N: number of information to be recovered.

For this case, the initial threshold for the learning phase must be a large value. In our experiment, we use 5 (see [2] for more details).

3. If the recognition rate (Tr) is smaller than 95%, and the data quantity stored is bigger than (number of memory cells/ 2) then:

$$\text{threshold}(t) = \text{threshold}(t-1) + (100 - Tr) * \bullet \qquad (3)$$

- For this case, the initial threshold of the learning phase must be a small value. In our experiment, we use 3 (see [2] for more details).

The equations (1) to (3) are used iteratively until to improve the recognition rate *(Tr)* of the previous learned pattern. Then, we restart the learning phase of the SDM with the new threshold.

IV. EXPERIMENTS

In our experiment we use an Applet in Java to simulate the SDM. In addition, we compare our results with [1, 4]. We use the next set of parameters: the size of the input and output binary vectors of the SDM, the number of memory cells (NLA), initial threshold and the number of input patterns (N).

A. First Experiment

In this experiment, NLA is 15, N is 5 and the size of the input and output binary vectors of the SDM is 10 bits. During the learning phase, we learned the next set of information with threshold=5: {0111110000, 0011111000, 0001111100, 0000111110, 1000001111}. The recognition rate of these learned patterns, with threshold=5, is equal to 83% (see [2]).

Because Tr = 83 % ≤ 95 %, we recalculate the threshold according to the equation (2),

Threshold(t) = 5 − (100−83)*0.1 = 3,3 ≈ 3

In this case, the recognition rate, with threshold = 3, is equal to 88%. Because Tr = 88 % ≤ 95 %, we recalculate the threshold according to the equation (2),

Threshold(t) = 3 − (100−88)*0.1 = 1,8 ≈ 2

Now the recognition rate, with threshold = 2, is equal to 83%. Because Tr = 83 % < 88 % with threshold = 3, the optimal value of the threshold is 3. We relearn the SDM with the threshold=3 and we obtain a recognition rate of the previous learned patterns equals to 95%. If we introduce some noise during the recognition phase, we obtain the next results:

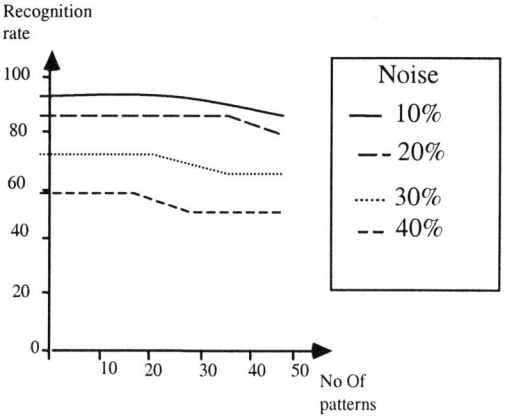

Fig. 1. Recognition rate Vs noise

Now, in this phase we compare the performance of our approach with [1] and [4]. For each case, we have developed 30 experiments.

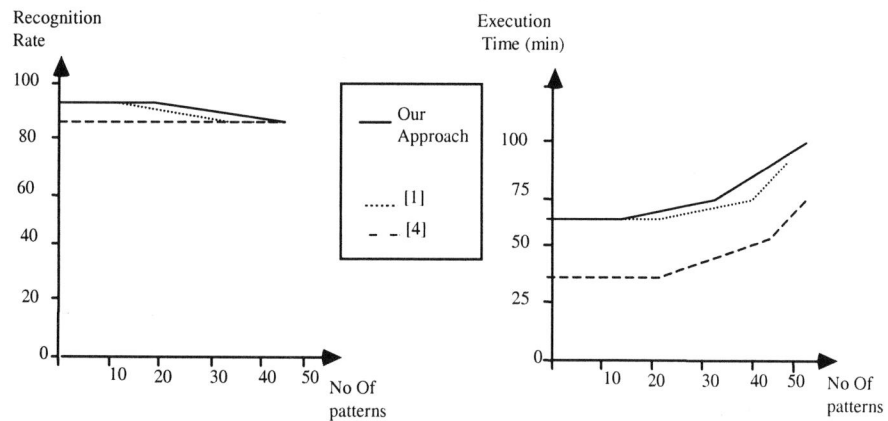

Fig. 2. Comparison of the Recognition rate and execution time for a noise = 10%

We improve the results obtained in [1, 4]. The reason is because our approach can adapt its procedure to the quality of the figures using the adaptive threshold. The execution time is very close to the evolutionary approach.

B. Second Experiment:

With a number of input patterns (N) = 10, we use the next set of data during the learning or written phase with an initial threshold = 3: {0111110000, 0011111000, 0001111100, 0000111110, 0000011111, 1000001111, 1100000111, 1110000011, 1111000001, 1111100011}. The recognition rate of previous learned patterns, with threshold=3, is equal to 91% (see [2]). Because Tr = 91 % ≤ 95 %, we recalculate the threshold using equation (3),

threshold(t) = 3 + (100−91)*0.1=3,9 ≈ 4

In this case, the recognition rate, with threshold = 4, is equal to 92%. Because Tr = 92 % ≤ 95 %, we recalculates the threshold using the equation (3),

threshold(t) = 4 + (100-92)*0.1=4,8 ≈ 5

In this case, the recognition rate, with threshold = 5, is equal to 86%. Because Tr = 86 % < 92 % with threshold = 4, the optimal value of the threshold is 4. We relearn the SDM with the threshold=4 and we obtain a recognition rate of the previous learned patterns equals to 93%. If we introduce some noise during the recognition phase, we obtain the next results:

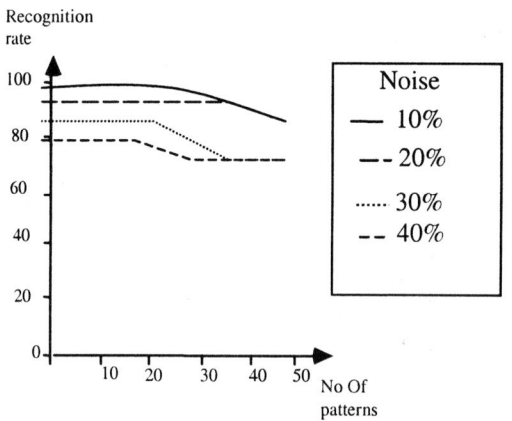

Fig. 3. Recognition rate Vs noise

Now, in this phase we compare the performance of our approach with [1] and [4].

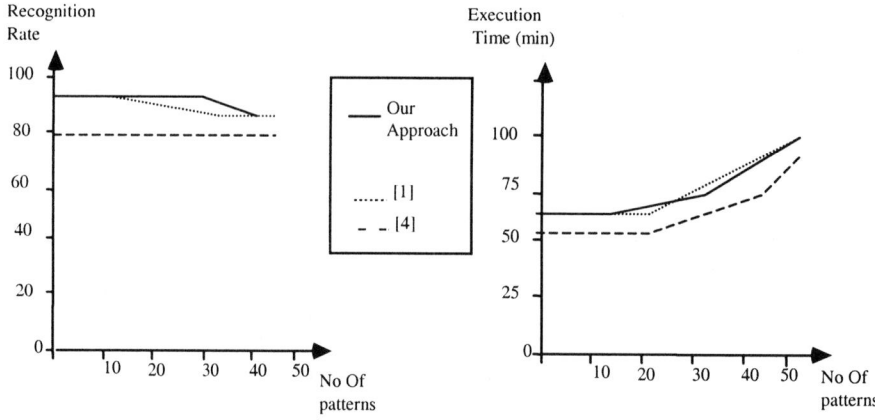

Fig. 4. Comparison of the Recognition rate and execution time for a noise = 10%

Similar to previous results, our approach improves the performance of previous work because we have obtained the optimal value of the threshold.

C. Third Experiment

In this part, we compare the performance of our approach for different number of bits of the input patterns. We suppose NLA=15 and N=10.

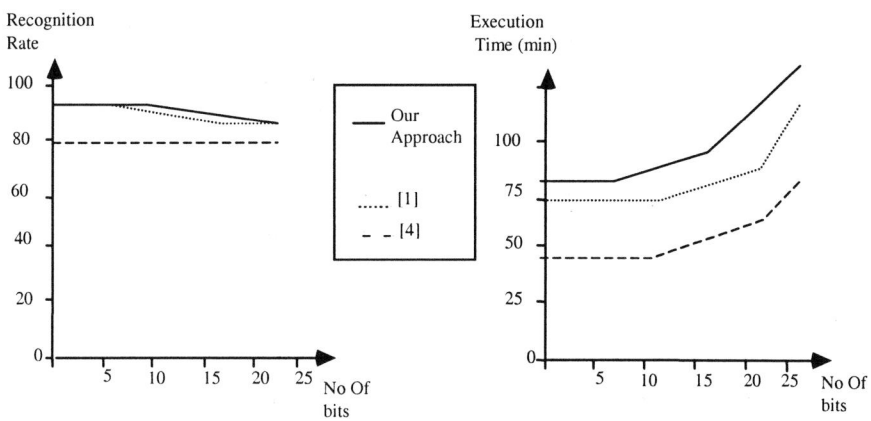

Fig. 5. Comparison of the Recognition rate and execution time for a noise = 10% and different number of bits of the input patterns

In this case, the pattern size doesn't affect the performance of our approach. The problem is with our execution time, this increases when the number of bits is large.

V. CONCLUSIONS

The experimental results show that if we use an adaptive threshold in the SDM we can improve the performance of the recognition phase with respect to the classical SDM approach. In general, we obtain similar performance than the evolutionary approach proposed in [1]. But the recognition rate is the best for large N (one of the main capabilities of the SDM approaches is that). The execution time is increase because we relearn the SDM with the optimal value of threshold. We are going to extend our experiments for more complex problems (images recognition with a large number of bits, etc.).

REFERENCES

[1] J. Aguilar, A. Colmenares, "Resolution of Pattern Recognition Problems using a Hybrid Genetic/Random Neural Network Learning Algorithm", *Pattern Analysis and Applications*, vol. 1, pp. 52-61, 1998.

[2] J. Aguilar, "Some experiments on the Sparse Distributed Memory", Technical Report 22-02, CEMISID, Universidad de los Andes, 2002.

[3] F. Grebenicek, "Data coding for Sparse Distributed Memory". *Mosis'98 Proceedings*, pp. 34-40, 1998.

[4] F. Grebenicek, "Self-Organized Sparse Distributed Memory- an Application: Pattern Data analysis". Technical Report 124, Ostrava University, 2000.

[5] P. Kanerva, *Sparse Distributed Memory*. The MIT Press, Cambridge, Massachussetts, 1990.

Modular Neural Networks for Solving High Complexity Problems

Hazem M. El-Bakry

Faculty of Computer Science &Information System
Mansoura University - Egypt
helbakry1@hotmail.com

ABSTRACT

In this paper, we introduce a powerful solution for complex problems which required to be solved using neural nets. This is done by using modular neural nets (MNNs) that divide the input space into several homogenous regions. Such approach is applied to implement XOR functions, 16 logic function on one bit level, and 2-bit digital multiplier. Compared to previous non- modular designs, a salient reduction in the order of computations and hardware requirements is obtained.

1. INTRODUCTION

Modular Neural Nets (MNNs) present a new trend in neural network architecture design. Motivated by the highly-modular biological network, artificial neural net designers aim to build architectures which are more scalable and less subjected to interference than the traditional non-modular neural nets [1]. There are now a wide variety of MNN designs for classification. Non-modular classifiers tend to introduce high internal interference because of the strong coupling among their hidden layer weights [2]. As a result of this, slow learning or over fitting can be done during the learning process. Sometime, the network could not be learned for complex tasks. Such tasks tend to introduce a wide range of overlap which, in turn, causes a wide range of deviations from efficient learning in the different regions of input space [3]. Usually there are regions in the class feature space which show high overlap due to the resemblance of two or more input patterns (classes). At the same time, there are other regions which show little or even no overlap, due to the uniqueness of the classes therein. High coupling among hidden nodes will then, result in over and under learning at different regions [8]. Enlarging the network, increasing the number and quality of training samples, and techniques for avoiding local minina, will not stretch the learning capabilities of the NN classifier beyond a certain limit as long as hidden nodes are tightly coupled, and hence cross talking during learning [2]. A MNN classifier attempts to reduce the effect of these problems via a divide and conquer approach. It, generally, decomposes the large size / high complexity task into several sub-tasks, each one is handled by a simple, fast, and efficient module. Then, sub-solutions are integrated via a multi-module decision-making strategy. Hence, MNN classifiers, generally, proved to be more efficient than non-modular alternatives [6]. However, MNNs can not offer a real alternative to non-modular networks unless the MNNs designer balances the simplicity of subtasks and the efficiency of the multi module decision-making strategy. In other words, the task decomposition algorithm should produce sub tasks as they can be, but meanwhile modules have to be able to give the multi module decision making strategy enough information to take accurate global decision [4].

In a previous paper [9], we have shown that this model can be applied to realize non-binary data. In this paper, we prove that MNNs can solve some problems with a little amount of requirements than non-MNNs. In section 2, XOR function, and 16 logic functions on one bit level are simply implemented using MNN. Comparisons with conventional MNN are given. In section 3, another strategy for the design of MNNS is presented and applied to realize, and 2-bit digital multiplier.

2. COMPLEXITY REDUCTION USING MODULAR NEURAL NETWORKS

In the following subsections, we investigate the usage of MNNs in some binary problems. Here, all MNNs are feedforward type, and learned by using backpropagation algorithm. In comparison with non-MNNs, we take into account the number of neurons and weights in both models as well as the number of computations during the test phase.

2.1 A simple implementation of XOR problem

There are two topologies to realize XOR function whose truth Table is shown in Table 1 using neural nets. The first uses fully connected neural nets with three neurons, two of which are in the hidden layer, and the other is in the output layer. There is no direct connections between the input and output layer as shown in Fig.1. In this case, the neural net is trained to classify all of these four patterns at the same time.

Table 1 Truth table of XOR function.

x	y	O/P
0	0	0
0	1	1
1	0	1
1	1	0

The second approach was presented by Minsky and Papert which was realized using two neurons as shown in Fig. 2. The first representing logic AND and the other logic OR. The value of +1.5 for the threshold of the hidden neuron insures that it will be turned on only when both input units are on. The value of +0.5 for the output neuron insures that it will turn on only when it receives a net positive input greater than +0.5. The weight of -2 from the hidden neuron to the output one insures that the output neuron will not come on when both input neurons are on [7].

Using MNNs, we may consider the problem of classifying these four patterns as two individual problems. This can be done at two steps:
1- We deal with each bit alone.
2- Consider the second bit Y, Divide the four patterns into two groups.

The first group consists of the first two patterns which realize a buffer, while the second group which contains the other two patterns represents an inverter as shown in Table 2. The first bit (X) may be used to select the function.

Table 2 Results of dividing XOR Patterns.

X	Y	O/P	New Function
0	0	0	Buffer (Y)
0	1	1	
1	0	1	Inverter ($\overline{Y}$)
1	1	0	

So, we may use two neural nets, one to realize the buffer, and the other to represent the inverter. Each one of them may be implemented by using only one neuron. When realizing these two neurons, we implement the weights, and perform only one summing operation. The first input X acts as a detector to select the proper weights as shown in Fig.3. In a special case, for XOR function, there is no need to the buffer and the neural net may be represented by using only one weight corresponding to the inverter as shown in Fig.4. As a result of using cooperative modular neural nets, XOR function is realized by using only one neuron. A comparison between the new model and the two previous approaches is given in Table 3. It is clear that the number of computations and the hardware requirements for the new model is less than that of the other models.

Table 3 A comparison between different models used to implement XOR function.

Type of Comparison	First model (three neurons)	Second model (two neurons)	New model (one neuron)
No. of computations	O(15)	O(12)	O(3)
Hardware requirements	3 neurons, 9 weights	2 neurons, 7 weights	1 neuron, 2 weights, 2 switches, 1 inverter

2.2 Implementation of logic Function using MNN

Realization of logic functions in one bit level (X,Y) generates 16 functions which are (AND, OR, NAND, NOR, XOR, XNOR, $\overline{X}$, $\overline{Y}$, X, Y, 0, 1, $\overline{X}$ Y, X $\overline{Y}$, $\overline{X}$ +Y, X+ $\overline{Y}$). So, in order to control the selection for each one of these functions, we must have another 4 bits at the input, thereby the total input is 6 bits as shown in Table 4.

Table 4 Truth table of Logic function (one bit level) with their control selection.

Function	C1	C2	C3	C4	X	Y	O/p
AND	0	0	0	0	0	0	0
	0	0	0	0	0	1	0
	0	0	0	0	1	0	0
	0	0	0	0	1	1	1
⋮							
X+ $\overline{Y}$	1	1	1	1	0	0	1
	1	1	1	1	0	1	0
	1	1	1	1	1	0	1
	1	1	1	1	1	1	1

Non-MNNs can classify these 64 patterns using a network of three layers. The hidden layer contains 8 neurons, while the output needs only one neuron and a total number of 65 weights are required. These patterns can be divided into two groups. Each group has an input of 5 bits, while the MSB is 0 with the first group and 1 with the second. The first group requires 4 neurons and 29 weights in the hidden layer, while the second needs 3 neurons and 22 weights. As a result of this, we may implement only 4 summing operations in the hidden layer (in spite of 8 neurons in case of non-MNNs) where as the MSB is used to select which group of weights must be connected to the neurons in the hidden layer. A similar procedure is done between hidden and output layer. Fig. 5 shows the structure of the first neuron in the hidden layer. A comparison between MNN and non-MNNs used to implement logic functions is shown in Table 5.

Table 5 A comparison between MNN and non MNNs used to implement 16 logic functions.

Type of Comparison	Realization using non MNNs	Realization using MNNs
No. of computations	O(121)	O(54)
Hardware requirements	9 neurons, 65 weights	5 neurons, 51 weights, 10 switches, 1 inverter

3. IMPLEMENTATION OF 2-BITS DIGITAL MULTIPLIER USING MNNS

In the previous section, to simplify the problem, we make division in input, here is an example for division in output. According to the truth table shown in Table 6, instead of treating the problem as mapping 4 bits in input to 4 bits in output, we may deal with each bit in output alone. Non MNNs can realize the 2-bits multiplier with a network of three layers with total number of 31 weights. The hidden layer contains 3 neurons, while the output one has 4 neurons. Using MNN we may simplify the problem as:

$$W = CA \quad (1)$$

$$X = AD \otimes BC = AD(\overline{B} + \overline{C}) + BC(\overline{A} + \overline{D})$$
$$= (AD + BC)(\overline{A} + \overline{B} + \overline{C} + \overline{D}) \quad (2)$$

$$Y = BD(\overline{A} + \overline{C}) = BD(\overline{A} + \overline{B} + \overline{C} + \overline{D}) \quad (3)$$

$$Z = ABCD \quad (4)$$

Equations 1, 2, 3 can be implemented using only one neuron. The third term in Equation 3 can be implemented using the output from Bit Z with a negative (inhibitory) weight. This eliminates the need to use two neurons to represent $\overline{A}$ and $\overline{D}$. Equation 2 resembles an XOR, but we must first obtain AD and BC. AD can be implemented using only one neuron. Another neuron is used to realize BC and at the same time oring (AD, BC) as well as anding the result with ($\overline{ABCD}$) as shown in Fig.6. A comparison between MNN and non-MNNs used to implement 2bits digital multiplier is listed in Table 7.

Table 6 Truth table of 2-bit digital multiplier.

Input Patterns				Output Patterns			
D	C	B	A	Z	Y	X	W
0	0	0	0	0	0	0	0
0	0	0	1	0	0	0	0
0	0	1	0	0	0	0	0
0	0	1	1	0	0	0	0
0	1	0	0	0	0	0	0
0	1	0	1	0	0	0	1
0	1	1	0	0	0	1	0
0	1	1	1	0	1	1	0
1	0	0	0	0	0	0	0
1	0	0	1	0	0	1	0
1	0	1	0	0	1	0	0
1	0	1	1	0	1	1	0
1	1	0	0	0	0	0	0
1	1	0	1	0	0	1	1
1	1	1	0	0	1	1	0
1	1	1	1	1	0	0	1

Table 7 A comparison between MNN and non-MNNs used to implement 2-bits digital multiplier.

Type of Comparison	Realization using non MNNs	Realization using MNNs
No. of computations	O(55)	O(35)
Hardware requirements	7 neurons, 31 weights	5 neurons, 20 weights

4. CONCLUSION

We have presented a new model of neural nets for classifying patterns that appeared expensive to be solved using conventional models of neural nets. This approach has been introduced to realize different types of logic problems. Also, it can be applied to manipulate non-binary data. We have shown that, compared to non MNNS, realization of problems using MNNs resulted in reduction of the number of computations, neurons and weights.

REFERENCES

[1] J, Murre, Learning and Categorization in Modular Neural Networks, Harvester Wheatcheaf. 1992.

[2] R. Jacobs, M. Jordan, A. Barto, Task Decomposition Through Competition in a Modular Connectionist Architecture: The what and where vision tasks, Neural Computation 3, pp. 79-87, 1991.

[3] G. Auda, M. Kamel, H. Raafat, Voting Schemes for cooperative neural network classifiers, IEEE Trans. on Neural Networks, ICNN95, Vol. 3, Perth, Australia, pp. 1240-1243, November, 1995.

[4] G. Auda, and M. Kamel, CMNN: Cooperative Modular Neural Networks for Pattern Recognition, Pattern Recognition Letters, Vol. 18, pp. 1391-1398, 1997.

[5] E. Alpaydin, , Multiple Networks for Function Learning, Int. Conf. on Neural Networks, Vol.1 CA, USA, pp. 9-14, 1993.

[6] A. Waibel, Modular Construction of Time Delay Neural Networks for Speach Recognition, Neural Computing 1, pp.39-46.

[7] D. E. Rumelhart, G. E. Hinton, and R. J. Williams, Learning representation by error backpropagation, Parallel distributed Processing: Explorations in the Microstructues of Cognition, Vol. 1, Cambridge, MA:MIT Press, pp. 318-362, 1986.

[8] K. Joe, Y. Mori, S. Miyake, Construction of a large scale neural network: Simulation of handwritten Japanese Character Recognition, on NCUBE Concurrency 2 (2), pp. 79-107.

[9] H. M. El-bakry, and M. A. Abo-elsoud, Automatic Personal Identification Using Neural Nets, The 24th international Conf. on Statistics computer Science, and its applications, Cairo, Egypt, 1999.

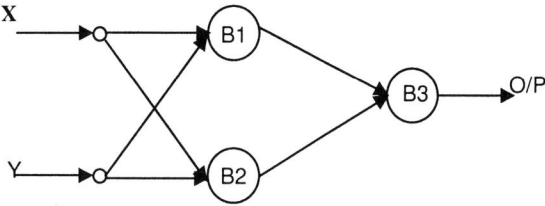

Figure 1. Realization of XOR function using three neurons.

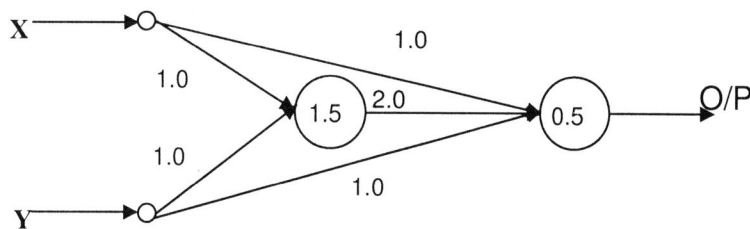

Figure 2. Realization of XOR function using two neurons.

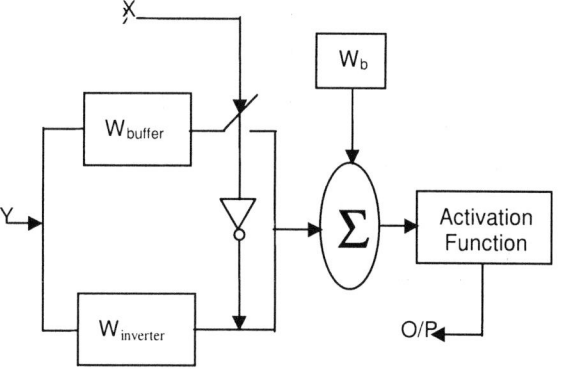

Figure 3. Realization of XOR function using modular neural nets.

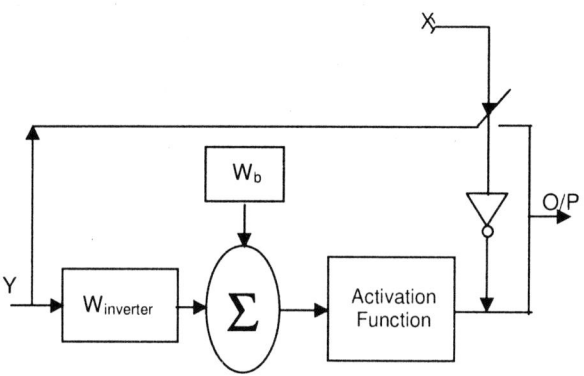

Figure 4. Implementation of XOR function using only one neuron.

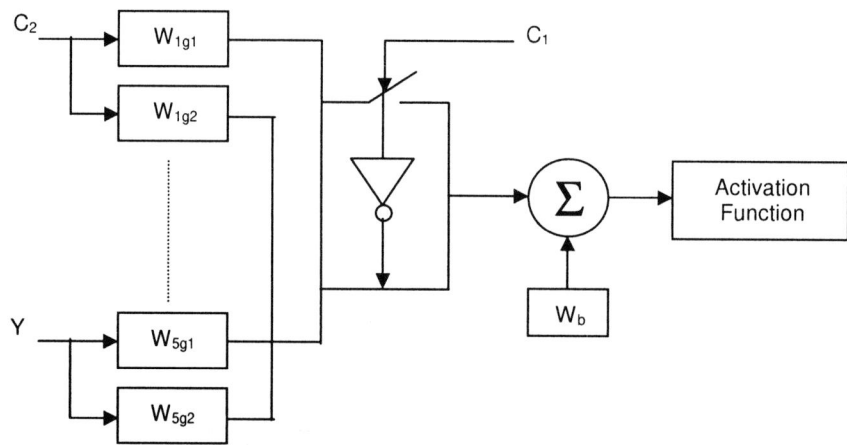

Figure 5. Realization of logic functions using MNNs (the first neuron in the hidden layer).

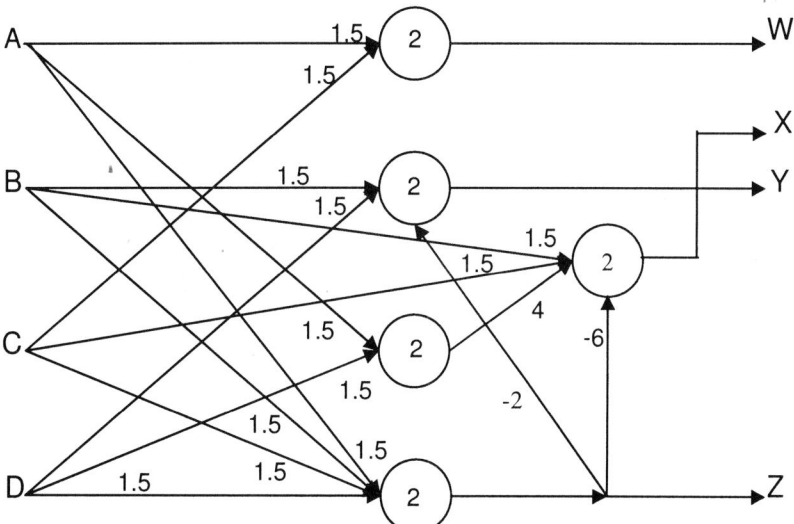

Figure 6. Realization of 2-bits digital multiplier using MNNs.

Human Face Recognition Based On Radial Basis Probabilistic Neural Network

Lin Guo   De-Shuang Huang

Institute of Intelligent Machines, Chinese Academy of Sciences,
P.O.Box 1130, Hefei, Anhui , China.
Emails: lguo@mail.iim.ac.cn, dshuang@mail.iim.ac.cn

Abstract- **In this paper, a novel human face recognition method based on radial basis probabilistic neural network (RBPNN) is proposed. The orthogonal least square algorithm (OLSA) is used to train the RBPNN and the recursive OLSA is adopted to optimize the structure of the RBPNN. The Olivetti Research Laboratory (ORL) facial database, which is preprocessed by wavelet transformation, is used to test the proposed approach. The experimental results show that the RBPNN achieves higher recognition rate and better classification efficiency with respect to radial basis function neural network (RBFNN) and BP neural network.**

I. INTRODUCTION

Human face recognition is one of most important and inherent abilities of human visual system. There are many applications in modern society for a successful face identification system: non-intrusive identification and verification for credit cards and ATM transactions, non-intrusive access control to buildings and restricted area, monitoring of ports of entry for terrorists and smugglers, and etc. For the designers of pattern recognition algorithms, face recognition is a very challenging problem. Many methods, such as the nearest feature line method [1], the fisher classifier [2], the support vector machine (SVM) [3], neural networks method [4]-[5], and etc., have been proposed. This paper focuses on using a novel radial basis probabilistic neural network (RBPNN) model [6] to perform face recognition task.

The RBPNN model [6], as shown in Fig.1, was derived from the radial basis function neural network (RBFNN) and the probabilistic neural network (PNN). Hence, it possesses the advantages of the above two networks while lowers their demerits. From Fig.1, this network consists of four layers. The first hidden layer is a nonlinear processing layer, generally consisting of selected centers from training samples. The second hidden layer selectively sums the first hidden layer outputs. Generally, the corresponding weight values of the second hidden layer are 1's. For pattern recognition problems, the outputs in the second hidden layer need to be normalized. The last layer for RBPNN is just the output layer.

This work was supported by NSF of China and the Grant of "Hundred Talents Program" of Chinese Academy of Sciences of China

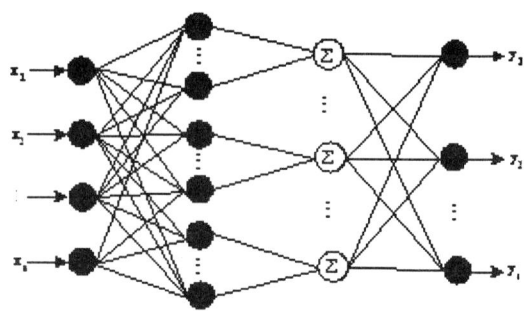

Fig.1. The topology scheme of RBPNN.

II. TRAINING ALGROITHMS FOR RBPNN

In mathematics, for input vector x, the actual output value of the ith output neuron of RBPNN, y_i^α, can be expressed as the following equation:

$$y_i^\alpha = \sum_{k=1}^{M} w_{ik} h_k(x) \qquad (1)$$

$$h_k(x) = \sum_{i=1}^{n_k} \phi_i(x, c_{ki}) = \sum_{i=1}^{n_k} \phi_i(\|x - c_{ki}\|_2) \quad k = 1, 2, \cdots M \qquad (2)$$

Here $h_k(x)$ is the kth output value of the second hidden layer of RBPNN; w_{ik} is the synaptic weight between the kth neuron of the second hidden layer and the ith neuron of the output layer of RBPNN; c_{ki} represents the ith hidden center vector for the kth pattern class of the first hidden layer; n_k represents the number of hidden center vector for the kth pattern class of the first hidden layer; $\|\bullet\|_2$ is Euclidean norm; and M denotes the number of the neurons of the output layer and the second hidden layer, or the pattern class number for the training samples set; $\phi_i(\bullet)$ is the kernel function, which is generally Gaussian kernel function. $\phi_i(\|x - c_{ki}\|_2)$ can be written as,

$$\phi_i(\|x - c_{ki}\|_2) = \exp(-\frac{\|x - c_{ki}\|_2^2}{\sigma_i^2}) \qquad (3)$$

where σ_i is the shape parameter for Gaussian kernel function.

From the viewpoint of classification for labeled patterns, the RBPNN is a kind of outer-supervised learning feed-forward neural network. Namely, when pattern samples from the kth class training set Ω are input into the RBPNN with one output neuron for one class, the corresponding teacher signal $[0,\cdots,\underset{k}{1},\cdots,0]^T$ is set up at the output layer.

The purpose of training the network is to assure the synaptic weights to change along with the direction of minimizing the squared error between the teacher signal and the actual output. Generally, the training algorithms for the RBPNN include orthogonal least square algorithms (OLSA) and recursive least square algorithms (RLSA), etc. These two methods have the common advantages of fast convergence and good convergent accuracy. The RLSA, which requires good initial conditions, however, is to fit for those problems with the large training samples set. As the OLSA make full use of matrix computation, such as orthogonal decomposition algorithm of matrices, its training speed and convergent accuracy is faster and higher than the ones of the RLSA. So the OLSA is preferred in this paper.

For L training samples, (1) can be written as:

$$\begin{bmatrix} y_{11}^a & y_{12}^a & \cdots & y_{1M}^a \\ y_{21}^a & y_{22}^a & \cdots & y_{2M}^a \\ \vdots & \vdots & & \vdots \\ y_{L1}^a & y_{L2}^a & \cdots & y_{LM}^a \end{bmatrix} = \begin{bmatrix} h_{11} & h_{12} & \cdots & h_{1M} \\ h_{21} & h_{22} & \cdots & h_{2M} \\ \vdots & \vdots & & \vdots \\ h_{L1} & h_{L2} & \cdots & h_{LM} \end{bmatrix} \begin{bmatrix} w_{11} & w_{12} & \cdots & w_{1M} \\ w_{21} & w_{22} & \cdots & w_{2M} \\ \vdots & \vdots & & \vdots \\ w_{M1} & w_{M1} & \cdots & w_{MM} \end{bmatrix} \quad (4)$$

or:
$$Y^a = H \times W \quad (5)$$

According to [7], it can be known that the synaptic weight matrix W between the output layer and the second layer of the RBPNN can be solved as follows:

$$W = R^{-1} \times \hat{Y} \quad (6)$$

where $R, \hat{Y}$ can be respectively obtained as follows:

$$H = Q \times \begin{bmatrix} R \\ \cdots \\ 0 \end{bmatrix} \quad (7)$$

$$Q^T \times Y = \begin{bmatrix} \hat{Y} \\ \tilde{Y} \end{bmatrix} \quad (8)$$

where Q is an $L \times L$ orthogonal matrix with orthogonal columns satisfying $Q \times Q^T = Q^T \times Q = I$, and R is an $M \times M$ upper triangle matrix with the same rank as H. In (7), $\hat{Y}$ is an $M \times M$ matrix and $\tilde{Y}$ is an $(N-M) \times M$ matrix.

Equations (7)-(8) express the orthogonal decomposition of the output matrix H of the second hidden layer of RBPNN.

III. STRUCTURE OPTIMIZATION OF RBPNN

Two methods of the structure optimization of RBPNN can be found in literature [8]-[9]. An optimization method based on genetic algorithms (GA) was proposed in literature [8]. Another optimization method based on recursive orthogonal least square algorithm (ROLS) was proposed in literature [9]. Compared with ROLS, GA is a global search method, and it can usually obtain a more parsimonious network. However, GA requires more computations and takes a longer training time. On the other hand, the ROLS is a backward selection algorithm. The philosophy of this method is to sequentially remove from the network, one hidden node at a time, i.e., the center that causes the smallest increase in training error. The details of ROLS method have been described in literature [9]. In this paper the ROLS is preferred.

The key point of optimizing the RBPNN is to select the hidden centers of the first hidden layer. Generally, selecting the hidden centers of the first hidden layer of the RBPNN is not only involved in how many the number of the hidden centers being selected, but also in what space locations the hidden centers being located at. Usually, we wish the number of selected centers to be as small as possible for the fewer hidden centers will not only simplify the training and the testing of the network but also improve the generalization capability of the network. On the other hand, the locations of the hidden centers in space are of utmost importance to the performance of the network. In the case of the number of the hidden centers being fixed, different locations for the hidden centers can lead to different network performance. In this paper, the ROLS is used to select the hidden centers of the first hidden layer of the RBPNN and to optimize the structure of the RBPNN.

In addition, for labeled pattern recognition problem, the number of the second hidden layer's neurons of RBPNN is generally set as the pattern class number of training samples set.

Another important parameter of RBPNN is the shape parameter of Gaussian kernel function. Generally, the shape parameters for all Gaussian kernel functions are chosen the same values. In the case of hidden centers being fixed, different shape parameters for kernel functions can lead to different classification performance and generalization capability. The shape parameter σ of the kernel functions of RBPNN is usually set according to the following heuristic relationship [10]

$$\sigma = \frac{d_{\max}}{\sqrt{K}} \quad (9)$$

where $d_{\max}$ is the maximum Euclidean distance among all the training samples, and K is the total number of the training samples.

IV. SIMULATION RESULTS FOR FACE RECOGNITION

We take the widely used Olivetti Research Laboratory (ORL) facial database, available from http://www.orl.co.uk/facedatabase.html [11], to verify our proposed approach. This database includes 400 images from 40 individuals. Each individual has 10 images that have various expressions, appearances and illuminations. Each image with 256 grey scales is in the size of 92×112. 200 images taken from 40 different individuals are used as training samples and the other 200 images as testing samples. Namely, each individual has 5 images for training samples and 5 images for testing samples. There was no overlap between the training and testing sets. A subset of the images (16 images from four different individuals) is shown in Fig.2.

First, the face images are preprocessed by twice discrete wavelet transformation. The size of each image is reduced from 92×112 to 23×28. As a result, we can not only decrease the computational complexity but also increase the recognition rate, as shown as in Table I. Then we select all the 200 training samples as the hidden centers of the first hidden layer. The number of the second hidden neurons is set as 40. The number of output layer neurons is also 40. According to (9), the shape parameter σ is set as 650. We use the OLSA to train the RBPNN. Consequently, the recognition rate of the testing samples is 95.5%.

In order to optimize and prune the RBPNN, likewise, by using the parameter similar to the one mentioned above we use the recursive orthogonal least squares algorithm to optimize the structure of RBPNN. As a result, the selected hidden centers number of the first hidden layer is reduced from 200 to 74 and the recognition rate of testing samples is still 95.5%.

Compared with the RBPNN, with the same training and testing samples, by selecting all the training samples as the hidden centers, the maximum recognition rate of RBFNN is 93.0% where the shape parameter of Gaussian kernel function of the RBFNN is about 9000.

The recognition rate of BP neural network (BPNN) to this data is about 93% according to [4], [12]. Thus, it can be seen that the recognition rate of the RBPNN is higher than both that of the RBFNN and that of the BPNN.

TABLE I
RECONGITION RATES WITH/WITHOUT ONCE/TWICE DISCRETE WAVELET TRANSFORMATION

Method	Without	With	
		Once	Twice
RBPNN	94.5%	95.0%	95.5%
RBFNN	88.0%	90.5%	93.0%

TABLE II
THE TESTING RESULTS WITH NOISY SAMPLES
Here the recognition rate is the average recognition rates of 20 different experiments. σ is the square root of noise variance.

Noise variances	$\sigma = 0$	$\sigma = 20$	$\sigma = 40$	$\sigma = 60$
Recognition rates	95.50%	95.20%	94.53%	94.10%

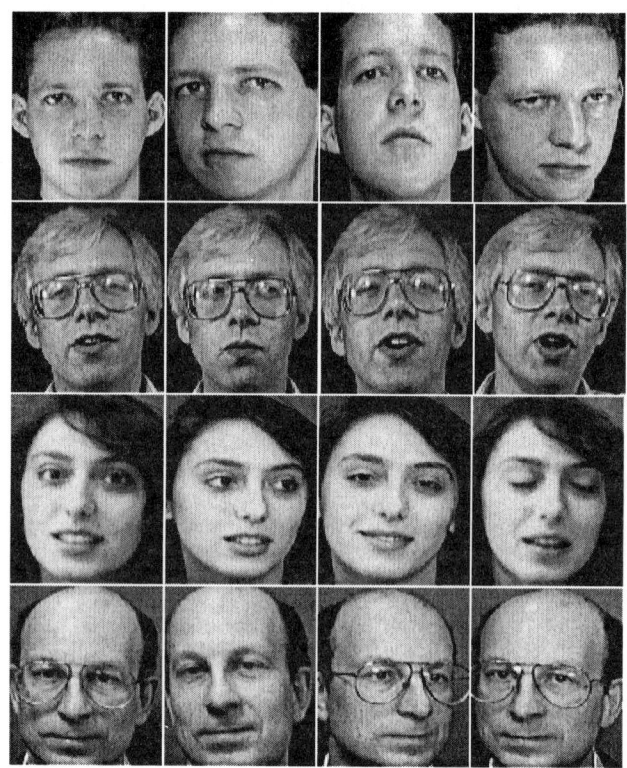

Fig.2. A subset (16 samples) of the images of ORL face database

TABLE III
TRAINING AND CLASSIFICATION CPU TIMES FOR THE ORL DATABASE

Method	Training CPU time	Classification CPU time
RBPNN	2.3s	0.015s
RBFNN	2.7s	0.012s
BPNN	>10min	> 0.1s

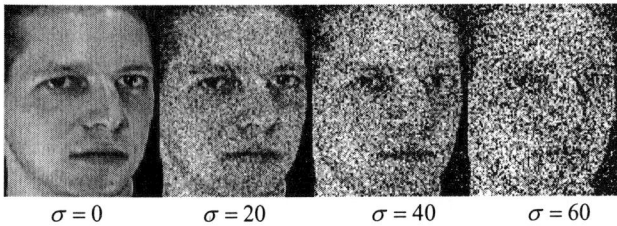

Fig.3. Example of testing samples with different noises

In order to test the generalization capability of the RBPNN, we test the trained networks with noisy testing samples. The noises generated are Gaussian white noises with zeros-mean and four different variances. The four testing images with noises are plotted on Fig.3. Likewise, we preprocess all the images with twice wavelet transformation. The test results are shown in Table II.

From Table II, it can be seen that the RBPNN also has good performance in noise toleration and in generalization capability.

On the other hand, in experiment, it was found that the training speed and testing speed with the RBPNN are also very fast. The algorithm was programmed with MATLAB 6.0, and it was run on Pentium IV with the clock of 1.7 GHz and the RAM of 256M under Microsoft Windows 2000 environment, preprocessing the images with twice wavelet transformation, the CPU time needed to recognize one face image with the RBPNN is only about 0.015 seconds and the training CPU time needed about 2.3 seconds. As far as the face recognition based on the BPNN is concerned, the training time and classification time are much longer than the ones of the RBPNN, as shown in Table III.

From the above experimental results, it can be observed that our face recognition method based on the RBPNN not only achieves higher statistical recognition rate but also are of faster training speed and testing speed.

V. CONCLUSIONS

This paper proposed a human face recognition method based on radial basis probabilistic neural networks (RBPNN). The orthogonal least square algorithm (OLSA) is used to train the RBPNN and the recursive OLSA is adopted to optimize the structure of RBPNN. By preprocessing the ORL images with discrete wavelet transformation, our method achieves higher recognition rate and faster training speed. The experimental results obtained show that our approaches are effective, efficient and feasible, which greatly support the claim that RBPNN is a very promising neural network model in practical applications.

Future research works will focus on how to use some effective feature extraction methods together with our RBPNN classifier to achieve better recognition performance.

REFERENCES

[1] S. Z. Li and J. Lu, "Face recognition using the nearest feature line method," *IEEE Trans. Neural Networks*, vol. 10, pp. 439-443, Mar. 1999.

[2] C. Liu and H. Wechsler, "A shape- and texture- based enhanced fisher classifier for face recognition," *IEEE Trans. IMAGE PROCESSING*, vol. 10, No. 4, Apr. 2001.

[3] Y. K. Zhang, P. Du, and C. Q. Liu, "A face recognition method based on principal component analysis and support vector machine," *Journal of Shanghai Jiaotong University*, vol. 36, No. 6, Jun. 2002.

[4] Z. Jin, Z. S. Hu, and J. Y. Yang, "A face recognition method based on the BP neural networks," *Journal of Computer Research and Development*, 1999, 3 (3): pp.274-277.

[5] S. Lawrence, C. L. Giles, A. C. Tsoi,and A. D. Back, "Face recognition: A convolutional neural-networks approach," *IEEE Trans. Neural Networks*, vol. 8, pp. 98-113, Jan. 1997.

[6] D. S. Huang, "Radial basis probabilistic neural networks: Model and application," *International Journal of Pattern Recognition and Artificial Intelligence*, 13(7), pp. 1083-1101, 1999.

[7] J. B. Gomm and D. L. Yu, "Selecting radial basis function network centers with recursive orthogonal least squares training," *IEEE Trans. Neural Networks*, vol. 11, No. 2, Mar. 2000.

[8] W. B. Zhao and D. S. Huang, "The structure optimization of radial basis probabilistic neural networks based on genetic algorithms," in *IJCNN2002*, pp.1086-1091, Hilton Hawaiian Village Hotel, Honolulu, Hawaii, May. 12-17, 2002.

[9] W. B. Zhao and D. S. Huang, "Application of recursive orthogonal least squares algorithm to the structure optimization of radial basis probabilistic neural networks," in *ICSP 2002*, pp. 1211-1214, Beijing, China, Aug, 26-30, 2002.

[10] S. Haykin, "Adaptive filter theory," *Upper Saddle River, NJ Prentice-Hall*, 1996.

[11] S. M. Lucas, "Continuous n-tuple classifier and its application to real-time face recognition," *IEE Proc.-Vis. Image Signal process.* vol. 145, No .5, Oct. 1998.

[12] H. T. Su and R. C. Zhao, "Face recognition based on wavelet transform and multiple classifier," *Computer Applications*, vol. 22, No. 8, Aug. 2002.

Classification of the Italian Liras Using the LVQ Method

Sigeru Omatu[+], Toshihisa Kosaka[++], and Masaru Teranisi[+++]

[+]Osaka Prefecture University, Sakai, Osaka 599-8531, Japan
[++]Glory TD Himeji, Hyougo 670-8567 Japan
[+++]Nara National Technical College, Yamato-Koriyama, Nara 639-1080

Abstract- For the pattern classification problems the neuro-pattern recognition which is the pattern recognition based on the neural network approach has been paid an attention since it can classify various patterns like human beings. In this paper, we adopt the learning vector quantization(LVQ) method to classify the various money. The reasons to use the LVQ are that it can process the unsupervised classification and treat many input data with small computational burdens. We will construct the LVQ network to classify the Italian Liras. Compared with a conventional pattern matching technique, which has been adopted as a classification method, the proposed method has shown excellent classification results.

I. INTRODUCTION

Bill money classification by transaction machines has been important to make progress the office automation [1]. Since sizes of bills are different according to kinds of bills, the measurement data of bills include various variations. Human being can classify the bills correctly even if they are suffered from those variations such as rotation and shift. But usual pattern recognition using a conventional transaction machine cannot give us the correct classification result under such cases since the basic method is a pattern matching principle. Furthermore, the conventional pattern matching method requires many template patterns for many kinds of bills, which takes much time and needs much experience [1].

Recently, neural networks which are based on the biological mechanism of human brain have been focused since they have intelligent pattern recognition ability [2]. In this paper, we will apply the neural network approach to classify the bill money under various conditions by using transaction machines. The learning vector quatization (LVQ) has been used to classify the bills since it can treat highly dimensional input and has simple learning structure[3]. The LVQ network adopted here has 64x15 units in the input layer and many units at the output layer. The bills are Italian Liras of of 8 kinds, 1,000, 2,000, 5,000, 10,000, 50,000 (new), 50,000 (old), 100,000 (new), 100,000 (old) Liras with four directions A,B,C, and D where A and B mean the normal direction and the upside down direction and C and D mean the reverse version of A and B. The simulation results show that the proposed method can produce the excellent classification results compared with the conventional method..

II. COMPETITIVE NEURAL NETWORKS

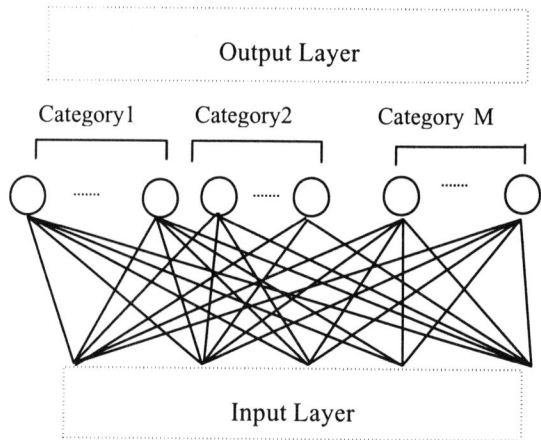

Fig. 1. Structure of the LVQ networks.

We will explain the competitive neural networks that are used to classify the bill money. The structure of a LVQ competitive network is shown in Fig. 1. The input for the LVQ is bill money data where an original image consists of 128x64 pixels and the input data to the network is compressed as 64x15 pixels to decrease the computational load. The output of the network consists of the Italian Liras of 8 kinds, 1,000, 2,000, 5,000, 10,000, 50,000 (new), 50,000 (old), 100,000 (new), 100,000 (old) Liras with four directions A, B, C, and D where A and B mean the normal direction and the upside down direction and C and D mean the reverse version of A and B.

In the input layer the original bill money data are applied and all the units at the input layer are connected to all the neurons at the output layer with connection weight W_{ij}. W_{ij} denotes the connection weight from the unit j in the input layer to unit i in the output layer. The output layer will output only one neuron which is called winner neuron. The winner neuron is selected as the neuron with the minimum distance between an input vector and its connection weight vector. The connection weights W_{ij} are set by the random number at the beginning. Here, we set the mean vector of the cluster plus small random number. Then the following learning algorithm of the connection weight vector is used.

LVQ algorithm

Step 1. Find the unit c at the output layer which has the minimum distance from the input data **x** (t)

$$\|\mathbf{x}(t) - \mathbf{W}_c\| = \min_i \|\mathbf{x}(t) - \mathbf{W}_i\|$$

where $\| \ \|$ denotes the Euclidean norm and t denotes

the iteration time.

Step 2. If the input **x**(t) belongs to Category c, then
$$\mathbf{w}_c(t+1) = \mathbf{w}_c(t) + \alpha(t)(\mathbf{x}(t) - \mathbf{w}_c(t))$$
$$\mathbf{w}_i(t+1) = \mathbf{w}_i(t), \quad i \neq c$$
and if the input **x**(t) belongs to the other Category j (j ≠ c), then
$$\mathbf{w}_c(t+1) = \mathbf{w}_c(t) - \alpha(t)(\mathbf{x}(t) - \mathbf{w}_c(t))$$
$$\mathbf{w}_i(t+1) = \mathbf{w}_i(t), \quad i \neq c$$
where $\alpha(t)$ is a positive function and denotes learning rate.

In the the usual LVQ $\alpha(t)$ is given by $\alpha(t) = \alpha_0(1 - \frac{t}{T})$ where ($0 < \alpha_0 < 1$) is a positive and T is a total number of learning iteratuions.

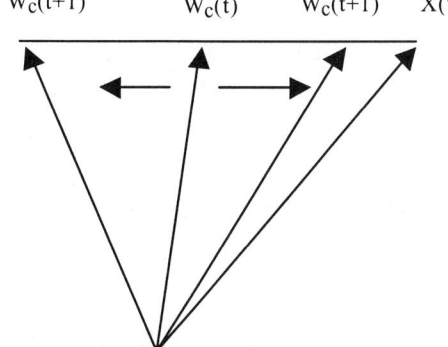

Fig.2. Principle of the LVQ algorithm where the right hand side shows the same category case of **x**(t) and Category c and the left hand side denotes the different category case.

The above algorithm for selection of new weight vector Wc(t+1) can be explained graphically as Fig. 2. In the above LVQ algorithm, the learning rate $\alpha(t)$ plays an important role for convergence. To adjust the parameter, Kohonen has proposed an optimization method without proof as follows:

$$\alpha_c(t) = \frac{\alpha_c(t-1)}{1 + s(t-1)\alpha_c(t-1)}$$

where s(t) =1 if **x**(t) belongs to the same Category c and s(t)=-1 if **x**(t) does not belong to the same Category c. Here, $\alpha_c(t)$ denotes the learning rate for the pattern of Category C. In what follows, we will prove the above relation. From the learning rule of the LVQ, we have
$$\mathbf{w}_c(t+1) = \mathbf{w}_c(t) + s(t)\alpha_c(t)(\mathbf{x}(t) - \mathbf{w}_c(t))$$
$$= (1 - s(t))\alpha_c(t)\mathbf{w}_c(t) + s(t)\alpha_c(t)\mathbf{x}(t)$$
and
$$\mathbf{w}_c(t) = \mathbf{w}_c(t-1) + s(t-1)\alpha_c(t-1)(\mathbf{x}(t-1) - \mathbf{w}_c(t-1))$$
$$= (1 - s(t-1))\alpha_c(t-1)\mathbf{w}_c(t-1)$$
$$+ s(t-1)\alpha_c(t-1)\mathbf{x}(t-1)$$
Substituting the latter equation the former one, we have

$$\mathbf{w}_c(t+1) = (1 - s(t)\alpha_c(t))(1 - s(t-1)\alpha_c(t-1))\mathbf{w}_c(t-1)$$
$$+ s(t)a_c(t)\mathbf{x}(t) + s(t-1)a_c(t-1)(1 - s(t)a_c(t))\mathbf{x}(t-1).$$

We assume that the optimal rate adjusts the effect of x(t) and x(t-1) equally within the absolute value, that is,
$$\alpha_c(t+1) = \alpha_0 \quad \text{if } \alpha_c(t+1) > 1.$$
Then we have
$$\alpha_c(t) = \frac{\alpha_c(t-1)}{1 + s(t-1)\alpha_c(t-1)}.$$

From the above equation, we can see that the value of $\alpha_c(t)$ become larger than 1 when s(t-1)=-1, which may make the learning algorithm unstable. Thus, we must fix the $\alpha_c(t)$ to a boundary value α_0 when it becomes larger than 1.
$$\alpha_c(t+1) = \alpha_0 \quad \text{if } \alpha_c(t+1) \rangle 1.$$
Using the above OLVQ1 algorithm, we will classify the Italian bills in the following section.

III. PREPROCESSING ALGORITHM

The images obtained by transaction machine, there are variations such as rotation or shift. Therefore, we must adjust the images such that the variations may be reduced as much as possible by using the preprocessing. The flow char of the preprocessing procedure is illustrated in Figure 3. In this figure, the original image with 128x64 pixels are observed at the transaction machine in which rotation and shit are included. After correction of these effects, we select a suitable aria which show the bill image and compressed as the image with 64x15 pixels to the neural networks. Although the neural network of the LVQ type could process any order of the dimension of the input data, the small size is better to achieve the fast convergence result. Thus, we have selected the above size of the image.

IV. ITALIAN LIRA CLASSIFICATION

The bills used here are Italian liras, which have 8 kinds such as 1,000 Liras, 2,000 Liras, 5,000 Liras, 10,000 Liras, new 50,000 Liras, old 50,000 Liras, new 100,000 Liras, and old 100,000 liras. Those Lira bills are used at the input of the transaction machine where four directions such as A, B, C, and D appear since normal direction, reverse direction, and their upside down directions occur at the input as shown in Fig.4.The typical images of 1,000 Lira for four directions are shown in Fig.5. Thus, thirty-two bill images are one set of the classification pattern of the experiment. Total number of data sets is 30 and 10 data sets are used for training of the network and the remaining 20 data sets are used to test the network. In order to reduce the misclassification, we have set the threshold value d_θ such that if $d_c > d_\theta$, unit c is not fired. This means that if the minimum distance is not less

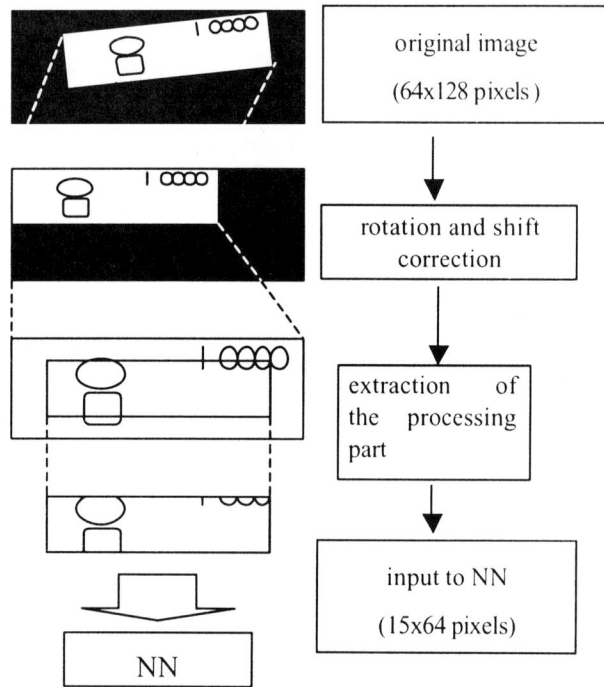

Fig. 3. Preprocessing algorithm.

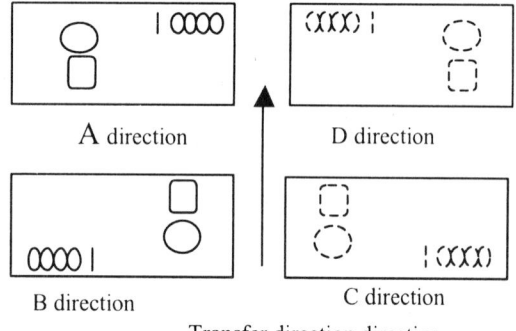

Fig. 4. Four directions of bill money.

(a) A direction of 1,000 Lira

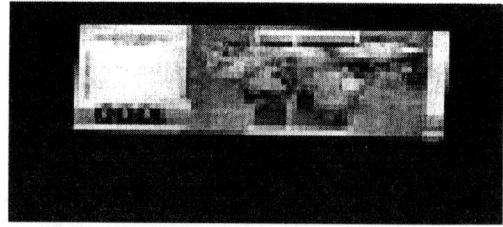

(b) B direction of 1,000 Lira

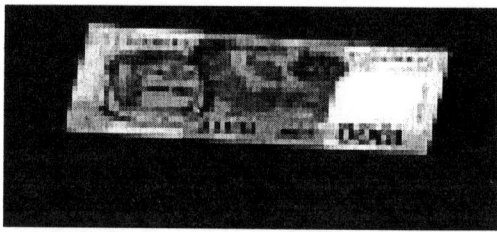

(c) C direction of 1,000 Lira

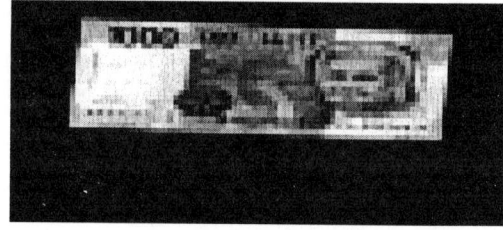

(d) D direction of 1,000 Lira

Fig.5. Image of four directions of 1,000 Lira.

than d_θ, the input data is not classified. The parameters of the neural network used here are as follows:

Number of units in the input layer=960.

Number of units in the output layer in the initial state=32 where every 50 iterations the number has been adjusted.

Total learning timeT=150.

$\alpha_i(0) = 0.5$, $i = 1, \cdots M$.

Initial values of the weight vectors=mean vectors for training patterns.

$d_\theta = \min_c (m_c + 4.5\sigma_c)$.

From the original image data we can see that the difference between 50,000 Lira old and new is slight and the difference between old and new 100,000 Liras. Therefore, it is rather difficult to recognize them so perfectly. but in this case the misclassification like old and new bills within the same values is not serious. Thus, we have regarded these misclassification as the correct one.. Furthermore, we have introduced the threshold value to prevent from occurring the misclassification. Thus, even if the minimum distance criterion results in the correct classification, we have decided these bells are unknown. Without these threshold constraints, we could obtain 100% recognition rate in any case. TABLE I shows the initial recognition rate which has been obtained by the conventional pattern matching method [1]. TABLE II shows the number of bills which are not classified(unfired bills). TABLES III and IV show the classification rates and the corresponding number of unfired neurons after learning, respectively. TABLES V denotes the number of codebook vectors. .From the results we can see that the classification rates have been improved by learning and the unfired numbers of neurons have been decreased compared with the conventional pattern matching method.

V. CONCLUSIONS

We have proposed a new classification method of Italian Liras by using the OLVQ1 algorithm. The experimental results show the effectiveness of the proposed algorithm compared with the conventional pattern matching method as shown in TABLES I-V.

REFERENCES

[1] S. Fukuda, T. Kosaka, and S. Omatu: Bill Money Classification of Japanese Yen Using Time Series Data, Trans. IEE of Japan, Vol.115-C, No.3, pp.354-360, 1999(in Japanese).
[2] J. Dayhoff: Neural Network Architectures: An Introduction, International Thompson Computer Press, New York, 1990.
[3] T. Kohonen: Self-Organizing Maps, Springer, Berlin, 1995.

TABLE I
RECOGNITION RATE(%) AT t=0

		Directions			
		A	B	C	D
Italian Liras	1,000	100	100	100	100
	2,000	100	100	100	100
	5,000	100	100	100	100
	10,000	100	100	100	100
	50,000(new)	100	100	100	100
	50,000(old)	85	100	80	95
	100,000(new)	100	100	90	100
	100,000(old)	100	100	95	90

TABLE II
NOT FIRED RATE(%) AT t=0

		Directions			
		A	B	C	D
Italian Liras	1,000	20	15	15	10
	2,000	5	10	25	25
	5,000	15	20	5	0
	10,000	10	10	10	5
	50,000(new)	5	0	20	5
	50,000(old)	0	0	0	0
	100,000(new)	0	0	0	0
	100,000(old)	0	5	0	0

TABLE III
RECOGNITION RATE(%) AT t=160

		Directions			
		A	B	C	D
Italian Liras	1,000	100	100	100	100
	2,000	100	100	100	100
	5,000	100	100	100	100
	10,000	100	100	100	100
	50,000(new)	100	100	100	100
	50,000(old)	100	100	95	95
	100,000(new)	100	100	90	100
	100,000(old)	100	100	95	90

TABLE IV
NOT FIRED RATE(%) AT t=160

		Directions			
		A	B	C	D
Italian Liras	1,000	5	0	5	0
	2,000	0	10	25	25
	5,000	15	20	5	0
	10,000	10	0	0	5
	50,000(new)	5	0	0	0
	50,000(old)	0	5	0	0
	100,000(new)	0	0	0	0
	100,000(old)	0	5	0	0

TABLE V
NUMBER OF UNITS AFTER LEARNING

		Directions			
		A	B	C	D
Italian Liras	1,000	2	2	2	2
	2,000	2	1	1	1
	5,000	1	1	1	1
	10,000	1	2	2	1
	50,000(new)	2	1	1	1
	50,000(old)	2	1	3	1
	100,000(new)	1	1	1	1
	100,000(old)	1	1	1	1

A Method of Biomimetic Pattern Recognition for Face Recognition

Wang Zhi-hai   Mo Hua-yi   Lu Hua-xiang   Wang Shou-jue

Lab of Artificial Neural Networks, Institute of Semiconductors, CAS, Beijing 100083, China

Abstract-A new method of face recognition, based on Biomimetic Pattern Recognition and Multi-Weights Neuron Network, had been proposed. A model for face recognition that is based on Biomimetic Pattern Recognition had been discussed, and a new method of facial feature extraction also had been introduced. The results of experiments with BPR and K-Nearest Neighbor Rules showed that the method based on BPR can eliminate the error recognition of the samples of the types that not be trained, the correct rate is also enhanced.

Key Words-Face Recognition   Biomimetic Pattern Recognition   Multi-Weights Neuron Network   Facial Feature Extraction

I. INTRODUCTION

Face recognition has been a very active research field in recent years, and its technologies have been widely applied in various fields such as ID verification and authority controls [1][2]. Current face recognition methods, which derive from the idea of "division" in the traditional pattern recognition, including methods based on face geometrical features [3][4], template-matching or neural networks [2][5][6], are all based on dividing existing face types in the face recognition systems, therefore can not avoid the following two drawbacks:

The first, these methods are unable to solve the problem that the high false acceptance rate for untrained samples. In a traditional face recognition system, the system is trained according to the existing various types of face samples, and the training ends till the samples are divided satisfyingly [6]. However, if a face sample of untrained type is introduced, the system will place the sample into one of the divided sample subspaces, thus recognized it falsely. For example, in the system showed in figure 1, A and B are trained sample subspaces, and if a sample of untrained type is introduced, it will be divided into A or B and false acceptance occurs.

The second, when a new type of face samples is added into a face recognition system deriving from the idea of "division" of the traditional pattern recognition, it is necessary to retrain the whole system, in other words, redivide all types of samples. The repeating retrainings cause long training time, which brings many inconveniences in the face recognition systems, especially a large one.

To avoid these drawbacks, a new theory of Biomimetic Pattern Recognition (BPR) [7] was proposed by Wang Shou-jue, a member of CAS. The purpose of the paper is to apply the theory to a face recognition system, and overcome these drawbacks existing in the traditional face recognition systems.

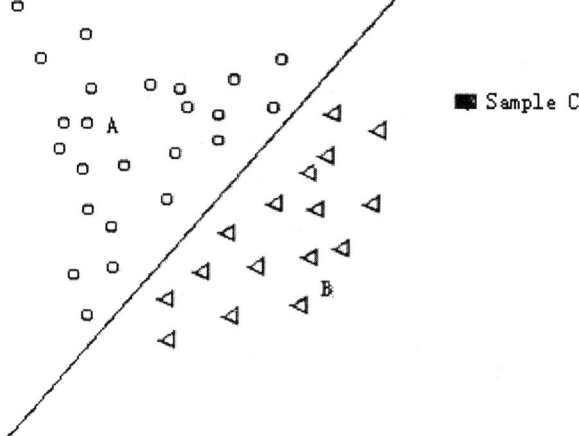

Fig.1. The traditional patter recognition method, the A subspace and the B subspaces are the two classes. The sample C is the one to be recognized, and it belongs to either A or B.

II. BRIEFLY INTRODUCTION OF BIOMIMETIC PATTERN RECOGNITION

Traditional Pattern Recognition methods, most typically, Support Vector Machine (SVM) theory [8], aim at the optimal division of the samples of different types in the feature space, while BPR aim at the optimal coverage of the samples of the same type. In other words, in BPR theory, the construction of the sample subspace of each type of samples depends only on the type itself, while on the contrary, it depends on the relations between various types of samples in traditional pattern recognition. More detailedly, in BPR theory, the construction of the subspace of a certain type of samples depends on analyzing the relations between the trained types of samples and utilizing the methods of "coverage of objects with complicated geometrical forms in the multidimensional space" [7][9]. For example, in Fig.2, the triangles represent the samples to be recognized, and the small circles and crisscrosses represent the samples of the other types. Then the broken lines represent the division methods of Pattern Recognition based on BP network, the large circles represent those of RBF network (these methods are equal to the ones based on template matching), and long ellipses represents the "recognition" methods of BPR [10].

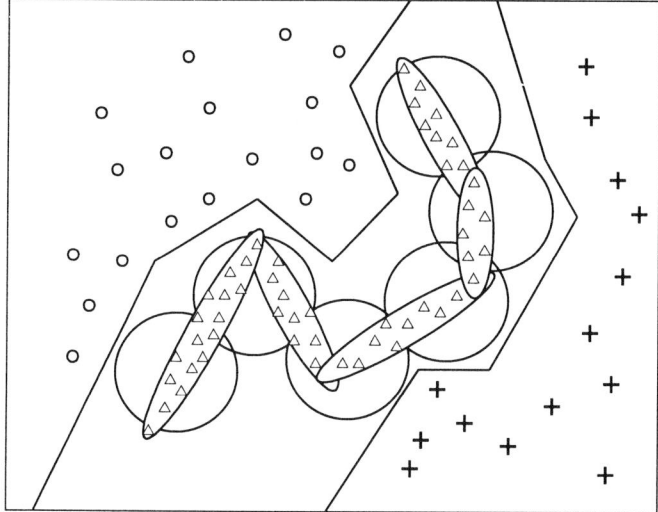

Fig. 2. The Biomimetic Pattern Recognition and The Traditional Pattern Recognition.

III. FACIAL FEATURE EXTRACTION

Facial feature extraction is an important step in face recognition. Because the faces used in our experiments are all obverse (the two eyes visible) and upright (the two eyes located in the same horizontal level), we choose a method based on differential and locating the two eyes to extract the facial features. Finally, we get a 512-dimensional vector for each face. The procedure is as following.

1). Find the two eyes on the face, and assign two points A'$(x_{a'}, y_{a'})$, B'$(x_{b'}, y_{b'})$ to represent the left eye and the right one, respectively. In fact, if the face is upright, $y_{a'} = y_{b'}$.

2) Take P as the center, shrink or enlarge the face image to a 255*255 image in the ratio of $|x_{a'} - x_{b'}| : 30$. Then transform the face image into a 85*85 one. The coordinates of P are determined by:

$$x_p = \frac{3}{2}(x_{a'} - x_{b'}) - 1$$
$$y_p = 3y_{a'} + 2|x_{a'} - x_{b'} - 1|$$

Based on points A (x_a, y_a) and B (x_b, y_b), which represent the positions of the two eyes in the transformed 85*85 image, C, D and E can be determined by

$$x_c = \frac{1}{2}(x_a + x_b), y_c = y_a + 25$$
$$x_d = \frac{1}{2}(x_a + x_b), y_d = y_a + 40$$
$$x_e = \frac{1}{2}(x_a + x_b), y_e = y_a$$

(A, B, C, D, E are showed in Fig.3).

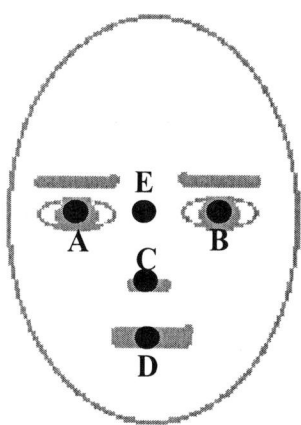

Fig. 3. The base points of facial feature extraction.

Taking A, B, C, D and E as the base points and extracting the face features referring to the parameters in Table, 1, we can get a 512-dimensional vector representing the face showed in Fig.3. In Table 1, the orientations of the parameters are 0, 45, 90, 135, 180, 225, 270, 315 degrees, respectively; the feature numbers represent the numbers of the features extracted by calculating the difference of the gray scale values of the two adjacent points in the orientation, and the base points represent the start points of the facial feature extraction. For example, if K(m,n) represents the gray scale

TABLE 1.

PARAMETERS FOR FEATURE EXTRACTION

Base points	Orientations	Numbers
A	0	15
	1	15
	2	15
	3	15
	4	15
	5	15
	6	15
	7	15
B	0	15
	1	15
	2	15
	3	15
	4	15
	5	15
	6	15
	7	15
C	0	15
	1	15
	2	24
	3	15
	4	15
	5	6
	6	7
	7	6
C'	0	8
	4	8
D	0	23
	1	8
	2	8
	3	8
	4	23
	5	8
	6	8
	7	8
E	1	15
	2	15
	3	15
	5	7
	7	7
Total		512

value of the point at (m, n), and we want to extract three features in the orientation of 0 degree with the point at (m, n) as the base point, then the three features should be

K(m+1,n)-K(m,n),

K(m+2,n)-K(m+1,n),

K(m+3,n)-K(m+2,n),

similarly, the three features extracted in the orientation of 45 degrees with the point at (m, n) as the base point should be

K(m+1,n+1)-K(m,n),

K(m+2,n+2)-K(m+1,n+1),

K(m+3,n+3)-K(m+2,n+2),

and so on.

Note that the point C' represent the point three pixels higher than the point C in the table, and we have:

$$x_{c'} = x_c$$
$$y_{c'} = y_c - 3$$

Reduce the influence of the environment lights. Assuming vector $\vec{F}$ is the one extracted in former steps, it can be written as:

$$\vec{F} = (f_1, f_2, f_3, ..., f_{512})$$

To reduce the influence of the environment lights, we recalculate $\vec{F}$ in the following equation:

$$\vec{F} = \vec{F} - \vec{I}(\frac{\sum_{i=1}^{512} f_i}{512} + 256)$$

Here, $\vec{I}$ represents a 512-dimensional vector, of which the subvalue in each dimension is 1:

$$\vec{I} = (1,1,1,...,1)$$

IV. THE FACE RECOGNITION SYSTEM BASED ON BPR THEORIES

1. Face Recognition Models

In this paper, we study the issue about the recognition of basically upright and obverse faces. In such issue, the two eyes of the faces are visible, the fronts of the faces are basically obverse to the scenes, the angles of elevation of the faces basically remain constant (small changes of the angles are regarded as the system noises), and only small rotations in horizontal level are permitted. Such prerequisites are available for common access control systems and face recognition systems. Some series of face images meeting the prerequisites above are showed in Fig.4.

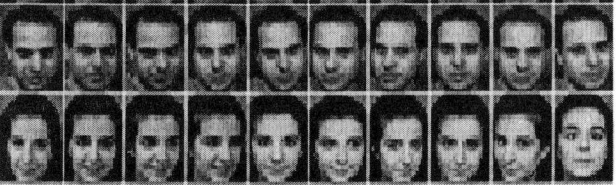

Fig. 4. Some face images for training feature subspace.

Since the rotations from left to right (or from right to left) of the faces are continuous processes, the variations of the corresponding images (feature points, which are the images formed by mapping the faces to the multidimensional space) must also be continuous. This case accords with the basic principle of BPR—the continuity law of the whole samples of the same type in the feature space [7]. Because we assume that the variations of the specific faces are limited in the horizontal level, there is only one variable. As a result, the distributions of corresponding image (feature point) sets in the multidimensional space should be one-dimensional manifolds [7]. Considering the small disturbances in other orientations, the coverage form of a certain type of samples in the feature space should be the topological product of a one-dimensional manifold congeneric with the broken lines and a 512-dimensional hypersphere, and thus the close subspace of such type of samples is formed. Assuming the broken line is A and the radius of the hypersphere is R, the subspace of this type of samples P_a can be written as:

$$P_a = \{x \mid \min(\rho(x,y)) < R, y \in A, x \in R^{512}\}$$

Assuming the number of trained samples of each type (each person) is K, the trained sample set can be written as:

$$S = \{x \mid x = s_1, s_2, s_3, ..., s_K\}$$

Here $s_1, s_2, s_3, ..., s_k$ are the samples collected in the sequential orientations

To cover the subspace P_a with limited neuron in the neural network, we utilize several lines to approximate the broken line A, and thus get a new broken line B. Then, we acquire P_b, the topological product of a 512-dimensional hypersphere and B, and which is the approximation of P_a and the final subspace acquired. Because there are K trained samples, we can use K-1 lines, each of which is represented by $B_i (i = 1, 2, ... K - 1)$, to approximate A, thus we have:

$$B_i = \{x \mid x = \alpha s_i + (1-\alpha)s_{i+1}, \alpha \in [0,1], s_i \in S, x \in R^{512}\}$$

$$B = \bigcup_{i=1}^{K-1} B_i$$

The coverage of each neuron is:

$$P_i = \{x \mid \min(\rho(x,y)) \leq R, y \in B_i, x \in R^{512}\}$$

To cover P_i, the following structure of the neurons is adopted:

$$y_i = f[\Phi(s_i, s_{i+1}, x)]$$

In the equation above, s_i, s_{i+1} is the feature vector of the ith and (i+1)th trained sample, respectively, x is the input vector, in other words, the feature vector of the sample to be recognized, and y_i is the output of the ith neuron.

Φ is a function with multi-vector inputs [7], one scalar quantity output and determined by the multi-weight vector neuron, and it can be written as:

$$\Phi(s_i, s_{i+1}, x) = \min(\rho(x,y)), y \in \{z \mid z = \alpha s_i + (1-\alpha)s_{i+1}, \alpha \in [0,1]\}$$

And f is a nonlinear transfer function, here we adopt the step function:

$$f(x) = \begin{cases} 1 & x \leq R \\ 0 & x > R \end{cases}$$

The sample subspace consisting of the coverage of all K-1 neurons is:

$$P_b = \bigcup_{i=1}^{K-1} P_i$$

2. Trainings Of The Samples.

According to the principle of BPR—determining the subspace of a certain type of samples basing on the type of samples itself, the training of the type of samples needs only the samples of the type itself, and if a new type of samples is added, it is not necessary to retrain anyone of the trained types of samples. The training procedure of a certain type of samples (faces of a specific person) is as following:

extract the features of each face and acquire K feature vectors;

Train the neurons covering the spaces P_1 (corresponding to the broken lines consisting of the 1st and the 2nd vectors), P_2 (similarly, corresponding to the broken lines consisting of the 2nd and the 3rd vectors),..., P_i ,..., P_{k-1} in sequence. Store the parameters of the K-1 neurons, and end the training.

3. Sample Recognition

According to the comments in 4.1, it can be concluded that the feature subspace of each type of faces consists of K-1 neurons, which can be written as:

$$y_i = f[\Phi(s_i, s_{i+1}, x)]$$

And the discriminant function of this type is:

$$F_m(x) = F(\sum_{i=1}^{K-1} y_i)$$

Note: here m is the symbol number of this type, and F is the step function

$$F(x) = \begin{cases} 1, x > 0 \\ 0, x \leq 0 \end{cases}$$

Therefore, if the output of $F_m(x)$ is 1, sample x belongs to type m, if not, sample x doesn't.

V. THE EXPERIMENT RESULTS AND ANALYSIS

In our experiments, we collected four types of samples (faces of four persons), trained three of them, and tested all. We also do experiments with K-Nearest Neighbor Rules using the same samples. The data of the experiment results are showed as follows in Table 2 and Table 3.

By analyzing the data in Table.2 and Table 3, the following results can be acquired: in the face recognition system based on BPR stated in this paper, the correct acceptance rate for the samples of the same type reaches 97%, and the refusal rate is 3%, while the two elements of KNN are 89.82% and 10.18%, respectively; in the other hand, the refusal rate of samples of different types reaches 99.7%, and the false acceptance rate is 0.3%, while the two elements of KNN are 97.94% and 2.06%, respectively. The results show that the face recognition system based on BPR has a very high correct acceptance rate and very low false acceptance rate, and therefore it is much more advanced than those based on traditional pattern recognition methods, such as KNN.

TABLE 2
THE RESULTS OF THE EXPERIMENTS WITH BPR

Type	Trained Samples	Sets of tested samples in this type			Sets of tested samples not in this type		
		Total	Correct	Refuse	Total	False	Refuse
A	30	55	55	0	263	2	261
B	30	110	107	3	208	0	208
C	31	61	58	3	257	0	257
Total	91	226	220	6	728	2	726

TABLE 3
THE RESULTS OF THE EXPERIMENTS WITH KNN

Type	Trained Samples	Sets of tested samples in this type			Sets of tested samples not in this type		
		Total	Correct	Refuse	Total	False	Refuse
A	30	55	49	6	263	3	260
B	30	110	93	17	208	12	196
C	31	61	61	0	257	0	257
Total	91	226	203	23	728	15	713

VI. CONCLUSIONS

The results above show:

(1) The false acceptance rate of untrained samples of the face recognition system based on BPR is very low, only 0.3%. If more rigorous threshold value is adopted, the false acceptance rate can be reduced to nearly zero, however, the refusal rate of trained sample will increase.

And the following conclusions can be drew:

(2) In the face recognition system based on BPR, each type of samples is trained and recognized independently [7], and the new type added will not influence the trained ones.

(3) In the face recognition system based on BPR, for a certain type of face samples, its topological characters in multidimensional space must be known first, and then the method of "coverage of objects with complicated geometrical form in the multidimensional space" is adopted to construct

its subspace.

(4) In our experiments, the training data must be sequential and continuous, which is the prerequisite of the face recognition system based on BPR [7]. In this case, without enough support, we can't test the system in a large database environment.

(5). In our experiments, the application of BPR on face recognition was researched and satisfying results were acquired. It shows that the application of BPR on face recognition is really a new and promising research field.

REFERENCE

[1] A. Samal and P. A. Iyengar. Automatic recognition and analysis of human faces and facial expressions: A survey. *Pattern Recognition*, 25:65–77, 1992.

[2] D. Valentin, H. Abdi., A. J. O'Toole, and G. W. Cottrell. Connectionist models of face processing: A survey. *Pattern Recognition*, 27:1209–1230, 1994.

[3] R. Brunelli and T. Poggio. Face recognition: Features versus templates. *IEEE Transactions on Pattern Analysis and Machine Intelligence*, 15:1042–1052, 1993.

[4] A. J. Goldstein, L. D. Harmon, and A. B. Lesk. Identification of human faces. *Proceedings of the IEEE*, 59(5):748–760, May 1971.

[5] R. Chellappa, C. L. Wilson, and S. Sirohey. Human and machine recognition of faces: A survey. *Proc. IEEE*, 83:705–741, May 1995.

[6] G. Guo, S. Li, and K. Chan, Face recognition by support vector machines, Proc. of the International Conferences on Automatic Face and Gesture Recognition, 196-201, 2000.

[7] Wang Shou-jue, Chen Xu and Wu Yan, "Biomimetic Pattern Recognition—A New Model of Pattern Recognition Theory and Its Applications", Acta Electronica Sinica Vol.30 No.10 Oct. 2002

[8] Vladimir N. Vapnik, **Nature of statistic learning theory**

[9] Wang Shou-jue and Wang Bai-nan, Analysis and Theory of High-Dimension Space Geometry for Artificial Neural Networks. Acta Electronica Sinica Vol.30 No.1 Jan. 2002

[10] Wang Shou-jue and Xu jian etc. Multi-camera Human-face Personal Identification System Based on the Biomimetic Pattern Recognition. Acta Electronics Sinica, Vol. 31, No.1, 2003.

NEURAL INTERPOLATOR FOR IMAGE RECOGNITION IN THE PROCESS OF MICRODEVICE ASSEMBLY

O. Makeyev, *Student Member, IEEE*
Kyiv National Taras Shevchenko University, Ukraine,
64, Volodymyrska str., 01033 Kiev, Ukraine
mckehev@baidyk.kiev.ua

Abstract-The neural interpolator for the image recognition system is proposed. This system is developed and used for the microassembly process. The system permits us to increase the assembly process precision. A pin-to-hole insertion task was used to test the developed system.

I. INTRODUCTION.

The task of microassembly automation is becoming more and more important in microtechnology [1] – [4]. The main approaches to microdevices production are the technology of micro electromechanical systems (MEMS) [5], [6] and microequipment technology (MET) [7] - [10]. To realize all the advantages of these technologies it is important to have advanced packaging and assembly technologies.

The problem of microfilter assembly is solved [7], [8]. The microfilter contains a large number of microrings inserted in special microchannels. To insert the microring in the microchannel we put it onto a pin. Therefore the position search problem is equal to the conventional pin-hole task.

II. APPROACH TO THE MICROASSEMBLY

Here we consider the assembly task: to install the pin into the hole.

The main idea of this approach is to replace the stereovision system, which requires two video cameras, with a system based on one TV camera for teleconferences, with a cost of 50 - 70 dollars, and four light sources. The shadows from the light sources permit us to obtain the 3-D position of the needle with the microring relative to the hole.

In Fig. 1 the prototype of the visual controlled assembly system is shown.

It is necessary to know the displacements (dx, dy, dz) of the pin tip relative to the hole. It is possible to evaluate these displacements with a stereovision system, which resolves 3D problems and demands two TV cameras. To simplify the control system we propose the transformation of 3D into 2D images preserving all the information about mutual location of the pin and the hole. This approach makes it possible to use only one TV camera.

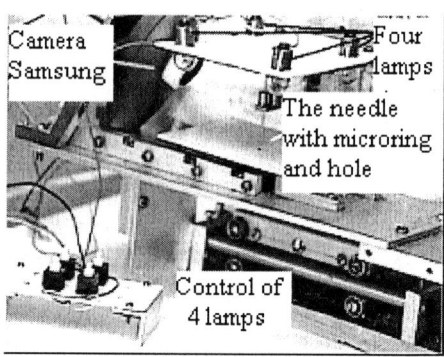

Fig. 1. The prototype of visual controlled assembly system

Four light sources are used to obtain pin shadows. Mutual location of these shadows and the hole contains all the information about the displacements of the pin relative to the hole. The displacements in the horizontal plane (dx, dy) could be obtained directly by displacements of the shadows center points relative to the hole center. Vertical displacement of the pin may be obtained from the distance between the shadows. To calculate the displacements it is necessary to have all the shadows in one image. We capture four images corresponding to each light source sequentially. Then it is necessary to extract contours and to superpose contour images (Fig. 2).

The image in Fig. 2 is similar to an optical character. It can be interpreted and treated as a symbol (resemblance to letters or numbers). For optical character recognition it was developed a Random Threshold Classifier and Random Subspace Classifier [11], [12], [13] which present the modified Rosenblatt perceptron. The classifier was adapted to recognize the position of the pin [14].

The experiments were made with the pin, the ring and the hole having the following diameters:
- Diameter of the pin 1mm;
- Outer diameter of the ring 1.2 mm;
- Inner diameter of the hole 1.25 mm.

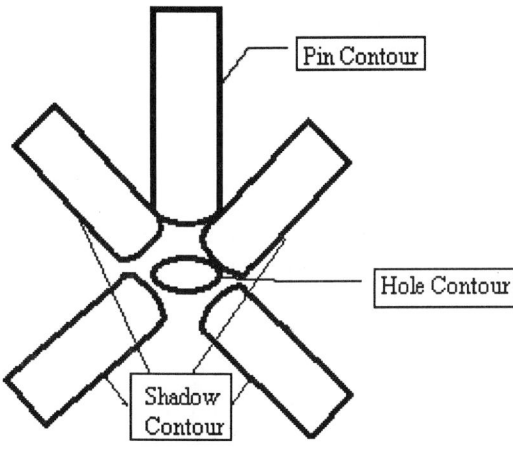

Fig.2. Shadows contours together

In this prototype we have measured only two coordinate displacements (X, Y). The images were taken from the 441 positions in the plane X-Y around the hole. The positions were located as a 21 x 21 matrix and the distance between neighboring positions was 0.1 mm. This distance corresponds to approximately 1.8 pixels in the X-coordinate and to approximately 1 pixel in Y-coordinate. An example of the original image, created with four different light sources, is presented in Fig. 3.

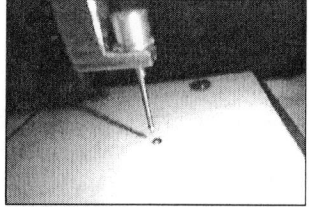 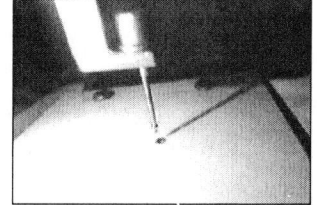
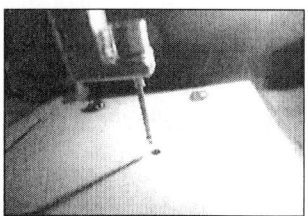 

Fig.3. An example of the images from initial database.

The image after preprocessing (contour extraction and combination) which is the input for neural interpolator is presented in Fig. 4.

III. NEURAL INTERPOLATOR FOR PIN-HOLE POSITION DETECTION.

The neural interpolator is based on the Random Subspace Classifier, which has the modified 3-layer perceptron structure: the S-layer is the receptor layer, the A-layer is the associative layer and the R-layer is the output layer.

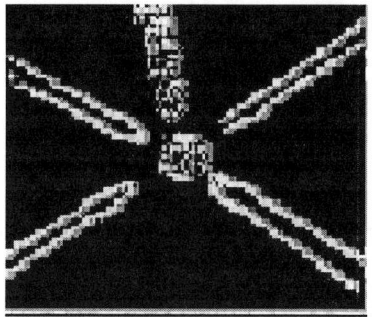

Fig.4. Input image for neural classifier.

The neural classifier outputs contain: 21 classes for X coordinates and 21 classes for Y coordinates (i.e. one R-layer has 21 neurons for X and the other R-layer has 21 neurons for Y).

Every neuron from each R-layer has 512 000 connections with the previous layer (i.e. the A-layer has 512 000 neurons).

The connections between S-layer and A-layer are untrainable connections and are formed with the random procedure ones for all the training and test session. The connections between S-layer and R-layer are trainable.

To improve the results obtained with Random Subspace Classifier the neural interpolator was worked out.

The neural interpolator differs from the neural classifier as follows: the excitations of the output neurons are considered as a set of values of continuous functions $f(dx)$ and $\varphi(dy)$. To determine the functions $f(dx)$ and $\varphi(dy)$ we use a parabolic regression equation, which is built on the base of five values selected from output neuron excitations.

We use the quadratic approximation:

$$y = a_0 + a_1 x + a_2 x^2 . \qquad (1)$$

To know the coefficients a_0, a_1, a_2 it is necessary to solve the system of the equations:

$$\begin{cases} s_0 a_0 + s_1 a_1 + s_2 a_2 = s_5 \\ s_1 a_0 + s_2 a_1 + s_3 a_2 = s_6 \\ s_2 a_0 + s_3 a_1 + s_4 a_2 = s_7 \end{cases}, \qquad (2)$$

$s_0 = n;\ n = 5;$

$$s_1 = \sum_{i=0}^{n-1} x_i \ ;\ s_2 = \sum_{i=0}^{n-1} x_i^2 \ ;$$

$$s_3 = \sum_{i=0}^{n-1} x_i^3 \ ;\ s_4 = \sum_{i=0}^{n-1} x_i^4 \ ; \qquad (3)$$

$$s_5 = \sum_{i=0}^{n-1} y_i \ ;\ s_6 = \sum_{i=0}^{n-1} y_i \cdot x_i \ ;$$

$$s_7 = \sum_{i=0}^{n-1} y_i \cdot x_i^2 ;$$

$$a_0 = s_2^3 - 2 \cdot s_1 \cdot s_2 \cdot s_3 + s_0 \cdot s_3^2 + s_1^2 \cdot s_4 - s_0 \cdot s_2 \cdot s_4 ;$$

$$a_1 = \frac{s_1 \cdot s_4 \cdot s_5 + s_2^2 \cdot s_6 - s_0 \cdot s_4 \cdot s_6 + s_0 \cdot s_3 \cdot s_7}{a_0} - \frac{s_2(s_3 \cdot s_5 + s_1 \cdot s_7)}{a_0} ; \qquad (4)$$

$$a_2 = \frac{s_2^2 \cdot s_5 - s_1 \cdot s_3 \cdot s_5 + s_0 \cdot s_3 \cdot s_6 + s_1^2 \cdot s_7}{a_0} - \frac{s_2(s_1 \cdot s_6 + s_0 \cdot s_7)}{a_0} ;$$

To find y_{max} it is necessary to find derivative y' and compare to zero. Then

$$x = -\frac{a_1}{2a_2} \qquad (5)$$

Five values y are selected according to the following rule. As a central point we selected the point with maximal value of the excitation E_{max} (Fig. 5a). In addition to this point two points to the left and two points to the right of E_{max} are selected. If point E_{max} is located at the edge of the point sequence, additional points are obtained as a mirror reflection (Fig. 5b) of the points, which are situated on the other side of E_{max}.

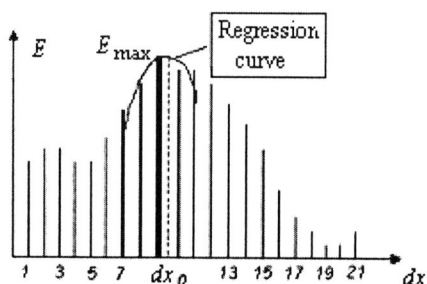

Fig.5, a. Parabolic approximations.

After determination of the functions $f(dx)$ and $\varphi(dy)$ the parameters dx_0 and dy_0, under which the functions $f(dx)$ and $\varphi(dy)$ have maximal values are determined. The parameters dx_0 and dy_0 are considered as recognized pin-hole displacements.

The interpolator training algorithm also differs form the classifier training algorithm. In this case the training rule is the following:

The modification of the weights is carried out at every step. They are modified according to the equation:

$$W_{ij}(t+1) = W_{ij}(t) + a_i * (\Delta w_j + \delta w_j), \qquad (6)$$

where $W_{ij}(t)$ is the weight of the connection between the i-neuron of A-layer and the j-neuron of R-layer before reinforcement, $W_{ij}(t+1)$ is the weight after reinforcement, a_i is the output signal (0 or 1) of the i-neuron of the A-layer.

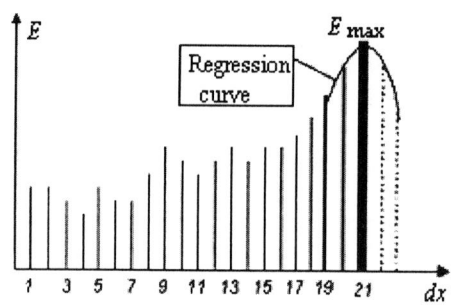

Fig.5, b. Parabolic approximation at the edge.

$$\Delta w_j = \frac{1}{(dx_j - dx_c)^2 + \varepsilon} ;$$
$$\delta w_j = -\frac{1}{(dx_j - dx_0)^2 + \varepsilon} \qquad (7)$$

where dx_c – correct pin-hole displacement; dx_0 – recognized pin-hole displacement, Δw and δw – positive and negative training factors for the j-th neuron; dx_j – pin-hole displacement which corresponds to the j-th neuron (Fig. 6).

For coordinate Y similar formulas are used.

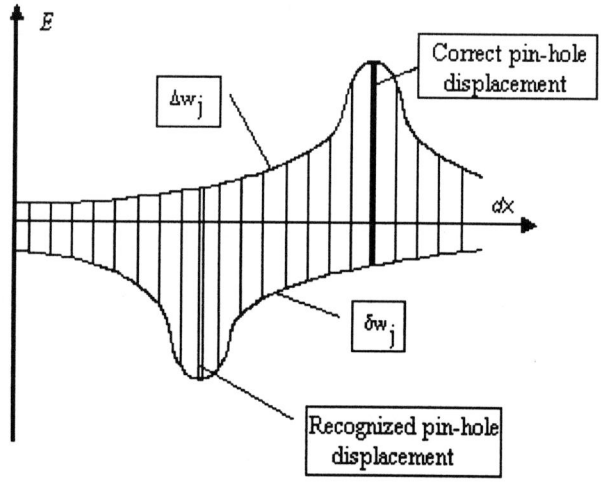

Fig.6. Correct and recognized pin-hole displacements.

IV. RESULTS.

To examine the developed method of pin-hole position detection we made a prototype of the microassembly device (Fig. 2).

It is known [15], that the recognition rate may be increased if during the training cycle the images are represented not only in the initial state but also with shifted image positions (so called distortions). We investigated the classifier with 9 distortions.

From 441 images the training and the test sets were formed. The "chessboard" rule was used to divide the initial database into training and test datasets. The initial database was considered as a 21 x 21 chessboard. The "black" cells were considered as training samples and the "white" ones as test samples.

The investigation of neural interpolator showed the following results: For coordinate X the results are in Table 1.

TABLE 1
THE RESULTS FOR X COORDINATE OF INTERPOLATOR INVESTIGATION

ε for recognition	$X\pm0.025$ mm		$X\pm0.05$ mm		$X\pm0.075$ mm		$X\pm0.1$ mm		$X\pm0.15$ mm	
	X	$X\%$	X	$X\%$	X	$X\%$	X	$X\%$	X	$X\%$
Error	74	33.6	25	11.4	4	1.8	0	0	0	0
Correct recognition	146	66.4	195	88.6	216	98.2	220	100	220	100

For coordinate Y the results are in Table 2.

In Tables 1, 2 average results for six independent experiments are presented.

TABLE 2
THE RESULTS FOR Y COORDINATE OF INTERPOLATOR INVESTIGATION

ε for recognition	$Y\pm0.025$ mm		$Y\pm0.05$ mm		$Y\pm0.075$ mm		$Y\pm0.1$ mm		$Y\pm0.15$ mm	
	Y	$Y\%$	Y	$Y\%$	Y	$Y\%$	Y	$Y\%$	Y	$Y\%$
Error	101	45.9	48	20.9	11	5	0.3	0.14	0	0
Correct recognition	119	54.1	172	79.1	209	95	219.7	99.86	220	100

V. DISCUSSION

The equipment for automatic assembly of microdevices must have high precision because the tolerances of microdevice components are very small. To increase the precision of the microequipment we use feedback based on computer vision principles. We propose an image recognition method based on neural interpolator. The neural interpolator is used to obtain relative positions of micropin and microhole. The neural classifier gives a finite number of relative positions [8]. The neural interpolator serves as an interpolation system and gives an infinite number of relative positions. The image database of relative positions of microhole and micropin of diameter 1.2 mm was used for the neural classifier and the neural interpolator testing. This database contains 441 images. In this paper the recognition results of the relative positions are presented for the neural interpolator.

A special prototype was made for the examination of the proposed method. With this prototype 441 images were obtained. The distance between neighboring images corresponds to 0.1 mm displacement of the pin relative to the hole. At the image this displacement corresponds to 1.8 pixels in the X-direction and 1 pixel in the Y-direction.

The experiments show that the computer vision system can recognize relative pin-hole position with a 0.1 mm tolerance. The neural classifier for this tolerance gives the correct recognition in 100% of cases in X and 86.7% cases in Y [16]. The neural interpolator gives for axis X 100% (Table 1) and for axis Y – 99.86% (Table 2). The neural interpolator also permits us to obtain data for smaller tolerances. For example, for axis X tolerance 0.05 mm it gives 88.6% and for axis Y tolerance 0.05 mm it gives 79.1%. The experiments show that the neural interpolator gives better results in estimation of the pin-hole relative positions.

It is interesting to mention that the 0.05 mm tolerance for Y axis is less than one pixel in the image. In this case, the recognition rate 79.1% shows that the recognition possibilities are not limited by the resolution of one pixel. This result could be explained by the fact that each object in the image contains many pixels and these pixels give much more detailed information than one pixel.

VI. Conclusion

A computer vision system for improvement of the microassembly device precision is proposed. The neural interpolator was tested in the task of pin-hole relative position detection. The neural classifier permits us to recognize the displacement of the pin relative to the hole with 1 pixel tolerance [8]. The neural interpolator permits the recognition of the pin displacement relative to the hole with 0.5 pixel tolerance. The absolute values of detectable displacements depend on the optical channel resolution. In our case, one pixel corresponds to 0.05 mm X-axis displacements and 0.1 mm Y-axis displacements. This precision is sufficient for many cases of assembly processes.

ACKNOWLEDGEMENT

The author thanks to Dr. E.Kussul and Dr. T.Baidyk for the database and useful discussions of related topics.

REFERENCES

[1] T.Ofeifer, G.Dussler, Process observation for the assembly of hybrid micro systems. *2002 IEEE International Symposium on Micromechatronics and Human Science.* – pp.117-123.

[2] J.Y.Kim, H.S.Cho, Visual sensor-based measurement for deformable peg-in-hole tasks. *Proceedings of the 1999 IEEE/RSJ International Conference on Intelligent Robots and Systems*, pp.567-572.

[3] Q.M. Jonathan Wu, M.F. Ricky Lee, Clarence W. de Silva. Intellihgent 3-D sensing in automated manufacturing processes. *2001 IEEE/ASME International Conference on Adevanced Intelligent Mechatronics Proceedings*, 2001, Italy, pp. 366-370.

[4] H.Bleuler, R.Clavel, J.-M. Brequet, H.Langen, E.Pernette. Issues in precision motion control and microhandling. *Proceedings of the 2000 IEEE International Conference on Robotics & Automation*, USA, 2000, pp.959-964.

[5] Micromechanics and MEMS. Classsical and seminal papers to 1990. Ed. by W.S.Trimmer, IEEE Press, New York, 1997, pp. 701.

[6] Madni A.M., Wan L.A. Micro electro mechanical systems (MEMS): an overview of current state-of-the art. *Aerospace Conference, 1998 IEEE*, V.1, pp 421-427

[7] E. Kussul, T. Baidyk, L. Ruiz-Huerta, A. Caballero, G. Velasco, L. Kasatkina, Development of micromachine tool prototypes for microfactories, *J. of Micromech. and Microeng.*, **12**, 2002, 795-813..

[8] Kussul E., Baidyk T., Ruiz L., Caballero A., Velasco G. Development of Low'cost Microequipment. *2002 International Symposium on Micromechatronics and Human Science*, Oct. 20-23, 2002, Nagoya, Japan, pp. 125-134.

[9] Friedrich C.R. and Vasile M.J. Development of the micromilling process for high- aspect- ratio micro structures. *J. Microelectromechanical Systems*, 1996, **5**, pp 33-38.

[10] Naotake Ooyama, Shigeru Kokaji, Makoto Tanaka and others. Desktop machining microfactory. *Proceedings of the 2-nd International Workshop on Microfactories*, Switzerland, Oct.9-10, 2000. pp.14-17.

[11] E. Kussul, T. Baidyk, Neural Random Threshold Classifier in OCR application", *Proc. of the Second All-Ukrainian Intern. Conf.*, Kiev, Ukraine, 1994, 154-157.

[12] E.Kussul., T. Baidyk, V. Lukovitch, D. Rachkovskij, Adaptive high performance classifier based on random threshold neurons, in R. Trappl (Ed.) *Cybernetics and Systems'94* (Singapore: World Scientific Publishing Co. Pte. Ltd., 1994) 1687-1695.

[13] E. Kussul, T. Baidyk, Improved method of handwritten digit recognition tested on MNIST database, *15-th Intern Conf. on Vision Interface,* Calgary, Canada, 2002, 192-197.

[14] T.N. Baidyk, E.M. Kussul, Application of neural classifier for flat image recognition in the process of microdevice assembly, *IEEE Intern. Joint Conf. on Neural Networks*, Hawaii, USA, Vol. 1, 2002, 160-164.

[15] L.Bottou, C. Cortes, J. Denker, H. Drucker, L. Guyon, L. Jackel, J. LeCun, U. Muller, E. Sackinger, P. Simard, V. Vapnik, Comparison of classifier methods: a case study in handwritten digit recognition", *Proc. of 12th IAPR Intern. Conf. on Pattern Recognition,* 1994, V. 2, 77-82.

[16] Baidyk T., Kussul E., Makeyev O. Image recognition system for microdevice assembly. *IASTED International Conference on Applied Informatics AI2003,* Innsbruck, Austria, February 10-13, 2003, p.1-6.

A Neuro-Fuzzy Graphic Object Classifier with Modified Distance Measure Estimator

R.A.Aliev, *Member IEEE,*
B.G.Guirimov,
R.R.Aliev

Dept. of Control Systems
Azerbaijan State Oil Academy
Baku, Azerbaijan

Abstract—The paper analyses issues leading to errors in graphic object classifiers. The distance measures suggested in literature and used as a basis in Traditional, fuzzy, and Neuro-Fuzzy classifiers are found to be not very suitable for classification of non-stylized or fuzzy objects in which the features of classes are much more difficult to recognize because of significant uncertainties in their location and gray-levels. The authors suggest a Neuro-Fuzzy graphic object classifier with modified distance measure that gives better performance indices than systems based on traditional ordinary and cumulative distance measures. The simulation has shown that the quality of recognition significantly improves when using the suggested method.

I. State of the Problem. Existing Systems Overview

The problem of optical recognition is not new – it exists many decades or even more. There are many good results and many theories have been developed [1]. Many examples of applications are known – extending from automated digital conversion of handwriting used in banks and offices to vision systems used in robotics and space systems, and to diagnostic and expert systems for micro-biology [2,3]. Despite of significant successes in the development of Artificial Intelligence systems, the optical recognition of fuzzy graphic objects still presents significant difficulties to machines. The human way of solving this problem, which seems for them to be not a problem at all, is very difficult to discover and mimic in artificial brains.

Let's give a simple definition and state in general the classification problem.

Definition 1. Let $X = (x_1, x_2, ..., x_N)$ be a graphic object described by N features ($X \in \Re^N$, a space of object features), and $C = (c_1, c_2, ..., c_S)$ be a set of S classes. Then a classifier is a function $F_{class}(X): \Re^N \to C$. The classifier partitions the feature space into S mutually exclusive areas.

It is not surprising to tell that the quality of classification depends on how well we can compare any two different objects. We call the tool used to compare graphic objects a Distance Measure Estimator (DME). The DME estimates the distance between (or similarity degree of) two objects. After the training of the classifier, its knowledge base KB (usually based on Neural Network, Fuzzy Rules, or combined Neuro-Fuzzy model) stores knowledge of the relations between the classes and the features. For every class there is a set of associated features in KB that uniquely identify the class. Then the classifier can make its decision about what the class of the input object is based on the value of some kind of DME. After the distance values between the input object and every class contained in the KB have been calculated, the class that produces the minimum value of distance with the input object is considered the best match.

In DME to classify fuzzy objects we have to implement some metric that will measure normalized fuzzy distance between instance vectors. The most widely used distance measures are Euclidean and Manhattan metrics [4]:

$$d(x,y) = \sqrt{\sum_{i=1}^{N} (x_i - y_i)^2} \; ; \qquad (1)$$

$$d(x,y) = \sum_{i=1}^{N} |x_i - y_i|, \qquad (2)$$

where $X = (x_1, x_2, ..., x_N)$ and $Y = (y_1, y_2, ..., y_N)$ are N-dimensional fuzzy feature vectors of two compared objects.

There are also a lot of modifications of traditional metrics [5]. Depending on the type of classes and their features different metrics should be used.

Because both the Euclidean and Manhattan distances are calculated separately for each dimension (standing for a specific feature), they are not very good distance measures for similarity between objects that have correlated and ordered features [4].

Reference [4] introduces cumulative distance measures for such cases. The cumulative Euclidean distance measure looks as follows:

$$d(x,y) = \sqrt{\sum_{i=1}^{N} \left(\sum_{u=1}^{i} x_u - \sum_{u=1}^{i} y_u \right)^2} . \qquad (3)$$

The cumulative Manhattan distance measure, called also

Landmover distance, is calculated as follows:

$$d(x,y) = \sum_{i=1}^{N} \left| \sum_{u=1}^{i} x_u - \sum_{u=1}^{i} y_u \right|. \quad (4)$$

The drawback of the suggested measures is that the features are not considered equal. As can be seen, the lower number features count more in the final value than the higher number ones. This leads to bad results when features are weakly related or not equally important [4].

An improvement for the distance measure in case of not equally important and fuzzy features is to attach a weight parameter to each feature:

$$d(x,y) = \sum_{i=1}^{N} |x_i - y_i| w_i \quad (5)$$

and to apply an *equivalent* feature aggregation as in:

$$d(x,y) = \frac{1}{N!} \sum_{u=1}^{N!} \sum_{i=1}^{N} \left| \sum_{v=1}^{i} x_{r_{uv}} - \sum_{v=1}^{i} y_{r_{uv}} \right|, \quad (6)$$

where $R = \{(r_{uv}), u = \overline{1, N!}, v = \overline{1, N}\}$ is the matrix the rows ($u = \overline{1, N!}$) of which are all possible combinations of the series $\{1, 2, ..., N\}$.

Another problem with classifiers, especially the classifiers implemented on the base of neural networks, is that following the traditional *definition 1*, the classifier partitions the feature space into S mutually exclusive areas. In many applications, especially, in case of fuzzy objects, the definition of the feature space is rarely complete. Also the boundaries of the partitions may partially overlap.

Disabling mandatory classification of an object into any class, i.e. applying so-called distance reject, introduced in [5], can significantly reduce the misclassification risk. In traditional neural networks with the "winner takes all" principle there is no way to reject the input object as not belonging to the allowed object space. For example, the neural network classifier learned to recognize the 26 English letters will classify into the same class set all figures and symbols from Russian and Greek character sets. This is because a neural network's learning set contains only allowable class samples and there is no way to provide any disabled samples because this would make the learning set infinite.

Fuzzy classifiers can provide a more trustable distance measure that would allow more quality recognition. Allowing human expertise with viewable and editable rules defining classes is essential for effective and rapid learning (knowledge one-step conversion) as well as human-like performance. However it would be more loss than profit to ignore the advantages of learning from experience, excellent performance, and the generalization ability all intrinsic to neural networks. The best solution is to mix these two techniques in the most effective way – in a Neuro-Fuzzy classifier [9,10].

II. NEURO-FUZZY MODEL. THE FUZZY RULES REPRESENTATION

We define a Neuro-Fuzzy system as an interrelated and mutually complementing intelligent combination of neural and fuzzy subsystems. Here the neural subsystem performs primarily functions of learning, tuning, and optimization of the parameters of the fuzzy subsystem. The parameters of the fuzzy subsystem are datasets able to represent the fuzzy rules defining the overall system operation. The model is designed such that it supports both fuzzy IF-THEN rules and connectionist-based representations via some explicit conversion procedure that regenerates them from the unique system knowledge base. Such a Neuro-Fuzzy system can be easily applied to develop graphic object classifiers.

The considered below Neuro-Fuzzy model was first introduced in [6] and then improved in [7].

Assume that in the considered environment we have N features to define M classes of graphic objects:

$$E = \{C_1, C_2, ..., C_M\}$$

Also for simplicity we suppose we can use only one fuzzy rule to describe every class. So the number of rules is also M.

The fuzzy rules for the classification of graphic objects are represented as follows [7]:

IF F_{11}/w_{11} AND F_{12}/w_{12} AND ... AND F_{1N}/w_{1N} THEN $O = C_1$;

IF F_{21}/w_{21} AND F_{22}/w_{22} AND ... AND F_{2N}/w_{2N} THEN $O = C_2$;

.... (7)

IF F_{i1}/w_{i1} AND F_{i2}/w_{i2} AND ... AND F_{iN}/w_{iN} THEN $O = C_i$;

....

IF F_{M1}/w_{M1} AND F_{M2}/w_{M2} AND ... AND F_{MN}/w_{MN} THEN $O = C_M$,

where $F_{ij} := (f_j \text{ IS } x_{ij})$, we denote a term expressing the degree of presence in an object O some feature (f_j) which makes it be interpreted as the class labeled by index i (C_i); x_{ij} is the constant fuzzy value from the set of features $X = \{x_1, x_2, ..., x_m\}$ used to define the value of feature f_j in the class C_i. F_{ij}/w_{ij} means that an object of class i should have the feature f_j with importance w_{iN}. (For example, a

Figure 1. Areas with higher importance (circled)

feature of graphic symbol 'A' might be: "the associated objects have a horizontal bar of dark color with the length of about a half the object's width, located somewhere in the middle of the object's height, approximately the same distances from the left and right sides.") .

The feature weights w_{ij} are intended to consider different importance of particular features in recognition of different classes. This helps significantly improve quality in case the environment contains classes with similar pictures having slight distinctions disseminated over small regions. For example, in Fig. 1 the circled areas (i.e. the related features) must be paid more attention than others when classifying the object into 'C' or 'O'.

Note that a feature is a combination of fuzzy constants expressing both locations and gray-levels (or colors). The same feature can be used in description of more than one class. The minimization of the number of features is part of the learning procedure and may be required in order to optimize the system knowledge base and to improve overall performance and interpretability.

A fuzzy constant defining the location has a membership function $\mu_D(d_x, d_y)$ of two orthogonal coordinates (Fig. 2, only one coordinate shown).

A gray-level constant for a fixed location (d_X, d_Y) is represented by a membership function $\mu_G(g)$ of an argument g representing the gray-level normalized into [0,1] (Fig. 3).

The truth value to which a particular feature i exists in the input object, T_{fi}, is calculated as:

$$T_{fi} = \max{}_{(d_x,d_y)} \{\min{}_2 \{\mu_{Di}(d_x, d_y), \mu_{Gi}(g, d_x, d_y)\}\} . \quad (8)$$

The truth values of all features are aggregated to obtain an overall truth value using a kind of t-norm. The appropriate choice of this t-norm is very crucial for quality classification. As can be seen, this aggregation (conjunction) operation is closely related in the meaning to the distance measure concept discussed in the first section. We will show in the next section how we implement the DME for a Neuro-Fuzzy classifier.

The output value O, determining the classified object, obtained from all rules is represented as a fuzzy set:

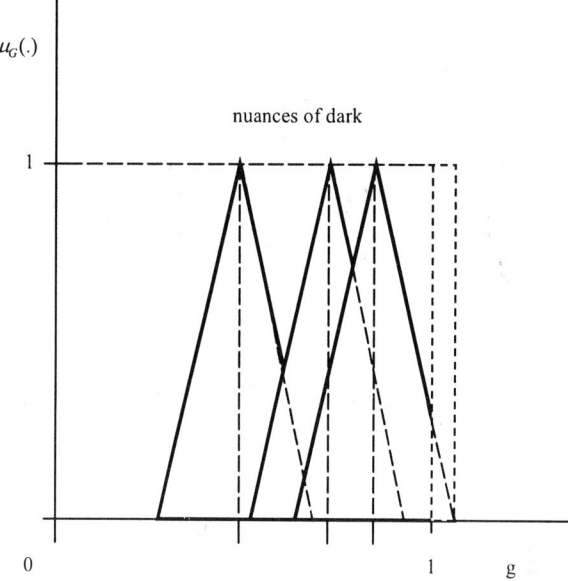

Figure 3. Constants of gray-level

$$O = \{C_1/T_1, C_2/T_2, ..., C_i/T_i, ..., C_M/T_M\}, \quad (9)$$

where T_i is the calculated truth value of the object to be treated as class C_i.

The final goal is to obtain the appropriate class label. We mentioned it above that the classifier must reject the objects having no associated class in the considered environment.

$$C = O_{defuz} = \begin{cases} L(\arg\max{}_i \{T_i\}), & \text{if } \max{}_i \{T_i\} > T_{min} \\ rejected, & \text{elsewise} \end{cases}, \quad (10)$$

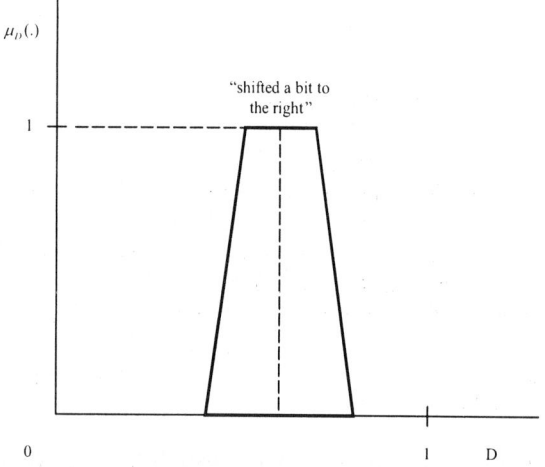

Figure 2. A location constant

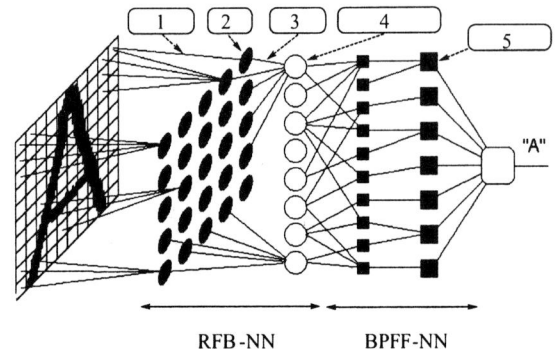

Fig. 4. The Neuro-Fuzzy classifier
(1 – location constants; 2 – gray-level values; 3 – gray-level constants;
4 – overall mismatch; 5 – final class mismatch)

where T_{min} is the minimum allowable truth value for classes in the environment E and $L(c)$ is the label for the class with the index c.

III. NEURO-FUZZY MODEL. THE NETWORK REPRESENTATION

The connectionist structure of the proposed Neuro-Fuzzy classifier is shown in Fig. 4. The network consists of 6 layers. Each layer performs different functions and uses specific processing units (neurons). The first layer is the receptive field. It just receives a single object in 2-color binary matrix form. In the second layer the locations (regions) responsible for particular features are retrieved. Each neuron in the second layer is related to a particular location constant. The output of these neurons contains information about the gray-level inside the region defined by the constant. The third layer neurons have accumulated in their parameters the information about the features used to classify the objects. These neurons actually implement the DME function (6) where instead of membership degrees we use error (or mismatch) values:

$$\varepsilon = w_{(i,j)} \min_{(D_x, D_y)} \{\max_2 \{\varepsilon_{\min(i,j)}(D_x, D_y), \varepsilon_{f(i,j)}(D_x, D_y)\}\}.$$

A neuron in this layer outputs the distance (mismatch) value between the input object and the class the neuron is related to. The remaining layers are for the purpose of defuzzification and are implemented as a Back-Propagation Feed-Forward Neural Network (BPFF-NN).

A more detailed description of the neural network and learning algorithms can be found in [7,8]. Here we just want to note that the learning is done by both supervised and unsupervised algorithms. The proposed Neuro-Fuzzy system also supports Human expertise, revision and one-step knowledge conversion.

IV. SOFTWARE IMPLEMENTATION AND SIMULATION RESULTS

On the basis of the suggested Neuro-Fuzzy classification system a software package has been developed [7,8]. The software system was intended for recognition of human handwriting characters. A sample text is shown in Fig. 5. In our further modification of this software we tried the modified DME suggested in this paper (6).

We have compared the performance indices of several recognition systems on the sample text (Fig. 5). Figure 6 show the output texts from 3 widely used recognition application software (a – Fine Reader Version 4; b – Fine Reader Version 6; c – HP Precision Scan). Figure 7 shows the system's output screen. Table 1 shows the comparison results shown by five systems. FR (Fine Reader for handwritten character recognition) is the leading commercial system used for optical character recognition. DME1 and DME2 are versions of the software implemented on the basis of DME implemented by formula (5) and (6), respectively. As can be seen the use of DME2 gave a noticeable improvement in the quality of recognition. Note that the performance index given in this table is calculated as the ratio of the number of correctly recognized characters to the number of all of the characters in the text.

Fig. 5. Sample handwritten text to test the system

TABLE I
COMPARISON OF PERFORMANCE OF THREE SOFTWARE SYSTEMS

Package	Performance %
Fine Reader Version 4	93.9
Fine Reader Version 6	95.8
HP Precision Scan	93,3
Uncon DME1	95.04
Uncon DME2	97.2

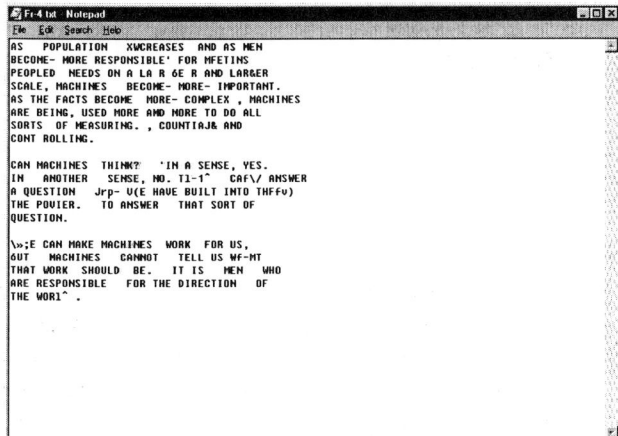

a. Fine Reader Version 4

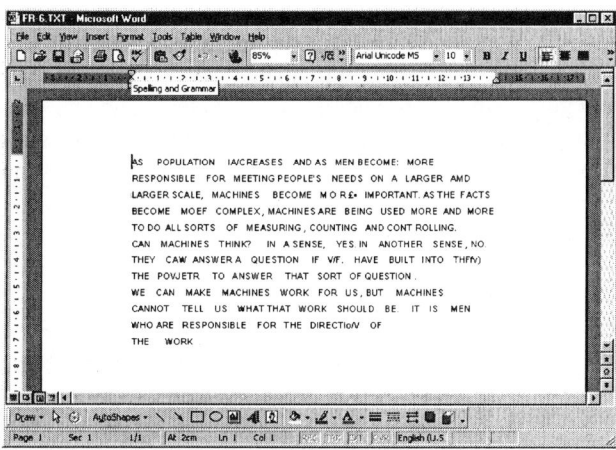

b. Fine Reader Version 6

c. HP Precision Scan

Figure 6. Recognition results from three application software packages imported to text editors

Also take into account that in the fuzzy rulebase there was used only one rule for every character class. Increasing the number of rules would give further improvement in quality.

Fig. 7. Handwritten recognition system's output screen

V. CONCLUSION

The researches of various classification techniques and practical experiments show that the quality of recognition of fuzzy graphic objects can be improved by choosing appropriate feature aggregation method or a DME by other words. The suggested Neuro-Fuzzy Object Classifier with modified DME has shown better quality of recognition compared with existing application systems when applied to handwritten text.

REFERENCES

[1] J.Bezdek and S.Pal (ed.), "Fuzzy models for pattern recognition," New York: IEEE Press, 1992.
[2] X.Ye, C.Suen, and M.Cheriet, "A generic system to extract and clean handwritten data from business forms," in P rof. Int. Workshop on Frontiers in handwriting Recognition, Amsterdam, 2000, pp. 63 -72.
[3] R.A.Aliev and R.R.Aliev, "Soft Computing and its applications," World Scientific Publishing Co. Pte. Ltd, 2001, p. 444.
[4] K.Saastamoinen, V.Könönen, and P.Luukka, "A classifier based on the fuzzy similarity in the Lukasiewicz structure with different metrics," in proceedings of IEEE International Conference on Fuzzy Systems, FUZZ-IEEE'02, vol. 1, 2002, pp. 363-367.
[5] H.Bandemer and W.Näther, "Fuzzy data analysis," Theory and Decision Library, Series B: Mathematical and Statistical Methods, Vol.20, Cluwer Academic Publishers, 1992, pp. 67 -71.
[6] L.Mascarilla and C.Frélicot, "Combining rejection-based pattern classifiers," in 19th International Conference of the No rth American Fuzzy Information Processing Society – NAFIPS, PeachFuzz 2000, 2000, pp. 114-118.
[7] R.Aliev and B.Guirimov, "Handwritten image recognition by using neural and fuzzy approaches," Intelligent Control and Decision Making Systems, No 1, Thematic Collected Articles, Baku, Publishing House of Azerb. State Oil Academy, 1997, pp. 3 -7.
[8] R.Aliev, B.Guirimov, K.Bonfig, and Steinmann, "A neuro-fuzzy algorithm for recognition of non-stylized images," in proceedings of Fourth International Conference on Application of Fuzzy Systems and Soft Computing, ICAFS'2000, Siegen, Germany, 2000, pp. 238 -241.
[9] S.Halgamuge and M.Glesner, "A fuzzy neural approach for pattern classification with generation of rules based on supervised learning," in proceedings of Nuro Nimes 92, 1992, pp. 165-173.
[10] V.Uebele, S.Abe, and M.Lan, "A neural-network-based fuzzy classifier," IEEE Transactions on Systems, Man, and Cybernetics, Vol. 23, No. 3, 1995, pp. 353-361.
[11] R.Yager, "A general approach to rule aggregation in fu zzy logic control," Appl. Intelligence, 2, 1992, pp. 333 -351.
[12] R.Yager, "On a general class of fuzzy connectives," Fuzzy Sets and Systems, 4, 1980, pp. 235-242.

Combinative Neural-Network-Based Classifiers for Optical Handwritten Character and Letter Recognition

Gao Daqi, Xie Chao, Nie Guiping

Department of Computer, East China University of Science & Technology, Shanghai 200237, China
State Key Laboratory of Bioreactor Engineering, ECUST, Shanghai 200237, China

Abstract–this paper compares the similarities and differences between multilayer perceptrons (MLPs) and radial basis function (RBF) neural networks, proposes the method of how to decompose a large-sample and multiple-category training set into many small-sample and two-class training subsets. Furthermore, we take single-hidden-layer perceptrons and RBF networks as the basis units to construct combinative neural-network-based classifiers. This kind of combinative classifiers has higher classification accuracy and better generalization performances than their component parts. The results for recognizing the handwritten numerals and English letters show that the presented combinative classifiers are quite effective for solving the large-sample, high-dimensional and multiple-category classification problems.

I. INTRODUCTION

Real classification tasks are often quite complicated and changeable, and the sample distribution regions in one class are of all forms. In order to acquire more information, many features are often extracted. In other words, the feature dimensions for overall describing an objective thing are often comparatively high. For example, the number of dimensions of handwritten digits are several hundreds or even over one thousand. In particular, maybe the samples from the same category lie in different regions, and the distribution situations between classes are perhaps over-lapping and jigsaw-like. When the number of dimensions is over 3, there no exists a simple and convenient method to judge how the sample distribution regions and shapes are. Generally speaking, one classifier that is available for the small-sample, limited-category and low-dimensional problems can not be simply generated to the large-sample, multi-class and high-dimensional problems. Despite there are many kinds of classifiers, it is far from enough for a single kind of them to effectively solve the complicated classification problems. Therefore, the viewpoint that combines several kinds of classifiers together is presented. Reference [1] combined the averaged posterior-probability Bayesian, *k*-nearest-neighbor (*K-NN*) and distance classifiers for recognizing totally unconstrained handwritten numerals, and got a comparatively good result. Reference [2] took polynomial, Bayesian, *K-NN*, segmentation-based and symbol classifiers together to distinguish the degraded machine-printed characters. Reference [3] used multiple linear classifiers, which were called the weak classifiers in the literature, to solve the Proben1 Data Sets and handwritten digits. One common characteristic of the above methods is that simple classifiers are taken to make up of superior and complicated classifiers, namely combinative classifiers. Because of composed by some simple-performance units, such combinative classifiers are of limited generalization performances.

This paper focuses attention on the following problems: (A). Decompose a large-sample, multiple-category and high-dimensional problem into many small-sample, limited-category simple problems. (B). Select suitable neural networks as modules to construct combinative classifiers. This paper is organized as follows. In Section II, we compare the similarities and differences of two kinds of classifiers, the single-hidden-layer perceptrons and the RBF networks, and take them as the basis units to construct a good-generalized combinative classifier. In Section III, we propose how to divide large-sample and multiple-category training sets into many small-sample and two-class training subsets. Furthermore, In Section IV, the methods for optimally determining the structures of combinative neural-network-based classifiers are introduced in details. In Section V, the presented combinative classifier is used to recognize the optical handwritten numerals and English letters. Section VI comes to our conclusions.

II. COMBINATIVE NEURAL NETWORK CLASSIFIERS

A. Comparison of Single-Hidden-Layer Perceptrons and RBF Networks

Without lose of generality, we take the single-hidden-layer perceptron shown in Fig. 1*a* and the RBF network in Fig. 1*b* as examples to compare their similarities and differences. Both networks have the same structure, namely 2×2×1 in topology. Let the classification thresholds be $\vartheta=0.5$. The decision boundary, namely the equiponential surface, of the 2×2×1 perceptron in the input space is determined by the following equation:

$$f(x_1,x_2) = \frac{v_1}{1+\exp(-(w_{11}x_1+w_{12}x_2+\theta_1))} + \frac{v_2}{1+\exp(-(w_{21}x_1+w_{22}x_2+\theta_2))} + \theta = 0 \quad (1)$$

In fact, (1) is a general equiponential curved surface.

Around $x_0=0$, the Taylor expansion of standard sigmoid activation function $f(x)=(1+\exp(-x))^{-1}$ is

---

*This work is supported by the National Science Foundation of China (NSFC) under Grant No. 60275017 and the Key Science and Technology Development Foundation of Shanghai, China, under Grant No. 025115028

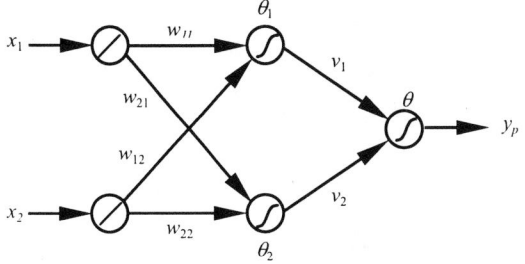
(a). A feedforward single-hidden-layer perceptron

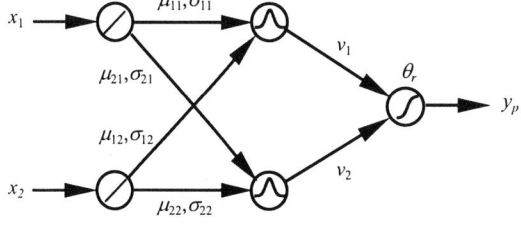
(b). A standard RBF network

Fig. 1. A perceptron and a RBF network with the same structure of 2×2×1

$$f(x) = \frac{1}{2} + \frac{1}{4}x - \frac{1}{8 \times 3!}x^3 + \frac{1}{4 \times 5!}x^5 - \frac{17}{16 \times 7!}x^7 + \cdots \quad (2)$$

Obviously, $f(x)-1/2$ is an odd function. Under the circumstances that (x_{10}, x_{20}) meets

$$\begin{cases} w_{11}x_{10}+w_{12}x_{20}+\theta_1 = 0 \\ w_{21}x_{10}+w_{22}x_{20}+\theta_2 = 0 \end{cases} \quad (3)$$

the Taylor expansion of (1) can be written as:

$$f(x_1,x_2) = A + Bx_1 + Cx_2 + Dx_1^2 + Ex_2^2 + Fx_1x_2 + \cdots \quad (4)$$

In fact, (5) is a general equiponential curved surface.

The basis functions, namely the net input of one hidden or output unit, are linear in perceptrons, under the circumstances that the classes are located to the border regions in the input spaces, the equiponential curved surfaces are open. Not only that, the equiponential curved surfaces are not unique. Therefore, sometimes the generalizing results of perceptrons are not trustworthy. Let us take the 2×2×1 perceptron shown in Fig. 1a to solve the 2-dimensional binary Exclusion-OR (XOR) problem. The four samples are (0, 0), (1, 0), (0, 1), (1, 1). When $(w_{11}, w_{12}, \theta_1, w_{21}, w_{22}, \theta_2, v_1, v_1, \theta)$=(4.6175, 4.6187, -7.0868, 6.4596, 6.4645, -2.8726, -10.2935, 9.6099 -4.4518), the real outputs of the perceptron are 0.0190, 0.9836, 0.9836, 0.0169 for the above 4 samples, but y=0.0059 for pattern (5, 10). At the moment, sample (5, 10) may be regarded to belong the same category with (0, 0) and (1,1). On the other hand, on condition that $(w_{11}, w_{12}, \theta_1, w_{21}, w_{22}, \theta_2, v_1, v_1, \theta)$=(6.9793, -6.8412 3.4844 -6.2838 6.5207 3.1672 -8.2865 - 8.3541 12.287), the real output of perceptron are 0.0225, 0.9746, 0.9748, 0.0204 for the 4 training samples, but y=0.980 for pattern (5, 10). At present, (5, 10) is considered in the same class with (1, 0) and (0, 1). The above two generalization regions are shown in Fig. 2. Generally speaking, the classification results of perceptrons are often either-or. It is the reason why neural networks are sometimes considered not able to say "No". According to the support vector machine (SVM) theory, the optimal hyperplanes can only get empirical risk minimization for the training set, not guarantee their generalization results to be definitely believable [7]. This kind of phenomenon that looks right but really wrong shows that it is not impeccable to depend only upon multilayer perceptrons to implement complicated classification tasks.

Not only that, multilayer perceptrons still exist some other defects, such as difficulty determining suitable number of hidden nodes, long learning time, unduly easy being caught in local points, etc [8-10]. Details are omitted here.

For the standard RBF network shown in Fig. 1b, the equiponential surface is determined by

$$g(x_1,x_2) = v_1 \exp\left(-\frac{1}{2}\left(\frac{x_1-\mu_{11}}{\sigma_{11}}\right)^2 - \frac{1}{2}\left(\frac{x_2-\mu_{12}}{\sigma_{12}}\right)^2\right)$$
$$+ v_2 \exp\left(-\frac{1}{2}\left(\frac{x_1-\mu_{21}}{\sigma_{21}}\right)^2 - \frac{1}{2}\left(\frac{x_2-\mu_{22}}{\sigma_{22}}\right)^2\right) + \theta_r = 0 \quad (5)$$

The standard Gaussian function $g(x)=\exp(-x^2)$ can be expanded in the Taylor series around $x_0=0$:

$$g(x) = 1 - x^2 + \frac{1}{2}x^4 - \frac{1}{3!}x^6 + \frac{1}{4!}x^8 - \frac{1}{5!}x^{10} +$$
$$+ \cdots + (-1)^n \frac{1}{n!}x^{2n} + \cdots \quad (6)$$

According to the theory of multivariate differentiation, (5) can be written in the form of (4), too. And $g(|x-\mu|/\sigma>3)<0.011$. Because the local nature of Gaussian functions, the equiponential curved surfaces determined by (5) are approximate to two regular ellipse-types when the between-class distances are lager. The equiponential curved surfaces are quite

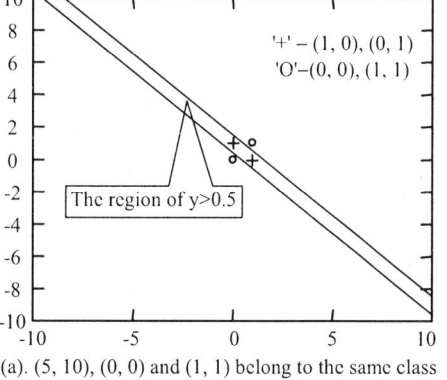
(a). (5, 10), (0, 0) and (1, 1) belong to the same class

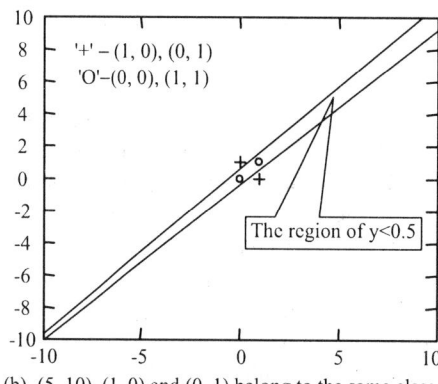
(b). (5, 10), (1, 0) and (0, 1) belong to the same class

Fig. 2 Two generalization regions of a 2×2×1 perceptron for the XOR problem

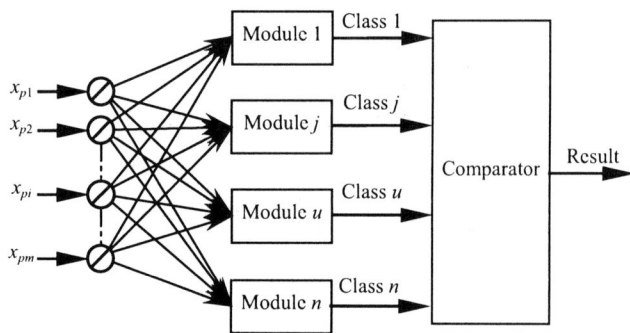

Fig. 3. Structure of A combinative neural network classifier

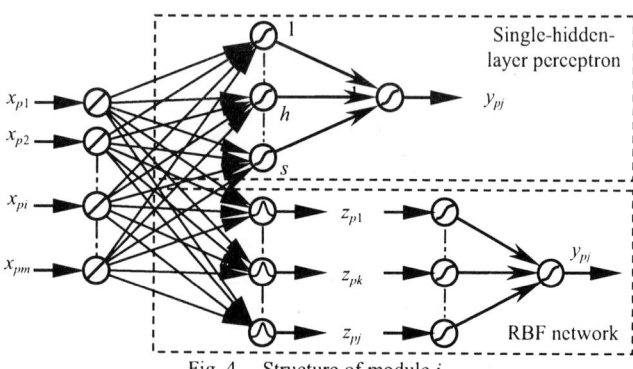

Fig. 4. Structure of module j

complicated if the sample distributions between two classes are jigsaw-like.

The multilayer perceptrons have advantages at simple structures, easy applications, comparatively ideal classification results for those low-dimensional, small-sample and few-category problems. But the trustworthy degrees of their generalizing results are not so high as expected. Compared with that, the strong points of RBF networks are fast learning speeds, high believable degrees of generalizing results. Therefore, we think that sometimes the generalizing results of RBF networks are a little more trustworthy than that of perceptrons. One of the main defects of RBF networks is that it is quite difficult to determine suitable number, locations and widths of kernels.

B. Combinative Neural Network Classifiers

Equation (2) is close to an odd function, and (6) wholly a mean function. The equiponential curved surfaces determined by (2) are not wholly coincident with that by (6). Combining (2) and (6) together can bring about a general polynomial function and form complicated decision boundaries, and is able to implement complicated classification tasks. Based on the above analysis, this paper presents a kind of combinative classifier, which takes single-hidden-layer perceptrons and RBF networks as its basic units, shown in Fig. 3. Figure 4 gives the detailed structure of Module j.

It is the most ideal situation if the single-hidden-layer perceptrons and RBF networks simultaneously judge that a certain pattern belongs to one certain class or not. Sometimes it is not so. With the combinative classifiers, we have to consider the following situations.

(I). The RBF network definitely determines that a certain pattern belongs to one given class, but the single-hidden-layer perceptron says "No". Under the circumstances, the result of RBF network is thought correct.

(II). The perceptron tells that a certain sample belongs to one category, but the real outputs of all kernels in the corresponding RBF module are below the classification thresholds, says $\vartheta=0.5$ in this paper. At the moment, there exist the following statuses. (A). If the real output of one corresponding RBF kernel is over 0.1, the result of the perceptron is admitted. (B). If the real outputs of all the corresponding RBF kernels are below 0.1, the final answer is still negative.

III. DECOMPOSITION OF LARGE-SAMPLE TRAINING SETS

When the number of samples in the training set is so numerous that surpasses the permissible range of a computer's memory capacity, it is not realistic to take all of them to attend in learning. Under many circumstances, it is not necessary to do so. In theory, multilayer perceptrons can implement the classification tasks of numerous categories. In fact, the convergence performance of multilayer perceptrons will be poor when the number of classes surpasses a certain limit, say 20. The examples for multilayer perceptrons to classify more than 20 categories are quite fewer in the literatures. For the large-sample, multiple-category and high-dimensional classification problems, multilayer perceptrons are almost powerless. Intuitively, the decision boundary for a class that is located on the border region in the input spaces is a half-open region; on the contrary, the separate hypersurface for a class that is wholly surrounded by other categories is a close region. In other words, perhaps some other classes are quite far from the decision boundary of a category. Therefore, those categories that are partitioned by its neighbor classes may not attend in deciding a certain separate boundary.

According to the above analyses, this paper presents the following steps to decompose a large-sample, multiple-category and high-dimensional classification problem into a large number of comparatively simple tasks.

(A). Transform an n-class training set into n 2-class training subsets one after another. In the ith subset, the target outputs for the ith class are 1, and that for the other categories 0.

(B). Divide the 2-class training set into a training subset and a cross-validation set. When determining the decision boundary of the jth class, namely training the jth module, the training subset first consists of the jth class and its 10 nearest classes according to the mean Euclid distances. The cross-validation set is made up of the other categories in the training set. Here, it is only empirical to select the 10 nearest classes. If growing from fewer categories, the finally training subset can only consist of the most necessary number of samples.

(C). After learning, if the classification error for a certain category in the cross-validation set goes beyond the given limit, say 2%, the category is taken out of the cross-validation set and added into the training subset.

Repeating the above three steps until every training subset is formed, on condition that the subset consists of as less samples as possible. A part of categories in the original large-sample training set that have less contribution to determine a certain corresponding decision boundary will not attend in learning. In the way, however many the samples and categories may be in the training sets, we can divide them into some comparatively simple subsets. The networks that are trained with the subsets have as good generalization performance as trained with the wholly training set.

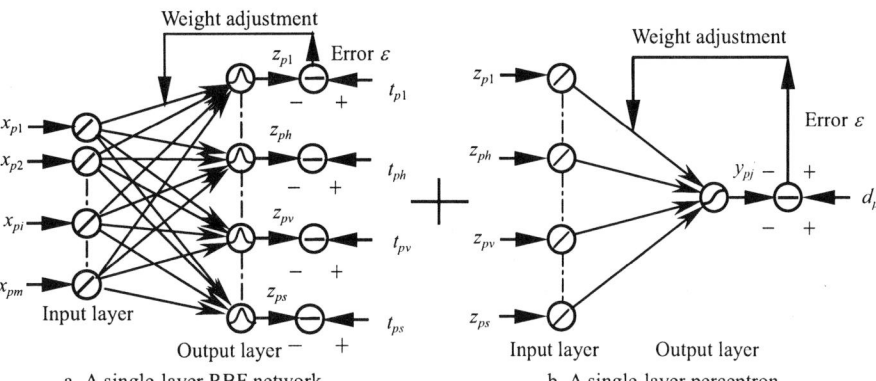

Fig. 5. A part of Module j–Structure of the RBF-type network

IV. DETERMINING STRUCTURES OF MODULES

A. Single-Hidden-Layer Perceptrons

The initial structure of single-hidden-layer perceptron is determined by the following formula:
$$s_0 = \lceil 2\log_2(m+n-1) \rceil \geq 2 \qquad (7)$$
where m and n are the number of input and output nodes, respectively. Its final structure depends upon the singular valves of the output matrix Z_j of hidden nodes. The deleted number of hidden nodes is equal to that of the singular values that are below 5% of $\|Z_j\|_F$. Here, $\|\cdot\|_F$ is the Fronbenius norm.

If the number of categories is not more than 15, the original training set is not decomposed, otherwise it is divided into n two-class problems. In order to improve the trustworthy degrees and convergence of single-hidden-layer perceptrons, the absolute maximums of input components are amplified to be 5.0, and the target values of output nodes are in the range of $\{0, 3\}$. The activation functions of hidden and output nodes are modified to be $f(x)=3(1+\exp(-x/3))^{-1}$, correspondingly. The reason for that sees Ref. [11].

B. RBF-Type Networks

The structures of RBF-type networks are shown in Fig. 5. When determining the structure of one RBF-type network in module j, the initial training subset is just the same as that used in the corresponding perceptron unit.

The initial structure of RBF-type network in module j is $m \times 1 + 1 \times 1$, where m is the number of input dimensions. At the moment, the initial location of the first kernel may be the center of the corresponding class, say class j, and its initial widths the maximum absolute differences between all the corresponding within-class individuals and the center. The back-propagation (BP) algorithm is first used to adaptively adjust the locations and widths of the kernel, then to determine the weights of the successive single-layer perceptron which takes the real output of the trained single-layer RBF network as its inputs.

If the classification error for the training subset surpasses the permissible limit, say 5% of the number of samples in class j, the first kernel is discarded, and new kernels come into being one after another. At first, a new kernel only contains the first sample in numeral order in class j that is not included by the existing kernels, then those patterns that are neighboring to it and in the same original class are admitted into in turn. The growing process keeps until the kernel makes one or more samples of the other categories produce responds that surpass the allowable threshold set in prior.

If only one sample in a subclass is misclassified, the sample itself makes up a new subclass. At this moment the center of the new kernel is in its position, and its widths are equal to half the Euclidean distances between it and the nearest neighboring pattern, and the centers and widths keep unchanged in all the learning stage.

The pruning process of RBF-type network is made up of the following two parts. (A). The mergence of kernels. In order to avoid "isolated islands", after a learning run, an existing kernel should contain as many patterns as possible according to the actual output values of the single-layer RBF network for the training set. At this moment, not only can the single-sample kernels be merged, but also those patterns in the multi-sample kernels can be added into an existing kernel as many as possible on condition that they belong to the same original class. As a result, some multi-sample kernels may be overlapping in part. (B). The pruning of kernels. After a learning run is finished, a kernel whose samples have been all contained by several other kernels in the same original category should be cut out.

Repeating in the above way until the optimal structures of RBF networks in one module are found, which should have satisfactory classification accuracy for both the training and the test set. Generally speaking, after put in a new pattern, a present RBF kernel only needs learning finite epochs again, namely 30 times in our experiments, because the adjustable ranges of widths and centers are limited after all.

V. APPLICATION EXAMPLES

A. Recognition of Optical Handwritten Digits [12]

We use the optical handwritten digit database from [11]. '0' to '9' 10 digits in total were written by 43 people, 30 of them contributed to the training set and the other 13 to the test set. Every handwritten numeral was digitized in bilevel on a 32×32 bitmap and divided into non-overlapping blocks of 4×4. The number of "on" pixels was counted in each block. This generates an input vector of 8×8 where each element is an integer in the range from 0 to 16, namely the dimensionality of input vectors reduce from 1024 to 64. The number of samples is 3823 in the training set and 1797 in the test set, respectively. We set the initial structure of the single-layer RBF-type network to be 64×10+10×10. Let the learning rate η_1=0.55 and the momentum factor α_1=0.075 for the RBF network, and η_2=0.018 and α_2=0.074 for the single-layer perceptron. After 200+2,000 epochs and 405.08+347.48 sec (by a PIII450 PC, the same below), the root-mean-square (RMS) errors are 0.1632 for the RBF network and 0.091 for the perceptron. As a result, the RBF-type network reaches only the classification correct rate of 3555/3823=92.99% for the training set and 1609/1797=89.54% for the test set. An interesting fact is that (64×2×10×200)÷((10+1)×10×2000)= 1.164≈405.08/356.08=1.138. It shows that the computing complexity degree of a RBF node is approximately equal to that of a unit with sigmoid activation function.

Because the classification result of the above RBF-type network is not very ideal, modules come into being one after another. RBFs in one module are produced in pattern sequence. Because the number of samples in the training set are not too many, all of them are present to determine the structures and parameters of each RBF network. During deciding the centers and widths of RBF nodes, although one pattern after another is put in, it is enough to just iterate 30 epochs for an existing kernel. In fact, a 30-epoch iteration takes only 5.13 sec. The wholly learning process takes 17,948.22 sec. As a result, the RBF network reaches a classification accuracy of 100% for the training set, but that of 91.03% for the test set.

Next, the single-hidden-layer perceptron starts learning. According to (7), the number of hidden nodes is selected to be 12. Therefore its structure is 64×12×10. Let the learning factor be η=0.00018, and the momentum parameter α=0.0075. After 20,000 epochs and 26,259 sec, the RMS error is 0.1019. As a result, the perceptron gets the best recognizing accuracy of 91.76% for the test set. In fact, in order to cope with the handwritten-digit recognizing problems effectively, the structure as well as the learning and momentum factors must be carefully selected.

TABLE I
CONFUSION MATRIX FOR THE PROPOSED METHOD WITH RESPECT TO THE TEST SET

Class	0	1	2	3	4	5	6	7	8	9	Recognizing rate
0	177	0	0	0	1	0	0	0	0	0	99.44%
1	0	178	2	0	0	0	0	0	2	0	97.80%
2	0	7	165	0	0	0	0	0	5	0	93.22%
3	0	0	1	177	0	1	0	2	1	1	96.72%
4	1	4	0	0	173	0	2	0	1	0	95.58%
5	0	0	0	2	0	179	0	0	1	0	98.35%
6	0	1	0	0	1	0	179	0	0	0	98.90%
7	0	0	0	0	1	0	0	174	2	2	97.20%
8	0	6	0	0	0	2	0	1	163	2	93.68%
9	0	2	0	2	1	1	0	2	0	172	95.55%
Average											96.66%
Num. of kernels	7	26	31	21	27	14	9	17	33	29	

Table I reports the final confusion matrix for the proposed combinative classifier with respect to the test set. The final recognizing rate is higher than any one of its component parts. The average recognizing accuracy is a little lower than that with k-NN classifiers using the Euclidean distance as the metric [11]. What is notable is that many RBF kernels have no contribution to improve the recognizing correct rate of the test set, although they enhance the classification accuracy of the training set.

B. English Letter Recognition [12]

The objective is to identify each of a large number of black-and-white rectangular pixel displays as one of the 26 capital letters (A to Z) in the English alphabet. The character images were based on 20 different fonts and each letter within these 20 fonts was randomly distorted to produce a file of 20,000 unique stimuli. Each stimulus was converted into 16 primitive numerical attributes (statistical moments and edge counts) which were then scaled to fit into a range of integer values from 0 through 15. We typically train on the first 16,000 samples and then use the resulting model to predict the letter category for the remaining 4,000 (the test set). Classification difficulty stems from the fact that the characters are generated from 20 different fonts, are randomly warped, and only simple features such as the total

TABLE II
CLASSIFICATION RESULTS OF COMBINITIVE CLASSIFIER

Letters	A	B	C	D	E	F	G	H	I	J	K	L	M
Number of kernels	30	82	63	64	74	70	73	79	40	46	77	38	36
Number of misclassification	9	6	8	7	5	8	7	18	8	9	9	13	7
Recognizing accuracy (%)	94.23	96.59	94.37	95.81	96.71	94.77	95.73	88.08	95.15	93.92	93.84	91.72	95.14
Letters	N	O	P	Q	R	S	T	U	V	W	X	Y	Z
Number of kernels	71	66	58	75	80	60	61	54	59	53	83	70	60
Number of misclassification	11	8	9	13	10	11	9	10	7	4	10	11	8
Recognizing accuracy (%)	93.37	94.24	94.64	92.26	93.79	93.17	94.04	94.05	94.85	97.12	93.71	92.42	94.94

number of "on" pixels, and the size and position of a box around the "on" pixels, are used.

It is enough to have only a part of the training set take part in deciding one module. The first 10 letters nearest to 'A', for example, are "J", "L", "R", "H", "O", "Q", "X", "K", "I", "G", in turn, 6664 samples in total. In other words, the 6664 samples are first taken to train module "A". According to (7), the initial structure of single-hidden-layer perceptron is 16×8 ×1. Let η=0.00025 and α=0.0075. After the first learning round, "N", "M", "W", "Y", "V" and "T" are added into the training sunset. The SVD result shows that the structure of perceptron may be 16×7×1. Next, "P" and "U" are admitted. Through the third round, "S" and "Z" also attend. As a result, the training subset "A" is made up of 21 categories, namely 12,900 samples. Finally, perceptron "A" reaches the recognizing accuracy of 141/156=90.38% for 156 samples of class "A" in the test set. Only one pattern, namely No. 1682 from class "L", is erroneously labeled, and class "L" has been included in the training subset.

For class "M", the first 10 nearest classes are "N", "H", "W", "O", "K", "R", "Q", "U", "D" and "G" in turn. Thus, the initial training subset consists of 11 classes and 6772 patterns. The generalization result of a 16×7×1 perceptron is that the correct rate is 137/144=95.14% for class "M" of the test set and 8 samples from the other categories are mislabeled. The result is already comparatively ideal.

The learning parameters of the single-layer RBF networks are η_1=0.015 and α_1=0.075. As a result, the biggest kernel consists of 442 samples, but the smallest ones include only three or two patterns. On the premise that the recognizing correct rate for the training set is 100 percent, Table II shows the structures and classification results of the module RBF-type network. The average accuracy is 91.85% for the test set. The number of RBFs in various module are different each other, which is entirely different with the C-mean cluster methods that require to artificially determine the number of clusters in prior.

The number of samples and categories in the training sunsets are different each other, and none of the subsets includes all the samples in the original training set. That shows that the above decomposition method is effective. As a result, the combinative classifier attains the classification correct rate of 3765/4000=94.13%.

VI. CONCLUSIONS

The experiment result for letter recognition shows that it is available to take only a part of categories to form training subsets. Through learning the smallest subsets, the combinative classification modules can have the same generalization ability as that learning the entire training set. The combinative classifiers made up of single-hidden-layer perceptrons and RBF-type networks can form more complicated separate hypersurfaces, so have higher classification accuracy and better generalization performances than any of their component units does. The proposed method is available for those large-samples, multiple-category and high-dimensional classification tasks.

REFERENCES

[1] Lei Xu, A. Krzyzak, C. Y. Suen. "Methods of combining multiple classifiers and their applications to handwriting recognition," *IEEE Transactions on Sys., Man, and Cyber.* Vol. 22, pp. 418-435, 1992.

[2] T. K. Ho, J. J. Hull, S. N. Srihari. "Decision combination in multiple classifier systems," *IEEE Transactions on Pattern Analysis and Machine Intelligence*, Vol. 16, pp66-75, 1994.

[3] C. Ji, S. Ma. "Combinations of Weak Classifiers," *IEEE Transactions on Neural Networks*, Vol. 8, pp. 32-42, 1997.

[4] F. Kimura, M. Shridhar. "Handwritten numerical recognition based on multiple algorithm," *Pattern Recognition*, Vol. 24, pp. 969-983, 1991.

[5] V. D. Mazurov, A. I. Krivonogov, V. L. Karantsev. "Solving of optimization and identification problems by the committee methods," *Pattern Recognition*, Vol. 20, pp. 371-378, 1987.

[6] E. M. Kleinberg. "Stochastic discrimination," *Ann. Math. Artificial Intelligence*, Vol. 1, pp. 207-239, 1990.

[7] V. N. Vapnik. "An overview of statistical learning theory," *IEEE Transactions on Neural Networks*, Vol. 10, pp. 988-999, 1999.

[8] T. Poggio, F. Girosi. "Networks for approximation and learning," *Proceedings of IEEE*, Vol. 78, pp. 1481-1495, 1990.

[9] R. P. Lippmann. "Pattern classification using neural networks," *IEEE Communication Magazine*, Vol. 11, pp. 47-64, 1989.

[10] C. M. Bishop. Neural networks for pattern recognition. *Clarendon Press, Oxford*, 1998.

[11] Gao Daqi, Yang Genxing. "Influences of variable scales and activation functions on the performances of multilayer feedforward neural networks," *Pattern Recognition*. 36(4), pp. 869-878, 2003.

[12] ftp://ftp.ics.uci.edu/pub/mechine-learning-databases or http://www.ics.uci.edu/~mlearn.

[13] Sung-Bae Cho. "Neural-network classifiers for recognizing totally unconstrained handwritten numerals," *IEEE Transactions on Neural Networks*, Vol. 8, pp. 43-53, 1997.

[14] J. Kittier, M. Hatef, R. P. W. Duin, et al. "On combining classifiers," *IEEE Transactions on PAMI*, Vol. 20(3), pp. 226-239, 1998.

[15] W. P. Kegelmeyer, K. Bowyer. "Combination of multiple classifiers using local accuracy estimates," *IEEE transactions on PAMI*, Vol. 19(4), pp. 406-410, 1997.

[16] L. Lam, C. Y. Suen. "Application of majority voting to pattern recognition: an analysis of its behavior and performance," *IEEE Transactions on System, Man, and Cybernetics-Part A*, Vol. 27(5), pp. 553-568, 1997.

[17] R. Anand, K. Mehrotra, C. K. Mohan, et al. "Efficient classification for multiclass problems using modular neural networks," *IEEE Transactions on Neural Networks*, Vol. 6(1), pp. 117-124, 1995.

[18] B. L. Lu, M. Ito. "Task decomposition and module combination based on class relations: a modular neural network for pattern classification," *IEEE Trans. on Neural Networks*, Vol. 10(5), pp.1244-1256, 1999.

[19] M. Demirekler, H. Altincay. "Plurality voting-based multiple classifier systems: statistically independent with respect to dependent classifier sets," *Pattern Recognition*, Vol. 35, pp.2365-2379, 2002.

[20] H. Altincay, M. Demirekler. "Undesirable effects of output normalization in multiple classifier systems," *Pattern Recognition Letters*, Vol. 24, pp. 1163-1170, 2003.

[21] Y. Lu, C. L. Tan. "Combination of multiple classifiers using probabilistic dictionary and its application to postcode recognition," *Pattern Recognition*, Vol. 35, pp. 2823-2832, 2002.

Document Clustering using Hierarchical SOMART Neural Network

M. F. Hussin [1], and M. Kamel [2]

[1] Dept. of Computer Science & Automatic Control, University of Alexandria, Alexandria, Egypt
[2] Dept. of Systems Design Eng., University of Waterloo, Waterloo, Ontario, Canada
{mfarouk,mkamel}@pami.uwaterloo.ca

Abstract- **Availability of large full-text document collections in electronic form has created a need for tools and techniques that assist users in organizing these collections. Document clustering is one of the popular methods used for this purpose. In this paper, we propose the neural network based document clustering method by using a hierarchically organized network built up from independent Self-Organizing Map (SOM) and Adaptive Reasonance Theory (ART) neural networks. We present clustering results using the REUTERS corpus and show an improvement in clustering performance using both entropy and F-measure as evaluation measures.**

I. INTRODUCTION

Document clustering attempts to identify inherent groupings of text documents, such that given a set of documents it is able to separate them into a number of clusters, where each cluster contains documents about the same topic. It has been used in a number of applications. In information retrieval systems, document clustering has been used to improve the precision and recall performance [1] and as an efficient way of finding the nearest neighbours of a document [2]. It has also been proposed in browsing a collection of documents [3], and organizing the results of a search engine query [4]. Document clustering has also been used to automatically generate hierarchical grouping of documents [5].

A common approach to document clustering is to use unsupervised artificial neural networks. Neural networks are highly suited to textual input, being capable of identifying structure of high dimensions within a body of natural language text. Neural networks work better than other method even when the data contains noise, has a poorly understood structure and changing characteristics.

The self-organizing map (SOM) [6],[7] is one of the most versatile unsupervised neural network architectures. It is capable of ordering high-dimensional statistical data in such a way that similar input items are grouped spatially close to one another.

The Adaptive Reasonance Theory (ART) [8] is another unsupervised neural network architecture used in clustering. It appears to be particularly suitable because of its well-defined interface as well as features that most other networks lack. In specific, ART networks have the ability to create new output nodes (i.e. category) dynamically, and do not suffer from the problem of forgetting previously learned categories if the environment changes. They, however, can only develop input categories at a given level of specificity, which depends on a global parameter called vigilance.

In this paper, the emphasis will be on using hierarchically neural network architecture, based on SOM, and ART to improve the quality of clusters. First SOM is used to partition the collection of documents until reaching a suitable partition size then ART is used to cluster all partitions.

The reminder of the paper is organized as follows. Section II describes the related work. Section III describes the hierarchical SOMART document clustering method. In Section IV we show experimental results and their evaluation. The conclusion is given in section V.

II. RELATED WORK

From the wide range of proposed architectures of artificial neural networks we regard the unsupervised models as especially well suited for document clustering. This is due to the fact that in a supervised environment one would have to define proper input-output-mappings anew when the text archive changes; and such changes should be expected to happen quite frequently. A number of successful applications of hierarchical unsupervised neural networks to document clustering have already been implemented. One of the most successful hierarchical unsupervised neural network is the hierarchical feature maps (HFM), as outlined in [9],[10],[11].

The key idea is to apply a hierarchical arrangement of several layers containing two-dimensional self-organising maps [6],[12]. In HFM, the architecture of the system has to be defined in advance, i.e. the number of layers as well as the size of the maps on each layer have to be specified prior to training. This turns out to be difficult for document clustering, where the precise nature and topic distribution of a collection might be unknown. Furthermore, some topics may be present more prominently than others, thus requiring more map space for representation.

Another hierarchical modification of the SOM is constituted by the Tree Structure (TS-SOM) [13],[14]. Yet, the focus of this model lies primarily with in speeding up the training process by providing faster winner selection using a tree-based organization of units. However, it does not focus on providing a hierarchical organization of data as all data are organized on one single flat map.

Dettenbach, and Merkl [15], presented the Growing Hierarchical Self-Organizing Map (GHSOM), which allows an automatic creation of hierarchical organization of a set of documents. This allows the network architecture to determine the topical structure of the given document repository during the training process, creating a hierarchy of Self-Organizing Maps, each of which provides a topologically sorted representation of a topical subset.

Another group of hierarchically unsupervised neural network based on Adaptive Resonance Theory (ART) type is the Modular Hierarchical ART (HART) models. There are two versions of HART, the first version is a HART-J implementing an agglomerative clustering method. The second is HART-S implements a divisive clustering method [16], [17]. Hung et al[18], presented a cascade of Fuzzy ART networks that develop hierarchies of analogue and binary patterns through bottom-up learning guided by a top-down search process. It has been applied to model-based 3D object recognition. Ishihara et al [19], presented the arboART. In this network, the prototype vectors at each layer are used as input to the following layer (agglomerative method). The architecture is similar to HART-J. It has been applied to automatic rule generation of kansei engineering expert systems.

III. HIERARCHICAL SOMART

The key idea of the hierarchical SOMART is to build a hierarchically organized combined SOM and ART neural network with layered architecture where each layer consists of a number of independent SOMs or ARTs as shown in Fig. 1. This idea is based on, combining the fast learning capability of SOM to generate compact clusters with the accuracy of the clusters produced by ART [20].

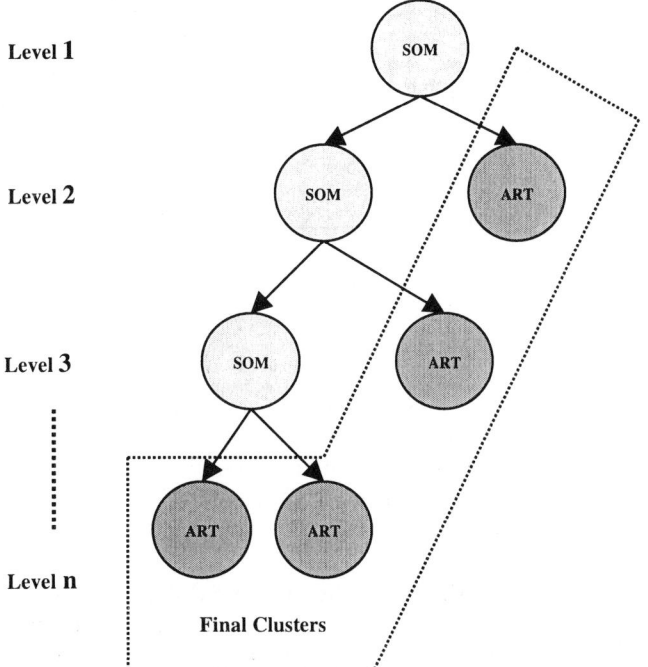

Fig. 1. Architecture of a hierarchical SOMART.

More precisely, for each SOM map unit in one layer, a SOM or ART is added to the next layer, based on the size of unit "number of documents in the unit". This network is trained sequentially from the first layer downwards along the hierarchy until the ART networks of the last layer are reached. Hence, as soon as the first layer SOM has reached its stable state, training continues with the SOMs or ARTs in the second layer based on the size of each unit in the first SOM. In this layer, however, each map is trained only by using the patterns mapped onto the corresponding unit of the layer above. Moreover, on the transition from one layer to the next, the input patterns may be shortened by omitting those components that are equal in the patterns mapped onto the same unit. This feature is of especial importance when dealing with text as the underlying input data because first text documents are represented in a very high dimensional feature space and second, some of these features are common to each text belonging to a particular topic, i.e. cluster. Thus, the pattern reduction inherent to hierarchical SOMART with high quality cluster output is expected to play an important role during the learning process. The recursive algorithm for document clustering using hierarchical SOMART is summarized in table I.

TABLE I
ALGORITHM FOR HIERARCHICAL SOMART
DOCUMENT CLUSTERING

Given a set of documents S,
1. Prepare the vector space representation of set S.
2. Apply SOM technique to partition S into m units, (s_1, s_2, ..., s_m).
3. Loop
   For each unit of s_i
     If size of unit s_i in suitable ART dimension Then
       apply ART technique to output the cluster.
     Else
       Repeat from **1** to **3** on s_i
     End if
Until s_i is finished.

A highly valuable property of hierarchical SOMART is the remarkable speed-up of the training process as compared to SOM, and the enhancement of clusters quality as compared to HFM (Hierarchical Feature Map).

IV. EXPERIMENTAL RESULTS

In order to test the effectiveness of the hierarchical SOMART to SOM and HFM, we used the REUTERS test corpus. This is a standard text clustering corpus composed of 21 578 news articles. From this corpus, 1 000 documents were selected and used as the test set to be clustered. Each document is processed by removing a set of common words using a "stopword" list, and the suffixes are removed using a Porter stemmer.

The binary word representation will be used to make a vector space model of the set of 1000 document, the vector space size is 1000X7293.

Two measure are widely used in text mining literature to evaluate the quality of the clustering algorithms: cluster entropy and F-measure [2]. Both of these techniques rely on labeled test corpus, where each document is assigned a class label. The measures compare the resulting clusters to the labeled classes, and measure the degree to which the documents from same classes are assigned to the same clusters.

The cluster entropy uses the entropy concept from information theory and measures the ``homogeneity'' of the clusters. Lower entropy indicates more homogeneous cluster and vice versa. Consider the results of a clustering experiment, and let $P(i,j)$ be the probability that a document has a class label i and is assigned to cluster j. Then the entropy E_j for a cluster j is given as:

$$E_j = -\sum_i P(i,j) \log_2 P(i,j) \quad (1)$$

The total entropy for a set of clusters is calculated as the sum of entropies for each cluster weighted by the cluster size:

$$E = \sum_j \frac{n_j}{n} E_j \quad (2)$$

where n_j is the number of documents in cluster j and n is the total number of documents.

The F-measure combines the precision and recall concepts from information retrieval, where each class is treated as the desired results for the query, and each cluster is treated as the actual results for the query. To evaluate the queries, precision and recall for class i and cluster j is given as:

$$\text{Recall}(i,j) = \frac{n_{ij}}{n_j}$$
$$\text{Precision}(i,j) = \frac{n_{ij}}{n_i} \quad (3)$$

where n_{ij} is the number of documents with class label i in cluster j, n_i is the number of documents with class label i, and n_j is the number of documents in cluster j, and n is the total number of documents. The F-measure for class i and cluster j is given as:

$$F(i,j) = 2 \left[\frac{\text{Recall}(i,j) \text{Precision}(i,j)}{\text{Recall}(i,j) + \text{Precision}(i,j)} \right] \quad (4)$$

The F-measure for all the clusters is given as a weighed sum of the maximum F-measures for each class as:

$$F = \sum_i \frac{n_i}{n} \max_j F(i,j) \quad (5)$$

In the test corpus, some document have multiple classes assigned to them. This does not affect the F-measure, however the cluster entropy can no longer be calculated. Instead of cluster entropy, we define the class-entropy[21], which measures the homogeneity of a class rather than the homogeneity of the clusters.

For every cluster j and class i, we compute $P(j|i)$, the probability that a document is assigned to cluster j given that it belongs to class i. Using these probabilities, the entropy for a class i is given as:

$$E_i^* = -\sum_j P(j|i) \log_2 P(j|i) \quad (6)$$

We use the conditional probabilities, rather than joint probabilities (as in Eq.1), because the probabilities are normalized over the summation, i.e. $\sum_j P(j|i) = 1$
Therefore, Eq.6 is a true entropy expression, while Eq.1 is not a true entropy expression, because $\sum_i P(i,j) \neq 1$.
The overall class-entropy E^* is calculated as a sum of the entropies E_i^*, weighted by the class probabilities:

$$E^* = \sum_i \frac{n_i}{n} E_i^* \quad (7)$$

where n_i is the number of document in class i, and n is the total number of documents.

Our hierarchical SOMART document clustering has been implemented by using the following component:
- SOM-PAK the self-organizing map program package developed by Kohonen's team [22].
- The ART gallery simulation package developed by Lars Liden [23].

Two experiments have been conducted, first we studied the execution time of the two different techniques ART and SOM with the same number of output clusters according to the number of documents as shown in Fig. 2, the SOM neural network was trained using 0.02 learning rate, and the ART neural network with ART1 style was trained using vigilance value ranging from 0.01 to 0.04 and 0.9 learning rate. It is obvious that ART is better than SOM when number of documents is small, and SOM is better than ART when number of documents is increased to 500.

Second, we investigated the enhancement of hierarchical SOMART over SOM and HFM. The organization of these document clustering techniques was as follows:
- The hierarchical SOMART consists of two layers the first layer is SOM with dimension 2X3 using 0.02 learning rate, and the second layer was organized from giving each resulting unit in the first SOM layer ART1 using 0.03 vigilance value and 0.9 learning rate. The resulted number of clusters is 23.
- The HFM consists of two SOM layers, the first layer with dimension 2X3 and the second layer was organized from giving each resulting unit in the first layer another SOM with dimension 2X3, the learning rate is 0.02 for all SOM layers. The resulted number of clusters is 24.
- Finally SOM was used with dimension 4X6, and 0.02 learning rate. The number of clusters from this network is 24.

Basically we would like to maximize the F_measure, and

minimize the Entropy of clusters to achieve high quality clustering. The results listed in table II, and fig 3 show the improvement on the clustering quality using a hierarchical SOMART compared with SOM and HFM.

The percentage of improvement ranges from 16.7% to 40.8% drop in the class-entropy measure and from 12.5% to 16.9% increase in the F_measure. It is obvious that the hierarchical SOMART provides enhanced quality measures over the SOM and HFM. It also speed-up the time of the clustering process over the SOM.

V. Conclusion

We presented a neural network based document clustering method, composed of hierarchically combined SOM and ART components. First SOM is used to partition a set of document collection into subsets, then ART is applied to refine the quality of the clusters. The performance was evaluated by testing the hierarchical SOMART on the REUTERS test corpus, and comparing it to SOM and HFM using both Class-entropy and F_measure. The experimental results show that the hierarchical SOMART achieves a better quality clustering than SOM and HFM. It also shows that it is more efficient in terms execution time.

VI. References

[1] C. J. van Rijsbergen, "Information Retrieval," Butterworth, London, UK, 1979.

[2] M. Steinbach, G. Karypis, and V. Kumar, "A comparison of document clustering techniques," KDD'2000, Workshop on Text Mining, 2000.

[3] D. R. Cutting, D. R. Karger, J. O. Pedersen, and J. W. Tukey,. "Scatter/gather: A cluster-based approach to browsing large document collections," In SIGIR'92, pp. 318 - 329, 1992.

[4] O. Zamir, O. Etzioni, O. Madani, and R. M. Karp, "Fast and intuitive clustering of web documents," In KDD'97, pp. 287 - 290, 1997.

[5] D. Koller and M. Sahami, "Hierarchically classifying documents using very few words," In Proc of the 14th Int'l Conf on Machine Learning (ICML), pp. 170 - 178, 1997.

[6] T. Kohonen, "Self-organizing maps," Springer Verlag, Berlin, 1995.

[7] D. Merkl, "Lessons Learned in Text Document Classification," In Workshop on Self-Organizing Maps, 1997.

[8] G.A. Carpenter and S. Grossberg, "A massively parallel architecture for a self-organizing neural pattern recognition machine.," Computer Vision, Graphics, and Image processing, vol. 34, pp. 54-115, 1987.

[9] R. Miikkulainen, "Trace Feature Map: A Model of Episodic Associative Memory," Biological Cybernetics, Vol. 66, pp. 273-282, 1992.

[10] R. Miikkulainen, "Subsymbolic Natural Language Processing: An integrated model of scripts, lexicon, and memory," MIT-Press, Cambridge, MA, 1993.

[11] J. Lampinen and E. Oja, "Clustering properties of hierarchial self-organizing maps," Journal of Mathematical Imaging and Vision, pp. 261-272, 1992.

[12] T. Kohonen, "Self-organized formation of topologically correct feature maps," Biological Cybernetics, Vol. 43, pp. 59-69, 1982.

[13] P. Koikkalainen and E. Oja, "Self-organizing, hierarchical feature maps," In Proc Int'l Joint Conf Neural Networks, San Diego, CA, pp. 279-285, 1990.

[14] P. Koikkalainen, "Fast deterministic self-organizing maps," In Proc Int'l Conf Neural Networks, Paris, France, pp. 63-68, 1995.

[15] M. Dittenbach, and D. Merkl, and A. Rauber, "Hierarchical Clustering of Document Archives with the Growing Hierarchical Self-Organizing Map," In Proc of the Int'l Conf on Artificial Neural Networks (ICANN01), Vienna, Austria, pp. 21-25, August 2001.

[16] G. Bartfai, "An ART-based Modular Architecture for Learning Hierarchical Clusterings," Neurocomputing, Vol.13, pp.31-45, September 1996.

[17] G. Bartfai, and R. White, "Adaptive Resonance Theory-based Modular Networks for Incremental Learning of Hierarchical Clusterings," Connection Science, Vol.9, No.1, pp.87-112, 1997.

[18] H. L. Hung, H. Y. M. Liao Lin, S. J., Lin, W.C. and Fan, K. C, "Cascade fuzzy ART: a new extensible database for model-based object recognition," In Proc of the Int'l Society for Optical Engineering, vol.2727, pt.1, pp.187-198, March 1996.

[19] K. Ishihara, S. Ishihara, Y. Matsubara, M. Nagamachi, "arboART: ART based hierarchical clustering and its application to questionnaire data analysis," In Proc of the IEEE Int'l Conf on Neural Networks, Vol.1, pages 532-537, 1995.

[20] Ji He, Ah-Hwee Tan, Chew-Lim Tan, "ART-C: A Neural Architecture for Self-Organization Under Constraints," In Proc of Int'l Joint Conf on Neural Networks (IJCNN), 2002.

[21] J. Bakus, M. F. Hussin, and M. Kamel, "A SOM-Based Document Clustering using Phrases," In Proc of the 9th Int'l Conf on neural information processing, Singapore, pp. 2212-2216, November 2002.

[22] T. Kohonen, J. kangas and J. Laaksonen, " SOM-PAK: the self-organizing map program package ver.3.1," SOM programming team of Helsinki University of Technology, Apr. 1995.

[23] L. Liden, "The ART Gallery Simulation Package ver.1.0," Dept. of cognitive and neural systems, Boston University, 1995.

Table II
Hierarchical SOMART clustering improvement

	Quality Measures			Improvement		
	F_measure	Entropy	Time	F_measure	Entropy	Time
SOMART	0.457	2.00	40			
HFM	0.406	2.40	40	+12.5%	-16.7%	
SOM	0.391	3.38	50	+16.9%	-40.8%	-20.0%

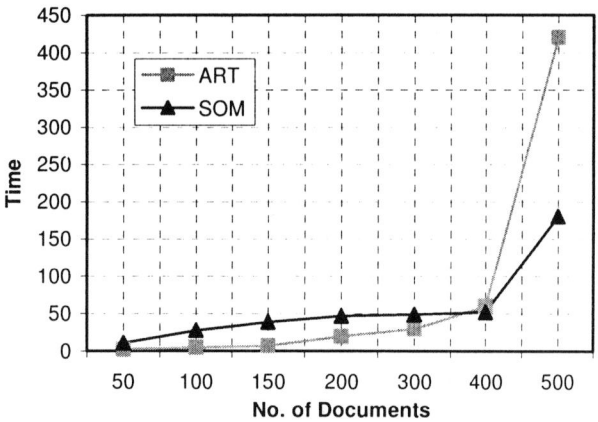

Fig.2. Execution time comparison between SOM and ART according to number of documents in the document set.

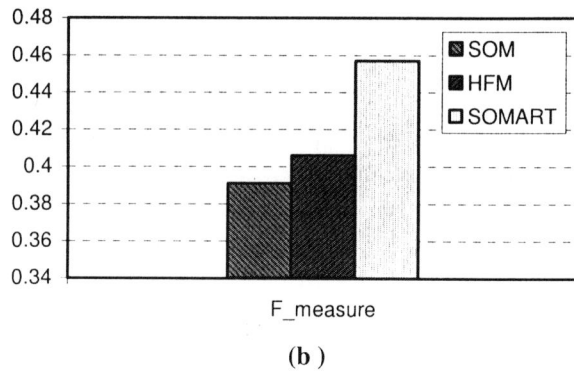

(b)

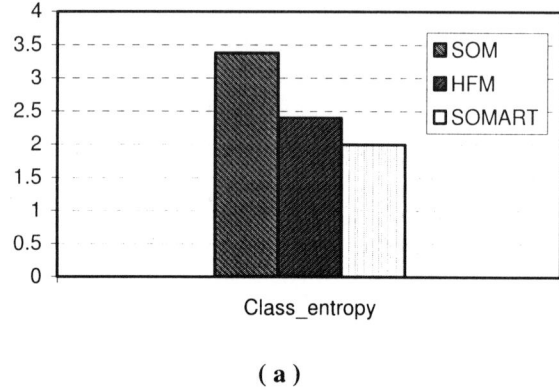

(a)

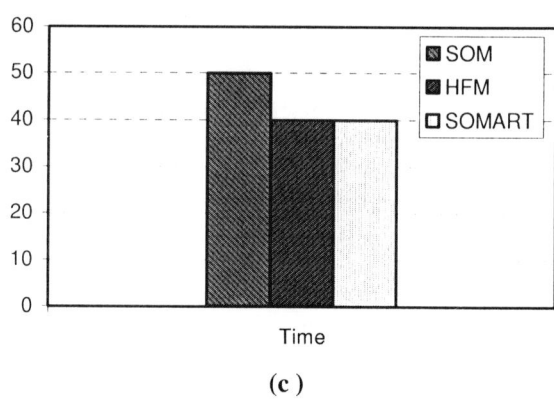

(c)

Fig.3. Hierarchical SOMART compared to HFM, and SOM
(a) Class-entropy, (b) F_measure, and (c) Execution time.

Facial Expression Recognition Combined with Robust Face Detection in A Convolutional Neural Network

Masakazu Matsugu, Katsuhiko Mori, Yusuke Mitari, Yuji Kaneda

Canon Research Center
5-1, Morinosato-Wakamiya, Atsugi, 243-0193 Japan

ABSTRACT

Reliable detection of ordinary facial expressions (e.g., smile) despite the variability among individuals as well as face appearance is an important step toward the realization of perceptual user interface and the next generation imaging system with autonomous perception of persons. We describe a robust facial expression recognition system using the result of face detection by a convolutional neural network and rule-based processing. In this study, we address the problem of subject independence as well as translation, rotation, and scale invariance in the recognition of facial expression. The result shows reliable detection of smiles with recognition rate of 97.6% for 5600 still images of more than 10 subjects. The proposed algorithm demonstrated the ability to discriminate smiling from talking based on the saliency score in the proposed algorithm. To the best of our knowledge, it is the first facial expression recognition model with the property of subject independence combined with robustness to variability in facial appearance.

1. INTRODUCTION

Facial expressions as manifestations of emotional states, in general, tend to be different among individuals. For example, smiling face as it appears may have different emotional implications for different persons in that 'smiling face', perceived by others, for some person does not necessarily represent truly smiling state for that person. To the best of our knowledge, only a few algorithms (e.g., [4]) have addressed robustness to such individuality in facial expression recognition. Furthermore, in order for facial expression recognition to be used for human-computer-interaction, for example, that algorithm must have good ability in dealing with variability of facial appearance (e.g., pose, size, and translation invariance).

Most algorithms, so far, have addressed only a part of these problems [12]. In this study, we propose a system for facial expression recognition that is robust to variability that originates from individuality and viewing conditions.

Recognizing facial expression under rigid head movements was addressed by Black and Yacoob [1]. Neural network model that learns to recognize facial expressions from an optical flow field was reported in Rosenblum et al. [11]. Rule-based system was reported in [13] and [2], in which primary facial features were tracked throughout the image sequence.

Convolutional neural network (CNN) models [8] as well as neocognitron [7] known as one of biologically inspired models, have been used for pattern recognition specifically for face recognition and hand-written numeral recognition. The network includes feature detecting (FD) layers, each of which alternating with a sub-sampling layer (pooling layer) to obtain properties such as translation and deformation invariance. Recently, Fasel [5] has proposed a model with two independent convolutional neural networks, one for facial expression and the other for face identity recognition, which are combined by an MLP.

The proposed model in this study turns out to be much more efficient and compact than Fasel's model. In addition, our model comes with the property of subject independence. Moreover, the proposed system can detect smiling or laughing faces based on difference in local features between a normal face and those not.

In Section 2, we introduce a modular convolutional network architecture for robust face detection and facial expression recognition involving module-based learning based on a variant of BP. In Section 3, we propose a rule-based algorithm that utilizes differences of specific local features, extracted in the CNN, between neutral and emotional faces. We show that the proposed scheme attains not only subject independence but also position independence in facial expression recognition. In Section 4, we discuss the properties of proposed scheme that adds to the conventional neural networks for facial expression recognition.

2. ROBUST FACE DETECTION USING CNN

As in the previously proposed model [9], internal representation of face is provided by a hierarchically ordered set of convolutional kernels defined by the local receptive field of FD neurons. Face model is represented as a spatially ordered set of local features of intermediate complexity, such as eyes, mouth, nose, eyebrow, cheek, or else, and all of these features are represented in terms of a fixed set of lower and intermediate features.

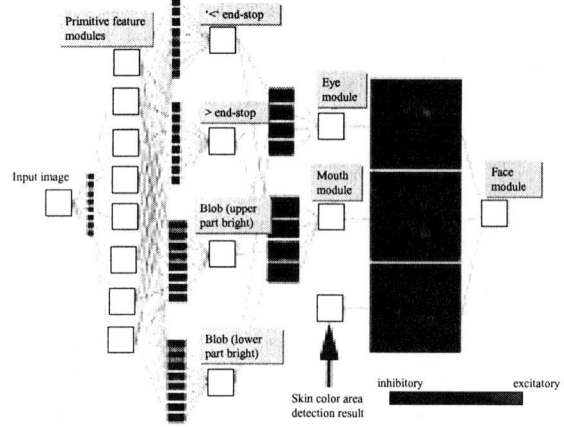

Fig.1. Convolutional architecture (feature pooling layers are not shown for simplified illustration) for face detection.

The lower and intermediate features constitute some form of a fixed set of figural alphabets in our CNN. Corresponding receptive fields for the detection of these *alphabetical* features are learned in advance to form a local template in the hierarchical network, and once learned, they would never be changed during possible learning phase for object recognition in upper layers.

Our CNN model is different from the original model [8] in three ways. First, training of the proposed model proceeds module by module (i.e., for each local feature class) only for FD_k (k>1) layers. Second, we do not train FP (or sub-sampling) layers (FP neurons perform either maximum value detection or local averaging in their receptive fields). Third, we use a detection result of skin color area as input to the face detection module in FD4. The skin area is obtained simply by thresholding of hue data of input image in the range of [-0.078,0.255] for the full range of [-0.5,0.5], which is quite broad indicating that skin color feature plays merely auxiliary part in the proposed system.

The training proceeds as follows. In the first step, two FD layers from the bottom, namely FD1 with 8 modules and FD2 with 4 modules, are trained using standard back-propagation with intermediate local features (e.g., eye corners) as positive training data sets. Negative examples that do not constitute the corresponding feature category are also used as false data. Specifically, we trained the FD2 layer, the second from the bottom FD layer to form detectors of intermediate features, such as end-stop structures or blobs (i.e., end-stop structures for left and right side and two types of horizontally elongated blobs (e.g., upper part bright, lower part bright) with varying sizes, rotation (up to 30 deg. with rotation in-plane axis as well as head axis). These features for training are fragments extracted from face images.

More complex local feature detectors (e.g., eye, mouth detectors, but not restricted to these) are trained in the third or fourth FD layer using the patterns extracted from

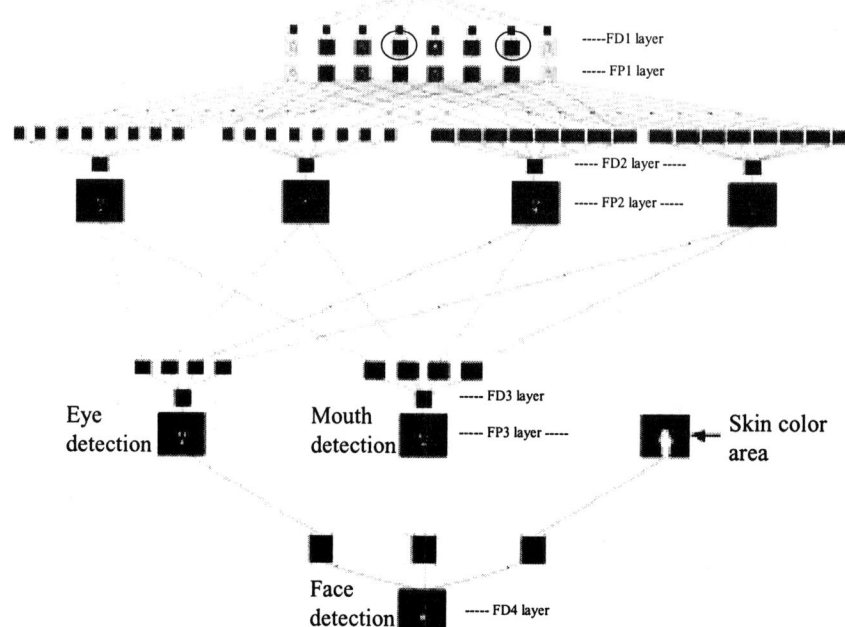

Fig. 2. Face detection by proposed convolutional NN with the results of intermediate feature detection.

transforms as in the FD2 layer. As the result of these training sequences, the top FD layer, FD4, learns to locate faces in complex scenes.

Fig.3. Face detection results in complex scenes.

The performance for other face images than the training data set was tested for over 200 face images under varying image capturing conditions. The tested images of face are of different size (from 30x30 to 240x240 in VGA image), pose (30 deg. rotation in head axis rotation or in-plane rotation), and contrast. The convolutional network demonstrated robust face detection with 1% false rejection rate and 6% false acceptance rate with quite good generalization. Fig. 2 shows a simulation result of the face detection in our model. Information concerning locations of eyes and mouth detected by the CNN is fed to the rule-based module so that our facial analysis system can deal with variability in position, size, and pose.

3. RULE-BASED ANALYSIS OF FACIAL EXPRESSIONS USING LOCAL FEATURES DETECTED BY CNN

In the following, we propose a rule-based processing scheme to enhance subject independence in facial expression recognition. We found that some of lower level features extracted by the first FD layer of CNN were useful for facial expression recognition. Primary features used in our model are horizontal line segments made up of edge-like structures similar to step and roof edges (extracted by 2 modules in FP1 layer, circled in Fig.2) representing parts of eyes, mouth, and eyebrows. For example, changes in distance between end-stops (e.g., left-corner of left eye and left side end-stop of mouth) within facial components and changes in width of line segments in lower part of eyes or cheeks are detected to obtain saliency scores of a specific facial expression. Primary cues related to facial actions adopted in our rule-based facial analysis for the detection of smiling/laughing faces are as follows:

(1) Distance between endpoints of eye and mouth gets *shorter* (lip being raised)
(2) Length of horizontal line segment in mouth gets *longer* (lip being stretched)
(3) Length of line segments in eye gets *longer* (wrinkle around the tail of eye gets longer)
(4) Gradient of line segment connecting the mid point and endpoint of mouth gets *steeper* (lip being raised)
(5) No. of step-edges in mouth get *increased* (teeth get appeared)
(6) No. of edges in cheeks *increased* (wrinkle around cheeks gets grown)

Each cue was scored based on the degree of positive changes (i.e., designated changes as given above) to the emotional state (e.g., happiness). For example, given a positive change in some cue with *a* % to the feature value in neutral face, then we give Ca points (C is some constant) to that feature.

Saliency score of specific emotional state is calculated with weighted summation of respective scores for features, which is then thresholded for judging whether the subject is smiling/laughing or not.

4. RESULTS AND DISCUSSION

Our model extracts only differences in local features between a neutral face and *emotional* faces, instead of using differences between adjacent frames. So, unlike other approaches, the proposed system requires no explicit estimation of motion parameters over image sequences, which is required by a number of conventional methods.

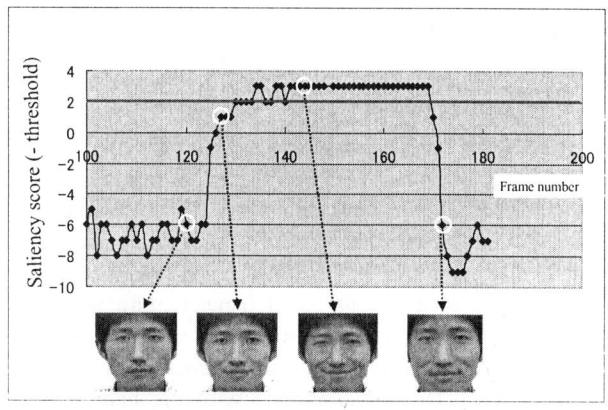

Fig.4 Normalized saliency score subtracted by constant value for smiling face detection.

Fig.4 shows a sequence of normalized saliency scores indicating successful detection of smiling faces with an appropriate threshold level.

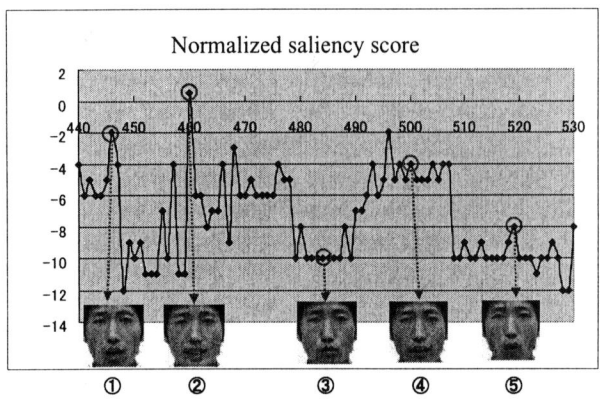

Fig.5. Talking faces can be discriminated from laughing face. Note that the second face obtained higher score due to similarity to laughing face.

As shown in Fig.5, the network demonstrated the ability to discriminate smiling from talking based on the saliency score proposed in Section 3. In addition, we obtained results demonstrating reliable detection of smiles with recognition rate of 97.6% for 5600 still images of more than 10 subjects.

In contrast to a number of approaches [3], invariance properties in terms of translation, scale, and pose, inherent in our non-spiking version of CNN [9], brings robustness to dynamical changes both in head movements and in facial expressions without requiring explicit estimation of motion parameters. Because of the topographic property of our network which preserves the position information of facial features from bottom to top layers, the translation invariance in facial expression recognition is thus inherently built into our convolutional architecture with feedback mechanism for locating facial features.

Specifically, intermediate facial features such as eyes and mouth are detected and utilized for tracking useful primitive local features extracted by the bottom layer FD1 for facial expression recognition. Location information of eyes and mouth detected in the CNN are used, through the feedback loop from the intermediate layer FP3, to confine the processing area of rule-based facial feature analysis, which analyzes differences in terms of at least six cues.

It turned out that the system is quite insensitive to individuality of facial expressions with the help of the proposed rule-based processing using single but individual normal face. Incorporating fuzzy rules may enhance robustness. Because of the voting of scores for various cues in terms of differences of facial features in neutral and emotional states, individuality is averaged out to obtain subject independence.

Moreover, as regards compactness and efficiency, it is evident in that our model uses single CNN, whereas Fasel's requires two CNNs in tandem.

In conclusion, our model is the first facial expression recognition system with subject independence combined with robustness to variability in facial appearance.

5. REFERENCES

[1] Black, M., Yacoob, Y. "Tracking and Recognizing Rigid and Non-rigid Facial Motions Using Local Parametric Models of Image Motion" In *Proc. IEEE Fifth Int. Conf. on Computer Vision* (1995) 374-381

[2] Black, M., Yacoob, Y. "Recognizing Facial Expressions in Image Sequences Using Local Parameterized Models of Image Motion" *Int. J. of Computer Vision* vol.25 (1997) 23-48

[3] Donato, G., Bartlett, M.S., Hager, J.C., Ekman, P., Sejnowski, T. "Classifying Facial Actions" *IEEE Trans. Pattern Analysis and Machine Intelligence* vol.21, (1999) 974-989

[4] Ebine, H., Nakamura, O. "The Recognition of Facial Expressions Considering the Difference between Individuality" (in Japanese) *Trans. IEE of Japan*, vol.119-C, (1999) 474-481

[5] Fasel, B. "Robust Face Analysis Using Convolutional Neural Networks" *Proc. Int. Conf. on Pattern Recognition* (2002)

[6] Földiák, P. "Learning Invariance from Transformation Sequences" *Neural Comput.* 3 (1991) 194-200

[7] Fukushima, K. "Neocognitron: A Self-Organizing Neural Networks for a Mechanism of Pattern Recognition Unaffected by Shift in Position" *Biol. Cybern.*, vol.36, (1980) 193-202

[8] Le Cun, Y., Bengio, T. "Convolutional networks for images, speech, and time series" In: Arbib, M.A. (ed.) *The Handbook of Brain Theory and Neural Networks.* MIT Press. (1995) 255-258

[9] Matsugu, M., Mori, K., Ishii, M., Mitarai, Y. "Convolutional Spiking Neural Network Model for Robust Face Detection" *Proc. The 9th International Conf. on Neural Information Processing* (2002) 660-664

[10] Matsugu, M. "Hierarchical Pulse-coupled Neural Network Model with Temporal Coding and Emergent Feature Binding Mechanism" *Proc. International Joint Conf. on Neural Networks* (2001) 802-807

[11] Rosenblum, M., Yacoob, Y., Davis, L.S. "Human Expression Recognition from Motion Using a Radial Basis Function Network Architecture" *IEEE Trans. Neural Networks*, vol. 7. (1996) 1121-1138

[12] Wallis, G., Rolls, E.T. "Invariant Face and Object Recognition in the Visual System" *Prog. in Neurobiol.* Vol. 51 (1997) 167-194

[13] Yacoob, Y., Davis, L.S. "Recognizing Human Facial Expression From Long Image Sequences Using Optical Flow" *IEEE Trans. Pattern Analysis and Machine Intelligence,* vol.18. (1996) 636-642

Hierarchical Learning of Optimal Linear Representations

Qiang Zhang and Xiuwen Liu
Department of Computer Science, Florida State University, Tallahassee, FL 32306-4530
Email: {zhang, liux}@cs.fsu.edu

Abstract—Due to their efficiency, linear representations are widely used in apperanace-based recognition. However, frequently used ones, such as PCA, ICA, and FDA, do not provide optimal performance as empirical studies have reported contradictory conclusions in the literature. To overcome this problem and provide an algorithm for finding the optimal linear representations for different applications, a Monte Carlo Markov chain based optimization algorithm was recently proposed and its effectiveness has been demonstrated on a number of datasets [4]. By formulating the problem on Grassmann manifolds, the algorithm is computationally efficient when the image size is relatively small. When images in typical applications are used, the optimization process is time consuming. In this paper, to speed up the algorithm, we propose a hierarchical learning one. The proposed algorithm decomposes the optimization in the given image space into several stages organized according to hierarchical layers. Given an image space, first its dimension is reduced using a shrinkage matrix and the optimization is then performanced in the reduced space. By expanding the obtained optimal subspace in the reduced one in a specified way, we show analytically that the performance is maintained. By applying the decomposition procedure recursively, a hierarchy of layers can be formed. This speeds up the original algorithm significantly as the search is done mainly in reduced spaces. The effectiveness of hierarchical learning is illustrated on a popular database, where the computation time is reduced by 600,000 factors compared to the original algorithm.

I. INTRODUCTION

Due to its simplicity, analytical tractability, and reported success on datasets for appearance-based object recognition, recently linear subspaces have become a popular choice for recognition. However, commonly used representations such as principal component analysis (PCA), Fisher discriminant analysis (FDA), and independent component analysis (ICA) are not optimal for a given application. Theoretically, PCA and ICA are designed for optimal reconstruction and statistical independence and thus are not directly related to recognition performance. While FDA is designed for optimal recognition performance, the optimality is valid only when the underlying probability distributions are Gaussian and linear discrimination functions are used[4]. As probability distributions of natural images are very different from Gaussian [7] and nonlinear discrimination functions are almost exclusively used in recognition applications, FDA is not optimal for recognition using images. This has been supported also by empirical evidence as contradictory conclusions are reported in the literature (e.g. [5], [1]). As recognition performance is critical for many applications, finding linear representations with optimal recognition performance for applications using images becomes an important topic. By formulating the problem of linear representation of images for recognition on a Grassmann manifold, Liu et al. [4] proposed a Markov chain Monte Carlo (MCMC) type algorithm that has been shown to be effective on all the used datasets and demonstrated significant improvement over commonly used bases. However due to its complexity, the algorithm is computationally effective only when the image size is relatively small. When datasets in typical applications are used, the algorithm is very time consuming as the search is done in a high dimensional space.

In this paper, we propose an algorithm that can speed up the original one [4] significantly. The key idea is to perform the search in shrinked image space and due to an analytical result the obtained performance in reduced space can be maintained if we expand the obtained linear representations in a particular way. To be effective, the requirement of the dimension shrinkage is that the optimal performance in the resulting space should be as high as possible. In this paper, this is achieved through a heuristic-based algorithm, which is named as *adaptive K-means algorithm*. The procedure can be repeated and a hierarchy can be formed. Thus the method is named as *hierarchical learning*.

This paper is organized as follows. In Section *II* we overview the problem of optimizing the recognition performance over the set of subspaces. The analytical result of hierarchical learning is shown in Section *III* and experimental results are given in Section *IV*. Section *V* concludes the paper with a discussion.

II. COMPUTING OPTIMAL LINEAR REPRESENTATIONS

Obtaining the optimal linear representation of images in terms of actual application performance requires the search in the linear representation space. Here we assume that the recognition performance depends only on the linear subspace and does not depend on the choice of bases in the given subspace. In other words, we assume the recognition performance on U is the same for any basis in the following set

$$[U] = \{UO | O \in \mathbb{R}^{d \times d}, O^T O = I_d\} \in \mathcal{G}_{n,d},$$

where U is a d-dimensional orthogal basis and O a $d \times d$ rotation matrix. For a given d, all the d-dimensional subspace in $\mathbb{R}^n$ is called a Grassmann manifold [2], denoted by $\mathcal{G}_{n,d}$. Thus the problem of finding optimal linear subspaces becomes an optimization on the Grassmann manifold. While there exist different optimization algorithms to solve this problem, a stochastic optimization process that maximizes the performance function over all subspaces is used in [4], given by,

$$\hat{U} = \underset{U \in \mathcal{G}_{n,d}}{\operatorname{argmax}} F(U) , \quad (1)$$

in which $F : \mathcal{G}_{n,d} \mapsto \mathbb{R}_+$ is the performance function, and U is one basis of the given subspace.

Since the set $\mathcal{G}_{n,d}$ is compact, if F is a smooth function, then the optimizer $\hat{U}$ is well defined. The search is performed in a probabilistic framework by defining a probability density function

$$f(X) = \frac{1}{Z(T)} \exp(F(X)/T) , \quad (2)$$

where $T \in \mathbb{R}$ plays the role of temperature and f is an induced density on the set $\mathcal{G}_{n,d}$.

The algorithm requires an estimation of the recognition performance F for a given subspace. Because the recognition performance is not a smooth function, a smoothed performance measure related to the recognition performance using the nearest neighbor rule is introduced in [4]. Specifically, let there be C classes to be recognized from the images; each class has k_{train} training images (denoted by $I_{c,1}, \ldots, I_{c,k_{train}}$) and k_{test} test images (denoted by $I'_{c,1}, \ldots, I'_{c,k_{test}}$) to evaluate the recognition performance measure.

$$F(U, \beta) = \frac{1}{Ck_{test}} \sum_{c=1}^{C} \sum_{i=1}^{k_{test}} h(\rho(I'_{c,i}, U) - 1, \beta), \quad (3)$$

where $h(\cdot, \cdot)$ is a monotonically increasing and bounded function in its first argument, and

$$\rho(I'_{c,i}, U) = \frac{\min_{c' \neq c, j} d(I'_{c,i}, I_{c',j}; U)}{\min_j d(I'_{c,i}, I_{c,j}; U) + \epsilon}, \quad (4)$$

where $d(I_1, I_2; U) = \|\alpha(I_1, U) - \alpha(I_2, U)\|$, $\alpha(I, U) = U^T I$ and $\epsilon > 0$ is a small number to avoid division by zero. In our implementation, following [4], $h(x, \beta) = 1/(1 + \exp(-2\beta x))$ is used, where β controls the smoothness of F. When we let $\beta \to \infty$, F is precisely the recognition performance of the nearest neighbor classifier [4].

In [4], a Markov chain Monte Carlo (MCMC) type gradient-based algorithm is used to find the optimal subspace $\hat{U}$. At each iteration, the gradient vector of F, which is a skew-symmetric matrix, is computed. By following the gradient, a new solution is generated, which is used as a proposal and is accepted with a probability that depends on the performance improvement. If the performance of the new solution is better than the current solution, it is always accepted. Otherwise, the worse the new solution's performance, the lower the probability the solution is being accepted. In the original implementation used in [4], the computation complexity C_n of each iteration of this algorithm is $C_n = O(d \times (n - d) \times k_{test} \times k_{training} \times n \times d)$, where $d \times (n - d)$ is the dimension of the gradient vector. For each dimension, to evaluate the performance measure, for each test image, the closest image in the same class and the one in different classes in the training set need to be computed as given by Eqn. 4, which requires to compute the representations using a perturbed subspace. The complexity for one iteration can be obtained easily according to Eqn. 3. The overall computation complexity is $C \times t$ where t is the number of iterations.

III. HIERARCHICAL LEARNING

From the above analysis, the computation at each iteration depends on several factors and the complexity is $O(n^2)$ in terms of n. For typical applications, n, which is the number of pixels in the image, is relative large. For example, in the face dataset (See Sect. IV), n is 2,576. Thus the algorithm can be very time consuming. Also when n gets larger, the dimension of the Grassmann manifold gets larger, resulting a search space with larger dimension. As the other factors in the complexity can not be avoided, here we propose an algorithm by shrinking the dimension of the search space first and performing the search in the reduced dimension. This reduces the complexity at each iteration and also the dimension of the search space.

There are several issues that needs to be addressed. First we are interested in finding optimal linear subspaces in the original space not the shrinked space, how can we use the obtained optimal subspace in the shrinked space? This question is answered by an analytical result, stating that there exists a way to expand the subspace in the shrinked space so that the performance of resulting basis in the original space is the same as the obtained performance in the shrinked space. In other words, if we can find an acceptable solution in the shrinked space, we can immediately get a solution in the original space. Note that the success of the procedure depends on the condition that the performance of the optimal solution in the shrinked space is acceptable. Ideally, this condition requires a search of different shrinkage matrices (see below). To be computationally efficient, this condition is replaced by finding good shrinkage matrix based on heuristics, where an adaptive K-means algorithm is proposed in this paper. Under this setting, the optimal performance achieved in the shrinked space may not be acceptable; however the search will improve the performance and thus can provide a better initial condition for the search in the original space, which can reduce the number of required iterations.

In the section, we first show an analytical result between the performance in shrinked space and the one in the original space. Then we present an adaptive K-means algorithm to find a shrinkage matrix with good performance.

A. Hierarchical Learning Algorithm

Before we present the hierarchical learning algorithm, we first state the following result that gives a specific way to expand a basis in a shrinked space to the original space so that the performance is maintained.

Theorem: *Suppose $N_1 = m \times N_2$ where $N_1, N_2, m \in \mathcal{N}$. Let $\hat{U} \in \mathbb{R}^{N_2 \times d}$, $U \in \mathbb{R}^{N_1 \times d}$, $d \in \mathcal{N}$, $I_1 \in \mathbb{R}^{N_1}$, $I_2 \in \mathbb{R}^{N_1}$, $\hat{I}_1 \in \mathbb{R}^{N_2}$, $\hat{I}_2 \in \mathbb{R}^{N_2}$, $A = [a_{ij}]_{N_2 \times N_1} \in \mathbb{R}^{N_2 \times N_1}$, in which $a_{ij} \in \{0, 1\}$ for $i = 1, \ldots, N_2; j = 1, \ldots, N_1$;*

$$\sum_{j=1}^{N_1} 1(a_{ij}) = m, \quad \sum_{i=1}^{N_2} 1(a_{ij}) = 1.$$

$$1(x) = \begin{cases} 0 & \text{if } x=0 \\ 1 & \text{otherwise} \end{cases}$$

If $\hat{I}_i = \frac{1}{m}AI_i$, for $i = 1,2$; $U = \frac{1}{m}A^T\hat{U}$.
Then $d(I_1, I_2; U) = d(\hat{I}_1, \hat{I}_2; \hat{U})$.

Proof:

$$\begin{aligned}
\alpha(I_i, U) &= U^T I_i \\
&= \frac{1}{m}\hat{U}^T A I_i \\
&= \hat{U}^T \hat{I}_i \\
&= \alpha(\hat{I}_i, \hat{U}),
\end{aligned} \quad (5)$$

for $i = 1, 2$.
So

$$\begin{aligned}
d(I_1, I_2; U) &= \|\alpha(I_1, U) - \alpha(I_2, U)\| \\
&= \|\alpha(\hat{I}_1, \hat{U}) - \alpha(\hat{I}_2, \hat{U})\| \\
&= d(\hat{I}_1, \hat{I}_2; \hat{U}).
\end{aligned} \quad (6)$$

EOP.

In the above theorem, we get the result without using the conditions $\sum_{j=1}^{N_1} 1(a_{ij}) = m$ and $\sum_{i=1}^{N_2} 1(a_{ij}) = 1$. The reason we put them there is that the adaptive kmeans algorithm(see below) requires A be that form.

Now let's consider how to compute the optimal basis $U \in \mathbb{R}^{N_1 \times d}$ in a more efficient way. Given the training and test images of size N_1, we can shrink their size to N_1/m by left multiplying matrix $(1/m)A$ with original training and test images, where A is a matrix that satisfies the conditions stated in the theorem. We call the dimension reduction process *shrinking the dimension* by a *shrinking factor* m through a shinkage matrix A. With the resulting new training and test images, we apply the optimization algorithm to search for $\hat{U} = \arg\max_{U \in \mathcal{G}_{N_1/m,d}} F(U)$. After $\hat{U} \in \mathbb{R}^{N_1/m \times d}$ is computed, we get $U \in \mathbb{R}^{N_1 \times d}$ by the equation $U = (1/m)A^T\hat{U}$. We call it *expanding basis* $\hat{U}$ to U. As the theorem states, $d(I_1, I_2; U) = d(\hat{I}_1, \hat{I}_2; \hat{U})$. As long as the performance function F is invariant with the distance between the representation of training and test images, the recognition rate will be unchanged. In this paper, F satisfies the above condition, because the nearest neighbor rule is used as the classifier. Thus we can get the basis $U \in \mathbb{R}^{N_1 \times d}$ by searching for basis $\hat{U} \in \mathbb{R}^{N1/m \times d}$.

For each iteration, the computation complexity with images of size N_1 is $C_{N_1} = O(d \times (N_1 - d) \times k_{test} \times k_{training} \times N_1 \times d)$. While the computation complexity with images of

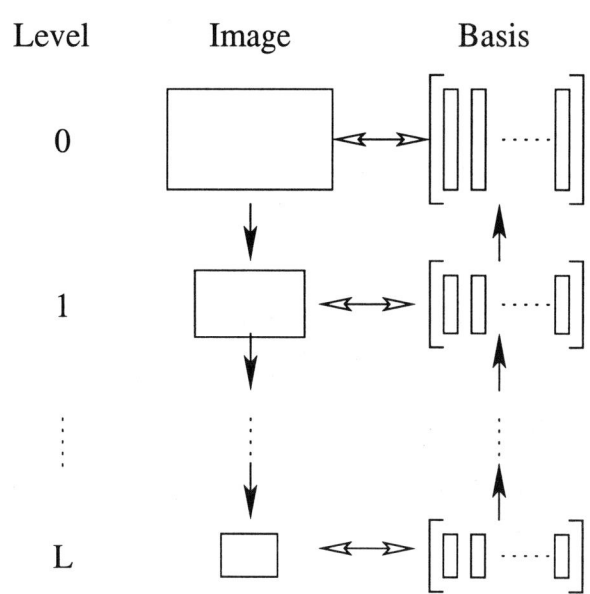

Fig. 1. Hierarchical search process. Image size is shrinked as level number grows. Firstly, the optimal basis U_L is got at level L. We obtain basis $\bar{U}_{L-1}$ of level $L-1$ by expanding U_L. $\bar{U}_{L-1}$ and U_L have the same performance. We use $\bar{U}_{L-1}$ as an initial point to perform the search at level $L-1$ with images of size $\frac{n_0}{\hat{m}^{L-1}}$. The 'search – expand basis – search' process goes on till we get the optimal basis for level 0.

size N_1/m is

$$\begin{aligned}
C_{N_2} &= O(d \times (\frac{N_1}{m} - d) \times k_{test} \times k_{training} \times \frac{N_1}{m} \times d) \\
&= \frac{N_1 - md}{m^2(N_1 - d)} C_{N_1} \\
&\approx \frac{1}{m^2} C_{N_1},
\end{aligned} \quad (7)$$

considering the fact $N_1 >> d$.

From the above analysis we see that we can save time significantly on the search if we do dimension shrinking on the original images using a large shrinking factor m. However the best achievable performance using these shrinked images can be much lower than that in the original space. To get the optimal basis, we have to search again with images of original size, which is potentially time consuming if the performance in the shrinked space is considerably low.

Inspired by [6], to overcome this problem, we propose to perform the search hierarchically at different levels. The basic idea is as follows. Instead of choosing large m to shrink dimension only once, we can choose relatively smaller shrinking factor $\hat{m}$ to shrink the original images for k times to get the training and test images at level k, in which k is from 1 to L. The size of images at level k is $\frac{n_0}{\hat{m}^k}$ where n_0 is the size of the original images. The search begins from level L with dimension-shrinked images of size $\frac{n_0}{\hat{m}^L}$. The computational complexity at this level is $\frac{1}{\hat{m}^{2L}} C_{n_0}$ for each iteration. The search can be effectively done. After getting an optimal basis U_L at level L, we obtain basis $\bar{U}_{L-1}$ of level $L - 1$ by expanding U_L. Based on the above discussion we know that $\bar{U}_{L-1}$ and U_L have the same performance. If we use $\bar{U}_{L-1}$ as an initial point to perform the search at level $L - 1$ with images of size $\frac{n_0}{\hat{m}^{L-1}}$, the search can be performed relatively effectively. The computational complexity at this level is $\frac{1}{\hat{m}^{2(L-1)}}C_{n_0}$ for each iteration. The search result of this level will be used to obtain a basis $\bar{U}_{L-2}$ of level $L-2$, which is used as an initial point for further search at level $L-2$. This process is repeated until we have reached level 0. This process is illustrated in Fig. 1. The hierarchical learning algorithm is given below.

Hierarchical Learning Algorithm: Suppose we have $L+1$ levels, and the shrinking factor is m. The original image size is n_0. Our aim is to find the optimal basis of level 0.

1) Choose the dimension shrinkage matrices A_k, for $k = 1, \ldots, L$. Then prepare new training and test images at each level i: shrinking the image dimension on the training and test images for i times by multilplying $\frac{1}{m^i}\prod_{k=i}^{1} A_k$ with the original images.
2) Search for the optimal basis U_L at level L with training and test images of size $\frac{n_0}{m^L}$.
3) For each $k = L-1, \ldots, 0$, let $\bar{U}_k = \frac{1}{m}A_{k+1}^T U_{k+1}$, using $\bar{U}_k$ as the initial point, search for the optimal basis U_k at level k with training and test images of size $\frac{n_0}{m^k}$.

B. Pixels Grouping Through Adaptive K-means

For the hierarchical search algorithm to be effective, the best achievable performance in the original space should be kept as much as possible. There are many different ways to group pixels, i.e to choose dimension shrinkage matrix A, when doing dimension shrinkage. As an illustrative example, Fig. 2 shows two methods on two 4×4 images. In this simple example, one method is very effective in that any performance achievable in the 4×4 image space can be achieved in the shrinked space and the other one is useless in that the shrinked images do not provide any information for recognition any more.

Based on the example, we argue that we should group pixels with similar values in the original image together and represent them in the dimension shrinked images by their mean. To achieve this, we propose a pixel grouping algorithm called adaptive K-means, which is an adaped version of original K-means algorithm [3]. This method is used in the hierarchical learning algorithm to generate shrinkage matrix A_i. As all the training images should be shrunk in the same way, we put all of them in a matrix M of size $n \times N_1$ with each row of M is an image where n is the number of training images. N_1 is the size of the image, $N_1 = mN_2$ where m is the shrinking factor. We want to get a matrix $\bar{M}$ of size $n \times N_2$ where each column is the mean of m columns of M.

Let $M = [M_1 M_2 ... M_{N_1}]$ where $M_i(i = 1, .., N_1)$ is the i-th column of M. Treating M_i as a point in $\mathbb{R}^n$, we give the following algorithm to group the N_1 points $M_i(i = 1, .., N_1)$ to N_2 clusters $\bar{M}_i(i = 1, \ldots, N_2)$.

Adaptive K-means Algorighm: Let $S = \{M_i | i = 1, \ldots, N_1\}$. Randomly choose N_2 points $\bar{M}_i \in \mathbb{R}^n, i = 1, \ldots, N_2$.

1) For each $\bar{M}_i$, choose the nearest m points in S, group them into cluster $\bar{M}_i$. Remove the chosen points from S.
2) For each cluster $\bar{M}_i$, compute variance $\bar{V}_i$ and mean $(\bar{M}_i)_{new}$, set $\bar{M}_i = (\bar{M}_i)_{new}$.
3) Let $S = \{M_i | i = 1, \ldots, N_1\}$. Sorting according to $\bar{V}_i$, get list $L: \bar{V}_{i_1} \leq \bar{V}_{i_2} \leq \cdots \leq \bar{V}_{i_{N_2}}$, in which $(i_1, \cdots, i_{N_2})$ is a permutation of $(1, \cdots, N_2)$.
4) According to L, for each cluster $\bar{M}_{i_k}$ we choose the nearest m points in S and put them into this cluster. Remove the chosen points from S.
5) For each cluster $\bar{M}_{i_k}$, compute variance $\bar{V}_{i_k}$ and mean $(\bar{M}_{i_k})_{new}$. If $(\bar{M}_{i_k})_{new} = \bar{M}_{i_k}$ stop, else go to step 3.

0	0	50	50
0	0	50	50
100	100	150	150
100	100	150	150

(a0)

100	100	0	0
100	100	0	0
150	150	50	50
150	150	50	50

(b0)

75	75
75	75

(a1)

75	75
75	75

(b1)

0	50
100	150

(a2)

100	0
150	50

(b2)

Fig. 2. An illustrative example for dimension shrinking. Two 4×4 images (a0) and (b0) are shrinked using different methods, giving two different 2×2 images. The optimal recognition performance using the two images given by (a1) and (b1) is much worse than that using the two images given by (a2) and (b2) as (a1) and (b1) are identical after dimension shrinkage.

IV. EXPERIMENTAL RESULTS

The database that has been used in our experiments: the ORL face recognition dataset[1]. The ORL dataset consists of faces of 40 different subjects with 10 images each.

We plot the recognition rate versus iteration and the distance between X_t and X_0 versus t, in which X_t is the basis of the subspace at iteration t. The distance between any two subspaces U_1 and U_2 is computed as: $\|U_1 U_1^T - U_2 U_2^T\|$.

1) We run the hierarchical learning algorithm on the ORL dataset with L=3, original image size n is chosen to be 2576, with the shrinking factor $m = 4$, $d = 10$, $k_{train} = 5$, and $k_{test} = 5$. Fig. 3 shows cases at

[1]http://www.uk.research.att.com/facedatabase.html

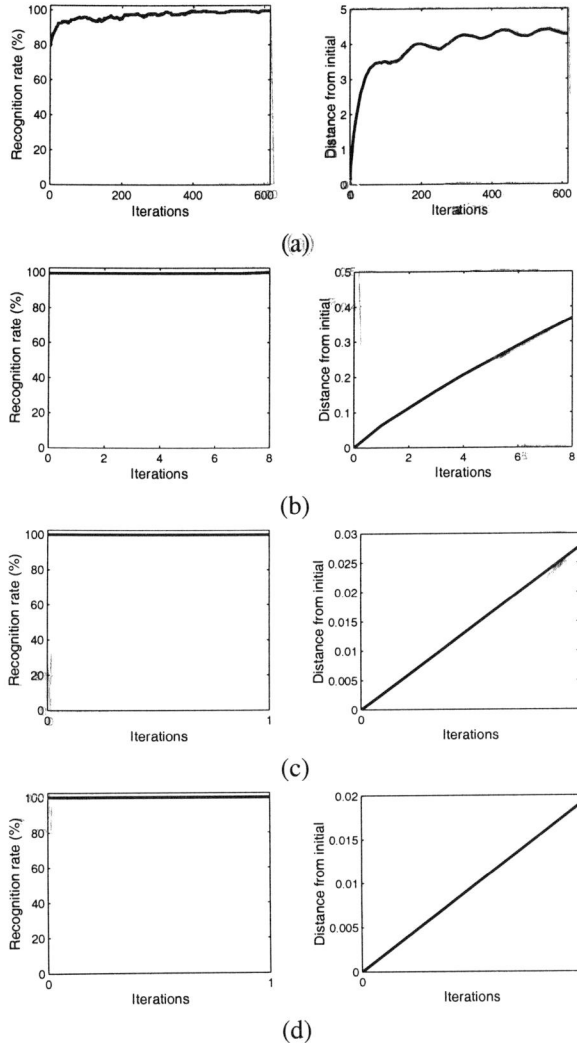

Fig. 3. Plots of recognition rate (left) and distance of X_t from X_0 (right) versus t for different level using it hierarchical search algorithm. (a) level 3, (b) level 2, (c) level 1, (d) level 0. For these curves, $L = 3$, $m = 4$, $n = 2576$, $d = 10$, $k_{train} = 5$, and $k_{test} = 5$. Database is ORL.

different levels. We can see that it costs 600 iterations to achieve a perfect performance at level 3 (a). Due to numerical error, when we get the initial basis at level 2 by expanding the optimal basis got at level 3 the performance goes down a little bit. It takes 8 iterations again at level 2 to achieve perfect performance (b). From (c) and (d) we see that it takes only one step to get the optimal basis at level 1 (c) and level 0 (d) respectively. This means that the performance is kept when expanding the optimal basis got at higher level to a basis at lower level. It's also worthy to note the plots of distance of X_t from X_0. At lower levels, it takes a small number of iterations with small moves from the initial point to get the optimal basis. Expending the basis from a higher level as the initial basis at the lower level does give a good guess of the optimal basis at the lower level.

2) Next, we have studied the time for searching for the optimal basis versus the level number L. Fig. 4 shows the

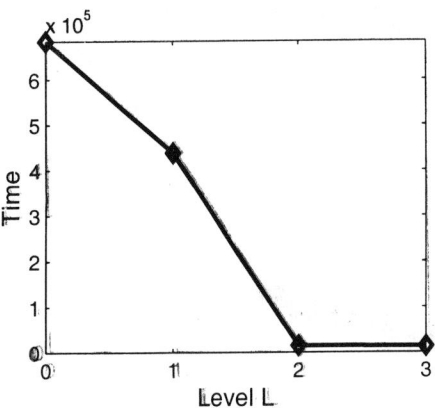

Fig. 4. Plot of searching time versus L. $n = 2576$, $m = 4$, $d = 10$, $k_{train} = 5$, and $k_{test} = 5$.

result, which highlights the effectiveness of hierarchical learning algorithm. In this experiment, the ORL database is used. n is chosen to be 2576, shrinking factor $m = 4$, $d = 10$, $k_{train} = 5$, and $k_{test} = 5$.

3) Fig. 5 shows the different cases when using a different level number L. In these experiments, we use the ORL dataset, n is chosen to be 2576, with the shrinking factor $m = 4$, $d = 10$, $k_{train} = 5$, and $k_{test} = 5$. All the cases converge to a perfect classification solution regardless of the level number. One point to mention is that after doing the dimension shrink, the recognition rate may be even higher than that of the original images. For instance, in Fig. 5 the initial recognition rate is 73% with dimension shrinked images(c), but the initial recognition rate is 60% with the original images (a).

V. DISCUSSION

In this paper, we have proposed a hierarchical learning algorithm for finding optimal linear representation. By grouping pixels using an adaptive K-means algorithm, we speed up the original search on the dataset significantly. This makes it computationally feasible and effective to find optimal linear representations for typical applications with large images. The significance of this work is that now it is possible to study generalization and other fundamental issues in linear representations systematically.

Note that the efficiency is gained by decomposing the search on a large Grassmann manifold to a number of hierarchically organized Grassmann manifolds with small dimensions. The effectiveness of the algorithm depends on the best achievable performance in the shrinked dimension. While the proposed adaptive K-means algorithm is shown to be effective for the dataset we have used, its effectiveness is not guaranteed. The conditions under which the algorithm is effective needs to be further investigated. Another future research issue is to find better pixel grouping algorithms to generate the shrinkage matrix A.

Acknowledgments This research was supported in part by an NIMA grant (NMA201-01-2010).

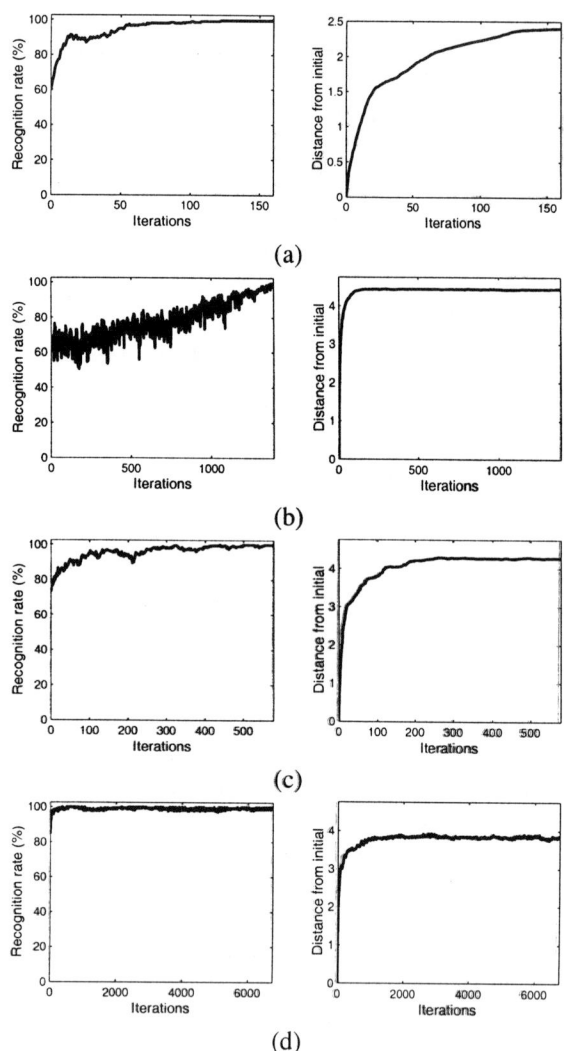

Fig. 5. Plots of recognition rate (left) and distance of X_t from X_0 (right) versus t at the highest level for different L. (a) $L = 0$, level 0, (b) $L = 1$, level 1, (c) $L = 2$, level 2, (d) $L = 3$, level 3. For these curves, $n = 2576$, $m = 4$, $d = 10$, $k_{train} = 5$, and $k_{test} = 5$.

REFERENCES

[1] P. N. Belhumeur, J. P. Hepanha and D. J. Kriegman, "Eigenfaces vs. fisherfaces: Recognition using class specific linear projection," *IEEE Transactions on Pattern Analysis and Machine Intelligence*, Vol. 19(7), pp. 711–720, 1997.

[2] W. M. Boothby, *An Introduction to Differential Manifolds and Riemannian Geometry*, Academic Press, 1986.

[3] D. A. Forsyth and J. Ponce, *Computer Vision, A Modern Approach*. pp. 315-317. Prentice Hall, 2003.

[4] X. Liu, A. Srivastava and K. Gallivan, "Optimal linear representations of images for object recognition," in Proceedings of *IEEE Computer Society Conference on Computer Vision and Pattern Recognition*, 2003.

[5] A. M. Martinez and A. C. Kak, "PCA versus LDA," *IEEE Transactions on Pattern Analysis and Machine Intelligence*, vol. 23(2), pp. 228–233, 2001.

[6] A. Rosenfeld, "Image analysis: problems, process and prospects," *Readings in computer vision*, pp. 3–12, Morgan Kaufmann Publishers, 1987.

[7] A. Srivastava, A. B. Lee, E. P. Simoncelli and S. C. Zhu. "On advances in statistical modeling of natural images," *Journal of Mathematical Imaging and Vision*, vol. 18(1), 2003.

GA-SVM Wrapper Approach for Feature Subset Selection in Keystroke Dynamics Identity Verification

Enzhe Yu and Sungzoon Cho
Department of Industrial Engineering, Seoul National University
San 56-1, Shillim Dong, Kwanak-Gu, Seoul 151-744 Korea
Email: {enzhe | zoon}@snu.ac.kr

Abstract— Password is the most widely used identity verification method in computer security domain. However, due to its simplicity, it is vulnerable to imposter attacks. Keystroke dynamics adds a shield to password. Password typing patterns or timing vectors of a user are measured and used to train a novelty detector model. However, without manual pre-processing to remove noises and outliers resulting from typing inconsistencies, a poor detection accuracy results. Thus, in this paper, we propose an automatic feature subset selection process that can automatically selects a relevant subset of features and ignores the rest, thus producing a better accuracy. Genetic algorithm is employed to implement a randomized search and SVM, an excellent novelty detector with fast learning speed, is employed as a base learner. Preliminary experiments show a promising result.

I. Introduction

Password is the most widely used identity verification method in computer security domain. However, due to its simplicity, it is vulnerable to imposter attacks. One way to add a shield to password is to employ keystroke dynamics in password typing. Keystroke dynamics is a biometric-based approach that utilizes the manner and rhythm in which each individual types password. It measures the keystroke rhythm of a user in order to develop a template that identifies the authorized user. When a user types a word, for instance a password, the keystroke dynamics can be characterized by a "timing vector", consisting of the durations of keystrokes and the time intervals between them. The owner's timing vectors are collected and used to build a model that discriminates between the owner and imposters. This idea comes originally from the observations that a user's keystroke pattern is highly repeatable and distinct from others'.

In 1980, Gaines et al. [3] first proposed the approach using keystroke dynamics for user authentication. Experiments with a population of 7 candidates were conducted. Later on, Leggett et al. [4] conducted similar experiments by applying a long string of 537 characters, and reported a result of 5.0% False Acceptance Rate (FAR: the rate that an imposter is allowed access) and 5.5% False Rejection Rate (FRR: the rate that a legitimate user is denied access). Recently, through the use of neural networks, a comparable performance of 12% to 21% was achieved using short strings such as real-life names [4]. Obaidat and Sadoun reported a 0% error rate in user verification using 7-character-long login name [6]. However, the assumptions were impractical. First, both the imposter's typing patterns and the owner's patterns were used in training.

In case of "password typing," the imposter patterns are not available. Second, a huge training data set of 6,300 owners and 112 negatives were used. Third, the training and test patterns were not chronologically separated. In [1], a novelty detection model, i.e. 2-layer AaMLP, was built by training owner's patterns only, and was used to detect imposters using some sort of a similarity measure, and a 1.0% FRR and 0% FAR was reported. However, 2-layer AaMLP usually works well for linear patterns, while performs bad for nonlinear data. Recently, Yu and Cho [10] applied non-linear models, i.e. 4-layer AaMLP and support vector machine (SVM) [7], [8] and reported improved results.

Novelty detection models are built under the assumption that the owner's typing follows a consistent pattern. But usually there are some problems with the original data due to owner's inconsistency. Irrelevant or redundant features are generated, thus lead the novelty detector to bad performance. One usual way to tackle such problems is by manually preprocessing data, i.e. removing noises or outliers from training patterns [10]. However, data preprocessing is subjective, and is not allowed in automated identity verification. Practically, identity verification allows no human intervention to deal with the owner's raw pattern, and an automated process is preferred. Without manual preprocessing, even the best-so-far method resulted in a relatively poor performance of 15% FRR when FAR was set to 0%. One way to improve the performance is to employ an "automatic" preprocessing process.

In this paper, we propose a feature subset selection process that can automatically selects a relevant subset of features and ignores the rest, thus resulting in a more comprehensive model. In particular, a Genetic Algorithm-Support Vector Machine (GA-SVM) based "wrapper" approach for feature subset selection was applied to keystroke dynamics identity verification problem. Experimental results from the proposed approach were compared with the results from the approach without feature selection.

This paper is structured as follows. In session 2, descriptions on the proposed GA-SVM wrapper approach are presented. Session 3 explains the data and experimental settings, and experimental results. A conclusion and limitation of the current work then follows.

II. GA-SVM based Wrapper Approach

Feature subset selection is essentially an optimization problem, which involves searching the space of possible features to identify one that is optimum or near-optimal with respect to certain performance measures (e.g., accuracy, learning time, etc.) Various ways to perform feature subset selection exist.

Let us consider them in terms of two different perspectives. First, according to the characteristics of the search strategy, feature subset selection algorithms can broadly be classified into three categories [9]: (a) *Exhaustive search*, which is computationally infeasible in practice, except in those rare instances where the total number of features is quite small; (b) *Heuristic search*, which is often used in conjunction with branch and bound search. But heuristic search assumes that the performance criterion is monotone, therefore it only works well with linear classifiers, and shows bad results with non-linear classifiers such neural network; (c) *Randomized search*, which uses randomized or probabilistic steps or sampling processes. Prominent among the randomized search algorithms is genetic algorithm, which does not require the restrictive monotonicity assumption.

Second, feature subset selection algorithms can be classified into two categories based on whether or not feature selection is done independently of the learning algorithm used to construct the classifier. If feature selection is performed independently of the learning algorithm, the technique is said to follow a filter approach. Otherwise, it is said to follow a wrapper approach. Filter approach is generally computationally more efficient than the wrapper approach, its major drawback is that an optimal selection of features may not be independent of the inductive and representational biases of the learning algorithm that is used to construct the classifier. The wrapper approach on the other hand, involves the computational overhead of evaluating candidate feature subsets by executing a selected learning algorithm on the dataset represented using each feature subset under consideration. This is feasible only if the learning algorithm used to train the classifier is relatively fast [9].

A. SVM for Novelty Detection

SVM is commonly used to solve two-class classification. But, recently, Schölkopf et al. [7], [8] extended the support vector machine methodology to "one-class" classification, i.e. novelty detection problem. Other support vector data description (SVDD) approaches such as [12] used a concept of *balls* to describe the data in a feature space. For Gaussian kernels, these two approaches can be proved to be equivalent.

Our approach is based on the one-class classification algorithm which was proposed by Schölkopf et al.[7], [8]. The idea is to map the data into the feature space corresponding to the kernel, and to separate them from the origin with a maximum margin. The algorithm returns a decision function f that takes the value +1 in a 'small' region capturing most of the normal data, and -1 elsewhere. For a new point x, the value $f(x)$ is determined by evaluating which side of the hyperplane it falls on in the feature space.

Let $x_1, x_2, ..., x_l \in X$, where $l \in N$ denotes the number of normal data, and X a compact subset of R^N corresponding to the one class. Let Φ be a feature map X $\rightarrow$ F, which transforms the training data to a dot product space F such that the dot product in the image of Φ can be computed by evaluating some simple kernel

$$k(x,y) = \big(\Phi(x) \cdot \Phi(y)\big). \quad (1)$$

In case of Gaussian kernel,

$$k(x,y) = e^{-\|x-y\|^2/s}. \quad (2)$$

To separate the normal data set from the origin, one needs to solve the following quadratic programming problem:

$$\min_{w \in F, \xi \in R^l, \rho \in R} \frac{1}{2} \| w \|^2 + \frac{1}{\nu l} \sum_i \xi_i - \rho. \quad (3)$$

subject to $\big(w \cdot \Phi(x_i)\big) \geq \rho - \xi_i, \xi_i \geq 0.$

Since nonzero slack variables ξ_i are penalized in the objective function, it can be expected that if w and ρ solve this problem, then the decision function

$$f(x) = sgn\big(w \cdot \Phi(x) - \rho\big). \quad (4)$$

will be positive for most examples x_i contained in the training set, while the SV type regularization term $\| w \|$ will still be small. The trade-off between these two goals is controlled by $\nu \in (0, 1)$.

Deriving the dual problem, and (1), the solution can be shown to have an SV expansion

$$f(x) = sgn\bigg(\sum_i a_i k(x_i, x) - \rho \bigg). \quad (5)$$

(patterns x_i with nonzero a_i are called support vectors), where the coefficients are found as the solution of the dual problem:

$$\min_a \frac{1}{2} \sum_{ij} a_i a_j k(x_i, x_j), \quad (6)$$

subject to $0 \leq a_i \leq \frac{1}{\nu l}, \quad \sum_i a_i = 1.$

If ν approaches 0, the upper boundaries on the Lagrange multipliers tend to infinity, thus the problem then resembles the corresponding hard margin algorithm. If ν approaches 1, then the constrains only allow one solution, that where all a_i are at the upper bound $1/(\nu l)$. In this case, for kernels with integral 1, i.e. Gaussian kernel, the decision function corresponds to a Parzen windows estimator with threshold [5], [8], [12].

In our research, we used used Chang and Lin's toolbox LIBSVM[2], which was based on the "one-class" SVM algorithm developed by Schökolpf et al. As for the parameters, since we evaluate the feature subset and training model according to FRR when FAR=0, therefore a heuristic search was applied for tuning parameters.

B. Genetic Algorithm

GAs are stochastic search techniques based on the mechanism of natural selection and genetics. A typical GA starts with an initial set of random solutions called *population* and each individual in the population is called a *chromosome*. A chromosome is usually, but not necessarily, a binary string and represents a solution to the problem on hand. Chromosomes evolve through successive iterations, called *generations*. During each generation, the chromosomes are evaluated, using some measures of fitness. To create the next generation, new chromosomes, called *offspring*, are formed either by *(a)* merging two chromosomes from the current generation using a *crossover* operator, or *(b)* modifying a chromosome using a *mutation* operator. A new generation is formed by: *(a)* selecting some of the parents and offspring according to their fitness values, and *(b)* rejecting the rest so that the population size is kept constant. In the process, fitter chromosomes have a higher chance of being selected. After several generations, the algorithm converges to the best set of chromosomes, which hopefully represent the optimum or near optimal solution to the problem. Table I describes the general structure of GA, where *P(t)* and *C(t)* denote the parents and offspring or children set in the current generation.

GAs are becoming popular as a technique for solving optimisation and search problems mainly because of three distinct advantages they have over their competition [11]: (1) GAs do not involve sophisticated mathematics; (2) The operators' ergodicity of evolution makes GAs very effective at performing global search; (3) GAs are flexible in that they readily allow for hybridization with domain dependent heuristics, which can result in a more powerful search routine for a specific problem.

TABLE I
GELETIC ALGORITHM

```
Procedure: Genetic Algorithm
    Begin
        t ← 0;
        Initialization P(t);
        Evaluation P(t);
        While (not termination condition)
        Do
            Recombine P(t) to yield C(t);
            Evaluation C(t);
            Selection P(t+1) from P(t) or P(t)+C(t);
            t ← t+1;
        End
    End
```

C. GA-SVM Wrapper

Our choice is the randomized wrapper approach. Specifically, we chose genetic algorithm paradigm for randomization and SVM as a base learner in wrapper approach. In other words, a population of feature subsets are evolved through the mechanism of genetic algorithm and a feature subset is evaluated through training and testing a SVM with the data set. GAs are stochastic search techniques based on the mechanism of natural selection and genetics, and are generally quite effective for rapid global search of large search spaces in difficult optimization problems. Previous researches have reported the feasibility of GA for wrapper approach to feature subset selection [9]. SVM also suits as a base learner well due to its quick training capability. In our previous study, SVM novelty detector was found to result in a comparable performance with that of neural network, but the learning time is much faster than that of neural network, i.e. less than 1/1000 times of neural network's learning time [10]. An initial population is made up of diversified binary strings indicating the features selected.

These candidates undergo crossover and mutation, evaluated by the SVM base learner. Only those that are selected according to the specified multi-criteria fitness are put back into the population and the process is repeated for a fixed number of generations. The best solutions are achieved in the end (see *Fig. 1*).

In the proposed GA-SVM wrapper approach, a Gaussian kernel is used for the induction algorithm, i.e. SVM, and the parameters were tuned through some heuristic method. The GA was implemented with the following settings. The chromosome is a binary string where each bit denotes whether the corresponding feature is present (1) or absent (0). The population size was generally set at 30, but when the population diversity resulted in an unsatisfactory performance, it was modified up to 50. The crossover rate of 0.6, and the mutation rate of 0.01~0.02 were adopted with corresponding mechanisms being two-point crossover and uniform mutation, respectively. Selection provides the driving force in the evo-

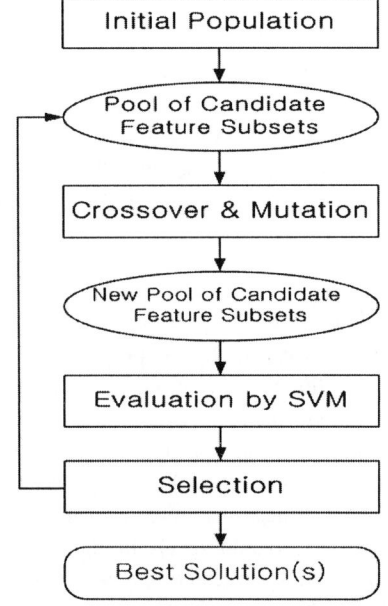

Fig. 1. GA-SVM Wrapper Feature Subset Selection

lutionary process, and the selection pressure is critical. At the early stage of evolution, a low selection pressure is preferred for a wide exploration of the search space. At the end of evolution, where the population is near convergence, however, a high selection pressure is taken to exploit the most promising regions of the search space [11]. As for the sampling space, a regular one was chosen, which has the size of the specified population and is made up of all the offspring and only part of parents. The sampling mechanism follows the probabilistic roulette wheel selection. In order to discriminate among the similar strong individuals in the last 10%~20% generations, a linear scaling method was applied to deal with the selection probability.

The fitness function combined three different criteria, i.e. the accuracy of the novelty detector, the learning time used, and the dimension reduction ratio. One definitions of the fitness function emphasized more on the accuracy:

$$Fitness(x) = \frac{1}{DimRat(x)} + \frac{1}{100 \times LrnT(x)} + 10 \times Acc(x). \quad (7)$$

where $Fitness(x)$ is the fitness of the feature subset represented by x, $Acc(x)$ is the test accuracy of the SVM novelty detector using the feature subset represented by x, and $LrnT(x)$ is the time taken to train the SVM.

Although usually the test accuracy is the only most important criterion, we also include dimension reduction ratio and training time into the fitness function in that when the model show comparable results, the model with least training time which is important in practical application, and the feature subset with the smaller dimension which is less suspectable to introduce irrelevant or redundant features, are more preferred. In fact, proper tradeoff values among the multiple objectives have to be based on the knowledge of the problem domain or the experimental results.

III. EXPERIMENTS AND RESULTS

Experiments were implemented using the GA-SVM wrapper approach with the data set identical to that of [10]. The goal was to observe the effect of the feature subset selection. A comparison of the model performances was made between the results of before- and after- feature subset selection.

A. Data Collection

The data was captured by a program in X window environment on a Sun Sparc-Station, in which the keystroke duration times and interval times was measured. The keystroke duration and interval times were captured at the accuracy of milliseconds (*ms*). A timing vector consists of keystroke duration times and interval times. A password with *n*-character long would result in the timing vector of dimension ($2n+1$), with the Enter key included. For instance, a password *abcd*, which is 4-character long ($n = 4$), together with the *Enter* key, results in a timing vector of 9 dimension.

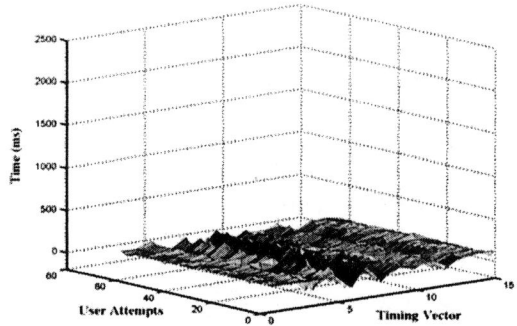

Fig. 2. Example of Owner's Patterns

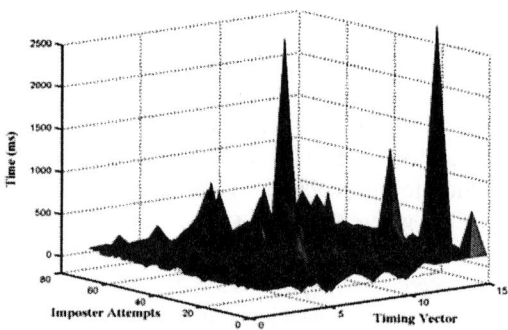

Fig. 3. Example of Impoters' Patterns

An example of a timing vector is [30, 60, 70, 135, 60, -35, 75, 40, 55]. A negative keystroke interval time results when a next key is stroked before a previous key is released.

The owners' data was collected from 21 participants with different passwords, whose length ranges from 6 to 10. Each participant was asked to type his password 150 to 400 times, and the last 75 timing vectors were collected for testing, whereas the remaining ones were used as training patterns.

As for the novelty data, 15 imposters were given passwords beforehand, and were asked to practice typing these passwords. After that, they type each of the given 21 passwords 5 times, resulting in 75 impostor timing vectors for each password. We call these imposters as "*imposters with practice.*" Together with the owners' test patterns mentioned above, two groups of 75 patterns, i.e. normal and novelty, are collected for each password.

When compared to other problems, the test data set is quite small, this is due to the limited participants in the data collection process. However, these imposters practiced typing the given password in many ways and can be regarded as somewhat representative of the practical situations, although these test sets still need to be extended in terms of diversity. Fig. 2 and Fig. 3 illustrated timing vectors of a certain password for the owner and "imposters with practice", respectively.

B. Experimental Results

Experiments were carried out on the 21 datasets as was described in the previous section. Since it can be assumed that the "imposters with practice" resemble the owners more than those "imposters without practice" in the way they type, and are more representative of practical situations, we evaluated the model performance by using the data collected from the owners and the corresponding "imposters with practice".

In the proposed GA-SVM approach, the novelty detector, i.e. SVM, is built by using the owner's pattern only, and GA makes a large number of evaluations in the evolutionary process, a certain number of validation sets for evaluation are required. This was solved by conducting cross-validation method in the experiments.

Table 2 compared model performance with raw data and the data after feature subset selection. Raw data contained noise or outliers, and resulted in bad performance without data cleaning or feature selection. Experiments reported an average FRR of 15.78%, with minimum FRR of 5.3% and maximum FRR of 20.38%. Wrapper approach greatly reduced the dimension of the timing vector, and improved the model accuracy as well. The average dimension of the feature subset is 5.86, the smallest feature subset was reduced even down to 3. Different features were selected for different passwords. For "atom" password dataset, for instance, the dimension was reduced from 15 to 5, with corresponding feature subset being "100100001100100." Only three keystroke durations and two keystroke intervals were selected. For other passwords, different features were selected. Model accuracies were all improved with the selected feature subset. The average FRR was reduced from 15.78% down to 3.54%.

IV. CONCLUSION

In this paper, we proposed GA-SVM based wrapper approach for feature subset selection for keystroke dynamics identity verification. SVM showed its excellence in both accuracy and learning speed, and was proved to be a suitable learner in the wrapper approach. A comparison was made between the performances of before- and after- feature subset selection and promising results were achieved.

Further investigation is necessary regarding the following issues: first, practically the users are unwilling to type passwords hundreds of times, thus result in insufficient training data. In such a situation, existing approaches may not work so well. A new method has to be studied to deal with such circumstances. Second, in order for a benchmark study, standard keystroke dynamics data like UCI data is called for.

ACKNOWLEDGMENT

This research was supported by Brain Science and Engineering Research Program sponsored by Korean Ministry of Science and Technology, and (in part) by KOSEF through Statistical Research Center for Complex Systems at Seoul National University. The authors would like to thank...

TABLE II
FRR WHEN FAR=0 (DIMENSION) BEFORE- AND AFTER-FSS

Owner ID	FRR (Dimension)	
	Before-FSS	After-FSS
Atom	19.32 (15)	2.68 (5)
Bubugi	19.75 (17)	4.39 (4)
Celavie	14.87 (17)	4.55 (4)
Crapas	19.82 (19)	3.60 (5)
Dry	19.88 (19)	4.23 (7)
Flower	15.15 (13)	3.25 (7)
Gmother	19.80 (17)	1.25 (11)
Gusegi	20.26 (15)	3.45 (6)
Jmin	14.85 (17)	3.25 (7)
June	5.30 (17)	1.97 (6)
Jywoo	12.40 (15)	4.35 (4)
Megadeth	10.53 (17)	4.68 (5)
Oscar	10.14 (17)	4.61 (6)
Perfect	12.79 (17)	3.49 (8)
Shlee	12.62 (17)	3.18 (7)
Sjlee	11.71 (13)	4.39 (3)
Woo	13.29 (13)	2.81 (5)
Wooks	19.74 (17)	3.95 (5)
Yanwenry	19.44 (17)	2.78 (4)
Ysoya	20.38 (17)	3.85 (6)
Zeronine	19.26 (21)	3.71 (8)
Minimum	5.30 (13)	1.25 (3)
Maximum	20.38 (21)	4.68 (11)
Average	15.78 (16.52)	3.54 (5.86)

REFERENCES

[1] S. Cho, C. Han, D. Han, and H. Kim, Web-based keystroke dynamics identity verification using neural network, *Journal of organizational computing and electronic commerce 10(4)*, 295-307, 2000.

[2] C. Chang, C. Lin, LIBSVM - A Library for Support Vector Machines, http://www.csie.ntu.edu.tw/ cjlin/libsvm/.

[3] R. Gaines, W. Lisowski, S. Press, and N. Shapiro. Authentication by keystroke timing: some preliminary results. Rand Report R-256-NSF. Rand Corporation, 1980.

[4] J. Leggett, G. Williams, M. Usnick, and M. Longnecker, Dynamic identity verification via keystroke characteristics, *International Journal of Man-Machine Studies*, vol. 35, pp. 859-870, 1991.

[5] L. M. Manevitz, Malik Yousef, One-Class SVMs for document classification, *Journal of Machine Learning Research 2*, 139-154, 2001.

[6] M. Obaidat and S. Sadoun, Verification of computer users using keystroke dynamics, *IEEE Transactions on Systems, Man and Cybernetics, Part B:P Cybernetics*, vol. 27, no. 2, pp. 261-269, 1997.

[7] B. Schölkopf, J. Platt, J. Shawe-Taylor, A.J. Smola, and R.C. Williamson. Estimating the support of a high-dimensional distribution, Technical Report MSR-TR-99-87. Microsoft Research, Redmond, WA, 1999.

[8] B. Schölkopf, R. C. Williamson, A.J. Smola, J. Shawe-Taylor and J.C. Platt. Support vector method for novelty detection. *Advances in Neural Information Processing Systems 12*, 582-588. (Eds.) S.A. Solla, T.K. Leen and K.-R. Mller, MIT Press, 2000.

[9] J. Yang, V. Honavar, Feature subset selection using a genetic algorithm, Feature Extraction, *In Construction, and Subset Selection: A Data Mining Perspective*. Motoda, H. and Liu, H. (Ed.) New York: Kluwer, 1998.

[10] E.Yu, S.Cho, Novelty detection approach for keystroke dynamics identity verification, *Fourth International Conference on Intelligent Data Engineering and Automated Learning*, 2003.

[11] Gen, M., Cheng, R., Genetic algorithm & engineering design, John Wiley & Sons, Inc.

[12] D.M.J. Tax and R.P.W. Duin, Outliers and data descriptions. *Proc. ASCI 2001, 7th annual conference of the advanced school for computing and imaging (Heijen, NL, May 30-June 1)*, ASCI, Delft, 234-241, 2001.

Biomimetic (Topological) Pattern Recognition—

A new Model of Pattern Recognition Theory and Its Application

Wang Shou-jue[1] Chen Xu

Artificial Neural Networks Laboratory, Institute of Semiconductors
Chinese Academy of Sciences
P.O.Box 912, Beijing 100083, P.R.China
([1]wsjue@red.semi.ac.cn)

Abstract–A new theoretical model of Pattern Recognition principles was proposed, which is based on "matter cognition" instead of "matter classification" in traditional statistical Pattern Recognition. This new model is closer to the function of human being, rather than traditional statistical Pattern Recognition using "optimal separating" as its main principle. So the new model of Pattern Recognition is called the Biomimetic Pattern Recognition (BPR)[1]. Its mathematical basis is placed on topological analysis of the sample set in the high dimensional feature space. Therefore, it is also called the Topological Pattern Recognition (TPR). The fundamental idea of this model is based on the fact of the continuity in the feature space of any one of the certain kinds of samples. We experimented with the Biomimetic Pattern Recognition (BPR) by using artificial neural networks, which act through covering the high dimensional geometrical distribution of the sample set in the feature space. Omnidirectionally cognitive tests were done on various kinds of animal and vehicle models of rather similar shapes. For the total 8800 tests, the correct recognition rate is 99.87%. The rejection rate is 0.13% and on the condition of zero error rates, the correct rate of BPR was much better than that of RBF-SVM.

Key words–Pattern Recognition, neural networks, biomimetic, high dimensional geometry

I. INTRODUCTION

Pattern Recognition has been developed for dozens of years. In the 1930s, Fisher proposed a discriminatory analysis method, which used the probability distribution functions of two kinds of known vectors to define a decision rule classifying two kinds of vectors [1]. And then with the development of statistical Pattern Recognition, it is considered that the role of Pattern Recognition is to choose the pattern class with the minimum average risk. Therefore, classification problem is just the same as statistical decision theory [2].

As early as 1974, Vapnik put forward the concept of "optimal classification hyperplane" [3], and proposed Support Vector Machine (SVM) [4] model firstly. It has been attracted much attention in recent years. For years, almost all studies on Pattern Recognition are based on optimal pattern separation of several classes.

In this paper, Pattern Recognition is based on "pattern cognition" instead of "pattern classification". In another word, Pattern Recognition is rooted on "cognition of all sample classes one by one" than on "the classification of many kinds of samples". So, the basic mathematical model of this novel method is definitely different from the traditional Pattern Recognition with the concept of "optimal classification surface".

II. THE DIFFERENCE IN RECOGNITION METHODS BETWEEN THE HUMAN BEING AND THE TRADITIONAL PATTERN RECOGNITION

In the countryside, a child can recognize many things such as cow, sheep, horse, dog, tree, house and so on. But

---

[1] This work was supported by the National Natural Science Foundation of China (No.60135010).

when he suddenly sees a car, which he has never seen before, what will he think of it? Whether he will compare it with the things that he can recognize (for example cow, sheep, horse, dog and so on) and choice the one that looks most like it (as the way of the traditional Pattern Recognition)? He will never think in this way. On the contrary, he will think "I have never seen this object" and "I don't recognize it". This is just the difference between cognition of our human beings and traditional Pattern Recognition. When the human beings recognize, they put particular emphasis on "cognition" and only consider "distinction" seriously in very few cases (such as to tell the distinction between the wolf and the dog or between the horse and the donkey). However, the traditional Pattern Recognition only paid attention to "distinction" and overlooked the concept of "cognition". The novel method proposed in this paper just concentrates on "cognition". Since this idea is greatly distinguished from traditional Pattern Recognition, a new term—"the Biomimetic Pattern Recognition (BPR)" has been introduced to stress the difference. Where "Biomimetic" emphasizes that the view point of the function and mathematical model of Pattern Recognition is the concept of "Cognition", which is much closer to the function of human being. But in respect of hardware or software realization, the new method doesn't embody the concept of "Biomimetic". The distinction between the BPR and traditional Pattern Recognition are showed in Table I.

TABLE I
COMPAREATION OF TRADITIONAL PATTERN RECOGNITION AND BPR

Traditional Pattern Recognition	Biomimetic Pattern Recognition
The optimal classification of many classes of sample	Cognizing different classes of sample one by one
The distinction between one class of sample and limited classes of known sample	The distinction between one class of samples and unknown unlimited different classes of samples
Based on the distinct of samples in different classes	Based on the connection of samples in the same class
To find the optimal classification hypersurface	To find the optimal covering of samples in the same class

This paper proposed the basic idea of the BPR, which is "covering in the hyperspace with the hyper-ellipsoid or hyper-sausage". In the next section, this discipline will be discussed in detail.

III. THE PRINCIPLE OF HOMOLOGY- CONTINUITY OF SAMPLES IN THE SAME CLASS

In real world, if two samples of the same class, the difference between them must be gradually changed. So a gradual change sequence must exist between the two samples (the process of feature abstracting must be continuous mapping). This principle of continuity among samples of the same class in the feature space is called the Principle of Homology-Continuity (PHC). We can get the mathematical description of PHC as follows:

In the feature space R^n, suppose that set A be a point set including all samples in class A. For if $x, y \in A$ and $\varepsilon > 0$ are given, there must be Set B

$$B = \{x_1, x_2, \cdots, x_n \mid x_1 = x, x_n = y, n \subset N, \rho(x_m, x_{m+1}) < \varepsilon, \varepsilon > 0, n-1 \geq m \geq 1, m \subset N\}, B \subset A$$

In the feature space R^n, PHC among samples of the same class is beyond the basic assumption in the traditional Pattern Recognition, but it is a real fact in the real world. It can improve the cognition ability greatly.

Traditional Pattern Recognition aims at get the optimal classification of different classes of sample in the feature space. However, the BPR intends to find the optimal covering of the samples in the same class. The case in two-dimensional space is illustrated as Fig.1. It can be seen that the basic method of BPR is to analyze the relation of training sample in the same class in feature space. And the PHC of sample distribution in the feature space makes it possible.

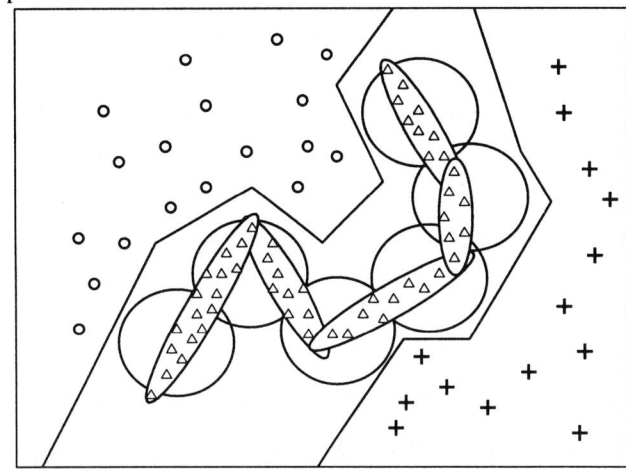

Fig. 1 The schematic diagram of the difference of BP, RBF, and BPR

In Fig.1 the triangles represent samples in one class to be recognized. The circles and crosses represent samples in other different classes. Polygonal line represents the classification manner of traditional Back Propagation (BP) networks. Big circle represents the classification manner of Radial-Basis Function (RBF) networks (which is the same as the template matching). The ellipses as well as sausage-like curves represent "cognition" manner of BPR.

IV. THE MATHEMATICAL TOOLS OF THE BIOMIMETIC PATTERN RECOGNITION

The Principle of Homology-Continuity in the feature space is introduced in the BPR. "Cognizing" one class of matters is essential to analyzing and "cognizing" the shape of infinite points set made up of all samples of the same class. In a mathematical work [5] written by pre-Soviet academician, A.D.Aleksandrov, he pointed out "The concept of topological space is very general, and the science about topological space — topology — is the most general mathematical branch about continuity." The mathematical tool of the BPR is just the method to analyze the manifold in point set topology. So, the BPR is also called the Topological Pattern Recognition (TPR).

In the Biomimetic (Topological) Pattern Recognition, point set of samples of the same class in the feature space R^n is a closed set, denoted by A, which is made up of the mapped "images" (it must be continuous mapping) of corresponding samples in the same class in original sample space. Set A can be a different dimensional manifold varying with the application of the BPR. But stochastic noise will be doubtlessly produced during collecting the training samples and recognizing objects. So, in practical BPR, Set A, the covering set for "cognition" should be replaced with Set P_a.

$$P_a = \{x \mid \rho(x, y) \leq k, y \in A, x \in R^n\}$$

Where k denotes selected distance constant.

Set P_a is n-dimensional. The task of the BPR is to judge whether the mapped "image" of the cognizing object, in the feature space R^n, belongs to set P_a, or not.

V. THE HIGH-DIMENSIONAL SPACE COVERING METHOD FOR RECOGNITION WITH ARTIFICIAL NEURAL NETWORKS

In actual application with BPR, to judge whether the points belong to set P_a, a n-dimensional geometrical shape, covering set P_a, needs to be constructed in the feature space. The geometrical shape is a union of infinite n-dimensional hyperspheres with constant k as radius and infinite points in set A as centers of spheres. In mathematical term, it is the topological product of set A and n-dimensional hypersphere with radius k.

According to dimension theory [6], to divide n-dimensional space into two parts, the interface must be a $(n-1)$-dimensional hyperplane or hypersurface. A neuron in Artificial Neural Networks (ANN) can construct a $(n-1)$-dimensional hyperplane or hypersurface in n-dimensional space. Moreover, a neuron can construct various types of complex closed hypersurface [7]. Therefore, ANN is a very appropriate tool to implement the BPR.

For easier developing the BPR with ANN, hyperspace geometric analysis method for ANN, as a practical tool, has been introduced in our previous published paper [8]. Where, the relations among the point, the line, the surface, the hyperplane, the circle, the sphere and the hypersphere in n-dimensional space were discussed. But hypersurface besides hypersphere wasn't involved. An applied example using n-dimensional hyper-ellipsoid and hyper-sausage in the BPR will be introduced in the following context.

In the experiment, cognized objects (such as naval ship, tank, bus, bow, horse, and sheep) on horizontal plane or sea level are cognized from different directions. Sampling process is to collect the bmp images sampled from different directions (continuous mapping). Then these images were compressed into 256-dimensional samples in feature space. Since observational directions are horizontal, the direction can only vary in one dimension. So, the samples distribution in the feature space is approximate one-dimensional manifold (set A). Considering about the small changes on other directions, the covering shape of the sequence in the feature space can be regarded as a topological product of the one-dimensional manifold and a hypersphere (set P_a). Then, we got

$$S = \{x \mid x = S_i (i = 1, 2, \cdots \text{the total number of samples})\}$$
$$P_a = \{x \mid \rho(x, y) \leq k, y \in A, x \in R^n\}$$

Where:

$$A = \{x \mid x = x_i, i = (1, 2, \cdots, n), n \subset N, \rho(x_m, x_{m+1}) < \varepsilon,$$
$$\rho(x_1, x_n) < \varepsilon, \varepsilon > 0, n - 1 \geq m \geq 1, m \subset N\}, A \subset R^n, S \subset A$$

We can sample the train data set along with the one-dimensional manifold, on the condition that the distances of every two adjoining samples in feature space are approximately near a constant value, which varied from 1/26 to 1/50 of the total length of one-dimensional manifold. We can find the union of some line segments (sets B_i) approximately to the one-dimensional manifold. So the union of hyper-sausages, the topological product of line segments and hyperspheres, can be a suitable basic shape (sets P_i) to cover the region of samples of the same class in the feature space approximately (set P_a').

Consider the original samples set S, let S' be a subset of S with j elements, as follows:

$$S' = \{x \mid x = S_i' (i = 0, 1, 2, \cdots, j), \rho(S_i', S_{i+1}') \leq d \leq \rho(S_{i-1}', S_{i+1}'),$$
$$\text{where d is selected constant}, S_0' = S_j'\}, S' \subset S$$

Let j neurons cover P_a approximately, and then the covering of $i-th$ neuron P_i is:

$$P_i = \{x \mid \rho(x, y) \leq k, y \in B_i, x \in R^n\}$$
$$B_i = \{x \mid x = \alpha S_i' + (1 - \alpha) S_{i+1}', \alpha = [0-1]\}$$

The covering of all j neurons is: $P_a' = \bigcup_{i=0}^{j-1} P_i$

VI. EXPERIMENTS AND RESULTS

In the experiments, the following eight objects were used: lion, rhinoceros, tiger, dog, tank, bus, car, and pumper as shown in Fig.2. The sampling was done while rotating each object through 360 degrees. For each object, we got 400 samples. These total 3200 samples are called the First Samples Set. Later, the sampling was done in the same way and provided us the Second Samples Set with another 3200 samples.

Subsequently, other six object models were used for rejection testing. They are cat, pug, zebra, lionet, polar bear, and elephant as shown in Fig.3. Each object was sampled 400 times in the same way mentioned above. So the Third Samples Set has 2400 samples.

The main steps and results of the experiments are as follows:

1) According to the different distances of every two adjoining samples in the First Samples Set, different numbers of samples are selected from every class as training samples. The number varied from 26 to 50. So, we have eight classes of training sets with totally 338 samples. The SVMs were also trained by LIBSVM-2.35 library [9] as control. For the polynomial kernel (rank 3) SVMs, the parameters were "-s 0 –c 1000 –t 1 –g 1 –r 1 –d 3 –w1 7 –w-1 1", and testing was done with the training set which contained 338 samples.

2) The recognition neural networks of eight classes of objects — $P_a, P_b, \cdots$, etc. were constructed with unified distance parameter k. And the number of neurons is equal to the number of samples in the training set (338).

3) All 8800 samples in three sample sets are regarded as testing samples for calculating error recognition rate. And in all cases, the error recognition rate is 0.

4) All 6400 samples in the First and Second training set were regarded testing samples for calculating correct recognition rate. The result of BPR is that the total number of samples correct recognized is 6392. Therefore, the correct recognition rate is 99.87%. 8 samples are rejected. So the rejection rate is 0.13%.

5) In the same condition, the correct rate of RBF-SVM was only 99.72% and the sizes of the network trained by SVM are 2598, which is almost 7 times larger than BPR (338).

Fig. 2 Cognition Objects

Fig. 3 Rejection Testing Objects

VII. Discussion and Conclusion

From the above experiment results, we can get following conclusions:

1) Any untrained object will not be recognized incorrectly with the BPR. (In the experiment, even if the outlines of animal's back are very similar, the error recognition rate is 0.) That is just the feature of recognition function of human being and the weak point of traditional Pattern Recognition.

2) In the BPR, each class of samples is trained to be "cognized" one by one. The training of additional class put no affect on the previously acquired knowledge, which is a noticeable advantage of the BPR.

3) In the experiment, the correct recognition rate is 99.87%. The rest 0.13% samples are rejected. (No error recognition) In actual application, such result will be attractive. On the condition of zero error rates, the correct rate of BPR was much better than that of RBF-SVM.

4) From above analysis, we see that, the BPR created a new hopeful way for Pattern Recognition. Our method showed significant improvement and could be used in practical problems in future.

References

[1] Fisher R.A, *Contributions to Mathematical statistics*, J.Wiley, New York, 1952.

[2] Chen JiGao, translated by Qiu BingZhang, Qiu Hu, *Statistic Pattern Recognition*, Beijing institute of Post and Telecommunications publishing company, 1989.

[3] Vapnik V.N and Chervonenkis A.Ja, *Theory of Pattern Recognition*, Nauka, Moscow, 1974.

[4] Boser B, Guyon I and Vapnik V.N., "A Training Algorithm for Optimal Margin Classifiers", Fifth Annual Workshop on Computational Learning Theory, Pittsburgh ACM, 1992, pp. 144 -152.

[5] A.D.Aleksandrov. etc., *Mathematics, Its Essence, Methods and Role*, Vol.3, USSR Academy of Sciences publishing company, Moscow, 1956.

[6] Ryszard Engelking, *Dimension Theory*, PWN-Polish Scientific Publishers-Warszawa, 1978.

[7] Wang Shoujue, Li Zhaozhou, Chen Xingdong, Wang Bainan, "Discussion on the Basic Mathematic model of Neurons in General Purpose Neurocomputer", Acta Electronica Sinica, Vol.29 No.5, May 2001, pp. 577-580.

[8] Wang Shoujue, Wang Bainan, "Analysis and Theory of High-Dimension Space Geometry for Artificial Neural Networks", Acta Electronica Sinica, Vol.30 No.1, Jan 2002, pp. 1-4.

[9] Chih-Chung Chang and Chih-Jen Lin, LIBSVM : a library for support vector machines, 2001. Software

A Feature Extraction of the EEG During Listening to the Music Using the Factor Analysis and Neural Networks

Shin-ichi Ito
University of Tokushima
2-1, Minami-Josanjima
Tokushima, 770-8506, Japan
Email: itwo@is.tokushima-u.ac.jp

Yasue Mitsukura
Okayama University
2-1, Tsushima
Okayama, 700-8530, Japan
Email: mitsue@cc.okayama-u.ac.jp

Minoru Fukumi and Norio Akamatsu
University of Tokushima
2-1, Minami-Josanjima
Tokushima, 770-8506, Japan
Email: fukumi,akamatsu@is.tokushima-u.ac.jp

Abstract

Recently in the world, the research of the electroencephalogram (EEG) interface is done, because it has the possibility to realize an interface that can be operated without special knowledge and technology by using the EEG as a means of the interface. As one of the EEG interface, as for a goal for the final of this research, the EEG control system by any music is constructed. However, the EEG control by music is very difficult because it does not know the music and the causal relation of the EEG clearly. Therefore, the EEG analysis and music analysis is absolutely imperative in this system. In this paper, the EEG analysis method by using the FA and the NN is proposed. The FA is used for extracting the characteristics data of the EEG. The NN is used for estimating extracted the characteristics data of the EEG. Moreover teacher signal data of the NN uses the data of the characteristics data of the music. The characteristics data of music is extracted by using the Bark scale analysis. Finally, in order to show the effectiveness of the proposed method, classifying the EEG pattern is done computer simulations. The EEG pattern is 4 conditions, which are listening to Rock music, Schmaltzy Japanese ballad music, Healing music, and Classical music.

I. INTRODUCTION

Recently in the world, the research of the electroencephalogram (EEG) interface is done, because it has the possibility to realize an interface that can be operated without special knowledge and technology by using the EEG as a means of the interface. The EEG is activities of electric potential inside the brain recorded from the top of the scalp. The EEG is a time series signal to change by the internal factor, which is human's thinking and conditions, or the outside stimulus those are the light and sound [1]-[4]. Moreover, the EEG is the time series signals that more than one factor was intricately intertwined, and the EEG is different by the measurement points of the EEG. Therefore, taking account of these, we must think the EEG analysis method and the measurement point of the EEG.

In this paper, taking account of the EEG interface, we propose the method, which is focused attention on in three points of the following. First of all, the EEG is analyzed by the information of one measurement point because we assume that the information of some measurement points is unfitted in using the EEG interface [4],[5]. Second, the Factor Analysis (FA) is used for the EEG analysis. Because the EEG is the time series signals that more than one factor was intricately intertwined and the EEG contains much noise, the EEG has the information, which is difficult to obtain from direct observation data. Therefore, taking account of the correlation of the time transition of each frequency spectrum of the EEG, the latent structure, which explains that correlation, is analyzed by using the FA. We have attempted to extract the characteristics data of the EEG by using the FA. Finally, the Neural Networks (NN) is used for the EEG analysis. The NN is possible that the non-line relations, which more than one factor was intricately intertwined, are expressed. The NN is used for estimating extracted the characteristics data of the EEG.

In other words, taking account of the EEG interface, we propose the EEG analysis method, which is using the FA and the NN. In order to show the effectiveness of the proposed method, classifying the EEG pattern does computer simulations. The EEG pattern is 4 conditions, which are listening to Rock music, Schmaltzy Japanese ballad music, Healing music, and Classical music.

II. MEASUREMENT OF THE EEG

In this paper, as for a goal for the final of our research, the EEG control system by any music is constructed. This system uses human's physiologic and mental effect, which the music stimulus gives to human. There is causal relationship between the EEG and the music, for instance, α waves appear by listening to Classical music, and β waves appear by listening to Rock music. This system adjusts the outputs of the music automatically by that causal relationship. Moreover, the EEG is controlled by listening to that music, which is adjusted the output of, in this system. In the constructing this system, the EEG analysis and the music analysis are absolutely imperative. The most important part of this system is that the EEG analysis. Therefore, the EEG analysis is done in this paper.

A. The EEG patterns

In this paper, as basic research of constructing the EEG control system, some genre of the music is classified by the EEG. The EEG patterns are 4 conditions, which are listening to Rock music, Schmaltzy Japanese ballad music, Healing music,

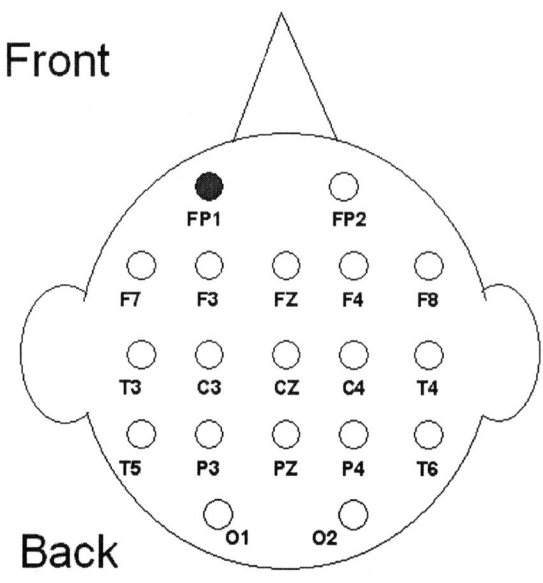

Fig. 1. Measured points of the EEG

and Classical music. We used the following questionnaire to decide the EEG pattern because classifying the genre of the music becomes easier. In addition, the questionnaire is done 20 people, who are boys and girls of twentysomething.

B. Measurement conditions of the EEG

The subjects of this paper were 5 people who are 4 boys (The average age: 22.3 years old) and a girl (age: 23 years old). The electroencephalograph used simple electroencephalograph of the band type. This simple electroencephalograph can be measured under the practical environment. This simple electroencephalograph is made by Brain Function Research & Development Center in Japan. Measurement part place is electrode arrangement FP1 in international 10/20.

As for the data, FFT is being done, and frequency analysis is carried out to 24Hz at intervals of 1Hz by attached analytic software. As a measuring condition, the EEG measuring is carried out in the laboratory with some noise. Then subjects wear a sensor band and headphone. Measuring time is for four minutes in each condition. In addition, the data of using frequency components are from 4Hz to 22Hz. Fig.1 shows measured points of the EEG.

III. THE PROPOSED METHOD

A. The procedure of the proposed method

In this paper, we propose the EEG analysis method, which is using and the FA and the NN. The FA is used for extracting the characteristics data of the EEG. The FA is one of the statistical methods. Then the information that each variate (frequency components) with the correlation has is summarized in small number of latent factor. The FA can be denoising, dimensional compression, latent structure analysis that structure lurks behind each variate with the correlation. In this paper, the model of the FA, which is shown Fig.5, is cross-factor model because we assume that common factor, which responds to particular stimulus, is identified when extracted common factor is noncorrelated [6],[7]. Moreover, taking account of measurement conditions of the EEG, the first common factor shows 'the EEG changing by the music', we think. The common factor is extracted by using principal factor analysis method. In this paper, the characteristics data of the EEG is the data of first factor loading. Then the NN is used for estimating extracted the characteristics data of the EEG. The NN, which is 3-layer class pattern, is used for learning the characteristics data of the EEG, and the EEG pattern classification. Then Back-propagation (BP) method is used for the way of learning the characteristics data of the EEG, and leave-one-out cross-validation (LOOCV) method is used for test method. In addition, Fig.2 shows that the structure of the EEG analysis method.

The EEG analysis method is as follows:

Step1 : The data matrix is composed. In this paper, the line of the data matrix is frequency components and the sequence of the data matrix is time.

Step2 : The correlation matrix R is calculated from the data matrix.

Step3 : The estimate which is entered into diagonal ingredient of the new correlation matrix R* is calculated. In this paper, the estimate is squared multiple correlation coefficient. Then the new correlation matrix R* is composed.

Step4 : The common factor is extracted. In this paper, the method that extracted the common factor by using the principal factor analysis. In addition, the characteristics data of the EEG is the data of the first factor loading. Fig.3 shows the sample of the characteristics data of the EEG.

Step5 : The data of the first factor loading is given as input data of the NN. Then the NN is used for estimating extracted the characteristics data of the EEG.

B. Teacher signal data

In preceding researches, teacher signal data is given 0 or 1 to each output layer unit of the NN to be easy to classify. Table.1 shows when teacher signal data is given 0 or 1. However, when teacher signal data is given 0 or 1, it lacks a generality. Because when classified patterns increased, the number of output layer units of the NN increases. Then as for a goal for the final of this research, the EEG control system by any music is constructed. In this system, the characteristics of music are adjusted automatically with the EEG, and listening to that music controls the EEG. So, the teacher signal data of that music are necessary. However, when teacher signal data is given 0 or 1(0 or 1 teacher signal data), teacher signal data of that music can't be made. Therefore, the versatile teacher signal data are necessary.

We propose giving teacher signal data the characteristics data of the music in this paper. The characteristics data of the

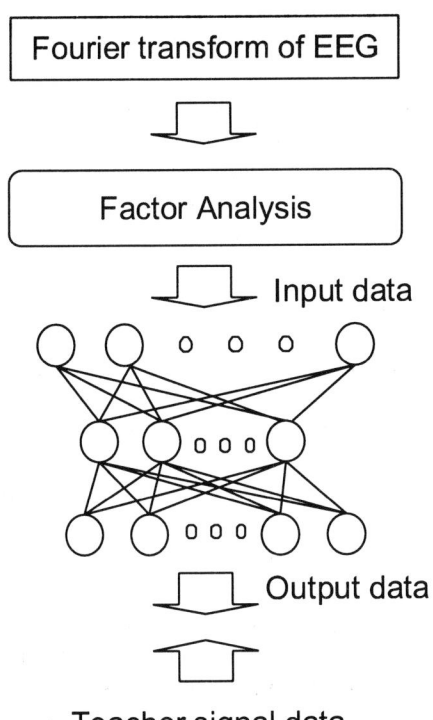

Fig. 2. The structure of the proposed method

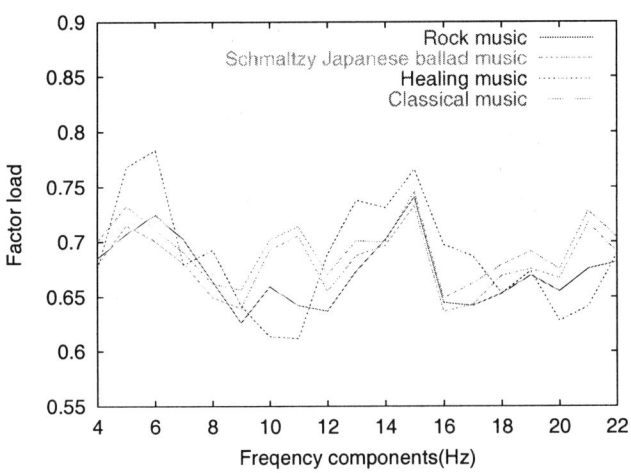

Fig. 3. The characteristics data of the EEG

TABLE I
0 OR 1 TEACHER SIGNAL DATA

	Rock	SJ ballad	Healing	Classical
Output layer unit[1]	1	0	0	0
Output layer unit[2]	0	1	0	0
Output layer unit[3]	0	0	1	0
Output layer unit[4]	0	0	0	1

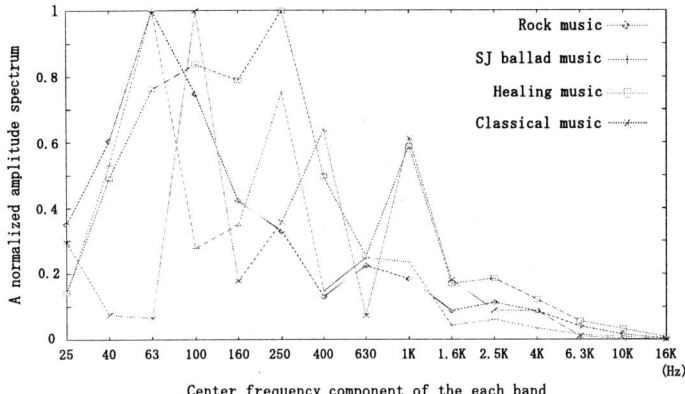

Fig. 4. The Bark scale teacher signal data

music. Consequently, new teacher signal data is the normalized amplitude spectrum of center frequency component of each band (Bark scale teacher signal data). In addition, each bands cope with each output layer unit of the NN. Fig.4 shows the Bark scale teacher signal data.

The judgment method of the classification when using the Bark scale teacher signal data is as follows:

Step1 : The learning data are learned by using the NN.
Step2 : Test data are input to the NN that learning is finished. Then output of test data is computed.
Step3 : The total square error of that output and each teacher signal data is calculated. Then teacher signal data of minimum total squared error is looked for.
Step4 : Teacher signal data of minimum total squared error is set to X. Then the pattern that test data shows is set to Y.
Step5 : When X conforms to Y, it considers that it succeeded in the classification.

C. The conventional method

The conventional method is using a time domain analysis. Time domain analysis is the method of analyzing the time series data from the beginning to the end in accordance with time. There is the method such as (RR50) finding the difference from the data that it was located next to each other, and (average value) of asking the average of the data, and (dispersion or standard deviation) of finding each data and the size of the difference in mean. In others, the band path filter which passes only a certain specific frequency for the time series data, and obtaining with-time change of a specific frequency ingredient further.

music is extracted by using the Bark scale analysis (BSA). The BSA is the method that the frequency components of the music that frequency is analyzed is divided into the band based on the Bark scale. In addition, The Bark scale is defined so that the critical bands of human hearing have a width of one Bark. In this paper, the frequency components of the music that frequency is analyzed are divided 15 bands based on the Bark scale (25Hz, 40Hz, 63Hz, 100Hz, 160Hz, 250Hz, 400Hz, 630Hz, 1kHz, 1.6kHz, 2.5kHz, 4kHz, 6.3kHz, 10kHz, 16kHz). Then the normalized amplitude spectrum of center frequency component of each band is the characteristics data of the

TABLE II
THE PARAMETER OF THE NN

The number of input layer units	19
The number of hidden layer units	5
The number of output layer units	4 or 15
The number of learning	50,000
The step size	0.1-0.3

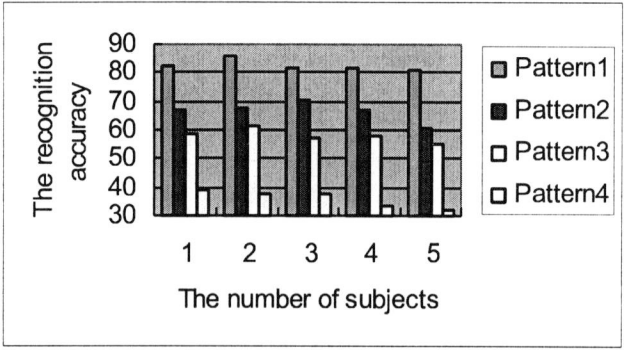

Fig. 5. The recognition accuracy

The time transition of each frequency spectrum of the EEG, which is given by the simple electroencephalography, is different by each EEG pattern. Then the dispersion of each frequency spectrum of the EEG is different by each EEG pattern, too. Therefore, a simple technique in the time domain analysis of asking the dispersion of the time is used in this paper [8].

IV. COMPUTER SIMULATIONS

In this simulation, the EEG pattern is classified. The EEG pattern is 4 conditions, which are listening to Rock music, Schmaltzy Japanese ballad music, Healing music, and Classical music. In addition, the subjects of this paper were 5 people who are 4 boys (the average age: 22.3 years old) and 1 girl (age: 23 years old).

Furthermore, the parameter of the NN is shown in the Table 2. In addition, the step size and the number of hidden layer in parameter of the NN are being found experientially. The number of output layer is 4 or 15. When using 0 or 1 teacher signal data, the number of output layer is 4. When using the Bark scale teacher signal data, the number of output layer is 15.

V. THE RESULT AND CONSIDERATION

Fig.5 shows the result of simulation. In addition, shown the result is used for total 4 patterns. Pattern 1 is in the case of using the proposed method and using teacher signal data is given 0 or 1. Pattern 2 is using the proposed method and using teacher signal data is the Bark scale teacher signal data. Pattern 3 is using the conventional method and using teacher signal data is given 0 or 1. Pattern 4 is using the conventional method and using teacher signal data is the Bark scale teacher signal data.

When the proposed method (Patttern1 or Pattern2) is compared with the conventional method (Pattern3 or Pattern4), the recognition accuracy of the proposed method is better than the recognition accuracy of the conventional method. This result suggests that the noise contained in the EEG was removed to some extent by using the FA, because using the characteristics data of the EEG, which is the data of the first factor loading, taking account of measurement of the EEG. Then, this result suggests that abstracted factor loading of first factor have characteristics of the EEG. Moreover, this result suggests that considering the time transition of each frequency spectrum of the EEG has a beneficial effect on extracting the characteristics data of the EEG. When 0 or 1 teacher signal data (Pattern1 or Pattern 3) is compared with the Bark scale teacher signal data (Pattern2 or Pattern4), the recognition accuracy of the Bark scale teacher signal data is worse than the recognition accuracy of 0 or 1 teacher signal data. The Bark scale teacher signal data is able to be the versatile teacher signal data. However, the distance between teacher signal data or the relation between teacher signal data is not fixed. For this reason, the portion that overlaps between teacher signal data arises, and incorrect recognition is caused.

VI. CONCLUSION

In this paper, taking account of the EEG interface, the simple electroencephalograph of the band type was used to measure the EEG. Additionally, we propose the EEG analysis method, which is using and the FA and the NN. The FA is used for extracting the characteristics data of the EEG. The NN is used for estimating extracted the characteristics data of the EEG. Moreover, teacher signal data of the NN is using the Bark scale teacher signal data. In order to show the effectiveness of the proposed method, classifying the EEG pattern is done. The EEG pattern is 4 conditions, which are listening to Rock music, Schmaltzy Japanese ballad music, Healing music, and Classical music. When the proposed method (Patttern1 or Pattern2) is compared with the conventional method (Pattern3 or Pattern4), the recognition accuracy of the proposed method is better than the recognition accuracy of the conventional method. When 0 or 1 teacher signal data (Pattern1 or Pattern 3) is compared with the Bark scale teacher signal data (Pattern2 or Pattern4), the recognition accuracy of the Bark scale teacher signal data is worse than the recognition accuracy of 0 or 1 teacher signal data.

When 0 or 1 teacher signal data is compared with the Bark scale teacher signal data, the recognition accuracy of the Bark scale teacher signal data is worse than the recognition accuracy of 0 or 1 teacher signal data. For this reason, the portion that overlaps between teacher signal data arises, and incorrect recognition is caused. Therefore, that problem should be solved. The future direction of this study will be to solve that problem.

REFERENCES

[1] O. Fukuda. T. Tsuji. and M. Kaneko. Pattern Classification of a Time-Series EEG Signal Using a Neural Network, *IEICE (D-II)*, *vol.J80-D-II*, *No.7*, pp.1896-1903, (1997)

[2] H. Tanaka. and H. Ide. Intention Transmitting by the Single-Trial MRCP Analysis, *T.IEE Japan*, *vol.122-C*, *No.5*, (2002)

[3] S. Yamada. Improvement and Evolution of an EEG Keyboard Input Speed, *IEICE (A)*, *vol.J79-A*, *No.2*, pp.329-336, (1996)

[4] T. Shimada. T. Shina. and Y. Saito. Auto-Detection of Characteristics of Sleep EEG Intergrating Multi Channel Information by Neural Networks and Fuzzy Rule, *IEICE (D-II)*, *vol.J81-D-II*, *No.7*, pp.1689-1698, (1998)

[5] S. Tasaki. T. Igasaki. N. Murayama. and H. Koga. Relationship between Biological Signals and Subjective Estimation While Humans Listen to Sounds, *T.IEE Japan*, *vol.122-C*, *No.9*, pp.1632-1638, (2002)

[6] L. R. Tuckey. and R. C. MacCallum. *Exploratory Factor Analysis*, Ohio State University, Columbus, (1997)

[7] A. L. Comrey. and H. B. Lee. *A First Course in Factor Analysis*, Lawrence Erlbaum Assoc, (1978)

[8] S. ITO. Y. MITSYKURA. M. FUKUMI. and N. AKAMATSU. The EEG Detection System Using Neural Networks Based on Genetic Algorithm, *IEICE Tech. Report NC2002-29*, pp.61-651, 2002.

Gene Expression Data Analysis Using Support Vector Machines

Feng Chu and Lipo Wang

School of Electrical and Electronic Engineering
Nanyang Technological University
Block S1, Nanyang Avenue, Singapore 639798
E-mail: elpwang@ntu.edu.sg

Abstract—Cancer classification is an important problem both for clinical treatment and for biomedical research. Considering the good performance of support vector machines (SVMs) on solving pattern recognition problems, we use a C-SVM to process the B-cell lymphoma data. Principal Components Analysis (PCA) is used for gene selection. A voting scheme is used to do multi-group classification by k(k-1) binary SVMs. The classification results show that SVMs are effective tools for this problem.

Index Terms—Cancer Classification, Gene Expression Data, Microarry, Principal Component Analysis, Support Vector Machine

I. Introduction

Microarrays are also called DNA chips. Through this newly appeared technology, researchers are able to analyze expression information of thousands of genes simultaneously. One of the important applications of microarrays is cancer classification. For example, lymphoma, a kind of cancer, has several subtypes. The clinical treatment to different subtypes should also be different. Unfortunately, traditional methods are not able to give a reliable classification of these subtypes. Therefore, microarry has been used in this field in recent years. [1]-[2]

Support Vector Machines (SVMs) pioneered by Vapnik and his colleagues [3]-[5], try to find optimal hyperplane for separable patterns. Compared with other kinds of supervised learning techniques, SVMs pay much more attention to the points (vectors) with shortest distance to the optimal separation hyperplane, i.e., the support vectors. Among the whole dataset, only very small parts are support vectors. That means only a small set of crucial vectors play key roles in classification. This feature makes SVM a powerful tool in pattern recognition. Actually, SVMs have already been used in the fields such as handwritten character recognition, human face recognition, radar target identification, and gene expression data analysis as well. [11]-[14]

In this paper, SVMs will be used to classify the lymphnoma microarray dataset from Alizadeh and et al. [6]. In this set of data, samples belong to three classes, i.e., diffuse large B-cell lymphoma (DLBCL), follicular lymphoma (FL), and chronic lymphocytic lymphoma (CLL). The objective of the work is to classify these three kinds of lymphomas by using SVM. All the data is available on the web site (http://llmpp.nih.gov/lymphoma). This paper is organized as follows. Section II describes the formation and pre-processing of the Microarray dataset. The method fulfilling gene feature selection is elaborated in the subsequent section. In section IV, foundations of SVMs are provided. Experimental results and discussions are given in sections V and VI. Finally, conclusions are made and some future works are suggested.

II. Microarry Dataset

A. Dataset

One microarry experiment (one sample) usually conducts several thousands hybridizations. One hybridization process means one specific gene takes part in the experiment. To get meaningful results, in one microarray dataset, there are usually several tens to over one hundred experiments. One experiment can be seen as an input vector. The number of genes will determine the dimension of the input vector. In the dataset we use, there are 4026 genes. Therefore, the input vector's dimension is 4026. The whole dataset contains 62 experiments (samples). Among these samples, we randomly chose 31 to train the SVM classifier; we use the rest 31 samples to test the classification result. In the samples for testing, 21 belong to DLCL, 4 belong to FL, and 6 belong to CLL.

Because not all the genes take part in all the experiments and because not all the hybridization process are successful, it is very common for microarray to have some missing data in the input vectors. We put zero to the places where data are missing.

B. Normalization

To limit the influence of different distributions of the input vectors on classification, we normalize all the input vectors with the below methods:

$$\overline{X(j)} = \frac{X(j)}{Max(X_j) - Min(X_j)}$$

Where $\overline{X(j)}$ is normalized j-th attribute of vector X, $Max(X_j)$ and $Min(X_j)$ are the maximum and minimum of the j-th attribute in the dataset. X(j) is the original value.

III. Gene (Feature) selection

According to Cover's theorem on the separability of patterns [7], vectors in a higher dimensional space are more likely to be separated than vectors in lower dimensional space. However, using too high dimensional input vectors will require much more computing resources. Therefore, casting the input vectors to a space with reasonable number of dimension is an important preprocessing before classification.

In our approach, principal components analysis (PCA) [8] is used for feature selection.

PCA is a classical dimension reduction method. It transforms the data set into a new space described by principal components (PC's). All the PC's are orthogonal and they are ordered according to the absolute value of their eigenvalues. The k-th PC is the vector with the k-th biggest eigenvalue. In fact, the PC's indicate the directions with largest variations of input vectors. Because PCA choose vectors with biggest eigenvalues, it can cover most of directions in which big variations happen in the input dataset. PCA also rejects some directions, because vector variations in these directions are very small, therefore, such variations can be looked as "noise" Furthermore, by calculating the sum of all the absolute values of all the PC's eigenvalues, we can estimate the percentage of the newly obtained dataset compared with the original dataset.

In microarray data analysis, PCA can be used both for experiments and for genes. In lymphoma dataset, because the genes greatly outnumber the experiments, we use PCA to select genes. After this preprocessing, 62 genes with greatest eigenvalues are chosen. The eigenvalues and their tendency of change are showed in Fig 1.

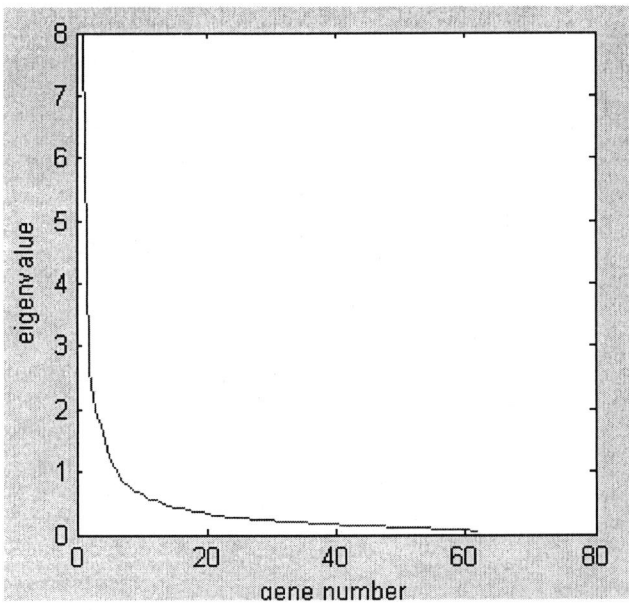

Fig 1. The variation of PCs' eigenvalues.

IV. Support Vector Machines

A. Binary SVM classifier

Support Vector Machines are comparatively new learning method. Just like multilayer perceptrons (MLP) and radial basis function (RBF) networks, SVMs are universal approximators. Their good performance on pattern recognition classification attracts researchers to work on them.

In our approach, we use a C-SVM. The basic idea of this C-SVM can be described as below. [15]

Given training vectors $x_i \in R^n, i=1,...,l,$ in two classes, vector $y \in R$ and $y_i \in \{1, -1\}$, C-SVM can solve the following primal problem:

Find the optimum values of weight vector w and bias b such that they satisfy the constraint

$$y_i(w^T \phi(x_i) + b) \geq 1 - \xi_i,$$
$$\xi_i \geq 0, i = 1,...,l.$$

Where $\phi(x_i)$ is a function mapping i-th pattern vector to a potentially much higher dimensional feature space. Also, the weight vector w and the slack variables ξ_i should minimize the cost function:

$$\psi(w,\xi) = \frac{1}{2} w^T w + C \sum_{i=1}^{l} \xi_i$$

Where C is a positive constant term.

This primal problem also has a dual:

Find the Lagrange multipliers $\alpha_i, i=1,...,l$, that minimize the objective function:

$$\theta(\alpha) = \frac{1}{2} \alpha^T Q \alpha - e^T \alpha$$

Subject to the constraints:

$$0 \leq \alpha_i \leq C,$$
$$y^T \alpha = 0,$$

Where e is the vector of all ones, C (>0) is the upper bound, Q is a l x l positive semi-definite matrix, $Q_{ij} \equiv y_i y_j K(x_i, x_j)$, and $K(x_i, x_j) \equiv \phi(x_i)^T \phi(x_j)$ is the kernel. Here training vectors x_i are mapped into a higher dimensional space by the function ϕ.

The decision function that discriminates different pattern classes can be expressed as:

$$sign(\sum_{i=1}^{l} y_i \alpha_i K(x_i, x) + b)$$

B. Multi SVM classifiers

In practical applications, it is very common that there are more than two classes in the dataset. Therefore, binary SVM classifiers are usually not enough to solve a whole problem.

In these cases, a group of binary SVM classifiers are used. Each classifier is responsible for classifying two classes. For any two classes, there must be one (and only one) classifier taking charge of the classification. Therefore, for a dataset with k classes, k(k-1)/2 binary classifiers are used. To get the ultimate result, a voting scheme is used. [9] For every input vector, all the classifiers give their votes so there will be k(k-1)/2 votes, when all the classification (voting) finished, the vector is designated to the class gets highest number of votes. If one vector gets highest votes for more than one class, it is randomly designated to one of them.

V. Classification results

We randomly divide the whole 62 samples into two parts, 31 for training and 31 for testing. To find the classification results using different gene groups, first, we feed the data with only one gene to the SVM. After the SVM finish the classification, we add one gene to the input data, and then do classification again. We do this "classification then add gene" again and again until all the genes are fed to the SVM. We feed the genes in the order given out by PCA. The first gene is the one whose eigenvalue has biggest absolute eigenvalue.

The classification results are shown in Table 1. In this table, Gen No. is the number of genes fed into the classifier. The numbers showed under DLCL, FL, CLL are the numbers of the samples correctly classified in these classes. As mention in the former part, among the testing samples, there are 21 DLCL, 4 FL, and 6 CLL. The rate in the chart gives the classification accuracy (Fig 2).

Table 1. Classification Accuracy Vs. the Number of Genes Included.

Gen No.	DLCL	FL	CLL	Accuracy
1	21	0	0	0.677419
2	21	0	0	0.677419
3	21	0	0	0.677419
4	19	0	0	0.612903
5	13	0	0	0.419355
6	13	0	0	0.419355
7	13	0	0	0.419355
8	9	0	1	0.322581
9	11	0	1	0.387097
10	10	0	1	0.354839
11	14	1	1	0.516129
12	12	1	1	0.451613
13	12	1	1	0.451613
14	13	1	2	0.516129
15	12	0	2	0.451613
16	13	0	2	0.483871
17	13	0	2	0.483871
18	13	0	2	0.483871
19	13	0	1	0.451613
20	15	1	1	0.548387
21	15	1	1	0.548387
22	16	1	1	0.580645
23	16	1	1	0.580645
24	19	1	1	0.677419
25	18	1	1	0.645161
26	18	1	3	0.709677
27	18	1	1	0.645161
28	19	1	1	0.677419
33	21	1	1	0.741935
37	21	1	1	0.741935
40	21	1	1	0.741935
41	21	1	2	0.741935
44	21	1	2	0.741935
47	21	1	2	0.741935
53	21	1	2	0.741935
54	21	2	2	0.806452
55	21	2	2	0.806452
56	21	3	2	0.83871
58	21	3	2	0.83871
60	21	3	2	0.83871
61	21	3	2	0.83871
62	21	4	6	1

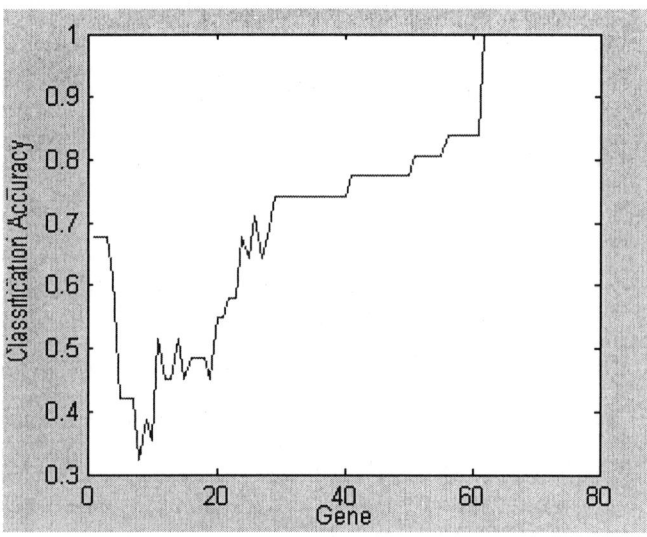

Fig 2. Classification Results Vs. the Number of Genes Included.

From Fig 2, it is can be seen that although there is drop when the number of genes fed in less than 10, the classification accuracy (the accuracy of the number of correctly classification to the number of testing samples, 31) increases gradually when more genes are fed in. At last, when all the 62 genes are fed in, the classification accuracy reaches 100%.

VI. Discussion

Compared with the popular acute myeloid leukemia (AML) and acute lymphoblastic (ALL) data, the B-cell lymphoma data is a relatively new dataset. Robert Tibshirani et al [10] have used "nearest shrunken centroids" method on this dataset. They got 100% classification accuracy with a dataset of 48 genes. From this point of view, their method is successful. Our approach is an much different approach. Compared with statistical classification methods, SVMs are more convenient to use. It is because after a SVM classifier has been trained, the user do not need to train it again when use it for classification. However, for statistical classification methods, all the needed factors must be calculated for every classification. Considering the similar classification accuracy and similar gene numbers to get the optimal result, it can be concluded that using SVMs is more convenient than statistical approach is.

VII. Conclusion and Future Work

Cancer classification based on gene expression data is an important and relatively new pattern recognition problem. From our application of SVM classifiers to B-cell lymphoma gene expression data analysis, it is found that SVMs are a promising tool for this problem. In addition, principal component analysis (PCA) is proved to be an effective way for feature selection in this problem.

In our classification approach, there are still some improvement can possibly be achieved in some aspects. First of all, we can find from the classification results that the classification accuracies show great difference between DLCL, FL and CLL. The unbalanced numbers of DLCL, FL and CLL in training dataset may have caused this. We will consider the unbalance in our future classifiers. In addition, we now replace the missing data with 0, in the future; we will try to find some better methods to handle missing data. Last, in the voting scheme, when more than one highest votes appear, we now randomly designate the sample. We will try to find more appropriate ways for this problem.

We will also use RBF neural networks for processing gene expression data.

REFERENCES

[1] T.R.Golub, D.K.Simon, P.Tamayo, et al, "Molecular Classification of Cancer: Class Discovery and Class Prediction by Gene Expression Monitoring" Science, vol. 286, pp. 531-537, Oct. 1999

[2] Bittner,M et al, "Molecular classification of cutaneous malignant melanoma by gene expression profiling" Nature, vol. 406, pp 536-540, Aug. 2000

[3] Boser. B, I.Guyon, V.N.Vapnik, "A training algorithm for optimal margin classifiers" Fifth Annual Workshop on Computational Learning Theory, pp. 144-152. San Mateo, CA, 1992

[4] Cortes.C, V.Vapnik, "Support vector networks", Machine Learning, vol. 20, pp. 273-297, 1995

[5] V.N.Vapnic, "Statistical learning theory", New York, Wiley, 1998

[6] Ash A. Alizadeh, et al, "Distinct types of diffuse large B-cell lymphoma identified by gene expression profiling" Nature, vol. 403, pp 503-511, Feb. 2002

[7] Cover. T.M., "Geometrical and statistical properties of systems of linear inequalities with applications in pattern recognition", IEEE Transactions on Electronic Computers, vol. EC-14, pp. 326-324, 1965

[8] Simon. Haykin, "Neual networks, a comprehensive foundation" 2nd Editon, New Jersey, Prentice Hall, 1999

[9] B. Scholkopf, C.J.C. Burges, A.J.Smala. "Advances in kernel methods-support vector learning", Cambridge, MA, MIT Press

[10] Robert Tibshirani, Trevor Hestie, et al, "Class prediction by nearest shrunken centroids, with application to DNA microarrays" http://www-stat.stanford.edu/~tibs/research.html

[11] Li Zeyu, Tang Shiwei, Wang Hao, "Fast recognition of handwritten digits using pariwise coupling support vector machine", Neural Networks, 2002. IJCNN'02. Proceedings of the 2002 International Joint Conference on, Volume:1, pp. 878-883, 2002.

[12] Ng, J., Shaogang Gong, "Multi-view face detection and pose estimation using a composite support vector machine across the view sphere", Recognition, Analysis, and Tracking of Faces and Gestures in Real-Time Systems, Proceedings, pp 14-21. 1999.

[13] Zhao, Q., Principe, J. "Support vector machine for SAR automatic target recognition." IEEE Transactions on Aerospace and Electronics, 37(2). Apr. 2001.

[14] Michael P. S. Brown, William Noble Grundy, David Lin, Nello Cristianini, Charles Sugnet, Terrence S. Furey, Manuel Ares, Jr., David Haussler. "Knowledge-based Analysis of Microarray Gene Expression Data Using Support Vector Machines", Proceedings of the National Academy of Sciences. pp262-267. 1997.

[15] Vorgetleg von, "Support vector learning". Oldenbourg Verlage, Munich, 1997.

Robust Recognition Based on Adaptive Combination of Weak Classifiers

Guoping Wang, Misha Pavel and Xubo Song

OGI School of Science & Engineering
Oregon Health & Science University
20000 NW Walker Road
Beaverton, OR 97006
{gpwang@bme, pavel@bme, xubosong@ece}.ogi.edu

Abstract—We describe a novel adaptive method that achieves robustness in pattern classification by combining a large number of weak classifiers. The individual classifiers are trained on subsets of features of the training samples and the output classification is obtained by a weighted sum of the individual weak classifiers. When the classifier is applied to the test set, the combination weights are adaptively adjusted in accordance with the agreement among the individual classifiers. We evaluated the performances of several different combination methods using simulated data and the results proved to be robust.

1. Introduction

A fundamental feature of an intelligent system is its ability to adapt to dynamic and unpredictable conditions. Unlike the biological system that is quite robust when confronted with complex and unpredictable world [1], existing engineering systems are sensitive to the contextual and environmental changes. These systems are typically designed to perform well in well-defined situations and contexts, but exhibit undue sensitivity to irrelevant changes. For example, whereas pattern recognition based on image processing algorithms has been successfully applied in numerous specific domains, the general problem of object recognition is plagued by its dependency on the specific representation, pose and lighting condition.

One possible explanation of the robustness of biological systems is due to their ability to use diverse information from a variety of sources, ranging from their sensory inputs to their prior knowledge. Such representation is redundant and not statistically efficient, but it provides a mechanism to achieve robustness. In contrast, the traditional approach to statistically optimal pattern recognition strives to exploit as much as possible the information in the training data and remove any redundancy. This approach, based on optimal use of training data, will perform poorly when information that is reliable in the training set is compromised in the test set.

Our approach is based on a collection of relatively weak classifiers, each using a different subset of input information. By combining multiple weak classifiers, we are able to compensate for the possibilities that during real-life applications, some of the input information can be lost or masked by noise. As a result, the fused classifier based on a collection of weak classifiers will be more resistant to noise when presented with unseen data and thus achieve robustness.

The critical aspect of our robust system is a rapid adaptation during the test phase in the mismatched environment that is not well represented by the training set. We argue that the analysis of feature subsets by individual classifiers may increase robustness because the system could dynamically adjust the weights in response to the changing conditions as demonstrated in the automatic speech recognition (ASR) systems from the recent work of Hermansky et al. [2] and Bourlard et al. [8]. One problem with these approaches is that the adaptation requires supervised learning. In our algorithm, each weak classifier is trained using only a subset of the features. In this way, whenever a feature subset of the input data is contaminated by noise, only the classifiers that use those particular features will be affected. Robustness is achieved by unsupervised adaptation of the weights associated with the classifiers.

2. Description of the Algorithm

2.1. Formulation of the Problem

We consider pattern classification problems with a large set of input measurements to be classified into a small set of discrete categories. We designate the input measurements by a vector,

$$\mathbf{x} = (x_1, x_2, ..., x_M), \qquad (1)$$

and the category labels associated with each input measurement vector by $c(\mathbf{x})$.

Fig.1 illustrates the formulation of the problem. The measurement vector defined in (1) is one input point in the feature space. The input feature vector is divided (nonexclusively) into separate streams and each stream is classified by a separate classifier module. For example, in a typical speech recognition system, the input acoustic waveform is separated to critical bands and the output of each critical band is an element of the input measurement vector. In our system, the vector of measurements is processed by a number of classifier modules $h_i(\mathbf{x})$, for $i = 1...N$, and the final output is computed by a weighted combination

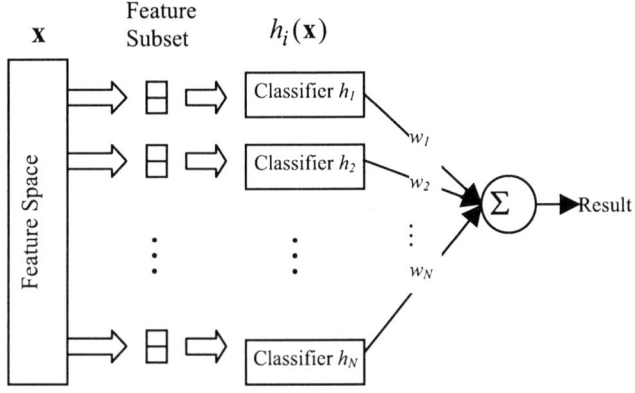

Fig.1. Model of the proposed system

$\sum_{i=1}^{N} w_i h_i(\mathbf{x})$. In the context of the speech-recognition example, the individual modules have access only to a subset of the input measurements. The performance of each classifier module is then limited by the information presented in each sub-band instead of all the features. The desirable performance of the pattern-recognition system is achieved by combining the outputs of the individual classifier modules.

A key assumption underlying this work is that the classifier modules are conditionally independent, given the input class. Formally:

$$P\{h_i(\mathbf{x}) | h_j(\mathbf{x}), c(\mathbf{x})\}$$
$$= P\{h_i(\mathbf{x}) | c(\mathbf{x})\}, \text{ for } i, j = 1...N \quad (2)$$

where $c(\mathbf{x})$ defined the true label of $\mathbf{x}$. The conditional independence assures that each classifier module provides somewhat independent information and the correlation among classifiers is then governed only by the input class. Conditional independence of the classifier modules can be approximated by training on independent subsets of data and using independent measurements.

One of the consequences of the conventional feature space reduction, based on the data in the training set, is that redundant or noisy features are either completely eliminated or the corresponding weights are greatly reduced. This may be the case even for informative features if those features are more variable in comparison to the ones retained. Referring to the speech-recognition example, suppose there are high and low frequency bands that contain similar but noisier information than the middle frequency bands. In this case, the middle frequency bands are assigned higher weights. Now suppose that in a real-life application, the middle bands are contaminated by band-limited noise. These middle-frequency bands will, therefore, loose their superiority for speech recognition. If the weighting is fixed by the training set, the middle frequency bands will determine the overall performance of this classifier, and thus the resulting performance will be quite poor.

In this situation, performance could be improved if the system could automatically reduce the weights of the contaminated classifier modules and increase the weights associated with the others. This adaptation of weights must be accomplished by unsupervised learning in real time. The consequence of the conditional independence assumption is that the classification modules that are more likely to be correct will produce more coherent responses to sequences of inputs [4,5]. The general approach described in this paper consists of computing some measure of coherence and then estimating the value of the weights from this measure.

In Section 2.2 and 2.3, we will describe the training and unsupervised adaptation algorithm in detail.

2.2. Training

The training of our system consists of two stages. In the first stage, we train the individual modules on clean data and the performance of each classifier module depends on the amount of information at the input to the classifier. If the modules are conditionally independent then the optimal combination is a weighted sum of the modular classifier outputs [3]. In the second stage, we determine the optimal weights for combining the individual classifier modules to achieve optimal performance on the training set [3].

2.3. Unsupervised Adaptation

Now, let us describe the adaptation algorithm. The initial weights are those from the training set. During the test, the sample $\mathbf{x}$ is classified by each classifier module h_i, yielding a vector of N outputs $[h_1(\mathbf{x}),...,h_i(\mathbf{x}),...,h_N(\mathbf{x})]$. For simplicity of the computation, we arrange these N outputs in a column vector. After t sample points are classified, we get a $N \times t$ response matrix G, where the element on the ith row and j^{th} column $G(i,j)$ is the output of classifier h_i for the jth point.

In our algorithm, the coherence among the classifier modules is evaluated using pair wise correlation coefficients. For this purpose, we compute a correlation coefficient matrix R that contains the correlation coefficients among classifiers (the row vectors of the response matrix G). The correlation coefficient among the outputs of classifier h_i and h_j is defined as:

$$R(i,j) = \frac{C(i,j)}{\eta_i \eta_j}, \quad i,j = 1...N. \quad (3)$$

where $C(i,j) = E\left\{\left[h_i(\mathbf{x}) - \overline{h_i(\mathbf{x})}\right]\left[h_j(\mathbf{x}) - \overline{h_j(\mathbf{x})}\right]\right\}$

$\approx \sum_{l=1}^{t}\left\{\left[G(i,l) - \frac{1}{t}\sum_{k=1}^{t} G(i,k)\right] * \left[G(j,l) - \frac{1}{t}\sum_{k=1}^{t} G(j,k)\right]\right\}$ is the covariance of the outputs of h_i and h_j, and $\eta_i^2 = E\left\{\left(h_i(\mathbf{x}) - \overline{h_i(\mathbf{x})}\right)^2\right\} \approx \sum_{l=1}^{t}\left[G(i,l) - \frac{1}{t}\sum_{k=1}^{t}G(i,k)\right]^2$ is the variance of the outputs of classifier h_i.

Correlation techniques have been used in previous work, e.g., of Oza and Tumer [9]. In contrast, our algorithm is using the correlation among the classifiers instead of the features.

An alternative (computationally simpler) approach to using the correlation is to use the Hamming distances among classifiers to assess their coherence. In particular, we compute the Hamming distance matrix D, in which the ith row, j^{th} column element $D(i,j)$ is the hamming distance of the responses of h_i and h_j on the training set. We then compute the reciprocal of each element of the distance matrix to form the agreement matrix of the classifiers. The resulting matrix approximates the correlation matrix.

The next step is to use these measures of coherence to compute the weights for different classifier modules. The correlation matrix will be used to increase weights of classifiers that are highly correlated with other classifiers. Therefore, prior to using the correlation matrix, we replace its diagonal elements, representing autocorrelations, by zeros. The resulting weight is computed by a so called "correlation max" method illustrated as follows.

To compute the weights, our algorithm first searches for the largest correlation, for example, $R(i,j)$. The corresponding classifier modules are assigned the weights $w_i = w_j = R(i,j)$. Then, we determine the next classifier h_k that has the largest average correlation $\max_k\{[R(i,k)+R(j,k)]/2\}$ with h_i and h_j, and assign this correlation coefficient to h_k's weight, i.e., $w_k = \frac{R(i,k)+R(j,k)}{2}$. This procedure is repeated until all the weights are assigned; the final weights are normalized so they sum to one.

Similarly, for computational simplicity, we can use the agreement matrix derived from Hamming distance instead of the correlation coefficient matrix and apply the previous procedure, then we can get the "Hamming max" method.

Once we have the weights for all the classifiers, we can use them to get the final decision by linearly combining all the decisions from the individual classifiers.

3. EVALUATION BY SIMULATION

We evaluate our algorithm formulated in Section 2 by simulating a 2-category classification problem such that $c(\mathbf{x}) \in \{0,1\}$.

In our simulation, we assume that the signal variances are the same for all the features. We then can use the variances of the features to represent their informativeness. The variances on the test and training sets are chosen to illustrate the condition that a subset of the features is more informative because they have lower variances than the remaining features.

The data set consists of input vectors with M elements $(x_1, x_2, ..., x_M)$ that are independent, normally-distributed random variables, where $x_i \sim N\left(\mu_i^{(c)}, \sigma_i^{TR(c)}\right)$ or $x_i \sim N\left(\mu_i^{(c)}, \sigma_i^{TE(c)}\right)$, depending on whether it is drawn from training or test set. The prior probabilities for both categories are equal. The test set has the same means as the training set, but some features are contaminated by large noise represented by large variances. In particular, we assume that the category means are the same for the training set and test set:

for category 0, $\quad \mu_i^{(0)} = 0, \quad i = 1...M,$ (4)

for category 1, $\quad \mu_i^{(1)} = 5, \quad i = 1...M,$ (5)

The variances of the training set and test set are different: for category 0 and category 1 in the training set:

$$\sigma_i^{TR(0)} = \sigma_i^{TR(1)} = \begin{cases} 3, & \text{for } i = 1...K; \\ 1, & \text{for } i = K+1...M; \end{cases} \quad (6)$$

and for category 0 and category 1 in the test set:

$$\sigma_i^{TE(0)} = \sigma_i^{TE(1)} = \begin{cases} 3, & \text{for } i = 1...K; \\ 1+\varepsilon, & \text{for } i = K+1...M; \end{cases} \quad (7)$$

where $\varepsilon \sim N(100,10)$ is a normally-distributed random variable representing the noise added to the feature.

To simplify this simulated example, we designed the classifier modules so that each module depends only on one feature. In other words, the number of classifier module N and the number of features M are identical. By design, in the training set, the first K classifiers use the more variable (noisier) features and the remaining $M-K$ use the less variable features.

Since each classifier operates on a single normally-distributed feature, the design of the optimal classifier, which maximizes the probability of correct classification $h_i(\mathbf{x}) = c(\mathbf{x})$, is quite simple. We start by denoting the grand mean of the two categories of the ith feature by: $\alpha_i = \frac{\mu_i^{(0)} + \mu_i^{(1)}}{2}, \quad i = 1...M$, where $\mu_i^{(0)}$ is the mean of the ith feature in category 0 as defined in (4), and $\mu_i^{(1)}$ is the mean of the ith feature in category 1 as defined in (5). Then, the M optimal classifiers $H = \{h_i, i = 1...M\}$, can be written in terms of a decision based on the value of each feature:

$$h_i(\mathbf{x}) = \begin{cases} 1, & \text{if } x_i > \alpha_i \\ 0, & \text{otherwise} \end{cases}, \quad i = 1...M \quad (8)$$

The discriminating performance of each classifier is limited by the fact that it can use only one feature instead of all the features. The output of combined classifier is determined by a weighted combination of the individual classifier modules. The optimal weights for the training set are determined by first assessing the performance of each classifier module in terms of the probability of true positive and the probability of false positive and then the weights are given by [1,3,6,7]:

$$w_i(\mathbf{x}) = \log \frac{p_i(\mathbf{x})(1-q_i(\mathbf{x}))}{q_i(\mathbf{x})(1-p_i(\mathbf{x}))} \qquad (9)$$

where $p_i(\mathbf{x}) = P\{h_i(\mathbf{x}) = 1 | c(\mathbf{x}) = 1\}$ is the probability of true positive response and $q_i(\mathbf{x}) = P\{h_i(\mathbf{x}) = 1 | c(\mathbf{x}) = 0\}$ is the probability of false positive response.

Equation (9) is derived by assuming conditional independence of each classification module. The weights obtained using (9) are optimal in that they maximize the probability of correct classification. Even with the optimal weights, the overall performance is less accurate than the optimal Bayesian classifier because of the nonlinear, discrete output of each modular classifier. This difference, however, diminishes with the increasing number of features and dimensions.

Having generated Gaussian distributed data with the parameters specified by (4), (5), (6), (7) and used the aforementioned procedure to get the optimal weights after the training, we then apply the adaptation algorithm described in Section 2 on the test set and the results are shown in Fig.2, From the results shown in Fig.2, it is clear that our "correlation max" algorithm can quickly adapt the weights to optimal – increase the weights of the uncontaminated classifiers and at the same time reduce the weights associated with the others, without any knowledge of the true label of the sample point. However, the error rate is very high when using the fixed weights trained from the training set. Another observation is that our algorithm greatly outperformed the majority rule.

Here, we use a very simple example to illustrate this point. We assume that among M classifiers, K classifiers are perfect (100% correct), the other $M-K$ classifiers just randomly guess, and then what will the error rate look like? In this case, the correct probability of the majority rule is:

$$Pc(K,M) = P\left\{\left(K + \sum_{i=K+1}^{M} h_i(x_i)\right) \geq \frac{M}{2}\right\}$$

$$= P\left\{\sum_{i=K+1}^{M} h_i(x_i) \geq \frac{M}{2} - K\right\}.$$

Because $h_i(x_i)$ is just random guess for $i = K+1...M$, $\hat{H} = \sum_{i=k+1}^{M} h_i(x_i)$ has a binomial distribution $\beta(M-K, 0.5)$. Thus, the correct probability $Pc(K,M)$ can be calculated as follows:

$$P\{\hat{H} \geq \frac{M}{2} - K\} = 1 - P\{\hat{H} < \frac{M}{2} - K\}$$

$$= 1 - \sum_{i=0}^{\frac{M}{2}-K-1} \binom{M-K}{i} 0.5^i * 0.5^{M-K-i} \qquad (10)$$

$$= 1 - 0.5^{M-K} * \sum_{i=0}^{\frac{M}{2}-K-1} \binom{M-K}{i}$$

To make it clearer, let us draw a figure of $Pc(K,M)$ as a function of K and M in Fig.3.

In Fig.3, from left to right, each line represents the correct rate of majority rule with the number of classifiers M varying from 10 to 100, step by 10. Fig.3 shows that even there are K classifiers that act perfectly, when K is small, the correct rate of the classifier is not very high.

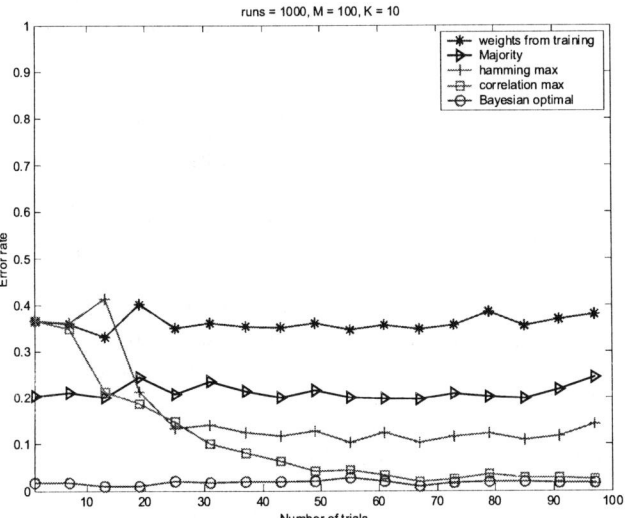

Fig.2. Performances of the different algorithms. The number of the features/classifiers M = 100; the number of the features uncontaminated in the test set K = 10. The curves are obtained by averaging the results $runs$ = 1000 times.

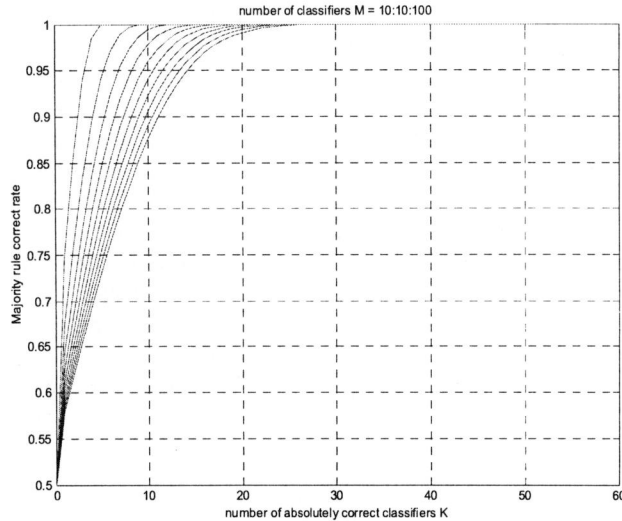

Fig.3. Theoretical performances of majority rule with different number of total classifiers M and perfect classifiers K.

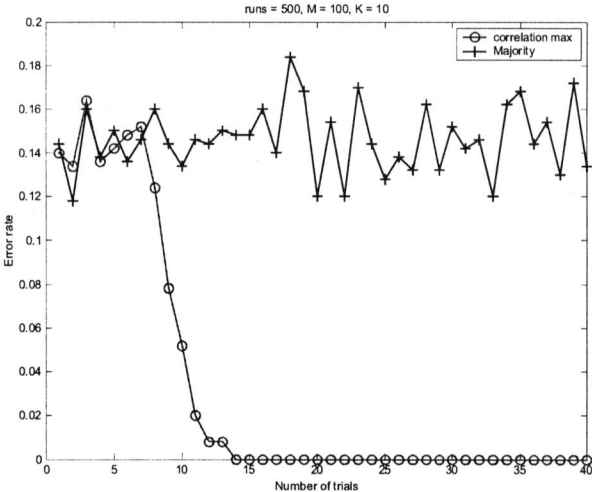

Fig.4. Compare the performance of the majority rule and correlation max with an example. The number of total classifiers $M = 100$. The number of perfect classifiers $K = 10$, the other $M-K = 90$ classifiers only randomly guess. The curves are obtained by averaging the results $runs = 500$ times.

Now we simulate this situation, and compare the performances of the correlation method and the majority rule. From the results shown in Fig.4 we can see that the "correlation max" method can quickly adapt the weights to the good classifiers, but the majority rule can not because it only uses the information in that specific trial and gives the classifiers equal weights without considering the agreement in the history as the correlation method.

4. CONCLUSIONS

In this paper, we have examined a novel adaptive algorithm with improved robustness to changing reliability of inputs. The robustness in pattern classification is achieved by unsupervised adaptation of fusion of a large number of weak classifiers. The unsupervised adaptation is based on the assumption of conditional independence and uses the correlation among the classifiers to determine the combination rule. The general scheme is to decompose the input measurements into multiple subsets (streams), perform classification on the streams and then use the adaptive combination to obtain the resulting classification. Using simulation with simple examples we conclude that:

- Robustness can be achieved in new conditions where some of the features are severely contaminated, because our algorithm can adapt the weights from time to time.
- The performance of our adaptive algorithm in the simulated situations is close to Bayesian rule and is significantly better than the commonly used majority rule combination method.
- Our algorithm is more practical because no *a prior* knowledge is required in terms of the accuracy of each classifier and the quality of the features.

ACKNOWLEDGMENTS

This research was supported by a NASA Grant NCC2-1218 to Oregon Health & Science University. We are grateful to Tomer Hertz for fruitful discussions.

REFERENCES

[1] M. Pavel and H. Hermansky, "Information Fusion by Human and Machine," *First European Conference on Signal Analysis and* Prediction, Strahov Monastery, Prague, Czech Republic, June 24~27, 1997.

[2] H. Hermansky, S. Tibrewala, and M. Pavel, "Towards ASR on Partially Corrupted Speech," *the Fourth International Conference on Spoken Language Processing*, Philadelphia, PA, USA, Oct.3~6, 1996.

[3] R.O. Duda and P.E. Hart, *Pattern Classification and Scene Analysis*, John Wiley & Sons, Inc., 1973

[4] K. Tumer and J. Ghosh, "Classifier Combining: Analytical Results and Implications," Working notes from the Workshop *Integrating Multiple Learned Models, National Conference on Artificial Intelligence*, Portland, Oregon, USA, Aug.4~5, 1996.

[5] K. Tumer and J. Ghosh, "Error Correlation and Error Reduction in Ensemble Classifiers," *Connection Science, Special issue on combining artificial neural networks: ensemble approaches,* Vol. 8, No. 3 & 4, pp. 385-404, 1996.

[6] J. Chen and N. Ansari, "Adaptive Fusion of Correlated Local Decisions," *IEEE Trans. on Systems, Man, and Cybernetics*, Vol. 28, No. 2, pp. 276-281, May 1998.

[7] Z. Chair and P. Varshney, "Optimum Data Fusion in Multiple Sensor Detection Systems," *IEEE Transactions on Aerospace and Electronic Systems*, Vol. 22, No. 1, pp. 98-101, 1986.

[8] H. Bourlard, S. Bengio, and K. Weber, "New Approaches towards Robust and Adaptive Speech Recognition," In T.K. Leen, T.G. Dietterich, and V. Tresp, editors, *Advances in Neural Information Processing Systems, NIPS 13*. MIT Press, 2001

[9] N. C. Oza and K. Tumer, "Input Decimation Ensembles: Decorrelation through Dimensionality Reduction," *Second International Workshop on Multiple Classifier Systems,* Cambridge, UK. 2001

Optimizing Radial Basis Probabilistic Neural Networks Using Recursive Orthogonal Least Squares Algorithms Combined with Micro-Genetic Algorithms

Wenbo Zhao[1,2]   De-Shuang Huang[2]   Lin Guo[2]
1. Department of Automation, University of Science and Technology of China
2. Institute of Intelligent Machines, Chinese Academy of Sciences,
P.O.Box 1130, Hefei, Anhui 230031, China.

Abstract: The paper focuses on discussing how to train and optimize the radial basis probabilistic neural network (RBPNN) structure by Recursive Orthogonal Least Squares Algorithms (ROLSA) combined with Micro-Genetic Algorithms (μ-GA). First, the previous ROLSA, used for optimally selecting the hidden centers of the RBPNN, was improved in two aspects, i.e., adopting new double error criterions and new stop condition. Secondly, the micro-genetic algorithm, used for optimizing the controlling parameter of kernel function, was incorporated in the improved ROLSA in order that the structure of RBPNN can be entirely optimized. Finally, to demonstrate the power of our approach, two examples, i.e., both two spirals classification problem and IRIS classification problem, were employed to validate the performance of the classification. The experimental result showed that, for the two spirals problem the structure of the RBPNN with 200 initial hidden centers was considerably compressed into the one with 30 hidden centers, and for the IRIS classification problem only 9 hidden centers among 75 initial hidden centers were selected for the optimized RBPNN structure. Whereas for the Radial Basis Function Neural Network (RBFNN), under the same condition, for the two spirals problem, there were still 46 hidden centers left, and for the IRIS problem 15 hidden centers were selected into the optimal structure of the RBFNN. Moreover, the experimental results also illustrated that the generalization performance of the optimized RBPNN for the two examples was obviously better than the one of the optimized RBFNN.

1. INTRODUCTION

The radial basis probabilistic neural network (RBPNN) model [1] is in substance developed from the radial basis function neural network (RBFNN) [2] and the probabilistic neural network (PNN) [3]. Therefore, the RBPNN possesses the common characteristic of the original two networks, i.e., the signal is concurrently feed-forwarded from the input layer to the output layer without any feedback connections within the three layers network models. On the other hand, the RBPNN, to some extent, decreases the two original models' demerits. The network structure of the RBPNN, as shown in Fig.1, comprises four layers: one input layer, two hidden layers and one output layer. The first hidden layer is a nonlinear processing layer, which consists of the hidden centers selected from the input training samples set. The second hidden layer selectively sums the output of the first hidden layer according to the categories, which the hidden centers belong to. Namely, the connection weights between the first hidden layer and the second hidden layer are 1's or 0's. The output layer fulfills the nonlinear mapping such as classification, approximation and prediction. In fact, the first hidden layer of the RBPNN takes the vital role in performing the task of the problems solving.

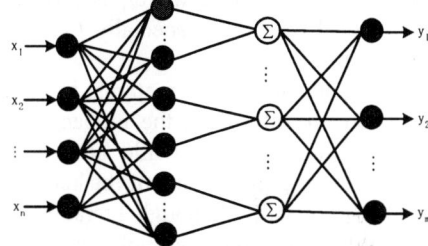

Fig.1 The structure of radial basis probabilistic neural network

Similar to the RBFNN, the hidden centers number and locations as well as the controlling parameters (or the shape parameters) of kernel function in the RBPNN are quite important indices. Over hidden centers will lead to so lengthy training and testing time while too few hidden centers can lead to quite great convergent error. So an appropriate number of hidden centers are very important for the RBPNN to be used to solve the specific problem. In addition, the controlling parameter of kernel function, also referred to as the receptive width, is another important index of the RBPNN. Similar to human visual nervous system, if the width value is chosen to be too great, the particular of an objection can be lost. Especially, from Fig.1, it can be seen that the hidden centers are correlative with the controlling parameters in the RBPNN structure. In fact, the first hidden layer of RBPNN accomplishes the hyper-separation and overlay for training samples space. We have experienced that the different number and locations of hidden center vectors can require especial controlling parameter in order to realize the entire overlay of training samples space. On the other hand, the chosen controlling parameter can corporate with especial

---

This work was supported by NSF of China and the Grant of "Hundred Talents Program" of Chinese Academy of Sciences of China

number and locations of the hidden center vectors to satisfy the entire overlay requirement. The tightly correlative characteristic between the hidden center vectors and controlling parameters determines that while investigating the structure optimization these factors must be simultaneously considered.

As for the selection of the hidden centers, literature [4] proposed applying the genetic algorithm (GA) to optimize the number and the location of the hidden centers. It is well known that the inherent merit of the GA is its potential global searching ability in theory, but when solving a practical problem, time and computation consuming problem still requires consideration. To optimize the RBPNN, [5] introduced a useful algorithm called the recursive orthogonal least square algorithm (ROLSA), which was first successfully used to train and optimize the RBFNN structure in [6]. Literature [5] showed that the telling-two-spirals-apart problem had been perfectly classified, and the initial hidden centers had been sufficiently well compressed and optimally selected in number and locations by this ROLSA. Compared with the GA [4], the computational complexity of the ROLSA is much smaller. The latter, however, is prone to converge toward a poor local optimum, especially for those problems with multiple extremums.

Nevertheless, both introduced methods in [4] and [5] had only investigated on optimizing the hidden centers number and locations of the RBPNN, while how to concurrently optimize the controlling parameters of the kernel function has not been so far discussed. Although literature [7] offered a heuristic relation equation for solving the controlling parameters, our experience shows that the equation is impossible to be widely applied into all real-world problems. This paper will be intended for entirely optimizing the RBPNN structure (including hidden centers number and locations as well as the controlling parameters) by means of an approach combining the ROLSA with the GA. In other words, a new ROLS-GA is proposed in this paper to implement the optimization of the neural networks like the RBPNN.

II. THE IMPROVEMENT OF ROLSA USED FOR SELECTING THE HIDDEN CENTERS

Assume that Y_d, H and $J(W)$, respectively, denote the desired signal matrix, the output matrix of the second hidden layer and the cost function of the RBPNN. In the form of F-norms, the cost function of the RBPNN can be given by

$$J(W) = \|Y_d - HW\|_F^2 \quad (1)$$

with the signal $\|\bullet\|_F$ representing the F-norm, and W the weight matrix between the second hidden layer and the output layer. By conducting the orthogonal decomposition operation, H can be expressed as

$$H = Q[R, 0]^T \quad (2)$$

with Q representing an orthogonal matrix corresponding to H, and R an upper triangle square matrix. By using Q^T to in left-hand multiply the desired signal matrix Y_d, there gives:

$$Y_d = Q[\hat{Y} \quad \tilde{Y}]^T \quad (3)$$

with $\hat{Y}$、$\tilde{Y}$ respectively denoting the orthogonalized desired signal matrix and the residual error matrix.

Substituting (2) and (3) into (1), yielding:

$$J(W) = \left\| Q\left([\hat{Y} \quad \tilde{Y}]^T - [R,0]^T W \right) \right\|_F^2 \quad (4)$$

Since the F-norm of a matrix is preserved by an orthogonal transformation, (4) is equivalent to the following equation.

$$J(W) = \left\| \begin{bmatrix} \hat{Y} \\ \tilde{Y} \end{bmatrix} - \begin{bmatrix} R \\ 0 \end{bmatrix} W \right\|_F^2 = \|\hat{Y} - RW\|_F^2 + \|\tilde{Y}\|_F^2 \quad (5)$$

By minimizing the cost function $J(W)$ of (5), W can be given by

$$W = R^{-1}\hat{Y} \quad (6)$$

The term $\|\tilde{Y}\|_F^2$ of the right hand of (5) is the residual error of $J(W)$, and it is also written as:

$$e = \|Y_d - HW\|_F^2 = \|\tilde{Y}\|_F^2 \quad (7)$$

For pattern classification problems, (7) can be further written as

$$e' = \|Y_d - round(HW)\|_F^2 \quad (8)$$

with $round(\bullet)$ representing the round operation. Equation (8) means that when the desired signal matrix Y_d is a unit matrix, the value of e can be $0,1,2,3,\cdots,N$ (N is the total number of the training samples). In the paper, (7) is also called the residual error (RE), while, (8) is named the classification error (CE). Both the RE and CE will be adopted into our algorithm, which is also called the double error criterions.

For large samples set, the orthogonal decomposition of H requires a large amount of computations. In order to decrease the computation complexity, a recursive algorithm is introduced to obtain the updating weight matrix W and the double errors. That is, from the decomposition of H at $t-1$ instance, we can deduce the one at t instance, where t denotes the previous t samples. The further details can be referred to [5].

In [5] the fundamental philosophy of the RBPNN structure optimization can be summarized as below. While the currently existing hidden centers or initial hidden centers of all pattern classes are removed independently one by one, the RBPNN constructed by the left hidden centers will be trained to the converged RE by ROLSA. The above operations are executed repeatedly until each existing center is once undergone removing. In sequence, the hidden centers combinations with the minimum RE are selected to keep as the initial hidden centers of next iteration. Until the optimized network structure could not correctly classify the training samples, the above iteration procedure will be terminated. For those optimization problems with multiple extremums, however, the above procedure can trap into the local optimum. In order to overcome this demerit, this paper proposes an improvement. Assume that there exist M labeled pattern classes for given problem, and initially there are M_i ($i=1,2,\cdots,M$) hidden centers involved for each pattern class. The improvement strategy includes two aspects, (1) The improvement of the error criterion, (2) The modification of the stop condition.

In [5], only the RE was employed to construct the ROLSA. The disadvantage for merely using the RE is that even if at some iteration, the RE reaches the local minimum, it could not guarantee the designed network completely to correctly classify all the training samples. So another error criterion, i.e., the CE, is introduced into our algorithm to examine whether the RBPNN, formed by the left hidden centers with the minimum RE, can accomplish completely & correctly classifying the training samples task. Namely, only if the CE is equal to zero, the corresponding selection for hidden centers is satisfied. The RE is, however, only used to evaluate which removing of the existing hidden centers is best, by means of searching for the minimum value of the REs. In summary, at one iteration, for each when currently existing hidden centers is removed, its RE needs to be computed, then the CE of the left hidden centers with the minimum RE is also to be calculated. The double error criterions (the RE and the CE) adopted ensure the optimized RBPNN to possess better classification performance.

In literature [5], the ROLSA was terminated as soon as the RE suddenly turned large from a smaller value. Thus this stop condition can make the searching procedure trapped into the local optimal solutions. Therefore, to avoid the demerits, the improper stop condition should be here modified. In our algorithm, the searching procedure can be directly implemented until a unique hidden center for each pattern class is kept, then the CE at each iteration will be inspected so as to search for the final turning point close to the last iteration, where the output error starts to upspring from zero. The RBPNN determined by the selected hidden centers corresponding to the final turning point is the optimal solution obtained by our improved algorithm.

III. SOLVING THE CONTROLLING PARAMETER OF KERNEL FUNCTION BASED ON THE μ-GA

It is well known that the computational complexity of the GA is determined by the designed population size. By means of some theoretical analyses, Goldberg [8] pointed out, however, that the GA with small population size (e.g., the population size is 3) and re-initialization is sufficient to ensure GA convergence. Specifically, the GA with small population size and re-initialization is generally referred to as micro-genetic algorithm (μ-GA). Krishnakumar [9] firstly reported applying the μ-GA to optimizing two stationary functions and one non-stationary function. By comparing the μ-GA with the simple GA (with a population size of 50, a crossover rate of 0.6 and a mutation rate of 0.001), Krishnakumar reported that the μ-GA had a significant advantage in the training speed and the searching ability. As stated above, the appropriate evaluation of the controlling parameter of kernel function is very important procedure for optimizing the RBPNN. For ROLSA, however, the controlling parameter is generally given beforehand. In this case, it can cause that the selected hidden centers are optimal combinations only matching the pre-given controlling parameter, but not the best selection considering the optimal controlling parameter. Generally, the controlling parameter is a function of many relative factors, and it is difficult to solve using the traditional methods. Therefore, the best method is to use the GA to optimize. In order to void by implementing a standard GA bring up a great deal of computational cost, μ-GA is here preferred into solving the controlling parameter of kernel function.

Assume that only one controlling parameter without any prior knowledge is used into the improved ROLSA (or OLSA) mentioned above, and that the elitist strategy is used into our μ-GA. The decoding strategy adopts the real number method, by which the searching for optimal solution can span the overall space of positive real number. Due to the sole real number being used as the gene in chromosome, the crossover operation seems to be redundant. In this way the mutation operation effects the main contribution in the μ-GA. Moreover, a Gaussian mutation operation is adopted into our algorithm, i.e.,

$$\sigma' = \sigma + a\sqrt{f_m}\mu(0,1) \tag{9}$$

with σ and σ' respectively representing the original genetic value and the mutated genetic value, and a a real number between -1 and 1, and $\mu(0,1)$ the random number generator of standard Gaussian distribution, and f_m the maximum fitness of the current group, i.e., $f_m = \max_{i=1}^{n} f_i$, where n denotes the group size, f_i is the fitness of individual

i, which is a function of individual RE, that is,

$$f_i = \frac{1}{e_i + eps} \quad (10)$$

with e_i denoting the RE of individual, and the *eps* a positive constant.

The procedure for solving the controlling parameter of kernel function by μ-GA can be summarized below.

1. Produce a population of size 5 randomly or 4 randomly and a best individual inherited from any previous generation.
2. Evaluate the fitness and determine the best individual, label it as individual 5 and carry it to next generation (the elitist strategy).
3. Choose all individuals (including individual 5) for the mutation operation. Since the population size is so small, the average law does not hold good. So the mutation strategy is kept purely deterministic. Namely, all of individuals take part into the mutation operation.
4. Check the nominal convergence (a reasonable measure based on either the genotype convergence or the phenotype convergence). If converged, go to next step, else, go to step 2.
5. Check if the given training error criterion is satisfied, if satisfied, stop the procedure, else, go to step 1.

IV. OPTIMIZING THE RBPNN BY ROLSA - μ-GA

We incorporate the μ-GA into the improved ROLSA to train or optimize the structure of the RBPNN. The μ-GA is used to evaluate the controlling parameter matching the selected hidden centers at each iteration precedure of our improved ROLSA. Therefore, our proposed algorithm is also called the ROLS-μ-GA, by which the RBPNN can be entirely optimized by means of ROLS-μ-GA. The implementation procedure is described as follows.

1. Initially select the hidden centers of the RBPNN.
2. By the μ-GA compute the optimal or appropriate controlling parameter matching currently selected hidden centers.
3. When those currently selected hidden centers are removed independently one by one, compute and save the respective RE of the converged RBPNN consisting of the left hidden centers, then find out the left hidden centers combinations with the minimum RE, and again compute the CE, meanwhile save the CE so as to plot the error curve. Moreover, the hidden centers combinations with the minimum RE are also used as the initial hidden centers of next iteration.
4. If only one hidden center exists in each pattern class, go to next step, else, go to 2.
5. Search for the final CE turning point, where corresponds to the optimal structure of RBPNN, then exit.

Finally, note that if the training samples set is not too large, all training samples can be selected as the initial hidden centers, otherwise, some heuristic method, i.e., *k-means clustering*, can be adopted to initially selecting these useful hidden centers from the training samples set.

V. EXPERIMENTAL RESULTS AND DISCUSSIONS

A. Two Spirals Classification Problem

In order to validate the performance of our approach, the two spirals classification problem [10] is addressed. For this example, not only the RBPNN but also the RBFNN are employed to perform the classification task. Assume that Gaussian function is used as the kernel functions of the two networks, and that the experimental data is generated according to the method of [4]: the sampled length and sampled step of each spiral is respectively 100 (form zeros to 100) and 1. Consequently, there are 200 samples generated for the training sample set. The experimental results show that the optimized RBPNN consists of 30 hidden centers and the optimal controlling parameter is 0.0319. From the CEs plotted in Fig. 2., it can be observed that there exist 4 turning points (upspring from zeros). According to the above analysis the initial three turning points are mostly local optimal solutions, but the 4th turning point is just the best solution. Under the same condition, the optimized RBFNN comprises of 46 hidden centers (as shown in Fig. 3) and the corresponding optimal controlling parameter is 0.1637. By our approach the compressing rate of the RBPNN is greater than the one of the RBFNN.

To further discuss the performance of the two networks optimized by our algorithm, the same testing sample sets (20 groups and 1982 samples per group), which are generated by mixing 20 groups of Gaussian white and zero mean noise signals with different variances of ($0, 0.001, 0.002, \cdots, 0.019$) into the original testing sample set produced by the approach of [5], are used to take part into the testing. The attained testing result is shown in Fig. 4. Clearly, in generalization ability, the RBPNN with 30 hidden centers is not worse but a little better than the RBFNN with 46 hidden centers. It fully illustrates that by our approach the largely compressed RBPNN do not cause too much losing the network performance.

B. IRIS Classification Problem

In addition, IRIS classification problem [11] is used to validate the algorithm presented in this paper. According to [11], the original data consists of three species of plants, which are setosa, versicolor and virginica. Three species of the IRIS plants, which were respectively measured in their sepal lengths, sepal widths, petal lengths and petal widths, include 150 samples (each species of the IRIS plants contains 50 samples) with the space size of 4. Assume that these samples are averagely divided into 75 training samples and 75 testing samples (where 25 samples are respectively taken out from each species). The RBPNN and the RBFNN are adopted to fulfill the classification task of the IRIS plants. The ROLS-μ-GA is applied to optimize the structures of two neural networks. Initially, assuming all the training samples to be selected as the hidden center vectors, the two neural networks implementing the classification task of the IRIS plants have all 4 input neurons, 3 output neurons, and the Gaussian kernel functions. The experimental results show that the optimized RBPNN consists of 9 hidden centers and the corresponding controlling parameter is 0.2993 as shown as Fig. 5. The curve of the CE *vs* the iterations is shown in Fig. 6. From it, it can be seen that the algorithm reaches the first turning point (local minimum) at iteration 62, then, it reaches the second or final turning point (global minimum) at iteration 66, which corresponds to the optimal solutions of the hidden centers and the controlling parameter of the RBPNN. Under the same conditions as the RBPNN experiments, however, the optimized RBFNN is composed of 15 hidden centers (as shown in Fig. 7) and the controlling parameter obtained is 0.7504 (as shown in Fig. 8). Compared with the optimized RBPNN, the reduced rate of the optimized RBFNN is lower.

To further validate and compare the performance of the RBPNN and the RBFNN optimized by our proposed algorithm, the testing samples sets formed by the original 75 testing samples, mixed with 20 groups of Gaussian zero mean white noises with the variances sampled in $[0,1)$, are used to test the generalization capability of the two network models. Consequently, the experimental results are plotted in Fig. 9. Obviously, from this figure, it can be found that in the sense of generalization capability, the RBPNN optimized by our algorithm is better than the RBFNN optimized by the same algorithm.

VI. CONCLUSIONS

This paper proposed a new improvement strategy on the ROLSA stated in [5] so that the local optimal solution can be successfully escaped. The proposed approach advantage is that is able to solve those problems with multiple extremums. Furthermore, by our ROLSA-μ-GA, not only the hidden centers can be optimally selected, but also, the controlling parameter matching the selected hidden centers can be simultaneously solved, so that the RBPNN structure can be entirely optimized. The experimental results show that our proposed algorithm is feasible and efficient. The future research work will include how to extend our algorithm to more real-world problems.

REFERENCES

[1] D.S. Huang, "Radial basis probabilistic neural networks: Model and application", International Journal of Pattern Recognition and Artificial Intelligence, 13(7), 1083-1101, 1999.
[2] D. Lowe, "Adaptive radial basis function nonlinearities and the problem of generalization", *First ICANN*, London, 171-175, Oct., 1989.
[3] D.F.Specht, "Probabilistic neural networks", *Neural Networks*, Vol.3, 109-118, 1990.
[4] W. B. Zhao, D. S. Huang, "The structure optimization of radial basis probabilistic neural networks based on genetic algorithms," in *WCCI2002 (IJCNN2002)*, Hilton Hawaiian Village Hotel, Honolulu, Hawaii, May 12-17,2002, p1086-1091.
[5] W. B. Zhao, D. S. Huang, "Application of recursive orthogonal least squares algorithm to the structure optimization of radial basis probabilistic neural networks," *ICSP'02* Proceeding, Beijing, China, Aug. 26-30, 2002, pp. 1211-1214
[6] J.Barry Gomm, Ding Li Yu, "Selecting Radial Basis Function Network Centers with Recursive Orthogonal Squares Training", IEEE Trans. Neural Networks, vol.11, NO.2, March 2000.
[7] S. Haykin, *Adaptive Filter Theory*, 3rd ed., Upper Saddle River, NJ: Prentice-Hall, 1996.
[8] David E. Goldberg, "Sizing Population for Serial and Parallel Genetic Algorithms", Proceedings of the Third International Conference on Genetic Algorithms, San Mateo, California, 1989, p70-79.
[9] K. Krishnakumar, "Micro-Genetic algorithms for stationary and non-stationary function optimization." In SPIE proceeding: Intelligence Control and Adaptive System., p289-296, 1989.
[10] Zhihua Zhou, Shifu Chen, Zhaoqian Chen, "FANNC: A Fast Adaptive Neural Network Classifier", Knowledge and Information Systems, pp 115-129, Feb. 2000.
[11] R. A. Fisher, "The use of multiple measurements in taxonomic problems", *Annals of Eugenics*, 7: 179-188, 1936.

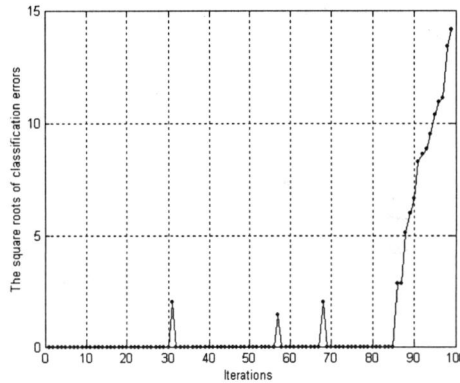

Fig. 2 The curve of CEs *vs* iterations for optimizing the RBPNN for the two spirals classification problem.

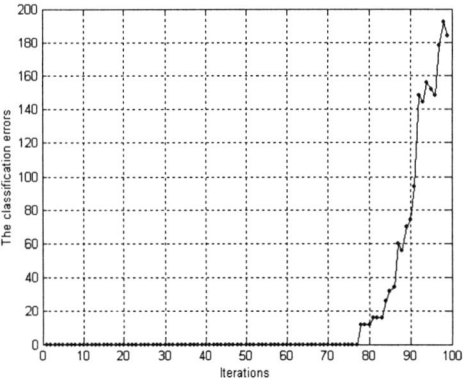

Fig. 3 The curve of CEs *vs* iterations for optimizing the RBFNN for the two spirals classification problem.

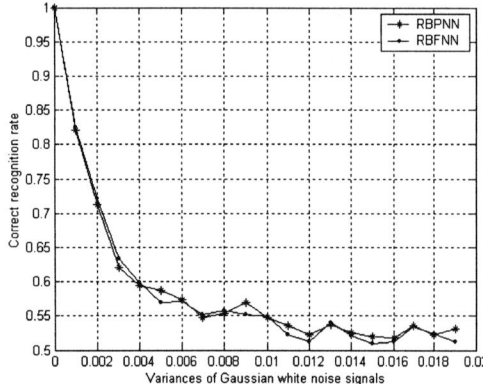

Fig. 4 The generalization capability comparison between the optimized RBPNN and the optimized RBFNN for the two spirals classification problem.

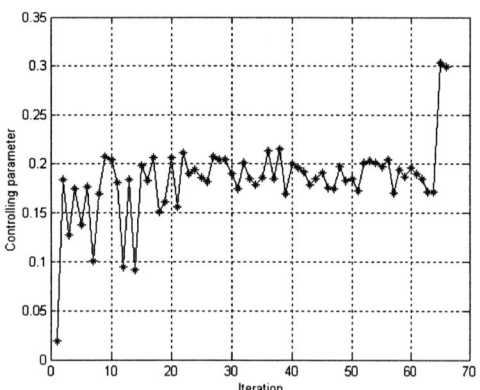

Fig.5 The learning curve of the controlling parameter for optimizing the RBPNN for the IRIS classification problem

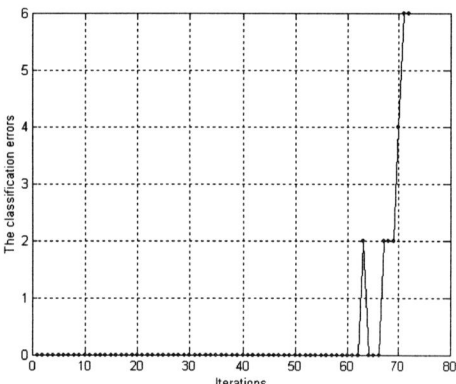

Fig.6 The curve of CEs *vs* iterations for optimizing the RBPNN for the IRIS classification problem.

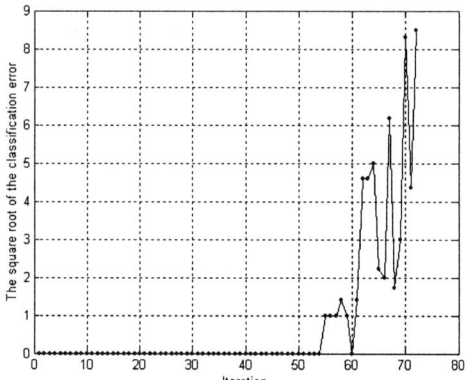

Fig.7 The curve of CEs *vs* iterations for optimizing the RBFNN for the IRIS classification problem

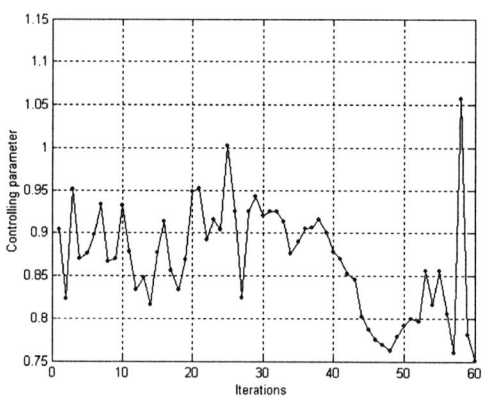

Fig.8 The learning curve of controlling parameters *vs* iterations for optimizing the RBFNN for the IRIS classification problem

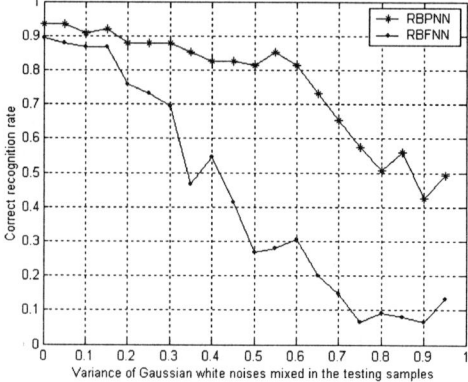

Fig. 9 The generalization capability comparison between the optimized RBPNN and the optimized RBFNN for the IRIS classification problem.

Using Artificial Neural Networks to Identify Headings in Newspaper Documents

Wei Zhang and Timothy L. Andersen
Computer Science Department, College of Engineering
Boise state University
Boise, ID 83725 USA

Abstract- Several features for Neural Network based document region identification are tested. Specifically, this paper examines features for headline and subheadline region identification. The Neural Network based region identification algorithm is a key component of a document recognition system that segments a document into regions, classifies them into text, graphic, photo, and other region types, and then uses this classification to guide the processing and analysis of the image. The input data are unusually challenging: low quality images of newspaper documents obtained from microfilmed archives. Experiments on several newspaper documents show that the features used are capable of robust and accurate headline identification.

1. Introduction

Document image analysis and recognition attempts to automate the process of extracting information from images of documents and interpret the information in a document in the same way that a human would. One of the major steps in document image analysis involves recognizing headline, paragraph, graphics and pictures in images. This paper focuses on the problem of distinguishing headlines and sub-headings from the rest of the text in a document. Textual processing and non-textual processing are two categories of document image analysis dealing, respectively, with the text components and non-text components of a document image. For text components, the goal is to separate them into headline and paragraph components, link them together according to article and correct word ordering, and recognize the text through an OCR system. The goal for non-text components is to separate them into graphics/drawings (non-halftone) and photo(halftone) categories and apply different algorithms to these regions in order to improve their display quality. The identification and elimination of non-text regions from the document also makes it possible to remove these regions from the image before presentation to the OCR system, thereby increasing OCR accuracy and speed. In addition, identification of headline regions is the first step to link headlines and paragraphs together to create the article index. Therefore, region classification in general and headline classification in particular is an important step in document image analysis.

An important question with any image analysis algorithm is determining the point (or points) at which to classify things as headline, text, graphics, etc. For example, one could choose to identify things at the connected component level – simply find the connected components and classify them. A disadvantage of this approach is that it can be difficult to classify things at the component level because there is often not enough information at that level to make a decision, and also it is possible for noise to connect what would otherwise be two or more components from differing types of regions. Another oft-used approach is to attempt to segment the page into homogenous regions, and then classify each of these regions. Ideally, with this approach one would like each segmented region to contain as much pertinent information as possible before attempting to classify it. For example, this means that one would like a headline region to contain the entire headline. Unfortunately, this is generally not possible to achieve in practice and one must over-segment the page to a certain extent in order to guarantee that regions are homogenous.

Numerous ways to segment regions have been proposed in the literature, ranging from purely top-down approaches that recursively split a page into smaller components, to purely bottom-up approaches that attempt to cluster individual connected components into larger and larger entities, with many variations in between.[3] [5] The bottom-up approaches usually classify each image pixel first and then group the pixels into regions. The texture Co-occurrence Spectrum technique [4], convolution [1], wavelet packets[9], multi-scale texture segmentation[15], texture discrimination masks [13], mask based local textural characteristics extraction [11], etc. are some of the techniques which can be used to classify each image pixel. Some bottom-up approaches [2][10] that are based on geometric relations group the pixels according to various patterns and then use simple statistical features to classify them.

The segmentation method used in this paper is a top-down approach that over-segments the page into homogenous regions before the classification stage. Once homogenous regions are produced by the segmentation process, various features are extracted from the region and used to classify it into an appropriate category. A number of different features have been proposed for region classification. Some of these include the area of the connected component, the number of black pixels in the block on the original document image, the mean horizontal black run lengths of the original image within the region, component width height ratio, component density, mean length of black intervals to the mean length of white intervals, the number of black intervals over a certain length, feature-based interaction map [12], texture discrimination masks[3], periodicity measure[14], the measures of visual attention (legibility, complexity, attractiveness, etc.) [6][7][8], and so on.

Since it is important to know how we produce the regions that are being classified, we will first introduce our segmentation algorithm in the next section (section 2). Section 3 talks about the important problem of test set generation. Section 4 defines the features that are used to classify headlines, and section 5 discusses our empirical results. Conclusion is given in section 6.

2. Our Approach

Our approach is based on a modified recursive X-Y cut projection algorithm [16][17], which is based on the horizontal and vertical projection profile, recursively using different thresholds (a local peak detector) to detect local peaks (corresponding to thick black or white gaps at which the cuts are placed) and cut the page into different regions. The steps of the algorithm proceed as follows: First, the gray scale image is binarized and deskewed. Second, the modified recursive X-Y cut projection algorithm oversegments the binarized image into regions, using horizontal and vertical projections of the page to detemine where to split regions. (Because of the free format of newspaper documents, with overlapping and mixed text and non-text areas, the recursive X-Y cut projection algorithm can not create homogenous regions in a mixed area if it does not oversegment the image.) Third, a neural network is used to classify the small, over-segmented regions created by the segmentation step. Fourth, the small, over-segmented regions are coalesced into larger regions. At the end, an xml document is created to store the pertinent information for each region (bounding box location, region type, relationship of regions).

In the classification step, the algorithm extracts features from the oversegmented regions and uses a neural network based classifier. In the first phase of classification, regions are first separated into text and non-text regions, then the text regions are separated into headline and paragraph regions. The neural networks used in the classification step are standard multiplayer perceptrons and are trained with the back-propagation algorithm.

There are several reasons for choosing a neural network based classification scheme for the task of region identification. First, neural networks are very general and robust, and any feature, such as legality, complexity or attractiveness of visual attention, can be utilized by the neural network to perform its decision task. Second, as new features are designed, the neural network can be retrained with these features to increase the accuracy of classification. Third, the system is much less dependent on user defined parameters and does not require a programmer or expert to fine tune the system to new data (such as newspaper documents from different eras or publishers). Rather, if a different newspaper needs to be processed, then the only human effort required is to manually zone and label a representative sample of documents from that newspaper. This manually labeled sample can then be used to automate the production of a training set, and a new set of networks can be trained to label the regions for that paper.

3. Training And Test Set Creation

The test and training sets are created in the following manner. First, we use a proprietary, interactive program to manually zone each newspaper page. Each region is bounded by a single rectangle and is labeled with one region type. All of this information is stored in one xml file (one xml file per newspaper page).

Next, we use a modified recursive X-Y cut algorithm [16] to oversegment the newspaper pages and to create the regions with rectangle boundary and various extracted features. The segmentation algorithm used in this step is the same as that used to segment images by the production system. This segmentation algorithm works independently of the classification algorithm.

Third, look through the ground truth that is created by the first step, and assign a region type for each machine generated region based on region boundary geometry relationships.

At the end, extract those machine generated regions whose region type is headline, subheadline, or paragraph. (In this paper, we exclude regions from advertisements and define both headline and subheadline to belong to the headline category) Finally, all of the extracted machine generated regions are randomized and separated into training and test sets according to a user chosen split rate.

4. FEATURE SELECTION

The features we used are based on the region and connected components in the region or touching the region. In the experiments, many different features beyond those features that are listed below, almost 80 features in all, were tested. In order to ease the selection of which features to use for the neural network, we developed a visual tool that incorporates a fast decision tree learning technique to assist in the selection of a good combinations of features.

The following definitions are used in the feature definitions. Here x refers to connected components that are bounded by rectangular bounding boxes and rect refers to region block produced by the segmentation process.

$$surface(x) = \text{the surface area of } x \quad (1)$$
$$weight(x) = \text{the number of pixels for } x \quad (2)$$
$$height(x) = \text{the height of } x \quad (3)$$
$$area(x) = \text{the size of } x \quad (4)$$
$$bigComp(x, \theta) = \begin{cases} 1 \text{ if } weight(x) \geq \theta \\ 0 \text{ otherwise} \end{cases} \quad (5)$$
$$numBigComp(rect) = \sum_{x \in rect} bigComp(x, \theta) \quad (6)$$
$$numComp(rect) = \text{sum of components} \quad (7)$$

Some of the good features for differentiating between pictures and regular text, and regular text and headlines, are what we refer to as "cheesiness" features. Cheesiness is the surface area of a component divided by its weight. Usually, a headline region will have components with a smaller cheesiness factor than a paragraph region. With the local adaptive thresholding algorithm used to binarize the images for these experiments, text areas often differ from graphics and pictures in the binarized image in terms of the surface area to mass ratio of connected components. When viewed at the pixel level, a connected component from a picture region, or a noise component, will often look similar to "Swiss cheese", while a text component has a more solid appearance and smoother edges. The "cheesiness" features capture this notion and are calculated as follows:

$$avgBigCompCheesiness(rect) = \frac{\left(\sum_{x \in rect} bigComp(x,\theta) surface(x)/weight(x)\right)}{numBigComp(rect)} \quad (8)$$

$$avgCompCheesiness(rect) = \frac{\left(\sum_{x \in rect} surface(x)/weight(x)\right)}{numComp(rect)} \quad (9)$$

$$regionCheesiness(rect) = \frac{\left(\sum_{x \in rect} surface(x)\right)}{\left(\sum_{x \in rect} weight(x)\right)} \quad (10)$$

Other features that were found to be useful for identifying headline regions include the average height of components in a region, number of components divided by region area, the average length of vertical black runs in a region, and the standard deviation of component heights within the region. These are listed below.

$$avgBigCompHeight(rect) = \frac{\sum_{x \in rect} bigComp(x, \theta) height(x)}{numBigComp(rect)} \quad (11)$$

$$BigCompRatio(rect) = \frac{\left(\sum_{x \in rect} bigComp(x,\theta)\right)}{area(rect)} \quad (12)$$

$$avgVBRunLength(rect) = \frac{\text{sum of the lengths of vertical black runs}}{\text{total number of black runs in region}} \quad (13)$$

$$stdevCompHeight(rect) \quad (14)$$

5. EXPERIMENTS

In these experiments, we used networks composed of 20 nodes in one hidden layer, and one output node. Because the number of headline regions is far less than the number of paragraph regions, the positive samples and negative sample set are separated into two distinct pools. Every training cycle, a sample is randomly chosen from one of these pools based on the balance rate. The balance rate is set so that it forces an equal number of positive samples and negative samples to be presented to the network.

Table 1. classification results of headline and paragraph region on Chicago newspaper

	Headline	Paragraph	Total	Accuracy(%)
Headline(real)	1298	23	1321	98.26
Non-headline(real)	117	19338	19455	99.40
Total			20776	99.33

Table 2. classification results of headline and paragraph region on all newspaper

	Headline	Paragraph	Total	Accuracy(%)
Headline(real)	2864	52	2916	98.22
Non-headline(real)	364	39722	40086	99.09
Total			43002	99.03

The document images we used in the training and test sets were provided by iArchives. These pages included 220 pages from the "Chicago Daily Tribune", 1928, 124 pages from "The Dallas Morning News", 1928, 55 pages from "The Washington Post", 1997, and 13 pages from "The Austin American", 1941. All of these pages were scanned from microfilm and as such have a great deal of noise and are of relatively poor quality in general.

After the small regions are created by the modified recursive X-Y cut projection algorithm and the text regions are labeled (headline, subheadline and paragraph) based on the ground truth, they are randomized and are split into a training and test set, where the training set contains 70% of the regions and test set contains 30%.

The first results given below are restricted to pages from "Chicago Daily Tribune", 1928. The accuracy for this set is given in table 1. The accuracy for all of the pages in the dataset is given in table 2. 6. DISCUSSION

Because the data in the training and test sets are from different sources, which have different formats and styles, the accuracy for all newspapers should be lower than that from Chicago Tribune. Therefore, even though the data that contains all of the documents has more training samples, the accuracy on this data is a little bit lower than the single source.

Because the accuracy and efficiency of classification approaches depends to some extent on accurate segmentation of the documents into homogenous regions, the segmentation error influences the classification error. It is likely that with better segmentation and especially less over-segmentation it would be possible to achieve higher accuracy rates.

While it is important to have high classification accuracy on the initial identification of regions after segmentation, during the coalescing process it is possible to correct some misclassifications based on context information obtained by examining the surrounding regions. Thus, it should be possible to increase classification accuracy of our approach during the phase when the many small regions are coalesced into articles.

7. CONCLUSIONS AND FUTURE WORK

We have demonstrated the saliency of several features for newspaper headline and subheadline identification using a neural network. The accuracy of these features during the initial classification phase (no coalescing and not using context information) is good and expected to be improved in the coalescing process.

In addition, It is possible that the results reported in this paper could be improved if we use a soft decision, which means using multiple output nodes (one node represent headline, the other node represent paragraph) in the neural network, we can classify some regions as not homogenous, in other words as containing part of headline and part of paragraph. According to this information, we can then re-partition this type of region into homogenous parts. This should make it possible for the classification pass to correct some of the mistakes from the initial segmentation pass.

REFERENCES

[1] D. Patel, "Page segmentation for document image analysis using a neural network," Opt. Eng. 35(7) 1854-1861 (July 1996)

[2] P. E. Mitchell, "Document page segmentation based on pattern spread analysis," Opt. Eng. 39(3) 724-734 (March 2000)

[3] T. N. Pappas, S. H. Tsng and D. A. Kosiba, "A robust and efficient algorithm for bilevel document block classification," International Conference on Image Processing 2001. Proceedings, Vol. 1, pp. 1122-1125

[4] J. S. Payne, T. J. Stonham, D. Patel, "Document segmentation using texture analysis," 12th Int. Conf. Pat. Rec., Jerusalem, Israel, Oct. 1994, 2, 380-382.

[5] J. Wieser and A. Pinz, "Layout and analysis: finding text, titles, and photos in Digital Images of Newspaper pages," Proceedings of the 2nd International Conference on Document Analysis and Recognition, Oct 20-22 1993. pp. 774

[6] G. Maderlechner, A. Schreyer and P. Suda, "Extraction of relevant information from document images using measures of visual attention," Pattern Recognition, 2000. Proceedings. 15th International Conference on, Vol. 4, 2000. pp. 385-388

[7] W. Eglin, and A. Gangneux, "Visual exploration and functional document labeling," Document Analysis and Recognition, 2001. Proceedings. Sixth International Conference on, 2001. pp. 816-820

[8] V. Eglin, S. Bres, and H. Emptoz, "Printed text featuring using the visual criteria of legibility and complexity," Pattern Recognition, 1998. Proceedings. Fourteenth International Conference on, Vol. 1, 1998. pp. 942-944.

[9] K. Etemad, D. Doermann, and R. Chellappa, "Page segmentation using decision integration and wavelet packets," Pattern Recognition, 1994. Vol. 2 – Conference B: Computer Vision & Image Processing., proceedings of the 12th IAPR International. Conference on, Vol. 2, 1994. pp. 345-349

[10] P. E. Mitchell, and H. Yan, "Newspaper document analysis featuring connected line segmentation," Document Analysis and Recognition, 2001. Proceedings. Sixth International Conference on, 2001. pp. 1181-1185.

[11] P. S. Williams, and M. D. Alder, "Generic texture analysis applied to newspaper segmentation," Neural Networks, 1996., IEEE International Conference on, Vol. 3, 1996. pp. 1664-1669

[12] D. Chetverikov, J. Liang, J. Komuves, R. M. Haralick, "Zone classification using texture features," Pattern Recognition, 1996., Proceedings of the 13th International Conference on, Vol. 3, 1996. pp. 676-680

[13] A. K. Jain, and Y. Zhong, "Page segmentation using texture discrimination masks," Image Processing, 1995. Proceedings., International Conference on, Vol. 3, 1995. pp. 308-311

[14] D. Ryu, S. Kang, and S. Lee, "Parameter-independent geometric document layout analysis," Pattern Recognition, 2000. Proceedings. 15th International Conference on, Vol. 4, 2000. pp. 397-400

[15] V. Wu, R. Manmatha, and E. M. Riseman, "TextFinder: An automatic System to Detect and Recognize text in images," IEEE Transaction on Pattern Analysis and Machine Intelligence, Vol. 21, No. 11, November 1999 pp. 1224-1229

[16] J. Ha, R. Haralick, and I. Phillips, "Recursive X-Y cut using Bounding Boxes of Connected Components," Proceeding of the 3rd ICDR, Montreal, pages 952-955, 1995

[17] G. Nagy, S. Seth, and M. Viswanathan, "A prototype document image analysis system for technical journals," Computer, 25(7):10-22, July 1992

"FreeCell" Neural Network Heuristics

Alphonsus Dunphy, Malcolm I. Heywood

Dalhousie University,
Faculty of Computer Science,
6050 University Avenue, Halifax, Nova Scotia. B3H 1W5

Abstract— In areas, such as planning, state space searches are often conducted to find solutions. Usually, the heuristic is derived from knowledge of the domain. In many cases the knowledge of a domain is limited or the domain is so complex that an effective heuristic cannot be formulated. As an alternative, machine-learning techniques such as neural networks may be used to derive the heuristic. The game of FreeCell was selected as a suitable benchmark domain, in which "knowledge based heuristics" and "neural heuristics" were employed to find solutions for randomly generated games. An amalgamation of the two, in which the neural network developed a heuristic from several knowledge based heuristics, was also used. Of the neural derived heuristics, the best-case architecture did not employ the "knowledge based heuristics." Moreover, neural heuristics were not able to improve upon those defined *a priori*.

Index terms—Benchmarking, State Space Search, Search heuristics, MLP, SOM.

I. INTRODUCTION

FreeCell is a popular card solitaire game invented by Paul Alfille in 1978 [1]. Its inclusion in PC operating systems has enhanced its popularity and there are several tournaments in which FreeCell enthusiasts participate. Its simplicity of rules and its diverse number of games and solutions make it suitable for heuristic search techniques. Since games are diverse, with 1.68038×10^{66} possible initial card layouts, basic searches such as breadth and depth first are ineffective.

The playing rules of FreeCell game are straightforward. The deck is the standard deck of 52 cards. The cards – ace, deuce, three to ten, jack, queen, king – are ranked 1 to 13 respectively, with 1 being the lowest rank. The color of the suits, ♥hearts and ♦diamonds, is red; the color of the suits, ♠spades and ♣clubs, is black. The arrangement of the cards is as follows:

- 8 container stacks or columns of unlimited size, into which a standard deck of 52 cards is, at the beginning of the game, randomly placed face up with 7 cards in the first four stacks and 6 in the remaining four.
- 4 free cells, which are allowed to contain a single card.
- 4 collector stacks into which all cards are eventually collected.

In FreeCell literature the stacks and cells are often referred to as tableau piles, cells, and foundation piles respectively [2]. The object of the game is to relocate all cards of the container stacks to the collector stacks. Each card may be moved according to the following rules:

- A card may be moved from a free cell or container stack into a second container stack if the receiving container stack is empty *or* if the card is different in color and one rank below the top card of the receiving stack.
- A card may be moved from a container stack (or a free cell) to a free cell if the free cell is empty.
- A card may be moved from a container stack or free cell to a collector stack if the card is an ace and the receiving stack is empty *or* if the card is of the same suit and one rank above the top card in the collector stack.

Once a card has been placed in a collector stack it cannot be removed.

Many programs, with diverse names such as *FreeCell Pro* [3], *Xcell* [4], *FreecellTool* [5], and *AutoFree* [6], have been written to automatically solve FreeCell. Some use specifically developed algorithms, while others use state space searches such as heuristic search and A* Search. Normally, the heuristic is based on knowledge of the FreeCell game. Few, if any, use machine-learning techniques such as neural networks. Since games are diverse and a large number of attributes are necessary to describe a layout, it would be difficult to train a neural network to solve the game directly by predicting a move for each possible layout. An alternative would be to train a neural network to calculate a heuristic to direct a best-first search. In a similar fashion, Chellapilla and Fogel use neural networks to evaluate board positions in the game of checkers [7, pp 1482-1495]. This is the approach employed here. Moreover, the specific interest is to identify the significance, if any, of different neural network architectures, relative to a baseline of performance established by *a priori* defined heuristics or "knowledge based heuristics", in both places applied in conjunction with a state space search.

The paper is organized as follows: Section II defines the state space approach within the context of the FreeCell game, and introduces the "knowledge based" heuristics. Section III provides the methodology utilized to define the neural network architectures and representation of the input space. The associated neural network learning algorithms are defined in Section IV, whereas Section V describes the results. Conclusions are drawn in Section VI.

II. STATE SPACE SEARCH

FreeCell was 'solved' by a best-first or heuristic search. The heuristic search is a state space search conducted through a tree or graph of nodes. In FreeCell, each state or node is a card layout of the game. The initially dealt hand is the start node or first node of the search. The goal node is the node at which all cards have been placed in the collector stacks and which signifies that a solution has been found. Successor nodes are the possible card layouts that can be generated from a node by making all legal moves. The parent node is the node from which successor nodes are generated. The heuristic value of a node is the estimated cost of reaching the goal node from the node. In FreeCell the cost of a move is unity and, hence, the heuristic value is generally the number of moves required to reach the goal node. However, it may also be an arbitrary value that tends to decrease as the distance from the goal node decreases.

An open node is one that has not been reached in the search, while a closed node is one that has been searched. OPEN and CLOSED are lists of nodes. A solution is the path from the start node to the goal node.

A simplification of a best-first search is as follows [8, pp 92-93]:
1. Start with OPEN = start node;
2. While (node ≠ Goal) OR (OPEN == ∅)
   a. Pick node on OPEN with best heuristic value and move node to CLOSED;
   b. Generate Successor Nodes;
   c. For (all Successor Nodes)
      i. Calculate heuristic value and add node to OPEN;
      ii. If generated before, change the parent node for a better path;
3. A solution, if it exists, is the path from the start to the goal node.

Only single moves were used to generate successor nodes. Super or meta moves were not used. A super or meta move is a series of several legal single moves, which can transport a sequence of several cards from one collector stack to another. Naturally, the performance of the best-first search is strongly influenced by the heuristic employed. To this end the following 5 knowledge-based heuristics are defined.

A. Number of Cards Collected (NCC)

The number of cards that have been collected is an indicator, albeit a weak one, of progress in the search for a solution. The negative of the number of cards that have been moved to the collector stacks can serve as a heuristic.

B. Distance of Node from Goal (NfG)

This metric basically sums the number of cards between the position of each card in the node under consideration and the position of that card in the goal node. When the distance has been calculated for a card, that card is considered removed from the container stack of the node under consideration and will not be used in calculations for the remaining cards. A card that has already been moved from a container stack is obviously not blocking any others. If the node already has cards in the collector stacks, then the distance for these cards is 0. If the node has a card in a free cell, than the distance for that card is 1.

C. Rank Order (RO)

Games, which have a high degree of card order in the container stacks, tend to be easier to solve and, hence, closer to the goal node. One means of estimating the order or (lack of order) is to estimate the difficulty to sort the cards in the collector stacks. Hence, the card order heuristic is the sum of the number of moves that it would take to sort the cards of each container stack in ascending order of rank (from top to bottom) ignoring card suit.

D. Sequence Order (SO)

This heuristic measures the order of the cards in the container stacks of the node in terms of both rank and color. To do so, the sum of costs of the cards is estimated as follows:
1. If, in a container stack, a card and the one above is in proper rank and color sequence such as a black 2 on a red 3, a negative cost equal to the depth of the card is assigned;
2. If the rank sequence is correct but the color sequence is incorrect, then (the difference in rank + 1) assigned as a cost;
3. If the rank sequence is incorrect and the above card is higher in rank, (the difference in rank − 1) × the depth of the card is assigned as a cost.
4. If the rank sequence is incorrect and the above card is equal or lower in rank, (the difference in rank + 1) is assigned as a cost.

E. Problem Reduction (PR)

Often a good heuristic for a search is the number of moves required to complete the search for a simplified version of the node. One means of simplifying a FreeCell node is to add an unlimited number of free cells. To solve the simplified version, low ranking cards are collected after continually moving covering cards to free cells. Each movement of a card from a container stack or free cell to a collector stack or from a container stack to a free cell is considered a single move. The heuristic of the original node is the number of moves it would take to reach the goal node from the simplified node. Since the heuristic is close to being admissible, this heuristic is useful in finding short solutions via an A* Search [8, pp 96-101].

III. NEURAL NETWORKS

Instead of using the above knowledge-based heuristics, neural networks were used to calculate the heuristic value. That is to say, the search for a FreeCell solution is conducted in exactly the same manner as described previously, with the neural network calculating the heuristic value used in the search. Training data for the neural network would consist of previously solved FreeCell games with a coding scheme to describe the current state and the number of moves to complete the game as the target. Naturally, many options exist in terms of different neural network learning algorithms. However, in this work, our principle interest lies in the contribution of different architectures and the input space employed. To this end, three different architectures are considered.

Firstly, architecture 1, a single neural network, is used to find suitable search heuristics based on the card layout. This represents the neural network base line, as no *a priori* information to encourage modular problem solving is incorporated [9]. Architecture 2 uses the knowledge-based heuristics from Section II as the input to the neural network. The question being, can a neural network learn to combine heuristics without recourse to the card layout? A combination of card layout and heuristics is considered to result in an undesirably large input space. In the final case, architecture 3, card layout is retained as the input, but two neural networks are employed, one to perform feature extraction and one to make the heuristic.

In all the above architectures, Multi-layer Perceptrons (MLP) with one hidden layer are employed for identifying the heuristics; Architectures 1 and 2. Architecture 3 utilizes a Self Organizing feature Map (SOM) to perform the feature extraction. Moreover, the SOM output provided to the following MLP takes the form of the quantized (real valued) SOM outputs, Section IV.

A. Encoding the Input Space

The selection of attributes of the domain is critical to the performance of a neural network. The training time, the ability of the network to generalize, and the minimum mean square error (MSE) are affected by the choice of attributes. FreeCell is, especially, problematic since there are numerous ways of encoding to produce layout patterns. In the case of this work we consider there to be two basic schemes: cell content or card location.

The FreeCell game is described in terms of labeled cells that can contain a card. The attributes are variables describing the card in a particular location. For a cell content encoding, two attributes are used to describe the card in a cell. One integer describes the suit of a card and a second describes the rank of the card. In the case of the card location scheme, there is one attribute per card, which identifies the card location.

Experiments using various coding schemes were conducted. The most successful and the one chosen to encode the training and test data for FreeCell was the Cell Content scheme, in which 2 attributes described the location of all cards, including those in the collector stacks. The success of the Cell Content scheme as compared to the Card Location scheme is not surprising, if we view the schemes in human terms. The Cell content scheme clearly displays the sequence of cards in the stacks; whereas in the Card Location scheme the sequences are not apparent.

B. Training and Test Data

Generating FreeCell solutions to train neural networks is a cumbersome process. Ideally, solutions should be perfect, that is, the solutions should contain the minimum number of moves. A breadth first search would generate optimal solutions. However, these are impractical on a FreeCell game using the full 52-card deck. Even with reduced games of 24 and 32 card configurations, which contain cards of 3 suits in rank ace to 8 and cards of 4 suits in rank ace to 8 respectively, breadth-first search is unfeasible. That is, tens of thousands of nodes would be generated requiring unattainable memory and CPU requirements. However, for the 24 and 32 card configurations it was still relatively easy to generate test data. An A* Search using the PR heuristic attains nearly optimal solutions. Only on rare occasions, less than 1%, in testing on the simple 14-card game would a solution be one greater than that found by a breadth first search. Therefore, the 32 Card Deck, which is sufficiently complex, was chosen as the domain for analysis.

C. 32 Card Deck Domain

The layout of the 32 Card FreeCell game and the number of attributes in the Cell Content coding scheme required to describe each state is as follows:

- 5 container stacks, each large enough to contain at least 8 cards. The number of attributes = $(5 \times 8 \times 2) = 80$.
- 4 free cells. The number of attributes = $(4 \times 1 \times 2) = 8$.
- 4 collector stacks, each to contain the 8 cards of each suit for the solved game. The number of attributes = $(4 \times 8 \times 2) = 64$.

A total of 152 attributes are required.

IV. LEARNING ALGORITHMS

A. Self-Organizing Feature Map

Kohonen's Self-Organizing Feature Map (SOM) algorithm is an unsupervised learning algorithm in which an initially 'soft' competition takes place between neurons to provide a topological arrangement between neurons at convergence [10]. The learning process is summarized as follows,

1. Assign random values to the network weights, w_{ij};

2. Present an input pattern, *x*, in this case a series of taps taken from the shift register providing the 'reconstruction' state space on which the SOM is to provide a suitable quantized approximation.
3. Calculate the distance between pattern, *x*, and each neuron weight w_j, and therefore identify the winning neuron, or

$$d = \min_j \{\|x - w_j\|\} \quad (1)$$

where $\|\cdot\|$ is the Euclidean norm and w_j is the weight vector of neuron j;
4. Adjust all weights in the neighborhood of the winning neuron, or

$$w_{ij}(t+1) = w_{ij}(t) + \eta(t) K(j,t)\{x_i(t) - w_{ij}(t)\} \quad (2)$$

where $\eta(t)$ is the learning rate at epoch *t*; and $K(j, t)$ is a suitable neighborhood function, in this case of a Gaussian nature;
5. Repeat steps (2) – (4) until the convergence criteria is satisfied.

Following convergence, presentation of an input vector, *x*, results in a corresponding output vector, *d*, the Euclidian distance between each neuron and input or quantization error. It is this concept of quantization error at each neuron which is forwarded to the following MLP.

B. Multilayer Perceptron

Various learning algorithms where evaluated including the LMS algorithm with adaptive learning rates and momentum and second order derivative approaches [11]. In this case, best results where achieved using second order derivatives as estimated using the Levenberg-Marquardt quasi-Newton method ('trainlm' in Matlab™ [12]). Specifically, the back propagation algorithm popularized the utilization of gradient methods for training MLP networks [13]. Weight updates, Δw, take the form of a gradient vector, *J* – changes in the sum square error, *E*, with respect to weights, *w* – and expanded in terms of the chain rule to provide the 'back propagation' across multiple layers. However, second order methods have the potential to provide a faster learning algorithm if efficient estimation of the Hessian matrix, *H*, is possible. In this case the gradient vector, $H \approx J^T J$, approximates the Hessian. The Levenberg-Marquardt algorithm [14] then employs a combination of this Hessian approximation with a quasi-Newton gradient update scheme and a suitable annealing schedule to control the adaptation of the learning rate parameter, η, as follows,

$$\Delta w \approx -[J^T J + \eta I]^{-1} J$$

The selection of the learning rate parameter, η, enables variation between the special cases of gradient decent ($\eta \to 1$) or Newton's method ($\eta \to 0$), where the latter is most desirable when an error minimum is encountered. The Matlab™ 'trainlm' routine employs one of two multipliers to update the learning rate at each epoch [11], depending on whether the last epoch resulted in an error decrease ($\eta(t+1) = \alpha \times \eta(t)$) or an error increase ($\eta(t+1) = \beta \times \eta(t)$).

V. RESULTS

For neural training purposes 101 games comprised of 4852 patterns, generated using the Reduction heuristic of Section II.E, were utilized. Each pattern represents a node or move in a game. An additional 1000 games, again generated with the Reduction heuristic, served as data to test the networks. If the search was not completed before 5000 nodes were generated, the search was terminated and the search deemed to have failed. Normally, the unit of testing is the pattern, in which a neural network is judged by the proximity to which it calculates the target from a pattern. However, in FreeCell a network is judged by performance on solving FreeCell games. In all cases the Neural Network toolbox of Matlab™ was employed [12].

A. Performance metrics

The performance of any approach – knowledge based or neural network – is evaluated in terms of two basic search parameters: Efficiency and Effectiveness.

1) Efficiency: expresses the number of *nodes closed* as the number of nodes from which successor nodes have been generated and which have been placed in the CLOSED list of nodes. A closed node is the one with the best heuristic value of those that have yet to be expanded. The 'total number of nodes' is the actual number of nodes that have been generated. Efficiency, therefore, measures the quality of the search algorithm and the heuristic.

2) Effectiveness: measures the number of nodes contained in the solution or solution length. In FreeCell the solution length is the quality of the solution and corresponds to the number of moves to complete the game. The breadth-first search and A* Searches will find the optimal solution, if a solution exists. The "number of games solved" is the number of games that could be solved within the prescribed time frame (node generation limit of 5000).

B. Network Topology

Neural Network heuristics based on the MLP all utilize three hidden layer neurons, tansig activation function, and a single linear output neuron. MLP#1 excludes attributes for the cards that have been placed in container stacks, whereas the patterns for MLP#2 include these attributes. Both MLP#1 and #2 are representative of architecture 1.

In the case of architecture 2, six knowledge-based heuristics are employed in conjunction with a multilayer perceptron, MLP#3. The first three are the Distance from Goal, Rank, and Sequence and the remaining three are variations of the Rank and Sequence heuristics. (Note the PR heuristic is used for directing the best-first search during creation of the datasets and, hence, cannot be employed as training data.)

Architecture 3 also utilizes a MLP with 3 hidden layer neurons. Three alternative SOM configurations – SOM#1, #2 and #3 – are considered. SOM#1 excludes attributes for the cards that have been placed in container stacks, whereas the patterns for SOM#2 and SOM#3 include these attributes. The topology of the map for SOM#1 and SOM#2 was 15 × 7 hexagonal grid, whereas the topology of the map for SOM#3 was a 105 × 1 linear grid.

C. Static Analysis

Table I details the test set performance in terms of *nodes closed*, *nodes open*, and solutions found for heuristic and neural solutions. The simplest heuristic, the Number of Cards Collected Heuristic managed to solve 970 of the 1000 test games, albeit it was the least effective. On average it searched 406.5 nodes to find solutions of average length 152.2. The number of *nodes closed* is equivalent to the number of nodes searched. The other knowledge-based heuristics performed much better with the PR heuristic searching an average of 205.5 nodes to find solutions of average length 63.1. It solved 992/1000 or 99.2% of the games.

TABLE I
COMPARISON OF SEARCH HEURISTICS ON 1000 TEST GAMES

Heuristic	Avg. Nodes Closed	Avg. Nodes Open	# Solution Found	Avg. Solution Length
Knowledge Based Heuristics				
NCC	408.6	878.5	970	152.2
NfG	205.5	448.7	994	64.4
RO	203.0	494.9	990	64.7
SO	251.2	543.9	972	70.7
PR	181.5	441.1	992	63.1
Architecture 1 – Card layout, no independent feature extraction				
MLP#1	285.8	683.4	979	70.7
MLP#2	353.2	960.4	983	93.7
Architecture 2 – Heuristics, no input partitioning				
MLP#3	211.6	542.5	991	64.0
Architecture 3 – Card layout, independent feature extraction				
SOM#1	241.1	600.4	990	67.0
SOM#2	234.6	554.0	996	65.5
SOM#3	208.4	502.8	992	62.7

The performance of the architecture 1 neural networks – MLP#1 and #2 – was significantly less than that of the knowledge based heuristics. MLP#1 searched through an average of 285.8 nodes or 57% more than the PR heuristic. The higher performance of MLP#1, in comparison to MLP#2, on *nodes closed* and *nodes open* was probably attributable to having fewer attributes on which to converge. Architecture 2, MLP#3 – an amalgamation of 6 heuristics – tended to be biased toward the better performing heuristics.

Architecture 3, the introduction of an SOM, is an improvement over a single MLP, whether the MLP is based on the card layout or heuristics. SOM#3 performs at a level approaching that of the "knowledge based heuristics." The corresponding average *nodes closed*, 208.9, is near that of the Distance from Goal and Rank heuristics, whilst providing more and shorter solutions. SOM#2 and SOM#3, in which patterns contained attributes for all cards including those in the collector stacks, performed better than SOM#1.

D. Generalization

Further experiments were conducted on 100 randomly selected games with the objective of assessing the degree of generalization provided by SOM#2. To do so, new games were created from the original games, by swapping randomly selected pairs of cards. For each of these 100 games, new games were generated by randomly swapping from 1 to 5 pairs of cards from the original game configuration, and then measuring performance in terms of *nodes closed*.

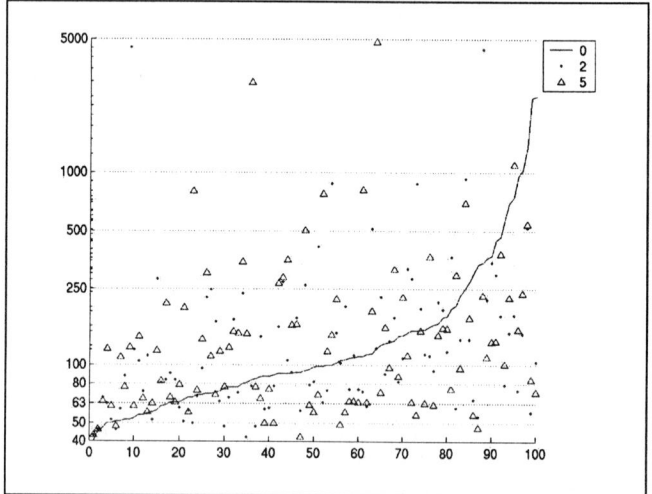

Fig. 1. Performance of SOM#2 following Random Swapping of cards. X Axis: game i.d. Y Axis: $\log_{10}$ *number of nodes closed*.

Figure 1 summarizes the experiments. The solid line represents the performance of SOM#2 on the original 101 games with 0 cards swapped. Altered games with 2 and 5 cards swapped are identified as '•' and 'Δ' respectively. Easy games are games that can be solved with a low number of *closed nodes*. Swaps to easier games such as games 1 to 10 in Figure 1, result in comparable or more difficult games, require an equivalent or greater number of *nodes closed* to solve and generally fall above the solid line. As the original games become more difficult (games 10 to 80, Figure 1), the swapped cards result in both more difficult and easier games. The '•' and 'Δ' points fall both below and above the line. Swaps to the most difficult (games 80 to 100, Figure 1) tend to result in easier games. Most '•' and 'Δ' points fall below the line. In summary, easy games become more difficult and more difficult games easier as cards are swapped. This supports the premise that the networks are providing general solutions that do not appear to be overtly sensitive to specific game layouts.

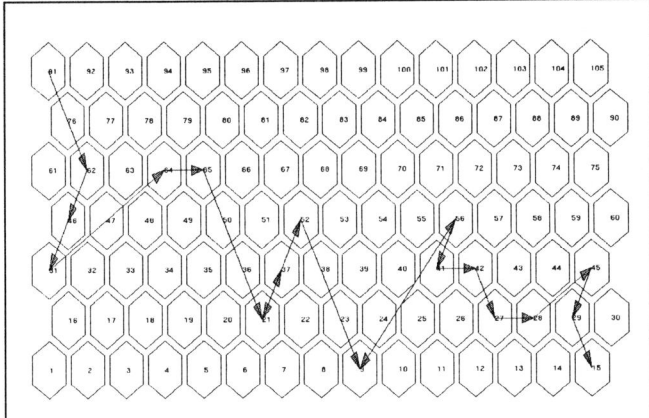

Fig. 2. SOM#2 on Nodes Closed for a 'Simple' Game.

E. SOM dynamics

Searches on 15 games were traced from neuron to neuron through the SOM identified as SOM#2. As each node is searched, the winning neuron for that node is calculated. Figure 2 and 3 contain traces of 2 games, one game solved in a low number of moves and a second game solved in a large number of moves. The SOM, used in training, was a 15 × 9. Numbers from 1 to 105 were arbitrarily used to label the neurons. Arrowheads indicate the direction of the solution. Consider a simple game. The initial card layout or node is located at neuron 91. The next node searched is located at neuron 62. The search gradually progresses through the SOM and eventually reached the final or goal at neuron 15. The most interesting feature of the trace is that solutions normally start at neuron 91, move across the SOM, and exit at neuron 15. It is understandable why the last winning neuron is always 15, since the goal node is always the same. However, a simple explanation for why solutions always start at neuron 91 is not obvious. Perhaps, the fact that the start node of all games has the same card positions filled may influence the assignment of the winning neuron. Moreover, the initial configuration also represents the least organized, where this is identified by one neuron performing an averaging function.

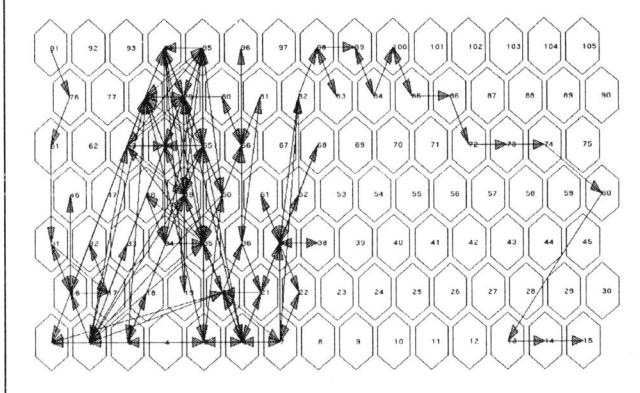

Fig. 3. SOM#2 on Nodes Closed for a 'Difficult' Game.

Complex or longer solutions, Figure 3, have many feedback and internal loops. The loops are generally in the early part of the solution. Once the solution approaches the winning goal the trace becomes less complex. This suggests that neurons may be overworked. Any technique that would spread the organization of attributes more evenly over the SOM would likely improve performance.

VI. CONCLUSION

Performance of neural network architectures is evaluated against a set of *a priori* selected knowledge based heuristics on a 32-card version of the FreeCell game. Particular emphasis is given to the evaluation and identification of appropriate neural architecture. A combination of SOM and single hidden layer multiplayer perceptron is found to provide competitive performance with the knowledge based heuristics. Trace analysis of the SOM once trained indicates that the SOM clearly partitions the problem into different stages of play. Moreover, the SOM may well benefit from the ability to encode temporal relationships in an attempt to provide additional context to the current spatial encoding of the input space.

In short, we believe that the FreeCell game provides a good benchmarking environment for a wide range of learning algorithms, providing both a concise definition and interesting spatial and temporal learning problems.

REFERENCES

[1] History of FreeCell, http://www.solitaire-freecell.com/history_of_freecell.htm.
[2] Solitaire Games Week – FreeCell, http://www.solitairegames.com/freecell.html
[3] FC Pro, http://home.earthlink.net/~fomalhaut/fcpro.html.
[4] Xcell, http://www.gamesdomain.com/directd/2154.html
[5] FreecellTool - Program Detail - WindowsPC.com, http://www.windowspc.com/games_misc/FreecellTool.htm
[6] Windows 95/98 » Games, http://www.bookcase.com/library/software/win9x.games.html
[7] Chellapilla K and Fogel DB (1999) "Evolution, Neural Networks, Games, and Intelligence," Proc. IEEE, Vol. 87:9, Sept., pp. 1471-1496.
[8] Russell, Stuart J. and Norvig, Peter, *Artificial Intelligence A Modern Approach*, New Jersey: Prentice Hall.
[9] J.F. Kolen, A.K. Goel, "Learning in Parallel Distributed Processing Networks: Computational Complexity an Information Content," IEEE Transactions on Systems, Man, and Cybernetics. 21(2), pp 359-366, March/ April 1991.
[10] T. Kohonen, Self-Organizing Maps, 3rd Ed., Springer-Verlag, ISBN 3-540-67921-9, 2000.
[11] Widrow B., Lehr M.A., "Adaptive Neural Networks and Their Applications," International Journal of Intelligent Systems," 8, pp 453-507. 1993.
[12] Demuth H., Beale M., Matlab – Neural Network Toolbox, Users Guide 4.0; http://www.mathworks.com
[13] D.E. Rumelhart, J.L. McClelland, et al., Parallel Distributed Processing – Explorations in the Microstructure of Cognition. Volume 1: Foundations, MIT Press, ISBN 0-262-68053-X, 1986.
[14] R. Fletcher, Practical Methods of Optimization. 2nd Edition. John Wiley and Sons, ISBN 0-471-91547-5, 1987.

Layered Neural Network training with Model Switching and Hidden Layer Feature Regularization

Keisuke Kameyama
Tsukuba Advanced Research Alliance
University of Tsukuba
Tsukuba, Ibaraki 305-8577, Japan
Email : kame@tara.tsukuba.ac.jp

Kei Taga
Doctoral Program in Risk Engineering
Graduate School of Systems and Information Engineering
University of Tsukuba
Tsukuba, Ibaraki 305-8573, Japan

Abstract—This work introduces a scheme of layered neural network training, which incorporates a dynamical model alteration during training, and regularization of the features extracted in the hidden layer units. So far, use of Model Switching (MS), which is a simultaneous search scheme for an optimal model and parameter, proved to improve training efficiency and generalization ability as a side effect. In MS, the operation to switch the network to a different model involve orthogonalization of the features extracted in the hidden layer. Assuming that the orthogonalization contributes to the observed merits, joint use of MS and orthogonalization of the hidden layer feature by introducing a regularization term in the training, is introduced. The network trained by the proposed training scheme is applied to a pattern recognition problem, and some improvement in training efficiency and generalization ability were observed.

I. Introduction

Regression or pattern recognition by supervised learning can be formalized as an acquisition of an approximate map of the true map $y = f(x)$, where x and y are the input and the output vectors.

Supervised learning in doing this usually assumes a model which is a set of functions $o = f_p(x; w)$, with varying parameter vector w. It tries to approximate f by selecting the optimal parameter vector w.

In selecting the values of the parameters, a set of ideal input-output pairs (training set) $\{(x_m, y_m)\}_{m=1}^{M}$ will be used. A classical strategy in the context of pattern recognition would be to approximate the class probability density function (PDF) and to apply a decision rule derived from the Bayes' theorem [1]. Other means such as direct estimation of the decision border in the feature space, in a distribution-free way [2] [3] is also being actively developed.

When a suitable function class which f belongs to is known, a model F_p including the class can be selected, and with an appropriate selection of the training set, the best parameter vector may be obtained. When the class of the true map f is unknown, an approximating function f_p must be selected from model $\hat{F}_p$ that possibly include the true map f. If the ability of the selected function class is sufficient, generally the approximation map can be tuned to an arbitrary closeness to the true map f measured by a certain distance metric, provided that a training set of sufficient size can be selected at will.

In most cases of real world applications, however, the function class to which f belongs to is unknown, and the

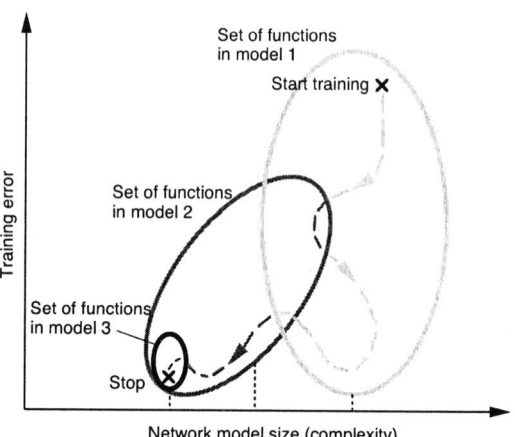

Fig. 1. The schematic of simultaneous determination of the model and the map by Model Switching. Each oval denote a set of functions included in a single model. All functions included in a model have the same model complexity, or model size. The dashed line denotes the locus of training in the function space. Although the training process is not tied to a single model, the search path is continuous in the function space.

size and the selection of the training set are limited. In these cases, all we can do is to predetermine the model $\hat{F}_p$, tune the parameter vector so that fulfills the mapping relation at the sample points in the training set. Some *a priori* information on the smoothness of f can help selecting the model $\hat{F}_p$. Naturally, the approximation function can differ in accordance to the model selection.

The layered neural network can be regarded as implementing a vector function of $o = f_N(x; w)$ with w being the vector of all the tunable connection weights. By altering the weight vector w, the network can implement various maps. The weight vector w can be determined by various means; one of the most well-known methods is the backpropagation (BP) training rule [4] which practically implements the gradient descent learning.

The issue of model selection renders itself as the problem of choosing the number of layers, the number of units within each layer, and the type of unit activation functions. These factors all affect the mapping ability, the readiness of training, and the computational cost for training and using the network. The requirements from these conditions tend to be contradictory, which makes the system trained in a predetermined function model sub-optimal at best. In this work, we will limit the discussion to networks with two active layers and an input layer.

Selection of the network model can affect various aspects of constructing and using the pattern recognition machine. First, it affects the efficiency of the training. Selection of the model is selecting the mapping ability of the possible set of functions, which determines the trainability of the network to a particular problem. It also affects the possibility of the training to be caught in the local minima of the error landscape [5]. Second, it can also affect the generalization ability of the pattern recognition machine, namely a desired ability to correctly classify an unseen input.

In order to solve the issues pointed above, the authors have jointly used the conventional stepwise training methods and occasional model transfer. The method of transferring the model, called *Model Switching* (MS) has been proposed, and have been used in several pattern recognition applications [6] [7] [8]. Among the findings in using MS was the improved training efficiency and generalization ability, compared with the networks trained in a predetermined model.

In this work, we analyze the merit of using MS in training, and conjecture that this nature comes as a side effect of the local operations used when switching from one model to the other. By repetitive use of this MS operation called *unit fusion* which locally unifies the hidden neurons that have similar functions, the features extracted in the hidden layer tends to be orthogonalized. However, in conventional MS, this operation affected the learning only when the model was switched.

In this work, we try to introduce an explicit orthogonalization in the stepwise training, and jointly use it with occasional MS operations.

In Sec. 2, the scheme of network training with MS will be reviewed. Then, modification to the BP training rule, which induces the orthogonalization of the features extracted by hidden layer units, by way of additional penalty term in the error function will be introduced in Sec. 3. The proposed learning method is applied to a pattern recognition problem in Sec. 4, and the paper will be concluded in Sec. 5.

II. NEURAL NETWORK TRAINING WITH MODEL SWITCHING

A. Model Switching and Map Distance

In order to solve the issues of training which is confined to a single network model, training involving dynamical model alteration have been developed. In Fig. 1, the aimed scheme, where the training process is not tied to a single function model is illustrated. When the training is proceeding in a model, it can be managed using a conventional training method such as BP. The critical point is when the training alters the model. On this operation, the authors have introduced a model alteration method named *Model Switching*, which is defined as follows.

Definition 1 (Model Switching): On altering the neural network model, methods which determine the moment or the

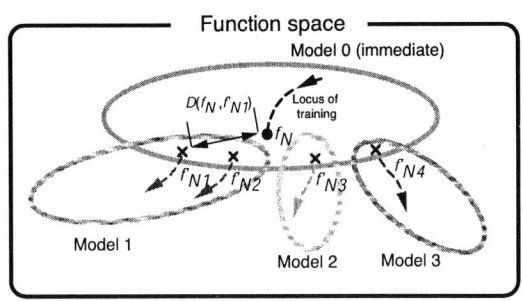

Fig. 2. Evaluation of the switchable candidates $f'_{N1}, \ldots, f'_{N4}$ (shown in "x"'s) by the map distance criterion. Switching will occur toward the candidate which gives the smallest map distance between the current map f_N.

occasion of model alteration, by taking into account the two factors in the following :

1) The nature and fitness of the new model and the initial map by the new model.
2) The status of the immediate model and map.

will be referred to as Model Switching.

In order to keep the search path in the function space as continuous as possible, inheritance of the map is important. In evaluating the map discrepancy (before and after the switch), measure *Map Distance* is used.

Definition 2 (Map Distance): The map distance between two mapping vector functions $g_1(x)$ and $g_2(x)$ trained with the training set $\{(x_m, y_m)\}_{m=1}^{M}$ is defined as,

$$D(g_1, g_2) = \frac{1}{M} \sum_{m=1}^{M} \|g_1(x_m) - g_2(x_m)\|^2, \quad (1)$$

where M is the number of the training pairs.

While training a network, candidates of switchable maps in other models are always monitored. When the map distance to one of the candidates is less than a certain threshold, switching of the model occurs. The idea of this operation is illustrated in Fig. 2.

B. MS by Unit Fusion and Unit Installation

Various types of operations to the network is conceivable in switching the model. Among them, an operation of particular interest is *unit fusion*, which either unifies the roles of two hidden layer units into one unit, or attributes the role of a hidden layer unit to the bias channel [6] [7].

Unit fusion implements a reduction in the model complexity as in *network pruning* [9]. For the precise description of the unit fusion operation, especially the manipulations of the weights in the network, see [6] and [7].

The relation between the nature of the fused unit pair (or the unit and the bias), and the map distance resulting due to the switch in the model, has been derived in the following theorem.

Theorem 1: Let the vector map of a three layered network be denoted by g_1, and the map of the same network with one hidden unit j pruned by fusing with unit i, be denoted by g_2. By denoting the distance of the two maps by $D_{ij}(g_1, g_2)$,

$$D_{ij}(g_1, g_2) \leq \frac{2}{O}(\sum_{k=1}^{O} w_{kj}^2)(S'_{max})^2 \sigma_j^2 (1 - |r_{ij}|), \quad (2)$$

holds using the following notations.

- O: Number of output layer units.
- S'_{max}: Maximum derivative of the unit transfer function.
- w_{kj}: Connection weight between the k-th output unit and the j-th hidden layer unit.
- σ_j^2: Output variance of the j-th hidden layer unit.
- r_{ij}: Correlation coefficient of the outputs of the i-th and the j-th hidden layer units.

When unit j is to be fused with the bias,

$$D_{bj}(g_1, g_2) \leq \frac{1}{O}(\sum_{k=1}^{O} w_{kj}^2)(S'_{max})^2 \sigma_j^2, \quad (3)$$

holds instead. See [6] and [7] for proofs.

According to the above theorem, fusion of unit pairs with response correlation of $r_{ij} \approx \pm 1$, and fusion of the bias and a unit having response variance of $\sigma_j^2 \approx 0$ will reduce the map distance. The former amounts to fusing the hidden layer units that have similar roles to one, and latter to fusing the unit with constant output with the bias. In [6] and [7], MS operation by unit fusion which resulted in a minimum estimated map distance was always selected.

The expansion of the model can be done by adding a hidden layer unit with random weights between the input and hidden layers, and zero-valued weights between the hidden and output layers. This *unit installation* will always allow MS with zero map distance.

C. Scheduling of MS

Various applicable MS operations can be selected according to the types of MS scheduling set for the training process. Network *pruning* and *growing* are one of the common approaches to override the limitations of a single model [9] [10] [11]. In case of *unlimited model scheduling*, where pruning and growing are jointly used, the training process is allowed to change the model as necessary, possibly driven by some internal triggers. In [12], an MS scheme controlled by the the monitoring measure reflecting the progress of training for automatic model selection is introduced.

When applying the training with MS to real world problems, preparing a system which allows various models can be costly. In such cases, training with MS can aid for an efficient training within the limited model. In *limited model scheduling*, the switching operation will be a composite one, to switch to a larger model and again to switch to a different map in the former model. When the training is caught in a local minima of the error potential function, the new map should enable to escape from it. Also, the composite switching operation to

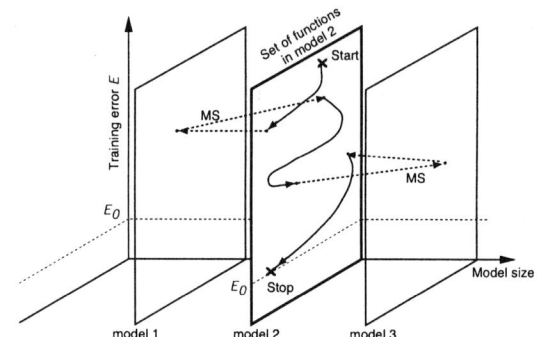

Fig. 3. The scheme of the change of the model and the map in the BP training with MS employing the limited model scheduling.

switch to a smaller model and again to switch to a different map within the former model, can be effective when there are redundancies in the extracted features during fast error convergence. By switching to a smaller model to remove the redundancy, and again switching to the original model by adding degrees of freedom may contribute to extraction of novel features. The change of the map by MS in the limited model scheduling is illustrated in Fig. 3.

D. The effect of MS operations

The findings in the experiments were that, in joint use of BP training and MS by unit fusion, the required training epochs were reduced and the generalization ability of the trained network was improved, in comparison with the networks trained in a single model.

Fusion of hidden layer units that have correlation $r_{ij} \approx \pm 1$ will work to eliminate duplicate feature extraction, and therefore the extracted features will be orthogonalized. It can be considered that, when the number of hidden layer unit is limited, this will enlarge the dimension of the space spanned by the hidden layer unit basis, and would be effective for efficient training. Elimination of near-zero variance units amounts to pruning the basis elements that have no effect to the training set (null space), that may have harmful effects on generalization.

III. Learning with Hidden Layer Regularization and Model Switching

Inspired by the results of applying networks trained by BP with MS, the orthogonalization of the hidden layer feature extraction will be further put forward by introducing a penalty term in the error function.

The new error function is defined as,

$$E = E_0 + \lambda E_1, \quad (4)$$

with

$$E_0 = \frac{1}{2MO} \sum_{p=1}^{M} \|y_p - o_p\|^2, \quad (5)$$

and
$$E_1 = \frac{1}{2}(\sum_{s=1}^{N}\sum_{t=1}^{N} r_{st}^2 - N) \quad (6)$$

Here, r_{st} is the correlation of the outputs of the s-th and t-th hidden layer units, each of which falls in $-1 \leq r_{st} \leq 1$. N ad O are the number of the hidden and output layer units, respectively. In Eq. (6), the value N is subtracted since the autocorrelation ($s = t$) will be always 1. Also, the whole sum is halved to compensate for the duplicated summation (r_{st} and r_{ts}). Parameter λ in Eq. (4) is a constant which determines how much the added penalty affects the learning.

The modification to the weights in the steepest descent method would be,

$$w_{mn}(t+1) = w_{mn}(t) + \Delta w_{mn}, \quad (7)$$

where t denotes the time, and

$$\Delta w_{mn} = \eta(\frac{\partial E_0}{\partial w_{mn}} + \lambda \frac{\partial E_1}{\partial w_{mn}}), \quad (8)$$

with parameter η being the training gain constant. Parameter λ determines the relative significance of the error factor E_1.

The term $\partial E_0 / \partial w_{mn}$ will be identical to those for the conventional batched backpropagation [4] [13]. The term $\partial E_1 / \partial w_{mn}$ is formulated as follows.

For the weights connecting the j-th hidden layer unit and the k-th output layer unit,

$$\frac{\partial E_1}{\partial w_{kj}} = 0, \quad (9)$$

holds since E_1 determined by the hidden layer unit response, is not a function of w_{kj}. For the weights between the i-th input channel and the j-th hidden layer unit, we have

$$\frac{\partial E_1}{\partial w_{ji}} = \frac{1}{2}\frac{\partial}{\partial \mathbf{h}_j}\sum_{s=1}^{N}\sum_{t=1}^{N}r_{st}^2 \cdot \frac{\partial \mathbf{h}_j}{\partial \mathbf{u}_j} \cdot \frac{\partial \mathbf{u}_j}{\partial w_{ji}} \quad (10)$$

$$= \mathbf{d}_j^T \cdot S'_j \cdot \mathbf{i}_i, \quad (11)$$

where $\mathbf{h}_j = [h_{j1}h_{j2}\ldots h_{jP}]^T \in \mathbf{R}^P$ and $\mathbf{u}_j = [u_{j1}u_{j2}\ldots u_{jP}]^T \in \mathbf{R}^P$ denote the outputs and the potentials of the j-th hidden layer unit for all of the training inputs. Here, $h_{jp} = s(u_{jp})$ holds with s being the unit transfer function. The details of $\mathbf{d}_j \in \mathbf{R}^M$, $S'_j \in \mathbf{R}^{M \times M}$, and $\mathbf{i}_i \in \mathbf{R}^M$ are given in the Appendix.

Note that this learning method can be defined assuming the batch mode training only, since the responses of the hidden layer units to the whole training set is required to calculate the regularization modification in Eq. (11).

IV. EXPERIMENTS

The proposed training method was applied to a simple character recognition problem. A set of 26 alphabet character fonts defined in bitmaps with dimension of $7 \times 7 = 49$ were used in the training to be recognized by the neural network (Fig. 4). In the test phase, original fonts with 5 random positions among the 49 bits flipped (0 to 1 or 1 to 0), were used to evaluate the generalization ability of the trained network.

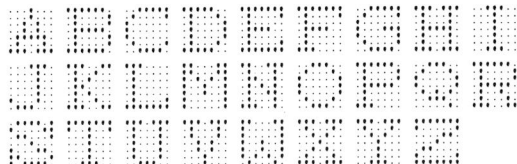

Fig. 4. The alphabet character bitmaps used in the experiment.

The networks had 49 input channels and 26 output units with various initial number of hidden layer units (N). All the units employed a sigmoidal activation function. The output of the j-th unit was defined as,

$$o_j = (1 + \exp(\sum_i w_{ji}o_i))^{-1}. \quad (12)$$

Experiments were conducted with the following conditions varied.

1) Model : Single model, Pruning by MS, and Limited Model by MS.
2) Regularization (λ in Eq. (4)) : 0.0, 0.001, 0.01, and 0.1.
3) Hidden layer (N) : 8, 12, and 18.

In all the trainings, batch training with the gain factor of $\eta = 5.0$ and the momentum factor of $\alpha = 0.9$ [13] was used to achieve $E_0 = 0.001$. For the training sessions employing model alteration by MS, switching candidates had to fulfill effective map distance [7] of $D \leq 0.005$, and MS operations were inhibited during 200 epochs initially, after unit fusion and unit installation.

In Fig. 5, the epochs required to train the networks and the recognition rate for the test set are shown. Each result is an average of 100 trials with random initial conditions. It is observed that use of regularization with λ factor of $0.001 \sim 0.01$ improves both the speed of training and the generalization ability. However, a larger value of λ becomes harmful to these performances.

This result shows that excessive uniform penalty for orthogonalization can be harmful to the training and generalization ability. Truly duplicated use of learning resource (hidden layer feature extraction) can be an issue with networks with limited resource, especially at the early stage of the training process. The situation can be avoided by applying the regularization term to decrease the correlation between unit pairs that are highly similar. Therefore, an alternative regularization error measure of,

$$E'_1 = \frac{1}{2}(\sum_{s=1}^{N} r_{sk(s)}^2), \quad (13)$$

$$k(s) = argmax_t(r_{st}^2) \quad (14)$$

may be used.

V. CONCLUSION

This paper introduced a scheme of layered neural network training, which incorporates model alteration during training, and regularization of the features extracted in the hidden

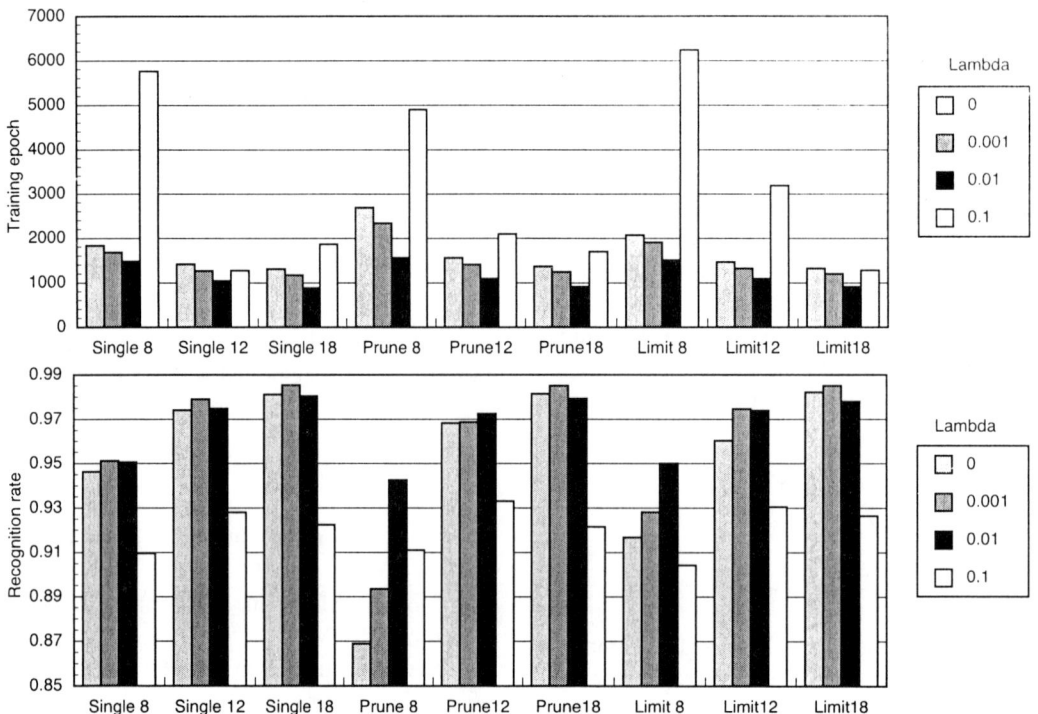

Fig. 5. Comparison of the training epochs (above) and the recognition rates (below). "Single", "Pruning", and "Limit" denote the model alteration strategy, and the numbers denote the initial number of hidden layer units. All experiments were tried for four different values of regularization parameters.

layer units. The use of Model Switching (MS), which is the operation to switch the network to a different model involved the orthogonalization of the features extracted in the hidden layer, proved to improve training efficiency and generalization ability in the previous works. Assuming that the orthogonalization contributes to the observed merits, joint use of MS and orthogonalization of the hidden layer feature by introducing a regularization term in the training, was introduced. The network trained by the proposed training scheme was applied to a pattern recognition problem, and some improvements in the training efficiency and generalization ability, were observed.

APPENDIX

Further details of the formula in Eq. (11) are given here. Term d_j will be derived as,

$$\begin{aligned}
d_j &= \frac{1}{2}\frac{\partial}{\partial h_j}\sum_{s=1}^{N}\sum_{t=1}^{N}r_{st}^2 \\
&= \frac{\partial}{\partial h_j}\sum_{s=1}^{N}r_{sj}^2 \\
&= [d_{j1}\ldots d_{jp}\ldots d_{jM}]^T \in \mathbf{R}^M, \quad (15)\\
d_{jp} &= \sum_{s=1}^{N}\frac{\partial}{\partial h_{jp}}r_{sj}^2, \quad (16)
\end{aligned}$$

and

$$\begin{aligned}
\frac{\partial}{\partial h_{jp}}r_{sj}^2 &= \frac{\partial}{\partial h_{jp}}\left(\frac{\sigma_{sj}^4}{\sigma_s^2\sigma_j^2}\right) \\
&= \frac{2r_{sj}^2}{M}\left\{\frac{(h_{sp}-\bar{h}_s)(1-\frac{1}{M})}{\sigma_{sj}^2} - \frac{h_{jp}-\bar{h}_j}{\sigma_j^2}\right\},
\end{aligned}$$
(17)

where $\bar{h}_i$, σ_i^2, and σ_{ij}^2 denote the average, variance and covariance of the hidden layer unit outputs.

Matrix S'_j and vector i_i are obtained as,

$$S'_j = \begin{bmatrix} s'(u_{j1}) & & 0 \\ & \ddots & \\ 0 & & s'(u_{jM}) \end{bmatrix} \in \mathbf{R}^{M\times M}, \quad (18)$$

and

$$i_i = [o_{i1}\ldots o_{ip}\ldots o_{iM}]^T \in \mathbf{R}^M, \quad (19)$$

respectively. Here, s' is the derivative of the unit transfer function s, and o_{ip} is the output of the i-th unit in the previous layer for the p-th training input.

From Eqs. (17),(18) and(19), we have,

$$\begin{aligned}
\frac{\partial E_1}{\partial w_{ji}} &= d_j^T S'_j i_i \\
&= \sum_{p=1}^{M}\sum_{s=1}^{N}\left[\frac{2r_{sj}^2}{M}\left\{\frac{(h_{sp}-\bar{h}_s)(1-\frac{1}{M})}{\sigma_{sj}^2}\right.\right.
\end{aligned}$$

$$\left. -\frac{h_{jp}-\bar{h}_j}{\sigma_j^2}\right\} \cdot s'(u_{jp}) \cdot o_{ip}\Bigg]. \tag{20}$$

ACKNOWLEDGMENT

This work was supported by Grant-in-Aid for Encouragement of Young Scientists, Japan Society for the Promotion of Science (JSPS), project number 12750362.

REFERENCES

[1] K. Fukunaga, *Introduction to Statistical Pattern Recognition*. Academic Press, 1972.
[2] C. Cortes and V. Vapnik, "Support-vector networks," *Machine Learning*, vol. 20, no. 3, pp. 273–297, 1995. [Online]. Available: citeseer.nj.nec.com/cortes95supportvector.html
[3] V. N. Vapnik, *The Nature of Statistical Learning Theory*, 2nd ed. Springer, 2000.
[4] D. E. Rumelhart, J. L. McClelland, and the PDP Research Group, *Parallel distributed processing*. MIT Press, 1986, vol. 1.
[5] M. Gori and A. Tesi, "On the problem of local minima in backpropagation," *IEEE Transaction on Pattern Analysis and Machine Intelligence*, vol. 14, no. 1, pp. 76–86, 1992. [Online]. Available: citeseer.nj.nec.com/gori92problem.html
[6] K. Kameyama and Y. Kosugi, "Model switching by channel fusion for network pruning and efficient feature extraction," 1998, pp. 1861–1866.
[7] ——, "Neural network model switching for efficient feature extraction," *IEICE Transations on Information and Systems*, vol. E82-D, no. 10, pp. 1372–1383, 1999.
[8] ——, "Semiconductor defect classification using hyperellipsoid clustering neural networks and model switching," 1999, p. No.569.
[9] R. Reed, "Pruning algorithms - a survey," *IEEE Transactions on Neural Networks*, vol. 4, no. 5, pp. 740–747, 1993.
[10] G. Castellano, A. M. Fanelli, and M. Pelillo, "An iterative pruning algorithm for feedforward neural networks," *IEEE Transactions on Neural Networks*, vol. 8, no. 3, pp. 519–531, 1997.
[11] S. E. Fahlman and C. Lebiere, "The cascade-correlation learning architecture," in *Advances in Neural Information Processing Systems*, D. S. Touretzky, Ed., vol. 2. Denver 1989: Morgan Kaufmann, San Mateo, 1990, pp. 524–532. [Online]. Available: citeseer.nj.nec.com/fahlman91cascadecorrelation.html
[12] K. Kameyama and Y. Kosugi, "Automatic fusion and splitting of artificial neural elements in optimizing the network size," vol. 3, 1991, pp. 1633–1638.
[13] S. Haykin, *Neural Networks - A Comprehensive Foundation*, 2nd ed. Prentice Hall, 1999.

Multi Class Support Vector Machine Implementation To Intrusion Detection

Tarun Ambwani
(Final Year Student)
Bachelor Of Computer Engineering,
K. K. Wagh College Of Engineering,
University of Pune, Nashik, INDIA.
Email: digicom_inc@yahoo.co.in

Date: 27/01/2003

Abstract

Despite advances in security practices the threat to information assurance is on the rise. Due to the growing number of malicious usage, attacks, stealing of sensitive information and sabotage, information security has become one of the prime concerns for many governments as well as corporate organizations, the world over. There exists a constant need for improvement and innovation in detection of intrusions and adoption of efficient countermeasures against security breaches. In a new approach, this paper focuses on applying multi class support vector machine classifiers, using one-versus-one method, for anomalous as well as misuse detection to identify attacks precisely by type. Evaluation has been done over a benchmark dataset used in the Third Knowledge Discovery and Data mining competition (KDD'99). The results obtained are comparable to some of the best in the contest.

1. Introduction

Technological developments over decades have led to a highly integrated electronic world - the realm of the Internet. Despite advances in security practices the threat to information assurance is on the rise. Due to the growing number of malicious usage, attacks, stealing of sensitive information and sabotage, information security has become one of the prime concerns for many governments as well as corporate organizations, the world over. Over the years various response teams have been created to counter such incidents. Statistics collected over time suggest that there exists a constant need for improvement and innovation in detection of intrusions and adoption of efficient countermeasures against security breaches, in order to prevent widespread information warfare.

In a new approach, this paper focuses on applying multi class support vector machine classifiers, using one-versus-one method, for anomalous as well as misuse detection to identify attacks precisely by type. The research has been conducted using a software tool LIBSVM Version 2.35 (see [2]). Evaluation has been done over a benchmark dataset used in the Third Knowledge Discovery and Data mining competition (KDD'99), which originated from MIT Lincoln Labs and was developed by the DARPA.

2. Intrusion Detection

In the context of information systems, intrusion refers to any unauthorized access, unauthorized attempt to access or damage, or malicious use of information resources [17]. The identification of such accesses or attempts is known as intrusion detection.

The concept of intrusion detection has been around for over twenty years but has witnessed dramatic rise in popularity recently. The notion of intrusion detection was born in 1980 with James Anderson's seminal paper written for a government organization [12]. Since then different approaches have been implemented in the research community, some of these are presented in [1,11,13,14,16,17].

Intrusions can be classified mainly in two types - anomaly and misuse. Anomaly detection refers to identification of deviations from the normal usage patterns. Misuse detection, on the other hand, primarily searches for recognized patterns of attacks. Usually, misuse detection is simpler than anomaly detection as it uses rule based or signature comparison methods whereas anomaly detection requires storage of normal usage behavior and operates upon audit data generated by the operating system.

Intrusion detection systems(IDSs) today are regarded as state-of-the-art measures for perimeter defense. Many of these systems built so far are based on the general model proposed by D. Denning [7]. IDSs can be mainly distinguished into two types - network based systems, which scan network traffic over a subnet to identify possible attacks using misuse detection approaches and host based systems, which detect possible attacks on individual computers usually relying on information provided by the operating system.

Almost all commercial intrusion detection systems today use signature based or rule based approaches to intrusion detection, this leads to high overhead of maintaining up to date signature databases. Adaptable, cost effective and real time intrusion detection is the goal of the researches in the field.

3. Support Vector Machine

3.1. Introduction

Support vector machines(SVMs) are learning machines that conceptually implement the following idea – input vectors are mapped to a high dimensional feature space through some non-linear mapping chosen a priori [5,6]. In this feature space a decision surface (a.k.a. hyperplane) is constructed. Special properties of this decision surface, ensures high generalization ability of the learning machine. SVMs are based on structural risk minimization principle, which minimizes the generalization error [4].

Support vector machines avoid the "curse of dimensionality" by placing an upper bound on the margin between different classes. The classification problem is viewed as a quadratic optimization problem. To classify data a set of support vectors, which are members of the training data outlining the hyperplane in the feature space, is determined.

For describing the optimal separating hyperplane in the feature space (pre-Hilbert or inner product space) and estimating the corresponding coefficients of expansion of separating hyperplane, the inner product of two vectors in the feature space is estimated as a function of two variables in the input space [19]. Such functions are known as kernel functions. SVMs are the most well known class of algorithms, which use the idea of kernel substitution. With suitable choice of kernel the data can become separable in the feature space despite being non separable in the input space. Some popular kernel functions are - linear, polynomial and radial basis functions(RBF).

3.2. Multi class Support Vector Machines

The standard method for an N-class SVM is to construct N SVMs. The i-th SVM is trained with all the examples in the i-th class with positive labels, and all other examples with negative labels. SVMs trained in this way are known as one-against-rest or one-against all SVMs. Another method to construct N-class classifiers is by combining two-class classifiers. All possible two-class classifiers from a training set of N classes are constructed, each classifier being trained only on two out of N classes. Thus, there are K=N(N-1)/2 classifiers in all. This method of constructing N-class SVMs is commonly known as one-versus-one approach [15].

One-versus-one approach for multi class classification has been shown to perform better than one-versus-rest [3,9,10]. In this case classification is done using the former approach. The first use of this strategy on SVM was can be found in [8,18].

4. DARPA Evaluation and KDD'99 contest

The 1998 DARPA Intrusion Detection Evaluation Program was prepared and managed by MIT Lincoln Labs which, set up an environment to acquire nine weeks of raw TCP dump data for a local-area network (LAN) simulating a typical U.S. Air Force LAN. They operated the LAN as if it were a true Air Force environment, but peppered it with multiple attacks.

The raw training data was about four gigabytes of compressed binary TCP dump data from seven weeks of network traffic. This was processed into about five million connection records. The two weeks of test data yielded around two million connection records. Each connection record (approx. 100 bytes) was labeled as either normal, or as an attack, with exactly one specific attack type.

A standard set of data to be audited, which included a wide variety of intrusions simulated in a military network environment, was provided. The 1999 KDD intrusion detection contest used a version of this dataset [20].

For this research, the labeled 10% training and test datasets were used. The training dataset comprises of 22 attack types and the test data consists of 37 attack types, which can be arranged into 4 categories namely - Probe, DOS, U2R and R2L (description in [17,20]). In addition to these both datasets contain patterns belonging to normal activity.

The percentage distribution of both the training and test datasets with respect to the 5 categories is shown in Table 1.

Each connection record comprised of 41 features, shown in Table 3.

Table 1: % Distribution -taken from [22]

Category	% Distribution Training Data	%Distribution Test Data
Normal	19.69%	19.48%
Probe	0.83%	1.34%
DOS	79.24%	73.90%
U2R	0.01%	0.07%
R2L	0.23%	5.20%

The winning entry achieved an average cost of 0.2331 per test example, using cost matrix in Table 4, and obtained the following confusion matrix in Table 2.

Table 2: Winner's Resultant Confusion Matrix [22]

	Normal	Probe	DOS	U2R	R2L	% Correct
Normal	60262	243	78	4	6	99.5
Probe	511	3471	184	0	0	83.3
DOS	5299	1328	223226	0	0	97.1
U2R	168	20	0	30	10	13.2
R2L	14527	294	0	8	1360	8.4
% Correct	74.6	64.8	99.9	71.4	98.8	

Table 3: Features - taken from [21]

Feature Name	Type
duration	Continuous
protocol_type	Symbolic
service	Symbolic
flag	Symbolic
src_bytes	Continuous
dst_bytes	Continuous
land	Symbolic
wrong_fragment	Continuous
urgent	Continuous
hot	Continuous
num_failed_logins	Continuous
logged_in	Symbolic
num_compromised	Continuous
root_shell	Continuous
su_attempted	Continuous
num_root	Continuous
num_file_creations	Continuous
num_shells	Continuous
num_access_files	Continuous
num_outbound_cmds	Continuous
is_hot_login	Symbolic
is_guest_login	Symbolic
count	Continuous
srv_count	Continuous
serror_rate	Continuous
srv_serror_rate	Continuous
rerror_rate	Continuous
srv_rerror_rate	Continuous
same_srv_rate	Continuous
diff_srv_rate	Continuous
srv_diff_host_rate	Continuous
dst_host_count	Continuous
dst_host_srv_count	Continuous
dst_host_same_srv_rate	Continuous
dst_host_same_src_port_rate	Continuous
dst_host_srv_diff_host_rate	Continuous
dst_host_serror_rate	Continuous
dst_host_srv_serror_rate	Continuous
dst_host_rerror_rate	Continuous
dst_host_srv_rerror_rate	Continuous

Description of features can be found in [20]

Table 4: Cost Matrix - taken from [22]

	Normal	Probe	DOS	U2R	R2L
Normal	0	1	2	2	2
Probe	1	0	2	2	2
DOS	2	1	0	2	2
U2R	3	2	2	0	2
R2L	4	2	2	2	0

In rank order, the average costs obtained by all 24 entries were:

Table 5: Results KDD'99 - taken from [22]

0.2331	0.2474	0.2552	0.3344
0.2356	0.2479	0.2575	0.3767
0.2367	0.2523	0.2588	0.3854
0.2411	0.2530	0.2644	0.3899
0.2414	0.2531	0.2684	0.5053
0.2443	0.2545	0.2952	0.9414

It was concluded that all the first seventeen entries had performed well [22].

5. Implementation

Step I - Data preparation for training

As mentioned earlier, the trainings and testings were conducted using LIBSVM. In order to transform the KDD formatted data into the format accepted by LIBSVM a collection of C++ modules were written. The functions performed by the code were:

- Determining different types of alpha numeric strings (values taken by protocol_type, flag, service are strings) along with the various types of attacks present in the training as well as the labeled test data. This was done since LIBSVM can accept only numeric values for features.

- Converting the KDD dataset into format accepted by LIBSVM by assigning numeric values to the strings and class labels to the different types of attacks (as shown in table 6: Blank entries indicate 'not present').

- Determining precise distribution of attacks as shown in table 6.

- Constructing confusion matrices and determining cost per test sample in the testing stage (for 5 categories using cost matrix in table 4).

Step II - Training & Testing

After conversion, the training and test datasets were scaled in the interval of 0 to 1. The training data consisted of 22 types of attacks plus data belonging to normal category. Thus, in all the training was done for 23 classes. Multi class implementation of LIBSVM, which uses the one-versus-one approach, was utilized for this purpose [2]. The Radial Basis Function (RBF) kernel option was selected and value of C was varied, at first, keeping the gamma value set to the default of 1/41(no-of-features). Due to large difference in the probability distribution of the two datasets cross validation was not considered suitable. For few parameters C having the lowest cost per test sample Gamma (of RBF kernel) was varied. Testings were done for all the parameters selected. The goal was to achieve minimum cost per test sample. The results of both training and testings are presented in table 7.

Table 7: Training and Testing

Parameter Value	Total Support Vectors	Accuracy Detection (23 class)	Cost Per Test Sample (5 Category)
Variation of C for Gamma = 1/41 = 0.0243902			
150	1909	91.4738%	0.264458
200	1790	91.4719%	0.264451
300	1665	91.4744%	0.264004
400	1619	91.4773%	0.263770
500	1561	91.4847%	0.263104
600	1533	91.487%	0.262882
700	1500	91.487%	0.262747
800	1482	91.4857%	0.262699
900	1447	91.487%	0.262477
1000	1435	91.4876%	0.262130
1500	1368	91.4944%	0.261217
2000	1336	91.4953%	0.260969
4000	1248	91.5027%	0.260227
8000	1167	91.6403%	0.254475
10000	1153	91.6497%	0.254089
12000	1139	91.6484%	0.254018
14000	1129	91.6477%	0.253963
15000▶	1125	91.6493%	**0.253864**
18000	1128	91.6484%	0.253867
VARIATION OF GAMMA FOR C = 15000			
0.07	1065	91.6767%	0.252947
0.08	1056	91.6699%	0.252883
0.09▶	1090	91.6738%	**0.252854**
0.1	1073	91.6683%	0.252925
0.11	1070	91.6574%	0.252928
0.13	1071	91.6439%	0.253031
0.15	1082	91.6397%	0.252954
0.19	1076	91.6178%	0.252980
0.21	1066	91.596%	0.253497
0.25	1054	91.5789%	0.254243

*Due to space constraints all variations are not shown.

Table 6: Distribution Of Patterns

Class Label	Category And Attacks	No. Of Patterns	
		Training Data	Test Data
17	NORMAL	97277	60593
	PROBE	**4107**	**4166**
8	ipsweep	1247	306
12	mscan		1053
16	nmap	231	84
21	portsweep	1040	354
25	saint		736
26	satan	1589	1633
	DOS	**391458**	**229851**
1	apache2		794
2	back	2203	1098
9	land	21	9
11	mailbomb		5000
15	neptune	107201	58001
20	pod	264	87
22	processtable		759
28	smurf	280790	164091
33	teardrop	979	12
34	udpstorm		
	U2R	**52**	**230**
3	buffer_overflow	30	22
6	httptunnel		158
10	loadmodule	9	2
18	perl	3	2
23	ps		18
24	rootkit	10	13
32	sqlattack		2
40	xterm		13
	R2L	**1126**	**16189**
4	ftp_write	8	3
5	guess_passwd	53	4367
7	imap	12	1
13	multihop	7	18
14	named		17
19	phf	4	2
27	sendmail		17
29	snmpgetattack		7741
30	snmpguess		2406
31	spy	2	
35	warezclient	1020	
36	warezmaster	20	1602
37	worm		2
38	xlock		9
39	xsnoop		4
TOTAL:	**39 Attacks**	**494020**	**311029**

Note: In the *training data* 2 patterns, one each of Neptune and Normal were found corrupted even after repeated downloading of the dataset from the UCI archive. These patterns were discarded and the above table was created.

Table 8: Confusion Matrix obtained after Multi Class SVM Classification

	2	3	4	5	7	8	9	10	13	15	16	17	18	19	20	21	24	26	28	31	33	35	36
17		2	1			1		1	1	2		60330		1	15	65	2	131			37		4
8						298						5							3				
12										255		549				222		27					
16											83	1											
21						1				12		32				308		1					
25								100				18						618					
26												167				7		1459					
1	439											355											
2	90											1008											
9							8					1											
11												4967						33					
15										57856		10				135							
20												2			85								
22										5		364				5		24	361				
28												5						3	164083				
33																					12		
34											1	1											
3		1										16	2				3						
6												149			2			7					
10												1	1										
18												2											
23												15											1
24												12	1										
32													1				1						
40		2						1				10											
5												4365						2					
4												2											1
7												1											
13												18											
14								1				16											
19												1		1									
27												11					2						4
29												7736						5					
30												2403				3							
36			75		1				59			930						1				17	519
37												2											
38												8						1					
39												3	1										

*Different categories (in order - Normal, Probe, DOS, U2R and R2L) are shown separately. The figure is just a confusion matrix without the % column. Leftmost column and topmost row indicate class labels of test data and training data, respectively. The entries marked in red are those that have been correctly detected. Blank entries indicate **0(zero)**.*

Step III - Results and Calculations

As shown in Table 7, the lowest cost was obtained at regularization parameter(C) value of 15000. The Gamma value for the same was 0.09. Optimization was done for 6757969 iterations. Total number of kernel evaluations were 313136024. Total number of support vectors were 1090. CPU runtime for training was measured to be 31 minutes and that for testing was 14mins. The machine used for the complete duration of all trainings and testings was running Pentium III - 933 MHz processor with 256MB of RAM.

The percentage accuracy in detection, 23-class classification, was obtained to be 91.6738 (Table 7) and exact classification result is shown in Table 8. The lowest cost per test sample calculated (Table 7) was **0.252854,** which is slightly better than the cost achieved by the entry at the 10th rank (refer table 5). The confusion matrix obtained, after arranging the classes into categories, is shown in table 9.

Table 9: Result Matrix (5 category)

	Normal	Probe	DOS	U2R	R2L	% Correct
Normal	60330	197	54	5	7	99.6
Probe	772	3124	270	0	0	75
DOS	6713	201	222578	0	361	96.8
U2R	205	9	0	12	2	5.3
R2L	15496	8	3	6	676	4.2
% Correct	72.2	88.3	99.9	52.2	64.6	

6. Conclusion

Statistical learning methods are being used more extensively in recent intrusion detection systems, owing to their adaptability and generalization capability regarding new attack signatures. Intrusion detection requires identification of attacks specifically by type. Earlier researches conducted using support vector machines fail to achieve this and have been done over small datasets [14,16,17]. The work presented in this paper has been done primarily to detect and identify attacks by type along with determining the suitability of the chosen approach. Although, the results obtained can be judged to be statistically little less significant than the winning entry in the contest, they can be bettered with more exhaustive research. Since the datasets are unbalanced determining and setting proper weight parameters may result in improvement. Support vector machines hold high potential against traditional approaches like Artificial Neural Networks due to their scalability, faster training and running times. Application of support vector machines to the task of intrusion detection shows promising results and this work is a contribution to the researches done in the field.

7. Acknowledgements

I would like to acknowledge helpful advice given to me by Prof. Chih Jen Lin (National Taiwan University).

8. References

[1] Anup K. Ghosh and Aaron Schwattzbard - A study in using neural networks for anomaly and misuse detection. *Proceedings of the 8th USENIX Security Symposium* (Aug 23-26, 1999).
[2] Chih-Chung Chang and Chih-Jen Lin - LIBSVM: a library for support vector machines.
[3] Chih-Wei Hsu and Chih-Jen Lin(2002) - A comparison of methods for multiclass support vector machines.
[4] Christopher J. C. Burges(1998) - A tutorial on support vector machines for pattern recognition.
[5] Colin Campbell(2000) - Kernel Methods: A survey of Current Techniques.
[6] Corinna Cortes and Vladimir Vapnik(1995) - Support Vector Networks.
[7] D. Denning (1987) - An intrusion detection model. *IEEE transactions on software engineering*, 13(2)
[8] J. Friedman (1996) - Another approach to polychotomous classification. Technical report, Department of Statistics, Stanford University.
[9] J. Weston and C. Watkins (1998). Multi-class support vector machines. Technical Report CSD-TR-98-04, Royal Holloway.
[10] J. C. Platt, N. Cristianni and J. Shawe Taylor(2000) - Large margin DAGs for multiclass classification in *Advances in Neural Information Processing Systems*, Volume 12, MIT Press.
[11] Jake Ryan, Meng-Jang Lin and Risto Miikkulainen - Intrusion detection with neural networks in *Advances in Neural Information Processing Systems*, Volume 10 (MIT Press, 1998).
[12] James Anderson, Computer Security Threat Monitoring and Surveillance. James P. Anderson Co., Fort Washington, Pa., 1980.
[13] James Cannady(1998) - Artificial Neural Networks for intrusion detection.
[14] John S. Baras and Maben Rabi - Intrusion detection with support vector machines and generative models, Institute of Systems Research (May 24, 2002).
[15] S. Knerr, L. Personnaz and G. Dreyfus(1990) - Single layer learning revisted: a stepwise procedure for building and training a neural network. In J Fogelman(Ed.), *Neurocomputing Algorithms, Architectures and Applications*. Springer-Verlag.
[16] Srinivas Mukkamulla, Guadalupe I. Janoski and Andrew H. Sung - Intrusion detection using support vector machines.
[17] Srinivas Mukkamulla, Guadalupe I. Janoski and Andrew H. Sung - Intrusion detection using neural networks and support vector machines.
[18] U. Krebel (1999). Pairwise classification and support vector machines. In B. Scholkopf, C. J. C. Burges, and A. J. Smola (Eds.), *Advances in Kernel Methods - Support Vector Learning*, Cambridge, MA, pp. 255-268. MIT Press.
[19] Vladimir N. Vapnik(1999) - An overview of statistical learning theory. *IEEE transactions on Neural Networks, Vol. 10.*
[20] http://kdd.ics.edu/datbases/kddcup99/task.html
[21] http://kdd.ics.edu/datbases/kddcup99/kddcup.names
[22] http://www.cs.ucsd.edu/users/elkan/clresults.html

On the efficiency of OLS reduced probabilistic neural networks for aircraft-flare discrimination

Gilles Labonté
Department of Mathematics and Computer Science
Royal Military College of Canada
Kingston, Ontario, Canada K7K 7B4
Email: labonte-g@rmc.ca

Abstract - Probabilistic neural networks (PNN) are the instruments of choice when it comes to critical decision making. Indeed, their output is not a simple yes-or-no decision; they are able to produce the probability that the features received as their input correspond to an object of any one of many classes. In work reported elsewhere, we have devised such a network for the discrimination of aircrafts from their decoy flares. It is very efficient, consistently exhibiting a recognition success rate of the order of 98-99%. However, because these neural networks are based on the Parzen-windows method, they must contain a very large number of neurons in order to be efficient. This can represent a serious disadvantage when they are to be incorporated in a real time system. It is thus advantageous to be able to reduce their size, without affecting appreciably their performance. We report in this article on the success we have had with adapting and applying an Orthogonal Least Squares (OLS) reduction method to the probabilistic neural network we built previously. We show that this method allows for a reduction of the number of neurons by as much as 81.9% with a decrease in performance of only 0.6%. Even a drastic reduction of 97.7% of number of neurons still produces a network with a 93.5% success rate. A side benefit of the application of this method to PNNs, is an ordered list of the images that the neural network considers as the best representatives of their class of objects.

I. INTRODUCTION

We report results concerning our work on an automatic decision system to differentiate between aircrafts and the decoy flares they deploy. The Defense Research and Development Canada establishment at Valcartier (DRDC-Valcartier) has developed an infrared tracker for the purpose of investigating relevant image processing and target tracking methods. This system is described in details in Morin and Lessard [1]. At its heart is an infrared camera that produces an image of 256×256 pixels of gray-scale intensities. The various objects present in this image then have to be recognized, and one of them has to be selected for tracking. Fig. 1 shows an example of such an image. In this particular one, the flare is rather easy to recognize, but this is not always the case; some flares produce shapes that make them difficult to differentiate from aircrafts. However, the challenge in this problem comes from the fact that the system has to function in real time. Thus, in order to minimize the computing time, the number of features extracted from the images is kept very small. The pattern recognition

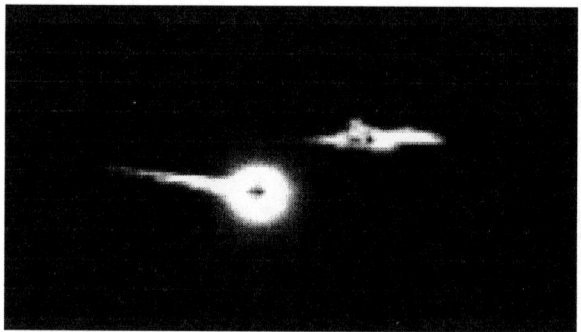

Fig. 1. Gray scale infrared image of an aircraft deploying a flare

algorithms therefore have to be able to function with little information.

Previous work we did on this problem, reported in Cayouette, Labonté and Morin [2], resulted in a probabilistic neural network (PNN) that can very successfully discriminate between aircrafts and flares. PNNs were first described by Specht [3], [4] and are explained in many books on neural networks such as, for example, in Section 4.3.5 of Duda, Hart and Stork. [5] and Section 7.3.1 of Fausett [6]. We chose this particular type of neural networks because, when given as input a set of features of an object, they can be made to output the probabilities that this object belong to any one of the possible classes. For the application at hand, in which critical decisions have to be taken, this makes the PNN far superior to all other neural networks that simply output a yes or no decision or even some "confidence index", the relation of which to the actual probability is unknown. Indeed, the information supplied by the PNN allows the user to take advantage of Bayes' theory [7] that provides an optimal and sound mathematical basis for decision-making. Chapter 2 of [5] and Sections 1.8 and 1.9 of [6] provide clear discussions of this point. Another major advantage of PNNs is their short training time. They are ready to perform their classification task after being shown, only once, a set of exemplars of objects of the various classes to be learned.

Paradoxically, the main disadvantage of PNNs stems from that which provides their remarkable efficiency. Indeed, these neural networks construct an estimate of the probability density functions, according to the Parzen-windows method [8], by summing the outputs of radial basis function neurons.

The probability theory underpinning this method states that this estimate can be expected to be valid only when there is a very large number of neurons. In real world situations, such as the one we are dealing with, there is frequently 1,000 or more neurons. When the neural network has to be integrated in a real time system, as in our case, there is a definite advantage in the neural network having as few neurons as possible. Indeed, if it is realized on a small number of processors, as for the DRDC-Valcartier system, a decrease in the number of its neurons is immediately translated into a decrease in processing time. This is not the case if the network is realized on a parallel computer, with perhaps as many processors as there are neurons. Nevertheless, in that case, being able to concentrate more knowledge in a smaller number of processors still means that a much better performing network or more networks can be realized on the same hardware.

A. Problem Considered and Solution

As mentioned above, we already possess a PNN that performs remarkably well, with a success rate that is consistently close to 98.7% of correct identification of aircrafts and flares. Furthermore, in most cases where it makes mistakes, it outputs odds close to 50-50 for the object seen to be either an aircraft or a flare. It is difficult to imagine that a network of another type could do better. However, because, it has a large number, namely 955, neurons, while it has to be incorporated in a real time system, we wanted to examine the possibility of building a new neural network, with fewer neurons, but similar performances as the one we already have.

We solved this problem by adapting to PNNs the Orthogonal Least Squares (OLS) method described by Chen Cowan and Grant [9] and in Section 3.6.3 of Ham and Kostanic [10]. Accordingly, we constructed a new neural network with fewer neurons that imitates the behavior of our PNN that performs so well. This new network is obtained by adding to it one neuron at the time, selecting the best neuron to add next as that which minimizes the most the error made by the new network. It is interesting to note that this construction method provides, as a side benefit, an ordered list of the exemplars that the neural network considers to be the best representatives of their class of objects. This, in itself, is worthwhile because an analysis of these images could yield hints at how to train networks more efficiently.

II. INITIAL NEURAL NETWORK

The image processing stages of the DRDC-Valcartier system have been described by Morin [11]. They can be summed up as follows. In a first stage, a low-pass filter is applied in order to remove much of the noise. The images are then segmented into blobs with the help of an intensity thresholding technique. For each blob in an image, a particular set of characteristics is extracted. In [2], we explained how, from these characteristics, we defined variables that are invariant under translations and rotations, and thus, correspond to intrinsic features of the objects. We then determined the discriminating power of these features, by examining their individual probability density functions. This resulted in our choosing the following 8 variables as components of the input vectors for our neural network.

- The normalized average intensity I_{av}/A, where A is the area of the blob.
- The ratios $\sqrt{M_{max}}/A$ and $\sqrt{M_{min}}/A$ where M_{max} and M_{min} are respectively the maximum and minimum moment of inertia about an axis through the blob's centroïde.
- The ratios $D_{max}/\sqrt{A}$ and $D_{min}/\sqrt{A}$, where D_{max} and D_{min} are respectively the maximum and the minimum of the radial distances of the blob, i.e. the distances between the blob's centroïde and its perimeter.
- The normalized variance of these radial distances: μ_D^2/A.
- The angle of orientation of the blob's principal axis of minimum moment of inertia.
- The roundness, i.e. the ratio $\frac{P^2}{4\pi A}$, where P is the blob's perimeter.

It is worthwhile recalling here, before we describe the reduction method, the basic ideas underlying PNNs and the particularities of the one we used. At the start, we consider that, when presented with the image of an object, the a priori probabilities that it be an aircraft P_{AC} or a flare P_F are equal. We let, as usual, $p(\mathbf{x}|\omega)$ denote the conditional probability that an object of a given class ω (our classes are here labeled ω = AC for aircrafts and ω = F for flares) has feature vector $\mathbf{x}$ and $p(\omega|\mathbf{x})$ that for an object with characteristics $\mathbf{x}$ to belong to the class ω. Then, according to Bayes' theorem,

$$p(\omega|\mathbf{x}) = \frac{p(\mathbf{x}|\omega)}{p(\mathbf{x})} \qquad (1)$$

where $p(\mathbf{x}) = p(\mathbf{x}|AC) + p(\mathbf{x}|F)$.

The PNN constructs an estimate of the probability $p(\mathbf{x}|\omega)$ by the Parzen-windows method [8] (see also Section 4.3 of [5]) as follows. Let $\mathbf{x}_1, \mathbf{x}_2,..,\mathbf{x}_n$ be feature vectors for objects in a same class ω. Then, according to Parzen, if n is large enough, an estimate of the probability density function $p(\mathbf{x}|\omega)$ is obtained as

$$p(\mathbf{x}|\omega) = \frac{1}{n}\sum_{i=1}^{n}\phi_i(\mathbf{x}) \qquad (2)$$

where $\phi_i(\mathbf{x}) = \phi(\mathbf{x}-\mathbf{x}_i)$, ϕ being a "window function" that serves to interpolate between the measured values $\{\mathbf{x}_i, i=1$ to $n\}$. We have taken for ϕ, the commonly used Gaussian:

$$\phi(\mathbf{x}) = \frac{1}{(\sqrt{2\pi}\sigma)^d} \exp(-\frac{\mathbf{x}^2}{2\sigma^2}) \qquad (3)$$

in which σ is the spread parameter and d is the dimension of the vector $\mathbf{x}$. This Gaussian is normalized such that its integral over all $\mathbb{R}^d$ is equal to one. Parzen's formula (2), combined with Bayes' formula (1), are realizable in a radial basis function neural network that has the structure shown in Fig. 2.

The particular network shown in this figure would have been constructed from n exemplars of aircraft images and m exemplars of flares. It is a 3-layer network. Its first layer consists of two independent sets of radial basis function neurons. The weight vectors of the neurons in the first and second sets are respectively the n feature vectors for aircrafts: $\mathbf{x}_i$, i=1 to n, and the m feature vectors for the flares: $\mathbf{x}_i$ i = n+1 to n+m. For an input vector $\mathbf{x}$, the output of the i'th neuron in the first layer is $\phi_i(\mathbf{x})$.

The second layer consists of only three neurons. One of them receives its inputs from all the neurons of the aircraft set, through connections of weights 1/n. This neuron's transfer function is the identity. Thus, it simply sums all of its inputs and returns as output, according to (2), an approximation of $p(\mathbf{x}|AC)$. Another neuron in the second layer plays exactly the same role, with respect to the flares, as the above one plays with respect to the aircrafts. Its output is an estimate of $p(\mathbf{x}|F)$. Finally, the third neuron receives all the inputs of the above two neurons. Its transfer function f has for value f(x) = 1/x. Its output is therefore $1/p(\mathbf{x})$.

The third layer has two neurons. The first one receives the output of the aircraft neuron and that of the third neuron of the second layer, which it multiplies together. Its transfer function is the identity so that, according to (1), its output is $p(AC|\mathbf{x})$, the probability that the feature vector $\mathbf{x}$ correspond to an aircraft. The second neuron of the third layer plays the same role as the first one, with respect to the flare neuron of the second layer. Its output is therefore $p(F|\mathbf{x})$, the probability that the feature vector $\mathbf{x}$ correspond to a flare.

Such a neural network is trained by a single presentation of the exemplars. During this presentation, it retains all the feature vectors of a same class of objects, which it uses as reference vectors for as many radial basis function neurons in the first layer. Thus, its learning is very fast. However, as is easily realized, they will contain a large number of neurons. For example, in our application, the data consisted in a set of 1264 images, 758 of aircrafts and 506 of flares. These were extracted from video sequences showing aircrafts coming and going in various directions. We divided this data into a training set of 584 vectors and a validation set of 174 vectors for aircrafts and a training set of 371 vectors and a validation set of 135 vectors for flares. These sets were obtained by randomly distributing vectors in the validation sets with a probability of 25%. Thus, our PNN had 955 neurons in its first layer.

III. ORTHOGONAL LEAST SQUARES REDUCTION

Since, in the PNN shown in Fig. 2, the sub-networks that build the probability density functions for the various classes are independent, the network reduction process can be applied to each of these sub-network separately. Thus, we shall hereafter describe this method in terms of only one sub-network.

Let Φ be the n×n matrix, the columns of which are the vectors $\phi_i \in \mathbb{R}^n$ defined as:

$$\phi_i = [\varphi_i(\mathbf{x}_1), \varphi_i(\mathbf{x}_2), \ldots, \varphi_i(\mathbf{x}_n)]^T$$

The components of this vector are the outputs of the same i'th first layer neuron, for the n exemplars. We also define the vector $\mathbf{p} \in \mathbb{R}^n$, the components of which are the outputs of the second layer single neuron for these n exemplars:

$$\mathbf{p} = [p(\mathbf{x}_1|\omega), p(\mathbf{x}_2|\omega), \ldots, p(\mathbf{x}_n|\omega)]^T$$

Thus, the n equations obtained by evaluating (1), at the points $\mathbf{x}_i$: i=1,2,..,n, can be written as

$$\mathbf{p} = \Phi \mathbf{W}_0. \qquad (4)$$

where $\mathbf{W}_0$ is the vector of $\mathbb{R}^n$ with components all equal to 1/n.

The reduction process that we shall use consists in selecting m (m<n) neurons of the first layer, and finding new weights W_i i=1,2,…,m, for their connections to the second layer, such that the output of the second layer neuron is as close as possible to what it was in the initial large network.

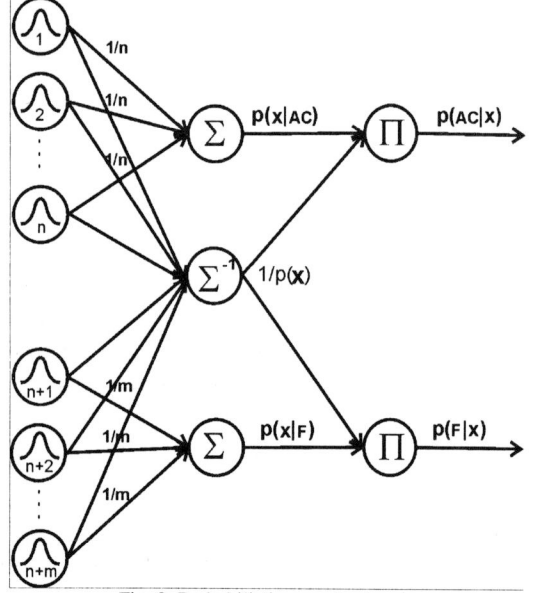

Fig. 2. Probabilistic neural network.

Letting $\mathbf{W} = [W_1, W_2, ..., W_m]^T$, the equivalent of (4) for the reduced network can be written as:

$$\mathbf{p} + \mathbf{e} = \Phi_m \mathbf{W} \quad (5)$$

in which Φ_m is the matrix, made up of the m columns of Φ that correspond to the m neurons that have been selected for the reduced network, and $\mathbf{e} \in \mathbb{R}^n$ is the vector of the errors made by the reduced network when it receives the inputs $\mathbf{x}_1, \mathbf{x}_2, ..., \mathbf{x}_n$.

Suppose that the reduced network construction is at the stage where N neurons have already been selected for it. Because the construction process is accompanied by a Gram-Schmidt orthogonal basis construction, we dispose at this point of a factorization for the matrix Φ_N as the product BA, in which B is a n × N matrix whose column vectors are mutually orthogonal, and are denoted $\mathbf{b}_i$: i=1,...,N, and A is N × N upper triangular matrix, with ones on its diagonal. Equation (5) can then be written as:

$$\mathbf{p} + \mathbf{e} = B\mathbf{g} = \sum_{i=1}^{N} g_i \mathbf{b}_i \quad \text{with} \quad \mathbf{g} = A\mathbf{W} \quad (6)$$

Thus
$$\|\mathbf{e}\|^2 = \mathbf{e}^T \mathbf{e} = (\sum_{i=1}^{N} g_i \mathbf{b}_i^T - \mathbf{p}^T)(\sum_{i=1}^{N} g_i \mathbf{b}_i - \mathbf{p}) \quad (7)$$

If $\{\mathbf{b}_1, \mathbf{b}_2, ..., \mathbf{b}_N, \mathbf{b}_{N+1}, ..., \mathbf{b}_n\}$ is a basis in $\mathbb{R}^n$ (Note that at this point, the vectors $\mathbf{b}_i$, with i=N+1, ...n, need not have already been constructed), $\mathbf{p}$ can be written as $\sum_{i=1}^{n} p_i \mathbf{b}_i$ so that it follows from (7) that

$$\|\mathbf{e}\|^2 = \sum_{i=1}^{N} (g_i - p_i)^2 \|\mathbf{b}_i\|^2 + \sum_{i=N+1}^{n} p_i^2 \|\mathbf{b}_i\|^2 \quad (8)$$

From this equation, one can see what the value of the weights $W_1, W_2, ... W_N$, should be, for the quadratic error to be minimum. Since the right hand side is a sum of positive terms, it will be minimum when

$$g_i = p_i = \frac{\mathbf{b}_i^T \mathbf{p}}{\|\mathbf{b}_i\|^2} \quad \forall \ i=1,...,N \quad (9)$$

Once $\mathbf{g}$ is known, (6) allows one to calculate the weights as
$$\mathbf{W} = A^{-1} \mathbf{g} \quad (10)$$

Given its triangular form, matrix A is always easy to inverse. With this choice of weights the total quadratic error is:

$$\|\mathbf{e}\|^2 = \sum_{i=N+1}^{n} p_i^2 \|\mathbf{b}_i\|^2 = \|\mathbf{p}\|^2 - \sum_{i=1}^{N} p_i^2 \|\mathbf{b}_i\|^2 \quad (11)$$

and the relative quadratic error is

$$\frac{\|\mathbf{e}\|^2}{\|\mathbf{p}\|^2} = 1 - \frac{\sum_{i=1}^{N} p_i^2 \|\mathbf{b}_i\|^2}{\|\mathbf{p}\|^2} \quad (12)$$

If this error is too high, one can simply add another neuron. Equation (11) tells us which one to add next so as to decrease the error as much as possible. Because a neuron corresponds to each $\mathbf{b}_i$, it should be the neuron for which the associated term $p_i^2 \|\mathbf{b}_i\|^2$ is maximum. Since, at this point, the basis vectors $\mathbf{b}_i$, i=N+1,...,n are not yet defined, we might as well construct $\mathbf{b}_{N+1}$ to be this vector. Thus, all non-committed neurons are tried, one after another, as candidate in the definition of $\mathbf{b}_{N+1}$. More precisely, one calculates, for all ϕ_i, with i the index of a non-committed neuron, the candidate next Gram-Schmidt basis vector

$$\mathbf{b}(i) = \phi_i - a_{1i} \mathbf{b}_1 - a_{2i} \mathbf{b}_2 - .... - a_{Ni} \mathbf{b}_N \quad \text{with} \quad a_{ji} = \frac{\mathbf{b}_j^T \phi_i}{\|\mathbf{b}_j\|^2}$$

For each $\mathbf{b}(i)$, the value of $p_i^2 \|\mathbf{b}(i)\|^2$ is calculated and the index of the next neuron to add will be that index i for which this quantity is maximum. The process of adding a neuron is repeated until one is satisfied with the relative error of the reduced network. This algorithm is easy to implement and its complexity is only of order n^2.

IV. TEST RESULTS

We have applied the above-described algorithm to reduce the probabilistic neural network that we initially built with 955 neurons. We have actually constructed 3 reduced networks that correspond respectively to relative errors, with respect to the initial network output, of less than 10%, 5% and 1%. Table 1 shows the success rate of these networks, when asked to identify images from our four data sets. The success rate is here defined as the proportion of correct identification with respect to the total number of input vectors in the set. Table 2 shows the global success rates, calculated with respect to the number of vectors in all four sets.

Then, in order to demonstrate that such a neural network could readily be used in a real time system, we measured its computing time. We found that, when calculating sequentially, on a Hewlett-Packard Pentium 4 PC at 2.53GHz, a Matlab implementation of it performed over 5,300 image recognitions per second.

A. Learning Curves

Because the reduced networks are constructed by adding neurons to them, one at the time, and their relative error is calculated at each step, it is easy to accumulate the sequence of these successive errors. The graphs in Fig. 3 and 4 show how this error evolves as a function of the number of neurons in the network.

TABLE 1
PERFORMANCE OF REDUCED PROBABILISTIC NETWORKS

Network /Relative Error / Number of neurons	Data Set	Number of Errors	Success Rate
Initial	Train AC	3	99.5%
Relative $e_{rms} = 0\%$	Val AC	1	99.4%
584 ac-neurons	Train F	6	98.4%
371 flare-neurons	Val F	6	95.6%
Reduced Net # 1	Train AC	6	99.0%
Relative $e_{rms} = 10\%$	Val AC	1	99.4%
14 ac-neurons	Train F	45	87.9%
8 flare-neurons	Val F	10	92.6%
Reduced Net # 2	Train AC	6	99.0%
Relative $e_{rms} = 5\%$	Val AC	1	99.4%
28 ac-neurons	Train F	44	88.1%
14 flare-neurons	Val F	12	91.1%
Reduced Net # 3	Train AC	6	99.0%
Relative $e_{rms} = 1\%$	Val AC	0	100%
102 ac-neurons	Train F	9	97.6%
71 flare-neurons	Val F	7	94.8%

In the second column, "Train AC" and "Train L" stand for "Training set for Aircrafts" and "Flares" and "Val AC" and "Val F" for "Validation set for Aircrafts" and "Flares".

TABLE 2
OVERALL SUCCESS RATES OF THE PNN

Network	Success Rate
Initial net with 955 neurons	98.3%
Reduced net #1 with 22 neurons	93.5%
Reduced net #2 with 42 neurons	93.5%
Reduced net #3 with 173 neurons	97.7%

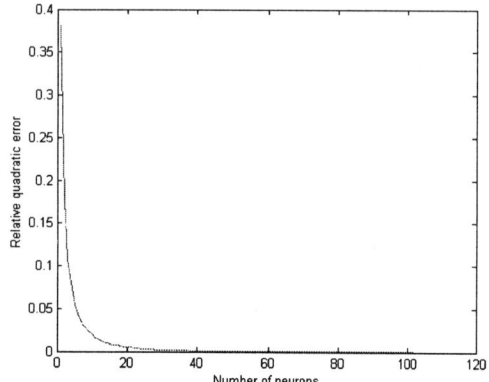

Fig. 3. Evolution of the relative quadratic error of the aircraft recognition sub-network as neurons are added to it.

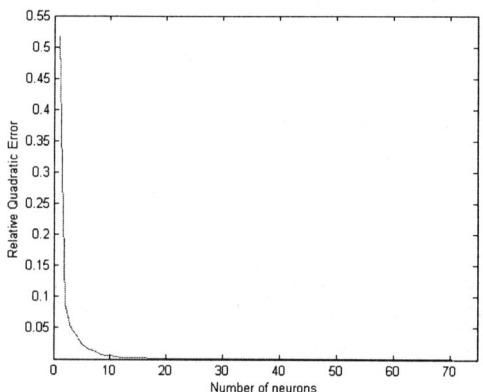

Fig. 4. Evolution of the relative quadratic error of the flare recognition sub-network as neurons are added to it.

V. CONCLUSION

We have tested a variant of an orthogonal least squares method that constructs a neural network with fewer neurons, from an initial probabilistic neural network that has a large number of neurons. The results we obtained with a particular real life practical application are quite remarkable. From an initial neural network with 955 neurons that has a target identification success rate of 98.3%, it produces a reduced network with only 22 neurons, which still has an identification success rate of 93.5%. This smaller network represents a reduction by a factor of 97.7% with respect to the initial network. A network with 173 neurons, which is a reduction by 81.9% of the initial network, shows a target identification success rate of 97.7%, only 0.6% below that of the initial network. These results provide a good indication that the two step procedure that consists in first rapidly creating an accurate but large network, and then reducing it with the OLS algorithm is very efficient and worthwhile.

We showed the graphs of the evolution of the relative square error made by the new network being constructed, as neurons are added to it. These graphs indicate that the error decreases dramatically at the start of the construction process. As mentioned above, it suffices of 14 aircraft-neurons and 8 flare-neurons, for this error to go below 0.01.

It is interesting to look at the images that correspond to the reference vectors of those neurons that are the first to be included in the reduced network, i.e. the neurons that decrease the most the quadratic error of the network. Fig. 5 shows, in order, the images that correspond to the first 3 neurons selected for the reduced aircraft recognition sub-network. It is very instructive to see that the neural network prefers these rather fuzzy images to much clearer ones, as representative of their class. This is understandable because such prototypes are effectively similar to more images in their class, than a clearer image would be. We don't show the corresponding images for flares because their characteristics are not so visually recognizable.

Finally, we report being able to identify over 5,300 images per second, with our 173 neurons network, realized in Matlab on a 2.53GHz, Pentium 4, PC.

Fig. 5. The three most representative aircraft images.

References

[1] A. Morin and P. Lessard, "An infrared imaging seeker emulator for countermeasure studies", *Proc. SPIE Acquisition, Tracking and Pointing XIII*, vol. 3692, pp.255-268, 1999.

[2] P. Cayouette, G. Labonté and A. Morin, "Probabilistic neural networks for infrared imaging target discrimination", to appear in *Proc. SPIE AEROSENSE Conference 2003, Automatic Target Recognition XIII*, SPIE Press, 2003.

[3] D.F. Specht, "Probabilistic Neural Networks for Classification, Mapping, or Associative Memory", *Proc. IEEE International Conference on Neural Networks*, San Diego, CA, I, pp. 525-532, 1988.

[4] D.F. Specht, "Probabilistic Neural Networks", *Neural Networks*, vol. 3, no. 1, pp.109-118, 1990.

[5] R.O. Duda, P.E. Hart and D.G. Stork, *Pattern Classification*, John Wiley & Sons, Inc., Toronto, 2001.

[6] L.V. Fausett, *Fundamentals of Neural Networks*, Prentice Hall, Upper Saddle River, NJ, 1994.

[7] T. Bayes, "An essay towards solving a problem in the doctrine of chances", *Phil. Trans. Roy. Soc. London*, vol. 53, pp. 370-418, 1763.

[8] E. Parzen, "On estimation of a probability density function and modes", *Annals of Mathematics and Statistics*, vol. 33, pp. 1065-1076, 1962.

[9] S. Chen, C.F.N.Cowan and P.M. Grant, "Orthogonal Least Squares Learning Algorithm for Radial Basis Function Networks", *IEEE Trans. Neural Networks*, vol. 2, pp.302-309, 1991.

[10] F.M. Ham and F. Kostanic, *Principles of Neurocomputing for Science & Engineering*, McGraw-Hill, New York, NY, 2001.

[11] A. Morin, "Adaptive spatial filtering techniques for the detection of targets in infrared image seekers", *Proc. SPIE, Acquisition, Tracking and Pointing XIV*, vol. 4025, pp. 182-19, 2000.

A Multivalent Logic Approach to Risk Estimation of Learning Machines

Bojan Novak
Faculty of Electrical Engineering, Computer Science and Informatics
Laboratory for Information Science
University of Maribor
Smetanova 17
2000 Maribor
Slovenija
Email: novakb@uni-mb.si

Abstract—A multivalent logic approach to estimating the risk of error on test samples of learning machine is developed and compared to the bivalent approach based on VC dimension, cover and entropy numbers of sets. The multivalent approach leads to more simple expressions for predicting bounds on the risk estimation which are computable in a short time and use a reasonable amount of computer memory. The results of testing reveal that multivalent logic algorithm outperforms Support Vector Machines.

I. INTRODUCTION

The currently available theories for predicting a bound on the risk estimation of learning machines for pattern recognition stems from the bivalent approach [3], [11]. This approach is a heritage of Aristotelian logic, which is the main underlying principle of today's thought. Unfortunately in practice it hits its limit very quickly. Only two class problems will be discussed here because most of the theory and solution methods are developed for such cases.

First, a short description of different SVM is presented because most of the theories for predicting a bound on the risk estimation have been developed for them. An important concept for solving nonlinear problems is a transformation that maps the original nonlinear problem into the linear problem in feature space. Next is presented a capacity concept for the set of indicator functions - the Vapnik Chervonenkis (VC) dimension. In the original form VC dimension is inadequate so a very sophisticated improved theories for the estimation of the risk bound based on covering and entropy numbers of sets were developed thereafter. A new multivalent approach is introduced that leads to simple and effective expressions for selecting an optimal model of a learning machine. A multivalent logic approach is the base for a new type of algorithms for pattern recognition that are much more effective than SVM.

In the experimental part a new risk bound estimation definition is used to define an optimal structure of new learning method. A comparison between different methods are given for the USPS data set. Multivalent logic algorithm outperforms Support Vector Machines.

II. SUPPORT VECTOR MACHINES AND THE FEATURE SPACE

The idea behind the support vector machines (SVM) approach is the following: for a two class problem (Fig. 1) a maximal margin is searched that separates data points into one (a member is marked with a rectangular) or another group (a member is marked with a circle) which is a typical bivalent logic approach. The points (painted black) lying on the margin are support vectors. Other points can be removed but the margin doesn't move, so they are sufficient to describe the problem. More formally, for given k, observations, each consisting of a pair: $\mathbf{x}_i$, y_i, where $\mathbf{x}_i \in \Re^n$, $i = 1, \ldots, k$, is the input vector and y_i is the associated output having values -1 or 1. The learning machine is actually building up a mapping ability $f(\mathbf{x}, p)$ during the learning process. The functions $f(\mathbf{x}, p)$ themselves are labeled by adjustable parameters p. For the artificial neural networks (ANN) the factor p represents weights and biases. For the SVM according to Fig.1 (without the two points lying on the wrong side) the following algorithm was developed [11]

$$\mathbf{x}_i \cdot \mathbf{w} + b \geq +1 \quad for \ y_i = +1 \qquad (1)$$

$$\mathbf{x}_i \cdot \mathbf{w} + b \leq -1 \quad for \ y_i = -1 \qquad (2)$$

or combined into one set of inequalities

$$y_i(\mathbf{x}_i \cdot \mathbf{w} + b) - 1 \geq 0 \quad \forall i \qquad (3)$$

a separation of two classes can be performed with an optimal hyperplane

$$\mathbf{x} \cdot \mathbf{w} + b = 0. \qquad (4)$$

The margin

$$r = \frac{2}{\|\mathbf{w}\|} \qquad (5)$$

can be maximized by the following primal Lagrangian model

$$\min_{\mathbf{w},b} L_p \equiv \frac{1}{2}\|\mathbf{w}\|^2 - \sum_{i=1}^{k} \alpha_i y_i(\mathbf{x}_i \cdot \mathbf{w} + b) + \sum_{i=1}^{k} \alpha_i \qquad (6)$$

subject to the constraints

$$\alpha_i \geq 0. \qquad (7)$$

Unfortunately, this is true only in the ideal cases. But in practice some points often lie on the "wrong" side (Fig. 1) because of inadequate knowledge of the problem, measurement error, etc. problem (6) and (7) has not feasible solution, so the bivalent logic approach becomes questionable. To solve this situation in a bivalent manner, additional variables ξ_i

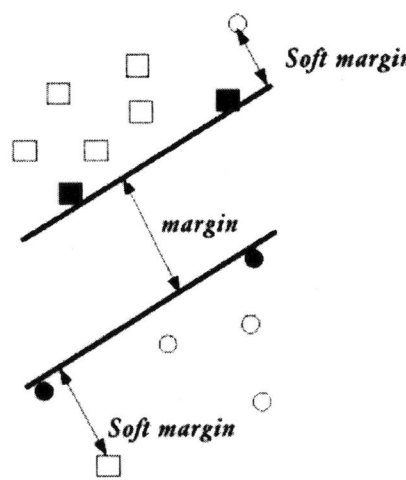

Fig. 1. Quasi soft margin classifiers

were introduced to make (6) and (7) solvable. The term "soft margin" was introduced, which is inadequate because one can not make a multivalued approach out of a bivalent logic. The correct term would be "quasi soft margin". Actually, the whole idea of margin is suspicious because it can not give the correct class label to the points inside the margin. This will be discussed in details latter. ξ_i is added to the constraints (1) and (2)

$$\mathbf{x}_i \cdot \mathbf{w} + b \geq +1 - \xi_i \quad for \ y_i = +1 \qquad (8)$$

$$\mathbf{x}_i \cdot \mathbf{w} + b \leq -1 + \xi_i \quad for \ y_i = -1 \qquad (9)$$

The model (6) and (7) is expanded to force the positivity of ξ_i. Following Lagrangian has to be minimized:

$$L_p \equiv \frac{1}{2}(\|\mathbf{w}\|)^2 + C\sum_{i=1}^{k}\xi_i$$
$$- \sum_{i=1}^{k}\alpha_i\{y_i(\mathbf{x}_i \cdot \mathbf{w} + b) - 1 + \xi_i\} - \sum_{i=1}^{k}\mu_i\xi_i \quad (10)$$

subject to the constraints

$$\alpha_i, \mu_i, \xi_i \geq 0. \qquad (11)$$

where C penalizes errors and its value is chosen by user.

An error occurs when ξ_i exceeds the unity and the summation of ξ_i presents an upper bound on the number of training errors (second term in (10)).

There are a lot of problems that are not linearly separable, such as the XOR problem. For such cases even the improved model (10) and (11) is not adequate. Fortunately there exist transformations that transform a problem that is nonlinear in the input space into a linear one in the feature space. This can be represented with the following transformation

$$\phi : \Re^n \to \mathsf{H}. \qquad (12)$$

Due to Hilbert-Schmidt theory the inner product in a Hilbert space has an equivalent presentation

$$\sum_{i=1}^{\infty}\phi(\mathbf{x})_i\phi(\mathbf{y})_i = \mathbf{K}(\mathbf{x}\cdot\mathbf{y}) \qquad (13)$$

where $\mathbf{K}(\mathbf{x}\cdot\mathbf{y})$ is a symmetric function satisfying Mercer conditions

$$\int \mathbf{K}(\mathbf{x}\cdot\mathbf{y})g(\mathbf{x})g(\mathbf{y})d\mathbf{x}d\mathbf{y} \geq 0 \qquad (14)$$

$$\int g(\mathbf{x})^2 d\mathbf{x} \quad is \ finite. \qquad (15)$$

For a specific kernel selection it may not be easy to check the fulfillment of Mercer's condition, but for a polynomial kernel of a degree p

$$\mathbf{K}(\mathbf{x}_i \cdot \mathbf{x}_j) = (\mathbf{x}_i \cdot \mathbf{x}_j + 1)^p \qquad (16)$$

condition (14) holds. For an example of the transformation from an input to a feature spaces for $\mathbf{x} \in \Re^2$ and a kernel of the form

$$\mathbf{K}(\mathbf{x}_i \cdot \mathbf{x}_j) = (\mathbf{x}_i \cdot \mathbf{x}_j)^p \qquad (17)$$

it is possible to find the space H generated by (17) and $\phi(\mathbf{x})$ defined as

$$\phi(\mathbf{x}) = [\mathbf{x}_1^2, \sqrt{2}\mathbf{x}_1\mathbf{x}_2, \mathbf{x}_2^2]^T. \qquad (18)$$

The dimension of a polynomial in the feature space H with the dimension n in the original space and the order p is

$$dim\mathbf{H} = \binom{n+p-1}{p} \qquad (19)$$

Dimension H reaches extremely high values very quickly with the growing values of n and p.

III. BIVALENT APPROACH TO THE BOUNDS ON THE GENERALIZATION PERFORMANCE OF A LEARNING MACHINE

In the late 1960s Vapnik and Chervonenkis defined conditions where the uniform law of large numbers held for a given set of events and the bounds on the nonasymptotic rate of uniform convergence. They introduced a capacity concept for the set of indicator functions - the VC dimension, which characterizes the variability of the set of indicator functions. The maximum number of different binary (values -1 or 1) partitioning (or shattering) of k samples is 2^k (Fig. 2).

The growth function is defined as

$$G(k) \leq k\log 2. \qquad (20)$$

If for an indicator function the expression (20) is valid for any k, then such a function is able to split any sample of arbitrary size in all possible ways without error. This is the well-known problem of over-fitting. The requirement for an indicator function is that after some finite value of k its growth is less than $k\log 2$. This value is the VC dimension h (VC = Vapnik Chervonenkis) [11]. Then the growth function is logarithmically bounded

$$G(k) = k\log 2 \quad if \ k \leq h$$
$$G(k) = h(1 + \log\frac{k}{h}) \quad if \ k > h \qquad (21)$$

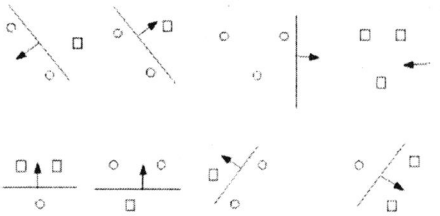

Fig. 2. Shattering and VC dimension (circle = first class and square = second class)

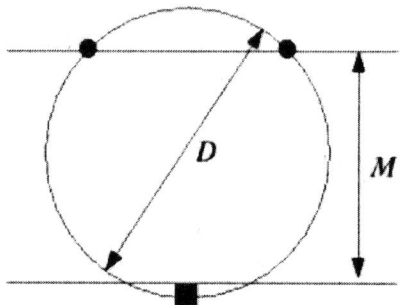

Fig. 3. A gap tolerant classifier

where G(k) is the growth function of a set of indicator functions $f(\mathbf{x}, p)$, and p represents the capacity ability. For the example it could be the order of the polynomial chosen from the finite set of orders p. Three points can be linearly shattered in the two dimensional plane, but four points no longer can be linearly separated. VC dimension for this case is 3. But this is an ideal case that seldom happens in practice because of the imprecision of the information [13]. Some counter examples were developed [3] that showed some serious drawbacks of the VC dimension. The first one was counter example from [3], where an example of infinite VC dimension for a indicator function of just one parameter $f(\mathbf{x}, p) = I(\sin(px))$. The second one was that this function can't shatter four equally spaced points on the line despite of the infinite VC dimension.

The expectation of the test error for the trained machine is

$$R(p) = \int \frac{1}{2}|y - f(\mathbf{x}, p)| dP(\mathbf{x}, p) \qquad (22)$$

where $R(p)$ is the expected risk. The measured mean error rate on the finite number of observations is "empirical risk"

$$R_{emp}(p) = \frac{1}{2k} \sum_{i=1}^{k} |y_i - f(\mathbf{x_i}, p)|. \qquad (23)$$

$R_{emp}(p)$ is fixed for the particular choice of p and for the selected training set $\{\mathbf{x}_i, p\}$ $i = 1, 2 \ldots, k$. The probability is not included in the equation. The quantity $\frac{1}{2}|y_i - f(\mathbf{x}_i, p)|$ is a loss function. The empirical risk minimization does not imply a small error on a test set if the number of training data is limited. The structural risk minimization is one of the new techniques for handling efficiently a limited amount of data. For a chosen confidence interval $\eta : 0 \leq \eta \leq 1$ the bound holds

$$R(p) \leq R_{emp}(p) + \phi(h, \eta, k) \qquad (24)$$

where η is defined as

$$\phi(h, \eta, k) = \sqrt{\frac{h(\log \frac{2k}{h} + 1) - \log \frac{\eta}{4}}{k}} \qquad (25)$$

The parameter h is the Vapnik Chervonenkis (VC) dimension [11]. It describes the capacity of a set of functions implemented on the learning machine. According to (24), the risk could be controlled by two quantities: $R_{emp}(p)$ and $\phi(h, \eta, k)$. The value of the second term in (24) is small when η and VC dimension are small enough, and the number of samples is large. Optimal values are chosen from a class of functions (for example polynomials of different order). The empirical risk R_{emp} and VC dimension depend on the choice of the optimal function $f(\mathbf{x}, p)$ applied in the learning machine. The optimal value for p is selected so as to minimizes (24). This is a principle of the structural risk minimization (SRM). Practical experiences with (24) and VC dimension have clearly shown that the bound is not tight and that the values for VC dimensions are too high, so the optimal values achieved by SRM can be far from optimum [9].

One of the further attempts to get a better bound was the introduction of gap tolerant classifiers (Fig. 3). For a data in $\Re^n$ the VC dimension h of a gap tolerant classifier of the minimum margin M_{min} and maximum diameter D_{max} is bounded above

$$min\left(\lceil \frac{D_{max}^2}{M_{min}^2} \rceil, n\right) + 1 \qquad (26)$$

Gap tolerant classifiers were actually the first attempt to relax the strict bivalent approach, introducing some "gray" area. Because this is not a multivalued approach, where a sample point can be a member of both classes at the same time, this approach can not concisely answer the question: to which class does a test point that lies in the gap belong? If all such points are simply assigned to the fixed class (for example +1) than the bound on the VC dimension would be higher than that in (26). A new range $\{-1, +1, 0\}$ of classes was introduced to be able to fulfill the conditions in the (26), where class $\{0\}$ is for the points that lie in the gap. This is actually a three-valued logic. Because the diameter D_{max} is computed from the training points some of the test points can lie outside the diameter D_{max} and the bound in (26) is again violated. In practical applications mostly nonlinear problems are encountered, so the bound in (26) is computed in the feature space (12). Unfortunately the points now cover a different shape. Because data cover some elliptical slanted area, the circle D_{max} does not cover points tightly anymore and VC dimension is overestimated. The enclosing box is constructed from eigenvectors of the kernel in the feature space. The data in the feature space are inside the parallelepiped with the lengths proportional $2C\sqrt{\lambda_i}$ where C

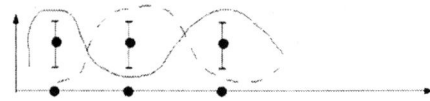

Fig. 4. A level fat shattering principle

is some constant and λ_i is the i-th eigenvalue. Theoretically, at least for a small data set a transformation that reshape the data in feature space in more circular form is possible [4].

Some improvement of VC dimension estimation was achieved by introducing fat shattering VC dimension [10]. The idea is presented in Fig. 4. Instead of using a strict bivalent division by a hyperplane, the thickness of the hyperplane is widened (The hyperplane has got some fat on it). The functions pass over or below the bars. In Fig. 4 is presented only one function out of 2^3 possible. Such a definition actually means that the behavior of a function class is lowered to a certain resolution. Some better bounds on the actual risk were achieved in practice. The estimation of the risk bound was computed in a very sophistic manner with the help of covering and entropy numbers of sets [9].

IV. MULTIVALENT APPROACH TO A BOUND ON THE GENERALIZATION PERFORMANCE OF A LEARNING MACHINE

The bivalent logic approach to the bound on the generalization performance of a pattern recognition learning machine has produced very complicated and imprecise bounds on the risk estimation. Considering that the multivalent approach allows a point to be a member of different classes at the same time, a different approach is possible. Instead of the large margin classifier approach it is a better idea to make a fuzzy soft division of classes based on a membership of data points. Instead of generating the support vectors, the whole data set contributes to the definition of soft separation between two classes. Only polynomial kernels are used because the mathematical theory is well developed for them. There is also no evidence that other kernels are superior. Some authors are actually claiming that some better results were achieved by radial basis functions. But the truth is that for some optimal width of a radial base more numerically stable iterative procedures were achieved than for the polynomial kernels.

The basis for setting a nonlinear model in the feature space is following transformation

$$\mathbf{H}_k = \frac{(\mathbf{X}_s\mathbf{X}^T+1)^p((\mathbf{X}_s\mathbf{X}^T+1)^p)^T}{((\mathbf{X}_s\mathbf{X}^T+1)^p)^T(\mathbf{X}_s\mathbf{X}^T+1)^p} \quad (27)$$

that performs mapping (12) selecting a polynomial kernel of the form (16). The matrix $\mathbf{X}_s$ presents a selected set of input samples from the matrix $\mathbf{X}$. The selection of the particular row vector $\mathbf{x}_i$ from the matrix $\mathbf{X}$ is performed on the basis of the explained variance of the fitted value $\hat{y}$

$$V = \sigma^2(1 - h_{ii}) \quad (28)$$

where h_{ii} is the element of the matrix $\mathbf{H}_k$ for the $\mathbf{x}_i$. The σ is is defined as

$$\sigma = \frac{\sum_{i=1}^{k}(K(\mathbf{X}_s \cdot \mathbf{x}_i) - \mu)^2}{k} \quad (29)$$

and μ is defined as

$$\mu = \frac{\sum_{i=1}^{k}(K(\mathbf{X}_s \cdot \mathbf{x}_i))}{k}. \quad (30)$$

A prediction of test values is computed by

$$\hat{\mathbf{y}} = \mathbf{H}_k\,\mathbf{y_s}. \quad (31)$$

The results from (31) are projected into the fuzzy space defined by overlapping fuzzy sets (Fig. 5) presenting linguistic PH=POSITIVE HIGH, PM=POSITIVE MEDIUM and PL=POSITIVE LOW confidence in the predicted value for the first class [+1] and NH=NEGATIVE HIGH, NM=NEGATIVE MEDIUM and NL=NEGATIVE LOW confidence in the predicted value for the second class [−1]. The vertical line on the Fig. 5 presents a hypothetic hard division which is unrealistic because (31) never produces zero values for any of its elements. In the case of zero value a point would be the member of both classes with each membership value equal to 0.5. In the vicinity of the zero, points to the left of the vertical line have greater membership values in the set PL for the first class than for the set NL for the second class. Points on the right side of the vertical bar have greater membership values in the set NL for the second class than for the set PL for the first class. This approach gives correct explanation for every point which is unlikely for the gap tolerant classifiers. The result does not give only the answer to which class a predicted point belongs but also a linguistic confidence value about the result [12], [13], [14]. Risk estimation is performed by

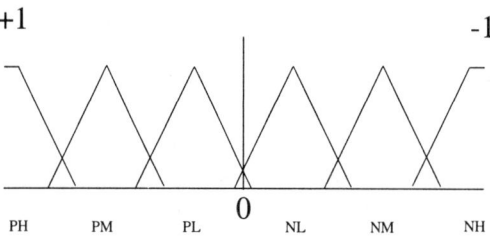

Fig. 5. Soft separation

$$R(p) = t\sqrt{\hat{\sigma}(1 + H_k)} \quad (32)$$

where $\hat{\sigma}$ is defined as

$$\hat{\sigma} = \frac{\sum_{i=1}^{k} f(y_i - \hat{y}_i)}{k - p} \quad (33)$$

and

$$f(y_i - \hat{y}_i) = (y_i - \hat{y}_i)^2 \quad if\ sign(y_i) \neq sign(\hat{y}_i). \quad (34)$$

In general $t = f(\eta, k)$. The coefficient η is a confidence level. In our experiment $t = 2$ because the number of samples is large enough. In the contradiction to the bivalent approach where errors are actually counted (22) in the multivalued logic approach errors are measured. The number of test errors does not bring enough information about the quality of the prediction. It is also necessary to include information about the distances of violations. Larger they are more likely errors will appear in the test phase.

V. COMPARISION OF RESULTS

The USPS handwritten number recognition problem [11] is one of most popular test for testing the performance of pattern recognition programs where SVM are supposed to clearly show their supremacy. A program named SEAL was developed on the basis of the multivalent logic approach [8], [6], [7]. The optimal degrees of polynomials were selected using (32). Predictions of new values were computed with (31). A test error of 1.3 % on the raw data set was achieved with SEAL, while a 2.3% test error was achieved with the best variation of the SVM algorithm by Jian-Xiong Dong [5]. In Table I a comparison of performances for different methods is given. The second order polynomial kernel was the best

TABLE I
PERFORMANCES OF DIFFERENT METHODS ON THE USPS DATA SET

Error	Method
5.10%	LeNet
4.00%	polynomial SVM
2.90%	sparse polynomials SVM p=4
2.70%	tangent distance (nearest neighbor)
2.34%	heroSVM
1.34%	SEAL fuzzy

in all cases for SEAL, which confirms Vapnik's theoretical predictions that the machine with the minimal complexity should achieve the minimal error. For the same size of the input and the same kernel, the complexity of the machine is the same. Unfortunately, none of the SVM algorithms is able to achieve these theoretical predictions as yet.

All methods except polynomial SVM and SEAL use inclusion of a priori informations that improves the results significantly (see SVM against heroSVM). However, it is not always evident how to perform such an inclusion for a different kind of problems. Better results were achieved with the SEAL despite the fact that heroSVM has additionally improved its performances with the inclusion of a priori information about the problem. Of course this could be done also for the SEAL, but then the comparison of the methods would no longer be fair. To compare the performances of different methods only the tests on the raw data set are fair.

VI. CONCLUSION

To achieve better bounds on the risk estimation one has to break with the Aristotelian logic and build up a new approach based on the multivalent logic. The currently available theories for predicting a bound on the risk estimation stems from the bivalent approach that in practice hits its limit very quickly. This is also true in the case of pattern recognition problems. The multivalent approach leads to different more simple expressions for predicting the bounds on the risk estimation and an extremely simple algorithm which is computable in a short time and uses a reasonable amount of computer memory. The USPS handwritten number recognition problem [11] is one of the most popular test for testing the performance of pattern recognition problems, where SVM are supposed to clearly show their supremacy. A program named SEAL was developed on the basis of the multivalent logic approach [8]. It has achieved a test error of 1.3 % on the raw data set, while a 2.3% test error that was achieved with the best variation of the SVM algorithm. Better results were achieved with SEAL despite the fact that SVM has additionally improved its performances with the inclusion of a priori information about the problem. Of course this could be done also for SEAL, but then the comparison of the methods would no longer be a fair. To compare the performances of different methods fairly the tests should only be performed on the raw data sets.

REFERENCES

[1] www.kernel-machines.org
[2] G. Baudat and F. Anouar,"*Kernel-based methods and function approximation*", In International Joint Conference on Neural Networks, Washington, DC July 15 - 19, pp. 1244 – 1249, 2001.
[3] C. J. C. Burges, "*A Tutorial on Support Vector Machines for Pattern Recognition*", Knowledge Discovery and Data Mining, 2(2), 1998.
[4] O. Chapelle and V. Vapnik," *Model selection for support vector machines*", In Sara A. Solla, Todd K. Leen, and Klaus-Robert Müller, editors, Advances in Neural Information Processing Systems 12. Cambridge, Mass: MIT Press, 2000.
[5] J. X. Dong, www.cenparmi.concordia.ca
[6] B.Novak, "An efficient method for selecting the optimal structure of a fuzzy neural network architecture". CIT. J. Comput. Inf. Technol., vol. 9, no. 2, pp. 113-122, 2001.
[7] B. Novak, "*Soft computing on small data sets*". Informatica, vol. 25, no. 1, pp. 83-88, 2001.
[8] B. Novak,"*SEAL*", BISC Berkeley Seminar, UC Berkeley, 10. Dec. 02. 2002.
[9] B. Schölkopf, J. Shawe-Taylor, A. J. Smola, and R. C. Williamson, "*Generalization bounds via eigenvalues of the Gram matrix*", Technical Report 99-035, NeuroCOLT, 1999, Short conference version: *Kernel-dependent Support Vector error bounds*, Ninth International Conference on Artificial Neural Networks, pp. 103 - 108, IEE Conference Publications No. 470, London.
[10] J. Shawe-Taylor and N. Cristianini. "*Margin distribution and soft margin*", In A.J. Smola, P.L. Bartlett, B. Schölkopf, and D. Schuurmans, editors, Advances in Large Margin Classifiers, pp. 349-358, Cambridge, MA, MIT Press, 2000.
[11] V. Vapnik, *Statisitical Learning Theory*, 1st ed. John-Wiley & Sons Inc., 1998.
[12] Yager R. and Filev D., "*Generation of Fuzzy Rules by Mountain Clustering*", Journal of Intelligent and Fuzzy Systems, Vol. 2, No. 3, pp. 209 - 219. 1994.
[13] L. A. Zadeh, "*The Role of Fuzzy Logic and Soft Computing in the Conception, Design and Deployment of Intelligent Systems*", Invited lecture at Computer Based Medical Systems 97, Maribor, June 1997.
[14] L. A. Zadeh, "*From computing with numbers to computing with words-from manipulation of measurements to manipulation of perception*", IEEE Trans. Circuit Systems 45, 105-119. 2000.

Toward A Modular Connectionist Model of Local Chlorophyll Concentration from Satellite Images

Edmondo Trentin	Letizia Magnoni	Alfio Andronico
Dip. di Ingegneria dell'Informazione	Dip. di Ingegneria dell'Informazione	Dip. di Ingegneria dell'Informazione
Università di Siena	Università di Siena	Università di Siena
V. Roma, 56 - Siena (Italy)	V. Roma, 56 - Siena (Italy)	V. Roma, 56 - Siena (Italy)
Email: trentin@dii.unisi.it	Email: magnoni@unisi.it	Email: andronico@unisi.it

Abstract— Monitoring the values of physical variables in water at ground level (in a river, lake or ocean) on the basis of noisy images acquired from a geostationary satellite is a relevant and challenging task. This paper introduces a *3-module* neural system that allows for automatic monitoring of the local concentration of chlorophyll in presence of clouds and turbid water at specific locations. The system relies on images in four different wavelength intervals taken by the satellite over specific points of the lake surface. Module (1) estimates the probability of presence of clouds over dots in the image, possibly applying the reject option, and feeding this information into the following nets. Module (2) estimates the *turbidity* of water, i.e., its transparency, on a dot-by-dot basis. Finally, module (3) is a neural network with adaptive amplitude of activation functions, featuring a combination of linear and nonlinear terms, that realizes a regression model to describe the relationship between its inputs (i.e., a 4-bands dot in the satellite image plus the corresponding outputs from the previous two modules) and the desired concentration of chlorophyll in the corresponding location of the lake. Eventually, a *global tuning* of the whole system parameters is possible. Experiments involving noisy data, sampled from the water of Lake Montepulciano in Tuscany (Italy), are presented. The problem of the limited availability of "target" training data, i.e. physical measurements obtained by sampling from the lake surface on boats, is addressed. Results are compared with standard multivariate linear regression models.

I. INTRODUCTION

Prediction of physical features of ground and water surfaces on the basis of satellite images is a challenging, as well as practically relevant task [1]. Monitoring the environmental sustainability requires the acquisition and evaluation of such features as the level of chlorophyll or pollution of the water in lakes or rivers. Sampling the data by hand on the field is a slow and expensive process. In addition, traditional analysis approaches allow only for an intrinsically limited coverage of sampling areas w.r.t. the whole geographic extension of the territory to be monitored. As a consequence, adequate models of the relationship between the satellite images and the physical values of those environmental features are sought.

In the present research we deal with the problem of information extraction from images acquired via satellite reflection over water surfaces. The goal is to realize a regression model in the form $y = \phi(\mathbf{x}) + \epsilon$, where ϵ is a Normal random variable with zero mean. The regression explains the relationship ϕ between the 4-dimensional feature vector $\mathbf{x}$ of color values in a given point of satellite images (taken in four different wavelength intervals, or bands) of the lake surface, and the corresponding value y of chlorophyll present in water in that point. An Artificial Neural Network (ANN) may be applied to estimate the regression, learning a non-linear model of ϕ from the data.

Unfortunately, the above regression task in often hardly hypothesizable, due to the severe presence of noise within satellite images. Two major sources of noise are quite common: the presence of clouds that may partially, or even totally, cover the image itself [2]; and the *turbidity* of water [3]. In fact, experts usually classify the water in oceans and lakes into two broad categories, known as Case 1 and Case 2. Case 1 water is the typical deep-blue, clean and transparent water of outer oceans. Case 2, on the contrary, refers to situations where the water is *turbid*. This happens in a spontaneous manner in proximity of coasts, where mud, sand, clay and human effects are (more or less intrinsically) present. Also the presence of decomposed organic residuals increases turbidity. In other circumstances, turbidity may be a straightforward consequence of rain, hurricane wind, off-shore pollution. The level of turbidity can be quantified through direct measurement over samples of water collected from the surface of the sea/lake.

While prediction of physical features of Case 1 water, e.g. the concentration of chlorophyll, from satellite images at different bands may be feasible, Case 2 water tends to reflect light in a way similar to clouds, saturating images and perturbing the accuracy of predictions.

This paper proposes a *3-module* neural system that allows for automatic monitoring of the approximate concentration of chlorophyll in presence of clouds and turbid water, according to the following hierarchical scheme:

1) a neural classifier $\mathcal{D}$ is trained to discriminate between areas that are actually covered by clouds or not, respectively. As an alternative, instead of a bare (binary) classifier, a probabilistic approach may be taken by estimating the Bayesian posterior probability [4] of the presence of clouds given the input pixel $\mathbf{x}$ at a specified location.

2) A connectionist model $\mathcal{T}$ of the turbidity level of water is developed. It has to be trained only over the datapoints where the classifier $\mathcal{D}$ detects no clouds. On the other end, if the Bayesian perspective is chosen for $\mathcal{D}$, training is accomplished over all datapoints,

involving a weighted contribution from each point on the overall training process. The weighted contribution is proportional to the estimated posterior probability of "having no clouds".

3) Another neural net $\mathcal{C}$ is finally trained to estimate the level of chlorophyll over the datapoints that are not covered by clouds and the turbidity of which is below a given threshold τ_C. More precisely, a Bayesian probabilistic variant is taken into account: the chlorophyll estimate relies also on the turbidity estimated by $\mathcal{T}$ and on the knowledge – yielded by $\mathcal{D}$ – concerning the "density" (presence) of clouds.

At test time, the same hierarchical scheme is applied, by first evaluating via $\mathcal{D}$ whether a portion of the satellite image is covered by clouds or not. If so, the *reject option* [5] may be taken; otherwise, its turbidity is estimated by applying $\mathcal{T}$. Again, if the estimate is below τ_C a rejection may occur. Otherwise, the chlorophyll level is eventually estimated via $\mathcal{C}$. Again, the above Bayesian probabilistic variant implies not to reject, but to apply $\mathcal{C}$ relying also on the estimates yielded by $\mathcal{D}$ and $\mathcal{T}$. The next Section formalizes these ideas.

II. Modular Architecture and Training

The first module ($\mathcal{D}$) is trained to estimate the probability $\Pi(\mathbf{x})$ of presence of clouds at a given point of the image having visual features $\mathbf{x}$. Training is accomplished by computing $\frac{\delta \Pi(\mathbf{x})}{\delta w}$ for each pattern $\mathbf{x}$ (on-line learning), where w is a generic connection weight, and backpropagating the derivatives according to the rule $\Delta w = \eta \frac{\delta \Pi(\mathbf{x})}{\delta w}$ whenever $\mathbf{x}$ is covered by clouds (i.e., when the probability has to be maximized), or $\Delta w = -\eta \frac{\delta \Pi(\mathbf{x})}{\delta w}$ when $\mathbf{x}$ is a clean point (thus, when the probability has to be minimized). This scheme for connectionist probability estimation is similar to that proposed in [6]. This requires a pre-labeled training set of datapoints where presence or absence of clouds is pointed out. In addition, in order to ensure that the network output actually *is* a probability, a sigmoid, which ranges in the $(0, 1)$ interval, is applied as the output activation function. A standard 2-layer Perceptron (MLP) [7], having 4 hidden units, was used in the experiments. The topology of the MLP (as well as the architecture of all the modules described in the following) was defined via cross-validation techniques [5] during a preliminary experimental step.

The second module ($\mathcal{T}$) estimates the turbidity of water, determining its reflectivity properties and accounting for the reliability of optical algorithms aimed at estimating the concentration of chlorophyll. A nonlinear regression model of turbidity in the form $z = \psi(\mathbf{x}, \Pi(\mathbf{x})) + \epsilon$ is learned from the data. Such a model explains the relationship ψ between the color vector $\mathbf{x}$, the corresponding estimated probability $\Pi(\mathbf{x})$ of presence of clouds in a given point of the lake surface, and the actual value z of turbidity of water in that point.

In the present paper, $\mathcal{T}$ is a 2-layer MLP with 5 inputs, one sigmoid output unit, and 5 sigmoids in the hidden layer. The i-th sigmoid, $\sigma_i(a_i)$, is in the form $\sigma_i(a_i) = \frac{1}{1+e^{-\frac{a_i-b_i}{\theta}}}$,

where b_i is the adaptive unit-specific bias, a_i is the input to neuron i and θ controls the slope of the sigmoid. By writing the overall input to the network as $\mathbf{x}' = (\mathbf{x}, \Pi(\mathbf{x}))$, then the resulting regression model takes the following form:

$$\psi(\mathbf{x}') = \sigma(\sum_i w_i \sigma_i(\sum_j w_{ij} x'_j)) \qquad (1)$$

where w_i denotes the connection weight between i-th hidden unit and the output unit, w_{ij} is the weight of the connection between j-th input unit and i-th hidden unit, and $\sigma(.)$ is the output sigmoid.

Finally, the third module ($\mathcal{C}$) is an ANN with adaptive amplitude of activation functions [8], featuring a combination of linear and nonlinear terms, that realizes a regression model $y = \phi(\mathbf{x}, \Pi(\mathbf{x}), z) + \epsilon$ to describe the relationship between its inputs ($\mathbf{x}$, $\Pi(\mathbf{x})$ and z) and the desired concentration y of chlorophyll.

$\mathcal{C}$ is a 2-layer MLP with 6 inputs, one linear output unit, and 9 sigmoids in the hidden layer. The i-th sigmoid, $\sigma_i(a_i)$, is in the form $\sigma_i(a_i) = \frac{\lambda}{1+e^{-\frac{a_i-b_i}{\theta}}}$, where λ is the gradient-learnable amplitude of activation nonlinearities [8] that improves learning and generalization [7] capabilities. Skip-layer weights [9] were introduced, connecting the input layer to the output layer directly (i.e., an additive linear regression term). By writing the overall input to $\mathcal{C}$ as $\mathbf{x}'' = (\mathbf{x}, \Pi(\mathbf{x}), \psi(\mathbf{x}))$, then the resulting regression model takes the form:

$$\phi(\mathbf{x}'') = \sum_i w_i \sigma_i(\sum_j w_{ij} x''_j) + W\mathbf{x}'' \qquad (2)$$

where W denotes the row vector of the skip-layer weights, and the other symbols have the same meaning as in Equation (1).

Both $\mathcal{T}$ and $\mathcal{C}$ are trained in a supervised manner, using target outputs measured on the field. It is interesting to observe that, once all the three modules are trained, they may be merged into a single, non-fully connected multi-layered network, having input $\mathbf{x}$ and output $\phi(\mathbf{x})$. The output from $\mathcal{D}$ simply feeds the input to $\mathcal{T}$ in the following layer (along with direct input $\mathbf{x}$) and the input of $\mathcal{C}$ in subsequent layers; the output from $\mathcal{T}$, in turn, feeds the input to $\mathcal{C}$ (again, along with direct input $\mathbf{x}$). Further backpropagation of partial derivatives through the whole unified model results in a global training scheme that allows for a final tuning of all parameters of the modular machine, aimed at improving the model ϕ.

III. The Dataset and the "Limited Sampling" Problem

Satellite monitoring of the concentration of chlorophyll is usually carried out by averaging over wide geographic areas [3]. The data analyzed and presented herein, on the contrary, refer to a rather small area, namely the Lake Montepulciano (Siena, Italy). Four different images are recorded by the satellite, corresponding to four distinct wavelength intervals: blue, green, red, and infrared. Satellite images are represented as 1024×1024 pixel matrices. For each point of the lake, i.e.

for each pixel in the satellite images, these color values are arranged into a single 4-dimensional feature vector **x**.

In order to discover the relationship ϕ, real sampling on the field is needed to be put in correspondence with the values of **x**. In practice, while the satellite takes a picture of the lake, samples of water are collected at certain points in the lake (using small boats). Although images are acquired instantaneously while sampling in the lake takes a certain amount of time, a realistic assumption is made that the average physical properties in a given point do not vary significantly in the short term. This represents an intrinsic drawback, affecting the precision of regression models to some extent. The samples are analyzed later, in laboratory.

The data used in the present experiments were acquired on September 27, 2001, by researchers of the Dipartimento di Scienze e Tecnologie Chimiche e dei Biosistemi of the Università di Siena. Four images of the Lake Montepulciano were acquired (one for each wavelength interval) from the Ikonos geostationary Satellite. The lake was partially covered by clouds. Sampling the water was accomplished over 13 distinct points over the lake surface. The distribution of the corresponding feature vectors is shown in Fig. 1, after projection along their first 2 principal components. The turbidity and the concentration of chlorophyll were then measured in laboratory. The turbidity values, expressed in NTU (Nephelometric Turbidity Units), were measured using a nephelometer and ranged in the (29.33 − 37.00) NTU interval, implying quite turbid water (water is usually considered turbid when its turbidity value is > 5 NTU). The chlorophyll values were measured by filtering the water samples through a glass fiber filter, and analyzing the filter using a spectrophotometer. Values ranged within (186.00 − 483.99) micrograms per liter, i.e. a significantly high concentration of chlorophyll with high variability.

The nature of such a dataset was hardly adequate for the ANN training, since 13 feature vectors **x** are definitely insufficient to draw significant, as well as separated, training and test sets. This problem was tackled according to a 2-step procedure:

1) for each of the 13 real samples (now on called *centroids*), a closed interval of points centered in the corresponding pixel was considered. This increases the size of the training set, since each interval contains 25 points, i.e. a 5×5 interval. Figure 2 shows the projection along the first two principal components [10] of the overall dataset obtained this way. Target outputs for the points within the interval that differ from the centroid were synthetically generated as follows. Level curves were first generated via the ERDAS geographic imaging software package[1], using a second-degree polynomial regression. In so doing, approximate values of chlorophyll in the points of the interval were obtained. These values are not reliable enough to use them directly as target outputs. Nevertheless, they may be used to infer an estimate of the *gradient* of the chlorophyll value w.r.t. the location over the surface of the lake. Such an estimated gradient was applied to compute synthetic targets starting from the (known) value of chlorophyll in the centroid of the interval.

2) A leave-one-out [5] evaluation strategy was applied to the enlarged dataset. In practice, 13 training-test steps were repeated by leaving one of the 13 intervals out of the training set and using its centroid for evaluating the performance of the regression model trained on the remaining 12 intervals. Final results are reported by averaging partial results over the 13 distinct training-test runs.

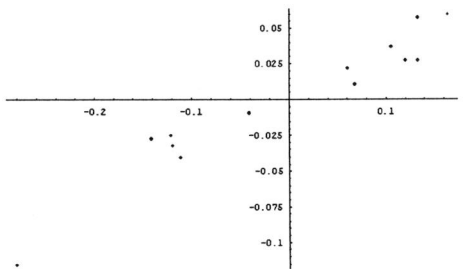

Fig. 1. *Projection along the first two principal components of the 13 normalized feature vectors (in the 4-bands feature space) corresponding to samples collected on the field.*

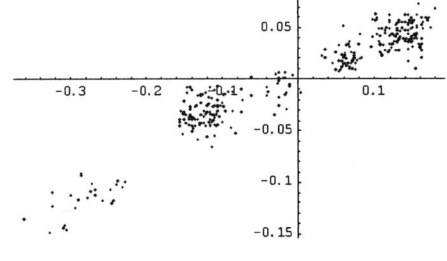

Fig. 2. *Projection along the first two principal components of the feature vectors (in the four bands, normalized) of the overall enlarged dataset.*

[1]ERDAS IMAGINE is a product (C) by Leica Geosystems.

IV. EXPERIMENTS

Input and target output data were normalized before feeding them into the ANNs, in order to improve convergence of the learning algorithm and to tackle numerical problems in the computation of derivatives along the tails of the sigmoids. Data were normalized as follows: a mixture of logistics was estimated as a parametric model of the overall distribution of all datapoints (one mixture for each component of the feature space). A mixture of sigmoids modeled the corresponding cumulative distribution function. For each component of each feature vector, the proper mixture of sigmoids was evaluated and the obtained value was taken as the "normalized" value. This normalization turned out to be particularly effective. It yields a uniform distribution of data over the $[0, 1]$ interval along each one of the dimensions of the feature space, and it allows for applying the same ANN architecture over different datasets.

The weights of the ANNs were initialized at random in the $[-0.001, 0.001]$ interval. The weights, as well as each bias of the sigmoids, were then optimized applying the usual backpropagation algorithm [11]. A fixed learning rate of 10^{-4} was applied for 100 epochs of online gradient descent over the training set. All the modules were trained and evaluated by applying the leave-one-out strategy described in Section III.

Module $\mathcal{D}$ was trained and evaluated first. It was observed that, after training, it was able to classify all datapoints that were completely covered ($\Pi(\mathbf{x})$ close to 1.0), or uncovered ($\Pi(\mathbf{x})$ close to 0.0) by clouds without any errors. In the points that were partially covered, an intermediate value for $\Pi(\mathbf{x})$ was estimated.

Module $\mathcal{T}$ was then trained to estimate ψ, either by using the estimate yielded by the cloud-detection module $\mathcal{D}$ or not. Results are presented in Table I in terms of average error w.r.t. the actual values of turbidity over the whole 13-points dataset. A standard multivariate linear regression model [10] was estimated as a comparison baseline for the connectionist model, too, under the same conditions (enlarged training set or not, leave-one-out). The first row of the Table refers to models trained on the bare satellite data, namely $\mathbf{x}$. Results obtained with the introduction of the value of $\Pi(\mathbf{x})$ estimated via $\mathcal{D}$ are reported in the second row. The reject option was not applied. It is seen that the connectionist estimate of turbidity shows a 13.36% relative error reduction w.r.t. the linear regression model. Both models took benefit from the knowledge of $\Pi(\mathbf{x})$.

Feature space	Linear regression	Neural model
Without cloud detection $\Pi(\mathbf{x})$	1.901	1.866
With cloud detection $\Pi(\mathbf{x})$	1.512	**1.310**

TABLE I

Turbidity estimation: average error obtained with the linear regression and the connectionist regression models.

Finally, we trained $\mathcal{C}$ to estimate the model ϕ of the chlorophyll concentration. All the following models for ϕ

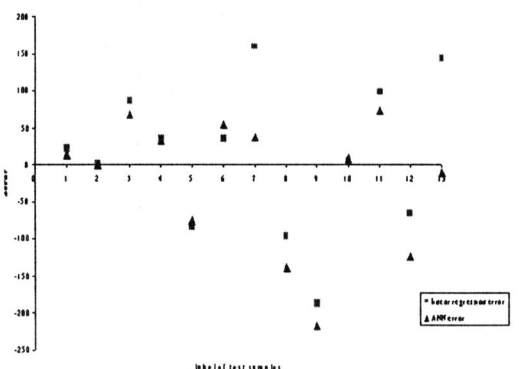

Fig. 3. Plot of errors (difference between estimated and actual chlorophyll vales) over the 13 samples for the linear regression (boxes) and the connectionist regression (triangles) models.

were trained and tested either by using the extended feature space (including the estimates for $\Pi(\mathbf{x})$ and $\psi(\mathbf{x})$) or not. Again, we started by training and evaluating neural and linear regression models over the original 4-dim feature space of dots in the satellite images. Figure 3 plots the errors (difference between estimated values and actual chlorophyll values) over the 13 samples for both regression models. Complete results are presented in Table II in terms of average error w.r.t. the actual concentration of chlorophyll over the whole 13-points dataset. Although the ANN allows for an improvement over the multivariate linear regression, it is seen that the absolute errors are satisfying only to a limited extent.

A significant gain in performance is obtained by extending the feature spec to include the estimate of $\Pi(\mathbf{x})$ (rows three and four in the Table), as well as the estimate of $\psi(\mathbf{x})$ (last two rows in the Table). The application of the global tuning of the modular system yields further gain. Although the value of the average error is not accurate yet, it is satisfying if we consider: (i) the limited amount of training samples that were measured on the filed; and (ii) the fact that the sampling of water with boats took a few minutes, while the satellite images were taken instantaneously, affecting the correlation between the input and the target output variables.

Regression model	Average error
Standard linear regression	91.13
Bare neural regression	65.59
Linear regression with cloud detection $\Pi(\mathbf{x})$	51.23
Neural net with cloud detection $\Pi(\mathbf{x})$	44.18
Complete modular system	29.16
Complete modular system with global tuning	27.57

TABLE II

Chlorophyll estimation: average errors obtained with the different models.

V. Conclusions

Estimating the relationship between the information contained in images of ground and water surfaces acquired by geostationary satellites, and the corresponding values of physical variables is a relevant and difficult task. The problem is even more challenging if we consider that data are intrinsically noisy. Noise is mostly introduced by the presence of clouds that may cover, or distort, the image; as well as by the turbidity of water. The latter is an index of its transparency and determines its reflectivity properties. This paper proposed a modular connectionist architecture that is a promising attempt to tackle such problems. It relies on: (1) a cloud-detector, i.e. a network trained to estimate the probability of presence of clouds covering the image; (2) a nonlinear connectionist regression model of turbidity; and on (3) a neural network trained to estimate the chlorophyll concentration from the original data and from the contribution from the previous modules. Eventually, the resulting architecture can be interpreted as a single multi-layered network that may be further tuned via a global training scheme. Furthermore, we proposed a viable technique to deal with the "limited sampling" problem, i.e. the limited amount of water samples that are actually collected from the water surface and analyzed in laboratory w.r.t. (a) the whole geographic area covered by the satellite image, and (b) the requirement of having enough data for ANNs training. Validation of the approach was favorably carried out on a real-world 13-point dataset from Lake Montepulciano (Siena, Italy).

Acknowledgment

The authors would like to thank Steven Loiselle and Andrea Cognetta at the Dipartimento di Scienze e Tecnologie Chimiche e dei Biosistemi of the University of Siena. Fabrizio "Briccone" Santini and his friend are gratefully acknowledged.

References

[1] R.W. Johnson and R.C. Harris, "Remote sensing for water quality and biological measurements in coastal waters," *Photogrammetric Engineering and Remote Sensing*, vol. 46, no. 1, pp. 77–85, 1980.

[2] Jr. Chavez, P.S., "Image-based atmospheric corrections - revisited and improved," *Photogrammetric Engineering and Remote Sensing*, vol. 62, no. 9, pp. 1025–1036, 1996.

[3] R.C. Smith and K.S. Baker, "Oceanic chlorophyll concentrations as determined by satellite," *Marine Biology*, vol. 66, pp. 269–279, 1982.

[4] R. O. Duda and P. E. Hart, *Pattern Classification and Scene Analysis*, Wiley, New York, 1973.

[5] K. Fukunaga, *Statistical Pattern Recognition*, Academic Press, San Diego, second edition, 1990.

[6] E. Trentin and M. Gori, "Continuous speech recognition with a robust connectionist/markovian hybrid model," in *Proceedings of ICANN2001, International Conference on Artificial Neural Networks*, Vienna, Austria, August 2001.

[7] C. M. Bishop, *Neural Networks for Pattern Recognition*, Oxford University Press, Oxford, 1995.

[8] E. Trentin, "Networks with trainable amplitude of activation functions," *Neural Networks*, vol. 14, pp. 471–493, May 2001.

[9] J. Hertz, A. Krogh, and R. Palmer, *Introduction to the Theory of Neural Computation*, Addison Wesley, 1991.

[10] K.V. Mardia, J.T. Kent, and J.M. Bibby, *Multivariate Analysis*, Academic Press, London, 1994.

[11] D.E. Rumelhart, G.E. Hinton, and R.J. Williams, "Learning internal representations by error propagation," in *Parallel Distributed Processing*, D.E. Rumelhart and J.L. McClelland, Eds., vol. 1, chapter 8, pp. 318–362. MIT Press, Cambridge, 1986.

Improved Defect Detection Using Support Vector Machines and Wavelet Feature Extraction Based on Vector Quantization and SVD Techniques.

D.A. Karras

[1]Hellenic Aerospace Industry, University of Hertfordshire (UK) and Hellenic Open University, Rodu2, Ano Iliupolis, Athens 16342, Greece, e-mails: dakarras@hol.gr, dkarras@haicorp.com, dakarras@usa.net

Abstract.

This paper aims at investigating a novel solution to the problem of defect detection from images using the Support Vector Machines (SVM) classification approach, that can find applications in the design of robust quality control systems for the production of furniture, textile, integrated circuits, etc. The suggested solution focuses on detecting defects for manufacturing applications from their wavelet transformation and vector quantization related properties of the associated wavelet coefficients. More specifically, a novel methodology is investigated for discriminating defects by applying a supervised neural classification technique, namely SVM, to innovative multidimensional wavelet based feature vectors. These vectors are extracted from the K-Level 2-D DWT (Discrete Wavelet Transform) transformed original image using Vector Quantization techniques and a Singular Value Decomposition (SVD) Analysis applied to these wavelet domain quantization vectors. The results of the proposed methodology are illustrated in defective textile images where the defective areas are recognized with higher accuracy than the one obtained by applying two rival defect detection methodologies. The first one of them uses all the wavelet coefficients derived from the k-Level 2-D DWT and involves SVM again in the classification stage, while the second one uses again all the wavelet coefficients derived from the k-Level 2-D DWT but involves a Multilayer Perceptron (MLP) neural network in the classification stage. The promising results herein shown outline the importance of judicious selection and processing of 2-D DWT wavelet coefficients for industrial pattern recognition applications as well as the generalization performance benefits obtained by involving SVM neural networks instead of other ANN models.

I. INTRODUCTION

A novel methodology is developed for defect detection employing the SVM approach along with a new feature extraction procedure applied to the k-Level wavelet domain. This feature extraction approach considers multidimensional vectors of wavelet coefficients having as components suitably selected windows of these coefficients from their associated QMF channels. The K-Level wavelet domain is, therefore, composed as the space of all these vectors by using the suggested methodology. A vector quantization algorithm is subsequently applied to this new vector space and the associated codebook vectors are extracted. The vector quantization algorithm used is the Kohonen topology preservation map (SOM) and the resulting codebook vectors are the corresponding SOM weight vectors. An SVD analysis of the codebook matrix associated with these codebook vectors provides the components of the feature vectors, which feed the supervised SVM architectures of the classification stage of the proposed defect detection system. The proposed defect detection system is favorably compared with one system involving as feature vectors the set of all 2-D DWT wavelet coefficients and as the corresponding pattern classifier a SVM. In addition, it is favorably compared with another defect detection system involving as feature vectors the set of all 2-D DWT wavelet coefficients again and as the corresponding pattern classifier an MLP. The promising results herein obtained set the baseline for the future work of the author, which is currently focused on building a real world defect detection system for the textile industry instead of the prototype investigated in this paper.

The SVM approach is an efficient ANN classification methodology and although there exist several research efforts concerning their applications to real world pattern recognition problems, there is lack of a systematic account with regards to the defect detection problem in manufacturing process. The first contribution of this paper lies exactly on investigating SVM defect detection performance and proving that it is better than the one obtained by applying MLP models as alternative in the classification stage of the suggested and outlined defect detection system. The second and major novelty and contribution of this work is the proposed feature extraction methodology, applied to the K-Level wavelet domain, which produces multidimensional wavelet vectors efficient for defect discrimination and demonstrates the significance of properly selecting and processing the wavelet domain coefficients in designing successful real world pattern recognition systems.

Defect recognition from images is becoming increasingly significant in a variety of applications since quality control plays a prominent role in contemporary manufacturing of virtually every product. Despite the lot of interest, little work has been done in this field since this classification problem presents many difficulties. However, the resurgence of interest for neural network research has revealed the existence of powerful classifiers. In addition, the emergence of the 2-D wavelet transform [1],[2] as a popular tool in image processing offers the ability of robust feature extraction in images. Combinations of both techniques have been used with success in various applications [3].

Therefore, it is worth attempting to investigate whether they can jointly offer a viable solution to the defect recognition problem. To this end, we propose a novel methodology in detecting defective areas in images by examining the discrimination abilities of their K-level wavelet coefficients based features and by subsequently classifying them using SVM. Besides neural network classifiers of the SVM type and the K-Level 2-D wavelet transform, the tools utilized in such an analysis are vector quantization and Singular Value Decomposition related analysis [4] of the vectors quantizing the K-Level wavelet domain of an image window. There are several reasons for involving SVM techniques instead of more traditional neural approaches.

More specifically, Support Vector Machines [4] are an attractive approach to data modeling through applying neural systems. They combine generalization control with a technique to address the curse of dimensionality. The formulation results in a global quadratic optimization problem with box constraints, which is readily solved by interior point methods. The kernel mapping provides a unifying framework for most of the commonly employed model architectures, enabling comparisons to be performed. In classification problems generalization control is obtained by maximizing the margin, which corresponds to minimization of the weight vector in a canonical framework. The solution is obtained as a set of support vectors that can be sparse. These lie on the boundary and as such summarize the information required to separate the data. The minimization of the weight vector can be used as a criterion in regression problems, with a modified loss function [4]. Out of these properties, the most important reason to use SVM in the defect detection problem is actually the generalization control capability they offer and thus, the avoidance of overfitting. These properties seem to be very important concerning the required sensitivity and specificity to be exhibited by defect detection systems in manufacturing quality control. For instance minimization of false alarms is an absolute must, while on the other hand even the slightest defects should be detected if an automated real world quality control system is to be realized.

The problem of defect detection can be clearly viewed as image segmentation one, where the image should be segmented in defective and non-defective areas only unlike its conventional consideration. Concerning the classical segmentation problem, that is dividing an image into homogeneous regions, the discovery of a generally effective scheme remains a challenge. To this end, many interesting techniques have been suggested so far including spatial frequency techniques [5] and relevant ones like texture clustering in the wavelet domain [5]. Most of these methodologies use very simple features like the energy of the wavelet channels [5] or the variance of the wavelet coefficients [6].

Our approach stems from this line of research related to the wavelet domain judicious processing. However, there is need for much more sophisticated wavelet feature extraction methods if one wants to solve the segmentation problem in its defect recognition incarnation, taking into account the high accuracy required. Following this reasoning we propose to incorporate in the research efforts multidimensional wavelet features, unlike the previously presented scalar feature extraction methodologies in the wavelet domain [6,5]. These multidimensional features, coming from the application of the K-Level 2-D DWT, are, in the sequel, processed using vector quantization and SVD methodology, which offer the accurate tools for describing transformed image characteristics and especially complex second order ones [4]. More specifically, SVD of a matrix analysis is well known to provide second order information, while Vector Quantization algorithms provide the means for efficient vector space encoding. Two are the main stages of the suggested system. Namely, efficient multidimensional feature selection in the wavelet domain and SVM neural network based classification. The viability of the concepts and methods employed in the proposed approach is illustrated in the experimental section of the paper, where it is shown that our methodology is very promising for use in the quality control field, by comparing its performance in defective areas classification accuracy with the one obtained by two rival defect detection techniques.

II. STAGE A: EFFICIENT MULTIDIMENSIONAL FEATURE EXTRACTION IN THE K-LEVEL WAVELET DOMAIN

The problem of defect discrimination, aiming at segmenting the defective areas in images, is considered in the wavelet domain, since it has been demonstrated that discrete wavelet transform (DWT) can in general lead to better image modeling, as for instance to better encoding (wavelet image compression [7,8] is one of the best compression methodologies) and to better texture modeling [7]. Also, in this way, we can better exploit the known local information extraction properties of wavelet signal decomposition as well as the known features of wavelet de-noising procedures [9]. We use the popular 2-D discrete wavelet transform scheme ([1], [2] etc.) in order to obtain the wavelet analysis of the original image data containing defects. Other possibilities for applying the wavelet analysis in the problem of defect detection are offered by adaptive wavelets [10], adaptive wavelet packets [11] or rotated wavelet filters [12]. The proposed approach, however, could be considered as a meta-wavelet analysis focused on further analyzing the wavelet coefficients obtained by applying any wavelet transform, in order to conduct efficient dimensionality reduction balanced with the preservation of the important results of the wavelet analysis. Therefore, it presents a new approach in defect detection by transforming the raw features of the wavelet analysis into powerful classification characteristics.

It is expected that the images considered in the wavelet domain should be smooth but due to the known time-frequency localization properties of the wavelet transform, the defective areas- whose statistics vary from the ones of the image background- should more or less clearly emerge from the background. We have experimented with the standard 2-D Wavelet transform using nearly all the well known wavelet bases like Haar, Daubechies, Coiflet, Symmlet etc. as well as with Meyer's and Kolaczyk's 2-D Wavelet transforms [2]. However, Daubechies and Haar wavelets have exhibited similar and the most accurate results and we employ them in the experimental section of the paper.

The proposed methodology involving multidimensional wavelet features obtained from the K-Level 2-D DWT, with application to defect detection, can be outlined in the following steps.

1) The N X N image is raster scanned by M X M sliding windows
2) Each such window is transformed into the wavelet domain using the K-Level 2-D DWT. As a result, the wavelet coefficients organized in $3*K+1$ channels (or bands) are obtained. (See Figure 1)
3) Starting from the channel LL_K (the upper left window in Figure 1, which represents the Low Pass filtered image), the multidimensional vectors V_j are formed from the wavelet coefficients, having as components $3*K+1$ windows (each one associated with one channel) of $2^{(K-\text{MAX\_LEVEL\_INDICATED\_IN\_QMF})} * 2^{(K-\text{MAX\_LEVEL\_INDICATED\_IN\_QMF})}$ points. These points comprise a sub-window of wavelet coefficients belonging in the corresponding channel, and the position of this sub-window, as defined by its upper left point, is exactly the point in the QMF window under consideration associated with the LL_K channel point comprising the first component of vector V_i. For instance, concerning the three-level DWT of figure 1, each V_j is comprised of 10 main components, which are windows of wavelet coefficients. Each such window includes $2^{(3-\text{MAX\_LEVEL\_INDICATED\_IN\_QMF})} * 2^{(3-\text{MAX\_LEVEL\_INDICATED\_IN\_QMF})}$ of wavelet coefficients. For the LL_3, HL_3, LH_3, HH_3 QMFs we have MAX_LEVEL_INDICATED_IN_QMF = 3 and, thus, 1 DWT coefficient is considered. For the HL_2, HH_2, LH_2 QMFs we have MAX_LEVEL_INDICATED_IN_QMF = 2 and, thus, $2*2$ DWT coefficients are considered. Finally, for the HL_1, HH_1, LH_1 QMFs we have MAX_LEVEL_INDICATED_IN_QMF = 1 and, thus, $4*4$ DWT coefficients are considered. Therefore, a total of $4*1 + 3*4 + 3*16 = 64$ wavelet coefficients comprise each multidimensional wavelet vector V_j, in the case depicted in figure 1. The above mentioned sub-windows are illustrated in figure 1.
4) Obviously, the K-Level 2-D DWT space is spanned by the vectors V_i. In the sequel, the K-Level 2-D DWT domain is quantized using the vector quantization method of Kohonen Self Organizing Feature Map (SOFM) [4], which produces topology preserving codebook vectors [4]. These codebook vectors encode the topological space of the DWT domain by preserving input vectors probability distribution and are estimated as the associated with the SO map weight vectors [4]. Let's Cb1, Cb2,.. Cbn stand for these codebook vectors, where n<<r, if r is the multitude of Vi input vectors, that span K-Level 2-D DWT domain.
5) After estimating each such Cbi, we formulate the codebook matrix of all n Cbi codebook vectors, where its ith column is occupied by Cbi only. To this codebook matrix the well known SVD technique [4] has been applied and the maximum p singular values S1, S2, ..., Sp singular values have been extracted. Such a set of singular values derived from a data matrix plays a significant role in quantifying its properties [4].

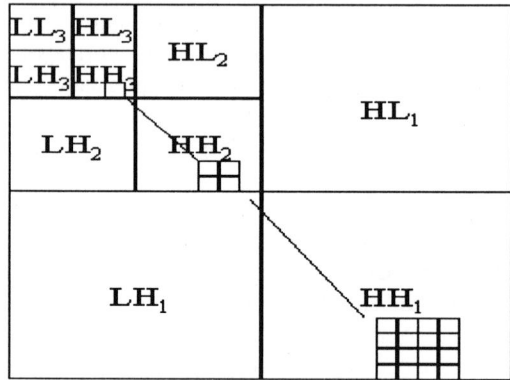

Figure 1. Illustration of a sample of the corresponding wavelet coefficients sub-windows taking place in the formation of vectors Vi that span K-Level Wavelet domain. Three such windows are shown out of a total of 10 (one for each QMF channel).

6) All the p above calculated singular values from the codebook matrix form the input vectors for the SVM neural classifiers of the subsequent stage B.

The practical aspects of the above proposed feature extraction approach, are next presented.

a) We have experimented with 256 x 256 images and we have found that M=32 is a good size for a sliding window raster scanning them and capable of locating defective areas (step 1).
b) A two-level 2-D DWT wavelet decomposition of these sliding windows associated images has been performed for each such window, resulting in seven main wavelet channels (step 2).
c) Step 3 above leads to vectors Vi having $4*1 + 3*4 = 16$ wavelet coefficients as components. There are 64 (since LL_2 channel includes $8*8$ coefficients) such vectors Vi that span the 2-Level wavelet domain. A total of 1024 wavelet coefficients comprise this domain, which is a large number of features to be employed in the classification stage of the proposed defect detection approach, since the curse of dimensionality obviously arises [4]. A judicious

compression of this 64 vector space is therefore, required.

d) This is achieved through applying step 4 depicted above. To this end, a Kohonen SOM neural network involving 16 component (the wavelet coefficients) input vectors Vi as inputs and a 4 X 4 map of 16 output neurons compresses this vector space. The associated codebook vectors compressing the input space of 64 vectors are the 16 corresponding SOM weight vectors.

e) The codebook matrix is formed from the above determined codebook vectors, having 16 rows (the number of wavelet coefficients belonging to each codebook vector) and 16 columns (the number of codebook vectors). In step 5 above the p=16 maximum singular values of the codebook matrix are extracted, that is all its singular values.

f) The input vectors of the neural based classification stage that follows, constructed by the suggested feature extraction technique, therefore, comprise 16 elements, i.e the singular values of the codebook matrix.

Thus, using the above in detail outlined feature extraction procedure, we have obtained 16 feature input vectors efficiently describing spatial distribution in the wavelet domain of each 32 x 32 sliding window raster scanning the images. These 16 features uniquely characterize such sliding windows and the corresponding feature vectors feed the SVM neural classifiers of the subsequent stage of the suggested methodology, next defined.

III. STAGE B: SVM NEURAL NETWORK BASED SEGMENTATION OF DEFECTIVE AREAS.

After obtaining the wavelet domain based characteristics of each M X M sliding window raster scanning the N X N image, involving the above defined methodology, we employ a supervised neural network architecture of the SVM type with RBF (and polynomial) kernels and in parallel, as baseline for comparison we, also, consider Multilayer Feedforward models (MLP), trained with the conjugate gradients algorithm (Polak-Ribiere variation) [4]. The goal for both supervised training procedures is to decide whether such a sliding window covers a defective area or not. The inputs to the networks are the 16 (or 1024) components of the feature vectors extracted from each such sliding window as previously defined. The desired outputs during training are determined by the corresponding sliding window location. More specifically, if a sliding window belongs to a defective area the desired output of the network is one, otherwise, it is zero. We have defined, during SVM/MLP training phase, that a sliding window belongs to a defective area if the majority of the pixels in the 4 x 4 central window inside the original 32 X 32 corresponding sliding window belongs to the defect. The reasoning underlying this definition is that the decision about whether a window belongs to a defective area or not should come from a large neighborhood information, thus preserving the 2-D structure of the problem and not from information associated with only one pixel (e.g the central pixel). In addition and probably more significantly, by defining the two classes in such a way, we can obtain many more training patterns for the class corresponding to the defective area, since defects, normally, cover only a small area of the original image. It is important for the effective neural network classifier learning to have enough training patterns for each one of the two classes but, on the other hand, to preserve as much as possible the a priori probability distribution of the problem. We have experimentally found that a proportion of 1:3 for the training patterns belonging to defective and non-defective areas respectively is very good for achieving both goals.

IV. RESULTS AND DISCUSSION.

The efficiency of our approach in recognizing defects in automated inspection images, based on utilizing wavelet domain information, is illustrated by applying it to the textile images shown in fig. 2,3,4 which contain various types of defective areas. Two other rival methodologies are applied to these images too. The former of them uses all the 32 X 32 (=1024) wavelet coefficients obtained by the 2-D DWT transformation of each 32 X 32 sliding window without any further processing and involves as defective area classifier a SVM, while the latter uses the 32 X 32 (=1024) wavelet coefficients again, corresponding to the same sliding window, and an MLP model instead. Therefore, the first defect detection procedure used in this experimental study is the suggested novel one outlined in section II, which involves 16 components feature vectors followed by a SVM pattern classifier. The second and the third procedures as mentioned above, involve 1024 components feature vectors and therefore, the curse of dimensionality might appear. The three images shown in figures 2,3,4 are of 256 x 256 dimensions and their associated 2-Level 2-D DWT are shown in figures 2, 3, and 4 respectively. The QMF channels shown in these figures have been obtained through applying the 2-D DWT with Daubechies wavelet bases to the original images. Obviously, the defective areas are preserved and enhanced in the corresponding wavelet domains and this explains the selection of the 2-D DWT as the baseline for the herein presented feature extraction methodology. There exist 50625 sliding windows of 32 x 32 size for each original image. The three rival defect detection procedures used in this study are applied to every such sliding window, yielding the corresponding feature vectors along with their classifications. Therefore, for each image a set of 50625 training and test patterns is derived.

The neural networks corresponding to the classification stage (stage B) of the first two defect detection systems under comparison are of the SVM type. Concerning the third such system an MLP network trained with the conjugate gradients algorithm (Polak-Ribiere variation) has been utilized. The best MLP architecture found and compared with the SVM is the 1024-64-32-1. For an image involved in the study, the SVM/MLP has been trained with its corresponding training set (obtained from the specific image) containing 1500 patterns extracted from the associated sliding windows as described above. On average (for the three images) 480 out of these 1500 patterns belong to the defective areas, while the rest belong to the class of non-defective areas. Each SVM/MLP has been tested on all 50625 patterns from which its training set comes from. The results obtained by involving our methodology are shown in fig. 5, 6 and 7 and clearly are very favorably compared, in terms of defect classification performance, to the two other defect detection methodologies.

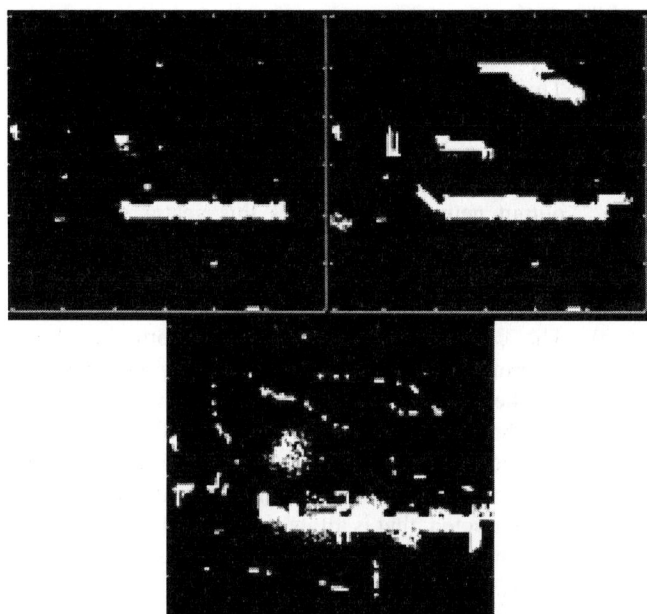

Figure 5. Defect Detection results for the first textile image. From left to right the results obtained using the proposed feature extraction method+ SVM, the 32 X 32 wavelet coeff. + SVM and the 32 X 32 wavelet coeff. + MLP, as described in section IV.

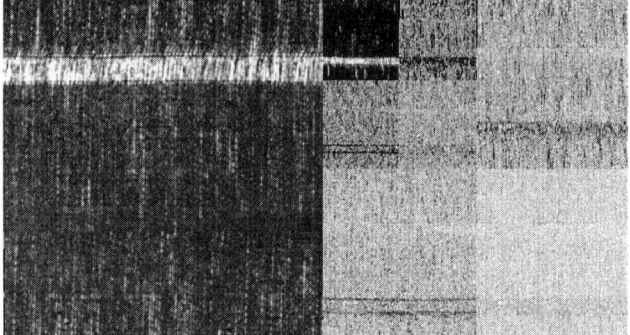

Figure 2. First original textile image containing a defect and the 2-Level 2-D Wavelet transformation of this image

Figure 3. Second original textile image containing a defect and the 2-Level 2-D Wavelet transformation of this image

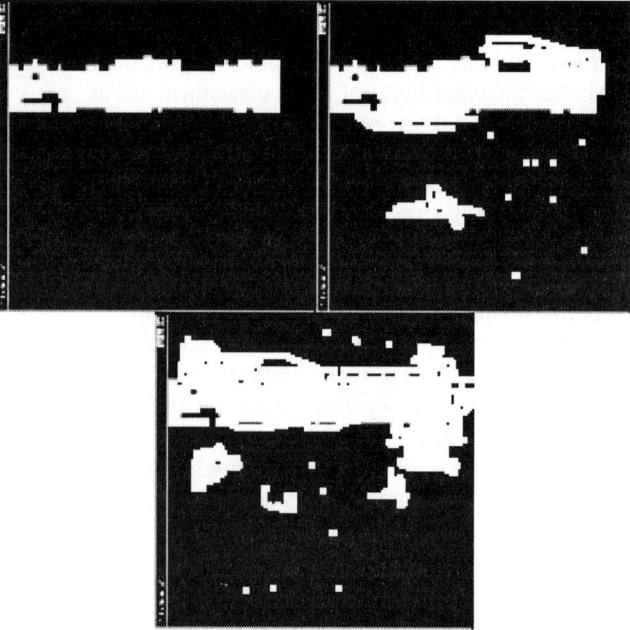

Figure 6. Defect Detection results for the second textile image. From left to right the results obtained using the proposed feature extraction method+ SVM, the 32 X 32 wavelet coeff. + SVM and the 32 X 32 wavelet coeff. + MLP, as described in section IV

Figure 4. Third original textile image containing a defect and the 2-Level 2-D Wavelet transformation of this image

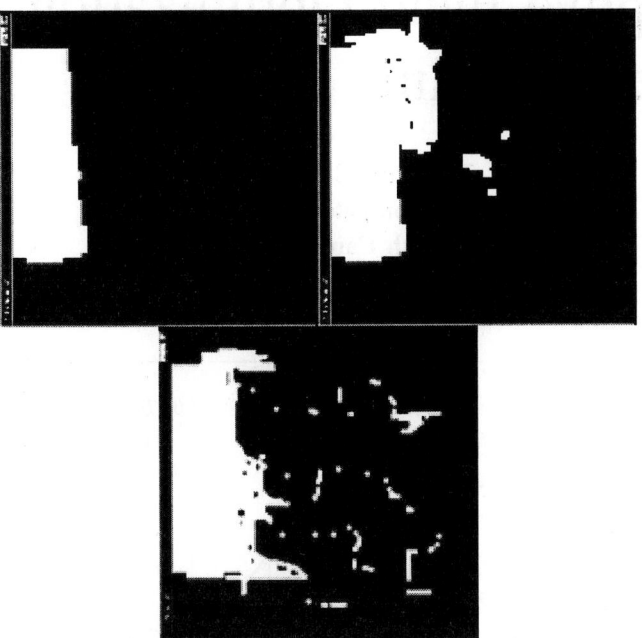

Figure 7. Defect Detection results for the third textile image. From left to right the results obtained using the proposed feature extraction method+ SVM, the 32 X 32 wavelet coeff. + SVM and the 32 X 32 wavelet coeff. + MLP, as described in section IV

V. CONCLUSIONS

A novel methodology is developed for defect detection employing the SVM approach along with a new feature extraction procedure applied to the k-Level wavelet domain. This feature extraction approach considers multidimensional vectors of wavelet coefficients having as components suitably selected windows of these coefficients from their associated QMF channels. The K-Level wavelet domain is, therefore, composed as the space of all these vectors by using the suggested methodology. A vector quantization algorithm is subsequently applied to this new vector space and the associated codebook vectors are extracted. The vector quantization algorithm used is the Kohonen topology preservation map (SOM) and the resulting codebook vectors are the corresponding SOM weight vectors. An SVD analysis of the codebook matrix associated with these codebook vectors provides the components of the feature vectors, which feed the supervised SVM architectures of the classification stage of the proposed defect detection system. The proposed defect detection system is very favorably compared with one system involving as feature vectors all the 2-D DWT wavelet coefficients and as the corresponding pattern classifier a SVM. In addition, it is very favorably compared with another defect detection system involving as feature vectors the 2-D DWT wavelet coefficients again and as the corresponding pattern classifier an MLP. The promising results herein obtained set the baseline for the future work of the authors, which is currently focused on building a real world defect detection system for the textile industry instead of the prototype investigated in this paper.

REFERENCES

[1] Meyer, Y. "Wavelets: Algorithms and Applications", Philadelphia: SIAM, 1993

[2] Kolaczyk, E. "WVD Solution of Inverse Problems", Doctoral Dissertation, Stanford University, Dept. of Statistics, 1994

[3] Lee, C. S., et. al, "Feature Extraction Algorithm based on Adaptive Wavelet Packet for Surface Defect Classification", to be presented in ICIP 96, 16-19 Sept. 1996, Lausanne, Switzerland.

[4] Haykin, S. "Neural Networks, A comprehensive foundation", Prentice Hall, Second edition, 1999.

[5] Porter, R. and Canagarajah, N. "A Robust Automatic Clustering Scheme foe Image Segmentation Using Wavelets", IEEE Trans. on Image Processing, April 1996, Vol. 5, No. 4, pp.662 - 665.

[6] Unser, M. "Texture Classification and Segmentation Using Wavelet Frames", IEEE trans. Image Processing, Vol. 4, No. 11, pp.1549-1560, 1995

[7] Ryan, T. W., Sanders, D., Fisher, H. D. and Iverson, A. E. "Image Compression by Texture Modeling in the Wavelet Domain", IEEE trans. Image Processing, Vol. 5, No. 1, pp. 26-36, 1996.

[8] Antonini, M., Barlaud, M., Mathieu, P. and Daubechies, I. "Image Coding Using Wavelet Transform", IEEE trans. Image Processing, Vol.1, pp. 205-220, 1992.

[9] Donoho, D. L. and Johnstone, I. M. "Ideal Time-Frequency Denoising." Technical Report, Dept. of Statistics, Stanford University.

[10] W. J. Jasper, S. J. Garnier, H. Potlapalli, "Texture characterization and defect detection using adaptive wavelets", Optical Engineering, Vol. 35, Iss. 11, pp. 3140-3149, November 1996.

[11] C.S. Lee-CS, C.H. Choi, J.Y. Choi and S.H Choi, "Surface defect inspection of cold rolled strips with features based on adaptive wavelet packets", IEICE Trans. Inf. Syst, Vol. E80D, Iss. 5, pp. 594-604, 1997.

[12] Nam-Deuk Kim and Satish Upda, "Texture classification using rotated wavelet filters", IEEE Trans. SMC-Part A., Vol. 30, Iss. 6, pp. 847-852, 2000.

Three Heuristics for Receptive Field Optimization for Ensemble Encoding

Ashraf M. Abdelbar, Deena O. Hassan,
Dept. of Computer Science,
American University in Cairo,

Gene A. Tagliarini, Sridhar Narayan
Dept. of Computer Science,
University of North Carolina, Wilmington

Abstract— Ensemble encoding is a biologically-motivated, distributed data representation scheme for MLP networks. Multiple overlapping receptive fields are used to enhance locality of representation. The number, form, and placement of receptive fields has a great impact on performance. We present three heuristics, two based on descriptive statistics, and one based on clustering, for optimizing receptive field configuration, and compare their performance on three benchmark data sets. Performance varies among the benchmarks, but on one benchmark, the clustering heuristic yields a 56% improvement in test set classification over unencoded data, and a 48% improvement over symmetrical-placement three-receptor ensemble encoding.

I. INTRODUCTION

Ensemble encoding [23] is a distributed data representation scheme for MLP networks trained by backward error propagation, that has been found to improve learning in a number of applications [19], [21], [22]. Multiple overlapping receptive fields are used to enhance locality of representation and improve localized learning. The number, form, and placement of receptive fields has a great impact on the success of the ensemble encoding technique. Previous work has investigated the use of genetic algorithms [20] and simulated annealing [1] in the optimization of receptive field configuration. In this paper, we present three heuristics, two based on descriptive-statistics, and one based on clustering, for optimizing receptive field configuration, and compare their performance empirically on three benchmark data sets: protein localization site prediction on *e. coli* bacteria, contraceptive method usage prediction, and breast cancer diagnosis.

Section II reviews the ensemble encoding representation and its biological motivations. Section III introduces our three heuristics. Section IV describes the experimental methodology employed in our empirical study and presents experimental results on each of the three data sets. Finally, Sections V and VI, respectively, present discussion of the results and concluding remarks.

II. ENSEMBLE ENCODING

Robert Erickson [8] has described Young's theory of color vision [26] as a unifying principle in neurobiology, with application to sensation and movement, as well as memory, emotion, and motivation. Young hypothesized the existence of different types of receptive cells in the eye. It is now known that there are rod cells and cone cells. Rod cells are sensitive to the intensity of light. Cone cells are sensitive across the

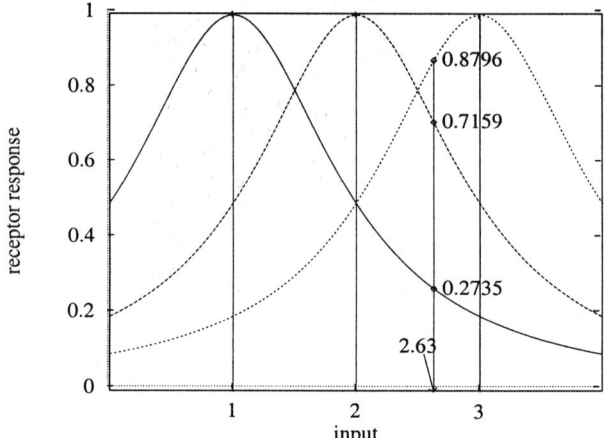

Fig. 1. Ensemble encoding of values from 0 to 4.

complete spectrum, but, each cone cell will produce a maximal response when stimulated with light of a particular color. Helmholtz [10] described colors as being encoded according to the ratio of responses across an ensemble of receptors. As Erickson [8] indicates, the idea of encoding sensory input based on responses of a population of receptors has relevance to hearing [6], smell [16], and taste [4], [7].

In a manner analogous to the way in which cone cells encode color, multiple receptors can be used to encode inputs to MLP networks. For instance, Hancock [9] and Lorquet *et al.* [15] have studied preprocessing schemes in which overlapping, Gaussian response curves were used to encode the inputs to MLP networks. Narayan *et al.* [23] proposed a data representation scheme termed ensemble encoding that uses multiple, overlapping receptive fields to generate a distributed representation for network inputs.

Consider the function

$$f(x,\alpha,\beta) = \frac{1}{1 + (\frac{x-\alpha}{\beta})^2} \quad (1)$$

which forms a receptive field model for a stimulus x that provides maximal response when x=α and a diminished response as x moves away from α. The function f(x,α,β) may be viewed as a fuzzy membership function that represents the degree to which a given x is a member of the set of x's that are close to α. The parameter α defines the center of the receptive field and β determines the degree of localization of the field. The parameter β is referred to as the half-width of a receptive field since $f(x,\alpha,\beta) = 1/2$ when $x = \alpha \pm \beta$. By using multiple receptors with overlapping fields, a distributed representation of an input x can be created. Figure 1 shows how three receptors might be used to encode values of x ranging between 0 and 4. The response curves in Figure 1 were generated using Equation (1) with α=1,2,3 and β=1. As illustrated in Figure 1, every receptor responds to every input but the degree of response depends upon how close x is to the center of each receptive field. The collective response of the receptors is an ensemble code for the input x. Using the receptive fields illustrated in Figure 1, the ensemble code for 2.63, for example, is (0.2735, 0.7159, 0.8796).

When ensemble encoding is used to encode the inputs to an MLP network, each input is individually encoded using a set of receptive fields and an MLP network receives the ensemble code for each input. For instance, if the number 2.63 (referenced above) was an input to an MLP network, and the coding scheme shown in Figure 1 was used, the network would now receive three inputs instead, with values 0.2735, 0.7159 and 0.8796, respectively.

In [23], Narayan *et al.* used three receptors for every attribute, set two of the α values to the maximum and minimum for that attribute, and set the third α to the midpoint of the range for that attribute, *i.e.*, to $min + \frac{max-min}{2}$. Values of beta were chosen so that the receptive field functions had half-widths halfway between the alphas. We will refer to this as the symmetrical placement approach.

In the present work, we have allowed the number of receptors to increase to up to five receptors per attribute. Although humans have only three types of cone cells, there is biological evidence [5] suggesting that some bird and reptile retinas have cone cells with more than five different spectral responses [24].

III. HEURISTIC APPROACHES

We present three heuristics which are based on a pre-specified maximum number of receptors but allow the number of attributes per receptor to be lower than the maximum. The three heuristics compute the receptive field center, α, differently, but compute the half-width, β, similarly. We therefore describe the determination of β separately at the end of the section.

As an example to be used in subsections below, suppose the set of values for a given attribute are $(0, 25, 17, 69, 79, 3, 45, 10, 0, 5, 0)$, and three receptors are used to encode each attribute. Let (α_1, β_2) refer to the parameters of the first receptor, (α_2, β_2) refer to the parameters of the second receptor, and so on.

A. Means Approach

The means approach can be applied for any number of receptors per attribute, although we have only experimentally investigated the cases for 3, 4, and 5 receptors. Suppose, first, that three receptors are to be used. The mean value for the attribute, let it be denoted y, is determined and we set $\alpha_2 = y$.

The data is then partitioned into values greater than the mean and values less than the mean. The mean of values below the mean (let it be denoted x) and the mean for values above the mean (let it be denoted z) are determined. We set $\alpha_1 = x$ and $\alpha_3 = z$.

Now, suppose, we are to use four receptors. First, we compute x, y, and z, as defined in the paragraph above. We then set α_1 to the mean of values below x, set α_2 to the mean of values within the range (x, y), α_3 to the mean of values within the range (y, z), and α_4 to the mean of values greater than z. If either the range (x, y) or the range (y, z) is empty, then only three receptors are produced.

Finally, suppose we are to use five receptors. We compute x, y, and z, as above. We set α_1 to the mean of values below x, set α_2 to the mean of values within the range (x, y), set $\alpha_3 = y$, set α_4 to the mean of values within the range (y, z), and set α_5 to the mean of values greater than z. If either of the ranges (x, y), or (y, z) is empty, then fewer than five receptors are produced.

The procedures described above can be generalized to more than five receptors.

In the numerical example described at the beginning of the section, symmetrical placement for three receptors would produce the three receptor centers: 0, 39.5, and 79. The means approach would produce: 5, 13, and 54.25.

B. Median Approach

Suppose the number of training records is n, the number of attributes per record is m, and the number of receptors per attribute is r. If we are processing the jth attribute, we sort all records according to their value for attribute j. Then, for $1 \leq i \leq r$, we then set α_i to the value of the jth attribute for record number $\frac{ni}{r+1}$.

If, for a given attribute, this method results in more than one receptor with the same α value, then all but one of the receptors is removed for that attribute.

In the numeric example described at the beginning of the section, the median approach would produce: 0, 10, and 45.

C. Clustering Approach

The c-means algorithm [13], [17] is used to cluster the values for the attribute being encoded into up to five clusters. The centers of the clusters are taken as the values of α.

We briefly review the c-means algorithm here; for a fuller exposition, the reader is directed to [12, Chapter 15]. c-means can be used to cluster a set of vectors, but we will restrict our attention to clustering a set of scalars (*i.e.*, values of given attribute). Given a collection of n values $x_1, \ldots, x_n$, we begin by randomly assigning each value to one of c clusters. We take the center c_j of each cluster j to be the mean of the values that are currently assigned to the cluster. For each data value x_i, we determine the distance $|x_i - c_j|$ for $j = 1, \ldots, c$, and re-assign each data value to the minimum-distance cluster. We then re-compute the cluster centers, and, again, re-assign each data value to the cluster to whose center it is closest. This process is repeated until no changes occur in the cluster assignments

TABLE I

RESULTS OF DIFFERENT APPROACHES AND NUMBERS OF RECEPTORS INDICATING TRAINING ERROR, TEST ERROR, AND PERCENTAGE IMPROVEMENT IN TEST SET ERROR, ON THE *e. coli* DATA SET AT THE END OF 100 EPOCHS

Approach	Arch.	Train. Err.	Test Err.	imp.
Clustering (3 rec.)	19-25-8	0.02713	0.02793	56.0%
Clustering (5 rec.)	29-18-8	0.02779	0.02932	53.8%
Clustering (4 rec.)	24-21-8	0.02835	0.02941	53.7%
Means (4 rec.)	26-19-8	0.02922	0.02995	52.8%
Median (5 rec.)	27-19-8	0.02877	0.02996	52.8%
Symmetrical (5 rec.)	35-15-8	0.02892	0.03000	52.7%
Means (5 rec.)	31-17-8	0.02947	0.03073	51.6%
Median (4 rec.)	22-22-8	0.02929	0.03089	51.4%
Means (3 rec.)	21-23-8	0.03026	0.03120	50.9%
Symmetrical (4 rec.)	28-18-8	0.03055	0.03130	50.7%
Median (3 rec.)	17-27-8	0.02997	0.03150	50.4%
Symmetrical (3 rec.)	21-23-8	0.05175	0.05403	14.9%
Unencoded	7-45-8	0.06428	0.06352	—

of all data values. If there are any clusters to whom no data values are assigned, then that cluster is eliminated.

In our experiments, the c-means algorithm is applied with $c = 3$, $c = 4$, and $c = 5$. But, in many instances, the number of clusters returned by the algorithm is less than the specified upper limit and is sometimes as few as 2.

D. Determination of β Parameter

Suppose we have n receptors, and $\alpha_1, \ldots, \alpha_n$ have already been determined. The β parameters are computed as follows:

$$\beta_1 = \frac{|\alpha_1 - \alpha_2|}{2}, \quad (2)$$

$$\beta_i = \frac{1}{2}\left[\frac{|\alpha_i - \alpha_{i-1}|}{2} + \frac{|\alpha_{i+1} - \alpha_i|}{2}\right] \text{ for } i \in [2, n-1], \quad (3)$$

$$\beta_n = \frac{|\alpha_n - \alpha_{n-1}|}{2}. \quad (4)$$

If the heuristic approach produces only one receptor for a given attribute, which happens occasionally with the median approach, then β for that receptor is taken as one-half of the receptor's center α.

IV. EMPIRICAL RESULTS

We used three popular benchmark datasets available from the UCI Repository [18]:

- *E. coli* [11]: Predicting protein localization sites in *e. coli* bacteria. Number of training patterns: 336. Number of attributes: 7. Number of classes: 8.
- Contraceptives [14]: Predicting current contraceptive method choice based on demographic and socio-economic characteristics. Number of training patterns: 1473. Number of attributes: 9. Number of classes: 3.
- Breast cancer (Wisconsin) [25]: Classifying breast cancer clumps as benign or malignant. Number of training patterns: 683 (the original data set contains 699 patterns, but 16 of these had missing attribute values and were

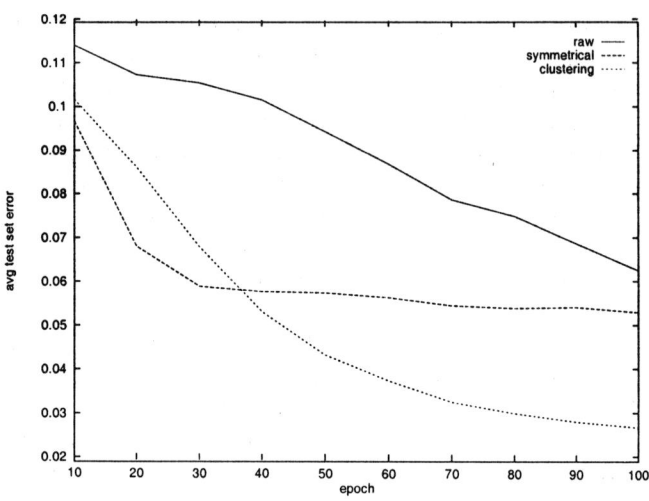

Fig. 2. Test set error curve for 3 receptors on the *e. coli* data set using unencoded data, the symmetrical placement approach, and the clustering approach

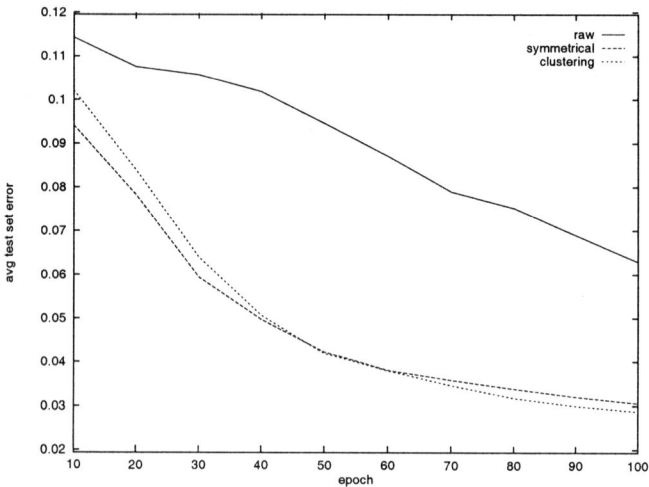

Fig. 3. Test set error curve for 4 receptors on the *e. coli* data set using unencoded data, the symmetrical placement approach, and the clustering approach

TABLE II

RESULTS OF DIFFERENT APPROACHES AND NUMBERS OF RECEPTORS INDICATING TRAINING ERROR, TEST ERROR, AND PERCENTAGE IMPROVEMENT IN TEST SET ERROR, ON THE CONTRACEPTIVES DATA SET AT THE END OF 200 EPOCHS

Approach	Arch.	Train. Err.	Test Err.	imp.
Means (4 rec.)	31-15-3	0.12130	0.12352	28.8%
Clustering (5 rec.)	29-16-3	0.12217	0.12424	28.4%
Clustering (4 rec.)	27-18-3	0.12216	0.12439	28.3%
Means (5 rec.)	37-13-3	0.12071	0.12465	28.1%
Clustering (3 rec.)	24-20-3	0.12274	0.12536	27.7%
Median (5 rec.)	25-19-3	0.12429	0.12662	27.0%
Median (4 rec.)	23-20-3	0.12423	0.12712	26.7%
Median (3 rec.)	20-23-3	0.12504	0.12761	26.4%
Means (3 rec.)	27-18-3	0.12624	0.12887	25.7%
Symmetrical (5 rec.)	45-11-3	0.13429	0.13435	22.6%
Symmetrical (4 rec.)	36-13-3	0.13517	0.13510	22.1%
Symmetrical (3 rec.)	27-18-3	0.13594	0.13631	21.4%
Unencoded	9-45-3	0.17380	0.17346	—

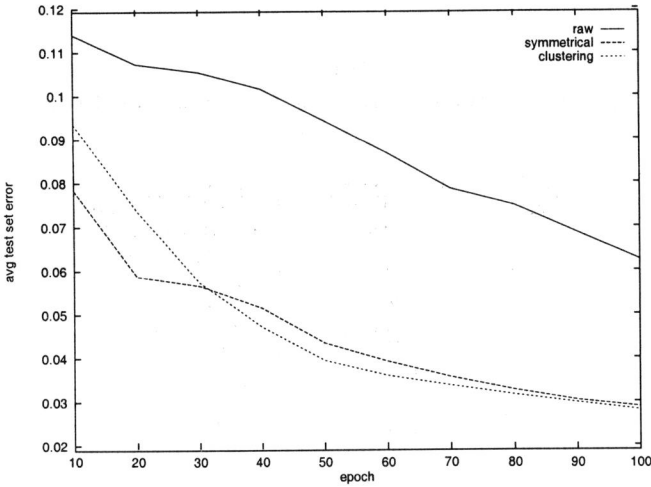

Fig. 4. Test set error curve for 5 receptors on the *e. coli* data set using unencoded data, the symmetrical placement approach, and the clustering approach

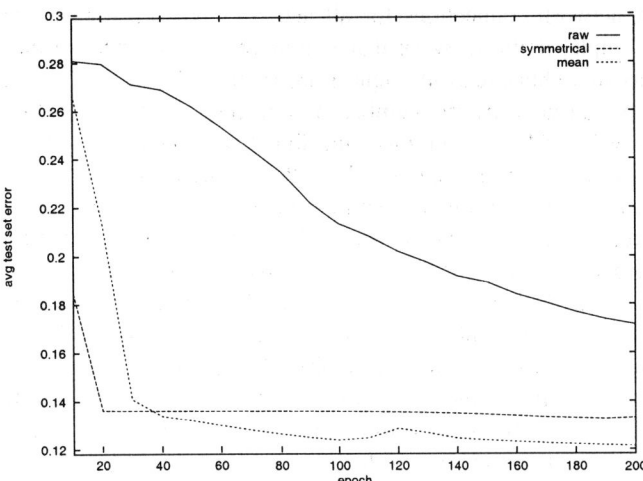

Fig. 6. Test set error curve for 4 receptors on the contraceptives data set using unencoded data, the symmetrical placement approach, and the means approach

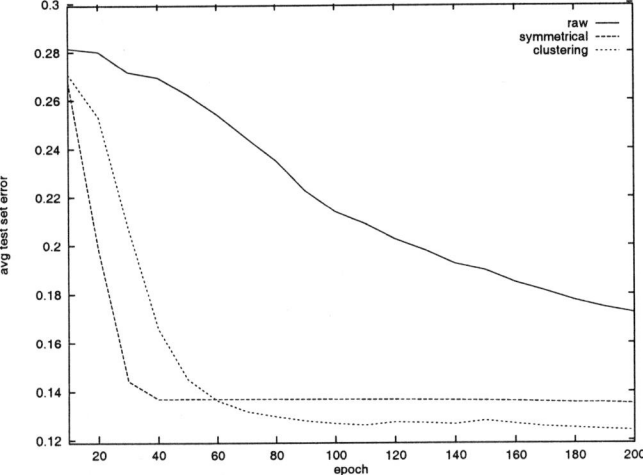

Fig. 5. Test set error curve for 3 receptors on the contraceptives data set using unencoded data, the symmetrical placement approach, and the clustering approach

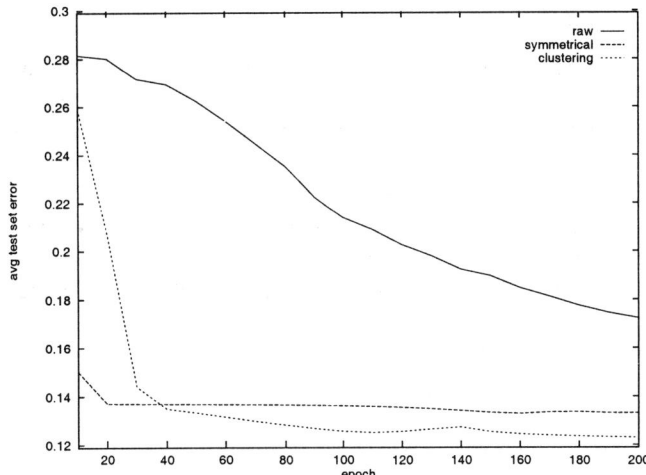

Fig. 7. Test set error curve for 5 receptors on the contraceptives data set using unencoded data, the symmetrical placement approach, and the clustering approach

TABLE III

RESULTS OF DIFFERENT APPROACHES AND NUMBERS OF RECEPTORS INDICATING TRAINING ERROR, TEST ERROR, AND PERCENTAGE IMPROVEMENT IN TEST SET ERROR, ON THE BREAST CANCER DATA SET AT THE END OF 200 EPOCHS

Approach	Arch.	Train. Err.	Test Err.	imp.
Symmetrical (3 rec.)	27-22-2	0.03669	0.03682	60.3%
Clustering (3 rec.)	27-22-2	0.03698	0.03701	60.1%
Means (4 rec.)	34-18-2	0.03691	0.03716	59.1%
Symmetrical (4 rec.)	36-17-2	0.03867	0.03852	58.4%
Clustering (4 rec.)	36-17-2	0.04036	0.03980	57.0%
Means (5 rec.)	43-14-2	0.04387	0.04382	52.7%
Clustering (5 rec.)	44-14-2	0.04629	0.04599	50.4%
Median (5 rec.)	29-21-2	0.04637	0.04623	50.1%
Median (4 rec.)	25-24-2	0.04719	0.04693	49.3%
Symmetrical (5 rec.)	45-14-2	0.04879	0.04923	46.9%
Means (3 rec.)	27-22-2	0.05439	0.05380	41.9%
Median (3 rec.)	19-31-2	0.06667	0.06689	27.8%
Unencoded	9-60-2	0.09282	0.09265	—

eliminated). Number of attributes: 9. Number of classes: 2.

For each data set, the experimental methodology was identical. An MLP network was trained by backpropagation for a fixed number of epochs using a fixed set of training parameters. Leave-one-out cross-validation was used: for each data set, the entire data set except for one training pattern is used for training, and that excepted pattern is used for testing; this process is repeated, re-initializing the network with random weights each time, for the entire data set, and the average training and test set error over the entire set is taken as descriptive of network performance.

Using ensemble encoding increases the number of network input neurons by a factor of the number of receptors used. For a fair comparison of the performance of different techniques, we adjusted the number of hidden neurons so that the number of network connections for all networks is comparable. For example, if the network that is trained with unencoded data has an architecture of 9 input neurons, 45 hidden neurons, and 3 output neurons, the number of connections will be $9 \times 45 + 45 \times 3 = 540$ connections. Encoding these inputs with three symmetrically placed receptive fields would result in 27 input neurons. Therefore, we would reduce the number of hidden neurons to 18 so that the network trained using the encoded data would have $27 \times 18 + 18 \times 3 = 540$ connections.

For each data set, we applied backpropagation, with leave-one-out cross-validation, for unencoded data, and for ensemble encoding with symmetrically-placed 3-, 4-, and 5-receptors, with the means approach with 3-, 4-, and 5-receptors, with the median approach with the maximum number of receptors set to 3, 4, and 5, and with the clustering approach with the maximum number of receptors set to 3, 4, and 5. Overall, a total of 32,396 MLP networks were trained for a total of 6,042,400 epochs in order to obtain the results described in this section.

A. Results on E. coli

On this data set, we used a learning rate of 0.05 and allowed training to proceed for 100 epochs. Table I shows the performance of each method, and indicates the percentage improvement, in test-set classification, over a comparable network trained with unencoded data. For methods which use a maximum of three receptors, Figure 2 shows a plot of average test set error versus epoch number for three networks: one trained with unencoded data, one trained with symmetrically placed fields as used by Narayan et al. [23], and one trained with the best-performing of our three techniques. Figures 3 and 4 show the corresponding plots for four and five receptors.

B. Results on Contraceptive Usage

We used a learning rate of 0.009 and allowed 200 epochs for training. Table II shows the performance of each method, and Figures 5-7 show test set error curves for three, four, and five receptors, respectively.

C. Results on Breast Cancer

We used a learning rate of 0.001 and allowed 200 epochs for training. Table III shows the performance of each method. Of the three data sets, this data set is unusual in that none of our heuristics outperformed the symmetrical approach. This might be because the symmetrical approach, in itself, performed much better on this data set (60% improvement over unencoded data) than any of the heuristic methods performed on any of the other data sets.

V. Discussion

An examination of the results presented in the previous section yields the following observations:
1) In most cases, clustering outperformed the means and median heuristics. The exceptions were in 4-receptor contraceptives, and four- and five-receptor breast cancer.

TABLE IV
(α, β) FOR 3-RECEPTOR SYMMETRICAL AND 3-RECEPTOR CLUSTERING FOR E. COLI

Attribute Name	Symmetrical	Clustering
Mcg	(0,0.25)	(0.263232,0.097963)
	(0.5,0.25)	(0.459158,0.107326)
	(1,0.25)	(0.692535,0.116689)
Gvh	(0,0.25)	(0.36336,0.074471)
	(0.5,0.25)	(0.512303,0.098609)
	(1,0.25)	(0.757797,0.122747)
Lip	(0,0.25)	(0.48,0.26)
	(0.5,0.25)	(1,0.26)
	(1,0.25)	
Chg	(0,0.25)	(0.5,0.25)
	(0.5,0.25)	(1,0.25)
	(1,0.25)	
Aac	(0,0.25)	(0.373364,0.072818)
	(0.5,0.25)	(0.519,0.079472)
	(1,0.25)	(0.69125,0.086125)
Alm1	(0,0.25)	(0.292609,0.099932)
	(0.5,0.25)	(0.492472,0.119164)
	(1,0.25)	(0.769266,0.138397)
Alm2	(0,0.25)	(0.292232,0.079842)
	(0.5,0.25)	(0.451917,0.121533)
	(1,0.25)	(0.778365,0.163224)

TABLE V
(α, β) VALUES FOR 3-RECEPTOR SYMMETRICAL AND 3-RECEPTOR CLUSTERING FOR BREAST CANCER

Attribute Name	Symmetrical	Clustering
Clump Thickness	(1,2.25)	(1.880546,1.463894)
	(5.5,2.25)	(4.808333,1.744863)
	(10,2.25)	(8.86,2.025833)
Uniformity of Cell Size	(1,2.25)	(1.107656,1.542724)
	(5.5,2.25)	(4.193103,1.975169)
	(10,2.25)	(9.008333,2.407615)
Uniformity of Cell Shape	(1,2.25)	(1.143564,1.546052)
	(5.5,2.25)	(4.235669,1.904683)
	(10,2.25)	(8.762295,2.263313)
Marginal Adhesion	(1,2.25)	(1.128603,1.461624)
	(5.5,2.25)	(4.051852,1.978159)
	(10,2.25)	(9.041237,2.494693)
Single Epithelial Cell Size	(1,2.25)	(1.895238,0.951115)
	(5.5,2.25)	(3.797468,1.461905)
	(10,2.25)	(7.742857,1.972694)
Bare Nuclei	(1,2.25)	(1.069444,1.527006)
	(5.5,2.25)	(4.123457,2.122345)
	(10,2.25)	(9.558824,2.717683)
Bland Chromatin	(1,2.25)	(1.516129,0.970568)
	(5.5,2.25)	(3.457265,1.552622)
	(10,2.25)	(7.726619,2.134677)
Normal Nucleoli	(1,2.25)	(1.076923,1.565499)
	(5.5,2.25)	(4.207291,1.991734)
	(10,2.25)	(9.04386,2.417969)
Mitoses	(1,2.25)	(1,0.936047)
	(5.5,2.25)	(2.872093,1.845588)
	(10,2.25)	(8.382353,2.75513)

2) The symmetrical approach was outperformed by one of the three heuristics in all cases except for 3-receptor breast cancer.
3) In general, the best performance of clustering was on *e. coli* and the best performance of symmetrical placement was on breast cancer. To explore the causes of this, we examined the (α, β) parameters pairs produced by the two approaches for three receptors for the two data sets; these are shown in Tables IV and V. An examination of the tables indicates that the parameters produced by the two methods are more similar for breast cancer than for *e. coli*. Indeed, with *e. coli*, there are two attributes for which clustering produced only two receptors; this allowed for two additional neurons in the hidden layer, since the total number of network weights is kept constant.
4) In two of the data sets, the best performance was obtained with three receptors. It was only with the contraceptives data set that the best performance was obtained with 4-receptor means followed closely by 5-receptor clustering.

VI. Conclusion

We have presented three heuristic techniques for optimizing the number, form, and placement of receptive fields for MLP networks with ensemble encoded data. In general, the best performance was obtained with the *c*-means based clustering approach. We would recommend setting the maximum number of clusters to 5, and letting the algorithm determine the most appropriate number of receptors for each field.

The more uneven the data distribution within the range of a given attribute, the more likely it is that clustering will perform better than the symmetrical placement of receptive fields. We have experimented briefly with clustering based on the fuzzy *c*-means [3] algorithm, but did not obtain a performance improvement over standard *c*-means. A Kohonen self-organizing map might be able to obtain better clustering than *c*-means, but we felt the difference in processing time was too great to be warranted.

References

[1] A. M. Abdelbar and S. Narayan, "Using simulated annealing to optimize receptive fields for MLP networks with ensemble encoding," *Proceedings International Joint Conference on Neural Networks*, 1999.

[2] N. Aerrabotu, G. A. Tagliarini, and E. W. Page, "Ensemble encoding for time series forecasting with MLP networks," *Applications and Science of Neural Networks III, Proc. SPIE*, Vol. 3077, pp.84-89, 1997.

[3] J.C. Bezdek, *Pattern Recognition with Fuzzy Objective Function Algorithms*, Plenum Press, New York, 1981.

[4] V.G. Dethier, "A Surfeit of Stimuli: A Paucity of Receptors," *American Scientist*, Vol. 59, pp. 706-715, 1971.

[5] J.E. Dowling, *The Retina*, The Belknap Press of Harvard University Press, Cambridge, Massachusetts, 1987.

[6] L.M. Eisenman, "Neural Encoding of Sound Location: An Electrophysiological Study in Auditory Cortex (A1) of the Cat Using Free Field Stimuli," *Brain Res.*, Vol. 75, pp. 203-213, 1963.

[7] R.P. Erickson, "The 'Across-Fiber Pattern' Theory: An Organizing Principle for Molar Neural Function," in: W.D. Neff, ed., *Contributions to Sensory Physiology*, Vol. 6, pp. 79-110, Academic Press, 1982.

[8] R. P. Erickson, "On the neural bases of behavior," *American Scientist*, Vol. 72, pp. 233-242, 1984.

[9] P J B Hancock. Data representation in neural nets: an empirical study. In D S Touretzky, G Hinton, and T Sejnowski, editors, *Proc. of the 1988 Connectionist Models Summer School*, pages 11–20, San Mateo CA, 1988. Morgan Kaufman.

[10] H. von Helmholtz, *Helmholtz's Treatise on Physiological Optics*, Third Edition, Vol. 2, 1860. (Translated and edited: J.P.C. Southall, Optical Society of America, Rochester, 1924-25.)

[11] P. Horton, and K. Nakai, "A Probablistic Classification System for Predicting the Cellular Localization Sites of Proteins," *Intelligent Systems in Molecular Biology*, pp. 109-115, St. Louis, USA 1996.

[12] J.-S.R. Jang, C.-T. Sun, and E. Mizutani, *Neuro-Fuzzy and Soft Computing*, Prentice-Hall, 1996.

[13] P.R. Krishnaiah, and L.N. Kanal, eds., *Classification, Pattern Recognition, and Reduction of Dimensionality*, Volume 2 of *Handbook of Statistics*, North-Holland, Amsterdam, 1982.

[14] T.-S. Lim, W.-Y. Loh, and Y.-S. Shih, "Comparison of Prediction Accuracy, Complexity, and Training Time of Thirty-Three Old and New Classification Algorithms," *Machine Learning*, Vol. 4, No. 3, pp. 203-228, 2000.

[15] V Lorquet, P Puget, R Gillemaud, and J Niez. Improving half distributed coding methods: a filtering process approach applied to data representation in neural nets. In *Artificial Neural Networks*, pages 931–936. Elsevier, 1991.

[16] A. MacKay-Sim, P. Shaman, and D. Moulton, "Topographic Coding of Olfactory Quality: Odorant-Specific Patterns of Epithelial Responsivity in the Salamander," *Journal of Neurophysiology*, Vol. 48, pp. 584-596, 1982.

[17] J. Makhoul, S. Roucos, and H. Gish, "Vector Quantization in Speech Coding," *Proceedings of the IEEE*, Vol. 73, pp. 1551-1588, 1985.

[18] P.M. Murphy, and D.W. Aha, *UCI Repository of Machine Learning Databases*, University of California, Irvine, Department of Information and Computer Science, URL: ftp://ftp.ics.uci.edu/pub/machine-learning-databases/.

[19] S. Narayan, "Enhancing incremental learning in MLP networks using ensemble encoding of network inputs," *Proceedings International Joint Conference on Neural Networks*, 1999.

[20] S. Narayan and E.W. Page, "Optimizing locality of data representation in MLP networks," *Proc. IEEE International Conference on Neural Networks*, Vol.1, pp.50-54, 1994.

[21] S. Narayan, G.A. Tagliarini, and E.W. Page, "Enhancing neural network functionality with ensemble encoding," *Proc. IEEE Southeastcon*, 1993.

[22] S. Narayan, G.A. Tagliarini, and E.W. Page, "Accelerating learning in a neural network for sonar signal classification," *Science of Artificial Neural Networks II*, Proc. SPIE 1966, pp.236-240, Orlando, FL, 1993

[23] S. Narayan, G.A. Tagliarini, and E.W. Page, "Enhancing MLP networks using a distributed data representation," *IEEE Transactions on Systems, Man and Cybernetics (Part B: Cybernetics)*, Vol.26, pp. 143-149, 1996.

[24] T. Ohtsuka, "Spectral Sensitivities of Seven Morphological Types of Photoreceptors in the Retina of the Turtle, *Geoclemys reevesii*," *J. Comp. Neurol.*, Vol. 237, pp. 145-154, 1985.

[25] W.H. Wolberg, and O.L. Mangasarian, "Multisurface Method of Pattern Separation for Medical Diagnosis Applied to Breast Cytology," *Proceedings of the National Academy of Sciences, U.S.A.*, Vol. 87, pp. 9193-9196, 1990.

[26] T. Young, "On the Theory of Light and Colours," *Phil. Trans. Royal Soc. of London*, Vol. 92, pp. 12-48, 1802.

A General Projection Neural Network for Solving Optimization and Related Problems

Youshen Xia and Jun Wang
Department of Automation and Computer-Aided Engineering
The Chinese University of Hong Kong, Shatin, New Territories, Hong Kong

Abstract—In this paper, we propose a general projection neural network for solving a wider class of optimization and related problems. In addition to its simple structure and low complexity, the proposed neural network include existing neural networks for optimization, such as the projection neural network, the primal-dual neural network, and the dual neural network, as special cases. Under various mild conditions, the proposed general projection neural network is shown to be globally convergent, globally asymptotically stable, and globally exponentially stable. Furthermore, several improved stability criteria on two special cases of the general projection neural network are obtained under weaker conditions. Simulation results demonstrate the effectiveness and characteristics of the proposed neural network.

I. Introduction

Many engineering problems can be formulated as constrained nonlinear optimization problems and complementarity problems [1]. Real-time solutions of these problems are often needed in engineering systems, such as signal processing, system identification, and robot motion control [2-4]. The numbers of decision variables and constraints are usually very large and large-scale optimization problems are even more challenging when they have to be solved in real time to optimize the performance of dynamical systems. For such applications, conventional numerical methods may not be adequate due to the problem dimensionality and stringent requirement on computational time.

A promising approach to solving such problems in real time is to employ artificial neural networks based on circuit implementation [5]. As parallel computational models, neural networks possess many desirable properties such as real-time information processing. Therefore, neural networks for optimization, control, and signal processing received tremendous interests. In the past two decades, the theory, methodology, and applications of neural networks have been widely investigated (see [5-18] and references therein). Tank and Hopfild [5] first proposed a neural network for solving linear programming problems that was mapped onto a closed-loop circuit [6]. Kennedy and Chua extended [7] their work and proposed a neural network for solving nonlinear convex programming problems. Having a penalty parameter, the true minimizer could be obtained only when the penalty parameter is infinite. Moreover, their network has both the implementation and deconvergence problem when the penalty parameter is very large. To avoid using penalty parameters, some significance work have been done in recent years. Rodríguez-Vázquez et al. proposed a switched-capacitor neural network for solving nonlinear convex programming problems, where the optimal solution is assumed to be inside of the feasible set [8]. Zhang et al. proposed a second-order neural network for solving a nonlinear convex programming problem with equality constraints [9]. The second-order neural network is complex in implementation due to the need for computing varying inverse matrices. Bouzerdoum and Pattison presented a neural network for solving quadratic convex optimization problems with bounded constraints [10]. Recently, we developed several neural networks: primal-dual neural networks for solving linear and quadratic convex programming problems and monotone linear complementary problems, a dual neural network for solving strictly convex quadratic programming problems, and a projection neural network for solving a class of nonlinear convex programming problems and monotone nonlinear complementary problems [12-16].

In this paper, based on a generalized equation in [20] we propose a general projection neural network for solving a wider class of optimization and related problems. The proposed neural network is a significant generalization of existing neural networks for optimization such as the primal-dual neural network, the dual neural network, and the projection neural network. In addition to its low complexity for implementation, the proposed neural network is shown to be stable in the sense of Lyapunov and globally convergent, globally asymptotically stable, or globally exponentially stable, under different mild conditions. Moreover, several improved stability conditions for two special cases of the general projection neural network are obtained under weaker conditions. Illustrative examples demonstrate the performance and effectiveness of the proposed neural network.

This paper is organized as follows. In the next section, a general projection neural network and its advantages are described. In Section III, the global convergence properties of the proposed neural network, including global asymptotic stability and global exponential stability, are studied, respectively under some mild conditions. In Section IV, several illustrative examples are presented. Section V gives the conclusions of this paper.

II. Model Description

We propose a general projection neural network with its dynamical equation defined as

$$\frac{du}{dt} = \Lambda\{P_X(G(u) - F(u)) - G(u)\}, \quad (1)$$

where $u \in R^n$ is a state vector, $\Lambda = diag(\lambda_i)$ is a positive diagonal matrix, $F(u)$ and $G(u)$ are continuously differentiable vector-valued functions from R^n into R^n, $X = \{u \in R^n \mid l_i \leq u_i \leq h_i, i = 1, ..., n\}$, $P_X : R^n \to X$ is a projection operator defined by $P_X(u) = [P_X(u_1), ..., P_X(u_n)]^T$, and $P_X(u_i)$ is given by

$$P_X(u_i) = \begin{cases} l_i & u_i < l_i \\ u_i & l_i \leq u_i \leq h_i \\ h_i & u_i > h_i. \end{cases}$$

The dynamic equation described in (1) can be easily realized by a recurrent neural network with a single layer structure as shown in Fig. 1. The projection operator $P_X(\cdot)$ can be implemented by using a piecewise activation function. It can be seen that the circuit realizing the proposed neural network consists of $2n$ summers, n integrators, n piecewise linear activation functions, and n processors for $G(u)$ and $F(u)$. Therefore, the network complexity depends only on the mapping $G(u)$ and $F(u)$.

In addition to its low complexity for realization, the general projection neural network in (1) has several advantages. First, it is a significant generalization of some existing neural networks for optimization. For example, let $G(u) = u$, then the proposed neural network model becomes the projection neural network model [16] given by

$$\frac{du}{dt} = \Lambda\{P_X(u - F(u)) - u\}. \quad (2)$$

In the affine case that $F(u) = Mu + p$ where $M \in R^{n \times n}$ is a positive semi-definite matrix and $p \in R^n$, the proposed neural network model becomes the primal-dual neural network model [13]

$$\frac{du}{dt} = \Lambda\{P_X(u - (Mu + p)) - u\}. \quad (3)$$

Let $F(u) = u$, then the proposed neural network model becomes

$$\frac{du}{dt} = \Lambda\{P_X(G(u) - u) - G(u)\}. \quad (4)$$

In the affine case that $G(u) = Wu + q$ where $W \in R^{n \times n}$ is a positive semi-definite matrix and $q \in R^n$, the proposed neural network model becomes the dual neural network model [15]

$$\frac{du}{dt} = \Lambda\{P_X(Wu + q - u) - Wu - q\}. \quad (5)$$

Next, the general projection neural network in (1) is useful for solving optimization and related problems. This is because it is intimately related to the following general variational inequality (GVI) [20]: find $u^* \in X$ such that $G(u^*) \in X$ and

$$(u - G(u^*))^T F(u^*) \geq 0, \quad \forall u \in X. \quad (6)$$

From [20] it can be seen that solving GVI is equivalent to finding a zero of the generalized equation

$$P_X(G(u) - F(u)) - G(u) = 0. \quad (7)$$

Therefore, the equilibrium point of the general projection neural network in (1) solves GVI. This property shows that the existence of the equilibrium point of (1) is equivalent to the one of the solutions of GVI. This implies that there is at least an equilibrium point of (1) when GVI has a solution. As for the existence of the solutions of GVI, the reader is referred to related papers [19,20]. It is well known that GVI has been viewed as the general framework of unifying the treatment of many optimization, economic, and engineering problems [22-24]. For example, GVI includes two useful models: the variational inequalities and general complementarity problems. The variational inequality problem is to find an $u^* \in X$ such that

$$(u - u^*)^T F(u^*) \geq 0, \quad \forall u \in X. \quad (8)$$

The general complementarity problem is to find an $u^* \in R^n$ such that

$$G(x) \geq 0, \quad F(u) \geq 0, \quad G(u)^T F(u) = 0. \quad (9)$$

Because solving GVI is equivalent to finding an equilibrium point of (1), the desirable solutions to GVI can be obtained by tracking the continuous trajectory of (1). Therefore, the proposed neural network in (1) is attractive alternative as a real-time solver for many optimization and related problems.

III. Convergence Results

We establish the following results on the general projection neural network.

A. General Case

Theorem 1. Assume that $F(u)$ is G-monotone at an equilibrum point, u^*, of (1):

$$(F(u) - F(u^*), G(u) - G(u^*)) \geq 0, \forall u \in R^n,$$

where $(\cdot, \cdot)$ denotes an inner product. If $\nabla F(u) + \nabla G(u)$ is symmetric and positive semi-definite in R^n, then the general projection neural network in (1) is stable in the Lyapunov sense and is globally convergent to an equilibrium points of (1). Specially, the general projection neural network in (1) is globally asymptotically stable if the equilibrium point is unique.

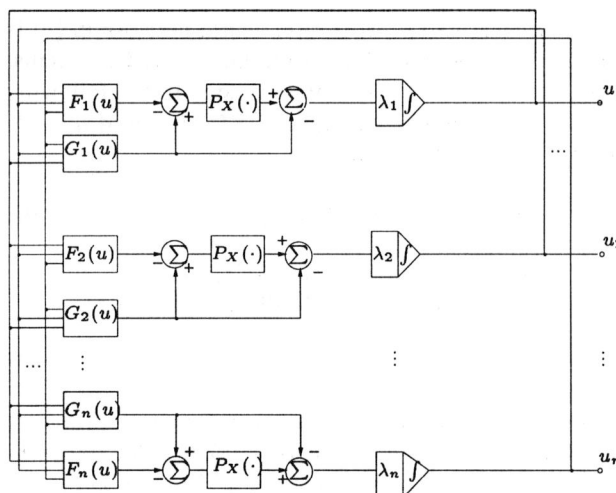

Fig. 1. A block diagram of the general projection neural network in (1)

Theorem 2. Assume that $F(u)$ is G-strongly monotone at u^*:

$$(F(u) - F(u^*), G(u) - G(u^*)) \geq \beta \|u - u^*\|^2, \forall u \in R^n,$$

where $\|\cdot\|$ denotes the l_2-norm of R^n and $\beta > 0$ is a constant. If $\nabla F(u) + \nabla G(u)$ is symmetric and positive semidefinite, and has an upper bound in R^n, then the general projection neural network in (1) is globally exponentially stable at u^*.

As an immediate corollary of Theorems 1 and 2, we have the following results.

Corollary 1. Assume that $F(u) = u$. If $\nabla G(u)$ is symmetric and positive semidefinite, then the neural network in (4) is stable in the Lyapunov sense and is globally convergent to an equilibrium point of (4). If $\nabla G(u)$ is symmetric and uniformly positive definite and has an upper bound in R^n, then the neural network in (4) is globally exponentially stable.

As a special case the $G(u) = Wu + q$, where $W \in R^{n \times n}$ is symmetric and positive semidefinite and $q \in R^n$, the result of Corollary 1 is presented in [15].

B. Two special cases

As for the projection neural network of (2), we have two further results below.

Theorem 3. Assume that $\nabla F(u)$ is positive semidefinite in R^n. If

$$\begin{cases} F(u)^T(u - u^*) = 0 \\ (P_X(u - F(u)) - u)^T \nabla F(u)(P_X(u - F(u)) - u) = 0 \end{cases}$$

implies that u is a solution to (8), then the projection neural network in (2) is stable in the sense of Lyapunov and globally convergent to an equilibrium point of (2).

Theorem 4. If $\nabla F(u)$ is uniformly positive definite in R^n, then the projection neural network in (2) is globally exponentially stable.

In the affine case that $F(u) = Mu + q$, $G(u) = Nu + c$, $M, N \in R^{n \times n}$, and $q, c \in R^n$, the neural network model becomes

$$\frac{du}{dt} = \Lambda \{P_X((N-M)u + c - p) - Nu - c\}. \quad (10)$$

As for the convergence of (10), we have the following results.

Theorem 5. Assume that matrix $\Lambda = N^T + M^T$. The neural network in (10) is globally convergent to an equilibrium point of (10) when $M^T N$ is positive semi-definite, and is globally exponentially stable when $M^T N$ is positive definite.

As an immediate corollary of Theorem 5, we have the following result, which is presented in [13].

Corollary 2. Assume that $N = I$ and $\Lambda = I + M^T$. The neural network in (10) is globally convergent to an equilibrium point of (10) when M is positive semi-definite, and is globally exponentially stable when M is positive definite.

IV. ILLUSTRATIVE EXAMPLES

In order to demonstrate the effectiveness and performance of the general projection neural network, in this section, we give several illustrative examples.

Example 1. Consider the implicit complementarity problem (ICP) [28] : find $u \in R^n$ such that

$$u - \Phi(u) \geq 0, \ F(u) \geq 0, \ (u - \Phi(u))^T F(u) = 0,$$

where $\Phi(u) = \Theta(Mu + q)$, $F(u) = Mu + q$, $q = [1, ..., 1]^T \in R^n$,

$$M = \begin{pmatrix} 2 & -1 & 0 & \cdots & 0 \\ -1 & 2 & 2 & \cdots & 0 \\ 0 & -1 & 2 & \cdots & 0 \\ \vdots & \vdots & \vdots & \ddots & \vdots \\ 0 & \cdots & -1 & 2 & -1 \\ 0 & \cdots & 0 & -1 & 2 \end{pmatrix}_{n \times n},$$

and

$$\Theta(u) = \begin{pmatrix} -1.5u_1 + 0.25u_1^2 \\ -1.5u_2 + 0.25u_2^2 \\ \cdot \\ \cdot \\ \cdot \\ -1.5u_{n-1} + 0.25u_{n-1}^2 \\ -1.5u_n + 0.25u_n^2 \end{pmatrix}_{n \times 1}.$$

It can be seen that the ICP can be viewed as the GNCP where $G(u) = u - \Phi(u)$ and $F(u) = Mu + q$. The general projection neural network in (1) is thus applied to solve the above ICP, and its state equation is given by

$$\frac{du}{dt} = \Lambda \{(u - \Phi(u) - F(u))^+ - u + \Phi(u)\}, \quad (11)$$

where $(u)^+ = [(u_1)^+, ..., (u_n)^+]^T$ and $(u_i)^+ = \max\{0, u_i\}$ for $i = 1, ..., n$. All simulation results show

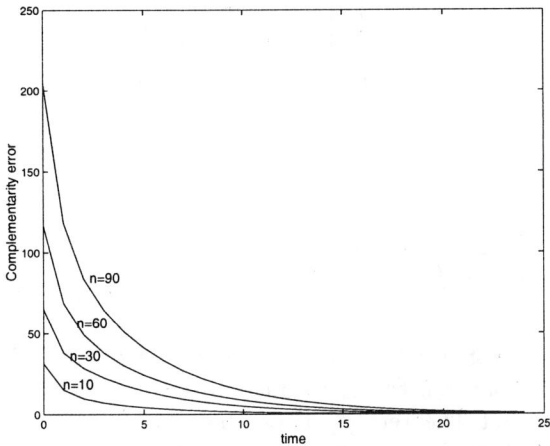

Fig. 2. The complementarity error based on the proposed neural network in (11) for solving ICP in Example 1.

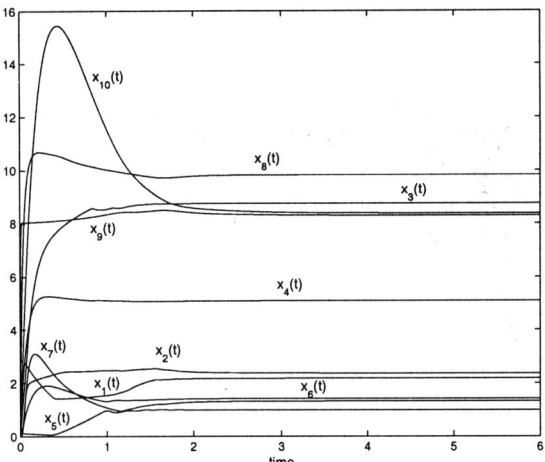

Fig. 4. Global convergence of the proposed neural network in (13) for solving GNCP in Example 2.

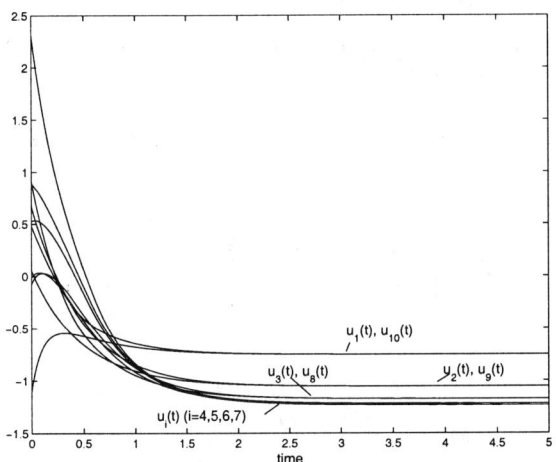

Fig. 3. Global convergence of the proposed neural network in (11) for solving ICP in Example 1.

that the trajectory of (11) always is globally convergent to a solution to ICP. For example, let $\Lambda = 2I$ and let the initial point be random. Fig. 2 shows the transient behaviors of the implementarity error $(u - \Phi(u))^T F(u)$ based on (11) with $n = 10, 30, 60, 90$. Fig. 3 shows the transient behavior of the proposed neural network with $n = 10$.

Example 2. Consider the variational inequality problem (VIP) with nonlinear constraints: find $x \in R^{10}$ such that

$$(x - f(x^*))^T x^* \geq 0, \quad \forall x \in X, \quad (12)$$

where $X = \{x \in R^{10} \mid h(x) \leq 0, x \geq 0\}$, and

$$f(x) = \begin{pmatrix} 2x_1 - 14 + x_2 \\ x_1 + 2x_2 - 16 \\ 2(x_3 - 10) \\ 8(x_4 - 5) \\ 2(x_5 - 3) \\ 4(x(6) - 1) \\ 10x_7 \\ 14(x_8 - 11) \\ 4(x_9 - 10) \\ 2(x_{10} - 7) \end{pmatrix},$$

$$h(x) = \begin{pmatrix} 3(x_1 - 2)^2 + 4(x_2 - 3)^2 + 2x_3^2 - 7x_4 - 120 \\ 5x_1^2 + (x_3 - 6)^2 + 8x_2 - 2x_4 - 40 \\ (x_1 - 8)^2/2 + 2(x_2 - 4)^2 + 3x_5^2 - x_6 - 30 \\ x_1^2 + 2(x_2 - 2)^2 - 2x_1 x_2 + 14x_5 - 6x_6 \\ 4x_1 + 5x_2 - 3x_7 + 9x_8 - 105 \\ 10x_1 - 8x_2 - 17x_7 + 2x_8 \\ 12(x_9 - 8)^2 - 3x_1 + 6x_2 - 7x_{10} \\ -8x_1 + 2x_2 + 5x_9 - 2x_{10} - 12 \end{pmatrix}.$$

This problem has an optimal solution given in [27]

$$x^* = [\ 2.172, 2.364, 8.774, 5.096, 0.991,$$
$$1.431, 1.321, 9.829, 8.280, 8.376]^T.$$

By the Kuhn-Tucker condition [1] we see that there exist $y \in R^8$ such that x solves the above VIP if and only if $u = (x, y) \in R^{18}$ solves the GNCP where $F(u) = u$ and

$$G(u) = \begin{pmatrix} f(x) + \nabla h(x)y \\ -h(x) \end{pmatrix}.$$

The general projection neural network in (1) is thus applied to solve the GNCP, and its state equation is

$$\frac{du}{dt} = \Lambda\{(G(u) - u)^+ - G(u)\}, \quad (13)$$

where $(u)^+ = [(u_1)^+, ..., (u_3)^+]^T$ and $(u_i)^+ = \max\{0, u_i\}$ for $i = 1, ..., 18$. All simulation results show the trajectory of (13) always is globally convergent to $u^* = (x^*, y^*)$. For example, let $\Lambda = 2I$ and let the initial point be zero. A solution to the GNCP is obtained as follows

$$x^1 = [\ 2.178, 2.368, 8.743, 5.09, 0.991,$$
$$1.430, 1.322, 9.823, 8.286, 8.371]^T,$$

where time parameter $t = 6$. Fig. 4 shows the transient behavior of $x(t)$ with a random initial point.

Example 3. Consider the nonlinear complementarity problem (NCP)

$$u^T F(u) = 0, F(u) \geq 0, u \geq 0, \quad (14)$$

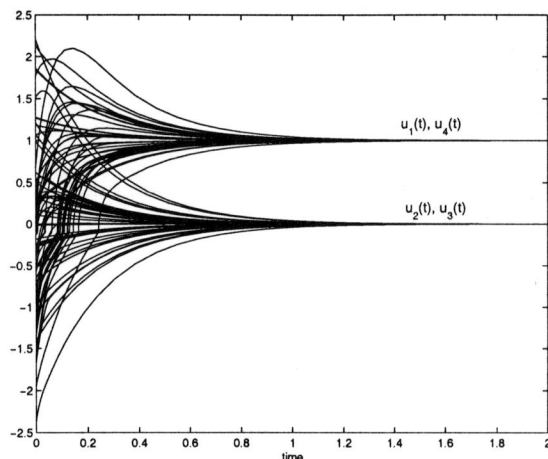

Fig. 5. Global Exponential stability of the projection neural network in (2) for solving VIP in Example 3.

where
$$F(u) = \begin{pmatrix} 2u_1 \exp(u_1^2 + (u_2-1)^2) + u_1 - u_2 - u_3 + 1 \\ 2(u_2-1)\exp(u_1^2 + (u_2-1)^2) - u_1 + 2u_2 + 2u_3 + 3 \\ -u_1 + 2u_2 + 3u_3 \end{pmatrix}$$

This problem has only one solution $u^* = [0, 0.167, 0]^T$ and $F(u^*) = [0.833, 0, 0.334]^T$. According to [19], u^* is a solution to the above NCP if and only if u^* satisfies the following equation

$$P_X(u - F(u)) = u, \quad (15)$$

where $X = R_+^3$, $P_X(u) = [(u_1)^+, ..., (u_3)^+]^T$, and $(u_i)^+ = \max\{0, u_i\}$ for $i = 1, 2, 3$. It can be seen that $F(u)$ is strongly monotone on R_+^3. We use the neural network in (2) to solve the above NCP. All simulation results show that the corresponding neural network in (2) always is globally exponentially stable at u^*. For example, Fig. 5 displays the exponential stability of the trajectory of (2) with 20 random initial points, where $\Lambda = 4I$.

Example 4. Consider the general linear-quadratic optimization problem (GLQP) [29]

$$\min_{x \geq 0} \max_{y \geq 0} \quad f(x,y) = q^T x - p^T y + \frac{1}{2} x^T A x$$
$$- x^T H y - \frac{1}{2} y^T Q y \quad (16)$$
$$\text{subject to} \quad 0 \leq Bx \leq b, 0 \leq Cy \leq d$$

where
$$A = \begin{pmatrix} 2 & 1 & 1 \\ 1 & 2 & 0 \\ 1 & 0 & 1 \end{pmatrix}, H = \begin{pmatrix} 1 & 0 & 0 & 1 \\ 0 & 1 & 0 & 0 \\ 0 & 0 & 1 & 0 \end{pmatrix},$$

$$Q = \begin{pmatrix} 2 & -1 & 0 & 0 \\ -2 & 1 & 0 & 0 \\ 0 & 0 & 2 & 1 \\ 0 & 0 & 1 & 1 \end{pmatrix}, B = \begin{pmatrix} 1 & 1 & -1 \\ 1 & 1 & -1 \\ -1 & 1 & -1 \end{pmatrix},$$

$$C = \begin{pmatrix} 1 & -1 & 0 & 0 \\ 1 & -1 & 0 & 0 \\ 0 & 0 & 1 & -1 \\ 0 & 0 & 2 & -2 \end{pmatrix},$$

and
$$q = \begin{pmatrix} -4 \\ -3 \\ -2 \end{pmatrix}, p = \begin{pmatrix} -0.5 \\ -1.5 \\ 0.5 \\ -0.5 \end{pmatrix}, b = \begin{pmatrix} 2 \\ 1 \\ 5 \end{pmatrix}, d = \begin{pmatrix} 1 \\ 5 \\ 5 \\ 1 \end{pmatrix}.$$

This problem has an optimal solution $(x^*, y^*) = (0.5, 1.5, 1, 0, 0, 0)$. According to the well-known saddle point Theorem [1], it can be seen that the above GLQP can be converted into an general linear variational inequality (GLCP): find $z^* \in X$ such that

$$(z - Nz^*)^T(Mz^* + l) \geq 0, \forall z \in X,$$

where $z = (x, y, s, w) \in R^3 \times R^4 \times R^3 \times R^4$, $z^* = (x^*, y^*, s^*, w^*)^T$,

$X = \{(x, y, s, w) \in R^{14} | x \geq 0, y \geq 0, 0 \leq s \leq b, 0 \leq w \leq d\}$,

$$N = \begin{pmatrix} I_1 & 0 & 0 & 0 \\ 0 & I_2 & 0 & 0 \\ B & 0 & 0 & 0 \\ 0 & C & 0 & 0 \end{pmatrix}, l = \begin{pmatrix} q \\ -p \\ 0 \\ 0 \end{pmatrix},$$

and
$$M = \begin{pmatrix} A & -H & B^T & 0 \\ H^T & Q & 0 & C^T \\ 0 & 0 & -I_1 & 0 \\ 0 & 0 & 0 & -I_2 \end{pmatrix},$$

where $I_1 \in R^{3 \times 3}$ and $I_2 \in R^{4 \times 4}$ are unit matrice. The proposed neural network in (10) is applied to solve the above GLCP, and it becomes

$$\frac{dz}{dt} = \lambda(M^T + N^T)\{P_X(Nz - Mz - l) - Nz\}. \quad (17)$$

All simulation results show the trajectory of (17) always is globally convergent to z^*. For example, let $\lambda = 2I$ and let the initial point be zero. A solution to GLCP is obtained as follows

$$(x^1, y^1) = (0.499, 1.504, 1.004, 0.012, 0.012, 0, 0),$$

where time parameter $t = 5$. Fig. 6 shows the transient behavior of $(x(t), y(t))$ with an random initial point.

V. CONCLUSION

Optimization has found wide applications in various areas such as control and signal processing. In this paper, we have proposed a general projection neural network, which has a simple structure and low complexity for implementation. The general projection neural network includes existing neural networks for optimization, such as the primal-dual neural network, the

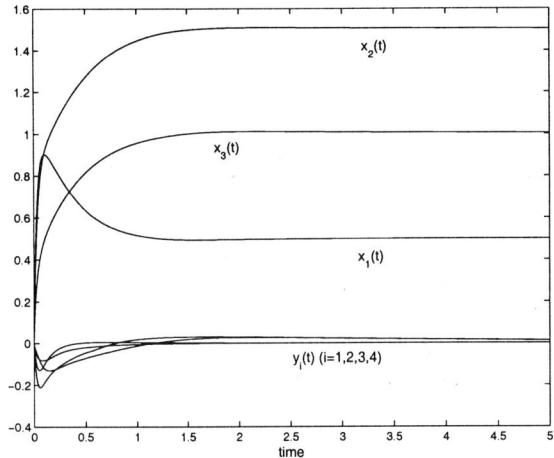

Fig. 6. Global convergence of $(x(t), y(t))$ based on the neural network in (17) in Example 4.

dual neural network, the projection neural network, as special cases. Moreover, its equilibrium points are able to solve a wide variety of optimization and related problems. Under mild conditions, we have shown the general projection neural network has a global convergence, a global asymptotic stability, and a global exponential stability, respectively. Since the general projection neural network contains existing neural networks in (2)-(5) as special cases, the obtained stability results naturally generalize the existing ones for a special case of such neural networks. Furthermore, we have obtained several improved stability results on two special cases of the general projection neural network under weaker conditions. The obtained results are helpful for wide applications of the the general projection neural network. Illustrative examples with application to optimization and related problems show that the proposed neural network is effective in solving these problems. Further investigations will be aimed at the improvement of the stability conditions and engineering applications of the general projection neural network to robot motion control and signal processing, etc.

ACKNOWLEDGMENT

This work was supported by the Hong Kong Research Grants Council under Grant CUHK4174/00E.

REFERENCES

[1] M. S. Bazaraa, H. D. Sherali, C. M. Shetty, *Nonlinear Programming: Theory and Algorithms* (2nd Ed.), John Wiley, New York, 1993.

[2] T. Yoshikawa, *Foundations of Robotics: Analysis and Control*, MIT Press, Cambridge, MA, 1990.

[3] N. Kalouptisidis, *Signal Processing Systems, Theory and Design*. Wiley, New York, 1997.

[4] B. Kosko, *Neural Networks for Signal Processing*, Prentice-Hall, Inc., USA, 1992.

[5] J. J. Hopfield and D. W. Tank, "Neural computation of decisions in optimization problems," *Biological Cybernetics*, vol. 52, no. 3, pp. 141-152, 1985.

[6] D. W. Tank and J. J. Hopfield, "Simple 'neural optimization networks: an A/D converter, signal decision circuit, and a linear programming circuit," *IEEE Transactions on Circuits and Systems*, vol. 33, no. 5, pp. 533-541, 1986.

[7] M. P. Kennedy and L. O. Chua, "Neural networks for nonlinear programming," *IEEE Transactions on Circuits and Systems*, vol. 35, no. 5, pp. 554-562, 1988.

[8] A. Rodríguez-Vázquez, R. Domínguez-Castro, A. Rueda, J. L. Huertas, and E. Sánchez-Sinencio, "Nonlinear switched-capacitor 'neural networks' for optimization problems," *IEEE Transactions on Circuits and Systems*, vol. 37, no. 3, 384-397, 1990.

[9] S. Zhang, X. Zhu, and L.-H. Zou, "Second-order neural networks for constrained optimization," *IEEE Transactions on Neural Networks*, vol. 3, no. 6, pp. 1021-1024, 1992.

[10] A. Bouzerdoum and T. R. Pattison, "Neural network for quadratic optimization with bound constraints," *IEEE Transactions on Neural Networks*, Vol. 4, No. 2, pp. 293-304, 1993.

[11] A. Cichocki and R. Unbehauen, *Neural Networks for Optimization and Signal Processing*, Wiley, England, 1993.

[12] Y. Xia, "A new neural network for solving linear programming problems and its applications," *IEEE Transactions on Neural Networks*, vol. 7, pp. 525-529, 1996.

[13] Y. Xia "A new neural network for solving linear and quadratic programming problems," *IEEE Transactions on Neural Networks*, vol. 7, no. 4, pp. 1544-1547, 1996.

[14] Y. Xia and J. Wang, "A general methodology for designing globally convergent optimization neural networks," *IEEE Transactions Neural Networks*, vol. 9, 1331-1343, 1998.

[15] Y. Xia and J. Wang, "A dual neural network for kinematic control of redundant robot manipulators," *IEEE Transactions on Systems, Man and Cybernetics - Part B*, vol. 31, no. 1, pp. 147-154, 2001.

[16] Y. Xia, H. Leung, and J. Wang, " A projection neural network and its application to constrained optimization problems," *IEEE Transactions on Circuits and Systems - Part I*, vol. 49, no. 4, pp. 447-458, 2002.

[17] C. Y. Maa and M.A. Shanblatt, "Linear and quadratic programming neural network analysis," *IEEE Transactions on Neural Networks*, vol. 3, no. 6, pp. 580-594, 1992.

[18] W. E. Lillo, M.H. Loh, S. Hui, and S. H. Żak, "On solving constrained optimization problems with neural networks: A penalty method approach," *IEEE Transactions on Neural Networks*, vol. 4, no. 6, pp. 931-939, 1993.

[19] D. Kinderlehrer and G. Stampcchia, *An Introduction to Variational Inequalities and Their Applications*, Academic Press, New York, 1980.

[20] J.-S. Pang and J.-C. Yao, "On a generalization of a normal map and equation," *SIAM J. Control and Optimization*, vol. 33, pp. 168-184, 1995.

[21] M. Fukushima, "Equivalent differentiable optimization problems and descent methods for asymmetric variational inequality problems," *Mathematical Programming*, vol. 53, pp. 99-110, 1992.

[22] T. L. Friesz, D.H. Bernstein, N.J. Mehta, R.L. Tobin, and S. Ganjlizadeh, "Day-to-day dynamic network disequilibria and idealized traveler information systems," *Operations Research*, vol. 42, pp. 1120-1136, 1994.

[23] M. C. Ferris and J. S. pang, "Engineering and economic applications of complementarity problems," *SIAM Review*, vol. 39, pp. 669-713, 1997.

[24] L. Vandenberghe, B. L. De Moor, and J. Vandewalle, "The generalized linear complementary problem applied to the complete analysis of resistive piecewise-linear circuits," *IEEE Trans. Circuits and systems*, vol.36, no.11, 1382-1391, 1989.

[25] R. K. Miller and A. N. Michel, *Ordinary Differential Equations*, Academic Press, New York, 1980.

[26] J. M. Ortega and W. G. Rheinboldt, *Iterative Solution of Nonlinear Equations in Several Variables*, Academic Press, New York, 1970.

[27] C. Charalambous, "Nonlinear least pth optimization and nonlinear programming," *Mathematical Programming*, vol. 12, pp. 195-225, 1977.

[28] R. Andreani, A. Friedlander, and S. A. Santos, "On the resolution of the generalized nonlinear complementarity problem," *SIAM Journal of Optimization*, vol. 12, no. 2, pp. 303-321, 2001.

[29] R. T. Rockafellar and R. J. B. Wets, "Linear-quadratic programming and optimal control," *SIAM Journal of Control and Optimization*, vol. 25, pp. 781-814, 1987.

Extended Simulated Annealing for Augmented TSP and Multisalsemen TSP

Chi-Hwa Song*, Kyunghee Lee** and Won Don Lee*
*Dept. of Computer Science, Chungnam National University,
220, Koong-Dong, Yusung-Ku, Daejeon, Korea
**Dept. of Computer Science, PyungTaek University,
111, YongI-Dong, PyongTaek-City, KyungKi-Do, Korea

Abstract-An extended simulated annealing (ESA), based on grand canonical ensemble (GCE), is proposed. An ESA is used to solve the augmented traveling salesman problems (ATSP) and the multiple traveling salesmen problems. Experimental results show that ESA has salient features such as simplicity and ability to find high-quality solutions as simulated annealing has.

Ⅰ. Introduction

The traveling salesman problem (TSP) is one of the hardest combinatorial optimization problems and remains NP-hard. Up to now, many researchers tried to solve large-scale multiple traveling salesmen problems for real world applications such as multi-depot vehicle routing problems and topological design of computer networks using many heuristic methods, connectionist models and annealing processes [1].

Most of the heuristic methods use a local search algorithm that depends on a neighborhood structure or a complex transform scheme [2][3]. Simulated annealing (SA) is powerful algorithm for solving combinatorial problems [4]. SA is applied to the standard TSP and some good results are reported. But SA can be applied only to the case of standard TSP because SA is based on the canonical ensemble, which has the properties of fixed number of molecules with fixed volume.

Ⅱ. Ensemble

An ensemble is simply a collection of a very large number of systems, each constructed to be a replica on a thermodynamic level of the actual thermodynamic system whose properties we are investigating. We can find mechanical volume average of Microsystems in ensemble average. In ensemble, Microsystems can have same variable about the number of molecules(N), volume(V), temperature(T), energy(E) or chemical potential(μ) in the system. The ensemble is divided into three cases: micro canonical ensemble, canonical ensemble or grand canonical ensemble by limiting variables N, V or E.

1. Micro canonical ensemble

In a micro canonical ensemble, the systems of the ensemble are distributed uniformly with equal probability or frequency over the possible quantum states consistent with the specified value of N, V and E.

2. Canonical ensemble

A system in a canonical ensemble has a fixed volume V, fixed number of molecules N, and is immersed in a very large heat bath at a certain temperature T. The entire ensemble is an isolated system with total volume nV and a total energy Et, where n is the number of systems in the ensemble. The probability of the state i with energy E is

$$P_i(N,V,E) = \frac{\exp(-E_i(N,V)/kT)}{\sum_j \exp(-E_j(N,V)/kT)} \quad (1)$$

Each system in a canonical ensemble has fixed volume V and fixed number of molecules N, but the energy of the system can fluctuate. A typical example of problem that Simulated Annealing can be applied is TSP. TSP is the problem which searches the minimum cost when the number of city is fixed. Because there is a fixed number of cities to make a tour in a TSP and because each tour has a total tour length as energy, a TSP can be regarded as a system in a canonical ensemble.

3. Grand Canonical Ensemble

The number of molecules of a system in a grand canonical ensemble can fluctuate; where as a system in a canonical ensemble has a fixed number of molecules. Hence each system in a grand canonical ensemble has fixed V, T and μ, but is open with respect to energy and the number of molecules. The probability of state i having energy E with N molecules is

$$P_i(N;\mu,V,E) = \frac{\exp(-(E_i(N,V) - \mu N)/kT)}{\sum_N \sum_j \exp(-(E_j(N,V) - \mu N)/kT)} \quad (2)$$

The above expression applies to a one-component system. But, it can be easily extended to any number of components as follows:

$$P_i(N_1, N_2, \cdots; V, T, \mu_1, \mu_2, \cdots)$$
$$= \frac{\exp(-(E_i(N_1, N_2, \cdots, V) - \sum_k \mu_k N_k)/kT)}{\sum_{N_1}\sum_{N_2}\sum_{\cdots}\sum_j \exp(-(E_j(N_1, N_2, \cdots, V) - \sum_k \mu_k N_k)/kT)} \quad (3)$$

The probability is related not only to the energy $E_i(N,V)$ but also to the chemical potential μ_k. Therefore, grand canonical ensemble is suited in studying an open system which varies on the number of particles as well as the energy.

III. Grand Canonical Ensemble, ATSP, and MTSP

The augmented traveling salesman problem(ATSP) and the multiple traveling salesman problem(MTSP) are extensions of the well-known TSP. In ATSP, n customer cities with their own profits are given. A salesman at a base city is required to visit k customer cities, k≤n, and return to the base city. A cost is incurred and a profit is gained if a salesman visits customers. The ATSP is to determine the travel route to maximize the total benefit acquired from visited cities. The benefit function and the cost function for solving the MTSP are defined as the following equations:

$$B_{ATSP} = \sum_i \mu_i N_i - \alpha C_{ATSP}, \quad (4)$$

$$C_{ATSP} = \sum_{i=1}^{n-1} d(i, i+1) + d(n,1). \quad (5)$$

where μ_i, N_i, and α denote the profit of the city i, the number of appearance of cities with the profit μ_I in the travel route, and the weighting factor of the cost, respectively. $d(i,j)$ denotes the (Euclidian) distance between city i and j.

The MTSP can itself be generalized to a wide variety of routing and scheduling problems. In MTSP, there are n customer cities with m salesmen. Each salesman at a base city is required to visit k customer cities, $k \leq n-m+1$, and return to the base city and each customer city is to be visited by one salesman only. A cost is incurred if a salesman is actively used to visit customers. The MTSP is to determine the travel route to maximize the total benefit acquired by all the salesmen.

$$B_{MTSP} = \sum_i \mu_i N_i - \alpha \sum_{i=1}^{m} C_{MTSP}^i, \quad (6)$$

$$C_{MTSP}^i = \sum_{j=1}^{n-1} d(j, j+1) + d(n,1) - \beta S_i, \quad (7)$$

$$S_i = -\left(\frac{|L_i|}{\sum_{i=1}^{m}|L_i|} \times Log_{10} \frac{|L_i|}{\sum_{i=1}^{m}|L_i|}\right) \quad (8)$$

where m denotes the number of salesmen. S_i is the entropy term to make the salesmen's workload be distributed equally, and β is the weighting factor. L_i denotes the number of cities that salesman i has visited.

IV. Extended Simulated Annealing by Grand Canonical Ensemble

In GCE the states of the system are to form a Markov chain by changing the number of molecules. GCE is an open system and this gives rise to the following four perturbation schemes to decide a next state of the system with N molecules:

(i) Increasing scheme : make a system to have *N+1* molecules. It is needed to select one molecule from the other system and add it to a system.
(ii) Decreasing scheme : make a system to have *N-1* molecules. It is needed to delete one molecule from a system.
(iii) Internal swapping scheme : make a system to have a same number of molecules. It is needed to interchange one molecule with another molecule in a system.
(iv) External swapping scheme : make a system to have the same number of molecules by exchanging a molecule from a system with a molecule in the other system.

These perturbation schemes are used in the following ESA algorithm for the TSPs.

Step 1: Set initial and final temperature values.
Step 2: (In case of the ATSP) Select one of the above perturbation schemes(i,ii,iii,iv) randomly and perturb a current tour route *s* with *n* cities to *s'*, by the scheme.
(In case of the MTSP) Perform one of the following steps(2.1, 2.2) randomly.
2.1 Select two tour routes randomly, perturb a route by the perturbation scheme(ii) and the other one by the perturbation scheme(i) to make the route *s'*. It should be noted that the city to be deleted in one route must be added into the other route.
2.2 Select one system randomly and perturb a current state by the perturbation scheme(iii) to be the state *s'*.
Step 3: Compute the benefit *B(s')*, the difference between the profit and the cost, and compare it with the *B(s)* of the current state *s*, and let the state *s'* be the new state with probability

$$P(s' \leftarrow s)$$
$$= \begin{cases} 1 & \text{if } B(s') \geq B(s) \\ \exp(-(B(s')-B(s))/kT) & \text{if } B(s') \langle B(s) \end{cases} \quad (9)$$

Step 4: Repeat step 2, 3 until the equilibrium state occurs.
Step 5: Anneal with an annealing schedule.
Step 6: Repeat step 2, 3, 4, and 5 until final temperature is reached.

V. Experimental Results

An ESA algorithm is tested with 25 cities of ATSP and 400 cities of three-salesmen MTSP, denoted by circles, having their own profit values(μ_i) on the ATSP and the MTSP. The tests are performed on an IBM PC-586(400MHz). The MTSP take less than 51 minutes to output the result of the tests with the starting temperature=$1.0*10^3$, the final temperature =$1.0*10^{-2}$, α=1.0, respectively. The temperature(T) is decreased as $T = 0.95T$.

Fig.1 shows the effectiveness of the ESA in solving the 25 cities ATSP. There is, in the beginning, a large degree of randomness at high temperature, and as the temperature is decreased the system converges to a stable state. The same result comes out when different initial tours are tried.

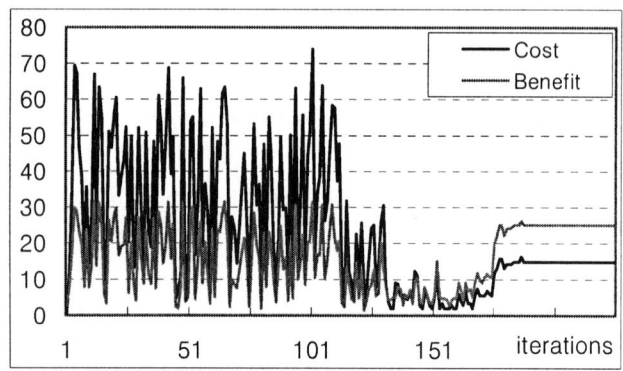

Fig.1. Progress of the convergence(ATSP)

Fig.2 is a final solution of 25 cities ATSP. It should be noted that some cities(dark gray colored cities) with the profit value of greater than 1.0 are not included and some cities(light gray colored cities) with the profit value of less than 1.0 are included in the final tour. This shows that a city is included in the tour not just because of its high profit and low cost but because of the high profits of its neighborhood included in the tour.

Fig.3~Fig.8 shows the result of MTSP with 3 salesman. The convergence of benefit, cost and number of visited cities are shown in a salesman unit in Fig.3 ~ Fig.5. The total benefit of salesman is in Fig.6 and Fig.7 shows changes of entropy caused by annealing. Fig.8 tells final your rout of salesman.

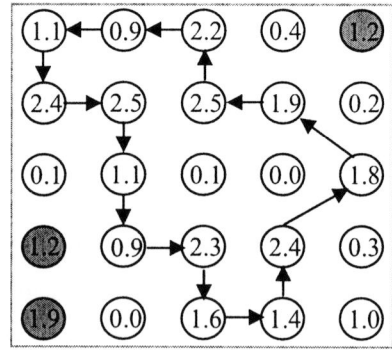

Fig.2. Result of ATSP

The parameters used in this test are the same as the ones used before except μ_i=1.0 and β=80.0 Fig.8 shows that the entropy plays a role to help the convergence. As expected, the cost is minimized and the benefit is maximized by ESA for MTSP with 3 salesmen. It is also noted that ESA can solve the MTSP without any transformation into a standard form, unlike most heuristic algorithms.

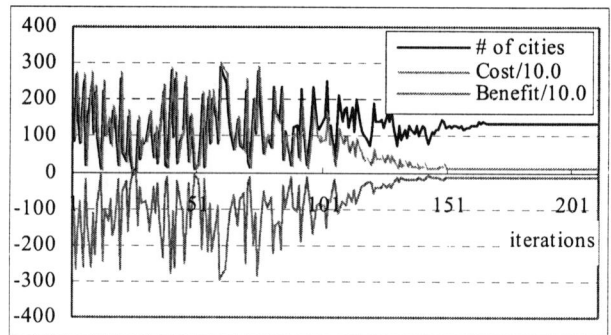

Fig.3 Salesman-1(MTSP)

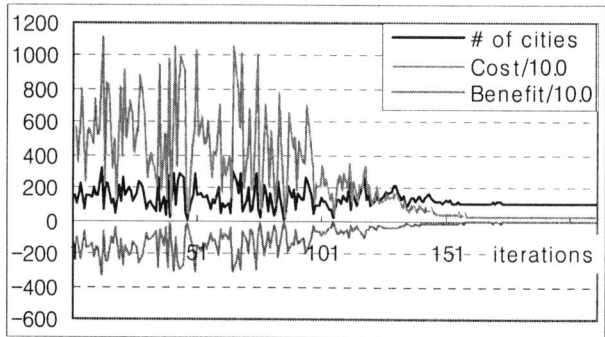

Fig.4 Salesman-2(MTSP)

Discussions

In this paper we propose ESA, based on GCE, and show how ESA can be used to solve the ATSPs and the MTSPs for real world applications. Experimental results show that ESA has salient features such as simplicity and ability to find high-quality solutions as SA has. By adding the entropy constraints to the energy function, MTSPs can be solved by ESA effectively.

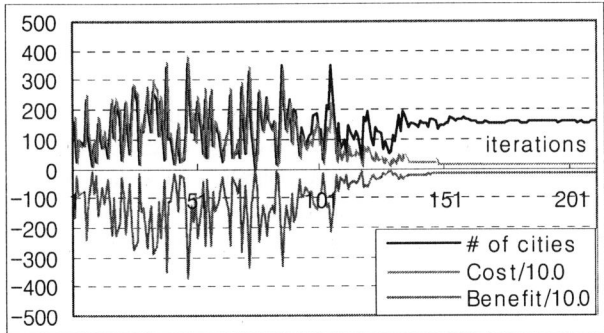

Fig.5 Salesman-3(MTSP)

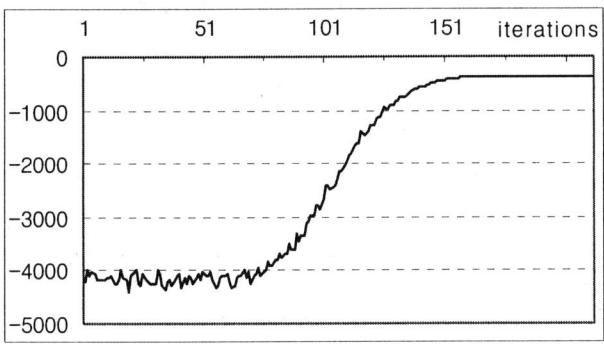

Fig.6 Total Benefit(3 salesmen)

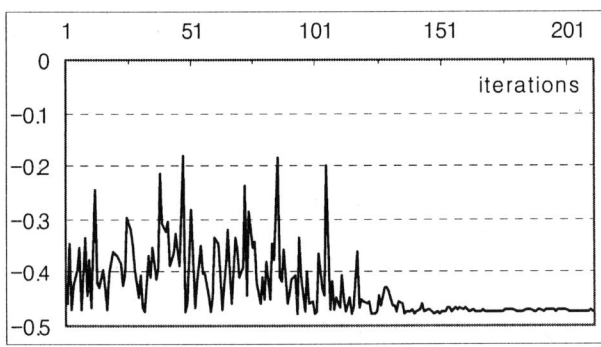

Fig.7 Total Entropy(3 salesmen)

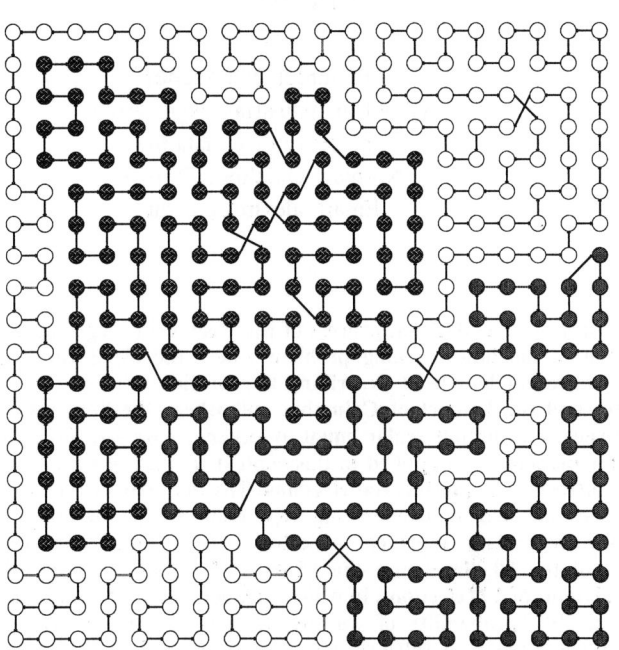

Fig.8. Result of MTSP

References

[1] PETERSON,C. : 'Parallel Distributed Approaches to Combinatorial Optimization −Benchmark Studies on Traveling Salesman Problem', Neural Computation 2, 1990, pp. 261-269.

[2] GU,J., and HUANG,X. :'Efficient Local Search With Search Space Smoothing: A Case Study of the Traveling Salesman Problem(TSP)", IEEE Trans. on SMC, 1994, 24, (5), pp. 728-735.

[3] GUOXING,Y. : 'Transformation of multidepot multisalesmen problem to the standard traveling salesman problem', European Journal of Operational Research 81, 1995, pp. 557-560.

[4] KIRKPATRIK,S., and GELATT,C., and VECCH,M. : 'Optimization by simulated annealing", Science, 1983, 220, pp. 671-680.

Support Vector Machines and the Electoral College

Alexander Malyscheff
School of Industrial Engineering
University of Oklahoma
Norman, Oklahoma 73019
Email: alexm@ou.edu

Theodore Trafalis
School of Industrial Engineering
University of Oklahoma
Norman, Oklahoma 73019
Email: ttrafalis@ou.edu

Abstract— The decision process of the electoral college can be seen as a machine learning problem where the input consists of a vector of length 51 describing the election outcome in 50 states and the District of Columbia and where the final result is given as an output scalar equal to either $+1$ or -1. Support vector machines are applied in this context to a set of simulated and historic U.S. presidential elections. The decision surface can best be modelled by a separating hyperplane where the weights of the hyperplane represent a scaled level of importance for each of the 50 states and the District of Columbia. For 100 simulations of 100 elections, in which Democrats and Republicans had a 50% probability of winning each state, support vector machines appear to retrieve a large-state bias. For a historic dataset covering the last 22 U.S. presidential elections no large-state bias could be detected.

I. INTRODUCTION

Since presidential elections in the United States are based on the electoral college system, a significant number of studies have investigated whether the "One-person, one-vote" rule applies across all 50 states and the District of Columbia. Banzhaf [1] suggests that voters in large states have a significant advantage compared to voters in smaller states to decide an election. Various studies, however, suggest that in addition a state's competitiveness ("toss-up state") is an important factor to determine the chance of a single voter to cast the deciding vote [6], [8], [9]. In particular, it is criticized that Banzhaf assumed that the probability that a vote is cast for a Republican or a Democrat is exactly 50% in all 50 states and the District of Columbia. These studies conclude that no large-state bias exists in the electoral college. Nonetheless, various articles have attempted to include competitiveness into Banzhaf's model and continue to support the existence of a large-state bias [4], [7].

Support vector machines (SVM) are employed here to analyze the electoral college from a machine learning perspective. Contrary to the traditional perceptron, support vector machines maximize the margin of the training data, therefore, they yield a very low generalization error. We briefly review SVMs in section II. In section III we shall cast the data for U.S. presidential elections into a form suitable for support vector machines and provide a theoretical argument as to why the decision surface discriminating the election data can best be modelled by a separating hyperplane (i.e. a linear classifier). In section IV we will elaborate on the linear classifier and compute the resulting weights for each voting area for 100 simulations of 100 elections and for historic election data, thus providing a ranking of importance of the 50 states and the District of Columbia. For the average of the simulations (which were based on a 50% probability for either party to win a particular state) a large-state bias appears to have been recorded, while for a historic dataset including the last 22 U.S. presidential elections no large-state bias could be observed.

II. SUPPORT VECTOR MACHINES IN PATTERN CLASSIFICATION

The support vector machine learning problem corresponds to solving the following (primal) optimization problem

$$\min \quad \frac{1}{2}\|\mathbf{w}\|^2 \quad (1)$$

subject to :
$$y_i\left(\mathbf{x}_i^T\mathbf{w}+b\right) \geq +1 \quad \forall i=1,...,l,$$

where the $\mathbf{x}_i \in \Re^d$ represent the input data and the $y_i \in \{-1,+1\}$ represent the labels. SVM learning computes $\mathbf{w} \in \Re^d$, the optimal weight vector, along with an offset b.

Moreover, support vector machine learning can easily be extended to pattern classification problems, which can only be solved using a nonlinear decision surface.

We can achieve this by mapping a classification problem that can not be linearly separated in input space to a so-called feature space using a function $\phi: \mathbf{x} \rightarrow \phi(\mathbf{x})$. The mapping creates the corresponding classification problem in feature space, which can be solved employing linear techniques. The price we have to pay is to significantly increase the number of dimensions. Thus a nonlinear problem behaves in feature space as if it was linearly separable.

Unfortunately, very often the function $\phi(\mathbf{x})$ is not available, can not be computed, or does not even exist. However, for certain functions the inner product of two vectors can be computed, both, in pattern and in feature space. In other words, while $\phi(\mathbf{x})$ might not be available, we can still compute the inner product $\phi(\mathbf{x}_1)^T\phi(\mathbf{x}_2)$ in feature space. This inner product can be expressed by the kernel function

$$k: \Re^d \times \Re^d \rightarrow \Re : k(\mathbf{x}_1,\mathbf{x}_2) = \phi(\mathbf{x}_1)^T\phi(\mathbf{x}_2).$$

For this reason it is more convenient to operate on the dual of (1). For each of the l constraints we introduce a set of nonnegative Lagrangian multipliers $\mathbf{\Lambda} = (\lambda_1, \lambda_2, ..., \lambda_l)^T$. Then, the dual problem can be written as follows:

$$\max \quad \sum_{i=1}^{l} \lambda_i - \frac{1}{2} \sum_{i=1}^{l} \sum_{j=1}^{l} \lambda_i \lambda_j y_i y_j \mathbf{x}_i^T \mathbf{x}_j \quad (2)$$

$$subject\ to:$$
$$\sum_{i=1}^{l} \lambda_i y_i = 0$$
$$\lambda_i \geq 0 \quad \forall i = 1, ..., l.$$

Here, the only unknowns are the dual variables $\lambda_1, ..., \lambda_l$. Note also that the input vectors $\mathbf{x}_i$ are given solely in terms of inner products. Very often the dual is also given in closed form. Let $\mathbf{e}^T = (1, 1, ..., 1) \in \Re^l$, $\mathbf{y}^T = (y_1, ..., y_l) \in \Re^l$, $D_{ij} = (y_i y_j \mathbf{x}_i^T \mathbf{x}_j)$, therefore $\mathbf{D} \in \Re^{l \times l}$, and keep in mind that $\mathbf{\Lambda} = (\lambda_1, \lambda_2, ..., \lambda_l)^T$. Then the dual optimization problem for support vector machine learning reduces to:

$$\max \quad \mathbf{\Lambda}^T \mathbf{e} - \frac{1}{2} \mathbf{\Lambda}^T \mathbf{D} \mathbf{\Lambda}^T \quad (3)$$

$$subject\ to:$$
$$\mathbf{\Lambda}^T \mathbf{y} = 0$$
$$(\mathbf{\Lambda})_i \geq 0 \quad \forall i = 1, ..., l.$$

The decision function, in higher dimension also referred to as decision surface, can be computed from:

$$f(\mathbf{x}) = sign\left(\sum_{i=1}^{l} \lambda_i y_i \mathbf{x}_i^T \mathbf{x} + b\right). \quad (4)$$

The reader might verify that all information pertaining to the classification problem in equation (2) can be formulated using solely inner products. These inner products are then mapped yielding a linear classification problem in feature space. Thus, for nonlinear instances we can reformulate the optimization problem:

$$\max \quad \sum_{i=1}^{l} \lambda_i - \frac{1}{2} \sum_{i=1}^{l} \sum_{j=1}^{l} \lambda_i \lambda_j y_i y_j k(\mathbf{x}_i, \mathbf{x}_j) \quad (5)$$

$$subject\ to:$$
$$\sum_{i=1}^{l} \lambda_i y_i = 0$$
$$\lambda_i \geq 0 \quad \forall i = 1, ..., l.$$

In other words the only necessary change to move a problem from input space to feature space consists of rewriting the data matrix $D_{ij} = (y_i y_j k(\mathbf{x}_i, \mathbf{x}_j))$.

The decision function to test for a new pattern $\mathbf{x}$ can now be formulated and calculated based only on the information contained in the set of λ_i's:

$$f(\mathbf{x}) = sign\left(\sum_{i=1}^{l} \lambda_i y_i k(\mathbf{x}_i, \mathbf{x}) + b\right). \quad (6)$$

Possible kernel functions include polynomial kernels such as $k(\mathbf{x}_1, \mathbf{x}_2) = (\mathbf{x}_1^T \mathbf{x}_2 + 1)^p$, with p indicating the degree of the polynomial or exponential kernels as for example $k(\mathbf{x}_1, \mathbf{x}_2) = \exp\left(-\frac{\|\mathbf{x}_1 - \mathbf{x}_2\|^2}{2\sigma^2}\right)$, with σ determining the width of the radial-basis functions.

III. THE ELECTORAL COLLEGE FROM A SUPPORT VECTOR MACHINE PERSPECTIVE

A. General Observations

The electoral college was originally devised as a compromise between direct election of the President and an election through Congress. The number of votes allocated to each state corresponds to the size of its congressional delegation, that is, the sum of its House members and Senators. This Senate add-on feature was a provision to allocate more power to the smaller states (small-state bias). In most states the winner-takes-all rule (unit rule) applies, which implies that even if one party achieves only a very narrow majority in a given state, this party will carry all of the state's votes. It is this aspect of the electoral college voting process which triggers – supposedly – the large-state bias [1], [5]. The prevailing two-party system in the United States suggests to employ a two-class machine learning model where each party is represented by a different class.

Upon a completely arbitrary and random coin toss by one of the authors the Republican party was assigned the value $R = +1$, while the Democratic party was represented by $D = -1$. For the case that no election was held in a particular territory (no statehood) or that a third party won a state the corresponding outcome was set equal to zero, $I = 0$. Thus if a particular state is won by the Republican party, we assign the value of $+1$ to this state, if it is won by the Democratic party we assign the value -1. Repeating this procedure for all 50 states and the District of Columbia we obtain a sequence of -1's, $+1$'s, and possibly 0's. For all elections we disregarded unfaithful electors. Thus, the input data consists of a vector of length $d = 51$ containing the results for each state in alphabetical order encoded as described above. The output value is given by the overall winner of the election. This value can be described by a scalar y_i assuming values -1 or $+1$. For the historic dataset we incorporated 22 elections from 1916 to 2000, consequently, there are $l = 22$ data samples. More precisely, the problem data can be formulated using the set $T = \{(\mathbf{x}_j, y_j)_{j=1}^{l}\} \subset \Re^d \times \{-1, +1\}$. The election results were taken from [2]. We also evaluated a simulated dataset, a random collection of 100 coin tosses in each of the 50 states and the District of Columbia, thus, for this experiment we have $l = 100$.

As an example let us consider the simplified case in which the electoral college consists of only 3 states, X, Y, and Z. We might allocate 2 votes in the electoral college to the states X and Y, while Z has only one vote. Table I illustrates the various possible outcomes for this "reduced" electoral college.

The data samples live in the space $\Re^3$, that is $d = 3$. One might consider each of the eight scenarios as a different

TABLE I
ELECTION OUTCOMES FOR THREE STATES

X (2)	Y (2)	Z (1)	+1	-1	Winner
-1	-1	-1	0	5	-1
+1	-1	-1	2	3	-1
-1	+1	-1	2	3	-1
+1	+1	-1	4	1	+1
-1	-1	+1	1	4	-1
+1	-1	+1	3	2	+1
-1	+1	+1	3	2	+1
+1	+1	+1	5	0	+1

election year. The optimal separating hyperplane for this situation is given by $x_1 + x_2 + x_3 = 0$. In other words a linear decision surface correctly classifies all data samples.

Moreover, it can be shown that there will always be a separating hyperplane that correctly classifies all training points. Consider the vector $\mathbf{a} = (a_1, ..., a_{51})^T \in \Re^{51}$, an input sample $\mathbf{x}_k \in \Re^{51}$ and the corresponding label $y_k \in \{-1, +1\}$. Let the a_i's represent the actual number of delegates that each state has in the electoral college. Then, following our previous notation of counting +1 for the Republican votes and -1 for the Democrat votes the difference of votes for the election described by $\mathbf{x}_k$ is given by $\mathbf{a}^T\mathbf{x}_k$. For the example discussed in subsection III-A consider the fourth election scenario (obviously, for this particular case the vectors are now living in $\Re^3$) with $\mathbf{x}_4 = (+1, +1, -1)^T$ and $\mathbf{a} = (2, 2, 1)^T$. We find for $\mathbf{a}^T\mathbf{x}_4 = 2 + 2 - 1 = 3$. In other words the vector $\mathbf{a}$ itself serves as the normal vector of a possible separating hyperplane, since it is the expression $sign(\mathbf{a}^T\mathbf{x}_k)$ which is used to determine the outcome of an election. Note also that this hyperplane is passing through the origin as there is no offset in the calculation of the vote difference.

For further illustration consider the following situation. Suppose an artificial electoral college consists of only two states. State A is represented by 2 delegates, while 3 delegates belong to state B. Table II displays all possible election outcomes.

TABLE II
ELECTION OUTCOMES FOR TWO STATES

A (2)	B (3)	+1	-1	Winner
-1	-1	0	5	-1
-1	+1	3	2	+1
+1	-1	2	3	-1
+1	+1	5	0	+1

Thus, the elections for which the second state votes -1 precipitate an overall election win of -1. In contradistinction, points with a positive second component result in an election win of $+1$ regardless of the outcome in state A. Support vector machine learning will take this constellation into consideration when the optimal separating hyperplane is computed. In fact, for this example, one finds $H_{SVM} : x_2 \geq 0$ with a normal vector $\mathbf{w}_{SVM} = (0, 1)^T$. Machine learning will "recognize" that the decisive vote will take place in state B. As pointed out before, the hyperplane $H_{del} : 2x_1 + 3x_2 \geq 0$ based on the number of available delegates in each state will separate

the two classes, however, this hyperplane is not the optimal hyperplane. In other words, H_{del} does not take into account the distinct integer character of the $\mathbf{x}_i$ which describe the voting process.

B. The Support Vector Machine Classifier is not identical to the Electoral Votes of the State

Following the discussion in section III-A one might suppose that in the limit, after all electoral outcomes are included in the machine learning analysis, the support vector solution might converge asymptotically to the vector of votes in the electoral college. More precisely, we examine $\mathbf{w} \to \mathbf{a}$ for $l \to 2^d$?

For this purpose we conducted three experiments on a reduced electoral college. For each of the three experiments seven states were randomly selected and all $2^7 = 128$ possible election scenarios were included in the support vector machine analysis. We emphasize the random nature of these experiments, since the state of Florida was selected in all three instances.

TABLE III
ELECTORAL COLLEGE WEIGHT VERSUS THE SVM SOLUTION

Exp. 1			Exp. 2			Exp. 3		
State	Votes	SVM	State	Votes	SVM	State	Votes	SVM
CA	54	7	FL	25	5	FL	25	5
FL	25	2	NJ	15	3	VA	13	2
GA	13	2	MO	11	2	AZ	8	2
MO	11	2	TN	11	2	NE	5	1
TN	11	2	MS	7	1	WV	5	1
CO	8	1	KS	6	1	DC	3	1
OR	7	1	RI	4	1	VT	3	1

Table III shows the results of these experiments with the name of the selected state followed by the electoral college votes and the computed weights of the support vector machine algorithm. The experiments indicate a large-state bias in the SVM solution and the results are presented in descending order of electoral college votes. Nonetheless, the computed weights are not identical to the electoral college votes. For the second and third experiment the two solutions differ roughly by a common factor of 5, however, this proportional behavior does not hold in the first dataset.

It should be pointed out that for this analysis *all* possible election outcomes were included in the training of the learning machine. For an electoral college consisting of 51 states this analysis is rather unpractical, which means that smaller samples of the overall population have to be considered. We shall do so by analyzing 100 datasets of 100 randomly simulated elections and one dataset comprising the last 22 U.S. presidential elections. We emphasize that support vector machines have demonstrated a powerful generalization performance being able to generalize well on small datasets [10].

IV. EXPERIMENTS

In subsection III-A we have provided evidence suggesting that the decision surface of the electoral college can be approximated by a hyperplane. Since nonlinear behavior can be excluded, no kernelization is necessary, hence $k(\mathbf{x}_1, \mathbf{x}_2) = \mathbf{x}_1^T \mathbf{x}_2$. Note that a kernel representing a simple inner product can be separated ($\Phi(\mathbf{x})$ exists), such that the weight vector **w** discriminating the two classes (parties) can be easily computed for this case. We solved these problems using a slightly modified version of Steve Gunn's MATLAB code [3], which is essentially based on MATLAB's built-in quadratic programming solver. We shall employ two different approaches and compare the resulting normal vectors of the optimal hyperplane. Recall that the 51 components of the normal vectors are a measure for the weight of a particular state.

The first dataset, simulation, consists of 100 realizations of 100 simulated elections. For each dataset realization one might imagine a collection of 100 coin tosses in each of the 50 states and the District of Columbia assuming therefore a probability of 50% for either party to win a state. The overall winner for each of the simulated elections was computed using the current electoral votes (1990 census). The solution was then averaged over all 100 realizations. In addition, the optimal hyperplane was computed for a dataset historic, which contains information of the last 22 U.S. presidential elections from 1916 to 2000. In subsection III-A it was argued that the optimal hyperplane separating all data samples pass through the origin. However, the experiments conducted here allow for a nonzero offset. But since it was observed that the normal vectors change only marginally when the separating hyperplane is forced to pass through the origin, we shall limit the reported results to those allowing for a nonzero offset.

Table IV displays the six states with the highest voting power all of which are identical to the ones found in [5]. It can be seen that apparently the weights computed from the simulation favor the larger states such as California, New York, and Texas. Thus, the simulated election dataset appears to display a large-state bias. Keep in mind, however, that we assumed a 50% probability for each state to vote either Republican or Democrat.

TABLE IV

AVERAGE STATE VOTING POWER, SIMULATION

simulation $b = -0.0127$	Average Hyperplane Weights
California	0.97
New York	0.55
Texas	0.52
Pennsylvania	0.41
Illinois	0.40
Florida	0.38

Turning our attention to the historic dataset the results are somewhat different. Although only one experiment was performed, it appears as if no large-state bias can be reported here. The six states with the highest voting power are shown in Table V. Based on available data support vector machine learning suggests that the highest voting power can be found in Missouri, Nevada, Ohio, Delaware, New Mexico, and West Virginia.

TABLE V

STATE VOTING POWER, HISTORIC

historic $b = 0.0743$	Hyperplane Weights
Missouri	0.19
Nevada	0.14
Ohio	0.12
Delaware	0.10
New Mexico/ West Virginia	0.08

V. CONCLUSION

State voting power has been subject to various studies investigating whether each voter has the same chance to cast the decisive vote in a U.S. presidential election. Banzhaf [1] computes a significant bias towards the larger states. Margolis [6] and others criticize that Banzhaf assumed a 50% probability that a vote is cast for either party in all 50 states and the District of Columbia while Rabinowitz and MacDonald [7] insist that a large-state bias still exists.

Machine learning can be applied in two-class classification problems to assign a collection of input parameters to either one of two classes. The electoral college along with the two-party system has been formulated as a linear machine learning problem.

Using this linear learning machine the separating hyperplane was computed for 100 simulated and for one historic dataset. The simulated datasets were based on random coin tosses indicating a 50% chance for either party to win the election in a given state. For the average of the simulated datasets a large-state bias appears to have been recorded in accordance with the Banzhaf-study. For the historic dataset comprising the last 22 U.S. presidential elections from 1916 to 2000 no large-state bias was detected. The Banzhaf study assumed a 50% probability that either Republicans or Democrats win a particular state and concluded that a large-state bias exists. Other studies were questioning this assumption unable to detect a large-state bias and suggesting instead that a state's competitiveness might also be an important factor to determine the chance of single voter to cast the deciding vote [6], [8], [9]. In this paper the simulated datasets were based on a 50% probability for either party to win a state. The support vector machine solution seems to confirm a large-state bias for this model. In contradistinction, no large-state bias could be detected for the historic dataset. Thus, our research sides with Margolis, Sterling, and Uslaner suggesting that other factors (competitiveness) might exist, which determine the importance of a single state for U.S. presidential elections.

ACKNOWLEDGMENT

In the present work the authors have been partially supported by the National Science Foundation, NSF Grants ECS-9978813 and 01-02 0099378.

REFERENCES

[1] J. F. Banzhaf III, "One Man, 3.312 Votes: A mathematical analysis of the electoral college," *Villanova Law Review*, vol. 13, pp. 304-332, 1968.

[2] Congressional Quarterly Inc., *Congressional Quarterly's Guide to U.S. Elections*, Washington, DC: Congressional Quarterly Inc., 1985.

[3] S. R. Gunn, "Support Vector Machines for Classification and Regression," Technical Report, Image Speech and Intelligent Systems Research Group, University of Southampton, 1997.

[4] J. E. Kallenbach, "Our Electoral College Gerrymander," *Midwest Journal of Political Science*, vol. 4, no. 2, pp. 162-191, 1960.

[5] L. D. Longley and J. D. Dana, Jr., "The Biases of the Electoral College in the 1990s," *Polity*, vol. 25, no. 1, pp. 123-145, 1992.

[6] H. Margolis, "The Banzhaf Fallacy," *American Journal of Political Science*, vol. 27, pp. 321-326, 1983.

[7] G. Rabinowitz and S. E. MacDonald, "The Power of the States in U.S. Presidential Elections," *American Political Science Review*, vol. 80, no. 1, pp. 65-87, 1986.

[8] C. W. Sterling, "The Electoral College Biases Revealed: The Conventional Wisdom and Game Theory Models Notwithstanding," *Western Political Quarterly*, vol. 31, pp. 159-177, 1978.

[9] E. M. Uslaner, "Spatial Models of the Electoral College: Distribution Assumptions and Biases of the System," *Political Methodology*, vol. 3, pp. 355-381, 1976.

[10] V. Vapnik, *The Nature of Statistical Learning Theory*. Springer Verlag, 1995.

Mixed Analog/Digital System for Quadratic Assignment Problems

Yukihiro Kobayashi, Takehiko Koyama, Satoshi Matsui and Yoshihiko Horio
Dept. of Electronic Engineering
Tokyo Denki University
Tokyo 101–8457, Japan
Email: yukihiro@ckt.d.dendai.ac.jp

Kazuyuki Aihara
Dept. of Mathematical Engineering
The University of Tokyo
Tokyo 133–8656, Japan

Abstract— We propose a mixed analog/digital system architecture of a chaos driven exponential tabu search for quadratic assignment problems. We construct a small size evaluation system using switched-capacitor chaotic neuron ICs and programmable logic devices. The experimental results from the system verify the validity and hardware compatibility of the proposed architecture.

I. Introduction

Superior performance of chaotic dynamics in solving combinatorial optimization problems has been demonstrated [1]-[4]. The quadratic assignment problem (QAP) is one of the Nondeterministic Polynominal (NP)-hard problems [5]. It should be noted that even a small size QAP is very difficult to solve; the optimum solution of the QAP with size more than 30 is unknown [5]. Main reason for the difficulty is an impractical computational time. Therefore, a heuristic algorithm that obtains a near optimal solution in moderate time is desired.

One of such methods is a 2-opt algorithm. Taillard has proposed a tabu search method for the QAP based on the 2-opt algorithm [6]. The tabu search introduced a finite inhibition period for the 2-opt exchanges on previously assigned exchange candidates.

Hasegawa et al. have implemented the tabu search on an artificial neural network [3], [4]. Moreover, they have extended the tabu search to an exponential tabu search using chaotic neurons [8] in the network [1]-[4]. In this approach, the 2-opt algorithm is driven by chaotic dynamics avoiding traps in local minima. Furthermore, the relative refractory effects in the chaotic neuron naturally implement an exponential decay of the tabu strength. Even though the chaos driven exponential tabu search shows superb performance in solving the QAP, it still requires a large computational power. Therefore, efficient hardware for the above algorithm is demanded.

By the way, the chaotic dynamics should be implemented with an analog circuitry since complexity in real numbers is essential for chaos. The analog circuits can faithfully handle real numbers, while digital circuits cannot compute almost all real numbers. In this respect, Tanaka et al. have modified the Hasegawa's method for an analog integrated circuit implementation [7].

In this paper, we propose a mixed analog/digital system architecture for the modified Hasegawa's method. The chaotic neuron model [8] has been fabricated as an integrated circuit form using sampled-data analog circuit techniques such as switched-capacitor (SC) [10], [11] and switched current (SI) circuits [9]. Especially, the SI chaotic neurons are small in area and operate at high frequency, thus they are suitable for optimization problems hardware. However, the SC chaotic neuron chips [10] which have been fabricated for a large-scale chaotic neuro-computer are used in this paper to evaluate the system architecture, since a dedicated SI chaotic neuron chip is still under fabrication.

The system is designed for size-10 QAPs. However, the evaluation system is built for a size-4 QAP, because the use of the general purpose SC chaotic neuron chip limits the system size. Note that irrespective of the size, all the functionality of the proposed system architecture can be evaluated with the small system. Moreover, the evaluation system boards are designed so that the SC chaotic neuron chips can be readily replaced by the SI counterparts. Other components in the system are implemented by means of programmable logic devices (PLDs).

II. Quadratic Assignment Problem

The quadratic assignment problem (QAP) is shortly reviewed in this section. The QAP of size n consists of n locations and n units. An $n \times n$ "distance" matrix denotes the mutual distances among these locations. In addition, another "flow" matrix defines the mutual relationships among these units. We should find the assignment of the units to the locations that gives the minimum sum of the products, $F^{\boldsymbol{P}}$, given by

$$F^{\boldsymbol{P}} = \sum_{i=1}^{n}\sum_{j=1}^{n} a_{ij} b_{p(i)p(j)}, \quad (1)$$
$$\boldsymbol{P} : (p(1), p(2), \cdots, p(n)), \quad (2)$$

where $\boldsymbol{P}$ is a one dimensional permutation with n elements, $p(i)$ is the ith element of the permutation $\boldsymbol{P}$, a_{ij} is a distance from the ith location to the jth location, and $b_{p(i)q(i)}$ is a flow from the $p(i)$th unit to the $p(j)$th unit.

III. Modified Chaos Driven Exponental Tabu Search

In this section, the modified chaos driven exponential tabu search is shortly reviewed [3], [4], [7]. For a QAP of size n, a chaotic neural network with $n \times n$ neurons is prepared as shown in Fig. 1(a). When the (i,j)th neuron in the network fires, we assign the ith element in the permutation P to the jth index as shown in Fig. 1(b). At the same time, the element at jth index, $p(j)$, is moved to the $q(i)$th index where the ith element originally resided. This set of operations is referred to as the (i,j)-assignment in this paper. As a result of the (i,j)-assignment, the element i at the index $q(i)$ and the element $q(i)$ at the index j are exchanged as shown in Fig. 1(b), that is, one set of the 2-opt exchange is executed.

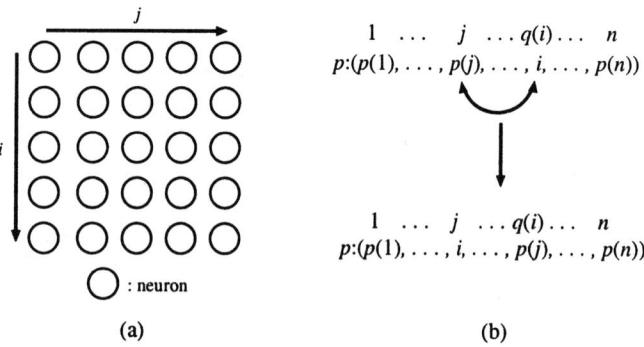

Fig. 1. (a) A neural network with $n \times n$ network, and (b) the (i,j)-assignment.

The chaotic dynamics of the (i,j)th chaotic neuron in the network is defined as follows:

$$\xi_{ij}(t+1) = \beta\{F_1^P(t) - F_{ij}^P(t)\}, \quad (3)$$

$$\eta_{ij}(t+1) = -W\sum_{k=1}^{n}\sum_{l=1}^{n} x_{kl}(t) + k_r \eta_{ij}(t) - \alpha x_{p(j)q(i)}(t) + \theta, \quad (4)$$

$$\zeta_{ij}(t+1) = k_r \zeta_{ij}(t) - \alpha x_{ij}(t) + \theta, \quad (5)$$

$$x_{ij}(t+1) = f\{\xi_{ij}(t+1) + \eta_{ij}(t+1) + \zeta_{ij}(t+1)\}, \quad (6)$$

where ξ_{ij} is an internal state which evaluates an improvement with the (i,j)-assignment, η_{ij} is a sum of a feedback input from constituent neurons in addition to a tabu strength for assigning the $p(j)$th element to the index $q(i)$, ζ_{ij} is a tabu strength for assigning the ith element to the index j, x_{ij} is an output of the (i,j)th neuron, and $f(\cdot)$ is a nonlinear output function of the neuron. Moreover, $F_1^P(t)$ is the object function at time t, $F_{ij}^P(t)$ is the object function after the (i,j)-assignment, and β is a scaling parameter. Furthermore, α is a scaling parameter and k_r is a decay parameter for the tabu effects. Finally, θ is an external bias.

In Hasegawa's method, each neuron state is updated asynchronously (sequentially) from the (i,j)th neuron to the (n,n)th neuron. We denote a set of this update sequence as one iteration. Furthermore, when $x_{ij} \geq 0.5$, the (i,j)th neuron is considered to be fire, and then the permutation P is updated with the (i,j)-assignment performed.

IV. SIMPLIFIED GAIN CALCULATION

Equation (3) gives a gain resulting from the (i,j)-assignment. By substituting P of (1) to (3), the gain can be calculated by the following equation [12]:

$$\begin{aligned}F_1^P(t) - F_{ij}^P(t) =\ & a_{p(i)p(i)}(b_{p(j)p(j)} - b_{ii}) \\ & + a_{jq(i)}(b_{p(j)i} - b_{ip(j)}) \\ & + a_{q(i)j}(b_{ip(j)} - b_{p(j)i}) \\ & + a_{q(i)q(i)}(b_{ii} - b_{p(j)p(j)}) \\ & + \sum_{k=1, k\neq i,j}^{n} a_{kj}(b_{p(k)p(j)} - b_{p(k)i}) \\ & + a_{kq(i)}(b_{p(k)i} - b_{p(k)p(j)}) \\ & + a_{jk}(b_{ip(k)} - b_{p(j)p(k)}) \\ & + a_{q(i)k}(b_{ip(k)} - b_{p(j)p(k)}),\end{aligned} \quad (7)$$

where a_{ij} and b_{ij} are the i,jth elements of the distance matrix and the flow matrix, respectively.

V. SYSTEM ARCHITECTURE

We propose a mixed analog/digital system architecture for the modified chaos driven exponential tabu search for the QAP explained in the previous sections. The QAP system is composed of eight blocks as shown in Fig. 2; 1. main block, 2. element extraction block, 3. gain calculation block, 4. feedback block, 5. element exchange block, 6. memory block, 7. neuron select block, and 8. chaotic neural network block.

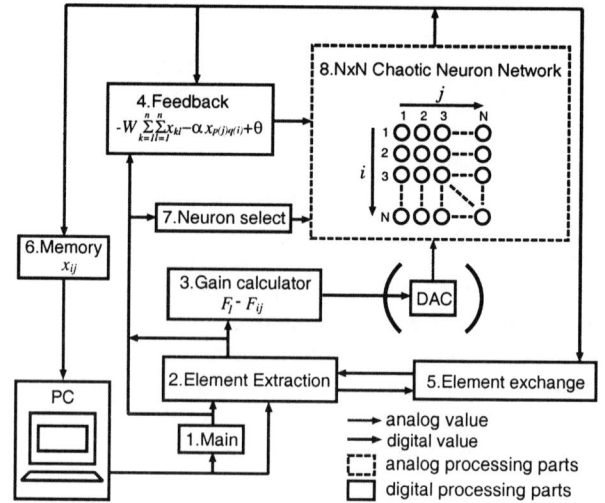

Fig. 2. A mixed analog/digital system architecture of the modified chaos driven exponential tabu search for the QAP.

A. Main Block

The main block provides control clocks for other blocks. In addition, the block has a two-dimensional sequential counter, (i,j)-counter, for i and j for distance matrix and flow matrix, respectively. The counter counts up from 1 to n in a manner that $(1,1), (1,2),..., (1,n), (2,1), (2,2),..., (2,n), (3,1),..., (i,j),..., (n,n)$. The output of the (i,j)-counter is used in other blocks as a reference. Moreover, the main block has an iteration counter which holds the number of iterations elapsed.

B. Element Extraction Block

The element extraction block refers to the value of the (i,j)-counter in the main block, and reads out, from its memory, $p(j)$, $q(i)$ for the permutation P, and corresponding elements of the distance and flow matrices required for the gain calculation of (7). The data are then sent to the gain calculation block. In the evaluation system, which will be mentioned in section IV, all these data are 4-bit. The 4-bit resolution, which is suitable for hardware, has been justified using exhaustive numerical simulations [7].

C. Gain Calculation Block

The gain calculation block executes (7). The result is passed to the chaotic neural network. This completes (3).

D. Feedback Block

This block stores the latest outputs from all neurons. This block also calculates (4). The i, j, $p(j)$ and $q(i)$ for the calculation are provided by the element extraction block, while W, α and θ are from the PC.

E. Element Exchange Block

The element exchange block exchanges the elements of the permutation P as shown in Fig. 1(b) if the (i,j)th neuron fires. Therefore, this block keeps the current permutation. The result of the exchange is sent to the element extraction block.

F. Chaotic Neural Network Block

The block contains $n \times n$ chaotic neurons. The chaotic neural network calculates (3) to (6) with its analog chaotic neurodynamics.

G. Neuron Select Block

This block drives one neuron in the neuron block at a time by providing control clocks for the SC neuron circuits. The block achieves the sequential updating of the neurons in the neural network.

H. Memory Block

Finally, the on-board memory block stores a time history of the neuron outputs. The data in this block is read out by the PC after scheduled iterations are over. This avoids the overhead with the slow communication between the PC and the system during the operation.

VI. SYSTEM VERIFICATION

A size-4 QAP system based on the system architecture in Fig. 2 has been constructed with a mixed analog/digital circuit technique onto two circuit boards as shown in Fig. 3. The purpose of the system is to verify the proposed system architecture.

The small board in the figure is the control board and the large one is the neural network board. The control board contains the block 1 to block 6 in Fig. 2, while the neural

Fig. 3. The evaluation system boards. The on-top small one is a control board, and the bottom one is a SC chotic neuron network board.

network board implements the block 7 and 8. An external PC is used to program the board and to collect the final results from the board. The system is driven by a 15 MHz clock.

In the evaluation system, the chaotic neurons from the general purpose SC chaotic neuron ICs are employed [10], [11]. However, a SI chaotic neuron IC which has been specially designed for the QAP system is under fabrication. The evaluation system boards are designed such that the SC chaotic neuron chips are readily replaced by the SI chips with minimum modifications.

The SC chaotic neuron circuit, of which block diagram is shown in Fig. 4, realizes the following set of equations:

$$\xi_j(t+1) = k_e \xi_j(t) + A_{iA}(t), \quad (8)$$

$$\eta_j(t+1) = k_f \eta_j(t) + \sum_{j=1}^{n} w_{ij} h_j\{x_{ij}(t)\}, \quad (9)$$

$$\zeta_j(t+1) = k_r \zeta_j(t) - \alpha_i x_i(t) + \theta_i, \quad (10)$$

where $A_{iA}(t)$ is an analog external input and $h(\cdot)$ is a step function. We have adapted this circuit to our system as

$$A_{iA}(t) = \beta\{F_1^p(t) - F_{ij}^p(t)\},$$

$$\sum_{j=1}^{n} w_{ij} h_j\{x_{kl}(t)\} = -W \sum_{k=1}^{n} \sum_{l=1}^{n} x_{kl}(t)$$

$$-\alpha x_{p(j)q(i)} + \theta,$$

$$\theta_i = \theta,$$

$$k_e = 0,$$

$$k_f = k_r.$$

In the evaluation system, an optional A/D converter is used to generate a suitable analog input voltage for the SC chaotic neurons as shown in Fig. 2.

The matrices used in the experiments are;

results have demonstrated various system dynamics. These results confirm that the proposed system architecture physically implements the chaos driven exponential tabu search.

TABLE I
THE PARAMETERS FOR THE EXPERIMENTS

Parameter	Value
k_r	0.83
β	1
α	1
W	0.1
θ	0.47

VII. CONCLUSION

We have proposed the hardware system architecture of the chaos driven exponential tabu search for the QAPs. Based on the proposed scheme, we have constructed the small size evaluation system employing the SC chaotic neuron ICs and PLDs. The system has confirmed the validity and hardware compatibility of the system architecture. We are currently building a size-10 QAP system with the dedicated SI chaotic neuron ICs. The results from the system will be presented at the conference.

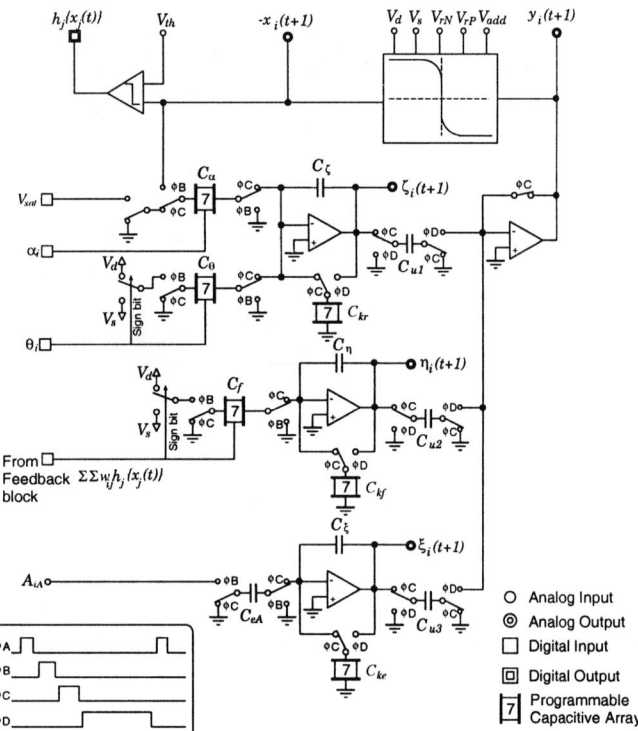

Fig. 4. SC chaos neuron circuit.

$$A = \begin{pmatrix} 0 & 15 & 8 & 9 \\ 15 & 0 & 11 & 8 \\ 8 & 11 & 0 & 11 \\ 9 & 8 & 11 & 0 \end{pmatrix}, \quad (11)$$

$$B = \begin{pmatrix} 0 & 1 & 8 & 4 \\ 1 & 0 & 13 & 9 \\ 8 & 13 & 0 & 5 \\ 4 & 9 & 5 & 0 \end{pmatrix}, \quad (12)$$

where A is the distance matrix and B is the flow matrix. An initial permutation has been randomly generated. 1000 iterations are done for one trial. The parameters in Table. 1 have been used.

Fig. 5 shows the time evolution of the object function value in (1). Because the problem size is 4, the object function can take 24 different values. These values are arranged in ascending order, and the order, 0 to 23, are assigned on the ordinates in Fig. 5. Namely, the best solution is expressed by 0, while the worst one is 23. The abscissas in Fig. 5 are iteration numbers. The time evolution of the neuron outputs are shown in Fig. 6. In the figure, the number of the neurons are assigned as $4i + j - 1$. These results illustrate the chaotic search dynamics of the system.

We have conducted many experiments with different sets of system parameters. We do not have enough space in this paper to show the results from these experiments, however, the

REFERENCES

[1] M. Hasegawa, T. Ikeguchi and K. Aihara, "On the relation between chaotic neural network approach and tabu search approach for combinatorial optimization," Tech. Rep. of IEICE, NLP'97-49, pp. 73–80, 1997.
[2] M. Hasegawa, T. Ikeguchi and K. Aihara, "A new modern heuristic approach using chaotic dynamics for quadratic assignment problems," Tech. Rept. of IEICE, NLP'97-8, pp. 613-616, 1997.
[3] M. Hasegawa, T. Ikeguchi and K. Aihara, "A novel chaotic search for combinatorial optimization," in Proc. International Symposium on Nonlinear Theory and its Applications, pp. 613–616, 1997.
[4] M. Hasegawa, T. Ikeguchi, K. Aihara and K. Itoh, "A novel chaotic search for quadratic assignment problems," in European Journal of Operational Research, pp. 543–556, 2002.
[5] R. E. Burkard, S. E. Karisch and F. Rendl, "QAPLIB - A quadratic assignment problem library," available via world wide web to http://www.opt.math.tu-graz.ac.at/qaplib/.
[6] E. Taillard, "Robust taboo search for the quadratic assignment problems," Parallel Computing, pp. 443–445, 1991.
[7] K. Tanaka, Y. Horio and K. Aihara, "A modified algorithm for the quadratic assignment problem using chaotic-neuro-dynamics for VLSI implementation," in Proc. IJCNN'01, pp. 240–245, 2001.
[8] K. Aihara, T. Takebe and M. Toyoda, "Chaotic neural networks," Phys. Lett. A, vol. 144, pp. 333–340, 1990.
[9] R. Herra, K. Suyama and Y. Horio, "IC implementation of a switched-current chaotic neuron," IEICE Trans. Fundamental, vol. E82-A, no. 9, pp. 1776–1782, Sept. 1998.
[10] Y. Horio, K. Aihara,"Chaotic neuro-computer," in "Chaos in circuit and systems," G. Chen, and T. Ueta, eds, pp. 237–255, World Scientific, 2002.
[11] Y. Horio and K. Aihara, "Neuron-synapuse IC chip-set for large-scale chaotic neural networks," IEEE Trans. Neural Networks, 2003, to appear.
[12] E. Taillard, "Comparison of interactive searches of the quadratic assinment problem," Location Science, vol. 3, pp. 240–245, 2001.

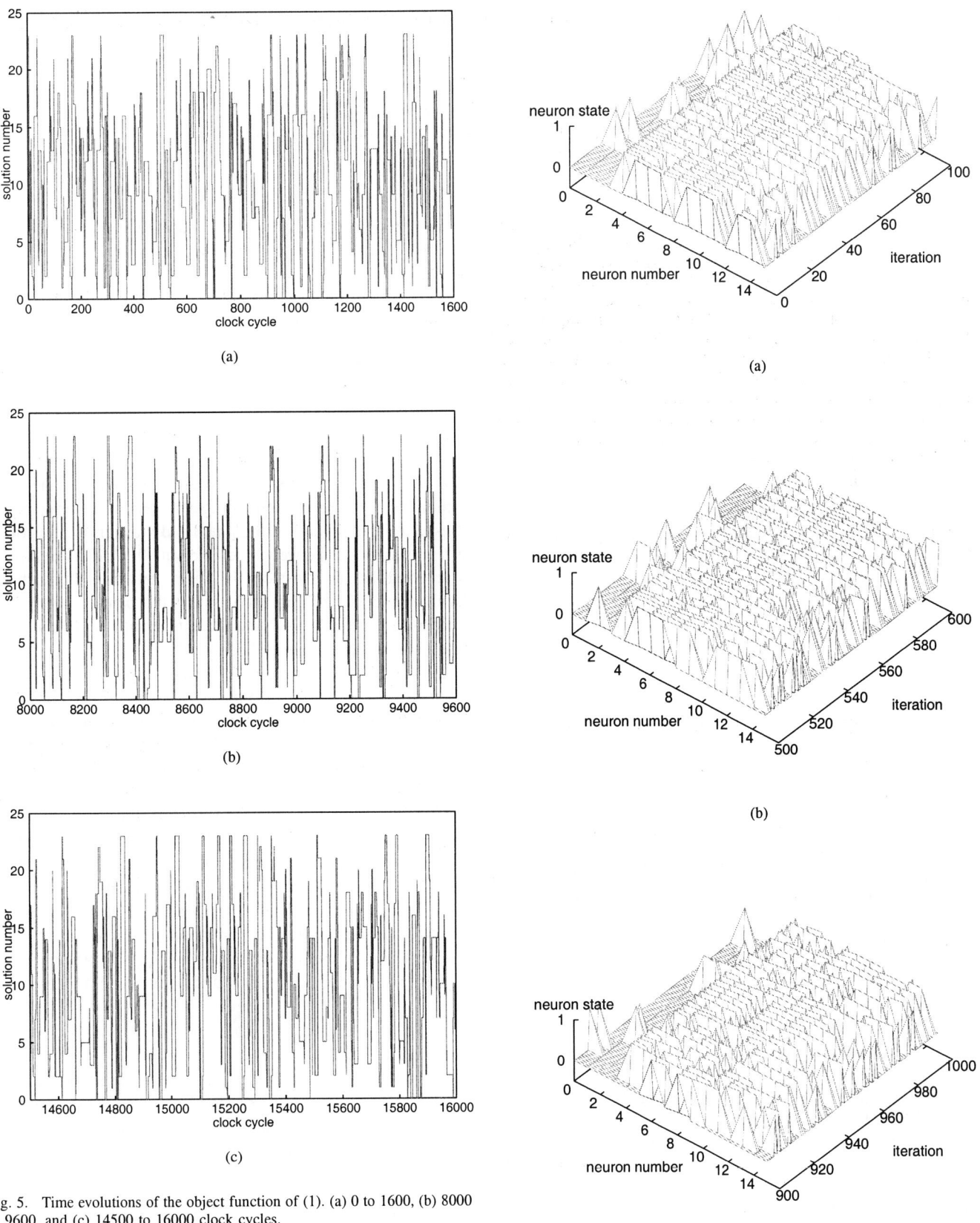

Fig. 5. Time evolutions of the object function of (1). (a) 0 to 1600, (b) 8000 to 9600, and (c) 14500 to 16000 clock cycles.

Fig. 6. Time evolutions of the neuron outputs. (a) 0 to 100, (b) 500 to 600, and (c) 900 to 1000 iterations.

Distribution Approximation, Combinatorial Optimization, and Lagrange-Barrier

Lei Xu
Department of Computer Science and Engineering
The Chinese University of Hong Kong, Shatin, Hong Kong
Email: lxu@cse.cuhk.edu.hk

Abstract—In this paper[1], typical analog combinatorial optimization approaches, such as Hopfield net, Hopfield-Lagrange net, Maximum entropy approach, Lagrange-Barrier approach, are systematically examined from the perspective of learning distribution. The minimization of a combinatorial cost is turned into a procedure of learning a simple distribution to approximate the Gibbs distribution induced from this cost such that both the distributions share a same global peak. From this new perspective, a new general guideline is obtained for developing analog combinatorial optimization approaches. Moreover, the Lagrange-Barrier iterative procedure proposed in Xu (1994, 1995a) is further elaborated with guaranteed convergence on a feasible solution that satisfies constraints.

I. INTRODUCTION

Many combinatorial optimization problems can be usually formulated as follows:

$$\min_V E_o(V), \quad V = \{v_{ij}\}_{i=1,j=1}^{N,M},$$
$$subject \ to$$
$$C_e^{col}: \sum_{i=1}^{N} v_{ij} = D_j^{col}, j = 1, \cdots, M,$$
$$C_e^{row}: \sum_{j=1}^{M} v_{ij} = D_i^{row}, i = 1, \cdots, N;$$
$$C_b: \quad v_{ij} \ takes \ either \ 0 \ or \ 1, \quad (1)$$

where $D_j^{col}, j = 1, \cdots, M$ and $D_i^{row}, i = 1, \cdots, N$ are given constants. Moreover, C_b can also be a general binary constraint that v_{ij} takes either a constant θ_0 or θ_1. Without losing generality, it is always easy to use a one-to-one mapping to normalize it back to the case of C_b given in eq.(1).

A typical example is the traveling salesman problem (TSP) with $N = M, D_i^{row} = 1, D_j^{col} = 1$ and

$$E_o(V) = \sum_{i=1}^{N} \sum_{j \ne i}^{N} \sum_{k=1}^{N} d_{ij} v_{i,k}(v_{j,k-1} + v_{j,k+1}) \quad (2)$$

where $d_{i,j}$ are known parameters. Other examples and a number of algorithms for the problem eq.(1) can be found in [9], [10], [13].

In the past decade, many efforts have been made in the literature of artificial neural networks on the problem eq.(1) of quadratic $E_o(V)$ by analog optimization since the work by [8]. Some detailed reviews of the efforts can be found in [2], [17], [1].

[1]The work described in this paper was fully supported by a grant from the Research Grant Council of the Hong Kong SAR (project No: CUHK4336/02E).

According to their features on dealing with the constraints C_e^{col}, C_e^{row} and C_b, these efforts can be roughly classified into three categories:

(1) The constraints C_e^{col} and C_e^{row} are transformed into a quadratic penalty term, e.g.,

$$G(V) = \sum_{j=1}^{M}(\sum_{i=1}^{N} v_{ij} - D_j^{col})^2 + \sum_{i=1}^{N}(\sum_{j=1}^{M} v_{ij} - D_i^{row})^2, \quad (3)$$

that can be merged into $E_o(V)$ via a weighted sum and results in a new quadratic $E(V)$ from which the connection weights of a classic Hopfield network [8] are obtained. The network minimizes $E(V)$ by implementing a system of dynamic equations in a parallel way, with C_b realized via sigmoid functions that constrain v_{ij} between the interval $[0,1]$. This approach is referred as the classical Hopfield network approach. A disadvantage of this approach is that the penalty strength is difficult to control, which often results in unfeasible solutions that violate the constraints C_e^{col}, C_e^{row}.

(2) The connection weights of the Hopfield network are obtained based on the original $E_o(V)$, with the constraint C_b still realized by sigmoid functions. Instead, the constraints C_e^{col}, C_e^{row} are considered as the Lagrange terms which add on biasing constants to the Hopfield network that minimizes $E_o(V)$ and the Lagrange terms under the fixed Lagrange coefficients. Moreover, another set of dynamic equations implement the maximization of $E_o(V)$ to settle the appropriate values of the Lagrange coefficients [14], [1]. The approach is referred as the Hopfield-Lagrange network approach.

(3) In a conference paper [17], a general cost $E_o(V)$, which can be either quadratic or nonquadratic, is considered and extended into a Lagrange-Barrier cost $E(V)$ by adding in the Lagrange terms for C_e^{col}, C_e^{row} and a barrier term

$$B(V) = \sum_{i,j} v_{ij} \ln v_{ij} \quad (4)$$

that constraints v_{ij} as an interior point between the interval $[0,1]$. Particularly, for a quadratic $E_o(V)$, this $E(V)$ becomes the cost used in [20] and the cost used under the name of maximum entropy approach [5], [7], [6]. Moreover, in [18] the barrier term

$$B(V) = \sum_{i,j}[v_{ij} \ln v_{ij} + (1 - v_{ij}) \ln(1 - v_{ij})] \quad (5)$$

has been studied. Also, the link has been set up between the leaking energy term in the Hopfield network and a family of barriers that includes eq.(4) and eq.(5), and thus we know that the above Hopfield-Lagrange network is one specific way for minimizing a Lagrange-Barrier cost. Furthermore, Xu in [17], [18] also proposed a new general approach for minimizing the Lagrange-Barrier cost. It consists of iterative updating equations obtained from $\frac{\partial E(V)}{\partial v_{ij}} = 0$, that updates v_{ij} with a particular emphasize on the satisfaction of the constraints C_e^{col}, C_e^{row}. This satisfaction is refined immediately after each updating on v_{ij}, through updating the Lagrange coefficients by an inner iterative loop. The approach is referred as the Lagrange-Transformation or the Lagrange-Barrier approach.

Though having the favorable parallel implementable feature, almost all the neural network motivated approaches share one unfavorable feature that these intuitive approaches have not been satisfactorily explained from a theoretical point of view. Basically, there is neither theory to support naturally the intuitive concept and to guarantee the convergence of a proposed algorithm, nor theory to relate this concept to computational complexity as traditionally developed in the discrete settings.

This paper aims at tackling partly these problems. The above neural network motivated approaches are systematically examined from a new perspective. The deterministic minimization of $E_o(V)$ is turned into a sequence of finding a simple distribution to approximate the Gibbs probabilistic distribution induced from $E_o(V)$ under the related constraints, such that the Gibbs distribution and the approximate distribution share a same global peak. In Sec. II, the basic idea of this distribution estimation theory is proposed. Particularly, it is shown that two special cases not only relate to the classical Metroplois sampling technique [12] but also interpret and justify the maximum entropy approach and the Lagrange-Barrier approach, as well as the Hopfield-Lagrange network via a link previously built [18]. In Sec.III, we further elaborate the Lagrange-Barrier iterative procedure proposed in [17], [18], with a guaranteed convergence on a feasible solution that satisfies constraints. Two simulation examples are demonstrated to illustrate the effectiveness of the iterative procedure. Finally, concluding remarks are given in Sec.IV.

II. Distribution Approximation and Optimization

A. The Basic Idea

The problem of finding a global minimization solution of $E_o(V)$ under a set of constraints is equivalent to the problem of finding a global peak of the following Gibbs distribution:

$$p(V) = \frac{e^{-\frac{1}{\beta}E_o(V)}}{Z_\beta}, \quad Z_\beta = \sum_V e^{-\frac{1}{\beta}E_o(V)}, \quad (6)$$

subject to the constraints, since $\max_V p(V)$ is equivalent to $\max_V \ln p(V)$ or $\min_V E_o(V)$.

Usually this $p(V)$ has many local maximums, it is difficult to the peak V_p. To avoid this difficult, we propose to use a simple distribution $q(V)$ to approximate $p(V)$ on a domain D_v such that the global peak of $q(V)$ is easy to find and that $p(V)$ and $q(V)$ share the same peak $V_p \in D_v$.

To do so, we adopt the following two types of measures for implementing this approximation:

$$Type\ (a): \quad \min_q KL(p,q),$$
$$KL(p,q) = \sum_{V \in D_v} p(V) \ln \frac{p(V)}{q(V)},$$
$$Type\ (b): \quad \min_p KL(q,p),$$
$$KL(q,p) = \sum_{V \in D_v} q(V) \ln \frac{q(V)}{p(V)}. \quad (7)$$

Given a D_v that contains V_p, the smaller the D_v is, the easier for a simple $q(V)$ to approximate $p(V)$, and thus the more likely $q(V)$ and $p(V)$ share a same global peak. This D_v is considered via the following support of $p(V)$:

$$D_\varepsilon(\beta) = \{V : p(V,\beta) > \varepsilon, \ a\ small\ constant\ \varepsilon > 0.\} \quad (8)$$

under the control of the parameter β. For a sequence $\beta_0 > \beta_1, \cdots > \beta_t$, we have $D_\varepsilon(\beta_t) \subset, \cdots, D_\varepsilon(\beta_1) \subset D_\varepsilon(\beta_0)$ that keep to contain the global minimization solution of $E_o(V)$, since the equivalence of $\max_V p(V)$ to $\min_V E_o(V)$ is irrelevant to β.

Therefore, it follows from eq.(7) that we can find a sequence $q_0(V), q_1(V), \cdots, q_t(V)$ that approximates $p(V)$ on the shrinking domain $D_\varepsilon(\beta)$. For a large β_t, $p(V)$ has a large support and thus $q(V)$ adapts the overall configuration of $p(V)$ in a big domain $D_\varepsilon(\beta)$. As β_t reduces, $q_t(V)$ becomes more and more concentrating on adapting the detailed configuration of $p(V)$ around the global peak solution $V_p \in D_\varepsilon$. As long as β_0 is large enough and β reduces slowly enough towards to zero, we can finally find the global minimization solution of $E_o(V)$. Strictly speaking, whether the global solution can be found relates to the selection of the distribution form of $q(V)$, and the selection of β_0, the reducing rate of β as well as the value of β at which the searching procedure stops.

B. Type (a) in Two Typical Cases

For the problem eq.(1), we consider $q(V)$ in the following special cases

$$q_1(V) = Z_1^{-1} \prod_{i,j} e^{v_{ij} \ln q_{ij}}, \quad 0 \leq q_{ij} \leq \infty,$$
$$Z_1 = \sum_{i,j} \prod_{i,j} e^{v_{ij} \ln q_{ij}},$$
$$q_2(V) = \prod_{i,j} q_{ij}^{v_{ij}}(1-q_{ij})^{v_{ij}}, \quad 0 \leq q_{ij} \leq 1; \quad (9)$$

and from the constraints in eq.(1) we have

$$C_e^{col}: \quad \sum_{i=1}^{N} <v_{ij}> = D_j^{col}, j=1,\cdots,M,$$
$$C_e^{row}: \quad \sum_{j=1}^{M} <v_{ij}> = D_i^{row}, i=1,\cdots,N;$$
$$<v_{ij}> = \begin{cases} q_{ij}\frac{Z_{ij}}{Z_1}, & \text{for } q_1(V), \\ q_{ij}, & \text{for } q_2(V), \end{cases}$$
$$Z_{ij} = \sum_{k \neq i, l \neq j} \prod_{k,l} e^{v_{kl} \ln q_{kl}}; \quad (10)$$

where $<x>$ denotes the expectation of the random variable x. When N, M are large, we have $Z_{ij} \approx Z_1$, and we also have $<v_{ij}> \approx q_{ij}$ also for the case of $q_1(V)$.

If not considering the constraints C_e^{col}, C_e^{row}, the global peak solution of $q(V)$ by eq.(9) is simply estimated by

$$v_{ij} = \begin{cases} 1, & \text{if } q_{ij} > 0.5, \\ 0, & \text{otherwise}. \end{cases} \quad (11)$$

Moreover, we can either consider the constraints C_e^{col} and get the global peak solution by

$$v_{ij} = \begin{cases} 1, & \text{if } j = arg\max_k q_{ik}, \\ 0, & \text{otherwise}. \end{cases} \quad (12)$$

or we can similarly consider the constraints C_e^{row}.

Next, we consider the problem of estimating q_{ij}, according to the two types of approximations given in eq.(7).

From eq.(7), Type (a) approximation is equivalent to the minimization of

$$H_0(\{q_{ij}\}) = -\sum_{V \in D_v} p(V) \ln q(V)$$
$$= \begin{cases} -\sum_{ij} p_{ij} \ln q_{ij}, & q_1(V), \\ -\sum_{ij}[p_{ij} \ln q_{ij} + (1-p_{ij}) \ln(1-q_{ij})], & q_2(V); \end{cases}$$
$$p_{ij} = \sum_V v_{ij} p(V),$$

under the constraints C_e^{col}, C_e^{row} given in eq.(10). Considering Lagrange approach, we have

$$H(\{q_{ij}\}) = H_0(\{q_{ij}\}) + \sum_{j=1}^M \lambda_j^{col}[\sum_{i=1}^N q_{ij} - D_j^{col}]$$
$$+ \sum_{i=1}^N \lambda_i^{row}[\sum_{j=1}^M q_{ij} - D_i^{row}], \quad (13)$$
$$\frac{\partial H(V)}{\partial q_{ij}} = \begin{cases} -\frac{p_{ij}}{q_{ij}} + \lambda_j^{col} + \lambda_i^{row}, & \text{for } q_1(V), \\ -\frac{p_{ij}}{q_{ij}} + \frac{1-p_{ij}}{1-q_{ij}} + \lambda_j^{col} + \lambda_i^{row}, & \text{for } q_2(V). \end{cases}$$

We have two methods for solving this problem:

(1) The Method I. If we have already get the mean field p_{ij} in eq.(13) under the Gibbs distribution $p(V)$, it follows from $\frac{\partial H(\{q_{ij}\})}{\partial q_{ij}} = 0$ that

$$q_{ij} = \begin{cases} \frac{p_{ij}}{\lambda_j^{col} + \lambda_i^{row}}, & \text{for } q_1(V), \\ a\ root\ of\ the\ equation\ below, & \text{for } q_2(V). \end{cases}$$
$$(\lambda_j^{col} + \lambda_i^{row})q_{ij}^2 - (1 + \lambda_j^{col} + \lambda_i^{row})q_{ij} + p_{ij} = 0,$$
$$0 \leq q_{ij}^r \leq 1 \quad (14)$$

By putting it into the constraints C_e^{col} and C_e^{row} given by eq.(10), we update the Lagrange coefficients $\lambda_j^{col}, \lambda_i^{row}, j = 1, \cdots, M, i = 1, \cdots, N$ to satisfy :

$$C_e^{col}: \sum_{i=1}^N q_{ij} = D_j^{col}, \quad C_e^{row}: \sum_{j=1}^M q_{ij} = D_i^{row}. \quad (15)$$

Thus, we encounter a problem of solving $N + M$ nonlinear equations. Particularly, for the case of $q_1(V)$ with $D_j^{col} = D_i^{row} = 1$, we use the following iterative algorithm to solve it:

$$(\lambda_i^{row})^{new} = (\lambda_i^{row})^{old} \sum_{j=1}^M q_{ij}^e(\{(\lambda_i^{row})^{old}, (\lambda_j^{col})^{old}\}),$$
$$(\lambda_j^{col})^{new} = (\lambda_j^{col})^{old} \sum_{i=1}^N q_{ij}^e(\{(\lambda_i^{row})^{old}, (\lambda_j^{col})^{old}\}),$$
$$i = 1, \cdots, N, j = 1, \cdots, M, \quad (16)$$

where $q_{ij}^e(\{(\lambda_i^{row})^{old}, (\lambda_j^{col})^{old}\})$ denotes q_{ij} by eq.(14) for the case of $q_1(V)$.

The remaining problem is to get the mean field p_{ij} of the Gibbs distribution $p(V)$, which can be made by a well known classical stochastic approximation approach called Metroplois sampling technique [12]. That is, we let β to start from a value large enough and then reduces to a value low enough. Under each given β, the Metroplois sampling is used to get eq.(13) at each β. Finally, at the lowest β value we can obtain a solution by eq.(14) and eq.(16). In fact, this procedure can be regarded as a combination of the Lagrange approach and a variant of the widely studied simulated annealing technique [11].

(2) The Method II. Even using the Metroplois sampling technique, it still needs quite a long sampling period to get a stationary process that can be used for estimating p_{ij}, because the Gibbs distribution $p(V)$ in eq.(6) is usually complicated with many local minimums. Alternatively, we get a set of samples $V_t = \{v_{ij}^{(t)}\}, t = 1, \cdots, N_t$ from its approximation $q(V)$, and then estimate

$$p_{ij} = \sum_{t=1}^{N_t} v_{ij}^{(t)} p(V_t) / q(V_t), \quad (17)$$

which is much easier to compute. Next, we use the same approach given in the above eq.(14) and eq.(16) to get a new set of estimates on q_{ij} for a new estimate $q(V)$, based on which we can again get new estimates on p_{ij} by eq.(17). The process can be iterated until it converges.

C. Type (b) in Two Typical Cases

We further consider Type (b) approximation in eq.(7). From eq.(9), we have

(a) for $q_1(V)$ $\sum_V q(V) \ln q(V) = -\ln Z_1 +$
$$\sum_{ij} q_{ij} \frac{Z_{ij}}{Z_1} \ln q_{ij} \approx -\ln Z_1 + \sum_{ij} q_{ij} \ln q_{ij};$$

(b) for $q_2(V)$, $\sum_V q(V) \ln q(V) =$
$$\sum_{ij}[q_{ij} \ln q_{ij} + (1-q_{ij}) \ln(1-q_{ij})]. \quad (18)$$

Moreover, we consider the cases that satisfy the condition:

$E_o(V)$ *is quadratic with respect to* V *and* $\frac{\partial^2 E_o(V)}{\partial^2 v_{ij}} = 0$.
$\quad (19)$

which is satisfied by the TSP problem eq.(2) and also by a number of concave costs [9].

In these cases, it follows from eq.(9) that $<\sum_{k\neq i, l\neq j} v_{ij} v_{kl} w_{ijkl}> = \sum_{k\neq i, l\neq j} <v_{ij}><v_{kl}> w_{ijkl}$ which is true due to the independence in $q_2(V)$ and can be regarded as being true approximately for $q_1(V)$. Thus, $-\sum_V q(V)\ln p(V)$ becomes

$$\ln Z + \frac{1}{\beta}\sum_V q(V)E_o(V) = \ln Z +$$
$$\begin{cases} \frac{1}{\beta}E_o(\{q_{ij}\})\frac{Z_{ij}}{Z_1} \approx \frac{1}{\beta}E_o(\{q_{ij}\}), & \text{for } q_1(V), \\ \frac{1}{\beta}E_o(\{q_{ij}\}), & \text{for } q_2(V). \end{cases} \quad (20)$$

After ignoring the irrelevant terms $\ln Z_1, \ln Z$ and putting eq.(18) and eq.(20) together, we get that Type (b) approximation is equivalent to

$$\min_{q_{ij}} E(\{q_{ij}\}), \; subject \; to \; eq.(10),$$
$$E(\{q_{ij}\}) = \frac{1}{\beta}E_o(\{q_{ij}\}) + \quad (21)$$
$$\begin{cases} \sum_{ij} q_{ij}\ln q_{ij}, & \text{for } q_1(V), \\ \sum_{ij}[q_{ij}\ln q_{ij} + (1-q_{ij})\ln(1-q_{ij})], & \text{for } q_2(V). \end{cases}$$

The case for $q_1(V)$ interprets the Lagrange-Barrier approach with the barrier eq.(4) discussed under the category (3) in Sec.I. In fact, it justifies the intuitive treatment of simply regarding the discrete v_{ij} as an analog variable between the interval $[0,1]$, previously used in [17] under the name of Lagrange-Transform (LT) approach, in [20] under the name of statistical physics, and in [7], [5], [6] under the name of maximum entropy approach.

From this new perspective, we do not regard the analog variables as the direct targets that we want to optimize. These analog variables are the parameters of the simple distribution that we use to approximate the Gibbs distribution induced from the cost $E_o(V)$ of the discrete variables. Instead, the discrete solution will be recovered from these analog parameters according to one of eq.(11) and eq.(12).

Similarly, the case for $q_2(V)$ interprets and justifies the Lagrange-Barrier approach with the barrier eq.(5), also discussed under the category (3) in Sec.I. In [18], this barrier is intuitively argued to be better than the barrier eq.(4) because it gives a U-shape curve. Here, this intuitive preference can also be justified from eq.(10), by noticing that there is an approximation $Z_{ij} \approx Z_1$ used for the case $q_1(V)$ during the transformation from the discrete random variable v_{ij} into the analog parameter q_{ij}, but no approximation for the case $q_2(V)$.

Moreover, the barriers eq.(4) and eq.(5) are respectively the special cases (a) $S(v_{ij}) = v_{ij}$ and (b) $S(v_{ij}) = v_{ij}/(1-v_{ij})$ of a family of barrier functions as follows [18]:

$$B(v_{ij}) = \int_0^{v_{ij}} \ln S(v_{ij}) dv_{ij}, \; S(0)=0, S(1)=+\infty,$$
$$S(v) \; monotonously \; increases \; within \; (0,1), \quad (22)$$

where $g^{-1}(v) = \ln S(v)$ has a shape similar to $tg(v)$, and thus its inverse $g(v)$ has a shape similar to $tg^{-1}(v)$. That is, $g(v)$ is a type of sigmoid function. In other words, such a barrier term has a form of

$$\sum_{i=1}^N \sum_{j=1}^M B(v_{ij}) = \beta \sum_{i=1}^N \sum_{j=1}^M \int_0^{v_{ij}} g^{-1}(v_{ij}) dv_{ij}, \quad (23)$$

which is exactly the leaking energy term in the Hopfield network [8]. In other words, imposing a barrier term of the family eq.(22) is equivalent to minimizing the leaking energy in the classical Hopfield network. This link was first discovered in [18]. With this link, we can see that the Hopfield-Lagrange network studied by [14], [1] can also be interpreted as one specific implementation for minimizing $E(\{q_{ij}\})$ in eq.(21), though whether this implementation gives a converged solution remains an open question.

Being different from the specific implementation by the Hopfield-Lagrange network and also from the algorithms in [20], [7], [5], [6], a general iterative procedure is proposed firstly in [17] and then refined in [18] for minimizing $E(\{q_{ij}\})$ in eq.(21), with a guaranteed convergence on a feasible solution that satisfies constraints, as will be further recommended in Sec.III.

III. LAGRANGE-BARRIER ITERATIVE PROCEDURE

A. Lagrange-Barrier Iterative Procedure

We consider the Lagrange-Barrier costs:

$$E(\{q_{ij}\}) = \frac{1}{\beta}E_o(\{q_{ij}\}) + \sum_{j=1}^M \lambda_j^{col}[\sum_{i=1}^N q_{ij} - D_j^{col}]$$
$$+ B(q_{ij}) + \sum_{i=1}^N \lambda_i^{row}[\sum_{j=1}^M q_{ij} - D_i^{row}], \; B(q_{ij}) =$$
$$\begin{cases} \sum_{ij} q_{ij}\ln q_{ij}, & q_1(V), \\ \sum_{ij}[q_{ij}\ln q_{ij} + (1-q_{ij})\ln(1-q_{ij})], & q_2(V). \end{cases} \quad (24)$$

For the case of $q_1(V)$, by following the methods used in [17], [18], from

$$\frac{\partial E(\{q_{ij}\})}{\partial q_{ij}} = \frac{1}{\beta}\frac{\partial E_o(\{q_{ij}\})}{\partial q_{ij}} + \lambda_j^{col} + \lambda_i^{row} + 1 + \ln q_{ij} = 0,$$

we get

$$q_{ij}^e = \frac{1}{a_i b_j exp(\frac{1}{\beta}\frac{\partial E_o(\{q_{ij}\})}{\partial q_{ij}})}, \quad (25)$$
$$a_i = exp(\lambda_i^{row} + 0.5), \; b_j = exp(\lambda_j^{col} + 0.5).$$

Similarly, for the case of $q_2(V)$, from

$$\frac{\partial E(\{q_{ij}\})}{\partial q_{ij}} = \frac{1}{\beta}\frac{\partial E_o(\{q_{ij}\})}{\partial q_{ij}}$$
$$+ \lambda_j^{col} + \lambda_i^{row} + \ln\frac{q_{ij}}{1-q_{ij}} = 0,$$
$$\frac{\partial E(\{q_{ij}\})}{\partial q_{ij}} = \frac{1}{\beta}\frac{\partial E_o(\{q_{ij}\})}{\partial q_{ij}}$$
$$+ \lambda_j^{col} + \lambda_i^{row} - \ln(q_{ij}^{-1} - 1) = 0,$$

we get

$$q_{ij}^e = \frac{1}{1 + a_i b_j exp(\frac{1}{\beta}\frac{\partial E_o(\{q_{ij}\})}{\partial q_{ij}})},$$

$$a_i = exp(\lambda_i^{row}), \quad b_j = exp(\lambda_j^{col}). \quad (26)$$

Under the condition eq.(19), $\frac{\partial E_o(\{q_{ij}\})}{\partial q_{ij}}$ is irrelevant to q_{ij} and $\frac{\partial^2 E(\{q_{ij}\})}{\partial^2 q_{ij}} > 0$. Conditioning on that other variables are fixed at their old values, $E(\{q_{ij}\})$ is minimized at $q_{ij} = q_{ij}^e$ given by eq.(25) or eq.(26). Therefore, we can update q_{ij} in either of the following two manners:

(a) *The sequential manner* That is, with other variables fixed, we update q_{ij} one by one with

$$q_{ij}^{new} = q_{ij}^e, \quad (27)$$

which will reduce $E(\{q_{ij}\})$ monotonically, as discussed as above.

(b) *The parallel manner* To the current values $\{q_{ij}^{old}\}$, each $q_{ij}^e - q_{ij}^{old}$ is obviously a descent direction of $E(\{q_{ij}\})$. Thus, with a stepsize $\eta > 0$ small enough, we can move all $\{q_{ij}\}$ in parallel along the direction $\{q_{ij}^e - q_{ij}^{old}\}$ that is

$$q_{ij}^{new} = q_{ij}^{old} + \eta(q_{ij}^e - q_{ij}^{old}), \quad (28)$$

which will also reduce $E(\{q_{ij}\})$ monotonically.

From eq.(27) and eq.(28), we can see that the constraints C_e^{col}, C_e^{row} given by eq.(10) are satisfied by q_{ij}^{new} as long as they are satisfied by both q_{ij}^{old} and q_{ij}^e. Therefore, what we need to do is to enforce that C_e^{col}, C_e^{row} are satisfied by q_{ij}^e through updating the Lagrange coefficients $a_i, b_j, j = 1, \cdots, M, i = 1, \cdots, N$, as follows:

$$C_e^{col}: \sum_{i=1}^{N} q_{ij}^e = D_j^{col}, \quad C_e^{row}: \sum_{j=1}^{M} q_{ij}^e = D_i^{row}. \quad (29)$$

That is, we encounter a problem of solving $N+M$ nonlinear equations of $a_i, b_j, j = 1, \cdots, M, i = 1, \cdots, N$, or equivalently a problem of finding the global minimum zero of the penalty

$$P(\{q_{ij}\}) = \sum_{j=1}^{M}(\sum_{i=1}^{N} q_{ij}^e - D_j^{col})^2 + \sum_{i=1}^{N}(\sum_{j=1}^{M} q_{ij}^e - D_i^{row})^2. \quad (30)$$

To solve it, we need another inner iteration loop, which is denoted as ENFORCING-LAGRANGE.

In a summary, a problem of eq.(1) that satisfies the condition eq.(19) can be solved by the following *Lagrange-Barrier Iterative Procedure*:

Step 0: Initialize $\{q_{ij}\}$ such that they satisfy all
the constraints.
Step 1: Update q_{ij}^{old} into q_{ij}^{new}
(a) Either sequentially $q_{ij}^{new} = q_{ij}^e$ by using
eq.(25) for the case of $q_1(V)$ or eq.(26)
for the case $q_2(V)$;
(b) Or in parallel by eq.(28).
Step 2: Update $a_i, b_j, j = 1, \cdots, M, i = 1, \cdots, N$ by
an ENFORCING-LAGRANGE loop to ensure
the satisfaction of eq.(29).
Step 3: Check whether the procedure is converged, if yes,
stop; otherwise, go to Step 1.

Since Step 1 reduces $E(\{q_{ij}\})$ monotonically, as long as the ENFORCING-LAGRANGE loop in Step 2 can ensure the satisfaction of eq.(29), the whole procedure will reduce $E(\{q_{ij}\})$ monotonically with the constraints C_e^{col}, C_e^{row} satisfied, until it converges to a local minimum of $E(\{q_{ij}\})$.

However, there remain two important problems. First, the satisfaction of the condition eq.(19) is required. Second, an effective algorithm for the ENFORCING-LAGRANGE loop needs to be designed. Though a direct use of the existing techniques in literature for solving nonlinear equations eq.(29) or for minimizing eq.(30) can be considered, we highly expect a simple iterative procedure that can be implemented in a parallel way.

Both the two problems have been solved in [3], [4]. First, the direction by $\{q_{ij}^e - q_{ij}^{old}\}$ is also proved to be a descent direction of $E(\{q_{ij}\})$ for a general $E_0(\{q_{ij}\})$ that the condition eq.(19) may not be satisfied, and thus the above Step 1(b) applies to any general cases. Second, a surprisingly simple and parallel implementable algorithm for the ENFORCING-LAGRANGE loop has been proposed as follows:

$$a_i^{new} = a_i^{old} + \mu a_i^{old}(\sum_{j=1}^{M} q_{ij}^e(\{a_i^{old}, b_j^{old}\}) - D_i^{row}),$$
$$b_j^{new} = b_j^{old} + \mu b_j^{old}(\sum_{i=1}^{N} q_{ij}^e(\{a_i^{old}, b_j^{old}\}) - D_j^{col}),$$
$$i = 1, \cdots, N, \quad j = 1, \cdots, M, \quad (31)$$

where $q_{ij}^e(\{a_i^{old}, b_j^{old}\})$ denotes q_{ij}^e by eq.(25) for the case of $q_1(V)$ or eq.(26) for the case $q_2(V)$ at $\{a_i^{old}, b_j^{old}\}$. Moreover, it has been also mathematically proved in [3], [4] that the iterative algorithm eq.(31) guarantees to converge a solution of nonlinear equations eq.(29).

B. Simulation Examples

A large number of simulation examples on TSP instances have been provided in [3] on the cost $E(\{q_{ij}\})$ in eq.(21) for the case $q_1(V)$ and in [4] on the cost $E(\{q_{ij}\})$ in eq.(21) for the case $q_2(V)$, through the Lagrange-Barrier Iterative Procedure that consists of Step 1(b) and Step 2 given by eq.(31). Here, we only demonstrate the results on two TSP instances obtained from the well-known TSPLIB on WWW, in order to illustrate the effectiveness of the iterative procedure and to further confirm our preference on the cost $E(\{q_{ij}\})$ for the case p_2 over that for the case p_1 with the reason discussed in Sec.II.B.

In the simulations, the parameter β starts at 100 and is reduced by a factor of $\frac{8}{10}$ gradually, μ in eq.(31) is taken to be one, and η in eq.(28) is obtained with a line search. The iteration terminates as soon as a feasible solution is generated.

The first example is made by an instance (bays29.tsp) of 29 cities. The iterative procedures are made both on the cost $E(\{q_{ij}\})$ in eq.(21) for the case $q_1(V)$ and the case $q_2(V)$, resulting a same near optimal tour. The ratio of the distance of the near optimal tour to that of an optimal tour is equal to 1.02, as shown in Fig. 1. However, the convergence on the cost $E(\{q_{ij}\})$ for the case $q_1(V)$ is much slower than on that for the case $q_2(V)$, by 1778 iterations in comparison with 344 iterations. Thus, it confirmed our preference discussed in Sec.II.B. Here, one iteration consists of one circle from Step 1 to Step 3.

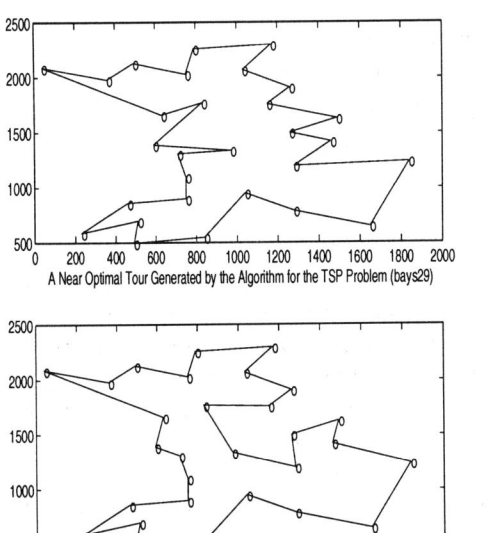

Fig. 1 Near Optimal Tour versus Optimal Tour (bays29.tsp)

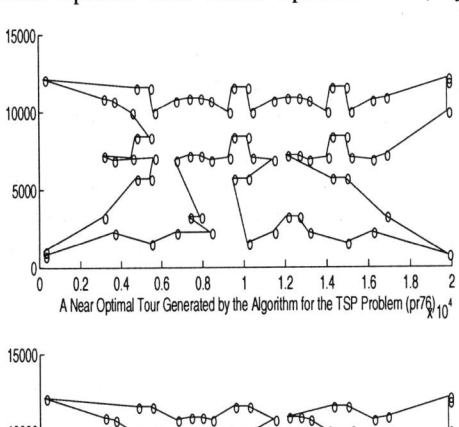

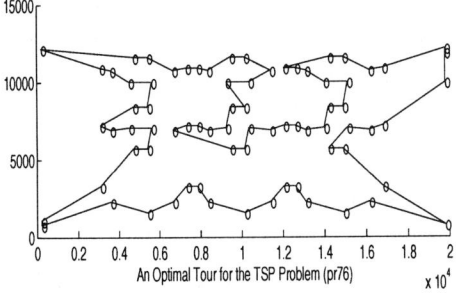

Fig. 2 Near Optimal Tour versus Optimal Tour (pr76.tsp)

The second example is made by an instance (pr76.tsp) of 76 cities. The iterative procedure is made on the cost $E(\{q_{ij}\})$ in eq.(21) for the case $q_2(V)$ only, resulting in a near optimal tour within 509 iterations. The ratio of the distance of the near optimal tour to that of an optimal tour is equal to 1.05, as shown in Fig.2.

IV. CONCLUDING REMARKS

The minimization of a combinatorial cost is turned into a process of learning a simple distribution to approximate the Gibbs distribution induced from this cost such that the Gibbs distribution and the resulted approximation distribution give a same global solution. From this new perspective, the treatment of simply regarding a binary v_{ij} as an analog variable, intuitively used in all the existing analog optimization approaches, can be interpreted and justified. Particularly, the Lagrange-Barrier iterative procedure is recommended because it always gives a guaranteed convergence on a feasible solution that satisfies constraints. Moreover, it has been shown via experiments in [3], [4] that this Lagrange-Barrier iterative procedure is significantly superior to the modified soft-assign algorithm [15], [16] in computational time, with the quality of solutions being similarly or even slightly better.

REFERENCES

[1] J. van den Berg (1996), "Neural Relaxation Dynamics", PhD Thesis, Erasmus University of Rotterdam, The Netherlands.

[2] A. Cichocki and R. Unbehauen (1993) *Neural Networks for Optimization and Signal processing*, John Wiley & Sons, New York.

[3] C. Dang and L. Xu, (2001a), "A globally convergent Lagrange and barrier function iterative algorithm for the traveling salesman problem", *Neural Networks*, Vol.14, No.2, pp217-230, 2001.

[4] C. Dang and L. Xu (2001b), "A Lagrange Multiplier and Hopfield-Type Barrier Function Method for the Traveling Salesman Problem", *Neural Computation*, Vol. 14 , No. 2 , pp303 - 324 .

[5] J. Eriksson (1980), "A note on solution of large sparse maximum entropy problems with linear equality constraints", *Mathematical Programming 18*, 146-154.

[6] S. Erlander (1981), "Entropy in linear programs", *Mathematical Programming 21*, 137-151.

[7] S. C. Fang and H.-S. J. Tsao (1995), "Linearly-constrained entropy maximization problem with quadratic cost and its applications to transportation planning problems", *Transportation Science 29*, 353-365.

[8] J. J. Hopfield and D. W. Tank (1985), "Neural computation of decisions in optimization problems", *Biological Cybernetics 52*, 141-152.

[9] R. Horst and P. M. Pardalos (1995), *Handbook of Global Optimization, Nonconvex Optimization and its Applications 2*, Kluwer Academic Publishers.

[10] B. Kalantari and J. B. Rosen (1987), " An algorithm for global minimization of linearly constrained concave quadratic functions", *Mathematics of Operations Research 12*, 544-561.

[11] S.Kirkpatrick, C.G.Gelatt Jr., and M.P. Vecchi (1983), "Optimization by Simulated Annealing", *Science 220*, pp671-680.

[12] N. Metroplois, et al, (1953), "Equation of State Calculations for fast Computing machines", *Journal of Chemical Physics 21*, 1087-1092.

[13] P. M. Pardalos and J. B. Rosen (1987). "Constrained Global Optimization: Algorithms and Applications", *Lecture Notes in Computer Science 268*, Springer-Varlag.

[14] E. Wacholder, J. Han and R. C. Mann (1989). "A neural network algorithm for the traveling salesman problem", *Biological Cybernetics 61*, 11-19.

[15] Rangarajan, A., Gold, S., & Mjolsness, E. (1996). "A novel optimizing network architecture with applications". *Neural Computation, 8*, 1041-1060.

[16] Rangarajan, A., Yuille, A., & Mjolsness, E. (1999). "Convergence properties of the softassign quadratic assignment algorithm", *Neural Computation, 11*, 1455- 1474.

[17] L. Xu (1994), "Combinatorial optimization neural nets based on a hybrid of Lagrange and transformation approaches", *Proc. of World Congress on Neural Networks*, San Diego, 399-404.

[18] L. Xu (1995a). "On the hybrid LT combinatorial optimization: new U-shape barrier, sigmoid activation, least leaking energy and maximum entropy", *Proc. of Intl. Conf. on Neural Information Processing (ICONIP'95)*, Beijing, 309-312.

[19] L. Xu. (1995b), "YING-YANG Machine: a Bayesian-Kullback scheme for unified learnings and new results on vector quantization", *Proc. of Intl. Conf. on Neural Information Processing (ICONIP'95)*, 977-988.

[20] A. L. Yuille & J. J. Kosowsky (1994), "Statistical physics algorithms that converge", *Neural Computation 6*, 341-356.

Synthesis of a k-winners-take-all neural network using linear programming with bounded variables

L. V. Ferreira, E. Kaszkurewicz and A. Bhaya

Department of Electrical Engineering, NACAD–COPPE/Federal University of Rio de Janeiro
P.O Box 68504, 21945-970, Rio de Janeiro, RJ, BRAZIL
E-mail: {lvalente,eugenius}@coep.ufrj.br, amit@nacad.ufrj.br

Abstract— A k-winners-take-all (KWTA) problem is formulated as a linear programming (LP) problem with bounded variables. The solution set of the LP problem determines the winners. The LP problem is converted into an unconstrained optimization problem with two exact penalty functions, that is solved by using a gradient descent method implemented as a neural network. Theoretical results ensuring the convergence to the correct solution are provided.

I. Introduction

The k-winners-take-all problem is that of determining the k largest components of a given vector $\mathbf{c} \in \mathbb{R}^n$. This problem appears in competitive network learning and pattern recognition. Many networks have been proposed to solve this problem, and these networks are referred as KWTA networks.

To solve this problem we propose a KWTA neural network designed on the basis of an LP problem with bounded variables, using the penalty function method. A nonsmooth computational energy function is associated to this LP problem. This converts the original LP problem into an unconstrained nonlinear optimization problem. This new optimization problem is solved by a gradient system, which represents the KWTA neural network that, in turn, minimizes the given energy function.

Convergence conditions for this system are obtained through an analysis that uses nonsmooth diagonal type Lyapunov functions and a gradient system represented in Persidskii type form [1], [2].

This formulation is inspired partially by the one presented by Urahama & Nagao [3], where this problem is formulated as an integer programming problem, which is mapped into a nonlinear programming problem, and solved by minimizing an associated Lagrangian function.

We modify the latter approach as follows. Instead of using the integer programming approach proposed in [3], we relax it to a LP problem with variables confined to the interval $[0, 1]$. An exact penalty method applied to the relaxed LP problem produces a so called computational energy function. The latter is minimized using a gradient (descent) system. Compared with the approach proposed in [3], the approach using linear programming has advantages. The gradient of the energy function provided by the penalty method is easily derived, leading to the development of simple convergence conditions. In addition, the corresponding neural circuit is very simple and can be implemented using resistors, amplifiers and switches. As suggested in [4], the transient time of this network can be adjusted by introducing a time scale factor in the model, making the proposed network suitable for real time operation. Moreover, simulation examples indicate that the network obtained presents better separability resolution than the circuit proposed in [3].

The penalty functions used are exact, thus ensuring that there exist finite values of the penalty parameters for which the exact solution of the LP problem can be found. The nondifferentiability of the penalty functions is not a drawback, since appropriate mathematical tools for dealing with this are available. We obtain constant penalty parameters that ensure global convergence of the network trajectories to the equilibrium state, which corresponds to the unique minimizer of the energy function.

The convergence analysis carried out here follows the same framework presented in [5] and [6] by the present authors, i.e., diagonal type Lyapunov functions are used and the systems of differential equations are described, equivalently, in Persidskii type form. Persidskii type systems and diagonal type functions are discussed in [1] and [2]. For reasons of space, some proofs are omitted and can be found in the technical report [7].

Utkin [8] also uses exact penalty functions and sliding modes in the design of gradient dynamical systems that solve optimization problems; his analysis is carried out by using the so-called equivalent control method. In this context, the contribution of this paper is a Lyapunov function analysis of the same class of gradient dynamical systems, leading to simple conditions on the penalty parameters for global convergence to the optimum.

In this paper we denote column vectors by boldface lowercase letters like $\mathbf{c}$. Scalars are represented by lowercase italic letters, like k and n. Matrices are denoted by uppercase boldface letters, like $\mathbf{P}$. Vector functions are denoted by $f(\mathbf{x})$ which, unless otherwise specified, are diagonal type functions, i.e.,

$$f(\mathbf{x}) = (f(x_1), \ldots, f(x_n))^T,$$

for $j = 1, \ldots, n$, x_j are the components of vector $\mathbf{x}$.

II. THE LP PROBLEM

Consider the following LP problem with bounded variables:

$$\text{Maximize } z = \mathbf{c}^T \mathbf{x} \quad (1)$$
$$\text{Subject to } \mathbf{1}\mathbf{x} = k$$
$$\mathbf{0} \leq \mathbf{x} \leq \mathbf{1}^T.$$

where $\mathbf{c} = [c_1, \ldots, c_n]^T$, $\mathbf{1} = [1, \ldots, 1] \in \mathbb{R}^{1 \times n}$, $k \leq n \in \mathbb{N}$ is a nonnegative integer and $\mathbf{x} \in \mathbb{R}^{n \times 1}$.

Notice that the LP problem (1) is always feasible. Moreover, the feasible set is closed and bounded, which ensures that its solution set is limited and bounded.

A solution of the LP problem is a vector $\mathbf{x}^*$ such that $\mathbf{x}^* = \arg\max(z)$, where $\mathbf{x}^* \in \{\mathbf{x} : \mathbf{1}\mathbf{x} = k\} \cap \{\mathbf{x} : x_i \in [0, 1], i = 1, \ldots, n\}$.

If the components of vector $\mathbf{c}$ are distinct, the solution of (1) possesses two properties that make the synthesis of a KWTA neural network possible:
1. The solution $\mathbf{x}^*$ of the LP problem (1) has k components equal to 1 and $n - k$ components equal to 0.
2. The k nonzero components of the solution $\mathbf{x}^*$ correspond exactly to the k largest components of the vector $\mathbf{c}$ of the objective function.

This can be summarized in the following proposition.

Proposition 1: Consider the LP problem (1), and let the components of vector $\mathbf{c}$ be distinct. Then, the solution of the LP problem (1) is unique and presents k components equal to one, which multiply the k largest components of vector $\mathbf{c}$ in the objective function z, and the $n - k$ remaining components are equal to zero.

Proof: Let $\mathcal{C}$ be the set of the k largest components of vector $\mathbf{c}$ and define the sets of indices $I := \{i : c_i \in \mathcal{C}\}$ and $J := \{i : c_i \notin \mathcal{C}\}$. Without loss of generality, let $c_1, c_2, \ldots, c_k$ be the k largest components in vector $\mathbf{c}$.

The feasible set of problem (1) corresponds to a hyperplane $\Pi := \{\mathbf{x} : \sum_{p=1}^{n} x_p = k\}$ inscribed in the hypercube defined by $H := \{\mathbf{x} : x_p \in [0, 1], p = 1, \ldots, n\}$. The vertices of the hypercube H intersected by hyperplane Π are only those ones that present k components equal to one and the remaining $n - k$ components equal to zero. Moreover, no edges of the hypercube are cut by the hyperplane Π, this is so because given the fact that each point on an edge of the hypercube H is described by a component $x_q \in]0, 1[$, for some index q, and the remaining $n - 1$ components $x_p \in \{0, 1\}$, for $p \neq q$, then, for such points the sum $\sum_{p=1}^{n} x_p$ does not yield an integer value. Thus, for $k \in \mathbb{N}$ the hyperplane Π does not cut any edges of the hypercube H.

Since the coefficients c_p, $p = 1, \ldots, n$ are distinct, the hyperplane described by the objective function of the LP problem (1) is not parallel to the hyperplane Π. This implies that the solution of the LP problem (1) is unique and is one of the vertices of the hypercube H intersected by the hyperplane Π, then it is a vector of k ones and $n - k$ zeros. Consequently, since $c_i > c_j$, for all $i \in I$ and $j \in J$, it is immediate that the vector that maximizes z, while satisfying the constraints of the LP problem, is $x_i^* = 1$, for $i \in I$ and $x_j^* = 0$, for $j \in J$. Then, the vector $\mathbf{x}^*$ that solves the LP problem (1) is a vector, such that its k components equal to 1 correspond to the k largest components of vector $\mathbf{c}$ and the remaining components are equal to zero. This concludes the proof. ∎

Comparing with the formulation using integer programming considered in [3], that is obtained by replacing the constraints on vector $\mathbf{x}$, in problem (1), with $x_i \in \{0, 1\}$, $i = 1, \ldots, n$, Proposition 1 states that LP problem (1) and the integer programming problem have the same solution $\mathbf{x}^*$.

Based on the preceding proposition, we can build a neural circuit that solves the LP problem (1), or, in other words, design a neural classifier that selects the k largest signals from vector $\mathbf{c}$. Such a network is presented in the next section and it is referred as a *KWTA network*.

III. MATHEMATICAL FORMULATION OF THE KWTA NEURAL NETWORK

Our aim, in this section, is to synthesize a neural network that solves problem (1). We use the *penalty function method* [9] with two exact penalty functions, each one corresponding to a different set of constraints of this LP problem.

After converting problem (1) into a minimization problem, by means of the penalty function method, we obtain the associated unconstrained optimization problem:

$$\text{Minimize } E(\mathbf{x}, \gamma, \rho) = -\mathbf{c}^T \mathbf{x} - \gamma \sum_{j=1}^{n} \min(0, x_j) +$$
$$\gamma \sum_{i=1}^{n} x_j^+ + \rho |\mathbf{1}\mathbf{x} - k| \quad (2)$$

where, for each j

$$x_j^+ = \begin{cases} x_j & \text{if } x_j > 1 \\ 0 & \text{if } x_j \leq 1. \end{cases}$$

Observe that E is constituted by the objective function of the original problem plus two penalty terms, each one acting on a different set of constraints.

According to the penalty function method, there exist finite values of γ and ρ, for which the solution of problem (2) corresponds exactly to the solution of problem (1).

The objective function E of problem (2) is convex, which ensures that E has a unique global minimum and that its minimizer can be found by means of a gradient descent method [4], [9]. Consider the gradient system $\dot{\mathbf{x}} = -\nabla E(\mathbf{x})$, that minimizes E, which is given by:

$$\dot{\mathbf{x}} = \mathbf{c} - \gamma[\,\text{hsgn}(\mathbf{x}) + \text{uhsgn}(\mathbf{x})\,] - \rho \mathbf{1}^T \text{sgn}(\mathbf{1}\mathbf{x} - k) \quad (3)$$

where for each j:

$$\text{hsgn}(x_j) = \begin{cases} -1 & \text{if } x_j < 0 \\ 0 & \text{if } x_j > 0 \end{cases}$$

$$\text{uhsgn}(x_j) = \begin{cases} 0 & \text{if } x_j < 1 \\ 1 & \text{if } x_j > 1 \end{cases}$$

$$\text{sgn}(\mathbf{1}\mathbf{x} - k) = \begin{cases} -1 & \text{if } \mathbf{1}\mathbf{x} - k < 0 \\ 1 & \text{if } \mathbf{1}\mathbf{x} - k > 0 \end{cases}$$

The system of differential equations (3) describes a modified Hopfield network that, for γ and ρ sufficiently large, is capable of selecting the k largest signals from the vector $\mathbf{c}$, which are referred to as the *winners*. The functional block diagram of the network is depicted in figure 1.

The network, shown in figure 1, consists of a parallel array of neurons, which receive, as input signals, the output signal of a perceptron neuron with synaptic weights equal to unity and the penalty parameters, γ and ρ, can be interpreted as network gains. The k largest input signals c_p, where p is the index of each of the k winners, are indicated by the k neurons that remain active.

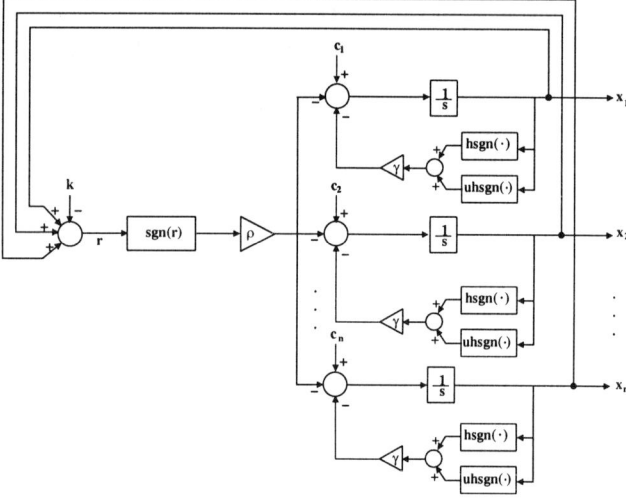

Fig. 1. Neural circuit described by the system of equations (3).

Two different terms can be identified in figure 1, each one acting on a corresponding set of constraints:

$$\mathbf{l}_1 = \rho \mathbf{1}^T \text{sgn}(\mathbf{1}\mathbf{x} - k)$$
$$\mathbf{l}_2 = \gamma[\,\text{hsgn}(\mathbf{x}) + \text{uhsgn}(\mathbf{x})\,],$$

For γ and ρ sufficiently large, the term $\mathbf{l}_1$ is responsible for keeping the trajectories within the set $\Delta := \{\mathbf{x} : \mathbf{1}\mathbf{x} - k = 0\}$. At the same time, the term $\mathbf{l}_2$ is responsible for maintaining trajectories within the intersection of the sets $\{\mathbf{x} : x_j \in [0, 1]\}$ and Δ.

Since for γ and ρ sufficiently large the trajectories of (3) converge to the solution of the LP problem (1), which satisfies Proposition (1), the circuit modeled by (3) presents KWTA property.

Notice also that the right-hand side of system (3) is discontinuous. This is due to the presence of exact penalty functions in the energy function (2), which are nondifferentiable at the feasible set of the LP problem. For this reason, solutions of (3) are considered in the sense of Filippov [10].

Some comments are necessary about the formulation of LP problem (1) and its consequences in the design of the neural network modeled by (3). Urahama & Nagao [3] propose an integer programming problem of the same type as (1), with $\mathbf{x} \in \{0,1\}^n$, which means that each component of vector $\mathbf{x}$ is 0 or 1.

Such a formulation is also possible with our model. We can regard the LP problem (1) as a problem with three equality constraints, and the penalty functions for this problem are $\gamma_1 \|\mathbf{x}\|_1$, $\gamma_2 \|\mathbf{x} - \mathbf{1}\|_1$ and $\rho|\mathbf{1}\mathbf{x} - k|$, where $\gamma_1 \neq \gamma_2$. The introduction of the parameter γ_2 is necessary, for if $\gamma_1 = \gamma_2$, the violation of the constraint $\mathbf{x} \in \{0, 1\}^n$ is not penalized for variables in the interval $]0, 1[$. However, the introduction of two penalty functions with different penalty parameters, in order to penalize the violation of the constraint $\mathbf{x} \in \{0, 1\}$, does not bring any benefits to the analysis and implementation of the neural network modeled by (3). The introduction of an extra parameter makes convergence analysis more complex, since it also has to be adjusted.

As far as practical implementation of the neural circuit is concerned, as suggested in [11], a large number of connections constitutes a major bottleneck for VLSI CMOS implementation of such neural networks, and an extra parameter, which is interpreted as a network gain, demands at least n extra components plus wiring to connect these components. Thus the use of linear programming with bounded variables is more convenient than using integer programming.

IV. CONVERGENCE ANALYSIS

The presence of discontinuous functions in the system of equations (3) requires that convergence of its trajectories to be understood in the sense of sliding modes. Once the trajectories reach the LP problem feasible set, a sliding motion is initiated and its trajectories "chatter" within a neighbourhood of the unique minimizer of the function E, where they remain confined. The *chattering* phenomenon is described as a high frequency switching around the feasible set of the LP problem, which is the surface of discontinuity of the dynamical system described by (3). Detailed expositions concerning differential equation with discontinuous righthand sides and theory of sliding modes can be found, for instance, in [10], [12], [8], [13], [14], [15].

Due to the phenomenon of chattering, the trajectories are said to converge to the *equilibrium set* of system (3), which consists of a neighbourhood of the solution $\mathbf{x}^*$ of the optimization problem (2).

Convergence analysis of the system described by equation (3) is divided into two steps. First, we prove convergence to the feasible set of problem (1), which is given by the intersection

$$\Omega := \Delta \cap \Phi \quad (4)$$

where $\Delta := \{\mathbf{x} : \mathbf{1}\mathbf{x} - k = 0\}$ and $\Phi := \{\mathbf{x} : x_j \in [0,1], \text{ for each } j\}$.

Once in the feasible set, it is necessary to prove that the trajectories converge to the solution of problem (1). This analysis results in sufficient conditions that the penalty parameters ρ and γ must satisfy in order to ensure convergence of the trajectories of equation (3) to the solution set of the LP problem (1). Equivalently, this analysis provides guidelines to set the gains ρ and γ such that the solution of LP problem (1) belongs to the equilibrium set of (3), and to guarantee that the trajectories converge globally to this set and remain in it thereafter.

Convergence results are obtained using a Lyapunov function V. It is possible to show finite time convergence; this means, for example, that there exists $\varepsilon > 0$, such that $\dot{V} < -\varepsilon$. For a detailed exposition on Lyapunov theory see, for instance, [16], [17], [14].

The following lemma states sufficient conditions that ensure convergence of the trajectories of system (3) to the feasible set of problem (1).

Lemma 1: Consider the system of ordinary differential equations (3) and assume that it admits solutions in the sense of Filippov. For any initial conditions, if γ and ρ satisfy

$$\rho > \frac{\|\mathbf{c}\|_2}{\sqrt{n}} + \gamma \quad (5)$$

$$\gamma > \frac{n}{2}\|\mathbf{c}\|_2 \quad (6)$$

then the trajectories of system (3) reach the set Ω, defined in (4), in finite time and remain in this set thereafter.

Proof: For brevity, we present only the basic ideas of this proof. See complete proof in [7]. Let ν be the subgradient of $P_\Phi(\mathbf{x}) = \sum_{j=1}^n \min(0, x_j) + x_j^+$. Premultiplying system (3) by vector $\mathbf{1}$ we get:

$$\dot{r} = \mathbf{1}\mathbf{c} - \gamma \mathbf{1}\nu(\mathbf{x}) - \rho \mathbf{1}\mathbf{1}^T \, \text{sgn}(r). \quad (7)$$

Notice that the equations (3) and (7) form the following Persidskii type system [1], [2], [5], written in vector notation:

$$\begin{pmatrix} \dot{\mathbf{x}} \\ \dot{r} \end{pmatrix} = \begin{pmatrix} \mathbf{c} \\ \mathbf{1c} \end{pmatrix} - \begin{pmatrix} \mathbf{I}_n & \mathbf{1}^T \\ \mathbf{1} & \mathbf{1}\mathbf{1}^T \end{pmatrix} \begin{pmatrix} \gamma \nu(\mathbf{x}) \\ \rho \, \text{sgn}(r) \end{pmatrix} \quad (8)$$

where $\mathbf{I}_n$ denotes the identity matrix of order n.

Consider also the following nonsmooth diagonal type candidate Lyapunov function associated to this system:

$$V(\mathbf{x}, r) = \gamma \sum_{j=1}^n \int_0^{x_j} \nu(\tau) d\tau + \rho \int_0^r \text{sgn}(\tau) d\tau. \quad (9)$$

Due to the presence of discontinuous terms in the righthand side of (3) the proof is divided into two steps. In step 1 we suppose that the trajectories do not belong to the set $\Delta = \{\mathbf{x} : \mathbf{1}\mathbf{x} = k\}$, which means that no sliding motion occurs and the solutions of system (3) are considered in the usual sense. In step 2 we consider $\mathbf{x} \in \Delta$, in this case sliding motion occurs, and the solutions are considered in the sense of Filippov.

Step 1: $\mathbf{x} \notin \Delta$. Then, the time derivative of function (9) along trajectories of system (8) is given by:

$$\dot{V} = -\|g(\mathbf{x})\|^2 + \|g(\mathbf{x})\|_2^T \mathbf{c}, \quad (10)$$

where $g(\mathbf{x}) = \gamma(\text{hsgn}(\mathbf{x}) + \text{uhsgn}(\mathbf{x}))$.

Once the gain ρ satisfy inequality (5), we assure $\dot{V} < 0$ and this concludes the first step.

Step 2: If $\mathbf{x} \in \Delta$ and $x_j \notin \Phi$, for some j. In this case, function (9) reduces to:

$$V(\mathbf{x}) = \sum_{j=1}^n \int_0^{x_j} h(\tau) d\tau. \quad (11)$$

The time derivative of function (11) is given by:

$$\dot{V} = \nabla V^T \dot{\mathbf{x}} = \nu(\mathbf{x})^T \mathbf{P}(\mathbf{c} - \gamma \nu(\mathbf{x})),$$

where $\mathbf{P}$ is the projection matrix onto the null space of the row vector $\mathbf{1}$.

Inequality (6) being satisfied with the corresponding parameter (gain) γ we assure $\dot{V} < 0$. This concludes step 2. It is easy to show that the trajectories of system (3) converge to the feasible set of the LP problem (1) in finite time and remain in it thereafter. ∎

Notice that when trajectories are confined to the set Ω, the penalty terms of the energy function (2) go to zero and it is reduced to the objective function of the original LP problem, described by (1).

Lemma 1 says that for parameters ρ and γ satisfying inequalities (5) and (6), respectively, the system trajectories reach the feasible set of LP problem (1), but it is still necessary to prove two other auxiliary results – first we must show that if ρ and γ satisfy the bounds of lemma 1, then the LP problem (1) and the unconstrained problem (2) have the same solution $\mathbf{x}^*$; this is necessary in order to validate our arguments, we are proposing a neural classifier on the basis of the unique solution of LP problem (1), so we need the network modeled by (3) to converge to the solution set of the original LP problem. Second, it is necessary to show that, if γ and ρ satisfy lemma 1, then the system trajectories converge to the solution of the LP problem (1); this is necessary because lemma 1 does not ensure convergence to the solution of the LP problem (1), but to its feasible set. This is taken care of in the following lemmas.

Lemma 2: If the network gains ρ and γ satisfy the bounds of lemma 1, then the LP problem (1) and the unconstrained problem (2) have the same solution.

Proof: Since E is convex for every $\mathbf{x}$, a local minimum of E is, in fact, a global minimum. We only need to prove that the minimizer of E belongs to Ω, since $E(\mathbf{x}) = z$, $\forall \mathbf{x} \in \Omega$, where Ω is defined in (4).

We prove this lemma by contradiction. Let $\mathbf{x}^* \notin \Omega$ be the minimizer of E and suppose that ρ and γ satisfy the bounds of lemma 1. Then, there exists at least one trajectory of system (3) that does not belong to Ω, which is a contradiction, since by lemma 1 all the trajectories of system (3) converge to Ω in finite time and remains in it thereafter. Thus $\mathbf{x}^* \in \Omega$, concluding the proof. ∎

This lemma ensures that the LP problem (1) and the problem of minimizing E have the same solution set, provided that ρ and γ satisfy the bounds of lemma 1. It remains to be shown that the trajectories of (3) converge to the solution of the LP problem, provided that the conditions of lemma 1 are verified. This result is stated in the next lemma.

Lemma 3: If the network gains ρ and γ satisfy the bounds established in lemma 1, then the trajectories of system (3) reach the solution of the LP problem (1) in finite time and remain in it thereafter.

Proof: See reference [7]. ∎

The previous three lemmas complete our convergence analysis. The key result is lemma 1 and all the other lemmas rely on it. Lemma 2 ensures that the minimizer of the computational energy function E, given in (2) is the maximizer of the LP problem (1), and lemma 3 states that the trajectories of system (3) converge to the solution of the LP problem. These results, together with proposition 1, ensure that the neural network modeled by the gradient system (3) is a k-winners-take-all network. We now have all the elements needed to enunciate the theorem below, which is the main result of this paper.

Theorem 1: Consider the neural network modeled by the system of ordinary differential equations (3) and assume that the network gains γ and ρ satisfy the bounds of lemma 1. Then, given a vector $\mathbf{c} \in \mathbb{R}^{n \times 1}$, with distinct components, and a positive integer $k \leq n$, the neural network described by (3) is a KWTA network. □

This Theorem states that our KWTA network is capable of extracting k winners from a given vector $\mathbf{c}$. Based on the fact that the solution of the LP problem (1) satisfies Proposition 1, convergence of the trajectories of (3) to the solution of the LP problem (1) provides our circuit with a KWTA property.

The bounds stated by Lemma 1 are simple and their derivation is straightforward. This occurs for two main reasons: (i) the use of an adequate diagonal type Lyapunov functions and Persidskii type system representation, and (ii) the use of exact penalty functions with analytical expressions for their gradients.

In order to illustrate the theoretical results presented in this paper, in the next section we present some examples with the corresponding computer simulations.

V. Simulation examples

In this section we present some examples to illustrate the theoretical results presented in the previous sections.

Example 1: Consider the vector

$$\mathbf{c} = \begin{pmatrix} 1.23 & 1.32 & 1.25 & 1.47 \end{pmatrix}$$

from which we wish to extract the two largest signals, that is $k = 2$.

Using Theorem 1 the bounds for the penalty parameters are $\gamma > 5.28$ and $\rho > 6.61$. Let $\gamma = 5.30$ and $\rho = 6.70$.

The simulation results are shown in figure 2, with initial conditions chosen (arbitrarily) at the origin. The components $x_2 = x_4 = 1$ correspond to the two largest components of vector $\mathbf{c}$ – the winners; and the remaining ones, $x_3 = x_4 = 0$, correspond to the losers.

In this example, in order to have faster convergence, we used a time scale factor $\mu = 10$ which was chosen empirically and is introduced in equation (3), which takes the form $\dot{\mathbf{x}} = -\mu \nabla E(\mathbf{x})$. Other techniques for choosing μ are discussed in [4, Section 3.1.4].

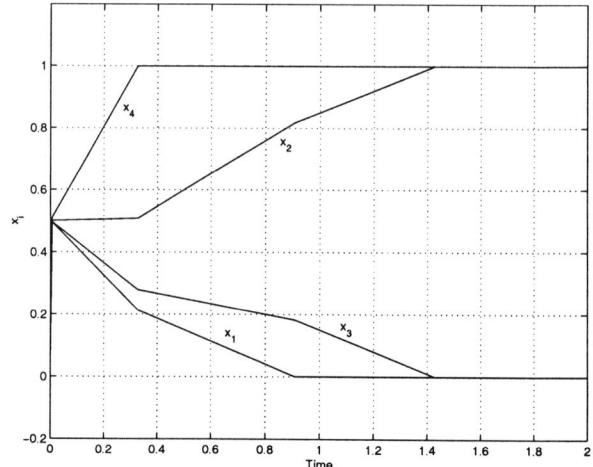

Fig. 2. Trajectories of example (1), showing correct classification of the two winners.

Example 2: (Adapted from [3, page 777]) In [3] it is considered a circuit with $n = 10$ and $k = 3$, where $c_j = j/2$ V, for $j = 1, \ldots, 9$ and circuit outputs are evaluated for c_{10} varying from 0 to 5 V. For this example, let us consider $c_{10} = 3.3V$, that is:

$$\mathbf{c} = \begin{pmatrix} 0.5 & 1 & 1.5 & 2 & 2.5 & 3 & 3.5 & 4 & 4.5 & 3.3 \end{pmatrix}$$

In this case, the winners are c_7, c_8 and c_9. Using Theorem 1, we get $\gamma > 45.32$ and $\rho > 48.19$. Let $\gamma = 45.35$ and $\rho = 48.20$. As in the previous example, in order to accelerate convergence, we used a time scale factor $\mu = 10$. Simulation results are shown in figure 3.

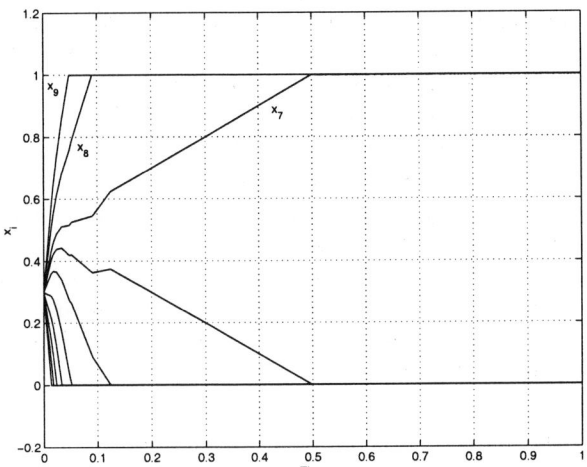

Fig. 3. Trajectories of example (2), showing KWTA behaviour.

Urahama & Nagao [3] show that, for this example, their circuit has resolution limit is 0.5 V and if the difference between the smallest winner and the largest loser is less than this limit, like in this example, then the outputs of their circuit become fuzzy. As shown for this case, our network produces correct classification of the entries of vector $\mathbf{c}$, showing a better separability resolution.

In the preceding examples, the discontinuous terms in equation (3) cause the trajectories shown in graphics 2 and 3, to chatter in a neighbourhood of the feasible set of the LP problem. Chattering happens when trajectories converge to the surface of discontinuity of system (3), which consists of the whole feasible set of the LP problem (1).

VI. Concluding remarks

In this paper we propose a new k-winners-take-all neural network designed on the basis of a linear programming framework with bounded variables. The theoretical formulation of the network is based on the fact that the solution set of the LP problem can be designed to coincide with the equilibrium set of a KWTA gradient type neural network.

Convergence analysis proceeds by representing the system of differential equations that models the network in a suitable Persidskii-like form, and using a diagonal type Lyapunov function.

Compared with the network based on a nonlinear programming relaxation framework proposed in [3], our network has the advantage of being synthesized from a simple linear programming problem. Performance of our network depends on the correct adjustment of the parameters γ and ρ, which, however have to be calculated only once.

Urahama & Nagao [3] claim that their model achieves almost instantaneous convergence with no transient phase, as opposed to Hopfield type models. However, we have shown that our network provides convergence in finite time. Also, Cichocki & Unbehauen [4] claim that in Hopfield type models the transient can be made shorter by choosing appropriate time scales, which can be chosen in such a way that the convergence time can be determined a priori. This is also the case for our network, making it suitable for real time operation.

References

[1] S. K. Persidskii, "Problem of absolute stability," *Automation and Remote Control*, vol. 12, pp. 1889–1895, 1969.

[2] E. Kaszkurewicz and A. Bhaya, *Matrix Diagonal Stability in Systems and Computation*. Birkhäuser, Boston, 2000.

[3] K. Urahama and T. Nagao, "K-winners-take-all circuit with o(n) complexity," *IEEE Transactions on Neural Networks*, vol. 6, pp. 776–778, May 1995.

[4] A. Cichocki and R. Unbehauen, *Neural Networks for Optimization and Signal Processing*. John Wiley and Sons, 1993.

[5] L. V. Ferreira, E. Kaszkurewicz, and A. Bhaya, "Convergence analysis of neural networks that solve linear programming problems," in *IJCNN 2002*, vol. 3, pp. 2476–2481, May 2002.

[6] L. V. Ferreira, "On using neural networks for solving linear programming problems," Master's thesis, COPPE/UFRJ, April 2002. In Portuguese.

[7] L. V. Ferreira, E. Kaszkurewicz, and A. Bhaya, "Synthesis of a k-winners-take-all neural network using linear programming with bounded variables," tech. rep., NACAD/COPPE/UFRJ, January 2003.

[8] V. Utkin, *Sliding Modes in Control and Optimization*. Springer-Verlag, Berlin, 1992.

[9] D. G. Luenberger, *Linear and Nonlinear Programming*. Addison-Wesley, 3rd ed., 1984.

[10] A. F. Filippov, *Differential Equations with Discontinuous Righthand Sides*. Kluwer Academic Publishers, Dordrecht, 1988.

[11] A. Cichocki, R. Unbehauen, K. Weinzierl, and R. Hölzel, "A new neural network for solving linear programming problems," *European Journal of Operational Research*, no. 93, pp. 244–256, 1996.

[12] A. F. Filippov, "Differential equations with discontinuous righthand sides," *American Mathematical Society Translations*, vol. 42, no. 2, pp. 191–231, 1964.

[13] C. Edwards and S. K. Spurgeon, *Sliding mode control: Theory and Applications*. Taylor & Francis, 1998.

[14] D. Shevitz and B. Paden, "Lyapunov stability of nonsmooth systems," *IEEE Transactions on Automatic Control*, vol. 39, no. 9, 1994.

[15] R. A. DeCarlo, S. H. Żak, and G. P. Matthews, "Variable structure control of multivariable systems: A tutorial," *Proceedings of the IEEE*, vol. 76, pp. 212–232, March 1988.

[16] H. K. Khalil, *Nonlinear Systems*. Macmillan Publishing Company, 1992.

[17] J. J. E. Slotine and W. Li, *Applied Nonlinear Control*. Prentice-Hall, 1991.

Regularization and Feedforward Artificial Neural Network Training with Noise

Pravin Chandra
School of Information Technology
G.G.S. Indraprastha University
Kashmere Gate, Delhi-110006, India
Email: pc_ipu@yahoo.com, pchandra@ipu.edu

Yogesh Singh
School of Information Technology
G.G.S. Indraprastha University
Kashmere Gate, Delhi-110006, India
Email: ys66@rediffmail.com, ys@ipu.edu

Abstract— Regularization is a method used for controlling the complexity of models. Explicit regularization uses a modifier term, incorporating *a-priori* knowledge about the function to be approximated by Feedforward Artificial Networks, that is added to the risk functional and implicit regularization where noise is added to the system variables during training, are two of the commonly used techniques for model complexity control. The relationship between these two type of regularization is explained. A regularization term is derived based on the general noise model. The interplay between the various noise mediated regularization terms is described.

I. INTRODUCTION

Feedforward Artificial Neural Networks (FFANN's) can be interpreted as a non-linear (semi-)parametric approximation set, $\mathcal{F}_{\text{ann}}(\mathcal{W}, x)$. The parameter $\mathcal{W}$ refers to the set of all adjustable parameters of the FFANN, collectively known as the weights of the FFANN. One hidden layer FFANN's, with sigmoidal activation in the hidden layer and pure linear activation in the output layer, have been shown to be universal approximators of continuous function [1]–[5]. The universal approximation results are existential results. That is, they provide the assurance that given a function to be approximated, there exists a FFANN that approximates it arbitrarily well, but leave the task of actually finding the network unsolved (even the constructive proofs make assumptions about the function to be approximated that cannot be satisfied in practice). This task is solved by the FFANN training algorithms (the standard backpropagation algorithm [6] being a prime example, see Haykin [7] and Ham and Kostanic [8] for further references and details).

The FFANN training algorithms are a realization of the supervised learning paradigm. The training process, for the supervised learning paradigm, may be defined as the process of establishing an unknown input(s) to output(s) functional dependency using a finite number of observation samples or exemplars of input-output pairs [6]–[10]. The FFANN training algorithms work by implementing a procedure for minimization of the risk functional defined as:

$$\mathcal{R}(\mathcal{W}) = \int\int \mathcal{E}\left(\mathbf{y}, \mathbf{F}\left(\mathcal{W}, \mathbf{x}\right)\right) p(\mathbf{x}, \mathbf{y}) \, d\mathbf{x} \, d\mathbf{y} \quad (1)$$

where $\mathbf{y}$ is the desired output corresponding to the input $\mathbf{x}$, $\mathcal{E}$ is a measure of the distance between the desired value and the output from the FFANN and is usually taken to be positive and is called the error function.

Let the function to be approximated be $\mathbf{y} = \mathbf{f}(\mathbf{x})$. The training algorithms minimize the risk functional to estimate the "true approximate" function, $\mathbf{y} = \mathbf{F}\left(\mathcal{W}_0, \mathbf{x}\right)$. With finite data, one cannot expect to find the function $\mathbf{F}\left(\mathcal{W}_0, \mathbf{x}\right)$ exactly, what can be found is an estimate of it, $\mathbf{F}\left(\mathcal{W}_0^*, \mathbf{x}\right)$, using the finite data and some training algorithm. The problem of recovery of the original function from the exemplar data set is an inherently ill-posed problem. That is, there are an infinite number of functions that fit the given data, arbitrarily well. In order to select one particular function from this infinite set, one needs to incorporate a-priori information/knowledge about the function to be approximated or to create a model/function selection criteria/methodology.

Explicit regularization (modifying the risk functional) and implicit regularization (induction of noise during training) has been used as a model selection method. In the current paper we investigate the role of noise introduction in the phase space consisting of the input variables, the parameters of the network and the output variables, as a technique for complexity control. The introduction of noise in the input variables have been studied by Bishop [11], Neunier and Zimmermann [12] etc. while the role of parameter noise has been studied by Murray and Edwards [13] and Wu and Moody [14] etc. This paper attempts to bring all types of noise introduction into a coherent theory and explain their relation to each other. Section 2 provides a summary of some existing techniques for model selection in FFANN's. Section 3 describes the regularization method. The relation between the regularization effect of different types of noises is studied in Section 4 while we present our conclusions in Section 5.

II. COMPLEXITY CONTROL METHODS

The training data tuples ($\mathbf{x}$, $\mathbf{y}$) are assumed to be independently and identically distributed (i.i.d.) according to the joint probability distribution function (pdf) as:

$$p(\mathbf{x}, \mathbf{y}) = p(\mathbf{x}) \, p(\mathbf{y}|\mathbf{x}) \quad (2)$$

where $p(\mathbf{x})$ is the probability density function of the occurance of $\mathbf{x}$, while $p(\mathbf{y}|\mathbf{x})$ is the conditional probability function of $\mathbf{y}$ assuming $\mathbf{x}$ has already occurred and $\mathbf{F}$ denotes the output(s) from the FFANN.

The error function generally used is the squared error function:

$$\mathcal{E}_1 = \|\mathbf{y} - \mathbf{F}\|^2 \quad (3)$$

where $\|\cdot\|$ denotes the Euclidean distance measure. Though, in principle, any distance measure can be used in (3).

The training for supervised learning is performed over a finite sample set of P-exemplars, we use the index p to label the exemplars, then the joint pdf may be written as:

$$p(\mathbf{x}, \mathbf{y}) = \frac{1}{P} \sum_p \delta(\mathbf{x} - \mathbf{x}^p)\, \delta(\mathbf{y} - \mathbf{y}^p) \quad (4)$$

where $\delta(\cdot)$ is the Dirac's delta function(al).

Usage of (4) in (1) gives the risk functional as:

$$\mathcal{R}(\mathcal{W}) = \frac{1}{P} \sum_p \mathcal{E}(\mathbf{y}^p, \mathbf{F}(\mathcal{W}, \mathbf{x}^p)) \quad (5)$$

And, then using (3) in (5) we get the sum-squared risk functional (6)(using $\mathbf{F}^p = \mathbf{F}(\mathcal{W}, \mathbf{x}^p)$).

$$\mathcal{R}_1(\mathcal{W}) = \frac{1}{P} \sum_p \|\mathbf{y}^p - \mathbf{F}^p\|^2 \quad (6)$$

A. Complexity Control Mechanisms

Some of the techniques of model selection that are used are early stopping or cross-validation [9], [15]–[17], minimum descriptor length [9], [10], [18]–[21], regularization techniques [7], [9], [10], [22]–[24] which may be implemented as a Bayesian technique [25], [26], weight decay [7], [9], [10], [27]–[30], noise in the input and/or outputs [11], [12], [14], [31], [32], and noise in the parameter [12], [13]. Pruning and constructive techniques are also used for complexity control (see Reed [30] and Haykin [7], for further references).

The early - stoppage or cross-validation [9], [15]–[17] works by splitting the sample data set into a training set and a validation set. The network is trained using the training set while periodically the error on the validation set is measured. When the validation set error starts increasing, the inference is made that overfitting of data has started and the training is stopped. The tendency to overfit is inherent in the training mechanism as the samples are presented at discrete points only. It has been said that early stopping can be viewed as having an effect similar to weight decay [14]. Early-stoppage has been empirically shown to be useful in controlling complexity of large networks [15]. Early - stoppage may be interpreted as a form of penalization, where the penalty is defined on a path in the parameter space corresponding to the successive model estimates obtained during FFANN training [9], [16].

The minimum descriptor length (MDL) principle [18], [19] is based on Kolmogorov's algorithmic complexity concept for the characterization of randomness of a data set [9], [10], [20] and works on the concept that the best model of a data is one that minimizes the "cost" of encoding the data together with the error of encoding [9], [10], [21]. Hinton and van Camp [21] provide a methodology for the implementation of this procedure using artificial gaussian noise injection in the training data.

We use a one hidden layer network with sigmoidal activation and pure linear output layer. Without loss of any generality, we treat only one output networks here. The network layers are fully connected to adjacent layers without any lateral or short-cut connections. We investigate the role of noise introduction during training in context to this form of FFANN's where the training loss/performance function is taken to be the mean squared error (*mse*, eq. 6). For the sake of brevity we do not consider the case of other risk functionals (for example the cross-entropic error).

III. REGULARIZATION

One of the major issue in FFANN training is to control the complexity and provide good generalization capabilities. One of the assumptions that is generally made in complexity control is that the desired function should be *smooth*, in the sense that the "nearby" input points lead to "nearby" output points. As pointed out by Geman et al. [33] the problem of complexity control may be related to the bias/variance dilemma in FFANN's. Regularization is the method which tries to strike a balance between the model bias and model variance by incorporating a-priori knowledge in the model selection (risk functional). Or, the problem is of locating an optimum architecture, of the number of parameters and as well as of parameter values. Due to this reason, the methods of complexity controls for FFANN's can be broadly divided into two classes, (a) methods that impose structural constraints (that is on constraints on the number of hidden nodes, layers, weights etc.) and (b) methods that impose constraints on the values of the parameters of the FFANN's to control complexity. Network growing algorithms and pruning algorithms belong to the first class of methods while methods that modify the error term to impose a constraint on the parameters of the model belong to the second class. The first class of methods are not investigated in this paper, the second method(s) of complexity control is also known as the method of *regularization*. This method makes an explicit modification to the risk functional. The relation of this methodology with the method of training with noise (which makes an effective change in the risk functional) is investigated in this paper.

The method of regularization modifies the risk functional $\mathcal{R}$ by adding a penalty/regularization term Ω to obtain a modified risk functional $\widetilde{\mathcal{R}}$.

$$\widetilde{\mathcal{R}}(\mathcal{W}) = \mathcal{R}(\mathcal{W}) + \gamma\, \Omega(\mathcal{W}, \mathbf{x}, \mathbf{y}, \mathbf{F}) \quad (7)$$

Equation (7) explicitly reflects that the regularization term may depend not only on the parameters of the FFANN but also on the input-output exemplar pairs and the output from the network. The Ω term may be provided as an explicit function, as in weight decay procedures where the commonly used penalty terms are given by (8) [27] and (9) [28] or as an implicit penalty term (in noise mediated regularization).

$$\Omega = \sum_{w \in \mathcal{W}} w^2 \quad (8)$$

$$\Omega = \sum_{w \in \mathcal{W}} \frac{(w/w_o)^2}{1 + (w/w_o)^2} \quad (9)$$

where, w_o is a preassigned parameter. [7], [9], [10], [16], [27]–[30].

The penalty term incorporates the a-priori knowledge about the behaviour of the function to be approximated. One of the problems of explicit regularization is the choice of the parameter value γ (also known as the *regularization parameter*). Too high a value for this parameter implies that the penalty term decides the function that is estimated while a low value may effectively lead to no effect (of the penalty term) on the solution found. Bayesian methods have been developed for the estimation of the regularization parameter while training is being performed [25], [26].

IV. Training with noise

The implicit regularization procedure does not explicitly employ a penalty term. Early stopping has been shown to be effectively implementing a regularization scheme [9], [16]. The same holds true for the case of training with input noise [11], [12], [14], [31], [32] or with parameter noise [12], [13].

To study the effect of training with noise, we assume that the training of the FFANN occurs with clean data (that is, the training exemplars are not contaminated with noise). Moreover the results are derived in the large sample limit. The introduced noises are assumed to be additive gaussian with zero mean and fixed variance.

A. Noise Types

At the time of training, noise may be introduced in the following parts of the FFANN system:

- Inputs to the FFANN
- Parameters ($\mathcal{W}$) of the FFANN
- Desired output(s) from the FFANN
- Hidden node(s) outputs

Since we consider the *mse*, we do not consider the case of noise introduction in the output of the FFANN as it is equivalent to noise introduction in the desired output/target. The noise introduced in the system, is assumed to be gaussian with mean zero and finite variance. Training noise in inputs is equivalent to (Tikhonov's) regularization [11], [12], [14], [31], [32]. Murray and Edwards [13], Neunier and Zimmermann [12] and others have described the regularization effect of synaptic noise. We do not know of a work detailing the effect of noise in hidden node output. Target noise introduction should not be confused with the function noise (assumed to be) present in regression studies. The former as shown below has a regularization effect, while the latter makes the task of function identification more difficult. Noise in inputs and outputs has been used to artificially create a effective larger training set with the aim of controlling the complexity of the model [12], [34]. Input noise has the effect of "smearing" the input data points, and thus prevents the FFANN from fitting the data point exactly [11]. Intuitively, similar arguments may be extended for the case of any type of noise usage in training.

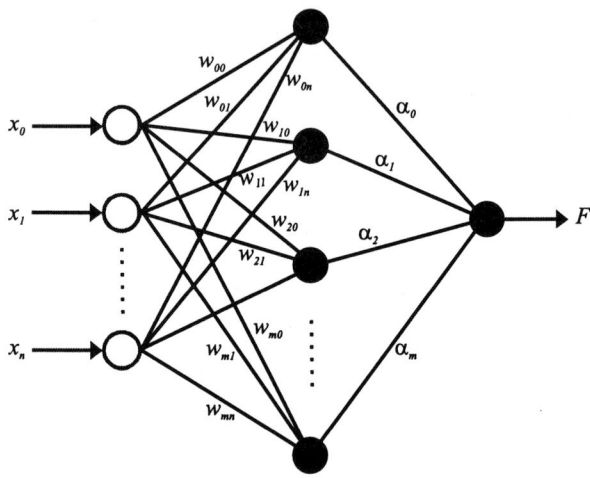

Fig. 1. Single hidden layer FFANN with m hidden nodes, n number of input nodes. The biases are explicitly shown as weights (w_{i0}'s and α_0 corresponding to the pseudo-nodes.

B. FFANN Structural Model

To quantify the above argument, we consider a one output FFANN, with the training exemplars being given as $\{y^p, \mathbf{x}^p\}$, where p is the pattern index, $k \in \{1, \ldots, P\}$, where P is the number of clean training pairs. We consider a FFANN with one hidden layer of sigmoidal hidden layer, the output from the FFANN (Fig. 1) is given by

$$\mathcal{F}(\mathbf{x}, \mathcal{W}) = \sum_{i=0}^{m} \alpha_i \sigma \left(\sum_{j=0}^{n} w_{ij} x_j \right) \quad (10)$$

$$= \sum_{i=0}^{m} \alpha_i \mathcal{O}_i \quad (11)$$

where

$$\mathcal{O}_i = \begin{cases} 1, & i = 0 \\ \sigma \left(\sum_{j=0}^{n} w_{ij} x_j \right), & i \in 1, \ldots, m \end{cases} \quad (12)$$

is the output from the ith hidden node, $\mathcal{O}_0 = 1$ acting as a pseudo-hidden node and α_i's for $i \geq 1$ are the weights from the ith hidden nodes' to the output nodes' while α_0 is the output node bias, and w_{ij}'s for $j \geq 0$ are the weights from the jth input node to the ith hidden node, $x_0 = 1$ acts as a constant pseudo-input while w_{i0}'s for $j = 0$ acts as the bias of the ith hidden node. The function $\sigma(\cdot)$ is a sigmoidal function usually taken to be the log-sigmoid (13) or the hyperbolic tangent function (14). We use the symbol σ for the noise variance also, the usage is apparent from the context.

$$\sigma_{\text{logsig}}(x) = \frac{1}{1 + e^{-x}} \quad (13)$$

$$\sigma_{\tanh}(x) = \tanh(x) = \frac{e^x - e^{-x}}{e^x + e^{-x}} \quad (14)$$

C. Noise Modification to the Risk Functional

We use the mean squared risk functional (6). The noise introduced are represented as δx's, δy, $\delta \mathcal{O}$'s, $\delta \alpha$'s and δw's corresponding to the inputs, the targets, the hidden node outputs, the weights between the hidden layer and the output node and the input and the hidden layer respectively. Let $\widetilde{\mathcal{R}}$ denote the value of the risk functional after noise introduction and taking into account the gaussian nature of the noise and component wise independent nature of the noise (the details of the derivation mechanism is similar to the one used by Bishop [11], the range of the indices is apparent from usage and the independence of the noises and their gaussianity is freely used in the derivation below) and introducing the noises in (6) and then expanding to the second order we may write;

$$\widetilde{\mathcal{R}} = \mathcal{R} + \frac{1}{2}\left[\frac{\partial^2 \mathcal{R}}{\partial y^2}\sigma_y^2 + \sum_j \frac{\partial^2 \mathcal{R}}{\partial x_j^2}\sigma_{x_j}^2 \right.$$
$$\left. + \sum_i \frac{\partial^2 \mathcal{R}}{\partial \mathcal{O}_i^2}\sigma_{\mathcal{O}_i}^2 + \sum_i \frac{\partial^2 \mathcal{R}}{\partial \alpha_i^2}\sigma_{\alpha_i}^2 + \sum_{i,j}\frac{\partial^2 \mathcal{R}}{\partial w_{ij}^2}\sigma_{w_{ij}}^2\right] +$$
$$+ \text{ higher order terms} \quad (15)$$

where σ's in the above equation represents the variance of the noise introduced in the appropriate parameter(s).

We can easily obtain the following relations:

$$\frac{\partial^2 \mathcal{R}}{\partial y^2} = 1 \quad (16)$$

$$\frac{\partial^2 \mathcal{R}}{\partial x_j^2} = \frac{1}{P}\sum_p\left[\left(\frac{\partial \mathcal{F}^p}{\partial x_j}\right)^2 + (\mathcal{F}^p - y^p)\frac{\partial^2 \mathcal{F}^p}{\partial x_j^2}\right] \quad (17)$$

$$\frac{\partial^2 \mathcal{R}}{\partial \mathcal{O}_i^2} = \frac{1}{P}\sum_p\left[\left(\frac{\partial \mathcal{F}^p}{\partial \mathcal{O}_i}\right)^2 + (\mathcal{F}^p - y^p)\frac{\partial^2 \mathcal{F}^p}{\partial \mathcal{O}_i^2}\right] \quad (18)$$

$$\frac{\partial^2 \mathcal{R}}{\partial \alpha_i^2} = \frac{1}{P}\sum_p\left[\left(\frac{\partial \mathcal{F}^p}{\partial \alpha_i}\right)^2 + (\mathcal{F}^p - y^p)\frac{\partial^2 \mathcal{F}^p}{\partial \alpha_i^2}\right] \quad (19)$$

where in the above equations, the pattern label for x, and $\mathcal{O}_i$ is implicit.

$$\frac{\partial^2 \mathcal{R}}{\partial w_{ij}^2} = \frac{1}{P}\sum_p\left[\left(\frac{\partial \mathcal{F}^p}{\partial w_{ij}}\right)^2 + (\mathcal{F}^p - y^p)\frac{\partial^2 \mathcal{F}^p}{\partial w_{ij}^2}\right] \quad (20)$$

From equation (14)-(16) we have:

$$\frac{\partial \mathcal{F}}{\partial x_j} = \sum_i \alpha_i \mathcal{O}'_i w_{ij} \quad (21)$$

where $\mathcal{O}'_i$ is the derivative of the output of the ith hidden node w.r.t. the net input to the node.

$$\frac{\partial^2 \mathcal{F}}{\partial x_j^2} = \sum_i \alpha_i \mathcal{O}''_i w_{ij}^2 \quad (22)$$

where $\mathcal{O}''_i$ is the second derivative of the output of the ith hidden node w.r.t. the net input to the node.

$$\frac{\partial \mathcal{F}}{\partial \mathcal{O}_i} = \alpha_i \quad (23)$$

$$\frac{\partial \mathcal{F}}{\partial \alpha_i} = \mathcal{O}_i \quad (24)$$

$$\frac{\partial^2 \mathcal{F}}{\partial \alpha_i^2} = 0; \quad \frac{\partial^2 \mathcal{F}}{\partial \mathcal{O}_i^2} = 0 \quad (25)$$

$$\frac{\partial \mathcal{F}}{\partial w_{ij}} = \alpha \mathcal{O}'_i x_j \quad (26)$$

$$\frac{\partial^2 \mathcal{F}}{\partial w_{ij}^2} = \alpha_i \mathcal{O}''_i x_j^2 \quad (27)$$

Using equation (16)-(27) in (15), we obtain

$$\widetilde{\mathcal{R}} = \mathcal{R} + \underbrace{\frac{1}{2}\sigma_y^2}_{\mathcal{R}_y} +$$
$$+ \underbrace{\frac{1}{2}\sum_{pij}\left[(\mathcal{F}^p - y^p)\alpha_i \mathcal{O}''_i + \alpha_i^2(\mathcal{O}'_i)^2\right]w_{ij}^2 \sigma_{x_i}^2}_{\mathcal{R}_x}$$
$$+ \underbrace{\frac{1}{2}\sum_{pij}\left[(\mathcal{F}^p - y^p)\alpha_i \mathcal{O}''_i + \alpha_i^2(\mathcal{O}'_i)^2\right]x_j^2 \sigma_{w_{ij}}^2}_{\mathcal{R}_w}$$
$$+ \underbrace{\frac{1}{2}\sum_{pij}\alpha_i^2 \sigma_{\mathcal{O}_i}^2}_{\mathcal{R}_{\mathcal{O}}} + \underbrace{\frac{1}{2}\sum_{pij}\mathcal{O}_i^2 \sigma_{\alpha_i}^2}_{\mathcal{R}_\alpha} \quad (28)$$

The risk functional is modified by the presence of noise mediated terms. The term $\mathcal{R}_y$ reflects the presence of the noise in the output/target. The risk functional modifier $\mathcal{R}_x$ is also given by Bishop [11] and Webb [32], this term is the modifier due to the noise in the inputs. The risk functional modifier $\mathcal{R}_w$ is also given by Murray and Edwards [13] and reflects the modification to the risk functional due to noise in the input to hidden nodes weights. The modifications, $\mathcal{R}_\alpha$ and $\mathcal{R}_{\mathcal{O}}$ reflect the presence of noise during training in the hidden nodes' to the output layer node and the output of the hidden nodes', respectively. In general, $\mathcal{R}_x$ and $\mathcal{R}_w$ are not positive definite due to a term that depends on the mismatch between the obtained output from the FFANN and the desired target value. The other modifier terms are positive (semi-)definite by definition.

D. Interpretation of Noise Induced Modifiers

From the equation (28) it is clear that inclusion of noise induces an equivalent regularization term given by:

$$\gamma \Omega = \mathcal{R}_y + \mathcal{R}_x + \mathcal{R}_w + \mathcal{R}_\alpha + \mathcal{R}_{\mathcal{O}} \quad (29)$$

where the regularization parameter, γ, is not required to be estimated, or equivalently we may take $\gamma = 1$. We define the positive definite components of equation (28) or (29) as:

$$\mathcal{R}_+ = \frac{1}{2}\sigma_y^2 + \frac{1}{2}\sum_{pij} \alpha_i^2 \left(\mathcal{O}_i'\right)^2 w_{ij}^2 \sigma_{x_i}^2 +$$
$$+ \frac{1}{2}\sum_{pij} \alpha_i^2 \left(\mathcal{O}_i'\right)^2 x_j^2 \sigma_{w_{ij}}^2 +$$
$$+ \frac{1}{2}\sum_{pij} \alpha_i^2 \sigma_{\mathcal{O}_i}^2 + \frac{1}{2}\sum_{pij} \mathcal{O}_i^2 \sigma_{\alpha_i}^2 \qquad (30)$$

while the non-positive definite part may be written as:

$$\mathcal{R}_- = \frac{1}{2}\sum_{pij} (\mathcal{F}^p - y^p)\, \alpha_i\, \mathcal{O}_i'' \left(w_{ij}^2 \sigma_{x_j}^2 + x_j^2 \sigma_{w_{ij}}^2\right) \qquad (31)$$

The interpretation of the term $\mathcal{R}_+$ is that it is the Tikhonov's regulizer term with respect to the variables of the phase space of the system (the phase space may be taken to be the space formed by weights, FFANN inputs, FFANN outputs and the hidden layer outputs). This term may physically be interpreted as a *drive towards smaller weights and smaller average output and smaller derivatives of the hidden layer, or more evenly distributed weights, and hidden node outputs and their derivatives, thereby trying to reduce the actual error*. As has been noted elsewhere [13], this may lead to not only better generalization but also better fault - tolerance.

The interpretation of the $\mathcal{R}_-$ term is more difficult. We may make the assertion that near the optimum model, this term would be negligible (a proof for the case of input noise, which can be easily generalized, is given by Bishop [11], see also Murray and Edwards [13]). But, as pointed out by Murray and Edwards [13] for the case of weight noise this term can actually lower the error locally via noise-injection in the weights, this assertion remains valid even when noise is injected to any component of the phase space of the FFANN. This term sculpts the error - surface during the initial phases of training. And, as concluded by Murray and Edwards [13] for the case of weight noise, this might reduce training time. We conjecture that this may happen for the noise in any parameter of the FFANN system.

In the above we have considered that the introduced noise is independent for every component of the phase space and has a separate variance. But consider the following:

$$\sigma_y^2 = \frac{1}{mn}\sum_{ij} \frac{\sigma_y^2}{w_{ij}^2} w_{ij}^2 \qquad (32)$$

where the zero weights are not summed over and then correspondingly the term nm is decreased. This term is similar in form to the second term of (30). In the usual discussions on the variance of the output/target noise, it is recommended to simply drop it, but the above expression establishes that even this term may contribute to the modification of the weight update rules. The primary question is not where the noise is introduced, but what variables it affects during training. Similar expressions allowing the explicit mmodelingof one type of noise introduction in terms of noise in other variables can be found for the other terms. Thus, the inclusion of any type of noise can be modelled by any or all terms of (28) or (30). This reflects our feeling that when noise is introduced during training in any parameter/variable of the FFANN system, during training it is iintrinsicallymodelled as a noise contamination in every variable.

Therefore, to explicitly model any type of noise used during training, we suggest the usage of all terms of the equation (30). The above relation implies that the overfitting tendency of the FFANN is used in a reversed role to control the complexity of the model. The introduced noises effectly smears the training point, so that the model found provides output which are "nearby" for any set of nearby points in the general phase space. This interpretation allows us to conjecture that the *networks trained with the established regularization function Ω or $\mathcal{R}_+$ will be more resistant to noise in any or all components of its phase space and will also posses better generalization capability.*

Equation (27), (29) and (30) also provide an explanation of the usual heuristic used in weight decay procedures where it is suggested that the regularization parameter for the weights of the different layers should be different (if make the assumption that the noise variance in each layer parameters is equal within the layer). From these equations it is apparent that the input noise is the "dual" to the regularization in the input to hidden nodes' weights while the hidden to output layer weights can be considered as "dual" to the outputs of the hidden layer nodes, (28) and (30). This "duality" means that the introduction of noise in one variable leads to regularization of the other.

The weight corrections may be found by any one of the following equivalent ways [11]:

1) Minimize the risk functional, and add noise to the phase space variables during training.
2) Minimize directly the regularized risk functional of (28). But this can be cumbersome and impractical due to the presence of the third derivative term[1], therefore, we may use the regulizer given by (30).
3) Perturbative evaluation of the weight corrections can also be done, and involves the calculation of the Hessian of the risk functional. For an example involving only the case of $\mathcal{R}_x$, see Bishop [11], this approach can easily be extended for any phase space variable term in (28) or (30). The remarks for the direct minimization of the regularized risk functional holds for this case also (See footnote on this page) and we suggest the usage of $\mathcal{R}_+$ (30) only.

V. DISCUSSIONS AND CONCLUSIONS

We have considered the introduction of noise during the training process in all variables of the phase space (consisting of the inputs, outputs, targets, and the parameters of the FFANN). This introduction was established to be equivalent

---
[1] As the second derivative term is present in the regularization term, this will give rise to a third derivative term in the weight update rule

to explicit regularization with a penalty term given by (29). We have established that noise introduction in any component of the phase space, acts an regulizer for all variables of the phase space. Thus, not only should one term of (28) be used if noise introduction (in even one phase space variable) is to be modeled explicitly, but all terms must be used. We have established that under small average performance error (of the FFANN) condition, the obtained regulizer is positive definite. We have also argued that the effective role played by all types of noises during training is equivalent.

We have also asserted that the non-positive definite part of the penalty term obtained (29) may lead to faster training in the early part of the training, but as these terms will require the evaluation of the third order derivative, the weight update rule can become cumbersome to evaluate. This term also decreases and becomes negligible as the system reaches towards the optimum point. Before its effect becomes negligible, we suggest that explicit noise should be introduced during the early part of the training in at least the inputs or the inputs to the hidden nodes weights, and after the performance measures shows a regularity, or converges to a point near a satisfactory/local minima, training should be resumed with clean data samples (without noise) and use should be made of the established regulizer $\mathcal{R}_+$ which is bounded below by zero or is positive.

Similar results can be established for the case of cross-entropic measure. The case of the vector valued FFANN can also be treated in exactly the same fashion as the case of single output FFANN. In an entirely analogous manner as the case of linear output FFANN's, we may treat the case when the output layer is also sigmoidal in nature.

Due to the paucity of space, we have not explicitly considered any activation functional form other than assuming the sigmoidality of the activation function. The perturbative weight update rule has not been presented explicitly, we refer to the paper by Bishop [11] for an exposition of this technique in context to input noise introduction.

Experimental validation of the conclusions of this paper must be conducted. This is more true for the conjecture that the introduction of noise only in the output may also have a regularization effect.

REFERENCES

[1] G. Cybenko, "Approximation by superposition of a sigmoidal function," *Math. Control, Signals, and Systems*, vol. 2, pp. 303–314, 1989.

[2] K. Funahashi, "On the approximate realization of continuous mappings by neural networks," *Neural Networks*, vol. 2, pp. 183–192, 1989.

[3] K. Hornik, M. Stinchcombe, and H. White, "Multilayer feedforward networks are universal approximators," *Neural Networks*, vol. 2, pp. 359–366, 1989.

[4] A. R. Barron, "Universal approximation bounds for superpositions of a sigmoidal function," *IEEE Trans. on Inf. Theo.*, vol. 3, pp. 930–945, 1993.

[5] F. Scarselli and A. C. Tsoi, "Universal approximation using feedforward network: A survey of some existing methods and some new results," *Neural Networks*, vol. 11, pp. 15–37, 1998.

[6] D. E. Rumelhart, G. E. Hinton, and R. J. Williams, "Learning internal representations by error propagation," in *Parallel Distributed Processing: Explorations in the Microstructure of Cognition*, D. E. Rumelhart and J. L. McCleland, Eds., vol. 1, chapter 8. MIT Press, Cambridge, Mass., 1986.

[7] S. Haykin, *Neural Networks - A Comprehesive Foundation*, Prentice Hall International, Inc., New Jersey, 2 edition, 1999.

[8] F. M. Ham and I. Kostanic, *Principles of Neurocomputing for Science & Engineering*, McGraw Hill Co., Singapore, 2001.

[9] V. Cherkassky and F. Mulier, *Learning from data: Concepts, Theory, and Methods*, John Wiley & Sons, Inc., New York, 1998.

[10] V. N. Vapnik, *Statistical Learning Theory*, John Wiley & Sons, Inc., New York, 1998.

[11] C. Bishop, "Training with noise is equivalent to Tikhonov regulariation," *Neural Computation*, vol. 7, no. 1, pp. 108–116, 1995.

[12] R. Neuneier and H. G. Zimmermann, "How to train neural networks," in *Neural Networks: Tricks of the Trade*, G. Orr and K. Muller, Eds., pp. 373–423. Springer Verlag, Berlin, 1998.

[13] A. F. Murray and P. J. Edwards, "Synaptic weight noise during mlp training: Enhanced mlp performance and fault tolerance resulting from synaptic weight noise during training," *IEEE Trans. Neural Networks*, vol. 5, no. 5, pp. 792–802, 1994.

[14] L. Wu and J. Moody, "A smoothing regularizer for feedforward and recurrent neural networks," *Neural Computation*, vol. 8, no. 3, pp. 463–491, 1996.

[15] A. S. Weigend, B. Huberman, and D. Rumelhart, "Predicting the future: A connectionist approach," *Int. J. of Neural Systems*, vol. 3, pp. 193–203, 1990.

[16] J. H. Friedman, "An overview of predictive learning and function approximation," in *From Statistics to Neural Networks*, V. Cherkassky, J. H. Friedman, and H. Wechsler, Eds., number 136 in NATO ASI Series. Springer Verlag, New York, 1994.

[17] S. Amari, K. Yoshida, K.-R. Muller, M. Finke, and H. Yang, "Statistical theory of overtraining – is cross-validation asymptotically effective?," in *Advances in Neural Information Processing*, vol. 6, pp. 176–182. MIT Press, Cambridge, MA, 1996.

[18] J. Rissanen, "Modeling by shortest data descriptor," *Automatica*, vol. 14, pp. 465–471, 1978.

[19] J. Rissanen, *Stochastic Complexity and Statistical Inquiry*, World Scientific, Singapore, 1989.

[20] A. N. Kolmogorov, "Three approaches to the quantitative definitions of information," *Problems Inf. Transmission*, vol. 1, no. 1, pp. 1–7, 1965.

[21] G. E. Hinton and D. van Camp, "Keeping neural networks simple by minimizing the description length of the weights," in *Proc. Sixth Annual ACM Conference on Computational Learning Theory*, Santa Cruz, CA, July 1993, vol. 1, pp. 5–13, ACM Press.

[22] A. N. Tikhonov, "Solution of incorrectly formulated problems and the regularization method," *Sov. Math. Dokl.*, vol. 4, pp. 1035–1038, 1963.

[23] A. N. Tikhonov and V. Y. Arsenin, *Solutions of Ill-Posed Problems*, W. H. Winston, Washington, DC, 1977.

[24] F. Girosi, M. Jones, and T. Poggio, "Regularization theory and neural network architectures," *Neural Computation*, vol. 7, pp. 219–269, 1995.

[25] D. J. C. MacKay, "Bayesian interpolation," *Neural Computation*, vol. 4, no. 3, pp. 415–447, 1992.

[26] D. J. C. MacKay, "A practical Bayesian framework for backpropagation networks," *Neural Computation*, vol. 4, no. 3, pp. 418–472, 1992.

[27] G. E. Hinton, "Connectionist learning procedures," *Artificial Intelligence*, vol. 40, pp. 185–234, 1989.

[28] A. S. Weigend, D. E. Rumelhart, and B. Huberman, "Generalization by weight-elimination with application to forecasting," in *Advances in Neural Information Processing Systems*, vol. 3, pp. 875–882. Morgan Kaufmann, San mateo, CA, 1991.

[29] F. Hergert, W. Finnoff, and H. G. Zimmerman, "A comparision of weight elimination methods for reducing complexity in neural networks," in *IJCNN'92*. 1992, vol. 3, pp. 980–987, IEEE Press, NJ.

[30] R. Reed, "Pruning algorithms – a survey," *IEEE Trans. Neural Networks*, vol. 4, pp. 740–747, 1993.

[31] K. Matasuoka, "Noise injection into inputs in back-propagation learning," *IEEE Trans. Sys., Man and Cybernetics*, vol. 22, pp. 436–440, 1992.

[32] A. R. Webb, "Functional approximation by feed-forward networks: A least-square approach to generalization," *IEEE Trans. Neural Networks*, vol. 5, pp. 480–488, 1994.

[33] S. Geman, E. Bienenstock, and R. Doursat, "Neural networks and the bias/variance dilemma," *Neural Computation*, vol. 4, pp. 1–58, 1992.

[34] G. N. Karystinos and D. A. Pados, "On overfitting, generalization, and randomly expanded training sets," *IEEE Trans. on Neural Networks*, vol. 11, no. 5, pp. 1050–1057, 2000.

Hybrid Adaptive Fuzzy Control Wing Rock Motion System with H^∞ Robust Performance

Chin-Teng Lin #   Tsu-Tian Lee #   Chun-Fei Hsu #   Chih-Min Lin *

#Department of Electrical and Control Engineering, National Chiao-Tung University,
Hsinchu 300, Taiwan, Republic of China
E-mail: ctlin@fnn.cn.nctu.edu.tw

*Department of Electrical Engineering, Yuan-Ze University,
Chung-Li 320, Taiwan, Republic of China
E-mail: cml@ee.yzu.edu.tw

Abstract

In this paper, a hybrid adaptive fuzzy control (HAFC) system is developed for a wing rock motion system. The design of HAFC system contains three parts: one is an indirect controller, the other is a direct controller and the last is a robust controller. A weighting factor α, which can be adjusted by a tradeoff between plant knowledge and control knowledge, is adopted to sum together the control efforts from the indirect and direct controllers. The robust controller is designed to achieve favorable control performance with a desired robustness. Simulation results demonstrate that the HAFC system can achieve favorable desired tracking performances for unknown the wing rock motion dynamics.

KeyWord: Adaptive fuzzy control, Robust control, Fuzzy approximator, Wing rock motion system

I. Introduction

Most current techniques for designing control systems are based on a good understanding of the plant dynamics even under its environment. However, in a number of instances, the controlled plant is too complex and the basic physical processes in it are not fully understood. To tackle this problem, adaptive control techniques are developed to the control these kinds of dynamic systems [1]. However, adaptive control theory can only deal with the systems with known system dynamic structure but unknown system parameters. Recently, fuzzy control using linguistic information is another model-free approach [2]. The fuzzy modeling rules are fuzzy If-Then rules describing the behavior of the system. The fuzzy control rules are fuzzy If-Then rules specifying appropriate control action. Though there have been many successful applications in using fuzzy control; however, it has not been viewed as a rigorous approach due to the lack of formal synthesis techniques that can guarantee the system stability. To tackle this drawback, some researches have been directed at the use of the Lyapunov synthesis approach to constructing the so-called adaptive fuzzy control [3, 4]. The success key element is the fuzzy approximation theory [3], where the parameterized fuzzy estimator can approximate the unknown plant dynamic model or the ideal control law.

Some combat aircraft often require operating at subsonic speeds and high angles of attack. At sufficiently high angles of attack, these aircraft become unstable due to oscillation, mainly a rolling motion known as wing rock [5]. Because of the modern combat aircraft is difficult to isolate the various flow phenomena created by the forebody, strake, wing and their relationship to the wing rock, the behavior of the wing rock motion system is not clear understood. Recently, several theoretical and experimental studies have been performed to understand the dynamics [5, 6]. Moreover, a series of papers have considered the control of the wing rock motion system based on output feedback linearization theory and adaptive control technique [7-9]. In the feedback linearization design approaches, the feedback control gain should be pre-selected to achieve the design performance by trial-and-error; however, this tuning procedure is time-consuming [7, 9]. In the adaptive control techniques, the adaptive control requires knowledge of the structure of the aerodynamic functions; however, this structure is difficult to obtain [8].

In this paper, a hybrid adaptive fuzzy control (HAFC) system is developed for a wing rock motion system. Both the adaptive fuzzy control approach and the H^∞ control technique have been employed together to design the HAFC. The developed HAFC system is comprised of an indirect controller, a direct control, and a robust controller. Simulation results demonstrate that the proposed HAFC system can achieve favorable tracking performances for unknown the wing rock dynamics. Moreover, it is a flexible design methodology by tradeoff between the plant knowledge and control knowledge. If fuzzy control rules are more important and reliable than fuzzy descriptions, chose smaller weighting factor; otherwise choose larger weighting factor.

II. Problem Statement and Control Objective of Wing Rock Motion System

The differential equation describing the wing rock is given by [8]

$$\ddot{\phi}(t) = (pU_\infty^2 Sb/2I_{xx})C_l(t) + u(t) \quad (1)$$

where $\phi(t)$ is the roll angle, an over-dot denotes a derivative with respect to time, $u(t)$ is the control effort, p is the density of air, U_∞ is the freestream velocity, S is the wing reference area, b is the chord, I_{xx} is the mass moment of inertia, and $C_l(t)$ is the roll moment coefficient written as

$$C_l(t) = c_0 + c_1\phi(t) + c_2\dot{\phi}(t) + c_3|\phi(t)|\dot{\phi}(t)$$
$$+ c_4|\dot{\phi}(t)|\dot{\phi}(t) + c_5\phi^3(t). \quad (2)$$

By defining the state vector $\boldsymbol{\varphi} = [\phi(t),\dot{\phi}(t)]^T$ and substituting Eq. (2) into Eq. (1), the dynamic system in Eq. (1) can be rewritten in a state variable form as

$$\ddot{\phi}(t) = f(\boldsymbol{\varphi};t) + u(t) \quad (3)$$

where

$$f(\boldsymbol{\varphi};t) = b_0 + b_1\phi(t) + b_2\dot{\phi}(t) + b_3|\phi(t)|\dot{\phi}(t)$$
$$+ b_4|\dot{\phi}(t)|\dot{\phi}(t) + b_5\phi^3(t) \quad (4)$$

and the parameters b_i, $i = 0,1,...,5$ are given by

$$b_i = (pU_\infty^2 Sb/2I_{xx})c_i. \quad (5)$$

For observing the qualitative natural behavior of the wing rock motion system, the open-loop system time response with $u(t) = 0$ was simulated for two initial conditions: a small initial condition ($\phi(0) = 6\,\text{deg}$, $\dot{\phi}(0) = 3\,\text{deg/sec}$) and a large initial condition ($\phi(0) = 30\,\text{deg}$, $\dot{\phi}(0) = 10\,\text{deg/sec}$) is shown in Fig. 1.

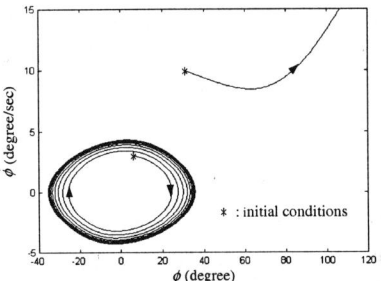

Fig. 1 Phase-plane portraits of the uncontrolled wing rock motion system.

III. Fuzzy Approximator Theorem

Assume that there are m rules in the fuzzy rule base as following form [2]

Rule i: If x_1 is F_1^i and ... x_n is F_n^i

Then y is w_i (6)

where x_j, $j = 1,2,...,n$, and y are the input and output variables of the fuzzy system, respectively, and F_j^i and w_i, $i = 1,2,...,m$ are the labels of the fuzzy sets. The defuzzification of the output is accomplished by the method of center-of-gravity [2]

$$y = \sum_{i=1}^{m}\varsigma_i \times w_i / \sum_{i=1}^{m}\varsigma_i \quad (7)$$

where ς_i is the firing weight of the ith rule. If w_i is chosen as adjustable parameters, Eq. (7) can be rewritten in the vector form as

$$y = \mathbf{w}^T \boldsymbol{\Theta} \quad (8)$$

where $\mathbf{w} = [w_1, w_2, ..., w_m]^T \in R^m$ is a parameter vector and $\boldsymbol{\Theta} = [\xi_1, \xi_2, ..., \xi_m]^T \in R^m$ is a regressive vector with ξ_i defined as

$$\xi_i = \varsigma_i / \sum_{i=1}^{m}\varsigma_i. \quad (9)$$

It has been proven that there exists a fuzzy system of Eq. (8) such that it can uniformly approximate any nonlinear even time-varying function Ω. By the universal approximation theorem, there exists an ideal fuzzy system y^* such that [3]

$$\Omega = y^* + \varepsilon = \mathbf{w}^{*T}\mathbf{\Theta} + \varepsilon \quad (10)$$

where $\mathbf{w}^*$ is the ideal vector of $\mathbf{w}$ and ε denotes the approximator error. In fact, the ideal vector that is needed to best approximate a given nonlinear function Ω is difficult to determine and might not even be unique. Thus, an estimated fuzzy system is defined as

$$\hat{y} = \hat{\mathbf{w}}^T\mathbf{\Theta} \quad (11)$$

where $\hat{\mathbf{w}}$ is the estimated vector of $\mathbf{w}^*$. Define the estimated error $\tilde{y}$ as

$$\tilde{y} = \Omega - \hat{y} = y^* - \hat{y} + \varepsilon = \tilde{\mathbf{w}}^T\mathbf{\Theta} + \varepsilon \quad (12)$$

where $\tilde{\mathbf{w}} = \mathbf{w}^* - \hat{\mathbf{w}}$. In the followings, an update law will be derived to on-line tune the estimated vector of the fuzzy system to achieve favorable estimation of the fuzzy modeling in the indirect controller and the fuzzy controller in the direct controller.

IV. Hybrid Adaptive Fuzzy Controller Design

The control objection of a wing rock motion system is to find a control law so that the roll angle $\phi(t)$ can track a desired command $\phi_m(t)$. Define the tracking error as

$$e(t) = \phi_m(t) - \phi(t). \quad (13)$$

If the system parameters in Eq. (3) are well known and measurable, an ideal controller can be obtained [10]

$$u^*(t) = -f(\boldsymbol{\varphi};t) + \ddot{\phi}_m(t) + k_1\dot{e}(t) + k_2 e(t). \quad (14)$$

Substituting Eq. (14) into Eq. (3) gives

$$\ddot{e}(t) + k_1\dot{e}(t) + k_2 e(t) = 0. \quad (15)$$

If k_1 and k_2 are chosen to correspond to the coefficients of a Hurwitz polynomial, it is imply that $\lim_{t\to\infty} e(t) = 0$. However, the system dynamics $f(\boldsymbol{\varphi};t)$ in Eq. (3) is a nonlinear time-varying function and it can not be exactly obtained, so the ideal controller $u^*(t)$ can not be implemented. To overcome this drawback, the design concept block diagram of the hybrid adaptive fuzzy control (HAFC) for the wing rock motion system is shown in Fig. 2. The control law is developed as

$$u_{hc}(t) = \alpha u_I(t) + (1-\alpha)u_D(t) + u_R(t) \quad (16)$$

where $u_I(t)$ is a indirect controller, $u_D(t)$ is a direct controller, $u_R(t)$ is a robust controller, and $\alpha \in [0,1]$ is a weighting factor for chosen by a control designer based on the understand level of the plant knowledge and control knowledge. From adaptive fuzzy control approach, the fuzzy approximator is used as fuzzy modeling of the plant in the indirect adaptive fuzzy controller, and the fuzzy approximator is used as a fuzzy controller in the indirect adaptive fuzzy controller. Thus, the indirect controller can be defined as

$$u_I(t) = -\hat{f} + \ddot{\phi}_m(t) + k_1\dot{e}(t) + k_2 e(t) \quad (17)$$

where the system dynamic estimator is chosen as

$$\hat{f} = \hat{\mathbf{w}}_f^T\mathbf{\Theta}_f \quad (18)$$

with $\hat{\mathbf{w}}_f$ is the estimated vector and $\mathbf{\Theta}_f$ is the regressive vector of the fuzzy modeling, respectively. Similarly, the direct controller is defined as

$$u_D(t) = \hat{\mathbf{w}}_u^T\mathbf{\Theta}_u \quad (19)$$

where $\hat{\mathbf{w}}_u$ is the estimator vector and $\mathbf{\Theta}_u$ is the regressive vector of the fuzzy controller, respectively. Applying Eqs. (14) and (16) into Eq. (3) and after some simple manipulations, the error dynamic equation can be obtained as

$$\ddot{e} = -k_1\dot{e} - k_2 e - \alpha(f - \hat{f}) \\ + (1-\alpha)(u^* - u_D) - u_R. \quad (20)$$

From Eq. (20), we shall define the estimator errors based on the universal approximation theorem as [3]

$$\tilde{f} = f - \hat{f} = \tilde{\mathbf{w}}_f^T\mathbf{\Theta}_f + \varepsilon_f \quad (21)$$

$$\tilde{u} = u^* - u_D = \tilde{\mathbf{w}}_u^T\mathbf{\Theta}_u + \varepsilon_u \quad (22)$$

where $\tilde{\mathbf{w}}_f = \mathbf{w}_f^* - \hat{\mathbf{w}}_f$, $\tilde{\mathbf{w}}_u = \mathbf{w}_u^* - \hat{\mathbf{w}}_u$, and ε_f and ε_u are the approximator errors. Defined the tracking error vector $\mathbf{e} = [e(t), \dot{e}(t)]^T$, thus Eq. (20) can be rewritten in the vector form as

$$\dot{\mathbf{e}} = \mathbf{A}_m\mathbf{e} + \mathbf{b}_m[-\alpha\tilde{\mathbf{w}}_f^T\mathbf{\Theta}_f + (1-\alpha)\tilde{\mathbf{w}}_u^T\mathbf{\Theta}_u \\ + \varepsilon - u_R] \quad (23)$$

where $\mathbf{A_m} = \begin{bmatrix} 0 & 1 \\ -k_2 & -k_1 \end{bmatrix}$, $\mathbf{b_m} = [0,1]^T$, and $\varepsilon = -\alpha\varepsilon_f + (1-\alpha)\varepsilon_u$. While ε appears, the following H^∞ tracking performance is requested [11]

$$\int_0^T \mathbf{e}^T \mathbf{Q} \mathbf{e}\, dt \leq \mathbf{e}^T(0)\mathbf{P}\mathbf{e}(0) + \frac{1}{\kappa}[\tilde{\mathbf{w}}_f^T(0)\tilde{\mathbf{w}}_f(0)$$

$$+ \tilde{\mathbf{w}}_u^T(0)\tilde{\mathbf{w}}_u(0)] + \rho^2 \int_0^T \varepsilon^2\, dt,$$

$$\forall T \in [0,\infty), \quad \varepsilon \in L_2[0,T] \quad (24)$$

for given weighting matrices $\mathbf{Q} = \mathbf{Q}^T \geq 0$ and $\mathbf{P} = \mathbf{P}^T \geq 0$, an adaption gain κ, and a prescribed attenuation level ρ. If the system starts with initial conditions $\mathbf{e}(0) = 0$, $\tilde{\mathbf{w}}_f(0) = 0$, $\tilde{\mathbf{w}}_u(0) = 0$ and $\mathbf{Q} = \mathbf{I}$, then the robustness control performance in Eq. (24) satisfies

$$\sup_{\varepsilon \in L_2[0,T]} \frac{\|\mathbf{e}\|_\mathbf{Q}}{\|\varepsilon\|_2} \leq \rho \quad (25)$$

where $\|\mathbf{e}\|_\mathbf{Q}^2 = \int_0^T \mathbf{e}^T \mathbf{Q} \mathbf{e}\, dt$ and $\|\varepsilon\|_2^2 = \int_0^T \varepsilon^2\, dt$, i.e., the L_2-gain from ε to the tracking error $\mathbf{e}$ must be equal to or less than ρ. That is an arbitrary attenuation level can be obtained, if ρ is adequately chosen. Therefore, the following theorem can be stated and prove.

Theorem 1: Consider the wing rock motion system presented in Eq. (3). If the hybrid robust indirect and direct adaptive fuzzy controller is designed as in Eq. (16), in which the indirect controller $u_I(t)$ is given in Eq. (17), the direct controller $u_D(t)$ is given in Eq. (19) and the robust controller $u_R(t)$ is given in Eq. (28) with the adaptive laws given in Eqs. (26) and (27):

$$\dot{\tilde{\mathbf{w}}}_f = \eta_1 \mathbf{e}^T \mathbf{P} \mathbf{b_m} \Theta_f \quad (26)$$

$$\dot{\tilde{\mathbf{w}}}_u = -\eta_2 \mathbf{e}^T \mathbf{P} \mathbf{b_m} \Theta_u \quad (27)$$

$$u_R = \frac{1}{\kappa} \mathbf{b_m}^T \mathbf{P} \mathbf{e} \quad (28)$$

where η_1 and η_2 are the learning rates with positive constants, κ is a positive adaption gain, and positive matrix $\mathbf{P} = \mathbf{P}^T$ is the solution of the following Riccati-like equation

$$\mathbf{P}\mathbf{A_m} + \mathbf{A_m}^T\mathbf{P} + \mathbf{Q} - \frac{2}{\kappa}\mathbf{P}\mathbf{b_m}\mathbf{b_m}^T\mathbf{P} + \frac{1}{\rho^2}\mathbf{P}\mathbf{b_m}\mathbf{b_m}^T\mathbf{P} = 0$$

(29)

Then, the H^∞ tracking performance in Eq. (24) can be achieved for a prescribed attenuation level ρ.

Proof: Define a Lyapunov function as

$$V(\mathbf{e}, \tilde{\mathbf{w}}_f, \tilde{\mathbf{w}}_u) = \frac{1}{2}\mathbf{e}^T\mathbf{P}\mathbf{e} + \frac{\alpha}{2\eta_1}\tilde{\mathbf{w}}_f^T\tilde{\mathbf{w}}_f + \frac{(1-\alpha)}{2\eta_2}\tilde{\mathbf{w}}_u^T\tilde{\mathbf{w}}_u \quad (30)$$

Differentiating Eq. (30) with respect to time and using Eqs. (23), (26) ~ (28), it is obtained that

$$\dot{V}(\mathbf{e}, \tilde{\mathbf{w}}_f, \tilde{\mathbf{w}}_u) = \frac{1}{2}\mathbf{e}^T\mathbf{P}\dot{\mathbf{e}} + \frac{1}{2}\dot{\mathbf{e}}^T\mathbf{P}\mathbf{e}$$

$$+ \frac{\alpha}{\eta_1}\tilde{\mathbf{w}}_f^T\dot{\tilde{\mathbf{w}}}_f + \frac{(1-\alpha)}{\eta_2}\tilde{\mathbf{w}}_u^T\dot{\tilde{\mathbf{w}}}_u$$

$$= \frac{-1}{2}\mathbf{e}^T(\mathbf{A_m}^T\mathbf{P} + \mathbf{P}\mathbf{A_m})\mathbf{e}$$

$$+ \mathbf{e}^T\mathbf{P}\mathbf{b_m}(\varepsilon - u_R) \quad (31)$$

Using robust controller (28) and Riccati-like equation (29), Eq. (31) can be rewritten as

$$\dot{V}(\mathbf{e}, \tilde{\mathbf{w}}_f, \tilde{\mathbf{w}}_u)$$

$$= \frac{1}{2}\mathbf{e}^T(-\mathbf{Q} - \frac{1}{\rho^2}\mathbf{P}\mathbf{b_m}\mathbf{b_m}^T\mathbf{P})\mathbf{e} + \frac{1}{2}\varepsilon\mathbf{b_m}^T\mathbf{P}\mathbf{e} + \frac{1}{2}\mathbf{e}^T\mathbf{P}\mathbf{b_m}\varepsilon$$

$$= \frac{-1}{2}\mathbf{e}^T\mathbf{Q}\mathbf{e} - \frac{1}{2}(\frac{1}{\rho}\mathbf{b_m}^T\mathbf{P}\mathbf{e} - \rho\varepsilon)^T(\frac{1}{\rho}\mathbf{b_m}^T\mathbf{P}\mathbf{e} - \rho\varepsilon) + \frac{1}{2}\rho^2\varepsilon^2$$

$$\leq -\frac{1}{2}\mathbf{e}^T\mathbf{Q}\mathbf{e} + \frac{1}{2}\rho^2\varepsilon^2 \quad (32)$$

where $\varepsilon\mathbf{b_m}^T\mathbf{P}\mathbf{e} = \mathbf{e}^T\mathbf{P}\mathbf{b_m}\varepsilon$ is used since it is a scale. Integrating the above equation from $t = 0$ to $t = T$ yields

$$V(T) - V(0) \leq -\frac{1}{2}\int_0^T \mathbf{e}^T\mathbf{Q}\mathbf{e}\, dt + \frac{1}{2}\rho^2\int_0^T \varepsilon^2\, dt \quad (33)$$

Since $V(T) \geq 0$, the above inequality implies the following inequality

$$\frac{1}{2}\int_0^T \mathbf{e}^T \mathbf{Q}\mathbf{e}\, dt \le V(0) + \frac{1}{2}\rho^2 \int_0^T \varepsilon^2 dt \quad (34)$$

Comparing with Eq. (24) the hybrid adaptive fuzzy control system can achieve the H^∞ tracking performance.

V. Simulation Results

The aerodynamic parameters b_i parameters for the model in Eq. (4) are given by $b_0 = 0$, $b_1 = -0.01859521$, $b_2 = 0.015162375$, $b_3 = -0.06245153$, $b_4 = 0.00954708$, and $b_5 = 0.02145291$. It should be emphasized that the derivation of the HAFC system does not need to use the aerodynamic parameters and the structure of the aerodynamic functions. The aerodynamic parameters are utilized only for simulations. In the indirect controller, the fuzzy system approximator is viewed as the fuzzy modeling. In the direct controller, the fuzzy system approximator is used as the fuzzy controller. For simulations, two initial conditions (a small initial condition and a large initial condition) are examined to illustrate the effectiveness of the proposed HAFC. The learning rates are selected as $\eta_1 = \eta_2 = 10$. The simulation results of the HAFC system for small and large initial conditions are shown in Fig. 3 for $\kappa = 1.0$. The state responses are shown in Figs. 3(a) and 3(c); and the associated control efforts are shown in Figs. 3(b) and 3(d), respectively. Simulation results show that the robust tracking performance of the HAFC system has been achieved for the different initial conditions.

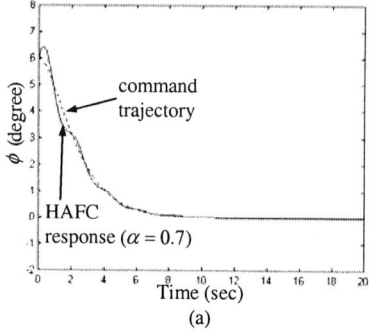

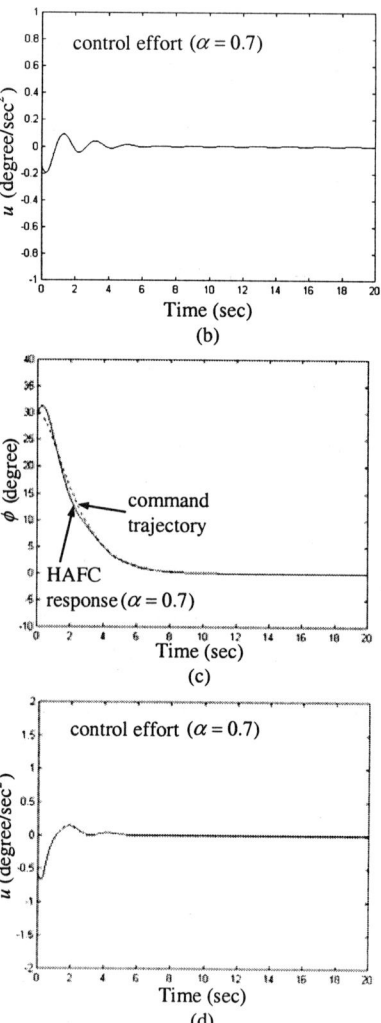

Fig. 3 Simulation results of HAFC wing rock motion system for $\kappa = 1.0$.

VI. Conclusions

In this paper, a hybrid adaptive fuzzy control system is developed to control a wing rock motion system. The hybrid control system is comprised of an indirect controller, a direct control, and a robust controller. A weighting factor is a tradeoff between plant knowledge and control knowledge to sum together the control efforts from indirect controller and direct controller. The robust controller is designed to achieve an arbitrarily attenuation level caused by the unmodeled dynamics and approximator error. The major contributions of this paper are (1) the successful development of the bridge between the indirect and direct adaptive fuzzy control using a weighting factor; (2) the successful development of the H^∞ control technique into the adaptive fuzzy control approach to achieve favorable control performance with desired robustness; (3) the successful application of the proposed HAFC to control the wing rock motion system.

Acknowledgment

This work was supported by the National Science Council of the Republic of China under Grant NSC 91-2213-E-009-035.

References

[1] Sastry, S., and Bodson, M., *Adaptive Control – Stability, Convergence, and Robustness*, Prentice-Hall, Englewood Cliffs, New Jersey, 1989, pp. 19-22.

[2] Lee, C. C., "Fuzzy Logic in Control Systems: Fuzzy Logic Controller-Part I/II," *IEEE Transactions on Systems, Man, and Cybernetics*, Vol. 20, No. 2, 1990, pp. 404-435.

[3] Wang, L. X., *Adaptive Fuzzy Systems and Control - Design and Stability Analysis*, Prentice-Hall, Englewood Cliffs, NJ, 1994, pp. 140-154.

[4] Wang, S. D., and Lin, C. K., "Adaptive Tuning of the Fuzzy Controller for Robots," *Fuzzy Sets and Systems*, Vol. 110, No. 3, 2000, pp. 351-363.

[5] Nayfeh, A. H., Elzebda, J. M., and Mook, D. T., "Analytical Study of the Subsonic Wing-Rock Phenomenon for Slender Delta Wings," *Journal of Aircraft*, Vol. 26, No. 9, 1989, pp. 805-809.

[6] Tan, S. Y., and Lan, C. E., "Estimation of Aeroelastic Models in Structural Limit-Cycle Oscillations from Test Data," *AIAA Journal*, Vol. 35, No. 6, 1997, pp. 1025-1029.

[7] Shue, S. P., and Agarwal, R. K., "Nonlinear H_∞ Method for Control of Wing Rock Motions," *Journal of Guidance, Control, and Dynamics*, Vol. 23, No. 1, 2000, pp. 60-68.

[8] Singh, S. N., Yim, W., and Wells, W. R., "Direct Adaptive and Neural Control of Wing-Rock Motion of Slender Delta Wings," *Journal of Guidance, Control, and Dynamics*, Vol. 18, No. 1, 1995, pp. 25-30.

[9] Monahemi, M. M., and Krstic, M., "Control of Wing Rock Motion Using Adaptive Feedback Linearization," *Journal of Guidance, Control, and Dynamics*, Vol. 19, No. 4, 1996, pp. 905-912.

[10] Slotine, J. J. E., and Li, W. P., *Applied Nonlinear Control*, Prentice-Hall, Englewood Cliffs, NJ, 1991.

[11] Chen, B. S., and Lee, C. H., "H^∞ Tracking Design of Uncertain Nonlinear SISO Systems: Adaptive Fuzzy Approach," *IEEE Transactions on Fuzzy Systems*, Vol. 4, No. 1, 1996, pp. 32-43.

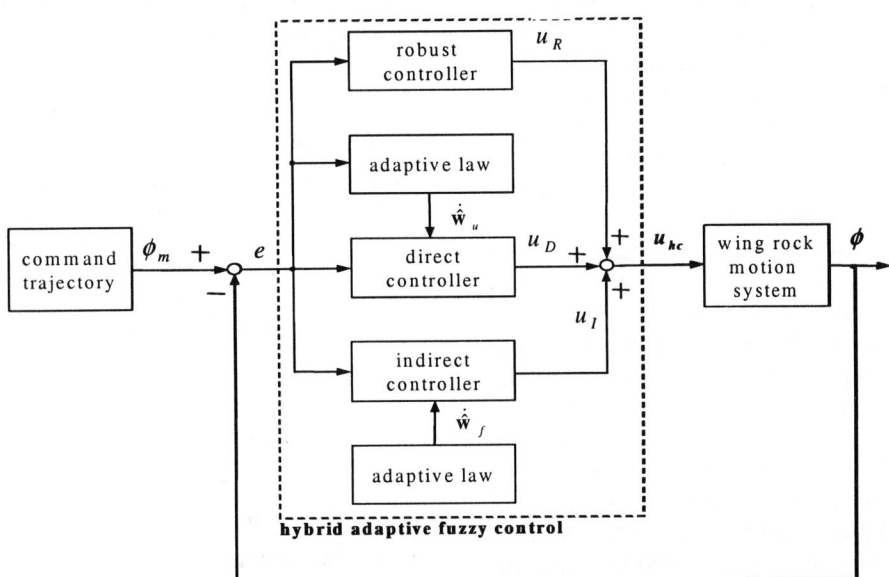

Fig. 2 The block diagram of hybrid adaptive fuzzy control wing rock motion system.

Parameter Plane Analysis of Neurocontrol Vehicle Systems for Limit Cycle Prediction

Bing-Fei Wu, Jau-Woei Perng and Tsu-Tian Lee
Department of Electrical and Control Engineering, National Chiao Tung University
1001, Ta Hsueh Road, Hsinchu, 30050, Taiwan, R.O.C.
Tel: +886-3-5712121 ext. 54428
Fax: +886-37-470647
E-mail: jwperng0@ms24.hinet.net

Abstract—The main purpose of this paper is to predict the limit cycles of neurocontrol system with perturbed parameters by combining the approaches of stability equation, describing function and parameter plane. The neurocontroller is first linearized by using the describing function method. The stability of equivalent linearized system is then analyzed by using stability equations and the parameter plane method. According to this procedure, the amplitude and frequency of limit cycles can be figured out clearly in the parameter plane. Moreover, the limit cycle may be suppressed by adjusting the control parameters carefully. Finally, a vehicle model is illustrated to demonstrate its validity.

I. INTRODUCTION

Limit cycle analysis of a nonlinear control system has been considered in many industrial applications. The linearizd system based on describing function method has been widely employed in the analysis of nonlinear control system. The hydraulic and robot control systems with friction were discussed in [1,2]. In [3], the car steering control with actuator rate limit was concerned. On the other hand, Amato et al. dealt with the analysis of pilot-in-the-loop oscillations due to position and rate saturations [4]. Based on the gain-phase margin tester technology, the limit cycle analysis of nonlinear control with multiple nonlinearities was proposed by Chang et al [5-6].

The robust analysis of uncertain parameters in linear control system is often dealt with parameter plane method or parameter space method [7-11]. In [12], limit cycle analysis of PID engine control in parameter plane has been studied. A set of control parameters can be chosen carefully in order to yield the suitable characteristics of limit cycles. Recently, the describing functions of neurocontroller have been considered in [13]. Due to the results in [13], we extend some basic approaches to analyze the neurocontrol system with perturbed parameters for limit cycle prediction. Ultimately, a vehicle control system is cited to verify this approach.

II. BASIC APPROACH

In this section, a basic approach to analyze the nonlinear system with adjustable parameters for limit cycle prediction is given. Based on describing function method, a general linearized system with multiple nonlinear elements is considered and shown in Fig. 1,

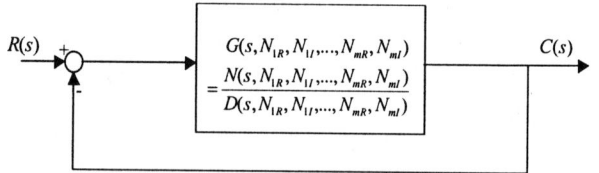

Fig. 1. Block diagram of a general linearized nonlinear control system.

where $G(s, N_{1R}, N_{1I}, \cdots, N_{mR}, N_{mI})$ is the open loop transfer function. $N_{1R}, \cdots, N_{mR}$ and $N_{1I}, \cdots, N_{mI}$ are real parts and imaginary parts of the describing function (N_i) of $n_1, n_2, \cdots, n_m$, respectively, which can be expressed as the following equation

$$N_i(A,\omega) = N_{iR}(A,\omega) + jN_{iI}(A,\omega) \qquad (1)$$

where $i = 1, \cdots, m$, A and ω are the amplitude and frequency of sinusoidal input to one of the nonlinearities.

The characteristic equation of this equivalent linear system can be expressed as

$$\begin{aligned}&1 + G(s, N_{1R}, N_{1I}, \cdots, N_{mR}, \cdots, N_{mI}) \\ &= 1 + \frac{N(s, N_{1R}, N_{1I}, \cdots, N_{mR}, \cdots, N_{mI})}{D(s, N_{1R}, N_{1I}, \cdots, N_{mR}, \cdots, N_{mI})} \\ &= 0,\end{aligned} \qquad (2)$$

which is equivalent to

$$\begin{aligned}f(s) &\triangleq D(s, N_{1R}, N_{1I}, \cdots, N_{mR}, \cdots, N_{mI}) \\ &\quad + N(s, N_{1R}, N_{1I}, \cdots, N_{mR}, \cdots, N_{mI}) \; . \\ &= 0\end{aligned} \qquad (3)$$

Let $s = j\omega$, one has

$$f(j\omega) = f(\alpha, \beta, \gamma, \cdots, j\omega) = 0, \qquad (4)$$

where $\alpha, \beta, \gamma, \cdots$ are variables which consist of the items (N_{iR}, N_{iI}) of describing functions and/or adjustable parameters of the linear portion of the system. Notice that the designer can define these variables arbitrarily in order to analyze the effect of system parameters. When only two parameters α and β are chosen to concern, Eq. (4) is arranged as the following equation

$$f(j\omega) = f(\alpha, \beta, \gamma, \cdots, \omega)$$
$$= X \cdot \alpha + Y \cdot \beta + Z \quad (5)$$
$$= 0,$$

where X, Y and Z are functions of $\gamma, \cdots$ and $j\omega$.

Let Eq. (5) be partitioned into two stability equations with real part (f_R) and imaginary part (f_I) and written in the following [5-6]

$$f_R(\alpha, \beta, \gamma, \cdots, \omega) = X_1 \cdot \alpha + Y_1 \cdot \beta + Z_1 = 0, \quad (6)$$

and

$$f_I(\alpha, \beta, \gamma, \cdots, \omega) = X_2 \cdot \alpha + Y_2 \cdot \beta + Z_2 = 0, \quad (7)$$

where X_1, Y_1, Z_1 and X_2, Y_2, Z_2 are real and imaginary parts of X, Y and Z. Therefore, α and β are solved from linear functions of (5) and (6), one has

$$\alpha = \frac{Y_1 \cdot Z_2 - Y_2 \cdot Z_1}{\Delta} \quad (8)$$

and

$$\beta = \frac{Z_1 \cdot X_2 - Z_2 \cdot X_1}{\Delta}, \quad (9)$$

where $\Delta = X_1 \cdot Y_2 - X_2 \cdot Y_1$. Note that if Eqs. (6) and (7) are not linear, but independent with α and β, they can be solved theoretically [10].

III. NEUROCONTROL VEHICLE SYSTEM DESIGN

The Static Neural Network (SNN) shown in Fig. 2 can be used as a controller (neurocontroller). The network structure is 1-m-1 and does not have bias weights [13]. The parameters g_k and h_k are the neural network weights and m is the number of hidden neurons.

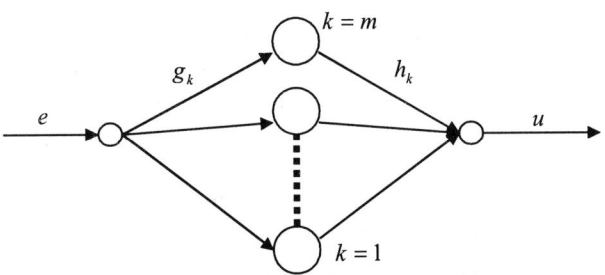

Fig. 2. Static Neural Network (SNN).

Based on the stability analysis in [13], the describing function of neurocontroller with sigmoid function tanh may be represented as

$$N_1(A) = \sum_{k=1}^{m} g_k \cdot h_k \left\{ 1 - \frac{g_k^2 \cdot A^2}{6} \right\}, \quad (10)$$

where A is the amplitude of limit cycle.

In this section, the limit cycle prediction of neurocontrol vehicle system with perturbed parameters is adduced and the block diagram is depicted in Fig. 3.

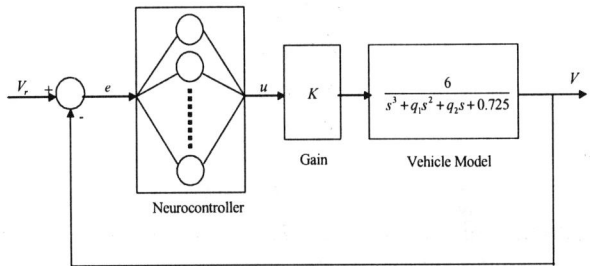

Fig. 3. Block diagram of neurocontrol vehicle system.

The vehicle model is given in the following [14]

$$H(s,q) = \frac{V(s)}{V_i(s)} = \frac{6}{s^3 + q_1 s^2 + q_2 s + 0.725}, \quad (11)$$

where $8.2 \leq q_1 \leq 14.8, 10.6 \leq q_2 \leq 19.5$. Note that V_i is the voltage applied to the throttle valve and V is the forward velocity of the vehicle. The boundaries of perturbed region are plotted in Fig. 4 and four vertex points are represented as $p_1(8.2, 10.6)$, $p_2(14.8, 10.6)$ $p_3(8.2, 19.5)$ and $p_4(14.8, 19.5)$. In Fig. 3, we assume that the input signal to neurocontroller is $e(t) = A \sin \omega t$.

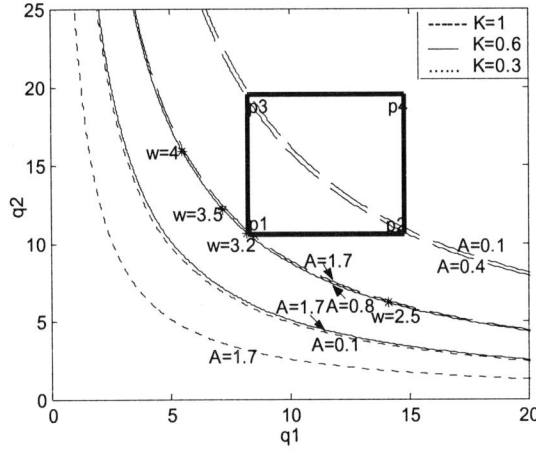

Fig. 4. Limit-cycle loci in the parameter plane with different control gain.

The overall open loop transfer function is

$$G(s) = \frac{6KN_1}{s^3 + q_1 s^2 + q_2 s + 0.725}, \quad (12)$$

where K is an adjustable parameter. After some manipulations, the characteristic equation is

$$\begin{aligned} f(s) &= s^3 + q_1 s^2 + q_2 s + 0.725 + 6KN_1 \\ &= s^2 q_1 + s q_2 + s^3 + 0.725 + 6KN_1 \\ &= X \cdot \alpha + Y \cdot \beta + Z \\ &= 0, \end{aligned} \quad (13)$$

where

$$\alpha = q_1,$$
$$\beta = q_2,$$
$$X = s^2,$$
$$Y = s,$$

and

$$Z = s^3 + 0.725 + 6KN_1.$$

Substituting $s = j\omega$ into Eq. (13), α and β are determined from Eqs. (6)-(9), which can be plotted by the boundaries with fixed amplitude A and gain K (varying ω from 0 to ∞) in the q_1 vs. q_2 plane. In the following, two cases are illustrated to study by this approach.

Case 1: The network parameters are chosen as:
$$g_1 = g_2 = g_3 = 1, h_1 = h_2 = h_3 = 9, \quad m = 3.$$

Let $K = 1$, the simulation results of output signal $v(t)$ and input signal $e(t)$ operating at the two vertex points are shown in Fig. 5. We can find that the limit cycle are generated when operating at p_1 but is not at p_4. If we change A from 0.1 to 1.7, some limit-cycle loci are plotted in Fig. 4, which confirm the results of Fig. 5. To give an example, the amplitude A and frequency ω of limit cycle at p_1 are 1.7 and 3.2 rad/sec, respectively. The dashed line in Fig. 5 proves this outcome.

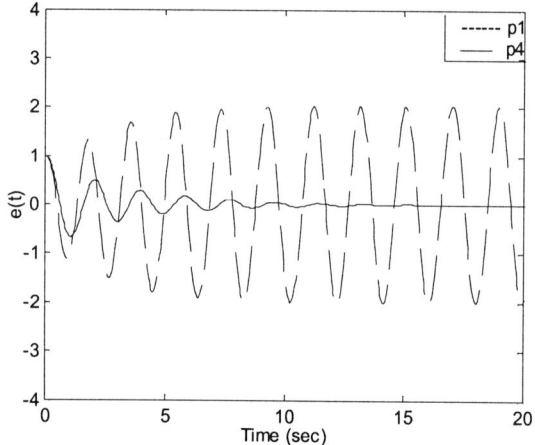

Fig. 5. Input signals operating at two points.

Besides, from Fig. 4, the amplitude of limit cycle may be reduced when the gain K is decreased to 0.6 and the amplitude A is 0.8. Finally, if the gain K is again decreased to 0.3, the limit cycle is indeed vanished. Figure 6 shows these results. On the other hand, the unit-step responses of four vertex points with $K = 0.3$ are displayed in Fig. 7. It is clear that the better performance could be acquired in this situation.

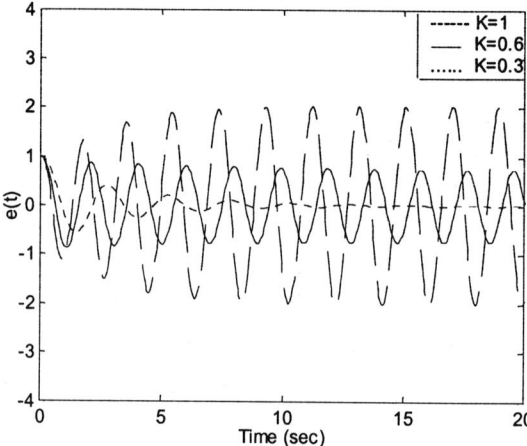

Fig. 6. Input signals at point p1 with different control gain.

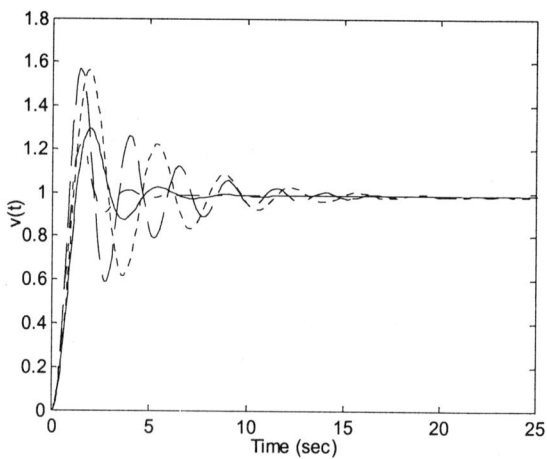

Fig. 7. Unit-step responses of four vertex points with K=0.3.

Case 2: The network parameters are chosen as:
$$g_1 = 2, g_2 = 0.8, g_3 = 1, h_1 = 2, h_2 = 1, h_3 = 3, \quad m = 3.$$

By adjusting the gain K from 1 to 7.5, the parameter plane may be redrawn in Fig. 8 with $A = 0.1$. The results show that the limit cycle can be restrained with $K = 1$. The curve of K passing through the point p_1 is 1.85. Fig. 9 shows the input signals $e(t)$ operating at different K, which are matched with Fig. 8. Notice that the amplitude of limit cycle will step up when K is increased. According to the above analysis, in fact, the generation of limit cycle could be avoided since the parameters of neurocontroller and gain K are adjusted carefully.

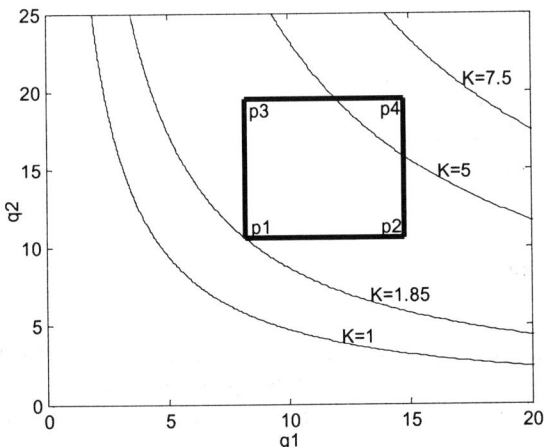

Fig. 8. Limit-cycle loci in parameter plane with $A = 0.1$

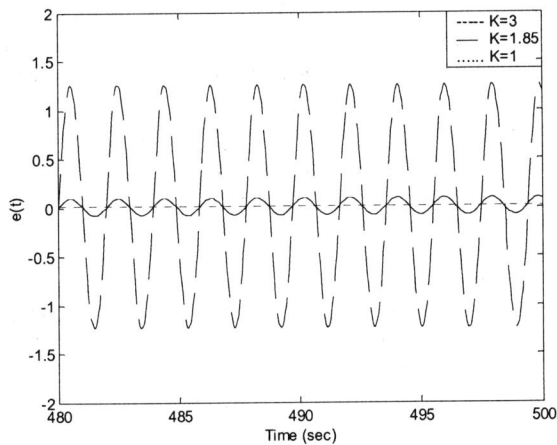

Fig. 9. Input signals at point p1 with different control gain.

IV. CONCLUSIONS

In this paper, the limit cycle analysis of neurocontrol system is achieved by utilizing the methods of stability equation, describing function, and parameter plane. A vehicle control system with adjustable parameters is illustrated to study. Simulation results show that more information about the characteristic of limit cycle could be acquired by this approach. In addition, the limit cycle analysis of neurocontrol system with multiple nonlinearities can be viewed as the future research topic.

ACKNOWLEDGEMENTS

The authors would like to thank Prof. K. W. Han for his kindly guide and suggestion. This paper was supported by 91X104 EX–91–E-FA06-4-4.

REFERENCES

[1] C. S. Cox, and I. G. French, "Limit cycle Prediction Conditions for Hydraulic Control System," *ASME Journal of Dynamic Systems, Measurement, and Control*, Vol. 108, 1986, pp. 17-23.

[2] H. Olsson, and K. J. Astrom, "Friction Generated Limit Cycles," *IEEE Transactions on Control Systems Technology*, Vol. 9, No. 4, 2001, pp. 629-636.

[3] J. Ackermann, and T. Bunte, "Actuator Rate Limits in Robust Car Steering Control," *IEEE Conference on Decision & Control*, 1997, pp. 4726-4731.

[4] F. Amato, R. Iervolino, M. Pandit, and L. Verde, "Analysis of Pilot-in-the-Loop Oscillations Due to Position and Rate Saturations," *IEEE Conference on Decision & Control*, 1999, pp. 3564-3569.

[5] M. K. Chang, C. H. Chang, and K. W. Han, "Gain Margins and Phase Margins for Nonlinear Control Systems with Adjustable Parameters," *IEEE Transactions on Industry and Application Society Conference*, 1993, pp. 2123-2130.

[6] M. K. Chang and C. H. Chang, "Analysis of Gain Margin and Phase Margin of Nonlinear Reactor Control System" *IEEE Transactions on Nuclear Science*, Vol. 41, No. 4, 1994, pp. 1686-1691.

[7] K. W. Han and G. J. Thaler, "Control System Analysis and Design Using a Parameter Space Method," *IEEE Transactions on Automatic Control*, Vol. 11, No. 3, 1966, pp. 560-563.

[8] K. W. Han, *Nonlinear Control Systems - Some Practical Methods*, Academic Cultural Company, California, 1977.

[9] D. D. Siljak, "Analysis and Synthesis of Feedback Control Systems in the Parameter Plane," *IEEE Transactions on Industry and Application*, Vol. 83, 1964, pp. 466-473.

[10] D. D. Siljak, *Nonlinear Systems - The Parameter Analysis and Design*, New York: Wiley, 1969.

[11] D. D. Siljak, "Parameter Space Methods for Robust Control Design: A Guide Tour," *IEEE Transactions on Automatic Control*, Vol. 34, No. 7, 1989, pp. 674-688.

[12] A. T. Shenton, "Parameter Space Design of PID Limit Cycle Controllers," *Proceedings of the American Control Conference*, 1999, pp. 3342-3346.

[13] A. Delgado, "Stability Analysis of Neurocontrol Systems Using a Describing Function," *IEEE International Joint Conference on Neural Network Proceedings*, 1998, pp. 2126-2130.

[14] A. S. Hauksdottir and G. Sigurdaraottir, "On the Use of Robust Design Methods in Vehicle Longitudinal Controller Design," *ASME Journal of Dynamic Systems, Measurement, and Control*, Vol. 115, No. 3, 1993, pp. 166-172.

PARAMETER SENSITIVITIES OF A NEURO-BASED ADAPTIVE CONTROLLER WITH GUARANTEED STABILITY

M. B. Menhaj and Swakshar Ray
School of Electrical and Computer Engineering
Department of Computer Science
Oklahoma State University, Stillwater
OK-74078-5032, USA
Fax: 405-744-9097
Tel. 405-744-2283
menhaj@okstate.edu

ABSTRACT

This paper provides a detailed analysis and study on the parameter sensitivities and domain of attraction of the novel neuro-based adaptive controller based on the previously published paper [1,2]. The special learning algorithm similar to back propagation provides better stability and wide domain of attraction for the controller provided that the neural network parameters are chosen carefully. The controller acts as a direct adaptive controller and the weight and bias matrices are updated online without any prior offline training. It is easy to implement in real time due to less complexity in terms of absence of several neural networks and robustifying terms. This paper reveals the domain of attraction based on different parameter values and the sensitivities of the error surface with respect to designed parameters. We have tested the controller on a two link robot arm system and extensive simulation results show the dependence and effectiveness of the controller with respect to parameters of the designed neural network. This gives a better insight of the controller that has been investigated with systems of the form $\dot{x} = f(x) + u + w$ and $\dot{x} = f(x) + g(x)u(t) + w$. The theoretical proof on the stability of the closed loop nonlinear systems with the adaptive controller has been investigated in detail in this paper. The paper also summarizes the potential advantages, disadvantages, prospective developments and real life applicability of the controller scheme at the end.

1. INTRODUCTION

Although there are many different ways to use neural networks(NN) for controlling a dynamic system but the main issue still remains that whether the NN is trained with sufficient data to control the system over a larger domain. So, the responsibilities lie on the designer to use the learning rules such that NN can control the system over greater regions and maintain stability while dealing with the dynamic behavior. In a classical control, the nonlinear system should be known to design a controller with output feedback linearization or similar type of technique. But neural network can be used for any system with unknown dynamics using the set of input and output data point collected from the system during operation. So the neuro-controller should be carefully designed to be stable and bounded within the operating region and hence we need to impose certain constraint on the parameters as well as on the system itself to use the well driven classical control theory.

In 1990's some achievements on stability of neuro-controllers have been reported. Tzirkel-Hancock et al. [14] designed a direct neuro-controller scheme for a special class of minimum phase nonlinear systems through input/output linearization and state feedback control mechanism in which instead of employing the Lie-derivatives the neural network approximations are used. The design of neuro-controllers along with its stability and convergence analysis have been continued by Chen et al. [7][8][9], Lewis et al. [10][11], Sadegh [13]…

For real time use of neural netwok controllers as intelligent systems, two main factors are important, it has to be easy to implement and response time has to be fast as delays will cause the controller lagging behind the plant; this intern might cause stability problems. Several radial basis neural networks have been dealt with in the literature [15],[16],[17], but MLP neural networks have some advantages over radial basis network in certain situations. As it is much difficult to prove the stability of MLP neural network theoretically, MLP networks have been studied less. In this paper, we consider a special type of MLP neural network with single hidden layer, a pre-processing block and a linear output layer which uses a special type of BP-like learning rules to adjust parameters in the neural network. The controller is basically a direct adaptive controller which does not need any pre-learning and the training is done online while controlling the plant in accordance with desired trajectories given by some reference model. It is assumed that all the state of the plant is available for measurement and the linear reference model is chosen by the designer. No additional controller is required. Stability analysis shows both tracking error and neural network weights remain bounded if the plant disturbed by a bounded disturbance input signal. Parameter sensitivities, tested by simulations can be seen fom theoretical study of the stability by Lyapunov criteria.

The rest of the paper is organized as follows. Section 2 presents the neuro-based adaptive controller. The performance of the controller is illustrated by some simulation examples along with some discussion on results in section 3. Section 4 gives a detail stability analysis with simulation data and theoretical back ground. Finally section 5 summarizes the paper.

2. THE PROPOSED NEURO-ADAPTIVE CONTROLLER

2.1 General Problem Statement

This paper addresses the model following control problem for a special class of dynamical systems with the following dynamical equation:

$$\underline{\dot{x}}(t) = \underline{f}(\underline{x}) + \underline{u}(t) + \underline{w}(t) \qquad (1)$$

where, $\underline{f}: \mathbb{R}^n \to \mathbb{R}^n$ is an unknown smooth non-linear function, $\underline{u}$ and $\underline{w}$, which represents the model uncertainties and state noise, are the system's control and disturbance signal vectors, respectively. It is assumed that states are available and the additive disturbance $\underline{w}$ is bounded. Though during the simulation we will show that the controller is also capable to control class of dynamical system $\underline{\dot{x}} = \underline{f}(\underline{x}) + g(\underline{x})\underline{u} + \underline{w}(t)$.

The objective is to design a neuro-adaptive controller so that the plant (1) follows asymptotically a desired trajectory given by the following reference model:

$$\underline{\dot{x}}_d = A_d \underline{x}_d + B_d \underline{r}(t) \qquad (2)$$

In the above, the matrix A_d is asymptotically stable.

Figure 1 represents the overall closed loop neuro-control system. The control signal is defined as:

$$u = A_d \underline{x}_d + \underline{u}_{NN}(\underline{x}, W_1, b_1, W_2, b_2) + B_d \underline{r}(t) \qquad (3)$$

where

$$\underline{u}_{NN}(\underline{x}, W_1, b_1, W_2, b_2) = W_2 f_1(W_1 f_0(W_0 \underline{x}) + b_1) + b_2,$$

W_1, W_2, b_1, b_2 are tunable weight matrices and biases of the multilayer perceptron neural network, and f_0, f_1 are any nonlinear smooth squashing functions (i.e., sigmoidal type functions).; that is

$$\underline{f}_1(y) = [f_1(y_1) \ldots f_1(y_n)]^T; \underline{y} \in \mathbb{R}^n$$
$$|f_1(z)| < 1, \forall z \in R$$

Note that the first layer represents a preprocessing block.

Universal approximation property of MLP neural network assures the existence of weight and bias matrices W_1, W_2, b_1, b_2 so that

$$\left| \underbrace{\underline{f}(\underline{x}) + \underline{u}_{NN}(\underline{x}, W_1, b_1, W_2, b_2)}_{\varepsilon(\underline{x})} \right| < \bar{\varepsilon}, \forall \underline{x} \in B \subset R^n$$

with $\|W\| \equiv Trace(W^T W) \leq \bar{W}$. Now the tracking signal error will be $\underline{e} = \underline{x} - \underline{x}_d$, $\underline{\dot{e}} = A_d \underline{e} + \underbrace{(\underline{u}_{NN} - \underline{u}^*_{NN})}_{\underline{\tilde{u}}_{NN}} + \underbrace{\underline{u}^*_{NN} + \underline{f}(\underline{x})}_{\varepsilon(\underline{x})} + \underline{w}$

(4)

$\tilde{W} = W_i - W^*_i, i = 1, 2, \ldots$. In this context note that the neural network control signal $\underline{u}_{NN}$ is approximating $-f(x)$.

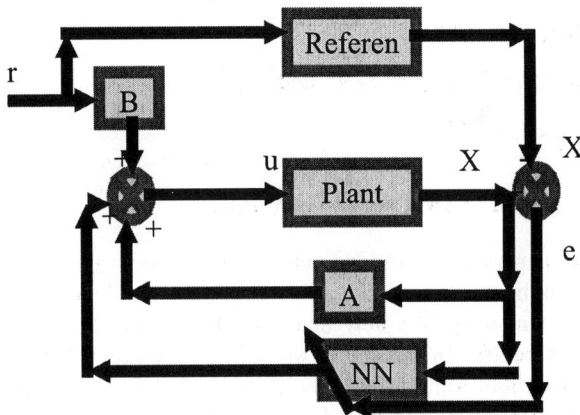

Figure 1. Block Diagram Representation of the MLP Based Closed-loop Control System.

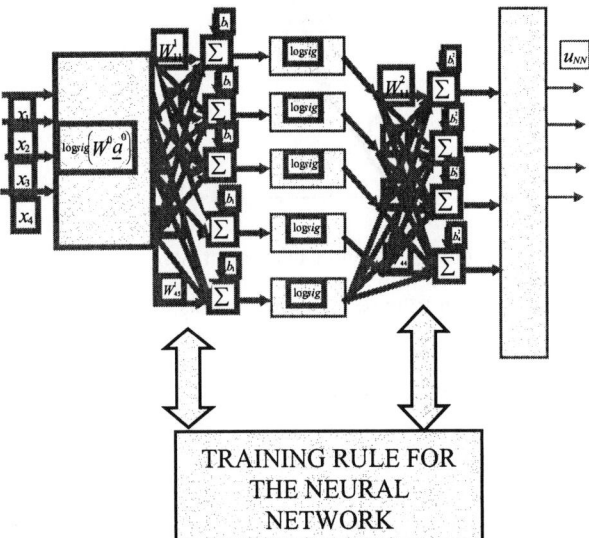

Figure 2: MLP Neural Network Diagram

2.2 Learning Rule for Parameter Adaptation

From (3) and Figure 1, one may easily notice that the control system is nothing but a direct adaptive control with parameters $W_1, W_2, \underline{b}_1$ and $\underline{b}_2$. The following BP-like learning rules are proposed for adjusting the parameters of the controller

$$\dot{W}_1 = -\Gamma_1 \gamma\, W_1 - \frac{1}{1+|\underline{e}|\|W_2\|}\Gamma_1 \dot{F}_1^T(n_1) W_2 P \underline{e} f_0^T(x)$$

$$\dot{b}_1 = -\Gamma_1 \gamma\, b_1 - \frac{1}{1+|\underline{e}|\|W_2\|}\Gamma_1 \dot{F}_1(n_1) W_2 P \underline{e} \quad (5)$$

$$\dot{W}_2 = -\Gamma_2 \gamma\, W_2 - \Gamma_2 P \underline{e} f_1^T(x)$$

$$\dot{b}_2 = -\Gamma_2 \gamma\, b_2 - \Gamma_2 P \underline{e}$$

where the matrices Γ_i are positive definite, $\gamma_i > 0$, the positive definite matrix P is the solution of the Lyapunov equation $A_d^T P + P A_d + Q = 0$ for an arbitrary positive definite matrix Q to be selected by the designer and

$$\dot{F}(y) = [\dot{f}(y_1) \ldots \dot{f}(y_n)]^T, y \in R^n \text{ and } \|\dot{F}(y)\| \le 1 \text{ as }$$
$$\|\dot{f}(y)\| < 1, y \in R^n$$

3. SIMULATION RESULTS

Earlier papers[1,2] provided simulation results in detail for some nonlinear systems including single and two link robot arm system using the new neuro-adaptive controller (bias terms ignored). In this paper, we will be provide test on a two link robot arm system from paper [1] with the neuro-adaptive controller proposed in section 2.1 and 2.2. The unstable nonlinear system for two link robot arm is shown below:

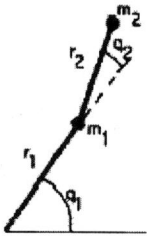

Figure 3.   Two Link Robot Arm

The parameters for the robot are chosen as follows:

$r_1 = 1m, r_2 = 0.8m$
$m_1 = 0.5kg, m_2 = 6.25kg$
$J1 = J2 = 5kg - m$
$g = 9.8 m/s^2$

The neuro-based adaptive controller was designed with the following parameters:

$\Gamma_1 = \Gamma_2 = 200*I$, $\gamma = 0.2$, Q=200*I,

$$A_d = \begin{bmatrix} 0 & 0 & 1 & 0 \\ 0 & 0 & 0 & 1 \\ -10 & 0 & -20 & 0 \\ 0 & -10 & 0 & -30 \end{bmatrix}, \underline{x}(0) = [-3;3;0;0], x_{d0} = [0;0;0;0]$$

No of neurons used in the hidden layer is 5. Figure 4.a shows how well the plant can follow the reference trajectory (angular positions) and figure 4.b presents the output of the controller which is reasonable considering the dynamic behavior of the plant.

Next we considered a variable load and changed its value from 6.25 kgs to 10 kgs. Figure 5. shows the simulation results. Still the response of the neuro controller is satisfactory. In figure 6, we can see the effect of the value of Q on the tracking error. A higher Q yields smaller tracking error. Figure 7 shows the effect of Γ_1 and Γ_2 on the tracking error. A higher Γ_1, Γ_2 gives a better tracking. We have also done extensive simulations to show the effect of eigenvalues of reference model and different values of Q on the tracking error. The error signals depicted in figures 8 and 9 is the norm of the tracking error vector. Finally, figure 10 exhibits the robustness of the tracking performance of the proposed neuro-based adaptive controller with respect to initial tracking error. All the simulation show the remarkable performance of the proposed controller. The theoretical foundation for the simulation results will be discussed in the next section.

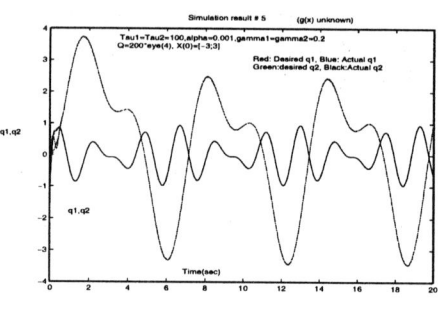

(a) State Trajectories

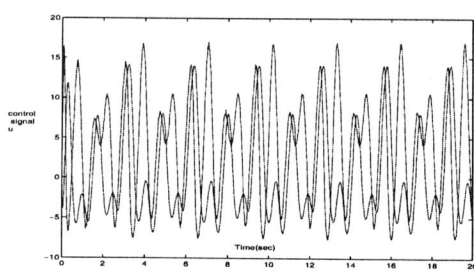

(b) Control signal

Figure 4 Performance of the neuro-based adaptive controller for the two link robot arm system

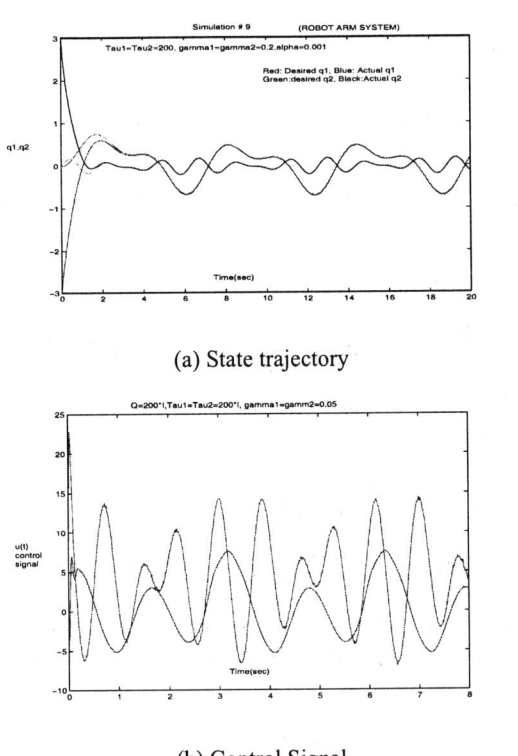

(a) State trajectory

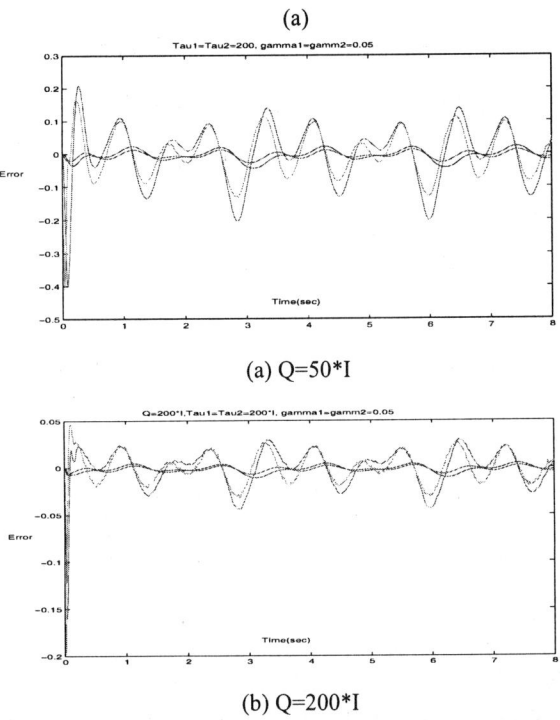

(b) Control Signal

Figure 5. Close loop Response for the two link robot arm problem

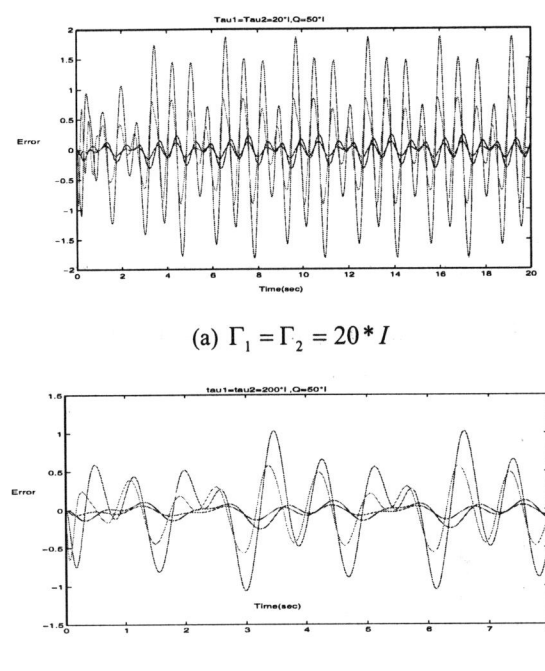

(a) $\Gamma_1 = \Gamma_2 = 20 * I$

(b) $\Gamma_1 = \Gamma_2 = 200 * I$

Figure 7 Error Trajectories with different $\Gamma_1 = \Gamma_2$

(a)

(a) Q=50*I

(b) Q=200*I

Figure 6 Tracking Error trajectories for different Q

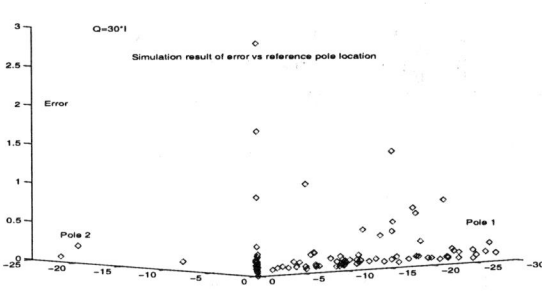

(a) Reference model Poles Vs Error

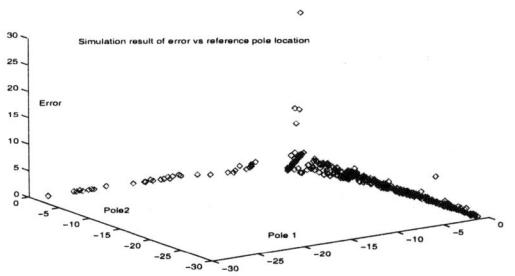

(b) Reference model poles vs Error

Figure 8 Effect of Eigenvalues of reference model with Tracking Error

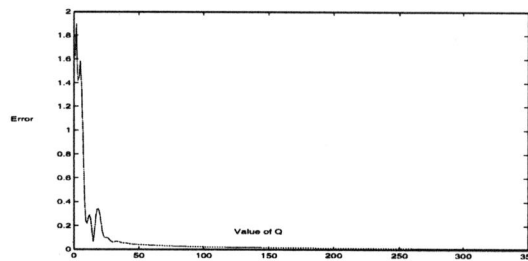

Figure 9 Effect of Q on the Tracking Error

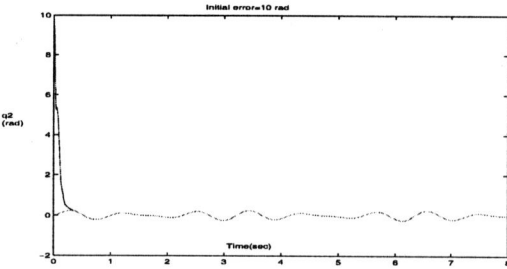

Figure 10 Close loop response of two link robot arm system with large initial error

4. PARAMETER SENSITIVITY AND STABILITY STUDY

To investigate the stability of the neuro-based adaptive controller proposed in this paper, we used Lyapunov's criteria. The Lyapunov function was chosen as:

$$V = e^T Pe + Trace\left(W_1^T \Gamma_1^{-1} W_1 + W_2^T \Gamma_2^{-1} W_2 + b_1^T \Gamma_1^{-1} b_1 + b_2^T \Gamma_2^{-1} b_2\right)$$

$$= V_e + V_{W_1} + V_{W_2} + V_{b_1} + V_{b_2} \qquad (7)$$

Now, taking the derivative w.r.t time, we can write:

$$\dot{V} = \dot{e}^T Pe + e^T P\dot{e} + \frac{d}{dt}\left[Trace\left(W_1^T \Gamma_1^{-1} W_1 + W_2^T \Gamma_2^{-1} W_2 + b_1^T \Gamma_1^{-1} b_1 + b_2^T \Gamma_2^{-1} b_2\right)\right]$$

$$= \dot{V}_e + \dot{V}_{W_1} + \dot{V}_{W_2} + \dot{V}_{b_1} + \dot{V}_{b_2} \qquad (8)$$

Now, the 1st term can be extended as

$$\dot{V}_e = \dot{e}^T Pe + e^T P\dot{e}$$
$$= \left(A_d e\right)^T Pe + \left(\varepsilon^T + w^T\right)Pe + e^T P\left(A_d e\right) + e^T P\left(\varepsilon + w\right)$$
$$= e^T \left(A_d^T P + P A_d\right)e + \left(\varepsilon^T + w^T\right)Pe + e^T P\left(\varepsilon + w\right) \qquad (9)$$
$$= -e^T Q e + \left(\varepsilon^T + w^T\right)Pe + e^T P\left(\varepsilon + w\right)$$
$$\leq -\lambda_{\min}(Q)\|e\|^2 + 2\left(\overline{\varepsilon} + \overline{w}\right)\|P\|\|e\|$$

and the 2nd term can be bounded as follows:

$$\dot{V}_{W_1} = Tr\left(\widetilde{W}_1^T \Gamma_1^{-1} \dot{\widetilde{W}}_1 + \dot{\widetilde{W}}_1^T \Gamma_1^{-1} \widetilde{W}_1\right)$$

$$= -\gamma Tr\left(\widetilde{W}_1^T \Gamma_1 \Gamma_1^{-1} \widetilde{W}_1\right) - \gamma Tr\left(\frac{1}{1+\|e\|\|W_2\|} f^0(\underline{x}) e^T P\dot{F}(y) W_2 \Gamma_1 \Gamma_1^{-1} \widetilde{W}_1\right)$$

$$= -\gamma Tr\left(W_1^T W_1\right) + \gamma Tr\left(W_1^T W_1^*\right) - \frac{1}{1+\|e\|\|W_2\|} Tr\left(f^0(\underline{x}) e^T P\dot{F}(y) W_2 W_1\right)$$

$$+ \frac{1}{1+\|e\|\|W_2\|} Tr\left(f^0(\underline{x}) e^T P\dot{F}(y) W_2 W_1^*\right)$$

$$\leq -\gamma \|W_1^T W_1\| + \gamma n\|W_1^T W_1^*\| - \frac{1}{1+\|e\|\|W_2\|}\|f^0(\underline{x}) e^T P\dot{F}(y) W_2 W_1\|$$

$$+ \frac{n}{1+\|e\|\|W_2\|}\|f^0(\underline{x}) e^T P\dot{F}(y) W_2 W_1^*\|$$

$$\Rightarrow \dot{V}_{W_1} \leq \gamma n\overline{W}^2 + \frac{n\overline{W}^2}{1+\|e\|\|W_2\|}\|P\|\|e\| \qquad (10)$$

$$\leq \gamma n\overline{W}^2 + n\overline{W}^2\|P\|\|e\| \quad as, \|f^0(\underline{x})\| < 1 \text{ and } \|\dot{F}(y)\| \leq 1$$

We can get the bound for other terms in the similar way. Due to space constraint all the detail analysis could not be shown here. So we can write,

$$\dot{V}_e \leq -\lambda_{\min}(Q)\|e\|^2 + 2\left(\overline{\varepsilon} + \overline{w}\right)\|P\|\|e\|$$
$$\dot{V}_{W_1} \leq 2\gamma n\overline{W}^2 + 2n\overline{W}\|P\|\|e\|$$
$$\dot{V}_{W_2} \leq 2\gamma n\overline{W}^2 + 2n\overline{W}\|P\|\|e\| \qquad (11)$$
$$\dot{V}_{b_1} \leq 2\gamma n\overline{b}^2 + 2n\overline{b}\|P\|\|e\|$$
$$\dot{V}_{b_2} \leq 2\gamma n\overline{b}^2 + 2n\overline{b}\|P\|\|e\|$$

Finally, $\dot{V} \leq -\lambda_{\min}(Q)\|e\|^2 + 2\left(\overline{\varepsilon}+\overline{w}\right)\|P\|\|e\| + 2\gamma n\overline{W}^2 + 2n\overline{W}\|P\|\|e\| +$

$$2\gamma n\overline{W}^2 + 2n\overline{W}\|P\|\|e\| + 2\gamma n\overline{b}^2 + 2n\overline{b}\|P\|\|e\| + 2\gamma n\overline{b}^2 + 2n\overline{b}\|P\|\|e\|$$

$$\Rightarrow \dot{V} \leq -\lambda_{\min}(Q)\|e\|^2 + 2\left(\overline{\varepsilon}+\overline{w}\right)\|P\|\|e\| + 4\gamma n\overline{W}^2 + 4n\overline{W}\|P\|\|e\| \qquad (12)$$
$$+ 4\gamma n\overline{b}^2 + 4n\overline{b}\|P\|\|e\|$$

$$\Rightarrow \dot{V} \leq \underbrace{-\lambda_{\min}(Q)\|e\|^2}_{1st} + \underbrace{\left[2\left(\overline{\varepsilon}+\overline{w}\right)+4n\overline{W}+4n\overline{b}\right]\|P\|\|e\|}_{2nd} + \underbrace{\left[4\gamma n\overline{W}^2 + 4\gamma n\overline{b}^2\right]}_{3rd}$$

It is obvious from the final expressions (12) that the Lyapunov stability will be valid under certain boundary space for controller parameters such as $Q, A_d, \Gamma_1, \Gamma_2, \gamma$. The controller is very stable with respect to initial error if controller parameters are chosen properly, though more energy will be required for the control signal if the initial error is too high. The Lyapunov stability of the composite system mainly depends on the proper selection of these parameters. From the expression (12), we can see that a large Q will make the 1st term in the expression more negative while γ should be selected as small as possible to make the positive 3rd term small. Also the positive 2nd term, which depends on P, needs to be small so that the right hand side of (12) is negative; this will guaranty asymptotic stability even with a large initial error. As selection of the reference model will yield P matrix, we can see that minimum eigenvalue for A_d should be high to make norm (P) small i.e. the poles of the reference model ought to be selected as distant from the imaginary axis as possible. As all these parameters are designer's choices and can be controlled depending on the energy constraint on control signal generation, the proposed MLP based adaptive controller can be very stable, fast and easy to implement.

5. SUMMARY

This paper presented a neuro-based adaptive controller for a special class of dynamical systems. The control scheme can be viewed as a direct adaptive controller. No off-line training phase for neural network is required. A BP-like learning rule adjusts the weights of the MLP-based NN and keeps them as well as the tracking error ultimately bounded, starting from any initial value in some compact bounded set in $\mathbb{R}^n$. The stability analysis of the neuro-control system and the parameter sensitivities of the proposed MLP based controller has been discussed in detail. Considering real time application, the proposed controller is fast, reliable and easy to implement which certainly gives it a edge over other complex adaptive controller. More study on the proposed controller and its application in different real life systems is going on and will be published in future.

REFERENCES:

1. *Menhaj, M.B.; Rouhani, M.;* "A novel neuro-based model reference adaptive control for a two link robot arm" ,Neural Networks, 2002. IJCNN '02. Proceedings of the 2002 International Joint Conference on , Volume:1,2002,Page(s): 47 -52

2. *Menhaj, M.B.; Rouhani, M.;* "A neuro-controller with guranteed stability", Presented on IEEE Midwest Conference, 2002

3. *Wang, Q.; Broome, D.R.;* "A novel neural adaptive controller for robots" ,Control, 1994. Control '94. Volume 1., International Conference on , 21-24 Mar 1994 Page(s): 486 -491 vol.1

4. *Meyne, Ph.; Houkari, M.; Barret, C.; Martinez, J.M.; Garassino, A.; Tormo, P.;* "A neural adaptive controller", Systems, Man and Cybernetics, 1993. 'Systems Engineering in the Service of Humans', Conference Proceedings., International Conference on , 17-20 Oct 1993 Page(s): 80 -84 vol.4

5. Jeffrey T. Spooner, Manfredi Maggiore, Raul Ordonez and Kevin M. Passino; "Stable Adaptive Control and Estimation for Nonlinear Systems", A John Willey and sons, Inc Publication.,2002.

6. *Hagan, M.T.; Menhaj, M.B.;* "Training feedforward networks with the Marquardt algorithm",Neural Networks, IEEE Transactions on , Volume: 5 Issue: 6 , Nov 1994 Page(s): 989 -993

7. Tzirkel-Hancock E., and Fallside F. "A Stability Based Neural Network Control Method for a Class of Non-Linear Systems". *IEEE Inter. Joint Conf. on N.N.*, 2, pages 1047-1052, 1991.

8. Chen F-C., and Khalil H. K. "Adaptive Control of Nonlinear Systems Using Neural Networks". *Int. J. Control*, **55**, 1299-1317, 1992.

9. Chen F-C, and Liu C-C. "Adaptively Controlling Nonlinear Continuous-Time Systems Using Neural Networks". *IEEE Trans.on AC,* 39(6), 1306-1310, 1994.

10. Chen F-C., and Khalil H. K. "Adaptive Control of a Class Of Nonlinear Discrete-Time Systems Using Neural Networks". *IEEE Trans. on AC,* 40(5), 791-801, 1995.

11. Lewis F. L., Yesildirek A., and Liu K. "Neural Net Robot Controller with Guaranteed Stability". 3rd *Inter. Conf. on Indus. Fuzz. Cont.*, pages 103-108, 1993.

12. Lewis F. L., Liu K., and Yesildirek A. "Multilayer Neural Net Robot Controller With Guaranteed Tracking Performance". *IEEE Trans. on Neural Networks*, 6(3), 703-715, 1995.

13. Sadegh N. "A Perceptron Network For Functional Identification and Control of Nonlinear Systems". *IEEE Trans. on Neural Networks,* 4(6), 982-988, 1993.

14. Tzirkel-Hancock E., and Fallside F. "A Stability Based Neural Network Control Method for a Class of Non-Linear Systems". *IEEE Inter. Joint Conf. on N.N.*, 2, pages 1047-1052, 1991.

15. Sanchez, E.N.; Vega, V.; "Stability of neurofuzzy controllers",American Control Conference, 1995. Proceedings of the , Volume: 6 , 21-23 Jun 1995 Page(s): 4251 -4252 vol.6

16. Meyer-Base, A.; Watzel, R.; "Relevant features selection with radial basis neural networks",Neural Networks, 1995. Proceedings., IEEE International Conference on , Volume: 2 , Nov/Dec 1995 Page(s): 963 -967 vol.2

17. Karayiannis, N.B.; Weiqun Mi; "Growing radial basis neural networks", Neural Networks,1997., International Conference on , Volume: 3 , 9-12 Jun 1997 Page(s): 1406 -1411 vol.3

Maximum Entropy Utility Equilibrium of Mobile Agents with Aggregated Statistical Behaviours

Alexandru Murgu
Department of Mathematical Information Technology
University of Jyvaskyla, FIN-40351 Jyvaskyla, FINLAND
E-mail: murgu@julia.math.jyu.fi

Abstract—Mobile agent technology is a service logic where the programs are implemented as mobile agents and thus, are not constrained to control an intelligent information network from a central location. The mobile agents can migrate and control the networking operations locally. The service logic programs are dragged by cloning or replication to the appropriate locations in response to the excess processing or signaling loads. In this paper, a mathematical view of the networking operations such as traffic aggregation and behavioural pattern discrimination of the differentiated service granularity using mobile agents is presented. The selection of behavioral patterns of the traffic streams is regarded as an optimization problem. Entropy type of utility models for the mobile agents cooperation are considered in order to describe the time separability for the group resource allocation in order to perform the stochastic aggregation of the networking resources.

I. Introduction and Motivation

There are two fundamental principles of organizing the information streams in a network which are motivated by the travel times from sources to destinations on the information propagation paths:

User optimized streams is the first principle used to obtain the traffic equilibrium where the travel times on all routes effectively used are equal.

System optimized streams is the second principle which states that the average travel time should be minimum.

The first principle is mostly used in practice since it implies that an equilibrium situation in which no entity can reduce its travel time by choosing a new route will occur. However, the second principle is the most efficient behavioural pattern in networking terms since it leads to the minimization the total travel time in the network. For user optimized traffic equilibrium, there exists an equivalent minimization problem ([1]). Consider a flow network with the node set N and the oriented arc set A. A node represents an origin, a destination or a transit point along the path from source to destination. A duplex link is represented by directed arcs of opposite orientation. The number of trips that occur from origins p to destinations q are given by a function $g_{pq}(u_{pq})$, when u_{pq} is the cost of the trip from p to q. On each link of the network, the congestion effects generated by user population accumulation in the transit points are represented as the link volume delay functions, $s_a(v_a)$, $a \in A$, which are convex increasing functions of the link streams v_a. At the network level, the demand function $g_{pq}(u_{pq})$ allows a local description of the route streams $h_{k,pq}$, where all the streams must be conserved, that is,

$$\sum_k h_{k,pq} = g_{pq}(u_{pq}) \quad (1)$$

for all (p,q). The link streams are related to the route streams by the following aggregation relation

$$v_a = \sum_p \sum_q \sum_k \delta_{ak,pq} h_{k,pq} \quad (2)$$

where for all $a \in A$,

$$\delta_{ak,pq} = \begin{cases} 1, & \text{if } a \text{ is on path } k \text{ for pair } (p,q) \\ 0, & \text{otherwise} \end{cases} \quad (3)$$

subject to the nonnegativity constraints

$$v_a \geq 0, \quad h_{k,pq} \geq 0 \quad (4)$$

The first principle can be stated as follows

$$\sum_a \delta_{ak,pq} s_a(v_a) = u_{pq} \quad \text{if} \quad h_{k,pq} > 0 \quad (5)$$

$$\sum_a \delta_{ak,pq} s_a(v_a) \geq u_{pq} \quad \text{if} \quad h_{k,pq} = 0 \quad (6)$$

The implicit assumption made is that the travel time on a route is the sum of the link times that form the route. The previous equations can be interpreted as the Kuhn-Tucker conditions of an equivalent minimization problem as follows

$$\min \left\{ \sum_a \int_0^{v_a} s_a(x)dx - \sum_{(p,q)} \int_0^{g_{pq}(u_{pq})} w_{pq}(y)dy \right\} \quad (7)$$

where $w_{pq}(g_{pq})$ is the inverse of the demand function $g_{pq}(u_{pq})$, subject to the constraints (1)-(4). When the demand function $g_{pq}(u_{pq})$ is a decresing function in u_{pq}, the objective function (7) is convex, which implies that the solution of this optimization problem is unique and stable.

The equilibrium state implies that a steady state is reached when the various streaming demands give rise to aggregatted flow patterns and the conditions that maintain the demand patterns stable ([6]). The actual computation of the equilibrium state is a difficult task since the collection of data and the estimation of the demand functions is an exceedingly difficult problem in practice. Estimation of the streaming demand is acheieved by using a sequence of *trip generation, trip distribution* and *modal split* models. Trip generation produces mathematical models that relate the number of trips originating in a_p and ending in b_q in a congestion region using statistical and economical characteristics. Trip distribution produces mathematical models that relate the streams $\bar{g}_{pq}$ to a_p and b_q, where the trips are originating and terminating into the congestion regions. Modal split models produces choices among the streams for the given service characteristics. Streaming trips produced by all modes $\bar{g}_{pq}$ are split into a set of behavioural classes. These models are relatively easy to calibrate against the flow patterns measured for some base interval. The goodness of the calibration serves as a substitute to provide the predictive ability of these models. The output of the first three stages of the flow planning process is a fixed streaming matrix which serves as input to the trip assignment stage. This describes the way in which the fixed streaming demands give rise to traffic streams on the network links. The relation of trip assignement to the traffic equilibrium problem is close, that is, rather than being given by the demand functions $g_{pq}(u_{pq})$, the demand is fixed at the value $\bar{g}_{pq}$ and the traffic assignment problem can be stated as

$$\min \left\{ \sum_a \int_0^{v_a} s_a(x) dx \right\} \tag{8}$$

subject to the constraints (2)-(3) and

$$\sum_k h_{k,pq} = \bar{g}_{pq} \tag{9}$$

for all (p,q). Because of the similarity of this problem with the general equilibrium problem, it became known as the traffic equilibrium problem with "fixed demand". The general problem is usually referred to as the equilibrium problem with variable or "elastic demand". Another approach to reach the equilibrium state is to incrementally load the network until the equilibrium conditions are approximatively satisfied. Generalizations of the traffic equilibrium models can be used for multiclass-user in user optimized flow systems handling switched averages of populations of traffic entities (e.g., packets, frames).

II. Entropy Utility Models of Mobile Agents

The mobile agents are used in the networking technologies as self-balancing instruments in contrast to the centralized nature of the more traditional information flow networks. The mobile agents are able to react to the external stimuli and exhibit a dynamic behavior because they can control their migration and execution processes. The mobile agents carry data which can preserve the state information and perform computations while migrating through a number of network locations. The network equilibrium is related to the concept of entropy in analyzing the zonal mobile agents distributions in controlling the traffic streams based on the disaggregation of behavioral patterns of travel demands. The ranking of the different service levels is based on the observable entropy which replaces the unobservable utility provided that a unique relationship between the entropy and the total costs associated to various behaviour patterns exists. The utility functions are compatible with the suggested relationship regardless of how various treads and services or trips to different locations for different purposes are grouped together into variables over which the utility is defined and the entropy is measured ([2]). In system analysis, a complete description of the system may be given as a microstate description. The distribution of such microstates can be seen as a kind of macrostate description because it is less complete in information granularity. Thus, many miscrostates may give rise to the same macrostate. In an econometric analogy, the entropy maximization can be viewed as an alternative modelling approach to the analysis of aggregates of mobile agent choices under a given set of market conditions. Utility maximizing systems have formed the basis for analysing the selection of behaviour patterns in economics. Let us denote by $X_1, X_2, ..., X_N$ the non-negative set of attributes describing the behavioural patterns $1, 2, ..., N$, where a mobile agent may select at fixed non-negative penalty costs $P_1, P_2, ..., P_N$. Let I be a fixed parameter denoting the mobile agent's *return on action* which is assumed to be equal to the total resource budget. Assuming the preferences are expressed by means of an utility function and that the total return on action I is spent on the N mobile agent selected streams, the usual utility maximizing problem can be stated as follows

$$\max U = U(X_1, X_2, ..., X_N) \tag{10}$$

subject to the budget constraint

$$\sum_{i=1}^{N} P_i X_i = I \tag{11}$$

Since the penalty costs and the return on action are fixed parameters while the quantities $X_1, X_2, ..., X_N$ are endogeneous variables, it follows that the knowledge of budged shares implies and is implied by the knowledge of these quantities. The usual maximizing analysis in terms of $X_1, X_2, ..., X_N$ is equivalent to the analysis of the budget shares

$$\alpha_i = \frac{P_i X_i}{I} \tag{12}$$

for $i = 1, 2, ..., N$, where

$$\sum_{i=1}^{N} \alpha_i = 1 \tag{13}$$

The quantities α_i are interpreted as probabilities, that is, the chance that a budget unit selected at random from the mobile agent's return on action will be spent on the ith seleted stream is equal to α_i. The essential state properties of the system can be described by the means of system entropy defined as

$$H(\alpha) = -\sum_{i=1}^{N} \alpha_i \log \alpha_i \tag{14}$$

The entropy is non-negative and zero if and only if one of the α_i is 1 and all other are 0. Let us maximize the entropy of the static utility model subject to the budget constraint and certain constraints imposed on the maximized problem in order to exclude certain budget share distributions from the set of possible solutions.

In economic terms, habit formation, or more generally, preferences, may impose similar restrictions that should be taken into account when formulating the entropy maximizing problem. We introduce K such constraints ($K > N$), written in the general form

$$f_k(x_1, x_2, ..., x_N) = g_k, \quad k = 1, 2, ..., K \quad (15)$$

We can formulate the entropy maximizing problem using the Lagrangian technique as follows

$$L = H(\alpha) + \sum_{k=1}^{K} \mu_k(g_k - f_k) + \lambda \left(\sum_{i=1}^{N} \alpha_i - 1 \right) \quad (16)$$

where $\mu_1, \mu_2, ..., \mu_K$ and λ are the Lagrangian multipliers. The alternative presented here involves the replacement of the explicit utility function by the system's entropy and by certain constraints on how the mobile agent can spend the resources under the given behavioral properties and the utility maximizing model. This assumption leads to

$$U = H(\alpha) + \sum_{k=1}^{K} \mu_k(g_k - f_k) \quad (17)$$

which is identified as the utility function since it is a function of the mobile agent's budget shares and preferences.

III. BEHAVIORAL PATTERN SELECTION THEORY

Classical utility theory implies a positive marginal utility of the real return on action. By increasing the real return on an action, it is possible to spend more resources of at least one stream which has a positive marginal utility without reducing the spending of any other resource. At a very low level of the real return on action, only the selected streams necessary for filling the minimal mobile agent's role will be selected. The list of the potentially selected streams by the mobile agents will contain zero budget shares for all selected streams except the most urgent priorities. By increasing the real return on action (thus the utility), the equilibrium distribution of the mobile agent selected streams will even out and the budget shares of the basic priority resources spending will decline. The more proritary selected streams will enter the budget and will increase their budget shares. The entropy of an utility maximizing system increases when the real return on action increases, that is,

$$\frac{dH}{dI} = -\sum_{i=1}^{N} \alpha'_i \log \alpha_i > 0 \quad (18)$$

where

$$\alpha'_i = \frac{d\alpha_i}{dI} \quad (19)$$

and

$$E_i = \frac{\partial X_i}{\partial I} \cdot \frac{I}{X_i} \quad (20)$$

is the *Engel elasticity*. Thus, we have

$$I \frac{dH}{dI} = \sum_{i=1}^{N} e_i H_i \quad (21)$$

where

$$e_i = E_i - 1 \quad (22)$$

$$H_i = -\alpha_i \log \alpha_i \quad (23)$$

Entropy and Utility Changes. We are interested to study the conditions under which the following inequality holds

$$\frac{dH}{dI} > 0 \quad (24)$$

or equivalently

$$\sum_{i=1}^{N} e_i H_i > 0 \quad (25)$$

Since $0 < H_i < N^{-1} \log N$, all the e_i values cannot simultaneously have a negative sign. On the othe hand, if all the e_i values are positive simultaneously, then $dH/dI > 0$. Such special cases are incompatible with the demand patterns, since

$$\sum_{i=1}^{N} \alpha_i E_i = 1 \quad (26)$$

is violated. Compatible demands means that some stream groups must be demand-inelastic with respect to return on action (or total resource budget), i.e., $E_i < 1$, whereas others must be return on action-elastic, i.e., $E_i > 1$. The entropy will increase with the return on action if and only if the budget shares become more equal as the return on action rises, i.e., the lower shares rises and the larger shares decline. A low return on action maximizes the utility by spending the return on action so that some budget shares are high and others are low. As return on action increases, the budget shares become more equal. The maximization of the utility is obtained by spending more equal amounts on the N-stream groups than in the non-maximizing case. Let us assume that the resource budget on X_i can be divided in two parts:
1) contracting of a fixed quantity T_i in order to ensure the minimal level of satisfaction;
2) constant fraction β_i of what is left of the budget after the minimal quantities of all selected streams are ensured.

This yields the following demand patterns

$$X_i = T_i + \frac{\beta_i}{P_i} \left(I - \sum_{k=1}^{N} P_k T_k \right) \quad (27)$$

which are equivalent to

$$X_i = a_{i1} \frac{P_1}{P_i} + \cdots + a_{ii} + a_{iN} \frac{P_N}{P_i} + b_i \frac{I}{P_i} \quad (28)$$

One of the utility functions leading to these demand functions is

$$U = \sum_{i=1}^{N} \beta_i \ln(X_i - T_i) \qquad (29)$$

where

$$\sum_{i=1}^{N} \beta_i = 1 \qquad (30)$$

This utility model is defined for return on action levels which satisfy the inequality

$$I \geq \sum_{k=1}^{N} P_k T_k \qquad (31)$$

Proposition 1. Assuming constant penalty costs, the budget shares of the model α_i converge to β_i for all $i = 1, 2, ..., N$ as the return on action approaches infinity. In the special case where $\beta_i = 1/N$ for $i = 1, 2, ..., N$, the utility model takes the form

$$U = \sum_{i=1}^{N} \beta_i \ln(X_i - T_i) = \frac{1}{N} \sum_{i=1}^{N} \ln(X_i - T_i) \qquad (32)$$

where

$$a_i = -\frac{1}{T_i} \qquad (33)$$

All the budget shares approach $1/N$ as the return on action approaches infinity. This utility model is *compatible* with the hypothesis that the entropy increases with return on action.

Proposition 2. The Engel-elasticies of the model in Proposition 1 are given by

$$E_i = \frac{\partial X_i}{\partial I} \cdot \frac{I}{X_i} = \frac{I}{NP_i X_i} = \frac{1}{N\alpha_i} \qquad (34)$$

Since the budget shares α_i approach β_i values as the return on action approaches infinity, the following inequality holds

$$H_T = -\sum_{i=1}^{N} \frac{P_i T_i}{\sum_{i=1}^{N} P_i T_i} \log\left(\frac{P_i T_i}{\sum_{i=1}^{N} P_i T_i}\right) < H_\beta \qquad (35)$$

where

$$H_\beta = -\sum_{i=1}^{N} \beta_i \log \beta_i \qquad (36)$$

Let X_i denote the number of trips by a particular mobile agent to a location i and let P_i be the cost of a round trip from home basis to location i (separability assumption in the utility model). Performing the utility maximization for the travel time separable from the other locations will yield the same resource allocation as the overall analysis showed (homogeneous separability can be assumed) ([3]). The problems facing the analyst choosing the entropy as the new utility measure are the following:

1) Empirical maximum entropy functions has one or several local maxima at finite in return on action levels. There are returns on action groups with a negative marginal entropy with respect to return on action (or group resource budget).

2) Critical level is independent of the degree of stream aggregation. The entropy concept is useful in analyzing phenomena at the aggregate level. The entropy models serve as a means of stochastic aggregation which lead to aggregate accessibility measures that can serve as proxy variables for zonal and group level.

IV. AGGREGATING THE STATISTICAL EQUILIBRIUM

The utility function approach serves to map the mobile agents action patterns to an econometric model and to point the various restrictive assumptions underlying the more conventional network models. The problem of modelling the transportation demand and supply involves the explanation of aggregate streams of travelers on paths of the flow networks in term of individuals' decision making for establishing a behaviour pattern. Individual decisions include the issue of whether or not to make a trip at a particular time, to what destination, by what mode of transportation and by what route. The approach provided in this section attempts to establish a direct correspondence between the demand and supply equilibria and to measure the efficiency which can be obtained in evaluating the alternative systems. Since the basic building block here is the individual mobile agent, the problem lies within the general class of disaggregate travel demand models ([5]). The the individuals' rational choice of transportation-related activities can be described in utility terms. An action is chosen for which the utility is a net maximum subject to certain explicit constraints. It is assumed that the locations can be stratified into s mutually exclusive and exhaustive classes with respect to the homogeneity of their utility functions. This stratification can be accomplished via multivariate statistical analyses of data services on the transport-related stimuli. Let us introduce x_{ik}^s as the trips from origin i to destination k by an mobile agent of type s; H_i^s as the number of mobile agents of type s residing at location i; y^s as the disposable reward of mobile agent s; z^s as the total leisure time of mobile agent s; p_{ik} as the cost of a trip from i to k by the best network path (i.e., route); t_{ik} as the time spent on a trip from i to k by the best route. The utility for a mobile agent residing at location i is specified by the function of nontravel loss, nontravel leisure time and the satisfaction of travel purposes at various destinations

$$u_i^s = u^s\left(y^s - \sum_k p_{ik} x_{ik}^s,\; z^s - \sum_k t_{ik} x_{ik}^s\right) \qquad (37)$$

This equation outlines a "short-run" transportation decision function. Trip generation, trip distribution and the route choice decisions are determined through optimization of this function. A network will be described in terms of nodes (vertices) i, k and links (edges) gh. A link gh between the nodes g and h is considered to run two ways: $gh = hg$. The basic variables in the network are the streams X_{gh}, travel times t_{gh}

and the travel costs p_{gh} on the links gh. It is necessary to decompose the observable aggregate streams X_{gh} on a link gh by origin, destination and type of traveler. The resulting variable is $x^s_{i,gh,k}$ denoting the flow of all travelers of type s on link gh having originated at i who are bound for location k over network link gh, that is,

$$x^s_{i,gh,k} = H^s_i x^s_{i,gh,k} \tag{38}$$

From the basic flow variable we can derive the following aggregate flow variables

$$X_{gh} = \sum_{s,i,k} x^s_{i,gh,k} \tag{39}$$

which represents the total flow on the link gh and

$$x^s_{ik} = \sum_h x^s_{i,ih,k} \tag{40}$$

which is the travel generated by a representative mobile agent of a class s at the location i intended for the destination k. Similarly, for aggregate streams, we have

$$X^s_{ik} = \sum_h X^s_{i,ih,k} = H^s_i \sum_h x^s_{i,ih,k} \tag{41}$$

Define also

$$X_{kk} = -\sum_{i \neq k} X_{ik} \tag{42}$$

The mathematical formulation of the selection problem the best routes requires that the flow variables are substituted for the trip variables in the cost parts of the utility function

$$u^s_i = u^s \left(y^s - \sum_{gh,k} p_{gh} x^s_{i,gh,k},\ z^s - \sum_{gh,k} t_{gh} x^s_{i,gh,k} \right) \tag{43}$$

The utility maximizing problem for a single mobile agent has the following formulation

$$\max_{x^s_{i,gh,k}} u^s \tag{44}$$

In the absence of effective capacity limits, there are no constraints. The limitations of streams on the actual network is implicit in the sums. Considering the problem of many mobile agents making trips and route choices simultaneously, it is of interest to describe the behavior and to predict the resulting streams (assignment problem) ([4]) leading to the optimum utilization of the information network. The maximization of the total reawrd cab be expressed as the sum of the individual utilities

$$\max_{x^s_{i,gh,k}} \sum_{i,s} H^s_i u^s \tag{45}$$

In a network model without capacity limits and congestion effects the travel time, t_{gh} and the travel costs P_{gh} on the various links are constant. Therefore, the maximization with respect to one set of variables $x^s_{i,gh,k}$ for fixed i, s is independent of the maximization with respect to other sets of these variables. The order of maximization and the summation over i and s can be interchanged leading to

$$\max_{x^s_{i,gh,k}} \sum_{i,s} H^s_i u^s = \sum_{i,s} \max_{x^s_{i,gh,k}} H^s_i u^s \tag{46}$$

which means that the overall maximum problem can be decomposed into a set of separate maximization problems, one for each pair (i,s).

This principle of decomposition leads to the following economic viewpoint: a system optimum is achieved if every individual seeks his own optimal path. The decision making process can be decentralized. No planning is needed at the level of users' utilization of the existing network. It is of interest to know that this principle continues to be reliable under traffic congestion and capacity constraints. The utility maximum problem in terms of the individual streams $x^s_{i,gh,k}$ can be restated in terms of aggregate streams for all mobile agents of a given type s residing at a given origin i. A sufficient condition for this to hold is that the utility function is homogeneous, that is,

$$u(\lambda c_1, \lambda c_2) = \lambda^\beta u(c_1, c_2) \tag{47}$$

where β is the *degree of homogeneity*. Consequently,

$$H^s_i u^s \left(y^s - \sum_{gh,k} p_{gh} X^s_{i,gh,k},\ z^s - \sum_{gh,k} t_{gh} x^s_{i,gh,k} \right) =$$
$$(H^s_i)^{1-\beta} u^s \left(Y^s_i - \sum_{gh,k} p_{gh} x^s_i,\ Z^s_i - \sum_{gh,k} t_{gh} X^s_i, \right) \tag{48}$$

where

$$X^s_{i,gh,k} = H^s_i x^s_{i,gh,k} \tag{49}$$

$$Y^s_i = H^s_i y^s \tag{50}$$

$$Z^s_i = H^s_i z^s \tag{51}$$

are the streams, return on actions and the time budgets aggregated over all agents of type s at location i, respectively.

Proposition 3. If u is linear homogeneous and $\beta = 1$, then the H^s_i terms can be eliminated entirely and the individual utility maximization is equivalent to the maximization of the same utility function in terms of the aggregate streams. If all the mobile agents are of the same type, the utilities are a function of the aggregate streams only.

The relevance of the above result consists of characterizing the Differentiated Service (DiffServ) networking strategy which advocates a model based on different "granularity" of service classes at network edges and within the network. Network devices as edge/core routers are only required to act on a few aggregates that are meant to offer a predefined set of service levels. The stream aggregation raises a number of questions for end-to-end services characterization, in particular when crossing domain boundaries where actions on return may be applied. Individual and bulk services built on top of the Expedited Forwarding (EF) per-hop-behavior (PHB) allow new usages embodied in service level agreements between users and providers. DiffServ framework relies on a small number of service levels or per-hop-behaviors (PHBs) that each specifies how a router should treat the corresponding traffic streams.

DiffServ models are highly scalable and rise questions such as aggregating traffic into a small number of packet treatments in terms of the conformance of flows as they exit a DiffServ domain. Conformance is measured in relation to a policer that controls the volume and timing of packet transmissions and provides a simple reference point for estimating the level of stochastic perturbations imposed on flows by their interactions with other flows with which they are aggregated. Interactions can be within a PHB or across PHBs. The dominant effect in terms of service level conformance of a stream is its internal packet variability. The impact of having a large packet within a stream, even if the average packet size remains unchanged is much more substantial than the potential increase in network perturbations caused by the variable packet sizes from cross streams (the impact of the packet size distribution of cross streams is minimal). Highler network loads increase the magnitude of network perturbations and they can contribute to the formation of larger bursts. Higher loads mean larger queues that prevent large intrinsic bursts from propagating undisturbed through the network. At high loads, the network can have a "smoothing" effect that limits the impact of aggregating multiple streams.

Increasing the number of cross streams can improve the situation by ensuring that large aggregate bursts are broken up, but this only holds when the increase does not negatively affect the smoothing effect of the network or contribute to substantially levels of network interferences. A similar trade-off is present when increasing the hop count: increasing the hop count values affects the relative impact of other parameters in a number of ways. An increase in the number of cross traffic streams can either improve or worsen the conformance depending on the hop count value. While increasing the number of cross streams can be beneficial, i.e., by ensuring that large bursts are broken up, it can also be detrimental because it contributes to larger levels of network interferences (the impact of the latter increases with the hop count). Increases in the hop count typically improve the performance, while increases in the number of cross streams usually degrade the performance. This shows that a trade-off exists between the greater level of network perturbations that higher hop counts or the number of cross streams induces and the greater likelihood that aggregate bursts will be broken up as they traverse the network. At low link loads, changes in either parameter have little or no effect and the differences emerge as the link load increases due to the greater impact of traffic interactions in the network. For homogeneous streams, the break-up of aggregate streams caused by crossing a larger number of hops is the dominant effect, hence the improvement in the after-aggregation conformance, while the negative impact of the perturbations created by the larger numbers of cross streams is the more influential effect (this is sensitive to the selected configuration).

V. CONCLUDING REMARKS

The contribution of this paper is to provide a mathematical basis on which we can investigate the issue of aggregated statistical behaviors in the context of EF PHB based services. We assume that the user EF traffic is shaped on the access point in the network in order to conform to a single token bucket filter that controls the long term rate and burst size. The wide range of traffic interactions in an heterogeneous network helps to break-up the intrinsic bursts formed by aggregating multiple streams. This wider range of interactions also leads to a number of differences with an homogeneous environment (these are mostly representative of how different trade-offs appear in these diverse conditions). As the number of cross traffic streams increases, the large number of independent interferences combined with the higher speed of the link and hence the lower relative magnitude of those interferences, ultimately improves the performance. This phenomenon is not present in the homogeneous case because of its lower initial burstiness. It is not observed at high network loads, because the decrease in network smoothing due to the larger number of cross-traffic streams is the dominant effect.

Mobile agents are used in order to provide the information needed for action on return traffic reshaping and filtering via behavioral patern selection identified as an important feature in support of services based on EF PHB. This feature adds complexity, especially on high speed adapters because of the need to compute conformance times and to hold packets until they become conformant. The non-work-conserving nature of shapers also requires additional buffers and contribute to higher delays. Extensions of the mathematical framework presented in this paper can include the variable rate streams and packet variability within streams where the bandwidth of an individual stream affects the variation of inter-packet spacing it experiences (having an impact on the network utilization). When the input traffic is smoother than a Poisson process and it only interacts with similar traffic, it retains that smoothness when crossing a network. Bunching of traffic using mobile agents keeps the burstiness of the traffic to controllable levels similar to Poisson processes.

REFERENCES

[1] U. Derigs, *Programming in Networks and Graphs. On the Combinatorial Background and Near-Equivalence of Network Flow and Matching Algorithms*, Springer-Verlag, Berlin, 1988.
[2] R.S. Ellis, *Entropy, Large Deviations and Statistical Mechanics*, Springer-Verlag, New York, 1985.
[3] A.V. Gheorghe, *Decision Processes in Dynamic Probabilistic Systems*, Kluwer Academic Publishers, Dordrecht, 1990.
[4] A. Murgu, "Fuzzy Successive Averaging Method in Multistage Optimization Systems", in *Proceedings of International Joint Conference on Neural Networks*, IJCNN-2001, July 15-19, 2001, Washington, D.C., USA, pp. 2206-2211.
[5] A. Murgu, "Fuzzy Aggregation of Input-Output Service Level Dynamics in Multimedia Networks", in *Advances in Computer Cybernetics*, Vol. XI, G.E. Lasker (ed.), pp. 54-62, 2002.
[6] A. Murgu, "Multicalls Service Dynamics Replication Using Evolutionary Selection Games", in *Proceedings of 10th International Symposium on Dynamic Games*, ISDG-2002, St. Petersburg, Russia, pp. 652-656.

Robust Tracking Control of Uncertain Nonlinear Systems with An Input Time Delay

Chiang-Cheng Chiang* and Tzu-Ching Tung
Department of Electrical Engineering,
Tatung University,
40 Chung-Shan North Road, Sec.3,Taipei, Taiwan, Republic of China,
E-mail: ccchiang@ctr3.ee.ttu.edu.tw

Abstract-In this paper, a robust dynamic controller design algorithm for nonlinear systems with unmatched uncertainties and an input time delay is provided. For many practical systems, the existence of time delay is common in control practice. Therefore the problem of controlling such systems becomes more complex and sometimes degrades the control performance. We will propose a feasible method to deal with the problem of unmatched uncertainties and an input time delay. Based on the Lyapunov theory and the concept of functional analysis, the conditions of the robust stability of the overall closed-loop system with unmatched uncertainties and an input time delay will be derived. Finally, some examples and simulation results are provided to illustrate the versatility and performance of the proposed method.

I. INTRODUCTION

In recent years, the research and development has led to a great deal of advance on the nonlinear control theory. Time delay can be found in various engineering systems such as chemical processes, pneumatic/hydraulic systems, biological systems, and economic systems. The central concept of this approach is to transform algebraically the nonlinear system dynamics into an equivalent linear system, such that the conventional linear control techniques also can be applied. A detailed development can be found in excellent text [1-3].

Generally, the feedback linearization technique requires the accurate mathematical model of the plant to achieve exact linearization of the closed-loop system. However, for many real processes, there exist inevitable uncertainties in their constructed models. The uncertainties may include parameter uncertainties, modeling error, and input disturbances. Generalized uncertainties include matched uncertainty and unmatched (mismatched) uncertainties. But for many practical systems, unmatched uncertainties are common in control practice. Therefore the design of a robust controller that deals with significant unmatched uncertainties of a nonlinear system is an important subject.

Several methods have been used together to conduct the systematic design of feedback linearizable system without the matched conditions. These include, adaptive control [4], Lyapunov-based control [5,6] and variable structure control [10], to increase the robustness and improve performance of the controlled nonlinear system. However, the above-mentioned methods are only valid for a class of minimum-phase and/or weakly non-minimum-phase nonlinear systems without time-delay.

Unfortunately, for some practical systems, the intrinsic process time delay resides. The existence of time delay degrades the control performance and sometimes makes the system stabilizing difficult. The Smith predictor [11] is usually used to improve the control performance of linear time delay systems. Several theses deal with the control problem of the time-delay systems via predictor-based controllers [24], [25], and [26]. Under a predictor-based controller, therefore, a time-delay system can be transformed into a delay-free system in which the delay is eliminated from the closed loop system. For uncertain nonlinear systems, treating time-delay problems with the use of feedback linearization techniques usually encounters the difficulty of exactly predictive action or the limitation of the Smith predictor framework. Therefore the problems of robust compensation for nonlinear systems with input time delay are rarely investigated. Though the Smith predictor can help to overcome the time delay problem, this method requests that the model of the controlled process be known accurately and the system have to be locally open-loop stable. Shyu and Yan [14], and Luo and de la Sen [15] employ the concept of variable structure control to only deal with the stabilizing of uncertain systems with state delays. Velasco *et al.* [16] deal with the approximate disturbance-decoupling problem of nonlinear systems with an input time delay. Recently, robust stabilization for time-delay systems has received considerable attention. The main object of this paper, a systematic analysis and a simple design method for a class of nonlinear systems with modeling errors and an input time delay are proposed. The so-called matching conditions [12] for controlled nonlinear systems and the Smith predictor are not necessary. System uncertainty is considered as the non-vanishing case in the desired operating condition. Using the coordinate transformation, the original nonlinear system can be transformed into a classical singular perturbation problem. When the lumped nonlinearity, including uncertainty and input time delay, is the local Lipschitz condition [7], its effect on the output trajectory can be effectively suppressed using the proposed technique.

II. PRELIMINARIES AND PROBLEM FORMULATION

Consider a class of the single-input single output uncertain nonlinear system with an input time delay as follows:

$$\dot{x} = f(x(t)) + \Delta f(x(t)) + g(x(t))u(t-\theta) + \Delta g(x(t))u(t-\theta) \quad (1)$$
$$y = h(x(t))$$

where $x \in R^n$ is the states variable, $u \in R$ is the manipulated input, $\theta > 0$ is a delay time in the manipulated input, $y \in R$ is the output. $f(\cdot), g(\cdot), \Delta f(\cdot)$, and $\Delta g(\cdot)$ are smooth vector fields on R^n, and $h(\cdot)$ is a smooth output function. $f(\cdot), g(\cdot) \in R^n$ are known function. The corresponding system without uncertainties, called the nominal system, is defined as follows:

$$\dot{x}(t) = f(x(t)) + g(x(t))u(t) \quad (2)$$
$$y(t) = h(x(t))$$

It is assumed that $f(x)$ and $g(x)$ are known functions and smooth vector fields on R^n. These has been a great deal of excitement in recent years over the development of a rather complete mapping of the nominal system (2) using state feedback, for explicitly linearizing the input between output. Now we induce the Lie derivative, which is described as follows. A more general treatment of the differential geometric approach to nonlinear control systems can be found in advanced textbook, such as Bank [19], Isidori [1], or Nijmeijer and van der Scharft [2]. The Lie derivative of $h(x(t))$ with respect to $f(x(t))$ is defined as:

$$L_f h(x(t)) = \frac{\partial h(x(t))}{\partial x(t)} f(x(t)) \quad (3)$$

We can recursively define
$$L_f(L_f^{i-1}h(x(t))) := L_f^i h(x(t)) \quad \text{for} \quad i = 1, \cdots n,$$
with $L_f^0 h(x(t)) = h(x(t))$. Similarly, $L_g L_f^i h$ denote $L_g(L_f^i h)$.

Definition 1 [1]: A nonlinear system of the form (2) is said to have a constant *relative degree* r, if there exists a positive integer $1 \le r < \infty$, such that
(i) $L_g L_f^k h(x) = 0 \quad k < r - 1$
(ii) $L_g L_f^{r-1} h(x) \ne 0$

for all $x \in R^n$ and $t \in [0, \infty)$.

Definition 2: The system (2) is said to have a strong relative degree in an open set D if it has the same relative degree at every point $x^0 \in D$.

Throughout this thesis, we assume that the nominal system (2) possesses a strong relative degree. Based on this assumption, it has been shown [1] that there exists a neighborhood U of the operating point x_s such that the mapping
$$\varphi : U \to R^n \quad (4)$$
defined as
$$\varphi_i(x(t)) = z_i(t) = L_f^{i-1}h(x(t)), \quad i = 1, 2, \cdots, r \quad (5)$$
$$\varphi_k(x(t)) = \eta_k(t), \quad k = r+1, r+2, \cdots, n \quad (6)$$
and satisfying
$$L_g \varphi_k(x(t)) = 0, \quad k = r+1, r+2, \cdots, n \quad (7)$$
is a diffeomorphism onto image.

Proposition 1: Suppose a system has a strong relative degree $r \le n$, let

$$z_1(t) = h(x(t))$$
$$z_2(t) = L_f h(x(t)) \quad (8)$$
$$\vdots$$
$$z_i(t) = L_f^{i-1}h(x(t)) \quad i = 1, \cdots, r$$

If r is strictly less than n, it is always possible to find $n - r$ smooth functions $\eta_{r+1}, \cdots, \eta_n$ satisfying
$$L_g \eta_j = 0 \quad \text{for all} \quad r+1 \le j \le n \quad (9)$$

Now, we set
$$z = [z_1, \cdots, z_r]^T$$
$$= [h(x), L_f h(x), L_f^2 h(x), \cdots, L_f^{r-1} h(x)]^T \quad (10)$$
$$\eta = [\eta_{r+1}, \eta_{r+2}, \cdots, \eta_n]^T$$

According to **Proposition 1**, there exists a diffeomorphic coordinate transformation $(z, \eta) = \varphi(x)$ which transforms system (2) into the normal form:

$$\dot{z}_1(t) = \frac{\partial \varphi_1}{\partial x} \frac{dx}{dt} = \frac{\partial h(x(t))}{\partial x} \frac{dx}{dt} = L_f h(x(t))$$
$$= \varphi_2(x(t)) = z_2(t)$$
$$\dot{z}_2(t) = \frac{\partial \varphi_2}{\partial x} \frac{dx}{dt} = \frac{\partial L_f h(x(t))}{\partial x} \frac{dx}{dt} = L_f^2 h(x(t)) \quad (11)$$
$$= \varphi_3(x(t)) = z_3(t)$$
$$\vdots$$
$$\dot{z}_r(t) = \frac{\partial \varphi_r}{\partial x} \frac{dx}{dt} = \frac{\partial L_f^{r-1} h(x(t))}{\partial x} \frac{dx}{dt}$$
$$= L_f^r h(x(t)) + L_g L_f^{r-1} h(x(t))u(t)$$

The above equation could be rewritten as
$$\dot{z}_r = b(z(t), \eta(t)) + a(z(t), \eta(t))u(t) \quad (12)$$

where
$$b(z(t), \eta(t)) := L_f^r h(x(t))|_{x = \varphi^{-1}(z(t), \eta(t))} \quad (13)$$
$$a(z(t), \eta(t)) := L_g L_f^{r-1} h(x(t))|_{x = \varphi^{-1}(z(t), \eta(t))}$$

And due to (7),
$$\dot{\eta}_k(t) = \frac{\partial \varphi_k}{\partial x} \frac{dx}{dt}$$
$$= \frac{\partial \varphi_k}{\partial x}(f(x(t)) + g(x(t))u(t)) \quad (14)$$
$$= L_f \varphi_k(x(t)) + L_g \varphi_k(x(t))u(t)$$
$$= L_f \varphi_k(x(t)), \quad k = r+1, r+2, \cdots, n.$$

The transformation of system (11) and (14) in the new coordinates is considered as follows.
$$\dot{z}_i(t) = z_{i+1}(t), \quad i = 1, 2, \cdots, r-1$$
$$\dot{z}_r(t) = b(z(t), \eta(t)) + a(z(t), \eta(t))u(t) \quad (15)$$
$$\dot{\eta}_k(t) = q(z(t), \eta(t))$$
$$y(t) = z_1(t)$$
where

$$q(z(t),\eta(t)) = L_f \varphi_k(x(t))|_{x=\varphi^{-1}(z(t),\eta(t))}, \quad k = r+1, r+2, \cdots, n$$

and $z(t) \in R^r$, $\eta(t) \in R^{n-r}$

As $a(z,\eta)$ is bounded away from zero, its inverse is well defined. Thus the following linearizing feedback law can be represented by a nonlinear function

$$u(t) = \Phi(x(t), v(t)) = \frac{1}{a(z,\eta)}[-b(z,\eta) + v] \quad (16)$$

where $v(t)$ is a new auxiliary controller to be designed for the purpose to synthesize a state feedback controller (16) that can guarantee either exponential, or uniformly ultimately bounded stability of the nonlinear system (1). Notice that the control law (16) make the state vector $\eta(t)$ completely unobservable at the output, and $z(t)$ can be thought of as an external input vector of $\dot{\eta}(t) = q(z(t), \eta(t))$. It can be easily verified that the equations

$$\dot{\eta} = q(0, \eta) \quad (17)$$

are referred to as the zero dynamic. The stability properties of the zero dynamics are crucial because they determine whether or not $\eta(t)$ remains bounded when a tracking control is applied. The system in which the zero dynamics are asymptotically stable is referred as the minimum-phase system. Stable tracking requires a stronger stability criterion for the dynamics

$$\dot{\eta}(t) = q(z(t), \eta(t)) \quad (18)$$

be bounded-input bounded state (BIBS) stable. In addition to the relative degree assumption, a further property of the zero dynamic is required. This is illustrated in the following assumption:

Assumption 1: The zero dynamics (17) is exponentially stable in the domain of definition, the function $q(z(t), \eta(t))$ is Lipschitz in $z(t)$, and uniformly in $\eta(t)$.

Remark 1: Since the zero dynamics is exponentially stable by assumption therefore by a converse theorem of Lyapunov [7] [19], there exists a Lyapunov function $V_0(\eta(t))$ which satisfies the following inequalities:

$$\kappa_1 \|\eta\|^2 \le V_0(\eta) \le \kappa_2 \|\eta\|^2 \quad (19)$$

$$\frac{\partial V_0(\eta)}{\partial \eta} q(0, \eta) \le -\kappa_3 \|\eta\|^2 \quad (20)$$

$$\left\|\frac{\partial V_0(\eta)}{\partial \eta}\right\| \le \kappa_4 \|\eta\| \quad (21)$$

where $\kappa_1, \kappa_2, \kappa_3$, and κ_4 are some positive constants.

Remark 2: Since $q(z(t), \eta(t))$ is Lipschitz in $z(t)$, there exists a positive constant Γ such that

$$\|q(z(t), \eta(t)) - q(0, \eta(t))\| \le \Gamma \|z(t)\|, \quad \forall \eta(t) \in R^{n-r} \quad (22)$$

and Γ is called a Lipschitz constant of $q(z(t), \eta(t))$ [1].

III. Robust Tracking Controller Design and Stability Analysis

In this section we will propose a robust controller which can easily tackle the output tracking problem of uncertain nonlinear systems with an input time delay. The robust stability of the system to be controlled can be guaranteed by the proposed control method in the presence of unmatched uncertainties.

Applying the nominal change of coordinates and the nonlinear state feedback of (16) to the system (1) yields

$$z_1 = h(x(t))$$

$$\dot{z}_1 = z_2 + \frac{\partial h(x(t))}{\partial x(t)}[\Delta f(x(t)) + \Delta g(x(t))u(t-\theta)]$$

$$\vdots$$

$$\dot{z}_{r-1} = z_r + \frac{\partial L_f^{r-2} h(x(t))}{\partial x(t)}[\Delta f(x(t)) + \Delta g(x(t))u(t-\theta)]$$

$$\dot{z}_r = v(t) + \frac{\partial L_f^{r-1} h(x(t))}{\partial x(t)}[\Delta f(x(t)) + \Delta g(x(t))u(t-\theta) + g(x)[u(t-\theta) - u(t)]]$$

$$\dot{\eta}_{r+1} = q_{r+1}(z(t), \eta(t)) + \frac{\partial \phi_{r+1}(x(t))}{\partial x(t)}[\Delta f(x(t)) + \Delta g(x(t))u(t-\theta)]$$

(23)

and

$$\dot{\eta}_n = q_n(z(t), \eta(t)) + \frac{\partial \phi_n(x(t))}{\partial x(t)}[\Delta f(x(t)) + \Delta g(x(t))u(t-\theta)]$$

$$y(t) = h(x(t))$$

Taking advantage of the identities in the nominal transformations (15) and by some derivations, it can be easily verified that (23) can be transformed into

$$\dot{z}(t) = Az(t) + Bv(t) + \Delta A(x(t), u(t), u(t-\theta))$$

$$\dot{\eta}(t) = q(z(t), \eta(t)) + \Delta \Psi(x(t), u(t-\theta)) \quad (24)$$

$$y(t) = Cz(t)$$

where

$$z = [z_1, \cdots, z_r]^T$$

$$\eta = [\eta_{r+1}, \cdots, \eta_n]^T \quad (25)$$

$$\Delta A = [\Delta A_1, \cdots, \Delta A_r]^T$$

$$\Delta A = \begin{bmatrix} \frac{\partial h(x(t))}{\partial x(t)}[\Delta f(x(t)) + \Delta g(x(t))u(t-\theta)] \\ \vdots \\ \frac{\partial L_f^{r-2} h(x(t))}{\partial x(t)}[\Delta f(x(t)) + \Delta g(x(t))u(t-\theta)] \\ \frac{\partial L_f^{r-1} h(x(t))}{\partial x(t)}[\Delta f(x(t)) + \Delta g(x(t))u(t-\theta) + g(x)[u(t-\theta) - u(t)]] \end{bmatrix} \in R^{r \times 1}$$

(26)

$$\Delta \Psi = \begin{bmatrix} \frac{\partial \phi_{r+1}(x(t))}{\partial x(t)}[\Delta f(x(t)) + \Delta g(x(t))u(t-\theta)] \\ \vdots \\ \frac{\partial \phi_n(x(t))}{\partial x(t)}[\Delta f(x(t)) + \Delta g(x(t))u(t-\theta)] \end{bmatrix} \in R^{(n-r) \times 1} \quad (27)$$

$$A = \begin{bmatrix} 0 & 1 & 0 & \cdots & 0 \\ 0 & 0 & 1 & \cdots & 0 \\ \vdots & \vdots & \vdots & \ddots & \vdots \\ 0 & 0 & 0 & \cdots & 1 \\ 0 & 0 & 0 & \cdots & 0 \end{bmatrix} \in R^{r \times r}$$

$$B = \begin{bmatrix} 0 & 0 & \cdots & 1 \end{bmatrix}^T \in R^{r \times 1} \quad (28)$$

$$C = \begin{bmatrix} 1 & 0 & \cdots & 0 \end{bmatrix}^T \in R^{1 \times r}$$

Consider the reference model as
$$\xi(t) = A_0 \xi(t) + B_0 v_r(t) \quad (29)$$
$$y_d(t) = C_0 \xi(t)$$

where $\xi \in R^r$ is the state variable. $A_0 \in R^{r \times r}$, $B_0 \in R^{r \times 1}$, $C_0 \in R^{1 \times r}$, $v_r(t)$ is the external input, and $y_d(t)$ is the desired output trajectory.

Assumption 2: The desired output $y_d(t)$ and its first r derivatives are uniformly bounded, and satisfy
$$\| y_d(t) \ y_d^{(1)}(t) \ \cdots \ y_d^{(r)}(t) \| \le B_d \quad (30)$$
for some positive constant B_d.

Remark 3: The fact that the model reference must be relative order of r to avoid the use of differentiators in the controller. Furthermore, if the desired trajectory $y_d(t)$ and its derivatives are uniformly bounded, one can make the output tracking error $e_1 = y(t) - y_d(t)$, as minimize as possible and the whole system states locally stable.

Then, define the trajectory error to be
$$e_i(t) = z_i(t) - y_d^{(i-1)}(t), \ i = 1, 2, \cdots, r, \text{ and } e(t) \in R^r \quad (31)$$

and substitute (23) into above with control law (16),
$$\begin{aligned} \dot{e}_1 &= e_2 + \Delta A_1 \\ \dot{e}_2 &= e_3 + \Delta A_2 \\ &\vdots \\ \dot{e}_{r-1} &= e_r + \Delta A_{r-1} \\ \dot{e}_r &= v + \Delta A_r - y_d^{(r)} \end{aligned} \quad (32)$$

The system are transformed into the error state equation as
$$\dot{e}(t) = Ae(t) + B\left(v(t) - y_d^{(r)}(t)\right) + \Delta A \quad (33)$$
$$\dot{\eta}(t) = q(z(t), \eta(t)) + \Delta \Psi$$

Consider the algebraic Riccati equation
$$A_c^T P + A_c P + Q - \alpha P B B^T P = 0 \quad (34)$$

When $Q > 0$, $\alpha > 0$, and the solution P is a symmetric positive definite matrix. In order to design stable controller to compensate for uncertainties and an input time-delay, we propose the following robust compensation control

$$v = y_d^{(r)} - \alpha_1 e_1 - \alpha_2 e_2 - \cdots - \alpha_r e_r + u_c \quad (35)$$

Notice that $\alpha_1, \cdots, \alpha_r$, are chosen such that
$$S^r + \alpha_r S^{r-1} + \alpha_{r-1} S^{r-2} + \cdots + \alpha_3 S^2 + \alpha_2 S + \alpha_1 \quad (36)$$
is a Hurwitz polynomial and S is the Laplace operator.

Now we devise the compensation term $u_c(t)$ of the following form
$$u_c = -\beta B^T P e \quad (37)$$

So, it is easy to obtain the external control law
$$v = y_d^{(r)} - \alpha_1 e_1 - \alpha_2 e_2 - \cdots - \alpha_r e_r - \beta B^T P e \quad (38)$$

Then the closed loop system can be represented as
$$\dot{e} = Ae + B[-\alpha_1 e_1 - \alpha_2 e_2 - \cdots - \alpha_r e_r + u_c] + \Delta A \quad (39)$$

yields
$$\begin{bmatrix} \dot{e}_1 \\ \dot{e}_2 \\ \vdots \\ \dot{e}_r \end{bmatrix} = \begin{bmatrix} 0 & 1 & \cdots & 0 \\ \vdots & \vdots & \cdots & \vdots \\ 0 & 0 & \ddots & 1 \\ -\alpha_1 & -\alpha_2 & \cdots & -\alpha_r \end{bmatrix} \begin{bmatrix} e_1 \\ e_2 \\ \vdots \\ e_r \end{bmatrix} + Bu_c + \Delta A \quad (40)$$

Furthermore, we obtain a standard singularly perturbed system by the form:
$$\dot{e}(t) = A_c e(t) + B u_c(t) + \Delta A\left(x(t), u(t) u(t - \theta)\right) \quad (41)$$
$$\dot{\eta}(t) = q(z(t), \eta(t)) + \Delta \Psi\left(x(t), u(t-\theta)\right)$$

where
$$A_c = \begin{bmatrix} 0 & 1 & \cdots & 0 \\ \vdots & \vdots & \cdots & \vdots \\ 0 & 0 & \ddots & 1 \\ -\alpha_1 & -\alpha_2 & \cdots & -\alpha_r \end{bmatrix} \quad (42)$$

Assumption 3: The pair (A, B) is controllable.

Assumption 4 [23]: Consider that $W(e(t)) = e(t)^T P e(t)$ is a positive definite function, and P satisfies (34) algebraic Riccati equation. If there exist
$$W(e(t-\theta)) \le \rho^2 W(e(t)), \ \rho > 1,$$
then $\| e(t-\theta) \| \le \rho c^* \| e(t) \| \quad (43)$
where $\theta > 0$, and $c^* = \sqrt{(\lambda_{\max}(P) / \lambda_{\min}(P))} \quad (44)$

The minimum and maximum eigenvalues of a hermitian matrix is denoted as $\lambda_{\min}(\cdot), \lambda_{\max}(\cdot)$, respectively.

The result of (43) represents that if the current state $x(t)$ is bounded, the delayed state $x(t-\theta)$ is uniformly bounded. This assumption had been used in the literature for state-delayed systems [13, 14, 28]. With the aid of **Assumption 4**, we can further describe the state bound between the delayed control input $u(t-\theta)$ and the control law $u(t)$ by (16) as follows:

$$\begin{aligned} |u(t-\theta) - u(t)| &= |\Phi(x(t-\theta), v(t-\theta)) - \Phi(x(t), v(t))| \\ &= |-a^{-1}(z(t-\theta), \eta(t-\theta)) \times b(z(t-\theta), \eta(t-\theta)) \\ &\quad + a^{-1}(z(t), \eta(t)) \times b(z(t), \eta(t)) \\ &\quad + a^{-1}(z(t-\theta), \eta(t-\theta)) \times v(t-\theta) \\ &\quad - a^{-1}(z(t), \eta(t)) \times v(t) | \end{aligned} \quad (45)$$

By the mean-value theorem [7], the local Lipschitz property of Jacobian $\partial \Phi / \partial x$ near the origin, one can show that
$$|u(t-\theta) - u(t)| \le c_1 \| z(t-\theta) - z(t) \| + c_2 \| \eta(t-\theta) - \eta(t) \| + c_3 \le \kappa \quad (46)$$

for some positive constants c_1, c_2, c_3, and $\tilde{\kappa}$.

Assumption 5: There exist some positive constants $\gamma_1, \gamma_2, \gamma_3, l_1, l_2,$ and l_3 such that

$$\|2P\Delta A(x(t),u(t),u(t-\theta))\| \leq \gamma_1\|z\|+\gamma_2\|\eta\|+\gamma_3\tilde{\kappa} \quad (47)$$

and

$$\|\Delta\Psi(x(t),u(t-\theta))\| \leq l_1\|z\|+l_2\|\eta\|+l_3 \quad (48)$$

where P is defined in (34) for all $x \in U \subset R^n$;

$$\|z\| \leq \|e\|+B_d. \quad (49)$$

Theorem 1: Consider the uncertain system (1). Under **Assumptions 1~5**, suppose that the control signal $v(t)$ is applied by (38). Then the solution of the closed-loop dynamics controlled system (41) converges a residual set.

$$\Omega_f = \{e \in R^r : V(e) \leq \mu^{-1}\varepsilon\} \quad (50)$$

Here, ε and μ are defined as

$$\varepsilon = \frac{1}{2}\left[(\gamma_1 B_d+\gamma_3\tilde{\kappa})^2+\gamma_2 B_c^2\right] \quad (51)$$

and

$$\mu = \frac{\lambda_{\min}(Q)-\gamma_1-\frac{1}{2}\gamma_2-\frac{1}{2}}{\lambda_{\max}(P)} \quad (52)$$

Moreover, the compact set can be selected as small as possible by choosing the each kind of design parameter appropriately.

Proof: To obtain the boundedness result, we proceed with the following quadratic function

$$V(e) = e^T P e$$

Differentiating $V(e(t))$ along the trajectory of the system (41) and satisfying (34), we obtain

$$\dot{V} = \dot{e}^T P e + e^T P \dot{e}$$
$$= -e^T Q e + \alpha e^T P B B^T P - 2\beta e^T P B B^T P e + 2 e^T P \Delta A$$
$$\leq -e^T Q e - (2\beta-\alpha)\|e^T PB\|^2 + \|e\|(\gamma_1\|z\|+\gamma_2\|\eta\|+\gamma_3\tilde{\kappa}) \quad (53)$$

by choosing $\beta > \frac{1}{2}\alpha$

The state $e(t)$ and $\eta(t)$ are uniformly ultimately whenever $\|e(t)\|$ or $\|\eta(t)\|$ is large for all $t \geq 0$. To investigate the ultimate bound of tracking error, suppose that $B_c > 0$ exists such that $\|\eta(t)\| \leq B_c$. Applying the algebraic inequality $ab \leq \frac{1}{2}a^2+\frac{1}{2}b^2$, it yields

$$\dot{V} \leq -\lambda_{\min}(Q)\|e\|^2+\gamma_1\|e\|(\|e\|+B_d)+\gamma_2\|e\|\|\eta\|+\gamma_3\tilde{\kappa}\|e\|$$

$$\leq -\lambda_{\min}(Q)\|e\|^2+\gamma_1\|e\|^2+\gamma_1 B_d\|e\|+\frac{1}{2}\gamma_2\|e\|^2+\frac{1}{2}\gamma_2\|\eta\|^2+\gamma_3\tilde{\kappa}\|e\|$$

$$\leq -(\lambda_{\min}(Q)-\gamma_1-\frac{1}{2}\gamma_2)\|e\|^2+\frac{1}{2}(\gamma_1 B_d+\gamma_3\tilde{\kappa})^2+\frac{1}{2}\|e\|^2+\frac{1}{2}\gamma_2 B_c^2$$

$$\leq -\frac{\lambda_{\min}(Q)-\gamma_1-\frac{1}{2}\gamma_2-\frac{1}{2}}{\lambda_{\max}(P)}V+\frac{1}{2}\left[(\gamma_1 B_d+\gamma_3\tilde{\kappa})^2+\gamma_2 B_c^2\right]$$

$$\leq -\mu V+\varepsilon$$

where ε and μ are described as (51) and (52), respectively.

Due to $\dot{V} \leq -\mu V+\varepsilon$, it implies that

$$V(e(t)) \leq V(e(t_0))\exp(-\mu t)+(1-\exp(-\mu t))\mu^{-1}\varepsilon \quad (54)$$

It is clear that $V(e(t))$ decreases monotonically along any solution of the controlled system until the solution reaches the compact set Ω_f in (50). Hence, The solution $e(t,t_0,x_0)$ of the dynamics (54) will converge to the residual set Ω_f with a rate at least as fast as $\exp(-\mu t/2)$. Thus, we conclude that they are uniformly ultimately bounded with respect to the ultimate bound $\mu^{-1}\varepsilon$.

IV. An Example and Simulation Results

In this section, we particularize some examples to show the performance of the proposed controller in Section 2.3, and manifest the effectiveness by computer simulation results.

Example 1: Consider an uncertain nonlinear continuous system with relative degree less than the state dimension n,

$$\begin{bmatrix}\dot{x}_1\\\dot{x}_2\\\dot{x}_3\end{bmatrix} = \begin{bmatrix}x_1^2-x_2\\-x_2\\-x_3\end{bmatrix}+\begin{bmatrix}0\\-1\\1\end{bmatrix}u(t-\theta)+\begin{bmatrix}0\\\delta(x_1^2+x_1+x_2+x_3)\\\delta x_3\cos x_2 u(t-\theta)\end{bmatrix} \quad (55)$$

$$y(t) = h(x(t)) = x_1$$

where δ is the uncertain parameter that lies within $[-2.0 \quad +2.0]$.

Then, we can calculate a normal form by taking

$$z_1 = \phi_1(x) = h(x) = x_1$$
$$z_2 = \phi_2(x) = L_f h(x) = x_1^2-x_2 \quad (56)$$
$$z_3 = \eta_3 = x_2+x_3 \quad (57)$$

Based on coordinate transformation, the uncertain nonlinear system (47) can be formulated as:

$$\dot{z}_1(t) = z_2+\frac{\partial x_1(t)}{\partial x(t)}(\Delta f(x(t))+\Delta g(x(t))u(t-\theta))$$

$$\dot{z}_2(t) = L_f^2 x(t)+L_f x_1 g(x(t))u(t-\theta)+\frac{\partial L_f x_1(t)}{\partial x(t)}(\Delta f(x(t))+\Delta g(x(t))u(t-\theta))$$

$$= 2x_1^3-2x_1 x_2+x_2-\delta(x_1^2+x_1+x_2+x_3)+u(t-\theta)$$

$$y(t) = x_1(t) \quad (58)$$

Select the Hurwitz polynomial parameters $\alpha_1 = 50$, and $\alpha_2 = 5$, then let $Q = \begin{bmatrix}6 & 0\\0 & 4\end{bmatrix}$, $\alpha = 5$. By the Riccati equation (32), the solutions are given by

$$P = \begin{bmatrix}17.9304 & 0.0598\\0.0598 & 0.3505\end{bmatrix}. \quad (59)$$

Then the eigenvalue $\lambda_{\min}(P) = 0.3503$ and $\lambda_{\max}(P) = 17.9306$.

Then the system with the auxiliary control law can be expressed as

$$\dot{e}_1 = e_2 + \Delta A_1$$
$$\dot{e}_2 = -\alpha_1 e_1 - \alpha_2 e_2 - \beta B^T Pe + \Delta A_2 \quad (60)$$
$$= -\alpha_1 e_1 - \alpha_2 e_2 - \beta B^T Pe - \delta(x_1^2 + x_1 + x_2 + x_3) + u(t-\theta)$$

The initial values of the states are given as $x(t_0) = [0.2 \quad 1.5 \quad -0.5]$. The sampling time is $\Delta t = 0.002$ sec. The computer simulation results are showed in Figs. 1~2, respectively.

V. CONCLUSIONS

In this paper, the theory and application of input-output feedback linearization of nonlinear systems with uncertainties and an input time delay in the manipulated input by the approach of robust compensation control have been presented. For a general nonlinear system with uncertainties and an input time delay, we select the controlled output and calculate the coordinate transformation based on the nominal system. Then the nonlinear system can be transformed into an equivalent linear system. The proposed robust controller is then developed, which guarantees the robust stability and the tracking errors exponential convergence to a small bounded residual set. The size of this set depends on the bounds of the uncertainties and on some design parameters. Finally, an illustrative example is used to account for the design procedures and the computer simulation results show the efficiency of the proposed controller.

References

[1] A. Isidori, *Nonlinear control systems:* an introduction, 2nd ed., Springer-Verlag, New York, 1989.

[2] H. Nijmeijer and A. J. van der Schaft, *Nonlinear dynamical control systems*, Springer-Verlag, New York, 1990.

[3] J. -J. E. Slotine and W. Li, *Applied nonlinear control*, Prentice-Hall, Englewood Cliffs, 1991.

[4] I. Kanellakopoulos, P. V. Kokotovic, and A. S. Morse, "Systematic design of adaptive controllers for feedback linearizable systems," *IEEE Trans. Automat. Contr.*, vol. AC-36, pp. 1241-1253, November, 1991.

[5] T. L. Liao, L. C. Fu, and C. F. Hsu, "Output tracking control of nonlinear systems with mismatched uncertainties," *System and Control Letters*, vol. 18, pp. 39-47, January, 1992.

[6] K. Y. Lian, L. C. Fu, and T. L. Liao, "Robust output tracking nonlinear systems with weakly non-minimum phase," *Int. J. Contr.*, vol. 58, pp. 301-316, April, 1993.

[7] KHALIL, H. K.: "Nonlinear systems" (Macmillan, New York, 1992).

[8] J. -J. E. Slotine and J. K. Hedrick, "Robust input-output feedback linearization," *Int. J. Contr.*, vol. 57, pp. 1133-1139, October, 1993.

[9] W. Wu and Y. -S. Chou., "Output tracking control of uncertain nonlinear systems with an input time delay," *IEE Proc. -Control Theory Appl.*, Vol. 143. No. 4, July, 1996.

[10] J. -J. E. Slotine and S. S. Sastry, "Tracking control of nonlinear systems using sliding surfaces, with application to robotic manipulator," *Int. J. Contr.*, vol. 38, no. 2, February, pp. 465-492, 1983.

[11] SMITH, O. J. M.: "Closer control of loops with dead time," *Chem. Eng. Prog.*, 1957, 53, pp. 217-221.

[12] L. C. Fu and T. L. Liao, "Globally stable robust tracking of nonlinear systems using variable structure control and with an application to a robotic manipulator," *IEEE Trans. Automat. Contr.*, vol. AC-35, no. 12, pp. 1345-1350, December, 1990.

[13] MAHMOUD, M. S., and AL-MUTHAIRI, N. F.: "Design of robust controllers for time-delay systems," *IEEE Trans.*, 1994, AC-39, (5), pp. 995-999.

[14] SHYU, K. K., and YAN, J. J.: "Robust stability of uncertain time-delay and its stabilizing by variable structure control," *Int. J. Control*, 1993, 57, (1), pp. 237-246.

[15] LUO, N., and DE LA SEN, M.: "State feedback sliding mode control of a class of uncertain time delay systems," *IEE Proc. D*, 1993, 140, (4), pp. 261-274.

[16] VELASCO, M., ALVAREZ, J. A., and CASTRO, R.: "Approximate disturbance decoupling for a class of nonlinear time delay systems." *Proceedings of American Control Conference*, 1993, pp. 1046-1050.

[17] BARMISH, B. R., CORLESS, M., and LEITMANN, G.: "A new class of stabilizing controllers for uncertain dynamic systems," *SIAM J. Control Optim.*, 1983. 21, (2), pp. 246-255.

[18] W. Wu and Y. S. Chou, "A new systematic design of high-gain feedback for nonlinear systems with unmatched uncertainties," *Int. J. Contr.*, vol. 62, no. 6, pp. 1471-1489, December, 1995.

[19] Stephen P. Banks *Control systems engineering:* Modelling and simulation, control theory and microprocessor implementation. ed., Prentice-Hall International, 1986.

[20] H. Seraji, "Simple method for model reference adaptive control," *Int. J. Contr.*, vol. 49, no. 1, pp. 367-371, March 1989.

[21] D. Y. Yoo and M. J. Chung, "A variable structure control with simple adaptation laws for upper bounds on the norm of the uncertainties," *IEEE Trans. Automat. Contr.*, vol. 37, pp. 860-865, June 1992.

[22] I. Tunay and O. Kaynak, "A new variable structure controller for affine nonlinear systems with non-matching uncertainties," *Int. J. contr.*, vol. 62, no 4, pp. 917-939, June, 1995.

[23] J. HALE, "Theory of functional differential equations" (Springer Verlag, New York, 1977)

[24] FIAGEDZ, Y. A., and Pearson, A. E., 1986, Feedback stabilization of linear autonomous time lag systems. *IEEE Transactions on Automatic Control*, AC-31, 847-855.

[25] FURUKAWA, T., and SHIMEMURA, E., 1983, Predictive control for systems with time delay. *International Journal of Control*, **37**, 399-412.

[26] MANITIUS, A. Z., and OLBROT, A. W., 1979, Finite spectrum assignment problem for system with delays. *IEEE Transactions on Automatic Control*, **25**, 266-269.

[27] Young-Hoon Roh and Jun-Ho Oh, "Sliding mode control with uncertainty adaptation for uncertain input-delay systems," *Int. J. Contr.*, Vol. 73, No. 13, pp. 1255-1260, 2000

[28] E. CHERES, S. GUTMAN, and PALMOR, ZJ.: "Stabilization of uncertain dynamic systems including state delay", *IEEE Trans.*, 1989, AC-34, (11), PP. 1199-1203.

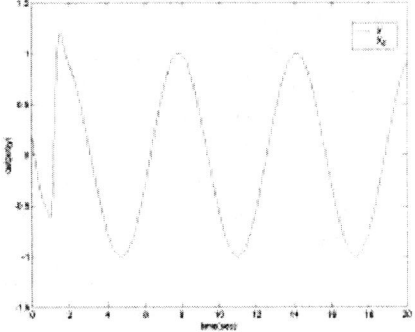

Fig. 1. The output $y(t)$ and the desired output $y_d(t)$ of the sinusoid case

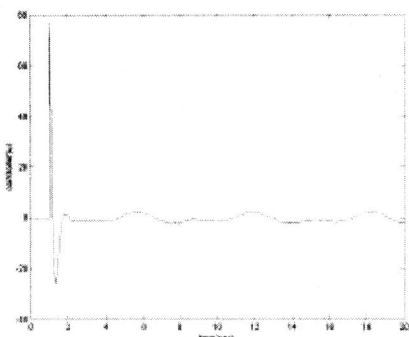

Fig. 2. The system input $u(t)$ of sinusoid case

Development of Autonomous Flight Control System for Unmanned Helicopter by Use of Neural Networks

Hiroaki Nakanishi and Koichi Inoue

Department of Aeronautics and Astronautics,

Graduate School of Engineering, Kyoto University, Kyoto, Japan, 606-8501

Email: hiroaki@kuaero.kyoto-u.ac.jp

Abstract

This paper describes methods to develop autonomous flight control systems for UAVs. The unmanned helicopter "RMAX" produced by YAMAHA Motor Co., LTD. is used in this study. It was difficult to develop flight control systems, because the dynamics of the helicopter is nonlinear. An efficient method to design controllers by training neural networks is proposed in this paper. It is easy to use trained neural network together with online training neural networks or adaptive controllers to compensate undesirable effects which are not modeled or sudden changes of the target and environment, therefore the control system can be highly reliable. Results of flight experiments are shown to demonstrate the effectiveness of our approach.

Figure 1: YAMAHA RMAX for autonomous flight

1 Introduction

Various kinds of UAV are developed in the United States and Europe for many purposes and many studies on UAV are also carried out. Most of them are aiming at military application. However, the most UAVs are produced and used in Japan, because it is quite common to use unmanned helicopters for chemical spray at rice paddy fields. If a unmanned helicopter can perform the chemical spray automatically, it will help to reduce work force in agriculture. But, to control the helicopter remotely, a pilot cannot be away from the unmanned helicopter, because the pilot must know the attitude, the velocity and the position by watching the helicopter. The skilled pilot can control the helicopter at a distance of 200 meters, but flying out of the sight isn't possible. Therefore, it is difficult to use the unmanned helicopter at dangerous area, because the pilot is exposed to danger. But attractive capabilities of unmanned helicopters, such as hovering, vertical landing and taking-off, are very important in observation or surveillance activities in an occasion of disaster such as large earthquakes and volcanic eruption. It is necessary to develop autonomous flight and semi-autonomous flight control systems to perform many activities at disasters. Therefore, the cooperated project to develop an autonomous unmanned helicopter between Kyoto University and YAMAHA Motro Co., LTD. was started, and the autonomous unmanned helicopter succeeded in surveillance and observation activities at erupting Mt. Usu, Hokkaido, Japan, in spring of 2000[1]. Figure 1 shows the unmanned helicopter YAMAHA RMAX for autonomous flight, which was used for observation activities at erupting Mt. Usu. A simple linear PD controller was used to control the heliconter, but it didn't have enough performance and robustness, therefore it is necessary to improve the flight control system for reliable autonomous flight.

In conventional methods, it is very difficult to develop autonomous flight control systems for UAVs because a control engineer must integrate knowledge of many experts and results of many experiments. Moreover, the dynamics of the helicopter is usually nonlinear, and includes uncertainties. Typical uncertainty which disturbs the flight is a wind, control systems should have robustness against the wind. But there wasn't effective method to develop nonlinear and robust control systems. To develop nonlinear and robust autonomous flight control systems, we propose a method to design control system by training a neural network. In the proposed method, a nonlinear flight simulator of the helicopter is used to train neural networks, and any knowledge about the dynamics of the helicopter isn't used in the training algorithm, so that the development can progress in distributed approach, and the efficiency of the development is also improved.

2 Autonomous Unmanned Helicopter

YAMAHA RMAX, which is used in our study, is a very small helicopter whose main rotor's diameter is 3.115m and the maximum payload is 30kg, so that it can perform many activities. The specification of RMAX can be found in the web pages(http://www.yamaha-motor.co.jp).

In this section, equipments for autonomous flight control are described. The helicopter equips an attitude sensor and a GPS sensor. The attitude sensor consists of a geomagnetic azimuth sensor, 3 gyros and accelerometers. To ensure the accuracy of measurement of position and velocity, a kinematics D-GPS is used. Velocity controllers based on simple PD controller was used in autonomous flight at erupting Mt. Usu, and the velocity of the helicopter was controlled automatically to the desired velocity which is calculated to fly along desired and programmed flight path.

To improve the performance and reliability of autonomous flight controllers, it is necessary to use more accurate states of the helicopter, such as the position, velocities, and the attitude. Therefore GPS-INS integrated navigation system using the extended Kalman Filter is developed. The integrated navigation system can cancel the effect of the offset of gyros and accelerometers and the effect of distance from the GPS antenna to the center of gravity respectively. Moreover, it is also able to compensate time delay in transmission of GPS measurement data. Much computation is required for the integrated navigation system and to use neural networks in the flight control, so that a note PC is also equipped on the helicopters. Real time processing is required in the computation, so that RT-Linux is used as the operation system. Because Note PC and RT-Linux are used, it is possible to reduce the total of the cost and time to develop flight control system Figure 2 shows the signal block diagram of the autonomous unmanned helicopter. In flight experiments, a Note PC, whose CPU is Intel Pentium III 650MHz, is used and it has enough capabilty to perform computation required in the flight control system. As the Figure 2 shows, the flight control system consists of two feedback loop, the inner loop and the outer loop. The outer loop is the positioning and velocity controller, which is computed by the Note PC. In our study, the outer loop controller is mainly discussed. The outer controller sends a signal to the inner loop as the desired attitude. In the inner loop, attitude controller was used the helicopter to track the desired attitude. The attitude controller is fixed and it have already programmed on the board computer. But outer controller can stop using the attitude controller, because the attitude controller may not have enough performance. If the attitude controller was turned off, the outer controller controls the helicopter directly. The flight simulator offered from YAMAHA Motor Co., LTD. can simulate the flight controlled by the flight control system described in Figure 2. But any information about the dynamics of the helicopter, such as aerodynamic coefficients, isn't open to public, so that the flight simulator was used only to check if the designed controller works or not. Even if a simulator can be used, it is almost impossible to design effective controllers without knowing the dynamics of the controlled object in conventional methods.

3 Control System by Training a Neural Network

As described in the previous section, even if we have the accurate flight simulator of the unmanned helicopter, it cannot be utilized for the design of a control system in conventional methods. In designing controllers, information about the dynamics of the controlled object is necessary, so that the designer must know the detail about the controlled object. To construct a simulator, information about detail dynamics of the controlled object is also necessary. If there is an effective method to fully utilize the simulator in designing controllers, it is not necessary to integrate much knowledge about the controlled object to design controllers, and it will improve the efficiency of the development.

We proposed to use neural networks in designing controllers[2], and the proposed training method can be built in any flight simulators without knowing anything about the dynamics. The proposed training method is based on Powell's conjugate direction algorithm[3], which can be applied to problems which include not-differentiable functions and is classified as off-line training method of neural networks. Neither any differential coefficients nor the teacher signal aren't necessary in training neural networks, therefore it is much suitable in developing controllers by use of neural networks.

Moreover in the training algorithm, any information about the controlled object, such as state equation, is not required, and only to calculate the performance index is required to train a neural network by use of the algorithm. It can easily be built in a flight simulator of

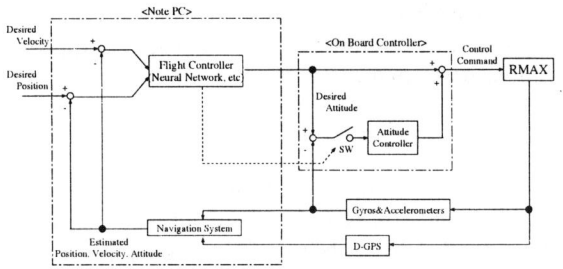

Figure 2: Block Diagram of Autonomous Flight Control System

UAV as a module. The flight simulator is fully used instead of integrating much information about UAV in designing controllers. Therefore much knowledge of many experts and results of flight experiments can be utilized easily in this designing method, and the development can progress in a distributed approach by using the flight simulator. Moreover it is very easy to design various controllers by the proposed method. But modeling errors are inevitable in any flight simulator. Moreover it is also impossible to remove disturbances, such as wind in real flights. Therefore robustness is essential to the autonomous flight controllers to improve the reliability.

3.1 Offline Training Algorithm to Design Robust Controllers

Generally speaking, some uncertainties are inevitable in developing controllers, so that designing robust control system becomes important. We had already proposed methods to design robust controllers by use of neural networks[4], but only deterministic uncertainties are considered in those methods. But stochastic disturbance is also one of the most typical uncertainties, so that controllers must be designed to reduce its influence on the performance. Our purpose in this section is to build method to design a robust neural controller against stochastic disturbances.

The most typical stochastic uncertainty[5] that exists in flight of UAVs is a wind, and time series of wind speed and its direction belong to stochastic process. Flight of an UAV is disturbed by a wind, so that a performance index of a sampled flight becomes stochastic. Training using a particular wind is quite danger because the trained controller doesn't have proper robustness. Any stochastic values cannot be used as the index for training. Therefore a statistical value of the stochastic process is suitable for the index for training. Even some statistical values, such as max or median, are not differentiable, but our training algorithm can use not-differentiable values as the index in training. To design robust controller against winds, we proposed to use a performance index described as (1)

$$L = \frac{1}{\gamma} \log(E[\exp(2\gamma J)]) \quad (1)$$

where J is a sampled index[5]. If the performance index (1) can be expanded about γ, we can obtain an approximated index described as (2).

$$L = E[J] + \gamma Var[J] + O(\gamma^2) \quad (2)$$

$\gamma \geq 0$ is a scalar parameter and it quantifies the robustness of the trained controller. γ is an induced L_2-gain from stochastic disturbances to reference outputs. From (2), it is shown that not only average but variance are considered in this method. The bigger γ is used in training, the smaller the variance of the performance is, that is, the trained neural network has robustness against

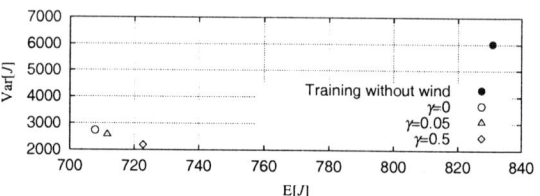

Figure 3: Average and Variance of Performance Index

stochastic disturbances. Therefore its robustness can be quantified by γ, and this is the most advantageous point of our method.

To confirm the effectiveness of the proposed method, it is assumed that only vertical wind exits and horizontal wind doesn't exist in simulations. Altitude controllers of RMAX, which are nonlinear state feedback controllers, are designed by use of neural networks. The sampled index J described as (3) is used in training, where d is the desired altitude.

$$J = \sum_{t=0}^{40sec} (z(t) - d(t))^2 + v_z^2(t) \quad (3)$$

Average and variance of the sampled index J are shown in Figure 3. Average indicates the performance of the controller, and variance indicates the extent of the influence of the disturbance, therefore these values are very important parameters for robust controllers against stochastic disturbances. Both average and variance of a neural network, which is trained without considering any winds, are big, therefore the network fails in reducing the influence of the wind, and the performances is not good enough. But both average and variance of neural networks trained by the proposed method are small, so that Figure 3 shows that neural networks trained by the proposed method have excellent robustness and performance. Moreover, this figure shows a designer can perform the tradeoff between robustness and performance by choosing γ. Quantified robustness against the stochastic disturbance is the most noteworthy property of the proposed method, and it can be combined with training for deterministic uncertainties very easily, so that more excellent training method will be brought.

But it is assumed that the origin of the plant is an equilibrium point in these design methods. This is because a feed-forward neural network is used and the trained neural network acts as a state feedback controller, not as a dynamical controller. In many cases, the average of the wind speed isn't 0 and the change of the weight of helicopter will cause the change of the trim. In order to cope with them, the controller, which has dynamics, is required. Moreover, something may break down during a flight. Robust controller is a fault tolerant controller, but if the failure is not considered in design or is bigger than expected, then the flight of the helicopter may be unstable. Therefore, for reliable autonomous flight, it is also necessary to cope with the change during a flight.

3.2 Online Training and Adaptive Control

To cope with the change that occurs after starting to use the plant, adaptive controllers are useful. Online training of neural network can be considered as a adaptive function, so that many studies are carried out to use neural networks in adaptive controllers. The Back Propagation is the most famous online training rule, but its training speed is very slow. Therefore before the adaptation is finished, it is possible that the plant may become unstable. Recently, training rule based on Lyapunov stability theorem and adaptive backstepping method were introduced to overcome the difficulty. Adaptation speed of these methods is very high. Moreover, the stability of these methods is proved. Therefore these online training methods are suitable to use in the autonomous flight control system. Figure 4 shows the control block diagram including online training controller, and [6] demonstrates the effectiveness of online training control systems.

The reference response has to be calculated in controlling the plant, because the error that measured from a certain reference is necessary in adaptive rules. That is because the error from the reference is a sign of the changing or failures, and to make the error equal to 0 even with failures or changes is the objective of the online training controllers. It is common that a linear model is used to calculate the reference response, because it is easy to compute. The model is chosen according to its properties, such as tracking speed and bandwidth and so on. If the online training is successfully finished, the actual flight path becomes equal to the reference model path.

3.3 Harmony of Online Training and Offline Training

As described in the previous section, even if some failures or changes occur, online training controller and adaptive controller can control the plant so that the response become equal to the model response. Although it is one of advantages that an adaptive system can reconfigure the control system using information collected after starting operation, information acquired before operation cannot fully be used, so that the performance is usually not good. From the viewpoint of the performance, an online training controller (an adaptive controller) is inferior to a controller that is trained offline. On the other hand, information acquired before operation is fully used in offline training of the controller, so that the offline trained controller has enough performance. But information collected after starting operation is never used in offline training, Therefore online training and offline training should be used together because they can compensate with each other. But if the purpose of control differs, it causes the conflict, not compensation. Since it is possible that using together with both controllers may be harmful, the purpose of each controller has to be identical. The purpose of the online training controller is to make the plant respond like a reference model, but the reference model isn't used in offline training. The purpose of the controller that is trained offline is to stabilize the plant. Especially in the nonlinear plant, the response isn't equal to the linear model in general, so that it causes the error between the actual response and the model response. In online training controllers, it is necessary to use the reference model in order to detect failures or changes, so that the purpose of the controller cannot be modified. Therefore offline training method in consideration of using together with an online training controller is discussed.

Consider a nonlinear system of n degrees freedom in general form:

$$\ddot{y} = f(y, \dot{y}, u) \tag{4}$$

where y and $\dot{y}$ are the state variables and u is the control variable. U is a pseudo-control variables, such that

$$U = f(y, \dot{y}, u) \tag{5}$$

If f is a known and invertible function with respect to control u, control u described as (6) can linearize the map between control and output.

$$u = f^{-1}(y, \dot{y}, U) \tag{6}$$

If the pseudo-control is chosen as (7), the closed loop dynamics can be expressed as (8) [7].

$$U = -K_p(y - d) - K_d\dot{y} \tag{7}$$

$$\ddot{y} = -K_p(y - d) - K_d\dot{y} \tag{8}$$

In this section, to develop a method to design a controller for feedback linearization, it is assumed that f is invertible but not known. A neural network is used as feedback linearizing transformation shown in Figure 5. But the block diagram shown in Figure 5 cannot be used in training directly, so that a block diagram shown

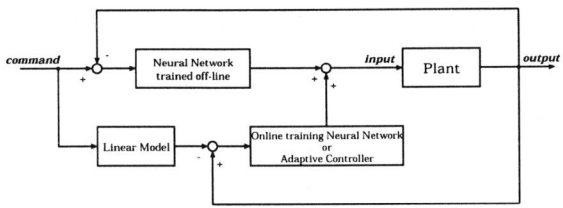

Figure 4: Block Diagram including Online Training Controller

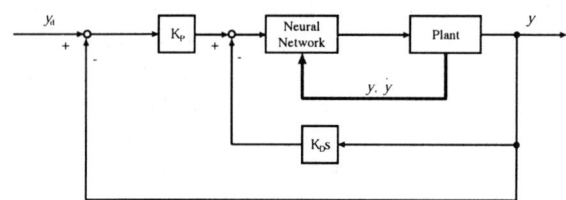

Figure 5: Controller for Linearization by a Neural Network

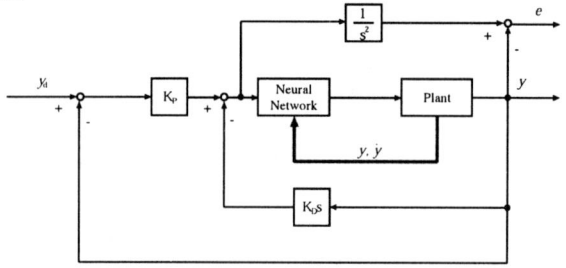

Figure 6: Block Diagram for Training a Neural Network

in Figure 6 is used in training the neural network. The performance index J described as (9)

$$J = \sum_{t=0}^{T} e^2(t) \qquad (9)$$

is used for training, where e is an inversion error. Training is equivalent to minimization of the performance index J. K_p and K_d are parameters that determine the response of the plant. After training is finished, the neural network can be used as the controller for linearizing the dynamics of the plant.

The transformed linear model(8) is selected according to tracking speed, bandwidth and so on. Moreover it is possible to select the same model as the reference model used in the online training controller, so that controllers trained by this method is used together with online training controllers so as to compensate with each other. Although the robustness isn't confirmed quantitatively, the robustness can be improved by using training methods for robust controllers together. Online training with a dead zone is often used as a robust adaptive rule because of the stability of the training, so that the performance index(10) can be useful in training controllers that are robust against wind.

$$J = \sum_{t=0}^{T} \phi(e(t))^2 \qquad (10)$$

$$\phi(x) = \begin{cases} x(|x| \geq E) \\ 0(|x| < E) \end{cases} \quad (E > 0) \qquad (11)$$

So far as possible, the online training controller doesn't work because of the controller trained by use of the performance index(10).

4 Flight Experiments

In this section, results of flight experiments using the flight control system designed by the proposed methods are shown. The proposed method can be applied to design various kinds of controllers, such as velocity controllers, positioning controllers and so on. Although we had already tested various controllers actually, only positioning control is demonstrated in this section because it is important in many activities at disasters. In flight experiments, 4 controllers, that is, elevator controller, aileron controller, yaw controller, and altitude controller, are used, and each controller is designed independently.

4.1 Positioning Control in a Horizontal Plane

Figure 7 shows the result of positioning control in a horizontal plane. The programmed path is a square of 10 meters. The helicopter is also controlled to keep the initial altitude and the initial direction. In Figure 7, xy axes direct forward and right respectively. Only controllers that were trained offline ware used in this experiment. The day of flight experiments was very windy, but the helicopter was controlled with enough accuracy but there was some steady-state error. The cause will be as follows. (1) The average of wind speed isn't 0 (2) Installation error angles of the main rotor (3) Error in trim Such steady-state error isn't desirable, but it is difficult to remove only by the state feedback controller that is trained offline.

4.2 Altitude Control

To check the performance in hovering, results of altitude control by 4 different controllers are compared with.
  [**A**] PD controller
  [**B**] Controller [**A**] + online training neural network
  [**C**] A neural network which is trained offline
  [**D**] Controller [**C**] + online training neural network
To determine the PD gain in [**A**] and [**B**], the optimal gain is searched using the flight simulator by try and errors. In the online training rule, sigma modification with dead zone is used. Figure 8 shows the results of each controller and it is proved that the performance of controller is much improved by adding online training controller. Moreover the neural network trained by the proposed method has good performance and robustness even without the online training controller. To confirm the effectiveness of the online training controller, the trim of collective was changed during the flight. This is the emulated experiment to check if the online training controller can reduce the influence of the gust, failures and so on. In Figure 9 and 10, responses to the change of trim are shown. Because Controller[**C**] is only a state feedback controller, the change of trim had a great influence on the altitude. But Figure 10 shows that the

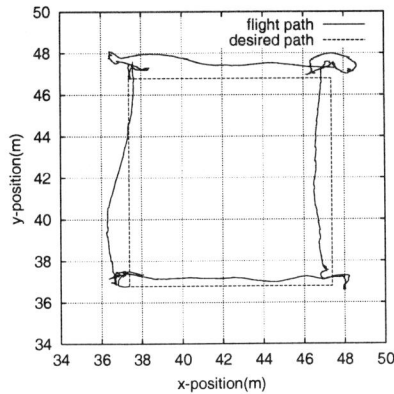

Figure 7: Flight Path in Horizontal Plane

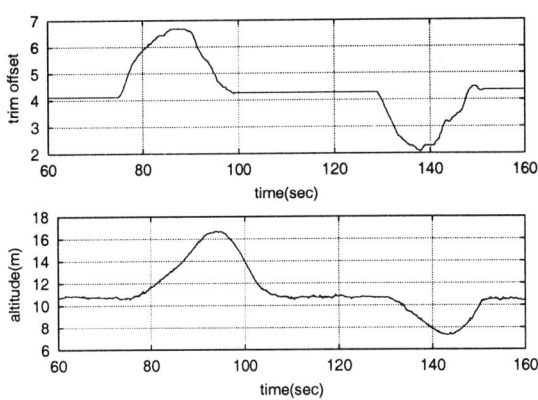

Figure 9: Response to Change of Trim(Controller[C])

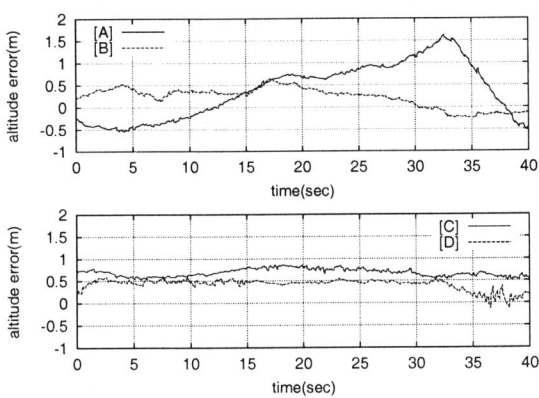

Figure 8: Results of Altitdude Controllers

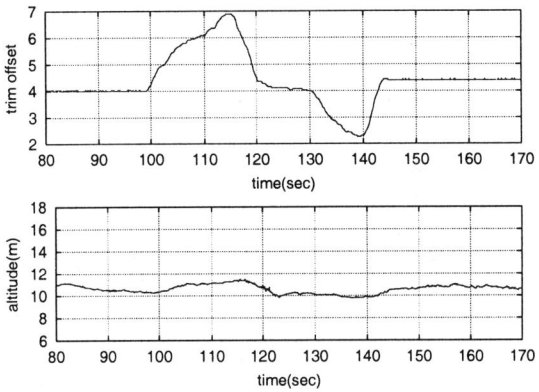

Figure 10: Response to Change of Trim(Controller[D])

online training controller can make the influence very small.

5 Conclutions

In this paper, a method to use online training controller and offline-trained controller together is proposed and the effectiveness is proved by flight experiments of autonomous unmanned helicopter. The proposed method not only can improve the reliability of the autonomous flight but also can be easily applied to general control systems design.

References

[1] Akira Sato: Research and Development and Civil Application of an Autonomous,Unmanned Helicopter; Proceedings of AHS International Forum 57, (2001)

[2] H. Nakanishi, T. Kohda and K. Inoue: A Design Method of Optimal Control System by Use of Neural Network: Proceedings of the 1997 International Conference on Neural Networks, *IEEE*, Vol. 2, pp. 871–875 (1997)

[3] M.J.D. Powell: An Efficient Method for Finding the Minimum of a Function of Several Variables Without Calculating Derivatives; Computer Journal, Vol. 7, pp. 155–162 (1964)

[4] H. Nakanishi and K. Inoue: Design Methods of Robust Feedback Controller by Use of Neural Networks; Proceedings of the International ICSC/IFAC Symposium on Neural Computation, pp. 731–736 (1998)

[5] H. Nakanishi and K. Inoue: Training Method of Robust Controllers against Stochastic Disturbance; Proceedings of the 2001 International Joint Conference on Neural Network, (2001)

[6] B.S. Kim and A.J. Calise: Nonlinear Flight Control Using Neural Networks: Journal of Guidance, Control and Dynamics, Vol. 20, No. 1, pp. 26–33

[7] M.W. Heiges, P.K. Menon and D.P. Schrage: Synthesis of a Helicopter Full Authority Controller: Proceedings of AIAA Guidance, Navigation and Control Conference, pp. 207–213

Constructive Neural Network in Model-Based Control of a Biotechnological Process

Luiz Augusto C. Meleiro
and Rubens Maciel Filho
School of Chemical Engineering
State University of Campinas - UNICAMP
Campinas, São Paulo, Brazil
Email: meleiro@lopca.feq.unicamp.br
maciel@feq.unicamp.br

Fernando J. Von Zuben
School of Electrical and Computer Engineering
State University of Campinas - UNICAMP
Campinas, São Paulo, Brazil
Email: vonzuben@dca.fee.unicamp.br
Telephone: +55 0 (19) 3788-3820
Fax: +55 0 (19) 3289-1395

Abstract—In the present work, a constructive learning algorithm is employed to design an optimal one-hidden layer neural network structure that best approximates a given mapping. The method determines not only the optimal number of hidden neurons but also the best activation function for each node. Here, the projection pursuit technique is applied in association with the optimization of the solvability condition, giving rise to a more efficient and accurate computational learning algorithm. As each activation function of a hidden neuron is optimally defined for every approximation problem, better rates of convergence are achieved. The proposed constructive learning algorithm was successfully applied to identify a large-scale multivariate process, providing a multivariable model that was able to describe the complex process dynamics, even in long-range horizon predictions. The resulting identification model is then considered as part of a model-based predictive control strategy, with high-quality performance in closed-loop experiments.

I. INTRODUCTION

Artificial Neural Networks (ANN) have been widely applied to the identification and control of nonlinear dynamic systems [20]. One of the main reasons for this success is the universal approximation capability of ANN, i.e., such models are able to approximate to arbitrary accuracy any continuous mapping defined on a compact (closed and bounded) domain [10], [15]. However, due to their generic structure, neural models usually require the estimation of a large number of parameters. Problems related to computational procedures necessary to achieve good results, including definition of the neural network dimension, choice of nonlinear activation functions, and the search for the optimum weight set, are still a drawback to a wider use of ANN [14], [9]. Another aspect to be considered is the generalization capability associated with supervised learning techniques when applied to universal approximators [8]. To get around these problems, Von Zuben & Netto [23] presented a Unit-Growing Learning (UGL) approach that corresponds to the Projection Pursuit Learning (PPL) in association with the optimization of the solvability condition. The improved PPL is a constructive learning algorithm [16] characterized by a more efficient and accurate computational procedure for nonparametric regression [24]. The solvability condition states that a neural network with one nonlinear hidden layer and one linear output layer is theoretically able to learn any input-output continuous mapping, given that the number of nodes of the hidden layer is capable of reproducing the dimensionality of the input space. In the present work, this constructive learning algorithm [24] is applied to model and control an important class of biotechnological process. The case study is a large-scale nonlinear Multi-Input/Multi-Output (MIMO) industrial plant to produce ethanol from sugar cane syrup [1]. The flexibility of the constructive learning approach should be properly explored to produce an effective tool for large-scale modeling. The resulting model must be able to describe the complex dynamics of the process, including long-range horizon predictions, which is one of the desired features for its use in model-based control strategies.

II. UNIT-GROWING LEARNING (UGL)

Although the problems related to a proper estimation of the weight set in conventional neural networks have been solved with relative success by using advanced first and second-order nonlinear optimization methods [3], the remaining two obstacles, i.e. definition of the neural network dimension and choice of the activation functions, are still solved heuristically in most applications, by exhaustive trial and error procedures. Bärmann & Biegler-König [2] presented a kind of unit-growing method that, along the learning process, enables additional neurons to be incorporated into the hidden layer by means of an iterative procedure, until the optimum network dimension (number of nodes) is achieved. However, this method uses monotonic functions determined arbitrarily, which does not guarantee the optimality of the set of activation functions. Hwang et al. [12] successfully applied parametric models using an orthonormal set of basis functions to solve the problem of searching for optimal activation functions. Von Zuben & Netto [23] discussed the solvability condition applied to constructive learning in neural networks, and developed an iterative procedure that conciliates nonlinear optimization, unit-growing learning and parametric activation function modeling, aiming at generating optimal neural network configurations for MIMO mappings.

A. The UGL Method

Consider the regression problem whose objective is to generate the best approximation of an unknown multidimensional model-free continuous function $G(\cdot)$ defined as

$$G(\cdot) : \Re^{1 \times m} \to \Re^{1 \times r} \qquad (1)$$

Starting from N pairs of input-output vectors derived from (1), and considering additive error such that

$$s_{(l)} = G(x_{(l)}) + \epsilon_{(l)} \quad (2)$$

we obtain, for $l = 1, \ldots, N$:

$$(x_{(l)}, s_{(l)}) = ([x_{l1}\ x_{l2}\ \cdots\ x_{lm}], [s_{l1}\ s_{l2}\ \cdots\ s_{lr}]) \quad (3)$$

The goal of the regression task is to construct an estimator, $\hat{G}(\cdot)$, that provides the best approximation of $G(\cdot)$ in such a way that it is able to predict $s_{(t)}$, given $x_{(t)}$ ($t \neq l$), as follows:

$$\hat{s}_{(t)} = \bar{s} + \hat{G}(x_{(t)}) \quad (4)$$

where $\bar{s} \in \Re^{1 \times r}$ is the sample average over all the desired output training data, given by

$$\bar{s} = [\bar{s}_1\ \bar{s}_2\ \cdots\ \bar{s}_r] = \frac{1}{N} \sum_{l=1}^{N} s_{(l)} \quad (5)$$

One-hidden layer neural networks can be used to estimate the matrix of output response, $S \in \Re^{N \times r}$, given the matrix of independent variables, $X \in \Re^{N \times m}$, as follows:

$$\hat{s}_{lk} = \bar{s}_k + \sum_{j=1}^{n} \left[w_{jk} f_j \left(\sum_{i=1}^{m} v_{ij} x_{li} \right) \right], \begin{array}{l} k = 1, \ldots, r \\ l = 1, \ldots, N \end{array} \quad (6)$$

where v_{ij} ($V \in \Re^{m \times n}$) denotes the hidden layer weight connecting the $i-th$ element of the input to the $j-th$ hidden node, w_{jk} ($W \in \Re^{n \times r}$) denotes the output layer weight connecting the $j-th$ hidden node to the $k-th$ output node, and $f_j : \Re \to \Re$ is the trainable activation function of the $j-th$ hidden node. Introducing an additional column of ones as the first column of X, we can denote by $v_j \in \Re^{(m+1)}$ the $i-th$ column of V, and $x_l \in \Re^{(m+1)}$ the column vector corresponding to the $l-th$ row of extended X, guiding to the following expression for the input signals to the output layer ($l = 1, \ldots, N$):

$$\begin{cases} \sigma_{l0} = 1 \\ \sigma_{lj} = f_j \left(\sum_{i=1}^{m} v_{ij} x_{il} + v_{0j} \right) = f_j(v_j^T x_l) \end{cases} \quad (7)$$

where the vectors v_j ($j = 1, \ldots, n$) represent directions of projection.

Using (6) and (7), the solvability condition [2] implies that the following system of linear equations

$$\Sigma \cdot W = S \quad (8)$$

where

$$\Sigma = \begin{bmatrix} \sigma_{10} & \sigma_{11} & \sigma_{12} & \cdots & \sigma_{1n} \\ \sigma_{20} & \sigma_{21} & \ddots & & \vdots \\ \vdots & \vdots & & & \vdots \\ \sigma_{N0} & \sigma_{N1} & \cdots & \cdots & \sigma_{Nn} \end{bmatrix},$$

$$W = \begin{bmatrix} w_{01} & w_{02} & \cdots & w_{0r} \\ w_{11} & \ddots & & \vdots \\ \vdots & & & \vdots \\ w_{n1} & \cdots & & w_{nr} \end{bmatrix} \text{ and }$$

$$S = \begin{bmatrix} s_{11} & s_{12} & \cdots & s_{1r} \\ s_{21} & \ddots & & \vdots \\ \vdots & & & \vdots \\ s_{N1} & \cdots & & s_{Nr} \end{bmatrix}.$$

has a solution.

Equivalently, this condition requires that every column vector of S, denoted s_k ($k = 1, \ldots, r$), lies in the linear subspace spanned by the column vectors of Σ, denoted σ_j ($j = 1, \ldots, n$). Notice that the weight matrix W does not contribute to solvability and that the ability to represent an arbitrary matrix S increases with the number n of column vectors of Σ (neurons in the hidden layer). A detailed discussion on the optimization of the solvability condition is found in [23]. The unit-growing learning is then presented as an alternative solution to this problem.

The great advantage of the constructive method proposed by Von Zuben & Netto [24], when compared to the Bärmann & Biegler-König's approach [2], is that the former uses hidden neurons with distinct activation functions. An iterative procedure that conciliates the optimization of the solvability condition and projection pursuit learning is carried out to determine an adequate activation function as well as the corresponding weight connections for each neuron, individually. This procedure generates single hidden layer networks with a reduced number of hidden neurons. While batch backpropagation methods apply optimization steps to estimate the weights of all layers simultaneously, the constructive learning method operates in a node-by-node fashion, starting with a single hidden layer neural network with only one hidden neuron and dynamically adding new hidden neurons until the approximation task is accurately accomplished. Denoting the $j-th$ row of W by $w_{(j)}$ ($j = 0, 1, \ldots, n$), (6) can be expressed as:

$$\hat{S} = \Sigma \cdot W = \sum_{j=0}^{n} \sigma_j w_{(j)} \quad (9)$$

with σ_0 a vector of ones and σ_j ($j = 1, \ldots, n$) being a column vector whose elements are defined in (7).

With $n = 0$, the linear least squares problem is solved

(where $\|\cdot\|$ is taken to be the L_2 norm):

$$\min_{\boldsymbol{w}_{(0)}} \|\boldsymbol{\sigma}_0 \boldsymbol{w}_{(0)} - \boldsymbol{S}\| \qquad (10)$$

For a given $n > 0$, let $\boldsymbol{D}_n$ be the matrix that contains the information not yet represented by a single hidden layer neural network with $n - 1$ neurons, i.e.

$$\boldsymbol{D}_n = \boldsymbol{S} - \sum_{j=0}^{n-1} \boldsymbol{\sigma}_j \boldsymbol{w}_{(j)} \qquad (11)$$

Then, the following optimization problem must be solved:

$$\min_{\boldsymbol{\sigma}_n, \boldsymbol{w}_{(n)}} \|\boldsymbol{\sigma}_n \boldsymbol{w}_{(n)} - \boldsymbol{D}_n\| \qquad (12)$$

which forces the solution $\boldsymbol{\sigma}_n^*$ to be optimally aligned with the columns of $\boldsymbol{D}_n$, regardless of $\boldsymbol{w}_{(n)}$. In the least-squares sense, the direction that gives the optimal alignment coincides with the principal component of the correlation matrix $\boldsymbol{D}_n \boldsymbol{D}_n^T$. Let $\boldsymbol{u}_n$ be this principal component, then $\boldsymbol{\sigma}_n$ is optimal for some $\boldsymbol{v}_n \in \Re^{(m+1)}$ and $f_n : \Re \to \Re$ maximizing the normalized scalar product

$$\boldsymbol{\sigma}_n^* = \arg\max_{\boldsymbol{\sigma}_n} \frac{(\boldsymbol{\sigma}_n^T \boldsymbol{u}_n)^2}{\boldsymbol{\sigma}_n^T \boldsymbol{\sigma}_n} \qquad (13)$$

The solution to this optimization problem is obtained by the following iterative process (see [24]): *i)* starting with a fixed $\boldsymbol{v}_n$, find an optimal f_n; *ii)* fixing f_n, determine an optimal $\boldsymbol{v}_n$, and *iii)* with this new $\boldsymbol{v}_n$ fixed, find a new optimal f_n, and so on. The iterative process should continue until convergence, which is guaranteed to exist [13].

Notice that, different from previous versions of projection pursuit learning [12], [21], this approach does not use any estimated value of $\boldsymbol{w}_{(n)}$ to obtain $\boldsymbol{\sigma}_n^*$.

The optimal value of $\boldsymbol{w}_{(n)}^*$ is obtained as follows. Given $\boldsymbol{\sigma}_n^*$ from (13), we set a value to $\boldsymbol{w}_{(n)}$ that solves the least mean squares problem in (12). This optimal value assumes the closed form:

$$\boldsymbol{w}_{(n)}^* = (\boldsymbol{\sigma}_n^{*T} \boldsymbol{\sigma}_n^*)^{-1} \boldsymbol{\sigma}_n^{*T} \boldsymbol{D}_n \qquad (14)$$

where $\boldsymbol{\sigma}_n^{*T} \boldsymbol{\sigma}_n^*$ is a scalar.

As a stop criterion, while $\|\boldsymbol{D}_{n+1}\| > \delta$, with δ a specified threshold, additional neurons are introduced in the hidden layer, freezing the parameters associated with existing hidden neurons.

Notice that the iterative process involving three groups of variables $[\boldsymbol{v}_n, f_n, \boldsymbol{w}_{(n)}]$, as done in [12] and [21], is now reduced to an iterative process in two groups of variables $[\boldsymbol{v}_n, f_n]$ followed by the calculation of the third group $[\boldsymbol{w}_{(n)}]$ in a closed and optimal form, with a guaranteed gain in computational performance and accuracy.

B. One-Dimensional Activation Function Modeling

In the multiple response regression problem, each response variable is estimated as a linear combination of the activations f_j $(j = 1, \ldots, n)$, as described in (6). For each j, an optimum smooth nonlinear activation function f_j is determined from linear combination of orthonormal functionals [12], freezing the weight vectors $\boldsymbol{v}_j \in \Re^{(m \times 1)}$.

For every j, given $\boldsymbol{u}_1^j \in \Re^{(N \times 1)}$ (the principal component of $\boldsymbol{D}_j \boldsymbol{D}_j^T$) and with fixed $\boldsymbol{v}_j \in \Re^{(m \times 1)}$, N input-output samples of the nonlinear mapping to be realized by the activation function f_j are obtained:

$$(z_l, y_l) = \left(\boldsymbol{x}_{(l)} \boldsymbol{v}_j, u_{1l}^j\right), l = 1, \ldots, N \qquad (15)$$

In order to define a smooth curve $\hat{f}_j$ that best approximates these N points, one-dimensional parametric models based on linear combinations of orthonormal functionals were used. Because of the easiness of calculation of the functional values and their derivatives, Hermite functions can be successfully applied [12]. A brief description of the Hermite polynomials used in this algorithm can be found in [23], [24], [18].

C. Determination of the Projections

In this subsection, the problem of finding an optimal direction of projection $\boldsymbol{v}_n^*$, that solves (13) for arbitrarily fixed f_n, is considered. As a first step, (13) is written in an equivalent form, using (7) and the fact that f_n is now a fixed function:

$$\boldsymbol{v}_n^* = \arg\max_{\boldsymbol{v}_n} \frac{(\boldsymbol{\sigma}_n^T \boldsymbol{u}_n)^2}{\boldsymbol{\sigma}_n^T \boldsymbol{\sigma}_n} \qquad (16)$$

The calculation of the functional values of Hermite polynomials and their derivatives can be done with low computational cost, making it easy to obtain first and second-order derivative information from the objective function in (16). The quality of the solution $\boldsymbol{v}_n^*$ usually depends on the initial value ascribed to $\boldsymbol{v}_n$.

D. The Backfitting Procedure

In order to determine the single hidden layer neural network dimension, every constructive learning strategy should be submitted to a backfitting procedure. In the single hidden layer neural network context, backfitting is the process that promotes the readjustment of the already introduced hidden neurons just after the introduction of a new one. Every newly introduced hidden neuron is guaranteed to be optimally defined for the actual neural network configuration. However, with the introduction of additional hidden neurons, what is optimal for the previous configuration will no more keep this condition for subsequent configurations. So, after the introduction of an additional hidden neuron, let's say the $n-th$ hidden neuron, all $j-th$ hidden neuron $(j = 1, \ldots, n)$ must be updated in sequence and cyclically, until convergence.

For all j $(j = 1, \ldots, n)$, the backfitting procedure will then sequentially solve the optimization problem

$$\min_{\boldsymbol{\sigma}_j, \boldsymbol{w}_{(j)}} \left\|\boldsymbol{\sigma}_j \boldsymbol{w}_{(j)} - \boldsymbol{D}_n^{[j]}\right\| \qquad (17)$$

with

$$\boldsymbol{D}_n^{[j]} = \boldsymbol{S} - \sum_{\substack{i=0 \\ i \neq j}}^{n} \boldsymbol{\sigma}_i \boldsymbol{w}_{(i)} \qquad (18)$$

The guarantee of convergence of the backfitting procedure comes also from the results in [13].

III. CASE STUDY

The case study considered in this work is an industrial plant for the production of ethanol. Technical features and economic importance of this process were discussed in [1].

The system is a typical large-scale industrial process composed of four tank reactors arranged in series and operated with microorganism recycling to produce ethanol from sugar cane syrup (Fig. 1). The process is fed with a mixture composed of sugars (Total Reducing Sugars - TRS) as well as sources of nitrogen and mineral salts, called feed medium. The feed medium is converted into ethanol by a fermentation process carried out using the yeast *Saccharomyces cerevisae*.

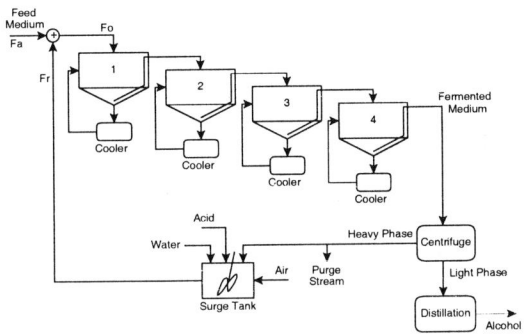

Fig. 1. Industrial plant for ethanol production.

IV. RESULTS

A. The Identification Procedure

Bioprocesses usually exhibit highly nonlinear dynamics, mainly due to the behavior of the microbiological kinetic. Considering these characteristics, the purpose of the study of this process is to generate identification models that can be used in advanced control strategies, in such a way as to maximize its efficiency.

Meleiro *et al.* [19] discussed the input, output, and disturbance variables of interest of this process and presented a detailed study on data generation, sampling frequency, and structure selection, i.e., the regression vectors.

In the present study, the same general structure was adopted; also the same data set was used in the learning and test steps. Considering these variables and the selected regressors, a MIMO model with seven inputs and three outputs, was identified.

The input variables considered are: feed flow rate, F_a, and recycle rate R. The main disturbance variable is the TRS concentration in the feed medium S_0. The output variables of interest are the substrate concentration S_4, ethanol concentration P_4, and microorganism concentration M_4 in the fourth tank.

A process simulator (validated with industrial data [1]) was used to generate a representative data set that contains the input and output signals related to 1500 hours (approximately 2 months) of the process operation. The proposed MIMO model was estimated with the constructive learning algorithm using data corresponding to 1000 hours.

The predictions of the three outputs provided by the model, generated from the learning process using the validation data (the remaining 500 hours), is shown in Figs. 2 to 4. These Figs. illustrate a good performance of the model for both one-step-ahead prediction (top), and recursive prediction or multi-step-ahead prediction (bottom), especially considering the long-range prediction horizons involved in the simulations.

Meleiro *et al.* [18] discussed the especial feature of a neural network architecture based on projection pursuit learning, i.e., the straightforward interpretability of the individual role of each neuron at the hidden layer.

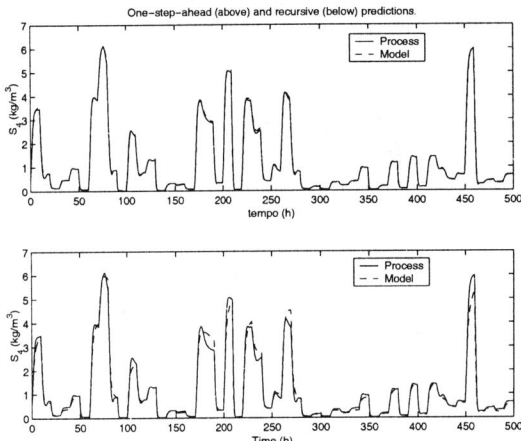

Fig. 2. Substrate concetration (S_4).

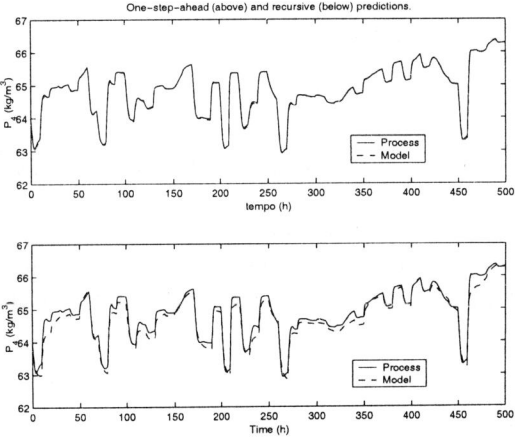

Fig. 3. Ethanol concetration (P_4).

B. Model Predictive Control of the Ethanol Production Process

Controllers of particular interest to chemical and biochemical processes, which usually exhibit slow dynamics and restrictive operational conditions, are the so-called Predictive Controllers (Model-Based Predictive Controllers - MPC) [5]. A controller of this type is considered in the sequel.

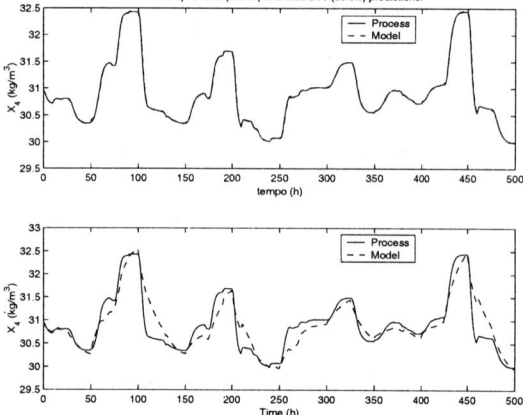

Fig. 4. Microorganisms concetration (M_4).

The aim of the controller is to select a set of future control actions in order to minimize the following objective function:

$$J = \sum_{i=N_1}^{N_y} (\hat{y}^c_{k+i} - w_{k+i})^2 + \lambda \sum_{i=1}^{N_u} (\Delta u_{k+i-1})^2 \quad (19)$$

where λ is the suppression factor, i.e., a tuning parameter that penalizes the control actions, Δu is the increment on the manipulated variable, N_1 is the initial horizon, N_y is the prediction horizon, N_u is the control horizon, w is the reference trajectory (or setpoint) and $\hat{y}^c$ is the corrected prediction of the UGL model, given by:

$$\hat{y}^c_{k+i} = \hat{y}_{k+i} + d_k, (i = 1, \ldots, N_y) \quad (20)$$

In equation (20), $\hat{y}_{k+i}$ is the model prediction of the controlled output of the process at the future sampling instant $k + i$ and d_k is a correction term, defined as:

$$d_k = y_k - \hat{y}_k \quad (21)$$

where y_k is the measured output at the present sampling instant and $\hat{y}_k$ is the respective model prediction (calculated at the previous sampling instant).

The optimization algorithm computes the increments Δu so as to minimize the objective function (19). The future control actions are then derived from the optimal control increments as:

$$u_{k+i} = u_{k+i-1} + \Delta u_{k+i}, (i = 0, \ldots, N_u - 1) \quad (22)$$

It is important to remark that only the first N_u control actions are optimized whereas the remaining ones are kept constant, i.e.:

$$u_{k+i} = u_{k+N_u-1}, (i = N_u, \ldots, N_y - 1) \quad (23)$$

The optimization problem is also subject to the following constraints:

$$y_{min} \leq \hat{y}_{k+i} \leq y_{max}, (i = 1, \ldots, N_y) \quad (24)$$

$$u_{min} \leq u_{k+i-1} \leq u_{max}, (i = 1, \ldots, N_u) \quad (25)$$

$$| u_{k+i-1} - u_{k+i-2} | \leq \Delta u_{max}, (i = 1, \ldots, N_u) \quad (26)$$

where y_{min} and y_{max}, u_{min} and u_{max}, and Δu_{min} and Δu_{max} are lower and upper bounds for y, u and Δu, respectively.

Finally, the *Receding Horizon* strategy is adopted [22], [4]. In this strategy, only the first control action u_k is implemented, and the optimization problem is solved again at the next sampling instant. Owing to the characteristics of the nonlinear equations which govern the model predictions, the (constrained) optimization problem is nonconvex and, accordingly, an appropriate methodology should be used to solve it. In this paper, the Successive Quadratic Programming (SQP) method is considered [6].

The UGL model derived for this process is used as the internal nonlinear model for the predictive controller. The operational constraints on the manipulated and controlled variables of the process are the following:

$$S_4(k+i) \geq 0, (i = 1, \ldots, N_y) \quad (27)$$

$$P_4(k+i) \geq 0, (i = 1, \ldots, N_y) \quad (28)$$

$$50 \leq F_a(k+i) \leq 150, (i = 0, \ldots, N_u - 1) \quad (29)$$

$$| F_a(k+i) - F_a(k+i-1) | \leq 50, (i = 0, \ldots, N_u - 1) \quad (30)$$

The controller is tuned as $N_1 = 1$, $N_y = 10$, $N_u = 2$ and $\lambda = 0.001$. In what follows, its closed-loop performance is evaluated for servo problems.

Figs. 5 and 6 present the closed-loop simulation and show that the proposed scheme is able to control the process output variables.

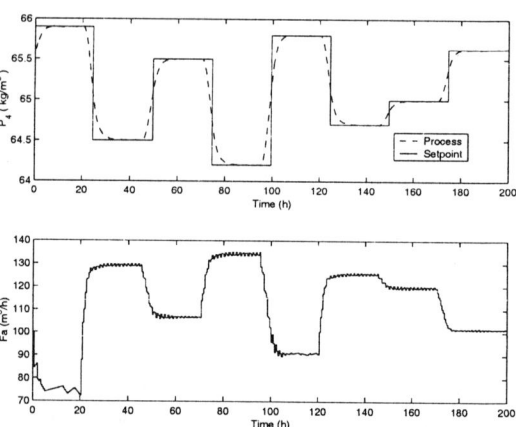

Fig. 5. Servo control for ethanol concentration, P_4. Reference and closed-loop process output (above) and manipulated variable (below).

C. Remarks on Results

The parsimony of the resulting neural network architecture is also significant, because the behavior presented in Figs. 2, 3, and 4 was produced by a neural network with just 4 neurons in the hidden layer. To obtain similar performance using a multilayer perceptron (MLP), it was necessary to use 10 neurons in the hidden layer [17].

Meleiro and co-authors [18], [17] have already reported the superior performance of the UGL algorithm, when compared

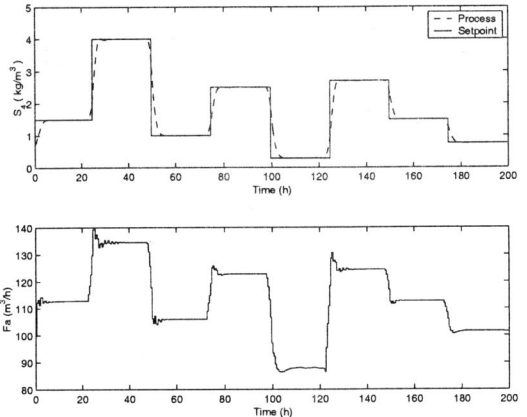

Fig. 6. Servo control for substrate concentration, S_4. Reference and closed-loop process output (above) and manipulated variable (below).

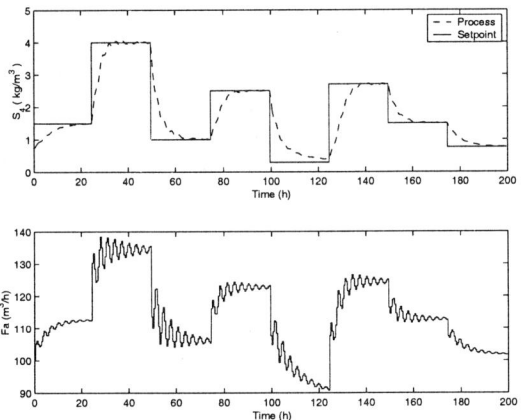

Fig. 7. Performance of Dynamic Matrix Control (DMC) for S_4.

with neural (MLP) and hierarchical fuzzy models, in the generation of the identification model.

With a higher-quality model-based prediction, the performance of the closed-loop control is fully consistent with what is expected from an implementation that takes into account the nonlinearity of the plant to obtain long-term horizon predictions.

The effect of the quality of the model predictions on the closed-loop performance of the controller, may be illustred by comparing Figs. 6 (MPC, based on UGL model), and 7 (DMC, based on linear convolution model).

V. CONCLUSION

The constructive learning algorithm using single hidden layer neural network has proven to be very efficient in generating a MIMO nonlinear identification model of the studied process. The unit-growing learning approach, based on projection pursuit learning associated with the solvability condition, presents the flexibility to search for the best activation function of each hidden neuron.

A nonlinear predictive controller using the UGL model as its internal model of the process has also been developed. This controller comprises constraints on manipulated and controlled variables and uses the Successive Quadratic Programming (SQP) algorithm to solve the optimal control problem at each sampling interval. The proposed control scheme has successfully been applied to control the substrate and ethanol concentrations in the outlet stream of the process, thus allowing an effective and economically feasible operation of the industrial plant.

REFERENCES

[1] S. R. Andrietta and F. Maugeri. "Optimum design of a continuous fermentation unit of an industrial plant for alcohol production". In *Advances in Bioprocess Engineering*. Kluwer Academic Publishers, 1994.

[2] F. Bärmann and F. Biegler-König. "On a Class of Efficient Learning Algorithms for Neural Networks". *Neural Networks*, 5(1): 139-144, 1992.

[3] R. Battiti. "First- and Second-Order Methods for Learning: Between Steepest Descent and Newton's Method". *Neural Computation*, 4(2): 141-166, 1992.

[4] E. F. Camacho and C. Bordons. *Model Predictive Control*, Springer-Verlag", 1999.

[5] D. W. Clarke. *Advances in Model Based Predictive Control*, Oxford University Press, 1994.

[6] T. F. Edgar and D. M. Himmelblau. *Optimization of Chemical Processes*, McGraw-Hill, 1988.

[7] J. H. Friedman and W. Stuetzle. "Projection Pursuit Regression", *Journal of the American Statistical Association (JASA)*, 76: 817-823, 1981.

[8] S. Geman, E. Bienenstock, and R. Doursat. "Neural Networks and the Bias/Variance Dilemma". *Neural Computation*, 4(1): 1-58, 1992.

[9] S. Haykin. *Neural Networks: A Comprehensive Foundation - 2nd Edition*. Prentice Hall, 1999.

[10] K. Hornik. "Multilayer feedforward networks are universal approximators". *Neural Networks*, 2(5): 359-366, 1989.

[11] P. J. Huber. "Projection Pursuit", *The Annals of Statistics*, 13(2): 435-475, 1985.

[12] J.-N. Hwang, S.-R. Lay, M. Maechler, R.D. Martin and J. Schimert. "Regression Modeling in Back-Propagation and Projection Pursuit Learning", *IEEE Transactions on Neural Networks*, 5(3): 342-353, 1994.

[13] L. K. Jones. "On a conjecture of Huber concerning the convergence of projection pursuit regression", *The Annals of Statistics*, 15: 880-882, 1987.

[14] B. Kosko. *Fuzzy Engineering*. Prentice Hall, 1997.

[15] B. Kosko. *Neural Networks and Fuzzy Systems: A Dynamical Systems Approach to Machine Intelligence*. Prentice Hall, 1992.

[16] T. Y. Kwok and D. Y. Yeung. "Constructive Algorithms for Structure Learning in Feedforward Neural Networks for Regression Problems", *IEEE Trans. on Neural Networks*, 8(3): 630-645, 1997.

[17] L. A. C. Meleiro. *Design and Applications of Linear, Neural, and Fuzzy Model-Based Controllers*, PhD Thesis (in Portuguese). 2002.

[18] L. A. C. Meleiro, R. J. G. B. Campello, R. Maciel Filho and F. J. Von Zuben. "Identification of a Multivariate Fermentation Process Using Constructive Learning". *Proc. SBRN'2002 - VII Brazilian Symposium on Neural Networks*, IEEE Computer Society. 2002.

[19] L. A. C. Meleiro, R. Maciel Filho, R. J. G. B. Campello and W. C. Amaral. "Hierarchical Neural Fuzzy Models as a Tool for Process Identification: A Bioprocess Application". In *Application of Neural Networks and Other Learning Technologies in Process Engineering*. Mujtaba, I. M. and Hussain, M. A. (Editors). Imperial College Press, 2001.

[20] G. W. Ng. *Application of Neural Networks to Adaptive Control of Nonlinear Systems*. Research Studies Press Ltd., John Wiley & Sons Inc., 1997.

[21] C. B. Roosen and T. J. Hastie. "Automatic Smoothing Spline Projection Pursuit". *Journal of Computational and Graphical Statistics*, 3: 235-248, 1994.

[22] R. Soeterboek. *Predictive Control - A Unified Approach*, Prentice Hall, 1992.

[23] F. J. Von Zuben and M. L. A. Netto. "Unit-growing learning optimizing the solvability condition for model-free regression". *Proceedings of the IEEE International Conference on Neural Networks*, 2:795-800,1995.

[24] F. J. Von Zuben and M. L. A. Netto. "Projection Pursuit and the Solvability Condition Applied to Constructive Learning". *Proceedings of the International Joint Conference on Neural Networks*, Houston - USA, 2: 1062-1067,1997.

Lyapunov Stability Analysis of the Quantization Error for DCS Neural Networks

Sampath Yerramalla, Bojan Cukic
Lane Department of Computer Science and Electrical Engineering
West Virginia University
Morgantown WV 26506
emails: syerrama@mix.wvu.edu, cukic@csee.wvu.edu

Edgar Fuller
Department of Mathematics
West Virginia University
Morgantown WV 26506
email: ef@math.wvu.edu

Abstract— In this paper we show that the quantization error for Dynamic Cell Structures (DCS) Neural Networks (NN) as defined by Bruske and Sommer provides a measure of the Lyapunov stability of the weight centers of the neural net. We also show, however, that this error is insufficient in itself to verify that DCS neural networks provide stable topological representation of a given fixed input feature manifold. While it is true that DCS generates a topology preserving feature map, it is unclear when and under what circumstances DCS will have achieved an accurate representation. This is especially important in safety critical systems where it is necessary to understand when the topological representation is complete and accurate. The stability analysis here shows that there exists a Lyapunov function for the weight adaptation of the DCS NN system applied to a fixed feature manifold. The Lyapunov function works in parallel during DCS learning, and is able to provide a measure of the effective placement of neural units during the NN's approximation. It does not, however, guarantee the formation of an accurate representation of the feature manifold. Simulation studies from a selected CMU-Benchmark involving the use of the constructed Lyapunov function indicate the existence of a *Globally Asymptotically Stable* (GAS) state for the placement of neural units, but an example is given where the topology of the constructed network fails to mirror that of the input manifold even though the quantization error continues to decrease monotonically.

I. INTRODUCTION

The learning process in most common Neural Networks (NN) evolves sequentially over time. This process of learning also being combinatorial and nonlinear in nature, it is a challenging task to evaluate the dynamic properties that govern the performance of a neural net over time. This kind of evaluation is needed, especially for safety critical system like, *The Neural Adaptive Flight Control System* [19]. Stability being considered as an important dynamic property, the question then is:

Is there an effective tool that can analyze the stability aspects of the dynamic learning process of the NN?

Even after decades of extensive research on neural networks and their widespread applications, the answer to this question still remains uncertain and contradictory. The objective of mathematical theory of non-linear stability analysis is often misunderstood as the process of finding a solution for the differential equation(s) that govern the dynamics, either analytically or numerically (simulation studies). Theoretically, there is no guarantee for the existence of a solution to a non-linear differential equation at all times, let alone the complicated task of solving them. In practice however, there exists a variety of techniques and tools that analyze the existence of stable states in non-linear systems, without actually the need for solving any differential equation [1], [4], [5], [6]. Almost all stability definitions for linear systems lead to a similar stability criterion (R-locus, eigenvalues, etc). Therefore defining a precise stability definition for linear systems can be relaxed. However, eigenvalue methods are not applicable to non-linear systems and so one needs to be careful while dealing with systems that have non-linear properties. It's often seen that if such systems are stable under one definition of stability they may tend to become unstable under other definitions [5]. This difficulty in imposing strong stability restrictions for non-linear systems was realized as early as a century ago by a Russian mathematician A.M.Lyapunov. Details on Lyapunov's stability analysis technique for non-linear discrete systems can be found in [1], [2], [6], [4]. The fact that *Lyapunov's Direct Method* or *Non-linear Theory of Stability Analysis* can be readily applied to validate the existence (or non-existence) of stable states in non-linear systems, intrigued us in using Lyapunov function in this stability analysis as a means to answer the question posed earlier. Dynamic Cell Structures (DCS) NN represents a family of Topology Representing Networks (TRN), used for both supervised and un-supervised learning. Some applications of DCS include vector quantization, clustering, dimensional reduction [17], [16]. In this paper we analyze the stability properties of neural unit positioning by DCS NN using Lyapunov theory and we present a qualified answer to the question

Is the learning process of DCS NN, stable?

Throughout this stability analysis we consider DCS NN as a sequentially evolving discrete logic system, closely related to the family of Logical Discrete Event Systems [2]. We also assume that the feature manifold being mapped by DCS, is fixed or stationary, meaning the manifold doesn't evolve over time.

The paper is organized in the following way. Section II provides an overview of the DCS algorithm as well as a description of the competitive Hebb rule and Kohonen-like rule that govern the learning process of the DCS NN. This description of the DCS algorithm is later used in Section III to present a state-space representation of the dynamics of the network. In Section IV, the construction of the Lyapunov function is described and we give a proof of the existence of a Globally Asymptotically Stable (GAS) learning state for the DCS NN. Simulation results are presented in Section V using a selected CMU benchmark of artificially generated data. Finally, some implications of the results are stated in Section VI based on the presented proof and simulation results. Foremost of these is the fact that while the error measure continues to decrease monotonically, the dynamical system describing the learning process of DCS neural net may pass through a local minima and maxima which represents a *fault* in the topological representation of the network.

II. DCS Neural Network

In 1994 Jorg Bruske and Gerald Sommer of the University of Kiel, Germany, introduced the concept of DCS as a family of topology representing self-organizing NN [16], [17]. This Topology Preserving Feature Map (TPFM) generation scheme was motivated by Growing Neural GAS algorithm developed by Fritzke and the former work on TRN by Martinetz [13].

DCS uses Kohonen-like adaptation to shift the weighted centers of the local neighborhood structure, closer to the feature manifold. This when applied in conjunction with Competitive Hebb Rule (CHR) to update lateral connections of the neighbors, produces a network representation that preserves the features of the input manifold. We believe that these two essential building blocks (rules) of DCS algorithm, play a key role in the generation of a TPFM. Before we proceed for an in-depth analysis of the DCS algorithm we need to study and formulate these competitive rules that govern the DCS dynamical system.

A. Competitive Hebb Rule (CHR)

DCS NN rests upon a Radial Basis Function (RBF) and an additional layer of lateral connections between the neural units [16]. These lateral connection strengths are symmetric and bounded in nature, $c_{ij} = c_{ji} \in [0, 1]$. The goal of CHR is to update the lateral connections by mapping neighborhoods in the input manifold to neighborhoods of the network. Thereby, avoiding any restrictions of the topology of the network [17]. For each input element of the feature manifold, CHR operates by setting the connection strength between the two neural units that are closer to the input than any other neuron pair, to a highest possible connection strength of 1. These two neural units are referred to as the Best Matching Unit (*bmu*) and Second Best Unit (*sbu*). CHR then proceeds to decay the strength of all other existing lateral connections emanating from the *bmu* using a forgetting constant, α. If any of these existing connections drop below a predefined threshold θ, they are set to zero. The set of all neural units that are connected to the *bmu* is defined as the neighborhood of the *bmu*, and represented by *nbr*. All other connections of the network remain unaltered. In this way CHR induces a Delaunay triangulation into the network by preserving the neighborhood structure of the feature manifold.

$$c_{ij}(t+1) = \begin{cases} 1 & (i = bmu) \wedge (j = sbu) \\ 0 & (i = bmu) \wedge (j \in nbr - sbu) \\ & \wedge (c_{ij} < \theta) \\ \alpha c_{ij}(t) & (i = bmu) \wedge (j \in nbr - sbu) \\ & \wedge (c_{ij} \geq \theta) \\ c_{ij}(t) & i, j \neq bmu \end{cases} \quad (1)$$

It was shown in [13] that algorithms utilizing CHR to update lateral connections between neural units generate a TPFM.

B. Kohonen-Like Rule (KLR)

Unlike feed-forward NN, the weight center $\vec{w}_i$ associated with a neural unit i of the DCS network represents the location of the neural unit in the output space. It is crucial to realize that these weighted centers be updated in a manner that preserves the geometry of the input manifold. This can be achieved by adjusting the weighted center of the *bmu* and its surrounding neighborhood structure *nbr* closer to the input element. For each element of the feature manifold, $\vec{m} \in M$, DCS adapts the corresponding *bmu* and its neighborhood set *nbr* in a Kohonen-like manner [12]. Over any training cycle, let $\Delta w_i = w_i(t+1) - w_i(t)$ represent the adjustment of the weight center of the neural unit, then the Kohonen-like rule followed in DCS can be represented as follows

$$\Delta w_i = \begin{cases} \varepsilon_{bmu}(\vec{m} - \vec{w_i}(t)) & i = bmu \\ \varepsilon_{nbr}(\vec{m} - \vec{w_i}(t)) & i \in nbr \\ 0 & (i \neq bmu) \wedge (i \neq nbr) \end{cases} \quad (2)$$

where $\varepsilon_{bmu}, \varepsilon_{nbr} \in (0, 1)$ are predefined constants known as the learning rates that define the momentum of the update process. For every input element, applying CHR before any other adjustment ensures that *sbu* is a member of *nbr* set for all further adjustments within the inner loop of the DCS algorithm.

C. Growing the Network

Like any other Self-Organizing Map (SOM), DCS has the ability to grow or shrink the map by increasing or decreasing the number of neurons of the network. A local error measure associated with the network, namely *Resource*, is used to determine if the network experienced a large enough cumulative error, meaning there is a requirement for an additional neuron in the network. In most cases Euclidean distance between the best matching unit (*bmu*) and the training input stimulus serves as a measure of the resource. After a cycle of adaptation (epoch), if needed an additional neuron is introduced into the network at the region between the highest and second highest resource neurons of the network.

D. DCS algorithm

Knowing the operational aspects of the individual building blocks, we now analyze the DCS training algorithm. As shown in Figure 1, the DCS algorithm is allowed to train on the input stimulus until the network has reached a specific stopping criteria. For each training input stimulus, the network is

```
while  stopping criteria is not satisfied
{
       for each training input stimulus
       {
              find bmu, sbu
              update connections using CHR
              adapt weights using KLR
              update resource error
       }
       compute cumulative network resource error
       if (cumulative network resource error) > (Predefined Error)
       {
              grow the network
              decrement all resource values
       }
}
```

Fig. 1. DCS Algorithm

searched for the two closest neurons, best matching unit (*bmu*) and second best unit (*sbu*). The lateral connection structure surrounding the *bmu* is updated using Hebb rule. Kohonen adaptation of the weights of the *bmu* and its neighbors (*nbr*) is performed.

The resource value of the *bmu* is updated correspondingly, marking the end of a training cycle (epoch). The cumulative resource error of the network is computed to determine the need for inserting an additional neuron into the network. Decreasing the resource values of all the neurons by a decay constant prevents the resource values from growing out of bounds.

III. STATE-SPACE ANALYSIS

The first step of any stability analysis lies in identification of the states involved with the dynamical system. State-Space representation is the most preferred method of representing the identified states of the dynamic system. This representation technique is very effective during the construction of a Lyapunov function for non-linear systems [6].

A. States of DCS Logic

The following equations give the representation of the states of DCS logic during CHR and KHR adjustment as discrete differences over a time step Δt.

1) Center State:
$$\frac{\Delta \vec{x_W}}{\Delta t} = f_W(\vec{x_W}, bmu, nbr, \varepsilon_{bmu}, \varepsilon_{nbr}) \quad (3)$$

2) Connection State:
$$\frac{\Delta \vec{x_C}}{\Delta t} = f_C(\vec{x_C}, bmu, nbr, \alpha, \theta) \quad (4)$$

Where $\vec{x_W}$ and $\vec{x_C}$ are the states of DCS learning that represents the spatial distribution of neural units and the lateral connection structure between the neural units respectively. $f_W, f_C : \mathbb{R}^I \to \mathbb{R}^O$ are continuous functions that provide the required adjustment to $\vec{x_W}$ and $\vec{x_C}$ respectively. $\mathbb{R}^I$ and $\mathbb{R}^O$ represent the input and output spaces of the DCS neural network.

B. DCS Output/Recall

When DCS NN is presented with a *test* input, $\vec{m^\star} \in \mathbb{R}^I$, the network is searched for the appropriate *bmu* and the closest of all neural units that is connected to the *bmu*. Note that the closest of all neural units connected to the *bmu* need not always be the *sbu*. We then apply linear interpolation technique between these two neural units to generate the estimated output vector $\hat{\vec{y}} \in \mathbb{R}^O$. The estimated output, $\hat{\vec{y}}$, is a function of the states $\vec{x_C}$, $\vec{x_W}$ of the DCS network as well as the location of the *bmu* and the topology of its neighborhood structure. This can be represented as $\hat{\vec{y}} = f(\vec{x_C}, \vec{x_W}, bmu, nbr, \vec{m^\star})$. If *bmu* is not connected to any other neural unit of the network then the estimated output is based solely on the *bmu*'s location. The output produced by the network with no neurons is zero.

C. DCS State Space Representation

We consider DCS neural net's approximation from any fixed input manifold $M \subset \mathbb{R}^I$. In this neural net, a set of neural units i for $i = 1 \ldots N$ with weighted centers $\vec{w_i} \in \vec{x_W} \subset \mathbb{R}^O$ and lateral connections $c_{ij} \in \vec{x_C} \subset \mathbb{R}^O$ represent the Nth order map generated by DCS, $A_{(N)} \subset \mathbb{R}^O$. It was proved by Martinetz and Schulten in [13] that this is a topology preserving operation in the sense that neighborhoods of $M \subset \mathbb{R}^I$ are preserved in $A \subset \mathbb{R}^O$.

Let $G_N(W, C)$ be the collection of N neural units of DCS having $W \in \vec{x_W}$ as their weighted center matrix and $C \in \vec{x_C}$ as their connection strength matrix, that represent the DCS map from a given input manifold $M \subset \mathbb{R}^I$ onto the output space $A \subset \mathbb{R}^O$. Then, $G_N(W, C)$ can be considered as an undirected graph of N multi-valent vertices.

Definition 1 (*DCS Mapping*): DCS Mapping, $G_N(W, C)$ is the Nth order neural unit representation of any given input manifold in the input space $M \subset \mathbb{R}^I$ onto the output space $A_{(N)} \subset \mathbb{R}^O$, gotten by assigning N neural in t_n steps of the DCS algorithm.

Considering DCS as a discrete time dynamical system, the following state-space representation can be formulated as follows:

$$\frac{\Delta \vec{x_W}}{\Delta t} = f_W(\vec{x_W}, bmu, nbr, \varepsilon_{bmu}, \varepsilon_{nbr})$$
$$\frac{\Delta \vec{x_C}}{\Delta t} = f_C(\vec{x_C}, bmu, nbr, \alpha, \theta)$$
$$y = G(W, C) \quad (5)$$

IV. LYAPUNOV'S STABILITY THEORY

We want to determine if the DCS algorithm will *reliably* learn a given fixed input manifold M on successive applications. Similar to the work done on backpropagation neural nets by Kaynak, et. al. [3], the question is then:

How much can the evolving DCS approximation of M, denoted by y_{t+1}, deviate from a previously learned version of M, denoted by y_t?

Since the DCS approximation process is a time-varying construction whose state changes according to the difference relations in (5), it is natural to use the Lyapunov formulation of stability for a dynamical system to answer this question. The relevant result of Lyapunov stability from [6] is the following

Theorem 1 (*Lyapunov Stability*): Given a system of differential equations

$$\frac{d\vec{X}}{dt} = f(x_1, \ldots, x_n, t) \tag{6}$$

if it is possible to find a *positive-definite* function V of $\vec{X}$ for which $V(0) = 0$ and $\frac{dV}{dt} \leq 0$ then the trivial solution of (6) is Lyapunov stable or locally stable.

The Lyapunov condition in the discrete case can be formulated as follows:

Theorem 2 (*Discrete Lyapunov Stability*): A solution of a discrete system of difference equations

$$\frac{\Delta \vec{S}}{\Delta t} = f(s_1, \ldots, s_n, t) \tag{7}$$

is stable in the sense of Lyapunov if there is a *positive-definite* function V for which $V(0) = 0$ and $\frac{\Delta V}{\Delta t} \leq 0$ for some time step $\Delta t > 0$ in some neighborhood of the solution in the state space of the system. If, in addition, $\frac{\Delta V}{\Delta t}$ happens to be *negative-definite*, $\frac{\Delta V}{\Delta t} < 0$, in this neighborhood, then the solution is said to be asymptotically stable there. Finally, if the region on which $V \to 0$ as $t \to \infty$ is the entire state space then the solution is Globally Asymptotically Stable (GAS).

A. Lyapunov Function for Neuron Placement

To set up a Lyapunov function for DCS, we measure how accurately a current state of the algorithm models any given fixed feature manifold in terms of the amount of geometry preserved in the output manifold. To measure the accuracy of the DCS approximation, Bruske and Sommer introduce the *Quantization Error* as defined in [17]. This measures the effectiveness of the placement of neural units by computing the Euclidean distance between each input element $\vec{m} \in M$ and its closest of all neural units (*bmu*). This is then averaged over the total number of neurons, N, during that state of DCS approximation. Throughout this paper, Q serves as a Lyapunov function V for the DCS neural net.

$$V(t) = Q(t) = \frac{1}{N} \sum_{\vec{m} \in M} \|\vec{m} - \vec{w}_{bmu(\vec{m},t)}\| \tag{8}$$

B. Neural Unit Placement by DCS is Lyapunov stable

With the above setup, it follows that

Theorem 3: The placement of the neural units, $\vec{w}_i$, assigned by the DCS approximation during learning of a fixed input manifold $M \subset \mathbb{R}^I$, is globally asymptotically stable in the sense of Lyapunov.

Proof: First of all we need to show that the Lyapunov function (8), constructed for the time-varying discrete system of DCS is valid. It is clear that $V(t) \geq 0$ since $\|\vec{m} - \vec{w}_{bmu(\vec{m},t)}\| \geq 0$. Also $V(0) = 0$, since there are no neurons in the DCS network during zero state $\vec{x}_C = \vec{x}_W = 0$. To show that $\frac{\Delta V}{\Delta t} < 0$, first note that since for an unit time step $\Delta t = (t+1) - (t) = 1 > 0$, the numerator ΔV will determine the sign in question. Computing using (8) we see that over any unit time interval $\Delta t = 1$, adjustments of the weighted centers $\vec{w}_i$ are determined by the Kohonen rule. Over any learning cycle, DCS adjusts the *bmu* and its neighbors for every $\vec{m} \in M$ according to the rule in (2). Let $\|\vec{m} - \vec{w}_{bmu(\vec{m},t)}\|$ be represented by $d(t)$, then we see that over a single training cycle

$$\begin{aligned}
\Delta V &= \frac{1}{N+1} \sum_{\vec{m} \in M} d(t+1) - \frac{1}{N} \sum_{\vec{m} \in M} d(t) \\
&= \frac{N \sum_{\vec{m} \in M} d(t+1) - (N+1) \sum_{\vec{m} \in M} d(t)}{N(N+1)} \\
&= \frac{N \sum_{\vec{m} \in M} [d(t+1) - d(t)] - \sum_{\vec{m} \in M} d(t)}{N(N+1)}
\end{aligned} \tag{9}$$

For any $\vec{m} \in M$, we need to show that either the corresponding portion of the numerator of (9) is negative or that some other portion compensates when it is positive. A neural unit after being updated as the best matching unit of $\vec{m} \in M$ at time t, $bmu(\vec{m}, t)$ can get updated again in three possible ways. It may get updated as

1) again as the best matching unit for $\vec{m} \in M$, $bmu(\vec{m}, t) = bmu(\vec{m}, t+1)$.
2) as the *bmu* of some other $\vec{m}' \in M$, $bmu(\vec{m}', t) = bmu(\vec{m}, t+1)$ or $bmu(\vec{m}, t) = bmu(\vec{m}', t+1)$
3) or as a neighbor of the best matching unit, $bmu(\vec{m}, t) = nbr(bmu(\vec{m}, t+1))$.

In the first case, to show that (9) < 0 it is sufficient to show that

$$d(t+1) - d(t) < 0 \tag{10}$$

Computing using (2) gives

$$\begin{aligned}
d(t+1) &= \|\vec{m} - \vec{w}_{bmu(\vec{m},t+1)}\| \\
&= \|\vec{m} - (\vec{w}_{bmu(\vec{m},t)} + \varepsilon_{bmu}(\vec{m} - \vec{w}_{bmu(\vec{m},t)}))\| \\
&= \|(\vec{m} - \vec{w}_{bmu(\vec{m},t)}) - \varepsilon_{bmu}(\vec{m} - \vec{w}_{bmu(t)})\| \\
&= \|\vec{m} - \vec{w}_{bmu(\vec{m},t)} - \varepsilon_{bmu}\vec{m} + \varepsilon_{bmu}\vec{w}_{bmu(\vec{m},t)}\| \\
&= (1 - \varepsilon_{bmu})\|\vec{m} - \vec{w}_{bmu(\vec{m},t)}\| \\
&= (1 - \varepsilon_{bmu})d(t)
\end{aligned}$$

Since $\varepsilon_{bmu} \in [0, 1]$,

$$d(t+1) < d(t)$$

which implies (10).

In the second case, the best matching unit for $\vec{m} \in M$, $bmu(\vec{m})$, may get updated as the best matching unit for some other $\vec{m}' \in M$, $bmu(\vec{m}')$. The update as $bmu(\vec{m}')$ can either precede or follow the update as $bmu(\vec{m})$ and the effect on V depends primarily on which input stimulus is closest to $bmu(\vec{m}) = bmu(\vec{m}')$. When m is farthest from $bmu(\vec{m})$, the triangle inequality for the euclidean metric implies that $d(t) > d(t+1)$ regardless of the order of update. On the other hand, if m' is farther from $bmu(\vec{m})$, $d(t)$ may be smaller than $d(t+1)$ but any increase in the distance from m to its *bmu* is smaller than the decrease in the distance from m' to the same neuron since m is closer to $bmu(\vec{m})$. Again, this follows from the triangle inequality for the euclidean metric. The net effect in all cases is a decrease in V.

The third and final case will have $\Delta V < 0$ since $\varepsilon_{bmu} \gg \varepsilon_{nbr}$ in general. Specifically, movement away from $\vec{m}$ caused by nbr adjustments will be an order of magnitude smaller in size than the movement towards $\vec{m}$. In case the two values ε_{bmu} and ε_{nbr} are comparable, the result follows instead from the same argument as in the second case above. As a result, the function V is a valid Lyapunov function for the weight state of DCS and furthermore since $\Delta V < 0$ and $V \to 0$ as $t \to \infty$ regardless of the initial placement of neurons, the stability is global and asymptotic. The strict decrease of V is due to the effect of the Kohonen rule as in case one. ∎

This result reflects the fact that DCS is geometry preserving since it is based on a Kohonen-like rule and the monotonic decrease in the Lyapunov function (quantization error) verifies this geometry preserving ability of DCS. Unfortunately, the quantization error does not completely correlate with the topology preserving nature of DCS. It is possible that while learning the structure of an input manifold the neural network may exhibit *faults* even though it ultimately preserves the topology of the manifold as a topology representing network as defined in [13]. An experimental demonstration is presented in the following section where the quantization error fails to detect local minima and maxima (fault) in the total state space of learning.

V. SIMULATION RESULTS

The fixed feature manifold $M \subset \mathbb{R}^I$ is the two-spirals as provided by CMU's archive for artificial neural net benchmark data [21], [20]. In order to provide a better understanding to this stability analysis, the parameters (density, radius) of the training data are set in a manner similar to that described by Bruske and Sommer in [17]. Thus, the density of the twin-spiral training data is 5 and the spiral radius is 6.5. The program *two-spirals.c* of [21], generates 962 input elements in the xy-plane.

Figure 2(a) is a snapshot of an order 51 DCS NN representation, $A_{(51)} \subset \mathbb{R}^O$, of the fixed twin-spiral feature manifold. A network that consists of relatively small number of neural units fails to produce an accurate representation of M in $A_{(51)}$. This is also indicated by a corresponding large value in the quantization error in Figure 2(b). As the neural units are incremented in number to 251, the network gradually evolved into a *topology preserved feature map*, as in Figure 3(a), meaning that the neighborhoods of M are preserved in order 251 DCS neural network representation, $A_{(251)}$. The relatively small quantization error in the network is indicated in Figure 3(b). However, if the simulation is

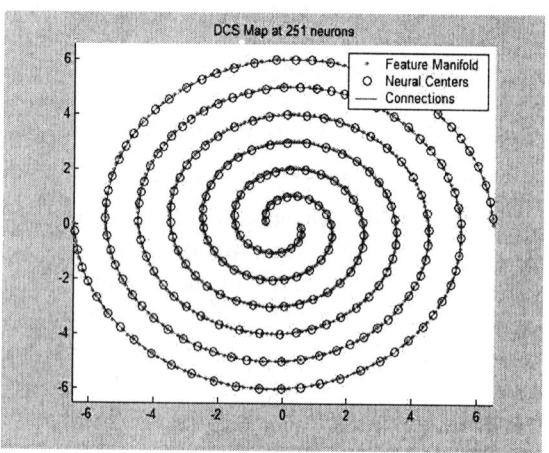

(a) DCS mapping at 251 neurons

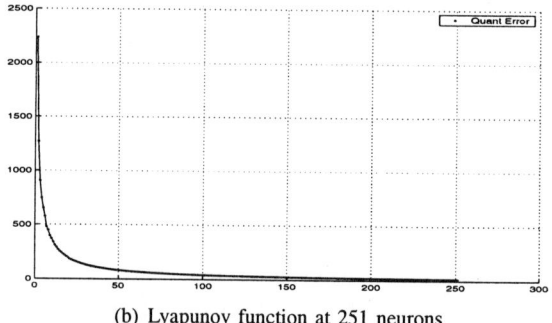

(b) Lyapunov function at 251 neurons

Fig. 3. Order 251 DCS Approximation of Two-spirals Data

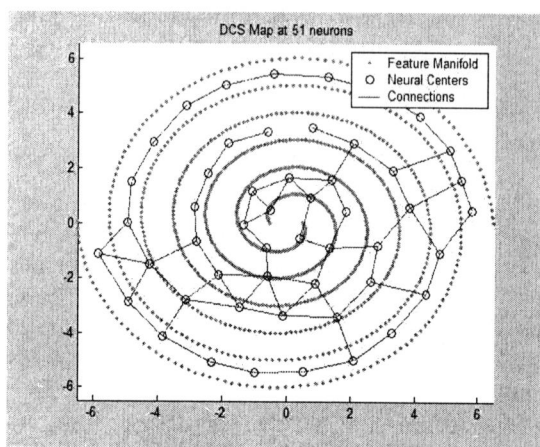

(a) DCS mapping at 51 neurons

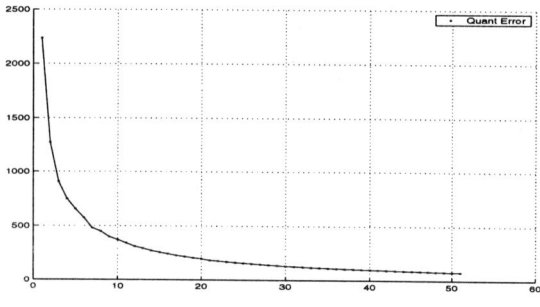

(b) Lyapunov function at 51 neurons

Fig. 2. Order 51 DCS Approximation of Two-Spirals Data

continued for another iteration as shown in Figure 4(a), a *fault* or a defective connection is developed in the network. In order to characterize this property of a defective network representation, we conclude our analysis with the following definition of a fault in DCS learning.

Definition 2 (*Fault*): We say that a fault, or a local minima followed by a maxima has occurred in the Nth order DCS neural net representation $A_{(N)} \subset \mathbb{R}^O$, if two neural units, $\{i,j\}$ of the network that are mapped to relatively *distant* input elements $\{\vec{m}_i, \vec{m}_j\} \in M \subset \mathbb{R}^I$, develop a a positive connection strength between them, $c_{ij} > 0$.

The faults, however, go undetected by the quantization error term of Figure 4(b), which continues to decrease monotonically.

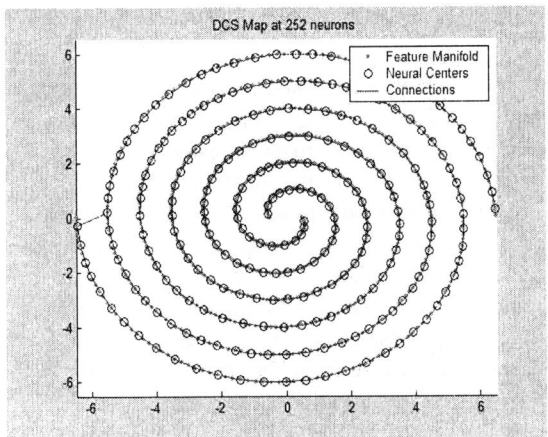

(a) Order 252 DCS Approximation With Fault

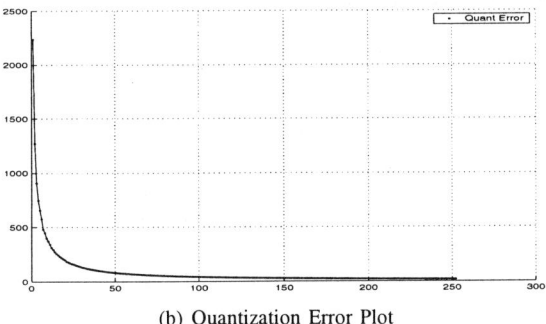

(b) Quantization Error Plot

Fig. 4. Faults in the DCS network at 252 neurons

VI. CONCLUSION

In this paper we proved through Lyapunov stability analysis, that the DCS NN mapping from a fixed input manifold is able to achieve a *globally asymptotically stable* learning state. The credit for this stable behavior is given to the design of the DCS approximating algorithm using Kohonen-like adaptation that adjusts the positions of weighted centers in conjunction with the competitive Hebb rule that updates the lateral connection structure to form a *topology preserving feature map*. It was proved through simulation study that the formation of an accurate representation of the input manifold onto the output manifold depends greatly on a precise moment where the the learning process needs to be stopped. The simulation study also proved that the quantization error, by itself does not indicate a local minima and maxima (fault) during the formation of an *accurate topology preserved feature map*, and thus cannot be used directly as a criteria for stopping the learning. We introduce the concept of a fault as a defective DCS NN connection in the representation of a feature manifold. Finally we propose the need for a simultaneous measure of the topology preservation in the network in terms of a *topology error*, operating in conjunction with the quantization error to provide a performance measure to the accuracy of DCS NN's approximation.

REFERENCES

[1] N.Rouche, P.Habets, and M.Laloy. *Stability Theory by Liapunov's Direct Method*, Springer-Verlag, New York Inc., 1997.
[2] Kevin M.Passino, N.Michel, and Panos J. Antsaklis. *Lyapunov Stability of a Class of Discrete Event Systems*, IEEE Tran. on Automatic Control, Vol. 39, No. 2, February 1994.
[3] Xinghuo Yu, M. Onder Efe,and Okyay Kaynak. *A Backpropagation Learning Framework For Feedforward Neural Networks*, IEEE transactions, No. 0-7803-6685-9/01, 2001.
[4] W. L. Brogan. *Modern Control Theory*, II Edition, Prentice Hall Inc., 07632.
[5] Bernard Friedland. *Advanced Control System*, Prentice Hall Inc., 1996.
[6] V. I. Zubov. *Methods of A. M. Lyapunov and Their Applications*, U.S. Atomic Energy Commission, 1957.
[7] Bernd Fritzke. *Growing Cell Structures - A Self-organizing Network for Unsupervised and Supervised Learning*, ICSI, Vol. 7, No. 9, Pages 1441-1460, May 1993.
[8] Bernd Fritzke. *Growing Self-organizing Networks - why?*, European Symposium on Artificial Neural Network, Pages 61-72, 1996.
[9] Bernd Fritzke. *A Growing Neural Gas Network Learns Topologies*, Advances in Neural Information Processing Systems, Vol. 7, pages 625-632, MIT Press, 1995.
[10] Bernd Fritzke. *Unsupervised Clustering With Growing Cell Structurea*, Proc. of the IJCNN, Pages 531-536, 1991.
[11] Bernd Fritzke. *Growing Grid - A Self-Organizing Network With Constant Neighborhood Range and Adaptation Strength*, Neural Processing Letters, Vol. 2, No. 5, Pages 9-13, 1995.
[12] Teuvo Kohonen. *The Self-Organizing Map*, Proc. of the IEEE, Vol. 78, No. 9, Pages 1464-1480, September, 1990.
[12] Jurgen Rahmel. *On The Role of Topology for Neural Network Interpretation*, Proc. of European Conference on Artificial Intelligence, 1996.
[13] Thomas Martinetz, and Klaus Schulten. *Topology Representing Networks*, Neural Networks, Vol. 7, No. 3, Pages 507-522, 1994.
[14] Lucius Chudy, and Igor Farkas. *Prediction of Chaotic Time-Series Using Dynamic Cell Structures and Local Linear Models*, Institute of Measurement Science, Slovak Academy of Sciences, Slovakia.
[15] Lucius Chudy, and Igor Farkas. *Modified Dynamic Cell Structures as a Thinning Algorithm*, Institute of Measurement Science, Slovak Academy of Sciences, Slovakia.
[16] Ingo Ahrns, Jorg Bruske, and Gerald Sommer. *On-line Learning with Dynamic Cell Structures*, Proc. of ICANN, Vol. 2, Pages 141-146, 1995.
[17] Jorg Bruske, and Gerald Sommer. *Dynamic Cell Structures*, NIPS, Vol. 7, Pages 497-504, 1995.
[18] Jorg Bruske, and Gerald Sommer. *Dynamic Cell Structure Learns Perfectly Topology Preserving Map*, Neural Computation, Vol. 7, No. 4, 845-865, 1995.
[19] Charles C. Jorgensen. *Feedback Linearized Aircraft Control Using Dynamic Cell Structures*, NASA Ames Research Center, ISSCI 050.1-0.50.6.
[20] Fahlman S.E. *CMU Benchmark Collection for Neural Net Learning Algorithms*, Carnegie Mellon Univ., School of Computer Science, machine-readable data repository, Pittsburgh, 1993.
[21] CMU Benchmark Archive.
http://www-2.cs.cmu.edu/afs/cs/project/ai-repository/ai/areas/neural/bench/cmu/, 2002.

An In-vehicle Virtual Driving Assistant Using Neural Networks

Anya Tascillo and Ronald Miller
Ford Motor Company
SRL MD2122
2101 Village Road
Dearborn, MI 48124
agetman @ ford.com

Abstract- A methodology has been developed that aids drivers by suggesting a safer following distance, through the use of sensors, and optionally, vehicle to vehicle communication. Given the restricted case where there is no option to swerve into another lane, a Matlab Simulink model varies vehicle dynamics, driver reaction delay, following distance, and initial speeds when a lead vehicle suddenly decelerates. Based upon the likelihood of collision, neural networks suggest a best following distance, and the benefits of reducing reaction delay with adaptive agents are quantified.

II. INTRODUCTION

The introduction of safety features such as seat belts, air bags, crash zones, and new vehicle structures has dramatically reduced the rate of crashes, injuries and fatalities [1,2,3]. Unfortunately, there is a limit to the number of roads we can add to our landscape to accommodate increasing numbers of vehicles on our roadways. With an aging population navigating ever more crowded streets, the probability of a collision increases. When faced with a possible dangerous situation, the driver has the option of taking a preliminary, or anticipatory, action to better prepare for collision avoidance. These options can include changing lanes, speeding up, or slowing down. Once it appears that a moving object is on a collision path with our driver, his or her reaction can vary widely. Drivers have their own default emergency behaviors, but even these can change with their familiarity with each vehicle they own or borrow. A sharp turn away might be best for a vehicle with a lower center of gravity. Acceleration might be preferable over braking for a vehicle with worn tires, for instance. Extra information provided by sensors, or using communication with intersections, businesses, or other vehicles, may or may not be useful to a driver who does not trust the technology, or is already suffering from sensory overload.

As a driving scenario increases in complexity (heavy traffic, driver distractions, etc.), an optimized artificially intelligent agent, employing telematics and local sensors, could improve the driver's odds of escaping injury, vehicle damage, and even traffic jams. Intelligent agents can be thought of as a combination of current awareness and a selective dissemination of information [4]. These agents already surround us in our everyday lives, as an integral part of search engines, database pattern extractors, mobile communication routing, email prioritization, topic collaboration, adaptive user interfaces, and even online shopping [5,6]. It is therefore not difficult, with telematics, global positioning, and sensors, to appreciate the benefit of a driving assistant that could effectively increasing a driver's peripheral vision to a full 360 degrees. This awareness of potential dangers, and navigable options, could help the driver avoid some less than desirable predicaments by suggesting more defensive, and defensible, positioning on the road [7,8,9].

To this end, we have developed an agent based virtual driving assistant to help reduce accidents through the use of auditory warning techniques. Our first application focuses on rear-impact collisions; however, the methodology is general and extensible to include a wide majority of accident scenarios and vehicle control such as brake assists or steer-by-wire. The virtual driving assistant uses adaptive algorithms that determine the optimal following distance between vehicles, reducing the likelihood of a rear-impact. The warning methodology and distancing between vehicles is partially constructed through the use of spatio-temporal safety zones. These safety zones consist of three regions, centered about each vehicle, whose spatial extent depends on the vehicle type and status, the driver, and on the roadway conditions. The three zones are Accident Mitigation (AM), Accident Avoidance (AA), and Accident Free (AF) which increase in radius concentrically from the vehicle's center. As multiple vehicles interact on the roadway, the safety zones from these vehicles intersect, and based upon their intersection, different countermeasures are applied to either lessen the severity of the accident (AM) or to avoid the accident (AA) altogether. In this paper, we discuss the analytical developments to characterize these spatio-temporal zones for rear-impact and the fundamental safety benefit from advance notification of impending threat on the roadway. Section II will describe how several vehicles are simulated, the case is limited to braking in one lane, and how a neural network is trained to detect a potentially unsafe following distance. Details of the results of this training, confirmed by previously unseen test vehicle interaction sets, are then discussed in Section

III. Conclusions, discussing possible future directions, are found in Section IV.

II. APPROACH

Given the acceleration and deceleration curves of a given vehicle, plus the tendencies of the driver inside that vehicle, one can estimate safety zones around that vehicle that define borders where countermeasures or warnings would be triggered to provide enhanced occupant safety. This zone boundary might or might not coincide with the moment that the human (and/or vehicle sensors) notices the possible threat, but it can be proportionally related. In this work the boundaries are modeled as two ellipses. The outer ellipse, separates the world that the vehicle may be aware of, from the world that the vehicle must pay close attention to, and may need to react to, to avoid a collision. Outside of this boundary, the vehicle might suggest that the driver modify its current trajectory to lessen its risk. The inner ellipse approximates the boundary between collision avoidance and mitigation.

A. Simulation

After the models of several vehicles are calibrated to their real world acceleration and braking data, a Matlab Simulink [10] simulation (flowchart representation in Fig.1) repeatedly emulates interaction of these vehicles for a rear-impact scenario.

With an original goal of following a target path through the driving scenario, each vehicle monitors the other objects (in this set of scenarios, other vehicles) in case it needs to react to them. Actions are prioritized with fuzzy logic, given calibratible barriers within a sensed accident scenario (e.g., rear-impact, head-on, T-bone, parallel), as well as the sensed relative speed. Once there are no longer any perceived threats, a vehicle returns to its original task of navigating, based on its present location. Initially configured to all be on a collision course, the driver-vehicle combinations are tracked for several seconds, and the final outcome (collide/not-collide) is recorded, as well as relative extra distance traveled, out of the way of a non-obstructed journey (an example is Fig. 2). Not only are driver variables (delays, rates), initial speeds, distances, and vehicle combinations varied, but so are the options allowed for each vehicle (accelerate, brake, steer/change lanes, no reaction at all).

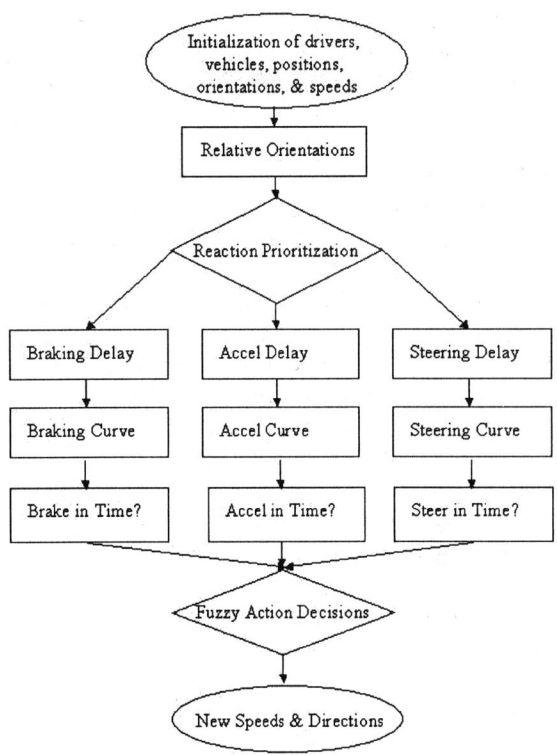

Figure 1. Flowchart of major simulation decisions. Algorithm Discussed is the Brake in Time block.

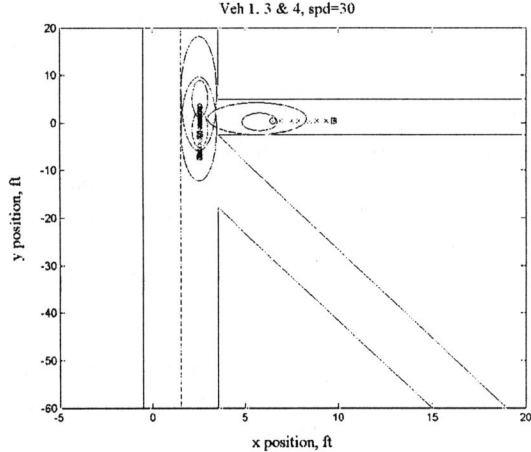

Fig. 2. Collision scenario, with no lane changes allowed. Note overlap of two of the inner envelopes.

B. Braking Within One Lane

To demonstrate the involvement of neural networks in adaptive collision behavior, a feed forward neural network approach is shown for the restricted case of one vehicle braking suddenly in front of another that follows it, with no option for either to swerve into another lane. Given today's hectic, crowded commutes, most drivers do not have the option to follow a safer two-second following rule (based on most vehicles' 60 to 0 mph braking distance [11]), which would allow for braking within a lane for many vehicles and conditions. Unfortunately, the space left by such a gap is often filled by a third vehicle. An additional concern is a driver's lack of awareness of vehicles behind oneself, increasing the possibility of a collision from behind, ironically while attempting to avoid one in front. Rear view glance frequency can easily vary from once every six seconds, to once every twenty seconds, due to distractions [12]. If an intelligent methodology is to be used in many uncertain multiple vehicle scenarios, it must consider, and allow for, wide variability in allowable following distances. Simulated reaction delay for the follower vehicle is varied to emulate a range of human reaction times, possibly enhanced by vehicle sensing and driver warning, in order to suggest an optimal following distance.

A one dimensional, lumped, stopping distance, S_T can be defined [13] as

$$S_T = V_1(t_r + t_a + \frac{t_b}{2}) + \frac{V_1^2}{2a_{max}} - \frac{a_{max}t_b^2}{24} \quad (1)$$

where V_1 = initial velocity, a_{max} = maximum achievable deceleration rate, which incorporates inertial effects; t_r = driver reaction time, due to distraction and musculo-nervous pathways; t_a = pedal application & actuation delay time, for the combined driver and vehicle; and t_b = deceleration build up time, due to frictional interaction.

For this demonstration, these parameters were calibrated experimentally using several representative in-service vehicles (a full sized truck, an SUV, a sports car, and a family sedan) with human driver delays. A flat, slightly gravelled road surface was assumed. Radial basis functions were trained to generalize the data for additional vehicle cases not specifically used for initial calibration.

C. Neural Network Adaptation

With this data, for a given driver-vehicle combination, not only can the relative contribution of a given collision sensing and warning technology be measured, but also optimal major and minor axes can be estimated for the safety zones around the vehicle. Radial basis function neural networks [14] separately categorize the driver-vehicle combination for both acceleration and braking. Then a feed forward neural network (Fig. 3) extracts this best following distance for a driver-vehicle combination from the data generated by thousands of simulated scenarios, ranking zone sizes higher which result in a lower rate of collisions. These neural networks base their conclusions on variables extracted from the driver-vehicle acceleration, braking, and turning mapping.

III. RESULTS

In order to test the generalization capability of the potential collision prediction feed forward neural network of Fig. 3, two data sets were generated, where driver-vehicle combinations were paired in a forward direction through the data for one set, then paired in reverse order for the second set. Although one set of pairings experienced a variety of speeds and following distances, a given feed forward neural net never saw other pairings for any of its training, only for its testing.

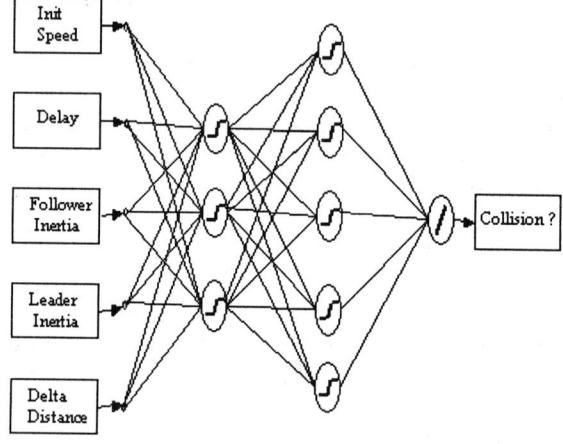

Fig. 3. Feed forward neural network employed to diagnose a collision-prone situation for one-dimensional braking.

One of the typical intersections is shown in Fig. 2 (with a collision) and Fig. 4 (with no collision). In this case 2 of the four vehicles shown are at rest, but the remaining two, headed toward the top of the map, are in the lane and following the exact same path. The first vehicle suddenly decelerates, and once a delay has passed, the second vehicle decelerates, based upon its following logic. Sometimes the follower will actually accelerate at first, if the vehicle awareness zones have not yet intersected. In these examples, "veh = 3&4" refers to vehicle 3 following vehicle 4, and "spd=30" indicates that the lead vehicle (who will decelerate first) was initially traveling at 30 ft/sec, or roughly 20 mph. In these two examples, the following vehicle starts at the same speed, but varies the distance behind, and delay until it is allowed to react.

Although a trace of vehicle position is illustrative of a given scenario, corresponding Fig. 5 and 6 plot distance between vehicles, and their respective speeds for these two instances. Once the two driver-vehicle combinations collide, their speeds combine, following the law of conservation of momentum, after which they exponentially slow to a stop. After 1800 scenarios were executed, a trend was observed, and a percentage of collisions (X) versus non-collisions (O) was computed, and compared for various driver-vehicle combinations, speeds, initial separation distances, and reaction delays. Fig. 7 shows the difference between a delay of 0.1 seconds (in these cases, near 50% collisions) and 0.4 seconds (in these cases, near 100% collisions) for a given range of following distances and speeds for 4 driver-vehicle combinations. Many non-collisions become collisions as the reaction delay increases. For comparison, Fig. 8 shows results for the reverse order of Fig. 7 interactions, which result in similar collision frequencies, but not for the same driver vehicle pairings.

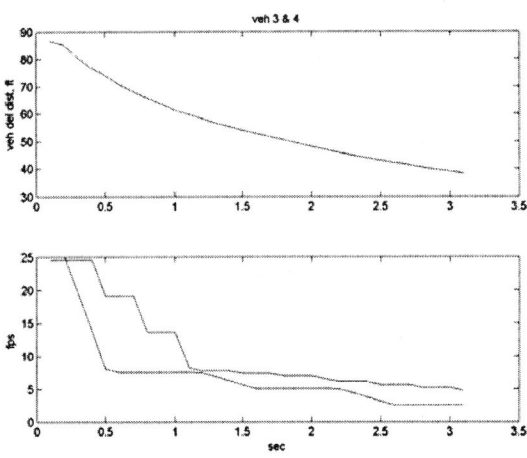

Fig. 6. Non-collision scenario, delta distance and speeds.

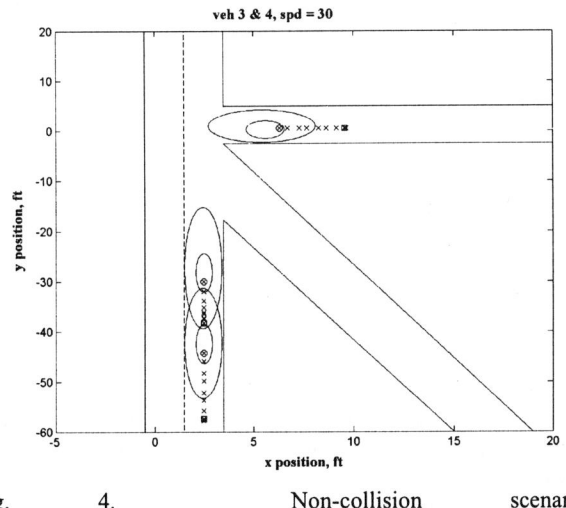

Fig. 4. Non-collision scenario.

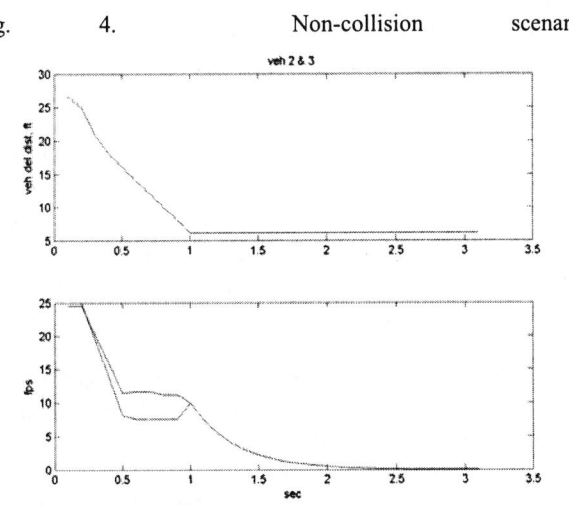

Fig.5. Collision scenario, following distance & speeds.

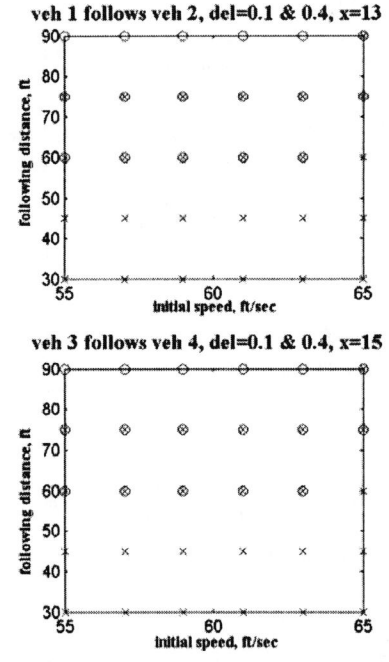

Fig. 7a. "Forward" driver-vehicle pairings, 0.1 and 0.4 sec follower reaction delay.

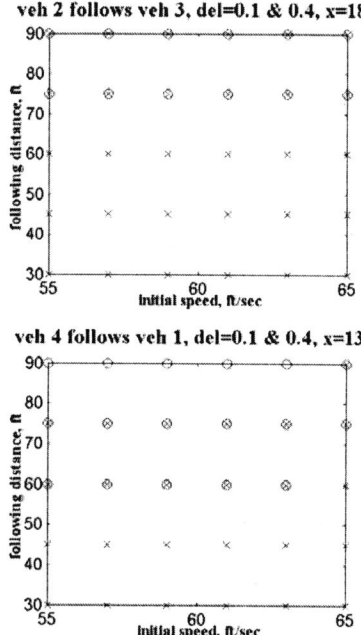

Fig. 7b. "Forward" driver-vehicle pairings, 0.1 and 0.4 sec follower reaction delay.

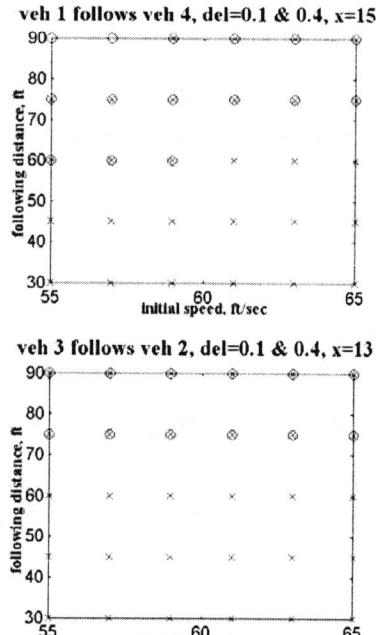

Fig. 8a. "Reverse" driver-vehicle pairings, 0.1 sec follower reaction delay.

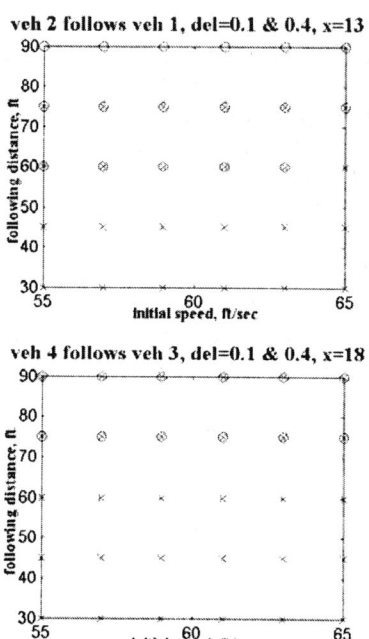

Fig. 8b. "Reverse" driver-vehicle pairings, 0.1 sec follower reaction delay.

Consistently, the feed forward neural networks, when trained to 1 for a collision, and 0 for a non-collision, would settle on a constant attractor value for non-collisions, and vary from that constant in an orderly fashion for collisions. When tested on the reverse driver-vehicle pairings, the exact same constant would emerge in every non-collision case. The trained collision output values can conveniently remain almost entirely on one side, as in this first net: min(non-collision) = 1.0916, max(non-collision) =1.0916, min(collision) = 1.0915, and max(collision) = 1.4035. The output values can also vary to both sides, as in this second net: min(non-collision) = -0.9535, max(non-collision) = -0.9535, min(collision) = -1.0108, and max(collision) = -0.7119.

Independent of one-sidedness (or lack thereof) in the outputs for a given network, trends were clearly defined in one direction for a specific driver-vehicle and following distance pairing, as shown in Fig. 9, where the first figure plots all following distances together, then with each successive plot toward the right, one following distance (30 ft first) is removed. Due to space limitations, the scale of each plot could not be shown, but the final attractor values for 75 and 90 feet are actually very close to the non-collision constant, nearly matching at 4 decimal places. This indicates that the likelihood of collision is low at these distances, independent of initial speeds. Therefore, in implementation, if the neural network indicates a value other than its favorite attractor, the driver might want to back off and not tailgate as closely, if s/he wants to be prepared for a sudden deceleration in the vehicle ahead.

This same neural network can be applied when the follower is initially traveling at a speed higher or lower than that of the leader. The training target for the output is modified via the following relationship:

$$L_C = 1 - e^{-\frac{m}{\tau}} \qquad (2)$$

where L_c = likelihood of collisions expected, m = the scale factor of follower/leader initial speed, and τ = a decay that is correlation-calibratible for a given vehicle-driver combination after a few braking maneuvers. If there is not enough data, the vehicle's last value can be used (or a general average value of 0.75).

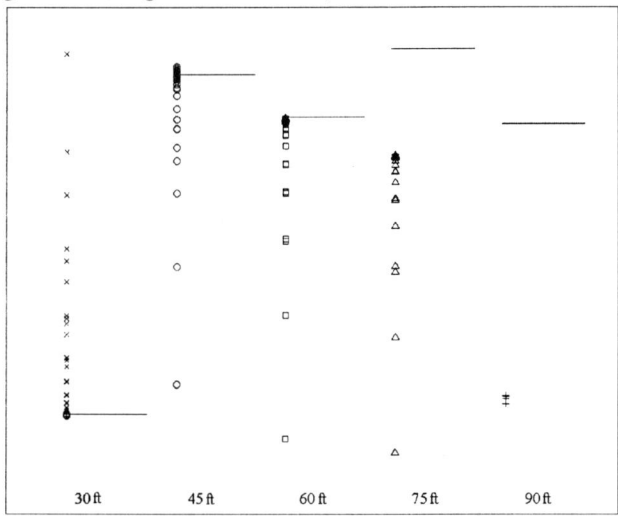

Fig. 9. Neural network outputs for largest vehicle, across initial following distances, as they relate to safe-distance target.

IV. CONCLUSIONS

Although ten percent white noise was added through the simulation, the neural network found the underlying dynamics of this simple one-dimensional braking case relatively uncomplicated to diagnose. Future work will remove the constraints on movement for both leader and follower, as well as allow other driver-vehicle combinations in as distractions. Most gross vehicle motion can be modeled by a relatively simple neural net (or captured at one set of operating parameters by a 3rd or 4th order polynomial). If past values are necessary to predict future states, a relatively small recurrent neural network can readily handle predictive diagnosis' and control scenarios [15]. Robots have been built to test these algorithms in hardware, with the eventual intent of vehicle testing. In parallel, human perception and acceptance studies will be run to better parameterize the complexity of integration into real world driving. For instance, driver perception of safe distances for following, lane change, and passing, decreases with increased traffic volume. However, this perception does not scale to compensate for the actual space needed, and is exacerbated as driver aggression and frustration increase [16].

ACKNOWLEDGMENTS

Many thanks are given to R. Basch for her braking insights, and Charles Wu and Gary Strumolo for their inspiration and support.

REFERENCES

[1] http://gulliver.trb.org/publications/trnews/rpo/rpo.trn145.pdf
[2] http://www.nhtsa.dot.gov/nhtsa/announce/NhtsaNow/v8-6/NNow8_6index.htm
[3] http://www.saferoads.org/Intersection-RLR/ITE factsheets Intersection RLR/problem.pdf
[4] Nwana, H.S. Software Agents: An Overview. Intelligent Systems Research AA&T, BT Laboratories, Ipswich, United Kingdom, 1996.
[5] Resnick, P., Zeckhauser R. and Avery, C. Roles for Electronic Brokers. United States, Cambridge, 1995.
[6] Etzioni, O. and Weld, D.S. Intelligent Agents on the Internet - Fact, Fiction, and Forecast. IEEE Expert - Intelligent Internet Services, number 4, page 44-49. August 1995.
[7] Newman, A., and Frazier, T. Intelligent Vehicle and Roadway System (IVRS): Research Exploration Framework (REF) for the DARPA ISO Taskable Agent Software Kit (TASK) Program. TASK Kickoff Meeting, October 3-5, 2000.
[8] Ehlert, Patrick. Intelligent driving agents: The Agent Approach to Tactical Driving in Autonomous Vehicles and Traffic Simulation. Master's Thesis, Delft University of Technology, Faculty of Information Technology and Systems, January 2001.
[9] Goldsmith, A. A New Methodology for Joint Design of Control and Communications. Path Program Wide Meeting, Stanford University, October 25, 2002.
[10] Mathworks, The. Matlab Simulink Neural Network Toolbox, Natick, Mass., Version 4.0.2 (R13). June 28, 2002.
[11] Tascillo, Anya. Neural Network Isolation of System Inputs for Transient Modeling and Control. ICNN97: Intelligent Estimation & Control. Westin Galleria Hotel, Houston, Texas, USA June 11, 1997.
[12] Tascillo, A. and Gearhart, C. A Neural Network Based Airbag Deployment Algorithm. ANNIE 2000: Smart Engineering Systems, Marriott Pavilion, St. Louis, Missouri, Nov. 6, 2000.
[13] http://www.nhtsa.dot.gov/cars/testing/brakes/
[14] Mapping Young Drivers in Behavioral Space. Stanley H. Schuman, M.D., and Donald C. Pelz, PhD.
[15] Limpert, R. Brake Design and Safety. Society of Automotive Engineers, Inc. Warrendale, PA, 1999.
[16] Hostetter, R. "Driver Passing Behavior on Two-lane Highways," Pre-crash Factors in Traffic Safety. The American Association for Automotive Medicine. 12th Annual Symp, 1968.

Transition between Position-Matching Control and Rhythm-Matching Control in Hand Tracking Task is Explained by a Phase Model for Hand Motion

Fumihiko Ishida
Graduate School of Information Systems
University of Electro-Communications
1-5-1 Chofu-ga-oka, Chofu,
Tokyo, 182-8585 Japan
Email: ishida@hi.is.uec.ac.jp

Yoshiki Kuramoto
Graduate School of Sciences
Kyoto University
Sakyo-ku, Kyoto, Japan
Email: kuramoto@ton.scphys.kyoto-u.ac.jp

Yasuji Sawada
Department of Communication
Tohoku Institute of Technology
Taihaku-ku, Sendai, Japan
Email: sawada@tohtech.ac.jp

Abstract— We recently reported a transitional behavior between position-matching control and rhythm-matching control in human hand tracking task. In this paper we present a phase model which successfully explains the transitional behavior. The present model is derived from a delayed feed-forward model which we recently proposed to understand proactive human percepto-motor control. The present model not only reproduced the systematic phase-lead of the hand-motion with respect to the target-motion in a finite frequency range but also the transition in the tracking modes from position-matching to rhythm-matching at a critical frequency of the target-motion experimentally observed in human hand tracking tasks.

I. Introduction

It is believed that the predictive mechanism should exist in order to compensate the delay or to generate appropriate motion by using internal model of the motor apparatuses or the external environment [1]–[5]. In relation to the predictive ability for compensation of the delay of processing, a number of hand or eye tracking experiments have been carried out [6]–[13].

The study on the phase-relation between the continuous motions of the target and the hand is important for understanding the strategy of catching moving objects by predictive mechanism. Although there exist a vast amount of research for hand tracking, phase-lead phenomena have not been reported systematically in hand nor eye tracking experiments in contrast to the discrete synchronization experiments [14]–[17].

We recently reported [18]–[20] by precise steady and transient experiments of hand tracking task that the hand-motion in steady motion runs does precede the target-motion statistically over a finite frequency range, and that the mean value of precedence in steady runs corresponds to the optimal value for which the transient error of the hand-motion with respect to the target-motion is minimum when the target-motion changes unexpectedly.

We also proposed a delayed feed-forward (DFF) model in order to understand the observed experimental results of proactive human control. It was shown that the model reproduced the main feature of the percepto-motor control system, except for the amplitude of the hand-motion due to the fact that this particular DFF equation we used was a linear equation in the hand-position. There would be two different approaches to take into the nonlinear effects. One is to introduce a lowest order nonlinear term when one wish to study the amplitude dynamics [21]. The other is to derive a phase equation when one wish to study the phase relation between the hand-motion and the target-motion [22].

In this paper we studied a phase equation derived from the delayed feed-forward model previously proposed, and report the possibility that the transition in the hand tracking modes from position-matching to rhythm-matching at a critical frequency of the target-motion experimentally observed is related to the phase instability caused by the delay of the signal transfer.

II. Hand Tracking Experiment

A. Protocol

The subject was seated at 50cm in front of a computer display. He was asked to trace a moving visual target in the display by his right hand. The position of the subject's hand during these tasks was measured as the position of a cursor. The target sinusoidally moved with a constant amplitude (75mm) on a horizontal line. In the steady state experiments, the target-frequency was kept constant. The target-frequency was selected in a random order from 0.1Hz to 1.8Hz by steps of 0.1Hz. All runs are continued over 45sec. The experimental data of a duration of 20sec from 10sec after the start was accumulated, in order to avoid the initial transient behavior of the subjects. The subjects carried out ten runs for each frequency. The data of seven subjects were used of this study. We also conducted the sudden frequency change transient experiments, and the detail was explained in [18]–[20].

B. Results

Here, we show the experimental results related to the mode transition of tracking.

Fig.1 shows the phase difference ψ between the hand-motion and the target-motion and the standard deviation taken from [18]. Fig.1(a) shows that the phase-shift value is nearly zero in the frequency range lower than 0.6Hz and is positive in the frequency range from 0.6Hz to 1.8Hz (positive value

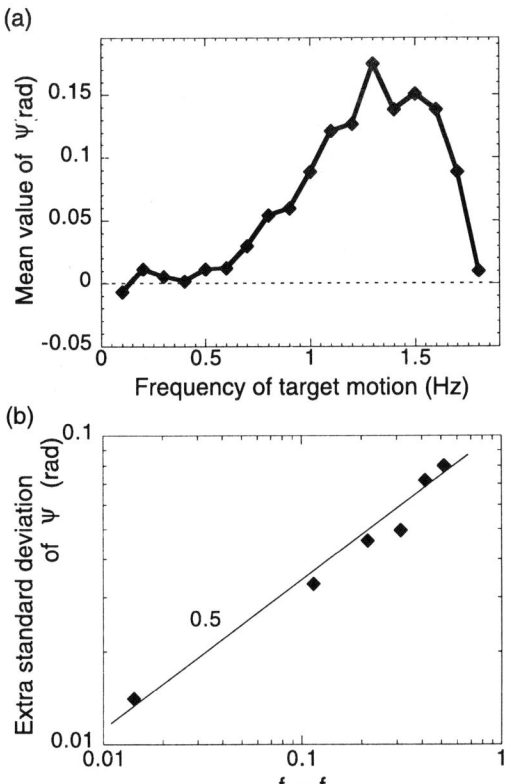

Fig. 1. The experimental data in the low frequency range taken from the reference [18]. The frequency dependence of the mean value of the phase difference ψ(a) and the extra standard deviation subtracted the intrinsic noise in percepto-motor control system from the observed standard deviation(b). The abcissa in Fig.1(b) is $f_0 - f$, for $f_0 = 0.61$Hz.

means that the hand-motion precedes the target-motion). This type of the frequency dependence of the phase-shift, which is nearly zero in low frequency range and is positive with precedence of the hand-motion in a finite frequency range, was also observed in synchronization tasks [15]. Thus, this frequency dependence may have a universality for human percepto-motor control system.

In the frequency range higher than 0.6Hz the standard deviation of the time difference between the hand-motion and the target-motion hardly depends on the target-frequency. On the other hand, in the frequency range lower than 0.6Hz it has some kind of frequency dependence [20]. This observation may be related to the mode change in percepto-motor control system between position-matching and rhythm-matching. Fig.1(b) shows that the extra standard deviation of the phase superimposed on the intrinsic noise in percepto-motor control system explained in [18] in the frequency range less than 0.6Hz, as,

$$\Delta\psi \propto (f_0 - f)^{1/2}, \quad (1)$$

where f_0 is 0.61Hz.

The aim of present research is to show how the standard deviation shows the behavior shown in Fig.1(b).

III. MODEL

A. A DFF model and a Phase model

It was reported that feedback of the positional error and feed-forward of the target-velocity might be important signal used to control the hand-motion in tracking task [10]. We have tried to reproduce the experimental results by the analytical model which has these minimum components for representation of the hand tracking behavior. The delayed feed-forward model

$$\dot{X}(t) = \frac{1}{\tau}\{T(t-\delta) - X(t-\delta)\} + \gamma\dot{T}(t-\delta), \quad (2)$$

previously proposed [19], [20] reproduces the main features of the experimental observation; the proactive control which minimizes the future dynamic error by phase-lead operation. In (2) X and T are the position of the hand and the target at t, respectively. This model includes the delay time δ of signal transfer time from retina to the computing section of motor command in the brain, a characteristic time τ of muscle and strength of connection weight of feed-forward loop γ. However, we were not able to discuss the apparent mode change of the tracking demonstrated by the break of the standard deviation around 0.6Hz [18]–[20].

A phase equation is derived from (2) by assuming that a nonlinear effect suppress any deviation of the amplitude of the hand motion from that of the target. Setting the deviation of the amplitude from unity, that is, substition of $X(t) = e^{i\phi(t)}$ and $T(t) = e^{i\omega t}$ in (2), we obtain the following phase equation for the hand-motion,

$$\tau\dot{\phi}(t) = \sqrt{1+(\gamma\omega\tau)^2}\sin[\omega t - \phi(t) - \omega\delta + \alpha] \\ - \sin[\phi(t-\delta) - \phi(t)], \quad (3)$$

where $\omega = 2\pi f$ and $\tan\alpha = \gamma\omega\tau$.

B. Stationary solution

Assumed that the phase model had a stationary solution $\phi(t) = \omega t + \psi_0$, stationary phase difference ψ_0 between the hand-motion and the target-motion can be obtained as follows,

$$\psi_0 = \alpha - \omega\delta - \sin^{-1}\left[\frac{\omega\tau - \sin\omega\delta}{\sqrt{1+(\gamma\omega\tau)^2}}\right]. \quad (4)$$

The stability of the stationary solution will be discussed below.

IV. RESULTS OF NUMERICAL SIMULATION

δ and τ should be in the range 100-300msec, estimated by reaction time from visual input to motion [10], [23]–[25]. γ was estimated to be in the vicinity of 2.5 as the optimum value for proactive control [19], [20]. Fig.2 shows the examples of the time evolution of $\sin\phi(t)$ calculated by (3) and the target-motion $\sin\omega t$. It was found that the hand-motion is clearly advanced with the target-motion in the high frequency range (Fig.2(a)). On the other hand, in the low frequency range the hand-motion fluctuated around the target-motion (Fig.2(b)).

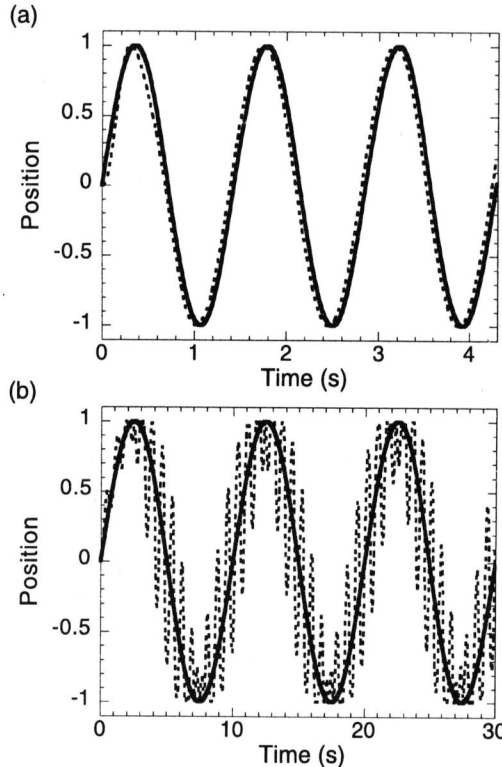

Fig. 2. The example of the time evolution of $\sin\phi(t)$ (the broken line) and $\sin\omega t$ (the solid line). The frequency of the target-motion in (a) or (b) is 0.7Hz or 0.1Hz, respectively. The parameter values (γ, τ, δ) were set as (2.5, 0.1, 0.2), respectively.

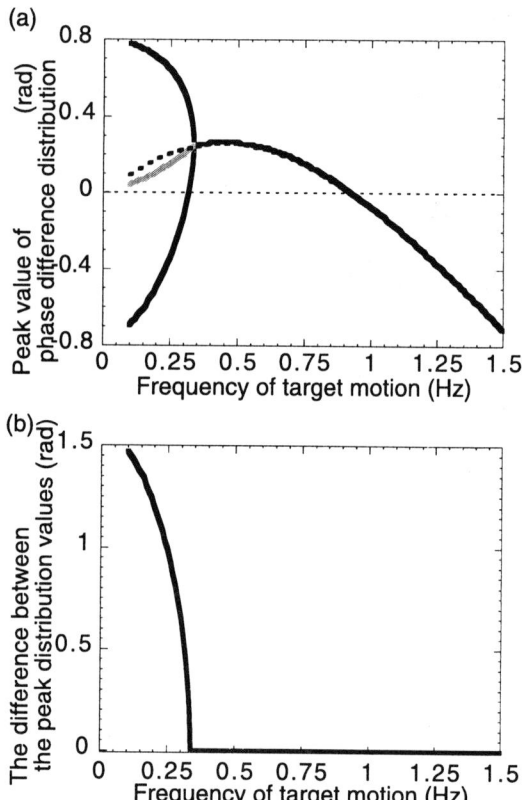

Fig. 3. The frequency dependence of the feature of the phase difference ψ of the hand-motion from the target-motion for the present phase model. (a). The black solid line shows the value of the phase difference where the distribution of the phase difference takes the peak value. The gray solid line in the frequency range less than 0.33Hz illustrates the averaged value of the phase difference at the peak of the distribution. The broken line shows the stationary phase difference ψ_0 given by (4). (b). The frequency dependence of the extent of the phase fluctuation $\Delta\psi$. The parameter values (γ, τ, δ) were set as (2.5, 0.1, 0.2), respectively.

In order to evaluate the fluctuation of the hand-motion in the low frequency range we calculated the histograms for the number of events with various phase differences ψ. Fig.3(a) illustrates the frequency dependence of the phase difference ψ with γ=2.5, τ=0.1sec and δ=0.2sec. This figure shows that the distribution of ψ has two peaks and the averaged value of ψ is smaller than the stationary phase difference ψ_0 given by (4) in the frequency range less than 0.33Hz. On the other hand, in the frequency range greater than 0.33Hz the average value of ψ corresponds to the stationary phase difference.

Fig.3(b) shows the frequency dependence of the extent of the phase fluctuation $\Delta\psi$. In this figure one can see that the frequency dependence is divided into two frequency range. One is the frequency range less than 0.33Hz; in this frequency range the hand-motion clearly shows phase instability around the target-motion like Fig.2(b). Another is the frequency range greater than 0.33Hz; here no phase instability was observed as seen in Fig.2(a).

V. DISCUSSION

A. Phase-lead control

Fig.3(a) illustrates that the phase equation (3), derived from DFF model by (2) reproduces phase-lead phenomena, characteristic to the proactive control, as expected. The frequency dependence of the phase-shift in the high frequency range is in reasonable agreement with our previous experimental result, except for the low frequency range part and the value of the cut-off frequency. However, with respect to the cut-off frequency the phase-shift would get better agreement by tuning the value of the parameters.

Furthermore, the present simulation of the phase model with the present value of the parameters showed that the system shows phase instability at around 0.33Hz, and that the fluctuation of the phase increases with decreasing frequency, as shown in Fig.3. Due to this phase instability, the value of the phase-shift itself may be modified to a lower value, as shown in Fig.3(a).

Fig.1(a) illustrates the experimental data of the averaged phase difference and shows that the phase-shift value is nearly zero in the frequency range less than 0.6Hz. This tendency was qualitaively explained by the phase instability which causes deviation from the stationary solution of the phase model by (3).

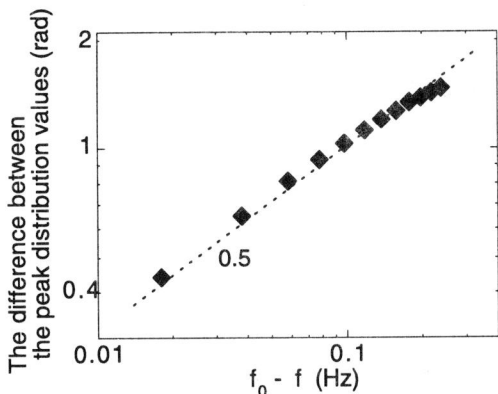

Fig. 4. The frequency dependence of the extent of the phase fluctuation at the low frequency range in the present phase model (3). The abcissa is $f_0 - f$, for $f_0 = 0.33$Hz.

Fig.1(b) shows the frequency dependence of the fluctuation of the phase difference observed experimentally. Although the value of the critical frequency in the phase model is different from that observed experimentally, it is interesting to note that this frequency dependence of the standard deviation of the phase-shift is reproduced almost exactly as shown in Fig.4. This is a strong evidence that the fluctuation of the hand-motion below 0.6Hz is caused by a phase instability of the percepto-motor control system.

B. Strategy change of hand tracking

The frequency dependence of the standard deviation of ψ in the present phase model is clearly divided into two frequency range at 0.33Hz in Fig.3 and reproduced our previously observed hand tracking experiments [18]–[20]. In the low frequency range the hand-position traces the target with no average phase deviation and may be called position-matching mode. In the high frequency range the hand moves proactively by rhythm-matching. The present paper clarified the nature of the position-matching mode in the frequency range lower than 0.6Hz.

VI. CONCLUSION

In this paper we report the analytical and simulation results of a phase equation for human hand-motion in tracking experiments. The present model is derived from a delayed feed-forward model previously proposed for proactive control. The model reproduced the systematic phase-lead of the hand-motion with respect to the target-motion in a finite frequency range and the change of tracking strategy from position-matching to rhythm-matching at a critical frequency of the target-motion experimentally observed in human hand-tracking tasks.

REFERENCES

[1] S.J. Blakemore, S.J. Goodbody and D.M. Wolpert, "Predicting the consequences of our own actions: the role of sensorimotor context estimation," *J. Neurosci.*, vol. 18, pp. 7511-7518, 1998.

[2] J.R. Flanagan and A.M. Wing, "The role of internal models in motion planning and control: evidence from grip force adjustments during movements of hand-held loads," *J. Neurosci.*, vol. 17, pp. 1519-1528, 1997.

[3] M. Kawato, "Internal models for motor control and trajectory planning," *Curr. Opin. Neurobiol.*, vol. 9, pp. 718-727, 1999.

[4] R.C. Miall, D.J. Weir, D.M. Wolpert and J.F. Stein, "Is the cerebellum a smith predictor?," *J. Mot. Behav.*, vol. 25, pp. 203-216, 1993.

[5] D.M. Wolpert and M. Kawato, "Multiple paired forward and inverse models for motor control," *Neural Networks*, vol. 11, pp. 1317-1329, 1998.

[6] G.R. Barnes, S.F. Donnelly and R.D. Eason, "Predictive velocity estimation in the pursuit reflex response to pseudorandom and step displacement stimuli in man," *J. Physiol.*, vol. 389, pp. 111-136, 1987.

[7] O. Bock, "Coordination of arm and eye movements in tracking of sinusoidally moving targets," *Behav. Brain Res.*, vol. 24, pp. 93-100, 1987.

[8] D.C. Deno, W.F. Crandall, K. Sherman and E.L. Keller, "Characterization of prediction in the primate visual smooth pursuit system," *BioSystems*, vol. 34, pp. 107-128, 1995.

[9] N.H. Drewell, "The effect of preveiw on pilot describing functions in a simple tracking task," *UTIAS Technical Note* 176, Institute of Aerospace Studies, University of Tronto, 1972.

[10] R.C. Miall, D.J. Weir and J.F. Stein, "Manual tracking of visual targets by trained monkeys," *Behav. Brain Res.*, vol. 20, pp. 185-201, 1986.

[11] S. Yasui and L.R. Young, "On the predictive control of foveal eye tracking and slow phases of optokinetic and vestibular nystagmus," *J. Physiol.*, vol. 347, pp. 17-33, 1984.

[12] L.R. Young and L. Stark, "Variable feedback experiments testing a sampled data model for eye tracking movements," *IEEE Trans. on Human Factors in Electronics*, vol. 4, pp. 28-51, 1963.

[13] R.S. Turner, S.T. Grafton, J.R. Votaw, M.R. Delong and J.M. Hoffman, "Motor subcircuits mediating the control of movement velocity: a PET study," *J. Neurophysiol.*, vol. 80, pp. 2162-2176, 1998.

[14] Y. Chen, M. Ding and J.A.S. Kelso, "Long memory processes ($1/f^\alpha$ type) in human coordination," *Phys. Rev. Lett.*, vol. 79, pp. 4501-4504, 1997.

[15] D.A. Engström, J.A.S. Kelso and T. Holroyd, "Reaction- anticipation transitions in human perception-action patterns," *Hum. Mov. Sci.*, vol. 15, pp. 809-832, 1996.

[16] M. Franek, R. Radil, M. Indra and P. Lansky, "Following complex rhythmical acoustical patterns by tapping," *Int. J. Psychophysiol.*, vol. 5. pp. 187-192, 1987.

[17] J. Mates and G. Aschersleben, "Sensorimotor sychronization: the impact to temporally displaced auditory feedback," *Acta Psychol.*, vol. 104, pp. 29-44, 2000.

[18] F. Ishida and Y.Sawada, "Proactive control in hand tracking: an error minimizing strategy in human beings," unpublished.

[19] F. Ishida, H. Ushioda and Y.Sawada, "Preceding motion in a hand tracking experiment," *Proc. 8th International Conference on Neural Information Processing*, vol. 2, pp. 971-974, 2001.

[20] F. Ishida and Y. Sawada, "Precedence of hand motion in a tracking task: a model of sensory-motor control system," *Proc. of 2001 International Symposium on Nonlinear Theory and its Applications.*, vol. 2, pp. 379-382, 2001.

[21] H. Haken, J.A.S. Kelso and H. Bunz, "A theoretical model of phase transitions in human hand movements," *Biol. Cybern.*, vol. 51, pp. 347-356, 1985.

[22] T.D. Frank and P.J. Beek, "Stationary solutions of linear stochastic delay differential equations; application to biological systems," *Phy. Rev. E*, vol. 64, 021917-1-12, 2001.

[23] J.R. Carl and R.S. Gellman, "Human smooth pursuit: stimulus-dependent responses," *J. Neurophysiol.*, vol. 57, pp. 1446-1463, 1987.

[24] S. Lisberger, E. Morris and L. Tyschen, "Visual motion processing and sensory-motor integration for smooth pursuit eye movements," *Ann. Rev. Neurosci.*, vol. 10, pp. 97-129, 1987.

[25] D.A. Robinson, J.L. Gordon and S.E. Gordon, "A model of the smooth pursuit eye movement system," *Biol. Cybern.*, vol. 55, pp. 43-57, 1986.

Applying Guided Evolutionary Simulated Annealing to Cost-Based Abduction

Ashraf M. Abdelbar
Dept. of Computer Science,
American University in Cairo

Heba Amer
Dept. of Computer Science,
American University in Cairo

Abstract— Guided Evolutionary Simulated Annealing (GESA) is a parallel simulated annealing (SA) technique that is based on competition among a population of independent SA chains. In each chain, each current state, called the parent state, iteratively, generates a number of child states using a domain-dependent neighborhood operator. The most fit child is deterministically determined, and then is allowed to replace the parent with a logistic probability. The number of child states that each parent is allowed to generate in each iteration is dependent on the quality of the solutions produced by this chain in the past. We show how this technique can be applied to cost-based abduction (CBA), an important AI formalism for representing knowledge under uncertainty. Performance is evaluated using a suite of 50 randomly generated CBA instances, containing 50 hypotheses and 70 rules.

I. INTRODUCTION

Guided Evolutionary Simulated Annealing (GESA) is a technique that belongs to a family of methods [1], [4], [5], [6], [10], [14], [18] that combine aspects of evolutionary computation (EC) [11], [13] and simulated annealing (SA) [12], [17]. The basic GESA technique was introduced in 1995 by Yip and Pao [22]; we have previously proposed [3] an extension of Yip and Pao's approach, based on what we have called heritage factors. In this paper, we apply the GESA technique (both with and without heritage factors) to cost-based abduction, an important problem in reasoning under uncertainty.

GESA is a parallel SA technique that uses the EC concepts of population and survival of the fittest. In GESA, a set of independent SA chains are maintained, with no recombination and no sharing of best solutions. In each chain, each current state, called the parent state, generates a number of child states using a domain-dependent neighborhood operator. The most fit child is deterministically determined, and is allowed to replace the parent with a logistic probability. The number of child states that each parent is allowed to sample in each iteration is dependent on the quality of the solutions produced by this chain in the past iteration.

We view this as modeling an evolutionary scenario in which there is survival of the fittest among competing families. The more affluent families have a greater number of children and, over time, this allows them to become more affluent. In the heritage factors extension, the number of children allocated to a parent is dependent on the quality of the last generation and on the past history of the family line (the family's "heritage").

Cost-based abduction is an important AI formalism for representing knowledge under uncertainty. In this formalism, evidence to be explained is treated as a goal to be proven. Proofs have costs based on how much needs to be assumed to complete the proof, and the set of assumptions needed to complete the least-cost proof are taken as the best explanation for the given evidence. The cost-based abduction problem is NP-hard, and current techniques have exponential time complexity in the worst-case. Computational intelligence approaches for this problem have not previously been explored.

Best-first search techniques were investigated by Charniak and Shimony [9], and Charniak and Husain [8]. In [20], [21], Santos presents an integer constraint satisfaction approach to cost-based abduction, and, in [2], Abdelbar shows how methods for cost-based abduction can be applied to the MAP problem on Bayesian belief networks.

The GESA technique and extension are described further in Section 2. Section 3 presents cost-based abduction and describes the neighborhood and fitness functions used for this problem. Experimental results are presented in Section 4, and Section 5 presents some concluding remarks.

II. GUIDED EVOLUTIONARY SIMULATED ANNEALING

In simulated annealing (SA), a single candidate solution is maintained. Every iteration, a neighboring solution is generated, and its fitness is compared to that of the present solution. If the new solution is more fit, it becomes the new current solution. Otherwise, if it is worse by a difference in fitness of Δ, then it becomes the new current solution with probability $\exp(-\Delta/T)$ where T is the temperature. The essence of simulated annealing is that the temperature starts out at a high value and then is gradually decreased, according to some annealing schedule. The SA process can be modeled by Markov chains, where the transition probability from one state s_i to another state s_j is $\min(1, \exp(-\Delta/T))$. In a well-known result, Geman and Geman [12] showed that the asymptotic convergence of an SA process to the globally optimal solution can be guaranteed if the temperature is decreased at a rate that is no faster than logarithmic. However, this theoretically-guaranteed schedule is generally considered too slow in practice, and the most commonly used schedule, first proposed by Kirkpatrick *et al* [17], is to periodically reduce the temperature by a fixed percentage.

In Yip and Pao's [22] Guided Evolutionary Simulated Annealing (GESA) technique, a number, say N, of independent SA chains are maintained but with a single global temperature for all processes. Let p_i denote the current state of SA process i. Each iteration, each process i samples m_i states from the neighborhood of p_i. The best of the m_i generated states, call them child states, is determined by a straightforward deterministic comparison of fitness. The best child state is then compared to the parent state p_i: if the best child state has better fitness, it replaces the parent; otherwise it replaces the parent with a logistic temperature-controlled probability.

The number of child states that SA process i is allowed to sample in the next iteration is affected by the fitness of the child states it sampled in the current iteration. Let $m_i^{(t)}$ denote the number of child states that process i is allowed to sample at time-step t. The number of child states generated in the first iteration, $m_i^{(1)}$, is set equal to some constant M for all the SA processes; in other words, all processes generate the same number of child states in the first time step. Then, the number of child states allocated to each SA process is made proportional to its *acceptance number*.

The acceptance number of a process i, denoted A_i, is determined by examining the fitness of each of the child states of process i. For each child, the acceptance number is incremented if the fitness of the child is better than the fitness of the parent; if not, it is incremented with probability $\exp(-\Delta/T)$ where Δ is the difference in fitness. The number of child states for the next iteration, $m_i^{(t+1)}$, is then determined according to

$$m_i^{(t+1)} = (MA_i/S) , \quad (1)$$

where

$$S = \sum_j A_j ; \quad (2)$$

thus, the total number of child states generated in any iteration, over all SA chains, is kept constant and equal to MN.

In Yip and Pao's GESA, the measure of neighborhood quality is based only on the previous time-step. When heritage factors [3] are employed, equations (1) and (2) are replaced by

$$m_i^{(t+1)} = \left(M \left[A_i + \alpha m_i^{(t)} \right] \right) / S , \quad (3)$$

and

$$S = \sum_j \left[A_j + \alpha m_j^{(t)} \right] ; \quad (4)$$

where $0 \leq \alpha < 1$ is a manually-tuned parameter we call the *heritage factor*. When $\alpha = 0$, of course, this reduces to pure GESA. This is similar to the use of momentum in backward error propagation networks [19], and inertia in particle swarm optimization [16]. It allows the decay of a family to occur more smoothly and gives a chance for a "good" family to recover from the effects of a single bad generation.

III. Cost-Based Abduction

Cost-based abduction [7], [9] (CBA) is a generalization of weighted abduction [15]. A cost-based abduction system is a 4-tuple $(\mathcal{H}, \mathcal{R}, c, \mathcal{G})$, where $\mathcal{H}$ is a set of hypotheses or propositions, c is a function from $\mathcal{H}$ to the non-negative reals where $c(h)$ is called the *assumability cost* of hypothesis $h \in \mathcal{H}$, $\mathcal{R}$ is a set of rules of the form

$$R : (p_{i_1} \wedge p_{i_2} \wedge \ldots \wedge p_{i_n}) \longrightarrow p_{i_k} ,$$

where $p_{i_1}, \ldots, p_{i_n}$ and p_{i_k} are all members of $\mathcal{H}$, and $\mathcal{G} \subseteq \mathcal{H}$ is the goal or the evidence. Some of the hypotheses in $\mathcal{H}$ will have infinite assumability cost, which means that they cannot be assumed, they can only be proved. The objective is to find the least cost proof (LCP) for the evidence, where the cost of a proof is taken to be the sum of the costs of all hypotheses that must be assumed in order to complete the proof.

In GESA, every state represents a candidate solution. We will represent each candidate solution by a vector of truth values. A solution vector will include a bit for every assumable hypothesis in $\mathcal{H}$. The neighborhood operator simply randomly toggles one bit.

The fitness function must first determine whether the hypotheses that are assumed by the solution vector are sufficient to prove the goal. This requires following the flow of logical inference within the CBA rules. If the goal cannot be proved, then the solution is not feasible. As a penalty, the cost of an unfeasible solution vector is multiplied by a constant (we used 100) so that it will not be preferred. For feasible solutions, the cost is determined by summing the assumability costs of the hypotheses which are assigned to true by the solution vector.

IV. Experimental Results

We used an experimental suite of 50 randomly-generated CBA instances. Each instance contained 50 hypotheses, and 70 rules. The maximum number of antecedents per rule was 12, and the average number of antecedents was half the maximum. The number of parents of the goal (called the subgoals) was randomly chosen to be approximately 20% of the number of hypotheses. Assumability costs were randomly selected with a uniform distribution within the range $[1, 1000]$. The data files for these 50 instances are available from the first author as a zipped file.

We used an initial temperature of 720, and the temperature was multiplied by 0.9995 after each iteration. These two parameters were determined by experimentation with pure SA. The maximum number of iterations allowed was 5000, and the run was terminated if 25 iterations went by without any change in the current state of any of the GESA chains.

We applied 10 different combinations of the following three GESA parameters: number of chains (N), the average number of children per chain (M), and the heritage factor α. We also applied pure SA for purposes of comparison. Table I shows each parameter combination, the average proof cost (for those instances for which a feasible proof was found), and the number of instances (out of the suite of 50 instances) for which a feasible proof was not found. Figure 1 shows a graphical representation of average proof cost for each parameter combination.

We note that, interestingly, the only parameter combination which always found a feasible proof was also the parameter combination with the worst average proof cost. No single

TABLE I
EXPERIMENTAL RESULTS

parameters (M, N, α)	avg proof cost	number of unfeasible sols
(pure SA)	4504.16	1
(5,30,0)	4406.67	1
(5,20,0)	4375.52	2
(10,30,0)	4313.66	3
(5,20,0.1)	4427.55	1
(5,20,0.15)	4416.45	1
(5,20,0.2)	4371.29	2
(5,20,0.25)	4382.27	2
(10,30,0.2)	4351.27	2
(5,30,0.2)	4482.18	0

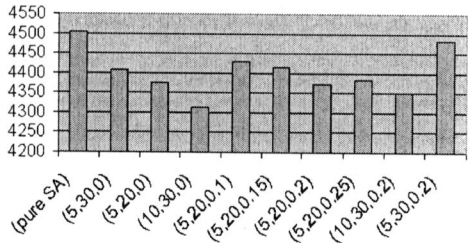

Fig. 1. Average proof cost for each (N, M, α) parameter combination

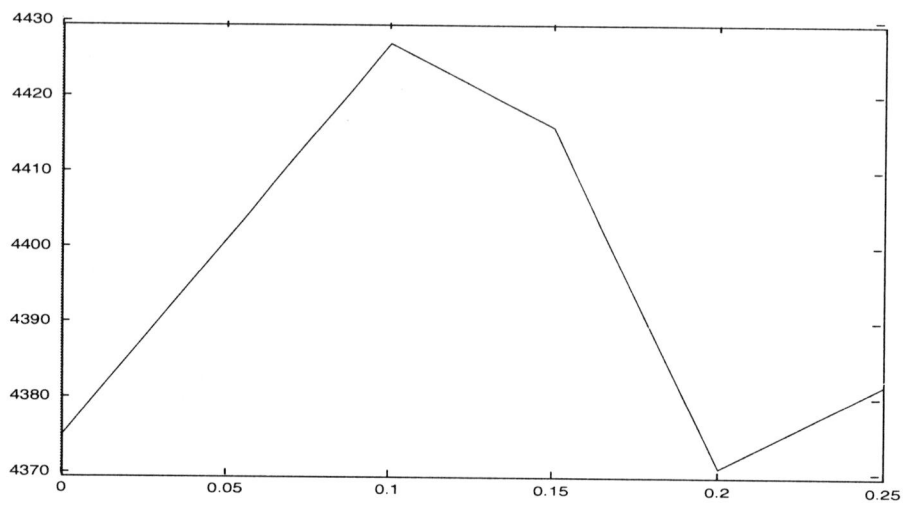

Fig. 2. Average proof cost versus α for runs with $N = 5$ and $M = 20$

parameter combination is best in both average solution quality and number of unfeasible proofs. The best balance is perhaps $(5, 20, 0.2)$ followed closely by $(5, 20, 0)$. We note that pure SA was outperformed by all GESA parameter combinations.

Five of the parameter combinations differ only in the value of α, with $N = 5$ and $M = 20$ for the five. The best α value for this combination is 0.2, which is the value of α we used for the other combinations of M and N. Figure 2 shows a plot of average proof cost versus α for those five runs.

The non-monotonicity of the plot suggests that performance is significantly affected by the choice of α.

V. CONCLUDING REMARKS

In this paper, we applied GESA, with the heritage factors extension proposed in [3], to cost-based abduction, an important problem in AI. Using a suite of 50 reasonably-sized randomly generated CBA instances, we found that GESA consistently found better solutions than simulated annealing alone. In the future, we would like to observe performance on a larger set of instances of varying sizes. It would be especially useful to identify characteristics of a CBA instance that make it particularly amenable to GESA solution. We are also currently investigating particle-swarm optimization approaches to the CBA problem.

REFERENCES

[1] A.M. Abdelbar, and S.M. Hedetniemi, "A Parallel Hybrid Genetic Algorithm Simulated Annealing Approach to Finding Probable Explanations on Bayesian Belief Networks," *Proceedings IEEE International Conference on Neural Networks,* Vol. I, pp. 450-455, 1997.

[2] A.M. Abdelbar, "An Algorithm for Finding MAPs for Belief Networks through Cost-Based Abduction," *Artificial Intelligence,* Vol. 104, 1998, pp. 331-338.

[3] A.M. Abdelbar, "Heritage Factors: Extending Guided Evolutionary Simulated Annealing," *Proceedings IEEE International Joint Conference on Neural Networks,* 2001.

[4] D. Adler, "Genetic Algorithms and Simulated Annealing: A Marriage Proposal," *Proceedings IEEE International Conference on Neural Networks,* Vol. 2, pp. 1104-1109, 1993.

[5] T. Boseniuk, and W. Ebeling, "Optimization of NP-Complete Problems by Boltzmann-Darwin Strategies Including Life Cycles," *Europhysics Letters,* Vol. 6, No. 2, pp. 107-112, 1988.

[6] D.E. Brown, C.L. Huntley, and A.R. Spillane, "A Parallel Genetic Heuristic for the Quadratic Assignment Problem," *Proceedings Third International Conference on Genetic Algorithms,* pp. 406-415, 1989.

[7] E. Charniak, and S.E. Shimony, "Probabilistic Semantics for Cost-Based Abduction," in: *Proceedings AAAI National Conference on Artificial Intelligence,* pp. 106-111, 1990.

[8] E. Charniak, and S. Husain, "A New Admissible Heuristic for Minimal-Cost Proofs," *Proceedings AAAI National Conference on Artificial Intelligence,* pp. 446-451, 1991.

[9] E. Charniak, and S. Shimony, "Cost-Based Abduction and MAP Explanation," *Artificial Intelligence,* Vol. 66, pp. 345-374, 1994.

[10] H.-J. Cho, S. Oh, and D.-H. Choi, "Population-Oriented Simulated Annealing Technique Based on Local Temperature Concept," *Electronics Letters,* Vol. 34, No. 3, pp. 312-313, 1998.

[11] D. B. Fogel, *Evolutionary Computation: Toward a New Philosophy of Machine Intelligence,* IEEE Press, Piscataway, 1995.

[12] S. Geman, and D. Geman, "Stochastic Relaxation, Gibbs Distribution, and the Bayesian Restoration of Images," *IEEE Transactions on Pattern Recognition and Machine Intelligence,* Vol. 6, No. 6, pp. 721-741, 1984.

[13] D.E. Goldberg, *Genetic Algorithms in Search, Optimization and Machine Learning,* Addison-Wesley, Reading, 1989.

[14] D.E. Goldberg, "A Note on Boltzmann Tournament Selection for Genetic Algorithms and Population Oriented Simulated Annealing," *Complex Systems,* pp. 445-460, 1990.

[15] J.R. Hobbs, M.E. Stickel, P. Martin, and D. Edwards, "Interpretation as Abduction," *Artificial Intelligence,* Vol. 63, pp. 69-142, 1993.

[16] J. Kennedy, and R. C. Eberhart, *Swarm Intelligence,* Morgan Kaufmann, 2001.

[17] S. Kirkpatrick, D. Gelatt, and M. Vecchi, "Optimization by Simulated Annealing," *Science,* Vol. 220, pp. 621-630, 1983.

[18] S.W. Mahfoud, and D.E. Goldberg, "Parallel Recombinative Simulated Annealing: A Genetic Algorithm", *Parallel Computing,* Vol. 21, pp. 1-28, 1995.

[19] J.L. McClelland, D.E. Rumelhart, and the PDP Research Group, *Parallel Distributed Processing: Explorations in the Microstructure of Cognition,* MIT Press, Cambridge, 1986.

[20] E. Santos Jr., "On the generation of alternative explanations with implications for belief revision," *Proceedings Seventh Conference on Uncertainty in AI,* 1991, pp. 339-347.

[21] E. Santos Jr., "A Linear Constraint Satisfaction Approach to Cost-Based Abduction," *Artificial Intelligence,* Vol. 65, 1994, pp. 1-27.

[22] P. Yip, and Y.-H. Pao, "Combinatorial Optimization with Use of Guided Evolutionary Simulated Annealing," *IEEE Transactions on Neural Networks,* Vol. 6, No. 2, pp. 290-295, 1995.

AUTHOR INDEX

A

Abdelbar, Ashraf M. 2328, 2428, 2803
Abe, Shigeo 102, 1599, 2043, 2054
Abe, Toshiro 1037
Abercrombie, David 809
Abramson, Myriam 1909, 2910
Acernese, Fausto 1356
Acevedo-Sotoca, Isabel 1441
Acha, Jose I. 726
Agabon, Shane 3128
Agostino, Diego D. 2631
Aguilar, Jose 1673, 2197
Aguilar, M. 2813
Ahmad, Zainal 2472
Ahmadi, Ali 1258
Aihara, Kazuyuki 942, 2349, 3161
Akamatsu, Norio 1227, 1253, 2130, 2263
Al-Dabass, David 919
Aldrich, C. 869, 2066
Alexander, William H. 2789
Alfredo, Jose 753
Aliev, R. A. 2227
Alonso-Betanzos, Amparo 2005
Alotaibi, Yousef A. 670
Alquézar, René 2181
Al-Rabadi, Anas N. 3112
Al-Rawi, Akram 2193
Al-Shaikhli, B. 1563
Alvarez, Ada 2083
Alvarez, M. R. 720
Alwazzi, Samir A. 2039
Amadio, V. 1458
Ambwani, Tarun 2300
Amemiya, Yoshihito 983
Amer, Heba 2428
Anagnostopoulos, Georgios C. 1987, 2782
Anastasio, Thomas 3201
Andersen, Timothy L. 2283
Anderson, G. 1290
Andonie, Razvan 1975
Andras, Peter 1385

Andrews, Emad A. M. 2803
Andronico, A. 2317
Anguita, Davide 1587, 2072
Ankaraju, Prashant 1476
Anstis, Stuart 11
Antani, Sameer 160
Aponte, Hugo 1673
Arakawa, Masao 1617
Araki, Osamu 2563
Arana, Nancy 2893
Araujo, Mariana 1673
Arellano-Baez, David R. 1280
Arita, Jun 3195
Arora, C. M. 2094
Artiklar, Mehmet 2552
Artiklar, Metin 2140
Arulampalam, Ganesh 1429
Asai, Hideki 2028
Asai, Tetsuya 983
Asari, Vijayan K. 1185, 2518
Ascoli, Giorgio A. 2831
Assadi, Amir 2899
Au, Francis T. K. 1873
Auer, Dorothee 601
Auner, Gregory 622
Azcarraga, Arnulfo P. 2528
Azimi-Sadjadi, Mahmood R. 1086, 1313
Azzerboni, B. 172

B

Badel, Stephane 977
Baek, Young-Hyun 1219
Bagnall, A. J. 1802
Baidyk, T. 2163
Balakrishnan, S. N. 1891
Balasubramanian, Mahesh 2100
Balya, D. 1492
Ban, Sang-Woo 119
Banerjee, Arindam 2697
Bang, Sung-Yang 1690
Barbalho, Jose Marinho 753
Barnard, J. P. 869

Barniv, Y. 2813
Barone, Fabrizio 1356
Barton, Alan J. 1945
Baruah, Pundarikaksha 2466
Baruth, Oliver 1249
Bassu, Devasis 914, 1553, 2497
Basu, Mitra 1623
Basu, Sumit 2797
Bauer, Christoph 81
Bauer, Kenneth W. 2807
Baumler, Wolfgang 81
Bayro-Corrochano, Eduardo 2881, 2893
Bean, Charlotte 3244
Beetner, Daryl 3157
Behnke, Sven 2758
Beiu, Valeriu 989, 1975
Berger, Theodore W. 666, 2848, 3134, 3146
Berlin, Matt 2795
Berno, E. 2637
Bersini, Hugues 3027
Bescoby, David J. 1132
Bharadwaj, Madan 2782
Bhaya, A. 2360
Bhumireddy, C. 432
Bhuyan, M. 404
Bi, Zeng 1933
Blumberg, Bruce 2795
Bo, C. M. 1054
Boger, Zvi 1065, 2643, 3095
Boggess, Lois 1678
Boni, Andrea 2072
Borghese, N. A. 1361
Bouchachia, Abdelhamid 1915
Bouslama, Faouzi 2193
Bouzerdoum, Abdesselam 1429, 2157
Bracco, Massimiliano 959
Brambilla, L. 2637
Brezak, Danko 310
Brier, Michael E. 71
Bruns, A. 1563
Bu, Nan 2661
Buchsbaum, Daphna 2795
Buchtala, Oliver 1025
Bullinaria, John A. 3207

Bullock, Daniel 3167
Burchiel, Kim 2837
Burd, Lyndsay 2770
Butz, Martin V. 1417
Byun, Hyeran 2175
Byun, Oh-Sung 1219

C

Caceres, Juan C. G. 841
Cafagna, Donato 61, 924
Caloba, L. P. 797
Calvo, Rodrigo 1340
Campenhout, Jan Van 2825
Canaparo, R. 2637
Cannon, Robert C. 1328
Canuto, Anne 316
Cardillo, John 2679
Cariani, Peter 1575
Carlson, Eric 2788
Carpenter, Gail A. 1396
Carroll, M. 3173
Carvalho, Alexandre X. 2916
Carvalho, Andre C. P. L. F. 1569
Casale, F. 2637
Casasent, David 1423, 1611
Casbon, James A. 3083
Castillo, Enrique 2005
Castillo, Oscar 1558
Caudell, Thomas Preston 1981, 3048
Cauwenberghs, Gert 2685
Cavalcante, Marco Aurelio P. 2493
Cavalcanti, George D. C. 2952
Cavicchi, R.E. 1065
Cawley, Gavin C. 1132, 1802, 2934, 2958
Chacon M., Mario I. 1195
Chacon, Oscar 2083
Chan, Andrew K. 1116, 3229
Chan, K. T. 1104
Chandra, Pravin 489, 2366
Chang, Bao Rong 254
Chang, Maiga 462
Changwu, Li 571, 2017
Chanyagorn, Pornchai 631
Chao, Xie 2232
Charumporn, Bancha 3185

Chaudhari, Narendra S. ... 450
Chen, C. L. Philip ... 432
Chen, Ke ... 1523
Chen, L. F. ... 1081
Chen, S. S. ... 1081
Chen, Sheng-Hao ... 1497
Chen, Tai-Cong ... 1873
Chen, Tianping ... 738
Chen, Xue-wen ... 1423
Chen, Yi ... 2710
Chen, ZhiHang ... 2860
Cheng, Chin-Hsing ... 2988
Cheng, Chiu-Hung ... 1497
Cheng, Lei ... 1324, 2146
Chengyin, Lin ... 571
Chennubhotla, Chakra ... 3083
Cherkassky, Vladimir ... 1143, 1581
Chermakani, Deepak P. ... 1999
Cheung, C. C. ... 1903
Cheung, Yiu-Ming ... 108, 513
Chi, Huisheng ... 3189
Chin, Cheng-Chung ... 1921
Chiang, Chiang-Cheng ... 2394
Chinnam, Ratna Babu ... 2466
Chiu, Kuo-Chuang ... 1043
Cho, Jeongho ... 34
Cho, Sung-Bae ... 28, 1702, 1708
Cho, Sungzoon ... 565, 2253
Cho, Yong B. ... 953
Choe, Yoonsuck ... 206, 1480
Choi, Jai ... 3007
Choi, Kwang-Ho ... 953
Choi, Seungjin ... 1690
Choudhury, Tanzeem ... 2797
Chow, Tommy W. S. ... 803
Chroston, P. Neil ... 1132
Chu, Feng ... 2268
Ciaramella, Angelo ... 708
Ciocchetta, F. ... 177
Cirrincione, G. ... 2106, 3106
Cirrincione, M. ... 2106, 3106
Civalleri, Pierpaolo ... 1486
Clanton, Carson ... 272
Clarkson, Brian ... 2797

Cochran, Jennie ... 2795
Coelho, Pedro H. G. ... 1153
Colaiocco, Barbara ... 1110
Colak, Sukru ... 627
Combs, W. E. ... 2995
Comes, Barbara ... 1714
Conery, J. S. ... 2574
Corinti, E. ... 1458
Corinto, Fernando ... 1486
Coskun, Nihan ... 1223
Costa, F. ... 753
Costa, M. ... 2637
Costantino, D. ... 166
Crespi, Valentino ... 266
Cripps, Al ... 1957
Crone, Sven F. ... 2460
Crossman, Jacob ... 2679
Crow, Mariesa L. ... 2964
Cucu, M. ... 154
Cukic, Bojan ... 2412
Cybenko, George ... 266

D

Dagher, Issam ... 1969
Dagli, Cihan H. ... 2905, 3218
Damiance Jr., Antonio P. G. ... 1569
Daqi, Gao ... 571, 1173, 2017, 2232
Davis, Bryan A. ... 332, 2558
De Placido, S. ... 2631
Deak, Gedeon ... 2788
Dekhtyarenko, O. K. ... 2579, 3031
Dell'Anna, R. ... 177
Demichelis, F. ... 177
Demmel, James W. ... 242
Denny, Gerald F. ... 1307
Denton, Stephen ... 272
Desai, Keyur ... 1862
Desai, Vishal ... 666
Dhananjaya, N. ... 692
Dhillon, A. P. ... 177
Dhillon, A. ... 177
Dibazar, Alireza A. ... 666, 3146
Diehl, Christopher P. ... 2685
Dilger, Werner ... 473, 1667
Dillon, Tharam S. ... 1243, 1746

Dimopoulos, Nikitas J. ... 2673
Ding, Runtao ... 930
Doboli, Alex ... 1126
Doboli, Simona ... 1126, 1643
Dong, Ming ... 2854, 3223
Dowding, George A. ... 1295
Downie, Marc ... 2795
Du, Yinggang ... 1104
Dua, Rohit ... 2667
Duch, Wlodzislaw ... 1735
Dudnikov, Evgeny ... 1138
Dudul, S. V. ... 1157
Dunn, N. A. ... 2574
Dunphy, Alphonsus ... 2288
Dutta, Ritaban ... 404

E

Eandi, M. ... 2637
Eckhorn, R. ... 1563
Eckmiller, Rolf ... 1249, 1832
Edwards, G. ... 1001
Eggen, C. ... 1290
Eggimann, Fritz ... 517
Eghbalnia, Hamid ... 2899
Eguchi, Hideo ... 2152
El-Bakry, Hazem Mokhtar ... 1284, 2202
Eleuteri, Antonio ... 1356, 2631
Eller, Vicki ... 2667
El-Sharkawi, Mohamed A. ... 1301, 3007, 3011
Elshaw, Mark ... 22
Eltoft, Torbjorn ... 523
Embrechts, Mark J. ... 1189
Engelbrecht, A. P. ... 1593
Erdogmus, Deniz ... 66, 332, 523, 1447, 2005, 2558
Espy-Wilson, Carol ... 675
Estrada, Steven ... 272
Evans, David ... 919

F

Fairhurst, Michael ... 316
Falck-Olsen, Ronny ... 698
Federici, Diego ... 3036
Feiden, Dirk ... 1149
Feldkamp, Lee A. ... 2860, 3017
Feldkamp, Timothy M. ... 3017
Feng, Chun-Bo ... 902
Feng, Xin ... 421
Fenwick, P. B. C. ... 276, 282
Fernandes, Cristiano ... 2493
Fernandez-Redondo, Mercedes ... 1752, 2655
Ferrari, S. ... 1361
Ferreira, L. V. ... 2360
Figueiredo, Mauricio ... 1340
Filho, J. B. O. Souza ... 797
Filho, R. Maciel ... 2406
Filho, Wedson T. de Almeida ... 1207
Finocchio, G. ... 172
Fitzpatrick, Paul ... 2703
Flanagan, John A. ... 3250
Fletcher, John T. ... 149
Floares, A. G. ... 154
Floares, Carmen ... 154
Fontenla-Romero, Oscar ... 2005
Foresta, F. La ... 172
Fox, Warren L. J. ... 1290, 1301
Foxall, Robert J. ... 2958
Fragopanagos, N. ... 298
Franks, J. G. ... 1059
Fraser, Andrew M. ... 3118
Freedman, Eric ... 230
Freeman, Walter J. ... 1373
Frezza-Buet, Herve ... 3054
Fujinaka, Toru ... 3185
Fujisaka, Hisato ... 2534
Fukuda, Osamu ... 2661
Fukuda, Osamu ... 3195
Fukumi, Minoru ... 1227, 1253, 2130, 2263
Fukushima, Kunihiko ... 2625
Fuller, Edgar ... 2412
Furlanello, C. ... 3077
Furuhashi, Takeshi ... 1729
Furukawa, Rogerio A. ... 1569
Fyfe, Suzanne K. ... 1019

G

Gail, A. ... 1563
Ganapathy, Senthil Kumar ... 936
Gangashetty, Suryakanth V. ... 686
Gao, Changjian ... 995

Gao, Dayong 2454
Garavaglia, Susan B. 75
García, Carlos A. Reyes 3140
García, Jose Orozco 3140
Garcia-Orellana, Carlos 1441
Gardner, J. W. 404
Garis, Hugo de 2589
Garrett, A. 2813
Gastaldo, Paolo 194
Gautam, Ramesh K. 1031
Gaweda, Adam E. 71
Genet, Marc C. Girod 814
George, Sageev 666
Georgiopoulos, Michael 1987, 2782
Gewehr, Jan E. 2940
Ghatol, A. A. 1157
Ghodsi, Ali 91
Ghosh, Joydeep 2697
Gilli, Marco 1486
Gillingwater, David 2023, 3256
Godfrey, A. 177
Goerke, Nils 660, 2609
Goh, Liang 1724
Gohara, Kazutoshi 825
Gomes, Diego de Miranda 1207
Gonzalez-Velasco, Horacio 1441
Goodman, Donald 1678
Gorban, A. N. 1826
Gorchetchnikov, Anatoli 1637
Gorelik, Vladimir A. 965, 2752
Gori, Marco 1351
Gothoskar, Gaurav 1126
Grassi, Giuseppe 61, 924
Graveron-Demilly, D. 596
Greco, A. 166
Grossberg, Stephen 8
Gruber, Christian 2482
Gudise, V. G. 468
Guimaras, Katia S. 2952
Guiping, Nie 1173, 2232
Guirimov, B. G. 2227
Gunay, Cengiz 224
Guo, Lin 2208, 2277, 3213
Guo, Wan-Yuo 616
Gupta, Madan M. 2615
Guruprasad, S. 577, 692
Gutierrez-Galvez, A. 341
Gutierrez-Osuna, R. 341
Guzelis, Cuneyt 45

H

Haijun, Zhu 1173
Halonen, Kari 1502
Hammerstrom, Dan 995, 1346
Han, Da-jian 1873
Han, Min 2146
Harley, Ronald G. 1879, 2964, 2976
Harvey, Richard 2934
Hashimoto, Setsuo 3151
Hassan, Deena O. 2328
Hasselmo, Michael E. 1328, 1470, 1637
Hassoun, Mohamad H. 2140, 2552
Hatanaka, Toshiharu 1013
Hayasaka, Taichi 478
Hayashi, Takuji 2563
Hayashi, Terumine 1048
He, Changming 1237
He, Ji 1684
He, Pingan 1535
Healy, Michael J. 1981, 3048
Heh, Jia-Sheng 462
Heileman, Gregory L. 1987, 2782
Hengartner, Nicolas W. 3118
Hernandez, Emilio Del Moral 353
Hernandez-Espinosa, Carlos 1752, 2655
Heynderickx, Ingrid 194
Heywood, Malcolm I. 781, 1780, 1808, 2288
Hickford, J. G. H. 582
Hild II, Kenneth E. 523
Hinamoto, Takao 1547
Hinde, Chris 2023, 3256
Hirahara, Makoto 2152, 2502
Hirano, Akihiro 1092, 1856
Ho, L. T. 1081
Ho, Shen-Shyang 1435
Hofmann, Alexander 415
Hohmann, S. G. 381
Homma, Noriyasu 2615
Honda, Katsuhiro 541, 732

Hong, Qin 948
Horace, H. S. 1098
Horio, Yoshihiko 942
Horita, Akihide 1092
Hornillo-Mellado, S. 726
Howells, Gareth 316
Hsieh, Jen-Chuen 616, 1081
Hsieh, William W. 759
Hsu, Chun-Fei 2372
Hu, PingZhao 1780
Hu, Xiao 3001
Hua, Liu 2017
Huang, De-Shuang 1098, 1868, 2208, 2277, 3213
Huang, Kaizhu 484
Huang, Kuan-Hsun 1497
Huang, Rongbo 513
Huang, Yaping 85, 704
Hua-Xiang, Lu 2216
Hua-Yi, Mo 2216
Huffel, S. Van 3106
Hulle, Marc M. Van 769
Hung, Chin-Pao 399, 2118, 2988
Hunter, David 2546
Hussain, Amir 2819
Hussin, M. F. 2238

I

Iancu, Laurentiu 2887
Ichihashi, Hidetomo 541, 732
Iftekharuddin, Khan M. 1201
Ikeda, Hitoshi 1268
Ikeguchi, Tohru 2563
Inoue, Koichi 2400
Ioannides, A. A. 276, 282, 287
Iordanova, Blaga N. 535
Ipsale, M. 172
Isaac, Kakkattukuzhy M. 2667
Ishida, Fumihiko 2424
Isik, Can 627
Ito, K. 2454
Ito, Kentaro 2077
Ito, Koji 2619
Ito, Shin-ichi 2263

J

Jacobs, Alfred A. 71
Jacobs, James H. 1295, 1307
Jagannathan, S. 1535
Jain, Brijnesh J. 1993
Jan, Tony 2478
Jankowski, Norbert 636
Jeffs, Janelle 1274
Jemwa, G. T. 2066
Jenssen, Robert 523, 2005
Jernigan, M. 200
Jian, Xu 948
Jiang, Hao 421
Jiang, Ju 1512
Ji-Xin, Qian 879
Johansson, Ulf 1798, 2866
Johnson, Michael R. 51
Johnson, Stanley 1007
Jorgensen, Chuck 3128
Joshi, Ameet 2928
Juang, Chia-Feng 1885
Juneja, Amit 675
Jung, Jae-Byung 1295
Jung, Jae-Byung 1307
Jurman, G. 3077

K

Kaburlasos, Vassilis G. 426, 1850, 1957
Kaieda, Kenichi 2043
Kakemoto, Yoshitsugu 852
Kalyani, R. P. 2982
Kambhampati, Chandra 3244
Kameda, Seiji 387
Kamel, Mohamed 1512, 2238
Kamenetsky, Max 2872
Kameyama, Keisuke 2294
Kamimura, Ryotaro 529, 2734, 3042
Kamio, Takeshi 885, 2534
Kananen, Asko 1502
Kanda, Akihiro 541
Kaneda, Yuji 2243
Kao, Yi-Hsuan 616
Karayiannis, Nicolaos B. 96, 517, 2100, 2722
Karras, D. A. 596, 1076, 1367, 2322

Karri, Sirisha S. 376
Kasabov, Nikola 438, 1724, 2124
Kasac, Josip 310
Kashimura, Hirotsugu 1268
Kashwan, K. R. 404
Kaszkurewicz, E. 891, 2360
Kato, Noriji 1268
Kawaji, Shigeyasu 642
Kayacik, H. Gunes 1808
Kazarlis, S. 426
Kecman, Vojislav 1232
Keerthi, S. Sathiya 2088
Kelemen, Arpad 654, 1714, 1769
Kellman, P. J. 2
Ken, C. K. Law 1098
Kenyon, Garrett 1274
Khairallah, Farid 2134
Khan, A. Nayeemulla 686
Khasawneh, Mohammed 2193
Khotanzad, Alireza 1071
Kiesling, Christian 393
Kijsirikul, Boonserm 1605
Kil, Rhee Man 507
Kim, Chan-Mo 953
Kim, Eunju 2175
Kim, Hyejin 1690
Kim, Hyoung Bae 1213
Kim, Jan T. 2940
Kim, Jeong Ha 1213
Kim, Kyung-Joong 28
Kim, Myeonghee 642
Kim, Sang-Hee 858
Kim, Sung-Phil 66
Kim, Tae-Hoon 444, 2011
King, Irwin 484
Kinouchi, Y. 2454
Kiselev, M. V. 2843
Kita, Hidehiko 1048
Kleffner, Matthew 2716
Ko, Jaepil 2175
Kobayashi, Yukihiro 2349
Koene, Randal A. 1328
Koh, Chung-Haur 260
Kohonen, Teuvo 3238

Kojima, Fumio 3151
Kong, Seong G. 149
Konig, Rikard 2866
Koo, Imhoi 507
Kopriva, Ivica 631, 747
Kosaka, Toshihisa 2212, 1258
Koshiba, Yoshiaki 2054
Kosko, B. 2740
Kostopoulos, G. K. 276
Koutnik, Jan 3233
Koyama, Takehiko 2349
Kozma, Robert 347, 831, 1476
Krause, Stefan 553, 2770
Kretzschmar, Ralf 517
Kristensen, Terje 698, 1718
Krout, D. 1290
Kubota, Naoyuki 3151
Kulkarni, U. V. 1939
Kumar, Kuldeep 2033
Kumarappan, N. 2112
Kuramoto, Yoshiki 2424
Kurino, Ryusuke 2512
Kussul, E. 2163

L

Labonte, Gilles 2306
Lai, D. 2060
Laiho, Mika 1502
Laine, Trevor I. 2807
Lan, Jing 764
Lan, Yuxuan 2934
Landa, J. 131
Lang, Elmar W. 81, 1318
Lange, Steffen 2691
Lansari, Azzedine 2193
Laurent, Patryk A. 1631
Laurentiis, M. De 2631
Law, Lap-Tak 108, 513
Lawhead, Pamela 1769
Laxdal, Erik M. 2673
Lazar, L. 154
Leblebici, Yusuf 977
Lee, Cheng-Ling 1921
Lee, Diana 3128
Lee, Hyeon-Cheol 206

Lee, Jaewook 410
Lee, Johnny 2716
Lee, Jong-Hwan 1453
Lee, Kyunghee 2340
Lee, Minho 119
Lee, Nung Kion 1746
Lee, P. L. 1081
Lee, Sin Wee 1412
Lee, Soo-Young 1453
Lee, Tsu-Tian 2372, 2378
Lee, Won Don 2340
Lendaris, George G. 2837, 2922, 3112, 3173
Leung, S. H. 1168, 1903
Levine, Daniel S. 272
Levinson, Stephen 2716
Levy, William B. 1469, 1625, 1631, 1655
Lewis, Rick 230
Li, Danfeng 2716
Li, Feng 1553
Li, Hailin 2905
Li, Haizhon 347
Li, J. 1054
Li, Jianyu 85
Li, Yuanhong 3223
Liang, Yulan 654, 1769
Lien, Sandra 2506
Likharev, Konstantin 365
Lin, Cheng-Jian 1921
Lin, Chih-Min 2372
Lin, Chin-Teng 2372
Lin, Li-Ju 371, 1497
Lin, Ruei-sung 2716
Lin, Weidong 2438
Lin, Wen-Lang 2988
Litvintchev, Igor 2083
Liu, Derong 902
Liu, L. C. 276, 282
Liu, W. 2970
Liu, Wenyao 2169
Liu, Xiuwen 182, 742, 1263, 1324, 2247
Liu, Yong 2540
Liu, Zhengping 836
Lo, James T. 914, 1541, 1553, 2497
Lockery, S. R. 2574

Long, L. Rodney 160
Long-hua, Ma 879
Lopez-Aligue, Francisco J. 1441
Lopez-Benavides, M. 582
Lu, Beiwei 759
Lu, C. 2106, 3106
Lu, Chun-Feng 1885
Lu, Wenlian 738
Ludermir, Teresa B. 143
Luk, Andrew 1903, 2506
Luo, Dingsheng 1523, 3189
Luo, Siwei 85, 704
Luo, Xiao 1786
Luo, Yun 2134
Lyons, Derek 2795
Lyu, Michael R. 484

M

M., Nagabhushan Kaliyur S. 2722
Ma, Junshui 1741
Ma, Yunqian 1143, 1581
Magalhaes, Kaiser M. C. 612
Maggini, Marco 1351
Magnoni, L. 2317
Magori, Yusuke 2534
Maida, Anthony S. 224
Majetic, Dubravko 310
Makeyev, O. 2222
Malaka, R. 125
Maldonado, Francisco J. 444
Maldonado, Javier F. 2011
Malinowski, Aleksander 2546
Malki, Heidar A. 2100, 2722
Maloof, Marcus A. 2764
Malsburg, Christoph von der 2994
Malyscheff, Alexander 2344
Manda, Prasad 622
Mani, N. 2060
Manian, Vidya 113
Mann, T. P. 1290
Manry, Michael T. 444, 2011
Marks II, Robert J. 1290, 1301, 2995, 3007, 3011
Marra, S. 2448
Marshak, David 1274

Martin-Clemente, Ruben	720, 726
Martinetz, Thomas	2940
Martins, Allan de Medeiros	3071
Massey, Louis	1402
Masulli, Francesco	791, 3089
Matsuda, Satoshi	873
Matsugu, Masakazu	2243
Matusi, Satoshi	2349
Matsunaga, Nobutomo	642
McCarthy, J.	3173
McClain, Matthew	2716
McLaren, I. P. L.	212
McNames, James	809, 2837
Mei, Jianfeng	3179
Meier, D. C.	1065
Meier, K.	381
Meleiro, L. A. C.	2406
Melin, Patricia	1558
Melo, Jeane C. B.	2952
Melo, Jorge Dantas de	3071
Menard, Olivier	3054
Meng, Hua	2146
Menhaj, M. B.	1963, 2382
Merler, S.	3077
Mertzios, B. G.	596
Metta, Giorgio	2703
Meyer-Baese, Anke	601, 3101
Milano, Leopoldo	1356, 2631
Miller, Earl K.	1
Miller, Richard L.	547
Miller, Ronald	2418
Mills, Britain	272
Minai, Ali A.	1643
Minchev, Stefan	2124
Mingolla, Ennio	16
Mitaim, S.	2740
Mitarai, Yusuke	2243
Mitchell, Matthew W.	1897
Mitman, Kurt E.	1631
Mitra, V.	1001
Mitsukura, Kensuke	1253
Mitsukura, Yasue	1227, 1253, 2130, 2263
Mittermeir, Roland	1915
Miyamoto, Robert T.	1301
Miyamura, Aiko	3161
Mizutani, Eiji	242
Mohagheghi, Salman	2964
Mohan, M. R.	2112
Molter, Colin	3027
Monaco, J. D.	1655
Monteiro, Luiz H. A.	337
Moon, Sung-Rung	1219
Moore, Bartlett	1274
Morabito, F. C.	166, 172, 2448
Mori, Katsuhiko	2243
Mori, Yoshio	541
Morisue, Mititada	885, 2534
Morris, Lori J.	590
Motter, Mark A.	34, 764
Movellan, Javier	2788
Mu, Xiaoyan	2140, 2552
Muckra, Ibrahim	365
Muezzinoglu, Mehmet Kerem	45
Mulder, Samuel	1408
Mulvaney, Rory	1774
Murata, Hiroshi	1757
Murgu, Alexandru	2388
Murphey, Yi Lu	2134, 2679, 2860
Murphy, Richard C.	2599
Musavi, Mohamad T.	590
Muselli, Marco	1844
Muthukkumarasamy, Vallipuram	1237
Mutihac, Radu	769

N

Nagano, Takashi	2152, 2502
Nakada, Kazuki	983
Nakamura, K.	1649
Nakanishi, Hiroaki	2400
Nakano, Ryohei	501, 2077
Nakasuka, Shinichi	852
Nakayama, Hirotaka	1617, 2049
Nakayama, Kenji	1092, 1856
Nam, Boo Hee	1213
Namarvar, Hassan H.	2848, 3134, 3146
Naranjo, Michel	2881
Narayan, Sridhar	2328
Narayanan, Sreeram	3007
Natarajan, Padma	39, 547, 590, 1019

Navarrete, Gorka 2181
Neocleous, C. 648
Neto, Adriao Duarte Doria ... 612, 753, 1207, 3071
Neto, Luiz Biondi 1153
Netto, Marico L. A. 753
Neumann, Dirk 1249
Neumann, Peter 1025
Neville, R. S. 1120
Ng, Geok See 1927
Ng, S. C. 1168, 1903
Nguyen, N. 1957
Niazi, K. R. 2094
Nicolelis, Miguel 66
Niklasson, Lars 2866
Ninomiya, Hiroshi 2028
Nishikawa, Ikuko 438
Nishikawa, Jun 825
Nishikawa, Tsuyoki 714
Nishiwaki, Takayuki 1856
Nitta, J. 1649
Noel, S. 131
Nomura, Hirosato 2523
Novak, Bojan 2312
Novakovic, Branko 310
Novokhodko, Alexander 1820
Nowicki, D. W. 2579
Nowicki, Robert 321
Nshimura, Kazuo 2604

O

O'Brien, Amy J. 606
Oezer, Tuna 3201
Ohashi, Gosuke 188
Ohta, Masaya 864
Okamoto, Keisuke 102
Oliveira, Rogério de 337
Omatu, Sigeru 1037, 1258, 1792, 2212, 3185
Ongsritrakul, Pedrudee 2488
Onoda, Takashi 1757
Ormondt, D. van 596
Ortiz-Gomez, Mamen 1752, 2655
Osana, Yuko 846
Osterloh, Bjorn 3157
Ozawa, Seiichi 102, 2583
Ozturk, Mustafa C. 332

Ozyilmaz, Lale 586

P

Paasio, Ari 1502
Paccanaro, Alberto 3083
Pachowicz, Peter 1909
Padhi, Radhakant 1891
Palaniswami, M. 2060
Palmer-Brown, Dominic 1412
Palmes, Paulito P. 478
Pan, Dong 971
Pan, Gang 2169
Panchal, Rinku 2033
Panigrahi, Suranjan 1031
Papadakis, S. E. 426
Paquet, U. 1593
Park, Chang-Hyun 2594
Park, Chanho 1702
Park, Jung-Wook 1879, 2964, 2976
Park, Won-Woo 858
Pasero, E. 2637
Patel, Ruben 1718
Patil, P. M. 1939
Pavel, Misha 2272
Peck, Michael W. 2958
Pegors, Teresa 2796
Pelillo, Marcello 55
Pentland, Alex 2797
Pepa, C. Della 2637
Perkins, Simon 1741
Perng, Jau-Woei 2378
Petrowski, Alain G. 814
Pezeshki, Ali 1313
Phatak, Dhananjay S. 1774
Phetkaew, Thimaporn 1605
Phua, Paul Kang Hoh 260, 2438
Phuan, Alex Tay Leng 1517
Piazza, Francesco 1110, 1458, 2819
Pilyugin, Sergei S. 3101
Ping, Wong Lai 1517
Piuri, V. 1361
Placido, S. De 2631
Poghosyan, ... 282
Polikar, Robi 553, 2770
Polk, Thad 230

Prasad, V. Shiv Naga 577
Prieto-Ortiz, Flavio A. 1280
Principe, Jose C. 34, 51, 66, 332, 523, 764, 1447, 2005, 2558
Prokhorov, Danil V. 3017
Pucci, M. 2106
Puljic, Marko 831
Puntonet, Carlos G. 720, 726, 1318
Puterman, Martin L. 2916
Putrus, May 2860

Q

Qi, Yingjian 85
Qidwai, Uvais 137
Quaglia, A. 177
Quek, Chai 1927

R

Randolph-Gips, Mary M. 96
Rao, K. Sreenivasa 686
Rao, Yadunandana N. 66, 1447, 2558
Rapaka, Arvind 1820
Ray, Monika 137
Ray, Swakshar 1963, 2382
Ray, Sylvian 1417, 3201
Rekeczky, Cs. 1492
Renganathan, S. 1007
Ressom, Habtom 39, 547, 590, 1019
Reznik, A. M. 2579, 3031
Rhodes, Bradley J. 3167
Ribeiro, Bernardete 1661
Ricalde, Luis J. 359
Ridella, Sandro 959, 1587, 2072
Ritter, Gerhard X. 2887
Rivepiboon, Wanchai 1605
Rivest, F. 559
Rivieccio, Fabio 1587
Roadknight, Christopher 1412
Robinson, Jonathan 1232
Robinson, Marc 1086
Rojas, F. 720
Rojas, Raul 3124
Romero, Enrique 2181
Rosa, Rosario De 1356
Rossi, Vivien 495, 2433
Rovetta, Stefano 791, 3089
Ruffino, Francesca 1844
Rutkowski, Leszek 321

S

Sadek, Nayera 1071
Saito, Toshimichi 787, 1391, 2569
Saito, Yasuo 1013
Salazar, Jaime 1086
Salem, Fathi M. 680, 775, 1862
Salmeron, M. 720
Samarasinghe, S. 582
Sanchez, Edgar N. 1280
Sanchez, Edgar N. 359
Sanchez, Justin C. 66
Sandwith, Rex 2187
Sansome, Gennaro 2631
Santiago, Roberto A. 2837, 2922, 3173
Saqi, Mansoor A. S. 3083
Sarti, Lorenzo 1351
Saruwatari, Hiroshi 714
Sasamura, Hiroki 787
Sasu, Lucian 1975
Sawada, Yasuji 2424
Sboner, A. 177
Scassellati, Brian 2704
Schaefer, Mark 473, 1667
Scharf, Louis L. 1313
Scheler, Gabriele 218
Schemmel, J. 381
Scherer, Rafal 321
Schieder, Thomas 1832
Schizas, Chr. 648
Schmid, Alexandre 977
Schrauwen, Benjamin 2825
Schumann, Johann 218
Schurmann, F. 381
Schuurmans, Dale 91
Seixas, J. M. 797
Sejnowski, Terrence 3261
Sekhar, C. Chandra 686
Sekiya, Yasuhiro 2523
Selamat, Ali 1792
Semancik, S. 1065
Semolini, R. 2946

Seow, Ming-Jung 1185, 2518
Serafini, M. 3077
Shaik, J. S. 1201
Shannon, Thaddeus T. 809, 2922
Sharkawi, M. A. El 1290
Shastri, Lokendra 1379
Shen, Haoming 188
Shepherd, Michael 781
Shervais, Stephen 3022
Shevade, Shirish K. 2088
Shi, Bertram E. 1506
Shi, S. Y. M. 1838
Shibata, Katsunari 2512, 2619
Shibata, T. 282
Shigeto, Kazuhide 1013
Shikano, Kiyohiro 714
Shimazaki, Masanao 2569
Shimizu, Masaaki 1268
Shimodaira, Yoshifumi 188
Shin, Hyunjung 565
Shin, Jang-Kyoo 119
Shou-Jue, Wang 2216
Shoujue, Wang 948
Shultz, T. R. 559
Sick, Bernhard 415, 1025, 2482
Silva, Carlos A. 612
Silva, Catarina 1661
Sim, Kwee-Bo 2594
Simen, Patrick 230
Simpson, Patrick K. 1295, 1307
Singh, Yogesh 489, 2366
Sitchov, A. S. 2579
Sivayoganathan, Siva 919
Skabar, Andrew 1814
Slade Jr., Wayne H. 547
Slepski, Joseph R. 3001
Snorek, Miroslav 3233
So, C. F. 1168
Sohn, Sunghwan 3218
Sokolov, Artem M. 2443
Soleimani, Masoud 1163
Song, Chi-Hwa 2340
Song, Qun 438
Song, Xubo 2272

Sonstrod, Cecilia 1798, 2866
Sontakke, T. R. 1939
Soonthornphisaj, Nuanwan 2488
Sopena, Josep M. 2181
Spiegel, Rainer 212, 908, 2746
Sporns, Olaf 2789, 2796
Squartini, Stefano 2819
Squire, Kevin 2716
Sriram, Ravichandra 2589
Srirangam, Siva 590, 1019
Srivastava, Anuj 182, 742
Stanley, R. Joe 160
Stiber, Michael 2728
Suganthan, P. N. 1838
Sugisaka, Masanori 2512
Sugiura, Nobukazu 732
Sullivan, David W. 1625
Sun, C. Y. 1054
Sun, Changyin 902
Surana, S. L. 2094
Sussner, Peter 236, 326
Swarup, Samarth 3201
Szatmari, I. 1492
Szu, Harold H. 131, 631, 747, 841, 3189

T

Taga, Kei 2294
Tagliaferri, Roberto 708, 1356, 2631
Tagliarini, Gene A. 2328, 2803
Taheri, Javid 456
Takada, Masaharu 501
Takaharu, Takeda 2540
Takano, H. 1649
Takao, Kenji 1547
Takase, Haruhiko 1048
Takatani, Tomoya 714
Takeuchi, Haruhiko 2734
Takeuchi, Ichiro 1729
Talevski, Alex 1243
Takimoto, Hironori 1253
Tan, Ah-Hwee 1684
Tan, Chew-Lim 1684
Tang, Bin 781
Tang, Jun 1143
Taniguchi, Takuya 942

Tascillo, Anya 2418
Taylor, J. G. 287, 292, 298
Teichert, J. 125
Teixeira, Marcelo 3065
Teng, Michael Mu Huo 616
Tepper, Jonathan 1412
Teranisi, Masaru 2212
Tetzlaff, Ronald 1149
Tham, L. G. 1873
Theiler, James 1274
Theis, Fabian J. 81, 1318
Thivierge, J. P. 559
Thoma, George R. 160
Thompson, Benjamin B. 1301, 3007, 3011
Timar, G. 1492
Titus, Albert H. 376, 936
Tivive, F. H. C. 2157
Tobinaga, Yoshikazu 2604
Tomita, Chikahiro 2028
Torikai, Hiroyuki 1391, 2569
Trafalis, Theodore B. 2039, 2344
Travis, Bryan 1274
Treeck, Bernd 698
Trentin, E. 2317
Triesch, Jochen 2788
Trujillo, Noel 2881
Tsuji, Toshio 2661, 3195
Tsujinishi, Daisuke 1599
Tsumori, Kenji 2583
Tsutsumi, Kazuyoshi 897
Tummarello, G. 1458
Tung, Tzu-Ching 2394
Turel, Ozgur 365
Tweedale, Wendy 590
Tymoshchuk, P. 891

U

Uchida, Osamu 529
Ulloa, Antonio 3167
Uosaki, Katsuji 1013
Usui, Shiro 478

V

Valdes, Julio J. 1945
Valentini, Giorgio 1844
Vallejo, Refugio 2893
Vapnik, Vladimir 1289
Vasquez, Ramon 113
Vaughn, M. L. 1059
Vazquez, Ernesto 2083
Vellasco, Marley M. B. R. 2493
Velloso, Maria Luiza F. 2493
Venayagamoorthy, Ganesh K. .. 468, 1879, 2964, 2970, 2976, 2982
Venkov, Gancho 2124
Verma, Brijesh 1237, 2033
Versaci, M. 166, 2448
Verzi, Stephen J. 1987, 2782
Vian, John 3001, 3007
Vicario, Elena 194
Vijila, C. Kezi Selva 1007
Vila, Jean-Pierre 495, 2433
Virnstein, Robert W. 590
Vixie, Kevin R. 3118
Voicu, Horatiu 1334

W

Wahab, Abdul 1927
Waheed, Khurram 680, 775, 1862
Wang, Bingchen 1037
Wang, C. 1001
Wang, Dali 39
Wang, DeLiang 182, 1574
Wang, Di 450
Wang, Dianhui 1243, 1746
Wang, Guoping 2272
Wang, Jun 2334
Wang, Lipo 2268, 3060
Wang, M. H. 399, 2118
Wang, Mang-Hui 2988
Wang, Qianyi 2523
Wang, Xiaohua 2438
Wang, Y. R. 1054
Waring, Christopher 1263
Washino, Koji 1617
Watkins, Andrew 1678
Watkins, Steve E. 2667
Watt, Peter 22
Watta, Paul 2140, 2552
Weaver, Kim 680

Wechsler, Harry 1435, 1909, 2910
Weijun, Li 948
Weinschenk, Jeffrey J. 2995
Wen, Ziyan 2679
Weng, Juyang 2710, 2928
Wermter, Stefan 22
Wesolkowski, Slawo 200
Widrow, Bernard 2872
Wilamowski, Bogdan M. 971, 2546
Wilks, Carsten 1832
Willey, J. 131
Wismueller, Axel 601
Wohlberg, Brendt E. 3118
Won, Hong-Hee 1708
Wong, H. S. 1098
Wu, Bing-Fei 2378
Wu, Chung-Yu 371, 1497
Wu, Sitao 803
Wu, Xihong 3189
Wu, Y. T. 1081
Wu, Yijun 2169
Wu, Yu-Te 616
Wu, Zhaohui 820, 2169
Wu, Zheng 1763
Wunsch II, Donald C. 248, 1408, 1696, 1820, 1826, 2667, 2970, 3001, 3157
Wysotzki, Fritz 1993

X

Xia, Youshen 2334
Xiao, Yunhai 1981, 3048
Xin, Jianguo 1189
Xu, Jianjun 930
Xu, Lei 2354, 2649
Xu, Peng 1116, 3229
Xu, Rui 1696
Xu, Wang Shoujue Chen 2258

Y

Yagi, Tetsuya 387
Yagoub, Mustapha C. E. 930
Yamada, Seiji 1757
Yamajo, Hiroaki 714
Yamamoto, Toru 1547
Yamanaka, Noriyuki 1729

Yamashita, Katsumi 864
Yamauchi, Koichiro 2776
Yamazaki, Akio 143
Yamazaki, M. 1649
Yan, Leipo 3060
Yanfeng, Qu 948
Yang, Wen-Chia 371
Yang, Yingchun 820
Yang, Yingjie 2023, 3256
Yao, Qiang 3157
Yap Jr., Teddy N. 2528
Yazama, Yuuki 2130
Ye, Zhengmao 622
Yegnanarayana, B. 577, 686, 692
Yeh, Tzu-Chen 616, 1081
Yen, Gary G. 1763
Yerramalla, Sampath 2412
Yildirim, Tulay 586, 1223
Yim, S.-B. 131
Ying, Huang 1933
Yong-Ling, Zheng 879
Yongquan, Yu 1933
Yoon, Min 2049
Yoshimori, Seiki 1227
Yoshioka, Michifumi 3185
Yoshioka, Horio 2349
Yu, Bo 1179
Yu, Enzhe 2253
Yu, Wen-Shyong 1951
Yuan, Chao 1611
Yun, Yeboon 2049

Z

Zaknich, Anthony 1464
Zamani, Morteza Saheb 1163
Zaverucha, Gerson 3065
Zhang, Chunlin 1512
Zhang, Jie 304, 2472
Zhang, Liming 1179, 3179
Zhang, Nian 248
Zhang, Q. J. 930
Zhang, Qiang 2247
Zhang, S. 1054
Zhang, Wanfeng 820
Zhang, Yilu 2710

Zhang, Zijun	2589
Zhange, Wei	2283
Zhao, Liang	841, 1569
Zhao, Qiangfu	2540
Zhao, Wenbo	2277
Zhao, Wenbo	3213
Zhao, Xueli	2454
Zheng, Thomas	1529
Zhi-hai, Wang	2216
Zhou, Hong	1769
Zhou, Xu-Shen	2854
Zhu, Shaojuan	1346
Zhu, Weiyu	2716
Zhu, Xiaotian	260
Zilles, Sandra	2691
Zimmerman S., Alejandro	1195
Zincir-Heywood, A. Nur	1786, 1808
Zinovyev, A. Yu.	1826
Zorkadis, V.	1076, 1367
Zuben, F. J. Von	2406, 2946
Zunino, Rodolfo	194, 959, 1587
Zurada, Jacek M.	45, 71
Zwick, Martin	3022